HANDBOOK OF THE BIRDS OF THE WORLD

Volume I

Ostrich *to* Ducks

Lynx Edicions

ICBP

HANDBOOK OF THE BIRDS OF THE WORLD

Volume I

Ostrich *to* Ducks

Josep del Hoyo
Andrew Elliott
Jordi Sargatal

<table>
<tr><td>José Cabot</td><td>Eloïsa Matheu</td></tr>
<tr><td>Carles Carboneras</td><td>Isabel Martínez</td></tr>
<tr><td>Anna Folch</td><td>Albert Martínez-Vilalta</td></tr>
<tr><td>Eduardo de Juana</td><td>Anna Motis</td></tr>
<tr><td>Francesc Llimona</td><td>Jaume Orta</td></tr>
</table>

Colour Plates by

Francesc Jutglar
Lluís Sanz
Àngels Jutglar
Juan Varela
Lluís Solé

Consultant for Status and Conservation Sections

Nigel J. Collar

Lynx Edicions

Barcelona

Citation:

del Hoyo, J., Elliott, A. & Sargatal, J. eds. (1992). *Handbook of the Birds of the World*. Vol. 1. Lynx Edicions, Barcelona.

Films by *Laser Press*
Colour reproductions by *Reprocolor Llovet, S.A., Barcelona*
Printed and bound in Barcelona by *Grafos, S.A., Arte sobre papel*
Dipòsit Legal: B-27.828-1992
ISBN: 84-87334-10-5

12599391

*a Ramón Mascort Amigó, que amb la seva confiança
ha fet possible un somni de molts anys.*

*to Ramón Mascort Amigó, whose confidence
has made possible a long-standing dream.*

Foreword

The study of birds represents a very special contribution to our appreciation of the world around us. Birds are better researched than any other group of animals or plants. They hold a special place within a large number of cultures throughout the world. They also act as biological indicators, showing us the implications of environmental change. To understand birds is to begin to understand the world.

There are more than 9000 species of birds. Today, over 1000 of these are threatened with extinction; another 5000 are declining. The facts hardly seem to do justice to the grim realities. Each of these species is unique. To lose one species is to deprive future generations of the opportunity to share our sense of wonder and joy. Once gone they will never return. For many of us the potential loss of a single bird species is sufficient to ring the alarm bell; yet there are excellent reasons why we should *all* concern ourselves with the conservation of our threatened and declinig birds. They are the small, visible tip of a large iceberg: for every threatened bird species there are numerous other, less conspicuous animal and plant species that inhabit the same ecosystem and are threatened by the same factors as the birds. Globally, at least one million plant and animal species are threatened. They represent an important proportion of the world's finite genetic resources. Today, mankind does have the power to stop this accelerating loss of species, but we all must show willingness to use that power.

I am delighted to endorse this marvellous Handbook on behalf of the International Council for Bird Preservation (ICBP). I have always believed that any contribution to our knowledge of birds is an additional step towards ensuring their conservation. I am particularly pleased to be associated with this series of volumes because it recognises that birds are not a national possession but a global treasure. When we start to acknowledge the world's birds as our own then we are recognising our responsibility to the whole planet. ICBP is a global organisation. We represent people from every continent. Together they constitute a deep appreciation for the role that birds can play in demonstrating the delicate balance in the environment. We upset that equilibrium at our peril.

We live on a small and vulnerable planet. Our actions as individuals can either contribute to the well-being of our collective home, or they can destroy it. Let us all learn to study and enjoy the birds of the world. In doing so we are adding to our ability to save the world.

Dr Christoph Imboden,
Director-General,
International Council for Bird Preservation.

CONTENTS

LIST OF PLATES

ICBP and the Conservation of the Birds of the World

We have every reason to acknowledge the foresight and vision that characterised the small group of people who gathered in London in 1922 to form the International Council for Bird Preservation (ICBP). International action to conserve birds was a unique and unheard of concept at that time. They met when the world had recently lost the last Passenger Pigeon and the Carolina Parakeet. The Eskimo Curlew stood on the edge of extinction while the Whooping Crane and the Trumpeter Swan were each reduced to a mere handful.

Over the following years the pressing need for international action to save birds has become ever more apparent. Since the 1950's, four major studies have identified the number of globally threatened bird species. It is clear that there has been a steady increase in that figure. Rising from 95 species in 1958 to 220 in 1971, 290 in 1979, and 1029 species in 1988. The latest information, without doubt, represents the most complete and reliable picture so far. In fact, earlier studies may well have underestimated the scale of the problems through lack of detailed information.

ICBP, as the principal organisation concerned with the birds of the world, establishes the status of every species. It is through painstaking research, frequently using ICBP's vast network of professional ornithologists and committed amateurs around the world, that the status of each species can be classified. Such information should be an impetus for conservation action. With each threatened species added to the list comes the stimulation to act both to save those species that are immediately threatened, and also to halt the decline of others.

The considerable increase in the number of species categorised as threatened reflects a disturbing trend for avifauna generally. It is estimated that approximately 5000 more bird species are declining. When added to the list of threatened birds this means that around two-thirds of all bird species are suffering long-term population reductions.

Seventy years on from that historic meeting to form ICBP, the problems facing birds and the environment have never been greater. How can we respond to such a challenge? For ICBP the answer is clear. The response must be based upon hard-headed research providing us with the ability to understand the problems clearly, and then deliver viable solutions. Inevitably this involves prioritisation. There are never enough resources to allow organisations such as ICBP to address all of the issues simultaneously. Difficult decisions have to be taken on the most effective way to act.

So what and where are the priorities for international bird conservation? In accordance with the World Conservation Strategy, and its successor Caring for the Earth, these priorities are concerned with the preservation of biological diversity, the maintenance of ecological processes and systems, and the sustainability of any utilisation of species and habitats. Therefore, priorities can be categorised in several ways.

The number of threatened species in each country or geopolitical unit can be assessed and then ranked. Such an approach provides us with a top three of Indonesia, Brazil, and China. Alternatively these units could be ranked for the number of threatened endemics only. Once again Indonesia and Brazil top the list, although by this method they are joined by the Philippines.

Another way of approaching the task is to identify the key groups of birds. In other words we can include those families and genera with a high proportion of threatened species. Among the obvious candidates for such a list are groups are parrots, which have a high degree of speciation and suffer heavy exploitation by trade, and raptors, which are major indicators for terrestrial ecosystems owing to their vulnerable position at the top of the food chain.

A further approach is through the selection of key sites for bird conservation. These can be determined, for example, by virtue of their holding more than one threatened species, by being sole home to one threatened species or by holding major populations of particular species, but also because they represent critically important areas for populations of certain species (notably in the case of wetlands).

Inevitably any decision on prioritisation will include a mix of the above criteria and take into account a number of other factors. For bird species, subspecies and populations to remain viable in the long term, substantial representative portions of the full range of the world's naturally occurring habitats and ecosystems require conservation. In practice it is essential to concentrate on tropical forests, both wet and dry, as the generally overriding priority, but with high recognition of wetlands, grasslands and islands as major custodians of the world's remaining biological diversity; also important are temperate old growth forests, in both Northern and Southern Hemispheres, which have become increasingly exploited and fragmented.

The difficult decisions on priorities must then be translated into action. For ICBP the key to success is creating links between organisations and people that transcend political boundaries. ICBP brings people together in collaboration and partnership, to take action wherever the need is greatest. This also necessitates the bringing together of developed and developing countries to work in cooperation and to transfer resources to where they are urgently required. ICBP plays a vital role in facilitating closer links between those who can provide those resources and those who need them most.

As a federation, ICBP has more than 360 member organisations, spanning 110 countries, with the backing of around ten million individual members. ICBP's direct conservation programme has in excess of 60 projects running in the field at any one time. These will range from survey work through to large-scale sustainable development projects. Through its member organisations, hundreds of conservation projects are taking action for birds throughout the world.

ICBP has achieved many notable conservation successes, but perhaps the story of the Seychelles Warbler is the best proof that even very small populations can be resurrected with careful management and wise use of resources. When ICBP bought Cousin Island, the last remaining home of the Seychelles Warbler in the 1960's, the world population had reached an all time low of just 30 individuals. But through careful habitat management the numbers began to increase, and by the early 1980's, the warblers had established a healthy population of some 400 individuals on the island.

Despite this early success, ICBP's project workers realised that while the birds were confined to just one island, the possibility of disease, or of a hurricane wiping out large areas of available habitat, meant that the species was still not completely safe.

So, in 1988, the decision to translocate 29 warblers to the nearby island of Aride was taken. The birds were closely monitored, and as the Cousin warblers bred in January, the new birds on Aride were expected to take a few months to settle in before the breeding season. In fact, as history reveals, they needed only two days to start building the first nest, and today, the population has climbed to more than 200 individuals. The warbler has now also been introduced to Cousine Island and is one of the few species actually to be removed from ICBP's list of threatened species.

ICBP is running a number of similar species-rescue projects covering priorities in all parts of the world. Amongst the birds which are benefiting from these initiatives are: Gurney's Pitta, confined to a tiny area of forest in southern Thailand; Bannerman's Turaco, known only from the montane forests of Cameroon's Bamenda Highlands; the Imperial Amazon parrot, endemic to Dominica's threatened rain-forests; the Seychelles Paradise Flycatcher, found only on the tiny island of La Digue; and many more.

Although birds remain the driving force behind ICBP's activities, much of the work to save the world's most threatened species depends upon the involvement of people and the protection of the broader environment. This is inevitable when one realises that the principal factors causing the serious decline of so many species are completely attributable to the behaviour of people. Habitat destruction, over-exploitation, introduced predators - the pressures driving birds towards extinction are numerous, and almost exclusively a result of human actions. Yet equally it is within our compass to act positively to halt the decline in distribution and abundance of so many of the world's birds.

ICBP represents a worldwide recognition of the value and importance of birds. Not simply for the sense of joy and wonder that they bring, but also for their role as indicators of the state of our common world. Birds provide us with an index to the health of the environment, locally, regionally, and on a global scale. In saving birds, we save our world, and ultimately ourselves. There can be no better incentive to act. ICBP has taken a lead, it falls to each of us to ensure that others follow.

ICBP

As a bird enthusiast, the best way you can help ICBP in its mission to save the world's birds is to become a member of the World Bird Club. Not only will you be contributing to ICBP's conservation programme, you will also receive updates on all the world's rarest birds and be kept in close touch with ICBP's priorities. Individual membership is (UK and rest of world) £25, (USA) $35. Subscriptions can be sent to

ICBP, 32 Cambridge Road, Girton, Cambridge CB3 OPJ, UK.

Many ornithologists, both professional and amateur, will undoubtedly have wished at some stage that they had a work illustrating and dealing in detail with all of the world's bird species, a work which allows an appreciation of their diversity on a global, rather than a regional, scale. This was, at any rate, the case of most of the participants in this project; as there were no signs of any such work appearing, we eventually decided to attempt it ourselves.

The initial stages of the project were begun in 1982, when one of the editors (JH) set out to put together a collection of all the major, and not so major, regional bird books, a collection which he had, in fact, already been gathering for some time, although rather less systematically. All this information was catalogued, and since 1985 has been computerized, species by species. This mass of information gave an indication that there were so many important gaps in our knowledge of the birds of the world that at first the project seemed almost impossible. However, after a few years of gathering information, the computerized reports started to show that the project could get under way, if suitable means were found, although these would have to be considerable, given the prerequisite that the project was only worth attempting if it could be carried out with rigorous levels of accuracy.

In 1987, two of the editors (JH and JS) met Ramón Mascort, a lawyer by profession who was able to provide the necessary financial backing, and together they formed Lynx Edicions, with the Handbook of the Birds of the World (HBW) as its main target. After a year's experience and the publication of five smaller books on wildlife, the decision to go ahead with HBW was approved in 1989.

The next steps involved co-opting a third editor (AE), building up a suitable group of authors and researchers, and forming a team of artists led by Francesc Jutglar, who had already done the artwork for the other books published by Lynx. At the same time, the internal structure of Lynx Edicions was substantially reformed to deal with this large-scale project. From the beginning, the success of the project has been totally dependent on a great deal of disinterested effort on the part of the staff at Lynx, and also, of course, of all the various contributors.

The final stage in the preparation of the project consisted of involving ICBP in the project, in the hope of making the work of the project more valuable, and ultimately, it is hoped, more international. We were delighted to find ICBP interested in HBW, and willing to participate actively, especially with the revision of the Status and Conservation sections for all of the species. It should be noted that the book has not been written by ICBP staff, so references in the text to ICBP's work and achievements should not be interpreted as the organization "blowing its own trumpet".

General Objectives

The objective of HBW is to provide an extensive reference work to what is probably the best known of all the classes in the Animal Kingdom. The work attempts to demonstrate the extraordinary diversity of the birds, covering aspects such as taxonomic relationships and, to some extent, evolutionary history, ecology, general habits, breeding strategies and the current status of populations on a global level. One of the main aims is to give comprehensive worldwide coverage from a genuinely international point of view. For this reason, wherever possible, in the selection of examples (and also of photos), preference has been given to poorly known areas and species, especially those of South America and Asia, rather than the more normal trend of concentrating on the best known species, most typically those of North America and Europe; nevertheless, there is obviously far more information available about the latter species, and equally there tend to be relatively fewer good photos of the former.

It must be made clear from the outset that, in a work that is planned to run to ten large, weighty tomes, the aim can not be to produce a sort of mammoth field guide. For this reason, it was decided not to illustrate the plumages of juveniles or subadults, nor those that are adopted outside the breeding season. This decision was not taken simply as a matter of convenience in order to reduce the work load, but also bearing in mind that an excessive number of illustrations for a single species would reduce clarity in two of the most important aims of the work: the possibility of direct comparison between different species; and the facility of an overview of a particular family or group as a complete entity, with all its component parts.

Last, but not by any means least, one of the most basic ideas behind HBW is to make some form of contribution towards the conservation of birds and their habitats, which explains the close links with ICBP. This work will be the first that attempts to analyse the status and conservation of all of the species, not just those that are known or thought to be threatened. The first Red Data Books were highly influential publications that had an important role in subsequent conservation planning around the world. Possibly their main achievement was highlighting how little was known about the status (and indeed all aspects of the lifestyle) of so many species. However, they had some serious deficiencies: the exclusion, mainly due to lack of data, of many species that turned out to be clear candidates for inclusion, such as the Greater Adjutant (*Leptoptilos dubius*); and the inclusion of some unsuitable species, notably the Peregrine Falcon (*Falco peregrinus*), which, with its immense range, gave the impression that it could not be so very seriously threatened on a global level, thus devaluing, to some extent, the peril in which other genuinely threatened species found themselves. In an important and influential paper, J. M. Diamond (*Conserv. Biol.* **1**: 77-79) proposed that a species might be better considered extinct unless proved extant, rather than the other way round. The publication by Collar & Andrew (1988) of a comprehensive list of all the species then considered to be globally threatened was a major step forward, as it highlighted the alarming numbers of species that were apparently in danger. One of the aims of HBW is to go a step further and examine, as far as is possible, the status of each one of the world's species, noting its conservation requirements and possible threats it faces, with an attempt to put these into perspective; again, the main value of this may be to highlight what is not known rather than what is. It is hoped that in this way there will be less chance of a species reaching the brink of extinction without its decline being detected.

Classification

First of all, it must be made quite clear that HBW has no pretensions as to being a definitive taxonomic list. The main aim in this sense has been to make a contribution by following, and therefore listing, what have been judged to be the most traditionally accepted versions, as well as summarizing the most significant alternatives. The decision on which classification to follow was not an easy one, especially given the major developments in this field in recent years.

The recent classification of Sibley & Monroe (1990), based on the principles and results laid out in Sibley & Ahlquist (1990), has been highly acclaimed and very well received in many quarters. However, it was considered both risky and irresponsible to base a series of ten volumes and many years' work on views that are so new and so revolutionary, and which seem bound to be subject to a certain amount of change in coming years. Furthermore, when the project was initiated, the definitive version of this classification had not yet been published. It should also be noted that this classification is not without its critics (e.g. *Auk* **106**: 508-512, or *Ibis* **134(2)**: 204-206).

As the intention of the series is to present a summary of what is known about many aspects of ornithology, it seemed appropriate to follow one of the more traditional versions. An examination of the possibilities led to the conclusion that the most suitable was that of Morony, Bock & Farrand (1975), hailed by K. H. Voous, in Campbell & Lack (1985), as the "most elaborate and well-balanced of recent lists"; a few minor amendments have been adopted, as detailed by Bock & Farrand (1980). The basic source for subspecies, as also for nomenclature and scientific descriptions, has been Mayr & Cottrell (1979).

To these major taxonomic works which have served as a base, several exceptions have been permitted. For instance, the views of acknowledged experts and authorities in certain groups, when at odds with the basic source references, have been given serious consideration and, in some cases, preference, although only when such views have met with widespread acceptance. Thus, the recent subdivisions of the families Procellariidae and Phalacrocoracidae involving the acceptance of many more species have been followed, in part because the relevant major authority for the area affected, in this case Marchant & Higgins (1990), has also accepted these changes. In terms of subspecies, considerably more leeway has been permitted in the acceptance of races, especially some of the newly described ones, and also in the removal of those that have been invalidated, usually as a result of more extensive research; it seems pedantic to maintain ideas that have fallen into disfavour. Nonetheless, when in doubt, the aforementioned basic sources have been adhered to. For instance, the comprehensive reorganization of Anseriformes proposed by Livezey (1986) has not been followed, although it has many supporters; it has been deemed more consistent to err on the side of caution.

While the decision of whether or not to follow certain new proposals has in many cases been difficult, the version followed does not claim to be definitive, but rather a necessarily subjective interpretation of the most widely accepted version. In the sections Systematics and Taxonomy of the family texts and species accounts respectively, all other major variations are mentioned, sometimes in detail, in order to make the alternatives quite clear, and at the same time indicate that they have not been ignored. For instance, where Sibley and Monroe differ from the version followed in HBW, in their placement of a taxon and its relationship with other groups or species, their alternative is mentioned. In these sections recent changes and former versions can also be mentioned.

At the end of the introductory chapter, Aves (Birds), two double-page tables have been included illustrating, in diagramatic form, both the classification of Morony, Bock and Farrand that has been followed, and that of Sibley and Monroe, simplified in an attempt to facilitate direct comparison between the two versions.

It should be noted that, in addition to its value as an important new classification, Sibley and Monroe's work has been a very valuable source reference on the taxonomic issues of each family, species, and, in some cases, subspecies.

The decision on which species should be treated as extinct has been awkward, and the result is possibly a certain degree of inconsistency. The most difficult cases included two species of grebe that are almost certainly extinct, but are included in HBW, each with its own species account, illustration and map (in these species of the former distribution); both species were treated as Endangered by King (1978/79) in the last complete edition of the Red Data Book. In contrast, two ducks considered Extinct by King, are here treated as such, and so do not have species entries, although one of them, the Crested Shelduck (*Tadorna cristata*) may yet be found to survive; both species are, in fact, illustrated and their cases discussed in the family text.

Family Texts

Although the title of the book might suggest that the intention is to produce a work equivalent to the important regional treatises which have appeared in recent years, notably those of Palmer (started in 1962), Bauer & Glutz von Blotzheim (1966), Cramp & Simmons (1977), Ali & Ripley (1978), Brown *et al.* (1982), Ilicev & Flint (1985) and Marchant & Higgins (1990), it should be emphasized that HBW does not attempt to emulate these works on a global scale. Treatment of species to that sort of degree would require some 50 volumes or more, while, on the one hand, the complete lack of information available for some species would leave their accounts much the same as in the present version, and, on the other, extensive treatment would usually only be possible for those species that are already exhaustively dealt with in the aforementioned works.

For these reasons, it seemed unrealistic to attempt to give such full treatment species by species, which would have implied numerous repetitions and an unmanageably long series, which only a very select few could have afforded, and which would probably have been finished by our grandchildren! It seemed far more appropriate to take the Family as the basic unit, as it normally presents a sufficient degree of homogeneity to allow a fair amount of detail in a general text, as opposed to the Order, which would be too vague for the kind of work planned.

Each chapter dedicated to a particular family has two clearly differentiated parts, which are, to a certain extent, complementary. First, there is the family text, which gives a fairly general view of the family, with numerous illustrative examples, which give a general idea of the members of the family, including to a certain extent, by extrapolation, even those species about which very little is known. Following this, however, each species is treated individually in a concise, but informative species account that accompanies the respective plate.

In some of the larger, more complicated families, sections may be treated more or less separately by subfamily, tribe or "natural group", which on occasions allows a more detailed examination of the different aspects, than if the whole family were necessarily dealt with as a single unit, which can sometimes demand a statement so generalized that it becomes almost meaningless. A certain amount of flexibility has been permitted in terms of the subjects dealt with in each section, in order to avoid the style becoming excessively repetitive.

Monospecific families receive slightly different treatment, as the species account becomes to a large extent a summary of the family text, but this slight duplication allows more direct comparison with species of other families. The bibliography is not divided into two parts, as it is in other families, with General Bibliography (family text) and Bibliography (species account); instead, all the references are lumped together in the Bibliography of the species account.

Within any one family, references are often made to other parts of the text of the same family, using the bracketed pointers e.g. (see Breeding); these refer exclusively to sections within the same family. References to other families are signalled using a page number e.g. (see page 338). No references are made from the family to the species account, but they are frequently made in the opposite direction, for example where the species account makes some reference to a conservation issue which is more fully explained in the family text, or where a feeding method is explained in greater detail in the family text, particularly when the name of the feeding technique is not particularly self-explanatory. References between families tend to be mostly related to matters of conservation or systematics.

Within the structure of the book, each order is separated from the preceding one by an order page. This gives a scheme showing the internal structure of the order, including all the families, and their relationships with each other through suborders.

Each family text is divided into the following sections: Summary-box; Systematics; Morphological Aspects; Habitat; General Habits; Voice; Food and Feeding; Breeding; Movements; Relationship with Man; Status and Conservation; and General Bibliography.

Summary-box

Each family text starts off with a summary-box, which summarizes the basic details of the family very briefly in a way that permits rapid interpretation. After the heading, which includes the higher taxa in which the family is placed, there is a succinct description of the most distinctive characteristics of its members. This is followed by the size range of the family, in terms of total length, in centimetres, from the tip of the bill to that of the tail, with the bird stretched out on its back. The size range is complemented by silhouettes of the largest and smallest members of the family placed alongside a human figure for reference: the full-length figure represents a man standing 180 cm (6') tall; in partial silhouette, he measures 90 cm (3') from his waist down to his toes; when only a hand appears, this measures 20 cm (8") from the wrist to the tip of the longest finger. This is followed by a brief summary of the family's range, which is illustrated by a world map, on which the red shading represents the whole area occupied, both during and outside the breeding season, although zones where members of the family may occur only irregularly are not included; the map of each family has been created by superimposing all the individual species maps. After a broad comment on the habitat characteristic of the family, there follows a list of its constituents in terms of the numbers of genera, species and taxa, which here is used rather freely to mean the sum of all the monotypic species added to the subspecies of polytypic species; this obviously follows the classification adopted for HBW. The summary-box closes with the total number of species currently considered threatened, as well as the number of species and subspecies extinct since 1600.

Systematics

This section deals with evidence and theories about the origins and evolution of the family, usually with brief reference to the fossil register. Important views as to the most closely related groups are also mentioned in connection with the relative situation of the family within its order, and reference is made to other alternatives proposed.

The internal structure of the family is usually discussed in greater detail, although there are, of course, cases which present few problems of internal organization. Whenever a family is divided into subfamilies and/or tribes the implications too are discussed, and, to permit easier interpretation, this is always accompanied by a diagramatic scheme. Subfamilies and tribes that have been proposed, but are not here accepted, are also mentioned and the reasons for their rejection discussed, although in a few particularly complicated cases, notably Anatidae, the subject can not be treated exhaustively quite simply for reasons of space, as so many variations have been proposed; in such cases reference has been made to the most significant alternatives. A few families are subdivided only into "natural groups", which tend to help in the treatment of other aspects of the family, although they have little or no taxonomic value.

The major sources for the taxonomy followed have been discussed above (see Classification). Thus, each family has been treated within this basic structure, but, in addition, works dealing with the systematics of the family in question, for instance monographs, have also been given due consideration, and some changes to the basic sources have been accepted, although only when the "new" version has received widespread support from recognized authorities. In this section such changes are discussed.

When the structure of a family is complicated, there may be a brief examination of the constituent parts, if appropriate, but there is not automatically a run through all the genera, as this has been considered superfluous. There is often a discussion genus by genus of controversial issues within or even between different genera, but in such cases not all the genera need necessarily be dealt with individually.

The section also deals with cases of subspecies that are sometimes considered species and vice versa, although clearly there are many cases which can not be given an exhaustive examination. When appropriate, the validity of certain races may also be discussed, although this is usually too detailed a matter to be dealt with in the family text, and is mentioned only in the species account, in the section Taxonomy. Another matter frequently discussed is the treatment of a particular species within one genus or another, although again such discussion is compulsory in the species account, but optional in the family, depending on its relative importance with respect to other issues and the space available.

Morphological Aspects

The main features in this section are the structure and external aspect of the members of the family. In general, matters of anatomical, skeletal or physiological detail are not normally discussed, except when their relevance to broader matters demands, for example when dealing with matters as diverse as systematics or thermoregulation.

The general physical characteristics of the members of a family are given and those of particular interest treated in more detail, usually with an attempt to interpret the significance of certain adaptations and their possible role in the evolution of the species; the benefits and limitations of such developments are also discussed. For instance, some birds, such as flamingos, prions or some ducks, have developed very special bills, which, in conjunction with a highly specialized feeding technique, are perfected to the exploitation of a particular food source; this, in turn, frequently limits the extent of suitable habitat, influences the timing of the breeding season, may be directly responsible for some or all of the bird's movements, and can, of course, have serious implications on its status and conservation, if the food supply shows signs of failing.

General tendencies of plumage colour are summarized, with comments, in some cases, on the significance of certain types of coloration to aspects of the bird's life. In this part of the section, comments are made on variations in plumage occurring with sex, age and season, so the existence of a distinct non-breeding plumage is mentioned, as is any variation in the colour of the bare parts.

This section includes a description of the various methods of locomotion used by the birds, as they are usually closely linked to the birds' physical make-up. For this reason, an attempt is made to link the morphological peculiarities of a particular bird or group with its lifestyle and habitat, for example the different adaptations of penguins, petrels and frigatebirds to a highly marine life.

Moult is dealt with in this section, though, being a fairly technical subject, it is generally permitted only a short summary of the strategies followed; it is obviously quite impractical to go into much detail. There are some exceptions in which the strategy is particularly interesting and important, notably in the case of the penguins, and in such cases the subject is dealt with in greater depth.

Habitat

A general comment is made about the typical habitat types used. Aspects that are considered include feeding, roosting and breeding habitats, and, in some cases, special habitats used during migration, when birds are often forced to use areas that they would otherwise pass by, or during moult. Breeding habitat, in particular, receives special attention. Generally speaking, this section deals with nesting habitat, whereas details of the actual nest-site are explained in Breeding. This separation appears quite clear in theory, but in practice it is very often difficult to draw the line between the two, for example if the nest is placed on a cliff ledge.

In many cases this section has been difficult to deal with, as the habitat types used by the members of a family are often very similar and limited, or quite the opposite, so diverse that it is difficult to make any sort of overall comment without it being so general as to be of limited interest, or effectively a list of related habitat types.

General Habits

As its name suggests, this section deals with a wide variety of topics; its scope can be rather flexible. Some form of consistency has, however, been imposed, but as different birds often have very different habits it seemed counter-productive to attempt a tendentious degree of unity. For this reason, General Habits is unavoidably a sort of hotch-potch, an all-purpose section, where all those matters that do not appear to fit in well elsewhere finally end up.

The aspects most typically covered include to what degree the members of the family are diurnal or nocturnal, and in what aspects of their lives, naturally commenting on any significant differences between the species. Another subject that is dealt with is the extent to which birds are gregarious, again stating how much this varies within the family, and what aspects of the birds' lives are involved. In some cases this leads on to social behaviour, but in most cases breeding behaviour, including territorial displays, is treated separately in Breeding; in a few cases, breeding behaviour has been considered so closely related to behaviour that is used in other aspects of the birds' lives that the two are treated together in this section, while reference is made to this section in Breeding. Sometimes intraspecific aggression that is not related to breeding appears in this part.

Another subject that is typically dealt with in this section is thermoregulation. On occasions it has been preferably treated in Morphological Aspects, as many birds have special morphological or physiological developments specifically designed to control the problems of excessive heat or cold. In other cases, it has been regarded as being more a question of behaviour than a particular physical development, and so is better placed in this section; in cases at both extremes of temperature thermoregulation is frequently a question of adopting a certain posture, which either retains or dissipates heat, as required.

Other commonly treated subjects include several activities often referred to as "comfort behaviour". These include preening, oiling, bathing, head-scratching and stretching exercises. Roosting and loafing activity is sometimes commented on, and in some cases it has been considered appropriate to detail the typical daily rhythm of members of a family or group.

Voice

This has probably been the most difficult section of all to deal with, and the least satisfactory in terms of the end-product. In most cases, the section has been used to describe the different ways in which a bird's voice can be important in its daily life, for instance by forming a part of displays. It is a very important system of enabling contact between adults and their young, sometimes before the latter have even hatched, for instance allowing an adult to locate its own chick in the midst of a noisy, bustling crèche. It is also used in some cases as a threat to birds invading a territory.

It has often been commented how difficult it is to put down on paper a useful rendering of a bird's call. In this case it is all the more difficult as the comments have to be applicable to the family in general, so only rather vague generalizations have been possible with respect to the actual sound of a call. Mechanical sounds, such as bill-clattering, where they occur, can be given more useful treatment, as the sound produced is more readily understood, and although these sounds have, by definition, nothing to do with the voice, they tend to be dealt with in this section, as being a form of "voice-substitute".

One of the proposals for improving the Voice section was the inclusion of sonagrams. While the sonagram has clear advantages over any other attempt to describe vocalizations, it also has certain drawbacks; although it is now being used in an increasing number of studies and publications, it still remains a form of data in highly technical form, which is fairly incomprehensible to a large proportion of the birdwatching public. Another serious problem is that several sonagrams would be necessary to do justice to any one species, and that only one or two for the whole family Anatidae, with its 147 species, would be pointless; sonagrams for each species would take up a good deal of space in the species account, which is already a highly compacted, and necessarily succinct, section; admittedly, this problem would presumably be reduced, by lack of availability for a large number of species.

Food and Feeding

General comments are made about the type of food consumed, although in some families there is a notable uniformity in diet, which permits a certain amount of detail within the generalization. Features that are commonly dealt with include food requirements, particularly those of nestlings which are often the most easily measured, and seasonal variations in diet, for instance species that are insectivorous for part of the year and herbivorous for the rest. The size of food items that are consumed is also dealt with on occasions.

The commonest foraging techniques are explained in some detail, and slight variations on the theme may be cited as illustrations. The more unusual and remarkable techniques are also described, typically those used by specialist feeders. Some of these unusual techniques involve physical adaptations, as in the two openbills (*Anastomus*), whereas others are based on behavioural developments, notably some of those used by the herons.

Breeding

General breeding strategy is mentioned where appropriate. Breeding seasons and factors determining the timing of the season are analysed, as are details of the strategy, such as the relevance of colonial or solitary breeding, polygamy or monogamy, the roles taken by the sexes, the duration of the season and the significance of its length, implications of chick development, chick-care, age of sexual maturity, nest-site, length of incubation stints, and so on.

The different stages in the course of a normal breeding season are followed, through procedures such as pairing, nest-site selection and defence, copulation, laying, incubation, hatching, chick-care, growth and development of the nestling, fledging, independence, and arrival at age of sexual maturity.

There is a brief description of the eggs, though the comment can only be fairly general; egg measurements given are length x breadth, not circumference. Overall tendencies in the down colour of the chicks are commented on. At all stages of the description, there is an attempt to interpret the significance of different parts of the strategy, and ask why it may differ between two species or groups, as well as examining the advantages of different strategies. In most cases, there is a reference to significant records of longevity. Details of breeding success are sometimes given, but it tends to be very variable, and can, in any case, be directly affected by the activity of researchers.

Names of displays appear in inverted commas and start with a capital letter, e.g. "Sky-pointing"; descriptions of displays are given very sparingly. In many cases the title of the display gives some indication of what goes on, as in "Head-up" or "Ritual Begging", but in others this idea is at best rather vague, for instance in "Billing" or "Scapular Action". The study of displays is very important in terms of studies of taxonomic relationships, behaviour and even ecology, but it has here been considered of limited interest to the non-expert; it can only be sufficiently interesting if the display is described and interpreted in sufficient detail, and this has not been considered one of the priorities of the work.

Movements

The explanation of movements varies considerably between families, mainly because the various strategies adopted require different treatment. Traditional usage has been followed in treating as "true" migration only those movements that are regular and seasonal, with predictable timing and destinations. Other movements may be classed as dispersive, nomadic, erratic and so on.

The form that migration takes is discussed, with birds travelling by day or night, flying at high or low altitudes, moving in flocks or singly, and in some cases making regular stops sometimes at known staging posts; attention is paid to the type of route taken, whether they move over inland areas, follow the coast or river valleys, or fly over the sea. Some migration involves only short distances, particularly that of altitudinal migrants, which generally move to lower levels to avoid the seasons of most inhospitable climatic conditions. Sometimes certain cases are discussed, usually because they are especially good, illustrative examples, or alternatively unusual cases which merit special consideration.

Attention may be given to daily movements, particularly in those species that do not perform large-scale movements; a typical example may be when species regularly commute between their breeding and feeding grounds, which can sometimes be a fair distance apart. In extreme cases, where very little is known about movements, or only very limited movements occur, even a bird's daily wanderings around its territory may be commented on, usually to illustrate the more limited mobility of such species, but equally to interpret the significance of these movements.

Relationship with Man

This section deals with the effects that the birds of the family in question have had on man, in a wide variety of ways. It thus contrasts with the following section, Status and Conservation, which in many cases is roughly equivalent to the influence that man has had on their populations, although its scope is actually somewhat broader and considers factors outwith man's control.

Relationship with Man typically mentions legends or popular traditions involving the birds. It can also include beliefs held about them and the part they play in the everyday life of some cultures. It frequently covers topics such as popular names for birds, for instance in seabirds, which often have popular names given to them by sailors, who were the only people that were familiar with many of them until relatively recently.

Another important aspect within the scope of this section is that of human exploitation of birds. In Relationship with Man, this is examined from the point of view of man, discussing, for example, how it has helped his economy, for instance with the commercialization of "muttonbirds", or of egret plumes or Ostrich eggs, and culminating in the case of the Peruvian "guano birds". The effects of such exploitation on the birds' populations is more appropriately described in Status and Conservation, but it is sometimes included here to prevent the whole story of a case of exploitation having to be repeated in both sections. One of the cases of human exploitation that does not appear to harm the birds is that of the collection of eider down.

Possible negative effects of some birds on human enterprises, for instance taking fish at fish farms may also appear in the present section, but there is a greater tendency for these to appear in Status and Conservation, as the offshoot is usually some persecution of the birds by the fishermen; in any case, research has often shown the effects to be exaggerated by the fishermen and on occasions to be quite untrue.

Another typical subject to be explained here is man's use of live birds, for instance his use of trained cormorants for fishing, or of frigatebirds as a form of homing pigeons. On a similar note, cases of domestication are dealt with in this section.

Status and Conservation

Within the structure of the book, this is considered to be one of the most important sections of all. First of all it runs through the overall status and trends of the family, and goes into some detail about the typical threats, which may well be virtually the same in most of the species in the family.

There is a comment on the species currently classified as threatened at a global level, and the text is often illustrated with a fairly full explanation of the decline of one or more threatened species, and an examination of what measures, if any, have been adopted to try to secure their survival, or at least to slow up declines. There is no attempt here to go into detail on the status and trends of all species, as this is dealt with in the species accounts, and in any case would be far too long in most families. Occasionally, for instance in the case of the Cattle Egret (*Bubulcus ibis*), the explanation is actually of a species expanding its range and increasing in numbers, but marked increases of this style are rather less common; in addition, more attention is generally paid to serious declines, for reasons which should be obvious.

The general factors responsible for the noted population trends are detailed and analysed. This typically means an evaluation of the relative importance of processes such as habitat destruction or degradation, which in a broad sense embraces a very wide range of processes, including forest destruction, water pollution, marine oil spills, salinization of freshwater lakes, drainage and so on. Other significant factors may be in the form of: direct human exploitation, particularly hunting and egg-collecting; competition with commercial fisheries, often related to the overfishing of stocks; competition with introduced fish; accidental mortality or injury as a result of human structures, including collisions with lighthouses, overhead power-lines, fishing gear or superstructure of ships, and drowning in gill-nets; mortality or injury caused by human rubbish, for instance the ingestion of lead originating from anglers' weights or hunters' pellets, or after the bird's neck becomes caught in the plastic can yokes. Human disturbance, especially in the region of breeding colonies, can also have very serious effects, and in recent years has often been related to leisure activities, such as water sports on what were previously remote, undisturbed lakes, or tourist visits to breeding colonies, disturbance caused by photographers, or even, in some cases, by birdwatchers. Then there are cases of mortality that are more indirectly linked with human activities, such as outbreaks of avian botulism that originate in an abundance of dead fish, which may have been killed by water pollution or changes in the water level.

On the positive side, some birds have benefited from the proliferation in many areas of artificial water bodies, although this tends to be at the expense of other habitat types, which are not always readily "expendable". Far more important are the positive actions directly destined towards the welfare of particular species; these may include the provision of artificial nest-sites, such as nestboxes, captive breeding programmes, active protection of nests or colonies, often by volunteers, the declaration of reserves and sanctuaries, legal protection, when effectively enforced, and so on.

General Bibliography

The family text, except in the aforementioned case of monospecific families, closes with a General Bibliography, normally including works which offer further information about the family in fairly general terms. Thus, throughout the book, the bibliographies that appear are not a list of the material used to compose the text, but rather that which is considered most relevant for further reading, although there is naturally a fair degree of overlap between the two.

Amongst the kinds of reference that regularly appear in the General Bibliography are monographs which treat each of the species in a family individually. The purpose of citing such works in this section is to avoid the repetition of the same reference in most or all of the species in the family, thus allowing room for more varied lists of references. However, in the individual Bibliography of little known species such monographs may also be cited, on the grounds that they are sometimes the only major source for a species.

Other kinds of reference that are typically included in this section are the proceedings of conventions and other technical publications dedicated mainly to a particular family or a group of families that are in some way related (not necessarily taxonomically), for instance seabirds or long-legged wading birds. These tend to be publications consisting of a series of articles by authors that are frequently not the same as the editors of the publication. In such cases, the whole publication is normally cited as a single unit and entered under the names of the editors, rather than each article being cited separately, quite simply to save space and allow more books or papers to be listed. In such cases, it should be understood that all (or most) of the articles are recommended for further reading. The only exception is when these more general works include an article of specific relevance to only one or a few of the species in the family; in this case, the article appears in the individual list of Bibliography at the end of the relevant species account.

Photographs

The general texts of the families are amply illustrated with photos, while at the start of each of the families that is internally divided into subfamilies or tribes or both, there is a diagramatic scheme designed to give a clear visual picture of the subdivisions, the internal structure of the family and the relationship between the different groups; beneath the representative figure for each group is the total number of species it contains and a list of all the genera it includes.

The photographs themselves have been selected primarily with the object of illustrating aspects of biology or ecology that are mentioned or explained in the text, for example showing methods of thermoregulation, feeding techniques or breeding behaviour. It is for this reason that straight portraits have been avoided as far as possible, even when they are of extremely high quality; they have been considered unnecessary, as all of the species already appear in the plates, where an attempt has been made to paint the birds in such a way as to show sufficient details of plumage and general morphology. The most obvious exceptions occur when dealing with photos of rare and little known species, and there are several cases of species that have probably never before had photographs published. In most of such cases, the species in question are threatened and dealt with in the section Status and Conservation, so that the photos serve to enrich one of the aspects of the work to which most attention has been paid.

In very special cases, where a photograph has great documentary value, it has been decided to include photos of considerably lower quality than the vast majority.

Within the structure of the family, the photos have been situated roughly in the order of the themes they have been selected to illustrate (following the order of sections used in the family texts). However, the restrictions of the lay-out do not permit the exact coincidence between all of the photos and the section they have been chosen to illustrate.

Plates

In the 50 bird plates, all of the species covered by this volume are illustrated. As explained above, the aim of HBW is not in any way to produce a field guide, so immature and non-breeding plumages are not illustrated. What the plates do show are all the major variations that occur between adults of the same species during the breeding season, in particular cases of noticeable sexual dimorphism, and the distinct morphs that are found in polymorphic species. Illustrations also appear of a considerable number of subspecies, especially those with major plumage differences, and also those that are sometimes considered full species, as this has been considered an important aid to a clear understanding of possible variations in the internal taxonomy of the family, one of the main aims of HBW. In contrast, it has not been considered of sufficient interest to clutter up the plate with illustrations of absolutely all the races, including many which have been described on the basis of scarcely appreciable differences, often in size or slight tones of coloration.

At least one bird has been painted for each of the living species covered by the volume. Plates follow the structure of HBW so that each plate deals only with one family.

All the birds appearing in a plate have been painted to the same scale, and this is indicated on each plate in centimetres and inches, to give a graphic idea of size. The scale need not be the same in different plates, even within the same family. In some cases it has been considered useful to add a second illustration for each species in order to emphasize important or distinctive aspects, such as the heads of albatrosses, or the aspect of gannets and boobies in flight, and in such cases, for obvious reasons, two different scales have been used on the same plate.

In order to facilitate reference between a plate and its accompanying species accounts, the distribution of species on the plate generally follows the systematic order of species adopted in HBW, although a certain degree of freedom has been permitted, so as not to cramp the illustrations or leave large gaps. Within these limitations, similar species tend to be positioned in such a way that direct comparison is easier.

Unless otherwise stated, the bird illustrated represents an adult male of the nominate race (where applicable) in breeding plumage. When there is a marked difference between breeding plumage and that of pre-breeding or courtship, the latter tends to be illustrated in cases where it constitutes differences in plumage, even though these plumage variations are only maintained for a very short time; a good example might be the white filoplumes on the head and neck of many cormorants. In cases in which courtship affects only the colours of the bare parts, the bird has been depicted in breeding plumage, as such colours tend to have a particularly brief duration, and can even vary considerably with the bird's mood, while they tend to give the bird a very different look, for instance in several species of the genus *Egretta*. Nevertheless, such changes are mentioned in the Descriptive notes of the relevant species accounts, in the part dealing with seasonal variation.

In a few exceptional cases, notably the tinamous, the female has been painted rather than the male, as in this family the roles are reversed and it is the former that has the more sightly plumage.

Where differences between the sexes or between different forms are marked, all the variations are shown, or at any rate the extremes. For example in the Little Pied Cormorant (*Phalacrocorax melanoleucos*) both pale and dark morphs are depicted, while the intermediate morph is merely mentioned in the Descriptive notes.

There is frequently a surprising amount of individual variation within the same species, even in monotypic species; the form depicted is that which has been considered to be the most representative. In cases of variation with sex or race where only the bird's head is shown, it should be interpreted that the rest of the bird is identical, or almost identical, to the bird that is depicted in full length.

Illustrations have been based on a wide selection of photographs of live wild birds, museum skins and captive birds. In the case of the tinamous, skins of all the species and many subspecies have been examined and used in painting the plates, as has been the case in other families with all rare species for which very few photos were available. In all cases full reference has been made to the descriptions in relevant literature.

Races and sibling species are depicted with a similar or even identical silhouette in order to make comparisons more useful. In general, a fairly standardized type of silhouette is used, although every effort is made to give the birds a "natural" look. In this sense, the aim has been to portray each bird with its characteristic jizz, which is often one of the main differences from other, similar species.

Species Accounts

Each species account opens with a heading covering the nomenclature of the species, starting with the vernacular name. Vernacular English names have been based on those selected, on the basis of extensive international correspondence, by B. L. Monroe, and published in Sibley & Monroe (1990); these have already been chosen to act as a basis for the standardization of English nomenclature planned for the 1994 International Ornithological Congress, and in future volumes the intention is to follow the official list adopted by the congress.

In general, there are very few departures from the aforementioned list, but some alternative versions have been preferred for a variety of reasons, in the most part to avoid what we consider possible cases of confusion. For instance, the use of American White Ibis for *Eudocimus albus* has been preferred to White Ibis on the grounds that, at any rate in Asia and Australia, the same name is applied to other species. Another case of possible confusion is the case of the name "Bald Ibis", which has been applied equally to *Geronticus eremita* and *G. calvus*; we have considered the most satisfactory solution to be the alternative names Northern Bald Ibis and Southern Bald Ibis. In the case of *Podiceps taczanowskii*, which is listed by Sibley and Monroe as "Puna Grebe", J. Fjeldså has pointed out that the species is found only on the periphery of the *puna*, and his alternative proposal, Junin Flightless Grebe, has been adopted here, as it has been considered more informative. Most other variations have been based on the same criteria, but in all such lists there is unavoidably a subjective element, and the list of names finally adopted in HBW is no exception.

The accepted English names of species are written without accents, hence Junin Flightless Grebe, Chiloe Wigeon, although the toponyms usually maintain the accent, e.g. Lake Junín. All species names of birds start with a capital letter, even in the plural, although in the text species of other life forms, such as fish, mammals or trees, do not start with a capital letter; this treatment is rather inconsistent, but it has been considered more practical, as this is essentially a book about birds.

Scientific names generally follow Mayr & Cottrell (1979), except in a few cases where names have since been emended, mostly as commented by Sibley & Monroe (1990). The International Commission on Zoological Nomenclature very kindly clarified the correct usage of the following: *Diomedea melanophris* as opposed to *D. melanophrys*; *Pelecanoides urinatrix* as opposed to *P. urinator*; *Cygnus melanocorypha* as opposed to *C. melanocoryphus*; *Anser canagicus* as opposed to *A. canagica*; and *Threskiornis molucca* as opposed to *T. moluccus*.

Names are also given for each species in French, German and Spanish. These three languages were selected as being considered the most widely spoken, after English, in ornithological circles, and because complete lists of names for virtually all of the world's species were available. The sources of these lists are:

— **Devillers, P.** (1976-1980). Projet de nomenclature française des oiseaux du monde. *Gerfaut* **66-70**. Modifications have been made by **Le Maréchal, P. & Dubois, P.J.** (LPO-France), **David, N.** (Canada) and **Géroudet, P.** (Switzerland).

— **Barthel, P.H.** (1992). Liste der Vögel der Erde. Pp. 366-412 in: *Die große Enzyklopädie der Vögel*. Mosaik, Munich.

— **Bernis, F., Ferrer, X., Fernández Cruz, M., del Hoyo, J., de Juana, E., Saez-Royuela, R. & Sargatal, J.** (1992). Lista de aves del mundo en lengua castellana recomendada por la SEO.

"Other common names" is not by any means a comprehensive list of alternative names, as this would be endless; one of its aims is to clarify possible confusion due to the use of similar or identical names for different species. Names that are considered to be "popular" are generally avoided, e.g. "Farmer's Friend" is not listed for the Straw-necked Ibis, although the name "Shoemaker", clearly of popular origin, is very much an accepted alternative name for the White-chinned Petrel, and so is listed. Names that are very similar to a listed one are also omitted, e.g. Ascension Island Frigatebird for Ascension Frigatebird.

In an attempt to include all the relevant names, some form of compression has been necessary. A slash mark means that the names on either side can be applied to the rest of the name, e.g. Dove Prion/Petrel, which means Dove Prion or Dove Petrel. Similarly, Streaked/Azara's/Pygmy Bittern, Little Red/Variegated Heron means that the other common names of the species are Streaked Bittern, Azara's Bittern, Pygmy Bittern, Little Red Heron and Variegated Heron. Where the name refers only to one race, it is separated by names of other races or of the species in general by a semi-colon, with the subspecific name in brackets; if it is the specific name that appears, this name refers to the nominate subspecies, and not the species as a whole, which would have no scientific name affixed. When the "other common name" is one that is applied to another species, the name is followed by a bracketed exclamation mark, to indicate the possibilty of confusion, e.g. Brushland Tinamou is the accepted name for *Nothoprocta cinerascens*, so under *Crypturellus cinereus* it is listed as Brushland Tinamou (!).

The section **Taxonomy** starts with the exact name (in italics) given to the species in the original description. This is followed by the author of the description (with or without initials, as listed), the year of the description, and the type locality; the reference of the original article of description can be found by turning to the section References of Scientific Descriptions.

Taxonomic problems or controversies are the main matter for discussion here. Although the superspecies is not a primary taxon, superspecific groups, especially those accepted by the main source authorities, are normally noted in this section. Subgenera have not generally been considered, as being a rather dubious category; only one case is mentioned, that of the "subgenus *Cookilaria*" within the genus *Pterodroma*, as it is frequently considered a useful aid to clarifying a rather difficult group. Note that the terms "race" and "subspecies" are used indiscriminately.

In polytypic species, in the section **Subspecies and Distribution**, the author of each subspecies is listed, along with the year, and once again the reference to the original article is listed at the end of the book, in References of Scientific Descriptions. Note that the author and year are placed in brackets in cases where the original description placed the taxon in a different genus, but not otherwise.

The section (Subspecies and) Distribution always includes breeding distribution. With many species, for instance in the Procellariiformes, a good deal of space would be required for sufficient explanation, and as there is a map included in the species account, it has not been deemed necessary to go into great detail. An attempt has been made to include the non-breeding range, where possible, although this has sometimes been difficult, especially in cases involving different races where the wintering range can not easily be separated, so the explanation is given in greater detail in the section Movements. Where the species has an introduced population, this is mentioned at the end of the section. Where a race has probably become extinct, this is indicated, but if the extinction is considered definite, the race is not listed, and is instead discussed in Taxonomy.

Throughout the species accounts the following abbreviations are used: N (North), S (South), E (East), W (West), C (Central), I/Is (Island or Islands), L/Ls (Lake or Lakes), and Mt/Mts (Mount/Mountain or Mountains). Nevertheless, these words are sometimes written in full, where abbreviations might leave room for confusion, or to avoid certain monstrosities. Thus, S South America is preferred to the rather ugly and confusing S S America; even worse, the distribution of *Eudyptula minor variabilis* might end up as the quite incomprehensible S N I S to N S I (from the southern part of North Island southwards to the northern part of South Island). When forming part of the name of a country, island, etc., the name is written in full, e.g. South Georgia, as opposed to S Georgia; this system helps to avoid confusion between South Africa, the country, and the southern part of the African continent, which appears as S Africa. Note that NC India is not the same as CN India; the former refers to the northern part of central India, for instance around Madhya Pradesh, while the latter is the central part of northern India, for example in the region of Uttar Pradesh.

Place names follow the Times Atlas of the World, although no attempt has been made to catch up with the latest political developments, so USSR is maintained rather than CIS. Accents have generally been respected, wherever possible, except in well known names, like Galapagos or Reunion, where it seems pedantic to use them, as these names really have accepted English versions. However, the decision as to which should be treated in this way is largely subjective; if the versions Galápagos and Réunion are to be adopted, then so should Perú.

Descriptive notes have largely been prepared by the artists. Once again it should be pointed out that HBW is not designed as an identification guide. The main aim of the Descriptive notes is to complement what is shown in the plates. The basic unit can be considered a male of the nominate race in breeding plumage, in relation to which all variations are detailed.

Measurements given attempt to give a minimum and maximum within the variability of normal adults of both sexes; when this is qualified, for instance, by the note "female smaller", this should be understood as "smaller within the given range". In cases where the difference in measurements between the sexes is sufficiently significant, the two are given separately. Subjects dealt with include the following: distinctive characteristics of the species, especially when they are not prominent or do not appear in the plate; the scope of individual variation with respect to the illustrated bird; colour morphs, especially when not illustrated; sexual dimorphism, especially if only one sex is illustrated and the differences are not obvious; differences in comparison with similar species; seasonal variations, including changes in bare part colours, for instance during courtship; significant variations due to feather wear, etc.; a brief summary of immature plumage, or in certain cases, a series of immature plumages, for instance in some albatrosses or frigatebirds; basis on which subspecies are differentiated, with reference to the nominate.

In the following four sections, **Habitat**, **Food and Feeding**, **Breeding** and **Movements**, relevant information is given in a very concise form. Uniformity has been attempted primarily within the same family, then within the same order or "group", and finally overall, but a degree of freedom in treatment is clearly desirable, as some aspects are of special interest in certain families. For instance, egg size in the Struthioniformes, moult in penguins, incubation stints in the Procellariiformes, and post-fledging care in some Pelecaniformes are of particular interest, and so are included in the respective groups. In little known families there is a tendency to permit some details that are not included elsewhere, for example in the tinamous egg colour is mentioned, to show at least to some extent what is known.

The punctuation of species accounts is rather variable, but, again, a degree of consistency is aimed at, especially within the same family or group. Phrases and clauses are often separated by a semi-colon to indicate the continuation of a theme, in order to avoid the repetition, for example, of "in Japan" with each part. For the same reason, within its own account, each particular species is referred to "species" or "present species". Other bird species that appear in an account are mentioned using the scientific name only, or the scientific and common names, if they belong to another family.

The section on Breeding normally deals with a fairly regular series of topics, obviously depending on the amount of information available. The following subjects are treated: season; strategy (where appropriate); colonial/solitary habits; nest-site; nest; number of eggs; incubation period; colour of chicks' down; fledging period; age of sexual maturity; longevity; and, in many cases, breeding success. Sexual maturity is taken to mean the age of first breeding, although in some cases, birds are, in fact, sexually in condition long before they breed. Limits are sometimes given, particularly for the number of eggs: "4-5 eggs (2-8)" means that the normal size of a completed clutch is four or five eggs, the minimum two, and the maximum eight. A general statement is given on the down colour of chicks, referring mainly to the upperparts, unless otherwise specified. Fledging refers to the completed growth of the first full coat of feathers; it is difficult to measure, and so in most birds it is most often taken as the first moment in which the bird flies. Comments on whether chicks are nidifugous or nidicolous, precocial or altricial, are usually explained in some detail in the family text, but not in the species account, as these aspects tend to be the same for all members of the family.

As has already been indicated, **Status and Conservation** is one of the chief themes of HBW, so considerable efforts have also been made to produce informative and up to date sections in the species accounts. The section always opens with the status of the species on a worldwide scale. In the case of threatened species, the official category is given in red, in capital letters. Categories are those listed in the 1990 IUCN Red List of Threatened Animals, updated as indicated by N. J. Collar, chief author of the latest edition of the ICBP/IUCN Red Data Book, who has revised all the Status and Conservation sections of the species accounts. The categories are as follows:

ENDANGERED — taxa in danger of extinction and whose survival is unlikely if the causal factors continue operating.

VULNERABLE — taxa believed likely to move into the Endangered category in the near future if the causal factors continue operating.

RARE — taxa with small world populations that are not at present Endangered or Vulnerable, but are at risk.

INDETERMINATE — taxa *known* to be Endangered, Vulnerable or Rare but where there is not enough information to say which of the three categories is appropriate.

INSUFFICIENTLY KNOWN — taxa that are *suspected* but not definitely known to belong to any of the above categories, because of lack of information. Some of these taxa are currently under review by ICBP and will be designated a category in the near future.

All the remaining species are classed in HBW as "Not globally threatened". Some of these are additionally signalled as "near-threatened", according to the list in Appendix 2 of Collar & Andrew (1988).

Wherever possible, overall population figures are given, normally followed by a selection of details such as estimates or counts for different parts of the species' range, paying special attention to important populations. Significant trends are noted and possible threats detailed, as well as references, where appropriate, to factors responsible for any declines or increases. An attempt has been made to deal with subspecies that may be threatened, even if the species as a whole is considered to be secure.

Maps

Without exception, each species account is accompanied by a distribution map. The main function of the map is to give a rough idea of the range of the species, as the size and scale of the map do not allow extreme precision; in an attempt to improve the level of detail given, the range of the background map is reduced to cover only the necessary area. The information imparted by the map should always be taken in conjunction with the section on Distribution, which often gives details of countries or geographical features that may help to clarify the exact distribution of the species within the shaded areas. In principle, the maps show the natural distribution of the species, omitting populations that are the result of introduction in other zones, even though these populations may be well established; a very few exceptions are permitted for species that have large, long-standing, fully consolidated populations that are well integrated into the avifauna of the respective areas, notably the Canada Goose (*Branta canadensis*) and the Black Swan (*Cygnus atratus*).

Three colours are used in the maps, yellow, blue and finally green, which is the sum of the other two. Yellow is used to indicate zones habitually occupied for breeding, but where the species is not normally present outside the breeding season; blue indicates zones occupied by the species, where it does not normally breed, or where breeding is suspected but has not definitely been recorded; thus, these colours should not be interpreted as summer and winter distributions, a regular practice in many bird guides, especially in temperate zones. In its turn, green is used to indicate areas where the species tends to be present all year round, although this does not preclude the possibility of erratic or dispersive movements, or even partial migration. On the maps of a few species, the only area shaded is blue; this means that in these species, usually seabirds, the general zone occupied is known, but the breeding grounds have not yet been located.

A great deal of effort has been made to base the maps on the most up to date information available, so the indiscriminate shading of large, continuous areas has been avoided in cases where this could apply to the original range of the species, but would give an unrealistically optimistic view of the present distribution. This is particularly true in the case of species that have undergone marked declines in recent decades; when sufficient information has been available, shading has been limited to those zones where the species has been recorded in recent years, even omitting those areas where the presence of the species is strongly suspected, although such cases are normally mentioned in the section on Distribution; similarly, blue has been used to signal areas where the species is known to occur, but where breeding has not been recorded, even if it is strongly suspected. In this respect, it has been decided not to follow the standard use of question marks on maps, as, except in a few very well known species, most of the world maps would be so cluttered up with question marks that the sign would lose much of the value it offers in works covering a more limited geographical area. In summary, we have tried to offer an approximation as close as possible to the present distribution of the species, based on the information available, although it is very possible that forthcoming research, especially in little known or totally unexplored areas, may indicate the necessity of adding to, or in some cases reducing, the areas indicated on the maps.

In some cases arrows are used to signal details of the distribution, particularly in the cases of some small islands, or in order to prevent small areas isolated from the main range from passing unnoticed. In the few cases of maps referring to species that are almost certainly extinct, but according to the criteria followed by CITES can not yet be officially designated as such, although a remote possibility of their rediscovery may remain, the last zones in which they were recorded are shaded grey, as their continued presence in these areas is most unlikely, and the vague chances of their survival seem marginally more possible in other, unstudied zones.

Bibliography

Each species account closes with a list of Bibliography, which aims to include all the most important literature about the species, be it in the form of articles, books or monographs, including doctoral theses and other academic works, or specific sections within regional handbooks, along with a series of less exhaustive publications which complement the information offered by the main references.

One of the main aims of the Bibliography is to offer the reader an idea of how much information is currently available on each species with an overview of the level of general knowledge, for which reason some references have been included without their having been revised personally by the authors. The Bibliography should not be considered a list of the material used in the elaboration of the species account, although almost all of the material which has ultimately contributed to the text is likely to be listed. In this way it is hoped that a certain amount of compensation is offered to the authors of source information for the absence of citations within the text itself, a sacrifice that was considered necessary for the sake of the palatability of the text. We are aware that this may be inconvenient for readers wishing to track down the source of a particular item of information, but have considered that the system adopted offered greater benefits for a wider proportion of readers.

In general, monographs or proceedings of congresses that deal with the entire family or order are not included in the Bibliography of the species account, as these references are included in the General Bibliography of the family, to avoid their repetition for most or all of the species. Thus, a reader wishing to consult all the information recommended for a certain species should refer not only to the Bibliography of the species account, but also to the General Bibliography of the family text, which in most cases contains works dealing with the species in question.

The preparation of the bibliographical lists has involved consideration of the 1500 or so books and the much larger number of articles consulted during the composition of the texts, as well as the references listed in the aforementioned literature. In addition, the Zoological Records and Wildlife Reviews covering the vast majority of publications over the last 12 years have been systematically checked through, while in some cases of little known species the search was continued right back into the 1930's. In some cases fairly exhaustive bibliographies have been published in recent years, and these too were consulted at great length.

Once the initial lists had been put together, it became necessary to make some sort of selection based on criteria aimed at achieving the highest possible degree of consistency, as in several species an exhaustive bibliography would have occupied several complete pages of the book. Nevertheless, these criteria have varied considerably, depending on the amount of information available for each species. Although there are intermediate cases, most species have tended to fall into one or other of the two opposite extremes: species that have been extensively, or even exhaustively, studied, resulting in hundreds of publications, as well, almost always, as inclusion in one or more of the major handbooks dealing with the regions which have traditionally been subject to the most intensive ornithological investigation; and, on the other hand, those species about which little if any research has ever been carried out, so that most, in some cases all, of the meagre information available can be found in general works, such as field guides, compendia and local check-lists.

In the case of the better known species, priority has been given to the inclusion of the most important original work, describing diverse aspects of the biology or ecology of the species, even, on occasions, when the publications are relatively old; similarly, priority has been given to the detailed accounts in regional handbooks, which are often, at least in part, the result of extensive revisions of all previous literature about the species. With respect to the less exhaustive works, recent work has been given preference, especially because such publications often refer, both in the text and in the listed references, to previous works of possible interest; again, publications on aspects that are dealt with in less detail by the major references are readily included. During the process of making the selection, an attempt has also been made to choose references dealing with a broad spectrum of themes, so that all of the aspects that are considered within the scope of HBW are covered as amply as possible. A similar attempt has been made to give a broad geographical selection, so that widely distributed species are represented, as far as is reasonably possible, by articles covering diverse localities. This explains the inclusion of some references that provide fairly limited information about a species in a zone where it is very poorly known, while a more extensive study may be omitted, on the grounds that it comes from an area in which the species is well known, and the information it offers is superceded by one of the major works already listed. In general, works dealing with regions in which the species is only accidental are not listed, except where this has some special relevance.

In species about which very little is known, the criteria followed in selecting bibliography have been far less restrictive, and in the most extreme cases, when there is hardly any other possible reference for consideration, field guides and local check-lists have been included, on the grounds that the information they give, usually included in and/or surpassed by the species text of the present work, refers to a particular area or even locality. In such cases, the Bibliography of a particular species may include references that can sensibly be listed for a species about which very little is known, but not for a well known species; there is no reason to suppose that a particular work need be cited systematically for all the species it deals with.

References are ordered alphabetically in the standard way, using the surname of the first author. In the lists General Bibliography of the family text and Bibliography of the species, in all articles written by two authors both names appear in the list. When there are more than two authors, only the name of the first appears, followed by the abbreviation *et al*. In these lists, only the surnames of the authors appear, although the initials are added after the appropriate surname, when this is necessary in order to be able to locate the reference with absolute certainty in the General List of References at the end of the book. Equally, to avoid confusion when looking up the full reference, in cases of more than one publication by the same author or group of authors in the same year, a letter is added at the end of the year. Again, in cases of articles written by more than two authors, it has been necessary on occasions to cite two or more of the surnames, with the same end of eliminating any possibility of duplication. In this way, the list has been prepared so that any one reference in the General Bibliography or the Bibliography can only lead to a single entry in the General List (of References).

Thus, apart from the aforementioned exceptions, the General Bibliography and the Bibliography are formed of references by one author only, by two authors, and by three or more authors, which normally appear as a name *et al*. When references of the same first author coincide, the first to be listed are those he or she has written alone; next come all those written with one other author, and finally those written with more than one other author, even though any or all of these may have a second author, whose name comes before that of the second author of one of the articles by two authors.

References

At the end of the volume is a section of References, which is divided into two parts. The first, titled References of Scientific Descriptions, contains the bibliographical details of the original descriptions of every genus, species and subspecies accepted in HBW. Their separation from the rest of the references has been determined by two factors. On the one hand, their grouping together will facilitate consultation by those readers interested in such works, without their having to wade through the far more extensive General List. On the other hand, it has been considered appropriate to treat these references in a different way from the rest: the only details listed are the surname (and, when required, initials), the year and the bibliographical reference of the publication in which the work appeared; the full title of articles does not appear, as this would take up extra space and the completion of the titles would require a considerable effort, while the extra information offered by the title would be of very limited use, as the general content of all the articles and the reason for their citation is obvious; articles of description that have been considered of sufficient interest in their own right, especially some of the more recent ones, are listed independently in the Bibliography of the species.

In the General List of References, however, it has been considered worthwhile, contrary to the practice of many major works on ornithology, to dedicate the effort and space necessary in order to be able to give the full title of each reference. The title normally makes the reference much more useful, as it tends to give a general idea of the real content of the article, typically indicating what aspect or aspects of the biology or ecology of the species or group of species is dealt with, where a study has been carried out, what other species are dealt with, and so on.

So that the order of the General List (of References) coincides totally with that of the General Bibliography of each family or the Bibliography of each species, the internal organization of the General List has been arranged in such a way that all the works headed by a particular author are classified in the following order: all articles by the author alone, in chronological order; all articles in conjunction with one other author (both names invariably appearing on all lists); and finally all those involving more than one other author (normally appearing in lists as the first author *et al.*). In the General List, the complete list of authors appears for each work, independent of their number.

In the presentation of the full references in the General List, it has been attempted to follow norms that unify their content, as detailed below. A large proportion of the references have been directly consulted by the editors, contributors or bibliographical researchers, who have participated in the project, so there has been no problem in verifying the correct citation of most of these. However, many other references have been gathered second hand from other lists and bibliographies, which have not always offered all the details required herein; in a few cases, in spite of the efforts made, it has been impossible to complete all of the details.

Each article is given in its original language when this uses the Roman alphabet. In cases using other alphabets, the title is given in English inside square brackets, followed by an indication of the language of the original and also a comment if there is a summary in other languages. It should be noted that the treatment of less common languages is an aspect in which many exceptions occur, as source bibliographies may simply give the reference translated into English, sometimes with no mention at all of the original language. In a few cases in which it has been deemed appropriate, the title of an article in its original language is followed by the title of the English summary in square brackets.

In formal aspects, such as the actual spelling and use of capitals in the original, we have respected the original version wherever possible.

The abbreviations used for periodical publications generally follow the versions used in other literature, although in cases of conflict preference has been given to the usage recommended by the publication itself.

Titles of books, monographs, theses and similar works appear in italics, to indicate that in general such works tend to be fairly extensive; italics are not used in brief reports, even if they are published separately. In contrast, the titles of extensive monographic works, even though published within a periodical publication, tend to appear in italics too.

When an article appears within congress proceedings, technical publications and other collective works which are themselves cited in the same General List, the reference includes only the page numbers and the name of the editor or editors of the publication, along with the year of publication. In such cases, the full reference can be reconstructed by looking up the latter reference; this system has been adopted to save extensive repetition of the full reference in all of the partial references.

Index

This indicates the page numbers for all orders, families, genera, species and sub-species treated in the volume. For orders, only the number of the order page is given; the family is signalled for the first page of the family text, and also the first page of the species accounts. The page number given for genera is the first in which a species of the genus in question occurs, although the species accounts often continue onto other pages; obsolete genera, synonyms or alternative names mentioned in the sections on Taxonomy are also included in the index. A species can be found in the index under the scientific and English names used in this work, all the synonyms appearing in its Taxonomy and all the alternative vernacular names listed in the section Other common names. Thus, the Great White Egret (*Egretta alba*) can be located by looking up any of the following entries: *alba*; *albus*; *Ardea*; *Casmerodius*; *Egretta*; *egretta* (race); *melanorhynchos* (race); *modesta* (race); Great American Egret; Great Egret; Great White Egret; Great White Heron; Large Egret. Species and subspecies that are definitely extinct, and therefore have no species account, are also indexed, in this case normally indicating the page in the family text that deals with the case in question. All the subspecies considered in the text appear in the index, even those that have not been accepted in the present work, but are commented on in the relevant Taxonomy section.

Acknowledgements

We are particularly grateful to Dolors Buxó, who undertook the mammoth task of processing and computerizing a large quantity of sources of ornithological information, a task that kept her occupied over a period of several years, and which was absolutely essential to the project eventually getting under way.

For the inspection of museum specimens we would like to thank the Smithsonian Institution in Washington, especially Gary R. Graves and J. Phillip Angle, and the American Museum of Natural History in New York, in particular Mary LeCroy. Equally helpful were the Museu de Zoologia of Barcelona (J. Piqué, J. C. Senar and M. J. del Valle), the Museo de Ciencias Naturales de Madrid (P. Barreiro), the British Museum of Natural History in Tring (M. P. Walters and G. Cowles) and the Muséum National d'Histoire Naturelle in Paris (C. Voisin).

In order to build up the abundant collection of material for consultation, many libraries have been visited. Of outstanding help have been those of the Museu de Zoologia of Barcelona (Margarida Cortadella), the Facultat de Ciències Biològiques of the University of Barcelona, the Sociedad Española de Ornitología in Madrid (Fernando Barrio), the Station Biologique de la Tour du Valat in the Camargue (L. Hoffman, J. P. Taris and J. Crivelli) and the Edward Grey Institute of Field Ornithology in Oxford (M. G. Wilson and E. Dunn).

For clearing up certain doubts and offering unpublished information, we have been particularly fortunate to count on the co-operation of W. Bokerman, M. C. Coulter, G. D. Field, J. Fjeldså, J. C. Guix, A. M. Paterson, A. R. Rahmani, G. Schleussner (Vogelpark Walsrode), and of P. K. Tubbs of the International Commission on Zoological Nomenclature. For the definitive list of French and German names, we thank P. Le Maréchal and P. Barthel respectively.

In the cases of certain very poorly documented species, we recognize the valuable contribution made by several people who kindly sent photos of live individuals, especially D. Williamson and X. Eichacker of the National Wildlife Research Center of Saudi Arabia, M. Marin of the Western Foundation of Vertebrate Zoology, D. G. Allen, M. Delano, M. P. Harris, J. B. Nelson and C. R. Schmidt.

In the preparation of the plates the team of artists have counted with the support of Antoni Brossa and Núria Ferrer, while in the elaboration of the maps the assistance of Bernat Garrigós, Rosa Llinàs, Mònica Martinoy, Gabriel Pujades, Deli Saavedra and also of Oriol Muntané, Jorge Puig and Francesc Farriols, has been most opportune.

On the administrative side, particularly in the promotion of the book, we are very grateful to Mike Parr and Eva Eckenrode, and to other members of the ICBP staff who have collaborated with great enthusiasm; equally the support from an early stage of Rob Hume, at RSPB, and Bernard Mercer has been extremely encouraging.

During the preparation of Volume 1, many other people have made important contributions in very different ways, from gathering information in the course of their travels to critical revision of the text and design of the work. We offer our sincere thanks to Maria Josep de Andrés, Ventura Boluda, Osvaldo Borcassa, Juan Antonio Cantí, Josep Maria Clausell, Alan Elliott, Sònia Frias, Maria del Mar Gispert, Francesc Kirchner, Toni Llobet, Susan Martin, Ralph Massanés, Gavin Melluish, Sílvia Muray, Maria Teresa Obiols, Xavier Portas, Mireia Riba and Montserrat Roldán.

Finally, a great many ornithologists and researchers have taken the trouble to send offprints of their work; they are too many to list here, but we would like to take this opportunity to thank all of them most kindly for their contributions.

Class AVES (BIRDS)

Class AVES (BIRDS)

There are many reasons for considering birds an evolutionary peak. They constitute a relatively recent branch of the vertebrates, characterized by their extreme adaptation to aerial life, with the power of flight. Due to this, and to the fact that they are warm-blooded animals, with considerable cerebral development, they are able to carry out a very active life in broad daylight, colonizing all kinds of environments, and occupying a great diversity of ecological niches. Of all the terrestrial vertebrates, birds are the class with the largest number of species, around 9000, approximately twice as many as mammals, and it has been estimated that the total number of individuals could be as many as 300,000 million.

From the poles to the equatorial forests, from the deserts to the centres of the oceans, from the highest mountains to the hearts of our cities, everywhere birds are amongst the most conspicuous forms of animal life, and to many they are the most spectacular and attractive. What probably fascinates us about birds is that they are warm-blooded, they have soft feathers, often with eye-catching colours, they have the enviable ability to fly, and also that many of their behavioural features, such as song, nests and migration are interesting and easily witnessed. In many different cultures since ancient times, they have frequently appeared in traditions, legends, religion, literature, music, painting and sport. They are domesticated and hunted, and make interesting pets, while in recent times the simple observation of birds in the countryside has become an extremely popular pastime in much of the world. This last factor has undoubtedly made a significant contribution to scientific knowledge.

Since the time of Aristotle, the study of birds has been singularly popular within the zoological sciences, and many important advances in evolutionary theory have been made by ornithologists (Ernst Mayr), ethologists (Oskar Heinroth, Konrad Lorenz and Niko Tinbergen), and ecologists (David Lack). In recent years, birds have played a special role as sensitive indicators of pesticide pollution and other environmental changes caused by man, so that ornithology, or simply birdwatching, has become an important factor in attempts to conserve nature.

General Characteristics

Birds constitute the zoological class Aves, in the phylum Chordata and the subphylum Vertebrata. Like the mammals and the reptiles, they are tetrapods and Amniota, and they have much in common with the reptiles, their evolutionary ancestors, so much so that some authors even feel justified in using a single class Sauropsida for both birds and reptiles.

Birds have some typically reptilian features, which are quite different from those found in the mammals, such as only one occipital condyle, and a lower jaw or mandible composed of several bones, whereas mammals have only one, the dentary. They also have a mandibular joint between the articular and quadrate bones, a single bone in the middle ear (the columella or stapes), a scleral ring in the eye, nucleated red blood cells and a kind of cleidoic egg, which is practically the same as in reptiles. Even last century Thomas Huxley stated that birds were merely "glorified reptiles".

The basic distinction between the two groups lies in an extremely obvious external characteristic, the presence of feathers in birds. This is an exclusive feature found in all species, and it has been ever since *Archaeopteryx*, the earliest representative of the birds so far discovered. In fact, it is the imprints of feathers in the fossil remains, extraordinarily well preserved by the fine grain Bavarian limestone, that allow us to place *Archaeopteryx* amongst the birds and not the reptiles (Archosauria), which in other respects it resembles very closely.

Apart from being a good diagnostic feature, feathers, which were originally modified reptilian scales, are such an extraordinary evolutionary advance that alone they explain much of the adaptive success of birds. In the first place, feathers allow more effective flight than the patagia of other vertebrates, such as bats (Chiroptera) or pterosaurs. Feathered wings are much more resistant to physical damage, as they are more easily repaired, and do not require long, fragile bones. Moreover, due to the feathers, birds' wings do not need to rest on the hind limbs, as in the case of patagia, which means that these limbs have been free to evolve in order to improve movement on land or in water, the capture of prey, the manipulation of objects and preening. Another difficulty with patagia is their large surface area, which leads to important heat loss due to radiation. This factor seriously limits bats as regards their geographical distribution and maintenance of year round activity.

Not only do feathers not lose heat, they are actually very effective in helping to conserve body heat, providing even better insulation than mammalian hair. This allows birds to maintain high and remarkably constant internal temperatures (homoiothermia), which in turn permit high levels of activity, even in environments with major climatic variations, whether these be daily or seasonal. Feathers, therefore, with their double function of enabling flight and helping to conserve heat, provide a unique evolutionary key, which explains the fundamental differences between the birds and their ancestors, the reptiles.

In many other aspects the evolution of birds has been influenced by flight and homoiothermia. Flight imposes singularly important structural modifications on the general model, and at the same time places clear limitations on possible

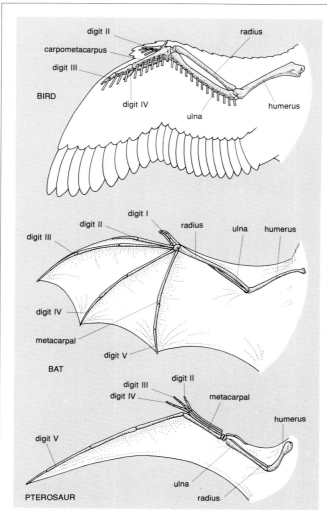

digit II
carpometacarpus
digit III
BIRD
digit IV
ulna
radius
humerus

digit I
digit II
digit III
radius
ulna
humerus
digit IV
metacarpal
digit V
BAT

digit II
digit III
digit IV
metacarpal
digit V
humerus
ulna
radius
PTEROSAUR

Comparison of the wings of a bird, a bat and a pterosaur.

[Figure: Xavier Ruiz]

Integument

Bird skin is comparatively thin and very flexible. The most conspicuous parts of the animal, especially the feathers, but also the horny coverings of the bill and of the hind limbs, the scales and claws, are all keratinized products of the epidermis.

Feathers are not only an outstandingly distinctive feature of the birds, in good measure explaining their evolutionary success; they also constitute the most complicated integumentary structure among the vertebrates, although their origin lies in the simple scales of the reptiles. They have many different functions. In addition to insulating the bird from water, cold temperatures and other external elements, they make flight possible and have colours, which are used in some cases as camouflage against predators, and in others as a means of visual communication. In spite of the proverbial lightness of feathers the total plumage normally weighs approximately two to three times more than the skeleton, and about 5-7% of the total body weight.

There are two basic types of feathers with somewhat different structures, the vaned feathers and the plumules, or down feathers. The vaned feathers are the most conspicuous, covering the exterior of the body and giving it its characteristic aerodynamic form. The down is situated underneath, forming an insulating layer. The vaned feathers have a central shaft with a broad, flat web on either side, forming the vane or vexillum. The shaft is divided into two parts, the calamus and the rachis. The calamus, the lower portion, is hollow, with an opening at either end, the upper umbilicus and the lower umbilicus. The rachis is solid and supports the vexillum, which is formed by parallel branches growing out from either side, the barbs, which in turn have two series of barbules. Normally, the barbules of the distal side of the barb have hooklets, called barbicels or hamuli, and those of the proximal side have a saw-toothed underside; the successive barbs of a feather hook up with one another constructing the flat, firm surface of the vanes.

In the contour feathers, on the underside of the rachis and level with the upper umbilicus, there is usually an auxiliary structure called the aftershaft or afterfeather (hypoptilum), which emerges with a rachis (hyporachis) and a series of barbs without barbicels. These do not connect with each other, and result in a loose, woolly appearance. The aftershaft is sometimes missing (Ostrich, pigeons, swallows), but in contrast in the Emu and the cassowaries it attains the same length and appearance as the main part of the feather. Its main function is to contribute to insulation, and in grouse of the genus *Lagopus*, it grows much longer in winter than in summer plumage.

Vaned feathers include the flight-feathers or remiges, which are attached to the rear portion of the wing bones, the tail feathers or rectrices, and the remaining contour feathers, which are distributed over the whole body. The remiges and rectrices are longer and stiffer, lack an aftershaft, and generally have an asymmetrical vexillum with the external vanes, those which cut through the air in flight, narrower than the internal ones. The rest of the contour feathers are more or less symmetrical, usually with a developed aftershaft and a portion of down (of barbs without hooklets) at the base of the rachis, normally hidden beneath other contour feathers, and this serves in thermal insulation.

The remiges have different names depending on their position on the wing, into which the long calami are deeply inserted. The primaries are connected to the hand bones, the secondaries to the ulna, and the "tertials", which seldom exist in the strict sense, to the humerus. The primaries are usually 11 in number, although the outermost one, the remicle, is either rudimentary or missing. However, there are exceptions, and while the Ostrich has 16 primaries, grebes, storks and flamingos have 12, and some modern passerines only nine. The number of secondaries depends amongst other things on wing length, and varies from only six in hummingbirds to no less than 32 in some species of albatross. On the leading edge of the wing, level with the first digit, there is a small group of 2-7 feathers, which constitute the alula, or bastard wing. In the tail, with few exceptions, there are usually twelve rectrices, six on either side.

divergence. This results in a marked uniformity within the class Aves, although certain birds, like the penguins and the Ostrich, have subsequently become flightless.

The skeleton, in particular, has undergone an important series of transformations, above all in the forelimbs, the wings, in the pectoral girdle, and in the sternum. These last two have been greatly developed in order to provide anchorage for the large mass of muscle that is required for flight. Similarly, the hindlimbs, the legs, have been modified, although to a lesser degree, for various modes of bipedal locomotion. Changes have also taken place in the vertebral column, which in comparison with that of reptiles is long and very flexible in the cervical region, and short and rigid in the thoracic, lumbar and caudal regions. In general, the skeleton forms an admirable combination of strength and lightness, by fusing some parts, eliminating others and making all as light as possible. In accordance with this, the skull has become particularly simple. The mandibles have been shortened, and the teeth suppressed, to form a hollow, toothless bill covered by a light, horny sheath.

Other important improvements that are required in order to sustain the intense activity of birds, particularly flight, have occurred in the respiratory apparatus. This consists of small, but very efficient lungs, which are elongated throughout the body to form the air-sacs. In the circulatory system, the heart is completely partitioned off, and a single aortic arch allows pulmonary circulation to be totally independent of the body's, as in the mammals, without mixing arterial and venous blood. The very high levels of activity in birds affect the brain and sensory organs, which have undergone exceptional development, particularly in those areas related to visual perception and hearing, co-ordination of movement and instinctive behaviour. Finally, birds also differ from reptiles in the important advances they have made in reproduction, with highly developed behaviour related to territoriality, nest building and care of the young.

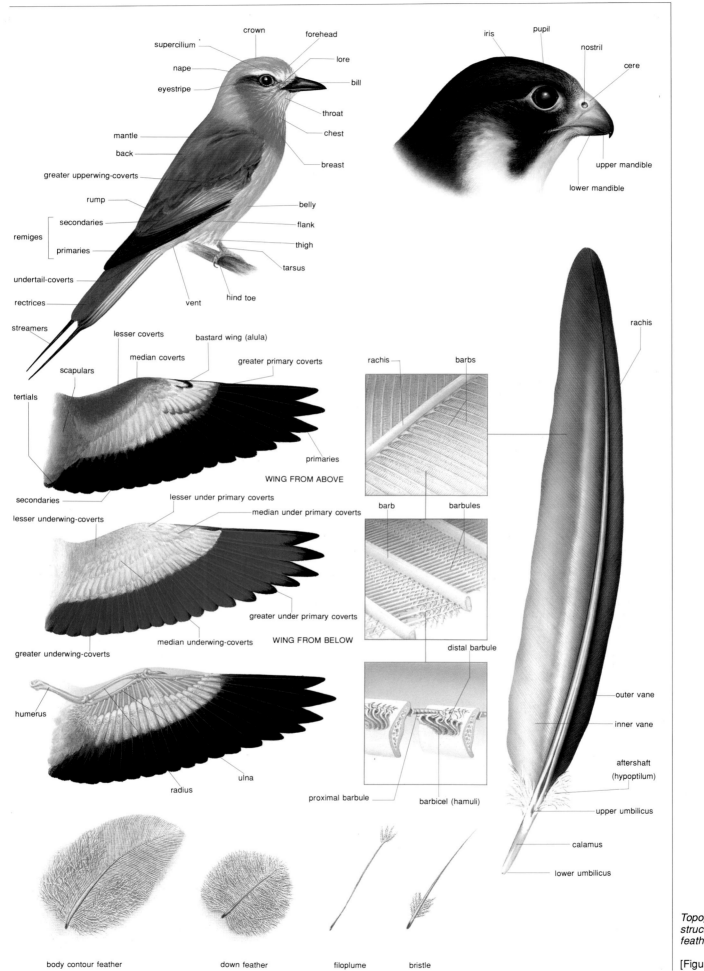

WING FROM ABOVE

WING FROM BELOW

body contour feather   down feather   filoplume   bristle

Topography of a bird: structure and types of feather.

[Figure: Lluís Centelles]

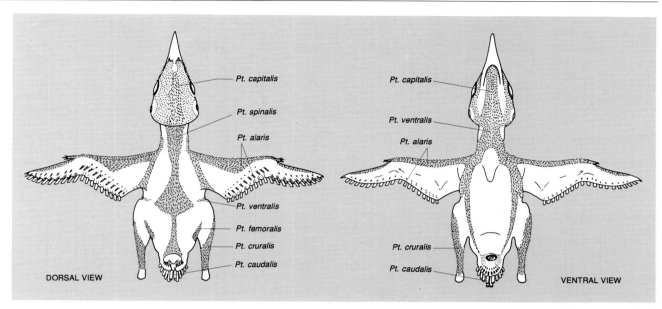

Dorsal and ventral views of the major pterylae.

[Figure: Xavier Ruiz]

DORSAL VIEW — Pt. capitalis, Pt. spinalis, Pt. alaris, Pt. ventralis, Pt. femoralis, Pt. cruralis, Pt. caudalis

VENTRAL VIEW — Pt. capitalis, Pt. ventralis, Pt. alaris, Pt. cruralis, Pt. caudalis

Contour feathers are distributed all over the body, in most cases not uniformly, but in groups along definite feather tracts, the pterylae, which are separated from each other by areas without feathers, known as apteria. The form and distribution of these areas, known as pterylosis, is easier to distinguish in young birds, and has a certain value in taxonomy. However, in Ostriches, penguins, screamers (Anhimidae) and mousebirds (Coliidae), the feathers are distributed more or less evenly, without apteria. In total, the number of contour feathers is usually several thousand, logically depending mainly on the size of bird. The known extremes appear to be the Ruby-throated Hummingbird (*Archilochus colubris*), with only 940 feathers, and the Tundra Swan (*Cygnus columbianus*), with 25,216.

The plumules, or down feathers, are much simpler, with short calami, a reduced or vestigial rachis, few barbs, and barbules without hooks. Their fluffy appearance is also due to the more or less circular cross-section of the barbs, which bend in all directions. The down feathers form the only covering during the first stages of growth, while in adults they have varying importance. They are well developed, for example, in waterbirds, but absent in pigeons and Coraciiformes.

Two other types of feather, filoplumes and bristles, are derived from contour feathers and probably have sensory functions. Both are hairlike in appearance and are connected with numerous sensory corpuscles in the skin around the feather base. Filoplumes have a long, fine rachis ending in a few barbs, and are distributed among the plumage in association with other feathers, particularly the flight-feathers. Their purpose appears to be to transmit information about the position of other feathers, so that they can be adjusted, if necessary. Flightless birds, such as the Ostrich, do not have filoplumes. Bristles have barbs only at the base and are found mainly on the head, especially around the mouth, eyes and nostrils, which they help to protect. They are more highly developed in insectivores which hunt on the wing, and particularly in nocturnal birds like nightjars.

Finally, powder-downs consist of a very special type of feather, which occurs amongst the ordinary down, sometimes forming special clusters, as in tinamous and herons. In these feathers, the tips of the barbules disintegrate into fine particles of keratin, forming a sort of talcum powder, which is used in preening.

Feather Formation and Renovation

Feathers are essentially formed in the same way as reptiles' scales. An epidermic germ, containing a dermal papilla with blood vessels, grows obliquely outwards, but later sinks low into the tissue, and develops into a follicle. While the dermal papilla acts as a kind of nutritious pulp, the epidermis gradually changes into a feather, growing from a ring-shaped germinative zone, called the collar. A series of barb-ridges, later to form the barbs of the feather, grow vertically out of the collar, and as they grow little by little they keratinize and become hollow. The dorsal area of the collar quickly elongates to form the rachis, on which the successive barb-ridges are situated, with those that formed first located at the tip. The outermost epidermic layer remains a thin corneous case, the periderm, which covers the developing feather, and when the feather reaches a certain length, this casing breaks at the end, allowing the barbs to push through. These then unfold, as they dry out and harden the bases of their respective barb-ridges. Finally, the dermal pulp retracts progressively from the calamus, leaving it empty, until the feather is an inert, dead structure, consisting of 90% keratin.

Feathers suffer wear and tear and have a limited life span. Normally they are replaced once or twice a year by new feathers, which form in the same revitalized follicles, and force the old feathers out. The renovation or moult of the plumage takes place periodically, is controlled hormonally, and is perfectly integrated into the annual cycle. In this way, the physiological disruption and the energy requirements caused by moult do not interfere with other efforts, such as breeding or migration.

Adult birds normally go through a complete post-breeding moult, which in temperate and cold climates normally occurs in summer. Birds pass the winter with this renewed plumage, and then, in spring, undergo a partial moult, which affects only the body-coverts, not the tail and flight-feathers. This pre-breeding moult leads to the breeding plumage, which is often more brightly coloured in one or other of the sexes, in conjunction with an intensification of secondary sexual characters. However, sometimes the change in appearance is not due to new feathers, but to wear of the feather tips, as in the House Sparrow (*Passer domesticus*), the Common Starling (*Sturnus vulgaris*), and the Eurasian Linnet (*Carduelis cannabina*).

The terminology used in this section, which was developed in temperate countries, tends nowadays to be substituted by another version, referring only to the successive generations of feathers, leaving out the possible relation with breeding or the seasons. According to the latter, the plumages referred to here as "winter" become "basic", those of spring "alternate", the pre-breeding moult "pre-alternate", and the post-breeding "pre-basic".

Before taking on the appearance of adults, immature birds pass through a major or minor series of plumages of greater or lesser importance. At hatching the chicks can be completely naked (Picidae, Alcedinidae), have a small number of plumules, which will afterwards become vaned feathers (Passeriformes in general), or be covered in a dense natal down with plumules, which later on will be substituted, either by vaned feathers, or by other plumules (ducks, Galliformes, gulls, waders). The first two cases refer to psilopaedic (or gymnopaedic) birds, and the third to ptilopaedic birds.

In all cases, with the pre-juvenile (post-natal) moult, the natal down is soon substituted by a first plumage of typical vaned feathers, the juvenile plumage. This is usually quite different from adult plumage, and often tufts of natal down can remain attached to the tips of some contour feathers for some time. In typically nidicolous species, such as the passerines or the raptors, the juvenile plumage is practically complete by the time the young birds abandon the nest. This plumage does not last long, and a post-juvenile moult (first pre-basic) soon gives way to the first winter plumage (first basic plumage), which is often very similar to that of adults. The next moult frequently results in the adult breeding plumage, although in many species this stage is not reached until the following year, or even several years later, as in large gulls, albatrosses and certain eagles. In this last case, the plumage is referred to as "immature", or "subadult" if it is already very similar to that of the adults.

Except perhaps in the very special case of penguins, where the plumage is shed in large irregular patches, moult usually occurs in a very orderly fashion. In each pteryla the dropping and renovation of feathers usually take place following a pre-determined sequence, which is particularly evident in the tail and flight-feathers. In the wings, the first feather to moult is usually the innermost primary, followed by each successive primary working outwards towards the wing tip in "descendant" order. However, there are other possibilities, and in birds of prey moult begins with the fourth primary, progressing thence in opposite directions, both inwards and outwards. When the moult of the primaries is half way through, that of the secondaries normally begins, this time starting with the outermost feather, and moving inwards in "ascendant" order. As some feathers are dropped when others have already begun to grow or are completely formed, the wing is always fully operative.

However, there is a series of bird families, normally aquatic birds (ducks, rails, grebes, divers, auks), in which the moult of all the flight-feathers occurs more or less simultaneously, leaving the birds flightless for several weeks. The temporary inability to defend themselves caused by this type of moult, is to a certain extent offset by the birds moulting on the open sea or in large lakes. In some species of duck, this entails special migrations and causes large concentrations of birds. Others protect themselves with a special, cryptic "eclipse" plumage.

Colour

The enormously varied and often eye-catching colours of birds are mostly related to the plumage. But sometimes the bill, feet and legs can also be brightly coloured, as can other areas of bare skin and various types of wattles or caruncles, from the combs of domestic cockerels (*Gallus*), to gular pouches in frigatebirds (*Fregata*) and prairie chickens (*Tympanuchus*). The colours are due to the presence of pigments (biochromes) and to different optical phenomena which produce structural colours. The most prevalent pigments are melanins, generally producing brown, black and grey colouring, carotenoids or lipochromes, which give yellow, orange or red colours, and porphyrins, which create various shades of red and green, like those present in turacos (*Tauraco*). All these pigments are produced in the dermis by special cells, for example in the case of melanin by melanoblasts, but are later incorporated into the feathers during their growth, often at more or less regular intervals, which explains the appearance of bands or speckles.

In some cases, structural colours are related to the dispersion of light through the numerous vacuoles (minute cavities) in the feathers, which, if there are no pigments, results in white or bluish tones. In other cases, the light plays on the successive layers of keratin producing iridescence and metallic reflections that change depending on the angle of incidence of the light. In many instances, particular colourings are due to a blend of pigmentary and structural colours. For example, many greens, as in the Budgerigar (*Melopsittacus*), are caused by the com-

bination of a blue structural effect and a yellow pigment coming from carotenoids.

On occasions, the presence of pigments in the feathers, particularly melanin, can help to give them greater resistance, and many species have the remiges or at least the tips coloured black. Pigments also appear to help in thermoregulation. However, in birds, as in almost all animals, colour has two main purposes, which are somewhat contradictory, concealment and exhibition. Cryptic coloration, which helps to hide or camouflage the animal from possible predators, has an obvious adaptive value. This is perhaps more evident in species that are forced to nest on the ground in the open, and in such cases the eggs, chicks and incubating adults can provide fantastic examples of protective colouring (thick-knees, woodcock, female ducks and pheasants, sandgrouse, nightjars, larks). In common with many members of the Animal Kingdom, birds show various types of camouflage or cryptic colours, such as disruptive patterns, which dissipate or "break up" the silhouette, or countershading, in which the white underparts counteract the potentially betraying shadows cast by the upperparts. Other special cases are the seasonal changes of colour, which occur with moult (*Lagopus*). Sometimes colours and patterns which at first sight appear to be very eye-catching can be perfectly cryptic in the natural environment, as in many pigeons, trogons and parrots in tropical forests. For these protective colourings to be effective it is very important for certain postures to be adopted and for the birds to remain immobile. A bittern points its bill skywards to mimic reeds, while steppe birds flatten themselves against the ground to eliminate shadows. In some cases cryptic colouring is used not so much to escape predators (procryptic function) but rather to guarantee a more dependable approach to prey (anticryptic function), for example the typical white colouring of the head, neck and underparts of many fish-eating birds.

On the other hand, phaneric colours try to make birds more eye-catching, sometimes with surprisingly effective results. These colours are mainly connected with behaviour, acting as visual communication mechanisms in mating, territoriality, colonial nesting and so on. Very often the same individual can have both cryptic and phaneric coloration, the latter normally relegated to areas that remain hidden while the bird is at rest, but which are suddenly displayed at take-off. These are the signal marks, very often a combination of black and white, which serve as alarm signals, or as signs for intraspecific recognition to help maintain groups. In several species bright colours are thought to be proaposematic, warning potential predators that the bird possesses unpleasant tasting flesh, as seems to be the case with many black and white birds, such as the Black-billed Magpie (*Pica pica*).

Plumage Care

Considering the importance of plumage for birds, it is not surprising that most of their maintenance activities are geared towards cleaning and caring for their feathers, and that it takes up a large proportion of their time. The most important activity is preening, which involves a bird using its bill to reorder the feathers and repair the vanes of the flight-feathers one by one. During this process it gathers an oily secretion from the uropygial gland, which is situated on the coccyx, and spreads it briskly over the feathers. The various components of the secretion (wax, fat, fatty acids) help to clean the feathers, as well as maintaining humidity and flexibility, and offering protection from fungus and bacteria. They do not make the plumage waterproof, as is often thought, but perhaps help to prevent it becoming soaked so easily, and it is true that the uropygial gland is usually more developed in waterbirds, while it is absent in pigeons, parrots and woodpeckers. For some birds, the powder-downs (see Integument) are more important in preening than the uropygial gland, and others occasionally treat their feathers with formic acid, which is obtained by gathering ants in the bill and rubbing them over their feathers, or by the bird settling on the ground in the midst of a swarms of ants, with its wings and tail spread and the body feathers fluffed up.

The Tawny Frogmouth and the Blue-necked Tanager provide good examples of cryptic and phaneric coloration respectively. These frogmouths show the characteristic alarm posture that members of the family adopt in daylight hours when danger threatens, and using this posture they manage a remarkable imitation of a broken branch; for the cryptic coloration to be completely effective, the bird must adopt a particular posture and then remain absolutely motionless. In contrast, the main function of phaneric coloration is obviously to make the bird conspicuous, which can have several biological functions, not only in relations between birds of the opposite sex, but also between rival males, between parents and their offspring and also in interspecific relations, for instance towards enemies or prey. In tangers, the brilliant coloration is mainly related with mating behaviour and territoriality.

[Above: *Podargus strigoides*, Queensland, Australia. Photo: Jen & Des Bartlett/ Bruce Coleman.

Below: *Tangara cyanicollis*. Photo: H. Rivarola/ Bruce Coleman]

The regions of the body which can not be reached with the bill, such as the head and the top of the neck, are treated to vigorous scratching with the feet. In order to scratch themselves, some birds pass their legs under the wing, "direct scratching", while others go over the wing, "indirect scratching", a behavioural aspect which has been apportioned certain taxonomic value. In herons, nightjars and pratincoles (*Glareola*), the internal edge of the middle toe is pectinated (toothed), which, at any rate in the case of the herons, is for combing the plumage. Another basic form of comfort behaviour is bathing, which is logically more common in summer and in hot countries. Certain birds, such as partridges, bustards, hoopoes, larks and sparrows, substitute bathing in water, where this is difficult, for dust baths in dry ground.

Skeleton

The skeleton is the part of the anatomy that best reflects the parallel adaptation of birds to flight and to bipedal locomotion. Starting from a basic reptilian form, numerous modifications have culminated in an authentic evolutionary marvel, with an impressive combination of strength and lightness. Many skeletal parts are suppressed, while others are fused. In general, bones are thinner and lighter and lack bone marrow, which is, however, present in flightless birds such as the Ostrich and penguins. Although hollow, the long limb bones are very strong, sometimes with internal struts known as the trabeculae. The cranial bones, the humerus and others are pneumatized, that is invaded by the air-sacs of the respiratory system. The skull is particularly simple and light, and in adults practically all parts are fused. Its form, far more rounded than that of reptiles, shows a notable increase in the size of the braincase and of the orbits.

An interesting characteristic of the avian skull is its capacity of cranial kinesis, whereby the upper mandible can move independently of the rest of the skull, which among other advantages allows the mouth to open wider. Kinesis is possible thanks to a fine, flexible nasofrontal hinge, the quadrate bones, which are capable of swinging forward like a pendulum, and the movement of the palates and zygomatic arches, all of which results in the lifting of the upper mandible. There is a real articulation in parrots, which show a particularly striking example of kinesis.

A comparison of the vertebral columns of birds and reptiles reveals significant differences. Firstly, in birds there is a very noticeable shortening of the regions which correspond to the trunk, so the body is far more compact and the centre of gravity is shifted towards the hind limbs. However, in a bipedal stance the vertebral column does not become vertical, as in man. Moreover, the central portion of the column is very rigid, with the last thoracic vertebrae fused with virtually all those of the lumbar region, the two sacral and several caudal vertebrae, to form a single bone, the synsacrum. Amongst other functions this allows the weight of the bird, when perching, to be distributed throughout the vertebral column. Sometimes a second group of vertebrae are fused in the thorax, constituting the os dorsale or notarium, for example in grebes, cranes and pigeons. The bird is largely compensated for the shortening and lack of mobility of the trunk, by having an extraordinarily flexible neck, due to its heterocoelous (saddle-shaped) vertebrae. The number of vertebrae is very variable, with as many as 25 in swans. In contrast with the neck, the tail is much reduced, with scarcely half a dozen independent coccygeal vertebrae, and a few others joined to create an end bone, the pygostyle, which carries the tail feathers.

An outstanding feature of the skeleton of flying birds is the large size of both the pectoral girdle and the sternum, where the pectoral muscles are situated. The sternum has developed a large keel (carina), to accommodate and offer points of insertion for the flight muscles, and the clavicles are fused into a single, characteristically V-shaped bone, the furcula or wishbone. Both the carina and the furcula are far smaller in flightless birds, in particular the ratites. Along with the ribs, the sternum

and the pectoral girdle help the chest to resist the strong pressure which the pectoral muscles exert during flight, and in this respect the powerful coracoids are particularly important. The ribs are fully ossified, in contrast with those of mammals, and are divided into dorsal and ventral segments. They are reinforced at the back by overlapping bony projections, the uncinate processes, which contribute to the strong, relatively rigid structure of the chest.

The fore limbs, the wings, are enormously transformed, particularly in the distal portion, where only the vestiges of three fingers remain, equivalent to the digits II, III, and IV of the reptilian limb. The corresponding wrist bones, the metacarpals, are fused with the main part of the carpals to form a single part, the carpometacarpus. Only two carpals remain free, one articulates with the ulna and the other with the radius. The enlarged head of the humerus has sizeable crests, to which the pectoral muscles are attached.

The bones of the pelvic girdle, the ilium, ischium and pubis, are partially fused with one another and with the synsacrum, whereas there are no ventral unions (symphysis) between the bones on either side of the pelvis. This is probably to help in the laying of eggs, which in birds are comparatively voluminous, rigid and fragile. Two large cursorial birds are exceptions, the Ostrich (*Struthio camelus*), with pubic symphysis, and the rheas (Rheidae), with ischiatic symphysis.

The hind limbs are also highly modified. Some of the tarsal (ankle) bones are fused to the tibia to form the tibiotarsus, which is usually longer than the very thin fibula. The rest of the tarsal bones are joined with one another and with the metatarsals to form the tarsometatarsus, which is commonly referred to as the "tarsus". For this reason, the joint which corresponds to the ankle in man is intertarsal in birds, and is not the usual one found between the tarsal bones and those of the leg, the tibia and the fibula. All that remains beyond the metatarsus are the phalanges of four fingers, which constitute the foot. The internal finger or hallux (I), is normally directed backwards and consists of two phalanges and a small residual metatarsal, while the other three toes (II, III and IV), normally face forwards, and have respectively three, four and five phalanges. However, there are many modifications to this basic pattern.

Musculature

The musculature has also been significantly modified by the requirements of flight and bipedal locomotion, and additionally as a result of the shortening and lack of mobility of the trunk. It is largely concentrated in two masses, one above the pectoral girdle, which in domestic fowl is known as the "breast", and the other above the pelvis, femur and the upper part of the tibiotarsus and the fibula, known as the "thigh". Only tough but very light tendons reach the distal parts of the legs, leaving the major mass of muscle very near the bird's centre of gravity.

The main muscle for pulling down the wings, undoubtedly the most costly movement during flight, is the pectoralis or pectoralis major, which on average comprises about 15·5% of the total weight of a flying bird. It originates in the furcula (wishbone), in the conjunctive raphe that connects the furcula to the sternum, and in the distal portions of the keel, and inserts on the crista pectoralis of the humerus. Underneath this is another large muscle, the supracoracoideus, which is attached to the sternum. Between the furcula, the scapula and the coracoid is a small hole, the triosseal canal, through which the tendon passes, before attaching to the surface of the humerus, not far from the deltoid crest. Although its position is ventral, it is not used for lowering the wing, but rather for raising it, by means of a pulley-like mechanism. The back muscles of birds, such as the scapulo-humeralis or the latissimus dorsi, collaborate from different angles in the lifting of the wing, but these muscles are comparatively very small, and have hardly any effect on the centre of gravity, which remains low.

The musculature of the hind limb is far less voluminous, but is also quite complicated. Its composition varies considerably, allowing the development of basic "formulas", depending

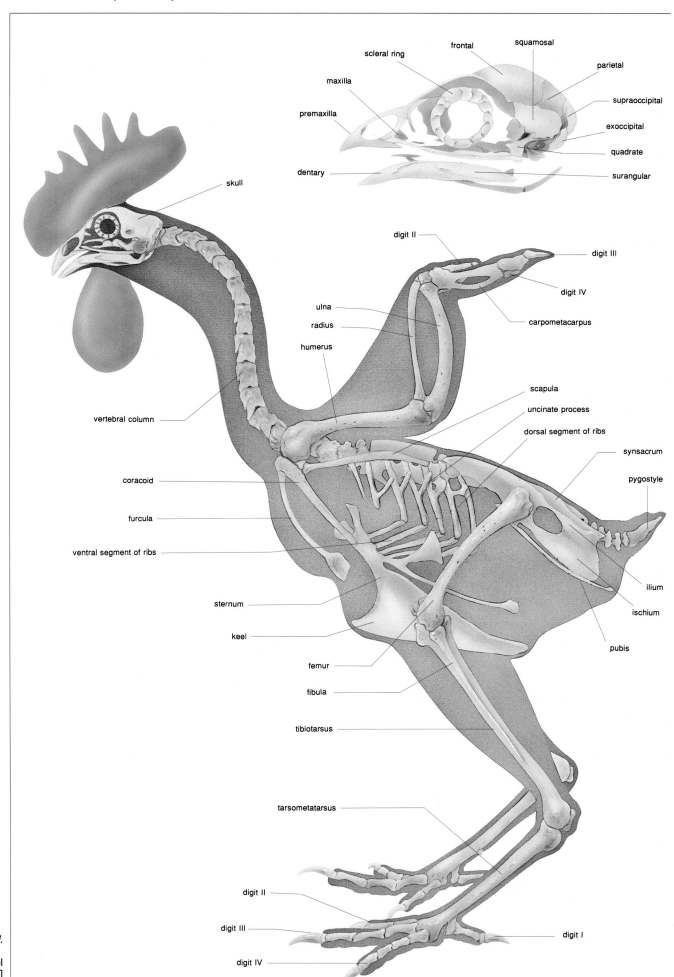

scleral ring
frontal
squamosal
maxilla
parietal
premaxilla
supraoccipital
exoccipital
quadrate
dentary
surangular

skull

digit II
digit III
digit IV
ulna
carpometacarpus
radius
humerus

scapula
uncinate process
dorsal segment of ribs

synsacrum
pygostyle

vertebral column

coracoid

furcula

ventral segment of ribs

ilium

sternum

ischium

keel

pubis

femur

fibula

tibiotarsus

tarsometatarsus

digit II

digit III

digit I

digit IV

Skeleton of a bird.

[Figure: Miguel Angel Castaños]

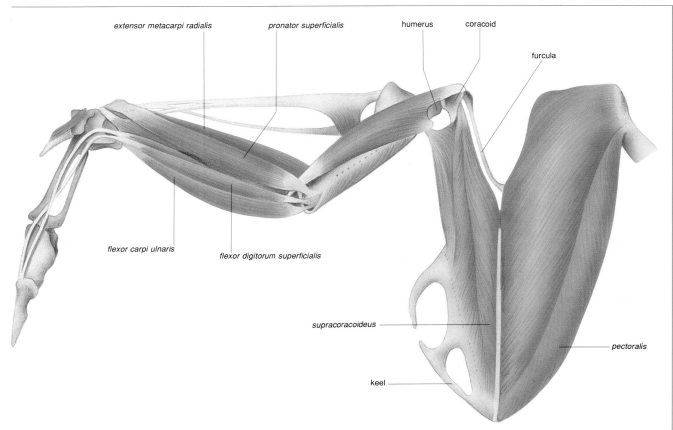

extensor metacarpi radialis

pronator superficialis

humerus

coracoid

furcula

flexor carpi ulnaris

flexor digitorum superficialis

supracoracoideus

pectoralis

keel

Main wing muscles.

[Figure: Miguel Angel Castaños]

on the presence or absence of certain muscles, and in this way it is useful in classification. Also of interest and some value in taxonomy is the system of tendons which reach the soles of the feet and are used to bend or stretch the toes. When birds perch on small branches or wires which they can encircle with their toes, as they fold their legs, the tendons running behind the tarsus are tensed, causing the toes to contract automatically, ensuring a firm grip, even while the bird is sleeping, without any energy being expended.

The lighter or darker coloration of the pectoral muscles provides information about the flying capacity of birds, as it indicates the type of muscular fibre. The red fibres metabolize mainly fats aerobically, for which they need high oxygen levels. This is achieved by the small size of each fibre, by a dense network of capillaries (whence the red colour), and by a high content of myoglobin and mitochondria. On the other hand, the white fibres metabolize sugars anaerobically, allowing for far quicker energy production, but lactic acid is also produced and quickly causes fatigue. Birds with red pectoral muscles, like pigeons, are therefore capable of long, sustained flight, while those with whitish pectorals, such as Galliformes, take off with tremendous force but tire very quickly.

Aerial Locomotion

Flight, which has been so important in conditioning the evolution of birds (see General Characteristics), is used in numerous activities, ranging from foraging and courtship to long migratory journeys. However, it demands substantial expenditure of energy, which the different species have had to optimize adaptively, depending on ecological factors, such as the type of habitat or food which they exploit. An examination of wing morphology can provide an initial indication of this. Wing shape is normally referred to using the aspect ratio, which is the wingspan squared, divided by the total wing area. Besides the aspect ratio, it is necessary to take into account the size of the bird, using body mass, and the weight per unit of wing area, the wing-loading. Large birds need comparatively far more wing surface than small birds, as body mass increases with volume, growing cubically, while the supporting surface area of the wings only squares.

For the same reason, large birds need to fly faster in order to remain airborne, and consequently experience more difficulties during take-off and landing. To take off successfully, many have to run along the ground or water surface, or let themselves drop from their perches, until they reach a minimum speed. For landing, they use different methods of braking, such as stretching the legs out below the body, which is more effective if the legs are long or if they have large webbed feet.

There are four basic wing types, although all the intermediate possibilities may also be found:

a) Elliptical wings. These are rounded, with a low aspect-ratio, and allow for easy manoeuvring in restricted spaces, so they are typical in forest birds such as hawks (*Accipiter*), woodcock (*Scolopax*), woodpeckers and passerines in general. However, within the passerines, migratory species tend to have more pointed wings. Capable of a high wingbeat frequency, this type of wing is also typical of Galliformes, which base their defence largely on an extremely fast take-off.

b) High speed wings. These are relatively short, but notably pointed, and are normally combined with heavy wing-loading and high wingbeat frequency, to achieve high speed at the cost of a high energy input. Good examples are the Peregrine Falcon (*Falco peregrinus*) and ducks in general. The case of the auks (Alcidae) and diving-petrels (Pelecanoididae) is very peculiar, as they use their wings to propel themselves under water, and consequently, because water is a far denser medium than air, have had to develop short, pointed wings, although this means that a great deal of energy is used during flight, as it demands furious flapping and considerable pectoral musculature.

c) High aspect ratio wings. These are far longer than they are wide. They normally have low wing-loading, to permit flight at low speeds or even at zero speed, in hovering, with the lowest possible energy cost (kestrels, terns, nightjars), or alternatively to specialize in gliding and soaring. The frigatebirds are an excellent example, as they are capable of remaining airborne in the weak thermals characteristic of tropical oceans. With their higher wing-loading and therefore higher speeds, the Procellariiformes glide over the sea extremely efficiently, sometimes almost at the level of the waves. The wings of swallows and especially of swifts also fall into this category, if one takes into account the allometric relationship. Contrary to popular belief swifts are not outstanding for their speed, but rather for being capable of flying slowly, when capturing insects, sleeping or even copulating in the air.

d) Soaring wings with slots. These are long, wide, rectangular wings, with deep slots between the successive primaries, in order to avoid turbulence around the wing tips. They are typical of the great soarers, such as eagles, vultures, storks and pelicans, birds that use thermals, rising air currents which originate when the land is heated up by the sun. In theory, they should be less well adapted for gliding than the high aspect ratio wings that are used for example by gliding aircraft, and their design may be to simplify the manoeuvres of take-off and landing, which are complicated in large species, such as albatrosses, which require very long runways, and these are not always available inland.

In recent years, thanks mainly to radar, it has been possible to obtain reasonably precise measurements of the cruising speeds of certain species. Large birds fly comparatively faster than small ones, and generally this is clearly reflected by the morphology of the wing. Indeed, amongst the fastest flyers are the ducks, with a maximum of 76 km/h recorded in the Common Eider (*Somateria mollissima*), and the falcons. Although precise measurements are lacking, it is estimated that the Peregrine Falcon can exceed 180 km/h during a stoop. Other fast flying birds include pigeons (50-60 km/h), for example the Common Wood Pigeon (*Columba palumbus*), and waders, such as the Eurasian Oystercatcher (*Haematopus ostralegus*), whereas birds with high aspect ratio and medium size, like the Herring Gull (*Larus argentatus*), the Common Tern (*Sterna hirundo*) and the Common Kestrel (*Falco tinnunculus*), move at only 30-40 km/h, the same speed that is normally reached by small passerines with elliptical wings, such as the House Sparrow and the Chaffinch (*Fringilla coelebs*). Common Swifts (*Apus apus*) have been recorded flying at 40 km/h during migration, but only at 23 km/h when foraging.

The wingbeat frequency is easier to determine and is also of great interest. Excluding the large soaring birds, which can continue in level flight for many minutes without a single wingbeat, the frequency varies from two to three beats per second in herons (*Ardea*), gulls (*Larus*) and crows (*Corvus*), to four or five beats per second in ducks (*Anas*), falcons (*Falco*), plovers (*Charadrius*), pigeons (*Columba*) and many passerines. There are, however, many birds which easily exceed these figures, such as the auks, with eight beats per second in the Black Guillemot (*Cepphus grylle*), and the pheasants, with nine beats per second in the Common Pheasant (*Phasianus colchi-*

cus). An exceptional case is that of the hummingbirds (Trochilidae), with a wingbeat frequency ranging from 22 per second in the larger species to more than 70 in the smallest ones, and even 78 in the Amethyst Woodstar (*Calliphlox amethystina*). This is related to a very special kind of flight, as the head of the humerus can be rotated to a remarkable degree, allowing these small birds to beat their wings equally towards the belly or the back, from a vertical position, in a continuous action with the wing tips describing a figure of eight. This complex wing action enables them to remain perfectly stationary in mid-air, or rise vertically like helicopters. The morphological features that make this phenomenon possible include a significant shortening of the humerus, radius and ulna, and the development of the supracoracoideus muscles, which are half as large as the pectoralis, whereas in other birds they are only about one tenth as large.

In contrast to highly aerial birds like swifts, several species, both terrestrial and aquatic, have lost the ability to fly. Becoming flightless represents a considerable saving, in terms of the energy required for developing and maintaining the flight apparatus, as the pectoral girdle, the sternum, the wings and associated muscles comprise most of the body weight of flying birds. It also allows the bird to increase in size. Flying birds can not weigh more than about 15 kg, whereas the Emperor Penguin (*Aptenodytes forsteri*) reaches 46 kg, the Ostrich 150 kg and the extinct Great Elephantbird (*Aepyornis maximus*) perhaps as much as 450 kg. However, flight would not be abandoned, if it were necessary either for foraging or for escaping from predators. In the absence of terrestrial predators, flightless forms have repeatedly appeared on oceanic islands, in many different orders. Some of these have already been exterminated by man or by animals he has introduced, like the moas (Dinornithidae) of New Zealand, the elephantbirds (Aepyornithidae) of Madagascar, the Dodo (*Raphus cucullatus*) and the Rodrigues Solitaire (*Pezophaps solitaria*) of the Mascarene Islands. Others are still extant today, such as the kiwis (*Apteryx*) and the Kakapo (*Strigops habroptilus*) of New Zealand, the mesites (Mesitornithidae) of Madagascar, the Kagu (*Rhynochetus jubatus*) of New Caledonia, and many rails of Pacific islands. Among cursorial birds, there are also continental forms that do not fly, including the Ostrich, the rheas (Rheidae), the Emu (*Dromaius*), the cassowaries (*Casuarius*), and in other geological epochs *Dyatrima*, *Phorusrhacos* and others. There are also flightless waterbirds, on the one hand wing-propelled divers, such as the Sphenisciformes and the

Characteristic wing types.

[Figure: Xavier Ruiz]

high aspect ratio wing

high speed wing

soaring wing with slots

elliptical wing

extinct Great Auk (*Alca impennis*) of the North Atlantic, and on the other foot-propelled divers, for example the Flightless Cormorant (*Phalacrocorax harrisi*) of the Galapagos, the Titicaca Flightless Grebe (*Rollandia microptera*) and most of the steamer ducks (*Tachyeres*) of South America. Already in the Cretaceous, some toothed birds, for example *Enaliornis* and *Hesperornis*, could have been flightless divers.

Terrestrial Locomotion

The ability to move on land varies widely, from species that are exclusively cursorial, to others incapable of supporting their own weight, as a result of extreme adaptation to aerial life (swifts), or to aquatic life (divers, grebes, shearwaters and auks).

As an adaptation to running, birds tend to have long, strongly muscular legs, especially in the tarsal area. The toes tend to be shortened, with short, robust claws. Often the hind toe is lost, for example in ratites, coursers (*Cursorius*), thick-knees (Burhinidae), and bustards (Otididae). The Ostrich has also lost the inner toe, and when running, it rests its weight on what was originally the middle toe. This has a very powerful claw, reminiscent of the odd-toed ungulates (Perissodactyla), such as horses. However, some highly terrestrial passerines, such as the larks (Alaudidae), the pipits (*Anthus*) and some buntings (Emberizidae), have short front toes, but a long hind toe, which boasts a long, fairly straight claw. The Greater Roadrunner (*Geococcyx californianus*) retains a tree-creeping trait of its order, Cuculiformes, with two toes facing forwards and two backwards, in spite of which it seems to reach speeds of about 34 km/h. Ostriches and Emus can manage over 50 km/h, in good measure due to their large size.

Aquatic Locomotion

Many birds depend on aquatic environments, either inland or marine, and have consequently developed special adaptations for movement in water. No less than 390 species, in nine orders, swim habitually, and many others do so occasionally. When swimming, they usually propel themselves using the feet, which in some orders have membranes joining the toes (divers, shearwaters, ducks, gulls and auks), and in others (Pelecaniformes) are "totipalmate", with an extra membrane between the hind toe and the inner toe. Other orders have distinctive horny lobes along the toes, (grebes, coots, finfoots and phalaropes). For efficiency, the legs tend to be situated well towards the rear, causing instability and clumsiness on land. Under the water, birds such as penguins, auks, and diving-petrels, are not foot- but wing-propelled, and in penguins the wings are like fins, with short flat bones, rigid joints and scale-like feathers.

In waterbirds the body is elongated, in comparison with that of land birds, in order to gain a more streamlined form. They are also better insulated with: well-developed layers of fat, especially in penguins; a thick coat of down; contour feathers with long barbules to retain a greater expanse of warm air; large uropygial glands; and capillary systems in the feet which help to reduce heat loss. Diving birds require further adaptations. To increase their weight and thus combat the upward push of water, they generally have heavier, less pneumatized bones, and a reduced system of air-sacs. Moreover, grebes and cormorants swallow pebbles to act as ballast, and cormorants have special barbs on their contour feathers, which allow the water to penetrate and soak the plumage, thereby reducing buoyancy. In order to achieve greater resistance to water pressure, the thoracic cage is reinforced, by the broadening of the ribs and the lengthening of the uncinate processes. Some birds, most notably the penguins, have special physiological adaptations which enable them to increase the duration of their dives, including high concentrations of myoglobin in the muscles and a certain capacity for anaerobic breakdown of glycogen. These adaptations, in conjunction with underwater propulsion using their wings and the large, heavy bodies they can afford to have, due to being flightless, allow penguins to perform remarkable feats in their dives and the Emperor Penguin has been known to make dives up to 18 minutes long and to a depth of 265 m.

Feeding and Digestion

The impressive scope that birds have for adaptation can be seen in the range of food sources that they are capable of exploiting. There are many adaptations that make this possible, but the well-known plasticity of their bills is an important factor. Because of the extreme specialization of the wings and legs, the bill is the principal, and often the only, part of the body that is used in the collecting and handling of food.

Different shapes of bill allow for a wide diversity of activities such as spearing fish, drilling holes in tree trunks, cropping grass, splitting open seeds, filtering mud, capturing aerial plankton, tearing off bits of flesh, and extracting nectar from the corollas of flowers. The sometimes subtle variations in form, length or strength help ecologists to explain the compatibility of the various different species present in diverse bird communities, whether they be of seabirds, seed-eaters, waders or forest insectivores. However, anatomically the bill is a very simple structure, formed by the mandible bones (the upper the maxilla, the lower technically termed the mandible), and by the corneous sheaths or rhamphotheca (rhinotheca the maxillar, and gnathotheca the mandibular sheath). Similar horny formations appear in tortoises and the platypus, a monotreme mammal, also related to a reduction in, or loss of, teeth.

In some bird orders, especially the Procellariiformes, the rhamphotheca is composed of various juxtaposed pieces. The nostrils open in the rhinotheca, sometimes in a bulbous proximal portion, an area softer than the rest which is called the cere in pigeons, birds of prey, and parrots. Normally the nostrils of the two sides are separated by a septum, but in other cases, for example in gulls and cranes, this is missing. In kiwis the nostrils are located at the bill tip which is related to their well-developed sense of smell. Gannets and boobies (Sulidae) do not have nostrils, an adaptation to a special diving technique consisting of plunging into the sea from a great height.

The tongue, although not very obvious, is also important and has many variations. In some groups it is rudimentary or vestigial, as in the Ostrich, pelicans, gannets, storks, ibises and hornbills, while in the woodpeckers and hummingbirds it is very long and can be protruded, in woodpeckers to extract wood-eating insects from tree trunks and in hummingbirds to obtain nectar from long corollas. It usually has papillae on the surface, with variations in development and degree of horniness, sometimes in the form of spines, hooks, barbs or brushes, with very different functions related to feeding modes and bill shape. In ducks and flamingos, lateral denticulations along the edge of the tongue work together with the lamellae of the ramphotheca to create a filtering apparatus. In grain-eating species the tongue is normally fleshy to help manipulate seeds and discard the shells. Parrots have extraordinarily meaty, mobile tongues with very well developed musculature, but they are exceptional, since normally the tongue only operates by means of the musculature of the hyoid apparatus. This explains, among other things, the surprising projection capacity of woodpeckers' tongues, where the long posterior horns of the hyoids completely encircle the cranium. The tongue is hardly used in sound production or phonation, although parrots are again an exception, their muscular tongues being capable of articulating very complex sounds including imitations of the human voice.

The salivary glands lubricate the food and help in the swallowing of large prey items, which birds are forced to ingest whole due to their lack of teeth. These glands are reduced in piscivorous species, perhaps because fish are already lubricated and therefore relatively easy to swallow, as long as they are swallowed head first, and not against the scales. They are enlarged in the case of woodpeckers, making the tongue sticky to help capture ants and other insects, and also in swallows and swifts, which use the saliva to construct their nests. Swifts of the genus *Collocalia* use hardly any other construction materials

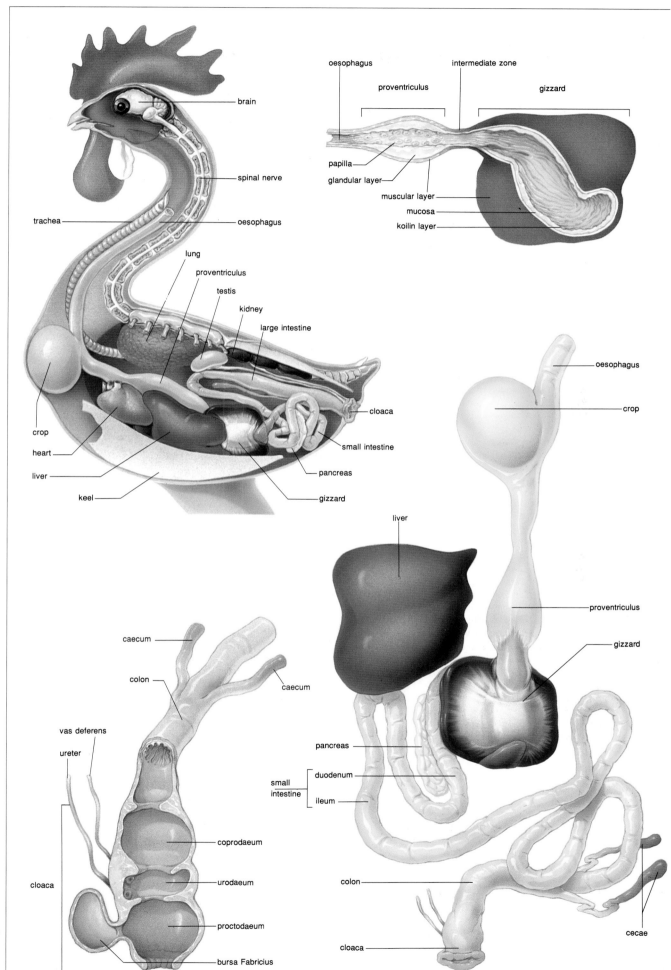

Anatomy of the digestive system of a bird.

[Figure: Joan Fors]

and their nests are therefore edible, the "birds' nests" of Oriental cuisine. In grain-eating species the saliva contains amylase, an enzyme which in fact starts the process of digestion.

The oesophagus is relatively wide and muscular, and is important both for storing food and for assisting in regurgitation when chicks are being fed, or for the ejection of pellets. Because of its storing function, the oesophagus often develops crops, special extensible sections, which are sometimes sack-like. These are usually found in seed-eating species, such as gallinaceous birds, pigeons and some passerines, where the rapid ingestion of food could have evolutionary value in places where danger from predators is high. Another function of the crop, in the case of pigeons, is the production of "pigeon milk", a special nourishing secretion of the crop walls, which are enlarged during the nesting period. This has a similar composition to mammal milk, apart from an almost total lack of carbohydrates. As in mammals, the hormone which starts milk production is the prolactin secreted by the hypophysis. The Greater Flamingo (*Phoenicopterus ruber*) and the Emperor Penguin also feed their young with similar oesophageal secretions.

The Hoatzin (*Opisthocomus hoazin*) has an enormous crop, which is so well-developed that the pectoral girdle has been transformed, in order to leave room for its various chambers and the thick muscular walls that help to digest the tough leaves that constitute its staple diet.

The stomach is composed of two parts, a glandular proventriculus or true stomach, and a muscular ventriculus or gizzard, the relative proportions of which can be related to dietary differences. The proventriculus is more developed in carnivores, and above all, in piscivorous species. The gizzard is more important in seed-eaters, where it has thick, striated muscles and the epithelium hardened with a coating of koilin, which, with the help of swallowed grit, grinds down the food, performing the function of molars in mammals. In fruit eaters, such as the tanagers (Thraupidae), the gizzard can become almost vestigial, while in the Bearded Parrotbill (*Panurus biarmicus*) important seasonal differences have been noted, for example in size, the thickness of the walls and grit content, which are all associated with a diet of seeds in winter and insects in summer.

The intestine can be subdivided into the small intestine, formed by the duodenum and the ileum, and the large intestine, composed of two caeca (rarely one or none), the colon and the cloaca. As in mammals, the intestine tends to be longer in herbivores, and relatively more so in the larger ones, although without reaching the extremes found in mammals, probably because of the limits imposed on weight by the capacity of flight. Birds like the Ostrich, tinamous and gallinaceous birds have well-developed caeca containing bacterial flora, which appear to be important for the digestion of cellulose-rich food. The cloaca, as in reptiles, has three chambers one after the other, the coprodaeum, the urodaeum and the proctodaeum, which receive the faeces, urine and genital products. The last chamber, the proctodaeum, has muscles which are used to eject faeces and urine, and also during copulation. Young birds have a dorsal diverticulum, the bursa Fabricius, which has an important immunological function, in some ways comparable to that of the thymus in mammals.

As would be expected from the high activity levels and homoiothermic metabolism, the digestive system is highly efficient. Food passes through the digestive tract in a surprisingly short time, an hour and a half on average in passerines, varying with the type of food. Shrikes (*Lanius*) need three hours to digest a mouse completely, while *Sylvia* warblers feeding on berries discharge the seeds in the faeces only a quarter of an hour later. It is said that a Lammergeier (*Gypaetus barbatus*) can completely digest a cow vertebra in two days.

Birds have very high assimilation rates: with 500 g of food growing European White Stork (*Ciconia ciconia*) chicks can gain 170 g daily, and domestic hens need only 1·9 kg of food to gain 1 kg.

Due to their high metabolic rates, birds generally have to feed frequently and abundantly, and spend a great deal of time and effort to this end. The amount of food required varies greatly, depending above all on the size of the bird and the

energy value of the type of food consumed. Given the unfavourable relation between surface and volume, small birds proportionally need much more food. In a group of four species of owl (Strigiformes), individuals, with the same environmental conditions and kind of diet, needed daily quantities of food which represented: 15·9% of body weight in the Burrowing Owl (*Speotyto cunicularia*), with a mean weight of 166 g; 12·7% in the Long-eared Owl (*Asio otus*), 295 g; 10·1% in the Barn Owl (*Tyto alba*), 598 g; and 4·7% in the Great Horned Owl (*Bubo virginianus*), 1333 g. Moreover, hummingbirds can consume up to double their own weight daily. As for the type of food, adult insectivorous passerines are known to ingest the approximate equivalent of 40% of their body weight daily, whereas seed-eaters need to consume only 10%.

Variations in feeding are also related to other factors, for example the amount of energy used to maintain internal heat, causing higher consumption in winter than in summer. Likewise, in boreal and temperate regions medium-sized birds consume about twice as much as their counterparts in tropical regions. The Village Weaver (*Ploceus cucullatus*) in captivity, at a temperature of 18°C, consumes the equivalent of 20% of its body weight daily, but this increases to 25% at 9°C and to 28% at 7°C. There are also periodic increases in food requirements, which are essential for reproduction or migration.

Other aspects related to feeding, such as the number of meals per day or the amount of time devoted to finding food, vary considerably. Some large birds such as vultures or albatrosses can fast for days or even weeks, and during the breeding period the male Emperor Penguin stops eating for almost four months, losing up to 45% of its initial weight. However, adaptation to flight normally restricts the build-up of large fat reserves, which, together with an intense metabolism, means that most birds must necessarily eat every day. In the Andes, hummingbirds visit from 1500 to 2700 flowers daily, and in winter many passerines in temperate latitudes use up to 90% of the daylight hours available searching for food.

Birds use a wide variety of techniques for acquiring their food, and these are related partly to morphological adaptations and partly to ethological aspects, which nowadays arouse a good deal of interest. Birds appear to adjust their feeding activity fairly precisely, in order to maximize the returns from the time and energy invested. They instinctively choose those types of food, habitat and search pattern (hours of activity, foraging speed, allocation of time to each food patch) that offer the highest yield of energy from the food taken, in comparison with the energy and time spent in its collection and consumption. However, sometimes the nutritional value of the food, such as its protein or mineral content, can be more important than its energetic value. In other situations, a feeding system that is favourable in terms of energy may be replaced by a less profitable one, for example in order to reduce exposure to predators.

The type of "decisions" which predict the theory of "optimal foraging" are closely related to the morphological characteristics of each species. Research shows that White Wagtails (*Motacilla alba*) taking flies (*Scatophaga*), capture larger proportions of medium-sized flies, although they are less abundant than larger, and therefore more nourishing ones. The explanation, it seems, is that it requires far more time to catch and swallow larger flies, causing the energy gained/time expended relation to be less profitable than with medium-sized flies. In a larger, stronger bird than the White Wagtail, the predicted strategy would probably be different. In the same way, in granivorous birds each species selects precisely the size of seed that best suits the size of its bill, even though smaller seeds are less nourishing. In this way, unusual morphological features can explain extremely specialized diets, as is the case of the Snail Kite (*Rostrhamus sociabilis*), which taking advantage of its abnormally long, hooked bill, feeds uniquely on water snails of the genus *Pomacea*. On the other hand, omnivorous birds, like gulls and crows, are normally characterized by unspecialized, multi-functional bills.

Also related to the morphological characteristics of the different species are the basic foraging techniques that they use. This, in turn, can often determine the type or types of food exploited. For example, amongst marine birds that normally capture their prey sitting on the water (petrels, albatrosses), cephalopods usually constitute a large proportion of the diet. Most of those that use high-energy techniques, like underwater diving (cormorants, auks), or hovering and diving (terns, gannets), eat little other than fish, which has a much higher energy content than cephalopods. Morphology, physiology and behaviour are thus closely related, and help to explain the paths which have led to the adaptive radiation of birds, and the ecological structuring of their communities.

Another fundamental aspect in birds' feeding activity is the formation of flocks. This appears to be closely related to the type of food consumed, and most seed or fruit eaters tend to form flocks, due to the spatial aggregation of these food types, while those that feed on animals, which are usually distributed in regular and therefore predictable patterns, are normally solitary and maintain territories. Flocks not only help in finding food, but also offer advantages against predators. Mixed-species flocks often occur, for example in tropical forests, where it is normal to find groups of 25-50 individuals of 5-15 species, or in temperate forests during winter, with the well known associations of tits, nuthatches, treecreepers, goldcrests and others.

Many insectivorous birds seek the company of larger birds, or of herbivorous mammals, and use them to flush their prey out into the open, or occasionally as perches. The Cattle Egret (*Bubulcus ibis*) is 3·6 times more efficient when feeding in the company of cattle than when feeding alone. Sometimes even closer associations are produced. The honeyguides (Indicatoridae), which feed on bees' and wasps' wax and honeycombs, lead mammals, such as man or the ratel (*Mellivora capensis*) to the nests and then wait for them to break open the nest and extricate the food. Ox-peckers (*Buphagus*) are specialized in delousing large mammals (mutualism). On the other hand, frigatebirds, skuas and gulls frequently exploit food found by other birds, harassing them until they drop or regurgitate their catch (kleptoparasitism). One of the Galapagos finches, the Sharp-beaked Ground-finch (*Geospiza difficilis*), sometimes feeds on the blood of moulting Red-footed Boobies (*Sula sula*), using its sharp bill to cut at the bases of the secondaries while they are growing (true parasitism).

Optimum feeding activity should also take into account fluctuations in the availability of different types of food. In many species, variations of diet may occur geographically, as well as seasonally. For example, the staple diet of many birds of prey in Central Europe is based on voles (*Microtus*), but in the Mediterranean region they depend almost entirely on the rabbit (*Oryctolagus cuniculus*). A seasonal change of diet is compulsory in temperate and boreal regions, both for sedentary birds, which often alternate between insectivorous and granivorous diets, and for migrants. However, different sedentary birds are capable of storing food, for example raptors, owls, shrikes, crows, tits, and nuthatches. This behaviour is particularly notable in nutcrackers (*Nucifraga*) and the Acorn Woodpecker (*Melanerpes formicivorus*). In the latter, groups of birds store acorns in small holes drilled for the purpose in the bark of certain trees. These form a communal larder, which can sometimes contain up to 50,000 acorns, and which is defended by the group against other birds. Diet can also vary in relation to the bird's maturity. For example, in its first few days a Mallard (*Anas platyrhynchos*) eats only small animals, such as insects, crustaceans and molluscs, which have proteins that may be essential for growth, but it quickly changes to an almost exclusively vegetarian diet. Similarly, there are many cases of adults feeding their nestlings different food from that which they themselves eat.

Excretory System

The elimination of nitrogenous waste products and the regulation of osmotic equilibrium take place in two metanephritic-type kidneys, as is normally the case in Amniota. These kidneys have a slightly irregular shape, normally trilobed, as there is limited space available, due to restrictions imposed by the pelvic and synsacral bones. The tubes that form the ureters lead the urine directly to the urodaeum of the cloaca; there is no urinary bladder. The nitrogen is excreted in the form of uric acid, rather than urea as in mammals, allowing for substantial economy of water, although the Henle loops (the part of the nephrons where water is reabsorbed) are much shorter in birds. To excrete the equivalent of 370 mg of nitrogen mammals need 20 ml of water, but birds scarcely require 1 or 2 ml. In addition, more water is recovered in the cloaca, in the large intestine and in the intestinal caeca, where part of the urine arrives by retroperistalsis. At the end of this process, the urine is not liquid but rather a dense whitish paste, sometimes containing only 50% water, which is discharged at the same time as the faeces.

It is not surprising that many birds never or hardly ever need to drink, as they acquire enough water from the animal or plant tissues they feed on, and from the liquid produced by metabolism. This is more frequently the case with frugivores, carnivores and insectivores, and not so often with granivores, as their food has a very low water content, although one budgerigar survived 150 days in perfect health without water, on an diet exclusively of seeds.

Water is also necessary for thermoregulation, as it is evaporated through the lungs, and to a limited degree through the skin. The amount lost increases rapidly with the ambient temperature, and in the Canyon Towhee (*Pipilo fuscus*), for example, it quadruples when the temperature rises from 30°C to 40°C. Because of this many granivorous birds (pigeons, parrots, sandgrouse, finches), especially in hot areas, are obliged to drink frequently. In arid areas, the presence of water-holes frequently decides the distribution of such birds, which on occasions must make long trips daily. To cope with this problem, sandgrouse (Pteroclididae) have developed a special adaptation, whereby they soak up water with the belly feathers, and then carry it to the chicks.

Another fundamental aspect of excretion is the maintenance of osmotic equilibrium, which is largely determined by the concentration of salt in the organism. Although small doses of salt can be lethal for some birds, others, mainly seed or fruit eaters, such as hens, pigeons, parrots, mouse-birds, finches and certain corvids, regularly visit places where they can find salt. An excess can normally be dealt with by the kidneys, as long as it is possible for the bird to drink fresh water, but obviously this is not the case for many seabirds. To this end, they have specialized excretory salt glands situated in shallow depressions above the eyes, and these glands allow them to drink even sea water without problems. These glands filter the blood through special capillaries in the ophthalmic arteries, and pass the resulting liquid through a system of ducts that lead to the nasal cavities. It then runs out in drops, trickles down the bill, and drips off the end. This liquid has a salt concentration of around 5%, compared with the 3% solution of sea water. The salt glands appear to be very effective, and after drinking a quantity of sea water equivalent to 10% of its body weight, a gull eliminates up to 90% of the ingested salt within three hours. There are glands of this type in at least 13 orders, but they are most developed in penguins, Procellariiformes, Pelecaniformes, gulls, auks and sea ducks. Within the same species, they can even be more highly developed in individuals that inhabit seas or salt lakes, than in others living in fresh water areas.

Respiration

The respiratory system must adapt to the demands of a most intense metabolism, and also help in the thermoregulation of the bird, which can suffer from overheating, especially during flight. It is certainly very efficient and is also quite original, based on rather different principles from those of the reptiles and the mammals. The lungs, the organs where the gas exchange takes place, are small and relatively immobile, because of the narrowness and rigidity of the chest, and because the diaphragm of birds is partial and membranous, not complete and muscular, as in mammals, and it is therefore not employed in the respiratory

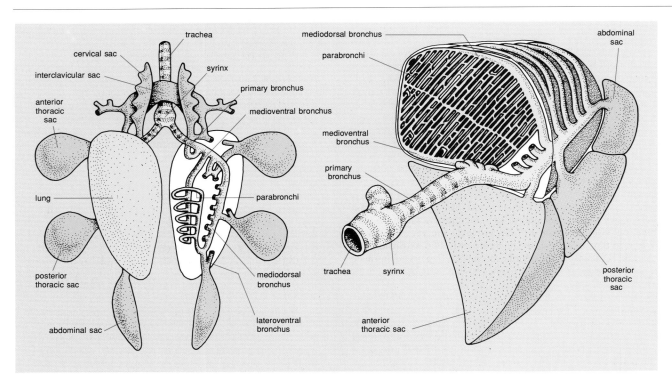

Anatomy of the respiratory system of a bird.
Right: cross-section of a lung.

[Figure: Xavier Ruiz]

movements. However, there is ample compensation for this in the development of a system of air-sacs, which extends throughout the body, and acts like bellows in connection with the lungs. While the lungs represent approximately 5% of the body volume in man, in a duck they only comprise 2%, but the air-sacs and the lungs together account for 20%.

These air-sacs are expansions of the bronchial walls, but they are situated outside the lungs and the thoracic cavity. They extend throughout most of the organism, passing in between the viscera, between muscles, under the skin and even invading the medullary cavity of some bones, thus pneumatizing them. Their walls are very thin, with only one or two layers of cells, and they contain elastic fibres, but hardly any muscles or blood vessels, so they can not be contracted, nor can they exchange gases. There are usually nine in all, named according to their position in the body, which (working backwards through the body) are the cervical, interclavicular, anterior thoracic, posterior thoracic and abdominal air-sacs, all of which are in pairs, with the exception of the interclavicular, which was, however, originally double. There are exceptions in the number, from species which have only six, such as the House Sparrow, to others with twelve, as usually occurs in storks and waders. Their form, symmetry and relative importance are also variable. As well as being essential for respiration, the air-sac system is important for cooling the body, and in swimming birds it offers buoyancy. In the latter case, the posterior thoracic and abdominal sacs are usually larger than in other birds. Some species use them in courtship, puffing out the neck, or even developing spectacular inflatable pouches, as in the frigatebirds and the Greater Prairie Chicken (*Tympanuchus cupido*).

The small lungs are dorsally placed in the chest cavity and not in a ventral position as in other terrestrial vertebrates. The air-sacs also tend to be situated dorsally, probably to help keep the centre of gravity low. They are moulded in amongst the ribs, to such an extent that they are marked with deep grooves. The principal or primary bronchi are subdivided according to a very definite pattern, with a medioventral series (4-6 bronchi), a mediodorsal one (7-10) and some other bronchi, which are labelled as lateroventral and laterodorsal. The secondary bronchi branch out to form the tertiary bronchi or parabronchi. However, these do not subdivide further, as in mammals, but connect the ventral to the dorsal series of the secondary bronchi. The end result is that the system, rather than having the form of a tree, as in mammals, is more like a radiator. The number of parabronchi can vary from 400 in domestic hens to approximately 1800 in pigeons and ducks, and, laid parallel to

each other, these form the true functional unit of the lung. Their walls are made up of hundreds of fine bronchi, and these in turn are repeatedly subdivided into smaller branches, which do not end in alveoli or air-sacs, as in mammals, but instead anastomose with one another, forming an intricate network of air capillaries, that allow the air to circulate freely. This network intertwines with blood capillaries, and it is here that the gases are exchanged, purifying the blood.

The air circulation in the respiratory apparatus follows a well defined direction. With each inspiration, the air passes through the principal bronchi directly to the large abdominal air-sacs. When the air is expelled, it flows through the lungs, circulating from the mediodorsal to the medioventral bronchi, through the parabronchi and their networks of air capillaries. It flows in the opposite direction from the blood in the blood capillaries, in a counter-current system that enhances gas exchange. As new air enters the abdominal sacs from the next inspiration, the used air from the lungs passes to the air-sacs in the front of the body, and with the next expiration, this air is ousted. The system functions like a pump with a double cycle, and the tubular, as opposed to alveolar, structure of the lung ensures a continuous flow of fresh air to the respiratory surfaces. It is enormously efficient, far more so than mammalian lungs, in which roughly 20% of the inhaled air never reaches the alveoli.

This structure explains the smaller relative volume of bird lungs, although their weight is similar to that found in mammals of the same size. An effect of its greater efficiency is that proportionally birds breathe more slowly, on average once every 7·5 heart beats, while mammals breathe once every 2·9 beats. Nevertheless, there is a great variety of respiratory rhythm between species, and also individuals, depending on size, age, sex, the amount of activity undertaken and external factors, such as the temperature. Logically, during flight the breathing rate increases, to supply the extra oxygen requirements (up to 20 times more than while resting) and to cool the body down. A duck passes from 14 breaths per minute while resting, to up to 96 per minute in flight. The respiratory rhythm does not coincide with the wingbeat as used to be thought, nor do the wing movements seem to help with breathing.

Syrinx

In birds, as in other animals, the respiratory system is largely responsible for the production of sound or phonation. However, sounds are not produced in the larynx, where the respiratory and digestive tracts meet, but in a special organ called the syrinx, situated where the trachea bifurcates to form the principal bronchi. The exact location can vary, and it is tracheo-bronchial in most birds, tracheal in primitive passerines, or even bronchial, and therefore double, as in cuckoos, nightjars and some owls. Some species lack a syrinx, for instance some ratites, storks and New World vultures.

Syrinx complexity varies widely between different groups. Sound production takes place in tympaniform membranes; these are held by tracheal or bronchial rings, which may be specialized to varying degrees, and they are tensed by muscles. The muscles can be extrinsic, originating and inserting on the trachea, or intrinsic, at any rate inserting on the syrinx, and originating either on the trachea or on the syrinx itself. These muscles control the tension of the membranes, which, in conjunction with the passage of air, produces the various sounds. While in the simplest cases there are only two extrinsic muscles, the Oscines or song birds can have 5-7 pairs of intrinsic muscles, the detailed arrangement of which has been used for taxonomic purposes.

Often the sounds or vocalizations coming from the syrinx are modified in other areas of the respiratory tract, especially in the trachea, which is sometimes markedly elongated and coiled, in order to amplify its resonance. In some swans and cranes the trachea is so long that some of its loops are coiled up inside the specially hollowed keel of the sternum.

Birds' vocal repertoires differ widely, and some species have as many as 20 different calls. Different types of voice are usually employed in different behavioural contexts, each apparently being used only for a particular function. There are voices for contact, alarm, flight, courtship, begging for food and other actions, covering almost all aspects of social behaviour, and constituting a real "language", of great ethological significance. Song is a special type of vocalization, normally more complex than the others (see Territory and Colony). The metallic sounds of the Oilbird (*Steatornis caripensis*) and the Uniform Swiftlet (*Collocalia vanikorensis*) are a special case, as they are used as part of an echo-location system that allows these birds to fly in complete darkness inside their caves.

Circulation

The circulatory system follows the basic reptilian plan, but the heart has four chambers, as the ventricle is completely partitioned off, and there is only one aortic arch. This permits a complete separation of the general and pulmonary circulatory systems, of arterial and venous blood respectively, resulting in a much more efficient system, which is closely related to birds' warm-blooded condition. Mammals have also adopted this solution from the original reptilian model, but the remaining aortic arch is on the left, whereas in birds it is on the right.

Compared to mammals of similar size, birds' hearts are 1·4 to 2 times larger, but have slower cardiac rhythms. Generally, the size of the heart is inversely proportional to the size of the body, constituting 1% of body volume in the Ostrich, but as much as 2·7% in some hummingbirds.

However, in some birds, particularly Galliformes and tinamous, the heart is relatively even more reduced, and in tinamous it makes up less than 0·25% of the body volume. This seems to be influenced by the kind of activity that is habitual in these birds. They feed on the ground and are only occasionally obliged to fly, and even then frequently only for short distances, as opposed to other birds which fly well and invariably have large hearts. Birds living in cold regions or at high altitudes also have proportionally larger hearts than their counterparts in more moderate climates.

The heart is distinctly asymmetrical, with the left side about three times the size of the right. This is related to the work performed by each side, for the right ventricle only has to pump the blood to the lungs nearby, while the left must drive it to the rest of the organism. The pressures generated by the right ventricle are 5 to 10 times less than those of the left.

Anatomy of the cardiocirculatory system of a bird. Below: cross-section of the heart.

[Figure: Xavier Ruiz]

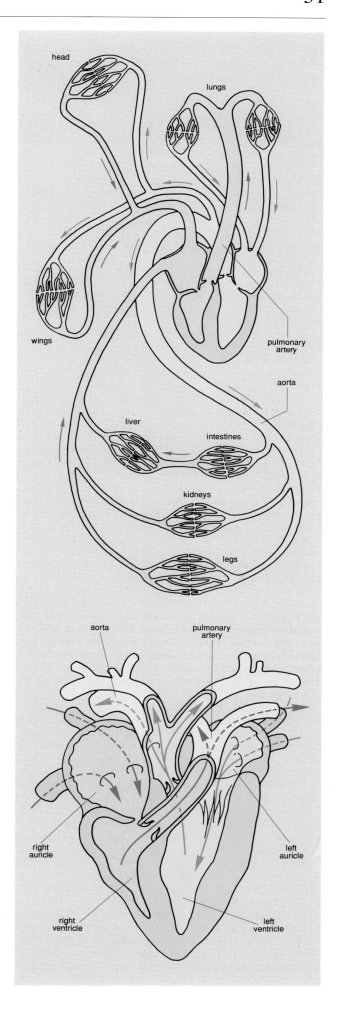

The heart rate at rest usually oscillates between 150 and 350 beats per minute in medium-sized birds, but it is much faster in smaller than in larger birds, with 60-70 in the Ostrich, about 500 in small passerines, and more than 1200 in small hummingbirds. During flight there is a significant acceleration, and the Herring Gull's rate of 130 beats per minute, while resting or gliding, rises to 625, when flapping, though the rate can also rise simply when the bird is excited or suffering from stress. On the other hand, it slows down to half or even less in birds such as penguins, auks and diving ducks, when they are under water.

Birds' blood has similar features to that of the reptiles, and is different from that of mammals, with relatively large red blood cells (particularly in those orders considered to be the most primitive), which are oval and have a nucleus.

Metabolism and Thermoregulation

In order to maintain their characteristic high levels of activity and constant temperatures, birds have a very high metabolism, which is comparable only with that of mammals, and they consume roughly 20-30 times more food than reptiles of the same weight.

As in other animals, metabolic rate is closely related to size. The basal metabolism is the minimum metabolic requirement, while resting quietly, with no digestive activity in a thermoneutral environment, in relation to units of time and body mass. Rates vary allometrically, according to logarithmic equations, in which the exponent, or slope of the curve, is 0·72, differing slightly from the 0·67 calculated from the simple relationship between surface and volume, and almost equal to the 0·75 corresponding to mammals. The equations that best display the variation observed in birds are different in passerines and non-passerines. The rates corresponding to the former can be approximately 1·65 times higher than those of the latter, in birds of similar sizes. There are also apparently less significant deviations in other orders, particularly in the ratites, which have lower rates than expected. Illustrative examples include: the Dwarf Cassowary (*Casuarius bennetti*), 29·3 Kcal/kg/day, with a body weight of 17,600 g; the Golden Eagle (*Aquila chrysaetos*), 34 Kcal, 3000 g; the feral pigeon, 113 Kcal, 150 g; the Common Quail (*Coturnix coturnix*), 235 Kcal, 97 g; the Great Tit (*Parus major*), 451 Kcal, 18·5 g; and Anna's Hummingbird (*Calypte anna*), 1,410 Kcal, 4·1 g. Man's basal metabolic rate is about 12·5 Kcal/kg/day. Metabolic rates as high as those in hummingbirds are otherwise found only in a group of small insectivorous mammals, the shrews. In both groups there are species with body weights of only 2 g, probably the minimum possible limit in homoiothermal animals. The basal metabolism is not fixed, but rather varies with individuals, in different seasons (higher in winter), and at different times of day (lower at night).

Any activity naturally causes an increase, over and above the basal metabolism, in the energy expended, for instance digestion, locomotion, growth, moult, egg formation and incubation. Flight demands an energy expenditure of around 2-25 times the basal metabolism, depending on the type of flight. Swifts and swallows use the least, and finches and hovering hummingbirds the most. When walking, a Greater Rhea (*Rhea americana*) uses 3·5 times more energy than when resting, and if it breaks into a trot, it uses 14 times more. A Mallard, swimming at its most economical speed, expends about 3·2 times more energy than while resting. Egg formation can use as little as half the daily basal metabolism in small passerines, or as much as the equivalent of 12 or 13 days' worth in the Brown Kiwi (*Apteryx australis*). Lastly, incubation can demand between 10% and 30% of a resting adult's basal metabolism.

In recent years a great effort has been made to discover the precise energy investment for each of these and other aspects of avian life. Some of the study methods include marking with radioactive isotopes, mainly doubly-labelled water, which allows the organism's production speed of carbon dioxide to be measured, and in this way the metabolic rates can be calculated under different conditions. Also, in biotelemetry, data

about the body temperature, and respiratory and cardiac rhythms can be transmitted over some distance using sensors. Already some relatively precise models have been constructed which indicate the time and energy that birds in the wild devote to different activities, such as foraging, defending territory, resting, preening, courtship and so on. These energy "budgets" permit the elaboration and analysis of very revealing ecological and evolutionary comparisons.

In accordance with birds' high metabolic rates, their internal temperature is very high, at around 40°C (38°-42°C), while in mammals it tends to be between 36°C and 38°C. As in mammals, daily temperatures usually fluctuate, and in diurnal birds it can reach 42°C during the day, but drop to 39°C at night, whereas in nocturnal species the opposite occurs.

Maintaining these internal temperatures within the more or less narrow limits imposed by homoiothermia depends on striking a balance between the heat generated by metabolism and that which is lost by conduction and radiation. The rates of heat loss can be regulated by varying the feather position or the intensity of the peripheral circulation, above all in the legs and feet. In cold weather, birds increase the angle of the feathers using special tiny cutaneous muscles, the "musculi pennati", so that the insulating layer of air within the plumage is augmented. When it is hot, they flatten the feathers against the body increasing conduction. In both water and land birds there is a dense network of capillaries ("rete mirabile") in the lower part of the tibiotarsus, which combats heat loss by means of a cross-current system called counter-current exchange. This system allows a fair proportion of the arterial blood heat to pass to the venous blood. The operation takes place while the arterial blood is moving outwards towards the feet and the venous blood is going back towards the centre. The arterial blood cools down before reaching the extremities, which thus maintain a temperature only a few degrees above freezing point, and in this way hardly any heat is dissipated. Sitting on the tarsi is another way of saving heat, and one or both feet may be positioned under the body, or the bill and part of the head may be tucked into the back feathers. In hot weather, expansion of the foot arteries allows the blood to bypass the capillary network and arrive at the feet more quickly, where excess heat can then be lost by radiation. Different species of cormorants, albatrosses, storks and New World vultures, for example, enhance heat loss by discharging highly liquid excrement over the legs and feet. Behaviour generally has a significant bearing on thermoregulation, for example in the location of suitable microclimates, with sun or shade, bathing, collective roosts and even the huddling together of individuals for protection against the cold.

These mechanisms are usually sufficient within certain environmental limits, but if these pass the "critical temperatures", the lower and upper limits generally of 18°C and 33°C, other mechanisms, which are physiological, come into play. The cold can be counteracted by continuous muscular shivering, particularly of the pectorals, to increase metabolic heat production. This causes oxygen consumption to increase and fat reserves to decrease. It is said that in winter some small birds lose half or more of their fat reserves each night, and are forced to make them up again the following day. If the upper critical temperature is exceeded the regulatory mechanism used is the evaporation of water. This takes place above all in the respiratory tracts, by panting, very often accompanied by a special throat vibration called gular-fluttering, which is activated by movements of the hyoid apparatus. Although birds do not have sweat glands, evaporation can sometimes take place through the skin, as in incubating sandgrouse, which manage to tolerate air and ground temperatures of 48°C and 73°C respectively, without panting. Evaporative cooling is obviously very effective, but it consumes metabolic energy, as well as water. Thus, when the temperature is either above or below the thermoneutral zone, energy expenditure increases, so that curves of oxygen consumption against ambient temperature display a characteristic U-shape, with the bottom section corresponding to the thermoneutral zone.

A last recourse to help birds tolerate extreme temperatures consists of renouncing homoiothermia partially and temporarily. The American Mourning Dove (*Zenaida macroura*) can allow its internal temperature to reach 45°C, incredibly near what is considered to be the lethal limit. More often the opposite occurs, with birds such as the Common Swift, which can reduce its body temperature to 20°-21°C, with a very much lower metabolic expenditure, on occasions when it is forced to fast, due to bad weather conditions, and it can resist several days in this way, while nestlings can survive thus for up to twelve days. One mechanism which undoubtedly saves energy is the lowering of internal temperature at night. This decrease is of around 2°-3°C in most birds, but in Andean hummingbirds it can be up to 20°C or 30°C, which is estimated to reduce the daily energy expenditure by up to 27%. In the Common Poorwill (*Phalaenoptilus nuttallii*), genuine hibernation has been recorded, and birds have been found to maintain internal temperatures of only 18°-20°C. In all these and other similar cases, the low body temperatures are associated with much slower cardiac rhythms and general states of sleepiness or lethargy. In the Blue-throated Hummingbird (*Lampornis clemenciae*) the heart rate lowers to 36 beats a minute, from the 480-1260 registered during different types of activity. Birds, especially nidicolous species, are also to a great extent poikilothermal during the first days of life.

One aspect related to this is long-term adaptation to extreme climates for instance in boreal, high altitude and desertic regions. In general, birds conform well to the classic ecogeographic rules that indicate increases in size (Bergmann's Rule) and shorter appendages (Allen's Rule) in colder climates. Other variations connected with climatic adaptation include the colour and density of the plumage. The number of body-coverts and especially of down feathers varies widely, not only geographically but also seasonally. In the House Sparrow, the weight of the plumage increases by some 70% after the autumn moult. Many birds of temperate or cold regions take a long time to complete their autumn moult, allowing the number of feathers to increase gradually, as winter approaches. In birds of warm regions, the number of feathers is not only relatively low, but is also fairly constant year round.

Nervous System and Senses

The active life that birds live demands a high degree of development in the nervous system and the senses. Both follow the general reptilian model, but with numerous notable improvements in various aspects. Apart from some rare exceptions, sight is the dominant sense and the eyes are relatively very large. In the Common Starling they make up 15% of its head mass, while in man they account for no more than 2%. The Ostrich has the largest eyes of all terrestrial animals (5 cm in diameter), and the eyes of many diurnal raptors and owls are larger than man's. They are generally situated well to the sides of the head, giving a very wide field of vision, of more than 300°, but the drawback of this is that the zone of binocular vision is very narrow. Binocular, stereoscopic vision is very important for calculating distances with precision, although many birds can do this by means of quick bobs of the head, viewing objects almost simultaneously from different angles. The field of binocular vision is particularly reduced in granivorous species (10-30°), wider in insectivores and raptors (35-50°), and widest in owls (60-70°) which have their eyes noticeably directed towards the front. There are, however, birds, such as woodcock, in which the eyes are set so far back that they allow for rear-view binocular vision. In connection with binocular vision, some birds have a second fovea (area of high receptor cell density) in the retina, called the temporal fovea, which is situated to one side of the central fovea, the only one present in mammals.

Externally the eyes are protected by a double eyelid and a nictitating membrane, which is used both for cleaning and protecting the ocular surface. As in reptiles, there is a scleral ring, which is formed of 12-15 small cartilaginous plates (ossicles) in the sclerotic layer. These plates provide the eye with a section of straight walls, which means that instead of being round, as in mammals, birds's eyes can have various different shapes, including flat (most species), globose (diurnal raptors), or tubular (owls). The scleral ring is, however, responsible for a certain immobility of the eyeball, even though birds too have the six pairs of extrinsic muscles that are found in all vertebrates. They compensate for this relative immobility by swivelling the head, and in owls this rotation can sometimes be of as much as 270°.

The lens is large, and normally very flexible with a surprising proficiency in focusing. This is effected by the two groups of striated muscles of the ciliary body, which are attached to the scleral ring. The first group alter the shape of the lens (Brücke's muscles), while the second group affect the curvature of the cornea (Crampton's muscles). Mammals only have muscles that change the shape of the lens. Focusing is very rapid, which is essential for flying animals, and it is also thought to be extremely powerful, producing changes of as much as 20 Diopters. By way of comparison, a human child achieves 13·5 and an adult far less. As an adaptation to diving, cormorants are capable of variations of between 50 and 60 Diopters.

The retina is unusually thick and has a high density of light receptor cells, not only in the foveae but all over the surface. The Yellow Wagtail (*Motacilla flava*) has 120,000 receptors per milimetre, compared to 10,000 in man. In the human fovea, density reaches roughly 200,000 receptors/mm, but this figure is half the number noted in the House Sparrow, and a fifth of those present in the Common Buzzard (*Buteo buteo*). Moreover, in birds practically every receptor is connected to a single bipolar cell, attached in turn to a single neuron. This means that the number of fibres in the optic nerve is almost double that in man's. It is believed that visual acuity in birds, although perhaps not as good as was thought in the past, must be at least as good as that of humans, and perhaps about two or three times better in diurnal raptors. In addition, birds have a larger field of sharp vision.

The most abundant receptors are the cones, which are linked with particularly good colour perception, and are capable of discriminating even polarized light, and colours from the ultraviolet light spectrum. As opposed to those of mammals, the cones found in birds each contain an oil droplet coloured by carotenoids, which probably enhances colour perception. In nocturnal species, as in other vertebrates with similar lifestyles or which live in dark environments, the retina has many more rods than cones.

A particularly curious feature of the avian eye is the pecten, a pleated sheet of tissue, which projects from the back of the eye into the vitreous body in the posterior chamber; reptiles have a more or less rudimentary pecten. Its main function seems to be to supply nutrients and oxygen to the retina, which, in contrast to the case of mammals, does not have blood vessels. However, many other theories have been proposed as to its possible functions.

The organ used for balance and hearing, the ear, is structurally simpler than that of mammals, with the pinnae (external part of the outer ear) missing, the middle ear containing only one small bone (columella), and the cochlea smaller and not coiled in a spiral. However, in the cochlea the number of sensory cells per unit of length is very high, and on the whole, it seems that the avian ear must be at least as sensitive as that of mammals, in terms of sharpness of hearing, discrimination of frequencies and sound location. Nevertheless, the frequency range is somewhat narrower, and it seems that most birds perceive properly only frequencies of 1-5 kHz, although the Oscines and some owls can hear frequencies of almost 8-12 kHz. At the other extreme, pigeons and guineafowl (*Numida*) register infrasounds of only 2-10 Hz, but the purpose of this capacity is not yet known.

Owls and some raptors, such as harriers (*Circus*) have unique adaptations to detect low intensity sounds, and in particular the precise location of these sounds. Amongst other things the eardrums, columella and cochlea are all enlarged, and there are discs of feathers on the face or covering the openings of the external ear that act as outer ears. The right and left ears are asymmetrical, a feature palpably reflected in the external shape of the cranium, and in the large quantity of specialized neurons that appear in the auditory centres of the brain. This asymmetry is used by birds like the Barn Owl to locate prey in complete darkness, with margins of error of only one degree in both the horizontal and vertical planes. The echo-location ability of cave-dwellers, like the Oilbird and the Uniform Swiftlet is also very striking, although it can not compare with the perfection of the bats.

The semicircular canals of the inner ear, on which the sense of balance depends, are very well developed. Their size is directly proportional, in fair degree, to the flying capacities of different groups and species, and they are notably larger, for example, in pigeons than in gallinaceous birds.

Generally the sense of smell is poorly developed, perhaps partly due to the regression of the upper jaw region of the cranium. The olfactory epithelium is practically limited to the posterior concha of the nasal cavities, next to the internal nostrils, and the large size of these possibly enables birds to smell food from inside the mouth. Experiments have shown markedly dissimilar olfactory capacities between different bird species, which are very closely related to the greater or lesser development of the olfactory lobes in the brain. Birds with a good sense of smell appear in very distant groups, among which stand out the kiwis, the Procellariiformes, and the New World vultures.

Relatively little is known about the sense of taste in birds, but in any case it does not seem to be very important. The taste buds are generally situated in the interior of the mouth, although they are sometimes at the tip of the bill, but their number appears to be relatively low, ranging from only a few dozen in passerines to several hundred in ducks and parrots. Mammals tend to have several thousand and man has about 10,000. On the other hand, birds' sense of touch is extremely keen. Apart from a large number of nerve endings distributed all over the skin that are sensitive above all to pain and temperature, there are many tactile corpuscles, which are characteristic of birds. Merkel's corpuscles appear on the skin, tongue and bill, while Grandry's corpuscles occur in the mouth and in the bills of owls and ducks. Herbst's corpuscles, the largest and most complex, are concentrated at the bill tip, especially in waders, on the tip of the tongue in woodpeckers, and in the gape flanges of nidicolous chicks. They also appear around the follicles of

the wing feathers, filoplumes and bristles, indeed these last two are specialized for sensory purposes.

Brain

The avian brain reflects and summarizes much of the development that birds have undergone in the sensory and nervous systems. It is at least as voluminous as that of small mammals, and about six to eleven times larger than in reptiles of comparable size. In the House Sparrow, the brain comprises 4·4% of total body weight of about 23 g, while in a vole (*Microtus*) or a lizard of equal weight, it represents 2·8% and 0·55% respectively. In the forebrain, or telencephalon, the olfactory lobes are generally small, but the cerebral hemispheres are well developed, as in mammals. However, whereas in mammals the growth is mainly in the cerebral cortex, in birds the most voluminous part is the corpus striatum at the base of the hemispheres. Traditionally it was thought that this difference in structure was responsible for the different levels of intelligence between the two groups, mammals being characterized by a greater capacity for learning, and showing much learnt or intelligent behaviour, whereas birds were seen as creatures of very complex instinctive behaviour, which were almost totally mechanical in their reactions. Nevertheless, the smooth, thin cerebral cortex of birds has hardly any importance at all. Pigeons in experiments were perfectly capable of mating and raising young successfully after having this part removed. Within the corpus striatum of birds there is a top layer or hyperstriatum, exclusive to the Aves, which is the source of intelligent behaviour and is to a certain extent comparable with the cerebral cortex of mammals. The learning capacities of birds such as crows or parrots, tested by laboratory experiments or by field observation, are quite exceptional and similar to, or even better than, those of many mammals. There are great differences between different species, which become apparent when brain volumes are compared, but above all when the sizes of their cerebral hemispheres are compared with those of the rest of the brain. The index thus obtained varies from 3 in pheasants and 4 in gulls, to 15 in owls, 19 in crows and 28 in macaws.

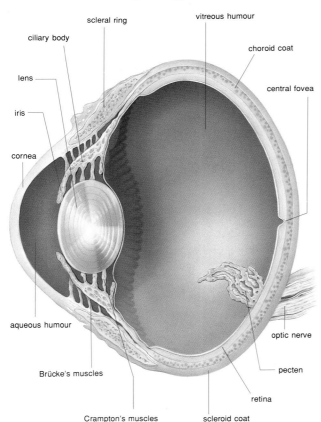

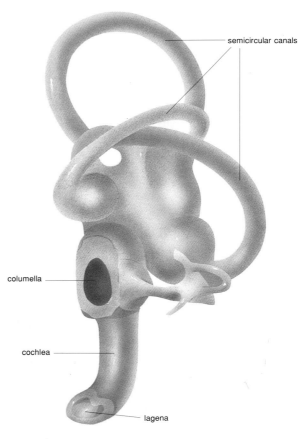

Horizontal cross-section of a bird's eye (left) and ear (right).

[Figures: Joan Fors & Miguel Angel Castaños]

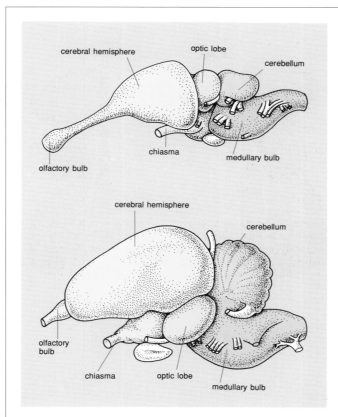

Lateral view of the brains of a lizard (above) and a bird (below).

[Figure: Xavier Ruiz]

The other parts of the corpus striatum (neostriatum, paleostriatum, ectostriatum and archistriatum), equivalents for which are found in reptiles and mammals, control instinctive behaviour. This is certainly very elaborate in birds and is involved in almost all aspects of activities such as locomotion, feeding behaviour, calls and song, nest building, the raising of young, and so on. Complex and intelligent as they may seem, in these operations birds usually behave automatically.

Two other brain areas with significant development are the optic lobes (mesencephalon), which are related to the great importance of sight, and the cerebellum (metencephalon), connected with the excellent muscular and locomotive co-ordination of birds, which is only to be expected from their perfect adaptation to flight. Another feature connected with flight is a distinctive thickening of the spinal cord, the brachial or cervical thickening, from which originates the plexus of nerves that control the wings. There is also a second thickening in the spinal cord related to the hind limbs, the lumbar or lumbo-sacral thickening, which is more developed in flightless cursorial birds, and has a gelatinous body, rich in glycogen and lipids of unknown function.

Reproductive System

Like the reptiles, birds are oviparous. This might be viewed as a disadvantage, in comparison with mammals, as regards the protection offered to the young during their foetal development. But it is compensated for to a certain extent by parental behaviour, which in birds includes building and guarding a nest. It is, however, advantageous for aerial life, as it frees them of cumbersome volume and weight, allowing them to lay each egg in turn as soon as it has been formed. Another adaptation to save weight is the uniquely seasonal development of the gonads and the gonoducts, which are atrophied outside the breeding season. In domestic quails the ovary weighs 15 mg and the oviduct 20 mg in winter, whereas in the breeding season they reach 6000 mg and 5000 mg respectively. In many species the size of the testes can multiply by 200-300 times in spring.

In males, the gonads or testes are normally bean-shaped and are situated on the roof of the abdominal cavity, in front of the anterior lobe of the kidney. The high internal temperatures of homoiothermic animals present a handicap for the rapid production of spermatozoa, a problem which in mammals is solved by a process in which the testicles abandon the coelomic cavity and are transferred to external scrotal sacs. Birds do not employ this mechanism, but instead use a form of air cooling in conjunction with the abdominal air-sacs, which almost completely surround the testes after they have swollen, and, secondly, they carry out spermatogenesis mainly at night, when body temperature is lower (see Metabolism and Thermoregulation).

The spermiducts have a fairly complicated proximal portion called the epididymis, which is followed by a deferent duct leading into the cloaca. Towards the end, each deferent duct widens into a seminal vesicle, which is not homologous to that of mammals, and is used for storing the semen temporarily. The progressive swelling of the vesicles leads to the formation of a protuberance on the exterior of the cloaca, which in many cases can be used for sexing birds externally. This protuberance apparently enables the stored spermatozoa to be kept at a temperature of about 4° less than that of the body. This cloacal protuberance also helps in copulation, which in birds is normally based simply on bringing the male's cloaca into contact with that of the female. There are, however, a series of species, in which the ventral wall of the cloacal proctodeum develops a peculiar structure that is used in copulation, an erectile, protrusible penis-like phallus, and this is found in ratites, tinamous, storks, flamingos, ducks, gallinaceous birds (especially the Cracidae) and thick-knees. In the Ostrich, the penis can reach a length of 20 cm. Some authorities consider this to be a primitive feature, related to the existence of similar copulatory organs in most present day reptiles, but other factors may intervene, and it is interesting to note the presence of a penis in the passerine genus *Bubalornis*.

In order to copulate the male stands on the female's back, keeping his balance by fluttering his wings. He squats on his tarsi, twists his tail aside and brings his cloaca towards the female's, while she collaborates by remaining crouched and practically immobile. Copulation tends to be brief, lasting scarcely a few seconds, but it is fairly frequently repeated. Many species copulate in the nest or in the immediate surroundings, others while swimming, and swifts in full flight.

Unlike the males, females normally have only one functional gonad on the left, while the right one is rudimentary. The existence of only one ovary could be interpreted as an adaptation to flight, taking into account its large size. However, many species of different orders, especially kiwis and raptors, frequently have two functional ovaries. Like the testicles, the ovary is situated in the roof of the abdominal cavity, in front of the kidney. The form is like a small bunch of different sized grapes, with each grape corresponding to an ovarian follicle. There can be hundreds or even thousands of follicles, although few of these ever develop into ovules. In the Carrion Crow (*Corvus corone*), up to 26,000 have been counted, with a normal clutch of only 4-5 eggs. The maturation of a follicle can take varying lengths of time, from 4-5 days in small passerines, to 16 days in some penguins. During this time the ovules, full of yolk, fall into the abdominal cavity, to be collected subsequently by the funnel of the infundibulum, the entrance to the oviduct.

The long oviducts of birds can be separated into various segments, each related to a different phase of egg formation. On entering the infundibulum, the ovule constitutes the part of the egg equivalent to the yolk. Here it remains for roughly 20 minutes, the interval during which fertilization must take place, before additional layers of the egg bar access to the spermatozoa. Remarkably, the spermatozoa swim the full length of the oviduct in under 30 minutes. After copulation, the spermatozoa remain viable for a long time, and they can survive for days or in some species even weeks.

The glandular section after the infundibulum is known as the magnum, and its job is to secrete the egg-white, or albumen, which will contain the water reserves of the egg. The albumen consists of 90% water and only 10% proteins. As the white is being deposited, in four different layers, the egg rotates slowly, causing the production of the chalazae, a series of twisted strands, which help to stabilize the yolk in position. After three

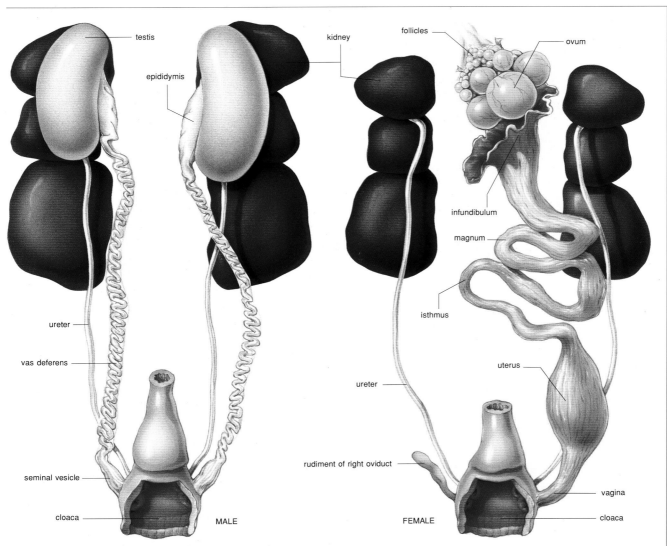

Anatomy of the reproductive system of a bird, male (left) and female (right).

[Figure: Joan Fors]

or four hours in the magnum, the egg passes through a narrow passage called the isthmus, where after barely an hour the two keratinous shell membranes are secreted.

The next process takes place in the uterus, which is quite different from the mammalian uterus, and consists of the production of the hard shell. Calcium carbonate is deposited in the form of calcite crystals, along with small quantities of organic matrix, phosphate and magnesium. The minerals are not laid down uniformly but leave numerous pores, about 7500 in a hen's egg, and these allow gas exchange with the exterior, though they do not allow the entry of micro-organisms. The shell represents 11-15% of the total egg weight.

The pigments responsible for colouring the shell are also deposited in the uterus. These are normally porphyrins (reds and browns) and cyanins (blues and greens), some of them deposited at the same time as the calcium carbonate crystals, giving the background colour, and others on the surface, creating various patterns such as spots, stripes or speckles. The egg normally stays in the uterus for 18 to 20 hours. A sphincter separates the uterus from the final segment, the vagina, a simple cavity with muscular walls, which opens out into the cloaca.

Breeding Behaviour

The raising of young in birds, as in all organisms, has evolved to optimize levels of breeding success, so that the significant investments of time, energy and physiological effort receive as full compensation as possible. This is reflected both in the number of healthy chicks fledged and in adult survival which enables the birds to breed in successive years, for the fitness of an individual is measured by the number of descendants it leaves throughout its life, and not only in one given breeding

season. Each of the many aspects of breeding behaviour, from the formation of pair-bond, to the type of nest constructed, should be scrutinized from this point of view.

The breeding season generally coincides with the times of year when food is most abundant, which means that the chicks can thus be fed better in terms of quantity or quality. However, breeding behaviour is usually initiated weeks or sometimes months before food abundance reaches its peak, so, although the seasonal variation in food abundance is the ultimate factor, which in evolutionary terms has conditioned a very precise seasonal breeding calendar in birds, it is not the proximate factor that triggers breeding activity.

As with other aspects of bird biology, breeding activity follows an innate, endogenous rhythm of approximately yearly (circannual) cycles, which is decided by a series of keys or external factors, the most important of which in temperate and cold regions seems to be the photoperiod. The progressive lengthening of the day as spring approaches appears to constitute the proximate factor that activates breeding behaviour, and in this way birds prepare themselves in advance for the period of maximum abundance of food, so that it coincides roughly with the moment when the chicks are in the nest.

Numerous experiments involving artificial modification of the photoperiod have demonstrated beyond doubt the determining role that this usually plays. However, other factors can intervene to a greater or lesser extent, giving rise to a finer adjustment, for example, temperature, rainfall (particularly in the tropics, or in arid regions), water levels in lakes and rivers (important for waterbirds), and indirectly food availability.

Breeding activity can be divided into a series of phases. There is a preliminary "refractory" period, in which birds appear to be insensitive to any stimulus, and can be interpreted to be resting after the previous breeding season, and during this period they devote their efforts to other activities, such as migration or moult. Subsequently, there is an acceleration phase, that coincides with the selection of the breeding biotope. This involves searching for a mate, with song and courtship, and sometimes the development of more pronounced secondary sexual characters, and this leads to the culmination phase, comprising nest building, copulation and ovulation. Birds are sensitive to artificial photoperiod modifications only during the second of these phases, while in the third they speed up or slow down, depending on different proximate factors, in particular, apparently, whether or not there is enough food for the female to form the eggs. Egg formation demands a very high energetic investment, and the laying of a complete clutch represents 45% of the female's body weight in the Common Pheasant and the Common Tern, 50% in the House Sparrow, 60% in the Mallard, and 130% in the Blue Tit (*Parus caeruleus*). Lack of food can cause a delay in the start of breeding activity, and consequently the time the chicks are in the nest will not coincide perfectly with the best days of the year, as regards food availability.

The artificial provision of food has often led to birds bringing forward their habitual breeding seasons, by up to a month in an experiment with Common Kestrels. Some birds develop adaptations to help to make egg-laying occur at the best moment, independent of the relative abundance of food at a given time. One of these adaptations is the development of fat deposits, for example in geese that breed in Arctic regions and begin laying as soon as they arrive at the breeding grounds, so that the young can be raised in the limited favourable time available. Others are courtship feeding, where the males pass sometimes very substantial quantities of food to the females, for instance in different birds of prey, terns, tits and others, or the food storing behaviour of nutcrackers, jays and woodpeckers.

The result of all this is that there is great variation in the timing of the breeding season between different birds, even within the same species. Geographical variability has been observed. Hopkins' Law calculates that in birds there is a delay of four or five days in the start of breeding for each degree of latitude going north, or for every 125 m of altitude climbed. Other variables are: meteorological, with breeding arriving sooner or later each year depending on the weather conditions; ecological, with variations within a region and breeding season, caused by different productivity in the various different habitats; or individual, with older and more experienced birds generally laying earlier. Due to the great stability of the ecosystems they form part of, some tropical seabirds breed in non-annual cycles. The Bridled Tern (*Sterna anaethetus*) breeds every eight months in the Seychelles, while the Sooty Tern (*Sterna fuscata*) breeds every nine and a half months on Ascension Island. On Christmas Island (Indian Ocean) the latter species breeds each year, but if the chicks die, birds lay again after only six months.

The length of the breeding season is also variable each year, depending both on the time taken over each part of the process and on the length of the favourable season. In northern and Arctic regions there is not time for more than one brood, and the same is usually the case in large species with slower development, to the point where some penguins, albatrosses, frigatebirds and condors are incapable of breeding more than once every two years. However, in passerines, pigeons and rails, especially in warm regions, two and even three broods are quite frequently raised.

Physiologically, the timing of breeding is controlled by hormones. The photoperiod is registered by the body in the hypothalamus of the brain, where there are photoreceptors that perceive light through the tissues, without the eyes being involved in the process. The length of the day is therefore evaluated in some way by an interior biological clock. Long days induce the release of different hormones in the pituitary gland, amongst which the most important are two gonadotrophins, the Follicle Stimulating Hormone (FSH) and the Luteinizing Hormone (LH), which are produced by the adenohypophysis. These are largely responsible for the seasonal growth of the gonads, and also cause them to start producing androgens and oestrogens, in the interstitial cells of the testicles (Leydig cells), and in the ovarian follicles. These, in turn, stimulate the development of secondary sexual characters and set off the instinctive behaviour related to breeding.

Territory and Colony

The diversity of the social behaviour found in birds becomes particularly obvious during the breeding season, although it is not exclusive to this period. It appears that birds are never distributed haphazardly, and they either form colonies, or tend to maintain territories, from which some individuals actively exclude others. In both cases, highly developed specific patterns of behaviour come into play, involving complex systems of communication, based on sounds or visual displays of various kinds.

Territorial behaviour can be explained by the limitations of certain resources which are essential for survival or successful breeding, such as food, nest-sites and sometimes individuals of the opposite sex. Maintaining a territory benefits the individual, as, by securing these resources for himself, he improves his chances of successful breeding, but this practice is, however, costly in terms of both time and energy. So the advantages depend in the first place on the relative abundance of such resources, which in turn determines the optimum size of territory to be defended. The benefits gained from a large territory increase only to a certain point, while the effort required to maintain it grow indefinitely. Likewise, they depend extensively on the way in which the resources are distributed, and territoriality only makes sense, if the distribution is more or less even, and therefore predictable. In general, this is more usual in insectivorous or predatory species, than amongst seed or fruit eaters (see Feeding and Digestion). The conditions sometimes change in the course of the year, and many pass-

Longitudinal section of a bird's egg.

[Figure: Xavier Ruiz]

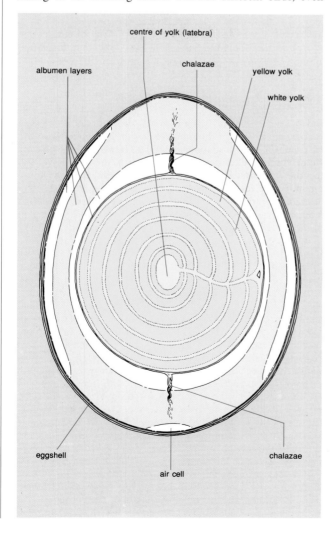

centre of yolk (latebra)

albumen layers

chalazae

yellow yolk

white yolk

eggshell

chalazae

air cell

erines that are insectivorous and territorial during the breeding season change to seed diets and form flocks in winter, while the few that continue primarily as insectivores establish winter territories, for instance the European Robin (*Erithacus rubecula*), the White Wagtail, and the Great Grey Shrike (*Lanius excubitor*) in Europe.

The signals that are used by birds to define their territories also appear, perhaps secondarily, to play a part in the attraction of a mate. These signals can be both acoustic and visual, and their efficiency varies with distance. They are often combined in such a way that, while singing, a bird may at the same time emit a long- and medium-range acoustic signal, and another of medium- and short-range, whilst showing off the combination of colours in its nuptial plumage by adopting certain postures.

Among large birds and those with open territories, visual signals predominate, whereas in forest, nocturnal or small species, sounds seem to be more important. This generally involves vocalizations using the syrinx, but they sometimes have other origins. Many birds beat their wings together or against the sides of their bodies (grouse, owls, nightjars, pigeons), while others take advantage of the air flow during flight, to produce sounds using modified wing or tail feathers (snipes, some bustards, hummingbirds). Some clatter or snap their bills (storks, owls), woodpeckers drum on hollow tree trunks with their bills, and some grouse and the Little Bustard (*Tetrax tetrax*) stamp noisily on the ground.

The very elaborate, clearly territorial vocalizations, normally made only by males, are those that we can accurately refer to as songs. They occur above all in passerines, but also in other groups, such as Galliformes, owls, nightjars, pigeons and cuckoos. The length, structure, tone, pitch and other attributes can be very different, allowing not only identification of the species, but also on occasions, in some species, individual recognition. In many songs there is a hereditary part that is completely innate, and another learnt by each individual. This helps to explain the existence of geographical "dialects" in the songs of some species like the Chaffinch, and the phenomenon of vocal imitation, which is very common (in 15-20% of Oscines in different parts of the world) with renowned specialists, such as the Northern Mockingbird (*Mimus polyglottos*), the Common Starling and the Marsh Warbler (*Acrocephalus palustris*).

Songs tend to be more complex in birds which live in dense growth of any kind (closed woods, reedbeds, thick undergrowth), where visual signals are ineffective, and consequently the most musical are usually those with cryptic plumage, like the Common Nightingale (*Luscinia megarhynchos*) and the Garden Warbler (*Sylvia borin*).

Singing activity usually follows a very regular pattern throughout the year, according to the breeding and hormonal cycles, and it is far more frequent during the initial phases of breeding activity, and in males that have not yet found a mate. Sometimes the sheer amount of vocalization can be astonishing, for example one every 7-15 seconds in the Chaffinch, or 22,000 a day in the Red-eyed Vireo (*Vireo olivaceus*). There are birds that also sing in autumn and winter, particularly those like the European Robin that maintain winter territories. But outwith the breeding season, normally only much simpler, weaker subsongs are heard, and these may also be uttered by females and immature males. There is also a daily pattern, with maximum singing around dawn and in the early hours of the morning, and minimum activity during the hottest hours. Particular meteorological conditions, such as rain, wind or temperatures, tend to affect the frequency of emission.

Colonial Breeding

Roughly 13% of bird species breed in colonies, and this tendency is especially marked in seabirds (93% of species), where both the main sources of food (concentrations of fish, squid or plankton) and the nesting grounds (cliffs and islands) usually favour aggregation. Colonies are also very common in freshwater fishing species (herons, pelicans, cormorants, terns),

granivorous birds (weavers, sparrows, parrots), carrion eaters (Old and New World vultures), and aerial insectivores (swifts, swallows, bee-eaters, some falcons). Colony size is enormously variable, from only a few pairs to millions, as in the King Penguin (*Aptenodytes patagonicus*), the Guanay Cormorant (*Phalacrocorax bougainvillii*) and the Red-billed Quelea (*Quelea quelea*).

The main advantages of colonies are related to obtaining food, and, amongst other possiblities, they may function as centres with information as to the whereabouts of good feeding areas, and this may also be the case of collective roosts. Colonies are also useful for reducing the danger of predation, through increased surveillance, and the possibility of co-operative defence (mobbing), and, with the synchronization of egg-laying, the requirements of local predators are quickly satisfied, and the latter can not take full advantage of a great source of food that is concentrated into a short time. However, colonies have the disadvantage of being easily located by predators, which makes protective colouring almost useless, at any rate in adults. In a form of compromise, various ground-nesting species, like terns (*Sterna*) and pratincoles, form very loose colonies, in which adults immediately abandon their nests, when predators appear, entrusting the fate of the widely scattered eggs or chicks to the effectiveness of their camouflage. Other more or less obvious inconveniences of colonies include increased competition for different resources, such as suitable nest-sites, building material for nests, or food in the surrounding area. Other disadvantages include the risk of cannibalism, among gulls for example, the higher risk of passing on ectoparasites or disease, and, perhaps most of all, the risk of mistakenly investing effort in looking after the eggs or chicks of other birds. These inconveniences generally compel the birds to perform territorial behaviour, at least on a small scale, which in turn creates minimum distances between and regular spacing of nests within the colony. Colonial birds must also be able to recognize their own eggs and chicks with complete certainty, memorizing their location, aspect or voice. In guillemots (*Uria*), which nest virtually touching each other, one adaptation seems to be an extraordinary variety in egg coloration.

Mating Systems

More than 90% of bird species are monogamous and form more or less stable relationships for breeding. In short-lived birds, like ducks and most passerines, the pair-bond tends to last only for one breeding season, but many other birds normally remain together year after year, especially if breeding has been successful, and birds like albatrosses, geese, swans and eagles have permanent relationships, with very low "divorce" rates. It seems that, amongst monogamous birds, the joint dedication of the two birds to the breeding tasks is normally the best way to optimize the breeding output of each individual. Sometimes it is obvious that the contribution of the males is essential, for example when the eggs or chicks can not be left alone for long, because of the threat of predation, for example in gull colonies, or when only one chick hatches each time, as in Procellariiformes and many vultures. If the female could successfully attend a chick by herself, then the pair could raise at least two, which would have resulted, in evolutionary terms, in a clutch of more than one egg. Polygamy is, in fact, rarer among nidicolous species, because the adults have to make a greater effort in transporting food to the nest, and this makes the participation of both parents necessary.

In cases where females can rear the brood successfully by themselves, for instance among nidifugous species like the Galliformes, or in very fertile environments such as marshes, males may find that an easy way of augmenting their own particular fitness is through polygamy. The mating of a male with more than one female is known as polygyny and it can occur simultaneously, with the male maintaining bonds with various females at the same time, or successively, with mating taking place in a rapid succession. In the first of the two cases, the male defends a wide territory and a greater or lesser number

The Eclectus Parrot offers one of the most extreme examples of sexual dimorphism in birds. It is so pronounced that, for many years, the male and female were regarded as separate species, until it was noticed that the green birds which were shot were always males and the red ones were always females. Another unusual feature of the plumage coloration in this species is the fact that it is the female that presents the more brilliant coloration; this is not due to a reversal of breeding roles, as in the case of the tinamous and the phalaropes, as only the female Eclectus incubates and both adults care for the chicks.

[Eclectus roratus. Photo: Hans Reinhard/ Bruce Coleman]

of females are attracted to this, depending on the quality of the territory, in other words the resources it contains. Females prefer to mate with a male that is already paired but holds a good territory, than with another, for herself alone, with a poor quality territory. This type of polygyny usually occurs in heterogeneous habitats like grasslands or marshes, where there are great differences in the productivity of adjacent areas, and this is often the case, for example, among the New World blackbirds (*Agelaius*). In successive polygyny, sometimes considered to be promiscuity, because in principle females can later pair with others males, males have to defend only a very small territory, where the females go solely for mating. Sometimes males group together very closely, forming areas known as leks or arenas, at fixed, traditional sites, as occurs in the Black Grouse (*Tetrao tetrix*) and the Sage Grouse (*Centrocercus urophasianus*), the Great Bustard (*Otis tarda*), the Ruff (*Philomachus pugnax*), the Kakapo, hermits (*Phaethornis*) and various families of passerines (manakins, cotingas, birds-of-paradise).

A far less frequent type of polygamy is polyandry, where the female mates with various males, and then leaves them to look after the eggs and chicks. This is typical in cassowaries, tinamous, button-quails (Turnicidae), jacanas, painted-snipes (Rostratulidae) and phalaropes (*Phalaropus*). Normally mating occurs successively, but in the Northern Jacana (*Jacana spinosa*) there is simultaneous polyandry, with females maintaining large territories within which live several males, each in charge of a nest and of a small private territory.

There is, of course, a clear relation between these different possible mating systems and the varieties of sexual dimorphism

in the birds. In monogamous species, sexes are usually similar in size and colour, and generally the roles played by male and female during courtship are also comparable. Conversely, almost all polygamous species are dimorphic, with one or other sex being larger and more brightly coloured, invariably the male in polygynous species, and the female in polyandrous species. This is the predictable result of Darwin's sexual selection, clearly imposed by these mating systems. At leks, it has been noted that generally almost all mating is performed by a few dominant males. This also leads to some very spectacular courtship behaviour, including that of the Western Capercaillie (*Tetrao urogallus*), the Ruff, and the birds-of-paradise. The more eye-catching colours of the males in some monogamous species, for example in many passerine families (Turdidae, Fringillidae, Emberizidae) could have developed basically in relation to territorial defence, which is normally the responsibility of the male. On rare occasions, some features of sexual dimorphism could be due to ecological factors, for example among hawks (*Accipiter*) where the much smaller males may be specialized in capturing fast prey. A similar case was that of the extinct Huia (*Heteralocha acutirostris*) of New Zealand, in which males and females had differently shaped bills.

Nests

Unlike the lower vertebrates, birds and mammals opt for producing a limited number of eggs or young, but in exchange they invest very intensive and costly parental care in them.

Consequently, the nest is a fundamental item in the adaptive strategy of birds, especially considering that the entire process of embryonic development takes place outside the female's body, in the nest. However, the Emperor Penguin is an exception, as the male incubates the single egg in an abdominal cutaneous bag, which enables him to be constantly mobile, and there is no nest, as such.

The most important function of the nest is to protect the eggs and chicks from predators. The degree of its efficiency hinges on various factors, the most important of which is the position. The nest is usually as well hidden and inaccessible as the habitat permits, marine birds selecting small islands or cliffs, whereas steppe birds are obliged to place their nests on the ground or in holes. Many species, in more than half of the orders, mainly use cavities in rocks or trees, where the level of predation is known to be less than in the open. However, cavities too have their limitations, and they can hamper the rapid escape of incubating adults, while the availability of suitable holes is often so low as to impose strict limits on the population size. Several other factors intervene in reducing predation as much as possible, from the use of materials which leave the outward appearance of the nest suitably camouflaged, to the behaviour of the adults, which may be designed so as not to disclose the location of the nest, or sometimes to distract the attention of predators through elaborate displays, such as the bird pretending to be injured. Many species of small tropical birds secure protection by placing their nests near or even inside those of termites, ants, bees and wasps.

The nest is also very important for creating a favourable microclimate for incubation, and for sheltering the chicks or even the adults, and it frequently offers shelter from the wind, rain and adverse temperatures. This last aspect is important, particularly for small birds like passerines or hummingbirds, which use a great deal of energy maintaining internal temperature (see Metabolism and Thermoregulation), and, in fact, these are the birds that usually construct the most complex nests, with various layers of different thicknesses, the innermost being of the finest and most effective material for insulation. The situation of the nest with respect to the sun or the prevailing winds can also be very important.

Nest complexity is enormously variable, from cases of simple scrapes in the ground, or holes or ledges where the eggs are lodged, to others that are true architectural marvels, for example the nests frequently found amongst the Ploceidae and Icteridae, which are shaped like hanging bags. Although the orders that are considered to be the most primitive tend to build simple nests, and passerines much more elaborate ones, there are many exceptions, and the degree of complexity generally tends to be more closely connected to ecological than to phylogenetic factors. Thus, although the Ciconiiformes normally make nests that are little more than piles of sticks, the Hamerkop (*Scopus umbretta*) constructs a large enclosed nest, with an entrance tunnel. Many birds that nest on the ground in open territory tend to use hardly any nesting material, for example plovers (*Charadrius*), thick-knees (*Burhinus*), sandgrouse (*Pterocles*) and nightjars (*Caprimulgus*); this is probably an aid to camouflage, as related genera in other environments usually do make more elaborate nests. Although parrots normally breed in holes in trees, and barely make a nest at all, various Monk Parakeets (*Myiopsitta monachus*) will co-operate to construct a large stick structure, in which several pairs nest at the same time, and this may be an adaptation to life on the treeless plains. Perhaps the very laborious, energy-draining flight of the auks has led to these birds bringing no material whatsoever to the ledges or holes where they nest, whereas at the opposite extreme, aerial birds such as hummingbirds, swifts and swallows can make hundreds of trips to transport little balls of mud or small feathers. In the construction of its nest, the Barn Swallow (*Hirundo rustica*) tends to make more than 1200 trips.

Additionally, activities related to the nest, such as site selection, transport of material and building, usually play important roles in the formation of the pair-bond. There are considerable variations between different groups and species, as regards the participation of the sexes in these tasks, with birds like ducks and Galliformes, in which all the work is undertaken by the female, and others, like some wrens (Troglodytidae) and weavers (Ploceidae), in which the males construct various nests until the female decides to accept one.

Eggs

Birds' eggs are cleidoic, as in reptiles, and they tend to be comparatively large. They vary in weight from 0·3 g in some hummingbirds to 1600 g in the Ostrich, and probably even 9000 g in the extinct Great Elephantbird. Weight also differs allometrically in relation to the female's body weight, by an exponent of 0·67, so that relatively large species tend to lay much smaller eggs than small species. Accordingly, the weight of an egg accounts for 25% body weight in a small hummingbird, but only about 1% in an Ostrich, with a normal range of variation of 2-5%. Nevertheless, there are many variations between the different bird orders. In birds of around 100 g: an egg weighs 4·5 g in a cuckoo; 6 g in a pigeon; 15 g in a pygmy falcon; and 21 g in a storm-petrel. These differences are related closely to the nature of the chicks, with large eggs corresponding to nidifugous species, and small ones to nidicolous species, but there are also other factors, for instance clutch size. Although their chicks are nidicolous, Procellariiformes have very large eggs, partly because they lay only one, and partly as an adaptation to the pelagic life of the adults. The chicks hatch with large reserves that allow them to survive long periods during which the adults are absent from the nest.

The normal egg shape is the oval shape typical of a domestic hen's egg, but there are quite a few exceptions. In many birds that nest in cavities, like petrels, owls and kingfishers, eggs tend to be spherical, which allows a saving in shell, for the same egg content. However, eggs of this form run the risk of rolling easily and perhaps this is why they are not usual in other types of nest. At the other extreme, the exceptionally conical form of guillemot eggs is usually explained as an adaptation to prevent them falling off the bare ledges on which they are laid. Gulls and waders also have fairly conical eggs, but in these cases it may be designed to enable the clutch of three or four eggs to fit into the nest better, with the sharp ends towards the centre, creating a minimum surface for adults to cover during incubation. Generally, there is also a certain correspondence between the form of the eggs and the form of the pelvis in different groups.

The coloration of eggs is very constant within the same species, and is clearly related to the location of the nest. Thus it is usually cryptic in birds that nest in the open, with background colours blending into those of the surroundings, and white in those that nest in cavities, where it is useful for them to be instantly visible to adults entering, thereby avoiding the risk of their being crushed. Similarly, they tend to be whitish in some birds, which, although they nest in the open, start to incubate from the moment of the laying of the first egg (herons, pigeons, owls), or in others that cover the clutch with down or vegetation each time they leave the nest (grebes, wildfowl, many gallinaceous birds). All of this goes to indicate that the ancestral colour was white. It appears that in some cases bright colours, or at least non-cryptic colours, are associated with low palatability, an unpleasant, normally very bitter taste. In some colonial species, such as guillemots, egg coloration can be useful for individual recognition of eggs by adults (see Colonial Breeding).

The number of eggs laid by different birds, the clutch size, can vary widely, from only one egg in Procellariiformes and several penguins, auks, vultures, condors and others, to a dozen or more in some ducks, Galliformes and tits, which is of great ecological and adaptive significance (see Demographic and Ecological Aspects of Reproduction). In many species the clutch size is fixed, leaving the birds unable to compensate for possible egg losses sustained during laying (determinate layers). In contrast, there are others which can continue laying even if the eggs are removed as they are laid (indeterminate layers), a feature that man has put to good use in the case of domestic fowl, with up to 365 eggs a year being collected from a single Japanese

Quail (*Coturnix japonica*). In the event of the loss of the entire clutch, most birds, apart from some albatrosses, large birds of prey and a few others, are capable of laying a replacement clutch, normally with fewer eggs than the original clutch, after a period of rest of several, or sometimes many days.

Many birds, including almost all passerines, lay their eggs at intervals of approximately 24 hours, but there are others that require a longer break between each egg, for instance up to 4-5 days in some kiwis, eagles, vultures and megapodes. Very often the eggs are laid early in the morning, perhaps because the relatively delicate process of shell formation is best accomplished during the night, while the female is immobile.

Incubation

The incubation of eggs is a very characteristic feature of birds, for in the reptiles, which are cold-blooded or poikilothermal, only some crocodiles and snakes provide heat for their eggs, and this is always in a very much less intense or constant way than birds. For this reason, in reptiles the time between the laying and the hatching of the eggs is very variable, depending mostly on the ambient temperature, while in birds the period of incubation has fairly strict time limits, which are characteristic in each species or group. The shortest period is 10 days in some woodpeckers, for example the Great Spotted Woodpecker (*Picoides major*), with 12-14 days in most passerines, 21 in the domestic hen, 30-50 in birds of prey, 40-60 in Procellariiformes in general, and up to 80 days in some albatrosses and kiwis. The length of the period depends on various factors, particularly egg size and the state of development in which the chicks hatch, which is extremely variable in different bird orders. It is also related to a particular rhythm that corresponds closely to the growth rates that chicks show later on, and probably also to the general metabolic rate of the species, which is faster, for example, in passerines than in other groups. Normally birds that raise their young in nest-holes have longer incubation periods than those that nest in the open, perhaps because the latter are accelerated in evolutionary terms, by a higher incidence of predation. On the other hand, the incubation period is usually shorter in temperate than in tropical regions, while in desert areas or at high altitudes species probably find themselves limited by the rate at which the eggs lose water through evaporation.

Incubation behaviour in birds appears to be set off by the tactile stimulus of the eggs on the belly, which prompts the secretion of hormones in the hypophysis (prolactin, oestrogen, progesterone), and these in turn are responsible, amongst other things, for the development of incubation or brood patches. These are areas of the abdomen, or the breast and abdomen, that are temporarily bare of feathers and highly vascularized, and the birds apply them directly to the eggs, in order to transmit heat more effectively. There can be one, two or three patches, the last case applying to waders, gulls and Galliformes, but there are sometimes none, as in penguins, gannets and boobies and Anseriformes. Ducks and geese pull out the ventral feathers with the bill, subsequently using them to line the nest, while gannets and boobies incubate the eggs under their large totipalmate feet, and penguins between the abdomen and the upper side of the feet.

Incubation manages to keep the eggs at a surprisingly constant temperature, and this is greatly affected by the relative lengths of the incubation stints and the rests in between, which as a whole is known as incubation constancy. In cold weather longer stints are necessary, whereas in hot weather adults sometimes limit themselves to standing in the nest providing shade. Many ground-nesting waders periodically cool their eggs by soaking their ventral feathers in water. Birds tend to shuffle their eggs regularly, as the temperature is higher in the centre of the nest than on the periphery, and they also turn them over one by one, to avoid the extra-embryonic membranes from sticking to the shell membrane. In artificial incubators, eggs that are not turned over at least once every day have a 15% lower hatching rate.

In 54% of bird families both sexes participate in incubation, compared with 25% in which only the female incubates, and 6% in which only the male incubates, and the remaining 15% where the three alternatives have been recorded. There is a logical relationship with the mating systems, so in polygynous species it is usually the female that incubates, and in polyandrous species the male, while in monogamous species males usually take their turns of incubation, or at least, in many passerines and birds of prey, help the females by fetching food for them, which is important as incubation generally requires 60-80% of the daylight hours. A male hornbill (Bucerotidae) imprisons his female in their tree-nest, by covering up the entrance hole with mud and excrement, leaving only a small hole, through which he will pass her food. In cases where both sexes incubate, the duration of stints can be very variable, from barely one or two hours, to several days, for example in many Procellariiformes. In pigeons and some waders of the genera *Calidris* and *Charadrius*, males incubate during the day and females at night, but sandgrouse and Ostriches do just the opposite. The change over at the nest is usually accompanied by special displays.

Incubation normally begins once the last egg has been laid, so that all the chicks hatch at the same time. This is very important in nidifugous species, as it allows them to abandon the nest simultaneously, and in nidicolous species because the stage of development will be more or less the same in all the chicks, enabling them to receive equal shares of food from the adults, thus avoiding possible death by starvation. However, in nidicolous birds, such as herons, owls, raptors and the Common Swift, incubation starts with the laying of the first egg, so later on the various siblings are all at different stages of development. Such asynchronous hatching is an adaptation in birds that depend on food supplies that are subject to considerable fluctuations. In this way, they can regulate the size of their brood depending on the availability of food each season. When food is scarce smaller chicks are liable to die of starvation, or be killed by their larger siblings.

In the Megapodes (Megapodiidae), a family of Australasian Galliformes, direct incubation has been substituted by other sources of heat. The majority bury their eggs in heaps of decomposing vegetation, as do some crocodiles, while some species bury their eggs in beaches of black sand, as these can absorb a great deal of heat, or in warm volcanic ground. In most cases, the adults constantly regulate the temperature of the eggs, either by depositing or removing material, as is necessary.

Lastly, there is a whole series of birds which save themselves the effort of having to incubate their eggs, and also feed their chicks, by the simple procedure of laying in the nests of other birds, a practice known as "brood parasitism". On an occasional basis, it is apparently relatively widespread among different species, but there are some specialized species that never incubate themselves, and that always exploit other birds. This is the case, not only of cuckoos (40% of the species in the Cuculidae), but also honeyguides, cowbirds (*Molothrus*), widows (Viduinae), and even the Black-headed Duck (*Heteronetta atricapilla*) of South America. In all, there are some 80 species that are habitual parasites, almost 1% of the total number of bird species. Such parasitism, which is also found in insects, has many obvious advantages, but in exchange demands significant adaptations, such as the ability to imitate the colour and even of the size of the host's eggs, a protrusible cloaca, to make laying in other nests easier, and a harder eggshell, to prevent the eggs from breaking as they drop. Sophisticated behaviour is also necessary, in both adults and chicks, normally including the direct elimination of the host's eggs or chicks.

Hatching

In order to help it emerge from the shell, the chick develops two special temporary structures, the egg tooth, a sharp horny point on the end of the rhinotheca, and the hatching muscle, or musculus complexus, which appears on the upper part of the hindneck. The chick first perforates the air chamber, which at the end of the incubation occupies a good deal of space in the blunt end of the egg, and then it pierces the shell in one place, which allows it to push out its bill and start breathing. The system of blood vessels of the allantoic sac, which until this moment have been supplying oxygen to the organism, now begin a rapid regression. Starting from the original hole, the chick continues to break the shell, by twisting its body and making new perforations in the shell, until it manages to free itself completely. The time this takes varies widely in different species, from twenty or thirty minutes, to hours or even days (3-4 days in many Procellariiformes).

The adults rarely assist in the process of hatching, but they do remove the shells quickly, once the operation has been completed, probably so as to avoid attracting the attention of predators. This behaviour occurs in nidicolous, but not in nidifugous species, where the most important concern is for all the chicks to abandon the nest quickly and simultaneously, and this is particularly true of species that nest in the open. While still in the egg, the chicks' contact calls are perfectly audible from the outside, and these induce the remarkable synchronized hatching of nidifugous species, chicks apparently influencing each other to accelerate or delay hatching, by the frequency of the call, which is fast in eggs that are just starting, and slow in more advanced ones.

Chicks

There is a noticeable dichotomy in birds as regards the relative state of development at hatching. Many birds, like the Ostrich, tinamous, ducks, gallinaceous birds and waders, hatch covered with down and with their eyes open, and are immediately capable of running and searching for food by themselves. Many others, for example pigeons, swifts, woodpeckers and passerines in general, hatch almost completely naked, with their eyes closed, and hardly able to move anything other than the neck and the mandibles, to accept the food brought by the parents. The first case refers to precocial chicks, which hatch with relatively large brains and hind limbs, while the second refers to altricial chicks, which tend to have the mouth and the intestine more developed. In precocial chicks the yolk reserves, which are the remains of the vitelline sac in the interior of the abdomen, form 12-25% of the body weight, whereas in altricial chicks they constitute only 5-10%. Logically the reserves last longer in the first case, for example six days in the Common Quail, as opposed to four in the Common Starling, and this is appropriate for species where the chicks have to find food for themselves. The eggs of precocial species initially have a larger proportion of yolk (about 35%) than altricial species (20%).

Precocial and altricial chicks are really two extremes of a continuous string of variations, with intermediate situations. Semi-altricial chicks are those, like the herons and raptors, which, although they hatch with down and with their eyes open, remain in the nest and depend on the food brought in by the parents. Semi-precocial chicks, like penguins, shearwaters, gulls and terns are very well developed when they hatch, and are able to move about easily, but remain in the nest or nearby, also to be fed by the parents. Sub-precocial chicks, for example grebes, rails and cranes, are those that abandon the nest in order to follow their parents around, but that are not capable of feeding themselves. Yet another category is that of super-precocial chicks, which are totally independent of their parents from the very beginning, such as the Black-headed Duck, a brood parasite, and also the megapodes, their chicks being capable of flying within 24 hours of leaving the nest. There is a very clear relationship with the type of food exploited by the different birds. Altricial, semi-altricial and semi-precocial chicks, which remain in or beside the nest (nidicolous), are fed on animal prey, which demands the strength and ability of adults for its capture, while the remaining chicks (nidifugous) usually eat plant matter, which they can obtain by themselves. However, some nidifugous species are fish eaters, for example divers (*Gavia*), grebes and most auks, and in these species, which are well adapted to diving, but consequently hampered by a very costly style of flight (see Aerial Locomotion), having nidifugous chicks probably saves the adults from having to fly long distances between the fishing areas and the nest.

The amount and type of parental care received by chicks after hatching is therefore very diverse. In nidicolous species, supplying food for the chicks undoubtedly involves the greatest effort. This normally demands the collaboration of both parents, and they must provide twice or thee times as much food as they require for themselves. The frequency of foraging trips varies widely from one species to another, depending on the size of bird, the number of chicks in the nest, the type of food, and also the way in which the trips are made. Great Tits have been known to feed their young 990 times in one day, while the large albatrosses (*Diomedea*) may only bring in food two or three times a week. The first are small insectivorous birds with an average clutch of 9-12 eggs, which carry prey in the bill, whereas the second are large birds, which feed their chicks exclusively on a very nutritious oily secretion of the oesophagus. In order to solicit feeding, nidicolous chicks exhibit special begging behaviour, with displays, some of which are normally acoustic (calling), tactile (pecking the tip of the adults' bills, as in gulls), or visual (among others, the buccal cavity sometimes has very sophisticated patterns, as in many passerines). These displays are usually brought about automatically by stimuli associated with the arrival of the parents at the nest.

Other forms of care invested in nidicolous chicks include defending them from predators, and cleaning the nest, for example the chicks of many birds, particularly passerines and Piciformes, excrete the faeces wrapped in a mucous membrane, the "fecal sac", which adults then remove in the bill, or may even swallow. They also regulate the temperature, providing heat or shade as necessary, and this is especially important among altricial birds, because the chicks are poikilothermal during the first few days (the first week in passerines), since they can not thermoregulate properly until they develop sufficient size and musculature.

In some 150 species, it has been noted that other birds may help the parents to look after their chicks, sometimes on an occasional basis and sometimes constantly, for example the *Turdoides* babblers of the Old World, and the *Aphelocoma* jays of Central and North America. The practice is most frequent in passerines, but is also common amongst rails, kingfishers, bee-eaters, wood-hoopoes and woodpeckers, almost always in hot regions and amongst sedentary birds. Research has shown, on several occasions, that the assistance of these helpers does, in fact, increase the number of young successfully raised, and even the survival rate of the parents through the breeding season. However, the advantages for the helpers are not immediately obvious, but, although it is sometimes quoted as an example of altruistic behaviour, co-operative breeding apparently provides clear benefits for the helpers too. Almost without exception, co-operative breeding appears in dense populations, which are governed by strict territorial organization, and in which young birds have very few possibilities of establishing territories and breeding successfully. By helping established pairs, they at least have the opportunity of sharing the advantages of the territory and the group, gaining experience, and perhaps being better equipped to compete later on for the same territory or a part of it. Moreover, as helpers are usually related to the breeding pair, and are normally offspring of one or the other, or both, a contribution towards the successful raising of related birds could be supposed to increase their own fitness (inclusive fitness).

A different case is that of the anis (*Crotophaga*), a group of Neotropical cuckoos, in which several monogamous pairs lay eggs in the same nest, and all individuals help in the incubation and care of the chicks. Rather than co-operative breeding, this case could be considered a form of communal breeding.

Growth

Like many other animals, birds grow slowly at first, quickly during intermediate phases and slowly again at the end of their

Two or three days after having perforated the air chamber of the egg, the developed chick produces the first openings in the eggshell with the help of its egg-tooth, a horny structure on the tip of the maxilla which can be seen in the first three photographs. After incubation, the eggshell is weaker than in the moment of laying because part of the mineral substances have been dissolved and transported by the blood to prepare the preliminary ossification of the bird's skeleton. In order to burst the shell open, the chick stretches its head and moves its legs, until its emergence is completed. The whole process can last a mere thirty minutes in small birds, whilst in larger ones it requires several hours, for instance eight to ten hours in the case of this Purple Heron. In this species, and apparently in most of those with nidicolous chicks, the fragments of shell are discarded over the side of the nest by the adults immediately after hatching is completed. This is thought to be a way of preventing the nest from becoming more conspicuous to predators.

[Ardea purpurea purpurea, Embalse de Azután, Toledo, Spain. Photos: Francisco Márquez]

development, when their size and weight are similar to those of adults, following typical sigmoidal curves. Occasionally, at the end of the period in the nest, chicks exceed the weight of adults, due to an accumulation of fat that bolsters the chances of their survival after leaving the nest. This occurs in some pelagic seabirds (Procellariiformes) and in consumers of aerial plankton (swifts and swallows), both of which are exposed to long periods of fasting.

Growth rates vary considerably between different species, and may be as much as 30 times more in some species than in others. In altricial or semi-altricial birds, for example, the period that chicks stay in the nest is typically 10-20 days in passerines, 20-30 in pigeons, 30-50 in small and medium-sized raptors, 70-90 in eagles, 100-150 in vultures, and 150-250 in albatrosses. Much of the variation in growth rates depends on the ultimate size of the adults, for growth is much slower in large than in small birds, with an allometric variation of 0·72 in terms of weight, very similar to that (0·76) which regulates the variation of the basal metabolism (see Metabolism and Thermoregulation). The rates are also closely related to the type of chick, with values three or four times higher in altricial than in precocial birds, perhaps because in the latter the fast maturation of the tissues is incompatible with the maintenance of fast post-natal growth. Growth rates also vary in relation to different ecological aspects, and they are, for example: higher in birds that nest in the open, and which are therefore particularly exposed to predation, than in hole-nesters; higher in birds of temperate regions than those of the tropics; and higher among coastal than pelagic seabirds. To a great extent, these rates represent the points of balance resulting from two counteracting selective influences: predation, which tends to select high rates of growth, as the risk of predation on chicks is positively correlated with the length of time they remain in the nest; and food availability, which normally tends to conserve low rates, as extremely rapid growth would entail excessive effort for the parents, or oblige them to raise fewer chicks.

There are also individual differences in the speed of growth, which can be ascribed principally to the quantity and quality of the food supplied by the parents, and to competition between siblings. Often the weakest chicks die, especially among birds with asynchronous hatching, in which the last chick to hatch can not compete for food effectively against its older siblings, unless they are already satiated. In some cases the death of the weakest chicks is caused by the direct action of its fellow nestlings, as is often the case among raptors, skuas and sulids (cainism, fratricide or siblicide).

Demographic and Ecological Aspects of Reproduction

Bird populations are regulated by various factors in such a way that they tend to maintain a more or less constant size. The main factors are the relative abundance of food at different times of year, and, to a lesser degree, the availability of sites for sheltering or breeding, and the incidence of disease and infestation by parasites. These factors operate through variations in mortality and breeding success, depending closely on the size of the populations in question. Density independent factors, such as the weather, appear to play a relatively unimportant role in birds. On the other hand, some aspects of social behaviour, especially the maintenance of territories, undoubtedly help to limit population sizes of birds, but as a consequence, rather than as a primary function.

For a given population to remain constant in size, in the absence of exchanges with others (immigration or emigration), it is necessary for there to be a balance between the mortality and birth rates. The data currently available, collected above all from ringing programmes, suggest that mortality is generally very high in young birds, but it then remains more or less constant with age, without showing particularly high increases in older birds. Average annual mortality ranges from 70% or more in small birds and some Galliformes, to less than 5% in

albatrosses, and probably also large eagles and vultures. These results show that mean life expectancy, once the juvenile phase is completed, ranges from slightly under a year to over thirty. The majority of small birds live two to five years on average. The records from captivity of longer-lived birds do not appear to be paralleled in the wild, where the greatest age recorded to date corresponds to a Royal Albatross (*Diomedea epomophora*), which lived to be over 58 years old.

Variations in the fecundity of birds apparently depend mainly on the normal clutch size, but the number of broods per year (rarely more than one), and the age of first breeding are also significant. Most birds already breed in their first year, but there are many exceptions, particularly in medium-sized and large birds, and in many seabirds and large raptors maturity is delayed until birds are over five years old (up to ten years in some large albatrosses). This delayed maturity is not, as is sometimes thought, altruistic behaviour designed to benefit the species or population as a whole, but rather an interesting adaptation, which serves mainly to improve the breeding success of the individual throughout its life in long-lived birds, which undergo obvious risks during breeding. For example, at their breeding colonies seabirds compete intensely both for food and very often for convenient nest-sites, which means that young birds breeding for the first time not only have limited chances of success, but also suffer much greater losses. In the Californian Gull (*Larus californicus*), birds that are 3-5 years old raise 0·76 chicks per year on average, while those of 7-9 years raise 0·80 chicks, and those of 12-18 years produce 1·5 chicks. In the Adelie Penguin (*Pygoscelis adeliae*) mortality decreases, from 75% among females breeding at three years old, to 10% among those breeding at eleven years old.

In addition, the clutch size of each species has undoubtedly evolved mainly to optimize reproductive success. According to Lack, in nidicolous birds this coincides with the clutch size that allows the maximum number of chicks to survive, which is related primarily to the amount of food the parents are capable of bringing to the nest. The general validity of this hypothesis has been proved repeatedly, even with experiments, but nevertheless, average clutches slightly smaller than those known to be more productive sometimes occur. This is perhaps a form of conservative strategy, designed to improve an adult's chances of survival after each breeding attempt, thereby enhancing the overall reproductive output of its entire life. These smaller clutches could also help to reduce the duration of breeding, when birds are most seriously exposed to predators.

In conjunction with their lower life expectancy, nidifugous species start breeding younger and lay larger clutches than nidicolous species, perhaps to compensate for the higher mortality of their chicks, which grow more slowly and are often late fliers (except the Galliformes and Turnicidae, which are able to fly at a very early age). In species with precocial chicks clutch size is not limited by the foraging ability of the parents, but rather, perhaps, by the amount of food or reserves of fat which the female has available at the moment of egg formation. In these species, the eggs are not only more numerous than in nidicolous species, but are normally larger, with a higher proportion of vitellus (see Eggs). Generally, there is more flexibility in the clutch size of nidifugous species.

Thus, from an ecological point of view, nidifugous birds, which eat mainly plant matter, base their systems of reproduction roughly on being "r-selected" species, as they suffer high losses from predation, have a short life, produce many descendants and have population sizes that fluctuate widely, without maintaining a close relationship with the carrying capacity of their environments. At the other extreme, some of the nidicolous birds that occupy the highest levels of the trophic pyramids, large predators or carrion eaters, such as eagles or vultures, and also albatrosses, are good examples of "K-selected" species, as they suffer almost no predation, are long-lived, produce few chicks and have very stable population sizes, closely connected to the carrying capacity of the environments they inhabit.

Although bird populations tend to remain more or less constant, nevertheless, like other animal groups, their long-term trends sometimes involve considerable increases, or alternatively declines, which can even lead to extinction. Such long-term variations are almost always the result of underlying environmental changes. Thus variations in climate on a global scale, such as the ice ages, entail inevitable expansions of range in many species, but contractions in others. For example, some recent range alterations in northern Europe are attributed to the amelioration of the climate in the last few decades. But especially important in this respect are the intense present day transformations of ecosystems by man, which variously reduce or extend the habitats of species, and create or eliminate sources of food and nesting grounds. This explains, on the one hand, the extinction of numerous species and, on the other, the spectacular increase and expansion of others, such as in Europe, that of the Northern Fulmar (*Fulmarus glacialis*), the Eurasian Collared Dove (*Streptopelia decaocto*) and various species of gull.

Migration

Although there are many groups of animals, both aquatic and terrestrial, that regularly undertake migrations, those of birds are the most striking in various ways. Birds as small as the Willow Warbler (*Phylloscopus trochilus*), weighing only 8 g, are capable of flying from Siberia or even Alaska to winter quarters in Africa beyond the Sahara, some 10,000-13,000 km away, and, furthermore, of returning with incredible precision to the same breeding grounds the following spring. The Arctic Tern (*Sterna paradisaea*) flies between areas of the Arctic and Antarctic during migrations of up to 15,000 km. The migrations of birds have caught the attention of man since ancient times, but only in the last few decades have different study techniques, especially ringing, made it possible to discover the details of migratory movements in a substantial number of species and to understand the basics of migration.

Not all kinds of movement undertaken by birds can be classed as "true" migration. Some affect only certain individuals among populations, without the geographical centres of the population changing, as happens, for example, in the very common cases of juvenile and post-breeding dispersal. Other movements are of an unpredictable nature, brought about by more or less sudden, non-cyclical changes in ecosystems, including: waves of cold weather, which lead to movements in the Northern Lapwing (*Vanellus vanellus*); prolonged droughts, affecting many aquatic birds; sudden crashes in the availability of food, which lead to irruptions of taiga birds, when the pine kernel crop fails, or of Rough-legged Buzzards (*Buteo lagopus*) and Snowy Owls (*Nyctea scandiaca*), when lemming populations slump; irregular rainfall in arid areas, causing nomadic movements of desert birds; and so on. Migration, in the strict sense, is characterized instead by its regularity and predictability, and because it affects entire populations. The birds move between breeding grounds and winter quarters that can be far apart, and that clearly differ from an ecological point of view. This spatial and temporal regularity allows migratory birds to take advantage of two different ecosystems, and therefore to maintain year round activity, without having to resort to torpor or hibernation in order to survive the winter, as other animals do.

In most cases migrations are latitudinal, from boreal or temperate regions to temperate or tropical regions, and vice versa on the return, but very often they also entail longitudinal or altitudinal components, for example birds from the interior of a continent, which winter in coastal areas, or those from the mountains that winter on the plains. Migration sometimes involves marked changes in habitat, as with many insectivores that breed in forests but winter in savannas, or for phalaropes and skuas, which breed on the tundra but winter on the open sea.

Migration affects an enormous number of birds. It is calculated that 40% of the species that nest in the Palearctic spend the winter outwith this region, some 5,000,000,000 birds wintering in the Afrotropical Region, without including waterbirds. The corresponding figures for the Nearctic-Neotropical migra-

Map of the world showing the main migratory flyways followed by many birds, in particular wildfowl, waterbirds and waders. These routes are usually followed more closely by species that nest in large concentrations than by those that are scattered over a wide area. Many passerines travel over large land masses on a broad front. The map also shows the major zoogeographical regions into which the world is divided; the avifauna of each region is much more homogeneous than that of each continent.

[Figure: Xavier Ruiz]

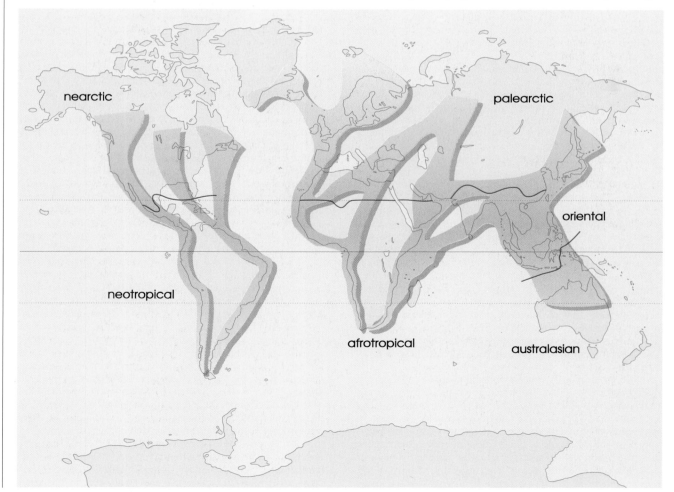

tion system are probably not very different. Many other species migrate within their zoogeographical region of origin, so that, for example, the number of boreal birds that do not migrate, at any rate to some extent, is fairly small. In Canada, out of 160 species of passerines, some 120 move off for the winter, as do most individuals in another 15 species.

Many bird species are only partial migrants, with varying proportions of sedentary and migratory individuals in a given population, and with migrants travelling very different distances. For example, many birds that are spread out all over Europe in the breeding season, have populations which are wholly migratory in the north of Russia, partially migratory in Central Europe and totally sedentary in the British Isles and Mediterranean countries.

There is a clear relation between the type of food exploited and the extent to which a species is migratory, so that birds that eat seeds, shoots or buds, which are available during the temperate winter, tend to travel much less than insectivores, for example. There is also a certain degree of correspondence with the morphology and consequent flight capacity of each species, and less migratory species normally have high wing-loading, as in the Galliformes, ducks and auks. The more migratory species normally have long, narrow wings, as in shearwaters, waders, terns, bee-eaters, swifts and swallows, or are good soarers, such as storks and certain raptors, and all of these birds have economical methods of flight. Within the same family or genus, those species that are more migratory tend to have narrower, more pointed wings, for instance in the Willow Warbler, which is a trans-Saharan migrant, as compared with the Eurasian Chiffchaff (*Phylloscopus collybita*), a partial, short distance migrant; to some extent the same tendency can also be found within the same species in different populations.

Migration clearly involves high risks for the individual. It has to make lengthy crossings of inhospitable environments, such as seas or deserts, with the possibility of gales or storms, probably an increase in predation, and, on arrival at the destination, competition with resident birds. However, as the practice has evolved in so many species, there must be great advantages. Many migrants, particularly those that cover long distances, belong to taxonomic groups that are essentially tropical, which suggests that migrants are birds of tropical origin that move off to breed in temperate or boreal zones. These regions have strongly seasonal, loosely structured ecosystems, which show outstanding increases in carrying capacity during spring and summer. In these zones birds encounter less competition, more daylight hours for foraging, greater availability of nest-sites and lower rates of predation, and all this combines to produce far higher breeding success than that achieved by related, non-migratory species in the tropics. On the other hand, birds of northern origin that migrate, normally only partial migrants, find advantages mainly in what is known as winter survival. Among these northern birds, the fact that some migrate, while others do not, can be explained by the improved breeding success in the most sedentary individuals. These can control the best breeding grounds in advance, and in this way compensate for the higher risks they run by remaining during the winter. In connection with this, it has frequently been noted that on average males cover far less distance than females, which is very obvious in the cases of the Chaffinch in Eurasia and the Dark-eyed Junco (*Junco hyemalis*) of North America. So, in general, migrants gain in reproductive output in comparison with sedentary tropical birds, though they suffer higher mortality, whereas in comparison with sedentary birds in cold countries, the opposite is true, as they improve their survival rates, but lose out in terms of breeding success.

As both survival during the winter and reproductive success during the breeding season ultimately depend closely on seasonal variations in the availability of food, it is obvious that such variations constitute the "ultimate factor" responsible for the evolution of migratory behaviour. However, it is definitely not one of the catalysts that sets it off, as migrants do not depart due to hunger; rather, their departure anticipates, sometimes well in advance, a real lack of food. Like breeding or moult, migrations are subject to a genetically programmed, endogen-

ous circannual rhythm which is conditioned by different external factors. The most important of these is the photoperiod, but other factors intervene in the fine adjustment of the date, including some meterological aspects, such as temperature, winds and cloud cover.

The first signs of migratory behaviour are displayed in a preparatory phase ("Zugdisposition"), at least among long distance migrants, by a large increase in food consumption, which is apparently caused by the action of the hormone prolactin, and leads to notable deposits of fat under the skin, in the muscles and in the peritoneal cavity. The maximum amounts of fat deposits are in the order of 3-5% of the total body weight among sedentary birds, but 13-25% in short distance migrants, and 30-47% in long distance migrants, such as some members of the Parulidae of North America or the Muscicapidae of Eurasia, which, from normal weights of 11-12 g, can reach 21-22 g in only a few days, while the Ruby-throated Hummingbird too can virtually double its initial weight of 3 g. These reserves of fat serve as an enormously effective fuel supply, and also as a store of water during long migration flights. It is calculated that small birds with fat deposits equivalent to some 40% of total body weight can fly for 100 hours without having to eat, covering as much as 2500 km, and that in the Dunlin (*Calidris alpina*), which increases its weight from 50 to 110 g, the resultant reserves are theoretically sufficient for a non-stop flight of 3000-4000 km. This explains the remarkable feats regularly accomplished by many birds, which cross the Mediterranean and the Sahara in one go, or fly non-stop from New England to Venezuela, and similarly the very frequent vagrancies of North American species to Europe or European species to North America.

The second phase of the migratory process ("Zugstimmung") induces the ethological changes that the bird must undergo, in order to "forget" its daily rhythm of activity, so that it is able to initiate and maintain prolonged migratory flights. In caged birds, this can be seen in migratory restlessness ("Zugunruhe"), whereby the birds remain in a particular corner of the cage, jumping about and beating their wings ceaselessly.

Between different groups and species there is a great deal of variety both in the way birds migrate and when they do so. Most migratory passerines move only at night, either alone or in small loose flocks, at a fairly high altitude (1000-5000 m, or more), and on a broad front, without taking into account the features of the terrain below. During the day they rest, and if the situation permits, they forage actively to replace as much as possible of their fat reserves. Many waders, rails and ducks also migrate at night. Conversely, swallows and swifts, which feed on the wing, and birds like storks, pelicans or raptors, which use thermals for soaring, migrate during the day and are therefore inclined to follow landmarks, such as mountain ranges and coasts, and at times large numbers concentrate at straits or other points of geographical note, for instance the Bosporus, Gibraltar, Cape May (New Jersey) and the Gulf of Aqaba.

How migratory birds navigate is one of the natural phenomena which has most fascinated and intrigued man, but until recently little was known. It now appears fairly certain that diurnal migrants use the position of the sun for orientation, and as its relative position changes throughout the day, birds compensate with the help of an internal biological clock, producing a form of genuine navigation. In a similar way, nocturnal migrants recognize and use the position of the stars. Several experiments in the 1970's demonstrated that many birds are able to use the earth's magnetic field (geomagnetism) for navigational purposes, which must obviously be enormously useful on cloudy days. For short distances, the ability to recognize landmarks on the ground is important, as is generally the case with large, long-lived birds that migrate by day, like cranes, geese or storks, and these birds learn geographical features, such as coastlines, mountains, major rivers or even cities. Finally, in the Procellariiformes the sense of smell is important, at least for locating the nest at the end of the journey.

The general compass direction followed by migrants is entirely innate, as are any variations in this direction that must be made during the journey. A caged Garden Warbler in Germany will align itself towards the south-west in the initial phases of "Zugunruhe", the direction which, under natural conditions, would lead it to the Iberian Peninsula, and it later changes automatically towards the south, and then towards the south-east, allowing the hypothetical journey to end in Africa and not in the midst of the Atlantic.

Research has recently been carried out into the genetic control of this innate behaviour. In partially migratory species, for example the Eurasian Blackbird (*Turdus merula*) and the European Robin, the descendants of more migratory individuals tend to travel further than those of more sedentary individuals, in other words, the tendency to migrate is inherited. On the other hand, while various features closely related to migration are inheritable, it appears that they may also be susceptible to a form of "hybridization". In the Blackcap (*Sylvia atricapilla*), for example, if highly migratory Central European birds are crossed with others that are totally sedentary, from the Canary or Cape Verde Islands, the resultant birds have intermediate values in aspects such as wing length, timing of the post-breeding moult, capacity to form fat deposits, and intensity and duration of migratory restlessness. The existence of a kind of genetic polymorphism would explain why in a particular species there are populations that are migratory or sedentary to different degrees, in the same way that in different human populations varying colours of skin or hair may predominate.

This would also help to explain the relative flexibility of migratory behaviour, which in some species has been known to vary in a short time. Such is the case of the European Serin (*Serinus serinus*), which is essentially sedentary around the Mediterranean, whereas it is migratory in areas of Central Europe that it has recently colonized. It is also apparent in some birds that exploit rubbish dumps in parts of Europe, such as the European White Stork, the Red Kite (*Milvus milvus*) and the Lesser Black-backed Gull (*Larus fuscus*), which are progressively becoming more sedentary. It is logical that migratory behaviour should be able to change fairly quickly, given its high adaptive value. The migratory patterns that we know nowadays must, in fact, have developed relatively recently in most species, for the the last ice age was at its zenith only 15,000 years ago.

Evolution of Birds

The evolutionary history of birds is comparatively poorly known in comparison with that of other terrestrial vertebrates, like reptiles or mammals. The fossil register is far less complete, mainly because birds' skeletons, particularly their skulls, are relatively fragile. Of the first known representative, *Archaeopteryx*, there are five specimens in museums, all from the same limestone quarries at Solnhofen in Bavaria, and dating back to the Upper Jurassic, about 150 million years ago. Further evidence does not appear until the Cretaceous, 70-130 million years later. One of the earliest and best preserved fossils from this period refers to *Hesperornis regalis*, and was discovered in Texas in 1870. It was a very large bird, about two metres long, that still retained primitive teeth, and was incapable of flight, as can be deduced from its very small wings and the weak structure of the sternum. It was clearly a diving bird, and probably bore a superficial resemblance to the present day divers (*Gavia*). Another dozen similar fossil species are known, which are sometimes considered to belong to the same genus *Hesperornis*, and there are others of different genera, which are sometimes included in the same taxonomic order, Hesperornithiformes. In addition, the seas of the Cretaceous contained at any rate other toothed birds, the Ichthyornithiformes, which could probably fly perfectly well, and were perhaps similar in appearance to gulls. Of the ten or so known species in this group, most are included in the genus *Ichthyornis*.

The presence of birds with such varied appearance suggests that by the Cretaceous an important initial adaptive radiation had already taken place in the class Aves. However, at the end of the period, along with the massive extinction of the dinosaurs, pterosaurs, ichthyosaurs and many other animal groups, the toothed birds also disappeared. All the fossil species of the Cenozoic or present day era are of toothless birds, and in the Eocene they were already very similar to those which have come down to the present day, and can generally be included in the same general groups (ostriches, penguins, albatrosses, herons, storks, pelicans, ducks, hawks, cranes, cuckoos, kingfishers, woodpeckers, and others). An exception perhaps are the small birds of the order Passeriformes, the most numerous nowadays, which must have diversified at a later stage, parallel to the diversification of the flowering plants and their accompanying insects. The second, virtually definitive radiation of birds in the Eocene produced, in addition, other forms which have not survived, like *Diatryma*, a flightless bird two metres tall, with a skull like that of a horse and an enormous hooked predatorial bill, or *Neocathartes*, which was similar to the present day New World vultures, but had long stork-like legs. Similar to *Diatryma*, and already present in the Oligocene and the Miocene, were *Phororhacos* and other closely related genera, which flourished in South America, probably due to the isolation of the continent around that time. Since then many other birds have, of course, come and gone during the evolution of the class, but most of them seem to have left no fossil remains behind. Some estimates suggest that in total about 150,000 bird species have existed, compared with the 9000 or so that have reached the present day.

Speciation

Evolution in birds, as in other animals, progresses by means of a process involving the gradual differentiation of new species from those that already exist, which is known as speciation. At a later stage, the complex, ever-changing ecological and geographical relationships that are established between species ultimately determine the extinction and renovation of fauna, which is reflected in the fossil register.

There appears to be general agreement that speciation, at least among higher animals, can not take place except in allopatric conditions, which means that for a new species to emerge from an already existing one, anterior geographical isolation is necessary in one of its populations, interrupting the genetic flow within the species. This is the only way in which the process of genetic divergence can, with time, and with different selective pressures in the different regions, give way to a genetic complex that is sufficiently distinctive to be considered a species in its own right. If this hypothesis is correct, it should be possible to see differences between geographical populations of present day species, and these differences should be directly related to the greater or lesser degree of isolation which these populations experience, or have experienced until recent times. Evidently this does occur in a general way, and these differences are normally used by taxonomists to describe subspecies, or geographical races, within a particular species. However, because speciation is a gradual process, the recognition of such subspecies is essentially artificial and subjective, because the phenotypic differences between populations of a given species, taking into account individual variation, are sometimes conspicuous, but on occasions they are very subtle. Ultimately, it depends on the criteria of the individual taxonomist, whether or not the differences are sufficient to merit classification as a subspecies. This is particularly difficult in species that are widely distributed over continental landmasses, where there are potential physical barriers like mountain ranges or deserts, but the differences tend to be relative, as these barriers slow down the genetic flow between populations, but do not halt it completely. Because of this, such species usually exhibit continuous variations in phenotypic characteristics, for example in body size, coloration or relative length of appendages, along geographical gradients. These gradual variations, or clines, make it very difficult or impossible to define the limits of the subspecies, however marked the differences may be between the two extremes of the gradient. This also explains why subspecies that are generally agreed upon are far more common in the faunas of islands or archipelagos.

ORDER	SUBORDER	FAMILY		
STRUTHIONIFORMES	STRUTHIONES	STRUTHIONIDAE	Ostrich	1
	RHEAE	RHEIDAE	rheas	2
	CASUARII	CASUARIIDAE	cassowaries	3
		DROMAIIDAE	Emu	1
	APTERYGES	APTERYGIDAE	kiwis	3
TINAMIFORMES		TINAMIDAE	tinamous	47
SPHENISCIFORMES		SPHENISCIDAE	penguins	17
GAVIIFORMES		GAVIIDAE	divers	4
PODICIPEDIFORMES		PODICIPEDIDAE	grebes	22
PROCELLARIIFORMES		DIOMEDEIDAE	albatrosses	14
		PROCELLARIIDAE	petrels, shearwaters	70
		HYDROBATIDAE	storm-petrels	20
		PELECANOIDIDAE	diving-petrels	4
PELECANIFORMES	PHAETHONTES	PHAETHONTIDAE	tropicbirds	3
	PELECANI	PELECANIDAE	pelicans	7
		SULIDAE	gannets, boobies	9
		PHALACROCORACIDAE	cormorants	39
		ANHINGIDAE	darters	2
		FREGATIDAE	frigatebirds	5
CICONIIFORMES	ARDEAE	ARDEIDAE	herons	60
	SCOPI	SCOPIDAE	Hamerkop	1
	CICONIAE	CICONIIDAE	storks	19
		BALAENCIPITIDAE	Shoebill	1
		THRESKIORNITHIDAE	ibises, spoonbills	32
PHOENICOPTERIFORMES		PHOENICOPTERIDAE	flamingos	5
ANSERIFORMES	ANHIMAE	ANHIMIDAE	screamers	3
	ANSERES	ANATIDAE	ducks, geese, swans	147
FALCONIFORMES	CATHARTAE	CATHARTIDAE	New World vultures	7
	ACCIPITRES	PANDIONIDAE	Osprey	1
		ACCIPITRIDAE	hawks, eagles	217
	SAGITTARII	SAGITTARIIDAE	Secretary Bird	1
	FALCONES	FALCONIDAE	caracaras, falcons	61
GALLIFORMES	GALLI	MEGAPODIIDAE	megapodes	12
		CRACIDAE	guans, chachalacas, curassows	44
		PHASIANIDAE	pheasants, grouse	213
	OPISTHOCOMI	OPISTHOCOMIDAE	Hoatzin	1
GRUIFORMES	MESITORNITHES	MESITORNITHIDAE	mesites	3
	TURNICES	TURNICIDAE	buttonquails	14
		PEDIONOMIDAE	Plains-wanderer	1
	GRUES	GRUIDAE	cranes	15
		ARAMIDAE	Limpkin	1
		PSOPHIIDAE	trumpeters	3
		RALLIDAE	rails, coots	133
	HELIORNITHES	HELIORNITHIDAE	finfoots	3
	RHYNOCHETI	RHYNOCHETIDAE	Kagu	1
	EURYPYGAE	EURYPYGIDAE	Sunbittern	1
	CARIAMAE	CARIAMIDAE	seriemas	2
	OTIDES	OTIDIDAE	bustards	24
CHARADRIIFORMES	CHARADRII	JACANIDAE	jacanas	8
		ROSTRATULIDAE	painted-snipe	2
		DROMADIDAE	Crab Plover	1
		HAEMATOPODIDAE	oystercatchers	7
		IBIDORHYNCHIDAE	Ibisbill	1
		RECURVIROSTRIDAE	avocets, stilts	13
		BURHINIDAE	thick-knees	9
		GLAREOLIDAE	coursers, pratincoles	16
		CHARADRIIDAE	plovers	64
		SCOLOPACIDAE	sandpipers, snipe	86
		THINOCORIDAE	seedsnipe	4
		CHIONIDIDAE	sheathbills	2
	LARI	STERCORARIIDAE	skuas	5
		LARIDAE	gulls, terns	90
		RYNCHOPIDAE	skimmers	3
	ALCAE	ALCIDAE	auks	23
COLUMBIFORMES		PTEROCLIDIDAE	sandgrouse	16
		COLUMBIDAE	pigeons, doves	283
PSITTACIFORMES		LORIIDAE	lories	55
		CACATUIDAE	cockatoos	18
		PSITTACIDAE	parrots	271
CUCULIFORMES	MUSOPHAGAE	MUSOPHAGIDAE	turacos	19
	CUCULI	CUCULIDAE	cuckoos	130
STRIGIFORMES		TYTONIDAE	barn owls	12
		STRIGIDAE	typical owls	134
CAPRIMULGIFORMES	STEATORNITHES	STEATORNITHIDAE	Oilbird	1
	CAPRIMULGI	PODARGIDAE	frogmouths	13
		NYCTIBIIDAE	potoos	5
		AEGOTHELIDAE	owlet-nightjars	8
		CAPRIMULGIDAE	nightjars	76
APODIFORMES	APODI	APODIDAE	swifts	82
		HEMIPROCNIDAE	tree-swifts	4
	TROCHILI	TROCHILIDAE	hummingbirds	338

Classification of the Class Aves, down to family level, based on Morony, Bock & Farrand (1975): Reference List of the Birds of the World. This is one of the most traditional and widely accepted classifications of the world's birds. In this scheme the background colour changes for each order. Each line ends with the number of species in the family.

[Figure: Xavier Ruiz]

ORDER	SUBORDER	FAMILY		
COLIIFORMES		COLIIDAE	mousebirds	6
TROGONIFORMES		TROGONIDAE	trogons	37
CORACIIFORMES	ALCEDINES	ALCEDINIDAE	kingfishers	90
		TODIDAE	todies	5
		MOMOTIDAE	motmots	9
	MEROPES	MEROPIDAE	bee-eaters	21
	CORACII	CORACIIDAE	rollers	11
		BRACHYPTERACIIDAE	ground-rollers	5
		LEPTOSOMATIDAE	Cuckoo-roller	1
	BUCEROTES	UPUPIDAE	Hoopoe	1
		PHOENICULIDAE	woodhoopoes	8
		BUCEROTIDAE	hornbills	44
PICIFORMES	GALBULAE	GALBULIDAE	jacamars	17
		BUCCONIDAE	puffbirds	34
		CAPITONIDAE	barbets	81
		INDICATORIDAE	honeyguides	14
		RAMPHASTIDAE	toucans	33
	PICI	PICIDAE	woodpeckers	204
PASSERIFORMES	DEUTERO-OSCINES	EURYLAIMIDAE	broadbills	14
		DENDROCOLAPTIDAE	woodcreepers	52
		FURNARIIDAE	ovenbirds	218
		FORMICARIIDAE	antbirds	228
		CONOPOPHAGIDAE	gnateaters	11
		RHINOCRYPTIDAE	tapaculos	30
		COTINGIDAE	cotingas	79
		PIPRIDAE	manakins	57
		TYRANNIDAE	tyrant flycatchers	374
		OXYRUNCIDAE	Sharpbill	1
		PHYTOTOMIDAE	plantcutters	3
		PITTIDAE	pittas	24
	OSCINES OR PASSERES	XENICIDAE	New Zealand wrens	4
		PHILEPITTIDAE	asities	4
		MENURIDAE	lyrebirds	2
		ATRICHORNITHIDAE	scrub-birds	2
		ALAUDIDAE	larks	77
		HIRUNDINIDAE	swallows, martins	80
		MOTACILLIDAE	wagtails, pipits	54
		CAMPEPHAGIDAE	cuckooshrikes	70
		PYCNONOTIDAE	bulbuls	123
		IRENIDAE	leafbirds, ioras, fairy-bluebirds	14
		LANIIDAE	shrikes	74
		VANGIDAE	vanga shrikes	13
		BOMBYCILLIDAE	waxwings	8
		DULIDAE	Palmchat	1
		CINCLIDAE	dippers	5
		TROGLODYTIDAE	wrens	59
		MIMIDAE	mockingbirds, thrashers	31
		PRUNELLIDAE	accentors	12
		MUSCICAPIDAE	thrushes, chats, log-runners, babblers, parrotbills, rockfowl, gnatwrens, Old World warblers, Australasian wrens, Old World flycatchers, wattle-eyes, batises, monarchs, fantails, whistlers	1423
		AEGITHALIDAE	long-tailed tits	8
		REMIZIDAE	penduline tits	10
		PARIDAE	tits, chickadees	47
		SITTIDAE	nuthatches	25
		CERTHIIDAE	treecreepers	6
		RHABDORNITHIDAE	Philippine creepers	2
		CLIMACTERIDAE	Australian creepers	6
		DICAEIDAE	flowerpeckers	58
		NECTARINIIDAE	sunbirds	116
		ZOSTEROPIDAE	white-eyes	83
		MELIPHAGIDAE	honeyeaters	171
		EMBERIZIDAE	buntings, cardinals, tanagers	558
		PARULIDAE	New World warblers	126
		DREPANIDIDAE	Hawaiian honeycreepers	23
		VIREONIDAE	vireos	43
		ICTERIDAE	New World blackbirds	95
		FRINGILLIDAE	finches	122
		ESTRILDIDAE	waxbills	127
		PLOCEIDAE	weavers, sparrows	143
		STURNIDAE	starlings	111
		ORIOLIDAE	orioles	28
		DICRURIDAE	drongos	20
		CALLAEIDAE	wattlebirds	3
		GRALLINIDAE	magpie-larks	4
		ARTAMIDAE	woodswallows	10
		CRACTICIDAE	butcherbirds	8
		PTILONORHYNCHIDAE	bowerbirds	18
		PARADISAEIDAE	birds of paradise	42
		CORVIDAE	crows, jays	105

ORDER	SUBORDER	FAMILY		
STRUTHIONIFORMES	STRUTHIONI	STRUTHIONIDAE	Ostrich	1
		RHEIDAE	rheas	2
	CASUARII	CASUARIIDAE	cassowaries / Emu	4
		APTERYGIDAE	kiwis	3
TINAMIFORMES		TINAMIDAE	tinamous	47
CRACIFORMES	CRACI	CRACIDAE	guans, chachalacas, curassows	50
	MEGAPODII	MEGAPODIIDAE	megapodes	19
GALLIFORMES		PHASIANIDAE	grouse, turkeys, pheasants, partridges, etc.	177
		NUMIDIDAE	guineafowl	6
		ODONTOPHORIDAE	New World quails	31
ANSERIFORMES		ANHIMIDAE	screamers	3
		ANSERANATIDAE	Magpie Goose	1
		DENDROCYGNIDAE	whistling-ducks	9
		ANATIDAE	stiff-tailed ducks / Freckled Duck / swans / geese / typical ducks	148
TURNICIFORMES		TURNICIDAE	buttonquails	17
PICIFORMES		INDICATORIDAE	honeyguides	17
		PICIDAE	woodpeckers, wrynecks	215
		MEGALAIMIDAE	Asian barbets	26
		LYBIIDAE	African barbets	42
		RAMPHASTIDAE	New World barbets / toucans	55
GALBULIFORMES		GALBULIDAE	jacamars	18
		BUCCONIDAE	puffbirds	33
BUCEROTIFORMES		BUCEROTIDAE	typical hornbills	54
		BUCORVIDAE	ground-hornbills	2
UPUPIFORMES		UPUPIDAE	hoopoes	2
		PHOENICULIDAE	woodhoopoes	5
		RHINOPOMASTIDAE	scimitarbills	3
TROGONIFORMES		TROGONIDAE	African trogons / New World trogons / Asian trogons	39
CORACIIFORMES	CORACII	CORACIIDAE	typical rollers	12
		BRACHYPTERACIIDAE	ground-rollers	5
		LEPTOSOMIDAE	Cuckoo-roller	1
	ALCEDINI	MOMOTIDAE	motmots	9
		TODIDAE	todies	5
		ALCEDINIDAE	alcedinid kingfishers	24
		DACELONIDAE	dacelonid kingfishers	61
		CERYLIDAE	cerylid kingfishers	9
		MEROPIDAE	bee-eaters	26
COLIIFORMES		COLIIDAE	typical mousebirds / long-tailed mousebirds	6
CUCULIFORMES		CUCULIDAE	Old World cuckoos	79
		CENTROPODIDAE	coucals	30
		COCCYZIDAE	American cuckoos	18
		OPISTHOCOMIDAE	Hoatzin	1
		CROTOPHAGIDAE	anis / Guira Cuckoo	4
		NEOMORPHIDAE	roadrunners, ground-cuckoos	11
PSITTACIFORMES		PSITTACIDAE	parrots and allies	358
APODIFORMES		APODIDAE	typical swifts	99
		HEMIPROCNIDAE	tree-swifts	4
TROCHILIFORMES		TROCHILIDAE	hermits / typical hummingbirds	319
MUSOPHAGIFORMES		MUSOPHAGIDAE	turacos / plantain-eaters	23
STRIGIFORMES	STRIGI	TYTONIDAE	barn and grass owls	17
		STRIGIDAE	typical owls	161
	AEGOTHELI	AEGOTHELIDAE	owlet-nightjars	8
	CAPRIMULGI	PODARGIDAE	Australian frogmouths	3
		BATRACHOSTOMIDAE	Asian frogmouths	11
		STEATORNITHIDAE	Oilbird	1
		NYCTIBIIDAE	potoos	7
		EUROSTOPODIDAE	eared-nightjars	7
		CAPRIMULGIDAE	nighthawks / nightjars	76
COLUMBIFORMES		COLUMBIDAE	pigeons, doves	310
GRUIFORMES	GRUI	EURYPYGIDAE	Sunbittern	1
		OTIDIDAE	bustards	25
		GRUIDAE	crowned-cranes / typical cranes	15
		HELIORNITHIDAE	Limpkin / finfoots	4
		PSOPHIIDAE	trumpeters	3
		CARIAMIDAE	seriemas	2
		RHYNOCHETIDAE	Kagu	1
	RALLI	RALLIDAE	rails, gallinules, coots	142
	MESITORNITHI	MESITORNITHIDAE	mesites	3

Classification of the Class Aves, down to family level, based on Sibley & Monroe (1990): Distribution and Taxonomy of Birds of the World. *This new classification, based on results of the modern technique of DNA-DNA hybridization used by the authors and J. Ahlquist, has caused a major stir in the field of systematics, as it advocates a series of surprising changes in numerous groups of birds with relation to the traditional classifications. It has been widely acclaimed as a major contribution to ornithology, although as yet it is far from receiving unanimous support. In the scheme the background colour changes for each order. Categories above ordinal level and the intermediate ranks infraorder, parvorder and superfamily have been omitted. Slashes indicate subdivisions into subfamilies or tribes within a family. Each line ends with the number of species in the family.*

[Figure: Xavier Ruiz]

ORDER	SUBORDER	FAMILY		
CICONIIFORMES	CHARADRII	PTEROCLIDAE	sandgrouse	16
		THINOCORIDAE	seedsnipe	4
		PEDIONOMIDAE	Plains-wanderer	1
		SCOLOPACIDAE	woodcock, snipe / sandpipers, curlews, phalaropes	88
		ROSTRATULIDAE	painted-snipe	2
		JACANIDAE	jacanas	8
		CHIONIDIDAE	sheathbills	2
		BURHINIDAE	thick-knees	9
		CHARADRIIDAE	oystercatchers / avocets, stilts / plovers, lapwings	89
		GLAREOLIDAE	Crab Plover / pratincoles, coursers	18
		LARIDAE	skuas, jaegers / skimmers / gulls / terns / auks, murres, puffins	129
	CICONII	ACCIPITRIDAE	Osprey / hawks, eagles	240
		SAGITTARIIDAE	Secretary Bird	1
		FALCONIDAE	caracaras, falcons	63
		PODICIPEDIDAE	grebes	21
		PHAETHONTIDAE	tropicbirds	3
		SULIDAE	gannets, boobies	9
		ANHINGIDAE	darters	4
		PHALACROCORACIDAE	cormorants	38
		ARDEIDAE	herons	65
		SCOPIDAE	Hamerkop	1
		PHOENICOPTERIDAE	flamingos	5
		THRESKIORNITHIDAE	ibises, spoonbills	34
		PELECANIDAE	Shoebill / pelicans	9
		CICONIIDAE	New World vultures / storks	26
		FREGATIDAE	frigatebirds	5
		SPHENISCIDAE	penguins	17
		GAVIIDAE	divers	5
		PROCELLARIIDAE	petrels, shearwaters, diving-petrels / albatrosses / storm-petrels	115
PASSERIFORMES	TYRANNI	ACANTHISITTIDAE	New Zealand wrens	4
		PITTIDAE	pittas	31
		EURYLAIMIDAE	broadbills	14
		PHILEPITTIDAE	asities	4
		Incertae sedis	Broad-billed Sapayoa	1
		TYRANNIDAE	mionectine flycatchers, antpipits / tyrant flycatchers / schiffornises / tityras, becards / cotingas, plantcutters, Sharpbill / manakins	537
		THAMNOPHILIDAE	typical antbirds	188
		FURNARIIDAE	ovenbirds / woodcreepers	280
		FORMICARIIDAE	ground antbirds	56
		CONOPOPHAGIDAE	gnateaters	8
		RHINOCRYPTIDAE	tapaculos	28
	PASSERI	CLIMACTERIDAE	Australo-Papuan treecreepers	7
		MENURIDAE	lyrebirds / scrub-birds	4
		PTILONORHYNCHIDAE	bowerbirds	20
		MALURIDAE	fairywrens / emuwrens / grasswrens	26
		MELIPHAGIDAE	honeyeaters, Australian chats	182
		PARDALOTIDAE	pardalotes / bristlebirds / scrubwrens / thornbills, whitefaces, etc.	68
		EOPSALTRIIDAE	Australo-Papuan robins, scrub-robins	46
		IRENIDAE	fairy-bluebirds, leafbirds	10
		ORTHONYCHIDAE	logrunners, chowchillas	2
		POMATOSTOMIDAE	Australo-Papuan babblers	5
		LANIIDAE	true shrikes	30
		VIREONIDAE	vireos, peppershrikes, etc.	51
		CORVIDAE	quail-thrushes, whipbirds / Australian Chough, Apostlebird / sittellas / *Mohoua* / shrike-tits, Crested Bellbird, Mottled Whistler / whistlers, shrike-thrushes / crows, magpies, jays, nutcrackers / birds of paradise, melampittas / currawongs, woodswallows, Peltops, Bornean Bristlehead / orioles, cuckooshrikes / fantails / drongos / monarchs, magpie-larks / ioras / bush-shrikes / helmet-shrikes, vangas, batises, wattle-eyes	647
		CALLAEATIDAE	New Zealand wattlebirds	3
		PICATHARTIDAE	rock-jumpers, rockfowl	4
		BOMBYCILLIDAE	Palmchat / silky-flycatchers / waxwings	8
		CINCLIDAE	dippers	5
		MUSCICAPIDAE	true thrushes, Black-breasted Fruit-hunter, shortwings, alethes / Old World flycatchers / chats	449
		STURNIDAE	starlings, mynas / mockingbirds, thrashers, catbirds	148
		SITTIDAE	nuthatches / Wallcreeper	25
		CERTHIIDAE	northern creepers / Spotted Creeper / wrens / gnatcatchers, Verdin, gnatwrens	97
		PARIDAE	penduline tits / tits, chickadees	65
		AEGITHALIDAE	long-tailed tits, bushtits	8
		HIRUNDINIDAE	river martins / swallows, martins	89
		REGULIDAE	kinglets	6
		PYCNONOTIDAE	bulbuls	137
		HYPOCOLIIDAE	Grey Hypocolius	1
		CISTICOLIDAE	African warblers	119
		ZOSTEROPIDAE	white-eyes	96
		SYLVIIDAE	leaf-warblers / grass-warblers / laughingthrushes / babblers / rhabdornises / Wrentit / *Sylvia* warblers	552
		ALAUDIDAE	larks	91
		NECTARINIIDAE	sugarbirds / flowerpeckers / sunbirds, spiderhunters	169
		MELANOCHARITIDAE	*Melanocharis* berrypeckers / longbills	10
		PARAMYTHIIDAE	Tit Berrypecker, Crested Berrypecker	2
		PASSERIDAE	sparrows, rock-sparrows, etc. / wagtails, pipits / accentors / weavers / estrildine finches / whydahs	386
		FRINGILLIDAE	Olive Warbler / chaffinches, Brambling / goldfinches, crossbills, etc. / Hawaiian honeycreepers / buntings, longspurs, towhees / wood-warblers / tanagers, Neotropical honeycreepers, seedeaters, flower-piercers, etc. / cardinals / troupials, meadowlarks, New World blackbirds, etc.	993

On occasions the external appearance or phenotype of the various subspecies can be so distinct that they may be referred to as "semispecies". So the question remains as to the point at which they constitute completely separate species. In principle, this is only the case once the genetic distance is such that interbreeding ceases to be feasible, at any rate in terms of producing perfectly fertile hybrids; that is to say, when the mechanisms of reproductive isolation have developed sufficiently to provide effective protection for their respective genotypic identities. If two geographically separate populations are reunited, for example due to climatic or geological changes which remove the geographical barrier, they can only perpetuate themselves as two different species, if they are already sufficiently isolated from the genetic point of view. If not, sooner or later a process of interbreeding will eliminate all the differences developed during the period of isolation. But even if these two populations already constitute "good" species, it is absolutely necessary, if they are to co-exist in a given area, that they be ecologically compatible, not occupying the same ecological niche (Gause's Rule). In fact, from the moment that they are together again, if one of the two does not die out, natural selection will tend to accentuate the morphological or behavioural differences that are connected with their use of the environment, in order to separate their niches as much as possible. For example, differences in bill size are likely to increase, and this in turn leads to varying levels of efficiency in the exploitation of different types of food. This serves not only to make the co-existence of the two species easier, but, as a consequence of such specialization, will also result in improved joint exploitation of the resources of the ecosystem. The repetition of this process of speciation followed by specialization leads to what is called adaptive radiation, and among the best known examples are the Galapagos finches (Geospizinae), comprising 14 species with different bill shapes and feeding habits, descended from an initial seed eating species, or the Hawaiian honeycreepers (Drepanididae), with 28 species in 15 genera, all descendants of an ancestral species of finch.

Sometimes speciation takes place without the morphological differences being very apparent, in contrast with the marked variations that may appear among the different races of a single species. This is the case of the "sibling species" (sometimes known as "cryptic species"), that are sympatric and perfectly isolated both reproductively and ecologically, although they hardly differ at all morphologically, giving rise to practical problems, such as the correct identification of birds in the field. Examples in Europe are the Willow Tit (*Parus montanus*) and the Marsh Tit (*P. palustris*), the Crested Lark (*Galerida cristata*) and the Thekla Lark (*G. theklae*), and the Thrush Nightingale (*Luscinia luscinia*) and the Common Nightingale, and in North America, the Least Flycatcher (*Empidonax minimus*), the Willow Flycatcher (*E. traillii*) and the Acadian Flycatcher (*E. virescens*).

Phylogeny and Classification

Contemplating the wide range of present day birds, there are clearly enormous differences between them, comparing, for example, penguins, hummingbirds, the Ostrich and eagles. Such a wide variety, however, extensive as it may seem, is simply the result of the accumulation, after millions of years, of the little differences that develop in the process of speciation. To date, biology does not know of other possibilities to explain the evolution of living beings. This means that if no species had ever died out, a reconstruction of the relationships between them all would produce a phylogenetic tree of birds showing a perfect, gradual gradation of characters, which through the different branches would lead without jumps from one extreme to the other, for example, from the hummingbirds to the Ostrich. It is the fact that only a small proportion of species have reached the present day that prompts the impression that the living species form a series of discrete units, which are separated more or less obviously. One of the essential objectives of zoology, and particularly of systematics, is to try to reconstruct

the family tree of animals, starting from these units; to provide a detailed history of their evolution.

As already indicated, the fossil register of birds is relatively incomplete. For this reason, research into their evolutionary or phylogenetic history depends principally on the detailed comparison of the characteristics of present day species, in an attempt to deduce the possible extent of their relationships, assuming that the more closely related species, those which have most recently shared a common ancestor, share a higher number of features than more distantly related species. In a second phase, groups of related species can be compared to try to define units of superior rank, which in turn can be compared and related internally or with other groups. This leads on to the creation of a classification of living birds depending on the similarity of their characters, with the final aim of reproducing the evolutionary process, as faithfully as possible. This is the ultimate objective of systematics, to achieve "natural" and not merely convenient classifications, although, of course, all classifications are in themselves of great value from a practical point of view, as they are essential instruments for ordering and transmitting the huge amount of accumulated scientific information.

To carry out classifications of animals, there is another science, Taxonomy. This has the practical aim of supplying all the norms and necessary procedures for naming the groupings of "taxa" which have been recognized (Nomenclature), and to assign them to the most appropriate compartments or taxonomic categories, including a genus, tribe, family, order, and so on (Classification). Perhaps it is not necessary to stress that, because the evolutionary process is gradual, these taxa and taxonomic categories are completely artificial and without biological significance in themselves, the opposite of what happens with the species.

Until quite recently, the only characters used in systematics were those provided by comparative anatomy or morphology. And these characters were very often useless for deducing phylogenetic relationships, as similarities could simply be due to adaptive convergences. For example, the common possession of a thick, conical bill does not necessarily imply a relationship between two species, because this could perfectly well have developed independently in two separate phylogenetic lines, as a basic adaption to eating seeds. If the similarities are due exclusively to functional, adaptive reasons, they are called "analogous" characters, whereas if they are related to a common ancestry, they are called "homologous" characters. Distinguishing homologous characters from analogous ones is the first and most important challenge for zoological systematics. In the case of birds the difficulties in this area have been tremendous. Ornithologists have thoroughly explored a daunting number of morphological characters, including: pterylosis, or the form in which the different tracts of the skin, feathered or bare, are laid out; the number and relative length of the remiges; the tarsal scutellation, the way in which the scales of the tarsometatarsus are arranged; the relative position of the toes and the possible relations established between them by membranes; the musculature and the tendons of the legs, wings, mandibles and various other parts of the body; the structure of the bony palate; the shape of the columella, a small bone in the middle ear; or the different types of syrinx. In more recent times attention has also been given to ethological characteristics, such as courtship display, or the manner of bathing, or of building the nest, and also to other physiological and biochemical aspects, including the degree of similarity of different enzymes and proteins, of carotenoids, or, recently, DNA. But the possibilities of adaptive convergence have shown themselves time and again to be extensive, and consequently, strange as it may seem, the classification of birds is still far from being universally agreed upon.

The first classification of birds was made in the seventeenth century by two Englishmen, Francis Willughby and John Ray (*Ornithologiae*, 1676). With a few modifications, the same base was used by Linneus in his *Systema Naturae* (1758). It was not until after Darwin (*On the Origin of Species*, 1859), that theoretical foundations existed for phylogenetic investigation and classification, and that some workers initiated the indefatigable search for useful taxonomic characters, which would in principle be less prone to the presence of hidden analogies. An excellent example in this respect was Thomas Huxley with his classic work on the lay-out of the palate bones of birds, published in 1867. Already towards the end of the nineteenth century very fruitful morphological studies had allowed the German Hans Friedrich Gadow (1892) to make a classification that was not very different from those which are considered as "modern": Stresemann (1927-1934); Mayr and Amadon (1951); Wetmore (1960); Peters (1931-1968); Storer (1971); or Morony, Bock and Farrand (1975).

Indeed, relatively little progress has been made since then, and there is a certain impression of defeat in the systematics of birds, when one considers the uncertainty that still hangs over the taxonomic situation of many different groups. For example, the flamingos are sometimes considered to be closely related to the ducks, but others place them with the storks and herons, or lately with the waders (Charadriiformes). In the ratites, it is argued whether the Ostrich, the rheas, the cassowaries, the Emu and the kiwis are related to each other or not, whereas others postulate that the penguins are perhaps descendants of primitive shearwaters.

It is only in the last ten years that a potential profound change in the systematics of birds has been outlined, with the modern DNA-DNA hybridization techniques used by Charles Sibley and Jon Ahlquist enabling the direct comparison between the genetic material of two different species, and even, to a certain extent, allowing a calculation of the time that has elapsed since the two lineages diverged. It appears that the findings presented by these techniques do in most cases corroborate what has already been established by traditional classification, and in some cases have supported recent suggestions, including the proximity of the New World vultures to the storks, and of the Shoebill (*Balaeniceps rex*) to the pelicans. However, some other conclusions are frankly novel, and will undoubtedly be the object of study and testing for some time to come.

An example of this is the fragmentation of the traditional Pelecaniformes, characterized by their "totipalmate" feet, with the four toes joined by membranes. It is now suggested that this feature has been acquired independently by the tropicbirds; by the pelicans, closely related to the Shoebill; by the cormorants, darters and gannets, relatives of the herons; and by the frigatebirds, in fact related to the petrels. Another is the case of the radical subdivision of the song birds or Oscines into two "parvorders", Passerida and Corvida, the second resulting from an independent radiation occurring in Australia, parallel to that which took place, amongst the mammals, with the marsupials.

For comparison, pages 68-71 include, in separate tables, two classifications of living birds down to family level, one of the widely used traditional type (Morony *et al.*, 1975), and another proposed by Sibley, Ahlquist and Monroe (1988), as a result of their research into DNA-DNA hybridization. There is obviously still a great deal to be learnt.

Bibliography

General
Austin & Singer (1961), Brooke & Birkhead (1991), Campbell & Lack (1985), Clements (1982), Dickson *et al.* (1979), Dorst (1971), Farner & King (1971-1975), Farner *et al.* (1982-1985), Fisher & Flegg (1974), Fisher & Peterson (1964, 1971), Gill (1990), Gilliard (1958), Gooders (1969-1971), Grassé (1950), Gruson (1976), Grzimek (1972-1973), Lack (1966, 1971, 1976), Loye & Buk (1991), Perrins (1990), Perrins & Birkhead (1983), Perrins & Middleton (1985), Newton (1896), Pettingill (1985), Pycraft (1910), Rand (1967), Ricklefs (1983a), Stefferud & Nelson (1966), Stresemann (1934), Thomson (1964), van Tyne & Berger (1976), Wallace (1963), Welty & Baptista (1988), Wolfson (1955).

Systematics
de Beer (1954), Bock & Farrand (1980), Brodkorb (1971), Cracraft (1973, 1981, 1986), Feduccia (1980), Eldridge & Cracraft (1980), Glenny (1955), Heilmann (1926), Howard (1950), Howard & Moore (1991), Lack (1947, 1974), Lambrecht (1933), Mainardi (1963), Martin (1983), Mayr (1969, 1970), Mayr & Amadon (1951), Mayr & Cottrell (1979), Morony *et al.* (1975), Olson (1985), Peters (1931-1987), Selander (1971), Sibley (1970), Sibley & Ahlquist (1972, 1983, 1991), Sibley & Monroe (1990), Sibley *et al.* (1988), Storer (1971a, 1971b), Voous (1973), Wetmore (1960), Wolters (1975-1982).

Morphological Aspects
Ames (1971), Baker (1984), Baumel *et al.* (1979), Berger & Hart (1974), Bock (1974), Burton (1990), Chamberlain (1943), Cooke & Buckley (1987), George & Berger (1966), Ginn & Melville (1983), Greenewalt (1975), Gwinner (1990), King & McLelland (1980-1988, 1984), Lindstedt & Calder (1976), Lucas & Stettenheim (1972), Marshall (1960-1961), Matthews (1968), O'Connor, R.J. (1984), Palmer (1972), Payne (1972), Paynter (1974), Pearson (1972), Pennycuick (1972, 1975, 1989), Phillips *et al.* (1985), Ricklefs (1983b), Romer (1970), Rüppell (1977), Schwartzkopff (1973), Shoemaker (1972), Sillman (1973), Stettenheim (1972), Storer (1948), Stresemann (1966), Sturkie (1986), Voitkevitch (1966), Walsberg (1983), Wenzel (1973), Ziswiler & Farner (1972).

Distribution and Habitat
Andrewartha & Birch (1954), Bernstein *et al.* (1991), Cody (1985), Collar & Stuart (1988), Darlington (1957), Dugan (1990), Fuller (1982), Gartlan (1989), Inskipp (1989), Keast (1990), Johnson (1988), Karr (1989), Lack (1971), MacArthur (1972), Moynihan (1979), Round (1988), Scott, D.A. (1982b), Scott, J.M. *et al.* (1986), Southwood (1977), Stuart (1986), Udvardy (1969), Vuilleumier (1975), Wallace (1876).

General Habits
Amlaner & Ball (1983), Armstrong (1965), Burton (1985), Cody (1974), Elkins (1988), Gwinner (1975), Hinde (1973), Howard (1920), Krebs & Davies (1991), Lorenz (1965), MacArthur (1971), Morse (1980), Orians (1971), Smith (1983), Skutch (1989), Tinbergen (1951), Wiens (1989a, 1989b), Wilson, E.O. (1975), Wittenberger (1981), Woolfenden & Fitzpatrick (1984).

Voice
Armstrong (1963), Busnel (1963), Catchpole (1979), Greenewalt (1968), Hinde (1969), Kroodsma & Miller (1983), Nottebohm (1975), Thorpe (1961).

Food and Feeding
Fisher, M. (1972), Kamil *et al.* (1987), Kear (1972a), Krebs & Davies (1991), Morrison *et al.* (1990), Morse (1980), Roberts (1979), Stephens & Krebs (1987), Storer (1971a).

Breeding
Deeming & Ferguson (1991), Birkhead & Moller (1991), Birkhead *et al.* (1987), Brown, J.L. (1987), Burley & Vadehra (1989), Burton (1987), Cody (1971), Collias & Collias (1984), Drent (1975), Immelmann (1971), Lack (1968), Lofts & Murton (1973), Makatsch (1950), Moller (1991), Murton & Westwood (1977), Newton (1989), Oring (1982), Romanoff & Romanoff (1949), Skutch (1976), Stacey & Koenig (1990), Westneat (1990).

Movements
Alerstam (1990), Baker (1978), Bernis (1966a), Berthold (1975), Dorst (1962), Emlen (1975), Gauthreaux (1982), Griffin (1974), Mead (1983), Moreau (1972), Papi & Wallraff (1982), Schmidt-Koenig (1979), Schmidt-Koenig & Keeton (1978).

Relationship with Man
Armstrong (1958), Bub (1991), Cott (1953, 1954), Lever (1987), Long (1981), Murton & Westwood (1976), Murton & Wright (1968), Rounds (1990), Rutgers & Norris (1970), Stresemann (1975), Wendt (1956), Woldhek (1980), Wright *et al.* (1980), Yapp (1981).

Status and Conservation
Avery *et al.* (1990), Beaufort (1983), Collar & Andrew (1988), Cooper (1989), Day (1981), Diamond & Filion (1987), Diamond & Lovejoy (1985), Diamond *et al.* (1987), Dollinger (1988), Fisher *et al.* (1969), Fuller (1987), Goriup (1988), Greenway (1967), Grimmett & Jones (1989), Halliday (1978), IUCN (1990), King (1978/79, 1980), Moors (1985), Mountfort (1988), Norton *et al.* (1990), O'Connor & Shrubb (1990), Perrins *et al.* (1991), Salathé (1991), Smart & Andrew (1985), Temple (1978), Terborgh (1989), Vincent (1966).

Order STRUTHIONIFORMES

Struthioniformes

Struthiones	Rheae	Casuarii		Apteryges
Struthionidae	Rheidae	Casuariidae	Dromaiidae	Apterygidae
Ostrich	rheas	cassowaries	Emu	kiwis

Class AVES
Order STRUTHIONIFORMES
Suborder STRUTHIONES
Family STRUTHIONIDAE (OSTRICH)

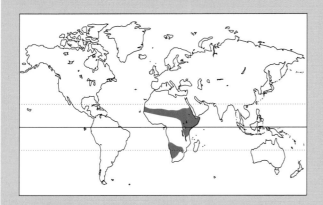

- Huge, flightless, two-toed terrestrial birds with long, powerful neck and legs.
- 175-275 cm.

- Afrotropical Region.
- Savannas, semi-arid and arid open areas.
- 1 genus, 1 species, 4 taxa.
- No species threatened; 1 subspecies extinct since 1600.

Systematics

The Ostrich family is related to all the other extant families of large, flightless birds, the rheas of South America, the cassowaries of Australia and New Guinea, the Emu of Australia and also the much smaller kiwis of New Zealand. Other close relatives included the now extinct moas of New Zealand and elephant birds of North Africa and Madagascar. The origin, phylogenetic relationships and systematics of these birds, often referred to as "ratites", have been studied and debated at great length, and the controversy is by no means over.

The physical similarity of members of these families caused many early taxonomists to group them together, but others claimed that these similarities were due to convergent evolution. As the theory of continental drift developed, it supplied a possible explanation for the origin of the ratites, starting from a common ancestor, with an ensuing period of dispersal throughout the Southern Hemisphere. This ancestor probably had a wide distribution in the ancient southern landmass of Gondwanaland and started to evolve into the distinct ratite families after the great continent began to split up towards the end of the Cretaceous, thus forming modern day Africa, South America, Australia and Antarctica. Subsequent studies of morphological, biochemical and genetic aspects have corroborated the theory that these families had a common origin.

However, their relationship with the rest of the birds remains unclear. Some authors consider that the ratites split off from the main branch of the birds at a very early stage and are thus among the most primitive of all, while others claim that they are actually quite advanced. The presence of vestigial wings is evidence that their isolation probably took place only after they had already evolved the ability to fly; the ratites subsequently lost this ability, as an evolutionary development to their terrestrial life, and the lack of a keel on their sternum is considered most likely a derived character, resulting from this adaptation of lifestyle, as a keel was no longer required to support the large flight muscles. Phylogenetically the closest relatives of the ratites are the tinamous, which share the same common ancestor, as indicated by certain derived anatomical features which are not found in any other birds, most notably the palaeognathous palate.

The debate continues and the ratites have been split up and grouped together in various different ways. For instance, some have divided them into two orders, while others have placed them all together in the same order, with the tinamous even thrown in too. The traditional classification places the five ratite families in four orders, emphasizing that they are really quite distinct from one another. However, current opinion advocates the lumping together of all five families in a single order, Struthioniformes; this has the advantage of showing that they are more closely related to each other than to any other birds, while their segregation along with the tinamous in a separate superorder, Palaeognathae, helps to emphasize that these two groups are quite different from all other members of the class Aves. The Ostrich is undoubtedly closest to the rheas, most notably in a series of skeletal features, and the two are sometimes placed in the same family.

Today the Ostrich is endemic to Africa, apart from an introduced population in parts of Australia (see Relationship with Man). However, the family was formerly found in southern Europe and Asia too, as fossils belonging to the genus *Struthio* have been found from Greece to the southern USSR, India and Mongolia, as well as all over Africa; the oldest of these was found in Pliocene deposits and dates back some 12 million years.

Nowadays, only one species remains and this is divided into four subspecies: the North African Ostrich (*Struthio camelus camelus*); the Somali Ostrich (*S. c. molybdophanes*); the Masai Ostrich (*S. c. massaicus*); and the South African Ostrich (*S. c. australis*). Fertile young have been produced by the hybridization both of *molybdophanes* and *massaicus*, and also of *australis* and *camelus*, and nobody now splits the Ostrich into more than one species. The Arabian Ostrich (*S. c. syriacus*) probably became extinct around the middle of this century (see Status and Conservation). A further race, the Dwarf Ostrich (*S. c. spatzi*), was proposed by Stresemann for populations of north-west Africa, on the grounds of its smaller size and different egg-pore structure, but it is not normally accepted.

Morphological Aspects

The Ostrich is the largest living bird and also the heaviest. Males stand 2·1-2·75 m tall and weigh 100-130 kg, or sometimes up to 150 kg, whereas females are about 1·75-1·9 m tall and weigh 90-110 kg.

Large size has obvious advantages for a flightless bird on the African plains, where predators abound. In the first place, the Ostrich's very height, combined with its excellent eyesight, mean that it can look over the top of a lot of vegetation and so detect its potential predators a long way off. Secondly, its long, stout legs enable it to cover great distances with the minimum of effort, when searching for its often sparsely distributed food. They also represent formidable weapons, armed, as each foot is, with a 10 cm long sturdy, flattened claw on the thick inner toe. Lastly, its long neck, which is almost bare, gives it access to a wide range of food at different heights.

The head is rather small in relation to the size of the bird, but its huge eyes, which are protected by long black eyelashes, are the largest of any terrestrial vertebrate, with a diameter of 50 mm. As well as for detecting predators, the Ostrich needs to see well, in order to be able to pick out conspecifics at a distance better than any potential enemies can, particularly in the breeding season, when a mate must be sought.

In common with the other ratites, the Ostrich has its skeleton and also its wing musculature simplified. One of the most significant characteristics of the group is that there is no keel on the sternum, hence the name "ratites", from the Latin, *ratis*, "a raft", in contrast to all other birds, which used to be termed "carinates", from *carina*, "a keel". Their feathers are also unusual, for the barbs are loose, due to the absence of hooks on the barbules (see page 37), and the Ostrich's plumage is soft and smooth. As they have no uropygial gland, ratites are unable to waterproof their feathers, which therefore tend to become sodden in rain. They have the unusually large number of 16 primaries, which may have developed in order to make their display more spectacular.

The Ostrich is the only species in which the toes have been reduced to two, the inner of which is thick and strong. All this shows a special adaptation for running, as the surface that comes into contact with the ground is much reduced, in order to gain speed. This helps to make it the fastest runner in the bird world and in terms of stamina it even defeats the mammals, as it can keep up a speed of 50 km/h for about half an hour. In a short sprint it may notch up 70 km/h, with strides of 3·5

m. At high speeds it uses its wings for balance, particularly if it swerves sharply to pull away from a pursuer.

The sexes are quite distinct in terms of plumage. The male is mostly pitch black, but the wings and tail are virtually pure white; the contrast is so striking that it can make the bird stand out at some distance. The female is an altogether drabber version of the male, presumably to make her less conspicuous during breeding. The body feathers are brown with pale fringes, while the wings and tail are dirty white. Juvenile plumage is similar to that of the female, but generally more uniform, in particular the wings and tail. It is thought that there is a complete moult between breeding seasons, but so far, evidence of this in wild birds is scant.

During the breeding season, male bare part colours are much brighter; this is most noticeable on the frontal shield of the tarsi and on the neck, both of which are normally dull pink or blue, depending on the subspecies. The Ostrich is one of fairly few birds in which the male has a penis, and this is displayed prominently during courtship.

Habitat

One of the typical inhabitants of the great African plains, the Ostrich is distributed over much of the continent. It can be found in a variety of different open habitats, ranging from savanna to desert.

In general it prefers open, semi-arid areas with relatively short grass, which provide it with an adequate food supply and also good visibility, to let it keep its distance from its enemies. It tends to avoid long grass that is over one metre high and areas that are densely shrouded in trees or bushes, but it may enter open woodland. Though absent from the belt of *Brachystegia* across southern central Africa, it may occur in Mopane woodland. It prefers to stick clear of true desert, where there

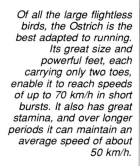

Of all the large flightless birds, the Ostrich is the best adapted to running. Its great size and powerful feet, each carrying only two toes, enable it to reach speeds of up to 70 km/h in short bursts. It also has great stamina, and over longer periods it can maintain an average speed of about 50 km/h.

[*Struthio camelus australis*, Etosha National Park, Namibia. Photo: Jen & Des Bartlett/ Bruce Coleman]

On the African plains it is vital to remain alert to the constant danger of attacks by predators. One of the standard ways of improving vigilance is to join other animals, and Ostriches often gather together in flocks when feeding, occasionally in the company of other species, such as these Thomson's gazelles (Gazella thomsoni).

[*Struthio camelus massaicus*, Kenya. Photo: Jonathan Scott/ Planet Earth]

is no vegetation at all, but its wanderings in search of food or water may take it through such zones.

It is, to some extent, adaptable to the hydrological conditions imposed by its environment and it does not actually require drinking water (see Food and Feeding). Thus, it has no problems surviving in areas where the annual rainfall is under 200 mm; notwithstanding, much of the sizeable East African population lives in areas with more than 800 mm per year.

General Habits

The daily activity of the Ostrich begins shortly before sunrise and ends soon after sunset, but it varies, depending on food availability; if food becomes scarce, birds have to spend a lot of time searching for it, and this may involve covering great distances (see Movements). Birds are most active during the first and last hours of the day, although they are quite capable of tolerating extreme heat and often walk out in the open in the midday sun.

At night they roost at regular communal sites, preferably with the wind in their favour, in case danger approaches. At such roosts individuals of a group are always within sight and hearing of each other, but they may be varying distances apart. They squat with their necks raised most of the night, although their eyes are closed. A deeper kind of sleep, when the bird rests its head and neck on the side of its body or stretched out on the ground in front of it, is limited to short intervals.

The Ostrich is gregarious, and this may well have evolved as a defence strategy (see Food and Feeding). Both the size and structure of its groups vary, depending on the habitat and the time of year. Outwith the breeding season, the group tends to consist of two to five birds, while single birds are also frequently seen. Alternatively, a variable number of immatures and adults of both sexes form groups of up to 100 birds, which individuals seemingly join or leave at will. In the

breeding season, however, birds form pairs or small harems (see Breeding). Each group has its own sites for feeding, roosting and dust-bathing, and tends to avoid contact with other groups. Nonetheless, in the dry season or in deserts large groups of up to 680 birds have been seen, congregating around water-holes.

Each group has a pecking order with dominant adult males and females, which are copied in their activities by the other members of the group, with the result that all of the birds tend to sand-bathe or preen at the same time. There are frequent social interactions between individuals, and they sometimes develop into short fights, though these are mostly restricted to disputes about social rank, or between individuals of the same sex during pair formation. Confrontations are usually settled by means of threatening noises (see Voice), or by one of the contestants adopting the dominant "Upright Display" posture. This involves the bird holding its head high, with its neck puffed out and its wing-tips and tail raised skywards. The bird thus threatened either flees or adopts the submissive posture, with its head held low, its neck kinked in a U-shape and the wings and tail pointing downwards. Sometimes there are short chases and the pursuer may peck or kick his rival.

The popular belief that Ostriches bury their heads in the sand, when in danger, is apparently erroneous, and it has never been recorded. However, when no other form of escape is evident, a bird may sit down, with its head and neck stretched out on the ground in front of it, and remain motionless, in the hope of being overlooked by its pursuer. This strategy is similarly adopted by an incubating bird, when it senses that danger is close, and this may have given rise to the myth.

Voice

The vocal repertoire of the Ostrich is quite extensive and includes whistling, snorting, guttural noises and "Booming" calls,

Although mainly occurring during the breeding season, aggressive encounters between males are frequent all year round, as a means of establishing the pecking order. This adult male is performing an "Upright Display", while the younger bird, on the right, has adopted a hostile attitude, as it makes a threatening cry.

[Struthio camelus australis, Zimbabwe. Photo: Jonathan Scott/ Planet Earth]

as well as non-vocal sounds, such as bill-snapping and stomach rumbling.

Among the most typical sounds made by the adults are the males' "Booming" calls, which are used to proclaim territory and during display. These consist of a deep "boo boo booooh hooo" repeated several times at short intervals, which sounds rather like a lion's roar, but without the final growl. At night, "Booming" can be triggered off by the presence of a predator or by unusual sounds, for example in a storm.

Males also frequently emit a soft "booh" or "twoo", which is normally used in disputes and accompanied by a threat, attack or retreat. Young birds make several different noises, which reflect their mood in a particular moment. Before hatching they make melodious contact calls, which are answered by their parents.

Food and Feeding

The Ostrich is omnivorous and what it eats depends mostly on whatever happens to be available, according to its environment and the time of year. However, generally speaking, most of its diet is made up of plant matter, for instance the roots, leaves, flowers and seeds of a great range of grasses, bushes and trees. The most typical items include succulent plants, seeds of *Acacia* and *Aloe*, and also figs (*Ficus*). These are sometimes supplemented with locusts, insects and small vertebrates, such as lizards or little tortoises.

As food is swallowed, it is collected in the crop, until a mass has accumulated; this then slides slowly down the neck, where it can clearly be seen stretching the skin on its way down. Many components of the Ostrich's diet are unpalatable to other animals, and to deal with such tough items, the Ostrich has formidable intestines that are all of 14 m long, which enable it to get the most out of what it consumes. Wild birds swallow pebbles and sand to help them break down food in their giz-

zards and they have a tendency to pick up small, bright objects. Stomachs of captive birds have yielded such diverse objects as coins, nails and bits of wire.

When searching for food, they peck with great precision at whatever they have picked out, most of which is within half a metre of the ground, but at times they browse at about head height.

While they are busy foraging, often with their heads lowered and hidden by the vegetation, they are liable to be surprised by their enemies, mainly lions, but occasionally leopards and cheetahs. To avoid such attacks, Ostriches have developed two strategies. Firstly, they look up and scan their surroundings at irregular intervals, so that a predator can not predict when they will next take a look. Secondly, they stick together in groups, thus reducing the vulnerability of the individual in the face of an attack, as each bird has a lower probability of being the chosen victim. This also allows them to concentrate more on feeding, as there are more pairs of eyes to spot a predator, and it has been noted that each individual pauses to look around less often, when in a group. An extension of this is their occasional association with herds of large herbivorous mammals, such as zebra and wildebeeste, which are on the look out for much the same predators.

Ostriches do not actually need to drink and most of their water is obtained from succulent plants, so these are particularly important in desert areas. They can also save a great deal of water by a special physiological adaptation, whereby they can increase their body temperature by 4·2°C on hot days, thus reducing water loss through transpiration.

Breeding

The breeding season of the Ostrich varies greatly from one part of Africa to another, depending on the rains. In wetter areas it tends to breed in the dry season, between June and October. In

When cornered, an Ostrich tries to escape detection by remaining immobile, with its body, neck and head flattened out on the ground. The same tactic is used by incubating birds, like this male, at the slightest sign of danger. This practice may well have given rise to the popular belief that Ostriches bury their heads in the sand when alarmed.

[*Struthio camelus australis*, Etosha National Park, Namibia.
Photo: Jen & Des Bartlett/ Survival]

arid zones it breeds more irregularly, usually taking advantage of the greater availability of food after the rains; thus, in the area by the Namib Desert in Angola, laying may occur at any time of the year.

Breeding strategy too varies from one place to another and different systems may be used, in accordance with the conditions of the environment. In isolated populations, where food is scarce, pairs tend to be monogamous, whereas the rule elsewhere is breeding groups, which tend to have a complex structure. These consist of the territorial male, the main female, or "major hen", and several secondary females, or "minor hens". The major hen mates with the territorial male, sometimes several years running and the two share the tasks of incubation and care of the young. The minor hens mate with several males and lay in different nests, but do not usually incubate. There are also some roving adult males, which mate with adult females, but have no territory or nest. This general structure is complemented by the fact that in most areas the sex ratio is biased in favour of the females.

The male defends a territory of 2-15 km² and, ever alert to the possibility of intruders, he patrols about, "Booming" (see Voice). On the approach of another individual, he sets off towards it in the dominant posture (see General Habits). If it is a male, he expels it from his territory, but if it is a female, he approaches, until all of a sudden he flops down on the ground, opens his wings and tail, and begins to shake each wing alternately and move his tail up and down. Meanwhile, his head and neck sway from side to side and beat rhythmically against his flanks. He then gets up and walks towards the female, with his wings open and his brightly coloured neck puffed out, stamping as he goes. Now, depending on her attitude, he either sits down again and repeats the ritual or goes to mount her. A female shows that she is ready for copulation by adopting the submissive posture (see General Habits) and by vibrating her primaries. During copulation the male grunts and groans and repeats his neck and wing movements. This spectacular performance is frequently enacted around dusk, though it may also occur in the heat of the day.

After mating with the major hen, the male leads her to one of the several nests he has prepared. These are shallow depressions about three metres across, which the male scratches out with his feet, at sites with good visibility roughly in the middle of the territory.

It is normally the major hen that starts a clutch, laying an egg every two days for about a fortnight in the chosen nest. From two to five, but as many as eighteen, other females lay in the same nest, on brief visits in the early afternoon. In cases where predators are a serious threat or it is excessively hot, the major hen guards the eggs during the day. If left unguarded, they may be eaten by jackals, hyenas or Egyptian Vultures (*Neophron percnopterus*); the last-mentioned have learnt to break the eggs by dropping stones on them.

The glossy white eggs are huge, averaging 159 x 131 mm, with a 2 mm thick shell, but despite their great size, they are actually rather small in relation to the size of the bird. An egg weighs about 1500 g, which is roughly equivalent to the weight of two dozen domestic hen eggs, but this is only about 1·5% of the adult female's weight. Although a sitting adult can cover no more than 19 to 25 eggs, most nests have more, after all the females have made their contributions. One nest in Nairobi National Park contained 78 eggs, but only 21 of these were incubated. When the major hen starts incubating, she shoves the excess eggs of the minor hens out of the nest, so they form a ring round it. Meanwhile, she situates her own eggs, which she seems to recognize by their size, weight or pore structure, right in the middle of the nest. Even thus, there is still plenty of room for several eggs of minor hens, as well as her own average of eight, so the other females benefit, despite the fact that they have neither a nest, nor a stable partner. The major hen also gains from this set-up, as the chances of her eggs being lost to predators are relatively lower, with so many other eggs to choose from.

Incubation is shared between the pair, with the more cryptically coloured female taking the daytime stint and the male sitting at night. After some six weeks the eggs all hatch simultaneously and it seems that the chicks are stimulated to break open the shell by vocalizations of the mother and also of other hatching chicks. When they hatch, they are already covered with a frizzy coat of down and within their first three days they leave the nest, in the company of their parents. After three months they start to gain their juvenile plumage, which is steadily replaced by adult-like plumage during their second year. At four or five months old, they are already about half the size of an adult bird, and after a year they reach adult height, but not till they are 18 months old will they be fully as heavy as their parents.

The adults look after their young, sheltering them under their wings from sun and rain alike. When potential predators threaten, adults perform a distraction display, where a bird first rushes back and forward at the predator and then drops down, waggling its wings and inflating its neck, perhaps pretending to be injured. In the mean time, the young birds either run for cover, normally accompanied by a female, or scatter and lie flat out on the ground, where they are difficult to see. Adults occasionally attack, if the situation so demands: men have had their skulls shattered by a kick, and even lions may be killed.

When two family groups with young come into contact, it seems that the parents normally dispute the guardianship with short chases, until one pair are victorious and make off with both broods. In this way, large groups of 100 to 300 chicks may be formed, and as many as 380 have been recorded. The chicks may be of different ages and from different areas and they tend to be escorted by one or more adults. These "Ostrich nurseries" make the chicks less vulnerable to predators than if they are in very small groups. Some adults generally stick with the young until the following breeding season, though they may stay together for up to 12 months, after which the immature birds move about in flocks of mixed ages. Sexual maturity is reached after three or four years and birds probably live 30 to 40 years, though in captivity they have lived up to 50.

Ostriches have a low level of breeding success, and only 10% of all eggs laid end up hatching. Similarly a large number of young birds perish in their first few months. In Nairobi National Park, it has been estimated that an average of 0·15 young per adult per year are successfully raised.

Movements

The Ostrich's movements are regulated by the availability of food and water. In deserts and semi-arid areas, it is more or less nomadic and must wander off frequently, in search of food and water, sometimes having to go a long way. On the other hand, in the wetter parts of its range, it is virtually sedentary and individuals tend to stay in the same area all year and also year after year, generally operating within a 10-20 km radius on any particular day.

Ostriches concentrate near water during dry periods, whereas they are more widely scattered when there is rain. However, their movements are not seasonal, as rainfall is highly irregular in the regions where they are nomadic. In parts of the Sahel, for instance, birds tend to move north when it rains, but, as the drought sets in again, they return to their more habitual areas further south.

Relationship with Man

Ostrich feathers have been used for adornment by man for at least 5000 years, as evidenced by both Mesapotamian and Egyptian art, and the Egyptians also used them as a symbol of justice, due to their perfect symmetry. The huge eggs have been put to manifold ends, and some African peoples, for instance the Sudanese and the Bushmen, still use them to make necklaces and bracelets, or as receptacles for carrying water in. In some places they have been invested with magical qualities, such as protecting houses against lightning. They are attributed force in certain rituals and frequently play a part in traditional death rites, while in Mali they are still collected for mosques.

Inevitably, it was the White Man who put the species at risk. During the eighteenth century the soft white feathers of the male's wings and tail came into fashion for ladies' hats, as the famous "aigrettes" and "ospreys", and this led to extensive persecution of the Ostrich, with the result that it was almost exterminated from the Middle East and North and South Africa. By the beginning of last century, the Ostrich feather trade had

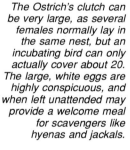

The Ostrich's clutch can be very large, as several females normally lay in the same nest, but an incubating bird can only actually cover about 20. The large, white eggs are highly conspicuous, and when left unattended may provide a welcome meal for scavengers like hyenas and jackals.

[*Struthio camelus australis*, Etosha National Park, Namibia. Photo: Jen & Des Bartlett/ Survival]

Incubation is carried out exclusively by the male and the main female, or "major hen". The eggs hatch almost simultaneously, thus reducing the overall incubation time and also increasing the efficiency with which the chicks can be attended. The chicks, already well developed at hatching, are soon able to leave the nest and follow their parents about in search of food.

[*Struthio camelus australis*, Etosha National Park, Namibia. Photo: Jen & Des Bartlett/ Survival]

become big business, and was well-established in Paris, London and other important cities.

Apart from for its feathers and eggs, the Ostrich has also been persecuted for its meat and its skin. Once Ostrich populations had decreased alarmingly, it was discovered that the birds could be farmed profitably, as indeed they had been by the ancient Egyptians and others. The first modern farm was set up in Cape Province, South Africa, in 1833, and others soon appeared all over South Africa, as well as in Algeria, Sicily, France, Australia and elsewhere. The business thrived until after the First World War, when demand dropped and most of the farms closed down. There are still at least 90,000 domesticated birds at Oudtshoorn in South Africa, which are now mainly used in the production of meat and high quality skin. Farming also remains in Florida, USA, but this is now basically a tourist attraction.

In southern Australia, there are some small feral populations of Ostriches, which have been left over from the abandoned farms. They are thought to belong to the southern race *australis*, though possibly crossed with the nominate *camelus*, as this crossbreed was used to produce better quality feathers; they are variously said to number hundreds or thousands.

The species has been kept in captivity for milennia and breeds regularly in zoos. Records show that 137 birds from only 16 zoos bred in 1984, and also that in 1979 a prodigious female laid 81 eggs in six and a half months!

Status and Conservation

Until last century, the Ostrich was common in most of Africa and south-west Asia, but intense persecution by man (see Re-

lationship with Man), coupled with habitat destruction, mostly in the form of overgrazing, has seen its range considerably reduced. Although not globally threatened, the species requires strict protection in certain regions.

In North and West Africa, Ostrich populations are already very small and at present they continue to decline, mostly due to hunting, disturbance and the collection of eggs and feathers. For this reason, most of these populations have now been included in Appendix I of CITES. In South Africa, the species is now confined to the extreme north-west of its historical range, although escapes have formed a substantial feral population of hybrids. In other parts, mainly in protected areas in East Africa, such as the Serengeti and Nairobi National Parks, there are still strong populations, with densities of 12-16 birds per 20 km², as opposed to 1-5 birds over a similar area in poorer regions.

The Near East had its own endemic subspecies *syriacus*, but this is now almost certainly extinct. The race used to inhabit an area ranging from the Syrian Desert to the Arabian Peninsula, and in 1977 along the coastal plain of Israel some eggs were found, which carbon-14 dating has subsequently shown to be in the region of 6000 years old. At the beginning of this century this race was still fairly common in places, but after the First World War the proliferation of firearms, coupled with the availability of motorized transport, led to the devastation of populations and the virtual extinction of the subspecies by 1941. The last record was of an individual found drowning in Jordan in 1966.

Attempts have been made to reintroduce the species in both Jordan and Israel, and eighteen chicks of the nominate *camelus*, the race most similar to *syriacus*, were introduced in the area of the Negev Desert, in southern Israel, in 1973.

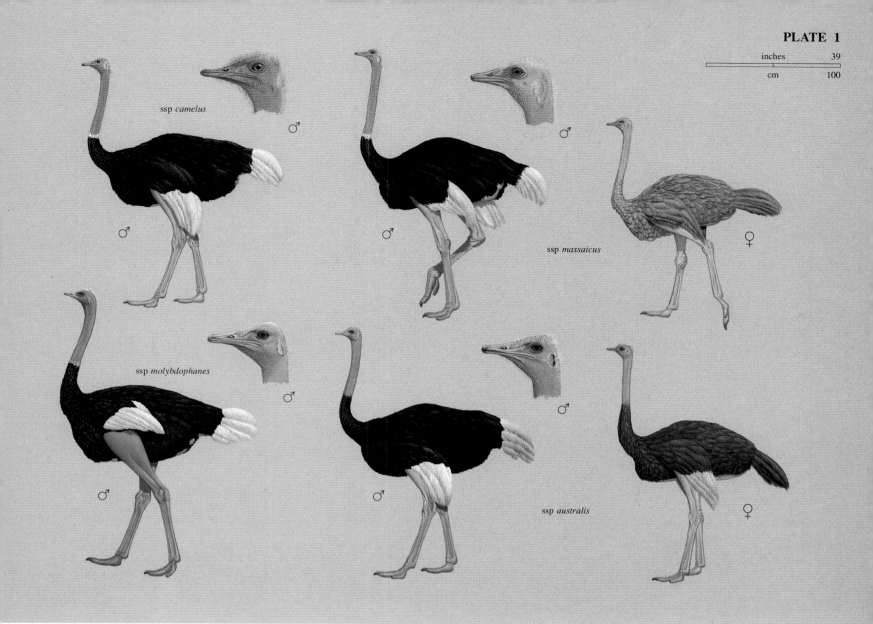

PLATE 1

| inches | 39 |
| cm | 100 |

Family STRUTHIONIDAE (OSTRICH)
SPECIES ACCOUNTS

PLATE 1

Genus *STRUTHIO*   Linnaeus, 1758

Ostrich
Struthio camelus

French: Autruche d'Afrique   **German:** Strauß   **Spanish:** Avestruz

Taxonomy. *Struthio camelus* Linnaeus, 1758, N Africa.
Race *molybdophanes* might be separate species; may be sympatric with *camelus* in NE Kenya. Race *syriacus* recently extinct; possible race *spatzi* of doubtful validity. Four subspecies recognized.
Subspecies and Distribution.
S. c. camelus Linnaeus, 1758 - W & S Sahara, Sahel.
S. c. molybdophanes Reichenow, 1883 - Somalia to Kenya.
S. c. massaicus Neumann, 1898 - S Kenya to Tanzania.
S. c. australis Gurney, 1868 - S Africa.
Introduced to S Australia.
Descriptive notes. Male 210-275 cm, 100-156 kg; female 175-190 cm, 90-110 kg. Unmistakable. Non-breeding male has much duller bare parts; white feathers of wings and tail may be stained brownish by soil. Females extremely variable even within same subspecies. Immatures similar to female, but darker. Races separated on colour of bare parts, bald or partially feathered crown, presence/extent of white neck-ring, and possibly, to some extent, egg-pore structure.
Habitat. A variety of open, semi-arid plains, from desert to savanna; also open woodland. Does not require standing water.
Food and Feeding. Mainly herbivorous, taking grasses, seeds and leaves; succulent plants very important in drier areas; also eats some insects and small vertebrates. Normally feeds in groups, browsing close to ground.
Breeding. Season and strategy vary with region. Normally "major hen" lays 5-11 eggs, and 2-5 "minor hens" lay 2-6 eggs each, in common nest. Nest is shallow scrape in ground; eggs yellowish, becoming white (average 159 x 130 mm); incubation 42-46 days; young have buff-coloured down

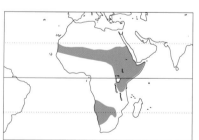

with some black lines and specks; fledging 4-5 months, fully-grown at c. 18 months; young form large crèches, which may be accompanied by one or more adults for about 9 months. Sexual maturity after 3-4 years, with life expectancy of 30-40 years.
Movements. Sedentary or nomadic, depending on habitat. In dry seasons or dry areas may travel long distances in search of food and water.
Status and Conservation. Not globally threatened. Frequent to abundant throughout most of range. Numbers and range diminished in W and N Africa; most N African populations included in CITES I. Range of wild population in S Africa reduced to NW of former range, elsewhere only feral birds, mostly hybrids of indigenous race *australis* and introduced *camelus*; still common in parts of E Africa. Middle East race *syriacus* probably extinct since 1966. Main damage caused by plume trade during 19th century and hunting/egg-collecting in 20th; also loss of habitat, which is currently main threat. Common exhibit in zoos worldwide, breeding well; Ostrich farms still exist in S Africa and Florida, USA; species introduced to S Australia from such farms.

Bibliography. Beaufort (1983), de Beer (1956), Bertram (1979a, 1979b, 1980, 1985), Bertram & Burger (1981), Bevolscaya & Tikhenov (1985), Bledsoe (1988), Bock (1963), van Bocxtaele (1988), Bolwig (1973), Brown *et al.* (1982), Bundy *et al.* (1989), Burger & Gochfeld (1988), Cho *et al.* (1984), Cloudsley-Thompson (1967), Cracraft (1974), Cramp & Simmons (1977), Crawford & Schmidt-Nielsen (1967), Davies (1976), Dollinger (1988), Elzanowski (1985, 1988), Etchécopar & Hüe (1964), Feduccia (1985), Fuller (1987), Gallagher (1988), Giordani (1988), Goodman (1989), Goodman *et al.* (1984), Greenway (1967), Guittin (1987), Handford & Mares (1985), Horwell (1990), Houde (1986), Hüe & Etchécopar (1970), Hurxthal (1979, 1986), Jarvis *et al.* (1985), Jennings (1986), Kock (1991), Kok (1980), Leuthold (1977), Lever (1987), Louw *et al.* (1969), Mackworth-Praed & Grant (1957-1973), Maclean (1985), Marchant & Higgins (1990), McGowan (1985), Negere (1980), Newman (1982), Parkes & Clark (1966), Paz (1987), Peters (1991), Prager *et al.* (1976), Pinto (1983), Rich & Balouet (1984), Robinson & Seely (1975), Rutgers & Norris (1970), Sauer (1970, 1972a, 1972b), Sauer & Rothe (1972), Sauer & Sauer (1966a, 1966b), Schüz (1970a), Sibley & Ahlquist (1981), Sibley & Frelin (1972), Siegfried & Frost (1974), Sinclair (1978), Smit (1973), Spreckels (1983), Thouless *et al.* (1989), Tyler & Simkiss (1959), Verney (1979), Vincent (1966), van der Walt & Retief (1984), Walters (1985), Wilson (1988).

Class AVES
Order STRUTHIONIFORMES
Suborder RHEAE
Family RHEIDAE (RHEAS)

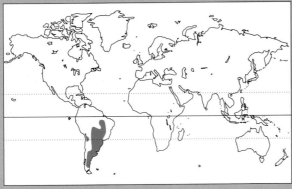

- Huge, flightless, three-toed terrestrial birds with long neck and legs.
- 92-140 cm.

- Neotropical Region.
- Grassland and open scrub, from sea-level up to 4500 m.
- 2 genera, 2 species, 8 taxa.
- No species threatened; none extinct since 1600.

Systematics

The Rheidae are endemic to the Neotropical Region. They probably first appeared around the beginning of the Tertiary, and fossils have been found dating back to the Eocene, approximately 40 million years ago. This situates them among the oldest birds in South America, and they are usually considered to be closely related to the tinamous, another exclusively South American family (see page 112).

However, their separation from the tinamous occurred a long way back in time and rheas actually belong with the outwardly more similar Ostrich, cassowaries, Emu and kiwis, all of which are far more remote in geographical terms. Their closest relatives are the Ostriches, and these two families probably evolved from a common ancestor when the African and South American plates definitively separated to form the present continents.

There is still a fair amount of disagreement over the systematics of the Rheidae, as indeed there is about the taxonomic status and situation of the ratites in general. The traditional version separates the Rheidae into a distinct order, the Rheiformes, while, at the other extreme, some systematists relegate the rheas to a subfamily within the Struthionidae. In recent years, yet another version has steadily been gaining support, that of lumping all the ratites together in the order Struthioniformes, and this version is followed here (see page 76).

Although fossils of four species in the genus *Rhea* have been found in Pliocene deposits, the present day family consists of only two species, the Greater Rhea (*Rhea americana*) and the Lesser Rhea (*Pterocnemia pennata*). Both species have several races, and the latter is sometimes considered to be two species, with the promotion of the Puna Rhea (*Pterocnemia (p.) tarapacensis*), which then includes the rather doubtful race *garleppi*.

Morphological Aspects

In external appearance the rheas recall the Ostriches, and for this reason on occasions they have been referred to as "South American Ostriches". However, there are obvious differences between the two, the most conspicuous of which is the rhea's smaller size; whereas some male Ostriches can be almost 3 m tall, the Greater Rhea only attains a height of 1·4 m, while the Lesser Rhea barely reaches 1 m.

Unlike its African relative, the rhea has its head and neck feathered. There is feathering too on the thighs, and it even extends down the upper part of the tarsus in the Lesser Rhea. The large, powerful feet have only three toes, as in the other ratites, except the Ostrich, where they are further reduced to two. The wings are proportionally larger than those of other ratites, and, although rheas too are flightless, their wings are not completely useless: they give the bird great manoeuvrability while it is running, to balance the fact that it has no

The male rhea performs his courtship display before a minimum of two, and a maximum of twelve females, which he first attracts into his territory. During the display, the male repeatedly approaches the females, with the feathers of his head, neck and body bristled up and his wings raised; he also puffs out his neck and produces a characteristic "Booming" call.

[*Rhea americana americana*, Das Emas National Park, Brazil. Photo: Günter Ziesler]

The breeding strategy of the rheas is based on polygamy: males are simultaneously polygynous; and females are serially polyandrous. The male copulates with several females, all of which lay eggs in the same nest, which he prepares beforehand. After laying these eggs, the females wander off in search of other males with which to mate.

[*Rhea americana americana*, Das Emas National Park, Brazil. Photo: Günter Ziesler]

rectrices; in addition, there is a strong claw on each wing, which can be used as an effective weapon.

Rheas are almost as good runners as Ostriches, despite the fact that their feet are not quite so specialized, and they can reach speeds of more than 60 km/h. They are also surprisingly good swimmers and can even cross rivers. Another important feature of their physiology is that they are endowed with both excellent eyesight and good hearing, which allow them to detect their enemies a long way off. As in the other ratites, the male has a penis, which is frequently visible.

The rhea's feathers are smooth and soft, as in the Ostrich, due to their unique structure (see page 77). The plumage is generally greyish, but the Lesser Rhea has varying amounts of white spots on its back, and such cryptic plumage allows the birds to blend into the vegetation easily, despite their great size; an interesting feature is that cases of albino Greater Rheas are not uncommon. Sexes are similar, but males are slightly larger and darker, and during the breeding season the Greater Rhea also has a prominent black ring at the base of the neck, which extends downwards like a stain. Juvenile plumage is similar to that of adults, but it is generally darker, and young Lesser Rheas have less white on their backs.

Habitat

The rheas live exclusively on the open plains of South America, although precise habitat preferences vary to some degree between the species.

The Greater Rhea is a characteristic bird in the tall grass steppe of the *pampas*, but it also occupies several other savanna-type habitats, such as those in the Chaco zone. In the *campos* of Brazil, areas of dense grassland and scrub with scattered trees, it is usually found on the edges of woods and near farmland. It tends to occur at low to moderate altitudes, though it reaches 2000 m in Argentina.

The Lesser Rhea, on the other hand, lives in areas of open scrub, for instance in the *puna* of Andean plateaux over 3500 m high, and also in the areas of steppe which extend over the eastern slope of the Andes and into the lowlands of Patagonia.

Although many of these typical habitats can be fairly arid, both species prefer to be in the vicinity of a river, lake or swamp for breeding.

General Habits

Rheas are gregarious and they generally live in mixed groups of males, females and juveniles, normally numbering 5-30 birds, although flocks of 50 and even more have been recorded. During the breeding season, however, females separate off into small groups, while males become territorial. Apparently a small percentage of males, on reaching an advanced age, go off on their own and live in seclusion.

While they are sociable birds, individuals have to keep a certain distance apart from one another and any violation of this code can lead to a "Head-forward" threat display. This consists of the bird throwing its head forward with its bill open, at the same time hissing repeatedly. The head is then rapidly flung back, so that the neck adopts an S-shape; such behaviour is most common when the bird is sitting, either during incubation or simply when it is resting.

Although rheas can easily outrun their predators, they have the strange habit, when chased, of retracing their steps, suddenly squatting down amongst the bushes and flattening the body against the ground, where, despite their size, they can pass totally unnoticed. They can also disconcert their pursuers by zig-zagging rapidly away from them, with frequent dodges to one side or the other, and even turning sharply at right angles. When making such abrupt changes of direction, a bird raises one wing vertically, meanwhile keeping its neck stretched out almost horizontally in front. The Lesser Rhea is quicker than the Greater but has less stamina and, instead of running normally with its neck up and its wings held open like the Greater, it often keeps its neck almost horizontal and its wings folded, in order to be able to pass more easily through the bushes which frequently litter its habitat.

Rheas are basically diurnal, although there is some suggestion that during very hot periods they rest for most of the day and devote the night to feeding. They sleep sitting on their tarsi with the neck stretched out horizontally in front or folded back to one side in an S-curve, and sometimes a bird may even lie flat on its belly, with its legs stretched out behind it.

Voice

The most common sound made by rheas is a deep, resounding "bu-up" or "nan-du", which is mainly produced by males during courtship display, although it can occasionally be heard at night too. Sounding more like the roar of a large mammal than a bird's call, it can be heard at great distances, and it is to this cry that the rhea owes one of the most widespread popular names by which both species are known, "Ñandú".

Outside the mating period, rheas utter hoarse cries of alarm, snorts to show their anger and also hissing threats. Young birds produce plaintive contact whistles, which help them to keep together in their groups, particularly when danger threatens.

Food and Feeding

The diet of the rhea family consists of assorted kinds of plant matter, such as roots, fruits, seeds and leaves, which may be taken from a great variety of plants, including thistles. Rheas also eat insects and small vertebrates and can catch flies and any small animals within their reach with great proficiency, although claims that they sometimes eat poisonous snakes have not as yet been substantiated.

Generally they drink little water since most of their liquid requirements are covered by succulent plants. Like the Ostrich, they ingest pebbles and small shiny objects to help grind down food in the gizzard.

Rheas tend to wander about ceaselessly while feeding, sometimes mixing with herds of pampas deer (*Dorcelaphus bezoarticus*), guanacos, vicunas, alpacas and even, where they are not persecuted by man, with cattle and sheep. The association of rheas with other wild herbivores is advantageous for both, since the combination of the former's good eyesight with the latter's excellent scent increases their efficiency in detecting enemies at a distance. In grazing lands they have been accused of competing with the cattle, but rheas also eat the weeds and other plants which the cattle reject, and their presence can even prove beneficial, because they often eat the burr-like seeds which get tangled up in the sheep's wool.

Breeding

The breeding season is fairly variable in the more northerly parts of the rheas' range, with laying between July and January, while in the extreme south, due to the stringent climatic restrictions, laying does not normally take place until November.

At the onset of the breeding season, males compete for territories in short fights, during which they intertwine necks, whilst running round in circles together, and they sometimes end up biting and kicking each other. The male that wins the contest expels the others from his territory and then tries to attract groups of females into his domain, by running quickly towards them with outspread wings. When he manages to assemble between two and twelve females, he begins the courtship display. In this display, he zig-zags around the group of females, giving voice in the characteristic courtship "Boom" (see Voice), with his neck erect and inflated, and his wings lifted up. Finally, he stands beside the females with his neck slightly lowered in a U-shape, and the feathers of his neck and head bristled up. Then he shakes his wings, before stretching them out to the sides, where he holds them motionless, so that the tips of the feathers quiver gracefully in the slightest breeze.

After copulation, the male leads the females to a nest which he has previously prepared. This is a depression about 1 m wide and 12 cm deep, which is covered with dried out vegetation. It is frequently hidden away amongst the bushes, although the male sometimes uproots all the vegetation within a radius of 2-3 m around the nest, apparently to isolate it, in case there is a fire. The females generally approach the nest as a group and, one after another, lay their eggs in the hollow, after which they leave the nest-site, also in a group. In the following weeks they return every two or three days to deposit their eggs.

Once laying is over at a particular nest, the females leave to mate with another male and to lay eggs in the corresponding nest; they may repeat this process several times during the three month breeding season. As a result, the male is left on his own

In both species of rhea the tasks of incubation and chick-care are left exclusively to the male. An incubating bird is well camouflaged, as he sits on about 13-30 eggs, taking care to cover them fully with his soft plumage. This Lesser Rhea shows a typical posture of repose, with the neck twisted back in an S-curve.

[*Pterocnemia pennata pennata*. Photo: Joseph van Wormer/ Bruce Coleman]

Young rheas spend up to six months under the constant supervision of the male. At this stage they are still quite vulnerable to predators, and the male tends to be particularly aggressive during this period. When moving at a leisurely pace the Lesser Rhea typically holds its head high, but in short sprints it stretches its neck out forwards, probably as an aid to balance.

[Pterocnemia pennata pennata, Torres del Paine National Park, Chile. Photo: Günter Ziesler]

to carry out the tasks of incubation and chick-rearing, in contrast with the case of the Ostrich, where these duties are shared between the male and a dominant female (see page 80).

The male begins incubation two to eight days after egg-laying has begun, and he normally continues for some 35-40 days. During this period he adopts a threatening attitude towards anything that comes near him. He hisses and snaps, as he performs the "Head-forward" display (see General Habits), at the same time spreading his wings sideways to cover the nest with them. He even threatens approaching females, which come to complete their egg-laying, with the result that they often end up having to leave their eggs somewhere around the nest; the male then rolls the nearest eggs into the nest with his bill, but many of them remain scattered around the edge and go to waste. Nonetheless, they are not completely wasted, since, in the process of rotting, they attract large numbers of flies, which provide a source of food for the male while he is incubating, and also for the newly-hatched chicks.

Once all the females have finished laying their eggs, the nest normally contains a total of 13-30 eggs, although extreme cases of 6 and 80 have been recorded. When the first chicks are ready to hatch, they start calling, which probably stimulates the others to break open their shells too, so that they all hatch synchronously in a period of 24-28 hours, emerging with a coat of down, which is greyish with dark stripes.

After a few days the chicks are led away from the nest by the male, and they keep together all the time by means of plaintive contact whistles; this is essential, for, once separated from their parent, they are likely to fall easy prey to any of a large number of potential predators, both avian and mammalian. In any situation of danger, chicks crouch down on the ground or hide under the male's wings, where they may also take refuge when it becomes too hot, or to shelter from the cold at night. The males are jealous guardians of their offspring, and even gauchos on horseback have been charged on occasions. Lost chicks are always liable to be adopted by another male with his own chicks, and this can lead to a fair disparity in ages between the members of a crèche. The period of parental care is about six months long, but the young birds, which by this stage are more than half the size of an adult, generally remain in their groups until they attain sexual maturity, at 2-3 years old.

Movements

Rheas are strictly sedentary. Unlike Ostriches and Emus, they do not need to move to areas far away from their usual home ranges to find water or food, as the characteristics of the climate in the regions they inhabit, where there is no very

The Puna Rhea is found only above 3500 m in the high Andes, where it is one of the typical inhabitants of the puna. Its numbers have been drastically reduced due to intense hunting pressure, and it is now reckoned to be endangered. It has received legal protection throughout most of its range, but is still the object of frequent attacks by hunters moving about over the open terrain in jeeps.

[*Pterocnemia pennata tarapacensis*, Chile. Photo: A. de Sostoa & X.Ferrer]

marked dry season, and the existence of abundant vegetation in their habitat mean that they generally have sufficient resources all year round.

Relationship with Man

Man's exploitation of rheas for food, both their meat and their eggs, probably dates back to the earliest times. They still constitute an important part of the diet of indigenous Indians in Patagonia and also other parts of the rheas' range. The gauchos had a peculiar method of hunting rheas: they used *bolas*, long intertwined strips of leather, which carried roundish stones at one end; if skilfully thrown, they got tangled up in the bird's feet or round its neck, causing it to fall.

Various parts of the rhea's body have been used for medicinal purposes, being considered to have therapeutic effects; an example of this is its fat, which is applied to venomous snakebites or used to treat rheumatism. Since the nineteenth century rheas have also been pursued for commercial ends, mainly for their feathers, which are used to make dusters, and these can be found throughout the rheas' range. The skin is sold to make rugs and also, more commonly, for burning, since it is believed that the resultant smoke has beneficial effects on the coca plantations.

In addition to the role rheas have played as a source of food for men, they are also deeply rooted in South American popular culture, and frequently appear in folklore, for example as a theme in popular songs, or through the use of their feathers in some dances. They can be kept in captivity and easily tamed, and they may even become quite docile. Although both species have been successfully bred in zoos, the Greater Rhea is present in many collections, whilst the Lesser Rhea is found in very few.

Status and Conservation

In most of the areas where the rhea was once abundant, its populations have declined dramatically, mostly due to extensive persecution, as it has been hunted either for food or for economic exploitation, as well as simply for sport at times.

At present, however, the main threat the rheas face is the reduction of their habitat, due to the conversion of the plains to farmland or pastures for cattle to graze. Ranchers accuse the rheas of competing with the cattle for food; other farmers accuse the birds of eating their crops, and they chase the rheas off their land, banishing them to the areas furthest away from civilization. In addition, the fences which are put up round fields block off access to what were formerly the rheas' feeding grounds, and many birds suffer serious injury when they get caught up in the barbed wire.

Although the Lesser Rhea, as a species, is not threatened, the Puna Rhea (see Systematics) is in serious danger of extinction in the short term. Considered endangered, it is rare in most of its range and its total population is thought to be of several hundred birds at the most, although there are no very precise estimates. The healthiest populations are found in Argentina, but there were thought to be only about 18 individuals left in Peru in 1983, while in northern Chile and on the *altiplano* of Bolivia numbers are also very low. Although protected by law in Peru, Bolivia and Chile, human pressure is still intense, and around mining centres in the Andes rheas are frequently hunted from jeeps, and their eggs are exhaustively collected by the Aymará Indians.

The Greater Rhea is not globally at risk, although its population has decreased considerably in recent years, especially in Argentina, where it has theoretically been protected since 1981. While neither species is reckoned to be in immediate danger, both have been listed as near-threatened, indicating that their future is far from secure.

Trade in specimens of both species of rhea, or in products obtained from them, has been regulated by CITES, which totally forbids any kind of trade in the case of the Lesser Rhea, and limits its volume in the case of the Greater Rhea.

General Bibliography
de Beer (1956), Blake (1977), Bledsoe (1988), Bock (1963), Bruning (1973b), Cho *et al.* (1984), Cracraft (1974), Elzanowski (1985, 1988), Feduccia (1985), Handford & Mares (1982, 1985), Horwell (1990), McGowan (1985), Meise (1963), Parkes & Clark (1966), Prager *et al.* (1976), Rich & Balouet (1984), Sauer (1972b), Sibley & Ahlquist (1981), Sibley & Frelin (1972), Sick (1985a).

PLATE 2

inches 20
cm 50

Family RHEIDAE (RHEAS)
SPECIES ACCOUNTS

PLATE 2

Genus *RHEA*   Brisson, 1760

1. Greater Rhea
Rhea americana

French: Nandou d'Amérique   **German:** Nandu   **Spanish:** Ñandú Común
Other common names: Common Rhea

Taxonomy. *Struthio americanus* Linnaeus, 1758, Sergipe and Rio Grande do Norte, Brazil, *fide* Marcgraf. Several races poorly known, classification remains provisional. Five subspecies recognized.
Subspecies and Distribution.
R. a. americana (Linnaeus, 1758) - NE to SE Brazil.
R. a. intermedia Rothschild & Chubb, 1914 - SE Brazil, Uruguay.
R. a. nobilis Brodkorb, 1939 - E Paraguay.
R. a. araneipes Brodkorb, 1938 - W Paraguay, E Bolivia, SW Brazil.
R. a. albescens Lynch Arribálzaga & Holmberg, 1878 - NE & E Argentina.

Descriptive notes. 127-140 cm; 20-25+ kg. Overall colour is very variable grey-brown; thighs feathered, but tarsi totally bare. Male slightly larger and darker than female. Juvenile plumage similar to that of adults. Races supposedly separated on extent of black on neck, colour of interscapular region and, to a lesser extent, size. Albinos frequent, particularly in race *albescens*.
Habitat. Typically found in *pampas*, *campos*, *cerrado* and open *chaco* woodland; normally in areas with at least some tall vegetation, tending to avoid open grassland. For breeding prefers to be close to river, lake or marsh.
Food and Feeding. Omnivorous. Plant matter includes leaves (even of thistles), seeds, roots and fruits. Also takes insects, especially grasshoppers, and small vertebrates, such as lizards, frogs, small birds and some snakes; sometimes catches flies which have gathered around carrion. When feeding, tends to be continuously on the move; ingests pebbles to help break down food.
Breeding. Aug-Jan, depending on region. Males simultaneously polygynous, females serially polyandrous; in Mato Grosso, females apparently outnumber males. Nest is shallow depression, usually sheltered in vegetation. Eggs start golden yellow, soon fading to dull white, average 132 x 90 mm and 600 g; normally 13-30 (up to 80 recorded) laid per nest, by as many as 12 different females. Incubation and chick-care carried out exclusively by male; incubation 35-40 days; chicks grey with dark stripes; almost half-grown by 3 months old. Sexual maturity at 2-3 years.
Movements. Sedentary. Outside breeding season, found in groups of 20-30, or even 100 birds.
Status and Conservation. Not globally threatened. Has declined markedly and now considered near-threatened. Decline due partly to hunting for meat, partly to colossal export of skins, with over 50,000 traded in 1980, most apparently originating from Paraguay, with Japan and USA leading consumers. Race *albescens* listed on CITES II, and all other races on CITES III for Uruguay; entire species should be listed on CITES II, to avoid confusion and curb excessive levels of trade. In recent years, conversion of habitat for agriculture has become increasingly important in some areas, including strongholds in *pampas* and *cerrado*; in former, still common in protected areas and on some ranches, where often semi-captive; healthiest populations now in parts of Chaco region.

Bibliography. Beaufort (1983), Beaver (1978), Belton (1984), Bevolskaya & Tikhenov (1985), Bruning (1973a, 1974), Bucher & Nores (1988), Cavalcanti (1988), Cracraft (1974), Davies (1976), Dollinger (1988), Ferrari *et al.* (1984), Gnam (1981), Hanagarth & Friedhelm (1988), Inskipp *et al.* (1988), Lever (1987), de la Peña (1986), Pinto (1964), Raikow (1968, 1969), Ruschi (1979), Rutgers & Norris (1970), Sick (1984), Vleck *et al.* (1985), Wetmore (1926), Willis & Oniki (1988).

Genus *PTEROCNEMIA*   G. R. Gray, 1871

2. Lesser Rhea
Pterocnemia pennata

French: Nandou de Darwin   **German:** Darwinnandu   **Spanish:** Ñandú Petizo
Other common names: Darwin's Rhea; Puna Rhea (*tarapacensis/garleppi*)

Taxonomy. *Rhea pennata* d'Orbigny, 1834, Río Negro, S Buenos Aires.
Race *tarapacensis* may merit consideration as full species; *garleppi* would also be included, but may not deserve subspecific status and possibly better fused into single (sub)species. *P. pennata* has been crossed with *R. americana* in captivity. Three subspecies recognized.
Subspecies and Distribution.
P. p. garleppi Chubb, 1913 - S Peru, SW Bolivia, NW Argentina.
P. p. tarapacensis Chubb, 1913 - N Chile.
P. p. pennata (d'Orbigny, 1834) - S Chile, WC & S Argentina.
Introduced (ssp. *pennata*) in Tierra del Fuego.

Descriptive notes. 92·5-100 cm; 15-25 kg. Feathering covers thighs and also top of tarsi (in front). Female generally duller and has fewer and smaller white spots on back. Juvenile browner, without white spotting; typical adult plumage gained gradually, in third or fourth year. Races *garleppi* and *tarapacensis* greyer, with reduced area of white spots and fewer frontal scutes on tarsi.
Habitat. N races in desertic salt *puna*, pumice flats, upland bogs and tola (*Lepidophyllum*) heath in *altiplano*, at 3500-4500 m. In S occupies shrub-steppe and grassland of floodplains, from sea-level up to 2000 m; normally breeds in upland areas with bunch-grass.
Food and Feeding. Omnivorous. Mostly plant matter, including seeds and grasses; also small animals, especially insects. Normally walks slowly along, with head held low, picking food off ground. Frequently associates with grazing llamas, guanacos or vicunas.
Breeding. Sept-Jan in N, starts July in Río Negro (Argentina), Nov in extreme S. Males simultaneously polygynous, females serially polyandrous. Nest is scrape, lined with dry grass or twigs. Eggs start yellowish olive-green, but fade to buff, averaging 127 x 87 mm (ssp. *pennata*); normally 10-30 (6-50) laid per nest, by several different females. Incubation and chick-care carried out exclusively by male; incubation c. 40 days; chicks greyish brown with blackish stripes and tarsi fully-feathered. Sexual maturity after 3 years.
Movements. Sedentary, but S populations mostly move into uplands for breeding. Normally in groups of 5-30 birds.
Status and Conservation. Not globally threatened. CITES I. Has declined markedly and now considered near-threatened. Puna Rhea (*tarapacensis/garleppi*) endangered, due to intensive hunting pressure (see page 88), which masks any possible effects of habitat alteration. Nominate race possibly still fairly common, perhaps due to inaccessibility and bleak conditions which prevail in much of range, though upland breeding habit might be result of agricultural development and hunting. In 1936 nominate race introduced to northern Tierra del Fuego, where now apparently well-established.

Bibliography. Beaufort (1983), Bonino *et al.* (1986), Cajal (1988), Cannon *et al.* (1986), Castañera & Mascitti (1986), Daciuk (1978), Diamond *et al.* (1987), Dollinger (1988), Fjeldså (1988a), Fjeldså & Krabbe (1990), Hanagarth & Friedhelm (1988), Johnson (1965), King (1978/79), Lever (1987), de la Peña (1986), Plenge (1982), Wetmore (1926).

Class AVES
Order STRUTHIONIFORMES
Suborder CASUARII
Family CASUARIIDAE (CASSOWARIES)

- Huge, flightless, three-toed terrestrial birds with long neck and legs, and prominent casque.
- 100-170 cm.
- Australo-Papuan Subregion.
- Rain forest and savanna woodland, from lowlands up to 3000 m.
- 1 genus, 3 species, 3 taxa.
- No species threatened; none extinct since 1600.

Systematics

The cassowaries are closely related to the Emu, which constitutes the only other family of very large, flightless birds found exclusively in Australasia. In the past, these two families were considered to form a separate order, Casuariiformes. However, the current trend is to group all the ratites together in the order Struthioniformes (see page 76), while the proximity of the Emu and the cassowaries is recognized by their being partitioned off in their own suborder, Casuarii.

The cassowaries and the Emu evolved in Australia from a common ancestor, but it is not clear when the two groups sep-

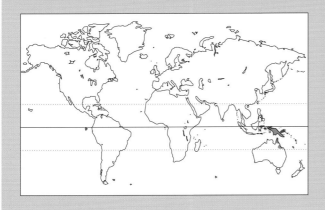

arated. Most of the fossils related to these families which have been turned up so far correspond to the Upper Pleistocene in Australia, some 5000-10,000 years ago, although there is one which dates back to the Pliocene, about four million years ago. Of the many fossils found, only one, from Pleistocene deposits in New South Wales, is clearly a member of the family Casuariidae, and it is probably the remains of a Dwarf Cassowary (*Casuarius bennetti*), a species which is nowadays restricted to New Guinea and neighbouring islands. The locality of the find indicates that this species, and perhaps also the family, were more widely distributed in the past, which may be because the climate was wetter, and rain forests therefore more extensive.

The family Casuariidae consists of only one genus, *Casuarius*, with three clearly distinguishable species, the Southern Cassowary (*Casuarius casuarius*), the Dwarf Cassowary and the Northern Cassowary (*Casuarius unappendiculatus*). Geographical isolation of different populations appears to have led to a large numbers of local variants, with slight differences in size, the formation of the wattles and neck colouring, and at least 42 subspecies have been described, based on this variability. Some twenty or so of these have traditionally been accepted, but museum collections are exceedingly incomplete and much of the information has come from captive birds of uncertain origin. So little is known about the nature and extent of physical variation with sex, age and individual that it seems safest to follow the recommendation of E. Mayr that all three species be considered monotypic, until good solid evidence of genuine racial variation can be produced.

Morphological Aspects

Cassowaries are amongst the largest birds in the world. The largest species, the Southern Cassowary, can measure up to 170 cm and weigh as much as 58 kg; only the Ostrich is heavier. The Northern Cassowary, is slightly smaller, whilst the Dwarf Cassowary only attains a height of 100-110 cm.

One of the most characteristic features of this family is, without doubt, the protuberance on the top of the head, which is known as the casque or helmet. It used to be thought that this was formed by a bony extension of the skull, covered with a horny growth. However, recent research on the Southern Cassowary has shown that there is no prolongation of the skull,

The geographical variation of the cassowaries is a matter of some discussion. There appear to be local differences, especially in the shape of the casque, the colour of the bare skin of the neck and wattles, and also the number and arrangement of the wattles, and upwards of 42 subspecies have been described. However, there is considerable variation between individuals, and this, in conjunction with the small sample size and uncertain origin of many birds, makes acceptance of subspecies very risky.

[Casuarius unappendiculatus, New Guinea. Photo: Alain Compost/ Bruce Coleman]

and that the centre of the casque consists of a very tough, elastic, foam-like substance.

The function of the casque has been debated at great length, but it remains a very poorly known subject. The standard version is that birds use the casque in the forest, both to force their way through dense vegetation, and also to avoid head injuries in the process. However, these possible functions do not appear sufficient on their own to justify the development of this curious structure, for the casque grows slowly throughout the bird's life and can only provide efficient protection in adults. Observations of captive birds using the casque as a shovel indicate a second possible function, that of searching for food hidden in leaf litter on the forest floor. In addition, the casque, like the wattle, is probably an indicator of dominance and age among individuals of the same species, and it may play an important role in social behaviour.

Wattles are another peculiar characteristic of the cassowaries. They are present in only two of the species, the Northern and Southern Cassowaries, which are alternatively known as Single-wattled and Double-wattled Cassowaries respectively. The wattles are folds of skin which hang from the bird's neck, either at the sides or the front, and, along with the head and part of the neck, are unfeathered and brightly coloured in different shades of red, blue, purple, yellow and white, depending on the species and, if accepted, subspecies. It is thought that this array of gaudy colours acts as a social signal in the dark rain forest; the colours of the bare parts can change with the bird's mood.

Plumage in the cassowary family is extremely hard and coarse, and this is believed to be another adaptation to protect the birds from the thorns, sharp leaves and humidity in the dense forest. As in the case of the related Emu, the feathers have an aftershaft, which is almost as long as the main feather; the structure is loose, due to the lack of interlocking hooks (see page 37). Again like the Emu, cassowaries lack rectrices, while their stunted wings are, in fact, proportionally smaller than those of any of the other large, flightless birds. In cassowaries, the remiges are reduced to five or six bare quills, which curve round under the bird's body, apparently protecting its flanks when it goes through dense vegetation.

Sexes are very similar and are frequently indistinguishable, although females tend to be larger and more brightly coloured, and have larger casques than males. Immature birds differ from adults in their dull, plain brown plumage. They lack the bright colouring on the head and neck, and have both the casque and the wattles smaller, as these develop slowly throughout a bird's life.

The legs and feet are robust and powerful, enabling birds to run at speeds of up to 50 km/h and jump up 1·5 m from a standing position. Cassowaries are also good swimmers, and can cross lakes and wide rivers without difficulties. Like many other terrestrial birds they have only three toes, each of which is equipped with a stout claw. In cassowaries, the inner toe has developed a 10 cm long, dagger-like claw, which converts its foot into a terrible weapon.

Habitat

Throughout their Australo-Papuan range, cassowaries are most typically found in rain forest. They prefer extensive expanses of forest, although in some hilly parts of inland New Guinea the Dwarf Cassowary has some rather scattered, disjointed populations. Birds normally flourish in virgin forest where they are relatively free from human disturbance, but such habitat is steadily receding (see Status and Conservation).

The three species are all found in fairly similar habitat in New Guinea, but they avoid competition largely by means of altitudinal segregation. The Southern Cassowary usually lives at medium altitudes, preferring dense tropical rain forest, but it

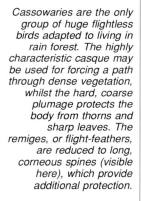

Cassowaries are the only group of huge flightless birds adapted to living in rain forest. The highly characteristic casque may be used for forcing a path through dense vegetation, whilst the hard, coarse plumage protects the body from thorns and sharp leaves. The remiges, or flight-feathers, are reduced to long, corneous spines (visible here), which provide additional protection.

[*Casuarius unappendiculatus*, Irian Jaya, New Guinea. Photo: Alain Compost/ Bruce Coleman]

As in the rheas and the Emu, it is the male cassowary that guards and incubates the eggs. However, in contrast to these other families, the male cassowary mates only with a single female, so she produces all of the eggs in a clutch. The Southern Cassowary normally lays three to five eggs.

[*Casuarius casuarius*, north-east Queensland, Australia. Photo: Frithfoto/ Bruce Coleman]

is also found in gallery and swamp forest and can be seen quite often around the forest edge, along river banks or crossing savanna. The Northern Cassowary is a low altitude species, and occupies riverine and coastal swamp forest. In contrast, the Dwarf Cassowary is a bird of higher altitudes and lives in montane forest up to 3000 m, although it will come down to sea-level in areas where no other species is present.

The Southern Cassowary, the only species found in Australia, is not surprisingly the best known. It sometimes remains in logged forest, as long as there is sufficient food. It has been recorded in a series of rather uncharacteristic habitats, such as canefields and *Eucalyptus* woodland, though it is never far from forest and may only pass such areas in transit between different pockets of its ever more fragmented habitat.

General Habits

Observation of wild cassowaries is extremely difficult, so as yet very little is known about their behaviour. On detecting an approaching human, a bird usually disappears into dense vegetation before it is seen, with the result that tracks and droppings are very often the only evidence of its presence.

Cassowaries are solitary except in the breeding season, and they appear to keep territories all year round. They are most active in the early morning and late afternoon, as well as on moonlit nights. In the middle of the day they tend to rest, using regular sites where they can sit in the sun, and where food is not far away. Most of their time is spent searching for food on the forest floor, and, as they apparently use regular feeding areas, they open up paths through the undergrowth; they also establish fixed points for crossing rivers.

Although they are usually shy birds, cassowaries can be quite aggressive during breeding, especially when accompanied by chicks, and also when cornered. An attack is generally preceded by a threatening "Stretch Display", in which the bird arches its body upwards, bristling up the feathers towards its rump, in an attempt to appear bigger. It then bends its neck downwards, with the bill pointing towards the ground, or towards the feet in the case of the Dwarf Cassowary, while it makes a deep "Booming" sound, with its neck puffed out and its whole body shaking. A male may use this display to expel other males from its territory during the breeding season, while the initial posture forms part of the courtship display. Females appear to be dominant, and a male will run away at the first signs of a threat from the larger, heavier female.

An attacking cassowary raises its body and kicks out at its adversary with both feet at once, or else races past, kicking out as it goes. In such confrontations the cassowary is a formidable opponent, and the long, sharp claw on the inner toe is an extremely dangerous weapon, which can inflict a mortal wound on a dog or even a man. However, open aggression is not the norm and, when alarmed, as when being pursued, a bird dashes through the thick vegetation with its body, neck and head stretched out horizontally forwards, protecting itself with its casque and the stiff primary quills.

Voice

Cassowaries produce a variety of different sounds, which vary with their mood and with the activity in which they are engaged. At present very little is known about this and many other aspects of their life history, but it is thought that outside the breeding season birds are usually silent.

The typical threat call is a rumbling sound, which is given as a warning to any bird approaching another's territory. Other vocalizations include hisses, whistles, low rumbling growls, bill-clapping as a threat, and loud roars during fights. During breeding, males utter low "boo-boo-boo" calls, which are produced most frequently at the start of the season, especially in the moment immediately prior to copulation, while they become steadily less frequent towards the end of the season. During the nine months or so in which the male stays with his chicks, he keeps in touch with them by means of a coughing contact call.

Food and Feeding

All three species of cassowary are essentially frugivorous, and their main food is fruit from trees and vines within the forest, especially of the families Myrtaceae and Lauraceae. Apart from fruit, they sometimes eat fungi, small vertebrates, snails, and some insects and other invertebrates. The Southern Cassowary has also been known to consume carrion.

They generally take only fruit which has fallen to the forest floor, often from the middle or upper canopy, but it may also be plucked directly from low branches, bushes or shrubs, when within reach. The dependence on fruit is great, and birds need forests where a wide diversity of plants produce fruit at different times of the year, so that there is sufficient available all year round. A study carried out in northern Queensland has shown that Southern Cassowaries consumed the fruit of at least 75 different species of forest plant. But not only do they need diversity, they also need a considerable quantity of food to nourish the massive body, and, particularly when food is scarce, they raid gardens and orchards, taking commercial crops, such as bananas and mulberries.

Foraging birds wander slowly along their regularly used tracks (see General Habits), picking up food with the bill, and tossing it up so that it falls directly into the throat and is then swallowed whole. In their wake, they leave copious multicoloured droppings, which are full of seeds and partially digested fruits. They visit regular feeding places in forest clearings, where fallen fruits are commonly found and may be consumed by several different birds, although individuals appear to feed independently and rarely, if ever, coincide.

Stones found in gizzards of the Dwarf Cassowary have probably been swallowed in order to help break down the food, as is habitual in other ratites. Cassowaries are known to drink water, either when standing or sitting, and they are frequently seen near forest streams, where they tend to be more visible.

Breeding

The little evidence available to date suggests that cassowaries tend to breed during the dry season, between June and October,

The cassowary's nest is a simple depression in the ground, which remains quite inconspicuous in the gloom of the rain forest. Nests are surprisingly hard to find, and it was not until September 1984 that a nest was finally photographed in the wild: a Southern Cassowary nest in north-east Queensland, Australia. This photo, one of the first, shows the male with day old chicks.

[*Casuarius casuarius*, north-east Queensland, Australia. Photo: Frithfoto/ Bruce Coleman]

which is the time when fruit is most plentiful in the forest. The Southern Cassowary has also been recorded breeding at the end of the wet season in New Guinea and there is a fair amount of evidence to show that the Dwarf Cassowary may breed at almost any time of year.

When the breeding season arrives, males appear to have clearly defined territories of 1-5 km², although there is no evidence that these are defended. When a female enters an occupied territory, the male repeatedly attempts to approach her, raising up the plumage along his back, until she gradually accepts him and lets him remain by her side. Later, the male begins the courtship display and circles round the female puffing out his throat and making a rumbling "boo-boo-boo" (see Voice). Sometimes it is the female that moves round in circles, with her own back plumage erected, and the male follows her. When the female is ready to copulate she crouches down, whereupon the male displays appeasement behaviour, such as pecking at the plumage on the female's back, "cleaning" her head, both in front and behind, or stroking one side of her body with one of his feet whilst he rests his weight on the other. Finally, he mounts the female and copulation takes place; as in the other ratites, the male has a penis.

The pair stay together for a few weeks during which the female lays three to five eggs in the nest which the male has prepared. This is a shallow depression scraped in the ground and lined with grass and leaves. Nests are well camouflaged and so hard to find that very few have been found in the wild, although egg-collectors have offered large sums of money for a complete cassowary clutch. Once laying is over, the female leaves the nest and usually goes off in search of another male to mate with, so on average most females lay two or three clutches during one breeding cycle. As in the cases of the Emu and the rheas, the male remains in charge of the eggs and the chicks.

Cassowary eggs are pale or dark green and elliptical, and those of the Southern Cassowary average about 135 x 90 mm, and weigh roughly 650 g. After 49-56 days of incubation by the male, the chicks hatch asynchronously with a coat of down striped buffish yellow and brown or black. They are precocial and nidifugous and are able to walk and feed by themselves only a few hours after hatching. A short time after this, about two days according to some observations, the male leaves the nest with his chicks. He accompanies them for about nine months, helping them to feed by picking food up off the ground for them, and protecting them from predators including mammals, birds of prey and large reptiles. In Australia eggs and chicks of the Southern Cassowary suffer heavy predation by feral pigs, and this seems to be having serious effects on the population.

After leaving their parent, juveniles probably remain together for some time. When they are three to six months old, young birds change into the uniform brown first year plumage, and by now each has a rudimentary casque. After one or two years they reach adult size and start to acquire the characteristic black plumage, a process which is not completed until they are three years old. The casque and wattles keep growing and bare parts start to gain their lurid colours. Sexual maturity is reached at three and a half years of age, although males can probably breed at two and a half. Virtually nothing is known about longevity, but wild birds are estimated to have a lifespan of at least 12-19 years, while in captivity birds have lived as long as 18-40 years.

Movements

If it is hard enough to make any sort of observation of cassowaries at all, it is hardly surprising that their movements remain a closed book. Their tracks and droppings can give some sort of idea of presence and numbers, but very little is known to date.

At Mission Beach in north-eastern Queensland, individual Southern Cassowaries were found in the same areas throughout the year, and these results suggest that here at any rate, and quite possibly elsewhere too, cassowaries are essentially sedentary and keep to a fixed territory all year round.

Nevertheless, in the dry season birds will move to residual waterholes to drink, or wander along river banks in search of water. Similarly, there are records of birds performing nomadic movements over great distances in search of food. Certainly the disruption of their habitat, be it due to a cyclone or human activities, is liable to cause dispersal, sometimes through atypical habitats.

Relationship with Man

Cassowaries have a long history of association with the forest tribes of New Guinea. They have been hunted mainly for their meat, which is considered a real delicacy by some tribes, and the sheer size of the adult means that one bird can provide food for several hungry mouths.

However, different parts of the cassowary's body are put to other uses, ornamental or practical. The feathers, for example, are used to decorate ceremonial headdresses, and the bare primary quills may be made into nose-pins or earrings. The razor sharp claws of the inner toes are used by some tribes of New Guinea for tipping their arrows, while leg bones can be made into long daggers, spoons or scrapers.

In New Guinea cassowaries are often kept in captivity, normally penned in behind high fences. Young birds can be seen roaming freely about the streets, but when they reach maturity they are usually shut in, as they can be very dangerous, and people have even been killed by cassowaries' kicks (see General Habits). The birds are fed until they are big enough to be eaten or sold to animal traders.

Trade in cassowaries has been going on with south-east Asia for at least 500 years, and it can apparently be very lucrative, as a cassowary has been exchanged for eight pigs, or even for a wife. Natives sometimes travelled great distances to take the birds to the traders, and this has greatly confused attempts to discover the original distribution of the present forms. It seems fairly likely that this was how the Southern Cassowary reached Seram, and the Dwarf Cassowary arrived in New Britain. In the sixteenth century, the trade spread to Europe, where the birds were bought by collectors to be displayed in their private menageries.

Nonetheless, cassowaries have not only been of economic importance to the people of New Guinea, they have also had great ritual and mystical significance. They appear in numerous

The male cassowary stays with his chicks for about nine months, protecting them from predators, as they learn foraging skills. By the time they become independent, the young birds have almost reached adult size and are quite capable of defending themselves.

[*Casuarius casuarius*. Photo: Hans & Judy Bespe/ Ardea]

Although none of the three species of cassowary is globally threatened, all suffer to some extent from habitat destruction and from hunting pressure. The Dwarf Cassowary of New Guinea is scarce throughout most of its range, and has disappeared or is very rare in many apparently suitable areas.

[*Casuarius bennetti*. Photo: Brian Coates/ Bruce Coleman]

legends and tribal tales and many strange beliefs are held about them. For the Kalam tribe of the Upper Kaironk Valley, in the Schrader Mountains, cassowaries are reincarnations of their female ancestors, for which reason it is forbidden to hunt or trade them or to keep them in captivity. The Ilahita Arapesh, in the Sepik River region of New Guinea, believe that the cassowary is their primal mother and it appears in many of their fertility rites.

Unlike their relatives the Ostrich, Emu and rheas, cassowaries do not breed readily in zoos, indeed they are difficult to rear. Although the first successful captive breeding, by a pair of Dwarf Cassowaries at London Zoo, took place as long ago as 1862, few zoos have managed to breed them successfully to date.

Status and Conservation

The main threat facing all three species is without doubt the loss of their natural habitat. Their strict ecological requirements mean that they are especially vulnerable to the reduction and fragmentation of the rain forests, as they need large, continuous expanses of forest, which must support a high diversity of fruiting plants.

The mass destruction of rain forest, whether for housing developments, road construction or agricultural projects, is mostly recent, but its speed is alarming. In Australia at present

the fragmentation is so far-reaching that cassowaries are often seen crossing roads to move from one patch of forest to another. The situation is particularly serious in the southern portion of their Australian range, where cattle regularly graze within the forest, producing serious alterations to the habitat. In Irian Jaya, the western, Indonesian sector of New Guinea, there are numerous projects to exploit mineral resources, or to intensify logging, and these represent serious threats to the extensive tracts of undisturbed rain forest and the cassowaries that inhabit them.

In addition to such destruction of habitat, human pressure has a negative influence in other, even more direct ways on cassowary populations. Birds are run over on roads or attacked by dogs, and in such situations chicks are particularly vulnerable. Feral pigs are a major problem in Australia, while in New Guinea the increase in the price fetched by cassowary feathers in native markets has led to an intensification of hunting pressure. Research carried out in Australia indicates that such factors are contributing towards a high annual mortality rate.

General Bibliography
de Beer (1956), Bledsoe (1988), Bock (1963), Bulmer (1967), Cho *et al.* (1984), Cracraft (1974), Davies (1976, 1985), Elzanowski (1985, 1988), Feduccia (1985), Handford & Mares (1985), Horwell (1990), Mayr (1979), MacGowan (1985), Parkes & Clark (1966), Reid (1982b, 1987), Rich & Balouet (1984), Sandell (1986), Sibley & Ahlquist (1981), Sibley & Frelin (1972), Stott (1981), Tyler & Simkiss (1959).

PLATE 3

inches   20
cm   50

possible ssp *aurantiacus*

1

2

3

PLATE 3

Genus *CASUARIUS*   Brisson, 1760

1. Southern Cassowary

Casuarius casuarius

French: Casoar à casque   **German:** Helmkasuar   **Spanish:** Casuario Común
Other common names: Double-wattled/Two-wattled/Australian Cassowary

Taxonomy. *Struthio Casuarius* Linnaeus, 1758, Seram.
Eight subspecies (*casuarius, tricarunculatus, bistriatus, lateralis, sclaterii, johnsonii, aruensis* and *bicarunculatus*) traditionally recognized, but good evidence for their validity lacking (see page 90). Monotypic.

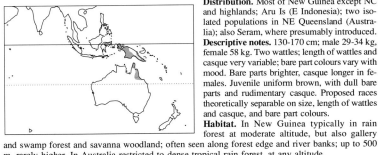

Distribution. Most of New Guinea except NC and highlands; Aru Is (E Indonesia); two isolated populations in NE Queensland (Australia); also Seram, where presumably introduced.
Descriptive notes. 130-170 cm; male 29-34 kg, female 58 kg. Two wattles; length of wattles and casque very variable; bare part colours vary with mood. Bare parts brighter, casque longer in females. Juvenile uniform brown, with dull bare parts and rudimentary casque. Proposed races theoretically separable on size, length of wattles and casque, and bare part colours.
Habitat. In New Guinea typically in rain forest at moderate altitude, but also gallery and swamp forest and savanna woodland; often seen along forest edge and river banks; up to 500 m, rarely higher. In Australia restricted to dense tropical rain forest, at any altitude.

Food and Feeding. Mainly fallen fruit (Lauraceae, Myrtaceae, Elaeocarpaceae, palms); also some fungi, invertebrates, small vertebrates and even some carrion. Fruit mostly picked up off forest floor, occasionally plucked off low bush. In captivity consumes 2·9 kg/day.
Breeding. Most data from Australia. Jun-Oct in Queensland; starts end of dry season in New Guinea. Females practise successive polyandry. 3-5 pale to dark green eggs (average 135 x 95 mm, 584 g). Incubation and chick-care carried out exclusively by male; incubation c. 50 days; chicks become independent at c. 9 months.
Movements. Presumably sedentary, with some evidence of irregular nomadic movements, especially in disturbed areas.
Status and Conservation. Not globally threatened. Fairly widespread in New Guinea, though presently rare or absent in many areas where formerly common; decline due to habitat destruction and hunting pressure. Apparently not uncommon in lowlands of C Seram; in coastal forests some birds taken as pets or hunted. In Australia limited to two (or three) isolated populations in rain forest of NE Queensland; density unknown, but clearly threatened at local level, due to habitat destruction and disturbance; feral pigs probably responsible for predation of eggs and young, competition for food and also habitat destruction; many run down on roads.
Bibliography. Beehler *et al.* (1986), Blakers *et al.* (1984), Bowler & Taylor (1989), Coates (1985), Coles (1986), Crome (1976), Crome & Moore (1988a, 1988b), Diamond, J.M. (1972), Fisher, G.D. (1968a, 1968b), Frith & Frith (1985, 1986), Hickey (1985), Marchant & Higgins (1990), Mathews & Walker (1983), Schodde & Tidemann (1988), Roberts (1977), Rich (1976), Rutgers & Norris (1970), Stocker & Irvine (1983), Tindale (1953), White (1975), White & Bruce (1986), Worrell *et al.* (1975), Wright (1988).

2. Dwarf Cassowary
Casuarius bennetti

French: Casoar de Bennett   **German:** Bennettkasuar   **Spanish:** Casuario Menor
Other common names: Bennett's Cassowary

Taxonomy. *Casuarius Bennetti* Gould, 1857, New Britain.
Seven subspecies (*papuanus*, *goodfellowi*, *claudii*, *shawmayeri*, *hecki*, *bennetti* and *picticollis*) traditionally recognized, but good evidence for their validity lacking (see page 90). Monotypic.

Distribution. New Guinea, Japen I (off NW New Guinea); also New Britain, where presumably introduced.
Descriptive notes. 100-110 cm; 17·6 kg. Feathering on foreneck extends higher up than in other species. Red "wart" on foreneck and pink of cheek may be absent; sometimes only one red patch at base of neck, which can be on hindneck and can extend downwards into plumage, as in *C. unappendiculatus.* Bare part colours brighter and casque generally tends to be longer in females. Juvenile has uniform brown plumage, dull bare parts and rudimentary casque. Proposed races theoretically separable on grounds of extensive variability of bare parts.
Habitat. Forests and secondary growth in hills and mountains, up to 3000 m. In NE New Guinea also found in lowland forests, where other species absent.

Food and Feeding. Mainly fallen fruit; also fungi, invertebrates and small vertebrates. Fruit mostly picked up off forest floor, occasionally plucked off low bush or heathy plant.
Breeding. Recorded both in dry and wet seasons. Nest normally between buttressed tree roots. 3-5 eggs. Incubation and chick-care carried out exclusively by male; incubation c. 7 weeks.
Movements. Presumably sedentary.
Status and Conservation. Not globally threatened. Generally scarce, though considered locally common in NE New Guinea. Rare or absent in many areas due to hunting pressure, which has increased with introduction of firearms.
Bibliography. Beehler (1978), Beehler *et al.* (1986), Body & Reid (1983), Coates (1985), Coles (1986), Diamond, J.M. (1972), Reid (1979, 1982a), White (1976).

3. Northern Cassowary
Casuarius unappendiculatus

French: Casoar unicaronculé   **German:** Einlappenkasuar   **Spanish:** Casuario Unicarunculado
Other common names: One-wattled/Single-wattled Cassowary

Taxonomy. *Casuarius unappendiculatus* Blyth, 1860, no locality.
Four subspecies (*unappendiculatus*, *occipitalis*, *aurantiacus* and *philipi*) or more traditionally recognized, but good evidence for their validity lacking (see page 90). Monotypic.
Distribution. N New Guinea, and nearby Japen I and Salawati I.

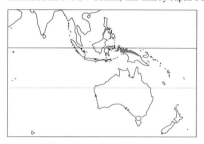

Descriptive notes. 120-150 cm. Small, but more or less prominent wart-like wattle at base of foreneck; some birds have more than one wattle; reddish brown mark on back of head sometimes missing; bare part colours known to vary with mood. Colour of neck and wattle(s) variable, as are size and shape of casque; casque can be as small as in *C. bennetti.* Bare part colours brighter and casque generally longer in females. Juvenile presumably as other species, with uniform brown plumage, dull bare parts and rudimentary casque. Proposed races theoretically separable on grounds of size, number and length of wattles and variability of bare part colours.
Habitat. Rain forest and swamp forest; mostly in lowlands, but locally up to 500 m.
Food and Feeding. Mainly fallen fruit; also fungi, invertebrates and small vertebrates. Presumably feeds in similar fashion to other species.
Breeding. Jun-Oct. Females polyandrous. Eggs grey-green to pale green, 139-160 x 93-105 mm. Incubation and chick-care carried out exclusively by male; incubation c. 50 days; chicks become independent at c. 9 months.
Movements. Presumably sedentary.
Status and Conservation. Not globally threatened. Generally scarce, though locally common. Threatened in some areas by destruction and fragmentation of forest; also by human pressure, especially in S of range.
Bibliography. Beehler *et al.* (1986), Coates (1985), Erftemeijer *et al.* (1989), Reid (1979, 1982a), Wennrich (1982a, 1982b, 1982c).

Class AVES
Order STRUTHIONIFORMES
Suborder CASUARII
Family DROMAIIDAE (EMU)

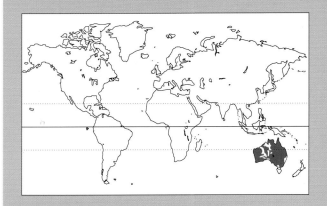

- Huge, flightless, three-toed terrestrial birds with long neck and legs.
- 150-190 cm.
- Australia.
- Open woodland and semi-arid plains.
- 1 genus, 1 species, 1 taxon.
- No species threatened; 2 species and 1 subspecies extinct since 1600.

Systematics

Emus belong to one of the oldest bird families of the Australasian Region. In prehistoric times, the common ancestor they share with the cassowaries gave rise to several different forms, most of which are now extinct. The oldest fossils of the present genus were found in Pleistocene deposits, and are some 5000-10,000 years old. They were discovered on King Island, off Tasmania, and belong to the island's own endemic species, the King Island Emu (*Dromaius ater*), which has since died out.

The Emu and cassowary families are placed together in the suborder Casuarii, because of their close phylogenetic relationship and morphological similarities. Along with the kiwis, they constitute the Australasian representatives of the Struthioniformes, an order which seems to have radiated from Gondwanaland through the southern landmasses (see page 76).

Only one species survives nowadays, the Larger or Spotted Emu, normally known simply as the Emu (*Dromaius novaehollandiae*); it is restricted to mainland Australia. Up to the beginning of the nineteenth century there were also three smaller single island forms off southern Australia, which have sometimes been lumped together as the Dwarf Emu. It is generally accepted that the King Island Emu and the Kangaroo Island Emu (*Dromaius baudinianus*) were authentic species, whilst the Tasmanian Emu is considered to have been a race of the mainland species, and is classified as *D. n. diemenensis*. However, very few remains of these extinct forms have been found, amounting merely to a few bones of the King Island Emu, and only one and three skins respectively of the Kangaroo Island and Tasmanian Emus. This, together with the fact that they are now extinct, has greatly hindered studies of their taxonomic relationships.

Morphological Aspects

Apart from the kiwis, all of the ratites are huge birds, and the Emu comes second in size only to the Ostrich (*Struthio camelus*). Within its range the only bird of comparable size is the Southern Cassowary (*Casuarius casuarius*), although there are also feral populations of Ostriches in southern Australia (see page 82). An adult Emu stands 150-190 cm tall, and generally weighs about 30-45 kg, or sometimes even as much as 55 kg, with females averaging larger and heavier than males.

Like other flightless birds, the Emu has a heavy, compact body, powerful feet for running, and rudimentary wings. The large, powerful feet, each ending in three toes, allow the bird to cover great distances with little effort, at a constant speed of 7 km/h. Furthermore, the reduced number of toes means that Emus are easily capable of reaching speeds of up to 48 km/h, with strides of around 2·7 m. They are also good swimmers, and readily bathe in either inland or coastal waters.

Another feature the Emu has in common with cassowaries is the double-shafted structure of its feathers, which have a highly developed hyporachis. The barbs are very widely spaced out and lack the usual interlocking hooks, giving the plumage an extremely loose, hair-like appearance, and it hangs down the sides of the bird's body from a conspicuous dorsal parting. The wings are very stunted and are hidden beneath the plumage, while there are no rectrices. Despite measuring only one tenth of the total body length, the wings have a significant part to play in keeping the birds cool (see General Habits).

Unique among the ratites is a cleft that the Emu possesses in the ventral region of the trachea; this is covered frontally by an expandable pouch, which measures some 30 cm in diameter, when inflated. The sound produced, when the air is intermittently driven through the cleft towards the pouch, re-echoes in turn in the cervical air-sacs, and creates the "Booming" and "Drumming" notes, which are characteristic of the Emu during the breeding season (see Voice).

Sexes are similar, and in adults the top of the head and the neck are black, while the body is brown mottled with black. After moulting, the new feathers are almost black, but with time and exposure to the sun they start to lose melanin, and take on a greyish brown shade. During the breeding season, the female's head and neck are more densely covered in black feathers, and the bare parts are more intensely blue than in the male. The juvenile can easily be recognized by its dark, finely barred head and neck.

Habitat

Emus can be found in most parts of Australia, and they live in a wide variety of habitats. Typically they occupy open sclerophyll forest and the semi-arid plains of the interior. In periods of torrential rain, or when food or water is scarce in their breeding areas, they may move to zones where they are not normally found, such as deserts or the outskirts of towns. Nevertheless, they do not enter tropical rain forest, which is the domain of the Southern Cassowary.

Density and distribution patterns are linked to climatic factors, which determine the availability of food and water in the critical seasons of the breeding cycle, autumn and winter. In some areas, human activities, such as the installation of fixed water points for sheep and cattle, and the erection of long fences to keep out predators, in particular dingos (*Canis familiaris*), have benefited the Emu, and have helped it to expand its range. For this reason, the highest densities nowadays are to be found in areas of sheep grazing, followed by those of cereal growing and cattle grazing, while the areas of lowest densities are those with no commercial value, in particular deserts.

General Habits

During both summer and winter, most of the Emu's time is spent in feeding. In this, as in other aspects of its life, the species is diurnal, starting soon after sunrise and finishing after sunset, though there is some activity on moonlit nights.

The daily routine varies slightly in pattern from one season to another. In winter, the first hours of the day are dedicated to foraging and moving about to all intents and purposes rather aimlessly. Around mid-morning or midday, they make their way slowly towards the drinking places, continuing to feed as they go along. After drinking, during the whole of the afternoon, activity is again limited mainly to feeding, although at a somewhat slower rate. In summer, less time is dedicated to feeding, as birds spend the hottest part of the day in the shade of the trees and return to the drinking places later in the afternoon, especially on very hot days. In very hot temperatures, Emus raise their wings up, baring the complex structure of surface veins underneath, and thus permitting heat loss through evaporation.

They normally sleep in open ground, although on cold winter nights they snuggle up in the shelter of bushes or tus-socks of grass. The same roost-site is used regularly while the birds remain in the same area, and usually it is only abandoned when food becomes scarce and they have to move on.

In general, Emus live alone or in pairs, although sometimes they form groups of four to nine birds. They are only gregarious when on the move, or in places where food or water are abundant. Large groups tend to congregate along fencelines and other man-made barriers, where their progress has been obstructed.

Different groups of Emus feeding in nearby areas pay little attention to each other. Within any particular group, ties between individual members are loose, and there is little social interaction. Birds tend to keep their distance, and are normally about 50-100 m apart, though they do not move more than 1 km away from the rest of the group. Antagonistic situations are frequently resolved with a threat display from the dominant bird; this consists of a simple grunt, with the neck stretched out forwards, and the bill pointed downwards. On occasions, birds may even peck, kick or chase their adversaries. The male uses similar behaviour during the nuptial display, and generally in the period before egg-laying. In addition, on encountering a strange object, females and also, less frequently, males perform another type of threat behaviour. The bird produces a repeated "Booming" call, with the neck arched and the cervical air-sacs inflated, whilst circling round the object.

As a rule Emus are pacific, except during the breeding season, when they are much more aggressive, and also on occasions when they are disturbed. They are very inquisitive, and frequently approach or even follow humans, apparently only to see what they are up to.

Voice

Outside the breeding season, Emus are normally silent, except during confrontations, or when they come across strange objects; on such occasions both sexes make "Grunting" and "Booming" sounds (see Morphological Aspects), although males "Boom" less often.

Emus are well adapted to living in the very arid areas prevailing over much of Australia, and they are quite capable of surviving droughts. Nonetheless, in normal circumstances, they tend to drink frequently, usually once or twice a day, and birds gather in fair numbers around regular drinking sites.

[*Dromaius novaehollandiae*, western New South Wales, Australia. Photo: Jen & Des Bartlett/ Bruce Coleman]

The "Grunt" is used by males in the breeding season in three main ways: as a threat and a territorial defence call in the presence of rivals; during courtship display; and before egg-laying. Both sexes "Grunt" during threat displays. Females mainly "Boom" during courtship display, to proclaim territory occupation, and also as a threat display. The fairly similar "High-intensity Booming" is exclusively produced by females, and can be heard up to 2 km away. The most characteristic of all the Emu's calls is the single low, resonant "Boom" known as "Drumming", which has been transcribed as "e-moo, e-moo". This curious sound is made only by females during the breeding season, probably to attract members of the opposite sex at first, and then peaking in intensity when the male starts to incubate.

Food and Feeding

The Emu is omnivorous, and its feeding routine consists of searching out and selecting highly nutritious food. The proportions of plant and animal items consumed varies at different times of year, although the former generally constitute a greater part of the diet.

Whenever possible, birds take the parts of plants containing the highest nutrient value, including seeds, fruits, flowers and tender roots. In summer they eat large quantities of insects, particularly caterpillars, beetles and grasshoppers, and also small vertebrates. In order to help grind down food in the gizzard, they swallow stones weighing up to 46 g. A primitive form of coprophagy also occurs, involving the ingestion of semi-digested portions of fresh droppings. This practice may play a significant part in avoiding dehydration and helping young birds to keep growing, for they sometimes have to survive in dry environments where food is very scarce.

During the day, Emus feed in open spaces, even in the heat of summer, a period when kangaroos and other inhabitants of Australia's semi-arid plains spend the day in the shade and feed at night. This prolonged exposure to the sun means that birds require a lot of water, so drinking is very frequent. Adults usually drink once a day, and sometimes twice in summer (see General Habits). Nevertheless, Emus possess a considerable capacity for resisting droughts, and in extreme conditions they can go several days without drinking, if succulent plants are available. Juveniles need to drink at much shorter intervals than adults, whilst chicks need water daily.

Prior to commencing incubation, the male builds up considerable reserves of fat, for he usually does not eat or drink at all during this eight week period. In order to counter dehydration during incubation, he goes into a sort of torpor, dropping his body temperature by 3-4°C, with the result that his water loss during this period is reduced to only a fifth of the normal rate.

Breeding

The breeding strategy of the Emu is based on successive polyandry of the females, with males taking on the full responsibility of looking after the eggs and subsequently the chicks.

Pairing occurs in December and January. The female starts to utter her characteristic "Drumming" call, probably with the purpose of attracting a male. The male starts collecting material and building nests within his territory, and the female gradually comes and joins him. During courtship display, the paired birds stand next to each other, with their heads lowered, and their necks bent and swaying from side to side. The male then performs a threat display (see General Habits). When the female sits down the male sidles up behind her and grabs the skin on her nape with his bill. Finally, copulation takes place, during which the male produces squeaking or purring sounds. As in other ratites, the male has a penis.

The nest is a shallow depression covered in twigs, leaves and grass, and is built by the male. It is frequently situated in the shelter of a bush or a tree, but always in a fairly open site, where the sitting male has a good view of the surrounding land. In spite of its large size, an incubating bird is well camouflaged and difficult to see. The female lays five to fifteen dark green eggs, with an interval of two to four days between each. Eggs average 130 x 90 mm and each weighs 450-650 g, which is about 1·5% of the female's body weight, one of the lowest proportions of all birds.

The pair stay together in the same territory for at least five months before incubation begins. As in the cassowaries and the rheas, the male alone performs the tasks of incubation and chick-care. While he is incubating, the female may remain in the vicinity, "Booming" loudly and showing particularly aggressive behaviour towards any intruders. Alternatively, the female may leave the territory to mate again and lay eggs for another male, or to undertake seasonal movements.

During the entire period of incubation, which lasts around eight weeks, the male does not eat, drink or defecate (see Food and Feeding). Although he never leaves the immediate vicinity of the nest, he gets up several times each day to turn the eggs, while the rest of his time is mainly spent tidying the nest, preening and dozing. Once a male has begun to incubate, he rejects the female aggressively, thus preventing her from laying more eggs, although cases of laying occurring up to 13 days later have been recorded.

After about 56 days of incubation, the eggs normally hatch synchronously, or a maximum of four days apart. The chicks are precocial and nidifugous, and are already able to walk after 5-24 hours. Weighing 440-500 g, newly-hatched chicks are covered in a thick coat of down striped cream, brown and black, and they blend easily into the vegetation. When they are two to seven days old, they leave the nest, accompanied by the male, and within a week they can run and swim competently.

The male looks after the chicks until they are about five months old, during which period he is extremely aggressive, and he may even drive away his own mate, as well as attacking any intruder. While a fully-grown adult has practically no enemies other than man, the undefended eggs and chicks are very vulnerable, and are sometimes taken by dingos, foxes or birds of prey. A male will allow chicks from other broods to join his group, as long as they are smaller than his own offspring.

After five months the bond starts to become looser, although males usually remain with their young for seven or eight months, and sometimes for as long as 18 months. At three to five months the young birds, now half the size of adults, lose the coat of down and assume juvenile plumage. After one year they are practically fully-developed and look like adults, though they still retain vestiges of their juvenile plumage. When they are two or three years old they reach sexual maturity, though there are actually records of birds in captivity breeding when only 20 months old.

Movements

When the circumstances permit, Emus can be totally sedentary. Otherwise, they are nomadic, and may cover great distances in search of food and water.

In Western Australia, results of studies involving ringing and recapture show that adults can travel up to 13·5 km per day and as much as 540 km in nine months. They generally move in small flocks containing birds of all ages, except in the breeding season, when birds usually move about in pairs.

Movements are markedly seasonal, and are related to the rains and the ensuing availability of food. In Western Australia, Emus migrate towards the coastal areas of the south in autumn and winter, returning towards the inland areas further north in spring and summer. Nevertheless, if the climatic patterns or the local availability of food vary in any particular year, the birds change their habits to adapt to the new environmental conditions.

Relationship with Man

Despite the fact that Emus have lived alongside man since way back into prehistoric times, it was not until the arrival of the

The male Emu is a very conscientious parent. He alone guards and incubates the eggs, and during the eight weeks of incubation he hardly ever eats, drinks or defecates. Each day he tidies the nest and turns the eggs, while the rest of his time is spent dozing or preening. The male is well camouflaged to make sure that he is quite inconspicuous and readily blends into the landscape during incubation, when he is exposed to danger for long periods. Note the characteristic "parting" down the back.

[*Dromaius novaehollandiae.* Photo: Jean-Paul Ferrero/ Ardea]

The male Emu stays with his chicks for five to seven months, by which stage the young birds are able to defend themselves. The male keeps in touch with his brood by means of a coughing contact call. Small chicks when left unattended are very vulnerable to attacks from dingos and foxes, and when alarmed the male may charge at his supposed assailants and kick out at them.

[*Dromaius novaehollandiae.* Photo: Jean-Paul Ferrero/ Ardea]

first European colonizers in Australia, that they started to suffer the sort of intense persecution that brought about the rapid extinction of the various different islands forms (see Status and Conservation).

Emu meat was appreciated by early settlers for its beef-like flavour, their eggs were eagerly sought after due to their great size, and Emu oil was used to fuel lamps. However, serious persecution only began when the birds started to come into conflict with man's economic interests. When extensive cereal growing areas were established in the coastal regions of Australia, Emus adapted their habits and their range, and they started to migrate in the dry season from the arid interior into farmlands, where they found abundant food and water. They broke into fields, destroying the crops and damaging property, and this soon led to farmers regarding them as a kind of plague, with the result that rewards were offered for killing them, and for the destruction of their eggs.

In 1932 the Australian government, under pressure from the farmers, sent an army artillery unit to Western Australia, in order to exterminate the 20,000 or so Emus that were causing such extensive crop damage. The tactics worked out for this "Emu War" involved driving the Emus along fences, until they were within the range of machine-guns and grenades. However, the birds proved to be more adept in terms of both camouflage and strategic retreat than the soldiers themselves, and they dispersed rapidly in small groups when they were shot at. After a month of endless and fruitless pursuit, during which it is reported that they only managed to kill 12 Emus, the Royal Australian Artillery had to admit defeat and they withdrew. In the wake of this fiasco, the farmers decided to build long, high, Emu-proof fencelines to stop the birds getting into their fields, and this seems to have been a more effective measure in the long run.

Emus are easy to keep and rear in captivity, and because of this they can be found in zoos all over the world. The species has been bred on farms in Western Australia since 1970, as a commercial proposition, mainly for the exploitation of its skin for leather.

Status and Conservation

In spite of the extensive persecution it has suffered, the Emu is widely distributed throughout Australia today and populations are considered to be fairly stable. In some zones numbers have actually increased, largely due to the changes in natural habitats which have been wrought by man (see Habitat). It is only in densely populated or heavily humanized areas that Emus have disappeared.

Their numbers are nowadays controlled by three main factors: the intensity of farming activities; the availability of water; and the density of dingos. In agricultural land, where they are in direct contact with man, there is a tendency to create "Emu sanctuaries", where the birds are completely protected, but are surrounded by high fences, which prevent them from moving out into the fields. In dry years such confinement can prove lethal for the birds.

If the overall situation of Emus on the Australian mainland can be considered fairly healthy, the same can not be said of the island representatives of the family. The Tasmania, Kangaroo Island and King Island forms (see Systematics) all became extinct in the 150 years following the arrival of the first European settlers in Australia; the causes of extinction are rather obscure. On Kangaroo Island, the endemic species died out probably because it was hunted by Flinders, the first settler on the island, who arrived in 1802, and also because its habitat was irreversibly altered by extensive burning. In any event, in 1836, when mass colonization began, the birds had already vanished. The King Island Emu disappeared at the beginning of the nineteenth century, before the arrival of settlers. The extinction of this species has been attributed to the same causes, although doubts have been expressed as to whether a handful of natives could have killed off the whole island population. All that remains of this species today are a few bones. In Tasmania, the birds were persecuted and were also forced out by the steady conversion of their original habitat into grazing lands. They were thus driven into the forests where, unable to adapt to such a different biotope, they soon died out.

♂

♀

PLATE 4

inches   20

cm   50

Family DROMAIIDAE (EMU)
SPECIES ACCOUNTS

PLATE 4

Genus *DROMAIUS*   Vieilott, 1816

Emu

Dromaius novaehollandiae

French: Emeu d'Australie   **German**: Emu   **Spanish**: Emú
Other common names: Larger/Spotted Emu

Taxonomy. *Casuarius N. Hollandiae* Latham, 1790, Sydney, New South Wales.
Race *diemenensis* of Tasmania extinct. Some authorities recognize three surviving races, *novaehollandiae*, *woodwardi* and *rothschildi*, while extinct species *D. ater* (=*minor*) and *D. baudinianus* (=*diemenianus*) have also been considered mere races of present species. Monotypic.
Distribution. Australia.
Introduced to Kangaroo I and Maria I (both off S Australia).

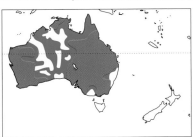

Descriptive notes. 150-190 cm; 30-55 kg. Appears wingless; plumage shaggy, with obvious dorsal parting. Females heavier and often appear darker than males, with brighter blue facial skin. Juvenile very dark, especially on head and neck.
Habitat. Wide variety of habitats, ranging from woodland and scrub to open country, at any altitude, both on coast and inland. Avoids arid inland areas, where rainfall is under 600 mm/year, and also heavily settled zones. Normally nests in grassland, woodland or heath.
Food and Feeding. Omnivorous. Seeds, fruits or shoots (*Acacia*, Casuarinaceae), grasses

(Poaceae), insects (e.g. grasshoppers, caterpillars). Some seasonal variation in preferences, generally reflecting availability. Plant matter normally plucked off living plant, though may be picked up off ground. Coprophagy also recorded. Most of day spent foraging; drinking normally regular, once or twice per day (see pages 99, 100).
Breeding. Pairing Dec-Jan; laying Feb-Jul, mostly Apr/May. Females practise successive polyandry. Nest is shallow depression in ground, 1-2 m wide, covered with leaves, twigs, grass; often situated by tree or bush. 5-15 eggs (maximum 24), average 130 x 90 mm, 450-650 g. Incubation and chick-care carried out exclusively by male; incubation usually 56 days; chicks have cream, brown and black striped down. Sexual maturity usually at 2-3 years. Known to have lived over 10 years in captivity. Little known of breeding success in wild, but only c. 40% hatching success; drought can cause breeding to be delayed or even abandoned.
Movements. Sedentary or nomadic, depending on local availability of food and water. In Western Australia makes seasonal N-S movements, following the rains. Exceptionally may cross shallow bays to coastal islands.
Status and Conservation. Not globally threatened. Population stable, with estimates (mid 1980's) of 100,000-200,000 birds in Western Australia, and 525,000 in rest of Australia, mostly in Queensland and New South Wales. Has probably benefited from many human alterations to environment, including increased water supplies and erection of fences to exclude predators, e.g. dingos; numbers may have increased about tenfold since European colonization. Present day threats limited, especially as fiasco of "Emu War" has shown that, unlike island congeners, this mainland species can withstand intense hunting pressure (see page 102). Successfully introduced to Kangaroo I and Maria I (both off S Australia), in 1957 and 1976 respectively; reintroduced to parts of Queensland, New South Wales and Victoria. Tasman race *diemenensis* extinct c. 1865, probably due to habitat destruction, shooting and poisoning.

Bibliography. de Beer (1956), Beutel *et al.* (1984), Bevolscaya & Tikhenov (1985), Blakers *et al.* (1984), Bledsoe (1988), Bock (1963), Brasil (1914), Buttemer & Dawson (1988), Buttemer *et al.* (1988), Calder & Dawson (1978), Caughley & Grice (1982), Caughley *et al.* (1980), Cho *et al.* (1984), Cracraft (1974), Curry (1979, 1985), Davies, S.J.J.F. (1968, 1972, 1975, 1976, 1977, 1978, 1983), Davies & Herd (1983), Davies *et al.* (1983), Dawson *et al.* (1984), Eastman (1968), Elzanowski (1985, 1988), Feduccia (1985), Fuller (1987), Greenway (1967), Grice *et al.* (1985), Handford & Mares (1985), Herd & Dawson (1984), Horwell (1990), Long (1959, 1965), Marchant & Higgins (1990), McGowan (1985), Meise (1963), Noble (1975), Parker, S.A. (1984), Parkes & Clark (1966), Prager *et al.* (1976), Quin (1984), Rich & Balouet (1984), Rutgers & Norris (1970), Sibley & Ahlquist (1981), Sibley & Frelin (1972), Slater (1978), Smith (1982), Tyler & Symkiss (1959), Willson (1989), Wilson, Hill & Barnes (1987).

Class AVES
Order STRUTHIONIFORMES
Suborder APTERYGES
Family APTERYGIDAE (KIWIS)

- Small to medium-sized, flightless terrestrial birds with rudimentary wings, no tail and shortish, stout legs.
- 35-65 cm.

- New Zealand.
- Mainly forests, also woodland and scrub, up to 1200 m.
- 1 genus, 3 species, 5 taxa.
- 1 species threatened; none extinct since 1600.

Systematics

Endemic to New Zealand, the kiwis form the oldest surviving family of birds on these islands. They share a common origin with the large, flightless birds, the Ostrich, the rheas, the Emu and the cassowaries, and together these five families, the ratites, constitute the order Struthioniformes (see page 76).

The forerunner of the kiwis separated from this common lineage at a very early stage, some time after losing the ability to fly. It lived on the ancient "supercontinent" of Gondwanaland, and reached the New Zealand Plate via western Antarctica, before the two became separated around 70 million years ago. From this early ancestor came two kinds of flightless birds, the moas and the kiwis, and the two followed quite separate evolutionary paths. The moas diversified into many different species, most of which became extinct before the end of the seventeenth century, although one small species probably survived until the beginning of the nineteenth. The kiwis, on the other hand, hardly diversified at all, and no recent species are known other than the extant three. The oldest kiwi fossil that has been found belongs to the Quaternary, but fossil footprints from the Upper Miocene have also been attributed to the Apterygidae. The close relationship of the kiwis with the moas has caused some to place the two families in the same order or suborder, while others have separated them into two distinct orders. Nowadays all of the ratites are normally grouped together in the same order.

The kiwi family comprises a single genus with three species, the Brown Kiwi (*Apteryx australis*), the Little Spotted Kiwi (*Apteryx owenii*) and the Great Spotted Kiwi (*Apteryx haastii*).

Morphological Aspects

In addition to being the smallest of the ratites, the kiwis are also the most atypical, and their morphology is quite different from that of the others. Body length ranges from 35 to 65 cm, depending on the species, with females being somewhat larger than males. They are also around 10-20% heavier, weighing anything from 3·5 kg or more, in the Brown Kiwi, to about 1 kg, in the Little Spotted Kiwi, and they are particularly heavy when carrying the huge egg.

The head is comparatively small, while the neck is long but strong and the thoracic muscles are greatly reduced. The

lower body, in contrast, is extremely robust, especially the pelvis, legs and feet, and all these proportions combine to give kiwis their characteristic pear-shape. The stunted wings are only 4-5 cm long, each with a claw at the end, and remain invisible beneath the body plumage. Kiwis do not have a tail, and the body ends in a small pygostyle.

Being basically nocturnal, kiwis are specially adapted to moving about at night amidst thick undergrowth in the forest (see General Habits). As a result of this, their senses of smell and hearing are very sharp, whereas their vision is poor, all characteristics more typical of a mammal than of a bird. Their eyes are small and lack the vascular membrane known as the pecten, and they can only see two feet in front of them in broad daylight, and only six feet at night. Their earholes are large, and birds can often be seen directing them in the direction of any sounds they hear.

The bill is long, flexible and slightly decurved, varying in colour from ivory to pink or brownish. In the Brown Kiwi it can measure as much as 20 cm, and in all species it is 25-30% longer in females than in males. The upper mandible is slightly longer than the lower and is somewhat swollen towards the tip. Birds often use the bill to help them adopt what is known as a "standing position", in which the bill tip is rested on the ground, thus forming a kind of tripod with the legs.

There are two small nostrils at the distal end of the bill, instead of at the base, as in most other birds, and these allow the kiwi to detect invertebrates in the leaf litter or even underground, using its well developed sense of smell. Towards the base of the bill there is a functional valve, which allows the bird to expel any water and impurities from the nostrils, by blowing air through them, and this produces a loud snuffling noise. The same valve enables them to feed in very wet areas, such as around the edge of a swamp. At the base of the kiwi's bill are a few rictal bristles, which are actually highly modified feathers with a tactile function. The tongue is horny and pointed.

The plumage has a crude, shaggy appearance from a distance, looking more like hair than feathers. In addition to lacking an aftershaft, the feathers, as in all the ratites, have no hooks on the barbs. The feather base is wide, soft and fleecy, whereas the distal end is hard, hair-like and waterproof. No detailed information is available about moult, but it can be continuous, at least in the North Island Brown Kiwi (*A. a. mantelli*), in which feather renewal has been observed practically all year round. There are no plumage differences between males and females, or between adults and young, except that young birds have softer plumage.

The strong legs have powerful muscles and are set quite far apart, which gives the birds a rather awkward gait. When running, they tend to stagger along, although their strides are forceful. The feet are also well developed, and have four toes, three in front and a small hind toe, unlike the other ratites, which only have two or three toes; each toe ends in a strong claw. Kiwis are good swimmers, and have no problems either wading or swimming across streams and shallow pools.

Habitat

The optimum habitat for kiwis is rain forest, which used to be extensive throughout New Zealand. Nowadays, due mostly to the destruction of a great deal of their original habitat, they are found in other ecotypes too. In addition to subtropical and temperate forests, they also inhabit shrubland, scrub, edges of grassland and so on. The Brown Kiwi even lives in some commercial pine plantations, indeed the largest surviving population of the North Island Brown Kiwi is to be found in such a plantation, whilst the species is in decline in its native forests (see Status and Conservation).

Kiwis have a broad altitudinal range, stretching from coastal areas at sea-level up to 1200 m in alpine regions. They live in areas with a warm subtropical climate, and always need a high level of relative humidity. Other environmental factors which are critical for all three species are the soil texture, its humus content, and the density of the vegetation, and these can all influence the ease with which birds dig their burrows. Burrows are normally situated in steep banks on the edges of forests, where the drainage is better and digging is easier. The same factors also affect the composition of the soil fauna, and consequently food availability.

There is no real evidence of any differences in the habitat preferences of the three species. Although the highest densities of Great Spotted Kiwis in South Island are found in subalpine and alpine forests, this is probably due to the fact that the populations which used to live in other environments have been decimated in recent years, rather than signalling a genuine preference for this habitat type.

General Habits

Kiwis are almost entirely nocturnal, and during the day they take refuge in their burrows or in natural hollows, only becoming active when the sun sets. When they eventually emerge, they are furtive and mostly move about amongst dense undergrowth in the forest, so it is not surprising that they are so difficult to see. Most of what is known about their behaviour and general biology has been discovered due to the major research efforts of recent years, sometimes with the help of night-viewing systems and radio-tracking equipment. Many questions, however, remain unanswered.

Kiwis are very set in their ways, and tend to live in pairs in the same territory all their lives. Solitary birds are generally juveniles or birds that have lost their partners. Territory size varies from one region to another, depending on the type of habitat, the abundance of food and the density of kiwis. In the Brown Kiwi a pair holds 5-50 ha, in the Great Spotted Kiwi 8-25 ha, and in the Little Spotted Kiwi some have been found to occupy as small an area as 2-3 ha. Both sexes are territorial, especially during the breeding season, when they expel any intruders, adult or immature, by calling and chasing, or very occasionally after a fight, which can include jumping and kicking and a fair deal of noise. The Brown Kiwi is more tolerant during the rest of the year, and home ranges can overlap widely. The attachment of birds to their territory is so strong that, even if their forest is cut down, they are liable to remain there for several weeks, until they are forced to move away, due to scarcity of food arising from the loss or drying out of the surface layer of soil.

Scattered about over their range a pair has numerous burrows, dug by both the male and the female, and these may be used both as the daytime shelters and also for breeding. Burrows normally have only one entrance, which is about 9-15 cm wide, and they vary considerably in length, from about 20 to 200 cm, ending in a chamber large enough to accommodate two kiwis. The entrance is usually well hidden by the vegetation, although some very conspicuous burrows have been found in open areas, where even the incubating bird can be seen from outside. Natural hollows, such as those found under tree roots and fallen branches, amongst dense vegetation, in fallen tree trunks, or in steep sand-banks, are also used as daytime shelters.

The patterns of the use of burrows and dens are very variable. They can be used individually or by the pair together, and birds can change roosts on successive nights, although the majority are used frequently and for many years. A remarkable habit of the kiwis, and one that is extremely rare in birds, is that of marking their territories and burrows with their droppings, which have a very pungent smell.

During the day a kiwi normally stays in its shelter, asleep, with its head turned backwards and its bill stuck in under the small, vestigial wings; sometimes a bird wakes up to preen, defecate, stretch, or, in wet weather, shake the water off its feathers. Some time normally 15-90 minutes after sunset, the birds venture out of their burrows in order to feed, each going its own separate way, and usually remaining active until dawn. In the Great Spotted Kiwi, activity has been recorded as much as an hour after daybreak in midsummer, while on Stewart Island, where nights can be extremely short, Brown Kiwis also use daylight hours for feeding.

Voice

Kiwis' calls are the commonest indication of their presence. They can be heard all year round, except on nights when there is a full moon or strong wind, or when the atmosphere is very dry. They begin soon after sunset, with maximum frequency during the first 1-3 hours of darkness, and are spread out irregularly throughout the rest of the night.

Calls play an important part both in territorial defence and in contact between partners, so the frequency of calls increases notably during breeding, whereas it decreases when the season ends. When calling, the bird adopts an upright position with the neck and legs fully stretched and the bill pointing upwards. Males call more than females, but duets between partners are common, with the two birds calling in unison, or one replying immediately after the other. Birds from neighbouring territories, especially males, very often answer, and vocal duels ensue. These can lead to aggressive encounters on territorial borders, and even to fights, involving snorting and bill-snapping, as well as other, more physical exchanges (see General Habits). When alarmed, or in aggressive mood, kiwis growl, hiss and loudly snap their mandibles.

The calls of the three species of kiwis are similar and can be heard hundreds of metres away, or even 1·5 km away in the case of the Brown Kiwi, in suitable weather conditions. The male Brown Kiwi makes long, loud, shrill whistles, in which the pitch first rises and then falls, and these have been described as "ah-eel". Calls consist of the repetition of these whistles up to 20 times or more. The female produces a series of notes which are shorter, harsher and more guttural than the male's, and these are quite unmistakable. Male Great and Little Spotted Kiwis make warbling whistles, which are quite different from the calls of the Brown Kiwi. The females' calls have the same general form, but they differ in both tone and tempo.

A pair that share a daytime burrow grunt and snuffle repeatedly for several minutes before coming out into the open, and this can continue when they are just outside the entrance. These sounds are also used as a form of greeting, and in the Little Spotted Kiwi they are also produced during the "Bill-to-bill Display" (see Breeding) and during copulation.

Other sounds include a snort, when a bird approaches an intruder or during fights, and "mewing" calls, which turn into a high-pitched "purr" during mating and copulation. Although chicks and juveniles are generally silent, they occasionally "peep", when in or out of the nest burrow, probably as a contact call or to convey distress or alarm; they also squeak and bill clack when alarmed.

Food and Feeding

Like most of the other ratites, the kiwis are omnivorous. Their diet consists chiefly of invertebrates and, to a lesser extent, vegetable matter, such as fruit, seeds and leaves.

They consume above all soil- and litter-dwelling invertebrates, including earthworms, millipedes, adult and larval beetles, larvae of moths and flies, large crickets and spiders. Remains of frogs, crayfish and fern sporangia have also been found in their droppings, but it is unclear whether these, like some other items of plant matter, are taken in deliberately or accidentally. The diet varies to a certain extent throughout the year, depending on the abundance of different types of invertebrates, which kiwis exploit as true opportunists.

In order to detect food, a kiwi uses its highly developed sense of smell and its sensitive bill, and, moving slowly through the undergrowth, it probes about in the earth with its bill. It is also able to hear the movements of large invertebrates. When it detects underground prey, it sinks its bill into the ground by moving its head back and forwards. Most attempts to capture prey are, however, unsuccessful, and all over its feeding area a bird leaves characteristic holes, which can be 15 cm deep and 1 cm wide. Prey is caught with the end of the bill, and earthworms are pulled out slowly and carefully, with short pauses, to avoid breaking them. Using the bill like tweezers, the bird also picks up fallen fruit and insects off the forest floor.

Kiwis have a great capacity for accumulating subcutaneous fat and in the North Island Brown Kiwi it may make up 30% of the body weight. This is important for males during the prolonged incubation period, for females with their high energy requirements before laying (see Breeding), and for all with the need to survive long periods when food is scarce during the summer.

Feeding sites are not fixed, and birds generally go to feed in a certain area several nights running, before changing to another one in another part of their territory.

Breeding

Unlike the rest of the ratites, most, if not all, kiwis are exclusively monogamous. Once a pair-bond has been formed it probably lasts until one of the partners dies, at which point the survivor may look for a new mate. In the Little Spotted Kiwi, pairs have been known to stay together for more than ten years.

The breeding season begins in spring, with most laying occurring from August to October. It can occur much later, in January or February, though this almost always refers to re-

In order to find its way about at night through the dense forest vegetation, a kiwi relies largely on its hearing and also its acute sense of smell; the bird's nostrils are situated towards the tip of the long bill, which has tactile bristles around the base, as a further aid to the efficiency of the senses. In contrast, the bird's eyes are small and beady, giving it fairly limited vision.

[Apteryx haastii.
Photo: Don Hadden/Ardea]

placement clutches. In captivity, eggs may be laid at almost any time of year.

Very few observations have been made of the pre-copulatory displays of kiwis, and most accounts are fragmentary. As in other aspects of their behaviour, there are few visual displays and the senses of hearing and smell predominate. During courtship display, birds carry out chases, jumps, hissing and "Close-contact Grunting". In the Brown Kiwi, the male calls, the female answers, and they then chase each other round in circles, before copulating. In the Little Spotted Kiwi there is a "Bill-to-bill Display", in which the pair face each other with bills crossed and pointing downwards, while they shuffle round each other and make short, soft grunts for up to twenty minutes. In the Brown Kiwi, copulation is preceded by the male gently tapping the female on the back and neck; when she bends over, the male climbs onto her back, leans on his tarsi, and keeps his balance by holding onto feathers on the female's back, while he makes a series of grunts.

Kiwis prefer to make their nests in burrows which they themselves have dug out, often in steep banks. Sometimes they use natural holes, such as hollow tree stumps, cracks in rocks, gaps in dense vegetation, and the like. Burrows are never used for breeding until months or even years after they have been dug, so that the surrounding vegetation has had time to grow and the entrance is thus well concealed. About two weeks before the eggs are laid, the male prepares the nest by bringing plant matter, especially moss, lichens and grass, into the nesting chamber. For replacement or second clutches, the nest-site is invariably changed.

Kiwi eggs are four times the expected size for a bird of their proportions. In the Brown Kiwi, the egg averages 129 x 78 mm, representing about 14-20% of the female's body weight, while in the Little Spotted Kiwi it constitutes about 25%, and such ratios are amongst the highest in the bird world. The size of the yolk is also exceptional, since it comprises 60% of the total volume of the egg. Before laying, the female has to walk about with her legs apart, and when she pauses her stomach sometimes touches the ground. Kiwis lay one or two eggs, rarely three, with an interval of about 25-30 days between the first and second in the Brown Kiwi, and of 2-3 weeks in the Little Spotted Kiwi. Up to three or four replacement clutches can be laid by the Brown Kiwi in a single breeding season, and occasionally birds attempt to raise two broods.

Incubation is normally carried out exclusively by the male, except in the Great Spotted Kiwi, where both sexes participate; in the Stewart Island Brown Kiwi (A. a. lawryi), the female may also help to incubate. After laying the second egg, and sometimes even after the first, the female leaves the nest burrow, but she remains in the surrounding area, sleeping in a nearby burrow. Once the young have hatched, she visits the nest quite regularly, probably to help the male with the brooding.

The timing of the start of incubation is rather variable. In general, it starts as soon as the female leaves the burrow, but it can begin up to 14 days later, and during the first 20-30 days incubation can be intermittent. The incubation period of 63-92 days is very long in relation to the size of the kiwi, which may be due to another of the bird's peculiarities, its low body temperature of 38°C, which is similar to that of a mammal rather than a bird.

The male goes out of his burrow every night to eat and defecate. He spends a variable amount of time outside, usually 4-5 hours in the Brown Kiwi, but on occasions as much as 20 consecutive hours. On leaving the burrow, he usually covers the entrance with sticks and leaves, but this does not prevent the eggs suffering heavy predation, mainly by Wekas (*Gallirallus australis*), which have even been known to eat eggs while they were still under the incubating bird! In the Great Spotted Kiwi, the female usually takes over from the male at night and stays in the nest until he returns.

Hatching takes two or three days with a 5-15 day interval between the first and second eggs, and chicks have to break the shell with their feet, as they lack an egg tooth. They hatch fully covered in feathers, like little replicas of the adult bird. The chick still has a large yolk sac attached to its stomach, and this can make up a third of the chick's weight at hatching; it will feed off this for around 10 days. Chicks are precocial and nidifugous, and can stand up after four days and walk after five or six. At this age they start to rove outside the nest, mainly at night, but also during the first and last hours of daylight, often leaving before and returning after the adult. They feed by themselves and, when out of the nest, are only loosely guarded by their parents. The male broods them during the day and part of the night for the first two or three weeks, sometimes with the female's help.

After 14-20 days, chicks are probably totally independent, but they remain within their parents' territory for some time, roosting apart from the adults. Nevertheless, adult Brown Kiwis have been recorded accompanying juveniles as much as a year and even three years old. Chicks and juveniles fall easy prey to introduced mammal predators, such as stoats (*Mustela erminea*), cats and dogs. When they are about 18 months old they reach adult weight. In the Brown Kiwi the earliest recorded breeding is at two years old for a female and 14 months for a male. Little is known about longevity, but they can live more than 20 years in captivity, and one Brown Kiwi even lived to be 35.

Movements

Kiwis are sedentary and, once a bird has occupied a territory, it usually stays there for life. Even if the habitat is destroyed, birds will remain in the territory as long as they can still find food, later settling in adjacent areas, if these are suitable.

At night, when searching for food, they can cover considerable distances. The Great Spotted Kiwi has been known to move up to three kilometres in a single night through thick vegetation and across rough ground.

Relationship with Man

Since way back into pre-colonial times, kiwis have been persecuted for their feathers and their meat. The first inhabitants of New Zealand, the Maoris, who had come there from Polynesia, regularly hunted them, and had already caused some local extinctions (see Status and Conservation).

Along with the Great White Egret (*Egretta alba*), the Kiwi occupied a place of honour in Maori traditions. It was believed to receive special protection from Tane, God of the Forest, and because of this, special rituals and chants were performed before each kiwi hunt. The Maoris used dogs in these hunts, and

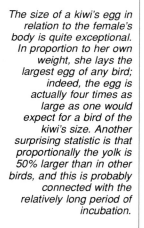

The size of a kiwi's egg in relation to the female's body is quite exceptional. In proportion to her own weight, she lays the largest egg of any bird; indeed, the egg is actually four times as large as one would expect for a bird of the kiwi's size. Another surprising statistic is that proportionally the yolk is 50% larger than in other birds, and this is probably connected with the relatively long period of incubation.

[Apteryx australis. Photo: Frances Furlong/ Bruce Coleman]

attracted the kiwis with pieces of bark smouldering to resemble glow worms, one of the kiwis' favourite foods, and also by imitating the birds' calls, by whistling through their fingers. The heart of the first kiwi to be caught was roasted and offered to the God Tane, in order to avoid his wrath.

The Maoris said that the kiwis' enormous eggs took so long to hatch that sometimes nearby roots grew and imprisoned the chicks. By weaving kiwi feathers into a base of flax, they made their most precious ceremonial cloaks, which were traditionally only worn by the tribal chiefs and persons of rank.

The white colonizers who later arrived on these islands also hunted kiwis abundantly, mainly for food, although the feathers were also highly valued, as they were used for trout flies. However, it was not until midway through the nineteenth century that really heavy persecution of kiwis began, in order to satisfy the demands of the European market, at that time avid for their feathers to make muffs and trimmings for clothes. At the time private collections of stuffed animals were popular in Europe, and a good number of kiwi skins ended up in these. According to records from this period one hunter declared in 1871 that he had killed 2200 kiwis single-handed, most of them Little Spotted Kiwis.

Today not only are kiwis strictly protected by law, but they have become the national emblem of New Zealand, and they are depicted on coins, stamps, army uniforms and commercial products from the country. New Zealanders even refer to themselves and also their dollars as "kiwis".

Status and Conservation

Although the New Zealand government passed a law banning the hunting, capture or killing of kiwis in 1908, and in 1921 the kiwi was declared an "absolutely protected bird", numbers have decreased drastically since then. In addition to direct pressure from hunting for food and feathers, kiwis have suffered from the relentless destruction of their habitat. This was begun by the Maoris, who cleared large areas of the forest by burning, and was intensified and spread further afield with the arrival of the Europeans, who substituted the original vegetation with farmland or exotic plantations in many regions. Such conversions are still going on at present, and pose the main threat to kiwis on North Island.

The introduction of predatory mammals also contributed greatly to the decline in populations, as kiwis were unaccustomed to having to elude such dangers. Stoats and weasels were introduced to combat the rabbit menace, whilst cats and dogs accompanied the human settlers. Many pets were abandoned after the decline of mining and associated activities at the end of the nineteenth century, and they were soon wreaking great havoc amongst the kiwi populations in these areas. Recently, a single dog ravaged a Brown Kiwi population in the Waitangi Forest, on North Island, and it was estimated that it had killed 500 birds out of a population of 900 in less than two months.

Another major cause of mortality has been the poisoned bait and gin-traps placed to catch the Common Brush-tailed Possum (*Trichosurus vulpecula*). Traps are now regulated by law, in such a way that it must not be possible for kiwis or other terrestrial birds to become trapped.

All these factors, in conjunction with the human pressure caused by the increase in population, have meant that the ranges of the three species of kiwi have shrunk notably. The Brown Kiwi is the only species to survive on North Island, and it is also found on South Island and the rather smaller Stewart Island. In general, its status can be considered fairly satisfactory, but the race *mantelli* of North Island is threatened by the steady felling of the remaining native forests on the island. In addition to this loss of habitat, kiwis face the direct threat of being roasted alive in the controlled burning which invariably follows logging, as they usually stay in their territories for some time after the forest has been cleared (see General Habits). Teams of dedicated volunteers carry out campaigns to capture the kiwis living in forests that are about to "get the chop" and move them to safer areas. However, catch-

The Little Spotted Kiwi is presently classified as Vulnerable. It has been exterminated from much, if not all, of its original range, and nowadays there is only one remaining viable population, on Kapiti Island off the south-west coast of North Island. The species has been successfully introduced to other islands, but its future continues to hang in the balance.

[*Apteryx owenii*. Photo: Eric & David Hosking]

ing the birds is no easy task, and it is quite impossible to cover the immense areas involved.

The Little Spotted Kiwi was formerly widely distributed over North and South Islands. It disappeared from the former for unknown reasons, even before the arrival of the European settlers about 150 years ago, whereas its extinction in the north and west of South Island coincided with the introduction of predatory mammals, especially the stoat. At present, it is considered Vulnerable, because there is only one remaining good population, which occurs on Kapiti Island, a nature reserve of 2000 ha. Its breeding success here is very low, with each pair producing only 0·08 chicks per year on average, and there is heavy predation by Wekas. In recent years, some birds from Kapiti Island have been transferred to other islands, in order to try to establish new populations that will assure the survival of the species. The status of the Great Spotted Kiwi, with only three isolated populations in South Island, is poorly known.

Fortunately, a good deal of action has been taken in recent years, involving captive breeding programmes, the protection of kiwi habitat and the establishment of new populations in reserves created specially for this purpose. In Northland, North Island, for example, several conservation organizations have banded together to buy an area of bushland that was going to be cleared, in order to create a special reserve for kiwis, the Tangiteroria Kiwi Reserve.

Keeping and breeding kiwis in captivity is not easy, indeed only the North Island subspecies of the Brown Kiwi is found in zoos in other parts of the world. The other two subspecies of the Brown Kiwi, and also the Little and Great Spotted Kiwis, are only kept in some zoos in New Zealand. The latter two species were recently bred in captivity for the first time in the Otorohanga Kiwi House and Nature Bird Park, a centre specialized in keeping and breeding kiwis, and in the National Wildlife Centre of New Zealand.

General Bibliography
de Beer (1956), Benham (1906), Bock (1963), van Bocxstaele (1983), Body & Reid (1987), de Boer (1980), Bull *et al.* (1985), Calder (1978, 1979), Calder & Dawson (1978), Calder & Rowe (1977), Colbourne (1981), Cracraft (1974), Davies (1976), Elzanowski (1988), Feduccia (1985), Folwell (1988), Francis (1982), Fuller (1987, 1991), Handford & Mares (1985), Horwell (1990), Houde (1986), Kinsky (1971), Kleinpaste & Colbourne (1983), McCann (1973), McGowan (1982, 1985), Morris & Smith (1988), Parkes & Clark (1966), Prager *et al.* (1976), Reid (1971a, 1971b, 1985), Reid & Rowe (1978), Reid & Williams (1975), Rich & Balouet (1984), Rowe (1985), Sibley & Ahlquist (1981), Sibley & Frelin (1972), Tyler & Simkiss (1959), Verheyen (1960a), Wenzel (1968), Williams, G.R. (1985), Williams & Given (1981).

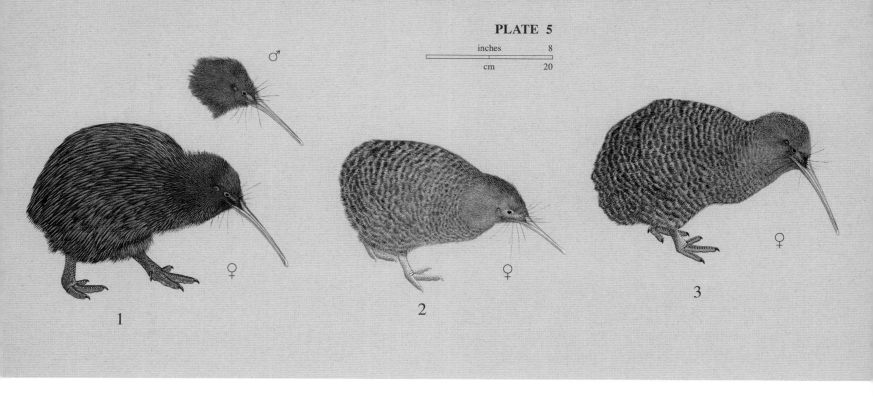

PLATE 5

inches 8
cm 20

Family APTERYGIDAE (KIWIS)
SPECIES ACCOUNTS

PLATE 5

Genus *APTERYX*   Shaw, 1813

1. **Brown Kiwi**

Apteryx australis

French: Kiwi austral   **German:** Streifenkiwi   **Spanish:** Kiwi Común
Other common names: Common Kiwi

Taxonomy. *Apteryx australis* Shaw, 1813, New Zealand.
Three subspecies recognized.
Subspecies and Distribution.
A. a. mantelli Bartlett, 1852 - North I.
A. a. australis Shaw, 1813 - South I.
A. a. lawryi Rothschild, 1893 - Stewart I.
Introduced (*mantelli*) to several small islands off North I.

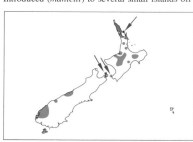

Descriptive notes. 50-65 cm; male 1440-3060 g, bill 110-155 mm; female 2060-3850 g, bill 130-205 mm. Plumage appears hair-like. Females larger and longer-billed. Juvenile similar to adult, but smaller. Race *mantelli* more heavily streaked, *lawryi* longer-billed.
Habitat. Subtropical to temperate forests and shrublands, especially wet forests of podocarps and hardwoods; also found nowadays in plantations, scrub and farmland.
Food and Feeding. Mostly invertebrates from soil and also leaf litter, especially insects (e.g. bugs and beetle larvae), spiders and earthworms; a small proportion of fruit, seeds and leaves. Searches ground and detects prey mainly by smell; bill then inserted using back and forth levering motion of head and neck (see page 106).
Breeding. Laying Jun-Feb, mainly Aug-Sept. Monogamous and solitary. Nests in burrows and natural cavities. 1-3 eggs, 115-137 x 70-83 mm, average 430 g, c. 14-20% of female's prelaying weight. Incubation by male 75-84 days; chicks hatch with similar, but softer version of adult plumage; leave nest nightly to feed alone after 5-6 days; independent at 14-20 days; fully-grown at 18-20 months. Sexual maturity at 14 months in males, 2 years in females. Success 0·5 chicks per pair per year to independence.
Movements. Sedentary. Ringing results show that some juveniles take territory nearby, within 2-5 km.
Status and Conservation. Not globally threatened. Range has shrunk, with extermination from E coast of South I and from S and SE of North I. Decline dates to period of European colonization, probably due to use of poison and traps for possums (*Trichosurus vulpecula*) and introduction of mammalian predators, e.g. cats, dogs, mustelids, feral pigs. Successfully reintroduced to Little Barrier I, and introduced to Kapiti I and D'Urville I; also introduced to Hen I in 1988, and planned for Tiri Tiri I, with intention of building up stable breeding populations. Race *mantelli* disappeared from much of North I due to destruction of native woodland; but largest counted population of this race 800-1000 birds in commercial plantation at Waitangi; has been bred in several zoos worldwide. Only one individual of race *lawryi*, and none of nominate, known to be held in captivity at present.
Bibliography. Bell (1984), Calder *et al.* (1978), Colbourne (1982), Colbourne & Kleinpaste (1983, 1984, 1986), Colbourne & Powlesland (1988), Corbett *et al.* (1979), Drey (1983), Falla *et al.* (1981), Goudswaard (1985, 1989), Klos & Reinhard (1990), MacMillan (1990), Marchant & Higgins (1990), McLennan (1988), McLennan *et al.* (1987), Potter (1989, 1990), Rasch & Kayes (1985), Reid (1977, 1981), Reid *et al.* (1982), Rowe (1974, 1978), Rutgers & Norris (1970), Silyn-Roberts (1983), Soper (1976), Sturmer & Grant (1988), Taborsky (1988), Taborsky & Taborsky (1991, 1992), Taranaki & Winter (1987), Watt (1971).

2. **Little Spotted Kiwi**

Apteryx owenii

French: Kiwi d'Owen   **German:** Zwergkiwi   **Spanish:** Kiwi Moteado Menor
Other common names: Little Grey Kiwi

Taxonomy. *Apteryx Owenii* Gould, 1847, New Zealand.
Monotypic.
Distribution. South I, W of main divide (probably extinct); Kapiti I, off SW coast of North I (possibly introduced). Introduced to three other islands.

Descriptive notes. 35-45 cm; male 880-1356 g, bill 63-72 mm; female 1000-1950 g, bill 75-94 mm. Greyish buff with slight yellowish tone and irregular bands of earthy brown or brownish black; bill appears straighter than in *A. haastii*; legs pale, claws whitish. Females larger and longer-billed. Juvenile similar to adult, but smaller.
Habitat. Evergreen or deciduous forest with dense undergrowth; also margins of forest-scrub and grassland. In temperate regions, from sea-level up to at least 1000 m, mainly in hills, though probably occurred formerly in plains and mountains.
Food and Feeding. Mostly invertebrates (generally of 5-40 mm), especially earthworms (Terricolae) and spiders, found in soil and litter; also fruit and fern sporangia. Searches for food in soil and natural hollows, e.g. rotten logs; prey probably detected mainly by smell.
Breeding. Laying mainly Sept-Oct, also Nov-Dec, and even Jan-Apr. Monogamous and solitary. Nests in burrows and natural cavities. 1-2 eggs, 105-113 x 68-76 cm, average 301 g, c. 25% of female's body weight. Incubation by male 63-76 days; chicks hatch with similar, but softer version of adult plumage; stay in burrow for 2-3 weeks. Sexual maturity probably at 2 years. Breeding success on Kapiti I, 0·08 chicks per pair per year reached independence, although sample small.
Movements. Sedentary.
Status and Conservation. VULNERABLE. Kapiti I, where possibly introduced this century, holds last remaining viable population, estimated at 1000 birds; low rate of breeding success, possibly due to its own population pressure and also predation by Wekas (*Gallirallus australis*); high fire risk in summer. Exterminated from North I, and probably also from South I, with last record in 1938; possibly also from D'Urville I, where only 4 birds seen in last 10 years, and these removed from island, due to serious threat of predation. Main causes of extinction from natural range include hunting, first by Maoris and later by European colonizers, burning of habitat, conversion of habitat for agriculture and pasture land, and introduced mammalian predators. Successfully introduced to Long I and Red Mercury I; also introduced to Hen I in 1988 and 1989, outcome not yet known. Successfully bred in New Zealand zoos in 1970 and 1989.
Bibliography. Atkinson & Daniel (1985), Bell (1986), Collar & Andrew (1988), Falla *et al.* (1981), Jolly (1983, 1985, 1989), Marchant & Higgins (1991), Reid (1978), Scarlett (1962a, 1962b), Sibson (1982), Williams & Given (1981).

3. **Great Spotted Kiwi**

Apteryx haastii

French: Kiwi roa   **German:** Haastkiwi   **Spanish:** Kiwi Moteado Mayor
Other common names: Great Grey Kiwi

Taxonomy. *Apteryx Haastii* Potts, 1872, Westland.
Monotypic.

Distribution. South I, mainly W of main divide.
Introduced to Little Barrier I.

Descriptive notes. 50-60 cm; male 1215-2610 g, bill 90-100 mm; female 1530-3270 g, bill 125-135 mm. Chestnut tinge to back; legs can be darker, and claws whitish. Greyer than *A. owenii*, with more regular pattern and larger black spots; thinner pale bands give overall appearance of darker plumage. Females larger and longer-billed. Juvenile similar to adult, but smaller.

Habitat. Variety of habitats, including tussock grassland, damp, mossy beech forests, dry, alluvial podocarp and hardwood forest, and scrub-covered coastal pasture. From sea-level up to 1200 m, mainly alpine and subalpine at 700-1100 m.

Food and Feeding. Mostly invertebrates, especially beetle larvae and earthworms, and in summer large crickets and spiders; freshwater crayfish taken, when they leave flooded streams. Searches for food by probing in soil and natural hollows; bill also used to pierce snail shells; access to higher levels may be gained by walking along trees leaning out from hillsides.

Breeding. Laying Jul-Nov (replacements Nov-Jan). Nests in natural hollows or short burrows. 1 egg, occasionally 2; 120-130 x 69-85 cm. Unlike other species, incubation by both sexes, period unknown; chicks hatch with similar, but softer version of adult plumage; age of independence unknown. Success 1 chick fledged from 11 eggs laid.

Movements. Sedentary.

Status and Conservation. Not globally threatened. Total numbers estimated at c. 8000 birds in 2 or 3 isolated populations, but little known. Decline dates to period of European colonization, probably due to use of poison and traps for possums (*Trichosurus vulpecula*) and introduction of mammalian predators, e.g. cats, dogs, mustelids, feral pigs. First captive breeding recently at National Wildlife Centre, New Zealand.

Bibliography. Eason (1988), Falla *et al.* (1981), Marchant & Higgins (1990), McLennan & McCann (1989), Potts (1871), Reid & Williams (1975).

Order TINAMIFORMES

Tinamiformes

|

Tinamidae

tinamous

Class AVES
Order TINAMIFORMES
Family TINAMIDAE (TINAMOUS)

- Small to medium-sized, plump terrestrial birds with short, strong legs and rudimentary tail.
- 15-50 cm.

- Neotropical Region.
- Forests or savanna/steppe, from sea-level up to 5300 m.
- 9 genera, 47 species, 149 taxa.
- 8 species threatened; none definitely extinct since 1600.

Systematics

The tinamous are endemic to the Neotropical Region and are among the oldest families in the New World. The earliest fossil evidence of the family to date comes from the Miocene in Patagonia, and is some 10 million years old. Caves in Brazil have also yielded fossil tinamous, which belong to the Upper Pleistocene, about 20,000 years ago.

The origin and the taxonomic affinities of the family have been a matter of debate for over a century and the discussion still continues at present. One of the most widely accepted theories is that the tinamous come from the same stock as the ratites (Struthioniformes), a group which subsequently spread to most of the southern landmasses (see page 76), and is still represented in South America by the rheas.

The tinamous were amongst the earliest of these birds and current thinking suggests that they probably became a distinct family before the ratites started to diversify. This argument is based on the fact that the tinamous retain both a keel on the sternum and fully developed wings, along with the ability of flight. The ratites have lost both of these features, as an adaptation to their specialized terrestrial lifestyle, and this indicates that their diversification came after they had already become separated from the tinamous; indeed, there are those who reckon that the ratites, far from being primitive, are actually quite an advanced group.

The two groups are closely related, as has become abundantly clear from studies of a whole series of diverse aspects: bone shape and structure, especially of the palate; musculature; calcite orientation in eggshells; ontogeny; karyotype (the structure is quite different in all other birds); DNA-DNA hybridizations; thermoregulatory and metabolic physiology, and so on. Comparisons on all of these points stress the phylogenetic proximity of the two groups and their remoteness from all other birds. Some taxonomists have even grouped tinamous and ratites in the same order, while their separation from all other birds in a private superorder Palaeognathae has received a good deal of support.

Neither fossil ancestors of the Palaeognathae, nor intermediate forms, which link them to the rest of Aves, have been found. The Palaeognathae, especially the tinamous, are normally supposed to be among the most primitive of birds, as they conserve certain reptilian features, such as their blood proteins and the shape of the palate, which are similar to those found in the dinosaur *Tyrannosaurus*.

The Tinamidae are usually divided into two subfamilies: the Tinaminae, with 29 species in the genera *Tinamus*, *Nothocercus* and *Crypturellus*; and the Rhynchotinae, with 18 species in the genera *Rhynchotus*, *Nothoprocta*, *Nothura*, *Taoniscus*, *Eudromia* and *Tinamotis*. The Tinaminae are found on the floors of tropical and subtropical forests and are characterized by having the nostrils half-way or more down the bill. The Rhynchotinae are sometimes known as "Steppe Tinamous" and have the nostrils at the base of the bill; this is probably connected with their habit of using the bill for digging.

The large genus *Crypturellus* is presently considered to comprise about 21 species, but the extreme interspecific similarity, combined with wide intraspecific diversity, has caused a lot of disagreement as to the number of species accepted. The complexity of the genus is well illustrated by the fact that several subspecies are variously assigned to different species. Future work using DNA-DNA hybridization and egg-white proteins to establish relationships is likely to cause a further upheaval within this difficult genus.

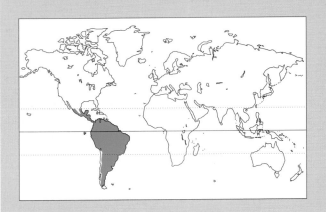

TINAMIDAE

TINAMINAE

RHYNCHOTINAE

forest tinamous
29 species
(Tinamus, Nothocercus, Crypturellus)

steppe tinamous
18 species
(Rhynchotus, Nothoprocta, Nothura, Taoniscus, Eudromia, Tinamotis)

FAMILY   SUBFAMILY

Subdivision of the Tinamidae.

[Figure: Lluís Sanz & Francesc Jutglar]

This White-bellied Nothura exhibits the most characteristic features of the tinamous: the compact form, slender neck, rather short, slightly decurved bill and the very short tail. The obvious similarity to gallinaceous birds is merely superficial, a result of convergent evolution. The tinamous' nearest relatives are actually the ratites, and some taxonomists place them in the same order.

[*Nothura boraquira*, Brazil. Photo: J. Dunning/Vireo]

Morphological Aspects

The external appearance of tinamous is reminiscent of the Old World partridges and this probably led the Conquistadores and early colonizers to name the tinamou "perdiz", which is Spanish for partridge, most typically the Red-legged Partridge (*Alectoris rufa*). The apparently similar habits, particularly of the more visible steppe tinamous, would have helped to promote this idea, but the similarities are nowadays considered by most authorities to be entirely superficial, reflecting convergent evolution.

There is a fair size range within the tinamous. The smallest is the Dwarf Tinamou (*Taoniscus nanus*) which, at 14·5 cm and 43 g, is about the size of a week-old domestic hen chick, whereas the Grey Tinamou (*Tinamus tao*) at 49 cm, and the Solitary Tinamou (*Tinamus solitarius*), at 1800 g, are equivalent to a medium-sized cockerel or a pheasant.

As befits smallish ground-dwelling birds, tinamous have a very compact build. The neck appears long and thin, because it is covered in very short feathers. The head is small and elongated and the slightly decurved bill is narrow and normally short, though in a few species it is quite long. Some species have a crest, which may be raised when the bird is alarmed, and this is most highly developed in the crested tinamous (*Eudromia*), which tend to direct the crest forwards when excited.

The tail is very short or rudimentary, with weak feathers which appear rather shaggy. When present, it is normally hidden under the uppertail-coverts and it is often difficult to distinguish from these. All this, in conjunction with the mass of feathers on the rump, help to give the bird its characteristic round look. The great accumulation of feathers on the back and the rump may have developed as an anti-predator mechanism: members of both Columbiformes and Galliformes in the Neotropics can drop their back and rump feathers with great ease, so that an attacking mammal or bird sometimes

ends up with a clawful of feathers, instead of catching hold of the bird itself.

The legs and feet are stout, as are the three front toes, whereas the hind toe is either raised well up the tarsus or absent. Tinamous spend virtually all of their time on the ground, for instance walking around their feeding grounds or searching for mates, and are thus among the most terrestrial of all flying birds. They walk along silently and meticulously, often pausing to examine something on the ground, when all the weight may be rested on one foot, and preferring always to skirt round any form of obstacle. They are good runners and, when alarmed, prefer to walk or run away, rather than fly (see General Habits). In several species with confusingly similar plumage, tarsus colour can be used for identification.

The rounded wings are small for the bird's size and so flight, though fast, is heavy and can not be kept up for long. A bird takes off, rising sharply with powerful wing-beats, and once it has gained height, it slips sideways, gliding along with its wings hanging down and only beating sporadically; from time to time it swerves or veers slightly. Before landing, it rises slightly and then brakes with powerful wing-beats, before landing in an upright posture, putting its feet down and stretching its neck upwards. As the tail is relatively inefficient for braking, some species, such as the Brushland Tinamou (*Nothoprocta cinerascens*), perform a sharp turn, almost at right-angles, just before landing, while another aid is to run along on landing and reduce speed less abruptly.

Another important function of a bird's tail is to act as a rudder, and again flying tinamous suffer from rather poor steering. Sometimes they lose control at take-off and fly into obstacles, which can have fatal consequences; birds have been known to perish after flying into branches, posts, wires and even houses. Many species, when frightened into flight, emit a harsh cry, which is reminiscent of that of partridges in similar situations. Birds normally fly only a short distance, rarely going more than 500 m before landing again. Steppe tinamous tend to glide with intermittent flaps, again in a manner recalling partridges.

Tinamous have poor circulation, because their blood vessels are very narrow; this gives their flesh a translucent, greenish white tone, but also, more significantly, precludes flight over a sustained period. The problem is aggravated by the fact that the lungs and heart are small; indeed, relatively speaking, no other birds have such a small heart, and, while a domestic cockerel's accounts for up to 12% of its total body weight, in tinamous the proportion is only 1·6-3·1%. This readily explains why fleeing tinamous quickly become exhausted, despite their considerable musculature. The latter makes up about 32% of their body weight, a proportion similar to that of those most tireless of birds, the hummingbirds (Trochilidae), though this ratio is certainly favoured by the fact that tinamous have a highly pneumatic skeleton.

Plumage is rather unspectacular, and tends to be striped, barred or mottled dark, thus helping the bird to blend into its surroundings. The predominant colours are dark brown, rufous, buff, yellow, grey and the like. Forest dwelling species tend to be darker and more uniform, while those of open areas, where there are few or no trees, tend to be paler grey, ochraceous or straw-coloured, normally speckled, barred or streaked dark, especially on the upperparts.

Some members of the genus *Crypturellus* are sexually dimorphic, the females being more heavily barred and brighter than males. Otherwise sexes are alike, except that females tend to be larger than males. There are also minor differences in size and plumage between different populations.

The microscopic structure of tinamou feathers differs from that of all other birds. The barbules are joined together solidly, rather than being hooked on, and this is particularly evident on the flight-feathers, with the result that they produce a whistling noise, when the bird flies. Little is known about moult in this family, but in *Eudromia* the chick quickly grows its primaries and these are mostly changed in the first complete moult, which starts when the bird is still only about six weeks old. This strategy is most celebrated in the Galliformes and in the buttonquails (Turnicidae).

Powder-downs, which the ratites lack, are extremely well-developed in the tinamous. These are feathers which grow continuously and disintegrate at the tip, producing a fine powder which the bird spreads all over its feathers, and this helps in waterproofing, as well as making the plumage more glossy. While most birds have powder-downs, they are only highly developed in the herons (Ardeidae), mesites (Mesitornithidae), wood swallows (Artamidae), parrots (Psittaciformes) and tinamous.

Males have a penis, which is not unlike that of the ratites or the ducks. In *Tinamotis* it is corkscrew-shaped, and is similar to the hemipenis of certain reptiles (*Squamata*), without the latter's characteristic fork. Females have a small phallic organ in the cloaca, and the difference between the two facilitates the determination of sex, when handling birds, especially during the breeding season, when these organs are enlarged.

Habitat

The tinamous are an exclusively Neotropical family and they reach their greatest diversity in tropical South America, especially in the Amazon Basin. The family just reaches the Tropic of Cancer in north-west Mexico and extends thence to southernmost parts of South America, although it has few representatives at these extremes.

Tinamous occupy a wide range of habitats, having conquered most of those available in South America. The exceptions are aquatic habitats, areas of permanent snow, deserts and the southernmost tip of the continent. They can be found in all forms of primary and secondary lowland forest in the tropics and subtropics, as well as in cloud forest on the slopes of the Andes. Elsewhere they occur in areas of bushes or scrub, xerophytic woodland, open prairies, dry and seasonally flooded grassland, arid and semi-arid steppe, *puna* and high-altitude Andean desert. They range from sea-level up to over 5000 m, where the Puna Tinamou (*Tinamotis pentlandii*) can be found. The greatest species diversity can be found in the lowlands or at moderate elevations in the tropics.

In northern parts of their range, they tend to be birds of forest and woodland, whereas further south most species live

The Tinamidae are usually divided into two subfamilies and one of the most obvious differences between the two is in the habitats they occupy. In the case of the Tinaminae, the typical habitat consists of the floor of more or less dense forests. This photo of a Great Tinamou also shows one of the most representative morphological features of the "Forest Tinamous": the nostrils are connected in the middle of the bill, or closer to the tip.

[*Tinamus major*, Mexico. Photo: A. de Sostoa & X. Ferrer]

in open habitats, with at most scrub or open woodland. *Tinamus* and *Crypturellus* are generally tropical forest dwellers, with *Nothocercus* occupying the higher altitude forests of the subtropical and temperate zones. The steppe tinamous are normally found in grassland, scrub or open woodland, but, while *Tinamotis* and *Nothoprocta* are typically found above the tree-line, the other genera generally have a wider altitudinal range.

The tinamous are the ground-dwellers *par excellence* in South America, with the widest distribution, the greatest diversity of species and the most complete adaptation to habitat types. The rheas (Rheidae) are only found in open habitats of the centre and south of the continent; the curassows and guans (Cracidae), a rather more arboreal family, are generally restricted to tropical lowland forests; lastly, the family Phasianidae, which has occupied this level so successfully in the rest of the world, is poorly represented with only thirteen species in scattered areas of northern South America. The tinamous have clearly managed to adapt themselves better to the wide variety of habitats, which is, in itself, rather surprising, given that these other families have all evolved much more recently.

This is even more remarkable, considering that they stick strictly to the ground in performing virtually all the functions of their life cycle. As they do not exploit higher levels within the vegetation gradient, the possibilities for the ecological segregation of species is markedly reduced. For this reason the tinamous have evolved mechanisms to avoid competition for space or food between congeners, which are always liable to be each other's strongest competitors, due to their similar morphology and habits. One such mechanism is a difference in size between sympatric species, which leads to different food preferences. Another is extremely precise habitat selection, which permits species to inhabit different sectors of the same habitat, occupying different plant communities, where the variations are scarcely perceptible, but are enough to prevent interference.

A species' restriction to a certain habitat type can be crucial to its survival, particularly if such habitat is not extensive and is subject to alterations by man; this is the chief problem facing threatened species (see Status and Conservation).

However, most species of tinamou are widespread and several are adapted to living in diverse habitats. The Red-winged Tinamou (*Rhynchotus rufescens*) is found in open savannas in Amazonia, but also in dry Andean valleys with thorn bushes and scattered trees. Similarly, the Brown Tinamou (*Crypturellus obsoletus*) lives in the Amazon Basin, as well as in humid montane forest on the slopes of the Andes.

Panama provides a good example of ecological separation within the tinamous: the Highland Tinamou (*Nothocercus bonapartei*) occurs in highlands throughout the country; the Great Tinamou (*Tinamus major*) prefers rain forest on the slopes; the Choco Tinamou (*Crypturellus kerriae*) uses similar habitat, but is restricted to the south-east of the country; and, finally, the Little Tinamou (*Crypturellus soui*) can be found in fairly dense secondary forest and thickets, above 1000 m on both the Pacific and Atlantic slopes. Although each species has its own preference, there is sometimes a certain amount of overlap, with two species occupying the same habitat. The Great and Little Tinamous are often found in the same zones, but the size difference means that they exploit different resources.

A similar size difference helps to separate the Red-winged Tinamou and the Spotted Nothura (*Nothura maculosa*), which share the same tropical savanna in Brazil; the former favours pastures with long grass, while the latter prefers it short.

Another interesting case of segregation, based on habitat and altitude in addition to size, can be seen in the Andean species of Bolivia. Darwin's Nothura (*Nothura darwinii*), a small species, is found in fields and pastures of temperate valleys at 2000 m, represented by the race *boliviana*. It co-exists with the larger Red-winged Tinamou, which prefers open ground with tall thornbush scrub, and with the Andean Tinamou (*Nothoprocta pentlandii*), which likes denser vegetation along streams. This last species extends up the steep slopes of the Andes through *Polylepis* woodland as far as the *puna*. Another race of Darwin's Nothura (*N. d. agassizii*) occurs at this level, where it affects open ground with bunch-grass, but another inhabitant of the *puna*, the Ornate Tinamou (*Nothoprocta ornata*) is less keen on grassland here, occupying instead rocky slopes and terraces of tola (*Lepidophyllum*) heath. The Puna Tinamou occurs higher than all the rest and lives mostly in tola heath just below the permanent snow-line, up to 5300 m, and also in desert areas of the southern *altiplano*.

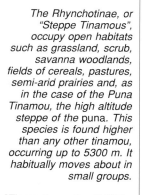

The Rhynchotinae, or "Steppe Tinamous", occupy open habitats such as grassland, scrub, savanna woodlands, fields of cereals, pastures, semi-arid prairies and, as in the case of the Puna Tinamou, the high altitude steppe of the puna. This species is found higher than any other tinamou, occurring up to 5300 m. It habitually moves about in small groups.

[*Tinamotis pentlandii*, Chile. Photo: A. de Sostoa & X. Ferrer]

The most obvious morphological feature separating the members of the subfamily Rhynchotinae from those of the Tinaminae is that they have the nostrils connected at the base of the bill, as can clearly be seen in this Andean Tinamou. This has normally been interpreted as an adaptation connected with using the bill to dig for food, and certainly such digging is much more frequent in these inhabitants of open spaces than in their forest relatives.

[*Nothoprocta pentlandii*. Photo: Kenneth W. Fink/ Ardea]

General Habits

Tinamous are generally shy and elusive and, when danger is imminent, they tend to stand stock still, in an attempt to pass unnoticed. An approaching human normally becomes aware of the presence of a tinamou by hearing either its far-carrying call, or an explosion of sound at his feet, as it flies off without even having been sighted, often with a harsh cry; it is thought that the sudden loud noise may cause momentary shock and hesitation to a potential predator.

When alerted to danger, a tinamou immediately freezes, either crouched down or with its neck stretched up in the air. If the source of danger approaches, a bird tries to avoid having to resort to flight, by walking stealthily away or running off, as tinamous are not particularly good fliers (see Morphological Aspects). In this way it may get out of the danger zone or find a suitable hiding place, for example under a bush or in dense grass. When chased over open ground, some species have been seen to take refuge underground, in burrows or holes made by other animals. Their skill in going unnoticed is such that, in forest areas where large birds such as guans have been hunted out, tinamous, for example the Grey Tinamou, very often survive. The furtive behaviour of an alarmed tinamou stands out in stark contrast with the normal reaction to danger of the much larger guans; they tend to flutter up trees, squawking noisily, and then stay still, offering an easy target to a hunter.

Tinamous frequently bathe in water and some species dust-bathe at regular sites; sometimes a bird's plumage gets so thickly impregnated with dust that it takes on the colour of the local soil. Some species are also known to sunbathe, resting on one leg and opening a wing.

In captivity, adult Solitary Tinamous normally defecate only once a day, and the act, though rapid, appears to require a fair effort, probably because the bird must be careful to move aside the dense plumage around its vent, to avoid its getting soiled.

The larger of the forest species, at least in the genus *Tinamus*, roost in trees, normally on fairly horizontal branches 2-5 m off the ground. The bird reaches the branch with a very laboured, noisy, vertical flight, and so tends first to look for some sort of opening where no branches will impede its path, and whence it can escape easily, if necessary. In areas of uneven ground, a downslope is preferred, as it means the bird can reach its perch with horizontal, and consequently fairly noiseless, flight, while a quick getaway down the slope is also available. It usually chooses a thickish branch, where it can rest comfortably on its folded legs, since it does not hold onto the branch; for this reason the back of the tarsus is rough in *Tinamus*, giving better grip, as opposed to other genera, where it is smooth. Birds regularly use the same roost and do not normally defecate here, to avoid giving away their whereabouts. Some hunters, specialized in taking Solitary Tinamous at their roosts, maintain that when a new bird takes over the vacant territory it very often adopts the same roost-site as the previous owner. Apparently tinamous become very wary as darkness approaches, and they have even been known to jump up onto their perches during an eclipse.

Like the smaller forest species, those of open areas roost on the ground, normally in the shelter of a bush. Both Elegant Crested (*Eudromia elegans*) and Ornate Tinamous appear to stick to the same roost-site on a regular basis, to judge from the abundant droppings which can be found beside scrapes made under plants.

Some species are strictly solitary, while others may gather in large groups, though the degree of gregariousness may vary at different times of year. The solitary species tend to be those of the forest, and in some cases the sexes only come together for displays, copulation and egg-laying; in others, the pair may stay together all year round. Some species, especially those of grassland and pastures, mostly go around in groups, and they tend to be more numerous than solitary species. Sometimes these groups are poorly structured and there is little interaction between individuals, apart from a short, sharp contact call. Group size in the Elegant Crested Tinamou varies with the time of year, reaching its maximum in winter, when as many as 50 or even 100 birds may be found together.

In many species, such as the Slaty-breasted Tinamou (*Crypturellus boucardi*), there is little movement around the middle of the day, when birds tend to doze or feed in a small area, and after dark all activity ceases. The Ornate Tinamou often climbs on boulders to sun itself, call and preen, while most of its time is spent wandering around, feeding or perhaps preening on the ground.

Voice

The calls of tinamous are among the most characteristic sounds of Central and South American tropical forests. They are clear and pure with a sweet tone, despite their simplicity. In some species they resemble the sound of an organ, whereas in others they sound like a flute, or like sad whistles. Some calls are uniform and monotone, while others are more varied, sometimes consisting of more than one phrase, and these may vary in intensity. A flushed tinamou often lets out a harsh trill, which is rather less appealing than the normal territorial call.

A male Highland Tinamou's call can be heard from several kilometres away, through the dense undergrowth of its montane forest habitat, though this is exceptional. Forest species tend to have a deep, loud call, which is designed to penetrate as far as possible through the forest environment, where a multitude of obstacles impede the progress of sound-waves. Plains-dwellers tend to have delicate, high-pitched calls, which are less melodious than those of the forest species, and sometimes resemble the rattle of crickets or grasshoppers. It is often very difficult to locate a calling bird, which may appear to be further away than it actually is.

The different calls are usually the easiest way to identify species in the field, and it is also the main means of intraspecific recognition. Each species has several kinds of call, which are generally composed of slightly different notes, and in the Solitary Tinamou as many as eleven distinct vocalizations have been detected, most of which are connected with territory, pairing or contact between parent and chicks. In most species both sexes call and in some species they can be distinguished by having different phrases, intensity or tone; females generally have a deeper call-note than males. In some species, especially members of *Crypturellus*, there is regional variation. Male Slaty-breasted Tinamous have sufficiently different calls for individuals to be recognized by the human ear, and during breeding neighbours quickly learn each others' calls (see Breeding).

Birds call more often during the breeding season, but while some tend to call more in the early morning and evening, others are vocally more active during the heat of the day, and calls can really be heard at any time of day or night. The frequency and insistence of calling is very variable between individuals and from day to day, and one male Brushland Tinamou called incessantly every few minutes from dawn to dusk, with some 500 calls being the maximum in a day. Regular calling sites may be used, at any rate by the genus *Crypturellus*.

Some species of open areas, which normally go around in more or less organized groups, continually emit a low peeping

The resonant calls of the "Forest Tinamous" are among the most distinctive sounds to be heard in tropical and subtropical America. They may be repeated every few minutes and calling is often kept up incessantly for hours on end. The most characteristic call of the Tataupa Tinamou, a species mainly of the forest edge, consists of a quick series of ringing trills with a downward trend which accelerates towards the end.

[*Crypturellus tataupa tataupa*, Paraguay. Photo: J. Dunning/Vireo]

One of the most common feeding methods of the tinamous consists simply of picking up seeds or small fruits off the ground. When searching for food, many rumage among fallen leaves with the bill, but unlike the gallinaceous birds they do not use their feet to scrape in the ground. The Elegant Crested Tinamou is an omnivorous species with a diet that includes seeds, fruits, buds, leaves and also many insects.

[*Eudromia elegans*, Argentina. Photo: Jeff Foott/ Bruce Coleman]

contact call, which maintains contact between individuals of the group, as well as notifying neighbouring groups that the territory is occupied. This type of communication is frequent among certain gallinaceous birds, such as *Odontophorus* and *Colinus*.

Food and Feeding

The tinamous' conquest of virtually all Neotropical habitat types (see Habitat) may be largely due to their feeding habits. Their diet is very variable and they are basically opportunists.

However, it must be realized that there have only been detailed studies of feeding in very few species, while information on other species has come from limited field observations and the stomach contents of a few birds. The little that is known to date indicates that almost all species have a mixed diet, which includes plant matter and small animals, particularly invertebrates. Nonetheless, some species have been found to be more herbivorous, while others are more carnivorous, and some eat more fruit than seeds and vice versa. The Red-winged Tinamou has been found to take mostly animal food in summer, when this is most abundant, but it switches to plant matter in winter, and this can lead to extensive crop damage (see Relationship with Man). Chicks tend to be more dependent on insects than adults, presumably due to the higher nutritional value that they offer the fast-growing bird.

The most typical constituents of their diets include the following plant matter: fruit, either fallen or plucked off the plant; seeds; green shoots; tender leaves; buds; flowers; tender stems; roots and tubers. Animals most commonly taken include: insects, such as ants, termites, beetles, grasshoppers, hemiptera, butterfly and moth larvae, etc.; small gastropods; worms; and small vertebrates, including amphibians, reptiles and, in the case of some of the larger species, small mammals.

Tinamous can be divided more or less into three groups, according to the vegetarian part of their diets. The genera *Tinamus*, *Nothocercus* and *Crypturellus*, which are all forest tinamous, eat a large proportion of fleshy fruits. Members of the genera *Nothura*, *Nothoprocta* and *Eudromia*, which are characteristically birds of meadows, pastures, high altitude grassland and arid or semi-arid scrub, take a greater proportion of seeds. Lastly, the high altitude species, such as the Puna Tinamou, or the Patagonian Tinamou (*Tinamotis ingoufi*), which occupy cold, bleak, inhospitable areas of open grassland, where primary production is low, have to eat more of the vegetative parts of the plants, such as leaves, shoots, buds, flowers and tender stems.

Food is normally taken off the ground itself or off plants that are within the tinamou's reach at ground level, although birds occasionally jump up one metre or so into the air to reach a fruit or an insect. Foraging normally involves walking about, pecking at the ground every few paces and looking up from time to time, just to keep an eye open for potential danger; the Ornate Tinamou regularly peeks out thus, from behind a clump of grass.

When dealing with large items, such as some fruits or tubers, the bird pecks at them on the ground, until they are broken up into smaller pieces for consumption. Seeds in pods or with wing-like appendages, which are too big to swallow whole, receive the same treatment. Most species frequently swallow pebbles, which help to grind down tough food in the gizzard.

When searching for roots or tubers, tinamous dig with their bills and sweep the soil away to the sides, but they do not use their feet, in the way many gallinaceous birds do. Digging is most frequent in the genera *Rhynchotus*, *Nothura* and *Nothoprocta*, which are birds of open country; the positioning of the nostrils at the base of the bill in these species is possibly an adaptation to this activity. The Red-winged Tinamou, with its stout, slightly decurved bill is very well equipped for digging, and consequently takes more tubers and underground animals than the altogether smaller, weaker Spotted Nothura.

Small insects are swallowed whole, while larger ones are pecked and killed first. Forest tinamous tend to rummage in the leaf litter with their bills, lifting leaves or twigs and turning them over, in the hope of finding insects or other invertebrates lurking underneath. They also tend to scratch around in damp ground to find worms or small molluscs. Forest species sometimes exploit the insects disturbed by army ants, and on such occasions they are usually found in the company of antbirds (Formicariidae) and furnariids. The Spotted Nothura, a species typically of pastures, often follows livestock, taking any grasshoppers, crickets or other insects that are disturbed by the beasts, as they amble along. It may also take ticks, when they fall off their hosts, bloated with blood.

Some species regularly drink water and so require a permanent source within their home range. The Solitary Tinamou normally drinks, but in some areas it has to undergo a lengthy dry season, to which its answer is to obtain water from succulent plants; species of arid or semi-arid areas seldom or never drink.

Breeding

Although there is a certain amount of variation between species and sometimes even within the same species, the general rule among tinamous is simultaneous polygyny for males and sequential polyandry for females. This kind of breeding strategy is considered to be among the most efficient, with polyandry leading to the most rapid proliferations, and certainly this idea is borne out by the abundance of tinamous in virgin habitat, where they do not suffer human persecution.

Like the rheas, but unlike most other birds, it is the male that carries out the tasks of incubation and subsequent chick-care, without any help from a female. So far few species have been studied, but it seems that normally males are polygynous, fertilizing several females, while females are polyandrous, that is fertilized by several males. However, some species, for instance the Ornate Tinamou, form stable pairs, and others, such as the Spotted Nothura are monogamous at first, but polygamous when older.

The breeding season varies with the species. Generally those of tropical forests, where there is little seasonal variation of climate, may breed at any time of year, although there are certain more favourable periods. In contrast, species that occupy areas which are subjected to marked seasonal variations in climate have a more restricted breeding season, which coincides with the period of greatest food availability. This is the case, for instance, in savannas with alternating periods of drought and flooding, or in more southerly latitudes, where winter weather can make life fairly difficult.

Both steppe and forest species are decidedly territorial, in some cases only during breeding, but in others all through the year. Territory is marked vocally, with birds calling from within their own territories and being answered by their neighbours; sometimes the whole forest echoes to their calls, especially those of *Crypturellus*. When an intruder calls, members of the same sex come to expel it and this can develop into a fierce tussle, with feet and wings being used as weapons. Both males and females defend their territory thus, though in each species it appears that only one of the sexes is regularly aggressive.

In the normal system of polygamy, a male attracts one, two or more females by his continuous calling. In some species, such as those of the genus *Tinamus*, when courting or intimidating rivals, a bird lowers its breast to the ground and, with its neck stretched forward, fluffs up its back end, trying to appear larger than it really is. When seen head on in this posture, all of the bird's back is in view, while the heavily marked under-tail-coverts are opened out and become very obvious to another bird standing at the side or behind. This display is similar to that of the rheas.

Tinamous always nest on the ground. In open areas, such as pastures and savanna, they usually situate their nests under the cover of a bush, in scrub or in a dense tangle of grass, so that the nest is invisible to any potential predator. In the forest, birds tend to place their nests at the bases of tree trunks in between projecting buttresses. The Highland Tinamou is exceptional in that it often nests in a cavity or under an overhanging rock on sloping ground.

Many species do not really build a nest, laying their eggs instead on a thin bed of dead leaves, which they have collected off the ground. However, other species, like the Ornate Tinamou, build a "proper" circular nest, using bits of grass on a base of earth and turf. There are indications, from captive Brushland Tinamous, that the male may start to scrape out nests when copulation begins, and that he is liable to prepare several, of which only one will eventually be used.

Tinamous' eggs are among the most beautiful in all the bird world. They are shiny and look like porcelain or polished metal. Their colour is very variable, including different tones of green, blue, turquoise, purple, violet, steel grey, chocolate and yellow;

In most if not all tinamous the incubation is carried out exclusively by the male. An incubating bird normally spends many hours sitting tight on the nest, and even the approach of an observer does not cause the bird to move until the interloper is within a few metres of the nest. In most species, the male only leaves his clutch once a day to feed, at which point he usually covers his eggs with leaves or feathers, presumably to hide them. Incubation lasts about 17 days in the Undulated Tinamou.

[Crypturellus undulatus, Peru. Photo: Günter Ziesler]

The tinamous' conspicuous eggs are amongst the most beautiful of all. They are usually highly glossed looking rather like porcelain, and they show a wide range of colours, including green, purple, wine red, chocolate and, as in the Highland Tinamou, turquoise. The chicks are covered in a thick coat of cryptically coloured down, so that when in danger, they just have to crouch low on the ground, where they become almost invisible.

[Nothocercus bonapartei frantzii, Costa Rica. Photo: Michael Fogden/DRK]

the colour varies with the species and sometimes with the subspecies. Eggs are normally uniformly coloured, without spots or speckles, but in *Tinamotis* they can be covered in tiny white dots. As incubation progresses, egg colour steadily fades, for example in the Red-winged Tinamou, where the eggs start off vinaceous purple, but end up leaden-coloured towards the end of the incubation period. This explains why differing descriptions have sometimes been made of eggs of the same species. The reason why tinamou eggs are so brightly and conspicuously coloured is not at all clear, but it has been suggested that the apparent disadvantages may not be significant, as the main threat to their safety probably comes from nocturnal predators, which rely more on scent than on sight.

The eggs are large in comparison with the size of the birds and have a characteristic shape, tending to be elliptical or spherical, rather than oval. The two ends of the egg are very similar, with the smaller end more flattened and less pointed than it is in most other birds, indeed, in some species it is very difficult to make out which end is which.

Once females have laid their eggs, they abandon them to the male for incubation, before setting off probably, in most species, to pair up with another male, and in this way they end up laying in several different nests. It is here that the efficiency of the system can be seen, as the clutch of conspicuous eggs is quickly laid, reducing the period of care required, and yet the females

are constantly available for mating with one male or another. One offshoot of this strategy is frequently a bias in the sex ratio: for example there can be as many as four male Variegated Tinamous (*Crypturellus variegatus*) for each female.

Up to 16 eggs may be laid, though in such cases this is probably because several females have laid in a nest. Normally the more mature males end up with more eggs than younger ones, as they can attract more females; thus, a male Brushland Tinamou can have as many as four mates. The Variegated Tinamou, in contrast, normally has a clutch of only one egg, though it occasionally has two. The Ornate Tinamou also has a clutch which is laid by a single female; this might be because in the high altitude ecosystems inhabited by this species food is scarcer, so females have to be more territorial and so will not allow another female to approach. In the larger species, females tend to lay every three or four days, whereas in smaller species they generally lay on consecutive days.

Incubation is relatively short, lasting about 16 days in *Crypturellus*, which includes some of the smallest members of the family, and 19-20 in *Tinamus* and *Eudromia*. During this period the male either calls very little and normally away from the nest, or is totally silent. If he breaks off incubation for a short while to feed, he usually covers the eggs with leaves or some of his own fallen feathers, so that the brightly coloured eggs are not so obvious.

The Brushland Tinamou is one of the few species of the family which has been studied in some depth. Each male occupies a fairly extensive home range, which overlaps widely with those of other, neighbouring males. Territorial behaviour apparently consists of no more than calling duels. Thus, one male only ventures deep into another's territory when the latter is not calling, or if it is calling from some way off. The calls of the territory owner as he approaches are usually sufficient to cause the intruder to leave the area, without producing any territorial chases.

[Nothoprocta cinerascens cinerascens. Photo: Kenneth W. Fink/ Ardea]

An incubating male remains absolutely motionless on the nest and is unbelievably tolerant of danger. An observer can approach very close or even brush gently against the bird with a twig, without causing the bird to abandon its incubation. In some species, in the presence of such a threat, a bird may flatten itself out on the ground with its head and neck stretched out in front of it and its back stuck up in the air. In this way the rump feathers stand up vertically and look not unlike a bushy plant and, if the posture is exaggerated the eggs may become visible behind. This posture has also been recorded for alarmed birds, which spread themselves out on the ground, in the hope of not being noticed, and such behaviour has close parallels in some of the ratites.

When a bird is frightened off its nest, it either flies away or moves off, performing a distraction display, in an effort to draw the predator's attention away from the eggs to itself. This means feigning injury, and involves hopping along and trying to fly but falling, as if attempting to take off, but being unable to; the same performance may be acted out to protect chicks. In general, tinamous do not seem to perform this distraction ritual as convincingly as many other birds.

Chicks hatch synchronously with a dense, drab coat of down, which is whitish, greyish or yellowish, with dark splodges to aid in camouflage. Within hours the male withdraws from the nest and, moving slowly about, calls his chicks after

him with a curious soft repeated call. When danger threatens, he freezes and hides his chicks under his belly and wings.

Newly-hatched chicks can actually feed themselves, but in the first few days the male usually captures insects and deposits them in front of his chicks for them to peck at and eat. At this stage chicks are very delicate, and it is difficult to believe that they can survive amidst the countless dangers of the tropical forest, or the tough climatic conditions that dominate the high Andes or Patagonia. Mortality is high at the beginning, but the chicks grow quickly and within a few days they already chase insects busily, and when only one to three weeks old, they can fly up onto branches about a metre off the ground. Slaty-breasted Tinamou chicks attain adult size within some twenty days, but it takes much longer to gain adult weight; for a young bird to move from 10% to 90% of its eventual weight requires about 85 days in the Spotted Nothura, and nearly 108 days in the Red-winged Tinamou.

It would appear that sexual maturity is normally reached at one year old, and although Spotted Nothuras may be physiologically prepared for mating at only about 57 days old, it is thought that they are unlikely to be successful at such an early age, partly because the act of copulation requires a fair degree of skill in order to be successfully performed.

Once the male has finished raising his brood and they have become independent, perhaps within 10-20 days, he starts calling again, in order to attract females and start another clutch. It is quite possible that he may mate again with the same females. This intensive breeding system has been recorded for Brushland, Highland and Slaty-breasted Tinamous.

Results show that immediately prior to the commencement of breeding, 54-62% of the females in a population of Spotted Nothuras were young birds from the previous season, indicating that this species has a very high rate of turnover. Nevertheless, the amount of recruitment varies from one year to another, even without the interference of hunters, and after a particularly good year, the population may exceed the carrying capacity of the area. When this occurs there are natural mechanisms to bring numbers back down to a sustainable level during late autumn and winter, before the next breeding season; this probably involves some natural mortality and dispersal to other areas where the habitat is not saturated.

Movements

Due to their terrestrial lifestyle and their limited flying skills, tinamous are strictly sedentary and do not perform any kind of migration. All movements are merely local, and in most species this refers to walking about in the normal pursuit of their daily activities.

Forest tinamous undertake short movements, when climatic conditions demand. The rainy season, flooding and drought can drive birds into areas where environmental conditions are more favourable. Thus, most Amazonian species move into *terra firme* forest, when the *várzea* forest becomes seasonally flooded.

Local bad weather can also make species move temporarily into climatically more comfortable zones. High in the Andes of northern Bolivia, the Puna Tinamou normally occupies the tops of ridges adjacent to the main range and also the slopes at the very edge of the permanent snow-line. However, in bad weather, for instance torrential rain, hail or snow, the birds tend to descend to the valley floors, where they are more sheltered and the weather is usually more clement.

Forest species, such as the Slaty-breasted Tinamou, maintain a large home range throughout the year and they move about erratically within it, in search of food. A male Brushland Tinamou has a home range of some 20 ha, although it may overlap considerably with those of his neighbours, as he only defends a much smaller territory. Females roam around the general area in groups of two to five birds, passing through a series of different home ranges and mating with different males.

The Ornate Tinamou, which lives in hilly parts of the *puna*, goes every morning and evening to the bottom of the slopes and ravines to feed and drink, which can involve flying to its feeding grounds, if they are far off. Some species which eat grain commute daily between their normal habitats and fields of cereals; in contrast, other species, for instance Darwin's Nothura, spend a long time in such feeding grounds, often staying put until the food supply runs out.

The species typical of open areas and also those of southern latitudes take up their territories for breeding, but afterwards leave them and join up in groups. They then move about apparently more or less at random over large areas until the next breeding season.

Relationship with Man

Tinamous play their part in the folklore of the native American peoples. Some forest tribes of Brazil and Colombia believe that the jaguar imitates the call of the Great Tinamou, in order to attract and catch it. A popular tale among the Guahibo Indians of Colombia tells how one day a native was going along a river in his canoe, close to the bank, trying to locate a tinamou that was calling. As he got closer, he noticed that the voice was very harsh and, his suspicions aroused, he turned back just in time to get away from an immense jaguar, the originator of the calls.

In Panama there is a tradition that, on seeing the original rainbow after the Flood, the Great Tinamou was so frightened by its bright colours that it fled from the rest of the birds in Noah's Ark and took refuge in the depths of the forest, where it has remained hidden ever since.

There is a Brazilian legend that explains the ecological separation of the Red-winged and the Undulated (*Crypturellus undulatus*) Tinamous. The story goes that the two species used to be inseparable and always went around together in the fields, the forest or wherever, until one day, as Fate would have it, they quarrelled and split up. The Undulated Tinamou entered the largest, densest, darkest undergrowth of the forest, while the Red-winged Tinamou went off to the open plains and sunny meadows. One day a long time afterwards, the Undulated Tinamou, feeling lonely and sad and longing to see his old friend, went to the edge of the forest and called out his sad song, "Vamos fazer as pazes?" ("Shall we make up again?") However, the other replied angrily, "Eu, nunca mais!" ("What, me? Never again!"). This story is symptomatic of the fact that the birds are much more often heard than seen. Indeed, their very name "tinamou" is a corruption of the local Argentinian name "inambú", which is probably a transliteration of a tinamou call, perhaps that of the Red-winged Tinamou.

During the present century there have been numerous attempts to introduce or reintroduce tinamous to certain regions for hunting. The favourite species for these purposes are those of open areas, as they are more likely to take flight, whereas forest species are wont to run away and hide, and adapt very poorly to open habitats. The Red-winged Tinamou has been reintroduced to the State of Rio de Janeiro, Brazil, where it used to have populations until they were exterminated around the beginning of the century. Attempts have been made to introduce the same species in France, Germany and Hungary, but without success.

Similar attempts to introduce tinamous in the USA have been equally fruitless: 473 Ornate and 110 Red-winged Tinamous in Oregon, 1966-74; 128 Spotted Nothuras in Florida (1966 and 1971), 47 in Alabama and 136 in Texas (1969); 164 Darwin's Nothuras in Colorado and 100 in Oklahoma in 1970; 256 Elegant Crested Tinamous in Nebraska (1971) and 217 (1969) and 1200 (1971-77) in California. In 1885 Chilean Tinamous (*Nothoprocta perdicaria*) were released on Easter Island, in the south-east Pacific, where the species still persists today. However, they have not prospered as much as they might have done, due to the introduction of the Chimango Caracara (*Milvago chimango*) in 1928.

No species of tinamou has been domesticated to date, despite the fact that they breed well in captivity. At the beginning of this century Red-winged Tinamous were acclimatized and bred on pheasant farms in France, Britain, Germany, Belgium and Denmark, with the intention of introducing them as game species, and vast sums were paid to the Argentinian suppliers. Today *Crypturellus* and Red-winged Tinamous are still bred in Rio Grande do Sul in south-east Brazil and these may be used to bolster populations for hunting. Hybridization between congeners has occurred in captivity, occasionally producing fertile offspring.

Tinamous are frequent in South American zoos. On some estates they are kept semi-domesticated with hens, normally after being taken as chicks or even unhatched, to be brooded by the hens.

Several species have the tendency of entering fields of wheat, barley, maize, rice (dry-grown), sorghum, millet and so on, in order to eat the grain. This is most frequent after reaping, when they feed on fallen grain, but they are also known to attack ears of grain that is still standing. Some species cause problems by digging up tubers and pecking away at them, most notably the Ornate and Andean Tinamous, which unearth potatoes on the *puna*. The Red-winged Tinamou raises similar havoc in peanut plantations. However, in some places members of the genus *Nothoprocta* are recognized to be helpful to farmers, as they take large numbers of the insects which often infest crops.

Status and Conservation

The status of species in this family is very difficult to determine, as there are many regions, such as the Amazon Basin or the high Andes, where access is extremely difficult, and they have consequently received relatively little attention from ornithologists. In addition, their habitat is often smothered with dense foliage and is sometimes marshy, while their secretive habits and their cryptic plumage have also added to the problems faced by anyone trying to perform any kind of census.

In areas of virgin forest, some species are known to be naturally more common than others, although all populations are assumed to be stable in such areas. The major threat facing these species is the deforestation on massive scale that is currently besetting all Neotropical forests. Immense areas of forest are clear-felled in order to commercialize the timber, or to make way for pastures or agricultural land, which is usually doomed to a very short period of productivity due to the poverty of the soil. In the wake of such changes, forest species, unable to adapt themselves to such a different environment, which lacks the protective shroud of the forest, have no chance of survival and simply disappear.

The massive destruction of the Amazonian rain forests, along with all its implications at global level, is among the most important issues confronting the modern world, and there is no need to enter into details here. It has at last awakened the world at large, and consequently the politicians, to look into the future with the idea that nature conservation is essential for everybody, even if it is not normally economically productive. Urgent action must be taken to save Amazonia, and as much as possible of tropical forests elsewhere, with a view to rational exploitation of their priceless resources in the future. It is difficult to know where to start when dealing with such a vast area and such widespread aggression, so to this end biologists have compiled maps of the priority zones for conservation, taking into consideration all forms of life, and it is now up to governments and investors to react responsibly.

A large proportion of the species of tinamous have populations in the Amazon Basin, often occupying hefty tracts. Although none of the eight threatened species of tinamou is Amazonian, it is obvious that all forest birds are bound to be declining in the area and will continue to do so, until decisive steps are taken to safeguard the forests from the chainsaw.

While some species are widely distributed, others are extremely restricted either to one region or to one habitat type. Obviously a restricted distribution means that habitat destruction takes on very serious implications, and the entire area of suitable habitat can disappear in next to no time. Such is the case of the Magdalena Tinamou (*Crypturellus erythropus saltuarius*), sometimes considered a full species, which is known

Although its loud piping trills are easy to hear, the Brown Tinamou, like other tinamous of dense forests, is a secretive bird which is extremely difficult to see. Most observations are of birds walking or running, singly or in pairs, along fairly open margins, for example by the sides of roads cut through thick forest.

[*Crypturellus obsoletus*, Brazil. Photo: J. Dunning/Vireo]

from a single specimen collected in 1943 in the Magdalena Valley in northern Colombia; as there have been no further records, it may well be extinct already.

It is not just in the tropical forests that habitat destruction is a serious problem. Virtually all habitat types of the continent are undergoing some form of conversion at the hands of humans, except perhaps the most remote parts of the Andes and Patagonia. There is still debate about how the vegetation of the Andes has been altered in historical times, but many experts think that much of what is now open grassland in the temperate zone was covered in elfin forest, before gradual clearance by the inhabitants. Both Kalinowski's (*Nothoprocta kalinowskii*) and Taczanowski's (*Nothoprocta taczanowskii*) Tinamous, of limited ranges in the high Andes of Peru, are now considered threatened, as the small remaining areas of their habitat are being destroyed by the cutting of *Polylepis* woods and the increasing amount of cultivation. There are no recent records of the former species and it too might already be extinct.

Another threatened species is the Dwarf Tinamou of open plains in eastern Brazil. Recent reports that it might actually be more common than had previously been thought seem to have arisen from a misidentification of its voice, due to confusion with that of the Ocellated Crake (*Micropygia schomburgkii*). Along with another threatened tinamou, the Lesser Nothura (*Nothura minor*), it inhabits the *cerrado* grasslands of central Brazil, where habitat destruction is again the chief threat. The establishment of the federal capital of Brasilia has meant the opening up of central Brazil for agricultural and economic development, as well as the rapid growth of the population and the improve-

ment of communications. Large areas of grassland and scrub have been cultivated, while a particularly harmful practice is the annual burning of such habitat in order to improve grazing for cattle; apart from the loss of habitat, Dwarf Tinamous have been seen to become intoxicated with the smoke, making them easy targets for any waiting predator.

One on the threatened list is the Solitary Tinamou; its race *pernambucensis* is confined to Atlantic forests in the Brazilian states of Alagoas and Pernambuco, where it is severely threatened both by habitat destruction and hunting pressure. It now has legal protection, and the Brazilian government has at last recognized the importance of these forests and has temporarily stopped issuing logging concessions for this zone, but a series of protected areas must be set up, if the rich endemic bird life of these forests is to survive much longer. The nominate race *solitarius* is also under extreme pressure, but a newly proposed reserve of about 4000 ha in north-east Argentina should at least secure one healthy population.

Other threatened tinamous which are generally rare with fairly limited ranges include the Black (*Tinamus osgoodi*) and Yellow-legged (*Crypturellus noctivagus*) Tinamous. Another species that is little-known and has a very limited range is the Tepui Tinamou (*Crypturellus ptaritepui*) of the Pantepui area in southern Venezuela. At present its cloud forest habitat appears to be intact, but its miniscule range means that it would take little to bring about its extinction.

As the forest steadily retreats, plains tinamous colonize new areas and many of these species are actually expanding their ranges. However, they have their own problems, and the main

Because of its considerable size and highly prized flesh, the Red-winged Tinamou is one of the most avidly hunted game species of South America. This is largely why it has declined or even disappeared in many areas, especially in parts of Brazil. However, it is still common, sometimes abundant, where hunting pressure is minimal, or at least suitably regulated. There have been several attempts to introduce this and other tinamous as game species in Europe and the USA, but these attempts have invariably been unsuccessful.

[Rhynchotus rufescens rufescens, Rocha, Uruguay. Photo: A. de Sostoa & X. Ferrer]

The race pernambucensis of the Solitary Tinamou is restricted to the coastal states of Alagoas and Pernambuco in eastern Brazil, where it occurs in the Atlantic forests. It is one of the most threatened forms in the family. Its habitat has suffered destruction on a massive scale in recent decades, and heavy hunting pressure has also played a major part in its decline. In 1971, the total population of this race was estimated at no more than 100 birds.

[*Tinamus solitarius pernambucensis*, Pilar, Alagoas, Brazil. Photo: Haroldo Palo/NHPA]

threat, at any rate for the medium-sized and larger species, is normally hunting. In places they are hunted systematically for sport, using guns and dogs. In open areas the dogs easily locate the birds and, as they have nowhere to hide, they are quickly shot down. This kind of hunting is frequent on the plains of Brazil, Uruguay, Paraguay, Argentina and Chile, and also in montane grassland in Ecuador, Peru and Bolivia.

Around the turn of the century there were real massacres of tinamous, especially of the Elegant Crested Tinamou and the Spotted Nothura in Argentina. A report to the Argentinian government in 1921 urged legal control of hunting, to prevent the extinction of several species including tinamous, which were sold in markets for food. The figures are horrendous, with more than 18 million tinamous sold between 1890 and 1899 in Buenos Aires markets alone. The same country also exported vast numbers of frozen birds to the USA, which were sold under the name of "South American partridges". A shipment of some 360,000 birds which arrived in New York provoked severe criticism on the part of Frank Chapman of the American Museum of Natural History, who warned Argentinian scientists that stocks would not last long, if the same rhythm of hunting were maintained. In the face of this alarming situation, conservationists in the United States launched a series of protests, until the importation of frozen tinamous was officially banned by law.

Tinamous were formerly so common in Brazil that they were sold at city fairs, for example in Rio de Janeiro. In Rio Grande do Sul, a business started up in 1935 with its own factory for the canning of Red-winged Tinamous. Even today, hunting pressure is intense, and a study of two areas in this same state showed some 25-40,000 Spotted Nothuras killed annually, without taking into account any of the many illegal forms of hunting; fortunately, control has recently been somewhat improved.

Tinamous remain to this day coveted trophies for hunters throughout Latin America, and they are still caught by native Indians who imitate their calls, or catch them in nooses or traps, as they have done for centuries; they are said to make very good eating! Hunting in itself need not have such drastic effects on populations, if it is properly controlled, but at present it is out of hand, and there are not the necessary means to provide adequate teams of wardens, for the enforcement of any suitable legislation, were it to be passed. Normally it is the hunting clubs themselves that establish the norms, and attempt to avoid overhunting, which in the long run means an end to their sport. However, not surprisingly, most hunters expect the others to make the necessary sacrifices, so they find themselves having to go further and further in order to find good hunting, as local populations decline and disappear.

Even worse are the hunters who do not accept the most basic hunting etiquette and use illegal systems, or hunt during the breeding season. It is difficult for species to survive such a concerted onslaught and some have thus been brought to the brink of extinction, as is the case of the Solitary Tinamou. In Brazil tinamous are hunted illegally at night, using torches, or using flutes which imitate their calls, during the breeding season. Poachers take advantage of their territoriality, using home-made whistles to lure the birds. They take males and females during different periods and can virtually exterminate a species from a particular area in this way.

General Bibliography

Blake (1977, 1979), Board & Perrott (1979), Boetticher (1934), Bruning & Dolenzek (1986), Cracraft (1974, 1981), Dunning (1982, 1987), Elzanowski (1987), Handford & Mares (1985), Hellmayr & Conover (1942), Hudson *et al.* (1972), Jehl (1971), Krieg & Schuhmancher (1936), Lahile (1921), McGowan (1985), Miranda Ribeiro (1938), Olalla & Magalhães (1956), Parkes & Clark (1966), Saiff (1988), de Schauensee (1982), Sibley & Ahlquist (1981), Sibley & Monroe (1990), Sick (1985b), Silyn-Roberts & Sharp (1985), Snow (1985), Verheyen (1960b), Ward (1957).

inches 10
cm 25

PLATE 6

1

2

3

ssp *castaneiceps*

4

ssp *robustus*

5

6

7

8

9

10

ssp *soui*

11

12

13

14

ssp *yapura*

ssp *undulatus*

ssp *modestus*

15

♀

♂

16

Subfamily TINAMINAE

Genus *TINAMUS* Hermann, 1783

1. Grey Tinamou

Tinamus tao

French: Tinamou tao **German**: Tao **Spanish**: Tinamú Tao
Other common names: Tao Tinamou

Taxonomy. *Tinamus tao* Temminck, 1815, Pará, Brazil. Four subspecies recognized.
Subspecies and Distribution.
T. t. larensis Phelps & Phelps, 1949 - C Colombia, NW Venezuela.
T. t. kleei (Tschudi, 1843) - SC Colombia and E Ecuador to E Bolivia and W Brazil.
T. t. septentrionalis Brabourne & Chubb, 1913 - NE Venezuela, (?) NW Guyana.
T. t. tao Temminck, 1815 - NC Brazil.

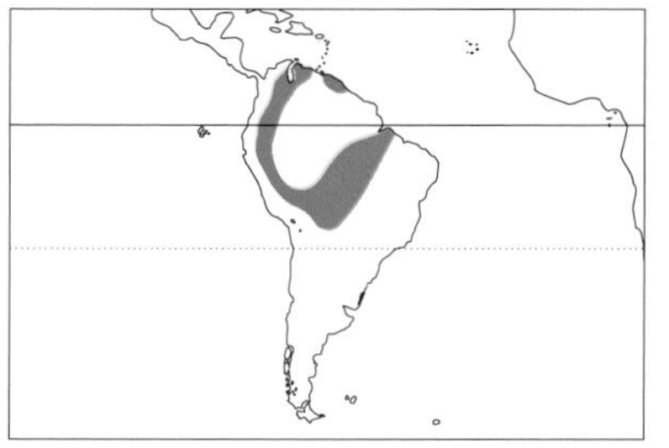

Descriptive notes. 42·5-49 cm; male 1325-1863 g, female 1430-2080 g. Sides of head freckled black and white, with fairly faint blackish band down side of neck; undertail-coverts reddish brown barred with blackish. Generally much greyer than *T. major*. Juvenile mainly fuscous brown above, much paler below. Races separated on size, coloration and extent of black barring on back.
Habitat. Tropical and subtropical rain forest on E slopes of Andes up to 1900 m; dense secondary forest; gallery forest in *cerrado* of Brazil, cloud forest in Venezuela. Forest floor of *terra firme* and less often *várzea*.
Food and Feeding. Mainly fruit, also seeds, insects, molluscs and a few small vertebrates.
Breeding. Jan-Mar in Colombia, Jun in Venezuela. Nest is slight depression lined with leaves, normally at foot of large tree, often in amongst protruding roots. 2-9 greenish blue or turquoise eggs.
Movements. Presumably sedentary.
Status and Conservation. Not globally threatened. Normally at low densities; common in some regions, rare and local elsewhere. Hunting important in some cases, otherwise deforestation of Amazonia is reducing overall numbers, as species requires pristine forest.
Bibliography. Amadon (1959), Hilty (1985), Hilty & Brown (1986), Olivares (1958, 1970), Osgood & Conover (1922), Pinto (1964), Ruschi (1979), de Schauensee & Phelps (1978), Schubart *et al.* (1965), Sick (1984), Terborgh *et al.* (1984), Wennrich (1983).

2. Solitary Tinamou

Tinamus solitarius

French: Tinamou solitaire **German**: Grausteißtinamu **Spanish**: Tinamú Macuco

Taxonomy. *Cryptura solitaria* Vieillot, 1819, Paraguay. Two subspecies recognized.
Subspecies and Distribution.
T. s. pernambucensis Berla, 1946 - EC Brazil.
T. s. solitarius (Vieillot, 1819) - E Brazil, SE Paraguay, extreme NE Argentina.

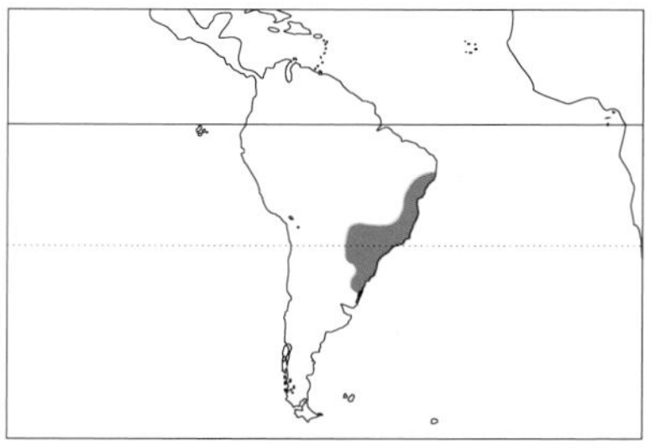

Descriptive notes. 42·5-48 cm; male 1014-1500 g, female 1710-1900 g. Crown tends to be darker than rest of upperparts, which have narrow black barring. Juvenile has variable amount of white spotting on upperparts, particularly on wings. Race *pernambucensis* paler and yellower, with more pronounced black markings on neck.
Habitat. Tropical and subtropical forest, preferably warm and moist, but also in areas with cold dry season; typically in Atlantic forests of Brazil. Prefers virgin forest with little undergrowth; fairly frequent over uneven ground. Each bird said to require c. 30 ha of primary forest.
Food and Feeding. Seeds (Rutaceae, Euphorbiaceae, Annonaceae), small fruit, berries and plant matter; also some insects and other invertebrates, and perhaps occasionally small frogs. Most feeding in evening; searches for fallen seeds in leaf litter.
Breeding. Nest is slight depression on ground, lined with leaves; site selection and construction by male. 6-14 greenish blue or turquoise eggs; incubation 19 days; chicks chestnut-cinnamon, paler on back. Remiges start growing at 2 days, rectrices at 8 days; juvenile plumage starts to replace natal at 25-28 days; fully replaced at c. 3 months. Has lived up to 12-15 years in captivity.
Movements. Presumably sedentary.
Status and Conservation. INSUFFICIENTLY KNOWN. CITES I. Apparently rare throughout its range and threatened due to hunting pressure and habitat destruction; has now disappeared from many parts of Brazil. Newly proposed reserve in Misiones, NE Argentina, will protect some 4000 ha of its habitat; more reserves may be established in this province. Race *pernambucensis* particularly at risk and range much reduced in recent years, due to rapid destruction of forest; not more than 100 individuals estimated in 1971; may previously have occurred in states of Sergipe and NE Bahía; only 3 or 4 skins in museums. Experience with species in captivity suggests reintroduction may be possible. See page 124.
Bibliography. Aguirre (1957), Amadon (1959), Anon. (1991), Belton (1984), Bokermann (1991), Coimbra-Filho (1971), Collar & Andrew (1988), Dabbene (1972), Grummt (1979), King (1978/79), Liebermann (1936), de Magalhães (1972), de la Peña (1986), Pinto (1954, 1964), Ruschi (1979), Schubart *et al.* (1965), Scott & Brooke (1985), Sick (1972, 1984), Sick & Teixeira (1979), Sick *et al.* (1981).

3. Black Tinamou

Tinamus osgoodi

French: Tinamou noir **German**: Schwarztinamu **Spanish**: Tinamú Negro

Taxonomy. *Tinamus osgoodi* Conover, 1949, Cuzco, Peru. Two subspecies recognized.
Subspecies and Distribution.
T. o. hershkovitzi Blake, 1953 - SC Colombia.
T. o. osgoodi Conover, 1949 - SE Peru.

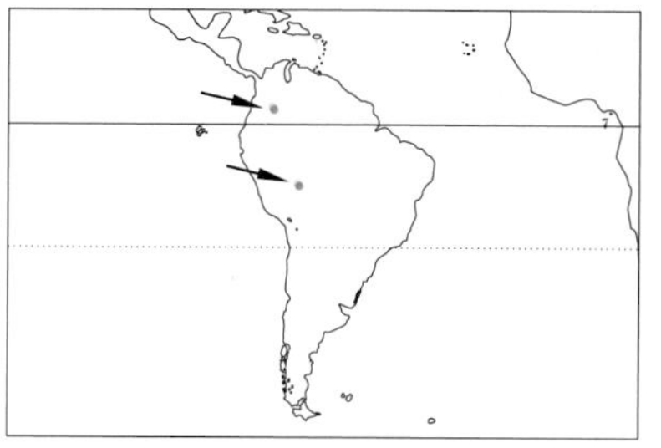

Descriptive notes. 40-46 cm. Females average slightly larger. Sooty brown belly and ochraceous to chestnut vent, with black speckling. Race *hershkovitzi* has wing-coverts blackish, similar to back, and darker chestnut rufous undertail-coverts.
Habitat. Mainly subtropical, in heavy, humid forest of E Andes 1500-2100 m, where epiphytes, tree ferns, bromeliads and moss all abundant.
Food and Feeding. No information available.
Breeding. One nest from Peru contained 2 glossy blue eggs.
Movements. Presumably sedentary.
Status and Conservation. INSUFFICIENTLY KNOWN. Very scarce in Peru, rare in Colombia. Only three specimens of *hershkovitzi* in museums and one recent sighting, this race being known only from type locality, while nominate *osgoodi* is known from a 100 km stretch of E Andean slope in Cuzco Dept. May never have been numerous, though apparently was once quite common in Peru, within its very limited range; main threat is probably habitat destruction.
Bibliography. Blake (1953), Collar & Andrew (1988), Hilty (1985), Hilty & Brown (1986), Olivares (1958), Orejuela (1985), Parker *et al.* (1982), Traylor (1952).

4. Great Tinamou

Tinamus major

French: Grand Tinamou **German**: Großtinamu **Spanish**: Tinamú Oliváceo

Taxonomy. *Tetrao major* Gmelin, 1789, Cayenne. Twelve subspecies recognized.
Subspecies and Distribution.
T. m. robustus P. L. Sclater & Salvin, 1868 - SE Mexico, E Guatemala, Honduras.
T. m. percautus Van Tyne, 1935 - SE Mexico, N Guatemala, Belize.
T. m. fuscipennis Salvadori, 1895 - N Nicaragua to W Panama.
T. m. castaneiceps Salvadori, 1895 - SW Costa Rica, W Panama.
T. m. brunneiventris Aldrich, 1937 - SC Panama.
T. m. saturatus Griscom, 1929 - E Panama, NW Colombia.
T. m. latifrons Salvadori, 1895 - SW Colombia, W Ecuador.
T. m. zuliensis Osgood & Conover, 1922 - NE Colombia, N Venezuela.
T. m. peruvianus Bonaparte, 1856 - SE Colombia, E Ecuador to NE Bolivia and extreme W Brazil.
T. m. serratus (Spix, 1825) - NW Brazil.
T. m. major (Gmelin, 1789) - E Venezuela to NE Brazil.
T. m. olivascens Conover, 1937 - Amazonian Brazil.

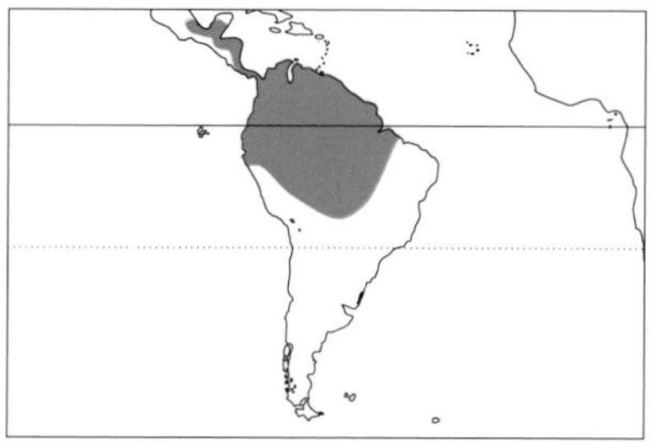

Descriptive notes. 40-46 cm; male 700-1142 g, female 945-1240 g. Overall coloration very variable, ranging from light to dark olive brown; whitish on throat and centre of belly. Juvenile darker than adult. Races separated on general coloration, crown colour and presence (and extent) or absence of occipital crest.
Habitat. Dense primary and secondary rain forest, both *terra firme* and *várzea*, in tropical and subtropical zones up to 1500 m; prefers tall, undisturbed forest, with fairly open forest floor, though sometimes found in dense undergrowth in wetter parts of forest.
Food and Feeding. Berries, fruits and seeds, especially Sapotaceae, Myrtaceae, Annonaceae and Lauraceae; also nuts and small terrestrial animals, including worms, insects, spiders, small lizards and frogs. Feeds while walking about on forest floor.
Breeding. Mostly Jan-Jul; even Sept in Surinam, where may nest all year round. Nest is scratch between buttress roots of large tree. Normally 3-6 (2-12) glossy, intense greenish blue, turquoise or violet eggs.
Movements. Presumably sedentary. Sometimes emerges into clearings or forest tracks.
Status and Conservation. Not globally threatened. Common to fairly common in much of range, where forest still relatively intact. Much appreciated as dish and is heavily hunted, both traditionally by indigenous peoples and also by settlers, having become rare near human settlements. More severely threatened by deforestation, especially in Amazonia (see page 123). Its furtive habits and its ability to pass unnoticed have helped it to survive in areas where other large game birds have been hunted out. Fairly scarce in Mexico.
Bibliography. Blake (1955), Chapman (1926), Edwards (1989), Haverschmidt (1968), Hilty & Brown (1986), de Kondo (1988), Lamm (1974), Leopold (1959), Lowery & Dalquest (1951), Mendez (1979), Monroe (1968), Olivares (1958, 1970), Osgood & Conover (1922), Pinto (1964), Ramos (1985a, 1985b), Ridgely & Gwynne (1989), Robbins *et al.* (1985), Ruschi (1979), Rutgers & Norris (1970), de Schauensee & Phelps (1978), Schubart *et al.* (1965), Sick (1984), Skutch (1959, 1983), Slud (1964), Smithe (1966), Stiles (1985), Stiles & Skutch (1989), Taibel (1938), Wetmore (1965).

5. White-throated Tinamou

Tinamus guttatus

French: Tinamou à gorge blanche **German**: Weißkehltinamu **Spanish**: Tinamú Moteado

Taxonomy. *Tinamus guttatus* Pelzeln (*ex* Natterer MS), 1863, Brazil. Monotypic.
Distribution. SE Colombia and S Venezuela to N Bolivia and E to NE Brazil.

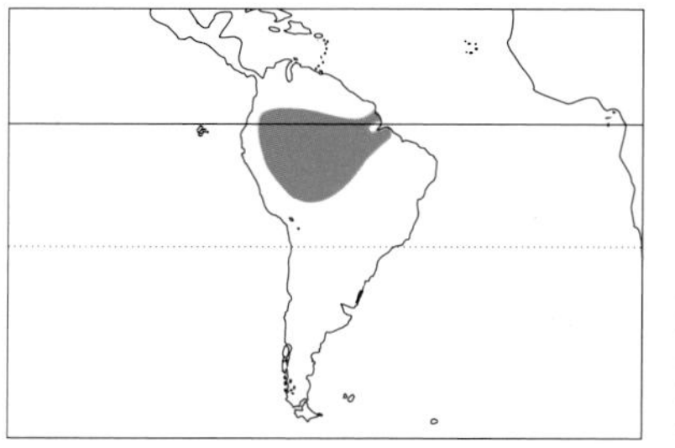

Descriptive notes. 32-36 cm; male 623-652 g, female 680-800 g. Throat occasionally buffy; back pale to dark chocolate brown, sometimes with black barring on lower back, rump and inner remiges; variable amounts of white or buff spotting on wing-coverts and inner remiges. Juvenile as adult, with heavier pale spotting on upperparts.
Habitat. Primary tropical rain forest up to 500 m, typically in *terra firme*.
Food and Feeding. Two stomachs from Brazil yielded 150 ants, 18 seeds and some fine sand.
Breeding. Mar-Apr in upper Orinoco area. 5-6 turquoise eggs.
Movements. Presumably sedentary.
Status and Conservation. Not globally threatened. Fairly common in places, though avoids contact with humans. Deforestation of Amazonia is main threat (see page 123).
Bibliography. Butler (1979), Hilty & Brown (1986), Olivares (1958), Parker *et al.* (1982), Pearson (1975), Pinto (1964), Remsen & Traylor (1989), Ruschi (1979), de Schauensee & Phelps (1978), Schubart *et al.* (1965), Sick (1984).

On following pages: 6. Highland Tinamou (*Nothocercus bonapartei*); 7. Tawny-breasted Tinamou (*Nothocercus julius*); 8. Hooded Tinamou (*Nothocercus nigrocapillus*); 9. Berlepsch's Tinamou (*Crypturellus berlepschi*); 10. Cinereous Tinamou (*Crypturellus cinereus*); 11. Little Tinamou (*Crypturellus soui*); 12. Tepui Tinamou (*Crypturellus ptaritepui*); 13. Brown Tinamou (*Crypturellus obsoletus*); 14. Undulated Tinamou (*Crypturellus undulatus*); 15. Pale-browed Tinamou (*Crypturellus transfasciatus*); 16. Brazilian Tinamou (*Crypturellus strigulosus*).

Genus *NOTHOCERCUS* Bonaparte, 1856

6. Highland Tinamou

Nothocercus bonapartei

French: Tinamou de Bonaparte **German**: Bergtinamu **Spanish**: Tinamú Serrano
Other common names: Bonaparte's Tinamou

Taxonomy. *Tinamus bonapartei* G. R. Gray, 1867, Aragua, Venezuela.
Five subspecies recognized.
Subspecies and Distribution.
N. b. frantzii (Lawrence, 1868) - Costa Rica, W Panama.
N. b. intercedens Salvadori, 1895 - WC Colombia.
N. b. bonapartei (G. R. Gray, 1867) - NC Colombia, W Venezuela.
N. b. discrepans Friedmann, 1947 - EC Colombia.
N. b. plumbeiceps Lönnberg & Rendahl, 1922 - EC Ecuador, extreme N Peru.

Descriptive notes. 35-41 cm; 850-1000 g. Slaty crown; thin blackish vermiculations all over body, especially on back. Throat ochraceous to bright rufous; primaries mottled or barred with cinnamon and black; variable amounts of small buffy-white spots on rump and wing-coverts. Juvenile as adult. Races separated on coloration, especially extent of rufous in plumage.
Habitat. Locally distributed mostly in subtropical zone, but also in tropical; from Amazonian rain forest up into cloud forest; in Colombia, at 1500-2200 m, but down to 500 m on E slope of Andes; above 2500 m in places. Within forest, prefers damp areas with dense vegetation, especially with seeding bamboo. Sometimes in dense secondary forest or near clearings.
Food and Feeding. Fallen fruits and also small animals. Often feeds in gulleys and marshy ground.
Breeding. Mar-Jul in Costa Rica, Jan-Jun in Venezuela, Feb-Nov in Colombia and Ecuador. Nest is small scratch lined with leaves and some thin plant stems, at base of tree trunk or in hollow on slope. 5-10 darkish turquoise-green eggs with violet gloss; laid in same nest, normally by more than one female. Downy chick has similar coloration to that of adults, with black stripes on face and crown.
Movements. Presumably sedentary.
Status and Conservation. Not globally threatened. Generally uncommon to rare. Widespread but rare in Costa Rica, where much reduced by hunting; recently very rare in Panama; possibly more frequent in Colombia, Ecuador and Peru.
Bibliography. Anon. (1953), Fjeldså & Krabbe (1990), Hilty (1985), Hilty & Brown (1986), McKay (1980), Mendez (1979), Miller (1963), Olivares (1958), Ridgely & Gwynne (1989), Schäffer (1954, 1975), de Schauensee & Phelps (1978), Slud (1964), Stiles (1985), Stiles & Skutch (1989), Stiles & Smith (1980), Wetmore (1965).

7. Tawny-breasted Tinamou

Nothocercus julius

French: Tinamou à tête rousse **German**: Gelbbrusttinamu **Spanish**: Tinamú Cabecirrojo

Taxonomy. *Tinamus julius* Bonaparte, 1854, Colombia. Monotypic.
Distribution. C Colombia and extreme W Venezuela to SC Ecuador; SC Peru.

Descriptive notes. 35-41 cm. Crown dull chestnut to sooty brown; olivaceous tones fairly variable between individuals. Juvenile has paler head and more rufous in underparts.
Habitat. Subtropical and temperate zones at 1700-3250 m, in rain forest and cloud forest with tree-ferns, and epiphytes, such as bromeliads, moss, lichens and orchids. Prefers slightly open areas with fairly small trees, sometimes in second growth; also in elfin forest of temperate zone just below tree-line; usually at higher altitudes than *N. bonapartei*.
Food and Feeding. No information available.
Breeding. Jun-Aug in Colombia. Downy chick has similar coloration to that of adults, with black markings on head.
Movements. Presumably sedentary; usually solitary or in small groups.
Status and Conservation. Not globally threatened. Fairly common in suitable habitat, but now local. Its habitat has become fragmented, due to deforestation and subsequent use of land for farming. Habitat still relatively intact on steep slopes, where human exploitation of forest is more difficult.
Bibliography. Blake (1955), Butler (1979), Chapman (1926), Fjeldså & Krabbe (1990), Hilty (1985), Hilty & Brown (1986), Olivares (1958), Parker *et al.* (1982), de Schauensee & Phelps (1978).

8. Hooded Tinamou

Nothocercus nigrocapillus

French: Tinamou à capuchon **German**: Kapuzentinamu **Spanish**: Tinamú Cabecinegro

Taxonomy. *Tinamus nigrocapillus* G. R. Gray, 1867, central Bolivia.
Two subspecies recognized.
Subspecies and Distribution.
N. n. cadwaladeri Carriker, 1933 - NW Peru.
N. n. nigrocapillus (G. R. Gray, 1867) - C Peru to Bolivia.
Descriptive notes. 32-35 cm. Dark head; fine vermiculations on upperparts, buffy white spots on wing-coverts forming bars; underparts occasionally with heavy barring, generally paler than upperparts. Race *cadwaladeri* has chest rufescent with only faint black vermiculations.
Habitat. Humid forest of subtropical and, less often, temperate zones, on E slopes of Andes, 2000-3000 m. Prefers damp areas without much undergrowth, but a thick layer of leaf litter; also in stands of bamboo.
Food and Feeding. Perhaps omnivorous; has been seen to take fallen bamboo seeds.

Breeding. No information available.
Movements. Presumably sedentary.
Status and Conservation. Not globally threatened. Little known, but apparently tends to occur at low densities, ranging from local and uncommon to fairly common. Its montane habitat has suffered less than lowland forest, but in some places deforestation has led to serious problems of erosion and landslides.
Bibliography. Blake (1977), Fjeldså & Krabbe (1990), Graves (1985), Parker *et al.* (1982), Remsen & Traylor (1989).

Genus *CRYPTURELLUS* Brabourne & Chubb, 1914

9. Berlepsch's Tinamou

Crypturellus berlepschi

French: Tinamou de Berlepsch **German**: Berlepschtinamu **Spanish**: Tinamú Tizón

Taxonomy. *Crypturus berlepschi* Rothschild, 1897, Esmeraldas, Ecuador.
Until recently considered race of *C. cinereus*, but now separated on grounds of ratio of toe and tarsus lengths, longer, heavier bill and conspicuous plumage differences. Monotypic.
Distribution. NW Colombia to NW Ecuador.

Descriptive notes. 29·6-32 cm; male 430-527 g, female 512-615 g. Plumage generally varies from brownish black to deep sooty brown; head and throat darker. Toes relatively longer, bill heavier and usually longer than in *C. cinereus*. Juvenile presumably barred below and on wings with cinnamon.
Habitat. Primary wet tropical forest; also in fairly mature secondary forest. Coastal lowlands and hills in Colombia, up to 500 m, once recorded at 900 m; avoids drier, more seasonal forests in area of Gulf of Urabá.
Food and Feeding. No information available.
Breeding. Very little known. Feb in Colombia.
Movements. Presumably sedentary.
Status and Conservation. Not globally threatened. Apparently quite common; as with other forest species, deforestation is probably main threat, although much of its range is still fairly inaccessible.
Bibliography. Blake (1977), Haffer (1975), Hilty & Brown (1958, 1986), Olivares (1958), de Schauensee (1964).

10. Cinereous Tinamou

Crypturellus cinereus

French: Tinamou cendré **German**: Grautinamu **Spanish**: Tinamú Sombrío
Other common names: Brushland Tinamou (!)

Taxonomy. *Tetrao cinereus* Gmelin, 1789, Cayenne. Monotypic.
Distribution. SE Colombia to N Bolivia and E to Guianas and NE Brazil.

Descriptive notes. 29-32 cm; male c. 435 g, female 549-602 g. Reddish tinge on crown and nape; throat appears very finely streaked with white. Browner than *C. berlepschi*. Juvenile darker, barred below and on wings with cinnamon.
Habitat. Tropical rain forest, especially in second growth, abundant in *várzea*; also in ecotone with savanna, in areas with bushes and scattered trees, and even in coffee and cocoa plantations. Prefers dense undergrowth.
Food and Feeding. Berries, fruits and seeds; also insects, including ants, mole-crickets and pentatomids.
Breeding. All year round, but mainly Aug-Oct; Jun in Colombia. No nest; normally 2 eggs laid in dense vegetation on forest floor. Egg-colour variously reported as salmon-violet or milk chocolate to dark chocolate. Chicks are dark brown with reddish speckling.
Movements. Presumably sedentary.
Status and Conservation. Not globally threatened. Relatively common in most of range; the commonest tinamou in Surinam, but uncommon in Peru. Habitat threatened by destruction of Amazonia (see page 123).
Bibliography. Butler (1979), Haverschmidt (1968), Hilty & Brown (1986), Olivares (1958), Parker *et al.* (1982), Pinto (1964), Remsen & Traylor (1989), Ruschi (1979), de Schauensee & Phelps (1978), Schubart *et al.* (1965), Sick (1984).

11. Little Tinamou

Crypturellus soui

French: Tinamou soui **German**: Brauntinamu **Spanish**: Tinamú Chico
Other common names: Pileated Tinamou

Taxonomy. *Tinamus soui* Hermann, 1783, Cayenne.
Fourteen subspecies recognized, several of which are clearly transitional.
Subspecies and Distribution.
C. s. meserythrus (P. L. Sclater, 1859) - S Mexico, Belize to SE Nicaragua.
C. s. modestus (Cabanis, 1869) - Costa Rica, W Panama.
C. s. capnodes Wetmore, 1963 - NW Panama.
C. s. poliocephalus (Aldrich, 1937) - W & C Panama.
C. s. panamensis (Carriker, 1910) - C & E Panama.
C. s. harterti (Brabourne & Chubb, 1914) - W Colombia, W Ecuador.
C. s. caucae (Chapman, 1912) - NC Colombia.
C. s. mustelinus (Bangs, 1905) - NE Colombia, NW Venezuela.
C. s. andrei (Brabourne & Chubb, 1914) - NE Venezuela, Trinidad.
C. s. soui (Hermann, 1783) - E Colombia to the Guianas and NE Brazil.
C. s. caquetae (Chapman, 1915) - SE Colombia.
C. s. nigriceps (Chapman, 1923) - E Ecuador, NE Peru.
C. s. inconspicuus Carriker, 1935 - C & E Peru to E Bolivia.
C. s. albigularis (Brabourne & Chubb, 1914) - N & E Brazil.
Descriptive notes. 21·5-24 cm; male c. 207 g, female 174-238 g. Very variable; blackish crown, nape and sides of head. Female usually more brightly coloured; male tends to be darker and less ochraceous. Juvenile has small black and white spotting on back and often underparts; undertail-coverts barred.

Races separated on coloration; some races have two plumage phases, one rufescent buff, the other greyish.

Habitat. Tropical and lower subtropical forest in dry or humid regions; prefers dense undergrowth of forest edge, young secondary growth, overgrown clearings; also thickets and plantations. Up to 1700 m on slopes of *tepuis* in Venezuela; up to 2000 m in Colombia. Affects bushy savanna and cocoa plantations on Trinidad and Tobago.

Food and Feeding. Fruits and berries, tubers and seeds, especially of Ciperaceae; also important are insects, including ants, termites and, to a lesser extent, Myriapoda, Acrididae, Curculionidae, Elateridae and larvae of butterflies and moths; occasionally frogs. Normally swallows lots of pebbles to help break down food.

Breeding. Throughout year in Costa Rica and Surinam; May/Aug/Oct on Trinidad and Tobago; Feb-Aug in Panama. Nest is slight depression under bush or at foot of tree, sometimes with a few leaves added. 1-4 eggs, reddish violet, pinkish brick or reddish chocolate depending on race; incubation c. 19 days; chick has brown down with pale speckles (*modestus*).

Movements. Presumably sedentary; often forms small foraging parties outside breeding season.

Status and Conservation. Not globally threatened. The commonest tinamou in C America. Main threat is habitat destruction. Legally protected in Panama, where intensively hunted for food; common in Colombia, abundant in *várzea* of upper Amazon.

Bibliography. Beebe *et al.* (1917), Chapman (1926), Edwards (1989), ffrench (1992), Haverschmidt (1966, 1968), Hilty & Brown (1986), Leopold (1959), Mendez (1979), Monroe (1968), Olivares (1958, 1970), Osgood & Conover (1922), Pinto (1964), Ridgely & Gwynne (1989), Robbins *et al.* (1985), Ruschi (1979), de Schauensee & Phelps (1978), Schubart *et al.* (1965), Scott & Brooke (1985), Sick (1984), Skutch (1963, 1983), Slud (1964), Smithe (1966), Stiles (1985), Stiles & Skutch (1989), Wetmore (1965).

12. **Tepui Tinamou**
Crypturellus ptaritepui

French: Tinamou des tépuis   **German:** Tepuitinamou   **Spanish:** Tinamú Tepuí

Taxonomy. *Crypturellus ptaritepui* Zimmer & Phelps, 1945, Bolívar, Venezuela. Monotypic.

Distribution. SE Venezuela.

Descriptive notes. 28·5-30 cm. Similar to *C. cinereus*, but smaller, with cheeks and throat more conspicuously sooty grey; rufescent breast; iris creamy white.

Habitat. Dense subtropical cloud forest, 1350-1800 m.

Food and Feeding. No information available.

Breeding. No information available.

Movements. Presumably sedentary.

Status and Conservation. Not globally threatened. Perhaps vulnerable, due to naturally small populations (see page 124). Habitat presently intact due to inaccessibility.

Bibliography. Blake (1977), de Schauensee & Phelps (1978).

13. **Brown Tinamou**
Crypturellus obsoletus

French: Tinamou brun   **German:** Kastanientinamu   **Spanish:** Tinamú Café
Other common names: Traylor's Tinamou (*traylori*)

Taxonomy. *Tinamus obsoletus* Temminck, 1815, São Paulo, Brazil. Race *traylori* may be distinct species. Nine subspecies recognized.

Subspecies and Distribution.
C. o. castaneus (P. L. Sclater, 1858) - EC Colombia to E Ecuador and N Peru.
C. o. ochraceiventris (Stolzmann, 1926) - C Peru.
C. o. traylori Blake, 1961 - SE Peru.
C. o. punensis (Chubb, 1917) - SE Peru, N Bolivia.
C. o. cerviniventris (P. L. Sclater & Salvin, 1873) - N Venezuela.
C. o. knoxi W. H. Phelps, Jr., 1976 - NW Venezuela.
C. o. griseiventris (Salvadori, 1895) - NC Brazil.
C. o. hypochracea (Miranda-Ribeiro, 1938) - SW Brazil.
C. o. obsoletus (Temminck, 1815) - SE Brazil, E Paraguay, NE Argentina.

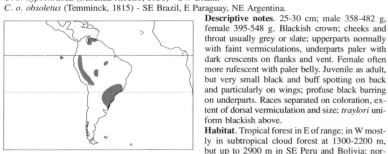

Descriptive notes. 25-30 cm; male 358-482 g, female 395-548 g. Blackish crown; cheeks and throat usually grey or slate; upperparts normally with faint vermiculations, underparts paler with dark crescents on flanks and vent. Female often more rufescent with paler belly. Juvenile as adult, but very small black and buff spotting on back and particularly on wings; profuse black barring on underparts. Races separated on coloration, extent of dorsal vermiculation and size; *traylori* uniform blackish above.

Habitat. Tropical forest in E of range; in W mostly in subtropical cloud forest at 1300-2200 m, but up to 2900 m in SE Peru and Bolivia; normally at forest edge or in glades, second growth or copses of *Alnus*.

Food and Feeding. Seeds (Lauraceae, Euphorbiaceae, Rutaceae); generally little known. Follows army ants, taking insects which try to escape them. Turns over leaves on forest floor to capture prey hidden beneath.

Breeding. Sept/Nov in SE Brazil, Oct in SE Peru. Nest at base of tree. 4-5 eggs, deep pink to dark reddish or chocolate depending on race; incubation 19 days (in captivity); chick tawny with dark crown.

Movements. Presumably sedentary; sometimes occurs at forest edge and by tracks.

Status and Conservation. Not globally threatened. Fairly common in lowlands, at lower densities in montane forest. In Brazil has increased notably in last century, perhaps due to decline of *T. solitarius*. Possibly extinct in Colombia.

Bibliography. Belton (1984), Dabbene (1972), Fjeldså & Krabbe (1990), Frisch & Frisch (1964), Hilty & Brown (1986), Liebermann (1936), Olivares (1958), Osgood & Conover (1922), de la Peña (1986), Pinto (1964), Rech (1984), Ruschi (1979), de Schauensee & Phelps (1978), Scott & Brooke (1985), Sick (1984), Sick *et al.* (1981), Willis (1983).

14. **Undulated Tinamou**
Crypturellus undulatus

French: Tinamou vermiculé   **German:** Wellentinamu   **Spanish:** Tinamú Ondulado
Other common names: Banded Tinamou

Taxonomy. *Tinamus undulatus* Temminck, 1815, Paraguay. Closely related to *C. cinnamomeus*. Six subspecies recognized.

Subspecies and Distribution.
C. u. manapiare Phelps & Phelps, 1952 - S Venezuela.
C. u. simplex (Salvadori, 1895) - SW Guyana, NC Brazil.
C. u. yapura (Spix, 1825) - SE Colombia, E Ecuador, E Peru, NW Brazil.
C. u. vermiculatus (Temminck, 1825) - E Brazil.
C. u. adspersus (Temminck, 1815) - C Brazil.
C. u. undulatus (Temminck, 1815) - SE Peru to N Argentina.

Descriptive notes. 28-32 cm; male 462-569 g, female c. 621 g. White throat; sooty crown, often with fine barring; wing-coverts tend to be paler, more olivaceous than back; flanks and undertail-coverts with ochraceous and black barring. Juvenile has black spotting on breast, sides and wing-coverts. Races fall into two main groups of coloration, brown and rufescent; separation within these according to crown colour and extent of black barring and vermiculations.

Habitat. Tropical zone, mainly in forest, dry scrub, *cerrado*, savanna, islands of forest in savannas, forest edge, *chaco* forest, *várzea*, open dry forest, moist gallery forest, river island forest; also in young secondary forest and near flooded areas. In *chaco* forest and *caatinga* of Brazil only found at edge, possibly because replaced here by species better adapted to dry conditions.

Food and Feeding. Small fruits, seeds and insects, especially Hemiptera, Odonata, beetles and beetle larvae.

Breeding. Feb-May in Colombia. 4-5 pale pink, wine pink or pale ash eggs; incubation 17 days (in captivity).

Movements. Presumably sedentary in general. Moves away from river islands during flooding; has been seen flying over small channels and lagoons on Amazon.

Status and Conservation. Not globally threatened. Generally common. Declining in *cerrado* region of C Brazil, due to extensive habitat deterioration and intense hunting pressure; also affected by mass-destruction of Amazonia (see page 123).

Bibliography. Cavalcanti (1988), Hilty & Brown (1986), Liebermann (1936), Narosky (1988), Olivares (1958), de la Peña (1986), Pinto (1964), Ruschi (1979), de Schauensee & Phelps (1978), Schubart *et al.* (1965), Short (1975), Sick (1984).

15. **Pale-browed Tinamou**
Crypturellus transfasciatus

French: Tinamou à grands sourcils   **German:** Brauentinamu   **Spanish:** Tinamú Cejudo

Taxonomy. *Crypturus transfasciatus* P. L. Sclater & Salvin, 1878, Manabí, Ecuador. Monotypic.

Distribution. W Ecuador to NW Peru.

Descriptive notes. 27-29 cm. Conspicuous whitish eyebrow, white throat; Male greyish olive to rufescent above, with pale barring on wing-coverts; female generally paler, with upperparts more heavily barred black and ochraceous.

Habitat. Humid tropical deciduous forest in lowlands.

Food and Feeding. No information available.

Breeding. Nov-Feb in Ecuador. Nest at foot of tree. Up to 7 eggs.

Movements. Presumably sedentary.

Status and Conservation. Not globally threatened. Natural tendency to be rare and currently considered near-threatened. Main threat is deforestation.

Bibliography. Blake (1977), Butler (1979), Marchant (1960), Parker *et al.* (1982).

16. **Brazilian Tinamou**
Crypturellus strigulosus

French: Tinamou oariana   **German:** Rotkehltinamu   **Spanish:** Tinamú Brasileño

Taxonomy. *Tinamus strigulosus* Temminck, 1815, Rio Madeira, Brazil. Recently proposed race *tambopatae* of doubtful validity; only known from one female. Monotypic.

Distribution. E Peru, NW Bolivia and S Amazonian Brazil.

Descriptive notes. 27-29 cm; male 332-464 g, female 388-500 g. Reddish brown back and cheeks; throat ranges from white to ferruginous. Male has faint black bars on rump and uppertail-coverts; female heavily barred black and ochraceous on wings and rump.

Habitat. Dense humid tropical forest of lowlands.

Food and Feeding. No information available.

Breeding. 4 eggs, pale purple with pinkish wash; incubation 13·5 days (in captivity).

Movements. Presumably sedentary.

Status and Conservation. Not globally threatened. Poorly known, but apparently uncommon. Main threat is undoubtedly destruction of Amazonian rain forest, as well as Atlantic forests of E Brazilian littoral (see pages 123, 124).

Bibliography. Blake (1959, 1960), Parker, Castillo *et al.* (1991), Parker, Parker *et al.* (1982), Pinto (1964), Remsen & Traylor (1989), Sick (1984).

inches 10
cm 25

PLATE 7

17

18

ssp *columbianus*

♂

♂ ssp *erythropus*

19

20

ssp *atrocapillus*

♂ ssp *saltuarius*

♀ ssp *cinnamomeus*

♂

ssp *garleppi*

♂

21

♀

ssp *occidentalis*

23

♀

ssp *goldmani*

♀

♂

22

24

25

26

27

28

29

17. Grey-legged Tinamou
Crypturellus duidae

French: Tinamou de Zimmer   **German:** Graufußtinamu   **Spanish:** Tinamú Patigrís

Taxonomy. *Crypturellus noctivagus duidae* Zimmer, 1938, Mt. Duida, Venezuela.
Considered by some a subspecies of *C. noctivagus*; also very close to *C. erythropus*. Monotypic.
Distribution. EC Colombia, S Venezuela.

Descriptive notes. 28·5-31 cm. White throat; crown rufescent brown, ochraceous underparts; grey legs. Male has faint black barring on rump and tail, heavier on flanks; female has thin buff barring on wing-coverts, rump and uppertail-coverts.
Habitat. Dense tropical rain forest and also open woodland with bushes; up to 500 m in Colombia, but only up to 200 m in Venezuela.
Food and Feeding. No information available.
Breeding. No information available.
Movements. Presumably sedentary.
Status and Conservation. Not globally threatened. Little known; species has very restricted range, but apparently not in danger at present.
Bibliography. Hilty & Brown (1986), Novaes (1978), Olivares (1958), de Schauensee (1964), de Schauensee & Phelps (1978).

18. Red-legged Tinamou
Crypturellus erythropus

French: Tinamou à pieds rouges   **German:** Rotfußtinamu   **Spanish:** Tinamú Patirrojo
Other common names: Red-footed Tinamou; Colombian Tinamou (*columbianus*); Magdalena Tinamou (*saltuarius*); Santa Marta/Perjita Tinamou (*idoneus*).

Taxonomy. *Tinamus erythropus* Pelzeln, 1863, Manaus, Brazil.
Sometimes considered subspecies of *C. atrocapillus* or *C. noctivagus* and much debate over status of several related taxa within this group. Races *columbianus*, *saltuarius* and *idoneus* have all been considered full species, or alternatively races of other species (e.g. *C. cinnamomeus*, *C. boucardi*, *C. noctivagus*); *cursitans* and *spencei* have also been ascribed to other species. Seven subspecies currently recognized.
Subspecies and Distribution.
C. e. columbianus (Salvadori, 1895) - NC Colombia.
C. e. saltuarius Wetmore, 1950 - Magdalena Valley, NC Colombia.
C. e. idoneus (Todd, 1919) - NE Colombia, NW Venezuela.
C. e. cursitans Wetmore & Phelps, 1956 - N Colombia, NW Venezuela.
C. e. spencei (Brabourne & Chubb, 1914) - N Venezuela.
C. e. margaritae Phelps & Phelps, 1948 - Margarita I (Venezuela).
C. e. erythropus (Pelzeln, 1863) - E Venezuela to NE Brazil.

Descriptive notes. 27·5-31·5 cm; male c. 485 g. Legs pink to reddish; throat usually white, sometimes rufescent; grey chest contrasts with reddish brown face and breast. Female brighter and more heavily barred on upperparts. Races separated on plumage tones, especially on crown and belly, and extent of markings; *margaritae* smaller.
Habitat. Tropical and lower subtropical zones, up to 1700 m; mostly in thorny thickets, open forest, second growth and dry to moist low deciduous forest; also grassland with bushes and few trees, open woodland and thorn scrub.
Food and Feeding. No information available.
Breeding. Jan-Sept in Colombia. Eggs light glossy pinkish brown, yellowish pink or reddish grey.
Movements. Presumably sedentary.
Status and Conservation. Not globally threatened. Complications of systematics have led to some confusion with other forms; apparently maintains low densities. Race *saltuarius* only known from holotype from middle Magdalena valley, N Colombia; rated Indeterminate and should perhaps be considered as anything from rare to extinct. Race *columbianus* currently considered near-threatened.
Bibliography. Blake (1977), Carriker (1955), Collar & Andrew (1988), Haverschmidt (1968), Hilty (1985), Hilty & Brown (1986), King (1978/79), Olivares (1958), Orejuela (1985), Ruschi (1979), de Schauensee & Phelps (1978), Sick (1984).

19. Yellow-legged Tinamou
Crypturellus noctivagus

French: Tinamou noctivague   **German:** Gelbfußtinamu   **Spanish:** Tinamú Patigualdo
Other common names: Wied's Tinamou

Taxonomy. *Tinamus noctivagus* Wied, 1820, Espírito Santo, Brazil.
Very similar to previous species, but separated by voice and colour of legs and eggs. Very close to several other species of *Crypturellus*, and may include *C. duidae* and *C. atrocapillus*. Two subspecies recognized.
Subspecies and Distribution.
C. n. zabele (Spix, 1825) - NE Brazil.
C. n. noctivagus (Wied, 1820) - SE Brazil.
Descriptive notes. 29-32·5 cm; male 533-602 g. Legs yellow to greenish; tawny or rufescent eyebrow; throat pale cinnamon to whitish; wings with tawny cinnamon barring; narrow black barring on rump,

uppertail-coverts and flanks. Juvenile thickly spotted buff on back; underparts brownish grey and ochraceous with darker brown markings. Race *zabele* distinctly paler.
Habitat. Tropical zone in forest, thorn scrub, savanna woodland and gallery forest.
Food and Feeding. Seeds, shoots, plant matter and insects, especially beetles and ants.
Breeding. Nov in S Brazil. 4 eggs; start off pale blue, becoming ashy after a few days; incubation 17 days (in captivity).
Movements. Presumably sedentary.
Status and Conservation. INSUFFICIENTLY KNOWN. Common to rare in natural state. Suffering intensely from both deforestation and hunting pressure, especially in Atlantic forests (see page 124), where now restricted to a few sites. Nominate race formerly common, but has also suffered extensive habitat destruction. Species adapts well to captivity, though with limited breeding success to date.
Bibliography. Belton (1984), Collar & Andrew (1988), Osgood & Conover (1922), Pinto (1964), Ruschi (1979), Schubart *et al.* (1965), Scott & Brooke (1985), Sick (1969, 1972, 1984), Sick & Teixeira (1979), Sick *et al.* (1981), Willis & Oniki (1981).

20. Black-capped Tinamou
Crypturellus atrocapillus

French: Tinamou à calotte noire   **German:** Schwarzkappentinamu   **Spanish:** Tinamú Capirotado
Other common names: Garlepp's Tinamou (*garleppi*)

Taxonomy. *Crypturus atro-capillus* Tschudi, 1844, Peru.
Has been considered subspecies of *C. noctivagus*. Race *garleppi* may be distinct species. Two subspecies recognized.
Subspecies and Distribution.
C. a. atrocapillus (Tschudi, 1844) - SE Peru.
C. a. garleppi (Berlepsch, 1892) - N Bolivia.

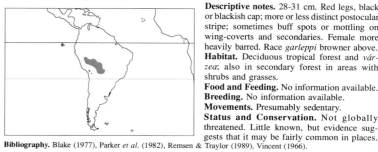

Descriptive notes. 28-31 cm. Red legs, black or blackish cap; more or less distinct postocular stripe; sometimes buff spots or mottling on wing-coverts and secondaries. Female more heavily barred. Race *garleppi* browner above.
Habitat. Deciduous tropical forest and *várzea*; also in secondary forest in areas with shrubs and grasses.
Food and Feeding. No information available.
Breeding. No information available.
Movements. Presumably sedentary.
Status and Conservation. Not globally threatened. Little known, but evidence suggests that it may be fairly common in places.
Bibliography. Blake (1977), Parker *et al.* (1982), Remsen & Traylor (1989), Vincent (1966).

21. Thicket Tinamou
Crypturellus cinnamomeus

French: Tinamou cannelle   **German:** Buschtinamu   **Spanish:** Tinamú Canelo
Other common names: Rufescent Tinamou

Taxonomy. *Tinamus (Nothura) cinnamomea* Lesson, 1842, El Salvador.
Possibly conspecific with *C. noctivagus* or *C. undulatus*; limited hybridization with *C. boucardi* in Honduras; perhaps close to *C. erythropus*. Nine subspecies recognized.
Subspecies and Distribution.
C. c. occidentalis (Salvadori, 1895) - CW Mexico.
C. c. soconuscensis Brodkorb, 1939 - SW Mexico.
C. c. mexicanus (Salvadori, 1895) - CE Mexico.
C. c. sallaei (Bonaparte, 1856) - S Mexico.
C. c. goldmani (Nelson, 1901) - SE Mexico, N Guatemala, N Belize.
C. c. vicinior Conover, 1933 - extreme S Mexico, C Guatemala, C Honduras.
C. c. cinnamomeus (Lesson, 1842) - S Guatemala, El Salvador, S Honduras.
C. c. delattrii (Bonaparte, 1854) - W Nicaragua.
C. c. praepes (Bangs & Peters, 1927) - NW Costa Rica.

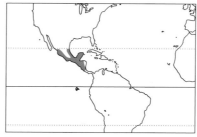

Descriptive notes. 25-30 cm; c. 440 g. White throat, cinnamon or rufescent cheeks and breast; blackish barring down back and on flanks and undertail-coverts. Female brighter, with upperparts more heavily barred than in male; often has narrow black barring on crown and upper breast. Races separated on size, plumage tones and extent of barring.
Habitat. Tropical and lower subtropical semi-arid zones; forest with undergrowth and bushes; also arid scrub, degraded secondary forest, islands of forest in savanna, occasionally in wetter forest. Prefers heavy undergrowth, especially with thorny bromeliads.
Food and Feeding. Fallen fruits, berries, seeds and small animals picked off forest floor. Insects include ants, termites, beetles, moths and butterflies.
Breeding. Mar-Aug in Costa Rica. Nest is shallow scrape, lined with leaves, at base of tree, usually in amongst low vegetation. Normally 3 eggs (up to 7), which are quite glossy purplish bronze to purplish pink; incubation 16 days; chicks become independent at c. 20 days.

On following pages: 22. Slaty-breasted Tinamou (*Crypturellus boucardi*); 23. Choco Tinamou (*Crypturellus kerriae*); 24. Variegated Tinamou (*Crypturellus variegatus*); 25. Rusty Tinamou (*Crypturellus brevirostris*); 26. Bartlett's Tinamou (*Crypturellus bartletti*); 27. Small-billed Tinamou (*Crypturellus parvirostris*); 28. Barred Tinamou (*Crypturellus casiquiare*); 29. Tataupa Tinamou (*Crypturellus tataupa*).

Movements. Presumably more or less sedentary, but in Costa Rica tends to occupy evergreen gallery forest for most of dry season.
Status and Conservation. Not globally threatened. Common in Mexico and Honduras. One of commonest tinamous of C America.
Bibliography. Dickey & van Rossem (1938), Edwards (1989), Janzen (1983), Lowery & Dalquest (1951), Monroe (1968), Ramos (1985a, 1985b), Schaldach (1963), Slud (1964), Smithe (1966), Stiles (1985), Stiles & Skutch (1989), Sutton (1951).

22. Slaty-breasted Tinamou
Crypturellus boucardi

French: Tinamou de Boucard **German:** Graukehltinamu **Spanish:** Tinamú Pizarroso
Other common names: Boucard Tinamou

Taxonomy. *Tinamus boucardi* P. L. Sclater (*ex* Sallé MS), 1859, Oaxaca, Mexico.
Known to have hybridized with *C. cinnamomeus* in parts of Honduras. Sometimes includes *C. erythropus* and *C. kerriae*. Two subspecies recognized.
Subspecies and Distribution.
C. b. boucardi (P. L. Sclater, 1859) - SE Mexico, Belize, N Guatemala, (?) NW Honduras.
C. b. costaricensis (Dwight & Griscom, 1924) - N & E Honduras, E Nicaragua to N Costa Rica.

Descriptive notes. 26-29 cm; 440-500 g. Blackish head, white throat, slaty breast and pink to bright red legs; back to uppertail-coverts ranges from blackish to deep chestnut. Female has conspicuous cinnamon barring on wings and rump; underparts paler, with heavier barring. Juvenile similar to adult. Race *costaricensis* has darker back and breast.
Habitat. Humid tropical and lower subtropical forest, from sea-level up to c. 1800 m; a variety of different forest types, typically with damp shrub layer, but sometimes quite open at ground level; also found in second growth and thickets. Usually near forest edge, but avoids paths and clearings.
Food and Feeding. Fallen fruit and seeds, e.g. of *Pseudolmedia spuria*, *Brosimum alicastrum*, *Protium* and also Sapotaceae; also ants (including army ants *Eciton burchelii* and *Labidus praedator*), termites (e.g. *Armitermes intermedius*), butterfly and moth larvae, beetles and other insects; also small lizards and frogs. Often looks for insects under twigs and leaves.
Breeding. Jan-Jun in Belize; Mar-Jul in Guatemala; Mar-Oct in Costa Rica. Male mates with 2-4 females; females not territorial, laying and then departing to mate with another male; male can incubate several successive broods during single breeding season. Nest is mat of leaves which is gradually pressed into ground, forming slight depression; usually placed at base of tree between buttresses, alternatively under a bush or in dense vegetation. Up to 10 purplish pink eggs; incubation 15-17 days; chicks have brown down; adult-like plumage acquired after only c. 20 days.
Movements. Presumably more or less sedentary. Moves erratically about territory, seeking food; moves maximum of c. 1 km in 1 day. Most activity in morning and evening, with no apparent seasonal variation.
Status and Conservation. Not globally threatened. Rare in Mexico, fairly common in Costa Rica. Local distribution may be heavily influenced by logging, plantation cutting and hunting.
Bibliography. Edwards (1989), Lancaster (1964a, 1964b), Land (1970), Lowery & Dalquest (1951), Monroe (1968), Ramos (1985a, 1985b), Slud (1964), Smithe (1966), Stiles (1985), Stiles & Skutch (1989).

23. Choco Tinamou
Crypturellus kerriae

French: Tinamou de Kerr **German:** Kerrtinamu **Spanish:** Tinamú del Chocó

Taxonomy. *Crypturus kerriae* Chapman, 1915, Chocó, Colombia.
Possibly conspecific with *C. boucardi*. Monotypic.
Distribution. Extreme SE Panama, NW Colombia.

Descriptive notes. 25-26·5 cm. Bright red legs; blackish crown, slate grey sides of head, whitish to grey throat; inconspicuous black barring on upperparts. Female darker above, with obvious black barring on wing-coverts; breast and sides slate grey.
Habitat. Heavy, humid tropical forest; low hills, 300-800 m.
Food and Feeding. No information available.
Breeding. No information available.
Movements. Presumably sedentary.
Status and Conservation. RARE. Very little known and not found in Panama until 1970. May be vulnerable due to restricted range.
Bibliography. Delgado (1985), Hilty (1985), Hilty & Brown (1986), Mendez (1979), Olivares (1958), Orejuela (1985), Ramos (1985a, 1985b), Ridgely & Gwynne (1989), Robbins *et al*. (1985), Wetmore & Galindo (1972).

24. Variegated Tinamou
Crypturellus variegatus

French: Tinamou varié **German:** Rotbrusttinamu **Spanish:** Tinamú Abigarrado

Taxonomy. *Tetrao variegatus* Gmelin, 1789, Cayenne.
Monotypic.
Distribution. Amazonian Brazil, Peru, Colombia, Venezuela and the Guianas; also littoral of E Brazil.
Descriptive notes. 28-31 cm; male c. 376 g, female 354-423 g. Black head, rufous neck and breast. Larger and brighter than *C. bartleti*. Juvenile as adult, with much fainter dorsal barring; underparts indistinctly spotted or barred.

Habitat. Forest and thickets of tropical and subtropical zones, 100-1300 m; rain forest and other forest types, often in clearings.
Food and Feeding. Seeds, fruits and insects.
Breeding. Apr in Venezuela; May/Jun (rainy season) in Guyana. 1 egg, rarely 2; colour variable, from brown washed with pinkish violet and purplish brown to pale chocolate.
Movements. Presumably sedentary.
Status and Conservation. Not globally threatened. Uncommon. Populations of E Brazil have declined appreciably, probably due mostly to habitat destruction; presumably also affected by forest destruction of Amazonia (see page 123).
Bibliography. Beebe (1925), Butler (1979), Hilty & Brown (1986), Olivares (1958), Parker, Castillo *et al*. (1991), Parker, Parker *et al*. (1982), Pinto (1964), Remsen & Traylor (1989), Ruschi (1979), de Schauensee & Phelps (1978), Sick (1984), Todd (1937), Willis (1983).

25. Rusty Tinamou
Crypturellus brevirostris

French: Tinamou rubigineux **German:** Rosttinamu **Spanish:** Tinamú Herrumbroso
Other common names: Short-billed Tinamou

Taxonomy. *Tinamus brevirostris* Pelzeln, 1863, Manaus.
May include *C. bartletti*. Monotypic.
Distribution. E Peru, NW Brazil; also French Guiana and extreme NE Brazil.

Descriptive notes. 25-28 cm. Crown ferruginous to dusky chestnut, often barred; throat white, vent and flanks pale ochraceous; thin black barring on flanks; yellowish legs. Juvenile duller than adult, upperparts pale brown with inconspicuous blackish barring; flanks with sparse black spotting or barring.
Habitat. Dense humid tropical forest, typically in *várzea*.
Food and Feeding. No information available.
Breeding. No information available.
Movements. Presumably sedentary.
Status and Conservation. Not globally threatened. Little known, but not apparently at risk; may be affected by destruction of Amazonia (see page 123).
Bibliography. Frisch (1981), Hilty & Brown (1986), Olivares (1958), Parker *et al*. (1982), Pinto (1964), Ruschi (1979), de Schauensee (1964), Sick (1984).

26. Bartlett's Tinamou
Crypturellus bartletti

French: Tinamou de Bartlett **German:** Bartlett-Tinamu **Spanish:** Tinamú de Bartlett

Taxonomy. *Crypturus bartletti* P. L. Sclater & Salvin, 1873, Río Huallaga, Peru.
Very similar to *C. brevirostris*, of which it has been considered a subspecies, but apparently some overlap in E Peru. Monotypic.
Distribution. E Peru, N Bolivia, W Brazil.

Descriptive notes. 25-28 cm. Crown and nape uniform blackish, throat whitish; sides of head grey or brownish, sometimes tinged ferruginous; most of upperparts heavily barred black and pale olive or reddish brown; breast pale buff to ochraceous, sometimes bright rufous at base of neck. Juvenile similar to that of *C. brevirostris*, with blackish crown; sparse black and white spotting on wing-coverts and breast; dark bars on flanks indistinct.
Habitat. Primary dense humid tropical forest; also recorded in shrubby thickets.
Food and Feeding. No information available.
Breeding. No information available.
Movements. Presumably sedentary.
Status and Conservation. Not globally threatened. Generally rare to uncommon throughout range, but fairly common in Peru; may be affected by habitat destruction in Amazonia (see page 123).
Bibliography. Hilty & Brown (1986), Olivares (1958), Parker *et al*. (1982), Pearson (1975), Remsen & Traylor (1989), Ruschi (1979), de Schauensee (1964).

27. Small-billed Tinamou
Crypturellus parvirostris

French: Tinamou à petit bec **German:** Kleinschnabeltinamu **Spanish:** Tinamú Piquicorto

Taxonomy. *Crypturus parvirostris* Wagler, 1827, Brazil.
Not obviously very close to any other species of *Crypturellus*. Monotypic.
Distribution. SE Peru, N & E Bolivia, Paraguay, NE Argentina and most of Brazil S of Amazon.
Descriptive notes. 20-32 cm; male 154-205 g, female 176-250 g. Crown, sides of head and neck range from brown to pale slate; undertail-coverts buff with dark centres; flanks reddish brown to black, with thin pale edges, giving bold scalloped appearance.
Habitat. Tropical forest (often secondary), riverbank vegetation, stands of bamboo, scrub, grassland with thornbush scrub, open fields and sometimes in cotton and millet plantations; typical species of both *cerrado* and *caatinga*.
Food and Feeding. Seeds of grasses, leguminous plants, Cyperaceae, Euphorbiaceae, Malvaceae, etc.; large amounts of termites and ants, also Hemiptera and other insects.

Breeding. 4-5 eggs, which are pale chocolate-coloured, with violet tint; incubation 19 days (in captivity).
Movements. Presumably sedentary.
Status and Conservation. Not globally threatened. Relatively common, although rare in Peru. Declining in *cerrado* of C Brazil, due to intense pressure of illegal hunting, but still quite common.
Bibliography. Belton (1984), Cavalcanti (1988), Dabbene (1972), Hoy (1980), Liebermann (1936), Navas & Bó (1988), Pearson (1975), de la Peña (1986), Pinto (1964), Ruschi (1979), Schubart *et al.* (1965), Scott & Brooke (1985), Short (1975, 1976), Sick (1984), Sick *et al.* (1981).

28. Barred Tinamou
Crypturellus casiquiare

French: Tinamou barré   **German:** Bindentinamu   **Spanish:** Tinamú Casiquiare

Taxonomy. *Crypturornis casiquiare* Chapman, 1929, Amazonas, Venezuela.
Monotypic.

Distribution. E Colombia and extreme S Venezuela.
Descriptive notes. 25·5-27 cm. Rufous head; upperparts boldly barred blackish and rufous; grey foreneck. Female larger and brighter. Juvenile has duller, browner barring on upperparts; rufous flecks on breast, white speckles on wing-coverts.
Habitat. Thick lowland forest, up to 200 m; apparently confined to sandy-belt forests of upper Orinoco/Negro basins.
Food and Feeding. No information available.
Breeding. No information available.
Movements. Presumably sedentary.
Status and Conservation. Not globally threatened. Next to nothing known about populations.

Bibliography. Hilty & Brown (1986), Olivares (1958), Orejuela (1985), de Schauensee (1964), de Schauensee & Phelps (1978), Vincent (1966).

29. Tataupa Tinamou
Crypturellus tataupa

French: Tinamou tataupa   **German:** Tataupatinamu   **Spanish:** Tinamú Tataupá

Taxonomy. *Tinamus tataupa* Temminck, 1815, Rio de Janeiro, Brazil.
Four subspecies recognized.
Subspecies and Distribution.
C. t. inops Bangs & Noble, 1918 - NW Peru.
C. t. peruviana (Cory, 1915) - C Peru.
C. t. lepidotus (Swainson, 1837) - NE Brazil.
C. t. tataupa (Temminck, 1815) - N & E Bolivia to C & SE Brazil and N Argentina.

Descriptive notes. 24·5-26·5 cm; male 169-229 g, female 189-298 g. Distinctly larger than *C. parvirostris*, with foreneck and breast bluish grey, upperparts much deeper, darker brown. Juvenile as adult, with black and white markings across wings. Races separated on size and coloration.
Habitat. Tropical and subtropical forest, in wet, densely vegetated gulleys, near forest edge; locally in grassy areas and scrub. Sometimes seen crossing paths.
Food and Feeding. Ants, small gastropods, seeds (Euphorbiaceae) and other plant matter.
Breeding. 4-5 eggs; olivaceous grey to pale chocolate with pinkish tinge; incubation 19 days (in captivity).
Movements. Presumably sedentary.
Status and Conservation. Not globally threatened. Generally common, but rare in Peru. May suffer from habitat destruction, but probably more adaptable than other members of genus. Scarce in Rio Grande do Sul, S Brazil. Relatively frequent in zoos; bred in captivity in France around turn of century.
Bibliography. Belton (1984), Dabbene (1972), Hudson (1920), Liebermann (1936), de la Peña (1986), Pinto (1964), Ruschi (1979), Rutgers & Norris (1970), Schubart *et al.* (1965), Scott & Brooke (1985), Seth-Smith (1904), Short (1975, 1976), Sick (1984), Sick *et al.* (1981), Speroni (1987).

ssp *rufescens*

ssp *maculicollis*

30

31

32

33

34

35

36

37

38

39

40

41

42

43

44

ssp *multiguttata*

ssp *albida*

45

46

47

PLATE 8

inches 8

cm 20

Subfamily RHYNCHOTINAE

Genus *RHYNCHOTUS* Spix, 1825

30. Red-winged Tinamou

Rhynchotus rufescens

French: Tinamou isabelle   **German:** Pampahuhn   **Spanish:** Tinamú Alirrojo

Taxonomy. *Tinamus rufescens* Temminck, 1815, São Paulo, Brazil.
Known from Pleistocene at Minas Gerais. Four subspecies recognized.
Subspecies and Distribution.
R. r. catingae Reiser, 1905 - C & NE Brazil.
R. r. rufescens (Temminck, 1815) - N Bolivia to E Brazil and S to E Paraguay, NE Argentina and Uruguay.
R. r. pallescens Kothe, 1907 - NE & C Argentina.
R. r. maculicollis G. R. Gray, 1867 - NW Bolivia to NW Argentina.

Descriptive notes. 39-42·5 cm; male 700-920 g, female 815-1040 g. Large, with stout, decurved bill; black crown patch, rufous primaries; neck sometimes black; underparts pale greyish brown to whitish; varying extent of black barring on flanks, abdomen and vent. Juvenile as adult. Races separated by coloration and shade of dorsal barring; *maculicollis* has conspicuous dark streaks on foreneck.
Habitat. Sea-level up to 2500 m and above; habitat varies with altitude. In tropical lowlands favours damp grassland and savanna woodland; race *maculicollis* occupies semi-arid, temperate valleys in Andes, with thorn-scrub and scattered trees, as well as fields of cereals, from 1000 m locally up to 3050 m.
Food and Feeding. Mostly animal in summer, vegetable in winter, when insects scarce. Seeds, fruits, shoots, roots, tubers and bulbs; also cereals and other crops (one stomach from Brazil produced 313 grains of rice, while another produced peanuts with their shells). Animals include insects (one stomach contained 707 termites); particularly keen on grasshoppers and occasionally takes reptiles, amphibians (*Rana*, *Bufo*) and small mammals. Uses bill to scratch away at ground and uncover insects, especially termites, also roots and bulbs; this activity has also been recorded in captivity, where it was not necessary as food was already supplied; can be agricultural pest, when unearths roots of cassava. Will jump up almost 1 m to peck an insect off vegetation. Captive birds seen to eat poisonous snakes (*Thamnophis*) over 35 cm long.
Breeding. Relatively little known. Timing probably varies throughout range; Aug onwards in Brazil. Nest is slight depression scratched in ground and lined with grass. Up to 5 eggs, wine red or reddish purple, though white eggs have been recorded; incubation 19-21 days; chick at hatching weighs c. 38 g and has red and white down with extensive black streaking; adult-like plumage acquired in c. 3 weeks.
Movements. Presumably sedentary.
Status and Conservation. Not globally threatened. Generally common, abundant in places, hunted out in others, such as Guaiba and Barra de Ribeiro regions of Brazil. Much appreciated for its meat and hence hunted heavily, and often illegally, hunted especially in proximity of civilization. Steady decline in Brazil, due to hunting pressure and perhaps poisoning by insecticides; also grassland often burnt to regenerate pastures, during breeding season. Marked decline too in *pampas* of Argentina, mostly due to hunting and agricultural development at expense of grassland; still fairly common, where protected on some ranches. Destruction of tropical forests to make way for pastures has helped this species to colonize new areas. Well-adapted to captivity and frequent in S American zoos; first captive breeding in France, 1869. Races *rufescens*, *pallescens* and *maculicollis* in CITES II, due to pressure from live animal trade. Species introduced to several European countries for hunting, but without success.
Bibliography. Belton (1984), Bucher & Nores (1988), Cavalcanti (1988), Dabbene (1972), Fjeldså & Krabbe (1990), Graham *et al.* (1980), Liebermann (1936), Menegheti (1983), Menegheti *et al.* (1985), de la Peña (1986), Pinto (1964), Ruschi (1979), Rutgers & Norris (1970), Sander (1982), Scott & Brooke (1985), Short (1975), Sick (1984), Sick *et al.* (1981), Weeks (1973), Wetmore (1926).

Genus *NOTHOPROCTA*

P. L. Sclater & Salvin, 1873

31. Taczanowski's Tinamou

Nothoprocta taczanowskii

French: Tinamou de Taczanowski   **Spanish:** Tinamú de Taczanowski
German: Taczanowskisteißhuhn

Taxonomy. *Nothoprocta taczanowskii* P. L. Sclater & Salvin, 1875, Junín, Peru.
N. godmani Taczanowski, 1886, may be immature of this species. Monotypic.
Distribution. C & SE Peru.
Descriptive notes. 32·5-36 cm. Long, thin, decurved bill; dark barring on upperparts with pale margins; inconspicuous dark bars on flanks, white spots on breast. Juvenile has breast and upperparts much browner; flanks light brown with black spotting.
Habitat. Temperate zone of Andes in pastures and semi-arid open rocky areas with scrub above tree-line, 2700-4000 m; typically in open woods of *Polylepis* and areas with great Andean bromeliad *Puya raimondii*, but not often in grassland. May frequent small fields of tubers.

Food and Feeding. No information available.
Breeding. Apr-May; chicks recorded in Junín and Puno provinces, in May and Oct respectively.
Movements. Presumably sedentary.
Status and Conservation. INSUFFICIENTLY KNOWN. Apparently rare within its limited range. Suffering from habitat destruction, with cutting and burning of grassland and *Polylepis* woodland, and increased cultivation.
Bibliography. Blake (1977), Collar & Andrew (1988), Fjeldså (1988a), Fjeldså & Krabbe (1990).

32. Kalinowski's Tinamou

Nothoprocta kalinowskii

French: Tinamou de Kalinowski   **Spanish:** Tinamú de Kalinowski
German: Kalinowskisteißhuhn

Taxonomy. *Nothoprocta kalinowskii* Berlepsch & Stolzmann, 1901, Cuzco, Peru.
Sometimes considered subspecies of *N. ornata*, but more probably distinct lower altitude species. Monotypic.
Distribution. NC & SE Peru.

Descriptive notes. 33·5-35 cm. Prominent blackish speckling on head and back. Darker and more rufous than *N. ornata*, with coarser black spotting above and shorter bill.
Habitat. Temperate zone of Andes, up to 3000 m and perhaps even to 4575 m; in arid parts with scrub and sometimes in cultivation, may not use grassland. (Recent record from forested area is misprint)
Food and Feeding. No information available.
Breeding. No information available.
Movements. Presumably sedentary.
Status and Conservation. INDETERMINATE. No recent reliable records; probably disappearing, though may survive locally in small numbers.
Bibliography. Ceballos-Bendezu (1985), Collar & Andrew (1988), Blake (1977), Fjeldså (1988a), Fjeldså & Krabbe (1990), Parker *et al.* (1982).

33. Ornate Tinamou

Nothoprocta ornata

French: Tinamou orné   **German:** Pisaccasteißhuhn   **Spanish:** Tinamú Pisacca

Taxonomy. *Rhynchotus ornatus* G. R. Gray, 1867, Bolivia.
Three subspecies recognized.
Subspecies and Distribution.
N. o. branickii Taczanowski, 1875 - C Peru.
N. o. ornata (G. R. Gray, 1867) - S Peru, W Bolivia, N Chile.
N. o. rostrata Berlepsch, 1907 - NW Argentina.

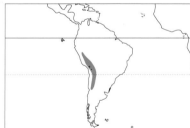

Descriptive notes. 31-35 cm; male 444-700 g, female 593-761 g. Thin, decurved bill; dark spotting on head and neck can be heavier; breast grey, often tinged pinkish buff. Bill less prominently decurved in female. Paler and less uniform than *N. perdicaria* and *N. pentlandii*. Juvenile browner above, with less spotting on face, and conspicuous black malar stripe. Races separated by size, coloration, bill length and extent of spotting and barring.
Habitat. High altitude steppe of *puna*, at 3500-4800 m, sometimes down to 2500 m. Mainly on hill slopes dominated by bunch-grass, less often on summits or flat ground; also found sometimes in areas of "tola" heath or open stands of *Puya* or *Polylepis*. Prefers to be near cultivation and water.
Food and Feeding. Clover, small leaves, fruits, shoots, tender buds, roots, grass seeds and pods, fond of damp, green grass around springs or areas of seepage; also caterpillars, beetles, grasshoppers and ants. Sometimes looks for insects under cowpats. Causes a fair amount of crop damage, particularly by digging up and eating potatoes; also eats ears of barley. Male normally precedes female in "Follow-feeding", which is common feeding practice, but also plays a part in typical courtship behaviour.
Breeding. Dec-Apr and Jun-Aug in Peru; southern spring and summer in Bolivia, Chile and Argentina. Apparently monogamous. Nest is round structure of twigs, grass and feathers on base of turf, placed under a clump of grass. 4-9 eggs, glossy violet-chocolate to vinaceous grey-brown, laid at daily intervals; incubation 22-24 days; chicks heavily streaked black and brown, leave nest c. 20 hours after hatching.
Movements. Presumably more or less sedentary. Regularly moves c. 200 m down slopes to feed and then returns. May fly to feeding grounds, to cross rivers or when alarmed. Normally walks from foot of slope to feeding grounds or to drink around dawn and dusk, alone, in pairs or in coveys, perhaps consisting of an adult and several young. During incubation breaks, male may wander far from nest to feed.
Status and Conservation. Not globally threatened. Widespread, but at moderate densities; common in places. Probably most severely persecuted Andean species: shepherds catch birds with nooses

---

On following pages: 34. Chilean Tinamou (*Nothoprocta perdicaria*); 35. Brushland Tinamou (*Nothoprocta cinerascens*); 36. Andean Tinamou (*Nothoprocta pentlandii*); 37. Curve-billed Tinamou (*Nothoprocta curvirostris*); 38. White-bellied Nothura (*Nothura boraquira*); 39. Lesser Nothura (*Nothura minor*); 40. Darwin's Nothura (*Nothura darwinii*); 41. Spotted Nothura (*Nothura maculosa*); 42. Chaco Nothura (*Nothura chacoensis*); 43. Dwarf Tinamou (*Taoniscus nanus*); 44. Elegant Crested Tinamou (*Eudromia elegans*); 45. Quebracho Crested Tinamou (*Eudromia formosa*); 46. Puna Tinamou (*Tinamotis pentlandii*); 47. Patagonian Tinamou (*Tinamotis ingoufi*).

and take eggs; also hunted with guns and dogs. In many places, such as parts of Bolivia where it is heavily hunted, close season not well-established, but in some cases local hunters control this efficiently. Other predators include Variable Hawk (*Buteo poecilochrous*) and Andean fox (*Dusicyon culpaeus*), as well as dogs belonging to local inhabitants. Much reduced by hunting in environs of civilization.

Bibliography. Bailey (1955), Cabot & Serrano (1988), Dabbene (1972), Fjeldså & Krabbe (1990), Johnson (1965), Liebermann (1936), Pearson & Pearson (1955), de la Peña (1986).

34. Chilean Tinamou
Nothoprocta perdicaria

French: Tinamou perdrix   **German:** Chilesteißhuhn   **Spanish:** Tinamú Chileno

Taxonomy. *Crypturus perdicarius* Kittlitz, 1830, Valparaíso, Chile.
Forms superspecies with *N. pentlandii* and *N. cinerascens*. Two subspecies recognized.
Subspecies and Distribution.
N. p. perdicaria (Kittlitz, 1830) - NC Chile.
N. p. sanborni Conover, 1924 - SC Chile.
Introduced (ssp. *perdicaria*) to Easter I, SE Pacific.

Descriptive notes. 29·5-32 cm. Cinnamon bars on wing-coverts and secondaries; breast fairly uniform, throat whitish. Juvenile as adult, breast browner with blackish spotting. Race *sanborni* considerably darker, with grey of breast weaker or lacking.
Habitat. Semi-arid prairies, grassland and scrub; also in fields of cereals. Frequently beside roads.
Food and Feeding. No information available.
Breeding. Dec. Nest is made of loose bits of grass and is situated under bush or clump of grass. 5-8 (-12) chocolate-coloured eggs, with porcelain-like aspect; chicks heavily streaked black and brown.
Movements. Presumably sedentary. Usually in small coveys.
Status and Conservation. Not globally threatened. Much reduced in recent years, especially in N of range; now scarce in N, commoner in S. Most prized game bird in Chile, where hunted with guns and dogs, but also trapped illegally. Race *perdicaria* introduced to Easter I, SE Pacific (see page 122).
Bibliography. Araya & Millie (1986), Fjeldså & Krabbe (1990), Glade (1988), Johnson (1965), Reed (1919), Withers *et al.* (1987).

35. Brushland Tinamou
Nothoprocta cinerascens

French: Tinamou sauvageon   **German:** Cordobasteißhuhn   **Spanish:** Tinamú Montaraz

Taxonomy. *Nothura cinerascens* Burmeister, 1860, Tucumán, Argentina.
Two subspecies recognized.
Subspecies and Distribution.
N. c. cinerascens (Burmeister, 1860) - SE Bolivia, NW Paraguay, NW & C Argentina.
N. c. parvimaculata Olrog, 1959 - NW Argentina.

Descriptive notes. 30-33 cm; male 457-493 g, female 540-615 g. Thinnish black dorsal barring. Generally whiter than *N. taczanowskii*, with shorter bill and black and white spotting on neck. Female slightly larger and darker, with breast more heavily barred. Juvenile browner. Race *parvimaculata* paler, with smaller breast spots.
Habitat. Fairly tolerant; typical species of Chaco region; only lowland *Nothoprocta*, found up to 2000 m, but rarely above 1000 m. Semi-arid ground with scattered bushes, xerophilous woodland, open thornscrub, grassy steppe and sometimes in flooded savanna; also in fields of sorghum, maize and alfalfa, preferably by hillsides. Nests in fairly open sites, but may feed in woodland or fields.
Food and Feeding. Largely animal, including insects (ants, cicadas, beetles), insect larvae and earthworms, which may be probed for in ground. Seeds of Compositae and maize; fruit taken off ground, or plucked off plant sometimes with little jump. Around drainage ditches, molluscs may constitute an important part of diet.
Breeding. Sept-Apr. Males polygynous, and each normally attempts to raise 2 or more broods every season. Nest is grass-lined scrape under bush. 8-11 glossy dark olivaceous or dusky purplish brown eggs; incubation 19-20 days.
Movements. Presumably sedentary. Males move erratically around territory, normally covering much less than 1 km in a day, though up to 4 km recorded; each male has basic home range, but may wander out of this into that of neighbouring male at times. Females may move around in unstable groups of 2 or more, roving through territories of different males.
Status and Conservation. Not globally threatened. Common. Range somewhat reduced, but effective protection on some large estates. Agricultural development may be main threat. Mammalian predators probably take fair numbers, and rattlesnakes (*Crotalus*) may account for some.
Bibliography. Cabot & Serrano (1988), Dabbene (1972), Lancaster (1964c), Liebermann (1936), Narosky & Yzurieta (1987), Partridge (1953), de la Peña (1986), Short (1975), Zapata & Martínez (1977).

36. Andean Tinamou
Nothoprocta pentlandii

French: Tinamou des Andes   **German:** Andensteißhuhn   **Spanish:** Tinamú Andino

Taxonomy. *Rhynchotus Pentlandii* G. R. Gray, 1867, Andes of Bolivia.
Seven subspecies recognized; a distinct subspecies, as yet undescribed, probably inhabits S coast of Peru.
Subspecies and Distribution.
N. p. ambigua Cory, 1915 - S Ecuador, NW Peru.
N. p. oustaleti Berlepsch & Stolzmann, 1901 - C & S Peru.

N. p. niethammeri Koepcke, 1968 - WC Peru.
N. p. fulvescens Berlepsch, 1902 - SE Peru.
N. p. pentlandii (G. R. Gray, 1867) - W Bolivia, extreme N Chile, NW Argentina.
N. p. doeringi Cabanis, 1878 - C Argentina.
N. p. mendozae Banks & Bohl, 1968 - WC Argentina.

Descriptive notes. 25·5-30 cm; 260-325 g. Slender, decurved bill; brownish grey back; neck and breast more delicately speckled white than in *N. taczanowskii*. Juvenile has pale spotting of breast mixed in with dark bars and vermiculations. Races form two groups, grey (in E) and brown (in W); details of plumage and bill length also significant for separation in some cases.
Habitat. Steep slopes of semi-arid valleys, mostly 1500-3600 m, but in places over 4000 m; typically in shrub-steppe, with coarse herbs (e.g. *Lupinus*), but often found in ravines, in dense vegetation along streams. Also near edge of cloud forest, areas of thornbush, columnar cactus (*Jatropa*) and sometimes in open *Polylepis* woodland, or with scattered *Carica* trees; also visits fields of crops, e.g. potatoes, alfalfa.
Food and Feeding. Seeds, shoots, buds and small fleshy fruits; crops, such as potatoes and barley, also insect larvae. One stomach of a bird taken near human habitation contained human excrement. Habitually swallows pebbles to help break down food.
Breeding. Austral spring/summer; also recorded in Jul/Aug in W Peru. Nest sited underneath bush; nest is depression 15 cm wide and 7 cm deep, lined with straw, thin stems and a few feathers. 5-8 (-14) eggs may be laid by different females; eggs glossy pale chocolate, tinged pinkish violet; chicks heavily streaked black and brown.
Movements. Presumably sedentary. Rarely moves out of cover of bushes or scrub.
Status and Conservation. Not globally threatened. Locally common. Tendency to hide away in dense vegetation, especially on steep slopes, has undoubtedly helped it to survive and prosper; much of its habitat is fairly inaccessible.
Bibliography. Dabbene (1972), Fjeldså (1988a), Fjeldså & Krabbe (1990), Johnson (1965, 1967, 1972), Koepcke (1968), Liebermann (1936), de la Peña (1986), Reed (1919), Salvador & Narosky (1984).

37. Curve-billed Tinamou
Nothoprocta curvirostris

French: Tinamou curvirostre   **German:** Krummschnabel-Steißhuhn   **Spanish:** Tinamú del Páramo

Taxonomy. *Nothoprocta curvirostris* P. L. Sclater & Salvin, 1873, Pichincha, Ecuador.
Two subspecies recognized.
Subspecies and Distribution.
N. c. curvirostris P. L. Sclater & Salvin, 1873 - C Ecuador to N Peru.
N. c. peruviana Taczanowski, 1886 - N & C Peru.

Descriptive notes. 26-29·5 cm. Bill fairly long, pointed and decurved; ochraceous-rufous underparts contrast with rest of *Nothoprocta*. Juvenile has breast and sides duller and less rufescent, with black spots. Race *peruviana* smaller and possibly paler above, with duller vermiculations and smaller spots.
Habitat. Humid and semi-arid zones of *puna* and *páramo*, at 2800-3700 m in Ecuador; on sandy plateaus with bunch-grass; in stands of evergreen Ericaceae, *Hypericum* and scrub dominated by Compositae; sometimes in slash-and-burn cultivation.
Food and Feeding. No information available.
Breeding. Jan-Aug. Eggs chocolate brown; chick heavily streaked black, whitish and brown.
Movements. Presumably sedentary.
Status and Conservation. Not globally threatened. Generally common; inaccessibility of habitat and apparent adaptability of species suggest no immediate threats of importance.
Bibliography. Blake (1977), Chapman (1926), Fjeldså (1988a), Fjeldså & Krabbe (1990).

Genus *NOTHURA*   Wagler, 1827

38. White-bellied Nothura
Nothura boraquira

French: Tinamou boraquira   **German:** Weißbauch-Steißhuhn   **Spanish:** Tinamú Ventriblanco
Other common names: Yellow-legged Nothura

Taxonomy. *Tinamus boraquira* Spix, 1825, Minas Gerais, Brazil.
Monotypic.
Distribution. NE Brazil to E Bolivia and NE Paraguay.

Descriptive notes. 26-28·5 cm. Similar to *N. darwinii*, but black markings on neck form broader, more clearly defined stripes, and different pattern on wing-coverts. Extent of vermiculation on flanks variable.
Habitat. Tropical zone; dry pastures and grassland, with thornbush scrub and scattered trees. In Brazil occupies both dense and more open parts of *caatinga*, as well as much of *cerrado* zone and part of Chaco.
Food and Feeding. No information available.
Breeding. 4 pale chocolate eggs.
Movements. Presumably sedentary.
Status and Conservation. Not globally threatened. Agricultural development important in much of its range; irrigation of much of xeric

caatinga supported by government subsidies, and agriculture steadily replacing traditional cattle and goat ranching.
Bibliography. Cavalcanti (1988), Pinto (1964), Ruschi (1979), Short (1975), Sick (1965, 1984).

39. Lesser Nothura
Nothura minor

French: Petit Tinamou   **German:** Wachtelsteißhuhn   **Spanish:** Tinamú Menor

Taxonomy. *Tinamus minor* Spix, 1825, Minas Gerais, Brazil.
Monotypic.
Distribution. SE Brazil.

Descriptive notes. 18-19·5 cm; male 158-174 g, female c. 158 g. Small; belly pale ochre; bill relatively long. Plumage very variable, especially on upperparts, ranging from rufescent to buff; these may constitute distinct colour phases.
Habitat. Grassland and scrub of tropical zone in dense *cerrado* and also more open *campo-cerrado*.
Food and Feeding. No information available.
Breeding. No information available.
Movements. Presumably sedentary.
Status and Conservation. INSUFFICIENT-LY KNOWN. Generally considered rare; very little information available. Steady transformation of habitat (see page 124), often with plantations of pines and eucalyptus, as well as cultivation of sugar cane and soybeans. In immediate danger in state of São Paulo, where agricultural development progresses rapidly, as land easily converted for cultivation. Predators include Burrowing Owl (*Speotyto cunicularia*).
Bibliography. Cavalcanti (1988), Collar & Andrew (1988), de Magalhães (1978), Pinto (1964), Ruschi (1979), Sick (1965, 1984), Willis & Oniki (1988).

40. Darwin's Nothura
Nothura darwinii

French: Tinamou de Darwin   **German:** Darwinsteißhuhn   **Spanish:** Tinamú de Darwin

Taxonomy. *Nothura Darwinii* G. R. Gray, 1867, southern Buenos Aires.
Sometimes considered subspecies of *N. maculosa*, but ranges overlap and songs quite different.
Five subspecies recognized.
Subspecies and Distribution.
N. d. peruviana Berlepsch & Stolzmann, 1906 - S Peru.
N. d. agassizii Bangs, 1910 - SE Peru, WC Bolivia.
N. d. boliviana Salvadori, 1895 - W Bolivia.
N. d. salvadorii Hartert, 1909 - W Argentina.
N. d. darwinii G. R. Gray, 1867 - SC Argentina.

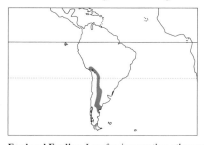

Descriptive notes. 25-27 cm; *boliviana* 179-200 g, *agassizii* 215-255 g. Slightly smaller than *N. boraquira*; lesser and median wing-coverts contrast with rest of wing to produce quite different pattern. Juvenile has paler, sometimes pure white throat; black spots, not stripes, on breast. Races separated by size and coloration.
Habitat. From subtropical lowlands up to 2600 m and locally up to 4300 m. In *puna*, occupies extensive plains with bunch-grass, also in tola (*Lepidophyllum*) heath; in temperate semi-arid Andean valleys uses grassland and cultivation of valley floor; also in subtropical lowland, open savanna and shrub-steppe.
Food and Feeding. Less frugivorous than other species; diet consists mainly of seeds and insects. In montane grassland tends to take seeds of bunch-grass, such as *Festuca*, in addition to some insects. In temperate valleys frequents fields of wheat, maize, barley and peas, especially after the harvest. Also eats seeds of other grasses and wild plants; very rarely leaves and green shoots. Ants, beetles and other insects taken too.
Breeding. Austral spring/summer; Nov/Dec in Bolivia. 4-6 eggs, lustrous reddish brown to greyish violet; chicks similar to those of *Nothoprocta*, but much less boldly marked.
Movements. Presumably sedentary.
Status and Conservation. Not globally threatened. Widespread and generally common, even in heavily humanized Titicaca area; presently expanding, due to agricultural conversion, while much of its natural habitat remains intact. Uncommon in most of Peru.
Bibliography. Bucher & Nores (1988), Bump & Bump (1969), Cabot & Serrano (1988), Daciuk (1980), Fjeldså (1988a), Fjeldså & Krabbe (1990), Liebermann (1936), de la Peña (1986), Short (1975), Tonni & Laza (1980).

41. Spotted Nothura
Nothura maculosa

French: Tinamou tacheté   **German:** Fleckensteißhuhn   **Spanish:** Tinamú Manchado

Taxonomy. *Tinamus maculosa* Temminck, 1815, Paraguay.
Eight subspecies recognized.
Subspecies and Distribution.
N. m. cearensis Naumburg, 1932 - NE Brazil.
N. m. major (Spix, 1825) - EC Brazil.
N. m. paludivaga Conover, 1950 - C Paraguay, NC Argentina.
N. m. maculosa (Temminck, 1815) - SE Brazil, E Paraguay, NE Argentina, Uruguay.
N. m. pallida Olrog, 1959 - NW Argentina.
N. m. annectens Conover, 1950 - E Argentina.
N. m. submontana Conover, 1950 - SW Argentina.
N. m. nigroguttata Salvadori, 1895 - SC Argentina.
Descriptive notes. 24-26·5 cm; male 162-303 g, female 164-340 g. Extremely variable, sometimes with very dark upperparts. Longer-legged than *N. darwinii*; larger than *N. minor*. Iris often dark

yellow in male, orange in female. Juvenile has weaker markings on upperparts, and black spots, not stripes, on breast. Races separated on plumage tones and, to some extent, size.
Habitat. Restricted to lowlands, except race *submontana* which reaches 2000 m, and also *pallida* which may be found up to 2300 m. Pasture land, grassy savanna, barren scrub, shrub-steppe, *caatinga*, hedgerows, *Larrea* semi-desert and fields of soybean, millet, wheat and rice (dry-grown); sometimes in open woodland.

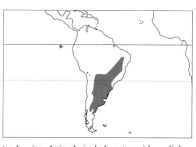

Food and Feeding. One of better known species. Omnivorous, with strong herbivorous tendencies. Animals include ants, spiders, diplopods, molluscs, myriapods and crustaceans. Plant matter comprises mostly seeds, especially Papilionaceae, Oxalidaceae, Malvaceae, etc., and fleshy fruits. In Argentina, seeds (e.g. of clover), large amounts of insects, such as larvae, caterpillars, chrysalises, Orthoptera and crickets; to a lesser extent, mole-crickets, beetles, Hemiptera, butterflies and moths, etc. Often in cultivation, especially after the harvest, taking oats, rice, sorghum, wheat, maize and soybeans; sometimes digs up tubers with beak. In Brazil follows grazing livestock, catching insects that are disturbed, especially grasshoppers; also takes cattle ticks.
Breeding. Sept-May in Brazil; further S probably limited more to austral spring/summer. Nest is small depression scratched out under bush, lined with leaves and twigs. 4-6 vinous brown or chocolate eggs.
Movements. Presumably sedentary.
Status and Conservation. Not globally threatened. Widespread, one of commonest tinamous, presently in expansion, due to deforestation and agricultural developments, e.g. in *pampas* of Argentina. Most commonly hunted species in Argentina and Brazil. Due to high reproductive potential, has capacity to recover quickly, if hunting temporarily banned for a few seasons; in Rio Grande do Sul, S Brazil, recent improved control and rotation of hunting areas favours healthy survival of species.
Bibliography. Belton (1982, 1984), Bohórquez & Carnevalli (1985), Bonetto *et al.* (1961), Bucher & Nores (1988), Bump & Bump (1969), Burger (1985), Dabbene (1972), Fabricio (1980), Fjeldså & Krabbe (1990), Grigera (1973), Höhn (1975), Hudson (1920), Jimbo (1957), Liebermann (1936), Menegheti (1981, 1983, 1984, 1985a, 1985b, 1985c, 1988), Menegheti & Arigony (1982), Menegheti & de Lourdes Abruzzi (1982), Menegheti & Marques (1981), Menegheti *et al.* (1981), de la Peña (1986), Pinto (1964), Ruschi (979), Seriè (1921), Short (1975), Sick (1984), Sick *et al.* (1981), Silva & Sander (1981), da Silveira & Menegheti (1981).

42. Chaco Nothura
Nothura chacoensis

French: Tinamou du Chaco   **German:** Chacosteißhuhn   **Spanish:** Tinamú Chaqueño

Taxonomy. *Nothura maculosa chacoensis* Conover, 1937, Paraguayan Chaco.
Sometimes considered subspecies of *N. maculosa*, but separated on grounds of sympatry in C Paraguay and N Argentina. Monotypic.
Distribution. NW Paraguay and extreme NC Argentina.

Descriptive notes. 23-25 cm. Neck less conspicuously marked than in other *Nothura*; underparts paler and more uniform ochraceous buff; much paler than *N. maculosa* in areas of probable sympatry.
Habitat. Arid and semi-arid grassland with thornbush thickets; also open woodland.
Food and Feeding. No information available.
Breeding. Austral spring/summer, Sept-Nov.
Movements. Presumably sedentary.
Status and Conservation. Not globally threatened. In Chaco region overgrazing has prevented natural cycle of fires and allowed invasion of woody plants; transformation of habitat to make way for pastures and also agriculture may well have adverse effects on populations of this species.
Bibliography. Blake (1977), Bucher & Nores (1988), Short (1975, 1976).

Genus *TAONISCUS* Gloger, 1842

43. Dwarf Tinamou
Taoniscus nanus

French: Tinamou carapé   **German:** Pfauensteißhuhn   **Spanish:** Tinamú Enano
Other common names: Least Tinamou

Taxonomy. *Tinamus nanus* Temminck, 1815, Misiones, Argentina.
Monotypic.
Distribution. SE Brazil and NE Argentina.
Descriptive notes. 14·5-16 cm; c. 43 g. Tiny; coloration very variable, ranging from ochraceous-rufous to ochraceous grey-brown; neck and back boldly patterned; brown barring on breast and flanks more or less intense.
Habitat. Secondary forest, savanna and *cerrado*, though more common in pastures with short grass under 2 m long and scattered bushes, than in *cerrado*. Sometimes found near cities and in burnt fields.
Food and Feeding. Omnivorous. Spends much time looking for small arthropods in amongst the vegetation; like *Rhynchotus*, digs termites (*Proconitermes araujoi*) out of their mounds. Also takes grass seeds.
Breeding. Little known. Sept/Oct in Brazil. Downy chicks similar to those of *Nothura*.
Movements. Presumably sedentary.
Status and Conservation. INDETERMINATE. May be much rarer than was thought; small and very difficult to see, even on burnt ground or paths. No recent records from NE Argentina, where may be extinct. Reported as frequent around Brasília, but these voice records due to confusion with Ocellated Crake (*Micropygia schomburgkii*). Formerly common in Minas Gerais, but no recent records; also disappearing from São Paulo state, due to agricultural development and overpopula-

tion; should be given legal protection, as should its habitat. Habitat giving way to plantations of exotic species, such as pines and *Eucalyptus*, as well as sugar cane and soybeans; burning of pastures also affects habitat. Predators include White-tailed Hawk (*Buteo albicaudatus*) and Aplomado Falcon (*Falco femoralis*), which are attracted to grass fires, where they prey on animals fleeing from the fire; present species frequently becomes groggy with smoke and can thus be captured easily by predators.
Bibliography. Cavalcanti (1988), Collar & Andrew (1988), Pinto (1964), Ruschi (1979), Silveira (1967, 1968), Sick (1965, 1984), Sick & Teixeira (1979), Teixeira & Negret (1984), Willis & Oniki (1981, 1988).

Genus *EUDROMIA* I. Geoffroy Saint-Hilaire, 1832

44. Elegant Crested Tinamou
Eudromia elegans

French: Tinamou élégant   **German:** Perlsteißhuhn   **Spanish:** Martineta Común

Taxonomy. *Eudromia elegans* I. Geoffroy Saint-Hilaire, 1832, southern Buenos Aires.
Ten subspecies recognized.
Subspecies and Distribution.
E. e. intermedia (Dabbene & Lillo, 1913) - NW Argentina.
E. e. magnistriata Olrog, 1959 - NW Argentina.
E. e. riojana Olrog, 1959 - NW Argentina.
E. e. albida Wetmore, 1921 - W Argentina.
E. e. wetmorei Banks, 1977 - W Argentina.
E. e. devia Conover, 1950 - SW Argentina.
E. e. numida Banks, 1977 - C Argentina.
E. e. multiguttata Conover, 1950 - EC Argentina.
E. e. elegans I. Geoffroy Saint-Hilaire, 1832 - C Argentina.
E. e. patagonica Conover, 1950 - S Argentina, S Chile.

Descriptive notes. 37·5-41 cm; *elegans* 402-512 g, *patagonica* 600-800 g. Lacks hind toe; leg colour varies from pale bluish to greyish brown. Long crest, normally carried backwards, with feathers twisted upwards; feathers of crest broader than in *E. formosa*. Juvenile has weak brown crest, and dull grey plumage with dark streaking. Races form three broad groups, pale (in N), intermediate and dark (further S), with extremes *albida* and *multiguttata*; distribution of dorsal spots and barring also significant in separation.
Habitat. Arid and semi-arid grassland, dry savanna, open woodland, dry Andean steppes, bare hills with isolated patches of bushes (e.g. *Larrea*) and cultivation; locally up to 2500 m, down to sea-level in S. In Patagonia prefers sheltered valleys; in temperate zone, normally in sandy areas with thornscrub and low evergreen bushes (e.g. *Verbena tridentata*).
Food and Feeding. Omnivorous. Plant matter includes: ears and grains of *Bromus* and *Hordeum*; fruit of *Erodium cicutarium*, *Lycium chilense* and *Condalia microhylla*; also leaves and buds. Insects include: *Trimeratropis pallidipennis*, *Dichroplus pratensis*, *D. elongatus*, *Scyllina variablis* and *S. signatipennis*. More insectivorous in summer, when prey abounds, predominantly herbivorous in winter. Ingests pebbles to help in breaking down food.
Breeding. Jun/Aug-Nov; most laying in Oct. Nest of plant matter, placed in shelter of bush. Polyandry and/or polygyny normal. 5-6 (-9) green or yellowish green eggs, shiny like porcelain; second or replacement clutches occur; incubation 20-21 days; chick resembles juvenile in coloration.
Movements. Moves about in groups over large areas in winter, when food is scarce; in Patagonia invades irrigated plantations, e.g. of alfalfa, in groups of 10-20, or even up to 50-100 birds. In spring and summer, when food more plentiful, tends to stick to smaller area. Otherwise presumably sedentary.
Status and Conservation. Not globally threatened. Widespread and not rare, but populations have declined appreciably due to hunting, and range reduced since beginning of century; still abundant in remote parts of range. In *monte* zone of W Argentina, several races have declined due mostly to intense hunting pressure. Mammal predators include skunks, foxes and wild cats; also taken by raptors, such as Red-backed Hawk (*Buteo polyosoma*). First recorded breeding in captivity in 1903 in Paris; large numbers exported to Germany at same time, with a view to its introduction as a game bird.
Bibliography. Banks (1975), Bohl (1970), Bucher & Nores (1988), Contreras (1975), Dabbene (1972), Daciuk (1978), Fjeldså & Krabbe (1990), Gallardo (1984), Gutmann (1989), Johnson (1965), Lehmann-Nitsche (1921), Liebermann (1936), Navas & Bó (1981), de la Peña (1986), Pereyra (1935), Rutgers & Norris (1970), Wetmore (1926).

45. Quebracho Crested Tinamou
Eudromia formosa

French: Tinamou superbe   **German:** Schmucksteißhuhn   **Spanish:** Martineta Chaqueña

Taxonomy. *Calopezus formosus* Lillo, 1905, Tucumán, Argentina.
Has been considered subspecies of *E. elegans*. Two subspecies recognized, though some confusion concerning overlap zone and may be better considered monospecific.
Subspecies and Distribution.
E. f. mira Brodkorb, 1938 - WC Paraguay.
E. f. formosa (Lillo, 1905) - NC Argentina.
Descriptive notes. 37·5-41 cm. Lacks hind toe. General coloration much brighter than *E. elegans*; crest feathers stiffer and narrower; characteristic, much less dense pattern, particularly on underparts. Upperparts of female more yellow and less grey than in male. Juvenile similar to adult. Race *mira* apparently somewhat browner.

Habitat. *Quebracho* woodland in arid areas; savanna and dry woodland of Chaco region.
Food and Feeding. No information available.
Breeding. Very little known; some birds collected in Feb in breeding condition.
Movements. Presumably sedentary.
Status and Conservation. Not globally threatened. Apparently frequent; may be adversely affected by degradation of Chaco region, due to agricultural development.
Bibliography. Banks (1975), Dabbene (1972), Liebermann (1936), Narosky & Yzurieta (1987), de la Peña (1986), Short (1975, 1976).

Genus *TINAMOTIS* Vigors, 1837

46. Puna Tinamou
Tinamotis pentlandii

French: Tinamou quioula   **German:** Punasteißhuhn   **Spanish:** Kiula Andina

Taxonomy. *Tinamotis Pentlandii* Vigors, 1837, Bolivia.
Monotypic.
Distribution. C Peru and W Bolivia to N Chile and NW Argentina.

Descriptive notes. 39-42·5 cm; 790-1000 g. Lacks hind toe. Large and bulky; striking pattern of white and blackish stripes on head and neck; deep rufous belly and vent. Juvenile has paler belly, less olive rump and heavier spotting on back.
Habitat. Grassland, bare steppe and desert of *puna*, at 4000-5300 m; highest altitude species. Prefers tola heath (*Lepidophyllum*), but also on sandy or stony areas, or pumice with scattered Yareta (*Larretia compacta*) and other cushion-plants, bunch-grass (*Festuca orthophylla*) and sometimes scattered stands of *Polylepis* shrub.
Food and Feeding. Apparently more herbivorous than other tinamous; three stomachs from Bolivia yielded leaves, fresh shoots, buds and flowers of *Adesmia* and a little grass, but no animal remains. This may indicate a scarcity of insects at such altitudes, but more evidence is required to confirm the tendency.
Breeding. Jun-Aug in Peru; austral summer in S of range, Nov in Bolivia, Sept/Oct and Jan/Feb in Chile. No real nest, eggs laid in shelter of surrounding vegetation. 4-7 eggs, yellowish green with spattering of white speckles; may start off greener and gradually become yellower. Chick similar to juvenile, with black/white head pattern. Normally several males accompany young which may come from different broods.
Movements. Presumably sedentary. Reported to descend from summits to valleys in bad weather, returning afterwards.
Status and Conservation. Not globally threatened. Generally scarce, but poorly known; fairly common in zone where Bolivia, Peru and Chile meet. Habitat not threatened by change for agricultural or pastoral ends, due to altitude and inaccessibility. Hunting pressure is likewise very limited for same reasons, though species might be more vulnerable in S of range, where present at lower altitudes. Possible predators include Andean fox (*Dusicyon culpaeus*), wild cats, skunks and the Variable Hawk (*Buteo poecilochrous*).
Bibliography. Fjeldså (1988a), Fjeldså & Krabbe (1990), Johnson (1965), Liebermann (1936), Morrison (1939a), Narosky & Yzurieta (1987), de la Peña (1986).

47. Patagonian Tinamou
Tinamotis ingoufi

French: Tinamou de Patagonie   **German:** Patagoniensteißhuhn   **Spanish:** Kiula Patagona

Taxonomy. *Tinamotis ingoufi* Oustalet, 1890, Santa Cruz, Patagonia.
Forms superspecies with *T. pentlandii*. Monotypic.
Distribution. S Chile and SW Argentina.

Descriptive notes. 33-37·5 cm. Lacks hind toe. Head pattern similar to but weaker than that of *N. pentlandii*; rufous flight-feathers; rich ochre belly and vent. Feathers of back and breast have less white, thus appearing generally darker. Juvenile similar to adult.
Habitat. Grassland and savanna steppes, at 200-800 m; also dry meadows, sheltered valleys with dense, low bushes of *Berberis*, *Pernetyia* and especially "mata negra" (*Verbena tridentata*), which invades overgrazed areas. Avoids open plains, where strong winds are prevalent; sometimes near coast, especially in winter.
Food and Feeding. Not well known. Mainly leaves and shoots of *Pernetyia pumila*, and seeds of box-leaved barberry (*Berberis buxifolia*).
Breeding. Nov/Dec. Nest is simple scrape in sandy soil. 8-15 eggs, dark olive-buff with many small speckles; chick similar to that of *E. elegans*, but lacks crest.
Movements. Tends to move near coast in winter, forming groups of up to 30-40 individuals.
Status and Conservation. Not globally threatened. Generally uncommon. Expanses of "mata negra", where species apparently common, steadily replacing long grass, due to overgrazing; this has been claimed to be beneficial to the species, but there is no evidence to support the claim.
Bibliography. Fjeldså (1988a), Fjeldså & Krabbe (1990), Johnson (1965), Liebermann (1936), Narosky & Yzurieta (1987), de la Peña (1986).

Order SPHENISCIFORMES

Sphenisciformes

Spheniscidae

penguins

Class AVES
Order SPHENISCIFORMES
Family SPHENISCIDAE (PENGUINS)

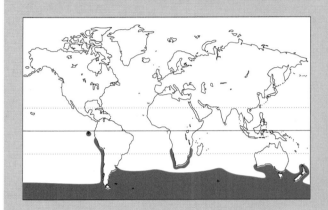

- Medium-sized to large, flightless seabirds with thick-set body, short, robust legs, and wings compressed to form flippers.
- 40-115 cm.

- Antarctic and Australasian Regions; marginal in Afro-tropical and Neotropical.
- Marine, mainly in cold waters of Antarctic and sub-antarctic.
- 6 genera, 17 species, 26 taxa.
- 3 species threatened; none extinct since 1600.

Systematics

Sphenisciformes is the only order within the class Aves in which all the species are both flightless and aquatic. It contains only one family, Spheniscidae.

The penguins are descended from ancestors which had the power of flight, but their evolutionary energy has been concentrated on adaptation to an amphibious lifestyle. They clearly originated somewhere in the Southern Hemisphere, but nobody is quite sure where. Their closest relatives appear to be the divers (Gaviiformes) and the petrels and allies (Procellariiformes), although no fossil has yet been found which sheds any light on these relationships. Studies using DNA confirm these traditional associations, but also suggest affinities with the highly aerial frigatebirds (Fregatidae).

The first remains of a fossil penguin were found in New Zealand in about 1859, and the species was named *Palaeeudyptes antarcticus* by T. H. Huxley. This bone, which is in the British Museum, shows the fusion of the tarsus and the metatarsus in a way peculiar to penguins (see Morphological Aspects), and its form can be used as a basis for separating the different species. Since this first find, many more fossils have been turned up in New Zealand, Australia, South America, various islands of the Antarctic and subantarctic, and more recently southern Africa.

There is fossil evidence of penguins from the late Eocene in Australia, New Zealand and the Antarctic. No definite penguin fossils from earlier periods have yet been found, although some remains from the late Paleocene or early Eocene might actually belong to penguins. The earliest evidence from South America dates back only as far as the late Oligocene or early Miocene, while none is known from South Africa before the late Miocene, and this could mean that these areas were colonized at a later stage, though it might simply reflect less exhaustive excavations.

The 21 genera and 32 species of extinct penguins now known to science show much greater diversity than the surviving species; they reached much larger sizes, but all were marine and have been found in the Southern Hemisphere. Four extant genera, *Aptenodytes*, *Pygoscelis*, *Eudyptula* and *Spheniscus* are known from fossil remains, whereas only one extant species, the Little Penguin (*Eudyptula minor*), appears in the fossil record.

Even today there is considerable disagreement about the number of extant species in the family, as the status of some species has been questioned. Here, the most widely accepted version of 17 species has been followed.

By far the most complicated genus in terms of systematics is *Eudyptes*. Both the Erect-crested Penguin (*Eudyptes sclateri*) and the Snares Penguin (*Eudyptes robustus*) have been included, as races, within the Fiordland Penguin (*Eudyptes pachyrhynchus*), while some taxonomists consider the three to form a superspecies. Nowadays they are generally accepted as three good species, on the grounds of morphological differences, allopatry, the different timing of their breeding cycles and the fact that no case of hybridization has been recorded. In contrast, the Rockhopper Penguin (*Eudyptes chrysocome*) is traditionally divided into three subspecies, of which one, *moseleyi*, is sometimes considered sufficiently different to qualify as a separate species, Moseley's Penguin.

Another controversial species complex is that of the Macaroni Penguin (*Eudyptes chrysolophus*) and the Royal Penguin (*Eudyptes schlegeli*). There are records of birds with white faces and throats in Macaroni colonies, for example at Crozet, Marion, Kerguelen and Heard Islands, but there is some dispute over the specific classification of these individuals. Many Royals have intermediate colouring; some have both face and throat black, a tendency that is more common in females than males, and also occurs more in the populations of the west than of the

The genus Eudyptula apparently represents a link between the penguins and the Procellariiformes. The internal organization of the genus is the source of some dispute, and there are those that consider the White-flippered Penguin, seen here, a separate species. The whitish leading edge to the flipper is the distinguishing feature of this form, but it can also be found in some populations of the nominate minor.

[Eudyptula minor albosignata, Banks Peninsula, New Zealand. Photo: A. Greensmith/ Ardea]

Penguins swim along under water moving their flippers in a way that closely resembles the wing movements of flying birds. However, the structure of the wings has been modified to deal with a medium that is much denser than air, with the result that they are correspondingly much less flexible. The tail and feet perform the function of a rudder.

[*Spheniscus mendiculus*, Isla Bartolomé, Galapagos Islands. Photo: D. Parer & E. Parer-Cook/Ardea]

east coast of Macquarie Island, the only breeding site of this species. Pale phase birds also tend to be larger than dark phase ones. It is not yet known if any of these birds are hybrids, and more detailed work is required to clarify the situation. Some authors prefer to separate these two species off into their own genus, *Catadyptes*, as the form of the crest and the number of rectrices differ from those of other members of *Eudyptes*.

Rockhoppers have been known to form mixed-species pairs with Erect-crested, Royal and Macaroni Penguins. Although such pairs apparently have only limited success, hybrids of Rockhopper X Macaroni have occurred.

Another contentious case is that of the Little Penguin. There is disagreement over the validity of several of its subspecies, while, at the other extreme, there are schools of thought that consider the race *albosignata* a valid species, the White-flippered Penguin; the latter view has recently fallen into disfavour, partly because *albosignata* has been found possibly interbreeding with another race, *variabilis*, and it seems that all the subspecies may form a north-south cline.

The propensity of some members of the genus *Spheniscus* to hybridize in captivity, in addition to the observation in the wild of individual Jackass Penguins (*Spheniscus demersus*) and Humboldt Penguins (*Spheniscus humboldti*) with a double pectoral band, suggests the presence of a recessive genetic character or perhaps some breeding contact with the Magellanic Penguin (*Spheniscus magellanicus*). Recent work on the genetics of these three species has shown that they are very closely related, and that, if they are indeed separate species, they have only differentiated relatively recently. Despite its double pectoral band, the Galapagos Penguin (*Spheniscus mendiculus*) is probably descended from the single-banded Humboldt Penguin.

Morphological Aspects

The penguins are a highly specialized group of seabirds. Their structure and physiology have been moulded both by their marine habitat and the climatological peculiarities of their environment. All penguin species are really quite similar, both in structure and coloration.

The body is streamlined, with a very short neck and long, flat wings, which are useless for flight. The tarsi are short and the legs are situated so far back on the body that the birds stand upright; the tail is short and stiff.

In general, penguins become steadily larger as one moves south into colder zones, a principle known as Bergmann's Rule, whereby optimum size changes with the increased energy requirements in colder zones. The widespread Gentoo Penguin (*Pygoscelis papua*) is, however, an exception, as its smallest representatives are those found in the southernmost, coldest parts of its range. The implications of this anomalous distribution are not yet understood, but it has been suggested that it could have originated from differences in diet (see Food and Feeding). Many species are sexually dimorphic to a very small degree, with males slightly larger than females; this is most marked in the genus *Eudyptes*.

The bill is composed of horny plates and its shape is adapted to suit the typical prey. Thus, the bill tends to be long and thin in species that are essentially fish eaters, but shorter and stouter in those that take plankton.

The eyes are basically adapted for underwater vision, though birds can see perfectly adequately when they are out of the water. Experiments on captive Humboldt Penguins indicate that this species, at any rate, may have a sense of smell. In common with the Procellariiformes, penguins have highly developed supraorbital glands, which enable them to deal with the extreme levels of salt in their diet. The excess salt is excreted in a concentrated saline solution, which tends to dribble down the bill.

Adult plumage is very similar in all species, with upperparts black or bluish grey and underparts basically white. All of the markings that serve to distinguish the different species are on the head and the breast, which are the parts that stick out of the water, when birds are swimming on the surface.

Penguins have a uniform covering of feathers over their bodies unlike most other birds, which have alternating feathered and bare tracts. Only during breeding is this cover interrupted, when feathers are dropped from the ventral region to make way for a brood patch.

The feathers of adult penguins are highly specialized. The bird is clothed in a thick coat of small, hard, stiff coverts, which

In order to reach their colony, these Royal Penguins have to pass through a group of dozing southern elephant seals (Mirounga leonina). *This poses no particular problem for the birds, but on occasions these enormous seals invade the penguins' colonies, causing considerable losses of eggs, chicks and young. Note that by no means all of the birds show the typical white face.*

[*Eudyptes schlegeli*, Macquarie Island. Photo: Ron & Valerie Taylor/ Ardea]

are lanceolate and slightly curved. The rachis is long and flattened, and out of it projects a hyporachis, which provides extra thickness and makes up for the absence of down. The feathers overlap each other, in order to improve their performance in both insulating and waterproofing the body. This plumage has high wind resistance and, even in winds upwards of 60 km/h, it remains smooth and compact.

The feathers of the upperparts are slightly longer and stiffer than those of the underparts, while the covering of feathers is denser on the upperwing than on the underwing. Irrespective of the size of the bird, relative feather length is quite different in tropical and polar species. Thus, the Adelie Penguin (*Pygoscelis adeliae*) of the Antarctic has the longest feathers, while the Galapagos Penguin of the equatorial zone has the shortest. Feathers become progressively longer as one approaches the South Pole, and this phenomenon is even discernible among different populations of the same species, for example in the Gentoo.

Chicks hatch covered in a dense coat of down, except in the genus *Aptenodytes*, where the down is sparse at first. After a period, for example of seven days in *Eudyptula* or twenty in *Megadyptes*, this first coat is changed for another, which is normally quite similar but thicker.

In most of the bird world, moult involves the old feather being dropped and a new one growing in its place, but in penguins the new feather grows under the rachis of the old one and forces it out, with the result that the old feathers are not totally discarded until the new ones are in place. Moult is rather patchy and this gives the birds a rather scruffy, moth-eaten look.

During moult both waterproofing and insulation are deficient, so penguins are forced to remain on land until their plumage returns to optimum condition. For this reason, before commencing their moult they must spend some time at sea, building up sufficient reserves of energy. The necessary period of preparation varies from one species to another, ranging from about 10 to 70 days. Birds are at their plumpest as they start their moult, but not surprisingly by the time they finish they have lost a lot of weight, up to 45% in the Emperor Penguin (*Aptenodytes forsteri*) or 39% in the Little Penguin; indeed, the daily expenditure of energy during moult is roughly double that used daily during incubation. Although they are largely inactive while moulting, they do not eat and have to use up more energy due to their reduced insulation, as well as in the process of generating new feathers.

The average length of the moult period varies between species, from 13 days in the Galapagos Penguin to 34 in the Emperor. These figures refer to the days spent on land until the new plumage is complete, though the new feathers apparently start to develop subcutaneously some days earlier, while the birds are still at sea. Immature Jackass Penguins have even been seen moulting the plumage of the head and breast, while they are still moving about in the water, just prior to coming ashore for their complete moult.

All penguins have a single complete annual moult, with the exception of the Galapagos Penguin, which can have two. In most species it is carried out after breeding, but the Galapagos Penguin's regular complete moult takes place before breeding. There are deviations, notably in the Jackass and King Penguins (*Aptenodytes patagonicus*), which breed at intervals of less and more than a year respectively; in these species, some individuals moult before and some after breeding. Immature birds tend to moult earlier than adults, while birds that lose their clutches can start their moult straight away. Plumage is at its brightest immediately following moult, after which it fades steadily, and by the end of breeding black feathers have turned dirty brown.

Immature plumage differs from that of adults by being duller, especially in the brightly coloured markings on the head or the distinctive crest feathers, which are generally shorter. Adult plumage is normally gained with the second complete moult, a year later, though certain features, such as the crests in *Eudyptes*, are still not fully-developed at this stage.

One of the most remarkable characteristics of the penguins is their capacity of thermoregulation in environments with very harsh temperatures, in some cases towards both extremes. Those species of temperate or tropical zones must be able to deal almost instantaneously with the radical contrast in temperature between the icy cold water and the shore under a hot sun. They are better adapted to regulating the temperature in the water, where conditions are more constant than on land. For this reason, when out of the water, they can have problems coping with excess heat, and the species that have to deal with high temperatures have additional methods of cooling, such as panting. These species also tend to have areas of bare skin by the bill or the eye, as in *Spheniscus*, or a fleshy gape, as in most members of *Eudyptes*. In contrast to this, the species that breed furthest south, the Emperor and the Adelie, have more feathering on the bill and feet.

Between the imbricate, highly weatherproof plumage and the important layer of subcutaneous fat there is a mantle of warmed air, which also helps in insulation. The complex vascularization of the wings is another feature that plays a very important part in thermoregulation, as a bird can manage to dissipate a good deal of heat by holding its wings away from its body and bristling up its plumage. The species of colder latitudes have shorter wings, as well as longer feathers.

The dark plumage of the upperparts is well designed for absorbing heat from the sun, and increasing body temperature. Another heat saving device is used by King and Emperor Penguins on land; a bird may tip up its feet, and rest its entire weight only on its heels and tail, in order to reduce contact with ice to an absolute minimum.

Unlike flying birds, penguins have solid, heavy bones, as they do not need to economize on weight. Normally body weight is just slightly less than the volume of water displaced, so less energy is used both in diving and in swimming on the surface.

The feet are webbed and the hind toe is vestigial. Unlike most other waterbirds, penguins do not use their feet as paddles, but instead, along with the tail, for steering, while it is the wings that provide the propulsion. These are moved as if the birds were really flying, and progress through a much denser medium than air has led to great development of the wing and breast muscles, to a degree comparable with those of flying birds. Penguins retain the same wing bones as flying birds, but these are far less flexible, because the only really mobile joint is that of the shoulder girdle with the humerus.

Another highly characteristic feature of the penguins is the form of the tarsometatarsus, which in penguins is short and thick, while in almost all other birds it is long and thin. It is the most distinctive of all the penguins' bones and has been very useful in the determination of fossils (see Systematics).

Penguins have three distinct modes of movement in the water: surface swimming; underwater "flying"; and "porpoising". Surface swimming is not very swift, as the birds are unable to flap fully, and turbulence causes them to lose speed, so the Jackass Penguin only moves at an average of about 1·5 km/h in this way. This kind of swimming is used for resting or toilet, and usually involves the head and sometimes the tail being raised up out of the water, whereas the whole body remains more or less submerged.

Underwater swimming is really a form of underwater flying. The depth at which birds swim depends basically on the location of prey, and this can vary seasonally or even daily. Members of the genus *Aptenodytes* are the deepest divers, with the King Penguin reaching a depth of 240 m, while the Emperor Penguin has been recorded at 265 m. Of course, penguins can not stay under water indefinitely, as they must come up to the surface to take a breath. Most species come up at intervals of a minute or less, but Gentoo and Adelie Penguins can stay under for seven minutes, and Emperor Penguins for 18, although two to eight minutes is the normal length for one of their dives.

Porpoising is a form of surface swimming, whereby the birds make an undulating movement, flopping in and out of the water at regular intervals. The Jackass Penguin spends 14 seconds under the water for every second it uses for taking a breath. Not all species use porpoising habitually, and while Emperors do not use it at all, it is infrequent in King Penguins and the genus *Spheniscus*, but common in the other genera. The advantages of this method of locomotion are unclear, but once a certain speed is reached, it reduces energy expenditure by cutting down the resistance of the water the bird displaces, as it is swimming near the surface. It also permits efficient breathing with a very low cost in terms of energy. Another possible benefit is that during a normal dive birds can lose part of the insulating layer of warm air between the skin and the feathers, so this has to be replaced periodically. It might also be a useful anti-predator manoeuvre, designed to confuse pursuers.

The fastest swimmers are the genus *Aptenodytes*. The Emperor Penguin can swim at 14·4 km/h, though it does not normally pass 10·8 km/h, while King Penguins move at 8·6 km/h. Other speeds recorded include the Adelie Penguin at 7·2 km/h, the Jackass Penguin at 7·4 km/h, and the Little Penguin at 2·5 km/h.

While they are expert swimmers, penguins also move about a fair bit on land, where they walk with an upright stance and short steps or hops, helping themselves at times on steep climbs with the bill or tail. The larger *Aptenodytes* penguins, however,

The species that breed in Antarctica, like these Emperor Penguins, have developed a special technique for moving over snow and ice known as "tobogganing". The necessary propulsion comes from the wings and particularly from the feet, with their long, thick, curved claws. Using this system the birds can move much faster, with a notable saving of energy.

[Aptenodytes forsteri, Antarctica. Photo: Joel Bennett/Survival]

One of the limiting factors for the location of penguin colonies is access to and from the sea. When the conditions of the site do not permit the birds to walk out of the water, they may be forced to make spectacular leaps, as in the case of this Adelie Penguin.

[*Pygoscelis adeliae*, Antarctica. Photo: Rick Price/Survival]

do not hop, and can only walk. Penguins are plantigrade, walking on the sole of the foot, as opposed to other birds, which walk on their toes. The shortness of the legs and their positioning mean that the birds walk with a rather clumsy, but very characteristic gait. It also means that they can not walk very fast, and an Emperor Penguin, for example, can only manage 1·4 km/h. It does, however, offer the advantage of allowing the birds to incubate an egg or brood a chick while standing, by placing it between its legs, as in *Aptenodytes*.

Antarctic species can move much faster over ice, by flopping down on their bellies and using their wings and feet to help them slide over the surface, a method known as "tobogganing".

Habitat

Penguins are highly marine and are only found in the Southern Hemisphere. They are not restricted to Antarctica, as is often thought, and the genus *Spheniscus* occurs in the tropics, with one species, the Galapagos Penguin, actually living on the equator.

Their distribution at sea is determined by the water temperature. Thus the species occurring in warmer climes are invariably found in zones affected by the cool currents originating from the Antarctic, the Humboldt and Falkland Currents of South America, and the Benguela of South Africa. They also require a relatively stable water temperature in general, though the temperature range of the family is remarkable, with the Galapagos Penguin occupying waters of 15°C to 28°C, while the Emperor Penguin occurs in temperatures ranging from –60°C to 0°C. No other family of birds can survive in such a wide diversity of temperatures.

Although all their food comes from the sea, and some species can spend months on end without leaving the water, nonetheless, there are two important parts of their annual cycle which necessitate the birds coming ashore, breeding and moult (see Morphological Aspects). Nesting habitat varies with distribution, but birds generally make use of the islands and coasts near their food supplies, wherever access is easy enough. Colonies may be situated in a wide variety of places, and while Emperors use frozen seas, Chinstrap Penguins (*Pygoscelis antarctica*) breed on fairly steep slopes. Some of the more surprising types of nesting habitat include the Fiordland Penguin in wet coastal rain forest, the Little Penguin in holes dug in sand and the Galapagos Penguin in volcanic caves or cracks in the rock.

General Habits

Penguins are sociable and gregarious, and carry out most of their life cycle in the company of conspecifics. They nest in colonies, which can be more or less dense, and may comprise hundreds or even thousands of birds, so individual recognition of partners and chicks is vital, and each bird must remember the exact location of its nest. Social behaviour too has an important part to play, especially in the densest colonies, those of *Pygoscelis* and *Eudyptes*, so territorial and courtship displays are highly developed. The complex mechanisms of visual and vocal communication permit the recognition of partners or the localization of an individual chick in the midst of a crèche (see Breeding).

The formation of crèches is an example of social behaviour during breeding which has crucial implications. It offers the advantages of collective defence against predators and insulation against adverse climatic conditions, whilst allowing both adults to go off in search of food, thus increasing the daily input of energy to the chick. It has also been found in Adelie Penguins that subadults guard the crèche, as may other adults that have failed in their own breeding attempts.

Virtually all species are territorial, though the degree of territoriality depends on the density of the colony. The only exception is the Emperor Penguin, which can reach densities of 10 birds/m^2 when incubating during the Antarctic winter. This social behaviour, in conjunction with the fact that activity is reduced to an absolute minimum, permits the birds to survive the extremely low temperatures with a minimum expenditure of energy (see Morphological Aspects).

Social behaviour at sea has been recorded for several genera including *Aptenodytes* and *Spheniscus*. The latter often form groups during the breeding season, for the purposes of movements or feeding, and they co-operate intraspecifically in the capture of prey. *Spheniscus* penguins occasionally prey on large shoals of fish in company with other species of birds, mammals or predatory fish (see Food and Feeding).

Penguins are capable of storing great reserves of energy in their layer of subcutaneous fat, which means that they can survive long periods without feeding at all. The length of time a bird can go without food depends basically on its weight at the beginning of the fasting period; the fatter the bird, the longer it can survive.

There are two periods when adults have to fast, which correspond firstly to courtship and incubation, and secondly to moult. During the former, it is the males that generally have to

The Little Penguin is the most nocturnal of the penguins, and all of its activity on land is invariably carried out at night. Birds tend to arrive on the beach in small groups, but they quickly disperse, each heading off towards its own nest.

[*Eudyptula minor*. Photo: Otto Rogge/ ANT/NHPA]

undergo longer periods of fasting, as they tend to arrive first at the colony, and often take the first incubation stint, immediately after the females have laid (see Breeding). The genus *Aptenodytes* take the longest stints, and while the male King Penguin may do 54 days, the male Emperor Penguin has a stint of 90-120 days, in contrast with the female's 30-45 days. A male Emperor can lose as much as 45% of its initial weight during this period. However, other species, such as the Gentoo, Rockhopper and Galapagos Penguins, have much shorter stints, so birds return to the sea much more frequently.

During the annual cycle a bird's weight varies enormously, with the maximum invariably occurring at the beginning of moult. Most species take 13-34 days to complete their moult, and lose 30-50% of their original weight in the process.

Penguin chicks too have to fast, normally around the time that they become independent, shortly before going to sea. The King Penguin is unusual in that the amount of food adults bring to their chicks drops drastically in winter when food is very scarce, and chicks consequently have to suspend growth, until conditions permit the adults to bring them enough food again (see Breeding).

A reduction in physical activity and perhaps an increase in the time spent sleeping are ways of diminishing unneccessary use of energy. In addition, penguins have a lower body temperature than other birds, which might also be an adaptation designed to save energy during these inactive periods of their annual cycle when feeding is impossible.

It appears that during periods of fasting only about half of what is consumed is fat, the rest consisting mostly of water. Thus it is important for some species, for instance the Rockhopper, to have fresh water near the colony, which it can use for drinking and washing in, especially during the periods of laying and incubation, when it is unable to go to the sea.

Voice

The constant stream of vocal exchanges means that penguin colonies tend to be very noisy, particularly the densest ones. As penguins are highly social birds, they have well developed systems of communication, both visual and vocal, and there are notable differences in voice at both interspecific and intraspecific levels.

Calls are individually separable, enabling partners to recognize each other and also their chick with complete certainty in the midst of a dense colony. In *Aptenodytes* there is sexual

dimorphism in voice, as the birds are physically identical, whereas other members of the family have certain slight differences, for instance in overall size or bill thickness. King Penguins, being territorial, can locate their mates more easily than Emperor Penguins, and, as a result of this, they have less marked vocal variation. Chicks too have to be recognized individually, and an Emperor chick's voice does not change during its first five months of life, whereas in the Adelie Penguin it changes when the chick is only ten days old.

There are three main kinds of vocalization in the Spheniscidae: the contact call of an individual; the display call used between partners at a colony; and the threat call. The first is usually used at sea, as an aid to visual recognition, in order to maintain the cohesion of the group, and the contact call of *Aptenodytes* can be heard a kilometre away. The display call is the most complex, as it has to communicate more information than the others, and must permit specific, sexual and individual recognition. The threat call is the least elaborate and is used for defending a territory, as well as for defence against predators.

The voice of the Jackass Penguin has given rise to its common name, as birds in a busy colony give off sounds not unlike an angry donkey. However, this type of voice is actually common to other *Spheniscus* penguins, and the species should perhaps more aptly be known as the African Penguin.

Food and Feeding

All penguins exploit marine zones that are rich in nutrients. Species of the Antarctic and the subantarctic basically feed on krill (*Euphausia*) and cephalopods, while those that live further north tend to eat fish.

Intake varies with the quantity and quality of food available from place to place at different times of year. The amount of time spent fishing, and likewise the speed and depth at which birds fish, normally depend on the ease with which prey can be located. The larger species are the best equipped for diving to greater depths (see Morphological Aspects).

Variations in marine productivity can cause serious problems for penguins, in terms of their very survival. The most extreme case of this is the phenomenon known as El Niño (see page 341), which can cause not only total breeding failure but also slumps in adult numbers of those species most directly affected, namely the Humboldt and Galapagos Penguins; it has even been found to have far-reaching effects in seabird colonies on the other side of the Pacific.

Typical penguin prey items include shoaling fish, cephalopods, especially squid, and crustaceans, especially krill. The genus *Spheniscus* take mostly anchovies (*Engraulis*), sardines, mullet and similar schooling pelagic fish, within a size range of 1-15 cm in the Galapagos Penguin, but up to 31 cm in the Jackass. *Aptenodytes*, in turn, take fish up to 15 cm long and cephalopods of over 30 cm.

Each genus normally exploits a particular kind of prey, but congeners tend to have slightly different preferences, a standard

evolutionary mechanism designed to reduce competition between similar species. Thus, in *Pygoscelis*, while Adelies feed mostly on small krill, Chinstraps eat large krill; the diet of Gentoos varies between populations, those in the south taking mostly large krill, while more northerly ones take more fish. In addition, the Gentoo dives deeper than the other two species. While crustaceans constitute the most frequent prey of *Eudyptes*, the Rockhopper seems to specialize in small prey, whereas the largest members of the genus, the Macaroni and Royal Penguins, take more fish and cephalopods than their congeners.

The sexual size dimorphism of *Eudyptes* is correlated with the size of prey taken, so that competition for food is further reduced, especially during the breeding season; this is a particularly important advantage, given the enormous colonies that this genus forms. Similarly, male Adelies take significantly larger prey items to their chicks than do females, although this species does not display the same extent of sexual size difference. In the South Shetlands, it has been found that male Gentoos take a higher proportion of fish than females, which seems to be connected with the males greater body size and heavier bill. As the species is sedentary at this locality, competition for food when it is scarce must undoubtedly be greater, and the reduction of intraspecific competition must help to alleviate this problem.

There is a great deal of interspecific variability in terms of the distance birds will stray from the colony in search of food, and some cover enormous distances. Apparently they head straight for a particular area, often in groups, and start looking around for food once they arrive. *Aptenodytes* and *Eudyptes* are offshore feeders, while the rest all feed in inshore waters. Fishing grounds can be surprisingly far from the colony, sometimes as much as 900 km in the King Penguin, and perhaps about 250 km in the Macaroni and the Rockhopper. In contrast, Adelie Penguins normally fish about 15 km away, though they may wander some 50 km, while Little Penguins tend to feed around 20 km from the colony.

Very little is known about the techniques used by penguins in prey capture. Once prey has been located, the birds tend to stay under water catching and swallowing it, probably until they have to come up to the surface for air. Most prey is swallowed head first, while the bird is swimming, but large items are brought up to the surface. The genera *Eudyptula* and

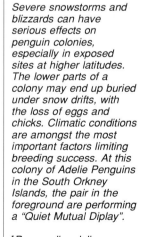

During breeding, when they have to spend very long spells on land, Adelie Penguins sometimes eat snow; a bird may even carry a mouthful of snow to its partner at the nest. Such activity is assumed to be simply a way of getting water, and certainly in warmer areas penguins are sometimes seen drinking water.

[Pygoscelis adeliae, Antarctica. Photo: M. P. Kahl/DRK]

Severe snowstorms and blizzards can have serious effects on penguin colonies, especially in exposed sites at higher latitudes. The lower parts of a colony may end up buried under snow drifts, with the loss of eggs and chicks. Climatic conditions are amongst the most important factors limiting breeding success. At this colony of Adelie Penguins in the South Orkney Islands, the pair in the foreground are performing a "Quiet Mutual Diplay".

[Pygoscelis adeliae, Signy I, South Orkney Islands. Photo: Rick Price/Survival]

Spheniscus have been recorded capturing fish, by swimming along underneath them, which probably makes the fish easier to see. It is thought that conspicuous colouring may help penguins to capture shoaling fish, by sowing panic amongst them, with the result that they break ranks in alarm and are easier to catch. The Little, Jackass and Magellanic Penguins have a specialized technique: when a bird locates a shoal of fish, it accelerates and swims round the fish in ever-decreasing circles, before suddenly dashing into their midst and snatching what it can. It is not known how penguins locate prey in the darkness, at great depths or at night, but they are undoubtedly helped by the fact that many pelagic cephalopods, crustaceans and fish are bioluminous.

The more piscivorous species are often seen fishing in groups, which may number more than 200 birds in the Galapagos Penguin, although most flocks contain less than 50 individuals. The movements of flocks tend to be closely synchronized, with birds moving in and out of the water in unison, though this tendency is most marked in smaller flocks, for example those of under 12 birds in the Jackass Penguin.

Some species, such as the Magellanic and Jackass Penguins, often feed in association with predatory fish, other seabirds and even sea lions (*Otaria byronia*). The Jackass, for example, regularly associates with feeding Cape Gannets (*Sula capensis*) and Cape Cormorants (*Phalacrocorax capensis*).

Breeding

Most penguins nest on islands to the south of or near the subtropical convergence and are strictly seasonal in their breeding. The most obvious exceptions are the Galapagos, Jackass and Humboldt Penguins, which inhabit subtropical to tropical zones and can nest at any time of year, so they adjust their breeding to tie in with the most suitable local conditions when food is most readily available. The Little Penguin is intermediate between these two extremes, as it does breed seasonally, but because it has a very long season, the timing of the beginning of breeding is rather variable.

The distribution of colonies is generally determined by two factors, the availability of sufficient food nearby and the existence of suitable nesting sites with good access.

All species are colonial to a greater or lesser degree, with the exception of the Yellow-eyed Penguin (*Megadyptes antipodes*). Gentoo, Fiordland, Little, Humboldt and Galapagos Penguins all nest in small colonies, which tend to be fairly loose, with nests widely dispersed. The other species form large colonies, which can at times reach gigantic proportions. In complete contrast, Yellow-eyed Penguins breed in isolated pairs or small, scattered groups of one to five nests per hectare, where pairs are usually far enough apart as to be out of sight of their neighbours.

Almost all penguin species are colonial, and some form vast aggregations. This colony at Punta Tombo in southern Argentina is the largest known of the Magellanic Penguin, holding an impressive 225,000 pairs. All four Spheniscus penguins typically nest underground, often in burrows, which provide them with shelter both from excessive heat and from predators.

[Spheniscus magellanicus, Punta Tombo, Argentina. Photo: Günter Ziesler]

Pygoscelis and *Eudyptes* penguins sometimes form mixed colonies or breed alongside two or more other species. In order to reduce interspecific competition for prey during the periods of greatest requirement, when chicks have to be fed, certain mechanisms come into play, such as staggered breeding cycles or the exploitation of different prey or different feeding zones (see Feeding). Clear evidence of this comes from the fact that mixed colonies of two species of *Eudyptes* are invariably formed of one large and one small species.

Colonies tend to be maintained year after year in most species. Some species, such as Adelie and Little Penguins, go further, and keep the same mate and even the same nest-site as the previous year. On the other hand, Gentoo colonies move slightly from year to year, though data from the Crozet Islands show that this shift tends to be less than 150 m per year. It may be a form of defence against parasites, or it might be a way of allowing the vegetation to regenerate, in the wake of heavy trampling and the accumulation of excreta.

Penguins are monogamous. In some species, for example Chinstrap, Royal and Magellanic Penguins, males arrive at the colony some considerable time before the females, and when the females eventually appear pairing is very quick. By the time female Rockhoppers reach their colonies, the nest tends to be half-built already. In other species, for instance the Adelie Penguin, males only arrive very slightly earlier, and the same partners from the previous season join up again at the same nest-site; the pair is reconstituted almost immediately. Many Gentoos apparently arrive at the colony already paired, while Yellow-eyed Penguins tend to be more or less sedentary, and the pair can be formed at any time of year.

Between pair formation and laying, there is a period dedicated to courtship. Most species tend to cease feeding during the courtship period and will not resume again until incubation permits, although there are exceptions, for instance the Gentoo and Yellow-eyed Penguins. Fasting at this stage may last anything from one or two days in Yellow-eyed Penguins to three and a half months in Emperors (see General Habits).

Of the subantarctic species, the spread of laying dates within a particular colony is greatest among Gentoo and King Penguins, and it can last as much as 154 days in the former. Laying dates for both of these species seem to depend directly on the success of the previous season's breeding attempt, but in different ways. King Penguins may start late due to the lengthy period of chick-care, whereas Gentoos may lay a late replacement clutch in the same season, if their initial attempt is unsuccessful.

The two *Aptenodytes* penguins make no nest, warming the egg and then the chick between their feet and folds of skin in the ventral region. This allows them a certain degree of mobility, which no other genus possesses, and adult Emperors can thus gather together in dense huddles during incubation, with as many as ten birds per square metre. In this way, they can maintain body temperature and save energy, for a lone individual loses twice as much energy as a bird in one of these snug huddles. Indeed, the temperature in the midst of one of these tight groups is some 10°C higher than the ambient temperature. The smallest colonies of this species are of about 300 birds, and it seems that successful breeding would probably not be possible for smaller groups.

The genera *Pygoscelis* and *Eudyptes* site their nests in the open or in amongst vegetation, while *Megadyptes*, *Eudyptula* and *Spheniscus* nest in hollows, caves or cracks, or alternatively under roots or vegetation, to avoid direct sunlight. The material used varies from place to place and with the species, but generally consists of pebbles, some kind of plant matter and old feathers. A medium-sized nest of the Gentoo Penguin was composed of some 1700 pebbles and 70 old tail feathers, whereas that of the more modest Chinstrap often has only a rim of eight to ten stones, whatever is necessary to prevent the egg from rolling away.

The members of *Aptenodytes* lay only one egg, and the Emperor has the smallest egg in relation to adult body mass of any bird. All other species lay two eggs, normally with an laying interval of three or four days, though on occasions more. Incubation generally starts with the laying of the second egg, but Gentoos incubate the first egg partially before the arrival of the second. Little, Jackass and Galapagos Penguins can successfully raise two broods in the one season.

Eudyptes penguins lay two eggs, but only one chick survives, almost always that of the second egg, which is laid three to eight days after the first. The first is much smaller and lighter than the second, indeed the size difference is the greatest found in any birds, while the larger size of the second is contrary to the normal tendency in other birds. The second egg is 20-70% heavier than the first, and tends to hatch first, so that when the first egg hatches there is such a size difference between the two

The King Penguin incubates its single egg under folds of bare skin between its legs. It has no nest and this gives it a certain amount of mobility during the incubation period, though in practice birds move very little. Each pair has a very small territory, extending only as far as the incubating bird can reach with its oustretched bill. Birds are territorial only during the courtship and incubation phases, and subsequently when brooding the chick.

[*Aptenodytes patagonicus*, Crozet Is. Photo: M. P. Harris]

chicks that the smaller bird can not compete for food and usually starves to death within a few days. The fact that the first egg is not incubated until the second has been laid only serves to diminish the slim chances of the first. Although the adults take turns in guarding the nest, some birds continue to bring material, and on occasions this can result in the egg being accidentally pushed out of the nest, and subsequently taken by a predator. Mortality is high during the incubation period, and a clutch of two eggs acts as an insurance policy, so that there is a better chance of at least one chick surviving.

It is thought that the smaller size of the first egg in *Eudyptes* may be directly connected with the fact that males are very aggressive during the early stages of the breeding season, which may mean that the first egg is far more likely to be lost, especially in very large, dense colonies. In support of this, it has been found that 54% of Macaroni Penguin pairs lose the first egg before the second has been laid, whereas in the Fiordland and Snares Penguins both eggs frequently hatch. Another hypothesis is that the genus is in the process of evolving towards a clutch of a single egg. However, the true significance of this strategy remains a matter for discussion.

The remaining genera, *Pygoscelis*, *Megadyptes*, *Eudyptula* and *Spheniscus*, lay two similar eggs, the first being only slightly larger and heavier, and both chicks may survive to fledging. Hatching is asynchronous, with the first egg laid hatching first, so that this chick, already the larger, will have been fed before the second hatches, with the result that the size difference between the two is magnified. This difference persists until the chicks reach independence: when the larger chick goes off to sea, the smaller one remains and is fed by the adults until it attains the necessary weight, and in this way the foraging effort of the adults is somewhat reduced, as it is spread out over a longer period.

Penguins do not feed while incubating (see General Habits), so they have to take turns, and while one bird remains at the nest, the other departs to feed at sea. The length of incubation stints varies with the species, but the first and second stints are normally the longest. If the foraging bird is absent too long, its mate will desert the nest and go off to sea to feed too.

Emperor Penguins start their breeding season a great distance from the open sea, on occasions as much as 200 kilometres or more. The male is left in charge of the incubation, and if the chick hatches before the female returns, the male, despite a lengthy period of fasting, is capable of feeding his chick with a form of curd secreted in the oesophagus, which is popularly known as "penguin milk". This ability is unique among penguins, and means that the chick can survive for up to two weeks more, awaiting the return of the female.

Chicks are fed by incomplete regurgitation. In the genera *Aptenodytes* and *Eudyptes*, the offshore feeders, chicks have to undergo long intervals between each feed, and so only one chick can be raised, but the remaining genera, which are all inshore feeders, can bring food to the chicks more frequently, and this means that two chicks can be raised. When food is in short supply, the adults only feed the larger chick, with the result that the smaller one soon dies of starvation, but in this way there is a better chance of the larger chick managing to survive to fledge. During breeding, penguins mostly feed diurnally, going off to sea at sunrise and coming back in the evening, though some birds may return early the next morning, or even after several days, if their feeding grounds are far off. In contrast, Fiordland, Little and Galapagos Penguins regularly return to their colonies at night.

King Penguins can only produce two chicks every three years, and the earliest nesters are invariably those that did not raise a chick the previous season. Chicks from the clutches laid latest do not survive, for, by the time the cold weather arrives, they have not grown big enough to endure the rigors of the long winter fast. The Emperor Penguin, on the other hand, breeds annually, and is unique in being the only species to breed in the Antarctic during its harsh, inexorable winter, when the temperature may drop below -60°C, winds can top 200 km/h, and for long spells the whole region is enshrouded in a cloak of darkness or half-light. The reasons behind this bizarre timing are not yet known, but some workers have speculated that it may have been adopted so that when the chick becomes independent after five months, in January or February, the climatic conditions are more favourable and food more plentiful. The northernmost populations of Gentoos are the only subantarctic penguins to lay their eggs at the beginning of winter, whereas Antarctic populations of the same species lay in spring like the other *Pygoscelis* penguins.

Chick-care is split into two separate phases. The first is the "Guard Phase", during which one adult stays with the chick or chicks, while the other is away searching for food; the second is the "Post-guard Phase", in which both adults go off to look for food. It is during this second phase that crèches are formed.

King Penguins look after their chicks for 10-13 months and this period can be divided into three distinct stages. The first starts with hatching, and continues through crèche formation, which takes place in the first month, and in all lasts three or four months, during which time the chicks are fed regularly, until they weigh about 10-12 kg. The second stage coincides with the austral winter, and during this period the chicks are left alone and are fed only infrequently, once every five or six weeks, or sometimes not at all for three or four months, so they lose something between a third and half of the maximum weight they

had managed to attain in the autumn. The third stage begins with the arrival of spring, when the adults once again feed their chicks regularly until their growth is completed.

The formation of crèches by the chicks seems to be directly related with the cold in *Aptenodytes*, whereas in *Pygoscelis* and *Eudyptes* the main reason seems to be defence against predators. The chicks of species that nest in holes do not normally form crèches, although in some species, such as the Jackass and Little Penguins, very small ones may assemble, usually consisting of no more than five or six birds. For the species that nest on the surface, the period of greatest chick mortality is the interval between the "Guard phase" and the formation of the crèche. As in other birds, each chick in a crèche is fed only by its own parents.

When they have finished growing, chicks undergo a complete moult (see Morphological Aspects), and after this has been completed, they are ready to become independent and go off to sea. Of all the penguins of the Antarctic and subantarctic, the Gentoo is the only species in which adults continue to take care of their chicks after they have gone to sea, and this can continue for anything between five and fifty days.

The level of predation in a colony is markedly higher around the periphery, and tends to involve eggs or chicks that are unattended. Other factors that cause loss of eggs or chicks include adverse weather conditions and lack of food.

The main predators of penguins at sea include leopard seals (*Hydrurga leptonyx*), killer whales (*Orcinus orca*), fur seals (*Arctocephalus*), sea lions (*Otaria*) and sharks (*Gliphis glaucus*). In and around the colonies, the important predators vary from one area to another, but include skuas (*Catharacta*), giant petrels (*Macronectes*), sheathbills (*Chionis*), gulls (*Larus*), Wekas (*Gallirallus australis*) and some coastal raptors. At some colonies, there is also "unnatural" predation by species introduced by man (see Status and Conservation).

The practice in some species, such as the Adelie, of subadults returning to the colony around the time when eggs are hatching has several possible explanations. It could be a communal defence strategy against predators. On the other hand, the non-breeders may help to maintain the cohesion of the crèches at this moment, when the breeding adults frequently leave the colony, in order to find food for the chicks. They may also help by incubating eggs or brooding small chicks that have been left unattended. Certainly, it must prove useful experience for immature birds, and may enhance their own chances of breeding successfully in the future.

It is known that breeding success is directly related to age in several species, including Adelie, Royal, Yellow-eyed and Little Penguins. Thus an inexperienced bird can have difficulty finding a mate or a suitable territory, or situating its nest in a safe place. Its laying capacity may be lower, and it may be inefficient in its chick-care. Sexual maturity is normally reached at two to seven years old.

Movements

To date, little has been discovered about penguins' movements, and the winter distribution of many species still remains largely unknown. In general, most species do not seem to be migratory. Populations inhabiting the warmer areas, such as the tropics, are basically sedentary, whereas those living in zones with a rather less congenial climate tend to travel northwards, with the Antarctic species at least moving out of the zones of pack ice. Not all populations of a particular species necessarily follow the same migratory strategy. In the Gentoo, for instance, with its relatively wide range, southern populations are migratory, while those of the north tend to be sedentary.

Young birds usually perform dispersive movements when they leave their colonies, and may wander far off. However, they generally return to the colony to moult and subsequently to breed. Subadults of some species, for example Adelies, have been found returning to the colony once breeding is already under way, in order to help adults with some of their tasks (see Breeding).

In stark contrast to traditional ideas about penguins, the typical nesting habitat of the Fiordland Penguin is wet coastal rain forest. The nest is a fairly shallow cup lined with plant matter at the base of a tree, under roots, amongst rocks or in caves. Note the diagnostic white lines across the cheeks which are not always visible.

[*Eudyptes pachyrhynchus*, Long Reef, Martin's Bay, New Zealand. Photo: Frances Furlong/ Bruce Coleman]

The Emperor Penguin, like its close relative the King Penguin, broods its chick between its feet and the folds of bare skin on its abdomen, so that the chick avoids direct contact with the ice. Using the same system, the male Emperor alone carries out the entire process of incubating the single egg, and if the chick hatches before the female's return, the male can feed his chick on a secretion popularly known as "penguin milk".

[*Aptenodytes forsteri*, Antarctica. Photo: Graham Robertson/ Ardea]

Chicks attain their maximum weight shortly before initiating their moult, and they can become notably fatter than the adults, as illustrated by these King Penguins. By the time the chick fledges, its weight has dropped to only about 75% of the adult's. Adults and young recognize each other's calls individually, which is particularly important for feeding during the crèche stage, but if a chick is very hungry it may beg for food from an adult other than its parent, though normally in vain. Note the moulting bird in the right foreground.

[*Aptenodytes patagonicus*, South Georgia. Photo: François Gohier/ Ardea]

Fishing or whaling vessels used to capture penguin quite frequently to carry as mascots, and in some cases the birds escaped or were set free later, far from their point of origin. For this reason, many records of birds found far from their colonies are considered of doubtful significance, and it can be difficult to ascertain whether or not genuine migration is really involved.

Relationship with Man

The first Europeans to see penguins were probably members of the expedition of Bartholomeu Dias de Novaes in 1487/88, as they were the first to round the Cape of Storms, later to be renamed the Cape of Good Hope. However, the earliest surviving written references to penguins come to us from Vasco da Gama's voyage of 1497/98, where the chronicler describes the penguins that were seen along the southern coasts of Africa. The second reference in literature belongs to Antonio Pigafetta, the historian who sailed with Magellan on his circumnavigation of the globe from 1519 to 1522. Despite the observations of these and later travellers, there was no scientific description of a penguin until Linnaeus described the Jackass Penguin in 1758.

The name "Penguin" actually came about as the result of confusion with another species of bird, the similarly-coloured and likewise flightless, but totally unrelated Great Auk (*Alca impennis*), which was once abundant in the North Atlantic. It became extinct in 1844, as a result of the commercialization of its fat, whence "Penguin", from the Latin *pinguis*, meaning "fat".

Penguins have constituted a very easy source of food for humans, largely due to their inability to fly, combined with their relative indifference, in the face of the relentless persecutions they have faced. These had devastating effects, particularly in the nineteenth century and at the beginning of the twentieth. The fact that penguins are geographically remote from their main persecutors, the Europeans, made their commercial exploitation rather difficult and this undoubtedly prevented even greater massacres. Nonetheless, whalers, fishermen and explorers found penguin colonies to be an important source of food, and they certainly did not waste their opportunities, loading as many eggs and birds on board their ships as they could.

Penguins have been put to many uses, apart from the extensive consumption of the flesh of adults and young birds. In some places, such as Amsterdam and St Paul Islands, in the southern Indian Ocean, fishermen still use penguins for bait. In the Falkland Islands, their eggs have been systematically collected in vast numbers since 1700, and this exploitation only ceased relatively recently. Many colonies have declined dramatically or even disappeared for this reason. On Dassen Island, off South Africa, some 300,000 Jackass Penguin eggs were collected per year around the end of last century, and enormous numbers were destroyed, in order to assure there would be plenty of fresh eggs on the next visit. Although banned in 1969, illegal egg-collecting continues today, though on a small scale.

Another form of exploitation which was to gain considerable economic importance was the extraction of their oil. This was obtained by killing and boiling penguins just at the moment when they are at their plumpest, when they return to land to moult. The industry took off in a big way. Between 1870 and 1918 the New Zealand government granted licences to capture penguins on Macquarie Island, for the extraction of their oil. This led to the annual killing of around 150,000 birds, the species involved being King and Royal Penguins. Between 1864 and 1880, some 2,000,000-2,500,000 birds were killed in the Falklands for their oil; most of these were Rockhoppers, though Gentoos also suffered, and King Penguins were actually exterminated from the islands. Fortunately the oil industry was discontinued due to protests by the general public, who believed that the penguins had to be thrown into the boiling-pots alive, for the oil to come out.

Guano is another product of penguins, and also of other seabirds, which has had great commercial value, and its use as fertilizer goes right back into Inca times. Between 1848 and 1875 Europe and North America together imported over 20,000,000 tonnes. However, such excessive exploitation could not continue, and around the beginning of the twentieth century it became necessary to rationalize the industry, by protecting the islands and the guano-producing birds, in order to ensure the continued renewal of the guano deposits (see page 338).

Penguin feathers too have been used in many diverse ways, for example as rugs, slippers, blankets, decorations on women's dresses, bags, hats and so on. Even moulted feathers can be collected for stuffing mattresses.

Zoos have played an important part in popularizing penguins, and they are among the birds most commonly featured in advertising or in children's comics. This popularity has helped to promote tourism to the Antarctic and the subantarctic. People are taken on organized trips to see round penguin colonies, all too often with a patent disregard of the disturbances caused; too many people going too close and making too much noise can have serious effects on a population (see Status and Conservation).

Status and Conservation

The exploitation of penguins on a massive scale up to the beginning of this century meant the sacrifice of millions of birds (see Relationship with Man). Likewise, the destruction of their breeding grounds during the course of guano mining undoubtedly caused a significant decline in some populations, and even, on occasions, the complete disappearance of whole colonies.

Right from the earliest scientific exploration of Antarctica, penguins have suffered frequent maltreatment, and this continues to the present day, with permanent politico-scientific bases frequently being located in the few areas suitable for breeding. Aircraft and helicopters flying over colonies spread panic, and both adults and chicks may stampede, causing many casualties, which are then easy meat for the opportunist predators. Quite recently 7000 King Penguins died on Macquarie Island due to one such stampede, and this seems to have been directly related to the low flights of an Australian Air Force Hercules. It can only be hoped that the measures already taken in some places to reduce the impact of humans will prove effective and will be applied more widely.

In general any disturbance of colonies can have very serious effects: birds can panic and trample eggs or chicks; if sitting birds leave the nest, predators quickly move in; even if they stay put, and are apparently unaffected, their alarm is liable to use up a lot of extra energy (see General Habits), which later in the breeding season may be found lacking, and this can result in possible breeding failure or death. In such ways, the results of disturbance may not always be immediate or obvious.

Zoos too have had a negative effect, as they have taken large numbers of birds for their collections. On Heard Island, for example, the few King Penguins which survived in 1949, after the ravages of the oil industry, were all removed to Australian zoos. Nonetheless, captive breeding programmes, with the aim of boosting natural populations could turn out to be of great importance to some species.

Any unattended egg or chick is quickly located and snapped up by the predators roving around the colony, the most efficient of which are the skuas (Catharacta). On occasions penguins practice communal defence, with several neighbouring adults joining forces to repel the intruder, as can be seen here with these Gentoo Penguins. Gentoos will, if necessary, charge skuas to drive them off.

[*Pygoscelis papua papua*, Falkland Is.
Photo: Rinie van Meurs/ Bruce Coleman]

The distinctive Yellow-eyed Penguin is one of the three penguin species that are currently considered to be globally threatened. The main threats to its future come in the form of habitat destruction, partly with the increasing conversion of land for agriculture, and partly as a result of the damaging effects that herbivores, both domestic and feral, can have on both the vegetation and the soil structure. The ravages of introduced predators are also highly significant, and in some years can plunder over 90% of the chicks hatched.

[Megadyptes antipodes, New Zealand. Photo: C. Carvalho/FLPA]

Man's introduction of predators has had disastrous effects in some places, causing great losses of adults, chicks and eggs. The worst offenders are rats, mustelids, dogs and pigs, and some of these can kill adults outright. All of the penguins' natural predators are basically opportunists, and there is none that relies exclusively on them as a source of food. A further problem is posed by introduced herbivores, such as sheep and rabbits, which cause serious deterioration of the habitat, and can eventually destroy a whole colony, as well as causing additional disturbance. Some eggs and chicks may also be lost due to trampling by large herbivores.

The dumping of rubbish, particularly of plastic objects, in the sea has caused problems, at any rate for Little Penguins. A bird may ingest articles, intentionally or accidentally, or get its neck stuck in can yokes, and this can cause serious injury or even death, for example because the bird may be unable to swallow its food.

Spills of crude oil affect penguins and other birds by spoiling the waterproofing of the plumage, and if a bird tries to clean itself, it invariably takes in some of the oil and become intoxicated. The layer of thermal insulation (see Morphological Aspects) is destroyed too, and this forces the bird to leave the water, where it finally dies, either of intoxication or of starvation. Jackass and Magellanic Penguins have suffered a fair deal with oil spills, though campaigns have been mounted in South Africa to clean up oiled birds, and these have had fairly satisfactory results.

Low concentrations of DDT and other chlorinated hydrocarbons have been found in the tissues of species living in very remote areas, such as the Adelie and Chinstrap Penguins, and it seems most likely that these pollutants have either been brought by ocean currents or by other animals. However, the significance of these finds is clearly the fact that such toxic substances have already reached Antarctica.

Census results indicate that several penguin populations have increased in number in recent decades, although it must be remembered that variations in the method of census or in its timing can affect the results, and figures are not always comparable, especially some of the older ones. The definitive termination of persecution on a large scale is clearly having its effects, but there are several other factors which can also affect numbers to a greater or lesser degree, such as climatic variations.

Another such factor is the activity of whalers during the first half of this century. The decimation of whale populations seems to have led to a boom in their main prey, krill, and this, in turn, has caused an increase in the numbers of some Antarctic penguins that feed on krill, most notably the Chinstrap. However, overfishing of krill, mostly destined for the Japanese market, could have a catastrophic effect on the food chains of the Southern Ocean.

Undoubtedly one of the most important positive steps taken in conservation in recent years was the re-signing of the Antarctic Non-exploitation Treaty in October 1991. This was one of the rare cases in which scientific and ecological arguments managed to prevail over those in favour of short-term benefits for a select few.

General Bibliography

Baudinette & Gill (1985), Burger (1991), Cairns (1986), Croxall (1982b, 1991), Croxall & Lishman (1987), Croxall, Evans, & Schreiber (1984), Croxall, Prévost et al. (1985), Davis & Darby (1988, 1990), Fordyce et al. (1986), Harrison (1985, 1987), Ho et al. (1976), Jouventin (1978, 1982), Kooyman & Davis (1987), Müller-Schwarze (1984), Nelson (1980), Peterson (1979), Pinshow et al. (1977), Simpson (1946, 1976), Sparks & Soper (1987), Stonehouse (1967a, 1970a, 1975), Tollu (1988), Watson (1975), Williams (1980d, 1981e), Williams, Cooper et al. (1985), Williams, Siegfried & Cooper (1982).

PLATE 9

inches 14

cm 35

1

2

3

4

5

6

7

8

ssp *moseleyi*

9

ssp *chrysocome*

10

11

12

ssp *minor*

13

ssp *albosignata*

14

15

16

17

Genus *APTENODYTES* J. F. Miller, 1778

1. King Penguin
Aptenodytes patagonicus

French: Manchot royal   **German**: Königspinguin   **Spanish**: Pingüino Rey

Taxonomy. *Aptenodytes patagonica* J. F. Miller, 1778, South Georgia.
Validity of division into subspecies sometimes questioned and species may be better considered monotypic. Some evidence of genetic differences between populations of Kerguelen and Crozet Is. Two subspecies normally recognized.
Subspecies and Distribution.
A. p. patagonicus J. F. Miller, 1778 - Falkland Is, South Georgia; formerly S tip of S America.
A. p. halli Mathews, 1911 - Southern Ocean from Marion I eastwards to Macquarie I.

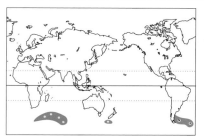

Descriptive notes. 94-95 cm; 9-15 kg. Bill relatively longer and auricular patches different shade and shape from those of *A. forsteri*. Juvenile has paler yellow auricular patches and duller mandibular plates. Races separated on length of bill and wing.
Habitat. Marine and pelagic in subantarctic and low latitudes of Antarctic, spending much time near breeding areas; not known to breed S of 60° S. Breeds on flattish beaches where no snow or ice, sometimes with tussock grass; normally near sea, with easy access. Offshore feeder.
Food and Feeding. Mostly fish, especially small Myctophidae (*Electrona carlesbergi*, *Krefftichthys anderssoni*); also cephalopods (*Moroteuthis*), small at Marion I, large at South Georgia. Captures prey by means of pursuit-diving, swimming at up to 12 km/h; 10% success rate in catching cephalopods. Normally fishes no deeper than 50 m, but sometimes dives more than 240 m down; probably fishes night and day, diving deeper during day.
Breeding. Arrival at colony Sept-Nov; laying Nov-Apr. Only 2 breeding cycles possible per pair every 3 years. Colonial; territory is c. 1 m²/pair; no nest. 1 egg; incubation by both sexes 52-56 days, with stints of 12-21 days; chicks hatch almost naked; 1st down pale grey or brown, 2nd down dark brown; crèche at c. 40 days; fledging 10-13 months. Sexual maturity at 5-7 years old. Breeding success 30·6% (Crozet), 36-47% (Macquarie). See pages 148-150.
Movements. Adults generally fairly sedentary, with some dispersive movements. Pre-moult period 17 days spent at sea in vicinity of colony, storing up reserves of fat. Post-breeding dispersal of juveniles mostly in pelagic zone; several juveniles from Crozet Is sighted at Marion I, c. 1000 km away. Feeding area of adults c. 80-418 km from colony, when chicks small, 77-902 km, when large. Vagrant to Australia, New Zealand and S Africa.
Status and Conservation. Not globally threatened. Total population estimated at over 1,000,000 pairs; presently stable or increasing. Largest colony in Cochons Is (Crozet), with c. 300,000 pairs; 240,000-280,000 pairs in Kerguelen Is; 228,000 pairs on Prince Edward Is in late 1970's. Suffered intense persecution during 19th and early 20th centuries: birds taken for extraction of oil; in some areas eggs collected. Most colonies have increased markedly in recent decades, e.g. Kerguelen 7% per year and Crozet 3% per year; however, some small colonies on South Georgia have disappeared. Exterminated from Heard I in period 1929-1948, probably by sealers, but recolonized in 1963 with 23 pairs, 600 pairs by 1980, 5700 pairs in 1989; exterminated from Falklands c. 1870, but subsequently recolonized, starting in 1933. At Macquarie I, sealers exterminated one colony and reduced the other to 5000 birds by 1911; numbers constant till 1930, since when prolific increase to 70,000+ pairs in 1980. Research stations built on some nesting grounds, e.g. by Australian National Antarctic Research Expedition on Macquarie I; some breeding grounds in Crozet Is ruined by construction of buildings and roads.
Bibliography. Adams (1987), Adams & Brown (1989), Adams & Klages (1987), Barrat (1976), Blake (1977), Cherel & Le Maho (1988), Cherel & Ridoux (1992), Cherel *et al.* (1987), Croxall & Kirkwood (1979), Derenne *et al.* (1979), Gales & Pemberton (1988), Gillespie (1932), Hindell (1988b), Howland & Sivak (1984), Hunter (1991), Johnson (1965), Jouventin & Weimerskirch (1991), Jouventin *et al.* (1988), Klages *et al.* (1990), Kooyman *et al.* (1982), Le Maho & Despin (1976), Lindsey (1986), Marchant & Higgins (1990), Niven & Abel (1991), Ridoux *et al.* (1988), Robisson (1990), Rounsevell & Copson (1982), Stonehouse (1960), Thibault & Guyot (1988), Tollu (1978), Warham (1985a), Watkins (1987), Vaucoulon *et al.* (1985), Viot (1987), Weimerskirch *et al.* (1992), Wilson, G.J. (1983), Woehler (1991).

2. Emperor Penguin
Aptenodytes forsteri

French: Manchot empereur   **German**: Kaiserpinguin   **Spanish**: Pingüino Emperador

Taxonomy. *Aptenodytes Forsteri* G. R. Gray, 1844, Antarctic seas.
Monotypic.
Distribution. Circumpolar; restricted to Antarctica, 66°-78° S.
Descriptive notes. 112-115 cm; 19-46 kg. Largest penguin. Pale yellow wash on underparts. Less brightly coloured than smaller *A. patagonicus*. Juvenile has whitish throat and auricular patches, and duller mandibular plates.
Habitat. Marine and pelagic, in Antarctic waters. Nests on ice floes near coast, or on the coast itself, but sometimes as much as 200 km from open sea; prefers areas of frozen sea with some elevation, to provide shelter from wind. Offshore feeder.
Food and Feeding. Mainly fish, especially Nototheniidae (*Pagothenia borchgrevinki*), normally 40-125 mm long, and *Pleuragramma antarcticum*; euphausiids important in places, and cephalopods also frequently taken. Captures prey by means of pursuit-diving, normally at depth of less than 50

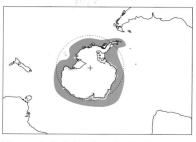

m, but recorded at 265 m; euphausiids typically taken by shallow dives under ice floes, cephalopods by deep dives, fish by both.
Breeding. Arrival at colony Mar-Apr; laying May/Jun. Annual breeding cycle. Colonial, but not territorial; no nest. 1 egg; incubation by male 62-66 days; chicks hatch almost naked; 1st down pale grey with black "helmet", 2nd down similar, but thicker and longer; crèche at c. 45 days; fledging c. 5 months. Sexual maturity normally at 5 years old for females, 6 for males. Total fledging success 64·4% (Pointe Géologie). See pages 148-149.
Movements. Probably dispersive, but little known. Few birds seen N of 60° S. Pre-moult period at sea 30 days. Vagrant to New Zealand, S parts of S America and several islands of subantarctic; record furthest N refers to 3 immatures off C Argentina.
Status and Conservation. Not globally threatened. Total population estimated at 135,000-175,000 pairs; stable, with some local fluctuations. Discovery of new colonies quite recently, due to increased winter exploration of coasts, rather than genuine increase in numbers; colonies where counts have been carried out in several different years appear stable. Some colonies apparently declining since 1970's, e.g. Cape Crozier; Pointe Géologie in Adelie Land held c. 6000 pairs in period 1950-1975, only 2500 pairs in 1982; problems include proximity of scientific bases and helicopters flying over colonies; climatic conditions can lead to early breaking up of sea-ice where colonies sited, causing deaths of adults and destruction of colony, whereas abnormal extension of sea-ice can also cause serious problems; frequency and significance of such cases not yet known.
Bibliography. Blake, E.R. (1977), Blake, R.W. & Smith (1988), Buchet *et al.* (1986), Budd (1962), Croxall & Kirkwood (1979), Croxall & Prince (1983), Deswasmes *et al.* (1980), Groscolas (1978), Groscolas & Clément (1976), Guillotin & Jouventin (1979), Isenmann (1971), Johnson (1965), Jouventin & Weirmerskirch (1991), Jouventin, Guillotin & Cornet (1979), Jouventin, Stahl & Weirmerskirch (1988), Klages (1989), Kooyman *et al.* (1971), Le Maho (1977, 1983), Le Maho, Delclitte & Chatonnet (1976), Le Maho, Delclitte & Groscolas (1977), Lindsey (1986), Marchant & Higgins (1990), Offredo & Ridoux (1986), Pinshow & Welch (1980), Pinshow *et al.* (1976), Prévost (1961), Prévost & Boulière (1975), Robisson (1990), Robisson *et al.* (1989), Stonehouse (1953), Stonehouse & Hempel (1987), Thomas (1986), Todd (1980), Warham (1985b), Wilson, G.J. (1979, 1983), Woehler & Johnstone (1991).

Genus *PYGOSCELIS* Wagler, 1832

3. Gentoo Penguin
Pygoscelis papua

French: Manchot papou   **German**: Eselspinguin   **Spanish**: Pingüino Juanito

Taxonomy. *Aptenodytes papua* J. R. Forster, 1781, Falkland Islands.
Two subspecies recognized.
Subspecies and Distribution.
P. p. papua (J. R. Forster, 1781) - subantarctic S to c. 60° S.
P. p. ellsworthi Murphy, 1947 - Antarctic Peninsula to South Sandwich Is.

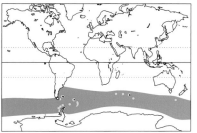

Descriptive notes. 76-81 cm. Appears browner in worn plumage. Small white flecks around large white supraorbital patch; whitish rump; fairly long tail. On reclining bird, white of underparts may reach through onto back in axillary region. Juvenile has smaller, less distinct white supraorbital patch; also thinner, often incomplete eye-ring and sometimes grey throat. Race *ellsworthi* separated on smaller size and proportions of bill.
Habitat. Marine; found much further N than other members of genus. Nests on rocky coasts, sometimes amongst vegetation; prefers flat ground; nesting grounds tend to shift very slightly from year to year. Inshore feeder.
Food and Feeding. Considerable variation with locality: S populations take large amounts of euphausiids, especially Antarctic krill (*Euphausia superba*), those further N taking more fish (e.g. *Electrona*, *Gymnoscopelus*) and different crustaceans; in smaller quantities cephalopods and polychaetes. Captures prey by means of pursuit-diving. When feeding on krill, most dives to less than 54 m down; when catching fish, dives down to 54-136 m.
Breeding. Arrival at colony varies with locality, Jun-Nov; earliest laying Jun/Jul in N, Nov in S. Least colonial of *Pygoscelis* penguins; normally in small colonies, sometimes mixed with congeners; nests well spaced out. Nest large, made with stones, tussock grass and moss. 2 eggs, but normally only one chick raised; one of few penguins to lay replacement clutch; incubation by both sexes 31-39 days, with stints of 1-7 days; 1st down grey, darker on head, 2nd down blackish grey-brown above, white below; crèche at 20-37 days; fledging at 85-117 days in N, 62-82 days in S; unique among penguins, juvenile fed by adults for further 5-50 days, with period becoming longer towards N. Sexual maturity at 2 years old. Total success to fledging 0·4-0·7 chicks/pair (Marion, Crozet, Kerguelen Is), 0·9+ chicks/pair (South Shetland, South Georgia, Macquarie Is).

On following pages: 4. Adelie Penguin (*Pygoscelis adeliae*); 5. Chinstrap Penguin (*Pygoscelis antarctica*); 6. Fiordland Penguin (*Eudyptes pachyrhynchus*); 7. Snares Penguin (*Eudyptes robustus*); 8. Erect-crested Penguin (*Eudyptes sclateri*); 9. Rockhopper Penguin (*Eudyptes chrysocome*); 10. Royal Penguin (*Eudyptes schlegeli*); 11. Macaroni Penguin (*Eudyptes chrysolophus*); 12. Yellow-eyed Penguin (*Megadyptes antipodes*); 13. Little Penguin (*Eudyptula minor*); 14. Jackass Penguin (*Spheniscus demersus*); 15. Humboldt Penguin (*Spheniscus humboldti*); 16. Magellanic Penguin (*Spheniscus magellanicus*); 17. Galapagos Penguin (*Spheniscus mendiculus*).

Movements. Partial migrant, with subantarctic populations tending to be sedentary, while those of Antarctic Peninsula are migratory. Pre-moult period at sea varies, 10-50 days, becoming steadily shorter towards N. In winter wanders to 43° S in Argentina; vagrant to Tasmania and New Zealand.

Status and Conservation. Not globally threatened. Total population estimated at 260,000-300,000 pairs; generally stable throughout 20th century, with substantial temporary fluctuations. Falkland Is hold 100,000-116,000 pairs, South Georgia 80,000-100,000 pairs; colonies of South Shetland Is known to have increased in period 1957-1965; in Kerguelen Is and Possession I (Crozet), colonies disturbed by scientific bases have declined. In Falkland Is, colonies have been affected by egg-collecting and capture of adults for extraction of oil, but overall numbers stable since 1933; colony of 50,000 pairs on Weddell I probably disappeared due to introduction of Patagonian fox (*Dusicyon griseus*). Some important local fluctuations have been associated with failure of food supply at beginning of breeding season.

Bibliography. Adams & Brown (1983, 1989), Adams & Klages (1989), Adams & Wilson (1987), Alvarez Cotelo *et al.* (1989a, 1989b, 1989c), Blake (1977), Bost (1987), Bost & Jouventin (1990, 1991), Conroy & Twelves (1972), Croxall & Kirkwood (1979), Croxall & Prince (1980a, 1983), Croxall *et al.* (1988), Davis, Croxall & O'Connell (1989), Davis, Kooyman & Croxall (1983), Despin (1972, 1977), Gales (1987b), Hindell (1989), Howland & Sivak (1984), Jablonski (1985, 1987a), Jouventin, *et al.* (1988), Klages *et al.* (1990), La Cock *et al.* (1984), Lindsey (1986), Marchant & Higgins (1990), Müller-Schwarze & Müller-Schwarze (1980), Murphy (1947), Reilly & Kerle (1981), Ridoux *et al.* (1988), Robertson (1986), Robertson *et al.* (1988), Stonehouse (1970b), Taylor (1986), Tollu (1978), Trivelpiece (1981), Trivelpiece, Bengston *et al.* (1986), Trivelpiece, Trivelpiece & Volkman (1985, 1987), Trivelpiece, Trivelpiece, Volkman & Ware (1983), Viot (1987), Volkman & Trivelpiece, S.G. (1980), Volkman & Trivelpiece, W.Z. (1981), Volkman *et al.* (1980), Warham (1985c), Williams, A.J. (1980e, 1980f, 1981f), Williams, A.J. & Siegfried (1980), Williams, T.D. (1990, 1991), Wilson, G.J. (1983), Wilson, R.P. (1989), Wilson, R.P. *et al.* (1991), Woehler (1991).

4. Adelie Penguin

Pygoscelis adeliae

French: Manchot d'Adélie **German**: Adeliepinguin **Spanish**: Pingüino de Adelia

Taxonomy. *Catarrhactes Adeliae* Hombron and Jacquinot, 1841, Adélie Land.
May form superspecies with *P. antarctica*. Monotypic.

Distribution. Circumpolar; largely restricted to Antarctica.

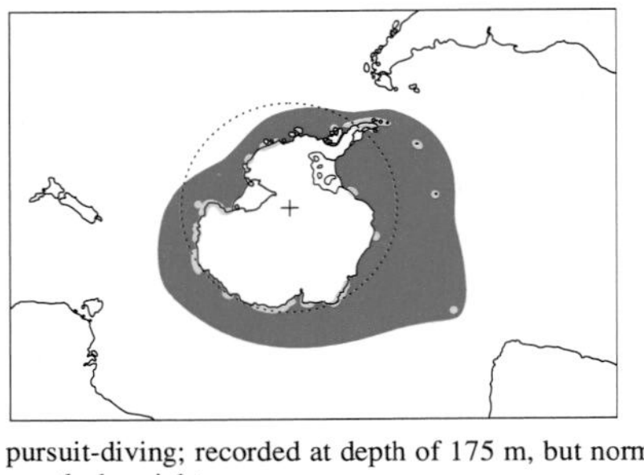

Descriptive notes. 71 cm. Much of bill covered in feathering; iris dark, white eye-ring; fairly long tail. Juvenile has chin and throat white, eye-ring black.

Habitat. Marine. Nests on ice-free rocky coasts, tending to occupy higher ground than *P. papua*; often in extensive open areas to accomodate typically large colonies. Colonies can be far from open sea. Inshore feeder.

Food and Feeding. Mainly krill (*Euphausia superba*, *E. crystallorophias*), with smaller quantities of fish, amphipods and cephalopods. Captures prey by means of pursuit-diving; recorded at depth of 175 m, but normally fishes less than 20 m down. May feed mostly by night.

Breeding. Arrival at colony Sept/Oct; most laying in Nov. Colonial, on occasions forming enormous aggregations; sometimes nests beside congeners, but usually in discrete sectors; nests very close together. Nest is small depression lined with pebbles. 2 eggs; replacement laying can occur, but with only 1 egg; incubation by both sexes 30-43 days, with stints of 7-23 days (females sometimes take shorter initial shift); 1st down pale grey, much darker on head, 2nd down dark brown; crèche at 16-19 days; fledging 50-56 days. Sexual maturity by 8 years old, possibly before; rarely at 5 and exceptionally at 3. Overall breeding success 50% (Cape Royds), 7·5-76·7% (Signy I).

Movements. Dispersive. Unlike most other species, adults do not moult at colony, but rather on ice floes; after breeding birds move N towards rich feeding grounds. Most immatures remain in zones of pack ice at least 2 years, and sometimes 3-5, before returning to natal colony; immatures normally return to colonies later than adults, with delay of up to 2-3 months. Accidental in S America, Falklands, Australia, New Zealand and several islands of Pacific and Indian Oceans.

Status and Conservation. Not globally threatened. Total population estimated at 2,000,000-2,610,000 pairs; stable or increasing. 1,100,000 pairs in Ross Sea sector; largest colony at Cape Adare, with c. 282,307 pairs; 177,083 pairs at Cape Crozier. Much the most studied penguin; however, installation of scientific stations near colonies has caused serious problems, with limitation of suitable ground for breeding, excessive frequency of visits to colonies, helicopters flying overhead, etc. In Ross Sea sector, census figures show number of breeding pairs has decreased; population at Cape Royds comprised 1500-2000 pairs in period 1907-1956, but with establishment of base at McMurdo Sound, down to 1100 pairs in 1962; 100 birds still killed annually at this site, for scientific purposes, but general decrease in human interference has caused recovery up to 3986 pairs; in 1916, collection of 2400 eggs at Cape Royds virtually eliminated colony. Enlargement of base on I of Petrels in Adelie Land has also led to decrease in breeding numbers. At Cape Hallett, colony of 8000-10,000 pairs evicted for construction of research station. Apparently very few colonies have increased (e.g. Haswell I), whereas most undisturbed colonies stable. Increase in tourist visits to some colonies liable to have detrimental effects. Some birds found oiled on Ross I; an increase in shipping traffic would clearly have negative effects.

Bibliography. Ainley (1970, 1972, 1978), Ainley & DeMaster (1980), Ainley & Emison (1972), Ainley & LeResche (1973), Ainley & Schlatter (1972), Ainley *et al.* (1983), Croxall & Kirkwood (1979), Croxall & Prince (1983), Davis (1982, 1988), Davis & McCaffrey (1986, 1989), Davis *et al.* (1988), Derksen (1977), Despin (1977a), Emlen & Penney (1964), Ensor & Basset (1987), Green & Johnstone (1988), van Heezik (1988b), Hui (1987), Jablonski (1985, 1987), Jouventin *et al.* (1988), Kooyman *et al.* (1976), LeResche & Sladen (1970), Lindsey (1986), Lishman (1983, 1985a, 1985b), Marchant & Higgins (1990), Müller-Schwarze & Belanger (1978), Müller-Schwarze & Müller-Schwarze (1977, 1980), Naito *et al.* (1990), Oelke (1978), Paulin & Sagar (1977), Penney (1967, 1968), Penney & Emlen (1967), Penney & Lowry (1967), Penney & Riker (1969), Robertson & Kinsky (1985), Sladen (1958), Speirs (1988), Spurr (1975a, 1975b), Stonehouse (1963), Tamiya & Aoyanagi (1982), Taylor (1962), Taylor & Wilson (1982), Tenaza (1971), Thomas (1986), Thompson (1977), Trivelpiece (1981), Trivelpiece & Volkman (1979), Trivelpiece, Trivelpiece, Geupel *et al.* (1990), Trivelpiece, Trivelpiece & Volkman (1985, 1987), Trivelpiece, Trivelpiece, Volkman & Ware (1983), Volkman & Trivelpiece, S.G. (1980), Volkman & Trivelpiece, W.Z. (1981), Volkman *et al.* (1980), Whitehead (1989), Whitehead, Johnstone & Burton (1990), Wilson, G.J. (1979, 1983), Wilson, R.P. (1989), Woehler & Johnstone (1991), Yeates (1971).

5. Chinstrap Penguin

Pygoscelis antarctica

French: Manchot à jugulaire **German**: Kehlstreifpinguin **Spanish**: Pingüino Barbijo
Other common names: Bearded/Ringed Penguin

Taxonomy. *Aptenodytes antarctica* J. R. Forster, 1781, South Shetlands.
May form superspecies with *P. adeliae*. Monotypic.

Distribution. Circumpolar, with bulk of population in S Atlantic.

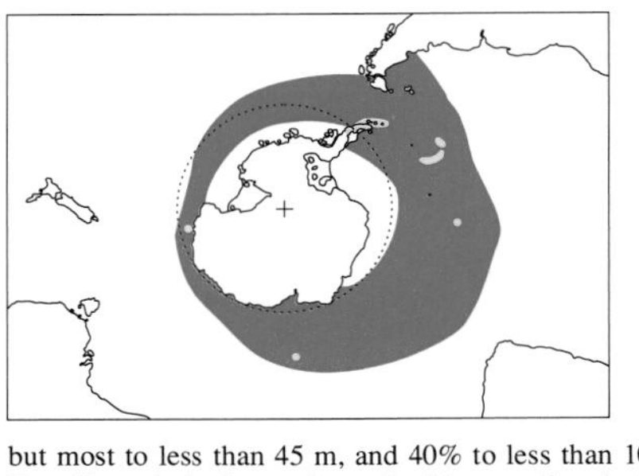

Descriptive notes. 68-77 cm. White of face reaches over eye; fairly long tail. Juvenile has black mottling on face, especially around eyes.

Habitat. Marine, mostly in zones with light pack ice (10-30% ice cover). Nests on irregular rocky coasts, in ice-free areas. Inshore feeder.

Food and Feeding. Almost exclusively Antarctic krill (*Euphausia superba*), normally in 4·0-6·5 cm size range; also takes a few fish and other species of crustaceans. Apparently captures prey by means of pursuit-diving; maximum depth of dives 70 m, but most to less than 45 m, and 40% to less than 10 m.

Breeding. Arrival at colony Oct/Nov; earliest laying Nov/Dec. Colonial, typically in huge colonies of hundreds of thousands of birds; often nests beside congeners. Nest is very simple round platform of stones. 2 eggs, rarely 1 or 3; incubation by both sexes 34-40 days, with stints of 1-18 days; 1st down pale grey, 2nd down pale grey, darker above and on chin; crèche at 23-29 days; fledging 52-60 days. Sexual maturity at 3 years old. Overall breeding success 0·36 chicks/pair (18·7%) in South Orkney Is, 1·06 chicks/pair in South Shetland Is.

Movements. Dispersive, wintering in zones of pack ice from Apr/May to Oct/Nov. Yearlings return to natal colony around Jan, remaining till Mar. Accidental in Australia and at Macquarie, Crozet and Gough Is.

Status and Conservation. Not globally threatened. Total population estimated at 6,500,000 pairs, with c. 5,000,000 pairs in South Sandwich Is. Appears to have increased markedly, with expansion of range, and also higher numbers at traditional colonies of South Georgia, Cooper Bay and Ice Fjord; increase apparently related to population explosion of krill, in turn caused by abusive levels of whaling. An increase in extent of commercial fishing in its feeding waters may have inverse effect.

Bibliography. Conroy *et al.* (1975), Croxall & Furse (1980), Croxall & Kirkwood (1979), Croxall & Prince (1983), Despin (1977a), Golombek *et al.* (1991), Jablonski (1985, 1987), Lindsey (1986), Lishman (1983, 1985a, 1985b), Lishman & Croxall (1983), Marchant & Higgins (1990), Müller-Schwarze & Müller-Schwarze (1980), Robertson (1989), Taylor (1986), Todd (1988), Trivelpiece (1981), Trivelpiece & Volkman (1979), Trivelpiece, Bengston *et al.* (1986), Trivelpiece, Trivelpiece, Geupel *et al.* (1990), Trivelpiece, Trivelpiece & Volkman (1985, 1987), Trivelpiece, Trivelpiece, Volkman & Ware (1983), Volkman & Trivelpiece, S.G. (1980), Volkman & Trivelpiece, W.Z. (1981), Volkman *et al.* (1980) Wilson, G.J. (1983).

Genus *EUDYPTES* Vieillot, 1816

6. Fiordland Penguin

Eudyptes pachyrhynchus

French: Gorfou de Fiordland **German**: Dickschnabelpinguin **Spanish**: Pingüino de Fiordland
Other common names: Thick-billed/Victoria/New Zealand/Fiordland Crested Penguin

Taxonomy. *Eudyptes pachyrhynchus* G. R. Gray, 1845, Waikowaiti, South Island, New Zealand.
Forms superspecies with *E. robustus* and *E. sclateri*; these 2 species have been considered races of present species. Monotypic.

Distribution. S and SW South I and offshore islands.

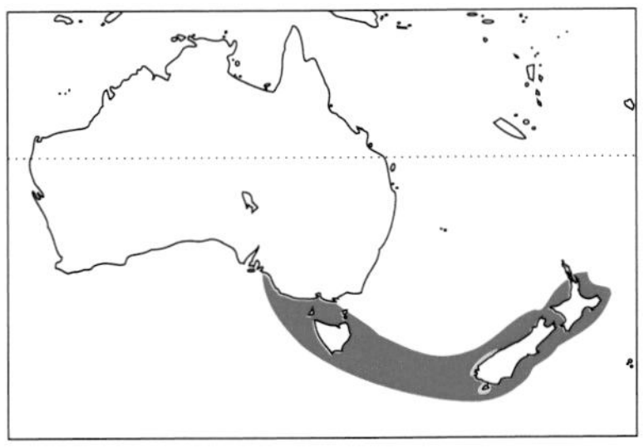

Descriptive notes. 55-71 cm. Feathers below eyes and bill black with white base, showing up as thin white lines when dishevelled. Male averages larger, with thicker bill. Juvenile has thinner yellow crest, white throat, grey flecking on cheek and brownish bill.

Habitat. Marine; probably pelagic outside breeding season. Typically nests on slopes in wet coastal rain forest, dominated by *Weinmannia racemosa*, *Metrosideros umbellata*, etc.; also along rocky coasts in hollows. Probably feeds closer inshore than congeners.

Food and Feeding. Diet variable with locality, with either small cephalopods (*Nototodarus sloanii*, *Moroteuthis ingens*, *Ocythoe tuberculata*) or fish (*Auchenoceros punctatus*, *Pseudophycis bachus*) predominating; also some crustaceans (*Nyctiphanes australis*). Captures prey by means of pursuit-diving. Solitary or in small flocks.

Breeding. Arrival at colony Jun/Jul; laying in Jul/Aug. Colonial, forming colonies of moderate size; nests not placed very close together. Nest under bushes, between tree roots or in holes; very little material. 2 eggs; incubation by both sexes 31-36 days, with stints of 5-13 days; 1st down dark brown above, dirty white below, 2nd down similar, but purer white below; crèche at 21-28 days; fledging c. 75 days, in Nov. Sexual maturity apparently at 5-6 years old. Estimated that c. 50% of laying pairs rear 1 chick to fledging.

Movements. Dispersive. Pre-moult period at sea 60-70 days; birds remain at sea from Mar to Jun/Jul, after completion of moult and before start of subsequent breeding season. Regularly

occurs off SE Australia and Tasmania; most records away from breeding grounds refer to moulting juveniles.
Status and Conservation. Not globally threatened. Currently considered near-threatened, though apparently stable. Total population estimated at 5000-10,000 pairs, although no census has included all colonies, due to difficult access and also poor visibility at some. Formerly had large colonies at Solander I (off S South I), but these have apparently declined. Introduced predators, especially dogs and stoats, cause frequent disturbances and casualties; rats may take chicks and eggs.
Bibliography. Chambers (1989), Falla (1935), Grau (1982), van Heezik (1989), Johnson, Bednarz & Zack (1987), Lindsey (1986), Marchant & Higgins (1990), Oliver (1953), Warham (1974a, 1985d).

7. Snares Penguin
Eudyptes robustus

French: Gorfou des Snares **German**: Snaresinselpinguin **Spanish**: Pingüino de las Snares
Other common names: Snares Crested Penguin

Taxonomy. *Eudyptes robustus* Oliver, 1953, Snares Islands.
Forms superspecies with *E. pachyrhynchus* and *E. sclateri*; has been considered race of former. Scientific name *E. atratus* formerly used, but was technically applicable to *E. sclateri*; name officially suppressed, to avoid confusion. Monotypic.
Distribution. Snares Is, to S of South I (New Zealand).

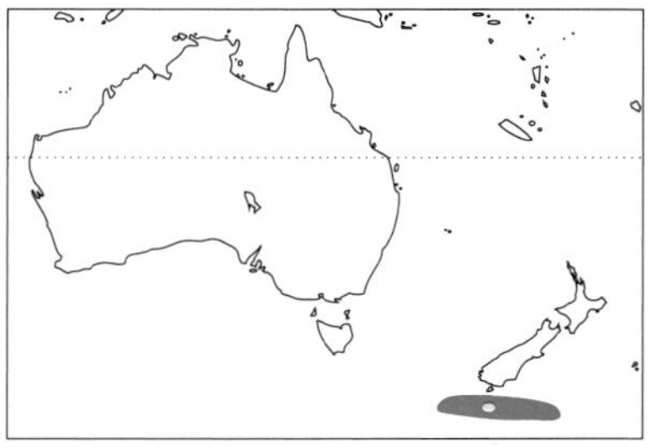

Descriptive notes. 56-73 cm. Differs from *E. pachyrhynchus* in fleshy pink skin around base of bill. Male averages larger, with thicker bill. Juvenile has thinner yellow crest, white throat with black mottling and brownish bill.
Habitat. Marine; probably pelagic outside breeding season. Typically nests in muddy forested areas, also on rocky slopes; colonies often shift, as vegetation killed off. Offshore feeder.
Food and Feeding. Mainly crustaceans, especially *Nyctiphanes australis*; also some cephalopods (*Nototodarus sloanii*, *Moroteuthis ingens*) and a few fish. Captures prey by means of pursuit-diving. Usually feeds in small flocks, often in company of Procellariiformes.
Breeding. Arrival at colony Aug/Sept; laying starts in Sept/Oct. Colonial, forming colonies of several hundred pairs. Nests under trees or bushes, though often with little shelter from sun. 2 eggs; incubation by both sexes 31-37 days, with stints of 5-25 days; 1st down dark brown above, dirty white below, 2nd down similar, but purer white below; crèche at c. 20 days; fledging at c. 75 days in Jan. Sexual maturity may be attained at 6 years old, but little known at present. Overall breeding success 41·2%.
Movements. Dispersive. Pre-moult period at sea c. 69 days; birds remain at sea from May to Aug, after completion of moult and before start of subsequent breeding season. Vagrant to SE Australia and Tasmania; record of adult at Falkland Is is only record outwith this immediate zone.
Status and Conservation. Not globally threatened. Total population estimated at c. 33,000 pairs. Marked increase between 1960's and 1980's, with 19,000 chicks reaching independence in 1984/85, as opposed to 6000 in 1968/69; presently stable. Access to Snares Is strictly controlled; no introduced predators.
Bibliography. Johnson, Bednarz & Zack (1987), Lindsey (1986), Marchant & Higgins (1990), Misquelly (1984), Oliver (1953), Stead (1948), Stonehouse (1971), Warham (1974b, 1985f), Watson (1971a).

8. Erect-crested Penguin
Eudyptes sclateri

French: Gorfou huppé **German**: Sclaterpinguin **Spanish**: Pingüino de Sclater
Other common names: Big-crested Penguin

Taxonomy. *Eudyptes sclateri* Buller, 1888, Auckland Islands.
Forms superspecies with *E. pachyrhynchus* and *E. robustus*; has been considered race of former. Scientific name *E. atratus* formerly applied, but now officially suppressed, owing to confusion with *E. robustus*. Monotypic.
Distribution. Islands to S and SE of New Zealand, with vast majority of population breeding almost exclusively on Bounty and Antipodes Is.

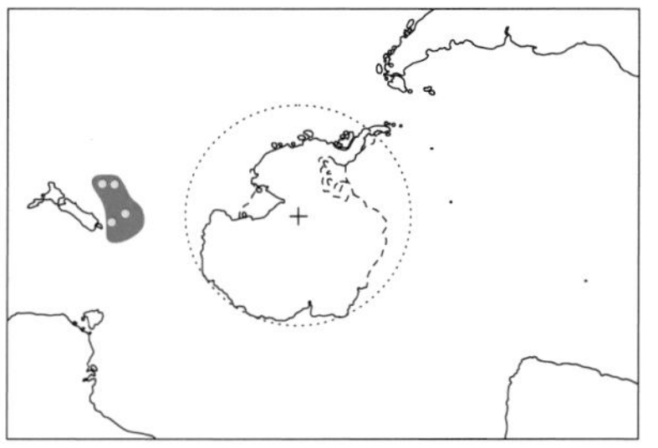

Descriptive notes. 63-68 cm. Yellow crest bristled up towards rear; starts beside gape, as opposed to between culminicorn and latericorn, as in *E. pachyrhynchus* and *E. robustus*; this is a distinctive feature for identification, especially when crest drenched. Male averages larger, with thicker bill. Juvenile has smaller yellow crest and whitish throat.
Habitat. Marine; probably pelagic outside breeding season. Nests on rocky coasts, cliffs or beaches, bare or with tussock grass, up to 75 m above sea-level. Offshore feeder.
Food and Feeding. Crustaceans and cephalopods.
Breeding. Arrival at colony Sept; laying starts Oct. Colonial, forming large colonies. Nest is small depression with rim of small stones. 2 eggs; incubation by both sexes c. 1 month; 1st down dark brown above, dirty white below, 2nd down similar, but purer white below; crèche at c. 21 days; fledging in Jan. Age of sexual maturity unknown.
Movements. Dispersive. Pre-moult period at sea c. 30 days; birds remain at sea from Apr to Sept, after completion of moult and before start of subsequent breeding season. Regularly occurs off E New Zealand; vagrant to S Australia, Macquarie and Chatham Is; also recorded in Falkland Is.
Status and Conservation. Not globally threatened. Total population estimated at over 200,000 pairs; Bounty Is hold c. 115,000 pairs, and Antipodes Is reckoned to support similar numbers; considered generally stable, although nesting not confirmed on Campbell I in recent years. Breeding habitat remains essentially intact and islands rarely visited by humans; rats may cause some loss of chicks and eggs.
Bibliography. Falla (1935), Johnson, Bednarz & Zack (1987), Lindsey (1986), Marchant & Higgins (1990), Napier (1968), Oliver (1953), Richdale (1941a, 1950a, 1951), Robertson & van Tets (1982), Warham (1972a, 1985e), Warham & Bell (1979), Watson (1971a).

9. Rockhopper Penguin
Eudyptes chrysocome

French: Gorfou sauteur **German**: Felsenpinguin **Spanish**: Pingüino Saltarrocas
Other common names: Southern Rockhopper Penguin (*chrysocome/filholi*); Northern Rockhopper/Moseley's Penguin (*moseleyi*)

Taxonomy. *Aptenodytes chrysocome* J. R. Forster, 1781, Falkland Islands.
Synonymous with *E. crestatus*. Known to have hybridized with *E. chrysolophus*. Race *moseleyi* sometimes considered separate species; validity of race *filholi* sometimes questioned. Three subspecies recognized.
Subspecies and Distribution.
E. c. chrysocome (J. R. Forster, 1781) - Cape Horn, Falkland Is.
E. c. filholi Hutton, 1879 - Southern Ocean, from Prince Edward Is E to Antipodes Is.
E. c. moseleyi Mathews & Iredale, 1921 - S Atlantic at Tristan da Cunha and Gough I, S Indian Ocean at Amsterdam and St Paul Is.

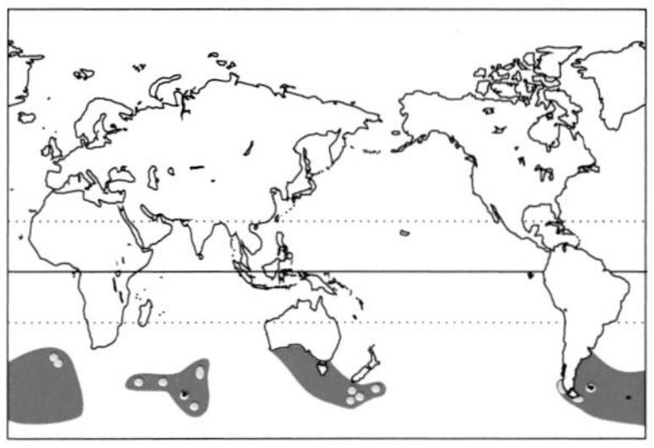

Descriptive notes. 55-62 cm. Yellow crest thin, often in two, nearly separate parts; margin of bill black. Black occipital crest. Male averages larger, with thicker bill. Juvenile has shorter yellow crest and duller bare parts. Race *moseleyi* larger, has longer, denser yellow crest; *filholi* has margin of bill pink and fleshy; pattern on underside of flippers also used for subspecific identification.
Habitat. Marine and apparently pelagic. Seems to have widest temperature tolerance of all *Eudyptes* penguins. Nests on slopes of scree, rocky shores, lava flows, etc., sometimes with tussock grass, and normally not far from coast. Offshore feeder.
Food and Feeding. Mainly euphausiids (*Euphausia vallentini*, *E. lucens*) and amphipods (*Themisto gaudichaudii*); also fish and cephalopods, especially in N. Captures prey by means of pursuit-diving.
Breeding. Season variable, with S populations generally starting later: at Tristan da Cunha birds arrive at colony in Sept, with first laying in Oct; at Macquarie I and Falkland Is birds arrive Oct/Nov, with first laying in Nov/Dec. Colonial, forming large colonies. Nest material includes grass, stones, bones, etc. 2 eggs; incubation by both sexes 32-34 days, with stints of 7-17 days; 1st down blackish grey, white below, 2nd down similar; crèche at c. 20 days; fledging at c. 10 weeks in Dec/Jan in N, Feb/Mar in S. Age of sexual maturity unknown. Breeding success 0·35-0·45 chicks/pair.
Movements. Pre-moult period at sea 20-35 days; birds remain at sea c. 6 months from Apr/May to Sept/Oct, depending on population, after completion of moult and before start of subsequent breeding season. Population of Falklands apparently moves to coastal Argentina, occurring N to 35° S. Vagrant to South Africa, New Zealand, Australia and Antarctica.
Status and Conservation. Not globally threatened. Total population estimated at c. 3,500,000 pairs; possibly stable. 2,500,000 pairs in Falkland Is, 300,000 pairs on Macquarie I; 284,000 pairs of race *moseleyi* at Tristan da Cunha and Gough I. Total of c. 12,000 eggs, including some of *P. papua*, collected in Falkland Is in 1980/81, but importance of traditional egg-collecting has decreased notably in recent decades. On Tristan da Cunha, egg-collecting almost led to eradication of species, but breeding grounds at Jews Point included in wildlife reserve in 1979. Intense human exploitation in Tristan da Cunha Group, with up to 62,000 eggs taken annually from uninhabited Nightingale I; each inhabitant of Tristan eats average of 146 eggs per year; penguins also taken for food, oil, bait, fertilizer, fire-lighters, feather mattresses, etc. Hundreds killed by oil spill at Marion I in 1980. Some populations decimated by introduced mammals, e.g. breeding grounds on Tristan da Cunha ravaged by pigs. Used as bait for catching crayfish (*Jasus paulensis*), e.g. at Amsterdam and St Paul Is. Impact of accidental capture by fishing vessels during drift-netting operations may be significant.
Bibliography. Adams & Brown (1989), Blake (1977), Boswall (1972), Brown, C.R. (1984, 1985, 1986, 1987a, 1987b), Brown & Klages (1987), Carins (1974), Croxall, Prince *et al.* (1985), Duroselle & Tollu (1977), Gales (1987b), Hindell (1988c), Horne (1985), Howland & Sivak (1984), Johnson, Bednarz & Zack (1987), Jouventin *et al.* (1988), Klages, Brooke & Watkins (1988), Klages, Gales & Pemberton (1989), Lindsey (1986), Marchant & Higgins (1990), Moors (1986), Napier (1968), Ryan & Cooper (1991), Ryan *et al.* (1990), Simpson (1985), Stahl, Derenne *et al.* (1985), Strange (1982), Tennyson & Miskelly (1989), Tollu (1978), Warham (1963, 1972b, 1985g), Warham & Bell (1979), Watkins (1987), Williams, A.J. (1980a, 1980b, 1980c, 1981a, 1981b, 1981c, 1981d, 1982), Williams & Siegfried (1980), Williams & Stone (1981), Wilson, G.J. (1983), Woehler (1991), Woehler & Gilbert (1990).

10. Royal Penguin
Eudyptes schlegeli

French: Gorfou de Schlegel **German**: Haubenpinguin **Spanish**: Pingüino de Schlegel

Taxonomy. *Eudyptes schlegeli* Finsch, 1876, Macquarie Island.
Sometimes considered subspecies of *E. chrysolophus* (see page 140); more often these two treated as superspecies. Monotypic.
Distribution. Macquarie I and adjacent islets.
Descriptive notes. 73-76 cm. Crest tinged orange with some black feathers admixed, sparse, starts on forehead (as in *E. chrysolophus*); larger and heavier-billed than *E. chrysolophus*. Male averages larger, with thicker bill; female often has greyer face. Juvenile has shorter crest and greyer cheeks and throat.
Habitat. Marine and apparently pelagic. Nests on beaches or slopes covered with tussock grass, up to 1·6 km from coast. Offshore feeder.
Food and Feeding. Mainly euphausiids (*Euphausia vallentini*, *Thysanoessa gregaria*) and amphipods (*Primno macropa*, *Themisto gaudichaudii*); also some fish (*Krefftichthys anderssoni*, *Electrona carlesbergi*) and cephalopods. Captures prey by means of pursuit-diving.

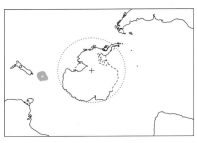

Breeding. Arrival at colony Sept; laying in Oct. Colonial, forming very large, dense colonies. Nest is shallow depression in stones or sand. 2 eggs; incubation by both sexes 32-37 days, with stints of 12-14 days; 1st down dark greyish brown, darker on head and white below, 2nd down similar, but blacker above; crèche at 21 days; fledging at c. 65 days in Jan. Sexual maturity at 7-9 years old, though some birds start breeding at 5 years old.
Movements. Presumably dispersive. Premoult period at sea c. 35 days; birds remain at sea from early Apr to Sept, after completion of moult and before start of subsequent breeding season. Juveniles stray further from colony in winter. Vagrant to SE Australia, Tasmania, New Zealand and Antarctica (once); several records further W on subantarctic islands of Indian Ocean, but of doubtful validity, due to uncertain separation from *E. chrysolophus*.
Status and Conservation. Not globally threatened. Total population estimated at 850,000 pairs, in 57 colonies; stable. Many killed for oil in period 1870-1918 (see page 152); end of exploitation in 1918, since when population has recovered steadily.
Bibliography. Berruti (1981a), Copson & Rousenvell (1987), Hindell (1988a), Horne (1985), Marchant & Higgins (1990), Lugg *et al.* (1978), Shaughnessy (1975), Simpson (1985), Voous (1963), Warham (1971a, 1985h).

11. **Macaroni Penguin**

Eudyptes chrysolophus

French: Gorfou doré   **German**: Goldschopfpinguin   **Spanish**: Pingüino Macarrones

Taxonomy. *Catarrhactes chrysolophus* Brandt, 1837, Falkland Islands.
Sometimes considered to include *E. schlegeli* (see page 140); more often these two treated as superspecies. Known to have hybridized with *E. chrysocome*. Monotypic.
Distribution. S Atlantic and S Indian Oceans, mostly on islands of subantarctic, but breeding in small numbers S to Antarctic Peninsula.

Descriptive notes. 70-71 cm. Crest tinged orange with some black feathers admixed, sparse, starts on forehead (as in *E. schlegeli*). Male averages larger, with thicker bill. Juvenile has shorter crest and greyer chin and throat.
Habitat. Marine and apparently pelagic. Colonies may be on flat ground or steep slopes, often amongst scree or on lava flows. Offshore feeder.
Food and Feeding. Mainly crustaceans, especially euphausiids (*Euphausia superba*, *E. vallentini*, *Thysanoessa*); also some fish (*Protomyctophum tenisoni*) and cephalopods, especially when feeding older chicks. Captures prey by means of pursuit-diving; by day fishes at depths of 20-80 m, by night not below 20 m.
Breeding. Arrival at colony Sept/Nov; laying in Oct/Dec. Colonial, forming compact, often large colonies. Nest often placed in shade under vegetation or rocks. 2 eggs; incubation by both sexes 33-40 days, with stints of 7-12 days; 1st down grey, white below, 2nd down blackish grey-brown above, white below; crèche at 23-25 days; fledging at c. 2 months in Feb/Mar. Age of sexual maturity unknown. Breeding success 0·43 chicks/pair.
Movements. Dispersive. Pre-moult period at sea variable with latitude, 12-14 days at South Georgia, 32 days further S; birds remain at sea from Apr to Jun, after completion of moult and before start of subsequent breeding season. Ranges to Antarctica, rarely to South Africa and Tristan da Cunha. Vagrant to S Brazil, Australia and New Zealand; possible confusion of records with *E. schlegeli*.
Status and Conservation. Not globally threatened. Total population estimated at 11,654,000 pairs; generally increasing. 5,400,000 pairs at 61 colonies on South Georgia; over 1,800,000 pairs on both Crozet and Kerguelen Is; c. 1,000,000 pairs on both Heard I and McDonald Is. Colony on Deception I seems to have been plundered by whalers. Increase in commercial fishing in its feeding waters could have adverse effects.
Bibliography. Adams & Brown (1989), Bonner & Hunter (1982), Brown, C.R. (1984, 1985, 1986, 1987a, 1987b), Brown & Klages (1987), Croxall & Furse (1980), Croxall & Kirkwood (1979), Croxall & Prince (1980a), Croxall *et al.* (1988), Davis, Croxall & O'Connell (1989), Davis, Kooyman & Croxall (1983), Downes (1955), Jablonski (1985), Johnson, Bednarz & Zack (1987), Johnson, Healey & Bednarz (1989), Jouventin *et al.* (1988), Klages *et al.* (1989), Lindsey (1986), Marchant & Higgins (1990), Mougin (1984), Ridoux *et al.* (1988), Stahl, Derenne *et al.* (1985), Tollu (1978), Watkins (1987), Williams, A.J. (1977, 1980a, 1980b, 1981a, 1981d, 1982), Williams, T.D. (1989), Williams & Croxall (1991), Wilson, G.J. (1983), Woehler (1991), Woehler & Gilbert (1990).

Genus *MEGADYPTES*   Milne-Edwards, 1880

12. **Yellow-eyed Penguin**

Megadyptes antipodes

French: Manchot antipode   **German**: Gelbaugenpinguin   **Spanish**: Pingüino Ojigualdo

Taxonomy. *Catarrhactes antipodes* Hombron & Jacquinot, 1841, Auckland Islands.
Monotypic.
Distribution. E & SE South I, Stewart I, Codfish I, Auckland I and Campbell I.
Descriptive notes. 66-76 cm. White of underparts continues onto leading edge of flipper. Juvenile has yellow head band incomplete, and paler throat.
Habitat. Marine. Nests in areas with dense vegetation near coast, mainly using slopes, gulleys or cliff tops. Occupies shallow coastal waters; inshore feeder.

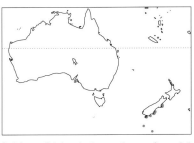

Food and Feeding. Mostly fish (*Pseudophycis bachus, Hemerocoetes monopterygius, Sprattus antipodum, Argentina australiae*); some cephalopods (*Nototodarus sloanii*) and a few crustaceans; diet varies with season and locality. Captures prey by means of pursuit-diving, diving down at least to c. 100 m, but usually only to c. 34 m.
Breeding. Nests occupied in Aug/Sept; laying in Sept/Oct. Solitary or in small, loose aggregations. Nest placed between roots or in midst of vegetation. 2 eggs; incubation by both sexes 39-51 days, with stints of 1-7 days; 1st down cocoa brown, 2nd down slightly paler brown; does not form crèches; fledging at 97-119 days in Feb/Mar. Sexual maturity at 2-3 years old in females, 4-5 years old in males. Breeding success 0·9-1·4 chicks/nest.
Movements. Adults mainly sedentary, occurring along coast near breeding grounds throughout year; some adults migrate N, as much as 500 km. Pre-moult period at sea c. 23 days. Juveniles disperse to N, up to 600 km from nesting grounds.
Status and Conservation. VULNERABLE. Total population estimated at 5133-6183 birds, including 1540-1855 breeding pairs, with 490-605 pairs on Campbell I. In last 40 years, population of South I has decreased by at least 75%, as habitat has receded at similar pace; by 1988 only three sites with over 30 pairs remained; South I population genetically isolated, so influx unlikely from healthier subantarctic populations, e.g. Campbell I. Mortality of at least one-third of population of 400 birds on Otago Peninsula in early 1990, for unknown reasons. Main threats include destruction of suitable nesting habitat, especially forested areas along coasts with shallow water; nesting birds require sufficient shade and tranquillity; habitat often removed to make way for farmland, and this implies additional disturbance. Introduced predators, e.g. stoats, dogs, cats and pigs, cause significant losses of both chicks and eggs; livestock can also have serious effects, due to trampling and general habitat deterioration, as well as disturbance. Frequently caught in fishing nets; may be indirectly affected by large-scale commercial fishing. Extensive research in recent years, but breeding habits make accurate census work difficult.
Bibliography. Chambers (1989), Collar & Andrew (1988), Darby (1984), Falla (1935), van Heezik (1988b, 1990a, 1990b, 1991), van Heezik & Davis (1990), van Heezik & Seddon (1989), Marchant & Higgins (1990), Richdale (1941b, 1951, 1955, 1957, 1985), Roberts & Roberts (1973), Seddon (1988, 1989a, 1989b, 1990), Seddon & Davis (1989).

Genus *EUDYPTULA*   Bonaparte, 1856

13. **Little Penguin**

Eudyptula minor

French: Manchot pygmée   **German**: Zwergpinguin   **Spanish**: Pingüino Enano
Other common names: Fairy/Blue/Little Blue Penguin; White-flippered Penguin (*albosignata*)

Taxonomy. *Aptenodytes minor* J. R. Forster, 1781, Dusky Sound, South Island, New Zealand.
Race *albosignata* has often been considered distinct species; some dispute concerning validity of races, and recent evidence points to N-S cline (see page 141). Six subspecies normally recognized.
Subspecies and Distribution.
E. m. novaehollandiae (Stephens, 1826) - S Australia and Tasmania.
E. m. iredalei Mathews, 1911 - N North I.
E. m. variabilis Kinsky & Falla, 1976 - S North I, Cook Strait.
E. m. albosignata Finsch, 1874 - E South I.
E. m. minor (J. R. Forster, 1781) - W & S South I, Stewart I.
E. m. chathamensis Kinsky & Falla, 1976 - Chatham Is.

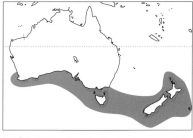

Descriptive notes. 40-45 cm; c. 1 kg. Smallest penguin. White trailing and sometimes leading edges of flippers. Male averages larger, with thicker bill. Juvenile duller. Races separated on dorsal coloration, bill size and weight; in male *albosignata*, white margins can meet to form patch on flipper.
Habitat. Temperate marine waters. Typically nests on sandy or rocky islands, often at base of cliffs or in sand dunes. Nests can be over 300 m from coast on land more than 50 m above sea-level. Inshore feeder.
Food and Feeding. Mainly pelagic shoaling fish (*Engraulis australis, Sardinops neopilchardus, Hyperlophus vittatus*); also cephalopods (*Nototodarus gouldi*) and occasionally crustaceans. Size range of prey 10-130 mm. Captures prey by means of pursuit-diving, frequently swimming round shoal of fish in concentric circles before plunging into midst; in shallow water pursues fish directly. Known to dive down to 69 m. Normally feeds alone.
Breeding. Season apparently depends on locality and year; breeding recorded in all months. Colonial; nests not closely packed together. Nest is burrow dug in sand, natural hollow or crack, under thick vegetation or even under human constructions. 2 eggs; 2 or 3 clutches may be laid per season, usually as replacement laying, but second attempts after successful breeding recorded; incubation by both sexes 33-37 days, occasionally over 43 days, with stints of 6 hours to 8 days; 1st down grey-brown, 2nd down dark brown or grey above, white below; sometimes forms small crèches of 3-6 birds at 30-35 days; fledging at 50-55 days. Sexual maturity at 2-3 years old. Overall breeding success 16-51%.
Movements. Sedentary. Adults, in particular, stray little from breeding colonies, and after moulting may return to colony sporadically. Pre-moult period at sea c. 40 days. On leaving colony, juveniles perform dispersive movements, with ringing recoveries up to 1000 km from

colony; some juveniles at 1-2 years old return to moult at natal colony, and subsequently to breed. Vagrant to Snares Is.
Status and Conservation. Not globally threatened. Total population very difficult to estimate, but Australia reckoned to hold under 1,000,000 birds. Particularly sensitive to human disturbance; has suffered from destruction of habitat by man and domestic animals; also killed by introduced predators. On De Witt I (Tasmania), three fires in 1975 and 1976 killed 1000 breeding adults and many chicks. On Phillip I (Victoria), predation by foxes particularly important since 1970's. Tourist motor launches pursue birds at night using powerful seachlights, thus disorientating and frightening them. Oil pollution can be problem around ports; rubbish dumped in sea can cause deaths (see page 153); some birds caught accidentally in fishing nets or kreels. Has been used as bait for catching crayfish.

Bibliography. Barton (1979a), Baudinette *et al*. (1986), Chambers (1989), Costa *et al*. (1986), Dann (1988), Dann & Cullen (1989), Gales (1985, 1987a, 1987b, 1988a, 1988b, 1988c), Gales & Pemberton (1990), Gales, Green & Stahel (1988), Gales, Williams & Ritz (1990), Hodgson (1975), Jones, G. (1978), Kinsky (1960), Kinsky & Falla (1976), Kinsky *et al*. (1985), Klomp & Wooller (1988a, 1988b, 1991), Klomp *et al*. (1991), Lindsey (1986), Lintermans (1989), Marchant & Higgins (1990), Meredith & Sin (1988), Montague (1982, 1984a), Montague & Cullen (1985, 1988), O'Brien (1940), Reilly & Cullen (1979, 1981, 1982, 1983), Richdale (1940), Schulz (1987), Stahel & Nicol (1982), Stahel & Gales (1987), Stahel *et al*. (1987), Waas (1988a, 1988b, 1990, 1991a, 1991b), Warham (1958a).

Genus *SPHENISCUS* Brisson, 1760

14. Jackass Penguin

Spheniscus demersus

French: Manchot du Cap **German**: Brillenpinguin **Spanish**: Pingüino del Cabo
Other common names: African/Black-footed/Cape Penguin

Taxonomy. *Diomedea demersa* Linnaeus, 1758, Cape of Good Hope.
Sometimes considered conspecific with *S. humboldti* and *S. magellanicus*; alternatively they may form superspecies (see page 141). Monotypic.
Distribution. South Africa and Namibia.

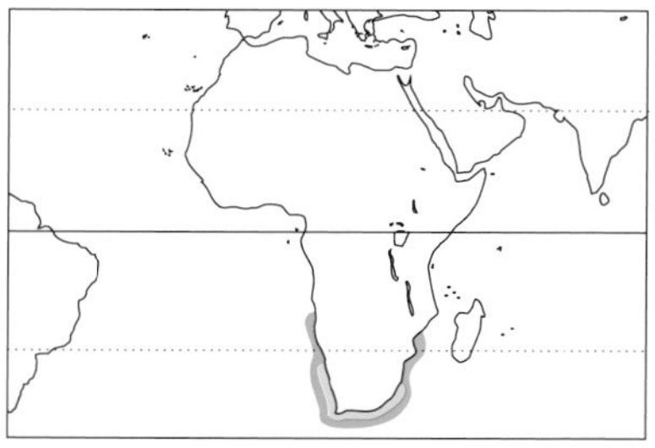

Descriptive notes. 68-70 cm. Black of face continues up behind eye and into white supercilium. Some birds have second black band on upper breast, as in *S. magellanicus*, though rarely more than incipient. Juvenile has grey head and incomplete breast band.
Habitat. Marine. Nests on inshore islands, or less frequently on mainland coast. Inshore feeder.
Food and Feeding. Pelagic school fish normally 50-120 mm (10-310 mm) in length; important prey species include *Engraulis capensis*, *Sardinops ocellata*, *Sufflogobius bibarbatus* and *Etrumeus teres*. Dives down to 130 m. Adults gregarious at sea, fishing communally; co-operative feeding at shoals recorded.
Breeding. Breeding occurs all year round, with local variations; peak laying in Nov/Jan in NW, May/Jul in SW and Apr/Jun in E. Colonial. Nest lined with material, and situated under rocks or vegetation or in burrows, where sheltered from sun. 2 eggs; laying of second clutch recorded; incubation c. 38 days, with stints of 1-2 days; 2nd down bluish grey above, turning brown, white below; may form small crèches of up to 5 birds; fledging 70-80 days. Sexual maturity at 4 years old. Success to fledging 15-50%.
Movements. Adults sedentary. Pre-moult period at sea 35 days; birds remain at sea for 4 months, after completion of moult and before start of subsequent breeding season. Juveniles, on becoming independent, disperse far from colony; birds from E head W, those from W and S move N. Most birds later return to moult and breed at natal colony. Recorded N to Gabon and Mozambique.
Status and Conservation. INSUFFICIENTLY KNOWN (under review). CITES II, due to live animal trade; collection of birds for zoos may have affected local populations. Total population at beginning of 20th century estimated at 500,000-1,000,000 pairs; since then steady decline, with loss of c. 75% of population, and current estimate of 50,000-171,000 pairs; slump particularly marked since 1960, especially in populations off SW Africa; a few local increases, but general decline continues. Cause seems directly related to commercial overfishing of its prey species. Importance of accidental catches of birds in fishing nets unknown. Large numbers die due to oiling; several campaigns carried out to rescue and clean up oiled birds, with fairly good results. In period 1970-1980 crude oil, and to lesser extent fish-oil, known to have affected at least 7088 birds. Construction of new ports also causing regression, with associated disturbance, e.g. blasting work; colonies particularly sensitive to human disturbance. Egg-collecting was serious problem in 19th century and early 20th century; nowadays continues illegally on small scale. Destruction of nest-holes during guano mining has led to greater vulnerability of both eggs and chicks, with ensuing lack of shelter from sun, flooding, aerial predators, etc.; now has to compete more and more for suitable breeding grounds with Cape fur seals (*Arctocephalus pusillus*); guano mining has been declared illegal. Suffers predation by introduced cats on Dassen I and Bird I.

Bibliography. Bennett (1990), Berruti (1986), Broni (1984, 1985), Brooke (1984), Brown *et al*. (1982), Collar & Andrew (1988), Collar & Stuart (1985), Cooper (1972, 1974, 1977, 1978a, 1980a), Cooper & Morant (1981), Cooper & Randall (1981), Crawford & Shelton (1981), Crawford *et al*. (1990), Duffy (1987a, 1990a, 1990b), Duffy, Berruti *et al*. (1984), Duffy, Wilson, Ricklefs *et al*. (1987), Eggleton & Siegfried (1979), Erasmus & Wessels (1985), Erasmus *et al*. (1981), Frost *et al*. (1975, 1976a, 1976b), Heath (1986), Heath & Randall (1985, 1989), Hockey & Hallinan (1981), Hui (1987), Jackson *et al*. (1976), King (1978/79), La Cock (1988), La Cock & Hänel (1987), La Cock *et al*. (1987), Morant *et al*. (1981), Nagy *et al*. (1984), Rand (1960), Randall (1983), Randall & Davidson (1981), Randall & Randall (1981, 1986a, 1986b, 1990), Randall, Randall & Baird (1981), Randall, Randall & Bevan (1980), Randall, Randall & Compagno (1988), Randall, Randall, Cooper & Frost (1986), Randall, Randall, Cooper, La Cock & Ross (1987), Randall, Randall & Erasmus (1986), Randall, Randall & Klingelhoeffer (1981), Ryan *et al*. (1987), Seddon & van Heezik (1991a, 1991b, 1991c), Seddon *et al*. (1991), Shaughnessy (1980), Shelton *et al*. (1984), Siegfried & Crawford (1978), Siegfried, Frost, Cooper & Kemp (1976), Siegfried, Frost, Kinahan & Cooper (1975), Sivak (1976), Westphal & Rowan (1971), Williams & Cooper (1984), Wilson, R.P. (1984, 1985a, 1985b, 1985c, 1885d), Wilson & Bain (1984a, 1984b), Wilson & Duffy (1986), Wilson & Wilson (1989), Wilson, La Cock *et al*. (1985), Wilson, Ryan *et al*. (1987), Wilson, Wilson & Duffy (1988), Wilson, Wilson & McQuaid (1986).

15. Humboldt Penguin

Spheniscus humboldti

French: Manchot de Humboldt **German**: Humboldtpinguin **Spanish**: Pingüino de Humboldt
Other common names: Peruvian Penguin

Taxonomy. *Spheniscus Humboldti* Meyen, 1834, Peru.
Sometimes considered conspecific with *S. demersus* and *S. magellanicus*; alternatively they may form superspecies (see page 141). Monotypic.
Distribution. Coasts of Chile and Peru, in region of Humboldt Current.

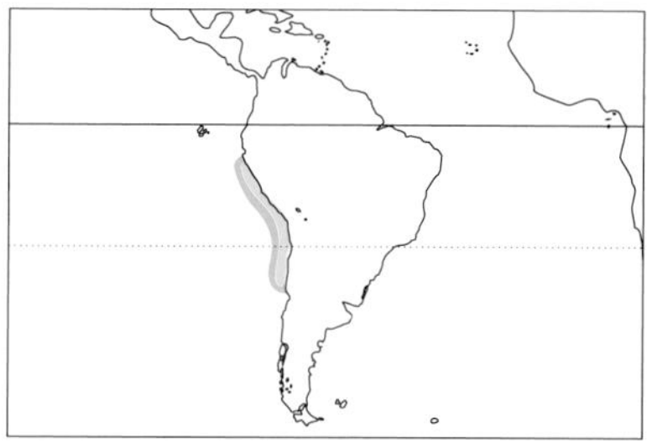

Descriptive notes. 65-70 cm. Only member of genus with large fleshy margins at base of bill. White supercilium much thinner than in *S. demersus* and *S. magellanicus*. Juvenile has grey head and lacks breast band.
Habitat. Marine. Nests on islands or on rocky stretches of mainland coast, especially in areas with cliffs. Inshore feeder.
Food and Feeding. Pelagic school fish and squid; size range of prey 36-270 mm long. Main prey species include *Engraulis ringens*, *Odonthestes regis* and *Scomberesox*.
Breeding. All year round. Colonial, normally in small colonies. Nest situated in holes, cracks or caves; occasionally in more open sites. 2 eggs; 2nd down dark grey above, white below. No further information available.
Movements. Virtually nothing known. Vagrant to Ecuador.
Status and Conservation. INSUFFICIENTLY KNOWN. CITES I, due to live animal trade. Total population estimated at c. 20,000 birds at beginning of 1980's, with 10,000-12,000 in Chile; occurrence of El Niño in 1982/83 (see page 341) caused loss of 65% of Peruvian population, subsequently estimated in 1984 at 2100-3000 adults; similar slump probably affected Chilean population, with no breeding in 1983, but partial counts in 1990 gave 8628 birds. General decline starting in mid-19th century, with intensive activity of guano collectors in traditional breeding grounds; this caused serious drop in quality of available nest-sites, and consequently in breeding success. In past hunted for food, oil or skin, while egg-collecting also significant; adults and chicks still taken for human consumption. Capture of birds for zoos or private collections has also had significant effect. Commercial overfishing in recent years likely to have reduced availability of prey; fair numbers thought to be caught in fishing-nets.

Bibliography. Araya (1983), Blake, E.R. (1977), Blake, R.W. & Smith (1988), Bowmaker & Martin (1985), Collar & Andrew (1988), Drent & Stonehouse (1971), Duffy (1990a, 1990b), Duffy *et al*. (1989), Edgington (1989), Hays (1984a, 1984b, 1985, 1986), Hui (1983, 1985, 1987, 1988), Martin & Young (1984), Scholten (1987, 1989a, 1989b), Sivak *et al*. (1987), Wilson *et al*. (1989).

16. Magellanic Penguin

Spheniscus magellanicus

French: Manchot de Magellan **German**: Magellanpinguin **Spanish**: Pingüino Magellánico

Taxonomy. *Aptenodytes magellanicus* J. R. Forster, 1781, Strait of Magellan.
Sometimes considered conspecific with *S. demersus* and *S. humboldti*; alternatively they may form superspecies (see page 141). Monotypic.
Distribution. S coasts of South America, from C Chile and C Argentina S to Cape Horn; also breeds in Falkland Is.

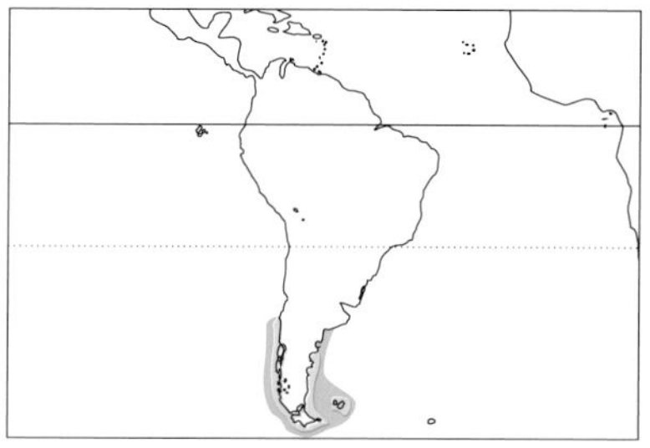

Descriptive notes. 70-76 cm. Head pattern very similar to that of *S. demersus*, but thin white line from under eye towards chin. Juvenile lacks bold pattern of adult on head and breast.
Habitat. Marine; pelagic on migration. Nests on beaches, hills of sand or clay, in forest or on grassy slopes. Inshore feeder.
Food and Feeding. Pelagic schooling fish, especially anchoveta (*Engraulis ringens*), and some squid; other important prey species include *Sprattus fuegensis*, *Engraulis anchoita*, *Ramnogaster arcuata*, *Merluccius hubbdi* and *Austroatherina smitta*. Size range of prey 25-160 mm. Co-operative feeding at shoals recorded.
Breeding. Arrival at colony Aug/Sept; laying in Sept/Oct. Colonial, sometimes in large colonies. Nest is placed underground, or in shade of vegetation, to avoid sun. 2 eggs; incubation by both sexes 38-42 days, with stints of 2-22 days; 1st down grey, 2nd down brownish grey above, whitish below; crèche at 20-23 days; fledging c. 80 days. Sexual maturity at 4-5 years old in females, 5-6 years old in males. Breeding success 0·02-1·36 chicks/pair.
Movements. Migratory, moving N from Apr to Aug, after completion of moult: in E reaching N Argentina and S Brazil at 23° S; in W as far N as 30° S. Pre-moult period at sea c. 1 month. Vagrant to NE Brazil, Australia, New Zealand and islands of S Atlantic.
Status and Conservation. Not globally threatened. Total population estimated at 4,500,000-10,000,000 birds; 4,500,000 in Atlantic sector, with 225,000 pairs at Punta Tombo and 70,000 pairs at Punta Clara; increasing in Argentina, status in Chile unknown. Has been hunted since 17th century, though nowadays pressure less intense. Marked decline since start of century, although expansion northwards, with new colonies, e.g. Punta Tombo, Punta Clara, Peninsula Valdés. Main causes of decline: egg-collecting; habitat deterioration, including destruction of burrows during guano mining, forcing birds to breed in unprotected sites; oil pollution, including spills and deliberate discharge by ships; industrial development; increase of commercial fishing; accidental capture of birds in fishing-nets; and other human activities in and around colonies, e.g. tourism and ranching.

Bibliography. Badano *et al.* (1982), Belton (1984), Bennett (1991), Blake (1977), Boersma (1986a, 1987, 1988), Boswall (1973), Boswall & Pryterch (1972), Bulfon *et al.* (1986), Capurro *et al.* (1988), Conway (1965a, 1971), Croxall, MacInnes, & Prince (1984), Daciuk (1976a, 1976b, 1977), Duffy (1990a, 1990b), Duffy *et al.* (1989), Gochfeld (1980), Gosztonyi (1984), Howland & Sivak (1984), Jehl (1975), Knaus (1990), Lindsey (1986), Marchant & Higgins (1990), Narosky *et al.* (1984), Perkins (1983, 1984), Pinto (1964), Robertson (1989), Scolaro (1978, 1980, 1983, 1984a, 1984b, 1984c, 1986, 1987a, 1987b, 1990), Scolaro & Arias de Reyna (1984a, 1984b), Scolaro & Badano (1986), Scolaro & Suburo (1991), Scolaro, Ares *et al.* (1981), Scolaro, Hall & Ximénez (1983), Scolaro, Hall, Ximénez & Kovacs (1979, 1980), Scolaro, Rodríguez & Monochio (1980).

17. Galapagos Penguin

Spheniscus mendiculus

French: Manchot des Galapagos   **Spanish**: Pingüino de las Galápagos
                    German: Galapagospinguin

Taxonomy. *Spheniscus mendiculus* Sundevall, 1871, Galapagos Islands.
Monotypic.
Distribution. Galapagos Is.
Descriptive notes. 48-53 cm. Much smaller than other members of genus, with more indistinct pattern, and black bands sometimes interrupted; underparts dirty white. Juvenile has grey upperparts and face lacks distinctive pattern.
Habitat. Marine. Nests in cracks or caves in lava, near sea-level. Inshore feeder in areas of upwelling of cool, nutrient-rich water; feeds closer inshore when water warmer.

Food and Feeding. Pelagic school fish, 10-150 mm long; recorded as taking sardines and mullet. Often forages in pairs; co-operative feeding at shoals recorded.
Breeding. All year round. Loosely colonial, in small groups or solitary. Nest shaded from sun. 2 eggs, but normally only 1 chick raised; more than 1 clutch per year can be laid, sometimes as replacement; incubation by both sexes 38-42 days, with stints of c. 2 days; fledging c. 60 days. Age of sexual maturity unknown. Breeding success averages c. 20% (0-54%).
Movements. Sedentary. Vagrant to Panama.
Status and Conservation. Not globally threatened. Currently considered near-threatened; included in first edition of Red Data Book (1966). Total population estimated at 6000-15,000 birds in 1977, and was fairly stable; dramatic decline, with loss of 77% of population due to El Niño in 1982/83 (see page 341); census of 1984 yielded maximum of 463 birds, with only 29 juveniles; slow recovery of population started in 1985. Main threats include disturbance by tourists and fishermen; also disturbance and predation by introduced mammals, including dogs, cats, rats, etc.
Bibliography. Boersma (1974, 1976, 1978), Duffy (1990a, 1990b), Duffy & Merlin (1986), Harcourt (1980), Harris (1977), Rosenberg *et al.* (1990), Rosenberg & Harcourt (1987), Valle (1986a), Valle & Coulter (1987), Vincent (1966).

Order GAVIIFORMES

Gaviiformes

|

Gaviidae

divers

Class AVES
Order GAVIIFORMES
Family GAVIIDAE (DIVERS)

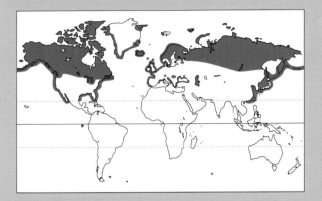

- Heavily-built waterbirds with narrow wings and body effectively streamlined for diving.
- 53-91 cm.

- Circumpolar in Holarctic.
- Stretches of open water, both inland and coastal.
- 1 genus, 4 species, 6 taxa.
- No species threatened; none extinct since 1600.

Systematics

The first recognizable fossils belonging to the Gaviidae date back to the Miocene, while the more remote ancestral forms *Gaviella* and *Colymboides* correspond to the Oligocene and the Eocene respectively. The origins of the order Gaviiformes have been traced even further back into the Paleocene, approximately 65 million years ago, making them amongst the most primitive of present day birds.

It appears that species diversification took place at two main centres within the upper latitudes of the Northern Hemisphere. The ranges of the Great Northern Diver (*Gavia immer*) and the closely related White-billed Diver (*Gavia adamsii*) overlap to some degree in the Nearctic, and both appear to have evolved from the Black-throated Diver (*Gavia arctica*). Presumably this species colonized North America, after which its population there was cut off and evolved into the two larger species. Then, at a later stage, the Black-throated Diver and the Red-throated Diver (*Gavia stellata*) underwent further range expansions, when they spread extensively over the Nearctic.

Diversification within the diver family has been limited, and, as the four species are very similar in most aspects, they are grouped in a single genus, *Gavia*. However, their relationship with other birds is far from clear and they are normally split off as the only family of the order Gaviiformes. For a long time it was believed that their closest relatives were the grebes (Podicipedidae), but similarities between the two families appear to be mostly superficial, and may be attributable to convergent evolution. Detailed studies have recently linked the divers more closely with the Charadriiformes, in particular with the gulls (Laridae) or the auks (Alcidae), although there is as yet insufficient evidence for these links to be considered definite. A totally different series of relationships emerges from studies using DNA, which place the divers alongside the frigatebirds, the penguins and members of the traditional order Procellariiformes.

The relationships between the different diver species are also complex. The Red-throated Diver is the species that clearly differs most from the others, be it in morphology, behaviour, breeding biology or ecology. The two larger species, the White-billed and Great Northern Divers, are obviously very alike in all of the aforementioned aspects, and it has been suggested that they may be allopatric forms of a single superspecies, although their ranges do overlap. The widely distributed Black-throated Diver can be situated half way between the two extremes. It is the only polytypic diver, and one of its three subspecies, the Pacific Diver (*G. a. pacifica*), is often considered to be a separate species. This form is visibly smaller than the Siberian race *viridigularis*, with which it is known to nest sympatrically at two sites. Further studies at these locations where both forms occur should shed more light on the taxonomic status of the Pacific Diver.

Morphological Aspects

Divers are large, bulky waterbirds. They range in size from 53 to 91 cm long and can weigh anything from about 1 to 6·4 kg. The sexes differ very little in structure, but on average males are slightly larger and more heavily-built than females.

The neck is thick, and the slightly elongated head tapers to a long, strong, sharp bill. This is uptilted in the Red-throated and White-billed Divers and ivory-coloured in the latter, but much darker in the other species. The nostrils are narrow and elongated, as an adaptation to diving. In all four species, the iris is reddish, most strikingly in adults during the breeding season.

Divers are exquisitely designed for swimming. Their short, strong legs are set far back on the body, and are thus ideal for

Divers are perfectly designed for diving. With their streamlined bodies, they propel themselves through the water using their large webbed feet. Unlike penguins and auks, which seem to "fly" along under the water, they only use their wings to help in turning manoeuvres.

[*Gavia stellata*, San Diego Harbour, California. Photo: R. F. Coomber/ Planet Earth]

This Pacific Diver or Pacific Loon (the North American race *pacifica* of the Black-throated Diver) illustrates some of the more characteristic morphological features of the diver family, including the thick neck, the slightly elongated head and the sharp bill. Divers are often to be seen riding low in the water, but they can, in fact, vary their buoyancy to the point of swimming with the entire body submerged, except for the upper part of the head.

[*Gavia arctica pacifica*, Arctic National Wildlife Refuge, Alaska. Photo: Johnny Johnson/DRK]

propulsion in water, although this design makes walking on land very difficult. The tarsi are laterally compressed, in order to offer the least possible resistance when the birds are moving forwards through the water, and the three front toes are joined together by webs. Unlike the grebes, divers have short, well-defined tails, which are generally carried level with the water surface.

All of the Gaviidae are expert divers and spend most of their lives in water. Their swimming and diving abilities, which are already evident in chicks of only one or two days old, can be equalled by few other birds. They are known to have reached depths of around 75 m and to have remained under water for as long as eight minutes, although most dives are to an average depth of 2-10 m and last around one minute. Most of the time they use only their laterally orientated feet for underwater propulsion, but the wings are occasionally extended to aid in manoeuvring. As a rule, they dive silently under the water from the surface by means of simple head-lowering and thrusting movements, usually with no previous spring actions, such as the hopping or jumping seen in cormorants (Phalacrocoracidae), or grebes (Podicipedidae). Divers are able to vary their buoyancy in order to remain under water, with the whole body submerged and only the eyes and bill visible above the surface.

They are extremely awkward birds on land, and progress with great difficulty, indeed they are quite incapable of standing upright for more than a few seconds. A diver does not walk along on its legs, but instead rests its weight on its breast and "frog-jumps" for a limited distance, kicking its legs out backwards. Despite these difficulties, the Red-throated Diver is known to cover considerable distances on land, and, when seriously disturbed, may even move to a new pool accompanied by young chicks.

The wings are relatively small and pointed, with wingspan reaching 106-152 cm, but, despite their heavy appearance and high degree of adaptation to aquatic life, divers are good fliers. They can cover large distances without stopping and perform considerable migrations, flying over land as well as water, often at great heights.

The three larger species require a long run along the surface of the water for take-off, but they take flight more readily and more frequently than some other waterbirds, such as grebes. They fly purposefully and swiftly, with the neck outstretched and held at a slightly lower level than the body, creating a

characteristic hump-backed silhouette, while the feet project beyond the tail. Landing too almost always takes place on water, with the approaching bird extending its webbed feet in order to skid along the surface, whilst using its wings for braking, before coming to rest on the water. Only the Red-throated Diver, the lightest and most agile species, with the largest wing-beat amplitude, is able to take off from the ground, or alight directly on it.

The plumage is thick and compact on the body, but soft and velvety on the head and neck. Breeding plumage is rather similar in the three larger species, with the upper body chequered black and white, as opposed to unspotted dark brown in the Red-throated Diver. The Great Northern and White-billed Divers have the head and upper neck mainly black with a purple or greenish sheen, while there are short white vertical stripes on the sides of the neck. The Black- and Red-throated Divers, on the other hand, have a greyish head and upper neck, with a large glossy coloured patch on the foreneck. Underparts are white and the tail is dark in all species and all plumages.

Divers have quite a distinct winter plumage. All have the face and foreneck pure white, with upperparts dark brownish, except in the Red-throated Diver, where the back is finely spotted with white, whence *stellata*. Sexes do not differ in plumage in any season, and immatures are similar to adults in winter, with some white scaling on the upperparts. Full adult breeding plumage is finally attained in the bird's third year.

Adult divers shed all their flight-feathers simultaneously, in late winter or early spring or, in the case of the Red-throated Diver, at the end of the breeding season; this renders them flightless for several weeks. The body feathers are moulted twice, in early autumn and early spring. Chicks, after hatching covered with greyish down, go through two moults before assuming juvenile plumage.

Habitat

True aquatic birds, divers are always found on or near water, breeding mostly at freshwater sites in the far north and wintering usually on sea coasts in temperate areas.

All four species breed on freshwater lakes of the subarctic and boreal zones, with a strong preference for undisturbed sites,

Although they have a considerable wingspan, divers are amongst the flying birds with the least wing surface area in proportion to their body weight. Because of this high wing-loading, they take off with some difficulty, after a long run over the water. The Red-throated Diver, the smallest, lightest species, needs the shortest run-up and is the only diver capable of taking off directly from the ground.

[*Gavia stellata*, Foula, Shetland Is. Photo: Günter Ziesler]

wherever possible. The White-billed Diver can also be found nesting in estuaries and along low-lying coasts of the Arctic Ocean, and is almost always restricted to treeless country. The Black-throated and Great Northern Divers usually nest on rather large, deep lakes, with or without a surrounding belt of trees, and where they have a choice of small islets, on which to site their nests. Red-throated Divers readily settle on stretches of still water ranging in size from small pools to large, deep lakes, and sometimes even nest on sheltered coasts.

The three larger species feed almost exclusively on their breeding lakes, although the Black-throated Diver may also feed on large expanses of water in the vicinity of its breeding grounds. The Red-throated Diver, on the other hand, habitually flies to larger bodies of water or to the sea in order to feed, a habit which permits it to breed on small, shallow stretches of water which can not produce enough fish to sustain a pair of divers and their brood.

After breeding, virtually all birds move to coastal waters, and they sometimes form large flocks on extensive inland lakes and reservoirs before leaving. The Great Northern Diver can be found on exposed rocky coasts, but the other species prefer sheltered shallow coastal waters and they frequently enter bays. In winter, few birds remain on inland waters, as these are usually frozen over in the northern latitudes inhabited by divers.

General Habits

Outwith the breeding season divers often gather in large flocks, of several hundred to a few thousand birds, in certain particularly rich feeding areas. At such localities the birds roost and feed communally and there may be signs of aggressive behaviour, although it seldom develops very far. Isolated pairs or individuals also occur irregularly along the coast in winter.

Like many other waterbirds, divers spend long hours in plumage care. Often, whilst preening their ventral parts on the water, birds roll over onto one side, sometimes waving a foot in the air, revealing their immaculate white belly feathers. They also bathe very frequently in a spectacular fashion, which involves much vigorous wing-shaking, rolling, diving and somersaulting.

Roosting mainly takes place on the water, but during the breeding season it sometimes occurs on land. A roosting bird does not place its bill under a wing, but rests it instead along its back.

Voice

During the breeding season divers can be very noisy at times, but for the rest of the year they tend to be silent, apart from the odd quack given in flight.

The characteristic yodel call is extraordinarily loud and can be heard a long way off. This, one of the most haunting sounds of the tundra, is used to proclaim the occupation of a territory to any neighbouring pairs or roving individuals. It is a long call, which sounds like a low-pitched whistle with some very clear notes interspersed; it is normally produced only by the male in the three larger species, but often by both mates at once in the Red-throated Diver.

Other territorial signals include a long wailing call and, in the Black-throated Diver, a short, intense one. When disturbed or threatened, the Red- and Black-throated Divers produce a raven-like croaking call of warning, whereas, in the two larger species, the alarm call is a strident, tremulous laugh. The low-pitched moaning contact call commonly used between parents and young is also uttered by males during copulation. Another call, produced only by the Red-throated Diver, is a short, frequently repeated, goose-like cackle, which it gives when flying over its own or neighbouring territories.

Food and Feeding

Divers obtain most of their food under water, at depths of 2-10 metres. When diving in search or pursuit of fish, they are mostly propelled by their feet, though the wings may be used too (see Morphological Aspects).

Prey is located visually, so divers favour clear waters for foraging. When the circumstances demand, they may search in fairly murky waters, but in such cases their prey is limited to slow-moving crayfish picked off the bottom. The same restriction means that they are not adapted to fishing by night.

Although formerly considered to be part of a courtship ritual, "Fencing" is actually an intense territorial display carried out mainly at the advent of intruders or during territorial confrontations. It consists of an upright posture, usually with the wings opened and flapping, and is often preceded by a long rush over the water. Aggressive and defensive behaviour in the diver family is generally a good deal more spectacular than the activities connected with courtship.

[*Gavia immer*, North America. Photo: Wayne Lankinen/ Bruce Coleman]

Their main prey is small, or medium-sized fish, which are usually caught after an underwater pursuit. Fish are generally swallowed before the birds surface, but, if too large or spiny, they may be carried out of the water, and disabled before being eaten.

Fish constitute a large proportion of the diet and are caught in large quantities at all times of year. The species chiefly taken in fresh water include trout (*Salmo trutta*), salmon (*Salmo salaris*), roach (*Rutilus rutilus*), char (*Salvelinus alpinus*) and perch (*Perca fluviatilis*). At sea, the principal prey are cod (*Gadus morhua*), herring (*Clupea harengus*), sprat (*Sprattus sprattus*), haddock (*Melanogrammus aeglefinus*), whiting (*Merlangius merlangus*), sand-eels (Ammodytidae), gobies (Gobiidae) and sticklebacks (Gasterosteidae).

Other recorded prey items include: fish spawn; frogs; crustaceans, including crabs, shrimps and prawns; molluscs, such as water snails and small cephalopods; annelids; and the larvae of aquatic insects. Plant matter has also been found in stomachs, on occasions in large quantities.

Divers are generally conservative in their diet, and when they find a suitable prey species in abundance they will exploit it to the full. A study of diet preferences in Minnesota, USA, showed that 20 out of 27 stomachs examined contained only one species of prey. On the other hand, they can adapt when necessary. Populations of Great Northern Divers in British Columbia, Canada, were found to be surviving comfortably in lakes where there were no fish, and the examination of the stomach contents revealed that they had switched to molluscs, amphipods and insects. Nevertheless, they will only take live prey, as has been seen with injured birds in rehabilitation centres, which refuse to touch dead fish that is thrown to them.

The size of prey taken is quite variable, but can be as little as about 30 g on average. A study of Great Northern Divers showed that around 80% of the trout they took measured 15-30 cm, with a maximum of about 45 cm, a fish weighing almost 1 kg. Birds have been known to take large numbers of hefty flounders (*Platichthys*), and in order to swallow such bulky prey they have a rather elastic oesophagus; however, this adaptation can have its disadvantages, and on occasions birds have been found suffocated after swallowing too large a fish.

It has been estimated that a pair of divers with two chicks consume about a tonne of fish during the 15 or so weeks of the breeding season. The impressive quantity they consume is related to their high level of energy expenditure, which in turn is probably due in part to their living in cold areas.

Breeding

Divers are monogamous and generally pair for life. They are also very faithful to a particular territory, and may use the same site for breeding several years running.

The point at which preparations for breeding get under way depends greatly on the timing of the spring thaw. As the signs of winter recede, birds begin flying inland to visit the previous year's territory, and they settle there as soon as the ice has withdrawn sufficiently.

Pairs already established from the previous season have probably remained together throughout the winter, and they start nesting early on, after a minimum of display. Even newly-formed pairs have a fairly simple courtship display. It consists of several synchronized movements, including mutual "Bill-dipping", "Splash-diving" and "Rushing" under water, and eventually leads to the female adopting a pre-copulatory inviting posture onshore, where she crouches motionless, or pecks repeatedly, as if she were gathering nest material.

On the whole, copulation takes place on dry land and is repeated frequently. The copulation period may begin on the very day of arrival, and it tends to continue till all the eggs have been laid. Sometimes the repeated use of the same platform results in its developing a distinctive nest-like shape. Such platforms, commonly known as "false nests", can often be found in territories occupied by Red- or Black-throated Divers, and also perhaps those of Great Northern Divers. However, unlike grebes, divers are not dependent on such mating-platforms for successful breeding.

In divers, the clutch normally consists of two eggs which are quite large considering the size of the birds, and though there can be marked differences in colour, even within the same clutch, the overall colour is normally olive brown. Unlike other birds, divers do not have true featherless brood patches, but under a feathered portion of the breast there are subcutaneous blood vessels that dilate during the incubation period. Thanks to this they can keep the eggs fairly warm at around 35°C.

[*Gavia arctica pacifica*, Manitoba, Canada. Photo: B. & C. Calhoun/ Bruce Coleman]

In general, it is the male that selects the nest-site. Where available, small islets are preferred, but birds may choose stretches of shallow water with ample views and a long, wide expanse of open water allowing them an easy escape in case of danger. In contrast to this, the Great Northern Diver's nest is often partially hidden by vegetation. As divers have great difficulty in walking, the nest-site is always close to water, indeed it is usually less than a metre from the shore. Although it is always on dry ground when selected, alterations of the water level may subsequently affect the site.

The nest is a simple structure, often consisting of a mere accumulation of plant matter, including moss and water weeds. Material is chiefly gathered by the male, and forms a 4-12 cm high mass with a shallow central depression. Throughout the incubation period, fresh material is added to it, particularly by the sitting bird.

The three larger species are highly territorial on their breeding grounds, as is often the case when solitary birds obtain virtually all their food from a limited territory around their nest-site. They do not tolerate the presence of any other adults within their field of vision, and will clearly demonstrate their ownership of the territory to any intruder. This is done using a wide range of aggressive postures.

A threatening bird generally starts by raising its neck, thus displaying the throat patch and neck markings. It may then indulge in various forms of territorial behaviour, such as "Circle-dancing", "Bill-dipping", "Splash-diving" and water chases with its wings flapping. Such behaviour may be accompanied by a variety of different territorial calls.

The typical pre-fight display involves the birds standing upright on the surface of the water, with their necks stretched backwards, whilst trampling noisily on the water; in this display the Great Northern and White-billed Divers, in particular, tend to hold their wings open. Although fights are infrequent, when they do occur, they are intense and violent, involving the use of the bill and wings, and can occasionally result in the death of one, or both, of the contestants, usually as a result of drowning or being speared.

Red-throated Divers are just as territorial as the other species, but they defend a much smaller area. Several pairs may breed semi-colonially, when there are only a few suitable tracts of fresh water within easy reach of their feeding areas. They therefore tolerate other pairs nearby and only defend the immediate vicinity of the nest, although they do this just as vigorously as the other species. Their repertoire of ritualized behaviour is fuller, and includes a series of stereotyped swimming ceremonies, which are performed by both partners. Both this species and the Black-throated Diver, which sometimes forages outside its nesting area, sometimes exhibit territorial behaviour on their feeding grounds.

Divers lay one to three eggs, normally two, at intervals of one to four days, exceptionally eight. The large, elongated eggs are slightly glossy olive brown with dark spots. They weigh between 83 g, in the Red-throated Diver, and 167 g, in the Great Northern Diver, so a normal clutch represents approximately 7-11% of the female's weight. Only one brood is raised, but if the eggs are lost early in the season, as often happens when the nest is flooded, a smaller replacement clutch is usually laid one or two weeks later.

The eggs are incubated by both parents, with the female spending longer periods on the nest than the male. Incubation begins with the first egg laid, so that the chicks hatch asynchronously after about four weeks. The resultant differences in both age and size, combined with the natural aggressiveness of sibling chicks towards each other, means that when food is scarce the older, larger chick obtains most of the food brought in by the parents, thus depriving its younger sibling of a fair share. Frequently, as a result of this, the younger chick starves to death in its first few days.

Very soon after hatching, young birds are able to swim, but they are generally brooded ashore for the first 1-3 days. Later they leave the nest and, up to the age of 2-3 weeks, spend most of their time swimming, or resting on their parents' backs. Although quite capable of swimming and diving from a tender age, they rely on their parents for food until they are fully-grown. Fledging takes place at around seven weeks in the Red-throated Diver and nine in the other species. At this stage the young birds are still fed irregularly by their parents, and this continues even after they leave the breeding area. Divers attempt to breed for the first time when they are about two or three years old.

In the studies carried out so far breeding success has been rather low. Of all the territory-holding pairs, only a small pro-

Although able to swim and even dive shortly after hatching, during the first weeks of life diver chicks spend up to 65% of their time resting on their parents' backs. Bearing in mind the fact that their body temperature is 3˚C lower than that of the adults, back-riding saves the chicks energy, as well as providing protection against predators, and increasing the adults' freedom of movement.

[*Gavia immer*, North America. Photo: Stephen J. Krasemann/NHPA]

portion laid eggs, and usually less than half of these hatched successfully. Only 50-75% of the young that hatched were successfully reared to fledging, and the overall figures of approximately 0·3-0·6 chicks fledged per territory-holding pair, are too low for populations to maintain numbers entirely on their own output in areas where human pressure is intense (see Status and Conservation).

Several factors contribute to this low productivity, one of which is the tendency of established pairs to take rest years, when they do not even attempt to nest, and, as a rule, most pairs breed in three out of every four years. Failure of attempted breeding can be due to any of a multitude of factors, including various different natural causes, such as infertile eggs, flooding of the nest, destruction of the contents of the nest or predation of small chicks. Skuas and gulls, racoons (*Procyon*), and mustelids are some of the most common predators, but cranes (*Grus*), sea eagles (*Haliaeetus*) and even large fish have also been reported to destroy eggs or, less often, take chicks.

Divers are long-lived, and most studies to date show that large numbers live over ten years. The oldest birds pass 20, and the Red-throated Diver has been known to reach 23, whereas the Black-throated Diver is recorded as reaching 28. The exception is the Great Northern Diver, and so far no individual has been known to live over eight years. Although few studies have been carried out on diver mortality, the death rate is known to be around 10-11% for adult Black-throated Divers, which gives them a life expectancy, on becoming adults, of a further eight or nine years.

Movements

All four diver species are both migratory and dispersive to some extent, although some populations obviously need to cover much greater distances than others to find ice-free waters.

In general, after breeding they move southwards and seawards, and there are some particularly impressive performances. The number of Great Northern Divers annually wintering along the western coasts of Europe clearly can not be accounted for merely by the small Icelandic population, and surely includes birds from Greenland and Canada. Another lengthy migration is performed by Siberian populations of Red-throated and Great Northern Divers, which have to fly hundreds of kilometres over land, perhaps following the major rivers, to reach their wintering grounds in the region of the Mediterranean, Black and Caspian Seas.

Large numbers take part in some of these movements, as amply demonstrated by the 1979 spring migration up the coast of California, where over one million (Pacific) Black-throated Divers were recorded passing through in about eleven weeks, with a peak of over 72,000 birds in one day. These figures are all the more dramatic, considering that most migration appears to take place at night and thus passes largely undetected.

As is frequent among long distance migrants, some of these regular movements may undergo considerable modifications in particularly cold weather, as birds move further south than usual in their search for ice-free waters, and all four species have been reported in subtropical waters. Unusual southerly occurrences include the Black-throated Diver in the Red Sea, the Red-throated off the coast of Pakistan and the Great Northern off southernmost Baja California. Such vagrants, struggling perhaps to find suitable habitat, often remain at a particular site for several weeks, or even months, before returning to areas within their normal range.

Relationship with Man

The breeding grounds of the divers tend to be in relatively remote areas and, as a result of this, over the centuries they have come into contact with man a good deal less than most other Holarctic birds. They have had to put up with a certain amount of human predation and disturbance, but are undoubtedly suffering more nowadays than ever before (see Status and Conservation).

Even today Eskimos still use diver skins to make ceremonial dresses, and in the legends of some of the native Indian tribes of North America the birds are linked with the creation of the world, or with pride and bravery, perhaps on account of the aggressive behaviour they use in territorial defence. In Scotland the ghostly qualities of a diver's yodel, echoing through

It has been estimated that a young diver's energy requirements are up to eight times greater than those of an adult. Although right from the very start it is able to search for prey on its own, its efficiency in catching fish is very low. Thus the majority of the food it consumes in the first weeks of life is provided by its parents. Adults often stimulate their offspring to learn fishing techniques by dropping a crippled fish in front of them.

[Gavia immer, North America. Photo: Wayne Lankinen/DRK]

the mist across a loch was regarded as an evil omen, more or less on a par with the howling of wolves.

In the past, significant numbers of divers were taken by human populations of the far north, and a limited amount of hunting continues today, but it does not seem to pose a serious threat to diver populations.

In North America divers are called "loons", a name also used in Scotland, though normally nowadays only for the Great Northern Diver. This name apparently comes from the Old Norse or Icelandic *lómr*, the Swedish *lom* or the Old Dutch *loen*, all of which mean something along the lines of "lame", "clumsy", "slow" or "a stupid fellow", probably referring to the difficulties the birds have moving about on dry land.

Status and Conservation

No species of diver is currently considered to be threatened, but despite the sizeable populations of all species that persist, there is no room for complacency about their future.

There are almost certainly in the order of many thousands of breeding pairs of each species, but, as their breeding grounds are mostly in remote areas where access is difficult, it is a laborious task to get precise figures of populations or trends, especially given that they are solitary breeders. However, at many of their more southerly breeding stations there is considerable cause for concern.

Direct human disturbance is responsible for most breeding failures, in addition to causing birds to abandon many territories which would otherwise be ideal for breeding. The increased use of lakes as recreational sites for water sports scares off many birds, as they are very sensitive to any form of intrusion into their territories. Equally, more and more lake shores are becoming cluttered up with holiday homes and, even if a house is only used irregularly, to divers it implies the permanent occupation of the lake and makes it a good deal less attractive for breeding.

There is a general increase in the extent of human presence and influence in some of these once remote areas, and this has indirectly helped populations of predators and opportunists, such as gulls, crows and some mammals, to proliferate. They feed off the great surplus of food found around human settle-

ments, and as they multiply rapidly, they exert more pressure on breeding divers and often have a negative effect on their breeding success.

At present, divers are losing much suitable nesting habitat, due more to disturbance than to actual destruction. However, the construction of reservoirs balances this to some extent, for, whilst some are being used for recreation, others remain largely undisturbed, and where the water level is fairly constant, divers have often moved in. In fact, some recent recoveries of local diver populations have been attributed to the birds establishing new territories on reservoirs.

Divers, like other waterbirds, have probably been hunted since prehistoric times. In the past, this presumably had little effect on their populations, as their breeding territories are spread far and wide, while much of the year is spent at sea. In modern times, however, many birds are shot merely for target practice or by overzealous trout fishermen, who accuse divers of taking large quantities of trout fry, and thus reducing fish stocks.

Major industrial development over the last few decades has generated a whole host of problems, particularly with chemical pollution affecting both inland and coastal waters. Windborne sulphates are released into the air in heavily industrialized zones, and these then join with moisture in the atmosphere and fall on the countryside in the form of acid rain, destroying lakeside vegetation and acidifying the lakes. The water becomes abnormally clear and deep blue, indicating extreme poverty of phytoplankton, and a new ecosystem emerges in which few organisms are equipped to survive. As algae populations decline, so too do those of zooplankton and insect larvae, and this in turn quickly brings about a slump in the numbers of amphibians and small fish. In no time at all the once rich lake loses most of its life.

This is particularly serious for young birds, which need to be fed on small prey items, mainly fish, and these are virtually unobtainable in such acidified lakes. Adults can feed on the larger fish, which generally survive for longer, but then they too have to resort to fishing in other, less contaminated lakes, where they can still find sufficient food. Continual transit between lakes carrying food, at times over a fair distance, can prove too exhausting for some birds, and the Great Northern Diver is the worst hit by this problem, perhaps due mostly to

The White-billed Diver is almost certainly the least numerous of the four species of divers. However, so little is known about the size and trends of its populations that its conservation requirements can not yet be established. Although it has been affected to some extent by oil spills, the fact that it breeds and winters in remote, less humanized areas than other members of the family suggests that its populations are unlikely to have declined significantly in recent times.

[*Gavia adamsii*, Arctic National Wildlife Refuge, Alaska. Photo: Johnny Johnson/ DRK]

its heavy build. Even if the adult numbers are not too badly affected at the moment, every year many chicks die in these polluted areas, so recruitment is severely reduced. Unfortunately, due to the birds' strong territorial sense and their fidelity to the previous year's nesting area, there is little chance that they will move to other, less affected lakes.

Other pollutants too are having serious consequences on diver populations, as well as on the rest of the ecosystem. Heavy metals dissolve very easily in acidic waters, so they pass rapidly into the food chain. High levels of mercury have been found in the tissues of divers washed ashore in both breeding and wintering areas. Fish-eating birds in particular are affected by this type of poisoning, since mercury dissolves in water in low concentrations, and then accumulates in the gills of fish. It is especially harmful, as it is released extremely slowly by living organisms, so the small amounts ingested through the consumption of contaminated fish remain in the bird's body for a long time, slowly building up, until the concentration is so high that it becomes lethal.

On some of the larger stretches of open water, another danger lies in wait for the migrating or wintering divers. Every year thousands of birds drown after becoming entangled in fishing nets; indeed nets are one of the chief causes of mortality outside the breeding season.

The other main cause is oil pollution, and divers are more adversely affected by oil slicks than most birds, for several reasons. The fact that they are flightless for several weeks makes them particularly vulnerable, and as they can cover fair distances under the water whilst searching for food, it is not unusual for a bird to surface in the midst of a slick, where it is doomed. The situation is all the gloomier given that in winter divers tend to gather in small flocks on sheltered coasts, so where one bird is oiled, others are liable to be affected too. The major oil disasters of the last few decades have severely affected several diver populations, some of which may take many

years to regain former levels. The vast quantities of oil spilt by the tanker Exxon Valdez off southern Alaska in March 1989 had disastrous effects on local bird populations, and divers were amongst those affected, with some 400-500 found dead in the ensuing six months; White-billed Divers appear to have suffered particularly severe losses. Even ignoring the major disasters, oil is a serious problem and survey work has shown that about two thirds of all the Red-throated Divers found dead on beaches around Britain in a normal winter are contaminated with oil.

A great deal of effort is being put into maintaining diver numbers, particularly in some of the more southerly parts of their breeding range, in Britain, the USA and Scandinavia. In some highly frequented areas, nest-sites are permanently guarded to ensure their safety. In other areas, floating islets have been launched on lakes that are potentially suitable for breeding, and these have proved quite successful as substitute nest-sites, especially in North America. Groups of enthusiasts, sometimes known as "Loon Rangers", help to bring the plight of divers to the attention of the general public. They hold public events to raise funds, which go towards the construction or restoration of suitable habitat, the maintenance of peace and quiet in the immediate vicinity of nests, the monitoring of breeding numbers and breeding success, and also towards public campaigns to stop the shooting of divers. The results of such efforts have been extremely encouraging and on occasions dramatic, and several local populations have already recovered former levels.

General Bibliography
Appleby *et al*. (1986), Barthel & Mullarney (1988), Boertmann (1990), Bourne (1968a), Butler & Jones (1982), Cracraft (1982), Eriksson (1985, 1987a), Harrison (1985, 1987), Johnsgard (1987), Mayr & Short (1970), Merrie (1978, 1979), Sibley & Monroe (1990), Sjölander (1985), Stegman (1974), Storer (1956, 1960), Stowe (1982), Townsend (1924), Woolfenden (1967).

PLATE 10

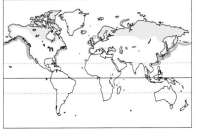

Family GAVIIDAE (DIVERS)
SPECIES ACCOUNTS

PLATE 10

Genus *GAVIA*   J. R. Forster, 1788

1. **Red-throated Diver**

Gavia stellata

French: Plongeon catmarin   **German**: Sterntaucher   **Spanish**: Colimbo Chico
Other common names: Red-throated Loon

Taxonomy. *Colymbus Stellatus* Pontoppidan, 1763, Tame River, Warwickshire, England. Monotypic.
Distribution. Holarctic, breeding generally N of 50° N and far into high Arctic; winters mainly along N coasts of Atlantic and Pacific, also in Great Lakes, and Black, Caspian and Mediterranean Seas.
Descriptive notes. 53-69 cm; 988-2460 g; wingspan 106-116 cm. Smallest, slightest diver, with uniform upperparts during breeding; bill slender, appears uptilted. Males average slightly larger, with heavier head and bill. Non-breeding adult brownish above speckled white, white below. Juvenile as non-breeding adult, with more extensive white spotting above.
Habitat. Breeds mostly on fresh water, typically in fairly open moorland, e.g. blanket bog; may occupy stretches of water of almost any size, and is often to be found nesting by small pools. Winters on inshore waters along sheltered coasts, occasionally inland.
Food and Feeding. Mostly fish, including cod (*Gadus morhua*), herring (*Clupea harengus*), sprat (*Sprattus sprattus*), sculpins (Cottidae), *Salmo* and *Salvelinus*; occasionally crustaceans, molluscs,

frogs, fish spawn, insects and sometimes some plant matter. Fish seized under water after pursuit dive; dives recorded to 2-9 m, averaging c. 1 minute.
Breeding. Starts May in S of range, dependent on spring thaw in N. Solitary or loosely colonial; nest is heap of plant matter near water's edge. 1-3 eggs, almost always 2; incubation c. 27 days; chicks have dark brown down, paler below; fledging c. 43 days. Sexual maturity at 2-3 years; known to have lived over 23 years in the wild. Success averages 0·45 young fledged per pair per year in Shetland Is (off N Scotland).
Movements. Migratory and dispersive; generally moves southwards and towards sea after breeding, shunning ice-covered water; large congregations of 200-1200 birds may occur. Accidental S to Tropic of Cancer.
Status and Conservation. Not globally threatened. Still numerous, though may be decreasing in some parts of range. In Nearctic, largest winter numbers apparently in E, though over 33,000 recorded on spring migration off California in 1979. In W Palearctic, c. 2000 pairs in Finland, c. 1200-1500 pairs in Scotland, c. 1000 pairs in Iceland, c. 1000 pairs in Norway, and fair numbers in Sweden; c. 10,000 winter in British waters. Fairly sensitive to human disturbance, and will desert breeding lake if too much human activity; also affected in places by alterations of water level. May suffer seriously from acidification of breeding waters and heavy metal pollution; highly vulnerable to oil spills, especially near rich fishing grounds where large concentrations of birds may form in winter;

On following page: 2. Black-throated Diver (*Gavia arctica*); 3. Great Northern Diver (*Gavia immer*); 4. White-billed Diver (*Gavia adamsii*).

201 birds found oiled in surveys of coastal Britain during 8 winters of 1970's. Some mortality in recent years at sea and on larger lakes, due to drowning in fishing nets set close inshore.

Bibliography. Ali & Ripley (1978), Anon. (1978), Barrett & Barrett (1985), Batten *et al.* (1990), Bauer & Glutz von Blotzheim (1966), Baxter & Rintoul (1953), Bent (1919), Bergman & Derksen (1977), Booth (1982), Brazil (1991), Brown *et al.* (1982), Bundy (1976), Buxton (1983), Bylin (1971), Camphuysen & Van Dijk (1983), Chandler (1981), Clapp *et al.* (1982), Cramp & Simmons (1977), Cyrus (1975), Davis (1972), Dementiev & Gladkov (1951c), Douglas & Reimchen (1988a, 1988b), Enquist (1983), Eriksson & Sundberg (1991), Eriksson *et al.* (1988, 1990), Furness (1981, 1983), Gomersall (1982, 1986), Gomersall *et al.* (1984), Grimmett & Jones (1989), Heubeck & Richardson (1980), Ilicev & Flint (1985), Jones *et al.* (1978), Kishchinskij *et al.* (1983), Krechmar (1966), Lokki & Eklöf (1984), Marchant *et al.* (1990), Merrie (1978, 1979), Norberg & Norberg (1981), Okill (1986), Pakarinen & Järvinen (1984), Palmer (1962), Parrack (1986a), Persson *et al.* (1986), Petersen (1976), Prater (1981), Reimchen & Douglas (1984), Richardson *et al.* (1982), Roalkvam (1985), Rutgers & Norris (1970), Schamel & Tracy (1985), Sharrock (1976), Sjölander (1977), Strong (1988), Stroud *et al.* (1989), Tasker *et al.* (1987), Thom (1986).

2. Black-throated Diver
Gavia arctica

French: Plongeon arctique **German**: Prachttaucher **Spanish**: Colimbo Artico
Other common names: Arctic/Black-throated Loon; Pacific Diver/Loon (*pacifica*)

Taxonomy. *Colymbus arcticus* Linnaeus, 1758, Sweden.
Nearctic race *pacifica* often considered separate species (see page 162). Three subspecies recognized.
Subspecies and Distribution.
G. a. pacifica (Lawrence, 1858) - extreme N & NW Nearctic; winters Pacific coast of N America.
G. a. arctica (Linnaeus, 1758) - W Palearctic E to R Lena; winters along coasts of NW Europe, also in Black, Caspian and Mediterranean Seas.
G. a. viridigularis Dwight, 1918 - E Palearctic E of R Lena; winters NW Pacific.

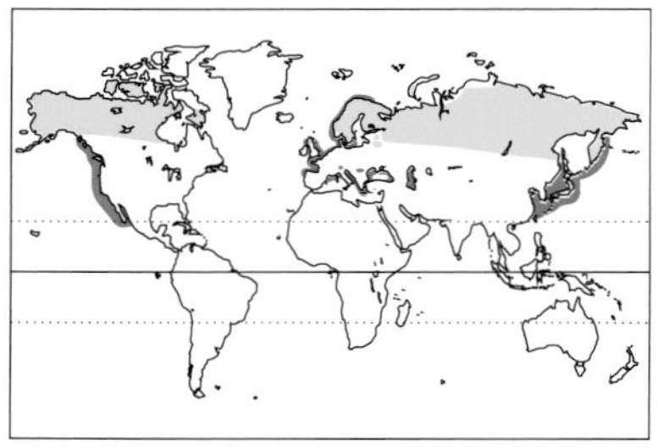

Descriptive notes. 58-73 cm; 1300-3400 g; wingspan 110-130 cm. Thicker neck and straighter looking bill than *G. stellata*. Non-breeding adult brownish grey above, white below with noticeable white patch on flanks. Juvenile as non-breeding adult, with indistinct buffy scaling on upperparts. Race *pacifica* smaller with head and hind neck paler and bill thinner; *viridigularis* differs from nominate in green throat patch.
Habitat. Breeds on fairly large, deep freshwater lakes, preferably with islets; more typically in taiga and boreal zone, less in arctic tundra than *G. stellata*. Winters on inshore waters along sheltered coasts, occasionally inland.
Food and Feeding. Mostly fish, including gobies (Gobiidae), sticklebacks (Gasterosteidae), herring (*Clupea harengus*), sprat (*Sprattus sprattus*), cod (*Gadus morhua*), perch (*Perca*), trout (*Salmo*), bleak (*Alburnus*); sometimes aquatic insects, molluscs, crustaceans and some plant matter. Fish seized under water after pursuit dive; dives recorded to 3-6 m, averaging c. 45 seconds.
Breeding. Starts May in S of range, dependent on spring thaw in N. Solitary; nest is heap of plant matter near water's edge. 1-3 eggs, almost always 2; incubation 28-30 days; chicks have sooty brown down, paler below; fledging c. 60-65 days. Sexual maturity 2-3 years; known to have lived over 27 years in the wild; annual mortality rate of adults c. 10%. Success averages 0·2-0·3 young fledged per pair per year in Scotland.
Movements. Migratory and dispersive; generally moves southwards and towards sea after breeding, shunning ice-covered water; often forms flocks of c. 50 birds. Accidental S to Tropic of Cancer.
Status and Conservation. Not globally threatened. World population probably large, in the order of several million birds, but generally decreasing throughout S of range. Over 1 million recorded on spring migration off California in 1979. Few data from W Palearctic: c. 2000 pairs in Finland, c. 150 pairs in Scotland; c. 1300 winter in British waters. Particularly sensitive to human disturbance, and reproductive output noticeably lower in much-frequented areas; also affected in places by alterations of water level, and less directly by some modifications of habitat, e.g. afforestation with conifers in Scotland. May suffer seriously from acidification of breeding waters and heavy metal pollution; highly vulnerable to oil spills, especially near rich fishing grounds where larger concentrations may be formed in winter. Some mortality due to birds drowning in fishing nets.

Bibliography. Ali & Ripley (1978), Andersson *et al.* (1980), Anon. (1978), Barrett & Barrett (1985), Batten *et al.* (1990), Bauer & Glutz von Blotzheim (1966), Baxter & Rintoul (1953), Bent (1919), Brazil (1991), Brown *et al.* (1982), Bundy (1979), Campbell & Mudge (1989), Campbell & Talbot (1987), Campbell *et al.* (1985), Camphuysen & Van Dijk (1983), Chandler (1981), Clapp *et al.* (1982), Cramp & Simmons (1977), Davis (1972), Dementiev & Gladkov (1951c), Dunker (1974), Eckert (1986), Eriksson (1986, 1987b), Eriksson & Sundberg (1991), Götmark *et al.* (1989, 1990), Grimmett & Jones (1989), Heubeck & Richardson (1980), Hunter & Dennis (1972), Ilicev & Flint (1985), Jones *et al.* (1978), Kirkham & Johnson (1988), Kishchinskij *et al.* (1983), Kochanov & Skokova (1967), Krechmar (1966), Lehtonen (1970, 1974), Lindberg (1968), Mackowicz & Nowak (1986), Madsen (1957), Marchant *et al.* (1990), Mudge *et al.* (1991), Nilsson (1977), Palmer (1962), Parrack (1986b), Petersen (1976, 1979, 1989), Prater (1981), Roalkvam (1985), Sharrock (1976), Sjölander (1978), Strong (1988), Stroud *et al.* (1989), Tasker *et al.* (1987), Thom (1986), Tove (1988).

3. Great Northern Diver
Gavia immer

French: Plongeon imbrin **German**: Eistaucher **Spanish**: Colimbo Grande
Other common names: Common/Black-billed Loon

Taxonomy. *Colymbus Immer* Brünnich, 1764, Faeroes.
Hybridization with *G. arctica* reported. Monotypic.
Distribution. Mainly Nearctic, where breeds between 48° N and Arctic Circle, in places S to c. 40° N, and N to c. 78° N; in N Atlantic also breeds in Greenland, Iceland, Bear I and very occasionally Scotland. Winters mainly along coasts of N Atlantic and NE Pacific, also stopping off in Great Lakes.
Descriptive notes. 69-91 cm; 2780-4480 g; wingspan 127-147 cm. Heavy, straightish bill; 15 stripes on each side of neck, pattern variable. Non-breeding adult brownish grey above with dark crown and nape, white below; bill greyish or whitish with dark brownish culmen. Juvenile as non-breeding adult, with indistinct buffy scaling on upperparts.
Habitat. Breeds mostly on rather large, deep freshwater lakes, in areas of coniferous forest or on open tundra; nests preferably on islets. Winters along coasts, frequenting both exposed, rocky headlands and sheltered bays; occasionally inland.

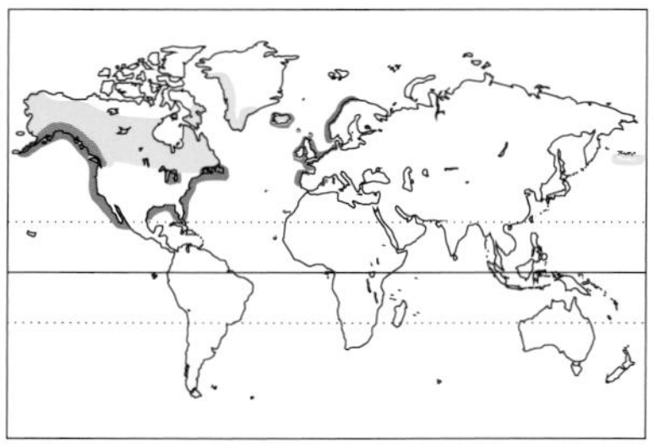

Food and Feeding. Mostly fish (c. 55-80%), including cod (*Gadus morhua*), haddock (*Melanogrammus aeglefinus*), herring (*Clupea harengus*), trout (*Salmo*), suckers (Catostomidae), minnows (Cyprinidae) and perch (*Perca*); some crustaceans (e.g. *Cambarus*, *Gammarus*), molluscs (e.g. *Planorbis*), aquatic insects, annelids, frogs and other amphibia; sometimes fair quantities of plant matter, e.g. pondweed (*Potamogeton*), willow shoots (*Salix*), roots, seeds, moss, algae (*Vaucheria*). Fish seized under water after pursuit dive; dives recorded to 70 m, though probably 4-10 m normally, maximum duration probably c. 1 minute.
Breeding. Starts May in S of range, dependent on spring thaw in N. Solitary; nest is heap of plant matter near water's edge. 1-3 eggs, almost always 2; incubation c. 24-25 days; chicks have dark brown down, paler or white below; fledging c. 70-77 days. Sexual maturity at 2 years; some individuals presumably live to 20 years old or more, as in other species, but to date no ringing record reaches 8 years. Average success 0·5 young per pair in Minnesota, USA.
Movements. Migratory, generally moving southwards and towards sea after breeding, shunning ice-covered water; large congregations of c. 300 birds may occur. Several thousand birds winter along western coasts of Europe, presumably originating from Iceland, but probably also from Greenland and Canada.
Status and Conservation. Not globally threatened. World population in the order of a few hundred thousand birds, but population levels have decreased steadily over much of this century in S of range. Palearctic breeding population essentially limited to 100-300 pairs in Iceland; c. 3500-4500 birds winter in British waters. Particularly sensitive to human disturbance, and many breeding lakes deserted after increase in human presence and activities. Sporadic mass mortality from type E botulism in region of Great Lakes, caused by accumulation of rotting organic matter. May suffer seriously from acidification of breeding waters and heavy metal pollution; highly vulnerable to oil spills, especially in areas of large winter aggregations, e.g. 146 killed after "Esso Bernicia" spill in Shetland (off N Scotland), in Jan 1979. Fishing nets cause significant mortality at sea and in larger lakes; alterations in water level and egg-collecting also important in places.

Bibliography. Alexander (1985), Alvo (1985, 1986, 1987), Alvo & Prior (1986), Alvo *et al.* (1988), Anon. (1978), Barr (1973, 1986), Barrett & Barrett (1985), Batten *et al.* (1990), Bauer & Glutz von Blotzheim (1966), Baxter & Rintoul (1953), Belant & Anderson (1991), Bent (1919), Blair (1990), Braekevelt (1986), Brown *et al.* (1982), Camphuysen & Van Dijk (1983), Chandler (1981), Clapp *et al.* (1982), Cramp & Simmons (1977), Christenson (1981), Croskery (1988, 1989), Daub (1989), Dulin (1988), Eberhardt (1984), Fair (1979), Fox *et al.* (1980), Grimmett & Jones (1989), Hammond & Wood (1976), Hands *et al.* (1989c), Haney (1990), Haseltine *et al.* (1983), Heimberger (1983), Heubeck & Richardson (1980), Hunter (1970), Hunter & Dennis (1972), Ilicev & Flint (1985), Jones *et al.* (1978), King (1976), Kirkham & Johnson (1988), Klein (1985), Lee (1987a), Line (1992), McIntyre (1974, 1975 1977a, 1977b, 1978, 1983, 1986, 1988, 1989), McIntyre & Barr (1983), Munro (1945), Olson (1951), Olson & Marshall (1952), Palmer (1962), Parker (1988), Parker *et al.* (1986), Parrack (1986c), Parslow & Everett (1981), Pichner & DonCarlos (1986), Powers & Cherry (1983), Prater (1981), Ream (1976), Richardson *et al.* (1982), Shoryer (1947), Sjölander & Agren (1972), Smith (1981), Sperry (1987), Strong (1985, 1988, 1990), Strong & Bissonette (1989), Strong, Bissonette & Fair (1987), Strong, Lavalley & Burke (1987), Sutcliffe (1978, 1979, 1980), Tasker *et al.* (1987), Thom (1986), Titus & van Druff (1981), Valley (1987), Vermeer (1973a, 1973b), Yeates (1950a), Yonge (1981), Zimmer (1979).

4. White-billed Diver
Gavia adamsii

French: Plongeon à bec blanc **German**: Gelbschnabeltaucher **Spanish**: Colimbo de Adams
Other common names: Yellow-billed Loon

Taxonomy. *Colymbus adamsii* G. R. Gray, 1859, Alaska.
Closely related to *G. immer*, with which sometimes considered to form a superspecies. Monotypic.
Distribution. Holarctic, breeding mainly along coasts of Arctic Ocean as far N as c. 78° N; winters in coastal waters of NW & NE Pacific and also off NW Norway.

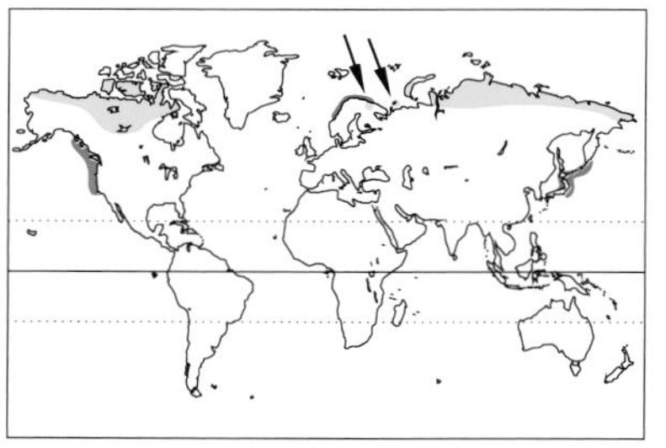

Descriptive notes. 76-91 cm; 4050-6400 g; wingspan 137-152 cm. Largest diver; pronounced bulge on forecrown, bill appears up-tilted; fewer stripes on sides of neck than in *G. immer*, pattern variable. Non-breeding adult brownish above, white below. Juvenile as non-breeding adult, with heavy buffy scaling on upperparts.
Habitat. Breeds preferably on freshwater pools or lakes of tundra; also on low-lying Arctic coast, rivers and estuaries; generally avoids forested areas. Winters on inshore waters along sheltered coasts.
Food and Feeding. Little known. Mostly fish, including sculpin (Cottidae), tomcod (*Microgadus proximus*) and cod (*Gadus morhua*); also crustaceans, molluscs and annelids. Fish seized under water after pursuit dive.
Breeding. Mostly starts early Jun, but largely dependent on spring thaw. Solitary; nest is heap of plant matter or turf near water's edge. 2 eggs; chicks have dark brown down, paler below. No information available on incubation and fledging periods, age of sexual maturity or success, though all probably similar to *G. immer*.
Movements. Migratory, generally moving southwards and towards sea after breeding, shunning ice-covered water; occurs S to c. 35° N off Japan, but otherwise only rarely S of 50° N. Fairly regular winter vagrant to N Scotland.
Status and Conservation. Not globally threatened. Very little known of numbers. In Palearctic, fairly common only in NE Siberia; Nearctic population apparently not very large. Relatively little human disturbance in its Arctic breeding grounds, so has probably not undergone steady decline of other species. Vulnerable to oil spills, especially in Beaufort Sea (to N of Canada), and also in several wintering zones (see page 170). Wintering birds might also be subject to pollution from heavy metals; some mortality through drowning in fishing nets, particularly in the N Pacific.

Bibliography. Anon. (1978), Cramp & Simmons (1977), Bent (1919), Brazil (1991), Camphuysen & Van Dijk (1983), Dementiev & Gladkov (1951c), Derksen *et al.* (1981), Dixon (1916), Dymond *et al.* (1989), Etchécopar & Hüe (1978), Gabrielson & Lincoln (1959), Godfrey (1966), van Ijzendoorn (1979), Ilicev & Flint (1985), Kishchinskij *et al.* (1983), North (1986), North & Ryan (1988, 1989), Palmer (1962), Piatt *et al.* (1990), Portenko (1981), Ramón (1987), Sage (1971), Sjölander & Agren (1976), Snyder (1957), Sutton (1963).

Order PODICIPEDIFORMES

Podicipediformes

Podicipedidae

grebes

Class AVES
Order PODICIPEDIFORMES
Family PODICIPEDIDAE (GREBES)

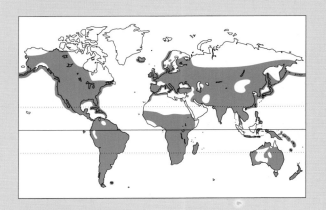

- Small to largish waterbirds with pointed bill, lobed toes and highly reduced tail.
- 23-74 cm.

- All regions except Antarctic; greatest diversity in New World.
- Freshwater habitats, in winter often on marine waters; mostly found in temperate zones.
- 6 genera, 22 species, 53 taxa.
- 5 species threatened; 2 of these probably extinct since 1600.

Systematics

Grebes constitute one of the oldest forms of birds, and they are particularly well represented in the fossil register of the New World. The oldest form, *Neogaeornis*, of the Upper Cretaceous in Chile, goes back 80 million years, while remains of the present day genus *Podiceps* have been found in deposits of the Oligocene, the Pliocene and the Pleistocene. From this last period, fossils of the living genera *Aechmophorus* and *Podilymbus* have also been found. The number and type of fossils found in southern South America suggest that the family originated in the Antarctic or in the Archiplatean, the southernmost of the three shields that by the start of the Tertiary made up what is nowadays South America. The most important centre of adaptive radiation is the Neotropical Region, in which 11 of the 22 species are present.

The grebes are the only family of the order Podicipediformes, and taxonomically they do not appear to be closely related to any other group. Various analyses of morphology and egg-white proteins conclude that their external similarity to the divers (Gaviidae), with which they were formerly associated, is due to convergent evolution. Instead, the celebrated studies based on DNA-DNA hybridization conclude that the grebes are derived from the same lineage that led to the traditional Ciconiiformes, Procellariiformes, Pelecaniformes and the penguins, and that all these groups should be placed in the infraorder Ciconiides.

The internal taxonomy of the group, which is fairly homogenous, is based on anatomical, morphological and ethological characteristics, the last-mentioned especially in terms of courtship and mating behaviour. In the last few years numerous systematic changes have been proposed, which are not accepted by all authorities; to these can be added two recent extinctions, but also the discovery of a new species in 1974.

The most diversified genus is *Podiceps*, with nine species, and these are normally divided into two main subgroups. The first is composed of the Great Crested Grebe (*Podiceps cristatus*), the Red-necked Grebe (*Podiceps grisegena*) and the Horned Grebe (*Podiceps auritus*), three species that are often sympatric. The second consists of five closely related species, that have on occasions been assigned a different genus, *Dytes*, in which the Horned Grebe has sometimes been included. The Black-necked Grebe (*Podiceps nigricollis*), the probably extinct Colombian Grebe (*Podiceps andinus*), often considered only a subspecies of the former, and the Silvery Grebe (*Podiceps occipitalis*) form a superspecies, which usually includes the Junin Flightless Grebe (*Podiceps taczanowskii*). However, this species is sympatric on Lake Junín, in Peru, with the Silvery Grebe's race *juninensis*, which has also been claimed as a distinct species, on the grounds of morphological and ethological differences with the nominate form. The fifth species of the subgroup is the Hooded Grebe (*Podiceps gallardoi*), rather surprisingly discovered only in 1974 and only known from Patagonia. It is very close to the other species of the subgroup, and has been reported to have hybridized with the Silvery Grebe. The remaining species of this genus, the Great Grebe (*Podiceps major*), differs significantly from the others, which makes it difficult to classify. For this reason, it has also been included in *Aechmophorus*, although it possibly represents a different genus, or at least a subgenus (within *Podiceps*), in which some authors also include the Red-necked Grebe.

All the other present day genera have also been included in *Podiceps*. The genus *Tachybaptus* includes several very similar species of the Old World. The Rusty Grebe (*Tachybaptus rufolavatus*) is virtually confined to Lake Aloatra in Madagascar, and is sometimes considered merely a subspecies of the cosmopolitan Little Grebe (*Tachybaptus ruficollis*), and the two have been hybridizing intensively since the recent expansion

The systematic position of the Great Grebe is one of the least clear of all the grebes. It was formerly included in the genus Aechmophorus, *but any similarity with the Western and Clark's Grebes is now considered to be purely superficial. The simple courtship rituals suggest that the species diverged from the* Podiceps *line at an early stage, and for this reason many authors believe it should be given a genus of its own.*

[Podiceps major, Argentina. Photo: Francisco Erize/ Bruce Coleman]

A grebe's body, as illustrated by this New Zealand Grebe, is perfectly adapted for diving. The front part, laterally compressed and rather pointed, penetrates the water with ease, whilst the hind part, rounded because of the extremely reduced tail, hardly produces any drag at all.

[Poliocephalus rufopectus, North Island, New Zealand. Photo: B. Chudleigh/ ANT/NHPA]

of the latter to Madagascar (see Status and Conservation). Likewise the Australasian Grebe (*Tachybaptus novaehollandiae*) was long considered another subspecies of the Little Grebe, but it was separated due to an overlap in breeding ranges, at least in northern New Guinea and possibly also in Java and the Lesser Sundas, apparently without hybridization. These three species form a superspecies, close to the Madagascar Grebe (*Tachybaptus pelzelnii*), another endemic of the island, which is also known to have hybridized with the Little Grebe. The fifth species of the genus, the Least Grebe (*Tachybaptus dominicus*), is the only New World representative, and is the most singular and difficult to classify. In support of this is the fact that it is still considered sometimes to belong to *Podiceps*, less often to *Poliocephalus*, or is even assigned the genus *Limnodytes* for itself.

The genus *Podilymbus* is restricted to America, and includes two species that constitute a superspecies, the widely distributed Pied-billed Grebe (*Podilymbus podiceps*) and the Atitlan Grebe (*Podilymbus gigas*). The latter was confined to Lake Atitlán, in the highlands of Guatemala, but it appears to be extinct now (see Status and Conservation). The first specimen of this interesting, but controversial species was collected in 1862, and it was considered to be a subspecies of the Pied-billed Grebe. In 1929, however, it was described as a distinct species, although this status has never had unanimous support. There are various hypotheses on its evolutionary history: according to one, it was the remnant population of an originally widely distributed species, which sheltered on mountain lakes during a period of climatic warming. An alternative explanation is that the Atitlan Grebe evolved from the Pied-billed Grebe, a species with migratory populations, and some individuals of these could easily have strayed to Lake Atitlán during the Pleistocene. The characteristics of the lake, which is very deep with precipitous banks and frequently with rough water, could have exercised adaptive pressure towards a larger and more powerful bird, and towards flightlessness, which would be a good example of evolutionary divergence in relation to isolation.

The genus *Rollandia* is at a primitive stage in the evolution of some displays. It comprises two South American species, the White-tufted Grebe (*Rollandia rolland*), of which two subspecies, *rolland* and *chilensis*, are sometimes considered distinct species, and the Titicaca Flightless Grebe (*Rollandia microp-*

tera), which is restricted to a few Andean lakes and was formerly assigned a genus of its own, *Centropelma*.

The genus *Poliocephalus* comprises a superspecies with well differentiated morphological and ethological characteristics, and is formed of two Australasian species, the Hoary-headed Grebe (*Poliocephalus poliocephalus*) and the New Zealand Grebe (*Poliocephalus rufopectus*). These species have at times been included in either *Podiceps* or *Tachybaptus*. Nowadays their nearest relatives are considered to be the genus *Rollandia* and the Great Grebe, which is still retained in *Podiceps*.

Finally, *Aechmophorus* of North America occupies the fish-eating niche of the Great Crested Grebe of the Old World. Until very recently, it was considered to consist of only one species, the Western Grebe (*Aechmophorus occidentalis*), with two colour morphs, sometimes treated as subspecies. However, it is now considered that the light phase constitutes a different species, Clark's Grebe (*Aechmophorus clarkii*), which is widely sympatric with the former, but shows differences in feeding behaviour, at any rate where the two coincide (see Food and Feeding), and these reduce the duplication of trophic requirements. At the same time, differences in the "Advertising-call" (see Voice) prevent hybridization, which means that interbreeding, although reported, is rare.

After extensive measurements and field studies in Europe, America and Australia, J. Fjeldså has suggested the operation in grebes of co-evolution, reciprocal evolutionary change in two or more interacting species. Accordingly, the Junin Flightless Grebe is characterized by a long bill that is specialized for capturing small fish, but the Silvery Grebes that also live on Lake Junín have a shorter bill in comparison with other Silvery Grebe populations, and this is appropriate for catching the midges that constitute their main food on this lake. The race *holboellii* of the Red-necked Grebe, which lives in eastern Siberia and North America, where the Great Crested Grebe does not occur, has a long bill, similar to the latter species, and this is suited to feeding on fish. On the other hand, the nominate subspecies, which coincides extensively with the Great Crested Grebe, has a smaller bill, more specialized for the capture of arthropods. But most interesting is that the populations of the nominate subspecies that live in the north of Europe, where the Great Crested Grebe is again absent, also have a long bill and the muscular development of their mandibles is similar to that of *holboellii*. So in both of these cases bill morphology is a good example of character displacement; the geographical overlap of closely related species intensifies the differences between them, with the purpose of allowing them to co-exist more easily.

Morphological Aspects

The different species of grebes vary in size from a minimum of 23 cm in the smallest species of the genus *Tachybaptus*, which weigh about 120 g and are the smallest of all diving birds, to 74 cm and 1500 g in the largest species. Although there are no obvious structural differences between the sexes, males average somewhat larger than females and also have slightly longer bills.

Their silhouette on the water is not unlike that of the divers, although the neck is relatively longer. The length of the neck and the shape of the body, short and round in the smaller species and longer in the larger ones, is related in each species to the type of diving it performs and the depth to which it dives. The same is true of the very variable shape and size of the bill, which depends on the diet and feeding habits. Therefore the bill is short and sturdy in the basically insectivorous species and quite long and pointed, similar to the divers, in the piscivorous species. The Atitlan Grebe is a special case, as its heavy, powerful bill and massive mandibular and neck musculature represent adaptations for capturing and crushing the large crustaceans that are abundant in Lake Atitlán, which is thought to have been fishless originally. The nostrils are narrow slits in all the species as an adaptation to diving.

In fact, the whole body of these almost exclusively aquatic birds is perfectly adapted to diving. The skeleton is not highly pneumatized, which means that they sit very low on the water. The streamlined body is well suited for coping with the upward pressure of the water and its resistance to rapid movement. The front of the body is laterally compressed and rather pointed, so it easily penetrates the water, while the rear, which is rounded due to the extremely reduced tail, creates very little resistance. Due to the lack of true rectrices, grebes appear to be virtually tailless, but they do in fact have a very short tail of small, soft, downy feathers.

The strong legs are set far back and are ideal for propulsion. At the same time they act as a rudder, replacing the rudimentary tail, which is useless for this task. This means that the hind part of the bird carries a good deal of weight, and it explains the typical outline with the low back that grebes present while swimming. The tarsi are laterally compressed to reduce water resistance. Unlike most other aquatic birds, the three front toes have broad independent lobes, which are only slightly interconnected by a small membrane at the base. The hind toe, which is raised above the others, has a small lobe. When the grebe is ready to submerge, it contracts its abdominal muscles, exhales and sleeks its plumage, thereby increasing specific weight and reducing buoyancy, and this helps it to dive. Then, apparently without much effort, it submerges head first, with a quick forward and downward movement of the neck and a very strong push with the feet. Birds sometimes jump, first pulling the head back, then using the legs to spring upwards so that the whole body comes out of the water before the bird dives under head first. It is thought that the reason for this type of "springing dive" is to enter the water at a steeper angle, in order to reach a greater depth.

While the birds are submerged, the wings are folded and tucked under the plumage of the flanks. Unlike penguins, they do not use them for propulsion, but only occasionally when they are swimming among dense vegetation, or when making a sharp change of direction.

Dives usually last 10 to 40 seconds, which usually gives them enough time to find food, but this depends on the species and on several other factors. In the first place, the larger species are better able to store oxygen and can therefore remain under water longer. Thus, in various studies carried out on the diminutive Australasian and Little Grebes, the average time of dives was found to be 8-20 and 10-25 seconds respectively,

As its name indicates, the Titicaca Flightless Grebe is quite incapable of flying; its wings are very short and the number of primaries is reduced. Flightlessness evolves readily in grebes when they are not forced to migrate by seasonal changes in the climate. The three species of flightless grebes are to be found on immense lakes mainly because of the stabilizing effects that large expanses of water have on the climate.

[*Rollandia microptera*, Lake Poopó, Bolivia. Photo: X. Ferrer & A. de Sostoa]

while the larger Great Crested and Red-necked Grebes dive for between 18-26 and 25-30 seconds. However, the maximum time registered in these four species is fairly similar, at about one minute, though dives of up to three minutes have been claimed for the medium-sized Horned Grebe.

Within the same species there is considerable variation in the duration of dives, and this can be explained by the influence of various other local factors, such as the depth of the water, the type of prey, whether they are invertebrates or fish, and their relative abundance. Thus, for example, in the New Zealand population of Great Crested Grebes, which live in environments with poorer feeding, maximum dives of 85 seconds have been recorded, while in the numerous studies conducted with the same species in Europe dives of over 56 seconds have not been recorded.

Again, the depth that grebes can dive to is also less than that reached by divers. They normally dive to depths of less than seven metres, and almost all the species normally dive to between one and four metres below the surface. Exceptionally they can reach far greater depths, as was apparently the case of a Great Crested Grebe found entangled in a fishing net 30 m down. Progress under the water is strong and regular, and birds can reach 2 m/second, with the propulsion being supplied solely by simultaneous strokes of the feet. They also display surprising agility, as a result of the flexibility of the tibiotarsal and tarsometatarsal joints, which allows them to manoeuvre easily. All these factors make it difficult to predict where a bird will emerge after a dive. While swimming on the surface a bird can adjust its buoyancy, and can even swim or sit with only the head visible.

The positioning of the legs well back on the body, which contributes so much to their diving ability, conversely reduces their proficiency in walking. For this reason, they hardly ever approach dry land, except sometimes to rest on the bank or very occasionally to reach a nest that may have been left high and dry due to a lowering of the water level. On such occasions, or when they climb up onto their typical floating nests, they adopt an erect posture with the body leaning slightly forwards and the tarsi at an angle of about 60° to it, and like this they can walk and even run short distances.

The small, narrow wings have curved primaries, which are held close to the body, and when folded the edges are covered by the body plumage and are almost invisible. In order to take off, a bird needs to run a long way along the surface of the water, at the same time beating its wings very quickly. As its wing-loading is relatively high, it has to keep beating its wings quickly throughout its flight, and the Great Crested Grebe registers 6·3 beats per second. Considering these adaptations, it is not surprising that in the face of any danger whatsoever, grebes prefer to dive rather than fly, with the possible exception of the Hoary-headed Grebe. Nevertheless, although they do not fly often, most grebes can fly quickly and for long distances, which explains how they manage to colonize new areas, and also the fact that some species migrate. Once in the air, their flight silhouette is characteristic with the neck stretched forward, held slightly lower than body level, and with the feet, which are also used to steer in the air, trailing conspicuously behind. Most of their flying is done by night and they are especially active when the moon is full, although the Hoary-headed Grebe also flies readily during the day.

On the other hand, their pectoral musculature is relatively poorly developed, and it seems that an atrophy of this occurs in some species after the arrival at the breeding grounds. This has been studied primarily in the Silvery Grebe, because it was suspected that nesting birds were incapable of flight. In fact, among the grebes there are three species which practically never fly, all of them inhabitants of mountain lakes in the Neotropical Region. These are the Titicaca Flightless Grebe, the only completely flightless species, which has a reduced number of primaries, and the Junin Flightless and Atitlan Grebes, which are permanently unable to take off and maintain level flight, although by running over the water and beating their wings rapidly, as the other species do for take-off, they can cover fair distances, and the Atitlan Grebe may move up to 300 m in this way.

Flightlessness in the grebes is not associated, as in the penguins, with the specialization of the wing for diving, but rather to the absence of the need to fly. This is due to the fact that these species occur at sites which are habitable all year round, as all three occupy large lakes at low latitudes with permanent food supplies. Thus the wings have lost their role in locomotion, but not their other typical functions, for instance in brooding and transport of chicks, or covering the feet when the bird is resting.

Interestingly, each of the three flightless grebes has a presumed sister species, which is capable of flying. Judging from morphological and behavioural criteria, the Titicaca, Junin and Atitlan Grebes seem to have evolved from the White-tufted, Silvery and Pied-billed Grebes respectively, presumably after being trapped in high altitude lakes, for example during glaciations. A comparison of all these species reveals several strongly convergent features in the three flightless species: a reduction in the relative length of the wings, tail, and primaries;

a reduction in the relative size of the pectoral muscles; and above all a marked increase in body mass. This last feature is more significant in males, so the biometrical differences between the sexes are also greater than in the flying species. The selective advantages that they obtain from these adaptations, apart from saving energy due to the reduced development of the pectorals and wings, are related firstly to the thermodynamic benefits of increased size, which can be important in high altitude lakes, secondly to feeding specialization (see Food and Feeding), and finally to a reduction of intraspecific competition for food due to the accentuated sexual dimorphism, which is also an important factor, given the extremely limited ranges of these species.

Two island forms, the Rusty Grebe of Madagascar, and the nominate race of the White-tufted Grebe of the Falkland Islands, also have a reduced ability to fly, and relatively shorter wings and tails than their closest relatives, although to a lesser degree. This indicates that on islands, as well as in mountain lakes, there are conditions operating that can lead to the loss of flight.

The grebes' plumage is extremely waterproof and offers the skin good protection against the wet; it is also very thick, and each bird has more than 20,000 feathers. It appears loose on the upperparts, downy on the rump and tail, and sleeker and smoother on the underparts. This silky appearance is due to the structure of the feathers, which is unique among birds, with only one in every two or three barbules of the inner barb clasping the next barb.

Grebes undergo a marked seasonal change in plumages. Outwith the breeding season their coloration is drab, with dark upperparts, usually brown or grey, and whitish underparts, while the breeding plumage is usually of various reddish or dark colours, especially on the head, throat, neck and breast. During breeding there are various characteristic markings, such as crests, tippets, ruffs, auricular fans, ear-tufts and hair-like filaments, which appear in both sexes, although they tend to be brighter in males.

Chicks have a distinctive design of clearly marked dark bands, particularly on the head and neck, in all genera except *Aechmophorus*, where they are more uniform. Remains of these marks are partially retained in the juvenile plumage and form the main difference with the plumage of non-breeding adults. Full adult plumage is acquired in the second calender year. A typical characteristic of grebe chicks is the presence of large loral patches and an inflatable outgrowth of bare, wrinkled skin

Sunbathing is a habit frequently observed among grebes living in cold parts or, as in the case of this Least Grebe, among the smaller species. Nevertheless, it is much more common on the water, where grebes spend almost all of their time, except when copulating or carrying out activities associated with nesting.

[Tachybaptus dominicus brachypterus, Mexico. Photo: Patricio Robles]

on the crown. These patches may be related to thermoregulation, but they also act as social signals for the parents when they fill with blood and quickly change colour (see Breeding).

Grebes drop all the flight-feathers simultaneously during the post-breeding moult or later, and are unable to fly for a period of about 3-4 weeks. During this period large concentrations of flightless birds, in the process of moulting, gather at sites that offer good feeding. Occasionally breeding birds have been seen moulting their flight-feathers, though these are usually late breeders. In fact, a partial moult of this kind requires less energy than a complete moult, and it has been suggested that, if compatible with the breeding activities, the breeding season could be a good time for moulting the flight-feathers.

The moult of the body feathers is also normally initiated at the end of the summer and is completed during the first part of the winter. It is quickly followed by a partial moult, with which the relevant species renew their tippets. In some Palaearctic species it has been found that the renovation of the white underparts slows down or stops in the middle of winter, when the birds need this thick protection, but the process continues constantly during most of the rest of the year. The almost continuous moult of some tracts, especially the flanks, may provide a permanent supply of feathers for their strange habit of swallowing them (see Food and Feeding).

Habitat

The grebes are strictly aquatic, and during the breeding season they usually occupy bodies of still fresh water, particularly shallow eutrophic lakes or pools, where there are ample amounts of floating, emergent or underwater vegetation, and mud, clay or sand on the bottom. They also breed at times on slow-flowing rivers, and occasionally even in sheltered bays along the coast, particularly the Western and Great Grebes. Some small species, such as the Least Grebe, are specialized in breeding on seasonal water bodies.

They generally stay well clear of snow and ice, and also very cold waters; likewise, they are rarely found in oligotrophic, deep or murky waters and avoid bare rock and gravel. However, there are exceptions, for instance the Hooded Grebe, which inhabits windswept Patagonia, where the rocky shores offer protection. In the Neotropical Region grebes are typically found on mountain lakes, and some species occur up to 4000 metres in areas of *páramo* or *puna*.

Although they are adapted to life in various depths of water, they usually forage in the top three or four metres of water, but occasionally they may dive much deeper in search of food (see

Food and Feeding). The size of the stretch of water occupied is very variable, and while some species prefer large bodies of water, in most cases size is not a strictly limiting factor. The smaller species can even occupy waters of less than one hectare.

The most important factors overall for breeding appear to be depth, distance to open water and density of vegetation, while the specific composition of the vegetation seems to be less significant.

Some Palearctic species are becoming adapted to life in humanized areas, by taking advantage of the eutrophication of water due to the disposal of organic waste, which increases the populations of cyprinid fish. They also take advantage of wetlands created by man, such as reservoirs, gravel pits, fish farms and stretches of water in built up areas, especially in some populations of the Great Crested Grebe in Central Europe.

Outside the breeding season, grebes may be obliged to migrate, due to particularly cold or dry weather. They may move to other inland lakes, normally large ones, or alternatively to the coast, generally without straying far from the coastline. However, some species, like the Red-necked and Great Grebes, can be found on the open sea in winter, many kilometres from the coast. During the moult of the flight-feathers, which renders them temporarily flightless, they can be found in large numbers on the coast. When on migration they are particularly tolerant and can occur in very diverse kinds of wetlands.

General Habits

In general, grebes tend not to be particularly sociable, indeed many species are often solitary. However, some species are gregarious, especially outside the breeding season, when they can form major concentrations during migration (see Movements) or in winter, and seven species habitually nest in colonies. These are the Hoary-headed, Black-necked, Hooded, Silvery, Junin Flightless, Western and Clark's Grebes. It seems that this high level of sociability is related to a form of feeding, whereby a gregarious tendency can facilitate the localization of food, and to open stretches of water, where dense grouping at the most sheltered sites may provide the most efficient protection for nests.

Grebes are fairly aggressive, especially when defending the nest. The Little Grebe for example, will chase a Mallard (*Anas platyrhynchos*) or a Common Moorhen (*Gallinula chloropus*) from near the nest, attacking the surprised intruders from the surface or under the water. Though infrequent, direct attacks between different species of grebe do take place and attacks by the Great Crested on the Little, Black-necked and Red-necked Grebes have been recorded.

Like other waterbirds, grebes spend most of their time foraging and resting, when they habitually pay a good deal of attention to cleaning and conditioning their plumage. During loafing breaks, after each feeding session and especially after diving, grebes clean their plumage conscientiously by spreading oil, from the oil gland on the back, with movements of the head. After oiling, the wings are held in a characteristic pose known as the "Wing Glide".

Grebes usually bathe, typically in sites that are sheltered from the wind, either by diving, or on the surface, wallowing in the water with the body vertical and the rear end submerged. Sunbathing is characteristic of the smaller species and of those that live in cold areas, such as the Junin Flightless, Hooded and Titicaca Flightless Grebes. By doing this they compensate for the loss of body heat and economize on energy. Early in the morning and also late in the evening they rest in the water exposing their backs to the sun, raising their wings slowly and bristling up the back feathers so that the sun's rays can reach the skin.

There are several characteristic postures that grebes adopt throughout the day, particularly while preening and resting. For resting and sleeping they adopt the typical "Pork-pie" posture, with the head pointed downwards, the closed bill mostly hidden in the feathers on the side of the neck, and one or both feet tucked up under the wings, which in turn are covered by the

Grebes' calls, a melodious whistle in the case of the Hooded Grebe, serve not only to proclaim a bird's species and sex, but also its individual identity. Hence, they play an important part in the formation and strengthening of the pair-bond, as well as in maintaining contact between birds in the same family group.

[Podiceps gallardoi, SW Patagonia, Argentina. Photo: Francisco Erize/ Bruce Coleman]

Most of the prey that grebes catch is swallowed under water. The only exceptions are items which, because of their size, or because they are heavily armoured or spiny, are much more difficult to ingest. Such prey is brought up to the surface to be dealt with, as can be seen here with the sizeable catfish which this Pied-billed Grebe has just caught.

[*Podilymbus podiceps podiceps*, Wisconsin, USA. Photo: S. Nielsen/DRK]

flank feathers. Characteristic movements are true yawning, jaw-stretching and direct head-scratching. Equally, on surfacing after a dive, a bird usually shakes its head from side to side to get rid of the water, or touches its throat in order to drain off water from the bill. The method of preening the underparts is especially eye-catching, for the bird rolls over on its side in the water, exposing the white plumage of the belly.

Grebes are essentially diurnal, and generally spend the night in their most recent loafing area, but normal daily activity can continue after sunset, especially when there is a full moon.

Voice

Grebes have a fair vocal repertoire, with marked variations depending on the species and the time of year. Thus, while some highly vocal species have a vocabulary of up to twelve different calls, others appear to be almost silent, even in the breeding season.

Grebes' voices have been described as a variety of barking, trilling, braying, whistling and wailing calls, whether in display, alarm or during aggressive encounters. The most distinctive vocalization is the "Advertising-call", which is particular in each species, and is generally made by individuals when they are alone. This voice announces not only the species, but also the sex, and even individual identity, and it plays an important role in pair formation and re-establishing contact with the bird's mate or chicks. In such cases, the bird that finds itself alone usually calls, and ceases only when visual contact is restored. In the case of the Western Grebe, it is known that each individual has its own call-frequence pattern, and it appears that the differences in the "Advertising-calls", double-noted in Western and single-noted in Clark's Grebes, prevents hybridization between these two, when they coincide.

Except for the genus *Tachybaptus*, grebes are generally silent outwith the breeding season. The most silent species of all is the extraordinarily colonial Hoary-headed Grebe, which has little need to use territorial voices, such as loud cries or trills, as it does not have to defend a territory. This species is only known to have an "Advertising-call" and some other, almost imperceptible sounds.

It has sometimes been thought that those species living in habitats with very dense vegetation are much more vocal. So it has been suggested that the Australasian Grebe is very vocal, and has developed very simple visual signals because it passes its life mostly concealed amongst the vegetation. However, after having studied and compared practically all species of grebes, Fjeldså has concluded that, as with the degree to which courtship is spectacular, there is no general correlation between vocal eminence and habitat. So the White-tufted Grebe is almost as silent as the Hoary-headed Grebe, although it uses habitats similar to those of the Australasian Grebe, while the Titicaca Flightless Grebe is very vocal, lives on open water and has very striking visual signals.

Food and Feeding

The diet of the grebes consists basically of aquatic animals, both fish and other organisms, in particular arthropods. The most piscivorous species, like the Great Crested or Western Grebes, have an elongated body, a slender neck and a long thin bill, while those that feed principally on invertebrates, like the Little or Least Grebes, are smaller, with a short, round body and a fairly short neck and bill (see Morphological Aspects). The grebes include some of the smallest diving birds, which are perfectly adapted to capturing small aquatic arthropods. Nevertheless, within a single species the trophic spectrum can also vary locally, and can be affected by the presence of competitor species. For example, the proportion of arthropods in the diet varies with the season, the site and the feeding method employed. Generally, the consumption of insects and larvae is especially important during the breeding season.

Most grebes feed on a large variety of species of freshwater fish, while in winter they also capture marine species. The list of fish species taken is interminable, largely because of the extensive range of the family and the variety of habitats occupied at different times of year. For example, in the diet of the European population of the Great Crested Grebe, the most studied species, more than 20 species of freshwater fish have been recorded, including both thin-bodied fish, such as eels (*Anguilla anguilla*), and deep-bodied coarse fish, such as roach

The "Rushing Ceremony" is characteristic of the Western Grebe, though it has been recorded in other species too. It is without doubt one of the most spectacular displays not only of grebes, but of all birds. It can be performed variously by two males, a male and a female, or several males and one female.

[*Aechmophorus occidentalis occidentalis*, USA.
Photo: G. Nuechterlein/ Vireo]

(*Rutilus rutilus*), gudgeon (*Gobio gobio*), tench (*Tinca tinca*), minnow (*Phoxinus phoxinus*), trout (*Salmo trutta*) and perch (*Perca fluviatilis*). During the winter, at sea, the spectrum is broadened to include young herring (*Clupea*), pipefish (*Signathus*), blenny (*Zoarces*), sandeels (Ammodytidae), butterfish (*Pholis*), goby (*Gobius*), cod (*Gadus*) and others.

In one day Great Crested Grebes are reckoned to require some 150-200 g of fish, a figure that is probably more or less valid for all the large grebes. The widest prey registered for this species is of 7·5 cm, while the maximum length is of 22 cm, corresponding to thin species like eels. When capturing prey to feed their chicks, birds go for much smaller prey items, and a study of the same species in New Zealand, showed that 84% of the prey offered to the chicks during their first week of life comprised fish 10-55 mm long, while those over 60 mm were rejected. Other items included midge pupae, waterweeds and insects.

Various studies show that species with a longer bill generally feed on larger fish. However, other factors are involved, as shown by the research of T. Piersma, on the IJseelmeer, in the Netherlands, where it was shown that the Horned Grebe, a smaller, shorter-billed species than the Red-necked Grebe, which is also present, captures the largest individuals of the main prey species, such as smelt (*Osmerus eperlanus*). The difficulty in capturing the larger individuals is related to the prey being able to swim faster, so food selection can in some cases be determined more by agility in diving and chasing, in which the Horned Grebe excels, than by the size of bill.

The less piscivorous species feed principally on the following: insects and their larvae, mayflies (Ephemoptera), stoneflies (Plecoptera), dragonflies (Odonata), waterbugs (Hemiptera), beetles (Carabidae, Ditiscidae); molluscs, including small bivalves and univalves, and snails (*Lymnaea*, *Valvata*); crustaceans, especially waterlice (*Asellus*), shrimps (*Gammarus*, *Artemia*), crayfish (*Astacus*) and waterfleas (Entomostraca); amphibians, including tadpoles and frogs; and also some small fish.

Some grebes are specialized for taking certain kinds of prey. The most extreme case is that of the Atitlan Grebe, with up to 56% of its diet made up of the sizeable freshwater crab *Potamocarcinus guatemalensis*. It is thought that its large strong bill and the strong muscles of the head, neck and mandibles were adaptations for capturing and consuming this prey. Even the characteristic large size of this grebe, which allowed it to dive to the necessary depth to capture its prey, could have been, at least in part, an adaptation to this specialized type of diet.

The plant matter that is often found in grebes' stomachs can be consumed both accidentally and intentionally. Seaweeds, stoneworts (Characea) and the leaves, stems and seeds of various aquatic plants have all been recorded.

Grebes generally seek out and chase their prey under the water, although some prey is captured on the surface. This may be by pecking on the surface, for instance to take flying insects, or gleaning amongst the aquatic vegetation, a practice which is more frequent in some species, especially the Black-necked Grebe. The most widely used method under the water is "Divehunting", which consists of swimming below the surface looking for prey, and, once it has been located, chasing it rapidly. Logically, this method is particularly appropriate in still, relatively deep waters, with only scattered patches of vegetation. However, in New Zealand, Great Crested Grebes can feed in rough waters, with waves up to 70 cm high, and poor visibility of under 20 cm. When they feed on the sea, if it is rough, or they are operating in the swell off the coast, they dive in a far more violent fashion than they do in calm waters. In a normal feeding session numerous dives are made with more or less regular short intervals. A feeding spell in the Great Crested Grebe can last for anything from a few minutes, with 5-10 dives separated by breaks of about 10 seconds, to 55 dives in 25 minutes.

However, feeding habits differ somewhat, even between morphologically similar species, and this can be useful for avoiding competition when such species coincide. Clark's Grebe tends to feed in areas further from the shore than the extremely similar Western Grebe. In turn, Clark's shows a far greater preponderance than the Western for making "springing dives" (see Morphological Aspects). These examples indicate that in this case the depth of the water may partition the niche between these two species.

In general, grebes feed alone and well spread out, but they can congregate, if abundant food supplies are found. This happens habitually in the Hoary-headed Grebe, a very gregarious species specialized in feeding on very small arthropods, which constitute an unpredictable, but sometimes abundant source of food. In this case, communal feeding is advantageous for locating the food, and at the same time reducing the risk of predation. Sometimes other, normally less gregarious species also form feeding groups, for instance the Horned Grebe, which can gather in flocks of up to 200 in the USA. This same species has also been seen associating with the Surf Scoter (*Melanitta perspicillata*), and the same feeding behaviour has been registered in the Little Grebe, with Mallards and Eurasian Coots (*Fulica atra*) in Europe, and with Cape Teal (*Anas capensis*) and several other African ducks. When feeding, these other waterbirds rummage in the vegetation, and the small invertebrates that sally forth are easily caught by the grebes, often simply by submerging the head, or even on the surface.

Grebes adapt their feeding times locally. In places where there is a marked variation in the vertical distribution of fish during the day, grebes can restrict their feeding time to the moment when the fish come near the surface. For this reason, the Great Crested Grebes that spend the moulting period at the IJsselmeer, where they depend mainly on smelt, feed basically in the twilight.

As in several other families of birds, small pebbles have been found in the stomachs of some species, such as the Western Grebe, and these are probably swallowed to help grind down food in the gizzard. Grebes are unique, though, in the habit of eating their own feathers, sometimes in large quantities. This is particularly common in the fish-eating species, and they have even been seen to give dowsed feathers to their chicks right from the day they hatch, sometimes even before feeding them for the first time. In general, this habit occupies a fair amount of time, and takes place during loafing breaks, after bathing and oiling. Birds concentrate on the small feathers of the breast, belly, and flanks, although some are also taken from the water. The feathers accumulate in the main compartment of the stomach, where they decompose and turn into a green, spongy, felt-like material, which is mixed with the food, basically fish, making a characteristic feather-ball that lines the gizzard. The balls, whole or in bits, are regurgitated periodically from the stomach in the form of pellets, along with the parts of the prey that are most difficult or impossible to digest, like fish bones and the chitinous hard parts of insects. Pellets have been recorded for the Pied-billed, Horned and Great Crested Grebes. Both the origin and purpose of this behaviour are still a matter of controversy. Apparently, in these primarily piscivorous birds the action of the gizzard is insufficient to crush the swallowed bones. The feather-balls protect the stomach,

wrapping up the fish bones and delaying their digestion, so that the sharp, pointed bones are fairly well dissolved by the time they pass into the intestine. In fact, remains of indigestible parts are hardly ever found in the intestine. Moreover, a feather-pad, formed by a small, more or less digested mass of feathers in the lower chamber of the stomach, blocks the entrance to the intestine, like a pyloric plug, and protects it from the indigestible remains.

Unlike the species that feed on fish, those that are mainly insectivorous, basically those of the genus *Tachybaptus*, do not have to defend themselves against sharp or indigestible objects like fish bones. Therefore, they eat only a small quantity of feathers, and simply regurgitate the inedible remains of the insects and other arthropods. Indeed, the Hoary-headed Grebe, which is specialized in feeding on tiny arthropods, does not swallow feathers. Another advantage of eating feathers is the prevention or minimization of infestations by endoparasites that are swallowed along with the fish. In fact, although this protection is not absolute, in comparison with other fish eaters, grebes generally suffer less from parasitic infestations. Another phenomenon that attracts attention is that some grebes eat their own tapeworms when they defecate them, and they even feed them to their chicks, in spite of the inherent risk of recycling parasites.

Breeding

Breeding is normally seasonal in grebes, especially in the species that live in high latitudes, but most have a lengthy season and are basically opportunists. In this way, the clutch is laid to coincide with the moment when the local conditions of the water level and the emergent vegetation, in which the nest will be built, are ideal to enhance the possibilities of successful breeding. In temperate regions, as pairs have to define and occupy their territories long before they start nesting in the spring, breeding activities are normally initiated during the winter, and in the Red-necked Grebe tentative nest building has occasionally been observed at the height of the winter cold.

During the course of the different phases of the breeding cycle, with the formation of the monogamous pair-bond, nest-site selection, definition of the territory, copulation and finally the rearing of chicks, grebes carry out various highly characteristic ritualized displays, in which the female plays almost as active a role as the male. This behaviour has been studied in detail by various ornithologists, starting with the pioneering research of J. Huxley in 1914 into the Great Crested Grebe. Classic works include those of K. E. L. Simmons on the same species, which established the basis for the description of courtship ceremonies, and of G. L. Nuechterlein on the Western Grebe. Other authors, such as R. W. Storer or J. Fjeldså, have extended the study of breeding behaviour to include most of the grebes of the world, paying special attention to the Andean species.

Many displays appear to originate from aggressive confrontations. They can be interpreted as ritual contests, where the male and female recognize each other individually by sight and by their "Advertising-calls". The female must check her impulse to flee when confronted by the aggressive behaviour of the male and at the same time pacify him, in such a way that the displays prepare, draw together, consolidate and maintain the pair, at the same time controlling, inhibiting and absorbing the aggression. Mutual displays have varying degrees of complication, with the male and female adopting similar roles simultaneously or reciprocally, or exchanging roles with each sex alternately taking the initiative. Nevertheless, in spite of these elaborate ceremonies, the pair-bond is often maintained only during the breeding season.

There are variations in the ritualization and complexity of the displays, so the comparative study of their procedure is of great phylogenetic interest. Normally, in the smaller and less highly ornamented species courtship is more vocal, often with duets, while most individual displays are simple. This is the case with the genera *Tachybaptus*, *Podilymbus*, *Rollandia* and

In grebes copulation occurs out of the water. This photo shows a pair of White-tufted Grebes copulating on the shore, but it is actually more common for birds to copulate on platforms built of water weeds specially for the purpose, or alternatively in the nest itself. At the start of the breeding season, reverse mounting (the female mounting the male) is very common; it is almost indistinguishable from authentic copulation, though it does not, of course, lead to fertilization.

[*Rollandia rolland rolland*, Falkland Is. Photo: Eric & David Hosking]

Poliocephalus, and also of the Great Grebe, an atypical member of the genus *Podiceps* (see Systematics). In the rest of the members of *Podiceps* and in *Aechmophorus*, behaviour is far more elaborate.

Various kinds of behaviour have been described which vary with the species, for example the Great Crested Grebe has five ceremonies, which consist of a series of highly ritualized displays. Generally they are performed after "Advertising-calls" by one partner or the other, or both, and take place in the water, or, in more advanced phases, on platforms that are also used for copulating. One of the most frequent is the "Head-shaking Ceremony", which is carried out to different degrees of intensity, and usually serves as an introduction to other, more elaborate ceremonies. In its most simple form, the two birds station themselves opposite one another, with their necks erect; both are silent, and they shake their heads, either quickly up and down, or slowly from side to side.

Some of the rituals practised by grebes are amongst the most spectacular in the world of birds. One of these, the "Weed Ceremony", is used by the Great Crested Grebe once the pair is already well established, and at the peak phase of sexual motivation. In a show demonstrating the perfect synchronization achieved by the members of the pair, both swim away from each other in an extremely ceremonious manner, with a contact "Twanging-call", until each slowly submerges. After several seconds, both reappear, one after the other, each with a billful of weeds, and they quickly move towards each other, before suddenly rising up vertically, breast to breast, treading water vigorously, in order to keep position, and rocking their heads quickly from side to side, to produce a beautiful dance.

Even more spectacular, if possible, is the "Rushing Ceremony" performed by the Western Grebe, which has also been observed in two species, such as the Horned Grebe. It can be performed by two males, a male and a female, or several males and one female. To the accompaniment of raucous cries and loud splashes, the male and female rush wildly across the water, with their necks bent stiffly, before diving under simultaneously.

Copulation usually takes place out of the water, normally on platforms, which are specially constructed in shallow water by both sexes, using underwater weeds. It involves one bird

going up onto the platform and inviting the other, by lying flat with its neck stretched forward and making intermittent calls. The bird in the water jumps up onto the back of the other, copulates quickly, and returns to the water, passing forwards over the head of its mate, and making typical calls throughout the process. Then the two birds often "Head-shake" together, one in the water and the other on the platform, with their tippets or ruffs splayed. All this sexual activity can start weeks or months before the clutch is laid, and during this period, reverse mounting, the female mounting the male, is very common. It is not authentic, functional mating, and only when the nesting season comes closer does the male do most of the mounting, and true copulation takes place, leading to insemination and ovulation.

During this period, aggression is to the forefront in the territorial behaviour of the grebes, sometimes producing territorial defence displays, chases and even fights, in which the male is the more active. However, seven of the 22 species of grebes almost always nest in colonies (see General Habits), while some that are habitually territorial nesters, like the Great Crested Grebe, occasionally breed in small colonies. Logically, in the colonial species, aggression and antagonistic behaviour are both simplified, but curiously, at least in the genus *Podiceps*, this does not imply an obvious decrease in the aggressive elements of the courtship rituals, which evolved in territorial ancestors, and have been maintained independent of the development of the social structure.

Several of the colonial species sometimes nest alongside other birds, such as terns or gulls. Some well known cases include the Western Grebe with Forster's Tern (*Sterna forsteri*) in North America, the Black-necked Grebe with the Common Black-headed Gull (*Larus ridibundus*) or the Whiskered Tern (*Chlydonias hybridus*) in Europe, and the White-tufted or Silvery Grebes with the Brown-hooded Gull (*Larus maculipennis*) in the wetlands of the *pampas* in southern South America. This type of association is advantageous for the grebes, as the terns and gulls act as aerial sentries, making up for the poor visibility that grebes have from the surface of the water. In fact, grebes react to the alarm calls of terns and gulls by abandoning the nest quickly. Another factor is that the feeding competition between these groups is not strong, as many gulls forage over land, and, in spite of some losses due to predation of eggs and chicks, these small species of gulls are less aggressive than the grebes. In some cases, these mixed colonies are known to have arisen as the result of grebes joining already formed colonies of gulls, and the grebes have even been seen to regulate their breeding procedure, so that they synchronize the laying of their eggs with that of the gulls.

The nest is generally constructed by both sexes, with leaves and bits of stems of aquatic plants. It tends to be partially floating, anchored to a clump of vegetation, but can also be built up from the bottom. In either case, it must always allow easy access to and from the water. Nests on dry land, next to the water, are exceptional and are generally due to a drop in the water level. Occasionally birds prefer not to situate the nest on the front line, but rather in the shelter of a fairly open reedbed, though on occasions nests are clearly placed in open water. The building and maintenance of the nest normally continues during laying and incubation, and in some species the same nest is used for successive clutches.

Although exceptional clutches of one or up to ten eggs have been recorded, grebes normally lay between two and seven eggs, with intervals of one or two days between eggs. The eggs are elongated, and, when freshly laid, are white, cream-coloured, or sometimes pale blue, particularly in the New World species. In all cases they quickly become stained brown.

Normally grebes have one or two broods a year, but the small species occasionally have three. The Hooded Grebe raises the fewest young per year, which is taken to be an adaptation to the harsh conditions of its habitat in Patagonia; it lays two eggs, but gives attention only to one chick, abandoning the second, if the first hatches successfully.

Incubation starts with the laying of the first or second egg, and is performed by both the male and the female, and both

Incubation is carried out more or less equally by the male and the female, and both have brood patches. It starts soon after the first or second egg has been laid, and lasts some 20-30 days, depending on the species. The incubation period of the Hoary-headed Grebe has not yet been determined, but it is believed to last a maximum of 25 days.

[Poliocephalus poliocephalus, Australia. Photo: R. Sclater/NPIAW]

birds have brood patches. It can last from 20 to 30 days. When the adult that is incubating has to leave the nest, before its departure it covers the eggs with material from the nest. This may be to protect them against predators, but it might only be a way of keeping the temperature constant, as it only occurs after the whole clutch has been laid. Grebes can lay replacement clutches after the loss of eggs or chicks.

Hatching is normally asynchronous, and when the last of the eggs has hatched, the adults abandon the nest and carry the chicks on their backs. The still damp hatchlings clamber up to the adult's rear end and thence towards a pocket formed by the wing and the dorsal feathers. While one adult serves as a floating nest, the other dives in search of food for the chicks. Occasionally they even carry the chicks on their backs while diving. The chicks are precocial and semi-nidifugous, and are straight away capable of diving to hide themselves, sometimes remaining submerged with only the bill showing. However, they depend on their parents for both food and heat. In some species the brood splits up, as in the Great Crested Grebe during the sixth week, and each adult takes charge of half the brood, by this stage normally only one chick each. In some species, such as the Black-necked Grebe, the young of different broods join together to form crèches. Juveniles have even been known to feed younger siblings of a later brood and lead them about.

The patch of bare skin on the crown of the recently hatched chick acts as a signal spot to indicate to the parents when it is hungry, alarmed, or needs attention. Normally when the chick is untroubled and satisfied the patch is pale yellow, but it changes colour to bright red, when it is excited or begging for food.

The fledgling period is variable depending on the species, with a range of 44-79 days. The young bird reaches independence about the time of fledging, or sometimes some days later. First breeding occurs at one or two years old.

The floating nest reduces the risk of predation by mammals, although in parts of America raccoons (*Procyon*) can cause severe losses. However, the main predators of nests are birds, such as gulls (*Larus*), crows (*Corvus*), harriers (*Circus*) and coots (*Fulica*). Large fish also take chicks, as in the well known case of pike (*Esox lucius*) in Europe, and even of salmonids, introduced to many lakes all over the world. Overall, although there is a lot of variation depending on particular local condi-

tions, breeding success appears to be quite low in the grebes, with less than one bird fledging per nesting attempt on average. On the other hand, the percentage of pairs that have suffered losses renesting is very high, and this may balance the high losses of eggs and chicks.

Adults are far less vulnerable to predation, although successful captures have been recorded by the Yellow-legged Gull (*Larus cachinnans*) of the Little Grebe, and by the Great Black-backed Gull (*Larus marinus*) of the Horned Grebe, and even of solitary Great Crested Grebes. Although there is very little data available, indications are that grebes are generally long-lived. Only in this way can the Hooded Grebe maintain its populations, with extremely low breeding success estimated at 0·12 young raised per adult per year. The oldest bird known from ringing was a Little Grebe of at least 13 years of age.

Movements

Although grebes fly little and appear to be permanently tied to their aquatic environments, a fair number of species, and especially those populations of high latitudes, are dispersive or truly migratory. The reverse is true for those that live near the equator; they rarely move, although in the Andes some species, such as the Silvery Grebe, do perform altitudinal movements. Nomadic local movements related to particular environmental changes, such as heavy rain, also occur. The Great Crested Grebe makes short term movements to large lakes, reservoirs or the coast in order to moult, and this can be expected in other species too.

When on migration, birds fly overland by night, or swim along the coast during the day. There is little data available from ringing programmes, and the studies of migratory routes are still not well advanced, but in Europe and North America it is supposed that they follow the coastline and to a lesser extent valleys and large rivers, like the Mississippi. As for the distances involved, in the case of the Great Crested Grebe, migrations of 1800-2000 km have been recorded between Denmark or Germany and the Black Sea.

During post-breeding migration there are large concentrations, such as those of the Great Crested Grebe at the

In most grebe species the chicks' down has a striking pattern of stripes which is particularly well defined on the head. Chicks are often carried by the adults in a pocket formed between the wing and the dorsal feathers, where they sometimes receive food from their parents, as can be seen with these Red-necked Grebes. Chicks are often transported in this way when the adult is swimming and even occasionally when it dives.

[*Podiceps grisegena holboellii*, USA. Photo: Bob & Clara Calhoun/Bruce Coleman]

IJsselmeer, in the Netherlands, where more than 20,000 individuals assemble, of which 25% are juveniles. In North America there are also concentrations at staging points involving several thousand Pied-billed, Western and Clark's Grebes, but the most spectacular migrant is the Black-necked Grebe. On Mono Lake, in California, peak numbers of up to 750,000 birds have occurred, and it is believed that at times this staging area for autumn migration, along with that of the Great Salt Lake, in Utah, can hold the entire North American population.

Proof that many species of grebes are better fliers than their habitual behaviour suggests comes in the ease with which they colonize new wetland areas, such as reservoirs. In this the Little Grebe stands out, with its ability to fly over unfavourable terrain if necessary, and explore new areas. The two members of the Australasian genus *Poliocephalus*, the New Zealand and Hoary-headed Grebes, tend to fly more than the rest of the family. Both are highly nomadic, especially the Hoary-headed Grebe, which often effects movements over great distances. In 1975, for example, some birds reached in New Zealand, where they managed to breed in subsequent years.

Not surprisingly, migratory species are reported in unexpected places with a certain regularity, and records of vagrants are especially frequent on islands. For example, stray Little, Horned, Great Crested and Pied-billed Grebes have turned up in the Azores; the Pied-billed Grebe has also been sighted in Britain. On the other hand there are doubts about two museum specimens of the Great Grebe, said to have been obtained in eastern Spain between 1900 and 1910. This South American species moves to coastal waters in winter and has been recorded at least six times in the Falklands, but it is most unlikely to have reached Europe unaided.

Relationship with Man

Members of this family have fascinated man since ancient times, for their appearance, and above all, for their behaviour, so it is not strange that they were amongst the first species to receive the attention of scientists. The courtship of the Great Crested Grebe was the object of the first experiment of co-oper-

ative study in the field of ornithology, directed by J. Huxley from 1920 onwards, with the participation of numerous students and members of ornithological societies, establishing the prototype for studies of this ilk.

But the relationship between man and grebes has not always been gratifying. The Great Crested Grebe, a species which is currently in a very healthy state, was intensely persecuted in the nineteenth century in Europe by waterfowl hunters and by fishermen, who saw it as a competitor, but most of all for its feathers. When the white "grebe-fur", the thick underpelt, became fashionable for ladies during the second half of the nineteenth century, especially for shoulder capes, while muffs were made of the "tippets", this and other species were hunted commercially on a large scale, to satisfy the demands of the millinery trade. Because of this, in 1860 a count in England yielded only 42 pairs. This situation led to combined efforts, and a series of Bird Protection Acts to save the grebes, which means that this species was also one of the first to receive attention from conservationists. In North America, the Western Grebe and to a lesser extent the Black-necked Grebe had the same luck for the same reason; thousands were killed to make coats and capes from their skins, until they were protected in the USA in 1918. Likewise, New Zealand Grebes were protected in mid-Victorian times.

Nowadays, grebes do not generally suffer serious hunting pressure, as their flesh has an unpleasant taste, and hunting on its own is not a cause for alarm. Egg-collecting used to be carried out intensively on Black-necked Grebes, but nowadays it only affects a few species in the Neotropical Region, like the Pied-billed and Least Grebes.

The English name grebe may be derived from *krib*, a Breton word meaning "crest". Other traditional popular names include "water witch" and "helldiver", both apparently related to the speed with which birds submerge.

Status and Conservation

The grebe family contains a high proportion of threatened species, with five out of the 22 recent species red-listed, constituting more than 25% of the total. Two of these, the Colombian and Atitlan Grebes, are almost certainly extinct, while two others, the Rusty and Junin Flightless Grebes, currently considered Endangered, are quickly heading in the same direction. The other currently threatened species, the Madagascar Grebe, is classified as Insufficiently Known, and it would appear to be slightly better off.

Negative factors that are common to several of these cases include the introduction of exotic species of fish, and the loss or degradation of habitat, often due to pollution. Hunting too is significant in some cases, while a less typical factor is hybridization with other grebe species, but each case has its own peculiar characteristics.

The case of the Atitlan Grebe is well documented, thanks to the studies of A. LaBastille, which were initiated in 1960, and show a pathetic course of events leading from a healthy population to total extinction. It appears that the population of this species, which was restricted to the volcanic Lake Atitlán of 130 km^2 in the highlands of Guatemala, was never numerous, with the maximum reckoned to be some 400 birds. Estimates made in 1929 (the year it was discovered), 1936 and 1960 all produced a figure of around 100 pairs. However, between 1958 and 1960 bass (*Micropterus*) were introduced to the lake, in order to lure tourist fishermen. The large fish competed directly with the grebes for crabs, small fish, snails and insects, and notably altered the food chain of the lake, so that, of the 19 species of autochthonous fish present before 1967, there were only six left by 1974. In addition, large bass of up to 12 kg preyed on the Atitlan Grebes' chicks and even larger young, and by 1965 the population had slumped to some 80 birds.

In response to this decline, various conservation measures were put into practice, mainly under the auspices of "Operation Poc", so-called from the local name for the bird. This involved the participation of the government of Guatemala along with various international organizations, such as ICBP, WWF, the Smithsonian Institution and the National Geographic Society. Guards were employed to prevent the theft of eggs and the poaching of waterbirds, which had been banned in 1959, but without the ban being effectively enforced until this time. The collection of reeds for the local weaving industry was also prohibited between May and August, as the reeds were indispensable to the grebe for nesting and shelter, and were proving to be another limiting factor. In 1968 a refuge of two hectares was also created, in which two pairs bred, the first birds to receive real protection, even though the lake had been declared

a National Park in 1955, a fact unknown to the local population. The efforts of the conservationists even managed to halt a large hydro-electric project proposed in 1969 that would have altered the condition of the lake irreversibly.

All these protective measures, and perhaps the adaptation of the bird to the presence of the bass, produced encouraging results, and the census of 1975 yielded 232 birds, which led to the belief that the species was saved. However, another factor seriously threatened the conservation of the habitat of Lake Atitlán. The local Indians sold their lands in the face of the growing demand for holiday homes. Therefore, the number of lakeside summer homes shot up, from 27 in 1960, to 315 in 1980, and the construction of luxury hotels soon followed. Many parts of the shore were destroyed to construct quays, boathouses and beach huts, and wide fringes of lakeside vegetation were eliminated to make the new estates safer and more salubrious. As though this were not enough, in 1976 a disastrous earthquake shook Guatemala and lowered the water level of Atitlán by almost 5 m, causing a notable expanse of the reedbed to dry out. In 1980 it was calculated that areas of shoreline suitable for the Atitlan Grebe had diminished by about 60%, while the population had dropped once more to 130 individuals.

In a last effort to regenerate habitat for the grebes, 75,000 reed bulrushes (*Scirpus*) and cat-tails (*Typha*) were planted, but the programme could not continue, due to the unstable political climate, which led the country into civil war. Sadly, the original promoter of the project, E. Bauer, was murdered in 1982. From this moment, the combination of problems caused by the drop in water level, the incessant destruction of the lake shores for building projects, and the reduction of vigilance and the ensuing lack of control of reed-cutting and hunting, all led to another inevitable decline, and in 1984 only 55 birds were counted.

In the census that was carried out two years later, Pied-billed Grebes were present on the lake. 32 grebes were counted, and 12 of these were captured alive, all of which turned out to be common Pied-billed Grebes, while there were no signs of their having interbred with Atitlan Grebes. In 1987 it was announced that, although one individual might perhaps survive, the Atitlan Grebe as a species was probably extinct. It remains to be ascertained whether the Pied-billed Grebe substituted it, once it had practically disappeared, or the arrival of this flying species was itself the final straw. Being capable of flight, it would probably be better able to adapt to the adverse conditions then affecting

Although adult Little Grebes also carry their chicks about on their backs, the practice is said to be less developed in this species than in the genus Podiceps, and the nest is often used as a resting spot out of the water. In fact, during the week after the hatching of the first chick, all the chicks remain in the nest most of the time, and one adult normally stays in the nest to brood them, whilst the other spends its time bringing the chicks the small items of prey that it captures by diving.

[*Tachybaptus ruficollis ruficollis*, Britain. Photo: J. A. Bailey/Ardea]

the lake, or it might even have hybridized with the last individuals, thus sealing the death sentence on the species.

The case of the Colombian Grebe is much less well known, and the species probably became extinct before it was possible to study its ecology and behaviour, so that it has not even been possible to determine with certainty its status as a separate species from the Black-necked Grebe. During the 1940's the species was assessed as abundant on Lake Tota, in south-east Boyacá, Colombia, and until the early 1950's it was sporadically sighted in various other lakes in the region of the Sabana de Bogotá. In 1968 there were apparently about 300 birds on Lake Tota, but there were only two records in the 1970's, one in 1972, and another in 1977 involving one to three birds. Detailed surveys in 1981 and 1982 did not manage to locate any birds, and the species was reckoned to be extinct.

This extinction has been attributed to the following: competition and predation of chicks by the rainbow trout (*Salmo gairdneri*), introduced to the lake in 1944; hunting, which probably led to the eradication of the last remaining survivors at the end of the 1970's; agricultural pesticides draining from the surrounding land into the lake; and the harvesting of reeds, which probably caused a marked decline in breeding success. However, lately it has been stated that the principal cause was the loss of habitat brought about partly by a drop in the water level of the lake of about one metre, due to a scheme in the 1950's to provide land for agriculture, and partly to the change in the composition of the aquatic plant community from 1960 on, due to a boom in onion-growing around the lake, which resulted in the application of large amounts of fertilizers and minerals. These changes drastically reduced the extent of shallow zones with floating vegetation, where the Colombian Grebe, a foliage gleaner, like the very similar Black-necked Grebe, obtained most of its food. This is thought to have reduced numbers markedly, making the population much more vulnerable to all the other adverse factors. It has even been suggested that the last records of the species, which were not reported first hand, could have been misidentifications, and that the extinction of the Colombian Grebe had already taken place at the beginning of the 1960's.

The population of the Junin Flightless Grebe, confined to Lake Junín in Peru, declined drastically from the several thousand estimated in the 1960's to about 300 in 1978. In the Red Data Book the species was only classed as Rare, but it had slid further to not more than 100 by 1987, and this portends a similar end for this species to that of the Colombian Grebe. In this case, the principal cause of the decline is thought to be the pollution caused by waste from nearby mines, and the regulation of the lake by a hydro-electric power station at the mouth of the lake. In 1969 the vegetation of Lake Junín already appeared to be dyed yellow with the breakdown products of sulphur acids and toxic fumes from the copper mine.

Since 1975 some conservation measures have been implemented: Lake Junín was declared a reserve and the Peruvian government nationalized the mines of Cerro del Pasco, in an attempt to free the lake from the effects of the mines. The use of the lake as a reservoir for Lima, although this led to the promise of an improvement in water quality, caused important periodical fluctuations in the water level, of more than seven metres, with the consequent reduction of suitable habitat for the grebes.

Given the serious situation, it was proposed that this grebe be introduced to one or more nearby lakes, like those of Carhuacayan or Punrun, and in recent years some projects of this type have been carried out, with the approval of the Peruvian government. Thus a small number of birds have already been successfully transported to a nearby lake, although it has been calculated that the other lakes near Lake Junín could not hold more than a maximum of 40 pairs, which would not guarantee the survival of the species.

Another grebe that appears to be on the verge of extinction is the Rusty Grebe, a small species endemic to Madagascar. It is very local and is limited basically to Lake Aloatra, although it has also been sighted in other wetlands fairly nearby. In this case, the principal threat is intensive hybridization with the invading Little Grebe, a species that probably forms the stock from which the Rusty Grebe was derived, after an earlier invasion. In this case the endemic species has clearly not evolved isolating mechanisms that prevent hybridization with the recolonizing Little Grebe. But this is an old problem, as indicated by the the fact that the type specimen was a hybrid, as were up to four others of the original series of 15, with which the species was described in 1929. However, the introduction of

There are few photographs of extinct species, and even fewer with the quality of this portrait of an Atitlan Grebe. The work carried out over almost 30 years by biologist Anne LaBastille has enabled the elaboration of a detailed reconstruction of how this species crashed from a healthy population to almost certain extinction. This comprehensive record constitutes an exceptional case within the history of ornithological research.

[*Podilymbus gigas*, Atitlan Lake, Guatemala. Photo: David Allen]

The Junin Flightless Grebe, endemic to Laguna Chynchaicocha, better known as Lake Junín, is liable to become extinct within the next few years, if its rapid decline is not halted. Numbers have dropped from several thousand in the 1960's to only 200-300 birds by the early 1990's. The slump has apparently come about mainly as a result of pollution and alterations of the water level in connection with a hydroelectric scheme.

[*Podiceps taczanowskii*, Lake Junín, Peru. Photo: M. P. Harris]

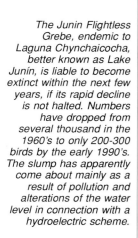

herbivorous fish (*Tilapia*) from 1945 onwards has facilitated the expansion of the Little Grebe, accelerating the process until it has become irreversible. At the end of the 1980's the total population was calculated at not more than 20 pairs, and, although it appears that more birds have recently been sighted in other places, this is not attributed to any recovery of the species, but rather to alteration of the habitat at Lake Aloatra. In fact, the vegetation that the Rusty Grebe uses for nesting in has been reduced by the presence of the *Tilapia*, at the same time as sectors of the lake continue to be transformed for rice cultivation. Furthermore, direct disturbance of the birds, basically through hunting and trapping, continues intensively on this lake.

The same factors that have carried the Rusty Grebe to its critical situation have also been bringing about a continuous decline, during the last 30 years, of the Madagascar Grebe. Thus, the introduction of exotic fish, competition and hybridization with the Little Grebe, and the reduction and alteration of wetlands have all been operating here too, with the difference that this species was originally widespread and common. It was distributed throughout the island, so a much larger population still survives, though its status is much more difficult to evaluate. This explains its present inclusion in the category of Insufficiently Known, given the paucity of studies in the wetlands of Madagascar.

The most surprising and heartening case in the recent history of this family is that of the Hooded Grebe. This species was discovered in 1974 by the Argentinian biologist Mauricio Rumboll, while he was studying the migration of South American wild geese. Initially, a population of 150 birds was located in the Laguna Los Escarchados, at an altitude of 743 m, in a region with an abundance of volcanic lakes in the south of Argentinian Patagonia.

From the moment of its discovery this species has been the object of intense conservationist activity on the part of the Fundación Vida Silvestre Argentina, with the help of the Zoological Society of New York and ICBP. Censuses have been carried out since 1978, and observation hides were constructed on the lakeshore to facilitate study of the birds. In January 1979 Los Escarchados was declared a wildlife reserve.

During the following two years, despite attempts, the Hooded Grebes failed to breed at this site. However, breeding occurred at two neighbouring small lakes, increasing the number of known breeding sites to three. In spite of all this, breeding success was negligible, probably due to the losses caused by Kelp Gulls (*Larus dominicanus*), which prey on the small chicks while the two parents are under the water search-

ing for food. Thus, the decline to 75 birds in 1981 was interpreted as an omen of inexorable extinction, unless there were other sites that still remained undiscovered. This hope was inspired by the fact that the winter quarters of these grebes, when the lakes are frozen over, were unknown.

A second breeding population of 250 birds was indeed discovered at the end of 1981, on a high plateau 120 km to the north of the original colony, and in 1984 the focal point of their distribution was located in the Meseta de Strobel, in the great caldera of Lakes Cardiel and Strobel. This area is formed of 1200 km^2 of lava plateaux, with heavily degraded bunch-grass heaths at 800-1200 m of altitude, and contains 560 small, scattered basaltic lakes and ponds. In 1986 the total population was estimated at 5000 or more individuals, and the species has recently been removed from the Red List.

The other species of grebe are not considered to be globally threatened, although the Titicaca Flightless Grebe was included in the first edition of the Red Data Book, due to its reduced range, limited to the basin of Lake Titicaca. Some species have actually expanded in recent years. This appears to be the case in northern Europe with the Great Crested, Red-necked and Little Grebes; it has been attributed above all to the climate improving during this century, as these species are very sensitive to harsh winters. Also, species which colonize easily have been favoured in some areas by human activities, such as the growth of fish farming, the increase in the number of ponds, gravel pits and reservoirs, where there are no marked fluctuations in water level, and also to the eutrophication of bodies of water with a subsequent increase in cyprinids.

Nevertheless, several consequences of modern human activities have an adverse effect on the conservation of grebes on a worldwide scale. Many local populations have undoubtedly declined because of the drying out or alteration of wetlands, which often involves the destruction of the lakeshore vegetation in which grebes nest. Another important factor is the increasing use of suitable habitat for recreation and water sports, which tend to disturb grebes and often oblige them to abandon the site.

Another alteration of the environment with obvious negative consequences is pollution. In the USA, for example, the decline in some populations of Western and particularly Red-necked Grebes has been put down to pesticides, especially organochlorines and PCB's that diminish breeding success, causing addled eggs or extremely thin eggshells. Pollution can also affect grebes through changes in the aquatic vegetation.

Oil spills, even small, localized ones, can have enormous impact on concentrations of wintering grebes at sea, for example in February 1978 a small oil spill occurred off Scotland, affecting 241 Great Crested Grebes, of which at least 200 died. In the early 1970's, a major oil spill in San Francisco Bay, California, caused the deaths of some 11,000 Western Grebes, which constituted about half of all the birds affected.

Some species become entangled in gill-nets and drown, as happens in winter to the Red-necked and Horned Grebes on the IJsselmeer, or with the Little and Great Crested Grebes in Mediterranean wetlands. For the same reason, the Great Crested Grebe has practically disappeared from some of its former haunts in East Africa since 1950.

The introduction of exotic fish all over the world has already proved disastrous for some species, and it has surely also influenced the status of many local populations of other, more widespread species. Thus, while introductions have favoured colonization by grebes in some cases, in others, especially when the fish in question are salmonids, they represent a threat to the grebes, through competition for food, direct predation of chicks or changes wrought in the aquatic vegetation.

General Bibliography

Borodulina (1977), Butler & Jones (1982), Cracraft (1982), Fjeldså (1978, 1980, 1982a, 1983a, 1985a, 1989a), Gotzman (1965), Harrison (1985), Ingram & Salmon (1941), Korzun (1981), Livezey (1989c), Nudds (1982), Sanders (1967), Sibley & Ahlquist (1972), Sibley & Monroe (1990), Simmons (1962a, 1985), Stegman (1974), Storer (1960, 1963a, 1967b, 1979), Storer *et al.* (1975), Townsend (1924), Vlug & Fjeldså (1990).

1

2

3

4

5

6

7

8

9

10

11

12

13

14

ssp *cristatus*

ssp *infuscatus*

15

16

17

ssp *occipitalis*

ssp *juninensis*

18

19

20

21

22

PLATE 11

inches 8

cm 20

Genus *TACHYBAPTUS* Reichenbach, 1853

1. Little Grebe

Tachybaptus ruficollis

French: Grèbe castagneux **German**: Zwergtaucher **Spanish**: Zampullín Común
Other common names: Common/Red-throated (Little) Grebe, Dabchick

Taxonomy. *Colymbus ruficollis* Pallas, 1764, Holland.
Formerly included in *Podiceps*. Forms superspecies with *T. novaehollandiae* and *T. rufolavatus*, both of which have been considered races of present species. Extensive hybridization with latter, and occasionally with *T. pelzelnii*. Validity of race *vulcanorum* doubtful. Nine subspecies recognized.
Subspecies and Distribution.
T. r. ruficollis (Pallas, 1764) - Europe E to Urals, NW Africa.
T. r. iraquensis (Ticehurst, 1923) - Iraq, SW Iran.
T. r. capensis (Salvadori, 1884) - Africa S of Sahara, Madagascar; Caucasus through India and Sri Lanka to Burma.
T. r. poggei (Reichenow, 1902) - SE & NE Asia, Hainan, Taiwan, Japan and S Kuril Is.
T. r. philippensis (Bonnaterre, 1791) - N Philippines.
T. r. cotabato (Rand, 1948) - Mindanao (SE Philippines).
T. r. tricolor (G. R. Gray, 1861) - Sulawesi to Seram and N New Guinea; Lombok to Timor.
T. r. vulcanorum (Rensch, 1929) - Java to Timor.
T. r. collaris (Mayr, 1945) - NE New Guinea to Bougainville I (Solomon Is).

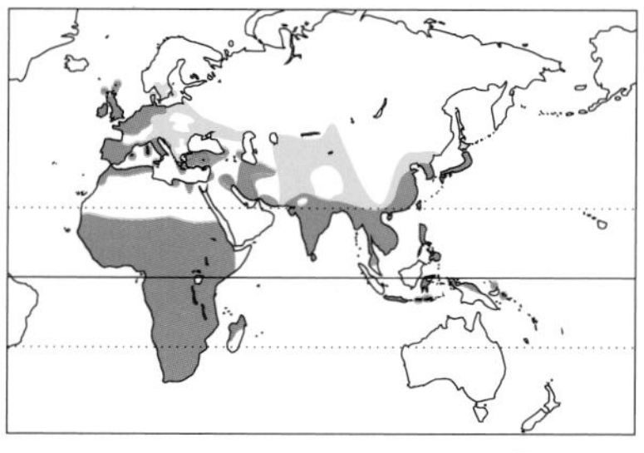

Descriptive notes. 25-29 cm; 130-236 g. As in most grebes, female marginally smaller. Chestnut throat, cheeks and foreneck separates from other *Tachybaptus*. Iris red-brown, yellow in E Asia. Non-breeding adult paler, especially on throat and foreneck, which lack chestnut. Juvenile similar to non-breeding adult, but head striped black and whitish. Races separated mainly on size, amount of white in secondaries; also slight differences in coloration.
Habitat. Wide range of wetlands, normally small and shallow, including small lakes, ponds, canals; also sheltered bays, vegetated shores of larger lakes and reservoirs. Outwith breeding season, occurs on more open waters; rarely on coast, in estuaries protected from large waves.
Food and Feeding. Mainly insects and larvae, especially mayflies, stoneflies, waterbugs, beetles, flies, caddisflies and dragonfly larvae; also molluscs, crustaceans and amphibians, mainly young, but also adults, e.g. small frogs, occasionally newts (*Triturus*); some small fish (*Cottus*, *Cyprinus*, *Gobio*). Largest prey are fish of up to 11 cm. Feeds mainly by diving for 10-25 seconds to depth of 1 m, rarely 2 m; also swims along with head and neck submerged or picks prey directly off emergent vegetation or water surface. Sometimes associates with ducks and coots, which stir vegetation and flush small invertebrates.
Breeding. Season very variable, depending on growth of emergent vegetation and water level: Feb-Sept in W Palearctic, with peak Apr-Jul; May-Jul, occasionally Oct-Feb in Japan; recorded all months in tropical Africa. Solitary; nest is floating platform of aquatic plants anchored to submerged vegetation. Usually 4 eggs (2-7); 2 broods, possibly 3 in warmer regions; incubation 20-25 days; chicks have dark down with pale stripes, paler below; fledging 44-48 days. Success of hatchlings to fledging 40% in Europe; probably less than 1 young reared per nest in Africa. Oldest ringed bird 13 years old.
Movements. Resident, dispersive or migratory, depending on winter temperatures of breeding grounds. Some birds winter in tidal estuaries and sheltered bays, but generally far less common in such habitats than other grebes. Frequent records outwith main range, even in unsuitable habitat, indicate considerable capacity for aerial reconnaissance and colonization of new areas. Nominate race recorded in N Norway, Azores, Madeira and Canaries.
Status and Conservation. Not globally threatened. Widespread and common in most of range. Well studied areas in Europe show fluctuations in numbers, related mainly to winter conditions: marked decline in Britain following cold winter of 1962/63, and similarly in Netherlands after that of 1984/85; increase in Scandinavia attributed to amelioration of climate during 20th century. Population of Britain and Ireland estimated at 9000-18,000 pairs in mid-1970's, with little evidence of subsequent change. Mid-winter counts in 1991 yielded 8450 in Kenya, 23,676 in India, 1359 in Pakistan, and 1035 in Japan. Some island populations may be very small; race *collaris* may be at risk. Negative effects of transformation of wetlands by destruction, pollution or recreational use offset by construction of man-made ponds and reservoirs, leading to expansion of species in many areas, e.g. E and S Africa. In Madagascar has benefited from introduction of herbivorous fish, to clear detriment of the two endemic species.
Bibliography. Ahlén (1966), Ali & Ripley (1978), Bandorf (1968, 1970), Bauer & Glutz von Blotzheim (1966), Becuwe (1971), Beissmann (1984), Benson (1971), Brazil (1991), Brichetti (1979), Brown *et al*. (1982), Broekhuysen (1973), Calvario & Sarrocco (1988), di Carlo & Laurenti (1988), Cheng Tso-hsin (1987), Coates (1985), Cramp & Simmons (1977), Dejonghe (1978), Dementiev & Gladkov (1951b), Etchécopar & Hüe (1978), Folkestad (1977), Fukuda (1986), Gilliéron (1974), Gyllin (1965), Hartley (1937), Ilicev & Flint (1985), Jacob (1982), Langrand (1990), Leuzinger (1966), Lippens (1983), Maclean (1985), Mann *et al*. (1987), Marchant *et al*. (1990), Medway & Wells (1976), Mester (1959), Paz (1987), Penry (1975), Pinto (1983), Rabosée (1983), Reichholf (1988), Reverdin & Géroudet (1979), Roberts (1991), Sackl (1982), Selous (1915), Sermet (1968), Simmons (1968a), Skead (1977d), Smythies (1986), Vinicombe (1982), White & Bruce (1986), Wood (1949).

2. Australasian Grebe

Tachybaptus novaehollandiae

French: Grèbe australasien **German**: Australischer Zwergtaucher **Spanish**: Zampullín Australiano
Other common names: Austral(as)ian (Little)/Black-throated Grebe, Dabchick

Taxonomy. *Podiceps novae Hollandiae* Stephens, 1826, New South Wales.
Formerly included in *Podiceps*. Forms superspecies with *T. ruficollis* and *T. rufolavatus*. Recently considered race of former, but breeding overlap in N New Guinea with no hybridization recorded. Validity of subspecies *timorensis* doubtful. Seven subspecies normally recognized.
Subspecies and Distribution.
T. n. novaehollandiae (Stephens, 1826) - Australia, Tasmania, New Zealand, S New Guinea.
T. n. leucosternos (Mayr, 1931) - Vanuatu and New Caledonia.
T. n. rennellianus (Mayr, 1931) - Rennell I (Solomon Is).
T. n. javanicus (Mayr, 1943) - Java.
T. n. timorensis (Mayr, 1943) - Timor.
T. n. fumosus (Mayr, 1943) - Sangir and Talaud Is (off NE Sulawesi).
T. n. incola (Mayr, 1943) - N New Guinea.

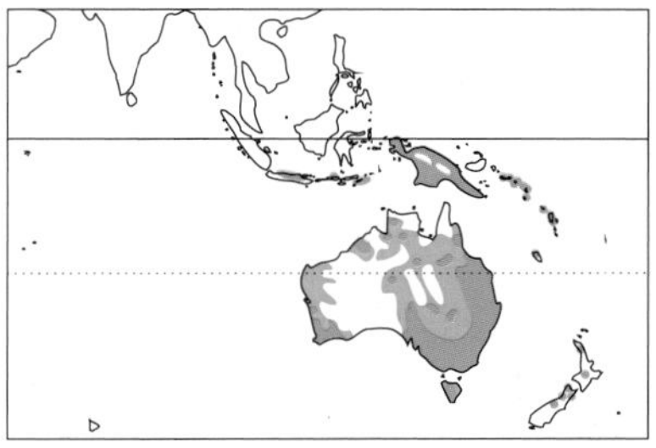

Descriptive notes. 23-27 cm; 100-230 g. Similar to *T. ruficollis*, but chestnut restricted to sides of upper neck and up behind eye; bare skin around gape yellower; iris orangish yellow. Non-breeding adult lacks chestnut; cheeks and foreneck whitish. Juvenile similar to non-breeding adult, but head and neck striped black and white. Races separated on slight differences in size and coloration.
Habitat. Wide range of water bodies, mainly freshwater and permanent or semi-permanent; often on temporary floodwaters; typically found on small reservoirs at farms. Especially during breeding, prefers vegetated shores.
Food and Feeding. Mainly small fish (*Philypnodon grandiceps*, *Gambusia affinis*, *Hypseleotris klunzingeri*), freshwater molluscs, aquatic insects and crustaceans. Catches prey with deep dives and surface chases; sometimes associates with ducks, coots and moorhens, capturing invertebrates that they flush.
Breeding. Season prolonged, laying Aug-Apr, due to opportunistic breeding on temporary waters; on permanent waters, mostly spring, laying Sept-Nov (SE Australia). Solitary; nest is floating platform of plant matter. Usually 4-5 eggs (1-9); 2 or 3 broods per season; incubation c. 23 days; chicks have dark brown down with pale stripes on upperparts, and white and grey-brown underparts; fledging c. 8 weeks. Breeding success thought to be relatively low.
Movements. Poorly known. Possibly resident in E and SW Australia, migratory in N and dispersive in arid interior; in very dry years, some birds move towards coast. Recent colonization of New Zealand and rapid occupation of temporory water bodies inland indicate extensive movements, with long distance flights, probably at night. Ringing records show movements of up to 338 km. Vagrant to Admiralty Is (Bismarck Archipelago) and Moluccas.
Status and Conservation. Not globally threatened. Generally common in Australia, where apparently stable. Small population in Tasmania, with less than 10 adults reported annually in 1972-1988. Small breeding population established in New Zealand during early 1970's, apparently now in decline. Common in New Guinea, with 264 censused in Papua New Guinea, Jan 1991. Rare in Java (except at Rakukak, where common) and Bali; status uncertain in Lesser Sundas. Much more widespread in Vanuatu than previously thought. Island races *rennellianus*, *javanicus*, *timorensis* and *fumosus* may have very small populations, and thus potentially at risk, especially *fumosus*, which may survive only with very small population in crater lake of Mt Awu, N Sangir I. In Australia, some local declines or extinctions due to human modifications of wetlands with e.g. drainage, increased salinity, exploitation of underground water supplies; however, widespread creation of artificial wetlands has undoubtedly benefited species.
Bibliography. Ashby (1933), Beehler *et al*. (1986), Bregulla (1992), Chambers (1989), Chance (1969), Clarke (1966), Coates (1985), Hannecart & Letocart (1983), Hobbs (1959), Lane (1978), Lauder & Murray (1978), Littlejohns (1936), Lyle (1973), Marchant *et al*. (1989), Marchant & Higgins (1990), Mayr (1945), Miller (1973), Pringle (1985), Schodde & Tidemann (1988), Sibson (1982), Slater (1987), Walters (1979), White & Bruce (1986), Wiegant & van Helvoort (1987).

3. Madagascar Grebe

Tachybaptus pelzelnii

French: Grèbe malgache **German**: Madagaskarzwergtaucher **Spanish**: Zampullín Malgache
Other common names: Madagascar Little/Pelzeln's Grebe, Madagascar Dabchick

Taxonomy. *Podiceps pelzelnii* Hartlaub, 1861, Madagascar.
Formerly included in *Podiceps*. Known to have hybridized with *T. ruficollis*. Monotypic.
Distribution. Madagascar occurring throughout island.

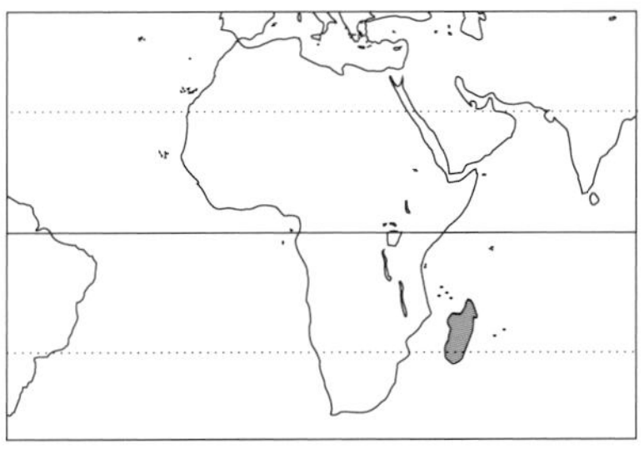

Descriptive notes. 25 cm. Characteristic combination of whitish throat and foreneck separated from dark cap and hindneck by reddish band; bill pale. Non-breeding adult duller and paler with less contrasted pattern. Juvenile resembles non-breeding adult, with irregular greyish brown striping on head and neck.
Habitat. Permanent or temporary water bodies, mainly freshwater, preferably with abundant aquatic vegetation, especially waterlilies (*Nymphaea*). Recorded on running water.
Food and Feeding. Small fish, but less piscivorous than *T. ruficollis* and *T. rufolavatus*; aquatic insects form important part of diet; also known to take crustaceans, at least occasionally.
Breeding. Mainly end of rains (Feb-Apr), but also spring (Aug-Oct). Nests may be close to each other; floating platforms of aquatic vegetation. 3-4 eggs.
Movements. Dispersive, when water bodies dry out or markedly reduced in size. Groups of over 150 birds recorded on L Ihotry in Aug 1983.
Status and Conservation. INSUFFICIENTLY KNOWN. In process of continuous, generalized decline, first noted in early 1960's; in early 1970's still considered common through most of Madagascar, though rare in area of Antananarivo, due to water pollution. At present is more numerous in W and N and on High Plateau. In 1988 recorded within six protected areas. Main threats are reduction of habitat to make way for rice fields and fish farms, and introduction of

On following pages: 4. Rusty Grebe (*Tachybaptus rufolavatus*); 5. Least Grebe (*Tachybaptus dominicus*); 6. Pied-billedGrebe (*Podylimbus podiceps*); 7. Atitlan Grebe (*Podylimbus gigas*); 8. White-tufted Grebe (*Rollandia rolland*); 9. Titicaca Flightless Grebe (*Rollandia microptera*); 10. Hoary-headed Grebe (*Poliocephalus poliocephalus*); 11. New Zealand Grebe (*Poliocephalus rufopectus*); 12. Great Grebe (*Podiceps major*); 13. Red-necked Grebe (*Podiceps grisegena*); 14. Great Crested Grebe (*Podiceps cristatus*); 15. Horned Grebe (*Podiceps auritus*); 16. Black-necked Grebe (*Podiceps nigricollis*); 17. Colombian Grebe (*Podiceps andinus*); 18. Silvery Grebe (*Podiceps occipitalis*); 19. Junin Flightless Grebe (*Podiceps taczanowskii*); 20. Hooded Grebe (*Podiceps gallardoi*); 21. Western Grebe (*Aechmophorus occidentalis*); 22. Clark's Grebe (*Aechmophorus clarkii*).

exotic fish: herbivorous species (*Tilapia melanopleura*, *T. zillii*) cause notable reduction of aquatic vegetation, favouring expansion of more piscivorous *T. ruficollis* and resultant competition and hybridization; predatory black bass (*Micropterus salmoides*) competes with species for food and takes chicks. Evaluation of current status required; conservation measures should probably include protection and maintenance of network of lakes and ponds with lush vegetation where introduction of exotic fish must be avoided.

Bibliography. Appert (1971a), Benson (1971), Benson *et al.* (1976), Collar & Andrew (1988), Collar & Stuart (1985), Dee (1986), Delacour (1933), Fjeldså (1983b), Langrand (1990), Milon *et al.* (1973), Rand (1936), Salvan (1971, 1972a, 1972b), Voous & Payne (1965).

4. Rusty Grebe

Tachybaptus rufolavatus

French: Grèbe roussâtre **German**: Delacourzwergtaucher **Spanish**: Zampullín del Aloatra
Other common names: Aloatra/Delacour's Little Grebe

Taxonomy. *Podiceps rufolavatus* Delacour, 1932, Lake Alaotra.
Formerly included in *Podiceps*. Forms superspecies with *T. novaehollandiae* and *T. ruficollis*. Sometimes considered race of latter, and intensive hybridization currently occurring. Monotypic.
Distribution. L Aloatra and immediate vicinity, NC Madagascar.

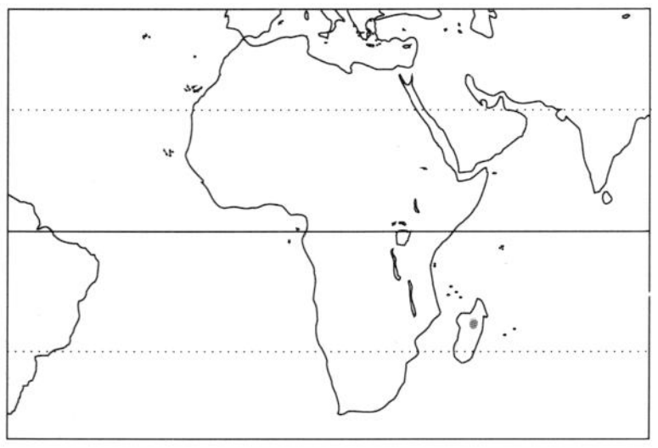

Descriptive notes. 25 cm. Differs from *T. pelzelnii* in throat and foreneck pale with cinnamon wash, mottled underparts, pale iris and dark bill. Non-breeding adult has paler, browner upperparts, with more mottling on pale parts of plumage. Juvenile as non-breeding adult, with dark patches on side of neck.
Habitat. L Aloatra is large but shallow lake; shores originally covered with dense vegetation, predominantly papyrus and reeds; numerous patches covered with waterlilies.
Food and Feeding. Almost exclusively fish.
Breeding. Season apparently variable: found breeding in Apr-Jun 1929; and in Jan-Mar 1960. No further information available.
Movements. Presumed strongly sedentary due to short wing and virtual restriction to L Aloatra. Increasingly recorded on other lakes and ponds of High Plateau in recent years implying some mobility, though movements may be caused by serious habitat alterations at L Aloatra. Doubtful records from further afield, in W and S Madagascar; could refer to hybrids with *T. ruficollis*.
Status and Conservation. ENDANGERED. In continuous decline since discovered in 1929; presently in apparently irreversible slide towards extinction due to hybridization with *T. ruficollis*. Total population reckoned scarcely to exceed 20 pairs in 1990. Process of hybridization, already at work when species described, has apparently intensified since 1945, when herbivorous fish (*Tilapia*) introduced to L Aloatra, favouring increased immigration of highly mobile *T. ruficollis*, with more widespread hybridization. Further threats include increased cultivation of rice in area and intensive hunting and trapping. Recently recorded at other sites; interpreted by some as expansion but more likely due to alteration of habitat at L Aloatra. Apparently doomed in wild; captive breeding programme might offer partial solution, but only possible if sufficient number of "pure" individuals survive; reintroduction would be pointless at present.

Bibliography. Benson (1971), Benson *et al.* (1976), Collar & Andrew (1988), Collar & Stuart (1985), Dee (1986), Delacour (1933), Fjeldså (1983b), King (1978/79), Langrand (1990), Milon *et al.* (1973), Rand (1936), Salvan (1971, 1972a, 1972b), Vincent (1966), Voous & Payne (1965), Wilmé (1990), Young & Smith (1989).

5. Least Grebe

Tachybaptus dominicus

French: Grèbe dominicain **German**: Schwarzkopftaucher **Spanish**: Zampullín Macacito
Other common names: American/Least Dabchick

Taxonomy. *Colymbus dominicus* Linnaeus, 1766, Dominica = Santo Domingo.
Sometimes included in *Podiceps*, less often in *Poliocephalus*. Alternatively separated in monospecific genus *Limnodytes*. Subspecies *brachyrhynchus* synonymous with *speciosus*; birds from W Ecuador sometimes placed in separate race *eisenmanni*. Four subspecies normally recognized.
Subspecies and Distribution.
T. d. dominicus (Linnaeus, 1766) - N Caribbean, from Cozumel I (off SE Mexico) to Virgin Is and N to Bahamas.
T. d. brachypterus (Chapman, 1899) - WC Mexico and S Texas S to Panama.
T. d. bangsi (van Rossem & Hachisuka, 1937) - S Baja California.
T. d. speciosus (Lynch Arribálzaga, 1877) - S America, S to N Argentina and S Brazil.

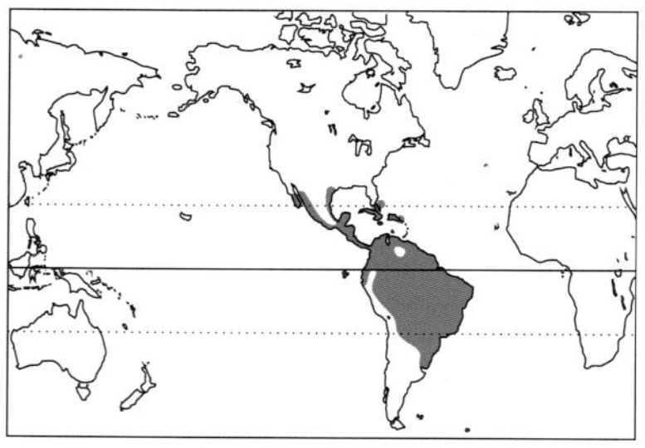

Descriptive notes. 21-26 cm; 116-130 g. Unmistakable, with fairly uniform greyish head and neck; yellow iris can be pale. Non-breeding adult has chin and throat white and pale flanks. Juvenile resembles non-breeding adult, with irregular stripes on sides of head.
Habitat. Wide range of inland bodies of fresh water, including lakes, pools, ponds, backwaters and roadside ditches, with special preference for breeding on small temporary waters. Generally occupies wetlands with abundant vegetation, sometimes almost completely overgrown. Breeding recorded up to 2700 m in W Andes of Colombia.
Food and Feeding. Generalist. Mainly larvae and adults of aquatic insects, especially beetles, true bugs and dragonfly larvae; also ants, spiders, crustaceans, tadpoles, frogs, small fish and some algae. Forages by diving; often picks insects or other food items off vegetation or surface of water. Opportunistic feeding habits related to adaptation to breeding on small, temporary water bodies, with limited invertebrate fauna.
Breeding. Throughout year, depending on local conditions: in Texas laying recorded all months, with peak Apr-Aug. Solitary, but occasionally loosely colonial; nest is floating platform of aquatic plants in shallow water, often anchored to submerged vegetation. Normally 4-6 eggs (1-10); 2 broods per season, possibly 3, or occasionally more; incubation c. 21 days; chicks have blackish brown down with white stripes on upperparts and white underparts. Breeding success apparently high, though no figures available.
Movements. Mainly sedentary, with local dispersal when pools dry out. Flies more readily than other grebes, and rapidly colonizes temporary pools and new wetlands. Outwith breeding season occurs on larger water bodies, forming small flocks; not necessarily family groups.
Status and Conservation. Not globally threatened. Often local or very local, but has extensive range and apparently quick to adapt to environmental changes, especially in water level. No population estimates available. Uncommon and local in S USA, at N limit of range. Not normally hunted for food or sport, though locally suffers some egg-collecting.

Bibliography. Belton (1984), Biaggi (1983), Blake (1977), Cottam & Knappen (1939), Fjeldså (1981b), Fjeldså & Krabbe (1990), Gross (1949), Hilty & Brown (1986), James (1963), Jenni (1969), Johnsgard (1987), Levy (1959), Lowery & Newman (1950), Monroe (1968), Palmer (1962), de la Peña (1986), Pinto (1964), Ridgely & Gwynne (1989), Ruschi (1979), de Schauensee & Phelps (1978), Scott & Carbonell (1986), Short (1975), Sick (1984), Slud (1964), Stiles & Skutch (1989), Storer (1975, 1976), Stott & Selsor (1960), Terres (1980), Voous (1983), Weller (1967a), Wetmore (1965), Zimmermann (1957).

Genus *PODILYMBUS* Lesson, 1831

6. Pied-billed Grebe

Podilymbus podiceps

French: Grèbe à bec bigarré **German**: Bindentaucher **Spanish**: Zampullín Picogrueso

Taxonomy. *Colymbus podiceps* Linnaeus, 1758, South Carolina.
Forms superspecies with *P. gigas*, with which may have hybridized. Three subspecies recognized.
Subspecies and Distribution.
P. p. antillarum Bangs, 1913 - Greater and Lesser Antilles.
P. p. podiceps (Linnaeus, 1758) - S & C Canada S to Panama; winters S USA, C America, West Indies.
P. p. antarcticus (Lesson, 1842) - S America, from E Panama S to SC Chile and SC Argentina.

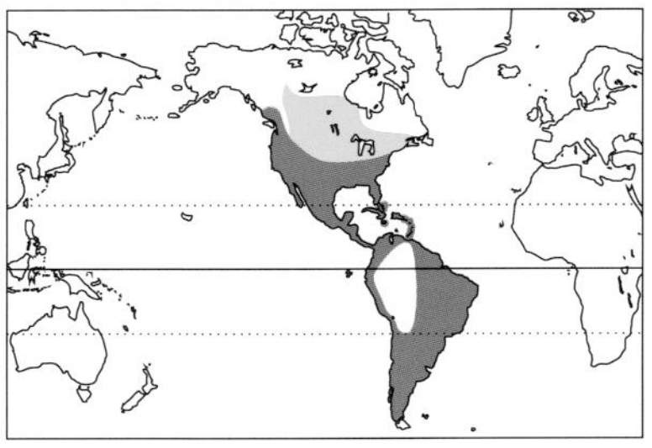

Descriptive notes. 30-38 cm; 339-458 g. Black throat. Overall coloration fairly variable. Female has less conspicuous pattern. Heavy build, especially of head and bill, distinctive; separates from all but *P. gigas*, which is considerably larger and darker. Non-breeding adult has whitish throat. Juvenile as non-breeding adult, with irregular striping on sides of head. Races very similar; *antarcticus* larger.
Habitat. During breeding, mainly shallow, stagnant fresh waters, marshy ponds, lakes, slow-flowing stretches of rivers. Prefers sites with abundant vegetation both emergent and along shores, with small patches of open water. Commonly breeds up to 3100 m in E Andes of Colombia. On migration and outside breeding season occurs on more exposed waters, including brackish waters along coast.
Food and Feeding. Opportunist. Wide variety of small aquatic insects, especially bugs, beetles and dragonfly larvae; also crustaceans, e.g. shrimps, crayfish and crabs, molluscs, amphibians and fish. Fish include heavy-bodied, armoured and spined fishes, up to 12 cm long. Locally leeches can be main prey during breeding. Normally forages by means of short dives averaging 7·58 seconds; related to fact that most prey is slow-moving, and can be captured quickly.
Breeding. Mainly May-Sept in N; Sept-Dec in S; all year round in tropical areas. Solitary; nest is fairly solid platform of aquatic vegetation anchored to reeds, rushes or bushes, sometimes built up from bottom. Usually 4-7 eggs (2-10); multiple-brooded, especially in tropics; incubation 21-27 days; chicks have black down with white stripes, paler below; fledging c. 35 days. Sexual maturity recorded at 13 months old; estimated hatching success 85%, with 37% mortality of hatched young before fledging (N America).
Movements. Mainly sedentary. Populations of extreme N move S, wintering S to Baja California, and C America. Most movement by night, alone or in pairs; concentrations of up to 20,000 birds occasionally recorded at Salton Sea, California, in Nov. Vagrant to Hawaii, N Alaska, Bermuda, Azores and W Europe; race *antarcticus* recorded on Grenada (Lesser Antilles).
Status and Conservation. Not globally threatened. Ubiquitous and very adaptable, at least in N America, where is most common grebe after *P. nigricollis*; less studied but equally common throughout much of Neotropical range. Partial census in Jul 1990 yielded 122 in Chile and 99 in Argentina; estimated 150-200 pairs at L Tota, Colombia, in 1982. Avoids open ocean, so not vulnerable to oil spills. Not normally hunted, but in parts of tropics suffers heavy pressure from egg-collectors; eggs often collected for sale.

Bibliography. Arnold (1989, 1990), Belton (1984), Biaggi (1983), Blake (1977), Bleich (1975), Borrero (1971), Cramp & Simmons (1977), Chabreck (1963), Davis *et al.* (1984), Deusing (1939), Faaborg (1976), Fjeldså (1981b), Fjeldså & Krabbe (1990), Forbes, M.R.L. (1986, 1987), Forbes & Ankney (1987, 1988a, 1988b), Forbes *et al.* (1989), Fugle & Rothstein (1977), Glover (1953), Haverschmidt (1968), Hilty & Brown (1986), Johnsgard (1987), Johnson (1965), Kirby (1976), Ladhams *et al.* (1967), Leck (1971), Mather (1967), McAllister & Storer (1963), Monroe (1968), Nores & Yzurieta (1980), Otto (1983), Otto & Strohmeyer (1985), Palmer (1962), de la Peña (1986), Pinto (1964), Prytherch (1965), Ridgely & Gwynne (1989), Ryan & Heagy (1980), de Schauensee & Phelps (1978), Scott & Carbonell (1986), Sealy (1978), Sick (1984), Simmons (1969), Slud (1964), Stiles & Skutch (1989), Storer (1961, 1976b), Terres (1980), Voous (1983), Wetmore (1949, 1965), Zusi & Storer (1969).

7. Atitlan Grebe

Podilymbus gigas

French: Grèbe du Lac Atitlan **German**: Atitlantaucher **Spanish**: Zampullín del Atitlán
Other common names: Giant (Pied-billed) Grebe

Taxonomy. *Podilymbus gigas* Griscom, 1929, Panajachel, north shore of Lake Atitlán, Guatemala; altitude 5,300 feet.
Sometimes considered race of *P. podiceps*, with which forms superspecies; hybridization may have occurred. Monotypic.
Distribution. L Atitlán, SW Guatemala (probably extinct).

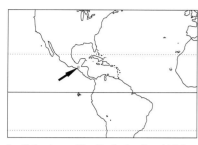

Descriptive notes. 42-52·5 cm. Browner with less grey than *P. podiceps*; bill whiter. Juvenile similar, with pale stripes on sides of head and neck.

Habitat. L Atitlán: waters near shore with thick emergent vegetation, especially beds of rushes, reeds and cat-tails.

Food and Feeding. Mainly fish up to 13 cm long; also insects, snails and crabs (*Potamocarcinus guatemalensis*). Powerful bill and strong muscles of head, neck and bill are adaptations to capture of crabs; *P. guatemalensis* abundant in lake before introduction of bass, and was probably main prey item. Prey caught by diving to considerable depths, for which large size important; dive averages of 34·9 seconds for males, and 27·1 for females, with respective maxima of 90 and 52 seconds. Juveniles recorded foraging at surface, picking hellgrammite and aphids off reeds.

Breeding. Starts Mar, with peak laying in Apr; nesting possibly throughout year on occasions. Solitary; nest is compact floating platform of aquatic vegetation always well anchored to submerged plants. 1-5 eggs; chicks have black down with white stripes, paler below; independent at 10-12 weeks. Estimated 1·36 young per brood to independence, implying survival rate of c. 47%.

Movements. Sedentary; practically flightless.

Status and Conservation. Almost certainly EXTINCT. CITES I. Maximum estimate of total population c. 400 birds in 1929; c. 100 pairs counted in 1960. Introduction of bass (*Micropterus*) to L Atitlán in 1958-1960 probably responsible for slump to c. 80 birds in 1965, with bass competing for food and taking chicks. Several protective measures (see page 185) and perhaps adaptation of grebes to presence of bass led to spectacular recovery with 232 birds counted in 1975. Destruction of lake shore and its vegetation, due to intensive urbanization of shores in 1960's and 1970's, aggravated by earthquake in 1976 as water level dropped by c. 5 m. In 1980 only 130 birds counted and suitable lake shore breeding habitat reckoned to have decreased by c. 60%; at same time exploitation of reeds and hunting became uncontrolled, and all factors forced species into irreversible decline. Only 55 birds counted in 1984; in 1986 *P. podiceps* observed on lake, since when species not definitely recorded. Uncertain whether *P. podiceps* responsible for disappearance of species due to competition or hybridization; may simply have substituted it, when extinction imminent. See page 185.

Bibliography. Blake (1977), Clark (1968), Collar & Andrew (1988), Diamond *et al.* (1987), Fisher *et al.* (1969), Griscom (1932), Hamilton (1970), Hunter (1988), King (1978/79), LaBastille (1965, 1969, 1974, 1978, 1983a, 1983b, 1984, 1990a, 1990b, 1992), LaBastille & Bowes (1962), LaBastille *et al.* (1973), Land (1970), Livezey (1989), Polunin (1969), Powers & LaBastille (1967), Prytherch & Everett (1988), Vincent (1966), Wetmore (1941), Zusi & Storer (1969).

Genus *ROLLANDIA*   Bonaparte, 1856

8. **White-tufted Grebe**
Rollandia rolland

French: Grèbe de Rolland   **German**: Rollandtaucher   **Spanish**: Zampullín Pimpollo
Other common names: Rolland's/Falkland Grebe (*rolland*); Chilean Grebe (*chilensis*)

Taxonomy. *Podiceps Rolland* Quoy and Gaimard, 1824, Falkland Islands.
Sometimes included in *Podiceps*. Mainland races often considered to form a separate species (*R. chilensis*). Three subspecies recognized.

Subspecies and Distribution.
R. r. morrisoni (Simmons, 1962) - C Peru.
R. r. chilensis (Lesson, 1828) - NW Peru and SE Brazil S to Cape Horn; winters on coast, some S birds moving N to Paraguay and S Brazil.
R. r. rolland (Quoy & Gaimard, 1824) - Falkland Is.

Descriptive notes. 24-36 cm. Only grebe with tuft of white feathers on head and rest of head and neck black; greenish gloss. Non-breeding adult browner, with white throat and underparts. Juvenile as non-breeding adult, with irregular blackish striping on cheeks. Races separated on size; nominate very large and almost flightless.

Habitat. Breeds on marshy ponds, lakes, roadside ditches, temporary pools and slow-flowing rivers. Prefers shallow water with mosaic of aquatic vegetation and open patches, but also frequent along thickly vegetated shores of more open lakes; not infrequent in coastal areas, e.g. fjords in extreme S. Generally common in *puna* at 3500-4500 m.

Food and Feeding. Generalist feeder: mainly fish, but also takes wide variety of largish arthropods. Normally feeds from surface, with head submerged; feeding dives average 18 seconds, rather sluggish.

Breeding. Mainly Sept to Jan, but at high altitudes delayed by up to 2 months, lasting until Mar; however, laying commonly occurs all year round, especially in N. Usually regarded as solitary and territorial, but colonies have been found; nest is small floating platform of aquatic plants anchored to adjacent vegetation. Normally 2 eggs (1-3), but up to 6 recorded; multiple-brooded; chicks have black and buff striped down. Sexual maturity within 1 year. At 6 colonies studied, 0-67% of nests hatched at least 1 egg, with higher success where colony mixed with gulls.

Movements. S populations migrate and winter up adjacent coasts, forming flocks in bays and at sheltered sites, often around floating rafts of seaweed.

Status and Conservation. Not globally threatened. Generally common or even abundant throughout range. In Argentina is most frequently observed grebe. Partial census in Jul 1990 gave 542 birds in Argentina, 266 in Chile and 150 in Lagunas de Mejía, S Peru; other recent counts in Argentina produced up to 5000 on Laguna La Margarita, up to 5000 on lakes in SW Córdoba and over 2000 at 4 other sites; in dry season up to 3500 on Laguna Pomacanchi, Asnacocha and Pampa Marca, in S Peru. Race *morrisoni* of L Junín also common, with estimated population of 1000-4000

birds; lake suffers pollution connected with mining in surrounding hills, and water level fluctuates as lake is used as reservoir for Lima. Use of water in energy production is additional threat and along with drought responsible for high mortality of species in 1983-1985. Nominate *rolland* widespread and fairly common in Falkland Is.

Bibliography. Belton (1984), Blake (1977), Burger (1974, 1984), Dott (1984), Dourojeanni *et al.* (1968), Fjeldså (1981b, 1985a, 1985b), Fjeldså & Krabbe (1990), Harris (1981), Humphrey *et al.* (1970), Johnson (1965), Narosky *et al.* (1988), Nores & Yzurieta (1980), de la Peña (1986), Plenge *et al.* (1989), Scott & Carbonell (1986), Short (1975), Simmons (1962b), Storer (1967a), Weller (1967a), Wetmore (1926), Woods (1988).

9. **Titicaca Flightless Grebe**
Rollandia microptera

French: Grèbe microptère   **German**: Titikakataucher   **Spanish**: Zampullín del Titicaca
Other common names: Short-winged/Flightless Grebe

Taxonomy. *Podiceps micropterus* Gould, 1868, Lake Titicaca.
Sometimes included in *Podiceps* or in monospecific genus *Centropelma*. Monotypic.
Distribution. SE Peru and W Bolivia, mainly in L Titicaca.

Descriptive notes. 28-45 cm. Distinctive. *P. taczanowskii* larger, with different bill shape, and lacks chestnut on nape and flanks. Non-breeding adult paler and duller, lacks crest. Juvenile greyer, with white on foreneck reaching breast; rufous stripes on sides of head.

Habitat. Large open lakes with reedbeds or floating vegetation, in high Andes over 3000 m. Breeds preferably in fairly open areas with patchy aquatic vegetation, and ready access to open water.

Food and Feeding. Mainly fish, estimated to comprise 97-98% (mass) of diet; takes some aquatic insects and other arthropods; frogs also recorded. Often forages far from shore, searching in patches of submerged vegetation. Better adapted to diving than *R. rolland*, with diving speed reaching 1 m/second; capable of capturing fish up to 15 cm long, typically after pursuit.

Breeding. Laying all year round, with peak in Nov/Dec. Solitary and territorial; nest is platform of plant matter. Usually 2 eggs (1-4); multiple-brooded; chicks have grey down, paler below, with rufous and white stripes on head and neck. Age of reaching sexual maturity unknown, but some birds manage to establish territories in first year.

Movements. Sedentary; flightless. Often runs over water flapping wings, sometimes over considerable distances.

Status and Conservation. Not globally threatened. Currently considered near-threatened. Included in first edition of Red Data Book (1966), because small, localized population reckoned to make it particularly susceptible to alteration of habitat or disturbance; was classed as very rare, but was thought to be stable, with no evidence of decline. Subsequent work has shown species to be common and locally abundant, with total population of several thousand. Has disappeared from some areas near Puno, due to pollution and excessive boat traffic, and from others due to intensive exploitation of reeds. Locally populations can disappear during years of severe drought, recovering in years with abundant rainfall and flooding.

Bibliography. Blake (1977), Fjeldså (1981b, 1981c, 1983b, 1985a, 1985b, 1986a), Fjeldså & Krabbe (1990), Livezey (1989), Niethammer (1953), Scott & Carbonell (1986), Villavisencio (1988), Vincent (1966).

Genus *POLIOCEPHALUS*   Selby, 1840

10. **Hoary-headed Grebe**
Poliocephalus poliocephalus

French: Grèbe argenté   **German**: Haarschopftaucher   **Spanish**: Zampullín Canoso
Other common names: Hoary-headed Dabchick

Taxonomy. *Podiceps poliocephalus* Jardine and Selby, 1827, New South Wales.
Formerly included in *Podiceps*, and less frequently in *Tachybaptus*. Forms superspecies with *P. rufopectus*. Monotypic.
Distribution. Australia and Tasmania; recent isolated breeding in New Zealand.

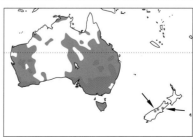

Descriptive notes. 27-30·5 cm; 220-260 g. Distinctive, with head characteristically finely streaked white. Lower neck and breast with variable amounts of brownish buff. Non-breeding adult appears capped, with throat and most of neck whitish, recalling non-breeding *Tachybaptus*. Juvenile as non-breeding adult, with black and white stripes on side of head.

Habitat. Prefers open, unsheltered wetlands, permanent or semi-permanent; also uses temporary wetlands, especially those occurring in normally arid Australian interior, after heavy rains. More common on large bodies of fresh water, but occasionally also found on small farm pools or tanks; also in brackish or saline waters of bays and estuaries, sheltered coasts, creeks and inlets, particularly in winter. Avoids waters with thick covering of water weeds.

Food and Feeding. Mainly small arthropods, both adults and larvae, e.g. corixid bugs, chironomids, cladocerans, amphipods, water beetles, moths, caddisflies, arachnids and damselflies; also takes small fish, but these only constitute c. 3% of prey. Adapted to feeding on wide range of prey types, taking advantage of those that occasionally abound in temporary waters. Main foraging method is deep diving, with average duration 17·5 seconds; on each dive usually explores only small patch of bottom, using numerous pecks. Sometimes also feeds at surface, but less than other grebes. Unlike other species, does not normally eat feathers.

Breeding. Traditionally stated as Oct to Jan, but season varies from year to year, normally after rains. Colonies of up to 400 nests, with each only c. 1 m apart, but sometimes semi-colonial or solitary; nest is small floating platform of aquatic plants loosely attached to submerged vegetation. 3-5 eggs (occasionally 6); no evidence of multiple broods; incubation 20-25 days; chicks have light brown down with blackish stripes, paler below. Abundance of drably coloured birds suggests delayed sexual maturity.
Movements. Poorly known. Some regular movements in coastal areas, at least in SE Australia, where large flocks gather during winter in bays and estuaries, or on perennial inland lakes. Highly dispersive in more arid parts of range, where flocks of thousands can turn up in swamps shortly after rise in water level. Some long distance movements, birds reaching remote lakes, and recent colonization of New Zealand; ringing records show movements of up to 572 km. Apparently shows stronger tendency to fly by day than other grebes.
Status and Conservation. Not globally threatened. In Australia common to abundant throughout most of range, rarer in drier areas. Large non-breeding flocks of up to 4900 birds recorded. Apparently stable, though in areas traditionally unsuitable due to aridity, expansion favoured by construction of artificial water bodies e.g. dams, reservoirs and purifying plants. Small influx to New Zealand in mid-1970's, with 1/2 pairs breeding each season in 1975-1978, since when sightings have continued, but no further breeding records. Vulnerable to oil spills in coastal waters.
Bibliography. Barlow (1976), Best (1976), Blakers *et al.* (1985), Braithwaite & Stewart (1975), Briggs (1977, 1979), Buddle (1939), Bull *et al.* (1985), Fjeldså (1983a, 1988b), Fooks & Reed (1978), Gosper (1981), Gosper *et al.* (1983), Hobbs (1958a), Marchant & Higgins (1990), Pringle (1985), Savage (1978), Schodde & Tidemann (1988), Storer (1987), Vestjens (1977c), Woodall (1985).

11. New Zealand Grebe
Poliocephalus rufopectus

French: Grèbe de Nouvelle-Zélande **German**: Maoritaucher **Spanish**: Zampullín Maorí
Other common names: New Zealand Dabchick

Taxonomy. *Podiceps (Poliocephalus) rufopectus* G. R. Gray, 1843, North Island, New Zealand. Formerly included in *Podiceps*, and less frequently in *Tachybaptus*. Forms superspecies with *P. poliocephalus*. Monotypic.
Distribution. North I (and formerly South I), New Zealand.

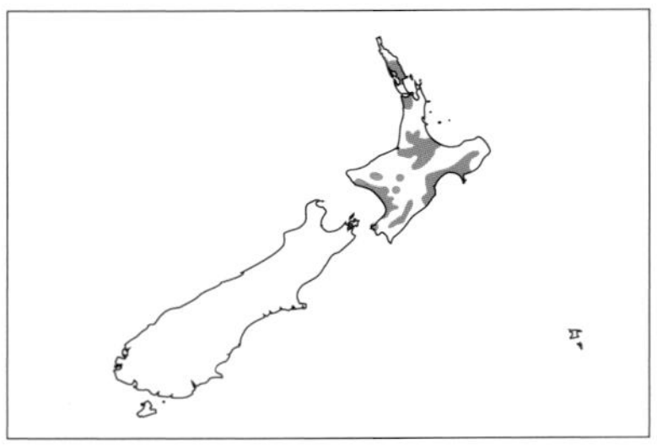

Descriptive notes. 28-30 cm; 232-271 g. Distinctive; fine white streaking on head, as in *P. poliocephalus*, breast and foreneck reddish, and iris usually pale yellow, though variable. Male averages larger, with longer bill. Non-breeding adult lacks chestnut on neck; chin and throat whitish. Juvenile has head and neck irregularly striped white, pale brown and blackish, giving mottled appearance.
Habitat. Freshwater lakes and pools, generally small and shallow, with dense vegetation, both emergent and along shore. Also occupies larger inland lakes with shallow inlets sheltered from waves, and artificial wetlands including farm water supplies and sewage ponds. Non-breeding flocks can occur on more open waters. Unlike other grebes, avoids estuarine and coastal waters.
Food and Feeding. Mainly aquatic invertebrates, including adults and larvae of insects, freshwater crayfish, molluscs and leeches; also some small fish and occasionally leaves of aquatic plants. Forages mainly by diving, with average duration of dives estimated at 24·8-33 seconds. Only large items brought up to surface, most prey swallowed under water. Sometimes pecks from surface and snatches midges and other flying insects. Unlike most other grebes, not recorded eating feathers.
Breeding. Breeding activity all year round, with peak laying late Aug-Jan. Mainly solitary, but semi-colonial where conditions favourable; nest is loose pile of aquatic plants, floating or grounded. 2-3 eggs; multiple-brooded; incubation 22-23 days; chicks have blackish brown down with paler stripes, white below; first flight c. 70 days. Success variable, but generally lower on large water bodies, probably due to fluctuation of water level, waves and disturbance by other birds.
Movements. Generally sedentary, with some local dispersal. Disperses freely in search of suitable sites when water conditions change; great facility for colonizing new water bodies. Particularly in S North I, many birds congregate after breeding, Feb-Sept, on large, more open lakes and oxidation ponds.
Status and Conservation. Not globally threatened. Gives some cause for concern, as total population estimated at only 1200-1500 birds. Disappeared from South I, where in mid-19th century was apparently widespread, though nowhere common; for unknown reasons marked decline started in second half of 19th century, continuing through 20th, until extinction in mid-1960's. In North I suffered with desiccation of many marshes and small lakes, perhaps responsible for decline in N of island; has benefited from creation of artificial wetlands and protection of some lakes for wildfowl shooting, leading to slight increase in S and E. Population of central Volcanic Plateau considered stable at estimated c. 500 birds. Tolerates moderate amount of human activity, e.g. breeding by built-up areas along shores of L Rotoiti. Usually ignored by hunters. If population in S of North I continues to increase, species might recolonize South I, where suitable breeding and wintering zones persist.
Bibliography. Buddle (1939), Bull *et al.* (1985), Chambers (1989), Edgar (1962), Fulton (1908), Heather (1985, 1988), Innes *et al.* (1982), Marchant & Higgins (1990), Lusk & Lusk (1981), Pierce (1980), Sibson (1982), Stidolph & Heather (1978), Storer (1971c, 1987), Tunnicliffe (1973), Westerskov (1974).

Genus *PODICEPS* Latham, 1787

12. Great Grebe
Podiceps major

French: Grand Grèbe **German**: Magellantaucher **Spanish**: Somormujo Macachón

Taxonomy. *Colymbus major* Boddaert, 1783, Cayenne; error.
Formerly placed in *Aechmophorus*, but similarity superficial. Probably represents distinct subgenus or perhaps even genus. Race *navasi* not universally accepted; if valid, name *leucopterus* may be applicable. Birds from coastal Peru suspected to constitute additional, undescribed race. Two subspecies recognized.
Subspecies and Distribution.
P. m. major Boddaert 1783 - NW Peru; Paraguay and extreme SE Brazil S to Patagonia and C Chile.
P. m. navasi Manghi 1984 - S Chile.

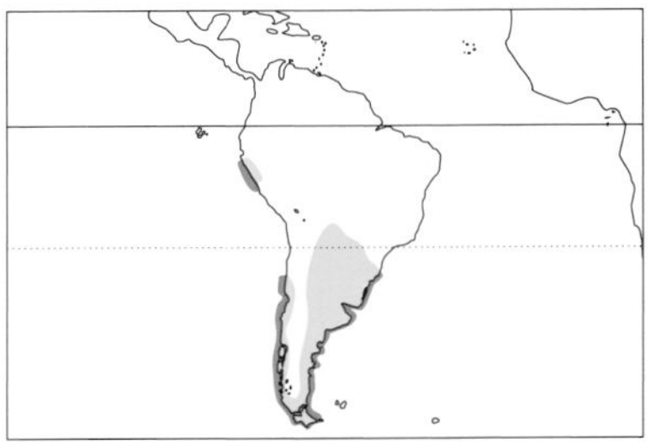

Descriptive notes. c. 67-77 cm; c. 1600 g. Distinctive, due to size, coloration and structure; iris red to dark brown. Non-breeding adult has whiter face, appearing as outsize *P. grisegena* with long neck. Juvenile probably paler. Race *navasi* larger, with blacker head.
Habitat. Occurs mainly in open water. Inlets fringed with vegetation on large lakes; low altitude lakes and sluggish rivers, especially in forested areas; estuarine marshes. Outside breeding season occurs along coast, frequenting estuaries, bays and areas with kelp (*Macrocystis*); non-breeders may occur here all year round; occasionally seen on open sea.
Food and Feeding. Apparently mainly fish. On R Paraná, Argentina, prey comprised fish (71%), insects (14%), crustaceans (10%) and molluscs (5%). Fish consumed include some species of open waters, others linked with aquatic vegetation. Takes fish up to 10·5 cm long, but mostly 2-5 cm, reducing competition with Neotropic Cormorant (*Phalacrocorax olivaceus*), which normally takes larger fish. In shallow, rocky coastal waters around mouth of R de la Plata, Uruguay, takes large quantities of small crabs (Decapoda, Brachyura), as well as small fish. Other prey items recorded include young of other waterbirds, e.g. coots (*Fulica*). Highly specialized for rapid diving in open waters.
Breeding. Season fairly irregular, some populations apparently breeding at any time of year; most laying Oct-Jan, becoming steadily later towards S; isolated Peruvian populations Sept/Oct, with possible second clutch Jan/Feb. Moderately sociable, frequently forming colonies; nest is floating platform of aquatic vegetation. 3-5 eggs (occasionally 6); may raise two broods or perhaps more; chicks have black and white striped down.
Movements. Generally spends non-breeding period in coastal waters, sometimes gathering in flocks of several hundred birds; at onset of breeding, birds move back from salt to fresh water. Strays onto open sea some distance from land, e.g. 1 bird c. 40 km off coast of NE Argentina; at least 6 records from Falklands. Two records from Spain 1900-1910 highly dubious; most unlikely to have reached Europe unaided.
Status and Conservation. Not globally threatened. Widespread and common throughout most of range. During partial census in Jul 1990, 257 recorded in Argentina and 283 in Chile. Isolated population of coastal Peru formerly merely considered accidental; very local, but fairly common in places, e.g. Bahía de Paracas, where regularly observed in 1974-1986, with up to 68 birds recorded. Much of its wetland habitat remains virgin or only slightly altered, especially in S of range.
Bibliography. Belton (1984), Beltzer (1983), Blake (1977), Cramp & Simmons (1977), Escalante (1980), Fjeldså (1982/83, 1985a), Fjeldså & Krabbe (1990), Gore & Gepp (1978), Greenquist (1982), Humphrey *et al.* (1970), Johnson (1965), Manghi (1984), Nores & Yzurieta (1980), de la Peña (1986), Pinto (1964), Plenge *et al.* (1989), Rieta Reig (1969), Ruschi (1979), Scott & Carbonell (1986), Short (1975), Sick (1984), Storer (1963b), Weller (1967a), Wetmore & Parkes (1954), Woods (1988).

13. Red-necked Grebe
Podiceps grisegena

French: Grèbe jougris **German**: Rothalstaucher **Spanish**: Somormujo Cuellirrojo
Other common names: Grey-cheeked Grebe; Holböll's Grebe (*holboellii*)

Taxonomy. *Colymbus grisegena* Boddaert, 1783, no locality; France designated.
Often erroneously spelt *griseigena*. Two subspecies recognized.
Subspecies and Distribution.
P. g. grisegena (Boddaert, 1783) - E Europe, W & WC Asia; winters from North Sea E to Caspian and Aral Seas.
P. g. holboellii Reinhardt, 1854 - E USSR, Manchuria, N Japan; W Canada, NW USA; winters from Japan and Korea through Aleutian Is to California; also E USA, S to Florida.

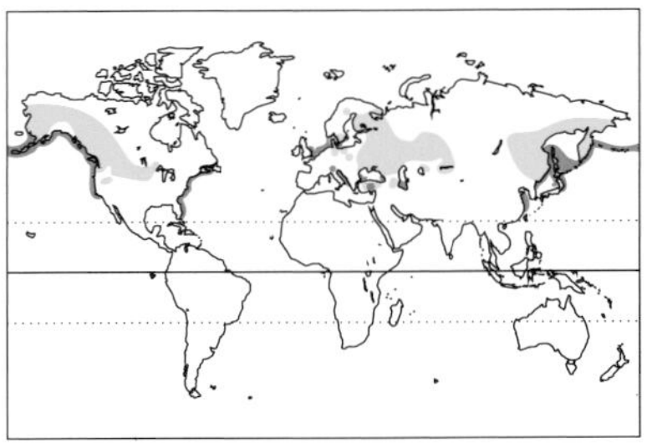

Descriptive notes. 40-50 cm; 806-925 g. Only grebe with black crown, greyish white face and chestnut neck. Non-breeding adult lacks reddish chestnut on neck, and generally greyer, especially on face. Juvenile as adult, but duller with foreneck tawny buff; sides of head striped black and white. Races separated on size.
Habitat. Breeds mainly on inland water bodies, typically fairly small (under 3 ha) and shallow (less than 2 m deep), with fair amount of emergent vegetation, but some stretches of open water; also breeds in backwaters of large rivers or estuaries and in pools cut off from sea. Generally prefers waters surrounded by forest, but in N also occupies areas of shrub tundra. Outwith breeding season affects open estuaries and other coastal waters with abundant supply of fish; particularly marine in winter, when occasionally found on open ocean.
Food and Feeding. Despite large size and strong bill, in Europe takes more aquatic arthropods (dragonfly larvae, waterbugs, beetles) than fish. Latter important only locally or seasonally: on IJselmeer (Netherlands), where large numbers congregate in winter, prey consists largely of smelt (*Osmerus eperlanus*). Captures prey by diving, but also takes insects from water surface or aquatic vegetation. Race *holboellii* of America (where *P. cristatus* absent) has longer bill and takes more fish, up to 55·5%; this has been interpreted as result of character displacement (see page 175).
Breeding. Apr/May to Jul/Aug, steadily later towards N. Normally solitary, but sometimes in loose colonies; nest is floating platform of aquatic plants anchored to vegetation. Normally 4-5 eggs (2-6); 1 brood, rarely 2; incubation 21-23 days, but up to 27 days in cold weather; chicks have down striped dark and light, more contrasted on head; fledging period unknown, but young independent at estimated 8-10 weeks. Sexual maturity not before 2 years old, though first year birds may form pairs and establish territories. Breeding attempts have success of estimated 70%; in Canada, in Aug average 0·65 young per adult, giving recruitment of c. 39%.
Movements. Migratory and dispersive. Winters along coasts, including inland seas, e.g. Black, Caspian and Aral Seas; in N America, occurs on Great Lakes mainly during migration. Migrates

alone or in small flocks, with concentrations at staging points e.g. Cape Cod, NE USA, where over 2000 birds may gather on spring migration. Nominate race occasionally reaches Ireland and W Mediterranean, accidental to Greenland; race *holboellii* recorded in Greenland, Iceland and Atlantic coasts of W Europe.

Status and Conservation. Not globally threatened. No figures available on overall population size and trends, but throughout range is apparently one of least common of Holarctic grebes. In Europe, thought to have increased and expanded towards W in second half of 19th century; presently increasing in places, e.g. in Schleswig-Holstein, N Germany, with 248 pairs in 1969, and 703 in 1990, and declining in others, especially at limits of range, no longer breeding in Austria or Greece; estimated 350-400 pairs in Denmark, 600 in Sweden, c. 2000 in Finland and 540-1000 in Poland. Census in Jan 1991 produced 175 in Iran, 120 in India, and 96 in Pakistan. Small numbers breed on Hokkaido, N Japan; numbers wintering in Japan seem to have decreased since 1963. One of least common grebes in N America; no figures available, but recently in decline, probably due to sterility of eggs and eggshell thinning caused by PCB's and other pesticides. During migration over 2000 birds may be seen off Cape Cod, NE USA. Other threats throughout range include modification of lakes and human disturbance, e.g. with water sports. Occasionally affected by oil spills, but widely scattered along coast in winter, so losses tend to be relatively insignificant.

Bibliography. Ahlén (1961, 1970), Andersson (1954), Axelsson (1988), Bacon (1974), Bauer & Glutz von Blotzheim (1966), Batten *et al.* (1990), Bezzel (1985), Brazil (1991), Brichetti (1979), di Carlo & Laurenti (1988), Cheng Tso-hsin (1987), Cramp & Simmons (1977), Chamberlin (1977), Chandler (1981), Davis & Vinicombe (1980), Dementiev & Gladkov (1951b), DeSmet (1982, 1983, 1987a), van der Elst (1987), Etchécopar & Hüe (1978), Evrard (1988), Fiedler & Freitag (1989), Fjeldså (1982b, 1983b), Folkestad (1978), Gallagher (1990), Gordienko (1981), Grenmyr (1984), Gunn (1951), Hemming (1968), Ilicev & Flint (1985), Johnsgard (1987), Karlsson & Kjellén (1984), Kevan (1970), Lawniczak (1982), Lönnberg (1936), Müller (1989), Munro (1941), Nielsen & Tofft (1987), Ohanjanian (1989), Onno (1960), Palmer (1962), Piersma (1988b), Roberts (1991), Sage (1973), Schmidt (1970), Scholl (1972), Schulze & Thinius (1982), Simmons (1970a), Struwe (1985), Terres (1980), Thomasson (1953), Tostain *et al.* (1981), Tuchscherer (1981a), Vlug (1985, 1986), Voet & Maes (1981), Wobus (1964a, 1964b).

14. **Great Crested Grebe**

Podiceps cristatus

French: Grèbe huppé **German**: Haubentaucher **Spanish**: Somormujo Lavanco
Other common names: (Southern) Crested Grebe (*australis*)

Taxonomy. *Colymbus cristatus* Linnaeus, 1758, Europe; restricted to Sweden.
Three subspecies recognized.

Subspecies and Distribution.
P. c. cristatus (Linnaeus, 1758) - Palearctic; winters in coastal zones, mainly in S of range.
P. c. infuscatus Salvadori, 1884 - scattered populations in E, S & WC Africa.
P. c. australis Gould, 1844 - SW & SE Australia, Tasmania; South I (New Zealand).

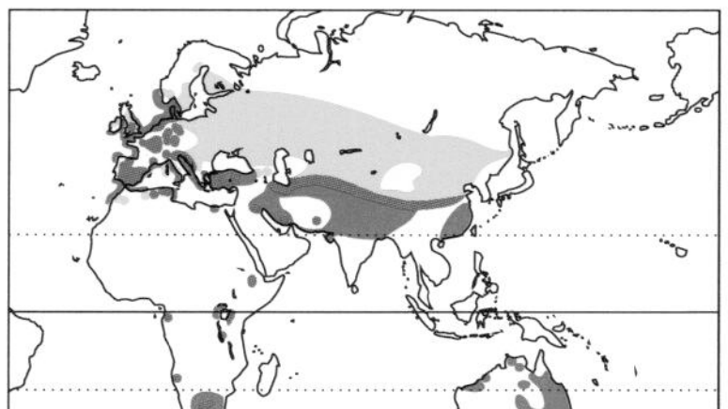

Descriptive notes. 46-61 cm; 596-1490 g. Unmistakable, with black crest and black tippets rufous chestnut at base. Non-breeding adult lacks tippets, and whiter on flanks. Juvenile similar to non-breeding adult, but head and upper neck striped blackish and white. Race *australis* similar to nominate, but tends to maintain breeding plumage throughout year; race *infuscatus* lacks white loral line, and also tends to lack seasonal variation.

Habitat. For breeding prefers fresh or brackish water, fringed by vegetation, with sizeable sheets of open water for foraging. Readily accepts artificial water bodies, including reservoirs, ponds, fish ponds, gravel pits and ornamental lakes; also on slow stretches of rivers with backwaters or pools. In tropical Africa, occurs on cold montane lakes, up to 3000 m and above; in New Zealand, occupies alpine and subalpine lakes up to c. 1000 m, where, in contrast to Palearctic birds, tolerates harsh conditions, including rough water and occasionally waters partially frozen over. Outwith breeding season, disperses to coasts, estuaries and large, exposed lakes and reservoirs.

Food and Feeding. Mainly sizeable fish, as much as 7·5 cm in diameter and 22 cm long, or even longer when thin species like eels; wide variety of species taken. Takes wide range of insects and other aquatic invertebrates, e.g. crustaceans, especially crayfish and shrimps, and molluscs, including snails; consumption of invertebrates highest in spring; also takes adults and larvae of amphibians. Main foraging technique is diving, typically with pursuit; dives average 18-26 seconds, performed in areas of open water or with scattered clumps of vegetation. Also feeds from surface (less than other grebes), with only head submerged, or picking insects off vegetation. Captive birds consume c. 150-250 g of food per day, c. 20% of body weight.

Breeding. Mainly Apr-Jul (Jan-Sept) in Europe; all months in tropical Africa, with peaks usually in or immediatly after long rains; in South Africa, mostly spring in W, autumn/winter in E; peak laying Nov-Mar in Australasia. Usually solitary or dispersed, sometimes in lax colonies; nest is platform of aquatic plants, either floating and anchored to vegetation or built from lake bottom. Usually 3-5 eggs (1-7); 1 brood, less commonly 2; incubation 25-31 days; chicks have down striped blackish and pale, paler below; fledging 71-79 days. Sexual maturity normally at 2 years old; some first year birds mate and establish territory, or even breed, usually late in season. Breeding success of 1·2-1·5 chicks reared per pair in Britain; success low in New Zealand, with range of 0·01-0·4 chicks per adult per year.

Movements. Migratory and dispersive, especially in N. After breeding, many make local movements to moult on large lakes and reservoirs; others moult on breeding waters. After moult, more marked movement towards coast; concentrations of up to 20,000 on IJsselmeer, Netherlands, and 20,000 on Turkish coast of Black Sea; in C Europe and Australia many winter on large lakes. Thought to migrate following coast and also over land, but little known. No true migration in Africa, where extensive dispersal related to rains. In New Zealand local post-breeding dispersal; occasionally performs large-scale movements. Nominate race vagrant to Senegal and Taiwan; race *australis* accidental to Moluccas.

Status and Conservation. Not globally threatened. Widespread decline in Europe during 19th century due to hunting for plume trade; has since recovered, and with amelioration of climate has expanded and increased in N and NW: in Britain, from 2810 adults in 1931 increased to 6000-7000 in 1979; in Denmark, from 4400-5000 in 1969 to 6800-7800 in 1978; in Sweden from 6000 in 1971 to 10,000 in 1976; in Finland, from 10,000 in 1958 to 50,000-60,000 in 1983. Main factors causing increase are widespread eutrophication of water, with consequent increase of cyprinid fish, and great adaptability of species to man-made wetlands. Apparently also on increase in Asia, though little information; formerly rare winter visitor to Japan, but more numerous since 1963, with 4610 birds counted in Jan 1991, and small breeding population in N Honshu, at least since 1972. African race *infuscatus* locally common, but generally sparse and absent from many apparently suitable sites; has virtually disappeared from several sites in E Africa because of gill-net fishing since 1950. Race *australis* generally uncommon but apparently stable in Australia; recent counts of 600-800 birds in Lachlan Swamps and 842 on L Gregory. In New Zealand on decline since arrival of Europeans and now threatened; apparently unable to recover from effects of past persecution, with low breeding success caused by poor food availability and modification of lakes for recreational purposes; now absent from North I and from several former strongholds on South I, but recent censuses suggest population stable at c. 240-250 birds on 28-32 lakes.

Bibliography. Ali & Ripley (1978), Asbirk & Dybbro (1978), Bauer & Glutz von Blotzheim (1966), Brazil (1991), Brichetti (1979), Brichetti & Martignoni (1983), Brown *et al.* (1982), Bujnowicz (1977), Büttiker (1985), Camphuysen & Derks (1989), Cheng Tso-hsin (1987), Commecy (1986), Cramp & Simmons (1977), Dean (1977), Dementiev & Gladkov (1951b), Emmerich (1982), Ferrer (1980), Fuchs (1978, 1982), Geiger (1957), Goc (1986), Hanzák (1952), Harrison & Hollom (1932), Hick (1966), Huxley (1914, 1924), Ilicev & Flint (1985), Jacob (1983), Keller (1989a, 1989b), Koshelev (1977), Lammi (1985), Leys & de Wilde (1971), Maclean (1985), Marchant, J.H. *et al.* (1990), Marchant, S. & Higgins (1990), Mayr (1986), McCartan & Simmons (1956), Melde (1973), Moskal & Marzalek (1986), Mundkur & Pravez (1986), Nilsson & Persson (1987), O'Donnell (1980, 1982), Paz (1987), Piersma (1984, 1988a, 1988c, 1988d), Piersma & van Eerden (1989), Piersma *et al.* (1988), Pinto (1983), Prest & Jefferies (1969), Ranftl (1980), Renevey (1987, 1988, 1989a, 1989b, 1989c), Roberts (1991), Ruwet (1984), Sagar (1981), Salonen & Penttinen (1988), Sarrocco (1986), Schifferli (1978), Simmons (1955, 1965, 1970b, 1974a, 1975, 1977a, 1989), Sobczyk (1975), Suetens (1960), Ulfvens (1988), Vlug (1976, 1979, 1980, 1983), Walravens *et al.* (1990), Westerskov (1977), Zang (1977).

15. **Horned Grebe**

Podiceps auritus

French: Grèbe esclavon **German**: Ohrentaucher **Spanish**: Zampullín Cuellirrojo
Other common names: Slavonian Grebe

Taxonomy. *Colymbus auritus* Linnaeus, 1758, Europe and America; restricted to Vaasa, Finland. Sometimes placed in genus *Dytes*, although actually closer to *P. grisegena* and *P. cristatus* than to other *Podiceps*. Subspecific differences slight and partly clinal; species sometimes considered monotypic. Two subspecies normally recognized.

Subspecies and Distribution.
P. a. auritus (Linnaeus, 1758) - Palearctic, from Iceland and Baltic to Kamchatka; winters from North Sea to Caspian and off Japan and China.
P. a. cornutus (Gmelin, 1789) - C Alaska to NW & NC USA; winters S to California and Texas.

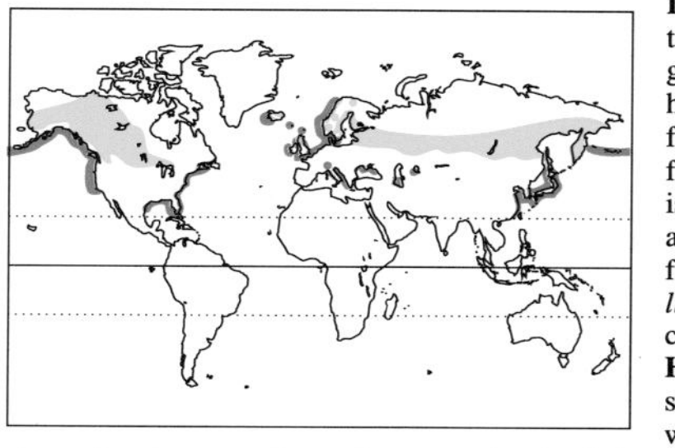

Descriptive notes. 31-38 cm; 300-470 g. Distinctive combination of reddish neck with golden yellow crest tufts. Non-breeding adult has extensive white on foreneck and face; differs from non-breeding *P. nigricollis* in whiter face, bill thicker and straight, and small whitish spot on lores. Juvenile as non-breeding adult, with separation of dark cap from whitish face less clearly demarcated, as in *P. nigricollis*. Race *cornutus* greyer above, especially on crown.

Habitat. Breeds on fresh water, occupying small pools and marshes with patches of open water, or secluded sectors of large lakes and rivers. In winter mostly marine, occurring in sheltered bays and occasionally on open sea; also on fresh waters in S of breeding range, especially on large lakes and river systems.

Food and Feeding. Arthropods normally predominate in number, but fish in weight. Highly adaptable, shifting to whatever food readily available: at autumn migration staging areas on Mono and Great Salt Lakes (USA), more than 90% of diet composed of brine-shrimps. Arthropods include adults and larvae of insects (beetles, dragonflies, mayflies, water bugs, damsel flies, caddisflies) and crustaceans (cladocerans, amphipods, decapods); also some molluscs and worms. Fish usually more important in winter, at sea, where crustaceans also taken. Remarkably agile under water, swimming at 1 m/second; this enables capture of sizeable fish. Main foraging method is diving, most dives averaging c. 20 seconds; also feeds from surface, taking floating and aerial prey, or snatching it off aquatic vegetation.

Breeding. Laying Apr-Aug (to Sept in Iceland and Norway), peaking in June. Usually solitary, sometimes loosely colonial; nest is platform of aquatic plants, usually floating and anchored to vegetation, but sometimes built from lake bottom or on rocks at water level. Usually 4-5 eggs (1-7); 1 brood, occasionally 2; incubation 22-25 days; chicks have typical striped down, most conspicuous on head and neck; fledging 55-60 days. Sexual maturity probably at 2 years old. Major study in Iceland gave 63% hatching success, with 53% of chicks surviving 20 days, after which pre-fledging losses minimal; success appears to vary considerably between years.

Movements. Migratory. Winters along coast on inshore waters, and to lesser extent on large lakes. Some populations dispersive, moving only to nearby seas. Overland migration by night, at least in N America; coastal migration often diurnal. Some stragglers, especially to S, with records from Bermuda and Hawaii; also Tunisia, Israel, Azores and Madeira.

Status and Conservation. Not globally threatened. In past may have had much wider distribution in NW Europe, but acidification and increased humus content of lakes probably led to range contraction; man-induced eutrophication of lakes has permitted general expansion during 20th century, but species currently declining in places. In 1970's estimated 500-750 pairs in Iceland, c. 500 pairs in Norway, c. 1000 pairs in Sweden and c. 500 pairs in Estonia; in Finland, c. 3000 pairs in 1958, but currently under 1500, again attributed to acidification and increased humus in breeding lakes, and also accidents in fishing nets. First recorded breeding in Scotland in 1908, with increase to maximum of 81 pairs in 1984, since when steady decline to 61-62 pairs in 1987; afforestation known to be responsible for loss of several pairs, as causes hydrological changes leading to reduced quantities of invertebrates. Widespread but apparently uncommon throughout its Asian range, where much less studied. In N America breeding range has contracted considerably, formerly reaching S and E to N Utah, N Indiana and S New England, and species apparently still declining; main threats include human disturbance, forestry operations around breeding lakes, fluctuating water levels and stocking of lakes with rainbow trout (*Salmo gairdneri*), which compete with grebes for aquatic insects. Particularly vulnerable to oil pollution: of 34,717 oiled birds killed in eight spills in S USA, 12·3% were present species; 8-16% of wintering population of Shetland Is killed after oil spill in 1978/79.

Bibliography. Arnold (1989, 1990), Bacon (1974), Bauer & Glutz von Blotzheim (1966), Batten *et al.* (1990), Brazil (1991), Cheng Tso-hsin (1987), Clase *et al.* (1960), Cramp & Simmons (1977), Dementiev & Gladkov (1951b), Dennis (1973), Dittberner & Dittberner (1977), DuBois (1919, 1920), van der Elst (1987), Etchécopar & Hüe (1978),

Ferguson (1977, 1981), Ferguson & Sealy (1983), Fjeldså (1973a, 1973b, 1973c, 1973d, 1974), Frantzen (1984), Gordienko (1981), Haupt (1981), Högström (1970), Ilicev & Flint (1985), Johnsgard (1987), Karlsson & Kjellén (1984), Lönnberg (1923), Løppenthin (1953), Mascher (1972), Nökleby (1963), Olsoni (1928), Onno (1960), Palmer (1962), Parkes (1952), Piersma (1988b), Potvliege (1978), Regnell (1981a, 1981b), Roberts (1991), Storer (1961, 1969), Sugden (1977), Terres (1980), Tuchscherer (1981b), Ulfvens (1988, 1989a, 1989b), Uusitalo (1969, 1976), Willgohs (1957), Wolk (1973), Woolfenden (1956), Ytreberg (1957).

16. Black-necked Grebe

Podiceps nigricollis

French: Grèbe à cou noir **German**: Schwarzhalstaucher **Spanish**: Zampullín Cuellinegro
Other common names: Eared Grebe

Taxonomy. *Podiceps nigricollis* C. L. Brehm, 1831, Germany.
Specific name *caspicus* obsolete. Often includes *P. andinus*. Sometimes placed in genus *Dytes*. Forms superspecies with *P. andinus*, *P. occipitalis* and *P. taczanowskii*. Three subspecies recognized.
Subspecies and Distribution.
P. n. nigricollis Brehm, 1831 - Europe to W Asia, wintering SW Palearctic; CE Asia, wintering E Asia; E Africa.
P. n. gurneyi (Roberts, 1919) - S Africa.
P. n. californicus Heermann, 1854 - SW Canada, W USA, NW & C Mexico; winters S to Guatemala.

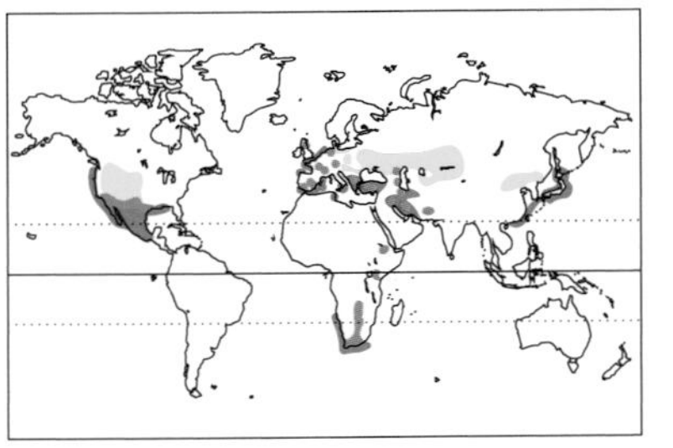

Descriptive notes. 28-34 cm; 265-450 g. Only grebe with yellow tufts on head and rest of head and neck black. Non-breeding adult can resemble *P. taczanowskii*, but contrast less marked. Juvenile as non-breeding adult, but throat and foreneck dirty white, with dark collar at base of neck. Races separated on slight plumage differences.
Habitat. Generally breeds on small, shallow, highly eutrophic water bodies, with lush vegetation and typically with stretches of open water; occupies ponds, fish ponds, sewage farms and quiet river backwaters, or areas of lakes and marshes with suitable conditions. Rather erratic: readily moves into newly flooded areas, but also abandons many sites after few years. Outwith breeding season, moves to open standing, generally saline waters, or coastal waters e.g. estuaries, bays, channels and arms of sea.
Food and Feeding. Especially during breeding season takes mostly insects, both adults and larvae, e.g. aquatic bugs, terrestrial and aquatic beetles, damselflies and dragonflies; also molluscs, crustaceans, amphibians (small frogs and tadpoles) and small fish. Plant remains frequently recorded in stomachs, but probably ingested accidentally. At Mono Lake, main migration staging point of N American population, brine-shrimps (*Artemia monica*) constitute over 90% of diet. During winter, in marine habitats, crustaceans can be as important as fish. Much food obtained by diving, with dives usually lasting under 30 seconds. Frequently practices foliage-gleaning, and feeds more from water surface than most grebes, picking objects off surface, submerging head while swimming, or occasionally capturing flying insects.
Breeding. Mainly May/Jun in Europe; season longer in N America, with laying Apr-Aug. Normally colonial, with very variable colony size, up to thousands in N America; amongst species that most frequently associates with small gulls and terns (see page 182); nest is floating platform of plant material anchored to vegetation. Usually 3-4 eggs (1-8); 1 brood, occasionally 2; incubation 20-22 days; chicks have brownish black down with paler stripes (darker than in other species), white underparts; fledging period unknown, with doubtful record of independence at only 21 days. Sexual maturity at 2 years old. Breeding success variable, with hatching success 5·4% in South Africa, 87·5% in Iowa, USA; apparently depends mainly on water conditions.
Movements. Mainly migratory and dispersive, though populations in S of range can be more or less sedentary. Highly gregarious on migration and in winter, forming concentrations of up to hundreds of thousands at certain sites in N America and Asia: at Great Salt Lake, Utah, and Mono Lake, California, sites for primary moult and migration staging; at Salton Sea, California, with c. 500,000 birds in winter; and in S Caspian Sea. Much movement apparently nocturnal, although diurnal migration also recorded in Palearctic. Straggler to Hawaii; also to Azores, Madeira and Canaries.
Status and Conservation. Not globally threatened. Widespread and locally abundant; probably most numerous of all grebes. In Europe has expanded N and W in last 100 years, colonizing most of C and W of continent; cause claimed to be invasions from E due to desiccation of lakes in steppe areas around Caspian Sea, though hard evidence lacking. In contrast, declining in S, e.g. in Italy, Spain and especially N Africa, where not known to have bred recently. Little known of Asian population; census in Jan 1991 yielded 620 birds in Pakistan, 1113 in India, 183 in South Korea and 1670 in Japan. Generally scarce in Africa, in many cases breeding sporadically when conditions suitable, but locally abundant. In N America suffered intense pressure from millinery industry and egg-collecting at dense colonies, but has now recovered and is commonest species; autumn concentrations of c. 750,000 birds at Mono Lake, California, may comprise majority of Nearctic population. May be vulnerable due to strong dependence on a few stable saline lakes outside breeding season. Throughout range some local declines attributed to loss of habitat and human disturbance, especially recreational activities on lakes; conversely, man-made aquatic habitats may have caused slight increase in African population. Vulnerable to oil pollution as frequently winters on coast; to date affected by few accidents, but amongst main sufferers of massive oil slick in Persian Gulf during conflict of early 1991, with estimated 30,000-100,000 birds, especially cormorants and grebes, killed; 17·3% of 1350-1500 birds attended in recovery centre were present species.
Bibliography. Ali & Ripley (1978), Anrys & Verhaegen (1986), Banks & Clapp (1987), Becuwe (1971), Blaser (1985), Bauer & Glutz von Blotzheim (1966), Bochenski (1961), Brazil (1991), Brichetti (1979), Brown *et al.* (1982), Broekhuysen (1962), Broekhuysen & Frost (1968a, 1968b), di Carlo & Laurenti (1988), Cheng Tso-hsin (1987), Cooper, Winkler & Lenz (1984), Cramp & Simmons (1977), Dementiev & Gladkov (1951b), Dennis (1973), Dickerman (1969), Dittberner & Dittberner (1984), van der Elst (1987), Etchécopar & Hüe (1978), Faaborg (1976), Fiala (1976), Fjeldså (1982a), Franke (1969), Frieling (1933), García Giménez & Calvo Sendín (1987), Gauckler & Krause (1968), Gordienko (1981, 1982), Ilicev & Flint (1985), van Impe (1969), Inskipp & Inskipp (1985), Jacobs (1953), Jehl (1988), Jehl & Bond (1983), Jehl & Yochem (1986), Jehl *et al.* (1987), Johnsgard (1987), Karlsson & Kjellén (1984), Land (1970), Lawniczak (1982), Lebreton *et al.* (1983), Maclean (1985), Mahoney & Jehl (1985), Mayol (1984), McAllister (1958), Nishikawa *et al.* (1984), Noll (1960), Ouweneel (1989), Palmer (1962), Pinto (1983), Prinzinger (1974, 1979a, 1979b), Regnell (1957), Roberts (1991), Robertson (1981), Schenk (1970), Sealy (1985), Shaughnessy (1983), Storer & Jehl (1985), Terres (1980), Wilson, Hernández & Meléndez (1988), Winkler & Cooper (1986).

17. Colombian Grebe

Podiceps andinus

French: Grèbe des Andes **German**: Andentaucher **Spanish**: Zampullín Colombiano

Taxonomy. *Colymbus caspicus andinus* Meyer de Schauensee, 1959, Lake Tota, Boyacá, Colombia; altitude 3015 metres.
Often considered subspecies of *P. nigricollis*. Sometimes placed in genus *Dytes*. Forms superspecies with *P. nigricollis*, *P. occipitalis* and *P. taczanowskii*. Monotypic.
Distribution. Boyacá and Cundinamarca, NC Colombia (probably extinct).

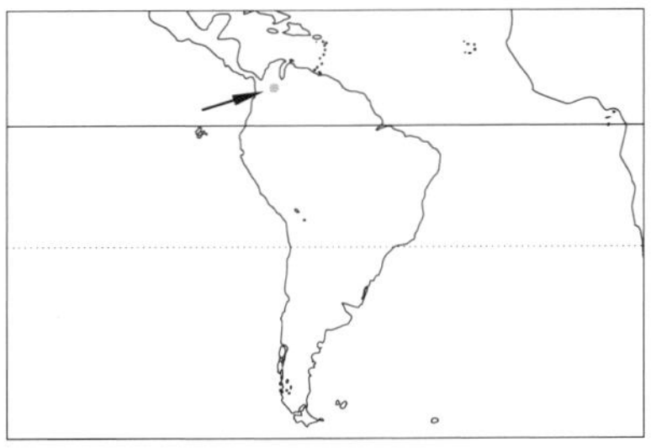

Descriptive notes. 33 cm. Differs from *P. nigricollis* in higher crown, more chestnut tone to head tuft and chestnut foreneck. Non-breeding adult has variable amount of white on throat and foreneck.
Habitat. Fresh waters and fairly open lakes, with tall reedbeds and stretches of shallow water with submerged and emergent vegetation. Last known population restricted to L Tota in Sabana de Bogotá at 3015 m; L Tota comprises 56·2 km^2 of open water with fringing vegetation, originally *Alnus* scrub along steeper banks and reed swamp in flatter parts, where floating vegetation abundant; changes caused by increased influx of agricultural fertilizer has reduced extensions of these macrophytes to relictual levels.
Food and Feeding. No information available; capture of insects by foliage-gleaning presumably important, as in closely related *P. nigricollis*; reduction of vegetation around L Tota may thus have been particularly significant.
Breeding. Virtually no data; several females found ready to lay in Aug, with main laying season possibly Aug-Sep.
Movements. No information available; probably sedentary.
Status and Conservation. Almost certainly EXTINCT. Considered abundant on L Tota in 1940's and periodically recorded on other lakes of Sabana de Bogotá up to early 1950's. Estimated c. 300 birds on L Tota in 1968, but only 1 bird in 1972, and 1-3 in 1977, last records of species. No birds seen during exhaustive surveys in 1981 and 1982. Suggested causes of population crash include introduction of rainbow trout (*Salmo gairdneri*) to L Tota in 1944, pollution of water with pesticides, harvesting of reeds and hunting; main reason may have been loss of suitable habitat due to artificial lowering of water level in mid-1950's for agricultural irrigation; this probably led to marked decline in numbers, making species much more vulnerable to other negative factors. Validity of last records of species has been questioned, and some consider species may have become extinct in early 1960's. See page 186.
Bibliography. Blake (1977), Collar & Andrew (1988), Fjeldså (1984a, 1985a, 1989b), Fjeldså & Krabbe (1990), Hilty & Brown (1986), King (1978/79), de Schauensee (1959), Varty *et al.* (1986), Vincent (1966).

18. Silvery Grebe

Podiceps occipitalis

French: Grèbe aux belles joues **German**: Inkataucher **Spanish**: Zampullín Blanquillo
Other common names: Crested/Silver Grebe; Junin Grebe (*juninensis*)

Taxonomy. *Podiceps occipitalis* Garnot, 1826, Falkland Islands.
Sometimes placed in genus *Dytes*. May form superspecies with *P. nigricollis*, *P. andinus* and *P. taczanowskii*, although race *juninensis* sympatric with *P. taczanowskii*. Hybridization with *P. gallardoi* recorded. Race *juninensis* may be distinct species, given morphological and ethological differences. Two subspecies recognized.
Subspecies and Distribution.
P. o. juninensis Berlepsch & Stolzmann, 1894 - C Andes of Colombia to N Chile, NW Argentina.
P. o. occipitalis Garnot, 1826 - C & S Chile, C & S Argentina, Falkland Is; winters in N of range.

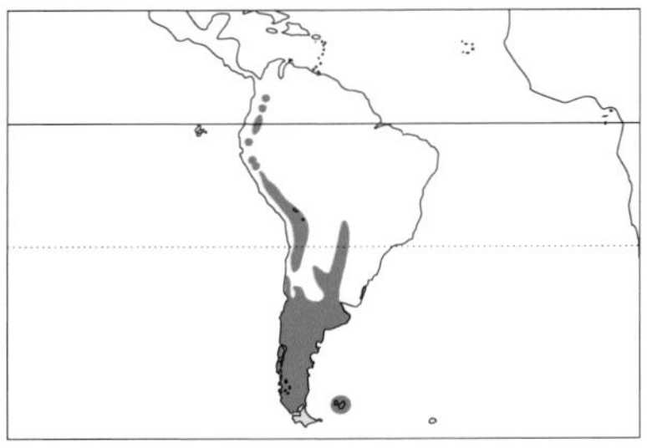

Descriptive notes. 23-28·5 cm; c. 340-400 g. Characteristic yellow facial tuft; nape black, foreneck white. Non-breeding adult lacks facial tuft. Juvenile as non-breeding adult, but nape grey. Race *juninensis* recalls *P. taczanowskii*, but neck clearly shorter, head more rounded and bill smaller.
Habitat. Breeds on open freshwater or slightly alkaline lakes, with ample areas of shallow water and dense reedbeds along shores; in highland areas, typically occurs on lakes with bare shores, nesting in open on submerged water weeds; also occupies pools and ponds. Prefers waters where submerged vegetation widely distributed, but not too dense. Particularly common in lowlands below 1300 m, but also inhabits *puna* at 3000-5000 m. Outwith breeding season can occur on salt-lakes, sometimes in fair numbers. Mainland birds only exceptionally seen on sea, but Falklands birds use coastal kelp patches in autumn and winter.
Food and Feeding. Mainly small arthropods, especially insects and their larvae (caddisfly, corixid bugs and beetles), and small crustaceans (freshwater shrimp); fish and plant matter also recorded. Often feeds by pecking from surface; dives average 17 seconds, rather clumsy and often stationary, as frequently used for underwater foliage-gleaning.
Breeding. Laying mainly Nov-Jan in S, sometimes later and rarely into Mar in *puna*; in Peru breeds Sept-Mar; in Colombia nests recorded in Feb. Colonial, with small nests almost touching and forming rafts, sometimes with several on same floating platform of loose weeds; colony of 400 pairs at Laguna de Caritaya, Chile, another of over 1000 nests on Río Fuego L (Tierra del Fuego); nest is floating platform of weeds and plant material. 1-4 eggs, mostly 2, but up to 6 recorded; normally 1 brood only; incubation c. 18 days; chicks have striped grey down, paler below. Age of sexual maturity unknown, but non-breeders numerous. Breeding success variable: at 8 colonies studied, 0-85% of nests hatched at least 1 egg, with higher success where colony mixed with gulls.
Movements. Migratory in S: arrives at Tierra del Fuego in late Sept, departing end of Mar or Apr; apparently moves by night. Falklands population resident, making some local movements.

Status and Conservation. Not globally threatened. Locally common in Falklands and abundant in Argentina, Chile, Bolivia and Peru, but local, rare, and probably declining in N of range. In partial census of Jul 1990, 1123 birds counted in Chile and 330 in Argentina; other recent surveys in Argentina yielded 2600 on lakes of Meseta de Strobel (1984), 2000 on Laguna La Margarita, 1500 at lakes in SW Córdoba and 1500 on Laguna Blanca (1982). In 1977 in S Peru, 1300 birds at Laguna Umayo and 700-800 on Laguna Lagunillas; in Bolivia, up to 400 counted on Laguna Alalay. Smaller numbers recorded in Ecuador, e.g. Laguna Cuicocha, with maximum of 44 adults counted, and L Yaguarcocha, with up to 25 birds. In Colombia restricted to small area in SW, e.g. at Lagunas La Cocha and San Rafael; has recently colonized Laguna del Otún, C Colombia, indicating northward extension of range.

Bibliography. Blake (1977), Burger (1974, 1984), Canales (1989), Dott (1984), Dourojeanni *et al*. (1968), Fjeldså (1981b, 1981c, 1982a, 1983b, 1985a, 1985b), Fjeldså & Krabbe (1990), Harris (1981), Hilsenbeck (1979), Hilty & Brown (1986), Humphrey *et al*. (1970), Johnson (1965), Keith (1970), Livezey (1989), Morrison (1939b), Nores & Yzurieta (1980), Nuechterlein & Storer (1989b), de la Peña (1986), Pettingill (1960), Scott & Carbonell (1986), Short (1975), Storer (1982), Woods (1988).

19. Junin Flightless Grebe

Podiceps taczanowskii

French: Grèbe de Taczanowski **German**: Punataucher **Spanish**: Zampullín del Junín
Other common names: Puna/Taczanowski's/Junin Grebe

Taxonomy. *Podiceps taczanowskii* Berlepsch and Stolzmann, 1894, Lake Junín, Peru.
Sometimes placed in genus *Dytes*. May form superspecies with *P. nigricollis*, *P. andinus* and *P. occipitalis*, although sympatric with *P. o. juninensis*. Monotypic.
Distribution. L Junín, C Peru; recently introduced to other nearby lakes.

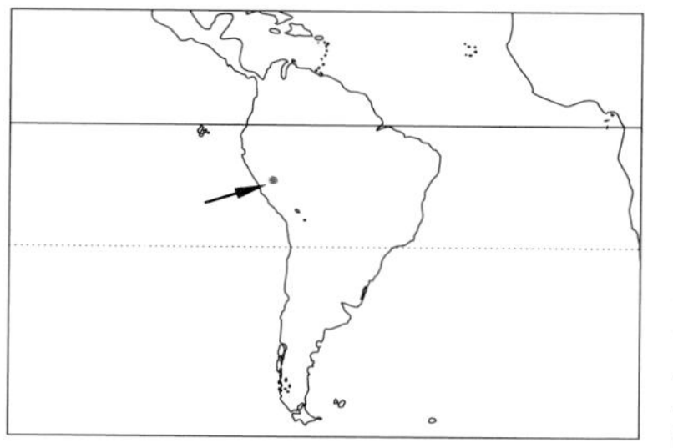

Descriptive notes. 33-38 cm. Bill fairly long and thin. Recalls non-breeding *P. nigricollis*, but larger, with whiter foreneck. Non-breeding adult lacks crest and black of hindneck. Juvenile as non-breeding adult.
Habitat. L Junín is large lake of 14,320 ha, at 4080 m above sea-level; bordered by extensive reed marshes, in places continuous, elsewhere forming mosaics with stretches of open water. Considerable areas of lake are shallow, where bottom covered in dense, uniform patches of *Chara*; centre of lake reaches depth of 10 m. When breeding, species frequents bays and channels in outer sector of lake generally within 8-75 m of reedbeds, but entering them only for nesting or roosting. In off-season shows strong preference for open water, occurring far from lake shore.
Food and Feeding. Mainly fish (*Orestias*), constituting c. 90% (mass) of diet. Small fish tend to predominate, with 62% of all fish taken under 25 mm long. Takes large quantities of chironomid midges and corixid bugs, although biomass only 2% and 6% respectively; also some amphipods and larvae and pupae of ephydriid flies. Fish become unavailable in Jan, as inaccessible amongst new reeds, and bugs act as reserve food supply. Main technique is diving, capturing fish by rapid pursuit; social feeding frequent, with several birds swimming along in line, all submerging together in time. Often snatches midges from surface; other methods of surface feeding exceptional, including swimming with head submerged or upending.
Breeding. Laying during rains: mostly Dec/Jan (late Nov-Mar). Colonial, with colonies of up to 20 nests; nests 2-4 m apart, sometimes only 1 m apart; nest is platform invariably in bed of tall reeds (*Scirpus*), often partially broken down by wind. Usually 2 eggs (1-3); probably 1 brood; chicks have grey down with paler stripes, whitish below. Low breeding potential probably related to highly predictable, stable environment: in 1979, in May when young are large, of 39 pairs observed, 1 had 3 young, 7 had 2 young, 13 had 1 young and 18 were without young; 37 adults remained single or in groups, thus 63·4% of all adult birds had no young; species presumably long-lived, in order to maintain population.
Movements. Sedentary; flightless. Tends to use different parts of lake in different seasons.
Status and Conservation. ENDANGERED. Dramatic decline during 20th century: abundant in 1938; common in 1961, with estimate of several thousand birds; currently only 200-300 birds remain, with extinction looming. Rapid slump brought about by pollution of L Junín by local mining activities, and variations of up to 7 m in water level, controlled by hydroelectric power station; less significant was introduction of trout in 1930's, replacing native fish species. Recent evidence shows species suffers heavy infestation of nematode parasites, ingested with food; causes unknown and impact unlikely to be important, but may indicate birds are in poor health. Another adverse factor is competition for food with much more numerous *R. rolland*. Since 1985 some pairs of present species introduced to nearby lakes, in attempt to increase total population, but probably only room for c. 40 pairs on water bodies near L Junín.

Bibliography. Balharry *et al*. (1989), Blake (1977), Collar & Andrew (1988), Diamond *et al*. (1987), Dourojeanni *et al*. (1968), Fjeldså (1981a, 1981b, 1982a, 1983b, 1984a, 1985a, 1986a, 1989b), Fjeldså & Krabbe (1990), Harris (1981), King (1978/79), Livezey (1989), Morrison (1939b), Mountfort (1988), Scott & Carbonell (1986), Sherrit (1969), Storer (1967a), Vincent (1966).

20. Hooded Grebe

Podiceps gallardoi

French: Grèbe mitré **German**: Goldscheiteltaucher **Spanish**: Zampullín Tobiano
Other common names: Mitred Grebe

Taxonomy. *Podiceps gallardoi* Rumboll, 1974, Laguna Las Escarchadas, 50 kilometres east and a little south of Calafate, Santa Cruz, Argentina.
Known to have hybridized with *P. occipitalis*. Monotypic.
Distribution. Extreme SW Argentina.
Descriptive notes. c. 32 cm. Unmistakable, with conspicuously contrasted plumage; as in other species, erectile crest can alter shape of head considerably. Juvenile similar to adult, with forehead white and head mainly duky grey, presenting indistinct pattern.
Habitat. Upland lakes in foothill mesetas at altitude of 500-1200 m, where small lakes abound; harsh environment, devoid of fringing reeds due to strong prevailing winds. In summer, young birds and non-breeders use larger lakes, more adequate for feeding; breeding attempted on small or medium-sized lakes, where shallow water allows growth of floating carpets of water weeds (*Myriophyllum*), important for breaking up waves and in nest building. Surface area and depth of

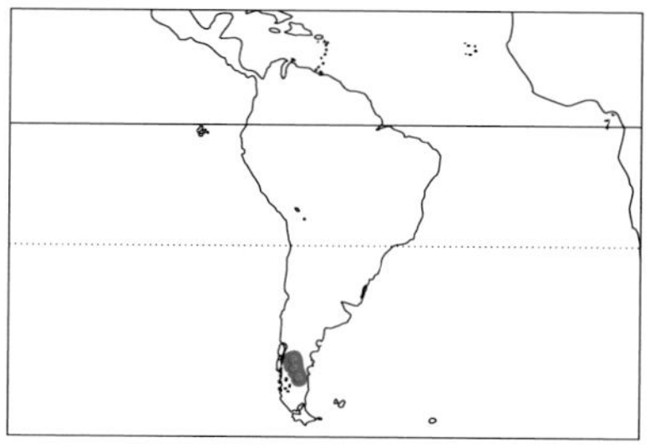

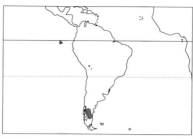

lakes depends on local snow fall; many suitable for breeding only in certain years; volcanic lakes surrounded by cliff walls more suitable for breeding, as more sheltered from wind and conditions generally more stable.
Food and Feeding. Small invertebrates: snails (*Lymnaea diaphana*) and to lesser extent amphipods are most important food items, at any rate when feeding young; also takes midge pupae, copepods, bugs and larvae of water beetles. Main feeding method is gleaning amongst water weeds, mostly in submerged vegetation, but also from surface along edges of floating vegetation; dives average 16 seconds.
Breeding. Laying in Dec/Jan, sometimes Feb. Colonial; colonies always in open areas and dense, with 5-75 pairs. Nest is weed platform, larger than in other grebes of comparable size, probably related to effects of waves and wind; built on thick floating carpets of water weeds; always 2 eggs, but only 1 chick hatches, as second egg abandoned if first hatches successfully; chicks have grey down with bold stripes, paler underparts. Sexual maturity possibly at 2 years old. Exceedingly low reproductive rate, with many pairs failing to rear single chick to fledging: average of 0·12 young reared per adult per year (including non-breeders); estimated 0·40-0·45 young per nesting pair.
Movements. Migratory. Much movement of flocks between lakes during summer; numbers vary from day to day, suggesting nightly movements. Birds leave before lakes freeze over in May: originally assumed to winter at sea, on Atlantic coast, or in fjords and channels of S Chile; but seems unlikely that they cover long distances; delayed discovery of species and almost complete absence of records away from upland plateaux suggest probable wintering close to breeding areas, perhaps on nearby lakes large enough to have permanently ice-free areas, e.g. L Islote, L Quiroga and L Strobel. Apparently may occasionally establish breeding colonies in areas marginal to main range. Casually near Paine, in Magallanes (S Chile).
Status and Conservation. Not globally threatened. Until very recently classified as Rare. Discovered in 1974, with 150 birds on Laguna Los Escarchados; site declared reserve in 1979. Found breeding on 2 nearby lakes, but by 1981 known population had dropped to 75 birds, due to breeding success of virtually nil, largely caused by predation of chicks by Kelp Gulls (*Larus dominicanus*). In 1981 second breeding population of c. 250 individuals discovered on Meseta de Tobiano, basaltic plateau 120 km to N; this population slid to only 45 birds in 1984, again due to predation by gulls. Species appeared to be heading towards extinction, despite intense campaign by conservationists involving control of predators, artificial incubation of eggs and captive breeding. In same year core area of species' range discovered on Meseta de Strobel, with c. 1500 pairs. Apparently populations previously known were marginal, undergoing regular fluctuations and breeding occasionally in S of main range. Total population estimated at minimum of 5000 birds in 1986, with far less worrying status. Meseta de Strobel well conserved at present due to remoteness and inaccessibility; only current threat is excessive grazing by sheep, causing erosion of shores of lakes and pools and limiting growth of emergent vegetation. See page 187.

Bibliography. Beltrán (1988), Collar & Andrew (1988), Conway (1980), Diamond *et al*. (1987), Erize (1981, 1983), Fjeldså (1982a, 1983b, 1984a, 1984b, 1984c, 1985a, 1986a, 1986b, 1989b), Fjeldså & Krabbe (1990), King (1978/79), König (1984), Lange (1981), Nuechterlein (1981e), Nuechterlein & Johnson (1980/81), Nuechterlein & Storer (1989b), de la Peña (1986), Rumboll (1974), Scott & Carbonell (1986), Simmons (1983), Storer (1980/81, 1982), Straneck & Johnson (1984).

Genus *AECHMOPHORUS* Coues, 1862

21. Western Grebe

Aechmophorus occidentalis

French: Grèbe élégant **German**: Renntaucher **Spanish**: Achichilique Común

Taxonomy. *Podiceps occidentalis* Lawrence, 1858, Fort Steilacoom, Washington.
Formerly included *A. clarkii*, which until recently considered a colour morph. Name *clarkii* was also applied to smaller southern race, including birds of both "colour morphs", now classified as *A. o. ephemeralis* and *A. c. clarkii*. Distribution limits of races not well established. Two subspecies recognized.
Subspecies and Distribution.
A. o. occidentalis Lawrence 1858 - SW & SC Canada, W & NC USA; winters Pacific coast S to Baja California.
A. o. ephemeralis Dickerman 1986 - CW & SC Mexico.

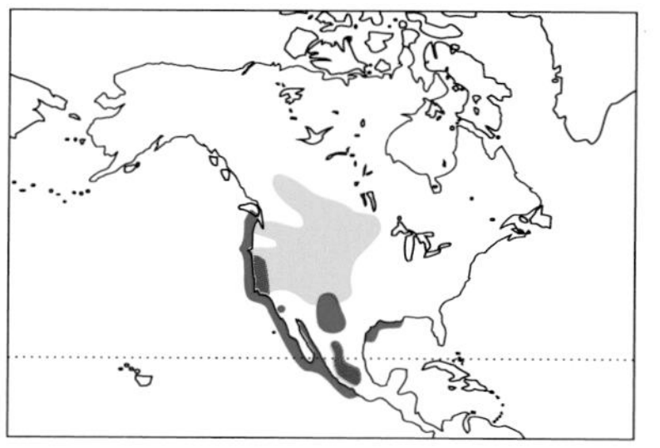

Descriptive notes. 51-74 cm; 550-1225 g. More black on face than *A. clarkii*, bill dirty yellow, back and flanks duskier. Females lighter. Non-breeding adult has crown and hindneck duller, less clearly demarcated from white throat and foreneck. Juvenile as non-breeding adult, but greyer, with transition between dark and light plumage more diffuse. Races separated on size.
Habitat. Breeds on freshwater, slightly brackish or brackish marshes, lakes, reservoirs and ponds; prefers sizeable sites with large stretches of open water, generally fringed with rushes. In winter favours brackish and salt waters, especialy at sea, in bays, estuaries and often out into deep offshore waters; sometimes on inland freshwater sites.
Food and Feeding. Mainly fish, both freshwater and marine, making up 81% to almost 100% of diet in mass; takes some very large fish, up to 20·5 cm long. Also feeds on aquatic insects, especially corixid bugs (much more important in spring and summer than winter), molluscs, crustaceans, marine worms and few amphibians. Main method is diving, with average duration of c. 30 seconds; more intensive at hours when underwater visibility greatest, when sun's rays strike water at high angle. Alternates rapid bursts of diving with longer periods at surface, suggesting feeding on schools of fish.

Breeding. Laying May-July in USA, but more extended in Mexico, with eggs May-Oct. Colonial, sometimes in large colonies, with hundreds or even thousands of nests, often mixed with *A. clarkii*; also single nests at times; nest is fairly solid mound of plant matter resting on bottom or floating. Usually 3-4 eggs, but up to 16 counted in single nest, undoubtedly due to joint laying, a common practice in *Aechmophorus* colonies; 1 brood; incubation 21-28 days; chicks have smokey grey down, whitish on head and underparts, lacking characteristic striped patterns of most grebe chicks; fledging c. 70 days (captivity). Success very variable, with 21-84% hatching success in different studies.

Movements. Migratory; almost entire population of USA and Canada winters down Pacific coast. Migration starts in Sept, with movements towards saltwater locations in W; gatherings of several thousand not uncommon at staging posts. Migration nocturnal over land, but partly diurnal along coast. Vagrant to Aleutian Is and Atlantic and Gulf coasts, as far as Tampa Bay, Florida. Mexican populations presumably fairly sedentary, with some local movements between different habitats, depending on season.

Status and Conservation. Not globally threatened. Common in several parts of range and locally abundant. At Marshy Point, Manitoba, breeding population estimated at c. 8000 birds in 1982. Many thousands killed in 19th and early 20th centuries for plume trade, until protected in 1918. Research has shown negative effects of pesticides on breeding success, and has practically disappeared from several Californian lakes that formerly held breeding populations. Marked gregarious tendencies make it highly susceptible to oil spills, as regularly winters on coast: c. 11,000 birds, half of all the birds affected, died after oil spill in San Francisco Bay in 1972. Has undoubtedly benefited from construction of reservoirs, especially in SW USA during 20th century.

Bibliography. Ahlquist *et al.* (1987), Burger (1971), Davis (1961), Dickerman (1973, 1986), Feerer (1977), Feerer & Garret (1977), Forbes (1985a, 1985b, 1988), Forbes & Sealy (1988, 1990), Gilliland (1984), Henshaw (1881), Herman (1973), Herman *et al.* (1969), James (1989), Johnsgard (1987), Kaufman (1979), Lawrence (1950), Lee (1967), Lindvall (1976), Lindvall & Low (1980, 1982), Nero (1959, 1960, 1972), Nero *et al.* (1958), Nuechterlein (1975, 1980, 1981a, 1981b, 1981c, 1981d, 1982, 1985, 1988), Nuechterlein & Buitron (1989), Nuechterlein & Storer (1982, 1989a), Palmer (1962), Paul (1969), Ratti (1977, 1979, 1985), Ratti *et al.* (1983), Scammell-Tinling (1983), Sibley, F.C. (1970), Storer (1965, 1989a), Storer & Nuechterlein (1985), Terres (1980), White & Ratti (1977), Williams, S.O. (1982), Ydenberg & Clark (1989), Ydenberg & Forbes (1988).

22. Clark's Grebe
Aechmophorus clarkii

French: Grèbe à face blanche   **German**: Clarktaucher   **Spanish**: Achichilique de Clark

Taxonomy. *Podiceps clarkii* Lawrence, 1858, California and New [*sic*] Mexico.
Recently separated from *A. occidentalis*, on grounds of wide sympatry with only rare hybridization; probably prevented by differences in advertising calls. Formely considered merely light phase of *A. occidentalis*. Name *clarkii* was also applied to smaller southern race, including birds of both "colour morphs", now classified as *A. o. ephemeralis* and *A. c. clarkii*. Distribution limits of races not well established. Two subspecies recognized.

Subspecies and Distribution.
A. c. clarkii Lawrence 1858 - Mexican Plateau from N Chihuahua to N Guerrero; Nayarit; (?) L Caballo (New Mexico).
A. c. transitionalis Dickerman 1986 - W USA, N to Utah and Colorado.

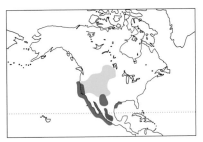

Descriptive notes. 51-74 cm; 550-1225 g. Differs from *A. occidentalis* in orangish yellow bill, more white on face and wing bar, and paler back and flanks. Females lighter. Non-breeding adult has crown and hindneck duller, less clearly demarcated from white face and foreneck. Juvenile as non-breeding adult, but greyer. Races separated on size.

Habitat. Generally uses same habitats as *A. occidentalis*; at sites where the two species coincide, present species usually tends to occupy more central parts of lakes and other, similar water bodies, where water is normally deeper. Winter habitat has not yet been clearly defined.

Food and Feeding. Probably very similar to *A. occidentalis*, with which often forms mixed feeding flocks: thus, mainly fish with some aquatic insects, especially during breeding season. Where both *Aechmophorus* coincide, present species tends to forage further from shore, and uses more springing dives; may feed at greater depth, thus reducing foraging overlap (see page 180). Nevertheless, research has shown that, while stomachs of female *clarkii* contained significantly smaller fish than those of female *occidentalis*, there were no significant differences between males.

Breeding. Laying May-July in USA, but more extended in Mexico, with eggs May-Oct. Colonial, sometimes in large mixed colonies with *A. occidentalis*, with hundreds or even thousands of nests; nest is fairly solid mound of plant matter resting on bottom or floating. Usually 3-4 eggs, though up to 7 counted in 1 nest, perhaps due to joint laying, a common practice in *Aechmophorus* colonies; 1 brood; incubation c. 23 days; chicks paler grey than in *A. occidentalis*, but similarly lacking characteristic striped patterns of most grebe chicks; fledging 63-77 days. Success variable and results from mixed colony gave higher success than for *A. occidentalis*: present species made up only 18·6% of total population, but 33·6% of all pairs with young successfully hatched; also has slightly greater clutch and brood size.

Movements. No information available; populations from USA probably winter along coast in company of *A. occidentalis*; in S of range, presumably sedentary with some local movements between habitats.

Status and Conservation. Not globally threatened. Much rarer than *A. occidentalis* in N of range, with under 1% of joint population in Canada and 12-18% in Utah; becomes steadily more frequent towards S, and is the more numerous breeder in California. Likely to suffer from same adverse factors as *A. occidentalis*, especially contamination of lakes and oil spills. In many lakes in highlands of C Mexico cutting of tule rushes (*Scirpus*) for local weaving industries probably has detrimental effects on grebe colonies; thought to be cause of apparent complete breeding failure on heavily exploited Lago de Pátzcuaro, in Michoacán. In highlands of N Mexico, species mainly breeds on reservoirs, and proliferation of these during 20th century has contributed to recent success of species in this region.

Bibliography. Ahlquist *et al.* (1987), Bunn (1986), Crabtree (1985), DeSmet (1987b), Dickerman (1963, 1973, 1986), Eckert (1989), Falk (1989), Feerer (1977), Feerer & Garret (1977), Henshaw (1881), Hunter (1985), Johnsgard (1987), Kaufman (1979), Labedz (1987), Lawrence (1950), Lindvall & Low (1982), Nuechterlein (1975, 1980, 1981a, 1981b, 1981c, 1981d, 1988), Nuechterlein & Buitron (1989), Nuechterlein & Storer (1982, 1989a), Palmer (1962), Ratti (1977, 1979, 1981, 1985, 1986), Ratti *et al.* (1983), Storer (1965, 1989), Storer & Nuechterlein (1985), Terres (1980), White & Ratti (1977), Williams (1982), Ydenberg & Clark (1989), Ydenberg & Forbes (1988).

Order PROCELLARIIFORMES

Procellariiformes

Diomedeidae	Procellariidae	Hydrobatidae	Pelecanoididae
albatrosses	petrels, shearwaters	storm-petrels	diving-petrels

Class AVES
Order PROCELLARIIFORMES
Family DIOMEDEIDAE (ALBATROSSES)

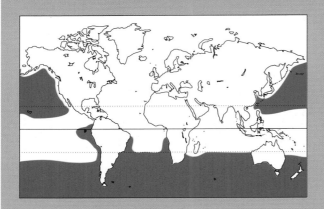

- Large, heavy seabirds with very long wings, long, heavy bill and "tubenose".
- 71-135 cm.

- Circumpolar in Southern Ocean, with outposts in North Pacific.
- Marine and pelagic.
- 2 genera, 14 species, 21 taxa.
- 2 species threatened; none extinct since 1600.

Systematics

The earliest recognizable albatrosses date back to Eocene times, some 50 million years ago. They probably originated in the Southern Hemisphere and subsequently spread northwards into the North Pacific, as is supported by the fact that the three species resident there, the Laysan Albatross (*Diomedea immutabilis*), the Black-footed Albatross (*Diomedea nigripes*) and the Short-tailed Albatross (*Diomedea albatrus*), breed during the local winter, which is the austral summer. There are also fossil records of an extinct species, *Diomedea anglica*, which was probably widespread in the North Atlantic during the Pliocene, since its remains have been found on both sides of the ocean, in Florida and in East Anglia, in eastern England.

The living forms are split into two quite distinct genera, *Diomedea*, with 12 living species and some 18-20 forms, and *Phoebetria*, comprising two relatively small, dark, long-tailed species, which are both monotypic.

Within the genus *Diomedea*, a distinctive group of species is formed by the three "great" albatrosses, the Wandering Albatross (*Diomedea exulans*), the Royal Albatross (*Diomedea epomophora*) and the Amsterdam Albatross (*Diomedea amsterdamensis*), all of which have exceptionally long breeding cycles that only allow them to attempt breeding once every two years. The Amsterdam Albatross, only described in 1983, might be better considered a race of the Wandering Albatross, and populations of the latter in the Antipodes Islands, off southern New Zealand, appear fairly similar. It has even been suggested that the lost type specimen for *D. exulans* could have been an Amsterdam Albatross, which would imply a considerable upheaval of the standard nomenclature, but it seems unlikely.

The great albatrosses share the high seas of the Southern Hemisphere with the "mollymawks", a group of five medium-sized, externally rather similar species, which have dark backs and often show bright colours on the bill. The only exclusively tropical species, the Waved Albatross (*Diomedea irrorata*) of the Galapagos Islands, is thought to be the most primitive extant species, due to its simple coloration and the fact that it does not build a nest.

Another group is formed by the three species of the North Pacific, which have parallel life histories but are markedly dissimilar in plumage. Like the Wandering and Royal Albatrosses, the Short-tailed Albatross undergoes a long sequence of immature plumages starting from an all dark juvenile and ending up as a white-bodied adult. The dark-backed Laysan Albatross, with its dark eye patches and tail, closely resembles the mollymawks, while the Black-footed Albatross is rather small and wholly dark.

Morphological Aspects

Albatrosses are amongst the largest flying birds and are characterized by their exceptionally long, narrow wings. These have enabled them to become amongst the most prodigious fliers of all, and their mastery of the air is unquestionable.

The great albatrosses have the largest wingspans of all birds, and that of the Wandering Albatross can exceed 350 cm. In the other species it is considerably smaller, though still impressive, for instance about 200 cm in the Yellow-nosed Albatross (*Diomedea chlororhynchos*). On stiff wings, albatrosses glide along, alternately rising and falling, in order to take advantage of the varying wind speeds at different heights. The wind creates the waves but moves faster than them, so most of its force rolls over the waves at greater speed. By dynamic soaring, albatrosses can cover enormous distances with a low expenditure of energy. A bird glides along the trough between two waves, and, as it loses speed, it turns into the wind, which lifts it over the oncoming wave and up to a height of 10-15 m, where the air-stream levels off. Thence it will drift down into a new trough and start the manoeuvre all over again. This process is repeated endlessly, night and day, when the bird is travelling long distances.

The wind is rarely so strong that albatrosses are unable to fly, and only the wildest storms keep them down on the water. Calm weather, in contrast, can leave them stranded either on the water or on dry land, when they can not take off. Albatrosses are heavy birds, and their very long, narrow wings are not suitable for powered flight. More than a few wingbeats in succession would quickly exhaust them, so when the surface wind speed drops below 18 km/h, the birds are forced to settle on the water.

Take-off is not an easy manoeuvre for an albatross, especially for the larger species. A bird sitting on the water needs a short run, helping itself with its feet, after which it can usually become airborne. It invariably attempts take-off facing into the wind, as this obviously helps to give lift. At breeding colonies, there is usually at least one "runway", which tends to consist of a long, narrow stretch of ground free of nests, and this is used for both take-off and landing. It is usually on some kind of a slope, and always on the windiest side of both the colony and the island. In order to get off the ground, a bird must run down-

This Waved Albatross illustrates many of the typical features of albatross morphology, the long, narrow wings, the compact body, and the shortish, rounded tail, in this case with the feet projecting beyond the tip. The head and neck are large and strong, to support the hefty hooked bill. The Waved Albatross is unique in having dark plumage with a pale head.

[*Diomedea irrorata,* Galapagos. Photo: Günter Ziesler]

hill into the wind with its wings spread. Then, with the help of a few wingbeats, it normally manages to take off, as long as the air-stream uphill is strong enough to keep it airborne.

Rapid manoeuvres are not easy for a flying albatross. One of the most difficult exercises can be landing at its breeding grounds, especially at the beginning of the season, when the bird is not yet familiar with the local air currents and has still not learnt how to use the particular eddies and updraughts of the site. There is very little a bird can do to evade an unforseen obstacle between it and its intended landing place, and serious accidents are not infrequent. Some involve humans, most notably collisions with aircraft (see Relationship with Man). Landing on water tends to be less complicated, and, of course, less dangerous. The bird flies low over the surface of the water and into the wind, stretching its wings backwards, before it touches down with its feet spread. Sometimes a few wingbeats are used to help with braking.

The bill and head are large, while the neck is thick and strong. The body is rather compact and great albatrosses can weigh almost 12 kg, making them amongst the heaviest of flying birds. In the genus *Diomedea,* the tail is rounded and short, most notably in the aptly named Short-tailed Albatross.

Amongst the most outstanding characteristics of albatross anatomy are the size and complex structure of the hooked bill, which is made up of several horny plates. In many cases it has some bright orange or yellow markings, while in others it is uniformly pinkish or dark. As in all Procellariiformes, or "tubenoses", there are external tubular nostrils on the bill. These are generally associated with a remarkable sense of smell, which is unusually acute for birds, and can be used for finding food or a bird's own nest; albatrosses may even be able to recognize each other individually by smell. The excess salt in the birds' diet, which is filtered by the salt glands above each eye, is excreted through the bill, and it can often be seen dribbling off the tip. Again, like other members of the order, albatrosses have a distinctive musty smell, which comes from the stomach oil (see Breeding).

The legs are short but powerful, and birds can stand and walk about comfortably on land. Due to the shortness of their legs,

they sway from side to side as they walk, and this movement has been adapted and exaggerated by the Waved Albatross to form part of its nuptial display. Albatrosses are buoyant and swim well. They use their large, webbed feet to propel themselves along the surface, and are able to cope with very rough seas.

Diomedea albatrosses mostly have the upperwing and the tail dark, whereas underparts tend to be pale, especially in adult plumage. Most species and plumages have both the head and rump whitish. The adult's face can be white, light yellow or grey, and many forms have a patch of dark feathers around and before the eye, resembling an eyebrow, for instance the Black-browed Albatross (*Diomedea melanophris*). By attracting sunlight, this patch improves vision, as it deviates sunlight that would otherwise strike the eye directly.

Immatures of most *Diomedea* species differ from adults only in that they have duller colours on the head or bill. They are virtually indistinguishable from adults in the Laysan (whence *immutabilis*) and Waved Albatrosses. On the other hand, young Wandering, Royal and Short-tailed Albatrosses undergo a long sequence of intermediate plumages, starting with a variable, mostly dark plumage, and gradually working up to the whitest forms, usually at a fair old age. At any rate some birds reach sexual maturity while still in what is understood as immature plumage, and a few have been known to breed successfully. Some individuals of these species, presumably very old males, are mainly white above and below, a plumage known as the "snowy stage". However, in all species the flight-feathers always retain their dark coloration. Albatrosses need to cover great distances every day when foraging, and dark feathers, with higher melanin content, are far more resistant to abrasion by salt water and sunlight than light-coloured ones. As the flight-feathers are moulted almost entirely at sea, very little is known about the mode of moult, and progress in this field of research is liable to be slow.

Phoebetria albatrosses are dark chocolate-brown all over, with variable amounts of greyish buff on the mantle and the breast and around the neck. They are similar in size to the mollymawks, but the wings are narrower and the tail is long and pointed. The bill is long and black, with a narrow line, or

Due to their enormous wingspan and more particularly their very high wing-loading, albatrosses can have considerable difficulty with both taking off and landing. Take-off often requires a substantial run-up, particularly if there is little wind to help. Landing can be hazardous, as the birds have little braking power and very limited manoeuvrability, due to the short tail, and it is not unusual for a bird to crash-land on its side or turn head over heels. Some colonies have special "runways" free from nests and other obstacles, which reduce some of these difficulties.

[Diomedea immutabilis, Midway Atoll, Hawaiian Is. Photo: Frans Lanting/ Bruce Coleman]

"sulcus", along the sides of the lower mandible; this is yellow or orange in the Sooty Albatross (*Phoebetria fusca*) and blue or purple in the Light-mantled Albatross (*Phoebetria palpebrata*). Both species have a narrow, but conspicuous, white eye-ring. Juvenile plumage is like the adult's, except for the duller sulcus and slightly greater extent of pale plumage.

Habitat

Among the most oceanic of all seabirds, albatrosses seldom approach land, except for breeding, and they commonly spend much of the time far out in the midst of the ocean. Most species wander thousands of miles on the high seas, shunning the relatively shallow waters over the continental shelf. However, they are attracted by the special richness of certain feeding areas, where they may gather in good numbers. This is the case of the Benguela Current off South Africa and Namibia, and of the Humboldt Current off western South America. The Black-browed, Black-footed and Waved Albatrosses are among the

least pelagic species, and all of them are known to occur regularly near coastal waters.

The stronghold of the albatross family is in the high latitudes of the Southern Hemisphere, where ten of the fourteen species are found. Here, in the Roaring Forties, as mariners called the zone due to the persistent strong winds, the conditions are ideal for the flying style of the albatrosses (see Morphological Aspects), in contrast with the calm of the doldrums nearer the equator. The albatrosses patrol the open ocean of the Roaring Forties, and forage far from land, even during the breeding season, and this has important implications on their breeding strategy (see Breeding).

Breeding colonies are usually established on remote oceanic islands. These are frequently sloping and windswept, and most of them lack tall vegetation, while some are completely bare. However, on Midway Island, in Hawaii, about 175,000 pairs of Laysan Albatrosses nest on the ground in the shelter provided by tall trees planted by men, and some nests are within a few metres of occupied houses and other buildings. The three great albatrosses and the Short-tailed Albatross nest on flat or sloping ground with tall grass. Most mollymawks and the genus *Phoebetria* build their nests on the grassy ledges of cliffs or steep slopes, and in places, Buller's Albatross (*Diomedea bulleri*) also occupies areas covered by bushy vegetation. Rocky islands strewn with boulders are sometimes used too, most notably by the Shy Albatross (*Diomedea cauta*) and by the Waved Albatross at its main breeding grounds on Española (Hood) Island in the Galapagos. Sandy beaches too may be used, and they form the typical nesting habitat of the Black-footed Albatross.

General Habits

At sea, albatrosses are solitary most of the time, though they sometimes move about in small flocks. Large congregations occur where food is abundant or at nesting grounds, but social interactions are generally less intense than in other seabirds, such as the Pelecaniformes. The only time when there is regular competition for food at sea is when they attend trawlers, but even then there is little threatening or actual fighting (see Food and Feeding).

Birds are often gregarious at their resting areas. Several hundred Royal Albatrosses may gather together in loafing areas, these

Despite the fact that it is one of the smaller species, the Sooty Albatross still has a very impressive wingspan of around two metres. The genus Phoebetria differs from Diomedea in having narrower, more pointed wings and a much longer, wedge-shaped tail. Other characteristic features of the former are the white eye-ring and the sulcus, a conspicuous pale line along the lower mandible.

[Phoebetria fusca, Gough Island. Photo: Clem Haagner/ Ardea]

birds tending to be the older immatures and other birds that have not yet bred. Adult Shy Albatrosses regularly form communal roosts in sheltered zones away from the nests, once their chicks are large enough to be left alone. In contrast, both of the *Phoebetria* albatrosses roost at or near the nest throughout the breeding season, while at other times they roost at sea. Buller's Albatrosses typically roost on the water fairly close to the colony. For roosting, albatrosses normally adopt a posture with the head resting down the back, often partly under a wing.

As albatrosses can not fly in totally calm weather (see Morphological Aspects), they may be forced to roost on the water when there is not enough wind. They often continue flying at night, and on moonlit nights can be seen following ships, indeed Wandering Albatrosses have been known to tail the same ship for six consecutive days and nights.

Voice

Although they are usually silent at sea, albatrosses make several croaking, shrieking or gargling sounds when competing for food, especially for offal from fishing boats.

On land, throaty cries, groans, grunts and moans normally accompany the various displays. All species produce a highly characteristic rattling sound by clappering the bill quickly and repeatedly, and this is used in various stages of courtship display, though it also serves as a threat to discourage potential intruders. Breeding colonies can be fairly noisy, and in the Light-mantled Albatross, for example, birds tend to call mostly during the day, almost invariably at the nest-site. As breeding progresses, the amount of calling tends to decrease, though immature Yellow-nosed Albatrosses usually remain vociferous long after adults have become silent.

Food and Feeding

Squid probably constitutes the most important type of prey for albatrosses in general, and many species depend heavily on it. Large shoals of squid perform vertical migrations usually by night, when they come up to surface waters, where the albatrosses can prey on them. As daylight spreads, the squid tend to move back down again, with the result that they remain out of reach of the surface-feeding albatrosses.

Another significant component of the albatross diet is fish, and a wide range of species are taken, varying with the locality. These include lampreys (*Gorea*), small flying-fish, pilchards (*Sardinops*) and rockfish (Scorpaenidae). Crustaceans too are important, in particular krill (*Euphausia*), although amphipods, copepods and crabs are also eaten. Other prey items that have been recorded include algae, sea urchins, fish spawn, medusae and barnacles. Some species, such as the Sooty Albatross, eat carrion, which they probably find floating on the surface of the ocean; stomachs have revealed pieces of prions, diving-petrels and penguins.

Man has helped albatrosses in many areas by providing easy and often reliable sources of additional food. One of the most typical of these is the refuse from ships' galleys, and albatrosses are particularly fond of animal fat. Many species regularly follow ships, partly for the aerodynamic advantages (see Relationship with Man), but partly also for the scraps thrown overboard; they also follow cetaceans on occasions, perhaps catching prey that is disturbed. The blubber of sea mammals is another extra form of food for albatrosses, and the whaling and sealing industries certainly made this more readily available.

Albatrosses normally obtain their food by sitting on the water, catching their prey by means of surface-seizing. The

Albatrosses have a style of flight that is highly efficient in the strong winds that prevail in the Southern Ocean. They frequently use dynamic soaring, first turning into the wind to gain height and then gliding in the desired direction and gradually losing height, before repeating the process over and over again. They are at home in the strongest of winds and take advantage of any eddies created as the wind rebounds off the waves. However, they are not well equipped for sustained flapping flight, and when there is no wind at all, they may remain becalmed on the water for some time, until the wind rises again and they can take off.

[*Diomedea chlororhynchos.*
Photo: M. P. Kahl/DRK]

Albatrosses typically feed by surface-seizing, sitting on the water and picking up food items with the bill. Several species regularly occur in commercial trawling grounds, where they feed on offal from the ships. In such cases they frequently occur alongside other Procellariiformes, like the Cape Petrels (Daption capense) that are feeding in the company of this Shy Albatross.

[*Diomedea cauta salvini*, off Kaikoura, New Zealand. Photo: A. Greensmith/ Ardea]

largest species, in particular, have difficulty manoeuvring on the wing, so it is only the most agile fliers that can pick up food in flight. Even around fishing boats, where food is plentiful, but birds are also numerous and competition for food is more intense, most albatrosses alight on the water before starting to feed, and birds may have to make short flights repeatedly to keep up with a boat. This procedure leads to the spacing out of feeding birds and prevents conflicts.

Like shearwaters, the smaller albatrosses sometimes make shallow plunges, going about a metre under the surface of the water, and this system has actually been recorded for the Wandering Albatross too. It is a technique that is often used for collecting fish scraps that have been thrown overboard and are slowly sinking. Another method observed in the Black-browed Albatross is underwater swimming, which can take the bird some five metres down.

Kleptoparasitism has been recorded, most notably in the Waved Albatross. It has been seen to attack boobies (*Sula*), as they take off after a successful dive, forcing them to regurgitate their recent catch.

Breeding

The breeding cycle of the great albatrosses is unusually long, lasting over one full year from nest building to the departure of the chick. In these species, therefore, when breeding is successful, it can only be attempted every two years. Amongst the mollymawks, several species have breeding cycles that are short enough to be fitted into less than one year, which would allow an annual repetition of the full cycle, but the Grey-headed Albatross (*Diomedea chrysostoma*), if successful, only breeds

every other year, as do the two *Phoebetria* species, perhaps the Short-tailed Albatross and possibly others.

Although birds are, in fact, sexually fertile at four to six years of age, they do not normally attempt breeding for the first time until they are rather older, on average at seven or nine. While the Waved Albatross may start at five or six years old, the larger species do not try until they are at least ten or eleven.

Most species nest in colonies of several hundred to a few thousand nests. Huge colonies of over 100,000 pairs are exceptional, and are only known for the Laysan and Black-browed Albatrosses. Nests are well spaced out even in the largest colonies, and the distance between nests ranges from 1·3 m in the smaller species to 4-25 m in the larger. This keeps sitting birds out of reach of each other, so the degree of interaction between individual albatrosses is much lower than in other seabirds.

Especially during the early stages of the breeding cycle, a pair of albatrosses defend their nest-site by bill-snapping at intruders, and short, violent fights are not infrequent early on. Ritualized territorial behaviour includes a number of postures, through which the occupant advertises its status to potential intruders. However, competition for nest-sites is not an essential procedure among low-density breeders which generally form small colonies. Albatrosses tend to lose their territorial instincts after just a few weeks of fighting, but any living creature that passes within close range of a sitting bird is liable to be pecked at, and a chick that strays too far from its own nest can receive a serious injury.

Albatrosses generally pair for life and have a very ample repertoire of courtship displays, mainly directed towards pair formation, and in many cases the pair is actually formed during the season prior to breeding. The birds spend much of their time performing a long sequence of stereotyped postures, which

The courtship display of the great albatrosses is highly spectacular. The "Ecstatic Ritual" involves "Wing-stretching", which in the Wandering Albatross may be accompanied by some "Bill-vibrating". At the climax of the display birds often produce a loud, braying whistle followed by an inhaled sigh, with the bill raised to vertical. Most displaying activity is performed by pre-breeders. At South Georgia there may be some 40-100 nests per hectare, but birds only defend a territory stretching for a metre or two around the nest.

[*Diomedea exulans exulans*, South Georgia. Photo: Francisco Erize/ Bruce Coleman]

are repeated over and over again. These include actions like "Bill-circling", "Sky-pointing", "Flank-touching" with the bill, an exaggerated "Head-swaying Walk", in the Waved Albatross, and full spreading of the wings in the great albatrosses, often accompanied by various calls, and usually performed with the birds facing each other. Such displays do not necessarily occur in the territory, and some may even be performed at sea. On occasions, there is a form of communal dancing, which can involve pairs that are in the active process of formation and also loose birds.

Confirmation of the pair-bond between a mated pair that have already attempted breeding in previous years does not require such elaborate displays. Their meeting point is already established at the nest-site of previous attempts, and here the male usually arrives some days before the female. They rejoin and perform a few greeting ceremonies, after which their breeding attempt is soon under way. "Divorce" is not common in albatrosses and is only liable to occur after a long series of failed breeding attempts, so under normal circumstances only death can rupture the pair. The surviving bird then has to go through the elaborate courtship display again, before pairing with a new mate, a process to which it will have to dedicate at least one full season.

All southern albatrosses build a proper nest, which may be reused in successive years. It is usually made of mud, grass and moss, in the form of a large truncated cone, with a shallow depression on top for the egg or chick and the sitting bird. The nest may be 15-90 cm high, depending on both species and location, being wider in the larger species and higher in wetter places. The three North Pacific albatrosses make more rudimentary nests: the Black-footed simply digs out a scrape in the sand; the Laysan builds up a substantial rim around the chosen

site by accumulating grass, twigs, sand, pebbles and many other items; and the Short-tailed builds a shallow structure of earth and some plant matter. The Waved Albatross, in contrast, is unique among albatrosses in that it builds no nest at all, laying its egg on the bare ground, with the result that it may be moved about a fair bit during incubation.

Invariably one egg only is laid. It weighs 205-487 g, about 5-11% of the female's body weight. The investment incurred in laying a relatively heavy egg can prove worthwhile, as it has a better chance of producing a healthy chick, but it takes a long time and a good deal of energy to produce. For this reason, there is normally no replacement laying, so a pair that loses its egg or an early chick will not attempt breeding again until the following year. Incubation is a lengthy process, lasting some 10-11 weeks on average, and is typically shared between the sexes, in stints of several days at a time.

The different roles played by the sexes are of vital importance to the successful development of the chick, and are worth examining. Having arrived at the nesting territory of the previous year, the male defends it against other males and waits for his partner, in the meanwhile rebuilding the nest or starting a new one. Upon the female's arrival a few days later, the birds display, choose a nest-site and copulate, after which they both go back to sea for the first time since they arrived on the island, in the case of the male one or two weeks earlier. At sea they feed and build up reserves, in the case of the female for making the egg, and for the male in order to start incubation. Both birds return shortly before the egg is laid, but the female returns to sea immediately afterwards, while the male stays on to take the first stint of incubation.

The male sits on the egg for days on end, without any food or water, until his mate arrives to relieve him. Once he is back

Like many other petrels, albatrosses form a permanent pair-bond, which normally lasts until one of the partners dies, although repeated breeding failures can lead to the separation of the pair. Wandering Albatrosses do not normally breed until about eleven years old on average, and some breed for the first time at sixteen. In this species copulation occurs 1-26 days before the egg is laid, always on land and usually at the nest. During this period males seem to be charged up and may attempt to mate with any passing female.

[Diomedea exulans exulans, Bird Island, South Georgia.
Photo: Julian Hector/ Planet Earth]

at sea, he has just enough time to put on enough weight before it is the female's turn to go off and feed. The length of incubation stints varies with the weather, availability of food, distance to foraging areas, and so on, averaging three to seven days in the smaller species, and two or three weeks in the great albatrosses. This repeated alternation of parental duties continues throughout incubation and until the chick is three to five weeks old and no longer needs to be brooded constantly. The chick is then left alone and both parents go off to sea to fetch food for it. At first parental visits are almost daily but they soon become more spaced out and occur only every few days. The growing chick often wanders freely about between such visits, but it rarely goes far, since it will be fed only at the nest-site itself, and not in the vicinity. There is no "desertion" period as in the Procellariidae (see page 227), and after a period of wing exercising, the chick simply flies out to sea on its own one day, between the visits of its parents.

The chick is fed a mixture of partly digested fish and squid, as well as stomach oil that the adults produce during the ordinary digestion of their food. A steady stream of oil squirts from the adult's mouth into the chick's bill, which is placed crosswise in its parent's. This foul-smelling oil is rich in fats, and it facilitates the task of gathering and transporting food to the chick, as adults often forage at several days' flying distance from the nest. This same factor explains the exceptionally long incubation and brooding stints, and the chick's extraordinary resistance to starvation. Although it is fed rather infrequently, the chick soon starts to put on weight and eventually becomes much heavier than its parents. However, much energy is consumed in the growth of the feathers, so by the time it fledges it weighs about the same as its parents.

Breeding success is generally quite high, with 30-60% of breeding attempts resulting in one chick successfully raised to fledging. Most of the losses take place during the early stages, when the egg or young chick, if left unattended, is most at risk of being taken by predators such as skuas (*Catharacta*) or

sheathbills (*Chionis*). When threatened, both adults and chicks may regurgitate the contents of their stomachs onto a predator. In most species, over 80% of the chicks hatched survive to fledge. The chances of raising a healthy chick are much reduced, however, when one of the parents is injured or dies, in which case the survivor rarely succeeds in rearing the chick, and this often starves to death. Healthy pairs too sometimes have poor levels of breeding success, for instance the Black-browed Albatross may produce hardly any young when the crustaceans that form its staple diet fail to form large swarms near the surface. The Waved Albatross, in turn, may desert eggs and young in abnormally wet years, due to the swarms of flies and mosquitos and the lush vegetation, as none of these are so abundant in normal, dry years.

Albatrosses are extraordinarily long-lived, and ringing results have yielded recaptures of individuals aged over 40 in several species. One of the oldest wild birds ever recorded was a Royal Albatross, which was still breeding at over 58. In fact, given the very low mortality rate of 3-11% among the adults of most species, a few birds should theoretically live over 80 years. To compensate for such longevity and the high breeding success to fledging, mortality is very high amongst immature birds, leaving only 10-20% to survive and breed; almost 70% of young Wandering Albatrosses die during their first year.

Movements

As they are unsuited to sustained flapping flight (see Morphological Aspects), albatrosses can not fly in totally calm weather, so the typically calm, windless conditions that prevail in the doldrums tend to prevent southern albatrosses from penetrating regularly into the Northern Hemisphere. However, some individuals are known to have reached northern latitudes, including Wandering and Yellow-nosed Albatrosses in the Atlantic and Wandering and Shy Albatrosses in the Pacific. In some cases,

The Waved Albatross is the only member of the family that lays directly on the ground without making any kind of nest at all. This means that during the two months or so of incubation the single egg may be moved about a good deal, on occasions as much as 50 metres. As a result of this, a fair number of eggs are lost, mostly through breakage or when they fall into cracks or hollows, from which the birds are unable to remove or incubate them.

[*Diomedea irrorata*, Española I, Galapagos. Photo: Dieter & Mary Plage/ Survival]

Unlike the four more northerly species, all of the southern albatrosses build a substantial nest. This is a heap of earth and grass piled up to form a truncated cone, with a shallow depression on top; sometimes a clump of tussock grass may be built into the structure. They frequently nest in exposed sites on high ground, like these Black-browed Albatrosses, in order to ease the problems they have with take-off.

[*Diomedea melanophris melanophris*, South Georgia. Photo: Julian Hector/ Planet Earth]

During their first few weeks of life albatross chicks are brooded more or less constantly, and adults take turns in much the same way as they do for incubation. Such protection is all the more necessary during inclement weather, as is well illustrated by this Grey-headed Albatross, which is protecting its chick from the rain.

[*Diomedea chrysostoma*. Photo: Ana F. Carvalho/ FLPA]

these birds have become stranded in the wrong hemisphere, where they are incapable of recrossing the doldrums, so they have remained "in exile" for many years. There are two particularly famous cases of Black-browed Albatrosses in the North Atlantic. One was shot in the Faeroes in 1894 at the gannetry where it had spent every summer since its arrival in 1860. Another bird visited the gannetry at Hermaness, in Shetland, where it even built a nest each season from 1972 to 1987, and this may have been the same bird seen in the period 1967-1969 at the gannetry on the Bass Rock, off eastern Scotland.

North Pacific albatrosses disperse widely, most heading northwards immediately after the breeding season, then gradually coming south again. The fact that the three species breed during the local winter means that, once breeding is over, they can visit the rich waters of the Bering Sea and the Gulf of Alaska when these are at their most productive. Laysan Albatrosses tend to be more abundant in the western Pacific, whereas Black-footed Albatrosses are more common in the eastern Pacific, although both species can be found in good numbers in both sectors. The once abundant Short-tailed Albatross used to be a regular visitor off the coast of North America as far south as California, after its stay in the Bering Sea, and a few recent sightings confirm that at least some of the few individuals that remain still visit these waters.

The only tropical species, the Waved Albatross, breeds mainly on Española in the Galapagos Islands. From January to March birds disperse eastwards to coastal Ecuador and Peru, to the cold, rich waters of the Humboldt Current.

The Southern Hemisphere albatrosses all have similar dispersal patterns. Their nesting grounds are situated between Tristan da Cunha, at 37° S, and Diego Ramírez, off Cape Horn, at 57° S. After breeding, young birds and to a lesser extent adults disperse widely over the Southern Ocean, chiefly from 65° S to the Tropic of Capricorn, but as far north as 15° S

following the Benguela Current, and 5° S along the Humboldt Current.

A few southern forms, however, seem to have regular patterns of migration and definite target areas. The Chatham Islands race of Buller's Albatross (*D. b. platei*), for example, crosses the southern Pacific eastwards to the coasts of Chile and Peru. Juvenile Shy Albatrosses of the races *cauta* and *salvini* migrate from the New Zealand area mainly to southern Africa and western South America respectively, whereas the race *eremita* is merely dispersive. Analysis of ringing recoveries of the Black-browed Albatross too has revealed that, though there is a general tendency to move northwards, the different populations have distinct destinations. On the other hand, non-breeders particularly of the great albatrosses scatter widely following the winds, and some individuals complete a circumpolar migration, taking under a year to do so.

Relationship with Man

Albatrosses are among the most legendary of all birds, even though their oceanic habits and their remote Southern Hemisphere range have rendered them largely inaccessible to man. They are much admired for their mastery of flight, and indeed are generally respected worldwide, to the extent that the killing of an albatross has always been a serious offence in many parts. Sailors used to believe that their souls were reincarnated in albatrosses, and nowadays it is still generally thought that to kill one will surely bring bad luck to the men on board a ship.

However, these beliefs were not strong enough to make albatrosses immune from persecution by man. In the early years of exploration, there was little human pressure on them, and generally only a few birds were occasionally taken by sailors, who had landed on the desolate islands of the Southern Ocean to look for food. In most instances, seals and sea-lions were preferred, and birds were only caught when the sailors failed to find more suitable food. But the more modern world produced a commercial demand for plumes, which developed during the late nineteenth century, and the large, thick, feathery coat of the docile albatrosses soon proved to be ideal for that growing industry. All over the world, breeding colonies were raided year after year and all the birds killed. As one might expect, the species that suffered most were those that had breeding stations within easiest reach. Many colonies were completely obliterated, whilst others were reduced to a very small fraction of their former size. More than a million Short-tailed Albatrosses were slaughtered by plume hunters between 1887 and 1903, and the species was brought to the brink of extinction (see Status and Conservation). Tens of thousands of Laysan and Black-footed Albatrosses were also killed in Hawaii, and the once huge colony of Shy Albatrosses on Albatross Island, off Tasmania, was reduced to only 300 nests by 1909.

Midway Island, in Hawaii, held around 100,000 pairs of Laysan and 9000 of Black-footed Albatrosses, but also a busy airport serving most of the North Pacific. The flat, treeless, grassy areas beside the runway offered ideal nesting habitat for the albatrosses, and so they gathered here in large numbers. In the period 1959-1963, there were some 300-400 collisions of birds and planes every year, with consequent risk to human life and great financial losses. Various attempts were made to shift the birds, using radar beams, smoke, smells, grids of electrically charged wires and the emission of a series of unpleasant sounds, such as sirens, explosions and distress calls; there was also large-scale destruction of nests, eggs and chicks, and some 54,000 adult Laysans were killed. But all proved futile, and the birds would not move. A thorough study subsequently indicated that it was mostly failed breeders or non-breeders that flew over the runway. A series of sand dunes contributed towards the production of updraughts, which helped the birds ride around above the runway, so these were levelled off to remove the air currents, while the grassy sides were covered over in tarmac, in order to prevent nesting. As a result of these measures, the

number of incidental collisions with aircraft immediately dropped. Albatross populations have gradually recovered, but even today strikes account for about 100 seabirds a year, most of which are albatrosses or Sooty Terns (*Sterna fuscata*).

Albatrosses have also benefited in some ways from man's activities, and many species habitually follow ships. The eddies in the air created by the ships as they advance are used by the birds to help them glide along effortlessly for hours on end. By following boats they also find some food, such as discarded fish and offal (see Food and Feeding), and large numbers may be attracted to commercial fishing grounds, where non-breeders in particular often spend several months.

The name "albatross" is probably a corruption of the Spanish or Portuguese "alcatraz", formerly used to designate any large seabird, but now mostly applied to gannets. The term "mollymawk" has its origins in the Dutch words "mal" (foolish) and "mok" (gull), and was at first applied to the Northern Fulmar (*Fulmarus glacialis*); it may have been used for albatrosses, because they have little fear of humans and readily allow themselves to be touched, although they can bite viciously, when handled! In Hawaii and the eastern Pacific, the albatross receives the local name "gooney" (simpleton), so the Laysan and Black-footed Albatrosses are known as the "White Gooney" and the "Black Gooney" respectively. The generic name *Diomedea* is in honour of Diomedes, the great Greek warrior and hero of the Trojan War, whose dead comrades were reincarnated in the form of large seabirds with long wings, which then accompanied him on his travels.

Status and Conservation

The population sizes of the various different species of albatross vary considerably, ranging from just a few birds to several million. Two species are threatened, the Amsterdam and Short-tailed Albatrosses, both of which are now restricted to single colonies, where they have very low rates of breeding success.

At least eleven islands are known to have been occupied by Short-tailed Albatrosses before vast numbers were slaughtered by feather hunters (see Relationship with Man). Although it probably never bred east of 143° E, the species must have been abundant and widespread in the past, in view of the many birds killed at their breeding islands off Japan, and also the number of remains found at many sites along the Pacific coast of North America. Feather gathering was banned by the Japanese government in 1906, but it continued illegally until 1932, when the last remaining stronghold at Torishima, off south-east Japan, was declared a bird refuge. By 1929, the population consisted of only 1400 birds, and on top of this, the island's volcano erupted in 1939 and again in 1941, destroying the village and covering the nesting areas with lava and ash. No birds at all were seen between 1946 and 1949, and the species was declared extinct. However, in 1950 a few birds returned, and in 1954 six pairs laid eggs, from which three young fledged. In this way the species embarked upon a slow but steady recovery. In 1986, 77 chicks fledged, making well over 750 since the reappearance, and the total world population is now thought to be in the region of 300-400 birds.

Breeding success in Torishima has been enhanced by the transplanting of native plants onto the slope where the birds currently nest, in order to make the nesting habitat more stable, and thus reduce losses of eggs or small chicks through the collapse of the nest structure. This vegetation should also provide the birds with new nest-sites. The island's population of rats is also being monitored, as there is some evidence that they may prey on the eggs or on newly-hatched young, while feral cats have now died out on Torishima.

The population of the Short-tailed Albatross has increased spectacularly in a short time, nearly doubling its size in the 15 years between 1967 and 1982, but the only breeding station is on an active volcano, which may erupt at any time. In April 1971, twelve birds were found sitting on the almost vertical cliffs of Minami-kojima, one of the Senkaku Islands, where the species formerly bred. No nesting has been confirmed yet, but

The Black-footed Albatross makes an extremely simple nest, usually a mere scrape in the sand that is most unlikely to survive to be reused the next season. As in most petrels, albatross chicks grow two successive coats of down, ranging in colour from grey to white. At hatching, the chick's bill is short, stubby and decurved, and at this stage it is made up largely of the maxillary and mandibular ungues, the sections that form the hooked tip of the bill in a fully-grown bird. In the albatrosses the nostrils are situated one on either side of the bill, separated by the culmen, whereas in the other "tubenoses" they are joined on top of the bill.

[*Diomedea nigripes*, Midway Atoll, Hawaii. Photo: Frans Lanting/ Bruce Coleman]

At first adult albatrosses feed their chicks on a pungent stomach oil, which is derived from the food itself rather than glandular secretions, as was previously thought. In the early stages chicks are fed almost every day, but as the season progesses feeds become steadily less frequent. The average feeding interval in Light-mantled Albatrosses is of about two and a half to three days.

[*Phoebetria palpebrata*, South Georgia. Photo: Annie Price/ Survival]

As the chick grows it is gradually fed on more solid food and less stomach oil; this well grown Black-browed Albatross chick is receiving an undigested squid. The young bird places its bill crosswise in its parent's and hard up against the adult's gape, to channel the food down its own gullet. It is thought that the adult may be able to control the size of meal delivered by constricting its throat.

[*Diomedea melanophris melanophris*. Photo: Cindy Buxton/ Survival]

The Japanese name for the Short-tailed Albatross means "stupid bird", a reference to the fact that incubating birds were so docile that they calmly allowed feather hunters to kill them at their nests. Around the turn of the century huge numbers were killed at their breeding grounds to the south of Japan, bringing the species to the brink of extinction. However, the efforts of Japanese conservationists appear to be leading to a slow but steady recovery.

[Diomedea albatrus.
Photo: B. L. Sage/Ardea]

their continuous presence on the island during the breeding season, alongside some immatures, suggests they might soon start breeding at this site. Numbers have increased steadily at Minami-kojima and now amount to over 50 birds. The establishment of a new breeding area, some way off from Torishima would clearly favour the growth, expansion and long term security of the species. In Japan, the Short-tailed Albatross was designated a Special Natural Monument in 1957, and a Special Bird for Protection in 1972, while the flora and fauna of Torishima were also given legal protection in 1965.

The Amsterdam Albatross was described as a new species as recently as 1983, by a group of French scientists, who had discovered it in 1978. In both coloration and size it resembles the immature Wandering Albatross, with which it had presumably been confused before, and some authorities maintain that it is, in fact, merely a race of the latter (see Systematics). It nests only on the highland plateau of Amsterdam Island, in the southern Indian Ocean, and like the other two great albatrosses, is a biennial breeder, with an average of only five pairs breeding each year. Its total population has been estimated at 44-63 birds, depending on the survival rate of immatures, making it one of the scarcest of all seabirds. About 30 of these birds are breeding adults, while about 15 are non-breeders that visit the colony. During the period 1978-1988, 34 chicks fledged successfully.

The species must have been much more numerous in the past, since its subfossil remains have been found on the island at a lower altitude than it occupies today, but only about 400 hectares are currently used for nesting, at an altitude of 470-640 m. A large herd of some 1200 feral cattle have destroyed all the vegetation cover at lower altitudes and were threatening the present nesting area, but in 1987 this was fenced off to keep the cattle out. Amsterdam Island also suffers heavily from fires started by humans, which destroy the vegetation and may even kill birds, for example many Yellow-nosed Albatross chicks were burnt alive in 1974. The Amsterdam Albatross has been legally protected by the French authorities, but its survival will require active management of the land, eventually leading to the creation of new areas suitable for nesting, and strict control of the remaining cattle.

Albatrosses are K-selected species, basing their strategy for survival on low adult mortality, relatively high breeding success, much deferred maturity and a long lifespan. Only a relatively small proportion of the total population is engaged in breeding at any particular time, while the remainder usually keep far out at sea. The large numbers of sexually fertile birds that have not yet attempted breeding, and those that take a rest year, form an essential stock of potential breeders. These help to keep the numbers of breeding birds fairly constant, and constitute a form of insurance policy against disasters. Thus, a species is equipped to survive most adversities and to recover after a significant drop in numbers.

But man has upset this delicate balance in many ways. Adult mortality at sea has increased considerably, with birds being killed accidentally in the course of fishing operations. Competition for food can be strong around fishing boats, and with hunger some birds become particularly tame. These birds are sometimes caught by fishermen using baited hooks, and they are not always released afterwards. A more frequent problem is birds dying as a result of a collision with fishing equipment, or after becoming entangled in fishing nets, and several thousand Laysan Albatrosses are killed each year in Japanese gill-nets, which are used for catching salmon in the North Pacific. Black-browed and Grey-headed Albatrosses have also been found to suffer their greatest mortality at commercial fishing grounds. The population of Wandering Albatrosses on South Georgia, in the South Atlantic, is currently in decline, due to increased mortality of both adults and juveniles, and it is thought that this has come about largely as a result of long line fishing for southern blue-fin tuna (*Thunnus maccoyii*). In addition, stocks of fish, squid and crustaceans are being overfished in many areas, and this is producing much lower breeding success in several species. Adults and chicks are still taken for food or for use as bait in places, for example

at Tristan da Cunha, in the South Atlantic, where Yellow-nosed and Sooty Albatrosses are the species affected.

Another serious threat is posed by alien predators, which have been introduced to breeding islands, sometimes intentionally, but often by accident. As the birds are not adapted to deal with such predators, they simply do not react to them. Polynesian rats (*Rattus exulans*) prey on eggs, young and adults of both Black-footed and Laysan Albatrosses, and on Kure Atoll, in Hawaii, they have been reported to attack adult Laysans on the nest, literally eating them alive as they incubate. However, sometimes adults and large chicks will try to defend themselves by spitting stomach oil onto the approaching predator. Nevertheless, feral cats, dogs, mustelids and foxes threaten the eggs and chicks of albatrosses in many areas, while the introduction of pigs to the Auckland Islands, off southern New Zealand, caused many Shy Albatrosses to move their nests to safer ground.

Large scale egg-collection in the past caused significant declines at many albatross colonies, and even nowadays it persists in some inhabited island groups, albeit very locally. Man is also responsible for causing a great deal of disturbance at nesting areas, which can very easily lead to breeding failures.

Oil does not appear to pose an immediate threat to albatrosses, since they are highly aerial and live mostly in the Southern Ocean, where the traffic of oil tankers is much less intense than in the Northern Hemisphere. Their size makes them less vulnerable to the cold or any loss of waterproofing due to the oiling of feathers. However, a few species have very large proportions of their total populations in just a few colonies; an oil spill near the nesting or feeding grounds of the Amsterdam, Short-tailed, Waved or Shy Albatrosses might have very serious implications.

Nine of the fourteen species of albatross have total populations of under 50,000 breeding pairs. The effects of artificially increased mortality amongst adults could be disastrous, and the survival of the species depends heavily on mortality being kept to its low, "natural" levels. The monitoring of colonies reveals that present trends are towards an overall maintenance of numbers, although slight decreases still continue in several areas. International effort should be directed towards the complete protection of breeding birds and their habitats, and also the reduction of adult mortality as a result of human activities.

General Bibliography
Alexander *et al.* (1965), Bang (1966), Barrowclough *et al.* (1981), Bourne (1985), Brooke, R.K. (1981), Brooke, M. de P. & Prince (1991), Croxall (1982b, 1987, 1991), Croxall *et al.* (1984), Furness & Monaghan (1987), Harrison (1985, 1987), Hector (1988), Hutchinson & Wenzel (1980), Jouanin & Mougin (1979), Löfgren (1984), Moors & Atkinson (1984), Nelson (1980), Prince & Morgan (1987), Reig (1988), Richdale (1950b, 1952, 1954), Schreiber (1984), Sibley & Monroe (1990), Tickell (1969, 1970), Tickell & Pinder (1966), Tuck & Heinzel (1978), Vermeer & Rankin (1984a), Warham (1990), Wilkinson (1969), Wilson, J.A. (1975), Wood (1973).

1

2

3

ssp *epomophora*

ssp *sanfordi*

4

5

6

7

8

ssp *impavida*

ssp *melanophris*

9

10

ssp *cauta*

ssp *salvini*

ssp *eremita*

ssp *chlororhynchos*

11

12

13

14

ssp *bassi*

Genus *DIOMEDEA* Linnaeus, 1758

1. Wandering Albatross

Diomedea exulans

French: Albatros hurleur **German**: Wanderalbatros **Spanish**: Albatros Viajero
Other common names: Snowy/White-winged Albatross

Taxonomy. *Diomedea exulans* Linnaeus, 1758, Cape of Good Hope *ex* Edwards.
Taxonomy and nomenclature confused; should perhaps include *D. amsterdamensis* (see page 198); type specimen lost, but probably not referable to race of Tristan da Cunha, as traditionally held; subspecific name *chionoptera* thus gives place to nominate. Populations of Antipodes Is and Campbell I, and of Auckland Is may represent two further subspecies. Two subspecies presently recognized.
Subspecies and Distribution.
D. e. exulans Linnaeus, 1758 - Southern Ocean, from South Georgia E to Antipodes Is.
D. e. dabbenena Mathews, 1929 - Tristan da Cunha, Gough I.

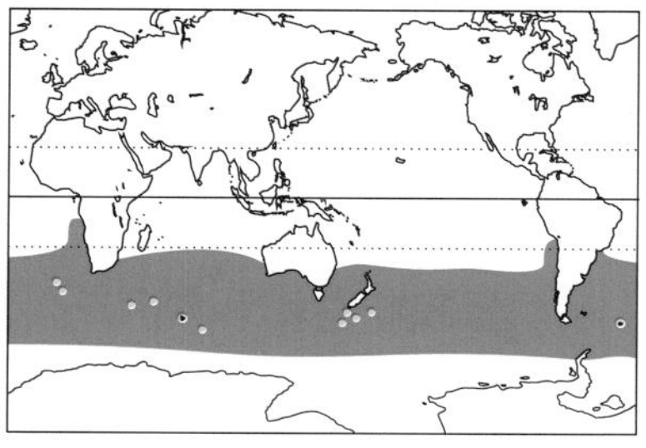

Descriptive notes. 107-135 cm; 6250-11,300 g; wingspan 254-351 cm. Plumage becomes whiter with age; illustrated bird shows plumage of old male, "snowy stage". Some birds have brownish grey crown; ear-coverts can be washed pink or orangish, or all white. Male slightly larger than female, as in most albatrosses; some females have weak greyish pectoral band; females do not normally reach "snowy stage", generally showing less white on upperwing and some black at edges of tail. Juvenile dark brown with white face; plumage progressively becomes whiter; upperwing whitens from centre outwards. Race *dabbenena* smaller, with wings shorter and darker above, some birds recalling *D. epomophora sanfordi*.
Habitat. Marine and highly pelagic; seldom approaches land except for breeding; in Australasian part of range occurs more frequently inshore. Nests on remote islands, typically on slopes with fairly sparse covering of tussock grass, at exposed sites to facilitate take-off; often on boggy ground.
Food and Feeding. Mainly cephalopods (*Kondakovia longimana*, *Sepia apama*, *Histioteuthis*, *Moroteuthis*); also fish (*Pseudochaenichthys*) and a few crustaceans. Feeds on carrion more often than other albatrosses. Captures prey mainly by surface-seizing, but occasionally makes shallow plunges, sometimes involving brief pursuit. Commonly catches squid at night, when more accessible. Often feeds in company of other Procellariiformes; sometimes follows cetaceans, typically taking their scraps. Habitually follows ships, feeding on offal and galley refuse.
Breeding. Biennial, starting Nov. Loosely colonial, in dispersed groups of few nests; nest is pile of mud and grass on ground. 1 egg; incubation c. 78 days with stints of 2-3 weeks; chicks have white down, brooded for 4-5 weeks; fledging c. 278 days. Sexual maturity at 9-11 years. Adult mortality c. 3% per year; estimated average life span 30-40 years, but in theory some birds may reach age of 80.
Movements. Disperses widely over Southern Ocean after breeding, most birds probably moving E, perhaps in circumpolar movement; race *dabbenena* probably stays mainly in S Atlantic and off South Africa; populations of Antipodes, Campbell and Auckland Is apparently remain in Tasman Sea and S Pacific. Several records in N Hemisphere, off Sicily, Portugal and California.
Status and Conservation. Not globally threatened. Considerable decline in past, which still continues slowly at present, though species may be recovering locally. World population c. 21,000 breeding pairs, perhaps over 100,000 birds; 7250 pairs at Auckland Is, c. 4300 pairs on South Georgia, and c. 2500 pairs on Prince Edward Is; possibly attempting to colonize Heard I. Last bred in Falkland Is in 1959, and at Tristan da Cunha (main island) in 1907, where probably eliminated due to human pressure. Declining steadily at South Georgia and Crozet Is, probably with increase in accidents associated with fisheries; higher mortality amongst females than males, due to habit of foraging further N, in areas with more long line fisheries. Many birds killed incidentally at commercial fishing grounds throughout range, though some albatrosses have probably benefited from greater availability of food in such areas. May be greatly affected by human disturbance and occupation of some of its nesting islands; eggs and young chicks occasionally lost to skuas, feral cats, pigs and other predators; a few birds still killed for fish bait in places. Low productivity of all albatrosses, especially larger species, makes population recoveries very slow; population of Macquarie I has never recovered from plundering by sealers.
Bibliography. Adams *et al.* (1986), Barrat *et al.* (1976), Barton (1979), Blake (1977), Bourne (1989), Bretagnolle & Thomas (1990), Brown & Adams (1984), Brown *et al.* (1982), Cramp & Simmons (1977), Croxall & Prince (1990), Croxall & Rothery (1991), Croxall, Evans & Schreiber (1984), Croxall, Rothery *et al.* (1990), Du Bost & Segonzac (1976), Fraser *et al.* (1988), Gibson (1967), Griffiths (1982), Imber & Russ (1975), Jameson (1958), Jehl *et al.* (1979), Johnson (1965), Jouventin & Lequette (1990), Jouventin & Weimerskirch (1990), Lequette & Jouventin (1991), Lequette & Weimerskirch (1990), Lindsey (1986), Marchant & Higgins (1990), Matthews (1951), Mougin (1970a, 1977), Murphy (1936), Paxton (1968), Pickering (1989), Richardson (1984), Rodhouse *et al.* (1987), Ryan *et al.* (1990), Sudbury *et al.* (1985), Swales (1965), Tickell (1968, 1980), Tickell & Gibson (1968), Tomkins (1983a, 1983b, 1984, 1985a), Voisin (1969, 1981), Watson (1975), Weimerskirch & Jouventin (1987), Weimerskirch, Jouventin & Stahl (1986), Weimerskirch, Jouventin *et al.* (1985), Weimerskirch, Lequette & Jouventin (1989), Weimerskirch, Zotier & Jouventin (1989), Woehler (1991), Woods (1988).

2. Amsterdam Albatross

Diomedea amsterdamensis

French: Albatros d'Amsterdam **German**: Amsterdamalbatros **Spanish**: Albatros de la Amsterdam

Taxonomy. *Diomedea amsterdamensis* Roux *et al.*, 1983, Amsterdam Island.
Recently described; may be better considered subspecies of *D. exulans* (see page 198). Monotypic.

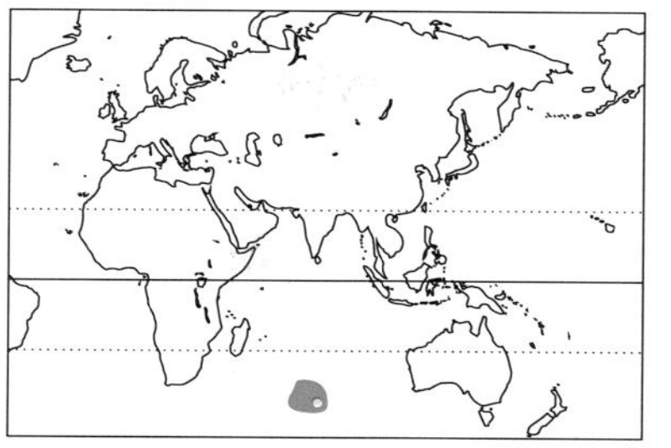

Distribution. Amsterdam I, S Indian Ocean.
Descriptive notes. 107-122 cm; 4800-8000 g; wingspan 300 cm. Only adult great albatross with upperparts all dark; extent of white on underparts variable. Virtually indistinguishable from juvenile *D. exulans*; dark bill tip and cutting edges diagnostic. All 3 great albatrosses can adopt characteristic flight posture illustrated for present species, with wings held pointing backwards.
Habitat. Marine and probably pelagic for most part. Nests on highland plateau at 470-640 m in area of peat bog with ample covering of moss; formerly nested at lower elevations on Amsterdam I.
Food and Feeding. Diet unknown, but probably variable proportions of fish, squid and crustaceans. Feeding habits presumably similar to *D. exulans*.
Breeding. Biennial, starts Feb. Only one breeding group known, consisting of 3-8 pairs. Nest is heap of mud and plant matter on ground. 1 egg; incubation c. 79 days; fledging c. 235 days. Adult mortality 4-5% per year; estimated average life span 30-40 years.
Movements. Pelagic range unknown. Plumage similarities with immatures of *D. exulans* may cause confusion at sea. A few possible records off New Zealand.
Status and Conservation. ENDANGERED. Tiny population estimated at only c. 44-63 birds, with only 5 pairs breeding per year on average; currently object of close study and several conservation initiatives. Has apparently declined considerably, presumably due to humans, with widespread use of fire and introduction of rats and cats. Cattle introduced in 1871 have been largely responsible for destroying vegetation of (presumed) former breeding area; perhaps also occasionally trampled nests and sitting birds; habitat further degraded with draining of peat bog on plateau. Nesting area fenced off from cattle in 1987, but some cattle to be kept as they maintain a vegetation firebreak; further proposals include management of vegetation to increase extent of ground suitable for nesting.
Bibliography. Bourne (1989), Collar & Andrew (1988), Collar & Stuart (1985), Harrison (1985), Jouventin & Weimerskirch (1991), Jouventin, Martinez & Roux (1989), Jouventin, Stahl *et al.* (1984), Roux & Martinez (1987), Roux *et al.* (1983), Thibault & Guyot (1988).

3. Royal Albatross

Diomedea epomophora

French: Albatros royal **German**: Königsalbatros **Spanish**: Albatros Real

Taxonomy. *Diomedaea* [sic] *epomophora* Lesson, 1825, no locality; probably Australian waters. Two subspecies recognized.
Subspecies and Distribution.
D. e. epomophora Lesson, 1825 - Campbell I and Auckland Is.
D. e. sanfordi Murphy, 1917 - New Zealand and Chatham Is.

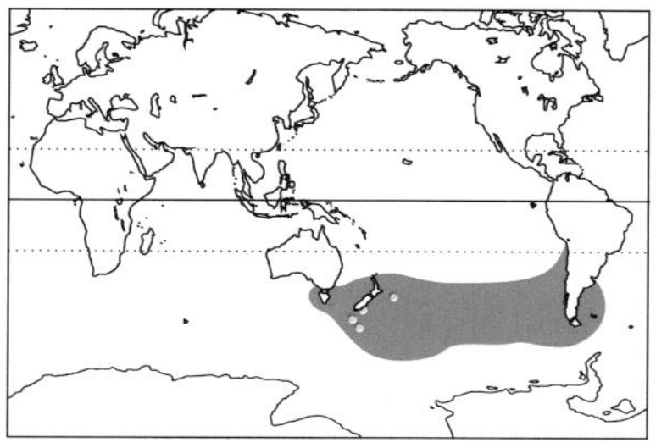

Descriptive notes. 107-122 cm; 9000 g; wingspan 305-351 cm. Long bill with black cutting edges to upper mandible diagnostic; black eyelid. Upperwing generally whiter than in *D. exulans*, and transition between white and blackish trailing edge less abrupt; tail all white except in first stage. Juvenile as adult, but upperwing mainly dark, progressively becoming white from leading edge backwards. Race *sanfordi* is considerably smaller and retains all-dark upperwing in full adult plumage.
Habitat. Marine, but apparently less pelagic than *D. exulans*. Nests on remote islands, typically on slopes with tussock grass providing some shelter, but often at exposed sites in order to facilitate take-off.
Food and Feeding. Mainly cephalopods (*Moroteuthis ingens*, *Kondakovia longimana*, *Histioteuthis atlantica*); also fish (*Macruronus novaezelandiae*) and a few crustaceans. Captures prey mainly by surface-seizing, but occasionally makes shallow plunges. Commonly catches squid at night. Often feeds in company of other Procellariiformes. Does not follow ships very often but regularly attends trawlers where feeds on offal.
Breeding. Biennial, starting Oct. Loosely colonial, in dispersed groups of few nests; nest is pile of mud and grass on ground. 1 egg; incubation c. 79 days with stints of 2-3 weeks; chicks have white down, brooded for 4-5 weeks; fledging c. 240 days. Sexual maturity at 9-11 years. Adult mortality c. 3% per year; known to have lived to over 58 years old in wild; in theory some birds may reach age of 80.
Movements. Disperses widely over Southern Ocean after breeding; most birds probably move E, perhaps in circumpolar movement; fair numbers occur off both coasts of S America, many apparently wintering in SW Atlantic; a few off S Africa (mainly *sanfordi*) and Australia, especially Tasmania. Not recorded N of equator.
Status and Conservation. Not globally threatened. Considerable decline in past, which still continues slowly at present, though species may be recovering locally; world population 10,000-20,000 pairs, with c. 7700 pairs at Chatham Is, c. 7500 pairs at Campbell I. Main threats include disturbance at breeding colonies and accidents at commercial fishing grounds, though likely to benefit with recent ban from New Zealand waters of trawlers using antiquated cable system. Well publicized population colonized Taiaroa Head, E South I, in c. 1919; protected for over 40 years, though still holds only 17 pairs; in past, most losses due to human interference, and also some predation by dogs and mustelids. Human exploitation at Enderby I (Auckland Is) led to disappearance of species by c. 1868; recolonized in 1940's, since when steady increase.
Bibliography. Barton (1979b), Blake (1977), Bourne (1989), Brown *et al.* (1982), Chambers (1989), Enticott (1986), Johnson (1965), Lindsey (1986), Marchant & Higgins (1990), Murphy (1936), Richdale (1939, 1942), Robertson (1985), Robertson & Bell (1984), Robertson & Kinsky (1972), Robertson & Wright (1973), Tickell (1968), Watson (1975), Westerskov (1960, 1963), Woods (1988).

On following pages: 4. Waved Albatross (*Diomedea irrorata*); 5. Short-tailed Albatross (*Diomedea albatrus*); 6. Black-footed Albatross (*Diomedea nigripes*); 7. Laysan Albatross (*Diomedea immutabilis*); 8. Black-browed Albatross (*Diomedea melanophris*); 9. Buller's Albatross (*Diomedea bulleri*); 10. Shy Albatross (*Diomedea cauta*); 11. Yellow-nosed Albatross (*Diomedea chlororhynchos*); 12. Grey-headed Albatross (*Diomedea chrysostoma*); 13. Sooty Albatross (*Phoebetria fusca*); 14. Light-mantled Albatross (*Phoebetria palpebrata*).

4. Waved Albatross

Diomedea irrorata

French: Albatros des Galapagos **Spanish**: Albatros de las Galápagos **German**: Galapagosalbatros
Other common names: Galapagos Albatross

Taxonomy. *Diomedea irrorata* Salvin, 1883, Callao Bay, Peru.
Possibly one of earliest forms to differentiate. Scientific name *D. leptorhyncha* officially suppressed. Monotypic.
Distribution. Española (Hood) I, Galapagos, and La Plata I, off Ecuador.

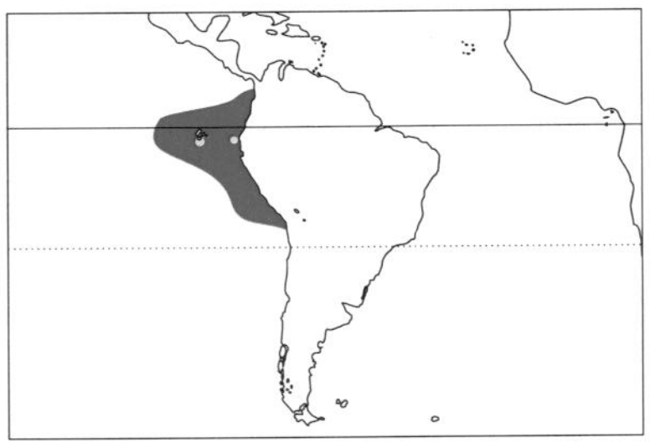

Descriptive notes. 85-93 cm; 230-240 cm. Unique combination of brown body and whitish head and neck tinged ochraceous yellow. Long bill. Juvenile has head whiter and bill duller.
Habitat. Marine and mainly pelagic, but may approach coast in zone of Humboldt Current. Only albatross restricted to tropics. Nests on bare lava amongst boulders, usually in fairly open zones surrounded by bushes.
Food and Feeding. Large fish and squid taken from water surface; also feeds on crustaceans. May feed mostly at night, when squid migrates closer to surface. Often feeds in loose rafts. Kleptoparasitism on boobies (*Sula*) recorded.
Breeding. Annual, starting Apr. Large aggregations, but nests spread out in loose groups; no nest, egg laid in depression on bare ground, may be moved about by incubating adult. 1 egg; incubation c. 60 days with stints of 5-22 days; chicks have blackish-brown down, often faded; fledging c. 167 days. Sexual maturity at 5-6 years, occasionally at 3. Adult mortality c. 4% per year; estimated average lifespan c. 30-40 years.
Movements. Birds from Galapagos leave islands Jan-Mar, dispersing E to waters of Humboldt Current off Ecuador and Peru, mainly between 4° N and 12° S. Immatures probably remain in this area until ready to breed.
Status and Conservation. Not globally threatened. Currently considered near-threatened. Population estimated at c. 12,000 breeding pairs, perhaps 50,000-70,000 birds; fairly stable in recent decades. Española I is effectively protected and has no alien fauna; tourism well regulated, with all groups accompanied by naturalist guides; efforts essential to avoid spread of introduced predators to the island. Population of c. 10-50 pairs nest on La Plata I, which is included in national park, but not sufficiently well managed at present; many rats and cats; also small population of goats presently being controlled; illegal collection of eggs and young probably still occurs.
Bibliography. Blake (1977), Coulter (1984), Duffy, Hays & Plenge (1984), Harris (1969a, 1969b, 1973), Murphy (1936), Prince & Morgan (1987), Rechten (1986), Ridgely & Gwynne (1989), Vincent (1966), Warham (1990), Wetmore (1965).

5. Short-tailed Albatross

Diomedea albatrus

French: Albatros à queue courte **German**: Kurzschwanzalbatros **Spanish**: Albatros Colicorto
Other common names: Steller's Albatross

Taxonomy. *Diomedea albatrus* Pallas, 1769, off Kamchatka.
May represent offshoot of ancient N Hemisphere stock of great albatrosses. Monotypic.
Distribution. Torishima I in Izu Is, off SE Japan; birds regularly seen on Minami-kojima in S Ryukyu Is. Formerly much more widespread in NW Pacific, E to Bonin and Izu Is.

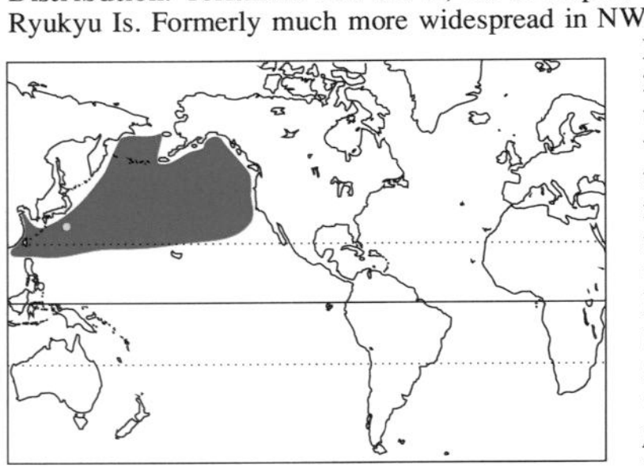

Descriptive notes. 84-94 cm; wingspan 213-229 cm. Tail has black terminal bar; upperwing pattern characteristic, but extent of white variable; bill tip pale blue. Yellowish orange tone to head can extend to foreneck. Juvenile fairly uniform blackish brown; much stockier than *D. nigripes*; immatures gradually gain white of adult plumage.
Habitat. Marine and pelagic, with concentrations in areas of upwelling. Breeds on fairly steep slopes of volcanic ash, thinly vegetated with *Miscanthus sinensis* and *Chrysanthemum pacificum*. At Minami-kojima birds sit on near vertical cliff c. 150 m high.
Food and Feeding. Mainly squid, fish and crustaceans. Also recorded taking galley refuse and offal. Squid probably taken at night.
Breeding. Possibly biennial when successful; starts Oct. Colonial. Nest made of earth with bits of vegetation. 1 egg; incubation c. 49 days; chicks have blackish grey down; fledging c. 180 days.
Movements. Present movements unknown, probably still disperses widely in N Pacific, reaching the Gulf of Alaska and W coast of N America, as in past; 3 recent records from Hawaii, including a ringed adult that has visited Midway I regularly since 1972.
Status and Conservation. RARE. CITES I. Formerly abundant in Izu and Bonin Is, S of Japan; disastrous decline around turn of present century due to feather collection and volcanic eruption, almost leading to extinction; further eruptions in 1939 and 1941; feather collecting banned in 1906, but continued into 1930's, when became uneconomical due to small size of albatross population. No breeding during 1940's, and species thought to be extinct; a few birds returned to Torishima in 1950 and made first breeding attempts in 1954. Population perhaps totals 300-400 birds at present, with maximum of c. 165 adults seen in 1987, and over 70 chicks reared successfully most years. Legal protection at breeding station since 1957, where vegetation managed to increase reproductive output, with stabilizing of steep slopes of volcanic ash. Main problems include fact that Torishima is an active volcano; also many rats in breeding zone, and formerly feral cats, which recently died out. Breeding also suspected on Minami-kojima in S Ryukyu Is; up to 50+ birds seen on almost vertical cliff, where safer from predators, though site perhaps unsuitable for breeding.
Bibliography. Austin (1949), Bent (1922), Brazil (1991), Cheng Tso-hsin (1987), Collar & Andrew (1988), Etchécopar & Hüe (1978), Fujisawa (1967), Harrison (1979, 1990), Hasegawa (1978, 1979, 1980, 1982, 1984a, 1984b), Hasegawa & DeGange (1982), King (1978/79), Melville (1984), Mountfort (1988), Palmer (1962), Rice (1984a), Rice & Kenyon (1962a), Thompson (1951), Tickell (1975), Vincent (1966).

6. Black-footed Albatross

Diomedea nigripes

French: Albatros à pieds noirs **German**: Schwarzfußalbatros **Spanish**: Albatros Patinegro

Taxonomy. *Diomedea nigripes* Audubon, 1849, Pacific Ocean, lat. 30° 44' N, long. 146° W.
Known to have hybridized with *D. immutabilis*. Monotypic.
Distribution. W Hawaii; small numbers in Izu, Bonin and S Ryukyu Is, to S of Japan.

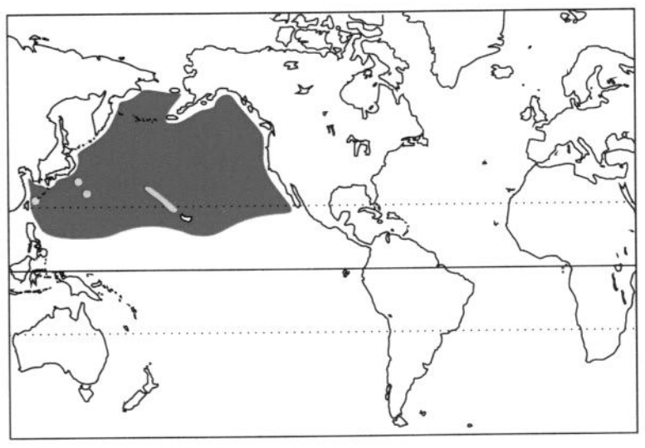

Descriptive notes. 68-74 cm; c. 3000-3600 g; wingspan 193-213 cm. Small and dark, recalling *Phoebetria*, but with proportions of *Diomedea*. Uppertail-coverts normally white; variable extent of white and pinkish grey or pale brown below eye, also extending from bill up towards crown. Bill blackish to earth brown with dark tip. Underparts can be paler than upperparts. Juvenile even more unifom brown.
Habitat. Marine and pelagic, seldom approaching land except at colonies. Breeds on mid-ocean islands on beaches or slopes with little or no vegetation.
Food and Feeding. Mainly fish and fish offal; also squid, crustaceans and some human refuse. Picks food from surface of water, may also plunge in from air. Feeds both by night and day. Follows ships persistently, especially along California Current; also attends trawlers.
Breeding. Annual, starting Nov. In colonies, usually associated with other seabird species, most typically *D. immutabilis* and *D. albatrus*. Nest very simple, usually scrape in sand with no rim. 1 egg; incubation c. 65 days with stints of c. 2 weeks; chicks have greyish brown down, soon fades; fledging c. 140 days. Sexual maturity at 8-10 years. Known to have lived to over 27 years old in wild; a few birds presumably live to greater age.
Movements. Disperses widely over N Pacific after breeding, regularly reaching Bering Sea; fairly large numbers off Pacific coast of N America. Also recorded in S Hemisphere, off Galapagos Is and New Zealand.
Status and Conservation. Not globally threatened. Has declined in numbers over past decades and has lost some colonies. Total world population, 37,000-50,000 breeding pairs, perhaps 150,000-200,000 birds; bulk of population in Hawaii, with 14,000-21,000 pairs at Laysan I; c. 500 pairs at Toroshima (Izu Is). Main threats are habitat destruction, human disturbance and predation by alien mammals. Essentially affected by same negative factors as *D. immutabilis*, though to lesser extent; heavily plundered in early 20th century by feather hunters, but has now recovered; adversely affected in same period by introduced rabbits on Laysan I and Lisianski I, causing instability of nesting substrate. Presently maintaining numbers at most colonies, with local increases at Midway I and Torishima, thanks to effective conservation management; apparently extirpated from Mariana Is during present century; formerly bred on several other Pacific island groups. Accidents at commercial fishing grounds probably account for some proportion of mortality. Many birds found to have ingested considerable quantities of plastic rubbish floating across N Pacific from Japan.
Bibliography. Bent (1922), Brazil (1991), Clapp & Wirtz (1975), Cheng Tso-hsin (1987), Etchécopar & Hüe (1978), Frings & Frings (1961), Gould *et al*. (1982), Harrison (1990), Harrison, Hida & Seki (1983), Harrison, Naughton & Fefer (1984), Howell & Bartholomew (1961a), Kenyon (1950), Kurochkin (1963), Kuroda (1955, 1988), Marchant & Higgins (1990), McHugh (1955), Miller (1940, 1942), Nakamura (1963), Palmer (1962), Reichel (1991), Rice (1984a), Rice & Kenyon (1962a, 1962b), Robbins & Rice (1974), Sanger (1974a), Sparling (1977), Starett & Dixon (1946), Thompson (1951), Yocom (1947).

7. Laysan Albatross

Diomedea immutabilis

French: Albatros de Laysan **German**: Laysanalbatros **Spanish**: Albatros de Laysan

Taxonomy. *Diomedea immutabilis* Rothschild, 1893, Laysan Island.
Known to have hybridized with *D. nigripes*. Monotypic.
Distribution. W Hawaii, mainly on Laysan I and Midway I; colony recently established on Bonin Is, off SE Japan; recent expansion in E too, on islands off W Mexico.

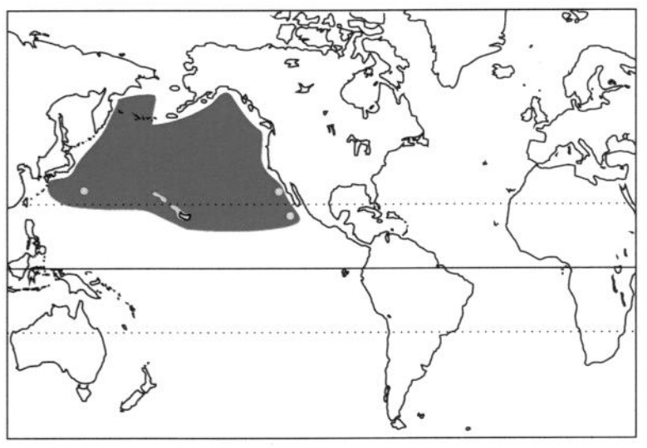

Descriptive notes. 79-81 cm; 2300-2800 g; wingspan 195-203 cm. Plumage resembles that of Southern Ocean mollymawks. Pattern of underwing variable, with black patches at wrist and "elbow"; latter can be isolated against white background in pale individuals, thus becoming even more prominent. From distance, grey patch on face can be indistinct, except around eye. Juvenile similar to adult.
Habitat. Marine and pelagic, rarely approaching land except at colonies. Breeds on oceanic islands with low vegetation or none; prefers flat ground with some cover from the wind.
Food and Feeding. Mostly squid; also fish, crustaceans and coelenterates. Squid taken at night when nearer surface. Does not often follow ships.
Breeding. Annual, starting Nov. Colonial; may form large aggregations, sometimes in company of *D. nigripes*. Nest is hollow with debris and sand added to form substantial rim. 1 egg; incubation c. 65 days with stints of c. 3 weeks; chicks have greyish down, darker when older; fledging c. 165 days. Sexual maturity at 7-9 years. Adult mortality 5-9% per year; known to have lived to 53 years old in wild.
Movements. Disperses over much of N Pacific after breeding, as far N as Bering Sea and eastwards to Pacific coast of N America. Most numerous on W side of N Pacific, with large concentrations off E Japan.
Status and Conservation. Not globally threatened. World population in the order of 320,000-360,000 breeding pairs, perhaps some 1,200,000-1,400,000 birds. Slaughter on massive scale by Japanese feather hunters around turn of century reduced numbers significantly, until banned in 1909; also suffered from extensive egg-collecting; population has probably recovered. Considerable increase over last 2 decades, following reduction in human pressure mainly at Midway I, where 54,000 killed by US Navy personnel in 1955-1964, during programme designed to reduce strikes with aircraft (see page 207). Recent expansion into E Pacific, with small breeding colony discovered

in 1986 on Guadalupe I, off W Mexico; apparently also in process of colonizing Revillagigedo Is. Mortality caused by birds flying into human constructions has diminished at breeding stations; but man-related mortality at sea has increased, with several thousand birds killed incidentally each year off Japan by gill-nets set for salmon. Some predation by rats, cats and dogs, but effects not significant overall; on Kure Atoll, rats eat incubating birds alive. Fledglings often swim away from nesting grounds, and large numbers taken by sharks; 1 shark stomach contained 13 fledglings. Many birds found to have ingested considerable quantities of plastic rubbish floating across N Pacific from Japan.

Bibliography. Bent (1922), Brazil (1991), Clapp & Wirtz (1975), Everett & Anderson (1991), Fisher, H.I. (1967, 1968, 1969, 1971, 1972, 1975a, 1975b, 1975c, 1976), Fisher & Baldwin (1946), Fisher & Fisher (1969, 1972), Frings & Frings (1961), Gould *et al.* (1982), Grant & Whittow (1983), Harrison (1990), Harrison, Hida & Seki (1983), Harrison, Naughton & Fefer (1984), Hasegawa (1984b), Howell & Bartholomew (1961a), Kenyon (1950), Kenyon & Rice (1958), Kenyon *et al.* (1958), Kepler (1967), Kurochkin (1963), Kuroda (1955, 1988), Lefebvre (1977), Meseth (1975), Palmer (1962), Pitman (1988), Rice (1959, 1984a), Rice & Kenyon (1962a, 1962b), Robbins & Rice (1974), Sanger (1965, 1974b), Sparling (1977), Thompson (1951), van Ryzin & Fisher (1976).

8. Black-browed Albatross

Diomedea melanophris

French: Albatros à sourcils noirs **German**: Schwarzbrauenalbatros **Spanish**: Albatros Ojeroso
Other common names: Black-browed Mollymawk

Taxonomy. *Diomedea melanophris* Temminck, 1828, Cape of Good Hope.
Emended to *melanophrys* by Temminck in 1839, but alteration unjustified. Races may constitute two full species, as sympatry recorded without interbreeding. Two subspecies currently recognized.
Subspecies and Distribution.
D. m. melanophris Temminck, 1828 - Southern Ocean, from Cape Horn E to Antipodes Is.
D. m. impavida (Mathews, 1912) - Campbell I, to S of New Zealand.

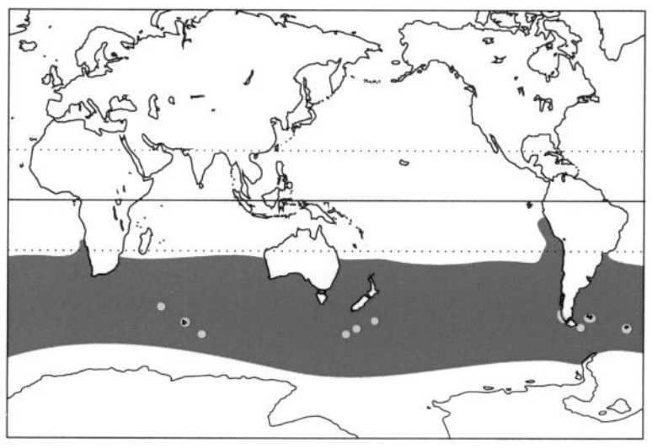

Descriptive notes. 83-93 cm; 3000-5000 g; wingspan 240 cm. Heavy build; wings often appear broad and blunt; fairly dark underwing, with variable white central stripe; black patches on underwing at joints can be more or less evident. Bill fairly uniform in colour, shorter than in *D. immutabilis*. Amount of black around eye fairly variable; some birds have stripe of bare pink skin below eye during courtship. Juvenile resembles adult, but underwing darker, dark bill and grey collar. Race *impavida* has pale iris, ranging from whitish to amber.
Habitat. Marine; to some extent pelagic, wandering over vast areas of sea sometimes 1000's of km from land, but also commonly near shore; more common on inshore waters than other albatrosses, entering fjords, bays and harbours, especially in stormy weather; even recorded feeding c. 35 km inland on freshwater lake at Tierra del Fuego; often feeds over continental shelf or shelf slope. Breeds on remote oceanic islands, normally on steep slopes with tussock grass; sometimes on cliff terraces.
Food and Feeding. Mainly crustaceans (*Euphausia superba*, *Munida*) and fish; also squid and carrion, e.g. penguin corpses. Captures prey mainly by surface-seizing, but sometimes by means of pursuit-plunging, surface-plunging or pursuit-diving. Feeds extensively on large swarms of krill and attends trawlers for discarded fish and squid. Often feeds in company of other Procellariiformes and other seabirds; off Chile steals fish from surfacing shags (*Phalacrocorax*); sometimes follows cetaceans (*Balaena*, *Globicephala*, *Lissodelphis*).
Breeding. Annual, starting Sept/Oct. Highly colonial; large nest of mud and grass. 1 egg; incubation c. 71 days; chicks have greyish white down, brooded for 1-4 weeks; fledging c. 120 days. Sexual maturity at 7-9 years. Adult mortality c. 7% per year; known to have reached at least 34 years old.
Movements. Despite extensive ringing, movements not very well understood. Strong migratory movement N, with young of different populations showing distinct target areas; perhaps also adults. Most common straggler of all S albatrosses into N Atlantic, with 41 records for Britain alone up to 1985 (see page 206); also recorded off Norway, Faeroe Is, Spitzbergen and Iceland; less common in NW Atlantic, where *D. chlororhynchos* more regularly recorded. Tradition of its capture as mascot for fishing vessels may have produced some of N Hemisphere records in past.
Status and Conservation. Not globally threatened. Probably most abundant and widespread species, with population of 550,000-600,000 breeding pairs, 2,200,000-2,400,000 birds; Falkland Is hold c. 400,000 pairs, with numbers fairly stable in recent decades; 65,000 pairs on South Georgia; 20,000 pairs on Diego Ramírez Is, S Chile; Heard I and McDonald Is hold 600-700 and 82-89 pairs respectively, both apparently on increase; first bred at Macquarie I in 1949/50, where population currently numbers 600-700 pairs; 74,825 pairs (*impavida*) at Campbell I. Main cause of mortality probably incidental takes at commercial fishing grounds, e.g. at Kerguelen where population in decline, and South Georgian birds wintering off S Africa; competition with fisheries also potentially significant, e.g. krill fishing in Scotia Sea and squid fishery off Falkland Is. Small numbers may be caught by fishermen for fish bait or to be kept as pets off S Africa and S America.

Bibliography. Amiet (1958), Andersen (1895), Astheimer *et al.* (1985), Barton (1979b), Blake (1977), Bourne (1977), Bretagnolle & Thomas (1990), Brooke & Furness (1982), Brown *et al.* (1982), Chambers (1989), Cramp & Simmons (1977), Croxall *et al.* (1984), Dymond *et al.* (1989), García (1972), Griffiths (1982), Hector *et al.* (1986), Humphrey *et al.* (1970), Jehl *et al.* (1979), Johnson (1965), Lindsey (1986), Marchant & Higgins (1990), Murphy (1936), Palmer (1962), Pascal (1979), Prince (1980b, 1985), Robertson (1985), Thompson (1992), Tickell (1964, 1967, 1976, 1984), Tickell & Pinder (1967, 1975), Watson (1975), Weimerskirch, Jouventin & Stahl (1986), Weimerskirch, Jouventin *et al.* (1985), Weimerskirch, Zotier & Jouventin (1989), Woehler (1991), Woods (1988).

9. Buller's Albatross

Diomedea bulleri

French: Albatros de Buller **German**: Bulleralbatros **Spanish**: Albatros de Buller
Other common names: Buller's Mollymawk

Taxonomy. *Diomedea bulleri* Rothschild, 1893, New Zealand.
Races occasionally treated as separate species, on grounds of differences in breeding season and migratory habits. Two subspecies recognized.
Subspecies and Distribution.
D. b. bulleri Rothschild, 1893 - Solander and Snares Is.
D. b. platei Reichenow, 1898 - Three Kings and Chatham Is.

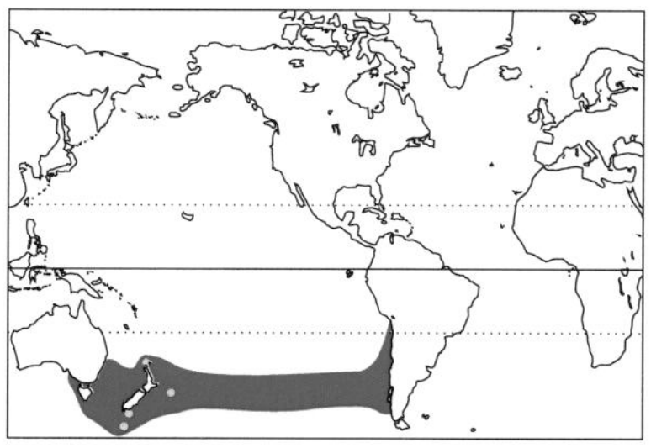

Descriptive notes. 76-81 cm; 2400-3100 g; wingspan 205-213 cm. Characteristic underwing pattern, with black bar thick on leading edge, thin on trailing edge. Upperwing shows grey base to primaries. Head grey, with marked capped appearance, due to white forehead and crown; more yellow on culmen and bill tip help to separate from *D. chrysostoma*. Juvenile as adult, but bill brownish and head more grey-brown. Race *platei* has darker head and broader bill.
Habitat. Marine and pelagic, rarely approaching land except at colonies. Breeds on remote islands on grassy slopes or among boulders, usually in areas with sparse vegetation; at Snares and Solander Is nests under *Olearia* forest.
Food and Feeding. Mostly cephalopods (*Nototodarus*, *Moroteuthopsis ingens*); also some fish (Moridae), tunicates (*Pyrosoma*) and crustaceans. Usually takes prey by surface-seizing; also known to make shallow dives from air or from water surface. Habitually follows ships.
Breeding. Annual, starting Oct (*platei*) or Jan (*bulleri*). Forms disperse colonies; nest is pile of grass and mud. 1 egg; incubation c. 72 days; chicks have whitish down; fledging c. 145 days. Sexual maturity at 7-9 years. Known to have reached over 30 years old in wild; one pair ringed in 1948, regularly controlled at nest in subsequent seasons and still breeding together at same site in 1971.
Movements. Race *bulleri* seems relatively sedentary, dispersing to adjacent waters and W to S Tasmania. Race *platei* apparently migratory, moving E across S Pacific to W coast of S America; probably returns by same route.
Status and Conservation. Not globally threatened. Population relatively small and localized. Race *bulleri* numbers 4750 pairs in Snares Is (late 1970's), and 4000-5000 on Solander I, with total of c. 50,000 birds; race *platei* c. 25,000 breeding pairs in Chatham Is, c. 100,000 birds; populations of both races seem fairly stable. Main cause of mortality at breeding stations may be predation by skuas (*Catharacta*) and giant petrels (*Macronectes*), e.g. at Snares Is; incidental mortality at commercial fishing grounds and competition with fisheries also likely to be significant.

Bibliography. Barton (1979b), Blake (1977), Lindsey (1986), Marchant & Higgins (1990), Murphy (1936), Richdale (1949), Richdale & Warham (1973), Robertson (1985), Robertson & Bell (1984), Warham (1982), Warham & Bennington (1983), Warham & Fitzsimons (1987), Warham & Richdale (1973), West & Imber (1986).

10. Shy Albatross

Diomedea cauta

French: Albatros à cape blanche **German**: Weißkappenalbatros **Spanish**: Albatros Frentiblanco
Other common names: White-capped Albatross (*cauta*); Salvin's/Bounty/Grey-backed Albatross (*salvini*); Chatham Albatross (*eremita*); Shy Mollymawk

Taxonomy. *Diomedea cauta* Gould, 1841, Bass Strait.
Sometimes split into three separate species on grounds of differences in coloration, ecology and non-breeding ranges. Population of Auckland Is have been assigned separate subspecies, *steadi*, but doubtfully valid. Three subspecies normally recognized.
Subspecies and Distribution.
D. c. cauta Gould, 1841 - Tasmania and Auckland Is.
D. c. salvini (Rothschild, 1893) - Crozet, Snares and Bounty Is.
D. c. eremita (Murphy, 1930) - Chatham Is.

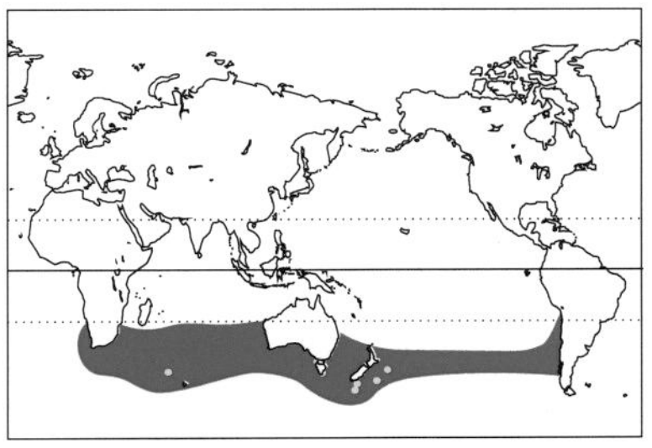

Descriptive notes. 90-99 cm; 3400-4400 g; 220-256 cm. Largest and stoutest-billed of mollymawks; dark eye patch gives characteristic stern look. Underwing white with narrow black edging; diagnostic squarish black patch where leading edge meets body. White cap more or less obvious, and most of head can be white. Juvenile as adult, but bill greyish with black tip. Races separated on head and bill colour; *salvini* has less white crown, appearing less capped and frequently more hooded; race *eremita* strongly hooded with smaller, yellow bill; both have dark under surface to primaries.
Habitat. Marine; less pelagic than many albatrosses, frequently occurring over continental shelf and even close inshore. Breeds on offshore islands occupying slopes or flatter ground, in areas with boulders but generally sparse vegetation.
Food and Feeding. Mostly cephalopods (*Nototodarus sloani*, *Sepioteuthis australis*) and fish (*Sardinops neopilchardus*, *Engraulis australis*, *Trachurus declivis*); also fish offal, barnacles and other crustaceans. Obtains food by surface-seizing or diving, often from air in shallow plunge. Some feeding occurs at night. Often feeds in company of other Procellariiformes, and sometimes follows cetaceans. Despite its name, attends fishing boats, where competes greedily for food.
Breeding. Annual in most instances, starting Sept. Forms colonies of variable density; nest is large mound of mud and grass. 1 egg; incubation 68-75 days with stints of 1-7 days; chicks have white down; fledging c. 4 months.
Movements. Race *cauta* occurs commonly off S Australia and South Africa, but migratory strategy and route not well known; race *salvini* moves E to W coast of S America, where is common in zone of Humboldt Current; race *eremita* virtually sedentary, dispersing only to waters around Chatham Is; breeding adults of migratory races probably do not disperse far from nesting grounds. Records in N Hemisphere off Pacific coast of N America (Washington) and in N Red Sea (Elat, Israel).
Status and Conservation. Not globally threatened. Population decimated around turn of century by plume hunters, especially off Tasmania, where only c. 300 nests by 1909; presently c. 3300 pairs at 3 colonies and population still recovering. 76,000 pairs at Bounty Is, 64,000 pairs at Auckland Is, and 4000 pairs at Chatham Is, giving total population of 800,000-1,000,000 birds. May suffer substantial mortality at commercial fishing grounds, but likely to benefit with recent ban from New Zealand waters of trawlers using antiquated cable system. Breeding grounds on mainland Auckland I visited by pigs; programme proposed for removal of these.

Bibliography. Bartle (1991), Barton (1979b), Blake (1977), Bretagnolle & Thomas (1990), Brown *et al.* (1982), Chambers (1989), García (1972), Johnson (1965), Jouventin (1990), Lindsey (1986), Maclean (1985), Marchant & Higgins (1990), Miskelly (1984), Murphy (1936), Palmer (1962), Robertson (1985), Robertson & Bell (1984), Robertson & van Tets (1982), Serventy *et al.* (1971), Slipp (1952), van Tets & Fullagar (1984), Watson (1975).

11. Yellow-nosed Albatross
Diomedea chlororhynchos

French: Albatros à bec jaune   **German**: Gelbnasenalbatros   **Spanish**: Albatros Clororrinco
Other common names: Carter's Albatross, Yellow-nosed Mollymawk

Taxonomy. *Diomedea chlororhynchos* Gmelin, 1789, Cape of Good Hope.
Sometimes considered monotypic. Two subspecies normally recognized.
Subspecies and Distribution.
D. c. chlororhynchos Gmelin, 1789 - Tristan da Cunha, Gough I.
D. c. bassi Mathews, 1912 - S Indian Ocean.

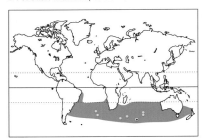

Descriptive notes. 71-81 cm; 2490-2930 g; wingspan 200-256 cm. Slim; bill long and thin, with narrow yellow band along culmen. More capped than *D. chrysostoma*, less so than *D. bulleri*, and less hooded than either; pattern on underwing intermediate between these species, with black on primaries reaching base. During courtship, all mollymawks can have thin stripe of bare skin stretching back from gape beyond eye; normally same colour as bare skin at base of bill. Juvenile as adult, but head all white and bill all black. Race *bassi* has head almost white and lacks capped appearance.

Habitat. Marine and pelagic, though occurs inshore in places. Breeds on remote oceanic islands, occupying slopes or cliffs, typically in bare, rocky areas, but sometimes with vegetation, e.g. tussock grass, ferns.
Food and Feeding. Mostly cephalopods (*Moroteuthis*, *Kondakovia*, Ommastrephidae) and fish (*Scomberesox saurus*, *Cheilopogon furcatus*, *Thyrsites atun*, *Sardinops*, *Engraulis*); also some offal and crustaceans, e.g. amphipods. Captures prey mainly by surface-seizing, diving and shallow plunges to c. 1 m deep, sometimes involving brief pursuit, using wings under water. When attends fishing boats, usually snatches food and flies away to consume it.
Breeding. Annual, starting Aug/Sept. Solitary or in loose groups, with greater density on flatter ground; large nest of mud and grass. 1 egg; incubation c. 71-78 days; chicks have whitish down; fledging c. 130 days. Sexual maturity at 9-11 years. Known to have reached 37 years old in wild.
Movements. Disperses over S Atlantic and Indian Oceans mainly between 15° and 50° S. Particularly numerous off South Africa and Argentina; abundant off S Australia and New Zealand; not recorded from W coast of S America. Sighted with increasing regularity off E coast of N America with 18 records from Quebec to Texas up to 1981; no reliable records for E side of N Atlantic, though recent British record presently under review.
Status and Conservation. Not globally threatened. World population estimated at 80,000-100,000 breeding pairs, or 450,000-550,000 birds. Amsterdam I holds 37,000 pairs, Prince Edward Is 7000 pairs, Crozet Is c. 4500 pairs. Colony on Amsterdam I, with c. 75% of race *bassi*, severely affected by human activities; fires caused by man have decimated tree cover; one fire in 1974 affected the colony directly, and several hundred chicks burnt to death; herd of c. 1200 feral cattle also represent threat to vegetation and nesting grounds (see page 209). Race *chlororhynchos* numbers 21,000-40,000 pairs at Tristan da Cunha Group and Gough I; several thousand adults, eggs and chicks still collected annually for food from Nightingale I; scale of harvest seems to have increased recently, so population could be in danger; decline led to halting of harvest on Tristan in 1930's; switch to Nightingale I led to renewed overexploitation, and fresh restriction in 1974; meanwhile Tristan population has recovered; survey of impact of harvest and stricter regulation required. Numbers apparently stable in most other colonies.
Bibliography. Amiet (1958), Barton (1979b), Blake (1977), Brown *et al.* (1982), Fraser *et al.* (1988), García (1972), Hagen (1952, 1982), Jouventin, Roux *et al.* (1983), Jouventin, Stahl *et al.* (1984), Lindsey (1986), Marchant & Higgins (1990), Murphy (1936), Palmer (1962), Pinto (1983), Richardson (1984), Rowan (1951), Ruschi (1979), Ryan *et al.* (1990), Sick (1984), Swales (1965), Thibault & Guyot (1988), Watson (1975), Weimerskirch, Jouventin & Stahl (1986), Weimerskirch, Jouventin *et al.* (1985), Weimerskirch, Zotier & Jouventin (1989), Williams (1984a).

12. Grey-headed Albatross
Diomedea chrysostoma

French: Albatros à tête grise   **German**: Graukopfalbatros   **Spanish**: Albatros Cabecigrís
Other common names: Flat-billed/Gould's/Grey-mantled/Yellow-nosed(!) Albatross, Grey-headed Mollymawk

Taxonomy. *Diomedea chrysostoma* J. R. Forster, 1785, vicinity of the Antarctic Circle and in the Pacific Ocean. Monotypic.
Distribution. Circumpolar in Southern Ocean, breeding from Cape Horn E to Campbell I.

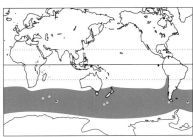

Descriptive notes. 81 cm; 3000-3750 g; wingspan 180-220 cm. Clearly hooded, but only indistinctly capped. Less yellow on bill than *D. bulleri*, with red at tip; underwing blacker than in *D. bulleri* or *D. chlororhynchos*, especially along leading edge, and incipient black marks at wrist and "elbow", more so than in *D. chlororhynchos*, but less than in *D. immutabilis*. Juvenile has blackish bill; pale ear-coverts and face give ring-necked appearance.
Habitat. Marine and pelagic, rarely approaching land except at colonies; favours much colder surface waters than most other albatross species. Breeds on remote oceanic islands occupying steep slopes or cliffs, generally with tussock grass.
Food and Feeding. Mainly cephalopods (*Todarodes*, *Kondakovia longimana*, *Histioteuthis eltaninae*) and fish (Myctophidae, *Channichthys rhinoceratus*, *Dysalotus alcockii*); also crustaceans (*Euphausia superba*) and carrion; lampreys (*Geotria australis*) locally important. High proportion of squid in diet at South Georgia may account for longer nesting period than *D. melanophris*, which takes mostly krill. Does not usually follow ships and attends fishing boats less regularly than other species.
Breeding. Biennial, when successful; starts Oct. Colonial, forming colonies of 15-10,000 pairs; large nest of mud and grass. 1 egg; incubation c. 72 days with stints of 5-15 days; chicks have

white or pale grey down; fledging c. 141 days. Sexual maturity at 8-10 years. Adult mortality of c. 7% per year suggests some birds may live to over 30 years old.
Movements. Disperses widely over Southern Ocean, mostly between 65° S and 35° S, reaching 15° S in zone of Humboldt Current. No reliable records fron N Hemisphere.
Status and Conservation. Not globally threatened. World population of c. 500,000 birds, with c. 80,000 pairs breeding in any one year; 38,000+ pairs at South Georgia, 11,530 pairs at Campbell I; c. 20,000 pairs in S Indian Ocean at Kerguelen, Crozet and Prince Edward Is. In early 20th century egg-collecting produced significant decline, but nowadays only occurs very rarely. Numbers apparently fairly stable at most breeding stations but significant recent decline at South Georgia; slight local decreases especially connected with habitat destruction and predation by alien mammals, e.g. cats, rats. In 1981, c. 20,000 birds at Diego Ramírez Is, off S Chile; decreasing here and threatened locally by launching of squid fishery and long line fishing for *Dissotichus*. Mortality has increased at commercial fishing grounds, especially off S Africa, where a few birds still deliberately taken, others die incidentally; at South Georgia, less affected by competition with fisheries than is *D. melanophris*.
Bibliography. Amiet (1958), Astheimer *et al.* (1985), Barton (1979b), Blake (1977), Bretagnolle & Thomas (1990), Brown *et al.* (1982), Croxall *et al.* (1984), Griffiths (1982), Hector *et al.* (1986), Jehl *et al.* (1979), Johnson (1965), Lindsey (1986), Marchant & Higgins (1990), Murphy (1936), Prince (1980b, 1985), Prince & Francis (1984), Tickell (1964, 1967, 1976, 1984), Tickell & Pinder (1967, 1975), Watson (1975), Weimerskirch, Jouventin & Stahl (1986), Weimerskirch, Zotier & Jouventin (1989), Woods (1988).

Genus *PHOEBETRIA*   Reichenbach, 1853

13. Sooty Albatross
Phoebetria fusca

French: Albatros brun   **German**: Rußalbatros   **Spanish**: Albatros Ahumado
Other common names: Dark-mantled Sooty Albatross

Taxonomy. *Diomedea fusca* Hilsenberg, 1822, Mozambique Channel.
Formerly regarded as conspecific with *P. palpebrata*, but differences in courtship display and timing of breeding prevent interbreeding at sites of overlap. Monotypic.
Distribution. S Atlantic and Indian Oceans, breeding from Tristan da Cunha and Gough I eastwards to Kerguelen Is and Amsterdam and St Paul Is.

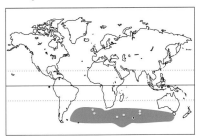

Descriptive notes. 84-89 cm; 2400-2700 g; wingspan 203 cm. Long, narrow, pointed wings and long, wedge-shaped tail distinguish present genus from *Diomedea*. Upperparts uniformly dark, but variable, leading to confusion with *P. palpebrata*; heavier bill, with pale line (sulcus) along lower mandible yellowish and perhaps slightly thicker; eye-ring narrower, more complete and perhaps less white. Juvenile more uniformly sooty black on bill and face; nape paler and paler fringes to feathers of mantle.
Habitat. Marine and pelagic, rarely approaching land except at colonies. Breeds on remote oceanic islands, occupying steep slopes or cliffs with vegetation, especially tussock grass; sometimes nests on flatter ground.
Food and Feeding. Mainly cephalopods (*Kondakovia longimana*, *Moroteuthis*), with small proportions of fish, crustaceans and carrion, e.g. penguins (*Eudyptes*); often scavenges corpses of birds found floating at sea. Apparently captures prey mainly by surface-seizing, but little known and possibly feeds mainly by night. Usually feeds alone, but sometimes in company of other seabirds or cetaceans. Readily follows ships and attends fishing boats.
Breeding. Biennial, when successful; starts Jul/Aug. Loosely colonial, usually in scattered small groups; low, conical nest of moss, grass and mud. 1 egg; incubation c. 70 days with stints of 3-14 days; chicks have greyish down; fledging c. 160 days. Sexual maturity at 9-15 years.
Movements. Disperses over temperate waters of S Atlantic and Indian Oceans 30°-60° S, normally from Argentina E to Tasmania, occasionally to New South Wales; vagrant to E Pacific, 90° W.
Status and Conservation. Not globally threatened. World population estimated at 15,000-21,000 pairs, 80,000-100,000 birds; 5000-10,000 pairs at Gough I, 4125-5250 pairs at Tristan da Cunha, 2732 at Prince Edward Is, and 2620 at Crozet Is. Major colony on Nightingale I (Tristan da Cunha) raided, with over 3000 chicks taken each year; such levels of exploitation can not be sustained for long. Introduced predators may be additional threat here and elsewhere; accidents at commercial fishing grounds also account for some deaths. As in some other albatross species, high losses caused by mass desertion of colonies for unknown reasons.
Bibliography. Berruti (1979, 1981b), Berruti & Harcus (1978), Brown *et al.* (1982), Fraser *et al.* (1988), Jouventin & Weimerskirch (1984), Jouventin, Monicault & Blosseville (1981), Jouventin, Stahl *et al.* (1984), Lindsey (1986), Marchant & Higgins (1990), Mougin (1970b), Richardson (1984), Roux (1987), Swales (1965), Watson (1975), Weimerskirch, Jouventin & Stahl (1986), Weimerskirch, Zotier & Jouventin (1989), Williams (1984a), Woods (1988).

14. Light-mantled Albatross
Phoebetria palpebrata

French: Albatros fuligineux   **German**: Graumantel-Rußalbatros   **Spanish**: Albatros Tiznado
Other common names: Light-mantled Sooty/Grey-mantled Albatross

Taxonomy. *Diomedea palpebrata* J. R. Forster, 1785, south of Prince Edward and Marion Islands. Formerly regarded as conspecific with *P. fusca*, but differences in courtship display and timing of breeding prevent interbreeding in areas of sympatry. Four subspecies described, but subsequently found to be invalid. Monotypic.
Distribution. Circumpolar in Southern Ocean, breeding from South Georgia E to Campbell and Antipodes Is.
Descriptive notes. 78-79 cm; 2800-3100 g; wingspan 183-218 cm. Mantle normally paler than in *P. fusca*, with dark head prominent. Sulcus line on lower mandible pale blue. At rest crown appears

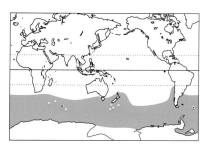

more angular, less rounded than in *P. fusca*. Juvenile as adult, but eye-ring, sulcus and primary shafts usually grey; can have paler fringes on mantle.

Habitat. Marine and pelagic, generally in much colder waters than *P. fusca*. Breeds on remote oceanic islands, occupying steep slopes or cliff ledges, often inland and amongst vegetation, especially tussock grass or ferns.

Food and Feeding. Mainly cephalopods (*Psychroteuthis glacialis*, *Kondakovia longimana*, *Teuthowenia*, *Histioteuthis*) and Antarctic krill (*Euphausia superba*); also takes other crustaceans, fish and carrion, including remains of birds found floating at sea. Catches prey by surface-seizing, but also by diving or surface-plunging. Perhaps mainly nocturnal feeder. Usually feeds alone, but sometimes in company of *D. exulans*; also known to associate with cetaceans. Occasionally follows ships and attends fishing boats.

Breeding. Biennial, when successful; starts Sept/Oct. Often solitary or very loosely colonial; low, conical nest of mud and vegetation. 1 egg; incubation c. 69 days with stints of 4-24 days; chicks have greyish down; fledging c. 141-170 days. Sexual maturity at 7-12 years.

Movements. Disperses widely over Southern Ocean, ranging from pack ice N to c. 33° S, reaching c. 20° S in zone of Humboldt Current; generally driven N in winter by expansion of pack ice. Normally keeps further S than *P. fusca*.

Status and Conservation. Not globally threatened. World population tentatively estimated at c. 30,000 breeding pairs, c. 150,000 birds; 5000-10,000 pairs in New Zealand area, 8000 pairs at South Georgia, 3000-5000 pairs at Kerguelen Is, and 2280 pairs at Crozet Is. Formerly exploited for food at some breeding stations, e.g. Kerguelen and Prince Edward Is. Main causes of breeding failure at South Georgia and Crozet Is were starvation of chicks and desertion by parents. Accidents in course of fishing operations presumably also account for some mortality.

Bibliography. Berruti (1979, 1981b), Berruti & Harcus (1978), Blake (1977), Bretagnolle & Thomas (1990), Brown *et al*. (1982), Croxall *et al*. (1984), Griffiths (1982), Humphrey *et al*. (1970), Jehl *et al*. (1979), Johnson (1965), Kerry & Colback (1972), Lindsey (1986), Marchant & Higgins (1990), Murphy (1936), Mougin (1970b), Sorensen (1950), Thomas (1982), Thomas *et al*. (1983), Watson (1975), Weimerskirch (1982), Weimerskirch, Jouventin & Stahl (1986), Weimerskirch, Zotier & Jouventin (1989), Woehler (1991), Woods (1988).

Class AVES
Order PROCELLARIIFORMES
Family PROCELLARIIDAE
(PETRELS AND SHEARWATERS)

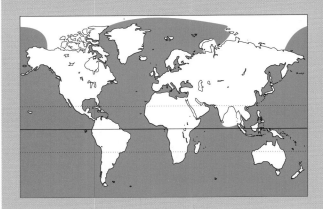

- Medium-sized to large seabirds with compact build, long, narrow wings and "tubenose".
- 25-99 cm.

- Cosmopolitan, in all oceans; greatest diversity in Southern Hemisphere.
- Marine and pelagic.
- 12 genera, 70 species, 109 taxa.
- 17 species threatened; 1 subspecies extinct since 1600.

Systematics

The taxonomy of the Procellariidae is extraordinarily complex, and it is consequently subject to frequent revisions, and more than its fair share of polemic. Two genera are especially controversial, *Pterodroma* and *Puffinus*, but other groups too have their problems. While many of its species are conveniently lumped together as "petrels", as in the title of the family, this name is otherwise used to refer to all members of the order.

Procellariiformes is amongst the most primitive of bird orders, and the Procellariidae, in particular, appear to display a rate of speciation that is much slower than that found in more recent bird groups. Thus some populations may spend longer than usual in an intermediate position before splitting up into different species, so that classification is not always straightforward. In addition, the life histories of many species are still poorly known, and in a few cases no nest has yet been found. It is not surprising therefore that, as knowledge of these birds is expanded, new theories to explain their origins and relationships are put forward.

The early origins of the Procellariidae are linked to those of the other Procellariiformes, from which they probably differentiated in Eocene times, some 40-50 million years ago. It seems that the family first appeared in the Southern Hemisphere, where most forms still live, and later colonized the north. Presently they occupy virtually all the world's oceans and seas, though they are not commonly found in landlocked seas. Nevertheless, there are several forms in the Mediterranean, one of which, the Yelkouan Shearwater (*Puffinus yelkouan*), also occurs in the Black Sea.

While there seems to be little doubt as to the monophyly of the Procellariiformes, their relationship with other orders is not altogether clear. It seems that they probably had a common ancestor with the penguins, and the Little Penguin (*Eudyptula minor*) shows a certain similarity in bill morphology to the typical "tubenose" bill of the petrels (see Morphological Aspects). They have long been linked with the Pelecaniformes too, though this relationship, if valid at all, certainly appears to be more distant. Recent work on DNA confirms the unity of the Procellariiformes, but reduces the four families to one, consisting of three subfamilies, the traditional Pelecanoididae having been swallowed up within the traditional Procellariidae. In this classification, the closest relatives of the petrels are the divers, penguins and frigatebirds.

The family is sometimes split into two subfamilies, Fulmarinae and Procellariinae. However, to all intents and purposes there appear to be four "natural" groups of species with similar characteristics and life histories, the fulmar-petrels, the gadfly-petrels, the prions and the shearwaters. It is convenient to use this division, as there is great uniformity within each group in most aspects of biology, with the partial exception of fulmar-petrels. While each group is distinct enough from the others to deserve separate consideration, there seems to be no doubt as to which forms belong in the Procellariidae. The main problem comes with the internal organization of these groups, and the number of forms that qualify as genuine species.

The fulmar-petrels are the least uniform of the four groups, as they show considerable variation in size and plumage, as well as in distribution, ranging from the Arctic to Antarctica,

Like their larger relatives the albatrosses, all of the Procellariidae are expert fliers. They use a fair amount of flapping flight, but often glide and some use dynamic soaring, with obvious savings in terms of energy. The White-chinned Petrel is a large, heavily built species that tends to have a rather laboured style of flight when there is not enough wind. In stronger winds, it typically glides swiftly along, alternately rising and falling.

[*Procellaria aequinoctialis*. Photo: Tony Howard/ ANT/NHPA]

but they perhaps differ less in diet and ecology. They include two groups of sibling species, the Southern Giant Petrel (*Macronectes giganteus*) and the Northern Giant Petrel (*Macronectes halli*), which were long considered conspecific, and secondly the Northern Fulmar (*Fulmarus glacialis*) and the Southern Fulmar (*Fulmarus glacialoides*). It is generally thought that the Northern Fulmar, now widespread in the Arctic and in northern sectors of the Atlantic and Pacific Oceans, and differentiated into three subspecies, had its origins in an early colonization of the Northern Hemisphere by the Southern Fulmar. The remaining three species of this group, the Antarctic Petrel (*Thalssoica antarctica*), the Cape Petrel (*Daption capense*) and the Snow Petrel (*Pagodroma nivea*), are each distinct enough to be placed in a separate, monotypic genus. The Cape Petrel has two subspecies differing slightly in size and in the extent of white on the wings and back. The Snow Petrel also has two subspecies that differ markedly in size; they breed sympatrically in places, and it has frequently been proposed that they be treated as separate species, but it seems probable that the two evolved in partial isolation, and have never become sufficiently distinct.

The gadfly-petrels are a group of rather similar medium-sized petrels that traditionally comprise the 23-34 species and over 38 forms of the genus *Pterodroma*, and the two species of the genus *Bulweria*. The Fiji Petrel (*Pterodroma macgillivrayi*) has been alternatively assigned to the genera *Bulweria* or *Pterodroma*, or isolated in its own genus *Pseudobulweria*, reflecting that its characteristics are intermediate between the first two genera. Within the genus *Pterodroma* are several of the world's least known seabirds, including species known only from a few specimens taken at sea long ago, and only recently rediscovered, after a lapse of over a century in several cases (see Status and Conservation). Many of these species are still very poorly known, and the breeding grounds of two have yet to be discovered, which, of course, adds to the intrinsic complexity of their taxonomy. In a major paper on the genus, M. J. Imber proposes several significant changes to the traditional classification, based on gut morphology. The Kerguelen Petrel (*Pterodroma brevirostris*) is ousted not only from the genus, but also from the gadfly-petrels, and it is placed in a monotypic genus *Lugensa* within the fulmar-petrels. In addition, the Tahiti Petrel (*Pterodroma rostrata*) and also the Mascarene Petrel (*Pterodroma aterrima*) join the Fiji Petrel in

the genus *Pseudobulweria*. The other species remain in *Pterodroma*, but are in turn divided between four subgenera, to represent different strands of radiation. Several of the new associations are quite revolutionary, for example the White-necked Petrel (*Pterodroma cervicalis*), formerly considered a race of the Juan Fernandez Petrel (*Pterodroma externa*) is not only raised to the status of polytypic species, but it is even placed in a different subgenus from its former ally, right at the other extreme of *Pterodroma*. However, these proposals have not yet received unanimous support, and it is perhaps safer to follow one of the more conservative versions.

The position of the genus *Bulweria* is not well understood, and while it has traditionally been associated with *Pterodroma*, for instance on skeletal grounds, it may really be closer to *Pachyptila* and *Procellaria*. Jouanin's Petrel (*Bulweria fallax*) has been considered to be merely an outsize race of Bulwer's Petrel (*Bulweria bulwerii*), but this now seems unlikely. One major reason for accepting them as different species is that each has its own unique species of *Halipeurus* feather louse.

The prions include the six externally similar species of the genus *Pachyptila* and the Blue Petrel (*Halobaena caerulea*). There is much discussion as to the number of full species within the genus *Pachyptila*, with three to six species and up to fourteen forms recognized. All look extremely alike and are found in the Southern Ocean. The Blue Petrel, sole member of the genus *Halobaena*, has a plumage pattern very like that of the *Pachyptila* prions, but it differs from them in some ecological aspects, and it has variously been assigned to each of the four "natural" groups.

The shearwaters are another large group with highly complex taxonomy. The group consists of four species in *Procellaria*, two in *Calonectris* and 15-20 species and around 34 forms in *Puffinus*. The semi-continuous distribution of some of these species, in belts around the world, suggests that they may have inhabited the "Middle Seas" that once encircled the globe, embracing both the Mediterranean and the Caribbean. As the shifting of landmasses isolated the different populations, these started a process of adaptation in each area, eventually leading to biological seclusion from each other, and thus specific divergence. One such case concerns the group of species related to the Manx Shearwater (*Puffinus puffinus*), which were formerly considered conspecific geographical replacements, but are now more often split into various different species. In contrast, both the Little Shearwater (*Puffinus assimilis*) and Audubon's Shearwater (*Puffinus lherminieri*) have forms spread over vast ranges, which are maintained as 7-8 and 9-11 subspecies respectively.

Morphological Aspects

In their morphology, as in many aspects of their lifestyle, the Procellariidae have much in common with the other members of the order Procellariiformes. They constitute one of the few exclusively marine orders, and are well adapted to a highly pelagic lifestyle.

One of the most remarkable features of the Procellariiformes is the long, hooked bill with tubular external nostrils. This bill is a conglomeration of horny plaques, and the arrangement of the plaques is often useful to scientists for identification in the hand. The sharp nail at the bill tip and the keen cutting edges are useful developments for dealing with awkward marine prey, and similar developments can be seen in other aquatic birds, particularly some Pelecaniformes. Except in the albatrosses, the nostrils are situated along the ridge of the culmen, and in some cases have only a single exit, when the cartilaginous division of the two nostrils occurs within. This "tubenose" seems to be related to a marked development of the sense of smell, which is probably used in the location of food, and birds may be able to detect food some way off at sea, by picking up the scent on the wind. This ability to smell is also used by a bird for locating its own particular nesting burrow within the colony even in complete darkness. Also characteristic of the species of this order is an intense musty smell, which permeates the plumage; this is the same odour that emanates from the stomach oil they produce during the breeding season.

In the Procellariidae coloration is mostly dull, with variable amounts of pure white, grey, bluish grey, brown and black, but the flight-feathers are almost always dark. Generally, there is no plumage variation between the sexes, but females tend to be slightly smaller and more lightly built.

Fulmar-petrels show great variation in size, from the giant petrels at around 5 kg, to the smallest Snow Petrels, which can

weigh as little as 250 g. Coloration is also extremely variable, ranging from pure white in the Snow Petrel, through a bold black and white pattern in the Cape Petrel, to wholly dark in the juvenile plumage of giant petrels and the dark phase of the Northern Fulmar, which is most typical of the Pacific race *rodgersii*. The two giant petrels are like small albatrosses, and in both species the wingspan approaches two metres. They are the only members of the family with strong legs, on which they can stand and walk without much difficulty. They use their huge, powerful bills to tear open the thick skin of the carcasses of seals, whales and penguins, on which they scavenge. In adult plumage they are mostly dark grey with whiter patches on face and neck, but the Southern Giant Petrel has a mostly white morph, with just a few dark feathers. The two fulmars are much smaller and are externally rather like large-headed gulls with broad wings. The Northern Fulmar occurs in two colour phases, dark greyish brown all over and light grey above with white on the head and underparts; Southern Fulmars are only known to occur with the latter plumage. Both the Antarctic and Cape Petrels have distinctive combinations of white and dark brown on the upperwing and tail, with a dark head and white underneath. These two medium-sized species are agile fliers and are very active on the water, while on land they manage better than most other procellariids. The Snow Petrel has pure white plumage, and shows great size differences of over 50% in weight, and up to 25% in wing length, which have led to the suggestion that there may be two species involved (see Systematics).

Gadfly-petrels are fairly large and have long wings. Most species are dark above, often combined with grey or white markings, and white below, with a white face. Many species show a distinctive band on the breast or neck. The two *Bulweria* petrels and a few *Pterodroma* species are dark all over, sometimes with paler areas on the wings. The former also have distinctive long, wedge-shaped tails, whereas in *Pterodroma* the tail is usually short and more rounded, especially in the larger species. All juveniles fledge with a plumage pattern indistinguishable from that of adults, and, as is typical of the Procellariiformes, there are no variations with sex or season, although several species are polymorphic, individuals with heavily worn and abraded plumages are quite frequent and

With its immaculate white plumage the Snow Petrel blends perfectly into the background of snow and ice that predominates in its Antarctic habitat. Its buoyant, erratic style of flight is probably not well suited to flying over long distances and the species is largely restricted to the zone of pack ice, where it can often be seen resting on ice floes. However, in places it breeds up to 300 kilometres inland, and in such cases it must obviously fly long distances to reach its foraging grounds.

[*Pagodroma nivea*. Photo: ANT/NHPA]

In calm conditions take-off can be a little laborious, and may require a run over the water, as demonstrated by this Manx Shearwater. This species has allies distributed mainly in the north-east Pacific, the New Zealand area and the Mediterranean, all of which were treated as races of the Manx until recently. Nowadays they are normally considered sufficiently distinct to be separated off as five, or even seven more species.

[*Puffinus puffinus*, near Isle of Rhum, Scotland. Photo: Rodney Dawson Trust/Bruce Coleman]

atypical plumages are by no means exceptional, so specific identification can be very difficult. Gadfly-petrels have rather short, stout, hooked bills with sharp cutting edges, which they use for seizing and cutting up small fish and squid. As they are quite inept on land, most species nest in burrows which they visit only by night.

Prions are bluish grey above and mostly white below, with a distinct dark M-shaped marking across the upperwing. The Blue Petrel also shows some white on the tail and dark patches on the head. *Pachyptila* prions are best distinguished by their characteristic bill shape, with broadened mandibles. The upper mandible is fringed with many lamellae, which function as filters so that, when water is forced out through them, they retain the small planktonic animals which constitute the birds' food. Prions vary greatly in the shape and dimensions of the bill, suggesting some differences in diet or in feeding technique. Another adaptation to plankton-eating is their unusual capability of distending the skin under the lower mandible to form a gular pouch, which facilitates the transport of food for the chicks. Prions are rather small and have comparatively short wings. They are very feeble on land, which forces them to visit their nest burrows in complete darkness.

Shearwaters vary greatly in size, from the Little Shearwater at 25 cm long, to the White-chinned Petrel (*Procellaria aequinoctialis*) at 55 cm long, with a wingspan of 140 cm. On the basis of their morphology, they can be distinguished in two groups that reflect different flight and feeding habits. The more aerial species, which cover great distances and feed on the wing, have longer wings and tail. These include *Calonectris* and most members of *Procellaria*, as well as the Wedge-tailed Shearwater (*Puffinus pacificus*) and Buller's Shearwater (*Puffinus bulleri*). The more aquatic shearwaters, which include the Grey Petrel (*Procellaria cinerea*) and most species of *Puffinus*, have the wings and tail relatively shorter and the body stockier. In shearwaters the bill is comparatively longer and thinner, with a smaller hook, than in any of the previous groups. The open nostrils situated above the bill are particularly conspicuous in all species. In *Procellaria* plumage is mostly blackish brown all over, with only a few white markings on the head and paler areas on the wings, except in the Grey Petrel, which is ashy grey above and mostly white below. Both the Streaked Shearwater (*Calonectris leucomelas*) and Cory's Shearwater (*Calonectris diomedea*) are grey-brown above with white underparts, and the former shows a conspicuous white face and forehead. Finally, amongst the *Puffinus* shearwaters some species are wholly dark, while others are mainly dark above

and white below. Buller's is unique in having grey upperparts with dark markings, recalling some of the *Pterodroma* petrels. Many species have a dark cap, and some are polymorphic within the same area.

All members of the family Procellariidae are good fliers, and they regularly use alternating periods of flapping and glides on stiff wings. Some of the larger species use dynamic soaring, like the albatrosses, but in contrast to them, the giant petrels feed mostly on land and can keep up sustained flapping flight for much longer. They are also more agile, and can manage take-off much more easily than albatrosses, either on land or at sea. The fulmars may spend hours on the wing, banking and gliding at different heights over land or sea, with just a few wingbeats. Their mastery of flight allows them to land and even build a nest on narrow cliff ledges. They are also buoyant on the water, even in very rough seas. The flight of the Antarctic and Cape Petrels is reminiscent of the fulmars, with perhaps more wing flapping and shorter glides. The Snow Petrel's style of flight is more fluttering and erratic, as dictated by the great unpredictability of the wind and the more constricted space of its pack ice habitat. It seldom alights on the water but frequently loafs on floating ice.

Gadfly-petrels fly very fast, sometimes low over the water, sometimes intermittently wheeling up into the sky, or "towering". They combine periods of rapid wingbeats with much gliding, with the wings held noticeably bent at the wrist and angled forward, but in calm weather, they flap and glide at lower speed, with less "towering". They generally feed on the wing, and do not normally dive, only rarely even alighting on the water.

The flight of prions is extremely active and erratic, and birds twist from side to side and do much weaving and manoeuvring at great speed, including a unique "looping-the-loop", which is typical of the Fulmar Prion (*Pachyptila crassirostris*). They feed by skimming the water with their lamellated bills, and some, including the Antarctic Prion (*Pachyptila desolata*), sometimes use a characteristic technique known as "hydroplaning" (see Food and Feeding).

The larger and more aerial of the shearwaters glide effortlessly above the waves, sliding down the troughs and taking advantage of the differences in wind speed at different levels, in a manner recalling the dynamic soaring typical of albatrosses. They are more agile and also flap more often than albatrosses, but like them they may be forced to roost on the water in absolutely calm conditions. The smaller, more aquatic shearwaters fly more swiftly in strong winds, banking widely

Perhaps rather surprisingly some procellariids nest in areas of forest, though they avoid closed canopy. Although it normally breeds in rocky ground or areas of tussock grass, the Mottled Petrel will also nest in open forest. An interesting practice in such cases is that the birds frequently climb trees, where take-off is obviously much easier, as they can launch themselves directly into the air.

[Pterodroma inexpectata, New Zealand. Photo: M. F. Soper/ ANT/NHPA]

and frequently showing off alternately dark upperparts and white underparts. In light breezes, they fly low over the water using whirring wingbeats alternated with frequent glides, to produce steady, fast progress.

Most members of the Procellariidae are very feeble on land, as their rather weak legs are set far back on the body, and are totally unsuitable for walking. Thus, instead of walking in the normal way, a bird tends to rest its weight on its breast, and work its way along, with the aid of the wings.

Moult is poorly known in the vast majority of species, but in general there appears to be a complete post-breeding moult. The primaries are moulted descendantly, and often several may be dropped simultaneously, but though flying ability is presumably impaired, the birds do not become totally flightless. Male giant petrels tend to start their moult around the time of egg-laying, but it is subsequently suspended, while the chicks are being raised. The smaller females start about two months later and do not require to suspend their moult.

Habitat

The procellariids are truly marine birds. The vast majority of their time is spent at sea and they have adjusted their morphology and lifestyles to it. The sea might seem much more homogeneous than land environments, but there are subtle variations in water temperature, salinity and primary production, which can make the same area suitable for two species with quite different requirements.

Fulmar-petrels all show a marked preference for cool or cold waters, where they may concentrate in good numbers, especially where food is plentiful. Sometimes they follow major cold currents into temperate and subtropical regions, and the Cape Petrel regularly occurs off the Galapagos Islands, at the equator, but in such areas they are restricted to the main fishing grounds. Several species are commonly found near the coast, for example the two giant petrels follow the coastline, in search of seal and penguin carcasses, whereas the Snow and Antarctic Petrels rarely wander far from the pack ice. The two fulmars and the Cape Petrel are more pelagic, and disperse extensively over oceanic waters. The diurnal habits of this group allow the birds to nest in the open, on cliffs and rocky slopes, and in this way they have access to a range of nesting sites that are not available to the rest of Procellariidae. The giant petrels, like many albatrosses, build their nests amongst the vegetation on grassy slopes. The other species of this group tend to choose a sheltered crevice or crack in the rock, especially in Antarctica, which naturally experiences the worst of the weather, or they may nest among boulders and on cliff ledges. The Northern Fulmar, which habitually nests on cliff ledges, during its great expansion over most of the temperate waters of the North Atlantic has occasionally bred in unusual sites, including buildings, roof tops and sand dunes.

Gadfly-petrels are highly pelagic and normally occur far from land. They can be found in many of the world's oceans and seas, one species often replacing another in different areas. The *Pterodroma* petrels are spread over a wide range of climatic zones, from tropical and subtropical to temperate and subantarctic waters, and a few species also reach the subarctic after the breeding season. They do not attend fishing boats, so their pelagic distribution is not affected by the presence of ships, but they are more abundant around the Subtropical and Antarctic Convergences. Gadfly-petrels nest in burrows and crevices, and several species originally occurred far inland on mountain tops and in forests. However, in many zones they have been displaced from such sites by introduced predators (see Status and Conservation). Where this has happened, nowadays the birds commonly nest on offshore islets. Due to their incompetence on land (see Morphological Aspects), birds tend to visit their burrows only by night, and it is only on islands that are free from predators that some species of *Pterodroma* will nest in the open and visit the colony by day, and even then it is unusual.

Prions inhabit the oceanic waters of the southern temperate, subantarctic and Antarctic zones. They are highly pelagic, usually keeping far out to sea, and may be found south to the vicinity of the pack ice. Their plankton diet attracts them to the rich areas of convergence, where they may gather in large flocks. They breed in burrows dug in soft soil or peat, in cavities under boulders and in crevices in steep rocky slopes, lava fields and cliffs.

As a group, the shearwaters are perhaps the most catholic of all the petrels in terms of habitat requirements. They are distributed over the world's oceans, occurring from the tropics to the high latitudes of both the Northern and Southern Hemispheres. In addition, many species are transequatorial migrants and can be found in much warmer waters than they usually frequent, on the way to their breeding grounds or their winter quarters. Other species spend the off season in waters with notably different characteristics from those they occupy during the breeding season. It is difficult, therefore, to generalize about their preferences. Most species only approach land for breeding, and keep well offshore the rest of the time. The larger, more aerial species, in particular, occur mainly on oceanic waters, and are attracted to the areas of convergence, where they may gather in large numbers alongside other petrels and many other seabirds. Food is plentiful in such areas, and the presence of trawlers, and also of tuna or whales, both of which may have the effect of driving fish up to the surface, can influence seabird distribution.

Like most other Procellariiformes, shearwaters are highly sensitive to the effects of terrestrial predators, so they tend to shun areas frequented by cats, rats and the like. Where these are present, the shearwaters lay their eggs in cracks and crevices on offshore islets or stacks, or alternatively on sheer cliffs or on the walls of large caves. Under normal conditions, they nest in burrows excavated or enlarged by themselves in soft soil, or in crevices, amongst boulders or hidden under dense vegetation or roots. They also use old rabbit burrows, and, where their density is very high, they may occupy almost every available site, although in such areas breeding success tends to be reduced. Colonies normally have direct access to and from the sea, but where terrestrial predators are few or absent, a colony may be established several kilometres inland, sometimes at a fair altitude.

General Habits

Most members of the Procellariidae are gregarious. They occur in small or large flocks, with the greatest aggregations occurring at particularly rich food sources. Many birds obtain supplementary food relatively easily by attending trawlers at fishing grounds, where competition for discarded fish and squid is strong and noisy scuffles are frequent. Each bird fights for a share, trying to displace the other birds, conspecifics or otherwise. Giant petrels are particularly aggressive, threatening even the larger albatrosses, and so too is the hefty White-chinned Petrel. Other birds especially fond of attending fishing boats are the Northern Fulmar, the Cape and Grey Petrels, the Great Shearwater (*Puffinus gravis*) and the Sooty Shearwater (*Puffinus griseus*). A few species actually follow ships, where they can glide along effortlessly, using the eddies created by the moving vessel. Only some of the larger fulmar-petrels and shearwaters, generally rather weak fliers, habitually do so, and they can remain on the wing for hours.

A typical aspect of the gregarious tendencies of most of these birds is their habit of forming large, sometimes huge, breeding colonies, which naturally leads to a fair amount of interaction amongst congeners. Mixed colonies are infrequent, and although

The Antarctic Petrel breeds only on mainland Antarctica and on nearby inshore islands and it frequently has to tolerate very harsh climatic conditions. It habitually nests in rather exposed sites where the wind should prevent an excessive accumulation of snow.

[*Thalassoica antarctica.* Photo: D. Watts/NPIAW]

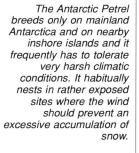

Many species of petrels and shearwaters are markedly gregarious, for example the Cape Petrel, which breeds colonially and forms large flocks at sea, especially in areas where food is abundant. To this end they regularly congregate on commercial fishing grounds, often in the company of other Procellariiformes and other seabirds. The same assemblages frequently follow cetaceans, feeding on their left overs, their faeces or prey that the huge mammals have disturbed.

[*Daption capense capense*. Photo: Peter Johnson/ NHPA]

several species may breed on the same island, they usually keep to different areas, and do not interfere with each other.

As a rule, it is only the fulmar-petrels that visit their breeding colonies by day, but where the colony is on an island unmolested by avian predators, the Black-winged Petrel (*Pterodroma nigripennis*), the Kermadec Petrel (*Pterodroma neglecta*) and the Herald Petrel (*Pterodroma arminjoniana*) may also do so, as does Cory's Shearwater on occasions. These diurnal visitors nest in the open, defend the nest-site as a territory, and have a series of visual displays to show their mood and intention (see Breeding).

Nocturnal species, on the other hand, usually nest in burrows or caves, where they hide during the day, and they tend to be very poor movers on land. They cannot use visual displays in order to communicate with conspecifics, so instead they have to resort to acoustic or tactile signals, or use their well developed sense of smell (see Morphological Aspects). The species that are essentially nocturnal on land include the prions, most of the gadfly-petrels and the shearwaters.

The main reason for the nocturnal habits of these birds at their colonies is their vulnerability. As most can only scramble or walk with great difficulty, they have little chance to defend themselves against more mobile predators, such as gulls, crows and raptors. In fact, many colonies are constantly patrolled by large gulls, which succeed in taking a heavy toll, even though the petrels only approach land when protected by complete darkness. However, while these birds may be strictly nocturnal on land, it does not necessarily follow that they are so at sea. Thus, many species that only visit the burrow in complete darkness can be found at sea in the middle of the day, perhaps feeding in strong sunlight. In contrast, some species take prey, such as squid, that occurs in surface waters mostly or exclusively during the night, so they are mainly night feeders too. After a few days or nights feeding at sea, adult shearwaters will concentrate in the immediate vicinity of their colony. There they sit on the water, forming large rafts, waiting for the hours of darkness. The vulnerability of some species is such that they may not visit the colony at all on moonlit nights.

Voice

At sea fulmar-petrels are usually silent when they are alone, but in large flocks they become very noisy, when there are disputes for food, making a variety of grunts and croaking sounds. Their repertoire of calls at the nest, although markedly poorer than that of most burrow-nesters, is still quite rich, for instance cackling, perhaps the most characteristic call in many species, and also droning, croaking and other guttural sounds. The giant petrels also make a cat-like mewing and hiss loudly.

Gadfly-petrels tend to remain silent at sea, but they are extremely vocal at night, when they visit the breeding grounds. While passing over the colony in communal courtship flights at dusk, they may produce various shrill cries that have been likened to the chatter of terns, the laugh of kestrels or the screams of swifts. Other high-pitched, squeaky calls are uttered by birds in flight over the burrows, and each species has its own vocabulary. Birds on the ground are known to give different crooning or growling notes, but most distinctive are the various moaning cries produced from inside the burrows, often accompanied by a few guttural sounds.

Prions too are usually silent at sea, even at feeding grounds, but several coos and harsh alarm notes have been recorded from birds captured at sea. At the colonies, the most typical call is a faint coo, which has given rise to the specific name of the Fairy Prion (*Pachyptila turtur*). Other calls include a variety of harsh gurgling, growling, guttural and throaty cries, squeaking notes and a piping whistle, this last given while the bird is in flight over the colony or inside the burrow.

Shearwaters follow the general rule of a strong tendency to be silent at sea, where only a few species make harsh, raucous cries and screams, when competing for food at fishing grounds. Again, they have a rich vocabulary at the colony, where a wide variety of sounds is produced by birds flying over the colony, and others on the ground, perhaps inside their burrows. Calls include a series of rapidly repeated crows, coos, croons, howls, cackles, wails, trills and moans, pig-like screams, cat-like mews and other almost human cries. Such sounds often elicit a response from a bird's mate, or from the owners of a neighbouring burrow, and especially during the period prior to egg-laying mated pairs may spend hours duetting from inside the burrow. There is evidence that, at least in the best known species, there is some variation both in voice and in the repertoire of calls with individual, sex and population.

In general, calling tends to be more intense during the early part of the breeding season. It is confined to the night, mainly to the first hours after dusk and the last before dawn; it is rare during the hours of daylight.

Food and Feeding

Given their marine habits and their general weakness on land, it is not surprising that almost all members of the Procellariidae feed exclusively at sea. The methods used and the type of prey taken are both related to the morphology of the different species.

The giant petrels are highly opportunistic, obtaining most of their food by scavenging on the carcasses of seals and penguins. Other, less important food items taken include krill (*Euphausia*) during the breeding season, and fish and squid in winter, when carrion is at its scarcest. The sexual dimorphism in size possibly accounts for the differences observed in diet, and the smaller females, which can be displaced from carcasses by the more dominant males, feed more on live marine prey. Giant petrels find most of their food on or near land, indeed they are unique among the Procellariiformes in feeding largely near the coast. They stand on their strong legs, tearing open the skin of carcasses with their heavy, powerful bills, and sometimes several dozen birds may gather at a particular carcass. Northern Giant Petrels also frequent commercial fishing grounds, where they feed on discarded fish and offal, for which they compete with albatrosses, shearwaters and other petrels.

The two fulmars feed mostly on fish, squid and planktonic crustaceans, but they also behave opportunistically, taking fish offal, whale blubber and carrion, whenever it is available. In fact, the increased availability of offal provided by the fishing and whaling industries is probably responsible for the remarkable spread of Northern Fulmars southwards over the Atlantic Ocean in recent times. Fulmars usually "surface-seize" their food items, while sitting on the water. They feed by day, but also by night, particularly when taking zooplankton. Very large numbers may concentrate around fishing vessels and at other abundant sources of food.

The remaining three members of this group, the Antarctic, Cape and Snow Petrels, feed mainly on crustaceans (mostly euphausiids), squid, fish, fish offal, carrion and medusae. The Cape Petrel may gather in the hundreds behind fishing boats, and its habit of sitting high on the water in a characteristic posture and pecking busily ahead and to the sides has earned it the name of "Cape Pigeon". All three species frequently feed on the wing, "dipping" or sometimes diving to catch their prey. The Snow Petrel alone is rather reluctant to alight on the water, preferring usually to rest on ice floes.

Little is known about the diets of gadfly-petrels, but squid seems to be the main item in all the species studied so far, complemented with variable proportions of small fish, crustaceans and other invertebrates. Evidence suggests that most of the squid, and perhaps fish too, is captured live at night, but a minor proportion is scavenged at sea. A remarkable feature of the gadfly-petrels is that they feed mainly on the wing, "dipping" whilst in flight; they seldom alight on the water and do not dive. Large flocks may form around sizeable shoals, but many species are mainly solitary feeders. Only occasionally do they attend fishing boats.

The diet of the prions consists mostly of zooplankton, especially euphausiid crustaceans, as well as squid and fish. The three larger species, the Antarctic Prion, Salvin's Prion (*Pachyptila salvini*) and the Broad-billed Prion (*Pachyptila vittata*), have specialized bills with comb-like lamellae in the upper mandible that act as filters, through which water is forced, and the small food items are strained out. Prions typically sit on the water to filter-feed but some use a peculiar technique called "hydroplaning", in which the bird rests lightly on the water and uses its feet to skim swiftly over the surface, with its wings outstretched, and the bill or even the whole head submerged. The smaller prions, for instance the Slender-billed Prion (*Pachyptila belcheri*), alternatively feed by "surface-seizing" from the water, by pattering over the surface or by "dipping", whilst on the wing. Their diet is largely similar,

Procellariids lack the spectacular ritualized courtship displays of the albatrosses, and this may be connected with the fact that many species only come to land at night, when visual displays are fairly useless. In most cases, courtship behaviour is very limited and may consist almost entirely of "Billing" in the burrow, during which oil may seep from the nostrils. Another regular practice is mutual preening, as demonstrated by these Wedge-tailed Shearwaters, and this is often a prelude to copulation.

[*Puffinus pacificus*, French Frigate Shoals, Hawaiian Isles National Wildlife Refuge. Photo: Frans Lanting/ Bruce Coleman]

Northern Fulmars do not normally form particularly dense colonies, and even in the densest, nests tend to be well spaced out, often one metre or more apart. For this reason there is not much territorial aggression, and intruders are normally seen off simply by means of a "Cackling-display", with the throat puffed out; if this is not sufficiently effective, the bird may eject stomach oil at its opponent. At the nest-site the "Cackling-display" has a series of other uses, and cliff colonies regularly echo to the sound of constant bickering.

[*Fulmarus glacialis auduboni*, Foula, Shetland. Photo: Günter Ziesler]

perhaps with greater proportions of fish and squid. All prions occasionally make shallow dives.

Due to their expansive range and extensive wanderings, shearwaters have a diet which varies considerably with species, region, time of year and the local abundance of certain types of prey. Generally they take mostly crustaceans and fish, as well as squid, amphipods and other invertebrates. Amongst the crustaceans, euphausiids seem to be of major importance, whereas amongst fish it seems that species of the herring type, that are often found in large shoals, such as pilchard (*Sardina*) and anchovy (*Engraulis*), are important prey. Discarded fish and offal are readily picked up astern of fishing boats by many species. The particular feeding technique of each species is partly determined by its morphology. Thus, some of the more aerial shearwaters often feed on the wing, whereas the bulkier species are well adapted to swimming under water, where they can reach depths of over 20 m, using their wings to "fly" under the water, in the same way as auks do. Most species can dive well from the air in shallow plunges that often develop into underwater pursuits, and "surface-seizing" is also a common method in this group.

At least some procellariids feed largely during the hours of darkness, especially those with a diet based on zooplankton and vertically-migrating squid. The "tubenoses" (Procellariiformes) are unusual in the world of birds in having a well developed sense of smell. There is good evidence that they use this in the location of food, as large numbers have been attracted from downwind, when substances smelling strongly of food were experimentally scattered at sea. The ability to detect food using the sense of smell is probably especially useful for night foraging.

Breeding

In common with most other members of the order, the Procellariidae tend to form large breeding aggregations. These colonies are usually situated strategically, with easy access to and from the sea, avoiding areas that abound in predators. In most species, a significant proportion of the total world population is concentrated at only a few traditional breeding sites, and only a few species breed in numerous colonies spread over an extensive area. Colonies are of vital importance, as these

birds spend most of their lives at sea, and their only contact with land normally takes place at night. With the safety of large numbers, the individual loses its fear of the land, where it is much more vulnerable than at sea, and joins in the noisy struggle to obtain a burrow and a mate.

Some colonies reach fantastic proportions, and the density of nests can be so high that disturbance by congeners accounts for a fair proportion of breeding failures. Huge breeding aggregations, sometimes of several million pairs, are known for various species. For example, over 6 million pairs of Short-tailed Shearwaters (*Puffinus tenuirostris*) breed in southern

One of the main foraging techniques used by Audubon's Shearwater is pursuit-diving, which involves swimming under water, usually not very deep, and using the wings for both propulsion and manoeuvring. Several species regularly lower the head below the surface of the water before embarking on a dive, presumably looking for prey to pursue.

[*Puffinus lherminieri*. Photo: L. Löfgren]

Australia and Tasmania, around 6 million pairs of Great Shearwaters nest at Tristan da Cunha and Gough Island, and one enormous colony of Sooty Shearwaters on the Snares Islands harbours over 2·5 million pairs; there are many other instances of procellariids that nest in large colonies. In contrast, this family also contains some of the scarcest seabirds in the world, and in some cases the number of nests known are not sufficient to constitute a "proper" colony. A few species are only loosely colonial, such as the Northern Giant Petrel, which is normally a solitary nester, and the Southern Giant Petrel, which breeds in small groups with nests well spaced out.

Breeding is annual in nearly all the species studied, and is necessarily so in all regions where latitude causes marked seasonal fluctuations in the availability of food. However, some species in tropical areas, like Audubon's Shearwater in the Galapagos, may attempt breeding every 9-10 months. Although there are some cases of winter breeding, most species breed during their local spring or summer, but, again, in parts of the tropics eggs may be laid irregularly throughout the year. Once an individual has attempted to breed for the first time, it will normally do so in successive seasons. However, a few birds each season take rest years, during which they do not even attempt to breed or visit the colony at all, though the reasons for this remain unknown. Such birds often resume regular breeding in the following years.

In the few species studied so far, ringing results show that, as with the other petrels, procellariids reach sexual maturity only after several years. The age of first breeding ranges from 3 years in the smallest petrels to 12 in some of the fulmar-petrels, but in most of the known cases it occurs at about 5-6 years. Many immature birds start visiting the colony long before they are able to commence breeding, late in the season at first but progressively earlier afterwards. By so doing, they become familiar with the structure of the colony and the activities of the breeding adults. These birds spend many nights on land out in the open, until they ultimately start to dig a burrow or claim an unoccupied site. This they visit assiduously,

evicting all intruders from it, as this is an important part in the process of obtaining a mate. Newly formed pairs commonly spend long periods of time at the nest, sometimes for more than one full season, before they actually start to breed.

Only a very few species nest in the open. Of these, the giant petrels pile up a rough mass of grass and other vegetation, or, where it is scarce, they may gather up small stones to form a mound with a shallow depression on top. The other fulmar-petrels nest on cliff ledges or in cracks in rocks, hollows or shallow crevices, with a degree of shelter that depends much on the local climate, so the birds of higher latitudes seek more protection. The nest itself is usually a small depression on the bare rock, often lined with small stones. Curiously enough, there are also two species of gadfly-petrel, the Kermadec and Herald Petrels, that tend to lay their eggs in a crevice among rocks, or in a depression in the soil lined with small bits of vegetation.

The burrow-nesters either dig their own hole using the bill and feet, or take up an abandoned rabbit burrow. Some species alternatively use natural cavities where these are available. Burrows can be of various different lengths and shapes, varying with species, type of soil, climate and density of nests; soft soil or peat is best, and as a rule, burrows are less protected in hotter, drier places. They range in length from about 30 cm to nearly 4 m, while they are often sloping and twisted, especially in wet areas, and the Great Shearwater's has a sharp turn just inside the entrance. In some cases, a primitive system of drainage helps to eliminate any incoming water and to prevent flooding. Not infrequently, the burrow splits into several branches after the entrance, each occupied by a different pair. The nest chamber is enlarged and may be bare or it may contain a rough nest made of leaves, twigs, feathers and debris. In a few species, the entrance to the burrow is littered with faeces, feathers and plant matter.

Unless there is a succession of breeding failures, the same nest is repeatedly used by the same pair over many years, as long as both birds survive, and the same pair of Northern

The giant petrels are the only members of the order that regularly forage on land and in line with this they are the only species that can walk well. They are perhaps best known for their habit of scavenging. Seals and penguins are amongst the commonest sources of food, and seal carcasses will be attacked within the first three or four days after death. However, they are also active predators and at sea they will even attack and drown small albatrosses. This Southern Giant Petrel is using the "Sealmaster Posture" to demonstrate its dominance at the carcass.

[Macronectes giganteus, St. Andrews Bay, South Georgia. Photo: Annie Price/ Survival]

Great Shearwaters are highly gregarious at sea, especially in areas of upwelling and near their main breeding grounds at Tristan da Cunha in the South Atlantic. They often form large rafts on the sea, when some birds may forage by pursuit-diving, although the main technique of this species is pursuit-plunging, from six to ten metres above the water.

[*Puffinus gravis*, Tristan da Cunha. Photo: M. P. Kahl/DRK]

Fulmars has been known to use a site for at least 25 years. "Divorce" is infrequent, but, should one of the members of the pair fail to turn up at the beginning of the breeding season, the surviving bird will try to find another mate, and occasionally may nest successfully during that same season. The nest is the meeting point for the pair, and the first bird to arrive usually waits patiently in the nest for the return of its mate.

Many species start visiting their nests long before egg-laying. This has a territorial function in the defence of the nest-site, and also helps maintain the pair-bond. For some weeks prior to the laying of the eggs, partners are commonly found together at the nest engaged in long sessions of duetting (see Voice), mutual preening and caressing. This is also the time when territorial conflicts are most intense. However, since few birds of pre-breeding age are present at the colony during the early part of the breeding season, such conflicts are soon resolved.

Displays are varied. Like other gadfly-petrels, the diurnal Black-winged Petrel nests at the end of a burrow. It has elaborate courtship flights, in which partners engage in a spectacular series of aerial chases, including high-speed swoops and "towering", accompanied by loud, shrill calls. The species that are exclusively nocturnal on land have less elaborate aerial chases, which may be communal with much screaming, and they have simpler display flights; they also lack any special markings that would make them conspicuous at night, such as the white rump found in many storm-petrels.

Fulmar-petrels defend their territories with "Head-waving" and a "Cackling-display", as well as loud hissing and various other harsh sounds, such as bill-snapping in the giant petrels. The fulmars also make use of their oil-spitting ability against their own congeners or other birds, in defence of the nest-site, whereas the rest of the diurnal petrels usually repel only predators in this way. Fulmars often spend much time on the wing, flying back and forth above their part of the colony, prospecting for a site or mate, or patrolling near the nest. Established birds usually respond to these potential rivals by "Head-waving" and swallowing conspicuously. In competition for nest-sites, giant petrels make use of a ritualized aggressive display, which generally inhibits actual fighting: the site owner spreads its wings and fans its tail forwards, swaying its head in large arcs at the same time. Fulmar-petrels develop, maintain or reinforce their pair-bonds by performing a number of stereotyped actions that include "Head-waving" at each other, nibbling, cackling and mutual preening. They often engage in "Mutual-billing", during which oil may seep from the nostrils.

In the nocturnal species, birds start flying over the colony in large numbers as darkness falls. Each bird calls loudly, in the moment it passes above its own burrow, eventually eliciting a response from its mate. Individual variations in voice and in repertoire of calls are thought to help the flying bird find its nest. Once the bird has located its burrow, it lands nearby and moves along to the entrance. Some species defend the whole burrow as their territory, evicting intruders with a combination of calls, hisses and threatening postures with the bill open, but more commonly only the nest chamber is defended, and several burrows may share the same entrance without conflicts. Initially, when two birds or pairs are disputing the ownership of a nest chamber, there may be some real fighting, but because they are so helpless on land, their fights are neither intense nor violent. They use only the bill, and even though it is powerful, there are few injuries. Most species do not usually make use of their spitting ability in territorial conflicts.

Most sexual activity between mates takes place inside the burrow, and courtship is rather simple in all members of the family. It consists largely of "Billing", with oil dribbling down the bill, and mutual preening. At this stage, both birds may engage in a series of long calls.

The Fairy Prion chick is normally fed every night by both adults and it is thought that the chick's nightly intake is some 30 grams, consisting mostly of euphausiids. At first, when the chick is still very small, the adults tend to bring it too much food. As in other members of the order, the chicks are fed by regurgitation.

[*Pachyptila turtur*. Photo: N. Brothers/NPIAW]

Not long after copulation has been effective, both members of the pair usually go back to sea to regain weight, after the long period spent on land in the construction or conditioning of the nest, territorial disputes and mating, and so as to build up reserves in order to be in good physical condition for the formation of the egg and subsequent long stints of incubation. This "honeymoon" period usually lasts about a fortnight, during which one of the pair, usually the male, may pay short visits to the nest, so that it is not thought by prospecting birds to be unoccupied.

Invariably, a single large white egg is laid. It represents a significant proportion of the female's weight, on average 12-16%, with the lowest figures of 6-8% corresponding to the heaviest females, the giant petrels, and the highest of 20-24% to the lightest birds, including prions and some gadfly-petrels. Such relatively heavy eggs can only be produced by females that are fit, after a period of abundant feeding. It is most improbable that the same female can lay twice in one season, and the few cases known are probably due to a change of partner during the course of the breeding season, while two eggs in the same nest are more probably the result of two females laying in the same burrow; this has been reported to take place, especially in very dense colonies, though it is apparently infrequent.

The incubation tasks are shared between the sexes, in turns of several days. The length of each incubation stint averages 2-14 days in most species, although it varies with species, food availability, distance to foraging area, intensity of moonlight in strictly nocturnal species, and so on. The male usually takes the first stint, but in the Northern Fulmar the female sits on the newly laid egg for the first day or so, after which the male normally incubates about seven days running. Each bird then sits for roughly 3·5 days, until, towards the end of the incubation period, they change over every 24 hours or so. The incubation period is extremely long in relation to body size, except perhaps in the larger species, with an average of 6-9 weeks, though it is 7-8 weeks in most species. The eggs have an extraordinary resistance to chilling, and the embryo will not die even after an interruption in incubation of several days, so it is easily resumed at virtually any stage. In such cases, the length of the incubation period can be notably increased, for instance in the Manx Shearwater, with an average incubation period of 51 days, one such egg took 63 days to hatch.

The newly hatched chick is covered in a coat of short, soft down, ranging in colour from pure white through variable tones of grey to wholly dark. It is tended by at least one of its parents for a period lasting 2-20 days, depending on the species and the type of nest, with burrow-nesters normally brooding for shorter periods. As soon as the nestling can regulate its own body temperature, it is abandoned during the day by its parents, which visit it only for feeding. The chick is fed an oily substance produced in the proventriculus of the adults, and resulting from the partial digestion of their ordinary food. The fat-rich, stinking oil is often greenish, and it tends to be the product of several days' foraging by the adult bird, facilitating the task of storing and transporting as much food as the chick needs. Fed on this, the chick soon becomes very fat, exceeding an adult's weight by 10-20% before it is fully-feathered. The chick is very resistant to starvation, and this counteracts the many difficulties its parents may encounter in gathering enough food for the chick and delivering it promptly, as well as feeding themselves. Feather growth consumes much energy, and the fat chick gradually loses weight. It is still fed regularly, but eventually, as it approaches fledging weight, it is abandoned by its parents.

The adults stop visiting the chick once it is fully-feathered, with perhaps only a few traces of down remaining; at this stage it is fully-grown, and is often still heavier than its parents. The chick will remain in the nest, waiting to be fed, unaware that it has been abandoned. Chicks that have stayed inside a burrow and those reared at an open nest alike have an instinctive urge to learn to fly, and all spend much time exercising their wings during this period. Those from burrows come out at night to practise, and hundreds of hungry chicks all over the colony stand at the entrances of their burrows, flapping away energetically. During the day, the chick hides in the nest, and one night, usually 6-15 days after its parents' desertion, it flies out to sea on its own.

Fledging is one of the most critical moments in the life of any bird, even more so if it has to find its way to the sea alone, with no flying experience, and especially if it is burrow-bred, in

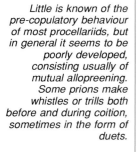

Little is known of the pre-copulatory behaviour of most procellariids, but in general it seems to be poorly developed, consisting usually of mutual allopreening. Some prions make whistles or trills both before and during coition, sometimes in the form of duets.

[*Pachyptila vittata*. Photo: Rick Price/Survival]

which case it flies exclusively at night. Some colonies have direct access to the sea, posing few problems to the unskilled fledging, but others are situated far inland, on mountain slopes or even in wooded country. The young bird sometimes has to cover distances of 30 km or more, before reaching the sea, and many such birds fall victim to the numerous predators that congregate near the colony around that time, including gulls, skuas, corvids and raptors. Others are incapable of finding their way out to sea, and many are found near human habitation, having been attracted by the bright lights and ending up dead in the jaws of a dog or cat, or run over by a car. Finally, violent weather may cause unexperienced fledglings that have succeeded in reaching the sea to be driven towards the coast, where they may die in hundreds, crashing against rocks or simply starving.

Breeding success is generally high, with 50-80% of the eggs laid hatching and 60% to almost 100% of all chicks hatched fledging successfully. These figures are, however, greatly reduced where a colony is subject to predation. Introduced mammalian predators, especially rats and cats, can reduce breeding success to virtually nil, and at the same time reduce the breeding population by killing large numbers of adults (see Status and Conservation). Except where there is heavy predation on the nesting grounds, members of the Procellariidae are generally long-lived. Several individuals are known to have lived for over 30 years, while a mean annual survival rate among adult birds of around 95% in many species suggests that the average life expectancy is of some 15-20 years.

Movements

Procellariids are highly mobile, and many species undertake long, complex migrations of several thousand kilometres, in which the whole population may be engaged for several months. Other species spend the whole year in the waters adjacent to the colony, dispersing only in its immediate vicinity. Some other species may show differences in their migratory habits depending on age, with the younger birds tending to wander far and wide, while the breeding adults stay within a few days' reach of the colony, which they may visit intermittently outside the breeding season.

Several shearwater species are amongst the greatest migrants, nesting on subantarctic islands and reaching the subarctic during their annual migration, with a range of about 120° of latitude. They travel at low energetic cost by making use of the prevailing winds. First they fly towards the windward side of the ocean, so that they can subsequently enjoy the maximum leeward range, before completing a wide loop. By flying in a figure of eight pattern they take the longest route but have side winds constantly guaranteed, and these allow them to cover great distances with little effort more or less continuously. The performers of these extraordinary migrations are, amongst others, the Short-tailed and Buller's Shearwaters in the Pacific, the Great Shearwater in the Atlantic and the Sooty Shearwater in both the Atlantic and the Pacific. Similarly, the Mottled Petrel (*Pterodroma inexpectata*) flies from New Zealand to the Bering Sea and back in a somewhat circular route.

Other species have more definite target areas, to which they fly without delay more or less directly. The Manx Shearwater, for example, leaves its British home waters for its winter quarters off eastern South America, which it reaches in just a few weeks. One fledgling, ringed at its nest at Skokholm in Wales, was found off Brazil, almost 10,000 km away, only 17 days after it was ringed. However, many of the Procellariidae are merely dispersive and nomadic after the breeding season, occurring more or less irregularly over a considerable area. Most Cory's Shearwaters, for instance, quit the Mediterranean and disperse over the Atlantic, arriving in good numbers both off the eastern seaboard of North America and in the waters of the Benguela Current off South Africa and Namibia. Many tropical species disperse after breeding over thousands of kilometres of sea within the tropics, and several of the species that nest on subantarctic islands spend the non-breeding season with a circumpolar distribution around the Southern Ocean. In nearly all cases, as seabirds take some years to reach sexual maturity, significant numbers of non-breeders spend all year in their winter range or may travel back only part of the way.

Procellariids have an extraordinary homing ability, which enables them to find their breeding island, sometimes a mere speck of land, in the midst of the ocean. This ability has been tested in one species in particular, the Manx Shearwater, with some spectacular results. Several individuals engaged in breed-

The Black-winged Petrel is one of a group of similar species often referred to as the subgenus Cookilaria. Very little is known about the breeding habits of this species, but it is known to nest in burrows 50-100 centimetres long, though it will similarly occupy rock crevices.

[*Pterodroma nigripennis*. Photo: T. & P. Gardner/ NPIAW]

The Short-tailed Shearwater has traditionally suffered intensive exploitation, and it is locally known as the Tasmanian Muttonbird. Nonetheless, it remains amongst the most numerous of the Procellariiformes, with vast breeding aggregations in the region of Tasmania. Around fledging time the colony is a seething mass, as all the chicks abandon their burrows and go off to sea by night over a period of about three weeks.

[*Puffinus tenuirostris*. Photo: Bernard Stonehouse/ Ardea]

ing, and thus with an urge to be back at the nest, were displaced from their colony at Skokholm, and subsequently released in different places. They were timed on their return to the colony: one bird returned from the Isle of May, off eastern Scotland, in 12 days, a distance of about 1400 km, assuming it travelled by sea; two birds returned from the Faroe Islands in 11 and 12 days respectively; several birds were taken out of the normal range of the species and also found their way back to their home island, and four birds flew back from Switzerland in 10-15 days; one crossed the Atlantic from Boston, over 5000 km away, in 13 days; and, most spectacular of all, one bird returned from Venice in 13 days, after a journey of about 6000 km, assuming it flew over the sea round by the Straits of Gibraltar, as is probable, or roughly 1500 km, if it flew directly over land.

Young birds of all species usually travel further afield than adults, and often occur in areas not usually frequented by the species. Northern Fulmars are known to cross the North Atlantic, from Britain to Newfoundland and from Greenland to Portugal. After fledging, giant petrels follow the main flow of the wind eastwards, and, like some albatrosses, may complete the circumnavigation of the Southern Ocean in a few months. Such large-scale movements may occasionally result in some birds drifting a long way away out of their normal ranges, and there are several exceptional records, including: a Manx Shearwater ringed as a nestling at Skokholm, and recovered 14 months later in Australia 16,675 km away; a Southern Giant Petrel recorded off Ushant, in northern France; a Jouanin's Petrel collected in Hawaii; Manx and Cory's Shearwaters off New Zealand; and Great and Buller's Shearwaters recorded in the north of the "wrong" ocean, the North Pacific and North Atlantic respectively.

In a few cases species are so closely tied to a particular habitat that they can not stray far from it, so they become relatively sedentary. This is an exceptional case among the Procellariidae, but is well exemplified by the Snow and Antarctic Petrels, which are particularly associated with pack ice. Only very occasionally are these birds driven away from their Antarctic haunts by long spells of bad weather and very strong winds.

Relationship with Man

Human exploitation has been and still is responsible for the extreme rarity of some species of the Procellariidae (see Status and Conservation). Due to their great vulnerability on land and occurrence in large breeding colonies, probably only a few species have been free from human exploitation, which has long affected virtually all inhabited islands and offshore islets within human reach. There is evidence of such ancestral ex-

ploitation by the Maoris in New Zealand, the Eskimos in the Arctic, the first Caribbeans, early Polynesians and many other indigenous cultures long before white settlement, while in parts of Europe too there has also been a great tradition of collecting seabirds. Even today, over 60,000 Short-tailed Shearwater chicks are taken annually off Tasmania. Over 50,000 Great Shearwater chicks are similarly collected on a regular basis at Tristan da Cunha, and the commercial exploitation of eggs and chicks is still of some importance in many places: Sooty Shearwaters on several of the islands off New Zealand; Cory's and Little Shearwaters on the Cape Verde Islands and Madeira; and Audubon's Shearwater in the Caribbean.

Direct exploitation by man has particularly affected some gadfly-petrels, several species of shearwater and the Northern Fulmar. Gadfly-petrels were mainly taken for food, and with pressure being greatest on the adult birds, there were swift declines in the populations. The use of shearwaters and Northern Fulmars has been more thorough, and in historical times eggs, chicks and adults were collected systematically, but this practice soon proved to be uneconomical, as it led to significant declines in numbers. Harvesting was then concentrated on the fat chicks, which provided feathers, down, flesh, fat and oil. Today, in Tasmania, the feathers and down of the young "muttonbirds", as Short-tailed Shearwaters in particular are known locally, are used in upholstery and in the manufacture of sleeping bags, while fat is used commercially as a food supplement for dairy cattle, and oil is greatly appreciated in the pharmaceutical industry. The flesh of young shearwaters is mainly salted and sold as food, but in Tristan da Cunha it is also used as bait for catching fish. Fortunately, in many areas strict control measures govern such traditional activities nowadays, for example in Tasmania harvesting is restricted to the chicks, which can only be taken by licensed operators during a period of just over a month. In the New Zealand area, the rights for harvesting are hereditary, and are enjoyed exclusively by Maoris.

The name "fulmar" comes from Icelandic and means "foul gull", in reference to the musty smell of its stomach oil. Similarly, several petrels are known to mariners as "stinkers", particularly, the giant petrels. The use of the term "gadfly", usually for the *Pterodroma* petrels, seems to allude to the impulse that drives these birds to fly swiftly in wide arcs above the waves, as if goaded on by a gadfly. Shearwaters received their name from their habit of flying high above the water and into wave troughs, alternately turning to one side and then the other, with the wings held perpendicular to the water surface, as if shearing the water. There are differing views concerning the origin of the name "petrel" (see page 264). Several other species have striking local names: the "Shoemaker" for the

Unlike the other three "natural" groups within the Procellariidae, the fulmar-petrels do not include any burrowers. The nest is usually above ground, although some species may occupy rocky crevices. Northern Giant Petrels collect a mass of grass, ferns, twigs and leaves; the size of the nest ultimately depends on the availability of material. The chick is brooded for anything from 14 to 24 days.

[*Macronectes halli*, Bird Island, South Georgia. Photo: Julian Hector/ Planet Earth]

White-chinned Petrel; the "Pediunker" for the Grey Petrel; and the "Moaning Bird" for the Wedge-tailed Shearwater. The attractive names "Cahow", "Taiko" and "Diablotin" (meaning "Little Devil") have been used as standard vernacular names respectively for the Bermuda Petrel (*Pterodroma cahow*), the Magenta Petrel (*Pterodroma magentae*) and the Black-capped Petrel (*Pterodroma hasitata*). The Cape Petrel, which is abundant off the Cape of Good Hope though it does not breed there, is also known as the "Cape Pigeon", in reference to its dove-like movements as it pecks its food from the water surface, and also as the "Pintado Petrel", since its chequered black and white upperparts appear to be painted; it seems rather fatuous that its generic name *Daption* was invented as an anagram of "pintado". Finally, some species, particularly the prions, are known as "Whale Birds", as they are often found at sea in association with whales, both feeding on swarms of planktonic crustaceans.

Status and Conservation

The family Procellariidae contains a striking contrast: at least 15 of its species have thriving world populations of over a million breeding pairs, while several others are among the least known of all seabirds, and are apparently hovering around extinction. The number of species considered to be threatened depends, of course, on how many and which species are accepted (see Systematics), and it is not surprising that those forms with the most obscure taxonomic affinities are those which are least known, least observed and probably amongst the most threatened. At present 19 forms are red-listed (two of which are here considered subspecies), while a further five have been placed on the list of near-threatened species.

The marked declines experienced by many of these species are mostly due to the same few factors, namely the effects of human exploitation, introduced predators and habitat deterioration. Some of the very little known species, such as the Fiji Petrel, might never have been much more numerous than at present. In some cases enormous numbers are concentrated in fairly limited areas (see Breeding), for instance Tristan da Cunha harbours virtually all the known breeding population of the abundant Great Shearwater. Other species have similarly limited ranges but much more reduced numbers, and the three islands of the Juan Fernández group, off western Chile, are the only breeding grounds of the Juan Fernandez Petrel and Stejneger's Petrel (*Pterodroma longirostris*), as well as holding substantial proportions of the world populations of the Mas a Tierra Petrel (*Pterodroma defilippiana*) and the Pink-footed Shearwater (*Puffinus creatopus*).

There is a clear connection between the breeding of procellariids on remote islands free from predators and their incompetence in terrestrial locomotion, though to what extent they are cause and effect is less obvious. In this respect it is of interest that some *Pterodroma* petrels visit their nests by day on predator-free islands, but are strictly nocturnal wherever there is a chance of predation. The lack of contact with predators seems to have made them excessively tame, a tendency which man has taken advantage of.

Several species were given up as extinct for many years until recent rediscoveries. The Bermuda Petrel, once an abundant breeder in Bermuda, was almost exterminated by the early colonists, who relied on it as an important source of food, and by 1621 it was believed to be extinct. Almost 300 years later another specimen was collected, and in 1951 the species was found breeding on a few small islets off Bermuda, where 41 pairs bred in 1991. The Mascarene Petrel was known only from four specimens collected and preserved at the end of the nineteenth century, until in 1970 and 1974 single birds were captured at Reunion, in the Indian Ocean, where a few more sightings have since been claimed, though the breeding haunts of the species have yet to be discovered. The Magenta Petrel of the Chatham Islands, off New Zealand, was exploited for food by the Maoris during the nineteenth century and was known to science only in the form of the abundant skeletal remains found on the island. It was suggested that the bird known to the Maoris as "Taiko" (see Relationship with Man) was in fact the same species as the single specimen of the Magenta Petrel, taken in the South Pacific in 1867, and this was confirmed in 1978, when two birds were captured and photographed by researcher D. E. Crockett. Since then more birds have been located, and in 1987 the first breeding grounds of the species were found; the total population is now estimated at some 50 birds. Another such case of rediscovery involves the Fiji Petrel, of which only one skin was known, collected on the island of Gau, in Fiji, in 1855. Fully 129 years later, in 1984, a second specimen was caught, photographed and released, since when there have been further records. While the nesting grounds have not yet been found, there would appear to be suitable habitat available, although feral cats may pose a threat.

Amidst all these cases of renewed optimism there is a much sadder one in the story of the Jamaican Petrel, a dark race of the Black-capped Petrel, which was also known locally as the "Blue Mountain Duck". Its breeding colonies were so heavily depleted that it was brought to the verge of extinction, and the introduction of mongooses to Jamaica in 1872 seems to have led to its definitive annihilation, though there are those that maintain that it might yet be found to survive. The nominate subspecies *hasitata* still breeds in small numbers mainly on Hispaniola and Cuba, though it too was long thought extinct, until its rediscovery in 1961.

Traditional exploitation of petrels can only be maintained nowadays, if it is rationally controlled (see Relationship with Man). As K-selected species, petrels are not equipped to deal with a substantial rise in the mortality of breeding adults, and the population soon crashes. The first birds are quickly replaced by the large stock of immatures and non-breeders, so that no significant changes can be appreciated at the colonies in the first few years, but as soon as this stock has been exhausted, no new birds are forthcoming. Any recovery is then slow and arduous, because even if the remaining birds are allowed to nest successfully for a few seasons, it still takes several years for their offspring to reach sexual maturity and breed.

However, an even greater threat to petrels than direct exploitation by man himself has been the series of associated mammalian predators which he has introduced, sometimes accidentally, but on occasions intentionally. This is undoubtedly the chief factor affecting the declines observed in procellariids and most of the other Procellariiformes. Rats, cats, dogs, foxes, mongooses, mustelids and pigs prey on eggs, chicks and adults of the helpless petrels, as do Wekas (*Gallirallus australis*). The birds are not able to respond to these new forms of aggression, and sometimes they are even unearthed from their burrows to be eaten. In addition, feral cattle, goats, sheep, deer, chamois, horses and donkeys cause disturbance and habitat destruction through grazing and the occasional trampling of the burrows. Rabbits compete with petrels for nest-sites in some places, though they also dig new burrows, which may later be abandoned. The combined effects of their intensive grazing and honeycomb burrowing have caused serious soil erosion in places, rendering the area unsuitable for nesting.

Historically, there are many cases of predators intentionally introduced to islands to control the numbers of pests, for example in the case of cats and rats. But sensible precautions were not always taken, for example on remote islands it would have been wise to introduce cats of only one sex. The predators, instead of preying on their intended victims, turned on the feeble petrels, which were plentiful and easy to catch on land, particularly as their foul smelling burrows, containing eggs or fat chicks, are easily located. In a very short space of time, petrel numbers were reduced to tiny fractions of their former levels on such islands. A well studied case of misjudgement is that of Marion Island, in the southern Indian Ocean, where five

As with many members of Pterodroma, very little is known about the breeding of the Kermadec Petrel. It nests above ground, scratching out a slight depression with its feet, usually in areas of fairly dense vegetation, such as grass or ferns. In the Kermadecs, most birds on Meyer Island breed some three months later than those at the formerly huge colony on Raoul Island. However, a few birds on Meyer follow the Raoul timing and it has been suggested that they may be a remnant group that emigrated from Raoul Island.

[Pterodroma neglecta, Meyer Island, Kermadec Islands. Photo: D. V. Merton/ NPIAW]

In order to solicit feeding petrel chicks peck at the side of the adult's bill around the gape. The adult typically stretches its head forward and raises its tail, and then starts to pump its folded wings up and down, as it starts to regurgitate the food. The chick now places its bill crosswise in the adult's, ready to receive its meal. The white morph of the Southern Giant Petrel occurs in up to 15% of some populations, but no equivalent is recorded for the northern species.

[*Macronectes giganteus*. Photo: Luiz Claudio Marigo/Bruce Coleman]

cats were introduced in 1948/49 to control the house mice at the newly-established meteorological station. By 1977 the cat population had risen to 3405, which preyed mostly on adults, chicks and eggs of Broad-billed Prions and Great-winged (*Pterodroma macroptera*), Kerguelen, Soft-plumaged (*Pterodroma mollis*), and White-chinned Petrels, occasionally taking Blue Petrels, diving-petrels and sheathbills. A total of over 455,000 birds were estimated to be taken by cats every year, whereas mice represented only 16% of all the prey in the cats' diet. Fortunately, important control measures have been adopted and the last cats were recently eliminated.

In recent years steps have been taken to eradicate as many alien mammals as possible on the islands used for breeding by seabirds. This has been particularly successful on several off-shore islands around New Zealand, in the Seychelles and in the Galapagos, but much remains to be done. The Black Petrel (*Procellaria parkinsoni*) of New Zealand is endemic to Little and Great Barrier Islands, where only a few hundred pairs bred during the 1970's. Cats took a heavy toll on chicks, for example killing about 65% of the chicks hatched in 1972, 90% in 1973, and 100% in 1974 and 1975, while they also ate breeding adults at the colony on Little Barrier Island, so numbers declined swiftly. An initial attempt to eliminate cats, by infecting them with the virus of feline enteritis, reduced their numbers by 80%, but their population soon recovered. A more thorough campaign of poisoning and trapping was carried out between 1977 and 1980, and this finally led to the eradication of cats from the island, followed quickly by a recovery in the numbers of the Black Petrel. The species currently breeds with great success on Little Barrier Island, whereas on Great Barrier Island, cats are still plentiful, though there is apparently little predation.

The Dark-rumped Petrel (*Pterodroma phaeopygia*) has a breeding range restricted to the archipelagos of Galapagos and Hawaii. Some 430 pairs still breed on montane ground on the Hawaiian island of Maui, where they suffer severe predation by rats, cats and mongooses, but intense trapping in 1980/81 resulted in breeding success being raised to nearly 70%. The population of the Galapagos was estimated at 35,000 breeding

pairs in 1984. However, predation by rats, cats and pigs was responsible for very low breeding success, generally of under 20%, which, repeated over a number of years and combined with a certain amount of predation on adults, has been causing a steady decline in numbers; on the island of Floreana the decline was of 25-30% every year during the 1970's and early 1980's. The present population may be very low, with perhaps no more than 1000 pairs. A good deal of effort is being exerted to save this species, through a programme designed to control predators on the petrel's breeding islands, and also by providing artificial nest-sites, some of which have been installed on islands that are free from predators.

Natural predation is also responsible for a certain amount of mortality, and it can be important in places. While many birds, including gulls, crows, raptors, Wekas and owls, readily prey on petrels, if they have the chance, few are as effective as skuas, which in some island groups eat almost exclusively seabirds. Among the most commonly recorded species are: prions and the Blue Petrel; several species of *Pterodroma*, such as the Soft-plumaged, White-headed (*Pterodroma lessonii*) and Kerguelen Petrels; the White-chinned and Grey Petrels; Little and Great Shearwaters; and several species of storm-petrel and diving-petrel. The skuas kill most of their prey at night, on the ground, but they will also dig birds out of their burrows. Some pairs of skua kill one or two petrels nightly throughout most of the breeding season, and feed them to their young.

In procellariids, the effects of habitat destruction are very often closely connected with introduced mammals. Where alien predation is combined with the destruction of nesting burrows, the results tend to be devastating, and these two factors appear to have caused declines, for example, in Pycroft's Petrel (*Pterodroma pycrofti*), the Westland Petrel (*Procellaria westlandica*) and Townsend's Shearwater (*Puffinus auricularis*). The habitat of the threatened Chatham Petrel (*Pterodroma axillaris*) has been recovering due to its management as a reserve since 1954, but it appears that the species is being ousted from its only known breeding grounds by the more aggressive Broad-billed Prion.

Given the extreme vulnerability of procellariids on land, their lengthy nesting periods, and the fact that adults normally forage far from their colonies, leaving the young bird unattended for long periods, it is essential that their breeding grounds be legally protected and managed appropriately. Legal protection should also be extended to the birds themselves, with strict control of the harvesting of eggs, young and fully-grown birds, in the cases where this may still be deemed acceptable. Extremely severe penalties have been proposed in an attempt to discourage the collection of eggs of the last 20 breeding pairs of the Madeira Petrel (*Pterodroma madeira*) or Freira. The Salvage Islands, in the subtropical northern Atlantic, used to hold the largest colony of Cory's Shearwaters in the Atlantic. For over a century some 18,000-22,000 chicks were taken annually by Madeiran islanders for their oil and flesh, or to be used as fish bait. The Portuguese government bought the islands in 1967 and declared them a national park in 1971, following a major decline in the population of shearwaters. Two wardens are permanently stationed on the Salvages, and the harvesting of shearwater chicks has decreased notably, but some exploitation still persists. The nearby Desertas are still frequently raided by Madeirans, who take many chicks of Little and Cory's Shearwaters and Bulwer's Petrels. Environmental education is important in such areas, and the raiding fishermen must understand that it is their loss in the long term. Nature tourism might be encouraged to provide a more substantial source of income for the islanders, at the same time involving the allocation of new protected areas.

Man's activities at sea have undergone significant changes in recent times. The potential range of most ships has been greatly increased in the last two centuries, allowing for exploitation of resources that were quite unreachable in former times. New fishing grounds are now worked and modern, more efficient techniques are applied. Although seabirds consume only a very minor part of the total biomass of sea animals potentially available, all species could easily be adversely affected by human overexploitation of these resources. The patchy distribution of food in many parts of the oceans requires much travelling about in order to find it, and when the reward is not enough to cover the energy cost, the balance soon goes against the birds. At present, two regions are causing particular concern, the tropics, where an excessive capture of tuna may render small fish unavailable for several species, including the Wedge-tailed Shearwater, and around New Zealand, where many species feed extensively on the highly prized arrow squid.

The increase in fishing activities over the last two centuries, especially intense in recent decades, has nevertheless had some beneficial effects for many petrel species, by providing them with a ready source of food in the form of offal and discarded

fish thrown overboard from ships. Several procellariids have made wide use of this easily available food, and their numbers have multiplied, while some have also expanded and colonized many new areas. While these species are thriving at present, this dependance on human fishing activities for food could lead to problems in the future, should this abundant artificial supply disappear. The flocking and avid feeding of large numbers of petrels around trawlers also poses threats to the individual bird, for many perish after accidental strikes with a part of a ship or its fishing gear, or becoming entangled in the nets, or after swallowing baited hooks on fishing lines. Others are captured for food, to be kept as pets or simply for "fun". Several hundred thousand shearwaters die each year in the North Pacific drowned in gill-nets set for fish and squid, with the Short-tailed and Sooty Shearwaters the main sufferers, although large numbers of Northern Fulmars are also killed; the highest mortality seems to occur on the Japanese fishing grounds. Abundant though these species may be, measures should be taken to minimize this unnecessary killing, before a substantial reduction in their numbers occurs.

Another form of habitat deterioration is the pollution of food supplies, which shows up in traces in most seabirds, even in Antarctica. Work on Macquarie Island indicates that both species of giant petrel reveal relatively high levels of mercury and DDE, and it has been suggested that this might be connected with a certain reduction in colony size recently noted in the more southerly species.

In general, oil does not seem to be a major threat to petrels, as many species are largely aerial, including the Snow Petrel and the various gadfly-petrels, which only rarely alight on the water. While several thousand shearwaters were found dead during survey work concerning the Exxon Valdez disaster of March 1989 off Alaska, it seems that these had mostly died of starvation, and that this mortality should not be attributed to the spill. Besides, there is evidence that petrels may be able to detect oil slicks, using their sense of smell (see Morphological Aspects), and thus avoid slicks. A further advantage is that their greatest numbers and diversity occur in the Southern Hemisphere, where the traffic of tankers is less intense. Nonetheless, there can be no doubt that an oil spill in the vicinity of one of those colonies that support a high percentage of a species' total population might well seriously endanger its future.

General Bibliography

Alexander *et al.* (1965), Atkinson (1985), Bang (1966), Barrowclough *et al.* (1981), Bourne (1967a, 1985, 1987a), Brooke & Prince (1991), Brown *et al.* (1978), Croxall (1982b, 1987, 1991), Croxall *et al.* (1984), Feare (1984a), Furness (1987), Furness & Monaghan (1987), Grubb (1972), Harper (1979), Harrison (1985, 1987), Hutchinson & Wenzel (1980), Imber (1976c), Jouanin & Mougin (1979), Kuroda (1954), Löfgren (1984), Matthews (1949), Moors & Atkinson (1984), Nelson (1980), Schreiber (1984), Sibley & Monroe (1990), Tuck & Heinzel (1978), Vermeer & Rankin (1984a), Warham (1964, 1971b, 1977a, 1977b, 1983, 1990), Warham *et al.* (1976), Williams *et al.* (1982).

Heinroth's Shearwater is one of a number of very poorly known procellariids. Its breeding grounds have not yet been discovered, but are suspected to be on Bougainville Island in the Solomons. Note the characteristic long, slender bill and, unusual in a petrel, the bluish iris.

[*Puffinus heinrothi*. Photo: Don Hadden/ Ardea]

The habitat of the Westland Petrel has deteriorated due to timber milling within its minute breeding range, and this means that the species is now probably more exposed to predation. No more than about 900 pairs remained in 1974, but the species seems to be recovering. One of the major factors is thought to be the improved food supply, as the amount of fish offal available in the bird's foraging zone has recently increased.

[*Procellaria westlandica*, Punakaiki, Westland, New Zealand. Photo: John Fennell/ Bruce Coleman]

PLATE 13

inches 18
cm 45

1

dark morph

white morph

2

3

light morph

4

dark morph

ssp *australe*

5

6

ssp *capense*

7

8

9

ssp *rostrata*

10

ssp *becki*

11

12

ssp *hasitata*

ssp *caribbaea*

13

14

Genus *MACRONECTES*   Richmond, 1905

1. **Southern Giant Petrel**
Macronectes giganteus

French: Fulmar géant   **German**: Riesensturmvogel   **Spanish**: Abanto-marino Antártico
Other common names: Antarctic Giant Petrel, Giant Fulmar, Stinker

Taxonomy. *Procellaria gigantea* Gmelin, 1789, Staten Island, off Tierra del Fuego.
Long considered conspecific with sibling *M. halli*, with which known to have hybridized on occasions; populations of Gough I and Falkland Is in S Atlantic may merit subspecific status. Monotypic.
Distribution. Circumpolar in Southern Ocean, breeding in Antarctica and from S Chile and SC Argentina E through subantarctic islands to Heard I and Macquarie I.

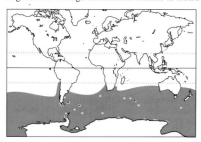

Descriptive notes. 86-99 cm; male 5 kg, female 3·8 kg; wingspan 185-205 cm. Head and breast fairly pale, underparts dark towards rear. Iris often dark brown. White morph occurs in up to 15% of individuals; diagnostic, as absent in *M. halli*. Female slightly smaller. Juvenile uniform blackish brown, with dark iris; progressively acquires more pale brown and white in plumage.
Habitat. Marine, ranging from coastal to pelagic waters; occurs S into regions of pack ice and N into subtropical zone. Breeds on open coastal plateaux and also headlands, usually occupying grassy or bare ground, often in exposed situations. Feeds along coast during most of year.
Food and Feeding. Carrion, especially carcasses of seals (*Arctocephalus*), penguins (*Eudyptes*, young *Aptenodytes*) and petrels (*Daption, Fulmarus, Thalassoica, Pachyptila, Pelecanoides*); some birds killed by battering or drowning, e.g. *Daption* and even immatures of some smaller albatrosses (*Diomedea*). Also takes cephalopods, krill, offal, discarded fish and galley refuse from ships. At sea feeds mostly by surface-seizing. Frequents trawling grounds.
Breeding. Starts Oct. Forms loose colonies of up to 300 pairs; nest is small mound of stones or rough pile of grass, with small depression on top. 1 egg; incubation 55-66 days, with stints of 2-12 days; chicks have white down with greyish markings, brooded for 2-3 weeks; fledging 104-132 days. Sexual maturity at 6-7 years.
Movements. Adults probably move little, dispersing only to adjacent waters and generally keeping further S than *M. halli*; juveniles may follow prevailing winds E around Southern Ocean. Immatures move further N than adults, regularly reaching tropics and typically following cold water currents off S Africa and W South America. Only definite record from N Hemisphere is 1 bird off Ushant, France, in Nov 1967; another giant petrel at Midway Atoll, Hawaii, in 1959, 1961 and 1962 not identified to specific level.
Status and Conservation. Not globally threatened. Total population c. 36,000 breeding pairs; 8755 pairs in South Orkney Is, 6185 pairs in South Shetland Is, but declining in both areas. Widespread, increasing in a few places, but has disappeared from some sites now much frequented by man, e.g. colony at Pointe Géologie (Adelie Land) down from 69 pairs in 1956 to 14 pairs in 1984, due to proximity of French base and associated disturbance; recent decline of at least 55% in Australian Antarctic Territory. Falkland Is hold c. 3200 pairs, but some still shot and eggs destroyed each year, as birds alleged to kill lambs. Population of Heard and McDonald Is c. 4500 pairs, but breeding success down by 43% since 1951. Future security of species probably closely linked with that of seal and penguin colonies, which are important source of food while breeding; however, main problems are vulnerability to disturbance and levels of incidental mortality in commercial fisheries.
Bibliography. Ainley *et al.* (1984), Blake (1977), Bourne & Warham (1966), Bretagnolle (1988a, 1988b, 1989), Bretagnolle & Thomas (1990), Brown *et al.* (1982), Burger (1978), Conroy (1972), Cramp & Simmons (1977), Croxall *et al.* (1984), Devillers & Terschuren (1980), García (1972), Humphrey & Livezey (1983), Humphrey *et al.* (1970), Hunter (1983a, 1983b, 1984a, 1984b, 1984c, 1987), Johnson (1965), Johnstone (1974, 1977, 1978), Langrand (1990), Lindsey (1986), Marchant & Higgins (1990), Milon *et al.* (1973), Mougin (1968), Murphy (1936), Parmelee & Parmelee (1987), Pinto (1983), Powlesland (1986), Richardson, M.E. (1984), Saiz & Hajek (1988), Swales (1965), Thomas (1986), Voisin (1968, 1976, 1978, 1982, 1988, 1990), Voisin & Bester (1981), Warham (1962), Watson (1975), Weimerskirch, Jouventin *et al.* (1985), Weimerskirch, Zotier & Jouventin (1989), Woehler (1991), Woehler & Johnstone (1991), Wood (1990b), Woods (1988).

2. **Northern Giant Petrel**
Macronectes halli

French: Fulmar de Hall   **German**: Hallsturmvogel   **Spanish**: Abanto-marino Subantártico.
Other common names: Hall's Giant Petrel

Taxonomy. *Macronectes giganteus halli* Mathews, 1912, Kerguelen.
Long considered conspecific with sibling *M. giganteus*; some hybridization in areas of sympatry, but differences in timing of breeding and social structure prevent higher degree of interbreeding. Monotypic.
Distribution. Circumpolar in Southern Ocean, breeding on subantarctic islands from South Georgia through S Indian Ocean to New Zealand area.
Descriptive notes. 81-94 cm; male 5 kg, female 3·8 kg; wingspan 180-200 cm. Variable extent of dark on head, giving slightly capped appearance. Underparts more uniform than in *M. giganteus*, paler than upperparts. Pinkish bill tip. Female slightly smaller. Both members of genus differ from

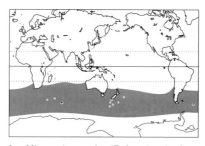

all albatrosses in structure, especially of bill. Juvenile uniform blackish brown, with dark iris, differing from *M. giganteus* only in bill; progressively acquires adult plumage.
Habitat. Marine, commonly occurring in coastal waters, especially by penguin rookeries; also far from coast, often at trawling grounds. Breeds on islands, occupying grassy slopes or rocky areas, usually with some shelter, e.g. from tussock grass (*Poa*). Feeds mainly along coast in summer.
Food and Feeding. Sexes differ markedly in preferred diet and habits. Males typically scavenge on carcasses of seals (*Arctocephalus, Mirounga*), penguins (*Eudyptes*) and a few petrels (*Pterodroma, Pachyptila, Puffinus, Pelecanoides*). Females mostly catch live prey at sea, especially krill and cephalopods, and some petrels; feed mainly by surface-seizing, but may dive down to 2 m. Birds also feed on offal, discarded fish and galley refuse from ships.
Breeding. Starts Aug. Generally solitary, only occasionally forming loose colonies, sometimes alongside *M. giganteus*; nest is irregular pile of grass c. 60 cm high with shallow depression on top. 1 egg; incubation 57-62 days; chicks have grey down, whitish below, brooded for 2-3 weeks; fledging 106-120 days. Sexual maturity at 6-7 years.
Movements. Disperses widely over Southern Ocean, normally N of Antarctic Convergence. Young birds more markedly dispersive, occurring off S Africa and Australia; adults may remain within vicinity of colony.
Status and Conservation. Not globally threatened. Total population 7000-12,000 breeding pairs; 3000 pairs at South Georgia, 1313+ pairs at Crozet Is, 1450-1800 pairs at Kerguelen Is, 1000-5000 pairs in New Zealand region. Increase at South Georgia related to increasing seal populations and greater availability of food, including both seals and penguins. Particularly vulnerable to disturbance, avoiding areas much frequented by man; very low breeding success on Possession I (Crozet) in 1975-1977, probably due to disturbance. Some eggs lost to natural and introduced predators, especially in areas of much disturbance. Accidents at trawling grounds may also account for increased mortality at sea.
Bibliography. Bourne & Warham (1966), Bretagnolle & Thomas (1990), Brown *et al.* (1982), Burger (1978), Croxall *et al.* (1984), Hemmings & Bailey (1985), Hunter (1983a, 1983b, 1984a, 1984b, 1984c, 1987), Johnstone (1974, 1977, 1978), Lindsey (1986), Marchant & Higgins (1990), Mougin (1985), Powlesland (1986), Voisin (1968, 1976, 1978, 1988, 1990), Watson (1975), Weimerskirch, Jouventin *et al.* (1985), Weimerskirch, Zotier & Jouventin (1989), Wood (1990b), Woods (1988).

Genus *FULMARUS*   Stephens, 1826

3. **Northern Fulmar**
Fulmarus glacialis

French: Fulmar boréal   **German**: Eissturmvogel   **Spanish**: Fulmar Boreal
Other common names: Arctic Fulmar

Taxonomy. *Procellaria glacialis* Linnaeus, 1761, within the Arctic Circle = Spitsbergen.
Forms superspecies with *F. glacialoides*. Birds from N Greenland sometimes considered to form separate race (*minor*); validity of race *auduboni* has often been questioned. Three subspecies normally recognized.
Subspecies and Distribution.
F. g. glacialis (Linnaeus, 1761) - high Arctic of N Atlantic.
F. g. auduboni Bonaparte, 1857 - low Arctic and boreal zones of N Atlantic.
F. g. rodgersii Cassin, 1862 - N Pacific.

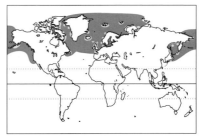

Descriptive notes. 45-50 cm; male c. 835 g, female c. 700 g; wingspan 102-112 cm. Fairly uniform grey upperparts, with head and neck white. Polymorphic, with several intermediate forms; dark morph differs from other dark members of family in robust structure and characteristic flight. Juvenile as adult. Races separated on length and thickness of bill and proportion of different colour morphs; race *rodgersii* has darkest dark morph and palest pale morph.
Habitat. Marine, mostly in waters over continental shelf; ranges from pack ice through Arctic and subarctic to temperate waters; avoids warmer regions. Typically breeds on cliffs and rock faces, occasionally on flatter ground, sometimes over 1 km inland; in places breeds near human habitation, sometimes even on occupied houses along seafront of towns.
Food and Feeding. Variable quantities of fish, squid and zooplankton, especially amphipods (*Thysanoessa, Hyperia, Gammarus, Themisto*); also fish offal and carrion, e.g. whale blubber. Most food obtained by surface-seizing; occasionally plunges. Feeds by both day and night; frequently attends trawlers, where large numbers may congregate.
Breeding. Starts May. Highly colonial; nests on narrow ledges or in hollows. 1 egg; incubation 47-53 days, with stints of 1-11 days; chicks have whitish to dark greyish down, tended for first 2 weeks; fledging 46-53 days. Sexual maturity mostly at c. 9 years old (5-12+). Several birds ringed as breeding adults still at nest 39 years later, so some probably c. 48 years old. Mean annual survival of adults 0·986; average adult life expectancy c. 34 years.

On following pages: 4. Southern Fulmar (*Fulmarus glacialoides*); 5. Antarctic Petrel (*Thalassoica antarctica*); 6. Cape Petrel (*Daption capense*); 7. Snow Petrel (*Pagodroma nivea*); 8. Great-winged Petrel (*Pterodroma macroptera*); 9. Mascarene Petrel (*Pterodroma aterrima*); 10. Tahiti Petrel (*Pterodroma rostrata*); 11. White-headed Petrel (*Pterodroma lessonii*); 12. Black-capped Petrel (*Pterodroma hasitata*); 13. Bermuda Petrel (*Pterodroma cahow*); 14. Atlantic Petrel (*Pterodroma incerta*).

Movements. N populations migratory, retreating S as sea freezes over, and mostly absent Nov-Feb. Further S dispersive, ranging widely, but not usually reaching zones of warm water; regularly occurs S to Baja California. Young birds may make transoceanic crossings and generally wander further than adults, which are less mobile. Has occurred in Mediterranean, at Madeira and far inland in Czechoslovakia.

Status and Conservation. Not globally threatened. Total population c. 4,000,000-16,000,000 pairs. Has undergone spectacular expansion over past 2 centuries, with massive increases of range and numbers; particularly well documented in Britain, with regular censuses since 1912. Expansion probably favoured by increased availability of food, especially fish offal, though other factors may be involved, e.g. changes in oceanic conditions. Still increasing at present in places, though more slowly. Subject to intensive exploitation for food in past, but only small numbers killed nowadays; heavy predation by foxes (*Alopex, Vulpes*), introduced to Kuril Is (S of Kamchatka) by Japanese fur farmers in early 20th century. May be affected by chemical pollution, especially in S of range; incidental mortality at commercial fishing grounds probably of some significance.

Bibliography. Anderson (1982), Baxter & Rintoul (1953), Bent (1922), Brazil (1991), Broad (1974), Brown, R.G.B. (1973, 1988a), Coulson & Horobin (1972), Cramp & Simmons (1977), Cramp *et al.* (1974), Croxall (1991), Croxall *et al.* (1984), Dott (1973, 1975), Duffey (1951), Dunnet (1986a, 1991), Dunnet, Anderson & Cormack (1963), Dunnet, Ollason & Anderson (1979), Enquist (1985), Fisher (1952, 1966), van Franeker & Wattel (1982), Furness & Todd (1984), Haney (1988), Hatch (1983, 1987, 1990a, 1990b, 1990c), Hatch & Hatch (1990), Hepburn & Randall (1975), Kay (1953), Lloyd *et al.* (1991), Macdonald (1977a, 1977b, 1980), Mercier (1987), Mougin (1967), Mudge *et al.* (1987), Ollason & Dunnet (1978, 1980, 1982, 1983, 1986, 1988), Palmer (1962), Pennycuick (1960), Pennycuick & Webbe (1959), Richards (1990), Rösler (1980), Salomonsen (1965), Shallenberger (1984), Sharrock (1976), Sifgusson (1990), Slater (1990), Tasker *et al.* (1987), Thom (1986), Voous (1949), Warham (1975), Watson (1981), Williamson *et al.* (1954), Wynne-Edwards (1939).

4. Southern Fulmar
Fulmarus glacialoides

French: Fulmar argenté **German**: Silbersturmvogel **Spanish**: Fulmar Austral
Other common names: Antarctic/Silver-grey/Slender-billed Fulmar, Silver-grey Petrel

Taxonomy. *Procellaria glacialoides* A. Smith, 1840, Cape seas.
Forms superspecies with *F. glacialis*. Monotypic.
Distribution. Antarctica and outlying islands, including Scotia Arc and N to Bouvetøya.

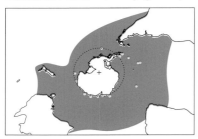

Descriptive notes. 46-50 cm; 800 g; wingspan 114-120 cm. Upperparts mainly pale grey, contrasting with dark trailing edge of wing and variable amounts of blackish on outer wing. Also differs from *F. glacialis* in longer, thinner bill. Juvenile as adult, but bill weaker.
Habitat. Marine and pelagic, normally linked with cold waters fringing pack ice, but rarely in midst. Breeds on steep rocky slopes and precipitous cliffs.
Food and Feeding. Mostly crustaceans (*Euphausia*), fish (*Pleuragramma antarcticum*) and cephalopods (*Psychroteuthis, Gonatus, Galiteuthis*), with proportions varying locally; also carrion and fish offal. Most food taken by surface-seizing; occasionally dives. Often feeds in flocks, sometimes with other seabirds. Attends trawlers and takes galley refuse from ships.
Breeding. Starts Nov. Highly colonial; nests on sheltered ledges or in hollows. 1 egg; incubation c. 46 days, with stints of 3-9 days; chicks have whitish down with grey markings, brooded for 3 weeks; fledging 48-56 days.
Movements. Migratory, ranging widely over Southern Ocean. Young birds commonly reach subtropical zone following cold water currents, especially off W South America; sometimes straggles N to South Africa, Australia and New Zealand.
Status and Conservation. Not globally threatened. Total population large, with very big colonies at South Sandwich Is, South Orkney Is and in nearby region; no evidence of change in recent decades. Main causes of mortality or lower breeding success are related to adverse weather conditions, e.g. freezing or flooding of nest; also some natural predation, mainly by skuas and sheathbills. Competition with fisheries could pose threat in long term; some birds killed at commercial fishing grounds.

Bibliography. Ainley *et al.* (1984), Blake (1977), Bretagnolle (1988a), Bretagnolle & Thomas (1990), Brown *et al.* (1982), Cooper (1979), Croxall *et al.* (1984), Fisher (1952), van Franeker *et al.* (1990), Furse (1976), Hudson (1966), Humphrey *et al.* (1970), Jehl *et al.* (1979), Jouventin & Weimerskirch (1991), Lindsey (1986), Luders (1977), Marchant & Higgins (1990), Mougin (1967, 1968), Murphy (1936), Pinto (1983), Powlesland (1986), Prévost (1964), Roux (1977), Thomas (1986), Voous (1949), Watson (1975), Weimerskirch (1990a, 1990b, 1990c), Woehler & Johnstone (1991), Woods (1988).

Genus *THALASSOICA* Reichenbach, 1853

5. Antarctic Petrel
Thalassoica antarctica

French: Fulmar antarctique **German**: Antarktiksturmvogel **Spanish**: Petrel Antártico
Other common names: Antarctic Fulmar

Taxonomy. *Procellaria antarctica* Gmelin, 1789, within the Antarctic Circle between lat. 36° S and 61° S.
Monotypic.
Distribution. Antarctica.
Descriptive notes. 40-46 cm; 510-765 g; wingspan 101-104 cm. Unmistakable pattern on upperparts in flight. From below resembles *D. capense*, but slighter and lacks dark speckles on underparts.

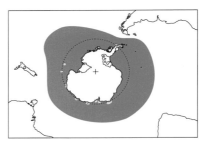

Female slightly smaller. As in other Procellariiformes, upperparts fade when worn. Juvenile as adult.
Habitat. Marine; prefers open waters in vicinity of pack ice, especially in areas with icebergs; style of flight probably unsuitable to pelagic foraging over long distances; largely pelagic outwith breeding season. Nests on snow-free cliffs and rock faces, mostly along coast or on offshore islands, but up to 250 km inland.
Food and Feeding. Mostly krill (*Euphausia superba*); also fish (*Pleuragramma antarcticum*), squid (*Gonatus antarcticus*) and medusae. Feeds mainly by surface-seizing, but also by plunging and dipping; also known to dive both from air and from surface. Often associates with whales (*Balaenoptera acutorostrata, Megaptera*) and seabirds, e.g. *Pagodroma* and Arctic Tern (*Sterna paradisaea*); concentrations of up to 5000-6000 birds recorded around whaling ships.
Breeding. Starts Nov. Forms colonies ranging in size from c. 100 pairs to over 1,000,000 birds; nests on cliff ledges or in hollows. 1 egg; incubation 40-48 days; chicks have pale grey down; fledging 42-47 days.
Movements. Little known; dispersive within normal extent of floating ice, rarely straying far; could be partially migratory. Some birds move N in winter, reaching Antarctic Convergence and sometimes beyond; others remain around edge of ice. Vagrant to South Africa, New Zealand and Tasmania.
Status and Conservation. Not globally threatened. Total population may number several million birds, though considerable disagreement, with estimates of 1,200,000 birds and only 380,000 breeding pairs; in contrast, estimated 1,500,000-2,500,000 pairs in Prydz Bay area, and estimated 3,900,000 pairs in Ross Sea sector (late 1970's). Restriction to bleak, icy habitat and breeding on mountains far inland imply few adverse factors, apart from rigors of climate. Could be affected by development of krill fisheries, as breeding success known to be related to levels of euphausiid and fish abundance.

Bibliography. Ainley *et al.* (1984), Bech *et al.* (1988), Beck (1970), Bretagnolle & Thomas (1990), Broady *et al.* (1989), Brook & Beck (1972), Brown *et al.* (1982), Croxall *et al.* (1984), van Franeker *et al.* (1990), Griffiths (1982, 1983), Haftorn *et al.* (1991), Johnson (1965), Lindsey (1986), Luders (1977), Marchant & Higgins (1990), Mehlum *et al.* (1986, 1988), Montague (1984b), Murphy (1936), Powlesland (1986), Thomas (1986), Watson (1975), Woehler & Johnstone (1991), Woods (1988).

Genus *DAPTION* Stephens, 1826

6. Cape Petrel
Daption capense

French: Damier du Cap **German**: Kapsturmvogel **Spanish**: Petrel Damero
Other common names: Cape Pigeon/Fulmar, Pintado/Pied/Spotted/Black-and-white Petrel

Taxonomy. *Procellaria capensis* Linnaeus, 1758, Cape of Good Hope.
Two subspecies recognized.
Subspecies and Distribution.
D. c. capense (Linnaeus, 1758) - Antarctica and islands of subantarctic from South Georgia E to Heard I.
D. c. australe Mathews, 1913 - islands of New Zealand area.

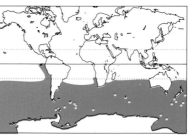

Descriptive notes. 38-40 cm; 340-480 g; wingspan 81-91 cm. Unmistakable pattern on upperparts, with varying amounts of white and blackish brown blotches. Underwing has some dark spotting and dark margin broader than in *T. antarctica*. Female slightly smaller. Juvenile similar to adult, but black feathers have grey wash in fresh plumage. Race *australe* smaller, and in fresh plumage has less white in upperparts.
Habitat. Marine and pelagic, especially in winter. In places occurs mainly over cold waters beyond continental shelf; elsewhere, during breeding, most commonly found on inshore waters not far from colonies; usually avoids pack ice. Breeds on cliffs or steep rocky slopes.
Food and Feeding. Mainly krill (*Euphausia superba, E. crystallorophias*); also fish (*Pleuragramma antarcticum*), squid, offal, carrion and galley refuse from ships. Apparently capable of locating some food by olfaction. Feeds by surface-seizing, pecking busily in pigeon-like manner; also by "hydroplaning" (see page 223) and by dipping while on wing; occasionally dives. Feeds both by day and by night. Often associates with whales (*Balaenoptera, Globicephala, Orcinus orca*) and also with other seabirds. Congregates in large flocks around trawlers.
Breeding. Starts Nov. Forms colonies of variable size, sometimes numbering thousands of nests; habitually solitary at some breeding grounds (e.g. Crozet Is); nests in shallow crevices, in scrape on rock ledge, on stable beds of gravel or among boulders. 1 egg; incubation 41-50 days, with stints of 1-11 days; chicks have greyish down, brooded for c. 19 days; fledging 47-57 days. Sexual maturity usually at 6 years old (3-10). Adult annual mortality c. 5%; mean life expectancy of adults 15-20 years.
Movements. Dispersive and perhaps partly migratory; absent from Antarctica Apr-Aug; in subantarctic some birds apparently fairly sedentary. Ranges widely over Southern Ocean and follows cool currents into tropics, especially off W South America; occurs regularly off Galapagos Is. Several records from N Hemisphere; in some cases probably referring to birds captured and kept on ships before subsequent release.
Status and Conservation. Not globally threatened. Abundant and widespread, with total population of several million birds; 100,000's-1,000,000's from South Sandwich Is to Antarctic Peninsula, 5000-10,000 pairs in New Zealand region, 3000-5000 pairs at Kerguelen Is. Highest mortality

probably from natural causes, especially severe Antarctic climate; some due to predation by skuas. Predation by rats and feral cats in places, e.g. Crozet Is, but most colonies too remote to be affected; accidents at commercial fishing grounds account for a few losses. More precise information required on population size and trends.

Bibliography. Ainley *et al.* (1984), Beck (1969, 1970), Bourne (1967b), Bretagnolle (1988a), Bretagnolle & Thomas (1990), Brown *et al.* (1982), Croxall *et al.* (1984), Despin (1977b), van Franeker *et al.* (1990), García (1972), Green (1986), Griffiths (1982), Humphrey *et al.* (1970), Imber (1983), Jehl *et al.* (1979), Johnson (1965), Jouventin & Robin (1984), Langrand (1990), Lindsey (1986), Marchant & Higgins (1990), Mougin (1968, 1985), Murphy (1936), Palmer (1962), Pinder (1966), Pinto (1983), Powlesland (1986), Prévost (1964), Robertson & van Tets (1982), Sagar (1979, 1985, 1986), Thomas (1986), Watson (1975), Weimerskirch, Jouventin *et al.* (1985), Weimerskirch, Zotier & Jouventin (1989), Woehler (1991), Woehler & Johnstone (1991), Wood (1990b), Woods (1988).

Genus *PAGODROMA* Bonaparte, 1856

7. Snow Petrel
Pagodroma nivea

French: Fulmar des neiges **German**: Schneesturmvogel **Spanish**: Petrel Níveo
Other common names: Snowy Petrel

Taxonomy. *Procellaria nivea* G. Forster, 1777, lat. 52° S., long. 20° E.
Races may constitute two separate species, as sympatry without interbreeding reported from E Antarctica (see page 217); alternative version claims most colonies are mixed, with extensive zone of hybridization; subspecific distribution confused and some authors prefer to recognize single monotypic species. Two subspecies normally recognized.
Subspecies and Distribution.
P. n. nivea (G. Forster, 1777) - Antarctica, South Georgia, Scotia Arc.
P. n. confusa Mathews, 1912 - Antarctica and adjacent islands; South Sandwich Is.

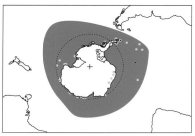

Descriptive notes. 30-40 cm; 240-460 g; wingspan 75-95 cm. Unmistakable; all white plumage with very small black bill. Female averages slightly smaller. Juvenile as adult, but has more extensive greyish barring on upperparts. Race *confusa* considerably larger and longer-winged; may have smaller eye patch.
Habitat. Marine; closely linked with pack ice, occurring mainly in areas with 10-50% ice cover; does not alight on the water, preferring to rest on icebergs or ice floes; style of flight perhaps unsuitable for long journeys into pelagic waters. Breeds on cliffs and rock faces up to 325 km inland, at altitudes of as much as 2400 m.

Food and Feeding. Mainly krill (*Euphausia*), fish, squid and carrion, e.g. whale blubber, seal carcasses and placentae, dead seabirds, excreta. Feeds on wing by dipping; also occasionally some diving and surface-seizing. Sometimes scavenges on land.
Breeding. Starts Nov in most areas. Forms colonies of variable size; nests in sheltered hollows or rock crevices. 1 egg; incubation 41-49 days; chicks have blue-grey down, white underneath, brooded for c. 8 days; fledging 41-54 days. Adult annual mortality 4-7%, giving mean adult life expectancy of 14-20 years.
Movements. Little known; relatively sedentary in places, most birds staying within vicinity of colony all year round, dispersing only to adjacent waters. Seldom strays far from pack ice except at northernmost breeding grounds (Bouvetøya, South Georgia).
Status and Conservation. Not globally threatened. Apparently abundant, with total population perhaps numbering several million birds, despite habitat restrictions; overall numbers stable and slightly increasing at present; estimated 2,000,000 birds at colonies around Ross Sea. Many eggs and chicks lost to skuas (*Catharacta*), but severe conditions of climate account for main mortality at breeding colonies.

Bibliography. Ainley *et al.* (1984), Beck (1970), Bretagnolle (1988a), Bretagnolle & Thomas (1990), Broady *et al.* (1989), Brook & Beck (1972), Brown, D.A. (1966), Cowan (1981, 1983), Croxall (1982a), Croxall *et al.* (1984), van Franeker *et al.* (1990), Griffiths (1982, 1983), Guillotin & Jouventin (1980), Haftorn *et al.* (1988), Hudson (1966), Isenmann (1970), Jouventin (1977), Jouventin & Robin (1984), Jouventin & Viot (1985), Jouventin & Weimerskirch (1991), Lindsey (1986), Lovenskiold (1960), Maher (1962), Marchant & Higgins (1990), Mehlum *et al.* (1988), Mougin (1968), Prévost (1964, 1969), Ryan & Watkins (1989), Somme (1977), Thomas (1986), Watson (1975), Woehler & Johnstone (1991), Woods (1988).

Genus *PTERODROMA* Bonaparte, 1856

8. Great-winged Petrel
Pterodroma macroptera

French: Pétrel noir **German**: Langflügel-Sturmvogel **Spanish**: Petrel Aligrande
Other common names: Grey-faced/Long-winged Petrel/Fulmar

Taxonomy. *Procellaria macroptera* A. Smith, 1840, Cape seas.
Has been considered conspecific with *P. lessonii*. Two subspecies recognized.
Subspecies and Distribution.
P. m. macroptera (A. Smith, 1840) - subantarctic from Tristan da Cunha E to Kerguelen Is; SW Australia.
P. m. gouldi (Hutton, 1869) - North I (New Zealand).

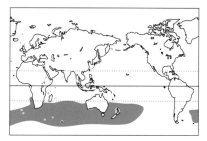

Descriptive notes. 41 cm; 460-750 g; wingspan 97 cm. Uniformly dark. Female slightly smaller. Resembles *P. ultima* and dark morph of *P. mollis*; compact body and short, robust bill separates from all-dark *Puffinus*; *Procellaria parkinsoni* slightly larger with two-tone bill. Juvenile has area around bill paler and greyish. Race *gouldi* slightly larger; resembles juvenile of nominate.
Habitat. Marine and highly pelagic; widespread, but sparsely distributed at sea. Breeds on oceanic islands, on ridges, slopes or flat ground, usually below 400 m, but up to 1400 m above sea-level at Tristan da Cunha.

Food and Feeding. Mostly squid (*Gonatus antarcticus*, *Histioteuthis*) with some fish (Gonostomatidae, Photichthyidae, Myctophidae) and crustaceans (*Gnathophausia*, *Eurythenes obesus*). Obtains most of its food by dipping and surface-seizing. Feeds mainly by night; may locate some cephalopods by bioluminescence. Associates with other Procellariiformes; occasionally follows cetaceans.
Breeding. Breeds in winter, starting Apr. Solitary or in loose colonies; nests in burrows or above ground in rock crevices, among tree roots or under scrub; same burrows may be used in summer by *Puffinus* or Little Penguins (*Eudyptula minor*). 1 egg; incubation 53-55 days, with stints of c. 17 days; chicks have dark brown down, brooded for 2-3 days; fledging 108-c.128 days. Sexual maturity at 7+ years old. Adult annual mortality c. 6%; mean adult life expectancy 18+ years.
Movements. Disperses widely in subtropical parts of Atlantic, Indian and W Pacific Oceans, mainly 25°-50° S; some birds near breeding islands all year round. Occasionally strays into the Antarctic zone.
Status and Conservation. Not globally threatened. Fairly widespread and numerous; 100,000-200,000 pairs at Kerguelen, c. 60,000 pairs around Australia. Race *gouldi* abundant, with 50,000-100,000 pairs, still legally taken for food by Maoris, although commercial exploitation banned; phasing out of harvesting may have caused recovery in Australasian Region in last 20 years. Substantial predation by cats, rats and skuas, leading to significant decreases and virtual disappearance of species from some areas, e.g. Little Barrier I; feral cats recently eradicated from Marion I, where in 1975 reckoned to be taking c. 48,000 individuals of present species per year. Introduced rabbits eject birds from burrows, e.g. formerly on Whale I (off N New Zealand). Populations should be monitored in order to detect significant changes; elimination of introduced predators highly desirable, e.g. at Kerguelen.

Bibliography. van Aarde (1980), Blake (1977), Brooke (1984), Brown, L.H. *et al.* (1982), Brown, R.G.B. (1988b), Cooper & Fourie (1991), Croxall *et al.* (1984), Cunningham & Moors (1985), Hagen (1952), Imber (1973, 1976b, 1984d, 1985a, 1985b), Johnstone & Davis (1990), Johnstone & Niven (1989), Jouventin *et al.* (1985), Lindsey (1986), Maclean (1988), Marchant & Higgins (1990), Murphy (1936), Newton & Fugler (1989), Powlesland (1987), van Rensburg & Bester (1988), Richardson, M.E. (1984), Schodde & Tidemann (1988), Schramm (1983, 1986), Serventy *et al.* (1971), Tennyson & Taylor (1990), Thibault & Guyot (1988), Warham (1956, 1957), Watson (1975), Weimerskirch, Zotier & Jouventin (1989), Wood (1990b).

9. Mascarene Petrel
Pterodroma aterrima

French: Pétrel de Bourbon **German**: Maskarenensturmvogel **Spanish**: Petrel de Reunión
Other common names: Mascarene Black/Reunion Petrel

Taxonomy. *Procellaria aterrima* Bonaparte, 1857, Réunion.
Sometimes placed in genus *Pseudobulweria*. Considered by some authors to be race of *P. rostrata*; external morphology and skeletal aspects indicate closely related. Monotypic.
Distribution. Reunion; subfossil remains suggest formerly occurred on nearby Rodrigues I.

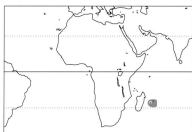

Descriptive notes. 36 cm. Uniformly dark. Somewhat smaller than *P. macroptera*; reminiscent of *Bulweria*, but larger, with tail rather shorter and slightly wedge-shaped. Gap between raised "tubenose" and swollen bill tip gives pinched appearance to middle of bill; bill noticeably heavy. Juvenile probably similar to adult.
Habitat. Very little known. Marine and probably pelagic; has been tentatively linked with cool waters. May breed in forest or on inland cliffs and ravines in mountainous parts of Reunion.
Food and Feeding. No information available.
Breeding. No information available. Breeding grounds undiscovered; assumed to nest in burrows or crevices.
Movements. No information available.
Status and Conservation. INDETERMINATE. Recently rediscovered (see page 230). Current population size unknown, but must be extremely small. Assuming species breeds in burrows, as seems likely, eggs, chicks and perhaps also adults likely to suffer predation by cats, dogs and rats; local people may take some for food (shearwaters commonly eaten on Reunion). Pesticide residues could be significant, as in case of *P. arminjoniana* at neighbouring Mauritius. Location of breeding grounds is immediate priority, followed by evaluation of numbers, major threats and conservation requirements.

Bibliography. Ali & Ripley (1968), Barré & Barau (1982), Collar & Andrew (1988), Collar & Stuart (1985), Feare (1984b), Greenway (1967), Imber (1985a), Jouanin (1970), King (1978/79), Mountfort (1988), Thibault & Guyot (1988), Vincent (1966).

10. Tahiti Petrel
Pterodroma rostrata

French: Pétrel de Tahiti **German**: Tahitisturmvogel **Spanish**: Petrel de Tahití
Other common names: Beck's Petrel (*becki*)

Taxonomy. *Procellaria rostrata* Peale, 1848, mountains about 6,000 feet on Tahiti, Society Islands. Sometimes placed in genus *Pseudobulweria*; forms superspecies with *P. macgillivrayi*. Race *becki* sometimes considered separate species on basis merely of smaller size; only known from two specimens and some recent sightings. *P. aterrima* may be better considered race of present species. Three subspecies recognized.
Subspecies and Distribution.
P. r. rostrata (Peale, 1848) - Society Is, Marquesas Is.
P. r. becki Murphy, 1928 - Bismarck Archipelago (?), Solomon Is (?).
P. r. trouessarti Brasil, 1917 - New Caledonia.

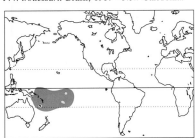

Descriptive notes. 38-40 cm; wingspan 84 cm. Central part of underwing has thin pale stripe. Smaller than *P. incerta*; slightly larger than *P. alba* and lacks pale throat. Juvenile as adult. Race *becki* considerably smaller, with thinner bill; *trouessarti* has larger bill.
Habitat. Marine and highly pelagic, rarely approaching land except at colonies. Breeds on volcanic islands, occupying hills and slopes usually with dense covering of trees and shrubs, at altitude of 200-2000 m, up to 12 km inland.
Food and Feeding. Probably feeds by surface-seizing. Has been recorded in association with other feeding seabirds and also with surfacing pilot whales (*Globicephala*). No further information available.
Breeding. Laying dates dispersed throughout year. Forms loose colonies; nests in burrows or rock crevices. 1 egg.
Movements. Very little known. Probably disperses in tropical and subtropical waters of Pacific, some birds occurring off NE Australia and New Guinea; also recorded off Taiwan and in E Pacific, between Mexico and Peru.
Status and Conservation. Not globally threatened. Poorly known; nominate race seen regularly, presumably breeding in fair numbers on several island groups of tropical Pacific; introduced rats and feral cats abundant on many island groups in this zone. Race *becki* classified as Indeterminate; breeding grounds thought to be in area of Solomon Is, but as yet undiscovered. Immediate priority is location of further breeding grounds, especially those of *becki*; details on population size and main threats also essential.
Bibliography. Beehler *et al.* (1986), Coates (1985), Collar & Andrew (1988), Garnett (1984), Holyoak & Thibault (1984), Imber (1985a), King (1978/79), Lindsey (1986), Marchant & Higgins (1990), Mountfort (1988), de Naurois (1978), de Naurois & Erard (1979), Thibault & Holyoak (1978).

11. **White-headed Petrel**

Pterodroma lessonii

French: Pétrel de Lesson   **German:** Weißkopf-Sturmvogel   **Spanish:** Petrel Cabeciblanco
Other common names: White-headed Fulmar

Taxonomy. *Procellaria Lessonii* Garnot, 1826, "Dans les parages du Cap Horn et de la mer Pacifique par 52° de lat. sept. [= austr.] et 85° de longit." Has been considered conspecific with *P. macroptera*, but timing of breeding cycles quite different; no mixed pairs reported despite extensive sympatry. *P. incerta* has been considered sibling species. Monotypic.
Distribution. New Zealand region at Macquarie, Auckland, Antipodes Is and possibly Campbell I; S Indian Ocean at Crozet, Kerguelen and possibly Prince Edward Is.

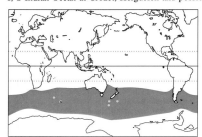

Descriptive notes. 40-46 cm; 580-810 g; wingspan 109 cm. Distinctive coloration, with all white head and conspicuous dark eye patch; only petrel with head, rump and tail whitish, contrasting with dark upperwing and back; dark underwing contrasts with whitish rest of underparts. Juvenile inseparable from adult.
Habitat. Marine and highly pelagic, rarely approaching land except at colonies; recorded on inshore waters in stormy weather. Breeds on subantarctic islands, near coast or inland, up to c. 300 m above sea-level; occupies flat or sloping ground, usually with some vegetation, e.g. tussock grass, ferns, shrubs; in places location of breeding grounds determined by competition with *Puffinus griseus*.
Food and Feeding. Apparently mostly squid and crustaceans; fish also recorded. Feeds mainly at night; mostly uses surface-seizing, but dipping also recorded. Associates with other Procellariiformes.
Breeding. Starts Oct. Forms loose colonies; sometimes solitary or in small groups; nests in burrows dug in soft soil or scree. 1 egg; incubation c. 58-60 days; chicks have greyish down, brooded for 2-3 days; fledging c. 102 days.
Movements. Disperses widely over Southern Ocean, probably in circumpolar range, generally S of 30° S; absent from colonies for only 2 months. Adults apparently less mobile than juveniles; large numbers in Straits of Magellan in Dec, thought to be immatures. Ranges S to pack ice, but also N into subtropical zone.
Status and Conservation. Not globally threatened. Total population probably c. 100,000 breeding pairs, though figures lacking for several areas; abundant at Kerguelen Is. Macquarie I held c. 7850 pairs in 1979, but currently declining, probably due to predation by feral cats, which have limited food available during breeding season of present species. Generally suffers much predation by cats, rats, skuas and Wekas (*Gallirallus australis*), which may lead to local extinctions; rabbits also ruin burrows and nesting grounds. Eradication of alien fauna on breeding islands should be complemented with regular monitoring of numbers and examination of other possible causes of decrease.
Bibliography. Barré (1976), Bretagnolle & Thomas (1990), Brothers (1984), Brown *et al.* (1982), Croxall *et al.* (1984), Imber (1983, 1985a), Jenkins (1982), Johnson (1965), Jouventin *et al.* (1985), Lindsey (1986), Marchant & Higgins (1990), Moors (1980), Powlesland (1987), Serventy *et al.* (1971), Watson (1975), Weimerskirch, Zotier & Jouventin (1989), Wood (1990b), Zotier (1990b).

12. **Black-capped Petrel**

Pterodroma hasitata

French: Pétrel diablotin   **German:** Teufelssturmvogel   **Spanish:** Petrel Antillano
Other common names: Diablotin, Capped Petrel; Jamaican Petrel (*caribbaea*)

Taxonomy. *Procellaria hasitata* Kuhl (*ex* Forster), 1820, no locality.
May include *P. cahow*. Race *caribbaea* sometimes considered to merit recognition as full species. Two subspecies recognized.
Subspecies and Distribution.
P. h. hasitata (Kuhl, 1820) - Cuba and Hispaniola; Guadeloupe, Dominica (possibly extinct) and (?) Martinique.
P. h. caribbaea Carte, 1866 - Jamaica (probably extinct).

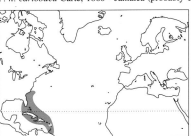

Descriptive notes. 40 cm; wingspan 95 cm. Unique dorsal pattern, prominent dark cap contrasting with broad white hind neck, rump and uppertail-coverts. Darkest individuals resemble *P. cahow*; from below, separable from slightly smaller *P. cahow* by narrow blackish half-collar on sides of breast. Juvenile as adult. Race *caribbaea* melanistic, recalling *P. aterrima*.
Habitat. Marine and highly pelagic, rarely approaching land except at colonies. Breeds mostly in mountainous areas, sometimes well inland, typically occupying cliffs with some vegetation.
Food and Feeding. Little known, but probably includes mostly squid and fish and perhaps also medusae.
Breeding. Starts Dec. Forms loose colonies; nests in burrows and rocky crevices. 1 egg; chicks apparently have yellow down.
Movements. Disperses over tropical and subtropical waters of Caribbean and Atlantic, ranging from NE Brazil to NE USA, where regular off Cape Hatteras, North Carolina. Two records from Britain, in 1850 and 1984.
Status and Conservation. RARE. Total population probably numbers a few thousand breeding pairs; highest density in Haiti, where still taken for food. In past suffered considerable human persecution by inhabitants of breeding islands, resulting in major reduction of breeding range with many local extinctions. Introduction of mongooses in 1870's, originally to control rat numbers, severely depleted populations and probably led to decline and possible extinction of *caribbaea*; rats also take heavy toll. Survival of species requires termination of human exploitation, extirpation of all introduced predators and effective protection of species and nesting grounds; programme of environmental education also desirable.
Bibliography. Bent (1922), Collar & Andrew (1988), Dymond *et al.* (1989), Evans, P.G.H. (1990), Garrido (1985), Greenway (1967), van Halewyn & Norton (1984), Haney (1987, 1989), Imber (1985a), King (1978/79), Mountfort (1988), Palmer (1962), Terres (1980), Vincent (1966), Voous (1983), Wingate (1964).

13. **Bermuda Petrel**

Pterodroma cahow

French: Pétrel des Bermudes   **German:** Bermudasturmvogel   **Spanish:** Petrel Cahow
Other common names: Cahow

Taxonomy. *Aestrelata cahow* Nichols and Mowbray, 1916, southeastern side of Castle Island, Bermuda.
Sometimes treated as race of *P. hasitata*. May be conspecific with *P. feae*, and individual of latter recently captured in Azores could be link; also linked to *P. madeira* on grounds of shared feather louse. Monotypic.
Distribution. Islets in Castle Harbour (Bermuda).

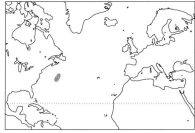

Descriptive notes. 38 cm; wingspan 89 cm. Dark upperparts contrast with narrow white rump, separating from all except very dark individuals of *P. h. hasitata*. Juvenile as adult.
Habitat. Marine and pelagic, seldom occurring near land except at colonies. Breeds on rocky offshore islets, having been driven there by abundant rats; formerly bred in very large numbers inland on hillsides and sandy dunes of main island.
Food and Feeding. Very little known. Apparently squid and crustaceans; probably also some fish.
Breeding. Starts Nov. Colonial; ideally nests in burrows dug in sandy or soft soil, but now on rocky islets with very little soil. 1 egg; incubation 51-54 days, with stints of 8-14 days; chick brooded for first 1-2 days; fledging 90-100 days. Success currently c. 50%.
Movements. Very little known; probably disperses N or NW in subtropical Atlantic, following warm part of Gulf Stream.
Status and Conservation. ENDANGERED. Suffered much exploitation for food in past, leading to near-extinction during early 17th century. Unknown for nearly 300 years until rediscovered at Bermuda, where breeding confirmed in 1951, with c. 18 pairs; 20 pairs in 1966, 35 in 1985, with 12-18 young fledged most years (21 in 1985); most recent figures available show that 41 pairs raised 19 young to fledging in 1991. Considerable efforts under way to save species: legal protection of birds and current breeding islets; periodical removal of rats; construction of artificial burrows with specially designed entrances, to prevent usurpation by White-tailed Tropicbirds (*Phaethon lepturus*); and special conditioning of predator-free Nonsuch I, in hope of inducing species to colonize.
Bibliography. Beebe (1935), Bent (1922), Collar & Andrew (1988), Diamond *et al.* (1987), Fisher *et al.* (1969), Fuller (1987), Greenway (1967), van Halewyn & Norton (1984), Halliday (1978), Imber (1985a), King (1978/79), Lever (1984), Mountfort (1988), Murphy & Mowbray (1951), Shufeldt (1916, 1922), Terres (1980), Vincent (1966), Wingate (1972, 1977, 1985).

14. **Atlantic Petrel**

Pterodroma incerta

French: Pétrel de Schlegel　　**German**: Schlegelsturmvogel　　**Spanish**: Petrel de Schlegel
Other common names: Hooded/Schlegel's Petrel

Taxonomy. *Procellaria incerta* Schlegel, 1863, "Mers australes, côtes de la Nouvelle Zélande, et Mers de l'Australie".
Has been considered sibling species of *P. lessonii*. Monotypic.
Distribution. S Atlantic, breeding at Tristan da Cunha and Gough I.
Descriptive notes. 43 cm; wingspan 104 cm. Only petrel of its size all dark with white lower breast and belly; undertail-coverts dark. Throat can be pale in worn plumage. Juvenile has greyish tips to mantle feathers in fresh plumage.
Habitat. Marine and probably pelagic. Breeds on oceanic islands, occupying ridges at altitude of 150-600 m.
Food and Feeding. Mostly squid, with some fish and crustaceans. Prey taken by surface-seizing.
Breeding. Breeds in winter, starting Mar. Colonial; nests in burrows dug in soft soil. 1 egg.

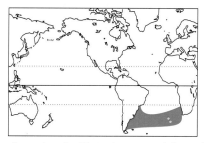

Movements. Disperses throughout S Atlantic, occurring off E coast of S America and rounding South Africa into Indian Ocean, N to at least 26° S.
Status and Conservation. Not globally threatened. Present population numbers few hundred breeding pairs at Tristan da Cunha and some thousands at Gough I. At Tristan, liable to suffer some human exploitation; several introduced predators, including rats and cats. On Gough I, house mouse is only potential predator introduced, but population of 6000-8000 skuas (*Catharacta*) feed almost entirely on seabirds, including large numbers of present species. Thorough census needed, as well as study of biology and ecology, to establish conservation requirements.

Bibliography. Belton (1984), Brown *et al.* (1982), Enticott (1991b), Fraser *et al.* (1988), Furness (1987), Griffiths (1982), Imber (1985a), Murphy (1936), Richardson, M.E. (1984), Ruschi (1979), Sick (1984), Swales (1965), Watson (1975), Williams (1984a), Woods (1988).

15

16

17

18

19

light morph

20

21

ssp *arminjoniana*
dark morph

22

ssp *mollis*

23

dark morph

ssp *heraldica*
light morph

ssp *dubia*

24

25

26

27

28

29

30

31

ssp *brevipes*

32

ssp *leucoptera*

PLATE 14

inches   14

cm   35

15. **Phoenix Petrel**

Pterodroma alba

French: Pétrel à poitrine blanche **German**: Phönixsturmvogel **Spanish**: Petrel de las Phoenix

Taxonomy. *Procellaria alba* Gmelin, 1789, Turtle and Christmas Islands = Christmas Island.
May include *P. magentae*. Monotypic.
Distribution. C Pacific, breeding at Tonga, Phoenix, Line, Marquesas, Tuamotu and Pitcairn Is.

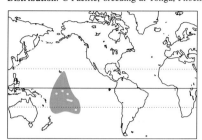

Descriptive notes. 35 cm; 269 g; wingspan 83 cm. Similar to *P. rostrata*, but slightly smaller; throat whitish and wings rather shiny, sometimes appearing to have pale patches. Juvenile apparently as adult.
Habitat. Marine and pelagic; occurs near land at colonies, which it regularly visits by day. Breeds on islands often under trees or bushes.
Food and Feeding. Mostly squid, with some fish and small quantities of crustaceans. Feeds mainly on wing by dipping; also uses surface-seizing and pattering.
Breeding. Thought to breed in any month. Nests in scrape on ground. 1 egg.

Movements. Disperses over wide range of tropical Pacific, occurring N to 24° N at Hawaii and S to 30° S at Kermadec Is.
Status and Conservation. Not globally threatened. Total population of some tens of thousands of breeding pairs; figures lacking for most island groups. Has decreased locally due to predation by rats, cats, dogs and mongooses, and may still suffer some human exploitation. Main priorities include more complete information on distribution and population size, protective legislation for birds and nesting habitats, elimination of introduced predators and environmental education programme.
Bibliography. Ashmole & Ashmole (1967), Bourne & David (1983), Gallagher (1960), Garnett (1984), Gould (1983), Harrison (1990), Holyoak & Thibault (1984), Imber (1985a), Marchant & Higgins (1990), Murphy & Pennoyer (1952), Ricklefs (1984), Schreiber & Ashmole (1970).

16. **Mottled Petrel**

Pterodroma inexpectata

French: Pétrel de Peale **German**: Regensturmvogel **Spanish**: Petrel Moteado
Other common names: Scaled/Peale's Petrel

Taxonomy. *Procellaria inexpectata* J. R. Forster, 1844, Antarctic Ocean.
Monotypic.
Distribution. SW South I (New Zealand), Stewart, Snares Is.

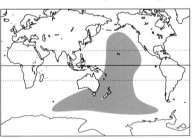

Descriptive notes. 33-35 cm; 247-441 g; wingspan 74-82 cm. Only member of genus in which underbody white with contrasting grey ventral patch. Upperparts show blackish open "M" across back and wings, similar to larger *P. arminjoniana*, but less prominent than in other *Pterodroma* species with same design. Juvenile has upperparts more heavily scaled.
Habitat. Marine and highly pelagic, rarely approaching land except at colonies. Breeds on islets and stacks, occupying rocky ground or tussock grassland up to 350 m above sea-level.
Food and Feeding. Mostly squid and fish; also some crustaceans. Feeds by plunging and surface-seizing. Sometimes associates with *Puffinus griseus*.

Breeding. Starts Oct. Forms dense colonies; nests in burrows or rock crevices. 1 egg; incubation c. 50 days, with stints of 12-14 days; chicks have grey down, brooded for 2 days; fledging 90-105 days.
Movements. Transequatorial migrant. During breeding season, common S to pack ice zone near Antarctica; probably main foraging area for nesting adults. After breeding, quickly moves N to Bering Sea, where concentrates off Aleutian Is and in Gulf of Alaska; uncommon off W coast of N America. A few records off extreme S America, dating back to times when more abundant. One record from N Atlantic, off North Carolina, USA.
Status and Conservation. Not globally threatened. Total population estimated at 10,000-50,000 breeding pairs. Formerly much more numerous and widespread, with breeding on North I and South I, New Zealand, where affected by forest clearance, and on Chatham, Bounty, Antipodes and Auckland Is. Local extinction from these island groups mainly due to predation by introduced mammals and Wekas, and harvesting for human consumption. Elimination of alien predators from present and former breeding stations advisable in order to maintain present numbers and encourage recolonization of former range.
Bibliography. Ainley & Manolis (1979), Ainley *et al.* (1984), Bretagnolle & Thomas (1990), Chambers (1989), Gould (1983), Humphrey *et al.* (1970), Imber (1985a), Lindsey (1986), Marchant & Higgins (1990), Nakamura & Tanaka (1977), Palmer (1962), Powlesland (1987), Robertson & Bell (1984), Shallenberger (1984), Terres (1980), Warham (1985i), Warham *et al.* (1977), Watson (1975).

17. **Providence Petrel**

Pterodroma solandri

French: Pétrel de Solander **German**: Solandersturmvogel **Spanish**: Petrel de Solander
Other common names: Brown-headed/Solander's Petrel, Bird of Providence

Taxonomy. *Procellaria Solandri* Gould, 1844, no locality = Bass Strait. Monotypic.

Distribution. Lord Howe I, and Philip I (Norfolk I).

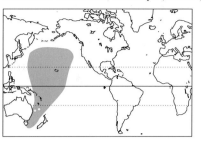

Descriptive notes. 40 cm; 500 g; wingspan 95-105 cm. Very similar to dark morph *P. neglecta*, but slightly paler on mantle, back, upperwing-coverts and ventral area, contrasting with dark head; less white on face and underwing and dark primary shafts on upperwing. Female slightly smaller. Juvenile as adult.
Habitat. Marine and pelagic, occurring well beyond the continental shelf. Breeds in mountainous ground, at altitude of 500-800 m, mainly in forested areas, but lower down in grassland.
Food and Feeding. Very little known. Fish, cephalopods, crustaceans and offal. Recorded fishing in groups, also at night and alongside *Puffinus bulleri*.
Breeding. Breeds in winter, starting Mar. Highly colonial; nests in burrows. 1 egg; incubation c. 8 weeks; partly diurnal on breeding grounds.
Movements. Transequatorial migrant, probably mainly moving into NW Pacific, with some birds occurring off Japan even during breeding season. When breeding occurs over W Tasman Sea.
Status and Conservation. Not globally threatened. Currently considered near-threatened. Total population 96,000 breeding pairs at Lord Howe I. Formerly abundant on Norfolk I, where establishment of penal colony led to convicts and garrison relying almost entirely on species for food and massive decline; introduction of pigs and goats helped bring about extirpation of species from Norfolk I in 1790-1800; small colony with at least 20 birds discovered on nearby Philip I in 1985. Colony on Lord Howe I has been subjected to predation by introduced rats, cats, pigs and dogs; also affected by grazing of cattle, goats and rabbits, and occasionally by trampling. Major efforts under way to eliminate all alien fauna and restore habitat.
Bibliography. Bailey *et al.* (1989), Brazil (1991), Imber (1985a), Kuroda (1955), Lindsey (1986), Marchant & Higgins (1990), Murphy & Pennoyer (1952), Nakamura & Tanaka (1977), Palmer (1962), Tanaka (1986), van Tets & Fullagar (1984), Wahl (1978), Wood (1990b).

18. **Kerguelen Petrel**

Pterodroma brevirostris

French: Pétrel de Kerguelen **German**: Kerguelensturmvogel **Spanish**: Petrel de las Kerguelen
Other common names: Little Black/Short-billed Petrel

Taxonomy. *Procellaria brevirostris* Lesson, 1831, no locality. Type from Cape of Good Hope.
Sometimes partitioned off in monotypic genus *Lugensa*. Monotypic.
Distribution. Tristan da Cunha, Gough I; Prince Edward Is, Crozet, Kerguelen Is.

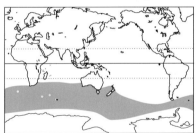

Descriptive notes. 33-36 cm; 331-357 g; wingspan 80-82 cm. Uniformly dark, but shiny plumage, especially on wings, often appearing as pale patches. Slightly smaller than other all dark *Pterodroma*, e.g. *P. macroptera*, *P. ultima*. Female slightly smaller. Juvenile as adult.
Habitat. Marine and highly pelagic, occurring mainly in cold waters. Breeds near sea on marshy ground; also higher up on volcanic ridges, up to 450 m.
Food and Feeding. Mostly squid (*Gonatus antarcticus*); also krill and fish. Squid captured by surface-seizing at night; also known to practise dipping.

Breeding. Starts Aug. Forms loose colonies; nests in deep burrows dug in soft, wet soil. 1 egg; incubation c. 49 days; chick has sooty brown down, brooded for first 2 days; fledging c. 59-62 days.
Movements. Frequents subantarctic and Antarctic waters S to pack ice all year round. Disperses widely over Southern Ocean to about 30° S; adults less mobile, some visiting colonies throughout year.
Status and Conservation. Not globally threatened. Abundant throughout range; total population probably numbers several hundred thousand birds; 30,000-50,000 pairs at Kerguelen, and tens of thousands each at Crozet and Prince Edward Is. Suffers extensive predation by rats and cats, e.g. in Crozet Is; skuas take some at Gough and Tristan, but more in Prince Edward Is. Regular surveys required to evaluate extent of predation, trends and conservation priorities; eradication of alien predators highly desirable.
Bibliography. Bourne & Elliott (1965), Brown, L.H. *et al.* (1982, 1986), Brown, R.S. *et al.* (1986), Clancey (1990), Fraser *et al.* (1988), Griffiths (1982), Harper *et al.* (1972), Imber (1984c, 1985a), Jehl *et al.* (1979), Jouventin, Mougin *et al.* (1985), Jouventin, Stahl *et al.* (1984), Lambert (1984), Lindsey (1986), Marchant & Higgins (1990), Mathews (1942), Mougin (1969, 1985), Richardson, M.E. (1984), Schramm (1983, 1986), Thibault & Guyot (1988), Watson (1975), Weimerskirch, Zotier & Jouventin (1989), Williams (1984a), Woehler (1990), Woods (1988).

19. **Murphy's Petrel**

Pterodroma ultima

French: Pétrel de Murphy **German**: Murphysturmvogel **Spanish**: Petrel de Murphy

Taxonomy. *Pterodroma ultima* Murphy, 1949, Oeno Island, south Pacific.
Monotypic.
Distribution. Austral, Tuamotu, Pitcairn Is.
Descriptive notes. 38-41 cm; wingspan 97 cm. Small whitish area around base of bill. Similar to *P. macroptera*, but legs pinkish, not uniformly dark. Juvenile as adult.
Habitat. Marine and pelagic, rarely approaching land except at colonies. Breeds on rocky islets off tropical oceanic islands.
Food and Feeding. Very little known; probably mostly squid.

On following pages: 20. Kermadec Petrel (*Pterodroma neglecta*); 21. Magenta Petrel (*Pterodroma magentae*); 22. Herald Petrel (*Pterodroma arminjoniana*); 23. Soft-plumaged Petrel (*Pterodroma mollis*); 24. Cape Verde Petrel (*Pterodroma feae*); 25. Madeira Petrel (*Pterodroma madeira*); 26. Barau's Petrel (*Pterodroma baraui*); 27. Dark-rumped Petrel (*Pterodroma phaeopygia*); 28. Juan Fernandez Petrel (*Pterodroma externa*); 29. White-necked Petrel (*Pterodroma cervicalis*); 30. Cook's Petrel (*Pterodroma cookii*); 31. Mas a Tierra Petrel (*Pterodroma defilippiana*); 32. Gould's Petrel (*Pterodroma leucoptera*).

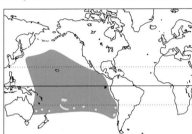

Breeding. First nests recently found in Austral Is; birds nesting on rocky cliffs of offshore stack; incubation during March.
Movements. Probably disperses within tropical Pacific. Recorded N to Hawaii and Oregon.
Status and Conservation. Not globally threatened. Currently considered near-threatened. Little known; discovered in late 1940's, and little studied since; rats abundant on some of breeding islands. Main priorities include thorough survey of potential breeding grounds, estimate of numbers and study of impact of introduced predators.
Bibliography. Bailey *et al.* (1989), Clapp (1974), Garnett (1984), Gould & King (1967), Imber (1985a), Murphy (1949), Pitman (1986).

20. Kermadec Petrel
Pterodroma neglecta

French: Pétrel des Kermadec **German**: Kermadecsturmvogel **Spanish**: Petrel de las Kermadec

Taxonomy. *Procellaria neglecta* Schlegel, 1863, Sunday Island = Raoul Island, Kermadec Group. Two subspecies recognized.
Subspecies and Distribution.
P. n. neglecta (Schlegel, 1863) - S Pacific, from Lord Howe and Kermadec Is E to Easter I.
P. n. juana Mathews, 1935 - Juan Fernández Is; San Félix and San Ambrosio Is.

Descriptive notes. 38 cm; 509 g; wingspan 92 cm. Polymorphic. Pale morph very similar to that of *P. arminjoniana*, but less white on underwing; above resembles other dark species, but head paler and bases of primaries partly white. Dark morph differs from *P. solandri* in being more uniformly dark, often with more white on face, pink legs and white primary shafts on upperwing, which also separate species from dark morph *P. arminjoniana*, which has whiter underwing. Several intermediate morphs. Juvenile as adult. Race *juana* slightly larger.
Habitat. Marine and highly pelagic, rarely approaching land except at colonies. Breeds on offshore islands, occupying cliffs or slopes with some vegetation.
Food and Feeding. Very little known. Squid and crustaceans recorded. Catches prey by dipping or surface-seizing; occasionally patters.
Breeding. Season variable, probably depending on locality; separate populations breed in summer and winter in Kermadec Is; elsewhere most birds breed during local summer. Forms loose colonies; nests on ledges, in scrapes, hollows or crevices, sometimes in open areas. 1 egg; incubation 50-52 days; fledging estimated at 110-130 days; visits colony by day.
Movements. Probably disperses over much of tropical and subtropical Pacific; occurs in N Pacific mainly Nov-Jan, recorded N to 42° N. Some populations may be fairly sedentary, especially adults.
Status and Conservation. Not globally threatened. Total population estimated at 5000-10,000 pairs. Known to suffer heavy predation by rats and cats, e.g. c. 500,000 birds on Raoul I (Kermadecs) in 1908 reduced now to near-extinction, and breeding success reduced to virtually nil on Henderson I; especially vulnerable due to habit of breeding in open or semi-open sites; extirpated from several islands with abundant mammalian predators, or displaced to offshore islets. Still locally exploited for food and bait; eggs collected, especially in E part of range, e.g. Easter I. Conservation priorities include campaigns to eradicate all introduced fauna from former and present breeding grounds, and programme of environmental education.
Bibliography. Bailey *et al.* (1989), Brooke (1987a), Coates (1985), Croxall *et al.* (1984), Bourne & David (1983), Gould & King (1967), Holyoak & Thibault (1984), Imber (1985a), Johnson (1965), King (1970), Lindsey (1986), Marchant & Higgins (1990), Murphy (1936), Palmer (1962), Pitman (1986), Tennyson & Taylor (1990).

21. Magenta Petrel
Pterodroma magentae

French: Pétrel de Magenta **German**: Magentasturmvogel **Spanish**: Petrel Taiko
Other common names: (Chatham Island) Taiko

Taxonomy. *Aestrelata magentae* Giglioli and Salvadori, 1869, Pacific Ocean, lat. 39° 38' S., long. 125° 58' W. Sometimes considered subspecies of *P. alba*. Monotypic.
Distribution. Chatham Is, to E of New Zealand.

Descriptive notes. 38-42 cm; 420-560 g; wingspan 102 cm. Recalls *P. incerta*, but slightly smaller and less contrasted plumage; head paler, throat pale and white of belly extends onto undertail-coverts; underwing also paler, with pale central stripe. Juvenile as adult.
Habitat. Marine and presumably pelagic, possibly foraging around Subtropical Convergence. Recently found breeding under dense bush forest on high ground or slopes, c. 5 km inland.
Food and Feeding. No information available. Perhaps mainly squid.
Breeding. Little known. Starts Oct. Solitary or loosely colonial; nests in burrows under bush forest. 1 egg; incubation probably c. 52 days; fledging c. 3 months.
Movements. Very little known. May disperse E over SC Pacific, perhaps reaching waters of Humboldt Current. During breeding, foraging range apparently to E or S in subantarctic waters.

Status and Conservation. RARE. Total population c. 50 birds and under 10 breeding pairs; rediscovered in 1978. Presumably plentiful in past, as Maoris took large numbers for food; probably already scarce when first predators introduced. At present many rats, cats, Wekas and pigs in Chatham Is; some adults, chicks and eggs may be lost to predation; grazing by feral cattle, sheep and possums has enormously reduced extent of bush forest. Priorities include: location of all nesting burrows; elimination of alien predators; removal of herbivores, or at least control by fencing off from breeding grounds; provision and protection of further areas with suitable habitat for nesting.
Bibliography. Bourne (1964), Collar & Andrew (1988), Chambers (1989), Crockett (1979, 1985, 1986), Eades & Rogers (1982), Ellis (1980), Fuller (1987), Imber (1985a), Johnstone (1985), King (1978/79), Marchant & Higgins (1990), Mountfort (1988), Müller (1988), Robertson & Bell (1984), Sibson (1982), Williams & Given (1981).

22. Herald Petrel
Pterodroma arminjoniana

French: Pétrel de la Trinité du Sud **Spanish**: Petrel de la Trinidad
German: Trinidadsturmvogel
Other common names: Trinidade Petrel (*arminjoniana*)

Taxonomy. *Aestrelata Arminjoniana* Giglioli and Salvadori, 1869, near South Trinidad (= Trinidade) Island.
Race *heraldica* sometimes considered separate species; at other extreme, validity of subspecific division has been questioned; birds of Easter I sometimes placed in separate race *paschae*. Two subspecies normally recognized.
Subspecies and Distribution.
P. a. arminjoniana (Giglioli & Salvadori, 1869) - S Atlantic, at Trinidad and Martin Vaz Is; Indian Ocean, at Round I (Mauritius).
P. a. heraldica (Salvin, 1888) - Raine I (NE Australia) and tropical Pacific E to Easter I.

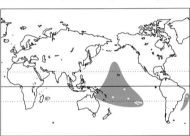

Descriptive notes. 35-39 cm; 318 g; wingspan 88-102 cm. Polymorphic. Dark morph similar to that of *P. neglecta*, but pointed tail and much more white on underwing. Pale morph likewise similar to that of *P. neglecta*, but less white on face and more on underwing; paler above, with dark open "M" as in *P. inexpectata*, but absent in *P. neglecta*. Several intermediate morphs. Juvenile as adult. Both races have pale, dark and intermediate morphs, with light to dark cline from W to E; race *heraldica* smaller, becoming steadily smaller still towards E.
Habitat. Marine and highly pelagic, rarely approaching land except at colonies. Breeds on oceanic islands, atolls or offshore stacks, occupying cliff ledges, ridges or rocky slopes up to 1000 m above sea-level, sometimes with dense vegetation of shrubs and grass.
Food and Feeding. Very little known; squid recorded. Has been seen to associate with *Puffinus pacificus*.
Breeding. Season variable, probably depending on locality; adults visit colonies almost all year round. Forms loose colonies; nests in rock crevices, on crag ledges or on ground. 1 egg; chicks have dark grey down; adults visit colonies by day.
Movements. Adults apparently fairly sedentary in much of range; immatures may be more mobile, dispersing over tropical and subtropical waters of Atlantic, Indian and Pacific Oceans; colonies at Raine I deserted Nov-Jan. In N Pacific occurs mainly Oct-Jan, recorded N to 39° N; in N Atlantic often seen after storms, recorded N to 42° N.
Status and Conservation. Not globally threatened. Widespread, but probably uncommon; few data available. Nominate race reported to be abundant at Trinidade and Martin Vaz Is, but no estimates of numbers; limited breeding range demands monitoring of population. Suffers predation by cats and rats at several colonies, e.g. breeding success reduced to virtually nil on Henderson I (S Pacific); adults, chicks and eggs taken for human consumption, especially on Round I (Mauritius). Conservation priorities include programme of environmental education, with a view to halting human exploitation, and eradication of introduced predators from breeding islands.
Bibliography. Antas (1991), Bailey *et al.* (1989), Bourne & David (1983), Burger & Gochfeld (1991), Croxall *et al.* (1984), Eades & Rogers (1982), Gardner *et al.* (1985), Gill *et al.* (1970), Gochfeld *et al.* (1988), Gould & King (1967), Holyoak & Thibault (1984), Imber (1985a), King (1970), King & Reimer (1991), Lee (1979, 1986), Lindsey (1986), Marchant & Higgins (1990), Murphy & Pennoyer (1952), de Naurois (1978), Palmer (1962), Pyle *et al.* (1990), Ruschi (1979), Sick (1984), Warham (1959).

23. Soft-plumaged Petrel
Pterodroma mollis

French: Pétrel soyeux **German**: Weichfeder-Sturmvogel **Spanish**: Petrel Suave
Other common names: Soft-plumaged Fulmar

Taxonomy. *Procellaria mollis* Gould, 1844, south Atlantic Ocean, lat. 20° S to 40° S.
Formerly included *P. feae* and *P. madeira*. Validity of subspecific division doubtful, due mainly to extent of individual variation and effects of plumage wear; race *dubia* should perhaps give way to alternative name *fusca*. Rare dark phase may result from hybridization with other species. Two subspecies normally recognized.
Subspecies and Distribution.
P. m. mollis (Gould, 1844) - Tristan da Cunha, Gough I; Antipodes I.
P. m. dubia Clancey *et al.*, 1981 - Prince Edward Is, Crozet, Kerguelen, Amsterdam Is.
Descriptive notes. 32-37 cm; 279-312 g; wingspan 83-95 cm (length and wingspan measurements refer to *P. mollis*, *P. feae*, and *P. madeira*; *mollis* large, but fairly short-winged). Underwing has pale central stripe. Very similar to *P. feae* and *P. madeira*, but darker on face and collar. Rare dark phase exists. Juvenile as adult. Race *dubia* often has collar thicker and more conspicuous, but much individual variation; upperwing darker, obscuring dark open "M" of nominate race; outer tail feathers grey as opposed to white.
Habitat. Marine and highly pelagic, rarely approaching land except at colonies. Breeds on oceanic islands, occupying steep slopes with tussock grass or ferns, usually along coast but occasionally inland.

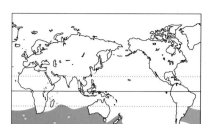

Food and Feeding. Mostly cephalopods (*Gonatus antarcticus*, *Discoteuthis*); also crustaceans and some fish. Prey apparently taken mainly by surface-seizing. Occasionally follows ships and cetaceans.
Breeding. Starts Sept. Colonial; nests in long burrows; burrow can be occupied by 2 pairs. 1 egg; incubation c. 50 days; chicks have grey down; fledging c. 90-92 days.
Movements. Little known; most birds apparently leave vicinity of colony after breeding; some populations may be largely sedentary, e.g. birds present around Amsterdam I throughout year. Disperses over S Atlantic and Indian Oceans; young birds may wander more widely than adults.
Status and Conservation. Not globally threatened. Total population thought to number tens of thousands of breeding pairs; 10,000's of pairs at Crozet Is, c. 1000 pairs each at Kerguelen and Prince Edward Is. Suffers considerable predation by rats and cats, producing severe declines in places; population of Marion I (Prince Edward Is) slumped from over 400,000 birds, with cats killing c. 38,000. Main conservation requirements include elimination of alien predators from breeding islands and legal protection to curtail human exploitation. Also frequently taken by skuas (*Catharacta*), especially on Gough I, where present species constitutes over 40% of birds taken by skuas.
Bibliography. Bourne (1983a), Brooke (1984), Brown *et al.* (1982), Cramp & Simmons (1977), Croxall *et al.* (1984), Eades & Rogers (1982), Enticott (1991a), Fraser *et al.* (1988), Furness (1987), Griffiths (1982), Hagen (1952), Harper (1973), Imber (1983, 1985a), Jehl *et al.* (1979), Jouventin *et al.* (1985), Lindsey (1986), Marchant & Higgins (1990), Murphy (1936), Powlesland (1987), Richardson, M.E. (1984), Ryan *et al.* (1990), Schramm (1982, 1983, 1986), Warham (1979), Watson (1975), Weimerskirch, Zotier & Jouventin (1989), Woods (1988).

24. **Cape Verde Petrel**

Pterodroma feae

French: Pétrel gongon   **German**: Kapverdensturmvogel   **Spanish**: Petrel Gon-gon
Other common names: Gon-gon, Fea's Petrel

Taxonomy. *Oestrelata feae* Salvadori, 1899, San Nicolas Island, Cape Verde Islands.
Until recently, considered conspecific with *P. mollis* and *P. madeira*. May be conspecific with *P. cahow*, and bird recently captured in Azores could represent link. Monotypic.
Distribution. Cape Verde Is and Bugio I (Desertas Is, off Madeira); might breed in Azores.

Descriptive notes. 32-37 cm; 295-355 g; wingspan 83-95 cm (length and wingspan measurements refer to *P. mollis*, *P. feae*, and *P. madeira*; *feae* largest). Like *P. mollis*, but white superciliary area highlights dark mask; collar faint. Juvenile as adult.
Habitat. Marine and pelagic. Breeds in rocky, mountainous areas, up to 2200 m above sea-level; also on steep slopes and vertical cliffs; formerly in woodland.
Food and Feeding. Little known; squid and small fish recorded.
Breeding. Starts Nov in Cape Verde Is, and Jun in Desertas Is. Colonial; nests in burrows or rock crevices. 1 egg; fledging mostly in May (Cape Verde) and until Dec (Desertas).
Movements. Disperses over subtropical and tropical waters of N Atlantic, although some birds present around breeding islands during much of year; may reach equator regularly, but probably does not range far into S Atlantic.
Status and Conservation. RARE. Total population estimated at a few hundred breeding pairs. On Bugio in Desertas Is (Madeira), heavy soil erosion caused by abundant goats and rabbits; possibly affected by significant human exploitation, but this is mainly directed towards other species. Cape Verde Is thought to hold a few hundred pairs in 1969; these suffer predation by cats, rats and monkeys; highly appreciated by islanders for fat, as attributed medicinal properties. Formerly bred in mountain woodland at Cape Verde Is; no woods remain and birds have been displaced to inaccessible sites on high ground. Survival of species depends on prompt termination of human exploitation and eradication of introduced predators.
Bibliography. Bannerman (1968), Bibby & del Nevo (1991), Bourne (1957, 1965, 1983a), Collar & Andrew (1988), Collar & Stuart (1985), Cramp & Simmons (1977), Croxall *et al.* (1984), Imber (1985a), James & Robertson (1985e), de Naurois (1969b), Zino & Zino (1986)

25. **Madeira Petrel**

Pterodroma madeira

French: Pétrel de Madère   **German**: Madeirasturmvogel   **Spanish**: Petrel Freira
Other common names: Freira

Taxonomy. *Pterodroma mollis madeira* Mathews, 1934, Madeira.
Until recently, considered conspecific with *P. mollis* and *P. feae*. Apparently linked with *P. cahow* by shared feather louse. Monotypic.
Distribution. Madeira.

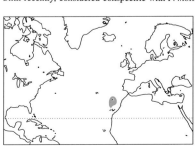

Descriptive notes. 32-37 cm; c. 204 g; wingspan 83-95 cm (length and wingspan measurements refer to *P. mollis*, *P. feae*, and *P. madeira*; *madeira* smallest). Similar to *P. feae*, but weaker white eyebrow produces less masked appearance; flanks heavily mottled grey. Juvenile presumably as adult.
Habitat. Marine and pelagic. Breeds inland, at foot of cliffs 1500 m above sea-level.
Food and Feeding. No information available.
Breeding. Starts Apr. Colonial; nests in burrows. 1 egg; fledging mostly in October.

Movements. No information available.
Status and Conservation. ENDANGERED. Total population estimated at only c. 20 breeding pairs at single colony. Breeding success affected by rat predation, but programme of rat poisoning recently begun. Undiscovered inland colonies might remain; all suitable habitat should be surveyed and known sites monitored regularly to detect significant changes. Urgently requires full protection of nesting grounds, or species may soon be extinct.
Bibliography. Bourne (1983a), Buckle & Zino (1989), Collar & Andrew (1988), Collar & Stuart (1985), Cramp & Simmons (1977), Croxall *et al.* (1984), Imber (1985a), King (1978/79), Zino & Zino (1986).

26. **Barau's Petrel**

Pterodroma baraui

French: Pétrel de Barau   **German**: Ba“Baraüsturmvogel”   **Spanish**: Petrel de Barau

Taxonomy. *Bulweria baraui* Jouanin, 1964, Saint-Denis, Réunion.
Monotypic.
Distribution. Reunion and Rodrigues I in W Indian Ocean.

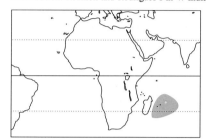

Descriptive notes. 38 cm; 400 g; wingspan 96 cm. From below resembles *P. cahow*, but from above easily separated by lack of white band across uppertail-coverts. Juvenile as adult.
Habitat. Marine and pelagic; not uncommon over continental shelf, but generally forages further offshore; normally comes to land only for breeding. Breeds inland in mountainous areas at 2700-2900 m, probably on inaccessible cliffs and peaks of volcanic cirque; only nest found on Rodrigues at 320 m above sea-level.
Food and Feeding. Very little known. Catches prey by surface-seizing or dipping. Associates with flocks of feeding seabirds; occasionally occurs by fishing boats.
Breeding. Starts Oct/Nov. Colonial; nests in burrows. 1 egg; fledging occurs mostly in April.
Movements. Little known, but seems to disperse N then E, following S Equatorial Current, reaching area of Cocos (Keeling) Is and Christmas I; recorded S to Amsterdam I, and E to Australia. Forages in zone of Subtropical Convergence to S of Reunion.
Status and Conservation. Not globally threatened. Currently considered near-threatened. Population figures lacking, but certainly numbers several thousand birds; not uncommon, though only discovered in 1963. Traditionally taken for food on Reunion and may still be subject to some human exploitation, but probably of minor importance nowadays. Assumed breeding grounds in cliffs, fairly inaccessible to people and also most mammalian predators. Most urgent priorities include complete survey of known colonies and all other suitable ground to determine population size and trends.
Bibliography. Barré & Barau (1982), van den Berg *et al.* (1991), Bretagnolle & Attie (1991), Croxall *et al.* (1984), Feare (1984b), Imber (1985a), Jouanin (1964b, 1987), Jouanin & Gill (1967), Marchant & Higgins (1990), Thibault & Guyot (1988).

27. **Dark-rumped Petrel**

Pterodroma phaeopygia

French: Pétrel des Hawaii   **German**: Hawaiisturmvogel   **Spanish**: Petrel Hawaiano
Other common names: Hawaiian Petrel; Galapagos Petrel (*phaeopygia*); Uau (*sandwichensis*)

Taxonomy. *Oestrelata phaeopygia* Salvin, 1876, Chatham Island, Galapagos.
Has been included in *P. hasitata*. Subspecies doubtfully distinguishable. Two subspecies currently recognized.
Subspecies and Distribution.
P. p. phaeopygia (Salvin, 1876) - Galapagos Is.
P. p. sandwichensis (Ridgway, 1884) - Hawaiian Is.

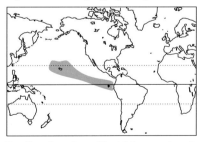

Descriptive notes. 43 cm; c. 434 g; wingspan 91 cm. Unique, amongst *Pterodroma* petrels with black line across underwing, in having black patch or stripe in axillary region and upperparts uniformly very dark, except forehead; sides of rump sometimes white. Juvenile as adult. Race *sandwichensis* closely similar and doubtfully separable.
Habitat. Marine and pelagic, normally keeping well away from land, except at colonies. Breeds on thickly vegetated high ground.
Food and Feeding. Mostly squid and fish. Prey taken by surface-seizing or caught on wing by dipping.
Breeding. Starts Jan or May (Galapagos, depending on locality), or Mar (Hawaii). Colonial; nests in burrows, or crevices and hollows in lava. 1 egg; incubation 52-56 days with stints of 10-13 days; fledging 110-117 days.
Movements. Probably disperses widely throughout Pacific, perhaps N towards boreal zone (*sandwichensis*), and E towards Humboldt Current (*phaeopygia*).
Status and Conservation. RARE. Total population c. 1500 pairs. Hawaiian population estimated at 400-600 breeding pairs, c. 2000 birds; almost wiped out in 1930's by intensive human exploitation and devastation by introduced mongooses. Only known colony at Haleakala Crater, Maui, still raided by mongooses, cats and rats, causing over 70% breeding failure in most years; intensive trapping of introduced predators has improved breeding success, but complete elimination of predators highly desirable. Rapid decline at Galapagos from thriving population to c. 1000 pairs, due to predation by dogs and rats, and also habitat destruction; breeding success under 20% in most seasons. Major conservation programme under way in Galapagos to save species; aims include complete eradication of alien predators, provision of safe nesting sites and transfer of chicks to predator-free islands, in attempt to found new colonies; also regular monitoring of numbers and productivity.

Bibliography. Bent (1922), Blake (1977), Collar & Andrew (1988), Coulter (1984), Coulter *et al.* (1981, 1985), Croxall *et al.* (1984), Cruz & Cruz (1987a, 1987b, 1987c, 1990a, 1990b), Gassmann-Duvall *et al.* (1988), Harris, M.P. (1970, 1974a, 1977), Harrison (1990), Imber (1985a), King (1978/79), Larsen (1967), Mountfort (1988), Murphy (1936), Phillips (1986), Pitman (1982), Richardson & Woodside (1954), Shallenberger (1984), Simons (1984, 1985), Simons & Whittow (1984), Tomkins (1985b), Tomkins & Milne (1991), Vincent (1966).

28. Juan Fernandez Petrel

Pterodroma externa

French: Pétrel de Juan Fernandez   **Spanish**: Petrel de las Juan Fernández
German: Salvinsturmvogel
Other common names: Pacific Petrel

Taxonomy. *Oestrelata externa* Salvin, 1875, islands of Más Afuera and Juan Fernández.
Often includes *P. cervicalis*. Has been considered subspecies of *P. hasitata*. Monotypic.
Distribution. Alejandro Selkirk I (formerly Más Afuera I) in Juan Fernández Is.

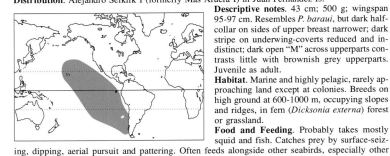

Descriptive notes. 43 cm; 500 g; wingspan 95-97 cm. Resembles *P. baraui*, but dark half-collar on sides of upper breast narrower; dark stripe on underwing-coverts reduced and indistinct; dark open "M" across upperparts contrasts little with brownish grey upperparts. Juvenile as adult.
Habitat. Marine and highly pelagic, rarely approaching land except at colonies. Breeds on high ground at 600-1000 m, occupying slopes and ridges, in fern (*Dicksonia externa*) forest or grassland.
Food and Feeding. Probably takes mostly squid and fish. Catches prey by surface-seizing, dipping, aerial pursuit and pattering. Often feeds alongside other seabirds, especially other *Pterodroma*; associates with cetaceans. Occasionally seen around fishing boats.
Breeding. Starts Oct/Nov. Colonial; nests in burrows. 1 egg; chicks have slate grey down; fledging mostly in May/Jun.
Movements. Transequatorial migrant, ranging over tropical and subtropical waters of E Pacific, N to Hawaii; occurs regularly off W Mexico. Vagrant to New Zealand and E Australia.
Status and Conservation. Not globally threatened. Total population may number over 1,000,000 pairs. Juan Fernández Is legally protected as national park since 1935, but abundant introduced predators, e.g. rats, cats and coatis (*Nasua nasua*); numbers apparently decreasing due to predation. Other alien fauna include cattle, rabbits and goats; sheep removed in 1983, but population of rabbits estimated at c. 52,000, and trapping has little effect.
Bibliography. Blake (1977), Brooke (1987b), Harrison (1990), Imber (1985a), Imber *et al.* (1991), Johnson (1965), Marchant & Higgins (1990), Murphy (1936), Schlatter (1984), Tanaka & Inaba (1981).

29. White-necked Petrel

Pterodroma cervicalis

French: Pétrel a col blanc   **German**: Weißnacken-Sturmvogel   **Spanish**: Petrel Cuelliblanco
Other common names: White-naped/Black-capped/Sunday Island Petrel

Taxonomy. *Oestrelata cervicalis* Salvin, 1891, Kermadec Islands.
Often included in *P. externa*. Has been considered subspecies of *P. hasitata*. Birds collected E of Vanuatu, SW Pacific, may represent undescribed race. Monotypic.
Distribution. Macauley I (Kermadec Is).

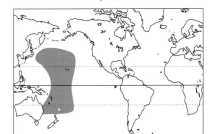

Descriptive notes. 43 cm; 380-545 g; wingspan 100 cm. Resembles *P. externa*, but tail paler and diagnostic white collar on hind neck. Juvenile as adult, but broader pale fringes on upperparts and front of dark cap.
Habitat. Marine and highly pelagic; often in areas of upwelling; rarely approaches land except at colonies. Breeds on oceanic islands, occupying higher parts of gentle slopes typically with low vegetation.
Food and Feeding. Very little known; squid recorded. Prey taken by surface-seizing, pattering and dipping. Sometimes feeds alongside other Procellariidae.
Breeding. Starts Oct-Dec. Colonial, alongside *P. nigripennis* and *Puffinus pacificus*; nests in burrows. 1 egg; chicks have pale grey down; fledging probably c. 100-115 days.
Movements. Transequatorial migrant, ranging over tropical and subtropical waters of NW Pacific, N to Japan; abundant in C Pacific May-Nov, where some birds occur all year round.
Status and Conservation. Not globally threatened. Total population estimated at 50,000 breeding pairs. Single breeding station on Macauley I, Kermadec Is; possibly increasing due to elimination of goats. Former colony on Raoul I (Kermadecs) probably wiped out by feral cats. More information required on numbers, productivity, trends and possible threats; establishment of another colony desirable.
Bibliography. Brazil (1991), Bregulla (1992), Falla *et al.* (1981), Imber (1985a), Marchant & Higgins (1990), Robertson & Bell (1984).

30. Cook's Petrel

Pterodroma cookii

French: Pétrel de Cook   **German**: Cooksturmvogel   **Spanish**: Petrel de Cook
Other common names: Blue-footed Petrel

Taxonomy. *Procellaria Cookii* G. R. Gray, 1843, New Zealand. Formerly included *P. defilippiana*.
Forms part of assemblage often referred to as subgenus *Cookilaria*. Monotypic.

Distribution. New Zealand area, breeding on Great and Little Barrier Is off North I, and Codfish I off Stewart I (to S of New Zealand).

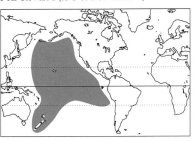

Descriptive notes. 25-30 cm; 190 g; wingspan 65-66 cm. Fairly pale above, lacking contrast of back with darker head and sides of breast found in *P. longirostris*. Outer tail more or less white. As in other similar species, upperparts darker when worn. Juvenile has paler feather tips on upperparts.
Habitat. Marine and highly pelagic in temperate and subtropical waters, mostly within temperature range of 15°-25°C; rarely approaches land except at colonies. Breeds on offshore islands, occupying thickly forested high ridges and slopes, up to 700 m above sea-level.
Food and Feeding. Mostly squid (Spirulidae, Cranchiidae); also crustaceans, fish and carrion. Feeds mainly by surface-seizing. Feeds by night.
Breeding. Starts Oct/Nov. Forms loose colonies; nests in burrows. 1 egg; incubation c. 47-51 days, with stints of 12-16 days; chicks have slate grey down, whitish from throat to belly; fledging c. 88 days.
Movements. Migrates to E Pacific; some birds occur in breeding and wintering areas all year round, perhaps due to poorly synchronized migration; ranges N to Aleutian Is and Hawaii, and E to California and W South America.
Status and Conservation. RARE. Total population numbers tens of thousands of pairs on Little Barrier I; relict populations of c. 100 pairs on Codfish I and 4 pairs on Great Barrier I. Codfish I formerly held c. 20,000 pairs, but major decline due to heavy predation by Wekas (*Gallirallus australis*); population of Little Barrier I also declined due to predation by feral cats; following removal of these predators, in 1980-1985 and 1976-1980 respectively, populations have started to recover; one of major successes in seabird conservation in recent decades. Large numbers of rats persist on Little Barrier I and Codfish I, and rats and cats on Great Barrier I. Formerly taken for food by Maoris.
Bibliography. Bourne (1983b), Bretagnolle & Thomas (1990), Chambers (1989), Collar & Andrew (1988), Ellis (1980), Falla *et al.* (1981), Imber (1983, 1984d, 1985a, 1985c), King (1978/79), Marchant & Higgins (1990), Mountfort (1988), Murphy (1936), Palmer (1962), Powlesland (1987), Roberson & Bailey (1991), Robertson & Bell (1984), Sibson (1982), Wood (1990b).

31. Mas a Tierra Petrel

Pterodroma defilippiana

French: Pétrel de Defilippe   **German**: Juan-Fernandez-Sturmvogel   **Spanish**: Petrel Chileno
Other common names: Defilippe's Petrel

Taxonomy. *Aestrelata defilippiana* Giglioli and Salvadori, 1869, off coast between Callao, Peru, and Valparaíso, Chile.
Formerly placed in *P. cookii*. Forms part of assemblage often referred to as subgenus *Cookilaria*. Monotypic.
Distribution. Juan Fernández Is, San Ambrosio and San Félix Is.

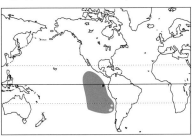

Descriptive notes. c. 26 cm; wingspan c. 66 cm. Very similar to *P. cookii*, differing mainly in stouter bill and darker eye patch; can have less white in tail, which is slightly longer. Juvenile probably similar to adult.
Habitat. Marine and probably pelagic. Breeds on islands, occupying sheltered cliff ledges, crevices and caverns; also amongst boulders at foot of lava cliffs.
Food and Feeding. No information available.
Breeding. Poorly known. Eggs Jul-Sept, chicks Oct, but also reported in Feb. Colonial; nests above ground, e.g. on ledges or in caves; nest can be lined with sticks and feathers. 1 egg; chicks have dark grey down; fledging in Jan/Feb. Visits colonies by day.
Movements. Little known, but apparently relatively sedentary. Some dispersal N in zone of Humboldt Current, and thence perhaps to C Pacific; absent from sea around breeding grounds, Mar-Jun.
Status and Conservation. VULNERABLE. Total population estimated at few hundreds, perhaps thousands of birds. Suffers considerable predation by introduced cats, rats and coatis (*Nasua nasua*). Juan Fernández Is legally protected as national park since 1935. Priorities include thorough survey to establish numbers and productivity; also elimination of all introduced fauna from Juan Fernández Is and San Ambrosio and San Félix Is.
Bibliography. Blake (1977), Bourne (1983b), Brooke (1987a), Collar & Andrew (1988), Imber (1985a), Johnson (1965), Roberson & Bailey (1991), Schlatter (1984).

32. Gould's Petrel

Pterodroma leucoptera

French: Pétrel de Gould   **German**: Weißflügel-Sturmvogel   **Spanish**: Petrel de Gould
Other common names: White-winged/Sooty-capped/White-throated Petrel; Collared Petrel (*brevipes*)

Taxonomy. *Procellaria leucoptera* Gould, 1844, Cabbage Tree Island, Port Stephens, New South Wales. Forms part of assemblage often referred to as subgenus *Cookilaria*. May form superspecies with *P. longirostris*, *P. pycrofti* and (?) *P. hypoleuca*. Race *brevipes* often treated as separate species. Three subspecies recognized.
Subspecies and Distribution.
P. l. leucoptera (Gould, 1844) - Cabbage Tree I (New South Wales).
P. l. caledonica de Naurois, 1978 - New Caledonia.
P. l. brevipes (Peale, 1848) - Fiji and Cook Is; possibly also Vanuatu, Samoa, Solomon Is.
Descriptive notes. 30 cm; 170-200 g; wingspan 70-71 cm. Similar to *P. longirostris*, but slightly larger with conspicuous black hood and white of forehead, cheeks and throat joined to white of

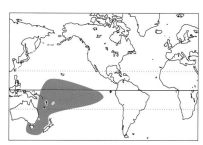

underbody. Juvenile as adult. Race *caledonica* larger with more white in outer tail; race *brevipes* has complete black collar separating white of face from white to grey underbody.

Habitat. Marine and generally pelagic, rarely approaching land except at colonies. Breeds on oceanic islands, on steep forested slopes and in gullies with palm forest.

Food and Feeding. Very little known, but apparently mostly squid; small fish also recorded.

Breeding. Starts Nov/Dec, slightly later in Fiji. Colonial; nests on ground in rocky crevices or where sheltered by thick foliage. 1 egg; incubation probably 6-7 weeks; chick has dark grey down; fledging probably c. 11-12 weeks, mostly Apr-Aug. Known to have lived over 20 years in wild.

Movements. Very little known. Race *brevipes* thought to be largely sedentary; other races apparently leave breeding zones, possibly dispersing E into tropical and subtropical Pacific; records from New Zealand and Galapagos.

Status and Conservation. Not globally threatened. Population rather small. Nominate race breeds only on Cabbage Tree I, off E New South Wales, where numbers low but apparently stable; no alien predators, but rabbits introduced in 1906; island used briefly for target practice in 1943; island protected as John Gould Nature Reserve in 1954. Many birds incapacitated after becoming entangled with seeds of bird-lime tree (*Pisonia umbellifera*). Little information available on other races; like most ground-nesting petrels, may be subject to heavy predation in most of range. Conservation priorities include further information on breeding grounds, numbers, productivity and population trends.

Bibliography. Bourne (1983b), Bregulla (1992), Bretagnolle & Thomas (1990), Garnett (1984), Fullagar (1976), Hindwood & Serventy (1941), Imber (1985a), Imber & Jenkins (1981), Johnson (1965), King (1978/79), Lindsey (1986), Marchant & Higgins (1990), de Naurois (1978), Powlesland (1987), Roberson & Bailey (1991), van Tets & Fullagar (1984), Watling (1986b), Wood (1990b).

ssp *aequinoctialis*

ssp *conspicillata*

PLATE 15

inches   12

cm   30

33. Bonin Petrel

Pterodroma hypoleuca

French: Pétrel des Bonin　　**German**: Boninsturmvogel　　**Spanish**: Petrel de las Bonin
Other common names: Stout-billed Petrel

Taxonomy. *Oestrelata hypoleuca* Salvin, 1888, north Pacific Ocean.
Usually forms part of assemblage referred to as subgenus *Cookilaria*. May form superspecies with *P. longirostris*, *P. leucoptera* and *P. pycrofti*. Has been considered conspecific with *P. nigripennis* or *P. axillaris*. Monotypic.
Distribution. Bonin and Volcano Is; W Hawaiian Is.

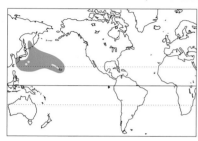

Descriptive notes. 30 cm; c. 182 g; wingspan 63-71 cm. Black bar across underwing-coverts heavier than in *P. baraui*; prominent carpal patch, unlike *P. nigripennis* and others. Upperparts mixed grey and dark greyish brown with weakish dark open "M" mark, as in *P. nigripennis* and *P. axillaris*, but nape blacker. Slightly masked appearance, as in *P. baraui*. Juvenile as adult.
Habitat. Marine and highly pelagic, rarely approaching land except at colonies. Breeds on oceanic islands, occupying areas of sandy soil or high sloping ground up to 918 m, usually amongst vegetation.

Food and Feeding. Unique amongst *Pterodroma* petrels in that diet probably consists mainly of fish, as well as some squid; also known to take shrimps and sea skaters (*Halobates sericeus*). Apparently feeds mostly by night.
Breeding. Starts Dec. Forms dense colonies; nests in burrows. 1 egg; incubation c. 49 days; fledging c. 82 days.
Movements. Disperses widely over subtropical N Pacific, though some birds remain in warm waters to E of Japan; recorded N to Sakhalin.
Status and Conservation. Not globally threatened. Abundant, with total population estimated at several hundred thousand breeding pairs; estimated 150,000-250,000 pairs on Lisianski I (1970's), 50,000-75,000 pairs on Laysan I; little known of Japanese populations, but reported to be numerous in S Volcano Is. In Hawaii, predation by rats has recently caused near-extinction on Midway I, and seriously affecting breeding success on Kure Atoll. Grazing of rabbits introduced to Midway, Laysan and Lisianski Is caused major soil erosion, leading to burrow collapse and many breeding failures; rabbits have now been eliminated. Competition for nest-sites with *Puffinus pacificus* also responsible for some reduction of breeding success, but probably not significant. Main conservation requirement is removal of all alien fauna from breeding islands.
Bibliography. Bent (1922), Bourne (1983b), Brazil (1991), Clapp & Wirtz (1975), Cheng Tso-hsin (1987), Etchécopar & Hüe (1978), Fisher (1961), Grant & Whittow (1983), Grant *et al.* (1981, 1983), Harrison (1990), Harrison *et al.* (1984), Hasegawa (1984b), Howell & Bartholomew (1961b), Imber (1985a), Pettit *et al.* (1982), Shallenberger (1984), Tanaka & Kaneko (1983), Tanaka *et al.* (1985), Tang Zi-ying (1981).

34. Black-winged Petrel

Pterodroma nigripennis

French: Pétrel à ailes noires　**German**: Schwarzflügel-Sturmvogel　**Spanish**: Petrel Alinegro

Taxonomy. *Oestrelata nigripennis* Rothschild, 1893, Kermadec Islands.
Forms superspecies with *P. axillaris*. Usually forms part of assemblage referred to as subgenus *Cookilaria*. Monotypic.
Distribution. SW Pacific, from Lord Howe I and (?) E Australia to Kermadec Is, extending N to New Caledonia and S to Chatham Is; also Austral Is (SC Pacific).

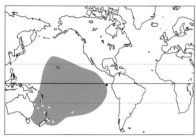

Descriptive notes. 28-30 cm; 140-200 g; wingspan 63-71 cm. Upperparts very similar to *P. axillaris*, from which differs in pale axillaries. Head and neck paler than in *P. hypoleuca*. Fairly obvious mask. Juvenile as adult.
Habitat. Marine and highly pelagic, avoiding land except during breeding. Breeds on oceanic islands, often on high ground inland and usually amongst scrub or tussock grass.
Food and Feeding. Little known; mainly cephalopods and prawns. Catches prey mainly by surface-seizing and dipping, with some pattering. Often recorded in feeding association with other Procellariiformes.
Breeding. Starts Nov. Colonial; nests in burrows, or sometimes in crevices. 1 egg; chicks have pale grey down; fledging mostly in Apr.
Movements. Migrates to N and E Pacific; common in NW Pacific, Jul-Nov, reaching 40° N; abundant between Hawaii and Peru.
Status and Conservation. Not globally threatened. Total population perhaps numbers a few hundred thousand breeding pairs; over 1,100,000 birds on Macauley I, in Kermadec Is. In process of notable expansion and increase in numbers, with recent (re)colonization of Philip I (Norfolk I), Lord Howe I and other islands in region; may be recovery after major declines in past, both before and after colonization by Europeans. Survey work under way in attempt to locate further breeding grounds on apparently suitable islands. In places suffers predation by introduced cats and rats, notably in Kermadecs; also disturbance and occasional trampling by feral pigs and goats (e.g. Lord Howe I), sheep and cattle; some local extinctions or near-extinctions, e.g. Raoul I (Kermadec Is). Elimination of all alien fauna from breeding islands recommended.
Bibliography. Bourne (1983b), Chambers (1989), Croxall *et al.* (1984), Gould (1983), Harrison (1990), Holyoak & Thibault (1984), Imber (1985a), Jenkins & Cheshire (1982), Lindsey (1986), Marchant & Higgins (1990), de Naurois (1978), Roberson & Bailey (1991), Serventy *et al.* (1971), Tanaka *et al.* (1985), Tennyson (1991), Tennyson & Taylor (1990, 1991), Wood (1990b).

35. Chatham Petrel

Pterodroma axillaris

French: Pétrel des Chatham　　**German**: Chathamsturmvogel　**Spanish**: Petrel de las Chatham

Taxonomy. *Oestrelata axillaris* Salvin, 1893, Chatham Islands.
Forms superspecies with *P. nigripennis*. Usually forms part of assemblage referred to as subgenus *Cookilaria*. Monotypic.
Distribution. Rangitira I (formerly South-east I) in Chatham Is.

Descriptive notes. 30 cm; 200 g; wingspan 63-71 cm. Only species of group with black bar on underwing extending onto axillaries. Juvenile as adult.
Habitat. Marine and presumably pelagic. Breeds on coastal lowlands and slopes, in areas with low forest, bracken or rank grass.
Food and Feeding. Very little known; cephalopods and fish recorded.
Breeding. Starts Nov. Colonial, alongside *Pachyptila vittata* and *Pelecanoides urinatrix*; nests in burrows. 1 egg; incubation shifts probably of 10-15 days; chicks have dark grey down; fledging probably in May/Jun.

Movements. Unknown; absent from colonies Jun-Nov. Single recent record outwith breeding grounds c. 120 km to S.
Status and Conservation. VULNERABLE. Total population estimated at c. 200-400 birds; only known to breed on Rangitira I (Chatham Is). Vegetation cover on Rangitira I devastated by abundant sheep and few cattle; island purchased by New Zealand government for reserve, and livestock removed by 1961. Nowadays vegetation has recovered well and no introduced mammals remain, but numbers of species not increasing; possible cause is competition for nest-sites with aggressive *Pachyptila vittata* and perhaps even with closely related *Pterodroma nigripennis*, a recent colonizer of Rangitira I; probably some predation by skuas (*Catharacta*), perhaps increased by depletion of vegetation cover. Formerly occurred on other islands of Chathams, where probably extirpated due to human exploitation and introduced predators. Research required to establish relationship with potential competitor species, and explain failure of present species to recover.
Bibliography. Bourne (1983b), Chambers (1989), Collar & Andrew (1988), Imber (1985a, 1985d), Johnstone (1985), King (1978/79), Marchant & Higgins (1990), Mountfort (1988), Robertson & Bell (1984), Sibson (1982), Williams & Given (1981).

36. Stejneger's Petrel

Pterodroma longirostris

French: Pétrel de Stejneger　**German**: Stejnegersturmvogel　　**Spanish**: Petrel de Más Afuera

Taxonomy. *Aestrelata longirostris* Stejneger, 1893, Province of Mutzu, Hondo, Japan.
Forms part of assemblage referred to as subgenus *Cookilaria*. May form superspecies with *P. leucoptera*, *P. pycrofti* and (?) *P. hypoleuca*. Sometimes includes *P. pycrofti*. Monotypic.
Distribution. Alejandro Selkirk I (formerly Más Afuera I) in Juan Fernández Is.

Descriptive notes. 26-31 cm; wingspan 53-66 cm. Black "M" across upperparts more poorly defined than in *P. cookii*; similar hooded appearance to *P. leucoptera*, but underwing whiter with very weak bar across underwing-coverts. Juvenile has stronger hooded effect due to greyer upperparts.
Habitat. Marine and highly pelagic. Breeds on oceanic islands, occupying slopes and ridges at 850-1100 m, in areas of dense fern forest.
Food and Feeding. No information available.
Breeding. Starts Nov. Forms mixed colonies with *P. externa*; nests in burrows. 1 egg; fledging mostly in Mar.

Movements. Transequatorial migrant, occurring in subtropical waters off Japan, Jun-Nov; might also be regular off California. Several records from New Zealand suggest widespread dispersal of non-breeders.
Status and Conservation. Not globally threatened. Total population estimated at 131,000 breeding pairs. Currently decreasing due to predation by introduced cats; at mixed colonies with *P. externa*, cats prefer to take present species; campaigns to eradicate all alien fauna recommended. Juan Fernández Is legally protected as national park since 1935.
Bibliography. Bourne (1983b), Brazil (1991), Brooke (1987a, 1987b), Falla *et al.* (1981), Imber (1985a), Johnson (1972), Marchant & Higgins (1990), Powlesland (1987), Roberson & Bailey (1991), Schlatter (1984), Tanaka *et al.* (1985).

37. Pycroft's Petrel

Pterodroma pycrofti

French: Pétrel de Pycroft　　**German**: Pycroftsturmvogel　　**Spanish**: Petrel de Pycroft

Taxonomy. *Pterodroma pycrofti* Falla, 1933, Taranga, Hen Island, New Zealand.
Sometimes placed in *P. longirostris*. Forms part of assemblage referred to as subgenus *Cookilaria*. May form superspecies with *P. longirostris*, *P. leucoptera* and (?) *P. hypoleuca*. Monotypic.
Distribution. NE North I, New Zealand.
Descriptive notes. 28 cm; wingspan 53 cm. Cap and nape darker than in *P. cookii*, but much less so than in *P. longirostris*, with masked rather than hooded aspect. Juvenile has whitish fringes to upperparts in fresh plumage.

On following pages: 38. Fiji Petrel (*Pterodroma macgillivrayi*); 39. Blue Petrel (*Halobaena caerulea*); 40. Broad-billed Prion (*Pachyptila vittata*); 41. Salvin's Prion (*Pachyptila salvini*); 42. Antarctic Prion (*Pachyptila desolata*); 43. Fairy Prion (*Pachyptila turtur*); 44. Fulmar Prion (*Pachyptila crassirostris*); 45. Slender-billed Prion (*Pachyptila belcheri*); 46. Bulwer's Petrel (*Bulweria bulwerii*); 47. Jouanin's Petrel (*Bulweria fallax*); 48. Grey Petrel (*Procellaria cinerea*); 49. White-chinned Petrel (*Procellaria aequinoctialis*); 50. Black Petrel (*Procellaria parkinsoni*); 51. Westland Petrel (*Procellaria westlandica*); 52. Streaked Shearwater (*Calonectris leucomelas*); 53. Cory's Shearwater (*Calonectris diomedea*).

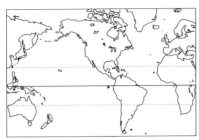

Habitat. Marine and probably pelagic. Breeds on offshore islands, occupying coastal slopes, cliffs and valleys under mature *Metrosideros excelsa* forest.
Food and Feeding. Very little known; small cephalopods recorded.
Breeding. Starts Nov. Colonial, sometimes alongside *P. macroptera*; nests in burrows. 1 egg; incubation c. 45 days, with stints of c. 5-14 days; fledging 77-84 days.
Movements. Very little known. Absent from colonies Apr-Oct; said to migrate to N Pacific, but only 1 record to date.
Status and Conservation. VULNERABLE. Total population estimated at no more than 300 breeding pairs, under 2000 birds. Subject to considerable predation by introduced rats and tuataras (*Sphenodon punctatus*); several eradication campaigns in progress, and total removal of alien fauna urgently required. Has also been affected by alterations of vegetation, and possibly by increase locally of larger, more aggressive *Puffinus bulleri*.
Bibliography. Bartle (1968), Chambers (1989), Collar & Andrew (1988), Dunnet (1985), Falla *et al.* (1981), Imber (1985a), Marchant & Higgins (1990), Powlesland (1987), Roberson & Bailey (1991), Robertson & Bell (1984), Tanaka *et al.* (1985), Williams & Given (1981).

38. **Fiji Petrel**
Pterodroma macgillivrayi

French: Pétrel des Fidji   **German:** Macgillivraysturmvogel   **Spanish:** Petrel de las Fiji
Other common names: MacGillivray's Petrel

Taxonomy. *Thalassidroma (Bulweria) Macgillivrayi* G. R. Gray, 1860, Ngau, Fiji Islands.
Often placed in genus *Pseudobulweria*, being considered intermediate form between *Pterodroma* and *Bulweria*. Monotypic.
Distribution. Gau I (Fiji); breeding grounds undiscovered.

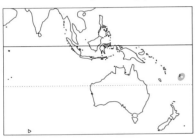

Descriptive notes. 30 cm. Head and neck more robust than in *B. bulwerii*, but less so than in *B. fallax*, which it resembles in lacking diagonal pale bar across upperwing of *B bulwerii*.
Habitat. Marine; presumably pelagic. Breeding grounds undiscovered; may be located in areas of undisturbed mature forest or on rocky, mountainous ground.
Food and Feeding. No information available.
Breeding. No information available.
Movements. No information available.
Status and Conservation. INDETERMINATE. Very little known; unrecorded for 129 years before rediscovery in 1984. Population on Gau I unlikely to be large, and species unknown to islanders; may suffer predation by numerous feral cats. Priorities include localization and protection of breeding grounds, and also information on biology, ecology and conservation requirements; research already in progress, but considerable efforts required due to apparently elusive nature of species.
Bibliography. Collar & Andrew (1988), Fuller (1987), Garnett (1984), Harrison (1985), Imber (1985a), King (1978/79), Thibault & Guyot (1988), Vincent (1966), Watling (1986a, 1987), Watling & Lewanavanua (1985).

Genus *HALOBAENA*   Bonaparte, 1856

39. **Blue Petrel**
Halobaena caerulea

French: Prion bleu   **German:** Blausturmvogel   **Spanish:** Petrel Azulado

Taxonomy. *Procellaria caerulea* Gmelin, 1789, "in oceano australi" = Southern Ocean, lat. 58° S. Monotypic.
Distribution. Subantarctic, from Diego Ramírez Is, Cape Horn and South Georgia eastwards through islands of S Indian Ocean to Macquarie I.

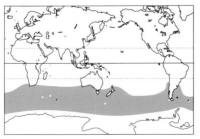

Descriptive notes. 26-32 cm; 170-230 g; wingspan 58-71 cm. Resembles *Pachyptila* in bluish grey coloration on upperparts with prominent "M" mark and white underparts, but differs in hooded aspect and white terminal bar on tail. Juvenile has greyer forehead and browner upperparts.
Habitat. Marine and pelagic, occurring in cold waters of subantarctic and Antarctic zones. Breeds on oceanic islands, occupying coastal slopes often with tussock grass.
Food and Feeding. In places takes mostly crustaceans, especially krill (*Euphausia*) and amphipods; elsewhere fish (Myctophidae, Nototheniidae); generally few cephalopods and even some insects. Feeds by surface-seizing and dipping; also dives and plunges. Often in flocks.
Breeding. Starts Sept. Colonial; nests in long burrows excavated in soft soil under grass tussocks. 1 egg; incubation 45-52 days, with stints of 1-16 days; chicks have bluish grey down, brooded for c. 3 days; fledging 43-60 days.
Movements. Adults perhaps mainly sedentary; visit colonies intermittently during winter and probably remain in surrounding area. Young birds more dispersive, occurring N to 20° S off Peru, and to 40° S in Atlantic and Indian Oceans; also S to zone of pack ice.
Status and Conservation. Not globally threatened. Abundant, with total population of several million birds; c. 2,000,000 breeding birds at Diego Ramírez Is (off Cape Horn), 100,000-200,000 pairs at Kerguelen, and tens of thousands each at Prince Edward and Crozet Is. Apparently highly vulnerable to predation by cats and rats, leading to extirpation of species from several breeding

islands; also suffers heavy predation by skuas (*Catharacta*), but unlikely to cause long-term reductions in population; some predation at sea by giant petrels (*Macronectes*) and even leopard seals (*Hydrurga leptonyx*). Research needed to determine trends, main threats and conservation requirements.
Bibliography. Ainley *et al.* (1984), Batchelor (1981), Blake (1977), Bretagnolle (1990b), Bretagnolle & Thomas (1990), Brothers (1984), Brown, L.H. *et al.* (1982), Brown, R.G.B. (1988b), Brown, R.S. *et al.* (1986), Carins (1974b), Croxall *et al.* (1984), Every *et al.* (1981), Fugler *et al.* (1987), Gartshore *et al.* (1988), Griffiths (1982), Jehl *et al.* (1979), Johnson (1965), Jouventin *et al.* (1985), Lindsey (1986), Marchant & Higgins (1990), Meeth & Meeth (1977), Murphy (1936), Prince (1980a), Schramm (1986), Steele & Klages (1986), Thibault & Guyot (1988), Watson (1975), Weimerskirch, Zotier & Jouventin (1989), Woods (1988).

Genus *PACHYPTILA*   Illiger, 1811

40. **Broad-billed Prion**
Pachyptila vittata

French: Prion de Forster   **German:** Großer Entensturmvogel   **Spanish:** Pato-petrel Piquiancho
Other common names: Blue/Broad-billed Dove-petrel, Long-billed/Common Prion, Icebird, Whalebird

Taxonomy. *Procellaria vittata* G. Forster, 1777, lat. 47° 10' S.
Often includes *P. salvini* and *P. desolata*; on occasions also includes *P. belcheri*. Monotypic.
Distribution. S South I (New Zealand) and Chatham Is; Tristan da Cunha and Gough I.

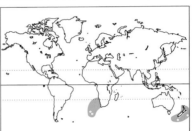

Descriptive notes. 25-30 cm; 160-235 g; wingspan 57-66. Heaviest-billed of prions. Black line behind eye well marked; grey of hind neck extends very little onto sides of upper breast. Juvenile similar to adult.
Habitat. Marine and probably pelagic, rarely approaching land except at colonies. Breeds on coastal slopes, flat lava fields, offshore islets and cliffs; also in dry rocky soil, caves or scree.
Food and Feeding. Mostly crustaceans, especially copepods (*Calanoides tonsus*), squid and some fish; apparently takes more crustaceans in summer and small squid in winter.
Feeds largely by hydroplaning (see page 223) and by filtering or surface-seizing.
Breeding. Starts Jul/Aug. Strongly colonial; nests in burrows, sometimes occupied by more than 1 pair. 1 egg; incubation c. 50 days; chicks have greyish down, much paler underneath; fledging c. 50 days.
Movements. Adults thought to remain in waters adjacent to colonies, which they visit intermittently in winter. Young birds more dispersive, occurring N to Australia and South Africa, reaching 10° S in tropical Indian Ocean.
Status and Conservation. Not globally threatened. Total population thought to number several hundred thousand birds; abundant on Gough I. Predation by rats and cats locally responsible for great reductions in numbers and some near-extinctions; also suffers heavy predation by skuas, but unlikely to cause long-term reductions in population. Introduced predators should be eliminated from all breeding islands; regular monitoring of populations recommended to detect any significant changes.
Bibliography. Batchelor (1981), Brown, L.H. *et al.* (1982), Brown, R.G.B. (1988b), Cox (1980), Croxall *et al.* (1984), Fitzgerald & Veitch (1985), Fleming (1941a, 1941b), Fraser *et al.* (1988), Furness (1987), Gartshore *et al.* (1988), Hagen (1952), Harper (1980), Lindsey (1986), Marchant & Higgins (1990), Milon *et al.* (1973), Powlesland (1989), Richardson, M.E. (1984), Richdale (1944b, 1965b), Roux & Martinez (1987), Roux *et al.* (1986), Swales (1965), Watson (1975), Woods (1988).

41. **Salvin's Prion**
Pachyptila salvini

French: Prion de Salvin   **German:** Kleiner Entensturmvogel   **Spanish:** Pato-petrel de Salvin
Other common names: Lesser Broad-billed/Little Broad-billed/Medium-billed/Marion Island Prion, Whalebird

Taxonomy. *Prion vittatus salvini* Mathews, 1912, Marion Island.
Often included in *P. vittata*. Race *macgillivrayi* has been ascribed to *P. vittata*; may be intermediate form. Two subspecies normally recognized.
Subspecies and Distribution.
P. s. macgillivrayi (Mathews, 1912) - Amsterdam and St Paul Is.
P. s. salvini (Mathews, 1912) - Prince Edward Is, Crozet Is.

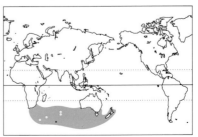

Descriptive notes. 25-28 cm; 168 g; wingspan 57-58 cm. Very similar to *P. desolata*, but has slightly less collar and bill longer and a little broader. Juvenile similar to adult with broader white tips to scapulars. Race *macgillivrayi* has broader bill and slightly longer wing.
Habitat. Marine, normally occurring offshore, except near colonies; outside breeding season occurs in areas of upwelling. Breeds on islands, usually inland on highland plateaus or on slopes with grass or shrubs; also in caves or crevices.
Food and Feeding. Mostly crustaceans, especially amphipods (*Themisto gaudichaudii*) and euphausiids; also squid and fish. Feeds largely by hydroplaning (see page 223); also by filtering and surface-seizing. Highly gregarious.
Breeding. Starts Oct. Forms huge colonies of up to 1,000,000+ birds; nests in burrows, often occupied by more than 1 pair. 1 egg; incubation 43-52 days; fledging 52-65 days.
Movements. Disperses widely over S Indian Ocean, ranging N to South Africa and Australia; some wander further E to New Zealand, apparently mostly immatures.
Status and Conservation. Not globally threatened. One of most numerous of all seabirds; 6,000,000-8,000,000 pairs at Crozet Is, and several hundred thousand pairs at Prince Edward Is. Main populations in Crozet nest on Est I, which is predator-free, and Cochons I, which has feral cats, but these too large to enter the prion burrows; islands should be declared reserve and human

access should be strictly limited. Heavy predation by rats and cats elsewhere has forced birds to establish new colonies above tree-line; cats formerly took vast numbers on Marion I (see page 231). Race *macgillivrayi* threatened by introduced rats and cats and deforestation. Despite large numbers, species breeds at few sites and introduction of rats at Est I would be disastrous; control or eradication of introduced predators desirable.

Bibliography. Adams & Brown (1984), Batchelor (1981), Berruti & Hunter (1986), Bretagnolle *et al.* (1990), Brown, L.H. *et al.* (1982), Brown, R.G.B. (1988b), Cox (1980), Fleming (1941a, 1941b), Gartshore *et al.* (1988), Harper (1980), Jouventin, Mougin *et al.* (1985), Jouventin, Stahl *et al.* (1984), Marchant & Higgins (1990), Mendelsohn (1981), Powlesland (1989), Roux *et al.* (1986), Thibault & Guyot (1988), Weimerskirch *et al.* (1985), Williams (1984).

42. Antarctic Prion
Pachyptila desolata

French: Prion de la Désolation   **German**: Taubensturmvogel   **Spanish**: Pato-petrel Antártico
Other common names: Dove Prion/Petrel, Bank's/Blue Dove-petrel, Dove-white Petrel, Whale-bird, Snowbird

Taxonomy. *Procellaria desolata* Gmelin, 1789, Desolation Island = Kerguelen Island.
Often included in *P. vittata*. Arrangement into subspecies highly confused, and populations apparently form cline; birds from Macquarie I sometimes placed in *alter*, or isolated in separate race *macquariensis*; birds from Heard I alternatively placed in *desolata*. Up to six subspecies variously accepted, but species may be best considered monotypic. Three subspecies normally recognized.
Subspecies and Distribution.
P. d. desolata (Gmelin, 1789) - Crozet, Kerguelen, Macquarie Is.
P. d. alter (Mathews, 1912) - Auckland, Heard Is.
P. d. banksi A. Smith, 1840 - Scotia Arc, South Georgia, South Sandwich Is; Scott I (Antarctica).

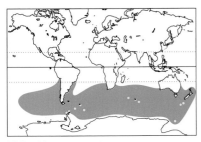

Descriptive notes. 25-27 cm; 150-160 g; wingspan 58-66 cm. Central portion of under-tail black, as in *P. belcheri*, but with thicker black terminal bar; incomplete dark grey pectoral band broad and distinctive. Juvenile as adult. Races supposedly separable on width of bill and length of wings and tail.
Habitat. Marine and highly pelagic, occurring in cold waters normally to N of pack ice; generally keeps away from land except at colonies. Breeds on slopes under grass tussocks, in rock crevices or scree, or on cliffs.
Food and Feeding. Mostly crustaceans, especially krill (*Euphausia superba*), copepods
(*Calanoides acutus*) and also amphipods (*Themisto*); small quantities of fish and squid. Feeds largely by surface-seizing; also filtering, hydroplaning and dipping.
Breeding. Normally starts Nov, but occasionally delayed by abundant snow. Forms dense colonies; nests in burrows, crevices or cracks. 1 egg; incubation 44-46 days, with stints of 1-5 days; chicks have blue-grey down, brooded for 3-5 days; fledging 45-55 days.
Movements. All birds leave colonies after breeding, probably moving N; species disperses widely over S Atlantic and S Indian Oceans, from pack ice to subtropical latitudes off S America, where recorded N to 12° S off Peru; also occurs off S Africa and Australia.
Status and Conservation. Not globally threatened. Abundant and widespread, with total population of many millions; c. 22,000,000 pairs at South Georgia, 2,000,000-3,000,000 pairs at Kerguelen. Some breeding islands free from predators; at South Georgia mainly breeds in areas without rats; cattle, pigs and Wekas affect numbers in places. Commercial exploitation of krill could have serious impact on populations, if excessive. Conservation aims are to preserve large populations, with protection of habitat and control or removal of introduced predators. Huge numbers do not imply total security or no need for protection.
Bibliography. Ainley *et al.* (1984), Batchelor (1981), Blake (1977), Bretagnolle *et al.* (1990), Brothers (1984), Brown *et al.* (1982), Cox (1980), Croxall *et al.* (1984), Fleming (1941a, 1941b), Fraser (1984), Fraser *et al.* (1988), Gartshore *et al.* (1988), Harper (1972, 1980), Jehl *et al.* (1979), Johnson (1965), Jouventin *et al.* (1985), Lindsey (1986), Marchant & Higgins (1990), Mougin (1985), Murphy (1936), Prince (1980a), Powlesland (1989), Ricklefs & Roby (1983), Serventy *et al.* (1971), Thomas (1986), Tickell (1962), Watson (1975), Weimerskirch, Zotier & Jouventin (1989), Woehler (1991), Woehler & Johnstone (1991), Zink (1981).

43. Fairy Prion
Pachyptila turtur

French: Prion colombe   **German**: Feensturmvogel   **Spanish**: Pato-petrel Piquicorto
Other common names: Fairy Dove/Blue/Dove/Gould Petrel, Short-billed/Narrow-billed Prion, Whalebird

Taxonomy. *Procellaria turtur* Kuhl, 1820, no locality.
Sometimes includes *P. crassirostris*, with which probably forms superspecies. Some authorities subdivide, accepting race *subantarctica* for populations to S of New Zealand. Monotypic.
Distribution. Subtropical and subantarctic, from Falkland Is and South Georgia eastwards through S Indian Ocean to SE Australia and New Zealand area.

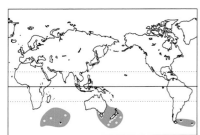

Descriptive notes. 23-28 cm; 90-175 g; wingspan 56-60 cm. Lacks blackish line behind eye. Bill relatively narrow with bulbous tip; thick black terminal band to tail. Closely resembles *P. crassirostris*. Juvenile as adult.
Habitat. Marine, apparently occurring mainly in offshore waters; may move inshore during stormy weather. Breeds in coastal sites on oceanic islands, occupying cliffs, rock falls and grassland with limited vegetation.
Food and Feeding. Mostly crustaceans, especially euphausiids (*Nyctiphanes australis*, *Euphausia superba*), but also copepods (*Rhincalanus gigas*) and amphipods (*Themis-*
to gaudichaudii); occasionally some fish or squid. Feeds mainly by surface-seizing and dipping; less often by surface-plunging and pattering. Often associates with other prions and storm-petrels when feeding around fishing boats.
Breeding. Starts Sept. Highly colonial; nests in burrows. 1 egg; incubation c. 55 days (44-56), with stints of 1-7 days; chicks have pale brownish grey down, brooded for 2-4 days; fledging 43-56 days. Sexual maturity at 4-5 years.

Movements. Most birds leave vicinity of colony, probably moving N into subtropical waters; most common off Australia and South Africa in winter. Some may disperse only to seas adjacent to colonies; birds occur at colonies on Crozet Is throughout winter.
Status and Conservation. Not globally threatened. Total population probably numbers several million birds; over 1,000,000 birds in New Zealand, tens of thousands at Crozet Is. Some breeding islands have abundant predators; cats especially harmful, e.g. at Cochons I (Crozet) and formerly Marion I; tuataras (*Sphenodon punctatus*) cause considerable losses at many islands around New Zealand, e.g. Stephens I; skuas also take many, but unlikely to have significant effects on population. Some colonies affected by soil erosion, and fires during breeding season. Control or eradication of introduced predators desirable; some campaigns already under way.
Bibliography. Batchelor (1981), Berruti (1981a), Bretagnolle *et al.* (1990), Brothers (1984), Brown *et al.* (1982), Cox (1980), Croxall *et al.* (1984), Fitzgerald & Veitch (1985), Fleming (1941a, 1941b), Harper (1976, 1980), Imber (1981, 1983, 1984b), Jones (1937), Jouventin *et al.* (1985), Lindsey (1986), Marchant & Higgins (1990), Mendelsohn (1981), Morgan & Ritz (1982), Mougin (1985), Owenden *et al.* (1991), Powlesland (1989), Prince & Copestake (1990), Richdale (1944a), Robinson (1961), Strange (1968), Watson (1975), Weimerskirch, Zotier & Jouventin (1989), Woods (1988).

44. Fulmar Prion
Pachyptila crassirostris

French: Prion à bec épais **German**: Dickschnabel-Sturmvogel **Spanish**: Pato-petrel Picogrueso
Other common names: Thick-billed Prion

Taxonomy. *Pseudoprion turtur crassirostris* Mathews, 1912, Bounty Island. Sometimes placed in *P. turtur*, with which probably forms superspecies. Race *pyramidalis* formerly current, now absorbed by nominate. In past, population of *P. turtur* at Kerguelen mistakenly ascribed to present species. Two subspecies normally recognized.
Subspecies and Distribution.
P. c. crassirostris (Mathews, 1912) - Snares, Bounty, Chatham Is.
P. c. eatoni (Mathews, 1912) - Heard, Auckland Is.

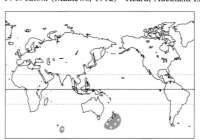

Descriptive notes. 24-28 cm; 99-147 g; wingspan 60 cm. Very similar to *P. turtur*, differing in shorter, stouter bill, "M" mark across upperparts broader and more conspicuous, and even wider black terminal bar to tail. Juvenile as adult, but can have white forehead. Race *eatoni* smaller, with slight differences in bill and tail.
Habitat. Marine, occurring in both pelagic and inshore waters. Breeds on coastal cliffs and boulder slopes, often without vegetation.
Food and Feeding. Mostly crustaceans, especially amphipods (*Hyperiella antarctica*, *Themisto antarctica*); also fish, squid and molluscs. Prey taken by surface-seizing and also shallow diving.
Breeding. Starts Oct. Colonial, sometimes alongside albatrosses; nests in rock crevices and cracks. 1 egg; chicks have grey down, white below; fledging mostly in Feb.
Movements. Largely sedentary, with adults roosting in nest virtually all year round, and regularly seen in surrounding waters. Unconfirmed records from Australia and South Africa.
Status and Conservation. Not globally threatened. Total population numbers c. 100,000 breeding pairs; 76,000 pairs of nominate race in Bounty Is; race *eatoni* numbers a few thousand pairs at various colonies. Some predation by skuas. Conservation priorities include elimination of introduced mammals, chiefly cats, rats and pigs, from breeding islands and also on adjacent islands that appear suitable for colonization; regular monitoring also required to discover trends and causes of any decrease.
Bibliography. Cox (1980), Fleming (1941a, 1941b), Harper (1980), Lindsey (1986), Marchant & Higgins (1990), Miskelly (1984), Powlesland (1987, 1989), Richdale (1965b), Robertson & Bell (1984), Robertson & van Tets (1982), Watson (1975), Woehler (1991), Williams (1984a).

45. Slender-billed Prion
Pachyptila belcheri

French: Prion de Belcher **German**: Dünnschnabel-Sturmvogel **Spanish**: Pato-petrel Picofino
Other common names: Narrow-billed/Thin-billed Prion

Taxonomy. *Heteroprion belcheri* Mathews, 1912, Geelong, Victoria.
Might hybridize with *P. desolata* at Kerguelen, though evidence largely circumstantial, based mainly on overlap in bill structure. Monotypic.
Distribution. Noir I (off S Chile), Falkland Is; Crozet, Kerguelen Is.

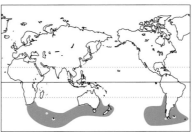

Descriptive notes. 25-26 cm; 150 g; wingspan 56 cm. Most distinctive of prions, with slender bill, black line behind eye, and longer white supercilium than other masked species; also has long blackish bar up centre of under-tail, and narrow black terminal band to upper-tail incomplete, as outer tail feathers whitish. Juvenile similar to adult.
Habitat. Marine and pelagic, but during breeding often feeds inshore or in shallow offshore waters, sometimes in areas of upwelling. Breeds in coastal areas, with soft or stony soil and low vegetation.
Food and Feeding. Mostly crustaceans, with heavy dependence on amphipods (*Themisto gaudichaudii*), but also some euphausiids; takes some small squid and fish. Feeds mainly by surface-seizing, dipping and pattering. Mainly feeds at night; gregarious.
Breeding. Starts Oct. Loosely colonial; nests in burrows. 1 egg; incubation 46-47 days, with stints of 4-9 days; chicks have grey down; fledging 43-54 days.
Movements. Disperses widely over Southern Ocean after breeding, absent Mar-Sept; birds from Falklands apparently move W, gathering in large flocks off W South America, and ranging N to 15° S; Indian Ocean birds move E, occurring regularly off Australia and New Zealand, but few records off S Africa.
Status and Conservation. Not globally threatened. Total population over 1,000,000 pairs; 1,000,000 pairs at Falklands, 700,000-1,000,000 pairs at Kerguelen. Largest known colony on New I (Falklands) has suffered heavy predation by cats; rats also abundant, as are rabbits in tussock

grass habitat where species breeds; recent elimination of introduced predators and revegetation apparently causing increase and expansion. Est I (Crozet Is) has neither cats nor rats but supports only small colony, presumably due to competition for nest-sites with superabundant *P. salvini*; population at Kerguelen suffers predation by cats. Colony on Noir I, off S Chile, reportedly large but no figures available. Skuas (*Catharacta*) dig birds out of burrows, especially in areas of soft peat. More information required on population sizes, trends and main threats; eradication of all alien fauna from breeding islands recommended.

Bibliography. Batchelor (1981), Blake (1977), Bretagnolle *et al.* (1990), Brothers (1984), Cox (1980), Croxall *et al.* (1984), Fleming (1941a, 1941b), Hamilton (1951), Harper (1972, 1980), Johnson (1965), Jouventin *et al.* (1985), Lindsey (1986), Marchant & Higgins (1990), Murphy (1936), Powlesland (1989), Ruschi (1979), Sick (1984), Strange (1980), Watson (1975), Weimerskirch, Zotier & Jouventin (1989), Woods (1988).

Genus *BULWERIA* Bonaparte, 1843

46. Bulwer's Petrel

Bulweria bulwerii

French: Pétrel de Bulwer **German**: Bulwersturmvogel **Spanish**: Petrel de Bulwer

Taxonomy. *Procellaria Bulwerii* Jardine and Selby, 1828, Madeira.
Sometimes considered to include *B. fallax*. Monotypic.
Distribution. Pantropical: in E Atlantic, from Azores S to Cape Verde Is; in Pacific, from E China and Bonin Is E to Hawaii, Phoenix and Marquesas Is.

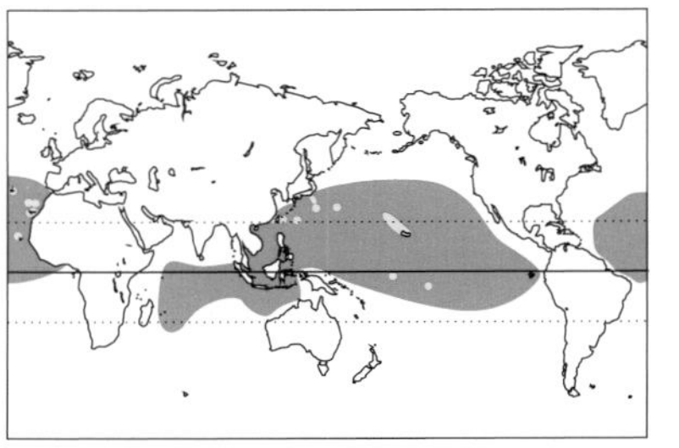

Descriptive notes. 26-28 cm; 78-130 g; wingspan 68-73 cm. Small head and pale bar across upperwing-coverts separate from similar species. Tail appears long, narrow and pointed, but is wedge-shaped when opened. Juvenile as adult.
Habitat. Marine and highly pelagic, usually far from land except at colonies. Breeds on barren offshore islands, occupying wide variety of habitats, from cliffs and boulder scree to sandy shores.
Food and Feeding. Mainly fish and squid, with minor proportions of crustaceans and sea-striders. Feeds largely at night by surface-seizing.
Breeding. Starts Apr/May. Colonial; nests in burrows, crevices, cracks or caves, under debris or vegetation cover. 1 egg; incubation c. 44 days, with stints of 8-14 days; chicks have blackish down; fledging c. 62 days.
Movements. Mostly absent from breeding grounds Sept/Oct-Mar. Disperses over tropical and subtropical waters: Pacific birds probably move into C and E Pacific, and also Indian Ocean, W to Maldives; Atlantic birds mostly move into W and S Atlantic, few reaching South Africa. Vagrant to Australia, British Isles and W Mediterranean.
Status and Conservation. Not globally threatened. Atlantic population thought to number several tens of thousands of breeding pairs; Pacific population must have over 100,000 breeding pairs, with estimate of over 400,000 birds in Hawaii. Heavy predation by cats and rats throughout range; large colony in Desertas Is (Madeira) suffers intense human exploitation for food or fish bait, as occurs at most other Atlantic sites, and several in Pacific; practice no longer affects large colony in Salvage Is, since declaration of islands as national park. Competition with commercial fisheries could prove significant at Hawaii. Barn Owl (*Tyto alba*) is significant predator in places. Conservation priorities include termination of all human exploitation and removal of alien predators.

Bibliography. Bannerman (1914), Bent (1922), Brazil (1991), Bretagnolle (1990a), Brown *et al.* (1982), Clapp & Wirtz (1975), Cheng Tso-hsin (1987), Cramp & Simmons (1977), Croxall *et al.* (1984), Etchécopar & Hüe (1978), Harrison (1990), Holyoak & Thibault (1984), James & Robertson (1985c), Jouanin *et al.* (1979), Marchant & Higgins (1990), Mougin (1989), de Naurois (1969b), Olson (1985b), Shallenberger (1984), Simpson (1973), Thibault & Holyoak (1978), Voous (1983), Zonfrillo (1986, 1988).

47. Jouanin's Petrel

Bulweria fallax

French: Pétrel de Jouanin **German**: Jouaninsturmvogel **Spanish**: Petrel de Jouanin

Taxonomy. *Bulweria fallax* Jouanin, 1955, north-western Indian Ocean, lat. 12° 30' N, long. 55° E.
Has been considered conspecific with *B. bulwerii*, but recent work suggests they are distinct species (see page 217). Monotypic.
Distribution. NW Indian Ocean, breeding grounds undiscovered; suspected to breed in Oman, either inland in desert mountains, or along coast, e.g. on Kuria Muria Is.

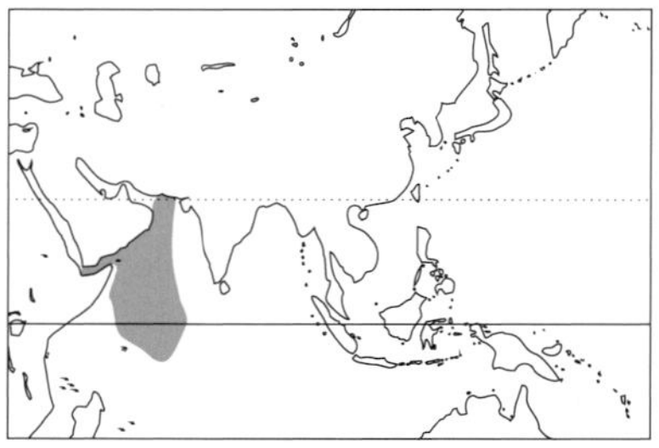

Descriptive notes. 30-32 cm; wingspan 76-83 cm. Larger version of *B. bulwerii*, with more robust head and bill; lacks pale upperwing bar, except in worn plumage, but never so conspicuous. Juvenile as adult.
Habitat. Marine and pelagic, mainly recorded far from land.
Food and Feeding. No information available.
Breeding. Virtually nothing known. Breeding grounds undiscovered; fledging in Nov/Dec.
Movements. Very little known. Recorded in S Red Sea, Gulf of Aden and well out into Arabian Sea; twice recorded S to Kenya. Exceptional cases of 3 birds in N Adriatic, and 1 bird captured in Hawaii.
Status and Conservation. Not globally threatened. Currently considered near-threatened. Breeding grounds as yet undiscovered, but sufficiently large numbers seen at sea to suggest population may be fairly healthy at present. Location of breeding grounds of primary importance, to enable study of biology, ecology and trends, and evaluation of possible threats.

Bibliography. Ali & Ripley (1978), Bailey (1966, 1968), van den Berg (1991), Bourne (1987b), Brown *et al.* (1982), Clapp (1971), Gallagher *et al.* (1984), Giol (1957), Hüe & Etchécopar (1970), Jouanin (1955, 1957), Olson (1975b, 1985b), van Oort (1912), Roberts (1991), Walker (1981), Zonfrillo (1988).

Genus *PROCELLARIA* Linnaeus, 1758

48. Grey Petrel

Procellaria cinerea

French: Puffin gris **German**: Grausturmvogel **Spanish**: Pardela gris
Other common names: Brown/Black-tailed/Bulky/Great Grey Petrel/Shearwater, Pediunker

Taxonomy. *Procellaria cinerea* Gmelin, 1789, within the Antarctic Circle = New Zealand seas, lat. 48° S.
Formerly isolated in monospecific genus *Adamastor*. Monotypic.
Distribution. Circumpolar in Southern Ocean, breeding from Tristan da Cunha and Gough I eastwards through S Indian Ocean to Campbell and Antipodes Is.

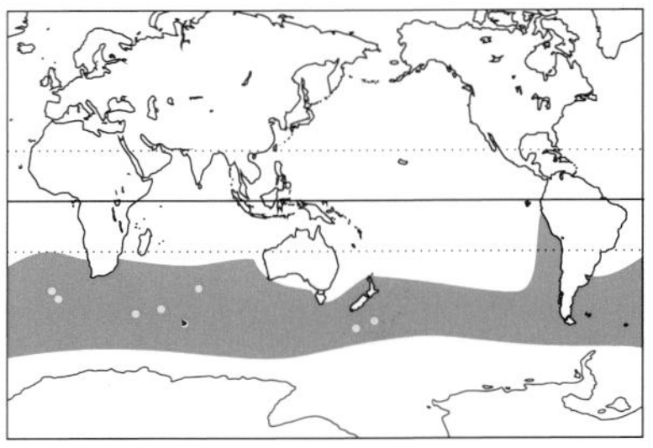

Descriptive notes. 48-50 cm; 900-1220 g; wingspan 115-130 cm. Bulky body. Distinctive pattern of whitish underbody contrasting with drab grey underwing and upperparts; slightly capped but transition to pale throat gradual. Female slightly smaller. Juvenile as adult.
Habitat. Marine and pelagic, occurring mainly in cold waters. Breeds on subantarctic islands, occupying steep vegetated slopes.
Food and Feeding. Mostly squid and fish, with some crustaceans, fish offal and galley refuse. Catches prey mainly by surface-seizing and pursuit-plunging. May feed alone or in large flocks; associates with cetaceans; regularly follows ships and scavenges around trawlers.
Breeding. Breeds in winter, starting Feb/Mar. Colonial; nests in burrows. 1 egg; incubation c. 52-61 days; chicks brooded for few hours; fledging 110-120 days.
Movements. Disperses over Southern Ocean, mostly 25°-60° S, but reaching subtropical zone by following cold Humboldt and Benguela Currents.
Status and Conservation. Not globally threatened. Total population size poorly known; 100,000's at Gough I, several thousand pairs at Prince Edward, Crozet and Kerguelen Is, 10,000-50,000 pairs at Campbell and Antipodes Is. Suffers much predation: notably by cats on Marion I until their recent eradication; rats take many chicks at Campbell I and Crozet Is; cats and Wekas probably caused extinction at Macquarie I; fair numbers also taken by skuas. Introduced predators represent main threat throughout range, and their elimination required at most sites; steps should also be taken to prevent their spread to other breeding islands. Small numbers breed at Tristan da Cunha on highland cliffs, but even there are probably subject to some human exploitation.

Bibliography. Barrat (1974), Bartle (1990), Blake (1977), Brooke, M. de L. (1986a), Brooke, R.K. (1984), Brown *et al.* (1982), Croxall *et al.* (1984), Despin (1976), Fraser *et al.* (1988), Imber (1983), Johnson (1965), Jouventin *et al.* (1985), Lindsey (1986), Marchant & Higgins (1990), Moors (1980), Murphy (1936), Newton & Fugler (1989), Palmer (1962), van Rensburg & Bester (1988), Richardson, M.E. (1984), Warham (1988b), Watson (1975), Weimerskirch, Zotier & Jouventin (1989), Woods (1988), Zotier (1990a).

49. White-chinned Petrel

Procellaria aequinoctialis

French: Puffin à menton blanc **German**: Weißkinn-Sturmvogel **Spanish**: Pardela Gorgiblanca
Other common names: Spectacled Petrel, Shoemaker

Taxonomy. *Procellaria aequinoctialis* Linnaeus, 1758, Cape of Good Hope.
Has been considered to include *P. parkinsoni* and *P. westlandica*. Four additional races have been proposed, but invalidated due to extensive individual variation. Two subspecies recognized.
Subspecies and Distribution.
P. a. aequinoctialis Linnaeus, 1758 - Falkland Is and South Georgia E through S Indian Ocean to Campbell and Antipodes Is.
P. a. conspicillata Gould, 1844 - Inaccessible I (Tristan da Cunha).

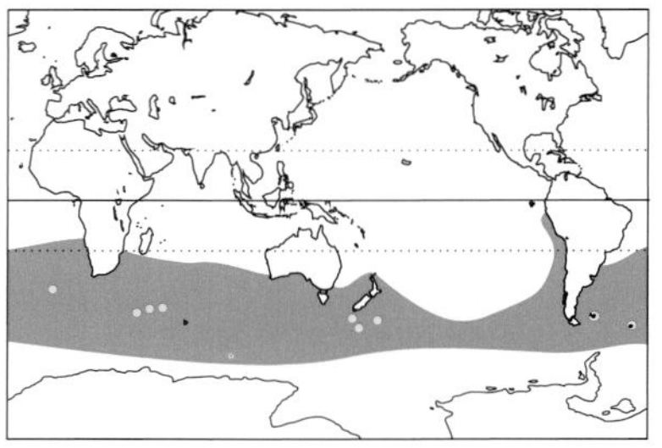

Descriptive notes. 51-58 cm; 1020-1420 g; wingspan 134-147 cm. Heavily built, especially around head and neck; legs project slightly beyond tip of tail. Bill pale with central part of culmen black. Chin ranges from white to dark. Very similar to smaller *P. parkinsoni* and *P. westlandica*, differing in heavy bill with bulbous tip and hunchbacked aspect. Female averages slightly lighter. Juvenile as adult. Race *conspicillata* has variable amounts of white on head, often irregularly distributed.
Habitat. Marine and pelagic; prefers offshore waters over continental shelf; frequents zones of convergence and upwelling. Breeds on subantarctic islands, occupying vegetated slopes or sometimes flat, waterlogged, peaty ground.
Food and Feeding. Mostly cephalopods (*Histioteuthis*, *Kondakovia*) with some crustaceans; fish and offal particularly important outwith breeding season. Feeds mainly by surface-seizing but also shallow dives and deep plunging. Regularly attends trawlers; also follows ships for refuse.
Breeding. Mostly starts Oct. Colonial; nests in burrows. 1 egg; incubation 57-62 days, with stints of 1-19 days; chicks have dark brown down, brooded for few hours; fledging 87-106 days.
Movements. Disperses widely over Southern Ocean, normally in zone c. 30°-55° S in Atlantic, Pacific and Indian Oceans; ranges N to c. 6° S following cold waters of Humboldt Current, and to c. 20° S following Benguela Current.
Status and Conservation. Not globally threatened. Total population presumably numbers several million birds; 2,000,000 breeding pairs at South Georgia, 100,000's at Kerguelen. Main threats include human exploitation, presumably responsible for low numbers breeding on Tristan da Cunha nowadays, and extinction from Chatham Is; also predation by cats, causing loss of large colony on Cochons I (Crozet Is) and considerable mortality on Marion I; rats significant predators too in places, e.g. Crozet Is, Campbell I. Maintenance of present numbers or recovery in places requires elimination of all alien predators, especially cats, from breeding islands. Suffers some predation by skuas and rats at several sites, but apparently without significant effects. Incidental mortality due to commercial fisheries may represent significant threat.

Bibliography. Berruti *et al.* (1985), Blake (1977), Bretagnolle & Thomas (1990), Brooke, M. de L. (1986a), Brown *et al.* (1982), Croxall *et al.* (1984), Fraser *et al.* (1988), García (1972), Griffiths (1982), Hagen (1952), Hall (1987), Humphrey *et al.* (1970), Imber (1983), Jackson (1986, 1988), Jackson & Ryan (1986), Jehl *et al.* (1979), Johnson (1965), Jouventin *et al.* (1985), Lindsey (1986), Marchant & Higgins (1990), Moors (1980), Mougin (1970c, 1971, 1985), Murphy (1936), Pinto (1983), Richardson, M.E. (1984), Rowan *et al.* (1951), Warham (1988b), Watson (1975), Weimerskirch, Jouventin *et al.* (1985), Weimerskirch, Zotier & Jouventin (1989), Woods (1988).

50. **Black Petrel**
Procellaria parkinsoni

French: Puffin de Parkinson   **German**: Schwarzsturmvogel   **Spanish**: Pardela de Parkinson
Other common names: Parkinson's Petrel, Black Fulmar

Taxonomy. *Procellaria parkinsoni* G. R. Gray, 1862, New Zealand.
Has been considered conspecific with *P. westlandica* and *P. aequinoctialis*. Monotypic.
Distribution. Little and Great Barrier Is, off NE North I, New Zealand.

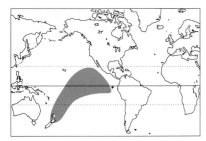

Descriptive notes. 46 cm; 680-720 g; wingspan 115 cm. Slightly smaller than *P. aequinoctialis*; wings narrower and body less robust; head more rounded, and weaker bill has black tip. Juvenile as adult.
Habitat. Marine and pelagic; usually occurs far from coast, avoiding inshore waters, except around colonies. Breeds on forested ridges in highlands.
Food and Feeding. Mostly cephalopods (*Ommastrephes bartrami*, *Histioteuthis*) with some fish and small proportions of crustaceans. Captures prey by surface-seizing; also dives and plunges. Feeds mainly by night. Often scavenges around trawlers; associates with other Procellariidae and also with cetaceans.
Breeding. Starts Nov. Colonial; nests in burrows amongst tree roots. 1 egg; incubation 56·5 days (1 record), with stints of c. 17 days; chicks have black down, probably brooded for under 1 day; fledging 96-122 days. Sexual maturity at c. 6-8 years. Known to have lived at least 17 years.
Movements. Migratory; most birds move E over C Pacific to W coasts of C and S America, where present Mar-Nov. Small numbers regularly occur off E Australia.
Status and Conservation. VULNERABLE. Total population now estimated at c. 1100 breeding pairs, c. 3300 birds. Slowly recovering after eradication of cats from Little Barrier I in 1980; heavy predation for over a century; cats killed 65% of all fledglings in 1972, 90% in 1973, and 100% in 1974 and 1975, as well as many adults; colony was in process of rapid decline, but saved when only a few hundred birds remained. Larger colony on Great Barrier I suffers little predation by cats and rats; a few may still be taken for food by Maoris. Formerly more widespread in New Zealand, breeding abundantly at several inland sites on North I, where subjected to human exploitation. Species saved from immediate extinction, but requires more suitable nesting habitat on other predator-free islands, to be able to build up adequate numbers; Great Barrier I seems suitable and efforts already being directed towards removal of cats. Some casualties amongst fledglings, when attracted to lights during first flight. Incidental mortality due to commercial fisheries may represent significant threat.
Bibliography. Chambers (1989), Collar & Andrew (1988), Imber (1976a, 1984d, 1985e, 1987), King (1978/79), Lindsey (1986), Marchant & Higgins (1990), Mountfort (1988), Murphy (1936), Pitman & Unitt (1981), Robertson & Bell (1984), Sibson (1982), Veitch (1985), Warham (1988b).

51. **Westland Petrel**
Procellaria westlandica

French: Puffin du Westland   **German**: Westlandsturmvogel   **Spanish**: Pardela de Westland
Other common names: Westland Black Petrel

Taxonomy. *Procellaria parkinsoni westlandica* Falla, 1946, Barrytown, Westland, South Island, New Zealand.
Has been considered conspecific with *P. parkinsoni* and *P. aequinoctialis*, but present species breeds in winter. Monotypic.
Distribution. NW South I (New Zealand).

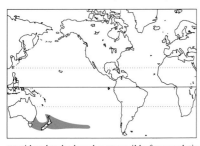

Descriptive notes. 50-55 cm; 800-1200 g; wingspan 135-140 cm. Similar to *P. aequinoctialis*, but has slightly lighter build; bill straighter with black tip. Juvenile as adult.
Habitat. Marine; during breeding occurs mostly in offshore waters; non-breeding distribution largely pelagic. Breeds in thick forest high on limestone bluffs.
Food and Feeding. Mostly cephalopods (*Histioteuthis*, *Teuthowenia pellucida*), with some fish (*Argentina*) and few crustaceans. Prey captured by surface-seizing, with some diving and plunging. Regularly attends trawlers, and increased availabilty of offal in recent years considered to be largely responsible for population recovery of species.
Breeding. Breeds in winter, starting Mar/Apr. Colonial; nests in burrows. 1 egg; incubation 57-65 days; chicks brooded for 1-2 weeks; fledging c. 120-140 days.
Movements. At close of breeding season birds migrate E of New Zealand into C Pacific, some reaching W South America; young birds may spend up to 10 years in zone of Humboldt Current. Small numbers cross Tasman Sea to E Australia; perhaps mainly young birds.
Status and Conservation. RARE. Total population estimated at 1000-5000 breeding pairs, possibly c. 20,000 birds. Main threats are predation by introduced mammals, especially cats, and intense timber milling activity in breeding area, with resultant clearings in forest and increased vulnerability to predators; some disturbance by birdwatchers noted. Combined effects of these two factors require further study to permit clarification of conservation requirements. Part of breeding grounds declared reserve; breeding population has subsequently increased from estimated c. 900 pairs in 1974, mainly attributable to increased availability of offal from trawlers. Enlargement of reserve necessary to include entire nesting area; cessation of all milling activities in area seems equally important.
Bibliography. Baker & Coleman (1977), Bartle (1985, 1987), Chambers (1989), Collar & Andrew (1988), Imber (1976a), Jackson (1958), King (1978/79), Lindsey (1986), Marchant & Higgins (1990), Mountfort (1988), Robertson & Bell (1984), Warham (1988b).

Genus *CALONECTRIS*   Mathews & Iredale, 1915

52. **Streaked Shearwater**
Calonectris leucomelas

French: Puffin leucomèle   **German**: Weißgesicht-Sturmtaucher   **Spanish**: Pardela Canosa
Other common names: White-faced/White-fronted/Streak-headed Shearwater

Taxonomy. *Procellaria leucomelas* Temminck, 1835, seas of Japan and Nagasaki Bay.
Monotypic.
Distribution. NE Japan, Izu and Ryukyu Is to Pescadores Is (Taiwan); islands off E China and Korea.

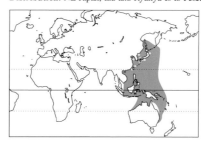

Descriptive notes. 48 cm; 440-545 g; wingspan 122 cm. Slender build; head small, with bill long and thin. Head mottled above giving way to pale forehead. In worn plumage can have white crescent at base of tail. Juvenile as adult.
Habitat. Marine and partly pelagic, also occurring over inshore waters. Typically breeds on offshore islands, occupying forested hills.
Food and Feeding. Mainly fish and squid. Prey captured by surface-seizing; also makes shallow plunges. Often associates with other seabirds, especially Procellariiformes. Follows fishing boats; attracted to anchovy crawls off Japan.
Breeding. Starts Mar. Colonial; nests in burrows. 1 egg; incubation c. 64 days; fledging c. 66-80 days.
Movements. Migrates S towards Australia: many ringing returns from Philippines; large flocks occur off New Guinea; recently found to be regular off N Australia, with some birds moving down W and E coasts to S Australia. Recorded E to California, and W to Sri Lanka and Maldive Is.
Status and Conservation. Not globally threatened. Abundant and widespread, with total population of several million birds; well over 1,000,000 pairs in Japan, under 150 pairs known in USSR. Human exploitation accounts for large numbers all over range, despite some protective laws; on many islands exploitation is traditional. Many birds die entangled in fishing nets; some predation by cats and rats. Protective measures required, e.g. effective legal protection of species, combined with programmes of environmental education; fishing activities could be made less harmful to birds with suitable regulations concerning areas, seasons, methods and gear.
Bibliography. Brazil (1991), Carter (1983), Coates (1985), Cheng Tso-hsin (1987), Etchécopar & Hüe (1978), Hasegawa (1984), Hayashi (1983), Jida *et al.* (1987), Lindsey (1986), Litvinenko & Shibaev (1991), Maesako (1985), Marchant & Higgins (1990), Melville (1984), Nakamura (1974), Okamoto (1972), Tan (1977), Yoshida (1962, 1973, 1981).

53. **Cory's Shearwater**
Calonectris diomedea

French: Puffin cendré   **German**: Gelbschnabel-Sturmtaucher   **Spanish**: Pardela Cenicienta
Other common names: Mediterranean/(North) Atlantic Shearwater

Taxonomy. *Procellaria diomedea* Scopoli, 1769, no locality; Tremiti Islands, Adriatic Sea.
Three subspecies recognized.
Subspecies and Distribution.
C. d. diomedea (Scopoli, 1769) - Mediterranean islands.
C. d. borealis (Cory, 1881) - Berlengas Is (WC Portugal) W to Azores and S to Canary Is.
C. d. edwardsii (Oustalet, 1883) - Cape Verde Is.

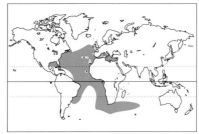

Descriptive notes. 45-48 cm; 560-730 g, *borealis* 817-956 g; wingspan 100-125 cm. More uniformly pale below than other similar species. Head more uniformly coloured than *C. leucomelas*; bill and overall aspect more robust. Can have pale crescent at base of tail. Juvenile as adult. Race *borealis* larger, with heavier bill; *edwardsii* smaller, with longer tail.
Habitat. Marine and pelagic, usually keeping well away from land, except at colonies. Breeds on barren offshore islands, occupying cliffs, caves and boulder fields; sometimes inland on rocky slopes.
Food and Feeding. Mostly fish, squid, crustaceans and offal. Feeds mainly by plunging and surface-seizing. Mainly nocturnal feeder.
Breeding. Starts Apr. Colonial; nests in burrows, rock crevices, natural hollows or cracks. 1 egg; incubation c. 54 days, with stints of c. 6 days; chicks have brown down, brooded for c. 4 days; fledging c. 97 days. Sexual maturity at 7-13 years.
Movements. Migratory. Mediterranean birds mostly come out into Atlantic, where move rapidly S; abundant off South Africa, occurring Nov-May. Race *borealis* winters off E coasts of N and S America, and probably in SW Indian Ocean, where species recorded in large numbers, Dec-Mar; vagrant to New Zealand. Race *edwardsii* also leaves breeding grounds, but winter quarters unknown.
Status and Conservation. Not globally threatened. Widespread and locally abundant, with total population numbering a few million birds; c. 500,000 pairs in Azores, 26,000+ pairs in Mediterranean. Mainly breeds in heavily populated areas and everywhere has suffered exploitation for food or fish bait, predation by introduced mammals, and a series of habitat modifications. Present location of colonies reflects degree of human pressure. In most areas human exploitation has ceased or is only occasional and some breeding islands have been declared reserves, where introduced predators may eventually be removed. Regular monitoring of colonies recommended.
Bibliography. Araujo *et al.* (1977), Bent (1922), Bretagnolle (1990a), Bretagnolle & Lequette (1990), Brichetti (1979), Brown, L.H. *et al.* (1982), Brown, R.G.B. (1990), Cramp & Simmons (1977), Croxall *et al.* (1984), Despin & Mougin (1988), Dymond *et al.* (1989), Finlayson (1992), Griffiths (1982), Guyot & Thibault (1988), Hamer & Read (1987), Haney & McGillivary (1985), Jouanin (1955), Jouanin & Roux (1966), Jouanin, Hémery *et al.* (1980), Jouanin, Roux & Mougin (1992), de Juana & Paterson (1986), de Juana *et al.* (1980), Lo Valvo & Massa (1988), Martin (1986), Massa & Lo Valvo (1986), Mayaud (1949-1950), Mayol (1986), Medmaravis & Monbailliu (1986), Michelot & Laurent (1988), Mougin & Stahl (1982), Mougin, Despin *et al.* (1987), Mougin, Jouanin & Roux (1987a, 1987b, 1987c, 1988a, 1988b, 1988c, 1990a), Mougin, Jouanin, Despin & Roux (1986), Mougin, Jouanin, Roux & Stahl (1984), Mougin, Roux *et al.* (1984a, 1984b), Mougin, Zino *et al.* (1986), de Naurois (1969b), Palmer (1962), Pulich (1982), Ristow & Wink (1980), Ristow *et al.* (1990), Round & Swann (1977), Sarà (1983), Tellería (1980), Thibault (1985), Vaughan (1980), Wink *et al.* (1982), Yésou (1982), Zino (1971, 1985), Zino *et al.* (1987).

inches 16
cm 40

PLATE 16

54

55

56

57 pale morph dark morph

58

59

60

61

62

63 ssp *mauretanicus*

64

65

66 ssp *auricularis*

ssp *newelli*

ssp *yelkouan*

67

68 ssp *assimilis*

68 ssp *boydi*

68 ssp *elegans*

69 ssp *lherminieri*

ssp *persicus*

70

Genus *PUFFINUS* Brisson, 1760

54. Pink-footed Shearwater

Puffinus creatopus

French: Puffin à pieds roses   **German**: Rosafuß-Sturmtaucher   **Spanish**: Pardela Patirrosa

Taxonomy. *Puffinus creatopus* Coues, 1864, San Nicolas Island, California.
Sometimes considered conspecific with *P. carneipes*, and may be merely pale phase at end of W-E cline; these two may form superspecies with *P. gravis*. Monotypic.
Distribution. Juan Fernández Is, breeding on Robinson Crusoe I (formerly Más a Tierra I), Santa Clara I and Morro Viñilla; Mocha I (off WC Chile).

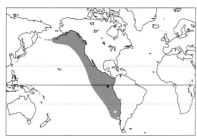

Descriptive notes. 48 cm; wingspan 109 cm. Robust. Polymorphic, with pale, dark and intermediate morphs; generally uniform greyish brown with underparts pale, mottled brown; extent of brown on underparts varies with morph. Bill flesh pink with dark tip. Pale morph of *P. pacificus* similar, but has dark bill and is cleaner white on underbody. Juvenile as adult.
Habitat. Marine and pelagic, preferring offshore waters over continental shelf. Breeds on oceanic islands, occupying hills or slopes, preferably forested.
Food and Feeding. Mostly fish and squid, with minor amounts of crustaceans. Feeds mainly by surface-seizing and pursuit-plunging.
Breeding. Starts Nov. Colonial; nests in burrows. 1 egg; fledging mostly in Mar/Apr.
Movements. Migrates up E Pacific to wintering areas off W coast of N America, some reaching Gulf of Alaska; returns by same route. Recorded NW to Hawaii and Line Is, and SW to SE Australia and New Zealand.
Status and Conservation. VULNERABLE. Size of population unknown, but presumably fairly numerous, given abundance in wintering zone; probably only a few thousand pairs remain in Juan Fernández Is; perhaps more abundant on Mocha I, off WC Chile. Decreasing at breeding grounds, mostly due to predation by coatis (*Nasua nasua*), with 30 found killed by one coati in single night in 1982; also predation by rats and cats. Elimination of such introduced fauna from breeding islands essential for this and other endemic petrel species; several eradication campaigns programmed by authorities of Juan Fernández National Park. Additional mortality in wintering zone, where birds die entangled in fishing gear.
Bibliography. Bent (1922), Blake (1977), Bourne *et al.* (1992), Brooke (1987a), Collar & Andrew (1988), Johnson (1965), Marchant & Higgins (1990), Murphy (1936), Palmer (1962), Schlatter (1984), Shallenberger (1984), Terres (1980).

55. Flesh-footed Shearwater

Puffinus carneipes

French: Puffin à pieds pâles   **German**: Blaßfuß-Sturmtaucher   **Spanish**: Pardela Paticlara
Other common names: Pale-footed Shearwater

Taxonomy. *Puffinus carneipes* Gould, 1844, small islands off Cape Leeuwin, Western Australia.
Sometimes considered conspecific with *P. creatopus*; these two may form superspecies with *P. gravis*. Birds from Lord Howe I and New Zealand may merit separation in race *hullianus*, on grounds of different migratory routes and slight size differences. Monotypic.
Distribution. St Paul I (S Indian Ocean) and SW Australia, with single isolated colony in South Australia; Lord Howe I (off E Australia) and North I (New Zealand).

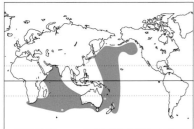

Descriptive notes. 40-45 cm; 580-765 g; wingspan 99-107 cm. Distinctive coloration of bill, pale horn with culmen and tip black. Differs from dark morph of *P. pacificus* in silvery primary bases on underwing. Juvenile as adult.
Habitat. Marine and pelagic; mainly in offshore waters over continental shelf. Breeds on vegetated hills or slopes facing sea.
Food and Feeding. Little known; squid and fish recorded. Prey mostly caught by pursuit-plunging; also uses surface-seizing and diving. Mostly diurnal feeder.
Breeding. Starts Sept/Oct. Colonial; nests in burrows. 1 egg; incubation (probably overestimated) c. 60 days; chicks have grey down, brooded for 2-3 days; fledging c. 92 days.
Movements. Migratory. Ringing results show that birds from Lord Howe I move N to winter off E Korea Apr-Jul; New Zealand population assumed to follow same route, but all ringing recoveries from within 645 km of colonies; species occurs N to Sea of Okhotsk, and in small numbers off N America. Another population, believed to be W breeders, winters in Indian Ocean, mostly in Arabian Sea, some birds occurring SW to South Africa; record of large numbers in Indonesia suggests at least some of W breeders may winter in Pacific.
Status and Conservation. Not globally threatened. Total population must number several hundred thousand birds; estimated c. 20,000-40,000 breeding birds on Lord Howe I. Main threat is rate of destruction of natural breeding habitat, dense forest on low flat ground or gentle slopes on offshore islands; birds now being displaced to higher ground. Tourism also contributes to local destruction of coastal sites. Suffers some predation by rats, cats, skinks, foxes and in past pigs; some human

exploitation in past. Maintenance of present numbers would be favoured by creation of reserves on offshore islands, with human access restricted; eradication of introduced predators also desirable.
Bibliography. Ali & Ripley (1978), Bent (1922), Brazil (1991), Brooke (1987a), Brown *et al.* (1982), Coates (1985), Croxall *et al.* (1984), Johnson (1965), Lindsey (1986), Marchant & Higgins (1990), Palmer (1962), Roux (1985), Shallenberger (1984), Warham (1958b), Watson (1975).

56. Great Shearwater

Puffinus gravis

French: Puffin majeur   **German**: Großer Sturmtaucher   **Spanish**: Pardela Capirotada
Other common names: Greater Shearwater

Taxonomy. *Procellaria Gravis* O'Reilly, 1818, Cape Farewell and Staten Hook to Newfoundland.
May form superspecies with *P. creatopus* and *P. carneipes*. Monotypic.
Distribution. Nightingale and Inaccessible Is (Tristan da Cunha), Gough I; Kidney I (Falkland Is).

Descriptive notes. 43-51 cm; 715-950 g; wingspan 100-118 cm. Unique combination of fairly pale underparts with poorly defined dark patch on belly. White band across uppertail-coverts and also across hindneck, emphasizing strongly capped appearance. Juvenile similar but greyer with paler fringes to feathers.
Habitat. Marine, frequenting cool offshore and pelagic waters. Breeds on sloping ground, mainly in areas of tussock grass or *Phylica* woodland.
Food and Feeding. Mostly fish, squid and fish offal; also some crustaceans. Prey taken mainly by plunge-diving from height of 6-10 m; also uses pursuit-diving and surface-seizing. Attends trawlers, sometimes in large numbers.
Breeding. Starts Oct. Highly colonial; nests in burrows or crevices among boulders. 1 egg; incubation 53-57 days; chicks have bluish grey down; fledging c. 105 days.
Movements. Transequatorial migrant. After breeding, moves NW to reach NE Canada in Jul/Aug; subsequently moves E, turning down past Britain and Iberia, and returning S towards breeding islands. Small numbers winter in S Hemisphere.
Status and Conservation. Not globally threatened. Abundant, with enormous total population; minimum 5,000,000 breeding pairs at Tristan da Cunha, 600,000-3,000,000 pairs at Gough I (1970), small numbers in Falklands. Highly restricted breeding range, with only 4 sites known. A few thousand adults and c. 50,000 chicks taken annually from uninhabited Nightingale I by Tristan islanders; such levels of exploitation could lead to collapse of population, and establishment of quota system recommended, to allow for rational exploitation. Research required into impact of harvesting, importance of other causes of mortality and population dynamics, in order to determine maximum sustainable levels of exploitation.
Bibliography. Bent (1922), Blake (1977), Broekhuysen (1948), Brooke (1988), Brown, L.H. *et al.* (1982), Brown, R.G.B. (1988a), Brown, R.G.B. *et al.* (1981), Collins & Tikasingh (1974), Cramp & Simmons (1977), Croxall *et al.* (1984), Fraser *et al.* (1988), Gräfe (1973), Griffiths (1982), Hagen (1952), Jehl *et al.* (1979), Johnson (1972), Lee & Grant (1986), Marchant & Higgins (1990), Martin (1986), Mayaud (1949-1950), Mees (1976), Murphy (1936), Richardson, M.E. (1984), Palmer (1962), Rowan (1952), Ruschi (1979), Ryan *et al.* (1990), Sick (1984), Stresemann & Stresemann (1970), Swales (1965), Thom (1986), Voous (1970, 1983), Voous & Wattel (1963), Watson (1971b, 1975), Woods (1970, 1988).

57. Wedge-tailed Shearwater

Puffinus pacificus

French: Puffin fouquet   **German**: Keilschwanz-Sturmtaucher   **Spanish**: Pardela del Pacífico

Taxonomy. *Procellaria pacifica* Gmelin, 1789, Pacific Ocean; restricted to Kermadec Island.
Several subspecies proposed, but considerable individual variation disrupts patterns. May form superspecies with *P. bulleri*. Monotypic.
Distribution. Tropical and subtropical Indian and Pacific Oceans: in Indian Ocean, breeds from Madagascar area E to W Australia; in Pacific, breeds from Japan S to E Australia, and E to Revillagigedo Is (off W Mexico), Marquesas Is and Pitcairn I.

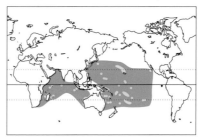

Descriptive notes. 38-46 cm; 300-570 g; wingspan 97-105 cm. Long wedge-shaped tail. Polymorphic: dark morph separable from *P. carneipes* by dark primary bases on underwing; pale morph distinctive, white below with mottling on underwing and flanks. Bill colour varies from whitish to dark grey. Juvenile as adult.
Habitat. Marine and pelagic, rarely approaching land except at colonies; frequents inshore waters off E Australia. Breeds mostly on offshore islands or atolls, typically occupying flat ground, slopes, plateaux or cliff tops, in areas of forest or grassland.
Food and Feeding. Mostly fish (Mullidae) with some cephalopods (Ommastrephidae); also insects and crustaceans in minor quantities. Feeds largely on wing, by dipping; also uses pursuit-plunging and surface-seizing. Around schooling fish often congregates with other seabirds, especially terns and boobies, and also with dolphins. Often attends trawlers and smaller fishing boats.
Breeding. Season very variable; mostly during local summer at extreme N and S of range. Colonial, often alongside other Procellariidae; nests in burrows. 1 egg; incubation c. 50-54 days; chick has ash-grey down, brooded for 2-3 days; fledging c. 100 days.
Movements. Some populations apparently largely sedentary, especially in tropics; others at extreme N and S of range tend to migrate to warm waters of tropical and subtropical Pacific and Indian Oceans, many crossing equator; regular N to Gulf of Aden and S off S Africa.

On following pages: 58. Buller's Shearwater (*Puffinus bulleri*); 59. Sooty Shearwater (*Puffinus griseus*); 60. Short-tailed Shearwater (*Puffinus tenuirostris*); 61. Christmas Shearwater (*Puffinus nativitatis*); 62. Manx Shearwater (*Puffinus puffinus*); 63. Yelkouan Shearwater (*Puffinus yelkouan*); 64. Hutton's Shearwater (*Puffinus huttoni*); 65. Black-vented Shearwater (*Puffinus opisthomelas*); 66. Townsend's Shearwater (*Puffinus auricularis*); 67. Fluttering Shearwater (*Puffinus gavia*); 68. Little Shearwater (*Puffinus assimilis*); 69. Audubon's Shearwater (*Puffinus lherminieri*); 70. Heinroth's Shearwater (*Puffinus heinrothi*).

Status and Conservation. Not globally threatened. Abundant and widespread, with total population of well over 1,000,000 breeding pairs. Numbers greatly reduced from former levels, with main causes including: direct exploitation by man, e.g. commercially significant harvesting of young birds in Seychelles and elsewhere in past; predation by alien fauna, with some local extinctions caused by cats, rats, dogs, foxes, pigs and mongooses; and destruction of nesting habitat by grazing rabbits and goats, leading to soil erosion. Competition with commercial fisheries may also be significant threat, as species relies heavily on tuna to drive fish prey up to the surface.

Bibliography. Ackerman *et al.* (1980), Ali & Ripley (1978), Bailey (1968), Beehler *et al.* (1986), Bent (1922), Blake (1977), Brazil (1991), Bregulla (1992), Brown *et al.* (1982), Clapp & Wirtz (1975), Coates (1985), Croxall *et al.* (1984), Dyer & Hill (1991), Everett & Anderson (1991), Feare (1984b), Gould (1967), Harrison (1990), Hill & Barnes (1989), Holyoak & Thibault (1984), Howell & Bartholomew (1961b), Jenkins (1979), King (1974), Langrand (1990), Lindsey (1986), Marchant & Higgins (1990), Milon *et al.* (1973), Munro (1940), Murphy (1936, 1951), de Naurois (1978), Pettit *et al.* (1984), Reichel (1991), Schreiber & Ashmole (1970), Shallenberger (1973, 1984), Swanson & Merritt (1974), Terres (1980), Whittow *et al.* (1987).

58. **Buller's Shearwater**

Puffinus bulleri

French: Puffin de Buller **German**: Graumantel-Sturmtaucher **Spanish**: Pardela Dorsigrís
Other common names: Grey-backed/New Zealand Shearwater

Taxonomy. *Puffinus bulleri* Salvin, 1888, New Zealand.
May form superspecies with *P. pacificus*. Monotypic.
Distribution. Poor Knights Is and perhaps two other islands off NE North I, New Zealand.

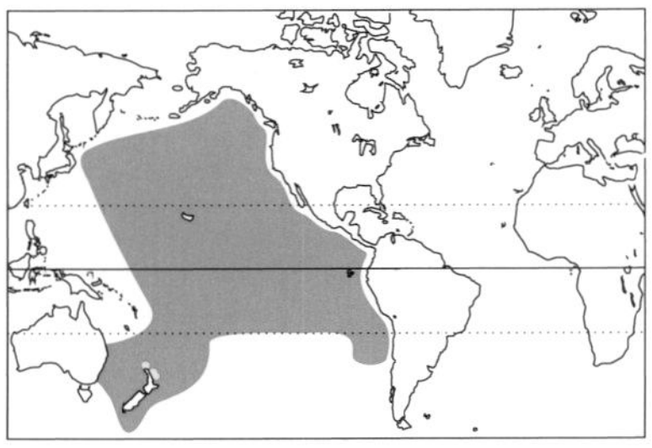

Descriptive notes. 46-47 cm; 342-425 g; wingspan 97-99 cm. Striking white underparts; distinctive pattern on upperparts makes it unmistakable, given quite different build from *Pterodroma*. Juvenile as adult.
Habitat. Marine and pelagic, showing marked preference for waters around Subtropical Convergence. Nests on densely forested slopes, or on cliffs or stacks.
Food and Feeding. Mostly fish, squid and crustaceans (*Nyctiphanes australis*). Feeds mainly by surface-seizing and dipping; rarely dives and plunges. May feed more at night than other shearwaters. Associates with other feeding Procellariidae; occasionally attends trawlers and smaller, fishing boats.
Breeding. Starts Oct. Colonial; nests in burrows or rock crevices or under roots. 1 egg; incubation c. 51 days, with stints of c. 4 days; chicks have grey down; fledging perhaps c. 100 days.
Movements. Transequatorial migrant. Most birds move N to winter in subarctic waters of Pacific; subsequently move S down W coast of N America, with large numbers off S California in Aug. Some, probably mostly immatures, spend breeding season in winter quarters, ranging S to Chile. Single record from N Atlantic, 1 bird off New Jersey, USA.
Status and Conservation. Not globally threatened. Total population estimated at 2,500,000 birds; c. 200,000 pairs on Aorangi I (Poor Knight Is). Intensely exploited for food by Maoris in past; also suffered heavy predation by feral pigs, but these removed from Aorangi in 1936, when declared reserve. In 1938 Aorangi population numbered c. 100 pairs, but has recently undergone spectacular increase; numbers still rising slightly, but restriction of entire breeding population to few islands renders species vulnerable to accidental introduction of alien predators. Species should be encouraged to colonize new areas.

Bibliography. Chambers (1989), Guzman & Myres (1983), Harper (1983), Harper & Imber (1985), Jenkins (1974, 1988), Johnson (1965), Lindsey (1986), Marchant & Higgins (1990), Murphy (1936), Nakamura & Hasegawa (1979), Palmer (1962), Robertson & Bell (1984), Shallenberger (1984), Sleptsov (1960), Terres (1980), Wahl (1985, 1986), Wohl (1975).

59. **Sooty Shearwater**

Puffinus griseus

French: Puffin fuligineux **German**: Dunkler Sturmtaucher **Spanish**: Pardela Sombría
Other common names: Sombre Petrel/Shearwater

Taxonomy. *Procellaria grisea* Gmelin, 1789, Southern Hemisphere between 35° S and 50° S = New Zealand. Monotypic.
Distribution. S Chile and Falkland Is; SE Australia and New Zealand area.

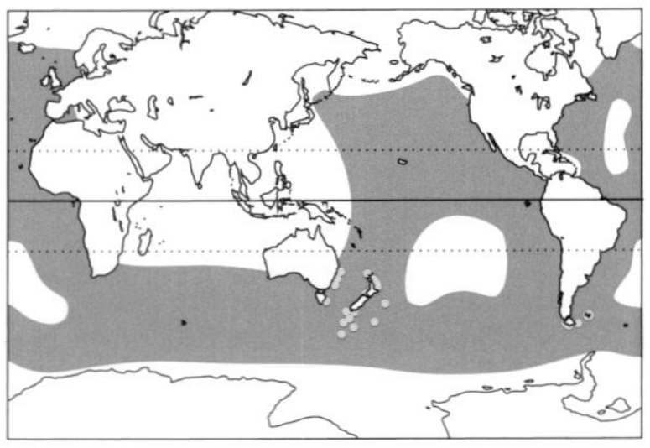

Descriptive notes. 40-51 cm; 650-978 g; wingspan 94-109 cm. All dark except for variable amount of white on underwing. Stocky build. Juvenile as adult.
Habitat. Marine; generally occurs in cold offshore and pelagic waters. Breeds on slopes, often covered with dense vegetation, mainly near sea but also inland, up to 1500 m above sea-level.
Food and Feeding. Mainly small shoaling fish, cephalopods (*Onychoteuthis*, *Gonatus*, *Loligo opalescens*) and crustaceans, proportions varying with season and locality; fish include anchovies (*Engraulis*), spawning capelin (*Mallotus villosus*), young of *Helecolenus*/*Neosebastes* and *Cololabis saire*. Feeds mainly by pursuit-plunging and diving, sometimes also by surface-seizing and hydroplaning. Frequently associates in large numbers with other seabirds, especially other Procellariiformes, penguins and terns. Birds sometimes attend trawlers, probably mostly juveniles.
Breeding. Starts Oct. Highly colonial; nests in burrows. 1 egg; incubation 53-56 days, with stints of 4-9 days; chicks have smoky grey down with paler underparts, brooded for 2-3 days; fledging 86-106 days. Sexual maturity probably at 5-9 years.
Movements. Transequatorial migrant, moving into N Pacific (where more abundant) and N Atlantic. Large numbers first head into NW sector of respective ocean, then progressively move E following prevailing winds to reach W coasts of N America and Europe late in local summer; many thus complete wide loop before returning to breeding islands. Most S American birds may move fairly directly up and down W coasts of Americas. Some birds remain in Southern Ocean over winter.
Status and Conservation. Not globally threatened. Abundant and widespread, with total population of several million birds. Probably 2,750,000 breeding pairs on Snares Is (1970/71). Only petrel species that can legally be sold in New Zealand area; important commercial exploitation, with up to 250,000 young taken yearly by local Maoris, mostly for food but also for soap and oil. Some predation by alien fauna, including cats, rats, pigs and Wekas. Several thousand birds drown in gill-nets in N Pacific each year. As with other abundant species that suffer high mortality due to man, numbers should be monitored so that any significant decreases can be detected in time. Elimination of introduced predators from breeding islands recommended.

Bibliography. Ainley *et al.* (1984), Bent (1922), Blake (1977), Brazil (1991), Bretagnolle & Thomas (1990), Briggs & Chu (1986), Brothers (1984), Brown, L.H. *et al.* (1982), Brown, R.G.B. (1988a), Brown, R.G.B. *et al.* (1981), Cramp & Simmons (1977), Chambers (1989), Croxall *et al.* (1984), Duffy (1983c), Fraser *et al.* (1988), García (1972), Griffiths (1982), Humphrey *et al.* (1970), Huyskens & Maes (1971), Jackson (1988), Jehl (1974), Johnson (1965), King *et al.* (1979), Lindsey (1986), Marchant & Higgins (1990), Murphy (1936), Ogi (1982, 1984), Oka *et al.* (1987), Palmer (1962), Phillips (1963), Pinto (1983), Richdale (1944c, 1963), Shallenberger (1984), Tasker *et al.* (1987), Thom (1986), Wahl (1980/81), Warham & Wilson (1982), Warham *et al.* (1982), Watson (1975), Woods (1988).

60. **Short-tailed Shearwater**

Puffinus tenuirostris

French: Puffin à bec grêle **Spanish**: Pardela de Tasmania
German: Kurzschwanz-Sturmtaucher
Other common names: Slender-billed Shearwater/Petrel, Tasmanian Muttonbird

Taxonomy. *Procellaria tenuirostris* Temminck, 1835, seas north of Japan and shores of Korea. Monotypic.
Distribution. Tasmania and S Australia (bulk of population in SE).

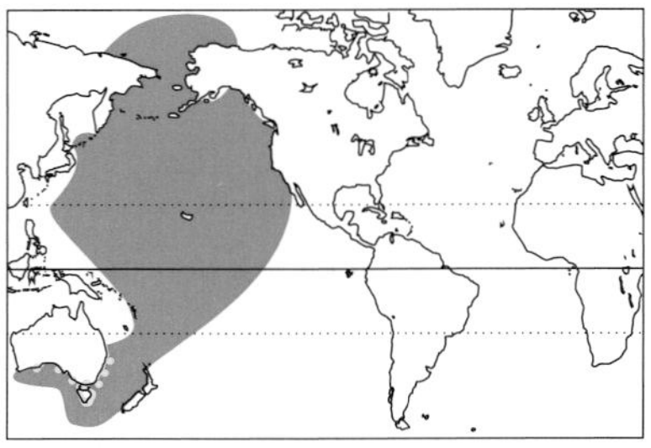

Descriptive notes. 40-45 cm; 480-800 g; wingspan 95-100 cm. Female slightly smaller. Similar to *P. griseus*, but underwing greyer, normally lacking white, though variable to some degree; bill shorter. Juvenile as adult.
Habitat. Marine; occurring in inshore, offshore and, to lesser degree, pelagic waters. Breeds mainly on coastal islands, typically in areas of grassland or other vegetation, but sometimes on cliffs or bare ground.
Food and Feeding. Fish (*Mallotus villosus*, *Ammodytes hexapterus*), crustaceans (*Nyctiphanes australis*, *Thyssanoessa raschii*, *Calanus cristatus*) and cephalopods (*Nototodarus gouldi*); proportions vary with season and locality. Feeds mainly by pursuit-plunging and surface-diving; other techniques include surface-seizing and hydroplaning. Feeds in flocks of up to 20,000 birds. Associates with cetaceans.
Breeding. Starts Oct. Markedly colonial; nests in burrows, with up to 2·4 burrows/m^2. 1 egg; incubation 52-55 days, with stints of 10-14 days; chicks have dark grey down, paler on underparts; brooded for 2-3 days; fledging c. 94 days (88-108). Sexual maturity at 4-6 years in males, and 5-7 years in females. Known to have lived to at least 30 years old.
Movements. Transequatorial migrant. After breeding most birds move N past Japan to winter off Aleutian Is, some moving N of Bering Strait; return route over C Pacific, some moving down W coast of N America. Apparently some regular movement into N Indian Ocean.
Status and Conservation. Not globally threatened. Abundant and widespread, with total population estimated at c. 23,000,000 birds at over 160 known breeding stations; population of Tasmania may number 5,600,000 pairs. Subject to commercial exploitation for food, down, oil and fat, with over 600,000 chicks harvested annually (see page 229); commercial activity now regulated but continues to flourish; trampling of burrows causes significant losses. Predation by introduced mammals, especially cats, responsible for some local extinctions, perhaps in combination with intense human pressure. Also suffers great mortality in N Pacific, especially off Japan, as many tens of thousands die each year entangled in gill-nets set for salmon. Maintenance of present numbers or recovery of huge former levels only possible with reduction of "useless" mortality; this demands elimination of introduced predators from breeding islands, and regulation of fishing equipment to prevent drowning of birds.

Bibliography. Bent (1922), Bradley, Skira & Wooller (1991), Bradley, Wooller *et al.* (1989, 1990), Brazil (1991), Bretagnolle & Thomas (1990), Callister (1991), Ford (1989), Harris & Bode (1981), Johnson (1965), Jones (1936), Kerry *et al.* (1983), King (1984), King *et al.* (1979), Lill & Baldwin (1983), Lindsey (1986), Marchant & Higgins (1990), Marshall & Serventy (1956, 1959), Montague *et al.* (1987), Morgan (1982), Morgan & Ritz (1982), Naarding (1980, 1981), Norman (1970, 1985), Ogi (1984), Ogi *et al.* (1980), Oka (1986, 1989), Oka & Maruyama (1986), Oka *et al.* (1987), Palmer (1962), Richdale (1948), Serventy (1963, 1967, 1974), Serventy & Curry (1984), Shallenberger (1984), Skira (1979, 1991), Skira *et al.* (1985), Sugimori *et al.* (1985), Terres (1980), van Tets & Fullagar (1984), Wahl (1980/81), Warham (1960), Watson (1975), Wooller *et al.* (1988, 1990).

61. **Christmas Shearwater**

Puffinus nativitatis

French: Puffin de la Nativité **Spanish**: Pardela de la Christmas
German: Weihnachtssturmtaucher
Other common names: Black Shearwater

Taxonomy. *Puffinus (Nectris) nativitatis* Streets, 1877, Christmas Island, Pacific Ocean. Monotypic.
Distribution. C Pacific, from Hawaii S to Phoenix Is, and thence E to Marquesas Is and Easter I.
Descriptive notes. 35-38 cm; 324-340 g; wingspan 71-81 cm. Uniformly dark, recalling *P. pacificus*, but smaller with rounded tail; smaller than *P. tenuirostris* and *P. carneipes*, with underparts uniformly dark. Juvenile as adult.
Habitat. Marine and pelagic; occurs over warm waters, generally keeping away from land, except near colonies. Breeds on oceanic islands, occupying slopes, often among rocks or in lava fields.
Food and Feeding. Mostly fish and squid, with only minor proportions of crustaceans. Feeds mainly by pursuit-plunging and pursuit-diving; also surface-seizes. Feeds in association with other shearwaters and also noddies (*Anous*).
Breeding. Season variable, starting in Mar in Hawaii. Colonial; nests in rock crevices or under dense vegetation. 1 egg; incubation 50-54 days; chick brooded for c. 7 days; fledging c. 96 days.
Movements. Presumably disperses over tropical and subtropical waters, though some populations are probably largely sedentary. After breeding, birds from Easter I may move E to coastal Peru.

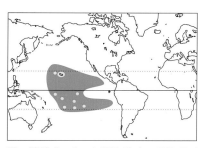

Status and Conservation. Not globally threatened. Widespread, with total population numbering several tens of thousands of breeding pairs; exact size of population, trends and conservation requirements very poorly known. Main threats are apparently direct human exploitation of eggs and chicks, and predation by introduced mammals on breeding islands, e.g. rabbits on Laysan and Lisianski Is, rats on Midway I (Hawaii). In many island groups, population under 1000 pairs and declining, which could lead to local extinctions unless corrective measures taken.

Bibliography. Ashmole & Ashmole (1967), Clapp & Wirtz (1975), Croxall *et al.* (1984), Harrison (1990), Harrison *et al.* (1983), Holyoak & Thibault (1984), Howell & Bartholomew (1961b), Johnson (1972), Marchant & Higgins (1990), Ricklefs (1984), Shallenberger (1984).

62. **Manx Shearwater**

Puffinus puffinus

French: Puffin des Anglais   Spanish: Pardela Pichoneta
German: Schwarzschnabel-Sturmtaucher

Taxonomy. *Procellaria puffinus* Brünnich, 1764, Faeroes and Norway.
Closely allied to *P. yelkouan*, *P. huttoni*, *P. opisthomelas*, *P. auricularis* and *P. gavia*, all of which have been considered races of present species. Monotypic.
Distribution. N Atlantic: islets off Massachusetts and Newfoundland; S Iceland S through Faeroes and British Isles to NW France; Azores though Madeira and Desertas Is to Canary Is.

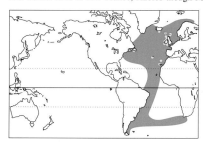

Descriptive notes. 30-38 cm; 350-575 g; wingspan 76-89 cm. Upperparts uniform blackish, contrasting sharply with white underbody and most of underwing; does not have white sides to rump. Juvenile as adult.
Habitat. Marine, occurring mainly on waters over continental shelf. Breeds on coastal or offshore islands or promontories, occupying flat hill tops or slopes, occasionally inland in mountainous terrain.
Food and Feeding. Mainly small shoaling fish (*Clupea harengus*, *Sprattus sprattus*) also some squid, crustaceans and offal. Feeds mainly by pursuit-plunging and pursuit-diving; also by surface-seizing. Normally feeds alone or in small flocks.
Breeding. Starts Mar. Colonial; nests in burrows. 1 egg; incubation 47-55 days, with stints of c. 6 days; chicks have grey-brown down, brooded for 2-3 days; fledging 62-76 days. Sexual maturity at 5-6 years. Annual mortality of adults 10%; average life span of adults estimated c. 10 years; known to have reached 30 years old in wild.
Movements. Transequatorial migrant. Most birds winter off E coast of S America, 10°-50° S; also occurs off South Africa. Small numbers may stray into Pacific; vagrant to Australia and New Zealand.
Status and Conservation. Not globally threatened. Widespread, with total population estimated at c. 250,000-300,000 breeding pairs. Numbers relatively stable in N of range, but considerable human exploitation continues at Azores and Madeira. Suffers predation by rats and cats on many islands. Rabbits compete for burrows, but also provide new ones; their grazing causes significant soil erosion, especially on arid islands. Several breeding islands are now bird sanctuaries, with regular control of introduced fauna.
Bibliography. Batten *et al.* (1990), Baxter & Rintoul (1953), Blake (1977), Brooke (1978a, 1978b, 1978c, 1978d, 1978e, 1986b, 1990), Brown *et al.* (1982), Cramp *et al.* (1974), Cramp & Simmons (1977), Croxall *et al.* (1984), Curtis *et al.* (1985), Harris (1965, 1966, 1972), Hernández *et al.* (1990), James (1985, 1986a), Lloyd *et al.* (1991), Lockley (1930, 1942), Matthews (1954), Mayaud (1931), Mazzeo (1953), Murphy (1936, 1952), Palmer (1962), Perrins (1966), Perrins & Brooke (1976), Perrins *et al.* (1973), Richards (1990), Sharrock (1976), Storey (1984), Storey & Grimmer (1986), Storey & Lien (1985), Tasker *et al.* (1987), Terres (1980), Thom (1986), Thomson (1965), Walker *et al.* (1990), Wormell (1976).

63. **Yelkouan Shearwater**

Puffinus yelkouan

French: Puffin de Méditerranée   Spanish: Pardela Mediterránea
German: Mittelmeer-Sturmtaucher

Other common names: Mediterranean Shearwater; Levantine Shearwater (*yelkouan*); Balearic Shearwater (*mauretanicus*)

Taxonomy. *Procellaria Yelkouan* Acerbi, 1827, the Bosphorus, opposite Bujukdere.
Often placed in *P. puffinus*. Sometimes split into two species. Two subspecies recognized.
Subspecies and Distribution.
P. y. yelkouan (Acerbi, 1827) - S France and E Algeria to Turkey and Bulgaria.
P. y. mauretanicus Lowe, 1921 - Balearic Is (W Mediterranean).

Descriptive notes. 30-40 cm; 349-416 g; wingspan 76-93 cm. Similar to *P. puffinus*, but upperparts paler, less clearly demarcated from pale underparts, with brownish wash, especially on flanks and undertail-coverts; in flight, feet project beyond shorter tail. Underwing paler than in *P. puffinus*. Juvenile as adult. Race *mauretanicus* larger and often darker below.
Habitat. Marine; mostly inshore waters. Breeds mainly on coastal or offshore islets or islands, but on occasions some distance inland from coast; sometimes nests on cliffs.
Food and Feeding. Mostly small shoaling fish (*Engraulis encrasicolus*) and squid. Feeds mainly by pursuit-plunging and pursuit-diving. Forms large feeding flocks. Attends trawlers.

Breeding. Starts Jan (*mauretanicus*) or Feb (*yelkouan*). Colonial; nests in rock crevices or ledges in caves. 1 egg; incubation c. 52 days; chick has slaty grey down, paler underneath; fledging c. 72 days.
Movements. Migratory. Race *yelkouan* apparently moves NE into Black Sea and disperses around Mediterranean, perhaps occurring in good numbers W to Gibraltar. Race *mauretanicus* tends to leave Mediterranean: moves N to coast of France and North Sea, but some birds move S towards South Africa; part of population fairly sedentary.
Status and Conservation. Not globally threatened. Balearic population small, estimated at 1800-2500 breeding pairs, though counts at sea suggest possibly more numerous; size of Levantine population not well known, but thought to number several thousand pairs. In past species suffered heavy persecution for eggs, meat and fat of chicks and for use as fish bait, causing many local declines. Main threats now are predation by rats and feral cats, and tourism, which leads to disturbance and habitat destruction. Research on breeding numbers, population trends and conservation requirements needed, especially in E Mediterranean.
Bibliography. Araujo *et al.* (1977), Ash & Rooke (1954), Baccetti (1989), Borg & Zammit (1986-87), Bourne *et al.* (1988), Brichetti (1979), Cade (1983), Cramp & Simmons (1977), Curtis *et al.* (1985), Finlayson (1992), Guyot & Thibault (1988), Huyskens & Maes (1971), de Juana (1984a, 1984b), de Juana & Paterson (1986), Mayaud (1932), Mayol (1986), Michelot & Laurent (1988), Nicholson (1952), Paz (1987), Vidal (1985), Yésou (1985, 1986), Yésou *et al.* (1990).

64. **Hutton's Shearwater**

Puffinus huttoni

French: Puffin de Hutton   German: Huttonsturmtaucher   Spanish: Pardela de Hutton

Taxonomy. *Puffinus reinholdi huttoni* Mathews, 1912, Snares Island.
Sometimes considered race of *P. puffinus*. Until quite recently, regularly placed in *P. gavia*. Monotypic.
Distribution. NE South I (New Zealand).

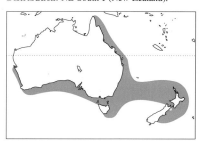

Descriptive notes. 36-38 cm; 365 g; wingspan 72-90 cm. Similar to *P. yelkouan mauretanicus*, but whitish on rear part of flanks extends upwards and is visible from above; bill weaker and underwing pale in centre only. Juvenile has whiter chin and throat.
Habitat. Marine; prefers waters over continental shelf, mainly offshore. Breeds well inland on mountain slopes 1200-1800 m above sea-level, in areas with tussock grass or scrub.
Food and Feeding. Mostly small fish (Clupeidae, Myctophidae) and crustaceans (*Nyctiphanes australis*). Prey mainly caught by plunge-diving and surface-diving. Apparently diurnal feeder for most part.
Breeding. Starts Sept. Colonial; nests in burrows. 1 egg; incubation estimated 50-60 days; chicks have mid-grey down; fledging estimated c. 80 days.
Movements. Migrates across Tasman Sea to Australia, where some birds apparently move up E coast while others follow S and then W coasts; birds may perform clockwise or anti-clockwise circumnavigation of Australia, although no evidence of extensive passage through Torres Strait.
Status and Conservation. Not globally threatened. Population little known; c. 160,000 breeding pairs at site in NE South I; only 2 sites known. Further surveys needed to locate undiscovered breeding grounds, and to determine trends and conservation requirements. Habit of breeding on mainland at inland sites makes species subject to considerable predation by introduced mammals, especially mustelids. Feral goats, deer and chamois commonly graze on unstable grassy slopes where burrows located, causing soil erosion and habitat destruction, as well as occasional trampling; increased hunting of mammals since 1970 has reduced scale of problem.
Bibliography. Chambers (1989), Halse (1981), Harrow (1965, 1976, 1985), Lindsey (1986), Marchant & Higgins (1990), Robertson & Bell (1984), Serventy *et al.* (1971), Tarburton (1981), Warham (1981), West & Imber (1985).

65. **Black-vented Shearwater**

Puffinus opisthomelas

French: Puffin culnoir   German: Schwarzsteiß-Sturmtaucher   Spanish: Pardela Culinegra

Taxonomy. *Puffinus opisthomelas* Coues, 1864, Cape San Lucas, Baja California.
Sometimes considered race of *P. puffinus*. Monotypic.
Distribution. Islands off W coast of Baja California.

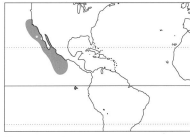

Descriptive notes. 30-38 cm; wingspan 76-89 cm. Similar to *P. yelkouan mauretanicus*, but underwing shows dark primaries; differs from *P. huttoni* especially in dark vent, and underparts more irregularly marked with dirty brownish. Juvenile as adult.
Habitat. Marine; mainly in warm inshore waters. Breeds on offshore islets, sometimes in caves.
Food and Feeding. Very little known. Mostly small shoaling fish.
Breeding. Starts Jan. Colonial; nests in burrows or caves. 1 egg; fledging mostly in Jun/Jul.
Movements. Disperses mostly N up W coast of N America to C California and rarely as far as British Columbia; some birds move S, with record of 288 birds just N of Galapagos Is.
Status and Conservation. Not globally threatened. Currently considered near-threatened, due to reduced breeding range and apparently small numbers; rough estimate of 2500 breeding pairs on Guadalupe I, 250-500 pairs at San Benito Is, and 5000-10,000 pairs on Natividad I. Substantial predation by cats, especially on Natividad I; possibly some incidental mortality related to recent development of gill-net fishery. Species poorly known and research needed to determine population size and extent of breeding range, present trends and conservation requirements; evidence already available indicates that protection and management of breeding islands essential, especially with elimination of introduced predators.
Bibliography. Croxall *et al.* (1984), Everett (1988), Everett & Anderson (1991), Jehl (1984), Jehl & Everett (1985), Shallenberger (1984).

66. Townsend's Shearwater

Puffinus auricularis

French: Puffin de Townsend   **German**: Townsendsturmtaucher   **Spanish**: Pardela de Townsend
Other common names: Newell's Shearwater (*newelli*)

Taxonomy. *Puffinus auricularis* C. H. Townsend, 1890, Clarión Island, Revillagigedo Group.
Sometimes considered race of *P. puffinus*. Race *newelli* has been classified as separate species.
Two subspecies recognized.
Subspecies and Distribution.
P. a. newelli Henshaw, 1900 - Hawaii.
P. a. auricularis C. H. Townsend, 1890 - Revillagigedo Is (off W Mexico).

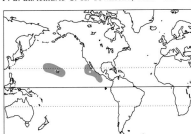

Descriptive notes. 31-35 cm; wingspan 76-89 cm. Marked contrast between dark brown upperparts and underparts mainly whitish. From above, differs from *P. puffinus* in white of flanks extending up onto sides of rump; from below, differs in blackish vent and undertail-coverts, and larger dark patch on sides of upper breast. Juvenile as adult. Race *newelli* slightly longer-winged, has vent and undertail-coverts white, and different form of black patch on sides of breast; blackish above as in *P. puffinus*, from which differs in white extending even more conspicuously onto sides of rump than in nominate race.

Habitat. Marine, occurring in warm subtropical offshore and pelagic waters. Breeds on islands, occupying mountain slopes; in Hawaii, areas with covering of ferns.
Food and Feeding. Little known; presumably mostly small fish and squid.
Breeding. Starts Mar/Apr. Colonial; nests in burrows. 1 egg; fledging mostly in Oct/Nov.
Movements. Little known; thought to disperse to adjacent seas; recorded S to waters just N of Galapagos Is.
Status and Conservation. VULNERABLE. Mexican population considered Endangered; restricted to Revillagigedo Is, with breeding only known on Socorro I (c. 1000 pairs) and Clarión I; suffers severe predation by feral cats at former and nest destruction and predation by c. 1000 feral pigs at latter; situation precarious. Hawaiian race *newelli*, sometimes considered separate species, classified as Vulnerable; population estimated at 4000-6000 breeding pairs; predation by cats, rats, pigs, mongooses and Barn Owls (*Tyto alba*) has seriously reduced numbers, causing some local extinctions, and species now restricted to Kauai I. Additional problem caused by street lights, which attract fledglings to built up areas where they suffer increased mortality; partial solution with programme based on public co-operation and c. 10,000 fledglings retrieved and released safely at sea in 15 years. Research needed to determine size and trends of populations and also conservation requirements; elimination of all introduced predators from present and former breeding islands is high priority, especially for Mexican population.
Bibliography. Bent (1922), Byrd *et al.* (1984), Collar & Andrew (1988), Everett & Anderson (1991), Harrison (1990), Harrison *et al.* (1984), Jehl (1982, 1984), King (1978/79), King & Gould (1967), Pratt *et al.* (1987), Shallenberger (1984), Sincock & Swedberg (1969), Terres (1980), Vincent (1966).

67. Fluttering Shearwater

Puffinus gavia

French: Puffin volage   **German**: Flattersturmtaucher   **Spanish**: Pardela Gavia
Other common names: Brown-beaked/Forster's Shearwater/Petrel

Taxonomy. *Procellaria gavia* J. R. Forster, 1844, Queen Charlotte Sound, New Zealand.
Sometimes considered race of *P. puffinus*. Until quite recently included *P. huttoni*. Monotypic.
Distribution. Islands off NE North I and in Cook Strait (New Zealand).

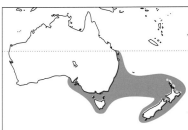

Descriptive notes. 31-37 cm; 225-425 g; wingspan 76 cm. Recalls *P. huttoni*, with similar incipient dark band at hind part of flanks, but slightly smaller; on underwing, primaries and axillaries paler; throat also paler, extending up behind ear-coverts. Upperparts have rusty tone in worn plumage. Juvenile as adult.
Habitat. Marine; more frequent than other shearwaters on inshore waters, frequenting small bays and harbours; only pelagic during migration. Breeds on coastal islands, occupying slopes, cliffs and rocky beaches, often with grass, shrubs or trees.
Food and Feeding. Little known; mainly small fish (*Engraulis*, *Sardinops*) and crustaceans (*Nyctiphanes australis*). Prey taken by pursuit-plunging, pursuit-diving and sometimes surface-seizing. Often associates with *P. carneipes* and *P. bulleri*, and also with Silver Gulls (*Larus novaehollandiae*).
Breeding. Starts Sept. Colonial; nests in burrows. 1 egg; fledging occurs mostly in Jan.
Movements. Partial migrant. Adults apparently fairly sedentary; immatures cross Tasman Sea to winter off SE Australia, where some stay over summer. Rarely occurs E to Chatham Is.
Status and Conservation. Not globally threatened. Total population unknown, but may number several hundred thousand breeding pairs; poorly known, although breeds on comparatively accessible islands. Partial decline in N of range due to competition with larger, more aggressive *P. bulleri*. Some human exploitation in past. Suffers some predation by introduced mammals, especially rats and cats; elimination of these from breeding islands recommended. Further research required on population size, trends and conservation requirements.
Bibliography. Bregulla (1992), Harper (1987), Imber (1985f), Lindsey (1986), Marchant & Higgins (1990), Robertson & Bell (1984), Schodde & Tideman (1988), Tarburton (1981).

68. Little Shearwater

Puffinus assimilis

French: Puffin semblable   **German**: Kleiner Sturmtaucher   **Spanish**: Pardela Chica
Other common names: Allied/Dusky Shearwater

Taxonomy. *Puffinus assimilis* Gould, 1838, New South Wales = Norfolk Island.
Sometimes considered to include *P. lherminieri* and *P. heinrothi*. Race *boydi* should perhaps be ascribed to former. Eight subspecies normally recognized.
Subspecies and Distribution.
P. a. baroli (Bonaparte, 1857) - Azores S to Canary Is.
P. a. boydi Mathews, 1912 - Cape Verde Is.
P. a. tunneyi Mathews, 1912 - islands off SW Australia.
P. a. assimilis Gould, 1838 - Lord Howe I, Norfolk I.
P. a. kermadecensis Murphy, 1927 - Kermadec Is.
P. a. haurakiensis Fleming & Serventy, 1943 - islands off NE North I (New Zealand).
P. a. elegans Giglioli & Salvadori, 1869 - Tristan da Cunha, Gough I; Chatham, Antipodes Is.
P. a. myrtae Bourne, 1959 - Rapa I in Austral Is (SC Pacific).

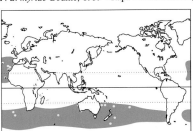

Descriptive notes. 25-30 cm; 170-275 g; wingspan 58-67 cm. Small; small bill. Similar coloration to *P. puffinus*, but white of face extends up around eye. Juvenile as adult. Races differ on colour of undertail-coverts and darkness of upperparts, which vary from brown to black; race *elegans* has black extending down face well below eye.
Habitat. Marine, occurring over warm, tropical and subtropical waters; often pelagic, but more frequent on inshore waters than other shearwaters. Breeds on offshore or oceanic islands on grassy slopes or amongst rocks, up to 15 km inland.
Food and Feeding. Poorly known. Squid, fish and crustaceans, including krill. Feeds mainly by pursuit-diving, pursuit-plunging and surface-diving; also by surface-seizing. Apparently mainly diurnal feeder.
Breeding. Mostly during local summer. Colonial; nests in burrows or rock crevices or among boulders. 1 egg; incubation 52-58 days, with stints of c. 2 days; chicks have variable grey down; fledging 70-75 days.
Movements. Most populations considered fairly sedentary, and birds may visit colonies throughout year; some dispersal, probably mostly of immatures. Race *elegans* thought to be partly migratory, with some birds from Antipodes Is moving E to coastal Chile.
Status and Conservation. Not globally threatened. Widespread and locally abundant, but few precise data; several races number only a few thousand breeding pairs, or perhaps tens of thousands; c. 100,000 pairs at Curtis I (Kermadec Is). Main threats include direct human exploitation for eggs or meat or for use as fish bait, and introduced predators, which account for many eggs, chicks and adults; many local populations may become extinct in near future, e.g. at Raoul I (Kermadecs), due to predation by rats and feral cats. Recommended measures include elimination of alien predators from breeding islands and cessation of all human exploitation.
Bibliography. Bannerman (1914), Blake (1977), Bourne (1959), Bretagnolle (1990a), Brown *et al.* (1982), Chambers (1989), Cramp & Simmons (1977), Croxall *et al.* (1984), Curtis *et al.* (1985), Dymond *et al.* (1989), Fraser (1984), Fraser *et al.* (1988), Glauert (1946), Holyoak & Thibault (1984), Imber (1983, 1985g), James (1986b), James & Alexander (1984), James & Robertson (1985a), Johnson (1972), Jouanin (1964a), Lindsey (1986), Marchant & Higgins (1990), Moors (1980), Murphy (1936), de Naurois (1969b), Palmer (1962), Richardson, M.E. (1984), Ryan *et al.* (1990), Sinclair *et al.* (1982), Swales (1965), Warham (1955), Watson (1975).

69. Audubon's Shearwater

Puffinus lherminieri

French: Puffin d'Audubon   **German**: Audubonsturmtaucher   **Spanish**: Pardela de Audubon
Other common names: Dusky-backed Shearwater; Bannerman's Shearwater (*bannermani*); Persian Shearwater (*persicus*); Baillon's Shearwater (*bailloni*)

Taxonomy. *Pufflnus* [sic] *Lherminieri* Lesson, 1839, Antilles.
Sometimes placed in *P. assimilis*; often includes *P. heinrothi*. Races *bannermani* and *persicus* may be distinct species. Race *P. assimilis boydi* often ascribed to present species. Ten subspecies normally recognized.
Subspecies and Distribution.
P. l. lherminieri Lesson, 1839 - Bahamas, West Indies; formerly Bermuda.
P. l. loyemilleri Wetmore, 1959 - SW Caribbean.
P. l. subalaris Ridgway, 1897 - Galapagos Is.
P. l. dichrous Finsch & Hartlaub, 1867 - C Pacific.
P. l. gunax Mathews, 1930 - Banks Is in Vanuatu (New Hebrides).
P. l. bannermani Mathews & Iredale, 1915 - Bonin and Volcano Is.
P. l. bailloni (Bonaparte, 1857) - Mascarene Is.
P. l. nicolae Jouanin, 1971 - NW Indian Ocean, from Aldabra to Maldives.
P. l. persicus Hume, 1873 - Kuria Muria Is (Arabian Sea).
P. l. temptator Louette & Herremans, 1985 - Mohéli I (Comoro Is).

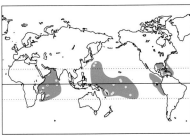

Descriptive notes. 27-33 cm; 150-230 g; wingspan 64-74 cm. Slightly larger than *P. assimilis*, with longer tail, longer, more pointed wings, larger bill and pink legs; less white on face and more brownish on underwing. Juvenile as adult. Races separated on slight differences in coloration, measurements and proportions; race *persicus* slightly larger, with longer bill and darker underwing and flanks.
Habitat. Marine; normally in offshore waters, but also pelagic and near land in vicinity of colonies; gathers in area of upwelling off SE Arabia. Breeds on oceanic islands, coral atolls and rocky offshore islets, occupying cliffs and earthy slopes.
Food and Feeding. Mainly fish, squid and crustaceans. Prey caught by pursuit-diving and pursuit-plunging, pattering and surface-seizing. Sometimes joins other feeding seabirds; occasionally attends small fishing boats.
Breeding. Season and length of cycle variable with locality. Colonial; nests in rock crevices or burrows. 1 egg; incubation 49-51 days, with stints of 2-10 days; chicks have greyish down above, white underneath, brooded for 3-7 days; fledging 62-75 days. Sexual maturity at c. 8 years. One bird ringed as adult known to have lived 11 years more.

Movements. Little known. Adults thought to be largely sedentary; immatures probably more dispersive. Vagrant to S Africa, Australia and NE Canada.

Status and Conservation. Not globally threatened. Widespread and locally abundant, with total population of several tens of thousands of breeding pairs. Intense human exploitation in past, which continues in places. Sedentary habits render distinct small populations more vulnerable to human exploitation and predation by introduced mammals; together with habitat destruction, these factors responsible for some local extinctions and near-extinctions.

Bibliography. Ali & Ripley (1978), Bailey (1966, 1968), Bent (1922), Blake (1977), Bourne (1960), Bregulla (1992), Brazil (1991), Brown *et al.* (1982), Croxall *et al.* (1984), Curtis *et al.* (1985), Furniss (1983), van Halewyn & Norton (1984), Harris (1969d), Holyoak & Thibault (1984), Jouanin (1987), Marchant & Higgins (1990), Murphy (1936), de Naurois (1978), Palmer (1962), Richardson (1990), Roberts (1991), Snow (1965a), Voous (1983), Wetmore (1965).

70. **Heinroth's Shearwater**

Puffinus heinrothi

French: Puffin de Heinroth   **German**: Heinrothsturmtaucher   **Spanish**: Pardela de Heinroth

Taxonomy. *Puffinns* [sic] *heinrothi* Reichenow, 1919, Blanche Bay, New Britain.
Often included in *P. lherminieri* and sometimes also in *P. assimilis*. Monotypic.

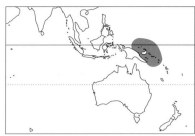

Movements. No information available.

Status and Conservation. INDETERMINATE. Very poorly known; breeding grounds not yet discovered. Research should be directed towards location of breeding grounds, and determining size of population, trends and most urgent conservation requirements.

Bibliography. Beehler *et al.* (1986), Coates (1985), Collar & Andrew (1988), Garnett (1984), Hadden (1981), King (1978/79), Mountfort (1988).

Distribution. Probably breeds in New Britain and Solomon Is.

Descriptive notes. 27 cm. Small and dark; bill noticeably long and slender, iris brown or blue; underbody brownish, usually with some white, but very variable. Underwing partly whitish, recalling *P. lherminieri*. Juvenile as adult.

Habitat. Marine, presumably pelagic. Probably breeds inland, as two birds reported in mountainous country on Bougainville I, Solomons.

Food and Feeding. No information available.

Breeding. No information available. No nests located to date.

Class AVES
Order PROCELLARIIFORMES
Family HYDROBATIDAE (STORM-PETRELS)

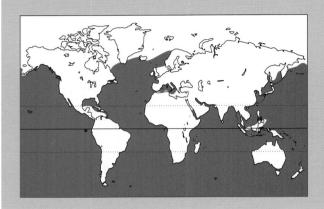

- Small, light, "tubenosed" seabirds with long legs and rounded wings, or shorter legs and more pointed wings.
- 13-26 cm.

- Cosmopolitan, in all oceans.
- Marine, mainly offshore and pelagic.
- 8 genera, 20 species, 36 taxa.
- 3 species threatened; 1 species extinct since 1600.

Systematics

The storm-petrels form a compact group of small species with a high degree of adaptation to aerial life in a marine environment. They represent a distinct evolutionary branch that must have differentiated from the rest of the petrels at an early stage, and are generally regarded as one of the most primitive families within the order Procellariiformes. Few fossil remains have been found, and to date storm-petrels can only be traced back to the Upper Miocene in California.

The family is often divided into two subfamilies, Oceanitinae and Hydrobatinae, which indicate their separate areas of origin in opposing hemispheres. It has been suggested that the group of northern genera, the Hydrobatinae, may have originated as a result of colonization of the north by some southern species, and one of the best candidates is Wilson's Storm-petrel (*Oceanites oceanicus*), a transequatorial migrant that winters abundantly in the Northern Hemisphere. The family has alternatively been called Oceanitidae, in order to emphasize the greater antiquity of the southern group, although this has yet to be proved definitively.

The southern subfamily Oceanitinae shows great taxonomic diversity, and the seven species commonly recognized are generally arranged into no less than five genera, of which three, *Garrodia*, *Pelagodroma* and *Nesofregetta* are monotypic. Of the remaining two genera, *Oceanites* comprises two distinct species, each with two subspecies, whereas the complicated genus *Fregetta* comprises about six distinct forms, which are usually grouped into two sibling species, but are occasionally treated as conspecific.

In the northern subfamily Hydrobatinae, the 13 species commonly recognized are normally grouped into three genera, of which two, *Hydrobates* and *Halocyptena*, are monotypic. The large genus *Oceanodroma* contains the remaining 11 species, which are distributed mainly throughout the Pacific Ocean, although two also breed in the Atlantic and two more are non-breeding visitors to the Indian Ocean.

There is still a great deal to be decided about storm-petrel taxonomy. For example, the validity of the genus *Halocyptena* has been much questioned lately, and it may be better to consider its sole species, the Least Storm-petrel (*Halocyptena microsoma*), a member of *Oceanodroma*. At least three of the currently accepted species in *Oceanodroma* may be no more than subspecies of others. Again, the Mediterranean population of the European Storm-petrel (*Hydrobates pelagicus*) may form a distinct subspecies, *melitensis*, but the differences in morphological aspects are generally regarded as insufficient to justify this.

Subdivision of the Hydrobatidae.

[Figure: Juan Varela]

Morphological Aspects

Storm-petrels are small to very small seabirds, ranging in length from 13 to 26 cm, with a wingspan of 32-56 cm. The wings are thus much shorter in relation to body length than in many other petrels, particularly the albatrosses, gadfly-petrels and shearwaters. They are, however, much broader and more appropriate for powered flight. The Oceanitinae have shortish, rounded wings, usually square tails and long legs, which often project beyond the tail in flight. The Hydrobatinae differ in having longer, more pointed wings, most species have forked tails, particularly in the genus *Oceanodroma*, and the legs are shorter; in this way they are better adapted for the calmer conditions of the northern seas.

Storm-petrels are agile, but restless fliers, with a purposeful style of flight, which can be buoyant and erratic. They fly low over the water, in a manner recalling swallows (Hirundinidae) or bats (Chiroptera). The Oceanitinae typically glide slowly, with their wings held level or in a shallow "V", and their legs

HYDROBATIDAE

OCEANITINAE

HYDROBATINAE

southern storm-petrels
7 species
(Oceanites, Garrodia,
Pelagodroma, Fregetta,
Nesofregetta)

northern storm-petrels
13 species
(Hydrobates, Halocyptena,
Oceanodroma)

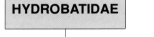

FAMILY   **SUBFAMILY**

dangling, while they dip their feet in the water repeatedly, and thus appear to hop or to walk on the surface of the water. The Hydrobatinae have a more active, busy flying action, which involves a good deal of flapping and hovering. They also bank sharply and glide, especially in strong winds.

Storm-petrels are extremely aerial seabirds, and they are rarely to be found settled on the water. Nonetheless, they swim well and some species may even form large rafts on the water. Occasionally they dive in search of food, normally making a shallow plunge directly from the air, quickly reappearing, and immediately taking off again. Their legs are relatively much longer than those of other petrels, with proportionately long tarsi, yet they are very weak and are equally unsuitable for walking on land. They can not sustain the bird's weight for more than a few steps, so progress on land is slow, clumsy and difficult, and requires the bird to stop frequently and rest on its breast. As they are so feeble and helpless on land, incoming birds usually avoid landing on large patches of open ground, where they would be very obvious to predators.

Despite their small size, storm-petrels spend most of their lives a long way out to sea, and only approach land for nesting. This lifestyle is possible, due to a number of adaptations, which they share with the other Procellariiformes. They have well-developed salt glands, excretory organs situated above each eye that filter the excess salt in the bird's blood and eliminate it through the bill. Their long, tubular external nostrils are generally associated with an extraordinary development of the olfactory part of the brain; it seems that, like other petrels, they are at least partly capable of detecting food by smell. The bill, made up of several horny plates and hooked at the tip, is well designed for dealing with such small, slippery prey as planktonic crustaceans, small fish and squid.

The flight-feathers are predominantly dark-coloured in all plumages, as dark feathers, with a higher melanin content, are more resistant to abrasion from salt water and sunlight. The rest of the plumage may be black, greyish or various shades of brown, with variable amounts of white on the face or underparts. Some species have a conspicuous pure white rump, and in a few species this also extends onto the undertail-coverts. Several species, especially those of the Southern Hemisphere,

may have more than one colour morph, and individual variations are not infrequent in some populations. However, there is no plumage variation between the sexes and immatures differ only slightly from adults. In the hand, adults have a different pattern of plumage wear, and during breeding they have large brood patches.

Although few species have been studied sufficiently, it appears that the norm is a complete post-breeding moult, which may start with the body feathers, shortly before the birds leave their colonies. Primary moult is serially descendant, and in the White-faced Storm-petrel (*Pelagodroma marina*), for example, the tail is often replaced only once the wing moult is almost finished. A strong, musty odour, which is characteristic of all Procellariiformes, pervades the whole plumage, and it persists in moulted feathers a long time after these have been shed.

Habitat

Storm-petrels are strictly marine, occurring mostly in pelagic or offshore waters. The different species and races can be found in zones with markedly dissimilar conditions of temperature and salinity. They inhabit nearly all the world's oceans and most of the main seas, and are only absent from the highest latitudes of the Northern Hemisphere and areas of brackish water. The largest concentrations can be found in cold waters around Antarctica and in the regions of upwelling off South Africa and western South America.

They establish their breeding colonies on remote, undisturbed, rocky islands or stacks. In general, they come inshore or to dry land exclusively at night, when fewer aerial predators are about, although the Wedge-rumped Storm-petrel (*Oceanodroma tethys*) is a diurnal visitor to its colonies in the Galapagos Islands. Nests tend to be in areas free from predators, or inaccessible to them, such as caves, crevices in amongst boulder scree, sheer cliffs or holes in walls and ruins. A few species dig their own holes or take up quarters in abandoned rabbit burrows, sometimes sharing them with other pairs, or even other petrel species, particularly shearwaters.

General Habits

Information on the habits and behaviour of storm-petrels is patchy and has mostly been obtained incidentally during biological and ecological studies at breeding colonies, so very little indeed is known about their behaviour at sea. This is hardly surprising, as they are markedly oceanic and spend most of their time well away from land; besides, they are small and occur in relatively low densities in the vastness of the oceans.

Storm-petrels are gregarious in all seasons, in particular when nesting, but also at sea, where they often gather in small feeding parties and loose groups. Much larger aggregations can occur at sites which are particularly rich in food, for example at whaling stations, and are especially typical of Hornby's (*Oceanodroma hornbyi*) and Wilson's Storm-petrels, which can collect in flocks of several thousand birds. However, most species are frequently solitary when at sea.

With the notable exception of the Wedge-rumped Storm-petrel in the Galapagos, all storm-petrels are exclusively nocturnal in their visits to land. The main reason for this is to reduce predation by gulls, skuas, crows and raptors, which nonetheless cause many casualties. It is interesting to note that the main predator of storm-petrels in the Galapagos is the Short-eared Owl (*Asio flammeus*), which hunts night and day, and that the other two storm-petrel species that breed there, the Madeiran (*Oceanodroma castro*) and Elliot's (*Oceanites gracilis*) Storm-petrels, follow the rule of being strictly nocturnal on land. Furthermore, the Peruvian race *kelsalli* of the Wedge-rumped Storm-petrel is said to visit its breeding colonies on the Pescadores Islands, north of Lima, in total darkness, so this deviation remains unexplained. The species that breed in high latitudes have to deal with continuous daylight in early summer, so they delay the start of their breeding season for some weeks, and visit their nests mostly in the hours when the sunlight is at its weakest.

Colony attendance at night seems to be greatly influenced by the weather conditions. Thus, when visibility is poor, for example in thick fog or drizzle, adults may arrive late and in small numbers, and when the wind is very strong, no birds at all may come. Moonlight seems to have variable effects on the species, with some, such as the European Storm-petrel, virtually unaffected, while others, such as Leach's, arriving late. In ordinary conditions, the first birds fly over the colony shortly after sunset, whereas in the morning the last birds disappear with daybreak. Peak activity tends to occur in complete darkness, mainly during the first part of the night. Many birds with breeding duties spend the night inside the burrow and fly out just before dawn. Those species that are essentially sedentary roost on land irregularly outside the breeding season.

Storm-petrels defend themselves by ejecting the contents of their stomach onto their potential predators. Adults produce this stinking oily substance during the period of chick rearing. It is generally greenish or orange-brown and can be spat out a fair distance by young birds as well as adults. However, it has little

The Galapagos race of the Wedge-rumped Storm-petrel is unique amongst the Hydrobatidae in that it can regularly be seen around land in broad daylight; this may be because it feeds mainly by night. Other species, and also the Peruvian race of the Wedge-rumped, only visit their breeding grounds at night, so as to avoid the attentions of patrolling predators.

[*Oceanodroma tethys tethys*, Galapagos. Photo: Francisco Erize/ Bruce Coleman]

Wilson's Storm-petrel is traditionally held to be one of the most numerous of all seabirds. It breeds in Antarctica and the subantarctic, but migrates far into the Northern Hemisphere, especially in the Atlantic. It uses several feeding techniques, of which pattering is the most common; the yellow webs to its feet may help to attract or disturb small fish or crustaceans.

[*Oceanites oceanicus*, Antarctica. Photo: Peter Johnson/ NHPA]

only the head comes into contact with the water. Some species actually patter on the surface of the water with their feet, notably the two members of the genus *Oceanites*, which have yellow webs on their feet. One theory is that the splashes, particularly with these brightly coloured webs, attract or frighten potential victims, making them easier for the birds to detect. It may be no coincidence that birds are commonly found with leg wounds or even with a leg missing, and it seems quite possible that these injuries are inflicted by predatory fish.

Foraging techniques vary somewhat from one species to another, to some extent in relation to the length and shape of the wings and tail. For example, the relatively large Leach's Storm-petrel (*Oceanodroma leucorhoa*), with its long wings and long, forked tail, does not often patter on the water, but instead hovers with deep wingbeats, whilst it moves around erratically. The White-faced Storm-petrel dances about from side to side, flopping down on its belly every few seconds. Wilson's Storm-petrel frequently patters, but it also uses other remarkable techniques, including "Walking" on the water, and "Standing", which involves the bird facing into the wind with its wings spread open and its feet tucked into the water acting as anchors, as it sails about gazing down and picking out prey. Storm-petrels do not normally surface-seize, whilst sitting on the water, in the way of many other Procellariiformes, and only rarely do they make shallow plunges or surface-dives.

Some species follow ships to feed in their wake and a few also attend trawlers. More commonly, they follow schools of dolphins, whales or fish, especially tuna, or other birds, in order to feed on the scraps of food they leave, or alternatively to catch small fish that are driven up to the surface.

There is some indication that, like other Procellariiformes, storm-petrels may be capable of detecting food by smell. Such an adaptation would be particularly useful for species that forage by night, although it would presumably be useful too for diurnal feeders, as a time- and labour-saving device.

effect against predators capable of capturing a bird in flight, such as some falcons, or those that catch them unawares, particularly straight after landing or as they emerge from their burrows. These are the moments typically used by skuas and owls.

Voice

Garrulous though they may be on or over land, storm-petrels are thought to be essentially silent at sea, where very few calls have been described. However, when competing for food, they can make a series of repeated peeping or chattering sounds, often not unlike those heard at colonies.

On land, they are extremely vocal and make a wide variety of calls and other sounds. Most of these are harsh, guttural, grating, moaning, cooing, purring, whistle-like, squeaky, twittering, or peeping notes rapidly repeated, sometimes for long periods. As in other petrels that are exclusively nocturnal on land and breed underground, a storm-petrel communicates its mood and intention using its voice. Flying birds may call during aerial pursuits or when flying over a particular nest-hole, in which they are interested. If the hole is occupied, the owner usually responds to this effect. It is believed that each bird can recognize its mate's voice and will respond to it even from inside the nest, which may help the overflying bird to locate it more quickly.

Food and Feeding

As it has a narrow gape, for the most part a storm-petrel takes correspondingly small food items. Birds feed mainly on planktonic crustaceans, in particular euphausiids and amphipods, as well as on squid and small fish. To a lesser extent they take molluscs, medusae, fish fry, offal, galley refuse from ships and cetacean faeces. They are particularly fond of oily and fatty substances.

In general, storm-petrels feed mostly in offshore or pelagic waters, over or beyond the continental shelf. A notable exception is Elliot's Storm-petrel, which is mainly an inshore feeder in Galapagos, where it commonly enters bays during the day.

Birds feed mostly on the wing, flying low over the water, with their long legs dangling, and often seizing their prey while

Breeding

As a rule, storm-petrels breed once every year more or less in the same season. Remarkably, though, in the Galapagos the Madeiran Storm-petrel has two laying seasons, which are about six months apart and correspond to distinct populations. Because birds occasionally take rest years, and in conjunction with the fact that a young bird takes several years to become sexually mature, only a small fraction of the total population of each species is engaged in breeding at any particular moment, although many of the non-breeders may pay regular visits to the colony.

Colony size ranges from a few dozen to tens of thousands of pairs, and a single Leach's Storm-petrel colony in Japan was said to contain about a million pairs in 1972. There is a great deal of interaction between birds around the colony, but the importance of territory varies between species, so that some, perhaps most, defend their site against all congeners from a stage long before breeding commences, whereas others, like the European Storm-petrel, allow any bird of their own species into the nest-chamber itself, at least until the hatching of the egg.

As in other petrels, the breeding season is long and begins very slowly. While species that are more or less sedentary may roost on land off and on all year round (see General Habits), the long distance migrants tend to arrive at their breeding grounds long before nesting activity actually starts, by which time the number of birds flying over the colony at night, calling loudly as they pass over the burrow entrances, has increased greatly. Some of these birds will have nested in the previous season and are now starting a new breeding cycle with the same partner, while others are seeking a site or a mate, but a fair proportion are non-breeding adults or immatures. Some birds may land and display on the ground, before eventually entering a burrow, and then later rejoining the frenzied mob, wheeling and calling above.

As part of their nuptial display, two or more birds often engage in aerial pursuits that consist of fast flying in circles above the nesting area, with one bird following the other closely, and both calling frequently and loudly. It is generally thought that the conspicuous rump patch on some species may be particularly helpful in this exercise, which is performed at great speed, and in almost total darkness. Eventually, one or both birds land in order to find, inspect and occupy a nest-site, after which they may stay there, or alternatively fly off again. Mid-air collisions are not infrequent during the busiest hours, the first two or three of complete darkness, and the victims often fall to the ground, at which point they either take off again or seek shelter in the nest-hole.

These "flighting" display activities are probably of major social significance, especially, it is thought, among pre-breeders, and at one colony nearly half the birds that visited burrows were not actively engaged in breeding at the time. Immature birds are easily attracted to the ground by tape-luring, and analysis of ringing recoveries has revealed that they travel extensively and quickly between colonies, so that by the end of the season individual birds may have visited a large number of colonies. In the process, they probably contribute to the survival of their species, as they spend a good deal of time out in the open, both in the air and on the ground, and are thus more likely to be taken by predators than are breeders. Breeders may fly directly into the nest-chamber, particularly if the entrance hole is wide, for example in a cave, and in this way they reduce the risk of predation. However, this kind of manoeuvre requires great flying skill, since it is performed in complete darkness, often with many other birds milling around in the same area.

There is no evidence of any sexual behaviour taking place at sea, and even mated pairs usually meet up at the nest. Unless they have been repeatedly unsuccessful, the same pair tends to breed at the same nest-site several years running; "divorce" is infrequent. Partners normally start to attend the site a few weeks before egg-laying, though on occasions this can begin over ten weeks before, and it is most intense in the period three to four weeks before laying. The female is usually absent for two to three weeks before laying, as she builds up the necessary reserves to make the remarkably large egg, which on average weighs 20-30% of her own body weight. The male continues to pay nightly visits to the nest-hole, and he sometimes remains there during the day too. Unlike the other members of the order, storm-petrels have no "honeymoon period", when both partners are out at sea putting on weight in preparation for the oncoming task.

Most of the sexual activity of the pair takes place actually inside the nest-chamber. There, they may devote hours to mu-

tual-preening, caressing, bill-touching or calling. In some species, for example Leach's Storm-petrel, partners engage in prolonged duets in the nest-hole, as occurs in many other petrels. In other species, however, only one bird calls and duets are unknown. The limited evidence available indicates that copulation takes place on the ground, usually inside the burrow. The male bites or preens the female's nape feathers, as he mounts her, and though some calling may precede copulation, birds are reported to be silent both during and after the act.

A single white egg is laid, which in some species is finely spotted red towards the larger end. As well as being relatively heavy, the egg is large in relation to the size of the adults, which presumably explains the great development of the brood patches in both sexes during breeding. This involves extensive vascularization and defeathering, which starts on average some 4-8 weeks before egg-laying; about a week after the chick has hatched, the feathers start growing again. It is not only breeding birds that develop a brood patch, but some of the non-breeders too that fly over the colony also drop a number of feathers, and a few even undergo full vascularization, which strengthens the idea that these birds are mainly pre-breeders, or birds that have bred in previous years, and are taking a rest year.

The female usually returns to the nest only one or two days before laying, or more commonly on the very night the egg is laid. If the male is present, he normally takes the first incubation spell and the female departs the following morning. If, however, the male is not there, she may sit on the egg for one or two days, after which she invariably leaves, even if her mate has not returned. Incubation is shared between the sexes and usually lasts about seven weeks. Stints average 2-8 days, depending largely on factors such as weather, distance to feeding areas, species and locality. As in other petrels, the eggs may be left unattended for long periods, because they are exceptionally resistant to chilling, which allows incubation to be resumed without the embryo having suffered damage, although the time necessary for hatching is prolonged.

The chick hatches with thick, greyish down, in some cases tinged brown, blue or black, and often paler on the underparts. It is brooded for one to six days, and fed most nights on a partly-digested paste of small fish and crustaceans. The fact that the pulp fed to the young is less pre-digested than in other "tubenoses" is usually taken to indicate that breeding storm-petrels forage much closer to their colonies, which would also explain the much higher frequency of feeding visits to the young in this family.

At six to eight weeks old, chicks reach their peak weight, up to 80% heavier than that of adults. Although feeding is rather infrequent during the last stages of chick growth, there is no complete desertion as occurs in the Procellariidae. Feather growth consumes a great deal of energy, so by the time the chick fledges, at 7-11 weeks old, it has lost a lot of weight, although it is still heavier than its parents. One night the young bird flies directly out to sea, where, if successful, it will probably live for 2-4 years, before joining a flock of pre-breeders.

Breeding success is rather low compared with other seabirds. Definite data are lacking for most species, but results available so far indicate one chick successfully raised from every two to four eggs laid. In normal circumstances, 50-60% of all eggs laid hatch, and 50-70% of all chicks hatched survive to fledging. The main causes of failure are infertility of eggs, chilling, intra- or interspecific competition for nest-sites and predation of adults and young. Again, in the few cases studied, most birds have been found to breed for the first time at four or five years old.

Storm-petrels are extraordinarily long-lived for their small size. This is especially true compared with landbirds of equivalent size, mostly passerines, which only exceptionally live more than 15 years, with a mean of little over five years at most. Among storm-petrels the mean annual mortality rate of adults is 5-15%, giving them a further life expectation of around 6-20 years. There is evidence that some individuals live many years, including a Leach's Storm-petrel that was 24 years old, when last recaptured in its nest-hole, and a European Storm-petrel, ringed when fully-grown, that must have been over 20 years old when it was retrapped 19 years later.

The very weak legs of the Grey-backed Storm-petrel are unsuited to digging, and as a result, unusually for a storm-petrel, it frequently nests above ground. The nest is hidden away in very dense vegetation, typically in a clump of tussock grass. The bird may increase its security by making access to the nest possible only through a small tunnel.

[Garrodia nereis. Photo: B. Chudleigh/Vireo]

Most storm-petrels normally nest in burrows or in cracks or crevices on rocky islands, in order to be as inaccessible as possible to their many potential predators, both terrestrial and aerial. In suitable areas, such as rock falls or scree, many pairs may nest in close proximity and a density of 3200 nests per hectare has been recorded for Wilson's Storm-petrel on South Georgia.

[*Oceanites oceanicus*, Antarctica. Photo: P. V. Tearle/ Planet Earth]

Movements

A wide variety of patterns of movement is used by the storm-petrels. Some species are more or less sedentary and may disperse only within the immediate vicinity of the colony. Others are transequatorial migrants, which abandon their home waters after breeding and spend the off-season in the opposite hemisphere. In some cases, different populations of a species follow different strategies.

Examples of species which are basically sedentary include Tristram's Storm-petrel (*Oceanodroma tristrami*) and the Ashy Storm-petrel (*Oceanodroma homochroa*) in the North Pacific, and the Grey-backed Storm-petrel (*Garrodia nereis*) in the Southern Ocean. The European Storm-petrel is both relatively sedentary and highly migratory in different areas. Its Atlantic population behaves as a transequatorial migrant, wintering mostly off South Africa and Namibia, while Mediterranean breeders are thought to remain mostly in the same waters throughout the winter.

Perhaps the most far-ranging of the transequatorial migrant storm-petrels is Wilson's Storm-petrel, which breeds in Antarctica and on several subantarctic archipelagos, and migrates northwards in all oceans, especially the Atlantic, where it normally occurs north to about 50° N. Leach's and White-faced Storm-petrels also undertake long distance migrations, as do Swinhoe's Storm-petrel (*Oceanodroma monorhis*) and Matsudaira's Storm-petrel (*Oceanodroma matsudairae*), which both regularly reach the western Indian Ocean from their breeding sites in the north-west Pacific. In most cases, birds winter in the tropics or the subtropics.

As storm-petrels are small and light, are weak fliers and are poor swimmers in rough weather, it is not surprising that large numbers are occasionally displaced and driven ashore by gale force winds. In such "wrecks", many birds may die after hitting objects or buildings, or may simply starve on a beach, quite unable to withstand the force of the wind and get back to the sea. The northern storm-petrels, with their more buoyant flight and more aerial habits, are generally more affected than their southern counterparts, and Leach's Storm-petrel is particularly prone to such disasters, for example in autumn 1952 birds were "wrecked" all over Europe, and even reached Switzerland.

Relationship with Man

Storm-petrels are small birds of the open seas that nest in burrows or tiny crevices on offshore islands and stacks. For this reason, they have come into direct contact with man less than many other seabirds, though they too have suffered at his hands.

In many areas, such as western North America, storm-petrels have been exploited for food, oil or fish bait. Their large breeding aggregations, often in the vicinity of other seabirds, have certainly made them more vulnerable. Although it is probable that they are rarely the prime targets, they have commonly been collected by those harvesting shearwaters or other petrels, which are nesting nearby. Large numbers have reportedly been taken on occasions, but three factors have helped to keep such exploitation at the level merely of an occasional activity: firstly, their small size means that very large numbers are required to make their exploitation worthwhile; secondly, their habit of nesting in every available nook and cranny means that many nests are inaccessible, sometimes simply because the entrance hole is too small for a human hand; and, thirdly, there is the fact that very often there are plenty of other, larger birds available.

At sea, storm-petrels and man often come into contact, though they interfere little with each other. Although some species are known to attend fishing boats, very few do so regularly or in significant numbers. Hence, incidental mortality on fishing grounds is low and probably has little effect on populations. Some species, notably Wilson's Storm-petrel, have benefited from the development of the whaling industry in the past, either directly, as they may feed on whale blubber, or indirectly, as the decreasing number of whales has left larger quantities of planktonic crustaceans available to the birds.

There is a general belief among sea-faring men of many areas that touching a storm-petrel, especially one that has strayed on board a ship, is a sure sign of bad luck, which may bring death to the man that has touched it or to his family. As with other Procellariiformes, storm-petrels are often seen as "soul birds". According to tradition, the souls of particularly cruel ships' captains were condemned to flutter over the seas for the rest of time, while those of drowned sailors are thought to be reincarnated in these birds. In some cultures, storm-petrels are known as "the birds of poets".

The name "petrel" is thought to come from French, as an abbreviated form of "péterelle", or "little Peter", referring to St Peter, who, according to biblical tradition, walked on the water. However, it is not clear that this is the genuine origin of the name, and it may in fact have come from the typical habit of birds of "pattering" on the water, or even from the voice of Leach's Storm-petrel, which has been transcribed as "petteret-teral". Another traditional name for storm-petrels among sailors is "Mother Carey's chickens", in reference to the Virgin Mary (*Mater cara*), to whom the protection of sailors was commended. The prefix "storm", which forms part of the name of members of the Hydrobatidae in many languages, refers to their irregular occurrence on land, linked with strong winds, although the popular belief that they can predict gales is most unlikely.

Status and Conservation

Due largely to the fact that they are difficult to observe, very little is known about the populations of most species of storm-petrel. While some species, such as Wilson's Storm-petrel, are said to be amongst the most numerous of all birds, three species are currently considered to be threatened on a global scale. These are Markham's (*Oceanodroma markhami*), Tristram's and Hornby's Storm-petrels, about all of which next to nothing is known, indeed the breeding grounds of Hornby's have yet to be discovered, while the first colony of Markham's was found as recently as 1987.

In addition, one species, the Guadalupe Storm-petrel (*Oceanodroma macrodactyla*), a former breeder on Guadalupe Island off north-west Mexico, is presumed extinct, as no individuals have been seen since 1912. Subsequent visits to the island have all proved fruitless, and the old burrows, which were still recognizable at the time of some of the earlier visits, have long since shown no signs at all of having been used. Cats are abundant on the island and are reported to have preyed extensively on this species, and they are thought to have been largely responsible for its downfall. Nonetheless, the species might still hang on, for no exhaustive search has been made in the appropriate season. Guadalupe is also home to a few thousand pairs of Leach's Storm-petrel, but most, if not all of these now breed on offshore rocks, where they are presumably safe from the cats.

Storm-petrels have a long list of natural predators that includes owls, especially the Barn Owl (*Tyto alba*) and the Short-eared Owl, gulls, skuas, crows and several raptors. Several small terrestrial predators, in particular mustelids and mongooses, also take many birds at sites where they breed on the mainland or on major islands. In most cases when natural predation on storm-petrels occurs, it is a few specialized individuals as opposed to the bulk of the predator population that capture most of the birds, although some inevitably fall victim to the non-specialized predators as well. Natural predation may be severe on some storm-petrel populations, and White-bellied Storm-petrels (*Fregetta grallaria*) and White-faced Storm-petrels together make up 33-50% of all prey taken by skuas (*Catharacta*) on Inaccessible Island, at Tristan da Cunha in the South Atlantic. Three colonies of Fork-tailed Storm-petrels (*Oceanodroma furcata*) in the Queen Charlotte Islands, off south-west Canada, disappeared after they were ravaged by American black bears (*Ursus americanus*) in 1947, though the species still breeds commonly in British Columbia, with almost 400,000 breeding birds estimated in 1991. In general, however,

In the Hydrobatidae incubation stints are relatively short, which presumably means that they can collect and transport sufficient food for themselves and the chick more quickly than most of the larger species of Procellariiformes, though it probably also indicates a lesser capacity for fasting. In the White-faced Storm-petrel incubation lasts for 50-56 days.

[*Pelagodroma marina.* Photo: J. R. Napier]

In areas with soft soil European Storm-petrels will dig out a burrow using their feet and bills, or they may use one excavated by other seabirds or by rabbits. There is normally a tunnel which may be up to three metres long, at the end of which the single egg is laid. In storm-petrels the egg is relatively large and is resistant to chilling, an important factor as the egg may be left unattended for some time if both birds are feeding.

[*Hydrobates pelagicus,* Mykines, Faeroe Is. Photo: Richard Vaughan/ Ardea]

In contrast with most other birds, almost all petrel chicks grow two coats of down. As in the penguins, the first coat is actually joined onto the second, and they may remain attached for some time after the appearance of the second coat. In Leach's Storm-petrel the second down differs from the first in being longer and somewhat darker.

[*Oceanodroma leucorhoa.* Photo: Richard Vaughan/ Ardea]

this kind of devastating predation is a rather local phenomenon and it is doubtful whether any natural predator can exploit a prey species so extensively as to produce significant effects in the long run.

Conversely, an alien predator introduced to an island with breeding seabirds finds abundant food and often no other predators, which might control its numbers, so that it quickly multiplies, and may eventually eradicate the prey species. Many storm-petrels have thus suffered local extinctions, and have had to seek refuge at other, inaccessible sites, which are free from predators.

It is a general rule in ecology that the larger the prey species, the fewer the predators that can prey on it. In the case of the storm-petrels, the smallest of all the seabirds breeding on many islands, this implies that the range of potential predators, and thus the pressure exerted, is greatest upon them, so even mice, which are harmless to albatrosses and the larger petrels and even to their chicks, are a significant danger for storm-petrels. Many thousands of mice, rats, cats, dogs, mongooses, mustelids and other mammals, as well as Wekas (*Gallirallus australis*) on the islands around New Zealand, now inhabit the oceanic islands that once housed vast numbers of breeding storm-petrels, while most seabirds are progressively being displaced towards the most isolated stacks. For example, until the 1960's huge numbers of the now threatened Tristram's Storm-petrel bred on Toroshima, in the Izus, to the south of Japan, but they were heavily plundered by cats and black rats (*Rattus rattus*), and they no longer breed on the island.

In addition to the action of predators, there are the secondary effects of overgrazing by imported herbivores. Intensive grazing contributes to a reduction of the vegetation cover, thus altering the character of the nesting grounds, and eventually perhaps leading to soil erosion and the definitive destruction of breeding habitat. The situation is critical on some islands where rabbits have been introduced, as their intense burrowing on slopes can open up broad areas bereft of vegetation that

eventually collapse after heavy rains. However, on islands where rabbits have lived for a long time, and are thus in harmony with the rest of the ecosystem, their burrowing may even have beneficial effects for storm-petrels, as it opens up new holes which may be abandoned later and left to the birds.

In many cases, the survival, recovery or maintenance of numbers of the different species requires the eradication, or at least control, of introduced mammals on breeding islands. This is a top priority for many seabirds, and several islands are currently being managed towards this end, although to date introduced predators have only been exterminated from a few small islands, mostly in the region of New Zealand.

Petrels in general suffer little from oil pollution, and they may be able to use their well-developed sense of smell to detect and therefore avoid oil slicks. As storm-petrels are highly aerial and only infrequently settle on the water, they should be even less susceptible to this danger than other, more aquatic petrels. Nonetheless, a major incident near one of the main breeding colonies around fledging time could have catastrophic results.

A great deal of effort is currently being made to restore natural conditions on oceanic islands. Further progress is being made with the establishment of numerous reserves and parks on islands, where human access has been banned, in order to prevent disturbance, exploitation and trampling of burrows. Several islands have been recolonized by storm-petrels, and overall numbers have increased almost everywhere.

General Bibliography

Alexander *et al*. (1965), Atkinson (1985), Bang (1966), Barrowclough *et al*. (1981), Bourne (1985), Crossin (1974), Croxall (1987, 1991), Croxall *et al*. (1984), Furness (1987), Furness & Monaghan (1987), Harrison (1985, 1987), Jehl (1972), Hutchinson & Wenzel (1980), Jouanin & Mougin (1979), Löfgren (1984), Moors & Atkinson (1984), Murphy & Snyder (1952), Nelson (1980), Vermeer & Rankin (1984a), Schreiber (1984), Sibley & Monroe (1990), Tuck & Heinzel (1978), Warham (1990).

ssp *oceanicus*

ssp *exasperatus*

pale morph

dark morph

1

2

3

4

5

6

7

8

9

10

11

12

13

14

15

16

17

18

19

20

PLATE 17

inches   8

cm   20

Subfamily OCEANITINAE

Genus *OCEANITES* Keyserling & J. H. Blasius, 1840

1. Wilson's Storm-petrel

Oceanites oceanicus

French: Océanite de Wilson   **German**: Buntfuß-Sturmschwalbe   **Spanish**: Paíño de Wilson
Other common names: Flat-clawed/Yellow-webbed Storm-petrel

Taxonomy. *Procellaria oceanica* Kuhl, 1820, South Georgia.
Possible race *maorianus* (taken off New Zealand) may be extinct. Two subspecies recognized.
Subspecies and Distribution.
O. o. oceanicus (Kuhl, 1820) - subantarctic islands, from Cape Horn E to Kerguelen Is.
O. o. exasperatus Mathews, 1912 - South Shetland, South Sandwich Is, coastal Antarctica.

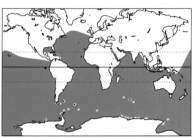

Descriptive notes. 15-19 cm; 34-45 g; wingspan 38-42 cm. Wings short with carpal bend indistinct; legs project beyond tail in flight. Broad white band on rump stretches to lateral undertail-coverts. Pale bars on upper- and underwing range from fairly prominent to faint. Juvenile very similar to adult. Race *exasperatus* has wings and tail slightly larger.
Habitat. Marine; prefers cold waters over continental shelf or inshore, especially during breeding season; wanders over pelagic waters after breeding; particularly abundant in plankton-rich areas. Breeds on rocky islets, on cliffs and among boulder scree, avoiding snow and ice.
Food and Feeding. Mostly planktonic crustaceans, especially krill (*Euphausia*), and fish (*Protomyctophum*); also small squid, polychaetes, gastropods and carrion. Feeds mainly on wing, by dipping and pattering; also from surface, by skimming over the water (see page 261). Can apparently detect food by smell. Follows ships and attends trawlers regularly; reported to follow cetaceans.
Breeding. Starts Nov/Dec. Loosely colonial; nests in burrows or rock crevices. 1 egg; incubation c. 43 days (38-59) in stints of c. 2 days; chicks have grey-brown down, brooded for 1-2 days; fledging c. 60 days, mostly in April. Mean annual survival of adults c. 90%.
Movements. Transequatorial migrant; spends off-season in middle latitudes of N Atlantic and N Indian Oceans; also in Pacific, where less abundant. May move clockwise round Atlantic.
Status and Conservation. Not globally threatened. Traditionally considered one of most abundant of all seabirds, with total population known to reach several million pairs; 1,000,000 pairs at South Shetland Is, 600,000 pairs at South Georgia, 200,000-500,000 at Kerguelen Is. Some colonies subject to predation, notably by rats and cats, e.g. Crozet and Kerguelen Is; others free from introduced predators. Main threat may be competition with commercial fisheries, especially large-scale commercial exploitation of krill; may have benefited indirectly from whaling (see page 263). Contamination with pesticides and heavy metals could be significant; breeding success often reduced by snow blocking off burrows.
Bibliography. Ainley (1984a), Ainley *et al.* (1984), Ali & Ripley (1978), Bailey (1968), Beck & Brown (1972), Bent (1922), Blake (1977), Bourne (1983c), Bretagnolle (1988a, 1989b), Bretagnolle & Robisson (1991), Bretagnolle & Thomas (1990), Brown (1988c), Brown *et al.* (1982), Coates (1985), Cramp & Simmons (1977), Croxall, Evans & Schreiber (1984), Croxall, Hill *et al.* (1988), Dymond *et al.* (1989), van Franeker *et al.* (1990), Huber (1971), Humphrey *et al.* (1970), Jehl *et al.* (1979), Johnson (1965), Jouventin *et al.* (1985), Lacan (1971), Langrand (1990), Lindsey (1986), Marchant & Higgins (1990), Milon *et al.* (1973), Murphy (1936), Nakamura, Tanaka & Hasegawa (1983), Obst (1986), Obst *et al.* (1987), Payne *et al.* (1983), Palmer (1962), Pefaur (1974), Phillips (1955), Pinto (1983), Roberts (1940, 1991), Ruschi (1979), Serventy (1952), Sick (1984), Thomas (1986), Voous (1983), Wasilewski (1986), Watson (1975), Weimerskirch, Zotier & Jouventin (1989), Woehler (1991), Woehler & Johnstone (1991), Wood (1990a), Woods (1988), Zink & Eldridge (1980).

2. Elliot's Storm-petrel

Oceanites gracilis

French: Océanite d'Elliot   **German**: Elliotsturmschwalbe   **Spanish**: Paíño de Elliot
Other common names: White-vented/Graceful Storm-petrel

Taxonomy. *Thalassidroma gracilis* Elliot, 1859, west coast of South America.
Two subspecies recognized.
Subspecies and Distribution.
O. g. gracilis (Elliot, 1859) - Ecuador S to C Chile, with breeding recorded only at Chungungo I off Chile, 29° S.
O. g. galapagoensis Lowe, 1921 - presumably breeds at Galapagos Is.
Descriptive notes. 15-16 cm. Small. Wings short and broad at base; legs project beyond tail in flight; very small bill. Centre of belly white; broad pale bar on underwing not well marked, but pattern distinctive. Juvenile probably as adult. Race *galapagoensis* averages larger with more white on belly.
Habitat. Marine and mainly pelagic; commonly occurs over cool waters, often quite near land. Breeding grounds mostly undiscovered.
Food and Feeding. Probably mostly small fish and crustaceans. Feeds mainly on wing, by pattering over the surface and dipping occasionally. Regularly follows ships and attends trawlers; reported to associate with cetaceans.
Breeding. No nests found in Galapagos, where species suspected to breed during cold season, Apr-Sept. Virtually nothing known of its breeding in Chile and perhaps Peru; found breeding in Aug.
Movements. May move little, dispersing only in zone of Humboldt Current along W coast of S America; suggested possible dispersal N to Colombia and Panama.

Status and Conservation. Not globally threatened. Known to be numerous, although only 1 nesting pair ever discovered; population of Galapagos estimated at many thousand birds. No threats known at present, but rats and fire thought to be causes of possible decline at only known breeding site; this site requires protection. Efforts should be directed towards finding further breeding grounds; research needed into requirements and population dynamics.
Bibliography. Blake (1977), Croxall *et al.* (1984), Harris, M.P. (1969c, 1974a), Hilty & Brown (1986), Johnson (1965), Murphy (1936), Ridgely & Gwynne (1989), Schlatter & Marin (1983).

Genus *GARRODIA* Forbes, 1881

3. Grey-backed Storm-petrel

Garrodia nereis

French: Océanite néréide   **German**: Graurücken-Sturmschwalbe   **Spanish**: Paíño Dorsigrís

Taxonomy. *Thalassidroma Nereis* Gould, 1841, Bass Strait, Australia.
Sometimes placed in *Oceanites*. Monotypic.
Distribution. Circumpolar in subantarctic, breeding from Falkland Is E to Chatham Is.

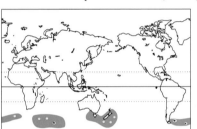

Descriptive notes. 16-19 cm; wingspan 39 cm. Well marked plumage; distinctive combination of white underparts from breast downwards, and grey rump and uppertail, with terminal black bar; prominent pale bar on upperwing. Legs project beyond tail in flight. Juvenile similar to adult.
Habitat. Marine; occurs in cool waters of subantarctic zone, generally over edge of continental shelf; apparently pelagic only during dispersal. Breeds on oceanic islands in coastal grassland and heath; sometimes in hollows in rocky areas.
Food and Feeding. Mainly immature barnacles (*Lepas australis*) of 1·7-5·4 mm, and other crustaceans; also small squid and occasionally small fish. Feeds mostly by pattering over the surface while in flight; also by dipping and shallow plunging; frequently hovers. Attends trawlers and occasionally follows ships.
Breeding. Starts Oct/Nov. Forms loose colonies; nest is burrow, tunnel in vegetation or crevice in rocks, usually above ground. 1 egg; incubation estimated c. 45 days with stints of 1-3 days; chicks have dark grey down; fledging mostly in Mar/Apr.
Movements. In most cases probably disperses only to waters adjacent to colony, but little known. Birds from Crozet Is absent in winter; species occurs regularly off SE Australia and Tasmania.
Status and Conservation. Not globally threatened. Widespread, with total population in order of 10,000-50,000 breeding pairs, mainly concentrated on islands around New Zealand; 3000-5000 pairs at Kerguelen Is, 10,000-12,000 birds at Chatham Is, population of Falklands may be sizeable. However, may be declining as suffers predation, mainly by cats and rats; probably facilitated by tendency to breed in fairly accessible sites. Eradication of introduced predators on all breeding islands seems desirable. Livestock also cause problems through trampling and general degradation of vegetation and nesting substrate. Requires monitoring and more ecological study.
Bibliography. Bennett (1930), Blake (1977), Brown *et al.* (1982), Croxall *et al.* (1984), Fraser *et al.* (1988), Humphrey *et al.* (1970), Imber (1981, 1983), Jehl *et al.* (1979), Johnson (1965), Jouventin *et al.* (1985), Lindsey (1986), Marchant & Higgins (1990), Murphy (1936), Richardson (1984), Swales (1965), Watson (1975), Weimerskirch, Zotier & Jouventin (1989), Wood (1990a), Woods (1988).

Genus *PELAGODROMA* Reichenbach, 1853

4. White-faced Storm-petrel

Pelagodroma marina

French: Océanite frégate   **German**: Weißgesicht-Sturmschwalbe   **Spanish**: Paíño Pechialbo
Other common names: Frigate Petrel

Taxonomy. *Procellaria marina* Latham, 1790, off the mouth of the Río de la Plata, lat. 35°-37° S.
Race *eadesi* should perhaps be included within *hypoleuca*; validity of race *albiclunis* has also been questioned. Six subspecies normally recognized.
Subspecies and Distribution.
P. m. hypoleuca (Moquin-Tandon, 1841) - Salvage Is.
P. m. eadesi Bourne, 1953 - Cape Verde Is.
P. m. marina (Latham, 1790) - Tristan da Cunha and possibly Gough I.
P. m. dulciae Mathews, 1912 - W & S Australia.
P. m. maoriana Mathews, 1912 - New Zealand area.
P. m. albiclunis Murphy & Irving, 1951 - Kermadec Is.

On following pages: 5. Black-bellied Storm-petrel (*Fregetta tropica*); 6. White-bellied Storm-petrel (*Fregetta grallaria*); 7. Polynesian Storm-petrel (*Nesofregetta fuliginosa*); 8. European Storm-petrel (*Hydrobates pelagicus*); 9. Least Storm-petrel (*Halocyptena microsoma*); 10. Wedge-rumped Storm-petrel (*Oceanodroma tethys*); 11. Madeiran Storm-petrel (*Oceanodroma castro*); 12. Swinhoe's Storm-petrel (*Oceanodroma monorhis*); 13. Leach's Storm-petrel (*Oceanodroma leucorhoa*); 14. Markham's Storm-petrel (*Oceanodroma markhami*); 15. Tristram's Storm-petrel (*Oceanodroma tristrami*); 16. Black Storm-petrel (*Oceanodroma melania*); 17. Matsudaira's Storm-petrel (*Oceanodroma matsudairae*); 18. Ashy Storm-petrel (*Oceanodroma homochroa*); 19. Hornby's Storm-petrel (*Oceanodroma hornbyi*); 20. Fork-tailed Storm-petrel (*Oceanodroma furcata*).

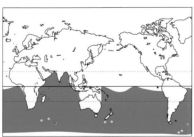

Descriptive notes. 20-21 cm; 60 g; wingspan 41-43 cm. Distinctive combination of white underparts, brownish grey upperparts and prominent head pattern, with white supercilium. Underwing broadly white, with dark trailing edge. Juvenile has head, rump and upperwing bar paler. Races separated by slight differences in size, proportions and coloration; *eadesi* has white collar on hind neck and more white on forehead; *maoriana* can have complete breast band.

Habitat. Marine and pelagic; both during and outwith breeding season normally occurs some distance from land, except at colonies. Breeds on isolated islands, often in flat, sandy areas with low herbaceous vegetation; also in rocky areas and on slopes.

Food and Feeding. Mostly planktonic crustaceans (*Nyctiphanes australis, Nematoscelis megalops, Cyllopus*; immatures of *Squilla armata, Nectocarcinus antarcticus*) and small fish, complemented with some squid. Feeds mainly on wing, by pattering and dipping; also flops into water (see page 261). May feed mostly at night. Rarely follows ships, but known to follow cetaceans.

Breeding. Generally breeds in local spring and summer. Colonial; nests in burrows. 1 egg; incubation c. 50-56 days, with stints of 3-5 days; chicks have pale grey down, brooded for first 2-4 days; fledging 52-67 days. Sexual maturity after at least 3 years. Known to have lived over 10 years in wild.

Movements. Variable with populations, migratory or dispersive. N Atlantic birds disperse after breeding, with several records from E coast of N America and 1 from Britain; nominate race disperses E to Africa, and W to S America; Australian birds migrate into tropical Indian Ocean, regularly reaching Arabian Sea; New Zealand birds move E over S Pacific to W coast of S America, where not uncommon N to Galapagos.

Status and Conservation. Not globally threatened. Total population large, with several million birds; well over 1,000,000 breeding pairs in New Zealand area; numerous along S coast of Australia. Race *hypoleuca* of Salvage Is estimated to number c. 500,000 birds (1965); questionable race *eadesi* of Cape Verde Is apparently breeds at several sites, though subject to considerable human pressure. In general, highly sensitive to human disturbance and locally subject to exploitation by fishermen; much predation by mice, rats, cats, owls, Wekas, skuas, large gulls, snakes, land crabs (*Ocypoda*), etc. Burrows sometimes trampled by man or livestock in parts of Australia; colony at Mud I, Victoria, legally protected as early as 1903. Human exploitation should be terminated; eradication of introduced predators on all breeding islands also recommended. In Chatham Is, c. 200,000 found dead in 1970, with legs tangled up and impeded by filaments of larval trematode *Distomum filiferum*, presumably picked up during foraging.

Bibliography. Bannerman (1968), Bailey (1968), Blake (1977), Bourne (1953, 1955), Bretagnolle (1990a), Brown *et al.* (1982), Claugher (1976), Cramp & Simmons (1977), Croxall *et al.* (1984), Cunningham & Moors (1985), Fraser *et al.* (1988), Furness (1987), Gillham (1963), Imber (1981, 1984a, 1984b, 1985h), Jones (1937b), Lindsey (1986), Marchant & Higgins (1990), Mougin (1988), Murphy (1936), Murphy & Irving (1951), de Naurois (1969b), Palmer (1962), Richardson (1984), Richdale (1943a, 1965a), Ryan *et al.* (1990), Serventy *et al.* (1971), Terres (1980), Watson (1975), Watson *et al.* (1986), Wood (1990a).

Genus *FREGETTA*   Bonaparte, 1855

5. Black-bellied Storm-petrel

Fregetta tropica

French: Océanite à ventre noir
German: Schwarzbauch-Sturmschwalbe
Spanish: Paíño Ventrinegro
Other common names: Gould's/Striped Storm-petrel

Taxonomy. *Thalassidroma tropica* Gould, 1844, equatorial regions of Atlantic Ocean.
Sometimes lumped together with sibling *F. grallaria*, its N counterpart; classification of species and subspecies in genus *Fregetta* is tentative, especially birds at Tristan da Cunha and Gough I; race *melanoleuca* may be invalid or may be referable to *F. grallaria*. Considerable individual variation in plumage tends to obscure geographical variation; most forms described as subspecies usually ascribed to *F. grallaria*. Two subspecies currently accepted.
Subspecies and Distribution.
F. t. tropica (Gould, 1844) - circumpolar, from islands of Scotia Arc through S Indian Ocean to Antipodes Is.
F. t. melanoleuca Salvadori, 1908 - (?) Tristan da Cunha and Gough I.

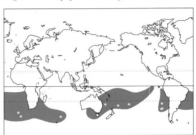

Descriptive notes. 20 cm; wingspan 46 cm. Plumage presents strong contrast of black and white; similar to *F. grallaria*, but darker above and often has blackish centre to underparts, though this feature very variable. Legs project beyond tail in flight. Whitish chin. Juveniles very similar to adults. Race *melanoleuca* has white belly.

Habitat. Marine and highly pelagic, rarely approaching land except near colonies; may be associated with cool currents. Breeds on offshore islands or stacks, often on bare rocky slopes, but also in thick vegetation or in peat; avoids snow and ice.

Food and Feeding. Little known; squid and small fish recorded. Feeds mainly on wing by pattering; dips and makes shallow plunges from the air. Can apparently detect food by smell.

Breeding. Starts Nov. Forms loose colonies; nests in rock crevices or burrows. 1 egg; incubation 38-44 days; chicks have pale grey down, are not brooded; fledging 65-71 days.

Movements. Migrates N into subtropical and tropical zones of Atlantic, Indian and Pacific Oceans, regularly occurring N to equator. Some confusion, as can be difficult to distinguish at sea from *F. grallaria*.

Status and Conservation. Not globally threatened. Widespread, with total population estimated at c. 100,000-150,000 breeding pairs. Suffers considerable predation; many colonies have moved to inaccessible offshore stacks, probably for this reason; at Macquarie I may have been eradicated

by introduced predators, before ever recorded. In order to maintain present numbers all introduced predators, including mice, should be controlled.

Bibliography. Ainley *et al.* (1984), Bailey (1968), Beck & Brown (1971), Blake (1977), Bretagnolle & Thomas (1990), Brown *et al.* (1982), Croxall *et al.* (1984), Harper (1987), Imber (1983), Jehl *et al.* (1979), Johnson (1965), Jouventin *et al.* (1985), Langrand (1990), Lindsey (1986), Marchant & Higgins (1990), Mathews (1933), Milon *et al.* (1973), Murphy (1936), Turner (1980a), Watson (1975), Weimerskirch, Zotier & Jouventin (1989), Wood (1990a), Woods (1988).

6. White-bellied Storm-petrel

Fregetta grallaria

French: Océanite à ventre blanc
German: Weißbauch-Sturmschwalbe
Spanish: Paíño Ventriblanco
Other common names: Vieillot's Storm-petrel

Taxonomy. *Procellaria grallaria* Vieillot, 1817, Australia.
Often treated together with sibling *F. tropica*, and classification of species and subspecies in genus *Fregetta* is tentative. Race *leucogaster* sometimes ascribed to *F. tropica*, may be invalid; race *titan* may be full species. Four subspecies currently recognized.
Subspecies and Distribution.
F. g. grallaria (Vieillot, 1817) - Lord Howe and Kermadec Is.
F. g. leucogaster (Gould, 1844) - Tristan da Cunha, (?) Gough I, St Paul and (?) Amsterdam Is.
F. g. segethi (Philippi & Landbeck, 1860) - Juan Fernández Is.
F. g. titan Murphy, 1928 - Rapa I in Austral Is (SC Pacific).

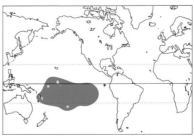

Descriptive notes. 19-20 cm; c. 60 g; wingspan 46 cm. Polymorphic, with several paler and darker variations. Back and upperwing paler than in *F. tropica*; well marked wing bar, as in *G. nereis*, but rump white. Underparts also resemble those of *G. nereis*, but more white on underwing. Juvenile plumage may be equally variable; 1 juvenile reported similar to light morph adult. Races supposedly separable on size and variations in colour.

Habitat. Marine and highly pelagic, rarely approaching land except near colonies; occurs in tropical waters with high salinity. Breeds on offshore islands or stacks, generally amongst boulder scree or on grassy slopes, up to 450 m above sea-level.

Food and Feeding. Very little known; mostly squid with some crustaceans. Feeds mainly on the wing, by pattering and dipping. Has been recorded feeding in company of other seabirds and following ships.

Breeding. Latter part of summer, starting Jan or before. Forms loose colonies; nests in rock crevices or burrows. 1 egg; chicks have dark bluish grey down.

Movements. Apparently disperses N to lower latitudes, but probably not as widely as *F. tropica*. In general, movements poorly known, as specific identification of these 2 species often very difficult, especially at sea.

Status and Conservation. Not globally threatened. Total population probably numbers a few thousand breeding pairs; lack of data for some of main sites indicates numbers might be higher. Has declined markedly as result of severe predation, chiefly by cats, rats and mice, at many of former breeding sites; several colonies have shifted to offshore stacks, e.g. at St Paul I, S Indian Ocean, where former large numbers devastated by cats and rats. Recovery of former numbers and recolonization of former sites not possible until predator pressure reduced or eliminated. Race *titan* of Rapa I, SE Pacific, thought to number only c. 500 pairs.

Bibliography. Blake (1977), Brooke (1987a), Brown *et al.* (1982), Coates (1985), Croxall *et al.* (1984), Fraser *et al.* (1988), Furness (1987), Hagen (1952), Holyoak & Thibault (1984), Johnson (1965), Lindsey (1986), Marchant & Higgins (1990), Mathews (1933), Murphy (1936), Palmer (1962), Richardson (1984), Ryan *et al.* (1990), Serventy *et al.* (1971), Terres (1980), Watson (1975), Wood (1990a).

Genus *NESOFREGETTA*   Mathews, 1912

7. Polynesian Storm-petrel

Nesofregetta fuliginosa

French: Océanite à gorge blanche
German: Weißkehl-Sturmschwalbe
Spanish: Paíño Gorgiblanco
Other common names: White-throated/Samoan Storm-petrel

Taxonomy. *Procellaria fuliginosa* Gmelin, 1789, Tahiti.
Polymorphism has led to description of several bogus subspecies. Monotypic.
Distribution. Tropical S Pacific, from Vanuatu (New Hebrides) and Kiribati (Gilbert Is) E to Marquesas and Gambier Is, and possibly Sala y Gómez.

Descriptive notes. 24-26 cm. Large. Characteristic wing shape, lacking marked bends on leading and trailing edges. Polymorphic: dark phase separable from other dark storm-petrels on size, wing shape, long, forked tail and short pale bar on upperwing; several intermediate phases; pale morph differs from genus *Fregetta* in size, long, forked tail, narrow white band on rump and dark breast band contrasting with white underparts.

Habitat. Marine and pelagic, seldom occurring near land except at colonies. Breeds among boulders or on vegetated ground on remote atolls, islands or stacks.

Food and Feeding. Diet very poorly known; said to take crustaceans, cephalopods and small fish. Feeds mainly on wing by pattering and dipping; also makes shallow dives.

Breeding. Breeds throughout year, with peak in Sept-Nov at Kiritimati (Christmas I); apparently Jul-Dec in Marquesas. Loosely colonial; nests in burrows or rock crevices. 1 egg.
Movements. Presumably disperses mainly over adjacent waters and E to warm waters of South Equatorial Current.
Status and Conservation. Not globally threatened. Various islands known to hold several thousand breeding pairs; sizeable populations in Phoenix and Line Is. More detailed information required on exact location, size and trends of colonies; details also required on breeding biology and ecology in order to establish conservation requirements. Presumably suffers some human exploitation and predation by introduced mammals.
Bibliography. Bregulla (1992), Garnett (1984), Pratt *et al.* (1987), Schlatter (1984), Warham (1990).

Subfamily HYDROBATINAE

Genus *HYDROBATES*   Boie, 1822

8. **European Storm-petrel**

Hydrobates pelagicus

French: Océanite tempête   **German**: Sturmschwalbe   **Spanish**: Paíño Europeo
Other common names: British Storm-petrel

Taxonomy. *Procellaria pelagica* Linnaeus, 1758, Sweden.
Mediterranean population might form distinct subspecies (*melitensis*). Monotypic.
Distribution. NE Atlantic, from S Iceland and W Norway S through N & W Britain to NW France, N Spain, Salvage and Canary Is; also in Mediterranean, from E Spain E to Greece and (?) Turkey.

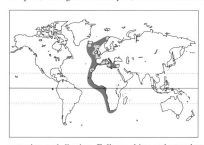

Descriptive notes. 14-18 cm; 23-29 g; wingspan 36-39 cm. Tail squarish as in *O. oceanicus*, but legs do not project beyond tip of tail and pale bar on upperwing narrow and weaker; white bar on underwing diagnostic for separation from *Oceanodroma*. Juvenile can have more prominent upperwing bar.
Habitat. Marine and pelagic, normally keeping well away from land, except near colonies. Breeds on rocky ground on offshore islands and stacks, occasionally on promontories.
Food and Feeding. Mainly small fish (*Sprattus sprattus*), squid and crustaceans; also medusae and offal. Feeds mainly on wing by pattering and dipping. Follows ships and attends trawlers occasionally.
Breeding. Starts May/Jun. Colonial; usually nests in crevices among rocks. 1 egg; incubation c. 41 days in stints of c. 3 days; chick has silvery grey down, brooded for 6-7 days; fledging c. 59-70 days. Sexual maturity at 4-5 years old. Adult mortality c. 12-13% per year; known to have lived over 20 years in wild.
Movements. Transequatorial migrant, wintering mainly off South Africa and Namibia. A few birds, especially of Mediterranean populations, may remain near colony throughout winter.
Status and Conservation. Not globally threatened. Total population estimated at 130,000-290,000 breeding pairs, mainly in Ireland, Faeroe Is and Scotland. Rat and cat predation responsible for some local extinctions and shifting of some colonies. Pollution significant in places. In Mediterranean also threatened by developing tourist industry, with extensive building along coast.
Bibliography. Araujo *et al.* (1977), Barrett & Strann (1987), Batten *et al.* (1990), Brichetti (1979), Brown *et al.* (1982), Clark, H. (1985), Cramp & Simmons (1977), Cramp *et al.* (1974), Croxall *et al.* (1984), Fowler (1985), Fowler & Swinfen (1984), Fowler *et al.* (1982), Furness & Baillie (1981), Griffiths (1981), Guyot & Thibault (1988), Hall-Craggs & Sellar (1976), Hemery (1980), James (1984b), Lambert (1983), Lloyd *et al.* (1991), Lockley (1932), Massa & Catalisano (1986), Medmaravis & Monbailliu (1986), Michelot & Laurent (1988), Myrberget *et al.* (1969), Pinto (1983), Richards (1990), Scott, D.A. (1970), Sharrock (1976), Slater (1991), Tasker *et al.* (1987), Thom (1986), Walmsley (1986).

Genus *HALOCYPTENA*   Coues, 1864

9. **Least Storm-petrel**

Halocyptena microsoma

French: Océanite minute   **German**: Zwergsturmschwalbe   **Spanish**: Paíño Menudo

Taxonomy. *Halocyptena microsoma* Coues, 1864, San José del Caba, Baja California.
Perhaps more appropriately placed in genus *Oceanodroma*. Monotypic.

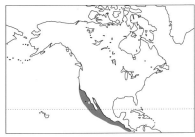

Distribution. Islands in Gulf of California and off W coast of Baja California.
Descriptive notes. 13-15 cm; wingspan 32 cm. Smallest storm-petrel; distinctive wedge-shaped tail. Dark underwing helps to separate from *O. homochroa*. Juvenile as adult.
Habitat. Marine and often pelagic, mainly occurring over warm waters away from land. Breeds on small islands or rocky stacks.
Food and Feeding. Mostly small planktonic crustaceans, particularly larvae of spiny lobster *Panulirus*. Feeds on wing, by pattering, and also by surface-seizing whilst sitting on water.
Breeding. Starts Jun/Jul. Colonial; nests in rock crevices. 1 egg.

Movements. Disperses S to winter off W coast of C America, reaching as far S as Colombia, Ecuador and possibly Peru.
Status and Conservation. Not globally threatened. Most abundant seabird in Gulf of California, with 100,000's or possibly 1,000,000's; c. 15,000 breeding birds at San Benito Is off Pacific coast of Baja California (1968). Introduced predators, especially rats and cats, on many islands in area. Surveys required to determine numbers, trends and threats; research on breeding biology and ecology also desirable to ensure future security.
Bibliography. Ainley (1984a), Bent (1922), Blake (1977), Everett & Anderson (1991), Jehl (1984), Palmer (1962), Ridgely & Gwynne (1989), Terres (1980), Wetmore (1965).

Genus *OCEANODROMA*   Reichenbach, 1853

10. **Wedge-rumped Storm-petrel**

Oceanodroma tethys

French: Océanite téthys   **German**: Galapagoswellenläufer   **Spanish**: Paíño de las Galápagos
Other common names: Galapagos Storm-petrel

Taxonomy. *Thalassidroma tethys* Bonaparte, 1852, Galapagos Islands.
Two subspecies recognized.
Subspecies and Distribution.
O. t. tethys (Bonaparte, 1852) - Galapagos Is.
O. t. kelsalli (Lowe, 1925) - Pescadores and San Gallán Is, off W Peru.

Descriptive notes. 18-20 cm. Much more white on rump and uppertail-coverts than any other storm-petrel. Pale centre to underwing; wings often angled forwards. Juvenile as adult. Race *kelsalli* averages smaller.
Habitat. Marine and pelagic, normally occurring well offshore, except near colonies; only species that regularly visits colonies by day (Galapagos). Breeds on cliffs or lava fields of remote islands and offshore stacks.
Food and Feeding. Mostly small fish, squid and crustaceans caught on wing, by pattering and dipping, or by surface-seizing while sitting on the water. Feeds mainly at night.
Breeding. In Galapagos, many birds present at colony in most months, but laying mainly in May/Jun. Colonial; nests in rock crevices or under vegetation cover. 1 egg; incubation in stints of c. 5 days; chick brooded for c. 2 days; fledging c. 76 days.
Movements. Some birds present throughout year at Galapagos, but most disperse following Humboldt Current, as do Peruvian population. Vagrant N to California.
Status and Conservation. Not globally threatened. Well in excess of 200,000 breeding pairs in Galapagos Is; exact numbers in Peru not known. Suffers predation by Short-eared Owl (*Asio flammeus*) in Galapagos; diurnal habits and location of breeding colonies make species particularly vulnerable to predation there. More research required, especially in Peru.
Bibliography. Ainley (1984a), Blake (1977), Coulter (1984), Duffy, Hays & Plenge (1984), Harris, M.P. (1969b, 1969c, 1974a), Johnson (1965), Murphy (1936), Ridgely & Gwynne (1989), Wetmore (1965).

11. **Madeiran Storm-petrel**

Oceanodroma castro

French: Océanite de Castro   **German**: Madeirawellenläufer   **Spanish**: Paíño de Madeira
Other common names: Band-rumped/Harcourt's Storm-petrel

Taxonomy. *Thalassidroma castro* Harcourt, 1851, Desertas Islets, Madeira.
Four birds caught at sea in Gulf of Guinea noticeably larger with less white on rump, might belong to undescribed subspecies. Monotypic.
Distribution. E Atlantic from Berlengas Is (off C Portugal) and Azores S to Ascension I and St Helena; also in Pacific, off E Japan, on Kauai (Hawaii) and at Galapagos.

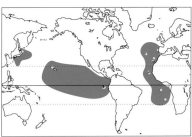

Descriptive notes. 19-21 cm; 29-56 g; wingspan 44-46 cm. Wing shape intermediate between *Oceanites oceanicus* and *Oceanodroma leucorhoa*; tail slightly forked, unlike *Oceanites* and *Hydrobates*, and underwing uniformly dark. Legs do not project beyond tip of tail in flight. Juvenile has more grey on greater upperwing-coverts.
Habitat. Marine and highly pelagic, occurring in warm waters; rarely approaches land except near colonies. Breeds on undisturbed islets, in flat areas near sea or inland on cliffs.
Food and Feeding. Mostly planktonic crustaceans, small fish and squid; also feeds on some human refuse. Feeds mainly on wing, by pattering and dipping; also surface-seizes. Most feeding by day.
Breeding. Season varies locally; in Galapagos two distinct populations breed annually, but 6 months out of phase. Colonial; nests in rock crevices or burrows. 1 egg; incubation c. 42 days with stints of 4-7 days; chick has pale grey down, brooded for c. 7 days; fledging c. 64-73 days. Estimated annual mortality of adults c. 6%; known to have reached nearly 11 years old in wild.
Movements. Apparently some birds largely sedentary, since colonies visited irregularly throughout year; others disperse widely, with records from Atlantic coast of N America, Britain, Cuba and Brazil.
Status and Conservation. Not globally threatened. Widespread, many islands holding several thousand breeding pairs; figures lacking for several areas. Main threats include direct exploitation by local fishermen, particularly on some Atlantic islands, and predation by introduced mammals, e.g. rats, cats, mice, mongooses; land crabs (*Ocypoda*) and Barn Owls (*Tyto alba*) kill many birds in Cape Verde Is.

Bibliography. Ainley (1984a), Allan (1962), Bent (1922), Blake (1977), Brazil (1991), Bretagnolle (1990a), Brown *et al.* (1982), Cramp & Simmons (1977), Croxall *et al.* (1984), Haney (1985), Harris, M.P. (1969b, 1969c, 1974a), Harrison (1990), Harrison *et al.* (1990), James & Robertson (1985b), Martín *et al.* (1984), McCaskie (1990), Mills (1968), Mougin *et al.* (1990b), Murphy (1936), de Naurois (1969b), Palmer (1962), Snow & Snow (1966), Teixeira & Moore (1983).

12. Swinhoe's Storm-petrel

Oceanodroma monorhis

French: Océanite de Swinhoe **German**: Swinhoewellenläufer **Spanish**: Paíño de Swinhoe

Taxonomy. *Thalassidroma monorhis* Swinhoe, 1867, near Amoy, China.
Sometimes considered subspecies of *O. leucorhoa*; these two may form superspecies with *O. homochroa*. Monotypic.
Distribution. Japan (N Kyushu, W Honshu) W to Yellow Sea off China and Korea, and N to extreme SE USSR. Recent records suggest possible breeding in N Atlantic.

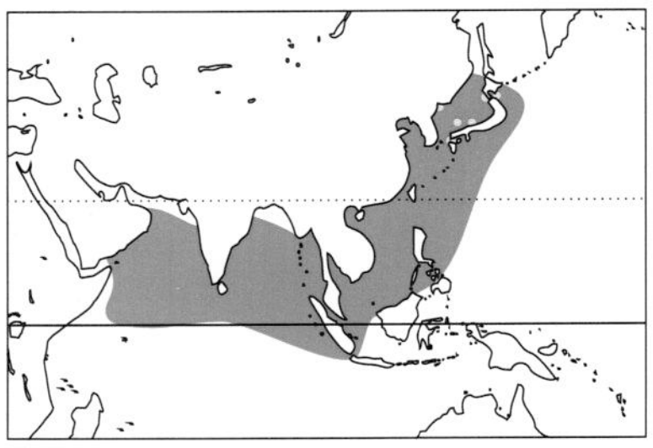

Descriptive notes. 19-20 cm; 38-40 g; wingspan 44-46 cm. Uniformly dark underwing separates from *O. homochroa*. Shallow fork to tail; different size from other all-dark species. Juvenile as adult.
Habitat. Marine and normally pelagic, but also occurs in coastal waters. Breeds on small offshore islands.
Food and Feeding. No information available on diet. Feeds mainly on wing by dipping; does not patter.
Breeding. Starts Apr. Forms loose colonies; nests in burrows. 1 egg.
Movements. Migrates S and W to winter in N Indian Ocean and Arabian Sea; irregular in Red Sea, straggling N to Elat in Gulf of Aqaba.
Status and Conservation. Not globally threatened. Largest known colony on Verkhovsky I, S of Vladivostok, with c. 7500 pairs; substantial predation by crows (*Corvus*) and migrating owls (*Asio*), but no mammals; frequent visits by tourists resulted in many nest losses, until protection of island in 1984. Minimum 1000 pairs in Japan; little known of populations in China and Korea. Much work required to determine population sizes and trends, main threats and conservation requirements.
Bibliography. Bailey *et al.* (1968), Brazil (1991), Bretagnolle *et al.* (1991), Brown *et al.* (1982), Cheng Tso-hsin (1987), Cramp & Simmons (1977), Croxall *et al.* (1984), Etchécopar & Hüe (1978), Gao Yu-ren (1984), James & Robertson (1985d), Litvinenko & Shibaev (1991), Netschajew (1969), Taoka & Okumura (1990), Taoka, Won & Okumura (1989), Won & Lee (1986), Zhao-Qing (1988).

13. Leach's Storm-petrel

Oceanodroma leucorhoa

French: Océanite culblanc **German**: Wellenläufer **Spanish**: Paíño Boreal
Other common names: (Leach's) Fork-tailed Storm-petrel (!); Socorro Storm-petrel (*socorroensis*)

Taxonomy. *Procellaria leucorhoa* Vieillot, 1818, maritime parts of Picardy.
Complex and confused, with major upheaval in recent years concerning status of birds down Pacific coast of N America; at present classification of birds in this zone is tentative. Birds of Guadalupe I (Mexico) particularly complicated, with three distinct populations breeding, possibly all belonging to different races; extensive individual variation adds to confusion. Some races have been treated as separate species; race *socorroensis* has been included in *O. monorhis*; traditionally recognized subspecies *beali* now generally regarded as obsolete. *O. monorhis* sometimes considered a race of present species; these two may form superspecies with *O. homochroa*. Four subspecies currently recognized.
Subspecies and Distribution.
O. l. leucorhoa (Vieillot, 1818) - N Pacific, from NE Japan N and E through Kuril and Aleutian Is to S Alaska, and SE to C California (USA); N Atlantic, from NE USA and E Canada E to Iceland, Faeroe Is, N Scotland and NW Norway.
O. l. chapmani Berlepsch, 1906 - San Benito and Coronados Is, off W Mexico.
O. l. socorroensis C. H. Townsend, 1890 - islets by Guadalupe I, off W Mexico (breeding in summer).
O. l. cheimomnestes Ainley, 1980 - Guadalupe I, off W Mexico (breeding in winter).

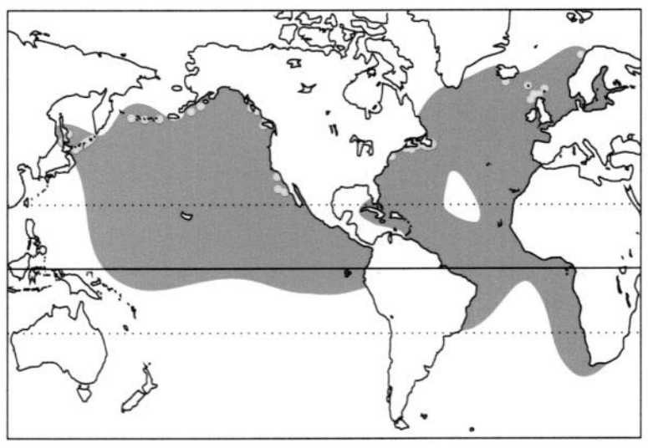

Descriptive notes. 19-22 cm; 45 g; wingspan 45-48 cm. Wings long and narrow, with sharp carpal bend; forked tail. Differs from other white-rumped species in combination of fairly well marked upperwing bar reaching forward to leading edge of wing, and less white looking rump due to dark median stripe. Some Pacific birds have dark rump. Juvenile can have even more prominent upperwing bar. Races separated on size and colour of rump.
Habitat. Marine and pelagic; often in areas of convergence or upwelling, or over continental shelf, rarely coming near land except at colonies. Breeds on offshore islands on high ground or slopes, usually among rocks but also in soft soil between tree roots.
Food and Feeding. Mainly small fish, squid, planktonic crustaceans and offal. Prey caught on the wing by dipping and skimming, or snatched from surface (see page 261). May feed both night and day. Sometimes follows marine mammals, feeding on left overs or faeces.
Breeding. Starts May in N Atlantic; at Guadalupe I (Mexico) different subspecies breed in summer and winter. Colonial; nests in burrows or rock crevices, nest sometimes lined with grass and twigs. 1 egg; incubation 41-42 days, with stints of c. 3 days; chicks have bluish grey down, brooded for 5 days; fledging 63-70 days. Sexual maturity at 5 years, occasionally at 4. Known to have reached 24 years old in wild.
Movements. N populations migrate S into tropics: N Atlantic birds occur S to South Africa and occasionally reach Indian Ocean; Pacific birds apparently winter mostly in equatorial zone of E Pacific. Several records from Australia and New Zealand; behaviour strongly suggesting possible breeding at Chatham Is.
Status and Conservation. Not globally threatened. Widespread and abundant, with total population of at least 10,000,000 birds; c. 4,000,000 in Alaska, c. 1,100,000 at over 40 sites in British Columbia, c. 350,000 birds on Kuril Is, off SE USSR (1972). Exact figures lacking for many breeding sites, especially in Europe, and recent trends not clear. Suffers severe predation chiefly by gulls, rats, cats, mice, mink, otters and foxes; these are responsible for some local declines, and some colonies having moved to predator-free offshore stacks; control of foxes on some of Aleutian Is has led to recolonization. Off NE USA some recolonization with help of artificial burrows and tape lures.
Bibliography. Ainley (1980, 1983, 1984a), Ainley *et al.* (1990), Batten *et al.* (1990), Bent (1922), Billings (1968), Blake (1977), Bourne & Jehl (1982), Brazil (1991), Brown, L.H. *et al.* (1982), Brown, R.G.B (1988c), Cramp & Simmons (1977), Cramp *et al.* (1974), Crossin (1974), Croxall (1991), Croxall *et al.* (1984), DeGange & Nelson (1982), Griffin (1940), Gross (1935), Grubb (1973, 1974, 1979), Hall-Craggs & Sellar (1976), Hatch & Hatch (1990), Hémery & Jouanin (1988), Imber & Lovegrove (1982), Jehl & Everett (1985), Lindsey (1986), Linton (1978), Lloyd *et al.* (1991), Marchant & Higgins (1990), Montevecchi *et al.* (1983), Morse & Buchheister (1977, 1979), Murphy (1936), Nakamura, Hori & Osaka (1983), Palmer (1962), Pinto (1983), Pitman & Ballance (1990), Place *et al.* (1989), Podolsky & Kress (1989), Power & Ainley (1986), Quinlan (1983), Randall & Randall (1986c), Richards (1990), Ricklefs *et al.* (1980, 1985, 1986, 1987), Sharrock (1976), Sklepkovych & Montevecchi (1989), Taoka, Sato *et al.* (1988, 1989), Tasker *et al.* (1987), Terres (1980), Thom (1986), Threlfall (1974), Vermeer *et al.* (1988), Watanuki (1985, 1986), Wilbur (1969).

14. Markham's Storm-petrel

Oceanodroma markhami

French: Océanite de Markham **German**: Rußwellenläufer **Spanish**: Paíño Ahumado
Other common names: Sooty Storm-petrel

Taxonomy. *Cymochorea markhami* Salvin, 1883, coast of Peru, lat. 19° 40' S, long. 75° W.
Sometimes considered conspecific with *O. tristrami*. Monotypic.
Distribution. SE Pacific, with breeding confirmed only on Paracas Peninsula (14° S), Peru, where first nests recently found; bulk of population probably nests on coast of Chile or Peru.

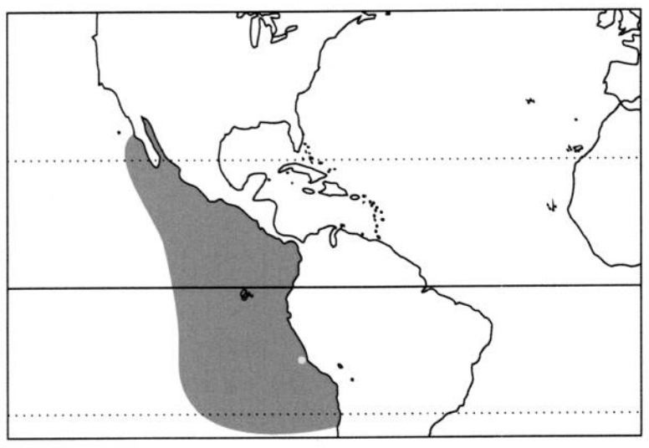

Descriptive notes. 23 cm. Forked tail. Pale bar on underwing reaches forward to leading edge of wing, in contrast to *O. melania*. Has more deeply forked tail than *O. tristrami* and generally browner, lacking blue-grey tinge. Juvenile as adult.
Habitat. Marine, occurring in cool offshore waters. Suspected to nest mainly down desert coast.
Food and Feeding. No information available.
Breeding. First nests found in August 1987. Next to nothing known of breeding biology.
Movements. Probably disperses along Humboldt Current, normally ranging between c. 15° N and 26° S; some birds apparently off coast of Peru all year round.
Status and Conservation. INDETERMINATE. Breeding grounds unknown until 1987. Virtually nothing known of population size, trends or main threats; research urgently required.
Bibliography. Blake (1977), Collar & Andrew (1988), Duffy, Hays & Plenge (1984), Harrison (1990), Johnson (1965), Murphy (1936), Schlatter (1984).

15. Tristram's Storm-petrel

Oceanodroma tristrami

French: Océanite de Tristram **German**: Tristramwellenläufer **Spanish**: Paíño de Tristram
Other common names: Sooty/Stejneger's Storm-petrel

Taxonomy. *Oceanodroma tristrami* Salvin, 1896, Sendai Bay, Honshu, Japan.
Sometimes considered subspecies of *O. markhami*. Monotypic.
Distribution. Tropical and subtropical C & W Pacific, breeding at three or more sites in Hawaii; also (formerly?) in Izu and Bonin Is, off SE Japan.

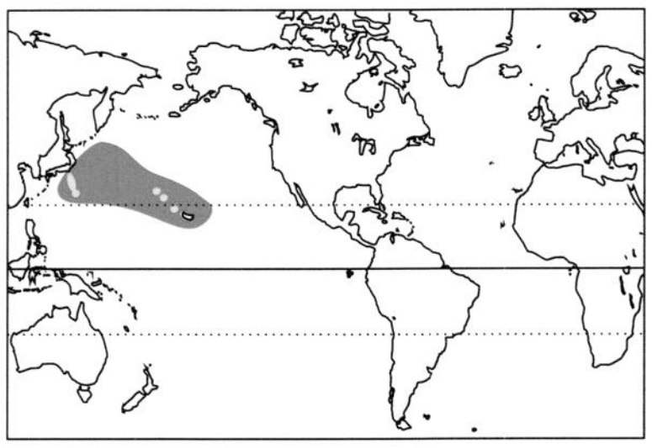

Descriptive notes. 24-25 cm; wingspan 56 cm. Prominent pale bar on upperwing reaches forward to leading edge. Plumage has bluish grey tinge, becoming browner with wear. Tail less deeply forked than in *O. markhami* and *O. matsudairae*.
Habitat. Marine and pelagic, rarely approaching land except at colonies. Breeds on volcanic offshore islands.
Food and Feeding. Mainly small fish and squid, with some planktonic crustaceans. Mostly caught on wing by pattering and snatching from surface.
Breeding. Mainly in local winter, with peak in Dec/Jan. Colonial; nests in burrows or recesses in scree. 1 egg; fledging by mid-May.
Movements. Thought to disperse only over adjacent seas; W populations may move short distance N up coast of Japan.
Status and Conservation. INSUFFICIENTLY KNOWN (under review). Population size not well known; at least 3500-7500 breeding pairs in Hawaii, but trends unknown; probably exterminated from Midway I by rats. Formerly bred in huge numbers on Torishima I (Izu Is), to S of Japan, but recently exterminated by cats and rats; little recent information from other Japanese former breeding islands, e.g. Bonin Is. Extensive research needed to determine population sizes, trends, main threats and conservation requirements.
Bibliography. Ainley (1984a), Bent (1922), Brazil (1991), Clapp & Wirtz (1975), Harrison (1990), Harrison *et al.* (1984), Hasegawa (1984), Rauzon *et al.* (1985).

16. Black Storm-petrel

Oceanodroma melania

French: Océanite noir **German**: Schwarzwellenläufer **Spanish**: Paíño Negro

Taxonomy. *Procellaria melania* Bonaparte, 1854, coast of California.
Possibly conspecific with *O. matsudairae*; these two sometimes isolated in separate genus, *Loomelania*, in view of long tarsi. Monotypic.
Distribution. Islands off W California (USA) and Baja California and in most of Gulf of California.

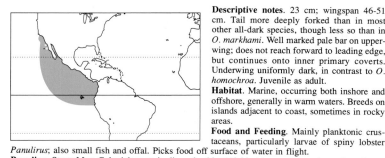

Descriptive notes. 23 cm; wingspan 46-51 cm. Tail more deeply forked than in most other all-dark species, though less so than in *O. markhami*. Well marked pale bar on upperwing; does not reach forward to leading edge, but continues onto inner primary coverts. Underwing uniformly dark, in contrast to *O. homochroa*. Juvenile as adult.

Habitat. Marine, occurring both inshore and offshore, generally in warm waters. Breeds on islands adjacent to coast, sometimes in rocky areas.

Food and Feeding. Mainly planktonic crustaceans, particularly larvae of spiny lobster *Panulirus*; also small fish and offal. Picks food off surface of water in flight.

Breeding. Starts May. Colonial; nests in disused auklet (Alcidae) burrows or rock crevices. 1 egg.

Movements. Disperses or migrates S to at least 8° S, to winter off W coasts of C and S America.

Status and Conservation. Not globally threatened. Little known of numbers and current status, but apparently numerous in Gulf of California; at 2 sites off Pacific coast of Baja California alternative estimates 10,000+ (1968) or 100,000's (1975). Suffers heavy predation by cats and rats on several breeding islands in Baja California. Only c. 150 birds nest at 2 colonies in California, USA. Information on populations needed to establish immediate conservation requirements.

Bibliography. Ainley (1984a), Bent (1922), Blake (1977), Everett & Anderson (1991), Harris, S.W. (1974), Jehl (1984), Palmer (1962), Terres (1980).

17. Matsudaira's Storm-petrel

Oceanodroma matsudairae

French: Océanite de Matsudaira   **Spanish**: Paíño de Matsudaira
                     German: Matsudairawellenläufer
Other common names: Sooty Storm-petrel

Taxonomy. *Oceanodroma melania matsudariae* [sic] Nagamichi Kuroda, 1922, Sagami Bay, Honshu, Japan. Sometimes considered subspecies of *O. melania*; these two sometimes isolated in separate genus, *Loomelania*, in view of long tarsi. Monotypic.
Distribution. Breeding at Kita-iwojima and Minami-iwojima in Volcano Is to SE of Japan.

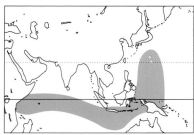

Descriptive notes. 24-25 cm; wingspan 56 cm. Deeply forked tail. Upperwing bar less conspicuous than in *O. tristrami*, but also reaches forward to leading edge, in contrast to *O. melania*. Differs from *O. markhami* and other dark species in white shaft bases of outer primaries contrasting markedly with dark remainder of outer wing. Juvenile probably similar to adult.

Habitat. Marine and pelagic, normally occurring far from coast; on migration often found over waters of continental shelf; frequently occurs in warm waters, but may be associated with local areas of upwelling and convergence. Breeds on high ground on offshore islands.

Food and Feeding. Little information available on diet; known to feed on galley waste from ships. Feeds mainly on wing, by dipping and snatching from surface. Sometimes follows ships.

Breeding. Starts Jan. Colonial; nests in burrows. Fledging occurs mostly in Jun.

Movements. Long distance migrant: after breeding, moves S across equator perhaps to Timor Sea off NW Australia, where turns W into Indian Ocean, wintering mostly in rich waters of equatorial belt around Seychelles and W to Somalia and Kenya; some birds may winter off NE New Guinea.

Status and Conservation. Not globally threatened. Little known, reported to breed on Kita-iwojima and Minami-iwojima in Volcano Is, to SE of Japan; no figures available, and Kita-iwojima not visited recently. Survey work required to determine population size, trends and main threats.

Bibliography. Bailey (1968), Bailey *et al.* (1968), Brazil (1991), Brown *et al.* (1982), Hasegawa (1984), Kuroda (1960), Lindsey (1986), Marchant & Higgins (1990).

18. Ashy Storm-petrel

Oceanodroma homochroa

French: Océanite cendré   **German**: Kalifornienwellenläufer   **Spanish**: Paíño Ceniciento

Taxonomy. *Cymochorea homochroa* Coues, 1864, Farallon Islands, California.
May form superspecies with *O. monorhis* and *O. leucorhoa*. Monotypic.

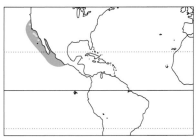

Distribution. Bird I, Farallon Is and Channel Is, off California (USA), S to Coronados Is (Mexico).

Descriptive notes. 18-21 cm; 38 g. Pale wash on underwing forms more or less distinct bar, separating from *O. monorhis* and other dark storm-petrels. Juvenile as adult.

Habitat. Marine and pelagic, normally staying well away from land, except at colonies. Breeds on offshore islands.

Food and Feeding. Limited distribution suggests may be food specialist; little information available, but diet seems to be based mainly on planktonic crustaceans and small fish, perhaps with some vegetable matter. Feeds mainly on wing, by dipping and snatching from surface.

Breeding. Start of season protracted, even within same colony, with eggs at least Jan-Aug. Colonial; nests in rock crevices or burrows. 1 egg; incubation c. 42 days; fledging c. 84 days, peaks Sept.

Movements. Thought to remain generally within adjacent seas, with some birds dispersing short distances to S. Absent from Farallon Is in Nov/Dec.

Status and Conservation. Not globally threatened. Total population c. 5200 breeding birds; apparently little change in recent decades. Part of population nests on protected islands off California, specially managed for the species. Small population implies species insecure; work required to determine factors keeping numbers low; protection of all breeding grounds desirable; also provision of additional predator-free areas into which species might expand.

Bibliography. Ainley (1984a), Ainley, Henderson & Strong (1990), Ainley, Morrell & Lewis (1975), Bent (1922), Everett & Anderson (1991), Jehl (1984), Palmer (1962), Terres (1980).

19. Hornby's Storm-petrel

Oceanodroma hornbyi

French: Océanite de Hornby   **German**: Kragenwellenläufer   **Spanish**: Paíño Acollarado
Other common names: Ringed Storm-petrel

Taxonomy. *Thalassidroma Hornbyi* G. R. Gray, 1854, west coast of South America.
Monotypic.
Distribution. SE Pacific; breeding suspected in coastal desert of S Peru and N Chile.

Descriptive notes. 21-23 cm. Pale upperparts; underparts white with characteristic grey collar. Only *Oceanodroma* storm-petrel with capped appearance; forehead and hindcollar white, but lacks white supercilium. Juvenile probably similar to adult.

Habitat. Marine and pelagic, normally occurring far from coast.

Food and Feeding. No information available on diet. Feeds mainly on wing, by pattering, dipping and snatching from surface.

Breeding. Breeding grounds remain undiscovered; might breed in coastal desert, possibly well inland.

Movements. Presumably disperses over waters of Humboldt Current adjacent to breeding grounds; seen Aug-Dec as far N as equator.

Status and Conservation. INSUFFICIENTLY KNOWN. As breeding grounds undiscovered, impossible to estimate population size, trends and conservation requirements; flocks of thousands recorded. Research priority must be location of breeding grounds.

Bibliography. Blake (1977), Collar & Andrew (1988), Duffy, Hays & Plenge (1984), Johnson (1965), Murphy (1936), Schlatter (1984).

20. Fork-tailed Storm-petrel

Oceanodroma furcata

French: Océanite à queue fourchue   **Spanish**: Paíño Rabihorcado
                     German: Gabelschwanz-Wellenläufer
Other common names: Grey Storm-petrel

Taxonomy. *Procellaria furcata* Gmelin, 1789, icy seas between America and Asia.
Two subspecies recognized.
Subspecies and Distribution.
O. f. furcata (Gmelin, 1789) - N Kuril, Commander and Aleutian Is.
O. f. plumbea (Peale, 1848) - W coast of N America, from Alaska S to N California.

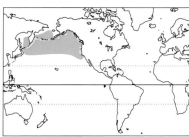

Descriptive notes. 20-23 cm; c. 59 g; wingspan 46 cm. Only grey storm-petrel; very pale underparts, forked tail and dark mask. Juvenile as adult. Race *plumbea* averages smaller and darker.

Habitat. Marine and pelagic, normally occurring over cold waters far from shore. Breeds on offshore islands, in grassy areas, on rocky hillsides or amongst trees; sometimes far from sea.

Food and Feeding. Mainly planktonic crustaceans, small fish and squid; also takes offal. Feeds on wing, by dipping and snatching from surface; also by seizing food whilst sitting on water. Follows ships and congregates around dead whales.

Breeding. Starts May/Jun. Colonial; nests in burrows or rock crevices. 1 egg; incubation c. 39 days; fledging c. 58 days.

Movements. Apparently disperses over adjacent waters, regularly occurring S to N Japan and S California, and N to Bering Strait.

Status and Conservation. Not globally threatened. Abundant, with total population estimated at c. 5,000,000 birds; most nest along coastal Alaska and Aleutian Is; c. 380,000 breeding birds at over 44 sites in British Columbia; c. 200,000 birds on Kuril Is, off SE USSR (1972). Subject to predation mostly by foxes, in particular, also gulls, rats, cats, mice, otters and even bears (see page 264). Disappearance of introduced predators on several islands has led to recolonization by species and overall increase in numbers; eradication of introduced predators highly desirable on other islands.

Bibliography. Ainley (1984a), Bent (1922), Boersma (1986b), Boersma & Wheelwright (1979), Boersma *et al.* (1980), Brazil (1991), Croxall *et al.* (1984), DeGange & Nelson (1982), Hatch & Hatch (1990), Litvinenko & Shibaev (1991), Palmer (1962), Quinlan (1983), Rodway (1991), Simons (1981), Terres (1980), Vermeer *et al.* (1988), Vleck & Kenagy (1980), Wheelwright (1987), Wheelwright & Boersma (1979).

Class AVES
Order PROCELLARIIFORMES
Family PELECANOIDIDAE (DIVING-PETRELS)

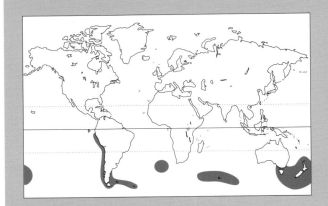

- Small, stocky seabirds with short wings and tail and "tubenose".
- 18-25 cm.

- Circumpolar in Southern Ocean.
- Subantarctic marine waters, inshore and offshore.
- 1 genus, 4 species, 9 taxa.
- 1 species threatened; none extinct since 1600.

Systematics

Within the Procellariiformes, the diving-petrels represent the highest degree of adaptation to an aquatic life. They form a distinct evolutionary branch, and, while all the other members of the order have perfected their flying abilities to the point of becoming highly aerial in most aspects of their lives, often to the detriment of other capabilities, diving-petrels have evolved towards the conquest of the water. Fossil evidence from the early Pliocene in South Africa sheds little light on the origins of the family, but it seems reasonable to surmise that diving-petrels may have differentiated in isolation somewhere around South America or Australasia and then spread widely into favourable areas of the Southern Ocean.

The taxonomy of the diving-petrels is a matter of some debate, and some systematists place them within the Procellariidae. Most workers recognize four species, two of which, the Peruvian Diving-petrel (*Pelecanoides garnotii*) and the Magellanic Diving-petrel (*Pelecanoides magellani*), have restricted ranges, while the South Georgia Diving-petrel (*Pelecanoides georgicus*) shows negligible geographical variation, even though it occurs in the Atlantic, Indian and Pacific sectors of the Southern Ocean. The Common Diving-petrel (*Pelecanoides urinatrix*) has the widest breeding range, overlapping partly with two of the other species, and it also shows the highest degree of geographical variation. At least six different races are commonly recognized, and on occasions some of these have been considered distinct species, for they differ almost as much from the nominate race as they do from the other species.

Morphological Aspects

Diving-petrels are small, stocky seabirds, with oval bodies, a short neck and rather short wings. While they clearly belong in the order Procellariiformes, as indicated by their "tubenose", they are remarkably similar in morphology and locomotion to the Northern Hemisphere auks (Alcidae), in particular the Little Auk or Dovekie (*Alle alle*) of the Arctic and North Atlantic, although the similarities are certainly due to convergent evolution, and the two families are quite unrelated.

The bill of the diving-petrels is short, broad at the base and hooked at the tip. As in the other Procellariiformes, it is formed by several horny plates and has external tubular nostrils (see page 218). These, however, open upwards, as opposed to forwards in other petrels, presumably as an adaptation for di-

ving. In common with plankton-eating auks, a diving-petrel is able to transport food, as it has a gular pouch, a distensible sac formed by the skin of the throat, which is used for storing food temporarily. Indeed, the generic name *Pelecanoides* comes from this pouch, as it was compared to the much larger and more spectacular ones of the pelicans.

As in the auks, the wings are short and strong, for efficient underwater propulsion, while flight is typically fast with whirring wingbeats, creating a marked contrast with all other Procellariiformes. Diving-petrels are unique in their extraordinary ability to "fly" through waves: they typically fly along low over the water and, on approaching an unusually high wave, do not hesitate to fly straight into it, emerging from the other side with no apparent alteration of speed or direction.

As in most other diving birds, the feet are webbed and the legs are set far back on their bodies, in the ideal position for swimming. However, walking on dry land is consequently difficult, and they scramble along slowly and clumsily. Diving-petrels are agile swimmers and divers, even in the roughest seas, and, in common with many of the auks, they sit rather high on the water, floating lightly on top of the waves. They usually dive from the surface, using their feet and tails as rudders and their wings as oars or propellers, thus "flying" under water, once again like auks.

There is evidence that, in common with the auks but unlike any other petrels, all of the flight-feathers are moulted simultaneously in the diving-petrels, leaving the birds flightless for a few weeks until the new feathers are fully-grown and suitable for sustained flight. Inconvenient though this may seem, the shape of the wing without the flight-feathers, when it closely resembles a penguin flipper, is ideal for propulsion under water, so the birds' feeding capabilities far from being reduced may actually be enhanced. In addition, diving-petrels normally prefer to escape from danger by diving rather than by flying, so it is only their long distance mobility that is affected by this temporary flightlessness.

Like many auks, the body weight of diving-petrels is near the limit that can be sustained by their small wing area, so they have to fly fast in order to defy the laws of gravity. As a consequence, any reduction in their wing area, however slight, but most notably during moult, or any increase of body weight beyond the limit, for instance after a heavy meal, can render them flightless, at any rate momentarily, until the balance is restored. Take-off can require a long run into the wind with much pattering on the water surface before they become airborne, though sometimes they appear to emerge from waves

The diving-petrels are perhaps the nearest equivalent in the south to the auks (Alcidae) of the Northern Hemisphere. They are much the most aquatic members of the large marine order Procellariiformes, and in order to get better propulsion their webbed feet are set far back on the body, as can clearly be seen on this Common Diving-petrel. The offshoot of this is that they find walking on dry land rather hard going, so like many other petrels they only visit their breeding colonies at night, so that the risk of falling prey to gulls or skuas is notably reduced.

[Pelecanoides urinatrix. Photo: Peter Steyn/Ardea]

Three of the four species are extremely similar, and this South Georgia Diving-petrel can only be safely separated from the Common and Peruvian Diving-petrels by its rather shorter, broader bill and the configuration of the nostrils. Note the highly streamlined body and the typical "tubenose" of the Procellariiformes.

[*Pelecanoides georgicus*. Photo: D. Garrick/NPIAW]

already in full flight. Landing on the water is generally more straightforward, as birds tend to plunge directly into the water. However, on dry land they tend to come down with a bump, and this can leave them stunned for a moment.

Plumage is dark grey or brown above, with some white fringes, and white below, from the throat to the undertail-coverts. There is no sexual dimorphism, and juveniles fledge with a plumage very similar to that of the adults. Only the Magellanic Diving-petrel has a notably different juvenile plumage, which lacks much of the adult's white fringing. The remarkable similarity of the species makes their identification at sea very difficult, even for experienced observers. In the hand, the most reliable features for use in identifying birds are overall size and bill shape, probably signalling differences in diet or feeding technique.

Habitat

Diving-petrels are strictly marine birds, occurring in both inshore and offshore waters. Although not exceptional far from land, the Common and Magellanic Diving-petrels appear to be primarily inshore feeders. They are generally found in coastal waters around their breeding islands, in bays, fjords or channels. In marked contrast, the South Georgia and Peruvian Diving-petrels commonly feed further offshore and may even forage in pelagic waters.

Breeding colonies may be placed on barren, rocky ground or where there is a certain amount of vegetation, though each species has its own preferences. Diving-petrel colonies are as vulnerable to predation as those of any other petrel species, and so are usually situated on sloping ground on offshore or oceanic islands. A slope facilitates take-off and landing manoeuvres, and reduces the average time spent out in the open by the incoming or outgoing birds, and this, in turn, reduces the risk of predation. The few colonies situated on the mainland are small and consequently of little significance to the total populations.

General Habits

Although often highly gregarious on land, where they form large, dense breeding aggregations, at sea diving-petrels are more commonly seen alone or in small rafts. When not actively feeding, they spend most of their time sitting on the water. They

show some reluctance to fly, and normally prefer to dive, if approached by a predator or a ship. They do not, as a rule, follow ships or attend trawlers to feed astern of them, so their interaction with members of other species is limited.

Diving-petrels generally roost at sea, but during the breeding season they spend the night in their burrows. Some populations are virtually sedentary, and in such cases intermittent roosting in the burrows outside the breeding season is not uncommon. They are strictly nocturnal on land, entering the colony in the dark and in numbers, in order to escape predation by gulls or skuas. For this same reason, they normally try to avoid coming to land on moonlit nights. Once on the ground, they may have to walk a few metres to the burrow entrance, and, this tends to be the moment chosen by skuas to prey upon them, as they are such inexpert walkers (see Morphological Aspects). If attacked by a predator on the ground, there is little a diving-petrel can do. On steep ground, there is a chance it can run downhill and fly away, but more often it will fall victim to the predator, and the available evidence suggests that there is normally a high degree of natural predation.

Voice

Diving-petrels are normally silent at sea. However, on their breeding grounds, they are extremely vocal, and make a large number of sounds including whistles, squeaks, moans, coos, mews and groans. These are uttered in the air above the colony, as well as inside the burrows, and, as in other petrels, probably help a bird flying over to locate its nest more easily.

There are also vocalizations to indicate that a bird is sexually receptive or ready to defend its nest-site. A vocal exchange can avert a fight and thus avoid the risk of having to alight on the ground, where the birds would be more exposed to predation (see General Habits).

Food and Feeding

The diet of diving-petrels consists principally of planktonic crustaceans, while they also take some small fish and cephalopods. Much the most common prey are euphausiids, such as Antarctic krill (*Euphausia superba*), and copepods, as well, to a lesser extent, as amphipod shrimps.

Preferences vary with species, locality and time of year. South Georgia Diving-petrels studied at South Georgia, in the

South Atlantic, were found to take 70% euphausiids in late February, but by the middle of March these constituted 100% of the birds' diet. In contrast, at Heard Island, in the southern Indian Ocean, copepods and amphipods were the most commonly taken prey. Results for Common Diving-petrels at South Georgia showed a decrease in copepods from 89% to 60% of their diet between early January and early February.

As their name indicates, diving-petrels catch most of their food under water by diving, either from the surface or plunging in directly from the air. Using their wings as flippers (see Morphological Aspects), they can reach great depths and cover fair distances under water. They may remain under for several minutes and make successive dives for hours. On occasions birds may eat so much, that they are temporarily unable to fly (see Morphological Aspects).

Records show that a considerable proportion of their food is caught during the hours of daylight, but there is evidence that some may be obtained at night, when large swarms of plankton migrate vertically and collect on surface waters.

Breeding

Like many other petrels, diving-petrels breed colonially. Their colonies can number many thousands of breeding pairs, which generally assemble on slopes on oceanic islands. The South Georgia Diving-petrel is remarkable in that some of its breeding colonies are situated well inland, often on high ground, and this obviously represents an extra effort for the adults, which have to travel longer distances loaded down with food for their young; it also means extra strain for the fledgling, which has a long way to fly on untried wings before it reaches the sea. However, there is compensation in the form of reduced predation, as such colonies are often situated in barren, inhospitable areas, in which few animals are adapted to survive.

Diving-petrels start visiting their breeding grounds long before the breeding cycle actually commences, though their visits are strictly nocturnal, as is the case of many of the Procellariiformes. As the season advances, the number of occupied sites increases. During the hours of darkness, territorial birds inside their burrows start calling, as do those flying over the breeding grounds. This establishes communication between the birds, indicating which territories are occupied and which birds

are looking for a mate. Throughout the breeding season, the colony is virtually always busy with birds flying over. During the early stages, these are mostly potential breeders, but later on they are joined by immatures and subadults, which spend long hours wheeling around above the nesting grounds.

The nest-site is a burrow dug by the birds themselves, for instance in soft soil, sand or guano. This is sometimes covered by some kind of vegetation, such as tussock grass or trees, but the hole may be dug in fine scree among rocks. The entrance to the burrow is very often hidden by a stone or tussock, or partly covered by twigs or plant debris. The burrow itself is usually less than 1·5 m long, but this depends largely on the locality, the type of soil and even the climatic conditions. It may be only a few centimetres wide, and is often twisted, ending in an enlarged nest chamber, which may on occasions be lined with feathers, grass or pebbles.

After a period of feeding abundantly at sea, the female lays a single large white egg, which is incubated by both sexes in alternate shifts for about seven or eight weeks. The relative proximity of the feeding grounds to the colony allows for a nightly switch-over of incubation duty, and this makes it the shortest incubation stint of all the Procellariiformes. The chick hatches with a fairly sparse covering of greyish down, through which the bare skin shows in places, especially on the face and throat. The brooding period is long for petrels, and can last up to 15 days, depending on species, locality, weather and food availability, amongst other things. As the adults forage near the colony, they can visit their chick most nights, and regularly feed it on a mixture of partly digested crustaceans and small fish. The chick rapidly starts to put on weight and soon begins to develop its plumage. Gradually the parents' feeding visits become less frequent, and then one night, when the chick is about eight weeks old, perhaps still with vestiges of down, it flies out to sea alone.

At this point a crucial period in the bird's life begins, during which it will have to learn all by itself where to find food and how to capture it, where danger lies, which animals are dangerous, how to survive bad weather, and so on. Many die during this period, but those that survive the first winter will probably join the flocks of immature birds that wheel above the colony. Sexual maturity and first breeding generally occur at two or three years of age in the diving-petrels, which is much earlier than in the rest of petrels, and suggests a shorter average lifespan.

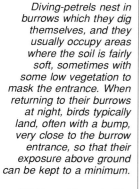

Diving-petrels nest in burrows which they dig themselves, and they usually occupy areas where the soil is fairly soft, sometimes with some low vegetation to mask the entrance. When returning to their burrows at night, birds typically land, often with a bump, very close to the burrow entrance, so that their exposure above ground can be kept to a minimum.

[Pelecanoides urinatrix. Photo: J. Warham/NPIAW]

Movements

Though little is known for sure, diving-petrels appear to be dispersive rather than migratory, and once breeding is over, they seem to scatter somewhat at random throughout the waters surrounding their breeding grounds.

The movements of an average bird are thought to be in the region of a few hundred kilometres at most each year, and many remain within the immediate vicinity of the colony, which they may visit intermittently outside the breeding season. Nevertheless, it is not unusual to see a few birds in mid-ocean, far from any nesting grounds, and this obviously indicates a certain amount of movement further away from the colony. At least part of the population, perhaps members of a particular age-class, undertake longer trips out to sea, and may occur well outside their normal breeding range. It is probable that, as in many other seabirds, it is the immature birds that are the most mobile.

Relationship with Man

The story of man's interactions with diving-petrels is short. As they are small and strictly nocturnal on land, and they often live in areas which are not frequented much by man, there is little tradition of their contact with humans, and for the same reasons the available information on their biology and ecology is recent and fragmentary.

It seems likely that, before the arrival of the White Man, the natives around some of the diving-petrels' breeding areas probably took some birds for food, particularly in the region of Cape Horn, where food must have been scarce. Today diving-petrels are still widely known in South America by the name "potoyunco" or "pato yunco", meaning "Yuncan Duck", a reference to a primitive tribe of the Peruvian coast, which may have exploited the birds for food. Sailors have traditionally known them as "firebirds", perhaps an allusion to their very fast flight.

Status and Conservation

Some species of diving-petrel, most notably the Common and South Georgia Diving-petrels, are among the world's most abundant seabirds, with breeding populations in the order of several million pairs. On the other hand, the Peruvian Diving-petrel is declining and is now listed as a threatened species. It serves as a reminder that very large numbers need not imply security when concentrated at few localities.

Peruvian Diving-petrels once formed huge breeding aggregations on the arid offshore islands along the coasts of Peru and Chile. Immense numbers of these and other seabirds were supported by the rich, cool waters of the Humboldt Current, although populations were decimated from time to time by the phenomenon known as "El Niño" (see page 341).

The commercial exploitation of guano as a fertilizer took off around the middle of the nineteenth century, with disastrous results for the seabird populations (see page 338). As the Peruvian Diving-petrels were used to digging their burrows in the guano, the extraction of such vast quantities of guano meant the destruction of their breeding grounds. In addition, large numbers of adults and chicks were found by the workers as they collected the guano, and these were commonly killed and eaten. In this way huge colonies could be almost completely wiped out in only a few weeks or months. Although the exploitation of guano is heavily restricted nowadays, only a few thousand pairs of Peruvian Diving-petrels still survive, nesting where they can on the barren islands. In Chile, until recently the species was still thought to be common, but it is apparently declining. Throughout its range it requires adequate protection, particularly of its breeding grounds, through a series of effectively patrolled reserves.

Perhaps the main global menace to diving-petrels is the same that affects the other Procellariiformes. Many remote oceanic islands had no terrestrial predators until the arrival of man. His colonization has meant the introduction of rats, cats, mice, dogs, mustelids, foxes, pigs, rabbits, goats, and others to these environments, with disastrous results. Entire breeding colonies, perhaps containing hundreds of thousands of breeding pairs, have been eaten out or have had to move to other, less convenient locations.

In the case of the diving-petrels, it is cats that are the worst offenders. In the southern Indian Ocean, Marion Island, which once held thriving colonies of South Georgia and Common Diving-petrels, probably no longer supports a single pair, after the island's 2200 or so feral cats, which killed over 455,000 seabirds each year, selected them as a major prey species. Meanwhile, on nearby Prince Edward Island, still without introduced predators, both species have continued to breed in large numbers. Likewise, in the Crozet Islands, it is Est Island that is free from introduced predators and consequently still supports millions of pairs of South Georgia Diving-petrels.

The most urgent measure to be taken towards the conservation not only of diving-petrels, but also of many other kinds of seabirds, is the eradication from the breeding islands of all introduced predators, as well as competitors, such as rabbits and goats, which through their grazing cause extensive soil erosion, and destroy the breeding habitat. Several campaigns have already been undertaken, particularly on islands around New Zealand, and these have developed effective methods of eliminating rats, cats and the like. It is to be hoped that these positive results will lead to further programmes of pest control, at least on those islands with important colonies.

Besides these introduced predators, diving-petrels have, of course, their natural predators, which include skuas, gulls and owls. However, the combined effects of all natural predation on a species can only rarely cause a long-term reduction in its numbers. Nevertheless, when a species is declining due to other factors, the impact of natural predation is merely to exacerbate the situation and accelerate the decline. Similarly, a reduction in numbers is liable to mean a decrease in density, and breeding success in many seabirds is known to be directly dependent on density; all such negative factors tend to influence each other.

Another potential danger to all seabird populations is competition from commercial fisheries. To date, this does not seem to have had significant effects on such specialized feeders as the diving-petrels, which base their diet on planktonic crustaceans. Nevertheless, excessive plundering of krill stocks may yet occur, before sustainable levels of exploitation have been established, and a slump in this crucial element in southern marine food chains could cause irreparable damage.

There is little evidence that diving-petrels suffer much unnatural mortality at sea. The areas they frequent are still not very heavily fished, so there is a relatively small risk of birds getting entangled in fishing nets. Besides, they do not approach ships in order to follow them or feed astern of them. There are a few casualties at night, however, when birds crash into ships, having been attracted by their lights.

Oil is not a significant threat to diving-petrels at present, as the main routes taken by tankers lie some distance away from their foraging grounds. Nonetheless, spills around southern South America, such as that of the Napier (270,000 barrels) in 1973, and that of the Metuia (330,000 barrels) in 1974, show that the danger is there. Certainly, their feeding technique suggests that, if there were a major oil spill in their range, birds would be liable to surface, after a long dive, in the midst of an oil-slick, as has already proved a disastrous tendency of the auks. Clearly, an oil spill near the diving-petrels' feeding areas could have devastating effects.

General Bibliography
Alexander *et al.* (1965), Bang (1966), Barrowclough *et al.* (1981), Bourne (1968b, 1985), Croxall (1991), Croxall *et al.* (1984), Cairns (1986), Furness & Monaghan (1987), Harrison (1977, 1985, 1987), Hutchinson & Wenzel (1980), Kuroda (1967), Löfgren (1984), Moors & Atkinson (1984), Murphy & Harper (1921), Nelson (1980), Pennycuick (1987), Prince & Morgan (1987), Tuck & Heinzel (1978), Warham (1990), Watson (1968).

PLATE 18

inches 4
cm 10

Family PELECANOIDIDAE (DIVING-PETRELS)
SPECIES ACCOUNTS

PLATE 18

Genus *PELECANOIDES* Lacépède, 1799

1. South Georgia Diving-petrel
Pelecanoides georgicus

French: Puffinure de Géorgie du Sud   **Spanish:** Potoyunco de Georgia
German: Breitschnabel-Lummensturmvogel
Other common names: Georgian Diving-petrel

Taxonomy. *Pelecanoides georgica* Murphy and Harper, 1916, Cumberland Bay, South Georgia.
Forms superspecies with *P. garnotii* and *P. magellani*. Monotypic.
Distribution. Circumpolar, with breeding at South Georgia, islands of S Indian Ocean and off S New Zealand.
Descriptive notes. 18-21 cm; 90-150 g; wingspan 30-33 cm. Possibly some variation in colour of tarsus and underwing. Reliably separable from *P. urinatrix* and *P. garnotii* only on configuration of bill and nostrils. Juvenile similar to adult.
Habitat. Offshore or pelagic in cool waters, commonly occurring further from land than other diving-petrels. Breeds on oceanic islands in amongst scree or volcanic ash above tree line, or under sand dunes in areas of relatively flat ground.

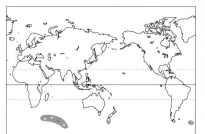

Food and Feeding. Mainly planktonic crustaceans, particularly krill (*Euphausia superba*), mostly of 10-13 mm; also copepods (*Paraeuchaeta antarctica*, *Calanoides acutus*, *Rhincalanus gigas*) and amphipods (*Themisto gaudichaudii*), and some small fish and young cephalopods. Prey caught under water in pursuit-dive from surface or after plunge, or seized whilst bird sits on water.
Breeding. Oct-Feb. Colonial, with 8-300 burrows/100 m^2; nests in burrows, averaging 80 cm long, with end chamber; no material. 1 egg; incubation 44-52 days; chicks have sooty grey down; fledging 43-60 days. Success to hatching 36-71%, then on to fledging 29% (much-handled birds).
Movements. Very little known; presumably sedentary, remaining throughout year in waters adjacent to colony, but movements at sea difficult to detect. Vagrant to SE Australia.
Status and Conservation. Not globally threatened. Abundant breeder on some oceanic islands: c. 2,000,000 pairs on South Georgia; large numbers of pairs in Crozet Is, with millions on Est I, c. 1,000,000 on Cochons I, and tens of thousands on Possession I; 1,000,000-2,000,000 in Kerguelen Is; 10,000+ pairs on Heard I. Also breeds on Prince Edward I and Codfish I (30-35 pairs). Other populations have been devastated by predation: probable extinction from Marion I due to large numbers of introduced cats; extirpated from Auckland I by Hooker's sea lions (*Phocarctos hookeri*).

On following page: 2. Common Diving-petrel (*Pelecanoides urinatrix*); 3. Peruvian Diving-petrel (*Pelecanoides garnotii*); 4. Magellanic Diving-petrel (*Pelecanoides magellani*).

Rats, dogs and in places Wekas (*Gallirallus australis*) have also contributed to decline, as have skuas (*Catharacta*); cattle, sheep and rabbits can cause serious damage to habitat, ultimately making areas unsuitable for breeding. Stricter control of grazing, together with eradication of introduced predators highly desirable, particularly on islands with large populations.

Bibliography. Croxall *et al.* (1984), Despin *et al.* (1972), Imber & Nilsson (1980), Jehl *et al.* (1979), Jouventin *et al.* (1985), Lindsey (1986), Marchant & Higgins (1990), Mougin (1985), Payne & Prince (1979), Ricklefs & Roby (1983), Roby (1989), Roby & Ricklefs (1983, 1984), Thibault & Guyot (1988), Watson (1975), Weimerskirch, Zotier & Jouventin (1989), West & Imber (1989), Woehler (1991).

2. **Common Diving-petrel**

Pelecanoides urinatrix

French: Puffinure plongeur   **German:** Lummensturmvogel   **Spanish:** Potoyunco Común
Other common names: Falkland/Berard's Diving-petrel (*berard*); Kerguelen/Subantarctic Diving-petrel (*exsul*); Tristan Diving-petrel (remaining subspecies)

Taxonomy. *Procellaria urinatrix* Gmelin, 1789, Queen Charlotte Sound, South Island, New Zealand. Races *exsul* and *berard* sometimes considered distinct species. Masculine form of species name (*urinator*) more accurate, but normally disregarded. Six subspecies recognized.
Subspecies and Distribution.
P. u. urinatrix (Gmelin, 1789) - SE Australia and Tasmania to N New Zealand.
P. u. chathamensis Murphy & Harper, 1916 - S New Zealand.
P. u. exsul Salvin, 1896 - South Georgia E to Antipodes Is.
P. u. dacunhae Nicoll, 1906 - Tristan da Cunha, Gough I.
P. u. berard (Gaimard, 1823) - Falkland Is.
P. u. coppingeri Mathews, 1912 - suspected to breed in S Chile.

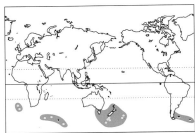

Descriptive notes. 20-25 cm; 86-185 g; wingspan 33-38 cm. Reliably separable from *P. georgicus* and *P. garnotii* only on configuration of bill and nostrils, though lacks white trailing edge of wing and variable grey tips to scapulars of other species. Juvenile similar to adult, but has smaller, weaker bill. Races separated on size and bill dimensions; also on extent of grey mottling on throat and sides of breast, though this character variable.
Habitat. Normally occurs on inshore waters more than *P. georgicus*, but also in offshore waters; during post-breeding dispersal, possibly occurs more in pelagic zone than other diving-petrels. Breeds on oceanic islands, on steep slopes, e.g. with dense covering of tussock grass; sometimes on flat ground, where snow may still persist at start of breeding; colonies normally coastal, but sometimes well inland.
Food and Feeding. Mainly planktonic crustaceans, particularly copepods (*Calanoides acutus*, *Rhincalanus gigas*); also euphausiids, including krill (*Euphausia superba*), amphipods (*Hyperiella antarctica*, *Hyperoche medusarum*) and some isopods. Prey caught under water in pursuit-dive from surface or after plunge, or seized whilst bird sits on water.
Breeding. Season variable according to locality, with laying late Jul (SE Australia) to Dec (Heard I); generally 1 month earlier than *P. georgicus* in zones of overlap. Colonial, with 50-60 or perhaps c. 1000-1500 burrows/100m²; nests in burrows, 25-150 cm long; no material. 1 egg; incubation 53-55 days; chicks have whitish or pale grey down; fledging 45-59 days. Success 87% to fledging, but high losses associated with fledging. Sexual maturity at 2-3 years; average life expectancy of breeder not more than 3·5 years.
Movements. Very little known; presumably fairly sedentary, remaining throughout year in waters adjacent to the colony, but movements at sea difficult to detect. Some dispersal northwards, e.g. from Falklands to N Argentina; may be more pelagic in dispersal than other species, and possibly even migratory to some extent.
Status and Conservation. Not globally threatened. Widespread and abundant breeder on some oceanic islands: 10,000 pairs in Falklands; c. 3,800,000 on South Georgia; millions of pairs in Crozet Is; abundant in Kerguelen Is; estimated 100,000-1,000,000+ pairs in New Zealand. Also colonies in Tristan da Cunha Group (100's-1000's), Prince Edward I, Heard I (1000+ pairs), Tasmania 500+ pairs. Numbers much reduced due to predation by introduced mammals: feral cats brought about extinction in once major breeding stations on Marion I, St Paul I and Amsterdam I; rats represent significant problem, e.g. in Crozet Is and islands round New Zealand. Cattle, sheep and rabbits can cause serious damage to habitat, ultimately making areas unsuitable for breeding. Stricter control of grazing, together with eradication of introduced predators highly desirable, particularly on islands with large populations. If split into three species, each retains secure and sizeable population.

Bibliography. Blake (1977), Brooke, M. de L. (1989), Brooke, R.K. (1984), Brothers (1984), Croxall *et al.* (1984), Fitzgerald & Veitch (1985), Furness (1987), Humphrey *et al.* (1970), Imber (1983), Jehl *et al.* (1979), Johnson (1965), Johnstone (1979), Jouventin *et al.* (1985), Lindsey (1986), Marchant & Higgins (1990), Mougin (1985), Murphy (1936), Norman & Brown (1987), Payne & Prince (1979), Richardson (1984), Richdale (1943b, 1945, 1965a), Ricklefs & Roby (1983), Roby (1989), Roby & Ricklefs (1983), Ryan *et al.* (1990), Schodde & Tidemann (1988), Serventy *et al.* (1971), Swales (1965), Thoresen (1969), Watson (1975), Weimerskirch, Zotier & Jouventin (1989), Woehler (1991), Woods (1988).

3. **Peruvian Diving-petrel**

Pelecanoides garnotii

French: Puffinure de Garnot   **German:** Garnot-Lummensturmvogel   **Spanish:** Potoyunco Peruano

Taxonomy. *Puffinuria Garnotii* Lesson, 1828, coast of Peru between San Gallán Island and Lima. Forms superspecies with *P. georgicus* and *P. magellani*. Monotypic.
Distribution. Breeds coasts of Peru and Chile, mainly between 6° S and 38° S.

Descriptive notes. 20-24 cm. Reliably separable from *P. georgicus* and *P. urinatrix* only on configuration of bill and nostrils. Juvenile similar to adult.
Habitat. Pelagic, in cool waters. Breeds on barren offshore islands; some nests at 400 m, but most less than 100 m above sea-level.
Food and Feeding. Mostly small fish and planktonic crustaceans. Prey caught under water in pursuit-dive from surface or after plunge, or seized whilst bird sits on water.
Breeding. Laying recorded in most months. Colonial, formerly in large, dense colonies, nowadays on San Gallán I 80% breed in groups of less than 10 pairs; nests in burrows dug in guano-covered slopes. 1 egg.
Movements. Disperses mainly over adjacent waters of Humboldt Current, regularly occurring S to 42° S.
Status and Conservation. INSUFFICIENTLY KNOWN. Has declined steadily from millions to probably only a few thousand pairs. In Peru, c. 1500 birds on La Vieja I and San Gallán I; of c. 1200 nests on latter only 30% active; poaching reduced, but casual tourism threatens colonies. In Chile, known to breed at Pan de Azucar I, with 220 active nests, and Choros I, with at least 300 active nests; heavy poaching pressure by fishermen threatens latter. Main cause of decline is commercial exploitation of guano, implying removal of layer of soft material in which burrows were dug; also a series of associated disturbances and many birds formerly taken to feed workers (see page 276). Rats, cats, foxes, etc. introduced to breeding islands, destroying many thousands of nests each season, and causing some local extinctions, e.g. no longer breeds on Chañaral I (NC Chile), where population of 200,000 birds in early 20th century devastated by introduced foxes. Survival of species requires complete cessation of guano extraction in breeding grounds, removal of all introduced predators and effective protection of islands, including their declaration as reserves, with efficient wardening; extensive research needed on biology and requirements of species.
Bibliography. Blake (1977), Collar & Andrew (1988), Duffy, Hays & Plenge (1984), Johnson (1965), Murphy (1936), Riveros-Salcedo & Aparicio (1990), Riveros-Salcedo *et al.* (1991), Schlatter (1984).

4. **Magellanic Diving-petrel**

Pelecanoides magellani

French: Puffinure de Magellan   **Spanish:** Potoyunco Magallánico
                 German: Magellan-Lummensturmvogel

Taxonomy. *Puffinuria garnotii magellani* Mathews, 1912, Strait of Magellan. Forms superspecies with *P. georgicus* and *P. garnotii*. Monotypic.
Distribution. Extreme S tip of S America, breeding off S Chile and Tierra del Fuego.

Descriptive notes. 19-20 cm. Most distinctive species, with extensive white fringes on upperparts and characteristic half-collar. Juvenile as adult, but lacks white fringes on scapulars, back and rump.
Habitat. Mainly inshore and offshore waters. Breeds on slopes with some vegetation, mostly occupying small inshore islands in channels and fjords.
Food and Feeding. Very little known. Feeds mainly by diving under water, especially from surface but also from air.
Breeding. Nov-Dec. Colonial; nests in burrows. 1 egg.
Movements. Presumably sedentary, with some dispersal over adjacent coastal waters; recorded up to 128 km from land.
Status and Conservation. Not globally threatened. Population reportedly large, although no figures available; common breeder on islets off S Chile. Extensive research and census work required. Main threats likely to be same as for other species, although remoteness of much of range suggests breeding areas probably less affected by human activities.
Bibliography. Blake (1977), Brown *et al.* (1975), Duffy *et al.* (1988), Humphrey *et al.* (1970), Jehl (1973a), Johnson (1965, 1972), Murphy (1936), Schlatter (1984), Woods (1988).

Order PELECANIFORMES

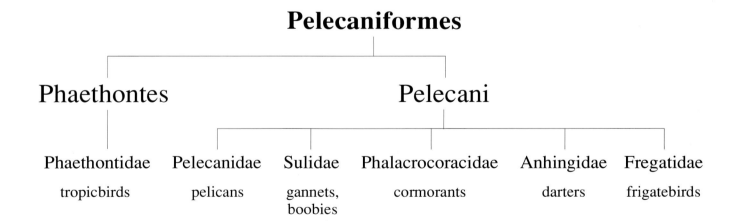

Class AVES
Order PELECANIFORMES
Suborder PHAETHONTES
Family PHAETHONTIDAE (TROPICBIRDS)

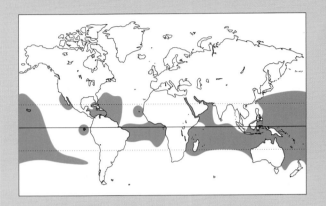

- Medium-sized seabirds with long, narrow wings and central tail feathers elongated to form streamers.
- 70-105 cm (including 30-56 cm tail streamers).

- Pantropical.
- Tropical and subtropical oceans, largely pelagic.
- 1 genus, 3 species, 12 taxa.
- No species threatened; none extinct since 1600.

Systematics

The tropicbird family consists of a single genus, *Phaethon*, containing three very closely related species, which may constitute a superspecies. The oldest fossil comes from the Lower Eocene, some 50 million years ago, in England, and corresponds to a fourth species which is now extinct.

Within the Pelecaniformes, the tropicbirds have been grouped with the frigatebirds, but it seems that their peculiarities are sufficiently marked to justify their isolation in a distinct, monofamiliar suborder, separate from the rest of the families in the order. In addition to certain skeletal differences, the gular pouch is extensively feathered, and chicks are covered with down at hatching.

Traditionally, all three species have been subdivided into several subspecies, but recent work indicates that many of these subspecies are bogus and should be considered mere colour morphs. The standard races of the Red-tailed Tropicbird (*Phaethon rubricauda*) appear to form a north-south cline in both plumage tone and measurements, with a fair amount of overlap; the White-tailed Tropicbird (*Phaethon lepturus*) has a very distinctively coloured race *fulvus* (see Morphological Aspects), which has always been designated exclusively to birds from Christmas Island in the Indian Ocean, but some are found elsewhere, while 7% or more of the Christmas Island birds are all-white. The proposed elimination of many subspecies seems likely to gain widespread acceptance.

Morphological Aspects

Tropicbirds are medium-sized seabirds, with a body approximately the size of a domestic pigeon, whereas their appearance, and likewise their behaviour, lie somewhere between the gannets and boobies (Sulidae) and the terns.

Both the Red-billed Tropicbird (*Phaethon aethereus*) and the Red-tailed Tropicbird can measure 50 cm or more, without counting their tail streamers, and they usually have a wingspan of over 1 m. The White-tailed Tropicbird is somewhat smaller and much lighter; it weighs little more than 300 g, less than half the weight of the other species, as the Red-billed can reach 700 g and the Red-tailed more than 750 g.

There is no seasonal variation in plumage, which is mainly white with contrasting black eye-stripes and black markings on

the wings. The white parts are sometimes slightly tinted, for example the Red-tailed Tropicbird, in fresh plumage, usually has a soft pink tinge, and in the case of the Christmas Island subspecies (see Systematics) of the White-tailed Tropicbird (*P. l. fulvus*), it is a strong golden apricot colour, which is reflected in the local name, Golden Bosunbird. Young of all three species have the upperparts heavily barred, as does the adult Red-billed. There are no plumage differences between the sexes, although tail streamers tend to be longer in males.

The main part of the tail is wedge-shaped, and adults have two extraordinarily long central tail feathers, which can exceed the entire length of the rest of the bird. These streamers are narrow and flexible and play an important part in the visual signals used in courtship display, in addition perhaps to acting as stabilizers during some of their more complicated aerial manoeuvres. In the Red-tailed Tropicbird they are bright red, whereas in the other two species they are white, though again in the Golden Bosunbird they tend to have a strong orange tinge. Moult lasts 19-29 weeks in the Red-billed Tropicbird, and in all species it tends to be suspended during breeding, although the tail streamers, due to their fragility, are constantly being replaced.

The long, stout bill is slightly decurved and ends in a sharp point, while the cutting edges are sharp and, in adults, finely serrated; unlike other Pelecaniformes, tropicbirds have well defined nostril slits. Bill colour varies with the species, ranging from yellow or orange to bright crimson, though it is generally much duller in young birds, being yellowish, or even, in the case of the Red-tailed Tropicbird, greyish-black.

The legs are very short and are set far back on the body. The feet are also small and, as in all other Pelecaniformes, totipalmate, the four toes being joined together by webs. The weakness of the feet and legs means that tropicbirds move about very awkwardly on land; they can hardly even stand up, and they shuffle along with their bellies scraping against the ground, so they can only move short distances. Their webbed feet are used to dig out the nest scrape, but are obviously more specifically designed for swimming, though tropicbirds are actually rather poor swimmers. However, they are a lot more proficient than the frigatebirds and, unlike the latter, can waterproof their plumage effectively, thanks to the feathered uropygial gland.

The wings are relatively long, narrow and pointed. The tropicbirds' typical flight is strong and direct, with forceful,

rapid wingbeats, which recall those of pigeons; they also glide or soar intermittently, but rather less frequently. They have an extraordinary capacity for sustained flight and, although some other seabirds, most notably Procellariiformes and frigatebirds, can seemingly keep flying endlessly, these groups use very different techniques, which depend basically on making use of wind and air currents to remain airborne and sail along, as opposed to the tropicbirds' powered flight.

The flight of the White-tailed Tropicbird, the most slender species, is correspondingly lighter, and birds tend to glide more and have a faster wingbeat, whilst the Red-tailed is the species with the least graceful flight, and it has proportionally shorter wings and a heavier body. All species can have a certain amount of difficulty in taking off, unless they have an elevated spot whence to launch themselves into the air, and similarly landing at the nest or on a perch may require several attempts.

Tropicbirds, like sulids and pelicans, have a network of air-sacs under their skin at the front of their bodies; these are built into the head, throat and neck, and absorb the blow the bird receives on hitting the water, when it is diving for fish. The bare gular pouch, such a typical feature of the other Pelecaniformes, is extensively feathered in Phaethontidae and is very inconspicuous.

Habitat

Members of the tropicbird family range widely over the warm tropical and subtropical waters of the Pacific, Atlantic and Indian Oceans. The Red-billed and the White-tailed Tropicbirds are found in the three great oceans, whilst the Red-tailed Tropicbird is not found in the Atlantic.

They are extremely aerial birds and this is undoubtedly linked with the fact that they habitually use the pelagic zone. Only very occasionally do they visit mainland coasts and they often wander hundreds of kilometres out to sea, to visit poor waters where seabirds in general are very scarce and widely dispersed; this is particularly true of the Red-tailed Tropicbird, the most oceanic species. They only come to land for breeding, and this almost always takes place on remote oceanic islands, where there are no terrestrial predators, or at inaccessible sites such as cliffs. Their nests also need some sort of shade, which may be provided by trees, bushes, ferns, overhanging rocks or the nesting cavity itself.

The smallest species, the White-tailed Tropicbird, occasionally coincides with one or other of the two larger species in the same breeding grounds. In such cases, as for example on Ascension Island in the South Atlantic, where it occurs alongside the Red-billed Tropicbird, there may be considerable competition for nest-sites (see Breeding). On the other hand, the two larger species have not, to date, been found breeding in the same place, which ties in with their similar size and feeding habits. In the hypothetical situation of the two co-existing, they would probably compete to the point of rendering impracticable the simultaneous and lasting usage of the same breeding or feeding grounds.

General Habits

At present, little is known about the habits and behaviour of this family, especially concerning their activities away from the breeding grounds. Tropicbirds spend most of their time flying over the sea at a height of 10-20 m or more, patrolling along in search of food. They usually forage alone or in pairs, and it is fairly rare to find birds in flocks, away from their island colonies.

They do not often sit on the sea, but when they do, they are fairly buoyant and rest or swim with their tails raised. Outside the breeding season, when they are wandering about over the open sea, they have to roost either on the water or possibly in mid-air.

Tropicbirds generally breed on fairly remote oceanic islands, locating their nests in the most inaccessible spots available, typically in crevices on precipitous cliffs. The main reason for these restrictions is security, and in many places man's introduction of predators, especially cats and rats, has had disastrous results on the populations of seabirds, including tropicbirds. Another advantage of nesting on cliffs is that take-off generally requires less effort, as the bird merely has to launch itself off the cliff.

[*Phaethon aethereus mesonauta*, Española (Hood) I, Galapagos. Photo: F. Köster/Survival]

Voice

Vocalizations are not highly specialized in the tropicbird family. Birds tend to call mostly when in flight and they are usually silent away from the immediate areas surrounding active breeding colonies.

However, during courtship flights they are particularly noisy, uttering strident, repetitive cries, which resemble a boatswain's pipe or a tern's shriek, especially those of the Red-tailed and Red-billed Tropicbirds. They also screech during fights, and both adults and chicks scream loudly, if disturbed at the nest. When bringing in food to nestlings, adults sometimes click or "chuck" softly, to which chicks may reply with guttural chirps, begging for food.

Food and Feeding

The tropical and subtropical waters inhabited by tropicbirds are generally very poor, and prey is usually distributed in a rather unpredictable way, especially in the pelagic zone, which can mean that birds are continually forced to embark on long journeys to find it. Concentrations of fish are rare, but even at these it is unusual to see groups of tropicbirds, although on occasions they join gatherings of other seabirds, such as Sooty Terns (*Sterna fuscata*) or shearwaters, which may be exploiting a shoal.

They feed mainly on flying-fish (Exocoetidae) and squid (Ommastrephidae), as well as other types of fish and cephalopods, and in some cases crustaceans. Most fishing takes place either early in the day, up to mid-morning, or around dusk, when squid swim near the surface of the water and are obviously easier to catch.

They capture their prey by plunge-diving from heights of up to 25 m or more, in a style resembling that of the Sulidae (see page 315). Often they detect the prey while hovering, like terns, before they plunge into the water with their wings half-closed. Prey is usually captured on, or very close to, the surface, although sometimes at a depth of several metres, and is not skewered, but instead is caught and held crossways in the bill. If birds dive under the water, they usually reappear within a few seconds, shake off any water and immediately take off again, having already swallowed their prey. On occasions flying-fish may alternatively be caught in the air.

The White-tailed Tropicbird tends to consume smaller prey than the other two species, perhaps due to the size of its bill, and therefore, in areas where it overlaps with another species of tropicbird, there is a certain differentiation in the prey selected. Around Aldabra Atoll, in the western Indian Ocean, the Red-tailed Tropicbird bases its diet on flying-fish and seems to feed in more pelagic zones than the White-tailed Tropicbird, whilst the latter feeds mainly on squid; in this way competition for food is reduced.

In the early stages, chicks are fed on small or semi-digested prey, but generally, as they grow, the prey they are given becomes progressively larger, while the amount of fish they consume may also increase proportionally.

Tropicbirds are sometimes attracted to boats, especially the White-tailed Tropicbird, which may even land on the rigging. However, they neither follow them for long, nor feed behind them, but are just inquisitive and circle around a few times crying noisily, before rapidly disappearing.

Breeding

Tropicbirds generally breed in colonies on oceanic islands. These colonies are not very large, and tend to be composed of loose groups, though the internal structure of the colony is obviously determined by the availability of suitable nest-sites.

Nests are normally sited in shady positions, which are secure from predators and where both landing and take-off are easy. This is why they tend to choose protected cracks or ledges

As the availability of suitable nest-sites is the main limiting factor to tropicbird breeding, territorial defence of the nest is fierce and can be extremely violent. Bloody struggles, like this one between two Red-billed Tropicbirds, are not infrequent and the sharp, pointed bills can cause serious injuries on the head and neck.

[Phaethon aethereus aethereus, Ascension I. Photo: Cindy Buxton & Annie Price/Survival]

tropicbirds can end up nesting quite far from the coast, and sometimes even several hundred metres above sea-level.

In most places there is a fairly well-defined breeding season. This varies from place to place, but in the extreme north and south of their range it tends to coincide roughly with spring and summer. In the Caribbean and nearby Atlantic zones, where the White-tailed and Red-billed Tropicbirds co-exist, the former lays between February and July, whilst the latter starts earlier, around December, but does not continue beyond April.

However, the breeding season can be much longer, and in some places eggs are laid in all months of the year. Where breeding is continuous, it seems to be the result of strong intraspecific, or on occasions interspecific competition, in places where there is a clear shortage of suitable nest-sites. Continuous breeding dilutes the negative effects of competition, and at the same time, more as a consequence than as an adaptation, it decreases the degree of competition for food in these particularly unproductive waters.

Another possible consequence of the great competition for nest-sites is that breeding can be more frequent than annual, which means that nests are overused. On Ascension Island, when the White-tailed and the Red-billed Tropicbirds breed successfully, they do so every 8-11 and 10-12 months respectively, while the interval between attempts is actually shorter, if a clutch is lost and no replacement is laid.

The tropicbirds' courtship displays are aerial, highly spectacular and very noisy. In general they display collectively, forming small, tightly-packed groups, which fly about the vicinity of the breeding area, circling around with loud screams. At a given moment, one pair (sometimes a trio) break away from the group and perform aerobatics in unison, with a surprising degree of synchronization.

In the White-tailed and Red-billed Tropicbirds these flights can be in zig-zag, or birds may carry out long downward glides, sometimes descending several hundred metres, with one bird

Tropicbirds perform tremendously spectacular, noisy courtship displays involving aerobatics that are way beyond the capabilities of most other seabirds. In the White-tailed Tropicbird the display starts off with a rowdy flock flying around, before a pair separates off to perform a series of breathtatking synchronized manoeuvres.

[Phaethon lepturus. Photo: Paul Pemberton/ Cornell Laboratory of Ornithology]

on cliffs, even though these need not necessarily be very high. The Red-tailed Tropicbird in particular sometimes breeds on more open ground, usually on sand under the shelter of vegetation. A strange deviation from these ground-nesting tendencies can be seen in the White-tailed Tropicbird, which nests in hollows and forks in trees at certain sites in both the Pacific and Indian Oceans. On Christmas Island (Indian Ocean) it uses trees in the forest on the high central plateau, situating its nests up to 3 km from the sea. Where there are high, impregnable cliffs in the interior of relatively large islands,

In much of its extensive Pacific range the Red-tailed Tropicbird has to breed on the ground, as there are no suitable cliffs. It tends to make a scrape in the sand and selects a site under the vegetation, where it receives shelter from the sun and some concealment, though at such sites it is particularly vulnerable to introduced terrestrial predators. The population of Midway Island is an important one, with around 4000-5000 breeding pairs. Hawaiian birds have been considered to form a distinct race, rothschildi.

[Phaethon rubricauda melanorhynchus, Midway I, Hawaii. Photo: Maurice Tibbles/ Survival]

flying immediately above the other; the bird on top lowers its wings and the one below raises its, so that the tips almost touch. In the White-tailed Tropicbird's flights, the bird on top may also lower its tail streamers, to touch its companion below.

The Red-tailed Tropicbird has an even more sophisticated courtship flight. In the pair which breaks away from the group, the bird below glides along, while the other starts to beat its wings rapidly, hovering, with its body almost vertical; it achieves a remarkable back-pedalling effect, with the bird rising backwards, possibly driven by the wind. At the same time the red tail streamers are lowered and shaken from side to side, and the feet are stretched out. A few seconds later, after the bird on top glides down, the roles are reversed, and this results in the pair describing a series of successive circles in the sky.

During their courtship flights, the birds inspect potential breeding sites, and thus pairs which are already formed end up flying to the selected nest, where copulation takes place with practically no preceding ritual. Probably the characteristics of the nests, and the tropicbirds' lack of agility on land, determine the fact that they do not perform complex displays on the ground.

The nest is a simple scrape that both members of the pair make using their bodies and feet when the substrate is soft, and it has little or no material. The owner of a nest often watches, as one or more tropicbirds settle nearby, with the intention of taking over the nest, and this generally ends up with the owner defending the nest decisively, attacking the intruder by pecking at him, and the two finally struggle around with their bills interlocked; as a result of these fights, many adults have scars on their heads and necks. On occasions, tropicbirds dislodge shearwaters from their breeding holes, as in the cases of the White-tailed Tropicbird and the Bermuda Petrel (*Pterodroma cahow*) on Bermuda, or the Red-billed Tropicbird and the Wedge-tailed Shearwater (*Puffinus pacificus*).

The female lays a single oval egg which is around 10% of her weight and, in contrast to the rest of the Pelecaniformes, is not white; instead it is very variable in both colour and markings, ranging from pale and uniform to red, brown, grey or purple with a variable spattering of speckles or blotches of assorted colours.

Incubation lasts 40-46 days and, as with frigatebirds and again contrasting with the rest of the Pelecaniformes, this is carried out using its body and not its webbed feet. Both sexes incubate in stints which normally last a few days, but which can, in the case of the Red-tailed Tropicbird, go on for as long as 16 days without the sitting bird being fed by its partner. On entering the nest adults leave their streamers outside, despite which they often get damaged during breeding and may end up snapping.

If an egg or chick is lost, a replacement may be laid, but this is rare, except perhaps when food is abundant. It occurs after an interval, which varies in length depending on the species and on the stage at which the egg or chick is lost.

Competition for nest-sites can occur between tropicbirds of the same or of different species, and sometimes it causes extensive breeding failure. Ascension Island provides an interesting example, as the White-tailed and the Red-billed Tropicbirds nest on the same cliffs and slopes. One study showed that, out of the total number of eggs laid by the White-tailed Tropicbird, 51·9% did not hatch, and later on 17·8% were lost as chicks, especially in the first two weeks, so that only 30·3% of all eggs produced young which were to fledge successfully. At the same location, the Red-billed Tropicbird, the larger of the two species and the dominant one in disputes between the two, lost only 30·8% of its eggs, with chicks from 51·5% of the clutches resulting in fledged young. On Aldabra, where the White-tailed and the Red-tailed Tropicbirds coincide but nest separately, the former's breeding success is higher than on Ascension Island, with 47·5% of all eggs laid producing fledged young.

Newly-hatched tropicbird chicks are covered with dense, silky down, which may be white, grey or fawn-grey; the chick of the White-tailed Tropicbird weighs a mere 30 grams. At first the chick is permanently brooded by an adult, but after a few days it tends to be left alone at the nest for periods that grow increasingly longer and thus after a few weeks the chick spends most of its time alone.

The White-tailed Tropicbird is far more catholic in its choice of nest-site than the other two species. It has been found nesting in hollow tree trunks, on limestone pinnacles and even on mining equipment at Christmas Island in the Indian Ocean. Nonetheless, it still prefers a site where it has enough room to park its lengthy tail streamers, though in all species these tend to receive fairly rough treatment and frequently snap.

[Phaethon lepturus lepturus, Cousin I, Seychelles. Photo: George Edwards/ Survival]

In general, the parents leave the colony before dawn, and some studies indicate that most feeding of chicks takes place in the morning. At the beginning, they are fed with small quantities of semi-digested food, regurgitated by the parents, and it is the adult that inserts its bill into the chick's gullet, once again in contrast with the other families of Pelecaniformes. As the chicks grow, they are steadily fed on more solid prey, and at the same time the frequency of feeds decreases.

The chicks grow slowly but, when only half way through the nestling period, they already attain adult weight, and they subsequently exceed it. Towards the end the parents' visits to feed the chicks become more spaced out and possibly stop altogether a few days before the young birds fly. The length of the nestling period varies, depending on the quantity and frequency of feeding; the first flight takes place when they are about 70-90 days old, at which point they immediately become independent and begin a prolonged period of post-fledging dispersal. The exact age at which birds reach sexual maturity is not known, although they apparently acquire full adult plumage, as well as definitive bill colouring, when they are two to

The tropicbirds differ from other Pelecaniformes in many ways. They are the only members of the order with clearly functional nostrils, and their gular pouch is feathered and inconspicuous. Another important difference is that their chicks hatch with a full covering of down, whereas in the rest of the order chicks hatch naked and only grow their coat of down after a few days.

[*Phaethon rubricauda melanorhynchus*, Tern I, Hawaii. Photo: Frans Lanting/ Bruce Coleman]

three years old, after passing through a transition plumage, which is quite similar to that of the adult.

Tropicbirds are monogamous and partners may stay together for years, especially if they manage to breed successfully. There is a strong instinct to reuse the nest from the previous breeding season, and this is probably determined by the fact that nest-sites are often scarce. The same nest is more likely to be reused if the same two partners coincide again, and seemingly they sometimes keep in touch at sea, even outwith the breeding period, an unusual practice among seabirds. Tropicbirds can live at least 16 years and possibly over 30.

Movements

Outside the breeding season, both adults and young leave the colony and wander far from land, where they lead a totally pelagic life. Adults moult before returning to the breeding grounds, whereas juveniles stay away for years, before returning as adults themselves.

Between breeding seasons tropicbirds disperse widely, but in general they do not perform true migrations. There are places, however, where they genuinely migrate, for example the White-tailed Tropicbird at its most northerly breeding grounds in Bermuda, where it arrives in February/March and leaves again in September/October, though timing varies to some extent from year to year, depending on the weather. In contrast, the same species is present all year round in the Lesser Antilles, for example, and at least some adults of both the other species can be seen near their colonies at any time of year.

Juveniles seem to disperse more than adults and thus, in many areas where tropicbirds are occasional visitors or vagrants, most records refer to juveniles. Good evidence of this comes from the Red-billed Tropicbirds observed off the Pacific coast of Costa Rica, as well as records from Israel and Pakistan, and similarly the observations of White-tailed Tropicbirds off

the east and west coasts of Australia. The Red-tailed Tropicbird appears to rove more widely than the other two species.

Storms can carry tropicbirds far out of their usual ranges, and sometimes even a long way inland, for example at least 19 Red-tailed and White-tailed Tropicbirds appeared in inland New South Wales, Australia, after a storm in March 1978. Likewise a White-tailed Tropicbird was found dying in Arizona, USA, in August 1981; it had probably been swept along by a hurricane from the Gulf of Mexico.

Relationship with Man

A series of popular names have been given to tropicbirds, and these indicate that they are strikingly visible birds. Some of their shrill calls have been likened to the sound of a boatswain's pipe, and this may have led to them being called "Bosunbirds" by British sailors. Another proffered explanation of this name is that the bird's long tail streamers resembled the boatswain's marlinspike, and this is certainly the origin of several other popular names, such as "Marlinspike", "Longtail" or "Strawtail".

The generic name *Phaethon* comes from Greek mythology: Phaëthon was allowed by his father, the sun God Helios, to drive the chariot of the sun for one day, and he almost set the Earth on fire. As a result of this Zeus, irritated by Phaëthon's clumsiness, struck him down with a thunderbolt.

In various regions tropicbird feathers have traditionally been highly valued for ornamental purposes, and Polynesians wear the Red-tailed Tropicbird's streamers in the hair and stuck through a hole in the nose. To this end, they capture nesting adults and pull out these feathers, without causing them any further harm.

However, there have been other more damaging forms of exploitation, which involved killing the birds, for example trade in their feathers for the once important millinery business. Egg-collecting and the killing of both chicks and adult birds for human consumption have been frequent since ancient times, and the Arawak and Caribbean Indians, for example, are known to have eaten fair numbers of White-tailed Tropicbirds, in addition to other birds. On Palmerston Island in Polynesia, until recently Red-tailed Tropicbird chicks were taken for human consumption, but there was only a single annual collection.

In modern times, such exploitation has continued in quite a generalized fashion in many parts of the tropics, and at times it has reached the level of seriously threatening some of their populations (see Status and Conservation).

Status and Conservation

None of the three species of tropicbirds is globally threatened, although local extinctions have occurred and a lot of suitable breeding sites have been lost. Present populations seem stable in many areas, and in some instances are even increasing. However, there is a general shortage of information about past populations, and it is often difficult to determine trends, while the quantity of data available at the various different localities is far from uniform. It is often difficult to carry out accurate census work, as nests may be tucked away in inaccessible parts of cliffs, and the bird that is not incubating is liable to be foraging hundreds of kilometres from the nest, and away for several days. Inaccessible in rather a different way are large numbers of islands in the Pacific, which are still awaiting the attentions of ornithologists and these may yet produce several large seabird colonies.

The main threats to tropicbird populations can be summarized as direct exploitation by man and the introduction of alien predators to breeding islands. In some places human exploitation of eggs, chicks and adults has caused a notable decrease in populations. The Red-tailed Tropicbird has declined seriously on Christmas Island (Pacific Ocean) due to the islanders' heavy consumption of chicks and adults, although the enforcement of protection laws since 1977 has brought about a spectacular recovery in the population. However, the same has not occurred everywhere, since the taking of both eggs and birds has frequently persisted after its prohibition. Among the main causes of this continued persecution are the low standard of living and the insufficient food supplies which often beset the local human populations.

A serious threat to many tropicbird populations comes in the form of the predators, such as cats and rats, introduced by man, sometimes deliberately but more often accidentally, to many oceanic islands which previously had no terrestrial predators. This has disrupted the peaceful conditions that tropicbirds require for nesting, with several consequences: a decrease in the number of suitable nest-sites; the death of considerable numbers of adults; a lower success rate for breeding pairs; and the restriction of nesting to the highest and least

To feed its chick the adult tropicbird places its bill in the chick's, whereas in other Pelecaniformes it is the other way round, the chick reaching into the adult's crop. Tropicbird chicks are constantly brooded at first, but after a few weeks they are left alone in the security of the nest while both adults are away foraging, and there is a fair amount of mortality due to the intrusions of other adult tropicbirds of the same or other species.

[Phaethon rubricauda melanorhynchus, Midway Atoll, Hawaii. Photo: Frans Lanting/ Bruce Coleman]

The Golden Bosunbird of Christmas Island was previously thought to be very rare, but recent observations suggest that this may have been due to difficulty in locating nests, and that it is actually numerous, with some 6000-12,000 pairs.

[Phaethon lepturus fulvus, Christmas I, Indian Ocean. Photo: J. B. Nelson]

vulnerable cliffs. For these reasons, many potential nest-sites have had to be abandoned, while the availability of suitable nest-sites is already a significant limiting factor for these species.

Cats are the worst predators of tropicbirds, and they even attack them on their nesting cliffs. Predation by the Polynesian rat (*Rattus exulans*) on the Red-tailed Tropicbird has also been observed, especially in years when plant food is scarce, and on Kure Atoll, in Hawaii, it was found to cause losses of eggs and chicks of up to 65% and 100% respectively in some years. It also preys upon adult White-tailed Tropicbirds, whereas the eggs of this species are in turn eaten by the black rat (*Rattus rattus*); the widespread brown rat (*Rattus norvegicus*) is apparently even more devastating in its effects than its two congeners. In Bermuda the White-tailed Tropicbird population was ravaged by rats, but with effective protection the species has recovered, and it once again breeds in large numbers.

Human constructions have also adversely affected tropicbirds on occasions. On Midway Island, in the central Pacific, the construction and subsequent use of military buildings and runways involved the destruction of Red-tailed Tropicbird nests and chicks, as well as the casualties which resulted from birds colliding with aeroplanes.

General Bibliography
Burger *et al.* (1980), Cracraft (1985), Croxall (1987, 1991), Croxall *et al.* (1984), Diamond (1978), Drummond (1987), Gibson-Hill (1947b), Harrison (1985, 1987), Howell (1984), Lanham (1947), Nelson (1980), Olson (1985c), Schreiber (1984), Stonehouse (1985a), van Tets (1965a), Tuck & Heinzel (1978).

PLATE 19

1

ssp *aethereus*

ssp *indicus*

2

3

ssp *lepturus*

ssp *fulvus*

PLATE 19

Genus *PHAETHON*   Linnaeus, 1758

1. Red-billed Tropicbird

Phaethon aethereus

French: Phaéton à bec rouge   **German:** Rotschnabel-Tropikvogel   **Spanish:** Rabijunco Etéreo

Taxomony. *Phaëthon aethereus* Linnaeus, 1758, Ascension Island.
Race *indicus* sometimes considered separate species, but differences slight and separation does not appear justified. Three subspecies recognized.
Subspecies and Distribution.
P. a. mesonauta Peters, 1930 - E Pacific, Caribbean and E Atlantic.
P. a. aethereus Linnaeus, 1758 - S Atlantic.
P. a. indicus Hume, 1876 - Persian Gulf, Gulf of Aden, Red Sea.
Descriptive notes. 90-105 cm (including 46-56 cm tail streamers); 700 g; wingspan 99-106 cm. Largest tropicbird; black mask slightly larger than in other species and sometimes joined across nape in worn plumage. Streamers of male average longer than those of female. Juvenile has yellow bill, lacks tail streamers, and black eyestripes meet on nape; otherwise resembles adult. Race *mesonauta* probably shorter-winged, has rosy flush in fresh plumage, and the dark areas of upperparts and flight-feathers are blacker; race *indicus* smaller, has orange bill with black cutting edges, and smaller black mask.

Habitat. Tropical and subtropical seas; mainly pelagic. Breeds on small, remote oceanic islands; prefers inaccessible spot on cliff, where take-off relatively easy.
Food and Feeding. Mostly small fish (10-20 cm), especially flying-fish (*Exocoetus volitans*, *Oxyporhamphus micropterus*), some larger, up to 25-30 cm; also squid. Diet varies locally, squid apparently more important in Indian Ocean populations. Most prey caught by plunge-diving, but flying-fish sometimes taken in flight.
Breeding. Seasonal in places, elsewhere can be more or less continuous. Loosely colonial. Nest is in rocky crevice, or scrape on ground; little or no material. 1 egg; incubation 42-44 days; chicks hatch with grey down; fledging 80-90 days (maximum 110); no post-fledging care. Age of sexual maturity unknown. Oldest ringed bird at least 10 years old.
Movements. No regular migration; some adults can be seen in vicinity of colonies all year round. Extensive dispersal, especially of juveniles, often over waters fairly near breeding grounds, e.g. birds from Cape Verde Is move to areas of upwelling off W Africa; but many disperse much further out to sea, and adults from Galapagos known to wander some 1500 km.
Status and Conservation. Not globally threatened. Probably least numerous of tropicbirds, and may number under 10,000 pairs. Healthiest populations probably in the Americas, with 1600+ pairs in Caribbean, 500-1000 pairs in Gulf of California, and several thousand pairs in Galapagos. South Atlantic may hold considerably less than 3000 pairs, with Brazilian population apparently

reduced to very small numbers, and predation by brown rats (*Rattus norvegicus*) reported; alarming decline in Cape Verde Is, where persecuted by fishermen; total population estimated at under 1000 birds in 1969, but in 1990 put at no more than 100 pairs. Race *indicus* possibly has only a few hundred pairs, but inaccessiblity of nests suggests they may be fairly secure and perhaps more numerous. Main threat throughout range posed by introduced terrestrial predators, especially cats and rats, though it has been suggested that aggressive nest defence behaviour may act as a deterrent to rats.

Bibliography. Ali & Ripley (1978), Blake (1977), Brown *et al.* (1982), Cramp & Simmons (1977), Croxall (1991), Croxall *et al.* (1984), Etchécopar & Hüe (1978), Furniss (1983), Gibson-Hill (1950), Harris (1969e), Johnson (1965, 1972), Korn (1989), Lee & Irvin (1983), Lee *et al.* (1981), Mackworth-Praed & Grant (1957-1970), Murphy (1936), de Naurois (1969b), Nelson (1968), Palmer (1962), Paz (1987), Pinto (1964), Richardson (1990), Roberts (1991), Ruschi (1979), Sick (1984), Snow (1965b), Steadman & Zousmer (1988), Stonehouse (1962a), Voous (1983), Wetmore (1965).

2. **Red-tailed Tropicbird**

Phaethon rubricauda

French: Phaéton à brins rouges   **German:** Rotschwanz-Tropikvogel   **Spanish:** Rabijunco Colirrojo
Other common names: Silver Bosunbird

Taxonomy. *Phaeton* [sic] *rubricauda* Boddaert, 1783, Mauritius.
Birds of C Pacific sometimes placed in separate race *rothschildi*. Recent work indicates that races form a N-S cline, and that species should probably be considered monotypic. Four subspecies recognized.
Subspecies and Distribution.
P. r. rubricauda Boddaert, 1783 - W Indian Ocean.
P. r. westralis Mathews, 1912 - E Indian Ocean.
P. r. roseotincta (Mathews, 1926) - SW Pacific.
P. r. melanorhynchus Gmelin, 1789 - W, C & S Pacific.

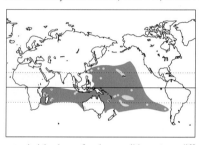

Descriptive notes. 78-81 cm (including 30-35 cm tail streamers); 600-835 g; wingspan 104-119 cm. Overall length similar to that of *P. lepturus*, due to much shorter tail streamers; appears relatively shorter-winged and heavier-bodied than other tropicbirds. Pink flush of fresh plumage often wears white. Juvenile has blackish bill, lacks tail streamers and is extensively barred blackish above (like other juvenile tropicbirds). Races separated on slight differences in length of bill and wing, and also intensity of pink flush of plumage.
Habitat. Tropical and subtropical seas; the most pelagic species. Breeds on small, remote
oceanic islands; prefers inaccessible spot on cliff, where take-off relatively easy.
Food and Feeding. Mostly fish, especially flying-fish (*Exocoetus volitans, Cypselurus*), up to 33 cm, and also large quantities of squid (Ommastrephidae); crustaceans also taken in places. Most prey caught by plunge-diving from height of 6-50 m, but flying-fish sometimes taken in flight. Where food scarce, immatures may learn techniques from adults. Sometimes follows ships, where may exploit flying-fish disturbed by vessel.
Breeding. Seasonal in places, elsewhere can be more or less continuous. Loosely colonial. Nest is in rocky crevice, or sheltered scrape on ground; little or no material. 1 egg; incubation 42-46 days; chicks hatch with grey or white down; fledging 67-91 days; no post-fledging care is probably standard (records of up to 30 days). Age of sexual maturity unknown. Oldest ringed bird 9 years old.
Movements. No regular migration known; some adults can be seen in vicinity of colonies all year round. Probably more extensive dispersal than in other species; birds from Hawaii recovered over 5000 km away to SE. S populations may perform some fairly regular transequatorial movements, following warm currents up E coasts of continents.
Status and Conservation. Not globally threatened. Populations generally considered stable. Most numerous in Pacific, with some 12,000 pairs in Hawaii, and probably large numbers in S Pacific, where known to breed on at least 9 island groups. Probably several thousand pairs in Indian Ocean, with 1380 pairs on Christmas I in 1984; 1000-3000 pairs breeding in Banda Sea, Indonesia. Has traditionally suffered extensive human exploitation for food, as well as extensive losses to rats (see page 287); in places, tends to nest more on flat ground under vegetation, as opposed to on cliffs, and this makes species more accessible to introduced predators. Introduced rabbits may remove protective vegetation and therefore suitable nest-sites, e.g. species ceased to breed on Laysan I (Hawaii) in 1920's. Tail streamers taken for ornamental purposes in much of its Pacific range. Some Pacific populations, largely dependent on areas of upwelling, adversely affected by Southern Oscillation of El Niño (see page 341).

Bibliography. Ainley *et al.* (1986), Ali & Ripley (1978), Ashmole & Ashmole (1967), Brazil (1991), Clark, Ricklefs & Schreiber (1983), Clark, Schreiber & Schreiber (1990), Coate (1989), Coates (1985), Croxall (1991), Croxall *et al.* (1984), Diamond (1975a), Dunlop & Wooller (1986), Dunlop *et al.* (1988), Fleet (1972, 1974), Gibson-Hill (1947a, 1949), Gould *et al.* (1974), Harrison (1990), Howell (1978), Howell & Bartholomew (1962, 1969), Langrand (1981, 1990), Marchant & Higgins (1990), Nelson (1972), Prys-Jones & Peet (1980), Schreiber & Ashmole (1970), Schreiber & Schreiber (1984a), Stokes (1988, 1990), Tarburton (1977, 1984, 1989).

3. **White-tailed Tropicbird**

Phaethon lepturus

French: Phaéton à bec jaune   **German:** Weißchwanz-Tropikvogel   **Spanish:** Rabijunco Menor
Other common names: Golden Bosunbird (*fulvus*); Yellow-billed Tropicbird

Taxonomy. *Phaëton* [sic] *lepturus* Daudin, 1802, Mauritius.
Recent opinion suggests races may be better considered merely colour morphs. Five subspecies recognized.
Subspecies and Distribution.
P. l. lepturus Daudin, 1802 - Indian Ocean.
P. l. fulvus Brandt, 1840 - Christmas I (Indian Ocean).
P. l. dorotheae Mathews, 1913 - W Pacific.
P. l. catesbyi Brandt, 1840 - Caribbean.
P. l. ascensionis (Mathews, 1915) - S & C Atlantic.

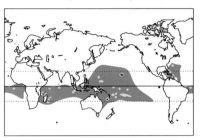

Descriptive notes. 70-82 cm (including 33-45 cm tail streamers); 220-410 g; wingspan 90-95 cm. Smallest tropicbird. Extent of black on primaries variable. Juvenile as other juvenile tropicbirds, but coarser barring on upperparts. Races separated on size and amount of black on primaries; *fulvus* has plumage tinged deep golden apricot.
Habitat. Tropical and subtropical seas; mainly pelagic, but in places frequents coast more than other tropicbirds, especially for feeding. Breeds on small, remote oceanic islands; prefers inaccessible spot on cliff, where take-off relatively easy, but more catholic in
nest-site selection than other species, and sometimes nests in hollows in trees; *fulvus* also breeds on limestone pinnacles in disused phosphate mines and even recorded on mining equipment.
Food and Feeding. Small fish, especially flying-fish (*Exocoetus volitans, Parexocoetus brachypterus, Cheilopogon furcatus*); also squid (Ommastrephidae), mostly 4-12 cm long and 3-79 g, and sometimes crustaceans, especially crabs. Local variations in diet: at Aldabra squid dominate, especially in wet season; in Seychelles mostly fish. In Bermuda, small chicks given gastropods. Generally takes smaller prey than other species, with low degree of overlap; large Caribbean population in zone where *P. aethereus* absent, perhaps due to unsuitable food supplies. Most prey caught by plunge-diving from height of up to 20 m, but flying-fish may be taken in flight.
Breeding. Seasonal in places, elsewhere can be more or less continuous. Loosely colonial. Nest is in rocky crevice, or sheltered scrape on ground, but also uses other sites; little or no material. 1 egg; incubation 40-42 days; chicks hatch with white, blue-grey or fawn-grey down; fledging 70-85 days; no post-fledging care. Age of sexual maturity unknown.
Movements. Resident and dispersive, with both adults and juveniles wandering extensively, sometimes as much as 1000 km. Migratory at some sites in higher latitudes, e.g. Bermuda (see page 285).
Status and Conservation. Not globally threatened. Most numerous of tropicbirds. Healthiest population probably in Caribbean, with 10,000+ pairs; population of Christmas I (Indian Ocean) must have declined slightly, due principally to loss of forest nesting habitat (see page 321), but is probably quite stable now and, at 6000-12,000 pairs, much higher than previously thought. Rest of Indian Ocean may hold some 5000 pairs, with good numbers at Aldabra, in Seychelles and to S and E of Java. Little known of numbers in Pacific, but must number several thousand pairs. S Atlantic reckoned to hold less than 3000 pairs. Main threats come from introduced rats, which probably cause considerable losses of both eggs and birds, e.g. formerly large numbers on Puerto Rico reduced now to a few pairs; also some human exploitation (see page 286).
Bibliography. Ali & Ripley (1978), Beehler *et al.* (1986), Blake (1977), Brazil (1991), Brown *et al.* (1982), Burger & Gochfeld (1991), Clapp *et al.* (1982), Coate (1989), Coates (1985), Croxall (1991), Croxall *et al.* (1984), Diamond (1975a), Dunlop (1988), Dunlop *et al.* (1988), Fuller *et al.* (1989), Furniss (1983), Gibson-Hill (1947a), Gross (1912), Harrison (1990), Kinsky & Yaldwyn (1981), Langrand (1990), Lee & Irvin (1983), Lee *et al.* (1981), Lindsey (1986), Mackworth-Praed & Grant (1957, 1970), Maclean (1985), Marchant & Higgins (1990), Murphy (1936), Nelson (1972), Palmer (1962), Pennycuick *et al.* (1990), Phillips (1987), Plath (1914), Prys-Jones & Peet (1980), Schaffner (1988, 1990a, 1990b), Stokes (1988), Stonehouse (1962a), Voous (1983).

Class AVES
Order PELECANIFORMES
Suborder PELECANI
Family PELECANIDAE (PELICANS)

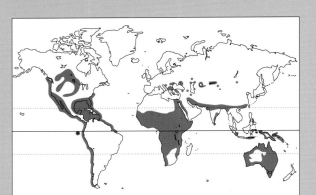

- Large waterbirds with long, heavy bill and voluminous distensible pouch.
- 105-188 cm.

- All regions except Antarctic.
- Stretches of open water, both coastal and inland, from tropical to warmer temperate zones.
- 1 genus, 7 species, 12 taxa.
- 2 species threatened; none extinct since 1600.

Systematics

The relationship between pelicans and the other families of the order Pelecaniformes is not very clear, and it is difficult to decide which groups are most closely related. It would appear that their nearest allies are the gannets and boobies, the cormorants and the anhingas, all of which used to be placed in the suborder Steganopodes, along with the pelicans and the frigatebirds. However, recent opinion suggests that the features considered to unify the order Pelecaniformes, such as the totipalmate foot, may be derivative, and that this order, long considered an unnatural grouping by some authorities, should be disbanded. Work on DNA implies that the closest relative of the pelicans is the Shoebill (*Balaeniceps rex*), which should actually be placed within the Pelecanidae.

As is the case of the other families of the Pelecaniformes, according to the traditional view, Pelecanidae comprises one genus only, in this case *Pelecanus*. At present, seven species are recognized and these can be conveniently divided into three groups: the first contains the Great White Pelican (*Pelecanus onocrotalus*), the Dalmatian Pelican (*Pelecanus crispus*), the Australian Pelican (*Pelecanus conspicillatus*) and the American White Pelican (*Pelecanus erythrorhynchos*), which are all large birds that nest and roost on the ground, form dense colonies and tend to be communal feeders; the second comprises the Pink-backed Pelican (*Pelecanus rufescens*) and the Spot-billed Pelican (*Pelecanus philippensis*), which are smaller birds that nest and roost in trees, form looser colonies and usually feed singly; finally, the Brown Pelican (*Pelecanus occidentalis*) is the only species that plunge-dives for its food.

The Great White Pelican, with its extensive Old World distribution, is replaced in North America by the American White Pelican and perhaps in Australia by the Australian Pelican. The Dalmatian Pelican used to be considered a subspecies of the Spot-billed Pelican, but nowadays they are recognized to be quite distinct in both morphology and habits, and are unlikely to be replacement species. However, this confusion has led to uncertainty concerning many records, for example in China, where both species are present.

When J. F. Gmelin, the translator of Latham and others, described the Spot-billed Pelican in 1789, he placed it alongside another species, the Rosy Pelican (*Pelecanus roseus*), and both were recorded from the Philippines. The two were later demonstrated to be synonymous, but the name *P. roseus* has

continued to cause confusion, latterly with another species. It has been claimed as a smaller, pinker subspecies of the Great White Pelican in parts of Africa and Asia, and at times this form has even been afforded full specific status in both regions. Recent studies invalidate *P. roseus*, both as a species and a subspecies, showing that size is very variable within the Great White Pelican and that the pink tinge is produced by a secretion of the uropygial gland (see Morphological Aspects).

The earliest of the ten or so known fossil species of pelican dates back to the Oligocene, some 30-40 million years ago. Most fossil species have been placed in the same genus, *Pelecanus*, as all the modern day pelicans, due to their very close anatomical similarities, and this suggests that pelican structure has changed very little over this lengthy period. Indeed, remains of extant species are plentiful in Pleistocene deposits, but the distribution of the family has certainly changed. The Dalmatian Pelican was widespread in Western Europe in Neolithic times, and sub-fossil remains have shown that New Zealand had its own large species of pelican.

Morphological Aspects

Pelicans are amongst the most distinctive of birds. Their huge, corpulent bodies, their long broad wings and, perhaps most of all, the unique arrangement of the long bill, with its voluminous distensible pouch, render them instantly recognizable and unconfusable.

They are amongst the heaviest flying birds. The largest of the pelicans is the Dalmatian Pelican, with an overall length of up to 180 cm, a 345 cm wingspan and a maximum weight of 13 kg. Although the Australian Pelican may measure as much as 188 cm, its wingspan has not been found to pass 260 cm. The Brown Pelican, in its more northerly forms, is the smallest member of the family, averaging 114 cm long, with a 203 cm wingspan, and weighing about 4 kg. Males tend to be larger, heavier and longer-billed than females, though the heaviest individuals are frequently young birds in the period shortly before fledging, when they need to be able to call on great reserves of energy to develop their muscles.

The bill is long and may measure 47·1 cm in the Great White Pelican, though in smaller races of the Brown Pelican it only averages 25·5 cm. The upper mandible has a ridged culmen, ending in a sharp nail at the tip, which may be used for gripping awkward fish. The nostrils are small, thin slits running along either side of the culmen and are probably obsolete. The lower mandible is loosely articulated and flexible to enable considerable distension of the enormous skin pouch which hangs from it. The tongue is very small, but it is the tongue muscles that control the pouch and permit the pelican to expel as much as 13·6 litres of water after a catch. Both the large bill and the massive pouch are evidently adaptations to the bird's requirement of catching a great quantity of fish. In addition, the bill is sensitive and can detect fish in murky water, while the upper mandible acts as a lid for the pouch, when it is used as a net (see Food and Feeding). The pouch is also very useful in hot weather, when it can be used to dissipate heat (see General Habits), while at times it is used for collecting rainwater. The neck is long, allowing the bird to rest its hefty bill on its breast, both while resting and while flying.

As the pelican is such a large bird, it is particularly important for it to economize on any unnecessary weight. Thus its bones are hollow and very light, contributing only about 1 kg to the total body weight of the heaviest birds. This is an important feature, as it helps the bird to fly long distances without tiring. It also helps, in conjunction with the extensive system of subcutaneous air-sacs, to make the pelican buoyant in the water. However, this buoyancy, combined with the fragility of the skeleton, precludes any possibility of the bird diving deep in the manner of its relatives the cormorants and anhingas.

The legs are short and are set far apart and well back on the body for efficient paddling at as much as 6 km/h. The feet, as in the other Pelecaniformes, are totipalmate, with the hind toe pushed forward and all four toes joined by webs, creating large, effective paddles. The underside of the body is well streamlined for swimming, but, although pelicans swim well, once out of water on dry land they look rather clumsy with their waddling gait.

At the onset of the breeding season, bare parts, especially the facial skin and the pouch, take on much more vivid colours, and sexes can sometimes be distinguished. The Great White Pelican, for example, has the facial skin pale yellow or pinkish in the male, but deep orange in the female, although these bright colours usually only last a few days, until the beginning of incubation. Most birds grow an occipital crest at this stage and there may be swellings or protuberances of bare parts, most notably in the case of the American White Pelican. In this species, both sexes sprout a horny knob on the upper mandible before pair formation and these knobs can grow to about 7·5 x 7·5 cm, although size depends on age and previous breeding experience; before the end of the breeding season, the knobs are shed.

Plumage in adults tends to be basically white, often with grey or pink tinges, and frequently with black or blackish flight-feathers; only the Brown Pelican is essentially brown. The pink tinges come from a secretion of the uropygial gland, which the bird speads all over its plumage during preening; it varies in intensity from place to place, depending on the diet. Young birds tend to be drabber than adults, with various mottled combinations of brown and grey and dull grey bare parts. Nestlings are born pink and naked and their first coat of down may be blackish brown or white.

Adults have a partial moult before breeding, when their shaggy crests are renewed, but the complete moult takes place after, or sometimes during, the breeding season; primary moult is serially descendant and can have three active centres at the one time. Pelicans often present a rather ragged appearance, as they frequently have one or more of the flight-feathers missing.

The lower arm is much longer than the upper, and, consistent with the tendencies of the order, the folded wing does not fit closely to the body. The wings are fairly long and broad, with eleven primaries, including a minute outer one, and over 30 secondaries. The short, rounded tail consists of 20-24 feathers.

This Australian Pelican obligingly offers an insight into the structure of its enormous bill and pouch. The gular pouch is present in all of the Pelecaniformes, but reaches its maximum expression in the pelicans, where it can be used as a kind of fishing net. The lower mandible is flexible, allowing the pouch to be distended to an extraordinary degree.

[*Pelecanus conspicillatus*, Australia. Photo: J. Cancalosi/DRK]

Pelicans are amongst the largest, heaviest flying birds, but despite their clumsiness on land, they are graceful fliers. As powered flight requires considerable expenditure of energy, in tropical areas they readily exploit thermals for movements of any great distance. A bird typically takes off and, with alternating flaps and glides, searches around for a thermal before spiralling up and setting off for its destination.

[*Pelecanus rufescens*, Tanzania. Photo: Jonathan Scott/ Planet Earth]

Due to the considerable size and weight of the birds, take-off from the water requires a lot of effort and quite a lot of room, unless they are assisted by the wind. They run over the surface of the water, beating their wings vigorously and pounding the water with their large webbed feet, until they become airborne; take-off from flat ground is equally demanding. Particularly in the tropics, they are dependent on thermals when they want to move long distances. For this reason, a newly-airborne pelican will often fly low over the ground, alternating flaps and glides, until it finds a thermal, whereupon it begins to spiral up and may rise to 1000 m or more, before setting off for its destination. They are expert and graceful fliers and have been recorded flying at altitudes of over 3000 m.

They are highly gregarious birds (see General Habits) and flights of any distance tend to be in flocks, often of 30 or more individuals. They almost invariably adopt a V-formation or fly in a staggered line, and it has been suggested that such systems may provide some aerodynamic advantages, though these are probably fairly limited. The typical flight consists of a few deep wingbeats followed by a longer glide. When flying in formation, all the birds flap in time with the leader, either in unison or, more commonly, in a regular succession. The Brown Pelican, the only truly marine pelican, normally flies low over the waves, but it too often soars high. It is also the only pelican that regularly plunge-dives (see Food and Feeding), and it seems somewhat surprising that its structure should be so similar to that of the other pelicans, when it uses such a radically different feeding technique.

Pelicans can fly up to 24 hours non-stop, and can cover about 500 km in a day, although their breast muscles do not permit sustained flapping flight. The flight posture is with the neck bent and the head drawn in between the shoulders, allowing the cumbersome bill to rest on the breast, where it is closer to the bird's centre of gravity. Their maximum reported air speed is about 56 km/h.

On arriving at a chosen site, descent is usually fairly abrupt, with perhaps some circling and side-slipping, before landing with heavy flaps and both tail and feet spread; the subcutaneous air-sacs may also help to cushion landing.

Habitat

Not surprisingly, like other waterbirds, pelicans are generally found on or near water. However, in the breeding season, due to their strict requirements both for nesting and feeding, they may find themselves having to commute long distances over inhospitable terrain, such as steppe or even desert. They generally prefer the warmer temperatures of tropical and warm temperate zones, but may be found in cold places, for example some desert areas, which can have very low temperatures at night. Lakes occupied by the Dalmatian Pelican in winter can be very cold, but they must be ice-free.

Because of their large size and their strong gregarious tendencies, pelicans need an abundant supply of fish, a requirement which severely restricts the potential range of most species. Thus they are most frequently found on large lakes and inland seas, as well as deltas and other extensive wetlands, including marshes. However, they need shallow water for their style of fishing, since they are unable to dive deep. Hence, they are locally abundant on several lakes of the Rift Valley, but are very rare on the steep-sided Lake Malawi. Pelicans are very rarely out of sight of land, whether they are on fresh or salt water.

Most species prefer freshwater sites, but may also be found in brackish lagoons or estuaries, and less frequently along the coast. The American White Pelican breeds almost exclusively in temperate freshwater sites, but winters in tropical marine zones (see Movements). The only truly marine pelican is the Brown Pelican of the Pacific and Atlantic coasts of America, where it has been recorded from Tierra del Fuego to Nova

Largely because of their hefty weight pelicans tend to find take-off very hard going. A bird runs along the surface of the water flapping heavily and pounding the water with both feet together until it manages to get airborne. Landing on the water is a good deal easier. The bird spreads its webbed feet and tail and splashes down, normally using its wings for a bit of back-pedalling and braking, before finally coming to rest on the water.

[Above: Pelecanus erythrorhynchos, USA. Photo: S. J. Lang/Vireo.

Below: Pelecanus occidentalis thagus, Chile. Photo: Günter Ziesler]

Scotia. It is most abundant in the area of upwelling off the Peruvian coast, where it breeds, in company with the other "guano birds", on small, rocky offshore islands, where mammalian predators cannot reach it. It is rarely found inland, and such occurrences are often due to hurricanes. Several species, such as the Australian Pelican, are particularly partial to small bare islands, either on the coast, or inland on large lakes.

In Africa, the Great White Pelican breeds on such islands off the south and west coasts of the continent, but it is mostly found on alkaline or freshwater lakes, or on alkaline mudflats. Ground-nesting species like this are extremely susceptible to disturbance from humans and other potential predators, and in the more developed zones, such as Europe, they often find themselves having to settle in dense reedbeds, in the middle of a swamp. Unfortunately, these are frequently areas which men want to drain, so that the land can be "reclaimed" for agriculture.

Some species, in particular the Spot-billed and Pink-backed Pelicans, may be found on smaller water bodies, including rivers, reservoirs and seasonal ponds, and this is probably connected with their smaller size and less gregarious tendencies. These tree-nesting species obviously need suitable wooded sites and can often be found breeding high up in tall trees, in mixed colonies with other waterbirds.

Several species, especially the more marine Brown and Australian Pelicans, affect man-made habitats and are often to be seen in and around fishing ports, searching for loose scraps of fish, following fishermen or snoozing on idle fishing boats. In the Danube Delta, Dalmatian Pelicans are attracted to commercial fish ponds, where they have made easy targets for those intent on shooting them. The Great White Pelican can also be seen scavenging on rubbish dumps in parts of Africa, while the Brown Pelican can be seen on freshwater sewage ponds in the Netherlands Antilles.

General Habits

Most pelican species are highly gregarious at all times. This includes breeding in colonies, the formation of crèches of young birds, communal feeding, communal roosting, and flying in formation in large flocks. However, some species, especially the Spot-billed and Pink-backed Pelicans, are less gregarious, for example in their feeding behaviour.

Fishing takes up only a rather small proportion of the day, so for instance the Great White Pelican, in Africa, has normally finished by about 8 or 9 a.m. This leaves the rest of the day for loafing, preening and bathing, which are frequently carried out in the company of cormorants, storks, other pelican species and other waterbirds, especially in the tropics. These activities usually take place on the same sites that are used for roosting, often on sandbars or small islands, and are frequently traditional sites which are used year after year.

More than 21 hours of the day may be taken up in roosting and loafing, whilst either standing or sitting. The long neck is normally drawn back and the bill rested on the breast, or alternatively, with the head turned round, the bill is placed lengthways down the bird's back, so that both head and bill are partly hidden under feathers. Preening occupies a lot of the bird's time and the long bill and neck make this a lot easier. Another common practice is direct head-scratching. Bathing, in freshwater streams or alkaline lakes, involves the vigorous ducking of the head and body, while the wings are flapped.

Pelicans often nest or loaf in very hot, exposed sites, where they have to endure long periods of intense heat. Temperature can be regulated by gular-fluttering: the gape is opened wide and the pouch distended and pulsated, a system similar to that of other Pelecaniformes, such as cormorants and frigatebirds. Another response to hot weather is wing spreading, although this does not constitute such a characteristic feature as in cormorants and anhingas. It has also been claimed that the subcutaneous air-sacs may play their own part in thermoregulation.

Some strange exercises are performed to stretch the gular pouch and throat tissues. These include holding the gape wide open, or tilting the head back to stretch the pouch, in "Bill-throw". Sometimes a bird may even invert its pouch completely, by forcing it over the protruded breast, a practice known as "Glottis-exposure".

Tree-nesting species can perch comfortably on trees and usually roost in them, but ground-nesters normally only land

Most species of pelican tend to be markedly gregarious in virtually all aspects of their daily activity. They breed colonially, fish communally and also tend to roost and loaf in large flocks. Australian Pelicans are occasionally solitary, but they normally occur in small or large flocks, sometimes of up to several thousand birds.

[*Pelecanus conspicillatus*, Australia.
Photo: Kelvin Aitken/ ANT/NHPA]

The Pink-backed Pelican is one of the less gregarious species and it habitually forages alone. Its main fishing technique involves looking out for prey, creeping up on it and then catching it with a rapid lunge. This juvenile is disputing the fishing rights with a Yellow-billed Stork (Mycteria ibis), and is intimidating it by means of a "Gaping" threat.

[*Pelecanus rufescens*, Kenya. Photo: Jane Burton/ Bruce Coleman]

in trees if forced to, perhaps by bad weather, as they have difficulty perching.

Pelicans are essentially diurnal and they tend to be inactive at night, though they occasionally fish on moonlit nights or with artificial light, or even in the dark. Despite the lack of help from thermals, they also do some flying by night.

Voice

Adult pelicans are usually silent away from their breeding colonies. As they have no syringeal muscles, they cannot produce true vocal sounds, although some of the noises they produce seem to belie this.

Breeding colonies are, however, exceptionally noisy, and a constant clamour of strange noises dominates the scene, in some cases continuing all through the night, though invariably becoming much louder around dawn. There is Oates' description of a colony of "millions" of Spot-billed Pelicans and Greater Adjutants (*Leptoptilos dubius*) in Burma in 1877, which, he remarks, were silent, apart from a whistling noise made by their wings. However, most other observers have commented on the general hubbub which is associated with large colonies. It should, perhaps, be noted that when a human is seen to approach a colony, all the birds may suddenly go silent.

Noises made by young pelicans, often when hungry, have variously been described as "groans, yelps, whines, screams, chattering, bleating, barking, squeaking, grunting" and so on. Such a broad spectrum seems to overlap amply with the adults' "moos, grunts, rattles, hissing, blowing, groaning, sonorous belching" and others. However, in general, noises made by young birds tend to be higher-pitched and are audible above the deeper sounds made by the adults.

Adults' noises may be connected with display, aggression or summoning their young. Some species, such as the Spot-billed Pelican, also participate in bill-clapping, with the head thrown back and the bill lifted skywards, in a display reminiscent of storks. This may be associated with defending a territory, but it has been recorded for both adults and young, and even on water and away from the colony.

The only other occasion when pelicans are sometimes noisy is in co-operative fishing, when they may create a stir in order to drive fish into the shallows (see Food and Feeding).

Food and Feeding

Pelicans eat almost exclusively fish, so their breeding colonies are typically found not far from an ample supply. As their colonies are often large, they may require an abundant source, for they do not seem able to adapt to other types of prey; if the fish run out, a colony is normally abandoned.

It has been estimated that the Great White Pelican in Africa needs about 1200 g per day, which is roughly 10% of its body weight. Thus, L. H. Brown and E. K. Urban calculated that the pelican population on Lake Nakuru in Kenya, averaging some 10,000 birds, eats 12,000 kg of fish per day, or 4380 t per year. An adult coming to feed nestlings at the Danube Delta was found to be carrying 3950 g of fish. However, the rather smaller Pink-backed Pelican, in contrast, probably needs only about 776 g per day. It has been calculated that some 80 kilos of fish may be required for the successful fledging of a single Brown Pelican chick in the USA.

North American pelicans have been shown to take mostly species of fish which do not interest commercial fisheries, such as carp (*Cyprinus carpio*) and chub (*Siphateles obesus*) in fresh water, and menhaden (*Brevoortia*) and silverside (*Menidia*) in salt water; indeed, in the south-east USA, menhaden constitutes 90-95% of the diet of the Brown Pelican.

However, there is a significant exception to this off the Pacific coast and similarly off western South America. In these areas, pelicans seem to be in direct competition with the important fisheries for their main prey species, anchovies (*Engraulis*) and sardines (*Sardinops*). Overfishing of the former off Peru coincided with guano bird numbers plummeting and it is feared that the same may happen soon with the latter (see page 341). Nor is this preference restricted to the Pacific, and one Brown Pelican stomach from the Caribbean contained over 250 small fish, most of which were anchovies.

At the Danube Delta, the two pelican species eat mostly cyprinids, again including carp, as well as bitterling (*Rhodeus sericeus amarus*), and perch (*Perca fluviatilis*). Pike (*Esox lucius*) are also taken, and the Dalmatian Pelican has been seen to catch them on hot days, when they swim near the surface. Asian preferences of the Great White Pelican include mullet (*Mugil*) in China and *Cyprinodon dispar* in India, where again most of the species taken are non-commercial. The commonest fish taken in Africa are the cichlids *Tilapia* and *Haplochromis*.

The American White Pelican is also known to eat salamanders and crayfish occasionally, while the Australian Pelican takes some crustaceans. There are also strange and presumably exceptional records of the Pink-backed Pelican eating figs and the Australian Pelican swallowing a female Grey Teal (*Anas gibberifrons*) along with her ducklings, and this species seems particularly prone to taking unusual prey items.

The size of fish taken varies from one species of pelican to another and also depends on availability. Thus, in Africa, the Great White Pelican normally takes larger fish, of up to 600 g, than the Pink-backed Pelican, which takes prey only up to 400 g. The latter's preference is for fish between 80 g and 290 g and lots of fry, whereas in Europe the former has been recorded with a carp weighing 1850 g. These differences in prey-size preference, as well as in their fishing techniques, mean that the two species can live together without severe problems of competition.

The youngest chicks are fed on regurgitated liquid matter, a sort of "fish soup". The parent lowers its inverted bill between its legs, and the red nail at the tip stimulates the chick to start pecking at it. By the time that the chicks are about two weeks old, they are fed on regurgitated fish, which the adult can retain undigested for up to 48 hours.

Young birds can be very noisy when hungry. They feed by thrusting their bills, and sometimes their heads too, into the parent's mouth, taking the food out of its gullet. Large young have been known to swallow fish of up to 600 g, and, shortly before fledging, they usually become larger and heavier than their parents and may even throw a parent about, when trying

Bathing is a fairly frequent form of comfort behaviour in pelicans. It is typically performed in fresh water and involves the bird ducking its head and shaking its wings energetically. After bathing, the bird normally removes to a loafing area where it will dedicate some time to feather care. Note the feathering on the forehead of this Dalmatian Pelican which forms a W-shape, as opposed to the pointed V-shaped finish in the Great White Pelican.

[*Pelecanus crispus*. Photo: Bruce Coleman]

to get at the food. A young Great White Pelican in India, weighing 11 kg, had 4 kg of fish in its pouch! Sometimes large young, on the point of becoming independent, can be seen eating rotting fish on the shore or in the water.

One of the most remarkable things about pelicans is their habit of communal fishing, one of very few cases of co-ordinated predation in birds. It is practised by all the species, although it is rare in the Brown Pelican. Typically a group of 8-12, or even as many as 40 birds, gather in a horseshoe formation in a lake and drive fish towards shallow water at the edge, opening their wings every 15-20 seconds as they advance, and simultaneously plunging their bills into the water in front of them to catch the fish. The Great White Pelican has a 20% strike rate with this method.

There are several variations on this theme, including one where a large number swim into the shallows in the same formation, but with their bills submerged all the time. As their bills are sensitive, they can detect fish without seeing them. Some species, such as the American White Pelican, also beat the water with their wings, to help drive the fish forwards into the shallows. Remarkably, a blind individual of this species was fed and kept alive for some time by its companions.

Another variation, usually used on rivers, is where two groups form up in parallel rows and swim towards each other, trapping the fish between them, or again driving them into the shallows, where they are more easily caught. During such manoeuvres the Dalmatian Pelican sometimes jumps up and then plunges under, in order to reach fish in deeper water. When a large shoal of fish is located, a seething mass of pelicans may mill about chaotically, with each bird helping itself plentifully. Once individuals are satisfied, they waddle ashore to loaf or preen, while others may join the feeding group, until all eventually end up together in the loafing zone.

Fish is hardly ever carried in the pouch. Immediately after a catch, any water is drained off from the pouch, the bill is tilted up and the fish is swallowed. Large fish may be siezed with the tip of the bill, before being tossed up in the air and swallowed head first. Once caught, a fish rarely escapes.

Three species, the Spot-billed, Dalmatian and Pink-backed Pelicans, prefer to fish singly, often in quiet backwaters with a fair amount of aquatic vegetation. The normal system involves the bird holding its head high, as it looks for prey. On locating this, it retracts its neck and swims slowly forward, before lunging out at the fish; the success rate is about 40-50%. The Australian Pelican uses this system too, whereas the American White Pelican sometimes flies along and, on spotting a fish, splashes down feet first, scooping up the fish in its pouch. These two species have also been recorded as simply standing or wading in shallow water and grabbing the passing fish.

A remarkable method is used by the Dalmatian Pelican in the Prespa Lakes in north Greece, in association with the Great Cormorant (*Phalacrocorax carbo*). One or more cormorants dive under the water from beside the the pelican, which then flutters forward low over the water, for about 10-20 metres, before flopping down and catching a fish; the cormorant soon reappears, often with its own fish. It seems that the cormorants seek out the pelican, perhaps in order to see better under its shadow, or because it may be better able to locate good feeding areas, whereas the pelican probably benefits from the cormorants chasing the fish up to the surface. This technique, which has not been recorded elsewhere, helps the pelicans to fish in the deep waters of these lakes.

The marine Brown Pelican habitually uses a totally different technique, which recalls that of the gannets and boobies (see page 315). It flies along and, when it sees a fish, dives down head first, from as much as 10-20 m. The wings are held in a "V" and the head and neck are stretched forward, as the pelican plunges steeply down. At the moment of impact wings and feet are thrust back to increase speed, and the bill is opened to encircle the fish. The bird may disappear completely under the water, but due to the layer of subcutaneous air-sacs, which probably also cushion the impact of the dive, it quickly bobs up again, always facing into the wind and ready for take-off. The water is then drained from its pouch, a process which can

be lengthy, as it can weigh more than the bird itself, and after this the fish is swallowed.

Each dive is made at only one fish, though more may be taken, especially when operating in shoals of small fish. Recent research shows that adult Brown Pelicans tend to dive from higher up and at a steeper angle than younger birds, and that they have a higher rate of success. It has been suggested that these refinements in technique may be designed to counteract the effects of refraction, and it is perhaps significant that they usually dive facing away from the sun.

In the Caribbean, a Laughing Gull (*Larus atricilla*) sometimes alights on the emerging pelican's head, waiting expectantly for any small fish that might escape or even just protrude from the pouch. Apparently the gulls prefer to kleptoparasitize juvenile pelicans, perhaps because they are more easily robbed, but in the Gulf of California adult Heermann's Gulls (*Larus heermanni*) prefer to attend adult Brown Pelicans. The adults have a higher success rate in their own captures than immatures, which may fail too often to make them worthwhile targets for the gulls. In some places the Brown Pelican is regularly found with the Magnificent Frigatebird (*Fregata magnificens*), although this species sometimes steals its fish.

In several parts of the world pelicans associate with fishermen, taking advantage of any scraps or unwanted fish, or even trying to rob them of their catch. In many cases the fishermen are quite tolerant and even favourably disposed towards the pelicans, but some see the birds as rivals and persecute them (see Status and Conservation).

Pelicans use several different fishing techniques of which two are particularly interesting. Co-operative fishing typically involves a small group of birds assembling in horseshoe formation on open water; the birds hound fish into the shallows, plunging their bills under the water in unison from time to time; any fish trying to escape is met with a barrage of living nets, and if it avoids one, it is likely to fall prey to another. The Brown Pelican (below) uses a radically different technique from all other pelicans, as it regularly plunge-dives like the gannets and boobies and the tropicbirds. The plummeting bird apparently dives at a pre-selected fish and uses its wings to alter course, but at the moment of impact it thrusts them backwards, to reduce drag, and opens its bill over the target fish.

[Above: *Pelecanus erythrorhynchos*, USA. Photo: Lee Rue/FLPA.

Below: *Pelecanus occidentalis*. Photo: A. R. Hamblin/FLPA]

Breeding

There are two important prerequisites for pelican breeding, a suitable place to breed, safe from terrestrial predators, and an adequate source of food to keep the colony supplied throughout the breeding season. There are a limited number of suitable nesting sites available, while food supplies are often only sufficiently abundant at certain times of year.

As one might expect, breeding is seasonal in temperate zones, but not normally so in the tropics. Most European birds start breeding in April, although the Dalmatian Pelican tends to begin about a fortnight before the Great White Pelican, with the last juveniles of both species fledging around the beginning of September. Northern colonies in America similarly start breeding in early spring.

In tropical climes breeding can occur all year round and some colonies are permanently occupied. In most of Africa laying tends to take place in the dry season, but in Kenya it usually coincides with the rains. Breeding can be triggered off by similar activity in other birds, particularly Ciconiiformes, such as herons, ibises and storks, and also flamingos.

Pelicans are almost always colonial, although ground-nesting species tend to form more densely-packed colonies than the tree-nesters. The latter frequently form mixed colonies with other species, especially Ciconiiformes and cormorants. Ground-nesters, on the other hand, tend not to form such mixed colonies, with the exception of the Brown Pelican, which, off the coast of Peru, breeds in large numbers alongside the Peruvian Booby (*Sula variegata*) and the Guanay Cormorant (*Phalacrocorax bougainvillii*). The Great White Pelican may breed alongside flamingo colonies in Africa or may oust them and take over their site. Dalmatian and Great White Pelicans sometimes share the same colony.

Colonies of "millions" of pelicans are sadly a thing of the past (see Status and Conservation) and the colony of Great White Pelicans at Lake Rukwa in Tanzania, which is probably the largest nowadays in the Old World, can only amass the much more modest figure of about 40,000 pairs, and this is itself exceptional. Large colonies contain discrete groups laying synchronously, probably as a result of "Peer-attraction", whereby, on seeing the breeding preparations of their neighbours, birds react by copying them. Such synchrony can be on a large scale, for example when, in 1973/74, some 14,000 pairs of Great White Pelicans bred in the colony at Lake Shala in Ethiopia, as many as 4000-6000 pairs were found breeding at the same time. Thus, as breeding groups overlap in timing, a colony can operate continuously for two years or more.

The first sign of breeding may be flocks flying over the breeding site. Soon males begin to display and look for mates, and this may occur at the breeding site or away from it. It is around this time that bare parts swell up and their colours become more vivid, while the crest has normally been moulted in by this stage.

Typical territorial displays, to ward off intruders or to strengthen the bond in pair formation, include a "Head-up", with the bill raised skyward and sometimes with the pouch swollen up like a balloon, "Gaping", "Bill-clapping", "Bowing", "Head-wagging" and "Bill-interlocking", amongst others. Details and frequency of these displays vary from one species to another. The bill is sometimes used by the male to attack interfering competitors during the breeding season, though often a wide-open gape threat is enough.

Pair formation is very quick, as are nest-site selection and often nest building, all of this sometimes taking as little as a few hours, though it can take about a week. The female Australian Pelican walks, swims or flies around, pursued by 2-8 males, until only one is left, and this she leads off to a suitable nest-site, where they copulate. A male Brown Pelican often perches on a branch and starts to display by "Head-swaying", at which point a female is quickly attracted; after this there is no further behaviour to confirm the pair-bond. To date there is no evidence to suggest that the pair-bond continues outside the breeding season, and it seems probable that a new pair is formed each year. In any case, not all mature adults breed every year, especially when food is in short supply.

The nest-site is selected by the female in most cases, though by the male in the Brown Pelican, and she stays there while the male brings material in his pouch. Normally he does not venture very far, collecting twigs and some grass, often from other nests, while softer lining materials, such as flamingo feathers, may come later or not at all. The Dalmatian Pelican has been known to collect up to 40 pouch-loads of material, but this is unusual.

Ground nests tend to be a fairly crude scrape sometimes made with the bill, although the American White Pelican may accumulate a substantial rimmed mound of debris, about 90 cm wide and 50 cm high. Normally, however, there is very little or even no material and only a slight depression, while sometimes a rim may be formed of the birds' excreta. Nests are usually contiguous and sitting birds may even touch, so it is only the immediate vicinity of the nest that is defended. A colony of several hundred pairs of Great White Pelicans in the Great Rann of Kutch in India had about 1 nest/m².

Tree nests, not surprisingly, are somewhat more elaborate structures. The Spot-billed Pelican builds a large, roughly circular nest, up to 75 cm in diameter and 30 cm or more thick, on the branches of large trees such as mango (*Mangifera indica*) and fig (*Ficus*), or alternatively on the low, horizontal

The Brown Pelican is the species that has best adapted itself to life alongside man. It is a frequent sight in fishing ports particularly up and down the Pacific coasts of the Americas, where it takes advantage of any scraps of fish discarded by the fishermen. In its spare time it often lounges on moored fishing boats.

[*Pelecanus occidentalis thagus*, Antofagasta, Chile. Photo: Günter Ziesler]

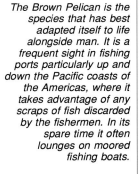

branches of palmyra (*Borassus*) and coconut (*Cocos*) palms. There is a thick twig base, which is sometimes covered with a lining of rice straw and decaying water weeds. As with the ground-nesters, other nests may be raided, material is added throughout breeding, and nests are very often contiguous.

The Pink-backed Pelican has a slightly smaller nest, which the sitting adult overflows. The nest is built 10-50 m off the ground and construction takes 7-8 days. It becomes solid with the droppings of the young, but an abandoned nest is usually dismantled by other pelicans or destroyed by the rains, so each year it is necessary to build a new one. Repeated nesting at the same site can kill the trees, but this normally results in the birds merely moving a short distance away.

Colonies of the Brown Pelican in the Netherlands Antilles are situated in *Rhizophora* mangroves. In each colony there are only up to about 20 nests, which are fairly small twig platforms, 4-9 m high in the trees. In contrast, the same species breeds on rocky sea cliffs at Tayrona in Colombia, and on low bushes in Venezuela.

Ground-nesting species need a site that is isolated from potential predators and disturbance, but tree-nesters are much more tolerant of man and sometimes nest in and around villages, where they can become quite tame (see Relationship with Man).

Copulation is frequent before laying, after which it stops. It is usually performed at the nest-site, but not always, and it may even be attempted in the water, though apparently without success.

One to six eggs are laid, with two being much the most frequent number. They vary in size from about 72 x 46 mm, in the Brown Pelican, to 106 x 64 mm, in the Dalmatian Pelican, weighing between 120 g and 195 g. They are oval and pale bluish or yellowish white, with a chalky covering, which starts white but soon discolours. They are normally laid at daily intervals, though sometimes there is an interval of up to four days. There is only one brood, but eggs lost in the first ten days are often replaced.

Incubation is carried out by both sexes and lasts 30-36 days. As in most other Pelecaniformes, there is no brood patch, so the eggs are rested on the feet for incubation, a system also used by the cormorants. Incubation begins with the laying of

the first egg, and each parent normally has a stint of about 24 hours, though this depends on various factors, including the availability of thermals. Nest-relief may be accompanied by grunting, "Bill-raising" and sometimes allopreening.

Hatching takes 24 hours and is asynchronous, so that, if there is a shortage of food, the eldest chick has a much better chance of survival than if all were the same age and size. Brood reduction may occur through "sibling-murder", as commonly happens in the Pink-backed Pelican, sometimes directly due to wounds inflicted, or with the smaller bird being pushed out of the nest, or alternatively through differential starving, where the larger chick monopolizes the food supply, as can happen for instance in the Brown Pelican.

The nidicolous chicks hatch naked and helpless, but after three to eight days they start to grow their coats of white or blackish brown down. After three or four weeks, the wing and tail feathers start to grow and at about eight weeks old the chicks are covered in feathers. After 10-21 days, brooding is only carried out at night, although there may be some shading from the sun's rays. At first, chicks may be fed up to 30 times daily (see Food and Feeding), but after about 40 days this may have been reduced to once a day or less. Young birds, when hungry, may bite at their own wings as a form of distraction behaviour, trying to entice their parents into feeding them. Alternatively, one chick may place its bill in another's pouch to imitate, and thus solicit, feeding.

The young of ground-nesting species tend to leave their nests after about four weeks and cluster together in crèches or "pods" of 10-100 individuals. The purpose of these crèches is probably thermoregulation, keeping the temperature down in the middle of the day and up at night, though it presumably also serves as an anti-predator device. Despite the writhing mass of youngsters, adults feed only their own young, and may look around for them before hauling them out of the midst of a large group.

Chicks are fully-fledged after 70-85 days and they become independent more or less immediately, or in some cases after another 20 days or so, during which time they join their parents at fishing and roosting sites. In tree-nesting species, it seems that the parents gradually stop bringing food to the nest, which eventually provokes the chicks into taking to the air for the first time, and ultimately becoming independent, although there is some dispute as to whether this is a genuine strategy or merely a coincidence, and that the adults might actually go on feeding their young, if these were to stay at the nest. Pelicans reach sexual maturity after three to five years.

In a successful colony, on average only one chick per pair or less (0·8) successfully reaches fledging. In the Brown Pelican, older birds have been found to nest earlier, with a higher proportion of chicks hatching.

Potential problems include mass-desertion due to disturbance, flooding or bad weather. In some species sibling aggression causes serious mortality, and in tree colonies once a chick is on the ground, it is rarely, if ever, attended or fed by adults, so it is likely to become prey to mammal or reptile predators, although some larger young may survive. Sibling aggression can also be a significant factor in the breeding success of the ground-nesting American White Pelican. Direct predation of eggs, for instance by Egyptian Vultures (*Neophron percnopterus*), or of chicks by eagles, or of both by *Leptoptilos* storks is reckoned to be uncommon, mostly at the edge of colonies and relatively unimportant, although it has been noticed that the Dalmatian Pelican often loses eggs to predators, such as corvids, when it leaves its nest in response to human disturbance. The vast majority of young birds do not survive their first year, so pelicans need a long time to build up numbers. They are fairly long-lived, and many survive at least 15-25 years in the wild, while in captivity birds have been known to reach the age of 54.

Movements

In most pelican species, once breeding has been completed, both adults and young tend to disperse extensively, in search of less busy feeding grounds. Some pelicans perform regular migrations, though not normally over the very long distances travelled by some of the more spectacular migrants.

The American White Pelican breeds mainly on inland lakes in North America, but most birds winter on the Gulf of Mexico. Although some move as far south as Guatemala, their route invariably sticks closely to the land, possibly because there are no thermals over the sea to ease their passage and help them regain lost height. As pelicans need thermals to gain height, periods of bad weather can delay migration, and even in favourable conditions they must wait until the sun has had time to generate thermals, if they are setting out on a long journey. Non-breeding birds of migratory populations sometimes spend the summer on their wintering grounds and are prone to erratic movements.

Some species are partially migratory, such as the Great White Pelican, for its European populations move over the land-bridge of Turkey and the Middle East into Africa, whereas African breeders are generally resident and dispersive.

The migration strategies of both European species are remarkably poorly known, considering the length of time that they have been familiar neighbours of civilized man. Recent work carried out by A. J. Crivelli and others, which even involved following migrating birds in a glider, as they flew south over Israel in one day, has already produced significant results. Around the turn of the century, the species wintered in large numbers in the Nile Delta in Egypt, but intense and increasing human pressure (see Status and Conservation) has forced it to seek alternative, more suitable winter quarters further south. As yet, it is not known where these winter quarters are, but they might be situated somewhere in the Sudd, in Sudan. As the numbers of migrating birds far exceeds that of the known breeding pairs, it has been suggested that non-breeders may well return north for the Palearctic summer, a theory which would tie in with wintering in the Sudd, as conditions there are unsuitable for the pelicans at that time of year. Much remains to be done, and it is hoped that southward-migrating pelicans could be monitored by satellite, in order to discover their main wintering zone, thus enabling more effective conservation planning.

The Dalmatian Pelican is really only dispersive, rather than truly migratory, except in Asia. It is probably a more northerly species in origin and even now it tolerates colder conditions, and winters in some numbers in the Balkans and Turkey, though mainly along the coast. It tends to undertake both spring and autumn movements a little earlier than the Great White Pelican, arriving at the Danube Delta in March and leaving in August.

Most pelicans eat almost exclusively fish and while small fish often make up the major part of a bird's diet surprisingly large ones may be eaten. It has been calculated that large piscivorous birds may need to eat about 10% of their body weight daily, while a Brown Pelican chick may require about 80 kg of fish in order to reach fledging successfully.

[Pelecanus occidentalis. Photo: Martin W. Grosnick/ Ardea]

Bare part colours intensify dramatically during the courtship period, which is also preceded by a partial moult, mainly affecting the feathers of the head and neck, including the short crest. The pouch can take on vivid coloration, as in these Californian Brown Pelicans, where the red base to the pouch plays its part in visual signals, for example in threats or in recognition of partners. Copulation usually occurs at the nest-site, but it even takes place on the water, where it is not, however, thought to be successful. The male normally seizes the female's nape and mounts, flapping his wings for balance. Birds tend to mate several times a day.

[*Pelecanus occidentalis californicus.*
Photos: François Gohier/Ardea]

In pelicans, as in most Pelecaniformes, chicks are fed by incomplete regurgitation and they must reach into the adult's throat, a remarkable habit, given the size of the chick's bill. Around fledging time the chick grows very large and may bundle the adult about in its attempts to get at the food. Note the feathering on the forehead ending in a pointed tip in this Great White Pelican, in contrast to the pattern found in the Dalmatian Pelican.

[*Pelecanus onocrotalus*, Lake Shala, Ethiopia. Photo: Goetz D. Plage/ Bruce Coleman]

An interesting early record of movements comes from Aristotle, who reports on pelicans travelling from their breeding grounds on the Danube to their winter quarters in Bulgaria.

In the tropics, most species are merely dispersive and make irregular movements, for instance between large lakes, often travelling by night. What prompts these movements is still unclear, but they could be related to food supplies failing, changes of water level or disturbance; whatever the reasons may be, they can occur at any time of the year. The Pink-backed Pelican does, in fact, make a regular movement north into sub-Saharan steppes, to coincide with the short summer wet season.

Due to their requirement of a breeding-site remote from potential predators, they often have to install themselves in a place where they are far from their other main need, namely an abundant food supply. Indeed, they may breed on small islands in lakes which have no fish, as is the case of the Great White Pelican on Lake Elementeita in Kenya, where up to 8000 breeding pairs have to travel to nearby Lake Nakuru for their fish. Sometimes the distances they have to commute are considerable, as happens with some American White Pelicans, which breed on islets in the Great Salt Lake and feed 160 km away on Utah Lake. In such cases, visits may be limited to once a day or even every two days per pair, and this naturally puts an additional strain on the business of breeding. When breeding is over, this commuting becomes unnecessary and all the birds are likely to move to good fishing grounds, which may or may not be the same as those used during breeding.

Erratic movements can be caused by droughts, for instance the 7000 Great White Pelicans that gathered on the Banc d'Arguin on the Mauritanian coast in August 1972, in response to successive years of drought affecting their habitual quarters in Senegal. In May-December 1978 there was a far-reaching irruption of Australian Pelicans, and birds appeared well beyond their normal range, reaching Sulawesi, western Java and possibly even Sumatra, with flocks of 300 individuals recorded in places. The movements of this species seem to be more or less nomadic, depending mostly on water levels. Thus, when the normally dry Lake Eyre was flooded in early 1990, large numbers of pelicans quickly colonized and started breeding. Brown Pelicans may be blown a long way inland by hurricanes, and on occasions they have been recorded in desert areas.

Amongst the most unusual cases lately was a pelican which flew into a central square of Beijing, China; the first pelican seen in the city since the 1930's, it was removed forthwith to the city zoo. Perhaps this was an escape, like several recent records in northern Europe.

Relationship with Man

The quite singular aspect of pelicans means that even a very rough drawing may be instantly recognized. For this reason they have appeared again and again in man's writing or artwork since the earliest times.

One of the most recurrent themes in legend is typified by a fable from India. A pelican once admonished her young so violently that she slew them. Overcome with remorse, she drew blood from her own breast, sprinkled it over them and brought them back to life again. Likewise, in Christian mythology, the pelican split open her breast to feed her starving youngsters and thus established herself as a paragon of altruism, in which role she found herself being drafted into many a coat of arms. These and similar legends may have originated from the bare gular pouch of the Dalmatian Pelican, which is blood red in the breeding season.

Pelicans were particularly common in medieval art, as a symbol of human mercy. In the modern world too, they make an important contribution, for they are amongst the most popular birds in children's comics or cartoons, and are frequently used in advertising all kinds of products.

The Brown Pelican
normally lays three eggs,
and as hatching is
asynchronous, there
tends to be a notable size
difference between the
chicks, to ensure that if
food is in short supply at
least one chick has a
better chance of
surviving. This species is
unusual in that it normally
nests on the ground, but
in some areas it nests in
trees. Interestingly, in its
tree-nesting populations
fledging takes longer, but
there is no post-fledging
care, as there is in
ground-nesting
populations.

[Pelecanus occidentalis
urinator,
Fernandina I, Galapagos.
Photo: Dieter & Mary Plage/
Survival]

The pelican has also been more directly exploited by man. Its pouch has for many centuries been used to make tobacco pouches and sheaths in south-east Europe. Young pelicans have been prized for their fat; in India the oil taken from this is highly valued as an embrocation against rheumatism. In China too, pelicans are considered to have medicinal qualities, while their feathers and skin are used to make camlets and leather respectively.

In the Sind area of Pakistan, fishermen were reported to use tethered pelicans as decoys, while others used their skins, disguised as live birds, with which to approach ducks or coots under water, and then capture them, pulling them under by their legs, one by one. Where they do not suffer persecution, some species, such as the Australian Pelican, often become quite tame and may beg for food at piers or even in urban parks.

By far the most important effects, in human terms, of any pelican are those related to the Brown Pelican off the coast of Peru, where the pelicans breed on the small, rocky Chincha Islands, in the company of the Peruvian Booby and the Guanay Cormorant. These are the famous "guano birds", which supply the raw material for the once massive local guano industry (see page 338).

In Karnataka, in southern India, there is a similar case on a much smaller scale, where a colony of 100-150 Spot-billed Pelicans breed in a small village. As the birds feed mainly on fish, their droppings are rich in phosphates and act as an excellent fertilizer. For this reason, the local people encourage the pelicans to nest in their village, so that they can collect the droppings and use them on their fields. It provides a good, cheap fertilizer and also a source of income for the guano collectors. The birds receive strict protection from the villagers, with heavy fines menacing any who persecute them, and the result is that the pelicans move about, quite relaxed, in amongst the local people and their dogs and cats. The inhabitants have learnt to live in harmony with the birds and to benefit from their presence, and they prefer to avoid publicity of their peli-

can colony, as the disturbance which might well ensue could might frighten the birds away from the village.

Status and Conservation

Like many large birds, pelicans are in a state of decline all over the world. Although only two species, the Spot-billed and Dalmatian Pelicans, are currently classified as threatened, most species have probably declined markedly in recent times.

The Dalmatian Pelican formerly had a much larger range, being present in southern Britain in the Neolithic period and breeding on the estuaries of the Sheldt, the Rhine and the Elbe in Roman times. There were "millions" in Romania in 1873, which by 1896 had become "thousands", and by 1909 only 200 pairs were left at the Danube Delta, the major site in the region. Despite some form of recovery to 1300 pairs in 1939, at present there are perhaps only 36-115 breeding pairs in the country, while the entire world population is now estimated at some 1926-2710 pairs at 21-22 colonies. However, the populations in China and the USSR are largely unknown, and the latter was quoted at 1500-2000 pairs in 1983, although it should be noted that the relatively large colony at the Volga Delta may still be on the decline. Sadly, the surprising record of over 2900 individuals seen in Pakistan in January 1988 turned out to be a misidentification, due to confusion with the Great White Pelican.

Undoubtedly, human activities, particularly agricultural developments and expansion, have been the major cause of the species' recession. The European populations of pelicans have been shrinking constantly, as man's alteration of the environment has consistently increased in both extent and degree of permanence, and both species are now limited to a tenuous foothold in the region.

It has become more and more difficult for pelicans to find an undisturbed site for breeding. Fish supplies have been heav-

Amongst the most impressive concentrations of birds anywhere are those of the "guano birds" of Peru and Chile, where vast numbers are supported by the very rich waters of the zone of upwelling. Guano bird numbers fluctuate notably, and while there were some 28 million in 1955, two years later numbers had plummeted to only 6 million; recent figures are generally much lower. The Peruvian or Chilean race of the Brown Pelican, sometimes considered a separate species, is one of the three major guano bird species.

[*Pelecanus occidentalis thagus*, Chile. Photo: Günter Ziesler]

ily plundered, and man now jealously guards and administers these exclusively for his own benefit. "Reclamation" of land, principally for agriculture, has been practised extensively, and vast areas of suitable habitat have thus been drained. In addition, alterations of the water level, sometimes man-induced, have led to the flooding of colonies or alternatively their exposure to terrestrial predators, and in both cases the colonies are liable to be abandoned immediately.

Fishermen have traditionally persecuted pelicans in many areas, as they claim that the birds rob them of their livelihood, but, like their American counterparts, the two Palearctic pelicans generally take only non-commercial fish. Nevertheless, in the Ambracian Gulf, in western Greece, during the breeding season Dalmatian Pelicans were found to take 13-18 tonnes of fish, of which about 90% were eels, and these are of commercial significance in the area; the proportion taken by the pelicans represents about 9-13% of the annual catch of eels by local fishermen, and a theoretical loss of US$ 11,600-17,000. But in most cases, while pelicans do take some of "their" fish, the fishermen's problems are usually due to mismanagement and overfishing in the past, in combination with the obvious impacts of large-scale drainage and deterioration of water quality, due to pesticides, waste products and the like. This does not stop fishermen killing pelicans, for example in Romania, despite legal protection. In 1983, fishermen destroyed one of the four remaining colonies in Turkey, killing the nestlings and later burning the nests, and many birds are still shot here every year. In addition, egg-collecting can still be a problem, as shown by the removal of at least six eggs from another Turkish colony by German collectors in 1987.

Clearly, some form of immediate action is necessary, if the Dalmatian Pelican is not to disappear totally. Environmental education is often the most important factor in attempts to save a species, and the recent attempts to promote conservation in Turkey are likely to be of great importance, but changes in attitude and tradition require time, and this is rarely available.

Even where there is no direct persecution of birds, their fight for survival is often an uphill struggle. Among the main problems affecting birds in Greece is the disturbance of colonies, very often by inquisitive tourists, with the help of overzealous tour operators. Furthermore, at Porto-Lago, in the north-east of the country, an alarming number of casualties were caused by collisions with electric power cables, until these were dismantled. A similar problem affected birds at Lake Mikri Prespa, but the positioning of plastic flags on the lines in 1988 promises to prove an effective solution, since no birds were killed thus in 1989, as opposed to 16 in the previous four years; it is certainly time that power lines were buried all over Europe.

The Dalmatian Pelican has at least been given legal protection in most countries, but this will not be sufficiently effective until the laws are enforced. Some breeding colonies have been included in protected areas, for example Lake Srebarna in Bulgaria which holds 70-90 pairs, and the recent protection of the Danube Delta should be a major step forward towards the recovery of its important pelican populations. Attempts to facilitate nesting include the installation of platforms in trees and floating or fixed rafts at the Volga Delta and at Lake Manyas in Turkey. Other proposed measures include: widespread construction of floodproof nesting platforms; protection of all surviving colonies and, where necessary, feeding areas; annual censuses; and investigation of possible effects of pesticides on breeding success. Meanwhile, in 1989, ICBP gave support for long-term ecological studies, with the intention of producing a sound recovery plan for the species in south-east Europe and Turkey.

The Spot-billed Pelican has suffered a similar disastrous decline, but this is more poorly documented. We have the testimony of Oates' visit to a vast colony in a swamp on the Sittang Plain in Burma in 1877. He talked of the pelicans breeding alongside Greater Adjutants (*Leptoptilos dubius*), and also referred to "millions" of birds. They were still there in 1910, but when B. E. Smythies visited the site in 1939, he found no signs at all of a colony. Nowadays the only known colonies are in Sri Lanka and south-east India, with some 900 and under 400 pairs respectively in 27 colonies. Fortunately, the Sri Lankan colonies are reported to be fairly stable, though some reduction in numbers has recently been noted.

The Spot-billed Pelican's decline seems to be even more recent than the Dalmatian Pelican's, though the causes are generally similar: human disturbance; destruction of nesting, roosting and loafing areas; a decline in the availability of fish; and an increase in the use of pesticides. In 1960, there was a thriving colony of 1500 pairs at Kolamuru in Andhra Pradesh, where the local villagers respected the pelicans and afforded them protection. However, by 1968 there were only 400 pairs, and by 1974 none were to be found at all, yet the causes of this local extinction remain unknown. Habitat loss or deterioration may well be responsible, and this bodes badly for other sites in India where the birds receive similar protection from the locals (see Relationship with Man). A colony discovered in 1961 near Kaziranga, in Assam, and still operating in the 1970's, has also apparently disappeared now, although the record of 2236 birds in Assam during a census in January 1990 is very encouraging.

Other, as yet undiscovered, colonies might exist, in China and particularly in Burma, where flocks are frequently present along the main rivers. Recent wetland surveys, between 1984 and 1990, along the east coast of Sumatra have repeatedly turned up a few individuals, and breeding somewhere in the area is suspected. Local inhabitants report that the pelicans breed there and an immature bird was seen in 1986, but to date no conclusive proof has been turned up. Certainly, it would imply a remarkable migration, if these birds had come from southern Indian or Sri Lankan colonies, especially given, on the one hand, the reluctance of members of this family to cross the open ocean (see Movements), and, on the other, the paucity of records from countries such as Thailand and Malaysia.

American pelicans, too, have had their own problems to face. Northern populations of the Brown Pelican were hit dramatically in the 1960's and 1970's by DDT and dieldrin contamination. The effects mostly reached the pelicans through their polluted marine food chain, causing extreme eggshell thinning, with the result that masses of eggs were broken in the nests. Some birds actually died as a direct result of poisoning, particularly when having to draw on their reserves of fat, where

such toxic substances accumulate, but this was undoubtedly less significant than the almost total lack of breeding success, and thus minimal recruitment. A fairly stable Californian colony of some 2000 birds dropped to 600 by 1969, and produced only 5 young that year. In the extreme north of its range, Brown Pelican numbers crashed by an astounding 90% in only two decades, and in 1973 the species was classified as endangered in the USA.

To make matters worse, sardine stocks off the Pacific coast were overexploited during the 1950's and 1960's, and only once suitable control was imposed have the sardines started a slow recovery. However, the North American Brown Pelican is one of the great conservation success stories, because DDT was discovered to be the major culprit and was subsequently banned. The pelican has undergone a spectacular recovery and now 75,000-90,000 birds can be seen off the Californian coast in autumn. The Louisiana population was exterminated, but the species has now been reintroduced and is recovering its former numbers. Many scientists are now advocating the reclassification of the species, as its present numbers are liable to make people sceptical of more critical cases, where species really are on the verge of local or global extinction.

There has been extensive scientific research and monitoring of populations since the crisis, and this has all helped to make this perhaps the best known of all the pelicans. Interesting demographic trends have emerged, and it seems that numbers naturally tend to fluctuate at each locality, as many colonies regularly shift. After the banning of DDT in 1972 and the improvement in fishing management, there was an increase in the population of the western USA, which rose from 3000 pairs in the late 1970's to a maximum of 7000 pairs in 1987. However, since then the number of breeding pairs has dropped back to 3000 again. The cause of this may be a large age-class of sardines in 1984, which probably led to massive immigration from Mexican colonies, followed by a corresponding emigration, once the proliferation of prey had died down. Other workers have found that colonies may shift locality due to acute infestations of ticks.

In South America, during most of this century, the Brown Pelican has been fighting quite a different war for survival, along with the other guano birds (see pages 338, 341).

The American White Pelican, which is partially sympatric with the Brown Pelican, has not suffered such drastic conse-

The Dalmatian Pelican has slumped dramatically over the last century or so, though its decline probably started many centuries ago with the spread of civilization, especially in Europe. The species has suffered extensive persecution and widespread loss of wetland habitat and its world population is now thought to consist of only 1926-2710 pairs. The ground nests of the species make it very vulnerable to the effects of a drop in the water level; one such drop led to this important colony at Lake Srebarna in Bulgaria being ravaged by wild boar (Sus scrofa).

[Pelecanus crispus, Lake Srebarna, Bulgaria. Photo: I. Vatev/FLPA]

The Spot-billed Pelican has also suffered a major decline and is currently considered to be threatened on a global scale. The causes of its slide are not well known, but habitat destruction seems to have been significant, involving both the loss of suitable trees for nesting and the deterioration and pollution of wetlands. Fortunately, the sizeable Sri Lankan population appears to be reasonably stable at present.

[Pelecanus philippensis, Sri Lanka. Photo: D. Zingel/FLPA]

quences from poisoning, maybe because its freshwater breeding sites are less affected by pesticides, although its eggshells too have become significantly thinner. It has recently gone into a major decline in California, due to habitat loss through the drainage of lakes, and this may be the chief threat facing this species. The total population in 1979-1981 stood at some 52,000 pairs, most of them in Canada, with the indication that numbers may be rising again after a gradual decline since the 1940's. This species is also persecuted by fishermen, especially in its wintering grounds off western Mexico, where it is said to take large quantities of shrimps. Studies show that pelicans do not generally eat the species of fish that men are interested in, and in any case Brown Pelicans off California have been calculated to consume less than 1% per year of the biomass of any single fish species. Nevertheless, attempts to encourage the Brown Pelican to recolonize the area at the mouth of the Mississippi were thwarted in May 1990, when fishermen stole 83 eggs from the first nests built there since the early 1960's; the men were reported and convicted, but the birds have not returned.

The Great White Pelican is regionally threatened in the Palearctic, for the same reasons as the Dalmatian Pelican, but it is not globally threatened, mostly due to its sizeable African population, which is thought to average some 40,000-75,000 pairs. In any case, it probably never ranged as far north or west as the Dalmatian Pelican, because the latter has a wider habitat tolerance, while in Europe the former is restricted to lowland areas for breeding. Most European breeders used to winter in Egypt around the beginning of this century, but intense human pressure, mostly in the form of drainage, agriculture and indus-

try has driven them further south (see Movements). Nonetheless, pelicans can still be found for sale in markets. One estimate was that a single market might sell 75 birds each season. It is to be hoped that the environmental education programme recently started in Egypt, with the backing of ICBP, will put a stop to this.

Tourism can also be a problem, as shown by the destruction in 1987 of a Brown Pelican colony in mangroves, on the island of Aruba in the Netherlands Antilles, in order to make way for recreational facilities. Tourist disturbance in the breeding season also contributed to the same species abandoning a major colony in Baja California over the period 1970-1975. The dangers of disturbance can not be overemphasized, and on several occasions scientists sampling eggs for traces of pesticides have noted with dismay that, despite their efforts not to disrupt the peace of the colony, breeding success may be lower in the parts of the colony that they have visited.

Pelicans are amongst the families most affected by pesticide poisoning and general contamination, and they can be useful indicators of pollution levels. The negative, or on occasions catastrophic, effects that have been produced by toxic substances should serve as a warning to man of the danger in allowing any further degradation of the environment.

General Bibliography
Burger *et al.* (1980), Cooper (1980b), Cracraft (1985), Crivelli & Schreiber (1984), Croxall (1987), Dorst & Mougin (1979), Drummond (1987), Grummt (1984), Harrison (1985, 1987), Lanham (1947), Nelson (1980, 1984), Sibley & Ahlquist (1972, 1988, 1990), van Tets (1965a), Tuck & Heinzel (1978), Urban (1985).

PLATE 20

inches 20

cm 50

(flying birds)

ssp *occidentalis*

ssp *thagus*

Genus *PELECANUS*   Linnaeus, 1758

1. Great White Pelican
Pelecanus onocrotalus

French: Pélican blanc   **German**: Rosapelikan   **Spanish**: Pelícano Común
Other common names: Eastern White/European White/Rosy Pelican

Taxonomy. *Pelecanus Onocrotalus* Linnaeus, 1758, Caspian Sea.
Some African and Asian populations have been classified as *P. (o.) roseus* (Rosy Pelican), but strong individual variation, and both subdivision and denomination now obsolete (see page 290). Monotypic.
Distribution. Breeds E Europe to W Mongolia, wintering (?) NE Africa and Iraq to N India; also resident in Africa S of Sahara and at single sites in NW India and S Viet Nam.

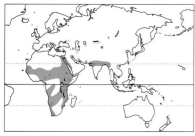

Descriptive notes. Male 175 cm, 9-15 kg, bill 347-471 mm; female 148 cm, 5·4-9 kg, bill 289-400 mm; wingspan 226-360 cm. Long-billed, legs pink, flight-feathers all black from below; feathering on forehead tapers to a point over bill. During breeding, facial skin pink-ish-yellow in male, bright orange in female, and legs tinged crimson; forehead swells out to form "knob". Non-breeding adult lacks pinkish tinge to plumage and yellow breast; bare parts duller. Juvenile greyish-brown above, dirty white below, with dull bare parts.
Habitat. In Eurasia, fresh or brackish water of lakes, deltas, lagoons and marshes, often requiring extensive reedbeds for breeding. In Africa, alkaline or freshwater lakes, sometimes marine; breeds on inselbergs in W Africa, also flat inshore islands off Banc d'Arguin. Fishing technique usually demands shallow, warm water. Generally in lowlands, except in E Africa; recorded at 1372 m in Nepal.
Food and Feeding. Fish, mostly 300-600 g. In Europe prefers carp (*Cyprinus carpio*); recorded taking mullet (*Mugil*) in China and *Cyprinodon dispar* in India; commonest prey in Africa are cichlids *Tilapia* and *Haplochromis*. In Africa, generally takes larger fish than *P. rufescens*, but can survive on abundant small fish; large fish may make up c. 90% of diet. At Walvis Bay, SW Africa, unfledged young take many eggs and chicks of Cape Cormorant (*Phalacrocorax capensis*), and decline of pelican apparently related to drop in cormorant numbers. Estimated daily food requirement 900-1200 g. Normally feeds in groups, often co-operatively, but solitary on occasions.
Breeding. Spring in temperate zones, all year round in Africa, starts Feb/Apr in India. Ground-nester, habitually in large colonies; nest is usually pile of reeds, sticks, etc., but sometimes nests directly on almost bare rocks in Africa. Average 2 eggs (1-3); incubation 29-36 days; chicks hatch naked, grow blackish-brown down; gather in "pods" 20-25 days after hatching; fledging 65-75 days. Success c. 0·64 chicks per attempt. Sexual maturity probably at 3-4 years.
Movements. Migratory in N populations; arrives Danube Delta late Mar/Apr, leaves Sept/early Nov; current wintering grounds of European population unknown (see page 301); many Asian breeders winter in Pakistan. Resident and dispersive in tropics and some S temperate sites. Regularly flies long distances from colony to feed, e.g. probably commutes 100's of km daily between colony at Mogodé, Cameroon, and L Chad.
Status and Conservation. Not globally threatened. Has declined dramatically in Palearctic over past century and now considered regionally threatened, although numbers thought to be fairly stable; total Palearctic population estimated at 7345-10,500 pairs at 23-25 colonies, with 3000-3500 pairs at Danube Delta in Romania, and c. 3070-4300 pairs in USSR; large colonies may exist in Iraq. Minimum of over 75,000 counted on autumn migration through Israel, late 1980's; winter counts of c. 10,000 in N India and Pakistan, in 1990 and 1991, with 25,000 in Pakistan alone in 1989, where up to 20,000 pairs may breed. Main threats are habitat destruction, depletion of food supplies, persecution and disturbance; pollution, flooding, disease, etc. could also have devastating effects, especially given typically large colonies. Still fairly numerous in Africa, and total African population may average up to 75,000 pairs: perhaps c. 40,000 pairs at L Rukwa, Tanzania, c. 10,000 pairs at L Shala, Ethiopia, 27,540 birds at L Nakuru, Kenya in July 1990; W Africa thought to hold up to 50,000 birds, with 11,000-17,000 pairs in Senegal and Mauritania; considered rare in South Africa, where c. 2000 pairs breed at 2 colonies. Persecuted for food in Egypt (see page 307).
Bibliography. Ali & Ripley (1978), Bartholomew & Pennycuick (1973), Bauer & Glutz von Blotzheim (1966), Berry *et al.* (1973), Britton (1980), Brooke (1984), Brown & Britton (1980), Brown & Urban (1969), Brown, Powell-Cotton & Hopcraft (1973), Brown, Urban & Newman (1982), Cooper, Williams & Britton (1984), Cramp (1983), Cramp & Simmons (1977), Crawford *et al.* (1981), Crivelli (1978b, 1979, 1981, 1984), Crivelli, Catsadorakis, *et al.* (1991), Crivelli, Leshem *et al.* (1991), Dementiev & Gladkov (1951), Din (1979), Din & Eltringham (1974a, 1977), Dragesco (1971), Dupuy (1976), Fossi *et al.* (1984), Goodman (1989), Grimmett (1987), Grimmett & Jones (1989), Guillet & Crowe (1981, 1983), Guillet & Furness (1985), Hatzilacos (1986), Jones (1979), Karpowicz (1985), Louette (1981), Maclean (1985), Mackworth-Praed & Grant (1957-1973), Milstein (1984), Parslow & Everett (1981), Perennou (1991a, 1991b), Perennou & Mundkur (1991), Pinto (1983), Pyrovetsi (1989), Roberts (1991), Romanov (1987), Rudinger (1984), Schreiber (1982), Scott (1989), Sutherland & Brooks (1981), Urban (1984), Verschuren & Dupuy (1987), Vesey-Fitzgerald (1957), Wirtz (1986).

2. Pink-backed Pelican
Pelecanus rufescens

French: Pélican gris   **German**: Rötelpelikan   **Spanish**: Pelícano Rosado

Taxonomy. *Pelecanus rufescens* Gmelin, 1789, West Africa.
Monotypic.
Distribution. Subtropical and tropical Africa from Senegal and Ethiopia to Natal (South Africa) and Botswana; also Madagascar (formerly) and recently SW Arabia.
Descriptive notes. 125-132 cm; 3·9-7 kg; bill 29-38 cm; wingspan 216-290 cm. Female slightly smaller. Pale greyish tinged plumage with pinkish back and, to lesser extent, underparts; leg colour

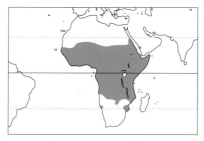

variable, ranging from grey to yellow or red-dish orange. Bare parts duller outside breeding season, especially pouch, and black patch in front of eye lacking. Smaller and shorter-billed than sympatric *P. onocrotalus*. Juvenile similar to adult, but browner above, with only faint pink tinges.
Habitat. Very variable. Prefers freshwater lakes, swamps, rivers and seasonal ponds; sometimes along coast, especially in bays, and also on alkaline lakes. Even in dry country, when locusts plentiful. Breeds in trees, often along waterfront, also sandy islands, mangroves and even by civilization; trees may be killed by repeated nesting. Roosts on cliffs, coral reefs, sand-dunes and sometimes piers or walls in areas where food abundant. More tolerant of humans than are ground-nesters.
Food and Feeding. Fish, mostly 80-290 g, but up to 400 g. Like *P. onocrotalus* prefers cichlids, especially *Haplochromis*, but takes plenty of fry and uses different techniques, frequently fishing alone (see page 297). Estimated daily requirement 900-1200 g.
Breeding. Breeds all year round, mostly starting late in rains. Tree-nester, in colonies mostly of 20-500 pairs; smallish stick nest (see page 300). Average 2 eggs (1-3); incubation normally 30 days; chicks hatch naked, grow white down; fledging averages 84 days; post-fledging care c. 21 days. Sexual maturity at 3-4 years; estimated adult breeding life of 6·25 years on average. Relatively high chick mortality due to sibling aggression (see page 300).
Movements. Mostly dispersive, especially juveniles, but some regular movement N into sub-Saharan steppes for wet season. Vagrant to Egypt and Israel. Local movements possibly related to water conditions or beginning of breeding. Less dependent on thermals than *P. onocrotalus*.
Status and Conservation. Not globally threatened. Widespread and common, locally abundant, especially in sub-Saharan zone. Difficult to estimate population, due to tree-nesting and less gregarious tendencies. Estimated 4200-6200 birds in Senegal and Guinea-Bissau, Oct-Dec 1983; 153 counted in Saudi Arabia, Jan 1991. In South Africa rare, breeding at only one colony, but no evidence that was ever more numerous, and presently on increase, due to conservation action by local landowners. Its greater tolerance of man makes it less susceptible to disturbance than some other species, and habit of solitary fishing may make it seem less of a competitor to fishermen. However, has declined markedly in Nigeria in recent years and now seeks out remote wooded wetlands for breeding; formerly bred in Madagascar, but only colony probably wiped out by villagers.
Bibliography. Berruti (1980), Britton (1980), Brooke (1984), Brown & Britton (1980), Brown *et al.* (1982), Burke & Brown (1970), Cooper, Williams & Britton (1984), Cramp & Simmons (1977), Din (1979), Din & Eltringham (1974a, 1974b, 1977), Elgood (1982), Hancock (1965), Jennings *et al.* (1982), Langrand (1990), Louette (1981), Mackworth-Praed & Grant (1957-1973), Maclean (1985), Perennou (1991a, 1991b), Pinto (1983), Verschuren & Dupuy (1987).

3. Spot-billed Pelican
Pelecanus philippensis

French: Pélican à bec tacheté   **German**: Graupelikan   **Spanish**: Pelícano Oriental
Other common names: Grey/Philippine Pelican

Taxonomy. *Pelecanus philippensis* Gmelin, 1789, Philippine Islands.
Confusion in past with now obsolete *P. roseus* (see page 290). Formerly included *P. crispus*, though now generally accepted that they are two quite separate species. Monotypic.
Distribution. Once widespread in S Asia, range now much reduced. Breeding now apparently limited to Sri Lanka and SE India, though also suspected in Sumatra.

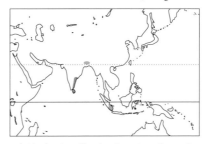

Descriptive notes. 127-152 cm; 5 kg (immature); bill 285-355 mm. Female slightly smaller. Smaller than other sympatrics, legs usually dark brown, though occasionally grey; plumage very variable, often tinged grey or brown above, primaries blackish; generally dingy appearance. Non-breeding adult has plumage duller and even dirtier looking, with crest less marked and facial skin drab yellow. Juvenile generally browner above, with legs grey.
Habitat. Watery tracts, including marshes, *jheels*, rivers, estuaries, reservoirs, tanks, flooded fields, large lakes, brackish lagoons, tidal creeks and along coast; often feeds in quiet backwaters. Requires large trees for nesting, normally in swamp forest or swampy savanna, but sometimes along margins of paddyfields, where undisturbed; trees also used for roosting, with certain preference for bare or dead trees.
Food and Feeding. Mostly fish, but poorly documented. Daily requirement reckoned to be around 1000 g. Normally feeds alone, though sometimes in groups.
Breeding. Oct-Mar, usually on traditional sites. Tree-nester, normally 3-15 nests per tree, often in mixed colonies with storks, egrets or cormorants; large stick nest (see page 299). 3-4 eggs; incubation 30 days; chicks hatch naked, grow snow-white down; fledging about 4 months.
Movements. Poorly known. Some local movements, other populations sedentary. In S India, birds reported to arrive at colony shortly before breeding in Oct/Nov or Jan/Feb, with most leaving site around May. Recorded as vagrant or even regular non-breeding species in SE China and parts of Indochina, as well as Sumatra and Java, but taxonomic confusion with both *P. onocrotalus* and *P. crispus* (see page 290) invalidates many of older records. Formerly found in Philippines, whence described.
Status and Conservation. INDETERMINATE. Possibly least numerous of all pelicans; only known to breed in SE India, with under 400 pairs at 4 colonies, and Sri Lanka, with c. 900 pairs in 23 colonies; 4245 birds counted in India and Sri Lanka, Jan 1990, with over half of these in Assam; similar overall numbers in 1991, but only 114 birds seen in Assam, with 3010 in Sri Lanka. Thought to be stable in Sri Lanka, though some reduction in numbers reported. Main threats reckoned to be pollution by organochlorine pesticides, hunting and habitat destruction. In Karnataka, S India, villagers protect breeding pelicans, which are consequently very tame (see page 304). In recent years regularly sighted in small numbers off E Sumatra, where breeding may well occur, but vast areas still await survey. Status in Burma unknown, though formerly abundant. See page 305.

On following pages: 4. Dalmatian Pelican (*Pelecanus crispus*); 5. Australian Pelican (*Pelecanus conspicillatus*); 6. American White Pelican (*Pelecanus erythrorhynchos*); 7. Brown Pelican (*Pelecanus occidentalis*).

Bibliography. Ali (1979), Ali & Ripley (1978), Collar & Andrew (1988), Etchécopar & Hüe (1978), Gee (1960), Guttikar (1979), He *et al.* (1984), Humphrey & Bain (1990), Karpowicz (1985), Martínez & Elliott (1990), Nagulu & Ramana Rao (1981, 1982), Nagulu *et al.* (1981), Neelakantan (1949, 1980), Neginhal (1976), Paulraj & Gunasekaran (1988), Paulraj *et al.* (1990), Perennou & Mundkur (1991), Roberts (1991), Saxena (1980), Scott (1989), Silvius (1986), Smythies (1986).

4. Dalmatian Pelican

Pelecanus crispus

French: Pélican frisé **German**: Krauskopfpelikan **Spanish**: Pelícano Ceñudo

Taxonomy. *Pelecanus crispus* Bruch, 1832, Dalmatia.
Has been considered subspecies of *P. philippensis*, but quite distinct in morphology and nesting habits. Monotypic.
Distribution. Breeds Yugoslavia to China, c. 30°-50° N; winters Greece to China, typically in Balkans, S Caspian Sea, floodplains of Indus and Ganges.

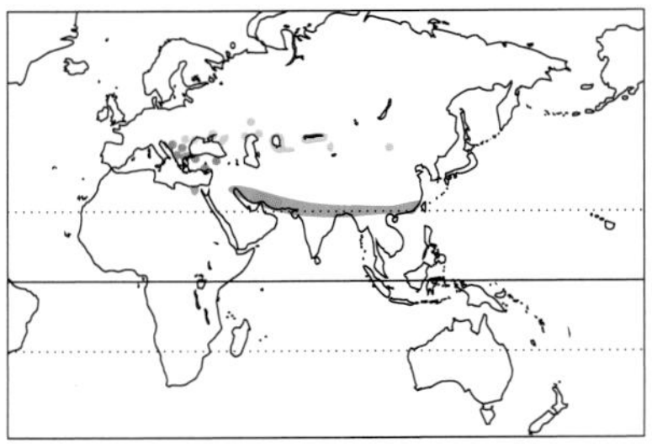

Descriptive notes. 160-180 cm; 10-13 kg; wingspan 310-345 cm; bill 370-450 mm. Female averages slightly smaller. Largest pelican; legs grey, only tips dark on underwing; feathering on forehead forms W-shape over bill. Non-breeding adult has bare parts much duller, with pouch dull orange and bill yellowish grey. Juvenile pale greyish-brown above, dirty white below, with dull bare parts.
Habitat. Rivers, lakes, deltas, estuaries. Similar to *P. onocrotalus*, but does not need lowlands and more readily breeds in smaller colonies; less opportunistic, tending to stick to traditional breeding locations. Nests on islands or in dense aquatic vegetation, e.g. extensive reedbeds of *Phragmites* and *Typha*. Typically winters on *jheels* and lagoons in India, on ice-free lakes in Europe. Sometimes fishes inshore along sheltered coasts.
Food and Feeding. Fish, especially carp (*Cyprinus carpio*), perch (*Perca fluviatilis*) and rudd (*Scardinius erythrophthalmus*); also pike (*Esox lucius*) up to 50 cm, and eels. Estimated daily requirement c. 1200 g. Normally solitary feeder or in small groups of 2 or 3 birds, typically swimming along and suddenly plunging head into water to catch fish; in co-operative groups on occasions; recorded fishing in conjunction with cormorants at Prespa, N Greece (see page 297).
Breeding. Spring, starting late Mar/Apr, earlier than *P. onocrotalus*. Ground-nester, often on floating islands of vegetation; can be solitary, but normally in colonies of up to 250 pairs, on occasions mixed with *P. onocrotalus*. Nest is pile of reeds, grass, sticks, etc., c. 1 m high and 63 cm wide; gradually cemented together by droppings. Average 2 eggs (1-6); incubation 30-34 days; chicks hatch naked, grow white down; gather in "pods" c. 6-7 weeks after hatching; fledging c. 85 days; independence at 100-105 days. Success c. 0·58-1·20 chicks per attempt. Sexual maturity probably at 3 or 4 years.
Movements. Dispersive in Europe, migratory in Asia; arrives Danube Delta during Mar, leaves Aug. European birds appear to move short distances, staying mostly in E Mediterranean zone; recoveries of birds ringed in USSR suggest movement W or WSW. Small Iranian population probably only dispersive.
Status and Conservation. ENDANGERED. CITES I. World population estimated in 1991 at only 1926-2710 pairs at 21-22 colonies; record of over 2900 individuals in Pakistan, Jan 1988, due to misidentification, and confusion with *P. onocrotalus*; 782 counted in Iran, Jan 1991; 1293 in N India and Pakistan, Jan 1990. About two-thirds of world total reckoned to breed in USSR, where population perhaps overestimated at 1500-2000 pairs. Alarming decline throughout range during 20th century, due mainly to habitat loss, through drainage of wetlands, disturbance of colonies and direct persecution by fishermen and sometimes also hunters; has probably been receding steadily, in the face of humanization of environment, since Neolithic times. Recent threat to colony in N Greece, where tourists taken towards pelicans in speedboats, until birds panic and scatter; many Greek birds also killed after collision with power lines. At several sites has bred on specially supplied artificial platforms; even when placed in trees at L Manyas, Turkey. See page 304.
Bibliography. Ali & Ripley (1978), Bauer & Glutz von Blotzheim (1966), Collar & Andrew (1988), Cramp & Simmons (1977), Crivelli (1978a, 1978b, 1981, 1984, 1987, 1988), Crivelli & Vizi (1981), Crivelli, Catsadorakis, *et al.* (1991), Crivelli, Focardi *et al.* (1989), Dementiev & Gladkov (1951), Diamond *et al.* (1987), Flint (1978), Goodman (1989), Grimmett & Jones (1989), Karpowicz (1985), Kenzhegulov (1974), King (1978/79), Korodi (1964), Mitchev (1981), Parslow & Everett (1981), Perennou & Mundkur (1991), Pyrovetsi & Daoutopoulos (1989), Roberts (1991), Scott (1989), Sutherland & Brooks (1981), Vizi (1975).

5. Australian Pelican

Pelecanus conspicillatus

French: Pélican à lunettes **German**: Brillenpelikan **Spanish**: Pelícano Australiano
Other common names: Spectacled Pelican

Taxonomy. *Pelecanus conspicillatus* Temminck, 1824, New South Wales.
Monotypic.
Distribution. Most of Australia and also Tasmania. Regular non-breeding visitor to New Guinea.
Descriptive notes. 152-188 cm; 4-6·8 kg; wingspan 230-260 cm; bill 409-500 mm in male, 346-408 mm in female. Female smaller, with much shorter bill. White panel on upperwing and white V on rump; legs dark slate blue. During courtship, orbital skin and distal quarter of bill orange, pouch dark blue, pink and scarlet; non-breeding adult has bill and eye-ring pale yellow, pouch pinkish. Juvenile plumage similar to adult, but black replaced with brown and white patch on upperwing reduced.
Habitat. Large stretches of open water lacking dense aquatic vegatation; both inland and coastal. Typically on large lakes, reservoirs, billabongs and rivers; also estuaries, swamps, temporarily flooded areas in arid zones, drainage channels in farmland, saltpans, coastal lagoons and humanized areas, such as fishing ports. Nests on small sandy islands or along shore of sea coast, lakes, swamps, etc., requiring remote, undisturbed site with adequate food supply nearby. Roosts and loafs at similar sites and also mudflats, sandbars, beaches, reefs, jetties and piles.
Food and Feeding. Probably mostly fish, including carp (*Cyprinus carpio*), *Carassius auratus*, *Leiopotherapon unicolor* and perch (*Perca fluviatilis*). Seems to be more catholic in taste than other pelicans, and recorded taking: insects; small crustaceans, e.g. decapod shrimps (*Macrobrachium*) and freshwater crayfish (*Cherax destructor*); occasional birds, e.g. Silver Gulls (*Larus

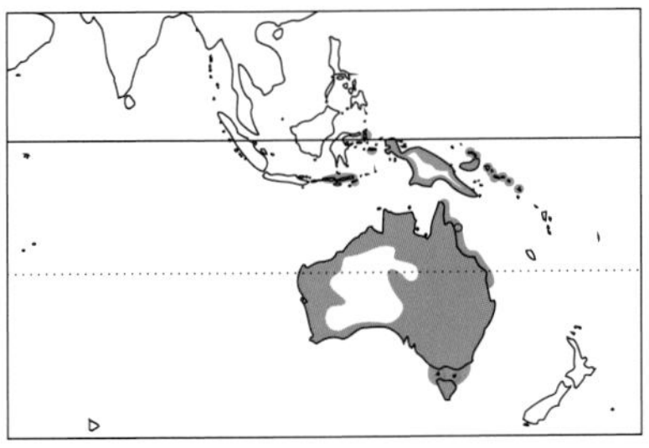

novaehollandiae*) and Grey Teal (*Anas gibberifrons*); some reptiles and amphibians; and probably even small dogs. Regularly feeds in groups, which may number up to 1900 birds, often co-operatively; also frequently solitary. Occasionally kleptoparasitic, robbing e.g. cormorants; also recorded plunge-diving from low down, close to surface of water.
Breeding. Poorly known, but apparently almost all year round in places; timing and duration largely dependent on rainfall and water levels. Nests on ground or on lignum bushes; nest is depression lined with plant matter and rubbish, slightly more elaborate on bushes. Average 2 eggs (1-4); incubation 32-35 days; chicks hatch naked, grow grey down; gather in "pods" c. 25 days after hatching; fledging c. 3 months.
Movements. Seasonal factors influence nomadic movements, with occasional mass movements during drought; also wind-blown on occasions. Irruption in 1978 into Indonesia, reaching Sulawesi, Java and possibly also Sumatra. Fairly regular visitor to S coast of New Guinea, also Bismarcks and Solomons; vagrant to New Zealand, Indonesia, Christmas I (Indian Ocean), Vanuatu and Fiji.
Status and Conservation. Not globally threatened. Generally stable and common in suitable habitat; over 200,000 found breeding on L Eyre in Mar 1990, taking advantage of flooding of the normally dry lake. Legally protected throughout Australia, and no evidence to date that species is suffering excessively from pollution. In many areas, associates with humans, though tends to prefer remote sites, particularly during breeding. Changes in water level often cause breeding failure, due to swamping of nests or greater accessibility to terrestrial predators. Readily adapts to artificial sites, such as reservoirs, while its traditional extensive open water habitat has suffered less from drainage than other wetlands throughout Australia.
Bibliography. Andrew (1986), Ap-Thomas (1986), Campbell & Sonter (1985), Coates (1985), Corrick & Norman (1980), Crawford (1987), Davies (1986), Eckert (1965), Fjeldså (1985), Garnett & Bredl (1985), Gosper (1981, 1983), Hobbs (1961), Lowe & Lowe (1976), MacGillivray (1923), Marchant & Higgins (1990), van Marle & Voous (1988), McCulloch (1987), Menkhorst *et al.* (1983), Mitchell (1986, 1989), van Tets (1978), Vestjens (1977a, 1977b, 1983), White & Bruce (1986).

6. American White Pelican

Pelecanus erythrorhynchos

French: Pélican d'Amérique **German**: Nashornpelikan **Spanish**: Pelícano Norteamericano
Other common names: Rough-billed Pelican

Taxonomy. *Pelecanus erythrorhynchos* Gmelin, 1789, Hudson Bay and New York.
Monotypic.
Distribution. Inland N America, from British Columbia to SW Ontario (Canada) and NE California to SW Minnesota, SE Texas (USA). Winters Pacific and Atlantic coasts from USA to Costa Rica.

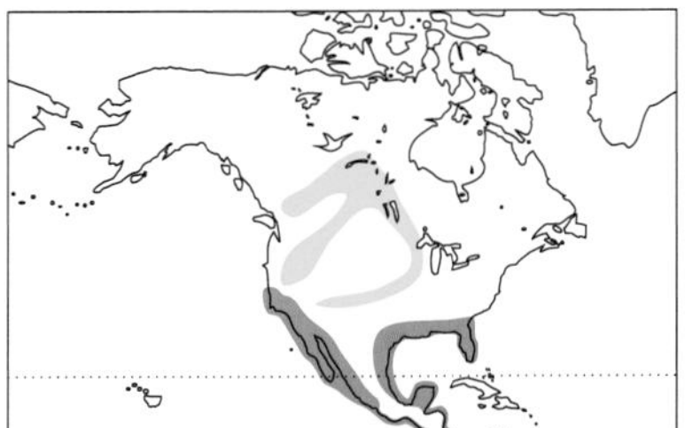

Descriptive notes. 127-178 cm; 5-8·5 kg; wingspan 244-299 cm; bill 320-365 mm in male, 265-320 mm in female. Female slightly smaller. Only white pelican in range; legs orange-red. Males average slightly larger. Non-breeding adult lacks yellow wash on upper breast; knob on upper mandible from late winter till after laying (Jun/Jul). Crown and nape grey in non-breeding plumage. Juvenile as adult, but nape and flight-feathers dark brown, bill and pouch grey.
Habitat. Rivers, lakes, estuaries, coast; mostly on open expanses of fresh water, but also brackish and salt water, especially on bays and inlets. Breeds on bare, remote islands of freshwater or alkaline inland lakes; also on Great Salt Lake. Susceptible to disturbance by humans.
Food and Feeding. Almost exclusively fish, normally species of little commercial value; typically carp (*Cyprinus carpio*), chub (*Siphateles obesus*), Sacramento perch (*Archoplites interruptus*) and rainbow trout (*Salmo gairdneri*); also takes salamanders (*Ambystoma*) and crayfish (*Astacus*). Habitually feeds in groups, often co-operatively, but solitary at times, especially in deeper water. Also kleptoparasitic, mainly on gulls and also conspecifics.
Breeding. Laying early Apr-early June. Ground-nester, in colonies of a few to about 5000 pairs; nest is usually slight depression with pile of reeds, sticks, debris. Average 2 eggs (1-6), but usually only 1 chick raised to fledging; incubation c. 29 days (c. 36 days from start of courtship to hatching); chicks hatch naked, grow white down; gather in "pods" 21-28 days after hatching; fledging c. 60 days; post-fledging care 20+ days. Recorded over 16 years old in wild; in captivity has lived to over 34 years old.
Movements. Regular N-S migration; all migration over land, at times over deserts or mountains, but avoiding long sea crossings. Arrives at most colonies Mar/Apr; after breeding, birds congregate at favourable sites, before departing S, mostly late Sept/Oct. Sedentary in S parts of range. Some non-breeders spend summer on wintering grounds. Populations breeding on unproductive alkaline lakes regularly commute over great distances for feeding.
Status and Conservation. Not globally threatened. World population surveyed in 1979-81 at c. 52,000 pairs: 33,000 nests at 50 colonies in Canada; 18,500 nests at 14-17 colonies in USA. Thought to be stable, perhaps increasing, after possible decrease in 1940's-1960's. Recovery probably due to increased protection and ban of harmful pesticides. Some effects of DDE, etc., and recently 70-84% of birds found dead in California revealed lethal levels of insecticide endrin; perhaps more problems from drainage of wetlands, and persecution by fishermen, who see it as competitor; general disturbance also significant. Degradation of shoreline on a breeding island in Colorado halted by installation, at great expense, of a nylon-encased concrete revetment.
Bibliography. Anderson, D.W. (1984), Anderson, J.G.T. (1991), Anon. (1983), Bartholomew *et al.* (1953), Beaver & Lewin (1981), Boellstorff *et al.* (1988), Bunnell *et al.* (1981), Cash & Evans (1986a, 1986b), Chapman (1988), Diem (1979), Evans, R.W. (1972, 1984, 1988a, 1988b, 1989, 1990a, 1990b), Evans & Cash (1985), Evans & McMahon (1987), Findholt (1986, 1987), Findholt & Diem (1988), Flannery (1988), Hall (1925), Johnson & Sloan (1976, 1978), Knopf (1975, 1976, 1979, 1980), Knopf & Kennedy (1981), Laycock (1979), Lies & Behle (1966), O'Malley (1980), O'Malley & Evans (1980, 1982a, 1982b, 1983, 1984), Palmer (1962), Paullin *et al.* (1988), Richards (1990), Ryder (1981), Schaller (1964), Sidle & Ferguson (1982), Sidle *et al.* (1985), Sloan (1973, 1982), Strait & Sloan (1974), Trottier *et al.* (1980), Vermeer (1970).

7. Brown Pelican

Pelecanus occidentalis

French: Pélican brun   **German**: Braunpelikan   **Spanish**: Pelícano Alcatraz
Other common names: Peruvian/Chilean Pelican (*thagus*)

Taxonomy. *Pelecanus occidentalis* Linnaeus, 1766, Jamaica.
Race *thagus* often considered full species. Subspecific status of birds on W coast of C America unclear. Six subspecies recognized.

Subspecies and Distribution.
P. o. occidentalis Linnaeus, 1766 - W Indies.
P. o. carolinensis Gmelin, 1789 - Atlantic coasts of tropical America, from S Carolina to Orinoco.
P. o. californicus Ridgway, 1884 - Pacific coast of America, from California to Mexico.
P. o. murphyi Wetmore, 1945 - Colombia to N Peru.
P. o. urinator Wetmore, 1945 - Galapagos.
P. o. thagus Molina, 1782 - C Peru to 33½° S in Chile.

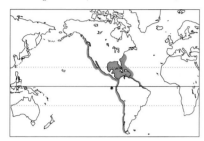

Descriptive notes. 105-152 cm; 3·5+ kg; wingspan 203-228 cm; bill 280-348 mm. Female slightly smaller. Only all dark brown pelican; feet and legs black. Non-breeding plumage similar, but head and neck generally white, most markedly in *thagus*. Juvenile dingy brown above, dirty brownish white below, with grey bill. Races separated on size, pouch colour and slight plumage differences; *thagus* much larger, has much brighter bare part coloration during breeding.

Habitat. Strictly marine, very rarely inland; only truly marine pelican. Prefers shallow inshore waters along coast, including estuaries and bays; avoids open sea. Breeds preferably on remote small, flat, bare islands or arid coasts, but sometimes on bushes or *Rhizophora* mangroves; requires isolation from disturbance and terrestrial predators. Often around fishing ports, feeding on fish scraps and roosting on fishing craft.

Food and Feeding. Mostly fish, with greatest congregations in areas with abundant anchovies (*Engraulis ringens* in S, *E. mordax* in N) and also sardines (*Sardinops sagax* in S, *S. caerulea* in N); otherwise mainly species of little commercial value, e.g. menhaden (*Brevoortia*). Also takes some shrimps and carrion or scraps discarded by fishermen; young birds recorded taking nestling egrets. Only pelican which regularly feeds by plunge-diving (see page 297). Frequently victim of kleptoparasites, especially Laughing Gulls (*Larus atricilla*) in NE part of range, and Heermann's Gulls (*L. heermanni*) in NW.

Breeding. Spring in extreme N of range, all year round in tropics, peaking variably at different sites. Colonial, with some colonies maintained over many years; in other areas, colonies frequently shift, probably due to disturbance, alteration in food supply or tick infestation. Mostly nests on ground, sometimes on cliffs, less often in small trees or bushes; ground nest is slight depression, normally with little material, while tree nest is a necessarily more elaborate stick platform. Eggs 2-3, usually 3; incubation c. 28-30 days; chicks hatch naked, grow white down; in ground-nesters fledging c. 63 days, post-fledging care c. 14+ days; in tree-nesters, fledging averages 74-76 days, no post-fledging care. Sexual maturity at 2-5 years. Recorded living to over 31 years old in captivity.

Movements. Most populations resident and dispersive; some migration, especially in N populations, but movements often erratic, depending on local conditions, and birds may even move N after breeding. Vagrant to British Columbia and Nova Scotia, Canada, and also to Tierra del Fuego.

Status and Conservation. Not globally threatened. Probably most abundant of all pelicans, with around 620,000-1,000,000 breeding individuals in Peruvian guano bird colonies; population fluctuates, due mainly to effects of El Niño and competition with local fisheries, but still some disturbance problems caused by egg-collectors. Other important populations include c. 35,000 pairs in Gulf of California, c. 5000 pairs on rest of W coast of N America, more than 13,000 pairs in SE USA, probably well over 6200 pairs in Caribbean, and a few thousand pairs in Galapagos. Serious decline in N America in 1960's and 1970's, due to pesticide contamination, resulting in reproductive failure and also deaths; banning of DDT seems to have solved the problem and populations recovering former levels (see page 306). Extensive research carried out and a series of conservation measures taken; main threats now considered to be disturbance of colonies by tourists and fishermen, particularly in Mexico, but even in USA (see page 307).

Bibliography. Anderson (1984, 1988), Anderson & Anderson (1976), Anderson & Gress (1981, 1982, 1983), Anderson & Keith (1980), Anderson, DeWeese & Tiller (1977), Anderson, Gress & Mais (1982), Anderson, Jehl *et al.* (1975), Anderson, Keith *et al.* (1989), Baldridge (1973), Barber & Chavez (1983), Bartholomew & Dawson (1954), Bildstein (1980), Blus & Keahey (1978), Blus, Cromartie *et al.* (1979), Blus, Lamont & Neely (1979), Blus, Neely *et al.* (1982), Brandt (1984), Briggs, Lewis *et al.* (1981), Briggs, Tyler *et al.* (1983), Carl (1987), Carroll & Cramer (1985), Clapp *et al.* (1982), Croxall (1991), Croxall *et al.* (1984), Duffy (1983a, 1983b, 1983c, 1988), Gress & Anderson (1982), Gress & Lewis (1988), Guzman & Schreiber (1987), Jehl (1973b), Jordan & Fuentes (1966), King, Flickinger & Hildenbrand (1977), King, Blankinship, *et al.* (1985), King, Keith *et al.* (1977), Kushlan & Frohring (1985), Leck (1973), MacCall (1982), McNeil & McNeil (1989), Mendenhall & Prouty (1979), Montgomery & Martínez (1984), Mora (1989), Murphy (1936), Orians (1969), Palmer (1962), Pennycuick (1983), Schnell *et al.* (1983), Schreiber (1975, 1976, 1977, 1979, 1980), Schreiber & Mock (1988), Schreiber & Risebrough (1972), Schreiber & Schreiber (1980, 1982, 1983), Schreiber, Belitski & Sorrie (1975), Schreiber, Woolfenden & Curtsinger (1975), Richards (1990), Tershy *et al.* (1990), Todd (1990), Tovar (1978), Tovar *et al.* (1987), Valdivia (1978), Vogt (1942), Voous (1983), Walsh (1978), Wetmore (1945).

Class AVES
Order PELECANIFORMES
Suborder PELECANI
Family SULIDAE (GANNETS AND BOOBIES)

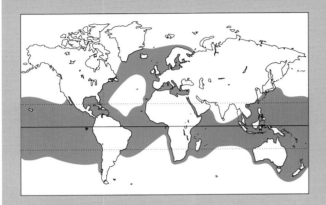

- Medium-sized seabirds with long, narrow, pointed wings and conical bill.
- 64-100 cm.

- All regions except Antarctic.
- Tropical, subtropical and temperate oceans, mainly offshore waters.
- 1 genus, 9 species, 19 taxa.
- 1 species threatened; none extinct since 1600.

Systematics

The Sulidae, comprising the gannets and the boobies, are most closely related to the cormorants and the darters. They belong to an ancient order, which probably originated in the late Cretaceous, more than 60 million years ago. The earliest recognizable sulid comes from France, and corresponds to the Lower Oligocene, over 30 million years ago, while other fossil sulids have been found in North America and Australia. Many of the fossil birds identified as belonging to this family, particularly those of the very early stages, show a greater adaptation to an aquatic way of life than the more aerial present day sulids.

It seems that the boobies were the first to appear, whereas the gannets probably split off at a later stage, perhaps around the Middle Miocene, about 16 million years ago. The gannets seem to have developed in the north and probably did not colonize the Southern Hemisphere until about the Middle Pliocene, and it is interesting to note that they apparently occupied the North Pacific until the latter part of the Pleistocene. The most ancient of today's sulids is reckoned to be Abbott's Booby (*Sula abbotti*), which may be the only extant representative of a different lineage.

Several authors have considered the family Sulidae to comprise two genera, and have saved *Sula* for boobies exclusively, giving gannets the generic name *Morus*. More recent studies, though, indicate that the differences between the gannets and the boobies are no greater than differences within the booby group itself, so that there is at present no reason strong enough to justify separate genera.

Even so, some species are undoubtedly more closely related than others, and it is possible to establish certain groups within the genus, of those species with the strongest taxonomic affinities. The three gannets, once regarded merely as geographical races of a single species, are now generally considered to form three distinct, yet very closely related, species; in order to indicate their proximity, they are placed together in a gannet superspecies. Another natural group of species is that of the so-called "pantropical boobies", the Brown Booby (*Sula leucogaster*), the Masked Booby (*Sula dactylatra*) and the Red-footed Booby (*Sula sula*). These species have adapted to living in similar environments and have comparable distributions and parallel life histories. The Blue-footed Booby (*Sula nebouxii*) and the Peruvian Booby (*Sula variegata*) of the eastern Pacific seaboard probably became separate species in the

near past, as many aspects of their biology and ecology still coincide. Finally, the peculiar Abbott's Booby, aberrant in many aspects, stands well apart from all the other species; the proposal to place it in its own monotypic genus, *Papasula*, may yet gain general acceptance.

Morphological Aspects

Gannets and boobies are birds of strictly marine habits, and so are well adapted to feeding and spending long periods of time away from land. The robust body is medium to large in size, and is characteristically cigar-shaped. This appearance is intensified by the strong neck muscles and the fairly long, wedge-shaped tail.

Sulids range in size from the male Brown Booby, which can measure only about 64 cm and weigh 724 g, to the Northern Gannet (*Sula bassana*), which at as much as 100 cm and 3600 g can be more than three times as heavy as most small boobies. Sexual dimorphism in size is readily appreciable in all boobies, with females averaging larger and heavier in virtually all species, but it is difficult to detect in any of the gannets.

The long, tapering bill is stout and conical and is specially designed for seizing fish, with is cutting edges serrated; unlike most other Pelecaniformes, however, there is no terminal hook, except in Abbott's Booby. As an adaptation to plunge-diving the external nostrils are closed, but beside the mouth sulids have developed secondary nostrils, which are automatically covered by moveable flaps when the bird plunges into the sea.

As with many other members of the order, there is extensive bare facial and gular skin, more noticeably so in boobies than in gannets. The adults of several species have their bare parts brightly coloured, especially at the beginning of the breeding season, and these often stand out in stark contrast to a rather unspectacular plumage. Bare parts can be important in displays, as in the cases of both the Red-footed and Blue-footed Boobies, and they are particularly important in ritualized heterosexual behaviour (see Breeding).

The eyes are situated right beside the bill and are orientated towards the front, giving the birds excellent binocular vision. This is particularly useful for calculating distances and is an advantage sulids share with most predatory birds; it also gives them an odd look when they face the observer. The iris is often strikingly pale-coloured and adds a lot to the handsome aspect of these birds.

The wings are long, narrow and pointed and are set quite far back on the body. They are very suitable for cruising along in a strong wind, but might be more specifically designed to play their part in the highly specialized fishing technique used by the family (see Food and Feeding). In normal flight, powerful flaps tend to be interspersed with gliding, and progress is fairly steady, especially in the larger species. Boobies, in particular, sometimes glide low over the waves, while in high winds the Northern Gannet may use dynamic soaring.

Take-off ability depends largely on the bird's weight. The large Northern Gannet has the most problems and usually requires a short run along the surface of the water; however, provided there is some wind, most species have little difficulty. Those that nest on flat ground, particularly the Cape Gannet (*Sula capensis*), often have to resort to the use of "runways", where they can gain the momentum and lift necessary for take-off. In absolutely calm conditions or after an exceptionally heavy meal, birds may have to wait several hours, before they can take off again.

Sulids normally land on the sea by diving in from low down. Alternatively a bird may glide low over the water, before spreading its feet forward and its tail downwards and settling on the surface. On land, due to relatively poor manoeuvrability, which stems from their narrow wings and resultant high wing-loading, landing can be awkward and may even result in accidents. Boobies tend to cope better than the bulkier gannets, and two species, Abbott's and the Red-footed Boobies, actually build their nests and rear their young on the unstable surface of treetops.

Sulids' legs are shortish and strong and their relatively large feet are totipalmate, or webbed between all four toes, a feature exclusive to the Pelecaniformes. They are set quite far back on their bodies, and this and the extent of the webbed area help the birds to swim well, so they are quite at home in the water. Although rather heavy, they are very buoyant and have little trouble riding even the roughest seas.

As a further adaptation to their distinctive fishing technique, gannets and boobies possess a series of air-sacs, which have been developed to an extraordinary degree. These sizeable extensions of the bronchi help to minimize the impact of a diving bird, in the instant that it crashes into the water.

As in most other aerial, fish-eating seabirds, the plumage of the family clearly reflects the compromise between two major

requirements: the first is the importance of being as near as possible invisible to potential prey, for which white underparts are best; secondly, in an environment where both the salt and the sun intensify the effects of feather abrasion, dark, melanin-rich feathers on the upperparts help to provide stronger resistance. Hence, all adults except the Brown Booby and brown forms of the Red-footed Booby are completely white on the belly and breast, while the primaries are dark in all plumages.

However, there are exceptions, and all three gannets and the Masked Booby are mainly white above. In these species the immaculate white plumage, which is even more conspicuous when contrasted against the dark blue of the sea, may serve as an indicator of food to conspecifics; when highlighted in their spectacular plunge-dives, it informs distant birds that a shoal of fish has been found. Large numbers of birds can be attracted in this way and there may be benefits from the presence of many predators (see Food and Feeding). However, this does not really apply to the Masked Booby, which normally feeds alone.

Juvenile plumage differs to varying degrees from that of adults in all species except Abbott's Booby. The general tendency is for juveniles to be darker, the extreme case being that of the Northern Gannet, where juveniles are very dark all over while the parents are mainly white. As in many other highly aggressive bird groups, such as gulls and some raptors, the juveniles' darkish plumage performs the function of inhibiting aggression from adult birds, which will readily attack, and even kill, any adult-looking bird that encroaches on their nest-site territory. Adult plumage is gained at approximately the same time as sexual maturity, when the bird is between three and six years old, depending on the species.

As sulids are highly aerial and obtain most of their food by plunge-diving, they need to be able to fly strongly and manoeuvre adeptly at all times. For this reason, their flight-feathers are moulted more or less continuously, to avoid periods of relative incapacity, although moult tends to be suspended during breeding. An average healthy bird has a few new feathers appearing most of the time, and each individual flight-feather is renewed yearly, or at most biennially.

In common with most other members of the Pelecaniformes, gannets and boobies lack brood patches, which might interrupt the birds' almost perfect streamlining and would certainly reduce insulation. So when it comes to incubation they

This Masked Booby illustrates the superb aerodynamic design of the Sulidae, with their cigar-shaped bodies and narrow wings. White underparts help to make the bird less obvious to its prey, while the all-important flight feathers are black, making them more resistant to wear.

[Sula dactylatra dactylatra, Ascension I. Photo: Annie Price/ Survival]

The three species of gannet are very similar and are sometimes lumped together in a single species; the long black gular stripe on this bird shows that it is a Cape Gannet. Like many predatory birds, sulids have binocular vision, which helps them to pinpoint their prey; this gives them a rather strange aspect, when seen head on. A further adaptation to their fishing technique is that their external nostrils have become obsolete.

[*Sula capensis*, South Africa. Photo: M. P. Harris]

must use the webs of their feet to transmit the essential heat, and to this end their webs are more extensively vasculated than in most other birds. Although when sitting a sulid might appear to incubate its eggs in exactly the same way as any other bird, it actually rests one or both of its webs on the eggs, instead of applying its breast directly to them.

Habitat

All gannets and boobies are well adapted to living at sea and may spend quite long periods without setting foot on land. Several species are generally confined to areas over the continental shelf and are rarely to be found in pelagic waters. The Brown and Blue-footed Boobies feed mainly in inshore waters, sometimes in water only 1 m deep or even less, near the shoreline of sandy beaches. On the other hand, the Red-footed and Abbott's Boobies are known for their long foraging trips, during which they may be encountered several hundred kilometres from the nearest land.

Boobies inhabit tropical and subtropical waters, where food availability depends little on any particular season, although it is often scarce and patchy. Gannets, on the other hand, affect more temperate waters, where the seasons dictate many significant factors, such as the weather and prey abundance. In a largely tropical family, only the Northern Gannet has managed to come to terms with the severity of subarctic conditions, where prey is abundant.

A variety of sites are used for breeding. The Blue-footed and Masked Boobies and the two southern gannets nest on flat ground on offshore islands, as may the Northern Gannet, albeit occasionally. The Brown Booby normally nests on a slope of some sort, while the true cliff nester is the Northern Gannet. The Peruvian Booby may use any of these types, though it prefers to nest on or around cliffs. However, off northern Peru, it tends to occupy areas of exposed, flat ground, while the Blue-footed Booby nests on cliffs at the same sites. The tree-nesting species are the Red-footed Booby, which may alternatively build its nest in low scrub, and Abbott's Booby, which is now restricted to the tall forest trees of Christmas Island in the Indian Ocean (see Status and Conservation).

General Habits

Gannets and boobies are highly gregarious and their intense social life has led to the development of a considerable amount of varied ritualized behaviour (see Breeding). All species, except Abbott's Booby, nest in colonies, where thousands of birds may gather. The largest colonies are those of the Peruvian Booby, which can number up to 750,000 pairs or perhaps even more, while colonies of around 100,000 pairs have also been reported for the Cape and Northern Gannets and the Red-footed Booby. Several species often breed in mixed colonies with other sulids and also other Pelecaniformes, such as frigatebirds and cormorants.

Sulids are basically diurnal birds, with the interesting exception of the Red-footed Booby, which often fishes at night, especially if there is plenty of moonlight. Outside the breeding season, gannets frequently spend the night on the sea, a habit which is not shared by the boobies, which normally return to land at roosting time.

Feather care is, of course, very important, especially oiling, which acts as a form of comfort behaviour. It involves the bird impregnating its plumage with the waterproofing secretion produced by the preen gland at the base of its tail. This activity is essential for most seabirds, in order to prevent the plumage becoming waterlogged. Also of basic importance, especially to tropical species, are the various heat-regulating techniques, such as exposing the webs of the feet or excreting on them for evaporative cooling. Gular-fluttering and hanging the wings loosely away from the body are other methods used to dissipate unwanted heat. However, the problem is not always of excess heat, and boobies in particular sometimes sun themselves with their wings held out backwards.

Voice

The fervent social life that sulids lead has forced them to develop highly intricate ritual behaviour and this also involves a fair variety of calls and sounds.

In most booby species, adult males and females produce different calls, sometimes markedly so, and there are structural differences between the sexes in both the trachea and the syrinx. Males tend to utter mild, plaintive whistles, whereas female sounds consist of resonant trumpeting quacks or honks. Young boobies' calls are similar to those of adult females and the typical voice of adult males is not acquired for several years.

Gannets have loud, raucous voices, which are virtually identical in male and female, especially in the case of the Northern Gannet. Among the various calls recorded for these species are: a series of harsh sounds uttered by birds at fishing concentrations; a rasping "arrah-arrah" made by a bird arriving at its nest; low moans and grunts; and a sighing "oo-ah" that normally accompanies both the "Sky-pointing" display (see Breeding) and take-off.

Variations in the voices of different individual gannets are probably recognized by their mates, neighbours and chicks, and this may be true of boobies too.

Food and Feeding

Gannets and boobies are well known for their spectacular plunge-dives, often from great heights; these enable them to penetrate to moderate depths, where they can exploit large shoals of fish or squid which are out of reach or too mobile for many other sea-birds. Each species has its own preferences, but among the

Sulids obtain most of their food by plunge-diving and they often forage in groups. The various stages in a typical dive are illustrated by this group of Peruvian Boobies: first the bird takes up position, with its wings held wide-open; then it starts its descent; in the latter part of the dive the wings are bent parallel to the body, allowing fine adjustments of the trajectory; finally, just before it hits the water, the bird thrusts its wings back and enters like a bullet. The Peruvian Booby is the most gregarious of all the sulids and forms vast colonies, with birds exploiting the huge quantities of anchovies and pilchards associated with the cool Humboldt Current.

[Sula variegata, Chile. Photo: Günter Ziesler]

commonest prey are mackerel (*Scomber*), pilchard (*Sardinops*), anchovy (*Engraulis*) and to a lesser extent sandeels (*Ammodytes*), while boobies only take large quantities of flying-fish (Exocoetidae) and squid (Ommastrephidae). In some cases birds take a wide range of prey species, but conversely the Peruvian Booby is almost entirely dependent on the anchoveta (*Engraulis ringens*). Despite the preferences of each species, all gannets and boobies are opportunists, and will feed on other prey or try other sources of food, should the occasion demand.

When foraging, they tend to fly higher than most seabirds, taking advantage of their binocular vision to locate prey. It is thought that they may select a particular target, even amidst a large shoal, before launching themselves. They normally plunge-dive from 10-30 m up, although sometimes from great heights, and dives from 100 m up have been estimated for the Masked Booby. The more heavily built gannets normally dive vertically and from a greater height than most boobies, which tend to dive at an angle and generally produce less impressive dives, often in shallower water.

Once a target has been selected, gannets in particular appear to stall, before hurtling into a dive, often adjusting direction slightly on the way down. The bird enters the water at top speed with its wings pushed backwards and parallel to its body. The heavy Northern Gannet can reach depths of up to 10 m, with the impulse of the dive alone. Once under water, birds sometimes use their wings to penetrate deeper, to 15 m or, exceptionally, 25 m down. Following a plunge the fish is usually captured when the bird is on its way up again, and it is normally swallowed under water, for, on the rare occasions when a big or poisonous fish is brought to the surface to be disabled, the bird may be intensely harassed by frigatebirds, gulls or skuas.

Although plunge-diving is the main feeding method used by all of the sulids, some species are also known to surface-dive, pursue prey by underwater swimming and even forage on foot in shallow water. Several boobies, in particular the Red-footed, are competent at capturing certain kinds of prey while in flight; flying-fish are frequently taken thus and squid are likewise whisked off the surface. Scavenging is probably not essential for any sulid, but several species use it as a viable alternative to fishing, and a trawler attended by a number of gannets or boobies is not an uncommon sight nowadays in many of the world's seas.

The high degree of social interaction in this family results in frequent communal feeding, though only the Blue-footed and, to a lesser extent, the Peruvian Boobies actually perform a kind of collaborative fishing. These species frequently fly along in small groups and when one bird, normally a male, whistles all members of the group dive in as one. The other species that often feed communally, the three gannets and the Brown Booby, simply seem to benefit from gathering together at a food source; a shoal of fish may be too large for a single individual to exploit effectively on its own, but the confusion created by a large number of predators attacking continuously may often result in more prey being taken per individual than if one bird tries to feed singly.

Breeding

Few species are tied down to laying regularly in the same season each year; these are the three gannets, particularly the Northern Gannet, and Abbott's and the Peruvian Boobies. The other boobies adapt their laying dates to food availability, local conditions, and the length or success of previous attempts.

The frequency of breeding varies with the species and also the area. It tends to be biennial in Abbott's Booby, when successful, and annual in the three gannets and the Peruvian and Masked Boobies. The other three species may attempt breeding at intervals of less than twelve months in some areas, whereas the Red-footed Booby sometimes breeds only every 15 months in the Galapagos.

Breeding density is relatively constant and rather high in the gannets, particularly in the Cape Gannet, which regularly nests on flat ground. For the boobies, it varies far more with the type of terrain (see Habitat), but in general it is much lower than in the gannets.

Social behaviour is highly developed in the sulids, and these Blue-footed Boobies show two fairly typical displays: "Foot-rocking" involves the bird making use of its vividly coloured feet, and showing them off to its partner; "Sky-pointing" is one of the most generalized displays, and has several different functions, for example in strengthening the pair-bond or in appeasement.

[Sula nebouxii excisa, Galapagos.
Photo: Dieter & Mary Plage/ Survival]

As large, dense colonies are typical of many sulids, displays have an extremely important part to play, for instance in establishing and confirming territory, and in boundary disputes. It is not surprising then that ritualized behaviour is richest in those species which breed at the highest densities. It is even richer in species like the Northern Gannet, which nest on steep cliffs, as there is always the danger of falling, so physical squabbles are to be avoided, if possible. In such cases, it is safer to resort to ritualized postures of menace and appeasement to sort out territorial conflicts, though this species can be notoriously violent.

In general, sulids' displays show a high degree of development, particularly those used to express site-ownership, or for heterosexual advertisement. Gannets, rather more than boobies, pair for life and reunite annually at the nest-site, after several months of wandering about at sea; for this reason, pair-bonding displays are particularly important and have thus become highly elaborate, sometimes lasting a couple of months before laying can begin.

Gannets' displays are generally much more ritualized than those of bobies, and have evolved sometimes into very complex stereotyped models, which probably started as simple, unintentional movements or postures. In order to communicate with others, a gannet makes use of its head in "Headshake", its bill in "Ritualized Menacing", its neck in "Sky-pointing" and, to a lesser extent, its wings in "Bowing" and the greeting ceremony. Boobies make extensive use of their wings and also their feet, and the Blue-footed Booby, for example, has a peculiar aerial greeting, in which an incoming bird stretches forward its conspicuous blue feet before landing.

Some ritualized postures are used to signal the intention of movement of an individual around its territory or away from its mate; this involves "Sky-pointing" in the gannets, and the "Bill-up-Face-away" posture in most boobies. For the purpose of inhibiting aggression, "Facing-away" and "Bill-tucking" are commonly performed. Courtship feeding, which is fairly standard practice in many other families, has not been recorded in the Sulidae, or indeed in any of the Pelecaniformes.

The nest is rudimentary in ground-nesting species, comprising a slight depression, which is often simply the result of the accumulation around the sitting bird of a rim of excreta, the famous guano. The tree-nesting Red-footed and Abbott's Boobies construct a fairly flimsy stick nest, which is stuck together gradually by the birds' droppings; nonetheless, these nests are always liable to be damaged in storms, especially when situated in exposed sites.

The number of young that parents can successfully raise to fledging determines brood size, so this is closely linked to food

supplies and the foraging effort required. The largest clutches correspond to the Peruvian and Blue-footed Boobies, which average three and two eggs respectively, in line with the fact that they nest close to the vast shoals of spawning anchovies off Peru. A different strategy is adopted by the Brown and Masked Boobies, which often lay two eggs; if both hatch, one chick is invariably lost, usually through "sibling murder", and the pair end up with a single chick just the same, the second egg acting as a kind of insurance policy.

The rest of the species all lay clutches of a single egg. In the case of the gannets, weight at fledging and the date at which this occurs are both known to have a great effect on further survival, so all efforts are directed towards the chick gaining as much weight as possible during a very short time; more than one chick would imply too great a burden for the parents and probably total failure of the breeding attempt, at any rate for the Australasian Gannet (Sula serrator) and the Cape Gannet.

Abbott's Booby faces a very arduous task even with its single egg, as the chick has an extremely long period of dependence on its parents, and this means that they have to keep it supplied with food during lengthy lean periods; it is hardly surprising that a large proportion of its chicks die of starvation.

Eggs are covered in a chalky layer and are pale blue, green or white, though this may get stained brown or even black during incubation. They are roughly oval, varying in size from about 53·3 x 36·7 mm in the Red-footed Booby to 82·2 x 49·7 mm in the Northern Gannet. Egg weight is a fairly low proportion of the female's body weight, representing 3-4% in most species, but 5% in the Red-footed Booby and 7·6% in Abbott's.

However, as not all species have single egg clutches, the weight of the whole clutch is a much higher proportion of the female's weight for these species, constituting over 7% in the Masked and Blue-footed Boobies, 8% in the Brown Booby and up to 9% in the Peruvian. This makes replacement laying more improbable in these species, as it obviously involves greater energy expenditure, so replacement clutches, when laid, tend to be smaller and the eggs themselves lighter, and this often means that the resultant chicks have less chance of surviving to fledge successfully. Replacement laying is fairly widespread among Northern Gannets, provided that the loss of the original egg does not take place more than 25 days after its laying, and it generally occurs about 15 days after the loss. In less seasonally dependant breeders like the pantropical boobies, replacement laying may occur, or a completely new breeding attempt may be started from scratch, implying all the necessary stages.

As sulids have no brood patch, they have to incubate by applying the webs of their feet to the egg or eggs (see Morphological Aspects). The eggshell has to be exceptionally thick, for the incubating bird rests its entire weight on the egg, actually standing on it.

Incubation lasts 41-45 days in all species except Abbott's Booby, which draws it out for 57 days. Incubation stints range from 12 to 60 hours, with the length depending on several factors, such as species, sex, distance to foraging area, climatic zone, presence of potential predators, and so on. In the Northern Gannet, the best known species in many aspects, the sexes share incubation duties more or less equally, although the male's stints are slightly longer.

Immediately after hatching, the near-naked chick is delicately placed on top of its parent's webs, where it will be brooded for the first few days. It is never left unattended until it is about a month old, by which stage it is capable of regulating its own body temperature. The chick takes its food directly from its parent's mouth, or by reaching into its throat. It gradually develops begging behaviour, which is variable according to the species and also the nesting terrain: it is frantic in the pantropical boobies and generally in species nesting on flat ground, but much more moderate in the Northern Gannet and in Abbott's Booby; in both of these species, any young which fall from the nest are doomed.

The different breeding strategies employed by the different species can be directly related to the growth rates of the chicks. The Peruvian Booby and the three gannets, which are all markedly seasonal, annual breeders, have fatter young at fledging and feed them more often, but over a shorter total period, than the other species, due to the extraordinary, though temporary, abundance of food. On the other hand, the far-foraging Abbott's Booby is a seasonal but biennial breeder, and its chick takes about five months to fledge. In all of the boobies, as in the frigatebirds, this is followed by a lengthy period of post-fledging care, in which the chick can fly about, but remains almost entirely dependent on its parents for food. Abbott's Booby chicks are fed very infrequently for part of the time, and their physiological response to this is very slow growth and a period of post-fledging care of five and a half to nine months; this slow growth enables them to put up with extended periods of starvation far better than the other species. The rest of the boobies range between these two extremes, sometimes varying

within the same species, depending on the breeding locality, on the availability of food and the foraging distance.

Chick production in all species, except Abbott's Booby, is generally rather high, since, in most cases, over 70 % of all clutches laid result in one chick fledged. However, among the three pantropical boobies and Abbott's, breeding success can in some cases fall below 20%, as a long spell of bad weather or an unusual scarcity of food can thwart most breeding attempts. The Peruvian Booby, normally the most productive of all the sulids, has an average production of 1·75 chicks reared per pair per year. However, the failure of food supplies, due to the phenomenon known as El Niño (see page 341), at irregular intervals can decimate bird populations, not only by frustrating all breeding attempts, but also by killing off large numbers of adults.

Sulids do not attempt breeding for the first time until they are 2-6 years old, depending on the species and partly also on the particular colony, as rapidly expanding colonies or sectors of colonies are more likely to take in inexperienced breeders than stable ones. In some species, it is apparently not unusual for birds to have rest years, in which the pair remains together, sometimes even holding a territory in the colony, without making a serious attempt to breed that season. Inter-colony movements have also been reported for some species, although this appears to be far from common.

Like most other seabirds, gannets and boobies are long-lived, which explains why they can afford relatively low chick production in comparison with other birds, as well as deferred maturity of up to 6 years. To balance these disadvantages, adult mortality is low, normally averaging under 10%. This gives a mean life expectancy of between 10 and 20 years for most species, with some individuals living to be well over 40.

In all species mortality is undoubtedly highest during the first year of life, but it also affects pre-breeders more than adult birds. For these reasons only a small proportion of the young produced in any one year survive to breed, but once they have reached this age they have a good chance of living for quite a few years more. There is some indication that, at least in some species, adult males may suffer slightly higher mortality than adult females. This is probably due to the different role played by each sex during the breeding season, since typically male

Cape Gannets often nest in dense colonies, such as this vast gannetry on Bird Island (South Africa). In such cases, where nests are very close together, aggressive encounters are frequent and quite violent at times. Notice the ground nests, which are formed basically as a collection of debris, cemented together by the birds' excreta.

[Sula capensis, Bird Island, South Africa. Photo: Jen & Des Bartlett/ Survival]

Australasian Gannets mating in a gannetry in New Zealand. During copulation, the male gannet "Nape-bites" the female and the whole affair is fairly violent. Boobies are much calmer during mating and rarely, if ever, perform "Nape-biting".

[*Sula serrator*, New Zealand. Photo: J. B. Nelson]

activities, such as fighting and displaying to defend the nest-site, or gathering nest material, imply more risk of an accident than those typically performed by females.

Movements

The three gannets, in particular the Northern Gannet, are the only members of the family that are truly migratory, but many adults do not leave their breeding zone. Boobies disperse widely over tropical waters, and some species may be found several hundred kilometres from land.

The three species of gannet show a similar pattern in their post-breeding movements. Soon after fledging, young birds fly off directly to tropical or subtropical areas, in order to avoid the hardships of winter conditions. Young Northern Gannets from the eastern Atlantic migrate almost to the equator off West Africa, while those from Canadian colonies head off to the Gulf of Mexico. Young Cape Gannets move north as far as the Gulf of Guinea, whereas juvenile Australasian Gannets from New Zealand cross the Tasman Sea and then, along with birds from the more westerly colonies, move along the east, south and west coasts of Australia.

The young gannets may stay on tropical waters during the summer, though most head part of the way back towards the breeding grounds of their origin. Older gannets, especially those that are to attempt breeding, only follow this pattern to some extent, as they do not travel so far from the colony and start their return much earlier. There is intense competition for the best nest-sites, so they stand a better chance of securing these optimum sites if they arrive early at the colony.

The movements of the various different booby species seem to be more directly linked with food availability, which tends to have fairly irregular variations in the tropics. In most cases, adults remain in the vicinity of the breeding grounds as long as food is plentiful, and this is most notably true of those species that inhabit the richest waters, the Blue-footed and Peruvian Boobies, which are virtually sedentary most years, but disperse widely when food becomes scarce. Adult pantropical boobies also stick more or less to their breeding areas for most of the year, attempting breeding when conditions seem favourable, and dispersing over adjacent waters when food becomes less readily available.

As with many other seabirds, vagrancy is known to occur in most species, as wind-blown individuals may drift far out of their normal ranges, giving rise to unusual records. There are several records of Australasian Gannets that must have flown across the southern Indian Ocean, and one found in a Cape Gannet colony off South Africa had even found a partner of the local species. Similarly, a Cape Gannet flew off in the opposite direction and turned up in a colony of Australasian Gannets near Melbourne, in south-east Australia.

Another interesting case, which demonstrates the exceptional mobility of a particular individual rather than vagrancy, is that of a female Northern Gannet. It hatched on Ailsa Craig off western Scotland, in 1966, and was found breeding four years later, and subsequently for several consecutive summers, in the Norwegian colony of Skarvlakken, well to the north of

The Red-footed Booby has several different colour morphs, including this, the white morph, but all are distinguished by their bright red feet, which, as in the Blue-footed Booby, are important in display. The Red-footed and Abbott's Boobies are the only sulids that nest in trees; here the male arrives with nest material, prior to copulation.

[*Sula sula rubripes*, Hawaii. Photo: M. J. Rauzon/Vireo]

the Arctic Circle; the same bird was later found dead, at 12 years of age, some 60 km east of Tripoli, on the coast of Libya.

The Brown Booby is possibly the most widespread and numerous of the three pantropical boobies, and perhaps of all the sulids, with a world population of several hundred thousand pairs. The plumage of most juvenile boobies is relatively similar to that of adults, possibly reflecting the fact that these species are relatively peaceful; the more aggressive gannets have a very distinct dark blackish juvenile plumage, in order to prevent adults confusing young birds with interfering adults and attacking them.

[Sula leucogaster plotus, Christmas I, Pacific Ocean. Photo: M. P. Kahl/ Bruce Coleman]

Relationship with Man

As gannets and boobies are large, conspicuous birds, which often breed in sizeable colonies, neighbouring human cultures have always been aware of them. From early times, many species of seabirds were heavily exploited by man for food, and whole communities grew up depending almost exclusively on seabirds for their sustenance and livelihood, most often on small islands. To the north-west of Scotland lie St Kilda and the Faeroes, and on both of these island groups the local inhabitants and their cultures revolved around the culling of adult and young seabirds, while the annual harvest of bird feathers helped the St Kildans pay the rent of their island. The islanders were well aware of the significance of the birds to their own survival and prosperity, and they also knew that overexploitation would lead to disaster both for the birds and themselves. Such human pressure was roughly equivalent to natural predation and might even be considered as such.

Present problems are somewhat different and adult sulids and their chicks are still regularly taken, especially in the tropics, but man now has much greater mobility and weaponry and, in conjunction with the population explosion, collection has quickly become excessive. Trade, mainly in eggs, has long been established in many parts of the world, and it still flourishes in places today. Wardens have now been posted at several breeding sites, for example in Peru, in an attempt to curb overexploitation, and it is hoped that with increased levels of environmental education the demand for birds' eggs will drop back to sustainable levels.

Human exploitation of sulids, their eggs, flesh and feathers and other parts of their bodies has also in the past been absolutely disproportionate in some instances. The massive slaughter carried out on Northern Gannet colonies in and around the Gulf of St Lawrence, off eastern Canada, during the 19th century led to the virtual eradication of the species from some of its former breeding strongholds; the colony at Bird Rocks, which is said to have contained 75,000-125,000 breeding pairs, making it the largest gannetry of the species ever recorded, was reduced to about 500 pairs by 1932; it has since partly recovered, and by

1984 held some 6700 pairs. No species has escaped irrational exploitation by man and even today there are records of gannets and boobies being shot for fun in many parts of the world.

Three species, the Peruvian and Blue-footed Boobies and the Cape Gannet, are among the world's greatest guano producers. The Peruvian Booby, in particular, was one of the major species responsible for building up the colossal guano industry, which played such an important part in the economic development of Peru (see page 338).

Many of the Sulidae have traditionally been the object of man's admiration, and written accounts of their talents abound in literary works, especially in Europe, though these tend to concentrate more on poetic rather than scientific aspects. They praise the birds' incomparable sight, which according to tradition weakens with age, and comment on their greediness and social foraging habits, as well as exciting interactions at their breeding colonies. Poets have seen in the Northern Gannet a symbol of the perfect marriage between wind and sea, waves and rocks, or of grace and force, and at the same time delicacy and strength, in a world where man feels vulnerable, and which gannets and boobies have conquered in spectacular fashion.

The name "Gannet" is a modified form of the Old English "gans", meaning "a goose"; this is parallelled by the traditional Scottish name for the Northern Gannet, "Solan Goose", while the Gaelic name is "Sula". The name "Booby" has its origins in the Spanish "bobo", which means "dunce" or "stupid", and refers to their lack of fear of man, making them easy to catch. In their remote breeding sites there was no need, until recent times, for them to develop such a fear.

Sulids have no brood patch, so incubation is carried out by means of the highly vasculated webs of the feet. The bird actually stands on the eggs, resting its entire weight on them. On a hot day, a sitting bird can resort to several techniques commonly used in thermoregulation, such as fluffing up the plumage, gular-fluttering and opening the mouth to let the heat out.

[Sula nebouxii excisa, Galapagos. Photo: F. Polking/FLPA]

Status and Conservation

Due to a close association with man from time immemorial, populations of all species of gannets and boobies have been steadily decreasing over the centuries. At present most are experiencing some form of recovery, largely because direct human exploitation has become less intense, but it still persists even at some sites in the North Atlantic. Despite this, the main threat to most species comes in the form of habitat destruction, notably in the tropics.

Every species has lost at least a few colonies in modern times, normally as a direct result of human activities, and again the most alarming cases are to be found in the tropics. Abbott's

Booby, the most acutely threatened of the sulids, lost three colonies on islands in the western Indian Ocean in the last 100 years, and it now breeds only on Christmas Island, in the eastern Indian Ocean.

The three gannets live in the temperate waters that border areas where the human populations enjoy a relatively high standard of living and, starting around the middle of this century, steps were taken to protect many gannetries. Thus, the human exploitation which beset colonies in the past has largely stopped, although a very limited amount is still allowed to continue. In some places, more nesting ground has been made available, in the hope of improving the breeding success of the colony. As a result of all this, the populations of all three gannet species have been increasing fairly steadily all over, and they have even recolonized some former sites, as well as founding new colonies, and have probably recovered their former levels. In the well-known case of the Northern Gannet, for example, the population has been increasing during most of the twentieth century, at an annual rate of around 3% in the period 1949-1969, and more recently (1969-1984/85) at about 2%.

In the case of the pantropical boobies, the picture is probably not so optimistic. Few colonies are properly protected and human pressure on them is still quite severe in some areas. In others, the slow but steady improvement in the standard of living of the local human population has reduced such activities as the collecting of eggs and chicks, or the shooting of adult birds, and the overall situation is slightly better now than it was some decades ago.

The Peruvian Booby has suffered from the same problems as the other "guano birds", the Peruvian (Brown) Pelican (*Pelecanus occidentalis thagus*) and the Guanay Cormorant (*Phalacrocorax bougainvillei*), and former population levels may never be recovered (see page 341). While there are still about one million Peruvian Boobies left, the future remains uncertain, given their dependence on a very localized food supply, and also the mass mortality that occurs when this supply fails.

By breeding close to the highly productive waters of the eastern Pacific, the Blue-footed Booby has probably suffered from much the same problems as the Peruvian Booby, though to a lesser extent. Its world population is much smaller, but it is also more stable, fluctuating less with local conditions. It establishes rather small colonies on offshore islands, and about one third of the total world population may nest on the Galapagos Islands, where they are undoubtedly afforded more protection than anywhere else in the tropics, although even there introduced

predators are always liable to wreak havoc. Much work is being done at present to minimize the danger and to eradicate alien species, or at least limit their effects on the native flora and fauna.

The pantropical boobies, the Brown, the Red-footed and the Masked, are treated together, as they are often found breeding on the same island or archipelago, over much of their respective ranges and thus face similar problems. In addition, they all have large, but very scattered, world populations and their juveniles disperse widely over the oceans, with the consequence that any local disasters are far less significant for the species at global level.

The main threats faced by these birds can be seen in the form of the intense level of human pressure on virtually any island group they inhabit. Many colonies are still being raided for eggs nowadays, and the rate of habitat destruction does not bode at all well for the future, especially in the case of the tree-nesting Red-footed Booby. Moreover, in the last few decades the growth of tourism in the tropics, especially to tropical islands, has opened up a multitude of possibilities in places where the local economy was all too often struggling around subsistence level. The concomitant development is usually carried out with no regard for the conservation of natural sites, in particular those on the coast, as well as implying increased disturbance of the birds. These boobies seldom form very large colonies, normally numbering a few hundred pairs, so their preservation does not arouse so much international concern, and colonies may disappear before much can be done to save them.

Abbott's Booby, the only sulid currently considered threatened, is classed as Endangered. It now breeds only on Christmas Island, in the eastern Indian Ocean, where on average under 1000 pairs initiate breeding each year, although the total population may be as many as 5000-8000 birds. The species used to be more widely distributed over the tropical Indian Ocean, and it is known to have occurred in western parts of the Ocean on a number of island groups around Madagascar. For instance, it nested on Assumption Island until 1930, and there are also old records of the species on Rodrigues and the Glorieuse Islands. However, the extensive destruction of forest on tropical islands has led to a dramatic shrinking of its range, and today only this relict population remains.

Abbott's Boobies face a long struggle to find enough food for their slow-growing chick, which normally relies on them for over a year before becoming fully independent (see Breeding). This, allied to the single egg clutch, with an average of

Sulid chicks are fed by incomplete regurgitation, and, as in most other Pelecaniformes, the chick has to thrust its head and bill right into the adult's mouth and gullet in order to get to its meal. The frequency of feeds is variable, presumably depending on food availability, and the Masked Booby's chick has to be able to withstand long periods of fasting, due to the pelagic foraging habits of the adults.

[Sula dactylatra dactylatra, Ascension I. Photo: Annie Price/ Survival]

Abbott's Booby is perhaps the most threatened of Christmas Island's endemic species. There has been extensive clearance of its tropical forest nesting habitat to get at the rich deposits of phosphates below, as can be seen in the background here. In addition, reproductive success is extremely low and the remarkably long period of post-fledging care means that many chicks are abandoned to starvation when almost fully-grown. Note the tree nest and the female's bill colour.

[Sula abbotti, Christmas I, Indian Ocean. Photo: J. B. Nelson]

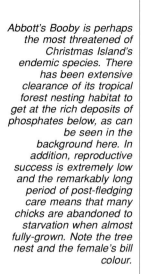

1·27 eggs laid per pair every two years, contrives to limit production to the alarming figure of one chick successfully raised to independence per pair every five years. Clearly the species has very little potential for recovery.

Christmas Island is rich in phosphate deposits, which were intensively mined for many years, until the operations were terminated by the Australian government in 1987. Mining affects the tree-nesting Abbott's Boobies through the stripping away of forests to provide access for machinery and support activities. A national park was established on part of the island in 1980 and it has subsequently been extended to encompass nearly all of the Abbott's Booby nests within its limits, although most of them are in areas of high grade phosphates. Abbott's Boobies are extremely conservative in terms of nest-site location, and will not colonize new areas when their nests are destroyed. Instead, they insist on building a new nest in the immediate vicinity of the previous one, so if this is in a fragmented part of the forest, the new nest is likely to suffer the same fate, and, for example, be blown down in a storm.

In order to save the last survivors of this ancient species, the entire area used for nesting by this and other endemic birds, such as the Christmas Frigatebird (*Fregata andrewsi*), the Golden Bosunbird (*Phaethon lepturus fulvus*) and several forms of small land birds, requires absolute and effective protection within the Christmas Island National Park. Reafforestation with autochthonous species should be carried out in those areas already cleared, so as to prevent the dessication of small islands of vegetation and instead favour their reintegration into the forest mass. Several programmes involving the monitoring of Abbott's Booby numbers, and also research on breeding success, habitat requirements, mortality and so on, are already in operation.

Apart from the particular factors which threaten each individual species, sulids as a group face a series of potential problems, the most important of which is competition from commercial fisheries, which sometimes reduce fish stocks to such levels that the birds have to struggle merely to survive; they hardly produce any young, and may themselves die of starvation. Overfishing is particularly dangerous, because its effects are usually large-scale and long-term. Huge concentrations of seabirds may be greatly reduced in only a few years, before the birds learn to adapt themselves to feeding on another prey type. International efforts should be made to control the

quantities and age-classes of the fish taken; stock management, if scientifically controlled, can provide large catches of fish, without seriously depleting stock.

Fishing vessels often catch more than their legal quotas and this usually results in the surplus fish being thrown overboard and thus being made available to birds, which have quickly learnt to exploit this new source of food. However, several birds are killed during such fishing operations, often after hitting or being hit by some metal part of the ship or the fishing gear; others drown after becoming entangled in the nets; some die as a result of swallowing hooked fish, which has been set for bait, and yet more perish at the colony, where pieces of rope, net or other abandoned equipment are favourite, but sometimes fatal, nest material, as chicks and even adult birds may get tangled up in them and be unable to free themselves.

The destruction of suitable breeding habitat also adversely affects populations, particularly in the tropics, where the species are continuously and more evenly distributed, but where there is also less awareness of the need for conservation. From the devastating destruction of vast areas of suitable habitat, particularly affecting the tree-nesting species, habitat destruction has now become more sophisticated, albeit equally harmful, through tourism.

Gannets and boobies, being mostly aerial, do not suffer greatly from oil pollution. They detect fish by sight and, as fish can not be seen through oily waters, they do not normally dive into such water, or even alight on it, and they generally prefer to move off elsewhere. However, it must be remembered that some Northern Gannet colonies are very close to the main oil fields of the North Sea, and there is always the danger of an oil spill; were this to occur late in the breeding season, it could result in the virtually flightless, newly-fledged young having their plumage impregnated with oil, and ultimately in thousands of deaths.

General Bibliography

Bourne *et al.* (1978), Burger *et al.* (1980), Cracraft (1985), Croxall (1987, 1991), Croxall *et al.* (1984), Diamond (1978), Dorst & Mougin (1979), Drummond (1987), Furness & Monaghan (1987), Harrison (1985, 1987), Löfgren (1984), Nelson (1966b, 1966d, 1970, 1977a, 1978a, 1978b, 1980, 1984, 1985b, 1986), Nettleship *et al.* (1982), Schreiber (1984), Sibley & Monroe (1990), Simmons (1972), van Tets (1965), van Tets *et al.* (1988), Tuck & Heinzel (1978), Warheit (1990).

PLATE 21

inches 10

cm 25

(standing birds)

1

2

3

4

5

6

7

8

9

♀

♂

white morph

brown morph

black-tailed white morph

ssp *leucogaster*

ssp *brewsteri*

white-tailed brown morph

white-headed and white-tailed brown morph

Genus *SULA* Brisson, 1760

1. Northern Gannet
Sula bassana

French: Fou de Bassan **German**: Baßtölpel **Spanish**: Alcatraz Atlántico
Other common names: (North) Atlantic Gannet

Taxonomy. *Pelecanus Bassanus* Linnaeus, 1758, Bass Rock, E Scotland.
Considered by some to form superspecies with *S. capensis* and *S. serrator*; others regard these two as subspecies of *S. bassana*; all three sometimes partitioned off in genus *Morus* (see page 312). Monotypic.
Distribution. Breeds both sides of Atlantic, 48°- 66° N on eastern side, reaching 72° N in Norway; more restricted on western side, 46°-50° N. Winters S down coasts, some reaching equator.

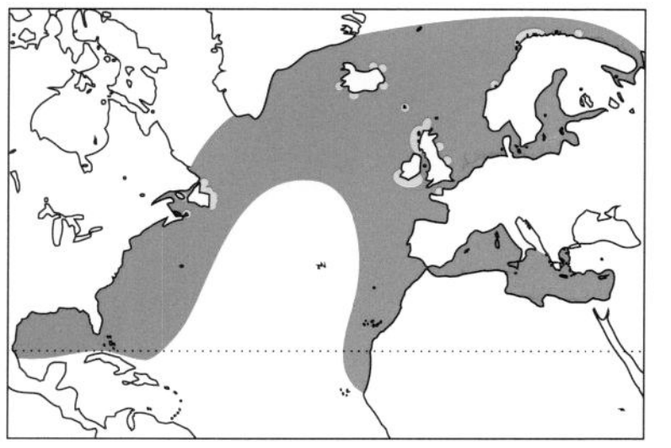

Descriptive notes. 87-100 cm; 2300-3600 g; wingspan 165-180 cm. Largest member of family; bill slightly stouter and head paler cream than in other gannets, though this colour brighter in breeding male. Juveniles start all dark brown, gradually gaining white feathers of adult plumage.
Habitat. Strictly marine. Wanders mostly over continental shelf. Nests on cliffs on offshore islands, sometimes also on mainland.
Food and Feeding. Shoaling pelagic fish, especially herring (*Clupea harengus*), mackerel (*Scomber scombrus*), sprat (*Sprattus sprattus*) and sandeels (*Ammodytes*). Mostly caught by spectacular plunge-dives from great heights. Also attends trawlers regularly; often forms large concentrations where food plentiful.
Breeding. Highly seasonal, starting Mar-Apr. Ground-nester, usually in large colonies, with density at around 1 nest/m^2; nest is large, dense mass of seaweed, grass, earth, etc. stuck together by excreta. Invariably 1 egg; incubation c. 44 days; chicks have white down on blackish skin; fledging c. 90 days. First breeds at 4-5 years. Known to have lived over 25 years in the wild. Annual mortality rate of adults c. 6%.
Movements. Well known, due to extensive ringing. Young birds migrate S, small numbers reaching equator; some spend summer too in winter quarters. Adults disperse less extensively, but regular in winter in Mediterranean and Gulf of Mexico.
Status and Conservation. Not globally threatened. Has been steadily increasing over much of present century, probably recovering former numbers, after earlier persecution by man. Population size well known by regular counts at the c. 40 gannetries, totalling over 263,000 breeding pairs and well over 600,000 birds in 1984/85. Over 60% of world population in British waters, where nearly all sites under protection. Continuous increase (c. 3% annually) has led to foundation of new colonies in recent years; total British population 54,500 pairs in 1939 to c. 160,000 pairs in 1989; c. 50,000 pairs on St Kilda. Norway colonized in 1946; now holds c. 2300 pairs. Huge colonies of NW Atlantic virtually wiped out by man in 19th century (see page 319); similar recovery here and present population c. 40,000 pairs. Increase throughout range probably due to marked decrease in human exploitation, and possibly also increase in prey species caused by intensive fishing of predatory fish. Main threat, however, may be overfishing, although population not seriously affected by Shetland sandeel stock crash in mid 1980's. Still taken for food in some places, e.g. small annual harvest carried out on Sula Sgeir, off NW Scotland. Frequent in captivity.
Bibliography. Barrett (1988), Batten *et al.* (1990), Bent (1922), Boyd (1961), Brun (1972), Chapdelaine *et al.* (1987), Cramp *et al.* (1974), Cramp & Simmons (1977), Croxall *et al.* (1984), Dunnet (1986b), Fisher & Vevers (1943-1944), Gardarsson (1989), Gurney (1913), Lack (1986), Leopold & Platteeuw (1987), Lloyd *et al.* (1991), Martin (1989), Montevecchi & Porter (1980), Montevecchi & Wells (1984), Montevecchi, Barrett *et al.* (1987), Montevecchi, Ricklefs *et al.* (1984), Murray & Wanless (1986), Nelson (1964a, 1964b, 1965, 1966a, 1966c, 1966d, 1978b), Nettleship (1976), Nettleship & Chapdelaine (1988), Palmer (1962), Sharrock (1976), Spano (1965), Tasker, Jones *et al.* (1985), Tasker, Webb *et al.* (1987), Terres (1980), Thom (1986), Thomson (1974, 1975), Wanless (1979, 1983, 1987), White (1971), White & White (1970).

2. Cape Gannet
Sula capensis

French: Fou du Cap **German**: Kaptölpel **Spanish**: Alcatraz del Cabo
Other common names: (South) African Gannet

Taxonomy. *Dysporus capensis* Lichtenstein, 1823, Cape of Good Hope.
Sometimes considered subspecies of *S. bassana*; alternatively considered to form superspecies with *S. bassana* and *S. serrator*; all three sometimes partitioned off in genus *Morus* (see page 312). Hybridization recorded with *S. serrator*. Monotypic.
Distribution. Breeds coasts of South Africa and Namibia; winters along African coasts, on W to Gulf of Guinea, on E to Mozambique, exceptionally to Kenya.

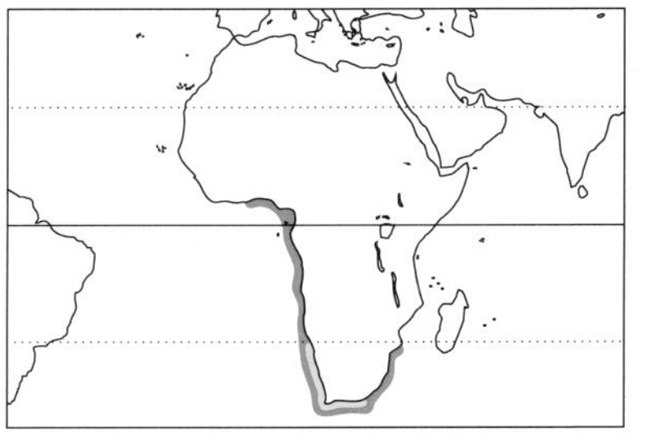

Descriptive notes. 85-90 cm; c. 2600 g. Black gular stripe longer than in other gannets; some birds (c. 10%) have one or more white tail feathers. Juveniles start all dark brown, gradually gaining white feathers of adult plumage.
Habitat. Strictly marine. Wanders over continental shelf. Nests on flat offshore islands, often in large colonies.
Food and Feeding. Mostly shoaling pelagic fish; about 90% of diet may consist of pilchard (*Sardinops ocellata*), anchovies (*Engraulis capensis*) and saury (*Scomberesox saurus*); also some mackerel (*Scomber japonicus*) and maasbankers (*Trachurus*). Prey caught by plunge-diving from c. 20 m above water. Regularly attends trawlers, where large aggregations occur.
Breeding. Highly seasonal, Sept-Apr. Ground-nester, usually in large colonies; nest is mound of debris with central depression, cemented together by excreta. 1 egg, very rarely 2; incubation c. 44 days; chicks have white down on blackish skin; fledging c. 97 days. Age of first breeding 3-4 years.
Movements. Adults range little from colony after breeding, most staying in adjacent waters. Young birds migrate N to Gulf of Guinea, also a few off Mozambique. May occur irregularly in European waters.
Status and Conservation. Not globally threatened. Heavily persecuted for food and for fish-bait in past, as well as suffering in exploitation of guano. Present numbers may be slightly increasing after severe decline; vast colony of over 100,000 pairs at Ichaboe, off SW Africa, in 1956. Only 6 breeding localities currently known, with total of over 80,000 pairs; world population may be up to 350,000 birds. Fully protected at gannetries, but still extensively persecuted by fishermen at sea. Incidental entangling with fishing nets also accounts for important mortality.
Bibliography. Adams & Walter (1991), Batchelor & Ross (1984), Berruti (1987), Broekhuysen *et al.* (1961), Brown *et al.* (1982), Cameron (1981), Cooper (1978b), Cooper, Williams & Britton (1984), Courtenay-Latimer (1954), Crawford *et al.* (1983), Duffy, Berruti *et al.* (1984), Furness & Cooper (1982), García (1972), Gibson-Hill (1948), Jarvis (1971a, 1971b, 1971c, 1972), Jarvis & Cram (1971), Mackworth-Praed & Grant (1957-1973), Maclean (1985), Navarro (1991), Paterson & Riddiford (1990), Pinto (1983), Rand (1959, 1963a, 1963b), Randall & Ross (1979), Venn (1982).

3. Australasian Gannet
Sula serrator

French: Fou austral **German**: Australtölpel **Spanish**: Alcatraz Australiano

Taxonomy. *Pelecanus serrator* G. R. Gray, 1843, from *Sula australis* Gould 1841 (preoccupied), Tasmania. Sometimes considered subspecies of *S. bassana*; alternatively considered to form superspecies with *S. bassana* and *S. serrator*; all three sometimes partitioned off in genus *Morus* (see page 312). Hybridization recorded with *S. capensis*. Monotypic.
Distribution. Breeds coasts of SE Australia, Tasmania and New Zealand; also small colony at Norfolk I. Winters on adjacent waters and up W and E coasts of Australia as far as Tropic of Capricorn.

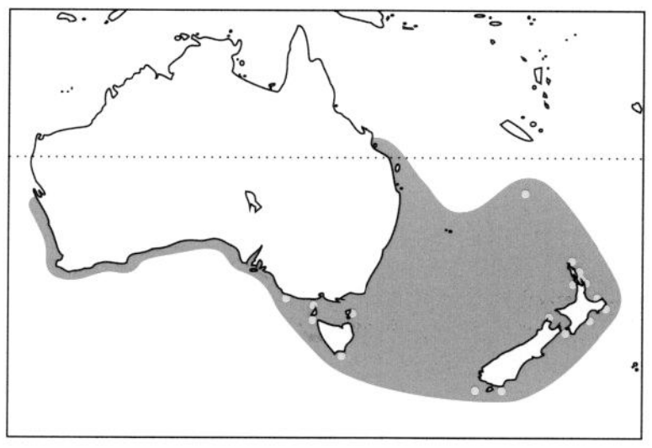

Descriptive notes. 84-91 cm; c. 2350 g; wingspan 160-170 cm. Four, occasionally more, central tail feathers black; orbital ring deeper blue than in other gannets. Juveniles start all dark brown, gradually gaining white feathers of adult plumage.
Habitat. Strictly marine. Wanders over continental shelf or inshore waters, seldom far from land. Nests on open offshore islets.
Food and Feeding. Mostly pelagic fish, especially pilchard (*Sardinops neopilchardus*), anchovies (*Engraulis australis*) and jack mackerel (*Trachurus novaezelandiae*); also garfish (*Hyporhamphus ihi*), other fish and some squid (*Nototodarus*). Prey caught by plunge-diving. Also attends trawlers regularly.
Breeding. Highly seasonal, Oct-May. Ground-nester, commonly in rather small but dense colonies; nest is rough mound of seaweed and grass, cemented together by excreta. 1 egg, exceptionally 2; incubation c. 44 days; chicks have white down on whitish skin; fledging c. 102 days. Age of first breeding 5-6 years. Known to have lived over 33 years in the wild. Annual mortality rate of adults c. 5%.
Movements. Adults stay within vicinity of colony after breeding. Young birds disperse: those from New Zealand move W across Tasman Sea to S Australian waters, where ringing results have shown they may cover 2600 km in a week; large numbers follow W and E coasts of Australia N as far as Tropic of Capricorn. Several records of individuals in colonies of *S. capensis* off S Africa (see page 318); vagrant to Brazil.
Status and Conservation. Not globally threatened. Numbers greatly reduced by human persecution during first half of the century. Population slightly increasing at present, but still least numerous of gannets, and total breeding population estimated at c. 53,000 pairs in 1980, with over 80% in New Zealand waters; colonies off Tasmania have declined markedly. About 33 gannetries known, some only established very recently; small colony of 1-3 pairs established in 1974 on Philip I, by Norfolk I in N Tasman Sea. Legally protected at colonies now, but eggs and chicks still taken at a few. Sometimes caught accidentally during fishing activities.
Bibliography. Bege & Pauli (1988), Cassidy (1983), Dyer (1990), Hawkins (1988), Hermes (1985), Lindsey (1986), McKean (1966), Marchant & Higgins (1990), Robertson (1989), Robertson & Bell (1984), Serventy *et al.* (1971), Sibson (1988), Soper (1976), Stein (1971), van Tets & Fullagar (1984), Warham (1958c), Wingham (1984a, 1984b, 1985), Wodzicki (1967), Wodzicki & Robertson (1953, 1955), Wodzicki & Stein (1958), Wodzicki *et al.* (1982).

4. Blue-footed Booby
Sula nebouxii

French: Fou à pieds bleus **German**: Blaufußtölpel **Spanish**: Piquero Camanay

Taxonomy. *Sula nebouxii* Milne-Edwards, 1882, Chile.
Two subspecies recognized.
Subspecies and Distribution.
S. n. nebouxii Milne-Edwards, 1882 – E Pacific, breeding NW Mexico and Panama to N Peru.
S. n. excisa Todd, 1948 – Galapagos.

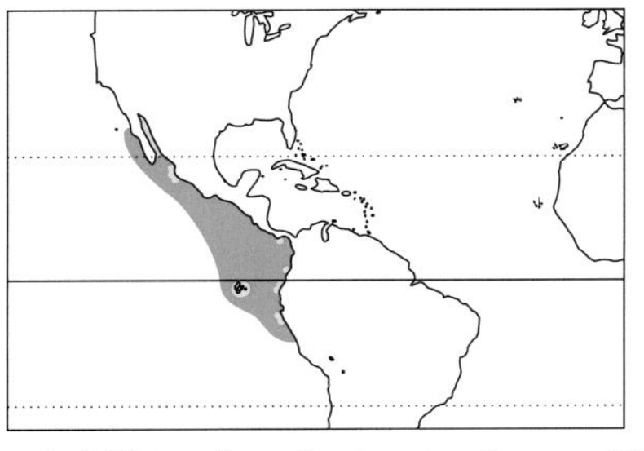

Descriptive notes. 76-84 cm; wingspan 152 cm. White patch on upper back. Females average larger and appear to have larger pupils due to dark inner iris. Juvenile browner on head and breast, with bare parts much duller. Race *excisa* larger and paler.
Habitat. Strictly marine. Nests along rocky coasts, on cliffs and islets, in areas with little or no vegetation. Feeds in adjacent inshore waters, tending to exploit cool, rich waters in areas of upwelling.
Food and Feeding. Fish, including sardina (*Sardinops sagax*), anchovies and mackerel (*Scomber japonicus*); also flying-fish (*Exocoetus*). Plunge-dives often in unison (see page 315), highly gregarious, feeding in groups of up

On following pages: 5. Peruvian Booby (*Sula variegata*); 6. Abbott's Booby (*Sula abbotti*); 7. Masked Booby (*Sula dactylatra*); 8. Red-footed Booby (*Sula sula*); 9. Brown Booby (*Sula leucogaster*).

to 200. Often feeds in shallow water; also seen to take flying-fish in air. May fish in company of *S. variegata*, and even alongside dolphins.
Breeding. Seasonal in places, otherwise opportunistic. Usually nests on ground, but sometimes in vegetation, and forms rather large colonies; nest is circle of accumulated excreta. Average 2 eggs (1-3), with no obligate brood reduction (see page 316); incubation c. 41 days; chicks have whitish down; fledging c. 102 days; post-fledging care c. 56 days. Age of first breeding probably 2-3 years.
Movements. Mostly related to distribution of food supplies: if food abundant, birds mainly stay in vicinity of colony; when scarce, may stray to N and S of breeding range, sometimes reaching California, USA, and N Chile.
Status and Conservation. Not globally threatened. Small world population estimated only c. 30,000 breeding pairs in 1970's. However, Gulf of California probably holds 10,000's-100,000's; population of Peru estimated at maximum 100,000 breeding individuals in 1984; c. 10,000 pairs breed in Galapagos, where numbers, breeding success and population dynamics regularly monitored. Vulnerable to alien predators in Galapagos. Earlier human pressure on this species has probably ceased.
Bibliography. Anderson (1989a, 1989b), Anderson & Ricklefs (1987), Bent (1922), Blake (1977), Brown, R.G.B. (1981), Coulter (1984), Dorward (1962a), Drummond (1988), Drummond *et al.* (1986), Duffy (1983b, 1984, 1987b), Duffy & Hurtado (1984), Duffy & Ricklefs (1981), Duffy, Hays & Plenge (1984), Everett & Anderson (1991), Gibbs *et al.* (1987), Harris, M.P. (1974a, 1984), Jordan & Fuentes (1966), MacCall (1982), Murphy (1925, 1936), Nelson (1968), Palmer (1962), Parkin *et al.* (1970), Ricklefs *et al.* (1984), Steadman & Zousmer (1988), Terres (1980), Tershy & Breese (1990), Tovar (1968).

5. Peruvian Booby
Sula variegata

French: Fou varié **German**: Guanotölpel **Spanish**: Piquero Peruano
Other common names: Variegated Booby

Taxonomy. *Dysporus variegatus* Tschudi, 1843, islands off Peru.
Perhaps closely related to *S. nebouxii*, though recent work suggests that they are more different than previously thought. Monotypic.
Distribution. W coast of S America, in area of Humboldt Current; breeding grounds N Peru to C Chile, with non-breeders dispersing as far as SW Ecuador.

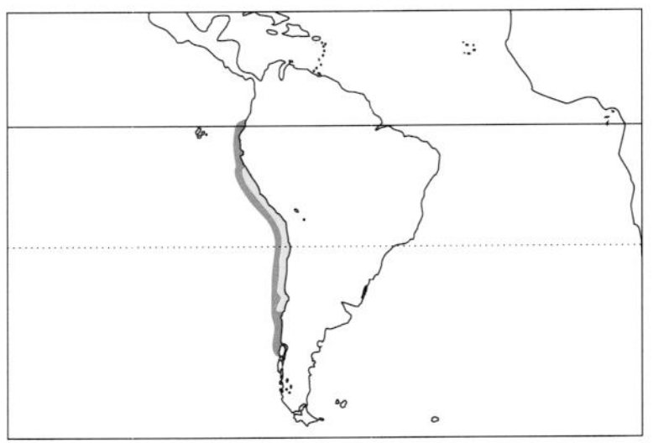

Descriptive notes. 71-76 cm. Females average slightly larger. Pale-tipped feathers of upperwing and back give mottled appearance to upperparts; white head and different underwing pattern separate from *S. nebouxii*. Juvenile has brownish head and underparts and drabber bare parts.
Habitat. Strictly marine. Feeds close to the coast in cool, rich waters of upwelling, where food extraordinarily abundant. Nests on bare, arid islets along rocky coast, mostly on cliff ledges in Chile, but in Peru prefers open, flat ground, with significantly lower temperatures than at nest-sites of *S. nebouxii*.
Food and Feeding. Used to feed almost exclusively on abundant supplies of anchoveta (*Engraulis ringens*), but after collapse of stocks (see page 341), may now have switched partially to sardina (*Sardinops sagax*); also takes some mackerel (*Scomber japonicus*) and other fish. Feeds by plunge-diving, usually from moderate height; almost invariably in groups, often of 30-40 or more individuals.
Breeding. Only loosely seasonal, mostly Sept-Feb in Peru; in Chile laying occurs Jan/Feb. Nests on ground in enormous colonies; nest is generally loose pile of seaweed, held together by droppings, but sometimes no nest at all. Average 3 eggs (1-4); incubation c. 42 days; chicks have whitish down; fledging c. 78-105 days; post-fledging care c. 62 days. Age of first breeding probably 2-3 years.
Movements. Largely sedentary, but occurrence of El Niño (see page 341) causes mass desertion of area and large-scale vagrancy N to Colombia or further S in Chile. Small numbers occur all year round off S Ecuador, though no breeding. Chilean population bolstered by influx of migrants, Mar-Oct.
Status and Conservation. Not globally threatened. Population much reduced during exploitation of guano, through disturbance and egg-collecting (see page 338); main problem subsequently commercial overfishing, causing 1972 crash of anchoveta stocks; although seems to be proportionally less affected by overfishing than other guano birds. Always susceptible to devastation by El Niño, and total population slumped from 2,690,000 breeding birds in 1981/82 to only 730,000 during Niño of 1982/83; partial recovery to 1,160,000 by 1985/86. Legally protected throughout range, but colonies still exploited for guano.
Bibliography. Aid *et al.* (1985), Barber & Chavez (1983), Blake (1977), Brown, R.G.B. (1981), Dorward (1962a), Drummond (1988), Duffy (1983a, 1983b, 1983c, 1987b, 1988), Duffy & Ricklefs (1981), Duffy, Hays & Plenge (1984), Johnson (1965), Jordan (1967), Jordan & Fuentes (1966), MacCall (1982), Murphy (1925, 1936), Schaefer (1970), Schlatter (1984), Tovar (1968, 1978), Tovar *et al.* (1987), Valdivia (1978), Vogt (1942), Walsh (1978).

6. Abbott's Booby
Sula abbotti

French: Fou d'Abbott **German**: Abbott-Tölpel **Spanish**: Piquero de Abbott

Taxonomy. *Sula abbotti* Ridgway, 1893, Assumption Island.
Possibly better separated from rest of family in monospecific genus *Papasula*. Monotypic.
Distribution. Breeding confined to Christmas I, E Indian Ocean. Dispersal and foraging over long distances, but very little information available. Formerly bred on several islands in W Indian Ocean; fossil remains recently found in Solomon Is, W Pacific.
Descriptive notes. 79 cm; 1460 g. Long, narrow wings. Bill pinkish in female, blue-grey tinged pink in male; bill slightly hooked, contrary to rest of family, and cutting edges highly serrated. Juvenile similar to adult in worn plumage, with grey bill.
Habitat. Strictly marine and pelagic. Nests on tall forest trees, preferably *Planchonella* or *Eugenia*, on central plateau of Christmas I, at about 160-260 m. Apparently forages in a rich upwelling area S of Java, but little known.
Food and Feeding. Poorly known. Flying-fish and squid. Presumably plunge-dives like other members of family. Undertakes long foraging trips to favourable feeding zones, and frequently away from nest for several days.
Breeding. Fairly seasonal, most laying May-July; biennial or even less frequent, when successful. Nests in tree-tops, fairly solitary, with maximum density of about 9 pairs/ha; nest is dishevelled stick platform. Invariably 1 egg; incubation c. 57 days; chicks have whitish down; fledging 140-175 days; post-fledging care 162-280 days. Age of first breeding 4-6 years. See page 317.

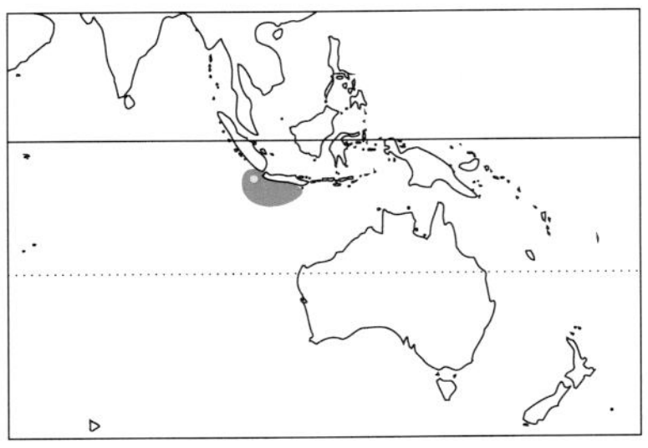

Movements. Very poorly known; adult birds probably largely sedentary, given exceptionally long breeding cycle, but perform lengthy foraging flights. Young and non-breeders largely absent from Christmas I; many may be in area of upwelling S of Java.
Status and Conservation. ENDANGERED. CITES I. Very small world population estimated at maximum of 1900 breeding pairs in 1989, with under 1000 initiating breeding each year. Breeding confined to single remaining colony, where phosphate mining has been causing destruction of forest habitat since late 1960's; mining ceased 1987 and no further forest clearance to be permitted. National park on Christmas I includes most of known nests, but many located in areas underlain by rich phosphates. Extremely reluctant to change location of nest-sites, despite degradation of forest; breeding success even lower at new sites, due to increased exposure to wind and crowding. Extirpated from other tropical Indian Ocean localities within historical times. Several projects currently in progress, investigating species, especially with a view to securing its survival. See page 320.
Bibliography. Anon. (1974), Becking (1976), Bourne (1976), Brouwer & Garnett (1990), Collar & Andrew (1988), Feare (1978, 1984b), Gibson-Hill (1947a), Gray (1981), King (1978/79), Lindsey (1986), Marchant & Higgins (1990), Mountfort (1988), Nelson (1971, 1972, 1974, 1975, 1977b), Nelson & Powell (1986), Olson & Warheit (1988), Ovington (1978), Ovington *et al.* (1981), Reville *et al.* (1987, 1990), Stoddart (1981), Stokes (1988), van Tets (1975), Vincent (1966), Warheit (1990).

7. Masked Booby
Sula dactylatra

French: Fou masqué **German**: Maskentölpel **Spanish**: Piquero Enmascarado
Other common names: Blue-faced/White Booby

Taxonomy. *Sula dactylatra* Lesson, 1831, Ascension Island.
Hybridization with *S. leucogaster* has been recorded. Five subspecies recognized; a sixth, *bedouti*, sometimes accepted.
Subspecies and Distribution.
S. d. dactylatra Lesson, 1831 – Caribbean and SW Atlantic.
S. d. melanops Heuglin, 1859 – W Indian Ocean.
S. d. personata Gould, 1846 – E Indian Ocean, W & C Pacific.
S. d. fullagari O'Brien & Davies, 1990 – N Tasman Sea.
S. d. granti Rothschild, 1902 – E Pacific.

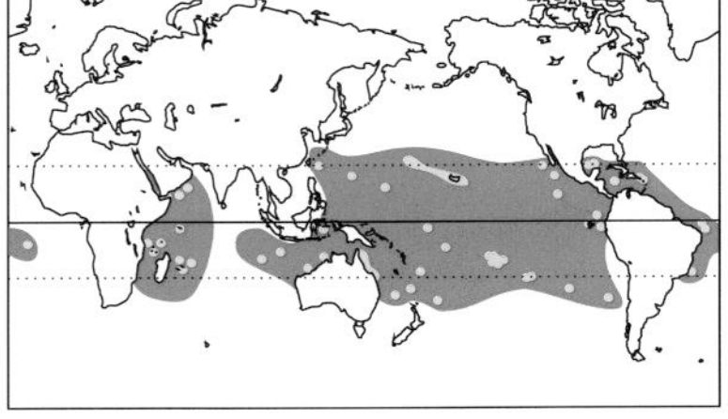

Descriptive notes. 81-92 cm; wingspan 152 cm. Largest booby. Legs yellow or grey; greater upperwing-coverts black, like secondaries. Bill usually bright yellow in males, dull greenish yellow in females; females average slightly larger. Juvenile similar to adult *S. leucogaster*, but paler brown above with white upper breast and white collar round upper back. Pacific races much larger than nominate; bare part colour variable, but not apparently reliable for subspecific determination.
Habitat. Strictly marine and fairly pelagic. Prefers deeper waters than other boobies; in Galapagos, feeds further from colony than *S. nebouxii*, although diet appears to be very similar. Nests on rocky islands offshore; prefers cliff ledge sites, where take-off is easier, but variety of sites used; occasionally on sandy islands, and even reported nesting in trees.
Food and Feeding. Shoaling fish, especially flying-fish (up to 28 cm long), generally taking larger prey than other boobies, including fish up to 41 cm long; only limited amounts of squid, perhaps due to small size of most available squid. Prey caught by plunge-diving from moderate to great heights. Normally solitary, or in small groups. Frequent victim of piracy by frigatebirds.
Breeding. Only loosely seasonal throughout most of its range. Small to medium-sized colonies of variable density. Nests on flat ground or, if possible, on slope or cliff; sometimes in midst of vegetation; nest is simple circle of accumulated excreta. Usually 2 eggs, but brood reduced to 1 chick; incubation c. 44 days; chicks have whitish down; fledging c. 120 days; post-fledging care c. 156 days. Age of first breeding probably 2-3 years. Known to have lived over 23 years in the wild. Annual mortality rate of adults c. 6%.
Movements. Most adults spend all year in vicinity of colony. Extensive dispersal of young, and sometimes adults too; may forage over 1000 km from nearest land.
Status and Conservation. Not globally threatened. Population widely dispersed throughout tropical waters and thus very difficult to estimate, but pantropical distribution suggests it may be large, comprising several hundred thousand individuals. Race *melanops* declining rapidly and the few remaining sizeable colonies are threatened; protection of at least some of these essential. Only 2500 pairs in Caribbean; 5000 in S Atlantic; but 25,000-50,000 in Galapagos and also fair numbers in S Pacific. Breeding colonies quite small and often subject to exploitation by local people, who take eggs or even kill adults. Also menaced by introduced predators and development associated with recent boom in tourist industry.
Bibliography. Ali & Ripley (1978), Anderson (1989a, 1989b), Anderson & Ricklefs (1987), Ashmole & Ashmole (1967), Bahamonde (1974), Blake (1977), Brazil (1991), Brown *et al.* (1982), Clapp *et al.* (1982), Coates (1985), Croxall *et al.* (1984), Croxall (1991), Diamond (1971), Dorward (1962a, 1962b), Drummond (1988), Duffy (1984), Feare (1978), Gibbs *et al.* (1987), Harris, M.P. (1974a, 1984), Harrison (1990), Harrison *et al.* (1984), Johnson (1965), Kepler (1969), Lindsey (1986), Mackworth-Praed & Grant (1957-1973), Marchant & Higgins (1990), Nelson (1967a, 1968), O'Brien & Davies (1990), Olson & den Hartog (1990), Palmer (1962), Rice (1984b), Ruschi (1979), Schreiber & Hensley (1976), Schreiber & Schreiber (1984c), Serventy *et al.* (1971), Sick (1984), Steadman & Zousmer (1988), Terres (1980).

8. Red-footed Booby
Sula sula

French: Fou à pieds rouges **German**: Rotfußtölpel **Spanish**: Piquero Patirrojo

Taxonomy. *Pelecanus Sula* Linnaeus, 1766, Barbados, West Indies.
Three subspecies commonly recognized, though validity doubtful.

Subspecies and Distribution.
S. s. sula (Linnaeus, 1766) – Caribbean and SW Atlantic.
S. s. rubripes Gould, 1838 – tropical W & C Pacific and Indian Oceans.
S. s. websteri Rothschild, 1898 – E Pacific.

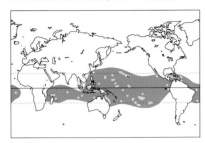

Descriptive notes. 66-77 cm; 900-1003 g; wingspan 91-101 cm. Polymorphic, including: white morph; black-tailed white morph (Galapagos); "golden" white morph (Christmas I, Indian Ocean); brown morph; white-tailed brown morph; and white-headed and white-tailed brown morph. Only booby with white tail, though in some morphs it is dark; larger eye than other boobies, possibly adapted to feeding by night. Females average larger. Juvenile all brown or greyish brown, with yellowish grey legs. Subspecies similar, *websteri* slightly smaller, *rubripes* slightly larger than nominate.

Habitat. Strictly marine and largely pelagic. Nests and roosts in trees, on islets with abundant vegetation; also recorded nesting on ground and on walls.

Food and Feeding. Mainly flying-fish (Exocoetidae) and squid (Ommastrephidae); mean prey length 8·8 cm. Caught by plunge-diving; flying-fish also taken in flight, especially when chased to surface by underwater predators. Frequently suffers piracy of frigatebirds. Partially nocturnal feeding habits, possibly because squid come to surface at night; with moonlight may fish all night. Often alights on ships, using them as vantage points.

Breeding. Not seasonal in most of range, and may start breeding in any month. Stick nest on tree or bush; highly gregarious, forming large colonies. 1 egg; incubation c. 45 days; chicks have whitish down; fledging 100-139 days; post-fledging care c. 190 days. Age of first breeding probably 2-3 years. Known to have lived nearly 23 years in the wild.

Movements. Pantropical distribution and long foraging trips obscure any regular movements, but probably mainly dispersive over tropical oceans; juveniles undertake the widest-ranging movements, sometimes hundreds of kilometres from nearest land. May forage up to 150 km from colony, often setting off before dawn and returning after dark.

Status and Conservation. Not globally threatened. One of most abundant and widespread of all sulids, but population widely scattered on myriad of small islands around the tropics; few colonies protected. Due to its tree-nesting habit, has suffered greatly from habitat destruction, especially in W Indian Ocean, where at least 12 colonies lost in last 100 years; also in S Atlantic, where only 100 pairs remain. Still numerous in Caribbean (14,000 pairs), Galapagos (250,000 pairs, including 140,000 on Genovesa), E Indian Ocean (12,000 pairs at Christmas I, 30,000 birds at Cocos (Keeling) Is) and S Pacific; population of Hawaii recovering from earlier loss of habitat. Other factors limiting numbers are egg-collecting, poaching, predation by rats and disturbance caused by tourism. Population greatly reduced in historical times, but, thanks to vast breeding range, still large, probably numbering well over 1,000,000 birds.

Bibliography. Ali & Ripley (1978), Anderson (1991), Ashmole & Ashmole (1967), Blake (1977), Brazil (1991), Cai Qi-Kan (1982), Coates (1985), Croxall *et al.* (1984), Croxall (1991), Diamond (1971, 1974, 1980), Dorward (1962a), Feare (1978), Gibson-Hill (1949), Harris, M.R. (1974a, 1984), Harrison (1990), Langham (1984), Lindsey (1986), Marchant & Higgins (1990), Monroe (1968), Nelson (1968, 1969a, 1969b, 1972), Palmer (1962), Rice (1984b), Ruschi (1979), Schreiber & Chovan (1986), Schreiber & Hensley (1976), Seki & Harrison (1989), Serventy *et al.* (1971), Sick (1984), Simmons (1968b), Steadman & Zousmer (1988), Terres (1980), Tunnell & Chapman (1988), Verner (1961, 1965), Voous (1983), Wetmore (1965).

9. Brown Booby
Sula leucogaster

French: Fou brun   **German**: Weißbauchtölpel   **Spanish**: Piquero Pardo
Other common names: White-bellied Booby

Taxonomy. *Pelecanus Leucogaster* Boddaert, 1783, Cayenne.
Known to have hybridized with *S. dactylatra* and these two species evidently very close; juvenile *dactylatra* closely resembles present species. Subspecies *brewsteri* formerly considered a full species. Four subspecies recognized.

Subspecies and Distribution.
S. l. leucogaster (Boddaert, 1783) – Caribbean and tropical Atlantic.
S. l. plotus (J. R. Forster, 1844) – Red Sea and W Indian Ocean to C Pacific.
S. l. brewsteri Goss, 1888 – NE tropical Pacific.
S. l. etesiaca Thayer & Bangs, 1905 – CE Pacific.

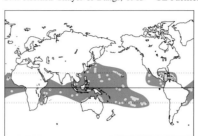

Descriptive notes. 64-74 cm; 724-1550 g; wingspan 132-150 cm. Bare part colour varies with race, especially in male; non-breeding male lacks blue on face. Females average larger. Juvenile as adult, but duller brown above with dirty white underparts. Race *plotus* larger and more uniformly dark above than nominate; male *etesiaca* has pale greyish forecrown; most of head greyish white in male *brewsteri*.

Habitat. Strictly marine. Feeds mostly on inshore waters. Not commonly seen sitting on water. Nests on bare, rocky islands or coral atolls, preferably on cliffs or slopes, but also on flat ground, sometimes where vegetation dense; in some areas roosts in trees.

Food and Feeding. Mostly flying-fish (*Exocoetus*, *Cypselurus*) and squid; some halfbeak (*Hemiramphus*), mullet (*Mugil*) and anchovy (*Engraulis*); mean prey length 9·4 cm. May be less dependent on flying-fish than other boobies. Prey usually caught by plunge-diving, from low over water and at oblique angle, but height and angle both appear to be variable; commonly uses feet and wings for underwater propulsion, though this may not be efficient enough to catch live, mobile prey; also snatches prey off surface of water in flight. Sometimes kleptoparasitic, especially on *S. dactylatra* and even on frigatebirds in one study; most attacks on *S. nebouxii* carried out by females. Feeds close inshore, sometimes in small groups, but generally more or less solitary.

Breeding. Seasonal in some areas, but elsewhere breeding opportunistic or more or less continuous. Usually nests on ground, but often in midst of vegetation; colonies tend to be smaller than those of other sulids; nest is small depression in ground, sometimes lined with twigs or grass. Normally 2 eggs, but brood reduced to 1 chick; incubation c. 43 days; chicks have whitish down; fledging 85-105 days; post-fledging care 118-259 days. Age of first breeding probably 2-3 years. Annual mortality rate of adults c. 6%.

Movements. Adults tend to stay more or less permanently around colony. Young and non-breeders disperse widely, and some records of inter-colony movements.

Status and Conservation. Not globally threatened. Possibly most numerous and widespread species, but population often scattered and thus difficult to estimate total numbers; must be several hundred thousand individuals, distributed over hundreds of small colonies. Large numbers off W Australia, including c. 20,000 pairs in Lacepede Is; c. 17,000 pairs in Caribbean; population more evenly spread out than in other pantropical boobies. Numbers severely reduced in historical times, mainly due to persecution by humans for food or bait, and long-established tradition of egg-collecting on regular basis, which still persists in places. Very few colonies have any kind of legal protection, and disturbance caused by increased tourism may also adversely affect breeding birds. Introduced predators have also caused problems, e.g. cats on Ascension I, S Atlantic.

Bibliography. Ali & Ripley (1978), Altenburg & van der Kamp (1989), Ashmole & Ashmole (1967), Bege & Pauli (1988), Brazil (1991), Bregulla (1992), Brown *et al.* (1982), Burbidge *et al.* (1987), Clapp *et al.* (1982), Cramp & Simmons (1977), Croxall *et al.* (1984), Croxall (1991), Diamond (1971), Dorward (1962a, 1962b), Drummond (1988), Duffy (1985), Coates (1985), Feare (1978), Gibson-Hill (1947a, 1949), Harrison (1990), Harrison *et al.* (1984), Humphrey & Bain (1990), Langrand (1990), Lindsey (1986), Mackworth-Praed & Grant (1957-1973), Marchant & Higgins (1990), Monroe (1968), Morris (1984), Nelson (1972), Palmer (1962), Polunin (1979), Rice (1984b), Ruschi (1979), Schreiber & Ashmole (1970), Serventy *et al.* (1971), Sick (1984), Simmons (1967a, 1967b, 1974b, 1977b), Slud (1964), Terres (1980), Tershy & Breese (1990), Voous (1983), Wetmore (1965).

Class AVES
Order PELECANIFORMES
Suborder PELECANI
Family PHALACROCORACIDAE (CORMORANTS)

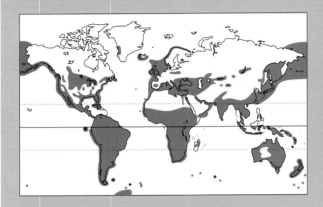

- Medium-sized to large waterbirds with elongated body, long neck and strong, hooked bill.
- 45-100 cm.

- Cosmopolitan, with greatest diversity in tropical and temperate zones.
- Stretches of open water, both coastal and inland.
- 1 genus, 39 species, 57 taxa.
- 11 species threatened; 1 species extinct since 1600.

Systematics

Phalacrocoracidae is the largest family in the Pelecaniformes, and in most versions it contains more than half the species of the order. However, there is a wide variety of opinions as to the exact number of species that should be recognized.

The total figure ranges from 26 to 40 species, with most of the discrepancies arising from the controversy that surrounds many closely related forms of the Southern Hemisphere. The problem is especially acute in the subantarctic and around New Zealand, where there are numerous allopatric forms that are restricted to particular island groups or stretches of coast, and most of these forms are usually differentiated at least to sub-specific level. Extensive chopping and changing has led to considerable confusion with scientific names, and even more so with vernacular names. D. Siegel-Causey's recent revision of the family, based on osteological analysis, has been largely responsible for a clarification of the general situation, and the acceptance of several new species. The most complicated case is that of the "blue-eyed shags", which have frequently been classified as only three or four species, *atriceps*, *albiventer*, *carunculatus* and usually *campbelli*. It now appears that it is probably better to split them into 13 different species: the collection of forms formerly grouped in *atriceps* and *albiventer* give rise to *atriceps* (incorporating *albiventer*), *bransfieldensis*, *georgianus*, *nivalis*, *melanogenis*, *verrucosus*, and *purpurascens*; *chalconotus* and *onslowi* are separated from *carunculatus*; and *campbelli* is divided into *campbelli*, *colensoi* and *ranfurlyi*. Other similar cases are the detaching of the form *featherstoni* from *punctatus*, and likewise that of *coronatus* from *africanus*.

Nor is there general agreement concerning the internal organization of the family. Many authors have placed all the species in a single genus, *Phalacrocorax*, though others add the monotypic genus *Nannopterum* for the Flightless Cormorant (*Phalacrocorax harrisi*). The so-called "microcormorants", which are small and relatively long-tailed, are frequently grouped in a distinct genus, alternatively named *Microcarbo* or *Halietor*, and including the species *melanoleucos*, *africanus*, *coronatus*, *niger* and *pygmaeus*. Some versions accept a total of five, or even nine, genera, though not always including *Nannopterum* and *Microcarbo* or *Halietor*.

Siegel-Causey also proposes the division of the Phalacrocoracidae into two subfamilies, labelled as the cormorants (*Phalacrocoracinae*), and the shags (*Leucocarboninae*). The latter have some derived characteristics, such as the form of the nasal gland depression, large and single-lobed, and the pattern of pneumatization of the skull; they are also characterized apparently by more pelagic tendencies and stronger flight. However, the subdivision into subfamilies and nine genera has not as yet received widespread support. Historically, the application of "cormorant" or "shag" in the coining of common names for the various different species has been fairly haphazard; in generalizations about the family it is the former term that is normally used.

The darters (Anhingidae) are clearly very closely related to the cormorant family, and in spite of some marked differences (see page 354), they are sometimes included within the Phalacrocoracidae. Fossils have been found in North America, which date back some 60 million years, and correspond to common ancestors of these two families, but not of the rest of the Pelecaniformes. Apparently, the differentiation of cormorants and darters occurred some 30 million years ago, or possibly even earlier.

Morphological Aspects

Cormorants are medium-sized to large aquatic birds, varying in length from about 45 to 100 cm. Plumage, morphology and size are similar in both sexes, although males are generally larger and heavier. This is especially true in the case of the Flightless Cormorant, the heaviest species, where the male weighs around 4 kg, over 1 kg more than the female. Nevertheless, a study of the Imperial Shag (*Phalacrocorax atriceps*) in Patagonia indicates that the characteristic that best differentiates the sexes is the depth of the bill, which tends to be greater in the male, at any rate in this species.

The body is robust and elongated, while the neck, head and bill are likewise long. The slender bill is laterally flattened and hooked at the tip, with the external nostrils completely closed. When perched, cormorants typically adopt an upright posture, often with the neck folded in an S-shape and the back hunched.

In many species plumage is basically black or very dark, usually with a metallic green or blue sheen, and the upperwing-coverts and scapulars are often grey or brown with black margins, which produce a scaly appearance. Most of the species of the Southern Hemisphere retain the dark upperparts, but have

The classification of the Phalacrocoracidae has undergone a considerable upheaval in recent years. The subantartic or "blue-eyed" shags constitute the most changed group, and detailed osteological analysis shows that there may be as many as 13 allopatric forms which until very recently were considered races of only three or four species, but are now regarded as full species. The situation has not yet been clarified, and the shags in this photograph provide a good example, as the population of the South Orkney Islands is at present only provisionally included within the South Georgia Shag, pending further investigation.

[*Phalacrocorax georgianus*, Signy Island, South Orkney Is. Photo: Roger Coggan/ Bruce Coleman]

white underparts, while three are predominantly grey, the Red-legged Cormorant (*Phalacrocorax gaimardi*), the Spotted Shag (*Phalacrocorax punctatus*) and the Pitt Shag (*Phalacrocorax featherstoni*). It has been noted that the two basic models of coloration could be designed to make these underwater pursuit-divers more inconspicuous to their prey: the species with white underparts could feed nearer the surface, as they would be less visible from below, whilst those that are uniformly dark would be bottom feeders, fishing well beneath the surface where there is less light. However, there is no such clear correspondence between each species' foraging zone and its plumage type, and the latter may simply have been determined phylogenetically.

In several species, there are populations which have more or less pronounced differences in plumage, but amongst the same population there are rarely true colour phases. Nevertheless, this does occur in the New Zealand race *brevirostris* of the Little Pied Cormorant (*Phalacrocorax melanoleucos*) and in the Stewart Shag (*Phalacrocorax chalconotus*), which contain some individuals with white underparts and others that are uniformly dark, while some birds have intermediate coloration. There are also some less marked plumage phases, for instance in the Imperial Shag in some areas, and variations in the juvenile plumages of the Red-legged Cormorant, the Rock Shag (*Phalacrocorax magellanicus*) and the Pied Cormorant (*Phalacrocorax varius*).

Cormorants have a complex moult, which is not well known in most species. As well as the complete moult, in which they obtain the basic non-breeding plumage, there is another, prior to breeding, which affects the feathers of the head, the neck and part of the body.

As in the majority of the Pelecaniformes, there is a bare, distensible gular pouch, which has various different functions. It can be used for holding on to large fish before they are swallowed, or in thermoregulation, and it can play a visual role in displays.

Before the breeding season, adults undergo changes that affect both the plumage and the bare parts. The naked skin of the face, the eye-ring, the gular pouch, the bill and the lining of the mouth can acquire bright colours, including varying shades of red, yellow, green and blue, depending on the species. In addition, crests are generally moulted in at this stage, as are

any long, white filoplumes, which may be found on different parts of the body, but mainly on the head and neck. In the Great Cormorant (*Phalacrocorax carbo*), Japanese Cormorant (*Phalacrocorax capillatus*), Pelagic Cormorant (*Phalacrocorax pelagicus*) and the Red-faced Cormorant (*Phalacrocorax urile*) a conspicuous white patch appears on the thighs. The decorative plumes and bright bare part colours are both lost as breeding advances, or sometimes even shortly after pair formation. Outwith the breeding season, as well as lacking these adornments, the whole plumage is duller.

Young birds are generally drab brown all over, though they tend to be somewhat paler on the underparts. In species with white underparts these may be tinged brownish in juveniles, and the contrast between the light and dark areas of the plumage is less clear than in adults. The eyes are brown in juveniles, but in adults they can become a brilliant blue, green or red.

The wings are rounded and relatively short, whilst the tail, long and wedge-shaped, is formed by 12-14 stiff, pointed rectrices. The wing area of cormorants is small in relation to their weight. Their flight is powerful and is almost always based on regular, continuous wingbeats, sometimes interrupted by the occasional glide, and, although they appear heavy, some species can reach speeds of up to 80 km/h. On occasions, with the help of the wind or thermals, they can glide and even soar. In flight, the neck is outstretched or slightly folded in, and the head may be held high or low.

Over water, they usually fly low over the surface, whereas over land or on long flights they fly at greater heights. When travelling in a flock, they may fly in a V-formation or in line. The marine species tend to avoid flying over land, even if this means lengthening the flight, so they often follow the coastline and only cross narrow strips of land.

A bird typically lands on the water, fanning out its tail, which is the first part to touch down, and stretching its feet out in front to brake, before coming to a complete halt. Take-off from the water in turn involves running along the surface, beating it with both feet at once, whilst flapping the wings energetically. Both at sea and on land, whenever possible, birds use the wind to help them land or take off, for example flying into the wind to make the most of its lift. Unlike the darters, they do not manoeuvre sufficiently well to be able to move

The filoplumes which adorn the head, and sometimes the neck and breast, of cormorants constitute an important feature of their nuptial plumage. This Great Cormorant, unmistakably in breeding dress, can clearly be recognized as the race sinensis with the characteristic expanse of white on the head and neck. In the cormorants, the males peform the task of collecting the nest material, while the females build the nest.

[Phalacrocorax carbo sinensis.
Photo: Marco Polo]

around small ponds and swamps that are closed in by high vegetation, so they prefer open waters without obstacles, where it is often windy and there is more room for manoeuvring.

The Flightless Cormorant has very reduced wings, which are roughly the size of penguin flippers. It has even lost the keel on its sternum, where birds' flight muscles are situated, and these too have become rudimentary in this species. Its ancestors colonized the Galapagos Islands and found an environment devoid of predatory mammals, where the ability to fly was not especially advantageous, and here they remained isolated. The birds evolved conditioned by these factors, until they lost the power of flight totally, while their swimming ability was improved; for example they developed stronger feet.

The short legs are set far back on the body, and the tarsi are thick and flattened. The totipalmate feet are large and are generally black, though in some species they are red, pink or yellow. On land cormorants waddle clumsily and heavily, due to the positioning and shortness of their legs. Several species habitually perch in trees, and some can even do so on cables.

As cormorants are compact and dense, birds swim quite low in the water, sometimes even with only the head and the raised neck protruding. The bill is held tilted and the tail stretched out horizontally on or beneath the surface of the water. Although they swim well, above all they are great divers, and they have several adaptations which reduce buoyancy, facilitating diving. In spite of the presence of a feathered oil-gland at the base of the tail, the structure of the feathers enables them to retain water, and thus the plumage can become soaked and increase the bird's density. At the same time, the bird has an insulating layer of air next to the skin, which limits heat loss. On emerging from the water, much of the water is efficiently repelled, and the insulating air can rapidly reoccupy the plumage to prevent the bird becoming cold. The structure of the bones is not highly pneumatic, and some marine species have been seen ingesting pebbles, in order to reduce buoyancy further.

The webbed feet give the bird powerful propulsion, and they are used alternately whilst swimming on the surface, but simultaneously for diving. The bird plunges down from the surface and many species start with a leap forward. The wings are not used to drive it along under the water, instead they are held close to the body to create a streamlined profile, and thus offer less resistance, as the bird moves forward. The tail can be used to steer the bird during diving. Although dives normally last for 20-40 seconds, sometimes they only last a few seconds.

In the Phalacrocoracidae, the surface area of the wing is small in relation with the bird's weight. Flight is powerful, normally consisting of fairly regular, continuous wingbeats, interspersed with occasional glides, and birds can reach speeds of up to 80 km/h. The Imperial Shag is one of 19 species with white underparts, while of the remaining species in the family, 18 are predominantly black, and only three are basically grey.

[Phalacrocorax atriceps,
Photo: Jen & Des Bartlett/ Bruce Coleman]

They are usually longer in the larger species, and when fishing is carried out in deeper waters. Although dives of up to four minutes have been claimed, the longest definitely recorded appear to be of some 95 seconds in the Crozet Shag (*Phalacrocorax melanogenis*) and the European Shag (*Phalacrocorax aristotelis*). Dives are alternated with rests, which in sum usually occupy only half or a third as much time as the total spent diving. The duration of rests can depend on several factors, such as the duration of the dive, the depth reached, whether or not the bird has inspected the seabed, and the characteristics of the latter.

Cormorants can reach considerable depths in their dives. Thus the Antarctic Shag (*Phalacrocorax bransfieldensis*) reaches depths of at least 25 m, and the Macquarie Shag (*Phalacrocorax purpurascens*), Brandt's Cormorant (*Phalacorcorax penicillatus*) and the Pelagic Cormorant may be able to reach depths of 50 m. Both the normal and the maximum depths attained in dives vary significantly with the species, and the small species usually fish at more modest depths, generally less than 10 m below the surface. Many species are benthic-foragers, descending towards the seabed at an oblique angle, but coming back up vertically. A study of the four marine species of southern Africa indicates a mean speed of 0·69-1·01 m/s in these descents. Once on the seabed, in the feeding area itself, the mean speed varies between 0·34 and 1·45 m/s, depending on the topography and also on each particular species.

Habitat

Apart from the darters, the cormorants are the most aquatic of the Pelecaniformes. Although they are not as closely tied to fresh water as the darters, they frequently occur inland, as well as along marine coasts.

The different species are habitually found on a wide variety of inland waters, such as lakes, open swamps, salt marshes, reservoirs and wide, slow-flowing rivers, and they also occur in lagoons and estuaries. Thus the family uses salt, brackish and fresh waters, but this apparently catholic taste is not by any means uniformly spread throughout all the species, indeed most are exclusively, or almost exclusively, marine, and are restricted to mainland or island coasts. In contrast, a few species occur only inland, mostly on fresh waters, especially the Little Cormorant (*Phalacrocorax niger*), the Pygmy Cormorant (*Phalacrocorax pygmaeus*), the Long-tailed Cormorant (*Phalacrocorax africanus*) and the Little Black Cormorant (*Phalacrocorax sulcirostris*). Finally, other species are more

adaptable, and in fact there is a small group of species that occupy marine and inland habitats almost indiscriminately, in particular the Double-crested Cormorant (*Phalacrocorax auritus*), the Neotropic Cormorant (*Phalacrocorax olivaceus*) and the Great Cormorant. The extreme versatility of the Neotropic Cormorant is particularly remarkable, as it lives in areas as different climatically and environmentally as coasts, from the southern part of North America to the extreme south of South America, wetlands, rivers with strong currents and even Andean lakes at altitudes of almost 5000 m.

Cormorants are distributed almost all over the world, and are present in all the oceans and large inland seas, as well as inland in all the continents except Antarctica. They are only absent from northern central Asia, the most northerly part of North America (though they occur on the coast of Alaska), the islands of the central Pacific and large, arid continental areas. The majority of the species live in tropical or temperate waters, although some reach the Arctic and the Antarctic.

While cormorants are absent from most small oceanic islands, there is the presence of the Flightless Cormorant in the Galapagos Islands, and also that of a series of species in the subantarctic islands roughly between the latitudes of New Zealand and the Antarctic Peninsula. These island groups, isolated, but with permanent sources of food, have favoured the process whereby colonizing birds become sedentary and differentiate into species. This has produced the extreme evolution of the Flightless Cormorant, and also the great specific diversification in the subantarctic shags (see Systematics). The Ice Ages may also have influenced the processes of speciation and subspeciation, by isolating populations for long periods, during which they were able to differentiate. This is presumably the case of the Japanese Cormorant, which probably originated from a population of Great Cormorants that was isolated during the glacial periods. Similarly, it may have caused some variations or plumage phases, like those in the Rock or Imperial Shags, which could be the result of later contact between populations, after they had been separated by the ice.

The extent of each species' distribution is very variable. While the Great Cormorant is nearly cosmopolitan, other species, such as the Neotropic and Long-tailed Cormorants, have extensive ranges. Yet, at the opposite extreme, many species are highly restricted in geographical terms, such as the Socotra Cormorant (*Phalacrocorax nigrogularis*), the Japanese Cormorant and the numerous island endemics.

The regions with the greatest concentrations of cormorants in the world are the coasts of Peru and northern Chile and the western coast of South Africa, the coasts washed by the Humboldt

Like most diving birds, cormorants have their legs set far back on the body, which makes underwater swimming much easier. As can be seen with this Double-crested Cormorant, the legs also play an important part in take-off from the water, as the bird has to run along the surface until it can gain sufficient speed to become airborne.

[Phalacrocorax auritus auritus, Forillon National Park, Gaspé Peninsula, Canada. Photo: John Eastcott & Iva Momatiuk/DRK]

Some members of the Phalacrocoracidae nest in trees or on the ground, while others build their nests on sea cliffs. This kind of site usually has the advantage of offering the birds a fair degree of protection, both by precluding access to predators and by reducing the risk of human disturbance. Nonetheless, the Chilean population of the cliff-nesting Red-legged Cormorant seems to be in decline at present, apparently due to raiding by egg-collectors.

[*Phalacrocorax gaimardi*, Paracas, Peru. Photo: Günter Ziesler]

and Benguela Currents respectively. These currents of cold, nutrient-rich water fertilize the oceans, creating some of the most productive marine areas on the planet, and permitting the extraordinary development of the seabird populations. Concentrated in enormous breeding colonies, these birds thus become prodigious guano producers (see Relationship with Man).

The marine species are almost always found within sight of land, partly because they are not particularly well equipped for lengthy flights, partly because they need to dry their plumage, so they require access to perches, and also due to the restricted depth at which they fish, as they often dive less than 5-8 m down. Moreover, many cormorants feed on benthic prey species, which they are only able to catch in shallow water, and this coincides with the coastal zone. In the areas they use for feeding, the nature of the seabed can vary considerably, and it may consist of rocks, sand, mud or kelp beds.

All species require the proximity of an adequate food supply, as well as suitable ground for nesting. Along sea coasts, this means cliffs or rocky islets, or alternatively tranquil islands, which need not necessarily be so steep or abrupt. Inland, they usually need some form of vegetation, on which they can perch, rest and build their nests (see Breeding).

Many species coincide with one or more other species of cormorant over extensive areas. Such is the case in southern Africa, where the Cape Cormorant (*Phalacrocorax capensis*), the Crowned Cormorant (*Phalacrocorax coronatus*), the Bank Cormorant (*Phalacrocorax neglectus*) and the Great Cormorant all co-exist, or in New Zealand, where there are mixed colonies of four species, the Pied, Little Pied and Little Black Cormorants and the Spotted Shag. Similar situations occur in Australia, Patagonia or on the Pacific coasts of America, and, to a lesser degree, in most of the remaining regions inhabited by the family.

Although a good deal of research is still required on the habitat and diet overlap of sympatric species, in general the studies carried out to date reveal more or less clear differences, which diminish competition and allow their co-existence. In this respect, there can also be differences in the timing of breeding, which mean that species nesting in the same area do not all breed at the same time.

In south-west Africa, the Bank Cormorant fishes above all in coastal kelp beds, whilst the Cape Cormorant feeds on pe-

lagic shoaling fish. In New Zealand, the smaller species, especially the Little Pied Cormorant, forage higher up in the water column. In temperate regions of Australia, this same species tends to fish alone in shallow waters, and to feed mainly on invertebrates, and it thus reduces competition with the Little Black Cormorant. The Pelagic, the Double-crested and Brandt's Cormorants can fish simultaneously in the same areas of the Pacific coast of North America, but they exploit different microhabitats, which in turn leads to their taking different prey; the Double-crested has a greater tendency to go for shoaling fish, while the others prefer bottom fish.

General Habits

The great sociability of this family is evident when birds form large flocks for roosting, at breeding colonies and in collective fishing (see Food and Feeding). In all cases many thousands of birds can assemble.

These gregarious tendencies and the often crowded nature of colonies have motivated the development of a complex and varied series of visual displays. These are, to a great extent, related to the need to announce their movements, including departures and arrivals on the wing, or moving about on foot, so that the bird does not alarm its mate or nearby birds, and conflicts are avoided.

The time spent in the water, basically dedicated to feeding, is quite short, so that birds have a fair amount of time for lazing around, preening or courting. Unlike other diving or swimming birds, they do not remain on the water when resting, but instead come ashore. Perches for diurnal use can be very simple, and birds can in fact use almost any protruding object, from a floating trunk to a buoy or, more typically, a post. Roosts are usually collective, and are situated in clear, safe positions, such as islands, rocks and sea cliffs. Although the marine species sleep on land all year round, the construction of offshore oil platforms has led to some species, such as the European Shag, sleeping on them occasionally. Many species also roost in trees, bushes or reeds, often surrounded by water, and some, like the Great, Brandt's, the Double-crested and the Neotropic Cormorants, are capable of perching on cables. Roosting sites and

breeding colonies are sometimes a considerable distance from the feeding area. This means the birds can spend several hours each day travelling, often in large flocks, flying in V-formations or in long, undulating lines.

Cormorants often bathe in a very vigorous and spectacular fashion, sometimes in groups. On coming out of the water, a bird will shake its plumage, and in this way it manages to get rid of a good deal of the water (see Morphological Aspects). Birds frequently use the uropygial gland for oiling the plumage with the bill.

The "Wing-spread" position is very characteristic of these birds, and is a posture they often maintain for long periods. The significance of the posture has been interpreted in various different ways: for thermoregulation; for drying the wings; to help the birds keep their balance in an upright stance; or for producing intraspecific signals, such as the announcement of successful fishing. However, studies of several species indicate that its only purpose seems to be for drying the wings. Hence, the thermoregulatory function in the "Wing-spreading" of the darters is lacking in cormorants, although the ultimate aim in cormorants might be to conserve energy.

In several Antarctic or subantarctic species, such as the Antarctic Shag, the Campbell Shag (*Phalacrocorax campbelli*), the Kerguelen Shag (*Phalacrocorax verrucosus*) and the Bounty Shag (*Phalacrocorax ranfurlyi*), no "Wing-spreading" has been observed. This has been interpreted as an adaptation to the extremely cold climate, in order to avoid the heat loss which this behaviour would imply. In contrast, when birds are too hot they can cool themselves by means of gular-fluttering.

In general, cormorants tend to be rather wary of man. This is not the case of the Flightless Cormorant, nor of some other species in areas where they have not been disturbed by humans and so are not afraid of them, as in the case of the Cape Cormorant at Hollam's Bird Island, in Namibia.

Voice

In general, outwith the breeding season cormorants are silent, and their voice is not highly specialized. Vocal displays are mainly produced at breeding colonies, and are associated with breeding behaviour. There are also frequent vocalizations at roosts, for example during disputes on perches, or during collective fishing in some species, such as the Neotropic Cormorant.

Overall, males are much more vocal than females, and they mostly make croaking, groaning, barking, ticking and gargling calls. In several species, females only produce soft, hoarse, hissing or puffing sounds, and often they are largely silent. Chicks generally make plaintive, monotonous, insistent calls when soliciting feeding.

Characteristic calls are usually produced in the distinct breeding displays, or in those related with take-off and landing, or threats and alarm. These vary with the species, and can also vary between the sexes, depending on the species or the display in question. These calls may be made only by the male, for example in the European Shag, which actually has a very limited vocal repertoire, and the female only makes throat-clicking and hissing sounds in the "Threat-gape" display.

The Great Cormorant has a very complex repertoire of loud, guttural and raucous calls, and this variety is quite outstanding, even amongst the Pelecaniformes as a whole. The females of this species have much softer calls, which become more similar to those of the males, as the breeding season advances.

Some species are especially noisy, such as the Pelagic Cormorant or the Indian Cormorant (*Phalacrocorax fuscicollis*), which is very vocal all year round, both at its breeding colonies and in its resting zones and roosts. The Neotropic Cormorant makes harsh grunts, which sound similar to those of a pig, and this has led to a series of very descriptive names for the bird in places. Other very distinctive sounds are the loud, guttural cries produced by the Bank Cormorant, when disturbed at the nest.

Food and Feeding

Fish is the main, and sometimes the only, component of a cormorant's diet. The prey eaten at each particular site can comprise a large number of species, but generally the birds' opportunism leads them to take mainly the most abundant and available small species, preferably slow-moving, benthic prey.

In addition to fish, many other aquatic animals can be consumed to a greater or lesser extent. Thus, they take inver-

This Neotropic Cormorant
is drying its wings using
the "Wing-spread"
posture. This posture is
highly characteristic of the
cormorants and the
darters, but, in contrast to
their close relatives,
cormorants do not seem
to use it for
thermoregulation. Several
other possible functions
have been suggested,
including intraspecific
signalling, for example
announcing successful
fishing, but there seems
to be little evidence of
this. In some Antarctic
and subantarctic species,
"Wing-spreading" has not
been recorded; this may
well be a response to the
extremely cold climate.

[Phalacrocorax olivaceus,
La Encrucijada, Mexico.
Photo: A. de Sostoa &
X. Ferrer]

tebrates, including crustaceans (crabs, shrimps, krill, crayfish, prawns, isopods, amphipods), cephalopods (squid, octopus) and other molluscs, polychaetes, nematodes and holothurians. On inland waters, they also consume amphibians, especially frogs and tadpoles, aquatic insects and sometimes water snakes and turtles. Exceptionally, the capture of small birds and mammals has been recorded.

The Heard Shag (*Phalacrocorax nivalis*) differs notably in its diet from the majority of the cormorants, and even from sibling species in nearby subantarctic waters. Although, like them, it bases its diet on benthic prey, nonetheless, invertebrates, particularly polychaetes, and to a lesser extent gastropods and octopods, predominate over fish in the Heard Shag's diet.

The diet can vary seasonally, depending on the availability of food in a particular area, or as a result of the birds' movements. In the majority of the species, the dominant prey are bottom-dwellers, which are caught in fairly shallow waters, whether these be marine or inland. The cormorants' opportunism often leads them to exploit mid-water prey, if these are easily obtained. For example, in some regions of the Canadian Atlantic coast, the Double-crested and Great Cormorants can feed off shoals of capelin (*Mallotus villosus*) and Atlantic herring (*Clupea harengus harengus*), which come to spawn near the coast.

A few species feed principally on active pelagic shoaling fish and can even be totally dependent on an abundance of such prey. Thus there is a close relation between the populations of Guanay Cormorant (*Phalacrocorax bougainvillii*) and the anchoveta (*Engraulis ringens*), and between the Cape Cormorant and the South African pilchard (*Sardinops ocellata*) and also the Cape anchovy (*Engraulis japonicus capensis*), all extremely abundant fish, which grow rapidly and breed frequently. These cormorants are very sensitive to changes in their food supply, and the scarcity of shoals of these fish, due to natural cycles or to overfishing by humans, has immediate repercussions on their populations and on those of other seabirds in these regions, including gannets, boobies and pelicans (see Status and Conservation).

The fish taken are usually small. For example, in the Great Lakes the Double-crested Cormorant mainly eats fish measuring 12-15 cm in length, in northern Norway the European Shag consumes sandeels (*Ammodytes*) measuring 5-14 cm and gadoids of 8-24 cm, and at the Prince Edward Islands the Crozet Shag eats fish up to 12 cm long. The pharyngeal section is, in fact, a limiting factor for the maximum size of prey that can be consumed. Nevertheless, on occasions very large prey are taken, and the Great Cormorant, for example, eats long, thin fish, such as eels up to 60 cm long, and bulky fish, such as a tench (*Tinca tinca*) 43 cm long, have exceptionally been recorded. There are even cases of cormorants which have choked to death, as a result of attempting to consume outsize prey.

The indigestible parts of prey, such as the bones and scales, are regurgitated in the form of pellets, at a rough rate of one per day, generally just before dawn and before leaving for the

A cormorant will often
capture and swallow a
fish that is longer and
wider than the diameter
of its own throat when in
its normal state; it is only
possible because the
walls of neck are highly
flexible. This Long-tailed
Cormorant is swallowing
a "squeaker", a species of
catfish, which, despite its
name, is of some
considerable size. Once
caught, a fish is always
manoeuvred into a
suitable position by
means of some deft
movements of the bill and
neck, so that it can be
swallowed head first to
prevent the scales and
any spines catching on
the throat and acting as a
brake or even causing
injury.

[Phalacrocorax africanus,
Chobe River, Botswana.
Photo: Richard Coomber/
Planet Earth]

The strong, hooked bill of the cormorants is a powerful but manageable weapon for catching fish and manipulating it before it is eaten, as illustrated by this Great Cormorant, which has just caught an eel (Anguilla anguilla), and is attempting to position it for swallowing. On occasions, a cormorant has been recorded taking a very large eel and forcing it into its crop, upon which the strong, slippery eel has managed to slither out again; this can lead to lengthy struggles between predator and prey.

[Phalacrocorax carbo sinensis. Photo: Gérard Lacz/ Marco Polo]

feeding grounds. Chicks start producing pellets around fledging time. Both adults and chicks may regurgitate food, if they are disturbed during the process of digestion.

Cormorants normally catch their prey by means of pursuit-diving. A bird dives from the surface, either slipping gently under the water with scarcely a ripple, or with a little leap forward. Prey is captured with the bill after active pursuit-diving, in which the bird propels itself along, using its totipalmate feet like oars. The prey is, however, not usually very fast-moving. After making a catch, the bird returns to the surface, especially if the prey is large, in order to manoeuvre it into a suitable position in the bill, by throwing it into the air to turn it round, if necessary, until it can be swallowed head first. With the exception of mid-water fish, catches are normally made when the bird is swimming around the benthos, and not during the descent or the return to the surface.

Neotropic Cormorants have also been recorded catching their prey by plunge-diving, both alone and in large, mobile groups. Unlike the rest of the family, they can plunge into the water obliquely, with the wings folded against the body, to pursue shoals of small surface fish. Even rarer are other types of behaviour, such as those observed in the European Shag, which can fish whilst standing in very shallow water, simply by upending, or in the Great Cormorant, which may steal food from gannets (Sula), or follow fishing boats which are throwing offal into the sea.

Fishing is normally carried out alone. However, in areas where food is abundant, flocks can form and these can even number thousands of birds. In such cases, many species, such as the Black-faced Cormorant (Phalacrocorax fuscescens), the Little Cormorant and several subantarctic shags, can perform truly co-operative fishing. This generally involves the birds being positioned close to each other in a fan-shape and advancing in a co-ordinated fashion, swimming and diving in unison, in order to gather together and shepherd the shoals of surface fish, whilst catching them at the same time. The stragglers at the back of the formation fly up to the front, to gain access to the fleeing fish, thus creating a rotating cycle of which birds are at the front. However, not always, nor in all species is communal fishing as organized as this, and gatherings can form over one particular shoal, where individuals act totally independently.

Prey can be detected from the air, either when the shoals of fish are conspicuous, or when their presence is given away by concentrations of other seabirds, which the cormorants can join in an opportunist manner. Such is the case of the Pelagic Cormorant on the coast of British Columbia, in western Canada, where seabirds form mixed-species feeding flocks, which feast on shoals of juvenile Pacific herring (Clupea harengus pallasii).

In coastal areas, cormorants usually feed inshore, although the breeding and roosting grounds are sometimes quite far from the foraging areas. In the European Shag, the maximum foraging range is normally 10-30 km. During breeding on the Isle of May, off eastern Scotland, the maximum is 17 km, although on average it is around 7, and feeding areas are always within 7 km of land and usually less than 2 km away from the colony.

They are very efficient in their fishing, so this occupies relatively little of their time. They generally feed at least once a day, though chicks tend to be fed more often. The duration of a foraging bout is short: in the Cape Cormorant, for example, it lasts half an hour or less; in the Bank Cormorant 30-60 mins; and also less than one hour in the Crozet Shag in the Prince Edward Islands. This short duration must be related to the fact that they are not adapted to roosting on the water, and in this way they avoid the risk of hypothermia, especially in cold waters.

Traditionally, these birds have been considered very voracious feeders, indeed their daily intake can constitute as much as one fifth of the bird's weight, or even more. For this reason, fishermen have often seen cormorants as competitors, and in some cases this has had serious effects on populations (see Status and Conservation).

Breeding

Cormorant colonies vary considerably in size, from a few pairs to hundreds of thousands of birds, for instance in the Guanay Cormorant. Colonies are very dense at times, and Guanay and Cape Cormorant colonies can have three nests per square metre. Both the size and the density of colonies are, to a certain extent, related to their distance from the foraging areas.

Several different species may breed together, or in the company of other seabirds, such as gannets, boobies, gulls, terns or penguins, and some, such as the Crowned Cormorant, even breed alongside fur seals. At inland colonies, cormorants frequently associate with other water birds, like herons, egrets, storks, ibises, spoonbills and darters.

Collective fishing is carried out by some species; it sometimes enables them to achieve high foraging success, for they can surround and attack large shoals of fish together. Pied Cormorants generally tend to be rather solitary, but near large marine colonies they sometimes gather in very dense concentrations, where they exploit large shoals of fish. In general, the species that fish near the surface tend to have white underparts which make them less visible from below, while the bottom feeders are normally the darker species.

[Phalacrocorax varius. Photo: Graeme Chapman/ Ardea]

The marine species breed on islands, rocky outcrops or rugged coasts, sometimes near the high tide line or the spray zone. In such areas, nests are almost always placed on the ground, though in a variety of situations, such as cliff ledges, grassy slopes, cliff tops, bare rocky platforms, or even on sand. Inland, they usually nest in trees, often emergent from or surrounded by water, or alternatively in bushes or reeds. The trees used for breeding may end up dying as a result of the droppings that accumulate underneath, and the birds must then move to others.

Some species, for example the Great Cormorant, are very adaptable in the location of their nests, whilst others have quite specific preferences. Nests are also built on human construc-

tions, such as jetties, or in south Africa on platforms specially designed for the purpose by the guano companies. In southern Africa, there are cases of Crowned, Cape and Great Cormorants breeding on wrecked ships and moored boats.

The breeding season is long, though it is much less spread out in high latitudes. In tropical species, birds can breed all year round, but there is always a pronounced peak. The Flightless Cormorant peaks between March and September, but it can breed twice in the same year; in general, however, there is only one brood annually in all species.

The male chooses a possible nest-site, which can be the one used in the previous year, and he generally displays from this spot, trying to attract a female, that he will later accept or reject. Many species perform "Wing-waving", which involves the repeated simultaneous lifting of the wing tips, with the primaries tucked in behind the secondaries. At the same time, with the bill pointing upwards and forwards to expose the brightly coloured skin of the throat, the head is lowered towards the back and raised again, in opposite time to the wings. In the species with a white display patch on the thigh, these wing movements alternately expose and cover the patch conspicuously.

Another very widespread display is "Gargling". A male throws his head back through a vertical arc, until the nape touches the rump. Meanwhile, he generally keeps his bill wide open and makes a special call.

Several species, such as the European Shag, have particularly bright colours in the lining of the mouth. The Flightless Cormorant's courtship has an aquatic phase, during which the male and female circle one another in a spiral, as they rise up in the water, fluttering their wings.

The displays end when one female lands beside the male and is accepted. The male then performs a "Greeting Display", which the pair later repeat during breeding, and he leaves the female guarding the nest-site, while he starts collecting nest material.

Normally the male brings the material and the female places it in the nest. This consists of plant matter and is cemented together with excreta. Inland, nests are mainly made of sticks and twigs, whilst in marine environments, they mostly consist of seaweed that is obtained by diving. Many other materials can be used, such as debris, feathers or bones, and there is often a lining of finer materials, like green grass or thin bits of seaweed.

The nest can be a simple depression in the sand or in gravel, as in the case of the Socotra Cormorant, or in guano. In the

During the breeding season, the bare skin of the face, the eye-ring, the gular pouch, the bill and the lining of the mouth can take on very bright colours, as is vividly demonstrated by this incubating Double-crested Cormorant, which is displaying a certain amount of apprehension as it adopts a defensive attitude. The family has a complex and varied series of visual displays, which have probably developed as a result of its gregarious tendencies, especially during breeding.

[Phalacrocorax auritus, USA. Photo: François Gohier/ Ardea]

Pelagic Cormorant, the nests, which are situated on narrow ledges, are made of grass, hay and seaweed, and are cemented together on their outer edges by droppings. The nests of the Imperial Shag, and other, closely related species of subantartic shags, are truncated cones of seaweed, held together by mud and excreta, and situated on flat ground. Nests can be sizeable, and in some species, because they are reused in successive years, they can become as much as 1 m deep; the Bank Cormorant's large nests of seaweed can weigh up to 6 kg. The Long-tailed Cormorant, on the other hand, usually builds nests only a few centimetres deep, and they regularly disintegrate, so a new nest must be built every year. Sometimes nests are made with unusual materials, as in the South Georgia Shag (*Phalacrocorax georgianus*), which sometimes builds nests exclusively from penguin's tail feathers, while some Flightless Cormorant nests contain a high proportion of sea urchin cases and starfish.

The duration of nest building varies, from about a week in the Long-tailed Cormorant and the Spotted Shag, to an average of five weeks in the European Shag and the Bank Cormorant, and at least two months in the Imperial Shag. The nest may be built quite a long time before the eggs are laid, but birds must take it in turns to guard the nest, as they must prevent other individuals, in search of building materials, from coming and taking it apart. In the Bank and Cape Cormorants, it has been calculated that around 20 hours are required for the birds to dive and gather all the material necessary for the construction of the nest.

Copulation takes place at the nest-site. Birds defend a small territory around the site, sometimes limited simply to the distance a bird can stretch out with its bill. If an intruder approaches the nest, this can trigger off threat displays, such as "Head-waving" with an open bill and an outstretched neck,

and the unwelcome bird may also be attacked and pecked. Fights occur mainly amongst males.

The clutch can be large, an unusual phenomenon amongst seabirds, and as many as six or seven eggs may be laid. However, the most common clutch size is of two to four eggs, very frequently three. Replacement laying occurs, if there is no shortage of food, and sometimes birds may even lay two more clutches.

The elongated eggs are pale green or blue, with a chalky surface, and are laid at intervals of 2-3 days. Incubation begins with the first egg, or in some species with the second, so the chicks hatch asynchronously. The parents take stints of equal length, incubating the eggs on the webs of their feet. New material is often added to the nest at the moment of changeover, and these additions can continue throughout breeding and right up to fledging.

After 23-35 days' incubation, the eggs hatch in the same order as they were laid in. The dark coloured, naked, helpless chicks can only raise and wave their heads. After a week, they are covered in black, brown or white woolly down.

Both parents brood, protect and feed their chicks. When very small, the chicks are brooded continuously, and later they are guarded until they can defend themselves. In hot weather they are shaded, in cold they are brooded. Adults may also bring moist seaweed to freshen up the nest.

The smallest chick has less possibilities of surviving, since it is at a clear disadvantage during feeds, and it usually dies in the first few days. It generally comes from a smaller egg, hatches later and is lighter, and in cases where it successfully reaches fledging, it also weighs less than the other nestlings. This phenomenon can actually affect more than one chick, and these chicks reinforce the brood only when the feeding conditions are good. In general, in successful broods, 1-3 chicks per nest are fledged.

This Antarctic Shag has just collected material with which to line its nest. Cormorants use three main types of nesting material: seaweed and algae torn from the bottom of the sea or found on the beach, washed up by the waves; bits of terrestrial plants, such as grass and sticks off bushes and trees; and diverse materials found on the beach or in neighbouring seabird colonies, especially feathers and bones. There are some curious cases, such as the South Georgia Shag, which sometimes builds its nest exclusively from penguins' tail feathers, whereas some Flightless Cormorant nests contain a high proportion of sea urchin "tests" and starfish.

[Phalacrocorax bransfieldensis. Photo: P.V. Tearle/ Planet Earth]

Where colonies are located on flat, open ground, the nest tends to be a truncated cone of seaweed and grass cemented together with excreta and mud. In places, cormorants breed in monospecific colonies, but they often form mixed colonies, and in coastal areas sometimes breed alongside gannets, boobies, gulls, terns, penguins and other cormorant species. In the background of the photo are some visiting Guanay Cormorants (Phalacrocorax bougainvillii), which have been attracted to this Imperial Shag colony.

[Phalacrocorax atriceps. Photo: Jen & Des Bartlett/ Bruce Coleman]

The chicks beg for food by raising their heads and calling with the bill closed. The very small ones receive regurgitated liquid food, which flows along the lower part of the adult's bill, and drips from the tip. Older chicks insert the head deep into the adult's throat in order to get at the food. In some species, such as the Double-crested, Long-tailed and Great Cormorants, chicks may receive water on hot days, and they beg for it silently, by lifting and waving their wide open bills.

The chicks grow rapidly. When Long-tailed Cormorant chicks are four weeks old, they can leave a tree nest and come back to it again without any difficulties, and when 35 days old, they are already able to fly. Nevertheless, most species fledge at around 50 days, and some do not fledge until they are 80 days old.

Fledglings often leave their nest-sites and concentrate in crèches, particularly in those species that breed in areas that are flat or have a gentle slope. In several species, fledglings return to the nest to be fed, but in others they are fed in their crèches. The latter is the case of the Red-legged Cormorant, for example, where it may be due to the difficulties involved in chicks returning to the narrow ledges where their nests are situated. In Brandt's Cormorant, crèches are very soon formed at the nesting grounds, even before the parents' continuous attendance is over, and three stages of crèching behaviour have been described: chicks in adjacent nests start to form groups after they are 10 days old; the medium-sized chicks then form larger groups; and, finally, chicks over 25 days old form crèches, which are maintained day and night, and from which the chicks periodically go into the sea, where they swim and dive.

The fledglings continue begging for food, and although the adults tend to lose interest in their chicks, they can continue feeding them for two or three months, or even for four, for example in the Long-tailed and Flightless Cormorants. In the latter species, towards the end only the male feeds the young birds, so that the female can breed again sooner and more often than the male.

The mortality rate is usually low, except in the first year. Adult plumage is acquired between the first and fourth years of the bird's life, depending on the species. A bird does not normally attempt breeding for the first time until its third or fourth year, but in some species, to a greater or lesser degree, it already occurs in the bird's second year. In the Flightless Cormorant, females have bred when only 17 months old, and most do so in their second year. In fact, in several species there is a clear tendency for females to begin breeding at an earlier age than males.

Cormorants are generally monogamous, but the pair-bond is not as strong as in many other waterbirds, and individuals often change partners from one year to another, for instance in the South Orkney Islands, 77% of South Georgia Shags change partner. Elsewhere 91% of Brandt's Cormorants change partners, and females are not particularly faithful to their nest-sites; the considerable lapse of time between the return of the male

Cliff nests normally require a larger mass of plant matter and a more complex structure than those built directly on the ground, and this Spotted Shag has certainly collected a considerable quantity of grass. This species habitually nests on cliff ledges and often collects nesting material from adjacent headlands. The nest is a carefully interwoven circular structure with a fairly deep depression in the centre.

[Phalacrocorax punctatus, New Zealand. Photo: Erwin & Peggy Bauer/Bruce Coleman]

and that of the female to the breeding grounds at the start of the season favours a change of partner. Polygamy is also recorded, and in the Farne Islands, off eastern England, where there are few suitable sites for nesting, in 3-5% of the nests of European Shags, many eggs are broken due to squabbles between the two females that occupy the same nest.

Movements

The great majority of the Phalacrocoracidae are sedentary or dispersive. After breeding, there is frequently a large-scale dispersal in no particular direction, which invariably affects juveniles more than adults. In the Bank Cormorant, for example, adults are markedly sedentary, but young birds can move several hundreds of kilometres away from their origins.

In high latitudes, particularly in the Northern Hemisphere, there is a tendency towards migration, to a greater or lesser extent. However, island species are totally sedentary. Several subantarctic species and also the Flightless Cormorant, have never been reported outwith the immediate surroundings of their respective island or archipelago. The Antarctic and South Georgia Shags sometimes perform local movements, driven by the necessity to find ample stretches of ice-free water. In winter, the Neotropic Cormorant, which is conspicuously sedentary in almost all of its range, leaves its most extreme localities in the Andes, where harsh conditions prevail. The Pelagic Cormorant is also basically sedentary and dispersive, but its northernmost populations, from north-east Siberia and north-west Alaska, move southwards in winter and do not start to return to these regions until the middle of May.

Great and Double-crested Cormorants can be either migratory or dispersive, depending on the case, and the former is even nomadic in some situations. The degree of migratory tendencies is very variable amongst the different subspecies and populations. Sometimes migratory contingents go to winter in areas occupied by sedentary populations, which may be members of the same subspecies. However, some populations do not migrate at all, for example the races *maroccanus* and *lucidus* of the Great Cormorant and most of the Double-crested Cormorant's race *floridanus* are only dispersive. The most migratory subspecies of the Great Cormorant is *sinensis*, although this too varies from place to place and with the harshness of

the winter; for example, the populations of the northern Caspian and the Baltic Seas are highly migratory. The same race can migrate overland, and a large number of birds reach the region of the Mediterranean, wintering also in northern Africa on the coast or inland. The nominate race *carbo* disperses widely, chiefly along the coasts or throughout its region of origin, although in the northern parts of North America it is more migratory, and moves southwards, reaching New Jersey and even Florida. In the Double-crested Cormorant the most migratory subspecies is the nominate *auritus*, which carries out extensive movements, both on the coast and inland, to its wintering grounds in Florida and the Gulf of Mexico. An exceptional case was that of an immature Double-crested Cormorant in 1989, which remained on a small pond in north-east England from early January to the end of April.

In inland areas movements can be carried out in response to severe droughts or alternatively to periodic flooding, which can encourage the temporary establishment, and even opportunistic breeding, of cormorants. Thus, large movements of populations occur in the Long-tailed Cormorant of Africa, and in the Little Pied, Pied and Great Cormorants in Australia, as a result of the inconstant nature of many water bodies in these continents.

A special case of large-scale dispersal occurs in the Guanay Cormorant, in the years when it is severely affected by El Niño and there is a dramatic crash in the populations of the prey species (see Status and Conservation). Faced with the lack of food, they wander up and down the coasts north and south of their breeding grounds in Peru and Chile, leaving the area of the cold Humboldt Current and roaming as far afield as Panama and the south of Chile, and also appearing inland.

Relationship with Man

The use of cormorants for fishing was formerly very widespread in the Old World, and in Britain it was even practised by members of the royal court in the seventeenth century. The custom is very ancient and dates back to the end of the fourth century BC in China, where it still goes on today. In Japan too, this type of fishing still occurs using Japanese and Great Cormorants, but it has now become a tourist attraction, which is subsidized by the Imperial Household because of its cultural

The Guanay Cormorant
was once the centre of a
great industry. Its vast
populations, along with
those of the Peruvian
Booby (Sula variegata)
and the Peruvian (Brown)
Pelican (Pelecanus
occidentalis thagus),
produced huge quantities
of guano, a natural
fertilizer, very rich in
nitrates and phosphates.
Guano is the end product
of the accumulation of
detritus produced by a
breeding colony, including
excrements, dead
animals, remains of prey
and of nests, feathers
and so on. Guano-mining
was at times intensive,
with the exploitation of
deposits that were almost
2000 years old, and in
places reputedly up to 90
metres thick.

[Phalacrocorax
bougainvillii.
Photo: Hans D. Dossenbach/
Ardea]

value. Exhibitions are performed at sunset, from a boat with a metal basket hanging from its prow. This basket contains burning wood, which produces light to attract the fish. Several cormorants are thrown into the water, although they are still controlled from the boat by a rein attached to a leather collar around each bird's neck, and, as fish are caught, they are taken back to the boat. The collar prevents the birds from swallowing the fish, which can thus be gathered by the fishermen, but after several catches the ring is removed to allow the birds to eat. Some specially trained birds can even fish like this without requiring the use of a collar.

The enormous breeding concentrations of some cormorants, sulids and pelicans on the western coasts of South America and South Africa have led to the accumulation of deep deposits of guano, some of which are more than 2000 years old. These deposits mainly form in desert areas, where there is hardly any rain, and where the nitrates are neither dissolved nor reduced. Because this guano is rich in nitrates and phosphates, it is of great value to man as a fertilizer. Before the Europeans arrived in America, the Incas used the guano islands for their fertility rites, indeed the word "guano" is of Quechua origin and means "excrement". The Spanish were only interested in the birds' eggs, which they used for mortar in their buildings, and it was not until the middle of the eighteenth century that the industrial exploitation of guano began. The first guano exported from Peru arrived in England in 1840, and its use rapidly spread all over the world. The high demand led exploitation to be extended to deposits in other countries, although the only other site of real importance was in south-west Africa. In the period 1848-1875 more than 20 million tons were shipped from Peru, mainly to Europe and North America. The quantities of money generated by the guano trade were phenomenal and led to the greatest producer, the Guanay Cormorant, being named "the most valuable bird in the world" or "the billion dollar bird". However, the Cape Cormorant, the Cape Gannet (Sula capensis), the Peruvian Booby (Sula variegata), the Peruvian (Brown) Pelican (Pelecanus occidentalis thagus), and to a lesser extent other cormorants, also played important roles as guano producers. In Peru, for over a century, it constituted the main source of the national income, but the constant, uncontrolled exploitation ended up depleting the reserves. In the Chincha Islands, where the greatest concentrations of "guano birds" were to be found, the vast deposits were totally exhausted, and at the end of the century this was the prevalent situation everywhere. At the same time, the continuous extraction of guano all year round, causing breeding failure amongst the seabirds, the destruction of the breeding habitat and the use of the eggs, chicks and adults to feed the workers, brought about a great decrease in the seabird populations and consequently in their annual guano production.

The paralysis of the extractions led to the revision of the systems used, so that excesses were curtailed. In 1909, the State Guano Company was created in Peru, with the aim of promoting the rational exploitation of the guano. Several measures in Peru and other guano areas led to the breeding colonies being protected and maintained: guards were stationed to prevent people entering the breeding colonies, and also to shoot at predators, such as condors; walls were put up to isolate the colonies from intruders and terrestrial predators; and the extent of available breeding surfaces was increased. These measures allowed extraction to continue, albeit at a limited level, much lower than in the nineteenth century, at the same time as it permitted the guano bird populations to recover. Nowadays guano is only collected during a short spell every one or two years, outside the breeding season, and this may even help the birds by reducing the vast numbers of ticks that infest them.

The history of the Peruvian guano industry is also a terrible example of the exploitation of human beings. On the Chincha Islands convicts were used at first for collecting the guano. However, because there were not enough of them to maintain a sufficiently quick extraction rate, it was decided to force thousands of Kanakas Indians to work as slaves on the islands. Due to the harshness of the work and the inhuman living conditions, especially in terms of hygiene and food, the Indians began to die in large numbers, until the mining ended up being done by paid workers. The effects on Peruvian society have been far-reaching. The first railway arrived in 1868 to transport the guano and link Lima with the rest of the country. As slavery was abolished, a large number of Chinese immigrants arrived to work in the guano extraction, and their descendants now represent a significant ethnic group.

The collection of eggs and the killing both of young and adults for human consumption has been practised extensively and still persists today, chiefly in the least developed regions. This consumption was already traditionally carried out by many primitive peoples, and sometimes assumed considerable importance. Thus, for some Indian tribes in British Columbia cormorants and other seabirds constituted 5-10% of their diet.

In America, the arrival on many islands and in coastal areas of a large number of new inhabitants, including seal hunters, guano miners, and so on, caused a far greater impact on the cormorant populations than that generated by the native peoples, with their traditional way of life. In the more industrialized countries the consumption of eggs and birds has also been very widespread, especially amongst fishermen, seafarers and people living on the coast. It might be added that cormorant flesh has a very strong taste, and to improve it the birds were usually hung or buried for some time before they were eaten.

Yet another use to which cormorants were put is derived from the medicinal values which have been attributed to the birds in many regions, and which continue to cause their exploitation in places such as China. In Argentina, it was believed that a good remedy for asthma was to open up a Neotropic Cormorant and spread it over the sufferer's chest. Other uses were probably rather more appropriate, including the eskimos' use of Pelagic Cormorant skins to make clothes.

One curious explanation for cormorants' wing-spreading behaviour comes from a legend of the Ona Indians, of Tierra del Fuego. According to the tale, a long time ago there was a violent fight between the Neotropic Cormorant and the Crested Caracara (*Polyborus plancus*), which were men in those days. In this struggle, both turned into birds and since that day the Neotropic Cormorant has suffered from a stiff back. Today it still hurts, and because of this, birds often open their wings, as if they were about to fly but unable to make up their minds about it.

The name "cormorant", of Latin origin, came into the English language by way of a French dialect. Because of their black plumage and their habitual presence on coasts, in Latin these birds were called *corvus marinus*, meaning "sea crow", a term still used to describe them today in several languages. The generic name *Phalacrocorax* is also very descriptive, this time of Greek origin, and meaning "bald raven", with reference to the bare facial skin.

Status and Conservation

The fate of the Spectacled Cormorant (*Phalacrocorax perspicillatus*) should serve as a warning to all. This large, not very mobile species was endemic to the Commander Islands of the Bering Sea, in the North Pacific, and it died out around 1850, little more than a century after its discovery by Steller in 1741, and less than 40 years after its scientific description by Pallas in 1811. The direct cause of this rapid disappearance was the widespread collection of the birds for human consumption, mainly by the sailors and workers who had settled on these islands.

Many living species of cormorant have very restricted ranges and small populations, in some cases of only a few hundred birds, but many of these populations are probably low by nature. Nonetheless, their scarcity makes them very vulnerable, despite the fact that generally they are not under any particular threat, nor apparently in regression. A good example of this is the Flightless Cormorant, which is classified as Rare, but is apparently more or less stable, and while its numbers fluctuate due to the periodic impact of El Niño, it has demonstrated a great capacity for recovery. After the 1982-83 occurrence of El Niño, the population was halved, but by the end of 1985 numbers had returned to normal, and there were an estimated total of 900-1200 birds.

Comparable low numbers, of under a thousand pairs, can be found in some of the southern island species, such as the Chatham Shag (*Phalacrocorax onslowi*), the Macquarie Shag, the Pitt Shag and the Heard Shag. The population of the Rough-faced Shag (*Phalacrocorax carunculatus*) consists of under 300 birds, and, while numbers were probably always low, it seems likely that many birds were killed by early ornithological collectors, and by hunting for the fashion trade, as well as illegally in recent years by fishermen; it is currently classified as Rare. Other populations which are only very slightly more numerous include the Auckland Shag (*Phalacrocorax colensoi*), the Stewart Shag, the Crozet Shag and the Bounty Shag.

Amongst the species with more numerous populations, those with continental populations have suffered considerable drops in numbers parallel to the destruction of their habitats, caused chiefly by the drying out of wetlands. Along with direct persecution by man, this is the main cause of the pronounced regression which has led to the Pygmy Cormorant being classified as threatened. It should be noted, however, that the increasing number of reservoirs has generally had the opposite effect for the most adaptable species, and has favoured their spread in inland areas. Thus, in 1986, 73% of the Double-crested Cormorant colonies in Wyoming, in the USA, were on reservoirs.

Abundant cormorant populations in Europe and North America were reduced during the nineteenth and part of the twentieth centuries by severe persecution, including the destruction of eggs, trapping, and so on, based on accusations that the birds' feeding had serious effects on fishing concerns. Nevertheless, several species have shown great powers of recovery, once the relevant negative factors disappear. After the birds were protected and DDT was banned, the Double-crested Cormorant has undergone a spectacular rise in numbers in North America, especially since the beginning of the 1970's. For example, in Massachusetts, after 1974 its population doubled every three or four years, and in Nova Scotia, the nesting population almost tripled between 1971 and 1982, by which time there were more than 12,100 breeding pairs. The Great Cormorant has shown varying tendencies, depending on the region, within its enormous range. In the second half of the present century, however, its numbers have increased considerably, basically in northern Europe, as human persecution has decreased. In Norway, a peak of 21,000 breeding pairs was reached between 1983 and 1986, but the population later dropped in some areas, partially due to the collapse in the stock of capelin (*Mallotus villosus*).

Once again, the issue has been raised as to whether or not the populations of some species of cormorants should be re-

The Rough-faced Shag is endemic to the Cook Strait area in New Zealand, breeding in only five colonies, all of which are in the Malborough Sounds, in the north-east of South Island. Its restriction to this area is such that, as yet, no sighting has been made even around nearby parts of North Island. The population of this species, calculated at less than 300 birds, is the least numerous in the whole family. It may always have been small, but early collecting by ornithologists, hunting for feathers, and more recently illegal shooting by fishermen, have probably had some effects on numbers.

[*Phalacrocorax carunculatus*, Cook Strait, New Zealand. Photo: M.F. Soper/NHPA]

duced, mainly due to their conflict with the growing fish farm industry. In 1989, the government of Quebec, in eastern Canada, approved a plan to kill 10,000 Double-crested Cormorants over several years and to destroy a large number of eggs on the islands in the St Lawrence River, in this case because of the damage the cormorants cause to the vegetation, and possible threats to other waterbirds.

Fishermen have traditionally had a strong antipathy towards cormorants and have seen them as insatiable, highly destructive competitors. However, this opinion is based on partial observations or on the impressive appearance that some of the

enormous breeding colonies can give, and it has always been man himself, who has depleted immense stocks of anchovies and pilchards, for example, to the point that their exploitation ceases to be economically viable. Tens of thousands of seabirds, on the other hand, fed off these same stocks without upsetting the natural balance, and their populations adjusted according to the abundance of prey.

Research into cormorants' feeding habits indicates that, except in very special cases, such as the guano cormorants, economically important fish form a very small part of the diet, and that the birds' impact on populations of commercial species is therefore minimal. The adults of these fish species are usually too large to appeal to them, and neither the young fish, nor the prey of the commercial fish themselves are consumed in excess. However, in some circumstances considerable damage can be caused, mainly in certain unnatural conditions, such as fish farms, hatcheries or pound nets, where there are dense concentrations of captive, easily caught fish. Even so, the production of fish farms is generally affected more by factors like fish diseases, or even the depletion of the oxygen content of the water, than by predation by cormorants, and diverse procedures, variable according to the situation, have been proposed to minimize these effects. One of these is the creation of buffer populations of crustaceans, in order to divert the cormorants' interest in the fish towards them.

Most species of cormorants are quite liable to become trapped accidentally in fishing-nets. The importance of the numbers of birds killed in this way is hard to evaluate, but in any case it is a difficult problem to avoid, since it involves a further clash with fishing interests.

Human disturbance can also cause great losses of chicks and eggs in colonies, when they are accidentally trampled on by alarmed adults, or taken by opportunist predators, such as gulls and other seabirds. These problems are on the increase in many areas, due to growing tourist developments and the proliferation of pleasure boats.

Domestic or feral animals occasionally pose a serious threat to these species, which are often ground-nesters. In this respect, on Isabela Island, in the Galapagos, feral dogs have been controlled, but there is always the possibility that a future expansion might lead them to spread to areas used for nesting by the very vulnerable Flightless Cormorant.

Like all diving seabirds, cormorants are highly sensitive to oil spills, whether they be the result of tanker disasters, leaks

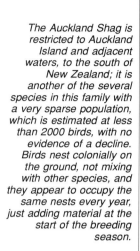

The Auckland Shag is restricted to Auckland Island and adjacent waters, to the south of New Zealand; it is another of the several species in this family with a very sparse population, which is estimated at less than 2000 birds, with no evidence of a decline. Birds nest colonially on the ground, not mixing with other species, and they appear to occupy the same nests every year, just adding material at the start of the breeding season.

[*Phalacrocorax colensoi*, Auckland Island, New Zealand. Photo: Francisco Erize/ Bruce Coleman]

from oil platforms, or other causes. As well as poisoning the birds, oiling renders them immobile and destroys the water-proofing of the feathers. Such incidents are relatively common in coastal areas, and usually result in mortality on a massive scale. In the Persian Gulf, which is already badly affected due to the presence of large numbers of oil tankers, several large oil slicks have occurred as a result of armed conflicts in the region. The most serious spills to date, at the beginning of 1991, affected more than 25,000 birds, including Great Cormorants and the endemic Socotra Cormorant, although not as seriously as was at first feared. In southern Alaska, the immense spill of the Exxon Valdez in March 1989 was probably responsible for the deaths of 100,000-300,000 marine birds, including significant numbers of Pelagic Cormorants.

Poisoning by pesticides or heavy metals has also affected this family. In the USA, the accumulation of DDT and other pollutants was a major factor in the decline of the Double-crested Cormorant in the period 1950-1970. During these same years, in Overijsseln, in the Netherlands, high concentrations of mercury residues and PCB's may have been partly responsible for a decline of the Great Cormorant and the delay in its subsequent recovery.

The enormous populations of the Peruvian "guano birds", the Guanay Cormorant, the Peruvian Booby and the Peruvian (Brown) Pelican (see Relationship with Man), are based on a profusion of shoaling pelagic fish in the cool waters of the Humboldt Current. The prevailing trade winds carry surface water away from the land and create an area of coastal upwelling, where the thermocline is raised, and cold, nutrient-rich water is brought up to the surface. The arrival of the nutrients in the euphotic zone, where there is sufficient light for growth, favours primary production on a massive scale, and this is the basis of the prodigious productivity all the way up the food chain.

However, periodically there is an anomaly in the behaviour of the marine currents, with an influx of warm water probably from the north, and, as the thermocline sinks, taking the nutrients further down with it, productivity slumps, even though the upwelling itself does not actually cease. This phenomenon, known as El Niño, "the child", as it tends to take place around Christmas, occurs in irregular cycles roughly every five years, and in severe years the guano birds' breeding fails totally and their populations can be decimated. Thus their numbers dropped from around 28 million birds in 1955, to only 6 million after the intense Niño of 1957/58, and from 5·75 million to about 2 million after that of 1982/83. The effects of this phenomenon are extremely far-reaching, and may even be related to the failure of monsoons in India; rather surprisingly, one of the first reports of consequences of the 1982/83 Niño came from the central Pacific, where thousands of boobies and frigatebirds abandoned their nests, due to a failure in the food supply.

The large seabird populations off south-west Africa are similarly supported by upwelling. However, in contrast with the situation off Peru, the massive mortality experienced by Cape Cormorants in 1985 coincided with the arrival of abnormally cold waters. Other cormorants with smaller populations, such as Brandt's Cormorant, in the area affected by the California Current, also reflect these considerable oscillations in production. The subsequent recovery of all such devastated populations is based on prolific breeding in the ensuing years.

Cormorant populations can be seriously upset by man's overfishing, although most species are not affected, as they take fish of no commercial value. However, the same "guano cormorants" have suffered greatly, because their main prey are the same fish that have been at the core of thriving industries. In Peru, for example, the anchoveta, the Guanay Cormorant's main prey, became the base for the world's largest fishery in the 1960's. After the occurrence of El Niño in 1971, combined with overfishing, there was a collapse in the anchoveta stock, and with it came an enormous reduction in the guano bird populations, especially that of the Guanay Cormorant. Even after the banning of its commercial fishing, the anchoveta has never recovered, and the subsequent switch, first by the guano birds, and later by the fisheries, to the sardina (*Sardinops sagax*) could easily lead to further overfishing for the fishmeal industry; one proposal is to abandon this production of fishmeal, which is mostly used as food for chickens and mink, and in cosmetics. In South Africa, similar situations have occurred with the overfishing of the South African pilchard and the Cape anchovy, which in its turn has reduced the populations of the Cape Cormorant and the Cape Gannet.

General Bibliography

Barlow & Bock (1984), von Boetticher (1937), Butler & Jones (1982), Cooper (1986a), Cracraft (1985), Croxall (1987, 1991), Croxall *et al.* (1984), Dorst & Mougin (1979), Drummond (1987), Harrison (1985, 1987), Malacalza (1991), Nelson (1980), Rijke (1968), Sibley & Monroe (1990), Siegel-Causey (1988, 1989a, 1990), Siegfried, Williams *et al.* (1975), van Tets (1965a, 1976, 1985a).

PLATE 22

inches 14
cm 35

ssp *auritus*

1

ssp *cincinatus*

2

3

ssp *carbo*

ssp *sinensis*

4

ssp *maroccanus*

4

ssp *lucidus*

5

6

7

8

9

10

11

12

13

14

15

16

17

Genus *PHALACROCORAX* Brisson, 1760

1. Double-crested Cormorant

Phalacrocorax auritus

French: Cormoran à aigrettes **German**: Ohrenscharbe **Spanish**: Cormorán Orejudo
Other common names: White-crested Cormorant

Taxonomy. *Carbo auritus* Lesson, 1831, New Zealand; error, North America.
Sometimes placed in genus *Hypoleucos*. Four subspecies recognized.
Subspecies and Distribution.
P. a. cincinatus (Brandt, 1837) - Aleutian Is to Alexander Archipelago (W Canada).
P. a. albociliatus Ridgway, 1884 - Vancouver I to Gulf of California.
P. a. auritus (Lesson, 1831) - Gulf of St Lawrence to Cape Cod and W to Utah.
P. a. floridanus (Audubon, 1835) - North Carolina and Florida S to Cuba.

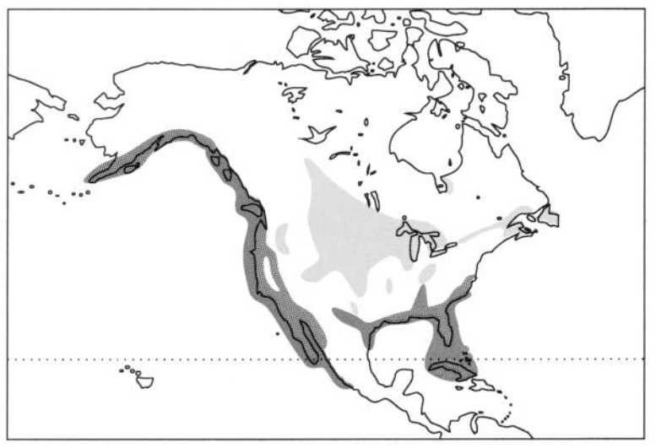

Descriptive notes. 76-91 cm; 1670-2100+ g; wingspan 137 cm. Orange facial skin; crest fairly inconspicuous. Male averages larger. Non-breeding adult duller, lacks crest. Juvenile light brownish, lightest on breast and foreneck. Races separated on general tone of coloration, amount of white in crest and small size differences.
Habitat. Occurs equally along coast or inland: affects sheltered marine waters, including estuaries, bays and mangrove swamps, and also rocky coasts and coastal islands, rarely far from coast; inland on lakes, rivers, swamps, reservoirs and ponds. Breeds on cliffs, reefs and islands, both marine and inland, on lakes and rivers; also slopes, rocky outcrops, abandoned wharves, wrecked ships; often nests on trees (live or dead) near or over water.
Food and Feeding. Almost exclusively fish, with a few crustaceans. At several sites along Pacific coast takes mainly schooling fish high over flat bottoms; along N Atlantic coasts mainly bottom-associated non-schooling fish, e.g. sandeels (*Ammodytes*), flatfish, gunnels (*Pholis*) and cunners (*Tautogolabrus adspersus*), but also some schooling fish, e.g. Atlantic herring (*Clupea harengus harengus*) and capelin (*Mallotus villosus*). Inland, prey species vary locally and regionally, but commercial species rarely important: on L Winnipegosis, Manitoba, hite sucker (*Catastomus commersoni*), yellow perch (*Perca flavescens*) and tullibee (*Coregonus artedii*); on L Superior, mainly small shallow-foraging species e.g. sculpins (*Cottus*), ninespine sticklebacks (*Pungitius pungitius*) and burbots (*Lota lota*); and at Pyramid L, Nevada, tui chub (*Gila bicolor*). Feeds mainly by pursuit-diving. Often fishes co-operatively, sometimes thousands of birds together. Can feed extensively at fish farms, e.g. taking catfishes at Mississippi Delta.
Breeding. Laying mainly Apr-Jul. Forms colonies, sometimes of thousands of pairs; sometimes in mixed colonies with other cormorant species, gulls, auks, herons, ducks. Nests on trees or on ground; nest of sticks and seaweed, lined with finer material; nests often reused. Usually 3-4 eggs (2-7); incubation c. 25-29 days; chicks naked, grow black down; fledging c. 42 days, independence c. 70 days. Average of 1·4-2·4 (occasionally 4·0) chicks fledged per nest; early and fringe nesters, probably younger birds, have lower success. Sexual maturity generally at 3 years old.
Movements. Northern and inland populations migratory, although N Pacific birds only slightly so: race *auritus* performs spectacular migrations along coast or inland, following river valleys, and winters in Gulf of Mexico and Florida; *cincinatus* winters along coast of British Columbia; *albociliatus* moves from upland areas of interior to lowlands or Pacific coast. Race *floridanus* fairly sedentary.
Status and Conservation. Not globally threatened. Severely affected in past by intense persecution and high levels of DDE and other pollutants, leading to population crash. Legal protection of species and banning of DDT led to spectacular recovery throughout range: at Great Lakes a few hundred nests in 1960's and early 1970's, but 1403 nests at 27 colonies in 1980, and 13,616 nests at 66 colonies in 1987; 4772 pairs in Manitoba (Canada) in 1969 increased to 22,681 pairs in 1979; similar figures elsewhere. Construction of reservoirs has permitted expansion to several inland areas. Largest Pacific colony at San Martín I (Baja California) formerly held up to 1,800,000 birds, but now almost totally abandoned, probably due to human disturbance and presence of domestic animals; disturbance caused by pleasure boaters probably responsible for decline of colony in Rose Islets (British Columbia) from 111 pairs in 1977 to 2 pairs in 1987. Campaign to control numbers initiated experimentally in Quebec at end of 1970's; if such campaigns stepped up, could lead to renewed decline.
Bibliography. Ainley (1984b), Ainley *et al.* (1981), Brechtel (1983), Carroll (1988), Casler (1973), Clapp *et al.* (1982), Craven & Lev (1987), Croxall (1991), Croxall *et al.* (1984), Desgranges (1982), Desgranges & Reed (1981), Desgranges *et al.* (1984), Dunn (1975), Durham (1955), Ellison & Cleary (1978), Findholt (1988), Gress *et al.* (1973), Hatch (1984), Hennemann (1984), Hobson *et al.* (1989), King *et al.* (1987), Kury & Gochfeld (1975), Kushlan & McEwan (1982), Leger & McNeil (1985, 1987a, 1987b), Lewis (1929), Lock & Ross (1973), Ludwig (1984), Matteson (1983), McNeil & Léger (1987), Mendall (1936), Milton & Austin-Smith (1983), Owre (1967), Palmer (1962), Pilon (1981), Pilon *et al.* (1983a, 1983b), Postupalsky (1978), Post (1988), Post & Seals (1991), Price & Weseloh (1986), Rijke *et al.* (1989), Robertson (1971, 1974), Ross (1973), Scharf & Shugart (1981), Siegel-Causey (1981), Siegel-Causey & Hunt (1986), Terres (1980), van Tets (1956), Vermeer & Rankin (1984b), Vermeer *et al.* (1989), Voous (1983), Watson *et al.* (1991), Weseloh & Struger (1985), Weseloh *et al.* (1983).

2. Neotropic Cormorant

Phalacrocorax olivaceus

French: Cormoran vigua **German**: Olivenscharbe **Spanish**: Cormorán Biguá
Other common names: Olivaceous/Bigua/Brazilian Cormorant; Mexican Cormorant (*mexicanus*)

Taxonomy. *Pelecanus olivaceus* Humboldt, 1805, banks of the Magdalena River, lat. 8° 55' N, Colombia.
Original name for species *P. brasilianus* recently revived, but acceptance and usage of *olivaceus* widespread, and former may be best considered "forgotten name". Sometimes placed in genus *Hypoleucos*. Two subspecies normally recognized.
Subspecies and Distribution.
P. o. mexicanus (Brandt, 1837) - NW Mexico and C America, S USA, Bahamas and Cuba.
P. o. olivaceus (Humboldt, 1805) - Panama to Cape Horn.

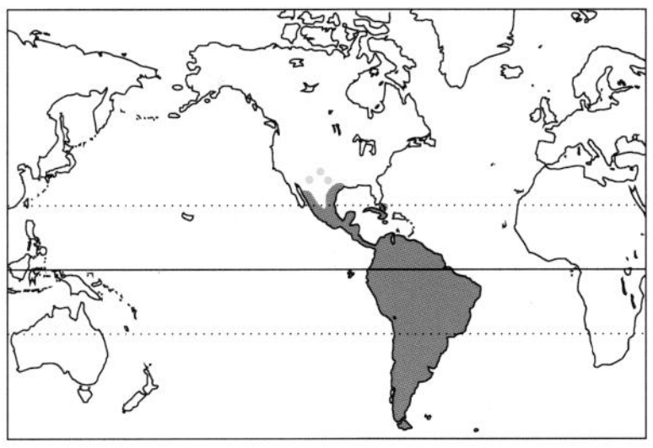

Descriptive notes. 58-73 cm; c. 1814 g; wingspan 101 cm. Characteristic white area around base of bill and gular pouch. Non-breeding adult duller, lacks tuft and scattered filoplumes on head and neck. Juvenile dusky brownish, paler below, especially on foreneck and breast. Races separated on slight differences in plumage and measurements.
Habitat. Wide variety of wetlands, in fresh, brackish or salt water. Sheltered parts of coast, including bays, inlets and estuaries; also lagoons, rocky coasts and islands, never far from land. Inland, occupies rivers, usually broad and slow-flowing, but also mountain streams; lakes, pools, marshes and swamps; common on Andean lakes up to 4000 m, occasionally up to 5000 m. Quick to colonize reservoirs and temporary wetlands in large numbers. Breeds on sea cliffs or rocky outcrops; also nests in trees (live or dead) or bushes.
Food and Feeding. Small fish, crustaceans, frogs, tadpoles and aquatic insects. In Argentina, takes large amounts of fish, especially *Aristromenidia bonariensis*, *Astyanax* and *Pilomedus*. On R Paraná (Argentina) takes fish mainly of 5-10 cm (2-30). Feeds mainly by pursuit-diving; only cormorant recorded plunge-diving, which is performed at sea, bird diving into surface shoals of small fish. Often fishes co-operatively, even on fast-flowing rivers.
Breeding. All year round, peak varying locally, sometimes coinciding with wettest months; May-Aug in USA. Colonial, sometimes in colonies of thousands of pairs; often in company of herons, egrets, spoonbills, darters or gulls. Nests in trees or bushes or on rocky ground; stick nest lined with grass or seaweed. Normally 3-4 eggs (2-6); incubation c. 30 days; chicks naked, grow blackish down. Average of 1·7 eggs hatch per nest; on occasions up to 3 chicks per nest may fledge.
Movements. Sedentary throughout most of breeding range, with some post-breeding dispersal. High altitude populations thought to move to lowlands in winter. Straggler to C and W USA.
Status and Conservation. Not globally threatened. Widespread and numerous. Common to abundant in Brazil, with many colonies of over 1000 pairs, especially in region of Pantanal; equally common in Argentina and Chile, where partial censuses in Jul 1990 yielded 2263 and 1901 birds respectively; 40,000 counted along stretch of R Paraguay (Paraguay) in Jan 1984; also common in Uruguay, but seems to have declined during 1980's. Apparently on increase in USA, where 4700 pairs at start of 1980's. In many areas construction of new reservoirs has increased amount of suitable habitat available. Suffers some persecution by fishermen off coast of Brazil.
Bibliography. Ainley (1984b), Bahamonde (1955), Belton (1984), Beltzer (1983), Blake (1977), Bó (1956), Browning (1989), Carp (1991), Clapp *et al.* (1982), Croxall (1991), Croxall *et al.* (1984), Fjeldså & Krabbe (1990), Hellmayr & Conover (1948), Hilty & Brown (1986), Humphrey *et al.* (1970), Johnson (1965), Lévêque (1964), Monroe (1968), Morrison (1977), Morrison & Slack (1977a, 1977b), Morrison, Hale & Slack (1983), Morrison, Shanley & Slack (1977, 1979), Morrison, Slack & Shanley (1978a, 1978b), Murphy (1936), Nelson (1903), Nores & Yzurieta (1980), Palmer (1962), de la Peña (1986), Pinto (1964), Ridgely & Gwynne (1989), Ruschi (1979), Scott & Carbonell (1986), de Schauensee & Phelps (1978), Sick (1984), Slud (1964), Skewes (1978), Stiles & Skutch (1989), Terres (1980), Voous (1983), Wetmore (1965).

3. Little Black Cormorant

Phalacrocorax sulcirostris

French: Cormoran noir **German**: Schwarzscharbe **Spanish**: Cormorán Totinegro
Other common names: Little Black Shag

Taxonomy. *Carbo sulcirostris* Brandt, 1837, New South Wales.
Sometimes placed in genus *Hypoleucos*. Division into two or three subspecies appears to be unjustified. Monotypic.
Distribution. Indonesia E to New Guinea, Australia, Tasmania and N New Zealand.

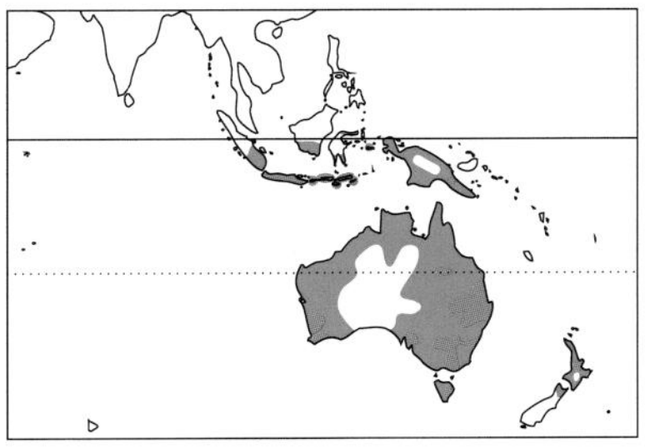

Descriptive notes. 55-65 cm; 520-1210 g; wingspan 95-105 cm. Non-breeding adult can be duller, lacks filoplumes and white nuptial feathering above eye. Differs from *P. fuscicollis* in dark facial skin. Juvenile browner.
Habitat. Mainly inland waters, including lakes and swamps; commonly on reservoirs and ponds, even in urban parks; also rivers and flood channels. Less frequent in sheltered coastal waters, including estuaries, inlets, lagoons, mangroves, salt-pans, etc. Inland, prefers open waters more than 1 m deep. Roosts on trees, bushes and rocks.
Food and Feeding. Mainly fish; also some crustaceans and other invertebrates. In much of Australia takes large quantities of introduced fish, e.g. carp (*Carassius auratus*), perch (*Perca fluviatilis*). On Magela floodplain, N Australia, takes almost exclusively fish, mostly under 4 cm, especially plotosid catfish *Neosilurus rendahli*, sail-fin perchlet (*Ambassis agrammus*) and *Melanotaenia splendida*; in estuaries of SW Australia mainly Atherinidae and Gobiidae. Feeds mainly by pursuit-diving. Frequently fishes co-operatively, sometimes with over 1000 birds together, efficiency increasing with number of birds; crayfish captured individually.
Breeding. All year round, depending on water conditions and food availability; Apr-Aug in N Australia. Normally forms small colonies of few pairs, but up to 1000; often in company of other cormorants, darters, egrets, herons or ibises. Nests in high forks in trees, often over water, or in bushes; nest of twigs and reeds, lined with leaves, grass and bark. Normally 3-4 eggs, but up to 6; chicks naked, grow black down.

On following pages: 4. Great Cormorant (*Phalacrocorax carbo*); 5. Indian Cormorant (*Phalacrocorax fuscicollis*); 6. Cape Cormorant (*Phalacrocorax capensis*); 7. Socotra Cormorant (*Phalacrocorax nigrogularis*); 8. Bank Cormorant (*Phalacrocorax neglectus*); 9. Japanese Cormorant (*Phalacrocorax capillatus*); 10. Brandt's Cormorant (*Phalacrocorax penicillatus*); 11. European Shag (*Phalacrocorax aristotelis*); 12. Pelagic Cormorant (*Phalacrocorax pelagicus*); 13. Red-faced Cormorant (*Phalacrocorax urile*); 14. Rock Shag (*Phalacrocorax magellanicus*); 15. Guanay Cormorant (*Phalacrocorax bougainvillii*); 16. Pied Cormorant (*Phalacrocorax varius*); 17. Black-faced Cormorant (*Phalacrocorax fuscescens*).

Movements. Mainly sedentary. Dispersive in Australia, with major movements related to droughts and temporary flooding; more common along coast when drought conditions prevail inland. In New Zealand may migrate to coastal waters of N for winter. Some movement between Australia and New Zealand, and also between islands of Indonesia. Vagrant to New Caledonia, Lord Howe I and Norfolk I.

Status and Conservation. Not globally threatened. Widespread in Australia, with colonies of up to 1400 nests. Has benefited in Australia from construction of dams and reservoirs, with increased habitat for both foraging and breeding. Less affected than most other species by transformation of wetlands, as mainly uses deeper waters and estuaries; some breeding grounds threatened by increased salinity, clearing, grazing, extraction of groundwater and burning. Feeds extensively on introduced fish species, and campaigns to remove such fish could have negative effects on species. Rare breeder and very common visitor to lowlands of New Guinea; partial census in Jan 1990 gave 1714 in Papua New Guinea. Locally common in Sulawesi. Has spread W to Java during present century.

Bibliography. Beehler *et al.* (1986), Bull *et al.* (1985), Chambers (1989), Coates (1985), Falla (1932), Falla *et al.* (1981), Garnett (1984), Lamm (1965), Lindsey (1986), Llewellyn (1983), Marchant & Higgins (1990), McClure (1974), McKeown (1944), McNally (1957), Miller, B. (1976, 1979, 1980), Perennou & Mundkur (1991), Potts, K.J. (1977), Schodde & Tidemann (1988), Serventy (1938, 1939), Serventy *et al.* (1971), van Tets & Fullagar (1984), van Tets *et al.* (1976), Trayler *et al.* (1989), Vestjens & van Tets (1985), White & Bruce (1986).

4. Great Cormorant

Phalacrocorax carbo

French: Grand Cormoran   **German**: Kormoran   **Spanish**: Cormorán Grande
Other common names: Common/Large (Black) Cormorant; European Cormorant (N America); White-breasted Cormorant (*lucidus*)

Taxonomy. *Pelecanus Carbo* Linnaeus, 1758, Europe.
May form superspecies with *P. capillatus*. Race *lucidus* often considered separate species. Race *novaehollandiae* may be good species; alternatively replaced by further races *carboides* (Australia) and *steadi* (New Zealand area). Race *hanedae* may be better considered synonymous with *sinensis*. Six subspecies normally recognized.
Subspecies and Distribution.
P. c. carbo (Linnaeus, 1758) - E Canada through Greenland and Iceland to Norway and British Is.
P. c. sinensis (Blumenbach, 1798) - C & S Europe E to India and China.
P. c. hanedae Nagamichi Kuroda, 1925 - Japan.
P. c. maroccanus Hartert, 1906 - NW Africa.
P. c. lucidus (Lichtenstein, 1823) - coastal W & S Africa, inland E Africa.
P. c. novaehollandiae Stephens, 1826 - Australia, Tasmania, New Zealand, Chatham Is.

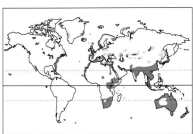

Descriptive notes. 80-100 cm; 1810-2810 g, female lighter; wingspan 130-160 cm. Very similar to *P. capillatus*. Non-breeding adult duller, lacks white patch on thighs and white filoplumes on neck. Juvenile brown, with underparts variably paler. Races separated on measurements and coloration: *sinensis* smaller and greener, normally with more white on throat and more filoplumes on neck; *lucidus* also smaller and greener, with white usually extending down onto breast or belly, but also has dark morph recalling *sinensis*; *maroccanus* intermediate between these two races.
Habitat. Most widespread species, ranging from Arctic to tropics. Open waters, both marine and inland, with preference varying regionally: race *carbo* is markedly marine, *sinensis* occurs mainly inland. At sea, rarely wanders far from coast, preferring sheltered areas and estuaries. Inland, occupies lakes, lagoons, reservoirs, wide rivers, salt pans and flood waters. Normally feeds in shallow water. Breeds on inshore islands, cliffs, stacks, amongst boulders and occasionally on wrecked ships and man-made structures; inland, nests on trees or bushes, in reedbeds and also on bare ground.
Food and Feeding. Mainly fish, with some crustaceans and amphibians. At sea, takes mostly bottom-dwelling fish from bare or vegetated seabed: in NW Europe takes flatfish, gadoids, viviparous blennies (*Zoarces viviparus*), sea-scorpions (Cottidae), sandeels (Ammodytidae), common eels (*Anguilla anguilla*), cod (*Gadus morhua*); on rocky coasts, wrasse (Labridae); on both sides of N Atlantic, sometimes takes schooling fish, e.g. herring, which make seasonal movements to coast to spawn. In estuaries of South Africa feeds on Cape silverside (*Atherina breviceps*) and estuarine round-herring (*Gilchristella aestuaria*). On inland lakes mainly roach (*Rutilus rutilus*) and perch (*Perca fluviatilis*); in Australia takes large quantities of introduced fish species, e.g. *Carassius auratus*, perch. Feeds mainly by pursuit-diving. Sometimes forms large fishing flocks. Fishes in close association with Dalmatian Pelican (*Pelecanus crispus*) in N Greece (see page 297).
Breeding. Season variable: laying mostly Apr-Jun in temperate parts of N Hemisphere; all year round in tropics. Colonial, often alongside other cormorants, darters, herons, spoonbills and ibises. Nests on cliff ledges, human structures, on ground amongst boulders, trees, bushes, reedbeds or bare ground; nest made of sticks, reeds and seaweed, lined with finer material; nests often reused. Normally 3-4 eggs (2-6); incubation 27-31 days; chicks naked, grow black down; fledging c. 50 days; post-fledging care c. 50+ days. Average 1·2-1·6 chicks fledge per pair. Sexual maturity at 3-5 years, occasionally at 2; known to have lived to 18 years old.
Movements. Migrant or partial migrant in most northerly populations, but sedentary or dispersive throughout most of range; migrants frequently winter within breeding range of species. Race *sinensis* fairly migratory, but variable with region and year: W populations move S towards Mediterranean, wintering inland and on coast, and reaching Persian Gulf. Nominate *carbo* widely dispersive, wintering mainly on coasts around breeding areas, though many inland in Ireland; populations of N North America and Greenland regularly move S, reaching New Jersey and sometimes Florida. In Australia, movements essentially nomadic and dispersive, related to cycles of flooding and drought.
Status and Conservation. Not globally threatened. Minimum total world population of 110,000-120,000 pairs at end of 1980's, with further tens of thousands of pairs in extensive zones where population estimates lacking. In Europe suffered heavy persecution in past, but generalized increase during present century due to protection and reduced direct persecution, leading also to extensive recolonization. Several important populations: 21,000 pairs in Norway; 14,100 pairs in Denmark, following recolonization in 1938; 13,600 pairs in Netherlands; 10,400 pairs in British Is in 1985-1987, as opposed to 8000 in 1969/70, with 142% increase in Ireland. Declining along Mediterranean coasts despite increased wintering population; has virtually disappeared from Faeroes. N America

holds several thousand pairs, Greenland 500-1500 pairs. Little known of population sizes in Africa and Asia, but censuses in Jan 1991 gave: 2746 in Senegal and 2906 at L Nakuru, Kenya; 7039 in Iran and 3683 in Oman; and 13,353 in Japan; also 5596 in India and 4697 in Pakistan in Jan 1990. Widespread in Australia, but little information on numbers, especially in inland areas; colony of 20,000 pairs at Blowering Dam (New South Wales) in 1974. Increasing conflicts with fish farms may lead to renewed persecution.

Bibliography. Ali & Ripley (1978), Barrett *et al.* (1990), Bauer & Glutz von Blotzheim (1966), Bezzel & Engler (1985), Brazil (1991), Brichetti (1982), Brooke *et al.* (1982), Brown *et al.* (1982), Builles *et al.* (1986), Coates (1985), Coulson (1961), Coulson & Brazendale (1968), Cramp & Simmons (1977), Cramp *et al.* (1974), Croxall *et al.* (1984), Debout (1987, 1988), Dementiev & Gladkov (1951a), van Dobben (1952), van Eerden & Munsterman (1986), Erskine (1972a), Etchécopar & Hüe (1978), Fukuda (1980), Goodman (1989), Grimmett & Jones (1989), Hansen (1984), Härkönen (1988), Harrison (1988), Hübner & Putzer (1985), Im & Hafner (1984), Jackson (1984), Janda & Musil (1990), Judin & Firsova (1988), Knief & Witt (1983), Kortlandt (1938), Lack (1945), Lindsey (1986), Litvinenko & Shibaev (1991), Llewellyn (1983), Lloyd *et al.* (1991), Lock & Ross (1973), MacDonald (1987), Mackworth-Praed & Grant (1957-1973), Madsen & Spärck (1950), Marchant & Higgins (1990), Marion (1983), van Marle & Voous (1988), Mikuska (1983), Mills (1965, 1969a), Milton & Austin-Smith (1983), Moerbeek *et al.* (1987), Oliver (1974), Olver & Kuyper (1978), Palmer (1962), Paz (1987), Perennou (1991a, 1991b), Perennou & Mundkur (1991), Pilon *et al.* (1983a, 1983b), Prokop (1980), Rae (1969), Roberts (1991), Ross (1973), Røv (1988), Røv & Strann (1986), Skead (1980a), Smythies (1986), Steven (1933), Stokoe (1958), Summers & Laing (1990), Urban (1979), Urban & Jefford (1974), West *et al.* (1975), Whitfield & Blaber (1979), Wilson & Wilson (1988).

5. Indian Cormorant

Phalacrocorax fuscicollis

French: Cormoran à cou brun   **German**: Braunwangenscharbe   **Spanish**: Cormorán Indio
Other common names: Indian Shag

Taxonomy. *Phalacrocorax fuscicollis* Stephens, 1826, Bengal.
Sometimes placed in genus *Hypoleucos*. Monotypic.

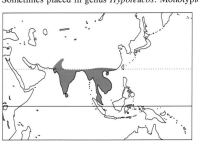

Distribution. Pakistan, India and Sri Lanka E to Indochina.
Descriptive notes. c. 63 cm; 600-790 g. Yellow gular skin. Upperparts more bronzed, less black than *P. sulcirostris*. Non-breeding adult duller and browner, with some whitish in region of throat; lacks filoplumes. Juvenile brown, with upperparts scaly, underparts whitish, mottled on flanks.
Habitat. Freshwater and marine habitats, including lakes, *jheels*, mangrove creeks, rivers, irrigation tanks and tidal estuaries. In Himalayas does not penetrate beyond foothills. Nests in trees, often over water.
Food and Feeding. Mainly fish. Feeds mainly by pursuit-diving. Often feeds in co-ordinated groups.
Breeding. Season very variable, depending on region, local water conditions and monsoon; laying mainly Jul-Feb. Colonial, often with other cormorants, darters, herons, egrets, storks, ibises and spoonbills. Nests in trees over water; nest of sticks and stems, sometimes lined with finer material. 3-6 eggs; chicks naked, grow brownish black down.
Movements. Sedentary; some movements over short distances in connection with local water conditions.
Status and Conservation. Not globally threatened. Widespread in India, with 5861 counted in Jan 1991, including 2836 in Tamil Nadu and 1540 in Andhra Pradesh; 1554 nests at Bharatpur in 1984. Common in Pakistan, with 18,879 counted in Jan 1991; greatest abundance in lower Sind and in estuarine waters; regular flocks of 100-200 in district of Jacobabad; in past reported to be abundant in Karachi harbour at certain times of year. Census of Jan 1991 produced 3820 in Sri Lanka. Local and uncommon in Thailand.
Bibliography. Ali (1979), Ali & Ripley (1978), Harvey (1990), Henry (1971), Lekagul & Round (1991), Perennou & Mundkur (1991), Ripley (1982), Roberts (1991), Scott (1989), Smythies (1986), Wildash (1968).

6. Cape Cormorant

Phalacrocorax capensis

French: Cormoran du Cap   **German**: Kapscharbe   **Spanish**: Cormorán del Cabo

Taxonomy. *Pelecanus capensis* Sparrman, 1788, False Bay, Cape of Good Hope.
Sometimes placed in genus *Leucocarbo*. Monotypic.
Distribution. Coasts of Namibia and South Africa.

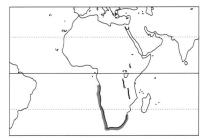

Descriptive notes. 61-64 cm; 1155-1306 g; wingspan 109 cm. Very black; short tail; bright yellow gular skin and around base of bill. Non-breeding adult browner, with some paler feathers on head and foreneck. Juvenile as non-breeding adult, but whiter on face and underparts.
Habitat. Almost exclusively marine. Fishes in cold waters of Benguela Current, generally less than 10 km from coast. More rarely in coastal lagoons, brackish waters of estuaries and harbours. Breeds on offshore islands and on mainland, mainly on cliffs and artificial guano platforms; occasionally on other man-made constructions, e.g. breakwaters, ruined buildings and even moored boats.
Food and Feeding. Mainly pelagic schooling fish, especially South African pilchard (*Sardinops ocellata*), Cape anchovy (*Engraulis japonicus capensis*), pelagic goby (*Sufflogobius bibarbatus*) and maasbanker (*Trachurus trachurus*); also other fish, e.g. hake (*Merluccius*), *Ammodytes*, and invertebrates, including crustaceans, squid and mussels. Diet can vary seasonally and regionally depending on relative abundance of different prey species. Pilchards less important since stocks crashed due to overfishing in mid-1970's. Feeds mainly by pursuit-diving. Normally feeds co-operatively in large flocks.
Breeding. Laying throughout much of year, mostly in Sept/Oct. Colonial, sometimes forming vast aggregations of over 100,000 pairs, with densities of up to 3 nests/m². Nests mostly on cliffs or

artificial platforms, usually on flat ground, ledges or bushes; nest of seaweed, sticks and stems. Normally 2-3 eggs (1-5); incubation 22-28 days; chicks naked, grow blackish down; fledging c. 9 weeks; post-fledging care of several weeks. Oldest ringed bird at least 9 years old.

Movements. Mainly sedentary; extensive post-breeding dispersal, with birds reaching mouth of R Congo and S Mozambique.

Status and Conservation. Not globally threatened. Abundant down coast of SW Africa; census in early 1980's yielded 280,000 pairs, 171,000 of which in Namibia; more than 60 breeding grounds known in mid-1980's. More numerous in past; recently on decline due to commercial overfishing and resultant collapse in stock of South African pilchard. Populations fluctuate with periodical mass-mortality and breeding failure produced by abnormal oceanographic conditions leading to failure of food supply (see page 341). In past guano mining caused considerable disturbance and produced decline, but species now favoured by rational exploitation of guano, with platforms specially constructed to increase extent of suitable breeding grounds.

Bibliography. Berry (1976a, 1976b, 1977), Brooke & Loutit (1984), Brooke & Milton (1980), Brown *et al.* (1982), Burger & Cooper (1982), Cooper & Brooke (1986), Cooper, Brooke *et al.* (1982), Cooper, Williams & Britton (1984), Crawford & Shelton (1978, 1981), Crawford *et al.* (1980), Duffy & Laurenson (1983), Duffy & Rudolf (1986), Duffy, Wilson & Wilson (1987), Duffy, Berruti *et al.* (1984), Furness & Cooper (1982), Mackworth-Praed & Grant (1957-1973), Maclean (1985), Pinto (1983), Rand (1960, 1963a, 1963b), Williams & Burger (1978), Wilson & Wilson (1988).

7. **Socotra Cormorant**

Phalacrocorax nigrogularis

French: Cormoran de Socotra   **German**: Sokotrakormoran   **Spanish**: Cormorán de Socotora

Taxonomy. *Phalacrocorax nigrogularis* Ogilvie-Grant and Forbes, 1899, Socotra.
Sometimes placed in genus *Leucocarbo*. Monotypic.

Distribution. Largely restricted to Persian Gulf and Dhofar (Oman); possibly also breeds in Gulf of Aden (Yemen) and on Socotra, although no hard evidence to date.

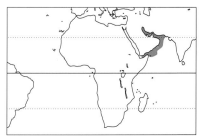

Descriptive notes. 76-84 cm; wingspan 102-110 cm. Very slim build; bill long and thin. Male averages larger. Non-breeding adult lacks most of filoplumes and white tuft behind eye. Juvenile grey-brown above, dirty white below.

Habitat. Exclusively marine, even to extent of preferring not to fly over land. Breeds on small desert islands. Rests on sandbanks, coastal cliffs and islets.

Food and Feeding. Probably mainly fish. Feeds mainly by pursuit-diving. Forms feeding flocks, sometimes immense, which can detect prey from air, and which fish collectively.

Breeding. Season very variable, with breeding recorded in most months, but each colony synchronized internally. Forms dense colonies, sometimes holding tens of thousands of birds. Nest is scrape in gravel or sand, or slightly raised mound. 2-4 eggs; chicks naked, grow white down.

Movements. Migratory or dispersive; poorly known. Disperses over Persian Gulf and Arabian Sea, where occurs all year round, reaching Gulf of Aden; vagrant to Red Sea coasts of E Africa in Somalia and Ethiopia, and also W India. Also performs some movements connected with feeding; moves in flocks, sometimes enormous; sometimes interpreted as migration.

Status and Conservation. Not globally threatened. Already considered near-threatened prior to war in Persian Gulf in early 1991. Major colonies include: Zakhnuniyah I, with 50,000 pairs in 1980; Huwar Is, with 50,000-250,000 breeding birds in 1981; and Az Zarqa' I, with 150,000 birds in (?)1972. Has very limited range in area of continual human conflict; particularly vulnerable to oil pollution which has repeatedly had serious effects in area; constant heavy traffic of oil tankers. Several spills related to armed conflicts in region; major spill in early 1991 reckoned to have killed a minimum of 25,000-30,000 sea-going birds, most of which were grebes and cormorants; present species was most affected of all, accounting for 37% of 1350-1500 birds attended in recovery centre; current carried slick S, but held up by Abu'Ali I and prevented from reaching Bahrain and major breeding colonies at Zakhnuniyah and the Huwar Is; 15,000 counted in Oman in Jan 1991, outside immediate zone of conflict. Shy and sensitive to human disturbance. Some of known breeding sites presently unoccupied; others hold very large colonies.

Bibliography. Bailey (1966), Brown *et al.* (1982), Bundy *et al.* (1989), Cramp & Simmons (1977), Gallagher *et al.* (1984), Hüe & Etchécopar (1970), Meinertzhagen (1954), Perennou & Mundkur (1991), Richardson (1990), Ripley & Bond (1966).

8. **Bank Cormorant**

Phalacrocorax neglectus

French: Cormoran des bancs   **German**: Küstenscharbe   **Spanish**: Cormorán de Bajío

Taxonomy. *Graculus neglectus* Wahlberg, 1855, islands off the coast of South West Africa.
Sometimes placed in genus *Compsohalieus*. Monotypic.

Distribution. Coast of S Namibia and W South Africa, from Swakopmund to Cape Agulhas.

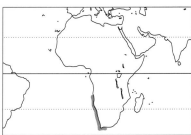

Descriptive notes. 76 cm; 1800 g; wingspan 132 cm. Corpulent; white rump. Eye often contrasts with dark head; iris brown above, green below, but appearing yellowish at distance. Non-breeding adult duller brown, lacks scattered nuptial plumes on head and neck, and also white rump. Juvenile as non-breeding adult.

Habitat. Strictly marine, occupying cold waters of Benguela Current. Prefers inshore waters, rarely fishing more than 10 km from land; range coincides with distribution of beds of kelp (*Ecklonia maxima*), where species usually forages. Breeds on offshore islands, islets, stacks and rocky outcrops; occasionally on breakwaters and other human constructions; often near high tide level and exposed to sea spray.

Food and Feeding. Wide variety of prey, including fish, crustaceans, cephalopods and molluscs; mean mass of prey items 59 g. On Ichaboe I and Mercury I (Namibia) takes large amounts of

pelagic goby (*Sufflogobius bibarbatus*), and also rock lobster (*Jasus lalandii*). Feeds mainly by pursuit-diving. Generally fishes alone or in small groups.

Breeding. Practically all year round, with peak laying in May-Jul. Normally in colonies of under 100 pairs. Nests on rocks or human constructions; nest of seaweed, sticks and feathers, cemented together with excreta; regularly reused and may grow very large, weighing up to 6 kg. Usually 2 eggs (1-3); chicks naked, grow sooty black down with some white on head; incubation 29-30 days. When breeding successful, 1 or 2 chicks tend to fledge.

Movements. Sedentary. Adults do not normally range further than c. 10 km from area of colony, thus only small distance beyond foraging range. Young birds can disperse over hundreds of kilometres, sometimes straying outwith limits of breeding range.

Status and Conservation. Not globally threatened. Currently considered near-threatened. Total population c. 18,000 birds at end of 1980's spread around c. 47 colonies; 12,800 on offshore islands of Ichaboe and Mercury (Namibia). Population could be negatively affected by expansion of commercial fishing activity in surrounding waters; some incidental mortality in fishing nets reported. Formerly considered threatened in South Africa, where now classed as species for monitoring.

Bibliography. Avery (1983), Brown *et al.* (1982), Clancey (1985), Collar & Stuart (1985), Cooper (1980c, 1984, 1985a, 1985b, 1986b, 1987), Cooper, Williams & Britton (1984), Crawford & Shelton (1978), Kriel *et al.* (1980), Maclean (1985), Rand (1960), Siegfried, Frost *et al.* (1976), Williams (1987), Williams & Burger (1978), Wilson & Wilson (1988).

9. **Japanese Cormorant**

Phalacrocorax capillatus

French: Cormoran de Temminck   **German**: Japankormoran   **Spanish**: Cormorán Japonés
Other common names: Temminck's Cormorant

Taxonomy. *Carbo capillatus* Temminck and Schlegel, 1850, Japan.
Synonymous with *P. filamentosus*. May form superspecies with *P. carbo*. Monotypic.

Distribution. Coasts of NE Asia from extreme SE coast of USSR and Sea of Japan to Sakhalin and South Kuril Is, and also S to Japan and Korea.

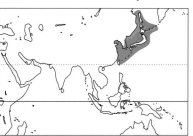

Descriptive notes. 92 cm; wingspan 152 cm. Differs from *P. carbo* in blackish green tone to plumage; also has more white on face. Non-breeding adult duller, lacks filoplumes on head and neck, and also white patch on thigh. Juvenile dull blackish brown, paler below, especially on throat and foreneck.

Habitat. Marine, occupying rocky coasts and islands; rarely found inland.

Food and Feeding. Mostly fish. Feeds mainly by pursuit-diving.

Breeding. Laying May-Jul in Japan. Colonial, sometimes alongside *P. carbo* and herons. Nests on cliffs or rocks, often on flat tops. 4-5 eggs; incubation c. 34 days; fledging c. 40 days. Mean brood size 2·5.

Movements. Dispersive. In Japan winters in warm regions; locally common during winter in Honshu and N Kyushu; returns to colonies in Apr. Winters in small numbers down coast of China, where vagrant to S.

Status and Conservation. Not globally threatened. Locally common in Japan, especially in Hokkaido which held c. 1900 pairs in 1980's; three major Japanese colonies amongst largest known, each with several hundred pairs; increasing disturbance caused by people fishing for sport, and as a result no longer breeds on Kyushu. Censuses gave 1199 in Japan in Jan 1991, and 825 in South Korea in Jan 1990. Total population of USSR under 16,000 birds, including not more than 8000 on Sea of Japan, and at least 7000 in Kuril Is in 1963. Largest known colony of species on Furugelm I (S of Vladivostok), with 1520 birds in 1985; in past ravaged by introduced Arctic foxes (*Alopex lagopus*). Intense human exploitation and persecution in 1940's and 1950's, involving shooting and egg-collecting; led to loss of all accessible colonies of Sakhalin I, nearby Moneron I and South Kuril Is; barely c. 100-120 birds on Sakhalin in 1980. All major colonies of USSR now included in protected areas.

Bibliography. Austin (1948), Austin & Kuroda (1953), Brazil (1991), Etchécopar & Hüe (1978), Golovkin (1984), Hasegawa (1984b), Litvinenko & Shibaev (1991), de Schauensee (1984), Scott (1989), Perennou & Mundkur (1991), Yamamoto (1967).

10. **Brandt's Cormorant**

Phalacrocorax penicillatus

French: Cormoran de Brandt   **German**: Pinselscharbe   **Spanish**: Cormorán Sargento
Other common names: Brown/Penciled/Townsend's Cormorant

Taxonomy. *Carbo penicillatus* Brandt, 1837, no locality.
Sometimes placed in genus *Compsohalieus*. Monotypic.

Distribution. Coasts of W North America, from SE Alaska to Baja California (Mexico).

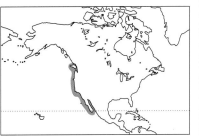

Descriptive notes. 84-89 cm; c. 2450 g; wingspan c. 124 cm. Throat cobalt blue, fringed by pale feathers. Female averages smaller. Non-breeding adult lacks white filoplumes on head, neck and upperparts. Juvenile dark brown above, paler below.

Habitat. Marine; restricted to rocky coasts and islands in region of California Current. Forages over rocky substrate, sometimes over sand or mud, but also in mid-water. In winter can occur in sheltered waters, e.g. bays and inlets. Roosts on rocks, islands and sandy beaches.

Food and Feeding. Mainly fish, both schooling and non-schooling. Typical prey species include rockfish (*Sebastes*), *Chromis punctipinnis*, northern anchovy (*Engraulis mordax*), *Oxyjulis californica*; also market squid (*Loligo opalescens*) and Pacific sanddabs (*Citharichthys sordidus*); in Gulf of California mostly *Apogon*, *Chromis*, Pomadasyidae, Serranidae. Feeds mainly by pursuit-diving. Sometimes fishes co-operatively, forming large aggregations.

Breeding. Laying mainly in Mar-Jul, earlier towards S. Colonial; sometimes alongside other seabirds, including other cormorants. Nests on ground, generally not in sheer cliffs, but rather on slopes, headlands and cliff tops; nests made of seaweed, grass, moss and debris, stuck together with excreta; can be reused. Normally 3-4 eggs (2-5); chicks naked, grow greyish down. When breeding successful, 1 or 2 chicks normally fledge per nest. Generally pair not maintained during successive seasons, but males tend to reoccupy same nest-site. Many females and some males breed at 2 years old; males can live to at least 12 years old, females 10.
Movements. Sedentary. Dispersal in autumn, with birds occurring S as far as Mazatlán (Mexico).
Status and Conservation. Not globally threatened. Bulk of population in California, USA, with 64,210 breeding birds in 1970's, and possibly increasing; also common in Oregon. May be stable in Baja California and Gulf of California, Mexico, though only 500-1000 pairs in Gulf; probably 10,000's along Pacific coast. Scarce in British Columbia (only 95 pairs in 1987) and in Alaska. Periodically suffers breeding failure or mortality related to El Niño (see page 341).
Bibliography. Ainley (1984b), Ainley & Boekelheide (1990), Ainley *et al.* (1981), Boekelheide & Ainley (1989), Carter & Hobson (1988), Croxall *et al.* (1984), Everett & Anderson (1991), Galbraith *et al.* (1986), Hodder & Graybill (1985), Hubbs *et al.* (1970), Manuwal & Campbell (1979), Palmer (1962), Richards (1990), Rodway (1991), Stirling & Buffam (1966), Talent (1984), Terres (1980), van Tets (1956), Williams (1942).

11. European Shag

Phalacrocorax aristotelis

French: Cormoran huppé **German**: Krähenscharbe **Spanish**: Cormorán Moñudo
Other common names: Common/Green Shag, Green Cormorant

Taxonomy. *Pelecanus aristotelis* Linnaeus, 1761, Sweden.
Sometimes placed in genus *Stictocarbo*. Race *riggenbachi* may be inseparable from *desmarestii*. Three subspecies recognized.
Subspecies and Distribution.
P. a. aristotelis (Linnaeus, 1761) - Iceland and N Scandinavia S to Iberian Peninsula.
P. a. desmarestii (Payraudeau, 1826) - C Mediterranean E to Black Sea.
P. a. riggenbachi Hartert, 1923 - coast of Morocco.

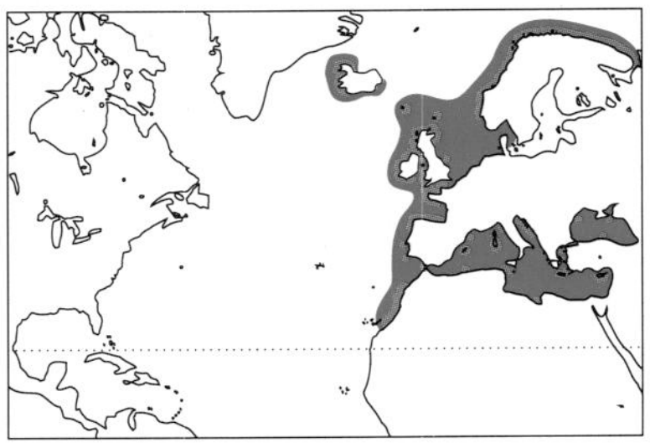

Descriptive notes. 65-80 cm; c. 2000 g; wingspan 90-105 cm. Length of crest very variable. Non-breeding adult duller, with pale chin and throat mottled brown; lacks crest. Juvenile brown, paler on side of head and underparts, but variable. Races separated on measurements and coloration: races *riggenbachi* and *desmarestii* both slightly smaller, with shorter crest and more yellow at base of bill.
Habitat. Marine; rarely in estuaries and only exceptionally inland. Has strong preference for rocky coasts and islands. Not normally far from land; forages over sandy or rocky seabeds and in mid-water. Breeds on sea cliffs, rocks and stacks or on ground under protection of boulders or bushes; also on open ground. Roosts on rocks and stacks, or at base of sea cliffs; far less often on beaches or harbour piers.
Food and Feeding. Almost exclusively fish, from bottom or mid-water: mainly Gadidae, sandeels (*Ammodytes*), Clupeidae, Cottidae, *Trisopterus*, Labridae. Feeds mainly by pursuit-diving. Normally fishes alone, and even where flocks form, birds do not fish co-operatively.
Breeding. Laying generally early, but dates vary with region, year and age of birds: Nov-Feb in Tunisia, Jan-Mar in Yugoslavia, Mar-Jun in Atlantic; youngest breeders start later, occupy sub-optimum nest-sites and have lower breeding success. Forms sparse colonies. Nests in crevices or caves, on ledges or amongst boulders, often a few metres above sea-level; nest of seaweed, lined with grass; nest frequently reused in successive seasons (93% in males, 41% in females), and pair-bond regularly maintained. Normally 3 eggs (1-6); incubation 30-31 days; chicks naked, grow brown down; fledging c. 53 days; post-fledging care 15-50+ days. Breeding success variable: at Lundy I (England) hatching success 69-73%, with 67-95% of hatched chicks fledging, giving 1·32-2·25 chicks per nest. Vast majority of young that survive return to breed at natal colony; some females breed in second year. Bigamy known to occur.
Movements. Sedentary, with post-breeding dispersal, mostly of young birds over short distances; some N populations more markedly dispersive, e.g. Norway and British Is (but not Iceland), birds moving up to 1000 km from colony. Some colonies totally deserted probably due to lack of food available locally. In Mediterranean and Black Sea limited dispersal. Generally irregular and rare from coast of Belgium to Denmark. Accidental to e.g. Israel, Egypt, Iraq and C Europe.
Status and Conservation. Not globally threatened. Total population may number c. 100,000 pairs. Great increase in British Is during present century, following decline in 19th century; increase of c. 40% in recent years, with 31,600 pairs in 1969/70, and 47,300 pairs in 1985-1987. Has also increased in other regions of Atlantic, e.g. Brittany and Normandy (France). Much less common in Mediterranean, perhaps with c. 10,000 pairs; declines in recent years at some major colonies, e.g. Sardinia and Balearic Is. Very scarce in N Africa.
Bibliography. Aebischer (1986), Amundsen (1988, 1990), Barrett & Furness (1990), Barrett, Strann & Vader (1986), Barrett, Røv *et al.* (1990), Bauer & Glutz von Blotzheim (1966), Brichetti (1982), Brown *et al.* (1982), Coulson (1961), Coulson, Potts & Horobin (1969), Coulson, Potts, Deans & Fraser (1968), Cramp & Simmons (1977), Cramp *et al.* (1974), Croxall *et al.* (1984), Dementiev & Gladkov (1951a), Galbraith, Russell & Furness (1981), Galbraith, Baillie *et al.* (1986), Géroudet (1972), Grimmett & Jones (1989), Guyot (1988), Guyot & Thibault (1988), Harris (1982), Harrison (1988), Johnstone *et al.* (1990), Judin & Firsova (1988), Lack (1945), Lloyd *et al.* (1991), Lumsden & Haddow (1946), Mills (1969b), Oliver (1974), Pasquet (1987), Pasquet & Monnat (1990), Potts, G.R. (1966, 1968, 1969, 1971), Potts, G.R. *et al.* (1980), Rae (1969), Røv (1990), Røv & Follestad (1983), Snow (1960, 1963), Steven (1933), Swann & Ramsay (1979), Tasker *et al.* (1987), Wanless, Burger & Harris (1991), Wanless, Harris & Morris (1991).

12. Pelagic Cormorant

Phalacrocorax pelagicus

French: Cormoran pélagique **German**: Meerscharbe **Spanish**: Cormorán Pelágico
Other common names: Pelagic Shag, Baird's Cormorant

Taxonomy. *Phalacrocorax pelagicus* Pallas, 1811, eastern Kamachatka and the Aleutian Islands. sometimes placed in genus *Stictocarbo*. Two subspecies recognized.
Subspecies and Distribution.
P. p. pelagicus Pallas, 1811 - N Pacific.
P. p. resplendens Audubon, 1838 - British Columbia to NW Mexico.

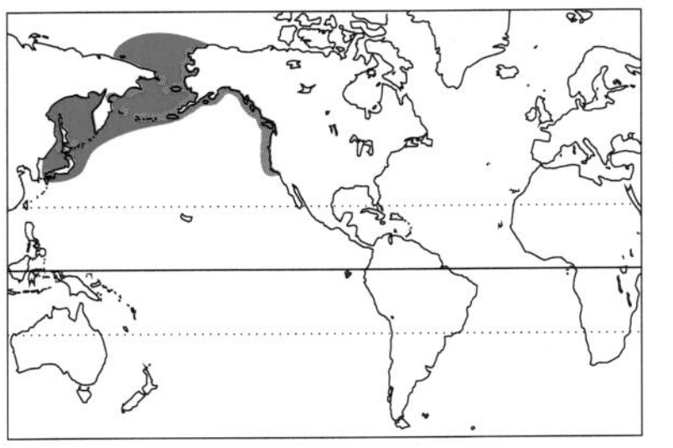

Descriptive notes. 63-76 cm; 1474-2438 g; wingspan c. 101 cm. Head slender and bill very thin; bill darker than in *P. urile*. Females average smaller. Non-breeding adult lacks white patch on flanks, scattered white filoplumes on neck and both crests. Juvenile dark brown, paler on breast and belly though without marked contrast; lacks crests. Race *resplendens* averages smaller.
Habitat. Marine. Feeds in sheltered coastal waters, including inlets and bays, and also on open sea. Breeds on rocky islands and coasts.
Food and Feeding. Mainly non-schooling fish captured over rocky substrates or kelp beds. Prey variable with region, including sandeels (*Ammodytes*), sculpins (Cottidae), Pholidae and rockfish (*Sebastes*); also shrimps and other crustaceans. Feeds mainly by pursuit-diving. Sometimes opportunistic, joining flocks of seabirds feeding on juvenile schooling Pacific herring (*Clupea harengus pallasii*).
Breeding. Laying May-Jul. Normally forms small colonies, sometimes solitary; neighbouring colonies can be used in alternate years. Nests on narrow cliff ledges, sometimes in caves; nest of grass, hay or seaweed, cemented together with excreta; reused in successive years, growing to be 1·5 m deep. Normally 3-4 eggs (2-7); incubation c. 31 days; chicks naked, grow sooty down. Up to 4 chicks per nest may fledge, but average 3 in years without shortage of food.
Movements. Mostly sedentary, with post-breeding dispersal; northernmost populations of NE Siberia and NW Alaska migratory. Winter visitor to Korea and China. Vagrant to Hawaii.
Status and Conservation. Not globally threatened. Apparently stable in general, with some fluctuations. Greatest abundance in Kuril Is, with 50,000-60,000 birds, including largest colonies; also c. 100,000 birds spread over Bering Sea (c. 50,000 birds), Aleutian Is and Alaska. Smaller numbers in British Columbia, with c. 8990 breeding birds, but increasing since start of century. Seems to be stable in California, where numerous colonies; c. 15,870 birds in 1970's; may suffer some mortality connected with gill-net fisheries.
Bibliography. Ainley (1984b), Ainley *et al.* (1981), Bayer (1986), Brazil (1991), Carter *et al.* (1984), Chilton & Sealy (1987), Croxall (1991), Croxall *et al.* (1984), Dementiev & Gladkov (1951a), Etchécopar & Hüe (1978), Hatch & Hatch (1990), Hobson & Wilson (1985), Hobson & Sealy (1985), Hodder & Graybill (1985), Judin & Firsova (1988), Manuwal & Campbell (1979), Palmer (1962), Richards (1990), Robertson (1971, 1974), Siegel-Causey (1981), Siegel-Causey & Hunt (1986), Terres (1980), van Tets (1956), Vermeer & Rankin (1984b), Vermeer *et al.* (1989).

13. Red-faced Cormorant

Phalacrocorax urile

French: Cormoran à face rouge **German**: Rotgesichtscharbe **Spanish**: Cormorán Carirrojo
Other common names: Red-faced Shag

Taxonomy. *Pelecanus Urile* Gmelin, 1789, Kamchatka.
Sometimes placed in genus *Stictocarbo*. Monotypic.
Distribution. N Pacific from Hokkaido (N Japan), Kuril and Commander Is eastwards to Aleutian Is and S Alaska.

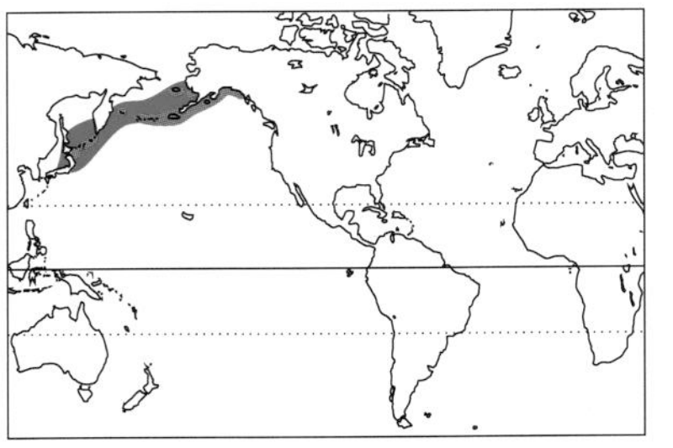

Descriptive notes. 71-89 cm; 1644-2552 g; wingspan 122 cm. Recalls *P. pelagicus*, but larger, with greater extent of red facial skin; bill almost ivory-coloured, crests longer and denser. Females average smaller. Non-breeding adult slightly duller, lacks white patch on flanks, white filoplumes and crests. Juvenile resembles non-breeding adult; dark brown, slightly paler below with brownish facial skin.
Habitat. Exclusively marine. Breeds along rocky coasts and on offshore islands.
Food and Feeding. Variety of small fish and crustaceans, including crabs and shrimps. Feeds mainly by pursuit-diving.
Breeding. Laying in May/Jun. Colonial. Nests on cliff ledges; nest is wide and well built, mainly of grass and seaweed. 3-7 eggs; mean brood size 2·8; chicks naked, grow dusky brownish down. Incubation said to last 21 days and fledging c. 60 days, but these reports unconfirmed.
Movements. Basically sedentary, dispersing over nearby coasts during winter.
Status and Conservation. Not globally threatened. Major increase in N Pacific during second half of century. Estimated c. 20,000-30,000 birds in Kuril Is and c. 174,000 in Bering Sea, Aleutian Is and Alaska. However, in Japan probably never abundant and seems likely to disappear as breeder in near future; may number no more than c. 10 pairs on Hokkaido.
Bibliography. Ainley (1984b), Armstrong (1983), Brazil (1991), Croxall *et al.* (1984), Dementiev & Gladkov (1951a), Hatch & Hatch (1990), Judin & Firsova (1988), Litvinenko & Shibaev (1991), Palmer (1962), Scott (1989), Squibb & Hunt (1983), Terres (1980).

14. Rock Shag

Phalacrocorax magellanicus

French: Cormoran de Magellan **German**: Felsenscharbe **Spanish**: Cormorán Magallánico
Other common names: Rock/Magellan(ic) Cormorant, Magellan Shag

Taxonomy. *Pelecanus magellanicus* Gmelin, 1789, Tierra del Fuego and Staten Island.
Sometimes placed in genus *Stictocarbo*. Monotypic.
Distribution. Pacific and Atlantic coasts of S South America, including Tierra del Fuego and Falkland Is.
Descriptive notes. 66-71 cm; wingspan 92 cm. Characteristic white patch on cheeks. Non-breeding adult has throat and foreneck white, lacks white cheeks, nuptial plumes of head and neck and also crest. Juvenile brown with white belly; underparts subsequently become darker.
Habitat. Marine; coasts, islands and channels. Apparently prefers colder waters, which are more prevalent in Atlantic part of range. Breeds on cliffs. Feeds inshore.
Food and Feeding. Very little known. Feeds mainly by pursuit-diving. Solitary feeder.
Breeding. Laying Oct-Dec. Forms small colonies. Nests on cliff ledges and rocks; nest is tight cup of seaweed, cemented together with excreta. Normally 3 eggs (2-4).

Movements. Some post-breeding dispersal towards northern limits of breeding range; some move N as far as Uruguay. Part of population of Tierra del Fuego moves to mainland coasts of Patagonia for winter.
Status and Conservation. Not globally threatened. Few colonies in Pacific; more abundant in Atlantic. Common in Chile, with no significant threats known at present; widespread in S Argentina. Locally distributed in Falkland Is, occurring mainly in E; small numbers, with c. 1550 pairs at 34+ colonies.
Bibliography. Bahamonde (1955), Blake (1977), Carp (1991), Croxall *et al.* (1984), Humphrey *et al.* (1970), Johnson (1965), Murphy (1936), de la Peña (1986), Rasmussen (1987), Schlatter & Riveros (1981), Siegel-Causey (1986b), Venegas & Jory (1979), Woods (1988).

15. **Guanay Cormorant**
Phalacrocorax bougainvillii

French: Cormoran de Bougainville   **German**: Guanoscharbe   **Spanish**: Cormorán Guanay

Taxonomy. *Carbo Bougainvillii* Lesson, 1837, Valparaíso, Chile.
Sometimes placed in genus *Leucocarbo*. Monotypic.
Distribution. Coasts of Peru and N Chile, with bulk of population off C Peru; SC Argentina.

Descriptive notes. 71-76 cm. Slim; has white gular stripe or streak. Non-breeding adult duller, lacks crest and white facial plumes. Juvenile as non-breeding adult but browner, underparts speckled brown and foreneck variably whitish.
Habitat. Marine. Feeds in open sea in cold waters of Humboldt Current. Breeds on headlands of mainland coast and offshore islands, notably those off C Peru; prefers gentle slopes.
Food and Feeding. Pelagic schooling fish, with almost complete dependence on anchoveta (*Engraulis ringens*): population of species tightly regulated by scarcity or absence of anchoveta. Feeds mainly by pursuit-diving. Often fishes co-operatively, sometimes several thousand birds together.
Breeding. All year round, with marked peak in laying in Nov/Dec. Forms very large, dense colonies, with up to 3 nests/m²; regularly breeds alongside Peruvian (Brown) Pelican (*Pelecanus occidentalis thagus*) and Peruvian Booby (*Sula variegata*). Nests on flat or gently-sloping ground; nest is pile of excreta, feathers and debris. Normally 3 eggs, sometimes 2. Breeding success extremely variable, with total failure when food supply fails.
Movements. After breeding spreads N to Ecuador and S to Valdivia (SC Chile). Mass dispersal when food supply fails due to occurrence of El Niño, birds straying far outside normal range, reaching Panama and extreme S tip of S America; some move inland following rivers.
Status and Conservation. Not globally threatened. Formerly superabundant, numbering c. 30,000,000 birds; has declined due to effects of guano extraction and overfishing. Population suffered greatly with irrational exploitation of guano, involving constant disturbance and considerable direct exploitation; subsequently recovered due to protection of species, creation of additional breeding grounds and regulation of guano mining. Since mid-1950's seriously affected by growth of commercial fisheries and resultant overfishing of anchoveta; this, combined with effects of El Niño, led to collapse of anchovy stocks in 1972, and dramatic slump in guano bird numbers; anchoveta stocks have not recovered, even though commercial exploitation has been paralysed. Total population of species c. 3,000,000 birds in 1981; in Peru reduced to 900,000 after Niño of 1982/83, and estimated c. 1,380,000 birds in 1985/86. Adaptation of species to cope with periodical population crashes under "natural" conditions suggests possibility of rapid recovery of former numbers, should anchoveta stocks eventually recover. See pages 338, 341.
Bibliography. Blake (1977), Devillers & Terschuren (1978), Duffy (1980, 1983a, 1983b, 1983c, 1988), Duffy, Hays & Plenge (1984), Erize (1972), Johnson (1965), Jordán (1959), Jordán & Fuentes (1966), Malacalza (1984b), Murphy (1936), de la Peña (1986), Ridgely & Gwynne (1989), Schlatter (1984), Tovar (1968, 1983), Tovar & Cabrera (1985), Tovar & Galarza (1983), Tovar *et al.* (1987), Walsh (1978).

16. **Pied Cormorant**
Phalacrocorax varius

French: Cormoran varié   **German**: Elsterscharbe   **Spanish**: Cormorán Pío
Other common names: Greater Pied/Large Pied/Yellow-faced/Black and White Cormorant/Shag, Pied Shag

Taxonomy. *Pelecanus varius* Gmelin, 1789, Queen Charlotte Sound, New Zealand.
Sometimes placed in genus *Hypoleucos*. Two subspecies recognized.
Subspecies and Distribution.
P. v. hypoleucos (Brandt, 1837) - Australia.
P. v. varius (Gmelin, 1789) - New Zealand.
Descriptive notes. 65-85 cm; 1300-2200 g; wingspan 110-130 cm. Female smaller, with shorter bill. Non-breeding adult similar, but duller. Juvenile dark brown instead of black, underparts streaked brownish grey. Race *hypoleucos* separated on slight differences in coloration, e.g. sheen on back blue as opposed to green.

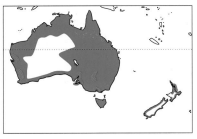

Habitat. Mostly marine, especially in W Australia, usually occupying sheltered waters of estuaries, bays and mangroves; also around offshore islands. In subcoastal and inland waters, regularly occurs in lakes, lagoons, reservoirs, rivers and swamps, preferring permanent open waters; absent from arid interior of Australia. Breeds on islands or in swamps; on trees or bushes, sometimes on ground.
Food and Feeding. Mainly fish, comprising 90% in both weight and number of prey items; also crustaceans, including prawns, shrimps and crabs, and a few molluscs and cephalopods. Wide variety in both species and size of prey taken. In estuaries of SW Australia, several introduced fish species important, e.g. carp, redfin and perch. Feeds almost exclusively by pursuit-diving. At sea, often forms feeding flocks.
Breeding. Sometimes throughout year; season varies considerably with region and year, depending on local water conditions; mostly autumn or spring in coastal areas. Generally colonial, sometimes in aggregations of several thousand birds; often in mixed colonies with other cormorants, Australian Pelicans (*Pelecanus conspicillatus*) and spoonbills (*Platalea*); colonies often transitory, due to damage caused to trees by excreta and peeling off of small branches. Nests on trees or bushes, sometimes on ground and occasionally on beacons; nest of twigs and seaweed, sometimes lined with grass; nests can be reused. Usually 3 eggs (1-5); incubation 25-33 days; chicks naked, grow dark brown down, white below; fledging 47-60 days; post-fledging care 80+ days. Breeding success 26·2%; average of 0·8 chicks fledged per nest. Sexual maturity at 2 years old or more, though some birds breed at 1 year old.
Movements. Adults basically sedentary, juveniles perform fairly extensive dispersal. Inland, temporary abundance related to local water levels. Vagrant to Tasmania and Lord Howe I (off E Australia).
Status and Conservation. Not globally threatened. Widespread in Australia. Less affected by destruction of habitat than several other species, as prefers coastal waters or permanent open waters inland, which are less subject to transformation than other wetland types. Has benefited from proliferation of artificial water bodies; also frequently uses man-made structures for perching and even breeding on. Feeds extensively on introduced fish species, and campaigns to remove such fish could have negative effects on species.
Bibliography. Bull *et al.* (1985), Chambers (1989), Cunningham & Moors (1985), Falla (1932), Falla *et al.* (1981), Ford (1963), Goodwin (1956), Lalas (1979), Lashmar (1987), Lindsey (1986), Marchant & Higgins (1990), McKeown (1944), McNally (1957), Millener (1972), Miller (1979), Moisley (1969), Norman (1974), Robertson & Bell (1984), Schodde & Tidemann (1988), Serventy (1938, 1939), Serventy *et al.* (1971), Soper (1976), Taylor (1987), van Tets & Fullagar (1984), van Tets, Waterman & Purchase (1976), van Tets, Milliner & Vestjens (1985), Trayler *et al.* (1989).

17. **Black-faced Cormorant**
Phalacrocorax fuscescens

French: Cormoran de Tasmanie   **German**: Schwarzgesichtscharbe   **Spanish**: Cormorán Carinegro
Other common names: Black-faced/Black and White Shag, White-breasted Cormorant

Taxonomy. *Hydrocorax fuscescens* Vieillot, 1817, "Australasie" = Tasmania.
Sometimes alternatively placed in *Leucocarbo* or *Compsohalieus*. Monotypic.
Distribution. Coasts of S Australia, with two independent populations: in S Western Australia; and in South Australia, Victoria and Tasmania.

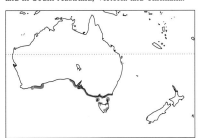

Descriptive notes. 61-69 cm; wingspan 93-107 cm. Has characteristic facial pattern and colour. Non-breeding adult lacks white plumes on head, neck and sides of rump. Juvenile has head more broadly dark; brown above, white below with brownish throat.
Habitat. Marine. Feeds in coastal waters, sometimes in sheltered places, including bays and inlets; sometimes enters rivers along coast. Breeds on islands, usually rocky; also on stacks, slopes and sea cliffs. Roosts on islands, rocks and sandbanks.
Food and Feeding. Variety of fish, including *Gymnapistes marmoratus*, Atherinidae and Clinidae. Feeds mainly by pursuit-diving. Forms feeding flocks of up to several thousand individuals.
Breeding. Season variable; probably mostly Aug-Jan, but also recorded Apr-Jun. Generally in colonies of up to 2500 pairs, sometimes very dense with nests only c. 1m apart; sometimes alongside other cormorants, gulls or terns. Nests on top of cliffs or rocky platforms, cliff ledges, stacks; nest of seaweed, grass, other plant matter and driftwood; possibly reused in different years. Normally 2-3 eggs (2-5); chicks naked, grow black down, white below.
Movements. Basically sedentary, with some dispersal of young birds. No records of movements between the two populations.
Status and Conservation. Not globally threatened. Total population probably numbers several 10,000's of birds; major colonies in South Australia, with 3000 nests at Winceby I and 1000+ at English I. Possibly in regression and range may have shrunk. Persecuted by fishermen, with regular shooting and use as bait for catching crayfish.
Bibliography. Angove (1982), Brothers (1983), Brothers & Skira (1983), Klapste (1977), Lane (1980), Lashmar (1987), Lindsey (1986), Marchant & Higgins (1990), McNally (1957), Norman *et al.* (1980), Pescott (1980), Schodde & Tidemann (1988), Serventy *et al.* (1971), van Tets & Fullagar (1984), van Tets & Marlow (1977), van Tets *et al.* (1976), Waterman (1968).

18

19   pale morph   dark morph   20   21

22   23   24   25

ssp *atriceps*   ssp *albiventer*

26   27   28   29   30

31   32   33

ssp *melanoleucos*

34   39

ssp *brevirostris*
dark morph   35   36   37   38

PLATE 23

inches   14

cm   35

18. **Rough-faced Shag**

Phalacrocorax carunculatus

French: Cormoran caronculé **German**: Warzenscharbe **Spanish**: Cormorán Carunculado
Other common names: (New Zealand) King Shag/Cormorant, Carunculated/Marlborough Sound/Cook Straits Cormorant

Taxonomy. *Pelecanus carunculatus* Gmelin, 1789, Queen Charlotte Sound, New Zealand, and Staten Island.
Often includes *P. chalconotus* and *P. onslowi*; these three sometimes considered conspecific with *P. campbelli* complex (*campbelli*, *ranfurlyi* and *colensoi*). Alternatively placed in *Leucocarbo* or *Euleucocarbo*. Monotypic.
Distribution. Restricted to area of Cook Strait (New Zealand), breeding in Marlborough Sounds, NE South I.

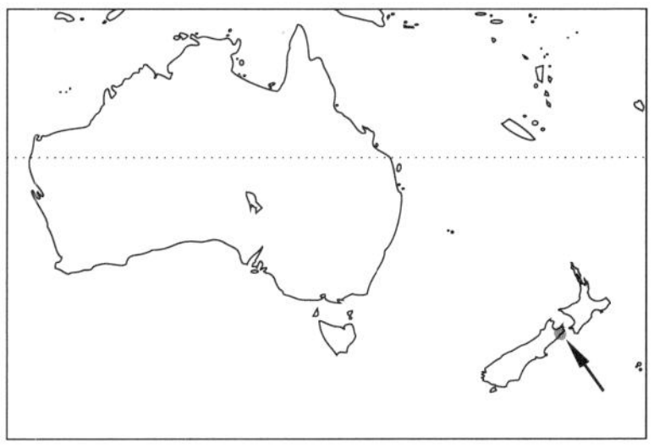

Descriptive notes. 76 cm; c. 2500 g. Bill long and thick, with caruncle clearly visible, though not prominent; two white dorsal patches sometimes apparent. Non-breeding adult duller, lacks crest. Juvenile similar to non-breeding adult, but brown above, as opposed to black.
Habitat. Marine. Forages in waters close to coast, in sheltered inlets and bays. Breeds on rocky islets and stacks, occupying flat ground or steep slopes. Roosts on bare rocks.
Food and Feeding. Probably benthic fish and crustaceans. Feeds mainly by pursuit-diving. Sometimes forms small feeding flocks.
Breeding. Mainly Mar-Dec, laying frequently in Jun/Jul; season varies between years and at different colonies; on occasions birds may apparently breed twice in same year; breeding cycle lasts c. 5 months. Forms colonies of up to 80 pairs. Nests on rocks, sometimes under shelter of bushes; on occasions only 1 m above high tide mark, but usually higher; nest of twigs and grass, cemented together by excreta; nest can be reused. Probably 1-3 eggs, normally 2; chicks naked, grow smoky brown down.
Movements. Sedentary. Very occasionally recorded elsewhere on South I, away from Cook Strait.
Status and Conservation. RARE. Total population under 300 birds, with estimates of 192-260 individuals in 1960's; restricted to 5 breeding localities. May neither be declining nor have declined since discovery in 1773, as is limited in both range and numbers by natural factors. Some egg-collecting in past for museums, and some hunting for feather trade; more recently shot at by fishermen. Highly susceptible to disturbance by humans. Protection started in 1924, and nowadays both species and breeding islands strictly protected.
Bibliography. Bull *et al.* (1985), Chambers (1989), Collar & Andrew (1988), Falla (1932), Falla *et al.* (1981), Fisher *et al.* (1969), King (1978/79), Nelson (1971), Marchant & Higgins (1990), Robertson & Bell (1984), Sibson (1982), Soper (1976), van Tets (1985c, 1985d), Vincent (1966).

19. **Stewart Shag**

Phalacrocorax chalconotus

French: Cormoran bronzé **German**: Stewartscharbe **Spanish**: Cormorán de la Stewart
Other common names: Bronze/Gray's Shag, Stewart Island Cormorant

Taxonomy. *Graculus chalconotus* G. R. Gray, 1845, Otago, South Island, New Zealand.
Often considered race of *P. carunculatus*. Some authors merge *carunculatus*, *chalconotus* and *onslowi*, and *campbelli*, *ranfurlyi* and *colensoi* into single species. Sometimes placed in *Leucocarbo* or *Euleucocarbo*. Monotypic.
Distribution. Restricted to SE South I and Stewart I (New Zealand).

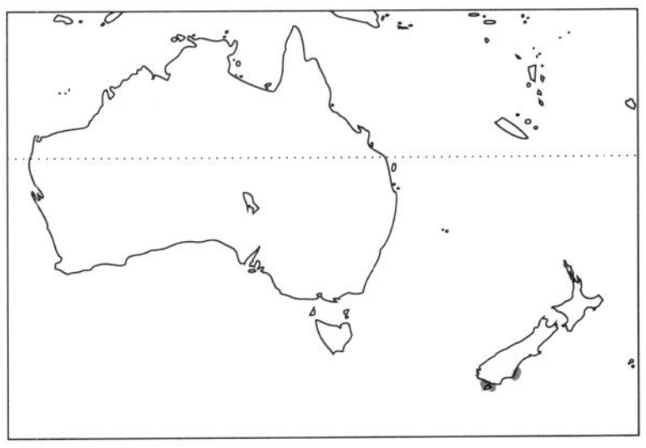

Descriptive notes. 65-71 cm; 1797-3875 g. Dimorphic; dark morph common. Base of lower mandible and gular pouch orange, not always conspicuous; can have white dorsal patch. Similar to *P. carunculatus*, but slightly smaller with shorter, thinner bill. Non-breeding adult duller, lacks crest and white filoplumes. Juvenile similar to non-breeding adult; similarly dimorphic, with dark brown replacing black.
Habitat. Marine. Preferably forages in sheltered coastal waters, including bays and inlets, but sometimes as much as 10-15 km offshore. Breeds and roosts in rocky coastal areas and on small islands or stacks near shore.
Food and Feeding. Mainly fish (70% of weight), including *Tripterygion*, *Rhombosolea*, *Arnoglossus*, *Peltorhamphus*; also crustaceans, cephalopods and polychaetes. Fish taken more in spring than in winter, when invertebrates, especially crustaceans, predominate. Feeds mainly by pursuit-diving. Sometimes gathers in small feeding flocks.
Breeding. All year round, varying with colony and from year to year, depending on local conditions. Forms monospecific colonies of up to several hundred pairs. Nests on bare sloping rock; nest of grass, peat and debris cemented together with excreta and lined with grass, sometimes over 1 m deep; experienced breeders tend to occupy optimum sites. Apparently 2-3 eggs; chick naked, grows grey down.
Movements. Sedentary; no observations far from Stewart I or breeding grounds on South I.
Status and Conservation. RARE. Under 5000 pairs; overall numbers may be only a few thousnad individuals. Much work needed on all aspects of biology in order to establish conservation requirements; susceptible to disturbance by humans.
Bibliography. Bull *et al.* (1985), Chambers (1989), Falla (1932), Falla *et al.* (1981), Marchant & Higgins (1990), Robertson & Bell (1984).

20. **Chatham Shag**

Phalacrocorax onslowi

French: Cormoran des Chatham **German**: Chathamscharbe **Spanish**: Cormorán de las Chatham
Other common names: Chatham Island Cormorant

Taxonomy. *Phalacrocorax onslowi* Forbes, 1893, Chatham Islands.
Often considered race of *P. carunculatus*. Some authors merge *carunculatus*, *chalconotus* and *onslowi*, and *campbelli*, *ranfurlyi* and *colensoi* into single species. Sometimes placed in *Leucocarbo* or *Euleucocarbo*. Monotypic.

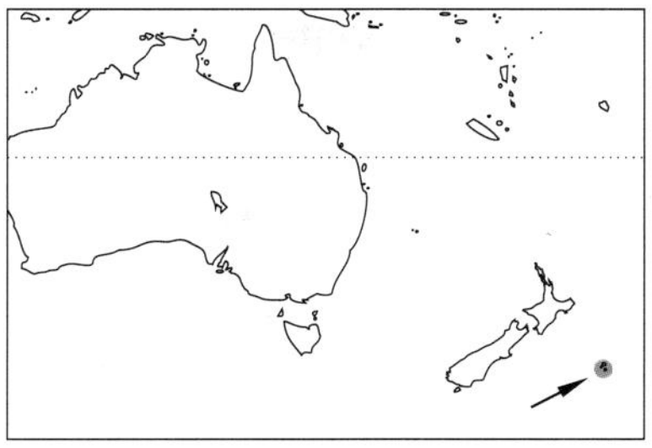

Distribution. Restricted to Chatham Is (New Zealand).
Descriptive notes. 63 cm; 1790-2525 g. Very prominent caruncle distinguishes from similar species; can have white filoplumes on neck and perhaps behind eye, as in *P. chalconotus*. Often without white on scapulars. Non-breeding adult duller, lacks crest and filoplumes. Juvenile brown above, white below; can have white wing patches.
Habitat. Marine. Forages near coast, no more than a few kilometres offshore, preferably in sheltered waters, including bays and inlets. Breeds in rocky coastal zones and on small islands, occupying flat areas, slopes or wide cliff ledges, sometimes very near high tide line. Roosts on rocks along coast.
Food and Feeding. Very little known. Probably small fish. Presumably feeds mainly by pursuit-diving. Sometimes forms small feeding flocks.
Breeding. Laying Sept-Dec, apparently with considerable variation even within same colony. Forms small monospecific colonies. Nests on flat or sloping bare rock; nest of ice-plant, grass and other plants. Said to lay 3 eggs; chicks naked, grow smoky brown down.
Movements. Sedentary; not recorded away from Chatham Is.
Status and Conservation. RARE. Very small population of under 1000 pairs. Disturbance of colonies can lead to stampede with loss of many eggs through breakage or ensuing predation by Silver Gulls (*Larus novaehollandiae*). Much work needed on all aspects of biology in order to establish conservation requirements.
Bibliography. Bull *et al.* (1985), Buller (1895), Cemmick & Veitch (1985), Falla (1932), Falla *et al.* (1981), Fleming (1939), Marchant & Higgins (1990), Robertson & Bell (1984), van Tets (1985e).

21. **Auckland Shag**

Phalacrocorax colensoi

French: Cormoran des Auckland **German**: Aucklandscharbe **Spanish**: Cormorán de las Auckland
Other common names: Auckland Island Cormorant

Taxonomy. *Phalacrocorax colensoi* Buller, 1888, Auckland Islands.
Often considered race of *P. campbelli*. Some authors merge *colensoi*, *campbelli* and *ranfurlyi*, and *carunculatus*, *chalconotus* and *onslowi* into single species. Sometimes placed in *Leucocarbo* or *Euleucocarbo*. Monotypic.
Distribution. Restricted to Auckland Is (New Zealand).

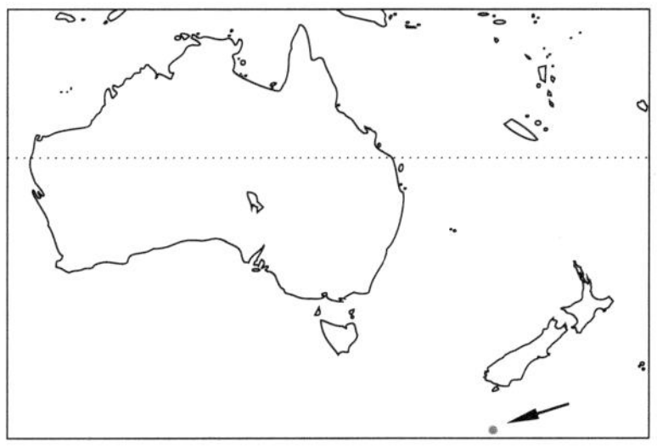

Descriptive notes. 63 cm; wingspan 105 cm. Upperparts can be wholly black; can have white on scapulars, and some males have white dorsal patch. Very similar to *P. campbelli*, but foreneck white, sometimes with black collar; facial skin paler and reddish, contrasting with orange eye-ring, and separating from *P. ranfurlyi*. Non-breeding adult duller, lacks crest. Juvenile resembles non-breeding adult, brown above, white below; can have foreneck brown and paler wing patch.
Habitat. Marine. Forages equally in open sea or in sheltered coastal waters, including bays or inlets. Breeds and roosts on ledges, tops of sea cliffs or in hollows; also on flat ground amongst grass tussocks or in shelter of overhanging rocks, bushes or trees.
Food and Feeding. Very little known. Probably crustaceans and fish. Presumably feeds mainly by pursuit-diving. Sometimes forms large feeding flocks.
Breeding. Laying Nov-Feb. Forms small or large monospecific colonies. Nests on ledges, cliff tops or on ground amongst tussocks; nest mainly of tussock grass, also seaweed, twigs, peat and debris. Apparently clutch normally of 3 eggs; chicks naked, grow grey down; incubation 28-32 days; brood normally consists of 2 chicks.
Movements. Sedentary; no records far from Auckland Is.
Status and Conservation. RARE. Very small population of under 2000 individuals; no evidence of decline. Nests sometimes washed away by high tides or storm waves.
Bibliography. Buller (1895), Falla *et al.* (1981), Marchant & Higgins (1990), Robertson & Bell (1984), van Tets (1985g).

22. **Campbell Shag**

Phalacrocorax campbelli

French: Cormoran de Campbell **German**: Campbellscharbe **Spanish**: Cormorán de la Campbell
Other common names: Campbell Island Cormorant

Taxonomy. *Urile Campbelli* Filhol, 1878, Campbell Island.
Often includes *P. colensoi* and *P. ranfurlyi*; these three sometimes considered conspecific with *P. carunculatus* complex (*carunculatus*, *chalconotus* and *onslowi*). Sometimes placed in *Leucocarbo* or *Euleucocarbo*. Monotypic.
Distribution. Restricted to Campbell I, to S of New Zealand.
Descriptive notes. 63 cm; 1600-2000 g; wingspan 105 cm. Black foreneck distinctive; lacks white on back and scapulars. Non-breeding adult has duller bare parts, lacks crest and filoplumes. Juvenile as non-breeding adult, but brown replaces black, and lacks wing patch.
Habitat. Marine. Forages equally in open sea or in sheltered coastal waters, including bays or inlets. Breeds and roosts on sea cliffs, stacks or islets, sometimes amongst tussocks.
Food and Feeding. Virtually nothing known. Probably shells and fish. Feeds mainly by pursuit-diving. Sometimes fishes co-operatively, forming flocks of up to 2000 individuals.
Breeding. Season not well known, possibly starting in Aug/Sept and lasting until Dec. Solitary or in small to medium-sized colonies; colonies sometimes mixed with gulls or terns. Nests on cliffs, occu-

---

On following pages: 23. Bounty Shag (*Phalacrocorax ranfurlyi*); 24. Imperial Shag (*Phalacrocorax atriceps*); 25. Antarctic Shag (*Phalacrocorax bransfieldensis*); 26. South Georgia Shag (*Phalacrocorax georgianus*); 27. Heard Shag (*Phalacrocorax nivalis*); 28. Crozet Shag (*Phalacrocorax melanogenis*); 29. Kerguelen Shag (*Phalacrocorax verrucosus*); 30. Macquarie Shag (*Phalacrocorax purpurascens*); 31. Red-legged Cormorant (*Phalacrocorax gaimardi*); 32. Spotted Shag (*Phalacrocorax punctatus*); 33. Pitt Shag (*Phalacrocorax featherstoni*); 34. Little Pied Cormorant (*Phalacrocorax melanoleucos*); 35. Long-tailed Cormorant (*Phalacrocorax africanus*); 36. Crowned Cormorant (*Phalacrocorax coronatus*); 37. Little Cormorant (*Phalacrocorax niger*); 38. Pygmy Cormorant (*Phalacrocorax pygmaeus*); 39. Flightless Cormorant (*Phalacrocorax harrisi*).

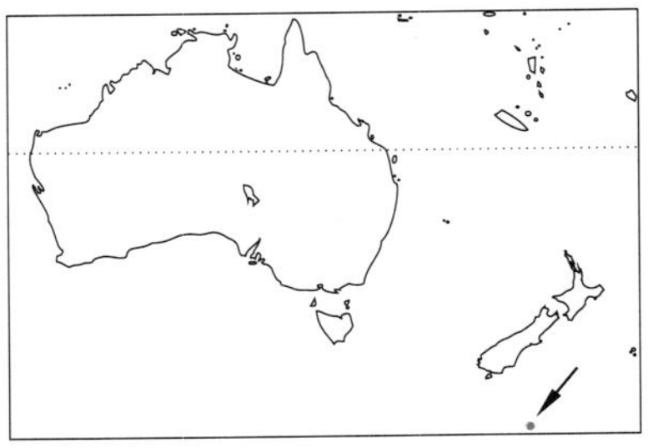

pying ledges, hollows or caves, or on flattish ground or on tussocks; nest mostly of tussock grass, with other plant matter and debris. Chick naked, grows grey down.
Movements. Sedentary; no records outwith waters in immediate vicinity of Campbell I.
Status and Conservation. Not globally threatened. Total population estimated at 2000 breeding pairs and 8000 individuals in 1975. Several species of mammal introduced to Campbell I, but not known to have any effects on present species; some eggs lost to skuas. Not apparently subject to any major threat.
Bibliography. Bailey & Sorensen (1962), Falla (1932), Falla *et al*. (1981), Marchant & Higgins (1990), van Tets (1980, 1985f).

23. Bounty Shag
Phalacrocorax ranfurlyi

French: Cormoran de Bounty **German**: Bountyscharbe **Spanish**: Cormorán de las Bounty
Other common names: Bounty Island Cormorant

Taxonomy. *Phalacrocorax ranfurlyi* Ogilvie-Grant, 1901, Bounty Islands.
Often considered race of *P. campbelli*. Some authors merge *colensoi*, *campbelli* and *ranfurlyi*, and *carunculatus*, *chalconotus* and *onslowi* into single species. Sometimes placed in *Leucocarbo* or *Euleucocarbo*. Monotypic.
Distribution. Restricted to Bounty Is (New Zealand).

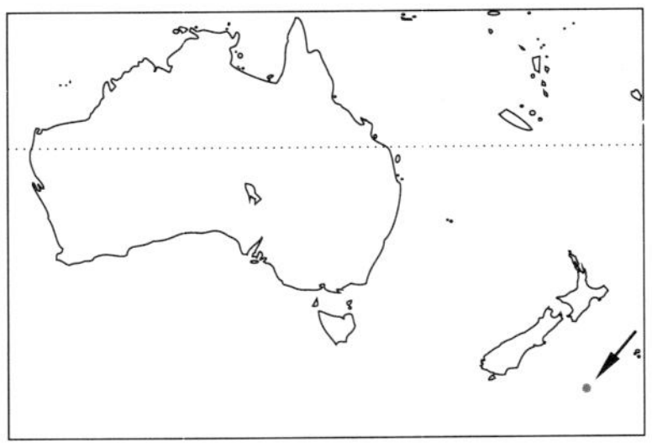

Descriptive notes. 71 cm; 2300-2900 g. Lacks white on scapulars; male can have small white dorsal patch; crest noticeably twisted forwards. Separated from other, similar species by having facial skin fairly uniform, orange to red. Non-breeding adult has duller bare parts and lacks crest. Juvenile as non-breeding adult, but brown replaces black, and more or less brown on foreneck; no wing patch.
Habitat. Marine. Forages out to sea and near coast. Breeds and rests on ledges and alcoves in sea cliffs and sometimes along narrow ridges.
Food and Feeding. Fish and invertebrates, including cephalopods, isopods, crabs and sea urchins. Feeds mainly by pursuit-diving. Sometimes forms feeding flocks of up to 300 birds. During breeding, female forages in morning, leaving after dawn and returning in middle of day; male forages in afternoon, after female's arrival, returning at dusk.
Breeding. Laying Oct/Nov. Forms monospecific colonies; centres of adjoining nests only c. 1 m apart. Nests on narrow cliff ledges and much less frequently on narrow skyline ridges; nest made of brown seaweed (*Marginariella*), epiphytes of seaweed, feathers, debris, pebbles and mud. 2-3 eggs.
Movements. Sedentary. Possible record of 2 birds at Antipodes Is (to S of Bounty Is) in 1950.
Status and Conservation. RARE. Very small population of 569 breeding pairs in 1978. Nesting space might be limited by competition with penguins and albatrosses, but this is considered unlikely. Small population requires constant monitoring, although no threats currently known.
Bibliography. Falla *et al*. (1981), Marchant & Higgins (1990), Robertson & van Tets (1982), van Tets & Robertson (1985).

24. Imperial Shag
Phalacrocorax atriceps

French: Cormoran impérial **German**: Blauaugenscharbe **Spanish**: Cormorán Imperial
Other common names: Imperial/Blue-eyed Cormorant

Taxonomy. *Phalacrocorax atriceps* King, 1828, Strait of Magellan.
Race *albiventer* formerly considered separate species, including birds of Falkland Is and parts of S America, but wide zone of sympatry where mixed pairs frequent, and no differences observed in either behaviour or osteology; thus *albiventer* only constitutes race or possibly even colour morph. Some authors also included *P. melanogenis*, *P. verrucosus* and *P. purpurascens* within *P. albiventer*. Present species has also frequently been considered to include *P. bransfieldensis*, *P. georgianus* and *P. nivalis*. Species sometimes placed in genus *Notocarbo*. Two subspecies normally recognized.
Subspecies and Distribution.
P. a. atriceps King, 1828 - S South America.
P. a. albiventer (Lesson, 1831) - Falkland Is.

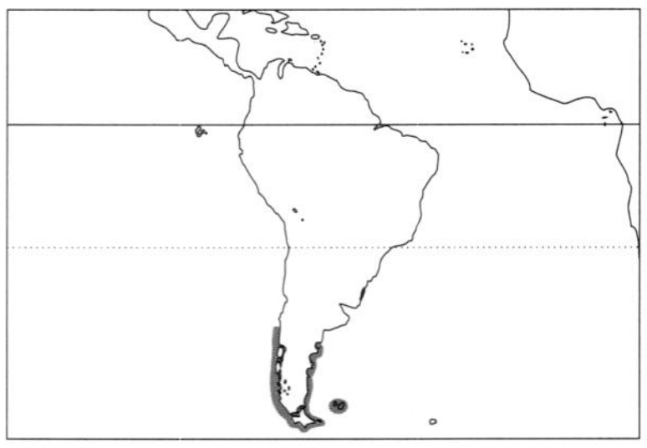

Descriptive notes. c. 68-76 cm. Large white dorsal patch. Limit between white and black starts between gape and eye, where moves upwards and backwards over ear-coverts. Non-breeding adult lacks crest, wing bar, head plumes and dorsal patch. Juvenile as non-breeding adult, but duller and browner on upperparts. Race *albiventer* lacks dorsal patch; black starts beside gape and moves straight backwards; sometimes has small reddish spot between eye and caruncle.
Habitat. Exclusively marine in most of range; forages in subantartic waters along coast and around islands. Breeds along coast, sometimes occupying islands in freshwater coastal lagoons, but commuting to sea for feeding. Locally inhabits large inland lakes in foothills of Andes at altitude of c. 800 m, where breeds on rocky islands.
Food and Feeding. Mainly fish and crustaceans, especially *Munida* in Falkland Is and also amphipods; other invertebrates include cephalopods. Feeds mainly by pursuit-diving. Can form large feeding flocks of thousands of birds out to sea.
Breeding. Laying starts Nov. Forms colonies, sometimes very dense, of hundreds of thousands of birds. Nests on flat tops of rocks or on small islands in sea or on lakes; nest is truncated cone of seaweed and other plant matter, mud and excreta; can be reused in successive years. Normally 3 eggs, often 2, occasionally up to 5; chick naked, grows brownish black down; fledging c. 7 weeks.
Movements. Basically sedentary, though wanders up coasts of Chile and Argentina to N of breeding zones. During austral winter may move up Atlantic coast as far as Uruguay.
Status and Conservation. Not globally threatened. Major populations both on mainland S America and in Falkland Is, with many large colonies. Common in Chile, though suffers some egg-collecting. Widespread in Falkland Is, especially in E; c. 19,900 pairs at 42-44 sites.
Bibliography. Bahamonde (1955), Behn *et al*. (1955), Blake (1977), Carp (1991), Croxall *et al*. (1984), Devillers & Terschuren (1978), Fjeldså & Krabbe (1990), Humphrey *et al*. (1970), Johnson (1965), Lindsey (1986), Malacalza (1984a, 1984b), Malacalza & Hall (1988), Murphy (1916a, 1936), de la Peña (1986), Rasmussen (1986a, 1986b, 1988b, 1988c, 1989), Rasmussen & Humphrey (1988), Siegel-Causey (1986a), van Tets & Vestjens (1985), Watson (1975), Williams & Burger (1979), Woods (1988).

25. Antarctic Shag
Phalacrocorax bransfieldensis

French: Cormoran antarctique **German**: Antarktikscharbe **Spanish**: Cormorán Antártico

Taxonomy. *Phalacrocorax atriceps bransfieldensis* Murphy, 1936, South Shetlands.
Often considered race of *P. atriceps*. Populations of *P. georgianus* in South Orkney and South Sandwich Is have frequently been ascribed to present species. Species sometimes placed in genus *Notocarbo*. Monotypic.
Distribution. Antarctic Peninsula and South Shetland Is.

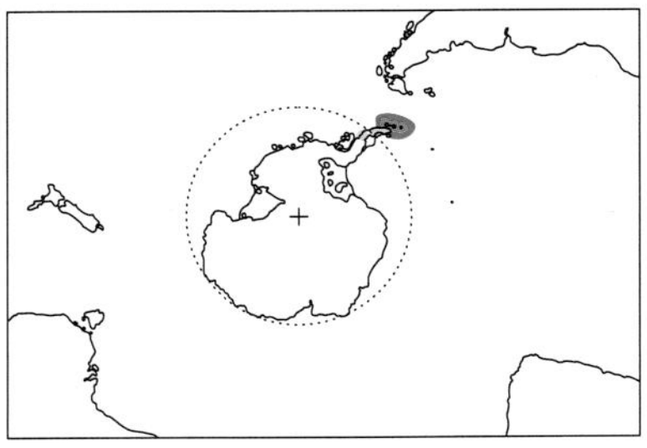

Descriptive notes. c. 75-77 cm (calculated); 2500-3022 g. Large; male heavier, with larger bill. Apparently has white dorsal patch. Limit between black and white begins as in *P. a. atriceps*, but passes higher over cheek and further back onto hindneck. Non-breeding adult duller, lacks crest. Juvenile as non-breeding adult but browner above.
Habitat. Marine. Inhabits coasts and islands, generally staying close to them or to pack ice. Breeds in rocky areas on coast or islets, including rocky outcrops and stacks, cliffs, slopes and flat ground.
Food and Feeding. Mainly fish (Nototheniidae, Chaenichthiidae) and benthic invertebrates, including crustaceans and cephalopods. Feeds by pursuit-diving. Generally forages alone or in small flocks; in winter forms larger flocks which move further out to sea.
Breeding. Laying Oct-Dec, varying between colonies. Normally forms small colonies, which can be very dense; sometimes breeds alongside penguins. Nests on ground in rocky areas; nest is truncated cone of seaweed and grass, cemented together with excreta; can be reused in successive years, and birds show marked tendency to breed in same part of colony each year, although evidence suggests usually with different partner. 2-3 eggs; males take greater share of incubation; chicks naked, grow brownish black down; fledging 40-45 days; post-fledging care occurs, but period unrecorded. Survival of chicks variable with year (44-83%). Sexual maturity at 4 years old, if not before.
Movements. Sedentary, tending to remain within vicinity of colony at all times. In winter may be forced to move short distances in order to find ice-free water for foraging; birds from Antarctic Peninsula thus move N.
Status and Conservation. Not globally threatened. Abundant: 10,000 pairs at 56 colonies on Antarctic Peninsula; 700 pairs at 21 colonies in South Shetland Is; 205 pairs at 14 colonies on Elephant I. Colony size can vary between years; breeding success thought to be closely related to food availability. Not subject to any particular threats.
Bibliography. Bernstein & Maxson (1981, 1982a, 1982b, 1984, 1985), Croxall *et al*. (1984), Devillers & Terschuren (1978), Marchant & Higgins (1990), Maxson & Bernstein (1982), Schlatter & Moreno (1976), Watson (1975).

26. South Georgia Shag
Phalacrocorax georgianus

French: Cormoran géorgien **German**: Südgeorgienscharbe **Spanish**: Cormorán de Georgia
Other common names: South Georgia Cormorant

Taxonomy. *Phalacrocorax atriceps georgianus* Lönnberg, 1906, South Georgia.
Often considered race of *P. atriceps*. Some authors restrict species to population of South Georgia, those of other zones being referred to *P. bransfieldensis*. Species sometimes placed in genus *Notocarbo*. Monotypic.
Distribution. South Georgia, South Orkney Is, South Sandwich Is and Shag Rocks (Scotia Sea).

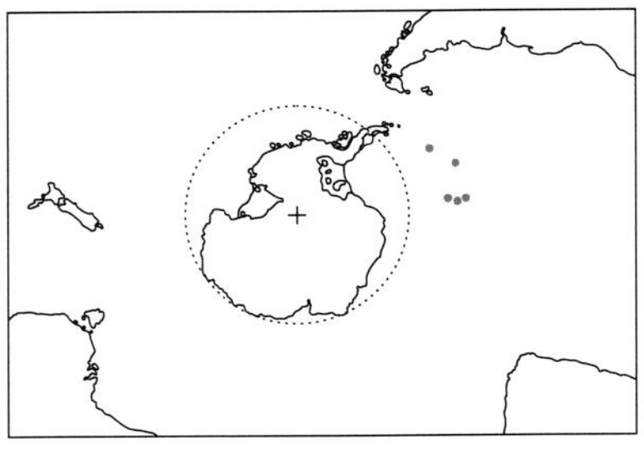

Descriptive notes. c. 75 cm (calculated); 2883 g. Can have white dorsal patch. Limit between black and white begins as in *P. a. atriceps*, but crosses ear-coverts; bill smaller and slightly more white on sides of neck than in *P. atriceps*. Non-breeding adult somewhat duller and more faded, lacks crest. Juvenile as non-breeding adult but dull brown above.
Habitat. Marine; inshore feeder. Breeds on islets and rocky zones, including ledges and terraces of sea cliffs and stacks; also on flat or gently-sloping ground, sometimes covered in tussock grass.
Food and Feeding. Benthic prey, mainly fish (Nototheniidae), up to 27 cm long. Feeds mainly by pursuit-diving. Generally feeds alone or in small flocks.
Breeding. Season short; laying Oct-Dec. Generally forms small colonies, but sometimes hundreds of pairs and sometimes very dense. Nests on ground, even on snow; nest is truncated cone of seaweed, grass, mud and excreta; some nests consist almost entirely of penguin tail feathers; nest-site often reused, but partners usually different, perhaps normally as result of one bird dying. 2-3 eggs; incubation 28-31 days; chick naked, grows dark grey down; fledging c. 65 days. Hatching success 85-91%; both hatching and fledging success lower with later laying. Sexual maturity at 3 years old; known to have lived to at least 12 years old.
Movements. Sedentary, with some movement over short distances in winter towards ice-free zones.
Status and Conservation. Not globally threatened. Total population of c. 7500 pairs, including almost 4000 at South Georgia, 2000 in South Orkney Is, 1000 at Shag Rocks and 100-1000 in South Sandwich Is. Frequently taken for food in past, as habitually flew very close over whaling ships where easily knocked down. Not subject to any particular threats at present.
Bibliography. Cobley (1989), Conroy & Twelves (1972), Croxall (1984), Croxall *et al*. (1984), Devillers & Terschuren (1978), Marchant & Higgins (1990), Prince & Croxall (1983), Shaw (1985a, 1985b, 1986).

27. Heard Shag
Phalacrocorax nivalis

French: Cormoran de Heard **German**: Heardscharbe **Spanish**: Cormorán de la Heard
Other common names: Heard Island Cormorant

Taxonomy. *Phalacrocorax (Leucocarbo) atriceps nivalis* Falla, 1937, Atlas Cove, Heard Island.

Often considered race of *P. atriceps*. Sometimes placed in genus *Notocarbo*. Monotypic.
Distribution. Restricted to Heard I, in SE Indian Ocean.

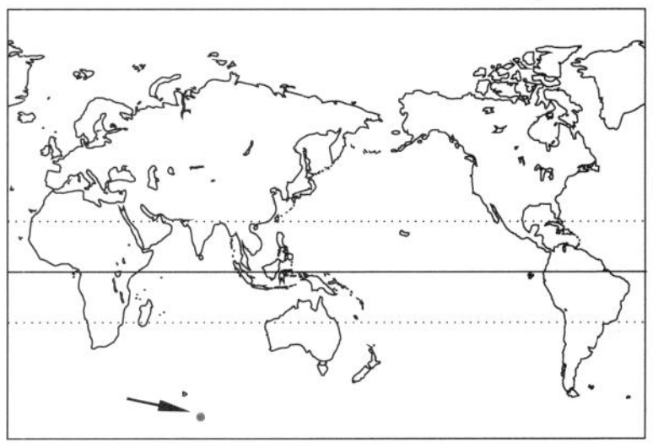

Descriptive notes. 77 cm; 2800-3300 g; wingspan 120 cm. Has white dorsal patch. One of largest and whitest of pied shags. Limit between black and white starts behind eye and continues substantially upwards and backwards. Non-breeding adult duller, lacks crest and filoplumes. Juvenile brown above, with variable pale wing patch.
Habitat. Marine. Forages in shallow coastal waters. Breeds on sea cliffs, in tussock grassland. In early 1980's bred on vegetated stack, but has now moved to mainland opposite, only c. 50 m from former colony. Roosts on cliff tops, offshore stacks, boulder beaches and in areas of volcanic sand.
Food and Feeding. Benthic prey, especially polychaetes and to lesser extent fish; also gastropods and octopods. Apparently differs from nearby subantarctic species in important quantities of invertebrates. Fish mainly Nototheniidae, especially *Notothenia cyanobrancha*. Proportions of different groups of invertebrates varies between years. Diet of breeding birds appears to be richer than that of non-breeders at roost. Feeds mainly by pursuit-diving. Can form small feeding flocks.
Breeding. Laying Oct/Nov. Forms small colonies, only 2 known. Nests in tussock grass on cliffs; nest of tussock grass compacted with mud and excreta. 2-4 eggs, average alternatively stated as 2·5 or 4; chicks naked, grow dark brown down. Breeding success very low: maximum of 43 chicks fledged from c. 90 nests in 1985/86; 7 chicks from c. 27 nests in 1986/87; and 94 chicks from 94 nests in late 1987.
Movements. Sedentary; no records even from McDonald Is and Shag I, respectively 40 km and 12 km from Heard I, nor anywhere far from Heard I. In mid-Feb, some internal movements of population at Heard I itself, from colonies in NW to roosts in SE.
Status and Conservation. VULNERABLE. Total population estimated at c. 600-1000 birds. Largest number observed was 548 individuals roosting at Stephenson Lagoon in 1985, but subsequent counts much lower. Overall numbers and also number of chicks fledged each year seem to vary considerably. Vulnerable due to very small size of population, restricted range and very limited number of breeding pairs; maximum of c. 90 pairs found breeding in any particular year since 1950's. Development of commercial fishing could have serious effects on survival of species.
Bibliography. Brouwer & Garnett (1990), Burton & Williams (1986), Devillers & Terschuren (1978), Downes *et al.* (1959), Falla (1937), Green, Williams *et al.* (1990), Johnstone (1982, 1985), Keage & Johnstone (1982), Kirkwood *et al.* (1989), Marchant & Higgins (1990), Pemberton & Gales (1987), Vining (1983), Woehler (1991).

28. Crozet Shag

Phalacrocorax melanogenis

French: Cormoran de Crozet **German**: Crozetscharbe **Spanish**: Cormorán de las Crozet
Other common names: Marion (Island) Shag

Taxonomy. *Hypoleucus melanogenis* Blyth, 1860, Crozet Islands.
Often considered race of *P. atriceps*. Sometimes placed in genus *Notocarbo*. Monotypic.
Distribution. Crozet Is and Prince Edward Is, in S Indian Ocean.

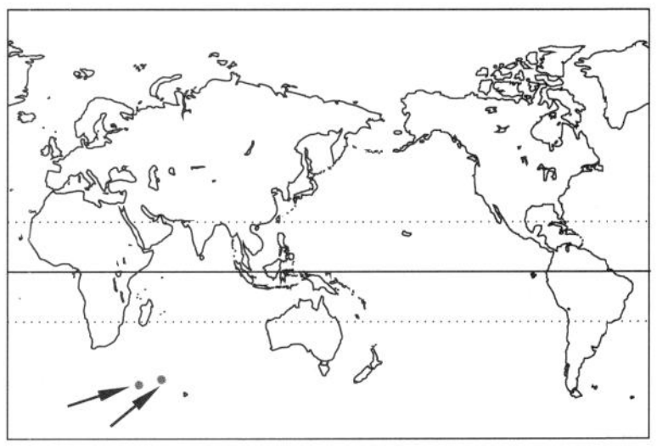

Descriptive notes. 70 cm; 1700-2700 g; wingspan 125 cm. No white on back, and only rarely on scapulars. Limit between black and white begins as in *P. atriceps albiventer*, but may have shorter neck; proportions intermediate between *atriceps* and *verrucosus*. Non-breeding adult duller, lacks crest and filoplumes. Juvenile as non-breeding adult, but black replaced by dark brown; lacks wing patch.
Habitat. Marine. Forages close inshore, at Marion I no more than 400 m from coast, at Crozet Is occasionally up to 6 km offshore over continental shelf. At Marion I, normally forages near fringe of thick beds of kelp (*Macrocystis pyrifera*), occurring within fringe in Dec. Breeds along coast, generally in areas sheltered from prevailing wind; occupies cliffs, slopes with or without vegetation, flat ground, rocky outcrops and sometimes boulder beaches. Roosts on cliff tops, headlands and stacks.
Food and Feeding. Bottom feeder, taking benthic prey: mainly fish, especially nototheniid *Notothenia squamifrons*; also crustaceans, especially shrimps (*Nauticaris marionis*), octopus, squid, polychaetes and holothurians. Fish most important in Feb-Mar, far less so in Apr-May. Feeds mainly by pursuit-diving. Forages alone or sometimes co-operatively in small flocks.
Breeding. Season varies between colonies, with laying Oct-Feb at Marion I and Crozets, but at Prince Edward I in 1984 some laying in Jun. Breeds alone or in small groups of up to 54 pairs; sometimes associates with penguins. Nests on bare ground or in vegetation, often in or near patches of *Cotula plumosa*; nest is truncated cone of *Cotula plumosa* and other plant matter, cemented together with mud and excreta; reused in successive years, but new pair each year, at any rate at Crozet Is. Normally 3 or 2 eggs (1-5); incubation 28-32 days; chicks naked, grow greyish brown down; fledging 50-63 days, exceptionally 75-80 days; post-fledging care c. 1 month. Hatching success 45-62% (Marion) or 56-65% (Crozet); overall breeding success 31-39% (Crozet).
Movements. Sedentary; not recorded far from respective island groups. At Crozet Is, some local movements over short distances of juveniles and of adults outwith breeding season, birds turning up at different colonies and roosts.
Status and Conservation. RARE. Total population over 1200 pairs, with at least 815 pairs in Crozet Is in 1981/82, and 405 pairs in Prince Edward Is (120 on Prince Edward I, 285 on Marion I). Some natural predation of eggs, but breeding failure apparently due mostly to rough sea conditions. At Crozet Is and Marion I some colonies deserted probably due to disturbance by humans; at present populations seem to be stable. Prince Edward I is restricted nature reserve.
Bibliography. Blankley (1981), Cooper (1985c), Derenne *et al.* (1976), Devillers & Terschuren (1978), Espitalier-Noel *et al.* (1988), Marchant & Higgins (1990), Rand (1956), Ryan & Hunter (1985), Williams & Burger (1979), Williams *et al.* (1979).

29. Kerguelen Shag

Phalacrocorax verrucosus

French: Cormoran des Kerguelen **German**: Kerguelenscharbe **Spanish**: Cormorán de las Kerguelen
Other common names: Kerguelen Cormorant

Taxonomy. *Halieus (Hypoleucus) verrucosus* Cabanis, 1875, Kerguelen.
Often considered race of *P. atriceps*. Sometimes placed in genus *Notocarbo*. Occasional occurrence of birds with white wing bars exclusively in E Kerguelen might suggest recent arrival of some individuals of *P. melanogenis* or *P. nivalis*, which might subsequently have hybridized with local birds. Monotypic.
Distribution. Restricted to Kerguelen Is, in S Indian Ocean.

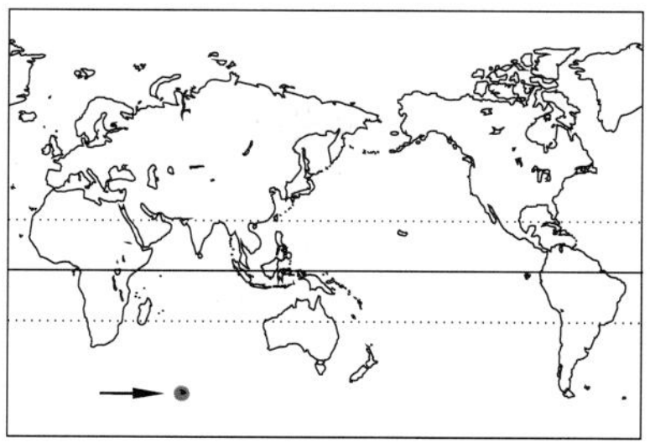

Descriptive notes. 65 cm; 1700-2240 g; wingspan 110 cm. Rarely has white wing bar and dorsal patch. Smaller and stubbier than other similar species, with leg colour drabber; duller, can have much more black on head. Non-breeding adult duller, lacks crest. Juvenile blackish brown, with variable amounts of white on underparts.
Habitat. Marine. Feeds in open inshore waters, mainly in bays and fjords of heavily indented shoreline of Kerguelen Is. Generally does not stray more than c. 6 km from coast. In summer feeds in kelp banks. Breeds along coasts of main island and on islands in gulfs or offshore; on exposed stretches of coast or in sheltered areas, e.g. heads of fjords.
Food and Feeding. Probably fish and sea urchins. Has occasionally been recorded feeding at surface alongside boats. Feeds mainly by pursuit-diving. In May-Oct sometimes feeds in flocks of up to several hundred birds; in Jan-Feb mostly solitary.
Breeding. Laying Oct-Jan, varying with colony. Normally breeds in small nuclei of 3-30 pairs, but on Courbet and Jeanne d'Arc Peninsulas, in E of main island, forms colonies of up to 400 nests; sometimes nests on periphery of penguin colonies. Nests on cliffs and rocky outcrops, occupying ledges and crevices; nest is truncated cone of seaweed and grass compacted with mud and excreta; if remains intact, can be reused in following seasons. Apparently 2-4 eggs (average 2·5); incubation probably c. 30 days; chicks naked, grow sooty brown down.
Movements. Sedentary; probably some dispersal around islands outside breeding season, although colonies are not totally abandoned. Some records, mostly of immatures, over continental shelf up to 80 km from Kerguelen Is.
Status and Conservation. Not globally threatened. Relatively abundant, with total population estimated at 6000-7000 birds in 1980's. Population apparently stable; not known to be affected by humans or introduced mammals; some natural predation of eggs and chicks by skuas, sheathbills and gulls.
Bibliography. Derenne *et al.* (1974), Jouventin *et al.* (1984), Marchant & Higgins (1990), Paulian (1953), Thibault & Guyot (1988), Thomas (1983), Voisin, J.F. (1970, 1973), Watson (1975), Weimerskirch, Zotier & Jouventin (1989).

30. Macquarie Shag

Phalacrocorax purpurascens

French: Cormoran de Macquarie **German**: Macquariescharbe **Spanish**: Cormorán de la Macquarie

Taxonomy. *Carbo purpurascens* Brandt, 1837, no locality.
Often considered race of *P. atriceps*. Sometimes placed in genus *Notocarbo*. Monotypic.
Distribution. Restricted to Macquarie I and nearby Bishop and Clerk Islets.

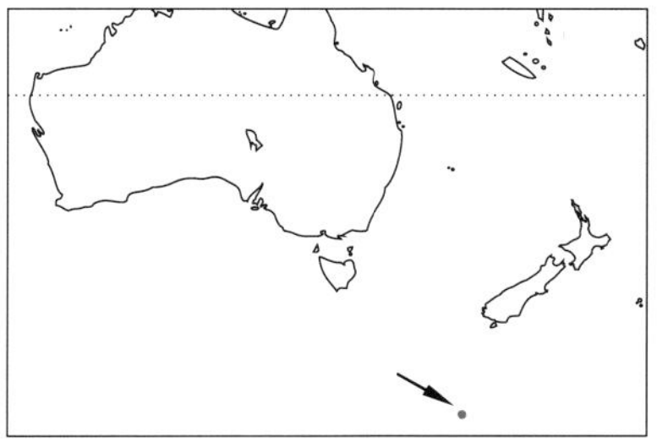

Descriptive notes. 71-75 cm; 2500-3500 g; wingspan 110 cm. Similar to *P. atriceps albiventer* and *P. melanogenis*, but bare skin at base of bill often conspicuously ochre yellow, and legs pinkish red with irregular dark spotting, especially on webs. Non-breeding adult duller, lacks crest and filoplumes. Juvenile similar to non-breeding adult, but brown above, with variable paler wing patch.
Habitat. Marine. Foraging zones conditioned by limited areas of shallow water; species thus forages close to shore, as seabed descends rapidly; suitable feeding grounds more extensive off W coast of Macquarie I, where largest colonies also occur. Major colonies along shoreline; also breeds on islets or stacks, mainly offshore.
Food and Feeding. Takes benthic prey, capturing it amongst rocks and kelp beds. Mainly fish, especially *Paranotothenia magellanica* and to lesser degree *Harpagifer bispinis*; also some invertebrates, including crustaceans, gastropods and polychaetes. Feeds by pursuit-diving. During breeding season feeds alone, but in off-season can form dense feeding flocks of up to 40 birds, which perform repeated simultaneous dives followed by short flights to new diving site.
Breeding. Laying mostly in Oct/Nov, but also in Jan. Forms colonies of 3-320 pairs; sometimes alongside penguins. Nests on ground often among boulders, near high tide line; nest is truncated cone of tussock grass held together with mud and excreta; strong competition for nest-sites, which males defend year after year, although nests do not survive between years and pairs frequently not renewed. 1-3 eggs, usually 3 and only rarely 1; incubation possibly 32-33 days; chicks naked, grow sooty brown down; quickly become independent. Mean fledging rate 1·0-1·9 chicks per nest, depending on year; breeding success 54-61%. Sexual maturity generally not until 4 years old, but sometimes at 2 years old; may pair at earlier age; known to have lived at least 13 years.
Movements. Sedentary; does not stray from home islands. At Macquarie I, birds that move between E and W coasts fly along coast, and thus avoid having to fly over land.
Status and Conservation. RARE. Very small population estimated at 760 pairs, including 100 pairs for Bishop and Clerk Islets, where no proper census has been carried out. Total of 23 colonies known, of which 19 active in period 1975-1979; numbers fluctuate, perhaps because of considerable movement between colonies. No major threats known; feral cats might take some chicks, but programme initiated to control cats.
Bibliography. Brothers (1985), Brouwer & Garnett (1990), Devillers & Terschuren (1978), Falla *et al.* (1981), Green, Williams & Slip (1990), Lugg *et al.* (1978), Marchant & Higgins (1990), Watson (1975).

31. Red-legged Cormorant

Phalacrocorax gaimardi

French: Cormoran de Gaimard **German**: Buntscharbe **Spanish**: Cormorán Chuita
Other common names: Red-footed Shag/Cormorant, Gaimard's Cormorant

Taxonomy. *Carbo Gaimardi* Lesson and Garnot, 1828, "Lima, au Pérou" = San Lorenzo Island, roadstead of Lima. Atlantic populations sometimes considered to form separate race *cirriger*. Sometimes placed in genus *Stictocarbo*. Monotypic.
Distribution. Coasts of S South America: in Pacific from near equator S to Chiloé I (SC Chile) and beyond; in Atlantic restricted to S Argentina.
Descriptive notes. 71-76 cm; wingspan 91 cm. Unmistakable. General coloration variable. Non-breeding adult similar, lacks white feathers behind eye. Juvenile browner overall, with throat and underparts variably pale.
Habitat. Marine. Breeds on rocky coasts and islands, often on cliffs.
Food and Feeding. Mainly fish. Feeds mainly by pursuit-diving. Habitually forages alone.
Breeding. Laying Oct-Jan in Chile; in tropics all year round. Solitary or in small groups. Nests in caves or on cliff ledges; large nests of seaweed. Generally 3 eggs, sometimes 4.

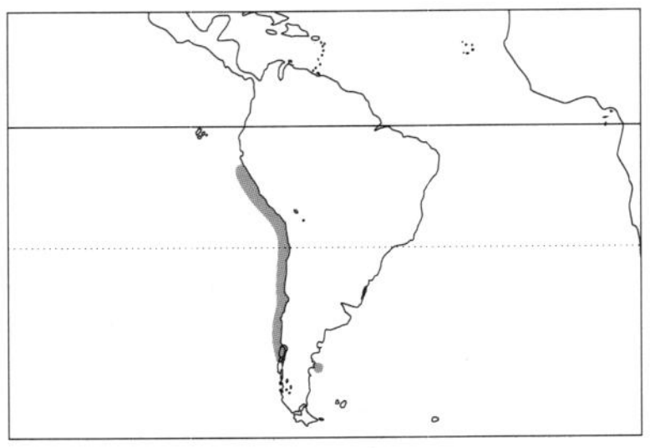

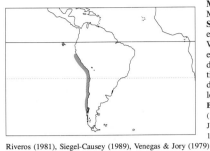

Movements. Little known. Vagrant to Straits of Magellan and S Ecuador.
Status and Conservation. Not globally threatened. Currently considered near-threatened. Widespread, but nowhere common in Peru, where estimated maximum of 10,000 breeding birds; does not suffer same severe fluctuations as partially sympatric *P. bougainvillii*. Uncommon and declining in Chile, where threats include egg-collecting.
Bibliography. Blake (1977), von Boetticher (1935), Carp (1991), Duffy (1983b), Duffy, Hays & Plenge (1984), Johnson (1965), Murphy (1936), de la Peña (1980a, 1986), Rasmussen (1988a), Schlatter (1984), Schlatter & Riveros (1981), Siegel-Causey (1989), Venegas & Jory (1979).

32. Spotted Shag
Phalacrocorax punctatus

French: Cormoran moucheté **German**: Tüpfelscharbe **Spanish**: Cormorán Moteado
Other common names: Spotted Cormorant, Crested/Ocean Shag; Blue Shag (*oliveri*)

Taxonomy. *Pelicanus* [sic] *punctatus* Sparrman, 1786, Queen Charlotte Sound, South Island, New Zealand. Often includes *P. featherstoni* as race. Sometimes placed in genus *Stictocarbo*. May be better regarded as monotypic, due to uncertainty caused by considerable variations in pre-nuptial and nuptial plumage. Two subspecies normally recognized.
Subspecies and Distribution.
P. p. punctatus (Sparrman, 1786) - New Zealand.
P. p. oliveri Mathews, 1930 - Stewart I; also Westland (South I).

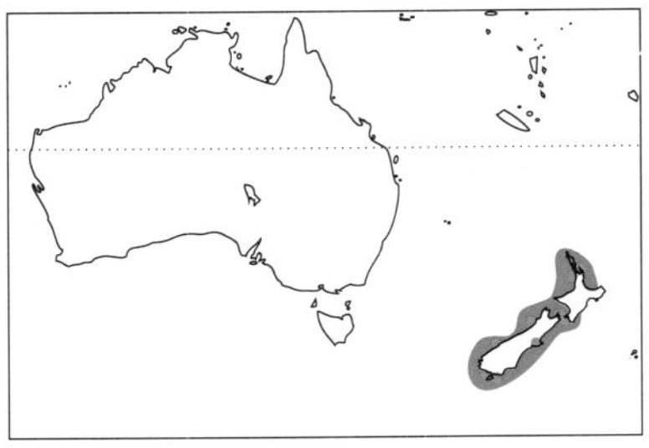

Descriptive notes. 64-74 cm; 700-1210 g; wingspan 91-99 cm. Underparts can be very pale grey. Non-breeding adult duller, lacks plumes of head, neck, rump and thighs; crest reduced. Juvenile grey-brown above, pale greyish below; as in most juvenile cormorants, bare parts duller. Races supposedly separated on whether or not white supercilium extends in front of eye.
Habitat. Marine. Forages in fairly deep offshore waters, up to 16 km from coast, but also along coast in bays, inlets and estuaries. Breeds on rocky coasts and inshore islands, often on cliffs. Uses offshore stacks, islands and breakwaters for roosting.
Food and Feeding. Very little known, but apparently fish, crustaceans and other invertebrates. Feeds mainly by pursuit-diving. Can form feeding flocks, sometimes numbering thousands of birds.
Breeding. Laying Sept-Nov in South I, but season longer in North I, with peaks in late Aug, Dec and Mar. Forms colonies of variable size. Nests on cliffs, occupying ledges or cracks; nest of seaweed, built in c. 1 week. Mostly 3 eggs (1-4); incubation 28-35 days; chicks naked, grow grey down; fledging 57-71 days. Breeding success at Otago (SE South I) 54·4%, with average of 2 chicks fledged per nest in successful pairs. Sexual maturity at 2 years old.
Movements. Mostly local movements, with dispersal along coasts in winter; birds breeding at Banks Peninsula (E South I) reach N tip of island in winter.
Status and Conservation. Not globally threatened. Total population estimated at 60,000-150,000 birds in early 1980's; locally abundant in South I, e.g. 10,000 nests on Banks Peninsula in 1960's. Has suffered much persecution through shooting and destruction of colonies; numbers at Noises Is (North I) greatly reduced at beginning of century by shooting. Some populations affected by disturbance associated with recreational boating and fishing; shooting continues in places.
Bibliography. Chambers (1989), Cunningham & Moors (1985), Falla (1932), Falla *et al.* (1981), Fenwick & Browne (1975), Marchant & Higgins (1990), Robertson & Bell (1984), Soper (1976), Stonehouse (1967b), van Tets (1985h), Turbott (1956).

33. Pitt Shag
Phalacrocorax featherstoni

French: Cormoran de Featherston **German**: Pittscharbe **Spanish**: Cormorán de la Pitt
Other common names: Chatham Cormorant (!)

Taxonomy. *Phalacrocorax featherstoni* Buller, 1873, Chatham Islands.
Often considered to be race of *P. punctatus*. Sometimes placed in genus *Stictocarbo*. Monotypic.
Distribution. Restricted to Chatham Is, to SE of New Zealand.

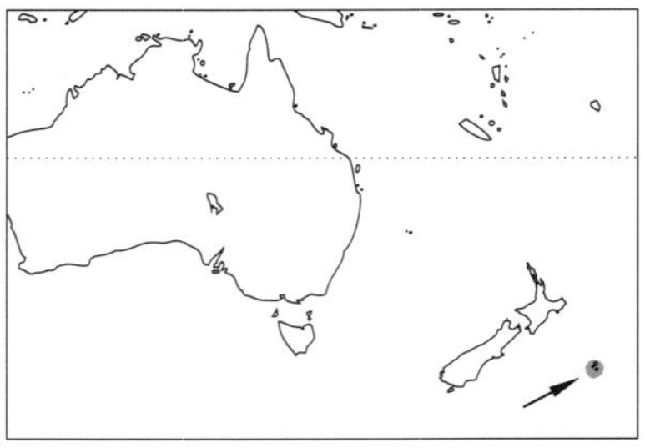

Descriptive notes. c. 63 cm; 645-1325 g. Markedly darker than *P. punctatus*, lacks extended white eyestripe. Non-breeding adult lacks plumes of head and neck. Juvenile dark brown above, paler brown below; darker than juvenile *P. punctatus*.
Habitat. Marine. Breeds on rocky coasts, typically on cliffs. Forages out to sea and also in sheltered inshore waters.
Food and Feeding. Probably small fish and crustaceans. Presumably feeds mainly by pursuit-diving.
Breeding. Apparently Aug-Dec. Forms small colonies. Nests on cliffs, occupying ledges and cracks; nests small, but well built of ice-plant (*Diphyma australe*) and other plant matter; reused in successive years. Average probably 3 eggs; chicks hatch naked.
Movements. Sedentary; no records outwith immediate vicinity of Chatham Is.
Status and Conservation. RARE. Very small population estimated at under 1000 individuals. Population requires monitoring, but not known to be subject to any particular threats at present.
Bibliography. Cemmick & Veitch (1985), Falla *et al.* (1981), Fleming (1939), Greenway (1967), Marchant & Higgins (1990), van Tets (1985i).

34. Little Pied Cormorant
Phalacrocorax melanoleucos

French: Cormoran pie **German**: Kräuselscharbe **Spanish**: Cormorán Piquicorto
Other common names: Little (Black and White) Cormorant/Shag, Little River/White-throated/Frilled Shag

Taxonomy. *Hydrocorax melanoleucos* Vieillot, 1817, "Australasie" = New South Wales.
Frequently placed in *Halietor* or *Microcarbo*. Polymorphic race *brevirostris* may be distinct species. Three subspecies normally recognized.
Subspecies and Distribution.
P. m. melanoleucos (Vieillot, 1817) - E Indonesia to Solomon Is and New Caledonia; Australia and Tasmania; Campbell I.
P. m. brevicauda Mayr, 1931 - Rennell I (Solomon Is).
P. m. brevirostris Gould, 1837 - New Zealand, Stewart I.

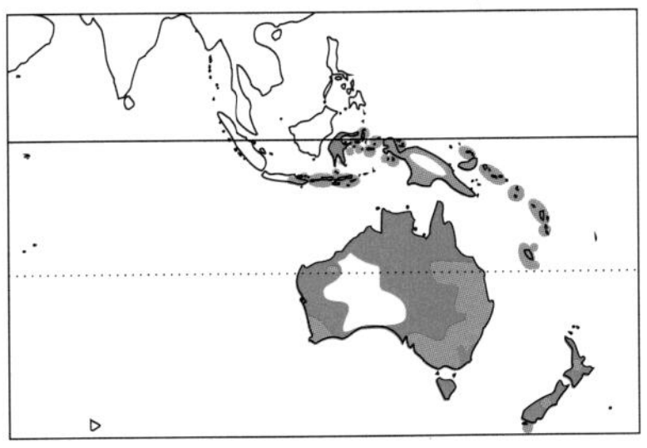

Descriptive notes. 55-65 cm; 487-900 g; wingspan 84-91 cm. Only small, long-tailed cormorant with pied plumage. White often stained reddish or orangish brown. Non-breeding adult lacks crests or frills on head. Juvenile duller, with dark on head extending below eye and dark thigh; juvenile of white-throated morph is all-dark. Races supposedly separated on measurements; race *brevirostris* polymorphic, with pied morph resembling nominate race, white-throated and dark morphs and intermediate morph, which has underparts white variably speckled black.
Habitat. Very adaptable, although prefers fresh water, frequenting swamps, lakes, pools, rivers, temporary flood waters, artificial impoundments; even in city, in ornamental ponds. Also in coastal waters, including lagoons, estuaries, mangrove swamps, sheltered harbours, salt-pans and offshore islands. Usually requires trees or bushes near or over water for breeding. On large water bodies, tends to fish along shallow margins.
Food and Feeding. Variety of fish and invertebrates, including freshwater crayfish, shrimps, prawns and aquatic insects; small amounts of frogs and tadpoles. Invertebrates, especially crustaceans, often important, e.g. in N Australia decapod crustacea, hemipterans, larvae of odonatans and other invertebrates constitute more than half of prey items, and 35% of dry weight; elsewhere even more important. Claws shaken off crayfish before consumed. In Australia, exotic fish species frequently form significant part of diet, especially carp (*Carassius auratus*) and perch (*Perca fluviatilis*). Feeds mainly by pursuit-diving. Generally feeds alone, and if flocks gather, birds do not tend to fish co-operatively.
Breeding. Season irregular, depending on local water conditions; possibly all year round; peak in Oct/Nov in places. Generally forms small colonies, often in company of other waterbirds, including other cormorants, darters, herons, etc. Nests on trees or bushes, occasionally on rocks; stick nest lined with leaves and grass. Usually 3-5 eggs, especially 4 (1-7); chicks naked, grow black down.
Movements. Basically sedentary, with extensive juvenile dispersal. Also moves in response to local water conditions on inland waters; more frequently on coast during severe droughts. Partially nomadic in interior of Australia.
Status and Conservation. Not globally threatened. Widespread in Australia, with hundreds of colonies; population of New Zealand estimated at 10,000-50,000 in early 1980's. Has suffered with destruction and alteration of wetlands; effects only partially offset by widespread colonization of reservoirs. In New South Wales, feeds extensively on introduced fish species, and campaigns to remove such fish could have negative effects on species. Partial census of Papua New Guinea in Jan 1990 gave 1121.
Bibliography. Beehler *et al.* (1986), Bregulla (1992), Bull *et al.* (1985), Chambers (1989), Coates (1985), Croxall *et al.* (1984), Dowding & Taylor (1987), Falla (1932), Falla *et al.* (1981), Galbreath (1989), Goodwin (1956), Hannecart & Letocart (1980), Harley (1946), Keast & D'Ombrain (1949), Kolichis (1977), Lindsey (1986), Llewellyn (1983), Marchant & Higgins (1990), Matthews & Fordham (1986), McKeown (1944), McNally (1957), Miller, B. (1976, 1979, 1980), Moisley (1960), Potts, K.J. (1977), Pratt *et al.* (1987), Schodde & Tidemann (1988), Serventy (1938, 1939), Serventy *et al.* (1971), Stonehouse (1967b), Taylor (1987, 1989), van Tets *et al.* (1976), Trayler *et al.* (1989), Vestjens *et al.* (1985), White & Bruce (1986), Whitlock (1921), Wooller & Dunlop (1981).

35. Long-tailed Cormorant
Phalacrocorax africanus

French: Cormoran africain **German**: Riedscharbe **Spanish**: Cormorán Africano
Other common names: Reed Cormorant

Taxonomy. *Pelecanus africanus* Gmelin, 1789, Africa.
Often includes *P. coronatus* as race. Frequently placed in *Halietor* or *Microcarbo*. Two subspecies recognized.
Subspecies and Distribution.
P. a. africanus (Gmelin, 1789) - Africa S of Sahara.
P. a. pictilis Bangs, 1918 - Madagascar.

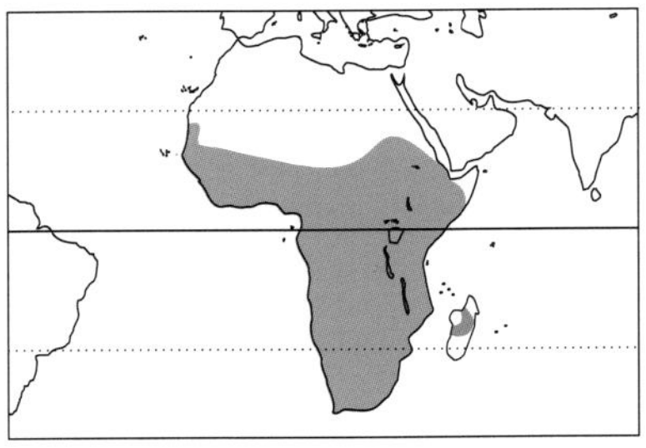

Descriptive notes. 50-60 cm; 680-685 g; wingspan 80-90 cm. White facial plumes quickly lost, thus giving very similar aspect to *P. coronatus*, but upperparts paler. Females average smaller. Non-breeding adult generally browner, with paler underparts and whiter throat and belly; lacks crest and white feathering over eye. Juvenile as non-breeding adult, but whiter underparts and less patterned upperbody. Race *pictilis* larger with bigger, less rounded spots on upperparts.
Habitat. Mainly inland waters: slow-flowing rivers, lagoons, swamps, ponds and even alkaline lakes. Also in freshwater wetlands along coast, estuaries, mangrove swamps and in parts of NW Africa truly marine waters. Quick to colonize temporarily flooded zones; during droughts concentrates on more permanent water bodies, e.g. large rivers. Often found in waters with fringing vegetation or emergent trees. Nests in trees or on ground, e.g. occupying rocky outcrops on coastal islands in Mauritania.
Food and Feeding. Mainly fish of up to 20 cm long, and usually of 3-4 g: cichlids, especially dwarf bream (*Pharyngochromis darlingi*) at L Kariba, Zimbabwe; fair quantities of Mormyridae in Zambia; sole (*Solea*) and cichlids (*Sarotherodon*) at L St Lucia, E South Africa. Also takes many frogs (*Xenopus*) and to lesser degree crustaceans and aquatic insects. Feeds mainly by pursuit-diving. Normally fishes alone.
Breeding. Season variable with region, with laying recorded in all months; sometimes opportunistic, after rains and flooding, e.g. 10,000 pairs bred in large mixed heronry at Chagana, W Tanzania, in 1962. Colonial, often alongside other waterbirds, including *P. carbo* and Darter (*Anhinga melanogaster*). Nests in trees, reedbeds, etc., sometimes on ground; thin stick nests lined with leaves and grass. Normally 3-4 eggs (2-6); incubation 23-25 days; chicks naked, grow jet black down; fledging c. 35 days. Hatching and fledging success c. 80% and 60% respectively; successful nest normally produce 2 chicks to fledging.
Movements. Essentially sedentary, with major irregular movements related to changes in local water conditions, especially with rising or falling water levels; this leads to local disappearances and colonization of new areas, sometimes on massive scale.
Status and Conservation. Not globally threatened. Widespread and common throughout much of range. Estimated minimum of 21,000 pairs in W Africa in mid-1980's, with over 17,000 pairs at Inner

Delta of R Niger and 2500-4000 pairs at Banc d'Arguin, Mauritania. During 19th century bred in Egypt.

Bibliography. Birkhead (1978), Bowen *et al.* (1962), Bowmaker (1963), Britton (1980), Brown & Britton (1980), Brown *et al.* (1982), Campredon (1987), Cramp & Simmons (1977), Crawford *et al.* (1982), Donnelly & Hustler (1986), Elgood (1982), Etchécopar & Hüe (1964), Goodman (1989), Jones, P. (1978), Langrand (1990), Mackworth-Praed & Grant (1957-1973), Maclean (1985), Milon *et al.* (1973), de Naurois (1987), Olver (1984), Perennou (1991a, 1991b), Pinto (1983), Salvan (1967), Skinner *et al.* (1987), Tarborton (1977), Whitfield & Blabler (1979).

36. Crowned Cormorant

Phalacrocorax coronatus

French: Cormoran couronné **German**: Kronenscharbe **Spanish**: Cormorán Coronado

Taxonomy. *Graculus coronatus* Wahlberg, 1855, Possession Island, South West Africa.
Often considered to be race of *P. africanus*, but fair geographical proximity without intergrading, and juvenile plumages different; may be more appropriately treated as forming superspecies. Frequently placed in *Halietor* or *Microcarbo*. Monotypic.
Distribution. Coasts of SW Africa, from C Namibia to Cape Agulhas (South Africa).

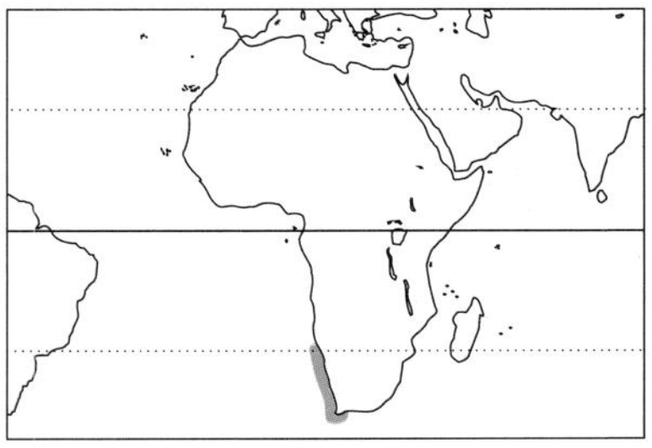

Descriptive notes. c. 54 cm, 800 g. Similar to *P. africanus*, but crest more conspicuous and retained throughout year; lacks white facial tuft; scapulars and wing-coverts darker, more bronzed and less grey, with smaller black tip. Non-breeding adult duller. Females average smaller Juvenile browner, darker than that of *P. africanus*.
Habitat. Markedly marine, occurring in cold waters of Benguela Current; does not stray more than 10 km offshore. Very rarely in estuaries. Breeds on rocky coasts and islands. Tends to feed close inshore along rocky coasts, often in kelp beds.
Food and Feeding. Mainly slow-moving benthic prey: fish including klipfish (Clinidae), pipefish (*Syngnathus*), sole or loose-skinned blennies (*Chalaroderma capito*); invertebrates include octopuses, shrimps, amphipods, isopods and polychaetes. Feeds mainly by pursuit-diving.
Breeding. Laying all year round, with peak in Sept-Jan, slightly later in Namibia. Forms small breeding groups of c. 4-150 pairs, often alongside other seabirds, or even Cape fur seals (*Arctocephalus pusillus*). Nests in wide variety of sites, including rocks, cliffs, bushes, small trees, kelp wracks, jetties, supports under guano platforms and wrecked ships; nest mostly of kelp and sticks lined with finer material. Normally 2-3 eggs (1-5); incubation c. 23 days (21-25); chicks naked, grow black down; fledging c. 35 days; independent at 45-60 days. Hatching success 48·2%; generally 2 chicks raised per successful nest.
Movements. Sedentary, with a few movements to N or E of breeding range.
Status and Conservation. Not globally threatened. Currently considered near-threatened. Very small population, but no proof of any decline; total population of c. 2700 pairs in early 1980's, including 1700 pairs in South Africa; over 40 breeding localities known. No apparent major threats, but sensitive to human disturbance; full protection of all colonies recommended. Formerly considered threatened in South Africa, where now classed as species for monitoring.

Bibliography. Berry (1974), Brooke & Loutit (1984), Brown *et al.* (1982), Clancey (1985), Collar & Stuart (1985), Cooper & Brooke (1986), Cooper, Williams & Britton (1984), Crawford *et al.* (1982), Kriel *et al.* (1980), Rand (1960), Maclean (1985), Shaughnessy (1979), Shaughnessy & Shaughnessy (1978), Siegfried, Frost *et al.* (1976), Williams & Cooper (1983), Wilson & Wilson (1988).

37. Little Cormorant

Phalacrocorax niger

French: Cormoran de Vieillot **German**: Mohrenscharbe **Spanish**: Cormorán de Java
Other common names: Javan(ese)/Pygmy(!) Cormorant

Taxonomy. *Hydrocorax niger* Vieillot, 1817, East Indies = Bengal.
Sometimes included in *P. pygmaeus*. Frequently placed in *Halietor* or *Microcarbo*. Monotypic.
Distribution. Indian and Indochinese Subregions, E to Java.

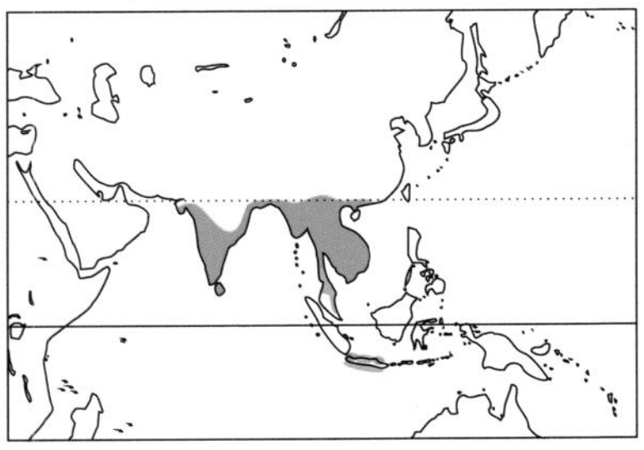

Descriptive notes. 51-56 cm, 360-525 g; wingspan 90 cm. Can have a few scattered white plumes on forecrown and sides of head. Generally similar to *P. pygmaeus*, but has fewer white plumes and lacks chestnut brown tone to head. Non-breeding adult duller and browner, with variable amount of white on throat. Juvenile as non-breeding adult, but duller and browner with paler scalloping on back; paler below, especially on throat and breast.
Habitat. Preferably occupies bodies of fresh water in lowlands, including ponds, rivers, lakes, swamps, canals and rice fields. Also along coast, occurring in estuaries and mangroves. During monsoons often occurs in temporarily flooded areas. Typically breeds in trees or bushes in flooded areas.
Food and Feeding. Mainly small freshwater fish; also frogs and tadpoles. Feeds mainly by pursuit-diving. Sometimes fishes co-operatively.
Breeding. Season variable with region, but mainly Jun-Aug. Colonial, sometimes with high density; often in company of other waterbirds, including herons, egrets, darters and other cormorants. Nests in trees over water, bushes, reedbeds, stands of bamboo; nest of sticks and leaves. Normally 4 eggs (3-5); chicks naked, grow dingy black down.
Movements. Basically sedentary; some movements related to local water conditions, including dispersal associated with monsoons.
Status and Conservation. Not globally threatened. Frequent to abundant in much of range. Censuses in Jan 1991 produced 35,876 in India, 16,731 in Sri Lanka, and 5054 in Pakistan (9193 in Jan 1990). Coverage generally much poorer further E and numbers less impressive, with 457 in Bangladesh, 770 in Burma and 848 in Thailand in Jan 1991; also 801 in Viet Nam and 570 in Indonesia in Jan 1990. Generally common in Thailand, but in Indonesia reported as common only in Java. Presumably suffering some negative effects of degradation of wetland habitats which is occurring on large scale throughout range.

Bibliography. Ali (1979), Ali & Ripley (1978), Harvey (1990), Henry (1971), Hüe & Etchécopar (1970), Inskipp & Inskipp (1985), Lekagul & Round (1991), Medway & Wells (1976), Perennou & Mundkur (1991), Ripley (1982), Roberts (1991), de Schauensee (1984), Scott (1989), Smythies (1986), Winkler (1983a).

38. Pygmy Cormorant

Phalacrocorax pygmaeus

French: Cormoran pygmée **German**: Zwergscharbe **Spanish**: Cormorán Pigmeo
Other common names: Little Cormorant(!)

Taxonomy. *Pelecanus pygmeus* [sic] Pallas, 1773, Caspian Sea.
Sometimes considered conspecific with *P. niger*. Frequently placed in *Halietor* or *Microcarbo*. Monotypic.
Distribution. Discontinuously from SE Europe and Turkey to region of Aral Sea; formerly N Africa.

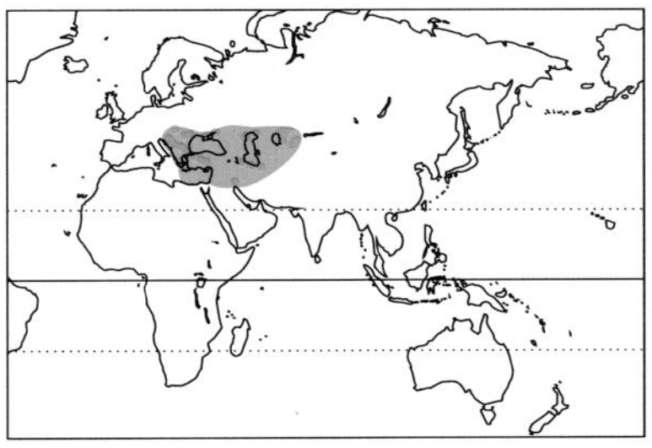

Descriptive notes. 45-55 cm; 565-870 g; wingspan 80-90 cm. Bill black, crest small. Females average smaller. As breeding season advances, black of head replaced by bronze or chestnut brown, and filoplumes steadily lost. Non-breeding adult has throat and foreneck pale brown, upperwing and mantle scaly. Juvenile as non-breeding adult, but underbody whitish.
Habitat. Lowland bodies of fresh water, including lakes, slow-flowing rivers, deltas and other wetlands. Sometimes in brackish or salt water, especially in winter. Requires emergent trees or reedbeds for roosting, resting and nesting.
Food and Feeding. Mainly fish, up to 15 cm long, averaging 15 g. At Danube Delta mostly Cyprinidae, e.g. rudd (*Scardinius erythrophtalmus*), roach (*Rutilus rutilus*), Crucian carp (*Carassius carassius*), loach (*Cobitis taenia*); also perch (*Perca fluviatilis*) and fish species of other groups. Feeds mainly by pursuit-diving. Normally fishes alone.
Breeding. Laying Apr-Jul. Forms colonies, often with *P. carbo*, egrets and herons. Nests near or over water, in trees, bushes or reeds; stick nest lined with finer material. Large clutch of 4-6 eggs, sometimes 7; incubation 27-30 days; chicks naked, grow dark brown down; fledging c. 70 days.
Movements. Partially migratory; most movements involve short distances, and species sedentary over large areas. Migration varies from year to year, but most marked in populations of Black Sea and especially N Caspian Sea; birds start to leave breeding grounds towards end of Aug, returning in Mar/Apr; major winter quarters in S Caspian Sea, with less important numbers along coasts of Adriatic, Aegean and NE Mediterranean. Accidental, occasionally irruptive in C Europe; also vagrant to Tunisia, Lebanon and Pakistan.
Status and Conservation. INSUFFICIENTLY KNOWN (under review). Has suffered major alterations to habitat, especially with drying out of wetlands for agriculture; also heavily persecuted by fishermen. Range has contracted, notably in SW Europe, with loss of colonies and also lower numbers, e.g. population of Prespa Lakes in N Greece slumped from 650 pairs in 1971 to 80 pairs in 1978. Formerly bred in Algeria in 19th century, and in Israel until middle of 20th. Population of USSR estimated at 3200-6600 pairs in early 1980's, with greatest numbers in zone of Caspian Sea. Numerous in Iraq in marshes of Euphrates; also at Danube Delta, Romania, with c. 12,000 pairs in mid-1980's; c. 2000 pairs at L Shkodra, Albania. Has recently bred in Hungary, after absence of over a century; has also bred in Italy, where increasingly regular in winter; has wintered irregularly in Israel in recent years. Censuses of Jan 1991 yielded 34 in Iran, 15 in Turkmenistan and 100 in Azerbaydzhan.

Bibliography. Bauer & Glutz von Blotzheim (1966), Benussi (1985), Brichetti (1982), Brown *et al.* (1982), Collar & Andrew (1988), Cramp & Simmons (1977), Dementiev & Gladkov (1951a), Géroudet (1972), Grimmett & Jones (1989), Hüe & Etchécopar (1970), Judin & Firsova (1988), McClure (1974), Paz (1987), Rutgers & Norris (1970), Scott (1989).

39. Flightless Cormorant

Phalacrocorax harrisi

French: Cormoran aptère **German**: Galapagosscharbe **Spanish**: Cormorán Mancón
Other common names: Galapagos Cormorant

Taxonomy. *Phalacrocorax harrisi* Rothschild, 1898, Narborough Island, Galapagos Archipelago.
Often separated from rest of family in monospecific genus *Nannopterum*; sometimes alternatively placed in *Leucocarbo* or *Compsohalieus*. Monotypic.
Distribution. Restricted to Fernandina I and N & W Isabela I, Galapagos Is.

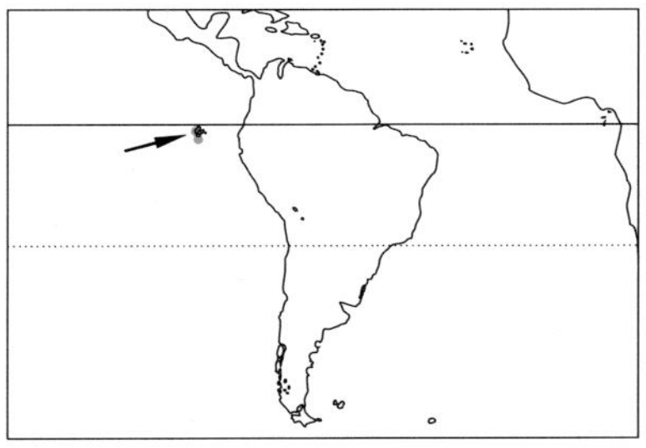

Descriptive notes. 89-100 cm; c. 2·5-4 kg, males heavier; wing c. 25 cm. Large head; flightless; unmistakable. Males average larger with heavier bill. No seasonal variation. Juvenile blacker, has brown iris.
Habitat. Marine. Feeds in cold, rich inshore waters connected with upwelling of Cromwell Current. Breeds on rocky coasts in fairly inaccessible sites.
Food and Feeding. Benthic prey: fish, including eels and rockfish; octopus and squid. Feeds mainly by pursuit-diving.
Breeding. Laying all year round, but mainly Mar-Sept; sometimes breeds twice in year; failure may be followed by fresh attempts. Forms small breeding groups of up to 12 pairs. Nests just above high tide limit, along rocky shorelines; nest voluminous, mostly of seaweed; normally each breeding attempt involves new nest-site and new partner. Normally 2-3 eggs (1-4); incubation c. 35 days; chicks naked, grow blackish down; fledging c. 60 days; post-fledging care 120 days; in later stages fed only by male, while female may initiate another breeding attempt. Normally only 2 eggs hatch; in 74% of successful nests only 1 chick fledged. Breeding success low, with only 0·6 chicks fledged per nest in years when food supply does not fail. Sexual maturity can be reached in second year, especially in females.
Movements. Limited by flightlessness, and completely sedentary, lacking even post-breeding dispersal. Strongly attached to breeding grounds, and rarely found more than 1 km away; movements between Fernandina I and Isabela I very rare.
Status and Conservation. RARE. Marked fluctuations of population, although stable overall. Potentially vulnerable to predation by introduced mammals due to limited mobility on land and lack of instinct to flee. Population periodically decimated when marine production fails, but species has shown itself capable of rapid recovery; thus, after El Niño of 1982/83 (see page 341) population halved due to high mortality and breeding failure, but only c. 18 months later population almost back to normal, with estimated 900-1200 birds by end of 1985. Traps and nets used for catching lobsters and tuna may pose threat; feral dogs almost eradicated on Isabela I, but might yet recover and move into areas occupied by species.

Bibliography. Collar & Andrew (1988), Coulter (1984), Davis & Friedmann (1936), Davies (1938), Fasola & Barbieri (1981), Gadow (1902), Greenway (1967), Harcourt (1980), Harris, M.P. (1974a, 1974b, 1979), Hennemann (1984), King (1978/79), Mountfort (1988), Rosenberg & Harcourt (1987), Shufeldt (1915), Snow (1966), Tindle (1984), Trillmich *et al.* (1983), Valle (1986a), Valle & Coulter (1987), Vincent (1966).

Class AVES
Order PELECANIFORMES
Suborder PELECANI
Family ANHINGIDAE (DARTERS)

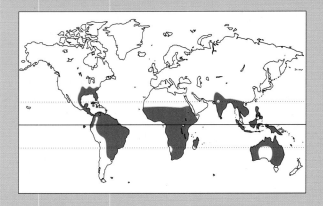

- Largish waterbirds with very long slender neck and long spear-like bill.
- 81-97 cm.

- All regions except Antarctic.
- Inland or coastal waters, preferably still or slow-moving.
- 1 genus, 2 species, 6 taxa.
- No species threatened; none extinct since 1600.

Systematics

Some authors have included the darters within the family Phalacrocoracidae, usually in their own subfamily, Anhinginae, but sometimes even without division into subfamilies. However, various morphological, ethological and ecological differences, such as the presence of only a single carotid artery in darters, or their quite distinct foraging behaviour, are considered sufficiently great to justify separating them off into distinct families within the order Pelecaniformes.

Darters, like other families in this order, differentiated in ancient times, and one must go back at least 30 million years to find a common ancestor with the cormorants. A fossil darter found in Florida, USA, dates back some 18 million years, whilst there is an older, Eocene one from Sumatra, although it is not altogether clear whether or not it can really be considered a darter. In both the Old and New Worlds, several fossil remains have been found from the Miocene onwards, and these correspond to various different species of darter, while for evidence of an extant species there are the remains of an Anhinga (*Anhinga anhinga*) from the Pleistocene in Florida.

The tendency nowadays is to recognize only two species, the Anhinga and the Darter (*Anhinga melanogaster*). The former is the single American representative of the family, while the latter is generally considered to encompass all the Old World forms. Nevertheless, on the grounds largely of plumage differences, the Darter is still frequently split up into three separate species, the African Darter (*Anhinga rufa*), the Oriental Darter (*Anhinga melanogaster*) and the Australian Darter (*Anhinga novaehollandiae*).

Morphological Aspects

Darters are fairly large birds, with an overall length of about 81-97 cm, and a wingspan of about 120 cm. In outward appearance they recall cormorants, although they are somewhat more drawn out, but certain morphological characteristics of the head, bill, neck and wings are closer to herons.

The head is very small and elongated, and is almost indistinguishable from the neck. The bill is straight, sharp and pointed, in the form of a dagger, and lacking the terminal hook present in cormorants. It is thin and elongated and, as in sulids and tropicbirds, the distal portions of the cutting edges are finely serrated, with the serrations pointing backwards. The nostrils are reduced, but not totally closed as in the case of cormorants. The neck, which is also long and thin, is undoubtedly one of the characteristic features of the family. The articulatory surfaces of the eighth and ninth cervical vertebrae have been modified to form a hinge mechanism, with which the neck can be bent back in an S-shape, and the powerful neck muscles, when taut, enable the bird to thrust its head forward with great force, like a harpoon (see Food and Feeding). The name "Darter" is derived from this action.

Sexes are similar in size, but the bill is generally somewhat longer in males. Adult male plumage is predominately black or dark, and it can be very glossy, especially during breeding. Adults, both males and females, have the scapulars long and lanceolate, and in the region of the upperwing-coverts there are some white, silver or buff stripes, forming a pale or silver band that stands out vividly on the wings. Females are generally less brightly coloured than males, and the juvenile plumage tends to be similar, but even browner and paler.

The Darter has a white stripe on the side of the head and the upper neck, which is most noticeable in the breeding male. The adult male Anhinga, in contrast, has an erectile crest of long black feathers on the hindneck, which he may ruffle up during display, as well as some slender white plumes on the sides of the upper neck.

The wings are long and broad, and the tail is very long with twelve broad, stiff rectrices. The outer webs of the two central tail feathers and also those of the two longest scapulars have transversal corrugations, which are not yet prominent in young birds. In flight, the tail is often fanned open, and this has led to them being known as "water turkeys" in the USA.

Darters are good fliers, and they alternate powerful flapping flight with glides, as opposed to the typical sustained flapping flight of the cormorants. They use thermals for soaring, and may rise up to a considerable height, before gliding on for example to another thermal. In gliding flight, the silhouette formed by the wings, the slightly kinked neck and the long tail resembles a flying cross. The tail is used for gaining height, steering or braking, according to the necessities of the moment, and, together with the flight-feathers, gives the bird the manoeuvrability necessary for moving about in quite closed and tangled environments, where swamps intermingle with forest.

Darters have short legs that are set well back on the body. They rarely walk, and do so very clumsily, with the wings half

opened, in order to help maintain balance. The feet have four long, webbed toes, giving them a large surface area for propulsion in the water. They are not really adapted for rapid diving chases, but rather for a slower kind of dive, that enables them to stalk their prey amongst submerged vegetation. When they dive, both feet are used simultaneously like oars, whereas they are moved alternately when the bird is swimming on the surface. When under water, the wings can be kept slightly open, although they are not used for propulsion (see Food and Feeding).

As in cormorants, the plumage very quickly becomes wet when in contact with the water, due to the microscopic structure of the feathers, rather than to any lack of waterproofing. In this way, they can reduce their buoyancy and diving is made much easier. Darters are even less buoyant than cormorants, as their skeletons are less pneumatic and their plumage sogs up relatively three times as much water. The body plumage becomes completely soaked, as they lack the insulating layer of air next to the skin which allows cormorants to keep the inner part of their feathers dry. For this reason, darters tend to swim very low in the water, with only the head and part of the neck sticking out of the water, like a periscope; in this posture they look not unlike swimming snakes, and this has led to the alternative name, "snake birds".

When diving, a bird keeps its bill slightly open, and, instead of leaping up before plunging, like cormorants and grebes, it stretches its head and neck forwards, and disappears quietly below the surface with hardly a ripple, so as to remain inconspicuous to prey or predators. A bird may dive from a perch beside the water or, more rarely, make a belly-landing on the water after a short glide from a perch. Occasionally a flying darter may dive directly into the water, though this generally occurs only as a hurried escape response. Dives last 30-60 seconds and there are normally very short intervals between each.

A darter is capable of taking off directly from the water, and it will shake the water out of its wings and tail, which, unlike the body plumage, are well waterproofed. However, this form of take-off is rare, and generally a bird settles first on the bank, a stone, or a floating tree trunk, or perches amongst the vegetation, where its plumage can dry out before it flies off.

The legs and feet are adapted for climbing up to perches and also for perching, so the claws are longer and more curved than in cormorants, and the hind toe is more opposable.

The Anhinga has a partial moult before breeding and a complete moult afterwards; the latter involves the simultaneous dropping and subsequent renewal of all the remiges, and in this darters differ from other Pelecaniformes. This means that they are temporarily unable to fly (see General Habits), as also occurs, for example, in the families Anatidae and Rallidae.

Habitat

Darters frequent a wide variety of wetlands with sheltered shallow waters, in particular at inland sites. They are widely distributed throughout tropical and subtropical zones of America, Africa, Southern Asia, Australia and New Guinea, and also occur in warm temperate zones. They are the least marine of all the Pelecaniformes and live mainly at fresh water sites with some open water, such as lakes, slow-flowing rivers, marshes and swamps. To a lesser extent, they can also be found in sheltered marine and brackish coastal waters, such as estuaries, mangrove swamps, shallow bays and coastal lagoons, or on alkaline lakes inland. They may also settle on reservoirs, as long as the local ecological conditions are suitable.

For roosting and breeding, they need adequate vegetation cover along the banks or on islets, in the form of forest, woodland or extensive stretches of emergent vegetation, for instance reedbeds. At the very least, they require somewhere to perch, for instance trees, bushes, posts or banks, where they can rest and dry out their plumage.

In many areas they live side by side with their close relatives the cormorants, and both families share a fish-based diet and catch their prey by diving. There are, however, marked differences between the fishing techniques used (see Food and Feeding) and the exact prey sought, and, as a result of this, there does not seem to be any serious competition between the two. Due to restrictions in their ability to conserve heat, darters can only inhabit warm regions (see General Habits, Movements), whilst cormorants have also occupied extremely cold waters.

General Habits

The general habits of the darters are very similar to those found in the cormorants. They spend most of the day resting on raised, exposed perches, sunning, digesting their food and preening. At these places they usually gather in small, loose flocks, although there may be concentrations of about 100 birds. However, they are far less sociable than cormorants, and tend to mix much more often with other waterbirds, such as herons or indeed cormorants, than with members of their own species. They can frequently be seen soaring in the company of ibises, herons or storks.

Perches are generally situated near water, on banks, in reed-beds and particularly in trees, especially where they stick out over the water, as well as on floating branches. Branches with or without leaves are used, and they may be thin enough for the birds to grasp with their feet. Birds hop or climb up to low spots, sometimes using the neck to help, while higher perches are normally reached by flying up, after taking off from a lower perch. Whilst birds are perched, the neck remains folded in an S-shape, with the bill pointing forwards. Preening occupies a fair amount of time, and the feet can be used for scratching the head and neck.

Darters are amongst the most territorial of the Pelecaniformes. In general, they do not tolerate other birds, especially conspecifics, too close to the nest, and conflicts may also occur at perches. Threats and attacks are most common amongst males: on the arrival of an intruding male near the nest, the occupying male approaches him making threatening gestures, walking or hopping over the branches with the wings partially spread and the bill open. Once he is near the intruder, he makes snapping movements with his bill. If the intruder does not leave, the two birds may fight, which normally consists of pecking at each other's heads and necks.

Before taking off from a perch, a bird announces its departure by partially spreading its wings, at the same time pointing its bill in the direction in which it intends to fly; a similar posture is adopted immediately after landing on a perch.

After diving, a bird settles on a perch with its wings spread wide open, in a manner reminiscent of cormorants, although the darters' open tail hangs more visibly, and the bird can remain thus for a long time. This posture is used for drying out the plumage, and in darters it is also for thermoregulation. As their plumage generally insulates less than that of the cormor-

ants (see Morphological Aspects), darters lose more heat, for they have to use up more energy in keeping warm. By absorbing heat from the sun, they can compensate for their low metabolic heat production and the cooling they suffer when they are wet and temperatures are low. The same posture can also be adopted when the plumage is dry, in order to increase body temperature. When they are too hot, they lose heat by panting, and by the rapid vibration of the bare gular pouch, as this rapidly cools the blood circulating in the dense network of capillaries in the throat.

Darters are wary birds, and when alarmed a bird generally swims in the characteristic, inconspicuous, half-submerged position, whereby only the head and the upper neck protrude above the surface of the water. If disturbed whilst perched, a darter may escape by dropping into the water as if it were dead. During the flightless period after the remiges have been dropped (see Morphological Aspects), they are even more cautious and vigilant: they do not usually perch in high places, and at the slightest possible danger, they slip quietly and unobtrusively into the water.

Voice

Away from the immediate vicinity of the nest, darters are generally silent, although they sometimes make clicking calls and shrill rattling sounds, either in flight or from a perch. They do not have an alarm call as such, but instead react to those of other birds.

In the nest, they produce harsh croaks, rattles and grunts. Before settling on the nest, a bird makes a rolling, repetitive call, which in males is harsher and more rapid. Prior to copulation, one or more explosive notes are produced, and these are different in males and females. Chicks are very noisy when begging for food, alternately squeaking and clicking.

Food and Feeding

Although the darters' diet consists mainly of fish, they also eat other aquatic animals such as amphibians, aquatic reptiles and invertebrates such as insects, crustaceans, molluscs and leeches.

The species of fish taken vary from place to place, depending on what is available. In different parts of Africa, for instance, darters have different preferences: at Lakes Victoria and Albert, in Uganda, the cichlid *Haplochromis*; at Lake Kariba, in Zim-

Darters usually nest in trees or amongst aquatic vegetation, always close to water. They sometimes breed alone or in small groups, but they are normally colonial, sometimes nesting beside cormorants, herons, egrets, ibises and storks. These resting African Darters illustrate several different postures of the charcteristic long neck, which has earned them the alternative name "snake birds" in several languages. Note also the conspicuous lanceolate scapulars which tend to be at their most attractive in breeding birds.

[*Anhinga melanogaster rufa*, Okavango Delta, Botswana.
Photo: Richard Coomber/ Planet Earth]

The Anhinga's long neck has a similar function to that of the herons, since in both families it is used as a powerful spring which can be thrust forward with great force and speed, due to a hinge mechanism situated between the eighth and ninth cervical vertebrae. The Anhinga's fishing technique involves diving with the neck folded, lying in wait and then pouncing on the fish with a rapid jab forward of the neck. The sharp, pointed bill is used as a very effective harpoon for spearing fish.

[*Anhinga anhinga*, USA. Photo: Fritz Pölking/FLPA]

babwe, other cichlids, *Pseudocrenilabrus*, *Sarotherodnon* and *Tilapia*; and at Katanga, in Zaire, the cyprinid *Barbus paludinosus*. Variety is also evident in Australia: in the Magela floodplain of Northern Territory, darters catch mainly fish of the family Plotosidae; in contrast, in inland parts of Victoria, the species taken include *Retropinna semoni*, *Perca fluviatilis* and *Nematolosa erebi* among others. At any one site the species of fish consumed can be very varied, but most are quite small, measuring less than 10 cm. Indeed, birds frequently capture fish only a few centimetres long, for example *Gambusia affinis* in the USA.

Darters fish alone, and even if concentrations can form where food is abundant, the birds never fish collectively. A fishing bird dives slowly, with its wings and tail extended and its neck cocked. It may hold its wings partially open under the water, attempting to attract fish into the apparent safety which the shade represents. This method is also found in the herons, although they only open their wings over the water, not in it.

Darters are not very active fishers and may forage in waters that are only 0·5 m deep. Whilst under water, instead of chasing prey, the bird waits for it to come and then jerks its neck forward from the initial S-shape position, folded between the shoulders. The fish are stabbed in the side and impaled on both mandibles, although with small fish apparently only the upper mandible is used. This spearing technique is again reminiscent of the herons, although darters usually start with the head under water. It is an extremely rapid action, which is made possible by the special adaptation of neck (see Morphological Aspects). This type of fishing technique, as well as their diving style, means that darters concentrate on catching slow-moving, preferably laterally flattened fish, that are neither too large nor too heavily armoured, and that live in shallow water.

Small items can sometimes be eaten under water, but after a catch the bird generally surfaces and shakes the fish vigorously until it comes off the bill. It then tosses it up in the air to turn it round, and catches it again in the bill, holding it securely with the serrated edges of the bill, and finally swallows it head first. Sometimes the fish is a bit big for the bird's bill or throat, and it may take a few minutes before it manages to position the prey suitably for it to be swallowed.

After fishing, a bird normally goes off to a perch where it can dry its plumage, so that it will be able to fly off more easily

to its colony or roost later on. Out of the water darters also catch small prey, such as insects, using the end of the bill like tweezers.

Breeding

In many areas darters breed in a well defined season, but this varies widely with the locality. It is normally quite lengthy and may even continue all year round, although there is always a pronounced seasonal peak.

Darters are monogamous, with the pair-bond possibly lasting for years, and birds can reuse the same nest each season. Nesting is usually solitary or in loose groups of several pairs, but occasionally they form large colonies of several hundred pairs. They often breed in company of other waterbirds such as cormorants, herons, egrets, ibises and storks.

At the start of the breeding season, males begin to display with soaring flights and glides. Later on, each selects a nest-site by placing a few leafy twigs in the fork of a tree or in an old nest, and establishes a territory around it, which can include the whole tree. Then the male performs different displays at the nest-site, with complex movements involving the body, head, neck, wings and tail. Displays include "Wing-waving", where the wings are raised alternately, and the neck is stretched out at various different angles; meanwhile, the bird lifts up its tail and may even point it forwards, or thrust its head and neck forwards to pick up a nearby twig with its bill. These displays intensify when a female flies over or perches near a displaying male.

After the pair has been formed, the nest is built, often in one day, while darters sometimes appropriate herons' nests in their absence. Material is mainly collected by the male, whereas the female is in charge of building the nest, and the end result is a bulky platform of interwoven sticks with a lining of green twigs and leaves. Nests are placed near water, often on overhanging branches, in emergent trees, live or dead, or alternatively in bushes or reeds. They can be built low down, close to the water, or up to six metres or more above it.

Copulation takes place on the nest, and during the act the male takes a stick or the female's bill in his own bill. The clutch consists of two to six eggs, most commonly four, and these are laid at one to three day intervals. Eggs are oval and are notice-

ably pointed at one end; they are pale green or bluish-white, sometimes with dark brown spots, and have a thin chalky covering. Incubation begins after the first egg is laid, and the adults take turns at the nest, incubating with their feet. During incubation, and in the first week after hatching, when the chicks are constantly brooded, the adults greet each other at the nest, when starting or ending their shifts, by means of calls and a complex display, including "Wing-waving" and "Snap-bowing", performed by the bird leaving the nest.

Incubation lasts 25-30 days, and hatching occurs at similar intervals to laying. Although chicks hatch naked, within two days their underparts are covered with white down, while a darker covering soon grows on the upperparts.

Chicks beg for food by reaching out as far as possible towards the adult, waving their heads and flapping their wings,

while they utter food-calls with the bill closed and the hyoids pushed forward, giving an angular appearance to the gular pouch. When begging for liquid, on the other hand, they remain silent and hold their mouths open to catch the fluid which trickles out of the adult's bill.

At first, chicks are fed at least six times a day on semi-digested and regurgitated fish, which dribbles, in liquid form, out of the adult's bill and into the chick's mouth. As in pelicans, the food is delivered through the upper part of the adult's bill, in contrast to the cormorants, which use the lower part. Older chicks obtain solid food by forcing the head and part of the neck into the adult's throat. The older chicks in each nest have an advantage in that they are able to get a greater proportion of the food at each feed. Fights between sibling chicks are frequent during feeding, and involve the birds pecking at each other.

Soon the chicks are able to jump from the nest into the water, whenever they feel threatened, and they can swim a fair distance, or dive, to escape from any possible threats. The larger the chick, the greater the chance it has of managing to return to the nest and climb back into it, with the help of its claws, feet, neck, bill and growing wings.

When they are three weeks old, the chicks begin to leave the nest and perch on nearby branches, where they can exercise their wings, while their plumage finishes growing. The adults only visit them at feeding times and these become progressively less frequent, until the chicks are fed only once a day. The Anhinga first begins to fly when it is around six weeks old, and the Darter when it is seven weeks old. The age for attaining sexual maturity is not known, but definitive adult plumage is acquired in the bird's third calendar year.

Movements

Throughout most parts of their extensive range, darters are sedentary. However, population fluctuations occur, involving local movements, mainly in response to droughts or temporary flooding, or as a consequence of the dispersal of young birds. There are also irruptions along coasts caused by the severe drying out of inland waters.

The northernmost populations of North America are migratory, arriving at their breeding grounds in March or April, and

In the Anhingidae, both the male and the female take part in the tasks of incubation and feeding the chicks. This female Australian Darter is about to feed her chicks on the food which can be seen in her crop, while they stimulate the process of regurgitation by begging. There can be intense competition between the chicks, especially when food is in short supply, and any size difference between siblings is quickly exaggerated, a natural mechanism designed to give the largest chicks the best possible chance of survival at the expense of the smaller ones.

[*Anhinga melanogaster novaehollandiae*, Victoria, Australia. Photo: I.R. McCann/ ANT/NHPA]

leaving at the beginning of October, before heading towards the extreme south of the USA or on to Mexico. Another northern population, which formerly nested in the marshes of southern Turkey, but is now extinct, was mainly migratory and wintered in Israel. The only remaining population of the Western Palearctic, which breeds in southern Iraq, appears to be sedentary, although there are reports of winter sightings in other parts of Iraq and in south-west Iran.

In the coldest parts of their range, darters have to expend a great deal of energy in keeping warm (see General Habits), and they can only spend the winter where there are sufficient hours of sunshine, so that heat thus absorbed can compensate for the considerable heat loss. Research carried out by W. W. Hennemann in the USA indicates that the Anhinga can be found in December in areas with an average temperature of 10°C, provided that there are at least 160 hours of sunshine during the month.

Relationship with Man

Darters rarely come into conflict with humans, and the fish they take are not usually of any commercial importance. In south-east Asia, Darters have been used for fishing, in the same way as the rather better known cases of some species of cormorant (see page 337). Nomadic tribes, for example in Assam and Bengal, use trained darters to catch fish, although the practice is now dying out.

They have also been exploited in many places for human consumption, and the eggs are considered a real delicacy in parts of Asia, while birds too are also taken. Sometimes, chicks are taken from the nests to be fattened up and then eaten later.

Status and Conservation

Both species of darter have very extensive ranges and neither is seriously threatened. Nonetheless, they have declined or even disappeared in many areas, especially in south-east Asia, mainly due to excessive pressure from egg collecting or birds being killed for food. In addition, their habitat has suffered, particularly with the worldwide conversion of wetlands. This has led to a general reduction in the amount of suitable areas available, although the decline is offset to some extent by birds settling on reservoirs.

Breeding success has been known to decrease due to contamination with DDT, a pesticide that is still legal and often used indiscriminately in many tropical countries. In the USA, even 12-13 years after the banning of DDT, Anhinga eggs containing high concentrations of DDE (a breakdown product of DDT) could still be found, for example at Yazoo, in Mississippi, and this was reckoned to be the cause of the low hatching success recorded in the area.

The Darter population of the Western Palearctic is now limited to southern Iraq, where the long term results of the 1991 Gulf War have yet to be evaluated. In the affected areas, all birds, especially the larger ones, are liable to have been subject to shooting either for target practice or for food, while the potential effects of disturbance, habitat destruction and pollution are incalculable.

The breeding population of Turkey disappeared relatively recently, following the drainage of the once extensive Lake Antioch, or Amik Gölü. However, plans have recently been put forward to reflood the area, in view of the biological importance it once had, and because the agricultural changes have not had the desired success.

In many parts of the world man has introduced fish species for commercial reasons or sport. Occasionally darters have taken readily to the new prey and this has led to an increase in darter numbers, as happened in the lowlands of New Guinea, after the introduction of the African cichlid *Tilapia*.

General Bibliography
Becker (1986, 1987), Brodkorb & Mourer-Chauviré (1982), Cracraft (1985), Drummond (1987), Forbes (1882), Harrison (1978), Martin & Mengel (1975), Miller (1966), van Tets (1985b).

ssp *melanogaster*

2

ssp *novaehollandiae*

2

♂

♀

2

ssp *rufa*

♂   ♀

2

PLATE 24

```
inches        10
┃━━━━━━━━━━━┃
cm            25
```

Genus *ANHINGA*   Brisson, 1760

1. Anhinga

Anhinga anhinga

French: Anhinga d'Amérique   **Spanish**: Anhinga Americana
                    German: Amerikanischer Schlangenhalsvogel
Other common names: American Darter, Snakebird

Taxonomy. *Plotus Anhinga* Linnaeus, 1766, Rio Tapajós, Pará, Brazil. Two subspecies recognized.
Subspecies and Distribution.
A. a. leucogaster (Vieillot, 1816) - USA (North Carolina to Texas) through C America to Panama; Cuba.
A. a. anhinga (Linnaeus, 1766) - S America from Colombia S to Ecuador and E of Andes to N
Argentina; Trinidad and Tobago.
Descriptive notes. 81-91 cm; c. 1350 g; wingspan c. 120 cm; bill 75-88 mm. Scapulars elongated
and lanceolate; bare part colours variable. Silvery grey more extensive on scapulars and upper-

wing-coverts than in *A. melanogaster*; male
has black erectile crest on nape. Juvenile similar to female, but generally browner, and lacks
most of silvery grey on upperparts. Race *leucogaster* smaller, with thinner pale tip to tail.
Habitat. Mainly still, shallow inland waters,
especially lakes, slow-flowing rivers and
swamps; less often estuaries or tidal inlets and
coastal zones with mangroves and lagoons.
Requires scattered emergent trees, forested
margins or islets with dense vegetation.
Food and Feeding. Mainly fish, including (in
USA) Centrarchidae, Poeciliidae, Cyprino-
dontidae and Mugilidae; also amphibians (e.g.
frogs, salamanders, newts, tadpoles and frogspawn), reptiles (e.g. snakes, terrapins, baby alligators),
crustaceans (e.g. crayfish, shrimps) and other invertebrates (e.g. aquatic insects and their larvae,
leeches). Prey normally speared under water, without active pursuit.
Breeding. Seasonal in some areas, at any time of year in others. Often colonial, sometimes with
cormorants or Ciconiiformes. Nest is platform of sticks and leaves, often 1-4 m above water. 1-5
eggs, usually 3-5; incubation 25-28 days; chicks naked, grow buffy tan down; fledging c. 6 weeks;

post-fledging care c. 2 weeks. Sexual maturity after at least 2 years. Known to have lived over 9 years in wild, and over 16 in captivity.

Movements. Basically sedentary. Migratory in extreme N of range, moving S for winter, as far as S Mexico.

Status and Conservation. Not globally threatened. Common in suitable habitat in S USA; fairly common locally in Colombia; little known of status throughout much of range, and solitary tendencies make census work more difficult. Main threats probably include conversion of habitat, with draining of wetlands and destruction of forests. In parts of USA, effects of DDT hang on in form of its breakdown product DDE (see page 359).

Bibliography. Allen (1961), Blake (1977), Burger *et al.* (1978), Casler (1973), Crutchfield & Whitfield (1987), Doig *et al.* (1989), Harriot (1970), Hellmayr & Conover (1948), Hennemann (1982, 1983a, 1983b, 1985, 1988), Jackson (1983), Leber (1980), Mahoney (1981), Ohlendorf *et al.* (1978a, 1978b, 1978c), Owre (1967), Palmer (1962), de la Peña (1980a), Pinto (1964), Ruschi (1979), Scott & Carbonell (1986), Sick (1984), Slud (1964), van Tets (1965a), Thibault & Guyot (1988), Virchow (1917), Wellenstein & Wiegmann (1986), Wetmore (1965), White *et al.* (1988).

2. Darter

Anhinga melanogaster

French: Anhinga roux   **German**: Schlangenhalsvogel   **Spanish**: Anhinga Común
Other common names: Oriental/Indian Darter (*melanogaster*); African Darter (*rufa*); Australian Darter (*novaehollandiae*); Snakebird

Taxonomy. *Anhinga melanogaster* Pennant, 1769, Ceylon and Java.
Sometimes included in *A. anhinga*. Often split into three species, *A. melanogaster*, *A. rufa* (incorporating race *vulsini*) and *A. novaehollandiae*; *A. rufa* is most distinctive of three. Four subspecies recognized.

Subspecies and Distribution.
A. m. melanogaster Pennant, 1769 - India to Philippines and Sulawesi.
A. m. rufa (Daudin, 1802) - Africa S of Sahara, Middle East.
A. m. vulsini Bangs, 1918 - Madagascar.
A. m. novaehollandiae (Gould, 1847) - New Guinea and Australia.

Descriptive notes. 85-97 cm; 1058-1815 g; wingspan 116-128 cm; bill 71-87 mm. Scapulars elongated and lanceolate; bare part colours variable. Juvenile similar to female, but white and black areas generally replaced by buff and brown. Races can be separated on variations in plumage of both male and female; female resembles male most closely in nominate *melanogaster* and least in *novaehollandiae*.

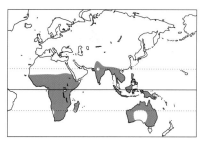

Habitat. Mainly still, shallow inland waters, such as freshwater or alkaline lakes, slow-flowing rivers, swamps and reservoirs; less often estuaries or tidal inlets and coastal zones with mangroves and lagoons. Requires scattered emergent trees, forested margins or islets with dense vegetation.

Food and Feeding. Mainly fish, including Cichlidae and Cyprinidae (Africa), Plotosidae (Australia); prey species vary with locality. Also takes amphibians, water snakes, terrapins and aquatic invertebrates, including insects, crustaceans and molluscs. Prey speared under water, without active pursuit.

Breeding. Seasonal in some areas, at any time of year in others. Usually colonial, often with cormorants or Ciconiiformes. Nest is platform of sticks and sometimes reeds, often c. 2 m above water. 2-6 eggs, usually 3-5; incubation 26-30 days; chicks naked, grow whitish down; fledging c. 7 weeks. Sexual maturity probably only after at least 2 years. Known to have lived over 9 years in wild, and over 16 in captivity.

Movements. Generally sedentary, with sporadic movements usually related to drought conditions.

Status and Conservation. Not globally threatened. Common to locally abundant in Africa, with 10,000 nests in colony at Chagana, in Tanzania, 1962; scarce and apparently declining in W Africa. In Middle East, formerly abundant in S Turkey, where has disappeared this century due to drying out of breeding grounds; now only breeds in S Iraq, where likely to have suffered during Gulf War of 1991; 110 counted in Iran, 1990. Generally uncommon in much of Oriental Region: regular in Punjab of Pakistan; 1260 censused in India, 1990; no longer breeds in Thailand, Malay Peninsula and perhaps Bali; has also declined in Borneo and Java; uncommon and local in Philippines. Common in lowlands of Sulawesi, late 1970's; 252 counted in Papua New Guinea, 1990. Widespread and common throughout much of Australia, with numbers decreasing from N to S; rare and erratic in arid interior. Main threats probably include habitat destruction and pollution.

Bibliography. Ali & Ripley (1978), Alletson (1985), Beesley (1976), Birkhead (1978), Bowen *et al.* (1962), Brown *et al.* (1982), Coates (1985), Cramp & Simmons (1977), Donnelly & Hustler (1986), Fothergill (1983), Hüe & Etchécopar (1970), Humphrey & Bain (1990), Langrand (1990), Lindsey (1986), Lockhart (1968), Manson (1969), Mackworth-Praed & Grant (1957-1973), Maclean (1985), Marchant & Higgins, (1990), van Marle & Voous (1988), Marshall (1972a), Milon *et al.* (1973), Mukherjee (1969), Paz (1987), Perennou (1991a), Perennou & MundKur (1991), Pinto (1983), du Plessis (1986), Rijke *et al.* (1989), Roberts (1991), Schodde & Tidemann (1988), Smythies .(1981, 1986), Tarborton (1975), van Tets (1965b), Vestjens (1975c), White & Bruce (1986).

Class AVES
Order PELECANIFORMES
Suborder PELECANI
Family FREGATIDAE (FRIGATEBIRDS)

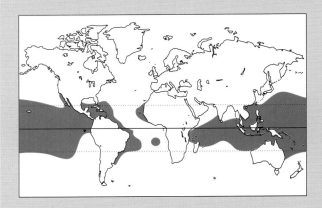

- Light, medium-sized to large seabirds with long, pointed wings and tail and long, hooked bill.
- 71-114 cm.

- Pantropical.
- Tropical and subtropical oceans, coastal and pelagic.
- 1 genus, 5 species, 11 taxa.
- 2 species threatened; none extinct since 1600.

Systematics

The frigatebirds form a small family of five species which are very closely related to one another and are thus grouped together in a single genus, *Fregata*. Similarities in plumage have led to a fair amount of confusion, and up to the beginning of this century most scientists considered that there were only two species, one large, which is now divided into four, and one small, which had been placed in a separate genus, *Atagen*. It was Mathews (1914), who finally sorted out most of the currently recognized species and subspecies, although even he included the Magnificent Frigatebird (*Fregata magnificens*) within the Great Frigatebird (*Fregata minor*).

Linnaeus had originally placed his frigatebird in the same genus as the pelicans and, as a result of this, the Great Frigatebird received its apparently contradictory scientific name, because it was, of course, substantially smaller than the pelicans. This, in turn, has led to a certain amount of confusion with the Lesser Frigatebird (*Fregata ariel*), as some authors have assumed that the name "Lesser" should be applied to the species labelled *minor*. The situation is further complicated by the fact that these species are extensively sympatric.

The extent of similarity between the species is illustrated by the fact that even today, with excellent field guides such as that of Harrison (1985), and very advanced optical equipment, it is still considered impossible to separate adult males of the Ascension Frigatebird (*Fregata aquila*) and the Magnificent Frigatebird in the field, while aberrant individuals preclude definite separation of the latter from an adult male Great Frigatebird. Such similarities, allied to a wide variation in immature plumage phases, make identification of the Fregatidae very difficult. It seems that, after evolving into distinct species, these birds have made only very limited changes in outward appearance. It is hardly surprising then that the recognition of five different species took such a long time to come about. Fortunately, identification difficulties are greatly eased by there being limited overlap of the species, partly because two out of five are single island endemics.

As is the case in the other families of the Pelecaniformes, the frigatebirds became a distinctive group at a very early stage, as is indicated by a fossil recognizable as a frigatebird, which was found in Wyoming, USA, and dates back some 50 million years to the Eocene. The family shares certain features with the tropicbirds (Phaethontidae), such as the form of the pelvis, but it would appear that they are actually less closely related to them than to the other families in the order (see page 280).

The results of recent studies on DNA change the relative situation of the frigatebirds substantially, placing them in the large superfamily Procellarioidea, alongside the families Spheniscidae, Gaviidae and Procellariidae. In this way the frigatebirds, a family of essentially non-swimming, highly aerial birds, end up beside the flightless, supremely aquatic penguins, some way off from their traditional allies of the Pelecaniformes.

Morphological Aspects

Of all the seabirds, the frigatebirds are perhaps the most exquisitely designed for a predominantly aerial life. They have a distinctive flight-silhouette, and are spectacular in both appearance and behaviour.

Four of the species are large and a Magnificent Frigatebird can be up to 114 cm in length, whereas a small male Lesser Frigatebird may measure as little as 71 cm. Their very size, combined with incredible manoeuvrability, makes them formidable opponents for any bird that gets involved in a skirmish with them.

Considering their large size, frigatebirds are surprisingly light, weighing about 600-1600 g, with females tending to be almost 25% heavier than males. This lightness is enhanced by their having highly pneumatic bones, which at the same time are quite flexible. The weight of all the bones together is less than 5% of the total weight of the bird, a feature unmatched in the world of birds. On the other hand, the large pectoral muscles weigh as much as all of the feathers, and together with the feathers account for half the bird's weight. Unlike any other group of birds, the frigatebirds have the bones of the pectoral girdle fused together, giving them added strength and solidity, which help them to perform their antics in the air.

The frigatebird's wings are also quite singular. They are long, narrow and angular and the wingspan is enormous, ranging from 175 cm to 244 cm, again in the Lesser and Magnificent Frigatebirds respectively. Their very low wing-loading, which reflects the low weight in contrast with the large wing area, is another record in the bird world, enabling them to be among the nimblest of fliers. It is due to this that they can keep up effortless dynamic soaring for hours on end, as well as executing some of the most breath-taking feats of aerobatics to be witnessed. With a fair breeze blowing, birds can take off from an exposed perch simply by opening their wings. They cruise at speeds of up to about 50 km/h, and can also hang motionless in the air for long periods. In contrast, they are not particularly well designed for sustained flapping flight and normally limit wingbeats to the odd one in the midst of a long spell of soaring or gliding, but on a totally calm day they can be seen in active flight with a series of deep, loose flaps. While preferring a stiff breeze, they are also capable of riding out heavy storms (see Movements).

The characteristic silhouette of the frigatebirds shows a marked bend at the carpal joint, producing the overall effect of an open "W". The long tail is deeply forked, but this is not always obvious, for it is often kept closed. It soon becomes apparent though, when the bird is engaged in awkward manoeuvres, as the tail is the indispensable rudder, controlling all the sharp turns and side-slips.

Yet another perfect adaptation to the frigatebird's needs for extreme aerial mobility is its svelte, streamlined body. The head is small and rounded and is normally tucked in over the shoulders in flight. The neck is relatively short, although it can be stretched out, for instance when snatching up prey. The bill is thin and markedly long, measuring up to 150 mm in the Great Frigatebird; it ends in a sharp hook, which undoubtedly assists when trying to catch hold of slippery fish and it may also help to persuade reluctant victims to "cough up" (see Food and Feeding). The bill is cylindrical and, as in most other Pelecaniformes, the rudimentary nostrils are probably obsolete.

As a result of the frigatebird's evolutionary dedication to superiority in the air, its legs and feet are somewhat stunted and weak, resulting in the bird's virtual inability either to walk or to swim. As in the other families of this order the feet are totipalmate, but in the frigatebirds this has been reduced to only a small, basal area of webbing, because they only swim very rarely. They mainly need their feet for perching and they have made the requisite adaptations, having strong, sharp, pointed claws, which enable them to grip tightly onto a branch.

Evidence that they are unsuited to settling on the water can be seen in the small uropygial gland, which allows only very inadequate waterproofing, so their plumage rapidly gets soggy; in addition to this, they are structurally unprepared for take-off from the water. Indeed for take-off under any circumstances they generally prefer assistance from the wind or some form of raised perch whence to launch themselves. Their long wings can be cumbersome when landing, particularly in the midst of other birds and if there is a strong wind blowing.

Perhaps the most spectacular feature of frigatebird anatomy is the preposterous scarlet inflatable gular pouch found in the males of all species. This comes into condition when the bird is getting ready for breeding and is fully blown up during display, in order to attract females. It takes some time for the air to escape, so a bird with its pouch inflated, when disturbed by an intruder, tends to fly off with its pouch deflating gradually. Sometimes males fly around displaying with the pouch inflated, though this is only at all frequent in the Lesser Frigatebird.

Plumage in this family is rather complex, as there is fairly little interspecific variation, yet such a variety of different plumages at intraspecific level as to baffle most observers. Apart from being among the few seabirds that present sexual dimorphism in plumage, as well as in size, they also present a series of confusing juvenile and subadult phases that may make identification extremely difficult and sometimes even impossible, despite an excellent view.

The predominant colour in frigatebirds is always black and this is most notably so in the case of adult males, where three of the species are almost entirely black, while the Lesser Frigatebird has white axillary "spurs" and the Christmas Frigatebird (*Fregata andrewsi*) a white lower belly; pale phase male Ascension Frigatebirds also have extensive white on the breast and belly, but it is far from clear that such birds are really adults. Some of the feathers, particularly the long scapulars, are often glazed with metallic green, blue or purple. Adult

The flight silhouette of the frigatebirds is highly characteristic, so they are easily recognizable at a distance. The wings are long, narrow and pointed, while the long tail has a deep fork, although this feature is not obvious when the tail is closed. Frigatebirds generally flap little, tending rather to glide or hang in the air, manoeuvring about on the air currents. The Christmas Frigatebird is the only species in which the male has a white belly.

[Fregata andrewsi, Christmas Island, Indian Ocean. Photo: P. Evans/ Bruce Coleman]

females have varying amounts of white mostly on the breast and belly and iridescent areas are much less vivid. Juveniles start off with the head white, tawny or freckled and quite a lot of white on the underparts. They then pass through various stages, before reaching adult plumage, probably after four to six years. There are no seasonal variations in plumage, but the Ascension Frigatebird has pale and dark morphs, which may not depend simply on age, and just add to the confusion. Bare parts too vary in colour with age, sex and population, though legs and feet tend to be black or brownish in males and red or whitish in females.

The pattern of moult in frigatebirds is not well known and there appears to be a lot of individual variation. Body moult is fairly continuous throughout the year, but flight-feathers are not moulted during breeding. There are 11 primaries, about 23 secondaries and 12 rectrices; primary moult is serially descendant and may take about three months to complete.

Habitat

Frigatebirds are strictly marine, affecting both coastal and pelagic waters. They have an ample distribution round the warm seas and oceans of the tropics and subtropics, which is conditioned by two main factors.

The first is a steady, abundant source of food, preferably flying-fish. The second is a suitable wind regime. As their entire lifestyle depends a lot on soaring and gliding, they require sufficient wind to be able to perform this. Hence, their distribution coincides approximately with that of the trade winds. These winds build up cumulus clouds with associated thermals, which are unusual in being over the sea, and continuing at night. Such a phenomenon is ideally suited to the frigatebirds' needs, as it enables them to travel far out to sea and by night, which obviously represents an important extension of their potential feeding grounds. Frigatebirds have traditionally been linked far more tightly with coastal waters than is actually the case, probably because they spend much of the time soaring high up, out of sight around the cloud base.

Most breeding occurs on small, remote islands, which offer the birds relative freedom from human disturbance and terrestrial predators. Some breeding colonies, particularly of the Magnificent Frigatebird, are found along mainland coasts, though this is much less common and is generally restricted to large tracts of mangroves where humans are rarely seen.

Mangroves are generally the favourite site both for nesting and roosting, though in both cases other kinds of trees and also bushes are frequently used. Interestingly, on Aldabra Atoll, off East Africa, both Great and Lesser Frigatebirds breed in mangroves, and whereas the former will nest on flat tree tops, the latter tends to use lower lateral branches, although both prefer intermediate situations. Lessers also use smaller *Pemphis acidula* bushes, thus avoiding fierce competition with the larger species which does not nest at all on these bushes on Aldabra, although it uses them extensively in the Cocos (Keeling) Islands of the eastern Indian Ocean.

When suitable vegetation is not available, birds may nest on bare, dry ground, as is the case of all breeding pairs of the Ascension Frigatebird and also the very small remaining population of Magnificent Frigatebirds on the Cape Verde Islands off West Africa, not presumably through preference but rather by force of circumstances.

General Habits

As many aspects of their lifestyle are only practicable during the daylight hours, frigatebirds tend to be largely diurnal. They spend much of the time in the air, usually in seemingly effortless soaring, and are better adapted to this medium than any other birds, except perhaps the swifts and hummingbirds (Apodiformes).

The typical day begins around dawn, when the birds leave their overnight roost and start to climb up into the sky. They sometimes rise very high, before setting off out to sea usually alone, in search of food. They disperse far and wide, foraging either singly or in small groups, at times forming mixed feeding flocks with other species of seabirds. They tend to return in the early afternoon and then spend hours hanging in the air over their roost, until they eventually come down just before dark.

Frigatebirds are highly gregarious in most aspects of their lives and this includes both their roosting and breeding. They frequently form mixed breeding colonies with other species of Pelecaniformes, as well as joining them for feeding or roosting. Recent work shows that such communal roosts probably arise from a lack of suitable sites on remote oceanic islands, rather than any particular benefit from the association. Sites typically used for roosting include trees, bushes, cliffs and sand-bars, but a secluded spot is almost always required and in suitable places birds may gather in their thousands. Large numbers of non-breeders usually hang around colonies and they tend to roost in or beside them. Multitudinous roosts far from colonies are almost always predominantly made up of juveniles. However, birds frequently spend all night on the wing, when there is sufficient wind, presumably dozing if conditions permit.

During the day frigatebirds often rest for hours on end on a variety of different perches, such as fishing posts, ships' masts and buoys, often in the full glare of the sun. Much of this time may be spent in preening, but birds can also be seen sitting idle for long periods.

Yet another aspect which separates the frigatebirds from most other seabirds is their habit of drinking fresh water when it is available. They drink on the wing, swooping down on pools and scooping up water with their bills. They also bathe in flight, splashing their bodies repeatedly onto the surface of the water and combining this with preening and scratching. Head-scratching is direct in flight, but indirect when the bird is perched, once again a peculiarity of this family with respect to other seabirds.

The "sunbathing" posture of the frigatebirds has long baffled scientists. Recent research on the Great Frigatebird has shown that, rather than basking in the sun, the bird actually uses this posture as a method of dissipating heat, a far more normal problem for tropical species like the frigatebirds. The wings are opened wide to expose the warm underwing, so that heat is lost to the slightly cooler atmosphere by convection, without having to resort to the more costly process of evaporative cooling.

[*Fregata minor*. Photo: Eichorn & Zingel/ FLPA]

Excess heat is a problem for many birds in the tropics, especially those that are regularly in exposed sites. Much the commonest solution in the Pelecaniformes is gular-fluttering and this is frequent in frigatebirds, but they also have other methods. Work carried out on the Great Frigatebird on Midway Atoll, in the central Pacific, has shown that these black birds incubating in the full glare of the sun, with air temperature at around 33°C, but environmental temperature at almost 52°C, can maintain their body temperature fairly stable at around 40°C. They manage this by adopting three main postures, one of which involves the wings being held wide open and inverted, which has led to it being labelled as "sunbathing". The main principle is that heat passes from the warmer body to the cooler air by convection, so the overheated underwing is unfolded and exposed to the sun, whereby heat loss is enhanced by radiation and perhaps also some evaporation. Feather ruffling lifts sunsoaked feathers further away from the body and lets any breeze penetrate as far as the skin, while the head may be moved into the shade of the wings in order to keep the brain cool. As birds may have to stay on the nest for several days at a time (see Breeding), it is important for them to conserve water by keeping evaporation down to a minimum. All this is apparently no great strain for them, as non-breeding birds with no constraint may sit for a day or more in similar exposed spots.

Voice

Although frigatebirds are generally silent, both in flight and when perched, their breeding colonies can be extremely noisy. Displaying males are particularly vociferous, and sometimes the noise of a colony is audible several kilometres away.

Males and females have separate vocalizations, which are most distinctive in their different alighting calls. Somewhat surprisingly, even the most ardent chases very rarely produce any sound. Typical frigatebird noises have been described as "twittering, reeling, drumming, rattling and whinnying", while young birds are said to squeal or chirp, mostly when begging for food.

All species indulge in a form of bill-clattering, with the mandibles being vibrated rapidly, for example by a courting male against his inflated pouch, which he uses as a sound box. Hungry juveniles perform a different variation, when trying to solicit food from adults.

Food and Feeding

Frigatebirds are notorious for their piratical habits, as their very name indicates (see Relationship with Man). However, the truth is that they actually obtain most of their food by means of direct capture.

Although there is a certain amount of local variation, all the species have similar food preferences and use the same methods to secure it. Their favourite prey is flying-fish, particularly of the genera *Cypselurus* and *Exocoetus*. They are also very keen on cephalopods, with a special predeliction for squid. Many other kinds of fish are taken and this depends largely on what is available to them with their specialized styles of fishing, but some species, such as menhaden (*Brevoortia*), can be locally important. Other fairly regular prey items include jellyfish and larger plankton.

Out to sea frigatebirds normally search for food alone or in pairs, but where prey is plentiful large concentrations may build up. On sighting prey, the birds circle or drift gradually down and snatch it off the surface of the water (surface dipping), hovering if necessary, but rarely immersing more than the bill and occasionally the head. Sometimes they skim along very fast, low over the water, snatching up prey in the process. They are quick to latch onto a school of dolphins or tuna chasing headlong in pursuit of flying-fish. In such situations, the flying-fish are liable to leap out of the water in a desperate attempt to evade their submarine predators, only to present a relatively easy target to the highly adept, agile frigatebird,

which gratefully siezes its gliding quarry. On occasions the birds themselves may pursue fish over short distances. All prey caught in this way is swiftly swallowed and the bird continues on its way. Young turtles and crabs are also frequently taken, especially when moving across the sand or floating on the surface of the sea.

The eggs and young of colonial seabirds, when left unprotected, are quickly snapped up by attendant frigatebirds, which swoop down and grab their prize in passing; occasionally a pirate lands to rob a nest. Terns are particularly susceptible to these marauding attacks and Sooty Terns (*Sterna fuscata*) on Christmas Island, in the Pacific Ocean, have been known to lose millions of eggs and young in one season, due to the combined attentions of feral cats and frigatebirds; in 1967, and again in 1983, a whole colony was virtually wiped out by just a few frigatebirds. Many other seabirds, such as boobies, petrels and shearwaters also sustain substantial losses due to such predation and frigatebirds even take eggs or young of their own species, particularly when a colony suffers frequent disturbances (see Status and Conservation).

Another important source of food for frigatebirds is that supplied indirectly by humans. Fishing boats are frequently followed and great concentrations of birds can build up in fishing ports, fighting to get at any unwanted fish or scraps thrown away after gutting. At Playas, in western Ecuador, Magnificent Frigatebirds have learnt to pilfer fish from tubs, which fishermen are carrying in from their boats. The men have to walk about 100 m across the beach and they brandish sticks to keep the birds off, but the birds still manage to steal a fair number of fish. Frigatebirds also congregate around slaughterhouses, and similar places where human waste products are dumped, thus exhibiting a fair degree of adaptability. Where large numbers gather, there is often fierce competition and several birds may squabble and chase each other for the paltriest of morsels.

Although their role as kleptoparasites has undoubtedly been overstated, it is nonetheless of great significance and it has been suggested that on occasions it may really be the main source of food. Almost all kinds of seabirds are liable to be harried and few, if any, can consistently stand up to the ardent attentions of a determined frigatebird. Boobies, in particular the widely distributed Red-footed Booby (*Sula sula*), are especially prone to attack, while tropicbirds are another favourite target. Terns, gulls, cormorants, shearwaters, petrels, noddies, pelicans and even Ospreys (*Pandion haliaetus*) are all considered fair game. Rather surprisingly, many of these species, in particular the Red-footed Booby, frequently install their nests right beside breeding frigatebirds, thereby inviting the predation that almost invariably follows.

After a plunge-dive out to sea, surfacing boobies are often robbed by waiting frigatebirds, but most piracy occurs around seabird colonies, where the potential victims are most numerous, and Blue-footed Boobies (*Sula nebouxii*) are even robbed at the nest, when in the act of delivering food to their chicks. The excessive importance given to frigatebird piracy is probably due to the fact that it is very spectacular, and also that it mostly takes place around the sites in which people normally see frigatebirds.

Several frigatebirds will soar over the periphery of the colony, patiently watching adult boobies, or other birds, return from their fishing trips. Once a victim has been singled out, perhaps because of its full crop or its heavy flight, one or more frigatebirds move off to intercept, and engage it in hot pursuit, often plunging down on it from above. Boobies and most other seabirds are easily outmanoeuvred by the agile frigatebirds, which tweak the feathers of the wings or tail, in an attempt to knock their victim off balance, until it disgorges part or all of its load. When this happens, the action breaks off immediately and, before the food hits the water, a frigatebird has normally caught it deftly. Physical contact in such strikes is normally very limited, but on occasions it can be quite violent and a determined frigatebird can cause serious injury to its victim.

However, a large proportion of attacks are fruitless, the frigatebird abandoning its pursuit and its intended victim

Frigatebirds generally forage alone or in pairs, but flocks occur in the vicinity of the colony and also where an abundant source of food has been located. Despite their notoriety as pirates, they actually obtain most of their food by direct capture, typically by dipping, flying low over the water and whisking prey off the surface, as demonstrated by one of these Lesser Frigatebirds.

[*Fregata ariel ariel*, Sunda Straits, Indonesia. Photo: Dieter & Mary Plage/Survival]

carrying on apparently unaffected. The effectiveness of the technique varies a lot, depending for example on place, time of year, species, age, sex and individual (of attacker, but maybe also of victim); it seems that some individuals are expert pirates and get their food almost exclusively from kleptoparasitism. Studies have shown that the attacks of Great Frigatebirds on Red-footed Boobies had a 63% success rate on Christmas Island (Pacific), as opposed to only 12% in the Galapagos. Three different studies showed that birds obtain less than 20% of their food from piracy. In most cases the larger, heavier females are more effective and the male Magnificent Frigatebird's attacks may be mainly limited to stealing nesting material from other conspecifics. However, there are also cases where most piracy is carried out by males, such as the Great Frigatebirds of Tower Island in the Galapagos, and males may benefit from their lower wing-loading and consequent greater manoeuvrability. General piracy may be easier to learn than the skills necessary for successful fishing, for young birds tend to hang around the colony, stealing eggs or young from unattended nests, picking up scraps, or attacking other species.

Frigatebirds very occasionally forage inland, for instance a Magnificent Frigatebird in Pennsylvania, USA, was found to have taken several different species of freshwater fish. Another, more remarkable, case was a Christmas Frigatebird which had its crop stuffed full of grasshoppers.

Breeding

The breeding cycle of the frigatebirds is amongst the longest of all seabirds, and the general pattern is that birds can only breed successfully every two years. The main factors behind this seem to be the slow development of chicks, the extraordinary length of post-fledging care and, at the root of it all, the difficulty adults have in obtaining sufficient food for their young over such a long period.

Breeding can start at a wide variety of different times, from one place to another, depending on a whole series of conditions. On Aldabra, for example, it tends to coincide with the onset of the dry season trade winds, which enable adults to range far and wide in search of food; thus large numbers of birds begin breeding synchronously. On Little Cayman, in the eastern Caribbean, the Magnificent Frigatebird starts breeding about a

month after the Red-footed Booby, perhaps to ensure a readier source of food when the frigatebird's own chicks are most at risk, in their first few weeks. The start of a dry season or a period of abundant food are factors that typically trigger off breeding. However, local variation is still tremendous and in the Galapagos, Great Frigatebirds have regularly been recorded with eggs in every month of the year. In any one colony there is normally a high degree of synchrony, with virtually all eggs being laid during a period of about two months and clear seasonal cycles are generally apparent.

Frigatebirds normally breed on islands in fairly large colonies, reaching a maximum of several thousand pairs. They often form mixed colonies with other species and nests may be contiguous with those of species that they parasitize. They normally nest at the top of trees, as much as 20 m up in the case of the Christmas Frigatebird. When optimum nest-sites are in short supply or non-existant, they make do with bushes or shrubs, or even nest on the ground; in such cases the preference tends to be for a cliff, which enables easy take off and makes the site less accessible to potential predators.

The courtship display of frigatebirds is the most spectacular of any seabirds, and is very similar in all of the species. It begins with males setting up shop, often in old, disused nests, usually in groups of up to thirty together. They show very little aggression towards each other, tolerating even physical contact during display. They spread open their wings, inverting them to reveal a silvery underwing. At the same time they inflate their scarlet gular pouches, tipping their heads back with bills pointing skywards. They are thus visible from a long way off, attracting the attention of females. When a female passes overhead, each male, in an ecstatic burst of excitement, quivers his wings and head, vibrating the bill against the fully inflated pouch, which produces a kind of drumming noise. It has been hypothesized that the different ventral patterns of females of the various species of frigatebird may have developed to enable displaying males to recognize females of their own species in these moments.

Eventually a female chooses a male and flies down to join him and certain pair forming rituals are performed, such as mutual "Head-snaking" or the male taking the female's bill in his own. Other males may move off to try their luck elsewhere, although it is quite normal for several of a group of suitors to attract females at much the same time, thus leading to well-synchronized breeding nuclei within a colony; indeed, a frigatebird "colony" is normally just a loose aggregation of synchronized nuclei.

Within two or three days the pair-bond has been cemented and nest building begins on the site of the successful display. It is interesting to note that the territory is only established once the pair has been formed, an unusual development arising from the lack of a permanent pair-bond, and hence nest-site. The nest-site is vigorously defended with bill-clattering or bill-grappling against intruders, who often try to steal material; squabbles may be noisy, but are never very violent. During this period copulation takes place intermittently, always at the nest-site and always preceded by a bout of "Head-waggling".

The male sets about the often difficult task of collecting material, which may take him far afield and away from his island. He will snap dead twigs or leaves off a tree as he flies over, or he may instead raid another bird's nest for material, and this is frequently a major contributor towards egg and chick losses. The male collects sticks, twigs, grass, seaweed, feathers and sometimes even human artifacts, and the female moulds these into a rough nest where she stands guard to see that no marauding males steal her material. Sometimes nesting material is so scarce that the nest may just be a scrape in the ground, as is the case of Ascension Frigatebirds.

When nest building is over, often about three weeks after the beginning of the male's displays, the female lays a single egg; this is dull white and weighs only about 5% of her body weight. There is recent evidence from Hawaii of two Great Frigatebird nests with two young each, but this is certainly exceptional and two such cases with Magnificent Frigatebirds in the Caribbean resulted in no young fledged.

Both parents have brood patches and incubate, taking stints of one to four days on average, although Great Frigatebirds have been known to sit for up to 18 days before being relieved.

These long stints on the nest are typical of pelagic feeders and almost certainly arise from the difficulty the absent bird has in finding food. Even within the same species there is variety, and stints average shorter where food is more readily available, while chick growth tends to be correspondingly faster. Many eggs, and later on chicks, are lost when adults abandon the nest due to hunger or have to defend it against raiders. Apart from those looking for food, there is another tendency noted in the Galapagos, where male Great Frigatebirds may ravage a nest and maul the chick; as yet there is no satisfactory explanation for this behaviour. If egg or chick is lost, breeding may be abandoned, although Ascension Frigatebirds probably lay a replacement in 20-25% of such cases of loss. Recent evidence for Great and Lesser Frigatebirds on Aldabra has shown that the same site is probably occupied and used by a new pair.

After 40-55 days a chick hatches, naked, wrinkled and helpless. It pecks away at the food brought in by its parents and within a few days it can beg for food by stretching its bill up and pecking at its parent's bill or gular area, in order to stimulate regurgitation. It soon grows a thick coat of white or whitish down. For the first few weeks it is permanently guarded in the nest, but as it starts to grow it becomes tough and, when about a month old, can fend off most intruders by itself and is often left alone. As time goes on, the nest is gradually cemented together by the chick's droppings.

Due to the difficulty adults have in finding food, the chick may have to wait three days or more between feeding sessions, although at times it can be fed as often as twice a day. The strategy of the family is to grow very slowly, so that young birds can stand up to protracted periods of starvation without dying or suffering deformity. As a result of this, fledging takes from about four and a half to seven months.

For the adults of many species the breeding duties are over at this stage, but not for the frigatebirds. The ensuing period

Unlike other frigatebirds, the Ascension Frigatebird nests exclusively on the ground, although this might actually be due to force of circumstance rather than preference: in the past it bred on Ascension Island itself, but it was probably driven from the main island as a result of intense predation by introduced cats, and it now breeds only on nearby Boatswainbird Islet. Perhaps somewhat surprisingly, frigatebirds' primary victims are often found breeding alongside them, as in the case of these Masked Boobies (Sula dactylatra).

[*Fregata aquila*, Ascension Island. Photo: Annie Price/ Survival]

of post-fledging care is the longest in any of the seabirds, with the partial exception of Abbott's Booby (*Sula abbotti*). It can last from four to an incredible fourteen months more, while Christmas and Great Frigatebirds have been recorded continuing for 15 and 18 months respectively. The normal period is probably between nine and twelve months. During this time the youngster frequently spends much time roaming around the colony, perhaps picking up the occasional titbit, such as scraps or unprotected chicks or eggs, but it consistently returns to the nest to beg for food from its parents; it is still heavily dependent on them and may still have to wait several days between feeds.

Adults have increasing difficulty finding enough food for themselves and what is now a fully-grown juvenile. Matters are not helped by the fact that the male tends to lose interest, most markedly in the case of the Magnificent Frigatebird, when the chick is only three or four months old, and the female is left with an even heavier burden to shoulder. Frigatebirds have a much smaller range of prey available to them than other Pelecaniformes, due to their specialized fishing methods and it is the perfectioning of this technique that demands the protracted period of parental care, so that the young bird can eventually fend for itself. Even so, despite many months of care, the time of emancipation is a very delicate one, and many chicks die of starvation soon afterwards. Many young birds loiter about the colony for months, in vain begging for food from any passing adult.

The protraction of the breeding cycle means that it can only be completed successfully on a biennial basis, although it has recently been suggested that success may be followed by a gap of three or four years, in which time the birds recover from their mammoth effort. A study by A. W. Diamond of the Magnificent Frigatebird on Barbuda, in the Lesser Antilles, showed that this species appears to differ from the others in its breeding strategy. Here, in its largest Caribbean colony, there is an unusually rich food supply close at hand, so birds do not need to wander so far off. This possibly makes the female better able to cope on her own, but in any case the male tends to abandon the rest of his family when the chick is only three or four months old. He then moves away from the colony, moults and possibly returns in time to breed the following season. This is

not feasible for the female, whose breeding cycle takes over a year. On finishing, she presumably leaves to moult and misses out on a year of breeding.

This pattern of males probably breeding annually, while females breed biennially is unparalleled in birds. It has recently been found to be the case off the coast of Belize too, but it is not yet known if this is the standard strategy of the species. As birds in the Barbuda colony have more food available, the strategy is considered to be an adaptation to maximize production, because the same male can serve two females. This theory is backed up by the facts, because two females are born for every male and male mortality is higher. In contrast to this, work on Aldabra suggests that each year there are more male than female Great Frigatebirds in breeding condition, while Lesser Frigatebirds have an equal sex ratio.

When attempting to breed, frigatebirds face prolonged hardships, so it is hardly surprising that they have a 75% failure rate. With the biennial breeding strategy, it would seem that there have to be two discrete breeding groups, starting on alternate years, but this is not so. Many of the birds that fail probably try again the next year and there may be some that try unsuccessfully several years running. Breeding numbers in a particular season may be directly related to the degree of success in the previous year or years.

Although they are monogamous during any one breeding attempt, it is most unlikely that any pair continue together after breeding or join the same partner for the next attempt, particularly as the nest-site is very likely to be occupied by other birds. Some male Great Frigatebirds have been known to return to the same nest, but with different females. In concordance with this, the pair-bond appears to be very weak after laying, and behaviour to strengthen the bond is poorly developed; once incubation is under way, the partners are together very little. A curious phenomenon of the frigatebird breeding strategy is that unpaired males often try to usurp an occupied nest-site, either with or without the resident female; this practice seems counterproductive towards the breeding effort of the population as a whole, and probably encourages the formation of the discrete synchronized nuclei, which are likely to represent a more formidable target for any potential usurper.

Courtship is highly spectacular in the frigatebirds. The male is endowed with an enormous, grotesque scarlet or carmine gular pouch, which is inflated like a balloon by the displaying bird. Males usually gather in "clubs", where several birds display together to the females flying overhead, until eventually each female selects a partner and flies down to join him. The striking visual display is made all the more impressive by the green, blue or purple iridescent tones on the upperparts, most notably on the long, lanceolate scapulars.

[*Fregata magnificens*, Galapagos. Photo: AGE FotoStock]

Frigatebirds have to guard their chick permanently for the first few weeks until it is large enough to take care of itself. The colony is regularly patrolled by conspecifics, mostly young birds, which will not hesitate to snatch any unattended egg or chick. Juveniles have extensive white on the head and underbody, which gradually gives way to the dark plumage of adults; this striking plumage difference is almost certainly a method of inhibiting possible attacks by adults, which are less likely to see them as possible rivals.

[*Fregata magnificens*, Curral I, Parana St, Brazil. Photo: L. C. Marigo/ Bruce Coleman]

Frigatebirds have extremely low productivity, due to their biennial breeding cycle, production of only one chick and the frequent failure even to raise this to independence. To join the ranks of the breeding population, it may have to wait six, seven or even eleven years and only about 5% of all chicks reach this stage. All this suggests that adults must probably live some 25 years on average, for the population to be maintained. The oldest bird known from ringing records was a Great Frigatebird which was calculated to have reached the age of at least 34 years old.

Movements

All five frigatebird species are essentially sedentary, spending most of the year in the vicinity of their colony. Some adults leave the colony to moult, but many undergo their moult in and around the colony, especially if food is still plentiful.

However, young birds, once they abandon the colony, disperse over vast areas. American birds tend to wander up and down both Atlantic and Pacific coasts, while Lesser Frigatebirds from the central Pacific seem to follow the prevailing winds clockwise round the south-west Pacific. There are many records of birds which have strayed over 6000 km from their colonies within a year of abandoning it, and with such lengthy movements, vagrancy is quite common. Adults outwith their breeding cycles can also be found wandering far off, in search of a better feeding station.

As food supplies are generally patchy in tropical waters and frigatebirds are not very versatile in their fishing methods, their search for food, especially when they have a hungry youngster to feed, can take them a long way from their colonies. To this end, they have developed a type of flight which is effortless under the right conditions, so they can travel enormous distances over the ocean.

Frigatebirds often ride along on the front of a storm, taking advantage of the wind, and this has led to the name by which

they are known to Australian aborigines, "rain-brothers", as they "bring" rain with them. Likewise, in Puerto Rico, when they are seen inland, this is taken to be an indication that there is a storm at sea. They are well-adapted to ride the fiercest of storms, but this often results in their being blown a long way off course. Most European records of Magnificent Frigatebirds almost certainly refer to American vagrants, as the entire east Atlantic population, which breeds in the Cape Verde Islands off West Africa, numbers only a handful of pairs. Despite its restricted breeding distribution around the tropics, this species has turned up in Ireland, Scotland and even Denmark. Even more impressive is the fact that both Great and Lesser Frigatebirds have been recorded in Siberia and New Zealand.

Frigatebirds sometimes move over land, indeed Magnificent Frigatebirds regularly cross the isthmus of Panama and, when work on the canal was going on, they quickly learned that fish could often be picked up following blasting operations. Occasionally birds follow large rivers some way inland, although most inland records refer to individuals carried in by heavy storms.

Relationship with Man

Due to their superb flying skills, but far more to their overrated tendency of attacking other birds, frigatebirds occupy a prominent place in seamen's lore. This violent habit is reflected in their vernacular name, which probably originates from a comparison with the fast, manoeuvrable warships that were most notoriously used by pirates to attack merchant vessels and relieve them of their cargoes; the same analogy is likely to have led to the alternative name of "Man-o'-war birds". Christopher Columbus was certainly impressed by their vigorous attacks and described them in his logbook, when on his way to the New World.

Frigatebirds have learnt the advantages of associating with fishermen, in order to pick up scraps, and this can at times

As in most other Pelecaniformes, frigatebird chicks are fed by incomplete regurgitation, the chicks reaching into their parents' gullets to get at the food. Young frigatebirds apparently take a remarkably long time to learn foraging skills and this has resulted in the imposition of a lengthy period of post-fledging care, during which the chick flies freely around the colony but still receives almost all of its food from its parents. In the Great Frigatebird, this period can last as much as eighteen months.

[*Fregata minor ridgwayi*, Galapagos. Photo: Konrad Wothe/ Bruce Coleman]

constitute an important source of food, where a colony is near a busy fishing port (see Food and Feeding).

When fed they can become quite tame, as islanders of Polynesia and Micronesia know well. They have a long-established tradition of taking Great Frigatebird chicks at about five months old and hand-rearing them. When setting off on a long fishing trip they take a frigatebird with them and, on arriving safely at their destination, they release the bird with a note attached to its leg. It invariably returns to the house where it was raised and thus carries the good news to its owner's family. Around the time of the discovery of America, frigatebirds were considered to represent good news, as they were thought to show sailors that land was not far off; those same men might have been alarmed, in retrospect, to learn of the long journeys out into the midst of the ocean that the same birds sometimes undertake!

Like other seabirds, frigatebirds have in many places traditionally supplied an important source of protein to the local population. Until quite recently, thousands were taken annually on Aldabra; in the Caribbean, first it was the indigenous fisherfolk, and later the boucan hunters, who harvested colonies of Magnificent Frigatebirds, taking eggs or young, to supplement their deficient diets. They were also used in medicine and even in voodoo, and the deep-rooted foundations of these practices have led to their persisting in places today.

Status and Conservation

Two species of frigatebirds are currently considered to be threatened. These are the Christmas and Ascension Frigatebirds, both of which are now probably restricted to single island populations, and indeed may never have been much more widespread.

By their very nature, single, small island endemics are highly vulnerable, because the concentration of the entire world population at a single site means that disease or a disaster,

whether it be natural or man-induced, can wipe out the species overnight. Similarly, genetic or demographic imbalances are more liable to affect such populations. For this reason, such species can rarely be considered really "safe", but both of the frigatebirds are classified as Threatened due to additional, more acute pressures.

The Christmas Frigatebird has been suffering from the same basic problem of habitat destruction, which has beset the other seabirds of Christmas Island, in the Indian Ocean, most notably Abbott's Booby (see page 321). By 1946 about 36% of the frigatebird's rain forest breeding grounds had been stripped away to facilitate mining for phosphates; it is no doubt fortuitous that it nests in areas of very poor quality phosphates. There was, in addition, a series of associated disturbances, one of which was the influx in the 1950's of Cocos-Malay people, many of whom were taken on as mining labourers; they took a heavy toll of seabird eggs and young to supplement their impoverished diets. In 1967, during his studies on the island, J. B. Nelson found the remains of 40 Christmas Frigatebirds killed under a single display area. However, improved living standards for the workers, together with legal protection for the birds helped to alleviate the problem and, with the general exodus of most of these people in the mid-1970's, hunting has now all but ceased.

Fortunately, the Australian government has taken steps towards preservation of the island and its unique species. Most of the breeding habitat of the Christmas Frigatebirds is now included in the Christmas Island National Park, and the species is legally protected, with a Government Conservator *in situ* since 1977. Mining operations were at last halted in 1987, and there is to be no further removal of rain forest, so these unique seabird colonies may yet be saved.

Nevertheless, the threat of mines being reopened, in areas which are already bereft of vegetation cover, may pose a major problem for the frigatebirds, as one of the main causes for their previous slump was the dust which had settled in a thick coat all over their nesting trees. Another cause of mortality in the past was the drowning of birds while trying to get a drink (see General Habits) from the mine slurry ponds, but it is thought that these ponds are unlikely to reappear.

Even without these problems so closely related to the mining, there are several other more natural hazards, for instance many eggs are lost when nests are blown down during cyclones, and this is undoubtedly more likely with the deterioration and shrinking of the birds' habitat. It is more difficult to see precisely why a large number of fledglings should be abandoned to starvation, but this frequently happens with Abbott's Booby too, and might imply that these species have recently had problems with food supply, although both have sympatric congeners which seem to cope better.

The most recent figures put the world population of the Christmas Frigatebird at around only 1600 pairs. The definitive closure of the mines could be crucial to their survival, and given the importance of the island for its endemic birds, especially its large, spectacular Pelecaniformes, it could be used for controlled tourism, as has happened in the Galapagos. It is certainly a sad paradox that human greed for short-term benefits should bring about the demise of the birds that originally created the resource, but this is a familiar story with the case of the Peruvian "Guano Birds" (see page 338).

As its name suggests, the Ascension Frigatebird used to breed on Ascension Island, in the South Atlantic, and it was said to have large colonies there in the eighteenth century. Although there may have been rats and mice since soon after the island's discovery in 1501, it was not till 1815 that the first human settlement was established and this spelt disaster for the birds, because it meant the introduction of the domestic cat. As the sparsity of the local vegetation forces the Ascension Frigatebird to breed on the ground, cats took a terrible toll and the species very quickly stopped breeding on the island. Ever since, it has only bred on Boatswainbird Islet, a flat-topped, precipitous rocky island of less than 3 ha, about 250 m off Ascension Island. The movements of this species seem to be restricted to the relatively small area of nutrient-rich waters around the islands.

No census of the species has been carried out since the BOU expedition in the late 1950's, which counted some 9000-12,000 birds, but several recent visitors have considered that the population appeared to be more or less stable. Feral cats remain the greatest threat and continue to account for large numbers of birds which roost on the coasts of Ascension Island. Thankfully cats have not yet spread to Boatswainbird Islet, and it is to be hoped that the rugged nature of the islet might be sufficient to preserve the birds' immunity there, but in any case it is quite clear that a determined effort to eradicate cats from the main island is most desirable, with a view to the re-establishment of the frigatebird there; without such a move, it is difficult to see the plight of the species improving.

In addition there are other problems. Towards the end of the 1960's, boatloads of visitors started visiting Boatswainbird Islet. With the expansion of government installations in 1982, human activity has increased notably and air traffic may represent a serious threat to the birds, as collisions with birds often lead to the authorities organizing culls of the "culprits". Even without this, birds are bound to be disturbed by low-flying aircraft, as they already have been by ships' horns, deliberately sounded to make the birds take flight and provide a good show for visitors. A large number of eggs and young can be lost to predators, when sitting adults are frightened off their nests, and this can even lead to a colony being abandoned, as happened on Aldabra. Tourists, photographers and even biologists visiting seabird colonies must be made aware of the damage that can be done. Fortunately, in 1977 pleasureboat visits to Boatswainbird Islet were banned and scientific work brought under stricter control. More recently the Islet was declared a bird sanctuary.

Habitat destruction or deterioration, disturbance of breeding colonies, the introduction of predators, and possibly direct human predation are the main problems facing most populations of frigatebirds. Overfishing of predatory fish, such as

Frigatebirds have learnt to benefit from man's presence by using his discards as an source of food. Magnificent Frigatebirds, in particular, tend to congregate in fair numbers around fishing ports, especially down the Pacific coast of South America, where they can regularly be seen following incoming fishing boats, fighting for scraps, or lounging on the masts of moored boats. Large numbers of these birds are juveniles, which probably have greater need of an easy food supply.

[Fregata magnificens, Esmeraldas, Ecuador. Photo: Isabel Martínez]

tuna, may have important repercussions too, as frigatebirds rely on these fish to chase their prey, especially flying-fish, up to the surface; if prey species stay lower down, obviously the frigatebirds can not reach them. The threat of intensive Japanese tuna fishing around Ascension Island could prove very serious for the entire local community of seabirds.

For the moment none of the other three species are in danger. World populations of Great and Lesser Frigatebirds probably add up to hundreds of thousands, due mostly to their large Pacific colonies, and Magnificent Frigatebird numbers may be of a comparable magnitude, though quantitative details for many parts of South America are lacking. Accurate, up-to-date figures of these species are available only for a few colonies, while deferred maturity, pelagic tendencies and the frequent practice among adults of non-breeding just serve to make it even more difficult to estimate overall numbers.

The same species have some survival problems at subspecific level. *F. magnificens lowei*, a rather dubious race found only in the Cape Verde Islands, is down to 10-12 pairs, with predation by local fishermen apparently being a major cause of its decline. The Martin Vaz Islands and Trinidade off eastern Brazil hold the only remaining populations of *F. minor nicolli* and *F. ariel trinitatis*. It seems that feral goats and cats, together with human activities, have virtually exterminated the birds from Trinidade, and light aircraft may contribute to their ultimate demise here; the Brazilian navy use the small, uninhabited Martin Vaz Islands for target practice. Census work is necessary and it is hoped that the government can be persuaded to take the appropriate measures to safeguard these last Atlantic populations of the two species, although it might already be too late.

Their dense colonies make frigatebirds highly vulnerable, as any disaster is quite liable to afflict all of a population, so great care must be taken to monitor numbers and react quickly to stem declines. The combination of very low productivity and the lengthy period necessary before birds reach sexual maturity means that they are very poorly prepared for recovery from a slump.

General Bibliography

Brockman & Barnard (1979), Burger (1980), Cracraft (1985), Croxall (1987, 1991), Croxall *et al.* (1984), Diamond (1978), Dorst & Mougin (1979), Drummond (1987), Harrison (1985, 1987), Lanham (1947), Nelson (1976, 1980), Olsen (1977a), Schreiber (1984), Sibley & Monroe (1990), Simmons (1972), Stonehouse (1985b), van Tets (1965a), Tuck & Heinzel (1978).

pale morph ♀   dark morph ♀

♂

1

♀   2   ♂

3 ♂   3 ♀   ♀ 4   ♂

5 ♀   5 ♂

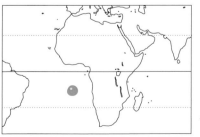

5 ♂

PLATE 25

Family FREGATIDAE (FRIGATEBIRDS)
SPECIES ACCOUNTS

Genus *FREGATA*   Lacépède, 1799

1. Ascension Frigatebird
Fregata aquila

French: Frégate aigle-de-mer **German:** Adlerfregattvogel **Spanish:** Rabihorcado de Ascensión

Taxonomy. *Pelecanus Aquilus* Linnaeus, 1758, Ascension Island.
Formerly included all four larger species of genus. Monotypic.
Distribution. Ascension I, S Atlantic, and surrounding waters; now breeds only on adjoining Boatswainbird Islet.
Descriptive notes. 89-96 cm; c. 1250 g; wingspan 196-201 cm. Typical male all-black with green gloss, inseparable in field from *F. magnificens*; typical female has dark brown collar and breastband (only female frigatebird without white); females average larger. Pale morph female exists, but poorly understood, and might refer to birds breeding in subadult plumage; pale morph male also said to exist. Complex series of immature plumages, with progressively decreasing amounts of white on head and underbody.

Habitat. Used to breed on volcanic slopes of Ascension I, where still roosts and forages; breeding now restricted to 4 loose colonies on Boatswainbird Islet, a flat-topped, steep-sided rock of 3 ha, about 250 m off main island. Feeds in surrounding waters, in pelagic zone, rarely straying more than 150 km from these islands.
Food and Feeding. Fish, especially flying-fish, including *Cypselurus*, *Hirundichthyes* and *Exocoetus volitans*; also some baby green turtles (*Chelonia mydas*) and Sooty Tern (*Sterna fuscata*) chicks. Fish mostly taken by surface dipping; kleptoparasitism probably only used by females, both adults and immatures.
Breeding. All year round, but mostly Apr-Nov/Dec, with peak laying in Oct. Biennial, when successful. Forms loose colonies, on ground, alongside other Pelecaniformes; nests mainly among rocks and guano deposits on flat top of islet, but also on cliff ledges. 1 egg; incubation 43-51 days (average c. 44); chicks naked, grow white down; fledging 6-7 months; post-fledging care 3-4 months (possibly more). Age of sexual maturity unknown. Success rate of only 15-20%.
Movements. Sedentary, rarely wandering more than 150 km from breeding grounds; vagrant to W coast of Africa. Moult mostly carried out at other end of islet, away from breeding grounds.

PLATE 2

inches
cm

Status and Conservation. RARE. Last census in late 1950's estimated population at 8000-10,000 breeding birds and 1000-2000 juveniles. More recent estimate of 1000-1500 pairs or less. Extirpated as a breeding bird from Ascension I itself by feral cats in early 19th century, and now confined to inshore stacks; reported to have been abundant on Ascension in past, though likelihood of this has recently been questioned. Chief threats related to increased human activity, especially since 1982 and establishment of permanent air force base; feral cats prevent recolonization of main island, while threat of their invading last remaining breeding grounds can not be dismissed. Recent control of disturbance, with declaration of Boatswainbird Islet as bird sanctuary, and also proposal to eradicate feral cats on main island. See page 370.

Bibliography. Anon. (1990b), Brown *et al.* (1982), Collar & Andrew (1988), Collar & Stuart (1985), King (1978/79), Mackworth-Praed & Grant (1970), Murphy (1936), Olson (1977b), Pinto (1983), Rose (1974), Simmons (1977), Stonehouse (1960, 1962b), Stonehouse & Stonehouse (1963), Vincent (1966), Williams (1984b).

2. Christmas Frigatebird
Fregata andrewsi

French: Frégate d'Andrews **German:** Weißbauch-Fregattvogel **Spanish:** Rabihorcado de la Christmas
Other common names: Andrews' Frigatebird

Taxonomy. *Fregata andrewsi* Mathews, 1914, Christmas Island, Indian Ocean.
Formerly included in *F. aquila*. Monotypic.
Distribution. Only known to breed on Christmas I, E Indian Ocean; feeds in surrounding ocean and disperses widely. Said to breed on Anambas Is, E of Malay Peninsula, but good evidence lacking.

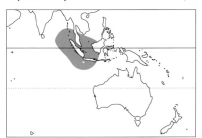

Descriptive notes. 89-100 cm; male c. 1400 g, female c. 1550 g; wingspan 205-230 cm. Male is only frigatebird all-black (glossed green) with white belly patch; female has white breast, belly and axillary "spurs"; females average larger. Complex series of immature plumages, with progressively decreasing amounts of tawny on head and white on underbody.
Habitat. Nests in tall trees, especially Indian almond (*Terminalia catappa*), preferably where sheltered from SE trade winds; nests and roosts in rain forest mostly on outer part of shore terrace, not far from human habitation, also phosphate dryers and golf course. Feeds in high temperature, low salinity waters of surrounding ocean, mainly in pelagic zone.
Food and Feeding. Little known. Mostly flying-fish and squid; also seabird eggs and chicks, carrion and even grasshoppers recorded. Surface dipping and, probably to a lesser extent, kleptoparasitism main systems for obtaining food.
Breeding. Laying mostly Mar-May. Breeding biennial, when successful. Loose colonies, usually in nuclei of 10-20 pairs; up to 38 nests in same tree; some overlap with *F. minor*. Nest is flimsy stick platform, c. 50 cm wide, 10-20 m up in fork of tree. 1 egg; incubation c. 50-54 days; chicks naked, grow white down; fledging normally 19-24 weeks; post-fledging care c. 5-10 months, maximum recorded 15. Sexual maturity at 5-7 years or more. Estimated 30% of eggs laid result in independent young.
Movements. Sedentary; non-breeders and immatures disperse widely throughout much of Indonesia, E to Timor, N to Borneo and SW Thailand. Vagrant to N Australia, Kenya, Hong Kong and possibly India.
Status and Conservation. ENDANGERED. CITES I. Population estimated at c. 1600 pairs, breeding at 3 colonies. Most of habitat protected by extension of national park in 1989, but very low numbers and poor reproductive output mean that any recovery is liable to be slow; protection of colonies presently excluded from park is essential. Habitat destruction, disturbance and human predation of birds and eggs have been main causes of decline; many eggs lost when nests blown down during cyclones, many young birds starve. Phosphate mining now halted, but planned resumption liable to cause problems, as dust from phosphate dryers probably prevented birds from nesting in past. See page 370.
Bibliography. Anon. (1974), Brouwer & Garnett (1990), Collar & Andrew (1988), Feare (1984a), Gibson-Hill (1947a, 1949), Gray (1981), Humphrey & Bain (1990), King (1978/79), Lindsey (1986), McKean (1987), Mann (1986), Marchant & Higgins (1990), van Marle & Voous (1988), Meeth & Meeth (1977), Nelson (1972, 1975a), Ovington (1978), Pocklington (1979), Rozendaal (1980), Smythies (1981), Stokes (1988), Stokes & Goh (1987), van Tets (1975), van Tets & van Tets (1967), White & Bruce (1986).

3. Magnificent Frigatebird
Fregata magnificens

French: Frégate superbe **German:** Prachtfregattvogel **Spanish:** Rabihorcado Magnífico

Taxonomy. *Fregata minor magnificens* Mathews, 1914, Barrington Island, Galapagos Archipelago. Formerly included in *F. aquila* and also in *F. minor*. Possible races *magnificens* (Galapagos), *lowei* (Cape Verde) and *rothschildi* (elsewhere) supposedly separable on length of wing, tail or bill; not generally accepted. Monotypic.

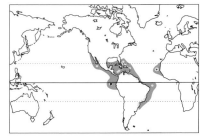

Distribution. Pacific and Atlantic coasts of America, from Baja California to Ecuador, including Galapagos, and from Florida to S Brazil; also relict population on Cape Verde Is, off W Africa.
Descriptive notes. 89-114 cm; c. 1100-1587 g; wingspan 217-244 cm. Largest, longest-billed species. Male all-black glossed purple/green, inseparable in field from male *F. aquila*, while a few have characteristic pale wingbar of *F. minor*; female has white breast band, greyish nuchal collar and thin white lines on axillaries; females average larger. Complex series of immature plumages, with progressively decreasing amounts of white on head and underbody.

Habitat. Tropical and subtropical seas, breeding on coasts and also small islands; nests often in mangroves (e.g. *Avicennia*), also in bushes and even on cactus (Galapagos); occasionally breeds on ground, where no vegetation available. Feeds in adjoining waters; less pelagic than other species.
Food and Feeding. Mostly flying-fish (Exocoetidae), and squid (Ommastrephidae) of 5-11 cm; also other fish e.g. menhaden (*Brevoortia*), and jellyfish, baby turtles, seabird eggs and chicks, offal and fish scraps. Fish mostly taken by surface dipping; kleptoparasitism probably mainly used by females, especially during post-fledging care period. Associates with fishermen (see page 365).
Breeding. Laying recorded all year round, with preference for local dry season, which often coincides with onset of trade winds. Possibly unique in birds in that, when successful, females breed biennially, while males may breed annually, at any rate on Barbuda, Lesser Antilles, and off Belize (see page 368). Colonial, often in mixed colonies alongside other species of Pelecaniformes. Nest is normally flimsy stick platform, c. 30 cm wide, 2-5 m up tree. 1 egg; incubation c. 40-50 days; chicks naked, grow white down; fledging 20-24 weeks; post-fledging care c. 5-7 months. Age of sexual maturity unknown.
Movements. Sedentary, with dispersal of immatures and non-breeders; one bird ringed in S Brazilian colony found on Dominica, E Caribbean. Vagrant to Argentina, Alaska and Newfoundland; also some European records, e.g. Scotland and Denmark, probably referring to vagrants from America.
Status and Conservation. Not globally threatened. World population probably several hundred thousand birds; main threats are habitat destruction and disturbance, in some cases also direct persecution. Caribbean population steadily decreasing since 16th century and now estimated at something over 8000 pairs at about 25 colonies. At least three colonies totalling up to c. 60,000 pairs in W Mexico. Still fairly numerous around S America, but few details available on population sizes or trends; common and widespread off S Brazil, with several thousand breeding pairs, including 2000 nests on Cagarras Is and 700 pairs on Currais I; may also breed off N coast. Population of Cape Verde Is down to perhaps 10 birds; direct persecution, particularly by fishermen, along with habitat destruction and disturbance, are chief causes of decline here.
Bibliography. Anon. (1985a), Bege & Pauli (1988), Belopolsky & Laskova (1986), Bent (1922), Blake (1977), Borin & Kokshaiskii (1983), Bourne (1957), Brown *et al.* (1982), Buckley & Tilger (1985), Clapp *et al.* (1982), Coello *et al.* (1977), Cramp & Simmons (1977), Croxall (1991), Croxall *et al.* (1984), Diamond (1972, 1973), Dujardin & Tostain (1990), Gibbs & Gibbs (1987), Gochfeld & Burger (1981), Gordillo (1981), Harrington *et al.* (1972), Harris (1969b), Janzen (1983), Kale (1978), Mackworth-Praed & Grant (1970), McNeil (1985), Moreno & Carmona (1988), Murphy (1936), de Naurois (1969b), Norton (1988), Palmer (1962), Pennycuick (1983), Rezende (1987), Pinto (1964), Ruschi (1979), Scherer Neto (1987), Schnell (1974), Schreiber & Schreiber (1984b), Sick (1984), Slud (1964), Trivelpiece & Ferraris (1987), de Visscher (1980), Voous (1983), Wetmore (1965).

4. Great Frigatebird
Fregata minor

French: Frégate du Pacifique **German:** Bindenfregattvogel **Spanish:** Rabihorcado Grande
Other common names: Pacific/Lesser (!) Frigatebird

Taxonomy. *Pelecanus minor* Gmelin, 1789, Christmas Island, E Indian Ocean.
Formerly included in *F. aquila*. Five subspecies normally recognized, though validity doubtful.
Subspecies and Distribution.
F. m. aldabrensis Mathews, 1914 - W Indian Ocean.
F. m. minor (Gmelin, 1789) - E Indian and SW Pacific Oceans.
F. m. palmerstoni (Gmelin, 1789) - W & C Pacific.
F. m. ridgwayi Mathews, 1914 - E Pacific.
F. m. nicolli Mathews, 1914 - S Atlantic.

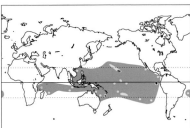

Descriptive notes. 85-105 cm; male 1000-1450 g, female 1215-1640 g; wingspan 205-230 cm. Male glossed green, usually separable from other all-black males by marked pale brown wingbar (but see *F. magnificens*); female has white breast and grey throat; females average larger. Complex series of immature plumages, with progressively decreasing amounts of tawny/white on head and breast and white on underbody. Races very similar, doubtfully separable on size and bare part coloration.
Habitat. Tropical and subtropical seas, breeding on small, remote islands, in mangroves (e.g. *Rhizophora*, *Bruguiera*) or bushes (e.g. *Scaevola*), occasionally on bare ground; on Christmas I (Indian Ocean) breeds on slopes further inland than *F. andrewsi*. Feeds in adjoining ocean, usually in waters over 22°C in pelagic zone, but within c. 80 km of colony or roost.
Food and Feeding. Mostly fish, especially flying-fish (Exocoetidae, including *Cypselurus*, *Exocoetus*, *Evolantia*) of 10-20 cm, and (flying) squid (Ommastrephidae) of 4-12 cm; also seabird eggs and chicks, hatchling turtles, carrion and fish scraps. Fish mostly taken by surface dipping; kleptoparasitism and nest robbery rarely used, mainly by males in Galapagos, by females and juveniles in Hawaii and Aldabra.
Breeding. Throughout year, varying with locality; some preference for laying in dry season. Probably biennial, when successful, although recent work with ringed birds in Galapagos shows that many females wait 3-4 more years before trying again. Colonial, with clusters of 10-30 synchronized pairs; often in mixed colonies alongside other species of Pelecaniformes, sometimes with *F. ariel*. Nest is stick platform, often c. 15 m up tree, though can be very close to ground, where taller vegetation lacking. 1 egg; incubation c. 55 days; chicks naked, grow grey/white down; fledging 17-23 weeks; post-fledging care 5-18 months. Sexual maturity probably at 8-10 years. Success (eggs to fledging) 19% Galapagos, c. 50% Aldabra.
Movements. Sedentary, with dispersal of immatures and non-breeders throughout tropical seas, mostly in Indian and Pacific Oceans; most birds probably return to natal colony to breed; Hawaiian birds tend to roam about archipelago or wander to nearby Johnston Atoll, but ringing recoveries from Philippines may indicate similar movements to those of *F. ariel*, though probably occurring later. Vagrant to Japan, Siberia, New Zealand and South Africa.
Status and Conservation. Not globally threatened. World population estimated at half a million to one million birds; main threats are probably habitat destruction and disturbance, in some cases also direct persecution. Several thousand pairs in Indian Ocean, including 4000+ at Aldabra and c. 3250 at Christmas I; at least 4 colonies in Indonesia, holding 1700-3500 pairs; 64,000 birds in

On following page: 5. Lesser Frigatebird (*Fregata ariel*).

Hawaii; large numbers in Galapagos, including c. 20,000 breeding birds on Genovesa (Tower) I; large numbers in SC Pacific, where both Line and Phoenix Is may hold tens of thousands of pairs, with possible breeding in another ten island groups; threats include introduced predators. El Niño Southern Oscillation can cause partial or total breeding failure both in Galapagos and C Pacific (see page 341). Atlantic race *nicolli* formerly bred on St Helena, now probably restricted to Martin Vaz Is and Trinidade off Brazil, but no recent breeding records and may be doomed; reasons for decline unclear (see page 371).

Bibliography. Barber & Chavez (1983), Belopolsky & Laskova (1986), Brazil (1991), Brown *et al.* (1982), Coates (1985), Coello *et al.* (1977), Conant & Collins (1983), Croxall (1991), Croxall *et al.* (1984), Diamond (1971, 1975b, 1979), Dunlop *et al.* (1988), Fairchild *et al.* (1985), Garnett & Crowley (1987), Gordillo (1980), Gray (1981), Harris (1969b), Harrison (1990), Hernández (1978), Hernández & de Vries (1985), de Korte & de Vries (1978), Langrand (1990), Lindsey (1986), Mackworth-Praed & Grant (1957), Mahoney *et al.* (1985), Marchant & Higgins (1990), van Marle & Voous (1988), Milon *et al.* (1973), Moore (1980), Nelson (1967b, 1968, 1985a), Newlands (1975), Olson (1975a, 1981a), Perry (1980), Pocklington (1979), Rauzon (1985), Reville (1980, 1983, 1988), Schreiber & Ashmole (1970), Schreiber & Chovan (1986), Schreiber & Hensley (1976), Schreiber & Schreiber (1984a, 1984b, 1988), Serventy *et al.* (1971), Stokes (1988), Stokes *et al.* (1984), Valle (1986b, 1988), de Vries (1981, 1984), Whittow *et al.* (1978), Williams & Rowlands (1980), Yépez (1979).

5. Lesser Frigatebird

Fregata ariel

French: Frégate ariel   **German:** Arielfregattvogel   **Spanish:** Rabihorcado Chico
Other common names: Least Frigatebird

Taxonomy. *Atagen ariel* G. R. Gray (*ex* Gould MS), 1845, Raine Island, Queensland.
Three subspecies recognized.
Subspecies and Distribution.
F. a. iredalei Mathews, 1914 - W Indian Ocean.
F. a. ariel (G. R. Gray, 1845) - C & E Indian, W & C Pacific Oceans.
F. a. trinitatis Miranda-Ribeiro, 1919 - S Atlantic.
Descriptive notes. 71-81 cm; male 625-875 g, female 760-955 g; wingspan 175-193 cm. Much the smallest species. Male unique, all-black, glossed blue/purple/green, with white axillary "spurs"; female has white upper breast and axillary "spurs"; females average slightly larger. Complex series of immature plumages, with progressively decreasing amounts of russet on head and white on underbody. Races very similar, separated on wing and bill length.
Habitat. Tropical and subtropical seas, breeding on small, remote islands, in mangroves or bushes/scrub (*Pemphis, Lepturus, Tournefortia*); more prepared to use lower vegetation than *F. minor* on Aldabra, and can even nest on ground, e.g. in Phoenix and Line Is (SC Pacific), Raine I (NE Australia). Feeds in adjoining ocean, usually in waters over 22°C in pelagic zone.

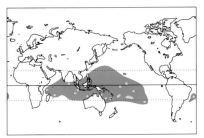

Food and Feeding. Mostly fish, especially flying-fish (*Cypselurus, Exocoetus, Evolantia*) of 10-20 cm, and squid (Ommastrephidae) of 4-12 cm; also seabird eggs and chicks, carrion and fish scraps. Surface dipping main system for obtaining food; kleptoparasitism used mostly by females. Food preference surprisingly similar to that of *F. minor* on Aldabra.
Breeding. Throughout much of year at different localities; some preference for laying in dry season. Probably biennial, when successful. Colonial, with sub-groups of up to 100 nests; often in mixed colonies alongside other species of Pelecaniformes, sometimes with *F. minor*. Nest is stick platform, usually up to 15 m up tree. 1 egg; incubation c. 45 days; chicks naked, grow white down; fledging 20-24 weeks; post-fledging care 4-6+ months. Age of sexual maturity unknown. Success (eggs to fledging) 12% Aldabra.
Movements. Sedentary, with dispersal of immatures and non-breeders throughout tropical seas, especially of Indian and Pacific Oceans. Results from ringing of some 13,000 juveniles in SC Pacific indicate that they follow prevailing winds W to Coral Sea, NE of Australia, before heading off N by New Guinea towards Philippines, with some reaching Japan; recent evidence suggests possible mixing with Australian birds, with some heading further W, e.g. to Cocos (Keeling) Is; may be trying to colonize Christmas I, Indian Ocean. Vagrant to Japan, Siberia, NE USA and New Zealand.
Status and Conservation. Not globally threatened. World population probably several hundred thousand birds; main threats are probably habitat destruction, disturbance and direct persecution by humans for food. Several thousand pairs in Indian Ocean, including 6000+ at Aldabra; minimum c. 15,000 pairs on islands off N and E Australia; most spectacular numbers in SC Pacific, where both Phoenix and Line Is may hold tens of thousands of pairs, with possible breeding in another ten island groups; El Niño Southern Oscillation can cause partial or total breeding failure in C Pacific (see page 341). Atlantic race *trinitatis* formerly bred on St Helena and possibly also Martin Vaz Is, now restricted to Trinidade, off E Brazil, where 25-50 pairs found breeding in 1975/76; reasons for decline unclear (see page 371).

Bibliography. Brazil (1991), Bregulla (1992), Brown *et al.* (1982),Burbidge *et al.* (1987), Coates (1985), Croxall (1991), Croxall *et al.* (1984), Diamond (1971, 1975b, 1979), Garnett & Crowley (1987), Langrand (1990), Lindsey (1986), Mackworth-Praed & Grant (1957), Marchant & Higgins (1990), van Marle & Voous (1988), Milon *et al.* (1973), Newlands (1975), Olson (1975a, 1981a), Perry (1980), Pocklington (1979), Reville (1980, 1983), Schreiber & Ashmole (1970), Schreiber & Schreiber (1984a), Serventy *et al.* (1971), Sibley & Clapp (1967), Staub (1976), Stokes & Dunn (1989), Stokes *et al.* (1984), White & Bruce (1986), Williams & Rowlands (1980).

Order CICONIIFORMES

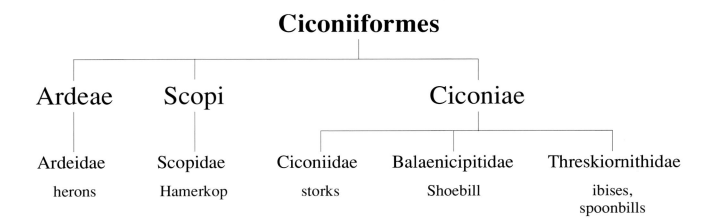

Class AVES
Order CICONIIFORMES
Suborder ARDEAE
Family ARDEIDAE (HERONS)

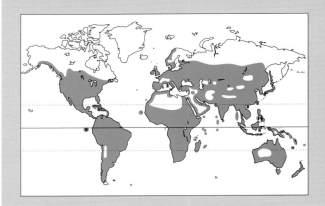

- Medium-sized to large wading birds with long bill, neck and legs.
- 27-140 cm.

- All regions except Antarctic, with greatest diversity in tropics.
- Wide variety of wetland habitats; a few species mainly terrestrial.
- 17 genera, 60 species, 149 taxa.
- 6 species threatened; 1 species and 1 subspecies extinct since 1600.

Systematics

The family Ardeidae belongs to the order Ciconiiformes. The origins of the family are ancient, dating back to the Lower Eocene, about 55 million years ago. Some of the present day genera are very old, for example *Ardea* is known from the late Miocene, over 7 million years ago, while *Nycticorax* is known from the early Quaternary. To date, 34 fossil species are known, many of which have been found in Europe.

The classification of this family has undergone many changes over the years and J. D. Ligon, basing himself on comparative, though incomplete, osteological analyses, even advocated a separate order, Ardeiformes, for the herons and their allies, as he maintained that the storks (Ciconiidae) actually belonged with the New World vultures (Cathartidae), rather than the herons.

The first revision of the Ardeidae which can be considered both sound and complete was that published by W. J. Bock in 1956, and this classification has served as a solid base, to which various modifications have subsequently been made. Traditionally, the Ardeidae were divided into two subfamilies, Botaurinae (bitterns) and Ardeinae (herons), reflecting two groups that are highly differentiated as regards morphological, structural and behavioural characteristics.

However, R. B. Payne and C. J. Risley carried out a comprehensive study of the evolutionary relationships of the family, based on numerical taxonomy using 33 skeletal characters, and complemented by ethological data, and this produced a substantial change in the standard classification. It indicated the existence of four equidistant natural groups, which correspond to the following subfamilies: Ardeinae (day-herons); Nycticoracinae (night-herons), incorporating the Boat-billed Heron (*Cochlearius cochlearius*); Tigrisomatinae (tiger-herons); and Botaurinae (bitterns), including the Zigzag Heron (*Zebrilus undulatus*).

Furthermore, these same criteria demanded an inversion of the systematic order. Previously, the bitterns were placed before the herons, on the grounds that they were more primitive, but, although there are some "primitive" characteristics in the tiger-herons and the bitterns, such as a simple vocal repertoire, allopatric and presumably relict distribution, and small clutches, they appear to have differentiated in the distant past, and subsequently to have undergone intense modifications. The day- and night-herons, on the other hand, are now considered to be more similar to the earliest ancestors of the family.

This same basic order emerges in recent work by F. H. Sheldon, based on the degree of similarity that appears from the DNA hybridization of different species. These results show that the differentiation of the day- and night-herons is adaptive as opposed to genealogical, and also that the bitterns are the sister taxon of the day- and night-herons at a tribal level, a totally new idea.

Over the years, the classification of the lower taxonomic levels has also undergone substantial changes. In the last 100 years, the family has been composed of anything from 15 to 35 genera, and 60 to 93 species. The practice of accepting a large number of monotypic genera has switched to a preference for grouping species together in a single genus. A further step in this direction can be seen in the recent case of the Little Egret (*Egretta garzetta*), which, according to some authors, has now absorbed both the Mascarene Reef-egret (*E. g. dimorpha*) and the Western Reef-egret (*E. g. gularis*), although others still consider them full species.

Although the different species of heron are morphologically very similar, there are some exceptions. The clearest is undoubtedly the Boat-billed Heron, an American species with such unique characteristics, in terms both of its habits and its displays, that some authors consider that it should even be given its own family. Note the unusual bill and the large eyes, which are an adaptation to the bird's crepuscular life style.

*[Cochlearius cochlearius, Mexico.
Photo: Patricio Robles]*

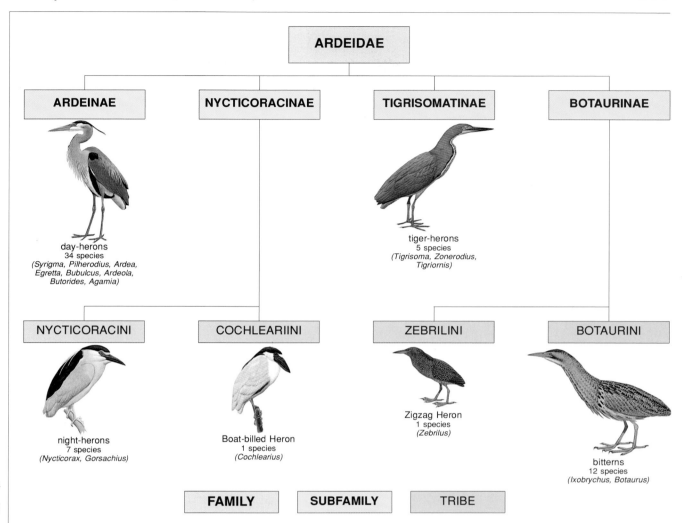

Subdivision of the Ardeidae.

[Figure: Francesc Jutglar]

The taxonomic situation of the Rufous-bellied Heron is a matter of some debate. During the first half of the century it was placed in the monotypic genus Erythrocnus; nowadays, while there are those that consider that it should be included in the genus Butorides, others place it in Ardeola, and it appears to show intermediate features between these two genera.

[Ardeola rufiventris, Chobe, Botswana. Photo: Richard Coomber/ Planet Earth]

Different classifications have alternatively situated the Whistling Heron (*Syrigma sibilatrix*) and the Capped Heron (*Pilherodius pileatus*) among the day-herons or the night-herons, but because of their behaviour and morphology it seems more convenient to keep them in the day-herons. The dividing line between the genera *Ardea* and *Egretta* is also unclear, and some authors actually include all the species of *Egretta* within *Ardea*. Some species are hard to place, such as the Purple Heron (*Ardea purpurea*), the Intermediate Egret (*Egretta intermedia*) and especially the Great White Egret (*Egretta alba*), and the intermediate characteristics of this last species have warranted its occasional inclusion in a monospecific genus, *Casmerodius*. Likewise, the Reddish Egret (*Egretta rufescens*), the Tricolored Heron (*Egretta tricolor*) and the Little Blue Heron (*Egretta caerulea*) were grouped together in a separate genus, *Hydranassa*. Another awkward species is the Cattle Egret (*Bubulcus ibis*), and some have situated it in the genus *Ardeola*, whilst others include it in *Egretta*, on the grounds of its great morphological and behavioural similarities with the typical egrets. The Agami Heron (*Agamia agami*) has some very peculiar features, which have even caused some doubt about its inclusion within the Ardeidae.

According to Payne and Risley, within the night-heron group, the Yellow-crowned Night-heron (*Nycticorax violaceus*) merits a separate genus (*Nyctanassa*), while all the remaining species should be placed in the genus *Nycticorax*. On the other hand, many authors prefer another genus, *Gorsachius*, for three of the species, the White-eared Night-heron (*Gorsachius magnificus*), the Japanese Night-heron (*Gorsachius goisagi*) and the Malayan Night-heron (*Gorsachius melanolophus*). However, K. Curry-Lindahl, in contrast, considered that it was the Malayan Night-heron that should be separated from all the other species.

Although the Boat-billed Heron is normally assumed to be related to the night-herons, it is difficult to classify because of its many peculiar features, including the form of the bill, some osteological features, plumage and behaviour. It is sometimes considered to be the sole member of a separate family, Cochleariidae. Likewise, the Zigzag Heron has been grouped along with the tiger-herons.

The status of some species has only recently been clarified, such as that of the Green-backed Heron (*Butorides striatus*), which used to be separated into several species, a view still supported by workers on DNA. Similarly, the Slaty Egret (*Egretta vinaceigula*) was formerly considered conspecific with the Black Heron (*Egretta ardesiaca*), whilst the specific limits of some other forms have not yet been determined.

In natural conditions, few cases of hybridization are known: the Grey Heron (*Ardea cinerea*) with the Little Egret in Belgium, the Grey Heron with the Great White Egret in Holland, the Indian Pond-heron (*Ardeola grayii*) with the Intermediate Egret in India, the Snowy Egret (*Egretta thula*) with the Little Blue Heron in Brazil, and the Black-crowned Night-heron (*Nyctico-rax nycticorax*) with the Rufous Night-heron (*Nycticorax caledonicus*) in the Philippines, Java and Sulawesi. In captivity, on the other hand, they hybridize easily, and on occasions produce fertile offspring, as in the cases of the Grey Heron with the Purple Heron, or the Little Egret with the Snowy Egret.

Undoubtedly, the most recent research and also future work on the evolutionary lineage of the family will lead to further changes in the classification. The work carried out on genetic affinities, for example, appears to situate the Boat-billed Heron and the Rufescent Tiger-heron (*Tigrisoma lineatum*) in the same subfamily, while the Cattle, Great White and Intermediate Egrets should perhaps be included within the genus *Ardea*. While work is going on to provide support for the new modifications, it seems most appropriate to follow the exhaustive revision of the family by J. Hancock and J. Kushlan, which drew on all previous studies, in addition to their own research, and was published in 1984. They propose a classification based on the four aforementioned subfamilies, with separate tribes for the Boat-billed Heron and the Zigzag Heron within the night-herons and bitterns respectively. They accept a total of 17 genera and 60 species, with eight superspecific groups.

Morphological Aspects

Herons are medium-sized to large birds, with long necks, legs and bills, short tails and rather long, broad wings. The day-herons are slim and graceful, with particularly long neck and legs. The night-herons and the bitterns, on the other hand, are plumper and have shorter necks.

The Ardeidae constitute a group of birds that are highly specialized in the capture of live prey, mainly in the water. The neck forms a characteristic kinked S-shape, due to the elongated structure of the sixth cervical vertebra. In general, the bird can retract and extend its neck with great ease, and it is usually drawn back into the body in flight. All this specialization of the neck is related to the use of the bill as a harpoon for capturing prey.

In this family there is no pronounced sexual dimorphism in terms of size. In the different European species for example, the

male's skeletal elements are only 2-4% larger than the female's, with the least variation occurring in the Great White Egret, and the greatest in the Little Bittern (*Ixobrychus minutus*).

The legs are strong and long or very long, as befits a group of birds adapted to spending most of the time standing motionless at the water's edge or wading in shallow water. The lower part of the tibia is bare, except in the Zigzag Heron, in which it is feathered. The herons have three toes pointing forwards and one backwards, all of which are long and thin. The middle toe is always the longest, and is joined to the shorter innermost toe by a short basal web, while the hind toe is directly opposite the middle one. The claw of the middle toe is pectinated. In some species that are specially adapted to walking on floating marsh vegetation, for example the Purple Heron, the toes are extremely long. In flight, the legs are stretched backwards and clearly project beyond the tail.

In general, the bill is long, straight and harpoon-shaped. In some species it is very long and fine, most notably in the Agami Heron. In others, it is also long, but thicker and robust, for example in the Grey Heron, or alternatively wide and rather short, as in the Black-crowned Night-heron. The Boat-billed Heron is an atypical species, with an extremely broad, thick bill.

The wings are long and broad, with 10-11 primaries, though the Boat-billed Heron has only nine, and there are 15 to 20 secondaries. The tail is short and squarish or slightly rounded, with ten rectrices in the bitterns and twelve in the other species. The undertail-coverts are long, and are more or less the same length as the rectrices.

The bare parts, the bill and the legs, are generally yellow, brown or black, and the lores too are featherless. In the Capped

The relationship of the Agami Heron with other species is not at all clear, but it is generally agreed that it is sufficiently distinctive to be awarded its own monospecific genus. It shows several peculiar morphological features, including a very short tibia, which gives it an unusual stance, a long and remarkably thin bill, and an extremely long neck recalling that of the darters.

[*Agamia agami*, Costa Rica. Photo: Manuel Marin]

Some species of herons have different colour morphs, which tend to be restricted to specific geographical areas. Populations living in tropical marine habitats tend to be white, as is the case of the Great Blue Heron, which, in the race *occidentalis* of the coasts of Florida and the Caribbean, regularly occurs in an all-white morph (above), instead of the more usual grey-blue plumage of the species. In the past, this white morph was regarded as a separate species, the Great White Heron. Another form, Würdemann's Heron (below), was described as a separate species in the middle of last century. It was later considered to be a hybrid between the two races of the Great Blue Heron found in Florida, Ward's Heron (A. h. wardi), and the Great White Heron (A. h. occidentalis), but more recently it has been regarded as no more than an atypical colour variant of Ward's Heron.

[*Ardea herodias*, USA. Photos: Stephen J. Krasemann/DRK (above) Larry Lipsky/DRK (below)]

Like almost all of the Ciconiiformes, herons have long necks and legs, and are basically adapted to living in aquatic environments. The heron family however, presents several unique features such as the spear-shaped bill, which is often grooved towards the tip, the S-shaped neck, the powder-down patches, the pectinated claw of the middle toe, and the lanceolate or filamentous display plumes on the head, neck, breast or back. Most species are slim and svelte, especially the day-herons, like this Cocoi Heron. The long legs and neck are useful adaptations for walking about and feeding in marshy areas, and have helped the herons to spread to practically all parts of the world, though they are especially abundant in the tropics.

[*Ardea cocoi*, Peru. Photo: Günter Ziesler]

Heron the featherless part of the face is more extensive and reaches beyond the eye. During the initial phase of breeding, the colours of the legs, the bill and the lores become brighter, in some cases strikingly so. The variations in colour indicate the bird's physiological state, for example during courtship in the nominate race of the Little Egret, the lores and feet, which are normally grey-blue and yellow respectively, both become red. The Grey Heron's bill also turns from its usual brownish yellow to a bright orange-yellow in the breeding season. The most spectacular colours usually occur during the courting and mating phases, and they rapidly lose intensity, once the birds start incubation or the brooding of their chicks, though their duration varies with the species.

Plumage is soft, with narrow feather tracts, and down is restricted to the apteria. Herons are basically black, brown, blue, grey or white, with complex colour patterns. In the day-herons, the majority of the species are not sexually dimorphic in their plumage, nor are there marked variations with age or at different times of year, except in the pond-herons. However, the Little Blue Heron is exceptional in that its white phase corresponds to birds that are less than a year old, but when they moult they acquire the dark grey-blue plumage typical of the adults. There are, on the other hand, clear geographical differences, and, particularly in tropical and subtropical zones, several species are dimorphic, with black and white phases, as in the case of the Western Reef-egret. However, these phases of coloration are not related to age, and both can live together in the same area. Mixed pairs have been found, for example, in the Great Blue Heron (*Ardea herodias*), although there appears to be a marked tendency for birds to mate with others of the same phase. Likewise, cases of aberrant plumage are recorded for some species, for example melanism in the Least Bittern (*Ixobrychus exilis*) or the Grey Heron, or Little Egrets with pied plumage. In some species there is marked geographical variation in the plumage, and the most extreme case is the Green-backed Heron, with 30 recognized races which differ principally in the colour of the foreneck, the breast and the upperparts. In the pond-herons, plumage is much more vivid during breeding than at other times of year, and immature birds are similar to non-breeding adults, although not indistinguishable from them.

In all of the night-herons, except the Japanese Night-heron, there is a marked difference between the adults, which have a highly contrasted plumage, basically black and grey or brown and black, and immatures, which are usually a very dull, striped brownish grey. In the tiger-herons of the genus *Tigrisoma*, and in two atypical species, the Zigzag and Boat-billed Herons, there are also marked differences between the plumage of adult and immature birds.

In the small bitterns, there is very pronounced sexual dimorphism, with males showing a much brighter, more contrasted plumage than females. In males, the predominant colours are black, cream and chestnut, whilst females are generally brownish, usually with some stripes.

Some species, especially the day- and night-herons, have ornamental plumes on the head, the lower neck, the breast and the back. Normally, these plumes appear during the prenuptial moult, before the start of breeding. These special feathers are of great importance during pairing and courtship, and they normally deteriorate or can even be lost during the breeding season. The kind of ornamental plumes present in each species and their positioning on the head, neck, breast or back are of great help in the identification of the different species during courtship. The ornamental plumes can be divided into three types, lanceolate, filoplumes, and "aigrettes". The lanceolate plumes are characterized by their great length in comparison with their width; the filoplumes are long and hairy with free barbs; the "aigrettes" have a looser appearance with loose, elongated barbs and barbules.

The presence of white lanceolate plumes on the head is typical of the genus *Nycticorax*, as well as the Great Blue Heron and the White-bellied Heron (*Ardea insignis*), the Little Egret, the Chinese Egret (*Egretta eulophotes*) and the Eastern Reef-egret (*Egretta sacra*), and also the Capped Heron. In different species of the genus *Egretta* and in *Butorides*, one can find the typical scapular filoplumes, or "aigrettes". The filoplumes are above all typical of the pond-herons, although they are most highly developed in the Reddish Egret. The Agami Heron is unique within the whole family in having characteristically short, fine, curved plumes on its neck.

Another typical feature of herons and of the Balaenicipitidae, a family traditionally considered to be closely related to

The small bitterns comprise the smallest species of the heron family, weighing between 100-200 g and with lengths of 27-58 cm. In this group are the only herons to present sexual dimorphism, the males showing a more contrasted and vivid plumage than the females. The Stripe-backed Bittern, however, is an exception, as both sexes have similar plumage.

[*Ixobrychus involucris*. Photo: H. L. Rivarola/ Bruce Coleman]

The modified feathers which normally appear on the head, breast and back during the pre-nuptial moult, play an important part in pair formation and generally in courtship behaviour. This Capped Heron sports three long white occipital plumes which in this species can measure up to 20 cm long. The buffy wash on the breast is thought to come from the powder-downs.

[*Pilherodius pileatus*, Pantanal, Brazil. Photo: Günter Ziesler]

The pond-herons are the only members of the Ardeidae to present a markedly different breeding and non-breeding plumage, the former being acquired by the pre-breeding moult of the body feathers and the inner secondaries. This Chinese Pond-heron, for example, is unmistakable in full breeding plumage, but in winter it is virtually indistinguishable from the Indian (Ardeola grayii) and Javan Pond-herons (Ardeola speciosa), with which it is partially sympatric.

[*Ardeola bacchus.* Photo: Michael Pitts/ Survival]

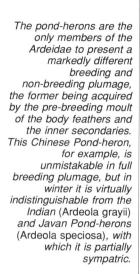

them, is the presence of powder-downs. These consist of a special kind of continuously growing down, which disintegrates to form powder, and this is used in preening, especially to remove grease from the feathers. A bird picks it up in the bill, passes it to the serrated claw of the middle toe, and thus proceeds to apply it to the feathers. All species in the family have several pairs of powder-downs situated on the breast, the rump and also sometimes on the back and thighs. There are normally three pairs, except in bitterns which have only two, and in the Boat-billed Heron and the American tiger-herons which have four. The oil gland is typically very small in herons.

The development of the plumage from the time the bird hatches until it gains adult plumage is variable. In some species there is a certain relationship between the colouring of chicks and that of adults, as for example in the egrets. The time required to gain adult plumage also varies, from one to two years in the species that mature most rapidly, such as the bitterns, to almost five years in the case of the Rufescent Tiger-heron.

The moult strategies of the different species are related to the environmental conditions of the areas they inhabit, and in some cases there can be variations within the same species. Moult is complex and relatively little is known; generally adults have a complete post-breeding moult, as well as a partial pre-breeding moult.

Frequently, the pre-breeding moult consists only of the development of the display plumes, and in some species it is practically non-existent. On the other hand, in some groups, especially the pond-herons, it is much more extensive as it brings in the markedly different breeding plumage of these species. In the Squacco Heron (*Ardeola ralloides*), for example, the pre-breeding moult occurs between January and June and involves the body-coverts, the wing-coverts and the innermost secondaries, but not the rest of the wings or the tail.

During the post-breeding moult, the display plumes are normally lost, except in the Rufous Night-heron, which retains the two white plumes on its head. In the Little Egret, for example, the post-breeding moult starts with the shedding of the head feathers, followed by the scapulars. Primary moult is generally irregular, but most typically the moult of the innermost primaries is descendant, while the outer primaries moult

irregularly. The moult of the tail is centripetal, starting from the outer rectrices and working its way inwards. Birds can continue to moult their body-coverts throughout the winter. In Europe, for example, adult Grey Herons carry out their post-breeding moult between June and November, starting before their chicks are fully-developed. Young Grey Herons, on the other hand, carry out a partial moult between September and February, changing most of the body coverts and some of the wing-coverts.

The flight of the herons is slow, rather heavy and not very agile, but strong. They generally use flapping flight, and can cover great distances both in migrations and in their comings and goings between feeding areas and breeding colonies or communal roosts. Speeds have been measured for different species, including about 28-51 km/h in the Great White Egret, or 32-56 km/h in the Black-crowned Night-heron. On long distance flights, the Great Blue Heron has been recorded flying at about 29-57 km/h and 48-56 km/h. The large species beat their wings slowly, for example the Great Blue Heron has a wingbeat frequency of 2·3-3·2 beats per second, while the Goliath Heron (*Ardea goliath*) makes 98 wingbeats per minute, and these species usually hold their wings distinctly arched. The smaller species logically have a faster wingbeat and the Slaty Egret, for example, flies with 190 wingbeats per minute. Despite the fact that their flight is not very agile, they are capable of landing on water and taking off again immediately, and they also carry out relatively acrobatic parachute descents. The night-herons and the bitterns have a flapping flight with faster wingbeats than day-herons of the same size. Herons have a characteristic flight silhouette, with the neck completely retracted so that it rests fully on the bird's back. When taking off, some species keep the neck stretched out for some time, as for example the White-faced Heron (*Egretta novaehollandiae*), but only one species, the Whistling Heron, flies without folding its neck back totally. This species also stands out because of its fast flapping flight with rapid wingbeats, in a style reminiscent of the Anatidae.

Herons have long, strong legs, and are good walkers. In fact, most species spend most of their time on the ground or perched on branches of trees. Some, such as the members of the genus *Ixobrychus*, are capable of moving with extraordinary agility through tangled marsh vegetation. The Eurasian Bittern (*Botaurus stellaris*), in spite of its relatively large size, is capable of moving easily through the vegetation and even of clambering through reedbeds.

Habitat

The herons are a group of waterbirds with a mainly tropical distribution, and they are spread out all over the world. Only the extreme latitudes, both in the north and the south, and many oceanic islands, remain outside their range.

Some species can live on high plateaux at a considerable altitude, for instance in New Guinea, Central Asia, Madagascar and particularly South America, where the Black-crowned Night-heron has been reported as occurring at a height of 4816 m in Chile. Nevertheless, they are more often birds of lower altitudes and usually avoid mountainous regions, although some species are normally found in zones of medium and low altitude mountains. The White-eared Night-heron, for example, lives in watercourses in forested areas of hills or moderately high mountains in China. Likewise, the Japanese Night-heron lives in areas of forest bordering watercourses in low hilly parts of Japan.

Herons are essentially non-swimmers that live on the margins of wetlands or aquatic zones of any kind, such as marine bays, tidal flats, mangroves, marshes, rivers and inland lakes. Their feeding behaviour, which consists of searching for prey whilst standing motionless at the edge of a flooded area, or walking through shallow water, means that they avoid deep water. However, not all of the species are linked to aquatic environments, and some can be found in areas far from water, such as the Whistling Heron, which lives in open savanna in South America, or the Black-headed Heron (*Ardea melanoce-*

phala), which can live on the grassy African savannas. The most terrestrial species in the family is the Cattle Egret, a widely distributed bird which adapts itself to a large variety of non-aquatic habitats, such as pastures, cultivated land and even suburban areas.

The day-herons are the largest and most diversified group, and they live in all kinds of wetlands. In this group there are a good number of very widely distributed species, such as the Cattle and Great White Egrets, and the Green-backed and Grey Herons. The Grey Heron is amongst the herons that can be found furthest north, and it occupies a fair proportion of the open wetlands of the Old World, in latitudes where there are four or five ice-free months per year. Quite a large percentage of the species live in open marshland with shallow water, but some prefer coastal areas, such as tidal flats or mangroves, as in the case of the Great-billed Heron (*Ardea sumatrana*) on the coasts of south-east Asia and Australia. One characteristic species of these coastal areas is the Chinese Egret, a very rare, local species of the Far East. Some day-herons, such as the Eastern Reef-egret, even inhabit coral reefs. Others, however, prefer freshwater wetlands and are not found on the coast, and these include the White-bellied Heron, which lives in the swamplands at the foot of the southern slopes of the Himalayas, or the Slaty Egret, which is found in the seasonal marshes of the Okavango Delta in southern Africa. The Rufous-bellied Heron (*Ardeola rufiventris*) occurs in similar surroundings to the bitterns, in large expanses of shallow, freshwater marshes with abundant vegetation. Some day-herons can be found in lagoons or areas of deep water, where they may settle on floating vegetation, most frequently on water-lilies, and this is especially common amongst the pond-herons. Likewise, there are some species, such as the Agami Heron, which live on small watercourses in the interior of dense tropical forests. In addition, the three aforementioned terrestrial species are all day-herons.

Herons can take off directly from the water. They fly with the neck folded back into the body, and their long, broad wings give them a powerful, albeit slow, style of flight, which allows them to cover great distances. After breeding, most species carry out dispersive movements and seasonal migrations, which often involve long journeys. The wingbeat frequency of the large herons, like this Great Blue Heron, is of two to three beats per second, and birds can reach speeds of over 50 km/h.

[*Ardea herodias*, USA. Photo: Scott Nielsen/ Bruce Coleman]

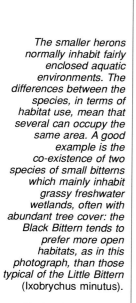

The smaller herons normally inhabit fairly enclosed aquatic environments. The differences between the species, in terms of habitat use, mean that several can occupy the same area. A good example is the co-existence of two species of small bitterns which mainly inhabit grassy freshwater wetlands, often with abundant tree cover: the Black Bittern tends to prefer more open habitats, as in this photograph, than those typical of the Little Bittern (Ixobrychus minutus).

[Ixobrychus flavicollis australis, Australia. Photo: A. Taylor/NPIAW]

The night-herons occupy both coastal and inland wetlands, and may be found in fresh, brackish and salt water. The Yellow-crowned Night-heron and the Boat-billed Heron are species which normally occupy coastal regions, and the race *falklandicus* of the Black-crowned Night-heron can even feed in marine waters some distance from the shore. They are nocturnal or crepuscular birds, which usually spend the daylight hours well hidden amongst the vegetation. For this reason, one of their most characteristic requirements is a dense covering of bushes or trees, preferably tall trees with safe perches, for instance mangroves, or riparian woodland. For feeding, they can use much more open spaces, such as marshlands or rice fields.

The tiger-herons chiefly live in river systems surrounded by forest in the tropical zone. Sometimes they also occur in more open wetlands, as in the case of the Bare-throated Tiger-heron (*Tigrisoma mexicanum*), which is found in the lagoons surrounded by marsh vegetation in the Usumacinta Delta in Mexico. This species and the White-crested Tiger-heron (*Tigriornis leucolophus*) are the only tiger-heron species usually found in coastal habitats, and the rest of the Tigrisomatinae are more typically found inland. Another species, the Fasciated Tiger-heron (*Tigrisoma fasciatum*), lives in montane rain forest, with streams or small, fast-flowing rivers.

Bitterns are normally found in freshwater wetlands between the latitudes 60° N and 40° S, and they occupy areas with a dense covering of marsh vegetation. The large bitterns live preferably in the temperate zones and normally select extensive areas of shallow water, where they can walk about with ease. They usually choose sites with a relatively constant water level and tall, dense vegetation, such as reeds, reedmace, rushes and the like, and some species such as the South American Bittern (*Botaurus pinnatus*) are also found in rice fields. The small bitterns live in similar areas, but will also use areas with abundant bush or tree cover. Two species, the Dwarf Bittern (*Ixobrychus sturmii*) and the Black Bittern (*Ixobrychus flavicollis*), usually occur near watercourses within dense forests. During migration periods or cold spells, the species in this group can occupy a wide variety of habitats, including small stretches of water or even coastal areas.

General Habits

Excluding the tiger-herons and the bitterns, which are solitary, most herons are sociable birds. The day- and night-herons are typically gregarious, breeding in colonies and concentrating in large roosts, although some species feed individually and defend their feeding grounds.

Many heron species form mixed communal roosts, which bring together diverse species of the family, as well as Pelecaniformes and other Ciconiiformes. Roosts are established at safe sites, for example in tall trees, small woods or reedbeds, and sometimes the birds assemble first at nearby pre-roosting areas, before finally making their way to the place where they will spend the night.

During the breeding season, most of the day- and night-herons are also gregarious. Some species breed in large mixed colonies, which can contain thousands of nests, whilst others breed in more modest-sized groups. Amongst the largest colonies known are those at Chagana in Tanzania, with 50,000 pairs of herons and other species, and at Koumbe Niasso in the Niger Delta where 23,000 pairs of seven species of heron nest, in the company of cormorants and Darters. Another large colony is the one at Dam Doi in Viet Nam where, in a 1979 census, 100,000 birds were recorded, including twelve species of heron. However, none can equal the former colony at Shark River in Florida, which held 1,000,000 birds in 1934. In some cases, birds show geographical variations in the extent of their sociability during breeding, with solitary nesting in some areas but colonies in others, for example the Green-backed Heron in North America. In general, the larger species such as the Goliath Heron, the Great-billed Heron and the White-bellied Heron tend to be solitary breeders.

Various suggestions have been put forward to explain why they are sociable. On the one hand, it has been suggested that their gregarious habits are associated with the exploitation of ephemeral and irregularly distributed food supplies, and allow them to benefit rapidly from the information passed on by congeners and quickly locate the areas where food is abundant. On the other hand, their social behaviour may constitute an

A specialization in the use of coastal environments, especially on rocky coasts and coral reefs, has led the Eastern Reef-egret to adapt its feeding rhythm to that of the tides. Although there is some evidence to the contrary, it appears that the white and blackish colour morphs are related to differences in habitat preference and feeding techniques. For example, survey results give equal proportions on rocky beaches and reefs, but ten dark birds for every white one in muddy creeks and rivers.

[*Egretta sacra*. Photo: Jean-Paul Ferrero/ Marco Polo]

adaptation to reduce the impact of predation. It has, for example, been noted that gregarious feeding in mixed-species groups facilitates the detection of predators by combining the diverse surveillance capacities of the different species. It is unclear which of these two factors has played the more decisive part in the development of their social conduct; some believe that the advantages of improved feeding efficiency do not seem to constitute a sufficient reason on their own. However, some of the studies carried out so far, for example in the Camargue, in southern France, have shown that the levels of predation on herons are not usually high. Nonetheless, a great number of predators have been recorded, from reptiles such as iguanas, snakes or crocodiles to various mammals, and a large number of birds. It appears that their main predators are the large birds of prey, which are reported to have caused considerable losses on occasions, of adults, chicks and eggs. It is believed that the scant presence of anti-predatorial defence behaviour in the herons is due to the fact that they are long-lived birds, which can breed many times during their lives, so they prefer to lose their eggs or chicks, rather than expose themselves to the danger of suffering injuries or possibly even death in confrontations with predators. Moreover, they are not very agile in flight (see Morphological Aspects), and this makes it difficult for them to compete with raptors in the air; indeed, one Grey Heron died after being attacked by Carrion Crows (*Corvus corone*). In any case, it has been suggested that the present day anti-predatorial adaptations of the herons may have evolved in situations where predators were much more numerous than they are today. In fact, in some tropical regions it has been found that the impact of predation on adults can be much more intense than was thought up to now, in view of the results of studies carried out mainly in temperate zones. Apart from these reasons, there are also the effects that social nesting can have on sexual stimulation, in shortening the courtship period and improving the synchronization of breeding. Recently, it has also been noted that colonial nesting might be important as it favours the selection of suitable partners, by increasing the choice available in species which probably take new partners every year.

Despite the fact that in a single colony the nests of different species are normally very similar and difficult to distinguish, detailed, quantitive behavioural studies show that there are small, but significant differences in the selection of nest-sites between the different species. Normally, the larger herons locate their nests in the highest parts of the colony. The main aspects influencing nest-site selection are the structure of the vegetation and, as a secondary consideration, the stability of the nest-site, which is necessary in order to avoid accidents during breeding.

The large roosts and breeding colonies act as centres of dispersal for the birds. Colonies exploit feeding areas that can be very extensive, and birds may have to travel great distances. For example, in the Mediterranean it has been found that for a mixed colony to exist, 8600 hectares of feeding grounds are required, and that a colony of 100 pairs of the Black-crowned Night-heron needs 5587 hectares. Similarly, in the Niger Delta, it has been shown that the birds forage within a radius of some 20-30 km of the colony, while the Grey Heron may wander off as much as 38 km away. Large roosts can receive birds from

The normal feeding habitat of the Dwarf Bittern consists essentially of flooded areas preferably with a fair amount of vegetation cover. This is a solitary species which is generally rather difficult to catch sight of, but it appears to be generally uncommon throughout its range. It is mainly active at night, although it can sometimes be seen feeding during the day, normally when the sky is overcast.

[*Ixobrychus sturmii*, Nangwa, Zambia. Photo: Steve Robinson/ NHPA]

even further afield, and the Cattle Egret has been known to commute over distances of up to 60 km in Africa, although the norm seems to be less than 20 km.

The bitterns form a typically solitary and unsociable group, especially the large bitterns, and with their highly cryptic colouring they usually remain hidden amongst the vegetation. A characteristic feature in birds of this group is the "Bittern-stance", which birds adopt in order to remain undetected when they are disturbed, and which they can maintain for several hours. In this position, birds remain motionless with the body erect and the neck and bill quite vertical, so that they are exceptionally well camouflaged amongst the vegetation.

Voice

Birds in this group have a limited vocal repertoire which is generally associated with courtship and agonistic behaviour, though vocal displays are more fully-developed in the solitary nesting species. Most species are usually silent outside the breeding season, especially the White-necked Heron (*Ardea pacifica*), the Reddish Egret, the Black Heron, the Intermediate Egret, the Squacco Heron and the Little Bittern. However, there are very vocal species, such as the Grey and Great-billed Herons, the Snowy and Little Egrets, the Green-backed Heron and the Least Bittern. Some have varied repertoires, as is the case of the Goliath Heron, the Great White Egret, the Tricolored Heron, the Black-crowned Night-heron or the Yellow-crowned Night-heron, the last of which has more than 20 different calls. However, there are still many species for which very little information is available concerning vocalizations.

In the colonial species, the noise produced by the breeding colonies is quite significant and consists of a continuous, fairly intense hubbub.

The vocalizations of herons have been described as a series of guttural honks, harsh sounds, croaks, coos and growls. Some sounds are produced by bill-snapping and bill-rattling, for example in the Black-crowned Night-heron. During flight, the Whistling Heron utters characteristic high frequency calls. The Boat-billed Heron has a varied repertoire of acoustic signals, including "popping" sounds made by bill-snapping, and a "Long Chant", which can lead to the formation of a chorus in breeding colonies.

The advertising call is one of the most conspicuous sounds in the family and it varies with the species. In the large bitterns it is very distinctive. They have a modified oesophagus, which can be inflated to form a soundbox, and by exhaling heavily they can produce their typical booming calls. Although these booms are generally produced by the birds when they are in amongst the vegetation, they are low frequency sounds which are transmitted over great distances, for instance up to 5 kilometres in the case of the Eurasian Bittern, and they serve to attract females and maintain territory, as these species nest in isolation; females reply with a similar call. Booms are generally made several times in succession at intervals of a few seconds, and they are especially frequent just before or during the breeding season, and in particular around dusk. The New Guinea Tiger-heron (*Zonerodius heliosylus*) and the White-crested Tiger-heron produce sounds similar to the large bitterns' booming. Although booms have also been reported in the Black Bittern in India and Sri Lanka, the small bitterns generally produce a long series of guttural cooings and croakings, when trying to attract females. In the Little Bittern, for example, the advertising call consists of the monotonous repetition of phrases of about 10 syllables at intervals of 0·5 to 10 seconds. The Yellow Bittern (*Ixobrychus sinensis*) has a call which closely resembles a tiger's grunt.

Food and Feeding

Herons are carnivorous birds, and they feed on live, normally aquatic prey. They have broad and variable diets related to the availability of prey in their habitat. Many species exploit abun-

The four species of large bitterns are typical of freshwater wetlands with constant water levels and dense vegetation cover, although during migration or in cold spells they can be found in practically any kind of wetland. Their cryptic plumage allows them to pass unnoticed amongst the reeds and rushes, especially when they adopt the "Bittern-stance", a posture they can hold for several hours. This South American Bittern illustrates this stance, although in this case its plumage does not provide any camouflage among the water hyacinths.

[*Botaurus pinnatus caribaeus*, Mexico. Photo: G. Lasley/Vireo]

dant resources, which are, however, irregularly distributed in terms of both space and time.

Some species, such as the Whistling and Black-headed Herons and, above all the Cattle Egret, are birds of relatively terrestrial habits, regularly feeding far from water. The Cattle Egret is well known for its habit of following herds of wild or domestic animals (see Relationship with Man), and it feeds off the insects or other animals which they disturb as they move along. There are some unusual examples of this feeding behaviour linked to large animals, one being the case of mutualism between the Cattle Egret and two species of sea mammals, the northern elephant seal (*Mirounga angustirostris*) and the Californian sea lion (*Zalophus californianus*). Commensalism is also known for other species, such as the Little Blue Heron with manatees (*Trichechus manatus*) in Florida. Apart from these three heron species, the rest capture their prey in or beside the water.

The diet consists chiefly of aquatic animals, such as fish, amphibians, reptiles, birds, small mammals and various aquatic invertebrates, including insects, crustaceans and molluscs. Although most herons have quite a varied diet, some species are relatively specialized, for example the Yellow-crowned Night-heron, which has a marked preference for crustaceans. Herons have also been known to feed on large prey on occasions, for instance a Grey Heron took a Common Coot (*Fulica atra*) in Belgium, while one Goliath Heron ate a fish weighing 1·4 kg. Some species plunder the nests and chicks of other species of birds, for example the Little Bittern has been seen robbing the nests of Reed Warblers (*Acrocephalus scirpaceus*) in Europe, while the Least Bittern reportedly eats Yellow-headed Blackbird (*Xanthocephalus xanthocephalus*) eggs and chicks in North America. Quite frequently, Black-crowned Night-herons consume the eggs and chicks of terns, ibises and even of other herons.

In the herons, and the Ciconiiformes in general, mixed feeding flocks are common. Some species habitually carry out commensalism, whereby they benefit from other species disturbing prey as they feed. On the right of this photo, a Snowy Egret can clearly be seen feeding alongside an American White Ibis (Eudocimus albus); the Snowy Egret has been found to have higher feeding efficiency when foraging alongside the ibises than when it feeds alone. This flock includes a Tricolored Heron (Egretta tricolor), a Reddish Egret (Egretta rufescens), several Double-crested Cormorants (Phalacrocorax auritus) and a Brown Pelican (Pelecanus occidentalis).

[Egretta thula, Sanibel I, Florida. Photo: Fritz Pölking/ Marco Polo]

Herons have also been reported to eat carrion very rarely. The White-faced Heron, for example, has been observed feeding off the carcasses of cattle in Australia, and in Kenya pellets from Black-headed Herons have been found to contain remains of duck and flamingo bones and fur from large mammals. The Cattle Egret, in particular, often feeds in rubbish dumps. Any ingestion of vegetable matter is probably accidental, although a Green-backed Heron was observed feeding on acorns in Florida. Again, in New Zealand the Cattle Egret has been seen feeding on barley grain and lucerne hay and peas in silos.

The daily food requirements are only known for very few species of heron. In captivity, adult Grey Herons need to consume a minimum of 330-500 g, and this species normally eats quite large-sized prey, preferably weighing 70-100 g, but occasionally, as much as 500 g. Other studies estimate that in piscivorous species adults need to consume around 16% of their body weight daily.

Herons use a wide variety of techniques for catching their prey. Both diet and hunting techniques are related to the structure of the different species. The size and shape of the bill are especially important, as it is used to harpoon the prey, and the length of the neck and the legs are related to the depth of water frequented by the different species. Other factors which influence the kind of foraging method used by the different species include the type of prey available, environmental conditions and the presence of other birds.

The commonest feeding technique, which is used by all species, consists of the birds standing motionless at the water's edge, or in shallow water, waiting until prey comes close enough for the bird to spear it with its bill. In this situation, there are two main postures, the "Upright" posture, in which the bird keeps the neck and body erect, and the "Crouched" posture, where the bird's neck and body are parallel to the ground. In the "Upright" posture the bird has a better field of vision, and this stance is associated with vigilance, agonistic behaviour towards other species, and the localization of prey. The "Crouched" posture, on the other hand, apart from being more cryptic, is chiefly related with the capture of prey, as it permits the bird to situate its bill closer to the intended victim. The large Ardea herons, the night-herons and the bitterns are all real specialists with this technique.

All species frequently capture prey in the water, and in order to catch it efficiently, they need to compensate for refraction. Because of this, the head and neck are moved both from side to side and back and forward, since this allows them to improve their binocular vision, and also to calculate the exact distance to the prey.

Other, more active foraging methods involve the birds moving about. The most common technique entails "Walking Slowly" about, searching for prey. This technique is also very widespread and is used by all species, on land and in shallow water, sometimes on aquatic vegetation or on the branches of trees. The speed at which birds move is variable, but is always less than 60 steps per minute. Some species, such as the Reddish, Little and Cattle Egrets, the Eastern Reef-egret and the Tricolored Heron, can move much faster and even run after their prey.

Much more rarely, Herons use aerial feeding techniques such as "Hovering", whereby they fly over the water, pausing in mid-air to capture prey. Sometimes a bird may strike the surface of the water with its legs, using the "Hovering Stirring" technique and trying to make the prey move. Other techniques include "Aerial Flycatching" to capture flying prey, or "Diving" which involves the bird plunging into the water from the air. The species with the largest repertoire of aerial techniques is the Snowy Egret, but many others have been observed using these methods, for example the Grey Heron, the Pied Heron (Egretta picata), the Great Blue Heron and the Black-crowned Night-heron. Likewise, cases of "Swimming Feeding" have been recorded, for example in the Black-crowned Night-heron.

The wings and legs are also commonly used during feeding. Occasionally a bird will open and close its wings to frighten prey, or spread its wings over its lowered head, in an attempt to attract prey into the shade thus created, or perhaps to reduce the glare and improve visibility. The most extreme case is the "Canopy Feeding" typical of the Black Heron, where the bird stretches its wings forwards until they touch and form a canopy over its head, with the tips of the wings reaching the surface of the water. In some species, especially the egrets, the feet are commonly used, and there are different kinds of movement designed to frighten prey, and enable the birds to localize their victims more easily. The birds normally move at an unhurried pace, from time to time sinking their feet slowly into the substrate, "Foot Probing". Another technique which they often use is "Foot Stirring", whereby the bird vibrates one of its legs. These foot movements are particularly used by species with brightly coloured feet, such as the Snowy and Little Egrets and the Black Heron, all of which have black legs and bright yellow feet.

Herons normally capture their prey by seizing it with the bill, and they sometimes impale their victims. Less frequently, they peck or probe about in the water or in the substrate. The Boat-billed Heron has been seen to use a special technique called "Scooping", which consists of the bird using its bill like a spoon to capture prey.

In the Green-backed Heron, there is a curious foraging method known as "Baiting", whereby a bird uses bait to attract its prey. This behaviour has been recorded in several parts of the species' extensive range, including South Africa, West Africa, Japan and North America, with birds using pieces of bread or insects as bait.

The digestive system of the herons is very efficient, and the only things they find indigestible are insects' chitinous exoskeletons and the keratin from mammal fur and bird feathers, and these materials have to be regurgitated in the form of pellets.

Generally speaking, herons eat their prey whole and they sometimes spend quite a long time dealing with large items before consuming them. Normally the shape and, above all, the size of the prey determine the swallowing time, and this is an important factor in terms of their feeding efficiency.

The different species have distinct feeding strategies. In areas where different species co-exist, birds usually diverge in the techniques they use to obtain food, in the prey they hunt or in their precise feeding grounds. There are both solitary and gregarious feeders. The solitary feeders defend their foraging grounds, and in the large species these territories can be extensive, for example in parts of Zambia the Goliath Heron has been found with densities of one bird per 4 km², whereas in South Africa the figure was one bird per 6 km². Other species are gregarious and can form groups of tens, and even hundreds of birds, and in Israel the Black-crowned Night-heron can feed in ponds in flocks of up to 400-600 birds. There is also the remarkable case of a flock of 40,000 egrets, mainly Cattle Egrets, feeding on swarms of grasshoppers in Tanzania. In some species, such as the Great Blue Heron, the gregarious tendency is an adaptation to the local feeding conditions, and they can forage individually or in groups, depending on the circumstances. Other species, like the Cattle Egret, are most markedly gregarious when the feeding conditions are particularly difficult. In this way, several species of heron can come together or even form mixed groups with ibises, spoonbills and others. Associations of herons with other birds have been recorded on many occasions, including the Snowy Egret, the Tricolored Heron, the Little Blue Heron and the Great White Egret with the American White Ibis (*Eudocimus albus*), which acts as a "beater" of their prey. In the Ciconiiformes in general, and the herons in particular, it has been repeatedly pointed out that white birds act as nuclei for the formation of mixed groups. The white birds are usually gregarious and live in open habitats. Some dimorphic species illustrate this well, such as the Western Reef-egret, as its dark phase is a solitary feeder in mangroves, whereas the white phase feeds in flocks in open areas.

Most species feed during the day and have a bimodal rhythm, with maximum activity in the early morning and the latter part of the afternoon, and the minimum levels around the middle of the day. Some species, such as the Grey Heron, also forage at night, and this is particularly common amongst a fair number of the birds which feed in tidal environments, for instance the Great Blue Heron, the Green-backed Heron and the Eastern Reef-egret. The comparative performances of foraging by night or by day vary in each case, and in the Great Blue Heron, for example, nocturnal feeding has on occasions been found to be much less profitable than diurnal. Nevertheless, in other birds which have been studied, such as the Grey Heron, no significant differences have been found. There are also some

The tiger-herons are generally speaking very secretive birds that are extremely difficult to observe, so most aspects of their biology and ecology remain poorly known. The Bare-throated Tiger-heron is the least wary of the three species that form the South American genus Tigrisoma *and it can regularly be seen resting on high, exposed perches usually in the vicinity of water. It is considerably larger than its congeners, but its bare throat can be quite inconspicuous.*

[*Tigrisoma mexicanum*, Mexico. Photo: Patricio Robles]

At the beginning of the breeding season, Grey Herons sometimes perform what has been called a "Dancing-display" which is reminiscent of those of the cranes, although it does not seem to have the sexual implications of true "dancing". On the arrival of a new bird at the day-roost, the birds will run or leap about with their wings open, bristling up their black head plumes aggressively. During such encounters bare parts can temporarily take on very vivid colours.

[Ardea cinerea.
Photo: Manfred Danegger/ NHPA]

species with mainly crepuscular or nocturnal feeding habits, such as the night-herons, and the White-backed Night-heron (*Nycticorax leuconotus*) stands out, as it appears to be strictly nocturnal. At the Camargue, the Black-crowned Night-heron feeds more efficiently at night than during the day, not because the prey is more skilfully caught, but because it is larger. By day this species forages in the same areas as the diurnal species, and it may be displaced by them, with the result that it avoids competition by feeding mainly at night.

Adults feed their chicks by regurgitating the prey whole, and in some cases this may be partially digested, for example in the Chinese Pond-heron (*Ardeola bacchus*), or the other pond-herons. Logically, during the chicks' first few days, the adults have to feed them with smaller prey items than those they themselves would eat, or else they have to break up larger items into small pieces. Grey Herons, for example, can not feed their chicks with prey of a size suitable for adults, until the young birds are 20 days old.

Food abundance has a direct influence on the breeding success of the herons, and this appears to be closely related to the size of the brood and the number of chicks which survive in large broods. The origin of sibling aggression, which is so typical of heron chicks, is the monopolization of the food, and this is directly related to the size of the prey which the adults bring to the nest. It is especially prevalent amongst those herons that feed their chicks with small prey items, which can easily be monopolized, but is lacking, or less pronounced, in species which feed their offspring with large prey. A good example of this comes from work done in Texas, which showed a high incidence of sibilicidal aggression in the Great White Egret, but not in the Great Blue Heron.

Breeding

Birds in this family follow a wide variety of breeding strategies. Most are monogamous, although there are a few records of polygamy in the Cattle Egret, the Intermediate Egret, the Grey Heron and more frequently in the Eurasian Bittern. Most species breed in fairly large, mainly mixed colonies, but there are some that breed alone or in semi-colonial groups. The day-herons are usually colonial, except for the larger species of the genus *Ardea*, such as the Goliath Heron, the White-bellied Heron and the Great-billed Heron. The Whistling Heron is normally a solitary breeder, but occasionally it can also breed semi-colonially, and other species, like the Grey Heron, the Great Blue Heron, the Green-backed Heron or the pond-herons can breed alone or colonially depending on the circumstances. The night-herons are likewise colonial, except for the members of the genus *Gorsachius*. The tiger-herons and the bitterns, on the other hand, are normally solitary nesters, and only the small bitterns sometimes breed in semi-colonial groups.

In temperate zones, birds generally breed in spring or summer, thus choosing the times when food is abundant. In the tropics, they can breed all year round, although normally they do not breed with the same intensity all the time, and there are clear differences between the species. At one colony in Costa Rica, for example, the Cattle Egret's nesting is related to the start of the rainy season, and there are usually two periods of increased activity. In the same colony, the Great White Egret, in contrast, has only one breeding period and it is not related to the start of the rains. In any case, if climatic conditions are unfavourable, with low temperatures or strong winds, the onset of breeding can be delayed and birds may even forego nesting, as occurs in the event of severe droughts.

Courtship and pair formation behaviour are quite complex and the nuptial plumes and colour changes of the bare parts play important roles in such behaviour (see Morphological Aspects). The male is normally the first to arrive at the nesting grounds and he begins to collect material for the construction or repair of the nest. At the same time, he tries to attract a female whilst defending his site from other males. In solitary breeding species, there are very important vocal displays, which act as advertising calls, such as the booming of the large bitterns or the small bitterns' calls (see Voice).

Most of this behaviour takes place at the nest or in the vicinity, and initially it consists of different types of aggressive displays or those in which males show off before the other birds.

One of the most typical and widespread displays is the "Stretch" display, in which the bird raises its head and neck vertically, with the bill pointing skywards, whilst displaying the nuptial plumes and the brightly coloured bare parts. Another is the "Forward" display, where the heron lifts up its wings, draws back its neck and pecks at the other bird. The characteristic "Snap" display involves the bird moving its head up and down with all its plumes bristling and the neck fully extended, and this is normally accompanied by "Bill-clappering". Aerial displays, such as the "Circle Flight" are also common, and in this the bird flies around the nesting area with its neck outstretched, whilst beating its wings very slowly, and in some species the legs hang down. Some displays are very spectacular, such as the Great White Egret's "Backward Stretch" display, where it continually shakes its long nuptial plumes, whilst making undulating movements with its neck and moving its tail. Once the male has managed to attract a female, there is some aggressive conduct, which gradually turns into less violent behaviour such as "Mutual Preening" or "Bill-clappering".

Once the pair has been formed, most of the time is taken up building the nest, and this is where copulation usually takes place. Normally the male brings the material to the female and she places it in the nest. However, in the small bitterns, for instance the Little Bittern and the Least Bittern, the nest is built exclusively by the male. During this period and also incubation and the rearing of the chicks, the pair only perform "Greeting Ceremonies", which are basically forms of recognition behaviour.

The Boat-billed Heron differs from the other species in that the birds pair before arriving at the nest. Because of this, males do not carry out advertising displays. Moreover, in this species, the "Crest Raising" display and vocalizations (see Voice) acquire great significance.

The nest is a platform built of sticks from trees or bushes or reed stems, and it generally starts off as quite a simple, rather flimsy structure. In many cases, it is just an agglomeration of sticks, which is so unsubstantial that the contents of the nest can be seen from below. However, the large species such as the Grey, Great Blue and Great-billed Herons, build nests in trees, which, with time, and after being reused annually, gradually become massive structures, measuring up to 1·5 m in diameter. Some species also nest in reedbeds, and the Purple Heron, for example, sometimes builds very large nests, which can be more than 1 m wide and about 1 m high.

The Ardeidae normally situate their nests near water, or on it, at variable heights above the ground (see General Habits). The species which breed in reedbeds and other types of marsh vegetation normally build low nests near the water, whereas those that build in trees, on the other hand, often construct the nest about 20-30 m up. The day-herons mainly nest in trees, although some species use bushes, normally near water or in flooded areas. Nesting grounds are often situated on wooded islands or in flooded woodlands, but, depending on local conditions, many species can also breed on large expanses of marsh vegetation. In Europe, for example, the Little Egret and the Black-crowned Night-heron normally breed in trees, but in the Iberian Peninsula some colonies are located in large reedbeds, for instance at the Ebro Delta or the Albufera of Valencia. On the other hand, other species, including the Purple Heron,

This Eurasian Bittern has adopted a threat display typical of the genus Botaurus. The bird crouches with its neck arched backwards and its bill pointing towards the intruder; the wings are spread and held slightly forwards, while the feathers of the crest are erected and those of the neck and the scapulars bristled up in order to make the bird appear larger. This display is performed in the presence of intruders, in this case the photographer, immediately prior to attack.

[Botaurus stellaris. Photo: Joe B. Blossom/ Survival]

Foraging behaviour in the herons consists of a wide variety of techniques, including even aerial methods. All species are capable of using various different techniques, which they combine to suit the conditions of the habitat and the prey. The Least Bittern tends to stalk its prey by means of "Walking Slowly" in the "Crouched" posture. The smaller species are quite at home walking about on the marsh vegetation.

[*Ixobrychus exilis exilis*, Florida, USA. Photo: Gordon Langsbury/ Bruce Coleman]

usually construct their nests in marsh vegetation. The tiger-herons generally nest in branches of trees overhanging water, while the bitterns prefer to build their nests in reedbeds or other kinds of aquatic vegetation. In some species, the nest has been known to be placed directly on the ground on occasions, as occurs in the Little Egret in parts of Kenya. In some populations, ground-nesting is normal, as in the race *falklandicus* of the Black-crowned Night-heron, or the race *monicae* of the Grey Heron on the coast of Mauritania. Usually, birds build a nest each year, although they can reuse the remains of previous years' structures. Birds which locate their nests in sheltered sites, for instance in trees, can reuse them year after year, so the Grey Heron, for example, which can use the same site for decades, may end up with an immense nest.

Some species, especially in tropical regions, can lay two or even three clutches per year, but herons normally only have one clutch. Two clutches per year have been recorded for the Grey and Purple Herons, the Chinese and Madagascar (*Ardeola idae*) Pond-herons, the Black-crowned and White-backed Night-herons and the Black Bittern. Cases of three clutches per year have been reported for the Green-backed Heron, the Little and Yellow Bitterns, and possibly also the Cattle Egret. The laying of replacement clutches, on the other hand, is widespread. The age at which birds breed for the first time depends on the species, but it normally occurs when they are one or two years old. Individuals of species which usually breed for the first time when two years old are frequently found nesting in the first year, when they have not yet acquired full adult plumage, and this is known for the Purple Heron and the Black-crowned Night-heron amongst others.

The clutch generally consists of three to seven eggs, although cases of up to ten are recorded in the small bitterns, and also exceptionally in some other species, such as the Grey Heron. Two little known species of tiger-herons, the New Guinea Tiger-heron and the White-crested Tiger-heron appear to lay only one egg, but this is exceptional within the family as a whole. The large bitterns have olive-brown coloured eggs, but in the rest of the family eggs are white or pale blue, normally without markings, and quite bright and glossy. In a few species, the eggs are speckled at both ends, for example in the genus *Tigrisoma*. The size of the eggs is not large in relation to the size of the female, and in the Purple Heron, for example, one egg represents approximately 5% of the female's weight and the complete clutch 20%.

Clutch size varies geographically, and increases with the latitude. Birds living in temperate zones, which are more pro-ductive and less stable, generally lay more eggs than those in tropical or equatorial regions. In the Cattle Egret, for example, clutch size ranges from 2·1 eggs in Botswana, to 2·6 in Ghana, 2·9 in Senegal, 4·05 in the Ebro Delta, in Spain, and 4·6 in the Camargue, in France. Again, birds breeding in coastal and marine environments have lower clutch sizes than those that breed inland. Similarly, clutch size normally decreases as the breeding season progresses, as happens in other birds, although the size of the eggs remains constant. The eggs are laid at two to three day intervals, or daily in the case of the small bitterns.

Incubation is usually performed by both sexes and begins after the first or second egg has been laid. The incubation period lasts 18-30 days in most species, although it is somewhat shorter in the small bitterns, lasting only 14-20 days. Little is known about many aspects of the breeding of tiger-herons, and the length of their incubation period in the wild is not yet known. Hatching is usually asynchronous, which means there are great size differences between chicks of the same brood. In the case of the Eurasian Bittern, the hatching asynchrony can be quite pronounced and the interval can be as much as 12-13 days. In this species, males can be polygamous and defend a territory where several females build their nests. In such cases, all the

One of the techniques most commonly used by the herons is that known as "Walking Slowly". It consists quite simply of a slow advance during which the bird searches for its prey. It can be carried out in the water, as in the case of this White-necked Heron, or on land, the bird normally taking some 20-30 steps per minute.

[*Ardea pacifica*, Australia. Photo: Hans & Judy Beste/ Ardea]

This Great Blue Heron gives a vivid demonstration of prey capture in the Ardeidae. This species specializes in "Standing", as in this sequence, and "Walking Slowly", and these two techniques account for over 90% of its foraging time. Its long legs enable it to wade into deeper water than most other sympatric species. The bird adopts the "Upright" posture (above left), which gives it a wide field of vision and enables it to combat glare and reduce any distortions caused by the effects of refraction, a particularly important factor in the moment of a strike. The heron may remain absolutely motionless for long periods waiting patiently for prey to approach. Once prey is within range and has moved into a suitable position for a strike to be attempted, the bird unleashes a lightning attack (above right), leaving its prey with only a fraction of a second to escape. Once captured (below left), the prey is manoeuvred into a suitable position for swallowing. In this case two small fish have been caught and these are easily swallowed whole (below right), given their small size.

[*Ardea herodias*, USA. Photos: Cornell Laboratory of Ornithology]

breeding tasks are carried out exclusively by the females, which have to take breaks from incubation in order to search for food, and especially to feed the first chick, which means that the hatching of the remaining eggs is delayed.

Heron chicks are nidicolous and when newly-hatched they are helpless, practically naked and have their eyes closed. The time the chicks stay in the nest varies, ranging from a minimum of 25-30 days in the small bitterns, to a maximum of 12-13 weeks in the large *Ardea* herons. However, the chicks begin to wander off from the nest about half way through their growing period.

The environmental conditions of wintering grounds are very important for these birds. For instance, the size of the Purple Heron populations which annually return to breed in the Netherlands is related to droughts in their winter quarters. Likewise, breeding success is closely related to environmental conditions, especially to the availability of food. There are three main aspects which affect breeding success. Firstly, there is clutch size, which varies each year, since birds seem able to make considerable adjustments, depending on how favourable the breeding season is. The other factors are the asynchronous hatching and the siblicidal aggression of chicks (see Food and Feeding). The chicks of a brood are intensely competitive for the food which their parents bring, and, in conjunction with the differences in size produced by hatching asynchrony, this favours the survival of the largest chicks, and means that when food is scarce the smaller chicks die. In the herons, breeding success seems to depend more on the phase of chick growth than on those of hatching or incubation.

Movements

Most members of the Ardeidae carry out seasonal migrations, which can involve the whole of a population, or only a part.

For example, whilst practically all the British population of the Grey Heron is sedentary, 70% of the Swedish and 25-45% of the central and east European populations are migratory. There is, however, a general tendency for herons to be sedentary, if the conditions are favourable. Thus, the amelioration of the climate in Europe has partially changed the Grey Heron's migratory tendencies into dispersive movements, and this species' African winter quarters have lost their former importance. Likewise, in years when the climate is milder, the extent of movements of species like the Great White Egret or the Eurasian Bittern are reduced.

Once breeding is over, and before true migration towards the winter quarters takes place, there are dispersive movements, especially of young birds, soon after they have become independent. This is a very widespread practice in this family and the purpose is to find new sources of food, thus reducing the density of individuals in the proximities of the colony. In addition, it allows the exploitation of resources which could not be reached in spring, as the areas in question were still frozen over, or because the conditions there were unsuitable for breeding. Furthermore, this may well be a mechanism for the colonization of new areas. Such dispersal is often very extensive and birds fly off in all directions, frequently in the opposite direction to that in which migration will occur. The average distance from the colony reached by young Grey Herons in June is 150 km and in August 250 km, and movements of 300-400 km are not uncommon. Little Bitterns may wander 220 km from the colony, while distances of 400 km are recorded for the Great White and Little Egrets, and Black-crowned Night-herons can stray as much as 800 or 1200 km away. These dispersals mean that birds can be observed far outside their usual ranges, and there are even cases of transoceanic movements.

Migration is mainly carried out at night, although it can occur during the day, even occasionally in crepuscular species,

These two Pied Herons are foraging by means of "Standing", the most frequently used technique in the herons and one that is employed by all the species. The birds stay still, waiting for their prey, while standing in the water, at the water's edge, or on land. The bird on the right is in the "Crouched" posture, with the legs flexed and the body parallel to the ground; this position is commonly adopted just before the bird strikes, although in this case it has been maintained after a successful catch.

[*Egretta picata*, Australia. Photo: Len Rue Jr/ Bruce Coleman]

All herons are basically carnivorous. The diet consists of a wide variety of live aquatic prey, ranging from crustaceans, molluscs and insects to amphibians and fish. They can, however, also prey on small birds and mammals. Often the prey caught is large in comparison with the size of the bird, as in the case of the Rufescent Tiger-heron in this photograph. Since the birds swallow their prey whole, the capture of a large item implies that a considerable amount of time is required to deal with it. The parts that are not digested are expelled in the form of pellets.

[*Tigrisoma lineatum marmoratum*, Pantanal, Brazil. Photo: Günter Ziesler]

The Whistling Heron normally feeds in open wet grasslands, notably in the vast expanse of the llanos *stretching between Venezuela and Colombia. Birds tends to feed alone or in pairs, and like many heron species, they appear to maintain feeding territories, which may be defended vigorously from rivals, by means of calling and jabbing, as well as "Crest Raising" and "Forward Displays". As in most other species, the diet is very varied and includes a selection of insects, fish, amphibians and reptiles.*

[*Syrigma sibilatrix fostersmithi*, in *llanos* of Venezuela. Photo: Mike Price/Survival]

such as the Black-crowned Night-heron or the Eurasian Bittern. Birds usually migrate individually or in small groups in a linear formation, so as to save energy. Nevertheless, large concentrations of birds can also occur, as indicated by the numbers involved in some migrating flocks, such as 200-250 Grey Herons, hundreds and up to 1000 Great White Egrets, or hundreds of Black-crowned Night-herons. As for the solitary species, such as the Little Bittern, it has been confirmed that in Israel migrant flocks normally consist of up to 40-50 birds, and sometimes over 100. Even flocks of 10 or more Eurasian Bitterns have exceptionally been seen. Mixed flocks also occur.

Herons have a strong style of flight (see Morphological Aspects), and they are capable of covering great distances without stopping. Grey Herons can maintain continuous, direct, flapping flight for more than 10 hours, at a speed of 32-50 km/h, alternating it with short glides. Ringing results show that one Little Egret completed the journey between the Camargue, in southern France, and Algeciras, in southern Spain, in less than 78 hours, and, assuming it flew along the coast, it must have covered 1500 km. This great stamina allows them to cross large seas and oceans, as in the case of migrants from south-east Asia which cross the South China Sea, and those from the Palearctic which cross the Mediterranean. Nor is it exceptional for vagrants to cross the great oceans. Although they are closely linked to water, and many species prefer to follow coastlines or rivers, they also cross deserts such as the Sahara, and some birds stop at oases, for instance the Purple Heron, the Little Egret and the Squacco Heron. The Little Bittern is known to be capable of crossing the Mediterranean Sea and the Sahara Desert in a single flight.

Populations of the Eastern Palearctic generally migrate, after breeding, to south and south-east Asia, as far as Malaysia and Indonesia. Of the birds from the Western Palearctic, some travel south-east to the Middle East or India, but most move in a south-westerly direction towards Central Africa. A few isolated cases are known of birds moving south of the equatorial rain forest belt, while some are known to remain in the area of the Mediterranean. Some Nearctic populations move to

southern North America, whilst the majority fly to Central America and tropical parts of South America. Little is known about the movements of the populations of the Southern Hemisphere, although it appears that they are regular, at least in some cases. For example, only 10% of Little Egrets and 20% of Cattle Egrets remain in South Africa outside the breeding season. The populations in Australia and New Zealand are basically dispersive, especially those dependent on freshwater habitats. Populations situated nearer the equator or in areas

The Green-backed Heron uses a wide variety of feeding techniques, and it has a great ability to adapt to local conditions. One of its main methods involves "Standing" in the "Crouched" posture, often, as in this case, on a branch low over the water. This sequence shows the extraordinary capacity that herons have for stretching their necks. Normally the neck is folded back in an S-shape, but, when the bird lunges out at prey, the kink in the neck acts as a kind of spring, giving extra force and speed to the thrust. The length of the neck also has another obvious advantage, in that it increases the bird's striking range.

[*Butorides striatus atricapillus*, Lake Nakuru, Kenya. Photos: M. P. Kahl/DRK]

where the climate is milder, display a less marked tendency to carry out migrations than those of temperate zones. The North American Bittern (*Botaurus lentiginosus*), for example, is sedentary in the southern part of its range, in Central America, but migratory in the northern part. Similarly, the tropical race *payesii* of the Little Bittern is basically sedentary, unlike its temperate counterpart *minutus*. Again, 59% of the young Great Blue Herons from populations between 34° N and 39° N are migratory, whilst none of those further south migrate.

During the return migration to the breeding areas, overshooting is frequent, and affects mostly immature birds and non-breeding adults. Thus, individuals are recorded in areas far from their breeding colonies. The Squacco Heron, for example, has been reported in Great Britain, Sweden and Central Europe between May and July, and the Little Egret in Scandinavia and northern Russia from April to November.

It is not uncommon for immature birds to remain in the wintering grounds all year round, for example Grey and Purple Herons, and the Madagascar Pond-heron on mainland Africa. In some cases, for example in the Little Egret, it is thought that such birds may end up breeding with the local population.

Apart from conventional migration, there are species which perform local movements basically linked to the availability of food, in connection with the rainy season or water levels. This occurs in the Black-headed Heron, the Intermediate Egret, the Pied Heron, the Rufous-bellied Heron and the Dwarf Bittern, amongst others. Totally sedentary species are, in fact, rare in this family, and include the tiger-herons and some populations of bitterns. Most species carry out dispersive movements at least, for example the Indian Pond-heron and the Rufous Night-heron, which move in direct response to diminishing food supplies, or the Eurasian Bittern, which is affected by low temperatures, such as those registered in the cold winters of 1962/63 and 1978/79, when birds from north-east Europe put in a rare appearance in Great Britain. The greatest distance known, from ringing, to have been covered by the Eurasian Bittern is some 2000 km, from Sweden to northern Spain. Some species that are essentially sedentary have migratory subspecies, for instance the races *virescens* and *amurensis* of the Green-backed Heron, or the race *violaceus* of the Yellow-crowned Night-heron.

Some species, in contrast, show a distinct trend towards vagrancy, for instance the White-necked, Goliath and Little Blue Herons. A pronounced nomadic tendency has facilitated the Cattle Egret's remarkably far-reaching colonization of new areas (see Status and Conservation). The greatest distance known to have been covered by this species is 4216 km, while some birds have even appeared in Antarctica. Sometimes birds

can also be carried great distances by strong winds. Thus, the Yellow Bittern has been observed in Australia because of a tropical cyclone. Other records include: the Least Bittern, the North American race *virescens* of the Green-backed Heron and the North American Bittern in western Europe; the Grey Heron and the Little Egret on the eastern coast of America; the Eurasian Bittern in Iceland, the Azores and the Canaries; and the White-necked Heron, the Great White Egret, the Snowy Egret and the Green-backed Heron at Tristan da Cunha and Gough Island in the South Atlantic.

Relationship with Man

As much for their large size and colourful plumage, as for their feeding habits or the fact that they breed in large, noisy colonies, herons have frequently been noticed throughout history. They are already mentioned in the Old Testament of the Bible, in the books of Deuteronomy and Leviticus, and some of the characteristics which Pliny used to describe the fabulous Phoenix are similar to those found in the Purple Heron. The peculiar booming of the bitterns has given rise to numerous legends, as in the case of the Australian aborigines with the Australasian Bittern (*Botaurus poiciloptilus*), and has often led them to be considered birds of ill omen. For example, old chronicles tell how, in the fifteenth century, a whole army at the Ebro Delta fled in terror one night, after hearing the booming of Eurasian Bitterns. Similarly, the inhabitants of Liberia attributed the bittern-like booming of the White-crested Tiger-heron to a giant snake which lived in the marshes. There are other kinds of symbolism, for example in Maori rhetoric it is considered a great compliment to compare someone with the Great White Egret, or "Kotuku", which is seen as a strange, but beautiful bird. In Japan, the Shoguns held herons to be sacred, and this led to the protection of some heronries.

The gastronomic qualities of the Eurasian Bittern are widely recognized, but other species too have been eaten regularly. In the Middle Ages, for example, the Grey Heron was one of the most highly appreciated table birds in Europe, while the Grey and Purple Herons were much sought after by the Mohana, a fishing people from the Sind, in Pakistan. They used to keep birds tied by one leg to a piece of floating wood, or to the prow of their boat, while they were fattened up. This fattening up of captive birds also occurred in the Seychelles and in Latin America. Another common practice has been the col-

lection of eggs and chicks. In many colonies exploited by local populations, the adults were not caught, thus ensuring an annual provision of eggs and chicks. This is the case in the colony at Danau Burung, now the Tanjung Puting reserve, in Borneo. The effects of this practice on bird populations were probably limited, as long as it was kept at a local level, but in some cases the birds were commercialized, and industry of this kind was still operating in Brazil and Malaysia in the 1970's. Today, some species are still exploited, such as the Chinese Pond-heron and the Green-backed Heron, which are exported from China to Hong Kong to be sold for food.

In the Middle Ages, herons were very widely sought after as quarry for falconry. One of the favourite prey species was the Grey Heron, and this led to its protection in parts of Britain. In the Netherlands the use of this species as prey for the Peregrine Falcon (*Falco peregrinus*) survived until the 1960's, and in Pakistan it was, and perhaps still is, used for this purpose, along with other species, such as the Great White, Little and Cattle Egrets.

Since ancient times, the beauty of heron feathers has led to their use by different peoples. The Maories used the Great White Egret's nuptial plumes as decorations in the chiefs' head-dresses, and they obtained them by plucking captive birds periodically. French colonels also used them for their stiff caps, or "shakos", and in some places the birds became known as "aigrette-colonels". Some of the native peoples of America used the Whistling Heron's feathers for bartering with. In New Zealand, the Australasian Bittern's feathers were particularly popular in making trout flies, and the birds were persecuted during the nineteenth century, until imitation feathers were brought in to replace the real ones.

However, the most significant form of exploitation of the herons' feathers, and the one which had the most serious and negative effects on the birds, was the large-scale trade in their plumes. In the nineteenth century, and at the beginning of the twentieth, they were used in the spectacular ladies' hats that were in fashion, especially in Europe and North America. London, Paris, New York, Berlin and Vienna became the principal trading centres for feathers from all types of birds, from gulls and albatrosses to condors, owls, parrots and even humming-birds. But the most coveted feathers of all were the long silky "aigrettes", or "ospreys", which appear on the backs of many species during courtship (see Morphological Aspects). Feather-collecting affected practically all the continents and reduced the populations of many of the species involved to alarming levels (see Status and Conservation). The most affected species were the Great White, Snowy and Little Egrets. One Great White Egret has 40-50 "aigrettes", so about 150 birds were needed to obtain 1 kg of "aigrettes", although other, less optimistic calculations reckon that approximately 1000 Snowy Egrets, 300 Great White Egrets and 250 Cocoi Herons (*Ardea cocoi*) were necessary. An idea of the magnitude of the industry can be drawn from the following facts: in Paris and the surrounding area alone, more than 10,000 people were employed in this business; in the first quarter of 1885, 750,000 bird skins were sold on the London market alone; and in 1887 one London dealer handled 2 million skins. Furthermore, in 1892, a merchant in Florida loaded 130,000 skins on board a ship bound

for New York, and in 1898 one and a half million birds were exported from Venezuela. The London Commercial Sales Rooms, a company specialized in this trade, sold 48,240 ounces of feathers in 1902, a quantity which, assuming that at least four birds are required to obtain an ounce of "aigrettes", means that a minimum of 192,960 Great White Egrets were slaughtered to supply the annual requirements of a single firm. Between 1899 and 1912 alone, 15,000 kg of feathers, especially of Great White and Snowy Egrets, were exported from Argentina, Brazil and Venezuela. To these enormous losses one must add the destruction of eggs and chicks, since the collection was carried out at the height of the breeding season, with adult birds being killed at their colonies. In 1903, a feather hunter in North America received 30 dollars per ounce, that is twice its weight in gold, and later prices rose to as much as 80 dollars per ounce. In 1914, in Europe, the price was about £15 per ounce.

In Pakistan, the Mohana people set up large productive farms for the exploitation of ornamental plumes of the Little Egret. The birds were forced to lay four or five successive clutches between March and September, and after the chicks had been hand-reared and had reached maturity, their feathers were extracted every three months, without the birds having to be killed. With this system, around 11·5 g of feathers were obtained per bird each year. Some of these farms were still operating in 1930 and in later years. On the Indian market, in 1914, the feathers were worth 10-28 times their weight in silver. Nevertheless, this type of farm exploitation did not prevent large-scale trade being carried out, with colonies of wild birds being massacred by hunters using snares and muzzle-loading guns, for instance in Burma, Malaysia and Indonesia. In China, many colonies had enjoyed local respect for centuries, and the birds were used to the presence of humans and even bred in temples and town gardens, but these colonies were now ravaged. Japanese hunters operated in Australia and in islands of the west Pacific. Several laws were passed to stop such massive killing of birds, for example the British Parliament passed the General Bird Protection Act in 1880, and the Seabird Protection Act in 1889, and some colonies were protected, but the consternation caused by the incessant sacrifice of millions of herons led, in 1898, to the creation in Great Britain of the Royal Society for the Protection of Birds. Likewise, in the USA, the American Ornithologists' Union (founded in 1883), the Audubon Society (founded in 1886), and other conservationist societies launched intense campaigns to halt the massacre. These efforts led to the murder of two of the Audubon Society's guards by poachers, but fortunately also to a change in women's fashion. In 1910, in New York state, the sale of feathers was declared illegal, in 1913 imports to the USA were banned, and in 1920 trade in plumes was prohibited in Great Britain. In spite of the fact that illegal trade still continued for a while, eventually it was completely eradicated.

Another factor which has caused herons to be hunted assiduously, is their consumption of fish, which has led to their being considered great competitors of fishermen and fish farmers, especially in Europe and North America. This belief induced great massacres from the end of the nineteenth century until well into the second half of the twentieth, and had particularly serious effects on some species, such as the Grey Heron, which was almost completely wiped out of Switzerland, and reduced to half its numbers in Germany. In Alsace, 3000 birds were killed in the period 1881-1917 for this reason, and in the late 1970's, at least 4600 birds were slaughtered annually in

Several species of heron have different colour morphs, which may sometimes occur at the same site and may even form mixed pairs, as is convincingly demonstrated by these Reddish Egrets, with a dark morph male and a white morph female. In most species, copulation takes place at the nest-site.

[*Egretta rufescens rufescens*, Rockport, Texas, USA. Photo: M. P. Kahl/ Bruce Coleman]

England. As a result of the conflict, many studies have been carried out to evaluate the effect the herons have on fish populations, and the results all reveal that this impact is minimal, indeed it can even be beneficial. In natural environments, the effect is negligible, since the majority of the birds' prey consists of non-commercial crustaceans, insects and small fish which are sometimes the main predators of the eggs and fry of the commercial fish. In general, effects on fish farms are very local, and are due especially to young, inexperienced birds. Exceptionally, greater effects can be caused when the natural feeding conditions are poor. Studies in the Camargue, for example, clearly show that the effect of the different species of heron on the fish farms is quite insignificant. Only the Grey Heron uses them as an occasional source of food, but the significance of this is negligible, in comparison with the comprehensive mortality of young fish, due to factors such as the weather, the oxygen content of the water or feeding problems. Likewise, research carried out into the impact of this species on fish ponds in Belgium and the Netherlands gave a maximum level of fish consumption by herons of 8% of the total yield, with the figure varying according to the density and availability of fish. It was considered that no significant losses were caused, except in regularly drained fish ponds, where the fish are very easily caught.

In spite of all this, some species have actually been helped by man. The Cattle Egret is, perhaps, the most obvious example (see Status and Conservation), since the generalized increase in pasturelands for cattle farming, to the detriment of woods and marshlands, has meant that the feeding habitat of this highly terrestrial species has been greatly increased. Furthermore, the species has been introduced by man in some regions, in order to control the populations of insects which attack crops. The Cattle Egret takes advantage of the presence of man's cattle to increase its feeding efficiency; it has been calculated that with this system a bird can make a 30% saving in energy and a 50% increase in the prey it catches (especially insects), in comparison to the levels achieved when feeding on its own. It

usually accompanies herds of cattle, which seem to be the hosts that provide it with the greatest yields of prey, although it can also feed with a large variety of wild animals and other domestic animals, such as sheep, pigs, horses, geese and so on. It sometimes associates with machines, or even working men, for example on sugarcane plantations in Cuba, or those cutting grass in India, where this habit sometimes occurs in the Indian Pond-heron too.

Other species have also adapted to living in very close contact with man. This is the case of the small Asian herons and bitterns, which live on the outskirts of towns and cities and feed in paddyfields, and many zoos and town parks have wild populations. This tendency has been noted in many other areas, and the Green-backed Heron nests near the metropolitan area of New York, without the traffic creating any problems for the colony. In Australia, the Pied Heron can be seen feeding amongst rubbish in drains and dumps, the Great White Egret is found in town parks, and the Rufous Night-heron has nested for years in the Melbourne Botanical Gardens and in gardens in Perth and other cities, very often sleeping in streets and city parks. The Rufous Night-heron's association with man and its crepuscular habits made it more vulnerable to mosquito bites, and it became the main carrier of the encephalitis virus during the epidemic which broke out in the Murray Valley in the 1970's. In Africa, the Black-headed Heron can often be found associating with man, nesting in cities such as Entebbe, or in the the Cattle Egret colonies at Fort Lamy, and it appears that it has benefited from human developments, which have created new open habitats and more water sources. In Europe, species such as the Grey Heron frequently nest in town parks, for example in Istanbul or Barcelona.

Status and Conservation

The large size, colonial nesting and very specialized habits of most members of this family, make them extremely vulnerable to any direct attacks and also to environmental changes. Nevertheless, due to their great capacity for survival, only a few of

During the period of incubation, it is of vital importance that the eggs be kept at a constant temperature. This Black-headed Heron is in the process of turning its eggs to make sure that the internal temperature of the eggs is homogeneous. Incubation lasts 23-27 days in this species, and, as in most species, is shared between the sexes.

[Ardea melanocephala, Kisumu, Kenya. Photo: M. P. Kahl/DRK]

In all of the herons, except the large bitterns, both parents take part in the tasks of guarding and feeding the chicks, and while they are still small, one of the adults must be with them at all times. They require feeding several times a day. The adult brings in the food and regurgitates it directly into the nestling's mouth. Prey is either delivered whole, or, in pond-herons like this Squacco Heron, partially digested. Each chick in turn grasps the adult's bill crossways in its own, in preparation to receive its meal.

[Ardeola ralloides, Czechoslovakia. Photo: Josef Mimok/ Survival]

them are seriously threatened at present, although man's activities have had, and are still having, significant effects on many species.

Apart from the factors linked with human activities, other, natural causes also influence heron populations, especially adverse climatic conditions. In America, populations of the race *occidentalis* of the Great Blue Heron are periodically decimated by hurricanes, like the one in 1935 that killed all but 150 individuals, or the one in 1960 that eliminated 60% of the population, which in 1966 stood at 1500 birds. The Eurasian Bittern is very sensitive to low temperatures. In Europe, the cold winter of 1962/63 caused a substantial drop in the populations of this species, which had already suffered losses because of hunting and habitat destruction. In 1976, the European population was estimated at around 2500-2700 pairs, spread over 21 countries, but the hard winter of 1978/79 reduced the population of north-east Europe, the largest, by 30-50%. Climatological effects are likewise evident in the Grey Heron, the most thoroughly researched species of the family. During the years of climatic amelioration, towards the middle of the present century, the species expanded its range towards the north of Europe. In Britain, where there have been annual censuses since 1928, the numbers of this species undergo great fluctuations in relation to cold winters, which are followed by a marked decrease in population levels. Numbers can take two or three years to recover their original levels, or even longer if the winter is particularly severe, as in 1962/63. In that same winter, numbers in Britain and the Netherlands were halved, and in the latter a short cold spell brought about a 19% decrease in the breeding population in 1976. In Alsace, protective measures led to a 40% annual increase in the population from 1979, until the cold winters of 1984/85 and 1985/86 caused a 35% drop in the number of pairs. Likewise, in the Netherlands, a correlation has been found between the numbers of breeding Purple Herons and the variations in the survival rates of birds after their first year, which depend on the extent of droughts in their wintering grounds in tropical Africa.

However, the main factors which determine changes in heron populations have generally been linked to human activity. The effects of intensive hunting for the plume trade, which raged in the nineteenth century and the beginning of the twentieth (see Relationship with Man), caused a significant decline in the populations of the most affected species, but since the winding up of the feather trade, many of these species have undergone spectacular recoveries. Nevertheless, although information on population sizes before persecution is limited, it seems clear that most populations have not yet regained former levels. In North America, the worst affected species were the Great White Egret and the Snowy Egret. The latter was particularly badly hit because it was more numerous, more widely distributed, less shy, and because its feathers were more eagerly sought. At the beginning of this century, it was almost extinct in places like Florida where it had previously been abundant. Today, its range is similar to that of the Great White Egret, and it nests further north than its original breeding grounds. The large colonies of the Great White Egret in the USA have, in turn, been replaced by small, scattered groups, as much a result of the effects of hunting, as of the destruction of its breeding and feeding grounds. Due to the protection the Great Blue Heron received, its numbers have recovered very well from the massacres. In addition, the Reddish Egret was exterminated in Florida at the beginning of the twentieth century, but a few birds are now nesting there, although white morphs only are found in the Bahamas. In Europe and Asia, the species most affected by the feather trade were the Great White, Little, Intermediate and Chinese Egrets, while others, such as the Cattle Egret and the Squacco Heron, were affected to a lesser degree. In New Zealand, the the Great White Egret population almost reached the point of extinction, with only 6 nests in 1877, but in the second half of the twentieth century it has gradually recovered. The Chinese Egret was also frequently hunted for its plumes, and this has had serious effects on its present status.

In addition to the effects of the plume trade, there are those connected with the destruction of aquatic habitats during the last

The feverish activity of the plume trade that took off in the latter part of nineteenth century almost all round the world had serious effects on the heron family, especially the white egrets. Those species with limited ranges were particularly badly affected, and the Chinese Egret was reduced to the verge of extinction. Although the species seems to be recovering, it still numbers only about one thousand pairs concentrated mainly around Korea.

[Egretta eulophotes. Photo: Morten Strange/ NHPA]

two centuries, which have been significant, for instance, for the Great White Egret, the Little Egret and the Squacco Heron. The plume trade brought Squacco Heron numbers in the Palearctic from an estimated 16,400 pairs in the period 1850-1900, to only 6800 in 1900-1920. Subsequently, habitat destruction has continued to affect the population, and the number of colonies fell from 115 (1900-1920), to 80 (1920-1940), with a population of around 6000 pairs. In the period 1940-60, a slight overall increase was registered, with a total of 8200 pairs, but the number of colonies was reduced to 71. Moreover, the persecution that some species suffered, due to supposed effects they had on natural fish populations and fish farms, has been of considerable significance in some cases. In Europe, such persecution has seriously affected the Grey Heron (see Relationship with Man), but it has also influenced other species in other areas, for example the Cattle Egret in Egypt, the White-faced Heron in New Zealand, or the Great Blue Heron in the USA.

One species of heron has become extinct in historical times. This was the Flightless Night-heron (*Nycticorax megacephalus*), which occurred on Rodrigues, one of the Mascarene Islands, in the Indian Ocean. It was mentioned in documents in 1708 and 1730, and its extinction, which occurred in the eighteenth century, was probably caused by hunting, particularly considering that it either flew very poorly or not at all. Studies of skeletal remains have placed the species among the night-herons. There are other records of herons from the Mascarene Islands, though they are very doubtful.

In addition, the race *crassirostris* of the Rufous Night-heron, formerly found in the Bonin Islands, south of Japan, also became extinct, though more recently. This form was discovered in the 1820's, and the last specimen was captured in Ogasawara in 1889; its extinction was probably due to human disturbance. Again, the race *novaezelandiae* of the Little Bittern, from South Island, New Zealand, which is known only from a few specimens taken last century, is now thought, in all probability, to be extinct. Although some authors actually consider it a distinct species, and it certainly appears to merit at least subspecific status, birds very similar to this extinct New Zealand form, have recently been found in Australia.

Six herons are currently considered to be threatened: the Madagascar Heron (*Ardea humbloti*); the White-bellied Heron; the Slaty Egret; the Chinese Egret; the White-eared Night-heron; and the Japanese Night-heron.

As its name suggests, the Madagascar Heron is found mainly in Madagascar, where, although widely distributed, it has probably never been common, and recently it has become alarmingly rare. Its large size and confiding character make it particularly vulnerable. The White-bellied Heron is restricted to the southern foothills of the Himalayas. There are no recent records in the western part of its range, and in general information about this species is very scarce. The Slaty Egret lives in a very restricted area of southern Africa, only nesting in the marshlands of the Okavango Delta and in parts of Namibia and Zambia. The size of its population is unknown, but it is thought to be small. Another Asian species, the Chinese Egret, only nests in a few sites on the coasts of China and especially Korea. It was apparently much more abundant and widespread last century, but came to the verge of extinction half way through the present century, due to the plume trade. Subsequently, the transformation of extensive areas of the coast, to make way for rice plantations, eliminated most of the habitat suitable for this

One of the several species with a highly restricted range is the Slaty Egret, which until the 1970's was considered to be merely a colour phase of the Black Heron (Egretta ardesiaca). In recent years, extensive transformations of its habitat have aggravated its already worrying situation, and have led, for example, to its disappearance from parts of South Africa.

[Egretta vinaceigula, Okavango Delta, Botswana. Photo: Clem Haagner/ Ardea]

decline in their numbers. A parallel situation exists in Africa with the Madagascar Pond-heron, the Rufous-bellied Heron, the White-backed Night-heron and the White-crested Tiger-heron. The Madagascar Pond-heron has declined dramatically since the middle of this century. Numbers at the best known breeding grounds at Antananarivo, in central Madagascar, dropped from 1500 birds in 1945, to 50 in 1970. This decrease in numbers, due to habitat destruction, also coincides with the colonization of the island by a competitor, the Squacco Heron. The status of species like the Capped Heron, the Fasciated Tiger-heron or the Rufescent Tiger-heron in South America, is not well known either. It is significant that the Eurasian Bittern, which is widely distributed throughout the Palearctic, is now threatened, as its numbers have dropped markedly since the nineteenth century, especially in Europe, partly due to climatic factors, but mainly because of the drainage and pollution of its habitat. Although a certain increase in numbers has been noted in some areas, especially with the creation of reserves, in other places, such as France, there was a decrease in the population of as much as 40% in 14 years, between 1970 and 1983.

The development of Cattle Egret populations has been in quite a different direction. Its ability to adapt, and also to perform extensive movements, as well as its association with humans (see Relationship with Man), have led it to colonize suitable new areas, where it has rapidly expanded. In Africa, from what appears to be its original range in the tropical and subtropical regions of the continent, it spread southwards around the end of the nineteenth century and the beginning of the twentieth. This expansion was associated with an increase in the number of irrigated areas and the proliferation of intensive cattle breeding, and the species even managed to breed in Cape Province in 1908. Although there are some previous references, it was at the end of the 1930's when the first birds began to colonize South America, covering the 2850 km from the African coast to the Guianas, at which point they dispersed. The first breeding in North America was confirmed in Florida in 1953, and probably involved migratory birds from the region of the Guianas. In the same way, they colonized Central America and the islands of the Caribbean. The birds spread rapidly across the USA, and arrived in Canada where breeding was first recorded in 1962. The Asian populations, in turn, spread towards the east and the south-east, reaching China, South Korea and Japan. They arrived in Australia, via New Guinea,

species, and the threat still persists. The present population is estimated at around 1000 pairs. Only very sporadic sightings of the White-eared Night-heron have been made this century, at sites in eastern China; it must be severely threatened, and some authors even claim that it is already extinct. The Japanese Night-heron is restricted, as a nesting bird, to the south of Japan. There is little information about its status or even its general biology, although it seems that numbers of this species have dropped throughout this century, parallel to the decrease in the amount of suitable habitat available. The Zigzag Heron, until recently considered to be threatened, is perhaps the least known of the herons in terms of biology or status.

There are, however, other species that are rare or thinly distributed, which require urgent attention, involving research and conservation. Little or nothing is known about the status and ecology of two Australasian species, the Great-billed Heron and the New Guinea Tiger-heron. The little information available concerning the population trends of these species and the progressive destruction of suitable habitat seems to point to a

at the beginning of this century, and by the 1950's their numbers had risen to millions. In 1963, they colonized New Zealand, where their rate of growth has also been phenomenal. In south-west Europe, the species seems to have had a similar distribution in the Iberian Peninsula during the sixteenth and seventeenth centuries to its present one, but it subsequently underwent a drastic decline, which led to its disappearance from many areas. Nevertheless, during the second half of this

century, it has recolonized the centre and east of the peninsula, and new colonies have appeared in other countries: in the Camargue, southern France, in 1968; in northern France in 1981; and in Italy in 1985. Total numbers in south-west Europe were calculated at around 50,000 pairs during the 1980's.

Populations of other species have also increased, although on a much more localized basis. The Intermediate Egret, for example, has increased both its numbers and range in West Africa since the 1950's. Also in Africa, the Black-headed Heron has benefited from changes made by man (see Relationship with Man). Again, the White-faced Heron has spread from Australia northwards into New Guinea, and as far as New Zealand, where it nested for the first time in 1941, and then, in the 1960's, underwent a demographic explosion; it is at present the most abundant of all the herons in New Zealand.

Nowadays, birds in this family are protected in many countries. The fact that hunting is now illegal has meant that mortality for this reason has been greatly reduced. In France, for example, before the hunting legislation was introduced, more than 30% of Little Egret mortality was due to the hunting of young birds in July and August. The breeding colonies, which are greatly affected by peaceful conditions and the absence of disturbance, have benefited notably from this proctective status in many areas, although disturbance is still a negative factor in other places. Moreover, human disturbance, often caused by tourist activities, also affects birds outside their breeding colonies, for example in the efficiency and time dedicated to feeding, as has been shown in the Snowy Egret, the Great White Egret or the Green-backed Heron in the USA, and this should also be taken into consideration when planning how best to protect these birds. Possible local effects on fish fry at fish farms can easily be eliminated by the use of several protective systems, ranging from a change in the structure of the pools, to the use of distress calls and other deterrents.

Local efforts have also been made to revive old populations. At Bermuda, the Yellow-crowned Night-heron was wiped out in the early 1940's, possibly because of the construction of an airport on Longbird Island, which destroyed a large area of the mangrove swamps inhabited by this species. In 1976, the Bermudan government encouraged the reintroduction of the

All three members of the genus Gorsachius *are uncommon species, about which little is known. Two of the species are endemic to the temperate regions of the Far East, while the Malayan Night-heron, illustrated here, inhabits India and south-east Asia. It is the only member of the genus that is not considered to be globally threatened, although is has been placed on the list of near-threatened species.*

*[*Gorsachius melanolophus, *Ujung Kulon, West Java, Indonesia. Photo: Alain Compost/ Bruce Coleman]*

Although it is not included in the World List of Threatened Animals, the Great-billed Heron is scarce in most of its range, and is generally not well known. It is one of the largest members of the family, and is typically found in mangroves and other coastal habitats. Its population appears to have been affected by the steady destruction of aquatic habitats within its range. This bird was photographed in Java, where the species is uncommon.

*[*Ardea sumatrana sumatrana, *Ujung Kulon, West Java, Indonesia. Photo: Dieter & Mary Plage/Survival]*

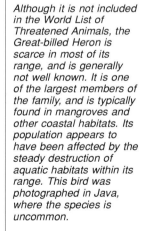

Widespread throughout tropical and subtropical regions of Central and South America, the Agami Heron is a rare, poorly known bird. It hardly ever comes out into the open, and its solitary, shy habits make it difficult to see in its dense tropical forest habitat. For this reason, it might not actually be quite as rare as the limited information available seems to suggest.

[*Agamia agami*, Cocha Cashu, Peru. Photo: P. Stein/Vireo]

Yellow-crowned Night-heron, in order to control the great plague of land crabs (*Gecarcinus lateralis*), and this was carried out using birds from Florida. Birds may have bred on Bermuda in 1978 or 1979, but it was confirmed in 1980, with the discovery of several nests, and since then numbers have risen. Research has shown that land crabs make up 95% of the Yellow-crowned Night-heron's diet on Bermuda.

There are, however, other aspects which are not at all favourable. Man's technological development this century has increasingly accelerated the alarming transformation of the aquatic habitats on which most herons are strictly dependent. This has brought about a drastic reduction in breeding grounds, and also in the extensive feeding areas which herons require for their survival (see Food and Feeding). Likewise, particularly in the tropics, nests and roosts in trees have been seriously affected by the accelerated destruction of forest, as well as by intensive drainage of wetlands, which is currently going on in these areas.

To these problems others must be added, which have also originated from human activity, such as water pollution and the uncontrolled use of pesticides. These birds are being affected by pollutants, especially through their diet of fish. High levels of mercury, selenium, chromium and chlorine compounds, such as dieldrin, endrin, heptachlor, oxychlordane, PCB's and DDT, have been found in the tissues, eggs and droppings of many species. The indiscriminate and abusive use of pesticides has almost led to the extermination of some local populations, as with the Purple Heron in the 1970's in the Ebro Delta, in Spain: in the 1960's there were more than 1000 pairs, but numbers dropped to only 60 pairs in 1973, and the species has still not fully recovered, with 475 pairs in 1990. Similarly, all the 1000 young Snowy Egrets of a colony in the Green Island Sanctuary, in Texas, were lost in 1976, for the same reason. Apart from the direct mortality that pollution can cause, and other effects such as abnormal behaviour in parent birds recorded in the Grey Heron, these pesticides produce a progressive thinning of eggshells. This phenomenon is particularly linked with concentrations of DDE (a breakdown product of DDT) in the eggs, and has been confirmed in several species, such as the Great Blue Heron, the Little Blue Heron, the Snowy Egret, the Greenbacked Heron and the Black-crowned Night-heron in the USA and Canada. It has also been noted in the Grey Heron in Britain,

where calculations indicate a 20% reduction in shell thickness since 1947. DDE concentrations have also been proved to affect the hatching success of the Black-crowned Night-heron. Furthermore, some data point to a gradual decrease in clutch size, since the start of the generalized use of pesticides, and although more research is required, it has been proved in several North American populations of the Great Blue Heron and the Black-crowned Night-heron.

Herons, and wading birds in general, are good biological indicators for monitoring the quality of habitats, as their breeding parameters are very sensitive to any modifications or deterioration that might occur in these areas.

Thus, despite their great ability to survive, herons, and other birds of aquatic environments, face a formidable menace, and in response to this, efforts are being made to conserve these birds. Already, in 1962, the MAR conference held at the Camargue under the auspices of IUCN, ICBP and IWRB, highlighted the importance of the great threat posed by wetland destruction, and led to the Convention on Wetlands of International Importance, especially as Waterfowl Habitat, passed in the conference at Ramsar, in Iran, in 1971. Up to 1990, the convention has been ratified by 53 states, which have designated 488 enclaves, involving more than 30,000,000 hectares of wetlands, that are subject to strict protection; unfortunately, however, this protection is not always carried out. Nevertheless, many important areas, and many countries, have still not signed this convention; it has only been ratified by five states in Latin America, seven in Asia and thirteen in Africa.

General Bibliography
Beaver *et al.* (1980), Bock (1956), Boer & Van Brink (1982), Boev (1987a, 1987b), Caldwell (1980, 1986), Curry-Lindahl (1968, 1971), Draulans (1988), Dubale & Mansuri (1969), Erwin (1985), Fasola (1986), Forbes (1989), Frederick & Collopy (1989a), Fuller (1987), Franchimont (1986), Gysels (1968), Hancock & Elliott (1978), Hancock & Kushlan (1984), Kent (1986, 1987), Kushlan (1977f, 1981, 1985), Meyerriecks (1960), Mock (1979, 1984, 1986), Mock *et al.* (1987), Murton (1971), Olson (1978), Payne (1979), Payne & Risley (1976), Percy (1951), Post (1990), Powell (1987), Sheldon (1987), Sibley & Monroe (1990), Spendelow *et al.* (1989), Sprunt *et al.* (1978), Vanden Berge (1970), Verheyen (1959, 1960c), Wiese (1978).

PLATE 26

inches 12

cm 30

dark morph

white morph

Subfamily ARDEINAE

Genus *SYRIGMA* Ridgway, 1878

1. **Whistling Heron**

Syrigma sibilatrix

French: Héron flûte-du-soleil **German**: Pfeifreiher **Spanish**: Garza Chiflona

Taxonomy. *Ardea sibilatrix* Temminck, 1824, Brazil and Paraguay.
Formerly placed with night-herons, but behaviour and morphology place it closer to day-herons; genetically seems closest to *Egretta*. Validity of race *fostersmithi* sometimes questioned. Two subspecies normally recognized.
Subspecies and Distribution.
S. s. sibilatrix (Temminck, 1824) - Bolivia to SE Brazil and NE Argentina.
S. s. fostersmithi Friedmann, 1949 - E Colombia, Venezuela.

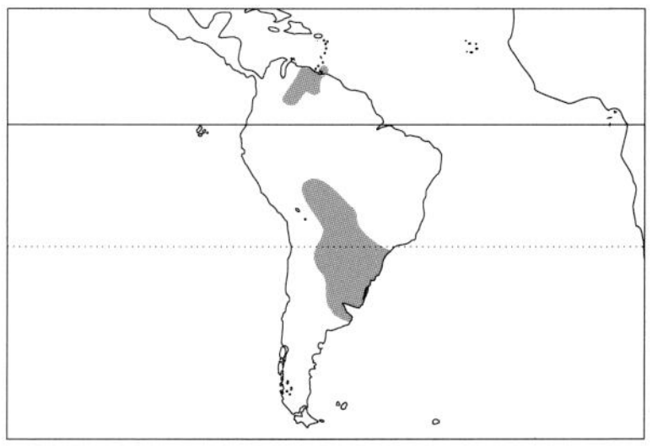

Descriptive notes. 50-61 cm. Plumes of hindcrown rigid; bill and lores duller outside breeding season. Juvenile duller, with some streaking on neck and wings. Race *fostersmithi* smaller, paler, longer-billed.
Habitat. One of the least aquatic of Ardeidae, normally occupies open, wet grasslands. In Argentina often seen along roadsides or perched on fence posts. Also found in shallow water in marshy areas, or in areas which have been soaked during the rains; also rice paddies, flooded woodland, lakeshores and by water courses.
Food and Feeding. Mostly arthropods, including dragonfly and beetle larvae, other invertebrates, frogs, eels, lizards and water snakes. Diurnal, territorial feeder, normally foraging singly or in pairs, though up to 25 recorded feeding together.
Breeding. Apr-Sept in N; varies with population in S, Sept-Jan in SE Brazil, peaks Jan in Uruguay. Solitary or loosely colonial; nest is stick platform normally 3-11 m up tree. 3 (sometimes 4) eggs; little else known, but incubation and fledging took total of two months in Corrientes, NE Argentina.
Movements. Sedentary; some local movements, connected with variations in local conditions. N populations may migrate, as absent from NE Venezuela Nov-Jan. Regularly flies off to roosts in trees, where shows more gregarious tendencies, with flocks of 100-200 seen flying to roost in *Eucalyptus* grove in Brazil.
Status and Conservation. Not globally threatened. Locally common, but distribution patchy. Seasonally common in *llanos* of E Colombia, occasionally in groups of 100+ birds. In Argentina, common in Chaco, Corrientes, Misiones and at Punta Lara, Buenos Aires; very common resident in Rio Grande do Sul, Brazil.
Bibliography. Belton (1984), Blake (1977), Boano (1981), Carp (1991), Devicenzi (1926), Di Giacomo (1988), Gallardo (1970), Gyldenstolpe (1945a), Hellmayr & Conover (1948), Hilty & Brown (1986), Humphrey & Parkes (1963), Kahl (1971f), Klimaitis & Moschione (1987), Kushlan *et al*. (1982), Nores & Yzurieta (1980), de la Peña (1980b, 1986), Pinto (1964), Ruschi (1979), de Schauensee & Phelps (1978), Scott & Carbonell (1986), Sick (1984), Wetmore (1926), Wilson, D.B. (1975).

Genus *PILHERODIUS* Bonaparte, 1855

2. **Capped Heron**

Pilherodius pileatus

French: Bihoreau blanc **German**: Kappenreiher **Spanish**: Garza Capirotada

Taxonomy. *Ardea pileata* Boddaert, 1783, Cayenne.
Has been placed with night-herons and even included in *Nycticorax*, but is not nocturnal feeder, lacks distinct juvenile plumage and morphologically closer to day-herons. Monotypic.
Distribution. Basins of Amazon and Orinoco; from E Panama, E through Guianas to E Brazil, and S through E Ecuador to S Bolivia and Paraguay.

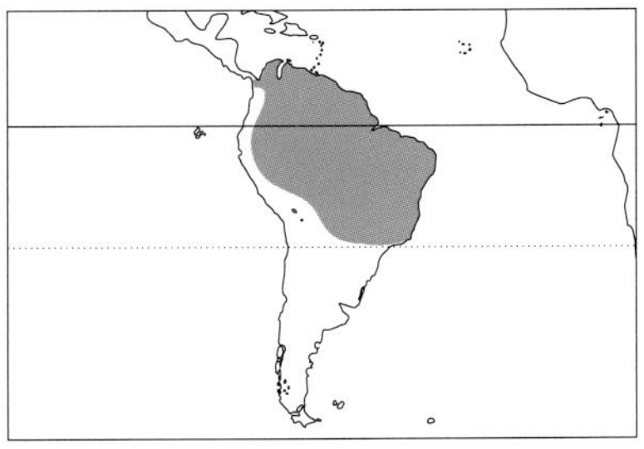

Descriptive notes. 51-61 cm. Back and wings pale pearl grey to variable extent; neck, breast and wings washed pale buff during breeding. Juvenile lacks occipital plumes and has some streaking on crown.
Habitat. Forested swamps, usually near rivers, streams or small pools, especially along muddy, grassy or rocky river banks in Colombia. Up to 400 m in upland tropical rain forest with streams and swamps in Pará, NE Brazil; in Venezuela, feeds in bare places in wet grassland; in Brazil, has recently colonized pools alongside the Transamazonian Highway; in Surinam, even found in coffee plantations, rice paddies and on sandbank in river.
Food and Feeding. Small fish, generally less than 5 cm long, aquatic insects, frogs and tadpoles. Diurnal, passive feeder; captures prey by Standing or Walking Slowly (see page 386) along edges of ponds or streams. Usually feeds alone, though occasionally joins loose feeding groups of other herons.
Breeding. Very little known. In Venezuela, birds in breeding condition taken in early Mar. Stick nest placed low in trees. Details from captive breeding in Miami, USA: 2-4 eggs; incubation 26-27 days; chick has white down.
Movements. Sedentary.
Status and Conservation. Not globally threatened. Poorly known; thinly but widely distributed and evidently scarce; uncommon in Brazil and Colombia.
Bibliography. Blake (1977), Haverschmidt (1958), Hellmayr & Conover (1948), Hilty & Brown (1986), Kushlan *et al*. (1982), Pinto (1964), Ridgely & Gwynne (1989), Ruschi (1979), de Schauensee & Phelps (1978), Schubart *et al*. (1965), Scott & Carbonell (1986), Sick (1984), Snyder (1966), Teixeira & Carvalho (1982), Thibault & Guyot (1988), Wetmore (1965).

Genus *ARDEA* Linnaeus, 1758

3. **Grey Heron**

Ardea cinerea

French: Héron cendré **German**: Graureiher **Spanish**: Garza Real

Taxonomy. *Ardea cinerea* Linnaeus, 1758, Europe; restricted to Sweden.
Forms superspecies with *A. herodias* and *A. cocoi*. Four subspecies generally recognized. Race *monicae* recently considered separate species by some authors.
Subspecies and Distribution.
A. c. cinerea Linnaeus, 1758 - most of Palearctic, thinly through Africa, India and Sri Lanka.
A. c. jouyi Clark, 1907 - Japan to N Burma and S to Java.
A. c. firasa Hartert, 1917 - Madagascar.
A. c. monicae Jouanin & Roux, 1963 - islands off Banc d'Arguin, Mauritania.

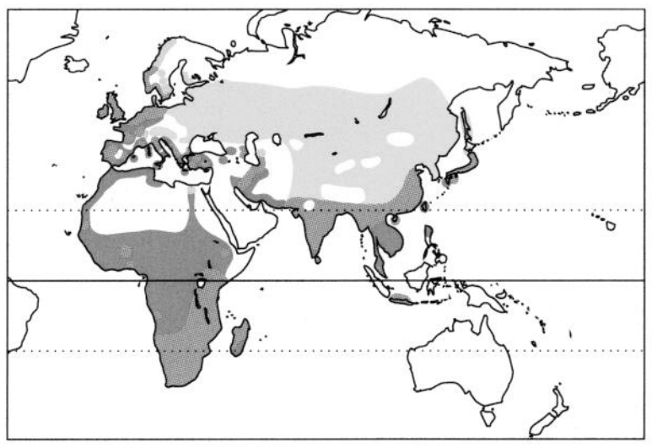

Descriptive notes. 90-98 cm: 1020-2073 g; wingspan 175-195 cm. Forehead and crown white. Normally differs from *A. herodias* in paler neck and thighs. Non-breeding adult has bill and legs brownish yellow, lacks long plumes of breast and scapulars. Juvenile more uniform grey, with duller bare parts. Races separated on size and tone of plumage on neck, back and wings; *monicae* much paler.
Habitat. Very variable; any kind of shallow water, fresh, brackish or salt, standing or flowing. Generally prefers areas with some trees, but can occupy very open areas; race *monicae* does not apparently use trees. Equally at home inland, where frequents rivers, lakes, marshes, floodplains, ricefields, irrigated areas and open grassland, or along coast, using deltas, estuaries, tidal mudflats or mangroves. From sea level up to 500 m or even 1000 m; occasionally much higher, breeding up to 2000 m in Armenia, and recorded at 3500-4000 m in Ladakh, NW India.
Food and Feeding. Mainly fish, but diet varies with habitat and season. Normally fish 10-25 cm long, but sometimes larger fish weighing up to 500 g, or eels up to 60 cm long. Also takes amphibians, crabs, molluscs, crustaceans, aquatic insects, snakes, small rodents, and some birds; plant matter also recorded. Adults require 330-500 g daily. Passive feeder; in some places feeds by day, mostly in morning and evening, in others feeds mostly by night and around dusk. Normally solitary feeder, each bird defending feeding territory; when conditions favourable, may feed in groups, e.g. at Ebro Delta, NE Spain, over 100 birds may feed together in a paddyfield in autumn, when ploughing tractors turn up abundant prey.
Breeding. Jan-May in Palearctic; more variable in tropics: mainly during rains in Africa (sometimes almost all year round) and Madagascar, Apr-Nov in Mauritania; in India, Jul-Oct in N, Nov-Mar in S, Mar-Jun in Kashmir; Jul/Aug in Sumatra. Normally colonial, often in mixed colonies of 100's or even 1000's of pairs; rarely lone nests, or 2 or 3 together. Nest is stick platform, 50+ cm wide, often reused in successive years, becoming vast; usually sited high in tall trees, up to 50 m off ground; also on ground (especially *monicae*) or cliff ledges, in reedbeds or bushes, exceptionally on houses, bridges, etc. 1-10 eggs, normally 4-5 in Europe, 3 in tropics; incubation 25-26 days (21 in tropics); chicks have brownish grey down, white below; fledging 50 days; chicks remain at nest 10-20 days more. Occasionally lays second clutch.
Movements. Populations of extreme N migratory, further S tend to be sedentary or dispersive; marked post-breeding dispersal (see page 392). In Palearctic, migratory tendency increases towards N and E; breeding populations of Iberian Peninsula, Britain and Ireland are sedentary, but others E to Siberia mainly migratory, though some individuals overwinter on breeding grounds; most migration towards SW, more rarely towards S or SE, starting Sept/Oct, with return starting in Feb. Birds of Far East migrate to S China; 2 birds ringed in SE Siberia recovered in N Thailand; partial migrant in Japan. Populations of Africa, India and SE Asia sedentary. Vagrant to Spitzbergen, Greenland, Lesser Antilles, Brazil. At Lac de Grand Lieu, W France, birds commute 2-38 km between colony and feeding territories.
Status and Conservation. Not globally threatened. In Europe heavily persecuted in past (see page 397); now common and expanding to both N and S, colonizing much of Scandinavia and Mediterranean in present century, e.g. Camargue (S France) in 1964, Albufera de Valencia (E Spain) in 1984. European population rising, and recent estimate of c. 50,000 pairs: France c. 2000 pairs in 1960's, 13,000 pairs in 1985; UK gradual increase since first censuses in 1920's, tempered by slumps following cold winters. Also common in USSR, with tenfold increase in some populations of Far East in period 1969-1982; 16,112 recorded in China, Jan 1990. In Africa widespread, particularly in E and S, but uncommon; apparently expanding in NW, and many new colonies in S; in Madagascar, commonest in W; c. 1000-1500 pairs of race *monicae* at Banc d'Arguin (Mauritania) in 1978/79. SE Asia fairly local: threatened in Thailand; only 2 colonies in W Peninsular Malaysia; apparently commoner in E Sumatra, with 242 nests found in 1986.
Bibliography. Ali & Ripley (1978), Altenburg *et al*. (1982), Baerends & van der Cingel (1962), Bauer & Glutz von Blotzheim (1966), Brown *et al*. (1982), Campos & Fernández-Cruz (1989, 1991), Campos & Fraile (1990), Cooke *et al*. (1976), Cramp & Simmons (1977), Custer *et al*. (1980), Dementiev & Gladkov (1951b), Draulans (1987), Draulans & van Vessem (1987), Duhautois & Marion (1982), Dupuy (1984), Etchécopar & Hüe (1978), Fernández & Fernández-Cruz (1991), Géroudet (1978a), Goodman (1989), Grimmett & Jones (1989), Harrison (1988), Knief & Drenckhahn (1984), Langrand (1990), Litvinenko (1982), Lowe (1954), Mackworth-Praed & Grant (1957-1973), Maclean (1985), Marchant *et al*. (1990), Marion (1989), Marion & Marion (1982), Marion & Marion (1987), van Marle & Voous (1988), Marquiss & Leitch (1990), Medway & Wells (1976), Milon *et al*. (1973), Milstein *et al*. (1970), Palmer (1962), Paz (1987), Perennou (1991a, 1991b), Perennou & Mundkur (1991), Pinto (1983), Prestt (1970), Roberts (1991), Round *et al*. (1988), Scott (1989), Silvius (1986), Smythies (1986), van Vessem & Draulans (1986), Voisin (1991), Walmsley (1975).

4. **Great Blue Heron**

Ardea herodias

French: Grand Héron **German**: Kanadareiher **Spanish**: Garza Azulada
Other common names: Great White Heron (white morph); Würdemann's Heron

Taxonomy. *Ardea herodias* Linnaeus, 1758, America = Hudson Bay.
Sometimes considered conspecific with *A. cinerea*; forms superspecies with *A. cinerea* and *A. cocoi*. Race *occidentalis*, mostly white morph birds, previously considered distinct species. Possible hybrid *occidentalis* x *wardi* with white head, described as different species, Würdemann's Heron (*A. wurdemanni*); recent opinion suggests it is merely colour morph of *wardi* or *occidentalis*. Five subspecies recognized.

On following pages: 5. Cocoi Heron (*Ardea cocoi*); 6. White-necked Heron (*Ardea pacifica*); 7. Black-headed Heron (*Ardea melanocephala*); 8. Madagascar Heron (*Ardea humbloti*); 9. White-bellied Heron (*Ardea insignis*); 10. Great-billed Heron (*Ardea sumatrana*); 11. Goliath Heron (*Ardea goliath*); 12. Purple Heron (*Ardea purpurea*).

Subspecies and Distribution.
A. h. fannini Chapman, 1901 - SE Alaska to coastal Washington.
A. h. herodias Linnaeus, 1758 - most of N & C America.
A. h. wardi Ridgway, 1882 - Kansas and Oklahoma to Florida.
A. h. occidentalis Audubon, 1835 - S Florida through W Indies to islands off Venezuela.
A. h. cognata Bangs, 1903 - Galapagos.

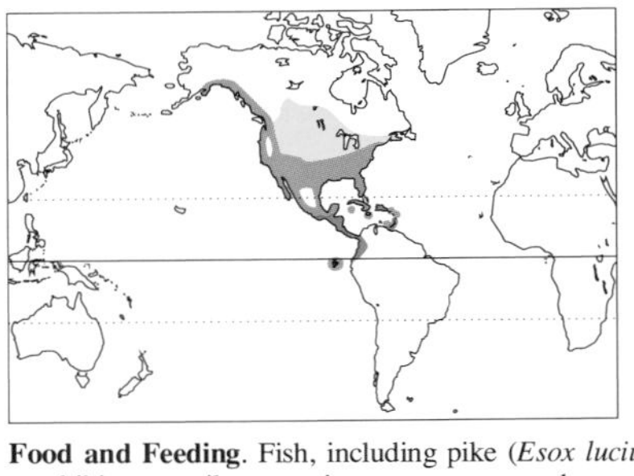

Descriptive notes. 91-137 cm; 2268-3629 g. Polymorphic, with all white form, differing from *Egretta alba* in heavier build, thicker bill and pale legs; some intermediate forms, with white head and neck and pale body. Juvenile darker, lacks crest, belly streaked, bare parts duller. Races separated on size and plumage tone.
Habitat. River and lake margins, wet meadows, marshes, swamps, fields, also mangroves and tidal mudflats; sometimes far from water. Up to 2600 m in Colombia and Ecuador. White morph strictly marine, found around keys, mangroves, tidal grass flats; after breeding occasionally found at freshwater sites.
Food and Feeding. Fish, including pike (*Esox lucius*) up to 30 cm, and smalltooth bass up to 28 cm, amphibians, reptiles, aquatic crustaceans, grasshoppers, dragonflies, aquatic insects, small mammals (e.g. shrews, rats, ground squirrels), rarely birds (as large as terns *Chlidonias*); scavenging also recorded. Fairly passive feeder; normally feeds alone, sometimes robbing other species, e.g. gulls. Normally feeds by day, mostly around dawn and dusk; some populations feed mostly by night, especially in tidal habitats.
Breeding. Feb-May in most of N America; all year round in Florida, peak in Dec-Jan; Mar-Jul in E Caribbean. Solitary or colonial. Nest is stick platform c. 1 m wide, often reused in successive years, becoming vast; typically in tallest trees in swamp, c. 40 m up, alternatively on ground, sea cliffs or shrubs. 2-7 eggs, average number decreasing from N to S; incubation 25-29 days; fledging c. 60 days; chicks leave nest at 64-91 days.
Movements. Marked post-breeding dispersal in N America. Populations of N migratory, those of S sedentary, sometimes with local movements. Autumn migration takes birds to S USA, Cuba, West Indies, C America and N parts of S America, though some birds winter as far N as S Canada. Accidental to Greenland; Hawaii, Azores. White morph sedentary, with some wandering and post-breeding dispersal.
Status and Conservation. Not globally threatened. Common and apparently stable in N America since 1930's, with 8016 breeding birds counted along US Atlantic coast in 1976, and 4000 pairs on US Gulf coast in 1975/76; increasing in places, e.g. New York State 1964-1981, due to reafforestation and reduced levels of cultivation; at L Michigan, increase of 61·7% in period 1977-1987. Also common in Mexico, e.g. 525 pairs at Usumacinta Delta and 250 pairs in Marismas Nacionales in 1979. Race *occidentalis* has limited breeding range and is considered rare; population periodically decimated by hurricanes, but recently on increase due to protection, with some 2500 adults in Florida (see page 399); probably extinct in Jamaica.
Bibliography. Allen (1962), Bent (1926), Blake (1977), Brandman (1976), Burkholder & Smith (1991), Byrd (1978), Cottrille & Cottrille (1958), Custer *et al.* (1980), Evans, P.G.H. (1990), Fjeldså & Krabbe (1990), Forbes, L.S. (1987), Forbes, L.S. *et al.* (1985), Heitmeyer (1986), Henny & Bethers (1971), Hilty & Brown (1986), Holt (1928), Hom (1983), Jenni (1969), Krebs (1974), McClung (1969), McCrimmon (1982), Meyerriecks (1960), Mock (1976a, 1976b), Ogden (1978), Powell & Powell (1986), Quinney (1982), Palmer (1962), Partch (1990), Pratt & Winkler (1985), Rodgers (1983), Scott & Carbonell (1986), Simpson *et al.* (1987), Slud (1964), Sullivan & Payne (1988), Terres (1980), Wetmore (1965).

5. Cocoi Heron

Ardea cocoi

French: Héron cocoi **German**: Cocoireiher **Spanish**: Garza Cuca
Other common names: White-necked Heron (!)

Taxonomy. *Ardea Cocoi* Linnaeus, 1766, Cayenne.
Forms superspecies with *A. cinerea* and *A. herodias*. Monotypic.
Distribution. Most of S America excluding Andes, from E Panama S to Aysén (Chile) and Chubut (Argentina).

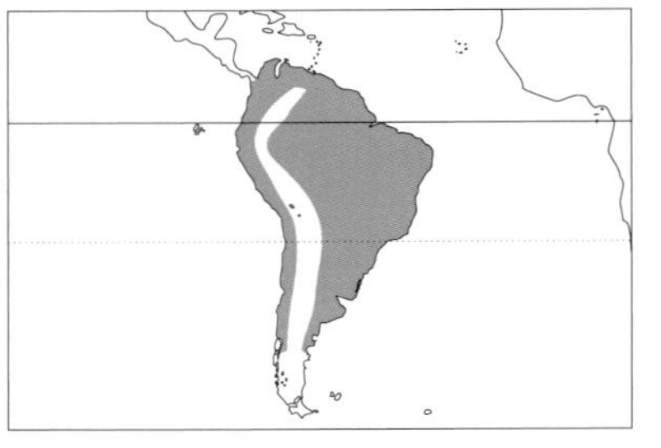

Descriptive notes. 95-127 cm. Black on head more extensive than on *A. cinerea* and *A. herodias*. Juvenile generally greyer, with streaked underparts.
Habitat. Very variable; any kind of wetland, including swamps, lake shores, rivers, flooded pastures and estuaries; absent from arid coasts and dense forest, though does occur in marshy areas surrounded by forest. Normally in lowlands, but straggles up to at least 2550 m in Cochabamba and Tarija, Bolivia.
Food and Feeding. Fish, frogs, aquatic insects; in coastal Brazil occasionally eats dead or dying animals; in Peru takes mostly large fish over 20 cm long. Passive feeder, most prey taken when Standing; in Chile mostly feeds by night, in Argentina often by day. Usually solitary and territorial, but occasionally feeds in large groups, e.g. 100-200 birds feeding in Lagoa do Peixe, Brazil, in Jan 1974, as water receded.
Breeding. Jul in Surinam; Aug-Nov SE Brazil and Argentina. Colonial; colonies sometimes large and may be mixed. Nest of reeds and twigs, lined with grass, and situated in trees, bushes or reedbeds. Up to 3 eggs in Argentina, but 2-4 chicks in Brazil. Incubation c. 24-26 days.
Movements. Generally sedentary, though birds in extreme S of range probably migrate N during winter. Also some post-breeding dispersal; occasionally reaches Strait of Magellan and Lake Kami in far S. Non-breeding vistor to Trinidad mainly Jan-Jun. Accidental to Falklands and Gough I.
Status and Conservation. Not globally threatened. Widespread in lowland S America. In early 1970's breeding population of Surinam estimated at 2500 pairs, but slump to 300-500 pairs in 1980's. Common but not abundant in Argentina; generally common in Chaco zone; census of R Paraguay in Jan 1984 yielded 4000 birds. Common in Darien, Panama, and along Caribbean coast of Colombia; scarce or absent along arid Pacific coast from Guayaquil (Ecuador) to Valparaiso (Chile).
Bibliography. Belton (1984), Blake (1977), Carp (1991), Devicenzi (1926), Fjeldså & Krabbe (1990), Haverschmidt (1968), Hellmayr & Conover (1948), Hilty & Brown (1986), Johnson (1965), Nores & Yzurieta (1980), de la Peña (1986), Pinto (1964), Plenge *et al.* (1989), Ridgely & Gwynne (1989), Ruschi (1979), de Schauensee & Phelps (1978), Scott & Carbonell (1986), Sick (1984), Spaans & de Jong (1982), Wetmore (1965), Woods (1988).

6. White-necked Heron

Ardea pacifica

French: Héron à tête blanche **German**: Weißhalsreiher **Spanish**: Garza Cuelliblanca
Other common names: Pacific Heron

Taxonomy. *Ardea pacifica* Latham, 1801, New South Wales. Monotypic.
Distribution. Australia and Tasmania; scarce, but probably regular, in S New Guinea.

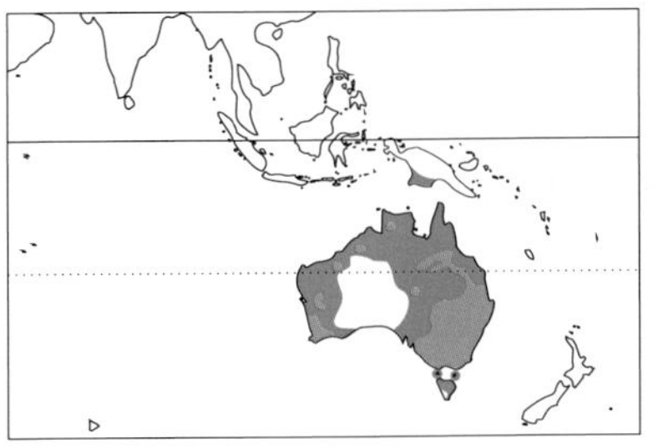

Descriptive notes. 76-106 cm; 860 g; wingspan 147-160 cm. Bare part colours vary, poorly understood. Non-breeding adult is duller, with streaked underparts and black spots on foreneck. Juvenile as non-breeding adult, but head and neck greyish.
Habitat. Shallow fresh water, flooded grassland, floodplains, ephemeral or fluctuating rivers or swamps, lagoons, pastures. Less frequent in salt or brackish water.
Food and Feeding. Small aquatic and terrestrial animals, fish (normally under 3 cm, largest recorded was catfish of 10 cm), amphibians, molluscs, crustaceans and aquatic insects. Diurnal, passive feeder; normally feeds alone or in pairs, sometimes defends territory, but also seen in loose feeding flocks.
Breeding. Usually Sept-Feb, during spring in S and summer rains in N; may occur all year round, depending on availability of food and water conditions. Normally colonial, in small colonies of 2-30 pairs, but up to several hundred; colonies often mixed with cormorants, spoonbills, ibises or other herons; occasionally solitary. Nest is stick platform, usually 15-40 m up tall tree, over or near water. Average 3-4 eggs (2-6); incubation 28-30 days; chicks have greyish white down; fledging c. 6-7 weeks.
Movements. Nomadic, moves about exploiting seasonality of Australian wetlands. Normally found along coast during dry season, moving to wetlands of interior during or after rains. Exceptional rainfall in arid areas can lead to irruptions, e.g. 1974 in SE Australia, 1975 in SW Australia and Tasmania, and 1978 and 1979 in E Australia; unusually abundant in Irian Jaya (W New Guinea) in 1978/79. Vagrant to New Zealand, Norfolk I and Tristan da Cunha.
Status and Conservation. Not globally threatened. Common in Australia, especially inland in SE; population stable, but has expanded to SW of Western Australia since 1950. Has benefited from deforestation carried out to create pastures or irrigation schemes, and also construction of reservoirs, etc. Uncommon and perhaps irregular in Tasmania and S New Guinea.
Bibliography. Beehler *et al.* (1986), Bull *et al.* (1985), Coates (1985), Crawford (1972), Lowe (1989), Marchant (1988), Marchant & Higgins (1990), Recher & Holmes (1982), Recher *et al.* (1983), Scott (1989), Serventy (1985).

7. Black-headed Heron

Ardea melanocephala

French: Héron mélanocéphale **German**: Schwarzhalsreiher **Spanish**: Garza Cabecinegra

Taxonomy. *Ardea melanocephala* Anon. = Vigors and Children, 1826, no locality; ? near Lake Chad.
Forms superspecies with *A. humbloti*. Monotypic.
Distribution. Africa S of Sahara, from Senegal to Ethiopia and S to South Africa.

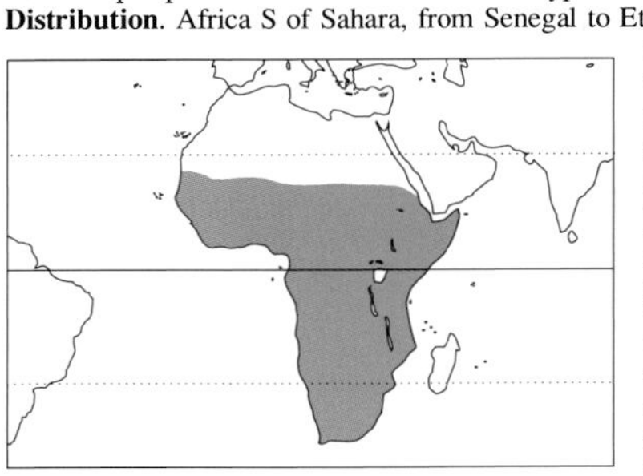

Descriptive notes. 92-96 cm. Somewhat variable: wings and back can be much paler, highlighting black of head and neck; extent of white varies, some birds lacking white spots on foreneck, others with no white at all. Juvenile has white underparts and brownish grey neck.
Habitat. Largely terrestrial and associated much less with wetlands than most herons; typically found in damp, open pastureland, sometimes far from water. Also moist grassland, marshes, margins of rivers and lakes, cultivation, estuaries, coastal areas and forest clearings. In S Africa feeds equally in terrestrial and semiaquatic habitats. Often nests in towns or cities, e.g. Nairobi, Kampala.
Food and Feeding. A wide range of vertebrates and invertebrates, mostly terrestrial but also aquatic; rodents, insects, lizards, snakes, frogs, birds, spiders, crabs, fish; also scavenges (see page 386). In S Africa takes mainly large rodents, but Dec-Jan also takes many birds, e.g. widowbirds *Euplectes*, doves *Streptopelia*, *Oena*. Birds feeding in wetlands take mainly fish and amphibians. Fairly passive feeder, partially nocturnal; generally solitary, though feeding assemblies recorded, e.g. in Zimbabwe.
Breeding. Mainly during rains; in places all year round, but peak still during rains. Colonial, normally in small mixed colonies, but sometimes 200 nests or more. Nest of sticks usually high in tree, less often in reedbeds or on ground. 2-6 eggs (average 2·3 Zimbabwe, 3·2 Nigeria); incubation 23-27 days; chicks have pale grey down; fledging 40-55 days; juveniles independent at 60 days.
Movements. Sedentary in equatorial zone; elsewhere apparently migratory, with movements related to dry seasons. In W Africa, moves N into Sahel for rains, May-Oct; in NE, E, C and SE Africa, birds migrate to drier zones during rains, e.g. in Welle District only present during dry season, moving N into Sudan to breed during rains. Vagrant to Algeria, SW Europe, Oman, Madagascar. May commute over 30 km between feeding grounds and roost.
Status and Conservation. Not globally threatened. Widespread and common, but with rather patchy distribution. Throughout most of Africa is commonest of large herons. Has probably benefited from some human alterations to environment, with increase in number and extent of open and irrigated areas.
Bibliography. Altenburg *et al.* (1986), Baccetti (1983), Beesley (1972), Benson & Benson (1975), Britton (1980), Brown & Britton (1980), Brown *et al.* (1982), Langrand (1990), Mackworth-Praed & Grant (1957-1973), Maclean (1985), O'Connor, T. (1984), Pinto (1983), Skinner *et al.* (1987), Stuart & Dürk (1984), Taylor (1948), Tomlinson (1975).

8. Madagascar Heron

Ardea humbloti

French: Héron de Humblot **German**: Madagaskarreiher **Spanish**: Garza Malgache
Other common names: Malagasy/Humblot's Heron

Taxonomy. *Ardea humbloti* Milne-Edwards and Grandidier, 1885, eastern Madagascar.
Forms superspecies with *A. melanocephala*. Monotypic.

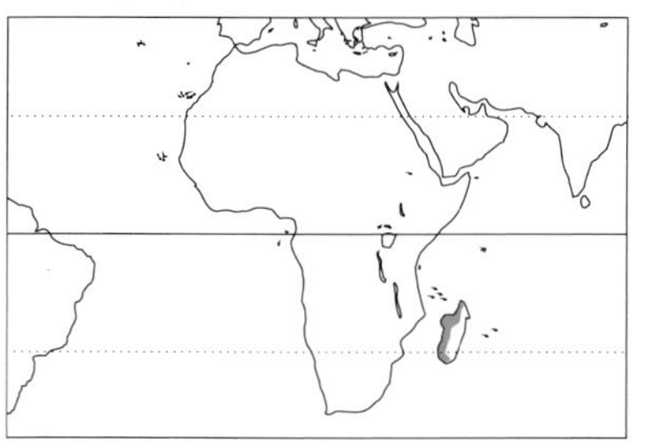

Distribution. Endemic to Madagascar, where occurs mainly in W; recent reports suggest possible breeding in Comoro Is.
Descriptive notes. 100 cm. Only member of *Ardea* with black chin; bare part colours apparently vary with season. Juvenile has white to brownish chin.
Habitat. Mainly along coast in fresh, brackish or salt water. Seems to prefer tidal areas or reefs, but also lakes, rivers, mangroves, estuaries, and rarely rice paddies. From sea level up to 1500 m.
Food and Feeding. Mainly medium-sized to large fish, up to 20 cm long (one eel 48 cm long); also crustaceans. Passive feeder, waiting station-

ary for long periods or walking slowly. Highly territorial, usually feeding alone; tends to be aggressive towards other heron species, though has been recorded feeding in mixed flocks.
Breeding. Little known. To date few occupied nests located, Nov and mid Jul. Solitary, or few pairs in colonies mixed with *A. cinerea* and other species. Stick nest in tree or rock hollow. 3 eggs.
Movements. Sedentary, though may perhaps disperse over long distances. Vagrant to Aldabra.
Status and Conservation. INSUFFICIENTLY KNOWN. Local and little known; probably never abundant, although still relatively frequent along N and W coasts and recorded in 4 protected areas; nowadays rare on central High Plateau and E coast, where most records refer to immature birds. However, improving observer coverage suggests species more secure than when classified Threatened in mid-1980's. Recent records from Comoro Is suggest possible breeding there on Mohéli and perhaps also Anjouan, as well as nearby Mayotte.
Bibliography. Collar & Andrew (1988), Collar & Stuart (1985), Dee (1986), Delacour (1932), Draulans (1986), Forbes-Watson (1969), Langrand (1990), Milon (1948), Milon *et al.* (1973), Norton *et al.* (1990), Rand (1936), Salvan (1970).

9. White-bellied Heron
Ardea insignis

French: Héron impérial **German**: Kaiserreiher **Spanish**: Garza Ventriblanca
Other common names: Imperial Heron

Taxonomy. *Ardea insignis* Hume, 1878, Sikkim terai, Bhutan duars, etc.
Alternative name *A. imperialis* not applicable, as senior name *A. insignis* is valid. Forms superspecies with *A. sumatrana*. Monotypic.
Distribution. Southern foothills of E Himalayas, from Nepal to NE India and Burma.

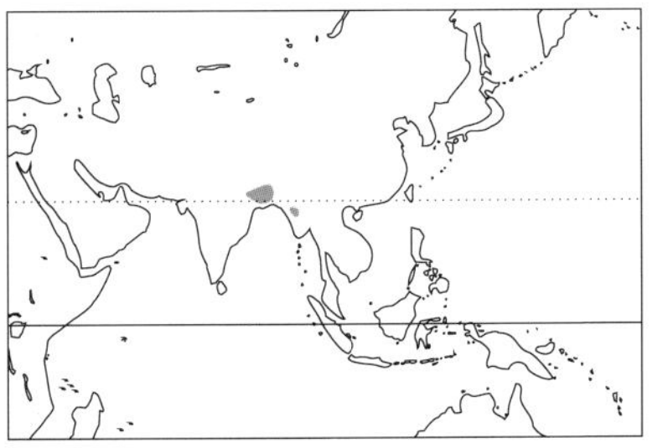

Descriptive notes. 127 cm; bill 152-176 mm. Robust bird with fairly uniform plumage contrasting with white belly. Juvenile as adult, but browner above and lacks streaks on underparts.
Habitat. Inland swamps, marshes, *terai* and stretches of rivers in forested zones.
Food and Feeding. Very little known, but probably specialized in large fish, and perhaps also amphibians, reptiles and small mammals. Probably territorial, normally feeding alone, though a few records of 4-5 birds feeding together.
Breeding. Very little known, only 2 nests described to date (none for over 60 years). Apr in Arakan (Burma), probably Jul-Aug in Indian *terai*, during SE monsoon. Solitary or colonial; nest is large stick platform placed high up tall tree. 4 eggs.
Movements. Mostly sedentary, but records from Toungoo and Pegu (SE Burma) and Tamil Nadu (S India), far from breeding grounds, may indicate some form of post-breeding dispersal.
Status and Conservation. ENDANGERED. Formerly resident all along foothills of E Himalayas, but seems to have declined in W of range: not recorded in Nepal this century; rare in NE India (where still breeds in a few small colonies in villages in Assam) and Bangladesh. Once considered common in parts of Burma, e.g. along Mali Hka and Irrawaddy rivers; little recent information, but habitat destruction seems to have been large-scale and devastating throughout Burma.
Bibliography. Ali & Ripley (1978), Collar & Andrew (1988), Hancock & Kushlan (1984), Mountfort (1988), Smith (1949), Smythies (1986), Stanford (1954), Stanford & Ticehurst (1939), Sugathan *et al.* (1987), Walters (1976).

10. Great-billed Heron
Ardea sumatrana

French: Héron typhon **German**: Rußreiher **Spanish**: Garza de Sumatra
Other common names: Dusky Grey/Sumatran/Giant Heron

Taxonomy. *Ardea Sumatrana* Raffles, 1822, Sumatra.
Forms superspecies with *A. insignis*. Validity of race *mathewsae* doubtful. Two subspecies recognized.
Subspecies and Distribution.
A. s. sumatrana Raffles, 1822 - Burma, Thailand and S Viet Nam to Indonesia, Philippines and New Guinea.
A. s. mathewsae Mathews, 1912 - N Australia.

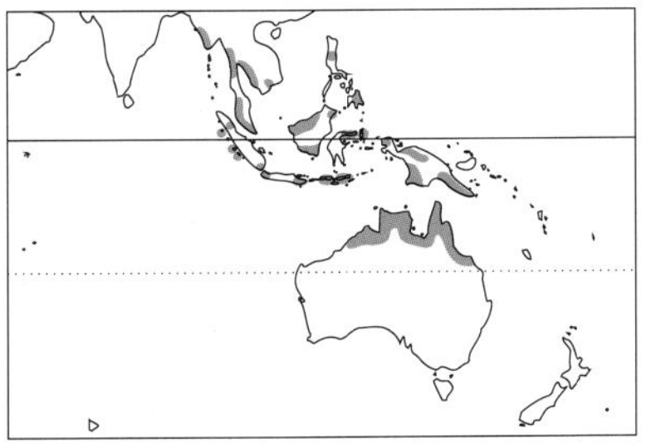

Descriptive notes. 100-115 cm; 1300-2600 g; bill c. 183 mm. Similar to *A. imperialis*, with more slender, slightly recurved bill and darker belly; elongated plumes on back more in evidence, nuchal crest longer. Juvenile more rufous, with heavier white streaks on neck and underparts. Race *mathewsae* browner, with shorter bill.
Habitat. Coastal, typically affecting mangroves, tidal mudflats and estuaries; also coastal swamps, rivers, beaches, (coral) lagoons and islets; occasionally follows large rivers inland for some distance.
Food and Feeding. Little known. In Australia, mainly fish, also crabs and other crustaceans; mudskippers taken in Borneo. Large size and huge bill suggest large prey probably taken. Territorial, solitary feeder, rarely in pairs or family groups. Feeds at low tide, flying back to trees as tide comes in.
Breeding. In any month in Australia, generally coinciding with monsoon, May-Jun in N, Sept-Jan in E; May-Jun (break in monsoon) in Singapore; Aug in W Java; Nov on Simuele I, off W Sumatra. Solitary nester, apparently forming stable pair, with several nests (up to 7), though may not breed every year. Stick nest often reused in successive years, becoming large, up to 1·3 m wide x 0·5 m deep; up to 10 m off ground in large tree. 2 eggs; chick fully-feathered at 63 days.
Movements. Apparently sedentary, although some records away from breeding grounds may indicate some post-breeding dispersal. Vagrant to NE New South Wales.
Status and Conservation. Not globally threatened. Currently considered near-threatened. Widespread, but at low densities. Information scarce and on occasions contradictory: in Australia, said by one authority to be "relatively common in suitable habitat", with densities of 2·5-5 birds/km, but by others to be "nowhere common" or "rare and apparently shrinking in numbers". Australian range appears to have contracted northwards during present century. Reportedly widespread in Malay Peninsula; may be relatively frequent in parts of E Sumatra; commonly sighted in W Sulawesi.
Bibliography. Beehler *et al.* (1986), Coates (1985), Dickinson *et al.* (1991), Gilliard & LeCroy (1970), Hoogerwerf (1949), Lansdown (1989), Larkins (1989), Marchant & Higgins (1990), van Marle & Voous (1988), Medway & Wells (1976), Mees (1982), Recher *et al.* (1983), Round *et al.* (1988), Seton (1973), Silvius (1986).

11. Goliath Heron
Ardea goliath

French: Héron goliath **German**: Goliathreiher **Spanish**: Garza Goliat

Taxonomy. *Ardea goliath* Cretzschmar, 1827, Bahr el Abiad = White Nile. Monotypic.
Distribution. Africa S of Sahara, S Iraq and S Iran, with some non-breeders along Red Sea; breeding also inferred at scattered sites on Indian Subcontinent from Pakistan to Bangladesh and S into Sri Lanka.

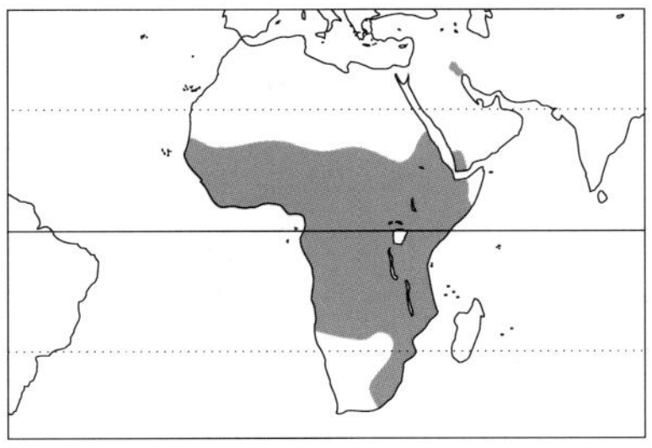

Descriptive notes. 135-140+ cm; wingspan 210-230 cm. Largest heron; very long tibia exaggerates this impression. Bill can be all blackish; occipital crest short and inconspicuous. Juvenile has head and neck paler and duller, with rusty buff edging above and paler underparts.
Habitat. Normally near water, fresh or salt; frequently found in shallow water along lake shores, also marshes, rivers, estuaries, reefs and mangrove creeks. From sea level up to 2100 m. Nest-site preferably surrounded by water.
Food and Feeding. Mainly large fish, also frogs, lizards, snakes, rodents, crabs, prawns and floating carrion. In S Africa, fish of 15-50 cm and 90-980 g, mostly c. 30 cm and 500-600 g. Diurnal and rather inactive feeder, mostly using Standing and Walking Slowly (see page 386). Solitary, normally alone or in pairs, rarely larger flocks; defends large feeding territory.
Breeding. Normally during rains; in some places all year, e.g. S Africa; on occasions does not breed each year, but only when conditions are favourable. Solitary, or rarely colonial; frequently colonial in Orange Free State, where 21·1% are solitary, 28·1% form monospecific colonies, and 50·8% nest in colonies mixed with darters, cormorants and other herons. Nest is large platform of sticks or reeds; placed 3 m or less up tree over water, on partly submerged trees, low bushes, mangroves, cliffs, sedges, papyrus or reeds. Average 3 eggs (2-5); incubation 24-30 days; chicks have grey brown down; nestling period variously reported as c. 42-81 days.
Movements. Sedentary; dispersive or nomadic movements in some areas in response to seasonal changes in conditions of habitat. No evidence of migration; vagrant to Egypt, Syria, Madagascar.
Status and Conservation. Not globally threatened. Generally frequent throughout Africa, locally common, e.g. in parts of Sudan and E Africa. Requires monitoring in South Africa, where formerly considered rare. CITES III, in Ghana. No recent breeding records from S Iraq, where nesting has probably ceased; probably also extirpated from Iran and Indian Subcontinent, where only record this century was in 1974.
Bibliography. Ali & Ripley (1978), Brown & Britton (1980), Brown *et al.* (1982), Cramp & Simmons (1977), Dean (1988), Dollinger (1988), Dowsett & de Vos (1965), Falzone (1989), Geldenhuys (1984), Goodman (1989), Hollom *et al.* (1988), Hüe & Etchécopar (1970), Langrand (1990), Mackworth-Praed & Grant (1957-1973), Maclean (1985), Mock & Mock (1980), Paz (1987), Perennou (1991b), Pinto (1983), Roberts (1991), Verschuren & Dupuy (1987), Whitfield & Blaber (1978).

12. Purple Heron
Ardea purpurea

French: Héron pourpré **German**: Purpurreiher **Spanish**: Garza Imperial

Taxonomy. *Ardea purpurea* Linnaeus, 1766, "in Oriente"; restricted to France.
Birds of Cape Verde Is sometimes considered separate race (*bournei*), or even distinct species, Cape Verde Heron. Three subspecies normally recognized.
Subspecies and Distribution.
A. p. purpurea Linnaeus, 1766 - W Palearctic, including parts of N Africa, E to Kazakhstan and Iran; Africa S of Sahara, Cape Verde Is.
A. p. madagascariensis Oort, 1910 - Madagascar.
A. p. manilensis Meyen, 1834 - S & E Asia, Indonesia, Philippines.

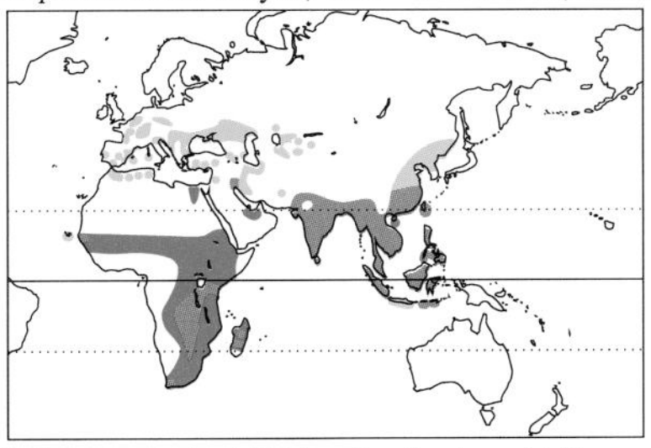

Descriptive notes. 78-90 cm; 525-1345 g, female lighter; wingspan 120-150 cm. Bill proportionally longer than in most members of *Ardea*. Juvenile more uniform brown and buff, with streaked breast, lacking neck stripes and elongated plumes of crown and scapulars. Races separated by extent of black streaking on neck; possible race/species *bournei* said to be uniformly paler.
Habitat. Open, shallow freshwater swamps with dense marshy vegetation. Typically reedbeds, also ricefields, lake shores, river margins, mangroves and coastal mudflats. In Cape Verde Is forages on dry hillsides. Lowlands and hills, up to 1500 m in Sumatra and 1800 m in Madagascar.
Food and Feeding. Fish (5-15 cm long, occasionally up to 44 cm), frogs, aquatic insects and crustaceans; also small birds and mammals, snakes and lizards. Passive feeder, normally waits motionless, half hidden in vegetation, waiting for prey to approach. Solitary, defends feeding territory. Feeds mainly at dawn and dusk, but also during day.
Breeding. Apr-Jun in W Palearctic; mainly during rains in Africa; in India, Jun-Oct in N, Nov-Mar in S. Colonial, usually small groups, but sometimes 100's, or up to 1000 at one Kenyan colony; often with other species; also solitary at times. Nest over or beside water, usually in flooded reedbeds at a height of up to 3 m; less often in bushes or trees, as much as 25 m up. 2-8 eggs (average: 2·1 S Africa; 3·3 Zimbabwe; 4·1 Ebro Delta, NE Spain; 5·1 C France); incubation 25-27 days; chicks have dark brown down, white below; fledging 45-50 days. Normally 1 clutch; possibly sometimes 2 in Africa.
Movements. Marked post-breeding dispersal. W Palearctic birds migratory, wintering in Africa S of Sahara but N of equator, especially in W Africa, a few in Mediterranean Basin, Middle East and Baluchistan, Pakistan; move S Aug-Oct, returning Mar-May, with some regularly overshooting into N and C Europe. Birds breeding in NE Asia migrate to Korea, S China, Thailand and Peninsular Malaysia. African and tropical Asian breeders sedentary, sometimes with local movements. Migration normally by day in small groups, but flocks of 350-400 birds in Turkey. Accidental to many islands of NE Atlantic, from Canaries to Iceland, also Brazil and Japan.
Status and Conservation. Not globally threatened. Widespread and locally common in Africa, common in Madagascar. Population of Cape Verde Is (possible race/species *bournei*) scarce, reckoned to be less than 20 pairs. In W Palearctic fairly scarce: tendency towards expansion in C Europe since 1940, colonizing new areas and increasing in Germany and Netherlands; most recent trends, however, suggest decline, e.g. in France, with numbers generally dropping in period 1974-1983, except along Atlantic coast; also declining in Spain (see page 403). Breeding population of Europe, excluding USSR and Black Sea, estimated at c. 6500 pairs. In E Palearctic: uncommon and local in Japan; common in China, e.g. 5000 breeding pairs in Zhalong. Threatened in Thailand, although abundant in places, e.g. Thale Noi, with 1000 breeding pairs; estimated c. 4000 at L Tempe, S Sulawesi, Jan 1990.
Bibliography. Ali & Ripley (1978), Bauer & Glutz von Blotzheim (1966), Brazil (1991), Brown & Britton (1980), Brown *et al.* (1982), Cavé (1983), Cramp & Simmons (1977), Duhautois (1984), Etchécopar & Hüe (1978), Géroudet (1978a), Goodman (1989), Grimmett & Jones (1989), Jongejan (1986), Kolbe & Neumann (1987), Kral & Figala (1966), Langrand (1990), László (1986), Ledant *et al.* (1981), Mackworth-Praed & Grant (1957-1973), Maclean (1985), van Marle & Voous (1988), Milon *et al.* (1973), Moser (1986), de Naurois (1966a, 1988), Paz (1987), Perennou (1991a, 1991b), Perennou & Mundkur (1991), Pinto (1983), Roberts (1991), Rodriguez dos Santos & Canavate (1985), Round *et al.* (1988), Rutgers & Norris (1970), Scott (1989), Smythies (1986), Tomlinson (1974a, 1974b), Voisin (1991).

ssp *alba*

13

ssp *egretta*

14

white phase

dark phase

15

16

17

18

19

ssp *intermedia*

ssp *plumifera*

20

21

ssp *garzetta*

22

23

ssp *schistacea*
white morph

ssp *gularis*
dark morph

24

25

dark morph

white morph

PLATE 27

inches   10

cm   25

Genus *EGRETTA* T. Forster, 1817

13. Great White Egret

Egretta alba

French: Grande Aigrette **German**: Silberreiher **Spanish**: Garceta Grande
Other common names: Great/Large Egret, Great American Egret, Great White Heron(!)

Taxonomy. *Ardea alba* Linnaeus, 1758, Europe.
Frequently placed in genus *Casmerodius*, less often in *Ardea*; work on DNA indicates closer genetic link with *Ardea* than with *Egretta*. Four subspecies recognized.
Subspecies and Distribution.
E. a. alba (Linnaeus, 1758) - C Europe to C Asia, S to Iran; winters N & C Africa and Persian Gulf to S China and S Korea.
E. a. modesta (J. E. Gray, 1831) - India, SE Asia, Japan and Korea S through Indonesia to Australia and New Zealand.
E. a. melanorhynchos (Wagler, 1827) - Africa S of Sahara, Madagascar.
E. a. egretta (Gmelin, 1789) - N, C & S America, from N USA to C Argentina.

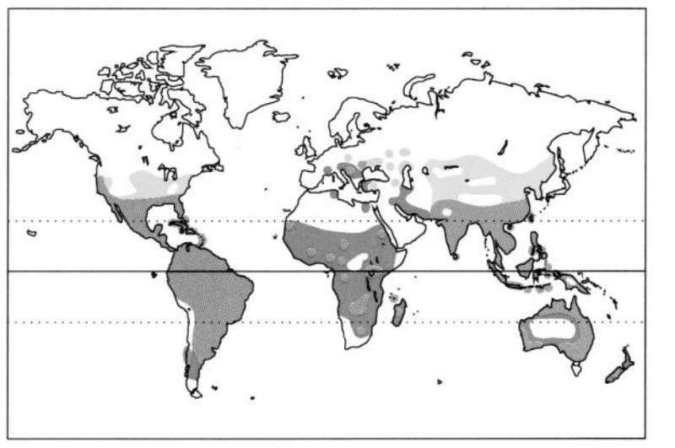

Descriptive notes. 80-104 cm; 700-1500 g; wingspan 140-170 cm. Characteristic S-shape of long neck. Bare facial skin reaches behind eye, in contrast with *E. intermedia*; white morph of *Ardea herodias* has heavier bill and yellow legs. Non-breeding adult has all yellow bill and dull greenish facial skin, and lacks ornamental plumes. Juvenile as non-breeding adult, but yellow bill has black tip. Races separated on bare part coloration, with varying extents of red and black on bill and legs during courtship.
Habitat. All kinds of wetlands, both inland and along coast, including marshes, floodplains, river margins, lake shores, salt-pans, estuaries, coastal swamps, mangroves and mudflats. Also agricultural land, especially rice fields and drainage ditches, occasionally dry pastures. Mainly in lowlands, but recorded nesting up to 1800 m in USSR; regularly wanders up to 3000-4000 m in N Andes, with breeding attempts at 4080 m in Junín, Peru.
Food and Feeding. Fish, amphibians, snakes, aquatic insects and crustaceans; also terrestrial insects, lizards and small birds and mammals. In South Africa, mostly fish 5-10 g (1-45); in Australia, mainly fish under 12 cm long. Mainly passive, diurnal feeder; feeds by "Walking Slowly" or "Stand and Wait"; mainly solitary, defends feeding territory aggressively; when food abundant may feed in flocks of hundreds of birds or more, e.g. 1000 birds at Benamba L, Madagascar.
Breeding. Season very variable depending on region. Tends to form colonies, sometimes mixed, with 10's, or up to 100's of pairs, e.g. 450 nests in mixed colony of 3000+ in Australia; on occasions solitary, nominate race showing greater tendency to breed alone or in small groups. Nests in reedbeds, bushes or trees, normally over water at height of up to 50 m. Normally 3-5 eggs (1-6); incubation 25-26 days; chicks have white down; fledging 6-9 weeks.
Movements. Extensive post-breeding dispersal. Populations of Palearctic and Nearctic partially migratory with some dispersive movements; tropical populations sedentary. E Asian birds migrate to SE Asia and Philippines, whereas birds from rest of Palearctic move to Mediterranean, Middle East, Persian Gulf and Pakistan. Birds of E USA winter S along coast to Bahamas and West Indies; W birds move S towards California, Mexico and C America; populations of Mississippi Basin move S to Gulf coast. Australian populations generally dispersive, although some regular seasonal movements occur, which might be migratory; sometimes irruptive, e.g. moving from interior to coast during droughts; occasionally to New Zealand; New Zealand population dispersive. Vagrant to islands of subantarctic, Seychelles, Canary Is, N and C Europe; several recent records of race *modesta* in Europe.
Status and Conservation. Not globally threatened. Intense persecution for plume trade in 19th and early 20th centuries led to crash in numbers and shrinking of range, but has now almost recovered to former numbers (see pages 396, 399). Abundant in N America, with rapid recovery in Florida since ban on plume trade: in 1912, largest colony contained only 400 nests; by early 1930's 80,000 birds in S Florida. Marked expansion N up Atlantic coast between 1930's and 1970's, since when stable, with estimated 15,000 pairs in 1975; 77,000 birds counted in Louisiana in 1976. Abundant in C and S America, e.g. 27,000 birds at Usumacinta Delta (Mexico), 2650 pairs at Palo Verde (Costa Rica) and 1000 pairs along coast of Surinam in 1970's. Due mainly to habitat loss, still threatened in W Palearctic, with c. 550 pairs in Europe (excluding USSR) at scattered localities; apparently expanding to W, and has recently bred in Netherlands and Italy. Local and uncommon in Africa, but common in some areas, e.g. 2800-3100 pairs at Inner Delta of R Niger in 1986/87; CITES III, in Ghana. Widespread race *modesta* relatively common, e.g. 10,940 counted in India and 5033 in Philippines, Jan 1990; scarce in New Zealand, with only c. 50 pairs at Okarito Lagoon.
Bibliography. Ali & Ripley (1978), Baccetti (1983), Bauer & Glutz von Blotzheim (1966), Belton (1984), Blake (1977), Brown *et al.* (1982), Byrd (1978), Carp (1991), Chambers (1989), Cramp & Simmons (1977), Custer & Frederick (1990), Custer & Peterson (1991), Custer *et al.* (1980), Dementiev & Gladkov (1951b), Dollinger (1988), Etchécopar & Hüe (1978), Evans, P.G.H. (1990), Fjeldså & Krabbe (1990), Frederick & Collopy (1989b), Géroudet (1978a), Goodman (1989), Grimmet & Jones (1989), Hom (1983), Johnson (1965), Langrand (1990), Mackworth-Praed & Grant (1957-1973), Maclean (1985), Marchant & Higgins (1990), van Marle & Voous (1988), Meyerrieks (1960), Mock (1976b, 1978, 1980), Monroe (1968), Ogden (1978), Palmer (1962), Paz (197), Perennou (1991a, 1991b), de la Peña (1986), Pinto, A.A.R. (1983), Pinto, O.M.O. (1964), Post (1990), Pratt & Winkler (1985), Recher *et al.* (1983), Roberts (1991), Rodgers (1983), Round *et al.* (1988), Ruschi (1979), Schlorff (1978), Scott (1989), Scott & Carbonell (1986), Shepherd *et al.* (1991), Sick (1984), Silvius (1986), Skinner *et al.* (1987), Slud (1964), Spaans & de Jong (1982), Terres (1980), Voisin (1983, 1991), Wetmore (1965), Wiggins (1991).

14. Reddish Egret

Egretta rufescens

French: Aigrette roussâtre **German**: Rötelreiher **Spanish**: Garceta Rojiza

Taxonomy. *Ardea rufescens* Gmelin, 1789, Louisiana.
Occasionally placed in monotypic genus *Dichromanassa*. White morph formerly considered separate species, Peale's Egret (*A. pealii*). Two subspecies recognized.
Subspecies and Distribution.
E. r. rufescens (Gmelin, 1789) - S USA and E Mexico through West Indies to N Colombia and N Venezuela.
E. r. dickeyi (van Rossem, 1926) - W Mexico.

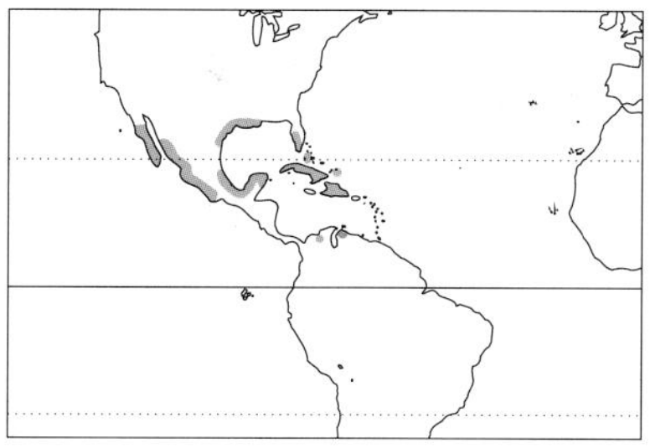

Descriptive notes. 66-81 cm; 450+ g; wingspan c. 117 cm. Polymorphic, with dark and white morphs, both of which somewhat variable; white morph separable from other egrets by size and bare part colours. Two-tone bill and shaggy neck distinctive. Bare part colours brighter during courtship, with lores bright violet. Juvenile greyish brown, pale below, with reddish tinge to neck faint or absent; bill mostly black. Race *dickeyi* has slightly paler head and neck.
Habitat. Typically in shallow coastal waters, salt-pans, open marine flats and along shore. Rarely recorded far from coast, almost always juveniles. Breeds on islands or in mangroves.
Food and Feeding. Mainly small fish, but also frogs, tadpoles and crustaceans. One of most active feeders of family; varied feeding behaviour, but generally chases prey by walking quickly or running; also uses "Hopping", "Open-wing Feeding" and "Foot-raking". Solitary feeder; defends feeding territory vigorously.
Breeding. Almost all year round in Florida, with peaks in Nov-Jan and Feb-May; Mar-Jun in Texas; summer in Baja California. Forms colonies alongside other herons, spoonbills or cormorants. On islands nests on low shrubs, cactus or ground, whereas in mangroves occupies trees or bushes, normally at least 5 m high. Normally 3-4 eggs (2-7); incubation 25-26 days; chicks of white morph have white down, while those of dark morph have smoky grey down with greyish cinnamon head and neck; fledging c. 45 days.
Movements. Pacific birds apparently sedentary, although records from California and Arizona. Population of Florida at least partially migratory; birds arrive in Dec; 1 ringing return from North Carolina. Texan birds move S to Yucatán, Guatemala and El Salvador, returning in Mar/Apr. Post-breeding dispersal along Gulf coast. Occasional in Honduras, Panama, Puerto Rico and N Colombia.
Status and Conservation. Not globally threatened. Formerly more widespread in N America, but suffered acutely from plume-hunting in USA and probably also further S (see pages 396, 399); for this reason disappeared from Florida at beginning of 20th century. Further decline in Texas during 1960's, with 3200 pairs in 1939 reduced to 552 pairs by 1965. Currently uncommon to rare in USA, with estimated 1400-1600 pairs during 1970's, 150 pairs in Louisiana, and 275 pairs in recolonized Florida. Uncommon in Mexico, except in NW Baja California; colony of 150 pairs at Mar Muerto, SW Mexico, in 1970's. In Belize, some small colonies of 5-12 pairs. White morph now survives only in Bahamas.
Bibliography. Allen (1954, 1955), Bent (1926), Biaggi (1983), Blake (1977), Custer *et al.* (1980), Dickey & van Rossem (1938), Hellmayr & Conover (1948), Hilty & Brown (1986), Meyerrieks (1960), Ogden (1978), Palmer (1962), Paul, Meyerriecks & Dunstan (1975), Paul, Kale & Nelson (1979), Recher & Recher (1980), Ridgely & Gwynne (1989), Rodgers (1983), de Schauensee & Phelps (1978), Scott & Carbonell (1986), Stiles & Skutch (1989), Terres (1980), Voous (1983).

15. Pied Heron

Egretta picata

French: Aigrette pie **German**: Elsterreiher **Spanish**: Garceta Pía

Taxonomy. *Ardea (Herodias) picata* Gould, 1845, Port Essington, Northern Territory.
Frequently included in genus *Ardea*. Monotypic.
Distribution. N Australia and S Sulawesi; also New Guinea, Moluccas and Tanimbar Is, where probably non-breeding visitor.

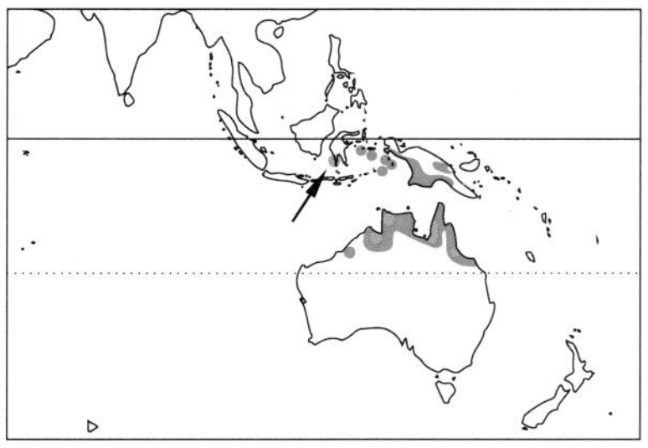

Descriptive notes. 43-55 cm; 210-372 g. Bare part colours brighter during courtship, with iris orange. Juvenile has head all white and white carpal patch, which is only visible in flight.
Habitat. Mainly coastal, occurring in grassland and swamps of salt or fresh water, mangroves, mudflats, sandbanks; also freshwater water courses, lakes, rice fields and sewage ponds. In New Guinea forms feeding aggregations on recently burnt land. Sometimes feeds on dry land away from water. Occasionally up to 1650 m in highlands of New Guinea.
Food and Feeding. Mainly aquatic insects, with crustaceans, amphibians, small molluscs and small fish. Sometimes scavenges or follows other waterbirds and forces them to regurgitate prey. Often feeds alongside livestock. Active feeder, not infrequently capturing prey by aerial techniques, e.g. "Hovering". Diurnal; usually feeds in loose flocks of 5-30 birds, but up to 1100 together at Balino, New Guinea; some records of solitary adults defending feeding territories.
Breeding. Nesting occurs during summer monsoon, mainly Feb-Apr, but sometimes Jan-Jun; at Adelaide R, fairly late in Mar/Apr, when flood waters receding. Generally forms large colonies with up to 1200 nests, often mixed with other herons, ibises or cormorants. Nest is small stick platform in tree, usually mangrove, 2-5 m above water. 2-4 eggs; chicks have yellowish brown to white down with dusky flanks.
Movements. Poorly known. In Australia, sedentary with some erratic movements; regular non-breeding visitor to Innisfail (Queensland) in Oct-Feb. Part of population peforms post-breeding dispersal or migration to Indonesia and New Guinea during Australian dry season between Mar/May and Dec/Feb. Occasional in SE Australia, during flood years; accidental to S Borneo.
Status and Conservation. Not globally threatened. Locally common or even abundant along coastal lowlands of N Australia; stronghold in floodplains threatened by invasion of *Mimosa* and other plants, and also by expansion of feral buffalo, which cause serious alterations to habitat. Has benefited from construction of artificial waterbodies. Locally common to abundant in lowlands of New Guinea, e.g. 2500 birds at Wasur and Rewa Biru, over 1000 on Kimaan I.

On following pages: 16. Slaty Egret (*Egretta vinaceigula*); 17. Black Heron (*Egretta ardesiaca*); 18. Tricolored Heron (*Egretta tricolor*); 19. Intermediate Egret (*Egretta intermedia*); 20. White-faced Heron (*Egretta novaehollandiae*); 21. Little Blue Heron (*Egretta caerulea*); 22. Snowy Egret (*Egretta thula*); 23. Little Egret (*Egretta garzetta*); 24. Chinese Egret (*Egretta eulophotes*); 25. Eastern Reef-egret (*Egretta sacra*).

Bibliography. Beehler *et al.* (1986), Coates (1985), Crawford (1972), Ely (1976), Frith & Davies (1961a), Gochfeld (1976), Marchant & Higgins (1990), Perennou & Mundkur (1991), Recher *et al.* (1983), Scott (1989), Serventy (1985).

16. Slaty Egret

Egretta vinaceigula

French: Aigrette vineuse   **German**: Braunkehlreiher   **Spanish**: Garceta Gorgirroja
Other common names: Brown-throated/Red-throated Egret

Taxonomy. *Melanophoyx vinaceigula* Sharpe, 1895, Potchefstroom, Transvaal.
Until recently considered merely colour phase of *E. ardesiaca*. Monotypic.
Distribution. Okavango Delta, N Botswana, and Caprivi Strip, NE Namibia, through NW Zimbabwe to Bangweulu Swamp, NE Zambia. Possibly also S Zaire and E Angola; formerly occurred in South Africa.

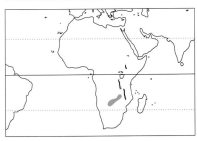

Descriptive notes. 43-60 cm; 340 g. Reddish throat becomes buff in worn plumage. Juvenile plumage undescribed.
Habitat. Marshes, floodplains; apparently prefers extensive shallow inundation zones, especially where water level dropping. Normally in areas with ample vegetation cover, and often feeds in long grass; does not normally venture into open water. Frequently perches on trees.
Food and Feeding. Mainly fish 5-10 cm long; occasionally dragonflies and snails. Normally forages alone or in small flocks of 2-8 birds, rarely in flocks of over 30 birds. Diurnal; feeds mainly by "Walking Slowly" and also "Foot Stirring".

Breeding. Little known; very few records. Breeding noted Mar-Jun. Forms small colonies, sometimes with other heron species, including *E. garzetta* and *Ardeola rufiventris*. Nests found in reedbeds or in thickets of fig (*Ficus verrucosa*), where nest 1-2·5 m off ground; stick nest without lining of reeds, c. 30-40 cm wide and 10-15 cm deep. 2-3 eggs; chicks have blackish down, paler below.
Movements. Apparently sedentary, but some local movements probably connected with seasonal variations in habitat conditions. Occasional in Malawi and Zimbabwe.
Status and Conservation. INDETERMINATE. Uncommon within its restricted, probably relict range; habitat that is thought to be suitable is widely available, and rarity of species as yet unexplained. In Zambia, flocks of up to 30 birds recorded; has disappeared from part of Kafue Flats, due to human control of flooding. Still fairly frequent in Okavango Delta, Botswana. In 1988, important colony of 26 nests in NE Namibia ravaged by pair of African Fish Eagles (*Haliaeetus vocifer*), reducing breeding success to nil.
Bibliography. Benson, Brooke & Irwin (1971), Brown *et al.* (1982), Clancey (1985), Collar & Andrew (1988), Collar & Stuart (1985), Diamond *et al.* (1987), Dowsett (1981), Fry *et al.* (1986), Irwin (1975), Maclean (1985), Mathews & McQuaid (1983), Milewski (1976), Norton *et al.* (1990), Penry (1986), Vernon (1971).

17. Black Heron

Egretta ardesiaca

French: Aigrette ardoisée   **German**: Glockenreiher   **Spanish**: Garceta Azabache

Taxonomy. *Ardea ardesiaca* Wagler, 1827, Senegambia.
Monotypic.
Distribution. Africa S of Sahara except Congo Basin and arid area around Kalahari; also found in Madagascar.

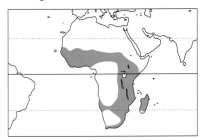

Descriptive notes. 42·5-66 cm. Blackest member of *Egretta*; broad flight-feathers are special adaptation to feeding technique; dense, shaggy nuchal crest. Feet red during courtship, but tarsi remain wholly black (not so in other yellow-footed egrets). Juvenile duller and browner, lacks long plumes.
Habitat. More common on fresh waters, shallow lakesides, ponds, marshes, flooded plains and rice paddies; also alkaline lakes, mangroves and tidal flats. Recorded up to 1500 m on High Plateau of Madagascar.
Food and Feeding. Mainly fish, but also crustaceans and aquatic insects. Catches prey by means of characteristic "Canopy Feeding" (see page 386); normally moves slowly about, intermittently spreading canopy; canopy maintained for 2-3 seconds, sometimes accompanied by "Foot Stirring". Feeds diurnally or around dusk, normally moving off to communal roost with other species. Some birds feed alone and defend territories; others form feeding flocks of 5-50 individuals or more, e.g. flock of 250 recorded at Benamba L, Madagascar.
Breeding. Generally peaks around onset of rains and period of flooding; laying Aug-Feb in Mali, Feb-Mar or May-Jun in Kenya, Feb-Apr or Jun in Botswana, Dec-Jan in South Africa, and Nov-Jun in Madagascar. Colonial: in Africa, normally with 5-50 nests scattered about colony mixed with other herons, ibises, cormorants or darters, sometimes in large colonies, e.g. 1500 nests of present species in huge mixed colony at Chagana, Tanzania; in Madagascar, more often in monospecific colonies, which were formerly huge, e.g. over 10,000 birds at Antananarivo in 1949/50. Nest of sticks usually up to 6 m up tree, but sometimes in bushes or reedbeds; always near or over water. 2-4 eggs; chicks have dark grey down.
Movements. Sedentary, especially in E and C Africa, with some local movements, e.g. present in Sierra Leone only Dec-Jun, and on Zimbabwe plateau Oct-Feb. Accidental to Gabon (Jan, Apr) and at Aswan, Egypt.
Status and Conservation. Not globally threatened. Generally scarce, though locally abundant, e.g. by L Victoria; patchy distribution. Unknown at many apparently suitable sites in E Africa, but seasonal concentrations of 100's at L Jipe and L Bilisa; rare S of Zambezi; in W Africa commoner along coast than inland, with 10,000-20,000 birds in Guinea-Bissau, Oct-Dec 1983. Seems to be particularly susceptible to disturbance during breeding, and many of the colonies studied have low breeding success. Found throughout Madagascar, though rarer in S; marked decline in last 30

years, especially in high central plateau; large colonies of past have disappeared due to human interference, and nowadays colonies rarely hold more than 40-50 pairs.
Bibliography. Altenburg & van der Kamp (1986), Britton (1980), Brown & Britton (1980), Brown *et al.* (1982), Elgood (1982), Langrand (1990), Mackworth-Praed & Grant (1957-1973), Maclean (1985), Milon *et al.* (1973), Milstein & Hunter (1974), Murton (1971), Perennou (1991a, 1991b), Pinto (1983), Pooley (1991), Skinner *et al.* (1987), Stronach (1968), Vandewalle (1985), Winkler (1983b).

18. Tricolored Heron

Egretta tricolor

French: Aigrette tricolore   **German**: Dreifarbenreiher   **Spanish**: Garceta Tricolor
Other common names: Louisiana Heron

Taxonomy. *Ardea tricolor* P. L. S. Müller, 1776, Cayenne.
Sometimes placed in genus *Hydranassa*. Birds of W Mexico often placed in separate race *occidentalis*. Two subspecies normally recognized.
Subspecies and Distribution.
E. t. ruficollis Gosse, 1847 - S & E USA to C America, W Indies, Colombia and NW Venezuela.
E. t. tricolor (P. L. S. Müller, 1776) - NE Venezuela and Trinidad to NE Brazil; Ecuador and extreme N Peru.

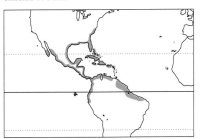

Descriptive notes. 50-76 cm; c. 300 g; wingspan c. 90 cm. Bill and neck proportionally very long and thin. Non-breeding adult has bill and legs yellow. Juvenile has brown neck and generally appears brown and white. Race *ruficollis* larger, has white line down foreneck.
Habitat. Generally occurs in coastal areas, rare inland; normally along shallow saltwater shores, frequenting mudflats, mangrove swamps and tidal creeks. Also freshwater swamps and river margins or lake shores. Up to 600 m in Honduras.
Food and Feeding. Mainly fish; also lizards, frogs, tadpoles, crustaceans, snails and aquatic insects. In South Carolina, USA, chicks fed mostly small fish (*Fundulus*) and some crustaceans. Diurnal; active feeder, with fair variation, using mostly "Walking Quickly", but also "Running", "Hopping" and "Open-wing Feeding". Normally solitary or territorial forager, but can occur in loose flocks of up to 25 birds.
Breeding. Mar-Jun in USA, Feb-Mar or Jun-Aug in Guianas, Nov in Ecuador. Colonial, in monospecific or mixed colonies, sometimes very large, e.g. mixed colony at Drum I (South Carolina, USA) held 1500 nests of present species in 1975. Nests on ground or more often in bushes or low trees, usually 2-4 m off ground; nest is stick platform, constructed by female. Normally 3-4 eggs (up to 7) in *ruficollis*, 2-3 in *tricolor*; incubation 21 days; chicks have dark grey down, white below; fledging c. 5 weeks.
Movements. N American populations generally migratory, wintering S USA to N South America, and returning to colonies of S USA in Mar-May; wintering population leaves Panama early Feb; some birds spend all year within nesting range. Nominate race sedentary. Post-breeding dispersal in populations of N less marked than in other N American herons. Accidental in Canada, Lesser Antilles, Brazil and Azores.
Status and Conservation. Not globally threatened. In USA: common on Gulf and E coasts, where is commonest heron; rare inland, although has bred in Kansas and both Dakotas; scarce in coastal California. Since 1930's has spread N up Atlantic coast, where population estimated at 29,100 birds in 1975, probably highest total this century; estimated 18,300 pairs in Louisiana and Texas in 1975/76. Widespread along coasts of Mexico, e.g. 680 pairs at Tamesi and Panuco Deltas, 300 pairs at Mar Muerto, and 600 pairs in SW Oaxaca. Uncommon to fairly common in Honduras, with winter influx of birds from N; not very numerous in Puerto Rico. One of commonest herons along coast of Surinam in 1970's, with estimated 10,000+ pairs; uncommon to fairly common on N and W coasts of Colombia.
Bibliography. Bent (1926), Biaggi (1983), Blake (1977), Custer *et al.* (1980), Frederick & Collopy (1989b), Hellmayr & Conover (1948), Hilty & Brown (1986), Meyerriecks (1960), Monroe (1968), Ogden (1978), Palmer (1962), Pinto (1964), Plenge *et al.* (1989), Post (1990), Ridgely & Gwynne (1989), Rodgers (1977, 1983), Rutgers & Norris (1970), de Schauensee & Phelps (1978), Scott & Carbonell (1986), Shepherd *et al.* (1991), Slud (1964), Spaans & de Jong (1982), Stiles & Skutch (1989), Terres (1980), Voous (1983), Wetmore (1965).

19. Intermediate Egret

Egretta intermedia

French: Aigrette intermédiaire   **German**: Mittelreiher   **Spanish**: Garceta Intermedia
Other common names: Yellow-billed Egret (*brachyrhyncha*); Plumed Egret (*plumifera*); Median/Smaller Egret

Taxonomy. *Ardea intermedia* Wagler, 1829, Java.
Sometimes placed in monospecific genus *Mesophoyx*, or alternatively in *Casmerodius*; work on DNA indicates closer genetic link with *Ardea* than with *Egretta*. Three subspecies recognized.
Subspecies and Distribution.
E. i. brachyrhyncha (A. E. Brehm, 1854) - Africa S of Sahara.
E. i. intermedia (Wagler, 1829) - SE Asia and W Indonesia N to Japan.
E. i. plumifera (Gould, 1848) - E Indonesia to New Guinea and Australia.
Descriptive notes. 56-72 cm; 400 g; wingspan 105-115 cm. Well developed breast plumes; bare facial skin does not pass eye, in contrast to *E. alba*. Bill black (*intermedia*) or red during courtship. Races *brachyrhyncha* and *plumifera* similar, differing from nominate in bill and tibia colour.
Habitat. Very varied; mainly inland habitats with abundant emergent aquatic vegetation, including freshwater swamps, pools, floodplains, rice fields, rivers and margins of freshwater, brackish and saltwater lakes. Less often in coastal habitats, e.g. mangroves, mudflats and tidal estuaries; also occurs in dry grassland near water, or among cattle in pastures. Lowlands up to 1000 m in Sumatra, or 1450 m in Nepal.
Food and Feeding. Fish, normally less than 10 cm long; also frogs, insects, crustaceans, sometimes terrestrial prey including grasshoppers and lizards; exceptionally birds, e.g. in Tanzania, 1 bird took nestlings of *Ardeola ralloides*. Diurnal; normally feeds alone, but sometimes in flocks of 15-20 birds, occasionally up to 250.
Breeding. Season very variable regionally: in Africa, during or just after rains, or in dry season; in India, Jul-Sept in N, Nov-Feb in S; in Java, Feb-Jul in W, Dec-Feb in E; in Australia, Dec-Mar

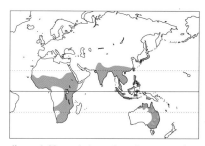

in N, Oct-Jan in SE. Colonial, often alongside other herons, ibises, spoonbills or cormorants; colonies sometimes contain 100's of nests of present species, up to 1500 in India, 2000 in Kenya; in Australia, occasionally single pairs. Nests on ledges, in reedbeds or bushes, or commonly in trees, normally at height of 3-6 m, but up to 20 m. 2-6 eggs, normally 2-3 in Africa, 3-4 in India and Australia; incubation 24-27 days in Africa and Australia, 21 days in India; chicks have white down; fledging 35 days. Bigamy recorded in Australia.

Movements. Mainly sedentary with some no-madic movements; extensive post-breeding dispersal. N populations of nominate race migratory: birds leave Japan in Sept/Oct to winter in Philippines and SE Asia, returning to colonies in Apr; often some birds overshoot and reach SE USSR or North Korea. Australian birds apparently sedentary, but great variations in numbers suggesting significant dispersal or perhaps migration, e.g. 1 bird ringed in Victoria recovered in Irian Jaya (W New Guinea), and possible movements N-S along central York Peninsula. In Africa, mainly sedentary, although some evidence of possible migration, e.g. 1 bird ringed in South Africa recovered in Zambia, and species is seasonal visitor to Sierra Leone and S Nigeria. Accidental to Cape Verde Is, C Asia, New Zealand and Marion I (S Indian Ocean).

Status and Conservation. Not globally threatened. In Africa, widespread and locally common, especially in E, e.g. estimated 2000 pairs on Tana R, Kenya in 1983; also common in some areas of S; relatively scarce in W Africa, but common at Inner Delta of R Niger, in Mali, with 800-875 pairs, and also in parts of Nigeria. Locally common in India, e.g. 1682 pairs at Bharatpur in 1983, and also in S China, Sumatra and Java; in Thailand, much less common than other egrets. Formerly commonest egret in Japan, but pollution and disturbance of colonies have caused marked decline since 1960's. Widespread in N and E Australia, but local inland. More shy and sensitive to human disturbance than other egrets.

Bibliography. Ali & Ripley (1978), Baxter & Fairweather (1989), Blaker (1969), Brazil (1991), Brown & Britton (1980), Brown et al. (1982), Coates (1985), Cramp & Simmons (1977), Dickinson et al. (1991), Etchécopar & Hüe (1978), Hazevoet (1990), Macdonald (1978), Mackworth-Praed & Grant (1957-1973), Marchant & Higgins (1990), van Marle & Voous (1988), McKilligan (1990b, 1991), McKilligan & McConnell (1989), Medway & Wells (1976), Perennou (1991a, 1991b), Perennou & Mundkur (1991), Pinto (1983), Recher et al. (1983), Roberts (1991), Round et al. (1988), Scott (1989), Skinner et al. (1987), Smythies (1981), Sodhi & Khera (1986).

20. White-faced Heron
Egretta novaehollandiae

French: Héron à face blanche   **German:** Weißwangenreiher   **Spanish:** Garceta Cariblanca
Other common names: Blue Crane

Taxonomy. Ardea novae Hollandiae Latham, 1790, New South Wales.
Formerly placed in genus Notophoyx, often alongside E. picata; may be close to Ardea. Validity of race parryi uncertain; birds of New Caledonia sometimes placed in separate race nana. Two subspecies usually recognized.
Subspecies and Distribution.
E. n. novaehollandiae (Latham, 1790) - New Zealand, Australia, S New Guinea, New Caledonia and S Indonesia; probably in process of colonizing Christmas I (Indian Ocean).
E. n. parryi (Mathews, 1912) - NW Australia.

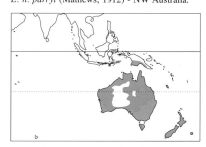

Descriptive notes. 65-69 cm; 550 g; wing-span 106 cm. Underwing appears barred due to white greater coverts. Bare part colours vary, probably with age and season, but not yet well understood. Female smaller. Non-breeding adult lacks plumes of breast and sca-pulars. Juvenile lacks reddish breast and grey plumes of back, underparts browner. Albinis-tic birds known to occur. Race parryi darker above and below. Birds from New Caledonia smaller.
Habitat. Very variable, including almost any kind of wetland with shallow water, fresh or brackish; inland and along coast, where occurs at estuaries, mangroves, tidal mudflats, reefs, offshore islands; also terrestrial habitats, including grassland, golf courses, city parks and orchards. Up to 1500 m, rarely 1700 m, in Baliem Valley, W New Guinea.

Food and Feeding. Generalist diet includes small fish, amphibians, aquatic insects, crustaceans, crabs, worms and snails; occasionally takes carrion (see page 386). Diurnal, feeding most busily early and late in day; active feeder, normally solitary and territorial, but occasionally forms feeding flocks of several 10's of birds, especially in more terrestrial habitats during winter; frequently associates with ibises.

Breeding. In Australia season related to rains and local flooding, mainly Oct-Dec in S, later in N; In New Zealand, starts Jun in N, peaks Oct in colder parts. Normally solitary, but occasionally in small or large colonies, which tend to be largest at flooded inland areas. Nests in trees, 5-22 m up, often over water but alternatively far off; at Chatham Is breeds on rocky promontories or crevices; small stick nest. Normally 3-5 eggs (2-7); incubation 24-26 days; chicks have grey down; fledging 38-42 days. Chicks fed at first every 40-70 minutes, after 3 or 4 weeks 6 times per day, and towards end only at dawn and dusk. Can lay 2 clutches.

Movements. Largely sedentary, with wide-ranging nomadic movements. Most birds from coastal parts of Victoria, Australia, move inland for breeding season. In New Zealand, during winter birds move from exposed coasts towards wet inland areas. Post-breeding dispersal towards S Wallacea, Mar-Oct, e.g. common in Lombok, Flores and Sumbawa. Accidental in Cocos (Keeling) Is, Su-lawesi, Tonga, Macquarie I.

Status and Conservation. Not globally threatened. Commonest heron in Australia; almost ubi-quitous. In Australia and New Zealand, has benefited from clearing of woodlands, conversion of land for agriculture and extensive irrigation. Has only colonized New Zealand relatively recently, with breeding first recorded in 1941; rapid increase during 1960's, and is now commonest heron. Widespread in lowlands of New Guinea and in Baliem Valley, although in 1960's was still only patchily distributed. Has recently spread to several islands of S Indian and Pacific Oceans: small resident population on Chatham Is since 1966; common and probably resident on Christmas I (Indian Ocean); breeding since 1938 on Lord Howe I, and well established on Norfolk I.

Bibliography. Beehler et al. (1986), Bregulla (1992), Bull et al. (1985), Carroll (1967, 1970), Chambers (1989), Coates (1985), Davis (1985a), Falla et al. (1981), Hannecart & Letocart (1980), Hemmings & Chappell (1988), Klapste (1991), Lo (1982, 1991), Lo & Fordham (1986), Louisson (1972), Lowe (1983a), Marchant & Higgins (1990), Mees (1982), Moore (1982, 1984), Recher et al. (1983), Scott (1989), Serventy (1985), Spurr (1967a, 1967b), Williams, M.J. (1985b).

21. Little Blue Heron
Egretta caerulea

French: Aigrette bleue   **German:** Blaureiher   **Spanish:** Garceta Azul

Taxonomy. Ardea caerulea Linnaeus, 1758, South Carolina.
Sometimes placed in monospecific genus Florida. Monotypic.
Distribution. N America, from Massachusetts to Florida and thence to E Mexico and W Indies; also from S part of Gulf of California through Central America into N half of South America, extending S to Peru, Bolivia and S Brazil.

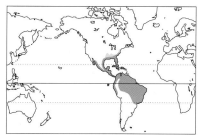

Descriptive notes. 51-76 cm; c. 352 g. General coloration varies in shade; mauve tinge on neck also varies in extent. Bill two-tone, broader at base than at tip, appears slightly decurved. Juvenile all white, with pri-mary tips normally slaty grey, and pale green-ish legs.
Habitat. Mainly inland, in freshwater pools, lakes, marshes, flooded grassland, paddy-fields; also in brackish waters and coastal habitats, e.g. mangroves. Up to 2500-3000 m in Andes, exceptionally to 3750 m.
Food and Feeding. Mainly invertebrates, crabs, crayfish and aquatic insects; also grass-hoppers, beetles, crickets, spiders, small fish 1·5-2 cm long (maximum 8 cm), frogs, lizards, snakes, turtles. Fairly passive feeder, catching prey mainly by "Walking Slowly". Can feed commensally, following e.g. ibises and manatee (Trichechus manatus). Diurnal; normally gregarious in flocks of 15-20 birds.

Breeding. In Florida Dec-Jun, but generally Apr-May in N America; in E Caribbean, Feb-Jul, sometimes to Sept. In small or large colonies, usually in nuclei around periphery of mixed colonies. Nests in trees, 0·5-12 m up, usually near or over water. Normally 4-5 eggs (3-6); incubation 22-24 days; chicks have pale grey down; move about nest at c. 13 days, fledging c. 30 days, but fed by parents until c. 50 days old.

Movements. In N America, extensive post-breeding dispersal towards N, especially of juveniles, with some birds reaching Canada and even occasionally Greenland. Population of USA migratory: birds from E move through Florida towards Cuba; those from W head towards Gulf of Mexico and Yucatán (SE Mexico); wintering birds occur from S USA to N South America. In Caribbean, at least some birds sedentary. Rare migrant to Paraguay, and accidental S into Argentina.

Status and Conservation. Not globally threatened. Common in USA, has had stable population throughout 20th century, although with considerable annual fluctuations; some expansion in New York, New Jersey, lower Mississippi Valley and W Gulf states. On Atlantic coast, 7126 breeding birds in 1976; estimated 81,000 breeding adults along N coast of Gulf of Mexico. Commonest heron in Puerto Rico and Honduras; common in E Caribbean. Fairly common in Colombia, particularly along coast; one of commonest species along coast of Surinam in 1970's, with estimated 10,000+ pairs.

Bibliography. Allen (1962), Belton (1984), Bent (1926), Biaggi (1983), Biskup et al. (1978), Blake (1977), Byrd (1978), Custer et al. (1980), Dickerman & Parkes (1968), Evans, P.G.H. (1990), Fjeldså & Krabbe (1990), Frederick & Collopy (1989b), Heitmeyer (1986), Hellmayr & Conover (1948), Hilty & Brown (1986), Johnson (1972), Monroe (1968), Niethammer & Kaiser (1983), Ogden (1978), Palmer (1962), Pinto (1964), Post (1990), Recher & Recher (1969), Ridgely & Gwynne (1989), Rodgers (1978, 1983), de Schauensee & Phelps (1978), Scott & Carbonell (1986), Slud (1964), Spaans & de Jong (1982), Sprunt (1954), Summerour (1971), Terres (1980), Voous (1983), Werschkul (1982), Wetmore (1965).

22. Snowy Egret
Egretta thula

French: Aigrette neigeuse   **German:** Schmuckreiher   **Spanish:** Garceta Nívea

Taxonomy. Ardea Thula Molina, 1782, Chile.
Forms superspecies with E. garzetta. Two subspecies recognized.
Subspecies and Distribution.
E. t. brewsteri Thayer & Bangs, 1909 - W USA, Baja California.
E. t. thula (Molina, 1782) - North, Central and South America: from NE USA through Caribbean to NE Argentina; and from NW Mexico to S Chile.

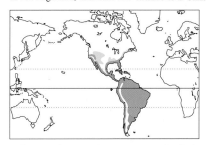

Descriptive notes. 47·5-68 cm; c. 370 g; wingspan c. 96 cm. Feet brighter yellow and, in breeding plumage, bushier crest and more upturned dorsal aigrettes than in E. garzetta. Bare parts brighter during courtship; non-breeding adult lacks ornamental plumes. Juvenile has shorter crest, lacks dorsal plumes. Race brewsteri larger.
Habitat. Wide variety of wetlands with fresh, brackish and salt water; inland and along coast; occasionally in dry grassland or bush. Regular up to 4000 m in Andes of Peru.
Food and Feeding. Shrimps, small fish, frogs, molluscs, crustaceans, aquatic insects, lizards, snakes, grasshoppers. Amongst most active feeders; mostly diurnal. Recorded using wider variety of techniques than any other heron: specialist in using feet to flush prey; typically uses aerial feeding; follows livestock fairly frequently, taking insects that are disturbed. Normally feeds in flocks.

Breeding. Laying Apr-Jun in N USA, Jan-Jul in Florida, Mar-May in Puerto Rico, Nov-Jan in Ecuador, and Oct-Nov in SE Brazil. Typically forms large colonies, sometimes with thousands of nests, often with other herons and ibises; can be solitary at limits of breeding range. Nests near water on ground, in bushes or low in trees, usually less than 3 m up; nest is stick platform 25-60 cm wide. Usually 2-3 eggs in tropics, elsewhere 3-5 (1-6); incubation 18 days; chicks have white down; fledging c. 30 days.

Movements. Migratory in USA, with marked post-breeding dispersal; winters along Gulf coast, in Florida, Caribbean, C America and N South America; some birds remain on Atlantic coast of USA, N to New Jersey; W birds winter in Mexico. Little known about movements of S populations of S America, but some evidence suggesting post-breeding dispersal; increasingly frequent records from Tristan da Cunha (S Atlantic) may indicate some true migration. Accidental to Canada, Alaska, Bermuda and Azores.

Status and Conservation. Not globally threatened. Suffered massive decline throughout range at beginning of 20th century, due to plume trade, and was considered endangered in USA (see pages 396, 399); due to protection, has now recovered former numbers, indeed probably now more numerous than at any other time in century. Nowadays common in USA, and breeding range has expanded northwards up E coast. Breeding population of Atlantic seaboard c. 23,000-32,000 birds in 1976; in Louisiana 26,000 pairs in 1976; in Texas 6000 pairs in 1972. Common in Mexico, with 30,000 birds at Usumacinta Delta in 1972, 3500 pairs at Mar Muerto and 2660 pairs at deltas of Tamesi and Panuco in 1970's. Scarce in E Caribbean and Honduras. Common along coast of Surinam in 1970's, with several thousand pairs; fairly common in coastal Colombia. Abundant in Brazil and N Argentina, e.g. 300,000-400,000 birds at Iguazú.

Bibliography. Allen (1962), Belton (1984), Bent (1926), Blake (1977), Carp (1991), Custer & Frederick (1990), Custer & Peterson (1991), Custer *et al.* (1980), Emlen & Ambrose (1970), Evans, P.G.H. (1990), Fjeldså & Krabbe (1990), Frederick & Collopy (1989b), Hellmayr & Conover (1948), Hilty & Brown (1986), Hom (1983), Itzkowitz & Makie (1986), Johnson (1965), Leck (1971), Meyerrieks (1960), Monroe (1968), Nores & Yzurieta (1980), Ogden (1978), Palmer (1962), de la Peña (1986), Pinto (1964), Post (1990), Ridgely & Gwynne (1989), Rodgers (1983), Ryder (1978), Scott & Carbonell (1986), Shepherd *et al.* (1991), Slud (1964), Spaans & de Jong (1982), Sprunt (1954), Stiles & Skutch (1989), Terres (1980), Terry (1991), Voous (1983), Wetmore (1965).

23. **Little Egret**

Egretta garzetta

French: Aigrette garzette   **German**: Seidenreiher   **Spanish**: Garceta Común
Other common names: Western Reef-egret, Western Reef Heron (*gularis/schistacea*); Mascarene/Madagascar Reef-egret, Dimorphic Heron (*dimorpha*)

Taxonomy. *Ardea Garzetta* Linnaeus, 1766, "in Oriente"; restricted to Malalbergo, north-eastern Italy.
Races *gularis/schistacea* and *dimorpha* often considered to form two separate species. Forms superspecies with *E. thula*. Six subspecies recognized.

Subspecies and Distribution.
E. g. garzetta (Linnaeus, 1766) - Palearctic, from France, Spain and NW Africa E to Korea and Japan; scattered in rest of Africa, Middle East, India and SE Asia.
E. g. nigripes (Temminck, 1840) - islands of SE Asia and SW Pacific.
E. g. immaculata (Gould, 1846) - N & E Australia and regular in New Zealand.
E. g. gularis (Bosc, 1792) - coastal W Africa, from Mauritania to Gabon.
E. g. schistacea (Ehrenberg, 1828) - coastal E Africa to Red Sea, Persian Gulf, W, S & SE India.
E. g. dimorpha Hartert, 1914 - Madagascar and outlying islands; also occurs on coast of E Africa, where has been recorded from S Kenya to N Mozambique.

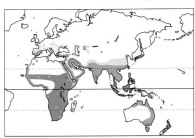

Descriptive notes. 55-65 cm; 280-638 g; wingspan 86-104 cm. Polymorphic, including dark grey morphs usually with white throat; also intermediate morphs with mixture of white and grey. Dark morphs paler than *E. ardesiaca*, with white throat and two nuchal plumes; legs longer, bill thinner, more white on throat than *E. sacra*. Non-breeding adult lacks ornamental plumes. Juvenile as non-breeding adult, but very variable; sometimes similar to intermediate morph adults, with admixture of some brown feathers. Races separated on colour of feet, legs, bill and lores; bill heavier in *gularis* and *schistacea*, and also longer in former.

Habitat. Wide variety, frequenting all kinds of open wetlands with shallow fresh, brackish or salt water, including margins of rivers and lakes, marshes, floodplains, rice fields, irrigated areas, salt-pans, sandy beaches, mudflats and mangroves; occasionally in dry fields, even following cattle. Normally in lowlands, but up to 1400 m in Nepal, 1740 m in New Guinea and 2000 m in Armenia. Races *gularis/schistacea* coastal, mainly on rocky or sandy shores and reefs; less frequently occupies estuaries, mudflats, salt-marshes, mangroves and tidal creeks, occasionally inland, e.g. Nigeria, Rift Valley lakes and Pakistan; in India, usually on muddy substrates, very scarce on pure rocky or sandy shores. Race *dimorpha* also mainly coastal, but also on dry inland savanna up to 1600 m.

Food and Feeding. Aquatic insects, crustaceans and small fish, usually under 1 g (Africa) or 20 g (Israel), and 1-4 cm long, but sometimes up to 10+ cm; also takes amphibians, molluscs, spiders, worms, reptiles, small birds; occasionally scavenges or follows cattle. Diurnal; active feeder, using wide variety of techniques, especially "Foot Stirring". Normally solitary, aggressively defending feeding territory, but frequently in loose flocks; coastal races more markedly solitary. During breeding season, may feed up to 7-13 km from colony.

Breeding. In Palearctic, Mar-Jul; in tropical Africa, most laying during rains; in India, Jul-Sept in N, Nov-Feb in S; in Viet Nam, Jun-Aug (rainy season); in Borneo May-Jun (start dry season); in Australia, Jan-Apr in N, Nov-Jan in SE; race *gularis*, Apr-Jul/Oct; race *schistacea* Apr-Aug. Forms colonies, often with other species, sometimes numbering thousands of nests; *gularis/schistacea* normally solitary or in small monospecific colonies of under 100 nests. Nests on ground or in reedbeds, bushes or trees, up to 20 m up; *gularis/schistacea* also on ledges or rocks or in mangroves. 2-6 eggs, averaging 4·2-4·5 in SW Europe and 2·4-2·9 in Africa, *dimorpha* lays only 2 eggs; incubation 21-25 days; chicks have white down; fledging 40-45 days.

Movements. Extensive post-breeding dispersal. Palearctic breeders partially migratory: W populations winter around Mediterranean, Middle East and particularly tropical Africa; E populations migrate to S of China, SE Asia and Philippines, although large numbers remain in Japan. Populations of Africa, India and Australia sedentary, with some dispersal or nomadism; birds ringed in E Australia recovered in New Zealand and New Guinea. Races *gularis/schistacea* apparently resident and dispersive; accidental to Europe and USA. Race *dimorpha* strictly sedentary. Migratory populations prone to overshooting in spring (see page 395).

Status and Conservation. Not globally threatened. Like other white egrets, seriously persecuted for plume trade; during 20th century, has recovered numbers and expanded range, due to protection (see pages 396, 399). Fairly common in Europe, with population (excluding Black Sea and USSR)

estimated at 19,000 pairs; has increased in France, Italy and Iberian Peninsula. In Israel has increased since 1950's to 2000 pairs in 1980. In Japan, colonies of 500 birds or less, with very few nowadays of 2000+ nests; some traditional colonies lost, e.g. one at Noda, known for over 200 years, disappeared in 1971. Common in Viet Nam; commonest egret in Thailand and Java, where 1000 pairs on Pulau Dua. Local and uncommon in N Africa; widespread and locally common in tropical Africa; CITES III, in Ghana. In Australia, widespread in E and along coasts of N and W, but nowhere common; range has expanded this century. Race *gularis* local in N parts of W Africa; c. 745 pairs on Banc d'Arguin, Mauritania; apparently expanding in Senegal; common breeding resident on coast of Sierra Leone; 80-110 pairs at Inner Delta of R Niger, Mali; not uncommon in Nigeria, with roost of 500-1000 birds at Bonny. Race *schistacea* apparently common throughout range; 130-200 pairs in Egypt; large colony of 1000 pairs at Bhavnagar, W India, 1980-1982. Race *dimorpha* common to locally very common, with 400 pairs in Antananarivo colony in 1981.

Bibliography. Ali & Ripley (1978), Balança (1987), Bauer & Glutz von Blotzheim (1966), Blaker (1969a, 1969b), Brazil (1991), Brown *et al.* (1982), Cezilly & Boy (1988), Cezilly *et al.* (1988), Coates (1985), Cramp & Simmons (1977), Davis (1985b), Dementiev & Gladkov (1951b), Dollinger (1988), Duhautois & Marion (1980), Erwin *et al.* (1985), Etchécopar & Hüe (1978), Fasola & Barbieri (1988), Fernández & Fernández-Cruz (1991), Fujioka (1985), Géroudet (1978a), Goodman (1989), Grimmett & Jones (1989), Hafner (1978), Hafner & Britton (1983), Hafner, Boy & Gory (1982), Hafner, Dugan & Boy (1986), Haneda & Iwasaki (1982), Inoue (1981), Katzir & Intrator (1987), Langrand (1990), Lotem *et al.* (1991), Mackworth-Praed & Grant (1957-1973), Maclean (1985), Marchant & Higgins (1990), Naik & Parasharya (1987), de Naurois (1982), Parasharya & Naik (1988), Paz (1987), Perennou (1991a, 1991b), Recher (1972), Recher & Recher (1972), Recher *et al.* (1983), Richardson (1990), Roberts (1991), Round *et al.* (1988), Rutgers & Norris (1970), Scott (1989), Terres (1980), Voisin (1985, 1991).

24. **Chinese Egret**

Egretta eulophotes

French: Aigrette de Chine   **German**: Schneereiher   **Spanish**: Garceta China
Other common names: Swinhoe's Egret, Yellow-billed White Heron

Taxonomy. *Herodias eulophotes* Swinhoe, 1860, Amoy, China.
Formerly thought to be a white morph of *E. sacra*. Monotypic.
Distribution. Breeds in Korea, E China and possibly also in E Siberia; non-breeders range from Japan to Sumatra and E to Philippines.

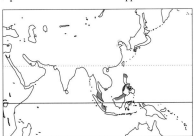

Descriptive notes. 65-68 cm. Separated from *E. sacra* during breeding by bare part colours and ornamental plumes; bill more slender, legs noticeably longer. Differs from *E. thula* in bare part colours, shorter tarsus, and denser, shaggy crest. Bare parts normally much brighter during courtship; non-breeding adult lacks ornamental plumes. Juvenile similar to non-breeding adult.

Habitat. Mainly coastal, in estuaries and bays, feeding in shallow water along margins of mangroves or on tidal mudflats; more rarely rocky coasts, rice fields, marshes, lagoons, salt-pans and rivers.

Food and Feeding. Apparently mostly fish, shrimps, crabs. Prey taken in shallow water, e.g. in Hong Kong, mainly feeds in water less than 7·6 cm deep. In Korea, chicks fed on sardines, shrimps and crabs on average 4·3 times per day. Very active feeder, following outgoing tide or chasing prey with wings open. Usually feeds alone or in small flocks, often occurring alongside other heron species.

Breeding. Starts Apr-Jun, depending on colony. Normally in or beside colonies of other species, forming dense aggregations. Since 1985 breeds only on offshore islands; nests in trees, up to 12-18 m up, but also in low trees, bushes on cliffs, or dense stands of mugwort, 0·4-3 m off ground; stick nest, sometimes with some grass. Normally 3 eggs (2-5); incubation 30-35 days, mostly by female; chicks remain in nest 36-40 days.

Movements. Migratory; probably also performs post-breeding dispersal. Arrives at colonies in Korea in early May, where remains till Sept; Apr-Aug in Hong Kong. After breeding moves off towards Japan and Ryukyu Is; in Japan is regular but rare migrant Apr-Jun and Jul-Aug. Recent data indicate main winter quarters in Philippines, on Luzon, Palawan and Bohol; also in Sarawak, Borneo, and Malay Peninsula, Singapore and Sumatra. Accidental to Aleutian Is, Burma, Sulawesi, Comoros Is, and erroneously recorded from Christmas I (Indian Ocean).

Status and Conservation. ENDANGERED. Total population estimated at about 1000 pairs. Threatened mainly by transformation of habitat; also by egg-collecting, although less important since declared protected species in N Korea. Formerly bred on coasts of China, in North Korea and on islands of Yellow Sea. Driven to verge of extinction by plume trade at end of 19th century, has not been able to recover former numbers (see page 400). Population on W coast of North Korea c. 500 pairs; colony of 429 nests located in South Korea in 1988; small breeding population on islands off Hong Kong discovered in 1956, but last bred 1985; 60 pairs at 2 colonies in Jiangsu Province, China. Now known to winter regularly in Philippines, with concentration of 635 birds roosting in mangroves in Bohol Province, April 1991; 39 birds recorded in Malaysia, Jan 1990; also 8 seen in Viet Nam, April 1991.

Bibliography. Anon. (1989d), Austin (1948), Brazil (1991), Collar & Andrew (1988), Diamond *et al.* (1987), Dickinson *et al.* (1991), Etchécopar & Hüe (1978), Fennell & King (1964), Gast & King (1985), Hails (1987), Howes (1986), Humphrey & Bain (1990), King (1978/79), Landsdown (1990), Medway & Wells (1976), Murton (1972), Norton *et al.* (1990), Perennou & Mundkur (1991), Round *et al.* (1988), de Schauensee (1984), Scott (1989), Thompson (1966), Smythies (1981), Sonobe & Izawa (1987), Vincent (1966).

25. **Eastern Reef-egret**

Egretta sacra

French: Aigrette sacrée   **German**: Riffreiher   **Spanish**: Garceta de Arrecife
Other common names: Pacific Reef-egret/Reef-heron

Taxonomy. *Ardea sacra* Gmelin, 1789, Tahiti.
Sometimes placed in genus *Demigretta*. Two subspecies recognized.
Subspecies and Distribution.
E. s. sacra (Gmelin, 1789) - coastal SE Asia to Japan, Indonesia, Philippines, SW & S Pacific, Australia, New Zealand.
E. s. albolineata (G. R. Gray, 1859) - New Caledonia, Loyalty Is.

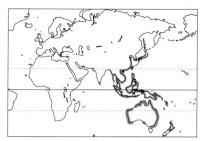

Descriptive notes. 58-66 cm; 330-700 g; wingspan 90-100 cm. Polymorphic, with white and dark grey morphs. Short stout legs and thick bill distinctive; short, inconspicuous crest. Non-breeding adult lacks ornamental plumes and has duller bare parts. Juvenile dark morph paler, white morph similar to adult. Race *albolineata* larger, bill can be partly black.

Habitat. Typically coastal, especially rocky shores, coral reefs and offshore islands; also estuaries, mangroves, mudflats and sometimes sandy beaches. Occasionally inland, but hardly ever far from sea; recorded c. 100 km from coast at L Taupo, New Zealand.

Food and Feeding. Mainly crabs and fish up to 15 cm long; less often molluscs, insects, lizards; also takes tern chicks, or forces adult terns to regurgitate prey. Feeds by day or night, depending on tide; active feeder. Usually feeds alone or in pairs; highly territorial, each bird defending feeding territory.

Breeding. In India, May-Jul, Sept; in Malaysia May, Jun and Nov; in W Java, Dec-Apr; in New Zealand, Sept-Dec; in Australia, all year round, peaking Sept-Jan. Nests singly or in small colonies, up to 20-70 pairs, or 200-300 birds in N Australia; sometimes in mixed colonies with other species; nests on ground, cliff ledges, bushes or trees, up to 3 m high. Normally 2-3 eggs (2-6), in Japan 3-5; incubation 25-28 days; chicks have dark grey down; fledging 5-6 weeks.

Movements. Sedentary, with some post-breeding dispersal: chick ringed at Pulau Dua (W Java) recovered 40 km away 3 months later; several birds ringed in Capricorn Is (off Queensland, E Australia) recovered on coast of Queensland. Some seasonal movements, e.g. large numbers reach Sentubong (Borneo) in spring, or New Zealand with large post-breeding congregations as late as Jun. Accidental to North Korea.

Status and Conservation. Not globally threatened. Relatively common, abundant in many islands of SW Pacific. In Japan, common along coasts with warm currents; still fairly common in Thailand; locally common to very common around Sumatra. In Australia, common along N coast and Great Barrier Reef, becoming steadily less frequent towards S. In New Zealand, more frequent in N, but has declined in last 30-40 years due to transformation of habitat.

Bibliography. Ali & Ripley (1978), Beehler *et al.* (1986), Brazil (1991), Bregulla (1992), Bull *et al.* (1985), Chambers (1989), Coates (1985), Dickinson *et al.* (1991), Edgar (1978), Etchécopar & Hüe (1978), Ewins *et al.* (1990), Falla *et al.* (1981), Gibson-Hill (1949), Hails (1987), Holyoak (1973), Jing Bo (1982), MacKinnon (1990), Marchant & Higgins (1990), van Marle & Voous (1988), Medway & Wells (1976), Perennou & Mundkur (1991), Pratt *et al.* (1987), Recher (1972), Recher & Recher (1972), Rohwer (1990), Round *et al.* (1988), de Schauensee (1984), Scott (1989), Serventy (1985), Smythies (1981), Wang Jiang-nan (1986), White & Bruce (1986), Williams, M.J. (1985c).

26

ssp *coromandus*

27

28

ssp *ibis*

31

32

29

30

ssp *atricapillus*

ssp *striatus*

33

ssp *sundevalli*

ssp *virescens*

ssp *patruelis*

33

ssp *stagnatilis*

ssp *solomonensis*

34

ssp *macrorhynchus*

PLATE 28

ssp *amurensis*

inches   10

cm   25

Genus *BUBULCUS* Bonaparte, 1855

26. Cattle Egret

Bubulcus ibis

French: Héron garde-boeufs **German**: Kuhreiher **Spanish**: Garcilla Bueyera
Other common names: Buff-backed Heron

Taxonomy. *Ardea Ibis* Linnaeus, 1758, Egypt.
Alternatively placed in *Egretta* or *Ardeola*; work on DNA indicates closer genetic link with *Ardea* than with *Egretta*. Race *coromandus* sometimes treated as allospecies. Validity of race *seychellarum* has been questioned; only one specimen in breeding plumage known from collections. Three subspecies recognized.
Subspecies and Distribution.
B. i. ibis (Linnaeus, 1758) - Africa and Madagascar; SW Europe to Caspian Sea; N, C & S America, from Canada to Guianas and N Chile; also NE Argentina and scattered parts of Brazil.
B. i. seychellarum (Salomonsen, 1934) - Seychelles.
B. i. coromandus (Boddaert, 1783) - S & E Asia to Australia and New Zealand.

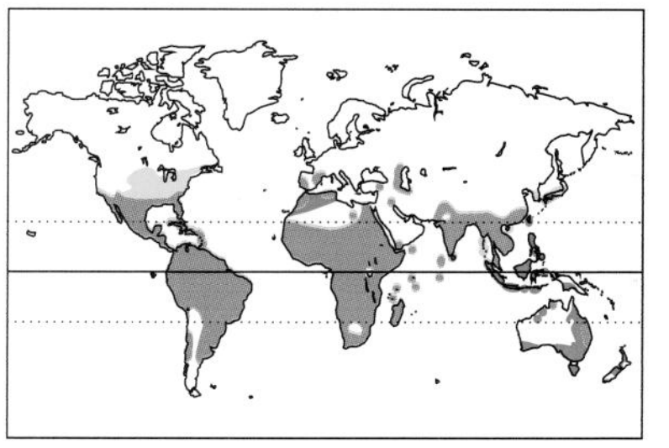

Descriptive notes. 46-56 cm; 340-390 g; wingspan 88-96 cm. Stubby aspect and shorter bill than other egrets. Bare parts brighter during courtship; non-breeding adult has duller bare parts and little or no reddish buff. Juvenile as non-breeding adult, with blackish legs. Races separated on extent and intensity of reddish buff plumage; *coromandus* also larger, with longer, heavier bill and longer legs.
Habitat. Open grassy areas, meadows, freshwater swamps, rice fields; rarely in marine habitats or thick forest. Least aquatic of herons, occurring regularly in wet pastures, dry, arable fields, semi-arid steppe; can remain for long periods in dry land far from water; sometimes in suburban zones or even in towns. From plains up to 1200 m in Sumatra, or 1500 m in India; in Andes, breeds up to 4080 m in Junín, Peru.
Food and Feeding. Mainly insects, locusts, grasshoppers and crustaceans; also frogs, tadpoles, molluscs, fish, lizards, small birds and rodents. Frequently takes wide variety of items at rubbish dumps; occasionally feeds on vegetable matter, e.g. palm-nut pulp. Active feeder, frequently following cattle, large mammals or tractors, whereby captures more prey than if feeding alone (see page 401); most successful when "Walking Slowly" following cattle. In C Africa attends forest and savanna fires, where captures fleeing insects. Diurnal; one of most gregarious of all herons, feeding mostly in loose flocks of a few dozen birds; where food abundant may gather in hundreds or even thousands.
Breeding. All year round in tropics, with different regional peaks (see page 388); in N America, Apr-May; in Palearctic, mainly Apr-Jul; in Africa, mainly during or just after rains; in India, Jun-Aug in N, Nov-Feb in S; in SE Australia, Sept-Feb. Colonial, often with other species; colonies from a few dozen to several thousand pairs, even up to 10,000 pairs in Africa. Nests in reedbeds, bushes or trees, up to 20 m off ground; sometimes in cities, and not necessarily near water. Normally 2-5 eggs (1-9), smaller clutch in tropics (see page 390); incubation 22-26 days; chicks have white down; fledging c. 30 days. Normally only 1 clutch, but up to 3 recorded.
Movements. Extensive post-breeding dispersal. Many populations in tropical parts of America, Africa and Asia essentially sedentary, with far-reaching dispersive movements in search of suitable feeding conditions, often in connection with rains. In N America, populations of E winter in C America, West Indies and N South America; those from SW move mainly towards Mexico. Populations of SW Europe partially migratory, wintering in S Iberian Peninsula and to lesser degree in N Africa. N African breeders fairly sedentary, with some movements S down coast. Birds breeding between Turkey and Caspian Sea apparently migrate to Middle East, Arabia and Iran. Populations of NE Asia migratory: birds ringed in Japan recovered in Philippines; others ringed in Taiwan have turned up in Japan, Philippines, Borneo and Carolinas Is; influx for winter noted in Thailand and Malaysia. Australian populations partially migratory, wintering mainly in SE Australia, Tasmania and New Zealand; some that breed in NW Australia move to SW. Highly prone to vagrancy over long distances, reaching Alaska, Scandinavia, Iceland, many oceanic islands and even Antarctica.
Status and Conservation. Not globally threatened. Has undergone enormous expansion this century, initially through Africa, SW Europe, S and E Asia, but has now colonized all continents except Antarctica (see pages 395, 401). In America is one of commonest herons of warm temperate inland areas, with 37,200-41,600 birds up Atlantic coast of USA, 43,460 pairs in Louisiana and Texas, 17,150 pairs in Pájaros I, Costa Rica; only seasonal migrant to Amazon Basin. Considerable increase in Europe, with 50,000 pairs in mid-1970's, but 80,000 pairs in Iberian Peninsula alone, by 1990. Locally common in N Africa; only widespread in S Africa since 1930's; particularly abundant in tropical Africa, e.g. 63,000-65,000 pairs at Inner Delta of R Niger, Mali, in 1986/87; CITES III, in Ghana. In Pakistan, common in Sind and Punjab; abundant in India, with 16,277 counted in Jan 1990. Common, though not numerous, in Thailand. Most abundant of herons on Java, e.g. 3500 pairs on Pulau Dua. In Japan formerly abundant, has declined since beginning of 20th century. Common in Australia and New Zealand, e.g. 2300 pairs in New South Wales in 1963/64. Has also spread to many islands of Pacific, Atlantic and Indian Oceans and even turns up regularly in Antarctic.
Bibliography. Ali & Ripley (1978), Arendt (1988), Bauer & Glutz von Blotzheim (1966), Blake (1977), Blaker (1969a, 1969b), Brazil (1991), Bredin (1984), Browder (1973), Brown *et al.* (1982), Burger (1982), Burger & Gochfeld (1982), Byrd (1978), Coates (1985), Cramp & Simmons (1977), Custer *et al.* (1980), Diamond *et al.* (1987), Dollinger (1988), Etchécopar & Hüe (1978), Fellows & Paton (1988), Fernández & Fernández-Cruz (1991), Fjeldså & Krabbe (1990), Franchimont (1986), Fujioka (1984), Géroudet (1978a), Goodman (1989), Grimmet & Jones (1989), Grusso & Secci (1986), Hafner (1978), Heather (1982, 1991), Johnson (1972), Langrand (1990), Lever, K.K. (1980), Lever, C. (1987), Maddock (1990) McKilligan (1984, 1990a), Maclean (1985), Marchant & Higgins (1990), Ogden (1978), Ohashi & Kimikuza (1988), Palmer (1962), Paz (1987), Perennou (1991a, 1991b), Ploger & Mock (1986), Post (1990), Roberts (1991), Round *et al.* (1988), Ruiz (1983, 1985), Ruschi (1979), Rutgers & Norris (1970), Scott, D. (1984), Scott, D.A. (1989), Scott & Carbonell (1986), Sick (1984), Siegfried (1971b, 1971c, 1972a, 1972b, 1978), Skinner *et al.* (1987), Slud (1964), Smythies (1986), Spaans & de Jong (1982), Summerour (1971), Telfair (1983), Terres (1980), Visscher (1978), Voisin (1983, 1991), Wetmore (1965), Woodall (1986), Woods (1988).

Genus *ARDEOLA* Boie, 1822

27. Squacco Heron

Ardeola ralloides

French: Crabier chevelu **German**: Rallenreiher **Spanish**: Garcilla Cangrejera

Taxonomy. *Ardea ralloides* Scopoli, 1769, Carniola.
Sometimes considered to form superspecies with *A. grayii*, *A. bacchus* and *A. speciosa*. Monotypic.
Distribution. SW & C Europe eastwards to region of Aral Sea and SE Iran; also Africa N & S of Sahara, Madagascar.

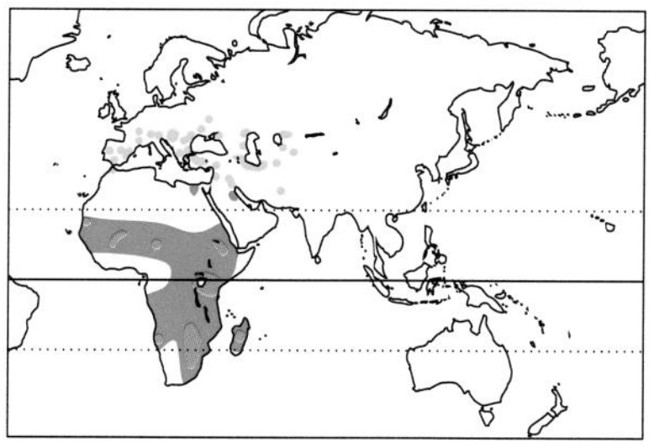

Descriptive notes. 42-47 cm; 230-370 g; wingspan 80-92 cm. Bare parts brighter during courtship, when legs can be reddish. Non-breeding adult dull brown with dark and light streaks, as in other members of *Ardeola*. Juvenile similar to non-breeding adult, but drabber, with more heavily streaked neck.
Habitat. Wide variety of preferably freshwater wetland habitats, including swampy plains, river valleys, deltas, lakes, ponds, canals, ditches and paddyfields, especially in areas with abundant covering of marsh vegetation. Rare in coastal areas, including estuaries, inshore reefs or islets. Generally in lowlands, although has bred on montane lakes at altitude of up to 2000 m.
Food and Feeding. Mainly insect larvae, with some fish and amphibians; generally small prey, up to 10 cm long; also grasshoppers, beetles, butterflies, spiders, crustaceans, molluscs and exceptionally small birds. Mainly crepuscular, but also feeds by day; generally solitary, but sometimes in small flocks with birds well spaced out. Normally passive feeder, hiding in vegetation and waiting for prey to approach; has been recorded using insects as bait.
Breeding. Apr-Jun in Eurasia and N Africa; mainly during rains in Africa S of Sahara, Jan-Aug in Kenya, Jan-May and Jul-Dec in South Africa; Oct-Mar in Madagascar. Usually in small or large colonies, of up to 2000 nests in Tanzania; typically forms small nuclei in mixed colonies. Nests near or over water, in reedbeds, dense thickets (e.g. of willow), or trees; generally low, less than 2 m up (but up to 20 m), and normally more effectively hidden amongst vegetation than in other herons; nest is well constructed platform. Average 2-3 eggs in Africa, more in Europe (4-7), e.g. average 4·4 at Ebro Delta (Spain); incubation 22-24 days in Europe, 18 days in Madagascar; chicks have grey, buff and white down; fledging c. 45 days, 35 days in Madagascar.
Movements. Palearctic populations migratory and dispersive: in Europe, post-breeding dispersal of juveniles from Jul, with birds moving on to winter quarters in Aug-Nov; return to colonies in Apr-May, some birds overshooting (see page 395). African populations mostly sedentary with some local movements; birds from Madagascar regularly cross over to Africa. Accidental from Azores to Cape Verde Is, Seychelles, and recently Brazil.
Status and Conservation. Not globally threatened. In Palearctic, population has shown marked fluctuations (see page 400); apparently on increase at present with total of c. 4000 pairs in Europe: in Italy 30 pairs in 1950, 270 pairs in 1981; in Spain 100-200 pairs in 1963, 800 pairs in 1990. Bred in Israel for first time in 1959, and estimated 100 pairs by end of 1970's. In Africa, frequent or common to locally abundant, with estimated 2000-4000 birds wintering in Guinea-Bissau, and 550-650 breeding pairs at Inner Delta of R Niger, Mali; more numerous S of equator. Common in Madagascar except in S, e.g. 1045 nests at Antananarivo in 1990.
Bibliography. Bauer & Glutz von Blotzheim (1966), Berthelot & Navizet (1986), Brown & Britton (1980), Brown *et al.* (1982), Cramp & Simmons (1977), Dementiev & Gladkov (1951b), Fernández & Fernández-Cruz (1991), Géroudet (1978a), Goodman (1989), Grimmet & Jones (1989), Hafner (1978), Hafner *et al.* (1982), Hüe & Etchécopar (1970), Josefik (1969, 1970), Langrand (1990), László (1986), Ledant *et al.* (1981), Mackworth-Praed & Grant (1957-1973), Maclean (1985), Milon *et al.* (1973), Perennou (1991a, 1991b), Pinto (1983), Skinner *et al.* (1987), Sterbetz (1962), Paz (1987), Prytherch (1980), Voisin (1980, 1991).

28. Indian Pond-heron

Ardeola grayii

French: Crabier de Gray **German**: Paddyreiher **Spanish**: Garcilla India
Other common names: (Indian) Pondbird/Paddybird

Taxonomy. *Ardea Grayii* Sykes, 1832, Deccan, India.
Forms superspecies with *A. bacchus*, *A. speciosa* and perhaps *A. idae*. Monotypic.
Distribution. N Persian Gulf E through Indian Subcontinent and Sri Lanka to Burma; also Laccadives and Maldives, Andamans and Nicobars.
Descriptive notes. 42-46 cm; 230 g; wingspan 75-90 cm. Legs greenish. Similar to *A. speciosa*, but back paler and lower neck browner, less cinnamon. Legs can become salmon pink during courtship. Non-breeding adult similar to congeners; head and neck streaked buff and dark brown, lacks plumes, upperparts drab brown. Juvenile as non-breeding adult, but bill darker.
Habitat. Very varied, including rivers, streams, lakes, marshes, paddyfields, reservoirs, tidal mudflats, mangroves; also in highly humanized areas. Shows certain preference for still waters of small extension. Mainly in lowlands, but up to 2150 m in Nilgiri Hills (S India). Sometimes nests in towns or even cities.
Food and Feeding. Small fish, frogs, crabs, other crustaceans, aquatic insects, grasshoppers, crickets, ants, baby turtles. Analysis of stomachs from Sunderbans (Bengal) has revealed substantial proportions (22%) of plant matter. Normally feeds by "Standing" or "Slowly Walking"; aerial

On following pages: 29. Chinese Pond-heron (*Ardeola bacchus*); 30. Javan Pond-heron (*Ardeola speciosa*); 31. Madagascar Pond-heron (*Ardeola idae*); 32. Rufous-bellied Heron (*Ardeola rufiventris*); 33. Green-backed Heron (*Butorides striatus*); 34. Agami Heron (*Agamia agami*).

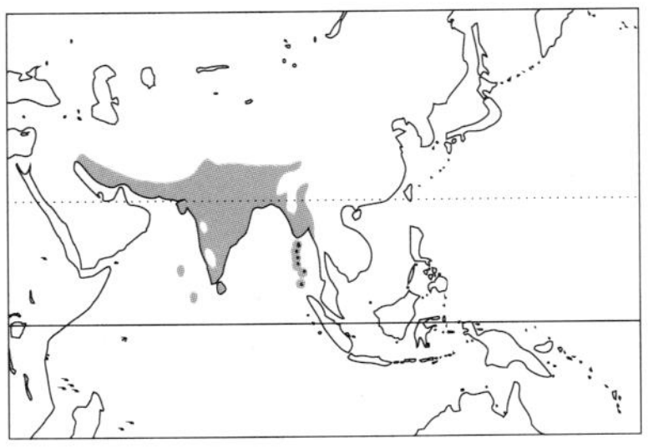

feeding recorded. Solitary or in small, loose flocks; sometimes gather in fair numbers at ponds in process of drying out. Feeds both day and night.

Breeding. May-Sept in most of range, Nov-Feb in S India and Sri Lanka. Colonial, normally in small, monospecific groups; also in colonies mixed with other herons and cormorants, where normally occupies marginal zones; sometimes solitary. Nests 2-16 m up in trees or bushes, not necessarily by water; where no disturbance, birds may use same colonies year after year. Normally 4 eggs (3-5); incubation 24 days.

Movements. Sedentary, with some local movements connected with flooding and droughts. Occasional records from Thailand, Saudi Arabia and Oman; once in Belgium, though origin of bird questionable.

Status and Conservation. Not globally threatened. Abundant throughout India, where is one of most familiar waterbirds; 15,314 counted in Jan 1990. Common in Nepal up to 1500 m; also common in Burma.

Bibliography. Ali & Ripley (1978), Bates & Lowther (1952), Boesman (1990), Cramp & Simmons (1977), Henry (1971), Hollom *et al*. (1988), Hüe & Etchécopar (1970), Inskipp & Inskipp (1985), Mukherjee (1971), Parasharya & Naik (1988), Perennou & Mundkur (1991), Richardson (1990), Roberts (1991), Scott (1989), Smythies (1986), Sodhi (1986).

29. Chinese Pond-heron

Ardeola bacchus

French: Crabier chinois **German**: Bacchusreiher **Spanish**: Garcilla China
Other common names: Paddybird

Taxonomy. *Buphus bacchus* Bonaparte, 1855, Malay Peninsula.
Forms superspecies with *A. grayii*, *A. speciosa* and perhaps *A. idae*. Monotypic.

Distribution. Breeds from Manchuria and E China W to Assam, N Burma and Andaman Is, and recently also Japan; winters in Malay Peninsula, Indochina, Borneo and Sumatra, and recently in Ryukyu Is.

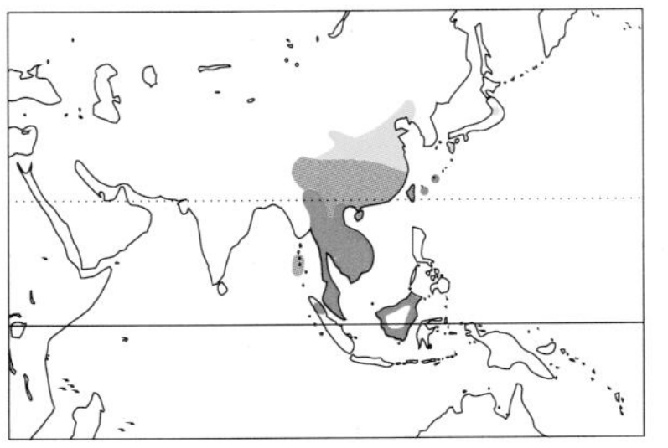

Descriptive notes. c. 45+ cm. Female differs from male in paler foreneck, shorter plumes and lack of slaty patch on breast. During courtship legs become intense pinkish red. Non-breeding adult similar to congeners, and lacks blue at base of bill. Juvenile brown, heavily streaked buff and dark brown, underparts whitish with brown streaking.

Habitat. Frequents paddyfields, swamps, ponds, riverbanks; also in mangroves and at tidal pools. In N Thailand recorded on streams at fairly high altitude; in dry grassland in Hong Kong and Thailand.

Food and Feeding. Small frogs, worms, aquatic invertebrates, fish, molluscs and some terrestrial insects. Little known about technique, but probably most commonly "Standing" and "Walking Slowly"; in Hong Kong recorded diving into ponds from overhanging perches up to 10 m high. Also in Hong Kong noted feeding more around dawn and dusk than in rest of day, although other records indicate regular feeding during day. Solitary or in pairs, sometimes in small flocks of up to 6 birds.

Breeding. In India, May-Jul, Aug; in China, nest records from Jun and Jul; in Hunan (SC China), lays in early May. Colonial, normally forming small colonies, sometimes with other herons; in extreme W of range can breed alongside *A. grayii*. Usually nests high in trees, c. 17 m up on average at Ichang (E China); also nests in bamboos; small stick nest sometimes lined with leaves and grass. Normally 4-6 eggs (2-8); incubation 18-22 days; fledging c. 30 days. Double-brooded.

Movements. Indian birds sedentary, with some local movements. N populations migratory: Chinese birds leave breeding grounds in Sept/Oct, returning in Mar/Apr; occurs in Malay Peninsula Sept-Apr, and in Borneo Sept-Feb. Occasional in Taiwan; vagrant to USSR and South Korea; single adult in Norway, autumn 1973.

Status and Conservation. Not globally threatened. One of commonest herons in E China; colony of 100-150 pairs in Hong Kong. In winter, common in Malay Peninsula, with 577 counted in Jan 1990; very common in Viet Nam and also in Thailand, where 1320 recorded in Jan 1990; apparently declining in Borneo in recent years. Large quantities of eggs and birds taken in parts of China for food; nonetheless, seems to have been expanding range during 1980's.

Bibliography. Ali & Ripley (1978), Brazil (1991), Dun Heng-qin (1987), Etchécopar & Hüe (1978), Flint *et al*. (1984), Li Yung-hsin & Liu Xi-yue (1963), van Marle & Voous (1988), Medway & Wells (1976), Murton (1972), Perennou & Mundkur (1991), Round *et al*. (1988), de Schauensee (1984), Scott (1989), Shen You-hui *et al*. (1987), Smythies (1981), Yan An-hou (1987), Zhu Xi (1986, 1989), Zhu Xi & Yang Chun-jiang (1988).

30. Javan Pond-heron

Ardeola speciosa

French: Crabier malais **German**: Prachtreiher **Spanish**: Garcilla Indonesia

Taxonomy. *Ardea speciosa* Horsfield, 1821, Java.
Forms superspecies with *A. grayii*, *A. bacchus* and perhaps *A. idae*. Two subspecies recognized.

Subspecies and Distribution.
A. s. continentalis Salomonsen, 1933 - C Thailand, S Indochina.
A. s. speciosa (Horsfield, 1821) - W & C Indonesia.

Descriptive notes. c. 45 cm. Back has stronger blackish tone than in *A. grayii*. Non-breeding adult similar to congeners. Juvenile as other juveniles of *Ardeola*, streaked buff and brown. Race *continentalis* separated on longer wing and bill.

Habitat. Mainly freshwater swamps, ponds, lakes, paddyfields and other flooded areas; less often in coastal areas, including mangroves and reefs. Up to 1500 m in Java.

Food and Feeding. Fish, frogs, tadpoles and aquatic insects; also grasshoppers, beetles, ants, termites and earthworms. Passive feeder, remaining motionless for long spells with body crouched and poised, and head retracted; habitually feeds around dusk. Normally solitary or in small flocks.

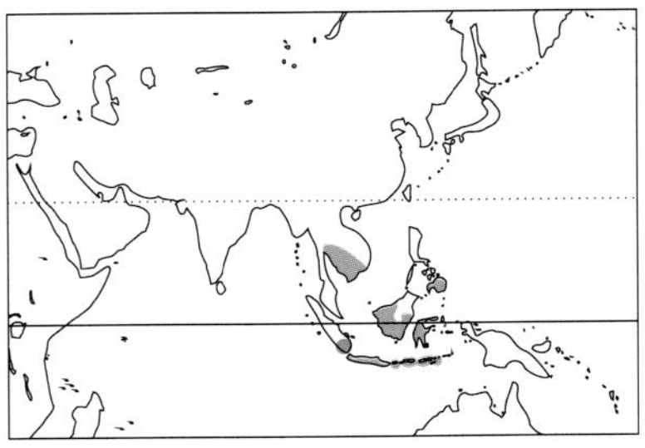

Breeding. Little known. In W Java apparently breeds Jan-Aug, in E Java Dec-May; in Borneo, eggs taken in Apr. Solitary or in small groups, or more normally in mixed colonies with other species. Nests on leafy branches of trees, often over water; nest is small stick platform. Often 3 eggs (2-5).

Movements. Mainly resident, with some local movements, e.g. fairly regular in S Sumatra where not known to breed. Occasional records from Malay Peninsula.

Status and Conservation. Not globally threatened. Race *continentalis* apparently frequent, especially in SC Thailand, e.g. 10,000 birds seen flying to roost at Bang Poo, Sept 1985. Said to be fairly common in Kampuchea, and also in S Viet Nam, e.g. roost of 300 birds at Bac Lieu in Mar 1988. Race *speciosa* very common at L Bangkau in SE Borneo, and common in Bali and Java, with 400-500 pairs breeding in 1970 at Pulau Dua (NW Java), and up to 900 pairs in other years; c. 8500 at L Tempe, S Sulawesi, in Jan 1990. Recently on increase in Philippines, where formerly considered accidental; now regular, e.g. 100 birds at L Buwan in 1982.

Bibliography. Delacour & Jabouille (1931), Hoogerwerf (1971), MacKinnon (1990), van Marle & Voous (1988), Perennou & Mundkur (1991), Round *et al*. (1988), Scott (1989), Smythies (1981, 1986), Sody (1930), White & Bruce (1986).

31. Madagascar Pond-heron

Ardeola idae

French: Crabier blanc **German**: Dickschnabelreiher **Spanish**: Garcilla Malgache
Other common names: Malagasy Pond-heron

Taxonomy. *Ardea Idae* Hartlaub, 1860, east coast of Madagascar.
May form superspecies with *A. grayii*, *A. bacchus* and *A. speciosa*. Monotypic.

Distribution. Madagascar and Aldabra; migrates to C and E Africa.

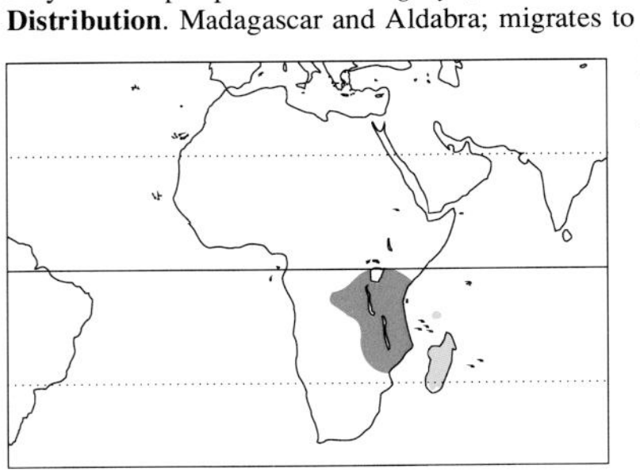

Descriptive notes. 45-48 cm. Typical two-tone bill of genus separates from *Bubulcus* and *Egretta*. Legs rose pink, feet green during courtship. Non-breeding adult similar to congeners, particularly dark on crown and nape and boldly streaked. Juvenile as non-breeding adult, but has fair amount of sooty brown on outer flight-feathers and tail.

Habitat. Shallow water bodies fringed with vegetation or with floating vegatation, including marshes, lakes, ponds, slow-flowing rivers and paddyfields. Typical forest species which takes refuge in trees when disturbed. Outside breeding season commonly along banks of small streams. Rarely found on coastal mudflats or in mangroves. From sea-level up to 1800 m in Madagascar.

Food and Feeding. In breeding zones, fish, frogs, skinks, geckos, grasshoppers and beetles. Secretive, solitary feeder, only rarely forming flocks. On Aldabra, adults feed mainly alongside other heron species. Prey caught mainly by "Walking Slowly" or "Standing" motionless at water's edge, in shallow water or on floating vegetation.

Breeding. Mainly Nov-Dec (Oct-Mar), at start of rains. Colonial, usually in mixed colonies, especially with *A. ralloides*; colonies formerly contained up to 1000 nests of present species. Nests in trees, bushes or shrubs near water, 0·5-4 m up; in mixed colonies, nests of present species tend to be in higher, safer situations than those of *A. ralloides*; nest of interlaced twigs. Normally 3 eggs (2-4); incubation c. 20 days; chicks have buffy yellow down; start to leave nest at c. 15 days, and can feed alone at under 4 weeks old. Normally single clutch, but a second may be laid in Feb-Mar.

Movements. Migrates to C and E Africa; a few birds remain in Madagascar, but away from breeding grounds; relatively common at such sites, May-Oct. First year birds apparently stay in Africa during breeding season. Vagrant to Comoros Is and Seychelles.

Status and Conservation. Not globally threatened. Currently considered near-threatened. Occurs throughout Madagascar; still considered relatively common, but more so in W than in E or S. Has declined dramatically in last 50 years; formerly bred throughout island, but now apparently only in W (see page 401). Decline thought to be due to competition with *A. ralloides*, which seems to be recent colonizer of Madagascar, and has adapted better to humanized landscape, e.g. with transformation of wetlands into paddyfields, and intensive deforestation. Population of Aldabra estimated at c. 100 birds in 1967/68. Uncommon to frequent in wintering zones in C and E Africa.

Bibliography. Benson & Penny (1971), Benson & Pitman (1962), Britton (1980), Brown *et al*. (1982), Burger & Gochfeld (1990), Dee (1986), Delacour (1932), Langrand (1990), Mackworth-Praed & Grant (1957-1973), Maclean (1985), Milon (1946), Milon *et al*. (1973), Pinto (1983), Rand (1936), Salvan (1972a), Thibault & Guyot (1988), Turner (1980b).

32. Rufous-bellied Heron

Ardeola rufiventris

French: Héron à ventre roux **German**: Rotbauchreiher **Spanish**: Garcilla Ventrirroja

Taxonomy. *Ardea rufiventris* Sundevall, 1851, Mooi River, near Potchefstroom, Transvaal.
Frequently placed in genus *Butorides*. Monotypic.

Distribution. Uganda and Kenya S to Natal (E South Africa) and W to Angola, N Namibia and N Botswana.

Descriptive notes. 38 cm. Female duller and browner with buffy white streak on throat and foreneck; lores paler and base of bill greenish or orange-yellow. Juvenile as adult female, with buffy brown streaking on sides of head, neck and upper breast.

Habitat. Seasonally flooded grassland, marshes and floodplains; shallow water along riverbanks, lake shores, stands of papyrus and reedbeds. habitually flies up into trees when disturbed.

Food and Feeding. Small fish, frogs, crustaceans, aquatic insects and worms. Apparently mostly uses passive techniques, especially "Walking Slowly", typically with horizontal stance. Feeds by day, but also said to be partially nocturnal. Usually feeds alone, but sometimes in small flocks of up to 5 birds, exceptionally 12. Sometimes alongside other heron species or other waterbirds.

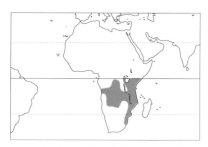

Breeding. During rains or floods: Apr-May in Uganda; Dec-Jan in Zaire; in Botswana, mainly Aug, but also Mar. Colonial, often alongside other herons, storks or darters, usually nesting in periphery of colony; normally forms small groups of 6-30 pairs, but up to 60-80 at L Bangweulu (N Zambia). Nests in small trees or beds of thick vegetation, 0·5-3·5 m off ground; nest is small platform of reeds, twigs and leaves. Normally 2-4 eggs (1-4); chicks have blackish grey down, grey below; fledging c. 24-32 days.

Movements. Basically sedentary, with some movements connected with seasonal flooding: occurs at L Bangweulu only Dec-Aug; at Katanga (SC Zaire) is regular Dec-Nov. Possibly partial migrant, with 2 records in Oct at Amboseli (S Kenya). Vagrant to Nigeria.

Status and Conservation. Not globally threatened. Local and generally scarce or rare. Strongholds in floodplains of W and N Zaire and Okavango Delta in Botswana; also found in coastal lowlands of Mozambique and e.g. in marshes at Salima, on W shore of L Malawi; common in extensive marshes of R Kagera, between Tanzania and Rwanda; 60-80 nests at L Bangweulu in Zambia. Only c. 10 pairs in South Africa, on floodplain of R Nyl in Transvaal; this area included in private nature reserve.

Bibliography. Brelsford (1942, 1947), Britton (1980), Brooke (1984), Brown & Britton (1980), Brown et al. (1982), Child (1972), Clancey (1985), Elgood (1982), Fry et al. (1986), Mackworth-Praed & Grant (1957-1973), Maclean (1985), Pinto (1983).

Genus *BUTORIDES*   Blyth, 1852

33. **Green-backed Heron**

Butorides striatus

French: Héron vert   **German**: Mangrovereiher   **Spanish**: Garcita Verdosa
Other common names: Green Heron (*virescens*); Striated Heron (*striatus*); Lava/Galapagos Heron (*sundevalli*); Little (Green) Heron (Asia); Red/Mangrove Heron, Red Mangrove-bittern (*rogersi*)

Taxonomy. *Ardea striata* Linnaeus, 1758, Surinam.
Sometimes placed in genus *Ardeola*. Races *virescens* and *sundevalli* often raised to full species; form "*patens*" of C Panama intermediate between *virescens* and *striatus*, might be result of hybridization. Thirty subspecies commonly recognized.
Subspecies and Distribution.
B. s. anthonyi (Mearns, 1895) - W USA, N Baja California.
B. s. frazari (Brewster, 1888) - S Baja California.
B. s. virescens (Linnaeus, 1758) - C USA and E Canada to Panama and Caribbean.
B. s. bahamensis (Brewster, 1888) - Bahamas.
B. s. striatus (Linnaeus, 1758) - E Panama and all S America S to N Chile and N Argentina.
B. s. sundevalli (Reichenow, 1877) - Galapagos.
B. s. atricapillus (Afzelius, 1804) - Africa S of Sahara and islands in Gulf of Guinea.
B. s. rutenbergi (Hartlaub, 1880) - Madagascar.
B. s. brevipes (Ehrenberg, 1833) - Red Sea and N Somalia.
B. s. crawfordi Nicoll, 1906 - Aldabra and Amirante Is.
B. s. rhizophorae Salomonsen, 1934 - Comoros Is.
B. s. degens Hartert, 1920 - Seychelles.
B. s. albolimbatus Reichenow, 1900 - Diego Garcia, Chagos and Maldive Is.
B. s. chloriceps (Bonaparte, 1855) - Indian Subcontinent, Laccadives, Sri Lanka.
B. s. javanicus (Horsfield, 1821) - Burma and Thailand S to Greater Sundas; Reunion, Mauritius and Rodrigues.
B. s. amurensis (Schrenck, 1860) - Manchuria E to Sakhalin, S to Shantung and Korea, Japan, Ryukyu and Bonin Is.
B. s. actophilus Oberholser, 1912 - E China to N Viet Nam and N Burma.
B. s. spodiogaster Sharpe, 1894 - Andamans, Nicobars and islands off W Sumatra.
B. s. carcinophilus Oberholser, 1924 - Taiwan, Philippines and Sulawesi.
B. s. steini Mayr, 1943 - Lesser Sundas.
B. s. moluccarum Hartert, 1920 - Moluccas.
B. s. papuensis Mayr, 1940 - NW New Guinea and Aru Is.
B. s. idenburgi Rand, 1941 - NC New Guinea.
B. s. rogersi Mathews, 1911 - NW Western Australia.
B. s. cinereus Mayr, 1943 - NE Western Australia.
B. s. stagnatilis (Gould, 1848) - NC Australia.
B. s. littleri Mathews, 1912 - SC New Guinea, NE Queensland.
B. s. macrorhynchus (Gould, 1848) - E Queensland, New Caledonia, Loyalty Is.
B. s. solomonensis Mayr, 1940 - Melanesia from New Hanover to W Fiji.
B. s. patruelis (Peale, 1848) - Tahiti, Society Is.
Descriptive notes. 35-48 cm; 135-250 g; wingspan 52-60 cm. Extensive variation in plumage, sometimes even within same race. Small size; sexes alike, except perhaps in race *stagnatilis*. Juvenile brownish, heavily streaked on neck and spotted whitish and buffish on upperwing. Most races separated essentially on coloration of head and neck, and on size, Australian races being larger; *macrorhynchus* and *stagnatilis* dimorphic, with grey and rufous morphs; *solomonensis* brownest, *sundevalli* all black with orange or red legs.
Habitat. Frequents fresh and salt water alike. Typically in mangroves, or in dense vegetation along streams, rivers, lakes, ponds or estuaries; sometimes in more open areas, including mudflats, tidal zones and even exposed coral reefs; also in reedbeds, grassy marshland, pastures, rice fields and other flooded cultivation. Mostly in lowlands, but up to 1500 m in Madagascar; in Andes, regular up to 3000 m in Colombia and Ecuador, and even recorded at 4050 m near Cuzco, Peru.
Food and Feeding. Varies considerably with region. Fish, especially mudskippers in some areas, amphibians, a variety of insects, spiders, leeches, crabs, prawns and other crustaceans, molluscs, small reptiles and even mice. Highly territorial, feeds alone; uses wide range of techniques,

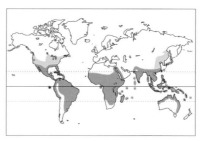

including "Baiting" (see page 387); also performs aerial feeding (see page 386). Generally tends to be crepuscular and nocturnal, although in places daily rhythm is regulated by timing of tides.
Breeding. Season very variable; in tropics related to rains. Generally breeds alone or in small groups, exceptionally forming colonies of up to 300-500 pairs; rarely alongside other species. Nest is well hidden amongst branches of trees or bushes, at height of 0·3-10 m over ground or water. Normally 2-5 eggs (2-8); incubation 19-25 days; chicks have pale grey down, white below; fledging c. 5 weeks. In some areas two clutches, in Galapagos sometimes three.
Movements. Majority of races sedentary, most northerly races migratory. Race *virescens* passes through USA mostly in Sept/Oct, wintering from Florida, S Texas and Mexico to West Indies and N South America, from Ecuador to Surinam; moves by day or night; both sexes return to breeding zones at same time, in Mar/Apr; *anthonyi* winters in W Mexico. In Asia, N race *amurensis* migrates S to winter from S China to Sumatra and Philippines; *actophilus* winters in S Nicobar Is, Sumatra and Borneo. In Africa, basically sedentary with some dispersal of Red Sea population: race *atricapillus* performs some local movements depending on rains, and is erratic seasonal visitor to South Africa. General tendency towards post-breeding dispersal, sometimes leading to irruptions. Also recorded as vagrant, race *virescens* crossing Atlantic or far into Pacific.
Status and Conservation. Not globally threatened. Generally common to locally abundant throughout almost cosmopolitan range; few details available on population sizes, and difficult to census accurately, e.g. 409 recorded in India, 1093 in Malaysia, 359 in Indonesia, Jan 1990; 332 pairs at Sine-Saloum Delta, Senegal, in 1977; race *sundevalli* common breeder on all islands of Galapagos. Rare in W parts of N America; several studies have shown it to be adversely affected by human disturbance and pesticides (see pages 402, 403). Taken for food in some areas (see page 396).
Bibliography. Allen (1962), Ali & Ripley (1978), Baccetti (1983), Belton (1984), Blake (1977), Brazil (1991), Brown et al. (1982), Coates (1985), Cramp & Simmons (1977), Custer et al. (1980), Dickinson et al. (1991), Etchécopar & Hüe (1978), Evans, P.G.H. (1990), Fjeldså & Krabbe (1990), Goodman (1989), Heitmeyer (1986), Higuchi (1986, 1988), Hilty & Brown (1986), Johnson (1965), Kaiser & Reid (1987), Kushlan (1983), Langrand (1990), Li Pei-xun & Zhu Lai-chun (1989), Mackworth-Praed & Grant (1957-1973), Maclean (1985), Marchant & Higgins (1990), van Marle & Voous (1988), Medway & Wells (1976), Meyerriecks (1960), Milon et al. (1973), Monroe (1968), Morris (1990), Niethammer & Kaiser (1983), Palmer (1962), Paton & MacIvor (1983), Payne (1974), Perennou (1991a), Perennou & Mundkur (1991), de la Peña (1986), Pinto (1964), Recher et al. (1983), Richardson (1990), Ridgely & Gwynne (1989), Roberts (1991), Round et al. (1988), Scott (1989), Scott & Carbonell (1986), Slud (1964), Smythies (1981), Stiles & Skutch (1989), Terres (1980), Thibault & Guyot (1988), Voisin (1983), Voous (1983, 1986), Wetmore (1965).

Genus *AGAMIA*   Reichenbach, 1853

34. **Agami Heron**

Agamia agami

French: Héron agami   **German**: Speerreiher   **Spanish**: Garza Agamí
Other common names: Chestnut-bellied Heron

Taxonomy. *Ardea Agami* Gmelin, 1789, Cayenne.
Behaviour suggests link with *B. striatus*. Monotypic.
Distribution. E Mexico through C America and N South America to E Bolivia and N and C Brazil.

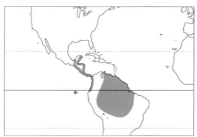

Descriptive notes. 60-76 cm. Unmistakable. Iris pale brownish red, orange or bright red; bill greenish yellow to bluish; legs yellow or greenish. Female smaller. Non-breeding adult lacks plumes of crest and back; bare part colours may vary seasonally. Juvenile drab brown above, blacker on crown and back; whitish underparts, streaked dark on lower breast.
Habitat. Swampy edges of lakes and margins of streams in midst of tropical forest; also seasonal marshes. Normally lowlands under 300 m, but recorded up to 2600 m in E Andes of Colombia.
Food and Feeding. Little known. Mainly fish, including cichlids (*Aequidens*) and in Peru characins (*Triportheus*, *Astyanax*). Feeds alone at edge of water.
Breeding. Little known. Season apparently related with rains: in Costa Rica, nest building at end of Jun; in Venezuela, downy chicks at end of Jul. Forms small colonies, e.g. 11 nests at colony in Costa Rica; sometimes with other species. Nests in trees (mangroves, figs) or bushes, only 1-2 m above water; stick nest with central depression. 2-4 eggs; chicks have sooty black down, skin pinkish with dark bluish area around eyes.
Movements. No evidence of migration. Occasional records in different areas, e.g. E Brazil and savannas in E Andes of Colombia. Absent from colonies in Venezuela and Costa Rica outwith breeding season, presumably moving into denser forest. Accidental to N America.
Status and Conservation. Not globally threatened. Currently considered near-threatened. Status very hard to determine, as rarely comes out into open areas and is difficult to see. Few data from C and S America: in 1960's considered widespread and common in Panama; rare in Colombia; apparently scarce in general, except perhaps along R Juruá in W Brazil; said to be one of commonest herons on oxbow lakes in SE Peru.
Bibliography. Blake (1977), Fjeldså & Krabbe (1990), Haverschmidt (1968), Hellmayr & Conover (1948), Hilty & Brown (1986), Marin (1989), Michener et al (1964), Pinto (1964), Ramo & Busto (1982a), Ridgely & Gwynne (1989), Ruschi (1979), de Schauensee & Phelps (1978), Scott & Carbonell (1986), Sick (1984), Slud (1964), Stiles & Skutch (1989), Wetmore (1965).

35

36

ssp *hoactli*

37

ssp *caledonicus*

ssp *nycticorax*

ssp *obscurus*

ssp *hilli*

38

39

40

41

44

45

ssp *cochlearius*

42

ssp *ridgwayi*

ssp *panamensis*

43

46

47

PLATE 29

inches 10

cm 25

Subfamily NYCTICORACINAE
Tribe NYCTICORACINI
Genus *NYCTICORAX*   T. Forster, 1817

35. Yellow-crowned Night-heron
Nycticorax violaceus

French: Bihoreau violacé   **German**: Krabbenreiher   **Spanish**: Martinete Coronado

Taxonomy. *Ardea violacea* Linnaeus, 1758, Carolina.
Often placed in monospecific genus *Nyctanassa*, for instance on skeletal grounds; this separation from rest of night-herons supported by work using DNA-DNA hybridization. Races *cayennensis* and *gravirostris* sometimes absorbed within *violacea* and *bancrofti* respectively. Six subspecies usually recognized.
Subspecies and Distribution.
N. v. violaceus (Linnaeus, 1758) - C & E USA, E Mexico to Honduras.
N. v. cayennensis (Gmelin, 1789) - Colombia to NE & E Brazil.
N. v. bancrofti (Huey, 1927) - Baja California to El Salvador, W Indies.
N. v. gravirostris (van Rossem, 1943) - Socorro I (W Mexico).
N. v. calignis (Wetmore, 1946) - Panama to Peru.
N. v. pauper P. L. Sclater & Salvin, 1870 - Galapagos Is.

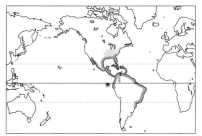

Descriptive notes. 51-70 cm; 652 g; wingspan 101-112 cm. Unmistakable; legs project beyond tip of tail in flight. Heavier bill than sympatric *N. nycticorax*. Non-breeding adult has crown yellower or rusty. Juvenile brownish, with underbody streaked cream and brown, and upperparts brown with narrow brown lines and spots. Races separated on size and proportions of bill, and darker or paler upperparts, with thinner or broader streaks; race *gravirostris* large-billed; race *calignis* has quite distinctive juvenile plumage, very dark and streaked on head; race *pauper* smaller and darker.

Habitat. Very varied, but most typically frequents mangroves, large cypress swamps, tidal mudflats, marshes, riverbanks, lakes, lagoons and rocky shores; also occurs on dry land on small islands. Habitually found along coast, but also inland on margins of rivers, freshwater lakes, pools and reservoirs. In Galapagos Is, inhabits rocky areas up to 800 m, and commonly nests on lava, sometimes even in caves. Roosts in tall trees, sometimes in parks and suburbs of cities, where breeding can also occur.
Food and Feeding. Specialist in crustaceans, particularly crabs, including marsh, mud, swimming, beach and land crabs in different areas; also crayfish, fish, aquatic insects, mussels, snails, leeches, frogs and small snakes; in dry areas takes arthropods, lizards, etc. Generally feeds alone; usually crepuscular and nocturnal, although can feed during day in conjunction with tides. Foraging behaviour adaptable to local conditions, which explains great success of species in occupying wide range of environments. Differences between races in dimensions of bill suggest evolution related to geographical variation in prey species.
Breeding. Laying Mar-Jun in N; continues later in tropics, mostly into Aug, and recorded in Oct in NC Venezuela. Solitary or in colonies of low density, sometimes with other species. Nests at variable height in bushes or trees, including mangroves, pines and cypresses; in Galapagos, race *pauper* occupies ledges in lava; stick nest lined with thin twigs, roots, grass or leaves; nests sometimes reused in successive years. 2-8 eggs, normally 2-3 in tropics, 4-5 in temperate zones; incubation 21-25 days; chicks have grey down; fledging c. 25 days.
Movements. Generally fairly sedentary. Majority of northern population of nominate *violaceus* migrates to Caribbean and C America, occurring S to Grenadines (S Windward Is) and Panama respectively; leaves colonies in Sept, returning in Mar. Subspecific ranges overlap considerably due to effects of post-breeding dispersal.
Status and Conservation. Not globally threatened. Common in USA, although less so than *N. nycticorax*; 540 birds counted along Atlantic coast in 1976; has spread northwards since 1930's, with first breeding recorded in Connecticut in 1953, in Rhode Island in 1972, and in Massachusetts in 1976. In Surinam c. 5500 pairs; common along Pacific coast of Panama, and probably also of Colombia. Exterminated from Bermuda in 1940's, but has been successfully reintroduced (see page 402).

Bibliography. Bagley & Grau (1979), Belton (1984), Bent (1926), Biaggi (1983), Blake (1977), Custer *et al.* (1980), Drennen *et al.* (1982), Evans, P.G.H. (1990), Harris, M.P. (1974a), Haverschmidt (1968), Hellmayr & Conover (1948), Hilty & Brown (1986), Laubhan & Frederick (1991), Lever (1987), Monroe (1968), Niethammer & Kaiser (1983), Palmer (1962), Pinto (1964), Ridgely & Gwynne (1989), Riegner (1982a, 1982b), Rodgers (1983), de Schauensee & Phelps (1978), Scott & Carbonell (1986), Slud (1964), Spaans & de Jong (1982), Steadman & Zousmer (1988), Stiles & Skutch (1989), Terres (1980), Thibault & Guyot (1988), Voous (1983), Watts (1988, 1989), Wetmore (1965), Wingate (1982), Wolinski (1988).

36. Black-crowned Night-heron
Nycticorax nycticorax

French: Bihoreau gris   **German**: Nachtreiher   **Spanish**: Martinete Común
Other common names: Black-capped Night-heron

Taxonomy. *Ardea Nycticorax* Linnaeus, 1758, southern Europe.
Forms superspecies with *N. caledonicus*, with which known to have hybridized in Java, Sulawesi and Philippines. Races *hoactli* and *falklandicus* sometimes absorbed within *nycticorax* and *obscurus* respectively. Four subspecies usually recognized.
Subspecies and Distribution.
N. n. nycticorax (Linnaeus, 1758) - C and S Europe eastwards to C and S Asia, extending N to Japan and S to Timor; Africa and Madagascar.
N. n. hoactli (Gmelin, 1789) - North, Central and South America from S Canada to N Chile and N Argentina.
N. n. obscurus Bonaparte, 1855 - N Chile and NC Argentina S to Tierra del Fuego.
N. n. falklandicus Hartert, 1914 - Falkland Is.

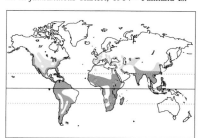

Descriptive notes. 56-65 cm; 525-800 g; wingspan 105-112 cm. Female smaller and lighter, has shorter nuchal plumes. Legs and lores red during courtship. Non-breeding adult has cap and back duller, lacks nuchal plumes. Juvenile spotted and streaked brown, grey, buff and whitish. Races separated essentially on size and plumage variations: *obscurus* is darkest race, large with greyer forehead and smoky brown underparts; *hoactli* has narrower supercilium, and legs salmon pink during breeding; *falklandicus* dimorphic, with"normal" and dark morphs.

Habitat. Extremely varied, using zones of fresh, brackish or salt water. Particularly in areas with aquatic vegetation or on forested margins of shallow rivers, streams, lagoons, pools, ponds, lakes, swamps, marshes and mangroves. Also frequents humanized zones, feeding in pastures, rice fields, reservoirs, canals and fish ponds. Particularly during migration occurs in dry land and along marine coasts. Recorded breeding up to 4816 m at L Cotacotani, Chile. Roosts in leafy trees with thick cover, e.g. oak, pine, mangroves, etc. or bamboo, sometimes gathering in hundreds or even thousands.
Food and Feeding. Opportunist feeder, with very varied diet, including fish, frogs, tadpoles, turtles, snakes, lizards, insects and their larvae, spiders, crustaceans, molluscs, leeches, small rodents, bats, and eggs and chicks of other species. Largely crepuscular and nocturnal, possibly due to competition with other herons (see page 388), but can feed during day, especially during breeding season. Mainly passive feeder, using variety of techniques, especially"Standing" and"Walking Slowly", but also including"Hovering" and"Swimming Feeding" (see page 386). Normally feeds alone and maintains territory, but sometimes forages in flocks, particularly race *hoactli*.
Breeding. Season varies considerably with region. Colonial, sometimes in very large colonies, e.g. 2500 nests in USSR, or 5000-6000 nests at Sungai Burung (Malaysia); sometimes with other species. Nest-site very variable, including trees (up to 50 m up), bushes, reedbeds, cliff ledges and even on gound, as commonly in race *falklandicus*; nest of sticks, rushes, reeds, etc., can be reused in successive years. Normally 3-5 eggs (1-8); incubation mainly by female 21-22 days (*nycticorax*), 24-26 days (*hoactli*); chicks have buffish brown down with darker crown, creamy white below; fledging 6-7 weeks. Sometimes lays second clutch. Sexual maturity at 2-3 years.
Movements. Extensive post-breeding dispersal in all directions, in Europe starting in Jun. N populations migratory. From Aug, W Palearctic birds cross Mediterranean and Sahara on broad front, reaching tropical Africa and possibly further S, e.g. bird ringed in Romania recovered in Mozambique; part of population remains to winter in Mediterranean Basin; birds return to breeding grounds Mar-May. Most N American breeders winter in S USA, C America and Caribbean, returning in Mar-May. NE Asian populations winter from SE China to Philippines and Indonesia. Tropical birds perform seasonal dispersive movements. Overshooting by N populations common in spring, birds occurring much further N than usual; vagrancy also frequent, with records from Alaska, Greenland, Iceland, Azores, Amsterdam I (S Indian Ocean), Micronesia, Galapagos, Hawaii, etc. Migration mainly takes place at night; typically solitary or in small flocks.
Status and Conservation. Not globally threatened. Common to locally abundant throughout most of range; very wide range makes overall population estimate very difficult. Increasing in some areas, mainly due to protection, e.g. at Kualakurau (Perak, Malaysia) up from 4000 birds in 1965 to 12,000 birds in 1986; at L Kinjhar, in Pakistan, population has risen to 5000 birds. Atlantic coast of N America held c. 6900 pairs in 1975; population of inland USA may have decreased; local declines, especially in NE, during period 1940-1970, due to habitat destruction and pesticides (see page 403). In Palearctic, small, scattered populations, but locally common; has increased in second half of present century, after decline in 19th and early 20th centuries, which led to its disappearance from several countries; main causes of decline were habitat destruction and direct exploitation, especially of chicks. Population of Europe, excluding USSR, estimated at c. 44,000 pairs; greatest concentration in N Italy with c. 17,000 pairs in 1981. Species seems to have been severely affected by drought conditions prevalent in Sahel during 1970's, with related drop in numbers at Camargue, S France; however, population seems to have adapted to conditions, and may now winter to S of Sahel; further decline at Camargue since 1983, perhaps due to increased salinity as result of reduced cultivation of rice. Census in Jan 1990 recorded 11,099 in India and Pakistan, 2529 in Malaysia, 2901 in Indonesia, 2404 in China and 1608 in Japan; numerous breeder on Pulau Rambut off NW Java, with estimated minimum of 4000 birds. Winter population of tropical Africa estimated at 70,000-100,000 birds, including c. 10,000 at Senegal Delta.

Bibliography. Ali & Ripley (1978), Bauer & Glutz von Blotzheim (1966), Belton (1984), Bent (1926), Blake (1977), Brazil (1991), Brown *et al.* (1982), Byrd (1978), Cramp & Simmons (1977), Custer & Frederick (1990), Custer & Peterson (1991), Custer *et al.* (1980), Dementiev & Gladkov (1951b), Duhautois & Marion (1982), Etchécopar & Hüe (1978), Fernández & Fernández-Cruz (1991), Fjeldså & Krabbe (1990), Géroudet (1978a), Goodman (1989), Grimmet & Jones (1989), Hafner (1978), Henry (1971), Hilty & Brown (1986), Hubbard (1976), Humphrey *et al.* (1970), Johnson (1965), Kale (1978), Langrand (1990), László (1986), Lever (1987), Mackworth-Praed & Grant (1957-1973), Maclean (1985), Marchant & Higgins (1990), McClure (1974), Medway

On following pages: 37. Rufous Night-heron (*Nycticorax caledonicus*); 38. White-backed Night-heron (*Nycticorax leuconotus*); 39. White-eared Night-heron (*Gorsachius magnificus*); 40. Japanese Night-heron (*Gorsachius goisagi*); 41. Malayan Night-heron (*Gorsachius melanolophus*); 42. Boat-billed Heron (*Cochlearius cochlearius*); 43. Bare-throated Tiger-heron (*Tigrisoma mexicanum*); 44. Fasciated Tiger-heron (*Tigrisoma fasciatum*); 45. Rufescent Tiger-heron (*Tigrisoma lineatum*); 46. New Guinea Tiger-heron (*Zonerodius heliosylus*); 47. White-crested Tiger-heron (*Tigriornis leucolophus*).

& Wells (1976), Meyerriecks (1960), Milon *et al.* (1973), Monroe (1968), Nelson (1975), Nores & Gwynne (1989), Ogden (1978), Palmer (1962), Parsons & Burger (1981), Paz (1987), Perennou (1991a, 1991b), de la Peña (1986), Pinto (1964), Post (1990), Prigioni *et al.* (1985), Qian Guo-zhen *et al.* (1986), Ridgely & Gwynne (1989), Roberts (1991), Round *et al.* (1988), Rutgers & Norris (1970), Scott (1989), Scott & Carbonell (1986), Sick (1984), Slud (1964), Smythies (1986), Spaans & de Jong (1982), Spanier (1980), Stiles & Skutch (1989), Terres (1980), Uttley (1987), Voisin, C. (1970, 1991), Watmough (1978), Wetmore (1965), White & Bruce (1986), Woods (1988).

37. Rufous Night-heron
Nycticorax caledonicus

French: Bihoreau cannelle   **German**: Rotrückenreiher   **Spanish**: Martinete Canelo
Other common names: Nankeen Night-heron

Taxonomy. *Ardea caledonica* Gmelin, 1789, New Caledonia.
Forms superspecies with *N. nycticorax*, with which has hybridized in Java, Sulawesi and Philippines. Race *crassirostris* of Bonin Is extinct. Five subspecies recognized.
Subspecies and Distribution.
N. c. manillensis Vigors, 1831 - Philippines, E Borneo and Sulawesi.
N. c. hilli Mathews, 1912 - Australia N to Java and New Guinea.
N. c. mandibularis Ogilvie-Grant, 1888 - Bismarck Archipelago to Solomon Is.
N. c. pelewensis Mathews, 1926 - Palau and Caroline Is.
N. c. caledonicus (Gmelin, 1789) - New Caledonia.

Descriptive notes. 55-59 cm; 550-900 g; wingspan 95-110 cm. Distinctive combination of black cap and rufous to dull brown back and wings. Very variable, even within same area. Overall coloration pale cinnamon to deep brown; legs range from bright yellow to dusky ochre-yellow. Legs can be bright pink and iris brilliant red during courtship. Non-breeding adult lacks nuchal plumes. Juvenile heavily spotted and streaked rufous, brown, buff and white. Races separated on colours of upperparts and of nuchal plumes; *mandibularis* lacks rufous-white eyebrow.

Habitat. Inland or coastal areas of fresh or brackish water, in areas permanently or semi-permanently flooded; normally in shallow water with forested margins, at swamps, lakes, pools, along rivers, estuaries fringed with mangroves, inlets of sea. Also places with less or lower vegetation cover, including wet meadows, flooded grassland, reedbeds, saltmarshes, dunes, rock or coral reefs and atolls. Up to 1600 m in New Guinea. Also in built-up areas, e.g. urban wetlands, ornamental ponds in gardens; at such sites may roost and even breed (see page 398).
Food and Feeding. Diet varied and adaptable. Great variety of fish, amphibians, crustaceans, molluscs, aquatic insects and their larvae; also eggs and chicks of other birds, newly-hatched sea turtles, mice during plagues and human rubbish. Generally feeds alone, apparently maintaining territory; uses passive techniques, especially "Standing" and "Walking Slowly"; sometimes even feeds by "Swimming". Mainly crepuscular and nocturnal, but can be partially diurnal when feeding chicks.
Breeding. In Australia, timing depends largely on food availability related to rainfall and water conditions; can occur all year round, but mainly Oct-Mar; recorded Feb, Mar, Jun in Java, Feb and May in Philippines. Highly gregarious, forming colonies of up to 250 pairs, or even 3000, but occasionally solitary; often with other species. Nests in trees or large bushes, 20+ m above water; also under rock overhangs, on piles of coral rock and even on ground or in caves, on islands without trees where predation negligible; nest of sticks lined with leaves. Normally 2-3 eggs (2-5); incubation c. 3 weeks; chicks have dark brown down, white on belly; fledging c. 6-7 weeks. Normally single-brooded, but record of pair breeding in winter and then in summer. Sexual maturity usually in third year.
Movements. Apparently essentially sedentary; post-breeding dispersal sometimes far-reaching, has presumably contributed to colonization of Sundas and Philippines. Also some movements connected with local water supply. At least part of population at S of range seems to move N fairly regularly in winter. Frequent visitor to New Guinea from Australia; vagrant to Tasmania, New Zealand and Christmas I (Indian Ocean).
Status and Conservation. Not globally threatened. In Australia, widespread and common in suitable habitat, some of which has suffered alterations. Locally common in New Guinea. One colony in Sulawesi contained minimum of 70 birds, alongside 10 *N. nycticorax* and some hybrids. Reportedly very rare in Java. Nominate *caledonicus* of New Caledonia said to be quite common. Race *crassirostris* of Bonin Is, to S of Japan, became extinct at end of 19th century (see page 400).
Bibliography. Beehler *et al.* (1986), Braithwaite & Clayton (1976), Brazil (1991), Bull *et al.* (1985), Coates (1985), Dickinson *et al.* (1991), Erftemeijer (1989), Falla *et al.* (1981), Greenway (1967), Hadden (1981), Hannecart & Letocart (1980), Hoogerwerf (1935a, 1952a, 1966), Hubbard (1976), MacKinnon (1990), Marchant & Higgins (1990), McClure (1974), Mees (1982), Recher & Holmes (1982), Schodde & Tidemann (1988), Scott (1989), Serventy (1985), Serventy & Whittall (1962), Slater (1987), Smythies (1981), Uttley (1987), White & Bruce (1986).

38. White-backed Night-heron
Nycticorax leuconotus

French: Bihoreau à dos blanc   **German**: Weißrückenreiher   **Spanish**: Martinete Encapuchado

Taxonomy. *Ardea leuconotus* Wagler, 1827, Senegambia.
Frequently placed in genus *Gorsachius*, but is apparently closer to *N. nycticorax*; formerly treated in separate genus *Calherodius*. Birds of South Africa occasionally differentiated in race *natalensis*. Monotypic.
Distribution. Scattered populations in Africa S of Sahara, from Senegal to N Angola, and through Zaire to Tanzania; S from Zambia and N Botswana to E South Africa.

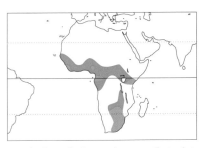

Descriptive notes. 50-55 cm. Inconspicuous white patch on back. Legs greenish to yellow-orange; iris from dark brown, red or chestnut to yellow or amber; leg colour varies seasonally, as may iris colour. Juvenile browner, with extensive white mottling and streaking; forehead and crown uniformly dark.
Habitat. Forested zones with dense vegetation along streams, islands in large rivers, wooded margins of marshes and lakes and also in mangroves; less frequently in reedbeds. Where local conditions suitable can occur in dry regions. In NE Gabon also occupies humanized areas, but generally tends to be very shy.
Food and Feeding. Little known. Apparently feeds on small fish, amphibians, molluscs, crustaceans, flying ants, flies and other insects. Solitary or in pairs, and strictly nocturnal; during day roosts high in trees.
Breeding. Season very variable; in equatorial zone, during rains or early in dry season, when floods highest. Solitary. Normally in trees, low over water or ground, but also uses bushes, rocks and reedbeds; nest of twigs and stalks lined with grass and leaves. Normally 2-3 eggs (2-5); incubation c. 23-26 days; chicks have olive brown down; fledging c. 6-8 weeks. Sometimes lays second clutch.
Movements. Very little known. Appears to perform seasonal movements related with onset of rains, but more evidence required.
Status and Conservation. Not globally threatened. Widespread; generally rare to uncommon, although frequent in some areas. Shy and rarely seen, due to nocturnal and solitary habits, so frequently overlooked; few data available, and real status difficult to assess. Apparent range contraction in South Africa, perhaps due to cutting down of waterside trees and silting up of clear pools used for foraging.
Bibliography. Anon. (1982), Benson & Benson (1975), Benson & Pitman (1966), Blasdale (1984), Bock & Medland (1988), Britton (1980), Brooke (1984), Brown & Britton (1980), Brown *et al.* (1982), Chapin (1932), Clancey (1985), Dupuy (1984), Elgood (1982), Forshaw (1988), Junor (1972), Louette (1981), Mackworth-Praed & Grant (1957-1973), Maclean (1985), Pinto (1983), Taylor & Taylor (1988), Shaughnessy & Shaughnessy (1980), Verschuren & Dupuy (1987).

Genus *GORSACHIUS*   Bonaparte, 1855

39. White-eared Night-heron
Gorsachius magnificus

French: Bihoreau superbe   **German**: Hainanreiher   **Spanish**: Martinete Magnífico
Other common names: Magnificent/Hainan Night-heron

Taxonomy. *Nycticorax magnificus* Ogilvie-Grant, 1899, Five-finger Mountain, Hainan.
Sometimes placed with all other night-herons in genus *Nycticorax*; formerly treated in separate genus *Calherodius*. Monotypic.
Distribution. E and S China, including Hainan; during present century, only recorded in provinces of Anhui, Zhejiang and Fujian (Fukien).

Descriptive notes. 54 cm. Can have white spots on lower back. Female has less contrasted pattern on head and neck, back and wings with more white mottling, and crest shorter. Juvenile has black plumage replaced with brown, and also buff or white spotting.
Habitat. Little known. Well watered areas of heavy forest, sometimes in bamboo; inhabits hills or mountains at moderate altitudes.
Food and Feeding. Very little known. Presumably nocturnal. Recorded feeding alone or in pairs, almost always on ground.
Breeding. Very little known. Almost certainly one nest in bamboo.
Movements. Little known. The few data available suggest that N population moves S in Oct to winter in Hainan (S China); no evidence of wintering further S. Vagrant to N Viet Nam.
Status and Conservation. ENDANGERED. Rare and local, with very few recent records; no information available on population size, distribution or general biology. Scarcity of recent records suggests decline, especially given vulnerability of its forest habitat. As in all members of *Gorsachius*, extensive research and surveys recommended, in order to evaluate status and establish conservation priorities.
Bibliography. Caldwell & Caldwell (1931), Collar & Andrew (1988), Chen Tso-Hsin (1973, 1987), Etchécopar & Hüe (1978), Hancock & Kushlan (1984), Mountfort (1988), Norton *et al.* (1990), de Schauensee (1984), Soothill & Soothill (1982).

40. Japanese Night-heron
Gorsachius goisagi

French: Bihoreau goisagi   **German**: Rotscheitelreiher   **Spanish**: Martinete Japonés
Other common names: Japanese Bittern

Taxonomy. *Nycticorax goisagi* Temminck, 1835, Japan.
Sometimes placed with all other night-herons in genus *Nycticorax*. May form superspecies with *G. melanolophus*. Monotypic.

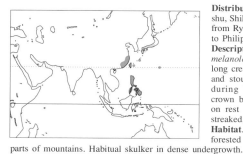

Distribution. Breeds in S Japan, on Honshu, Shikoku and possibly Kyushu; winters from Ryukyu Is, Volcano Is and SE China to Philippines.
Descriptive notes. 49 cm. Similar to *G. melanolophus*, but lacks black cap and long crest; flanks less mottled; bill shorter and stouter. Bill possibly all green-black during breeding season. Juvenile has crown blackish brown and is less rufous on rest of head; neck more spotted and streaked, wing-coverts paler.
Habitat. Rivers and swamps in thickly forested areas, generally occurring in low parts of mountains. Habitual skulker in dense undergrowth.
Food and Feeding. Very little known. Apparently mainly crabs and other crustaceans; also insects and small fish. Solitary or in small, loose flocks. Generally nocturnal, but sometimes feeds during day when dull and cloudy.
Breeding. Very little known. Eggs recorded in May and Jul. Solitary or in small groups. Nests in thick foliage 7-20 m up trees, especially conifers (cedars, cypresses), but also deciduous trees (oaks); nest is flimsy stick platform. 3-4 eggs; incubation 17-20 days; fledging 35-37 days. Can probably lay second clutch.
Movements. Some birds sedentary, but vast majority of population seems to migrate S in Sept/Oct, returning in early Apr. Record of exceptionally early migrant on Palawan (Philippines) on 5 Aug; following year recovered in S Honshu (Japan) on 28 Apr. Occasional records to N of breeding range on Hokkaido and Sado (N Japan), and also Sakhalin (off SE USSR). Sometimes diurnal during migration.
Status and Conservation. VULNERABLE. Uncommon to rare and very local throughout Japan; suitable habitat now extremely scarce. Little information available on status and general biology, due mainly to dense, tangled habitat, together with nocturnal habits. Marked decline in last 30 years; in 1957 still considered not uncommon on Miyake-jima, to S of Tokyo; seems to have been relatively common in places at beginning of century, as eggs and skins were sold cheaply; one such site was near what is now Tokyo's main airport. None recorded in Asian Waterfowl Census, Jan 1990. Uncommon winter visitor to Philippines; only 3 records in Sulawesi.
Bibliography. Austin & Kuroda (1953), Brazil (1991), Caldwell & Caldwell (1931), Collar & Andrew (1988), Dickinson *et al.* (1991), DuPont (1971), Etchécopar & Hüe (1978), Flint *et al.* (1984), McClure (1974), Norton *et al.* (1990), de Schauensee (1984), White & Bruce (1986).

41. **Malayan Night-heron**

Gorsachius melanolophus

French: Bihoreau malais   **German**: Wellenreiher   **Spanish**: Martinete Malayo
Other common names: Malayan/Tiger Bittern

Taxonomy. *Ardea melanolopha* Raffles, 1822, western Sumatra.
Sometimes placed with all other night-herons in genus *Nycticorax*. May form superspecies with *G. goisagi*. Monotypic.
Distribution. SW India, in Western Ghats, S to Nilgiris and S Kerala; Assam to S China and S through Indochina to Philippines; Nicobar Is. Winters in Sri Lanka, Malay Peninsula and Greater Sundas.

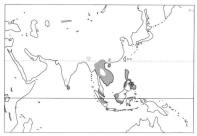

Descriptive notes. 49 cm; 417-450 g. Notable plumage variations between individuals; birds from Nicobar Is smaller. Flight-feathers blackish, tipped whitish. Lores and orbital skin may acquire reddish tone during breeding season. Juvenile densely and conspicuously spotted dark brown and whitish.
Habitat. Lowland wooded swamps, streams and marshes in dense tropical and subtropical forest in areas of heavy rainfall. Up to at least 800 m on plateaux, and to 1800 m in Sri Lanka. In Thailand, resident occurs in one zone of secondary scrub near reservoir. Sometimes forages along margins of cultivation, rice fields and pastures. Also found in reedbeds during migration.
Food and Feeding. Mainly insects, molluscs, frogs, lizards and probably to lesser extent small fish. Solitary feeder; generally crepuscular or nocturnal, but also recorded feeding by day.
Breeding. Very little known. Season during heavy rains; in Assam (NE India), mainly May-Aug during heavy rains; in SW India, May-Jun. Nests in fork 5-10 m up tree in dense forest, but occasionally in reedbeds; nest is fragile stick platform sometimes lined with leaves and grass. Normally 3 eggs (3-5).
Movements. Little known. Partial migrant: population of SW India apparently migrates in Oct/Nov to Sri Lanka; birds from N India and Burma move S in Aug-Oct, probably wintering in Malay Peninsula and Greater Sundas, where may be joined by birds from Thailand and Indochina which are absent from breeding areas between Oct and spring; passage through Malay Peninsula noted in Oct-Dec and Apr; wintering birds in Sumatra Nov-May. Post-breeding dispersal of E populations to Taiwan and Ryukyu Is, where species overlaps with wintering *G. goisagi*, as in Philippines, where present species sedentary. Vagrant to Shikoku I (Japan), Palau Is, Banggai Is (off NE Sulawesi) and Christmas I (Indian Ocean).
Status and Conservation. Not globally threatened. Currently considered near-threatened. Regarded as generally rare, though may be commoner in some areas than is thought. Difficult to see, due to impenetrable habitat and nocturnal habits. Said to be fairly frequent in China; uncommon and local in Japan; at risk in Thailand; 30 recorded in Indonesia, Jan 1990; uncommon resident in Philippines.
Bibliography. Ali & Ripley (1978), Bell (1901), Brazil (1991), Dickinson *et al.* (1991), Etchécopar & Hüe (1978), Henry (1971), Inskipp & Inskipp (1985), King *et al.* (1975), Lekagul & Round (1991), MacKinnon (1990), Marchant & Higgins (1990), van Marle & Voous (1988), Medway & Wells (1976), Perennou & Mundkur (1991), Round *et al.* (1988), de Schauensee (1984), Scott (1989), Smythies (1981, 1986), White & Bruce (1986), Yoshida (1986).

Tribe COCHLEARIINI

Genus *COCHLEARIUS*   Brisson, 1760

42. **Boat-billed Heron**

Cochlearius cochlearius

French: Savacou huppé   **German**: Kahnschnabel   **Spanish**: Martinete Cucharón
Other common names: Northern Boat-billed Heron (*zeledoni/phillipsi/ridgwayi*); Southern Boat-billed Heron (*cochlearius*)

Taxonomy. *Cancroma Cochlearia* Linnaeus, 1766, Cayenne.
Has been placed in separate, monospecific family Cochleariidae (see page 377). Traditionally linked with night-herons, but work with DNA indicates relationship with *Tigrisoma*. The three N subspecies sometimes considered a separate species, *C. zeledoni*; birds from NW Costa Rica, currently placed in race *panamensis*, intermediate between the two groups. Five subspecies normally recognized.
Subspecies and Distribution.
C. c. zeledoni (Ridgway, 1885) - WC Mexico.
C. c. phillipsi Dickerman, 1973 - E Mexico and Belize.
C. c. ridgwayi Dickerman, 1973 - S Mexico to W Honduras and El Salvador.
C. c. panamensis Griscom, 1926 - Costa Rica and Panama.
C. c. cochlearius Linnaeus, 1766 - E Panama to Guianas, and Amazonia S to NE Argentina.

Descriptive notes. 45-51 cm. Female has shorter occipital plumes. During breeding season, lining of mouth, lores and gular skin black. Juvenile has dull rufous back and wings, drab white below with buff or pinkish wash; shorter crest. Races separated on coloration: *cochlearius* palest; *panamensis* darkest; other races generally lavender grey above, buffy brown on throat and breast.
Habitat. Mangroves and other kinds of dense forest along coastal rivers, margins of freshwater creeks, lakes, marshes and swamps. Occasionally up to 650 m.
Food and Feeding. Variety of shrimps, insects, amphibians and fish; also small mammals. Passive feeder, capturing most of its prey using "Standing". Form of bill may be feeding adaptation, since regularly used as scoop, a technique unparallelled in rest of Ardeidae. Generally crepuscular and nocturnal, in line with large eyes; exceptionally feeds by day.
Breeding. Season related to rains: Jul in W Mexico; Jun-Oct in Trinidad; Nov in Brazil; in Veracruz and Campeche (Mexico) and tidal zones of Panama, where aquatic habitats persist during dry season, nesting recorded Feb-Apr. Solitary or in small groups of 5-6 pairs, sometimes in mixed colonies. Nests in mangroves or other trees, 0·4-10 m above ground or water; flat stick nest sometimes with fresh, leafy branches; nest fairly small, but can grow large if used repeatedly over years; nests of other species sometimes used. 2-4 eggs; incubation 23-28 days; chicks have thick, pale grey down, dull white below.
Movements. Basically sedentary. Evidence of some movements, with records outside breeding season along Peruvian coast S of Lima, and concentrations in mangroves in several areas. Casual visitor to N Argentina, and also recorded in Rio Grande do Sul (SE Brazil).
Status and Conservation. Not globally threatened. Widespread, generally found in all suitable habitat within range; no details available on real status and population sizes. Common breeder in parts of Mexico, e.g. Marismas Nacionales, delta of R San Pedro; 300 pairs counted on SW coast of Oaxaca. In Palo Verde National Park, Costa Rica, population estimated at 210 pairs in early 1980's; maximum 400 birds counted by Crooked Tree Lagoon, in Belize; common breeder in Nicaragua. Estimated few thousand pairs in Surinam; local in Colombia.
Bibliography. Biderman & Dickerman (1978), Blake (1977), Cracraft (1967), Dickerman & Juarez (1971), Fjeldså & Krabbe (1990), Haverschmidt (1969a), Hellmayr & Conover (1948), Hilty & Brown (1986), Janzen (1983), Lowe-McConnell (1967), Mock (1975), Monroe (1968), de la Peña (1986), Pinto (1964), Ridgely & Gwynne (1989), Ruschi (1979), Rutgers & Norris (1970), de Schauensee & Phelps (1978), Scott & Carbonell (1986), Sick (1984), Slud (1964), Smithe (1966), Spaans & de Jong (1982), Stiles & Skutch (1989), Thibault & Guyot (1988), Voous (1983), Wetmore (1965).

Subfamily TIGRISOMATINAE

Genus *TIGRISOMA*   Swainson, 1827

43. **Bare-throated Tiger-heron**

Tigrisoma mexicanum

French: Onoré du Mexique   **German**: Nacktkehlreiher   **Spanish**: Avetigre Mejicana
Other common names: Cabanis's/Mexican Tiger-heron/Tiger-bittern

Taxonomy. *Tigrisoma mexicana* Swainson, 1834, Real del Monte, Hidalgo, Mexico.
Upland population of Sonora and Sinaloa (S Mexico) formerly assigned separate subspecies *fremitus*. Monotypic.
Distribution. Coastal W and E Mexico through C America to NW Colombia.
Descriptive notes. 71-81 cm. Only *Tigrisoma* with bare throat, bright yellow to orange during breeding. Some individuals larger, with broader striping. Iris can be bordered with silver and black. Juvenile boldly barred and spotted cinnamon-buff and fuscous brown; wings and tail blackish with narrow white bars.

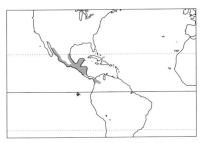

Habitat. Normally coastal zones of salt or brackish water, especially mangroves; also inland, in marshes, swamps of tropical zone, and on freshwater streams and wooded rivers in uplands. Up to 440 m on Sonora-Sinaloa border (S Mexico), and up to 1000 m in Honduras.

Food and Feeding. Fish, frogs and crustaceans. Generally feeds alone, but forms small flocks at favourable sites. Apparently crepuscular or nocturnal; feeds mainly by remaining motionless and waiting, or by "Walking Slowly".

Breeding. Season variable, ranging from Feb in Panama to Jul in El Salvador. Normally nests in trees, on horizontal branches 6-15 m over water, but also on low branches only 4 m up, in trees over sea cliffs; nest is large stick platform. 1-3 eggs; chicks have pale greyish white down.

Movements. Apparently sedentary.

Status and Conservation. Not globally threatened. No information available on overall status and population size. Widespread and fairly common in Honduras in 1960's; supposedly common in Belize, Guatemala and Nicaragua; also in Costa Rica, where 30 pairs breed at Estero Madrigal.

Bibliography. Blake (1977), Dickey & van Rossem (1938), Edwards (1989), Hilty & Brown (1986), Land (1970), Lowery & Dalquest (1951), Monroe (1968), Peterson & Chalif (1973), Ridgely & Gwynne (1989), Schaldach (1963), Scott & Carbonell (1986), Slud (1964), Smithe (1966), Stiles & Skutch (1989), Sutton *et al.* (1950), Wetmore (1965).

44. Fasciated Tiger-heron
Tigrisoma fasciatum

French: Onoré fascié   **German**: Streifenreiher   **Spanish**: Avetigre Oscura
Other common names: Salmon's Tiger-heron

Taxonomy. *Ardea Fasciata* Such, 1825, Brazil.
Three subspecies recognized.
Subspecies and Distribution.
T. f. salmoni P. L. Sclater & Salvin, 1875 - Costa Rica E to Venezuela and S to N Bolivia.
T. f. fasciatum (Such, 1825) - SE Brazil and NE Argentina.
T. f. pallescens Olrog, 1950 - NW Argentina.

Descriptive notes. 61-71 cm. Colour of facial skin variable; lower mandible can be yellowish green. Juvenile generally duller, more prominently banded blackish and pale buff; whiter below, recalling juvenile *T. lineatum*, but bill shorter and stouter, appearing more curved. Races separated on measurements, coloration and feathering on mandible: *pallescens* large, paler; has strip of feathering over base of lower mandible; *salmoni* smaller, lacks mandibular feathering.

Habitat. Occurs in wet premontane forest; generally found along creeks, streams and fast-flowing rivers with sand or gravel banks and forested margins.

Food and Feeding. Very little known. Stomach contents included armoured catfish (Loricariidae) and water bug. Normally feeds alone and is presumably nocturnal.

Breeding. No information available.

Movements. Sedentary. In Andes, regular dispersal, mostly of juveniles, to temperate zone; in Peru, occurs up to 3300 m in semi-arid valleys of Cuzco, and possibly also in Ayacucho and Apurimac.

Status and Conservation. Not globally threatened. Currently considered near-threatened, but no information available on overall status or population size; said to be local and uncommon; presence in some parts of supposed range has not yet been confirmed. Legally protected in Brazil. Rare and patchy in Colombia. Nominate *fasciatum* very rare or perhaps even extinct in many parts of its range in SE Brazil, due to forest destruction; evidence suggests may never have been numerous; included in previous Red Data Book (1978/79), where placed in category Indeterminate, due to scarcity of observations. Race *pallescens* of Salta and Tucumán Provinces, Argentina, even less known; may also be at risk.

Bibliography. Belton (1984), Blake (1977), Butler (1979), Eisenmann (1965), Fjeldså & Krabbe (1990), Hellmayr & Conover (1948), Hilty & Brown (1986), King (1978/79), Parker *et al.* (1982), de la Peña (1986), Pinto (1964), Remsen & Traylor (1989), Ridgely & Gwynne (1989), Ruschi (1979), de Schauensee & Phelps (1978), Scott & Carbonell (1986), Sick (1984), Slud (1964), Stiles & Skutch (1989), Todd & Carriker (1922), Vides-Almonacid (1988), Wetmore (1965), Yamashita & Valle (1990).

45. Rufescent Tiger-heron
Tigrisoma lineatum

French: Onoré rayé   **German**: Marmorreiher   **Spanish**: Avetigre Colorada
Other common names: Lined/Banded Tiger-heron

Taxonomy. *Ardea lineata* Boddaert, 1783, Cayenne.
Two subspecies recognized.
Subspecies and Distribution.
T. l. lineatum (Boddaert, 1783) - SE Mexico to W Ecuador and E through Amazonia to N Bolivia, E Brazil and NE Argentina.
T. l. marmoratum (Vieillot, 1817) - C Bolivia to E Brazil and S to NE Argentina.
Descriptive notes. 66-76 cm. Bare part colours very variable. Unmistakable, with rich chestnut head and neck, white-banded flanks and long tarsus. Juvenile bright cinnamon buff with black

barring; later as adult, but black barring on neck only disappears gradually. Race *marmoratum* larger, with gular feathering over base of lower mandible, as in *T. fasciatum*.

Habitat. Typically found along wooded banks of slow-flowing rivers, and in swamps and marshes of tropical zone; also in mangroves, and sometimes occurs in hilly areas.

Food and Feeding. Little known. Fish, aquatic insects, crustaceans, grasshoppers, water beetles and dragonfly larvae and imagines; occasionally colubrid snakes. Feeds by means of "Standing" in streams, creeks and patches of open water in marshes. Solitary or in pairs, rarely in flocks. Mostly crepuscular and nocturnal, but also feeds by day.

Breeding. Little known. Nests quite high up in trees, although ground-nest recorded in captive birds; nest in large platform of sticks. In captivity: 3 eggs; incubation 31-34 days, by female only; chicks have white down.

Movements. Sedentary.

Status and Conservation. Not globally threatened. No information available on overall status and population size. Said to be common breeder in parts of Nicaragua; estimated 15 breeding pairs at lagoons of R Cañas, in Costa Rica. Thinly spread over much of Colombia, but commoner in *llanos*; locally common too in *llanos* of Venezuela, and 64 individuals seen at Hato el Frio in 1984; uncommon in Peru.

Bibliography. Belton (1984), Blake (1977), Carp (1991), Haedo Rossi (1958), Haverschmidt (1968), Hellmayr & Conover (1948), Hilty & Brown (1986), Klimaitis & Moschione (1987), de Kondo (1987), Monroe (1968), de la Peña (1986), Pinto (1964), Power *et al.* (1989), Ridgely & Gwynne (1989), Ruschi (1979), de Schauensee & Phelps (1978), Scott & Carbonell (1986), Sick (1984), Slud (1964), Smithe (1966), Sobrinho (1932), Stiles & Skutch (1989), Wetmore (1926, 1965).

Genus *ZONERODIUS*   Salvadori, 1882

46. New Guinea Tiger-heron
Zonerodius heliosylus

French: Onoré phaéton   **German**: Bindenreiher   **Spanish**: Avetigre Papúa
Other common names: New Guinea/Forest/Zebra Bittern

Taxonomy. *Ardea Heliosyla* Lesson, 1828, New Guinea.
Monotypic.
Distribution. Restricted to New Guinea and some of larger islands adjacent to W coast, including Salawati; Aru Is.

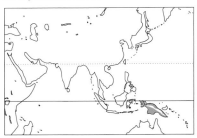

Descriptive notes. 65-71 cm. Whitish rump. No information available on seasonal variation or juvenile plumage. Little known, but has been claimed that female often has legs more uniform greenish yellow, lores and orbital skin greener and pearly greenish tinge below bill.

Habitat. Little known. Always found along streams and rivers or by pools and swamps in densely forested areas; mainly occurs at 100-300 m above sea-level, but recorded up to 1430 m.

Food and Feeding. Very little known. Diet includes crayfish and other crustaceans, small fish, beetles, snakes and lizards. Feeds alone at water's edge, hidden amidst vegetation.

Breeding. Very little information. Season presumably related to monsoon; in S of central mountain ridge, probably Apr-Jun. Nest discovered in N Irian Jaya in mid-Apr, containing single chick with yellowish white down; nest c. 12 m up tree beside stream; nest made of sticks and twigs.

Movements. No evidence of any kind of movements.

Status and Conservation. Not globally threatened. Now considered near-threatened. Presumably very rare and localized, with few, scattered observations throughout 20th century. Most records from extreme W of Irian Jaya, but no recent sightings in area of Port Moresby, where 3 specimens taken last century. See page 401.

Bibliography. Beehler (1978), Beehler *et al.* (1986), Coates (1985), Hancock & Kushlan (1984), Payne & Risley (1976), Peckover & Filewood (1976), Rand & Gilliard (1967), Soothill & Soothill (1982).

Genus *TIGRIORNIS*   Sharpe, 1895

47. White-crested Tiger-heron
Tigriornis leucolophus

French: Onoré à huppe blanche   **German**: Weißschopfreiher   **Spanish**: Avetigre Africana
Other common names: White-crested (Tiger-)Bittern, African Bittern

Taxonomy. *Tigrisoma leucolopha* Jardine, 1846, Old Calabar River or Bonny River, Nigeria.
Monotypic.

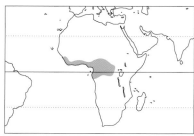

Distribution. Equatorial rain forest belt of W Africa, from Sierra Leone E to Cameroon, Gabon, Zaire and Central African Republic.

Descriptive notes. 66-80 cm. White crest often half-hidden by other feathers. Appears more slender than large bitterns. Female gives overall impression of being darker, due to narrower buff barring above; duller pinkish cinnamon below; bill and wings tend to be smaller. Juvenile has much broader barring; generally appears more sandy or rufous.

Habitat. Typically found at small streams, marshes or swampy areas inside dense primary forest. Also on forested riverbanks and in tangled mangrove swamps.

Food and Feeding. Small fish, crustaceans, spiders, insects, frogs, snakes and lizards. Solitary; partially nocturnal, and active mainly around dawn and dusk.

Breeding. Little known. Season varies locally, tending to coincide with rains; apparently mostly May-Jul in W of range, Nov-Jan in E, where period of chick-feeding coincides with peak water levels. Solitary. Only nest found to date was fragile platform of twigs 6 m up tree; contained 1 egg. Incubation at least 29 days, possibly more; chicks have yellowish down, soon replaced with white down.

Movements. Basically sedentary. Certain indications of vagrancy or some form of migratory movement.

Status and Conservation. Not globally threatened. Generally uncommon to rare, though apparently less so in parts of Gabon and basin of R Zaire. Very difficult to see, and consequently little information available on status, population size and general biology. Has disappeared from some localities in E Zaire due to habitat destruction.

Bibliography. Brosset (1971), Brosset & Erard (1986), Brown *et al.* (1982), Chapin (1932), Elgood (1982), Fishpool *et al.* (1989), Hancock & Kushlan (1984), Lippens & Wille (1976), Mackworth-Praed & Grant (1957-1973), Payne & Risley (1976), Pinto (1983), Soothill & Soothill (1982).

48

49

50 ♂ ♀

♀ ssp *minutus* ♂ 51 ♂ ssp *dubius* 52

♀ 53 ♂ 54 ♂ ♀

PLATE 30

inches 8

cm 20

55 56

57

58 59 60

Subfamily BOTAURINAE

Tribe ZEBRILINI

Genus *ZEBRILUS*   Bonaparte, 1855

48. **Zigzag Heron**

Zebrilus undulatus

French: Onoré zigzag   **German**: Zickzackreiher   **Spanish**: Avetigre Enana
Other common names: Vermiculated Heron

Taxonomy. *Ardea undulata* Gmelin, 1789, Cayenne.
Monotypic.
Distribution. Poorly known. Basins of Orinoco, Negro and Amazon: E Colombia through Venezuela to Guianas and NC Brazil, extending SW to E Peru and NE Bolivia.

Descriptive notes. 28-33 cm. Leg colour variable. Juvenile rufous, especially on dorsal vermiculations, forehead, face, side of neck and foreneck.
Habitat. Streams, pools, marshes and swamps in tropical evergreen forest; also recorded in mangroves.
Food and Feeding. Very little known. Recorded taking small fish and flying insects. Main activity apparently occurs during day. Typically fishes from branches hanging over water or emergent roots of trees, and also from within water; techniques unknown, but probably involve remaining motionless or moving slowly about; performs peculiar "Tail-flicking" during feeding sessions.
Breeding. No information available.
Movements. No information available.
Status and Conservation. Not globally threatened. Until very recently, considered Threatened, classed as Insufficiently Known. Scarce but widespread. Least known member of heron family, with few recent records. Nothing known of population size; rare and local in Colombia. Uncontrolled hunting may be a problem, e.g. in Venezuela.
Bibliography. Bates *et al.* (1989), Blake (1977), Collar & Andrew (1988), Davis *et al.* (1980), Hellmayr & Conover (1948), Hilty & Brown (1986), Mathews & Brooke (1988), Norton *et al.* (1990), Payne & Risley (1976), Pinto (1964), Ruschi (1979), de Schauensee & Phelps (1978), Scott & Carbonell (1986), Sick (1984), Snyder (1966).

Tribe BOTAURINI

Genus *IXOBRYCHUS*   Billberg, 1828

49. **Stripe-backed Bittern**

Ixobrychus involucris

French: Blongios varié   **German**: Streifendommel   **Spanish**: Avetorillo Listado
Other common names: Streaked/Azara's/Pygmy Bittern, Little Red/Variegated Heron

Taxonomy. *Ardea involucris* Vieillot, 1823, Paraguay.
Monotypic.
Distribution. N Colombia through N Venezuela, Trinidad and Guyana to Surinam; also S Bolivia and S Brazil to C Argentina and C Chile.

Descriptive notes. 28-33 cm. Only member of *Ixobrychus* with heavy streaking on back; outer quarter of primaries and secondaries cinnamon buff or rufous, rest darker.
Habitat. Areas with sedges and long grass; also reedbeds in tropical marshes. Recorded in rice fields in Rio Grande do Sul, Brazil.
Food and Feeding. Small fish, crustaceans, dragonflies, water beetles and other insects and their larvae. Feeds alone or in pairs; has been seen feeding by night.
Breeding. Little known. In Argentina nests in spring, Nov-Dec. Solitary. Nests in dense, impenetrable patches of rushes, only 30-60 cm above water; nest is conical mass of dry rushes or reeds. Normally 3 eggs, sometimes 4; chicks have buff down, greyer below.
Movements. Little known. Presumed to be sedentary in some areas where occurs all year round, e.g. Chile, S Brazil, Punta Lara (NE Argentina); some birds may migrate towards N, as species

absent from some nesting areas during S winter, and some records outside breeding range in NE Brazil.
Status and Conservation. Not globally threatened. Generally scarce, though appears common in places. Very difficult to see, due to size, skulking habits and habitat, so very little known about status, and no figures of population sizes available; seasonally fairly common at Hacienda Corocora in W Meta, Colombia.
Bibliography. Belton (1984), Blake (1977), Carp (1991), Haverschmidt (1968), Hellmayr & Conover (1948), Herklots (1961), Hilty & Brown (1986), Johnson (1965), Klimaitis & Moschione (1987), Nores & Yzurieta (1980), Olmos & Barbosa (1988), de la Peña (1986), Pinto (1964), Ruschi (1979), de Schauensee & Phelps (1978), Scott & Carbonell (1986), Sick (1984), Teixeira *et al.* (1986), Walter (1967).

50. **Least Bittern**

Ixobrychus exilis

French: Petit Blongios   **Spanish**: Avetorillo Panamericano
                German: Amerikanische Zwergdommel

Taxonomy. *Ardea exilis* Gmelin, 1789, Jamaica.
Forms superspecies with *I. minutus* and *I. sinensis*. Erythristic colour morphs were described as different species, Chory's Bittern (*I. neoxenus*); these morphs occur in races *exilis* and *erythromelas*. Subspecific status of birds from E Ecuador unclear; sometimes assigned separate race *limoncochae*. Five subspecies normally recognized.
Subspecies and Distribution.
I. e. exilis (Gmelin, 1789) - SE Canada and E USA, W USA to Baja California; C America and Caribbean.
I. e. pullus van Rossem, 1930 - NW Mexico.
I. e. erythromelas (Vieillot, 1817) - E Panama through Guianas to SE Brazil and Paraguay.
I. e. bogotensis Chapman, 1914 - C Colombia.
I. e. peruvianus Bond, 1955 - CW Peru.

Descriptive notes. 28-36 cm. Tips of alula, primaries, primary coverts and secondaries cinnamon, but less prominently than in *I. involucris*. Female has purplish brown instead of black, and dark streaks on foreneck. Juvenile as adult female but paler, with browner mantle and crown, and dusky streaks on lesser wing-coverts. Races generally separated on measurements, and especially on brighter or duller orangish tone, although there is considerable variation between individuals.
Habitat. Usually dense freshwater marshes with reeds, sedges, cat-tails or sawgrass on margins of lakes, pools, rivers and canals. Also brackish or saltwater swamps, especially during migration or in winter. Sometimes in areas markedly altered by man. Races *pullus* and *erythromelas* also occur in mangroves.
Food and Feeding. Mainly small fish; also aquatic insects, molluscs, crustaceans, leeches, tadpoles, frogs, salamanders and occasionally shrews and mice; recorded taking eggs and chicks of other birds. Usually solitary and crepuscular.
Breeding. In N of range, laying Mar-Jul (including second and replacement clutches), becoming progressively later towards N; normally later in tropics; race *bogotensis* found in breeding condition in Feb. Usually solitary, but forms loose groups in suitable habitat. Nests in dense marsh vegetation or in bushes low over shallow water; nest made of dead or live stalks of cat-tails or other aquatic plants. Normally 2-4 eggs in S and C of range, 4-5 in N (2-7); incubation mainly by female c. 17-20 days; chicks have buff down, whitish below; chicks remain within vicinity of nest for at least c. 25 days.
Movements. Nominate *exilis* performs widespread post-breeding dispersal, and also long distance migration from N of range, leaving in Sept-Nov and returning in Feb-Apr, or in May in extreme N; winters from S USA through C America and Caribbean to N South America; birds from W USA migrate through W Mexico as far as Costa Rica. Migration apparently takes place by night. Straggler to N of breeding range in British Columbia and Newfoundland; accidental to Iceland and Azores. Other races seem to be sedentary, though can apparently perform some movements due to failure of seasonal rains.
Status and Conservation. Not globally threatened. In USA, declining in many areas, especially in W, and considered threatened or of special concern in several states; difficult to estimate numbers, but e.g. density of 0·4 birds/ha in Horicon Marsh Wildlife Refuge, in Wisconsin. Uncommon to rare in parts of C America. Has colonized some islands in Lesser Antilles during 1980's. Locally common in Colombia; race *bogotensis* apparently declining, due to habitat destruction in Andes.
Bibliography. Adams (1989a), Allen (1915), Aniskowicz (1981), Benito-Espinal & Portecop (1935), Bent (1926), Biaggi (1983), Blake (1977), Cramp & Simmons (1977), Evans, P.G.H. (1990), Fjeldså & Krabbe (1990), Frederick, Dwyer *et al.* (1990), Hands *et al.* (1989a), Haverschmidt (1968), Hellmayr & Conover (1948), Hilty & Brown (1986), Johnson (1965), Kushlan (1973a), Mock (1976), Monroe (1968), Palmer (1962), de la Peña (1986), Pinto (1964), Rabenold (1987a), Ridgely & Gwynne (1989), de Schauensee & Phelps (1978), Scott & Carbonell (1986), Slud (1964), Stiles & Skutch (1989), Swift *et al.* (1988), Terres (1980), Varty *et al.* (1986), Weller (1961), Wetmore (1965).

51. **Little Bittern**

Ixobrychus minutus

French: Blongios nain   **German**: Zwergdommel   **Spanish**: Avetorillo Común
Other common names: Australian/New Zealand Little Bittern

Taxonomy. *Ardea minuta* Linnaeus, 1766, Switzerland.

On following pages: 52. Yellow Bittern (*Ixobrychus sinensis*); 53. Schrenck's Bittern (*Ixobrychus eurhythmus*); 54. Cinnamon Bittern (*Ixobrychus cinnamomeus*); 55. Dwarf Bittern (*Ixobrychus sturmii*); 56. Black Bittern (*Ixobrychus flavicollis*); 57. South American Bittern (*Botaurus pinnatus*); 58. North American Bittern (*Botaurus lentiginosus*); 59. Eurasian Bittern (*Botaurus stellaris*); 60. Australasian Bittern (*Botaurus poiciloptilus*).

Forms superspecies with *I. exilis* and *I. sinensis*. Race *novaezelandiae* often considered separate species, but very little known and now probably extinct (cause unknown); *payesii* and *podiceps* have been treated as two further species. Five subspecies normally recognized.

Subspecies and Distribution.

I. m. minutus (Linnaeus, 1766) - C & S Europe and N Africa E to W Siberia and through Iran to NE India; winters Africa to India.

I. m. payesii (Hartlaub, 1858) - Africa S of Sahara.

I. m. podiceps (Bonaparte, 1855) - Madagascar.

I. m. novaezelandiae (Potts, 1871) - South I, New Zealand (probably extinct).

I. m. dubius Mathews, 1912 - SW & E Australia; S New Guinea.

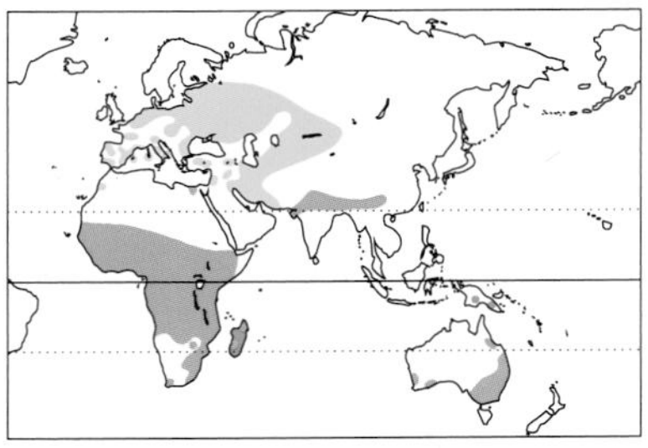

Descriptive notes. 27-36 cm; 59-150 g; wingspan 40-58 cm. Lores and base of bill range in colour from lemon yellow to orangish yellow; legs variable shade of yellow or green. Female can have more contrasted plumage, more similar to that of male. Juvenile as adult female, but more heavily streaked overall. Races separated on measurements and coloration of head, neck and upperwing; *dubius* has shorter, thicker bill.

Habitat. Very varied throughout extensive range, from dense forest to deserts; from lowlands to hills, up to 1500 m in Madagascar, or 1800 m in Vale of Kashmir (W Himalayas). Most commonly in freshwater marshes with reedbeds or other kinds of dense aquatic vegetation, preferably with bushes or trees; margins of lakes, pools, reservoirs, peat bogs, oases. Also in wooded swamps, overgrown banks of streams and rivers, wet grassland and rice fields; in places, frequents mangroves and margins of saline lagoons. During migration and in winter occurs on more open waters, and even in heavily humanized zones, as well as dry land including fields of cereals or sugar cane.

Food and Feeding. Varies with region and season. In places, essentially insectivorous, taking aquatic insects and their larvae, crickets, grasshoppers, caterpillars, etc. Also feeds on spiders, molluscs, crustaceans and small vertebrates, including fish, frogs, tadpoles, small reptiles and birds. Mainly active around dawn and dusk, but also feeds during day; race *payesii* apparently more strongly diurnal, with peak activity in middle of day in South Africa. Like all *Ixobrychus* feeds alone, either by standing motionless or "Walking Slowly" partially hidden amidst vegetation.

Breeding. In W Palearctic and India nesting mainly May-Jul; in tropical Africa season variable, generally related to rains; in South Africa Jun-Feb; in Australia Oct-Jan. Generally solitary, although sometimes forms small, loose groups in particularly favourable areas. Nest normally in aquatic vegetation, but alternatively low in bushes or trees (tea-trees, alder, willow), and in E Asia occasionally high in trees over dry land; nest has conical base and is shallow platform of reeds and twigs lined with leaves or finer stems. 2-9 eggs, normally 5-6 in *minutus*, mainly 3-4 in tropical and subtropical races; incubation 16-21 days; chicks have reddish buff down, white below; fledging c. 1 month. In W Palearctic usually 1 brood, sometimes 2; in South Africa often 2, sometimes 3; in Australia only 1 brood.

Movements. Race *minutus* undergoes post-breeding dispersal in all directions (see page 392); also migrates S from Palearctic towards tropical Africa and S to Cape, wintering mostly in S half of continent; migration mostly nocturnal, but can be diurnal; normally in small flocks (see page 393). Crosses Arabia and Sahara on broad front. Peak migration over N Africa in Aug-Oct and Apr-Jun. Birds regularly overshoot on return, with sightings N to Iceland and Scandinavia; regularly turns up in Azores, Madeira and Canaries. Populations of Middle East partly sedentary with influx in winter; resident in India, apparently with some local movements. Race *payesii* performs movements connected with fluctuations in water level; straggles to Canaries. Race *podiceps* occasionally moves from Madagascar to Africa during dry season. In Australia, race *dubia* moves from S to N Australia and perhaps on to New Guinea; part of population of N Australia apparently sedentary; only record from New Zealand was juvenile.

Status and Conservation. Not globally threatened. Has declined since middle of century in parts of W Palearctic, due to habitat destruction and pollution: in Belgium, 100-200 pairs before 1960, reduced to 60 pairs by end of 1970's; in France, 1260 pairs in 1970, down to 453 pairs in 1983, a drop of 64%; population of EEC countries presently estimated at 2700-4500 pairs. Frequent to uncommon in Africa; rare breeder in South Africa, probably with under 100 pairs; uncommon in Madagascar, where only known from a few localities. At Haigam Rakh, in Kashmir (NW India), c. 1000-2000 breeding pairs in area of 1400 ha. Apparently rare and local in Australia, though may be commoner than thought.

Bibliography. Ali & Ripley (1978), Batten *et al.* (1990), Bauer & Glutz von Blotzheim (1966), Brichetti (1983), Brooke (1984), Brown & Britton (1980), Brown *et al.* (1982), Coates (1985), Cramp & Simmons (1977), Dementiev & Gladkov (1951b), Duhautois (1984), Etchécopar & Hüe (1978), Gentz (1959), Géroudet (1978a), Goodman (1989), Grimmet & Jones (1989), Hoyer (1991), Hüe & Etchécopar (1970), Jaensch (1989), Langley (1983), Langrand (1990), Ledant *et al.* (1981), Mackworth-Praed & Grant (1957-1973), Maclean (1985), Marchant & Higgins (1990), Milon *et al.* (1973), Morel & Morel (1989), Paran & Shluter (1981), Paz (1987), Perennou (1991a, 1991b), Pinto (1983), Richardson (1990), Roberts (1991), Rutgers & Norris (1970), Scott (1989), Voisin (1991).

52. Yellow Bittern

Ixobrychus sinensis

French: Blongios de Chine **German**: Chinadommel **Spanish**: Avetorillo Chino
Other common names: Chinese Little/Long-nosed Bittern

Taxonomy. *Ardea Sinensis* Gmelin, 1789, China.

Forms superspecies with *I. exilis* and *I. minutus*. Monotypic.

Distribution. Indian Subcontinent through SE Asia to SE USSR and Japan; Indonesia, Philippines, New Guinea and Micronesia; Seychelles.

Descriptive notes. 30-40 cm; 50+ g. Bill long and slender; forehead brown. Female possibly has more streaking on lower neck. Juvenile browner and obviously streaked.

Habitat. Mostly in freshwater marshes; also reedbeds and other dense aquatic vegetation fringing lakes, in riverside shrubs, inland swamps, rice paddies and flooded fields; in parts of China occurs in mangroves. From lowlands into hills, occurring up to 900 m in India, 1200 m in Sri Lanka and 1500 m in Sumatra.

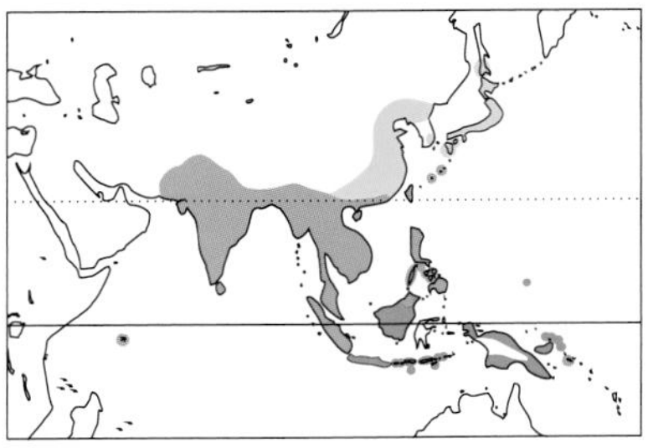

Food and Feeding. Mainly aquatic insects and their larvae; also small fish, crustaceans, frogs, molluscs, crickets. Sometimes catches flies in flight. Solitary and secretive; mainly crepuscular and nocturnal, but sometimes active on overcast days.

Breeding. Starts spring in N, May-Aug in Japan; Jun-Sept in India, related to monsoons; laying Jul-Oct in Malay Peninsula; Sept-Apr in Solomon Is. Normally solitary, but can form small groups at favourable sites. Nests usually less than 1 m above water or mud; nest light platform of grass and leaves, usually with canopy of foliage. Normally 4 eggs (3-7); incubation c. 22 days; chicks have pinkish down; start to clamber about nest at c. 15 days. Can have 2 or perhaps even 3 broods per year.

Movements. N populations (S to C China) migrate to S of range, to Philippines and Indonesia, some birds reaching Wallacea and New Guinea; leave in Oct and return in mid-Apr. Passes through Malay Peninsula Oct-Dec and Mar-Apr. Migration takes place by night. S populations (including some of S Japan, S China, N Burma and N Indochina) sedentary. Resident in India with some local movements related to water conditions; may perform some regular migration. Long distance migration has permitted colonization of remote Pacific islands and Seychelles. Accidental to Australia and Christmas I (Indian Ocean).

Status and Conservation. Not globally threatened. Common to frequent in many areas, e.g. Pakistan, Japan, Thailand, Borneo (winter), Philippines; 176 counted in China, c. 1400 at L Tempe, S Sulawesi, Jan 1990. In China and upland Borneo protected and considered beneficial by rice growers, as it eats stem-boring crickets in paddyfields. Population of Seychelles estimated at under 100 pairs at end of 1970's.

Bibliography. Ali & Ripley (1978), Beehler *et al.* (1986), Brazil (1991), Caldwell & Caldwell (1931), Coates (1985), Dementiev & Gladkov (1951b), Dickinson *et al.* (1991), Etchécopar & Hüe (1978), Flint *et al.* (1984), Hails (1987), Henry (1971), Herklots (1967), Jenkins (1983), Li Cheng-li (1986), Liu Huan-jin *et al.* (1986), Lu Xin & Liu Huan-jin (1987), Marchant & Higgins (1990), van Marle & Voous (1988), Medway & Wells (1976), Perennou & Mundkur (1991), Pratt *et al.* (1987), Roberts (1991), Round *et al.* (1988), de Schauensee (1984), Scott (1989), Smythies (1981), Watson (1980), Yan An-hou (1988).

53. Schrenck's Bittern

Ixobrychus eurhythmus

French: Blongios de Schrenck **German**: Mandschurendommel **Spanish**: Avetorillo Manchú

Taxonomy. *Ardetta eurhythma* Swinhoe, 1873, Amoy and Shanghai, China.

Monotypic.

Distribution. SE Siberia, Manchuria and Japan S to E China. Winters from S China, Indochina and Malay Peninsula to Greater Sundas, Sulawesi and Philippines.

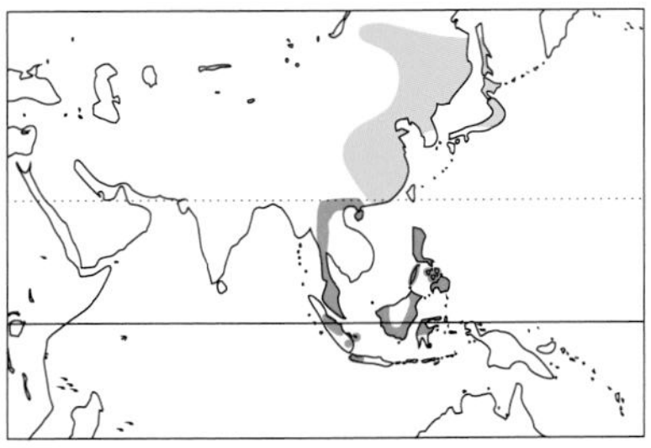

Descriptive notes. 33-39 cm; wingspan 55-59 cm. Tips of flight-feathers silvery grey. Only member of *Ixobrychus* in which female has prominent pattern, produced by black and white spotting. Juvenile as adult female, but less conspicuously patterned.

Habitat. Marshes with reedbeds, wet, grassy meadows, swamps in flat, open areas of river valleys and coasts; in some areas frequents cultivation, especially rice paddies. Sometimes nests close to human habitation beside village ponds. Can tolerate drier conditions and limited tree cover. In Japan, also breeds in dry pastures and areas of bushes.

Food and Feeding. Little known. Small fish, frogs, shrimps, isopods, variety of insects and their larvae. In uplands of Borneo takes mostly large ground crickets. Largely crepuscular, but sometimes active by day.

Breeding. Laying May-Jul in China and USSR; season May-Aug in Japan. Solitary. Nests in grass near water, often on or very close to ground, occasionally in thick vegetation c. 1 m above water; nest of dry stalks lined with dry grass and leaves, has clay base to prevent water seeping through. 3-6 eggs; incubation 16-18 days.

Movements. Migration towards winter quarters starts in Aug, with main passage through Hong Kong in Sept-Oct, and through Malay Peninsula in Oct-Nov; returns through Thailand in Mar-Apr and through Malay Peninsula in Apr-Jun, reaching breeding grounds of S in Apr-May and extreme N in Jun. Vagrant to Burma and Palau Is (Micronesia); two surprising records from Europe, in Germany and Italy, the latter at any rate not apparently bird escaped from captivity.

Status and Conservation. Not globally threatened. Currently considered near-threatened, but no information available on population sizes. Uncommon in USSR; uncommon and local in Japan, where no recent breeding records from Hokkaido; in Fukien Province, SE China, common, but not abundant breeder; rare winter visitor to Philippines.

Bibliography. Bauer & Glutz von Blotzheim (1966), Brazil (1991), Caldwell & Caldwell (1931), Cramp & Simmons (1977), Dementiev & Gladkov (1951b), Dickinson *et al.* (1991), Etchécopar & Hüe (1978), Flint *et al.* (1984), Herklots (1967), Lekagul & Round (1991), Liu Yi *et al.* (1988), van Marle & Voous (1988), Medway & Wells (1976), Round *et al.* (1988), de Schauensee (1984), Scott (1989), Smythies (1981), Tomek & Dontchev (1987), White & Bruce (1986).

54. Cinnamon Bittern

Ixobrychus cinnamomeus

French: Blongios cannelle **German**: Zimtdommel **Spanish**: Avetorillo Canelo
Other common names: Chestnut Bittern

Taxonomy. *Ardea cinnamomea* Gmelin, 1789, China.

Monotypic.

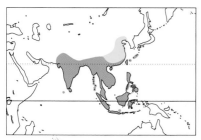

Distribution. Indian Subcontinent through SE Asia to NE China; also occurs in Maldives, Sri Lanka, Andaman and Nicobar Is; widespread throughout Greater Sundas, Sulawesi and Philippines.

Descriptive notes. 40-41 cm. Overall appearance uniform rich cinnamon. Lacks any contrast between upperwing-coverts and rest of upperparts. Female can be spotted, but less so than female of *I. eurythmus*. Non-breeding adult has bill greenish orange, lores yellow and legs yellowish green. Juvenile as adult female, but generally rather duller.

Habitat. Mainly flooded rice fields and grassy areas, often near human habitation; frequently active in paddyfields with people working nearby; also open freshwater swamps and reed marshes, as well as overgrown ditches, damp, scrubby thickets and patches of reeds along roads or margins of lakes and pools; in Kerala (SW India) occurs along coast, especially in mangroves. Occurs from lowlands up to at least 900 m in India, 1800 m in Sri Lanka, 1200 m in Sumatra and 1980 m in NE Borneo.

Food and Feeding. Fish, including eels up to 13 cm long, frogs, molluscs, insects, prawns, etc. Appears to be active mainly around dawn and dusk, but also frequently feeds by day. Generally feeds alone and defends feeding territory.

Breeding. Jun-Sept in India, starting with monsoons; in Sumatra eggs recorded Jan-Mar in lowlands, Oct-Dec in highlands; in Malay Peninsula Sept, Dec, Feb-Jul; in Java Oct-Jun. Can apparently breed in small groups, sometimes in loose association with other herons. Nests on flattened clump of reeds, in cane break or in emergent trees or bushes, usually c. 1m above water or mud, but sometimes even on ground; nest is platform of small sticks, reeds and sedges, lined with a few dead leaves and fine grass. Normally 3-5 eggs (2-6); chicks have pinkish chestnut down; at 10 days old can clamber about in reeds.

Movements. N populations spend non-breeding season in S of breeding range, apparently moving in connection with rainfall and high water levels of monsoon period; passes through Malay Peninsula in Sept-Nov and Feb-May. S populations (from Thailand to Philippines and Indonesia) sedentary, with influx of migrants from N in N winter. Birds of Pakistan and India also perform local movements and perhaps seasonal migrations in relation with water conditions. Recorded in Primorskiy Kray Territory, SE USSR.

Status and Conservation. Not globally threatened. Widespread and common in most of range; well adapted to man-made habitats, and most populations appear to be quite healthy. Widespread and common throughout areas with suitable habitat in Sumatra and Philippines; estimated 1070 birds at L Tempe, S Sulawesi, Jan 1990.

Bibliography. Ali & Ripley (1978), Brazil (1991), Dickinson *et al.* (1991), Etchécopar & Hüe (1978), Hails (1987), Henry (1971), Herklots (1967), Inskipp & Inskipp (1985), Lansdown (1988), Lekagul & Round (1991), Liu Huan-jin *et al.* (1982), van Marle & Voous (1988), Medway & Wells (1976), Mukherjee (1971), Perennou & Mundkur (1991), Roberts (1991), Round *et al.* (1988), de Schauensee (1984), Scott (1989), Smythies (1981, 1986), White & Bruce (1986).

55. **Dwarf Bittern**

Ixobrychus sturmii

French: Blongios de Sturm   **German**: Graurückendommel   **Spanish**: Avetorillo Plomizo
Other common names: African Dwarf Bittern, Rail Heron

Taxonomy. *Ardea Sturmii* Wagler, 1827, Senegambia.
Sometimes separated in monospecific genus *Ardeirallus*. Monotypic.
Distribution. Africa S of Sahara, avoiding arid zones.

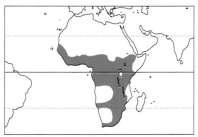

Descriptive notes. 27-30 cm; 142 g. Plumage variations very poorly known, but female paler, more rufous on belly. Juvenile more extensively buff and duller; upperparts tipped with buff.

Habitat. Wooded areas or bush with dense foliage along margins of freshwater rivers, streams, lakes and pools; also marshes with grass or reeds, seasonally flooded areas, mangroves, rice fields and swamps with grass, cat-tails or papyrus.

Food and Feeding. Insects, including water beetles and especially grasshoppers, and frogs; also small fish, crabs, spiders and snails. Feeds alone or in pairs; mainly nocturnal but also forages by day, especially in cloudy conditions.

Breeding. Season very variable, generally coinciding with rains, but sometimes early in dry season: Jul in Ghana; Apr in Ethiopia; May-Jun in coastal Kenya; Nov-Apr in Zimbabwe; and Dec-Mar in Transvaal, South Africa. Solitary, occasionally in small groups of few dozen pairs. Nests in trees or bushes on horizontal or hanging branches, c. 0·5-4 m above water; nest is flimsy stick platform lined with dry grass. Normally 3-4 eggs (2-5); incubation 14-15 days; chicks have ginger down; wander from nest at c. 1 week; remiges start to appear at 11 days.

Movements. African migrant, movements related with changes in water level due to seasonal rains. Equatorial populations probably sedentary, numbers boosted by arrival of migrants from N or S. Birds of southern third of Africa present Oct-Apr, presumably moving to equatorial zone during dry season; in South Africa erratic seasonal movements in Nyl floodplains only when they are totally flooded, roughly Jan-Jun. Apparently present in N of range only during rains, May-Sept. Recorded far outside usual range in Canary Is, and surprisingly in France, a bird of doubtful origin.

Status and Conservation. Not globally threatened. Widespread, but uncommon to rare throughout extensive range. Locally common during breeding, e.g. in NE Namibia, S Angola. Population of South Africa estimated at c. 200 pairs in wet season; no evidence of decrease.

Bibliography. Ash & Miskell (1983), Britton (1980), Brooke (1984), Brosset & Erard (1986), Brown & Britton (1980), Brown *et al.* (1982), Chapin (1932), Elgood (1982), Mackworth-Praed & Grant (1957-1973), Maclean (1985), Pinto (1983), Tarboton (1967).

56. **Black Bittern**

Ixobrychus flavicollis

French: Blongios à cou jaune   **German**: Schwarzdommel   **Spanish**: Avetorillo Negro
Other common names: Yellow-necked/Mangrove Bittern

Taxonomy. *Ardea flavicollis* Latham, 1790, India.
Often separated in monospecific genus *Dupetor*. Three subspecies recognized.
Subspecies and Distribution.
I. f. flavicollis (Latham, 1790) - SE Asia from Pakistan to SE China and S to Indonesia and Philippines.
I. f. australis (Lesson, 1831) - Moluccas, New Guinea and Bismarck Archipelago S to W, N & E Australia.
I. f. woodfordi (Ogilvie-Grant, 1888) - Solomon Is.

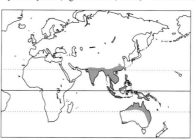

Descriptive notes. 54-66 cm; 300-420 g; wingspan 80 cm. Female browner and slightly paler. Juvenile variable shade of brown, from rufous to dark brown, with more or less scaling. Races separated on coloration and slight biometrical differences.

Habitat. Typically along densely forested freshwater streams and pools or other permanent wetlands. In Australia also frequents mangroves and *Melaleuca* swamps, margins of estuaries, lagoons, tidal creeks and mudflats. In India mainly in reedy swamps inland or overgrown *nullahs*, but not apparently mangroves. In Malay Peninsula and Borneo in winter occurs in reedbeds and other aquatic vegetation around lagoons, seasonal pools and reservoirs. In China frequents thickets of bamboo. Mainly in lowlands, but also in mountains, up to 1200 m in India and Burma.

Food and Feeding. Fish up to 15 cm long, frogs, molluscs, crustaceans and insects. Crepuscular and nocturnal, with peak activity at dusk and dawn; also feeds during day in rainy weather with sky overcast.

Breeding. Season related to monsoons in N of range: in India mainly Jun-Sept during SW monsoon, but varies locally with amounts of rainfall; Apr in Sri Lanka; May in Java; Feb in New Guinea; and mostly Sept-Jan in Australia. Usually solitary, but sometimes in small colonies. Nests in dense reeds, bamboo or bushes, or c. 1-15 m up tree over water; in China occasionally nests far from water; nest is platform of sticks, twigs and reeds with shallow central depression. Normally 4 eggs (3-6), but habitually 2 in New Guinea; chicks have white down with light brown tinges; wander from nest at c. 15 days. Generally single-brooded, but 2 broods in Fu-chou, S China, with laying in May and Jul.

Movements. In India, local movements depending on water conditions, although some migration may occur: 1 bird ringed in Malaysia in Dec 1965 recovered in Manipur (NE India) in Nov 1965; 1 bird ringed in India captured in Maldives. Population of S China migrates S to Malay Peninsula from Oct on, where remains till Apr-May; also winters in Greater Sundas and Philippines. Australian birds essentially sedentary, although sometimes forced by drought conditions to move about. Vagrant to Christmas I (Indian Ocean), Moluccas, Guam (Mariana Is) and NC Japan.

Status and Conservation. Not globally threatened. Probably much overlooked, due to secretive habits. In Australia, may still be fairly common, but has declined considerably over last 50 years, due to destruction of riverine habitats for agriculture and pastoral farming, and also salinization of rivers. Fairly common in Karnataka and Kerala, SW India, in areas of heavy rainfall; also in Sri Lanka, and Sanghar and Thatta districts of Pakistan. Common in winter on seasonal lagoons in SW Sarawak; uncommon in Sumatra and Philippines.

Bibliography. Ali & Ripley (1978), Beehler *et al.* (1986), Caldwell & Caldwell (1931), Coates (1985), Dickinson *et al.* (1991), Etchécopar & Hüe (1978), Herklots (1967), Marchant & Higgins (1990), van Marle & Voous (1988), McClure (1974), Medway & Wells (1976), Mees (1982), Perennou & Mundkur (1991), Rand & Guilliard (1967), Roberts (1991), de Schauensee (1984), Scott (1989), Serventy & Whittall (1962), Smythies (1981, 1986), White & Bruce (1986).

Genus *BOTAURUS*   Stephens, 1819

57. **South American Bittern**

Botaurus pinnatus

French: Butor mirasol   **Spanish**: Avetoro Mirasol
German: Südamerikanische Rohrdommel
Other common names: Pinnated Bittern

Taxonomy. *Ardea pinnata* Wagler, 1829, Bahia, Brazil.
May form superspecies with *B. lentiginosus*, and these two sometimes included within *B. stellaris* superspecies. Two subspecies recognized.
Subspecies and Distribution.
B. p. caribaeus Dickerman, 1961 - E Mexico.
B. p. pinnatus (Wagler, 1829) - SE Nicaragua to Ecuador and Guianas, S through Brazil to Paraguay and NE Argentina.

Descriptive notes. 63·5-76 cm. Female tends to be smaller, with tail brown as opposed to black. Juvenile more reddish ochre, less boldly barred on upperparts. Race *caribaeus* claimed to have longer bill, and shorter wings and tail; paler, with less streaking on throat.

Habitat. Shallow freshwater swamps and marshes with stands of tall, dense vegetation, including rushes (*Scirpus*), cat-tails (*Typha*) or reeds (*Phragmites*); generally in flat, open areas. Sometimes feeds in rice fields and plantations of sugar cane. From coastal areas at sea-level to inland savannas and lakes. Recorded at 2600 m in E Andes of Colombia.

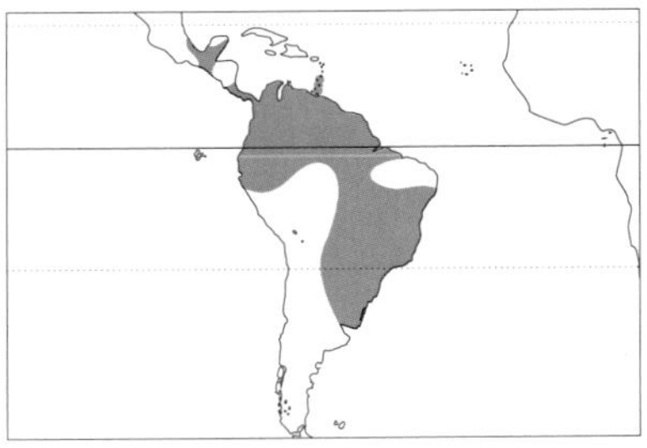

Food and Feeding. Little known. Fish (including eels), frogs, snakes, and insects. Largely nocturnal; usually solitary, although sometimes several birds birds feed fairly close together.
Breeding. Very little known. Jul-Oct in Trinidad and possibly Colombian Andes; May in Mexico; Jul in Costa Rica; Feb-Mar in Brazil. Nests in dense vegetation, close over water; nest is platform of reeds or other plants. 2-3 eggs; incubation apparently by female.
Movements. Little known. Appears fairly sedentary in Trinidad and Costa Rica, where recorded in off-season; in S of range, in Brazil, Paraguay, Uruguay and N Argentina, no records outwith breeding season.
Status and Conservation. Not globally threatened. Apparently rare or uncommon; rarely seen, due to secretive nature, and might be commoner than thought. Can be quite numerous in places, e.g. Usumacinta Delta, Mexico; local in Colombia.
Bibliography. Belton (1984), Blake (1977), Fjeldså & Krabbe (1990), Haverschmidt (1968), Hellmayr & Conover (1948), Herklots (1961), Hilty & Brown (1986), Orians & Paulson (1969), Paynter (1955), de la Peña (1986), Pinto (1964), Ruschi (1979), de Schauensee & Phelps (1978), Scott & Carbonell (1986), Sick (1984), Slud (1964), Stiles & Skutch (1989).

58. North American Bittern

Botaurus lentiginosus

French: Butor d'Amérique **Spanish**: Avetoro Lentiginoso **German**: Nordamerikanische Rohrdommel
Other common names: American Bittern

Taxonomy. *Ardea lentiginosa* Montagu, 1813, Piddletown, Dorset, England.
May form superspecies with *B. pinnatus*, and these two sometimes included within *B. stellaris* superspecies. Monotypic.
Distribution. N and C America, from S and C Canada to Panama; West Indies.

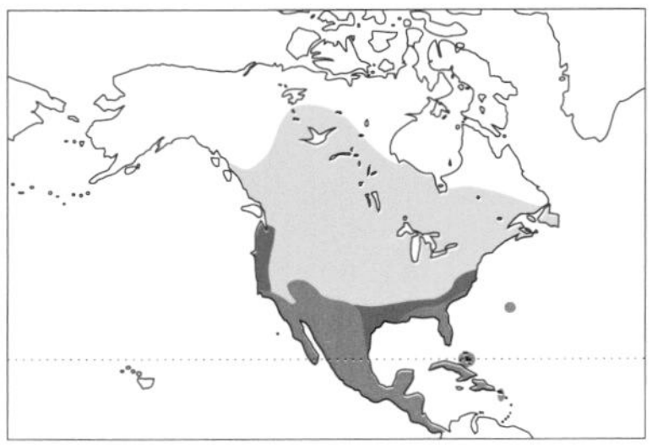

Descriptive notes. 56-85 cm; 372-571 g; wingspan 105-125 cm. Dark line through lores, contrasting with yellow facial skin around gape, and forming distinctive pattern of pale and dark lines. Overall plumage tone variable. Juvenile lacks black markings at sides of neck.
Habitat. Marshes and bogs with fresh, brackish or salt water; prefers good covering of vegetation, especially *Typha* and *Scirpus*. Unlike other bitterns, occurs in open areas, e.g. wet meadows and pastures, and even found in fairly dry grassland. Outside breeding season frequents freshwater swamps and occasionally mangroves.
Food and Feeding. Very variable, but mainly fish, including eels, catfish, perch, pickerel, suckers, killifish and sticklebacks; also frogs, salamanders, garter snakes, water snakes, crayfish, molluscs, insects and small mammals. Mainly crepuscular and nocturnal. Like other bitterns, usually solitary; mainly passive feeder, although more active than other *Botaurus*, and can feed by "Walking Quickly" and even "Running".
Breeding. Laying Apr-Jul, mostly May. Generally solitary and territorial; no conclusive evidence that males are polygamous. Nests low over water in areas with dense covering of reeds or rushes, in grassy parts of marshes or in wet meadows, sometimes on ground; nest is platform of reeds, cat-tails, sedges or other marsh plants. Usually 3-5 eggs (2-7); incubation c. 28-29 days; chicks have yellowish olive down, slightly darker below; start to leave nest at c. 2 weeks old.
Movements. Extensive post-breeding dispersal from Jul; in Sept-Nov birds migrate S, returning Feb-Mar or May in extreme N; migration basically by night. Fairly sedentary more temperate parts in S and W of breeding range. During migration, occasional anywhere from S Alaska to Panama; accidental to Greenland, Bermuda, S America and several times in W Europe, S to Canary Is.
Status and Conservation. Not globally threatened. Population levels difficult to estimate. Declining in USA, especially in central states, probably due to loss of marsh habitat; endangered in several states, e.g. Illinois, Indiana and Ohio, and of special concern in others.
Bibliography. Adams (1989b), Banks & Dickerman (1978), Bent (1926), Blake (1977), Cramp & Simmons (1977), Duebbert & Lokemoen (1977), Hands *et al.* (1989b), Holtz (1988), Middleton (1949), Palmer (1962), Rabenold (1987b), Ridgely & Gwynne (1989), Stiles & Skutch (1989), Stone (1965), Vesall (1940), Terres (1980), Wetmore (1965).

59. Eurasian Bittern

Botaurus stellaris

French: Butor étoilé **German**: Rohrdommel **Spanish**: Avetoro Común
Other common names: Great/Common Bittern

Taxonomy. *Ardea stellaris* Linnaeus, 1758, Sweden.
Sometimes considered to include *B. poiciloptilus*, with which forms superspecies. Two subspecies recognized.
Subspecies and Distribution.
B. s. stellaris (Linnaeus, 1758) - Palearctic and Oriental Regions and N Afrotropical Region.
B. s. capensis (Schlegel, 1863) - S Africa.
Descriptive notes. 64-80 cm; 867-1940 g, female lighter; wingspan 125-135 cm. Fairly variable; can be paler or darker than illustration. Colour of lores varies seasonally. Juvenile has cap and moustache paler, and dorsal pattern less defined. Race *capensis* darker above, recalling pale individuals of *B. poiciloptilus*.

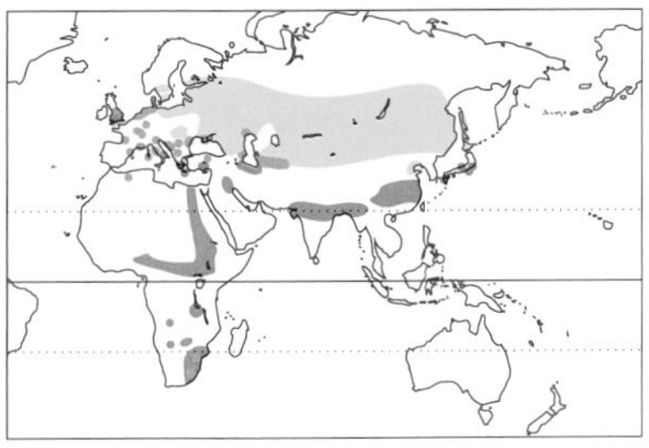

Habitat. Highly restrictive habitat requirements during breeding season: quiet, peaceful marshes around lakes and rivers with extensive reedbeds of *Phragmites*; these must be comprehensively flooded and fairly shallow, with little fluctuation in water level; with mixture of young and old reeds, and clearings where bird can fish undisturbed and unseen. Occupies sites with either fresh or brackish water. In places breeds in pure stands of rushes (*Scirpus*). Outwith breeding season uses much more varied habitat, including rice fields, grassy areas, beds of cress, gravel pits, fish farms, ditches, sewage farms, etc. In freezing conditions, may be found in open water and even in suburban areas.
Food and Feeding. Very variable, depending on place and season: mainly fish of of wide variety of species, particularly cyprinids and eels, and amphibians; other important items include insects and their larvae, spiders, crustaceans, molluscs; also takes snakes, lizards, birds and their nestlings, and small mammals. Feeds alone, usually in pools hidden away in dense vegetation. Main techniques include "Walking Slowly" in shallow water, interspersed with periods of "Standing". Mostly crepuscular and nocturnal, but also active by day.
Breeding. In Eurasia laying Mar-Jun, occasionally earlier, with records from Jan in Spain; in South Africa breeds during rains, Sept-Jan.Solitary and highly territorial; often polygamous, male mating with up to 5 females. Nests in midst of dense reedbeds near male's booming site and not far from open water; nest on mat of dead plants close over water or sometimes even floating on it; exceptionally nests in trees; nest is circular platform 30-40 cm wide, constructed of dead reeds, stalks and leaves, and lined with finer material. Normally 4-5 eggs (3-7); incubation 25-26 days; hatching asynchronous; chicks have brown down, rufous below; fledging c. 50-55 days. Female alone builds nest, incubates eggs and feeds chicks. Sexual maturity at 1 year old. Single-brooded.
Movements. Extensive post-breeding movements by juveniles, sometimes of hundreds of kilometres. Partial migration, affecting only most northerly populations of Eurasia, which move mostly to S and SE Asia, W and S Europe and Mediterranean Basin, while some cross Sahara and range S roughly to equator. In W Palearctic, juvenile dispersal from Jul and migration Sept-Nov, occasionally in Dec, with return in Feb-Apr. Migration tends to be mostly nocturnal. S populations basically sedentary except during freeze-ups, although birds sometimes stay and die of cold rather than moving. Vagrant to Iceland, Azores, Canary Is and Malaysia. Race *capensis* basically sedentary, peforms seasonal movements mainly towards SW at onset of rains, in order to congregate at breeding grounds.
Status and Conservation. Not globally threatened. Now considered near-threatened. General decline, especially in Europe, since 19th century, due to habitat destruction, pollution, hunting and collecting of eggs and chicks. Protection has eased situation in some countries. Decline continues in Netherlands, and also in France, where a drop of 40% was noted between 1970 and 1983. In 1911 recolonized Great Britain, but has declined markedly since 1970's. Populations further N affected by cold winters (see page 395). In Europe, excluding USSR, 2500-2700 "booming" males counted in 1976; present population of EEC estimated at 1020-1350 pairs. Winter census yielded 82 birds in India and 892 in China, Jan 1990. Race *capensis* apparently undergoing marked decline, due to loss of wetlands; no recent records from several areas where still bred up to 1970's; in South Africa, now probably only breeds in Natal and Transvaal; apparently only survives in any numbers in Zambia, where also rare.
Bibliography. Ali & Ripley (1978), Batten *et al.* (1990), Bauer & Glutz von Blotzheim (1966), Bibby (1981), Bibby & Lunn (1982), Brazil (1991), Brichetti (1983), Britton (1980), Brooke (1984), Brown *et al.* (1982), Clancey (1985), Cramp & Simmons (1977), Day, J.C.U. (1981), Dementiev & Gladkov (1951b), Duhautois (1984), Etchécopar & Hüe (1978), Flint *et al.* (1984), Gauckler & Krause (1965), Gentz (1965), Géroudet (1978a), Grimmet & Jones (1989), Harrison (1988), Hüe & Etchécopar (1970), Inskipp & Inskipp (1985), Ledant *et al.* (1981), Lekagul & Round (1991), Mackworth-Praed & Grant (1957-1973), Maclean (1985), Paz (1987), Pinto (1983), Roberts (1991), Rutgers & Norris (1970), de Schauensee (1984), Scott (1989), Smythies (1986), Voisin (1991).

60. Australasian Bittern

Botaurus poiciloptilus

French: Butor d'Australie **Spanish**: Avetoro Australiano **German**: Australische Rohrdommel
Other common names: Australian/Brown Bittern, Boomer, Bull-bird

Taxonomy. *Ardea poiciloptila* Wagler, 1827, New South Wales.
Sometimes considered mere race of *B. stellaris*, with which forms superspecies. Population of SW Australia has been held to merit consideration as distinct subspecies *westralensis*; birds from New Zealand have also been placed in separate race *maorensis*. Monotypic.
Distribution. SW and SE Australia, Tasmania and New Zealand; New Caledonia and Loyalty Is.

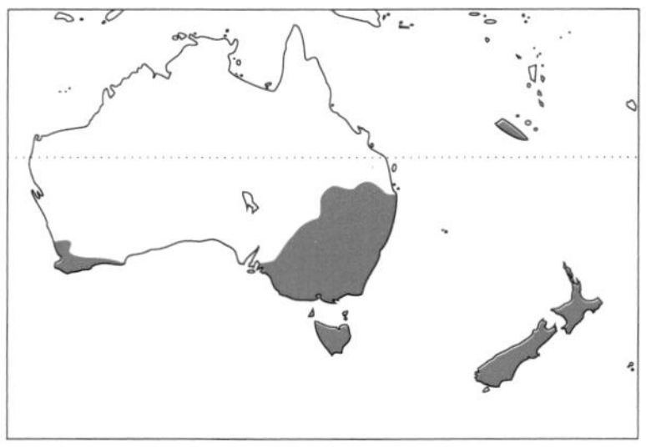

Descriptive notes. 66-76 cm; male 875-2085 g, female 571-1135 g; wingspan 105-118 cm. Plumage variable, with paler and darker birds; typically darker than *B stellaris*, especially on neck and back, with duller, paler cap. Juvenile paler.
Habitat. Wetlands with tall, dense vegetation of reeds (*Phragmites*), sedges, rushes (*Scirpus*, *Juncus*, *Eleocharis*) and cat-tails (*Typha*) along margins of rivers, pools, lakes and swamps; prefers still, shallow waters with little fluctuation in water level. Also occurs in wet paddocks with long grass and in rice paddies. Predominantly in fresh water, but also found in brackish water, in lagoons connected to sea or in estuaries; avoids coast. Only occasionally in open areas.
Food and Feeding. Fish, especially eels, amphibians, crustaceans, snails, insects and other arthropods, reptiles, small mammals and even birds; in New Zealand, introduced Australian tree frog (*Hyla aurea*) apparently constitutes main prey. Markedly nocturnal in feeding, but sometimes feeds by day. Solitary feeder, maintaining feeding territory and building several feeding

platforms by flattening clumps of reeds in dense parts of reedbeds; such sites often littered with remains of prey. Main foraging technique is "Quiet Stalking", but also known to use "Standing" on occasions; has been recorded using small bits of grass as bait for catching fish.

Breeding. Mainly breeds Oct-Dec (Sept-Feb) in Australia. Solitary; normally each male mated to only 1 female, but sometimes more, and up to 7 nests found in same reedbed. Nests a few centimetres above surface of water in area of dense vegetation; nest is thin platform of reeds and rushes 30-40 cm wide. Normally 4-5 eggs (3-6); incubation c. 25 days; chicks have dark brown down; fledging c. 7 weeks. Female alone builds nest, incubates eggs and feeds chicks.

Movements. Apparently sedentary, with post-breeding dispersal; regular short distance movements noted in winter in parts of Australia and in North I (New Zealand). Irruptive movements sometimes occur in response to particularly wet years, but such movements are not seasonal.

Status and Conservation. Not globally threatened. Rarely seen, due to secretive habits. Locally common in Australia, especially in Murray-Darling Basin. In SW Australia, has declined during 20th century, with under 100 pairs estimated in 1980's; may now be more or less restricted to W coastal plain, and a few sites on S coast. Widespread in Tasmania, particularly in E. In New Zealand, heavily persecuted during 19th century, as feathers used to make trout flies; slump has continued in recent decades, due to draining of wetlands; total population estimated at 580-725 birds in 1985; average density at wetlands of Whangamarino 1 bird/49 ha, with maximum of 1 bird/8·3 ha. May well be extinct on largest of Loyalty Is.

Bibliography. Bull *et al*. (1985), Chambers (1989), Falla *et al*. (1981), Hannecart & Letocart (1983), Macdonald (1988), Marchant & Higgins (1990), Miller & Miller (1991), Schodde & Tidemann (1988), Serventy (1985), Serventy & Whittell (1972), Soper (1976), Whiteside (1989), Williams, M.J. (1985d).

Class AVES
Order CICONIIFORMES
Suborder SCOPI
Family SCOPIDAE (HAMERKOP)

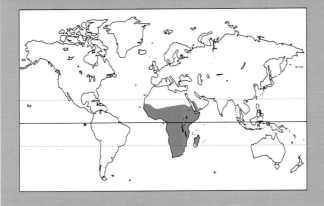

- Medium-sized wading birds with heavy bill and singular backward-pointing crest.
- 50-56 cm.

- Afrotropical Region.
- Woodland and wetlands.
- 1 genus, 1 species, 2 taxa.
- No species threatened; none extinct since 1600.

Systematics

The origins of the Hamerkop (*Scopus umbretta*) are extremely obscure and nobody really knows where its nearest affinities lie, though it is usually placed in the Ciconiiformes, alongside other large, long-legged water birds. The oldest evidence of the family is a fossil from the early Pliocene in South Africa.

Superficially the Hamerkop's bill recalls those of both the Shoebill (*Balaeniceps rex*) and the Boat-billed Heron (*Cochlearius cochlearius*), but this is normally attributed to convergent evolution. It has a pectinated middle toe as in the herons, a free hind toe as in the flamingos, egg-white protein like the storks and yet ectoparasites which are only otherwise found in plovers. To confuse matters further, its habits and behaviour are unique, leaving taxonomists with little option but to place it in its own monospecific family.

Work on DNA suggests that it should be placed between the herons and the flamingos, not far away from the storks and the Shoebill, its traditional allies. Most systematists consider it sufficiently distinctive to be placed in its own private suborder, Scopi.

Morphological Aspects

The Hamerkop's name is Afrikaans for "Hammer-head", one of its alternative English names. It owes this name to the strange aspect which results from its long, heavy bill being balanced by a curious backward-pointing crest.

The bill is deep, but laterally compressed and appears flattened and thin from the front. The ridged culmen is 80-85 mm long and ends in a slight hook. A groove runs along the side of the bill and here the nostrils are concealed. The terminal half of the lower mandible is very thin and may help in cutting up prey or vegetation or other tasks which require a delicate touch. This most peculiar bill is undoubtedly an evolutionary development in response to the bird's feeding requirements and, though it is perhaps comparable with that of the Shoebill, the Hamerkop's is clearly a much more lightweight version, which enables it to be far more selective and manoeuvrable in the moment of striking at prey (see Food and Feeding). Young birds start with a blunt, brown bill, but before they leave the nest the bill has acquired fairly similar proportions to that of the adults and is likewise black.

The Hamerkop stands about 56 cm tall and weighs about 470 g in the nominate race, while the dwarf West African race *minor* is obviously smaller, as well as a little darker. The plumage of the nominate race is rich sepia brown all over with a slight iridescent purplish gloss on the back; there are several darker brown bars on the tail. On emerging from the nest young birds already look very like adults. The legs are blackish, with feathering only extending down the upper half of the tibia. Both neck and legs are relatively short for a wading bird, so it is not surprising that it feeds mainly in shallow water.

The wings are broad and rounded and in flight the Hamerkop is reminiscent of an owl or perhaps a large moth. The neck is stretched out when soaring or gliding, as in most members of the stork family, but, being a smaller and more mobile bird, the Hamerkop indulges more in flapping flight, during which its head is partly retracted in towards its shoulders. It finds take-off much easier from some sort of elevated spot, but if from level ground, it is not nearly as difficult or awkward as it is for example for the Shoebill and many storks. Again there is no similar dependence on thermals for movement, principally, of course, because the Hamerkop is a much lighter bird.

Habitat

The Hamerkop is one of the most familiar birds of tropical Africa and it can be found throughout, in a variety of different types of wetland.

For feeding it requires shallow water, though the shallows themselves need not be extensive and may be along a lakeshore or the banks of a large river, as well as any small streams or seasonal pools; it can frequently be found on sandbanks, mud or floating vegetation, in estuaries, reservoirs, marshes and sometimes mangroves. Recently, in Tanzania, Hamerkops have even been seen foraging in rocky tidal pools on the coast, and this may represent a further extension of its feeding niche.

The other main requirement of the species is somewhere to build its enormous nest. Trees are normally favoured, but other possible sites include cliffs, and rocky hillslopes. When not breeding, Hamerkops still prefer to have trees nearby for roosting, although they may also roost in reedbeds. Typically they are found in open woodland, but they also occur in savanna and even in semi-desert, if there is water in the vicinity.

As it is not persecuted by man, the Hamerkop tends not to be wary of humans and it is frequently seen around villages. It actually seems to have benefited from his presence, having more suitable habitat for breeding and in particular for feeding, with the creation of fish ponds, paddyfields, dams and the like.

General Habits

Hamerkops have been thought to be largely nocturnal, but, although they are partly crepuscular, they are generally active only during the day. Like many birds in the tropics, they tend to be inactive during the heat of the day, preferring to rest in shady trees. In Mali nest building activity was found to have three peaks, one after sunrise, one in mid-morning and the last before sunset.

Birds are usually found alone or in pairs, though they sometimes congregate in groups of about 10, and at times up to 50 may occur together; such gatherings may be for communal roosting, for example in reedbeds.

A unique and extraordinary feature of Hamerkop behaviour is the "False-mounting" display. This involves one bird climbing on another's back, as if for copulation; however, there is no cloacal contact nor do there seem to be any clear sexual implications. It need not be performed by paired birds; indeed there can be a female above and a male below or two birds of the same sex involved, and the birds need not even be facing the same way. The purpose of this curious performance is unknown, but it would appear to be some form of social display.

Voice

The Hamerkop's vocal repertoire is fairly extensive, but is not as yet well understood. It is most expressive vocally when in the company of other conspecifics, and at times a group seems to get carried away with an impressive array of loud, nasal cackles such as "yik-yik-yik-yirrrr-yirrrr" or a repeated "wek-wek-wek-warrrk", accompanied by various social displays.

When alone, on the other hand, it is usually silent and the only sound that is commonly heard is the flight-call, a shrill, piping "nyip" or "kek". It does not perform bill-clattering and its vocal organs seem to be closest to those of herons.

Food and Feeding

Amphibians constitute a significant part of the Hamerkop's diet throughout most of its range, though they are not essential. In South and East Africa, clawed frogs (*Xenopus*) and their tadpoles are particularly favoured and provide an important source of nourishment for nestlings.

A substantial proportion of the prey consists of small fish, especially young of *Clarias*, *Barbus* and *Tilapia*, and Hamerkops have been found to take almost exclusively fish in Mali. Other items recorded include shrimps and other crustaceans, insects, worms and occasionally small mammals.

The normal method of feeding involves wading in shallow water, usually in amongst aquatic vegetation, and looking for individual prey items. The feet may be used for raking in the mud

The taxonomic position of the Hamerkop is an enigma. The species presents certain affinities with other long-legged wading birds, such as the herons and storks, and its unique bill has caused it to be associated with the Boat-billed Heron (Cochlearius cochlearius) and the Shoebill (Balaeniceps rex), although it does not really resemble either of these species any more than it does the herons or storks. More recently it has been linked with the waders or shorebirds of the Charadriiformes. It typically forages in shallow, freshwater wetlands, feeding mainly on frogs and small fish.

[Scopus umbretta. Photo: Tony & Liz Bomford/ Survival]

to disturb prey, or alternatively the wings may be flashed open to the same end. Unlike the Shoebill, the Hamerkop probes in the mud trying to locate prey, a practice to which its more manageable bill is better suited. Again, it does not engulf its prey with a great mass of vegetation, but rather picks it out with much more delicate precision, and often rinses it prior to consumption.

The Hamerkop also uses another system for catching its prey, which is very rare in the Ciconiiformes: it takes swarms of tadpoles or small fish from the water, while in flight. It flies into the wind, low over the water with slow wingbeats, and scoops its prey off the surface of the water, achieving a success rate of about 80%. It is able to perform this dexterous feat, thanks to its low wing-loading.

Like several other members of the order, the Hamerkop sometimes benefits from the presence of large herbivores. It has been recorded catching prey disturbed by the African buffalo (*Syncerus caffer*), even in the midst of a herd of about 200. It takes similar advantage of domestic cattle and may even hitch a ride on the back of a hippopotamus.

Perhaps because they do not rely on large prey items or any particular types of prey, Hamerkops do not normally seem to have problems with their food supply, and indeed spend relatively little time foraging. Their feeding pattern is commonly disrupted only by African Fish Eagles (*Haliaeetus vocifer*), which rob them of small fish and thus protract the task of finding sufficient food.

Breeding

Hamerkops are not colonial, although one might think so from the fact that many nests are often seen in close proximity, sometimes even in the same tree. This is because pairs have several nests in their home territory, some of which are never used, indeed some are not even completed. Also, a completed nest is remarkably strong and can support the weight of a heavy man, so nests may remain intact for many years.

The nest itself is undoubtedly one of the wonders of the animal world. The sheer weight of it is impressive enough, as it occasionally reaches more than 100 times the bird's own weight and it may be built with up to 8000 pieces. It averages about 1·5 m deep with a slightly smaller girth and takes three to six weeks to complete. Nest building is carried out by both sexes and almost all the material is collected within 100 m of the nest. Co-operative nest building with seven individuals involved has been recorded in Zimbabwe, but this is certainly not the rule.

The nest is normally placed about 9 m up in a major fork of a large tree, but it can also be sited on a cliff or even on the ground. The structure is extremely elaborate, though it starts off as a conventional enough stick platform nest; after this the rims are gradually built up with a mass of large sticks interwoven and glued together with mud and grass; the next stage is to raise a dome over the top, starting from the back; once

The function of the Hamerkop's curious "False-mounting" display remains a mystery. As its name suggests, it resembles copulation, and it can, in fact, be a prelude to it. However, there is no attempt to make cloacal contact. In addition, the display can be performed at any time of year, and with the female above and the male below, or between two birds of the same sex. It can even take place with the mounting bird facing backwards.

[*Scopus umbretta*. Photo: Alan Weaving/ Ardea]

this has been completed, a lot more material is added to the roof, leaving a very solid, near impenetrable structure. The only way in is a small opening from below, which complicates access for potential predators. The final touch is to fortify the entrance hole and then plaster this and the single inner nesting chamber with mud and leaves. The latter is some 40 cm wide by 60 cm high, while the entrance tunnel is 10-15 cm wide and 40-60 cm long. The roof often ends up adorned with an extraordinary collection of odds and ends, ranging from bits of skin and bone to paper, plastic, clothing and general rubbish.

When the nest is still at the early platform stage, it is sometimes taken over by Verreaux's Eagle Owls (*Bubo lacteus*), which the Hamerkops are powerless to chase away. Similarly, once finished, it is often usurped by other species, particularly Barn Owls (*Tyto alba*), which, in a study area of 150 ha in Mali, were found to have occupied 50 out of 70 Hamerkop nests. When Hamerkops abandon a nest, other birds frequently move in or on to breed, especially the Egyptian Goose (*Alopochen aegyptiacus*) and the Comb Duck (*Sarkidiornis melanotos*); other common tenants include the Grey Kestrel (*Falco ardosiaceus*), the African Pygmy Goose (*Nettapus auritus*) and the Speckled Pigeon (*Columba guinea*), and there is also a record of one being taken over by Black Storks (*Ciconia nigra*). Even when Hamerkops are in occupation, the vast structure is often used by small birds, such as sparrows, for building their nests in. Interestingly, Hamerkops may move back to a nest and even breed successfully, after it has been used by owls.

It is not only other birds that have learnt to take advantage of the Hamerkop's secure nest, it can also be used by honey bees or, mostly for sleeping or resting in, by genets (*Genetta*), mongoose (*Herpestes*), monitor lizards (*Varanus*) and a variety of snakes such as Spitting Cobras (*Naja nigricollis*) and pythons (*Python*).

The reason why the species invests so much energy in nest building is still obscure. It is evidently not for concealment, as nests stand out at some distance, and the above partial list of unwelcome visitors indicates that it is by no means an impregnable stronghold, so it does not mean that parents can safely leave the nest unguarded for any length of time; in any case, the proportion of young fledged to eggs laid is very low, so

protection is unlikely to be the answer. It does not seem to regulate heat or act as a sort of brood chamber and its main purpose might be to house a relatively large clutch.

An exhaustive study of the species in Mali, carried out by R. T. and M. P. Wilson, has shown that an average pair tends to build three to five nests every year. Over a period of about four and a half years one pair built eleven new nests and occupied two other old ones, rarely staying more than a few months in any one nest and "moving house" at least seventeen times. As nest building, or repair, was more or less continuous, it was not directly correlated with breeding, which could mean that the underlying object of such activity is to strengthen the pair-bond. The limited evidence available suggests that the pair do indeed stay together on a long-term basis.

Hamerkops are territorial, but are not actively aggressive towards intruders and territories may overlap extensively. In East Africa, a typical territory may be about 3 km of riverbank, whereas in Mali it was calculated as some 20-37 ha per pair. In a remarkable case in South Africa, five pairs all reared young successfully within an area of one hectare!

When breeding is to be attempted, copulation is frequent and it may occur on or by the nest, or alternatively on the ground, up to 100 m away. It is preceded by the male bobbing his wings and crest up and down at his mate and sometimes by a courtship flight accompanied by croaking; the same performance can also be the prelude to the "False-mounting" display, which itself may be performed at any time, even during breeding (see General Habits).

In East Africa laying occurs all year round, without any obvious preferences. Elsewhere it peaks at different times, but, rather surprisingly for a bird which takes almost exclusively aquatic prey, there appears to be a slight overall bias towards breeding in the dry season or around the end of the rains; nest building also tends to be less frequent during the rains.

The clutch is normally of three to six eggs, although in South Africa up to seven have been recorded. They are laid at intervals of between one and three days and start off chalky white, though they soon become stained brown with mud. Incubation is shared between the sexes, but it appears to be carried out mostly by the female. It lasts about 30 days and probably starts after the first egg has been laid, as chicks hatch asynchronously. The eggs

The Hamerkop's complicated nest structure is entered from below, through a tunnel which leads into the nest chamber. Within this chamber the chicks can carry out their development relatively secure from predators, although pythons and monitor lizards are often a threat. By the time the young birds are fully fledged and ready to emerge from the nest, they closely resemble the adults, and have both the bill and the crest well developed.

[*Scopus umbretta.*
Photo: Alan Root/Survival]

may be left unattended for fairly, long periods, and egg temperatures are surprisingly low during incubation.

The nidicolous chicks are covered with grey down, which is soon replaced with feathers. After six days chicks have developed a crest and after 30 their plumage is very similar to that of the adults. They are fed by both parents and are often left alone in the nest, while the adults are away foraging. They stay in the nest until they are about 47 days old and often return to roost there for about a month after fledging. The age at which sexual maturity is attained is not yet known.

Non-breeding is apparently quite a common practice in the Hamerkop and it has been estimated that, at any one time, 78% of all nests may not be used for breeding. Also, up to 50% of eggs may be lost and 30-40% of chicks hatched may not survive to reach fledging, many falling prey to invading monitor lizards. This gives the very low figure of 0·13 young per adult every year, which would imply that adults probably live on average for around 20 years. However, more complete information from a dense population in Mali indicates that pairs produce 0·5-0·9 young per year, a much more satisfactory figure.

Movements

The Hamerkop is strictly sedentary and there is no evidence of its regular migration anywhere, although in drier parts of its range there may be some dispersal during the wet season, if temporary feeding sites appear. In many cases a pair sticks to its home territory all year round, occupying and roosting in different nests every few months (see Breeding). As territories frequently overlap, small-scale local movements can bring several birds together.

Relationship with Man

In all parts of tropical Africa, the Hamerkop is held in a position of great respect, with the result that it does not suffer persecution at the hands of man. It has also been claimed that it is the origin of more legends and superstitions than any other bird.

It is considered a magical bird. This is probably largely due to the fact that it builds its impregnable, inaccessible and therefore mysterious nest, after which a whole host of different species of animals may emerge from it; this impression would undoubtedly have been enhanced, when some incautious investigator introduced a hand, only to be rewarded with a nasty bite from a cobra. Another feature which has probably helped the growth of this superstition is the varied collection of articles which can end up in the nest structure, including bones and human effects. The bird's strange appearance, crepuscular habits and weird calls, especially when in a noisy group, must also have contributed to its reputation of possessing supernatural powers.

It is not perhaps surprising then, that in some places it is also regarded as a bird of evil omen. Villagers have been known to abandon a hut, because a Hamerkop flew over it and croaked. If a Hamerkop is harmed, the offender can suffer in many ways: the hills round his house can melt; his cattle may be hit by an epidemic; lightning can strike his house; and he can even die as a result of his offence. The belief that to molest a Hamerkop brings bad luck has clearly helped the species to survive and flourish. For this reason, it can often be seen in villages or feeding in fish ponds alongside humans.

Status and Conservation

Throughout its range, the Hamerkop is frequent to abundant and it is probably on the increase at the moment, due to the greater availability of suitable feeding grounds (see Habitat), combined with its immunity from human interference. No estimate of the current world population is known to have been put forward.

Perhaps the greatest foreseeable threats for the future might be degradation of water supplies, as the Hamerkop's diet is composed almost entirely of aquatic prey; note the case of the White Stork (*Ciconia ciconia*) in Europe (see page 454). Another possible problem could be loss of its protected status, with the spread of Western values, however, it is to be hoped that local cultural traditions could withstand such an onslaught with the help of an understanding of conservation issues.

PLATE 31

inches 6
cm 15

ssp *umbretta*

ssp *minor*

Family SCOPIDAE (HAMERKOP)
SPECIES ACCOUNTS

PLATE 31

Genus *SCOPUS*   Brisson, 1760

Hamerkop
Scopus umbretta

French: Ombrette du Sénégal   **German:** Hammerkopf   **Spanish:** Avemartillo
Other common names: Hammerhead, Hammer-headed stork

Taxonomy. *Scopus umbretta* Gmelin, 1789, Senegal.
Origins and relationships obscure. Some affinities with Ardeidae, Ciconiidae, Balaenicipitidae, Phoenicopteridae and Charadriidae. Birds from Madagascar sometimes considered separate race, *bannermani*. Two subspecies normally recognized.
Subspecies and Distribution.
S. u. umbretta Gmelin, 1789 - most of tropical Africa, SW Arabia, Madagascar.
S. u. minor Bates, 1931 - coastal belt from Sierra Leone to E Nigeria.
Descriptive notes. 50-56 cm; 415-430 g. Unmistakable. Iridescent purplish gloss on back. Juvenile similar to adult. Race *minor* smaller and darker.
Habitat. Wetlands of a wide variety, including estuaries, riverbanks, lakesides, fish ponds, irrigation schemes; also along rocky coasts in Tanzania. Usually requires trees (e.g. *Khaya senegalensis*) for nesting and also for roosting.
Food and Feeding. Mostly amphibians, especially frogs and tadpoles of genus *Xenopus*; in Mali, almost exclusively small fish (e.g. young *Tilapia*); also takes crustaceans, worms, insects, etc. Normally wades in shallows; sometimes whisks prey off surface of water in flight.

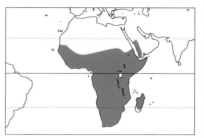

Breeding. All year round in E Africa, elsewhere peaks at different times, mostly late rains or dry season. Non-colonial. Extraordinarily elaborate large stick nest with central chamber, usually in fork of tree. Normally 3-6 eggs; incubation 28-32 days; chicks have grey down and broad, blunt bill; fledging 44-50 days; age of sexual maturity unknown. Breeding success variable, c. 0·3-0·9 chicks fledged per pair per year.
Movements. Sedentary, often with local movements; rarely occupies same nest for more than a few months. Some dispersal during rains, in drier areas.
Status and Conservation. Not globally threatened. Frequent to locally abundant in African range; widespread and locally common in Madagascar. Protected by native superstition. Probably increasing at present due to creation of artificial wetlands, though could suffer from deterioration of water quality caused by excessive use of pesticides.

Bibliography. Brown & Britton (1980), Brown *et al.* (1982), Campbell (1983), Cheke (1968), Clancey (1982), Coulter, Bryan *et al.* (1991), Cowles (1930), Crane (1987), Deane (1979), van Ee (1963, 1977), Frazier (1982), Gentis (1976), Goodfellow (1958), Grant (1914), Gray (1965), Hamilton (1972), Hanmer (1984), Hickman (1980), Hüe & Etchécopar (1962), Irwin (1984), Kahl (1967a, 1967b), Langrand (1990), Lewis (1989, 1990), Liversidge (1963), Lorber (1985), Louette (1981), Mackworth-Praed & Grant (1957-1973), Maclean (1985), Marshall (1972b, 1976), Milon *et al.* (1973), Nel (1966), van Niekerk (1985), Olson (1984), Pinto (1983), Rands *et al.* (1987), Richards (1979), Sibley & Ahlquist (1985), Siegfried (1975), Siegfried & Grimes (1985), Sievi (1975), Steyn (1972), Stowell (1954), Talbot (1976), Tree (1983), Uys (1967, 1986), Wilson, R.T. (1985, 1987), Wilson & Wilson (1984, 1986a, 1986b, 1988), Wilson, Wilson & Durkin (1987, 1988).

Class AVES
Order CICONIIFORMES
Suborder CICONIAE
Family CICONIIDAE (STORKS)

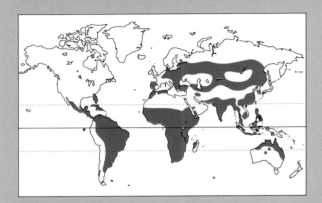

- Large wading birds with long neck and legs; bill long and sometimes heavy.
- 75-152 cm.

- All regions except Antarctic; marginal in Nearctic. Greatest diversity in tropics.
- Variety of wetlands, with some species in grassland and forest; generally warm continental areas.
- 6 genera, 19 species, 24 taxa.
- 5 species threatened; none extinct since 1600.

Systematics

The stork family is a well-defined group which was already distinctive around the beginning of the Tertiary, and the earliest remains identifiable as belonging to a stork come from the Upper Eocene in France. There is extensive fossil evidence, pertaining to some 30 species and the main radiation of the group seems to have taken place in the Oligocene. The modern day genera *Ciconia*, *Ephippiorhynchus* and *Leptoptilos* were all around in the Miocene, while of today's species remains of both the Wood Stork (*Mycteria americana*) and the Jabiru (*Jabiru mycteria*) have been found in late Pleistocene deposits, which were laid down some 140,000 years ago.

Tradition has long placed the storks alongside other large, long-legged wading birds in the order Ciconiiformes, but many recent taxonomists reckon that their closest relatives may actually be the New World vultures (Cathartidae). There is a fair amount of evidence to support this, including fossil remains of putative long-legged vultures, but the debate rages on and for the present the standard version is followed here.

Nineteen species are currently recognized, although there is still dispute over the taxonomic status of a few. Storm's Stork (*Ciconia stormi*) was for many years considered a subspecies of the widely distributed Woolly-necked Stork (*Ciconia episcopus*), mostly because very little was known about it. As both Storm's and the Indonesian race *C. e. neglecta* have red on their bills and both are rare and secretive, the separation of Storm's Stork as a good species has been tardy and laborious, but convincing proof has now been produced on the basis of different habitat preferences, in addition to the fact that physically the two are not really so very similar.

The Marabou (*Leptoptilos crumeniferus*) and its Asian counterpart, the Greater Adjutant (*Leptoptilos dubius*), used to be classified as the same species but important differences in their displays (see Breeding) indicate that they are sufficiently different to qualify as separate species. The last case of this type for consideration here is that of the Oriental White Stork (*Ciconia boyciana*), which is often ranked merely as a subspecies of the (European) White Stork (*Ciconia ciconia*). The Oriental is considerably larger and its bill is black as opposed to red; also it has not managed to adapt itself in the same way to the human environment and seems best considered as an independent species, with the caveat that it is evidently closely related to the European species.

As has happened with many other groups, the stork family has constantly been kept on the move by systematists; many of the changes have been due to differences in principle between "lumpers" and "splitters". In addition to the examples of specific status mentioned above, there has also been disagreement about the genus of several species. The Woolly-necked Stork was regularly placed in the now obsolete genus *Dissoura*; this was monospecific, although, of course, it also included Storm's Stork. The Maguari Stork (*Ciconia maguari*) similarly had its own monospecific genus, *Euxenura*. However, recent work in Venezuela has shown convincingly that this species does belong in the genus *Ciconia* and is, in fact, very close to the European White Stork. The Black-necked Stork (*Ephippiorhynchus asiaticus*) is probably best situated in the genus of the Saddlebill (*Ephippiorhynchus senegalensis*), although some authors still prefer to give it a genus of its own, *Xenorhynchus*. A few workers also include the Jabiru in *Ephippiorhynchus*.

The most remarkable case of nomenclature concerns the Yellow-billed Stork (*Mycteria ibis*) and its allies, the Milky Stork (*Mycteria cinerea*), the Painted Stork (*Mycteria leucocephala*) and the Wood Stork. The last-mentioned was originally the only member of this genus and all four at times have been placed in one or other of the genera *Tantalus* or *Ibis*. What is evident from the latter, as well as the formerly current English name of "wood ibises", is that they were confused with the "true" ibises (Threskiornithidae). Superficially they resemble this family, but their behaviour and several structural features are typical of the storks and are quite distinct from anything found in the ibis family, indicating that these were misnomers.

Extensive work by M. P. Kahl led to his division of the Ciconiidae into three tribes: the Mycterini; the Ciconiini; and the Leptoptilini. The Mycterini consist of the genera *Mycteria* (four species) and *Anastomus* (two species) and are typified by smallish size, breeding in colonies and specialization in bills, feeding techniques and prey. The Ciconiini, comprising the seven members of the genus *Ciconia*, are storks of medium size, which are solitary or loosely colonial breeders; they have general purpose bills and foraging techniques, suitable for taking a variety of prey types. There is the interesting exception of the apparently aberrant Abdim's Stork (*Ciconia abdimii*), which is decidedly small, breeds colonially and is a specialist feeder. The Leptoptilini, comprising the genera *Ephippiorhynchus* (two species), *Jabiru* (monospecific) and *Leptoptilos* (three species), are distinctive for their large size and their massive bills, which are designed for some specialized and some more generalized feeding; whereas *Leptoptilos* are almost invariably colonial, *Ephippiorhynchus* are solitary breeders, as is *Jabiru*, and some consider that the last two genera might be better placed in the Ciconiini.

Morphological Aspects

Storks are medium-sized to very large waterbirds with long bills, necks and legs and they thus constitute one of the most distinctive families. They are generally heavier-bodied birds than their relatives the herons, though superficially they have fairly similar structure.

The largest members of the family are among the largest flying birds. A male Marabou can be 152 cm tall and weigh as much as 8·9 kg, whereas Abdim's Stork only measures 75 cm and weighs about 1·3 kg.

Generally speaking, males tend to be a little larger than females, though this difference is more noticeable in some cases than in others, for instance the female Saddlebill averages 10-15% smaller than the male. There is no plumage difference between the sexes, and the only case of different colouration is that of the eyes of the two species of *Ephippiorhynchus*, where the male has a dull brown iris, as opposed to the female's strikingly bright pale yellow one.

The bill is invariably large, but in several species, such as the Marabou, it is really huge; in this species it grows continuously and may reach 34·6 cm long. The nostrils are normally small slits at the base of the bill.

The shape is very variable from one genus to another, according to feeding habits (see Food and Feeding). The seven members of the genus *Ciconia* have medium to fairly large bills, which are probably the least spectacular of the family. These are adaptable birds that take many different kinds of prey in very varied habitats and their bills are thus suited to their rather general foraging methods.

The genus *Ephippiorhynchus* and the Jabiru have very long, pointed, slightly upturned bills, which are used, rather as if they were daggers, for jabbing at fish in the shallows. The Jabiru's is the deepest of the three, but even this bulky bill is surpassed by the massive conical bills of the genus *Leptoptilos*. These huge meat-cleavers are among the most formidable weapons in the animal world, although it seems that they are not, in fact, particularly effective for opening up the carcasses, which represent an important part of the diet of the Marabou and the Greater Adjutant. Be that as it may, this bill is sufficiently formidable

to make the bird respected by other scavengers, both avian and mammalian. The skin of the head and part of the neck is bare or sparsely bristled with tough down, as an evolutionary development to avoid getting feathers caked in blood or mud.

However, the most unusual bills in the family are perhaps those of the genera *Mycteria* and *Anastomus*. The former have a long, tapered, slightly decurved bill, which is round in cross-section and has some sensitive parts towards the tip that enable the birds to fish under conditions that for many other species would be impossible. Like *Leptoptilos* and also the Jabiru, this genus has bare skin on the head and, in the case of Wood Stork, on the neck too, so as to avoid getting feathers dirty, when fishing in muddy water; the Wood Stork also has a bony plate on the top of its head, like the Lesser Adjutant (*Leptoptilos javanicus*), which has even been found to have green algae growing on its cap. In all cases bare skin takes on much more vivid colours during courtship and so helps to make displays more spectacular.

The two members of the genus *Anastomus*, the African Openbill (*Anastomus lamelligerus*) and the Asian Openbill (*Anastomus oscitans*) share a unique bill. As their name indicates, the bill has an opening between the two mandibles, giving it a distorted, somewhat deformed, appearance; indeed, this bill might well have developed when birds with slightly deformed bills found that they could use them effectively for getting snails out of their shells. Alternatively the technique used for extracting the snails may wear away or warp the bill and certainly young birds, while still in the nest, have more conventional, straight bills.

Whatever the explanation, it seems likely that this strange bill has been specially adapted for the very restricted diet of the genus. The upper mandible is almost straight and along the edges, near the tip there are 20-30 small columnar pads, which probably help the stork to grip a shell, while extracting its inhabitant. The lower mandible is distinctly recurved from about two thirds of the way along and is sometimes warped off to one side too, again possibly a deformity resulting from the special feeding technique.

As already indicated, the different species may have bare facial skin, in some cases extending down onto the neck. In others, such as Storm's Stork, it is limited to brightly coloured orbital skin, while some species have the whole face feathered. The neck has a series of large subcutaneous air-sacs and these reach their most remarkable development in the Greater Adjutant and the Marabou. They possess large, bulbous pendant air-sacs, one of which hangs from the throat, while another is much less obvious on the upper back. One of the old theories

Subdivision of the Ciconiidae.

[Figure: Francesc Jutglar]

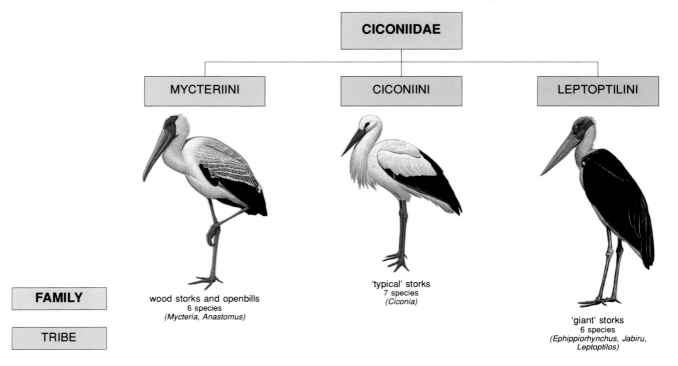

CICONIIDAE

MYCTERIINI — CICONIINI — LEPTOPTILINI

FAMILY

TRIBE

wood storks and openbills
6 species
(*Mycteria, Anastomus*)

'typical' storks
7 species
(*Ciconia*)

'giant' storks
6 species
(*Ephippiorhynchus, Jabiru, Leptoptilos*)

was that the former was for resting the bill on, as a kind of pad, but they are now known to be used basically in display and as cooling mechanisms. As with all the bare skin, during breeding they take on much more vivid colours and they are often distended to spectacular effect.

The neck is long in all species and, as with the long legs, shows a development for feeding, which enables a long reach and gives the bird a better chance of securing prey that is further away or that tries to escape. The long legs obviously give the bird a long stride, allowing it to cover ground relatively quickly, and also to wade into deeper water. The tarsus is reticulated and the shortish toes are basally webbed. The middle toe is not pectinated, as it is in the herons, while the hind toe is slightly raised, perhaps to put a little more spring into the bird's step. The normal pace is unhurried and rather stately with a decidedly upright stance, though birds sometimes dart rapidly after prey for short distances. It has been suggested that their normally slow, deliberate movements help to reduce nest losses through slipping and falling.

Storks have long, broad wings that are excellently suited to soaring. Being large and fairly bulky, they are heavily dependent on this method of flight, as they do not generally have the stamina necessary for sustained flapping flight. Unlike the pelicans, storks do not fly in any regular formations, whether in small-scale movements or during migration, although it has been reported in Brazil that Maguari Storks regularly fly in wedge-shaped formation.

The wingspan of the genus *Leptoptilos* has been claimed exceptionally to reach 320 cm, and this is only surpassed by the Wandering and Royal Albatrosses (*Diomedea exulans* & *D. epomophora*). However, some of the smaller species, for example the Black Stork (*Ciconia nigra*), do not rely quite so much on soaring and have a correspondingly smaller wing surface area. There are 12 primaries and 22 secondaries.

Unlike their relatives the herons, most storks fly with their necks outstretched, presenting a very distinctive silhouette and thus assisting in long-distance identification. The only exceptions are the members of the genus *Leptoptilos*, which usually retract their necks, probably in response to their huge bills having become so heavy, a tendency also evident in the pelicans and the Shoebill (*Balaeniceps rex*). The normal flight of storks consists of soaring alternated with some flapping, but some species can perform surprising feats of aerobatics, and the African Openbill may execute plummeting dives or even fly upside-down.

The tail is short, so the legs stick out behind it in flight, and elongated undertail-coverts sometimes partially obscure it, as happens in Storm's and the Woolly-necked Storks. It consists of 12 feathers and is normally squarish or slightly rounded, though it can be slightly forked, as in the Woolly-necked and Maguari Storks.

Plumage in the stork family tends to consist mostly of varying combinations of black or blackish grey and white and there are frequently iridescent tones to the black parts, most notably in the African Openbill and the Black and Black-necked Storks. The appearance is often enhanced by beautiful colours on the bill, legs and facial skin, such as in the Saddlebill, the Jabiru and the Yellow-billed Stork. Several species take on pinkish tones to their feathers in breeding plumage, none more so than the Painted Stork, but breeding plumage is normally just a brighter version of non-breeding plumage. Juvenile plumage tends to be drab grey or brown, while intermediate immature plumages are usually a rather watered-down version of adult breeding dress.

While they lack the elegant plumes of the Ardeidae, some species of storks have their own peculiar brand of unusual feathers. The genus *Ciconia* have an impressive neck ruff, which may be bristled out during courtship. The Woolly-necked Stork has this feature further developed than others and has its whole neck covered in soft, woolly down-like feathers, whence its common English name. As mentioned above, several species, such as the Black Stork, have spe-

The handsome Saddlebill is amongst the most colourful of all the storks. It is also one of the largest, with a wingspan that can stretch an impressive 270 cm. While it can take off quite easily from the ground with a few powerful wingbeats, like other storks it relies largely on soaring flight, so it is heavily dependent on the presence of suitable thermals in order to make movements of any distance. Note the characteristic flight posture, with the neck outstretched, and also the dark eye indicating that this bird is a male.

[*Ephippiorhynchus senegalensis*, Okavango Delta, Botswana. Photo: P. Evans/ Bruce Coleman]

cialized, very long, stiff undertail-coverts, which may be fluffed out in displays.

Moult in the stork family is poorly known, but there is normally one more or less complete moult per annual cycle, occurring either after breeding, as in the Marabou, or during breeding, as in the European White Stork. Primaries are replaced in descendant, serially descendant or irregular order, with several active centres. Juveniles moult into typical adult plumage during their second, third or fourth calendar year.

Habitat

The storks have a near cosmopolitan distribution, with representatives on six continents. However, only three species reach temperate areas and all of these migrate during the northern winter to the strongholds of the family in tropical parts of Asia and Africa. The storks do not reach nearly as far north as the heron family, indeed in the New World, where the family has diversified least, only one species actually makes it north into the USA and there it only has a foothold in the southern states.

Storks are fairly adaptable in terms of habitat. Like their allies the herons, they normally prefer to be near water and indeed some species are almost entirely dependent on aquatic prey, such as the genera *Mycteria* and *Anastomus*. However, most species are not so rigorously restricted to wetlands and many can live and feed in areas where water is scarce. The Marabou frequents drying pools, especially when searching for food on which to feed its young, but a lot of its life is spent over dryish, rolling savanna, scavenging around for carcasses, and at such times it may be far from water. Similarly, Abdim's Stork and others frequently forage in dry grassland. Most species prefer lowlands with warm, continental climates where persistent rain and cold are exceptional.

Typical stork habitats include various kinds of wetlands, such as swamps or marshes, paddyfields, flooded grassland, river or lake margins and irrigation schemes. They are frequently found in light woodland, savanna and fields, normally with shallow water for feeding in. Small ponds are favoured by many

species, as they tend to concentrate prey and also limit the chances of prey being able to escape. Other popular sites include shallow backwaters in rivers, marshes and wet meadows.

The more extreme habitat types used include the dry upland areas exploited by Abdim's Stork and the extensive forests of Eastern Europe, where the Black Stork reaches its highest densities. In general storks are not common in coastal habitats, although there are notable exceptions including Milky and Wood Storks and the Lesser Adjutant, which are typically found around mudflats, mangroves or lagoons.

Some species have undoubtedly benefited from man's impact on the landscape, most notably the European White Stork in Western Europe, where mass deforestation over the centuries opened up vast tracts of farmland which is ideal for the species, in areas that must previously have been totally unsuitable; indeed, it only started breeding in Denmark in the fifteenth century. It has also been supplied with an unending supply of suitable nest-sites on man's buildings.

However, one species' gain is another's loss and the Black Stork, which is still frequent in woodland in Poland must have been much more widespread and abundant over Western Europe in the past, when forests were larger and humans, which this species shuns, were less in evidence. As it is, both species are now declining alarmingly in the area (see Status and Conservation).

As most species normally breed in trees, they obviously need at any rate a few in their breeding area, although not necessarily many. In a famous colony of Asian Openbills at Wat Phai Lom in Thailand there are several thousand nests spread out over a few trees; however, such dense concentrations may be detrimental towards the very survival of the species (see Relationship with Man). Some form of removal from terrestrial predators is usually favoured and many species, such as Wood Storks, tend to nest in trees over water, preferably on islets.

Not all storks nest in trees, however, and the most celebrated case is unquestionably that of European White Stork, which throughout its European range nests most regularly on the roofs of buildings, though it also nests in trees. Abdim's Stork similarly installs itself in the roofs of native huts, where it again obviously benefits from the protection it is afforded by local superstitions; around Lake Chad people even put up basket-like structures for the storks to nest on. However, this species is also notable for the large colonies it forms on rocky islands, for example in Lake Shala in Ethiopia, with the nests being built on ledges or in amongst boulders. Several other species can sometimes be found breeding in towns, for instance Yellow-billed Storks in West Africa and Painted Storks in parts of India.

Other species show more limited adaptability. In Poland, large numbers of Black Storks nest in trees in fairly dense forest, but further south in Spain the species normally takes up residence on cliff ledges, sometimes in the company of Griffon and Egyptian Vultures (*Gyps fulvus* & *Neophron percnopterus*).

The Maguari Stork, the only New World representative of its genus, is remarkable in being the only stork that regularly nests on flat ground; it normally looks for a secluded spot in a marshy area, possibly in reedbeds. However, in Venezuela it prefers to use bushes or small trees and may only be a ground-nester when local circumstances demand.

Some species are attracted to rubbish dumps, especially the Marabou and the Greater Adjutant, which are renowned as scavengers. In south-west Spain concentrations of over fifty European White Storks sometimes gather at rubbish dumps along with various corvids and kites, like them presumably finding an abundant source of food, although whether this is limited to mice and insects or may also include food discarded by humans is not clear. Some pairs have even been seen to build their nests and begin breeding right beside such dumps.

Migrating storks frequently end up having to use habitat types which they would not otherwise visit, due to the large-scale reduction of some of their favourite habitats in certain areas; the most frequent cause of this is the conversion of wetlands for agriculture.

General Habits

Some species of stork are highly gregarious, notably the colonial breeders, such as the members of the genera *Mycteria* and *Anastomus*. However, although they may breed and roost in numbers varying from only a few to hundreds or even, in the case of Abdim's Stork, thousands, many of them habitually forage alone especially outside the breeding season. Other species are basically solitary, sometimes associating in loose flocks with conspecifics, for example at favourable feeding sites, or temporarily forming small family groups.

Migration usually takes place in sizeable flocks and large numbers of European White Storks can be seen gathering around either end of the Mediterranean, in preparation for crossing the Bosporus or the Straits of Gibraltar. The mass movements of Abdim's Storks in conjunction with the beginning of the rains are a similarly impressive sight.

Storks are basically diurnal, so the night is almost invariably dedicated exclusively to roosting, although Wood Storks may practice their tactile fishing by night. We have little detailed information about roosting, but it appears that in most species this normally takes place high up a tree, frequently near water, and often on small islands; cliffs may also be used. Colonial species often roost at regular sites in the company of other waterbirds, such as other stork species, herons, ibises, spoonbills, cormorants and the more arboreal species of pelicans, whereas the more solitary species are rarely found roosting in groups and associate far less with other species in all aspects of their lives; they very often roost at a site near their most recent nest. The Maguari Stork regularly roosts on the ground, probably because it is not able to grasp branches and so can only balance on a tree.

Temperate breeders are active throughout most of the daylight hours, especially during breeding, when they have to collect food for all the family. Tropical species, however, tend to feed mostly in the first and last hours of daylight and often spend most of the day loafing around, although larger birds like the Marabou must normally wait till thermals have formed, before taking flight in the morning. The daily timetable of coastal species like the Lesser Adjutant is often strictly regulated by tides and these birds tend to rest in mangroves at high tide.

Much of the time is spent in preening and general toilet which sometimes includes direct head-scratching and, for

Excess heat can be a major problem for many birds in the tropics, and several different systems of thermoregulation have been developed. One of the most typical among storks is panting, as demonstrated by the bird on the left. By exposing the overheated underwing these Woolly-necked Storks probably manage to lose heat to the atmosphere by convection. This posture may also serve, as in the vultures, for toning up the feathers which tend to become dishevelled after long periods of soaring.

[*Ciconia episcopus microscelis*, Malawi. Photo: Liz & Tony Bomford/ Survival]

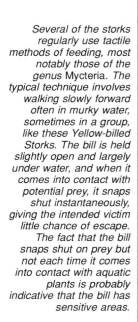

example in the Maguari Stork, bathing in water. It is interesting to note that in Venezuela this species was found to have exactly the same species of ectoparasite as that found on Asian Openbills in Thailand.

Both inter- and intraspecific aggression are rare outside breeding colonies and nest-sites, and individuals usually pay no attention at all to each other, although there may be some competition for a particularly choice morsel of food, as sometimes happens with Marabous. For most species, non-breeding aggression is limited to a "Forward-display" from the would-be aggressor and an answering "Upright-display" from the appeasing defender.

Extreme weather conditions, especially with regard to temperature can present problems for storks, especially during breeding. A cold, wet spring can result in the devastation of many European White Stork clutches both directly by destroying nests, eggs or young, and also indirectly by reducing food supplies or affording impoverished conditions for foraging. Somewhat surprisingly, adults of this species do not shelter their young from the rain, even when they happen to be nearby at the time. In contrast to this behaviour, in Venezuela, with a temperature that averages 5-15°C higher, the Maguari Stork will protect even large young, not only in heavy tropical showers, but also in light rain, and an adult may spend up to five hours sheltering its young.

Another problem which faces a lot of large waterbirds, especially in the tropics, is that of excess heat. Unlike many of these other birds, storks do not indulge in gular-fluttering, though it has been recorded in the Maguari Stork. Instead, they use other fairly common strategies, such as panting with the tongue raised, and ruffling up the feathers in order to separate the sun-heated surface from the body. Storks also practice urohydrosis, which involves defaecating directly onto the legs, thus favouring heat loss through evaporation. Many species use this system, but it is most celebrated in the *Leptoptilos* storks, which have repeatedly been described in the most unflattering terms, and this practice evidently adds to the repugnance that some people feel towards them. The Marabou and Greater Adjutant also use their pendant air-sacs to dissipate heat.

Other means of getting rid of unwanted heat that the Painted Stork, among others, commonly uses involves the wings being spread half-open, but bent at the wrists, in the form of a shield. Much the same posture is also used in sunning, with the opposite end in view, and this practice is known to help restore the curve to feathers after soaring has left them misshapen. Wing-spread postures may be adopted at times to shelter young from the direct rays of the sun. Adults of some species, for instance the Asian Openbill or the Saddlebill, empty a billfull of water over their eggs or young in order to cool them off.

Heat loss can also be a problem on occasions and two strategies have been developed to cut down on this. One involves standing on one leg only when resting, in order to minimize the exposed suface area of bare skin; this may also be used simply for resting a leg. The other method used by storks is only recorded for the genus *Ciconia*. It works on the same principle, but this time it is the bill that is tucked away into the feathers of the ruff to prevent the heat getting out. However, this should not be confused with the occasions when storks rest their bills on their retracted necks perhaps with the intention merely of taking the weight off their neck muscles.

Birds may often be seen resting on their tarsi, though this practice is most common in juveniles and nestlings, as it does not allow the bird to take off so quickly in an emergency. This habit is particularly common in some of the larger storks, for instance the Black-necked Stork.

Voice

Most adult storks are not voiceless, as has frequently been claimed, though it is certainly true that they are normally silent. The only time they tend to break this silence is at their breeding sites, where they produce a variety of vocalizations and also other noises.

Several different genera normally accompany their "Updown" greeting display (see Breeding) with some form of noise which may be more or less vocal. These range from *Mycteria*, which hiss or fizz, to *Anastomus*, which honk or croak, and

Leptoptilos which squeal and moo. *Ciconia* storks go in for varying extents of whistling, which is highly developed in the Black Stork, but rare and weak in the almost voiceless European White Stork.

Bill-clattering is another important part of this display, most notably in the genus *Ciconia* and it reaches its most advanced form in the European White Stork. This species throws its head right back, creating a resonance box in the lower neck, which provides a tremendous amount of amplification and helps the sound to carry much further. Where there are many nests nearby, a whole town can echo to these sounds well into the night, when the illumination may apparently keep them active much later. Even downy young of this species can produce a creditable version.

The other members of the genus are not such ardent bill-clatterers and it is much reduced for example in the Woolly-necked Stork. Nonetheless, most stork species perform a certain amount of bill-clattering, with the probable exception of the Saddlebill, which in addition seems to be genuinely voiceless after the nestling stage. The Yellow-billed Stork only bill-clatters during copulation and at other times it just snaps or rattles its bill.

In the Marabou bill-clattering is most commonly used as a threat display, although it is also common during breeding and may even be attempted, albeit without much success, by young birds. Both openbills are hampered by it being physically impossible for them to produce a normal bill-clatter; nevertheless, during copulation, they make a similar noise when the male rattles his bill against the side of his mate's.

The greatest variety in vocal repertoire seems to belong to the Marabou, which is reported to moo, whine, whistle, and hiccup during breeding and threat displays, while its young chitter, squawk or bray at varying stages. In addition, most of the sounds made by this species are said to be "impossible to syllabize in any known language".

Food and Feeding

It is reckoned that food availability is the most important limiting factor for storks in almost all aspects of their ecology, including distribution, longevity, breeding success and population numbers. Several species, such as the Maguari Stork, regularly travel long distances in search of food during breeding, in order to meet the demands of hungry chicks.

In the case of the Wood Stork, it has been shown that the state of food resources influences the time breeding begins, the proportion of the adult population that attempt to breed and the survival rates, first of fledglings, and later of young birds throughout their first year. In addition, it must be remembered that mere survival does not necessarily imply fitness for breeding when the time comes and this again depends largely on food.

All species are exclusively carnivorous and plant matter ingested at times is almost certainly taken by accident when prey is being caught. The typical food of the family includes smallish fish, frogs, insects and small rodents, but a great many other items occur with varying frequencies, depending on the different species.

As already mentioned in connection with bill structure (see Morphological Aspects), there is a great variety within the stork family in terms both of feeding techniques and food. It is perhaps most instructive to examine each of the genera separately.

The four species of *Mycteria* are specialist feeders, taking mostly smallish to medium-sized fish with some frogs, crustaceans and aquatic insects. The Wood Stork also takes some salamanders, small snakes and even baby alligators. On the vast mudflats of eastern Sumatra the Milky Stork seems to feed largely on mudskippers (*Periophthalmus*).

These species generally prefer to feed in shallow water with dense concentrations of fish, brought about sometimes by changes in the water level, indeed densities of almost 8000 fish/m² have been recorded in drying ponds in Florida. Breeding is usually synchronized with the periods when food is most readily available and abundant, but this occurs in different conditions from one place to another (see Breeding).

The shallow water frequented by this genus is very often murky and muddy and it is here that we see their highly specialized feeding method in action. A bird either stands still or, more normally, walks about in this shallow water moving its largely submerged bill from side to side as it goes. Sometimes the bird also stirs up the water or the mud on the bottom with one of its feet to make fish move about more, either through alarm or being attracted to the movements; to the same end they sometimes flash their wings open over the surface of the water.

When the bill comes into contact with prey, it snaps shut on it immediately and the combination of this speed, its accompanying force and the sharp edges of the mandibles mean that prey once caught rarely escapes. Kahl measured the time that elapsed between the first contact and capture in the Wood Stork and found it to be the astounding figure of only 25 milliseconds, making it one of the fastest reactions ever recorded in the vertebrate world.

The bill undoubtedly has some extremely sensitive areas, though it is not yet clear exactly which parts. It has also been surmised that it may work as a kind of trigger reaction, with the jaw muscle being activated by any sudden jolt. Nonetheless, when moving through tangled vegetation, the bird does not seem to get confused between fish and plants. Furthermore, fish over 3·5 cm are preferably taken, so it is clearly a system which is at least partly selective.

The system enables these storks to fish in conditions that would be impossible for any bird relying entirely on vision to capture its prey. Again Kahl carried out experiments to test this, using one bird with its forward view temporarily blocked out. He found that this bird was equally successful at catching fish in clear water as was another without its vision hampered, thus convincingly showing that capture was mostly tactile.

Much more work has been done on this species than on its congeners, undoubtedly due to its being the only North American stork and probably also because of its continuing struggle for survival on this continent (see Status and Conservation). The other three members of the genus are known to use much the same techniques and take fairly similar food.

The Milky Stork, when searching for mudskippers on mudflats, tends to look for a mudskipper's hole and then probes its bill in and around the hole up to 10-15 times, sometimes immersing the whole bill and the head in the mud. When a mudskipper is caught, it is hauled out, tossed up in the air until in the head first position and then swallowed alive. After capturing prey the bird normally rinses the mud off its bill. Unsuccessful probing usually results in the bird wandering off and trying elsewhere, before returning to try the same site again. Another, rarer alternative involves the bill being inserted into a hole and then pushed forward, opening up a runnel in the mud. In these cases, no experiment is necessary for us to realize that capture is tactile.

Another method known to be used by this species is where the bird stands perfectly still for up to 8 minutes with its bill held slightly open and about two thirds submerged in the water at the edge of the sea or alternatively in the mud, waiting for prey to come into contact with it, when it will be snapped shut in the usual way; again the only prey recorded as having been taken using this method were large mudskippers. The limited evidence so far collected would suggest that this species may take larger prey, on the whole, than its American counterpart, but perhaps fewer items. One estimate reckoned that, if the Milky Stork's requirements are equivalent to the Wood Stork's, then, even allowing for its larger size, it could catch its daily intake in about two hours. It has also been found that the Yellow-billed Stork can catch its immediate requirements in only a few minutes.

The amount of food required is obviously almost as crucial a factor as the amount available and it was calculated that at Keoladeo (Bharatpur), in north-west India, each individual Painted Stork fledgling consumed on average about 500 g of fish daily and that during the breeding season in this park the young of this species alone put away some 60 t. An alternative view of this, for the Wood Stork, is that during the breeding

Two storks are notable scavengers, the Marabou (Leptoptilos crumeniferus) and its close relative the Greater Adjutant, here seen feeding on a buffalo carcass in the company of three species of vulture (Gyps). The massive bill found in these storks is not actually much use for dismembering a carcass, so they tend to wait in the offing, nipping in from time to time to snatch a morsel from the vultures, which show a certain amount of respect for the stork's large bill. These two species are also unique among the storks in their possession of inflatable air-sacs, one hanging from the throat, another, less visible on the upper back.

[Leptoptilos dubius, Manas Tiger Reserve, Assam, NE India. Photo: Joanna Van Gruisen/Ardea]

season some 200 kg of fish are required to feed a single pair and the young they raise to fledging.

The openbills have developed one of the strangest of all bills, presumably as a feeding adaptation (see Morphological Aspects). The two species eat almost exclusively freshwater molluscs, though at times they also take other small marsh animals, such as frogs and crabs. Both species have a very strong preference for apple snails (*Pila*), large aquatic snails which can normally be found either in very muddy water or buried in the mud itself. This preference is so strong that captive young African Openbills had to be force-fed on any food other than snails.

Openbills frequently feed in small groups, normally in marshes or paddyfields, digging around in the mud or searching the aquatic vegetation for prey. The African Openbill may even hitch a lift on a grazing hippopotamus, waiting for its huge host to turn up a snail, which the bird then grabs and carries off to dry land or at least to the shallows to eat. Often a favourite site for consuming prey is used several days running and a pile of shells may accumulate. In Thailand large numbers of Asian Openbills are able to breed successfully in the dry season, thanks to their ability to take aestivating snails from the hard-caked mud of paddyfields; they sometimes follow tractors engaged in ploughing, which regularly churn up snails as they go along.

It used to be thought that snails were carried in the opening in the bill, but it is, in fact, the tip that is used for any such carrying. Another, rather more serious, misconception which prevailed for a long time was that this strange bill was used as a kind of nutcracker to shatter the shell and thus get at the snail. The real process is now fairly well known, but, as it happens very quickly and habitually takes place under water, there are still question marks hanging over the precise procedure.

The upper mandible is used to hold the shell steady against the ground during extraction. The snail is relatively secure against most potential predators with its operculum, a hard, bony shield, tightly shut over the entrance to the shell. The stork, however, eases the razor-sharp tip of its lower mandible under the operculum, cuts the snail's very strong columellar muscle and extracts the detached snail for immediate consump-

tion, without further ado. The Asian Openbill has also been found to produce a narcotic secretion in its saliva. When the shell is being gripped, saliva flows down the lower mandible and onto the operculum; this relaxes the snail's muscle and thus facilitates the introduction of the lower mandible.

During this process the shell, far from being cracked open, normally receives only a few scratches. The method for dealing with bivalves, or freshwater mussels (*Ampullaria*), is similar and involves inserting the lower mandible between the two parts of the shell near the hinge and, once again, cutting the muscles which keep the shell closed tight, allowing the bird to take its meal with scarcely any damage to the shell. Bivalves may also be left in the sun, which causes them to open up and expose themselves, but the storks rarely seem to resort to this method. During the dry season bivalves are the prey most readily available to the African Openbill and it is thought that they provide insufficient food to allow breeding, hence in Africa, as in India, openbills mostly start breeding around the onset of the rains, when the snails are beginning to emerge from their aestivation.

Although most food is consumed on the spot, it is quite normal for breeding birds to carry one snail back to the nest to be dealt with there. Thus large colonies have the floor littered with broken shells, which may have helped to promote the former ideas about their feeding method.

Exact food requirements are not known as yet, but a fifteen-day-old African Openbill in captivity ate 143 g of snails, virtually its own body weight, in 24 hours. The strong defences of the snails mean that the storks have few, if any, competitors for their main source of food, which in suitable conditions often abounds, but such reliance on one type of food always carries its concomitant risks, as a species may have little capacity to adapt if this particular food supply fails; a period of prolonged drought or the excessive use of pesticides could pose serious threats to these species. Likewise years of abundant snails will mean much greater breeding success, hence their relatively large clutch.

The feeding methods used by members of the other four genera are far more generalized, although they are not by any means without their own interest.

The two members of the genus Ephippiorhynchus often perform an attractive "Flap-dash" display on their feeding grounds, as demonstrated by this female Black-necked Stork. This display involves the bird rushing through the water, flashing open its wings, which are conspicuously patterned black and white. The display is thought to strengthen the pair-bond, as it is usually performed in the presence of the bird's mate, and closes with the active bird pausing in front of its mate and holding its wings open. It is only otherwise known for the Jabiru (Jabiru mycteria), the only other stork with extensive white in the flight-feathers.

[Ephippiorhynchus asiaticus australis, Kakadu National Park, Northern Territory, Australia. Photo: Jean-Paul Ferrero/ Ardea]

The genus *Ciconia* are really "all-purpose" storks in the aspect of feeding behaviour. They are basically opportunists with decidedly catholic taste, taking whatever kind of food happens to be most readily available at any particular time. Typical prey items include small fish, frogs, snakes, small mammals and a variety of insects. The amount of food required is probably variable, but young Black Storks were reckoned to consume 400-500 g of prey daily, comprising mainly fish.

The only exception is Abdim's Stork, which in fact differs from its congeners in several aspects of behaviour (see Systematics, Breeding). It is one of the most gregarious storks and it habitually congregates in large feeding flocks, especially at grass fires and around swarms of locusts and army worm (*Spodoptera exempta*) caterpillars. At such swarms it tends to feed very rapidly, gobbling down its prey as quickly as possible until it is sated. It takes a few more general prey items, in line with the other members of the family, but insects represent a very high proportion of its diet and it must be classified, at least to some extent, a specialist feeder. To date pesticide control of locust plagues does not seem to have had any noticeable effects on the numbers of the species, but this must be watched closely.

The other five members of the genus are much less dependent on any one particular kind of food and the feeding methods of all six are certainly generalized. It should be pointed out that there is a reservation to this statement in the form of Storm's Stork, which still remains largely unknown in many aspects. The only records of food taken by this species come from a nest in South Sumatra, where food brought to nestlings consisted mainly of fish.

A very wide variety of prey is taken by this genus and the same species may have different preferences in different places or at different times of year. Fish are important for several species, as are insects and their larvae. Like Abdim's Stork, the European White Stork is known in Africa as an instrument of control of the potentially devastating swarms of locusts, at which large numbers may congregate to gorge themselves on the temporarily abundant food supply. Both species are known in many parts of Africa as "grasshopper birds".

Amphibians, especially toads, frogs and tadpoles are frequently eaten, as are reptiles, especially snakes and lizards. Small mammals may also constitute an important part of the diet, but whereas the Maguari Stork takes mostly aquatic rodents, the European White Stork takes a wide variety, including voles (*Microtus*), moles (*Talpa europea*), hamsters (*Cricetus cricetus*) and even weasel (*Mustela nivalis*), young goat and cat. Chicks and eggs of ground-nesting birds are rarely eaten.

The typical foraging method of the genus consists of stalking, by walking about slowly with measured steps, normally in or by shallow water or alternatively in dry grassland, looking out for prey. When this is located, invariably visually, the neck may be cocked in preparation, before the bill is jabbed out and the prey grasped. In some cases there may be a short chase of a few steps, with the bird walking or running and sometimes flashing its wings open, although such a chase is rarely, if ever, protracted.

The genera *Ephippiorhynchus* and *Jabiru* take mostly fish of up to at least 500 g and have quite similar feeding habits. Other prey taken by the former includes frogs, reptiles, small mammals, molluscs, crustaceans and probably some insects and small birds. The Jabiru is also known to take young caimans (*Caiman crocodilus*), snakes and freshwater turtles (*Podocnemis*).

These species feed preferably in shallow water, for example margins of rivers and lakes, marshes, lagoons or mudflats, however they sometimes forage in grassland or open woodland. They normally feed alone or in pairs, though the Jabiru associates with other Ciconiiformes and is recorded as practising a form of communal fishing, where several birds walk side by side from deeper water towards the shore, thus frightening fish into the shallows where they are more easily caught.

The basic technique of these species involves walking about rather busily in the shallows, jabbing the bill repeatedly into the water. The purpose of this is to disturb fish, which are then quickly snatched up, but birds may dash around in circles in pursuit of evasive prey. A particularly difficult or large fish may be taken to dry land to be dealt with; if it is dropped here it is unlikely to be able to escape. After capturing and consuming its prey the stork frequently drinks water.

Another system used by the Saddlebill involves standing still in the water, waiting for prey to come within reach, when it is rapidly snapped up. The same species may also be seen probing around aquatic vegetation in murky water, sometimes shaking a foot to disturb fish, as in *Mycteria*; any successful captures made in this way are likewise probably tactile.

The Greater Adjutant and the Marabou have a very distinctive feeding preference which they do not share with any other storks. They feed extensively on carrion, obtaining much of their food from dead animals and also from human waste products. The Marabou competes on fairly equal terms with hyenas, wild dogs, jackals and several species of vultures at large herbivore carcasses on the African plains. Despite its huge bill, the stork can rarely dominate a carcass and normally stands by the much more numerous vultures and nips in from time to time to snatch morsels which are dropped by others, though Tawny Eagles (*Aquila rapax*) in turn often steal food from the stork. The bill is not apparently very effective for cutting up meat and dismemberment is normally carried out quite simply by pulling. Lumps of meat weighing up to 1 kg may be consumed whole.

However, while the Marabou has prospered through opportunism, the story in Asia is quite different. The Greater Adjutant was once abundant in much of southern Asia, especially Burma, but it has declined dramatically (see Status and Conservation). In Calcutta it was well known for feeding on human refuse and even for disposing of human corpses which had been abandoned in the streets, but with improved sanitation it has disappeared from the city and now almost from the whole sub-continent. The few recent records seem mostly to refer to birds scavenging in the company of vultures at carcasses of dogs or cows. The Lesser Adjutant has probably never been very interested in this source of food and it has never had the same close links with civilization.

Like most other storks, these three species often feed mainly on fish, along with some amphibians and crustaceans.

On the mudflats of eastern Sumatra, the Lesser Adjutant, like the Milky Stork, mostly seems to take mudskippers. Individuals forage along the edge of the sea, spaced out at intervals of about 50 m, each jabbing its bill repeatedly into the mud, trying to make contact with prey; again all the bill and head may disappear into the mud, as at times may as much as half of the neck, hence the unfeathered, bristled areas (see Morphological Aspects).

The Marabou is known to be fond of fishing in drying pools where fish are abundant and breeding is normally timed so that this highly nutritive food is available to the fast-growing nestlings. However, this species also preys on rats, army worms and, rather alarmingly from the point of view of conservation, on flamingos. Where flamingos are settled in large colonies, eggs and chicks are often taken and even adults may be killed. Normally a whole flock is frightened into flight and the Marabou picks out one bird which is stabbed in the back and brought down in the water and drowned. It is then torn up and disposed of by one or more storks in three or four minutes. Whole colonies of 4500 pairs of flamingos have been known to desert due to the presence and interference of a few Marabous.

The same species is frequently found hanging around fishermen, in the hope of picking up scraps; it also visits rubbish dumps, especially where entrails are served up. Indeed, one which regularly mopped up around a slaughterhouse in Kenya one day swallowed a butcher's knife; a couple of days later the knife reappeared sparklingly clean, while the stork went about its work as normal, with no apparent ill effects!

Breeding

As has already been seen, the genera *Mycteria* and *Anastomus* are highly gregarious and this is particularly true of their breeding habits. Of the other storks, the three members of *Leptoptilos* and Abdim's Stork are also normally communal breeders. All

The Jabiru is a solitary nester, building its huge stick nest at the top of a tree, often a palm tree. The pair may well stay together for life and they appear to reuse the same nest year after year, as occurs in the genus Ephippiorhynchus, a genus in which the Jabiru is sometimes included. In these species the repertoire of behaviour for strengthening the pair-bond is fairly limited, again suggesting a long-term bond that does not require continual confirmation. The extensive bare skin of the head and throat, the inflatable pouch and the heavy bill are features that link the species with the genus Leptoptilos.

[Jabiru mycteria, Pantanal, Brazil. Photo: Günter Ziesler]

of these species breed in colonies which range from a few pairs to several thousand, though most colonies must have been much bigger in the past, such as the giant mixed colony of "millions" of Greater Adjutants and Spot-billed Pelicans (*Pelecanus philippensis*) recorded in Burma in 1877 (see Status and Conservation). Mixed colonies are not unusual and in Africa may include Abdim's and Yellow-billed Storks, Marabous, Pink-backed Pelicans (*Pelecanus rufescens*) and several species of herons, egrets, ibises and cormorants. The commonest combination in Asia is Painted Storks with Asian Openbills, though Lesser Adjutants also mix with other species, for example the Milky Stork.

Three species, the Maguari and the European and Oriental White Storks, are loosely colonial, with several pairs often breeding very close to each other, within range of both sight and sound, though without showing any form of colonial behaviour, and almost completely ignoring neighbours. Maguari Storks often breed in small nuclei, where 5-15 nests may be close to each other. However, these same species can also be solitary breeders in the same areas. In south-west Spain, buildings or even large parts of towns may be festooned with nests, while a few kilometres away one pair may have set up a nest in a tree all alone; the mechanisms that determine the strategy adopted by each pair are not yet clear. The remaining two genera, *Jabiru* and *Ephippiorhynchus*, along with the Black, Woolly-necked and Storm's Storks, are almost exclusively solitary breeders.

Breeding tends to be seasonal in all species, though in different ways. As one would expect, the three species that breed in temperate areas start breeding in the spring and continue through the summer. Breeding in the tropics is usually linked with the water regime, although the significance may be different in different cases. However, it is always related to the effects that water has on relative food availability. For the same reason, breeding may not necessarily occur every year.

In the case of the Wood Stork, optimum feeding conditions occur during the dry season, when large amounts of prey are concentrated in small pools, as the water level subsides and the general area dries out. In contrast to this, Yellow-billed Stork populations breeding round the shores of Lake Victoria normally wait for the onset of the rains, when the lake overflows into previously dry areas, creating many shallow pools, in which fish are accessible to the species, as opposed to when they are in the much deeper, open waters of the main lake itself.

In most species the nest is always sited in a tree (see Habitat), sometimes high up it. The Jabiru often occupies the crown of a palm tree, and repeated nesting there usually kills the tree. The same nest-site tends to be used in successive years, where possible, and Marabous have been known to use the same colony for over 50 years.

In the colonial species it is normally the male that arrives first at the breeding site and he occupies and starts to defend a territory, which may just be a matter of about 1 m². His defence is fairly vigorous and can even become quite violent, resulting occasionally in deaths, as happens for instance with the Maguari Stork. Once males have occupied their territories, females start to approach too and, while they are at first met with the same aggression as encroaching males, they themselves remain subdued as though trying to appease their selected male.

Eventually the male accepts a female and various ritual greeting ceremonies become the order of the day. Storks have developed a complex series of displays many of which have been studied in detail.

There are variations from one species to another, but several general patterns emerge. Perhaps the most universal display is one called the "Up-down", which is used as a greeting within the pair and probably helps to strengthen the pair-bond. It occurs when one of the pair returns to the nest, and involves the head being raised and lowered, often to the accompaniment of some form of vocalization or bill-clattering (see Voice). An important reason for classing the Greater Adjutant and the Marabou as separate species is that their "Up-down" displays are different: in the former, the bill is clattered while the head is thrown back; in the latter, the head is thrown back with a grunt, then lowered again before bill-clattering. The "Up-down" also serves as a threat display for repulsing any would-be intruders.

Other displays include the "Advertising Sway" of the openbills, where the male rocks from one foot to the other, while standing on a branch, with his head held down between his legs. The Jabiru, Saddlebill and Black-necked Stork display at their feeding grounds with a "Flap-dash", where the bird dashes

At the beginning of the breeding season, male Painted Storks start to jostle for the best nest-sites in the treetops. At this time the colony echoes to the sound of bill-clattering and noisy wingbeats, as birds are constantly being displaced or refused "landing permission".

[*Mycteria leucocephala*, Keoladeo Ghana National Park, Bharatpur, India. Photo: Mike Price/ Bruce Coleman]

about in the water with violent flap of its wings. *Mycteria* storks go in for the more or less self-explanatory "Display Preening", "Flying Around" and "Gaping", all of which are connected with the confirmation of the pair-bond. *Ciconia* storks often precede their "Up-down" with a "Head-shaking Crouch", whereby the male normally solicits copulation.

The solitary breeders may well stay together all year and therefore form a more or less permanent pair, sometimes breeding in the same nest year after year. For this reason, and perhaps also due to the lack of competition at hand and the consequent facility of recognizing one's partner, these species tend to have far less elaborate courtship rituals, which take up less of their time. Colonial breeders appear to form new pairs every year and it seems very unlikely that the same bird may breed in the same nest two years running, if for nothing else, because their nests may be destroyed by storms or dismantled by other birds looking for nest material.

Nest building, or in some cases nest repair, begins once the pair has been formed and, even if the existing nest is in good condition, a certain amount of material is always added. In this work both sexes participate, with the male usually bringing material and the female putting it in place. In a densely-packed colony nests may actually touch each other, though they are normally at least 30 cm apart.

Nests are built largely of sticks, but other plant matter is also woven in. Many species, such as the Jabiru and the European White Stork, bring large clods of turf with which to line the nest, perhaps to make it more comfortable and to help to cement it together. The non-colonial species, when reusing a nest several years running, may end up on a gigantic platform, sometimes as much as 3 m deep in the European White Stork, and about 2 m across in the Saddlebill. The final touch in some species is a green, leafy twig which the male brings as the definitive decoration.

An interesting feature of large stork nests is that they are attractive nest-sites for other smaller species. The European White Stork is often joined by sparrows (*Passer*), starlings (*Sturnus*) and even rollers (*Coracias*). The sizeable structure constructed by the Jabiru also attracts many opportunists such as kiskadees (*Pitangus*), Monk Parakeets (*Myiopsitta monachus*), Chopi Blackbirds (*Gnorimopsar chopi*) and the Thrush-like Wren (*Campylorhynchus turdinus*). All of these help to solidify the nest by bringing their own nesting material, especially the wren, which brings mud and thus provides a filling of mortar. They are also extra guards to warn the stork of approaching danger.

Copulation is frequent during nest building and is habitually performed on the nest itself, while the male often indulges in bill-clattering (see Voice). Laying begins within a week of the start of copulation, with an interval of about two days between each egg. Normally three to five eggs are laid, but up to seven have been recorded in the European White Stork, while the Saddlebill often lays only one. They are roughly oval and are chalky-white, measuring from 84·5 x 62 mm in the Marabou to 54·6 x 45·3 mm in Abdim's Stork and weighing between 146 g in the Saddlebill and 58 g in Abdim's Stork.

Incubation usually begins with the first or second egg and is shared more or less equally by the sexes. It lasts about 25-38 days and constitutes a fairly peaceful time for the prospective parents in between two periods of frantic activity. In the event of a total loss early on in the season, Maguari Storks tend to lay a replacement clutch and this seems to be the general pattern.

Hatching is asynchronous and the nidicolous chicks start off with very little feathering. However, they are soon covered in a substantial coat of down, which is usually white or whitish, although in some cases, most notably in the Maguari Stork, the down is blackish, perhaps in order to make the chicks less conspicuous in a ground nest.

Both parents busy themselves about bringing in a constant supply of food for the ever hungry youngsters. Food is always regurgitated onto the floor of the nest, where even the smallest of young rapidly dispose of it. Like most chicks, young storks

Unique among storks, the Maguari Stork regularly breeds on the ground in dense reedbeds. In Venezuela it tends to nest in trees or bushes, which implies that the use of reedbeds elsewhere might be a habit acquired due to a lack of suitable trees in the pertinent areas, but the fact that the chicks have blackish down may be connected with the ground-nesting habit in helping to make the chicks less conspicuous to potential predators.

[*Ciconia maguari*, Corrientes, Argentina. Photo: M. P. Kahl/DRK]

consume enormous quantities, especially in the first few weeks, when they may put away 50-60% of their own body weight daily, and their growth is correspondingly quick.

After about three weeks the rate of body growth decreases, as the all-important flight-feathers start to sprout. Fledging normally takes at least 50 days in the smaller species, such as the African Openbill, but probably over 100 days in large species like the Marabou.

Young storks have to squat in the nest at first, resting on their tarsi, but they develop quickly. At 17 days old Marabou chicks can stand and flap their stunted wings, while after 21 days Yellow-billed Stork chicks are confident enough to take on any would-be intruders, thus allowing their parents more time for foraging. In colonies, a few young birds may fall from their nests; their parents will not help them, so they need to be well-developed to have any chance of survival. Cases of sibling aggression are generally rather rare, though this can involve a larger chick causing a smaller one to fall.

After they have overcome the basics of flying, young storks remain largely dependent on their parents for some weeks, often returning to the nest every night to roost, until their parents finally tire of the arduous task of finding food for them. Gradually the young birds start to forage for themselves, which is obviously essential if they are to survive the risky period of their emancipation.

Storks do not normally breed until they are 3-5 years old, although the European White Stork is known to breed occasionally at two or not until seven years old and it seems likely that this may also occur in other, lesser-known species. Again, the same species provides the record for the oldest known stork in the wild at 33 years old, but no other species have been so extensively ringed. It has been calculated that the oldest Marabous probably live over 25 years. In captivity, no less than eleven species have lived to over 30, while the Oriental White Stork has been known to reach 48 years old.

Accurate details of reproductive success are likewise limited to a few species, but probably range from under one young per pair per year in the larger species to a maximum annual average of about three in the smaller species, especially the opportunists, such as the Wood Stork and the Asian Openbill, which can raise larger broods when prey is abundant. Data for the European White Stork in Europe give it an average success rate of around two young successfully fledged per pair per year. However, adverse conditions can mean total failure in breeding and, if repeated, can present serious threats to the survival of a particular population.

Movements

Most species of stork can only travel over significant distances by extensive use of soaring flight and this requires the presence of thermals. Typically they fly around till they find a suitable thermal and then spiral up on it, sometimes to great heights, having been recorded up at 4500 m, though generally much lower, before setting off towards the desired destination. By flying so high, they gain some of the same advantages as the vultures, as they can sight prey from afar and particularly because they can often see other conspecifics or other birds or even mammals with similar prey requirements congregating in an area where food may have become temporarily available or abundant. Actually some of the smaller species, including the Black Stork, can maintain dynamic flapping flight over a fair period of time, but this is still of little importance when considering long distance migration. Research in Georgia, USA, has shown that when Wood Storks range more than 10 km from their colony, they tend to soar, whereas they use flapping flight over shorter distances.

Few storks are true migrants, but there are various kinds of movement in which the majority take part. Birds tend not to be totally sedentary, and most species carry out at least some local, nomadic movements.

Local movements tend to be connected with the food supply, as birds look for more favourable conditions when their food has ceased to be abundant in their home range. These movements may be more or less regular, as a local food supply

Small nestlings are particularly vulnerable to harsh extremes of the climate. In tropical species, the adults have several ways of alleviating this problem, one of the simplest of which is bringing water in the bill and unloading it over the chicks to help them cool off. Another system is to provide shade for the youngsters, for instance by adopting a shielding posture, like the bird on the right; this posture is particularly typical of the Painted Stork, and can also be used for sunning or dissipating heat. Urohydration, the practice of defaecating on the legs in order to lose heat by evaporation, is commonly used by most species, and tends to leave the legs stained white.

[*Mycteria leucocephala,* Keoladeo Ghana National Park, Bharatpur, India. Photo: Mike Price/ Bruce Coleman]

is liable to run out at about the same time every year, due to the same factors. However they can not correctly be termed migrations, given the opportunistic nature in which a new feeding site is likely to be chosen and also because a failure in the food supply at a regularly visited site or the discovery of an hitherto unknown site, for example with a temporary glut of prey, means that the birds will merely go elsewhere and may not even turn up at all at the regular site.

Some species are forced to commute over large distances between their breeding site and suitable feeding grounds. In colonial species this is most common half way or more through the breeding season, when feeding grounds closer to home have deteriorated and demand for food for the colony is reaching its peak. Wood Storks have been seen feeding 130 km away from the colony, which obviously involves a lot of extra time and effort. This problem is certainly more likely to arise for the specialist feeders, whereas a generalist like the European White Stork can adapt to whatever is closest to hand (see Food and Feeding) and so it rarely ventures even 3 km from its nest.

The largely solitary Saddlebill tends to be fairly sedentary in its home territory, but will move around within the immediate vicinity in search of the best pickings, as local conditions vary.

Both openbills make some regular movements, with large numbers of African Openbills breeding in the Southern Hemisphere during the wet season, but crossing the equator to join other more or less sedentary populations in the dry season; the motivation for this is as yet obscure. Juvenile Asian Openbills ringed in central Thailand have been seen to have a rather erratic dispersal, with most recoveries coming from the west in Bangladesh, but others from the north of Thailand and also one from Kampuchea, to the east. Similarly, young birds ringed at Keoladeo may disperse widely and have been recovered some 800 km to the east a few months later. This practice of juvenile dispersal is a strategy which gives a species more chance of spreading to new areas and colonizing them, and also favours the mixing of different gene pools.

One of the most famous migrants of all is the European White Stork, which has been known as such since biblical

times: Jeremiah mentions that the stork "knows its appointed time". The popularity and conspicuousness of this species, especially as it usually migrates in large flocks of up to 11,000, have helped to make its migration perhaps the best known of all birds.

As they rely heavily on soaring during migration, storks shun any lengthy crossings of large water bodies, where thermals are absent. For European birds there is clearly a complication in the shape of the Mediterranean, which stands between the African winter quarters and breeding grounds in Europe.

The European White Stork's response to this problem is to follow two well-defined routes round either end of the sea, with focal crossing points at the Straits of Gibraltar and the Bosporus, where vast concentrations gather in the company of other soaring birds, especially raptors, rising high on thermals before making the relatively short crossing. A very small proportion use a more direct route from northern Europe, passing through Italy or Greece. Interestingly there is a very precise divide in the breeding populations in Europe: those from the western section (estimated at some 35,000-50,000 in the late 1970's) use the western flyway and winter in West Africa; while all those from populations east of Alsace (e.g. 339,000 in autumn 1972; 167,000 in spring 1984) head off towards eastern and southern parts of Africa, by way of the Turkish route.

This species is also one of the large birds that travels furthest on migration, with some individuals notching up over 20,000 km in a year in going from Scandinavia to South Africa and back, very often returning to the same nest and usually not far from where they hatched.

Their aversion to crossing water is not matched with the other extreme, the desert, and birds regularly fly straight across the Sahara without stopping. However, in general when migrating, they tend to drop down to feed every day, for example in grasslands, as they can not build up reserves of fat to the same degree as small passerines. They also break up their journey into stages and eastern birds tend to pause for a couple of months in Sudan, preying on locusts, before most head south again in November; western migrants used to have similar

The mass movements of European White Storks have helped to make the species perhaps the most famous of all migrants. Extensive ringing campaigns have been going on for many years throughout Europe, and these have enabled an accurate study of matters such as the routes followed, the timing and changing trends in the migratory habits of this species. Most spectacular of all are the large concentrations that can be seen as birds prepare to cross the Straits of Gibraltar or the Bosporus.

[*Ciconia ciconia*, Bosporus. Photo: G. K. Brown/Ardea]

stages, but their pattern has been seriously disrupted in West Africa and more and more birds are tending to stay in Spain and North Africa over the winter (see Status and Conservation).

The other European stork, the Black Stork, follows a roughly similar pattern, though the population divide is not so strict, and different birds from the same brood in Denmark were found to use the different flyways. This species is apparently less averse to crossing large bodies of water and travels in much smaller flocks. In any case, few individuals go to West Africa and the bulk winter around north-east Africa and southern Asia, while a few appear to be resident in south-west Spain. In this last zone European White Storks frequently start to arrive around the end of December, but both species generally arrive in most of their European breeding range around March/April and migrate south again mostly between August and early November, with the European White Stork peaking two or three weeks earlier than the Black Stork in both of these migrations.

The migration of the Oriental White Stork is much more poorly known, but it does not have to face the same problem, as its route to its wintering grounds in south-east China are over land. Of course, vagrants that still turn up in Japan must inevitably have crossed the sea, as the species no longer breeds there. Records from the Indian sub-continent are now subject to reappraisal and, if the species occurs at all here, it is only sporadic. The gathering of large flocks for migration can be of great help when trying to estimate numbers (see Status and Conservation).

The only true tropical migrant is Abdim's Stork, which is mostly south of the Zambezi during the southern rains, from about November to March, after which it heads north, passing through East Africa during the heaviest rains. It ends up at its breeding grounds north of the equator from Senegal to Somalia in April or May, coinciding with the arrival of the rains there. The significance of this timing for the bird is that its favourite insect prey becomes abundant with the rains. The species often travels in vast flocks and, although the western breeders may fly over the extensive rain forests non-stop, again flocks normally come down to feed every day, sometimes plummeting out of the sky with breathtaking speed.

Like most migrants, storks sometimes go off course, which is one way in which a species' range can be expanded. Both

European species have several British records and the European White Stork may have bred in Devon in the last interglacial period, though the only definite British breeding record refers to a pair nesting on St. Giles' Cathedral in Edinburgh and dates back to 1416.

Relationship with Man

Due to the fact that they are large and conspicuous, almost everyone knows the stork, and several species are popular and respected. The most famous species and among the best-known of all birds is the European White Stork. It has been revered in Western Europe at least since the Middle Ages and it is even known from Tamil Nadu in southern India from a description in a 3000-year-old poem.

It seems to have been in northern Germany that the legend originated of storks bringing babies. It is interesting to note that storks start to arrive there about nine months after midsummer, which could mean that the legend goes right back into pagan times. It is certainly true that, until this century with its problems of overcrowding, most civilizations were very keen to have as high a birth-rate as possible, in order to have greater manpower for work and for fighting wars. The association of storks and babies was undoubtedly highly propitious for the bird, as people encouraged the birds to nest on their roofs, in the belief that they would bring fertility and prosperity to the house.

There is also another traditional legend, namely that storks look after their parents when they are old. Evidence of this comes to us from Ancient Greece, where there was a special law about taking care of one's parents called *Pelargonia*, coming from *pelargos*, "a stork".

It is quite clear that all these traditions have helped the bird to survive remarkably well in a very changed environment in which almost all large birds have been persistently persecuted. The bird is now associated with man and can be found on his buildings, in his fields and even around his rubbish dumps (see Habitat, Status and Conservation).

A somewhat similar tradition has also helped Abdim's Stork. It arrives at its breeding grounds north of the equator just as the rains begin and this has led to native folklore giving

it the title of the "Rain-bringer", in an area where the people depend on the rains for the success of their crops and ultimately their own survival in the face of starvation. Again, superstition demands the immunity of the bird from any form of disturbance and as a result they are quite tame and frequently install themselves in the roofs of native dwellings.

Another interesting case is the large colony of 8,000-14,000 pairs of Asian Openbills at the Buddhist sanctuary of Wat Phai Lom in Thailand. This species was probably widespread and common throughout the Oriental Region in the past, but many of its colonies have greatly diminished or disappeared, indeed in Thailand it is found nowhere else. Here the Buddhist laws which prevent the taking of any life, even that of the multitudinous ticks, have saved all life within the precincts of the sanctuary and the large colony of storks has survived and prospered. However, their great reproductive success in this confined area is leading to the death of the trees, due to urate accumulations in the soil, a common feature at tree colonies. The problem here is that, as nest-sites become scarce, the birds have nowhere else to go within the sanctuary, and outside it they are exposed to the usual threat of hunting, which has largely prevented them from spreading to other areas.

One suggested solution was a cull, in order to control numbers, but the paradox is that the Buddhist law which has saved the birds would not allow this, even if it could be demonstrated to be the only way for the species to survive there. As it is, this rather drastic suggestion seems totally unsuitable and fortunately the birds have found some form of relief by nesting in bamboos, and they have even set up three new smaller satellite colonies. However, inferior nest-sites lead to greater losses and lower productivity, while the habitat continues to degrade, making tree-planting and soil-washing highly desirable. Recent work, supported by the Brehm Fund, includes the installation of artificial nesting aids and feeding ponds; it is also planned to build an observation tower, for the use of both scientists and visitors.

Two members of the genus *Leptoptilos* frequently associate with man too, but they are not held in similar esteem. This is perhaps partly because they are rather ugly birds, especially with the pendant air-sacs that they carry and their large amount of bare, wrinkled skin. However, it may be equally due to their habits of defaecating on their legs, eating carrion and frequenting rubbish dumps.

In fact, these scavenging tendencies are a great service to man and also to the environment, as they help to prevent diseases breaking out and then spreading. In the last century the Greater Adjutant performed a very useful sanitary function in Calcutta by disposing of human corpses which had been left to rot in the street.

Some species have suffered direct exploitation by man and in some places chicks are still taken from the nest, usually to be fattened up first before consumption. This is certainly the case of the threatened Milky Stork and Lesser Adjutant in eastern Sumatra, and of the Maguari Stork in Venezuela. In Ancient Rome, unlike much of the rest of Europe, the European White Stork was not respected, except as an exquisite dish!

In many cases conspicuous birds receive vernacular names which appear to have been given tongue in cheek. The two Asian species of *Leptoptilos* are called Adjutants and it is easy to imagine this as a rather uncomplimentary nickname given to the birds by British soldiers in India. Maybe they found that the birds' fairly staid carriage and gruesome aspect reminded them of one of their officers. Rather more pertinent is the Hindi name for the Greater Adjutant in north-east India, "Hargila", meaning "Bone swallower".

The Woolly-necked Stork was similarly anthropomorphized in a former name, the Bishop Stork, which survives in its scientific name and may have come about because the bird appeared to be wearing a black cloak and cap, like a bishop.

Status and Conservation

As is the case with almost all large birds, storks are undergoing a general recession worldwide, with the possible exception of Africa. Although only five species are presently listed as Threatened, most species are struggling for survival over much of their reduced ranges and several more can be expected to join the red list soon. A recent overview of the family considered that 15 out of 19 species are regionally threatened and that the Black Stork should be added to the growing list of globally threatened species.

The exact causes for the regression obviously differ from one case to another, but they can be summed up as the typical causes affecting many other groups: habitat loss, often due to agricultural or fisheries development; excessive use of dangerous pesticides; disturbance or destruction of colonies; and direct persecution by man. In many cases, too little is known about numbers and ecological requirements, and this is always liable to lead to complacency.

All the species currently red-listed belong to Asia, mostly in overpopulated regions, where agricultural exploitation has been intense for centuries. The onslaught continues and suitable habitat is rapidly running out, while hunting is reaching more and more devastating levels. In Bangladesh people have been known to chop down trees with over 100 occupied nests in them, for firewood. In Africa, the other stronghold of the storks, all the species appear to be reasonably secure at present, but little is known about most populations and human pressure is increasing throughout. In the Americas, where the stork family has diversified far less, all three species are surviving thanks to relatively large numbers in areas with fairly difficult access. There is not the same tradition of agricultural exploitation, but recent large-scale changes, including the human colonization of previously wild areas, threaten the future of these species.

Conservation efforts are co-ordinated by the ICBP/IWRB Specialist Group on Storks, Ibises and Spoonbills, and symposia have been held to discuss problems and possible solutions. The main priorities include research on status and ecology, adequate protection of nest-sites, effective control of hunting and egg-collecting, and promotion of captive breeding, with a view to reintroductions in appropriate circumstances.

Very few stork species are regularly bred in zoos, but ideas are changing and an encouraging case is that of the Oriental White Stork, one of the globally threatened species. It breeds in south-east Siberia and north-east China, with most birds wintering in fairly remote parts of China. The Soviet population has been estimated at only 400-500 pairs and scientists are monitoring their populations and have been ringing nestlings since 1984. The record of 2729 birds on migration in Hebei province, south-east China, in autumn 1986, possibly refers to most of the remaining individuals.

Elsewhere there are a few records from the two Koreas, where the bird is sporadic in the south and apparently only a little more regular and numerous in the north. In 1971 a pair was surprisingly discovered nesting in South Korea and villa-

gers subsequently explained that storks had bred there for at least 40 years. However, within three days of this exciting discovery a poacher shot the male. The lone female showed remarkable resilience and even laid infertile eggs in 1977, before being taken into captivity in a Korean zoo, but the species is obviously doomed in this country, where it was once a locally common breeder.

In Japan it was formerly abundant, but in the last part of the nineteenth century it was heavily hunted, until it only survived on one hill, Tsuruyama, in west-central Honshu. Protection of this site produced a recovery to 50 birds, but poaching continued, and from 1957 the extensive use of pesticides containing mercury contaminated first the storks' favourite food, loaches, and ultimately the birds themselves, causing death or at least reproductive failure. The last successful breeding in Japan occurred in 1970, showing very clearly that protecting a species in itself is not enough, if its habitat and food supply are not safeguarded.

Captive breeding has been tried for many years in Japan and China without much success, as all the chicks that hatched died very young. The focus subsequently shifted to the Vogelpark Walsrode in Germany, where 11 fledglings were brought from the Amur Basin in 1980/81. In 1987 birds finally bred both in Walsrode and Shanghai, giving genuine hope to the feasibility of a reintroduction scheme that is planned for Japan and Korea. A studbook has now been prepared of the birds known to be kept in captivity, and the prospects of the species surviving now seem more encouraging, especially as this breeding success has been repeated.

The most dramatic crash of any stork must be that of the Greater Adjutant. In the last century there was a vast colony of "millions" in Burma, while not far away in Calcutta there was "almost one on every roof", perhaps referring to birds from the same population, as no large colonies have ever been known in India. Nowadays, the species may not breed at all in Burma and it no longer occurs around Calcutta or even in the Sundarbans. There are sightings ranging from annual to occasional from north-west India, Burma, Thailand and Viet Nam, but the bird is only regularly seen and only known to breed in Assam, north-east India. It may still be fairly numerous here and 75 nests were found in 1990, but unfortunately the whole region is experiencing a prolonged period of political turmoil and, as guerillas have now driven forest wardens out of the parks, poaching and illegal tree-felling have become rife. The Indian government consistently refuses to intervene and, unless it wakes up to the situation rapidly, it seems likely that the extraordinarily rich wildlife of the area will be devastated.

The species' decline has been so rapid that it was not even included in the 1979 Red Data Book. The causes of its decline are not clear, but the present threats in Assam have been highlighted as: hunting by a nomadic tribe; destruction of nesting trees by locals, usually for timber; lack of public awareness; and deterioration of feeding habitat. Among the most alarming findings of a survey, carried out in the area from 1987 to 1990, was the felling of a tree containing six nests; this meant the loss of 13 nestlings and three eggs. The Greater Adjutant is not generally persecuted and is valued in its role of cleaning up the countryside, so it is quite tame and its decline is particularly strange given the success of the very similar Marabou in Africa. The hope remains that as an yet unknown colony or colonies might exist in northern Bangladesh, Burma, Kampuchea or Laos, while the known population in Minh Hai, in southern Viet Nam, might still be viable. The WWG-SIS have proposed the localization and protection of existing nest-sites, along with suitably large areas for foraging. Projects in Assam include one of public awareness and another of long-term monotoring of colonies and nests.

The Lesser Adjutant was also excluded from the last Red Data Book and it appears to be considerably better-off at present than its congener, but it might be heading for the same kind of slump. It is still found throughout the Oriental Region, with 100 pairs in Sri Lanka, 140 pairs in Malaysia and other scattered small populations. Its stronghold is on the east coast of Sumatra, where a maximum of 1095 were counted in 1985.

The stronghold of the Milky Stork is nowadays down the east coast of Sumatra. However, human pressure is currently intense in this area, where the internationally important colonies of large waterbirds are in jeopardy. This juvenile, taken from the nest at an early age, was kept by villagers as a free-flying pet.

[Mycteria cinerea, Kubu, near Bagan siapi-api, E Sumatra. Photo: Isabel Martínez]

The same zone is also the most important area in the world for the Milky Stork and it is believed to hold some 5000 individuals, while three breeding sites were discovered here in 1988, totalling about 1000 occupied nests. A few other populations are spread out between Kampuchea and Sulawesi, but numbers appear to be very low in all of these.

Recent work, mainly by the Asian Wetland Bureau (AWB), has been aimed at pinpointing the most important sites for these species along Sumatra's swampy east coast. Although there has already been a good deal of government-organized transmigration to the area, the main centre for both these species seems to be in an area which would be very unsuitable for agricultural development, due to the high probability of rapid soil acidification. The threat of colonization remains, despite this being the most important site in the world for both of these stork species, and in addition for migrating Asian Dowitchers (*Limnodromus semipalmatus*); it also holds important populations of other threatened species, including the White-winged Wood-duck (*Cairina scutulata*) and possibly the Spot-billed Pelican and the Estuarine Crocodile (*Crocodylus porosus*). Unfortunately, to date, the government has taken no steps to secure the future of the area, and logging continues throughout Indonesia at a rate no less horrendous than the far more publicized "ecocide" of the Amazon Basin.

Commercial logging and clearance of the mangroves and freshwater and peat swamp forest to make room for fish ponds are perhaps the greatest dangers for both species, as they both prefer to nest in high trees in such habitat. An additional threat is that of the collection of eggs and young birds for consumption or sale in markets or to zoos. While this was kept at a very local level, it appeared to be of little significance, but with an already huge human population living along this coast and plans for the immigration of many more families, the extent of the menace is clear.

The AWB has been working steadily in conjunction with the PHPA (Indonesian Nature Conservation Department) on programmes of investigation and increasing public awareness and the Sriwijaya University of Palembang is also participating, but it will need quick, decisive action at high levels, if these sites and these species are to be saved; most attempts to survey wetlands with potential find that the logging companies have got there first.

The other threatened species, Storm's Stork, is very little-known, but it is reckoned to number possibly less than 300 individuals in Indonesia, which may hold virtually the entire world population. Its range is fairly extensive, but the bird appears to be scattered and very rare throughout. There are few recent records from Malaysia, where it may not even breed and a remarkable one from southern Thailand.

The first nest of the species was discovered here as recently as 1986, during operations organized to save stranded animals, as the new Chiew Larn reservoir was filling up and flooding one of the last sizeable tracts of lowland forest in the region, which, into the bargain, was in a "protected area"! Thus, it became a very surprising addition to the country's avifauna, extending its range northwards by over 500 km, but immediately went into the category of "possibly extinct" in Thailand.

Once again, one of the strongholds of Storm's Stork is south-east Sumatra, although Borneo, especially Kalimantan, supports a significant proportion of the known population. The solitary and secretive tendencies of the species make it very difficult to make an accurate estimate of densities, but being a bird of freshwater swamp forests and not of the coast, its main threats surely come from logging and perhaps also hunting. There is no evidence to suggest that it has ever been common, but it is certainly in decline and may perhaps be the most difficult species to save in the long run.

While these are the only species currently considered to be globally threatened, a brief glance shows us that most other species are regionally threatened. The Black-necked Stork has a much wider distribution than Storm's Stork, but again it is very sparsely scattered throughout and it is only thanks to substantial populations in Australia and New Guinea that the species can be considered safe. In the Oriental Realm it is fast disappearing and only remnant populations are left in a few countries, with the once large Indian population producing the alarming total of only 33 birds after a survey of 575 wetlands in 1989. Again, as the species is not very conspicuous and is rarely numerous, this decline has occurred almost without its being noticed. This fact should be noted and currently healthy populations in the south of its range must be carefully monitored, to avoid the possibility of future declines arriving similarly unheralded. The same latent danger exists for the closely related Saddlebill and Jabiru and again close vigilance of numbers

The situation of the Oriental White Stork (left) is alarming, and it is now classed as Endangered. One of the major breakthroughs in recent years was the first successful breeding of this species in captivity, which occurred in 1987, almost simultaneously at the Vogelpark Walsrode and Shanghai Zoo. It is hoped to build up a strong captive bred population with a view to reintroductions. While captive breeding may be a potential solution for some species, it is certainly not so at present for Storm's Stork (right), as the species is extremely rare in the wild, and the building up of a captive population can not be considered a feasible option.

[Left: Ciconia boyciana. Right: Ciconia stormi. Vogelpark Walsrode, Germany. Photos: Josep del Hoyo]

is called for. The Black Stork has likewise slumped in much of its range without receiving much attention.

As in many other cases, one of the main conservation measures proposed for the Black-necked Stork is a thorough survey, to be followed by the protection of appropriate sites. However, this is always less effective for the non-colonial species, as a reserve which may harbour thousands of pairs of a colonial species often supports only one or two pairs of a solitary species. On the other hand, a solitary species has a better chance of keeping the whereabouts of its nest-site secret, and discovery of all the nests in any one area obviously represents a much greater effort to anyone wanting to steal eggs or chicks or kill the adults.

Another feature of the predicament in which the Black-necked Stork finds itself is the irresponsible behaviour of many zoos. A selection of nine Indian zoos was recently discovered to have a total of 42 individuals, all of which must presumably have been taken from the wild, as there is no record of the species breeding in captivity. Given this lack of success and the fact that it is not a colonial species, it seems difficult to justify the presence of 13 individuals in one zoo. Nor is it merely a problem of local zoos, as some assorted and incomplete records show that during the 1970's zoos from Europe and the USA imported a bare minimum of 68 individuals from India alone.

The European White Stork, although still numerous and widespread, has been steadily declining in Western Europe in recent years. There has been a great deal of conjecture as to the causes and there appear to be several that have acted in concert.

Large-scale international censuses have been performed periodically since 1934, and the latest, in 1984, indicated a crash of about 76% over the 50 year period. However, figures show that in the past stork numbers increased regularly, when there were plagues of locusts in their wintering areas, and the extent of the overall decline is exaggerated, because 1934 was apparently a very good year for the storks. Nonetheless, the situation is far from satisfactory. The virtual eradication of locust swarms in West Africa more or less coincided with the species' steady

slide since the 1950's. The celebrated drought years in the Sahel, aggravated by overgrazing by farmers in previous very wet years, has made the situation far worse for wintering storks, so that many fail to survive and others arrive at their breeding grounds either late or in poor condition, or both.

One problem which has received considerable attention is that, when on migration through parts of Africa, many storks are killed by hunters. As long ago as 1822 a stork was found in Germany with an African arrow impaled in it, since when many more instances have been reported, but obviously the spread of firearms has altered the scale of things dramatically, increasing the toll to unacceptable numbers. One of the aims of ICBP's Migratory Birds Campaign is to make farmers aware of the beneficial role of storks in natural pest control and the importance of nature conservation.

However, the causes are not all to be found outwith Europe, where the modernization and intensification of agriculture have greatly limited the availability of suitable foraging grounds. Levels of pollution have increased, with pesticides adversely affecting prey. Further casualties occur every year, as a result of collisions with power cables, and these should now be buried all over Europe.

Due to the popularity of the species, much has been done to try to alleviate its plight, notably the widespread provisioning of artificial nest-sites. Reintroduction schemes have been going on in various countries since 1948, but with mixed results. Young birds are generally kept in captivity until they reach sexual maturity, when they are released and encouraged to breed at the desired site. Unfortunately, this has led to birds overwintering in northern Europe and becoming very tame; such "unnatural" stock is seen by some as equivalent to animals in a wildlife park, while these birds are also contributing to the increasing numbers that do not cross the Sahara for the Palearctic winter.

All three American species are widely distributed and are still fairly numerous in parts of their ranges, for example in the *llanos* of Venezuela and Colombia. However, the speed of destruction and reconversion of vast zones of South America has been well-publicized and these species could easily crash before the extent of their decline were really evident. A study of

Nowadays the Greater Adjutant is only known to breed in Assam, although it formerly had huge colonies in Burma. This nest, discovered by M. P. Kahl in 1967, was until very recently the only one known of the species this century. The causes of the species' decline are not at all clear, but they are likely to be connected with habitat destruction and persecution, particularly in poorly known Burma.

[Leptoptilos dubius, Kaziranga National Park, Assam, India. Photo: M. P. Kahl/ Bruce Coleman]

For many years the Milky Stork was only known to breed on Pulau Dua, a small island off north-west Java. It no longer breeds there now, but fortunately new colonies have been found in Sumatra and other parts of Java, and recently in Peninsular Malaysia; it may also breed in southern Sulawesi. As in many other storks, and indeed large waterbirds in general, the main threats seem to be habitat destruction and uncontrolled hunting.

[Mycteria cinerea, Pulau Dua, north-west Java. Photo: M. P. Kahl/ Bruce Coleman]

the Maguari Stork in the *llanos* of Venezuela carried out during the 1980's by B. T. Thomas indicated a significant decline in populations, in some cases reaching 90-100%.

The northernmost populations of Wood Storks, which breed in Georgia and Florida, USA, have slumped dramatically from, by some accounts, 20,000 birds in the 1930's, to some 10,000 in 1960, to only 5850 pairs in 1986. The species has disappeared as a breeder from Texas to Alabama and its desperate plight led to its being included on the list of birds endangered in the USA in 1984. The main reason for its regression seems to have been the conversion and degradation of its feeding grounds, indeed this century Florida has lost more than half of its wetlands to both urban and agricultural development. Areas in the Everglades that used to be permanently flooded now dry out in some years, and the larger fish, which the storks prefer, die off or never reach the shallow pools. In other areas water levels are raised too high, the fish disperse and the storks can end up abandoning their nests for want of food. In addition, many of the large cypresses in which the storks nested have been cut down, so they have to try to breed in less favourable sites.

A good deal of research and conservation action has been carried out, including the protection of present nest-sites, the construction of artificial feeding ponds, where water levels are specially controlled to suit the birds' needs and the stocking of these ponds with suitable prey species. Constant monitoring of populations has shown that numbers vary considerably from one year to the next and early records of high numbers may have come from particularly good years. At present numbers seem to be fairly stable, but productivity is low, with only 0·79 young fledged per pair per year.

The birds tend to disperse a little in summer after breeding, following the coast north and west, but they do not nowadays come into contact with the Mexican breeders which may straggle as far as Louisiana. In the past the populations all along the south coast of the United States presumably allowed a

certain amount of inter-colonial movement, but almost all of these colonies have now disappeared, breaking the link and effectively preventing any chance of recruiting new birds to this area through natural means.

Conservation efforts may be aimed at one particular species, but adequate protection for the species in question invariably implies the preservation of its ecosystem and a large number of plant and animal species. This is largely the rationale behind ICBP's current worldwide biodiversity project: by protecting important areas of avian endemism, the project aims to provide security at the same time for other, less popular or well-known forms of life, which naturally tend to have similar centres of endemism; the concentration on these centres will inevitably bring greater security for many of the more widespread species too. Storks may have an important role to play, as they are large, conspicuous, popular birds, which are ideal as "flagship" species, on which to mount conservation drives. Such an initiative has recently been taken in Belize, using the Jabiru, a species now listed by ICBP as near-threatened and which may have a total Central American population of under 100 individuals. The bird has appeared on posters and even on the money in Belize, making the general public more aware of its existence and also of its predicament. This should help to promote nature conservation at all levels in the country.

General Bibliography

Boer & Van Brink (1982), Coulter & Brouwer (1991), Coulter & Rodgers (1987), Coulter, Balzano *et al.* (1989), Coulter, Bryan *et al.* (1991), Cracraft (1981), Crandall (1927), Gysels (1968), Hancock (1984), Johnson & Luthin (1990), Johnson, Coulter *et al.* (1987), Kahl (1971a, 1971b, 1972a, 1978, 1979a, 1987a), King & Coulter (1989), Kushlan (1977f, 1981), Ligon (1967), Luthin (1984a, 1984b, 1987a), Ogden (1985c), Olson (1978), Sibley & Ahlquist (1985, 1988, 1990), Sibley & Monroe (1990), Soothill & Soothill (1982), Sprunt *et al.* (1978), Vanden Berge (1970), Verheyen (1959, 1960c), Wood (1983, 1984).

ssp *neglecta*

ssp *episcopus*

ssp *microscelis*

PLATE 32

inches 16

cm 40

Tribe MYCTERINI

Genus *MYCTERIA* Linnaeus, 1758

1. **Wood Stork**

Mycteria americana

French: Tantale d'Amérique **German**: Waldstorch **Spanish**: Tántalo Americano
Other common names: Wood Ibis (see page 436)

Taxonomy. *Mycteria americana* Linnaeus, 1758, Brazil *ex* Marcgraf.
Has been isolated from rest of genus (other three species placed in genus *Ibis*); but feeding and display behaviour very similar, with differences mainly in bare parts. Monotypic.
Distribution. SE states of USA, Mexico through C and S America to N Argentina.

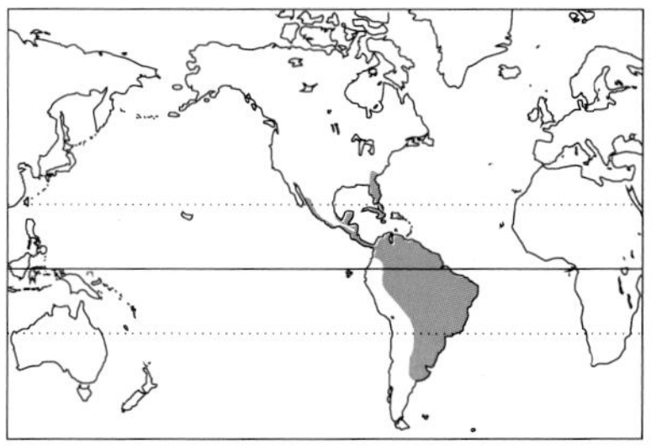

Descriptive notes. 83-102 cm; 2-3 kg; wingspan 150 cm. Head and neck unfeathered, bony plates on cap. Immature has head and neck brownish, with some feathering, and yellow bill.
Habitat. Wetlands, including mangroves, gallery forest, damp grassland, freshwater marshes and swamps; any shallow water, including estuaries, canals and ditches. Mostly in freshwater, but may exploit tidal waters when ample food available. Often nests in trees surrounded by water in order to be safe from terrestrial predators.
Food and Feeding. Mostly fish, including sunfish (*Lepomis*) and catfish (*Ictalurus*); also opportunistic, occasionally taking crayfish, amphibians, insects, small snakes and even baby alligators. Tactile feeding (see page 442), but may also take anything visually available, such as catfish walking in drying ditches; often feeds in small flocks, sometimes apparently in concert.
Breeding. (almost all data from USA) Related to water levels, in USA may occur Nov-Aug; in bad years not attempted or sometimes abandoned before completion. Colonial tree-nester, sometimes in mixed colonies e.g. with other Ciconiiformes; stick nest built in three days and lined with leaves, normally at top of tall cypress or mangrove, preferably on island or over water; up to 50 nests in same tree. Average 3 eggs (2-5); incubation 28-32 days; chicks have pale grey down; fledging 60-65 days. Sexual maturity at 4 years, though nesting not normally successful until 5th year. Oldest captive bird over 27 years old.
Movements. Post-breeding dispersal in USA and Mexico (see page 455); in tropical S America out of breeding season wanders about, looking for optimum conditions, e.g. regular movements between Orinoco and Amazon basins, but also up and down Amazon and even regularly across Andes of S Colombia at c. 2000 m; some N-S movement, with many birds passing southern summer in S Brazil, where absent in winter; flocks of 500-1000 recorded on migration, though larger ones may well occur. Can commute over large distances during breeding.
Status and Conservation. Not globally threatened. Population of USA has slumped to such an extent that species has been declared endangered at national level (see page 455). Major colony of 8000-10,000 pairs in Usumacinta Delta, SE Mexico considered to be healthiest population outside S America, but this and other Mexican populations declining, due mainly to collection of eggs and young, and more recently habitat destruction associated with development, e.g. rice fields. In rest of C America only one other large stable colony known, in Costa Rica. Still apparently quite common in Venezuela, with over 5500 birds recorded in *llanos* in Jul 1983; also fairly common in parts of Brazil, but quantitative data mostly lacking. Surveys in N Surinam produced 1750 birds recently at Ciénagas Bigi Pan and Wageningen, and 2550 birds at Ciénagas Braamspunt, Matapica and Motkreek, where c. 400 pairs bred in 1970. Partial census in Jul 1990 gave 476 birds in Argentina. Throughout range, habitat alteration is probably main threat; also hunting and egg-collecting in much of Latin America. Has occasionally bred in captivity.
Bibliography. Anon. (1986b), Baker (1982), Belton (1984), Bent (1926), Blake (1977), Bratton (1988), Bratton & Hendricks (1990), Bratton *et al.* (1989), Brook van Meter (1985), Browder (1976, 1978, 1984), Bryan & Coulter (1987), Clark, E.S. (1978, 1979, 1980), Comer (1985), Comer *et al.* (1987), Coulter (1986-1990, 1987), Coulter & Bryan (1988), Coulter *et al.* (1987), Fleming *et al.* (1984), Hagenrath & Ribera (1985), Hamel (1977), Heinzman & Heinzman (1965), Hilty & Brown (1986), Hodgson *et al.* (1988), Hopkins & Humphries (1983), Jensen *et al.* (1989), Kahl (1962, 1963a, 1963b, 1964, 1972c), Kahl & Peacock (1963), Kale (1978), Kushlan *et al.* (1975), Leber (1980), Lowe *et al.* (1990), McNeil *et al.* (1990), Meyers (1984), Monroe (1968), Morales (1990), Morales *et al.* (1981), Nores & Yzurieta (1980), Odom (1978), Ogden (1978, 1985d), Ogden & Nesbit (1979), Ogden & Patty (1981), Ogden & Thomas (1985a), Ogden, Kushlan & Tilmant (1976, 1978), Ogden, McCrimmon *et al.* (1987), Ohlendorf *et al.* (1978c), Palmer (1962), Pinto (1964), Ramo & Busto (1984), Ridgely & Gwynne (1989), Rodgers (1990), Rodgers *et al.* (1987, 1988), Ruckdeschel & Shoop (1987), Scott & Carbonell (1986), Short (1975), Sick (1984), Slud (1964), Spaans (1975a), Sprunt & Knoder (1980), Stangel *et al.* (1990), Stiles & Skutch (1989), Tate & Humphries (1980), Terres (1980), Thomas (1979a, 1985), Valdes Miro (1984), Walsh (1990), Wetmore (1965).

2. **Milky Stork**

Mycteria cinerea

French: Tantale blanc **German**: Milchstorch **Spanish**: Tántalo Malayo

Taxonomy. *Tantalus cinereus* Raffles, 1822, Sumatra.
Formerly placed in genus *Ibis*; less frequently in *Tantalus*. Monotypic.
Distribution. S Viet Nam, Kampuchea, Peninsular Malaysia and the Indonesian islands of Sumatra, Java and Sulawesi.
Descriptive notes. 95-100 cm. Black patch by base of bill. Non-breeding adult lacks milky tone to plumage; bare parts duller. Immature generally a good deal drabber, with more feathering on head and bare parts dull yellow.

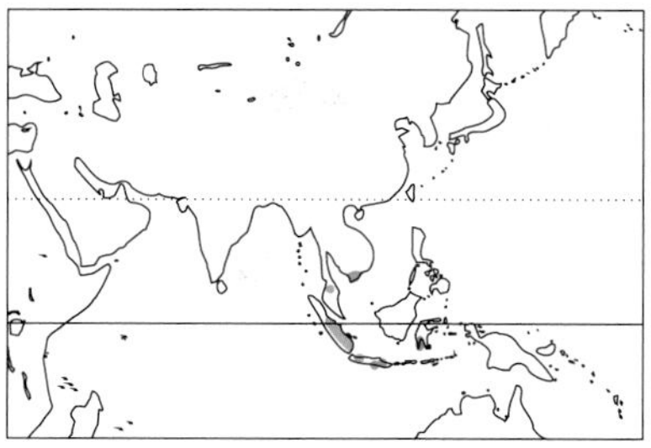

Habitat. Mostly coastal, feeding on extensive mudflats, and nesting in bordering mangroves or freshwater/peat swamp forest; also recorded from lakes, marshes, fishponds and paddyfields, up to 50 km inland; sometimes feeds near human settlements. Up to 1000 m.
Food and Feeding. Recorded taking large mudskippers (*Periophthalmus*) of 10-23 cm, also small fish, snakes, frogs. Most recorded methods of prey capture involve tactile use of bill; regularly probes in sediments (see page 442); occasionally locates prey by sight. Daily food intake estimated at around 630 g, which bird is reckoned to catch in only about two hours. Frequents shallow pools in mangroves, where high density of fish.
Breeding. Peak appears to be dry season, July-Aug, both in Sumatra and Java, although on Pulau Rambut, off N Java, evidence of breeding in Nov 1983, Mar 1984 and also in Aug 1984. Colonial tree-nester; nest usually 6-12 m up large tree. 1-4 eggs.
Movements. Very little known. Some seasonal movements are probable outside the breeding season; Sumatran breeders seem to disperse along coast, with some crossing the Sunda Straits in Sept to Java or maybe even further afield; return in Apr. Vagrant to Bali and Sumbawa, C Indonesia. Javan colony of Pulau Rambut probably visited irregularly by varying numbers throughout year. If necessary, breeders may commute over large distances.
Status and Conservation. VULNERABLE. CITES I. Considered endangered in Viet Nam (1 breeding colony) and Malaysia, where colony with 21 nests found in 1989; nothing known of Kampuchean population. Stronghold in E Sumatra, with about 5000 birds; up to c. 1000 nests found here in 1988; first Sumatran colony discovered in Jambi Province in 1985, had disappeared by 1989; possible causes include degradation of mangroves and probable plundering of nestlings for sale to zoos in SE Asia and Europe. Java still appears to hold some 600, though species no longer breeds at celebrated colony on Pulau Dua; resident, probably breeding, population discovered on Sulawesi in 1977, with up to 73 individuals subsequently being recorded. Destruction of suitable nest-sites for fish ponds, agriculture and timber extraction is main threat, as well as increased capture for food by growing human population and general disturbance. Measures proposed include further surveys, creation of reserves and public awareness campaigns; recovery plan proposed to Indonesian government by ICBP and Asian Wetland Bureau; recent success in Malaysia partly attributed to vigilance by wardens. Military activity in Viet Nam and Kampuchea is liable to have had adverse effects, such as destruction of about 50% of mangroves in Viet Nam due to herbicide spraying on a colossal scale by US forces; vast replanting scheme of 25,000 ha in operation, and system of parks proposed. Several recently taken into Asian zoos, should be used for breeding; species has recently bred in captivity in Kuala Lumpur, Malaysia, and San Diego, USA, and reintroduction planned for Malaysian reserve.
Bibliography. Allport & Wilson (1986), Andrew & Holmes (1990), Anon. (1989a, 1989b, 1990d), Baltzer (1990), Collar & Andrew (1988), Danielsen & Skov (1987), Duc & Thuy (1987), Erftemeijer & Djuharsa (1988), Erftemeijer *et al.* (1988), Grimmett (1985), Hoogerwerf (1947, 1949), Imboden & Parish (1986), Iskander (1985), Kahl (1972c), Karpowicz (1985), King (1978/79), Lambert & Erftemeijer (1989), van Marle & Voous (1988), Martínez & Elliott (1990), Medway & Wells (1976), Milton & Marhadi (1985), Morris (1989), Nisbet (1968), Parish (1985), Parish & Wells (1984), Scott (1989), Silvius (1986), Silvius & Verheugt (1989), Silvius, Steeman *et al.* (1987), Silvius, Verheugt & Iskandar (1985, 1986), Swennen & Marteijn (1987), Uttley (1987), Verheugt (1987), Wells (1985), White & Bruce (1986), Wilson & Allport (1985).

3. **Yellow-billed Stork**

Mycteria ibis

French: Tantale ibis **German**: Nimmersatt **Spanish**: Tántalo Africano

Taxonomy. *Tantalus Ibis* Linnaeus, 1766, Egypt.
Formerly placed in genus *Ibis*; less frequently in *Tantalus*. Monotypic.
Distribution. Africa S of Sahara, Madagascar; straggles into Palearctic Africa in Morocco, Tunisia and Egypt.

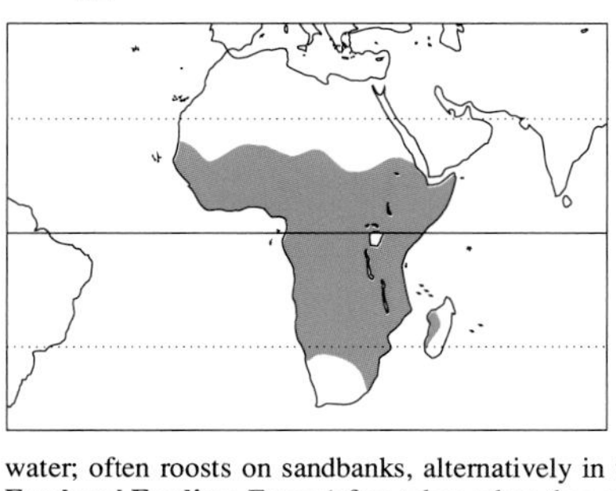

Descriptive notes. 95-105 cm; wingspan 150-165 cm. Males average larger. Non-breeding adult has plumage and bare parts duller. Immature duller, especially bare parts; juvenile all dingy brown, with dull green bare parts.
Habitat. Found in variety of wetland sites, including swamps, reservoirs, margins of rivers and lakes, waterholes, sandbanks, rice paddies, lagoons, alkaline lakes and marine mudflats, though preferably avoids areas of large-scale flooding (e.g. in Sudan); in W Africa sometimes nests in towns; rarer in areas of forest, though not uncommon in savanna woodland. Feeds mainly in relatively shallow water; often roosts on sandbanks, alternatively in trees.
Food and Feeding. Frogs (often taken when they emerge after rain), small fish, other small aquatic prey. Tactile feeding (see page 442); sometimes walks along, repeatedly probing into water with bill, or with head under water for some time. Has been known to scavenge fish regurgitated by cormorants. Little time normally spent feeding.
Breeding. Seasonal, mostly starts towards end of rains or in drier areas in dry season, with young fledging respectively in dry season or in rains. Colonial tree-nester, often with other species (see page 446); smallish stick nest, usually high up in *Acacia* or *Bombax*. Usually 2-3 eggs, rarely 4; incubation probably c. 30 days; chicks have pure white down; fledging c. 55 days. Sexual maturity probably at minimum of 3 years. Oldest captive bird over 19 years old.
Movements. Resident in most of range, sometimes with local movements. Non-breeding summer migrant to parts of S Africa, Oct-Apr; in W Africa moves N for wet season Oct/Nov-Mar, dry season in coastal swamps (Nigeria).
Status and Conservation. Not globally threatened. Throughout range is common to abundant and numbers generally stable, except perhaps in S Africa, where irregular with under 25 pairs. Locally

On following pages: 4. Painted Stork (*Mycteria leucocephala*); 5. Asian Openbill (*Anastomus oscitans*); 6. African Openbill (*Anastomus lamelligerus*); 7. Black Stork (*Ciconia nigra*); 8. Abdim's Stork (*Ciconia abdimii*); 9. Woolly-necked Stork (*Ciconia episcopus*); 10. Storm's Stork (*Ciconia stormi*); 11. Maguari Stork (*Ciconia maguari*); 12. European White Stork (*Ciconia ciconia*); 13. Oriental White Stork (*Ciconia boyciana*).

common in WC Madagascar. Figures from partial census in Jan 1991 include 302 birds in Cameroon, 229 in Senegal, 202 in Uganda, and 275 in Kenya, where 1621 birds counted at L Nakuru alone in Jul 1991; highest figures from W Africa in recent years include 650 birds in Senegal Basin, 1070 in Niger Basin, and estimated 500-1500 birds in Guinea-Bissau. Not generally subject to persecution, as shown by nesting in towns in W Africa. Before 1913 was regular in Egypt, May-Sept.

Bibliography. Baha El Din (1984), Bell-Cross (1974), Berruti (1980), Britton (1980), Brooke (1984), Brown & Britton (1980), Brown & Pomeroy (1984), Brown *et al.* (1982), Calder (1959), Castan & Olier (1959), Cramp & Simmons (1977), Feely (1964), Ford (1943), Fraser (1971), Goodman (1989), Goodman & Storer (1987), Johnson & Luthin (1990), Kahl (1968, 1972c), Kasoma & Pomeroy (1987), Kinzelbach (1986), Langrand (1990), Mackworth-Praed & Grant (1953-1973), Maclean (1985), Milon *et al.* (1973), Morel & Morel (1962), Pennycuick (1972b), Pinto (1983), Talent (1940), Taylor (1957), Tree (1982b).

4. **Painted Stork**

Mycteria leucocephala

French: Tantale indien **German**: Buntstorch **Spanish**: Tántalo Indio

Taxonomy. *Tantalus leucocephalus* Pennant, 1769, Ceylon.
Formerly placed in genus *Ibis*; less frequently in *Tantalus*. Monotypic.
Distribution. India and Sri Lanka to Indochina and S China.

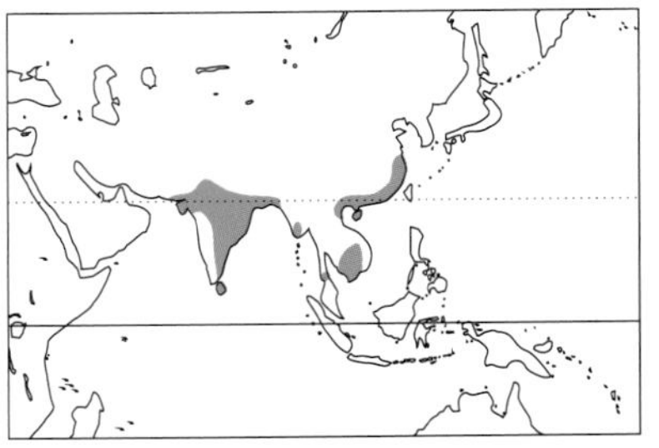

Descriptive notes. 93-102 cm; 2-3·5 kg. Only *Mycteria* stork with pectoral band. Non-breeding adult has plumage and bare parts duller. Immature pale brown, lacks pectoral band.
Habitat. Mostly in shallow freshwater of various wetland sites, such as lakes, grassy marshland, *jheels*, riverbanks and paddyfields, but also occasionally along coast and in salt pans. Normally nests on trees over or near water; may breed in towns.
Food and Feeding. Mostly fish, also frogs, reptiles, crustaceans, insects. Typical tactile feeding methods of the genus, commonly flicking wing as well as stirring mud with foot in order to disturb prey; also scythe-like movements of bill through water. Average daily food requirement for nestling reckoned to be about 500 g, made up of about nine fish in two separate helpings. Normally feeds in pairs or small groups, except when prey abundant, as when rivers swollen by monsoon.
Breeding. In India July/Aug-Oct in N, Nov-Mar in S; starting soon after beginning of monsoon. Colonial tree-nester, sometimes 70-100 nests in only five or six trees, commonly in babool (*Acacia arabica*), often over water; nests often almost contiguous; sometimes mixed colonies with *A. oscitans*, herons, ibises, cormorants, etc. Nest is large stick platform with central depression and lining of other plant matter. Normally 3-4 eggs (2-5); incubation c. 30 days; chicks have whitish down; fledging c. 60 days. Oldest captive bird over 28 years old.
Movements. Resident with local movements. After breeding, birds disperse in search of optimum feeding conditions. In recent years, in Thailand, flocks of 52 and 110 birds seen, in addition to regular small groups; may indicate dispersal from hitherto unknown colonies in Burma. Some birds also migrate to W Burma. Vagrant to Peninsular Malaysia.
Status and Conservation. Not globally threatened. One of most numerous and secure of Asian storks, but regionally threatened in SE Asia; colonies require protection. Still locally common in parts of India, e.g. 1749 breeding pairs at Keoladeo (Bharatpur), Rajasthan, in 1984, and 170 nests in Bavnagar city, Gujarat in 1983; abundant in Sri Lanka in 1984; census of Jan 1991 yielded 4599 birds in India and 659 in Sri Lanka. Scarce in Pakistan, with population of Indus Delta apparently declining rapidly, as fishermen raid only known colonies and sell chicks to animal exporters. Rare and threatened in Bangladesh. On verge of extinction in Thailand, where was once common; last remaining colony at Thale Noi was plundered, despite protected status, and only one pair remained in 1988. Has bred in captivity in Bangkok and reintroduction may be feasible in future; also large breeding group in Colombo Zoo, Sri Lanka. Four small breeding nuclei in what remains of mangrove and *Melaleuca* forests of Minh Hai, Viet Nam; must have suffered habitat loss, also some human predation. Status in Burma, Laos and Kampuchea unknown.

Bibliography. Ali (1979), Ali & Ripley (1978), Badshah (1963), Bain & Humphrey (1980), Bolster (1923), Cheng Tso-hsin (1987), Desai (1971), Desai *et al.* (1974, 1979), Etchécopar & Hüe (1978), Ewans (1989), Fei Dianjin (1986), Henry (1971), Hill (1943), Humphrey & Bain (1990), Kahl (1972c), Karpowicz (1985), Khan (1984, 1987), King & Brouwer (1991), Malhotra & Arora (1991), Medway & Wells (1976), Paulraj & Gunasekaran (1988), Roberts (1991), Round *et al.* (1988), Scott (1989), Shah & Desai (1972, 1975a, 1975b), Shah *et al.* (1977), Smythies (1986), Urfi (1989a, 1989b, 1990), Weinman (1940), von Wetten (1985).

Genus *ANASTOMUS* Bonnaterre, 1791

5. **Asian Openbill**

Anastomus oscitans

French: Bec-ouvert indien **German**: Silberklaffschnabel **Spanish**: Picotenaza Asiático
Other common names: Oriental/Asiatic Openbill, Openbilled Stork

Taxonomy. *Ardea oscitans* Boddaert, 1783, Pondicherry.
Monotypic.
Distribution. India and Sri Lanka to Thailand and Indochina.
Descriptive notes. 81 cm. Forked tail black, but usually hidden by long undertail-coverts. Immature smoky brownish grey with darker mantle, bill straightish.
Habitat. A variety of wetlands, including lakes, *jheels*, canals, rivers, marshes and occasionally mudflats; paddyfields also frequently used, even in dry season in Thailand when mud caked hard; also in newly ploughed fields. May nest near humans.
Food and Feeding. Almost entirely apple snails (*Pila*); occasionally other small aquatic animals, such as frogs, crabs and large insects. Specialized bill and technique enables species to exploit abundant source of food, which is inaccessible to most other potential predators. Snails extracted by inserting bill, virtually without damage to shells (see page 443).

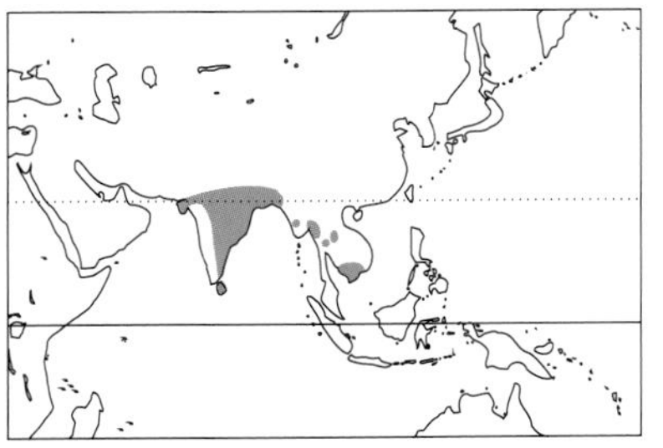

Breeding. Mostly July-Sept in N India, Nov-Mar in S India and Sri Lanka, starting at onset of rains; in dry season in Thailand, with most laying in Jan. Colonial tree-nester, sometimes in mixed colonies with herons, cormorants and *M. leucocephala*; smallish, unelaborated stick nest with central depression lined with leaves; nests often very close together, with 100's spread over a few large trees, but may also nest in smaller trees, e.g. *Avicennia*, or even bamboo. Normally 4 eggs (2-5); incubation 27-30 days; chicks have pale fawn-coloured down and normal bill; eggs and young may be taken by monitor lizards (*Varanus*), crows or raptors; fledging reportedly 35-36 days, probably averages more. Oldest captive bird only 7 years old.
Movements. Mostly local movements after breeding, depending on water conditions; probably also some juvenile dispersal. Thai birds recovered in Kampuchea, N Thailand and Bangladesh, undoubtedly accounting for many sight records in Burma; most of Thai population migrate W to deltas of Ganges and Brahmaputra during wet season, although some birds sedentary. Birds from NW India may also move E towards Bangladesh; several records of birds migrating on dark nights crashing into lighthouses in C and S India.
Status and Conservation. Not globally threatened. Commonest Asian stork, though regionally threatened in SE Asia. Still locally common at scattered sites throughout India, e.g. 5181 at Keoladeo (Bharatpur), Rajasthan, in 1981, and over 10,000 birds in Indian Sundarbans in 1977; tendency to be abundant under favourable conditions. Small breeding population in Sri Lanka. No evidence of regular breeding in Pakistan since early 1930's, and now considered rare visitor; formerly common in Sind. Virtually exterminated as a breeder from Bangladesh due to hunting pressure, disturbance and habitat destruction, though migrants still arrive. A few small colonies of 50-100 pairs remain in mangroves of S Viet Nam, where have legal protection, but this is inefficient and wardens now being trained, thanks to Brehm Fund; largest colony in Thailand, 8000-14,000 nests, where various research, conservation and monitoring projects are under way (see page 451); status unknown in Burma and Kampuchea. Mid-winter census of Jan 1991 yielded 9683 birds in India (5380 in Orissa, 2316 in Tamil Nadu), 804 in Sri Lanka, 1286 in Burma and 200 in Thailand. Main problems appear to be hunting and trapping, habitat destruction and possibly contamination through accumulation of pesticides in snails. Protection of often large colonies and nearby feeding grounds could be relatively easy and effective. Has been proposed as a potential indicator species of pollution levels.

Bibliography. Ali (1979), Ali & Ripley (1978), Amget (1986), Anon. (1990a), Bain & Humphrey (1980), Breeden & Breeden (1982), Chaudhuri & Chakrabarti (1973), Ewans (1989), Frédéric (1985), Harris (1988), Henry (1971), Humphrey & Bain (1990), Huxley (1960, 1962), Inkapatanakul (1986), Jackson (1938), Kahl (1971e, 1972e), Karpowicz (1985), Khan (1984, 1987), King & Brouwer (1991), Lauhachinda (1969), Law (1926), Luthin (1988), McClure (1974, 1989), McClure & Kwanyuen (1973), Mukherjee (1971, 1974), Mukhopadhyay (1980), Ogle (1986), Poonswad (1979), Roberts (1991), Round *et al.* (1988), Scott (1989), Sitwell (1984), Smythies (1986), von Wetten (1985).

6. **African Openbill**

Anastomus lamelligerus

French: Bec-ouvert africain **German**: Mohrenklaffschnabel **Spanish**: Picotenaza Africano

Taxonomy. *Anastomus lamelligerus* Temminck, 1823, Senegal.
Two subspecies recognized.
Subspecies and Distribution.
A. l. lamelligerus Temminck, 1823 - Africa, S of Sahara.
A. l. madagascariensis Milne-Edwards, 1880 - Madagascar.

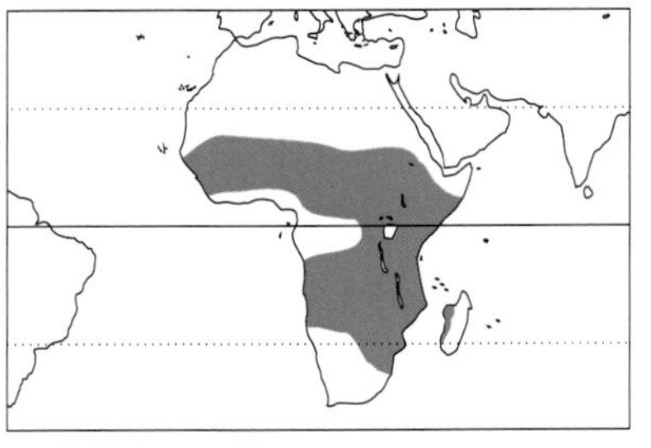

Descriptive notes. 80-94 cm; 1-1·3 kg. Males average larger. Mantle and breast glossy green, purple or brown; gap in bill 6 mm wide at most. Immature duller, bill almost straight. Race *madagascariensis* smaller, with thinner bill, which has more pronounced longitudinal ridges.
Habitat. Mainly found in extensive freshwater wetland habitats, typically in marshes and swamps, backwaters and margins of lakes or rivers, paddyfields and floodplains; sometimes in moist savanna or burnt grassland, occasionally in forest clearings.
Food and Feeding. Mostly aquatic snails (*Pila*, *Lanistes ovum*), also frequently freshwater mussels (*Ampullaria*); in Uganda recorded taking terrestrial snail *Limicolaria martensiana*; occasionally other prey, including frogs, crabs, worms, fish and insects. Highly specialized technique of extracting snail from shell and also of opening bivalves (see page 443); sometimes associates with hippopotami, which may expose snails when churning up water, mud or vegetation.
Breeding. Normally starts late in rains, probably when snails most readily available, having emerged from aestivation; in some cases at beginning of rains, or immediately before; opportunistic in terms of both time and place. Tree-nester in colonies of varying sizes, frequently over water; also in reedbeds. Nest small, only c. 50 cm wide, platform of sticks and reeds. Average 3-4 eggs (2-5); incubation estimated 25-30 days; chicks have black down and a normal bill, curvature developing over several years; fledging estimated at 50-55 days.
Movements. Some regular transequatorial movement, with fair numbers arriving in W Africa for dry season, while common in Sudan Nov-Apr; most birds breed in S Hemisphere, but migration not well understood. Normally migrates in flocks, riding on thermals, though can perform some sustained flapping flight. S African breeders resident while conditions favourable; juveniles wander far during foraging.
Status and Conservation. Not globally threatened. Common in suitable habitat throughout its range, often abundant round breeding colonies; in 1968, largest known colony of over 5000 pairs, in Tanzania. Population considered probably stable, possibly increasing in E Africa; perhaps the commonest stork in Africa. Mid-winter census of Jan 1991 yielded 201 birds in Nigeria, 165 in Uganda, and 160 in Zambia; highest figures from W Africa in recent years include 980 birds in Chad Basin. In S Africa under 100 pairs, breeding only in wet years. Race *madagascariensis* still rather common in WC Madagascar, but has declined in both range and numbers in recent years, due to destruction of colonies by villagers.

Bibliography. Anthony & Sherry (1980), Bell-Cross (1974), Bonvallot & Randrianasolo (1975), Braine (1974), Britton (1971, 1980), Brooke (1984), Brown & Britton (1980), Brown *et al.* (1982), Chapin (1932), Coverdale & Hancock (1983), Dutton (1972), Feely (1964), Ginn (1984), Hanmer (1985), van der Heiden (1973, 1974), Huxley (1960), Jacot-Guillarmod (1965), Jubb (1981), Kahl (1968, 1971e, 1972e), Kasoma & Pomeroy (1987), Klug & Boswall (1970), Langrand (1990), Macdonald *et al.* (1985), Mackworth-Praed & Grant (1957-1973), Maclean (1985), Milon *et al.* (1973), Newman & English (1975), Niven & Niven (1966a), Parsons (1974), Pennycuick (1972b), Pinto (1983), Root (1963), Steyn (1988).

Tribe CICONIINI

Genus *CICONIA* Brisson, 1760

7. **Black Stork**

Ciconia nigra

French: Cigogne noire **German**: Schwarzstorch **Spanish**: Cigüeña negra

Taxonomy. *Ardea nigra* Linnaeus, 1758, Sweden.
Apparently most primitive member of genus in both behaviour and morphology. Monotypic.
Distribution. Breeds across Palearctic, mostly c. 40°-60° N; winters in NE and E Africa and from W Pakistan, through N India to SE and E China; some birds probably resident in SW Spain. Also breeds in scattered populations from Malawi and Namibia to South Africa.

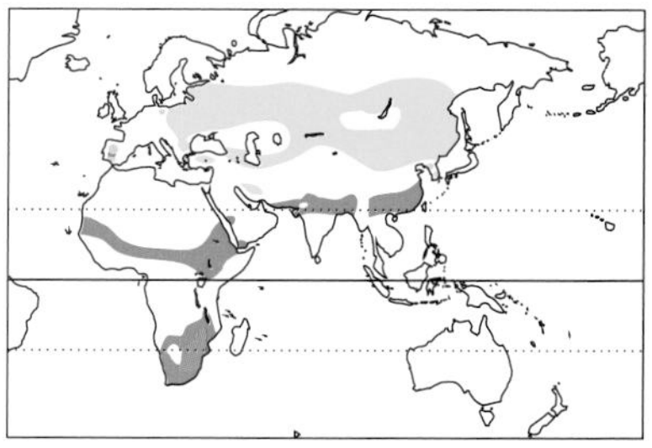

Descriptive notes. 95-100 cm; c. 3 kg; wingspan 144-155 cm. Males average larger. Upperparts have green and purple gloss; bill can appear slightly recurved. Juvenile browner and duller, with bill and legs greenish.
Habitat. Generally prefers undisturbed open woodland, feeding in streams, pools, marshes, riverbanks, occasionally grasslands, normally avoiding large bodies of water and closed forest; also shuns contact with humans. Not usually in extensive open areas, except e.g. Caspian lowlands and Ethiopian highlands. Breeds up to 850 m in Austria and 2000 m in S Africa.
Food and Feeding. Mostly fish, such as loaches (*Misgurnus*) and pike (*Esox lucius*); also amphibia, insects, snails, crabs and small reptiles, mammals and birds. Usually forages in shallow water; stalks prey, catching it with a sharp stab of bill; reported to shadow water with wings in Portugal. Young require 400-500 g of food daily.
Breeding. Starts spring in Palearctic and in Cape Province; further N in Africa mostly in cool dry season. Solitary nester, usually in trees in forest; on cliffs in S Africa and Spain. Large stick nest, c. 1·5 m wide, lined with moss, grass and leaves, and cemented together with earth; re-used in successive years; may take over nests of raptors, e.g. Black Eagle (*Aquila verreauxi*), and one record on nest of Hamerkop (*Scopus umbretta*). Average 3-4 eggs (2-6); incubation 32-38 days (reportedly up to 46 days); chicks have white down; fledging 63-71 days. Sexual maturity probably not before 3 years. Oldest ringing recovery of 18-year-old bird. Oldest captive bird over 31 years old.
Movements. Migratory; partially resident population in Spain; S African birds disperse after breeding with local, mostly altitudinal movements. W Palearctic birds mostly skirt Mediterranean, though less so than *C. ciconia*, because more capable of sustained flapping flight; few, if any, cross equator. Migration to and from Europe peaks in Mar/Apr and Sept, c. 2 weeks later than *C. ciconia*. Migration spread fairly evenly throughout day. In India mostly in small groups, often associating with *C. episcopus*. Reported foraging almost 10 km from nest in Poland.
Status and Conservation. Not globally threatened. CITES II. Has declined all over, most markedly in W Europe, where now threatened; disappeared from Belgium and parts of Germany in latter parts of last century and from Denmark and Sweden in 1950's; main problems include deforestation and persecution; in Africa, wetland conversion and pesticides probably worsen situation. In 1992, Spain held 300 pairs; over 30 birds known to have been shot illegally in Spain and Portugal during 1980's. Still common and even increasing in parts of E Europe, with Polish population of c. 800 pairs in 1980's, and Austrian population increasing from 3 pairs in 1960 to 60-65 pairs in 1983. Rare further E, with only c. 500 pairs in whole of USSR; very little known in China; mid-winter census in Jan 1991 gave 121 birds in India. Only known nest-site in South Korea, at Hak so dae, near Andong, may have been occupied by the species for over 400 years. Frequent, locally common in S Africa, with 50-70 pairs in Transvaal; probably over 200 pairs, stable, may be increasing. Slight decline in Zimbabwe may be due to conditions of extreme drought.
Bibliography. Ali & Ripley (1978), Anon. (1988), Babko (1987), Bauer (1952), Bauer & Glutz von Blotzheim (1966), Bednorz (1974), Bereszynski (1977), Bernis (1959, 1966b, 1980), Bloesch *et al.* (1987), Boev & Paspaleva-Antonova (1964), Brazil (1991), Brooke (1984), Brown *et al.* (1982), Cheng Tso-hsin (1987), Cramp & Simmons (1977), Creutz (1970, 1982), Dementiev & Gladkov (1951b), Einarsson *et al.* (1989), Etchécopar & Hüe (1978), Fei Dianjin (1986), Feldman (1965), Fincham (1971), Flint (1978), Fouarge (1987), Géroudet (1978a), González & Merino (1988), Goodman (1989), Gore & Won (1971), Grimmett (1987), Grimmett & Jones (1989), Hemetsberger (1989), Hubaut (1986), Humphrey & Bain (1990), Janez (1987), Kahl (1972d), Kasoma & Pomeroy (1987), Krapivni (1958), Kumerloeve (1966b), Lebedeva (1959), Lesniczak (1989), Litvinenko (1985), Liu Huanjin *et al.* (1985), Loiseau (1977), Lorber (1982), Maclean (1985), Madsen (1990), Moreau (1972), Muller-Scheessel (1964, 1965), Niethammer (1967), Paz (1987), Peterson (1976), Pierre (1988), Priklonskii (1958), Priklonskii & Galushin (1959), Rasmussen (1979), Roberts (1969, 1991), Robiller & Trogisch (1986a), Round *et al.* (1988), Roux & Dupuy (1972), Ryder & Ryder (1978), Sackl (1985), Schröder & Burmeister (1974), Scott (1989), Siegfried (1967a), Siewert (1932), Sklyarenko & Berezovikov (1987), Sonobe & Izawa (1987), Su Hualong *et al.* (1989), Takashima (1957), Tarboton (1977, 1982), Tilson & Kok (1980), Tree (1982a), Vergoossen (1983), Volrath (1987), Vondracek (1983), Won (1971), Yu Han (1963), Zhang Xinglu (1983).

8. **Abdim's Stork**

Ciconia abdimii

French: Cigogne d'Abdim **German**: Abdimstorch **Spanish**: Cigüeña de Abdim
Other common names: White-bellied Stork

Taxonomy. *Ciconia Abdimii* Lichtenstein, 1823, Dongola, Sudan.
Formerly placed in monospecific genus *Sphenorhynchus*. Monotypic.
Distribution. Africa S of Sahara and SW Arabia; breeds N of equator, with most birds spending rest of year in eastern and southern parts of Africa.

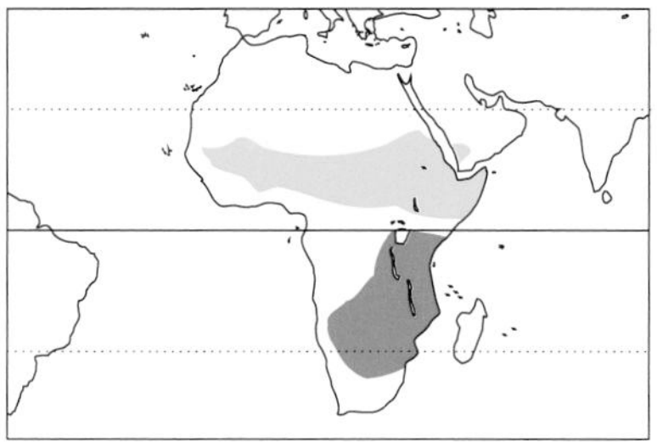

Descriptive notes. 75-81 cm; 1·3 kg. Male slightly larger. Upperparts glossed purple and green. Non-breeding adult has bare parts duller. Immature browner and duller.
Habitat. Normally found in open grassland, also in areas of cultivation; often near water, but also found in very dry zones, including semi-desert. Roosts on trees or cliffs and often rests beside marshes and pools. Also nests in villages, as protected from disturbance by superstition, consequently having little fear of man.
Food and Feeding. Almost exclusively large insects, especially swarming locusts and caterpillars of army worm (*Spodoptera exempta*); also grasshoppers, crickets and infrequently mice and small aquatic animals. Congregates in large flocks at swarms and grass fires, each bird gorging itself rapidly. Otherwise, walks along looking out for prey, which is located and then quickly snatched up.
Breeding. Usually early in rains, in May; earlier in W Kenya. Colonial in cliffs or trees, often with other species (see page 446); sometimes solitary at edge of range; may nest in roofs of native huts. 2-3 eggs, sometimes only 1; incubation 30-31 days (in captivity); chicks have light grey down; fledging probably c. 50-60 days. Oldest captive bird over 21 years old.
Movements. Trans-equatorial migrant; mostly May-Aug in breeding zones N of equator, Nov-Mar in S tropics, everywhere coinciding with the rains. Often travels in vast flocks of c. 10,000, landing daily to feed, except perhaps when over forests.
Status and Conservation. Not globally threatened. Common, locally abundant, with flocks of up to 10,000 in Uganda. Protected by local superstitions as bringer of rain; also welcomed as "grasshopper bird". Nesting in roofs of native huts sometimes encouraged by inhabitants, who erect a suitable basket-like structure, as the birds are supposed to bring them good luck. Pesticide control of locusts does not seem to have affected the species adversely as yet and numbers are considered to be relatively stable. Breeds well in captivity.
Bibliography. Ash (1981), Bigalke (1948), Blencowe (1962), Britton (1980), Brooke (1969), Brosset & Erard (1986), Brown & Britton (1980), Brown *et al.* (1982), Chapin (1932), Condy (1965, 1966), Dekeyser (1952), Duignan *et al.* (1988), van der Elst (1988), Ezealour (1985), Farnell & Shannon (1987), Gallagher (1986), Kahl (1968, 1971d, 1972d), Kasoma & Pomeroy (1987), Lohding (1987), Mackworth-Praed & Grant (1957-1973), Maclean (1985), Morel & Morel (1962), North (1940), Pinto (1983), Wilkins & Wilkins (1990).

9. **Woolly-necked Stork**

Ciconia episcopus

French: Cigogne épiscopale **German**: Wollhalsstorch **Spanish**: Cigüeña Lanuda
Other common names: White-necked/Bishop Stork

Taxonomy. *Ardea episcopus* Boddaert, 1783, Coromandel Coast.
Formerly placed in monospecific genus *Dissoura*. Sometimes includes *C. stormi*, but now generally regarded as separate species (see page 436). Validity of race *neglecta* disputed; some doubt as to geographical limits of subspecies in SE Asia. Three subspecies normally recognized.
Subspecies and Distribution.
C. e. microscelis G. R. Gray, 1848 - Tropical Africa.
C. e. episcopus (Boddaert, 1783) - India to Indochina and N Malay Peninsula; Philippines.
C. e. neglecta (Finsch, 1904) - Java and Wallacea.

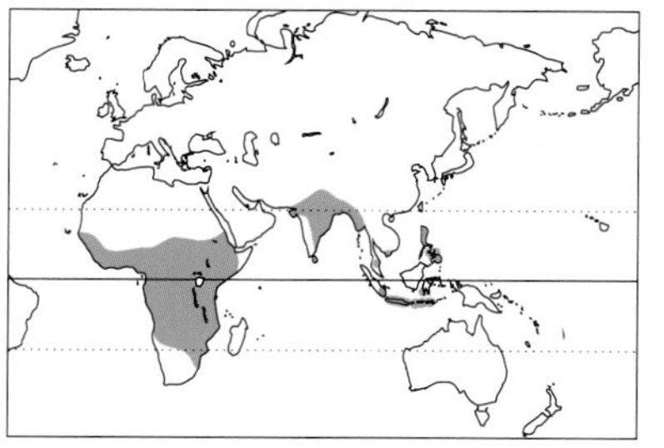

Descriptive notes. 86-95 cm. Neck feathers very soft, black of plumage glossed blue and purple; forked tail black, but usually obscured by long undertail-coverts. Immature duller and browner. Races separated on size, bill colour and extent of black cap.
Habitat. Usually in or by wetlands such as rivers, lakes, flood plains, marshes, *jheels*, paddyfields, drying ponds, flooded pastures, water-holes, lagoons, freshwater and peat swamp forest; prefers waterlogged ground in India; in E Africa mostly along coast, on mudflats or coral reefs, but also in savanna, grassland and cultivation, attending grass fires; normally avoids forest, but found in light woodland and forest clearings, usually by streams or rivers and also in forest marshes. Has been found at 1400 m in Sulawesi and up to 1250 m in Nepal.
Food and Feeding. Fish, frogs, toads, snakes, lizards, large insects, crabs, reptiles, molluscs, marine invertebrates; fibres of palm nut also found in some stomachs. Largely solitary, feeds by walking about slowly, picking up any prey encountered; rarely wades in water.
Breeding. In India, Jul-Sep in N, Dec-Mar in S; usually lays in dry season throughout Africa, but during rains in N Sudan. Solitary, though pairs may be close together in E Africa; tree-nester, typically 20-30 m up tall tree, such as silk cotton (*Salmalia*) in India, where often near village. Large stick platform, 1 m wide x 30 cm deep, with central depression lined with grass and rubbish. 2-4 eggs; incubation 30-31 days; chicks have grey down, with neck buff; fledging 55-65 days. Sexual maturity probably after 3 years in female. Oldest captive bird over 30 years old.
Movements. Mainly resident, but some regional N-S movements in Africa, at times collecting in flocks of up to several hundred. Only local movements in India. Vagrant to Iran; race *episcopus* apparently in Sumatra.
Status and Conservation. Not globally threatened. Widespread, but uncommon throughout and probably regionally threatened in SE Asia; main problem may be fragmentation of habitat. Uncommon to rare, but probably stable in Africa, possibly even increasing in E Africa; under 30 pairs in South Africa, where stable; estimated 400-600 birds in Guinea-Bissau. Still fairly common in much of India, with 363 birds counted in mid-winter census in Jan 1991; large numbers recorded in recent survey of N India, where species thought to be fairly secure. Very rare, if not extinct, in Pakistan. Near extinction in Bangladesh, Burma, Thailand and Viet Nam; status largely unknown throughout rest of SE Asia. Indonesian population estimated at about 1000 individuals, being most common on Sulawesi and E Java; race *neglecta* very poorly known, a lot of survey work required, especially to establish its habitat requirements.

Bibliography. Ali (1979), Ali & Ripley (1978), Ambedkar (1959), Andrew & Holmes (1990), Anthony (1977, 1978a), Baltzer (1990), Berruti (1983), Britton (1980), Brooke (1984), Brown & Britton (1980), Brown *et al.* (1982), Dickinson *et al.* (1991), Dixon (1970), Dunning (1977), Ewans (1989), Garland (1963), Harvey (1972), Henry (1971), Hitchins (1974), Holmes (1977a), Hoogerwerf (1949), Humphrey & Bain (1990), Kahl (1968, 1972d), Karpowicz (1985), Kasoma & Pomeroy (1987), Khan (1984, 1987), King & Brouwer (1991), Mackworth-Praed & Grant (1957-1973), Maclean (1985), van Marle & Voous (1988), McCann (1930), Medway & Wells (1976), Morris (1989), Pennycuick (1972b), Pinto (1983), Pitman (1931a), Roberts (1991), Round *et al.* (1988), Scott, D.A. (1989), Scott, J.A. (1972, 1975), Silvius & Verheugt (1989), Silvius *et al.* (1987), Smythies (1986), Steyn (1987), Verheijen (1964), Verheugt (1989), Wells (1985), Whistler (1918), White (1974), White & Bruce (1986).

10. Storm's Stork

Ciconia stormi

French: Cigogne de Storm **German**: Höckerstorch **Spanish**: Cigüeña de Storm

Taxonomy. *Melanopelargus episcopus stormi* W. Blasius, 1896, Pontianak, western Borneo.
Sometimes considered subspecies of *C. episcopus*, but now generally accepted as separate species (see page 436). Monotypic.
Distribution. Borneo, Sumatra (and Mentawai Is off W coast) and peninsular Malaysia; recently discovered in Thailand, although probably now extinct.

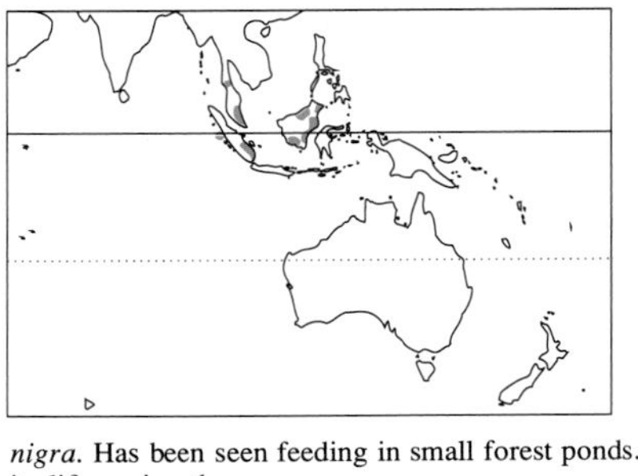

Descriptive notes. 85 cm. Bare facial skin far more extensive and brighter than in *C. episcopus*. Non-breeding adult has bare parts duller. Immature has duller plumage and bare parts.
Habitat. Undisturbed freshwater habitats, especially peat swamp forest; densely forested tracts, often seen by rivers, e.g. on muddy banks. Unlike *C. episcopus*, not normally found in open areas.
Food and Feeding. Apparently mainly fish, though very little known; probably also reptiles, amphibians, insects; feeding habits even less known, but probably similar to other *Ciconia* storks, such as *C. episcopus* and *C. nigra*. Has been seen feeding in small forest ponds. Probably tends to be solitary in this aspect of its life, as in others.
Breeding. Very poorly known, with only two nests so far discovered, both since 1986: one occupied Apr-July in S Sumatra; one with chicks hatched in mid Oct in Thailand. Solitary tree-nester; stick platform, 50 cm long x 15 cm deep, lined with dry leaves and some down; one nest some 20 m up a large *Dipterocarpus baudii*, the other in canopy of a *Rhizophora* mangrove. 2+ eggs; fledging over 45 days; chicks have white down.
Movements. Unknown. Possibly only irregular visitor to Malaysia.
Status and Conservation. INDETERMINATE. Should probably now be considered Endangered. Probably rarest of all storks after *L. dubius*. Most of world population in Indonesia, where recent estimate is of under 300 birds; recent records also from other parts of Borneo. Has probably never been abundant, but is now declining due to extensive logging activities all over its range; transmigration plans of Indonesian government, in conjunction with World Bank, threaten vast areas of habitat and should be seriously reconsidered. Not well adapted to disturbed habitat, although up to 12 were seen in E Kalimantan, Borneo, in an area where the swamp forest had been devastated two years earlier by fire. Solitary habits make it less openly vulnerable to human persecution, but also hamper research work on both feeding and breeding requirements, as well as on numbers and methods of effective protection of a viable population. Known nesting area in SE Sumatra included in large proposed reserve. In Malaysia, is either rare resident or irregular visitor. Recently discovered Thai population probably already exterminated or, if not, almost certainly doomed (see page 453).
Bibliography. Anon. (1986c, 1989c), Chasen (1935), Collar & Andrew (1988), Holmes (1969, 1977a), Holmes & Burton (1987), Kemp & Kemp (1976), Kidd (1978), King (1978/79), MacKinnon (1983), van Marle & Voous (1988), Medway & Wells (1971, 1976), Nakhasathien (1987), Nash & Nash (1985, 1988), Round & Treessucon (1986), Round *et al.* (1988), Scott (1989), Silvius & Verheugt (1989), Silvius *et al.* (1987), Smythies (1981), Verheugt (1989), Wells (1985), Westhuizen (1967), White (1974).

11. Maguari Stork

Ciconia maguari

French: Cigogne maguari **German**: Maguaristorch **Spanish**: Cigüeña Maguari

Taxonomy. *Ardea Maguari* Gmelin, 1789, north-eastern Brazil.
Formerly placed in monospecific genus *Euxenura*. Specific name *galeata* older, but indeterminable. Monotypic.
Distribution. S America E of Andes, from Venezuela to Argentina.

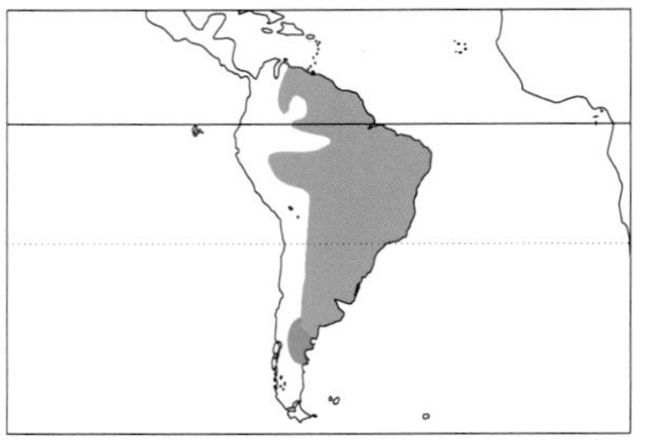

Descriptive notes. 97-102 cm. Male larger with slightly longer bill. Red orbital skin and creamy white iris; tail forked. Immature similar to adult, but black orbital area.
Habitat. Variety of freshwater wetland sites, including swamps, savanna areas with ponds, flooded pastures, reedbeds, ricefields; also in short, dry grass of fields and even on beach. Strays up to 2500 m in Bolivia.
Food and Feeding. Frogs and tadpoles, fish, especially eels, small aquatic rodents, snakes, crabs and aquatic insects. Typical generalized visual feeding method of the genus, though more closely linked with water, often foraging in dense aquatic vegetation and sometimes taking in some of this with prey. Feeds alone, in pairs, or more often in small groups, especially around drying ponds. Also searches for insects under dry cowpats.
Breeding. June-Nov in *llanos*, Aug-Oct in S Brazil. Loosely colonial, normally in clusters of 5-15 nests, which may be only 50 cm apart. Nests preferably isolated from predators, 1-6 m up on bushes or small trees; if these not available, on ground in dense reedbeds; nest-site always surrounded by water; stick nest up to 2 m wide and 75 cm deep, lined with grass. 2-4 eggs; incubation 29-32 days; first coat of down white, rapidly replaced with black one; fledging 60-72 days. Sexual maturity at 3 years in males, 4 in females. Oldest captive bird over 20 years old.
Movements. Little known. At breeding grounds studied in Venezuela birds arrive Mar-May, probably depending on rains, leaving again in Jan, when area dries up; normally travel in flocks of 50 or more; also some pre- and post-breeding dispersal. May feed up to 30 km from nest; reported to fly in wedge-shaped formations. Sometimes crosses Andes between Argentina and Chile.
Status and Conservation. Not globally threatened. Total Venezuelan population in 1987 reckoned to be under 5000 and decreasing, with declines of 90-100% in some places over last ten years or so; this might be due to agricultural developments, including excessive use of pesticides, and also to direct exploitation, with young birds still being taken from nests to be eaten. Little known of status in other countries: local in Colombia; stable in Brazil; stable, but uncommon in Bolivia; still widespread and abundant in much of Argentina, where partial census in Jul 1990 gave 206 birds.
Bibliography. Belton (1984), Blake (1977), Boer & van Brink (1982), Fernández (1929), Gabaldón & Ulloa (1980), Gyldenstolpe (1945), Haedo Rossi (1969), Hagenrath & Ribera (1985), Hellmayr & Conover (1948), Hilty & Brown (1986), Kahl (1971c, 1972d), King (1988), Kushlan *et al.* (1985), Morales (1990), Morales *et al.* (1981), Nores & Yzurieta (1980), Ogden & Thomas (1985a), de la Peña (1986), Pinto (1964), Ramo & Busto (1984), de Schauensee & Phelps (1978), Scott & Carbonell (1986), Short (1975), Sick (1984), Spaans (1975a), Thomas (1979a, 1979b, 1984, 1985, 1986, 1987, 1988), Wetmore (1926).

12. European White Stork

Ciconia ciconia

French: Cigogne blanche **German**: Weißstorch **Spanish**: Cigüeña Blanca
Other common names: White Stork

Taxonomy. *Ardea Ciconia* Linnaeus, 1758, Sweden.
Until recently considered to include *C. boyciana*, but now generally accepted as separate species (see page 436). Two subspecies recognized.
Subspecies and Distribution.
C. c. ciconia (Linnaeus, 1758) - Europe, W Asia, S Africa; winters mostly tropical Africa and S Africa.
C. c. asiatica Severtsov, 1873 - Turkestan; winters Iran to India.

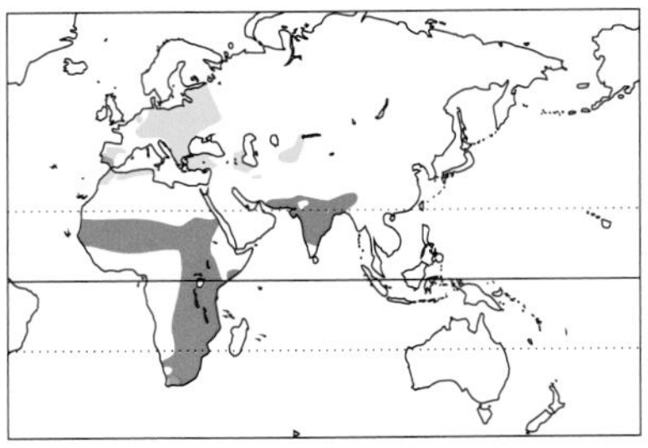

Descriptive notes. 100-102 cm; 2·3-4·4 kg; wingspan 155-165 cm. Males average larger. Black orbital skin, iris dark brown or grey; pale band on secondaries not normally apparent. Juvenile has duller plumage and bare parts. Race *asiatica* slightly larger than nominate.
Habitat. Open areas, frequently wetlands, but not necessarily; more aquatic in Palearctic, terrestrial in Africa; grasslands, steppe, savanna, cultivation, often near pools, marshy areas, slow streams or ditches; also water meadows, flooded or damp pastures, lakesides, lagoons; frequently with scattered trees, in which birds may nest or roost; a wide variety of human constructions and also rubbish dumps. Mainly in lowlands, rarely higher up in S Palearctic, e.g. at 3500 m in Caucasus. Avoids areas with persistent cold, wet weather and also tracts of tall, dense vegetation, such as reedbeds and forest.
Food and Feeding. Very varied, though entirely animal. Small mammals (e.g. *Microtus*, *Arvicola*), large insects (especially *Coleoptera*, *Orthoptera*), young and adult amphibians (*Rana*, *Bufo*), reptiles (snakes, lizards), earthworms, fish, etc.; some odd items also recorded (see page 444). In Austria takes diverse prey, especially rodents, Apr-Jun, but mostly grasshoppers Jul-Aug. Generalized foraging method of strutting about, locating prey by sight and snatching it up in bill, occasionally after very brief chase. Opportunistic, preying on whatever happens to be available, feeding very quickly; in Africa large numbers may concentrate at grass fires or swarms of locusts (e.g. *Locusta migratoria*), army worms (*Spodoptera exempta*), etc.
Breeding. Starts Feb-Apr in Palearctic, Sept-Nov in S Africa. Loosely colonial, with many nests often close together; sometimes solitary. Large stick nest, may be 2·5 m deep or more, lined with turf, dung, paper, etc.; usually in tree (always in S Africa) or on roof of building; otherwise on pylons, telegraph poles, strawstacks and other man-made sites, including structures specially erected for the birds; also on cliffs and even recorded on ground, among rushes; same nest regularly reused in successive years. Average 4 eggs (1-7); incubation 33-34 days; chicks have white down and black bill; fledging 58-64 days. Sexual maturity normally at 4 years (2-7). Bigamy recorded, e.g. one male paired with two females on different nests. Oldest ringed bird, male over 33 years old, which successfully raised 3 young at age of 32; in captivity over 35 years old.
Movements. Migratory. Highly dependent on soaring and thus thermals, crossing deserts, but avoiding large bodies of water and extensive forests. Migration of European birds very well known (see page 449); populations of race *ciconia* from SE Palearctic may winter mostly from Iran to India. Birds winter in India Sept/Oct-Mar/Apr; one stork ringed in Germany was recovered in NW India. Most migration takes place from mid-morning to early afternoon.
Status and Conservation. Not globally threatened. Currently considered near-threatened. World population in mid 1980's estimated at over 150,000 breeding pairs, with 33,000 in Poland in 1984, and some 47,000 in USSR in 1974, where may be increasing in places; increasing in Baltic region, e.g. in Estonia, with 1 pair in 1841, 1060 pairs in 1974. Protected by superstition in many parts of Europe and in Iran, and as being a useful pest-controller in parts of Africa, but persecuted in some places. Recently established S African population of under 10 pairs. Great decline in W Europe, where now regionally threatened: last bred in Switzerland in 1949, in Sweden in 1954; disappeared from Belgium in 1895, though started breeding again in 1972; in Netherlands from 316 pairs in 1939 to 1 pair in 1983; in Denmark 10,000 pairs pre 1857 to 14 pairs in 1985; strongest population in W Europe in Iberian Peninsula, with 7736 nests in 1989; captive breeding bolsters several populations. Apparently still fairly common in winter in parts of India, especially in N, but very little known. Problems include: habitat alteration, mainly drainage of wetlands and conversion of foraging areas; in some cases, shortage of nest-sites; excessive use of pesticides (e.g. Sudan and Tanzania); mortality due to eating of poison baits put out for large carnivores; collisions with power lines; and hunting. Hunting particularly important during migration: in 1985, 21 tethered wild decoys were found surrounded by hundreds of snares near Kano in N Nigeria, and storks can be found for sale in local markets; estimated c. 200 storks caught in Sahel in a single season, though shooting may be more serious problem than trapping; several thousand birds shot annually in Syria and Lebanon; sometimes hunted for fun in Sudan, where species not legally protected. Has been object of extensive research and considerable conservation effort for many years. Symposia held on this species in Germany in 1983 and 1985. Breeds well in captivity, but young mostly hand-reared, to protect from bad weather. See page 454.
Bibliography. Abduladze & Eligulashvili (1986), Ali & Ripley (1978), Allan (1984a, 1985a), Assfalg & Schüz (1988), Bairlein (1981), Bardin (1959), Bauer & Glutz von Blotzheim (1966), Bereszynski (1977), Bernis (1959,

1966b, 1980), Bloesch (1980, 1986), Boreiko *et al.* (1988), Brooke (1984), Brown *et al.* (1982), Cao Yupu & Xu Tielin (1983), Chozas (1983), Cramp & Simmons (1977), Creutz (1985), Dallinga & Schoenmakers (1987), Etchécopar & Hüe (1978), Fei Dianjin (1986), Fei Dianjin *et al.* (1983), Géroudet (1978a, 1978b), Glas & Porper (1986), Goodman (1989), Goriup (1990), Grimmett (1987), Grimmett & Jones (1989), Hall *et al.* (1987), Haverschmidt (1949), He Baoqing (1981), Hölzinger & Schmid (1986), Horin & Adar (1986), Hornberger (1967), Johnson (1985), Kahl (1972d), Kania (1985), Kasoma & Pomeroy (1987), Katz (1986), King (1988), Krapivni (1958), Kumerloeve (1966a), Lazaro *et al.* (1986), Lebedeva (1958, 1960a, 1960b), Lewis & Pearson (1981a, 1981b), Martínez (1987), Mendelssohn (1975), Moreau (1972), Niethammer (1967), Nowak & Berthold (1987), Paz (1987), Peterson (1976), Profus & Mielczarek (1981), Rheinwald *et al.* (1989), Roberts (1991), Round *et al.* (1988), Sackl (1987), Schneider (1988), Schüz (1936, 1942, 1960, 1979, 1984), Scott (1989), Seward (1987), Sklyarenko & Berezovikov (1987), Sutter (1984), Thiollay (1985), Vaidya (1986), Vicente (1984), Yan Fengtao (1987).

13. Oriental White Stork

Ciconia boyciana

French: Cigogne orientale   **German**: Schwarzschnabelstorch   **Spanish**: Cigüeña Oriental
Other common names: Eastern White Stork

Taxonomy. *Ciconia boyciana* Swinhoe, 1873, Yokohama.
Until recently included in *C. ciconia*, but the two now generally accepted as distinct species (see page 436). Monotypic.
Distribution. Breeds in SE Siberia and in parts of NE China; winters in S and SE China, with a few in Japan and Korea. Formerly bred in Japan and Korea.

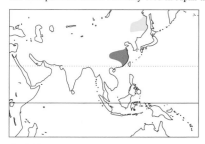

Descriptive notes. 110-115 cm. Males average slightly larger. Red orbital skin, iris whitish; bill very slightly recurved, much heavier than in *C. ciconia*, and legs deeper red. Silvery fringe along secondaries. Immature similar to adult, but duller.
Habitat. Marshes with scattered clumps of trees, wet grassland, river banks, preferably in woodland. In Japan used to forage extensively in cultivation, especially paddyfields, breeding in nearby woods. Does not associate with man in same way as *C. ciconia*, probably due to persecution; however, some evidence in USSR that species adapting to more humanized zones.
Food and Feeding. Variety of prey types: mainly fish, especially loach (*Misgurnus fossilis*), *Perccottus glehni* and Crucian carp (*Carassius auratus*); also insects, especially Orthoptera (*Mecostethus grossus*) and Coleoptera; amphibians, including Siberian frogs (*Rana amurensis*) and tree frogs (*Hyla japonica*); mammals, especially voles; gastropods; earthworms; and small birds.

In winter, recorded taking fish, shellfish and crustaceans; bamboo and other plant matter deliberately consumed. Daily intake estimated at c. 1500-3000 g. On land, prey located visually; in water, may use tactile foraging techniques; forages by walking slowly through water, or standing still. Catches fish mostly at base of tail, using terminal third of bill. Feeds alone or in flocks of up to 16 birds.
Breeding. Laying in Apr-May. Solitary or loosely colonial. Nests in trees, often dead trees with good visibility; also on buildings, but rather infrequently; same nest can be reused in successive years. 2-6 eggs; incubation c. 32-35 days; chicks have white down and orange bill; fledging c. 55 days. In USSR, up to 6 chicks may fledge from nest, but in poor years maximum 2. Oldest captive bird over 48 years old.
Movements. Migratory, mostly over little known areas of China; quits breeding grounds in Sept/Oct, returning in Mar/Apr. Most migration takes place from mid-morning to late afternoon. Vagrant to Tibet in 1922; also reported from NE India and Bangladesh, though some doubt about these records. In USSR, normally nests within 1-2 km of foraging areas.
Status and Conservation. ENDANGERED. CITES I. World population may be something over 3000 birds. Exterminated from Japan and S Korea, where used to be common even in towns; dramatic decline in Japan in latter part of 19th century, with proliferation of firearms. Population of USSR estimated at c. 700 pairs; research on nesting and feeding, and ringing of nestlings since 1985; healthiest populations in remote areas, making survey work difficult. Wetlands at confluence of Bureya and Amur threatened by drainage and agricultural development. Chinese population appears larger than previously thought; at Beidaihe, Hebei province (SE China), 2729 birds seen on migration in autumn 1986, with slightly fewer recorded in subsequent years; several hundred winter in or near a large, recently declared reserve by Chang Jiang (Yangtze) drainage system; census of Jan 1991 produced 121 birds in Hong Kong. Causes of decline include hunting, poisoning and habitat loss, due to agricultural conversion, peat extraction and tree felling. First successful captive breeding in 1987, when 38 birds known in captivity; further breeding groups being established in other parks and zoos with a view to reintroduction of the species in Japan and Korea (see page 452); attempts at captive breeding started in Japan in 1963, but no success to date. More surveys and ecological studies required, as well as effective protection, construction of artificial nest-sites and public awareness campaigns, such as posters distributed in China in 1987 and USSR in 1990 by Brehm Fund.

Bibliography. Ali & Ripley (1978), Andronov (1983), Archibald (1985, 1989), Archibald & Luthin (1985b), Archibald & Schmitt (1989), Austin (1948), Austin & Kuroda (1953), Boswall (1989), Brazil (1991), Cheng Tso-hsin (1987), Collar & Andrew (1988), Coulter (1990), Coulter, Qishan & Luthin (1991), Dementiev & Gladkov (1951b), Doguchi & Ushio (1973), Dymin & Pankin (1975), Etchécopar & Hüe (1978), Litvinenko (1985), Fei Dianjin (1986, 1989), Fennel & King (1964), Flint (1978), Fujimaki (1988), Gore & Won (1971), Hemmingsen (1951), Kahl (1972d), Kamel (1971), Karpowicz (1985), Kennerley (1987), King, C.E. (1988), King, C.E. & Patzwahl (1987), King, W.B. (1978/79), Kolbe (1988), Komine & Sugita (1990), Lebedeva (1977), Leonovich & Nikolyevski (1976), Litvinenko (1968, 1985), Luthin *et al.* (1986), Murata (1988), Myong (1967), Neufeldt & Wunderlich (1982), Ogasawara & Izumi (1977), Pankin & Neufeldt (1976), Rheinwald *et al.* (1989), Sakamoto (1966), Scott (1989), Shibaev *et al.* (1976), Smirenski *et al.* (1987), Sonobe & Izawa (1987), Takashima (1956), Utvinenko (1968), Wang Qishan (1987), Wang Yongjun & Zhou Wei (1989), Wennrich (1982d), Williams *et al.* (1986), Winter (1978, 1982), Won (1971), Yamashina (1962a, 1977), Yamashina & Takano (1959), Yoshii (1971).

PLATE 33

inches 16

cm 40

♀

14

♂

♀

15

♂

with throat sac inflated

16

17

18

19

with throat sac inflated

Tribe LEPTOPTILINI

Genus *EPHIPPIORHYNCHUS*
Bonaparte, 1855

14. Black-necked Stork
Ephippiorhynchus asiaticus

French: Jabiru d'Asie   German: Riesenstorch   Spanish: Jabirú Asiático
Other common names: Jabiru (!), Green-necked Stork (Australia)

Taxonomy. *Mycteria asiatica* Latham, 1790, India.
Sometimes placed in monospecific genus *Xenorhynchus*, but close similarity to *E. senegalensis* in breeding habits, behaviour and morphology demand their treatment as congeners. Two subspecies recognized.
Subspecies and Distribution.
E. a. asiaticus (Latham, 1790) - Oriental Region.
E. a. australis (Shaw, 1800) - S New Guinea, N and NE Australia.

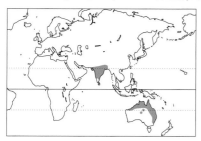

Descriptive notes. 110-137 cm; wingspan 190-218 cm. Black plumage glossed blue, greenish and purple; flight-feathers white. Genus *Ephippiorhynchus* unique among storks in showing sexual dimorphism in coloration: iris dark brown in male, yellow in female. Immature starts mainly dull brown, with white mottling on rump and lower back, breast and belly; juvenile plumage thought to give way gradually to full adult plumage. Race *australis* tends to have greener sheen to head and neck.
Habitat. Extensive, comparatively undisturbed freshwater wetlands, including
swamps, rivers, *jheels*, (oxbow) lakes, lagoons, flooded grassland, water meadows and *billabongs*; also dry floodplains, irrigated crops and open, grassy woodland; less often along coast, frequenting mangroves, mudflats, beaches, salt-marshes and tidal creeks. In arid parts of Australia, frequents small artificial water bodies, including farm water supplies, irrigation storages and sewage ponds. Nests in trees, usually in secluded part of swamp in S parts of range, but frequently surrounded by cultivation in India.
Food and Feeding. Mainly fish, including eels; also frogs, snakes, turtles, crabs, prawns, molluscs, beetles and arthropods; also recorded capturing Common Coots (*Fulica atra*), which are swallowed whole; snakes battered or skewered to death. Usually in shallow water, probing or sweeping bill from side to side and stabbing at prey; also waits motionless in areas with clear water; sometimes dashes around or jumps up in ungainly manner to snatch prey. Normally solitary or in pairs; also in small flocks.
Breeding. Mainly Apr-June in Australia, although surprisingly little known; varying Aug-Jan in different parts of India. Solitary tree-nester, building huge stick nest, almost 2 m wide x 1 m deep, lined with rushes, leaves and grass; nest near top of large, preferably isolated tree, commonly peepul (*Ficus religiosa*) in India, pine, *Eucalyptus*, *Melaleuca* in Australia; near water. Normally 2-3 eggs (2-5); chicks have grey down; fledging reported as 100-115 days. Oldest captive bird over 34 years old.
Movements. Basically sedentary, probably sticking to recognized feeding territories; young birds usually stay with adults for considerable time. Vagrant inland in Australia, even to Alice Springs. In the dry season in Irian Jaya (W New Guinea) many birds seem to cluster together at last remaining flooded areas.
Status and Conservation. Not globally threatened. Widespread, but nowhere common and probably never has been. Secure populations in Australia and S New Guinea, but threatened throughout most, if not all, of Asian range. Conversion of wetland habitat seems to be main factor in regression in S Asia, especially as each pair requires a large territory; successive years of drought have aggravated the situation, with many of the nesting trees having been cut down too. Small, scattered populations in India are mostly now too far apart ever to come into contact with each other, particularly as young birds do not tend to disperse very far; highly susceptible to disturbance; mid-winter census of Jan 1991 yielded 113 birds in India. Bred in mangroves at Indus Delta until late 1970's, but has since disappeared, and now only occasional straggler to Pakistan. No longer breeds in Bangladesh or Thailand, with only relict populations in Sri Lanka and Viet Nam. Recommended conservation measures include full-time protection of nesting trees, inclusion in CITES I and breeding of captive birds, which are numerous, with a view to bolstering natural populations; too many still taken for zoos, especially as the species has never yet bred in captivity (see page 454); full-scale surveys and studies of ecological requirements are also necessary. Much of its habitat in Irian Jaya (W New Guinea) is protected, in areas where hunting appears to be non-existent; 300 and 350 birds counted at two different localities in dry season of 1983. Australian population relatively large and stable, appears to be spreading S; conflict in New South Wales, where power lines being erected through midst of habitat. Has benefited from provision of artificial wetlands in many areas, especially in arid interior, but many natural wetlands lost through drainage. Other threats to habitat include: invasion of *Mimosa pigra* in wetlands in Northern Territory (Australia); salinization and siltation of wetlands due to intrusion of salt water caused by destruction of levees by feral buffalo; and probably increased disturbance due to spread of human development to previously remote areas.

Bibliography. Abdulali (1967), Ali (1979), Ali & Ripley (1978), Beehler *et al.* (1986), Bell (1963), Beruldsen (1972), Bishop (1984), Coates (1985), Ewans (1989), Field (1920), Goenka & Pandit (1986), Hancock (1989), Henry (1971), Humphrey & Bain (1990), Kahl (1973), Karpowicz (1985), Khan (1984, 1987), King & Brouwer (1991), Luthin (1988), Marchant & Higgins (1990), McCann (1930), McCulloch (1974), Morse (1965), Panday (1974), Rahmani (1987, 1989a, 1989b, 1990), Roberts (1991), Round *et al.* (1988), Salmon (1965), Scott (1989), Serventy (1985), Silvius & Verheugt (1989), Silvius, Lambert & Taufik (1991), Silvius, Steeman *et al.* (1987), Smythies (1986), Sridhar (1989), Sticklen & Sticklen (1981), Wells (1985), von Wetten (1985), Wikramanayake (1969).

15. Saddlebill
Ephippiorhynchus senegalensis

French: Jabiru du Sénégal   German: Sattelstorch   Spanish: Jabirú Africano
Other common names: Saddlebilled Stork, African Jabiru

Taxonomy. *Mycteria senegalensis* Shaw, 1800, Senegal. Monotypic.
Distribution. Tropical Africa from Senegal to Ethiopia and S to South Africa.

Descriptive notes. 145-150 cm; 6 kg; wingspan 240-270 cm. Males average considerably larger; both sexes have bare crimson "medal" on breast. Genus *Ephippiorhynchus* unique among storks in showing sexual dimorphism in coloration: iris dark brown in male, yellow in female. First year birds are dull grey, second year duller version of adult.
Habitat. Varied aquatic habitats, preferably large-scale, such as marshes, wet grassland, margins of large and small rivers and freshwater and alkaline lakes; often in open, semi-arid areas, generally avoiding forest.
Food and Feeding. Mainly fish of up to at least 500 g; also crabs, shrimps, frogs, reptiles, small mammals, young birds, and a few molluscs and insects, particularly large water-beetles. May search around vegetation in shallows, either standing still or walking slowly about; at more open sites tends to stab bill repeatedly into water, grabbing any prey that is contacted; also searches with bill in muddy water or vegetation, catching prey in tactile way reminiscent of *Mycteria*. Once fish caught, any spines may be snipped off, fish washed, swallowed head first, followed by drink of water. Has been known to scavenge fish regurgitated by cormorants. Solitary or in pairs, sometimes in groups of up to 12 and exceptionally a group of 100 at L Turkana, N Kenya.
Breeding. Mostly starts late in rains or in dry season; may be timed for young to leave nest at end of dry season. Solitary tree-nester; large, fairly flat stick nest, c. 2 m wide x 50 cm deep, lined with reeds, sedges, mud; on top of tree, often isolated from other trees and disturbance, and near water; occasionally on cliff. Normally 2-3 eggs (1-5); incubation estimated 30-35 days; chicks have white down; fledging estimated 70-100 days. Sexual maturity after at least three years. Does not necessarily breed every year. Oldest captive bird over 36 years old.
Movements. Basically sedentary, with some nomadic movements within or near home territory, in search of optimum feeding conditions. 1st and 2nd year birds often remain in natal range, tolerated by parents, until nearly adult.
Status and Conservation. Not globally threatened. Widespread, but usually uncommon. Population considered more or less stable, though probably susceptible to important changes in wetland areas, such as excessive use of pesticides, conversion for agriculture, etc. Very little known of populations, but census of Bangweulu swamps, N Zambia, in 1983 estimated 275 birds, with 1 bird/ 5.8 km^2; under 50 pairs in S Africa. Monitoring of numbers required, as species susceptible to disturbance and could easily become threatened. CITES III in Ghana.

Bibliography. Allan (1984b), Benson, Brooke, Dowsett & Irwin (1971), Berruti (1980, 1983), Berruti *et al.* (1977), Berry (1984), Boer & van Brink (1982), Britton (1980), Brooke (1984), Brown & Britton (1980), Brown *et al.* (1982), Elliott (1983), Howard & Aspinwall (1984), Kahl (1968, 1973), Kasoma & Pomeroy (1987), Lassus (1973), Logsdon (1971), Mackworth-Praed & Grant (1957-1973), Maclean (1985), McLean (1986), Morris (1979), Niven & Niven (1966b), Pennycuick (1972b), Pinto (1983), Pitman (1965), Vernon (1975), Walsh (1977), Wilson, R.T.A. (1983).

Genus *JABIRU* Hellmayr, 1906

16. Jabiru
Jabiru mycteria

French: Jabiru d'Amérique   German: Jabiru   Spanish: Jabirú Americano
Other common names: Jabiru Stork, American Jabiru

Taxonomy. *Ciconia mycteria* Lichtenstein, 1819, Brazil.
Sometimes included in genus *Ephippiorhynchus*, which it resembles in feeding and display behaviour, but seems to be intermediate between this and *Leptoptilos* in morphology. Monotypic.
Distribution. Neotropical Region, from Mexico through C America and N South America to N Argentina and Uruguay.

Descriptive notes. 122-140 cm; 8 kg; wingspan 230-260 cm. Male larger, with longer, deeper bill; amount of red variable.
Habitat. Large freshwater marshes, savanna, *llanos*, ranchland with ponds and lagoons, banks of large rivers and lakes with scattered trees, flooded cultivation, estuaries. In Venezuela, frequents rice fields, particularly outside breeding season; prefers shallow pools without vegetation during dry season, but somewhat deeper water of flooded fields in wet season.
Food and Feeding. Fish, frogs, snakes, insects, young caimans (*Caiman crocodilus*)
and turtles (*Podocnemis*). In *llanos*: in dry season, over 80% of diet is fish, including *Synbranchus marmoratus*, *Hoplosternum littorale* and *Hoplias malabaricus*; in wet season, eels predominate in weight, but amphibians, crabs (*Dilocarcinus dentatus*) and aquatic insects in number. Typically

On following pages: 17. Lesser Adjutant (*Leptoptilos javanicus*); 18. Greater Adjutant (*Leptoptilos dubius*); 19. Marabou (*Leptoptilos crumeniferus*).

bustles back and forth energetically in shallows, splashing bill into water at each step, in order to disturb prey; prey location tactile (35%), visual (37%), or mixed (28%). Any awkward fish usually carried to the shore, where it is easier to recapture, should it manage to slip out; large fish may be dismembered before consumption. Baby caimans may be located when emitting distress calls, and if necessary are beaten against logs. During dry season, often feeds in groups of 11-50 birds; sometimes apparently in concerted fashion, herding fish into the shallows where they are easier to catch; tends to be more solitary during wet season. May associate with other storks and ibises, and frequently kleptoparasitizes them, especially during dry season.
Breeding. Varies throughout range, starting Nov-Dec in parts of Colombia and Mexico, but July-Dec in Venezuela. Normally solitary or up to 6 nests together, but sometimes associates with mixed colonies of other Ciconiiformes. Typically nests on crown of tall palm tree, e.g. *Copernicia tectorum*; centre stamped down by one bird, while other looks on; tree may be killed off, particularly after successive years of nesting; also nests on tall mangroves. Nest of sticks and mud is added to each year, attaining dimensions of 2 m wide x 1 m deep. Normally 3-4 eggs (2-5); fledging 80-95 days; chicks continue to be fed by adults for up to 2 months. Oldest captive bird over 36 years old. Nesting success 47% in Venezuela, with 0·9-1·0 chicks fledged per nest.
Movements. Out of breeding season, small groups tend to congregate, often with other Ciconiiformes; much more scattered when breeding. Sometimes crosses Andes in Peru. Preliminary results of study using radio-tracking in Pantanal of Brazil suggests birds may move to Chaco zone of Argentina, Nov-Jun. Vagrant to Texas and Oklahoma, USA.
Status and Conservation. Not globally threatened. CITES I. Currently considered near-threatened. Regionally threatened C American populations very small, perhaps only 150-250 birds surviving, though has probably never been abundant here; northernmost population at Usumacinta Delta (Mexico) declining due to habitat destruction associated with development. Suffering from habitat degradation, hunting and disturbance. Widespread, but not abundant in Venezuela, where 223 individuals were found in aerial census in 1983; in study at Hato El Frio in *llanos*, main causes of breeding failure were: desertion of nest by adults; predation by Crested Caracara (*Polyborus plancus*); and collapse of nest. Recent survey gave 70 birds at Ciénagas Bigi Pan and Wageningen, N Surinam. Detailed information lacking for most other S American countries, but still considered widespread, abundant and relatively secure in Chaco-Pantanal of Brazil, Paraguay and Argentina. Popular for food on Amazon, especially fat young. See page 455.
Bibliography. Anon. (1983b), Arnold (1978), Bent (1926), Blake (1977), Camacho (1983), Clark (1982), Deignan (1933), Dott (1984), Gabaldón & Ulloa (1980), Gyldenstolpe (1945), Hagenrath & Ribera (1985), Hauckl & Kiel (1973), Hellmayr & Conover (1948), Hilty & Brown (1986), Hughes (1970), Kahl (1971c, 1973), Knoder *et al.* (1980), Kushlan *et al.* (1985), Luthin (1985a), McConnell & McConnell (1974), Monroe (1968), Morales (1990), Morales *et al.* (1981), Mott (1965), Naumburg (1930), Nores & Yzurieta (1980), Ogden & Thomas (1985a), de la Peña (1986), Pinto (1964), Ramo & Busto (1984), Richard & Laredo (1988), Ridgely & Gwynne (1989), Scott & Carbonell (1986), Shannon (1987), Short (1975), Sick (1984), Slud (1964), Spaans (1975a), Sprunt & Knoder (1980), Stiles & Skutch (1989), Thibault & Guyot (1988), Thomas (1979a, 1981, 1985), Wetmore (1926, 1965), Young (1972-1975).

Genus *LEPTOPTILOS* Lesson, 1831

17. **Lesser Adjutant**

Leptoptilos javanicus

French: Marabout chevelu **German**: Kleiner Adjutant **Spanish**: Marabú Menor
Other common names: Lesser Adjutant Stork, Hair-crested Adjutant

Taxonomy. *Ciconia Javanica* Horsfield, 1821, Java.
Monotypic.
Distribution. India and Sri Lanka to S China, Indochina and Indonesia.

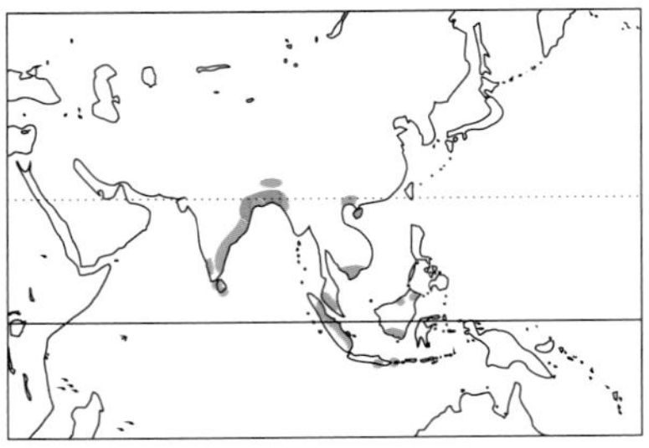

Descriptive notes. 110-120 cm. Bony plate on crown; lacks pendant air-sac. Differs from *L. dubius* in retaining dark slaty blue-black upperparts during breeding; inner greater upperwing-coverts narrowly edged white; undertail-coverts pure white (dark tipped in *L. dubius*). Non-breeding adult has bare parts duller. Immature has duller upperparts and more feathering on neck.
Habitat. Mangroves, mudflats, coastal swamp, marshes, flooded grassland, lakes, paddyfields; much more coastal than *L. dubius* and has never been associated with man in same way.
Food and Feeding. Fish, especially mudskippers (*Periophthalmus*), also frogs, reptiles, crustaceans, locusts, rats and some carrion. Walks, searches and probes, when trying to catch mudskippers; often thrusts head and even sometimes most of neck into mud when probing. On mudflats, tends to feed along water's edge, often one bird every c. 50 m.
Breeding. Nov-Jan in Assam; recorded in June in Sumatra, Oct in Borneo. Tree-nester in colonies, sometimes with other species, such as *M. cinerea* and *L. dubius*. Large stick nest, 1·5 m wide x 1·2 m deep, built 12-30 m off ground in large tree, such as silk cotton (*Salmalia*) or *Alstonia*; typically in mangroves. Normally 3 eggs (2-4). Oldest captive bird over 30 years old.
Movements. In India resident, nomadic and locally migratory. Probably some movements up and down E coast of Sumatra, possibly some birds crossing to Java.
Status and Conservation. VULNERABLE. Has declined greatly throughout range, due mainly to habitat destruction and direct persecution, as well as disturbance. Strongest world population in E Sumatra, where more than half the estimated Indonesian total of not more than 2000 birds have been recorded; same threats are imminent here with extensive logging of mangroves and swamp forest, massive human transmigration in progress, and birds frequently found for sale in markets (see page 453); at least 47 killed in single day at one site in Riau province, 1990; less common in Borneo. Small groups recorded at several sites scattered over India, such as Kaziranga and other parts of Assam, Indian Sundarbans (where probably still breeds) and Keoladeo (Bharatpur); large numbers recorded in recent survey of N India, where species thought to be fairly secure. Elsewhere numbers much lower: Sri Lanka, 100 pairs; Bangladesh, only about 200 birds; peninsular Malaysia, 140 pairs; Viet Nam, only one colony of about 50 individuals (some may be *L. dubius*); rare resident and occasional visitor in Thailand; very rare in Burma; occasional resident in Nepal; status unknown in Laos and Kampuchea. Mid-winter census of Jan 1991 yielded 59 birds in India, 202 in Sri Lanka and 68 in Malaysia. Effective protection of species and habitat essential; recommended for CITES I. Has never bred in captivity.
Bibliography. Ali & Ripley (1978), Bain & Humphrey (1980), Beadle & Whittaker (1985), Bruce (1982), Cheng Tso-hsin (1987), Collar & Andrew (1988), Danielsen & Skov (1987), Erftemeijer & Djuharsa (1988), Erftemeijer *et al.* (1988), Etchécopar & Hüe (1978), Galdikas & King (1989), Henry (1971), Hill (1943), Hoogerwerf (1949), Humphrey & Bain (1990), Iskander (1985), Kahl (1970, 1972b), Karpowicz (1985), Khan (1984, 1987), Kidd (1978), King & Brouwer (1991), MacKinnon (1983), van Marle & Voous (1988), Martínez & Elliott (1990), Medway & Wells (1976), Menon (1980), Morris (1988), Nash & Nash (1985), Nisbet (1968), Parish (1985), Parish & Wells (1984), Quy (1985), Rensenbrink (1981), Round *et al.* (1988), Saikia & Bhattacharjee (1989a, 1989b), Scott (1989), Silvius (1986), Silvius & Verheugt (1989), Silvius *et al.* (1987), Smythies (1981, 1986), Verheugt (1989), Wells (1985), von Wetten (1985), White & Bruce (1986).

18. **Greater Adjutant**

Leptoptilos dubius

French: Marabout argala **German**: Großer Adjutant **Spanish**: Marabú Argala
Other common names: (Greater) Adjutant Stork

Taxonomy. *Ardea dubia* Gmelin, 1789, India.
Formerly considered to include *L. crumeniferus*, with which forms superspecies. Monotypic.
Distribution. N India to Indochina; breeding now probably restricted to Assam.

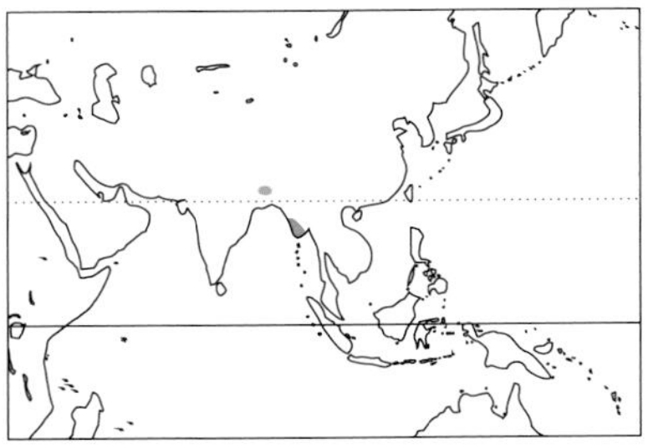

Descriptive notes. 120-152 cm. Head covered with dark scabs of dried blood. Legs dark, but appear whitish, due to urohydrosis, as in all *Leptoptilos* (see page 441). Much heavier bill than *L. javanicus*. Non-breeding adult has upperparts darker and blacker. Immature has duller upperparts and more feathering on neck.
Habitat. Marshes, lakes, *jheels*, paddyfields, open forest; often in dry areas, such as grassland and fields. Typically at carcasses and rubbish dumps at edges of towns and in open fields; formerly abundant in streets and on rooftops of Calcutta (see page 451), still known to perch on houses or wander about by markets. Nests usually near humans and not far from large wetlands.
Food and Feeding. Carrion and large fish; also frogs, reptiles (e.g. *Vipera russelli*, *Uromastix hardwickii*), large insects and crustaceans; also injured wild ducks. Recorded swallowing 2 buffalo vertebrae at least 30 cm long in c. 5 minutes. Often at drying pools; associates with other scavengers at carcasses and rubbish dumps (see page 445), such as kites and vultures, with several birds congregating where food plentiful; otherwise tends to be solitary.
Breeding. Oct-Dec/Jan in Burma and India. Preferably nests in large, sometimes mixed colonies (see page 446), but now restricted to a few small colonies and scattered solitary pairs; mixed colonies formerly of "millions" of birds, now largest known of 31 nests. Large, bulky stick nest, 2 m wide x 1 m deep, 12-23 m up in large tree, such as *Anthocephalus cadamba* or *Bombax ceiba*, with dense foliage; also on rock pinnacles. Normally 3 eggs (2-4). Average 2·2 young fledged per nest, Assam 1990. Oldest captive bird over 43 years old.
Movements. Nomadic and locally migratory; disperses widely after breeding, occurring irregularly in Nepal and various parts of N India, especially during rains; also almost annually in Thailand, perhaps indicating the existence of a breeding population in Burma or Kampuchea.
Status and Conservation. ENDANGERED. Recommended for CITES I. Has declined catastrophically and now on the verge of extinction. In 19th century abundant in Calcutta and Burma; still large flocks in 1940's and not uncommon in late 1960's in N India. Now only known to breed at a few sites in Assam, NE India; 75 nests in six colonies (a few solitary) discovered in the region in 1990, none inside protected areas, but future of all wildlife here jeopardized by tense political situation (see page 452). Causes of regression include destruction of potential nesting, feeding and roosting sites and probably poisoning by pesticides. Only colony in Viet Nam is mixed with *L. javanicus* and not known how many individuals there are of each species, but only 50 birds in total and no recent sightings of this species; even less known about Laos and Kampuchea, where breeding sites might still exist; may no longer breed in Burma, where vast areas of its forest habitat destroyed; probably only rare migrant now to Thailand and Bangladesh, although occurs almost annually. Conservation priorities include effective protection of remaining sites, exhaustive surveys in search of other populations and a serious attempt at captive breeding, with a view to reintroduction; has never bred in captivity.
Bibliography. Ali (1979), Ali & Ripley (1978), Bain & Humphrey (1980), Collar & Andrew (1988), Dathe (1970), Dover & Basil-Edwards (1921), Hancock (1989), Humphrey & Bain (1990), Kahl (1970, 1972b), Karpowicz (1985), Khan (1984, 1987), King & Brouwer (1991), Luthin (1988), Ogle (1986), Quy (1985), Rahmani (1989b), Rahmani *et al.* (1990), Rao & Murlidharan (1989), Roberts (1991), Round *et al.* (1988), Saika & Bhattacharjee (1990), Scott (1989), Singh & Singh (1960), Smythies (1986), Sridharan (1986), Wildash (1968).

19. **Marabou**

Leptoptilos crumeniferus

French: Marabout d'Afrique **German**: Marabu **Spanish**: Marabú Africano
Other common names: Marabou Stork

Taxonomy. *Ciconia crumenifera* Lesson, 1831, Senegal.
Formerly included in *L. dubius*, with which forms superspecies. Monotypic.
Distribution. Tropical Africa.
Descriptive notes. 115-152 cm; 4-8·9 kg; wingspan 225-287 cm. Males average larger. Only member of genus with dark iris. Immature has duller upperparts and more feathering on neck.
Habitat. Open dry savanna, grassland, swamps, river banks, lake shores, receding pools; rare in forest or desert. Typically in and around fishing villages; also frequents slaughterhouses and rubbish dumps. In E and S Africa commonly found around carcasses, in association with other scavengers, both avian and mammalian.
Food and Feeding. Carrion and scraps of fish and other food discarded by humans; also fish, termites, locusts, frogs, lizards, rats, mice, snakes and birds, including adult and young flamingos (see page 445). Bill is not well designed for dismembering carcasses, so normally steals scraps from vultures or snatches up morsels that are dropped. Fishes with submerged bill partly open, probably by touch, as in *Mycteria*; sometimes walks about shallows, repeatedly jabbing bill into water, like *Ephippiorhynchus*; also visual, like Ardeidae. Often gregarious; sometimes associates with herds of large mammals, which disturb insects by their movements.

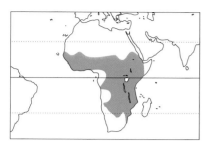

Breeding. In tropics normally begins in dry season and ends in rains; more variable in equatorial zone, where dry seasons much shorter. Colonies of 20-60 pairs, up to several thousand; often mixed with other species, especially other Ciconiiformes (see page 446). Nest usually in trees, 10-30 m off ground; also on cliffs and even in main streets of towns; stick nest, 1 m wide x 30 cm deep, lined with twigs and green leaves. Normally 2-3 eggs (1-4); incubation 29-31 days; chicks have pale grey, then white down; fledging 95-115 days. Sexual maturity is apparently reached after at least 4 years. Only about 20% of E African population thought to breed in any one year. Oldest birds reckoned to be over 25; in captivity over 41 years old.

Movements. Many sedentary, especially in urbanized districts, others locally nomadic. Populations furthest N and S generally move towards equator after breeding. In dry season in W Africa, some movement S into wetter savanna, probably of non-breeders. Vagrant to Israel; also in Spain (1990), though could have escaped from collection.

Status and Conservation. Not globally threatened. Throughout range is frequent, common or abundant; probably actually increasing, due to ability to exploit ever-increasing amounts of rubbish dumped by humans. Estimate of populations in mid 1980's include: Uganda c. 5000 birds, with some 2000 in Ruwenzori National Park; Kenya 1000-2000, with 797 birds counted at L Nakuru in Jan 1991. Highest figures from W Africa in recent years include 600 birds in Chad Basin, 280 birds in Niger Basin; 402 birds counted in Cameroon in Jan 1991. Irregular breeding of up to 10 pairs in S Africa, where main colony in Swaziland destroyed in 1960's to make way for for sugar cane plantation. Ugly appearance and habits may have made it less attractive to potential hunters, while sometimes appreciated for services rendered in cleaning up carcasses and rubbish, thus helping to control disease; may also be protected by local superstitions. CITES III in Ghana. Large numbers in captivity, but has bred only occasionally.

Bibliography. Akester *et al*. (1973), Alamargot (1976, 1984), Anderson, A.B. (1949), Anderson, D.J. & Horowitz (1979), Archer (1978), Bamford & Maloiy (1980), Boothroyd (1987), Britton (1980), Brooke (1984), Brooke & Masterson (1971), Brown (1958), Brown & Britton (1980), Brown & Pomeroy (1984), Brown *et al*. (1982), Chapin (1932), Cramp & Simmons (1977), Dean (1964), Din & Eltringham (1974b), Dupuy (1982), Easton (1975), Elwell (1970), Evans *et al*. (1981), Grummt (1981), Houston (1980), Jacob & Pomeroy (1979), Kahl (1966a, 1966b, 1968), Kasoma & Pomeroy (1987), Mackworth-Praed & Grant (1957-1973), Maclean (1985), Marshall (1982), Merz (1980), Mlingwa (1989), Mundy (1985), Mundy *et al*. (1988), North (1943), Pennycuick (1972b), Pinto (1983), Pitman (1957), Pomeroy (1973, 1977a, 1977b, 1978a, 1978b, 1978c, 1986), Post (1987), Saikia & Bhattacharjee (1989a, 1989b), Schneider (1952), Schurmann (1984), Seibt & Wickler (1978).

Class AVES
Order CICONIIFORMES
Suborder CICONIAE
Family BALAENICIPITIDAE (SHOEBILL)

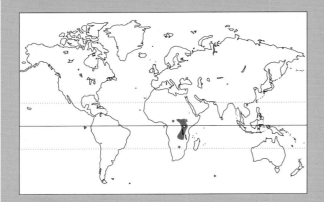

- Large, long-legged wading birds with huge, bulbous bill.
- 120 cm.

- East and Central Africa.
- Swamps, usually with papyrus.
- 1 genus, 1 species, 1 taxon.
- 1 species threatened; none extinct since 1600.

Systematics

The Shoebill (*Balaeniceps rex*) is normally placed in a monospecific family, and sometimes even in its own order, Balaenicipitiformes, as its antecedents are unclear and no close relative is known, either living or fossil.

It has been considered a stork, as indicated by the alternative names of Shoe-billed Stork or Whale-headed Stork, and has even been included in the Ciconiidae. However, though it shares several anatomical and behavioural characteristics with that family, it is more like the herons (Ardeidae) in its possession of powder-downs and in its habit of flying with its neck retracted; it is also closest to the herons in some of the most important skeletal aspects. To add to the confusion, its skull shares certain developments with that of the pelicans (Pelicanidae), but this could be due to convergent evolution: the resemblances may all be connected with its rather violent method of fishing, and pelicans and their allies may well have had to make similar developments. Certainly there is little in the Shoebill's behaviour to relate it to the pelicans. Nevertheless, this may yet prove to be the true origin of *Balaeniceps*, as work on DNA indicates that it should be placed alongside the pelicans, actually within the family Pelecanidae.

Most systematists still consider it to be closest to the storks, in particular to the genus *Leptoptilos*, but it is placed in its own private family, and sometimes in its own suborder, for the time being in the Ciconiiformes.

Morphological Aspects

The most obvious feature of the Shoebill's unique anatomy is its huge, bulbous bill, which together with its imposing stature makes it one of the most distinctive birds of African marshes.

The enormous bill is quite unlike that of any other bird. It is about 19 cm long, almost as wide, and also very deep, enabling the bird to take a colossal mouthful. The mandibles have sharp edges, which help in the decapitation of prey and also in discarding vegetation, after prey has been caught (see Food and Feeding). The upper mandible, as in the pelicans, is strongly keeled and ends in a sharp nail, which may help to secure slippery prey. It has been conjectured that the bill might be specially adapted to burrowing in the mud for dormant lungfish, but the Shoebill does not do this, and it seems more

likely that it is essentially designed to be powerful, for taking prey from the midst of dense aquatic vegetation. It has been reinforced to give added strength, and perhaps also to act as a kind of shock absorber, during fishing "Collapses", where the bird's entire weight is hurled at its prey and the bill receives most of the impact. One of its other uses is for carrying water and giving eggs or young a dowsing during hot weather.

The head is of necessity large, to support the massive bill, while the neck is rather short and thick. There is a small, shaggy nuchal crest, again resembling pelican morphology. The Shoebill is a large bird, standing 1·2 m tall or more.

The wings are broad and well suited to soaring, in which the Shoebill frequently indulges. In flight, the neck is retracted in order to bring the heavy bill closer to the bird's centre of gravity, a practice in common with pelicans and the *Leptoptilos* storks, which both have to deal with the same problem, and also shared by the lighter-billed herons. The powerful wings allow it to take off almost vertically, but take-off can be a little cumbersome, requiring a hefty leap and some deep, heavy wingbeats until a suitable thermal is found. The wings also play an important part in the aftermath of the Shoebill's unusual fishing technique (see Food and Feeding), as well as helping it to keep its balance, as it clambers over shifting masses of vegetation.

The legs are fairly long and, when moving about on floating vegetation, the bird often sinks in up to its tibia. However, it has very long toes which, as in the jacanas (Jacanidae), help to distribute body-weight over as large a surface as possible and thus reduce the extent of subsidence. Its moves about in a slow, deliberate, stately manner, with a gait far more reminiscent of a stork than of a heron.

The entire plumage is blue-grey with darker slaty-grey flight-feathers and a dull green gloss on the upperparts. The belly is white and there are some elongated feathers on the breast, which have dark shafts. Juvenile plumage is similar to that of adults, but darker grey with a brown tinge.

Habitat

The stronghold of the Shoebill is in the vast papyrus (*Cyperus papyrus*) swamps of the Sudd, in northern East Africa. Here it can most often be found in areas of overspill, where deep water is moving slowly down towards lakes, carrying with it large

The Shoebill is a solitary bird that is generally to be seen strutting about on the floating vegetation of swamps in East and Central Africa. It prefers fairly dense vegetation cover, although this need not be particularly high, as the bird's main requirement is concealment from potential prey below.

[*Balaeniceps rex*, near Lira, Uganda. Photo: M. P. Kahl/ Bruce Coleman]

quantities of fish. Further south, in Uganda, it is found along marshy edges of lakes, but almost always in places that are heavily overgrown with reeds, papyrus and grasses.

Despite its clear association with papyrus, it normally avoids pure stands, preferring a little variety, for example some *Phragmites*. It rarely wades into deep water, presumably as this would be unsuitable to its fishing techniques (see Food and Feeding), but can typically be seen lurking on floating islands of vegetation, waiting to spring on its prey. In areas of dense vegetation, it tends to make use of clear channels, which may have been opened up by the grazing or trampling of a hippopotamus or an antelope. Waters with a low oxygen content are particularly favoured, as fish have to surface more often in such places, and thus are more readily available as prey.

In general the Shoebill tends to avoid high, dense cover, which restricts its manoeuvrability; anyway, there tend to be very few fish in dense papyrus. While it is very wary of men and shuns contact with them, its main interest is normally to remain invisible to its potential prey below. It sometimes forages in open, shallow water, but only when this is murky.

Occasionally birds may be seen away from water in damp grassland, though always in places where vegetation is plentiful and the ground soft, as the Shoebill's violent technique of prey capture would surely result in head injury, if practised on hard ground.

The nest-site is invariably situated in the depths of a swamp, where the birds are free from disturbance. Here the vegetation is often dense and may stand as much as 7 m high over the surface of the water. Normally areas of deep water are favoured, as they take longer to dry out after the rains, and hence are inaccessible both to potential predators and returning farmers, with their cattle and fires, until the latter stages of the breeding season.

General Habits

The Shoebill is solitary for most of its life and even within the pair, birds often feed at opposite ends of their territory. At times several individuals may be seen feeding at the same site, but they invariably keep their distance (see Food and Feeding).

The species is basically diurnal and, despite some claims to the contrary, it appears to feed at night only rarely and if there is sufficient moonlight, or in pools illuminated by fishermen's fires. It generally passes most of its time in swamps, where it also tends to roost. It can often be seen perching or roosting in trees, but is normally found on the ground near water.

It is a rather slow-moving bird, except in the moment of catching its prey. Both during fishing and when resting, it may spend a lot of the time motionless. It appears somewhat reluctant to fly and, as it tends to rely mostly on thermals, its early morning flying is particularly limited. In this it again resembles the storks, as it probably also does in the habit of defaecating on the legs, in order to induce cooling by evaporation. However, like the pelicans and herons, and in contrast to the storks, it also indulges in gular-fluttering, as a means of heat reduction.

Voice

Shoebills are normally silent, but at the nest they perform bill-clapping, like storks; the sexes can be distinguished by a slight difference in tone. Adults are also recorded as "whining or mewing" at the nest, while young make a "hiccupping" noise, when begging for food.

Food and Feeding

The diet of the Shoebill consists largely of fish of varying sizes, especially lungfish (*Protopterus aethiopicus*), bichirs (*Polypterus senegalus*) and *Tilapia*. Other favourite prey items include water snakes, frogs, monitor lizards (*Varanus*) and young turtles. Young waterbirds and crocodiles (*Crocodylus niloticus*) and small mammals are also taken, but probably constitute a relatively insignificant proportion of its food.

When fishing, the Shoebill's movements are reduced to a minimum: it either stands perfectly still or moves slowly and deliberately through the vegetation, planting its feet with great care. These techniques of "Stand and Wait" and "Wade or Walk Slowly" are generally determined by the immediate surroundings, as deep water or dense vegetation can make the latter

when the floodwaters are going down, as in Sudan and Zambia, and in this way it is timed so that young birds fledge at the end of the dry season or early in the rains. However, in Uganda it coincides with the main rains.

As in other aspects of its life, the Shoebill is solitary in its breeding habits and, while there may be several nests in a particularly suitable area, they are always widely dispersed and never form colonies, indeed, birds foraging at the same place may have their nests up to 100 km apart.

Nest-sites are established and defended against conspecifics by means of a slowed down version of the "Collapse" (see Food and Feeding); bill-clattering also takes place and if the intruder is not repulsed, the site owner may jump up in the air to come crashing down on its opponent's back. Displays during pair formation are not well known, but include both bill-clattering and some up and down bobbing movements, which are similar to displays performed by storks. At times, either member of the pair may be seen soaring over the nest-site, and it is thought that this may be a form of territorial advertisement.

The nest is placed either on a platform of floating vegetation or on a true island, for example an exposed termite mound, and is fairly well concealed. First the birds trample down the selected area, and then plant matter is collected and sewn into the substrate, thus anchoring the base of what develops into a large, flat mound of aquatic vegetation. Material, collected nearby, is continually added during the breeding season and a floating nest gradually sinks deeper and deeper into the water. In the most secluded spots, the same nest may be used year after year.

The nest-site is defended against aerial intruders by means of bill-clattering and "Bill Hook Exposure", which involves partially opening the bill and raising the tip in the air. The territory can be roughly 2·5-3·8 km², or it might be, for example, 7 km long by 200 m wide. The pair will never forage within 200 m of the nest, which is normally situated more or less in the centre of the territory.

Shoebills lay one to three eggs, normally two, at intervals of up to five days; eggs measure 80-90 x 57-61 mm and are chalky bluish white, but soon become stained brown. Incubation lasts about 30 days, with duties being shared by both parents, and it probably starts with the first egg, as hatching is asynchronous. The eggs are frequently turned, using the feet or the bill, and on hot days they are dowsed, sometimes four or five times a day, to keep them cool, while water weeds are sometimes added in order to augment these cooling effects.

Chicks are covered in a thick coat of silvery grey down and already have a wide gape, although the bill itself is not particularly large, and does not start to swell out until the fourth week; even by fledging time it is still not fully swollen and is pinkish, as opposed to yellow in adults. The chicks are nidicolous and are brooded, shaded, fed and cared for by both parents. On hot days they too are liable to get a dowsing to cool them off, and older chicks usually manage to get a drink at the same time.

When chicks are newly-hatched, the adults chew up prey for them, as they cannot deal with it whole, but after about 30 days, the food is simply deposited in the nest for the young to swallow. At first chicks only need one to three prey items per day, but by the end of the fledging period they require to be fed five or six times a day. After some 35 days they start to grow feathers and fledging occurs at about 95-105 days. During these last days, they start to wander about near the nest and attempt to fly, but they remain dependent on their parents at least for another week and perhaps much more.

Exact figures for breeding success are not known, but more than one chick successfully fledged per pair is very rare, while losses, for various reasons, are not uncommon and a replacement clutch is not laid. It is not yet known how long Shoebills take to reach sexual maturity, but it is reckoned to be at least three years.

Even during the breeding season, Shoebills maintain their strong solitary tendencies and the members of a pair are only rarely found together. They tend to forage at opposite ends of the territory and will never do so in the vicinity of the nest. The massive bill seems to be designed essentially for power, as the bird typically secures its prey by lunging at it through a tangled mass of aquatic plants, so it must not be impeded by the tough stems.

[Balaeniceps rex. Photo: Wilhelm Möller/ Ardea]

impossible. The bird holds its bill pointing vertically downwards, so as to get the benefit of binocular vision, which is particularly important, as prey location seems to be entirely visual, although the hearing might also play a part.

When a fish is spotted, the bird jerks its head forwards, and the momentum of this lunge causes the bird to overbalance and "Collapse": the whole body lurches swiftly forwards and downwards, with the head plunging into the water, so that the bill engulfs the prey. A strike usually lasts less than one second and such is the force exerted in the "Collapse" that, if the prey is not caught, the bird can not normally gather itself together again in time to strike again quickly. The Shoebill now tosses its head backwards and exerts pressure against the substrate with its wings, and sometimes also its bill, until it can regain its feet; this procedure is all the more awkward, when the bird is grasping a fish.

In a normal strike, a fair amount of plant matter is taken in too, and once this has been ejected by moving the mandibles from side to side, the prey is swallowed head first, in some cases after being decapitated. A successful attempt is invariably followed by drinking. After each strike the bird tends to move on to try another site, which may be 5-200 metres away. On occasions, even a flying bird may perform a "Collapse".

Shoebills tend to feed alone and defend their favourite feeding grounds and platforms against other conspecifics. At times they fish relatively near others, for example in the dry season, when a lot of prey is concentrated in a few small pools. They have been said to practise communal fishing, but this is not true: when they feed near each other, there is no behavioural interaction.

Although they may start feeding soon after dawn, the vast majority of feeding takes place after 11 a.m. If necessary, as for example during incubation, Shoebills can survive for over four days without food.

Breeding

The Shoebill's breeding cycle starts in different months, depending on the area, but it is always related to local water levels. It generally starts at the beginning of the dry season,

Movements

Shoebills are strictly sedentary and are rarely to be seen outside their preferred habitat. The only time they tend to stray from their home territories is when changes in the water level mean that optimum feeding conditions can only be found elsewhere, for instance when prey is concentrated in a few pools, which are in the process of drying out; at such times several individuals may be seen in the same area.

Thus, in south Sudan there are regular seasonal movements between breeding and feeding zones. Again, records from south Rwanda and Lake Rukwa in Tanzania probably refer to an influx of birds from other areas looking for better feeding, as there are apparently no sites suitable for breeding in these zones. It was suggested that records from the Central African Republic pointed to regular migration, but this has been dismissed as highly improbable.

There is a recent record of a single individual on the Nyika Plateau, in northern Malawi, in quite unsuitable habitat; it has been suggested that the bird might have been en route to a swampy area on the Shire River near Liwonde, further south in the country, where there have been several unconfirmed sightings in recent years. This too appears to be a case of movement between favourable feeding grounds, and such movements may also be responsible for erratic occurrences. Nevertheless, the sightings reported from Lake Chad and the Okavango Delta both appear rather inconclusive and unlikely.

Relationship with Man

No native African peoples have any tradition of persecuting Shoebills, in some places because local folklore requires that they be protected and even feared. They are shy birds, shunning all contact with humans and it seems that the oldest, most experienced birds breed in the sites most remote from any contact with humans. Nevertheless, superstitions are losing their force and the species is suffering directly and indirectly from human activities, as the swamps are invaded by colonizers (see Status and Conservation).

The species was not described until 1850 and, although two birds were brought to London Zoo in 1860, it was still very little known outside Africa until relatively recently. However, its unusual appearance and strange name have helped it to become one of the most evocative of species, at any rate in ornithological circles. The origin of its common name appears to be local, having been copied in many languages perhaps from the Arabic name "Abu Marqub", meaning "Father of the shoe".

Sculptures from Ancient Egypt and, likewise, 3000-year-old paintings from Zimbabwe implied that the species may have been around in these countries a long time ago, but the evidence is by no means conclusive, indeed the possibility of its presence in Egypt has now been generally rejected.

Status and Conservation

The Shoebill is widespread, but local, and is thinly distributed throughout its range. It is classified as Insufficiently Known, and its status is under review, after having been designated a unique IUCN status, "of special concern"; despite a worrying trend, it does not yet appear to be in imminent danger of extinction.

Its total population was quite recently reckoned to be less than 1500 individuals, but this is now known to be a gross underestimate, as a survey of part of the Sudd in 1979 yielded no less than 3000 birds, giving an extrapolated total of some 10,000 for the zone, which was considered to be a slight overestimate. Numbers from an aerial census in 1984 put the Sudd total at about 5500 birds and the total for Sudan at some 7000. To these figures can be added those of 400-600 or more in Uganda in 1977, and probably at least 232 and over 300 at single sites in Zambia and Tanzania respectively. Next to nothing is known of other populations, for example in Zaire, but the species is certainly better off than had previously been thought, and in 1986 the world population was reckoned to number in the region of some 11,000.

The tasks of incubation and chick-care are shared between the parents. In the early stages of the chick's development, it is unable to deal with whole prey items, especially the larger ones, and this means that the adults have to mash up the food for the nestling. At first the small chick is brooded all night and most of the day, but after some 40 days the brooding only continues at night.

[*Balaeniceps rex*, Bangweulu, Zambia. Photo: Cindy Buxton/ Survival]

Heat can be a major problem for many tropical birds. In particularly hot weather, adults may go several times a day to collect a billful of water which it will shower over the eggs or chicks, although in this case its aim seems to have been rather indifferent. Often the chick will drink some of the water as it is poured out, or it may sip it off its down. Once the chick is about a month old, it can make its own way to the water's edge to drink.

[*Balaeniceps rex*, Bangweulu, Zambia. Photo: Cindy Buxton/ Survival]

The main threat the species faces is habitat destruction, which is occurring all too rapidly in its hitherto stronghold in the Sudd, as well as in Zambia and probably throughout its range. The greatest menace to the birds is that of general agricultural development, which invariably implies the draining of all wetlands and the "reclamation" of economically unproductive land. The most alarming of these schemes is the Jonglai Canal project, which plans to re-route the White Nile and might represent the definitive destruction of the Sudd.

Papyrus swampland is continuously being destroyed by fire to make room for cattle, while humans themselves are colonizing and converting other zones. Most of this destruction takes place in the dry season, when the water level is low, but in the rains the natural swamp vegetation is unable to regenerate after the onslaught from the cattle, so good habitat is steadily disappearing.

In addition to this loss of habitat, there is the concurrent problem of the disturbance caused to this very shy, retiring species. Fishermen, even though they do not usually persecute Shoebills actively, often do enough to upset birds that are nesting or fishing, and it is becoming increasingly difficult for the birds to find remote sites, especially as most breeding occurs in the dry season, which means that nests are all the more accessible. The species is legally protected throughout its range, but in many parts both adults and young are still captured and sold for food; officials are often unaware of the bird's protected status.

As the species is not colonial, protection even of a fairly large area of swamp may not actually safeguard the future of many individuals. It has been proposed that reserves in south Sudan should be enlarged and strict control should be maintained of cattle, fire and fishermen. It is also recommended that new reserves be set up in Zambia and Uganda, where swamps face the same threats of drainage and agricultural development.

Another important problem is the excessive number of young birds captured for zoos, with some 500 supposed to have been taken in 1978 alone, while more than 30 were available in the Netherlands in 1986/87. In order to meet the demand of zoos, villagers are offered large sums, which they can hardly be expected to refuse. As the species has a low rate of reproductive success, it can not sustain such losses for many years. The number of such captures is particularly difficult to justify, given that the species only recently bred in captivity for the first time, and its full protection by inclusion in Appendix I of CITES is regarded as essential.

PLATE 34

inches	12
cm	30

Family BALAENICIPITIDAE (SHOEBILL)
SPECIES ACCOUNTS

PLATE 34

Genus *BALAENICEPS*   Gould, 1850

Shoebill
Balaeniceps rex

French: Bec-en-sabot du Nil   **German:** Schuhschnabel   **Spanish:** Picozapato
Other common names: Shoe-billed/Whale-headed Stork, Bog Bird

Taxonomy. *Balaeniceps rex* Gould, 1850, Upper White Nile. Some morphological and behavioural affinities with Ardeidae, Scopidae and Pelecanidae. Has been considered a member of the Ciconiidae, but recent work on DNA suggests best situated within Pelecanidae. Monotypic.
Distribution. S Sudan and S Ethiopia to S Zaire and N Zambia.
Descriptive notes. 120 cm. Unmistakable, with unique, highly conspicuous bill; flight-feathers darker, dull green gloss on upperparts, iris variable, grey, whitish or yellow. Males probably slightly larger. Juvenile similar to adult, but plumage darker grey tinged brownish; bill pinkish and somewhat less swollen, even at moment of fledging.
Habitat. Swamps, overspill channels and marshy lakesides, especially with papyrus (*Cyperus papyrus*); floating vegetation favoured for both fishing and breeding. Infrequently forages in damp, overgrown grassland.
Food and Feeding. Mostly fish, especially lungfish (*Protopterus aethiopicus*), bichirs (*Polypterus senegalus*) and *Tilapia*, up to c. 500 g; also some amphibians, snakes and small young of other reptiles, birds and possibly mammals. Habitually fishes from floating vegetation, walking slowly or standing still, then pouncing on prey (see page 467). Solitary feeder.
Breeding. Linked with water levels, typically starting at beginning of dry season. Solitary nester; nest is flat mound of plant matter. Normally 2 eggs (1-3); incubation c. 30 days; chicks have greyish down, but not large bill; fledging c. 95-105 days; dependent on parents for food at least for another week, possibly much longer; normally only one bird per brood reaches fledging. Sexual maturity probably after 3 years or more. Has lived to over 36 years old in captivity.

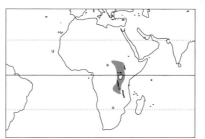

Movements. Sedentary. Small-scale displacements for feeding, related to changes in water levels. Recent record on Nyika Plateau in N Malawi, combined with other possible sightings at Liwonde, SC Malawi, suggest may be scarce but regular visitor, or possibly even breeder in this country. Many doubtful records, e.g. Lake Chad, N Cameroon, and Okavango Delta, Botswana.
Status and Conservation. INSUFFICIENTLY KNOWN (under review). CITES II. Widespread, but local, with most of population in S Sudan and N Uganda. Total population estimated at about 11,000 birds in 1986. Partial dependence on papyrus swamp makes it vulnerable in view of increasing amounts of habitat destruction and disturbance throughout its range, mostly due to pressure for agricultural development, especially large-scale drainage schemes and burning of papyrus to make room for livestock; problems particularly acute in the species' stronghold in the Sudd, but can not be considered safe anywhere in its range. Popularity and unique features of the species make it an attractive target for zoos; has only bred once in captivity, at Lubumbashi Zoo (Zaire).

Bibliography. Anon. (1986a), Benson (1961), Benson, Brooke, Dowsett & Irwin (1971), Boer & Van Brink (1982), Böhm (1930), Britton (1980), Brooke *et al.* (1982), Brown & Britton (1980), Brown *et al.* (1982), Burton & Benson (1961), Buxton *et al.* (1978), Collar & Andrew (1988), Collar & Stuart (1985), Cottam (1957), Coulter, Bryan *et al.* (1991), Cracraft (1985), Critchley & Grimsdell (1970), Dean (1963), Dechambre (1936), Duckworth (1974), Feduccia (1977), Fischer (1970), Fletcher (1979), Gordon (1959), Guillet (1978, 1979, 1984, 1985, 1987), Hanmer (1989), Hanmer & Roseveare (1989), Harrison & Walker (1982), Howard & Aspinwall (1984), Johnson, Coulter *et al.* (1987), Kahl (1965, 1967b, 1987a), Kasoma & Pomeroy (1987), Klös (1985), Kuehler & Toone (1989), de Lisle (1956), Louette (1981), Luthin (1987a), Mackworth-Praed & Grant (1957-1973), Maclean (1985), Mathews (1979), Mitchell (1913), Möller (1979, 1980, 1982a, 1982b), Nikolaus (1987), Olson (1978), Owen (1958), Parker, I.S.C. (1984a, 1984b), Preston (1976), Roseveare (1989), Saiff (1978), Schonwetter (1942), Sibley & Ahlquist (1972, 1985, 1988, 1990), Snow (1978), Urban (1967), Vande Weghe (1981).

Class AVES

Order CICONIIFORMES

Suborder CICONIAE

Family THRESKIORNITHIDAE
(IBISES AND SPOONBILLS)

- Medium-sized to large wading and terrestrial birds with longish neck and legs; long bill thin and decurved, or broad and flat.
- 46-110 cm.
- All regions except Antarctic, with greatest diversity in tropics.
- Variety of wetlands, with some species in forests, grassland and arid or semi-arid areas.
- 13 genera, 32 species, 47 taxa.
- 6 species threatened; 1 subspecies extinct since 1600.

Systematics

The earliest fossils of the Threskiornithidae date back 60 million years to the Eocene. From the Pliocene in South Africa come remains of the present genera *Geronticus* and *Threskiornis*, in the case of the latter only the end of a tibiotarsus that is indistinguishable from the present day Sacred Ibis (*Threskiornis aethiopicus*). In North America there are remains dating back to the same period which correspond to the modern genus *Plegadis*. Fossils clearly attributable to several of today's species have been found in Pleistocene deposits in different parts of the world.

Ibises and spoonbills are related to the storks. Indeed the *Mycteria* storks, with their slightly downcurved bills, were pre-

viously placed in a genus named *Ibis*, and until quite recently, they were frequently referred to as "wood ibises". In reality, their similarity to the true ibises is rather superficial, although some have suggested that this genus may form a link between the two families.

The Threskiornithidae are divided into two groups, which are easily distinguishable by their external features, and are generally regarded as two subfamilies. The subfamily Threskiornithinae comprises the ibises, which are characterized by a long, narrow, markedly decurved bill, whereas the subfamily Plataleinae is formed by the spoonbills, which have a long, wide bill with a flattened tip, giving them their common name. However, the relationship between the ibises and the spoonbills is actually very close, much more so than the striking differences in the bills might suggest, and several cases of hybridization have been reported, for example between the Black-headed Ibis (*Threskiornis melanocephalus*) and the Eurasian Spoonbill (*Platalea leucorodia*). This has led some authorities to reject the division into separate subfamilies.

The controversy of the internal taxonomy throughout this family is considerable. This is already apparent with the family name, as there are those that give precedence to the name Plataleidae. There is a good deal of disagreement about both the sequence of species and the assignation of genera, and also about the classification of several different taxa as species or subspecies. In fact, this debate affects almost all species, excluding only a few very well differentiated forms in monospecific genera.

The genus *Threskiornis* includes three very similar allopatric forms, the Sacred Ibis, the Black-headed Ibis and the Australian White Ibis (*Threskiornis molucca*), which may be considered to form a superspecies, though they are often reduced to subspecies of a single species. At the other extreme, some also regard the Madagascar Sacred Ibis (*T. aethiopicus bernieri*) as a full species, including the race *abbotti* of Aldabra. It is becoming increasingly customary for the Straw-necked Ibis (*Threskiornis spinicollis*) to be included in *Threskiornis*, even though it is still sometimes placed in a monospecific genus *Carphibis*.

One, two or three species, depending on the source, form the genus *Pseudibis*. Hence, in recent years the allopatric Indian Black Ibis (*Pseudibis papillosa*) and White-shouldered Ibis

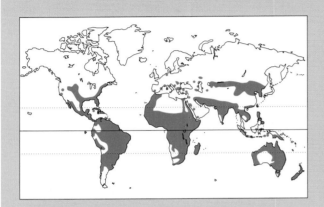

THRESKIORNITHIDAE

THRESKIORNITHINAE

PLATALEINAE

ibises
26 species
(Threskiornis, Pseudibis, Geronticus,
Nipponia, Bostrychia, Theristicus,
Cercibis, Mesembrinibis, Phimosus,
Eudocimus, Plegadis, Lophotibis)

spoonbills
6 species
(Platalea)

FAMILY

SUBFAMILY

Subdivision of the Threskiornithidae.

[Figure: Francesc Jutglar]

(*Pseudibis davisoni*), which were formerly placed in distinct genera, have often been linked as races of a single species. The Giant Ibis (*Pseudibis gigantea*), however, is still commonly assigned its own genus *Thaumatibis*.

It has also been suggested that the Northern Bald Ibis (*Geronticus eremita*) and the Southern Bald Ibis (*Geronticus calvus*) may be conspecific. Nevertheless, as the fossil register indicates that the two forms separated a long time ago, they are generally reckoned to constitute a well marked superspecies. In South Africa, where the Southern Bald Ibis presently occurs, fossils have been found that are closer to the Northern Bald Ibis, and it has been suggested that their ancestors may have been sympatric.

One particularly difficult genus is *Bostrychia*, which is restricted to Africa. Nowadays, it is usual to include the Wattled Ibis (*Bostrychia carunculata*), the Olive Ibis (*Bostrychia olivacea*), the Spot-breasted Ibis (*Bostrychia rara*) and the Hadada Ibis (*Bostrychia hagedash*). Nonetheless, the Hadada Ibis is often isolated in a monospecific genus, *Hagedashia*, whilst the Olive and Spot-breasted Ibises are sometimes still placed in *Lampribis*. In recent years, the threatened Dwarf Olive Ibis (*B. o. bocagei*) of São Tomé has sometimes been considered a full species.

The South American genus *Theristicus* is equally complex. The Buff-necked Ibis (*Theristicus caudatus*) and the Black-faced Ibis (*Theristicus melanopis*) are increasingly accepted as two distinct species, although they clearly form a superspecies. Some split this genus even further, by recognizing the Andean Ibis (*T. m. branickii*) as a full species. The other species of this genus, the Plumbeous Ibis (*Theristicus caerulescens*), is still quite commonly maintained in its own monospecific genus, *Harpiprion*.

The most widespread view regarding the American White Ibis (*Eudocimus albus*) and the Scarlet Ibis (*Eudocimus ruber*) is that they are separate species. However, they show obvious similarities in their feeding and breeding behaviour, and the relatively frequent cases of hybridization in Venezuela and Colombia, where their ranges overlap, have recently led to some authors considering them conspecific.

The Glossy Ibis (*Plegadis falcinellus*), the only cosmopolitan member of the family, and the White-faced Ibis (*Plegadis chihi*) coincide marginally in North America. They are usually considered to form a superspecies, though the latter is occasionally relegated to subspecific level within the former.

The spoonbills too share in the taxonomic problems of the family. Nowadays all six species are usually included in *Platalea*, but it is still common for the Yellow-billed Spoonbill (*Platalea flavipes*) and especially the Roseate Spoonbill (*Platalea ajaja*) to be isloated in monospecific genera, *Platibis* and *Ajaia* respectively. Again, the Royal Spoonbill (*Platalea regia*) is sometimes regarded as a subspecies of the Eurasian Spoonbill.

Morphological Aspects

Ibises and spoonbills are medium-sized to largish birds, ranging in length from just under 50 cm in the smallest species to 110 cm in the Giant Ibis. In some species, males are slightly larger than females.

The body is elongated, but robust, with a fairly long neck. The most distinctive element in the morphology of both the ibises and the spoonbills is unquestionably the bill. In the former, it is characteristically long, slender and decurved, perfectly adapted for probing in water or mud, or even in cracks in dry ground. In those species of drier habitats, the bill is generally shorter, but the fact that females generally have somewhat smaller, finer bills than males does not appear to imply differences in feeding behaviour between the sexes. In the spoonbills, the long, straight, flattened bill, with its broader distal end, provides the bird a wide surface, which is ideal for its typical feeding system involving the swinging of the head from side to side (see Food and Feeding).

The slit-like nostrils are located at the base of the bill, so that the bird can breathe whilst its bill is immersed in the water or mud. The head is also adapted for feeding, with the eyes positioned in such a way that the birds have binocular vision, which is either orientated downwards or directed towards the end of the bill. However, in spite of this development, it is more usual for the birds to feed in a tactile fashion.

In all species there are bare, featherless parts, for example on the face, throat or nape. The extent of these areas is very variable, ranging from only the lores and the chin, as in the

Plumbeous Ibis, to the whole of the head and nape, and even part of the neck, as in *Threskiornis*. This genus also has bare patches of skin on the breast which spread along the underside of the wings to the carpals.

In some species, the bare parts, sometimes including the bill and legs, show a striking change of colour during the period of pair formation. At such times, the bare skin on the breast and under the wings, which are flesh coloured outwith the breeding season, turn deep red in the Sacred, Black-headed and Australian White Ibises.

The longish legs are sturdy, and the lower half of the tibia is bare. The toes are of moderate length, longer than in storks, and the hind toe or hallux is slightly raised. The three forward toes are connected by a small basal membrane, and in some species, such as those of the genus *Plegadis*, the middle claw is pectinated, as in the herons. Ibises and spoonbills move about on foot with ease, and some species, such as the Northern Bald Ibis, even move comfortably about over quite rough terrain. Although they might appear poorly adapted, many ibises and spoonbills perch in trees without difficulty, even though they move about on them quite slowly. Occasionally spoonbills swim short distances, when in fairly deep water.

The wings are relatively long and broad, with 11 primaries and some 20 secondaries. The tail is short and wedge-shaped or slightly rounded, and it consists of 12 feathers. Ibises have a powerful, rapid flight, and birds can alternate flapping flight with glides, although in general they do not glide much. Spoonbills fly more slowly than ibises, but faster than the large

herons, and they too can use flapping flight or glides. Both groups fly with the neck and legs outstretched, even though in some ibises, such as the Hadada and Northern Bald Ibises, the legs do not reach the tip of the tail.

Those species that are notably gregarious generally fly in large flocks, either in a regular line or a V-formation, as these apparently provide aerodynamic advantages. On such occasions it is usual for all the birds to beat their wings in unison, and all pass from flapping flight to glides simultaneously. The American White Ibis, for example, flies in lines, which can be as much as about two kilometres long. Juveniles of this species normally fly alongside the flock of adults, but without joining the formation, and they acquire this tendency progressively from about two months after fledging. Glossy Ibises often fly in compact groups with the birds continually changing their relative position, so the group appears to be in a constant process of reorganization. However, there are exceptions, for example the Hadada Ibis, which tends to fly in a disorderly fashion, like storks, even in large flocks of 200 birds or more. This species has a very characteristic, irregular wingbeat, which is alternately strong and weak. Other species, such as the Roseate Spoonbill, prefer to fly in small groups, frequently in association with other species of large wading birds. The Northern Bald Ibis and some others fly in a circle when prospecting their feeding grounds.

Plumage colour is remarkably varied in this family, but it is usually uniform, and similar in both sexes. There are some totally white species, such as the American White, Sacred, Black-headed and Australian White Ibises and most spoonbills, while others are almost entirely black, including the Indian Black and White-shouldered Ibises. Between the two extremes there are various shades of brown and grey, often with green, bronze or purple metallic sheens, as well as the extremes of the deep pink of the Roseate Spoonbill and the bright red of the Scarlet Ibis.

The plumage coloration of the spoonbills, ibises and other Ciconiiformes has been related to their feeding behaviour by J. A. Kushlan, who indicates a general dichotomy between dark and light plumage. He suggests that two main factors may contribute to the development and persistence of plumage colorations: the advantage of going unnoticed by prey; and, in gregarious species, that of attracting other birds. It may also have a secondary function in reducing the amount of heat absorbed by birds that feed in environments with strong sunlight. In diurnal species of more open areas, those with pale upperparts should attract other birds to their foraging grounds more efficiently than those with dark plumage, whereas those with pale underparts should be less likely to frighten away prey than those that are dark below. In nocturnal species, or those that feed in enclosed, shady habitats, dark underparts should scare off prey less than pale underparts. On the basis of these hypotheses, predictions can be made of plumage colour: diurnal species which feed gregariously should have pale or brightly coloured upperparts; diurnal species that feed actively should have pale underparts, so that they can get close to their prey; those that feed at night or around dusk, or in shady sites, should have dark underparts; species that frequent very sunny habitats, especially in the tropics, should have white plumage, which would reduce the oppressive effects of the sun.

In fact, the plumage of ibises and spoonbills is quite consistent with these predictions, although there are exceptions, for example in the gregarious genera *Plegadis* and *Geronticus*, which are wholly dark. The colour of juveniles in some species, such as the American White Ibis, does not fit in with the expected patterns, perhaps because they are less gregarious than the adults.

Some species, notably the genus *Threskiornis* and the spoonbills, have a breeding plumage which differs from the non-breeding one by the presence of ornamental feathers, such as crests or specially modified feathers. In the case of the Japanese Crested Ibis (*Nipponia nippon*), there is also a marked difference in general coloration, and breeding plumage is a deep grey, as opposed to the usual white. Ignorance of this fact led to the description of a new race, *sinensis*, at the end of the

The bill is the morphological feature that best differentiates the two groups, generally considered subfamilies, into which the family Threskiornithidae is usually divided. This Yellow-billed Spoonbill clearly shows the typically long, straight, flattened bill of the spoonbills; the broader distal end provides the bird with a wide surface which is ideal for its characteristic feeding method. Note also the long legs, which allow it to wade into quite deep water, and the slit-like nostrils situated at the base of the bill, that permit the bird to continue breathing whilst the bill is under the water.

[Platalea flavipes, Lake Cowal, Australia. Photo: M.P. Kahl/DRK]

In ibises, the bill is characteristically long, slender and decurved, perfectly adapted for probing in water or mud, or even into cracks in dry ground. These Indian Black Ibises also display another characteristic that is common to all members of the family: the presence of unfeathered areas on the head, which usually play an important part in the formation of the pair. In adults of this species, the naked head is black, and the occiput is capped with a triangular patch of brilliant scarlet warts.

[*Pseudibis papillosa*, Gujarat, India. Photo: P. Evans/ Bruce Coleman]

Muddy areas are among the preferred habitats of ibises, as the soft substrate allows them to probe deeply with their bills and locate prey by touch. Wet savannas are a very characteristic habitat of the inland populations of the Scarlet Ibis. The rarely photographed Green Ibis (in the background) can also be found in the same habitat, although less commonly, as this shy species is more closely linked to forest habitats.

[*Eudocimus ruber*, *Mesembrinibis cayennensis*, Venezuela. Photo: X. Ferrer & A. de Sostoa]

nineteenth century, but this was none other than the normal form in nuptial plumage.

Juvenile plumage is generally darker than that of adults, with smaller bare patches on the head, and birds do not usually acquire adult plumage until they reach sexual maturity. However, in the Buff-necked Ibis, for example, young birds are paler than adults, while juvenile Roseate Spoonbills are predominately white with only a few pink tinges.

In this family there are two moults per cycle. The pre-breeding moult tends to be partial, involving only some small areas of the plumage, whereas the post-breeding moult is complete. Primary moult is descendant or serially descendant. Moult of the flight-feathers can be suspended during migration, after which it may be continued on arrival, unless the movement is followed by the start of the breeding season.

Habitat

The family Threskiornithidae is cosmopolitan, and both ibises and spoonbills are present in all the continents except Antarctica. They are mainly found in the tropics and subtropics, but are also represented in temperate zones.

Habitat requirements are very broad in some species and stringent in others. Even though all the spoonbills and a good number of the ibises are typical of wetland habitats, where they obtain their food, some of the latter are not linked to such sites, and even in the aquatic species, terrestrial environments can be of great importance.

All kinds of wetland may be used, though there is a general preference for standing or slow-flowing water. In coastal zones, typical sites include estuaries, marine intertidal flats, brackish coastal lagoons and mangroves. Inland, birds frequent marshes, floodlands, riverbanks, shallow margins and inlets of lagoons, lakes and reservoirs, and also rice fields. Some species are more typical of coastal wetlands, whilst others are characteristic of inland fresh waters. Nevertheless, both groups are liable to occur in both zones, and both on occasions visit drier zones, such as savanna or farmland.

Although ibises and spoonbills are more abundant in open areas, some species live exclusively in dense forests, where they use wetlands such as swamps, streams and rivers. These include the Spot-breasted and Olive Ibises of Africa, the Madagascar Crested Ibis (*Lophotibis cristata*), which occurs in a whole series of forest types that are peculiar to Madagascar, and the Green Ibis (*Mesembrinibis cayennensis*) of South

America. The Whispering Ibis (*Phimosus infuscatus*) is found mainly in flooded woodlands, although this association is less strict than in the preceding species.

A few species of ibis live in dry habitats, and are able to do without water completely. The Northern Bald Ibis inhabits arid or semi-arid regions, such as dried up beds of wadis, areas with steep, rocky slopes, and also dry farmland, meadows and pastures at relatively high altitudes. Its counterpart, the Southern Bald Ibis, is typical of grasslands and cultivated pastures in the highlands of southern Africa, and is particularly partial to recently burnt areas. Another African species that is typical

of dry habitats is the Wattled Ibis, which is confined to the upland regions of Ethiopia, where it even inhabits moorlands at 4100 m. In South America, the Buff-neck and Black-faced Ibises can also do without wetland habitats, and they live mainly in dry woods and savannas, though the latter species also occurs up to 5000 m on the Andean *puna*.

These are not the only ibises that are found at high altitudes, and the Puna Ibis (*Plegadis ridgwayi*) mainly frequents marshy areas of the *puna*, at altitudes of 3500-4800 m. Nevertheless, members of this family are generally more frequent in the lowlands, especially those species that depend more strictly on aquatic habitats, whether these be in open or forested areas. But there is even an exception here, for the race *akleyorum* of the Olive Ibis is typical of the montane forests of Kenya and Tanzania, where it reaches heights of 3700 m.

General Habits

In general, ibises and spoonbills are gregarious, both in their feeding and breeding, and also when they are resting during the day or at their roosts. They do not associate exclusively with conspecifics, but instead are regularly found in the company of other Ciconiiformes, such as storks, herons and egrets (see Food and Feeding).

However, the extent of social tendencies varies with the different species. The most remarkable aggregations are those of the genera *Threskiornis*, *Geronticus* and particularly *Eudocimus*, which can gather in flocks of hundreds or even thousands of birds. Other species, for instance the spoonbills, are not so gregarious, and even though they breed in colonies, they fly about and feed alone or in small flocks, in which there may also be other species of waterbirds. A few species are even less sociable and generally go about alone, in pairs, or at the most in small groups of under ten birds. This is the case of the Sharp-tailed Ibis (*Cercibis oxycerca*) and the Green Ibis, in South America, and of the Indian Black Ibis and the White-shouldered Ibis in the Oriental Region.

Ibises tend to feed during the day, and this normally involves walking and flying short distances, the groups moving from one place to another. Some spoonbills, on the other hand, can be more nocturnal, so the time they spend resting during the day is greater. The fully diurnal species also move in broad daylight to trees near their foraging grounds, in order to rest for a while. In general, birds feed more during the first hours of the day and at dusk, and they normally rest in the middle of the day. Nevertheless, there are factors that can change this behaviour, for example in coastal areas birds rest during high tide and start feeding again with the ebb tide. During breeding, or at other times when they have substantial energetic requirements, they have to spend more time feeding, so they often feed at high tide too, if necessary flying fair distances to reach areas that are unaffected by the tides.

When they are not foraging, apart from resting, they busy themselves with preening and cleaning their plumage, a task to which they sometimes dedicate considerable periods of time. Their comfort behaviour is quite similar to that of other waterbirds and includes direct head-scratching. Birds also bathe in shallow water, stretching the head and bill over the water, and simultaneously beating the water vigorously with the wings. During the day, birds commonly fly from the foraging grounds to nearby freshwater ponds to drink. In order to dispel excessive heat, ibises and spoonbills may carry out gaping or gular-fluttering, whereas eggs and nestlings may be sheltered by the adult drooping its wings.

Roosts are normally in trees, but are sometimes at ground level, and they may be several kilometres from the foraging grounds; they are often used many years running. In the highly gregarious species, the arrival at the roost around dusk can be very spectacular. Large flocks of American White Ibises fly in towards their roost from all directions, spiralling down once they have flown over it. At a former roost in the Everglades National Park, in Florida, which was destroyed by a hurricane in 1960, some 60,000-80,000 American White Ibises used to arrive in less than three hours. In parts of Brazil, the crepuscular flights of the White-faced Ibis are a wonderful sight, with birds coming and going in myriad streams, and later gathering in the fields to roost, where they form a single compact mass. During the breeding season, birds mainly rest in or beside the occupied nests, or in nearby fields, as occurs in the Northern Bald Ibis.

Most species of ibis, in particular all four of the genus Threskiornis, *are gregarious, both at their feeding grounds and at their roosting and breeding sites. This colony of Black-headed Ibises at Bharatpur, in north-west India, is one of the largest known for this species, with around 400 pairs. As is usual in this species, the colony is mixed; on the right are several well grown chicks of the Asian Openbill* (Anastomus oscitans), *the most numerous of Bharatpur's breeding Ciconiiformes.*

[*Threskiornis melanocephalus*, Bharatpur, India. Photo: Günter Ziesler]

Although it is one of members of the family that inhabits drier habitats, mainly high altitude grasslands, the Southern Bald Ibis often bathes at the fringes of reservoirs or in rivers, usually standing on submerged rocks. It also frequently comes to the water to drink after consuming a large prey item, a common practice among other ibises. Note the bright red bare, dome-shaped crown, and the whitish beige tone to the rest of head and upper neck, the features that best distinguish it from its close relative the Northern Bald Ibis (Geronticus eremita).

[Geronticus calvus, South Africa. Photo: M.P. Kahl/DRK]

Whilst resting, a bird usually keeps its neck retracted and often stands on one leg. Some of the less gregarious ibises prefer to rest alone, or in small groups in large trees, often with only one bird or a pair in each tree. This has been recorded for the Wattled, Spot-breasted and Olive Ibises, and these species generally use the same roosts the whole year round.

Aggressive behaviour in members of this family does not tend to be frequent, although on occasions disputes can be intense, for example rival Northern Bald Ibises peck at each other with open bills, generally in short bursts. Nevertheless, it is more frequent for one individual simply to touch another with the tip of the bill or to perform a threat display with feathers bristled up, especially those of the mantle. Similar threat behaviour also occurs between neighbours defending territorial boundaries.

Voice

In both ibises and spoonbills the vocal apparatus is not very highly developed, so they generally tend to be rather silent. The voice is mainly used during pair formation, the building and occupation of the nest, and upon entering and leaving the roost. Outside the colony or roost, birds are normally silent, except when flocks are alarmed. Most vocalizations consist of harsh, guttural, low, grunting or wheezing calls. Chicks are more garrulous than adults, and produce shriller sounds.

One particularly noisy species is the Hadada Ibis, and its common name is onomatopoeic, coming from its characteristic call, which can be heard at quite a distance. Hadadas typically call around dusk or sunrise, when they are returning to the roost or leaving it. One bird starts calling, followed immediately by the others, and in large roosts several groups may call simultaneously. During the breeding season, birds continue to call in flight, on occasions with both partners in unison.

Another species with a striking voice is the Wattled Ibis. It produces a deep, raucous call, which can be heard five kilome-

tres away or more. The species which are restricted to forest, like the Green, Olive and Spot-breasted Ibises, are normally discreet and hard to see, and they are more commonly detected by their characteristic calls emitted above all at dusk, but sometimes also during the night.

Ibises and, in particular, spoonbills also make some mechanical sounds, such as bill-snapping or bill-clappering, and these are mostly used when birds are excited, for example during confrontations. Otherwise, the spoonbills tend to be notably silent, producing weak murmurings that are audible only over short distances.

Some forms of intraspecific behaviour also involve sounds made with the bill and calls. Scarlet Ibises, for example, rattle their bills during disputes, whilst Spot-breasted Ibises clatter their mandibles during the change over at the nest, or when they are disturbed. When two male Sacred Ibises are defending their territories within the colony, they sometimes confront one another, repeatedly simulating attacks with the bill, whilst squealing, squeaking and producing a series of sounds by inhaling and exhaling. Similar sounds are also made by both sexes in heterosexual or antagonistic situations. During the final phase of nest building, the female Sacred Ibis, and perhaps the male too, utters a sharp call up to three times, and this is sometimes followed by copulation.

Food and Feeding

All spoonbills and most ibises feed in shallow water. Their diet consists of aquatic insects, insect larvae, crustaceans, molluscs, small fish and amphibians, including tadpoles. The species that feed in dry habitats, for instance the genus *Geronticus*, take terrestrial insects, including grasshoppers, locusts and beetles, and also spiders, scorpions, terrestrial molluscs, such as snails, and small vertebrates including amphibians, reptiles and small rodents. Occasionally, they feed on the eggs of birds or reptiles and even carrion.

As a result of their partly nocturnal feeding habits, spoonbills, like these Royal Spoonbills, often sleep during the day. This group illustrates several features of resting behaviour which spoonbills share with many other Ciconiiformes and other large waterbirds: they habitually rest or sleep standing on only one leg; in bad weather they rest with the body facing into the wind, so that it does not penetrate the plumage; and they habitually rest their long bills down their backs, tucked beneath the feathers on the back and scapulars, so they have to turn their heads roughly 165°, generally to the opposite side of the leg that is down.

[Platalea regia.
Photo: G.K. Brown/
ARDEA]

Although all species are preferably carnivorous, it is not unusual for them to include some plant matter in their diet, such as aquatic plants, and even berries, shoots and rhizomes, though this tendency is more frequent among the ibises of dry habitats.

All Ciconiiformes have apparently had to adopt one of two principal foraging strategies: visual foraging, generally carried out by the herons and most storks; and tactile foraging, performed particularly by the *Mycteria* storks and by the ibises and spoonbills. However, the tactile foragers occasionally use their sight to help in feeding, thus increasing their foraging niche, and this is again more frequent in dry habitats; nonetheless, tactile feeding may even be used in clear water.

Although both ibises and spoonbills are preferably tactile feeders, they have followed two different evolutionary paths. The former specialize in "Probing", with the long bill, quickly and repeatedly into the mud in shallow water or at terrestrial sites, whereas the latter use "Head-swinging", sweeping the bill from side to side through water and silt, while wading through shallow water. These distinct forms of specialization are closely linked with the most obvious structural adaptation, the characteristic bills, which so readily distinguish the ibises from the spoonbills (see Morphological Aspects). Nevertheless, the common ancestry of these distinctive groups is illustrated by the fact that spoonbills occasionally use the "Probing" technique and ibises that of "Head-swinging".

The feeding ecology and foraging behaviour of the large wading birds has been studied in depth by J. A. Kushlan, who has described 38 forms of feeding behaviour in herons, storks, ibises and spoonbills. Ten of these have been observed in seven representative species of the Threskiornithidae. "Standing", where the bird stands still in the same place, is one of the most frequent, and has been recorded in all the species of this family that have been studied, as well as in many other waterbirds. In birds which feed in a tactile manner, "Standing" involves certain types of active behaviour such as "Probing" and "Head-swinging". "Groping" has also been observed in ibises and spoonbills; this consists of a bird holding its open bill in the water and "Pecking", picking up items of food from the substrate. "Standing" may be carried out in the water, on a perch, on land, or amongst floating vegetation, and it some-

times involves short movements that merge imperceptibly with "Walking Slowly", another of the recognized forms of feeding behaviour.

Peculiarities of the spoonbills include "Running", where the bird moves rapidly, sometimes with wing movements for balance and to permit quicker movement, and "Hopping", consisting of flying short distances and alighting, and both of these systems have been classified as "Disturb-and-chase" feeding. Kushlan, however, considers that they may be primarily used for moving quickly from one place to another, better spot, or for overtaking moving prey. "Gleaning", taking prey off emergent plants above the water, has been observed in the Roseate Spoonbill, whilst "Forward Ploughing" has been recorded in the African Spoonbill (*Platalea alba*), and consists of walking with the bill pointing forwards under the water.

The ibises that feed in dry areas advance relatively quickly, pecking at the ground, and taking insects that are flushed from pastures, or probing with the bill in cracks in the ground, between stones or in clumps of vegetation. Another style of feeding behaviour has been observed in the Southern Bald Ibis, "Flipping", where the bird turns over objects, like rocks or dung, to find prey underneath.

Green Ibises have been seen feeding in water with one or both of the wings open, especially at dusk. This behaviour, which has also been recorded in herons and storks, has been interpreted as a means of gaining improved visibility to deal with certain types of prey which are more active on the surface of the water at dusk than during the day.

As might be expected, different types of feeding behaviour can be used by the same birds, depending on habitat or season, and a bird may even change from one moment to the next, as it forages in patches with slightly different conditions. For example, in just a few minutes, an American White Ibis can peck many times around the base of a plant, then move to a softer, muddy substrate, in which it can probe deeply, before finally moving to fairly deep waters and busying itself with "Head-swinging".

The method of catching the prey depends mainly on the shape of the bill and of the prey. The "Bill Snap" involves the rapid closing of the bill as a reflex reaction to the tactile stimulus generated by contact with prey; this method is typical of tactile feeders. On the other hand, when prey is dead or scarcely moves, ibises or spoonbills will seize it by means of a "Bill Grab" using the bill like tweezers.

Small prey items are normally swallowed immediately after capture, either by tossing the prey up in the air and catching it, or else by releasing it and moving the mouth forward to engulf it. With this second method, ibises can swallow their prey almost instantaneously, without altering their "Head-down" posture.

Large, heavy or dangerous items of prey, which cannot be swallowed in one go, are manipulated using various methods, and may be battered, shaken, kneaded or ripped apart; they can also be broken up and eaten in small morsels. The Australian White Ibis holds mussels against a rock with its feet whilst it stabs them. The capture of large or dangerous prey may take quite a long time and thereby increase the probabilities of the prey escaping. After consuming a large prey item, ibises usually drink, lowering the bill into the water.

Small differences in feeding behaviour can reduce interspecific competition between closely related species feeding in the same areas, and thus permit their co-existence. A good example is that of the Royal and Yellow-billed Spoonbills, which are sympatric in Australia. The former has a shorter, wider bill than the latter, with more papillae in the spoon; whilst the former zig-zags its bill several times in each sweep, the latter sweeps in a regular, slower pendulum fashion. This leads to some differences in their diet, and although both catch much the same prey, in the Yellow-billed Spoonbill it is more restricted to crustaceans and insects, whereas the Royal Spoonbill can capture larger, faster prey, which means that it can consume relatively larger quantities of fish.

Young birds have to learn to feed effectively. The most common feeding methods of each species are innate, and birds may use them frequently even before they fledge. Young ibises "Probe" in the area surrounding the colony, whilst spoonbills "Head-swing" in shallow waters adjacent to their colonies. Once independent, the young birds probably perfect their feeding techniques, and learn when to use each one by means of trial and error. Similarly, they learn to localize new foraging grounds and to detect potentially dangerous sites.

There is no difference between the foraging strategies of juveniles and adults, but the quantity of prey caught in relation to the number of attempts is greater in adults than in juveniles. Young birds therefore need to spend more time feeding, which may explain the fact that the proportion of juveniles feeding in

both the early morning and the late evening is greater than during the rest of the day. This also shows why juveniles arrive later at the roost than adults. It has been suggested that the fact that American White Ibises do not breed until the end of their second year could be related to an inability to obtain sufficient food. In general, juveniles tend to come to their foraging grounds and leave them in large flocks with other juveniles, and to feed alongside them. At an American White Ibis colony in Florida, the juveniles have been seen to supplement the food provided by their parents by feeding in the vicinity of the colony, in flocks formed solely of immatures.

Most species feed in large flocks, which can be monospecific or include other species of large wading birds. Perhaps not surprisingly, the diversity of these mixed flocks is highest in the tropics. Although some species are highly gregarious (see General Habits), others are much less so and feed in small groups or in pairs, or else exclusively on the periphery of feeding flocks.

The advantages of this type of foraging can be explained, in the first place, by the fact that flocks occur in places where there is a concentration of food. In addition, the performance of each individual is increased in this way, as long as its feeding behaviour is appropriate. This does not happen in species which use a methodical form of foraging, since they would be disturbed and at a disadvantage in flocks, but it does occur in those that feed by "Standing" or by slow, non-visual feeding. Thus, it is advantageous for these species to attract other birds, in order to increase foraging performance, which appears to be one of the purposes of the bright coloration of most of the gregarious species (see Morphological Aspects).

As birds mostly look downwards when they are feeding, another advantage of flocks could be that the risk of predation is lower. In fact, there is evidence that peripheral or isolated individuals in large flocks spend a fair amount of time on the look out, whilst the birds in the centre waste hardly any time in this, and so can spend more time feeding. The constituent members of large flocks are constantly on the move, changing position, and shifting from the centre to the edge or vice versa. There do not seem to be any social or sexual factors which determine the position of adults within large flocks, although there does appear to be a certain tendency for young birds to be positioned around the periphery. This may be explained by adult dominance, because this would be the least favourable position for catching prey, or because on the edge it is necessary for birds to be more alert. It has even been seen, again in the

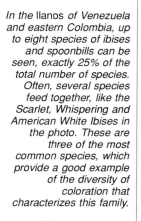

In the llanos of Venezuela and eastern Colombia, up to eight species of ibises and spoonbills can be seen, exactly 25% of the total number of species. Often, several species feed together, like the Scarlet, Whispering and American White Ibises in the photo. These are three of the most common species, which provide a good example of the diversity of coloration that characterizes this family.

[Eudocimus albus, Eudocimus ruber, Phimosus infuscatus, in llanos of Venezuela. Photo: Nellaine Price/ Survival]

Although their vocal
apparatus is not very
highly developed, ibises
can be rather noisy birds
in and around roosting
sites, and also during
courtship displays or nest
building. The Buff-necked
Ibis utters a loud, harsh,
very penetrating call,
which is often repeated
persistently by the same
individuals; at the climax
of a cry, a bird typically
stretches its neck right
back, so that its bill points
skywards.

[*Theristicus caudatus*,
Pantanal, Brazil.
Photo: Angelika Hofer/
Günter Ziesler]

well studied American White Ibis, that position in a flock can effect the feeding techniques used. So birds that are catching crabs on the edge of a large flock are more likely to hunt them visually, before they hide in the mud; the same is true when birds hunt crabs alone or in small groups. On the other hand, birds in the centre of a large flock catch the crabs using tactile techniques, since the prey is sure to be buried away under the mud, due to the considerable disturbance at this point.

Foraging in flocks also has negative aspects, such as theft of prey, which is common, especially with adults stealing from juveniles, although the latter also steal from each other. There are also cases of piracy at breeding colonies, especially where they are far from the foraging grounds. A roving adult may seize food from another, just as it is about to feed its chick, and in this way it can obtain a fair amount of food. There are also cases of commensalism, the best known involving the Snowy Egret (*Egretta thula*) and the Little Blue Heron (*Egretta caerulea*). When these species feed alongside American White Ibises, they capture more prey than when they forage alone, in the same habitat and with the same density of prey. Apparently the ibises facilitate prey capture for the herons, either because they locate it or because they cause the prey to move. When feeding in flocks, Glossy, White-faced and American White Ibises are all susceptible to kleptoparasitism by crows and grackles (*Quiscalus*). The victims of these attacks are most commonly birds that have caught large prey which requires a certain amount of time for manipulation, before it can be swallowed.

Adults feed their chicks on the same type and size of prey as that which they themselves consume. When the chicks are very young, rather than bringing them small prey, the adults give them semi-digested food. As the chicks grow, they are brought food that is either less digested or quite undigested. When a prey item is too large to be eaten by the chicks, the adults may reswallow it, but very often the chicks can deal with large prey, even if it is live.

In some cases, the chicks have requirements that determine the type of prey acceptable to them. In American White and Scarlet Ibis colonies situated in areas with brackish water, there is a change in the adults' diet after the chicks have hatched. Seemingly, the chicks are unable to eliminate salt through the excretory glands until they are five days old, and even after this they would not be able to tolerate a diet containing high con-

centrations of salt, without being given fresh water, and there is no evidence of this occurring in the Threskiornithidae. For this reason, adult Scarlet Ibises, which roost in coastal mangroves and normally feed on brackish water prey, such as crabs and polychaete worms, fly during the breeding season to freshwater areas inland, so as to find food for their chicks. On the other hand, in the same area non-breeders continue to feed on brackish water prey. The same tendency has been noted in American White Ibises, when they have chicks. Birds will fly to flooded inland areas, sometimes covering great distances, in order to capture the right kind of prey, such as crayfish. In this way, fluctuations in the numbers of ibises nesting in coastal colonies and their breeding success are directly related to the adults' ability to find suitable freshwater prey, and this, in turn, depends on the rainfall patterns. This may explain the poor levels of breeding success during periods of drought, as adults are forced to feed their chicks on prey with high salt concentrations.

Young ibises can regurgitate and eject food when disturbed, and adults also do so on occasions. This is thought to be an anti-predator mechanism, which may be used to keep predators away from the nest. However, Turkey Vultures (*Cathartes aura*), which sometimes kill American White Ibis chicks in the nest, have learnt to collect and consume regurgitated food. Digestion is rapid and selective in ibises and spoonbills, and adults expel balls of indigestible materials, such as bones, feathers and chitinous exoskeletons.

Due to their relatively large size, ibises and spoonbills require a considerable quantity of food to produce sufficient energy and particularly to breed successfully. There are numerous adaptations that highlight the importance of this aspect and the potential difficulties that they, and indeed Ciconiiformes in general, may have in obtaining enough food. These include social foraging, a gliding flight used in foraging, asynchronous hatching, cannibalism amongst chicks and the tendency to abandon the nest when there is a shortage of food.

Breeding

Most ibises and spoonbills nest in fairly dense colonies, often in association with other waterbirds, in particular herons, but also storks, cormorants or darters.

This White-faced Ibis is feeding by "Probing", the foraging technique that is most extensively used by ibises in general. This means of locating prey consists of moving the tip of the bill rapidly and repeatedly in and out of the substrate. While this feeding system is tactile, ibises are also capable of foraging visually, for example locating crayfish holes in which they probe, or picking food items off the ground. This species is most readily differentiated from the very similar Glossy Ibis (Plegadis falcinellus) by the red irides, facial skin and legs, and the white feathering which extends behind the eye and onto the chin.

[Plegadis chihi. Photo: Leonard Lee Rue/ Bruce Coleman]

Colonies are situated in trees, bushes, low vegetation such as sawgrass or bulrushes, or sometimes even on the ground, for example on islands. Colonies are generally near water or over it. The Northern Bald, Southern Bald and Wattled Ibises, however, nest on rocky cliffs beside rivers or coasts, or in piles of boulders, in small monospecific colonies, or even alone on occasions. The less gregarious species, including those that live in forests, such as the Olive, Spot-breasted and Madagascar Crested Ibises nest in isolation. Even the Hadada Ibis, normally gregarious at the roost, nests alone. On the other hand, although they are not highly sociable in other activities, most spoonbills nest in large colonies regularly containing thousands of pairs and often mixed. The exception is the Yellow-billed Spoonbill, which may nest in isolation or semi-colonially, with the few nests separated by distances of 30 m or more.

The species that nest in temperate zones breed annually and seasonally, in the spring. The start of breeding in these cases is influenced by environmental factors, such as an increase in the hours of daylight, temperature, and perhaps also relatively high humidity levels.

In the tropics, the main factor that induces nesting is not well known, but it is usually related to the hydrological patterns, although there is variation between the different species. Depending on the habitat, either the dry season or the wet correlates with a greater availability of the sort of prey that is suitable for the development of the chicks, and as a result most species tend to breed during the appropriate period in their area. In many tropical zones, prey is more abundant and accessible during the rainy season, whilst in subtropical regions the dry season is normally the period with the greatest availability of food in marshes.

The crucial role of the local water cycle in the availability of food is such that heavy rain in the dry season can cause breeding birds to abandon their colonies, whilst a drought can have the same effect on those which breed in the rainy season. Conversely, conditions of rainfall and water levels which are out of season occasionally cause some species to start nesting. The rainfall patterns also influence the number of birds that breed, for instance in Florida, where the number of American White Ibises in wet years is much higher than in dry years (see Food and Feeding).

In tropical parts of Africa and South America, the birds often nest and raise their chicks during the rainy period of three to four months, which occurs before the long dry season. The Sacred and Hadada Ibises have different breeding calendars throughout Africa, and these can vary each year, depending on seasonal precipitation. In years with deficient rainfall, the White-faced, Northern Bald and Southern Bald Ibises may fail to breed; in the last of these species, for example, the absence of rain reduces growth in grasslands, so that ultimately there are fewer insects for them to feed on. In Australia, the Straw-necked and Australian White Ibises depend on flooding far more than merely on the rains for successful nesting, so they are nomadic, moving about until they find the right conditions.

Ibises and spoonbills are monogamous, and in colonial species pair formation normally takes place at the colony. Often, males arrive first at the nesting grounds, where they establish small territories which they defend from other males with threat displays that include wing flapping, head stretching, pursuit flights and "Stretch-and-snap" displays. Displays between members of a pair have only been studied in a few species, and include "Bowing", intertwining of necks, presentation of nest material and "Mutual Billing", which consists of birds seizing one another's bill and shaking them in unison with movements of their heads. Other displays which have been observed include elements that are very similar to those of the herons, like the "Stretch" and "Snap" displays (see page 389).

Displays between partners not only strengthen the pair-bond, but also play an important part in the development of their sexual behaviour and the sexual stimulation of other birds in the colony. In captivity, for example, when young Northern Bald Ibises are stimulated by experienced adult birds, they can breed when three years old, but without this stimulation they do not breed until they are six. This tendency has also been observed in other species of ibises in captivity.

In general, the pair-bond is only maintained during the breeding season. In some species, including the Northern Bald and American White Ibises, before the eggs are laid there are numerous changes of partner and promiscuous copulation has been observed in some birds seeking new partners between breeding seasons. On the other hand, the fact that pairs sometimes rest together at the colony and carry out pairing displays outside the breeding season, and that some pairs only perform brief pair forming displays before nesting, appear to indicate that some pairs probably remain together all year long.

"Head-swinging" is the most characteristic feeding method of the spoonbills, and involves the bird moving its broad bill from side to side in long arcs through the water. The bill, open a few centimetres at the tip, is usually held almost vertical, and it can be partly or completely submerged. In this non-visual system, the bill closes only on objects that touch the inside of the spoon, which has numerous vibration detectors. The Roseate Spoonbill is clearly distinguished from the other five species of spoonbill by its pink plumage and its carmine lesser wing-coverts.

[Platalea ajaja. Photo: Stephen J. Krasemann/DRK]

Both sexes participate in nest building. In general, it is the female who actually carries out the building with materials brought to her by the male. The collection of material, its presentation to the partner and its manipulation in the nest are probably important in sexual stimulation. Some species, like the Hadada and the Northern Bald Ibises, perform ritualized manipulation of the nest material in what constitutes an elaborate display.

Normally a nest consists of a large accumulation of diverse materials, such as grass, rushes, branches and so on, which are roughly woven together. In the colonies, nests are usually placed very close to each other, separated by only some 15 cm. In general, copulation takes place on the small nest-site territory.

In colonies, birds normally start their egg-laying more or less simultaneously, some three weeks apart at the most. The oval eggs are laid at intervals of 1-3 days, and are white, pale green or blue, without spots or markings; they have a chalky coat and often a rough surface. Clutches of one to seven eggs have been reported, but the normal size is two to five. There is generally a single clutch, but replacement clutches can be laid, if the eggs are broken or lost.

Incubation lasts 20-31 days, depending on the species, and usually begins with the first egg, which leads to a pronounced asynchrony in hatching. Some species, however, such as the Sacred and Glossy Ibises, and the Roseate Spoonbill, do not begin incubation until all the eggs have been laid. Although both sexes incubate, the female probably spends more time on this task than the male. Change overs occur at least once every 24 hours, and normally much more frequently. In the Glossy and Spot-breasted Ibises, the female incubates at night and the male during the day. Several displays have been described that are related to the change over at the nest. In some species, such as the Spot-breasted and Glossy Ibises, these can be very elaborate, and involve the male bringing small branches and green leaves, which the female places in the nest with several ritualized movements.

Each pair defends only the immediate nest-site, from conspecifics and other species alike. This defence involves several threat displays, short pursuit flights and supplanting attacks, in which the bird flies towards its perched opponent and forces it to abandon its position. In the Northern Bald Ibis, a "Nest-covering" display has been described, which is carried out when an intruder approaches the nest. In this case, the bird half

raises its body and ruffles the body feathers, partially lowering the wings and stretching out the neck.

After the eggs have hatched, the eggshells are ejected from the nest by the adults. The semi-altricial, nidicolous chicks may be naked or covered in fine down. The chicks of the Scarlet, Hadada and Sacred Ibises have vestigial claws on their wings. Upon hatching, the bill of an ibis chick is straight, which has been interpreted as proof that its ancestors had straight bills, but as the chick grows the bill becomes increasingly decurved. Likewise, spoonbill chicks do not hatch with a spatulate bill similar to the adult's; instead it is short, stubby, soft and fleshy, as in ibis chicks, providing further evidence of their close relationship. When the spoonbill chick is about nine days old, its bill begins to flatten out at the tip, and at sixteen days old the shape of the bill already resembles the adult's.

For several weeks, chicks are defenceless and are looked after by both of their parents, which brood them almost continuously whilst they are small. There is always an adult in the nest, at least during the first few days. In the Glossy Ibis, at the beginning it is the female that stays in the nest and feeds the chicks, and food is brought in by the male. In the nest, a chick feeds by inserting its head and bill into the adult's mouth to obtain regurgitated food, an action which must be repeated several times a day (see Food and Feeding). As the chicks grow, the number of visits adults make to the nest gradually decreases, and in the later stages the latter may disgorge the food directly into the nest. The hungry chicks beg for their food using plaintive calls and rapid wing movements. During the nestling period, their excrements are dropped over the side of the nest. In some species, such as the Glossy Ibis, after about two weeks the chicks can leave the nest and move about in the surrounding area, though they return to be fed.

The fledging period is very variable, with a range of 28-56 days, depending on the species. At the start, the young birds feed with their parents and come back to the nest to rest, becoming independent one to four weeks after fledging. The young of some species, for instance the Japanese Crested Ibis, soon leave their parents and disperse away from the area in which they hatched. In other species, however, such as the Northern Bald Ibis, juveniles stay with their parents for quite some time, and from them they learn the feeding and migration patterns.

Most of what is known about the age of sexual maturity comes from data on captive birds, and this subject is poorly known in the wild. In general, it appears to occur when birds are two to four years old, but has even been recorded at eighteen months in the Sacred Ibis.

Breeding success is variable. Competition for food between siblings does not usually allow more than two chicks from each nest to reach fledging, although this does depend on the availability of food. In good years, up to 80% of the pairs in one colony manage to rear one, two or sometimes three chicks, with an average success rate of around one chick per pair. On the other hand, complete failure in a colony is not rare, when there are unexpectedly adverse feeding conditions or due to rises in water levels. Mortality is high during the first two weeks of life, because growth is very rapid during this period, there is often a considerable difference in size between chicks, and only one of the adults brings food, while the other remains on the nest. Falls from the nest can also constitute an important cause of mortality in these early days. Reptiles, such as snakes and iguanas, and birds, especially crows, raptors and grackles, plunder chicks and are also responsible for some egg losses.

Mortality is also high during the bird's first months of independence, but it starts to drop as the birds develop into adults. Thus, these birds generally have a good survival rate, as demonstrated by longevity records in the wild of over 14 years in the White-faced Ibis, 16 in the White American Ibis, and 28 in the Eurasian Spoonbill.

Movements

As a rule, ibises and spoonbills tend to be sedentary in the tropics, whereas in subtropical and particularly temperate zones, most carry out true migrations. Migration takes place by day and probably also by night; birds frequently fly at great altitudes, generally in a linear or V-formation, and often soar.

In temperate climates, the abundance of prey varies seasonally. Several temperate zone species migrate to the tropics or subtropics for the winter, and return to temperate latitudes to nest in the spring and summer, and in such cases cold weather is a limiting factor. This pattern is followed by the Glossy, American White and Japanese Crested Ibises, as well as the White and Black-faced (*Platalea minor*) Spoonbills, all of which breed in temperate areas of the Northern Hemisphere. The White-faced Ibis in America is generally sedentary, but the northerly populations of the USA migrate southwards, wintering in Mexico and Central America. In the Northern Bald Ibis, the western population which persists in Morocco only per-

forms irregular movements, while the practically extinct population which until recently nested in Turkey, and formerly in neighbouring countries, was seasonally migratory, apparently wintering mainly in Ethiopia and southern Arabia; this may have been a significant factor in the decline of the species.

In the Southern Hemisphere, there are movements similar to those recorded in the north, for example Glossy Ibises ringed at colonies in South Africa have been found 1000-1500 km to the north, in Angola and Zambia. In Australia, on the other hand, where the same species also breeds, movements are less clearly defined, and journeys from north to south within the continent are only registered in a few populations. Other Australian species, the Straw-necked and Australian White Ibises, are basically nomadic, as they depend on the aquatic food which becomes available in certain conditions of flooding. Thus, during dry periods, populations disperse widely, whilst they assemble to nest at intermittently flooded marshes, after heavy rains have produced an abundant supply of invertebrates.

Although they are primarily sedentary, the species that inhabit warmer zones also carry out dispersals and irregular movements. Most species have some kind of post-fledging dispersal of juveniles and a post-breeding dispersal of adults. In many populations which nest in warm regions, there is a tendency to disperse after breeding towards temperate marshes, where food is more abundant. It is likewise characteristic for some species of northern temperate regions to disperse northwards, especially individuals of younger age classes. For example, in Europe both Glossy Ibises and Eurasian Spoonbills have turned up in Iceland, the Faeroes, Norway and Sweden, well to the north of their normal ranges. Spoonbills too, especially young birds, carry out regular post-breeding dispersals, usually over short distances, though they occasionally involve long journeys.

The irregular movements that many species carry out on a regional level are interpreted as a response to seasonal changes, basically in rainfall patterns and water levels, due to the influence these have on food supplies and nesting grounds. When environmental conditions facilitate a succession of areas favourable for feeding, birds move on from one site of abundant food to another. In salt-marshes and swamps, the reactions of birds to drought conditions or excessively high water levels are proof of the importance of feeding conditions. Flocks of American White Ibises move along the vast inland swamps of northern Florida throughout the whole year, remaining where the water is shallow enough to permit feeding. When the flood water recedes in the dry season, they follow the subsiding

Although ibises sometimes feed by "Probing" in holes and cracks in dry ground or even in dense tufts of vegetation, more often they use this technique in soft, muddy ground, as in the case of this Sharp-tailed Ibis, which has its bill completely covered in mud. This species is not abundant, and is one of the most poorly known of the family. Its distinctive features are its very long tail and a characteristic facial pattern, with a whitish grey forehead and malar stripe, a bare orange throat and red facial skin.

[*Cercibis oxycerca*, in *llanos* of Venezuela. Photo: Mike Price/Survival]

waters, establishing a series of roosts near each of the successively used feeding grounds. These movements allow them to use most of their habitat all year round, and if the food supply lasts, a resting site can turn into a breeding colony.

Relationship with Man

The ancient Egyptians acknowledged the Nile as the source and protector of life, so the ibis, which appeared in the region during the annual flooding of the great river, was considered worthy of their adoration. For the Egyptians, the Sacred Ibis was the incarnation of Thoth, the god of wisdom and knowledge; there are numerous mummified specimens, as well as murals showing nesting ibises and young birds. It was probably the first bird in the world ever to be protected. Nonetheless, since about 1850 the Sacred Ibis has not been seen during the Nile's spates in Egypt, although it is still present in many parts of sub-Saharan Africa, where there is ample evidence of its tendency to associate with man; in places it uses inhabited villages for roosting.

However, before worshipping the Sacred Ibis, the ancient Egyptians had idolized the Northern Bald Ibis, which was apparently abundant in the past, as shown by its representation in hieroglyphics dating back 5000 years. It seems that the Sacred Ibis gradually replaced the Northern Bald Ibis as a holy symbol in the subsequent centuries.

Few examples of man's relationship with the animal world are as complex and dramatic as that of the Northern Bald Ibis. In 1555, a Swiss doctor, K. Gessner, described and illustrated in his *Historia Animalium*, a bird "larger than a hen, with black plumage, a naked face and a long bill", which arrived with the good weather, along with the storks, and bred in the mountains of Switzerland and Central Europe. Gessner called it the "Forest Raven". He commented on the tastiness of its flesh, especially that of chicks taken from the nest before fledging, and this fact must have contributed to the intense persecution suffered by the species in the following 200 years. There were two other factors, the progressive conversion into fields and pastures of the mountain meadows where it fed, and the cooling of the climate in Europe, which started during the second half of the sixteenth century. These three factors, especially the third, brought about the extinction of the "Forest Raven" in Europe, around the end of the seventeenth century.

The bird was soon forgotten since it was regarded as a species which had completely disappeared from the face of the earth. Gessner's description and drawing were even considered to be pure fabrication, since they did not coincide with any of the birds known in Europe, including the Glossy Ibis, which was present on the banks of the Danube.

But when, at the start of the twentieth century, the Northern Bald Ibis was discovered in North Africa and the Middle East, it was noticed that its appearance was surprisingly similar to that of the bird described by Gessner. Nevertheless, the scientists of the day did not believe that a bird from the Orient could have lived in the Alps, until osseous remains of an ibis were found during excavations in prehistoric deposits; the final proof came when the Swiss paleontologist H. G. Stehlin discovered a semi-fossilized specimen of what was unquestionably a Northern Bald Ibis. So Gessner's "Forest Raven" and the Northern Bald Ibis were quite simply one and the same species.

But the dramatic history of the Northern Bald Ibis and its relationship with man does not end there. When the news of the discovery of this species was divulged, all the European museums and collectors rushed to obtain specimens of this rare, mythical bird, until with the help of local hunters entire colonies were wiped out, including most of those that remained in Algeria and all those in Syria. In addition to this direct persecution there were other factors, such as the conversion into farmland of large expanses of its habitat, the proliferation of pesticides, and climatic changes involving increasingly intense and frequent droughts, so the species found itself in a very delicate situation at the middle of the century: there was a single eastern colony in Turkey, at Birecik, one small colony in Algeria and a few more in Morocco.

It was not pure coincidence that this particular Turkish colony was the only one that remained in the whole of the Eurasian continent. It survived because the inhabitants of Birecik, on the banks of the Euphrates, believed that Noah not only released a dove from the ark, as a symbol of peace, but also Abu Mengel, a black bird with a sickle-shaped bill, as a symbol of fertility. Abu Mengel, without a doubt the Northern

Ibises often feed in shallow parts of wetlands, generally by probing into the muddy bottom, as illustrated by these two Puna Ibises, which are feeding at a flooded meadow in the Peruvian Andes. The fine white streaks on the head indicate that these birds are in non-breeding plumage.

[*Plegadis ridgwayi*, Peru. Photo: Günter Ziesler]

The Black-faced Ibis is
one of the most
adaptable species in the
family with regards
nesting. It can nest alone
or, more frequently, in
colonies of very variable
density at a wide array of
locations. In addition to
using tree stumps and
other emergent sites in
the middle of marshes
and flooded areas, birds
can site the voluminous
nests in reedbeds, on
rocky outcrops or ledges
of gullies and cliffs, or
occasionally in trees in
patches of woodland.

[Theristicus melanopis,
Lago Roca, Parque
Nacional Los Glaciares,
Argentina.
Photo: A. de Sostoa &
X. Ferrer]

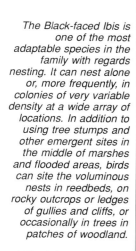

Bald Ibis, supposedly guided Noah and his children from Mount Ararat to a small house in a valley, and was venerated because of this and respected by everyone. The arrival of the ibises every February from Ethiopia and the south of Arabia was celebrated in a great annual festival.

Religious belief held that the aim of this bird's migration was to serve as a guide for the pilgrims that made their way each year to Mecca, a legend probably fostered by the repeated observation of the birds near the Holy City by pilgrims coming from the region of Birecik.

However, several events led to a gradual weakening in the veneration of the bird. The construction of a bridge over the Euphrates led to the disappearance of the boat which crossed the river, and with it the ferrymen who maintained the tradition of the sacred bird. Also, with the bridge, the growth of the population accelerated and immigrants arrived from other regions who did not share this belief. The annual ibis reception festival ceased to be celebrated from 1958, and as the town grew it invaded the nesting grounds, with the result that by 1960 local children could be seen throwing stones at the occupied nests. In spite of having been the target of one of the most widely publicized rescue campaigns, which still continues with captive birds *in situ*, the Northern Bald Ibis colony has now disappeared and the eastern population of this species can be regarded as extinct (see Status and Conservation).

Ibises and spoonbills have always been hunted by primitive peoples for food or sport, and particularly for their decorative feathers. Hunting for food has often been carried out by indigenous communities at sustainable levels, causing no great harm to the bird populations, with man acting as a normal predator integrated into the ecosystem. However, with the arrival of technology, civilization and colonizers, the impact of hunting can be far more serious on certain populations, and even on the total population of some forms with restricted ranges. This was the case of the race *abbotti* of the Sacred Ibis, otherwise known as the Aldabra Ibis, which had its population reduced to little over a hundred birds after it was hunted by temporary workers who moved to its islands.

Nowadays, the majority of the species in this family are protected in most parts of the world. However, poaching is favoured by the lack of control and guards in many breeding and wintering grounds, so it continues to have negative effects on many populations. Hunting to obtain the decorative plumes,

which was especially intense around the turn of this century, had a devastating effect on some species, especially the Japanese Crested and Scarlet Ibises and the Roseate Spoonbill. This last species was greatly admired, like the Scarlet Ibis, for its brilliant coloration, and it has enjoyed effective protection in the USA from the 1940's onwards. Thanks to this, it reappeared in parts of Florida and of the coast of Texas where the plume trade had caused it to disappear. The Japanese Crested Ibis, on the other hand, continues to flirt with extinction (see Status and Conservation). Such activity is not a thing of the past, for today in French Guiana there is a prosperous industry, which appears to be of great economic importance to the town of Sinnamary: the production of artificial flowers made from Scarlet Ibis feathers, for sale to tourists. The species may be hunted legally from the 1st of December to the 15th of February, and there is no kind of control over the sale of these flowers.

The striking features and the appeal of ibises and spoonbills have led to the commonest species being typical zoo exhibits in many parts of the world. However, until recently no special management or breeding programmes were applied to them. Despite this lack of concern, several common species bred fairly easily, which meant that details were learnt about successful captive breeding, and these can now be applied to the recovery of endangered species. Thus, the Northern Bald Ibis now has a captive population of more than 700 birds, far more than those remaining in the wild. The species breeds well at several zoos, and recovery programmes are being carried out based on breeding in captivity (see Status and Conservation). In the case of the Japanese Crested Ibis, on the other hand, breeding in captivity has proved extremely difficult in spite of intense efforts. In 1990, however, the first success was achieved (see Status and Conservation), and this is a cause for renewed hope in the plight of this extremely rare bird.

Status and Conservation

Seven members of the Threskiornithidae are currently listed as globally threatened, four of them, the Giant, Northern Bald and Japanese Crested Ibises and the Black-faced Spoonbill, in the Endangered category; it is very likely that the White-shouldered Ibis, at present considered Vulnerable, will soon join them. The subspecies *bocagei* of the Olive Ibis, which is in-

As in other members of the family, "Stick Presentation" is a characteristic procedure in the breeding behaviour of the Hadada Ibis; it is performed during nest building and also during incubation. In this species, the male is thought to collect the material while the female is left in charge of the construction of the nest, a task that usually requires roughly two weeks to complete. Typically, the bird at the nest jibbers its bill as the other approaches with a stick, which often precedes a change over at the nest during incubation. An unusual characteristic of the Hadada is that, although fairly gregarious when not breeding, it is a solitary nester.

[Bostrychia hagedash, South Africa. Photo: Clem Haagner/ Ardea]

creasingly regarded as a separate species, the Dwarf Olive Ibis, is included in the Indeterminate category, because of the lack of precise information about its present status, which is certainly precarious. In the short term, the situation of the Southern Bald Ibis gives less cause for concern, although its small total population and restricted range lead it to be considered Rare.

In contrast, two other ibises which were included in the second edition of the Red Data Book of 1978/79 are now deemed less worrying than was thought at that time. The Madagascar Crested Ibis, previously qualified as Vulnerable, is today considered near-threatened, whilst the race *abbotti* of the Sacred Ibis, a native of Aldabra, previously categorized as Rare, has benefited from adequate protective measures, thanks to which its survival is no longer in the balance.

Apart of these threatened species, the race *rothschildi* of the Olive Ibis, which formerly lived on the island of Príncipe in the Gulf of Guinea, is believed to have disappeared in recent times, although the reasons for this are not altogether clear. At the end of last century, it was already considered rare and was seen for the last time in 1901. There were several subsequent attempts to localize it in 1909, 1928 and 1948, but all failed. Although it is very shy and difficult to see, and the last reports came from virtually inaccessible areas, it does emit a low distinctive call, which makes it improbable that it could have eluded all the naturalists who have visited the island throughout this century.

The case of the related Dwarf Olive Ibis of São Tomé is more positive. It was probably never very numerous, but in the nineteenth century no less than five specimens, and probably eight or more, were collected in areas of continuous virgin forest, and perhaps in gallery forest too, always away from higher ground. Since then the species has evidently suffered a decline, probably related to the forest damage and destruction that is known to have occurred in lowland areas, notably between 1890 and 1915. This was mainly due to their conversion into cocoa, coffee, banana and coconut plantations. Other factors may include the introduction of diseases and of predatory mammals, like civets and weasels. The capture, in 1928, of one female in the south-west of the island was until recently the last record of the species, thus, following CITES criteria, it was considered to be extinct from 1978.

In 1987 and 1988, ICBP teams visited São Tomé and Príncipe. Although they were not able to observe the species themselves, during the second visit they heard first-hand accounts from two expert local guides explaining that the ibis still survived in the untouched forests of the south of the island. Apparently, unlike most of the remaining endemic species of São Tomé, the Dwarf Olive Ibis has not adapted to the regenerating secondary forest that grows up on abandoned plantations. In 1989 two German biologists working for the Geneva Museum saw five birds on lava beds along the Io Grande River, whilst a British ornithologist sighted another bird in 1990 in a small forest stream in the nearby valley of the Ana Chaves River. Whether these are the last survivors of a virtually condemned relict population, or whether a sufficient number still remain to make the bird's future viable, will only be known when some 200 km² of untouched rain forest that remain in the centre and south-west of the island have been explored from an ornithological point of view.

A much better known case is that of the Japanese Crested Ibis, one of the rarest and most threatened of all birds. In former times this species bred in south-east Siberia, Korea, Japan and north-east China. However, during the twentieth century, as a result of the human population explosion in China and Japan, several wars each with its own aftermath, deforestation and alteration of habitat, and hunting, the population and range of the species have been drastically reduced. There are no recent confirmed records from Siberia, where a few ibises were reported in the first half of the twentieth century. In Japan, around 1930 there were some 40 birds distributed over Sado Island and the nearby Noto Peninsula, in Honshu. In 1934 the Japanese government decreed the protection of the species, but the destruction of the forests continued, so that by 1953 only 31 birds were recorded, and only 10 in 1961. In 1962, a forest sanctuary was purchased by the government and created on Sado Island, and captive breeding facilities were installed there in 1965. Three young birds and the only survivor from Noto Peninsula were captured, but all but one died soon after, apparently as a result of being fed an unsuitable diet. Simultaneously the wild population continued to decline, and several young birds are known to have died as a consequence of poisoning by pesticides. In 1977 only eight birds remained and they did not subsequently

The African Spoonbill's nest is made of reeds when the colony is situated in reedbeds, or of sticks when in trees. Both types of colony are generally loose associations in which other waterbirds also breed, amongst which the Sacred Ibis (Threskiornis aethiopicus) is one of the most frequent. In both coloration and external appearance the sexes are alike, but in this case it is fairly certain that the male is the standing bird: firstly because its bill is noticeably longer; but also because in this species the female usually incubates almost all day long, whilst the male almost always takes the night shift, the change over rarely taking place during the day. The red facial skin and the red-fringed grey upper mandible are unique among spoonbills.

[Platalea alba.
Photo: Peter Steyn/Ardea]

breed. Finally, the five which still survived in 1981 were captured and united with the only other captive bird, so the species became extinct in the wild in Japan.

In China, the species was reported in 14 provinces during the 1930's, whereas by 1958 it was observed in only three, and in the 1960's, as none were reported, the ibis was thought to have died out in the whole country. In 1978, the Zoological Research Institute of the Chinese Academy of Sciences began a search for the species travelling 50,000 km throughout 13 provinces before in 1981 they found seven birds, including two breeding pairs, in Shaanxi Province. After the spectacular rediscovery, the Forestry Ministry established an Ibis Protection Station in the area and continued the search, with the result that by 1989 the known population comprised some 46 birds. Nonetheless, the species can hardly be considered out of danger unless the population reaches the region of 500 birds.

It is to be hoped that, in spite of the initial failures, breeding in captivity can play an important role in the recovery of this emblematic species. On Sado, the captive group formed by two males and two females, the survivors of the Japanese population and one bird donated by China, has not yet managed to breed, although the management of the birds has greatly improved. In Beijing Zoo, on the other hand, a group of five ibises taken from the wild just before fledging have all developed into healthy adults. The first pair formed in 1989, and two eggs were laid and hatched. One of the chicks was apparently killed by its parents and the other only survived one week, but the pair had just acheived sexual maturity and give hope for successful captive breeding in the near future.

Another of the better known endangered birds is the Northern Bald Ibis, which has been the object of several intensive recovery attempts. Until a few years ago, the species nested in several colonies in Morocco and Algeria and in one colony along the river Euphrates in Birecik in Turkey. The Algerian colony recently disappeared, whilst numbers in the Moroccan and Turkish colonies have been decreasing rapidly, and in 1989 the wild population in Turkey was reduced to one individual, so that technically it could also be considered extinct as a breeding bird.

The process of extinction of the eastern population of this ibis is very well known and is indicative of the danger in waiting too long before attempting to save an endangered species. In 1953, 530 pairs still nested in the cliffs at Birecik, but between 1956 and 1959 more than 600 individuals, about 70% of the birds at this colony, were found dead, due to poisoning by pesticides used against locusts, a favourite food of this ibis, and those used to control malaria. The effects of this poisoning were apparent for several years, since breeding success decreased notably amongst the surviving pairs, with the result that the colony did not produce any further young until 1972. Numbers thus dropped from 65 pairs in 1964, to 23 in 1973.

In an attempt to save this population, a recovery programme was begun in 1977 by several international conservation organizations, headed by the WWF. A colony of captive birds was created 2 km north of Birecik. One of the aims was to attract wild birds from the town centre to the colony, since it was considered that they were suffering excessive disturbance (see Relationship with Man). By 1982 all the free birds had abandoned their breeding site in the town, which had been used for at least a century, and had started to nest in the rocky walls over the artificial breeding station. During a period of seven years, 40 wild birds were captured, whilst 67 birds, hatched at the breeding station, were released, to bolster the wild population. However, most of the released birds did not integrate with the wild poplation, and they did not migrate, with the result that they died on the outskirts of Birecik during the winter. Errors committed during the capture of the birds, inadequate food, the tardy release of juveniles and the complete lack of action by the Turkish government, regarding the use of pesticides on crops in the surrounding area, led to a new pronounced decline in the population. In spring 1988, only four of the 18 birds which had migrated during the previous season returned, and in 1989 only three returned, two of which subsequently perished in accidents.

At present, the programme of captive breeding continues, but the main problem affecting this reintroduction is the lack of completely wild birds to lead the migration journey towards the winter quarters. Such birds are necessary because this species does not migrate instinctively, but instead each new generation is taught by its parents.

In the Straw-necked Ibis, as in other members of the family, the chicks are fed by both parents by means of incomplete regurgitation. On occasions, if the adult seems reluctant to feed it, a chick may wrap its wing over the adult's neck and pull its head down, so that the chick can reach into its bill. Note the spiny, yellowish feathers on the adult's foreneck that give this species its common name.

[*Threskiornis spinicollis*, Lake Cowal, Australia. Photo: M.P. Kahl/DRK]

This photograph of a Spot-breasted Ibis at its nest was taken during the first study of the breeding of this little known species. The two chicks in the small nest can be seen to be less than six days old, since at this age the first blackish brown down is replaced by a second, thicker, white coat.

[*Bostrychia rara*. Photo: A.R. Devez/ CNRS-Ecotrop]

In Morocco, the prospects are not very encouraging either. In 1987, the construction of a dam for irrigation and the intense farming of the species' foraging areas led to the disappearance of the famous Aulouz colony, where 33 breeding pairs had raised 44 young that very same year. Since then only six colonies have survived on the Atlantic coast, with 78 breeding pairs and a total of around 220 birds, which for the moment are not receiving any effective protection, despite the fact that three of the colonies are within the proposed Oued Massa National Park. For several years, the WWF and other organizations, under the initiative of U. Hirsch, have been urging the Moroccan government to create this park. Of the proposed area of some 76,000 ha, about 30,000 would be turned into a strict nature reserve, which would include the coastal cliffs where the ibises breed and one of the most important wintering grounds. In wetter winters, such as those at the end of the 1980's, the Moroccan ibises did not move too far from their breeding grounds and survival levels were good. It is feared, however, that the dispersals carried out in drier winters will lead them, especially the young birds, to areas where pesticides are extensively used to combat the plagues of locusts, and this has already proved to have fatal consequences. Another problem has now arisen in this area with children and shepherds throwing stones to flush the ibises, even at the breeding colonies, in order to get a tip from foreign visitors who are keen to see the birds.

At present, the number of captive Northern Bald Ibises, more than 700, is far greater than the number remaining in the wild, and this may prove the saving of the species, if birds can be successfully reintroduced and the factors responsible for the decline removed. There is enough captive stock for several reintroduction programmes, but priority should go towards restoring the Moroccan populations which have disappeared recently, or reinforcing the colonies that are still occupied but in regression. Secondly, the species could be reintroduced to other areas within its presumed former range. Some preliminary experiments are already being carried out in Israel by Tel Aviv University, which possesses the largest captive population of over 100 individuals; this work is being conducted in conjunction with Frankfurt Zoo. Several ibises have been released after breeding, in the hope that initially they may remain in the vicinity of the enclosure and progressively adapt to a semi-natural, and eventually a natural life. Up to now results have been poor, but if successful, introductions may proceed in other suitable areas, such as Mount Carmel. Some well protected and climatically suitable areas of the Iberian Peninsula, such as the Cabo de Gata Natural Park, have also been proposed for the introduction of the species, due to the great similarity of these areas with the birds' native territory in Morocco. Such introductions will become increasingly likely, if the situation in Morocco continues to be precarious.

Another endangered species which is apparently on the verge of extinction is the Giant Ibis. Although it has apparently always been uncommon and local, it formerly inhabited vast areas of south-east Asia. However, it is thought to have become extinct in most of the regions where it still survived in the 1970's, perhaps only remaining in the Dong Thap Muoi, an inland delta of the Mekong in Viet Nam. Agricultural development and the frequent wars which have devastated the zone are regarded as the probable main causes of its regression. The wars have also hindered field work so that the status of the species is not at all well known.

The White-shouldered Ibis has a fairly similar range to that of the Giant Ibis, and it has therefore been affected by much the same problems. It is also found in parts of Borneo, with most sightings on the middle reaches of the Mahakam River in East Kalimantan. Although there are few records on the island, large tracts of apparently suitable habitat remain to be surveyed, and the sighting of a probable flock of 12 in 1989 suggests that the species may still be numerous in places. All of the recent records were from Borneo until June 1991, when a group of ICBP ornithologists, who were carrying out a survey in Nam Bai Cat Tien National Park, in southern Viet Nam, saw two White-shouldered Ibises feeding along a small forest creek, from which they flew to a dead tree, where a third individual joined them, and the birds displayed. The species is well known to the local people, who claimed to have seen up to six birds in the same area earlier in the year. Unfortunately, the species and these wetlands are threatened by major disturbance from local fishermen living within the park. The authorities have planned to relocate several thousand outside the park, but this has led to some serious fighting, for instance a shoot-out in 1991 which resulted in the deaths of a fisherman and a park guard. The species formerly occurred in Thailand, where it is

The Turkish town of
Birecik was, for many
years, home to the most
celebrated population of
the Northern Bald Ibis.
During the early 1970's,
simple activities, like
hanging out the washing,
in the houses adjoining
the colony caused the
adults to leave their
nests, which considerably
increased chick mortality;
thus, in 1972, when this
picture was taken, of 64
chicks hatched only nine
reached fledging. By
1989 only one wild bird
remained, and the
eastern population of the
species was considered
effectively extinct,
although birds continue to
breed in semi-captivity at
Birecik, where 17 chicks
were reared in 1991. In
the same year, a group of
38 birds left the
enclosures in late July,
and have never been
seen again. This, together
with recent sightings of
apparently wild birds in
south-west Arabia, allows
some hope for the future
of this population.

[Geronticus eremita,
Birecik, Turkey.
Photo: Udo Hirsch]

now considered extinct, and in Laos and Kampuchea, where
there are no recent records, although there has been virtually
no ornithological exploration in these countries in recent years.

The Black-faced Spoonbill has the the most restricted range
of any of the the spoonbills, and it is the only one which is at
present considered to be globally threatened. Confined to the
eastern coasts of Asia, it was apparently common over much
of its range in the past. It is now only known to breed on a few
small, rocky islands off the west coast of North Korea, while
there are three wintering localities in Hong Kong, Taiwan and
Viet Nam, and a few other sites where it has been seen on
migration. The estimated world population of this species,
based upon maximum winter counts at all the known localities,
is 288 birds. The breeding population in North Korea does not
exceed 30 individuals, which implies that there must be another
colony, as yet undiscovered, perhaps in eastern China.

It is thought that the main cause of the decline of this
species is the destruction of its habitat, especially through the
"reclamation" of intertidal mudflats for agriculture, and more
recently for aquaculture and industrialization. The Korean War
(1950-1953) must also have had a negative effect on the
species, for the bird stopped breeding in South Korea at this
time. Meanwhile, in Japan, where it had been a common winter
visitor, it became notably scarce in this same period, and in
recent years no more than five birds have been recorded in any
particular winter.

At present, the species is reasonably well protected in North
Korea, where the offshore breeding islands have been declared
a Protection Area, with restricted access. Nevertheless, several
threats remain, especially in its wintering grounds. The demand
for land to be used in industry is great in the wintering grounds
in Taiwan, while those in Viet Nam are being converted to
shrimp ponds, even though they are within a reserve backed
by the Ramsar Convention. In Hong Kong, disturbance by

fishermen and shellfish collectors often prevents the birds from
feeding at low water. On top of all this, with the continued
expansion of the human population in eastern Asia, pollution
is likely to become an important problem.

The situation of the Southern Bald Ibis is apparently less
serious for the moment, but it has undergone a pronounced
decline in the twentieth century. Its present population comprises some 5,000-8,000 individuals, which are confined to the
highlands of South Africa, Lesotho and Swaziland. Pressure
was especially intense at the beginning of this century, when
there was a notable expansion of Karoo vegetation following
severe overgrazing of the grasslands used by this species. Other
factors include predation by man of adults, chicks and eggs,
for food, feathers and medicinal use. The species is now fully
protected within South Africa and its total population seems to
have remained stable since 1970. The greatest fear for the future
is a spread in the use of pesticides, which had such detrimental
effects on the closely related Northern Bald Ibis. In the case of
the Southern Bald Ibis, a captive breeding programme has also
been started, and this has already had success at Pretoria Zoo.

In general, the same causes that have led several species to
a situation where they are globally threatened are also responsible
for the threats that face numerous populations of other species
on a local or regional level. As ibises and spoonbills depend on
certain habitats, in particular wetlands, for breeding, feeding and
resting, they are particulary vulnerable to the massive transformations which have been carried out in these areas in the last
few decades. These include the alteration or complete disappearance of continental wetlands, their conversion into grazing or
agricultural lands, the proliferation of water weeds, which reduce
the area suitable for feeding, the canalization of water ways and
the creation of dams. On the coast, major damage has been caused
by the clearing or contamination of mangroves, the transformation of the habitat due to changes in the water cycle, the creation

The Madagascar Crested Ibis is currently considered near-threatened; it is intensively hunted for food and its forest habitats are rapidly disappearing. However, it is still reasonably widespread and shows a certain degree of adaptability to slightly degraded habitats. This well grown chick already shows the characteristic plumage of the species, most notably the white wings contrasting markedly with the rufous body; the crest, however, is still very short.

[*Lophotibis cristata cristata*, Madagascar. Photo: O. Langrand/ Bruce Coleman]

of harbours for yachting and an increase in disturbance produced by tourism, overfishing and so on.

In the *llanos* of Venezuela, for example, the important Scarlet Ibis population is in a state of regression, and in recent years many nesting grounds have been abandoned. In 1983, a census revealed 65,439 pairs at 22 colonies, whilst in the following year the number of colonies had crashed to seven with only 42,236 pairs. Seemingly, the desertion of some sites is related to the high water level, brought about by the construction of dykes which retain the water in the dry season. The construction of these dykes and drainage canals is constantly on the increase, and this could well have serious effects on the nesting grounds of the ibises and other waterbirds. The Scarlet Ibis constitutes a clear example of a species which, although not currently threatened, and still present in high numbers, is undoubtedly vulnerable due to its extensive loss of habitat, particularly given its patchy distribution and colonial tendencies, which also make it more susceptible to the increase in any kind of disturbance by man.

Poisoning by toxic products used in agriculture or dumping in wetlands is nowadays another of the main threats facing all

waterbirds. As they are predators situated at the top of a food chain, they accumulate persistent types of toxic matter previously ingested by their prey. The havoc that can be wreaked by pesticides has already been seen clearly in the case of the Northern Bald Ibis, but they are also affecting many other species that are not globally threatened. These include the White-faced Ibis, which has declined in the USA apparently for this reason. Large numbers of clutches have been lost due to high concentrations of pollutants, which can cause the thinning of eggshells, or the death of chicks.

Hunting has also had significant effects (see Relationship with Man), as have other forms of direct persecution, such as the collection or destruction of eggs and chicks, or the devastation of nests or even colonies, usually for food, to expand collections or on the grounds that the birds are pests. Some species are more vulnerable than others to human presence, and some will completely desert a colony at the slightest disturbance.

Occasionally, natural causes can be added to the numerous human factors that have negative effects on populations. In the 1970's, there were around 20,000 pairs of Scarlet Ibis nesting between the mouths of the Amazon and the Orinoco, of which 13,500 were in Surinam; by 1980, two colonies had disappeared and only one remained with 4000 pairs. The cause of this decrease was probably natural: the mangroves where these colonies were located had been modified by erosion or by natural succession, and were no longer suitable for nesting. As mangroves tend to operate in cycles, it is to be hoped that the situation will once again be favourable for the birds, once the young mangroves have built up adequate cover.

In spite of all the above cases, several species appear to be in good health and some even seem to be expanding in places. One example is the American White Ibis, which appears to be increasing its range in Venezuela, where it is competing with the Scarlet Ibis. The Glossy Ibis is currently in full expansion in North America, where it must have arrived around 1880, whilst in Europe it is considered endangered and in other areas, such as India, it is in decline.

This Black-faced Spoonbill, photographed in East Berlin Zoo, is one of the few individuals of this species currently held in captivity. The only threatened spoonbill and one of the most endangered of the Threskiornithidae, its total population numbered only 288 birds in 1991.

[*Platalea minor*, East Berlin Zoo, Germany. Photo: Josep del Hoyo]

General Bibliography

Archibald *et al.* (1980), Bennett *et al.* (1975), Bildstein (1990b), Boer & Van Brink (1982), Campbell *et al.* (1986), Coulter, Bryan *et al.* (1991), Eisenmann *et al.* (1984), Elliott (1877), Gysels (1968), Kushlan (1977f, 1981), Luthin (1983d, 1984a, 1984b), Ogden (1985a, 1985b), Olson (1978, 1981b), Rutgers & Norris (1970), Sibley & Ahlquist (1990), Sibley & Monroe (1990), Soothill & Soothill (1982), Sprunt *et al.* (1978), Steinbacher (1979), Vanden Berge (1970), Verheyen (1959, 1960c).

ssp *aethiopicus*

ssp *abbotti*

1

2

3

4

5

6

7

8

9

10

ssp *akleyorum*

11

ssp *bocagei*

12

13

ssp *olivacea*

14

Subfamily THRESKIORNITHINAE

Genus *THRESKIORNIS* G. R. Gray, 1842

1. **Sacred Ibis**

Threskiornis aethiopicus

French: Ibis sacré **German**: Heiliger Ibis **Spanish**: Ibis Sagrado
Other common names: Madagascar (Sacred) Ibis (*bernieri*); Aldabra (Sacred) Ibis (*abbotti*)

Taxonomy. *Tantalus aethiopicus* Latham, 1790, "Aethiopia" = ? Egypt.
Forms superspecies with *T. melanocephalus* and *T. molucca*; these two sometimes regarded as races of *T. aethiopicus*. Races *bernieri* and *abbotti* very similar, perhaps better considered single form (*bernieri* has priority), that some regard as distinct species. Three subspecies normally recognized.
Subspecies and Distribution.
T. a. aethiopicus (Latham, 1790) - Africa S of Sahara, SE Iraq; formerly Egypt.
T. a. bernieri (Bonaparte, 1855) - Madagascar.
T. a. abbotti (Ridgway, 1893) - Aldabra I.

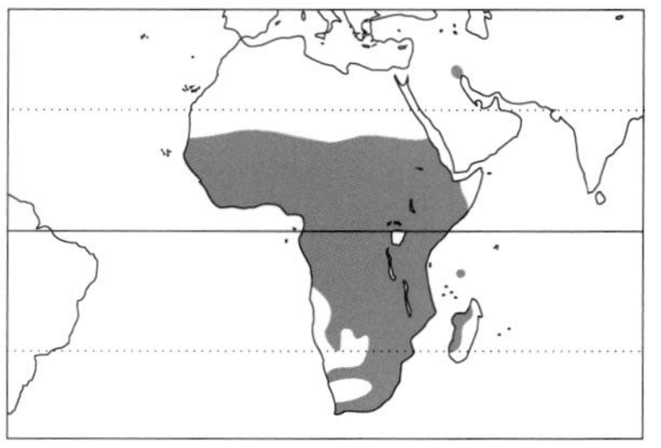

Descriptive notes. 65-89 cm; c. 1500 g; wingspan 112-124 cm. Thickest-billed of *Threskiornis*. Primaries and secondaries tipped black. In breeding plumage, separated from congeners by bare skin reaching base of neck, where loose sac of skin sometimes hangs; black ornamental plumes often more abundant and shaggier than in *T. molucca*. Immature has tertials blackish brown, not lacy; head and neck feathered, black mottled and streaked white. Races *bernieri* and *abbotti* more slender-billed, lack black trailing edge to wings, and have white (*bernieri*) and bluish (*abbotti*) irides.
Habitat. Very varied; mainly margins of inland freshwater wetlands, sewage works, grasslands, cultivated fields, coastal lagoons, intertidal areas and offshore islands. Also in human environments, like farmyards, abattoirs and dumps on outskirts of towns. Sometimes far from water, particularly in recently burnt areas.
Food and Feeding. Mainly insects including grasshoppers, locusts, crickets and aquatic beetles; also crustaceans, worms, molluscs, fish, frogs, lizards, and small mammals; sometimes eggs of birds and crocodiles, nestling birds, carrion, offal and seeds; in some areas visits rubbish dumps to feed on animal and vegetable refuse. Usually feeds during day in groups of 2-20 birds, occasionally up to 300; walks slowly, taking live prey by pecking or probing in mud or soft earth.
Breeding. Often starts during or shortly after rains, but in flooded areas also lays in dry season. Colonies of 50-2000 pairs, often with other Ciconiiformes. Nests in trees or bushes, or on bare ground on rocky islands; nest is large platform of sticks and branches, lined with leaves and grass. Usually 2-3 eggs (2-5); incubation 28-29 days; chicks have black down on head and neck, white on rest of body; fledging 35-40 days. Oldest ringed bird over 21 years old. Breeding success often very low, with less than 1 chick per nest fledging.
Movements. Nomadic or migratory. Movements of several hundred kilometres to breed during rains; birds N of equator move northwards, those S of equator southwards, both returning at end of rains or early in dry season. Birds captured in Angola and Zambia had been ringed 1000-1500 to S in South Africa. Little information available on Iraqi population; present all year round, though not necessarily sedentary; small numbers winter in Iran. Stragglers recorded in Kuwait and N Yemen.
Status and Conservation. Not globally threatened. Widespread and common to very common in Africa, with colonies of up to 2000 pairs. Fairly common in S Iraq in 1970's; abundant in Egypt in past, e.g. 1,500,000 birds entombed in catacombs at Saqqara; apparently common until early 19th century, but almost completely disappeared by 1850. Race *bernieri* uncommon, colonies probably raided. Race *abbotti* has very small population, estimated at 150-200 birds in 1968; has probably declined due to hunting and disturbance by temporary workers on Aldabra; considered Rare in Red Data Book (1978/79); effective legal protection and management have improved breeding success recently, with numbers reaching support level. CITES III in Ghana.
Bibliography. Altenburg & van der Kamp (1989), Barlow (1933), Becher (1967), Benson (1967), Benson & Penny (1971), Bolster (1931), Britton (1980), Brown & Britton (1980), Brown *et al.* (1982), Clark, R.A. (1979a, 1979b, 1979c), Clark & Clark (1979), Clay (1976), Comfort (1962), Cooke *et al.* (1978), Cramp & Simmons (1977), Cunningham-van Someren (1970), Cuvier (1804), Dowsett (1966a, 1969), Evans *et al.* (1981), Friendly (1973), Gaymer (1966), Gliddon (1850), Goodman (1988, 1989), Holyoak (1970), King (1978/79), Klug & Boswall (1970), Kushlan (1978), Langrand (1990), Lowe & Richards (1991), Lowe *et al.* (1985), Mackworth-Praed & Grant (1957-1973), Maclean (1985), Manry (1978a, 1978b), Milon *et al.* (1973), de Naurois (1966b), Nicoll (1906a, 1906b), Olson (1985d), Parsons (1977), Pennycuick (1972b), Pinto (1983), Rand (1936), Risdon (1971), Skead (1967), Smith (1943), Snow (1978), Stoddard (1971), Tandan (1976), Urban (1974a, 1974b).

2. **Black-headed Ibis**

Threskiornis melanocephalus

French: Ibis à tête noire **German**: Schwarzhalsibis **Spanish**: Ibis Oriental
Other common names: White/Oriental Ibis, Oriental/Indian/Asian White Ibis, Oriental/Indian Black-necked Ibis

Taxonomy. *Tantalus melanocephalus* Latham, 1790, India.
Forms superspecies with *T. aethiopicus* and *T. molucca*; sometimes considered race of *T. aethiopicus*. Monotypic.
Distribution. Breeds from Pakistan and Nepal through India to Sri Lanka; NE China; Viet Nam; Java and possibly Sumatra. Winters in S China, Burma, Thailand, Sumatra and Philippines. Formerly more widespread in E Asia.
Descriptive notes. 65-76 cm. Ornamental feathers grey, not black. Very little black on tip of primaries, and none on secondaries. Non-breeding adult largely lacks grey scapulars and neck

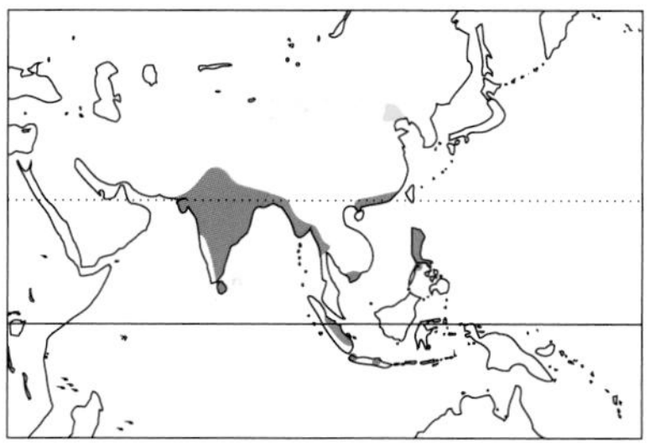

plumes. Immature has blackish, feathered head and neck; whitish on foreneck; bare skin of underwing black instead of red.
Habitat. Open country in marshes, swamps, flooded areas, margins of rivers and lakes, paddyfields and fallow land; also wet grasslands; less often intertidal mudflats, mangroves and brackish lagoons. Nests in wetlands; sometimes close to human dwellings.
Food and Feeding. Diet includes frogs, tadpoles, snails, adults and larvae of insects, and worms; also fish and crustaceans, probably more commonly when feeding in coastal areas; occasionally plant matter. Usually feeds in medium-sized to large groups; probes with bill in mud or shallow water; often submerges whole head and neck, when wading in shallow water; sometimes associates with grazing buffalo, possibly taking insects they flush.
Breeding. Jun-Oct in N India, Nov-Mar in S India and Sri Lanka; season varies depending on water conditions after onset of monsoon. Colonial, often with other Ciconiiformes and cormorants. Nest is small cupped platform of sticks, usually unlined; situated in trees or shrubs over or near water. Usually 3 eggs (2-4); incubation 23-25 days; chicks have black down on head, white on body; fledging c. 40 days. Heavy predation by crows, raptors and man reported at several colonies.
Movements. Throughout Indian Subcontinent, sedentary, with frequent nomadic movements related to water conditions; population of E China migrates in winter to SE China, occasionally to Taiwan. Rare winter visitor to Japan, with 77 records between 1874 and 1985; likewise rare S to Philippines. Commonly flies in single file or V-formation.
Status and Conservation. Not globally threatened. Declining in many areas due to increased pressure on habitat from growing human population; still numerous in places, e.g. Bharatpur, with 389 nests in 1984. Scarce in Pakistan, and now confined to lower Sind, where largest flock recently 100 birds in 1965. Censuses in Jan 1991 gave 2417 in India, 685 in Sri Lanka, 252 in Bangladesh and 730 in Burma. Formerly common in Thailand where bred, but now uncommon winter visitor. Few recent records in Malaysia, where formerly resident. Apparently abundant in past in Viet Nam, where still breeds at 4+ colonies, including 1500-2000 breeding birds at Dam Doi, 800-1000 at Bac Lieu and 500-600 at Cai Nuoc. Formerly numerous colonies in Java; now rare and local, still breeding at Brantas Delta (E Java). Sumatra reckoned to hold c. 2000 birds, but breeding not proved; 607 at Banyuasin Peninsula in 1985. Highly vulnerable to drainage and agricultural conversion, though commonly uses rice paddies; also affected by hunting and pesticide poisoning.
Bibliography. Ali & Ripley (1978), Austin & Kuroda (1953), Bhutia (1985), Brazil (1991), Cheng Tso-hsin (1987), Clay (1976), Dickinson *et al.* (1991), Dyegtyariov *et al.* (1990), Etchécopar & Hüe (1978), He (1979, 1987), Henry (1971), Holyoak (1970), Hoogerwerf (1935b, 1937), Humphrey & Bain (1990), Inskipp & Inskipp (1985), Iskander (1985), Itoh (1986), Karpowicz (1985), Khan (1984, 1987), Lowe & Richards (1991), Luthin (1984b), van Marle & Voous (1988), Medway & Wells (1976), Menon *et al.* (1979), Nisbet (1968), Roberts (1991), Round *et al.* (1988), de Schauensee (1984), Scott (1989), Sichiri (1980), Silvius & Verheugt (1989), Silvius *et al.* (1985, 1986), Smythies (1986), Snow (1978), Tandan (1976), Treesucon & Round (1990), Vo Quy (1975), von Wetten (1985), White & Bruce (1986).

3. **Australian White Ibis**

Threskiornis molucca

French: Ibis à cou noir **German**: Australischer Ibis **Spanish**: Ibis Moluqueño
Other common names: Australian White/Black-necked/Sacred Ibis

Taxonomy. *Ibis molucca* Cuvier, 1829, Moluccas.
Forms superspecies with *T. aethiopicus* and *T. melanocephalus*; sometimes considered race of *T. aethiopicus*. Population of Australia and S New Guinea has been separated in race *strictipennis*, but recent studies show it to be identical to birds from Moluccas, and indicate that the two should be synonymized. Validity of race *pygmaeus* questioned, but recent examination of specimens shows much smaller size than that to be expected from clinal variation. Two subspecies normally recognized.
Subspecies and Distribution.
T. m. molucca (Cuvier, 1829) - Australia through New Guinea to S Moluccas and E Lesser Sundas.
T. m. pygmaeus Mayr, 1931 - Rennell I and Bellona I (Solomon Is).

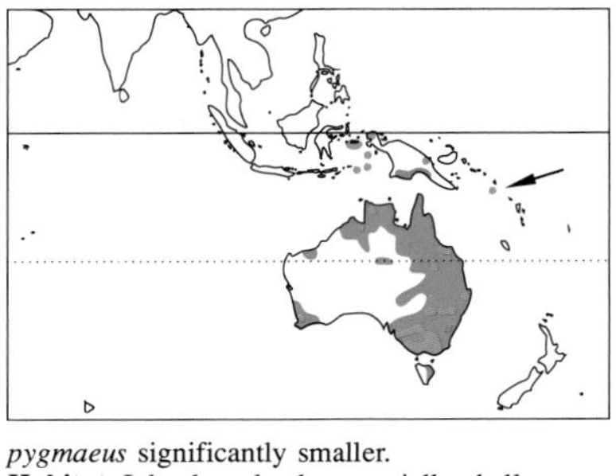

Descriptive notes. 63-76 cm; 1400-2500 g, female lighter; wingspan 110-125 cm. Male generally larger, with longer bill, as in most ibises. Narrow pinkish transversal nuchal tracts. Bill thinner and legs less intensely black than congeners; in breeding plumage easily separated from *T. aethiopicus* by extensive feathering up neck, with ornamental plumes on foreneck; black tips to primaries only. Non-breeding adult has tertials dull grey, less lacy, and lacks neck plumes; bare skin of underwing pink instead of red. Immature totally feathered on head and neck, variably dark; tertials greyish brown, not lacy. Race *pygmaeus* significantly smaller.
Habitat. Inland wetlands, especially shallow swamps with abundant vegetation, and floodplains; sheltered marine habitats, especially tidal mudflats, mangrove swamps, salt-pans and coastal lagoons; also grasslands, cultivation, open areas and recently burnt land, often far from wetlands. Reservoirs, farm ponds and sewage works widely used; also uses large gardens, rubbish dumps, abattoirs and other humanized areas. Breeds in reedbeds, shrubs or trees in wide variety of wetlands, occasionally in urban areas.
Food and Feeding. Diet very variable, depending on habitat. Main prey includes frogs, fish (*Gambusia*, *Perca*, *Arenigobius*, *Clinus*), freshwater crayfish (*Cherax*), mussels, crabs, shrimps, earthworms, crickets, grasshoppers and beetles; occasionally snakes and mice; also feeds on carrion. Usually forages in flocks of up to 40 birds, occasionally up to 200; on occasions solitary. Forages by walking slowly, probing in soft substrate or pecking at surface.
Breeding. Season very variable according to prevailing water conditions. Usually forms colonies of up to 20,000 pairs, sometimes with other Ciconiiformes; occasionally in single pairs. Nest is

On following pages: 4. Straw-necked Ibis (*Threskiornis spinicollis*); 5. Indian Black Ibis (*Pseudibis papillosa*); 6. White-shouldered Ibis (*Pseudibis davisoni*); 7. Giant Ibis (*Pseudibis gigantea*); 8. Northern Bald Ibis (*Geronticus eremita*); 9. Southern Bald Ibis (*Geronticus calvus*); 10. Japanese Crested Ibis (*Nipponia nippon*); 11. Olive Ibis (*Bostrychia olivacea*); 12. Spot-breasted Ibis (*Bostrychia rara*); 13. Hadada Ibis (*Bostrychia hagedash*); 14. Wattled Ibis (*Bostrychia carunculata*).

compact cup of sticks and twigs, lined with leaves and other soft materials; where breeds in swamps, nest built of reeds. 1-4 eggs, with clutches of 5-6 eggs recorded, but possibly laid by 2 females; incubation 20-23 days; chicks have blackish brown down on head and neck, white on body; leave nest at 30-48 days. Success varies annually: in study of 2025 breeding attempts, 51% failed; 1·73 young fledged per successful nest.
Movements. Most adults sedentary, although throughout range some irregular, nomadic movements occur, sometimes over long distances, and usually related to availability of water. Population of SW Australia partially migratory, apparently moving N in winter, returning S in summer. Young birds disperse widely. Irregular visitor to Tasmania and vagrant to New Zealand. Some movement recorded between NE Australia and New Guinea, and flocks of up to 500 birds have been recorded crossing Torres Strait.
Status and Conservation. Not globally threatened. Common in Australia, frequently forming large gatherings; largest colonies in S New South Wales and Victoria, occasionally with over 20,000 pairs. Population size and range in Australia have both apparently increased since European colonization: conversion of woodland for farming has increased available foraging grounds; adapts well to artificial habitats and even nests in cities. Sparse and very uncommon breeder in W and N New Guinea, locally common visitor to S; up to 37,000 birds recorded in Bensbach area, Papua New Guinea; ground and air surveys suggested minimum 45,000 birds in SE Irian Jaya in 1983, where colonies of c. 10,000 birds discovered at Wasur/Rawa Biru Reserve in 1988, but some disturbance from hunting. In Moluccas not uncommon on Seram, and recorded on other islands, but status uncertain.
Bibliography. Beehler *et al.* (1986), Bekle (1982), Beruldsen (1980), Carrick (1959, 1962), Clay (1976), Coates (1985), Cowling (1974), Cowling & Lowe (1980), Davis (1985a), Falla (1958), Fjeldså (1985c), Green (1959a), Hobbs (1957a), Holyoak (1970), Karpowicz (1985), Lalas (1974), LeSouef (1917), Lowe (1981, 1984), Lowe & Richards (1991), Marchant & Higgins (1990), Mees (1982), Morris, A.K. (1973), Morris, F.T. (1978), Pringle (1985), Purchase (1976), Schodde & Tidemann (1988), Scott (1989), Sharland (1957b), Silvius & Verheugt (1989), Slater (1987), Snow (1978), Tandan (1976), Vestjens (1973), White & Bruce (1986), Williams, M.J. (1985a).

4. Straw-necked Ibis

Threskiornis spinicollis

French: Ibis d'Australie **German**: Stachelibis **Spanish**: Ibis Tornasol

Taxonomy. *Ibis spinicollis* Jameson, 1835, Murray River, New South Wales.
Often placed in monospecific genus *Carphibis*. Said to have hybridized with *T. aethiopicus*, but no details given. Monotypic.
Distribution. Australia; also non-breeding visitor to southern parts of New Guinea; occasional visitor to Tasmania and several islands of Bass Strait.

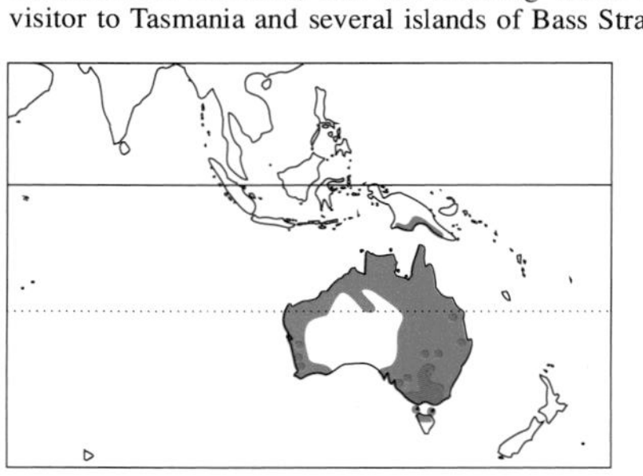

Descriptive notes. 59-76 cm; 1100-1500 g; wingspan 100-120 cm. Usually unmistakable, with highly iridiscent plumage, but can appear fairly uniform dirty dark brown in indifferent light. Male larger, with longer bill. No seasonal variation. Immature dark brown, less barred; head and neck feathered dark brown.
Habitat. Pastures, cultivation, irrigation areas, open forests and dry grasslands, often far from wetlands; also wetlands, especially shallow swamps or shallow parts of lakes and watercourses, and temporary floodwaters; rarely in coastal and saline habitats. Enters humanized areas including gardens, farms, rubbish dumps and abattoirs. Nests in wetlands, in reedbeds, shrubs and trees, or even on ground.
Food and Feeding. Diet consists mainly of insects (beetles, crickets, grasshoppers, caterpillars), spiders, freshwater crayfish (*Cherax*), snails, frogs and fish; occasionally toads (*Bufo marinus*), snakes, mice and rats; also takes human refuse. Forages in flocks of up to 200 birds; probes into soil, mud, crevices, vegetation or shallow water.
Breeding. Season very variable, much influenced by water conditions; more fixed in S, in Aug-Dec; recorded in all months in C and N. Breeds in colonies, often of several thousand pairs. Nest is shallow cup of sticks, reeds and rushes, sometimes lined with soft vegetation. 2-5 eggs; incubation c. 3½ weeks; chicks have blackish down, darker on head and neck.
Movements. Partially migratory: some birds sedentary; others make seasonal or irregular movements as water conditions vary. Seasonal migrations recorded from SE and N Australia, and from coast and inland wetlands in CE Australia; also across Torres Strait between NE Australia and S New Guinea. Vagrant to Norfolk I and Lord Howe I. Usually flies in line or in V-formation; at great heights during long distance movements.
Status and Conservation. Not globally threatened. Most widespread and abundant ibis in Australia, with several colonies of 10,000's; up to 150,000 nests at Bool Lagoon, South Australia, in 1963; and mixed colony with *T. molucca* at Narran L, New South Wales, of 400,000 pairs (both species) in 1983. Numbers in colonies fluctuate from year to year. Range in Australia has increased, due to conversion of forest to pastures, cultivation and irrigation schemes, but some natural wetlands formerly used for breeding destroyed or altered, while flood-mitigation works threaten frequent use of temporary waters. Common non-breeding visitor to S New Guinea, where several thousand birds regularly counted.
Bibliography. Beehler *et al.* (1986), Beruldsen (1980), Carrick (1959, 1962), Coates (1985), Cowling (1974), Cowling & Lowe (1980), Ellis (1958), Fjeldså (1985c), Green (1959b), Haffenden (1981), Hobbs (1957a, 1958b), Holyoak (1970), Hoogerwerf (1964), Karpowicz (1985), Lalas (1974), LeSouef (1917), Lowe (1981), Marchant & Higgins (1990), McKilligan (1975), Pringle (1985), Rose (1973), Schodde & Tidemann (1988), Schulz (1989), Scott (1989), Silvius & Verheugt (1989), Slater (1987), Stumpf (1978), Waterman *et al.* (1971).

Genus *PSEUDIBIS* Hodgson, 1844

5. Indian Black Ibis

Pseudibis papillosa

French: Ibis noir **German**: Warzenibis **Spanish**: Ibis Verrucoso
Other common names: Black/Red-naped Ibis

Taxonomy. *Ibis papillosa* Temminck, 1824, India and Ceylon.
Forms superspecies with *P. davisoni*, which is often considered race of present species. Monotypic.
Distribution. Pakistan, Nepal and India, southwards to Mysore and eastwards to Assam; perhaps also in Arakan (W Burma).

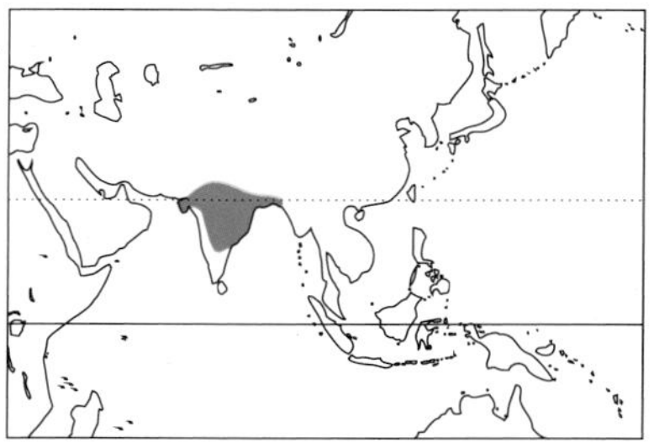

Descriptive notes. 60-68 cm; wingspan 90-115 cm. Crown and nape covered in bright red warts. White patch near shoulder of wing not always visible. Immature generally dull matt brown; has head feathered.
Habitat. Dry grassy areas, meadows, cultivated or fallow land and fields of stubble, often far from wetlands; also sandy banks of rivers and swamps, though less dependent on water than sympatric *Threskiornis melanocephalus*. Usually nests in tall trees, often at considerable distance from water.
Food and Feeding. Diet includes frogs, fish, earthworms, adults and larvae of beetles and other insects; also scorpions, crustaceans, lizards and small snakes; occasionally takes seeds, perhaps more frequently than other ibises, as adaptation to drier areas. Usually feeds in small parties of up to 10 birds, occasionally more; probes into substrate or picks up items from surface.
Breeding. Mar-Oct in N India, later further S, though season variable; in Nepal nest building recorded in Jan. Solitary; rarely in small colonies of up to 5 nests in same tree. Nest is large platform of twigs, lined with straw, built on palm tree or other leafy tree; often takes over disused nests of raptors. Usually 2-3 eggs (2-4); incubation 25-27 days.
Movements. Sedentary. Some nomadic movements related to rainfall; in recent times, rare visitor to SE Pakistan, mainly during monsoon season.
Status and Conservation. Not globally threatened. Still locally common in India and S Nepal, where censuses yielded respectively 654 and 134 birds in Jan 1990, and 1360 and 80 in Jan 1991. In India most common in Gujarat, Maharashtra and Orissa; in Jan 1987, 200 birds at Chandpata L, Madhya Pradesh, and 250 in wetlands of C and E Saurashtra, Gujarat. In Nepal flocks of up to 40 birds still occur at Chitwan National Park, Kosi Barrage and Kosi Tappu Reserve. In Pakistan common in 1920's with large flocks recorded, but now only irregular visitor, occurring mainly during monsoon. Appears to have been severely affected by schemes of wetland conversion and agricultural development.
Bibliography. Ali & Ripley (1978), Chavda (1988), Holyoak (1970), Inskipp & Inskipp (1985), Karpowicz (1985), Lathigara (1989), Luthin (1984b, 1987b), Roberts (1991), Salimkumar (1982), Salimkumar & Soni (1984), Scott (1989), Smythies (1986), Soni *et al.* (1989), Wennrich (1982e).

6. White-shouldered Ibis

Pseudibis davisoni

French: Ibis de Davison **German**: Weißschultesibis **Spanish**: Ibis de Davison
Other common names: Davison's Ibis

Taxonomy. *Geronticus Davisoni* Hume, 1875, Pakchan estuary, Tenasserim.
Often considered race of *P. papillosa*, with which forms superspecies. Monotypic.
Distribution. Once widespread from Burma to SW China and S to Indochina and Borneo, range now much reduced; apparently restricted to S Viet Nam and Borneo, though also suspected to occur in Kampuchea.

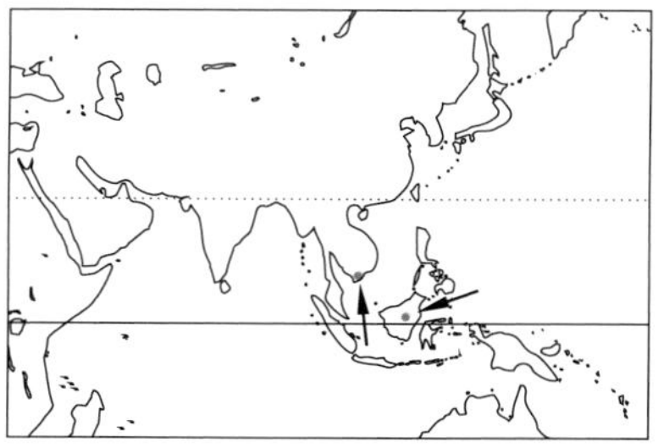

Descriptive notes. 60-80 cm. White patch on lesser wing-coverts very often not visible on standing bird. Slightly larger than very similar *P. papillosa*, with different head pattern. Immature has dull brown plumage; head feathered.
Habitat. Marshes, seasonally flooded areas, paddyfields and other cultivation, grasslands and edges of lakes and large rivers; recent sightings in Borneo associated with riverine forests.
Food and Feeding. Very little known. Old records indicate main food includes grasshoppers, cicadas and grain. Feeds singly, in pairs or in family groups.
Breeding. Solitary. Nest built in trees, at height of 5-10 m above ground. 2-4 eggs. No other information available about breeding habits, although probably very similar to those of closely related *P. papillosa*.
Movements. Presumably sedentary.
Status and Conservation. VULNERABLE. Probably better considered Endangered, given paucity of records in last few decades. Several recent sightings in Borneo, mainly along middle reaches of R Mahakam, E Kalimantan, where probable flock of 12 reported in 1989. In SE Asia no recent authenticated records until June 1991, when 3 birds seen in Nam Bai Cat Tien National Park, Viet Nam (see page 489). In Thailand, where formerly occurred in central plains, peninsula and once extensive marshes of far north, no confirmed records since 1937, and now considered extinct. Species never considered abundant; drainage and conversion of wetlands for agriculture on unrestrained scale throughout SE Asia must have had serious effects; succession of prolonged wars in region also likely to have contributed to decline. Nonetheless, shy nature of species and limited amount of survey work carried out in much of range suggest might be more common than is thought.
Bibliography. Archibald *et al.* (1980), Bain & Humphrey (1980), Cheng Tso-hsin (1987), Collar & Andrew (1988), Deignan (1945), Delacour (1928, 1929a), Delacour & Jabouille (1931), Eames (1991), Etchécopar & Hüe (1978), Holmes (1990a, 1991), Holmes & Burton (1987), Holyoak (1970), Humphrey & Bain (1990), Karpowicz (1985), King (1978/79), Luthin (1983d, 1984b, 1988), Medway & Wells (1976), Petersen (1991), Riley (1938), Round (1988), Round *et al.* (1988), de Schauensee (1946, 1984), Scott (1989), Silvius & Verheugt (1989), Smythies (1981, 1986), Treesucon & Round (1990), Vo Quy (1975, 1990), Wells (1985).

7. Giant Ibis

Pseudibis gigantea

French: Ibis géant **German**: Riesenibis **Spanish**: Ibis Gigante

Taxonomy. *Ibis gigantea* Oustalet, 1877, Mekong River, Cambodia.
Sometimes placed in monospecific genus *Thaumatibis*. Monotypic.

Distribution. Once widespread in Indochina, range now much reduced; apparently restricted to S Viet Nam, though also suspected to occur in Kampuchea.

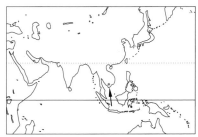

Descriptive notes. 104 cm. Unmistakable due to large size. Upper wing-coverts mainly silvery grey, contrasting with darker body and flight-feathers. Narrow black stripes across nape.

Habitat. Lowlands, occurring in lakes, swamps, seasonally flooded marshes, paddy-fields, open wooded plains, humid clearings and pools in deep forest. Said to congregate at permanent water holes during droughts.

Food and Feeding. Almost nothing known. One stomach contained crabs. Thought to feed in pairs or small flocks.

Breeding. No information available.

Movements. Presumably sedentary; records from peninsular Thailand in late 19th and early 20th centuries may have referred to migrants or vagrants.

Status and Conservation. ENDANGERED. Probably close to extinction. Formerly bred in C and SE Thailand, Kampuchea, S Laos and S Viet Nam, but seems always to have been uncommon and local throughout range; flocks of up to 40 birds in Kampuchea in 1920's. Recently seen at Dong Thap Muoi, inner delta of Mekong in Viet Nam, possibly last remaining site where species survives. In 1964 recorded on Kampuchea-Laos border and might still survive in wetlands around Tonle Sap (Kampuchea), largest lake in Indochina, where continued warfare has prevented surveys. Extinct in Thailand, with last confirmed record in 1913. Loss of wetlands probably one of main causes of decline: conversion for agriculture of central valley of Chao Phraya thought to have been instrumental in extirpation from Thailand. Large size probably makes it very vulnerable to hunting, and almost continuous war throughout much of range likely to have had negative effects.

Bibliography. Archibald *et al.* (1980), Bain & Humphrey (1980), Bangs & van Tyne (1931), Collar & Andrew (1988), Delacour (1928, 1929a), Delacour & Greenway (1940), Delacour & Jabouille (1931), Fisher *et al.* (1969), Holyoak (1970), Humphrey & Bain (1990), Karpowicz (1985), King (1978/79), Luthin (1983d, 1987b, 1988), Manry (1986), Medway & Wells (1976), Riley (1938), Round (1988), Round *et al.* (1988), Scott (1989), Treesucon & Round (1990), Vincent (1966), Vo Quy (1975, 1990), Wells (1985).

Genus *GERONTICUS* Wagler, 1832

8. **Northern Bald Ibis**

Geronticus eremita

French: Ibis chauve　　　**German**: Waldrapp　　　**Spanish**: Ibis Eremita
Other common names: Waldrapp/Hermit/Bald Ibis, Waldrapp

Taxonomy. *Upupa Eremita* Linnaeus, 1758, Switzerland.
Forms superspecies with *G. calvus*. Monotypic.

Distribution. Morocco and Algeria, S to W Sahara; apparently now breeds only in Morocco. Distribution of eastern population uncertain: until recently bred in SE Turkey, wintering in Arabia, Ethiopia and N Somalia, but extinct since 1989; recent records in SW Arabia and Yemen suggest existence of unknown colonies. Formerly more widespread in Near and Middle East; also in Alps, S Europe and Egypt.

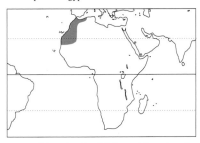

Descriptive notes. 70-80 cm; wingspan 125-135 cm. Bill can be deeper red. Differs from *G. calvus* in pattern and colour of face, and patent crest. Immature duller, less glossy, lacks coppery wing patch; feathered head and neck appear greyish, with less elongated nape feathers.

Habitat. Arid and semi-arid plains and plateaux with rocky escarpments; also cultivated fields, high altitude meadows and pastures. Nests and roosts in cliffs, adjacent to watercourses or along the sea. Sometimes in association with man, especially in past, nesting on top of old buildings like castles, walls and towers.

Food and Feeding. Mainly grasshoppers, locusts, crickets, beetles (adults and larvae) and small reptiles; also earwigs, ants and their eggs, caterpillars, woodlice, spiders, scorpions, snails, earthworms, tadpoles, frogs and fish; occasionally small mammals, nestling birds and vegetable matter, including rhizomes of aquatic plants, berries and young shoots. Usually feeds in small, loose flocks; pecks at ground, or probes into cracks and fissures, under stones and in tufts of vegetation, or into ground on sandy areas or on soft earth.

Breeding. Starts mid-Feb, laying in Mar-Apr. Colonies of 3-40 pairs, occasionally more in past; single pairs may well be last members of dying colony. Nest is loose platform of branches lined with grass and straw; situated in cliff, on ledge or in cave. Usually 2-4 eggs (1-6); incubation 24-28 days; chicks have greyish brown down above, paler below; fledging 43-47 days. Sexual maturity at 3 years, though does not usually breed until 6 years old; survival estimated at c. 25 years. In favourable years, breeding success of 2·5 young/nest recorded; in very dry years, no breeding may take place at all in some colonies.

Movements. E population migratory; colonies vacated late Jun or early Jul, but emigration rather later; wintering areas not well known, but largely in NE Africa, thought to be chiefly in highlands of Ethiopia. W population dispersive and erratic, generally moving S after breeding, but most birds winter in Morocco; young birds tend to move further, and especially in dry years can reach distant areas, e.g. Mauritania, and even across Sahara, to Mali.

Status and Conservation. ENDANGERED. CITES I. Formerly bred in Switzerland, Austria and Hungary, but disappeared from Europe by end of 17th century, perhaps due to climatic changes and collection of chicks for food. By early 20th century, species restricted to single populations in Asia Minor and NW Africa. E population had at least 5 colonies, but only 1 in recent years, at Birecik (Turkey): c. 3000 pairs in 1890, slumped to 530 pairs in 1953, 65 in 1964, 23 in 1973 and only 1 bird in 1989; main causes of decline were intensive use of pesticides and human disturbance. W population, with more, but smaller colonies, also declined markedly, from c. 1000 pairs in 1930's, to 198 pairs in 13 colonies in Morocco, and 8-12 pairs in 1 colony in Algeria in 1975; in 1990 only 6 colonies remained in Morocco, with 78 pairs and total population estimated

at c. 220 birds; habitat conversion for agriculture and direct persecution appear as main reasons for decline, but parallel slump in Asia and earlier extinction in Europe suggest undetermined natural factors may be responsible for declines, with human pressure exacerbating situation. Effective protection essential, with creation of long-awaited Oued Massa National Park (S Morocco) which would encompass 3 breeding colonies and also wintering habitat. Captive breeding readily achieved; could be important in recovery of surviving populations and for reintroductions, but so far unsuccessful in Turkey (see pages 485, 489). Recent records of wild birds indicate that unknown colonies exist: in Mar-Jul 1991, 24 birds seen near Taif, SW Saudi Arabia, suggesting colonies in Asia Minor or SW Arabia, perhaps in unexplored Asir Mts, where many remote wadis have suitable nesting cliffs and feeding habitat; possibly also in Yemen, where 14 birds, including 2 juveniles, seen several times in summer/autumn 1985.

Bibliography. Aharoni (1929), Akçakaya (1990), Ash & Howell (1977), Baris (1989), Bezzel & Wartmann (1990), Brown *et al.* (1982), Collar & Andrew (1988), Collar & Stuart (1985), Cramp & Simmons (1977), Danford (1880), DesFayes (1987), Dollinger (1988), Elbin (1990), Etchécopar & Hüe (1964), Fatio (1906), Flower (1922), Géroudet (1965), Hamel (1975), Heim de Balsac (1931), Hirsch (1976, 1978a, 1978b, 1979, 1980, 1983, 1991), Hirsch & Schenker (1977), Holyoak (1970), del Hoyo (1989), Hüe & Etchécopar (1970), Kasparek (1986), King (1978/79), Kumerloeve (1958, 1962b, 1965, 1967, 1969a, 1969b, 1978, 1983, 1984), Luthin (1984b), Manry (1978a), Mallet (1977), Michelmore & Oliver (1982), Oliver *et al.* (1979), Olson (1985d), Pala (1971), Parslow (1973), Parslow & Everett (1981), Paz (1987), Pegoraro & Malin (1990), Pegoraro & Thaler (1985), Peter (1991), Rands *et al.* (1987), Rencurel (1974), Robin (1973), Safriel (1980), Sahin (1982a, 1982b, 1983a, 1983b, 1983c, 1983d, 1986, 1988, 1990), Schenker (1977, 1979), Schenker *et al.* (1980), Siegfried (1972c), Smith (1970), Thaler *et al.* (1981), Valverde (1957), Vincent (1966), Wackernagel (1964), Wittmann & Ruppert (1984).

9. **Southern Bald Ibis**

Geronticus calvus

French: Ibis du Cap　　　**German**: Kahlkopfrapp　　　**Spanish**: Ibis Calvo
Other common names: Bald Ibis

Taxonomy. *Tantalus Calvus* Boddaert, 1783, Cape of Good Hope.
Forms superspecies with *G. eremita*. Monotypic.
Distribution. Restricted to highlands of SE South Africa.

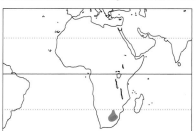

Descriptive notes. 78 cm. Depending on light, lesser upperwing-coverts can appear distinctly blue. Male slightly larger, with slightly longer bill and tarsus. Immature lacks coppery wing patch; head feathered, appearing greyish.

Habitat. High altitude grasslands, usually at 1200-1850 m; prefers to feed where grass lower than level of bird's belly, so occurs mainly in recently burnt, ploughed, mowed, or heavily grazed fields and cultivated land. Nests on cliffs in mountains; often near water, in river gorges or by waterfalls.

Food and Feeding. Insects, especially grasshoppers, beetles and caterpillars, taken live or fire-killed after burning; also earthworms, snails, frogs and small dead mammals and birds; carrion reported in past, but not recently confirmed. Recorded swallowing buttons, possibly mistaking them for beetles; maize stalk-borers found in good proportion (up to 33%) in stomach contents of young birds. Usually forages in flocks of up to 100 birds; probes in ground and turns over leaves and cattle dung.

Breeding. Starts Jul, laying Aug-Oct, during southern winter; this permits chick development during the season of grass burning, when maximum foraging ground available. Usually in colonies of 2-72 pairs, sometimes singly. Nest is platform of sticks lined with soft vegetation; placed on ledges or in potholes of cliffs. Usually 1-3 eggs (1-5); incubation period unrecorded; chicks have dark grey down, darkest on crown; fledging c. 55 days. Sexual maturity before 3 years of age; known to live to at least 11 years old. Breeding success variable: high in favourable years, e.g. in Transvaal, 0·6-0·8 young produced per pair per year in 1982/83; lower in drought years, sometimes with total failure.

Movements. Disperses in Dec-Jan after breeding, but movements apparently limited to relatively short distances, up to c. 18 km. Several records in outlying areas at beginning of 20th century, as far W as Cape Town, 1000 km W of present range; these suggest that more extensive wanderings took place in past, although at that time species probably bred in E Cape Province.

Status and Conservation. RARE. CITES II. Total population c. 5000-8000 birds; reckoned to be stable since 1970. Recent surveys have located previously unknown colonies, so previous censuses probably underestimates, but increase in Transvaal between 1969 and 1980's regarded as genuine. Major decline in early 20th century, leading to disappearance from Cape Province and Transkei, where apparently fairly widespread in 19th century. Main cause of decline seems to have been propagation of karoo vegetation following severe overgrazing of grasslands; in Transkei, drainage of wetlands may have been significant. Has suffered considerable human predation of eggs, chicks and adults, which still continues on small scale, despite full legal protection of species in South Africa. Breeds in several protected areas. Captive breeding programmes under way in Pretoria Zoo and in Cape Town, with primary objective of reintroduction to Cape Province.

Bibliography. Allan (1983a, 1983b, 1984c, 1985b, 1989), Bolster (1931), Brooke (1984), Brown *et al.* (1982), Clancey (1985), Clark, B. (1979), Collar & Andrew (1988), Collar & Stuart (1985), Cooper & Edwards (1969), Dollinger (1988), Grafton (1972), Holyoak (1970), van Jaarsveld (1979, 1980), King (1978/79), Kumerloeve (1978), Kushlan (1978), Luthin (1984b), Maclean (1985), Manry (1978a, 1982, 1983, 1984, 1985a, 1985b, 1985c), Milstein (1973, 1974), Milstein & Siegfried (1970), Milstein & Wolff (1973), Olson (1985d), Parnell (1942), Pocock & Uys (1967), Siegfried (1966a, 1966b, 1971d), Skead (1967), Snow (1978), Vincent & Symons (1948).

Genus *NIPPONIA* Reichenbach, 1853

10. **Japanese Crested Ibis**

Nipponia nippon

French: Ibis nippon　　　**German**: Nipponibis　　　**Spanish**: Ibis Nipón
Other common names: Japanese (White) Ibis, Oriental Crested/Oriental/Crested Ibis

Taxonomy. *Ibis nippon* Temminck, 1835, Japan.
Around end of 19th century race *sinensis* described, but this turned out to be same birds in breeding plumage. Monotypic.
Distribution. Once widespread in NE Asia and Japan, wintering S to Hainan, range now much reduced; only known population in Quinling Mts, Shaanxi Province, NE China.

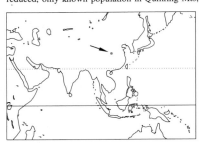

Descriptive notes. 55-78·5 cm. Non-breeding adult white, with orangish cinnamon tones in tail and flight-feathers.
Habitat. Marshes, streams, rivers, ponds, lakes, rice fields and other cultivation, surrounded by forested hills or near clumps of large trees, which are used for roosting and nesting. Only known surviving population lives at 875-1150 m.
Food and Feeding. Diet in Japan was freshwater fish (*Misgurnus, Carassius, Parasilurus*), amphibians (frogs, newts and salamanders), crustaceans (*Potamon, Cambaroides*), freshwater molluscs (*Viviparus, Cristaria*) and insects, especially grasshoppers and adults and larvae of aquatic beetles (*Hydrophilus, Cybister*); in China, eels also important. Intake of 300-500 g of food per day in captivity. Forages during day, in small flocks, though over 50 birds recorded together in 19th century; probes into mud or shallow water with bill, or picks up prey from ground.
Breeding. Surviving population in China starts late Feb to early Mar, with laying from mid Mar to early Apr; in Japan formerly started in Feb, with laying in Apr. Nowadays solitary; formerly in colonies, said to be small, but no information from period when species commoner; unconfirmed report of breeding in mixed colony with herons and cormorants in late 19th century in Aomori, Japan. Nest is flimsy stick platform, lined with small twigs, leaves and hay; built on branches of trees (pine, oak, chestnut or poplar), at height of c. 5-25 m. Usually 3 eggs (2-5); incubation 28-30 days in wild, 25 days in captivity; chicks have grey down, white below; young birds independent at 45-50 days. Sexual maturity apparently at 3 years old; captive bird in Japan lived to over 17 years old.
Movements. Populations of C China, including only known surviving one, sedentary; former populations of Siberia, Manchuria and N China wintered in SE China and Hainan. In Japan, birds that bred in C Japan apparently sedentary, while those from S Hokkaido and N Honshu migrated S in winter, with records as far S as Ryukyu Is. Flies in line or in V-formation.
Status and Conservation. ENDANGERED. CITES I. Formerly widespread in SE Siberia, NE China, Korea and Japan, and not uncommon in Japan according to medieval accounts and art; drastic decline during 20th century related to deforestation of pine woodland nesting habitat, human persecution, especially hunting, and contamination by mercury compounds and other pesticides applied to paddyfields during 1950's. Only known breeding population is in Shaanxi Province, China, where 2 pairs discovered in 1981, estimated at 46 birds in 1989. No recent records in Siberia and only scattered sightings in Korea since 1930. In Japan, population down to few dozen birds by c. 1920; extinct in 1981, when last 5 birds on Sado I taken into captivity. Shaanxi population receives effective protection, and supplementary feeding in winter. China and Japan collaborating with captive breeding programmes, but little success to date: in 1989 the first two chicks hatched in Beijing Zoo, but survived only one week. See page 488.

Bibliography. Archibald (1981), Archibald & Lantis (1979), Austin (1948), Austin & Kuroda (1953), Brazil (1991), Cheng Tso-hsin (1987), Collar & Andrew (1988), Dementiev & Gladkov (1951b), Diamond *et al.* (1987), Dollinger (1988), Dongchou *et al.* (1989), Etchécopar & Hüe (1978), Fan & Song (1991), Fan *et al.* (1991), Fennel & King (1964), Fisher *et al.* (1969), Flint *et al.* (1984), Gore & Won (1971), Hachisuka & Udagawa (1951), King (1978/79), Li Fulai (1990), Li Fulai & Gao Xijing (1989), Li Fulai & Huang Shiquiang (1986), Li Fulai *et al.* (1990), Luthin (1983d, 1984b, 1985b), Luthin *et al.* (1986), Manry (1986), Ogasawara (1985), Sato (1968), de Schauensee (1984), Scott (1989), Shi Dongchou *et al.* (1989), Simon & Géroudet (1970), Swinhoe (1863), Uchida (1970, 1974), Vaurie (1972), Vincent (1966), Won (1971), Yamashina (1962b, 1967, 1969, 1977, 1978), Yasuda (1984), Yinzeng (1982), Yoshii (1971), Zhang (1991), Zhi-Yen (1986).

Genus *BOSTRYCHIA*   Reichenbach, 1853

11. **Olive Ibis**

Bostrychia olivacea

French: Ibis olive   **German:** Olivenibis   **Spanish:** Ibis Oliváceo
Other common names: (African) Green Ibis; Dwarf Olive/Sao Tomé Ibis (*bocagei*)

Taxonomy. *Ibis olivacea* Du Bus de Gisignies, 1838, "côte de Guinée" = upper Guinea.
Sometimes placed in genus *Lampribis*, together with *B. rara*. Recent tendency to consider race *bocagei* a full species. Race *rothschildi* of Principé I extinct. Four subspecies recognized.
Subspecies and Distribution.
B. o. olivacea (Du Bus de Gisignies, 1838) - Sierra Leone, Liberia.
B. o. cupreipennis (Reichenow, 1903) - Cameroon, Gabon, Congo and Zaire.
B. o. bocagei (Chapin, 1923) - São Tomé I.
B. o. akleyorum (Chapman, 1912) - mountains of Kenya and Tanzania.

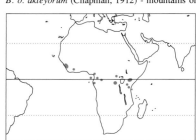

Descriptive notes. 65-75 cm. Leg colour variable. Dark facial skin and crest separate from other members of *Bostrychia*. Immature duller, with shorter crest. Races generally separated on overall coloration and form of crest; race *akleyorum* slightly larger and greener; race *bocagei* very small, more uniformly brownish.
Habitat. Dense forests of lowlands, occurring along streams and rivers, and in areas of swamp forest; in W Africa, sometimes found in mangroves, e.g. in Sierra Leone; in Gabon, recorded in regenerating forest over abandoned plantations. Race *akleyorum* inhabits montane forests up to tree-line, usually at 2000-3700 m, but at 160-1100 in East Usambaras, Tanzania.

Food and Feeding. Little known. Diet includes beetles, grubs, worms, snails, snakes and occasionally plant matter. Feeds quietly, usually singly, in pairs or in small flocks, frequenting glades in relatively open sections of forest and in swampy areas, taking food from forest floor.
Breeding. Little known. Old records of laying in Jun-Aug in Kenya; extinct race *rothschildi* was in breeding condition in Jan; as yet no records from W Africa. Solitary. Nest is platform of dead sticks constructed on tree limb; said to use holes in cliffs, but unconfirmed. 3 eggs; chicks have brownish black down.
Movements. Presumably sedentary.
Status and Conservation. Not globally threatened. Rare to uncommon throughout most of range, though retiring habits, dense forest habitat and limited survey work may partly account for scarcity of records; forest destruction is main threat. Race (possible species) *bocagei* threatened, classed as Indeterminate; not known ever to have been common, declined markedly after most of forest on island converted to plantations, mostly in 1890-1915; last record in 1928 until rediscovery, 5 birds seen in 1989 and 1 in 1990; c. 200 km² of virgin rain forest remain, but not yet known if viable population survives (see page 486). Race *rothschildi* of Principe I extinct for unknown reasons; last record in 1901 (see page 486).

Bibliography. Amadon (1953), Ash (1990), Atkinson, Dutton & Sequeira (1991), Atkinson, Peet & Alexander (1991), Bocage (1903), Bolster (1931), Britton (1980), Brosset & Erard (1986), Brown & Britton (1980), Brown *et al.* (1982), Chapin (1921, 1923), Collar & Andrew (1988), Collar & Stuart (1985, 1988), Correia (1928/29), Dubus (1838), Elgood (1982), Fry *et al.* (1985), Fuller (1987), Greenway (1967), Harrison & Steele (1989), Jones (1988, 1989), Jones & Tye (1988), Mackworth-Praed & Grant (1957, 1970), Manry (1978a), Meinertzhagen (1937), de Naurois (1973, 1983), Parker, I.S.C. (1982), Snow (1950).

12. **Spot-breasted Ibis**

Bostrychia rara

French: Ibis vermiculé   **German:** Fleckenbrustibis   **Spanish:** Ibis Moteado

Taxonomy. *Lampribis rara* Rothschild *et al.*, 1897, Denkera, Ghana.
Sometimes placed in genus *Lampribis*, together with *B. olivacea*. Monotypic.
Distribution. Liberia to Cameroon, Gabon, Zaire and extreme NE Angola.

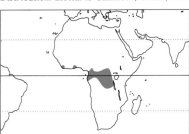

Descriptive notes. 47 cm. Characteristic small size; distinctive, with ochre-buff or cinnamon-buff centres to feathers of neck, breast and belly. Female as male, but turquoise-green spots and streak on face smaller; bill shorter and duller red. Immature duller, with shorter bill and crest.
Habitat. Lowland forests, always over or near water, along forest streams and rivers or in wooded swamps; in Gabon, often recorded in swampy areas with low, tangled vegetation in mouths of forest rivers or sites of confluence.
Food and Feeding. Diet includes beetles, larvae, grubs, aquatic snails and worms. Although small groups congregate at roosting sites, species usually feeds alone, or in pairs; probes in mud, in swamps and muddy banks of forest watercourses. Feeds by day, though occasionally active by night, especially in bright moonlight.
Breeding. Probably most of year, except during long dry season, when water levels lowest. Breeding only studied in Gabon: laying in all months except Jul/Aug, with peaks in Mar-May and Sept-Dec, corresponding to rainy seasons. Solitary. Nest is small platform of sticks, roots, lianas and twigs, lined with leaves and bits of epiphytes; situated in tree, 0·8-6 m above water or ground. 2 eggs; incubation c. 20 days; chicks have blackish brown down, replaced at 6 days by thicker white down.
Movements. Sedentary. At dusk, groups of 5-8 birds gather and fly around calling, generally moving to open parts of large watercourses.
Status and Conservation. Not globally threatened. Very little known. Uncommon throughout most of range, rare in Liberia. Has only been studied in any detail in Gabon, where common in NE, in basin of R Ivindo; in this area visiting fishermen known to take nestlings; probably suffers similar exploitation elsewhere. Preference for dense rain forest suggests that forest destruction, most intensive in W Africa, is probably main threat. CITES III in Ghana.

Bibliography. Bolster (1931), Brosset & Erard (1976, 1986), Brown *et al.* (1982), Chapin (1921), Fry *et al.* (1985), Lippens & Wille (1976), Louette (1981), Mackworth-Praed & Grant (1970), Manry (1978a), Pinto (1983).

13. **Hadada Ibis**

Bostrychia hagedash

French: Ibis hagedash   **German:** Hagedasch   **Spanish:** Ibis Hadada
Other common names: Hadada, Hadeda, Hadedah

Taxonomy. *Tantalus Hagedash* Latham, 1790, Cape of Good Hope.
Sometimes placed in monospecific genus *Hagedashia*. Birds from Somalia to Malawi sometimes assigned separate race, *erlangeri*. Three subspecies normally recognized.
Subspecies and Distribution.
B. h. brevirostris (Reichenow, 1907) - Senegal E to Zaire and Kenya, whence S to Zambezi Valley.
B. h. nilotica Neumann, 1909 - Sudan and Ethiopia to NE Zaire, Uganda and NW Tanzania.
B. h. hagedash (Latham, 1790) - S Africa S of Zambezi Valley.

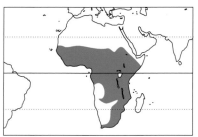

Descriptive notes. 65-76 cm; c. 1262 g. Distinctive with red base to culmen and lack of crest. General tone can be greyer or more olive brown depending on subspecies. As in members of genus *Threskiornis*, axillaries often project beneath folded wing of standing bird. Immature duller. Races separated on general coloration and size.
Habitat. Open grasslands and savanna, especially along wooded streams and river courses, and in cultivated land, large gardens and playing fields; less often marshes, edges of lakes and reservoirs, mangroves and beaches. Also occurs in open woodland and at forest edge; in Gabon and Cameroon recorded breeding in primary rain forest.

Food and Feeding. Mainly insects, especially Diptera, pupae of Lepidoptera and larvae of Coleoptera; also crustaceans, millipedes, centipedes, spiders, earthworms, snails and small reptiles. Forages by picking prey from surface or probing in soft ground.

Breeding. Lengthy season, usually peaking during and after main rains; in some areas, e.g. Gambia and Tanzania, mainly in dry season. Solitary. Nest is flimsy platform of sticks and twigs, lined with grass or lichens; situated on horizontal branch of tree 1-12 m (usually 3-6 m) above ground or water; sometimes in bushes or even on telegraph poles. Usually 2-3 eggs (2-4); incubation 25-28 days; chicks have rufous brown down; independent at 49 days. High breeding success recorded of 1·8 young per pair per year in one study in E Africa; high losses recorded in South Africa, especially as a result of eggs and chicks falling from nest, and only 3 young fledged from 17 nests with total of 67 eggs.

Movements. Mainly sedentary, but some local movements to wetter areas during droughts. Flocks of 5-30 birds, occasionally up to 200, wander several kilometres from roost.

Status and Conservation. Not globally threatened. Locally common throughout range, though more so in E and S Africa than in W Africa, where highest numbers recorded during international waterfowl censuses 1955-1990 were 90 birds in basin of R Niger, 70 in Gulf of Guinea and 20 in basin of L Chad. Around turn of century, species underwent marked decline over few years in South Africa, apparently due to hunting during period of colonial expansion. However, since 1910 has been expanding towards W, probably as result of: reduced human persecution following legal protection; proliferation of imported tree species, providing new sites for resting and nesting in formerly treeless areas; construction of reservoirs; increase in extent of irrigated land; and arrival of cattle in zones recently colonized by man, as cow dung favours expansion of coprophagous insects, frequent prey of species. CITES III in Ghana.

Bibliography. Amadon (1953), Anthony (1978b), Bell-Cross (1974), Berruti (1983), Bradfield (1967), Britton (1980), Brooke, R.K. (1986), Brosset & Erard (1986), Brown & Britton (1980), Brown et al. (1982), Capanna et al. (1982), Elgood et al. (1973), Fry et al. (1985), Kushlan (1978), Line (1941), Macdonald et al. (1986), Maclean (1985), Mackworth-Praed & Grant (1957-1973), Manry (1978a), Martin, R.J. (1972, 1984), Ossowski (1952), Ott & Joslin (1981), Pinto (1983), Pitman (1928, 1931b), Plowes (1967), Raseroka (1975a, 1975b), Richardson, D.M. (1984), Schüz (1970b), Skead (1951, 1966, 1967), van Someren (1956), Stander (1960), Symons (1924), Uys (1983), Uys & Broekhuysen (1966), Wennrich (1981, 1982e), Winterbottom (1972), Wolstenhilme (1961).

14. Wattled Ibis

Bostrychia carunculata

French: Ibis caronculé   **German**: Klunkeribis   **Spanish**: Ibis Carunculado
Other common names: Carunculated Ibis

Taxonomy. *Ibis carunculata* Rüppell, 1837, Taranta Mountains, Ethiopia.
Said to be link between *Bostrychia* and *Geronticus*, on basis largely of breeding habits. Monotypic.
Distribution. Restricted to highlands of Ethiopia.

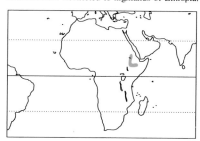

Descriptive notes. 65-75 cm. Very dark; conspicuous black and white upperwing-coverts. Pendant throat wattle often difficult to see. Immature duller and paler, with less white on wing; lacks wattle.

Habitat. Highlands of Ethiopia at 1500-4100 m. Most frequent along river courses with rocky cliffs; also in open country, including high altitude moorland, swamps, cropland and in open woodland, typically in olive or juniper woodland; occasionally in stands of *Eucalyptus*. Small flocks seen around human settlements, including Addis Ababa. Usually nests on rocky cliffs, less often in trees and buildings.

Food and Feeding. Diet unknown, but probably mainly worms and insects, including adults and larvae of coprophagous beetles; perhaps less often large insects, amphibians and small mammals. Usually feeds in flocks, which are often small soon after leaving roost, but build up to 50-100 birds, or more, as day goes on. Normally forages in open country, walking about deliberately, probing regularly in mud or soft ground; may locate some of its prey by ear. Searches dung for beetles, and sometimes accompanies herds of domestic animals.

Breeding. Laying mainly during short rains of Mar-May, and in main rains of Jul; occasionally in dry season, in Dec. Usually colonial, but sometimes solitary or in small groups of 2-3 pairs. Nest is platform of branches and sticks, lined with soft vegetation like grass stems, mosses and strips of bark; situated on ledges, bushes protruding from cliff faces; occasionally on tops of trees or on buildings, when nesting alone or in very small groups. 2-3 eggs; chicks have blackish brown down. Other aspects of breeding habits unrecorded.

Movements. Sedentary; probably some local altitudinal movements.

Status and Conservation. Not globally threatened. No quantitative details available, but seems to be locally common to very common, e.g. in Bale Mts, where feeding flocks of over 100 birds recorded. Has adapted well to living in humanized zones, visiting cultivation and plantations, sometimes associating with herds of livestock, and even breeding on ledges of buildings. Small flocks often seen in Addis Ababa, flying between large buildings in city centre.

Bibliography. Bolster (1931), Brown et al. (1982), Dorst & Roux (1972), Fry et al. (1985), Luthin (1984b), Manry (1978a), Mackworth-Praed & Grant (1957), Schüz (1970b), Smith (1957), Urban (1978).

PLATE 36

inches 12
cm 30

15

16

17

ssp *melanopis*

18

ssp *branickii*

19

20

21

22

ssp *urschi*

26

ssp *cristata*

23

24

25

Genus *THERISTICUS*   Wagler, 1832

15. **Plumbeous Ibis**

Theristicus caerulescens

French: Ibis plombé   **German**: Stirnbandibis   **Spanish**: Bandurria Mora
Other common names: Blue Ibis

Taxonomy. *Ibis caerulescens* Vieillot, 1817, Paraguay.
Sometimes placed in monospecific genus *Harpiprion*. Monotypic.
Distribution. Bolivia and C Brazil to Paraguay, N Argentina and Uruguay.

Descriptive notes. 71-76 cm. Unmistakable, due to very uniform coloration, bushy crest and white forehead.
Habitat. Open country, occurring in pastures, grassland and savanna; also frequents rice fields, ponds, marshes and swampy and seasonally flooded areas. Nests in large trees near water.
Food and Feeding. Diet includes insects, snails and aquatic molluscs (*Pomacea*). Feeds almost always singly or in pairs; probes into mud with long bill.
Breeding. Recorded in Aug-Sept in Pantanal, Brazil. Solitary. Nest is platform made with twigs, lined with grass and leaves; built on horizontal limbs of large trees, at 8-20 m. 2-3 eggs; incubation c. 28 days. Egg predation by capuchin monkeys (*Cebus apella*) and Greater Black Hawk (*Buteogallus urubitinga*) has been recorded in Pantanal.
Movements. Not well known, but appears to be mainly sedentary; some wandering, as occasional birds appear casually further S than normal range, in C Argentina.
Status and Conservation. Not globally threatened. Generally uncommon and little known, but fairly common locally, for instance in: Argentinian, Paraguayan and Bolivian Chaco; Río Yacuma area, NW Bolivia; Brazilian Pantanal; and N of Cerro Largo Province, N Uruguay. Partial census of Jul 1990 produced 95 birds in Argentina. Apparently increasing in frontier zones of N and W Paraguay; usually occurs in pairs, but flock of over 40 birds seen at Estancia San José (N Chaco) in 1989.
Bibliography. Belton (1984), Blake (1977), Brooks (1990, 1991), Cintra (1986), Dubs (1988), Gyldenstolpe (1945b), Hellmayr & Conover (1948), Klimaitis & Moschione (1987), Olmos (1990), de la Peña (1986), Perigo (1990), Pinto (1964), Remsen (1986), Ruschi (1979), Scott & Carbonell (1986), Short (1975), Sick (1984), Storer (1989b), Wetmore (1926).

16. **Buff-necked Ibis**

Theristicus caudatus

French: Ibis mandore   **German**: Weißhalsibis   **Spanish**: Bandurria Común
Other common names: White-throated Ibis

Taxonomy. *Scolopax caudatus* Boddaert, 1783, Cayenne.
Forms superspecies with *T. melanopis*, which was formerly considered race of present species. Two subspecies recognized.
Subspecies and Distribution.
T. c. caudatus (Boddaert, 1783) - Colombia and Venezuela to French Guiana, S to Mato Grosso, Brazil.
T. c. hyperorius Todd, 1948 - E Bolivia to SE Brazil, Paraguay, N Argentina and Uruguay.

Descriptive notes. 71-76 cm. Very similar to *T. melanopis*, but has part of wing white; buffish of breast does not extend so far down neck, and is not crossed by grey band. Immature has head and neck narrowly streaked brown. Race *hyperorius* has paler neck and less white on wing.
Habitat. Open country in savanna, ranchland, fields and open forests; also small marshes, flooded areas and shores of lakes, lagoons, ponds and watercourses, but often far from water; often found in burnt fields. Generally from sea-level up to c. 1000 m, occasionally wandering higher up; small breeding population at over 2000 m in mountains of Córdoba, NC Argentina.
Food and Feeding. Mainly insects; also spiders, centipedes, amphibians, small reptiles and occasionally small mammals; toads (*Bufo granulosus*), poisonous for most animals, have been recorded. Usually feeds in small, loose flocks, occasionally alone; walks about probing in soft soil, grassy pastures and wetlands.
Breeding. In *llanos* of Venezuela, contrary to most other Ciconiiformes in area, breeds more frequently during dry season; in Córdoba, NC Argentina, nests in spring (Nov-Dec). Colonial, in small, loose colonies, or solitary. Nest is bulky, flattish structure of branches, situated in trees or on cliff ledges, usually along rivers; one nest in Rio Grande do Sul was 10 m up tree. 2-4 eggs.
Movements. Possibly sedentary; some local movements occur. In Colombia, seems occasionally to wander W of Andes; accidental in E Panama.
Status and Conservation. Not globally threatened. Generally common throughout range. In Colombia, uncommon in E *llanos* and rare W of Andes, where has apparently decreased in recent

years. Widely distributed in *llanos* of Venezuela; record of 30 birds at Esteros del Mantecal in 1984. In Uruguay, formerly considered merely migrant, but nest discovered in N at Tacuarembó in 1987. In C Chaco of Paraguay, commonest where forest has been cleared for development of cattle ranching, supposedly because presence of cattle favours increase of insects, which form important part of diet of species. Normally receives protection from farmers, as recognized to help in biological control of noxious animals.
Bibliography. Antas & Cavalcanti (1988), Arballo (1990a), Belton (1984), Blake (1977), Brooks (1990, 1991), Gibson (1919), Gyldenstolpe (1945b), Hellmayr & Conover (1948), Hilty & Brown (1986), Hughes (1970), Luthin (1981), Morales (1990), Neto (1982), Nores & Yzurieta (1980), Ogden & Thomas (1985a), Olrog (1965), de la Peña (1986), Perigo (1990), Pinto (1964), Ruschi (1979), Salvador & Salvador (1988), Salvadori (1900), San Martín (1959), de Schauensee & Phelps (1978), Schulenberg & Parker (1981), Scott & Carbonell (1986), Serna (1990), Short (1975), Sick (1984), Snyder (1966), Thomas (1979a), Weller (1967a), Wetmore (1965), Zapata & Martínez (1972).

17. **Black-faced Ibis**

Theristicus melanopis

French: Ibis à face noire   **German**: Schwarzzügelibis   **Spanish**: Bandurria de Collar
Other common names: Andean/Puna Buff-necked/Branicki's Ibis (*branickii*)

Taxonomy. *Tantalus melanopis* Gmelin, 1789, "in insula *novi anni*" = New Year's Island, near Staten Island, *ex* Latham.
Formerly considered race of *T. caudatus*, with which forms superspecies. Race *branickii* sometimes regarded as full species, on basis mainly of ecological differences. Two subspecies recognized.
Subspecies and Distribution.
T. m. branickii Berlepsch & Stolzmann, 1894 - highlands of Ecuador, Peru, NW Bolivia and extreme N Chile.
T. m. melanopis (Gmelin, 1789) - S Chile and S Argentina, migrating outside breeding season to N Argentina; isolated population in coastal Peru.

Descriptive notes. 71-76 cm. Lacks white on wing; different proportions from otherwise similar *T. caudatus*. Immature has faint dusky streaks on neck, and scalloped wing-coverts, produced by buff feather edges. Race *branickii* paler, has less ochraceous foreneck and breast, and usually smaller area of bare skin on throat.
Habitat. Open country in fields, meadows, pastures, ploughed and cultivated fields, damp valleys in places with rushes, arid ranchland and upland bunch-grass heaths; also marshy areas and borders of lakes and rivers; sometimes in sandy habitats with very little vegetation; also in forest glades or in open forest without standing water. Usually nests in rocky gullies, on cliffs, in reedbeds, and occasionally in woods. From near sea-level up to 3000 m (race *melanopis*) or 5000 m in *puna* (race *branickii*).
Food and Feeding. Diet includes insects, worms, frogs, salamanders and occasionally rodents; large quantities of soil larvae and molluscs (*Mytilus*) have been recorded; stomach of large chick collected in Tierra del Fuego contained fragments of apparently complete shell of a sheldgoose (*Chloephaga*) egg. Feeds alone, in pairs or in small flocks of 3-12 birds, apparently in larger groups in winter; forages by walking slowly, probing bill into soil and vegetation.
Breeding. Laying Sept-Mar in C Peru, Sept-Dec in S Chile and Tierra del Fuego. Colonial, sometimes with Black-crowned Night-herons (*Nycticorax nycticorax*), or with cormorants in S of range; colonies of 10-30 pairs in Chile, over 50 pairs in colony in Tierra del Fuego; less often solitary. Nest is voluminous platform of dry branches and sticks, lined with grass or rush stems; when colony is in reedbeds, nest made of dry reeds; situated on rocky outcrops or cliff ledges, on ground near water, in reedbeds, or occasionally in branches of trees. 2-3 eggs; chicks have grey down, paler on head and below.
Movements. S populations of Chile and Argentina migrate to *pampas* in N Argentina. In Tierra del Fuego is breeding summer visitor; spring migration starts in late Aug and autumn migration in late Jan, with most birds leaving by end of Apr; very few records of birds overwintering in area. Flies in lines, in flocks of over 100 birds during migration, sometimes at great heights. Irregular vagrant to Falkland Is, in parties of up to 7 birds.
Status and Conservation. Not globally threatened. Common in S Chile and S Argentina, but uncommon to rare in coastal Peru and N Chile. Partial census in Jul 1990 yielded 158 birds in Chile. During migration, flocks of 123 and 112 recorded in S of Buenos Aires Province in 1967 and 1968 respectively. Race *branickii* uncommon and very local throughout range. Species redlisted as vulnerable in Chile, although common in S.
Bibliography. Blaauw (1917), Blake (1977), Fjeldså & Krabbe (1990), Hellmayr & Conover (1948), Hughes (1970), Humphrey *et al.* (1970), Johnson (1965, 1972), Nores & Yzurieta (1980), de la Peña (1986), Salvadori (1900), Scott & Carbonell (1986), Woods (1988).

Genus *CERCIBIS*   Wagler, 1832

18. **Sharp-tailed Ibis**

Cercibis oxycerca

French: Ibis à queue pointue   **German**: Spitzschwanzibis   **Spanish**: Ibis Rabudo

---

On following pages: 19. Green Ibis (*Mesembrinibis cayennensis*); 20. Whispering Ibis (*Phimosus infuscatus*); 21. American White Ibis (*Eudocimus albus*); 22. Scarlet Ibis (*Eudocimus ruber*); 23. Glossy Ibis (*Plegadis falcinellus*); 24. White-faced Ibis (*Plegadis chihi*); 25. Puna Ibis (*Plegadis ridgwayi*); 26. Madagascar Crested Ibis (*Lophotibis cristata*).

Other common names: Long-tailed/Bare-faced Ibis

Taxonomy. *Ibis oxycercus* Spix, 1825, "in Provincia Pará." Type from Amazonia.
Monotypic.
Distribution. E Colombia, Venezuela and Guyana; Amazonian Brazil to NW Mato Grosso.

Descriptive notes. 76-86 cm. Malar region can be dark brownish grey, and rather inconspicuous. Similar only to sympatric *Phimosus infuscatus*, but much larger, with different proportions and small, bushy nuchal crest.
Habitat. Savannas along margins of lakes, pools, rivers and streams; also open marshy regions, muddy rice fields and damp grassland. From sea-level up to 500 m.
Food and Feeding. No information available on diet, but presumably mainly invertebrates, as in other ibises. Feeds alone, in pairs or in small flocks; walks and probes in soft muddy areas.

Breeding. Virtually nothing known. Nests in trees.
Movements. Presumably sedentary.
Status and Conservation. Not globally threatened. Local and uncommon throughout range. Frequently observed in *llanos* of Venezuela, singly, in pairs or in small flocks; no records of large flocks. The least numerous ibis in Colombia. No evidence that low numbers due to anything other than natural causes; impact of man unknown; but species readily uses muddy rice fields.
Bibliography. Blake (1977), Chamberlain *et al.* (1956), Hellmayr & Conover (1948), Hilty & Brown (1986), Morales (1990), Ogden & Thomas (1985a), Pinto (1964), Ruschi (1979), de Schauensee & Phelps (1978), Scott & Carbonell (1986), Sick (1984), Snyder (1966), Thomas (1979a).

Genus *MESEMBRINIBIS*   Peters, 1930

19. **Green Ibis**

Mesembrinibis cayennensis

French: Ibis vert   German: Grünibis   Spanish: Ibis Verde
Other common names: Cayenne Ibis

Taxonomy. *Tantalus cayennensis* Gmelin, 1789, Cayenne.
Monotypic.
Distribution. E Costa Rica, Panama and Colombia; E of Andes, from S Venezuela and the Guianas S through E Ecuador, E Peru, E Bolivia and Brazil to Paraguay and extreme NE Brazil.

Descriptive notes. 48-58 cm; 715-785 g. Upperwing bronze olive with greenish reflections; bushy crest with green-turquoise gloss highly characteristic. Juvenile plumage is considerably duller overall, the head and neck being sooty, with little gloss.
Habitat. Wet, muddy forested areas, swampy woods and thickets, gallery forest and open, stony banks of forest streams and rivers; also in open marshes, thickets around lagoons and in wet savannas, usually near woodland. Recorded in mangrove swamps in Panama. Evidence seems to suggest it may be adaptable

to secondary forest.
Food and Feeding. Diet includes insects (Orthoptera, Homoptera, Coleoptera), worms and some plants. Usually feeds alone or in pairs, occasionally in small flocks of up to 9 birds; forages by walking about with head bobbing, probing methodically deep into soft mud, gravel or shallow water: probes in soft earthworm casts in forest; in Venezuela, has occasionally been recorded foraging with wings open, presumably as method of improving visibility.
Breeding. Nesting recorded in Jun-Jul in *llanos* of Venezuela, 1-2 months after onset of rains; single record of laying in late Apr in N Colombia. Solitary. Nest is rather sparse structure of twigs; built high in tree, usually over pools of water. 2-4 eggs; incubation period unrecorded; fledging 23-27 days.
Movements. Presumably sedentary, though local movements known to occur; isolated birds recorded passing through extreme SE Brazil.
Status and Conservation. Not globally threatened. Uncommon to locally fairly common throughout range. Areas where fairly common include: Brazilian and Bolivian sectors of Amazonia; Surinam; parts of Venezuelan *llanos*; coastal Limon, Costa Rica; Bocas del Toro, E Colon and Darien, Panama. In 1984, 80 birds censused at reservoirs of Jatira and Tacarigua, Venezuela. Usually solitary or in small groups, shy and rather hard to see and often undetected, so populations probably more numerous than thought. Marked decline in French Guiana where has practically disappeared from most accessible parts of all forest rivers, probably due to intense hunting pressure. Vulnerable to rapid destruction of forest habitat throughout much of range; however, in Surinam uses abandoned, overgrown coffee plantations, and in Costa Rica recorded in swamps surrounded by second growth and heavily logged forest.
Bibliography. Belton (1984), Blake (1977), Chubb (1916), Collins (1964), Emerson & Proce (1969), Haverschmidt (1962, 1968), Hellmayr & Conover (1948), Hilty & Brown (1986), de Jong *et al.* (1984), Luthin (1983a, 1983c), Narosky & Yzurieta (1987), Ogden & Thomas (1985a, 1985b), de la Peña (1986), Perigo (1990), Pinto (1964), Ridgely & Gwynne (1989), Ruschi (1979), de Schauensee & Phelps (1978), Scott & Carbonell (1986), Serna (1990), Sick (1984), Slud (1964), Snyder (1966), Soothill & Soothill (1982), Stiles & Skutch (1989), Thibault & Guyot (1988), Thomas (1979a), Wetmore (1965), Wood (1923), Young (1928).

Genus *PHIMOSUS*   Wagler, 1832

20. **Whispering Ibis**

Phimosus infuscatus

French: Ibis à face nue   German: Mohrenibis   Spanish: Ibis Afeitado
Other common names: Bare-faced Ibis

Taxonomy. *Ibis infuscata* Lichtenstein, 1823, Paraguay.
Three subspecies recognized.
Subspecies and Distribution.
P. i. berlepschi Hellmayr, 1903 - NE Colombia, E Ecuador and NW Brazil E through Venezuela to Guyana and Surinam.
P. i. nudifrons (Spix, 1825) - C, E & S Brazil, S of Amazon.
P. i. infuscatus (Lichtenstein, 1823) - E Bolivia through Paraguay to NE Argentina and Uruguay.

Descriptive notes. 46-54 cm. Considerably smaller and shorter-tailed than partially sympatric *Cercibis oxycerca*. Immature as adult, with white lores and black bill. Races separated by extent of red on face and colour of gloss.
Habitat. Open, wet meadows, pastures and savannas, marshes, rice fields and margins of lagoons, pools and rivers; also wooded swamps and streams. Nests in dense shrubs in brushy savanna, and in thickets of trees and shrubs surrounding lagoons. Usually near sea-level, but recorded at 1950 m in Venezuela and at 2600 m in Colombia.

Food and Feeding. Mainly insects, worms, freshwater clams and other small invertebrates; seeds and leaves recorded in Brazil. Usually feeds in small groups of 3-20 birds, less often singly or in pairs; walks slowly and probes in soft ground in grassy pastures, and in mud at wetlands and edges of shallow pools and lagoons. In areas grazed by cattle and horses, probes into mud exposed by their walking.
Breeding. Early in wet season in Venezuela and Colombia; rather continuous during all rainy season; early summer (Oct-Dec) in SE Brazil. Solitary or loosely colonial, in monospecific aggregations of 5-70 pairs, or even up to several hundred pairs in mixed colonies with other Ciconiiformes. Nest is small, rough, flattish platform of sticks and twigs; situated in low trees or shrubs, usually over open water. Usually 3-4 eggs (2-5); incubation 21-23 days; chicks have black down; fledging 27-30 days. Success limited by high losses to predators; in one colony in Venezuela, over 80% of eggs and young were lost.
Movements. Not well known, but movements related to rainfall seem usual to be throughout range; in Córdoba (NC Argentina) only occurs in very wet years, sometimes in fair numbers; in Brazil appears periodically in great numbers in some regions, e.g. Pantanal, Mato Grosso.
Status and Conservation. Not globally threatened. Generally common, but rather local, throughout range. In Colombia, most common ibis E and W of Andes. Periodically one of most numerous birds in Mato Grosso, Brazil. Similarly, one of most abundant ibises locally in Paraguayan Chaco. Up to 250 recorded at Laguna José Ignacio and Laguna Garzón, Uruguay. 370 at Esteros del Mantecal, in Venezuelan *llanos*. Frequently visits rice fields and other cultivation, where vulnerable to effects of pesticides.
Bibliography. Belton (1984), Blake (1977), Boano (1981), Brooks (1990, 1991), Brouwer & van Wieringen (1990), Collins (1964), Gibson (1919), Grant (1911), Hellmayr & Conover (1948), Hilty & Brown (1986), Luthin (1983a, 1983c), Morales (1990), Nores & Yzurieta (1980), Ogden & Thomas (1985a), de la Peña (1986), Perigo (1990), Pinto (1964), Ruschi (1979), de Schauensee & Phelps (1978), Scott & Carbonell (1986), Serna (1990), Sick (1984), Snyder (1966), Thomas (1979a).

Genus *EUDOCIMUS*   Wagler, 1832

21. **American White Ibis**

Eudocimus albus

French: Ibis blanc   German: Schneesichler   Spanish: Corocoro Blanco
Other common names: White Ibis

Taxonomy. *Scolopax alba* Linnaeus, 1758, America = Carolina *ex* Catesby.
Forms superspecies with *E. ruber*; recent proposal to merge them into single species, on basis of close morphological and ecological similirities and relatively frequent natural hybridization in zone of overlap in Venezuela, where over 40 mixed pairs recorded; another view is that they may simply be colour morphs. Monotypic.
Distribution. Baja California E to N Carolina and S through Mexico, C America and Greater Antilles to Colombia, NW Venezuela, W Ecuador and extreme NW Peru.
Descriptive notes. 56-71 cm. Distal third of four outer primaries black. During breeding, distal half of bill blackish. Non-breeding adult has bare facial skin reduced, with malar region feathered and less intensely coloured. Immature has head and neck streaked or spotted brown and grey or whitish; underparts, rump and underwing white; upperparts olive brown with variable amount of white.
Habitat. Wetlands with salt, brackish or fresh water; often in or near coast, especially frequenting estuaries, tidal mudflats and mangrove swamps; also grassy and ploughed fields, and swamp forests;

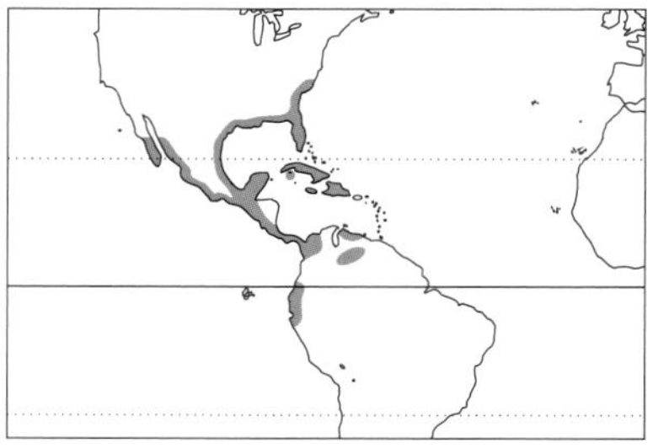

inland, near large water bodies or on flooded land. Nests on mangrove islands and on well vegetated islets on freshwater pools, lakes or marshes; in trees, bushes or cacti, or on ground; occasionally nests in grassy parts of rocky offshore islets, e.g. I Ballena (Costa Rica).

Food and Feeding. Mainly crustaceans, including crayfish (Cambarinae), fiddler crabs (*Uca*), mud crabs (*Sesarma*) and grass shrimps (*Palaemonetes*); also fish, frogs, snails, slugs and adults and larvae of insects, including aquatic beetles, grasshoppers and cockroaches; small snakes (*Agkistrodon*) often taken. Forages singly or in tight flocks; probes in soft mud, shallow water and among roots of plants, or picks up prey from surface.

Breeding. Spring in N of range, laying Mar-May; Jun-Oct, during rains, in Venezuela. Colonial, sometimes in aggregations of thousands of pairs. Nest is shallow platform of twigs and leaves, usually 2-3·5 m up, over mud or water, occasionally on ground. 2-3 eggs; incubation 21-23 days; chicks have brownish black down; fledging 45-55 days. Sexual maturity at 2 years old. Success variable: respectively 2·11 and 1·11 fledglings per successful nest in wet seasons of 1986 and 1987 in Everglades, Florida; major nesting failure caused by abnormal tides; predation usually less significant factor, but important at some colonies.

Movements. Essentially sedentary throughout range; post-breeding dispersal and seasonally some local movements, mainly related to conditions at feeding grounds. In Netherlands Antilles, several recent sightings of single birds in Dec-Jul, coinciding with dry season in the Venezuelan *llanos*. Commutes considerable distances between foraging areas and breeding colonies or roosts. Vagrant to Trinidad and inland areas of S America. Flies in lines or V-formations.

Status and Conservation. Not globally threatened. Still abundant locally in SE USA: from South Carolina to Florida, several large colonies of thousands of pairs and even up to c. 20,000 pairs; most abundant wading bird in Florida, but has declined considerably since 1940's; 4130 nests counted in Everglades in 1987. In Mexico, 14 small colonies with 20-600 nests along Pacific coast in 1972; several large colonies on E coast; recent counts include 2225 pairs at Tamesí and Panuco Deltas and Tampico Lagoons, 1000-1500 at Ascensión and Espíritu Santo Bays, and 1250 at Usumacincta Delta and Tabasco Lagoons. Also fairly common in C America, especially in Guatemala, Costa Rica and Panama, in coasts and lowlands of Pacific slope; recently, 400-500 pairs recorded in Northern Lagoon, Belize, and 1000 at Palo Verde, Costa Rica. Uncommon in Ecuador and Colombia. Apparently expanding in Venezuela, where is now competing with *E. ruber*, and some hybridization occurring; in 1983, at 9 mixed colonies in *llanos* present species estimated to comprise average 6·26% (c. 7600 pairs) of total numbers. Main threats throughout range are loss of breeding sites and feeding habitat, and also pollution.

Bibliography. Allen-Grimes (1982), Bateman (1970), Bent (1926), Bildstein (1983, 1984, 1987), Bildstein *et al.* (1990), Blacklock *et al.* (1978), Blake (1977), Burger *et al.* (1977), Christy *et al.* (1981), Custer & Osborn (1978), Edelson (1990), ffrench (1992), Frederick, P.C. (1985a, 1985b, 1986a, 1986b, 1987a, 1987b, 1990), Frederick & Collopy (1989b), Frederick & Shields (1986), Henderson (1981), Hilty & Brown (1986), Johnston & Bildstein (1990), Kale (1978), Kilham (1980, 1984), Kushlan (1973b, 1974, 1976a, 1976b, 1977a, 1977b, 1977c, 1977d, 1977e, 1978, 1979, 1986), Kushlan & Kushlan (1975), Kushlan & White (1977), Leber (1980), Luthin (1984b), Monroe (1968), Nesbitt *et al.* (1974), Ogden (1978), Ogden *et al.* (1980), Palmer (1962), Parkes (1955), Pennycuick & de Santo (1989), Petit & Bildstein (1986, 1987), Post (1990), Powel (1987), Ramo & Busto (1982b, 1984, 1987), Ridgely & Gwynne (1989), Ridgway (1884), Rudegeair (1975), de Santo *et al.* (1990), de Schauensee & Phelps (1978), Shepherd *et al.* (1991), Shields (1985, 1987), Shields & Parnell (1983, 1986), Slud (1964), Sprunt & Knoder (1980), Stangel *et al.* (1991), Stiles & Skutch (1989), Terres (1980), Thomas (1979a), Valdes Miro (1984), Voous (1983), Wayne (1922), Wetmore (1965), van Wieringen & Brouwer (1990), Wrege (1980).

22. Scarlet Ibis

Eudocimus ruber

French: Ibis rouge **German**: Scharlachsichler **Spanish**: Corocoro Rojo

Taxonomy. *Scolopax rubra* Linnaeus, 1758, America = Bahamas *ex* Catesby.

Forms superspecies with *E. albus*; recent proposal to merge them into single species, on basis of close morphological and ecological similiraties and relatively frequent natural hybridization in zone of overlap in Venezuela, where over 40 mixed pairs recorded; another view is that they may simply be colour morphs. Monotypic.

Distribution. N & E Colombia and E Ecuador to N Venezuela, the Guianas and coastal Brazil as far as Amazon Delta; non-breeding visitor to Margarita I and Trinidad, where formerly bred; formerly also coastal Brazil S to Paraná; recent recolonization of Santos Bay, São Paulo.

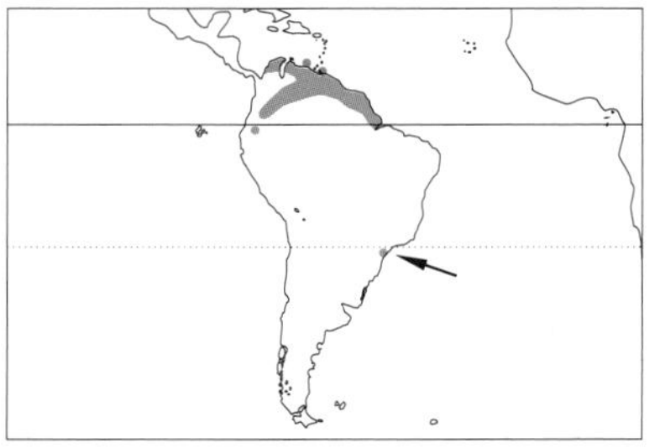

Descriptive notes. Distal third of four outer primaries black. Non-breeding adult has bill flesh pink or reddish, contrasting little with plumage. Immature has head and neck streaked or mottled brown and white; underparts and rump white; dark grey-brown above, can have pink mottling on white parts of plumage.

Habitat. Mangrove swamps, muddy estuaries and tidal mudflats; also freshwater marshes, shallow lakes, sewage ponds, lagoons, flooded areas, fish ponds and rice fields. Nests on islands with mangroves, often in or near river mouths; alternatively on trees and shrubs at inland wetlands.

Food and Feeding. Mainly crustaceans, especially fiddler crabs (*Uca*) and other crabs (*Aratus*, *Ucides*), molluscs, including snails (*Melampus*) and bivalves, insects and small fish (Cichlidae); also worms (*Nereis*). Forages in flocks of 30-70 birds; probes with bill in mud and shallow water.

Breeding. Season variable, especially along coast, but mainly during rains; laying Apr-Aug in Surinam; in *llanos*, apparently more dependent on local water conditions, breeding only after extensive rains; in Pará, Brazil, and formerly in Trinidad, at beginning of dry season. Forms large to very large colonies, of 50-5000 pairs in *llanos*, and even more along coast, often with other ibises and herons. Nest is small platform of sticks, 1-4·5 m up trees. Usually 2 eggs (1-3); incubation 21-23 days; chicks have thick black down; fledging 35-42 days.

Movements. Coastal birds supposedly resident, but subject to extensive local dispersals; in very dry season in Surinam, moves inland following rivers. Now only non-breeding visitor to Trinidad. Migrates from part of *llanos* in Venezuela during dry season, possibly N to coast; flocks fly at great heights, usually in V-formation. Flies long distances, sometimes several kilometres, from nesting or roosting site to foraging areas. Vagrant to West Indies; sightings in SE USA might involve only escapes, though some have occurred after tropical storms.

Status and Conservation. Not globally threatened. CITES II. Still common to abundant in places; has declined throughout most of range, though marked fluctuations occur. In Colombia, common resident in E *llanos* with flocks up to several hundred birds, but rare in lower Magdalena valley; breeding not recorded, but likely. In Venezuela, 22 colonies known in *llanos* in 1983, of which 15 abandoned in 1984, while census results dropped from 65,439 to 42,236 pairs; 1280 pairs counted at Orinoco Delta. On Trinidad, bred at Caroni Swamp until 1970, usually in thousands, but now non-breeding resident with peaks of up to 10,000 birds in autumn and winter. Also declining in Guyana: c. 600 breeding pairs near Mahaicony in 1972, only c. 300 in 1976 and by 1982 did not even breed. In French Guiana, c. 6000 pairs in coastal wetlands of Sinnamary in 1976, but only c. 300 in 1984; in 1991, 2 colonies remained, with c. 1200 pairs at Karouabo and c. 500 at Pointe Béhague. In Surinam, c. 10,500 pairs at swamps of Wageningen in 1971, down to c. 4000 in 1984; other large colonies at mouth of R Copename and in Wia-Wia, with recent counts of up to 6200 and 12,600 pairs respectively. In Brazil, formerly very common S to Santa Catarina, but now restricted to N of Amazonas Delta, where c. 7500 counted in 1982; in 1986 recorded in Santos Bay, São Paulo, where c. 100 birds and 2 breeding pairs seen in 1989, in apparent recolonization of SE Brazil. No recent information about status in E Ecuador. Main causes of decline are: alteration of habitat, with construction of drainage canals and containing dikes in *llanos*, and destruction of mangroves along coast; and human disturbance, including hunting. Pesticides could also become major threat.

Bibliography. Allen (1962), Anon. (1985b), Antas (1979), Belser (1989), Bent (1926), Betlem (1984), Betlem & de Jong (1983), Bildstein (1990a), Blake (1977), Bokermann & Guix (1987, 1990), Brouwer & van Wieringen (1985, 1986), Condamin (1979), Dujardin (1987, 1991), Evans (1983), Fad & Hall (1989), ffrench (1985a, 1992), ffrench & Haverschmidt (1970), Frederick, Morales *et al.* (1990), Haverschmidt (1967, 1968), Heimendahl (1985), Hilty & Brown (1986), Hughes & Owen (1988), de Jong (1983), Korsten & Lukken (1990), Lindblad (1969), Luthin (1983a, 1983c, 1984b, 1984c), Luthin *et al.* (1990), Marcondes-Machado & Monteiro Filho (1989, 1990), Monroe (1968), Palmer (1962), Pinto (1964), Ramo & Busto (1982b, 1984, 1985, 1987, 1988), Ridgway (1884), Risdon (1969), Roozendaal (1988), Ruschi (1979), de Schauensee & Phelps (1978), Serna (1990), Sick (1984), Simpson (1988), Spaans (1975b, 1982), Spaans & de Jong (1982), Spil *et al.* (1985), Stevenson (1972), Thibault & Guyot (1988), Thomas (1979a), Terres (1980), Voous (1983), van Wieringen *et al.* (1990), Wiersum (1971), Zahl (1950, 1954).

Genus *PLEGADIS* Kaup, 1829

23. Glossy Ibis

Plegadis falcinellus

French: Ibis falcinelle **German**: Sichler **Spanish**: Morito Común

Taxonomy. *Tantalus Falcinellus* Linnaeus, 1766, "Austria, Italia"; Neusiedler See, Lower Austria. Forms superspecies with *P. chihi*, which was formerly considered race of present species. Population of Philippines, Indonesia and Australia have been assigned separate race, *peregrinus*, but recent studies show that differences are not significant. Monotypic.

Distribution. Wide discontinuous breeding distribution from S Europe, Africa and Madagascar to C and S Asia, Philippines, Sulawesi and Java; S New Guinea and Australia. Also Atlantic coast of North America and West Indies; has bred in Venezuela. Occurs more widely as vagrant.

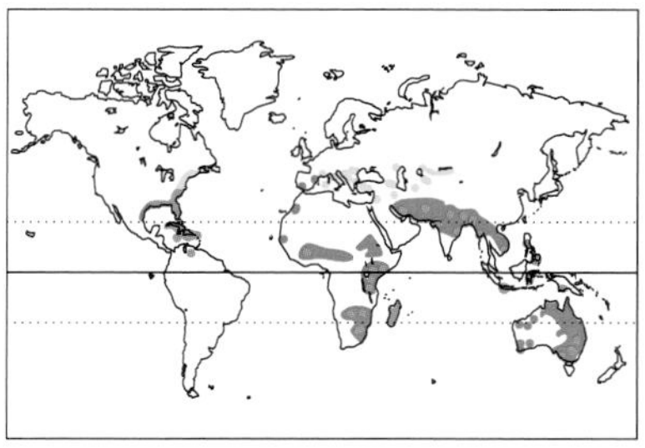

Descriptive notes. 48·5-66cm; 485-580 g; wingspan 80-95 cm. Leg colour varies from very dark brown to olive grey; bill colour also variable, grey or brownish. Differs from other *Plegadis* by facial pattern, and by colour of bill and legs. Non-breeding adult duller, dark brown, with head and neck finely but densely streaked whitish. Immature similar to non-breeding adult, with oily green sheen; head and neck browner, with variable amount of white on forehead, throat and foreneck; darker above than immature *P. chihi*.

Habitat. Shallow lakes, swamps, lagoons, sewage ponds, rivers, floodplains, wet meadows, rice fields and irrigated cultivation; less often in coastal lagoons, estuaries and other sheltered marine habitats; roosting sites in large trees often far from water. Nests in freshwater or brackish wetlands, usually in tall, dense stands of reeds or rushes, or in low trees or bushes over or near water.

Food and Feeding. Mainly adults and larvae of insects, including aquatic beetles, boatmen, dragonflies, flies, grasshoppers, crickets and caddisflies; also worms, leeches, molluscs, e.g. snails and mussels, and crustaceans, e.g. crabs and crayfish; sometimes small vertebrates, including fish, frogs, tadpoles, lizards and small snakes; 147 small snakes, most cottonmouths (*Agkistrodon*), recorded in 194 meals of young birds in Florida, USA. Usually forages in small flocks; walks slowly and probes bill into mud and shallow water, or takes prey from surface; sometimes submerges head completely, and occasionally runs after prey.

Breeding. In Black Sea area, most laying in May; Mar-May in E North America; in most of Africa lays during rains or just after, sometimes late in dry season; in New South Wales, Australia, Oct-Feb. Colonial, sometimes in large aggregations of thousands of pairs, almost always with other waterbirds. Nest is compact platform of twigs or reeds, lined with leaves and other soft vegetation; usually built less than 1 m above water, occasionally up to 7 m up. Usually 3-4 eggs (2-6);

incubation 20-23 days, usually 21; chicks have sooty black down, with some white on hindcrown and throat; fledging c. 25-28 days. Oldest known bird was over 21 years old. Success of 1·0 young (at 15 days old) per nest found in study of 64 clutches at Balranald, New South Wales, Australia.
Movements. Migratory and dispersive, notoriously nomadic. Post-breeding dispersal of adults and young birds (often in separate flocks) in all directions, with frequent records N of breeding range. In Europe, migrates S in autumn, probably mostly to sub-Saharan Africa. In South Africa, some birds sedentary, some disperse N after breeding as far as Zambia. In E Australia, birds breeding in S migrate N in winter; erratic local movements elsewhere, probably related to rainfall; vagrant to New Zealand. Tends to fly in formations.
Status and Conservation. Not globally threatened. Marked contraction of range in W Palearctic during 20th century; in Greece has crashed from 1840 pairs before 1970 to 50-71 pairs. Romania holds c. 1500 pairs in c. 20 colonies at Danube Delta; 260-1495+ pairs in Bulgaria; populations of Caspian Sea fluctuate, with 900-3000 pairs in Kirov Bay and 300-4500 pairs at Volga Delta. Notable increase in Turkey recently, with 730-1020 pairs at 4 known colonies; Israel colonized since 1969, and now holds 36 pairs in 2 colonies. Local in C Asia and India; mid-winter counts in early 1990's produced 517 birds in Iran, 953 in Saudi Arabia, 1410 in Pakistan and 4343 in India; marked decline in Assam since 1980. Much rarer in E Asia, with mostly old records in China and SE Asia, but recently 3 colonies with 1000-2000 birds in Viet Nam. Good numbers in Sulawesi, with flocks of up to 1000 birds, and 5000 counted at L Tempe; also in New Guinea, with 6500 birds in 1983 in SE Irian Jaya. In Australia generally uncommon, but locally common in N and in Murray-Darling Basin, with aggregations of up to 9000 birds and colonies of up to 4000 pairs. Uncommon to locally common in Africa, with Jan 1991 censuses of 644 in Senegal, 1001 in Cameroon, and 526 in Uganda; in South Africa expanding and increasing numbers. Fairly common in W Madagascar, but has declined since 1950. Reached N America in c. 1880, occupying Atlantic coast; has expanded to N especially since 1940's, and recently colonized E Canada (first record in 1986). Fairly common in Greater Antilles and apparently increasing. Records becoming more frequent on migration or in winter in Mexico, where strong evidence of breeding was for the first time obtained in 1988, C America and N South America, presumably connected with increase in N America and West Indies. Undoubtedly affected by habitat destruction, disturbance, hunting and pesticides, but dramatic changes in both distribution and numbers seem to be typical of species.
Bibliography. Ali & Ripley (1978), Bailey (1934), Bauer & Glutz von Blotzheim (1966), Baynard (1913), Beaver *et al.* (1980), Bent (1926), Blake (1977), Bordignon (1988), Brichetti (1982, 1986), Brown *et al.* (1982), Burger (1979), Burger & Miller (1977), Byrd (1978), Carrick (1962), Cheng Tso-hsin (1987), Coates (1985), Cowling & Lowe (1980), Cramp & Simmons (1977), Custer & Osborn (1978), Davis (1979), Dementiev & Gladkov (1951b), Edelson (1990), Géroudet (1978a), Gochfeld (1973), Goodman (1989), Grussu (1987), Heinzel & Martinoles (1988), Hilty & Brown (1986), Hoogerwerf (1953), Howell & Montes (1989), Humphrey (1987), Jozefik (1960), Kale (1978), Kolbe & Neumann (1991a), Kokshaisky (1959), Kumerloeve (1971), Kushlan & Schortemeyer (1974), Kyllingstad (1986), Langrand (1990), Lowe (1983b), Luthin (1984b), Maccarone & Parsons (1988), Maclean (1985), Manry (1978a), Marchant & Higgins (1990), McAlpine *et al.* (1988), Miller, L.M. (1976), Miller & Burger (1978), Milon *et al.* (1973), Ogden (1978, 1981), Palmer (1962), Parkes (1955), Parslow & Everett (1981), Paz (1987), Perennou (1991a), Portella (1986), Post *et al.* (1990), Prall (1976), Pringle (1985), Ridgely & Gwynne (1989), Roberts (1991), Pinto (1983), Saikia & Bhattacharjee (1991), Sanson *et al.* (1954), Sapetin (1968), Scott (1989), Shanholtzer (1970), Silvius & Verheugt (1989), Smythies (1986), Sprunt & Knoder (1980), Stiles & Skutch (1989), Suzuki (1980), Terres (1980), Valdes Miro (1984), Voous (1983), White (1974), White & Bruce (1986), Williams, J.W. (1973), Zook-Rimon & Dotan (1989).

24. White-faced Ibis

Plegadis chihi

French: Ibis à face blanche **German**: Brillensichler **Spanish**: Morito Cariblanco
Other common names: White-faced Glossy Ibis

Taxonomy. *Numenius chihi* Vieillot, 1817, Paraguay and campos of Buenos Aires, Argentina.
Forms superspecies with *P. falcinellus*, of which formerly considered race; hybrids reported in captivity, but not known under natural conditions in narrow zone of overlap in S Louisiana, USA. Monotypic.
Distribution. C California and NW USA S down both coasts of Mexico, wintering S to N Central America. Also SC South America, from SE Bolivia, Paraguay and S Brazil to NC Chile, NC Argentina and Uruguay.

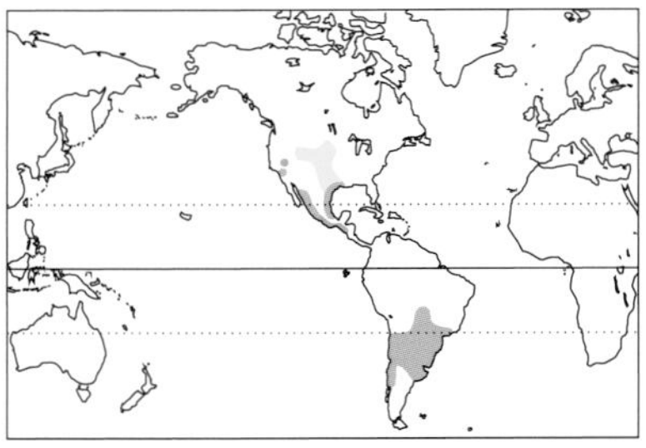

Descriptive notes. 46-66 cm. Some birds have more extensive white around pink-red facial skin than illustrated. Legs redder than in *P. falcinellus*. Non-breeding adult similar to that of *P. falcinellus*, but duller, with head and neck more or less heavily streaked whitish. Immature has head and neck strongly streaked white, underparts dull brown, faintly tinged purple.
Habitat. Mainly freshwater marshes, ponds, rice fields, flooded pastures, irrigated cultivation and margins of large water bodies; less often in areas of brackish water; occasionally in dry fields. Nests on well vegetated islands or around edges of ponds and marshes, usually in large beds of bullrushes or reeds.
Food and Feeding. Mainly insects, especially larvae of horseflies and dragonflies, beetles, grasshoppers and crickets; also crayfish, crabs and other crustaceans, leeches (Hirudinea), snails, frogs, newts and small fish; earthworms (Lumbricidae) main food in irrigated cultivation; fragments of aquatic plants also recorded. Feeds in flocks, sometimes very large, with more than 1000 birds; probes deep in soft soil or picks up prey from surface.
Breeding. Spring breeder in N and S of range, laying Apr-Jun in Texas, May-Jul in California; nesting recorded in Nov in SE Brazil and Dec in Chile. Colonial, in small to very large colonies of up to several thousand pairs, often in association with other Ciconiiformes, cormorants and gulls. Nest is deep cup of reeds, lined with grass; often built less than 1·5 m above water. Usually 3 eggs (3-5); incubation 21-22 days; chicks have dull black down. One bird lived 14 years in captivity. Success related to pesticide levels; in study in Utah, chick production declined from 1·76 chicks per nest with up to 1·50 ppm of DDE, to 1·25 chicks per nest when DDE level was over 3·00 ppm.
Movements. Considered resident in Neotropical portion of range, though irregular local movements occur on large scale throughout; birds ringed as chicks in Santa Fé, NC Argentina, recovered in Rio Grande do Sul, SE Brazil, 1400 km to NE; stragglers to Patagonia and Tierra del Fuego, and at 4300 m in Andes of Bolivia. N populations disperse N after breeding, reaching S Canada, before migrating S to winter in S USA, Mexico and rarely C America. Rare vagrant to Hawaii, though appears less prone to wandering over sea than *P. falcinellus*. Tends to fly in formations.
Status and Conservation. Not globally threatened. Locally abundant in S of range, where is commonest ibis. Uncommon to locally common in N America, where expanding W; said to have declined in USA during 20th century, but trends unclear because of marked fluctuations, probably due mostly to effects of pesticides and relocation of many birds; in Texas, DDE-induced eggshell thinning and mortality caused by dieldrin appear to have reduced population by 42% in period 1969-1976, but use of pollutants reduced and breeding success recovered; in N Utah, number of nests doubled in 1976-1979, after apparent decrease in levels of DDE detected in eggs from 1975; at Carson L, Nevada, colony of c. 3000 pairs disappeared in 1977 when water diverted from lake during drought, but subsequently reoccupied and increasing, with c. 2000 pairs in 1980, c. 3100 in 1983 and c. 5000 in 1985. In Mexico, 100 pairs recently seen at Tamesí and Panuco Deltas and Tampico Lagoons, and 500 birds at Usumacinta Delta and Tabasco Lagoons. Rare in C America and N South America, with few recent records. Flocks of several thousand still frequent in S South America; c. 12,000 pairs breeding at Taim Ecological Station, SE Brazil; in Uruguay c. 25,000 birds at Laguna Merín and Bañados de San Miguel, and minimum 30,000 near Cebollatí, Rocha; large numbers in N and C Argentina, including 20,000 birds at Bañados del Rio Saladillo, 300,000-400,000 at Cañada de Los Tres Arboles y Los Morteros, and 300,000-400,000 at Bañados del Río Dulce. Much less common in Chile, and only found in fair numbers in Cautín and Valdivia; has declined after drainage of swamps in C Chile, where now rare.
Bibliography. Belknap (1957), Belton (1984), Blacklock *et al.* (1978), Blake (1977), Booser & Sprunt (1980), Bray & Klebenow (1988), Burger (1979), Burger & Miller (1977), Capen (1977a, 1977b, 1978), Capen & Leiker (1979), Custer & Mitchell (1989), Davis (1989), Dinsmore & Dinsmore (1986), Eckert (1988), Findholt & Berner (1988), Flickenger & Meeker (1972), Gochfeld (1973), Henny & Bennett (1990), Henny & Herron (1989), Henny *et al.* (1985), Howell & Montes (1989), Hughes (1970), Ivey & Severson (1984), Ivey *et al.* (1988), Jobanek (1987), Johnson (1965, 1972), King *et al.* (1980), Kotter (1970), Nores & Yzurieta (1980), Ogden (1978), Olrog (1975), Palmer (1962), Parkes (1955), de la Peña (1986), Perigo (1990), Pinto (1964), Prall (1976), Rengstorf (1990), Rodgers (1976), Ruschi (1979), Ryder, R.A. (1967), Schmidt, R.A. (1980), Scott & Carbonell (1986), Short (1975), Sick (1984), Skadsen (1988), Stahlecker (1989), Sprunt & Knoder (1980), Steele (1980, 1984), Terres (1980), Voeks & English (1981), Voous (1983), Weller (1967a).

25. Puna Ibis

Plegadis ridgwayi

French: Ibis de Ridgway **German**: Punaibis **Spanish**: Morito de la Puna

Taxonomy. *Falcinellus Ridgwayi* J. A. Allen, 1876, Lake Titicaca, Peru.
Closely related to *P. falcinellus* and *P. chihi*, and might be considered member of same superspecies. Monotypic.
Distribution. Highlands of C Peru S to Bolivia, extreme N Chile and NW Argentina; non-breeding visitor to Peruvian coast.

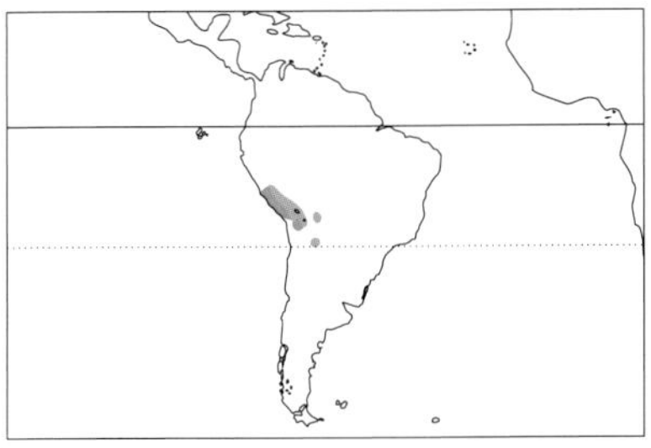

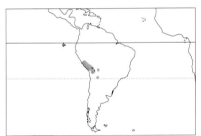

Descriptive notes. 56-61 cm. At some stages has fleshy bill, and legs can be dull red. In breeding plumage, differs from other *Plegadis* by darker overall colour, especially on back and scapulars, with less chestnut; bill and tarsi shorter. Non-breeding adult similar, but duller above; head and neck dark chestnut with fine white streaking. Immature as non-breeding adult, but duller above; some purple on underparts, which are more blackish than in *P. chihi*; dark brown iris and brownish bill.
Habitat. Swampy areas, rushy pastureland, mudflats, ponds and streams; also in coarse bunch-grass on hills, sometimes far from water. In *puna* at 3500-4800 m.
Food and Feeding. Diet unrecorded, but probably based on arthropods and other invertebrates. Usually feeds in flocks, often in fair numbers; mostly feeds by probing into mud in creeks and flooded areas.
Breeding. Season variable: laying peaks in Apr-Jul, but also recorded in Dec-Mar in Peru, and Nov in Bolivia. Colonial. Nest is platform of dry vegetation, built in tall reeds c. 0·5-1 m above water level. Usually 2 eggs (1-2); chick has dark brown down.
Movements. Visits Peruvian coast May-Sept. Vagrants recorded in N Peru.
Status and Conservation. Not globally threatened. Common in Peru and Bolivia: 8000 birds in late 1970's on L Junín, and 1300 at Laguna Arapa and wetland areas of Taraco, Peru; 105 birds at Laguna Alalay, Bolivia, and common resident in area of L Titicaca. Red-listed in Chile, where classed as vulnerable; until 1965 only two confirmed records of 1 and 3 birds, but some sizeable flocks subsequently recorded, e.g. 32 in marshes of Parinacota, Arica, and 40 near Isluga, Tarapacá, both in 1970. Isolated population in *altiplano* of Jujuy, NW Argentina, apparently not numerous.
Bibliography. Blake (1977), Carey *et al.* (1987), Fjeldså & Krabbe (1990), Hellmayr & Conover (1948), Hughes, M.R. (1984), Hughes, R.A. (1970), Johnson (1965, 1972), de la Peña (1986), Perigo (1990), Plenge *et al.* (1989), Scott & Carbonell (1986), Short (1975), Wennrich (1983).

Genus *LOPHOTIBIS* Reichenbach, 1853

26. Madagascar Crested Ibis

Lophotibis cristata

French: Ibis huppé **German**: Schopfibis **Spanish**: Ibis Crestado
Other common names: Crested Wood/Madagascar/White-winged Ibis

Taxonomy. *Tantalus cristatus* Boddaert, 1783, Madagascar.
Two subspecies recognized.
Subspecies and Distribution.
L. c. cristata (Boddaert, 1783) - E Madagascar.
L. c. urschi Lavauden, 1929 - W Madagascar.

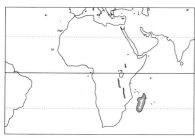

Descriptive notes. 50 cm. In some birds, crest shows more white than in the individual illustrated. Immature probably has duller bare parts, browner head and shorter crest. In western subspecies *urschi* crest appears to have blue (as opposed to green) gloss, with little or no white.
Habitat. All kinds of original woodland of Madagascar, including humid forest in E and N, and dry forest in W and S. In E of range seems able to adapt to slightly degraded and secondary forest, and also found in dense, shaded plantations, e.g. of vanilla or oil-palm. Occasionally sighted in mangroves. Recorded from sea-level to 2000 m, though mainly below 1000 m.

Food and Feeding. Diet presumably based on invertebrates, including adults and larvae of insects, as well as worms, spiders and snails; also small vertebrates including frogs and reptiles. Usually feeds in pairs, less often in small groups or alone; walks rather briskly, stopping frequently to probe deeply into humid forest soil, moss and thick leaf litter, or to pick up small items from surface.
Breeding. At start of rainy season, Sept-Jan. Solitary. Nest is fairly large platform made of branches; usually situated on major forks of trees, 7-15 m above forest floor. Usually 3 eggs (2-3).
Movements. Presumably sedentary. In past, claimed that E populations were probably migratory, but not corroborated.
Status and Conservation. Not globally threatened. Currently considered near-threatened; considered Vulnerable in Red Data Book (1978/79); its forest habitat is disappearing and species hunted for food, so numbers have dwindled throughout range. Race *urschi* still widespread and locally common in dry forests of W Madagascar. Nominate race of E, where deforestation more intense, shows certain degree of adaptability, using secondary forest and breeding in large trees shading vanilla plantations; formerly much more numerous. Despite legal protection, still suffers intensive trapping and hunting.

Bibliography. Andriamampianina & Peyrieras (1972), Appert (1966), Benson *et al.* (1976), Curry-Lindahl (1975), Dee (1986), Delacour (1932), Forbes-Watson (1972), Fradrich (1969), Keith *et al.* (1974), King (1978/79), Langrand (1990), Luthin (1983b, 1983d), Milon *et al.* (1973), Rand (1936), Safford & Duckworth (1990), Salvan (1972a, 1972b), van Someren (1947), Werding (1972).

PLATE 37

inches 12
cm 30

27

28

29

30

31

32

Subfamily PLATALEINAE

Genus *PLATALEA* Linnaeus, 1758

27. Eurasian Spoonbill
Platalea leucorodia

French: Spatule blanche **German**: Löffler **Spanish**: Espátula Común
Other common names: White/European/Common Spoonbill

Taxonomy. *Platalea Leucorodia* Linnaeus, 1758, Europe; restricted to Sweden.
Considered by some to form superspecies with *P. minor*, *P. alba* and *P. regia*; *P. regia* sometimes regarded as race of present species. Asian populations have been assigned separate race, *major*, but doubtfully valid. Three subspecies recognized.
Subspecies and Distribution.
P. l. leucorodia Linnaeus, 1758 - S Spain, Holland and SE Europe to C & E Asia, extending S to Persian Gulf, India and Sri Lanka; winters in W & E Africa and SE China.
P. l. balsaci de Naurois & Roux, 1974 - islands off coast of Mauritania.
P. l. archeri Neumann, 1928 - coasts of Red Sea and Somalia.

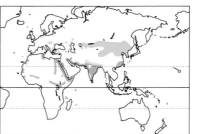

Descriptive notes. 70-95 cm; 1130-1960 g; wingspan 115-135 cm. Male somewhat larger, with longer bill and legs. Extent of yellow at base of neck variable, from only small patch in front to complete ring. Non-breeding adult lacks yellow and also crest. Immature similar to non-breeding adult, but bill initially pinkish; black tips to primaries. Races *balsaci* and *archeri* smaller; *balsaci* has bill wholly black, and usually lacks yellowish at base of neck.
Habitat. Shallow, usually extensive wetlands, including marshes, rivers, large water bodies and flooded areas; also, more often in wintering areas, in sheltered marine habitats, such as deltas, estuaries, tidal creeks and coastal lagoons. Usually nests on islands in lakes or rivers, occasionally off marine coast; alternatively in dense masses of emergent plants, especially reedbeds, often with scattered bushes or trees.
Food and Feeding. Adults and larvae of water beetles, dragonflies, caddisflies, locusts, flies and other insects; also molluscs, crustaceans, worms, leeches, frogs, tadpoles and small fish; sometimes algae, fragments of aquatic plants and other plant matter. Forages in small flocks, less often alone; wades about methodically in shallow water, sweeping bill from side to side; sometimes runs after prey. Partly nocturnal.
Breeding. Spring breeder in N of range, laying mainly from Apr in Spain, but occasionally in winter (Jan-Feb); season variable on Indian Subcontinent, depending on water conditions, mostly

Jul-Oct in N, Nov-Jan in S; Dec-Apr in Sri Lanka; African breeders mainly before or during rains. Typically forms monospecific colonies; in mixed colonies shows tendency towards segregation. Nest is platform of sticks, twigs, reeds or grass stems, lined to varying extent with grass and leaves; built on ground or on tufts of grass, when nesting on islands, or in reeds, bushes, mangroves or trees, up to 5 m above ground. Usually 3-4 eggs (3-7); incubation 24-25 days; chicks have sparse white down; fledging 45-50 days. Sexual maturity probably at 3-4 years old; oldest ringed bird over 28 years old. Success sometimes reduced to nil by rising water levels; in good years, mortality of chicks in nest may be as low as 17·2%.
Movements. Nominate race of Palearctic is migratory and dispersive: European population winters partly in Mediterranean Basin, partly in N tropical Africa; post-fledging dispersal to N in early autumn, exceptionally involving long distance movements; immatures ringed in Yugoslavia and Holland have been recovered in Scotland and Azores respectively. Birds nesting in N Asia winter in S Asia; birds ringed in Caspian region have been recovered in India; breeding populations of India and Sri Lanka sedentary and nomadic. Races *balsaci* and *archeri* sedentary and dispersive. Flies at considerable heights, generally in formation.
Status and Conservation. Not globally threatened. CITES II. Breeding range always discontinuous, but certainly reduced, especially in W Europe; marked declines in many areas, and many former colonies abandoned or only occasionally used; total European population estimated at 3100-4400 pairs. Still breeds regularly in SW Spain, where has increased from small numbers in 1960's, to 300-500 pairs in 1970's, and 500-700 pairs by end of 1980's; Netherlands hold 400 pairs; still fairly widespread in SE Europe; Turkish population 900+ pairs. No information on size of breeding populations in Asia, but mid-winter censuses in early 1990's yielded 508 birds in Iran, 401 in Oman, 438 in Saudi Arabia, 2543 in Pakistan, 4301 in India (1616 in Gujarat, 805 in Rajasthan), 545 in Sri Lanka, and 47 in Bangladesh. In China, over 1000 birds found wintering at Poyang L, Jiangxi; in Japan, perhaps fairly common winter visitor before 1870, but now rare, indicating probable decline in population of E Asia. In Africa, nominate race is uncommon to rare winter visitor, except in Senegal where 781 birds recorded in Jan 1991, and especially at Banc d'Arguin (Mauritania) where 8600-10,000 birds counted in Jan 1980, greatest concentration of present species anywhere; this probably included most of migratory European population; also majority of sedentary race *balsaci*, which is local but abundant, with breeding population estimated at c. 1200 pairs. Race *archeri* uncommon to locally common in Ethiopia, coastal Sudan (200-500 pairs) and Somalia; rare in Egypt (30-50 pairs). Declines throughout range related mainly to drainage of wetlands, pollution and human exploitation of eggs and nestlings in past.
Bibliography. Aguilera (1989, 1990a, 1990b), Aguilera & Alvarez (1989), Ali & Ripley (1978), Austin & Kuroda (1953), Bakewell & Young (1989), Boswall (1971), Bauer & Glutz von Blotzheim (1966), Bernis (1969), Beteille (1986), Brazil (1991), Brown *et al.* (1982), Browner (1964), Canova & Fasola (1989), Cheng Tso-hsin (1987), Cramp & Simmons (1977), Dementiev & Gladkov (1951b), Dollinger (1988), Dragesco (1961a, 1961b), Etchécopar & Hüe (1978), Galarza (1986), García *et al.* (1983), García-Oliva *et al.* (1979), Géroudet (1978a), Girard (1990), Goodman (1989), Goodman & Storer (1987), Hazevoet (1990, 1992), Holstein (1929), Hommonay (1959), Hopwood (1909-1910), Inskipp & Inskipp (1985), Jairaj & Sanjeev Kumar (1990), Kemper (1985, 1987, 1989), Khan (1984, 1987), Kokshaisky (1959), Kolbe & Neumann (1991b), Kortegaard (1973), Luthin (1984b), Marion & Marion (1982), Morel & Morel (1989), Muller (1984, 1987a, 1987b), de Naurois & Roux (1974), Parslow & Everett (1981), Paz (1987), Perennou (1991a), Poorter (1982), Pundt & Ringleben (1963), Roberts (1991), Robiller & Trogisch (1986b), Sapetin (1968), Scott (1989), Skokova (1959), de Souza & Gómez de la Torre (1980), Sutherland & Brooks (1981), Trotignon (1976), Trotignon & Trotignon (1981), Valverde (1960), Vespremeanu (1967, 1968), Weickert (1960), von Wetten (1984, 1985, 1986), von Wetten & Wintermans (1986).

28. Black-faced Spoonbill
Platalea minor

French: Petite Spatule **German**: Schwarzgesichtlöffler **Spanish**: Espátula Menor
Other common names: Lesser Spoonbill

Taxonomy. *Platalea minor* Temminck and Schlegel, 1849, Japan.
Considered by some to form superspecies with *P. leucorodia*, *P. alba* and *P. regia*. Monotypic.
Distribution. Formerly more widespread in E Asia, range now much reduced; breeding only known from N Korea, though also suspected in NE China. Winters in N Viet Nam, S China and Taiwan, occasionally in Japan.

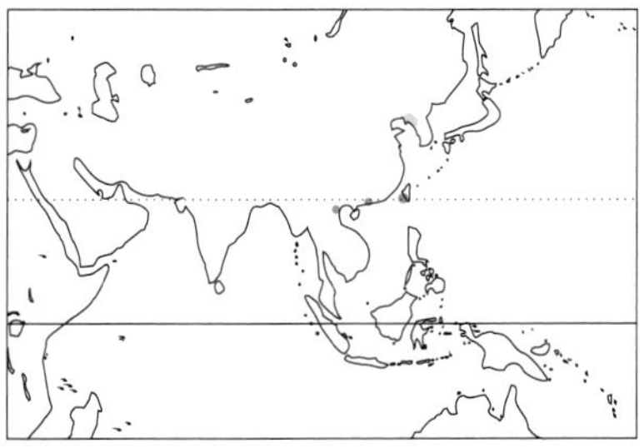

Descriptive notes. 60-78·5 cm. Differs from *P. leucorodia* in facial pattern and darker bill. Non-breeding adult lacks yellowish at base of neck and has shorter crest. Immature similar to non-breeding adult, but bill dark pinkish grey and tips of primaries dark.
Habitat. Marshes, wet rice fields, mangroves, fish ponds, tidal mudflats and estuaries. Nests on small offshore islets.
Food and Feeding. Mainly fish, shellfish, insects and crustaceans, including crabs and shrimps. Feeds in small groups, with 4-25 birds recorded together in Hong Kong; wades in shallow water, sweeping bill from side to side.
Breeding. Laying recorded in Jul in Korea. Colonial, in small groups of 2-3 pairs. Nest is platform made of twigs, built on cliff ledge. 4-6 eggs.
Movements. Migratory; arrives in Korea in Mar, and departs in Nov. Earliest arrival of wintering bird in Japan, end of Oct; wintering population in Hong Kong present late Oct-Mar, with some immatures staying throughout summer since 1987.
Status and Conservation. ENDANGERED. In 1930's was common winter visitor to coast of SE China; has undergone dramatic decline, probably due mainly to drainage of wetlands. Total population estimated at 288 birds, based on maximum counts at all known wintering localities in 1988-1990. Single breeding area known, off W coast of North Korea, but holds only c. 30 individuals; other, undiscovered colonies almost certainly exist elsewhere, probably in NE China, e.g. offshore islands of Liaoning (adjacent to Korean breeding area), where no recent surveys. Only three sites known to hold significant numbers in winter: Mai Po and inner Deep Bay marshes in Hong Kong, where numbers have increased after effective protection, from 3 in 1968 to 50 in 1989; estuary of R Tsen-Wen, SW Taiwan, where large flock discovered in 1985, since when has returned each winter, with 145 birds in 1989; and estuary of Red River in Viet Nam where 62 birds recorded in 1988; other sites in Japan, South Korea, China and Taiwan occasionally hold small numbers in winter. The recent discoveries in Taiwan and Viet Nam suggest that undiscovered wintering areas may exist; small numbers may well go unnoticed in large wintering flocks of *P. leucorodia*; few individuals detected thus in surveys carried out to date, e.g. at Poyang L, Jiangxi. The breeding area in North Korea is effectively protected, but drainage and general alteration of wetlands still threatens wintering sites, especially in Taiwan and Viet Nam (see page 490).
Bibliography. Anon. (1991b), Austin (1948), Austin & Kuroda (1953), Bakewell & Young (1989), Brazil (1991), Cheng Tso-hsin (1987), Chung (1986), Collar & Andrew (1988), Delacour & Jabouille (1931), Dickinson *et al.* (1991), Etchécopar & Hüe (1987), Gore & Won (1971), Hachisuka & Udagawa (1951), Karpowicz (1985), Kennerly (1987, 1990a, 1990b), Luthin (1983d), Mann (1989), Pinto (1983), Round *et al.* (1988), de Schauensee (1984), Scott (1989), Scott & Howes (1989), Sonobe & Izawa (1987), Swinhoe (1863), Vo Quy (1975), Won, H.G. (1966), Won, P.O. (1971).

29. African Spoonbill
Platalea alba

French: Spatule d'Afrique **German**: Afrikanischer Löffler **Spanish**: Espátula Africana

Taxonomy. *Platalea alba* Scopoli, 1786, Luzon, Philippines; error, Cape of Good Hope.
Considered by some to form superspecies with *P. leucorodia*, *P. minor* and *P. regia*. Monotypic.
Distribution. Senegal to Ethiopia, S to Cape Province; Madagascar.

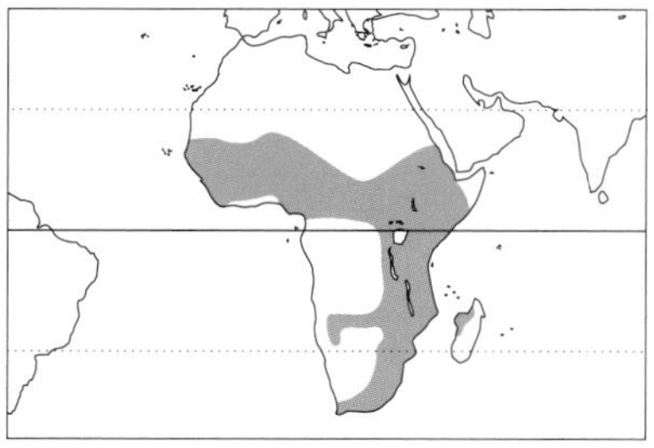

Descriptive notes. 90-91 cm; c. 1790 g. Unmistakable; only white *Platalea* with intense pink-red legs. Short crest. Male slightly larger. No seasonal variation. Immature has more feathering on forehead, smaller crest and blackish tips to primaries and underwing-coverts; bill duller, legs black.
Habitat. Lakes, marshes, reservoirs and other large, shallow inland waters; less often in coastal lagoons, salt-pans, creeks and estuaries.
Food and Feeding. Small fish and aquatic invertebrates. Usually feeds in small parties of up to 10 birds, sometimes singly; wades slowly into shallow water with bill partly or wholly submerged, sweeping it from side to side; also probes in mud and sometimes dashes about rapidly, chasing fish.
Breeding. From W Africa E to Sudan laying peaks in dry season; in E and C Africa mostly in rains, sometimes in dry season; in S Africa mainly winter to early spring. Colonial, in groups of up to 250 pairs, or even more, often with other Ciconiiformes, cormorants and darters. Nest is flattish, oval platform of sticks or reeds; situated on partly submerged trees, in bushes or reeds, or on rocky islets. Usually 2-3 eggs (2-4); chicks have white down; incubation 25-29 days; young birds independent at c. 46 days. Success of 0·8, and less than 1 chick fledged per pair, recorded in S and E Africa respectively.
Movements. Little known; probably nomadic throughout most of range and possibly migratory, at least in S Africa, where wanders considerable distances; ringing results show movements of several hundred kilometres from Transvaal to Zambia; apparently sedentary in Madagascar. Vagrants recorded in S Oman and S Yemen. Often flies in V-formation.
Status and Conservation. Not globally threatened. Generally uncommon and patchily distributed, but locally common, especially on Rift Valley lakes of Kenya, Tanzania and W Uganda. Resting flocks of up to 1000 birds recorded. In 1987, 300-400 pairs bred in colony at L Fitri, Chad, and 300-350 pairs at 2 colonies in Inner Delta of R Niger, Mali. Census of Jan 1991 gave 313 birds on L Nakuru (Kenya), 108 at L St Lucia (South Africa), 333 in Botswana, 130 in Senegal and 61 in Zambia. In Madagascar, still common around some lakes of W coast, particularly L Kinkony, L Bemamba and L Ihotry, but seriously threatened by destruction of breeding colonies; in recent years has declined notably at L Aloatra, where formerly frequent.
Bibliography. Altenbourg & van der Kamp (1989), Berruti (1980, 1983), Blaker (1967), Britton (1980), Brown & Britton (1980), Brown *et al.* (1982), Connor (1979), Coverdale & Hancock (1983), Elgood (1982), Kahl (1983), Kieser & Kieser (1977), Klug & Boswall (1970), Kushlan (1978), Langrand (1990), Liversidge (1955), Maclean (1985), Macleod *et al.* (1960), Mackworth-Praed & Grant (1957-1973), Milon *et al.* (1973), Morel & Morel (1961), de Naurois (1966b), Neame (1968), Parsons (1977), Perennou (1991a), Pinto (1983), Pooley (1968), Quickelberge (1972), Rand (1936), Reynolds (1965), Robiller & Trogisch (1986b), Skead (1954, 1967), Siegfried (1968a), Smith (1943), Snow (1978), Taylor (1957), Whitelaw (1968), Whitfield & Blaber (1979), Wilson (1957), Winterbottom (1958), Wylie (1982).

30. Royal Spoonbill
Platalea regia

French: Spatule royale **German**: Königslöffler **Spanish**: Espátula Real
Other common names: Black-billed Spoonbill

Taxonomy. *Platalea regia* Gould, 1838, east coast of New South Wales.
Considered by some to form superspecies with *P. leucorodia*, *P. minor* and *P. alba*. Sometimes regarded as race of *P. leucorodia*. Monotypic.
Distribution. Australia and New Zealand; Java and Sulawesi through Lesser Sundas and Moluccas to S New Guinea and Rennell I (Solomon Is).
Descriptive notes. 74-81 cm; 1400-2070 g; wingspan c. 120 cm. Bill and face more extensively black than in *P. minor*, with conspicuous yellow patches above eyes. Long crest. Males slightly larger, with longer bill, legs, and often crest. Non-breeding adult lacks crest and yellow at base of foreneck. Immature as non-breeding adult; has shorter, smooth bill, and lacks red and yellow patches on head; has black tips to primaries.
Habitat. Freshwater wetlands including swamps, flooded pastures, lagoons, sewage works, pools and shallow parts of lakes and reservoirs; also sheltered marine habitats, especially tidal mudflats, and less often coastal lagoons, salt-pans and mangroves. Nests in wetlands, on trees, shrubs and reeds, occasionally on ground.
Food and Feeding. At inland sites, mainly fish (*Gambusia*, *Arenigobius*, *Carassius*); on tidal mudflats, mostly shrimps (*Macrobrachium*); also takes other crustaceans (amphipods, isopods, crayfish), aquatic insects and molluscs; occasionally plant matter. Intake estimated at c. 1900 prey items/day. Usually forages alone or in dispersed parties of up to 50 birds; feeds by wading, sweeping bill from side to side in smooth lateral arcs. Feeds both day and night, taking different prey types.

On following page: 31. Yellow-billed Spoonbill (*Platalea flavipes*); 32. Roseate Spoonbill (*Platalea ajaja*).

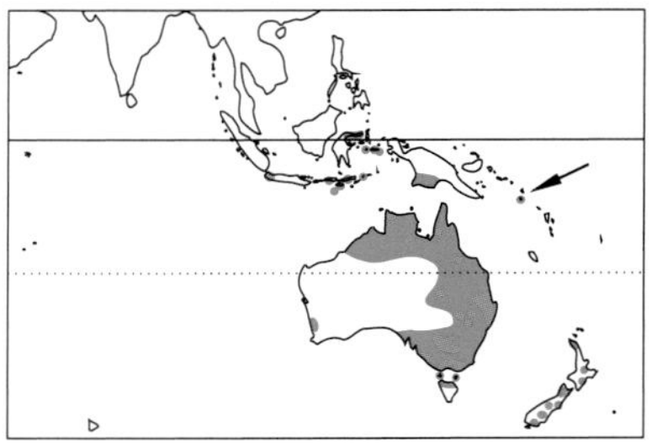

Breeding. Usually Oct-Mar in SE Australia, and Mar-May in N Australia, but season varies according to water conditions; laying in Nov in New Zealand. Colonial or semi-colonial, with up to 50 pairs; sometimes single pairs. Nest is shallow platform of sticks and twigs, lined with soft vegetation. Usually 3 eggs (2-4); incubation 20-25 days; chicks have white down. Success recorded of 0·4 and 0·55 chicks reared per pair.
Movements. Most coastal populations in Australia appear to be sedentary; irregular movements inland influenced by water conditions. Movements between Australia and S New Guinea recorded frequently. In New Zealand, disperses after breeding. Colonization of New Zealand and records of vagrants on several Pacific islands indicate occurrence of some long distance movements; one immature recovered over 1400 km from breeding site.
Status and Conservation. Not globally threatened. Generally common in suitable habitat in E and N Australia, rare in SW; may have become commoner in recent years in coastal New South Wales; recorded with increasing frequency in Tasmania, where formerly unknown. In New Zealand, was rare straggler, probably started to breed in early 1940's, with first confirmed record of 1 pair at Okarito, South I, in 1949/50, and has since increased, perhaps with further arrivals from Australia: 10-12 pairs by 1960 and 100 birds by 1972, but after disruption of breeding in Okarito only 49 in 1977; since 1978 new colonies established, up to 4 at the beginning of 1990's, all in South I; 157 birds counted in 1990 in survey of coast of Otago; regular winter visitor in small numbers to North I. In New Guinea, common in S, especially in Trans-Fly region; present throughout year, but thought to be non-breeding visitor from Australia; in 1988, flocks of up to 250 birds in SE Irian Jaya, where breeding might occur, and 800 birds counted in Bensbach R and Tonda Wildlife Management Area, Papua New Guinea. Status uncertain in Sulawesi, Moluccas and Lesser Sundas, where frequently sighted; possibly vagrants from Australia, but sporadic breeding seems likely. In Java small population bred at Pulau Dua, but in 1950's only 5 birds reported and no recent records. No recent information from Rennell I (Solomon Is), where was rare inhabitant of L Tengano in 1945. In Australia, many natural freshwater wetlands used by species have been altered by drainage, increased salinity and recreational activities; species very vulnerable to disturbance, especially when breeding. Construction of artificial wetlands has provided additional feeding habitat.
Bibliography. Anon. (1990c), Beard *et al.* (1942), Beehler *et al.* (1986), Beruldsen (1980), Boekel (1980), Bull *et al.* (1985), Chambers (1989), Coates (1985), Crawford (1980), Falla *et al.* (1981), Fjeldså (1985c), Ford (1989), Hannecart & Letocart (1983), Holdaway (1980), Hoogerwerf (1951, 1952b, 1964), Kahl (1987b, 1988), Karpowicz (1985), Lowe (1981, 1982), Marchant & Higgins (1990), Pringle (1985), Robertson & Preece (1980), Schodde & Tidemann (1988), Schulz (1989), Scott (1989), Sharland (1957a), Sibson (1982), Silvius & Verheugt (1989), Slater (1987), Vestjens (1975a, 1975b), White & Bruce (1986), Williams, M.J. (1985a), Wyndham (1978).

31. Yellow-billed Spoonbill
Platalea flavipes

French: Spatule à bec jaune **German**: Gelbschnabellöffler **Spanish**: Espátula Piquigualda
Other common names: Yellow-legged Spoonbill

Taxonomy. *Platalea flavipes* Gould, 1838, New South Wales.
Sometimes placed in monospecific genus *Platibis*. Monotypic.
Distribution. Australia.

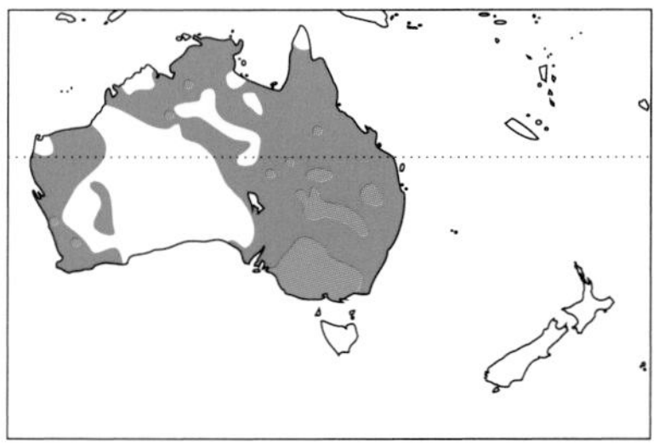

Descriptive notes. 76-100 cm; 1814-1928 g. Bill colour variable, from uniformly buffish to conspicuously spotted black on distal part. Male larger, with longer bill and legs. Non-breeding adult lacks or has shorter plumes on scapulars and base of foreneck; facial skin less strongly coloured. Immature similar to non-breeding adult, but somewhat smaller, with shorter, less spoon-shaped bill, and black tips to primaries.
Habitat. Inland wetlands with fresh or brackish water, including shallow swamps, flooded pastures, watercourses, channels, pools and shallow margins of lakes; rarely in tidal mudflats and other sheltered marine habitats. Visits small swamps, farm water supplies and pools more often than *P. regia*. Nests in wetlands, on trees, or in reeds or rushes.
Food and Feeding. Mainly aquatic insects, especially back-swimmers; also crayfish, shrimps, fish and occasionally molluscs and plant matter. Usually forages by wading slowly, sweeping bill from side to side; sweeps bill more slowly than sympatric *P. regia*, taking smaller, slower prey. Occasionally makes loping runs after prey.
Breeding. Sept-Apr in S of range, Mar-May in N; season varies markedly, depending on water conditions, especially inland areas. Solitary or in very loose colonies usually of few pairs. Nest is large, flattish platform of sticks and twigs, or with rushes and reeds where colony in reedbeds. Usually 3 eggs (2-4); incubation 26-31 days; chicks have white down. Success recorded of 0·75 and 1·37 chicks reared per pair.
Movements. Appears to be mostly sedentary in S of Australia; observations suggest regular movements in N of range and in inland New South Wales. Vagrant to Tasmania, New Zealand, Lord Howe I and Norfolk I.

Status and Conservation. Not globally threatened. Uncommon to locally common in suitable wetlands; stronghold of breeding population in New South Wales and Victoria. Natural freshwater wetlands used for feeding and breeding have been altered by drainage, clearing, grazing, increased salinity, burning and groundwater extraction. However, irrigation and construction of dams and channels have provided new feeding habitats, and range seems to have expanded during present century, especially in E and W Australia. Very vulnerable to human disturbance.
Bibliography. Beruldsen (1980), Billing (1977), Boekel (1980), Fjeldså (1985c), Ford (1989), Garstone (1973), Kahl (1988), Lowe (1981), Marchant & Higgins (1990), Pringle (1985), Schodde & Tidemann (1988), Slater (1987), Vestjens (1975a, 1975b), Williams, M.J. (1985a), Wyndham (1978).

32. Roseate Spoonbill
Platalea ajaja

French: Spatule rosée **German**: Rosalöffler **Spanish**: Espátula Rosada

Taxonomy. *Platalea Ajaja* Linnaeus, 1758, "in America australi" = Rio São Francisco, eastern Brazil, *ex* Marcgraf.
Often placed in monospecific genus *Ajaia*. Monotypic.
Distribution. SE USA and West Indies through Mexico and C America to S America: E of Andes, S to N Argentina; W of Andes in W Ecuador and NW Peru.

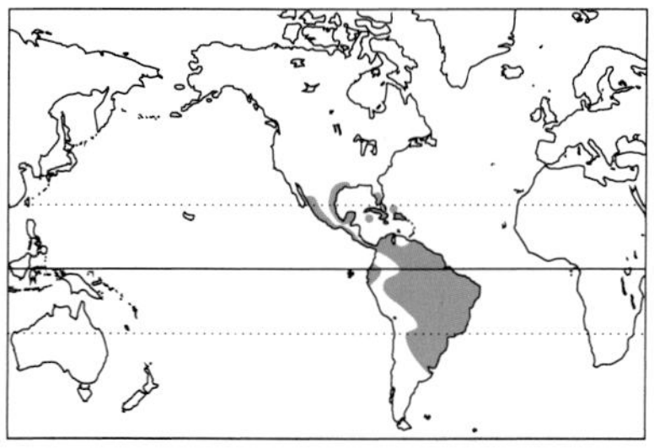

Descriptive notes. 68·5-86·5 cm; c. 1400 g. Only pink spoonbill. Bill uniform or spotted black. During courtship, facial skin partly orange-yellow. Immature has head feathered, white plumage variably tinged pink, outer primaries tipped and edged brown and yellowish bill.
Habitat. Tidal ponds, sloughs, mangrove swamps and other coastal areas with salt or brackish water; less often inland, on pools, marshes, rice fields and other freshwater wetlands in savannas and other open areas. Nests in wetlands and on coastal islands, on low trees, thick bushes, mangroves or reeds; occasionally on ground.
Food and Feeding. Small fish (*Zygonectes*, *Gambusia*, *Cyprinodon*) and crustaceans, especially shrimps (*Palaemonetes*, *Penaeus*); water beetles and other insects, molluscs and slugs; also some plant material, including fibres and roots of sedges. Forages alone or in small flocks; feeds by moving bill sideways in long arcs through water; sometimes immerses entire head and part of neck.
Breeding. Main laying period Nov in Florida, Apr in Texas; in Costa Rica, breeds from end of rains to dry season, starting Oct-Dec, depending on year. Colonial, usually with other Ciconiiformes and cormorants; nest is platform of sticks and twigs lined with grass and other soft vegetation. Usually 2-3 eggs (1-5); incubation 22 days; chicks have short white down; fledging c. 6 weeks. Sexual maturity at 3 years old at earliest. Average success of 1·5 chicks fledged per nest per year, at Nueces Bay, Texas (1977-1980).
Movements. Generally considered to be sedentary throughout most of range, though partially migratory in N; most birds breeding in Louisiana and Texas apparently winter in Mexico; seasonal movements also recorded between Cuba and Florida. Post-breeding dispersal of immatures and adults throughout range; single birds or flocks from Mexico occasionally reach S California. Movements very little known in S America; rare non-breeding visitors reach c. 52° S in Argentina and C Chile. Accidental to Falkland Is.
Status and Conservation. Not globally threatened. Uncommon to locally common throughout extensive range, though normally in lower numbers than other Ciconiiformes. In USA, was common along Gulf coast in early 19th century, but almost exterminated in 1930's by intense persecution for plume trade starting in 1880's; legally protected in 1940's, followed by recovery and in mid-1970's c. 1000 pairs in Florida and c. 2500 in Texas; now seems to be declining again due to mosquito control programmes and increasing alteration of breeding and feeding habitats. In Mexico, during 1970's, estimated c. 100 pairs on Pacific coast, and 3250 pairs on Gulf coast, including 1250 at Usumacinta Delta and Tabasco Lagoons. Largest C American colony at Palo Verde, Costa Rica, where up to 1000 pairs recently recorded; no recent evidence of breeding in Belize, Guatemala and Panama, where declining. In West Indies, c. 50 pairs breed on Great Inagua (Bahamas), small numbers on Hispaniola, and several colonies in Cuba. Status unknown in much of Amazonia; important colonies probably in Mato Grosso, Brazil; population of Pantanal apparently declining. Recent counts in S America include: 624 birds on L Maracaibo and along coast, 228 in *llanos*, and 92 at Orinoco Delta, Venezuela; 130 at estuary of Essequibo, Guyana; a few hundred birds and tens of breeding pairs in Surinam; 150 birds at Lagoa do Peixe, SE Brazil; 100 along R Paraguay, Paraguay; and 300-400 at Bajos Submeridionales, NE Argentina. Main threats throughout range are alteration of breeding and feeding habitats, hunting and pollution.
Bibliography. Allen (1942, 1947, 1962), Belton (1984), Bent (1926), Blacklock *et al.* (1978), Blake (1977), Brooks (1990), Burger (1979), Crawford (1979), Dunstan (1976), ffrench (1992), Griffith *et al.* (1946), Haverschmidt (1968, 1969b), Heinrich (1986), Hilty & Brown (1986), Hoyt (1906), Kale (1978), Kushlan (1978), Kushlan & White (1977), Leber (1980), Luthin (1984b), McDaniel *et al.* (1963), McNeil *et al.* (1990), Monroe (1968), Morales (1990), Morrison *et al.* (1978b), Nores & Yzurieta (1980), Ogden (1976a, 1976b, 1978), Olrog (1965), Palmer (1962), Parmalee & Perino (1970), de la Peña (1986), Perigo (1990), Pinto (1964), Powell (1987, 1989), Ramo & Busto (1984), Ramsey (1968), Ridgely & Gwynne (1989), Robertson *et al.* (1983), Robiller & Trogisch (1986b), Ruschi (1979), Russell, J.K. (1978), Russell, R.P. (1982), Scott & Carbonell (1986), Serna (1990), Shackford (1991), Sick (1984), Slud (1964), Smith & Breininger (1988), Sprunt (1939), Sprunt & Knoder (1980), Stiles & Skutch (1989), Stott (1959), Terres (1980), Thibault & Guyot (1988), Thomas (1979a), Valdes Miro (1984), Voous (1983), Weller (1967a), Wetmore (1965), White *et al.* (1982), Woods (1988), Zapata & Martínez (1972).

Order PHOENICOPTERIFORMES

Phoenicopteriformes

|

Phoenicopteridae

flamingos

Class AVES
Order PHOENICOPTERIFORMES
Family PHOENICOPTERIDAE (FLAMINGOS)

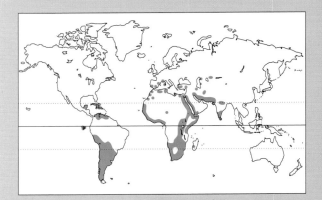

- Large waterbirds with long neck and legs, and unique downcurved bill adapted to filter-feeding.
- 80-145 cm.

- All regions except Australasian and Antarctic.
- Shallow waterbodies, normally saline, brackish or alkaline; coastal or inland, from sea-level up to c. 5000 m.
- 3 genera, 5 species, 6 taxa.
- No species threatened; none extinct since 1600.

Systematics

The flamingos form one of the most ancient bird families, and there are fossils of present day genera from the Oligocene, about 30 million years ago, while more primitive forms have been traced back to the Middle Eocene, more than 50 million years ago. Some fossils have been turned up in parts of Europe, North America and Australia where flamingos are not found today, indicating that their past distribution was a good deal wider than at present.

There is still very little consensus about the taxonomic situation of the flamingos. The most conservative view is to maintain them as a suborder of the Ciconiiformes. In favour of this are some anatomical similarities, such as the shape of the pelvis and the ribs, which are very similar in the storks; their egg-white proteins are, in turn, like those of the herons. However, there are other aspects, including behaviour, especially that of chicks, voice and feather-lice, which link them more closely with wildfowl (Anseriformes), especially geese. Like geese, they have webbed feet and waterproof plumage, while the structure of the bill is fairly similar. For all these reasons, there is a growing tendency, followed here, for flamingos to be designated a separate order, Phoenicopteriformes, placed between the Ciconiiformes and the Anseriformes.

In the early 1980's, a new hypothesis claimed that flamingos have common ancestors with some of the waders, including oystercatchers, avocets and stilts, and should, therefore, be included as a separate family within the Charadriiformes. This proposal is based on fossil evidence and on similarities, in both anatomy and behaviour, between flamingos and the Australian Banded Stilt (*Cladorhynchus leucocephalus*), while the resemblances with storks, herons and waterfowl are put down to convergent evolution.

The most recent studies of systematics, using advanced techniques, are equally varied in their results. Sibley and Ahlquist, basing their classification on DNA-DNA hybridization, include the storks, ibises, Shoebill, pelicans and New World vultures among the flamingos' closest relatives. They reckon that flamingos diverged from these relatives around 48 million years ago, and that similarities with geese are due to analogy rather than kinship. On the other hand, a recent study on the structure of biliary acids, another criterion used to determine evolutionary relationships in vertebrates, groups flamingos with the Anseriformes, in particular with the genus *Branta*, separating them off from the Ciconiiformes and the Charadriiformes.

The very slight differences between the six described forms of flamingo do not really appear to justify the classic division of the family into three distinct genera. The species can be separated into two groups according to the structure of the bill. The Greater Flamingo (*Phoenicopterus ruber*) and the Chilean Flamingo (*Phoenicopterus chilensis*) have a relatively primitive feeding apparatus, whereas, in contrast, the Lesser Flamingo (*Phoeniconaias minor*), the Andean Flamingo (*Phoenicoparrus andinus*) and the Puna Flamingo (*Phoenicoparrus jamesi*) are more specialized. The basic difference between the genera *Phoeniconaias* and *Phoenicoparrus* is the absence or presence of a hind toe. The three forms of *Phoenicopterus* have been considered three distinct species or alternatively races of a single species. Nowadays, however, the two larger forms are nearly always treated as well defined races of the same species, the Greater Flamingo, but when they are separated, rather confusingly it is the Old World race *roseus* that is almost invariably known as the Greater Flamingo, while the nominate race *ruber*, of the New World, is usually known as the Caribbean Flamingo. The Chilean Flamingo shows greater differences, especially in behaviour, and seems best considered a full species.

The isolated Galapagos population of Greater Flamingos is occasionally considered to form a separate subspecies, *glyphorhynchus*, on the basis of coloration and size, as well as its habit of breeding in small colonies on small lagoons, quite unlike any other populations of flamingos.

Morphological Aspects

Flamingos are quite unmistakable, due to their remarkably long legs and neck, and their distinctive pink plumage. They are large birds, standing 90-155 cm tall, and while males are larger than females, in some species this difference is not very noticeable. The body is oval and the head is rather small, in comparison with the long neck.

The neck and the legs are longer, relative to the body size, than in any other group of birds. The long legs allow them to wade to greater depths than the other large wading birds, while the long neck enables them to take food from the mud at the bottom. When feeding in shallow water, the long neck permits wide swinging movements of the bill, which increases foraging efficiency. There are 17 cervical vertebrae, not a particularly high number compared with 25 in swans, or 15-16 in geese. However, flamingos have elongated vertebrae which give the neck a stepped appearance, when it is bent.

The outlying population of
Greater Flamingo that
occurs in the Galapagos
Islands is the source of a
certain amount of
taxonomic controversy.
Although generally
included in the Caribbean
race ruber, some authors
consider that its slight
morphological differences,
basically the shorter
wings, bill and tarsi, along
with the paler overall
coloration, as well, in
particular, as its notable
ecological characteristics,
suggest its placement in
a separate subspecies.
One of the aspects which
most differentiates this
population is its tendency
to live in small groups,
even when breeding,
some colonies consisting
of only three pairs, and
with a maximum of 50, a
habit which has no
parallel within this highly
gregarious family.

[Phoenicopterus ruber ruber,
Isla Floreana, Galapagos.
Photo: A. de Sostoa &
X. Ferrer]

Another adaptation that increases the depth to which flamingos can wade is the reduced feathering on the tibia, which allows them to go in virtually up to the belly. The feet are comparatively small, with four toes, except in *Phoenicoparrus*, which lacks the hind toe. The three front toes are webbed, and this gives them extra support when walking along on mud, while it also allows them to swim with ease and to feed in areas where they can not stand up; they even upend, like many waterfowl, in order to feed at greater depths.

The pink and crimson plumage, with black flight-feathers, is unmistakable, and characteristic of all five species. The reddish coloration, which is fundamental in stimulating reproduction, comes from carotenoid pigments; these are substances synthesized by algae or other abundant organisms, which flamingos consume either directly or through the invertebrates that feed on them. The birds can break down the carotenoids with hepatic enzymes, in order to convert them into usable pigments, such as canthaxanthin, which has been found in the feathers, the bare skin and the egg yolks. Juvenile plumage is grey with brown and pink markings.

Very little is known about moult in flamingos. The moult cycle is extremely irregular, and can occur anything from twice a year to once every two years, or at even longer intervals. Both the frequency and the degree of completeness of moult vary, apparently with age, and in relation to breeding attempts, although this is not yet clear. Occasionally, especially in captive birds, the flight-feathers are moulted simultaneously which implies a period of flightlessness, as in the waterfowl, which lasts about three weeks in the Lesser Flamingo; otherwise moult is more or less continuous, with no flightless period.

A remarkable feature of flamingo morphology is the extraordinary bill, which allows the birds to feed in a manner comparable to that of whalebone whales (Mysticeti). The edges and inner part of the mandibles are covered in numerous lamellae, corneous structures which are set in rows and are generally covered in fine hairs which can be raised or flattened at will. The gap between the mandibles is occupied by the tongue, which moves back and forward like the piston in a pump. In order to avoid the ingestion of excessively large particles, flamingos keep their mandibles only partially open. The characteristic bend in the bill means that the opening be-

tween them is more or less equal along their entire length, whereas, if the bill were straight, the opening would be too big at the tip. When the tongue sucks in water, the inner lamellae are depressed, in order to let in all the food particles which have managed to cross the narrow opening. Afterwards, as the tongue expels the water, the inner lamellae are raised in order to trap the particles like a filter. The particles are then guided to the throat by the backward-pointing spines which cover the tongue and palate. The bills of the different species differ in internal shape and also in the number, dimensions and arrangement of the lamellae and hairs. Thus, when two or more species coincide in the same habitat, they feed on different food, and so avoid competition (see Food and Feeding).

Flamingos are graceful and agile in their movements; they walk easily and can run well when threatened. Take-off normally requires a short run up, with wings flapping, except when the wind is sufficiently strong. Flight, with the neck outstretched, as in storks and cranes but unlike herons, is swift and direct, and birds can manage speeds of 50-60 km/h. Wingbeats are quite rapid and are more or less continous, although they are sometimes interspersed with short glides. Flocks tend to fly in lines or in V-formations, like geese and cranes, and in this way, with each bird flying behind and slightly to one side of the preceding bird, they avoid the turbulence produced by their neighbours, and can also see them clearly so that any change of direction can be followed instantly. When landing is imminent, glides become longer and, as at take-off, landing birds run a few paces.

Habitat

The typical habitats of flamingos are rather specialized. They occupy large, shallow lakes or lagoons, which may be alkaline, with a pH value of as much as 10·5, or saline, sometimes with more than twice the salinity of sea water. Lakes may be far inland or near the sea, or even connected to it, and at such sites flamingos can be abundant.

Flamingos' resistance to the harsh conditions of their environment is quite remarkable. They can put up with high levels of chlorides, sodium carbonate, often sulphates and fluoride,

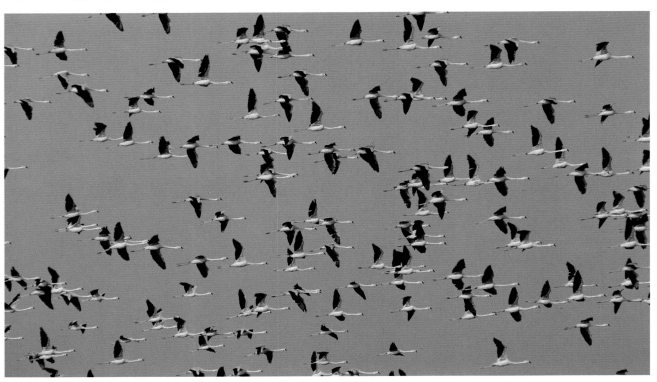

The flight silhouette of the flamingos is unmistakable, with the long neck stretched out in front and the equally long legs trailing behind. It is only in flight that the wings completely reveal the striking black and red coloration that, with slight variations, is shared by all species. The typical style of flight involves the wings being flapped fairly rapidly and almost continuously. As with nearly all their activites, flamingos' movements are carried out in large flocks, in which individuals generally follow one another closely, using a variety of formations, which afford them aerodynamic advantages.

[*Phoenicopterus chilensis*, Paracas, Peru. Photo: A. Greensmith/ Ardea]

together with temperatures of up to 68°C or more, and such conditions prove intolerable for most other animals. Flamingos, however, seem unaffected by the caustic nature of the water, and will drink it, even near the outlets of hot springs and geysers, where the water temperature is near boiling point, but the salinity level is somewhat lower. Often, the only other living creatures with them are algae, diatoms and several kinds of aquatic invertebrates, which can become abundant, due to the lack of competition. These constitute an extremely rich source of food almost exclusively for the flamingos (see Food and Feeding). The birds can survive the harsh winters of the *altiplano*, when night temperatures may drop to -30°C, due to the hot springs of volcanic origin, which are found in many Andean lakes. Around these the water is never frozen over, and groups of flamingos frequent them all winter, when the rest of the lake is completely frozen. This use of a highly specialized habitat may have helped these ancient birds to survive, as they have probably had to face relatively little competition from species of more recent origins.

Furthermore, altitude does not seem to be a limiting factor for flamingos. Thus, the Greater Flamingo is usually found at sea-level, but it also breeds at 3100 m in Afghanistan, at Lake Dasht-e-Nawar, whilst the three Andean species use high-altitude lakes, mostly at 3500-4500 m, although the Chilean Flamingo is also found at sea-level in places.

The presence or absence of fish, which is often related to the salinity of the water, could have a great influence on the use of lakes by some flamingos. This connection has been firmly established for the Chilean Flamingo by S. H. Hurlbert and other researchers, in a study carried out in 20 lakes in the Peruvian Andes, at altitudes ranging from 3700 to 4700 m. The Chilean Flamingo is scarce or absent in the lakes with fish, and present, generally in large numbers, where there are no fish to compete with them for their invertebrate prey. The lakes with no fish are almost always either saline or periodically dry, or both. However, the introduction of fish to some lakes has been encouraged by the authorities in recent years, for example in Peru, and this may seriously affect the distribution of this species. The same factor could also be critical in the case of the Greater and the Caribbean Flamingos, which also feed basically on invertebrates, although there are no data yet to prove this. It should not affect the other three species, as their main food is algae.

The flamingos' most characteristic habitats are these large lagoons and saline or alkaline lakes, which may be as much as 80 km wide, for instance the Salar de Uyuni, in Bolivia. They tend to be practically void of vegetation, especially those used for breeding, and surrounded by desert-like ground. However, there are some exceptions, and birds can occasionally be found feeding in fresh water. Since 1975, this habit has increased at the Camargue, in the south of France, perhaps due to the growth of the Greater Flamingo population in the preceding years, which may have forced the birds to exploit new habitats, and the same tendency has also been noted for the Chilean Flamingo in some Andean lakes. The Caribbean Flamingo in the Galapagos Islands constitutes another exception, for the birds use small saline lagoons next to the beach, and tiny colonies of 3-50 pairs even breed in them. The Greater Flamingo also uses mangrove swamps and salt-pans, including some which are still in operation, and it has even been found trying to nest at reservoirs with high salinity, in the Orange Free State, in South Africa. Purely marine habitats are also used on occasions, for instance the tidal flats in the Gulf of Gabès, in Tunisia, and at the Banc d'Arguin, in Mauritania, where the birds breed on sandy islands in the intertidal zone.

General Habits

Not only at their colonies, but also whilst feeding, resting and moving about, flamingos are amongst the most gregarious of birds. Groups of only a few individuals are rare, whilst it is not uncommon to find dense flocks of thousands or tens of thousands of birds, and in East Africa over a million Lesser Flamingos can gather together. This obviously provides greater security, and is possible only because, like most life forms in such specialized habitats, the algae and invertebrates on which they feed also tend to be concentrated in great profusion, so the birds do not have to compete for food.

The amount of daily activity varies with the circumstances, and in places the Greater Flamingo has been found to feed little during the day. A study at the Camargue has demonstrated that, while breeding birds show a certain amount of feeding activity at any time of the day or night, the large numbers of non-breeders feed almost exclusively at night, and spend the day sleeping or in comfort activities. Contrary to the previous belief that this was an adaptation to improve foraging efficiency, in connection with the diurnal vertical migration of the main prey, brine-shrimps (*Artemia*), it seems that it may have an anti-predator or thermoregulatory function, or that it might even be an

adaptation to avoid human disturbance. In East Africa, the Lesser Flamingo tends to feed more at night than the Greater, which could be explained by the former's need for calmer water for feeding (see Food and Feeding).

Starting several months before breeding and continuing afterwards, flamingos often devote considerable time to the performance of collective displays, which may be carried out by several hundred birds, or even thousands, in the case of the intensely communal displays of the Lesser Flamingo. They consist of a series of ritualized postures and movements: one of the most common, "Head-flagging", involves stretching the neck and the head up as high as possible, with the bill pointing upwards, and then rhythmically turning the head from one side to the other; in the "Wing-salute", the wings are spread for a few seconds, showing their strikingly contrasted colours, while the tail is cocked and the neck outstretched; the "Twist-preen" entails the bird twisting its neck back and appearing to preen quickly, with its bill behind a partly open wing; the "Wing-leg Stretch" consists of the leg and the wing on one side of the body being extended backwards; and "Marching" involves a large, tightly packed, synchronized flock walking in one direction, before turning tail abruptly.

Sometimes only one display is performed before the birds go back to feeding or other activities, but more often, especially as breeding approaches, the displays are carried out in stereotyped, predictable sequences, one of the most typical being the "Head-flag" - "Wing-salute" - "Twist-preen" series.

The purpose of these displays is to synchronize, by means of hormonal stimulation, the breeding attempts of as many birds as possible. In this way, the population can make the most of the periods when the conditions, particularly the water level and food availability, are suitable for nesting, for these conditions are often unstable, especially in tropical and subtropical zones.

Not all displays are performed identically by all the species, and some have not been recorded for certain species. The similarities observed reinforce the accepted taxonomic division of the genera, species and subspecies, as the similarities are greater between the more closely related forms.

Some of the displays recall other actions, such as the preening and stretching movements which are also performed daily for practical reasons of maintenance and comfort; this is the case of the "Twist-preen" and the "Wing-leg Stretch" displays. However, when used practically, they are carried out in an effective, non-ritualized, slower manner, lasting as long as is necessary, and at such moments they are less infectious to other birds. Comfort behaviour also includes bathing, preferably in shallow fresh water.

A characteristic feature of the flamingos is their resting position, which involves standing on one leg. In this way, the amount of heat lost through the leg and the foot on cold days is reduced, but this can not be the sole reason, for the posture is also used in hot weather. It is probably quite simply a comfortable position. A sleeping bird rests its head on the forward part of its body with the neck in a pronounced S-shape, or alternatively on its rump, with its neck along its back. In these postures, birds almost always stand facing the wind, so that the wind and rain can not penetrate the plumage.

A recent study at the main breeding and wintering grounds of the Caribbean Flamingo in Yucatán, in Mexico, has shown that feeding, preening and resting, in this order, are the main activities of both adults and immature birds for almost all the year. Birds spend 15-30% of their time preening, a high proportion in comparison with waterfowl, which rarely use more than 10% of the day. This could be explained by the hypersaline conditions of the area, which force the flamingos to clean accumulations of salt out their plumage quite regularly. In the same study, feeding decreased sharply in February, when courtship activities were reaching their peak, and also, though less markedly, during the nesting season in May and June, when more time was spent on activities associated with breeding. These results indicate that flamingos, like several species of geese, need to spend a good deal of time storing up nutrient reserves before the start of their courtship activity, when competition for mates can be intense. Further evidence of this comes from the Camargue, where breeding success is higher following a wet autumn, as there is apparently more food available.

Voice

Perhaps the most important role of the voice in flamingos is in keeping flocks together, and they are generally quite noisy birds. Sounds vary with a bird's activity, from the low gabbling produced by a feeding flock, to the nasal honking calls given in flight; other typical sounds include a deep grunting or growling, when displaying or showing aggression at the colony. There are differences between the voices of the various species, and the Lesser Flamingo's, for example, is much more high-pitched than the loud, goose-like calls of the Greater Flamingo, even though the message is probably very similar.

Flocks of several thousands are common in all species of the family, although it is the Lesser Flamingo which gathers in the greatest numbers; this compact group is in Etosha Pan, Namibia, where on occasions, a million birds have been recorded together, along with tens of thousands of Greater Flamingos (Phoenicopterus ruber). Numbers similar to these, or even higher, also occur in various East African lakes and are amongst the largest assemblies of non-passerine birds of any kind.

[Phoeniconaias minor, Etosha National Park, Namibia. Photo: Jen & Des Bartlett/ Survival]

The voice also plays an important part in ritualized displays (see General Habits), and certain postures or movements are accompanied by particular sounds, for example, loud calls are made continuously during "Head-flagging", but are immediately replaced with low grunting noises when the "Wing-salute" begins. Some calls also form part of the less spectacular displays which occur during the formation or strengthening of the pair-bond, or can be uttered by both birds when they change over at the nest during incubation, or after copulation.

During breeding, the voice becomes most important for the mutual recognition of parents and chicks, which is vital when the chicks gather together in large crèches (see Breeding). For this reason, chicks are very vocal from the start, and they begin cheeping several hours before they hatch; they are immediately answered by the adults, and this exchange continues for several days after the chicks have left the nest. Thus, when an adult approaches the crèche to feed its chick, the chick immediately recognizes its parent and calls out to it.

Food and Feeding

Flamingos feed on minute particles of food including algae, diatoms and several kinds of aquatic invertebrate. A bird normally obtains these organisms by wading, with the head lowered into the water and the bill horizontal and pointing backwards. It pumps water and mud in and out repeatedly, five or six times per second in the Greater Flamingo, but about 20 times per second in the Lesser, which takes in a much smaller measure of water each time. Filtering with its lamellae (see Morphological Aspects), it retains the appropriate food particles. However, there are pronounced interspecific differences which allow different species to co-exist without competition, for instance Greater and Lesser Flamingos in Africa or India, and Chilean, Andean and Puna Flamingos on the *altiplano* of the Andes.

The Greater Flamingo, like its congener the Chilean Flamingo, has a shallow-keeled bill, which means that the upper mandible is roughly oval in cross-section, but more flattened. When the bill is closed, the two mandibles do not fit tightly together, but instead leave a large gap, where there is enough room for the tongue. The inner lamellae are spaced approximately 0·5 mm apart, so the species mainly takes particles ranging in diameter from 0·5 mm to 4-6 mm, the width the bill is opened during feeding. Within these fairly broad limits, there are many aquatic invertebrates including small crustaceans,

molluscs, annelids and larvae of Diptera and other insects, as well as plant seeds and possibly small fish, so the birds can have a relatively varied diet. A partiality towards one kind or another of these organisms can depend on the locality: in Europe and North Africa there is a predominance of brine-shrimps (*Artemia*), which can survive in waters of up to 20% salinity; in the East African lakes chironomids and copepods are very important; whilst in the West Indies birds mainly take the larvae and chrysalids of brine-flies (*Ephydra*), or snails (*Cerithidea*, *Cerithium*). In addition, rapid changes of both salinity and water levels are common in flamingo feeding grounds, so the abundance of a particular prey, and consequently its importance in the birds' diet, can undergo marked periodical variations. All these organisms are normally found in the mud at the bottom of the water, so the Greater Flamingo, like the Chilean, almost always feeds with its head completely immersed and near the bottom, raising its head at 5-25 second intervals, in order to breathe. It usually walks steadily along, but sometimes stands and paddles or stirs up the mud with its feet, so that the food particles float free and can be picked up more easily.

In contrast, the Lesser Flamingo has a deep-keeled bill, which means that the cross-section of the upper mandible is like an equilateral triangle, with the vertex pointing downwards, so that when the bill is closed it hardly leaves any free space, and the tongue must be placed in a narrow cleft. Unlike the shallow-keeled bill, there are outer lamellae that act as excluders to particles that are too big. The spaces between these lamellae measure about 1·0 x 0·4 mm, so larger particles do not even enter the mouth. The inner lamellae are much closer together than in the Greater Flamingo and are covered in fine hairs, leaving gaps of no more than 0·01 x 0·05 mm, so there is virtually no overlap in the size of particles taken by the two species of flamingo. The Lesser thus takes only very small algae and benthic diatoms, concentrating particularly on blue-green algae of the genus *Spirulina*, which can form extremely dense blooms on the surface of the water in some African and Indian lakes. This specialized diet also entails a different feeding method, for, in order to catch the *Spirulina*, the birds have to filter almost at the surface of the water, with the bill only partially submerged, only 3-6 cm below the surface. This has led to another adaptation of the bill, for the lower mandible is notably bulbous and holds in a good deal of air, so it acts as a float. In this way the head is wafted about by ripples, originating from the swell which is often present on these lakes, and it constantly floats at a suitable depth. In spite of this, the Lesser Flamingo needs calmer waters for feeding than the Greater, so with high winds or choppy water, large flocks of Lessers gather along the shore, resting and preening.

In a similar way, the three species which co-exist in parts of South America also show differences which allow them to share food supplies at a particular site. The Chilean Flamingo has a shallow-keeled bill and a similar filtering system to that of the Greater Flamingo, and likewise it enjoys a mixed diet of various different invertebrates. The Andean and Puna Flamingos, on the other hand, have deep-keeled bills with finer filtering devices, so they feed on tiny diatoms. The Andean basically takes them 0·8 mm long, or a little more, while the Puna, with its even finer filtering system, takes diatoms of less than 0·6 mm.

The Chilean Flamingo walks about rapidly and purposefully when feeding, probably due to the greater mobility of its prey. It averages 40-60 steps per minute, quite unlike the Puna Flamingo and, to a lesser degree, the Andean Flamingo, which move about far more slowly and erratically, with 10-15 and 20-30 steps per minute respectively. This also accounts for the curious interaction observed between the Chilean Flamingo and Wilson's Phalarope (*Phalaropus tricolor*), a species which winters in huge numbers in the lakes of the central Andes. In groups of one to three, phalaropes feed, swimming rapidly around and through the legs of feeding Chilean Flamingos, whereas they ignore the Andean and Puna Flamingos which are also present, as the faster moving Chilean Flamingo stirs up invertebrates from the lake bottom more than the other species. The same type of interaction has also been observed on occasions at the Ebro Delta, in north-east Spain, between the Greater Flamingo and the Red-necked Phalarope (*Phalaropus lobatus*).

All species of flamingo at times feed while swimming, and this increases the amount of food available. The three larger species, in particular, sometimes upend like ducks, paddling with their feet alternately to maintain the position. In this way, the Greater Flamingo can reach down 120-130 cm, whereas a wading bird will go no deeper than 70-80 cm.

It is thought that flamingos occasionally swallow mud, so as to take in nutrients from all the organic matter, such as bacteria, protozoa, algae and organic salts, and these can constitute as much as 20% of the dry weight of the mud.

Daily requirements have been throroughly studied in the Caribbean and Lesser Flamingos. It has been estimated that a Caribbean Flamingo needs around 270 g (dry weight) of larvae or brine-fly chrysalids per day, which is equivalent to 32,000 chrysalids or 50,000 larvae. A flock of 1500 flamingos can consume 48 million chrysalids or 75 million larvae every day. A Lesser Flamingo requires 60 g per day of blue-green algae, a more nutritious form of prey, which means, for example, that the gatherings of 1 million birds or more on Lakes Nakuru and Bogoria in Kenya, can eat no less than 60 tons, of algae per day!

The vast quantities of food involved imply an extremely rapid rate of production by the prey species, and the feeding system of the flamingos also contributes to this acceleration. Indeed, water samples from the surface of some of the East African lakes used by Lesser Flamingos have concentrations of algae of about 3 g (dry weight) per litre, which means they have to filter some 20 litres of water a day to obtain the required 60 g. As the concentration decreases, due to the birds' feeding, they have to filter more water to obtain the same amount of food, until the concentration drops probably to about 1 g per litre, and the energy used in feeding is greater than that obtained from the food. Similarly, for Caribbean Flamingos it is calculated that feeding ceases to be worthwhile when the concentration of brine-fly is reduced to between a third and a quarter of the initial level. At this point, the birds have to move to another area, sometimes in the same lake, allowing the over-exploited zone to recover, as long as the organisms remain sufficiently numerous.

Flamingos have also been observed feeding with unusual methods, for example on Inhaca Island, at the entrance to Lourenço Marques Bay, in Mozambique. Greater Flamingos frequent a sandy strip inhabited by millions of crabs (*Dotilla fenestrata*), which they catch by pecking at them, while striding along with the head lowered half way down their legs. On occasions, they take unusual prey, for instance adult insects, or perhaps even small fish, such as *Cyprinodon*, when these are temporarily abundant.

Another peculiarity of the flamingos is that, like pigeons, they feed their chicks with milk that is secreted in the upper digestive tract. Its nutritional value, with a 8-9% protein and 15% fat content, is similar to mammal milk and, as in the latter, the secretion is regulated by the hormone prolactin. However, in the case of the birds, the milk is produced by members of both sexes. Apparently, the chicks' constant begging calls

Yet further proof of the flamingos' extreme gregariousness can be seen in the fact that their ritualized sexual displays are almost always performed in large groups, and this apparently plays an important part in synchronizing their breeding attempts. These Andean Flamingos are in the "Alert Posture", which consists of maintaining the neck fully stretched upwards, with the head held so that the bill is more or less horizontal; very often, the "Alert Posture" precedes the display known as "Head-flagging", where the birds move the head from side to side in horizontal arcs.

[*Phoenicoparrus andinus*, Salar de Atacama, Chile. Photo: Günter Ziesler]

This group of Caribbean (Greater) Flamingos, shows most birds "Head-flagging", but three individuals are performing the "Wing-salute", a display consisting of the bird opening its wings fully for a few seconds, whilst the bill is pointed forward, the scapular feathers spread and the tail cocked. The majority of the known displays are carried out by several or all species of flamingos, although there are some variations; thus, whilst in the "Wing-salute" performed by the Caribbean Flamingo the upper margin of the wing is held some 30° above horizontal, in the Greater (Phoenicopterus ruber roseus) and Chilean (P. chilensis) Flamingos this display is carried out with the wing held lower, practically horizontal.

[Phoenicopterus ruber ruber, Inagua, Bahamas. Photo: M. P. Kahl/DRK]

stimulate the production of prolactin, which in turn leads to a proliferation of the gland cells of the upper digestive tract. In captivity, non-breeding birds have also been known to produce milk, including seven week old chicks, which were able to feed orphaned birds.

Breeding

Strange as it may seem for large colonial birds, the flamingos' breeding habits are imperfectly known. Many colonies are in bleak, remote areas, which explains why, for example, the breeding grounds of Lesser Flamingos in East Africa were not discovered until 1954, even though their enormous concentrations were famous long before this, whilst no breeding site of Puna Flamingo was seen or described until 1957.

In temperate latitudes with well-marked seasons, flamingos usually breed in spring, as in southern Spain or the Camargue, or at the beginning of the rainy season, from the end of November in the Andean *altiplano*. In tropical or subtropical areas, on the other hand, breeding can take place at practically any time of the year. In the Galapagos, nests can be found in any month between February and December, while in Bonaire, in the Netherlands Antilles, the same colony site was used continuously over 18 months by at least four consecutive groups of birds, probably due to lack of available space. In India and East Africa, the same locations can be used successively at different times of year.

In general, flamingos are opportunists, breeding irregularly or even erratically, and they tend not to breed every year. In the Camargue, the flamingos have been monitored annually since 1914, and during a period of 76 years they attempted breeding in 54 years, although in several of these no chicks were fledged. Since 1969, however, breeding has been uninterruptedly annual, though diverse management schemes must have contributed to this, including the construction of an artificial island to prevent the colony being flooded (see Status and Conservation), whilst in the 55 years between 1914 and 1968, breeding was only attempted on 32 occasions. In East Africa, the Greater and Lesser Flamingos breed every two years on average, but this can mean several consecutive years of breeding followed by a few years during which there is no

attempt. Occasionally, flamingos will even breed at a new site, but, even if they are successful, they will not try again in the ensuing years. This happened at Lake St Lucia in South Africa in 1972, where some 6000 pairs of Greater Flamingos reared about 4000 chicks. Likewise, in 1988, for the first time several thousand pairs of Greater Flamingos were found breeding on Lake Shala, in Ethiopia.

Rainfall is undoubtedly the main factor, although not the only one, that determines whether or not flamingos breed at a particular site, and also the timing of breeding. An adequate water level implies sufficient food, areas with soft mud for building nests, and also extensive flooded areas around the colony, which protect it from terrestrial predators.

Flamingos are apparently monogamous, with a strong pair-bond which can be maintained from one year to the next. The displays used in pair formation are similar to some of those carried out when they are in groups (see General Habits), but much less flamboyant. Copulation does not take place until the pair have left the displaying groups, and pre-copulatory rituals are very inconspicuous. Both displays and copulation, and even preliminary nest-building, can sometimes occur at sites other than those of their eventual breeding grounds.

Flamingo colonies tend to be very large, and rarely consist of less than 50 pairs, except in the Galapagos (see Habitat). Colonies of at least a few thousand breeding birds are known for all six forms of flamingo, and enormous colonies have been recorded, like those of the Lesser Flamingo: at Lake Magadi, in Kenya, with about 1,100,000 pairs in 1962; at Lake Natron, in Tanzania, with some 500,000 pairs in 1957; and at Etosha Pan, in Namibia, with over 100,000 pairs in 1969. Similarly, the Greater Flamingo colony in the Rann of Kutch, in northwest India held more than 200,000 pairs in 1960.

One peculiarity of some of the colonies in the *altiplanos* of the Andes, such as the colony at Laguna Colorada in Bolivia, is that Chilean, Andean and Puna Flamingos can breed together without any apparent segregation between them. The Greater and Lesser Flamingos have also bred in association in Lakes Nakuru and Elementeita, in Kenya, and in Lake Natron, in Tanzania.

Colonies, particularly the largest ones, are normally situated on extensive mud-flats or salt-flats, which emerge when the water level of huge, shallow salt-lakes and pans drops. At

In the places where two or more species of flamingo coincide, their coexistence is favoured by several differences in feeding habits which allow them to exploit different trophic resources, and thus avoid or reduce competition between the two species. A good example of this is provided by the Greater and Lesser Flamingos, which overlap both in Africa and in India. The Greater Flamingo basically feeds on the invertebrates that live in the bottom of water bodies; this is why it usually forages with the bill practically touching the bottom, requiring total immersion of the head and neck when the bird is feeding in waters of a certain depth. The Lesser Flamingo's diet, on the other hand, mainly consists of microscopic algae which float near the surface, and this explains why they almost always feed with only the bill submerged. These dietary differences can, in turn, be explained by the distinct structure of the bills, allowing them to filter particles of quite different sizes.

[Above: *Phoenicopterus ruber roseus*, Fuente de Piedra Lagoon, Spain. Photo: Francisco Márquez.

Below: *Phoeniconaias minor*, Lake Bogoria, Kenya. Photo: John Downer/ Planet Earth]

In general, among flamingos copulation starts a few days after the pair stops participating in group displays. It is usually the female which, by walking around, invites the male, and he follows her closely with his neck outstretched. Suddenly, the female halts, lowers her neck, sometimes even completely submerging her head, and spreads her wings, whereupon the male jumps up, flapping his wings, and copulation takes place. Once ejaculation has occurred, the male stands up on the female's back and descends, jumping down in front of her.

[*Phoenicopterus ruber roseus*, Fuente de Piedra Lagoon, Spain.
Photo: Francisco Márquez]

such sites the precise location of the colony may shift from one season to the next, depending on the depth of the water. Smaller colonies tend to be established on flat islands in shallow bodies of water. The most common locations are muddy islands, devoid of vegetation, or with very little, but this is not always the case. They also use rocky islands, like those in Lake Elementeita, or at Lake Uromiyeh (formerly Rezaiyeh), in Iran; sometimes these are formed by hard incrustations of salt, for example in several South American salt-lakes, and they may occasionally be thickly covered in plants, including mangroves. In the Orange Free State, breeding was attempted on some reservoirs without islands, and nests were built on earth dams.

The typical nest consists of a pile of mud in the form of a truncated cone, with a shallow depression on top, and round the base a circular trench as much as 20 cm deep, which is excavated for building material and is frequently full of water. The dimensions of the mound vary greatly, depending on the nature of the ground, and clay sites have higher nests than at sandy or dry sites, but nest size also varies within the same colony, where it is difficult to find two exactly alike. The nest is 35-56 cm wide at the base, and 22-40 cm across at the top, with height averaging 30-45 cm, although some are much lower. This heap provides protection from rises in the water level and also from excessive heat. In East Africa, the temperature at the top of the nest was found to be 30-35°C, when the surrounding ground was at 50-55°C.

Nest-building is carried out by both partners in turn. A bird uses its bill to work mud, and also stones or plant debris when available, towards itself, and in between its feet. Apparently it is often the male that begins the task at a leisurely pace, and afterwards the female that takes over the task much more actively, as the egg is already forming. Once the egg has been laid, building continues, sometimes at a frenetic pace, to heighten the nest. After some repair and heightening, nests are often reused by other birds in subsequent breeding cycles.

In colonies on rocky islands, where there is no soft mud available, but no danger of flooding, nests are merely formed of a small circular rim of debris of any kind and small stones which the bird collects.

The distribution of nests within a colony is irregular, and there are usually some empty, or nearly empty, spaces, but high densities of nests elsewhere; the greatest densities have been found in the Lesser Flamingo, with up to 5 nests/m². Only the nest-site itself is defended, both during incubation and whilst the chick remains in the nest. Several threat postures may be performed, involving the bird swaying its neck and head from side to side, while spreading the scapulars and back feathers. In the most heated moments, there can be contact between neighbours' bills, but fighting generally only occurs during nest-site selection.

Flamingos lay a single chalky white egg, which sometimes has a pale blue tinge when it is newly-laid. It is quite large, ranging from about 78 x 49 mm and 115 g in the Lesser Flamingo, to about 90 x 55 mm and 140 g in the Greater Flamingo. Clutches of two eggs occur in a very low proportion of cases, generally under 2%, but it is thought that at least in some cases two separate females are involved. If the egg is destroyed by flooding or predators, a replacement second egg may be laid, but only if the loss occurs within a few days of the first egg being laid.

Incubation begins immediately after the egg has been laid, and is shared between the sexes, although neither possesses a brood patch. Stints on the nest can last from less than an hour to over 24 hours, often depending on the distance to the feeding grounds. Sometimes they last several days, but in the Camargue this is known to lower breeding success, and attempts almost always fail when shifts last four days or more. The change over at the nest is carried out rapidly, without elaborate ceremonies and hardly ever takes place at night. Incubation lasts 27-31 days in all species.

Hatching can be actively helped by the adults pulling off pieces of the eggshell. Initially the chick has a straight bill and is covered in grey down, which is replaced by a second, generally darker, downy plumage, when the bird is about four weeks old. After hatching, the chick remains in the nest, unless forced to leave, for 5-12 days, during which time it is often brooded, typically between the adult's wing and body, whence the chick may stick its head out to look around. When it leaves the nest, it can already walk and swim quite well and joins up with other chicks, forming large crèches of hundreds or thousands of birds, or even 300,000 in the Lesser Flamingo. These groups are looked after by a few adults, possibly birds which have lost their own clutch, in a decreasing ratio of one adult to ten chicks at the beginning, but one to several hundreds later on. The parents feed their chick with a secretion from their upper digestive tract (see Food and Feeding), both at the nest and once it has become part of the crèche, and the birds recognize each other by their calls (see Voice). The adult holds its bill over the chick's, dripping the liquid secretion into the chick's bill. At first this process lasts five minutes, but the time increases as the chick grows, until it lasts about 20 minutes in the final stages. The frequency of feeds, on the other hand, decreases, from every 45-90 minutes in the first few days, to roughly once a day at the end. Although chicks can obtain food by themselves when they are 4-6 weeks old, parental feeding is normally prolonged, on occasions until the chicks fledge, at about 10-12 weeks old. At this stage, the bill already has the typical bent shape of the adults' and is suitable for efficient filtering, but adult plumage is not attained for several years. In the Camargue, most successful breeders are seven years old or more, and younger birds, attempting at three years old, nearly always fail. Similarly, observation of ringed birds at the Fuente de Piedra Lagoon, in south Spain, showed that breeding success was much greater (86.4%) for birds six years old or more, than for the colony as a whole (44%), while younger birds had much lower success (13.6%). The greatest success (91.7%) was achieved by seven year olds, and success dropped off progressively again in older birds, with only 50% for nine year old birds.

However, breeding success varies considerably, averaging about 40% to fledging in Greater and Lesser Flamingos, excluding years of total failure. Some eggs and chicks are lost due to predation, especially by birds, such as raptors, crows and gulls, and a particular species can pose a serious threat to a colony. At the Camargue, for instance, Yellow-legged Gulls (*Larus cachinnans*) may account for half of the eggs and chicks in some years, and the gulls have developed methods, such as pecking the flamingos on the leg joints or pulling them by the bill, to force the incubating bird to get up, so that the egg or chick can be stolen. The Marabou (*Leptoptilos crumeniferus*) has also been responsible for great destruction in East Africa,

not only preying on eggs and chicks, but also making the nervous flamingos desert colonies of up to 6000 pairs. Recently, Great White Pelicans (*Pelecanus onocrotalus*) have also caused losses in some Greater Flamingo colonies in East and south-west Africa, by choosing the same enclaves for breeding, perhaps triggered by the flamingos' own breeding, which leads to the displacement of the lighter, weaker flamingos.

Another negative factor can be intraspecific interference, when large numbers of birds arrive at an active colony, causing disruption and sometimes the desertion of many nests. This was apparently the cause of low success at Fuente de Piedra in 1987, when there was a large influx of birds, probably from the large colony formed that year in the nearby marshes at Doñana.

Nonetheless, most breeding failure is caused by changes in the weather. Many colonies have been wrecked by flooding, while a drop in water level due to drought can drastically reduce food supplies, as well as admitting terrestrial predators. In the Camargue, dogs and foxes have disrupted breeding in the past, while more recently herds of wild boars invaded the colony at Doñana. Flamingo populations are, however, able to maintain their numbers, despite the relatively frequency with which breeding fails completely or is not even attempted. On Bonaire, for example, it has been calculated that the population maintains its numbers, if it breeds successfully three times every six or seven years.

Unlike chicks, adults suffer very little predation. On average they live more than 20-30 years, and it is not unusual for wild birds to live over 50 years.

Movements

Flamingos are not true migrants in the accepted sense, but they disperse widely. The populations which breed in high latitudes, or on high altitude lakes which freeze over in winter, move to warmer areas, but these movements are irregular or even erratic, with the number of birds involved varying greatly from year to year, depending on climatic conditions.

Although the majority of the flamingos' breeding colonies are situated in extensive mudflats completely devoid of vegetation, there are many exceptions, as in this colony of Chilean Flamingos in Peru. When the quantity of wet mud available for nest building is limited, the nests are much lower than the truncated cones of up to 40 cm typical of muddy areas; in some areas, colonies are even located in places without any mud, and in such cases the eggs are laid directly on the ground. Some colonies in the tropics are used continuously for long periods, so that groups of birds in different phases of breeding coincide; this explains the presence of well feathered young, downy chicks and incubating birds all together.

[*Phoenicopterus chilensis,*
Apurimac, Peru.
Photo: Günter Ziesler]

After about 28 days' incubation, the eggs begin to hatch, a process that lasts 24-36 hours. During hatching the chick cheeps persistently, and is frequently answered by its parents. Apparently, this precocious vocal exchange favours the surprising capacity for individual recognition between parents and offspring that flamingos maintain throughout the whole period of chick rearing. Note the atypical nest, consisting of little more than a slight depression surrounded by some debris; this abnormality can be explained by the rocky nature of the islands in Lake Elmenteita, which are totally devoid of mud.

[*Phoenicopterus ruber roseus*, Lake Elmenteita, Kenya.
Photo: Jane Burton/
Bruce Coleman]

Until recently, very little was known about flamingos' movements, but the extensive marking of Greater Flamingos in the Western Palearctic has clarified their strategy a great deal. At the Camargue, since 1977, birds have been fitted with plastic leg rings, which can be read at a distance, with the result that by 1988 there had been almost 70,000 resightings.

A fair proportion of the population leave in September, but several hundreds or thousands of birds of all ages stay in the area every winter. This tendency has increased, and during the 1980's, in some years up to 20,000 birds stayed on, even in very hard winters, for example in 1985, when 3500 birds died due to the cold. Some birds appear to be more or less sedentary, as they have not migrated in their first ten years.

Most of the flamingos that leave the Camargue head either south-west to winter in Spain and Morocco, or else south-east via Sardinia, where they often stop, and on into Tunisia and Algeria; a few birds continue even further, as far as Senegal or Turkey. It appears that the proportion of birds that go west or east depends on the direction of the prevailing winds in a bird's first autumn. In subsequent years, regardless of the wind direction, it remains faithful to these same winter quarters, and in Tunisia this is known to continue until the birds reach sexual maturity.

In Tunisia and Spain, breeding starts earlier, and an interesting offshoot of this is the arrival in the Camargue of juveniles from these colonies, before the local chicks have fledged. Similiarly, in May 1988 juveniles turned up in southern Spain, and these are thought to have come from Mauritania. In these

dispersive movements, young birds are usually accompanied by some adults.

Most birds return to their native colony to breed, although a fair proportion join neighbouring colonies. In 1986, of 642 birds ringed as chicks in the Camargue, about 87% had returned there to breed, whilst 13% were breeding in Fuente de Piedra, and one had even turned up in the colony at the Banc d'Arguin. Some of the birds found breeding in Spain had previously bred in the Camargue, indicating that a change of colony need not imply that the original site has become unsuitable.

Other movements are caused by climatic factors, such as the droughts which often affect the wetlands around the Sahara, and which give rise to reverse migration between August and October. This involves movement north across the Mediterranean at the same time as the post-breeding dispersal, which occurs in the opposite direction. Similar movements are also caused by severe cold, and in the winter of 1985 many birds moved south, including a flock of 150-200 birds, which arrived in Corsica, where the species is rarely recorded.

Flamingos perform their movements mainly at night, and they prefer to set off with a cloudless sky and favourable tail winds. Flock size has been found to range from two to 340 birds, with an average of 71.

Ringing data indicates that the population of the Western Palearctic is discrete from bhat of western Asia. Large numbers of birds have been marked at Lake Uromiyeh, in north-east Iran, and at Lake Tenghiz, in Kazakhstan, and results show a similar east-west split. Thus, Iranian birds have been recovered in Israel,

During their first days of life, the chicks are brooded by their parents for long periods in the nest; in this period, it is normal for the chick to be held by one of its parents, tucked between the adult's wing and body. In this position, the chick, with only its head protruding, is fed by the adult dripping liquid into the chick's straight bill; this is a rich secretion from the upper digestive tract, with nutritional value comparable to that of mammals' milk. This Greater Flamingo also demonstrates that it can bend its very long legs without problems while sitting in the nest, refuting the theories of some early naturalists who spread the belief that the flamingos incubated with their legs hanging over the sides of the nest.

[*Phoenicopterus ruber roseus*, Camargue, France. Photo: Hellio & Van Ingen/ NHPA]

Cyprus, Libya, Turkey and Greece, but also in Pakistan and India. Most of this population actually winters in the south of Iran, with a few hundred or so overwintering on their breeding grounds. Likewise, birds from Kazakhstan have been recorded from Egypt and Cyprus to the west, and Pakistan to the east.

The western Asian population has recently expanded, and since 1982 birds have bred in the area of Izmir, in western Turkey. There was also a surprising report from Turkey of 320,000 flamingos at Seyfe Golu, in September 1986; it is thought that the birds may have come from India, since such high numbers of Greater Flamingos had previously only been reported from the Rann of Kutch.

A minimal amount of exchange appears to occur between the two discrete Palearctic populations. A few birds from Iran and Kazakhstan have recently been sighted in France and Tunisia, while two birds ringed in the Camargue were recovered in Turkey. The dispersal ranges of the two populations overlap slightly, for example in Libya, where wandering immatures from the Camargue may join up with larger flocks from Iran, whence they may move eastwards with them in the spring. There may also be some contact between the Greater Flamingo populations of Iran and East Africa, although this is thought to refer almost exclusively to young birds.

Similarly, the Lesser and Greater Flamingos of Etosha Pan, in Namibia, are in contact with those of Makarikari Pan, in Botswana, some 960 km away. Breeding only seems to occur in Botswana, as a response to failure or unsuitable conditions in Namibia.

The Lesser Flamingo populations of East Africa and Botswana have traditionally been thought to be isolated from each other, as they are separated by at least 1440 km, but there may be some contact between them. A remarkable concentration of around a million birds at Makarikari Pan, in 1974, coincided with the sharp drop in the population of Lake Nakuru in Kenya, and aerial censuses of other lakes in the Rift Valley could not locate the missing birds. However, as flamingos travel by night, at about 50-60 km/h, they can not cover more than 600 km in one night, and there are no reports of large numbers stopping off between the two areas. Nevertheless, such movements

might be possible, for aircraft pilots have seen flamingos flying at great altitudes by day, perhaps in order to avoid predation by eagles.

Similar sightings of Lesser Flamingos at intermediate sites suggest some contact between the large East African population and the small, isolated nuclei in West Africa and India. In fact, breeding in both West Africa and India seems to be sporadic and may not, in itself, be sufficient to maintain the continuity of these populations. This implies the existence of undiscovered colonies or recruitment now and then from East Africa, or even from the south. The record of 800-1000 birds at the estuary of the River Como in Gabon, in 1981, indicates that birds certainly could arrive in considerable numbers. However, unknown colonies probably do exist, as a flock of around 6000 Lesser Flamingos in the Djoudj National Park, in 1988, contained about 100 recently fledged young, some of which were still being fed by adults. Likewise, a flock of 937 adults and 159 juveniles was seen in India in 1984, suggesting that breeding had occurred in India or Pakistan, and in 1989 a second Indian colony was found in the Little Rann of Kutch.

In Madagascar, both Greater and Lesser Flamingos are frequent visitors to lakes in the south-west, sometimes in large numbers, with up to 15,000 Greater and 20,000 Lesser on Lake Ihotry. It is not known whether these birds originate from the populations in East or southern Africa, but sporadic breeding may occur.

The best known of the American forms is the Caribbean Flamingo, and ringing recoveries indicate movements between the colony at Great Inagua, in the Bahamas, and Cuba and Hispaniola, whilst the Mexican population, which breeds at Río Lagartos in Yucatán, generally winters in the Celestun estuary, about 280 km to the west. Some 5000 of the 6000 or so birds that breed on Bonaire disperse after the breeding season, mainly along the coast of Venezuela, but also west into Colombia and east as far as the Amazon estuary. Since 1969, there has not been enough food on Bonaire to feed the whole colony during breeding (see Status and Conservation), so many birds make daily trips to coast of Venezuela, at least 70 km away, which has had no apparent ill effects on breeding success. In fact,

such movements also occur elsewhere, for instance at Fuente de Piedra, in southern Spain, where many of the breeding Greater Flamingos head off to feed in the marshes of Doñana, about 150 km to the west.

Very little is known about the movements of the other three American species. The Chilean Flamingo is clearly less sedentary than the Andean and Puna Flamingos, but there is nothing to suggest any long distance movements. The Chilean Flamingo leaves its breeding grounds at Lake Junín in Peru, when the water level is high between the months of February and May. It also performs some fairly regular movements between the high Andes and the Pacific coast, and also between southern Argentina and Tierra del Fuego. Moreover, problems with food supply, water level or nesting conditions often cause irregular movents of vast numbers of birds in the Andes.

There are frequent reports of flamingos in very unexpected areas, but many of these are undoubtedly due to escapes, as they are very common in captivity, where they often breed. Such is clearly the case of the Chilean and Caribbean Flamingos, which have turned up at the Camargue on several occasions, and have even bred. However, there are some erratic movements of wild birds, including Greater Flamingos seen in central Europe, Kampuchea and at the Cocos (Keeling) Islands, in the western Indian Ocean; there are also records of the Chilean Flamingo in the Falkland Islands and the Lesser Flamingo in Spain.

A remarkable case involved two Puna Flamingos seen in the Argentinian province of Chubut in 1973, some 2000 km south of the known range of this, the most localized species. Again, in 1989, an emaciated juvenile Andean Flamingo, ringed in northern Chile when five months old, was captured at the exceptionally low altitude of 1008 metres in Santa Catarina, in southern Brazil. Storms are a major factor in causing vagrancies, since water levels can rise and force the birds to fly off,

in search of more favourable sites. Some birds are then incapable of battling against the wind and are blown away off course. In November 1982, for example, after exceptionally strong winds in the Camargue, many birds were seen inland, 500 km or more from their normal haunts.

Relationship with Man

Man has long been fascinated by flamingos, perhaps due to their peculiar appearance, a strange mixture of the bizarre and the beautiful. An accurate cave painting of a flamingo in the south of Spain dates back to about 5000 BC. The ancient Egyptians used the silhouette of the flamingo as the hieroglyphic for the colour red, and it also represented the reincarnation of Ra, the Sun God.

At the beginning of the Christian era, many considered the flamingo to be the incarnation of the legendary Phoenix, the immortal red bird which was reborn from the embers of its own funeral pyre, which was symbolically related to the resurrection of Christ.

This fascination, and the legends and myths derived from it, did not safeguard the flamingos from direct, sometimes intense, persecution. One remarkable case was the massacre of flamingos by the Romans simply for their tongues, which were considered a real delicacy. The collection of eggs and birds, especially flightless young, for food, must have started long before, probably when man was still a hunter-gatherer, and it has continued up to the present day in many areas where colonies are not too remote. Several colonies of the three South American species are still exploited regularly by the local people, generally for food, but also for traditional medicines, for instance flamingo fat is considered to be a cure for tuberculosis in parts of the Andes. In many parts of the world where much of the human population lives at subsistence level, colonies have been exploited in recent years, for example in India, Turkey or Tunisia, even in areas where the flamingo only breeds sporadically. Indeed, traditional egg-collection only ceased within the last 20 or 30 years in some places with a much higher standard of living, such as France, Spain or the Netherlands Antilles.

The capture of flamingos for exhibition in zoos and private collections has affected, and continues to affect, many populations, and the effects are aggravated by mortality caused during the capture, transit and acclimatization of the birds. Flamingos have always been amongst the most popular species to exhibit, and even very recently all the birds on display were taken from the wild. Captive breeding proved impossible, until it was discovered that the pink colouring of the plumage was crucial, and a suitable diet was worked out. At present, several zoos have groups of Greater and Chilean Flamingos which maintain numbers on their own output, whilst the Andean Flamingo only breeds regularly at Slimbridge in south-west England and at West Berlin Zoo. Lesser and Puna Flamingos have still not bred in captivity, probably due to the difficulties in coping with their more specialized feeding habits.

In spite of their beautiful pink and red feathers, flamingos did not suffer particularly intense exploitation for the plume trade that decimated many egret populations during the nineteenth century (see page 396); this was probably because flamingo feathers, once shed, quickly lose their colour.

Flamingos have rarely come into conflict with economic interests, probably because of the remoteness of their habitat, and also their diet based on algae or invertebrates. However, at the Camargue rice fields have been proliferating around the areas used by flamingos, and in 1978 the birds started feeding by night in these fields, apparently due to an increase in the water levels, which reduced the salinity of the traditional feeding areas. Not surprisingly, the flamingos damaged the rice, not by eating it, as some farmers maintained, but by trampling on it, and this led to pressure being put on the authorities to shoot the birds, or pay high compensation. Fortunately, local biologists succeeded in scaring the birds off the fields, using flares and carbide bangers, and there were no further consequences.

Flamingo chicks continue to be fed by their parents until they are quite old, even when their bill is completely curved and capable of filtering, as shown by several of these Greater Flamingo chicks. Soon after leaving the nest, the chicks assemble in large crèches containing as many as several thousand individuals, to which both adults come to feed their chick. Individual recognition between adults and chicks appears to pose no problems.

[*Phoenicopterus ruber roseus*, Fuente de Piedra Lagoon, Spain. Photo: Hidalgo-Lopesino/ Marco Polo]

In almost all flamingo colonies, there is a certain amount of predation, especially by other species of birds, since, it is difficult for terrestrial predators to reach the breeding islands, unless the water level drops. In Africa, the Marabou (Leptoptilos crumeniferus) is the species that causes the greatest losses in both of the local flamingo species. One of the main causes of losses is the stealing of eggs and chicks, as attempted by this lone Marabou in the face of brave defence offered by the adult Greater Flamingos (above). Less important is the killing of adults, as in the case of this Lesser Flamingo, taken by two Marabous (below). However, the losses due to both of these factors are quantitatively insignificant. The greatest losses occur when the arrival of a group of Marabous at a colony causes the adults to panic; this happens most frequently when it coincides with the hatching period, leading many pairs to abandon their nests definitively.

[Above: *Phoenicopterus ruber roseus*, Lake Elmenteita, Kenya. Photo: Jane Burton/ Bruce Coleman.

Below: *Phoeniconaias minor*, Kenya. Photo: M. P. Kahl/Vireo]

Status and Conservation

Two species of flamingo, the Andean and Puna Flamingos, were, until recently, considered to be threatened, and both were classified as Insufficiently Known, although this has recently been amended to near-threatened.

The Puna Flamingo is reckoned to have a population of 30,000-50,000 birds, and, with its very restricted range, it has traditionally been considered the rarest member of the family. It was actually thought to be extinct from 1924 onwards, until its rediscovery in 1957 at Laguna Colorada, in the Andes of Bolivia. Nevertheless, recent estimates indicate that the Andean Flamingo, with its slightly larger range, is probably just as rare, or possibly even rarer. It has only one or two regular breeding

sites and a population certainly no greater than 50,000 birds, and perhaps much less, so previous estimates of 150,000, or even 500,000 birds can be discounted. Both species live in remote, inaccessible areas in the Andean *altiplanos*, where census work is difficult. In addition, these areas are often politically sensitive, for they are near the borders between Peru, Bolivia, Chile and Argentina, so simultaneous aerial censuses are impossible at present. Thus, population sizes and trends remain little known, while the very high survival rates of adults can give a false impression of stabilty, even when breeding success is very low, as may be the case at present.

Egg-collecting is undoubtedly one of the main threats to populations of these species, and is common among the Andeans (see Relationship with Man). It has been carried out for many years, probably even for centuries, and many colonies are seemingly able to withstand it. However, in addition to harvesting the eggs for themselves, some Indians, particularly in Bolivia, have recently started selling the eggs in neighbouring villages, especially in new mining towns, and this could have devastating consequences. The increase in the number of settlements and mining activities can seriously affect the birds' habitat, with water pollution and the diversion of streams for human purposes. The frequent introduction of fish to many lakes can also render them unsuitable for the flamingos, owing to competition for food (see Habitat).

Since the mid-1980's the prospects of the Andean species have been improving. In 1984, with the backing of the New York Zoological Society, a programme was begun, to protect the birds in the north of Chile, where the pressure exerted by mining activities is very high. Both adults and young birds are now ringed and the breeding colonies are monitored and guarded. The immediate results have been encouraging, with two very successful seasons producing 18,000 and 16,000 chicks of the three species in 1985/86 and 1986/87 respectively. At Laguna Colorada in Bolivia, an emergency plan was adopted, after the reports of high mortality of Puna Flamingos in 1986, as well as the alarming escalation in illegal egg-collecting; since 1987 two guards with motor-cycles have been protecting the colony.

The Chilean, Greater and Lesser Flamingos are all very numerous, with estimated populations of at least 200,000, about 800,000 and over 2,500,000 birds respectively. However, some local populations are small and, therefore, much more vulnerable, for instance that of the Lesser Flamingo in West Africa, where there are around 6000 individuals.

The future of the Caribbean race of the Greater Flamingo, with a total population of no more than 80,000-90,000 birds at four main colonies around the Gulf of Mexico, can not really be considered safe. Threats include direct persecution, for food or sport, and the continued capture of many birds for zoos. Planes flying low over colonies cause disturbance, and this factor was responsible for the disappearance in the late 1940's of the last flamingo colony on Andros, in the Bahamas, where up to 10,000 used to breed, as well as for substantial losses on Great Inagua. The desiccation or deterioration of much of their habitat, along with all these other factors, has brought about a marked reduction in numbers, and the species no longer breeds in Puerto Rico, the Virgin Islands, Haiti or Colombia. After a full-scale survey in 1950, Robert Allen reported that at least 15 flamingo nesting sites in the Caribbean had been abandoned in the previous 35 years. The outlying population in the Galapagos Islands is in a much more precarious state. This population, sometimes considered a different race (see Systematics), comprises no more than 500 individuals, perhaps because of the limited feeding areas. Such a small population is always liable to be wiped out by a disaster, natural or otherwise, although this was not the case after the occurrence of El Niño in 1982/83. Less food was available, due to the entry of enormous quantities of fresh water into the saline lagoons, and several nest-sites were flooded, but once normal conditions were restored, flamingo numbers had only dropped by about 12%. The

proportion of juveniles in the population was calculated to be 15%, as opposed to 9% in 1982, indicating a high rate of breeding success after El Niño.

Despite the massive destruction of wetlands in recent decades, the remoteness and high salinity of most of the flamingos' lakes have meant that flamingos have suffered less significant habitat destruction than other waterbirds. However, the development of salt and soda works has caused considerable problems, particularly in the Caribbean. In fact, these changes are not always detrimental to the flamingos, and they often use such sites for feeding, for example in Río Lagartos and the Camargue, where they benefit from the continual flooding. Nevertheless, sometimes the works destroy breeding islands, as happened to two of the three breeding sites at Río Lagartos. As water levels are artificially maintained throughout the year, the erosive action of waves is increased, and this can indirectly occasion similar destruction. Roads are often built to facilitate the exploitation, bringing additional human disturbance, and sometimes even blocking off lagoons.

On several occasions the popularity of flamingos has led to notably successful conservation efforts to make the presence of the flamingos compatible with the saltworks. On Bonaire, the saline lagoon where the Caribbean Flamingos breed was transformed into saltworks in the mid-1960's, but conservationists managed to convince the salt company to establish a reserve of 55 hectares, which had a dyke built round it and two pumps installed to control the water level. The flamingos rapidly accepted the sanctuary and bred there only a few months later, since when breeding has continued on a regular basis. However, in contrast to what has happened at other saltworks, the modifications carried out on Bonaire caused a decrease in the food available to the flamingos. The high salinity of the new pans

The Puna or James' Flamingo was until recently considered the rarest flamingo, but it now appears that the sympatric Andean Flamingo (Phoenicoparrus andinus) is in a similar situation, or perhaps even worse. Today, it is calculated that there are about 50,000 individuals of both species. They are subject to intense egg-harvesting which has been facilitated by the construction of roads for mining and oil-exploration; in the same way, the access of foxes and other terrestrial predators to the colonies has become easier. The morphological features which best differentiate this species include the bright red elongated scapulars, the broad band of carmine streaks on the breast and the orange-yellow and black bill, the most brightly coloured bill of all flamingos.

[Phoenicoparrus jamesi, Salar de Surire, Chile. Photo: Günter Ziesler/ Bruce Coleman]

led to the build-up of a thick crust of gypsum, which in turn prevented the breeding of brine-flies, the flamingos' main source of food. The birds, therefore, adapted their diet to feed on snails and tiny clams in the lagoons, which, perhaps because they are less nutritious, proved insufficient to maintain the whole population. As a result of this, many flamingos had to commute daily to Venezuela (see Movements). Presumably as a result of the sustained breeding success on Bonaire, a colony was established in Venezuela in 1987, and more than 2000 pairs bred successfully, the first breeding in the country for at least 40 years. This colony is on the north-west coast at the Ciénaga de Olivitos, where a new saltworks had been authorized the previous year.

Erosion has been a problem in the Camargue, as here too it increased with the saltworks, and the flamingos themselves contributed to it by digging up mud for nest-building. The result was that the island on which they had bred for many years began to disintegrate, and from 1962 to 1968 breeding success was almost nil. In 1969 the flamingos began to breed again on a new island, which was not big enough to accomodate the 7000 pairs. For this reason, a bulldozer was used to construct an artificial island of about 6200 m^2, rising some 40 cm above the water. Although four years went by before it was used, it later accomodated the main colony, and continues to do so today. Here the flamingos receive a good deal of attention, including vigilance day and night during the whole of the breeding season, to avoid disturbances of any kind, the control of the Yellow-legged Gull populations, which can cause considerable losses in colonies (see Breeding), the banning of light aircraft from flying over the breeding grounds, and, in some very cold winters, like that of 1985, the capture, penning and subsequent release of weak birds, in order to reduce the high mortality which occurs in such years. All these measures have contributed to an uninterrupted chain of successful breeding since 1969, and the steady growth of the population, with 19,926 pairs breeding in 1986. A similar increase has occurred

at Fuente de Piedra, with successful breeding in 10 out of 13 years since 1977, due to similar protective measures. However, these increases are causing concern and controversy, for the large numbers of flamingos walking about stir up sediments, even in lagoons that they rarely visited in the past, which is leading to the eutrophication of lagoons. Thus, less food is available for some threatened species, such as the White-headed Duck (Oxyura leucocephala) or the Red-knobbed Coot (Fulica cristata) in southern Spain.

Man has come to the rescue of flamingos on other occasions, for example when water levels drop disastrously half way through breeding. In 1962, the high concentration of salts in Lake Magadi, in Kenya, caused heavy rings of soda to form around Lesser Flamingo's legs, and of about 100,000 chicks affected, more than 27,000 were saved, in a large-scale rescue operation. About 200,000 more chicks were saved, by the pumping in of fresh water and also the relocation of the crèches from the areas with greatest soda concentrations. The same measures have been applied elsewhere, and in 1969 the transfer of chicks to areas with higher water levels similarly avoided the starvation of around 20,000 Lesser Flamingo chicks at Etosha Pan, in Namibia. At Fuente de Piedra, in the very dry year of 1984, water was pumped from wells and transported by lorry, to save the breeding season of the Greater Flamingo colony, and, in conjuction with other measures of vigilance and management, this also improved breeding success in subsequent years.

General Bibliography
Allen (1956), Bildstein (1990b), de Boer & Johnson (1984, 1986, 1988, 1989), Feduccia (1976a, 1976b, 1978, 1980), Haavie (1962), Hagey et al. (1990), Jenkin (1957), Kahl (1979b, 1980), Kear (1985, 1986), Kear & Duplaix-Hall (1975), Mainardi (1962), Ogilvie & Ogilvie (1986), Olson & Feduccia (1980a), Palmes (1981), Rutgers & Norris (1970), Sibley & Monroe (1990), Sibley et al. (1969), Studer-Thiersch (1964), Thiede (1987), Vanden Berge (1976), Visser (1987), Yeates (1950b).

ssp *ruber*

1

ssp *roseus*

2

PLATE 38

inches   14

cm   35

3

4

5

Genus *PHOENICOPTERUS* Linnaeus, 1758

1. Greater Flamingo

Phoenicopterus ruber

French: Flamant rose **German**: Rosaflamingo **Spanish**: Flamenco Común
Other common names: Caribbean/American/Cuban/West Indian Flamingo (*ruber*); Rosy Flamingo (*roseus*)

Taxonomy. *Phoenicopterus ruber* Linnaeus, 1758, Bahamas, *ex* Catesby.
Race *roseus* sometimes considered distinct species; occasionally referred to as *antiquorum*, but this name is obsolete. Some authors place population of Galapagos in separate subspecies, *glyphorhynchus* (see page 508). *P. chilensis* has been included in present species. Two subspecies normally recognized.
Subspecies and Distribution.
P. r. ruber Linnaeus, 1758 - Caribbean; Galapagos.
P. r. roseus Pallas, 1811 - S Spain and S France E to Kazakhstan; S through N, W and E Africa to South Africa and through Middle East to India and Sri Lanka.

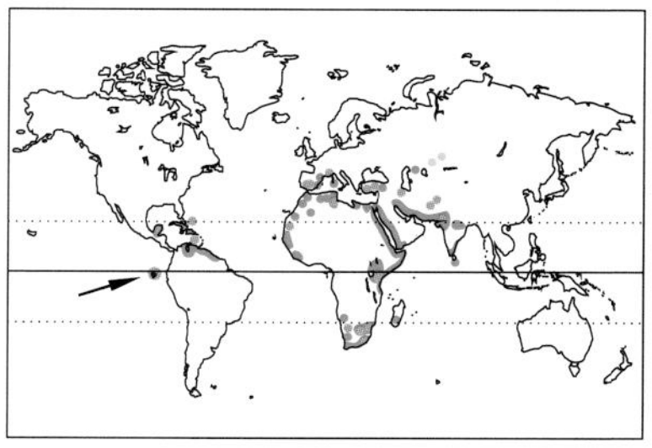

Descriptive notes. 120-145 cm; 2100-4100 g; wingspan 140-165 cm. Largest flamingo. Female up to 20% smaller and shorter-legged. Juvenile grey-brown with some pink in underparts, wings and tail; legs, feet and bill mainly brown. Variable subadult plumages during first 3 years or so. Race *roseus* paler and less brightly coloured.
Habitat. Saline lagoons and salt-pans; also (*roseus*) large, shallow, highly alkaline or saline inland lakes. Also sandbanks and mudflats in W Africa, e.g. Banc d'Arguin (Mauritania). Breeds on mudflats or islands of large water bodies and occasionally on bare, rocky islands; in Mauritania breeds on sandy islands of intertidal zone.
Food and Feeding. Relatively varied diet. Animal food consists of aquatic invertebrates, e.g. crustaceans (*Artemia*, *Gammarus*, copepods), molluscs (*Cerithidea*, *Cerithium*, *Paludestrina*, *Neritina*, *Gemma*, *Macoma*), annelids (*Nereis*) and insects, including larvae or chrysalids of Diptera (*Ephydra*, *Chironomus*, *Thinophilus*) and corixids (*Sigaria*, *Micronecta*); plant matter consists largely of seeds or stolons of marsh grasses (*Ruppia*, *Scirpus*, *Juncus*, *Cyperus*), also algae, diatoms and decaying leaves. Occasionally takes adult insects, e.g. waterbeetles (Coleoptera) or ants (Formicoidae); also crabs (*Dotilla*) and perhaps small fish (*Cyprinodon*). Sometimes ingests mud, in order to extract organic matter, especially bacteria. Normally feeds with head, and often most of neck, completely under water, while walking along steadily; only occasionally filters on surface, in style of *P. minor*. Also "treads" ground to loosen surface and bring out prey. See page 512.
Breeding. Laying Apr in S Europe, Feb-Mar in Tunisia, May in Kazakhstan and Mexico, Mar-Jun in Bahamas; variable in most of tropics and subtropics. Large, dense colonies of up to 20,000 pairs (up to 200,000 in India); in Galapagos small colonies of 3-50 pairs. Nest is normally truncated cone of mud with shallow bowl on top; on rocky islands without mud, nest is small pile of stones and debris. 1 egg, rarely 2; incubation 27-31 days; chicks have pale grey down, quickly replaced by second darker coat of down; fledging 65-90 days. Sexual maturity normally at 5-6 years, occasionally at 4 or even 3. Oldest ringed bird 33 years old, still breeding; oldest captive bird over 44 years old.
Movements. Partially migratory and dispersive. N populations perform fairly regular migrations, hardly ever involving whole population; complex pattern in W Mediterranean, but quite well known; some records of movements between discrete populations; migration apparently by night, with birds covering about 500-600 km per night between staging sites. In warmer climes dispersive, after breeding or in response to adverse climatic conditions. Daily movements during breeding between Bonaire I and Venezuela, in search of food (see page 519). The small Galapagos population is sedentary.
Status and Conservation. Not globally threatened. CITES II. Population of nominate race has declined markedly and now estimated at only c. 80,000-90,000 birds, at 4 main colonies, in Mexico, Cuba, Bahamas and Netherlands Antilles; all of these colonies are protected, but expansion of salt-pans in early 1980's removed 2 of the 3 nesting zones in Yucatán and has reduced amount of optimum habitat on Bonaire; several other former sites deserted, due to reclamation of land, drainage or disturbance. Isolated population of Galapagos estimated at only 400-500 birds; appears stable, but could be badly affected by natural disasters (see page 522). Race *roseus* numbers c. 800,000 birds, at c. 25 widely scattered breeding colonies, but no recent census in India, where up to 500,000 birds thought to occur. Population of W Mediterranean estimated at c. 80,000 birds in 1983 and increasing markedly, due to improved protection. Exterminated from Cape Verde Is, where last bred in 1898; also from islands off Kuwait, where last bred in 1922; until early 20th century, bred in several lakes of Nile Delta (Egypt). Thought to be threatened and declining in Kazakhstan. Over 65,000 counted in Iran, Jan 1990. In Egypt large numbers shot or captured to be sold in markets. Important steps taken towards conservation of both subspecies, including construction of artificial lagoons and islands (see page 523). Breeds fairly well in captivity.
Bibliography. Abdulali (1964), Ali (1945), Ali & Ripley (1978), Allen (1956), André & Johnson (1981), Bahena (1983), Bauer & Glutz von Blotzheim (1966), Berry (1972), Bharucha (1987), Blasco *et al.* (1979), de Boer (1979, 1981), Brichetti (1983), Britton *et al.* (1986), Brooke (1984), Brown (1955, 1958), Brown, Powell-Cotton & Hopcraft (1973), Brown, Urban & Newman (1982), Campredon (1987), Cramp & Simmons (1977), Dementiev & Gladkov (1951a), Dollinger (1988), Domergue (1950), Dupuy (1979), Espino-Barros & Baldassarre (1989a, 1989b), Fernández-Cruz *et al.* (1987), Foers (1984), Gallet (1949), Gerharts & Voous (1968), Géroudet (1978a), Green *et al.* (1989), Guzmán (1986), Haverschmidt (1970), Hernández & García (1976, 1979), Hoffman (1955-63), Johnson (1966, 1970-76, 1977, 1978, 1979a, 1979b, 1980, 1983, 1984, 1989a, 1989b), Johnson *et al.* (1991), Klockenhoff & Madel (1970), Kumerloeve (1962a, 1966c), Langrand (1990), Litvidinova *et al.* (1984), Mocci Demartis (1985), de Naurois (1969a), Niethammer (1970), Ottenwalder *et al.* (1990), Palmer (1962), Pearson (1924), Porter & Forrest (1974), Poslavski *et al.* (1977), Richter *et al.* (1991), Ridley *et al.* (1955), Roberts (1991), Robertson & Johnson (1979), Rooth (1965, 1976), Salathé (1983), Sánchez *et al.* (1985), Savage (1964), Sprunt (1976, 1988), Studer-Thiersch (1966, 1967), Tindle (1978), Trotignon & Trotignon (1981), Uys *et al.* (1961, 1963), Valle & Coulter (1987), Van Dijk (1986), Voous (1983), Wiley & Wiley (1979), Yeates (1950b), Zahl (1951, 1952).

2. Chilean Flamingo

Phoenicopterus chilensis

French: Flamant du Chili **German**: Chileflamingo **Spanish**: Flamenco Chileno

Taxonomy. *Phoenicopterus Chilensis* Molina, 1782, Chile.
Sometimes considered subspecies of *P. ruber*. Monotypic.
Distribution. C Peru southwards through Andes to Tierra del Fuego; extends eastwards to S Brazil and Uruguay.

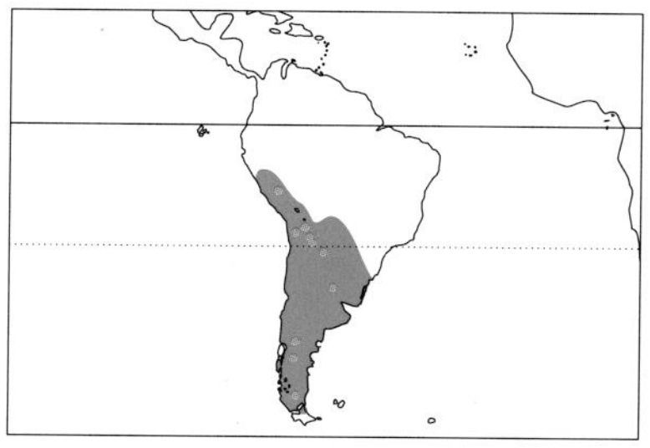

Descriptive notes. 105 cm; c. 2300 g. Yellowish-grey legs with contrasting red "knees" and feet. Black of bill tip extends beyond bend; rest of bill very pale. Immature grey with brown and pink markings.
Habitat. Coastal mudflats, estuaries, lagoons and salt-lakes from sea level up to 4500 m. On lakes with fish (often introduced by man), species scarce or absent, but normally abundant on lakes without fish; most lakes highly saline and/or dry periodically. Normally breeds on islands and islets of mud or gravel, but also on stony islands in Chile, and on margins of large, sediment-covered icebergs in Bolivia.
Food and Feeding. Generalist. Takes aquatic invertebrates, including: crustaceans, e.g. brine-shrimps (*Artemia*), copepods (*Boeckella*), cladocerans, ostracods and amphipods; larvae and pupae of Diptera, including chironomids (*Paratrichocladius*) and brine-flies (*Ephydra*); corixids; and snails. Almost always feeds at sediment/water interface, often with entire neck submerged, advancing steadily and almost in straight line. Also "treading" or "stomping" in same spot; apparently commoner in some lakes where aquatic plant *Ruppia* forms sparse carpet on bottom replete with invertebrates. Occasionally flocks swim to filter planktonic cladocerans right at water surface.
Breeding. Laying from Nov in S Argentina, Dec in Cordoba (C Argentina), Jan-Mar in *altiplano*, and Oct in extreme N of range at L Junín (Peru). Colonies of up to 6000 pairs; in Andes often alongside *P. andinus* and/or *P. jamesi*. Nest is usually truncated cone of mud with shallow bowl on top; on rocky islands without mud, lays on bare ground. 1 egg; incubation 27-31 days; chicks have pale grey down; fledging 70-80 days.
Movements. Birds breeding in high Andes winter along Pacific coast. Abandons L Junín (Peru) in Feb-May, when water level rises. In Sept, flocks fly N from Tierra del Fuego, where species not uncommon in winter. Dispersive movements between lakes outside breeding season. Vagrant to Falkland Is and Ecuador.
Status and Conservation. Not globally threatened. CITES II. Most numerous and widespread flamingo in S America. Probably subjected to intensive egg-harvesting, since arrival of man in S America; in recent years, egg-collecters responsible for partial or complete breeding failure of colonies in Bolivia. In mid-1970's total population estimated at 500,000 birds, but more recent figures: c. 100,000 in Argentina; up to 30,000 in Chile; and tens of thousands in Peru and Bolivia, where greatest concentrations occur, e.g. 100,000 at L Poopo, Bolivia, in 1972. Overall total not much more than 200,000 birds. Apparent decline since 1970's probably misleading, and may be put down to improved census methods; however, marked decline noted in C Chile and in moist *pampas* of Argentina, due to alteration of habitat. At Mar Chiquita, in Cordoba (N Argentina), 29,277 chicks fledged in 1977, after which species has bred no more, due to flooding of breeding areas. Breeds fairly well in captivity.
Bibliography. Belton (1984), Bennett (1987), Blake (1977), Canevari & Cabal (1988), Cordier (1965, 1968), Dabbene (1920), Davies, W.G. (1978), Dekker (1984), Dollinger (1988), Fjeldså & Krabbe (1990), Glade (1988), Harper & Drabble (1936), Hellmayr & Conover (1948), Hughes (1984), Humphrey *et al.* (1970), Hurlbert (1978, 1981, 1982), Hurlbert & Keith (1979), Hurlbert, Loayza & Moreno (1986), Hurlbert, Lopez & Keith (1984), Johnson (1965, 1967, 1972), Johnson *et al.* (1958), Lee (1987b), Markham (1971), Morrison (1968), Nores & Yzurieta (1980), de la Peña (1986), Peña (1962), Richter *et al.* (1991), Scott & Carbonell (1986), Shannon (1981), Sivelle (1984), Studer-Thiersch (1967), Vides-Almonacid (1990), Wackernagel (1959), Ward (1941), Wilkinson (1989).

Genus *PHOENICONAIAS* G. R. Gray, 1869

3. Lesser Flamingo

Phoeniconaias minor

French: Flamant nain **German**: Zwergflamingo **Spanish**: Flamenco Enano

Taxonomy. *Phoenicopterus minor* Geoffroy, 1798, no locality = Senegal.
In recent years, frequently included in genus *Phoenicopterus*, along with all other flamingos. Monotypic.
Distribution. Bulk of population in Rift Valley of E Africa; three further more or less discrete populations in Namibia/Botswana, Mauritania/Senegal and NW India/Pakistan.
Descriptive notes. 80-90 cm; c. 1500-2000 g; wingspan 95-100 cm. Smallest flamingo; bill long, very dark. Female slightly smaller. Juvenile grey-brown, slightly darker overall, with browner head and neck than juvenile *P. ruber*.
Habitat. Inland saline and alkaline lakes, and also coastal lagoons. Tolerates or actively seeks out more alkaline water than *P. ruber* due to specialized diet. Breeds on extensive mudflats usually far out from shore in large lakes or pans.
Food and Feeding. Highly specialized: almost entirely dependent on microscopic blue-green algae (*Spirulina*, *Oscillatoria*, *Lyngbya*) and diatoms (*Navicula*, Bacillariophyceae); to lesser extent small invertebrates, e.g. rotifers (*Brachionus*), which may partially substitute normal food in times of very low *Spirulina* densities in E African lakes. Usually feeds near surface in calm water, with bill only partly submerged; walks or very often swims, which is only way of reaching fair proportion of potential food supply in most lakes. Rarely feeds on bottom like *P. ruber*, possibly sifting diatoms from mud. Does not compete with *P. ruber* (see page 512).

On following page: 4. Andean Flamingo (*Phoenicoparrus andinus*); 5. Puna Flamingo (*Phoenicoparrus jamesi*).

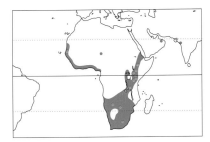

Breeding. Very irregular habits; does not attempt breeding every year, and at same locality can breed at different times of year; in E Africa, mainly late in dry season and during short rains; in Namibia and Botswana, apparently in dry season following years of high rainfall; in Mauritania, in Jun-Jul, during rains. Large colonies of many thousands of pairs (up to 1,100,000). 1 egg, rarely 2; incubation 28 days; chicks have whitish to dark grey down; fledging normally 70-75 days (65-90). Sexual maturity at 3 or 4 years old.

Movements. Extensive movements of vast numbers of birds; normally occur after several months at same lake, in response to adverse conditions. Some evidence of movements, at least occasionally, between populations of E and S Africa; irregular movements may also occur between E African and more distant W African and Indian populations (see page 519). Migrates by night. Vagrant to Morocco and Spain.

Status and Conservation. Not globally threatened. CITES II. The most numerous flamingo, with total population of 2,500,000-4,000,000 birds, or possibly even 6,000,000; discrepancy partly depends whether or not over 1,000,000 birds seen at times in Botswana considered part of E African population or not. Numbers in India poorly known, but estimated at tens of thousands; 5224 counted in India and 3150 in Pakistan, Jan 1990. W African population very small, only c. 6000 birds; breeding only confirmed in 1965, with 800-900 pairs at lagoons of Aftout es Samel, Mauritania, though probably also bred in 1988 at unknown colony. Difficult to breed in captivity, probably due to specialized feeding habits.

Bibliography. Ali & Ripley (1978), Alam (1982), Appert (1971b), Archibald & Nott (1987), Bernis (1966c), Berry (1972, 1975), Brooke (1984), Brown, H.D. (1957), Brown, L.H. (1955, 1959, 1971, 1973), Brown et al. (1982), Brown & Root (1971), Cramp & Simmons (1977), Dollinger (1988), Eltringham & Din (1976), Grobler (1981), Guillou & Pages (1987), Guillou & Vielliard (1969), Grzimek & Grzimek (1960), Johnson (1980a), Karpowicz (1985), Kumar (1986), Langrand (1990), Lippens & Wille (1976), Louette (1981), Maclean (1985), Merz (1980), Middlemiss (1958c), Milon et al. (1973), Morillo (1973), Mundkur (1984), Mundkur et al. (1989), de Naurois (1965), Palmes (1984), Pennycuick & Bartholomew (1973), Pinto (1983), du Preez (1973), Ridley et al. (1955), Roberts (1991), Robertson & Johnson (1979), Scott (1989), Thiede & Gloe (1987), Tuite (1978, 1979, 1980, 1981), Vareschi (1978).

Genus *PHOENICOPARRUS* Bonaparte, 1856

4. Andean Flamingo
Phoenicoparrus andinus

French: Flamant des Andes **German**: Andenflamingo **Spanish**: Parina Grande
Other common names: Greater Andean Flamingo

Taxonomy. *Phoenicopterus andinus* Philippi, 1854, salt lake near Altos de Pingopingo, Antofagasta, Chile.
In recent years, frequently included in genus *Phoenicopterus*, along with all other flamingos. Monotypic.
Distribution. Restricted to high Andes, from S Peru through Bolivia to N Chile and NW Argentina.

Descriptive notes. 102-110 cm; 2000-2400 g. Head, neck and upper breast tinged wine red; red spot between nostrils; only flamingo with yellow legs and feet. Lacks hind toe. On standing birds, large black triangle towards rear, formed by flight-feathers, more visible than in other species. Immature is dull greyish with conspicuous dark streaks on upperparts.
Habitat. High altitude salt-lakes, mainly between 3500 and 4500 m, but also down to 2500 m and up to 4950 m. Often coincides with *P. jamesi*, but present species apparently more numerous on lower altitude lakes, with slightly deeper, less alkaline water. Absent from lakes, where bottom consists of hardened sediments. Breeds on islands or islets of soft clay sediment or sand, in centre or along shores of salt-lakes.
Food and Feeding. Primarily diatoms (Bacillariophyceae), particularly of genus *Surirella*. Almost always feeds at sediment/water interface, and frequently upends where water slightly deeper. Walks fairly slowly, occasionally pausing. While feeding is normally distributed patchily about lake.
Breeding. Laying Dec-Jan. Colonies of up to thousands of pairs, often mixed with *P. chilensis* and/or *P. jamesi*. Nest is truncated cone of mud with shallow bowl on top. 1 egg; incubation c. 28 days; chicks have grey down. Full adult plumage attained at 3+ years.

Movements. Little known. Movements between lakes on *altiplano* related to changes in water level, and in food availability. In winter, some vertical migration between temporarily inhospitable *altiplano* and lower areas where food remains plentiful. In 1956, exceptional record of 15-20 birds at altitude of only 500 m in N Argentina. In 1989, first record in Santa Catarina (S Brazil), an individual ringed in N Chile.
Status and Conservation. Not globally threatened. Currently considered near-threatened; until very recently considered threatened, in category Insufficiently Known. CITES II. Population usually estimated at c. 150,000 birds, but recently considered overestimate; more realistic figure may be 50,000 birds. Only known regular breeding site at Salar de Atacama, in N Chile; also, less regularly, at other lakes in N Chile, Bolivia and N Argentina. Very low breeding success reported. Largest recorded concentration, 18,000 birds on L Uru-uru, Bolivia, in 1970. No precise figures to show trend, but have almost certainly declined in recent years. Habitat loss due to diversion of streams by man; egg-harvesting, in particular, facilitated by construction of roads for mining and oil-exploration, which have also permitted access of foxes to colonies, causing desertion of several colonies in Bolivia and Chile, and virtual halt of chick production in Salar de Atacama. Recent vigilance of colonies and establishment of national flamingo reserve of 73,000 ha, around Atacama and other saline lakes in high Andes of Chile, should improve situation. Very difficult to breed in captivity, probably due to specialized feeding habits.

Bibliography. Bege & Pauli (1990a, 1990b), Blake (1977), Collar & Andrew (1988), Conway (1965b, 1991), Cordier (1965, 1968), Dollinger (1988), Fjeldså (1985a), Fjeldså & Krabbe (1990), Glade (1988), Hellmayr & Conover (1948), Hurlbert (1978, 1981, 1982), Hurlbert & Chang (1983), Hurlbert & Keith (1979), Johnson (1965, 1967), Johnson et al. (1958), Kear & Palmes (1980), Klös (1975, 1976), Morrison (1968), Nores & Yzurieta (1980), de la Peña (1986), Peña (1962), Reinhard (1983), Scott & Carbonell (1986), Vides-Almonacid (1990).

5. Puna Flamingo
Phoenicoparrus jamesi

French: Flamant de James **German**: Jamesflamingo **Spanish**: Parina Chica
Other common names: Lesser Andean/James's Flamingo

Taxonomy. *Phoenicopterus jamesi* P. L. Sclater, 1886, Sitani, at foot of Isluga volcano, Tarapacá, Chile.
In recent years, frequently included in genus *Phoenicopterus*, along with all other flamingos. Monotypic.
Distribution. Restricted to limited zone in Andes, 15°-26° S, comprising extreme S Peru, W Bolivia, N Chile and NW Argentina. Most localized species.

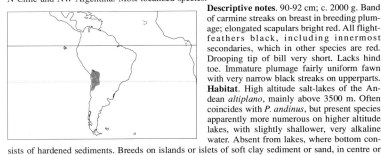

Descriptive notes. 90-92 cm; c. 2000 g. Band of carmine streaks on breast in breeding plumage; elongated scapulars bright red. All flight-feathers black, including innermost secondaries, which in other species are red. Drooping tip of bill very short. Lacks hind toe. Immature plumage fairly uniform fawn with very narrow black streaks on upperparts.
Habitat. High altitude salt-lakes of the Andean *altiplano*, mainly above 3500 m. Often coincides with *P. andinus*, but present species apparently more numerous on higher altitude lakes, with slightly shallower, very alkaline water. Absent from lakes, where bottom consists of hardened sediments. Breeds on islands or islets of soft clay sediment or sand, in centre or along shores of salt-lakes.
Food and Feeding. Highly specialized. Has shortest bill of any flamingo, with very small filtering area. Main food diatoms (Bacillariophyceae). Feeds by walking slowly and fairly aimlessly, often pausing. When feeding, individuals more widely scattered over lake than in *P. andinus*.
Breeding. Breeding grounds not discovered until 1957. Laying Dec-Feb. Colonies of up to thousands of pairs, often mixed with *P. chilensis* and/or *P. andinus*. Nest is truncated cone of mud with shallow bowl on top. 1 egg; chicks have grey down. Full adult plumage attained at 3 or 4 years.
Movements. Little known. At the end of summer, flocks seen leaving Laguna Colorada at 4500 m, probably moving to other salt-lakes at lower altitude. However, some birds remain throughout winter, probably thanks to presence of hot volcanic springs, which prevent surrounding water from freezing. Some other movements: exceptional record of 2 birds in S Argentina, more than 2000 km from normal range.
Status and Conservation. Not globally threatened. Currently considered near-threatened; until very recently considered threatened, in category Insufficiently Known. CITES II. Population estimated at c. 50,000 birds and usually considered rarest flamingo (but see *P. andinus*). Most important site is Laguna Colorada, SW Bolivia, where 26,000 birds recently counted, with up to 7000 breeding in 1960, alongside many *P. chilensis* and *P. andinus*; 6000 found breeding at Salar de Tara, Chile, in 1988. Has attempted breeding at 3 other lakes in Bolivia, 1 in Argentina and 3 in Chile. Egg-harvesting and loss or deterioration of habitat, due to pollution and diversion of streams for human purposes, have clearly had negative effects. Rare in captivity, where has never been bred.

Bibliography. Blake (1977), Collar & Andrew (1988), Conway (1960, 1961, 1965b, 1991), Cordier (1965, 1968), Dollinger (1988), Fjeldså (1985a), Fjeldså & Krabbe (1990), Glade (1988), Hellmayr & Conover (1948), Hurlbert (1978, 1981, 1982), Hurlbert & Keith (1979), Johnson (1965, 1967, 1972), Johnson et al. (1958), Kear & Palmes (1980), Morrison (1968, 1972), Patrick (1961), de la Peña (1986), Peña (1962), Scott & Carbonell (1986), Walcott (1925).

Order ANSERIFORMES

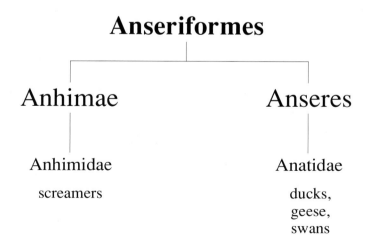

Class AVES
Order ANSERIFORMES
Suborder ANHIMAE
Family ANHIMIDAE (SCREAMERS)

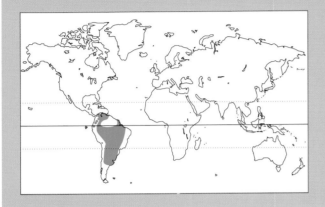

- Large, heavily-built waterbirds with long, robust legs and small head and bill.
- 76-95 cm.

- Neotropical Region.
- Marshes, forests and savannas.
- 2 genera, 3 species, 3 taxa.
- No species threatened; none extinct since 1600.

Systematics

Although the screamers had actually been known to science for some time, nobody appeared very interested in their origin and taxonomic relationships until the final decades of the nineteenth century. From then on they were considered to be directly related to the duck family (Anatidae), and they were even regarded as a missing link between the ducks and the gamebirds (Galliformes).

Nowadays, after more far-reaching studies, majority opinion still believes them to be primitive Anseriformes, probably very close in evolutionary terms to the Magpie Goose (*Anseranas semipalmata*) of Australia, indeed recent work using DNA suggests that the latter is actually closer to the screamers than it is to the rest of the Anatidae. Although it is generally felt that there is enough evidence for screamers to be designated a distinct family, they are usually retained within the Anseriformes, as they are living representatives of the evolutionary line which has led to the present day ducks, geese and swans.

The taxonomy of the Anhimidae has been studied in detail, particularly because of its relevance in attempts to discover the origin of the Anseriformes. From traditional opinions that related this order principally to the flamingos (Phoenicopteriformes) and the large, long-legged wading birds of the Ciconiiformes, or alternatively to the Galliformes, new opinions are emerging that place them with other groups. Due to the recent reappraisal of *Presbyornis*, an early Eocene fossil bird with a wader's body and a duck's head, some taxonomists believe that the Anseriformes could also be linked to the waders (Charadriiformes).

The earliest fossil remains of screamers come from the Pleistocene in Argentina, some 20,000 years ago, and since that time they seem to have diversified very little, in stark contrast to the Anatidae. The family comprises three exclusively South American species. Two of these, the Southern Screamer (*Chauna torquata*) and the Northern Screamer (*Chauna chavaria*), are extremely similar in morphology, habits, habitat requirements and several other aspects of their biology. The other species, the Horned Screamer (*Anhima cornuta*), is treated in a separate genus, as it has several marked physical peculiarities.

Morphological Aspects

Screamers are large, stocky birds, measuring up to 95 cm and weighing as much as about 5 kg. Superficially they look more like misshapen gamebirds than waterbirds, particularly with the small chicken-like head and bill.

Their relation with other Anseriformes can best be seen through various morphological details, especially internal ones, which show their close links with the Magpie Goose. For instance, the three front toes are basally webbed, with only a vestigial membrane between the toes. In addition, moult is gradual and does not interfere with their ability to fly, so they do not have to undergo the typical flightless period of the swans, ducks and geese. Like the Spur-winged Goose (*Plectropterus gambensis*) of Africa they have two extremely sharp, long, curved spurs that protrude from the bend of the wing. Their function seems to be related to intraspecific fighting, perhaps for a particular mate or territory, as remains of the horny covering have been

Due to their external appearance, mainly the disproportionately small head for the size of the bird, and the short, hooked bill, the screamers were for a long time classified as Galliformes. However, more detailed studies appear to indicate that they are, in fact, primitive Anseriformes, related in particular to the Magpie Goose (Anseranas semipalmata). In the Horned Screamer the "horn", present in both sexes, is formed from an unbranched, modified feather shaft and can be up to 15 cm long.

[Anhima cornuta. Photo: Kenneth W. Fink/ Ardea]

lamellate, as in the ducks, and the tongue is horny, as opposed to fleshy, both presumably adaptations for dealing with tough aquatic plants. In fact, there are rudimentary lamellae on the bill, and it has been suggested that these may indicate that the screamers are not so primitive after all, as they may have given up the technique of filter-feeding. All three screamer species have adornments on the head, in *Chauna* a tuft of feathers on the nape, and in *Anhima* a long, slender cartilaginous appendage that grows out of the forehead; this "horn" is presumably only for display purposes, as it is quite brittle and often breaks, although it does regrow.

The legs are fairly long and sturdy. The toes too are long and strong and the hind toe is elongated but not raised, so the bird is well adapted for making its way through marsh vegetation. Although screamers rarely swim, they are quite capable of doing so from an early age. They sit high on the water and are, in fact, fairly good swimmers; they are not, however, known to dive.

They have long, broad wings and, like most Anseriformes, are good fliers, although take-off is rather ponderous with heavy wingbeats. Nonetheless, once under way a bird can glide comfortably along with its neck outstretched, and the Southern Screamer regularly soars to great heights, a habit more typical of storks or pelicans than of wildfowl.

The plumage of the screamers is grey, brown or black, with some brighter white markings on the head, neck or wings. Differences between the sexes are not visible in the field, although females tend to be slightly smaller, and fully-grown juveniles are similar to adults. In general the plumage appears looser and more dishevelled than in the Anatidae.

found embedded in the breasts of other screamers. In any case, the spurs are renewed periodically, so their attachment to the wing can be fairly loose at times.

Certain features separate them from all other Anseriformes. For example, they lack feather tracts, so their feathers grow evenly all over the body without the normal separations between tracts. Again, their bones are far more pneumatic than in other birds, making the bone structure exceptionally light. Moreover, they have a complicated system of air-sacs beneath the skin, which, when contracted, can collapse rapidly with a distinctive cracking sound. Finally, screamers are the only birds that lack uncinate processes, rib projections which cover and reinforce the rib-cage in other birds.

The head is disproportionately small for the size and bulk of the bird, as is the short, strong, hooked bill. This is not

Habitat

The characteristic habitat of screamers includes extensive open areas, which may often be flooded to form marshes and swamps. They live and feed in open savanna, meadowlands, marshes and lakes with abundant vegetation. Both the Horned and Southern Screamers favour flat, uncultivated plains, where

Unlike the Anatidae, in the screamers the pair-bond usually lasts for several years, or even for life. During the breeding season, they are strongly territorial and dependent on wetlands, while outside this period they can assemble in flocks of up to several thousand individuals in the case of the Southern Screamer, and they are not rare in cultivation and habitats drier than those they use for nesting.

[*Chauna torquata*, Pantanal, Brazil. Photo: Günter Ziesler]

they may congregate in large groups. The Northern Screamer, in turn, prefers marshes with dense vegetation.

Screamers stick to such habitat all year round, although during the breeding season they are particularly keen to be as near water as possible, where the chicks are safer from terrestrial predators. In marshy areas, their long toes help them to walk on floating vegetation without sinking in, as is the case of other marsh birds, such as the jacanas (Jacanidae) and the Shoebill (*Balaeniceps rex*). In the non-breeding season they also visit drier sites, especially fields of crops, where they often feed alongside farm birds.

General Habits

Outside the breeding season, screamers may form groups of several dozen, hundreds or even thousands of individuals. This is especially true in the case of the Southern Screamer, and large flocks can be seen foraging alongside domestic animals, for example beside sheep in Rio Grande do Sul, in southern Brazil. In tropical areas, however, birds tend to be less gregarious, and the Horned Screamer is generally a good deal more solitary than the other two species.

Screamers are thought to be essentially diurnal, although the Horned Screamer will carry on feeding some time after dusk. Southern Screamers tend to gather together in large groups to roost, standing up in the shallow water of pools. Horned Screamers may also roost in shallow water, but it seems more likely that they usually spend the night in a tree.

All species spend long periods resting in trees, usually perched on the top, and thus, with their considerable bulk, all the more visible from far off. When a screamer feels threatened, it tends to fly straight up into a tree, where it begins to call out loudly in alarm. In spite of its corpulence and largely terrestrial habits, it has no difficulty perching in trees, and this is undoubtedly facilitated by the long toes and the virtual absence of webbing. A bird may also fly up to a tree top, whence to use its strident voice to proclaim its territory.

Voice

Screamers are extremely vocal, and owe their vernacular name to their very distinctive calls, which are extraordinarily loud and unmelodious, and may be repeated incessantly for hours on end. The Southern Screamer's popular names, "Chajá" or "Tachã" come from its harsh, double-noted trumpeting call, while the Horned Screamer is named "Mohooka" by some of the native peoples, also after its exceptional voice.

The most outstanding feature of a screamer's voice is its phenomenal volume, for it is audible as much as three kilometres away. This, together with the fact that one bird calling usually sparks off its neighbour or its mate, while duets can be seemingly interminable during the breeding season, has meant that they are sometimes regarded as unwelcome companions in the forests and savannas where they live. They are especially unpopular among hunters, as the alarm call of one bird immediately warns all other animals of human presence, making it difficult for them to take their intended quarry by surprise.

Screamers also call from the air, while rising or soaring in circles, and, when in large groups, can produce a deafening noise, as well as an unforgettable sight. They often produce a noisy chorus from the roosting site as night is falling.

There is little difference in voice between the sexes, that of the male being slightly lower-pitched. Both sexes can produce a gruff, almost guttural noise, which sounds like a kind of drumming or cracking. It appears that this sound is used to threaten at close range, and there is evidence that it may be produced not vocally, but by the sudden collapse of the subcutaneous air-sacs.

Food and Feeding

Screamers are almost entirely herbivorous, and their diet is based on the leaves, flowers, seeds and roots of various succulent aquatic plants. The consumption of small quantities of insects has been recorded, especially for the Horned Screamer, but these are mostly taken during the breeding season to feed the chicks, or by the chicks themselves. When actively feeding, a bird is likely to consume any arthropods or dead small animals that it comes across in amongst the plants it is eating.

The normal feeding method involves grazing, with the bird pecking at the fleshy parts of the plants as it goes along, sometimes half submerged amidst the aquatic vegetation in flooded areas. Another typical method of obtaining food, if not so frequent, is by digging in the mud of shallow waters; in this respect they are similar to the Magpie Goose, although it is not known if screamers filter-feed at all or simply seize food with the bill.

The Southern Screamer obtains a fair amount of its food by grazing in fields of crops, often alongside domestic birds. As they regularly mix with farm birds, sometimes in large numbers, in some areas they come into conflict with farmers, as they may be thought to compete with the domestic stock, damage crops or even bring in disease.

Breeding

As is often the case with tropical and subtropical species, screamers may nest at any time of year, and nests with eggs have been found in all months, but in higher latitudes in particular the main nesting season is during the southern springtime, and the first eggs tend to be laid in September and October.

Unlike most of the true waterfowl, the Anatidae, screamers usually keep the same mate for successive years or even for life, and in the same way they usually maintain a breeding territory, which they defend against intruders of all species. Although the information available on many aspects of the biology of the family is patchy, it seems that the Horned Screamer is probably the most territorial of the three. It uses its "Mohooka" call (see Voice) to mark and maintain territory borders, and to inform neighbouring pairs of the limits. When another bird encroaches upon the territory, it has to confront the threatening postures of the owner; these postures involve

Screamers always nest alone, near or over water, and build their nest from material which they generally gather from the surrounding vegetation. Both adults incubate and subsequently look after the chicks. The sexual dimorphism in the three species of this family is restricted to slight differences in size, which can clearly be seen in this pair of Southern Screamers, the female being somewhat smaller than the male.

[Chauna torquata, in pampas of Argentina. Photo: Clem Haagner/ Ardea]

the displaying of a reddish mark on the wing that is lacking in the other two species, while the wings are spread to show off the spurs.

Open fighting is probably not a rare occurrence in any of the three species, and the spurs appear to play an important role (see Morphological Aspects). Aerial pursuits are also relatively common, when the resident bird tries to chase away the intruder that has dared to fly over the territory, or has even tried to land in it.

The pair-bond is forged through long sessions of repeated calls in duet, and also by mutual preening. Other important displays include walking side by side, and a posture with the head thrust right back, until it almost touches the back. Territorial birds frequently repeat a low, hoarse sound from subcutaneous air-sacs in the side of the neck. Copulation takes place on land, with the male gently pecking the female on the nape and treading on her back; no post-copulatory display has been described.

Both sexes take part in the construction of the nest, which consists of a pile of weeds, reeds and sticks, normally collected in the area immediately around the nest. However, there is some evidence indicating that they also fetch material from further afield, a habit not shared by the Anatidae. The nest, once finished, can be quite large, and is situated either in shallow water, or on dry ground not far from water.

Two to seven eggs may be laid, with four or five being the usual number, though there is a general tendency towards more eggs in subtropical zones. The relatively large eggs, laid at intervals of about two days, are white with pale spots and have a granulated shell. Both sexes take part in incubation, and on occasions when the nest is left unguarded, the eggs are covered.

The chicks hatch after 42-45 days, covered in thick yellowish grey down, and are able to leave the nest immediately, but they remain close by and follow their parents about. During the first few weeks they spend a good deal of time in the water, as they are not yet able to run and look for a safe spot amongst the vegetation.

In captivity, adult Northern Screamers have been seen feeding their chicks actively, in a manner similar to that seen in the Magpie Goose. They have also been seen to gather food and then drop it, apparently with the intention of helping the chicks discover it.

Juveniles fledge after eight to ten weeks, and they become fully independent at 12-14 weeks old. However, it probably takes a fair time before they begin to breed, judging from the large numbers of non-breeders, which can often be seen in sizeable flocks, even during the breeding season.

Movements

In many parts of their extensive range, the precise distribution of screamers is poorly known, and information on their presence or absence in different seasons is often lacking. Consequently very little is known about the kind of movements they make, the distances involved, the routes or the destinations. Certainly, they are quite capable of soaring at great heights (see Morphological Aspects) and probably also of covering long distances.

Outside the breeding season, they can form large flocks (see General Habits), sometimes apparently containing birds from different areas. These flocks move about erratically during

Screamer chicks, which with their yellowish down resemble goslings, are precocial, meaning that they are active immediately after hatching. They usually remain in the nest for only a short time, and then wander about led by their parents. Note the vestigial web at the base of the adult's toes, one of the morphological details which have been taken into consideration when deciding to include this family in the Anseriformes.

[Chauna torquata, Rocha, Uruguay. Photo: X. Ferrer & A. de Sostoa]

the winter months, and these movements seem to be determined by the severity of the weather and the availability of food. However, this pattern is far less common in tropical areas, as screamers are less gregarious than they are further south, and they tend to move about less. The Horned Screamer usually remains in its breeding grounds almost all year round, in the company of its mate, or alternatively it moves in small groups of five to ten birds through the surrounding area.

Relationship with Man

Their vocal prowess, together with their size and relative abundance in natural conditions, has meant that screamers are well known to all neighbouring human populations, though in many cases they are to some extent regarded as pests.

In several areas they are quite tame and may be approached closely, and, as they are large birds and can often be found occupying conspicuous perches, they would seem to offer a tempting target to hunters. However, many people find the unusual, spongy flesh, with its extensive network of air-sacs, to be fairly repulsive. In addition, hunters trying to stalk game do not like to have screamers in the area (see Voice), while farmers too are often keen to keep them away from their fields (see Food and Feeding). The "horn" of the Horned Screamer has traditionally been attributed medicinal values, when ground down into powder, and is considered a powerful remedy against a venomous snake-bite, or alternatively a preservative.

Like most members of the Anatidae, the three species of screamer very easily become "imprinted" during the first weeks of life, and this has been a very important factor in their domestication, as chicks can readily be reared alongside farm birds. As chicks tend to follow their parents in the wild, in captivity they quickly get used to following hens, domestic geese or even humans. The fact that the chicks can feed by themselves and are not fussy about what they eat has also contributed to their rapid adaptation.

Above all they are especially prized for their powerful voices, which they unleash at the first sign of danger, whether this be a stranger or any kind of animal that could threaten them. They are excellent in the role of watchdogs, for they are constantly alert and give warning at the slightest suspicious movement.

Southern Screamers, in particular, are fairly frequent in zoos and bird collections, especially in South America, where they can often be seen in the parks and gardens of big cities.

Status and Conservation

Any evaluation of the status of the three species of screamers runs into a common problem with birds, and indeed other life forms in South America, that of insufficient data. Large tracts of the continent are still virtually unknown, while very few areas can really be considered at all well studied, and the speed of economic growth and development means that information quickly becomes outdated.

Nevertheless, both the Horned and Southern Screamers are still widespread and locally common at present, particularly in areas where their habitat remains more or less intact. The Northern Screamer, in contrast, has a fairly limited range, and the destruction of its habitat in some areas has caused sufficient concern for it to be considered a near-threatened species. Like the other species, it too is locally common, for example in the region of the national park of Los Katios, in north-west Colombia, where birds can regularly be seen perched in trees along the River Atrato. In Venezuela, it is restricted to the areas to the west and south of Lake Maracaibo, where the main population occurs around the Ciénaga de Juan Manuel, which is fortunately included in a state-owned reserve of over 200,000 hectares.

The general deterioration of habitat is clearly the main problem facing all of the species, and this can take different forms. In the case of the Horned Screamer, for instance, the

The Northern Screamer is considered near-threatened, partly due to its restricted range, limited to north Colombia and north-west Venezuela, making it more vulnerable to the alteration of its habitat, mainly through wetland drainage and deterioration of water quality. The two allopatric species of the genus Chauna appear very similar at first glance, although the longer neck of this species, almost entirely black and strongly contrasting with the white of its throat and the sides of its head, clearly differentiates it from the Southern Screamer (C. torquata), in which only the base of the neck is black.

[Chauna chavaria. Photo: Kenneth W. Fink/ Ardea]

mass felling of the Amazonian rain forest is bound to reduce both its local abundance and overall numbers, while the opening up of once remote areas makes them accessible to all the typical associated human developments, including increased levels of hunting pressure. In wetlands all over the continent poaching and egg-collecting have been reported as having serious effects on waterbird populations, and screamers are very likely to be among the sufferers.

In other areas it is the intensification of agriculture that poses the main threat. Wetlands are generally receding all over the world, as they are steadily being dried up, in order to make way for livestock or crops; in addition, screamers are always liable to be seen as competitors by farmers (see Food and Feeding). Water quality is also deteriorating in many areas, as pesticides and herbicides are sprayed about inadvertently, and this might yet prove a major threat to the Northern Screamer, as the human population is considerable throughout much of its range.

Extensive research into these little known species is essential, in order to clarify their numbers, densities and ecological requirements, and to enable their future to be secured. The speed of habitat conversion in much of South America is such that common species may well become rare or threatened overnight, before scientists have time to react, as is already becoming a familiar story all over the world.

General Bibliography
Gizels *et al.* (1969), Haffer (1969), Hellmayr & Conover (1948), Livezey (1986), Olson & Feduccia (1980b), Rutgers & Norris (1970), Stott (1982), Todd (1979), Weller (1985).

1

2

3

Family ANHIMIDAE (SCREAMERS)
SPECIES ACCOUNTS

PLATE 39

Genus *ANHIMA*   Brisson, 1760

1. Horned Screamer

Anhima cornuta

French: Kamichi cornu   **German:** Hornwehrvogel   **Spanish:** Chajá Añuma

Taxonomy. *Palamedea cornuta* Linnaeus, 1766, eastern Brazil.
Monotypic.
Distribution. Tropical S America, from Colombia through Brazil to N Argentina.

Descriptive notes. 84-94 cm; c. 3000-3150 g; wingspan 170 cm. "Horn" fairly long, though sometimes broken; second, lower spur often hidden; iris yellow to orange. Variable amount of white on neck and buff or white on fore-wing; latter is conspicuous, when not covered by scapulars. Juvenile duller, with short, stunted "horn".
Habitat. Moist tropical forest, swamps and grassy meadows near rivers; also in *llanos* of Venezuela. Nearly always near water, al-though in winter sometimes occurs in drier habitats.
Food and Feeding. Leaves, stems, flowers and roots of aquatic plants, with predilection for succulent parts. Also small proportion of insects, consumed particularly by chicks. Grazes like other Anseriformes.
Breeding. Mostly during austral spring or summer, with eggs in Nov/Dec, but also in other months. Solitary nester, each pair defends territory fiercely; nest is large accumulation of plant matter and debris. 2-7 eggs, usually 3-5; incubation 40-47 days; chicks hatch with thick greyish yellow down, white below; nidifugous, brooded only for first few days.
Movements. Apparently sedentary, with local movements outside breeding season, mainly of juveniles or non-breeders.
Status and Conservation. Not globally threatened. Widespread and locally common, though probably declining in most areas with intensive human pressure. Breeding range has decreased in historical times, probably mainly due to drainage of wetlands and destruction of suitable habitat. Also subject to certain amount of hunting pressure. Extensive studies required to obtain information on numbers, threats and immediate conservation requirements.
Bibliography. Allen (1962), Barrow *et al.* (1986), Blake (1977), ffrench (1985b), Gill *et al.* (1974), Herklots (1961), Hilty & Brown (1986), Lint (1956), Naranjo (1986), Ortiz (1988), Pinto (1964), Ruschi (1979), de Schauensee (1948, 1964), de Schauensee & Phelps (1978), Scott & Carbonell (1986), Sick (1984), Veselovsky (1986a, 1986b).

Genus *CHAUNA*   Illiger, 1811

2. Southern Screamer

Chauna torquata

French: Kamichi à collier   **German:** Halsband-Wehrvogel   **Spanish:** Chajá Común
Other common names: Crested Screamer

Taxonomy. *Chaja torquata* Oken, 1816, "in Paragai, um Plata".
Monotypic.
Distribution. Bolivia and S Brazil to N Argentina.

Descriptive notes. 83-95 cm; c. 4400 g. Second, lower spur often hidden; thin white neck-ring more or less obvious, depending on bird's posture; large white patch visible on upper-wing in flight. Juvenile as adult, but duller; lacks collar of naked skin, black collar faint, spurs short or absent.
Habitat. Tropical or subtropical wetlands, in-cluding lakes, lagoons, marshes, flooded fields and meadows. May occur in drier habi-tat than other species, particularly during winter, when not uncommonly in agricultural land.
Food and Feeding. Green parts of succulent, aquatic plants; seeds, leaves and stems of vegetables and other crops. Also a limited amount of animal food. Grazes like other Anseriformes.
Breeding. Mostly during austral spring, with eggs in Oct/Nov, but also in other months. Solitary and territorial; nest is large accumulation of plant matter and debris. 2-7 eggs, usually 3-5; incubation 43-46 days; chicks hatch with thick greyish yellow down, white below; nidifugous, brooded only for first few days.
Movements. Mostly sedentary; somewhat nomadic outside breeding season, when large flocks may form and wander erratically in search of food.
Status and Conservation. Not globally threatened. Apparently most abundant of screamers, but also most subject to human pressure, as inhabits some heavily populated regions; popular target for hunters. Presently suffering habitat destruction, mainly in form of drainage of wetlands, though has shown some adaptation to human pressure by foraging in cultivated fields. Extensive studies required to obtain information on numbers, threats and immediate conservation requirements. Commonly kept and bred in zoos and collections, particularly in S America; frequently domesti-cated in several parts of range.

Bibliography. Belton (1984), Blake (1977), Gore & Gepp (1987), Goszawski *et al.* (1989), Hudson (1920), Klimaitis & Moschione (1987), Parker, T.A. (1982), de la Peña (1986), Pinto (1964), Rumboll (1975a), Ruschi (1979), Scott & Carbonell (1986), Servat & Pearson (1991), Sick (1984), Soothill & Whitehead (1978), Stonor (1939), Veselovsky (1986a, 1986b, 1986c), Weller (1967a), Wetmore (1926).

3. Northern Screamer

Chauna chavaria

French: Kamichi chavaria   **German:** Weißwangen-Wehrvogel   **Spanish:** Chajá Chicagüire
Other common names: Black-necked Screamer

Taxonomy. *Parra Chavaria* Linnaeus, 1766, lakes near Río Sinú, south of Cartagena, Colombia. Monotypic.
Distribution. N Colombia and NW Venezuela.
Descriptive notes. 76-91 cm. Second, lower spur often hidden. Darker and somewhat slighter than *C. torquata*, with longer neck; black extends further up neck; white patch on throat and face, as opposed to middle of neck in *C. torquata*. Juvenile drabber version of adult.
Habitat. Swamps, marshes, lagoons, banks of slow-flowing rivers, often in areas surrounded by forest; also in seasonally flooded alluvial plains.
Food and Feeding. Exclusively vegetarian, taking roots, leaves, stems and other green parts of succulent, aquatic plants. Grazes like other Anseriformes.

Breeding. Most eggs Oct/Nov, but breeding throughout year. Solitary and territorial; nest is large accumulation of plant matter and debris. 2-7 eggs, usually 3-5; incubation 42-44 days; chicks hatch with thick greyish yellow down, white below; nidifugous, brooded only for first few days.
Movements. Probably sedentary; no evidence of long-range movements. Juveniles and non-breeders perhaps may wander, but species only exceptionally recorded outside normal range.
Status and Conservation. Not globally threatened. Currently considered near-threatened. Very little information available. Restricted range and relatively small population; no evidence that range may have been much wider in recent past. Locally common in both N Colombia and NW Venezuela, but human pressure increasing in many areas, implying further habitat loss (see page 533). Main threat is loss of habitat, through drainage of wetlands, deterioration of water quality, etc.; hunting pressure apparently less significant. Extensive work required to determine numbers, threats and immediate conservation requirements.
Bibliography. Bell *et al.* (1970), Blake (1977), Collar & Andrew (1988), DeMay (1940), Haffer (1975), Hilty & Brown (1986), Olivares (1970), de Schauensee (1948, 1964), de Schauensee & Phelps (1978), Scott & Carbonell (1986), Soothill & Whitehead (1978), Veselovsky (1986a, 1986b).

Class AVES
Order ANSERIFORMES
Suborder ANSERES
Family ANATIDAE (DUCKS, GEESE AND SWANS)

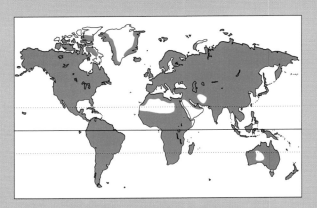

- Medium-sized to large waterbirds with plump body, short legs and flat, rounded bill.
- 30-180 cm.

- Cosmopolitan, all regions except Antarctic.
- Wide variety of aquatic habitats, mostly breeding on fresh water.
- 41 genera, 147 species, 238 taxa.
- 16 species threatened; 5 species and 3 subspecies extinct since 1600.

Systematics

The world's 147 living species of ducks, geese and swans, commonly lumped together under the rather vague term "wildfowl", form the large cosmopolitan family Anatidae. Their closest relations are the screamers (Anhimidae) of South America, and together these two families form the order Anseriformes. What is still none too clear, and subject to much debate, is the relationship of the Anseriformes with other bird orders.

According to some authors, the Anseriformes are most closely related to the Galliformes (gamebirds), and there are some indications of a common ancestor from the Cretaceous. These two orders share a number of characters in both morphology and behaviour, but the closest parallel is in breeding biology, including the following: large clutches; nidifugous young; little or no participation of the male in either incubation or brooding; and unstable pairs. However, the traditional view links them more closely with the Ciconiiformes (herons, ibises and storks) and Phoenicopteriformes (flamingos), and this view has been reinforced by the detailed studies carried out on the chemical composition of egg-white proteins.

The first fossil attributable to this family comes from the Upper Eocene, perhaps 40-50 million years ago. Amongst the living genera, the earliest fossil records correspond to *Mergus* and date back to Miocene times. The radiation of the Anseriformes probably started somewhere in the Southern Hemisphere, as the most primitive member of the Anatidae, the Magpie Goose (*Anseranas semipalmata*), is endemic to the Australasian Region, and its relatives the Anhimidae are restricted to South America.

The taxonomic division of the family Anatidae is rather complex and has been much disputed and revised. Most of the controversy is centred around the partition into subfamilies and tribes, whereas there is much more agreement on the total number of species and the taxonomic status of the different forms. The traditional classification of the Anatidae, put forward by J. Delacour and E. Mayr and subsequently modified by Delacour and then P. A. Johnsgard, has been followed by many others, such as F. S. Todd, although Johnsgard himself proposed several changes. A radically different view, based on the findings of B. C. Livezey, has recently been championed by S. C. Madge and H. Burn, while C. G. Sibley and B. L. Monroe, using DNA as a basis for classification, propose an alternative upheaval, so it must be understood that the order

followed here, that of Johnsgard, can scarcely be considered definitive.

Relationships within and between the different subdivisions of the Anatidae are generally based on factors such as: structure and proportions; plumage of adults and young; pattern of scales on the tarsus; voice; structure of syrinx and trachea; moult pattern; geographical distribution; and general behaviour. This last aspect is particularly important, as it includes courtship displays, which are species-specific and help to prevent interbreeding.

In the conventional view, the family is arranged into three subfamilies, Anseranatinae, Anserinae and Anatinae. The first is reserved for the primitive, aberrant Magpie Goose, in order to emphasize the differences in anatomy and way of life between this species and all other wildfowl. It is generally accepted that this ancestral form of goose represents an evolutionary link between the wildfowl and the much more terrestrial screamers, though its retention within the Anatidae indicates that it is closer to the wildfowl.

The other two subfamilies correspond roughly to the rather broad division of wildfowl into swans and geese (Anserinae) and ducks (Anatinae). The Anserinae are, in turn, subdivided into four tribes. The tribe Dendrocygnini contains the eight species of whistling-ducks (*Dendrocygna*) and the White-backed Duck (*Thalassornis leuconotus*), a peculiar African species formerly grouped with the stifftails (Oxyurini) but now generally accepted to be more closely allied to the whistling-ducks; nonetheless, some authors isolate it in its own tribe (Thalassornini) or even its own subfamily (Thalassorninae).

The largest tribe of the Anserinae is the Anserini. It includes all the swans, comprising seven species in the genera *Cygnus* and *Coscoroba*, and the "true" geese, comprising 15 species in the genera *Anser* and *Branta*. Some workers have split the Anserini in two, placing the swans in their own tribe, Cygnini, although this view has not received much support so far.

Treatment of the *Cygnus* swans has been quite varied. There are two southern species, the Black Swan (*Cygnus atratus*) and the Black-necked Swan (*Cygnus melanocorypha*), both of which are closely related to the Mute Swan (*Cygnus olor*) of the Northern Hemisphere. The other swans of the Holarctic, sometimes referred to as "wild swans", in contrast with the tame, semi-domesticated Mute Swan, show a great degree of similarity with each other, but little with the rest of the swans, to the point that the four forms commonly recognized have sometimes been separated in their own genus, *Olor*, or even treated as a single species, known as the Northern Swan. Few now dispute the idea that the Trumpeter Swan (*Cygnus buccinator*) is a good species, and not merely a race of the Whooper Swan (*Cygnus cygnus*), but conversely the Whistling and Bewick's Swans are still lumped together as races of a single species, the Tundra Swan (*Cygnus columbianus*).

The Cape Barren Goose (*Cereopsis novaehollandiae*) is an Australian endemic of disputed affinities. It was formerly considered an aberrant shelduck, and was thus included in the tribe Tadornini; nowadays, however, it is more commonly regarded as distantly related to the swans and true geese and is occasionally included in the tribe Anserini, but more often it is separated in its own tribe, Cereopsini. A similar case is that of another Australian endemic, the Freckled Duck (*Stictonetta naevosa*); it was traditionally included in the tribe Anatini with the dabbling ducks, but it seems more closely linked to the swans and true geese, so at present it is included in the subfamily Anserinae, where it is generally placed in its own tribe, Stictonettini.

The Anatinae, with eight tribes and 113 species, is the largest of the three subfamilies. Within the Anatinae, the shelducks and sheldgeese, which form the tribe Tadornini, show the closest affinities with the true geese of the Anserini, some species showing intermediate characters and certainly looking quite goose-like. This rather varied group includes the typical shelducks of the nearly cosmopolitan genus *Tadorna* (6 species), the sheldgeese of the endemic South American genus *Chloephaga* (5 species), an aberrant African "goose" (*Cyanochen*) and the monotypic genera *Neochen* and *Alopochen* of South America and Africa respectively.

As the Tadornini represent something of a transitional group, several species of unclear lineage are occasionally incorporated in this tribe, including the monotypic genera *Lophonetta*, *Malacorhynchus*, *Hymenolaimus*, *Cereopsis* and *Merganetta*. However, the inclusion of such assorted species in the Tadornini certainly reduces the homogeneity of the tribe, and some are often isolated in their own tribes, as they can not be shown to have close affinities with any other groups. Thus, the steamerducks (*Tachyeres*) of South America, traditionally considered an aberrant genus within the Tadornini, are now more commonly separated and placed in their own tribe, Tachyerini. These are large ducks that have partially lost the power of flight and comprise four very similar species.

The tribe Cairinini, for want of a better name, are rather loosely termed "perching ducks". With 13 species in nine genera, this tribe forms an extremely heterogeneous group, and its

Subdivision of the Anatidae.

[Figure: Francesc Jutglar & Àngels Jutglar]

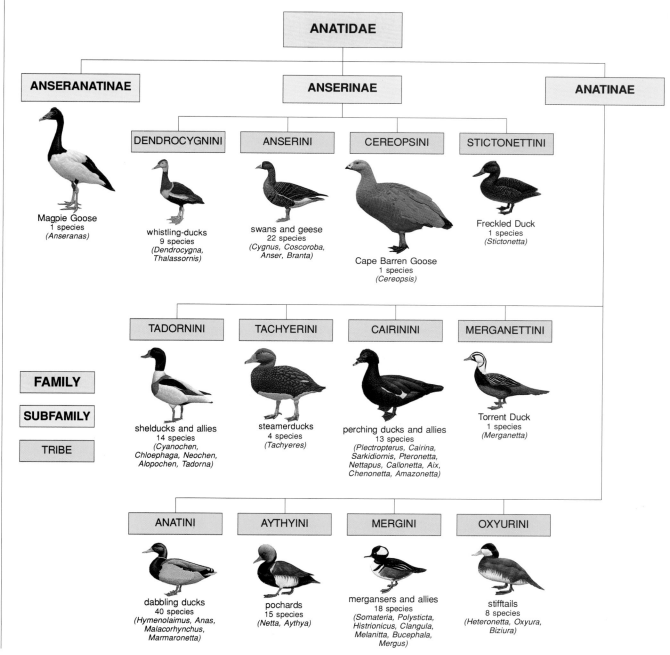

Its long legs, bare facial skin and robust bill with a large nail, make the Magpie Goose a very peculiar species, better adapted to terrestrial habitats than the rest of the Anatidae. Several peculiarities, for instance anatomical, biochemical or biogeographical, have led the bird to be considered an evolutionary link between the screamers (Anhimidae) and the Anatidae. Some authors prefer to place it in its own family, Anseranatidae, more closely related to the screamers.

[Anseranas semipalmata, Australia.
Photo: Eckart Pott/
Bruce Coleman]

validity as a genuine tribe has been seriously questioned, due to the great variations in structure, size and plumage between some of the species. However, these birds have more characteristics in common with each other than they have with the members of any other tribe, particularly in the aspects of general behaviour and breeding biology, so it seems advisable to maintain this tribe at the moment, on the grounds that it gives some sort of general indication of relationships between these awkward species. The group has a cosmopolitan distribution and is most closely related to the dabbling ducks, the Anatini, to which some of its members are occasionally assigned. Some workers argue in favour of separate treatment, and the Comb Duck (*Sarkidiornis melanotos*) has been placed in its own tribe, Sarkidiornini, whereas the Spur-winged Goose (*Plectropterus gambensis*) has even been given an exclusive subfamily, Plectropterinae.

The Torrent Duck (*Merganetta armata*) is a unique species that inhabits the fast-flowing rivers of the Andes. Its affinities are still unclear and, although it used to be grouped with the dabbling ducks, it is now more often regarded as distinct enough to deserve a tribe of its own, Merganettini. Some prefer to position it alongside the shelducks, the Blue Duck (*Hymenolaimus malacorhynchos*) and the steamerducks in the tribe Tadornini.

The tribe Anatini (dabbling ducks) is the largest of the family, with 41 species, 38 of them belonging to the large, cosmopolitan genus *Anas*, which includes many of the most abundant duck species in the world; there are also three monospecific genera, *Hymenolaimus*, *Malacorhynchus* and *Marmaronetta*. The Blue Duck almost certainly establishes a link, via the Torrent Duck, with the Cairinini and perhaps also

with the Tadornini, while the Marbled Teal (*Marmaronetta angustirostris*) links the dabbling ducks with the pochards (Aythyini). The situation of the peculiar Pink-eared Duck (*Malacorhynchus membranaceus*), yet another Australian endemic, has been much debated, and it is sometimes included within the Tadornini. However, the opinion that currently prevails is that it is more closely related to the Northern Shoveler (*Anas clypeata*), establishing a further link, via the Marbled Teal and the now almost certainly extinct Pink-headed Duck (*Rhodonessa caryophyllacea)*, between the dabbling ducks and the pochards. Salvadori's Teal (*Anas waigiuensis*), endemic to the highlands of New Guinea, should perhaps be given its own genus *Salvadorina*, while there are those who consider it to be closer to *Merganetta* and the Tadornini than to *Anas*.

Relationships within the genus *Anas* are rather intricate, as some species have very wide ranges and occur in a number of races, some of which may merit full specific status. The Eurasian Wigeon (*Anas penelope*), the American Wigeon (*Anas americana*) and perhaps also the Chiloe Wigeon (*Anas sibilatrix*) form a superspecies, as do the Northern Pintail (*Anas acuta*) and the Yellow-billed Pintail (*Anas georgica*), the Northern Shoveler and the Australian Shoveler (*Anas rhynchotis*), and likewise the Spot-billed Duck (*Anas poecilorhyncha*) and the Pacific Black Duck (*Anas superciliosa*). In contrast, the Common Teal (*Anas crecca*), the Mallard (*Anas platyrhynchos*) and the Northern Pintail again all provide cases of subspecies which might well be considered species. Clearly there are several series of closely related forms, and deciding whether two or more forms should be considered conspecific or regarded as distinct members of a superspecies is often simply a matter of personal preference.

A strange-looking bird with a large head and a very stubby body, the White-backed Duck at first glance does not seem to resemble any of the accepted tribes of waterfowl. Its taxonomic position is not clear. It vaguely recalls the stifftails, with which it is sometimes placed, but, for various reasons, including its behaviour, it is more often linked with the whistling-ducks. Some authors consider that it merits its own tribe or even its own subfamily.

[*Thalassornis leuconotos*, Amboseli, Kenya. Photo: Günter Ziesler]

In the tribe Aythyini (pochards), there are 15 species divided between the the genera *Netta* and *Aythya*. The latter is another mass of similar forms and includes several species pairs. However, most of the forms involved, although externally very similar in many cases, are usually distinct enough to be considered full species. The Pink-headed Duck presumably represented the link between this tribe and the dabbling ducks, and for this reason it is occasionally placed amongst them.

The Mergini are another fairly motley crowd, but there is little doubt that all the genera included are fairly closely related. The eiders are sometimes separated from the rest of the sea ducks in their own tribe Somateriini, as they form a very compact group. The three species of the genus *Somateria* are very closely related, while Steller's Eider (*Polysticta stelleri*) is rather more distinctive and probably represents the link between the eiders and the other sea ducks. The now extinct Labrador Duck (*Camptorhynchus labradorius*) was apparently fairly eider-like, and the Harlequin Duck (*Histrionicus histrionicus*) and the Long-tailed Duck (*Clangula hyemalis*) are generally supposed to be further links between the eiders and the rest of the tribe.

The three species of scoter (*Melanitta*) also form a close-knit group of northern sea ducks, as do another evolutionary branch, the three species of goldeneye (*Bucephala*). Finally, the sawbills (*Mergus*) are widely distributed over the Holarctic with two outposts in the Southern Hemisphere, the now extinct Auckland Merganser (*Mergus australis*) of New Zealand and the threatened Brazilian Merganser (*Mergus octosetaceus*). Despite their markedly different external appearance, the sawbills seem to be closest to the goldeneyes, and are linked to them by way of the Smew (*Mergus albellus*), which is sometimes isolated in its own genus *Mergellus*, and the Hooded Merganser (*Mergus cucullatus*), occasionally partitioned off too in a private genus *Lophodytes*.

The last tribe in the Anatinae is Oxyurini (stifftails); it comprises eight species, six of which belong to the cosmopoli-

tan genus *Oxyura*. The Black-headed Duck (*Heteronetta atricapilla*) shows some external similarities with the dabbling ducks, to which it has sometimes been ascribed, offering a possible pointer towards the early evolution of the stifftails, although other factors link them more closely to the sea ducks. The Masked Duck (*Oxyura dominica*) is probably the least typical of the *Oxyura* stifftails and has been separated by some in its own genus *Nomonyx*. Finally, the odd-looking Musk Duck (*Biziura lobata*) is a unique species, with complex social and breeding behaviour. Although obviously one of the stifftails, it has evolved in isolation and has become one of the most bizarre species of all the Anatidae.

Described in 1981, the White-headed Steamerduck is one of the four closely related species that make up the genus Tachyeres. *Their relationship with other wildfowl is somewhat unclear: formerly placed among the dabbling ducks, more often included in the tribe Tadornini, as a link between the Anserinae and the Anatinae, they are currently considered sufficiently different to constitute their own tribe, Tachyerini. Note that this species, although flightless, uses its wings when it has to carry out rapid movements, for example during chases, which are frequent due to its territorial character during breeding.*

[*Tachyeres leucocephalus*, Punta Tombo, Argentina. Photo: Günter Ziesler]

Livezey's revolutionary proposition, based on a comparative study of 120 morphological characters, recommends many significant changes, of which the following are among the most important: the isolation of the Magpie Goose in a separate family, Anseranatidae; the creation of new subfamilies for the whistling-ducks (Dendrocygninae), the White-backed Duck (Thalassorninae), the Freckled Duck (Stictonettinae), the Spur-winged Goose (Plectropterinae) and the shelducks and sheldgeese (Tadorninae); the separation of swans in their own tribe, Cygnini; the integration of the steamerducks within the tribe Tadornini; and the dissolution of the traditional tribe Cairinini, most of the members of which are assigned to the Anatini.

Sibley and Monroe's classification based on DNA-DNA hybridization recommends some significant innovations too, but also shows a fair degree of agreement with the traditional organization of the family. Some of the main changes proposed are: the isolation of the Magpie Goose in its own family, and alongside the screamers in a different infraorder from the rest of the wildfowl; the promotion of the tribe Dendrocygnini to family level; the division of the Anatidae into four subfamilies, Oxyurinae (the former Oxyurini), Stictonettinae (monotypic), Cygninae (swans) and Anatinae; the last remains quite similar in composition and sequence, with the addition of the true geese and the Cape Barren Goose, but is now split into only two tribes, with the partition falling down the middle of the traditional tribe Cairinini.

An additional problem in the classification of wildfowl is the fact that they are far more prone to hybridization in the wild than most other bird groups. This tendency is favoured by a number of factors, including the following: the close genetic proximity of many species; the peculiar mating systems, in which the pair-bond is generally renewed each year, and formed mostly during the winter, when the birds are often jumbled up in mixed species flocks; the relative similarity of courtship displays; and the fact that males participate little in the breeding tasks. In some genera, notably *Anas* and *Aythya*, hybridization is not at all exceptional and may affect a considerable proportion of the whole population. Some of the young produced are

fertile, which can add further to the intrinsic complexity of the taxonomic relationships within the wildfowl. The Marianas Duck, described by Salvadori as *Anas oustaleti*, is now thought to be a hybrid of the Mallard and the Pacific Black Duck, although neither of the "parent" species are recorded for its range. Unfortunately, this taxonomically interesting form may have died out, probably in part due to intensive hunting pressure by troops during the Second World War.

Nonetheless, hybridization in the wild remains infrequent, and it normally occurs only when a series of conditions are met. The vast majority of individuals in any given population are genetically pure, even in such plastic birds as wildfowl. Hybridization in wildfowl is largely a consequence of the close relationship between different species, but, except in some extreme cases, should not affect the specific status of sufficiently discrete populations.

Morphological Aspects

Most wildfowl typically spend much of the time sitting on the water, and their bodies are well designed for a highly aquatic life. However, each species has its own particular ecological niche, an optimum habitat, feeding method, mating system, and so on, and these specialities are often reflected in a number of specific adaptations. So most species are similar in many morphological aspects, but they differ widely in others. There are marked differences in size, for example, and male Trumpeter Swans can measure over 180 cm in length and over 240 cm in wingspan, whereas the female African Pygmy-goose (*Nettapus auritus*) is only some 30 cm in length. Differences in weight are also considerable, with a male Mute Swan sometimes reaching 22·5 kg, while a female African Pygmy-goose does not exceed 230 g.

Most of the Anatidae have a body that is broad and elongated, or more rounded in some of the specialized divers. This characteristic body shape improves buoyancy, though it helps to make walking on land awkward; nonetheless, they are much

Roughly half of all the species of wildfowl display pronounced sexual dimorphism. This is particularly strong among the eiders, as can be seen in this pair of Spectacled Eiders. The female shows strongly cryptic coloration, quite the opposite from that of the drake. This dimorphism undergoes variation during moult, when in this species the white part of the drake's plumage becomes grey. Despite the marked dimorphism, the female, and even chicks only a few days old, display a hint of the characteristic facial pattern, with the spectacled eyes.

[*Somateria fischeri*, USA. Photo: D. Roby/Vireo]

Some species of wildfowl sport special adornments. The most common are extensions of the highly coloured bare facial skin between the bill and the eye, and also the frontal knobs and caruncles. The most spectacular knob is that of the male Comb Duck (above); the fleshy protuberance over his bill becomes especially large during the breeding season. Apart from some seasonal variation in size, it is also typical for these structures to take on brighter colours in the different species, whereas they tend to be absent or reduced in females, with the exception of the Black-necked Swan (*Cygnus melanocorypha*). A unique case is that of the distendible gular skin of the remarkable Musk Duck (below), which is very small in the female, but is always conspicuous in the male, becoming turgid during display as in this photograph. It appears that these growths are related in some way to breeding behaviour.

[Above: *Sarkidiornis melanotos melanotos*, South Africa. Photo: Peter Pickford/DRK.

Below: *Biziura lobata*, Queensland, Australia. Photo: Patrick Fagot/NHPA]

Ducks are relatively heavy birds in relation to the surface area of their wings, so they need a powerful thrust in order to achieve the necessary lift for take-off. There are two kinds of take-off. The dabbling ducks are capable of taking flight thanks to the impulse of a single thrust of both feet, as is vividly portrayed by this drake Mallard. On the other hand, the anatomical particularities of the swans and the diving ducks, like these Buffleheads, force them to run short distances moving their feet alternately, whilst vigorously flapping their wings.

[Above: *Anas platyrhynchos platyrhynchos*, Wisconsin, USA. Below: *Bucephala albeola*, USA. Photos: Scott Nielsen/ DRK]

It is a well known fact that marshes are highly productive environments, offering a great quantity of food which can be exploited, for instance, by ducks, and still fresh or brackish waters constitute the favoured feeding sites of many species. These Spot-billed Ducks provide a good example, as they prefer the shallow waters, typically used by the dabbling ducks. Note the green speculum, which is visible on the individual in the background.

[*Anas poecilorhyncha poecilorhyncha*, Bharatpur, India. Photo: Günter Ziesler]

more efficient on the ground than many seabirds. Male Anseriformes are among the very few birds to possess a special copulatory organ, similar to the mammalian penis, which normally rests inside the cloaca and is evaginated by muscular action for coition.

The neck is relatively long in all species, particularly so in swans and geese but also in some ducks, and the head is generally small. The bill is broad and conical, with serrated lamellae in the interior, which are particularly well developed in plankton-filtering species, or along the cutting edges, especially in fish-eating species; among the most specialized are those of the sawbills (*Mergus*), which are serrated for catching fish. There is a shield-shaped horny tip to the upper mandible known as the "nail", which is harder than the rest of the sheath and is specially designed for the purposes of grazing or mollusc-eating. The bill may present a conspicuous knob-like projection in some species, with the noteworthy example of the Comb Duck; this knob may be horny or fleshy, temporary or permanent and may appear in males only or in both sexes, and in general it attains its fullest expression in males during the breeding season. In many species, the bill colour, particularly of the male, is also brightest at the onset of the breeding season. There are some particularly strange bills in this family, none more so than those of the Blue and Pink-eared Ducks.

Ducks, geese and swans have rather strong legs, the skin of which is fully scaled. The legs are comparatively shorter in *Cygnus* and in most of the Aythyini, Mergini and Oxyurini. They are set far back on the body, particularly in these same tribes, which are the most aquatic of all the family, and the wildfowl that have most problems walking on land. The hind toe is reduced and elevated and the three forward toes are fully joined by webs in most species, although the webbing is only partial in *Anseranas* and some of the *Anas* ducks. In the Hawaiian Goose (*Branta sandvicensis*), the webs have receded as an adaptation to its peculiar habitat of lava slopes on volcanic islands.

The wings are relatively short and pointed, and are very strong. Gaining or maintaining momentum in the air requires continuous, fast beating of the wings for such heavy birds with high wing-loading. For this reason, the wing muscles are necessarily large and well developed; they are deeply inserted on the highly keeled sternum and help give wildfowl their broad-breasted appearance.

In most species, the tail is fairly short and square or slightly rounded. In a few, though, it has a very distinctive shape, for instance it is thin and pointed in male Northern Pintails and Long-tailed Ducks, whereas in the stifftails (Oxyurini) it is long and narrow and is often held cocked, and is used as a rudder when diving under the water.

Ducks, geese and swans have a thick covering of feathers for insulation, which is particularly necessary for birds that are usually on the water. The feathers must always be in good condition in order to maintain their waterproofing effects, and birds spend many hours daily in the care of feathers. The oil-gland is feathered, and is highly developed in this family.

All species have salt glands, excretory organs in the head, situated above each eye, which filter the blood and eliminate excess salt in the form of a highly concentrated fluid that drips off the tip of the bill. However, it is only in the species, or individuals, that habitually spend long periods in coastal or brackish waters that they have achieved a development comparable to that of the truly marine birds, including penguins, petrels, sulids, and cormorants. This may result in a characteristic profile with the head obviously protruding, as in the eiders and scoters.

In many species, the males have specially designed tracheal and syringeal structures (bullae) that act as resonating tubes. These may be completely, or only partly, ossified and their particular structure is specific and characteristic in each major taxonomic group, and thus a major element in phylogenetic studies.

Some of the most variegated and brilliantly coloured of all birds are to be found amongst the wildfowl. At the same time, however, there are many very cryptic colour patterns.

In the subfamilies Anseranatinae and Anserinae, plumage differences between the sexes are generally insignificant. The prevalent colours are brown (*Dendrocygna*), grey (*Anser*), white (*Cygnus*) and a combination of black and white (*Branta, Anseranas*). Metallic sheens are rare and only the Black-bellied Whistling-duck (*Dendrocygna autumnalis*) shows a conspicuous wing bar, which in this case is white. Most geese (*Anser, Branta*) and the Fulvous Whistling-duck (*Dendrocygna bicolor*) have

some white markings on the rump or tail. The flight-feathers, particularly the primaries, are dark coloured in most species, for the higher melanin content makes them far more resistant to abrasion. However, this rule does not apply in *Cygnus*, in which even the Black Swan has all the primaries and many of the secondaries pure white, although otherwise the plumage is wholly black. In these two subfamilies, juvenile plumage is similar in pattern to that of adults, but is generally duller.

Most characteristic of the subfamily Anatinae is a high degree of sexual dimorphism, and, except in very few cases, adult male and female plumages are readily distinguishable in the field. A striking example is the Kelp Goose (*Chloephaga hybrida*), in which the male is all white, while the female is barred sooty brown, while its congener the Upland Goose (*Chloephaga*

picta) shows less spectacular differences. But the most remarkable case is that of the Paradise Shelduck (*Tadorna variegata*), which shows inverted sexual dimorphism, and it is the more brightly coloured female that has an eclipse plumage. In general, in the Anatinae males tend to be very brightly coloured with many patches of metallic sheen. Females are usually brown and inconspicuous, and in most cases they only show notable markings on the wings. The dull colours of the female at rest have an important survival value, in protecting her while she stays still sitting on the eggs. Since males take no part in incubation, their plumage is not subject to the same protective limitations, and it thus produces some of the most spectacular combinations of all birds, as in the American Wood Duck (*Aix sponsa*), the Mandarin Duck (*Aix galericulata*), the Baikal Teal (*Anas formosa*) and the King Eider (*Somateria spectabilis*). Competition with males of other species may have played an important part in the evolution of male duck coloration, and in populations of otherwise brightly coloured species that have become isolated and have lost contact with other duck species, such as those of Northern Pintail on the Crozet and Kerguelen Islands of the Indian Ocean, males have a tendency to lose their spectacular patterns and acquire a plumage that is similar to that of the female throughout the year. In such cases, the main differences from the females are in behaviour and size, with males usually larger, whereas there are fewer differences in plumage.

In the tribes Anatini, Tadornini, Merganettini and Cairinini, each species has its own distinctive speculum. This is a brightly coloured patch on the secondaries, which is generally metallic green, bronze or blue, often bordered by black or white bars, and sometimes with a white trailing edge. Both sexes and all ages exhibit the same pattern, which is peculiar to the species. Members of the Mergini frequently show white wing panels, a series of broad patches on the wings, whereas the Aythyini generally have a simple white stripe on the upperwing; there are no special markings on the wings in Oxyurini. Wing markings are thought to perform the function of maintaining cohesion within a group, particularly in flight, so they are more highly developed and well marked in migratory species.

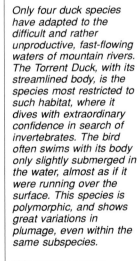

Although ducks are mostly associated with shallow inland waters, several species regularly exploit marine waters or deep lakes. The White-winged Scoter nests on freshwater lakes, but winters preferably at sea, which has the advantage of not freezing over so easily during winter.

[Melanitta fusca. Photo: A. Christiansen/ FLPA]

Only four duck species have adapted to the difficult and rather unproductive, fast-flowing waters of mountain rivers. The Torrent Duck, with its streamlined body, is the species most restricted to such habitat, where it dives with extraordinary confidence in search of invertebrates. The bird often swims with its body only slightly submerged in the water, almost as if it were running over the surface. This species is polymorphic, and shows great variations in plumage, even within the same subspecies.

[Merganetta armata leucogenis, Apurimac, Peru. Photo: Günter Ziesler]

In the Anatinae, juvenile plumage closely resembles that of the adult female, and in some cases they are virtually indistinguishable. Adult male plumage is normally acquired at one to three years old. Another distinctive mechanism that affects many species in this subfamily is the adoption of an "eclipse" plumage. Although males keep their breeding plumage during the best part of the year, towards the end of the summer they typically undergo a complete moult, during which they shed the brilliantly coloured feathers, temporarily assuming a much duller aspect, whereby they closely resemble the females. This eclipse plumage is worn by adult males for a period of a few weeks, until the new flight-feathers are grown, so that during the winter, when sexual activity starts off again, they are ready to exhibit their striking patterns of colours.

With the notable exceptions of the primitive *Anseranas* and at least some forms of the genus *Chloephaga*, all wildfowl moult their flight-feathers simultaneously and thus become flightless for a short period. On average, it takes three or four weeks until the new feathers have developed sufficiently to sustain these heavy birds in the air. In the many species in which the male takes little or no part in incubation and brooding, males gather in large flocks and move, sometimes over considerable distances, to quiet moulting sites, where they undergo a complete moult (see Movements). On the other hand, females tend to moult when the chicks are young, and they too become flightless for a while.

Three species, the Magellanic Steamerduck (*Tachyeres pteneres*), the Falkland Steamerduck (*Tachyeres brachypterus*) and the White-headed Steamerduck (*Tachyeres leucocephalus*), are to all effects permanently flightless, although they can actually fly very short distances on occasions, if the conditions are right. These are birds of coastal waters that have developed a way of life in which the ability to fly is totally unnecessary and perhaps even inconvenient. All the other species (but not two races) are capable of sustained flight at most times of year, although some require a tremendous effort to stay on the wing for more than a few seconds. Because they are heavy birds with compact bodies and a relatively small wing area, ducks, geese and swans need to beat their wings rapidly and ceaselessly in flight. Take-off perhaps demands the greatest effort, and in most cases it must be preceded by a lengthy run along the surface of

the water with the wings beating and a good deal of splashing before the bird can become airborne. This is particularly true in *Cygnus*, the Aythyini, Mergini and Oxyurini. Despite its name, the Flying Steamerduck (*Tachyeres patachonicus*) has serious difficulties in taking off, and some particularly heavy individuals can not fly at all. Only birds of the more terrestrial groups, such as geese, shelducks and dabbling ducks, can take off without a previous run along the water, or directly from land.

Once on the wing, wildfowl must maintain their particularly fast rate of wingbeats, so they can not soar, and they only tend to glide when coming in to land. When covering long distances, for example during migration, some species may fly very high, and on occasions they have been recorded at extraordinary heights, for example geese and swans have been seen at over 8000 m. By flying at such altitudes, they take advantage of the strong winds originating in the jet stream of the lower stratosphere, and they thus use less energy. The characteristic V-formations that they adopt when cruising also help to save energy, and when flying in one of these "skeins", the individual bird encounters less wind resistance, as the air displaced by the preceding birds creates a slipstream effect that reduces friction.

Coming down from the air can be almost as difficult as taking off for some species. Only the most agile species, including some geese, shelducks and dabbling ducks, can alight directly on the land. Others require a stretch of water, onto which they can skid down with their feet lowered and their webs fully spread, in order to reduce speed before the body makes contact. Not all ducks readily take to flight when they are threatened, and some species prefer to escape potential dangers by swimming away or diving instead.

Wildfowl do not find walking easy, and the combination of the broad body with the relatively short legs causes them to waddle rather clumsily. Only those species with relatively longer legs and slimmer bodies spend much time away from the water. In contrast, the diving ducks, sea ducks and stifftails, together with the larger swans, usually choose to nest in sites with immediate access from the water or directly from the air, so that the distance they have to walk is reduced to a minimum. They also tend to avoid setting foot on land outside the breeding season.

It is well known that wildfowl are good swimmers and, without exception, they are quite at home on the water. All

Sleeping during the day is very frequent in wildfowl, as they are often very active at night. In a roosting flock, at least one bird always remains awake, and will alert the rest if danger threatens. One of these Hottentot Teals shows the typical sleeping posture, with its head turned round resting on its back and its bill tucked into its feathers.

[*Anas hottentota*. Photo: A. J. Deane/ Bruce Coleman]

species are capable of diving under water, although some only do so in cases of extreme danger. The expert divers are the members of the Aythyini, Tachyerini, Merganettini, Mergini and Oxyurini, and these birds may remain submerged for over a minute, sometimes covering fair distances under the water. Some reach considerable depths, for instance the Long-tailed Duck has been recorded more than 150 m down. In most cases, only the feet are used for underwater propulsion, and many of the so-called "diving ducks" keep their wings close in to their bodies when swimming under water. However, some species are known to dive with partly opened wings, as an aid for steering or in order to "fly" under water in the manner of auks (Alcidae); this is particularly typical of eiders, steamerducks and scoters, but also occurs in such unspecialized divers as the Mallard and swans. The foot-propelled divers generally use the feet simultaneously when diving, but alternately when swimming on the surface. Most ducklings can swim and dive only a few hours after hatching, as soon as they have dried out. Moulting birds, even though flightless, retain their swimming and diving abilities quite unimpaired, and their plumage remains equally waterproof.

Habitat

Ducks, geese and swans are clearly linked to predominantly aquatic environments, and each species shows a preference for a certain kind of habitat, including lakes, marshes, streams, ponds or reservoirs. A series of factors, such as the depth and quality of the water, the presence and nature of emergent or fringe vegetation, the maintenance of a minimum water level throughout the year, the type of bottom material and the presence of a particular kind of food, generally decide whether or not a given water body can sustain a population of a particular wildfowl species.

Some species, especially geese, often use quite different areas for feeding, some distance away from the breeding or roosting sites. In other cases, there is a seasonal shift in habitat requirements, for instance many ducks that are strictly marine outside the breeding season establish their nesting territories well inland, for example on lakes in tundra or wooded country.

In general, the dabbling ducks belonging mostly to the tribe Anatini require much shallower waters than the diving ducks of the Aythyini, Mergini and Oxyurini. In conjunction with this, they also prefer more gently sloping land with some vegetation around it where they can build a nest or seek refuge in case of danger, and tend to occur on smaller water bodies than those preferred by diving ducks. Swans are most commonly found in marshes, shallow lakes or slow-flowing rivers, whereas geese inhabit grasslands, boggy tundra, damp meadows, large shallow lakes and flood plains. Shelducks tend to occur in areas with salt or brackish water, such as estuaries and mudflats, while sheldgeese frequent exposed grasslands, sometimes well away from water. Eiders and steamerducks are the most marine of the Anatidae, and they occur along the coast during most of the year. The Torrent Duck and the Blue Duck are highly specialized birds that live along fast-flowing rivers with rapids and waterfalls; their approximate ecological counterpart in the Nearctic Region, the Harlequin Duck, is found mainly in coastal waters during the winter.

The nature and type of vegetation surrounding the water or emerging from it constitute significant factors affecting the extent to which any locality is suitable for a particular species of wildfowl, especially if it is to be used as a nesting site. Relatively few species prefer open ground uncluttered by vegetation around the shores of the chosen stretch of water, and most of these nest in the tundra of the high Arctic. A covering of reeds or grass suits most whistling-ducks, sheldgeese, dabbling ducks, pochards and stifftails. Several groups of species require more forested surroundings, and some are virtually dependant on holes in trees for nesting, including the so-called "perching ducks" of the Cairinini and the tree-nesting Mergini. The Smew commonly uses old, disused nests of the Black Woodpecker (*Dryocopus martius*), and the Common Golden-

Preening behaviour is particularly important in the wildfowl, as their plumage has to remain perfectly waterproof during the long periods they spend in the water. The White-faced Whistling-duck, seen here in various postures, dedicates hours daily to the maintenance of its feathers. The individual on the left is preening the feathers on its side, whilst the birds in the centre are allopreening, one bird preening another's plumage in the regions that it can not reach itself; the significance of this mutual preening is largely social. Preening is composed of two complementary actions: combing all the feathers thoroughly, and coating them in an oily substance to make them waterproof. Note also the typical resting posture, which involves standing on one leg.

[*Dendrocygna viduata*, Lake Baringo, Kenya. Photo: Marie Read/ Bruce Coleman]

eye (*Bucephala clangula*) has recently expanded its breeding range where it has been provided with suitable nestboxes.

Man's daily requirement of large volumes of fresh water and the difficulties involved in storing it have resulted in the construction of many dams and reservoirs and extensive networks of canals and ditches. Many of these have been occupied by various species of wildfowl and have now become regularly used habitat. In Western Europe, gravel pits represent a similar case, as many are flooded and turn out to be excellent habitat for wildfowl. Other man-made sites widely used by wildfowl include rice fields, salt-pans and ponds and lakes in urban parks.

General Habits

Ducks, geese and swans are well known for their strong gregarious tendencies. They frequently gather together in flocks, which vary in size from a few dozen or less to several hundred thousand birds, depending largely on species composition, time of year and locality. The range of activities that are habitually performed socially includes feeding, roosting and loafing, either on water or on the ground, and moving about, for instance during migration. A significant proportion of sexual activity is also carried out socially in most species, mainly during the early stages, and activities such as pair formation, courtship display and so on often take place in groups. However, most species disperse afterwards in order to nest in solitary pairs or loose groups with little interaction between neighbouring pairs. Colonial or semi-colonial breeding is not unknown among wildfowl, and is the rule for several species of geese, the Black Swan and some eiders, as well as for some other sea ducks of the Mergini.

In most wildfowl, flocking occurs mainly outside the breeding season. In geese and swans particularly, but also in some ducks, the most typical flock is composed of one family party or occasionally a few; large flocks of other duck species often contain mostly birds of one sex, as males and females commonly

have separate distributions for much of the non-breeding season. Moulting flocks in many cases are also composed of one sex only, and they may reach extraordinary proportions, sometimes with huge concentrations of well over 100,000 birds, notably those of Common Shelducks (*Tadorna tadorna*) in the Helgoland Bight, off north-west Germany (see Movements).

The advantages of flocking are obvious in that it reduces the risk of predation and also facilitates the process of finding food. The individual in the flock may obtain food more easily by watching and closely following conspecifics that have been successful, instead of having to spend hours searching on its own. Equally, if a predator attacks the flock, it is less likely to be successful than when attacking an individual bird. One of the many alert individuals in the flock warns the others with an alarm call, which usually has a rapid effect, and the whole flock can be on the wing in seconds. In flight, a predatory bird has very little chance unless it manages to separate one individual from the flock, but the wildfowl try to avoid this and often succeed.

It is essential for a flock of birds to maintain its cohesion. Further advantages of flocking include maintaining a certain degree of uniformity in the behaviour of the individuals in the group and of facilitating the social integration of each bird, which seems to be of great value in this family, as birds take a new mate each season in most species. Two specific adaptations serve the purpose of keeping the group united: the species-specific wing specula (see Morphological Aspects), which help to maintain visual contact between conspecifics and are particularly useful when migrating or moving about; and "contact calls" (see Voice), by which a bird keeps in touch with other conspecifics in situations where visual contact may be difficult, for instance when travelling at night or in thick fog.

Mixed flocks are frequent amongst wildfowl, although some species are very catholic and will mix almost with any other species, while others are more discreet and prefer to join up with conspecifics only. There is a general tendency for closer relatives to occur more often together than distant ones, so dabbling ducks more commonly mix with dabbling ducks, and pochards with pochards. A few species are not at all sociable, particularly those that breed on rivers. In these species, there seem to be greater benefits in occupying a definite territory and defending it throughout the year, than having a nomadic life for several months. This strategy occurs in the Blue-winged Goose (*Cyanochen cyanopterus*), the Torrent Duck, the Blue Duck and Salvadori's Teal.

Due to their mostly aquatic habits, wildfowl require a thick coat of feathers that will insulate them against heat loss, but will not become waterlogged. In order to maintain their plumage in good condition, they have to spend a great deal of time and care in the daily maintenance of feathers. Wildfowl dedicate many hours to feather repair and preening, using the bill and coating the plumage with an oily substance produced by the enlarged uropygial gland, situated at the base of the tail. It is the combination of these two actions that gives wildfowl plumage its perfect waterproofing. Ducks, geese and swans also bathe regularly, often before long sessions of preening. They normally bathe while swimming in deep water, ducking the head under the water so that the water runs backwards down the neck, and making a series of thrashing movements with the wings to help spread the water throughout the plumage. During bathing they frequently somersault or dive below the surface with the wings open, reappearing immediately, before flapping the wings and diving again. Occasionally they make short flights between spells of bathing.

Many species are partly nocturnal in their feeding habits, and they may carry out a number of other activities at night, for instance several species perform an important part of their courtship display at night. For this reason, they have little time left for sleep while it is dark, so they commonly roost in the middle of the day. In estuarine habitats, the rhythms of daily activity are imposed by the tides, with birds feeding on the mudflats exposed at low tide and resting at high tide, in a sequence that is quite unrelated to the hours of daylight. Most species roost communally on the water or where undisturbed on small islets or on the shore. When sleeping on the water, a bird tucks its bill under its wing feathers. When resting on land,

birds often stand on one leg. A few birds always remain alert in a roosting flock, ready at the first sign of any possible danger to signal it to the rest of the group.

Voice

Vocal expression is extremely well developed in wildfowl, and constitutes an important means of communication, with a wide range of uses and functions. Calling has significant survival value for wildfowl as it plays a basic role in maintaining the necessary cohesion within a particular flock. Birds typically produce fairly strident, unmelodious calls, though there is a high degree of variation at specific or tribal level.

Ducks, geese and swans have a number of special anatomical adaptations with which they can produce loud, far-carrying sounds, which are especially useful as contact calls. The most spectacular contact calls are made by swans and geese. The Whooper and Trumpeter Swans, in particular, have exceptionally well developed bullae, special structures in the trachea and syrinx that act as resonating chambers and produce the loud, clear, trumpet-like sounds which are responsible for the birds' vernacular names. Typical contact calls of females and young are the harsher, lower-pitched notes with which they continuously announce their presence. This gives young birds more confidence to swim about in search of their own food, knowing that the female is nearby, even if they can not see her. A significant interruption in this calling quickly causes alarm in the female or the chicks, which scurry along towards each other seeking protection. A similar effect is produced by the female's alarm call, which is usually a short, high-pitched, easily audible note, which causes the chicks to flee towards cover amongst the vegetation, where they remain silent and immobile until the female restarts her continuous contact calling.

In all species of the Anatidae, there are some sounds directly related to particular displays or to sexual activity. In many cases, the adoption of an aggressive posture is accompanied by distinctive calls that tend to be loud and far-carrying. These, or other similar calls, are used in signalling the defended

A Canada Goose bathing. Whilst bathing, wildfowl often somersault and dive with the wings open, but they normally partially submerge the neck and wings, and then, with rapid movements, spray the water all over the body. Bathing, which often precedes a preening session, forms part of the daily routine of feather maintenance, which is carried out all year long.

[*Branta canadensis*. Photo: Sorensen & Olsen/ NHPA]

In the Anatidae, comfort behaviour is carried out both on the water and on dry ground. One of these Ruddy-headed Geese is performing a typical "Both-wings Stretching" display, with the wings partially folded, while the neck is stretched forward.

[*Chloephaga rubidiceps*, Falkland Islands. Photo: Rinie Van Meurs/ Bruce Coleman]

territory, often in association with a display indicating ownership of the territory. A variety of calls are made during the many stages of courtship, and at the moment of copulation. These are generally low-pitched notes and are distinctive in each species, so that they help to prevent interbreeding among closely related species.

The Magpie Goose is a highly vocal species, which utters loud honks, reminiscent of the true geese, in flight, from the water or on dry ground, and these often elicit the response of their mates or other conspecifics. The whistling-ducks owe their name to the thin, whistling calls they commonly make when feeding, resting on land or flying. The continuous repetition of these calls often results in a shrill twittering, with several birds in a flock calling together, though they sometimes make short, low, harsher calls. The White-backed Duck too produces a variety of high-pitched whistles, as well as a few short, low conversational calls.

The loud, resonant calls of the Trumpeter, Whooper and Tundra Swans are incessant, both when the birds are in flight and when at rest on the water or on land. The Coscoroba Swan (*Coscoroba coscoroba*) is also a vociferous species with a loud, trumpeting call, indeed its vernacular name is an onomatopoeic rendition of this call. In contrast, the Mute, Black and Black-necked Swans are relatively silent, uttering weak notes that are only audible nearby. Actually, the Mute Swan is by no means mute, but the fact that its voice is only very occasionally heard has led to this misnomer.

The true geese are renowned for their sonority, particularly when they gather in large flocks. They produce loud honking or barking calls, notably in flight, but also on land or water. Migrating flocks of geese can be heard from far off, especially as they often call from high in the air, so the sound carries further.

The Cape Barren Goose produces a series of loud guttural sounds, including a low-pitched grunt typically uttered by fe-

males and a trumpet-like honk made by males. The Freckled Duck's voice is rather inconspicuous, and its most frequent calls are a soft whistle and several weakish quacks.

Sheldgeese are peculiar in showing great sexual variation in their calls, although there is relative uniformity between the several species. Males make a high-pitched whistle that is repeated rapidly, whereas the characteristic calls of females are harsher, consisting of various loud cackles, growls, quacks and grating sounds. There is a similar degree of sexual variation amongst shelducks, with rather less consistency between the species. Typical female calls tend to be loud and raucous, often uttered in quick repetition, whereas males produce loud whistles and honks that may be heard over considerable distances.

Similarly, male steamerducks' calls consist of various high-pitched whistling notes that are generally clear, loud and far-carrying. These notes are repeated rapidly to produce a series of very characteristic calls, that are shrill in the Flying Steamerduck, or rasping in the three flightless species. Female steamerducks have a low-pitched, more grunting voice, with croaks, cackles and growls as their more frequent calls, but these too are often combined into a long series of rapidly repeated notes.

The great heterogeneity shown by the Cairinini in many aspects of their biology and ecology is also evident in the rhythm, tone, loudness, repertoire and general type of their calls. As a rule, however, they tend not to be very noisy species, with the exception of some of the pygmy-geese. Most species only tend to call with any form of regularity when they are displaying, alarmed or taking off, and normally they only make a few inconspicuous sounds the rest of the time. Males frequently have a higher-pitched voice, with a variety of whistles, hisses, wheezes and shrill notes; females' voices are generally more rasping and their range of calls includes quacking, honking, whistling and short moaning notes, which are weak and low-pitched.

This drake American Wood Duck is performing "Wing-flapping", or, more precisely, "Swimming-flapping". It consists of a series of flaps made without any intention of flying, sometimes accompanied by "Tail-wagging" or "Body-shaking". This behaviour can be used to dry the plumage, but it is more often a feather-settling movement.

[*Aix sponsa*, Wisconsin, USA.
Photo: Scott Nielsen/DRK]

The male Torrent Duck has a loud, high-pitched whistle, which is clearly audible above the noise of raging rivers. This sharp call can be heard over long distances and probably performs the function of signalling territory to neighbouring males. It may be produced in flight or by perched birds, and the same call may be directed to a bird's mate and chicks. The female's voice is not as loud, but is equally clear and high-pitched.

Dabbling ducks are not among the noisiest of all wildfowl, and many species remain relatively silent outside the breeding season. As in other groups of wildfowl, there is a fair degree of sexual variation in the voices of many of the *Anas* ducks, and it is the females that tend to be more vociferous. They have a loud, grating voice and produce a characteristic descending series of quacking notes, typically exemplified by the Mallard, but shared by most other members of the genus, with variable intensity and length. Males' calls are generally either a short, high-pitched, multisyllabic whistle, which is most distinctive in the wigeons, or a soft, rough note, like those made by the Common Teal, Mallard and Northern Pintail. A few species have added most distinctive calls to their vocabulary and use these particularly during their courtship displays, as they contribute to prevent interbreeding.

In the pochards, the calling of both sexes is virtually restricted to courtship displays and aggressive postures associated with breeding, and, while males make cooing, whistling and mellow notes, females produce two different kinds of sound, low growling notes and harsh, quacking calls. Eiders are also relatively silent, particularly outside the breeding season. The vocabulary of the males consists mostly of soft cooing sounds that may be heard at short distance during courtship display, while females have a variety of hoarse grunts and croaking sounds. Amongst the rest of sea ducks, males' vocalizations range from the noisy Long-tailed Duck, with its yodel-like calls, through the whistling of the scoters and the Harlequin Duck, to the peculiar mellow notes of the sawbills. These, together with the scoters and goldeneyes, remain relatively silent outside the breeding season. Females of most species produce a variety of harsh, frog-like, rattling calls and other rough sounds.

Stifftails are amongst the least vocal of all wildfowl, and females in particular have been considered to be almost mute. During courtship display males may produce grunts, low whistles and trumpeting sounds, while they are also known to produce mechanical sounds, and splashing noises in the water.

Several species can produce special sounds with certain parts of their bodies, particularly the wings. Thus, some whistling-ducks have specially designed feathers in their wings, which produce whistles with the friction caused by the rapidly passing air, whereas the Common Goldeneye and the Black Scoter (*Melanitta nigra*) similarly produce ringing sounds. These noises may serve the same purpose as contact calls, as does the rushing sound produced by the wings of flying Mute Swans.

Food and Feeding

The diversity of the wildfowl is reflected in a wide variety of diets. The availability of food in each area is, of course, fundamental, but such aspects as the proportion of plant and animal matter and the methods of obtaining it are generally consistent with the taxonomic groupings of species.

There are some purely vegetarian and other purely carnivorous species, but vegetarian diets predominate amongst fully-grown birds. In contrast, young chicks of most species feed mainly on small animal prey items for a certain period. This is favoured by the relative facility with which animal food is digested, in comparison with vegetable items, and by the increased abundance and availability of aquatic insects, molluscs and crustaceans during the period immediately after the chicks have hatched. Nonetheless, there are a few species with an entirely vegetarian diet throughout their lives, including geese and swans.

Another general rule is that wildfowl that live in estuarine or maritime environments, at any rate when in such habitats, tend to feed primarily on animal food items, particularly molluscs and crustaceans, whereas those species that occupy terrestrial habitats, and are thus distant from water for long periods, have a diet that is more vegetarian or exclusively so.

Wildfowl have several methods of foraging, the most important of which are surface-feeding, or dabbling, diving and grazing. In addition, they sometimes wade, probe with the bill, filter mud, upend, sieve the bottom debris, chase fish, reach for overhead grasses and seedheads, pick up acorns, chase small animals, break up termite nests and so on. The distinction between the dabbling ducks and the diving ducks has been based more on taxonomic divisions than ecological differences. The Anatini normally feed by dabbling at the surface, whereas the Aythyini are commonly regarded as diving foragers, so these tribes have often been labelled respectively the "dabbling" and "diving" ducks.

The daily pattern of foraging activity among wildfowl also varies according to species, season, general area, particular site, type of food and feeding method. Some species are mostly nocturnal, particularly in winter or when feeding in rice fields. The majority, though, are more crepuscular, feeding during the first hours of the morning, from dawn to just after sunrise, and during the hours immediately prior to nightfall; moonlit nights often prompt an increase in activity. Predators also play a role in determining a bird's pattern of daily activity. The flightless races *aucklandica* and *nesiotis* of the Brown Teal (*Anas aucklandica*), which are restricted to a handful of small islands in the New Zealand area, usually remain hidden inside petrel burrows or under vegetation for most of the day, and come out to feed principally at night, when they are less likely to be detected by the numerous skuas (*Catharacta*) that nest on the same islands.

Many wildfowl species eat large quantities of seeds and other matter that is difficult to digest, and they need the help of harder materials to grind these down. Thus they ingest small particles of stone or sand, the size usually depending on the coarseness of the food ingested, and birds may have to fly long distances on a regular basis to special places where they collect grit. Other species which eat thick-shelled molluscs, such as the eiders and scoters, may retain the harder parts of the food as it is passing through the stomach and use them as grit. Lead pellets are also used, particularly in areas with heavy shooting or angling pressure, where lead poisoning has become so frequent as to affect significant proportions of the population (see Status and Conservation). Like many other birds, wildfowl have salt glands (see Morphological Aspects), but in most species these are only incipient, so that, with a few exceptions, including the eiders, scoters and goldeneyes, birds have to drink fresh water regularly, which may force them to travel a considerable distance to a favoured source.

Seeds constitute most of the food consumed by Magpie Geese, which gather them on land, using their feet to bend down tall grasses and picking off the seedheads with the bill. Grazing and mud filtering are other feeding methods that have been recorded in this species. Its diet is almost entirely vegetarian, and is complemented with blades of grass and the bulbs of plants.

The various species of whistling-ducks are also mainly vegetarian, consuming bulbs, rushes, stems, buds, leaves, sedges, grass, seeds, grain, berries and small fruit. In places the distribution of some species is closely related to that of waterlilies, as the birds eat the roots, seeds, buds and leaves. Similarly, the Fulvous Whistling-duck is virtually dependent on rice in several areas. Various aquatic invertebrates, such as insects, molluscs and crustaceans, have been recorded for several species, but these only rarely form a significant part of the diet. Grazing seems to be the main system used by the Black-bellied and Plumed (*Dendrocygna eytoni*) Whistling-ducks, whereas the Wandering (*Dendrocygna arcuata*) and Fulvous Whistling-ducks are perhaps better structurally adapted for swimming and diving. The White-faced Whistling-duck (*Dendrocygna viduata*) dives, wades and dabbles at the surface of

Upending consists of tilting the body into a vertical position, with the head under the water, whilst searching for food, as the adult Black Swan on the left is doing. The swan's particularly long neck allows it to exploit a series of depths much greater than those normally reached by the dabbling ducks, using this same procedure. Despite the porous appearance of the young birds' down, it is interesting to note that it is, in fact, waterproof and permits them to swim without problems; they even dive more often than the adults.

[*Cygnus atratus*, Australia. Photo: Jean-Paul Ferrero/ Marco Polo]

the water. Most species of whistling-duck are largely nocturnal in their foraging habits, and some are strictly so, whereas the White-backed Duck is mostly crepuscular.

Swans are also mainly, but not exclusively, vegetarian, for they complement their diet of aquatic plants and algae with aquatic insects and molluscs of various kinds, amphibians, fish spawn and so on. They eat not only the greener parts of plants, such as leaves, buds or stems, but also seeds, roots and tubers, for instance potatoes are a favourite food. All such food is obtained mainly while the birds are on the water, and their long necks allow them to reach down to the bottom in shallow water by upending. They also graze on emergent plants along the shoreline and commonly dabble and wade in shallow water, but in general swans seldom dive, the exception being cygnets, which dive freely. Some species, particularly the northern swans, are much more comfortable on land than others, and may be found grazing on dry agricultural land, especially in winter.

Adult true geese are essentially vegetarian throughout the year, occasionally complementing their diet with small invertebrates. Such items are much commoner in the diet of young birds, which sometimes depend almost entirely on small aquatic insects, molluscs or crustaceans. Geese obtain a good deal of their food through grazing, taking mainly grass, sedges, herbs and mosses. Particularly during winter, they frequent drier agricultural land, where their food consists mostly of grain, bulbs and tubers, especially potatoes, which they unearth using the feet and bill. This habit, together with the predilection of certain species for tender shoots and the concentration of large numbers of birds in especially suitable areas, has turned some of them into pests locally (see Relationship with Man). Long flights of geese may travel considerable distances daily for grit and water, mainly during the winter months, when their diet contains a much higher proportion of seeds, grain and other dry, hard materials.

The Cape Barren Goose feeds mainly by grazing in pasture land with short grass. It feeds on tussock grass, sedges and grasses of all kinds, and on the leaves and seeds of broad-leaved plants. One peculiarity of this species is that it often lives a considerable distance from the nearest source of fresh water, but it seems to be able to survive on a minimal amount, probably obtaining the necessary liquid by filtering brackish water with its well developed salt glands or directly from its plant food.

The peculiar shape of the Freckled Duck's bill recalls those of the stifftails. It has an unusual feeding method, which is again parallelled only by the stifftails, using the bill to filter the bottom debris. Other foraging actions commonly reported include upending, wading along the shore, dabbling and filter-feeding at the water surface. Freckled Ducks are crepuscular rather than truly nocturnal. Their diet consists primarily of various types of algae, seeds of plants near the shoreline and smaller quantities of aquatic invertebrates, particularly insects.

Within the Tadornini some species are almost entirely vegetarian, including most sheldgeese and both the Ruddy Shelduck (*Tadorna ferruginea*) and the South African Shelduck (*Tadorna cana*). The Australian Shelduck (*Tadorna tadornoides*) and the Paradise Shelduck have a more varied and mixed diet, while the Common and Radjah (*Tadorna radjah*) Shelducks virtually depend on small animals. Vegetarian sheldgeese and shelducks feed on grasses, seeds, grain, bulbs, tubers, small sprouting plants and algae. The sheldgeese are so strictly vegetarian that even young chicks take almost exclusively vegetable food, but the Ruddy Shelduck, in contrast, has been reported to feed frequently on refuse, and possibly also on carrion. The Common Shelduck is a highly specialized predator on the salt water snail *Hydrobia*, while the Radjah Shelduck also feeds primarily on molluscs. Such food is obtained on land by probing with the bill or in shallow water, where the birds dabble, wade and upend. Inland foragers normally choose to be most active around twilight or in complete darkness, and they generally loaf during the day, whereas birds that feed on the coast have to adapt their activities to the rhythm of the tides.

The diet of steamerducks consists mostly of molluscs, particularly mussels (*Mytilus*) and crustaceans, such as amphipods, occasionally complemented with small fish. They obtain their food by diving, or by wading and probing at the water's edge. It seems that when on inland waters the Flying Steamerduck has to be primarily diurnal, but on the coast birds are more dependent on the tides, with most foraging activity taking place around high tide.

Vegetable matter is probably a major component in the diet of most perching ducks, although some species, notably the Muscovy Duck (*Cairina moschata*) are more omnivorous. The Spur-winged Goose and the Maned Duck (*Chenonetta jubata*) are typical grazers, with a varied but essentially vegetarian diet; the Green (*Nettapus pulchellus*) and African Pygmy-geese are virtually dependent on water-lilies, taking the flower heads and seeds, and the American Wood Duck has a specialized diet based on acorns. Amongst the more carnivorous species are Hartlaub's Duck (*Pteronetta hartlaubii*) and the Mandarin Duck, which take considerable proportions of invertebrates in spring, and the Muscovy Duck, which feeds on all sorts of small animals, with a strong predilection for termites. However, the Mandarin feeds mostly on acorns and other vegetable matter during the autumn and winter months. Only exceptionally will perching ducks dive when foraging, and most of their food is gathered by dabbling or upending, while the bird is on the water, or by grazing on land. As in many other features (see Morphological Aspects), there is little uniformity in the timing of feeding activity within this heterogeneous group; some species are essentially night foragers, such as the Maned Duck, whereas others, including the African Pygmy-goose, feed almost exclusively during the day.

The Torrent Duck is a specialized diver in the fast-flowing, turbulent waters of mountain rivers. Under the water it probes among the rocks, searching every nook and cranny mostly for the larvae of aquatic insects, but also for molluscs or perhaps small fish. In calmer, deep water it frequently swims and feeds on the surface; in shallow water it may upend.

The dabbling ducks include a large number of species, each of which has its own peculiar structural adaptations, ecological requirements, diet and foraging methods; despite the relative uniformity, a few species are quite distinctive. The Blue Duck and Salvadori's Teal, for example, although taxonomically linked with the dabbling ducks, occupy a habitat comparable to that of the Torrent Duck, or that of the Harlequin Duck in

summer, and both dive readily and feed mostly on the larvae of aquatic insects. The case of the African Black Duck (*Anas sparsa*) is similar, and it consumes much vegetable food but also dives for aquatic insects, crustaceans, molluscs, amphibians and fish spawn, in secluded rivers with abundant surrounding vegetation. The three species of wigeon are almost entirely vegetarian, feeding mainly by grazing on green grass. The shovelers, with bills specially designed for filter-feeding, collect most of their small planktonic food from the water surface, often feeding co-operatively, swimming in small circles to bring up small food particles and filtering the mud in one another's wake. The exceptional bill of the Pink-eared Duck reveals its specialization as a filter-feeder too, and its habits are much the same as in the shovelers.

The unspecialized species of dabbling ducks feed mostly by swimming along, dabbling and upending, or probing for food while standing, for example on mudflats. The members of the Anatini very rarely dive for food, with the remarkable exception of the Marbled Teal, which is to some extent intermediate between the dabbling ducks and the pochards. Many species have predominantly crepuscular or nocturnal feeding habits, particularly where they are disturbed, as on rice fields, so they tend to loaf during the rest of the day. In estuarine habitats, however, the timing of activities is directly controlled by the rhythm of the tides. Although some species are almost exclusively vegetarian, or less often carnivorous, most dabbling ducks have mixed diets consisting mainly of seeds, grain, green parts of aquatic plants and herbs, as well as a wide variety of tadpoles, small fish and aquatic invertebrates, including insects, molluscs and crustaceans.

The pochards, often known as the diving ducks, are specialized in diving under water for their food. In shallow water, they may also upend and dabble, and they occasionally forage on vegetation at the water's edge or strip seeds from plants overhanging the water. Their food consists mostly of the leafy parts, roots and seeds of submerged vegetation, in some species complemented with aquatic invertebrates, including insects, molluscs and crustaceans, though often these are apparently not consumed intentionally, but swallowed incidentally together with the vegetable matter. The largest proportions of animal food are consumed by those birds that winter in areas of brack-

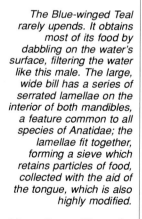

The Blue-winged Teal rarely upends. It obtains most of its food by dabbling on the water's surface, filtering the water like this male. The large, wide bill has a series of serrated lamellae on the interior of both mandibles, a feature common to all species of Anatidae; the lamellae fit together, forming a sieve which retains particles of food, collected with the aid of the tongue, which is also highly modified.

[Anas discors, Wisconsin, USA. Photo: Scott Nielsen/DRK]

Shallow waters are the Red-billed Duck's favoured feeding habitat. In many places, this type of environment tends to become covered in a layer of duckweed (Lemnaceae), a small floating plant with a seasonal cycle which forms part of the diet of many species of ducks. Note that these plants readily become stuck to the bill and to other parts of the birds, which, as a consequence of their movements, can act as dispersal agents for the duckweed.

[Anas erythroryncha, South Africa. Photo: Clem Haagner/ Ardea]

ish water along the coast, particularly the three scaups, the Tufted Duck (*Aythya fuligula*) and the Common Pochard (*Aythya ferina*).

Eiders have a characteristic diet consisting mostly of bivalve molluscs, especially mussels and periwinkles (*Littorina*), while other animal foods abundantly consumed include univalve molluscs, echinoderms, larvae of aquatic insects and crustaceans, such as amphipods and isopods. These are complemented with small quantities of vegetable matter, including algae, grasses, sedges and broad-leaved herbs. Eiders mainly forage by diving down to the bottom in shallow marine waters or in small ponds in their tundra breeding habitat. The Harlequin Duck breeds along mountain streams, where its diet and foraging methods resemble those of the Torrent Duck and its other ecological counterparts; it winters at sea, where its diet differs little from that of scoters and goldeneyes. These birds, in turn, take mostly bivalve molluscs, particularly mussels, and crustaceans, echinoderms, small fish and marine algae during the winter. In their breeding habitat they consume mainly insect larvae and freshwater crustaceans. Sawbills have a specially

designed bill adapted for handling fish, their main prey, while they also take small quantities of amphibians, crustaceans, molluscs and aquatic insects. Virtually all of the Mergini capture their prey under water, either by bottom feeding, as in the scoters, or after pursuit, as in the sawbills.

Stifftails dabble, upend and strain mud in shallow water, but their most characteristic feeding method consists of fairly long dives, lasting 20-40 seconds on average, during which they sieve the bottom debris with the bill. In this way they feed on submerged plants, algae, seeds and roots, as well as small molluscs, crustaceans, worms and insect larvae. The Musk Duck usually takes larger food items, most of which are animal, including even ducklings of some other species.

Breeding

In almost all species of wildfowl, birds attempt breeding only once a year, during the most favourable period. This is particularly true in regions with marked seasons, where the availability of both suitable habitat and food is more or less predictable. However, in a number of regions the climate is more constant throughout most of the year, generally dry with irregular bouts of rain. Such is the case in parts of northern and inland Australia, where the onset of breeding activities is generally triggered off by rainfall and the subsequent flooding of billabongs.

In temperate regions of both hemispheres, many wildfowl are essentially migratory, as many of the areas used for breeding, which abound in food and water in spring and summer, may freeze over during the winter and the few areas that remain ice-free are insufficient to support the increased populations after the breeding season. Furthermore, in high latitudes, where most birds breed, the spell of fine weather and abundant food is usually too short for a whole breeding cycle to be fitted in, so some of the activities connected with breeding, particularly pair formation and courtship displays, have to be performed while the birds are still in their winter quarters or on migration towards their breeding grounds.

In subtropical regions, where warm, dry weather extends for a much longer period of time, water often becomes the limiting factor for the breeding of wildfowl. As a result of autumn rains, many areas flood during winter, creating a multitude of small temporary lagoons, where many pairs establish themselves for breeding. But in such areas the birds are limited to relatively short breeding cycles to ensure that the brood has fledged before the area dries up completely, forcing the birds to move off and con-

Like all shovelers, this Northern Shoveler drake displays an especially long, wide, voluminous bill, which is extremely specialized in filter-feeding. This ability permits the bird to exploit adverse situations; in this case the bird is obtaining plankton by filtering on the water surface through holes in the ice.

[Anas clypeata. Photo: R. Carr/ Bruce Coleman]

centrate in much larger water bodies, sometimes leading to vagrancy and large-scale irruptions, in what has been referred to as the "summer drought exodus".

In the tropics, where day length and temperature are relatively constant throughout the year, one or more dry and rainy seasons can generally be distinguished. Most species of wildfowl adapt their activities so that they can start breeding with the first rains and thus rear their chicks when water is plentiful. Where water is not limiting, for instance on tropical rivers or where rainfall is abundant all year round, breeding tends not to be related to seasons, and it is often possible to find eggs in all months, even within the same species.

In most of the ducks of the Anatinae a new pair is formed each year, so that the bond is broken each season, usually just after egg-laying. In most species, while birds are still in their winter flocks, each selects a new partner and the new pair travel to the breeding grounds together, so that when they reach the nesting area they are already paired, thus saving time. Only in a few cases, particularly amongst eiders and some other sea ducks, do birds pair up again with the same mate in successive years.

The opposite strategy is shown by the larger and the more territorial species, including swans and geese, where the pair bond tends to be permanent and potentially life-long. An extreme case is that of the swans, particularly Bewick's Swans (*Cygnus columbianus bewickii*), and one study showed that over several years there was not a single case of "divorce" among 500 pairs that had produced young, while under 1% of 1000 repeatedly unsuccessful pairs ever changed mate. Similarly, less than 3% of Mute Swans that had bred successfully one year paired with a new mate in the following season, and only about 9% of those that had attempted to breed but produced no young changed their partner.

Permanent pair bonds seem to be essential in extremely territorial or purely sedentary species. Thus, it is the rule amongst the river specialists, the Torrent, Blue and African Black Ducks and Salvadori's Teal, as well as in the Mute Swan. These species maintain a territory throughout the year, expelling all conspecifics from it except their own mates and, to a lesser extent, the young from the previous year.

In contrast with most duck species, in which the male takes little or no part in the incubation or chick rearing, male birds of the species with permanent pair bonds generally have an active role in the breeding tasks, sitting on the eggs, when the female goes out to feed during incubation, guarding her while she incubates, accompanying the young, defending the territory necessary to provide enough food for all the family, and so on. This is the case of the various species of whistling-duck, in most of which the family depart from the breeding waters after the young have fledged and integrate in larger flocks. Even within the flock, however, it seems that the pair remain together until the conditions are suitable to attempt breeding again.

Geese follow a fairly similar strategy. They remain paired for life, even though they do not maintain a territory all year round. The male contributes to incubation and helps rear the brood, and when the young have fledged, the whole family normally join large flocks and make the journey together to the winter quarters, where the pair remain together into the following spring. In these species, a large proportion of juveniles remain with their parents throughout the winter and often fly back to the breeding grounds still in their company. The young birds do not establish a pair bond until their second winter, and in many cases the yearlings spend the summer of their second year in their parents' nesting territory, contributing to its defence and helping rear their much younger siblings.

Virtually all wildfowl are monogamous in any one season. However, males of certain species may copulate with unattended females occasionally, particularly in species where the female is deserted soon after the start of incubation, and especially in areas where the chances of complete nesting failure are highest. Such promiscuous behaviour is generally irrelevant in the long term, and only adds slightly to the chances of the eggs being fertilized properly, while it is unlikely to interfere with overall breeding success; in any case males typically leave to moult at an early stage, so only a few are involved.

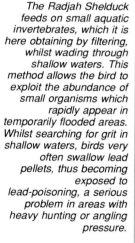

The Radjah Shelduck feeds on small aquatic invertebrates, which it is here obtaining by filtering, whilst wading through shallow waters. This method allows the bird to exploit the abundance of small organisms which rapidly appear in temporarily flooded areas. Whilst searching for grit in shallow waters, birds very often swallow lead pellets, thus becoming exposed to lead-poisoning, a serious problem in areas with heavy hunting or angling pressure.

[*Tadorna radjah rufitergum*, Fogg Dam, Northern Territories, Australia. Photo: Jean-Paul Ferrero/ Ardea]

Several species of ducks include fish in their diets, but the most markedly piscivorous are the sawbills (*Mergus*), represented here by two female Goosanders. The bill is sharply serrated along its cutting edges so that the bird can keep a firm grip on such slippery prey. The Goosander, an excellent diver, catches fish by direct underwater pursuit, moving along with its neck stretched forwards and propelling itself using only its feet, unlike some diving birds which mainly propel themselves using their wings, as in the case of the auks. Birds can remain submerged for two minutes, but normally resurface after less than 30 seconds. Once the fish has been caught, they can swallow it underwater if it is small, but, in general, they return to the surface, and, before swallowing the fish, turn it round so that it will enter head first, thus avoiding any injuries which the spiny fins of some fish can cause; they are capable of swallowing prey the size of an eel (*Anguilla*) 46 cm long.

[Above: *Mergus merganser*.
Photo: Richard & Julia Kemp/Survival.

Below: *Mergus merganser americanus*, Wisconsin, USA.
Photo: Scott Nielsen/DRK]

Courtship displays constitute a stereotyped series of ritualized movements accompanied by vocalizations; there is a unique sequence for each species, a strategy designed to prevent hybridization. This male King Eider is displaying in front of the female by performing the "Pushing-display" which involves the bird alternately pushing its head up with the bill tilted downwards, and then retracting it smoothly down again. During the process, the bird puffs up its chest and coos.

[*Somateria spectabilis*, Alaska. Photo: Erwin & Peggy Bauer/Bruce Coleman]

Only the Magpie Goose, the Maccoa Duck (*Oxyura maccoa*) and the Comb Duck are regularly polygamous. The Magpie Goose has a rather peculiar mating system, whereby males are often permanently paired with two females. Both females lay in the same nest and share incubation with the male, while he also participates in the rearing of the chicks. In the Maccoa Duck, the extremely aggressive males establish quite large territories, sufficient to accommodate more than one female, and these rear their young within its boundaries. Male Comb Ducks are often seen in the company of several females, to which they may be paired either simultaneously or in succession.

The numerous species of wildfowl show a wide range of strategies as far as breeding dispersion is concerned, from the highly territorial species that do not allow any other birds apart from their mates or young within the defended area, as is the case of the riverine species, particularly the Torrent Duck, to the truly colonial nesters. Breeding aggregations of wildfowl are never exceedingly large, and colonies of a few dozen or just over a hundred nests are probably the norm. In many cases, colonies are formed due to a scarcity of suitable breeding habitat, so that the birds simply coincide and concentrate in the few optimum areas. However, in other instances they gather in fairly dense colonies, even when there is plenty of suitable habitat nearby. This is particularly the case of many tundra-nesting geese, and their colonies have a primarily defensive function, as geese nesting in a colony suffer less predation than solitary nesters. Besides, the synchrony in breeding activities that accompanies colonial nesting tends to reduce the period of occupation of the colony and hence of vulnerability.

One of the main components of the early parts of the breeding season are the ritualized courtship displays, each species exhibiting a unique repertoire of movements and postures that, in theory, can only be properly interpreted and responded to by its conspe-

cifics. Furthermore, being unique in each species, courtship displays also help to prevent interbreeding, even though this is a relatively common phenomenon among wildfowl (see Systematics). There are, of course, a multitude of different displays in the wildfowl, but some general patterns emerge.

In many species, social interactions leading to the selection of a mate take place in groups, commonly in the winter flocks. It is generally the female that starts displaying amidst several already receptive males. She commonly performs a "Head-nodding" movement while swimming in circles around several males, and adopting a very flat posture that is typical of dabbling ducks. The males respond by adopting an "Uptilted" posture, in which the head is retracted, the plumage bristled up and the whole body stretched out, and at the climax of this movement, the bird shakes its plumage vigorously. Then it bends its neck well forward and produces a loud whistle followed by a grunting sound, as it recovers its original position. Finally, the various drakes engage in a "head-up-tail-up" swimming posture, which is mainly directed towards the selected mates.

Displays between paired birds affect only the two birds involved, although they may be performed in front of other birds. The female swims after the drake calling loudly, after which the male often preens behind his wing, then the two birds may face each other and drink. As a normal prelude to copulation, both birds raise their heads slowly and then lower them in jerks, in a display known as "Head-dipping" or "Pumping". Copulation almost always takes place on the water, one of the very few exceptions being the Cape Barren Goose, which invariably copulates on land. The male mounts his partner for some seconds, often biting her on the nape, after which he usually stretches his neck and utters a loud call, sometimes spreading his wings fully, in the "Triumph Ceremony", which is most highly developed amongst geese. After copulation, the

The breeding activity of the Red-crested Pochard begins with communal courtship, which involves a group of males surrounding a female, after which a rapid chase ensues. If the female takes flight, the display becomes an aerial chase, but this is less common. Such displays occur in autumn and winter, usually with the participation of 5-20 males.

[*Netta rufina*, Tablas de Daimiel, Spain. Photo: Oriol Alamany]

female normally bathes and preens for some time, while the male often swims away in a more or less stereotyped posture, for example, commonly with the bill tucked down in pochards.

Courtship display is generally much more elaborate in species that renew the pair bond each year. Amongst already mated pairs, it consists of simpler performances, or perhaps similar ritualized movements performed at much lower intensity. Ritualized feeding of the female by the male, an essential part of the courtship display in many other bird families, is exceptional amongst wildfowl, and the Red-crested Pochard (*Netta rufina*) is the only species known to do so regularly. Males, however, play an important role in the feeding efficiency of their mates, as they defend their feeding territories, and guard them as they forage. This is essential if the female is to build up reserves for the considerable efforts involved in nest building and especially egg-making.

The nest is usually a simple structure. Very often it consists of only a hollow or shallow scrape in the ground, sparsely lined with vegetation, including herbs, mosses and lichens, but frequently with some feathers. These come from the female's breast, and by plucking them she uncovers her extensive brood patches. These areas of bare skin, abounding in blood vessels, transmit heat more efficiently than any other part of the bird's body and are essential for effective incubation. The habit of lining the nest with down is particularly well developed in species that breed in high latitudes, especially the eiders, which are commonly farmed for this purpose (see Relationship with Man). The insulating properties of the breast down help maintain the warmth of the nest and prevent any chilling of the eggs when the female has to leave them for some time. In addition, the fact that females of many species cover the eggs with the down when they leave renders the nest inconspicuous and thus reduces the risk of predation.

Where flooding is a serious threat, especially in marshy areas, some species may gather up large amounts of plant material and build their nests in the form of large conical mounds, on top of which there is usually a shallow depression where the eggs are laid. Such nests are typical of swans and are typically found on the ground in reed beds or partially afloat.

Some species have more specific nest-site requirements, for instance those that nest in holes in trees, including the whistling-ducks, most perching ducks, goldeneyes and sawbills. Some of these species are adaptable, and may nest in other sites such as in hollows amongst boulders or under vegetation, for example Barrow's Goldeneye (*Bucephala islandica*), which breeds in treeless country in Iceland. But others depend almost exclusively on tree-holes, and the availability of these limits the breeding range of the species. The Common Goldeneye has expanded its range considerably in Scotland as the result of an intensive campaign during which many nestboxes were provided.

In the vast, barren expanse of the tundra, where terrestrial predators have direct access to nests, geese tend to breed on the tops of hills, on rocky outcrops or even on cliff faces, particularly the Barnacle Goose (*Branta leucopsis*) and to a lesser extent the Red-breasted Goose (*Branta ruficollis*). The latter species is also peculiar in breeding almost invariably in close association with the nests of Peregrine Falcons (*Falco peregrinus*) or Rough-legged Buzzards (*Buteo lagopus*). This is presumably an anti-fox device, as these raptors will expel any mammalian predator from the vicinity of their own nests, but are themselves too small to prey on the adult geese.

In most species, it is the female alone that builds the nest, but in the swans, the whistling-ducks and the Magpie Goose the male helps with the building, and in the Coscoroba Swan and Cape Barren Goose the nest is built entirely by the male. Some species make use of the abandoned nest structures of other birds, such as the Comb Duck and the Spur-winged Goose, which take over old Hamerkop (*Scopus umbretta*) nests, while the Egyptian Goose (*Alopochen aegyptiacus*) also uses empty heron nests. Several of the species that use holes in trees show a preference for occupying vacant holes excavated by large woodpeckers.

In territorial species males tend to defend the whole territory, and their antagonistic behaviour consists of a combination of ritualized postures, in which mainly the neck and wings are used to persuade an adversary to leave. The most typical actions include "Bowing", "Wing-flapping", "Head-jerking", "Chin-lifting", ruffling of feathers and, most characteristic of ducks, noisy chases and rushes on the water. Such actions are often accompanied by distinctive loud calls. Fighting is not infrequent, and it can occasionally be vicious in some species. The owner of the territory or site usually wins, sometimes after an intense, violent battle involving the use of the bill and the bend of the wing, and this can result in the death of one, or exceptionally both, of the opponents. Nearly 3% of all adult Mute Swans found dead in Britain were thought to have been killed in such disputes.

Females defend only the nest-site and its vicinity but in a more direct way, with less ritualized behaviour. They will chase and attack any intruder in the defended area, whether male or female, but such interactions seldom develop any further, and the intruding bird normally retreats quickly without offering any opposition. Especially in species with long-term pair-bonds, both partners sometimes co-operate in the defence of the territory or the nest. This is more usual when the established pair are disturbed by another pair searching for a site or are menaced by a predator.

Wildfowl lay sizeable clutches of fairly large eggs, so a great deal of energy is required to make them. In the Ruddy Duck (*Oxyura jamaicensis*), for example, the mean weight of the whole clutch is equivalent to the body weight of the female. Obviously, in the species where the weight of the clutch is highest in proportion with that of the female, part of the energy expended in forming the eggs is obtained by much more intense foraging. But even in the species that rely mostly on their reserves for egg formation and incubation, as in the swans, geese and eiders, the average clutch weight represents 20-30% of the female's body weight. However, in these species replacement laying is exceptional, since the female has not enough time to build up the necessary reserves within the same season.

Eggs are normally laid at daily intervals, and the average clutch size is of about 4-13 eggs. However, it is not unusual to find well over a dozen eggs in the same nest, and a single Red-crested Pochard's nest was found to contain 39, but these cases are normally attributed to dump laying by other females, generally of the same species. The smallest clutches are those of the swans, geese and eiders, which do not build up extra reserves, whereas the largest correspond to the dabbling ducks, perching ducks and pochards, followed closely by the sea ducks of the Mergini. The largest eggs relative to the size of the female, however, are laid by the stifftails, and their chicks lead a truly aquatic life immediately they are dry after hatching. Large eggs are essential in order to produce relatively large, well formed chicks that can leave the nest and fend for themselves soon after hatching. Furthermore, large eggs are more resistant to chilling, which can occur due to the flooding of the nest during incubation. In this way the wildfowl clutch represents a compromise between the necessarily large eggs and the minimum number of young required to ensure that enough chicks will reach fledging each year, so that the population may remain stable. Nidifugous chicks obviously suffer more losses than those that stay in the nest until they have fledged.

Ducks can lay replacement clutches if the first attempt fails within the early stages of incubation, but once past that point, it is very improbable that breeding will be attempted again within the same season, and it is generally put off until the following year. In the cases studied, replacement laying generally involves smaller clutches of lighter eggs, so the chances of survival of the resulting chicks are significantly reduced. The new eggs are laid after a variable period of 4-20 days or more, which is mostly determined by the time elapsed since the laying of the last egg of the original clutch. The longer the gap between the laying of the last egg and the loss of the clutch, the longer it will take and the more improbable it is that a replacement clutch will be laid.

Having precocial chicks that leave the nest soon after hatching and find food for themselves, it is essential for all the chicks in a brood to hatch more or less synchronously, within a period

*In the Anatidae, mating almost always takes place on the water, although the Cape Barren Goose (*Cereopsis novaehollandiae*) invariably copulates on land. Unlike most other birds, the males of this family have a penis-like copulatory organ. During the few seconds that copulation lasts, the male Mute Swan grips the female's nape. In swans, copulatory behaviour is also important in maintaining the pair-bond, as they copulate much more frequently than is necessary for efficient fertilization. Note the more developed knob in the male.*

[Cygnus olor, Wisconsin, USA. Photo: Scott Nielsen/DRK]

of no more than 24 hours, so incubation can not start until after the last egg has been laid and the clutch is complete. Incubation lasts from 22 days, in species like Common Teal, Garganey (*Anas querquedula*), Northern Pintail and Ross's Goose (*Anser rossii*), to 35 or 40 days in the Trumpeter and Black Swans respectively. The geese that nest in the high Arctic, such as the Greater White-fronted Goose (*Anser albifrons*), the Snow Goose (*Anser caerulescens*) and the Brent Goose (*Branta bernicla*), present a special case. As they have such a brief period of suitable weather for nesting, they are committed to a very short breeding cycle, so, despite their relatively large size, they have remarkably short incubation periods of less than 25 days in all cases, which are only comparable to those of small ducks in more southerly latitudes.

Incubation is carried out almost exclusively by the female, except in the Magpie Goose, the whistling-ducks and the *Cygnus* swans, in which both sexes contribute. In these species, the male usually stays in the vicinity of the nest while his mate incubates, though he may sit on the eggs when she leaves the nest to forage. Even though males in most species of the Anatidae have no brood patches and thus can not incubate actively, their sitting on the eggs while the female is away helps to prevent the chilling of the eggs and, at the same time, reduces the chances of nest predation.

The Black-headed Duck is unique amongst the Anatidae in being a true parasitic breeder that lays its eggs in the nests of various marsh birds, particularly several species of coot (*Fulica*) and the Rosy-billed Pochard (*Netta peposaca*). The egg or eggs are incubated amidst those of the host species, and, with an incubation period estimated at only some 21 days, they hatch some time before the host's. The young chick is extraordinarily precocial and leaves the nest where it hatched after only one or two days. It is capable of fending for itself from that tender age and does not interfere much with the rest of the brood, becoming independent almost immediately.

Three or four days before hatching, wildfowl chicks start calling inside the egg more insistently than chicks of other groups. It has been suggested that communication between the chicks at this stage helps all or most of them to hatch within a few hours, since the very weak or unusually delayed have to be abandoned at the nest, as those that have hatched need food. At the same time as the chicks start to peep inside the egg, the female at the nest also becomes much more attentive. In those species in which the male guards the female as she incubates, he also moves in closer to the nest at this stage.

The young hatch with their eyes open and can stand up, move about or swim almost immediately after they have dried out. However, until they are one or two days old their mobility tends still to be limited and they do not usually stray far from the nest. It is at this stage that their capacity to become imprinted is greatest. They have an innate tendency to follow their mother, or both parents, and they immediately become attached to the parental contact call. Thus the parent bird may lead them to new feeding or staging areas across fields, roads or whatever. The chicks that hatch in raised nests, such as in a tree-hole or on a steep cliff, have to face the additional problem of descending to ground level. First, they must find their way to the entrance of the hole or to a favourable part of the cliff, generally clambering with the aid of their feet and claws, and from this point they jump down onto the ground. They have only very rudimentary wings that are no use at all for trying to brake or parachute, but their soft, fluffy bodies absorb the impact, normally with no harm to the bird whatsoever.

Young wildfowl, led normally by the female alone, or by both parents, are capable of gathering food for themselves immediately they can swim. The role of the parent bird in the foraging of the chicks is based on a rather passive attitude, and consists mainly of leading the young birds to areas with plenty of food, where it stays alert and guards them from predators. Nevertheless, in some species the adults actually assist the chicks by actively showing them the food. Adult Magpie Geese and Musk Ducks go even further and present food to the chicks, holding it in the bill. Parent swans and geese have been seen to trample the water with their feet to stir up the bottom and bring food items up to the surface.

The young birds remain within sight and hearing of the parents, but once they have left the nest they are generally brooded only very occasionally, in bad weather or danger; adult

Several species of wildfowl have the habit of taking over old nests of other birds, as in the case of this Egyptian Goose, which has taken advantage of the enormous nest of a Hamerkop (Scopus umbretta). Such behaviour is also common in the Comb Duck (Sarkidiornis melanotos) and the Spur-winged Goose (Plectropterus gambensis). This nest illustrates another common habit of the Anatidae, in that the female has added down from her breast to cover the nest.

[Alopochen aegyptiacus. Photo: Joan Root/Survival]

Some birds have to nest in the open, in areas where they are exposed to many predators. When threatened by a potential predator, an adult goose may defend its clutch vigorously, as clearly illustrated by this Emperor Goose adopting an aggressive posture and emitting threatening cries. As an adaptation to the favourable season being very short, this and other species of the high Arctic have a reduced incubation period, which lasts only 24-25 days in the Emperor Goose.

[*Anser canagicus*, Alaska. Photo: Brian Hawkes/ NHPA]

swans often carry young chicks on their backs. It is not uncommon for the young of different broods to mix and interact, eventually becoming more attached to a female other than their own mother. In some species, this is a voluntary strategy with great survival value, in which the young of several broods are brought together in a larger aggregation, or crèche, under the attendance of a few adults. This strategy, which also occurs for instance in penguins, pelicans and flamingos, is particularly common among shelducks and eiders, and is thought to improve the chances of survival of the chicks, by concentrating them in the best feeding areas and by diminishing the individual risk of predation. It is also thought to have advantages for the females, as most of them are freed from breeding duties and can start moulting earlier in the season, so as to be ready for migration sooner.

Young ducks are mostly guarded by the female until they are fully-feathered and capable of sustained flight, which takes some 5-10 weeks, though only four in the Common Teal. However, stifftail chicks are abandoned by the female before they reach that age, and before they are fully-grown. Cygnets remain with their parents throughout the winter and in migratory species fly with them to the breeding grounds, or are evicted by the male as he starts showing territoriality for a new breeding attempt. Family bonds among geese sometimes go even further, and yearlings often fly to the breeding grounds still accompanying their parents, whom they may help partially with the breeding tasks. The bond is often not broken until the second or third winter, or exceptionally even later, which can lead to family groups of considerable size, as the young produced in one year mix with those produced in previous seasons.

Most duck species are sexually mature at about one year old, so they are capable of successful breeding in their second summer. In stifftails and sea ducks, however, maturity is deferred until birds are at least two years old. First breeding usually takes place at the age of one in whistling-ducks, two in shelducks, three in geese and occasionally swans, or up to five years old in male swans, although individual variation can

account for some birds breeding for the first time long before or after the normal age.

There have been many studies of the average chick production of different species of wildfowl in different parts of the world. Obviously, the results fluctuate greatly from one species to another, and within the same species between areas. In general, those pairs that attempt breeding, sometimes a small fraction of the total population, obtain medium to high overall hatching success, often 60-80% or higher in normal years. However, the number of surviving chicks decreases gradually as the season advances, as many are lost to predators or in bad weather, so that only a fairly small proportion reach fledging. In most species, 40-60% of the young that hatch die before they are fully-grown.

As in many other birds, mortality is highest during the first year of life, and over 80% mortality during the first 12 months after fledging is not uncommon. Although it decreases significantly in successive years, it never descends to levels comparable with those of other waterbirds or of seabirds. Being prey species in most cases, average life expectancy for many wildfowl is only a few months or at most a few years. This is particularly true of ducks, for only a fraction of the total population can expect to live one full year. However, once they have reached that age, they have a mean life expectancy of a further one or two years. In geese and swans, average mortality is often about 25% after the first year, so the mean life expectancy for those birds that survive one year is about four more years. However, these figures are extremely variable depending on the species, for instance swans are generally longer-lived; they also depend on the particular population, so they are only very rough estimates.

Many individuals are known to have lived many more years than the calculated mean life expectancy, both in the wild and in captivity. As regards wild birds, the record of longevity for any member of the Anatidae is 29 years 1 month for a Mallard ringed in North America; one Common Eider (*Somateria mollissima*) lived to be almost 23, and a Pink-footed Goose (*Anser brachyrhynchus*) more than 22.

The habit of using tree holes as nest-sites is not unusual in wildfowl, as is the case of the Goosander, or Common Merganser, as it is known in North America. Two days after hatching, these nestlings will jump out through the nest entrance; usually, the chicks' light weight, combined with their soft, dense plumage, prevents them suffering injury on their headlong descent.

[*Mergus merganser.*
Photo: Wayne Lankinen/
Bruce Coleman]

Movements

As in most other birds, those wildfowl that nest in high latitudes, where they can take advantage of the explosion of life and almost continuous sunlight during the local summer, generally fly to lower latitudes where they spend the non-breeding season, whereas those that nest in tropical or subtropical latitudes generally remain within the same region throughout the year. This is especially true of most of the species that breed on the tundra, since the spring thaw creates large stretches of uninterrupted wetlands, such as bogs, swamps and fens, where a great many birds will breed, yet the same area is covered in snow and ice for several months during the winter. Some birds manage to survive the non-breeding season in such conditions, but there is clearly not enough food in the area to sustain the whole population, so most are forced to leave.

Some species of wildfowl execute very precise migrations, with previously defined routes and target areas, as well as regular timing and points for breaking the journey. Others are more irregular, not actually moving until they are displaced by adverse weather conditions, and even then travelling just as far as the first suitable area. Typical examples of the former are geese, whereas the latter group is best exemplified by sawbills. In many species, however, certain individuals or populations are more migratory than others. Significant differences in the extent of migratory movements also occur between the sexes in many cases, and, as in most groups of birds, there is a tendency for immature birds to disperse more extensively than adults.

Most wildfowl of tropical and subtropical regions tend to spend the off-season months in the vicinity of the water body where they breed. The main problem they have to face is the great variation in water level of swamps and lakes. Where wetlands are liable to dry up, the breeding populations of wildfowl have to adapt their cycles, and when they have bred, they move on to more suitable areas, as soon as the water level starts to drop. Occasionally these movements, often known as "drought migrations", involve vast numbers of birds flying considerable distances, particularly when one of the temporary refuges in turn dries up and forces the birds to fly off again, in search of another suitable wetland. This can give rise to a high degree of vagrancy, and occasionally birds appear well outside their normal ranges in such circumstances.

Almost all ducks, geese and swans are temporarily flightless during the annual moult of the flight-feathers (see Morphological Aspects), and this is perhaps the time when adults are most vulnerable to predation. So they choose the quietest areas with an abundant food supply and concentrate there in great numbers, thus adding to the protection of the individual, with the result that some such particularly favoured areas attract birds from considerable distances. For example, the bulk of the population of Common Shelducks of north-western Europe, including most of the birds from Scandinavia, Britain, the Baltic states and much of north-central Europe, gather together to moult in the area of the Helgoland Bight off north-west Germany, whence they disperse to their wintering grounds or return to their breeding areas, after they have completed their moult.

In many cases, the off-season is spent not only at another locality but also in a completely different habitat. A good example of this is found in the sea ducks of the tribe Mergini, and it represents a different type of solution to the permanent problem of breeding areas becoming totally inadequate for sustaining the whole population of a particular species during the winter. By dispersing over marine waters, which do not freeze over so easily, these ducks can remain at much higher latitudes than most other species and do not need to develop a true migration. Nevertheless, the biological implications of this option are substantial, as the anatomy of the individual bird needs to be equally efficient in very diverse habitats, for example the Harlequin Duck occupies mountain torrents in summer and surf waters along rocky coasts in winter.

Relationship with Man

Wildfowl have been associated with man more closely and longer than any other group of birds, except perhaps the Galliformes. This intense relationship is reflected in the everyday life of many people and has affected many cultures. Nowadays, in the western world it is common to cover a bed with an eiderdown or to eat such delicacies as pâté de foie gras, while

some play "ducks and drakes", or use colourful expressions such as "to kill the goose that lays the golden egg", "to cook someone's goose", "to swan off to the races", to have "goose pimples", "like water off a duck's back", "all my geese are swans" and a "swansong"; cricketers try to avoid being out for a "duck".

This wealth of expressions, which is but a brief example of the many hundreds of similar sayings that exist in many languages, is the result of many centuries of co-existence with ducks, geese and swans. Wildfowl, in particular swans, have also been prominent in the traditions of many cultures. In Greek mythology, for instance, Zeus took the form of a swan to seduce Leda and beget Helen of Troy. In Europe, black swans were a symbol of evil long before the discovery of Australia and of the Black Swan; indeed, they represented an unnatural, impossible being. In contrast, the swan-maidens of many different Nordic and Celtic legends were famed for their purity. A typical version is that the swan-maiden possessed a special feather robe, which she removed to become the maiden, upon which a young man fell in love with her, hid the robe and the two married. Some time afterwards the robe was rediscovered, the maiden was forced to turn back into a swan and she flew off. This legend is thought to represent the swan's moult and migration.

The close relationship of wildfowl with man is undoubtedly connected with the fact that both are numerous and widespread, occurring in virtually every corner of the world, and almost everywhere they have come into contact. Ducks, geese and swans have been domesticated in Europe, Asia, Africa and America, they have been farmed for meat, eggs and down, they have been trapped, hunted and killed in many ways, they have been kept in collections and have become naturalized in places far from their original ranges. Nowadays, they are significantly affected by the conservation effort being invested in wetland habitats worldwide, but they often come into conflict with agriculture too.

It was probably soon after the advent of agriculture, when the sedentary life supplanted that of the hunter-gatherers, that the first wildfowl were domesticated. Ducks, geese and to a lesser extent swans proved to be ideal birds for domestication. In the first place, they are medium-sized to large and they readily lay down deposits of fat, an adaptation for improving insulation for their life in an aquatic environment. They generally have large broods and easily become imprinted, so that the first animate being that communicates sufficiently with them immediately after hatching is taken to be "mother" and the chicks will follow "her" about continuously. As geese and swans stay in their family groups into the first winter and often much longer, they are intrinsically prepared to maintain bonds with their relatives for a long time. From a practical point of view, wildfowl do not require special enclosures and they can live almost anywhere, often wandering around the farm during the day and sleeping under some sort of cover at night. They do not even require water, except for drinking, and will eat almost any food, for instance scraps or vegetable peelings, which they often complement by catching small invertebrates or amphibians.

It is not known when the first domestication of wildfowl took place. In the Old Kingdom of Egypt, which ended around 2300 BC, domestic Egyptian Geese were certainly widespread, and the Greeks and Romans had domestic ducks and geese, whereas in South America Muscovy Ducks were already common in captivity when the first Europeans arrived. However, it seems that the first species of wildfowl to be domesticated were probably the Mallard and the Swan Goose (Anser cygnoides), which are known to have been living with humans in China and south-east Asia from a very early date. The mechanism of domestication was probably very simple: wild birds would rarely breed in captivity, but it would certainly not be difficult to collect eggs from the wild and have them incubated and hatched by the already domesticated hens. The young hatched in this way could rapidly become imprinted by their surroundings and captive breeding by such birds would be far less difficult.

The only wildfowl species known to have been common formerly as a domestic bird, but now only found in the wild, is the Egyptian Goose. As a domestic bird, this species was probably never known outside the Nile Valley. It was regarded as the sacred bird of Geb, god of the land, its eggs being attributed a symbolic value according to which they could not be eaten. Its flesh, however, was extensively consumed, and some birds were force-fed in order to cause the degeneration of their liver tissues, with which a kind of foie gras was made. It seems that

Soon after hatching, wildfowl chicks will readily follow the female, or indeed any large moving object. This behaviour, known as "imprinting", was extensively investigated by Konrad Lorenz using the Greylag Goose (Anser anser). Here a female Redhead is being followed by "her" brood. This species normally lays about 9 eggs, so this is probably an example of dump-nesting, a form of parasitic nesting very frequent in the Redhead.

[Aythya americana, Malheur Refuge, Oregon, USA. Photo: Jeff Foott/ Bruce Coleman]

after the conquest of Egypt by the Persians in 525-524 BC, Egyptian Geese were no longer kept as domestic birds.

Domestic geese seem to have had a twofold origin. On the one hand, the European domestic goose seems to be derived directly from the Greylag Gooese (*Anser anser*), whereas all the Chinese breeds probably have a common ancestor in the Swan Goose. Both of these main types have undergone a complex process of genetic selection, which has included some interbreeding resulting in many different breeds, each specially adapted to a particular need. Geese make very good eating, and trade in them gained international importance as the main European cities started to become heavily populated. The geese were walked into the cities in large flocks of up to several thousand, sometimes from considerable distances. The breeders generally "shoed" them first, by walking them over several baths of tar and sand or sawdust, so that a thick layer was formed to protect their feet. Once in the city, they were sold at markets or at regular "goose fairs", that often attracted people from far afield.

Domestic geese have traditionally been force-fed in order to produce foie gras. This practice was common in several ancient cultures, and was fairly widespread over much of Europe, Israel, Turkey, Egypt and other countries; indeed the Greeks would sew up the eyes of swans and cranes so as to fatten them up more easily. In early times, the birds were overfed with carbohydrates, particularly ripe figs, kept in warm places and allowed very little exercise, so that the excessive fatty enlargement of the liver would soon develop into a cirrhosis, at which point the birds were killed. Nowadays, several breeds have been developed that will allow corn to be forced down their gullets with minimal resistance.

Whether bred for their flesh or foie gras, the geese provided the farmer with a thick coat of feathers that soon proved very useful for several purposes. Goose quills were highly appreciated as pens, and the Latin word "penna", from which the English "pen" is derived, means "a feather". They were also commonly used to make shuttlecocks, and, added to the shaft of an arrow, they permitted excellent flight. The rest of body feathers, particularly those of the breast, made fine stuffing for mattresses, quilts or pillows.

Geese are always alert and are naturally aggressive birds, so it is not surprising that they were also kept to guard property from intruders. Their eyesight is excellent and their hearing

acute, they are brave and defiant, and give out loud alarm calls. A group of geese saved Rome from an attack by the Gauls in 390 BC by alerting the garrison, and thus began the tradition of the sacred geese of the Capitol, one of the most respected emblems of ancient Rome. Even now, geese are often used to alert human guards of the presence of intruders. In Russia, aggressive geese were specially bred and selected for fighting between males, in which the birds had to use the bill and wings to draw blood from their opponents. This often resulted in the death of one of the birds, and such competitions were banned during the last century. Hungry goslings have also been used, even commercially, to free planted fields from fast growing weeds. The birds do so without damaging the commercial crops, as they find the green parts of these plants distasteful.

The Mallard is the direct ancestor of almost all the current breeds of domestic duck. These are numerous and have quite different characteristics, according to the main purpose for which they were selected. The Indian Runner, for example, has an unmistakable upright stance, due to the great development of its genital organs. This bird is an excellent layer, with the added quality that the female seldom becomes broody, so her production of eggs is not halted; thus fertilized eggs must be incubated artificially. The breeds specially developed for their meat tend to be bulkier and white all over, since white birds gain weight more quickly and can become heavier than dark birds, while these in turn lay eggs more regularly and for longer than white birds. Some breeds have intermediate characteristics and thus serve both purposes, whereas others have been developed for particular functions, like "Crested Ducks", which are beautifully feathered and purely ornamental, or "Call Ducks", which were bred small, noisy and white for use as decoys.

The remaining group of domestic wildfowl are all derived from the originally dark Muscovy Duck, from which several colour varieties but no recognised breeds have been obtained. It is a common bird in South America, where it is often kept in houses to control insects. This species shows noticeable sexual dimorphism, and the male, which puts on weight rapidly, is often used for food, whilst the female is generally a good layer, with a fairly long season. Muscovies are sometimes crossed with domestic ducks, and the resulting infertile hybrids, known as Mulards, are often crammed to produce foie gras, or used directly for food; their breast fillets are very popular in France, where they are served smoked or dried, as "magrets".

Not all forms of management of wildfowl for human interests require complete domestication of the bird. The semi-domesticated Mute Swan has been farmed and its stocks managed for centuries in many parts of Europe, but principally in Britain. Young cygnets were counted, pinioned and marked with their owner's special design on their bills in a special ceremony known as "swan-upping" that still survives. Nowadays the purpose of "swan-upping" is only to mark the birds, but in former times, some of the year's young were kept in captivity and fattened up to be eaten at Christmas or at wedding receptions. Owning swans was a privilege of the rich, and any unmarked swan was declared to be the property of the Crown.

The down of Common Eider ducks is the best insulating material known, as it combines its unparallelled capacity of temperature maintenace with a remarkable lightness and elasticity. Female eiders line their nests with their own breast feathers and, once the ducklings have hatched and departed for the sea, they do not use the nests again during that season, so the tradition of collecting the down after the whole brood have left the nest probably originated spontaneously. Later it was realized that the birds could be encouraged to breed near human habitation, where they form loose colonies, by keeping the area free from predators that might disturb the sitting females. Special devices have been designed, including small flags that flutter in the wind or metal objects that produce a whistle as the air passes through them, and these keep gulls away from the nests. Nowadays, the down is gathered twice during the season, soon after the start of incubation, which forces the female to replace the lining, and after the nest has been abandoned. Its commercial value is less important at present than it used to be, but the market price of eider down is still high and its trade continues to be the main or a secondary source of income in many places.

Wildfowl are common prey species for many predators including man. Particularly in the winter, when they gather in large flocks at suitable sites, man has traditionally caught, shot and killed them, first out of necessity, as they are rather large,

plump birds with tasty meat, and later for sport. In the early days, before guns came into widespread use, it was necessary to approach the confiding ducks, geese or swans at night, from under the water or on camouflaged boats, and the birds were snatched directly, netted or caught using sticks or in South America "bolas". They were also killed by hawking, or caught with baited fish hooks or birdlime. Evidently, wildfowling was already an important activity before the advent of shotguns.

Perhaps the most sophisticated device for catching ducks is the "decoy", in its original sense, developed in the Netherlands during the sixteenth century. It consists of a small pond,

preferably secluded in woodland, from which radiated one to eight "pipes", or lateral, curved, tapering extensions of the pool that were covered by netting. The operating principle of decoys was the natural attraction that some mammals, particularly foxes and dogs, cause among wildfowl, which swim towards the intruder in order to mob it. So, with the aid of a trained dog and some "call ducks", which helped by making the pool more attractive to overflying wild birds, it was possible to drive large numbers of ducks and other wildfowl through a pipe into its narrow end, which was closed and there the ducks were trapped and killed.

The use of decoys was fairly widespread in the Netherlands, Britain, parts of central Europe and in Asia until early in the present century. Long-term exploitation was apparently worthwhile, for it was not unusual for a good decoy, particularly in the Netherlands, to catch over 10,000 ducks, mostly juveniles, in a year. The destination of such birds was the market, and the growing demand for food in cities kept prices high. The use of decoys for killing ducks has now become more or less obsolete, but they are sometimes used as a trapping method by ringers. Decoys are probably not as efficient for ringing as they were for killing ducks, as the captured birds which are released apparently learn something of the method and are less likely to react in the same way to a dog again. Nevertheless, a few decoys are currently in use for ringing purposes, and have given reasonable results. The shooting of ducks, geese and, to a lesser extent, swans is still a major hobby in many areas, particularly where large flocks commonly congregate during the winter or migration (see Status and Conservation).

The breeding dress of the males of many species of wildfowl is amongst the most splendid of all birds. They are easily kept in captivity, and the common practice of pinioning one or both of the wings forces them to stay put on the same stretch of water, where they still have a more "natural" look than most other captive birds. It is therefore not surprising that they have been ideal objects of collectors, since antiquity, from China to Egypt. Wildfowl collections became particularly popular in Western Europe during the eighteenth and nineteenth centuries, especially the latter, and in the first decades of the present century, as more and more exotic birds could be obtained with the advances made in the field of transport and communications.

Some collections were extraordinary, containing birds that had become extremely rare in their original range; the last Pink-headed Ducks, for example, lived in captivity in England until 1936, when they had already become extinct in their original homeland in India. The most important collection nowadays is that of the Wildfowl and Wetlands Trust at Slimbridge in England. Founded by Sir Peter Scott during the 1940's, it now holds over 7000 birds at its various centres, representing the vast majority of living species and distinctive races of wildfowl. The importance of this collection is not only its size and genetic richness, but also the fact that it contributes to the welfare of endangered populations through a series of programmes of reintroduction. The Hawaiian Goose, or Nene, was saved from seemingly inevitable extinction by the reintroduction of captive-bred birds, in which the participation of the Wildfowl Trust was significant. Similarly, other threatened species are bred in captivity and their young released into the wild, such as the White-winged Wood Duck (*Cairina scutulata*), the Aleutian race *leucopareia* of the Canada Goose (*Branta canadensis*), the Brown Teal of New Zealand and some nearby islands and the White-headed Duck (*Oxyura leucocephala*). The degree of integration of such captive-bred individuals in the environment and with their surviving conspecifics seems to be reasonably good, and reintroduction may be the only solution for several of the currently threatened species, as long as it is combined with sensible habitat management and programmes to increase local awareness.

This splendid photograph of Barnacle Geese in flight gives an idea of the flying power of most of the Anatidae, which is fairly surprising in such large, heavy species. In areas with well defined seasons, many species perform important migrations to reach breeding, moulting or wintering grounds. The migrations of geese are particularly regular, sticking closely to fairly precise routes and dates. Adopting a characteristic V-formation, they often fly at high altitudes, sometimes over 8000 m, so they may be able to take advantage of jet stream.

[*Branta leucopsis*. Photo: John Downet/ Planet Earth]

The total population of the Hawaiian Goose was probably about 25,000 birds around the time that the first Europeans reached the archipelago. Predation on the species started with the introduction of dogs, pigs, cats and rats, but the major population crash began after the arrival of mongooses. In 1950, there were only 34 birds, including around 17 in captivity; this grave situation led to the protection of the wild population and the initiation of a programme of captive breeding and reintroduction. At present, about 350 birds remain in the wild, with populations increasing only where predator control is effective.

[*Branta sandvicensis*, Maui, Hawaii. Photo: Stephen J. Krasemann/NHPA]

The Cape Barren Goose is frequently found in coastal habitats. It is essentially a grazer, and in the past it was accused of causing a good deal of damage to grasslands, with the result that it was indiscriminately persecuted by farmers. Nowadays, its population may be recovering, in part due to the availability of suitable new habitats provided by agriculture.

[*Cereopsis novaehollandiae*, Mondrain Island, Western Australia. Photo: Patrick Baker/ Bruce Coleman]

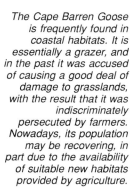

However, aviculture is also answerable for some rather unfortunate occurrences, as illustrated by the case of a few Ruddy Ducks that were taken from North America to Slimbridge from 1948 onwards. They were provided with suitable habitat and started to breed in the following season. The amazingly aquatic young took to water immediately after hatching, and catching them to clip their wings was soon a problem. Eventually, a few managed to escape the curator's efforts to catch them and became free flying, when they fledged. During the following years, they were seen in surrounding areas, but during the hard winter of 1962/63 they dispersed into neighbouring counties where they eventually established themselves and started to breed. By January 1989, the population had swollen to an estimated 2700 birds, with expansion as far as Scotland and Ireland, while birds now turn up regularly on mainland Europe, where breeding first occurred in France in 1988. The Ruddy Duck is a distinctive species that seems to be occupying a more or less vacant niche, so it competes little with the indigenous fauna, except perhaps for food with the Tufted Duck, and for nest-sites with grebes. Nevertheless, if the expansion of this species continues, it could well reach the few remaining areas frequented by its threatened relative the White-headed Duck, and contact between the two might lead to the extinction of the native species, either through direct displacement or through hybridization. Indeed, contact between the two is already occurring in southern Spain.

There are numerous cases of introductions of wildfowl, mostly affecting Western Europe, primarily Britain, North America, Australia and New Zealand. In many cases, the birds were obviously first taken to the new land for ornamental reasons, for instance the Mandarin Duck, which has established feral populations in Britain and California, the American Wood Duck in Britain, and the Mute Swan in parts of Europe, North America, South Africa, Australia and New Zealand. The Black Swan was introduced to New Zealand partly in an attempt to clear the rivers of watercress, which had in turn been brought in from abroad. There are probably well over 100,000 Black Swans in New Zealand at present, and their commercial exploitation on Lake Ellesmere, through shooting and egg-collecting, is of significant economic value. Another successful species, with flourishing populations that originated

from escapes, is the Canada Goose, which now breeds abundantly in parts of Western Europe, particularly Britain and Sweden, and also in New Zealand. The Egyptian Goose too has had free-flying populations in Britain for the last two centuries, and in the Netherlands since 1967. Their success, however, has been much less marked and there are at present only a few hundred individuals, which are not thriving as much as other alien wildfowl.

Introductions could yet prove to have value in the conservation of certain species, for instance the Mandarin Duck. Although unknown at the time of its importation into Britain during the eighteenth century, there is evidence suggesting that the species once lived in Western Europe as a wild bird, probably during the

The Freckled Duck is a very strange species that is difficult to classify. It is generally uncommon, and has suffered greatly from the destruction and modification of freshwater wetlands, as well as flood mitigation works, as it is adapted to an opportunistic way of life depending on changing conditions in different areas. During droughts, it usually concentrates in the southern parts of Australia, where hunting pressure is particularly high. Some measures have already been taken to reduce the amount of poaching to which this species has been subjected.

[*Stictonetta naevosa,* Australia. Photo: Joe B. Blossom/ Survival]

Middle Pleistocene. The Mandarin's preferred habitat of lakes and rivers surrounded by dense broad-leaved woodland was probably widespread in Britain at that time, and it is that kind of environment that it inhabits nowadays, perhaps occupying an ecological niche that it once left vacant. The importance of this situation is that the feral population in Britain was estimated in 1988 at some 1000 breeding pairs, or about 7000 individuals, a significant proportion of the total surviving world population. Indeed, the prospects of the Mandarin in Asia do not seem very optimistic, after a serious decline has reduced numbers in China to under 1000 pairs, with a further 600 pairs in the USSR. Only Japan has higher numbers, with an estimated population of around 5000 pairs. With the present rate of deforestation in the Far East, further declines are to be expected, and the British population may be the only one that remains healthy.

The large flocks that wildfowl tend to form during the winter have frequently brought the birds into conflict with human interests. Large flocks of wintering geese and swans descend on agricultural land where food is plentiful, and they can cause extensive crop damage, for instance to potatoes, which they unearth in large quantities, turnips, carrots and the like; they also plunder fields of winter wheat and barley. Since wintering geese and swans have adopted this habit only recently, no wholly efficient scaring methods have yet been developed. In contrast, down the west coast of Scotland a major problem involves geese feeding on winter grazing land, and this is certainly not a new habit. In places farmers are being reimbursed for their losses, a practice which could usefully be extended to other cases involving conflicts of birds with human interests.

On the other hand, it is sometimes claimed that some wildfowl species cause local damage to fish stocks on rivers or lakes. Sawbills have historically been persecuted on their breeding grounds for this reason, and the clash continues today. Although sawbills are protected throughout most of their breeding range, significant numbers are still killed, some by poachers but some also under legally issued licences, particularly at fish farms. Eiders also come into conflict with man's interests, as they feed on mussels that are farmed along the coast. At some such farms where Common Eiders are so abundant that they may cause significant damage, special shooting licences have been issued.

Status and Conservation

Although five species and three subspecies of wildfowl are reckoned to have become extinct in modern times and some 16 extant species are currently considered to be threatened on a global scale, the status of the Anatidae in general is a good deal more satisfactory than that of many other families of sizeable birds. This is particularly encouraging given the high levels of exploitation that wildfowl have traditionally suffered, and indicates that effective protection might be achieved with simpler measures than those required for many other birds. Many species have thriving populations of millions and occur on a great number of sites in different geographical regions.

The White-winged Wood Duck is a species which frequents well forested waters. Widespread during last century, it has probably declined by more than 95%, mostly through large-scale destruction of lowland tropical forests and due to hunting. As the current situation does not seem to be changing, a captive breeding programme will probably be necessary, and some captive-bred birds have already been released. However, the most urgent requirement is the effective protection of large patches of tropical forest.

[*Cairina scutulata.* Photo: J. A. Bailey/Ardea]

The Chatham Swan (*Cygnus sumnerensis*) probably became extinct between 1590 and 1690, long before the islands were inhabited by white men, and it seems to have been mostly due to excessive hunting by the previous colonizers, the Maoris. The extinction of this species left a vacant ecological niche that has been most successfully exploited by the introduced Black Swan (see Relationship with Man).

The Labrador Duck was probably never very abundant. Its peculiar bill indicates that it must have had a highly specialized diet, perhaps consisting of molluscs, that may have been obtained by dabbling, or by diving in the manner of other sea ducks. The bird was shot and commonly sold in markets but the small numbers involved are not thought to have been sufficient by themselves to have caused the extinction of the species. The reasons for this would perhaps have to be investigated at the bird's undiscovered breeding grounds, which may have been on a few islands, and these could have been invaded by a mammalian predator or visited regularly by bird fowlers or egg-collectors. The last individual recorded with certainty was shot at sea in autumn 1875 off Long Island, New York.

The Auckland Merganser was last recorded in 1902. Fossil evidence suggests that it was once widespread around New Zealand and that it may have occupied South Island. It was a specialized fish eater that inhabited large streams and areas of brackish water. It may have suffered from shooting to some degree, but its definitive demise was almost certainly brought about due to predation by alien mammals, including pigs, cats and rats, that were introduced to the main Auckland Island. A very small population might have survived on nearby Adams Island, which is free from predators, but the habitat is mostly unsuitable and there are no recent indications of the species surviving there, despite several searches specifically for the species.

The Pink-headed Duck is almost certainly extinct. The last definite sighting of the bird in the wild was in 1935, although there have been subsequent, inconclusive reports that suggest it might still survive in remote country somewhere around northern Burma, India and Tibet. Very small numbers were kept in captivity in England and France and probably in Calcutta, but they never managed to breed and the last one died in France in 1944. The species is said never to have been numerous, and the ultimate causes of its extinction are probably related to habitat destruction and excessive hunting, from which the population never managed to recover.

It is not clear whether the Crested Shelduck (*Tadorna cristata*) is extinct or still survives in very small numbers. For many years it was thought that the last individual had been caught in December 1916 in Korea. But there were sightings in March 1943 (2 individuals), May 1964 (one male and 2 females) and March 1971 (2 males and 4 females). The absence of further records for almost two decades, during which there were extensive searches was taken by some as a sign of their definitive extinction, but hope was renewed by the reports that the species is thought to survive at a site in Yunnan Province in south-west China, where some may have been seen by environmental officials in December 1990. More intensive surveys are required, but the lack of ornithological work throughout its presumed range suggests that the species may still survive in small numbers, and it is thought to occur occasionally in winter along the coasts of China, Korea and Japan.

The Madagascar Pochard (*Aythya innotata*) is classified as Endangered and is apparently very close to extinction. Its former range was Lake Alaotra in the northern central plateau of Madagascar, and perhaps some adjacent lakes and pools. Until recently, the last record was in 1970, despite many searches in subsequent years. Its dramatic decline started in the 1930's, due largely to the transformation of the lakesides into rice fields, with large-scale destruction of the stands of papyrus, and also to excessive hunting; even today the species is not legally protected. The introduction to the lake of several exotic fish

This photo shows the entire known population of the Madagascar Pochard in 1992, the last pair being recorded in 1970. No birds were sighted during a Wildfowl and Wetlands Trust survey in 1989, although drawings and questionnaires were distributed among the local people. In 1991, a fisherman snagged this drake in his net, and took it along live to Antananarivo; nowadays it lives in the Botanical Gardens. Meanwhile, the lake is suffering with the conversion of some parts into rice paddies, the effects of introduced fish and extensive silting up as a result of deforestation. The last hope for the species lies in an exhaustive search for more individuals, along with a major reduction in the threats to its habitat.

[Aythya innotata, Antananarivo Botanical Garden, Madagascar. Photo: Lucienne Wilmé]

inches   8
cm   20

Both the Crested Shelduck (Tadorna cristata), *left*, and the Pink-headed Duck (Rhodonessa caryophyllacea), *right*, were treated as Extinct in the last complete edition of the Red Data Book. Unconfirmed reports are occasionally made of both these birds, suggesting that they might still survive in remote areas; this seems more probable in the case of the former than of the latter. For more information on the Crested Shelduck see: Nowak (1983, 1984a, 1984b), O Myong Sok (1984), Rank (1991), Yuan Hai-ying (1984); and for the Pink-headed Duck: Ali (1960), Humphrey & Ripley (1962), Prestwich (1974).

[Figure: Àngels Jutglar]

species, including the black bass (*Micropterus*), and the increase in gill-netting amongst the growing human population around the lake, are other factors partly responsible for the decline. Indeed, it was a male caught in a gill-net that represented the rediscovery of the species in 1991. Somewhat less critical at present is the state of the Madagascar Teal (*Anas bernieri*), listed as Vulnerable, which is suffering from heavy persecution.

Several globally threatened species breed in poorly known parts of northern Asia, including the Lesser White-fronted Goose (*Anser erythropus*), the Baikal Teal, Baer's Pochard (*Aythya baeri*) and the Scaly-sided Merganser (*Mergus squamatus*). Scant information is often a problem and, while the White-winged Wood Duck continues to be sighted in very small numbers over a wide range, the West Indian Whistling-duck (*Dendrocygna arborea*), which was formerly considered Vulnerable, has now been upstaged to Rare, due partly to a recovery and partly to the discovery of a sizeable population. The Ruddy-headed Goose (*Chloephaga rubidiceps*) was similarly considered Vulnerable, due perhaps to loss of habitat and predation in southern South America and intense persecution in the Falkland Islands, but it has now been removed from the Red List, as its numbers in the Falklands are healthy and appear to be able to sustain the current levels of persecution, to the extent that it is still considered a major agricultural pest.

Like other waterbirds, wildfowl throughout the world are dependant on the success of wetland conservation. This is perfectly illustrated in the Western Palearctic by comparing the situation between north-western Europe and the Mediterranean area in the last few decades. While most of the major wetlands in north-western Europe have been preserved, protected and improved, and many new areas created, through the flooding of gravel pits, the construction of barrages, and so on, the drainage of wetlands and transformation of coastal sites around the Mediterranean have caused severe reductions in the already impoverished populations of some of its most characteristic species, such as the Ruddy Shelduck, the Marbled Teal, the Ferruginous Duck (*Aythya nyroca*) and the White-headed Duck, while other, more widespread species have also declined significantly in the area, including the Mallard and the Common and Red-crested Pochards.

Britain probably has the best system of protected wetlands in Europe, and the populations of the 20 or so wildfowl species that breed there in significant numbers have all either remained stable or increased in the last few decades, with substantial upward trends in at least 12 cases, the only exception being the Garganey, which is still in a long-term decline, mainly due to the loss of damp meadows and grasslands, its preferred breeding habitat.

Large-scale drainage of wetlands has affected, and is still affecting, nearly all regions of the world. As agricultural methods become more efficient, the demand for more land leads to the desiccation of such "wasted" ground as marshes and lagoons. In the past, marshland was generally classed as unhealthy and merely a focus for disease, particularly those, like malaria, that are transmitted by mosquitoes. The result was that hundreds of thousands of hectares were lost before the present century, mainly in Europe and North America, but also in Australia and Asia. Fortunately, the indiscriminate destruction of wetlands in Europe and North America was slowed up, and has been partially balanced by an increased interest in nature conservation and the restoration of some habitats. In Asia, as well as in Africa and South America, the destruction still continues, and there is widespread international concern that the same mistakes made in Europe and North America should not be repeated.

Pioneering efforts in the conservation of wetlands resulted in the establishment of the first national wildlife refuges in North America at the turn of the present century, while in Britain the first nature reserves were established by the RSPB during the early 1930's. Since these beginnings, many more wetland areas have been protected, both with public and private backing, mostly in the developed countries.

As the concern for wildlife conservation kept growing, it was soon realized that, birds being migratory, there was little use in trying to preserve and increase the population of certain species in one country when they could be killed in large numbers in another, so international co-operation was essential. The International Council for Bird Preservation (ICBP) was founded in 1922, and the International Union for the Conservation of Nature (IUCN) in 1948. A meeting was held in Iran in January 1971, under the auspices of the International Waterfowl and Wetlands Research Bureau (IWRB), and this resulted in the momentous Ramsar Convention on Wetlands of International Importance especially as Waterfowl Habitat.

Hunting is one of the main problems facing wildfowl conservation, and the annual toll of ducks, geese and, to a lesser extent, swans is considerable. In North America, for example, where wildfowl shooting is widespread, some 3 million registered hunters have been taking about 20 million birds, including over 2 million geese, annually during the last two decades. In Europe the "bag" is also huge, with more than 11 million wildfowl known to be shot each year, of which some 200,000 are geese. These figures are estimates for the late 1970's, but are considered highly representative of the true scale of hunting pressure on these populations. There are no estimates for other parts of the world, but the limited information available indicates that wildfowl are regarded as quarry species almost everywhere, and that certain species are bound to be undergoing severe hunting pressure in places. The annual kill on a global scale must be well in excess of 100 million birds.

Wildfowl have proved to be highly resilient in the face of intense hunting pressure, but some form of control is essential, so that a sufficient number of sexually mature birds survives to breed in the following season and replace those that have been shot. The most widespread method of control involves the enforcement of a close season embracing the breeding cycle, during which it is illegal to shoot wildfowl. In many areas it is legally possible to hunt only on certain days and there are often "bag" limits, which stipulate the maximum number of birds a hunter may kill in one day. Another possibility is to establish a "harvest quota" at the beginning of the open season, by which the season ends automatically as soon as a certain number of birds have been killed, or on a definite date, if the allowance has not been reached. Finally, there are systems that provide more protection for the females, and hence for the population as a whole, like the "points system", which rates each species and sex with a certain number of points and allows hunters to kill birds up to a given points total, but this sophisticated system requires genuine goodwill on the part of all the hunters and is difficult to operate successfully where there is not complete surveillance and wholehearted co-operation. Hunting regulations have become stricter in many parts of Eu-

rope, and this, together with the protection of the most sensitive areas, has presumably reduced the mortality due to shooting, but in North America, where many wetlands are also protected, hunting regulations are less strict and are locally and temporarily extremely variable.

Wildfowl hunting carries with it associated drawbacks that are responsible for equally significant mortality, and these are all the more deplorable for they serve nobody. One is the fact that not all the birds hit are fatally wounded; many suffer the impact of the pellets, but survive, crippled, for several days, weeks or months. It has been estimated that in North America 20-35% of the surviving birds at the end of a shooting season are crippled to some degree. Such birds are not usually included in the statistics of birds shot, though they almost inevitably die as a result of their wounds and so should be taken into account when quotas are being fixed. In recoveries of traditionally hunted species, such as the Mallard or the common goose species, lead pellets were found in the tissues of over 40% of the individuals recovered dead after colliding with an obstacle or starving in very cold weather, which had presumably been living normally up to their deaths. Perhaps more surprisingly, some 15-25% of legally protected species, such as Bewick's or Whooper Swans, were also carrying lead pellets.

Another associated problem is that the material shot at the birds is in the form of lead pellets. Lead is a mineral that, in significant quantities, becomes highly poisonous. After many years of intense hunting activity in the same area, the lead pellets accumulate at the bottom of the water. There they may remain unaltered for years, until a goose, duck or swan mistakenly swallows them, taking them for grit. Once in the bird's gizzard, the piece of lead takes part in the process of food grinding, but being much softer than grit it soon erodes. It is absorbed fairly slowly, but is released at an exceptionally slow rate, so it accumulates there, particularly in the vital organs and the bone marrow. Once the dose reaches a certain level, the bird starts to lose weight, appearing much less active, and it eventually becomes incapable of flying; highly contaminated birds suffer muscle paralysis and eventually die. It is estimated that as many as 10% of all wildfowl that use a heavily shot over area may die each year from lead poisoning. A single pellet is sufficient to cause the death of a

The Brown Teal has two flightless subspecies, one of which is very rare, with an estimated population of 30-50 birds on an islet off Campbell Island. Forms that are restricted to single small islands are permanently at risk, and tend to succumb rapidly to the effects of introduced predators, such as cats and pigs, or those of habitat modification by cattle and rabbits. This species breeds well in captivity, and there is a considerable captive stock, but the problem is that no predator-free islands can be found for their release.

[Anas aucklandica aucklandica, Auckland Islands. Photo: Eric & David Hosking]

Formerly more common, Baer's Pochard still has a fairly wide range, but numbers have decreased considerably. Its decline is attributed to wetland drainage and increased disturbance. The current situation of Baer's Pochard, along with four other Asian wildfowl species, is clear evidence of the dangerous mismanagement of resources currently affecting much of the continent.

[*Aythya baeri*.
Photo: Joe B. Blossom/
Survival]

medium-sized bird, while two or three will kill a Mute Swan, and in some areas, for example the Camargue, in southern France, lead was found in the gizzards of over 60% of the birds analysed. Birds that feed on grain are the most severely affected, presumably because they consume larger quantities of grit and are thus more at risk.

Not all the lead ingested by wildfowl comes from shotgun pellets, and in places it is mostly made up of the lead weights used and often lost or discarded by anglers. On the River Avon in England, where this problem was first detected, 85% of the Mute Swan population disappeared in a few years for this reason. The banning of lead weights in 1987 has already produced a partial recovery of English populations, and a much lower incidence of lead poisoning as the cause of death.

Several alternatives to lead have been proposed, but they have not been readily accepted either by hunters or by anglers, because lead apparently has its advantages. Some attempts are being made to ban the use of lead completely, not only for the sake of the birds, but also in view of the possible effects of lead poisoning on humans. In 1991 the use of lead for the hunting of wildfowl was prohibited in North America, where it was estimated that 1·6-2·4 million birds may have died of this single cause in 1987. It is to be hoped that equally prohibitive measures will soon be adopted by the European Community and other countries, whether or not lead poisoning has yet been detected.

There are other ways in which man increases wildfowl mortality. Large, heavy birds like swans and the larger geese suffer significant losses due to collisions with man-made artefacts, particularly power lines. Although the effects are most obvious in heavily industrialized zones, they are also significant in many of the less developed areas, and a large remote stretch of open moorland with power lines running across it can prove a lethal trap for birds, though the results are unlikely to be evident. With their high wing-loading and comparatively large bodies, wildfowl have little manoeuvrability in the air, and especially in adverse weather conditions, for instance in fog, strong winds or heavy rain, they may hit overhead wires and die either electrocuted or from the injuries produced by the impact. A study carried out in Britain in 1987 showed that in the Mute Swan, perhaps the species with the highest risk, collisions with power lines ranked second only to lead poisoning as a cause of mortality.

Several species of wildfowl spend part of their lives at sea or in coastal environments and would thus be heavily at risk of becoming oiled in the event of a major spill, especially if it were to coincide with their autumn moult, when they become

flightless and thus unable to fly away to safety. In March 1989, the oil tanker Exxon Valdez ran aground in Prince William Sound, Alaska, spilling 260,000 barrels of crude oil into the sea, the largest spill ever in the Arctic. The oil drifted some 750 km down the coast, eventually affecting more than 30,000 km² of coastal and offshore waters, in an area used by about a million seabirds. The total kill was estimated at 100,000-300,000 birds, including masses of auks, substantial numbers of eiders, scoters and Long-tailed Ducks, and a significant proportion of the local population of Harlequin Ducks. While the scientists monitoring this disaster were loath to exaggerate its magnitude, they reckoned that some populations would take 20-70 years to recover. The risk of oil pollution is considerable in many areas, and in a detailed analysis of birds found dead along the coasts of Britain, almost 27% of the Common Eiders and over 50% of the Black Scoters located were contaminated with oil. Some birds may have become oiled after death from some other cause, but in some areas like the North Sea, with perhaps over a million sea ducks at certain times of year and important oil fields, it is evident that the risk is greater.

The use of pesticides in agriculture is another cause of fatality for some wildfowl, especially when the chemical product is contained in the seed dressings that granivorous species may eat during the winter. There have been several incidents in developed countries, resulting in the death of several hundred birds and normally the product being withdrawn from the market to avert a major catastrophe, but health control is less strict in most developing countries, where there is also much less interest in nature conservation. In the tropics and subtropics, particularly where the dry season is severe, many wildfowl die

This is one of the very few photos known of the rare Brazilian Merganser. An inhabitant of mountain rivers, this bird is Endangered due to the modification of its fragile habitat. There are some populations in protected areas, but all consist of only small numbers.

[*Mergus octosetaceus*.
Photo: Mark Pearman/
ICBP]

A reduction in the amount of suitable habitat and excessive hunting at wintering grounds, have caused continuous declines of the White-headed Duck in Turkey, USSR and Pakistan, the strongholds of the species. There has recently been a certain increase in the western population; in Spain, numbers declined from 400 in 1950 to 22 in 1977, but the species was then protected and it increased up to 545 birds in 1991. Note the highly specialized bill and the raised, stiff tail, which is the origin of the vernacular name of the genus Oxyura.

[*Oxyura leucocephala*, Laguna del Rincón, Córdoba, Spain. Photo: Francisco Márquez]

each year as a result of contamination with chemical products dissolved in the water. These are normally found at levels that are relatively harmless to the birds while there is plenty of water, but as the water level drops, the concentration of chemicals increases. This problem is particularly acute in some areas because it tends to occur just at the moment when the birds are flightless and thus unable to move to other, healthier areas.

In similar conditions, avian botulism can kill millions of wildfowl, such as the outbreak of type C botulism in the western USA in 1952, which killed 4-5 million wildfowl. The disease is caused by the anaerobic bacterium *Clostridium botulinum*, which produces a toxin that infects the birds. The bacteria multiply profusely in residual water with decaying vegetation and dead animals, typically fish or other birds; the carcasses become maggot ridden, and the birds tend to consume both maggots and fish in large quantities, thus ingesting the toxin. A single wildfowl carcass can produce thousands of maggots, while the ingestion of two to four toxic maggots can be enough to intoxicate a bird. Every summer many ducks, geese and swans become contaminated and inevitably die. The disease is being fought in some places where it has traditionally occurred, but it seems that only early detection can effectively prevent large-scale mortality; management recommendations include avoiding fluctuations of the water level in summer and prompt and suitable disposal of vertebrate carcasses.

The same scale of wildfowl mortality now occurs in the USA due to another bacterial disease, avian cholera. This highly infectious, potentially virulent disease is caused by the bacterium *Pasteurella multocida*, and in its most acute form can kill in a matter of a few hours. A vaccine has been produced and tested on Canada Geese, with success, but this obviously remains a solution that is only operable on a small scale, and again the efficient removal of infected carcasses is the main recommendation.

Despite all these negative factors, wildfowl have their future guaranteed as long as their habitats are preserved and, where possible, restored. The present rate of wetland drainage is the most urgent threat to their survival throughout the world. The "reclamation" of land for agricultural purposes, the destruction of coastal lagoons to improve the attractiveness of an area for tourists, and the use of lakes and rivers for recreational purposes are factors that reduce the abundance and diversity of wildfowl, so protection of all appropriate sites worldwide is essential.

General Bibliography

Atkinson-Willes (1972, 1975), Ball (1934), Barber (1934), Bookhout (1979), Bottjer (1983), Boyd & Pirot (1989), Brush (1976), Butler & Jones (1982), Cross (1989), Delacour (1954-1964), Delacour & Mayr (1945, 1946), Dobrowolski (1969), Earnest (1982), Eyton (1838), Feduccia (1976a, 1978), Gollop & Marshall (1954), Halchreuter (1990), Harrison (1958), Heinroth (1911), Hochbaum (1955), Holm & Scott (1954), Hoyt *et al.* (1979), Hyde (1974), Ingram & Salmon (1941), Ives (1947), Jacob & Glaser (1975), Johnsgard (1960b, 1960c, 1961d, 1961e, 1962, 1963, 1965a, 1968a, 1978, 1979), Johnsgard & Kear (1968), Kear (1964, 1970, 1986, 1990, 1991), Lack (1967, 1974), Kolbe (1979), Livezey (1986, 1991), Lorenz (1941, 1951-1953), Madge & Burn (1988), Madsen *et al.* (1988), Mallory & Weatherhead (1990), McKinney (1953, 1965c, 1975, 1985), McKinney *et al.* (1990), Murton & Kear (1978), Myers (1959), Nichols (1990a, 1991b), Nichols & Johnson (1989), Nichols *et al.* (1984), Novakova *et al.* (1987), Olson & Feduccia (1980b), Owen (1980), Owen & Black (1990a), Phillips (1922-1926), Rogers *et al.* (1979), Rohwer (1988), Rutgers & Norris (1970), Ruthven & Zimmerman (1968), Scott, D.A. (1982a, 1982b), Scott, P. (1972, 1985), Sibley & Monroe (1990), Soothill & Whitehead (1978), Sowls (1955), Swanson & Meyer (1973), Thomson (1931), Todd (1979), Toft *et al.* (1984), Tyler (1964), Verheyen (1955), Weller (1975a, 1988), Woolfenden (1961), Yamashina (1952).

ssp *autumnalis*

ssp *discolor*

PLATE 40

inches 10
cm 25

inches 18
cm 45

ssp *bewickii*

ssp *columbianus*

Subfamily ANSERANATINAE

Genus *ANSERANAS*   Lesson, 1828

1. Magpie Goose

Anseranas semipalmata

French: Canaroie semipalmé   **German**: Spaltfußgans   **Spanish**: Ganso Urraco
Other common names: Pied/Semipalmated Goose

Taxonomy. *Anas semipalmata* Latham, 1798, Hawkesbury River, New South Wales.
A primitive, aberrant goose, sometimes thought to be sufficiently distinct to be placed in its own family, Anseranatidae (see page 540). Monotypic.
Distribution. N Australia and S New Guinea. Reintroduced in Victoria, SE Australia, where formerly widespread.

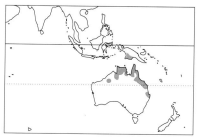

Descriptive notes. Male 75-90 cm, 2800 g, wingspan 130-180 cm; female 70-80 cm, 2000 g, wingspan 125-165 cm. Protuberance on head variable in size, but smaller in female. Uppertail-coverts and most of upperwing-coverts white. Juvenile greyer and more mottled.
Habitat. Swamps and grasslands in floodplains of tropical rivers, where great variations in water level commonly occur. Usually found not far from coast.
Food and Feeding. Almost entirely vegetarian diet, consisting mostly of blades of grass, seeds (Poaceae, Nymphaeaceae, Cyperaceae), bulbs and rhizomes; bulbs and rhizomes dug from ground using hooked bill; feeds also by grazing and mud-filtering; bends down tall grasses with aid of feet.
Breeding. Often polygamous, typically 1 male paired with 2 females. Starts at beginning of wet season, Feb-Apr in N, Aug-Sept in S. Forms fairly large colonies; nest is large floating mound of vegetation. Usually 5-11 eggs (1-16), laid by single female (average 8·6) or by both females in a trio (average 9·4); incubation 23-25 days; chicks have grey down, whiter below, with cinnamon head and neck; fledging c. 11 weeks. Sexual maturity at 2 years in females, 3-4 in males. Success can be markedly reduced by particularly severe dry seasons and by predators; 77% of nests at one locality completely or partly destroyed by predators.
Movements. Not truly migratory, but wanders extensively in relation to food and water availability. Occasionally reported outside normal range throughout much of Australia and even Tasmania, especially during dry season.
Status and Conservation. Not globally threatened. Nested abundantly in S and E Australia during 19th century, but has suffered substantial decline mostly due to habitat destruction and direct persecution by man. Now increasing both in natural conditions and through several rather unsuccessful reintroductions, e.g. in Victoria. Generally numerous, but subject to substantial fluctuations. Forms concentrations of up to 10,000 birds in wetlands of Irian Jaya (W New Guinea), where it is common to abundant. Partial census of Northern Territory in 1980 yielded 380,501 birds. Habit of visiting pastures and rice fields leads to its being hunted in farming areas. Legally hunted during open season in Northern Territory, but protected elsewhere, although may still be hunted in traditional way by aborigines. Breeding areas threatened by settlements, rice growing and uranium mining; also by draining or damming, and by water buffalos grazing or trampling vegetation and breaking down levees, allowing intrusion of salt water and also silting. Introduced *Mimosa pigra* forms dense shrubland unsuitable for breeding.
Bibliography. Bayliss (1989), Bayliss & Yeomans (1990), Beehler *et al.* (1986), Ciarpaglini (1983), Coates (1985), Davies (1962a, 1962b, 1963), Davies & Frith (1964), Dexter (1988), Frith (1961, 1967), Frith & Davies (1961b), Hoorgerwerf (1959, 1962), Johnsgard (1961a), Marchant & Higgins (1990), Roy (1988), Schodde & Tidemann (1988), Tulloch (1985), Tulloch *et al.* (1988), Whitehead & Tschirner (1990, 1991), Whitehead, Freeland & Tschirner (1990).

Subfamily ANSERINAE

Tribe DENDROCYGNINI

Genus *DENDROCYGNA*   Swainson, 1837

2. Spotted Whistling-duck

Dendrocygna guttata

French: Dendrocygne tacheté   **German**: Tüpfelpfeifgans   **Spanish**: Suirirí Moteado
Other common names: Spotted Tree Duck

Taxonomy. *Dendrocygna guttata* Schlegel, 1866, Celebes.
Superficially resembles *D. arborea*, but apparently linked most closely to *D. eytoni*. Monotypic.
Distribution. Mindanao (Philippines) and Sulawesi through Moluccas and Tanimbar (Lesser Sundas) to New Guinea and Bismarck Archipelago.
Descriptive notes. 43-50 cm; c. 800 g. Small white mark at base of lower mandible. Reminiscent of *D. arborea* though smaller and with blackish mask and grey face; round white marks on belly.

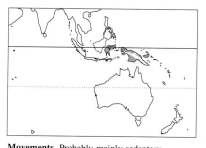

Juvenile duller, having white flank feathers broadly edged with black; irregular white streaks on sides.
Habitat. Margins of freshwater swamps, lakes, pools, marshes, creeks and rivers, surrounded by grasslands and scattered trees; only in lowlands.
Food and Feeding. Diet includes grass seeds and small snails. Food obtained by dabbling at water's edge, filtering surface and diving. Mainly nocturnal.
Breeding. Starts at beginning of wet season (Sept). Nests in hollow trees, generally standing in or near water. Normally c. 11 eggs; incubation c. 28-31 days; fledging c. 7 weeks.
Movements. Probably mainly sedentary.
Status and Conservation. Not globally threatened. Not usually found in large concentrations. Appears well represented within range, especially in parts of Indonesia, probably including Irian Jaya (W New Guinea), where is one of most common and widespread ducks. Recent partial censuses produced 116 in New Guinea, and 41 in Philippines.
Bibliography. Beehler *et al.* (1986), Coates (1985), Delacour (1954-1964), Dickinson *et al.* (1991), Johnstone (1960), Perennou & Mundkur (1991), Rand & Gilliard (1967), Weller (1980), White & Bruce (1986).

3. Plumed Whistling-duck

Dendrocygna eytoni

French: Dendrocygne d'Eyton   **German**: Gelbfuß-Pfeifgans   **Spanish**: Suirirí Australiano
Other common names: Plumed/Red-legged Tree Duck, Eyton's Whistling/Tree Duck, Grass Whistling Duck

Taxonomy. *Leptotarsis Eytoni* Eyton, 1838, northwestern Australia.
Hybridization with *D. bicolor* and *D. arborea* reported in captivity. Monotypic.
Distribution. N and E Australia.

Descriptive notes. 40-45 cm; 580-1400 g; wingspan 75-90 cm. Uppertail-coverts with dark marks. Only *Dendrocygna* with pale iris. Juveniles resemble adults but are paler with narrower and less distinct barring on sides.
Habitat. Typically associated with grassland, meadows and plains; also frequents edges of lagoons, pools and swamps.
Food and Feeding. Mostly plant matter, particularly grasses, herbs, sedges and seeds (*Fimbristylis*, *Echinochloa colona*). Feeds mainly on land at night.
Breeding. Starts at onset of wet season. Solitary; very simple nest on ground lined with soft vegetation, no down added (captivity). 8-14 eggs; incubation c. 28-30 days; chicks have yellowish buff and brown down, more or less streaked, especially on face.
Movements. Local movements depending on availability of water in different seasons: moves towards coast and larger lagoons in dry periods, and disperses more widely inland during wet season. Vagrant to Tasmania, New Guinea and New Zealand.
Status and Conservation. Not globally threatened. Generally widespread throughout range; has expanded breeding range in SE Australia. Agriculture and pastures have provided new feeding grounds, as species prefers short grass; construction of farm dams, sewage farms and reservoirs has allowed expansion, especially into semi-arid and arid zones. Often forms large concentrations at particularly favoured sites, e.g. 3000-5000 reported in area of Townsville (NE Queensland). Generates conflicts with farmers when feeds in rice fields, but does not usually attack mature crops unless they are of poor quality or neglected.
Bibliography. Beehler *et al.* (1986), Bell (1967), Bull *at al.* (1985), Falla *et al.* (1981), Frith (1967), Johnstone (1970), Kolbe (1979), Lack (1968), Marchant & Higgins (1990), Morton *et al.* (1990), Roy (1988), Schodde & Tidemann (1988).

4. Fulvous Whistling-duck

Dendrocygna bicolor

French: Dendrocygne fauve   **German**: Gelbbrust-Pfeifgans   **Spanish**: Suirirí Bicolor
Other common names: Fulvous Tree Duck, Large Whistling Teal

Taxonomy. *Anas bicolor* Vieillot, 1816, Paraguay.
Forms superspecies with *D. arcuata*. Hybridization with *D. arcuata* and *D. eytoni* reported in captivity. Population of S USA and N Mexico has been assigned separate race *helva*, but doubtfully valid. Monotypic.
Distribution. S USA southwards to N and E South America, as far as N Argentina; Africa S of Sahara from Senegal to Ethiopia S to South Africa and Madagascar; Indian Subcontinent E to Burma.
Descriptive notes. 45-53 cm; 621-755 g. Uppertail-coverts whitish. Female slightly duller and smaller. Larger than *D. arcuata*. Juvenile duller with uppertail-coverts tipped brown, paler underparts and little chestnut on upperwing.
Habitat. Various types of marshy habitats and swamps in open, flat terrain. Generally associated with good development of tall-grass vegetation. Particularly frequent in rice fields.
Food and Feeding. Almost entirely vegetarian, especially rice; also feeds on other seeds and fruits (*Nymphoides indica*, *Ambrosia maritima*, *Echinochloa stagnina*, *Nymphaea capensis*), grasses, bulbs and rushes, with minor quantities of animal food (only 1% dry weight in one study in Zambia). Forages by dabbling, with head immersed or upending; occasionally dives for food; mainly nocturnal.
Breeding. Season largely determined by water availability. In single pairs or loose groups; nest is mound of plant material amidst vegetation, or rarely hollow in tree, with or without down lining.

On following pages: 5. Wandering Whistling-duck (*Dendrocygna arcuata*); 6. Lesser Whistling-duck (*Dendrocygna javanica*); 7. White-faced Whistling-duck (*Dendrocygna viduata*); 8. West Indian Whistling-duck (*Dendrocygna arborea*); 9. Black-bellied Whistling-duck (*Dendrocygna autumnalis*); 10. White-backed Duck (*Thalassornis leuconotos*); 11. Mute Swan (*Cygnus olor*); 12. Black Swan (*Cygnus atratus*); 13. Black-necked Swan (*Cygnus melanocorypha*); 14. Trumpeter Swan (*Cygnus buccinator*); 15. Whooper Swan (*Cygnus cygnus*); 16. Tundra Swan (*Cygnus columbianus*); 17. Coscoroba Swan (*Coscoroba coscoroba*).

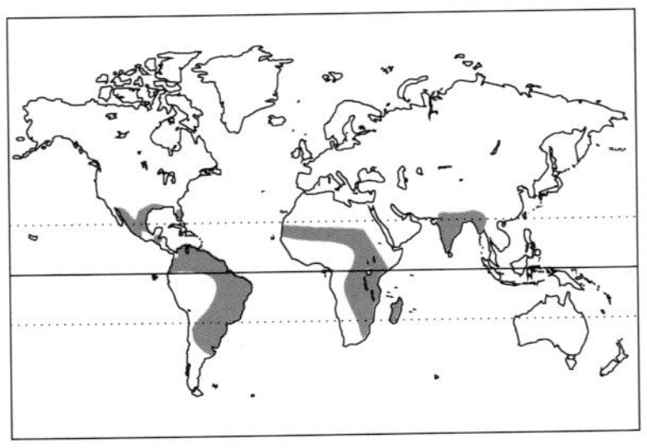

Generally c. 10 eggs (6-16); incubation c. 24-28 days; chicks have grey down, whitish below; fledging c. 63 days. Sexual maturity at 1 year.
Movements. Mostly sedentary but subject to seasonal movements according to availability of water and food. Has wandered N to SW Canada, NE USA, Hawaii, Morocco, Spain, S France and Nepal; Indian birds have occurred S to Sri Lanka.
Status and Conservation. Not globally threatened. Very widespread but rather local, concentrating in large numbers on suitable wetlands: 10,000 birds in January 1987 at Hail Haor, Bangladesh; 2820 at Lagunas de Topolobampo, Mexico. Counts of up to 1000 birds are not exceptional in S America. In Africa, population of Sahel estimated at c. 100,000 birds; up to 2300 counted on L Turkana, Kenya, in 1987; record of c. 12,000 birds at L Chuali, Mozambique. In Madagascar generally rare, but still locally common; has declined due to hunting pressure. Regularly hunted in many rice growing areas; particularly exposed to pesticides contained in dressings for rice seed. CITES III in Ghana and Honduras.
Bibliography. Acosta *et al.* (1988, 1989a, 1989b), Ali & Ripley (1978), Bellrose (1976), Belton (1984), Biaggi (1983), Bolen (1973), Bolen & Rylander (1973, 1983), Brickell (1988), Brown *et al.* (1982), Carp (1991), Clancey (1967), Clark, A. (1974a, 1976, 1978a), Dallmeier (1991), Dollinger (1988), Douthwaite (1977), Evans, P.G.H. (1990), Fjeldså & Krabbe (1990), Gómez & Mendoza (1981), Gómez-Dallmeier & Cringan (1989), Gooders & Boyer (1986), Johnsgard (1975), Johnson (1965), Langrand (1990), Mackworth-Praed & Grant (1957-1973), McCartney (1963), Meanley & Meanley (1958, 1959), Milon *et al.* (1973), Monroe (1968), Nores & Yzurieta (1980), Perennou (1991a, 1991b), de la Peña (1986), Pinto (1983), Roberts (1991), Rylander & Bolen (1970, 1974a, 1974b, 1980), Scott & Carbonell (1986), Siegfried (1973a), Smythies (1986), Stiles & Skutch (1989), Turnbull *et al.* (1989).

5. Wandering Whistling-duck

Dendrocygna arcuata

French: Dendrocygne à lunules **German**: Wanderpfeifgans **Spanish**: Suirirí Capirotado
Other common names: Wandering Tree Duck, Water/Diving Whistling Duck, Water Whistle Duck

Taxonomy. *Anas arcuata* Horsfield, 1824, Java.
Forms a superspecies with *D. bicolor*, with which it shows many similarities in morphology and behaviour, and hybridization has occurred. Three subspecies recognized.
Subspecies and Distribution.
D. a. arcuata (Horsfield, 1824) - Philippines, S Borneo, Sulawesi, Java, Lesser Sundas and Moluccas.
D. a. australis Reichenbach, 1850 - N Australia and S New Guinea.
D. a. pygmaea Mayr, 1945 - New Britain.
Birds of N New Guinea intermediate between *arcuata* and *australis*.

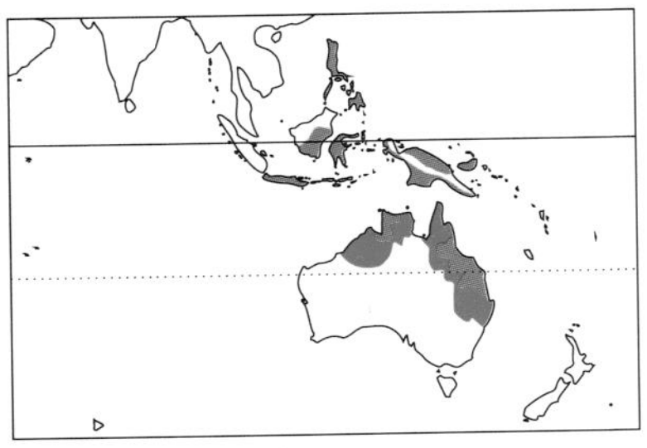

Descriptive notes. 40-45 cm; 453-986 g; wingspan 80-90 cm. Lateral undertail-coverts whitish. Black dots on sides of breast. Similar to *D. bicolor* but with more contrasting pattern on head and neck. Juvenile has less reddish underparts, little chestnut on upperwing and lacks broad pale edges to back feathers. Subspecies vary in size; *australis* slightly larger and *pygmaea* smaller.
Habitat. Eminently aquatic, frequenting bodies of relatively deep water with emerging vegetation, showing preference for lakes, lagoons, rivers, etc., where water is permanent.
Food and Feeding. Almost entirely vegetarian, mostly water-lilies (*Nymphaea*), sedges and other aquatic plants and grasses. Obtains most of food by diving; also on surface, by dabbling and pecking at plants.
Breeding. Starts at beginning of wet season. In single pairs; nest built with plant matter on ground, frequently among vegetation and away from water. 6-15 eggs; incubation c. 28-30 days; chicks have dark grey down, whitish below and streaked face; fledging c. 12-13 weeks. In one study broods reduced in size by 66% from average 10·7 after hatching to average 4·6 at flapper stage.
Movements. Dispersive; movements largely determined by variations in water level; concentrated in permanent waters during dry season, disperses widely in wet season.
Status and Conservation. Not globally threatened. Has decreased markedly in several areas. Nominate race particularly numerous in Philippines, where counts of 300 common in suitable wetlands, and up to 700 recorded at La Laguna Marsh; also common in Indonesia. Race *australis* widely distributed in New Guinea, where locally common, and also has large numbers in Australia: concentrations of as many as 40,000 reported in Northern Territory during 1960's. Race *pygmaea* still survives precariously in New Britain, but has almost certainly disappeared from Fiji. In Australia, favoured wetlands on floodplains of Northern Territory suffer salt-intrusion and accumulation of silt where feral water buffalos break down levees; floodplain systems may be threatened by agricultural, pastoral or urban development.
Bibliography. Beehler *et al.* (1986), Bolen & Rylander (1983), Coates (1985), Dickinson *et al.* (1991), Frith (1967), Marchant & Higgins (1990), van Marle & Voous (1988), Morton *et al.* (1990), Perennou & Mundkur (1991), Roy (1988), Schodde & Tidemann (1988), Weller (1980), White & Bruce (1986).

6. Lesser Whistling-duck

Dendrocygna javanica

French: Dendrocygne siffleur **German**: Javapfeifgans **Spanish**: Suirirí de Java
Other common names: Lesser/Javan Tree Duck, Indian/Javan Whistling Duck, Lesser Whistling Teal

Taxonomy. *Anas Javanica* Horsfield, 1821, Java.
Apparently most closely linked to *D. arcuata*. Monotypic.
Distribution. Pakistan, India and Sri Lanka E to SE China and Taiwan, and S through Indochina to Borneo, Sumatra and Java.
Descriptive notes. 38-40 cm; 450-600 g. Smallest of the whistling-ducks. Fairly uniform plumage; chestnut uppertail-coverts; inconspicuous yellow eye-ring. Juvenile duller.
Habitat. Generally found on small bodies of shallow water with abundant marshy vegetation and surrounded by trees, used for roosting.

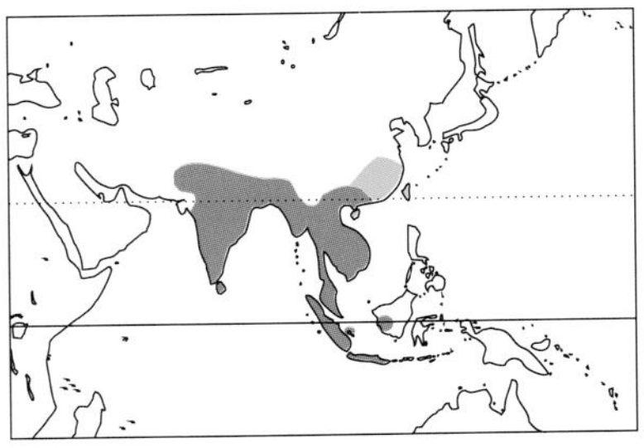

Food and Feeding. Mostly grasses, rice, seeds and shoots of water weeds (*Lymnophyla heterophyla*), but, in contrast with other whistling-ducks, complemented with small molluscs, particularly freshwater snails.
Breeding. Season determined by extent of rains, but tends to coincide with start of rainy period. Often in loose colonies; nests in trees, either in hollows or on disused nests of raptors or herons, also on ground. 7-12 eggs; incubation c. 26-30 days.
Movements. Mostly sedentary, except for northernmost Chinese population, which vacates breeding areas in winter. Resident birds in other zones may be subject to local movements related to water availability.
Status and Conservation. Not globally threatened. Abundant in much of range. Concentrations of thousands are common in India, where census in 1990 yielded 37,857 birds; equally common in Nepal, Bangladesh, Burma and especially Thailand, where estimated 50,000-100,000 winter on southern central plains. Numbers in India and Bangladesh indicate that species is 10 times as numerous as *D. bicolor*. Present in low numbers in Japan until end of 19th century; extinction probably came about as result of overhunting, which continues on some small islands in present range. Hunted in some places due to conflicts with rice growing.
Bibliography. Ali (1979), Ali & Ripley (1978), Brazil (1991), Delacour (1954-1964), Etchécopar & Hüe (1978), Inskipp & Inskipp (1985), Lekagul & Round (1991), van Marle & Voous (1988), Medway & Wells (1976), Perennou & Mundkur (1991), Qian Guo-zhen & Zhou Hai-zhong (1980), Roberts (1991), de Schauensee (1984), Smythies (1986).

7. White-faced Whistling-duck

Dendrocygna viduata

French: Dendrocygne veuf **German**: Witwenpfeifgans **Spanish**: Suirirí Cariblanco
Other common names: White-faced Tree Duck

Taxonomy. *Anas viduata* Linnaeus, 1766, Cartagena, Colombia.
A distinctive species, apparently most closely linked to *D. autumnalis*. Monotypic.
Distribution. Tropical America from Costa Rica S to N Argentina and Uruguay; Africa S of Sahara from Senegal to Ethiopia and S to South Africa; Madagascar and Comoro Is.

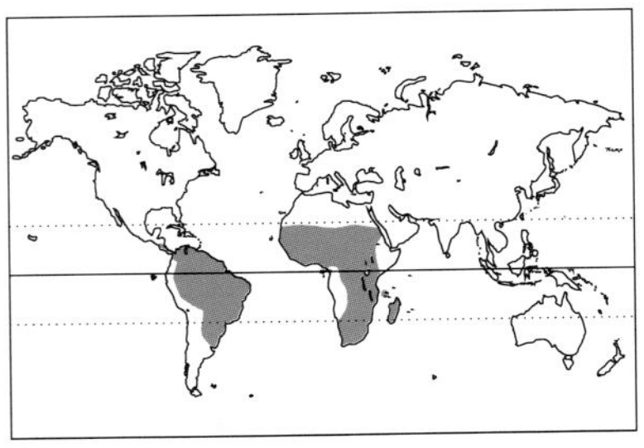

Descriptive notes. 38-48 cm; 502-820 g. Dorsal and scapular feathers longer than in other *Dendrocygna*. Juveniles have greyish buffy-white or ash-grey face, throat and underbody; breast less extensively and vividly chestnut.
Habitat. Wide variety of wetlands, including some artificial ones, and showing preference for fresh water in open country. Sometimes occurs in tiny water bodies.
Food and Feeding. More varied than in other whistling-ducks, consisting of vegetable matter (grass, seeds, rice) and also aquatic invertebrates (molluscs, crustaceans, insects); 92% dry weight of crop contents was *Ambrosia maritima*, *Nymphoides indica* and *Nymphaea* seeds and *Echinochloa stagnina* fruits, in one study in Transvaal, South Africa. Mainly a night forager, obtains food mostly by diving; also on surface, by wading and dabbling.
Breeding. Starts at beginning of rainy season. In loose colonies or small groups; nests made using surrounding vegetation with no down or only traces; on ground, in long grass or among reedbeds. 4-13 eggs; incubation 26-28 days; chicks have dark brown down above, yellow below; fledging c. 8 weeks.
Movements. Often subject to local movements caused by variations in availability of water, generally of only a few hundred kilometres at most. However, has occurred N to Spain and on several islands in the Caribbean Sea.
Status and Conservation. Not globally threatened. Fairly abundant, particularly in Africa, where may have benefited from protection of extensive areas. Most abundant of Afrotropical ducks in W Africa, where 200,000 birds recorded in Jan 1987 census. In Madagascar is commonest duck along with *Anas erythrorhyncha*. Concentrations of over 1000 are rare in Argentina; up to tens of thousands at Salto Grande Reservoir, Uruguay; 15,000 in Hato Masaguaral, Venezuela; common to very common in Brazil, Bolivia and parts of Colombia. CITES III in Ghana.
Bibliography. Belton (1984), Brickell (1988), Brown *et al.* (1982), Carp (1991), Clancey (1967), Clark, A. (1974a, 1976, 1978a), Dallmeier (1991), Dollinger (1988), Douthwaite (1977), Elgood (1982), Fjeldså & Krabbe (1990), Gómez (1979), Gómez & Rylander (1982), Gómez-Dallmeier & Cringan (1989), Hellmayr & Conover (1948), Hilty & Brown (1986), Jones, M.A. (1978), Langrand (1990), Mackworth-Praed & Grant (1957-1973), Maclean (1985), Madriz (1982), Milon *et al.* (1973), Nores & Yzurieta (1980), Perennou (1991a, 1991b), de la Peña (1986), Pinto (1983), Ridgely & Gwynne (1989), Ruschi (1979), de Schauensee & Phelps (1978), Scott & Carbonell (1986), Sick (1984), Siegfried (1973a), Slud (1964), Treca (1981b), Wetmore (1965).

8. West Indian Whistling-duck

Dendrocygna arborea

French: Dendrocygne à bec noir **German**: Kubapfeifgans **Spanish**: Suirirí Yaguaza
Other common names: West Indian/Cuban/Black-billed Tree Duck, Black-billed/Cuban Whistling-duck

Taxonomy. *Anas arborea* Linnaeus, 1758, America = Jamaica.
Despite its quite different plumage pattern, perhaps most closely related to *D. viduata*. Hybridization in captivity with *D. eytoni* recorded. Monotypic.
Distribution. Bahamas, Greater Antilles and N Lesser Antilles to Martinique.
Descriptive notes. 48-58 cm; c. 1150 g. Black and white ventral speckling becomes more streaky on flanks. Juvenile duller with less distinct spotting.
Habitat. Occurs mostly in swamps and marshes surrounded by abundant tree cover, particularly mangroves.
Food and Feeding. Primarily fruit (especially of royal palm, *Roystonia*), berries, seeds and grain, irregularly complemented with small amounts of animal food. Obtained basically at night, on ground or perching in trees; not known to dive.

Breeding. Season variable according to locality. Forms loose groups; nests in trees or on ground. 6-12 eggs; incubation c. 30 days. **Movements**. Resident, with only minor local movements recorded. Has occurred N to Bermuda. **Status and Conservation**. RARE. CITES II. Population widely scattered, occurring in small groups; in process of major decline. During 1970's bulk of population reckoned to be in Hispaniola and Cuba; at former, species was not protected and has since declined; at latter, now protected but has also declined greatly in wetlands of Jíbaro, where was common in rice fields, but in 1974 suffered due to programme designed to "control" ducks which damaged rice fields, although hunters actually caused more damage than ducks. In Bahamas, small but apparently secure populations on Andros and Great Inagua, with 10's of birds. One of most numerous populations is in Caiman Is, where more than 400 nested in 1986, with flocks of up to 32 birds, but species is still hunted illegally here. In Jamaica last refuge at Black River Lower Morass. Perhaps minor recovery in Puerto Rico, especially in *Pterocarpus* forest at Lagunas de Humacao, but still very rare. Population of Barbuda probably large. In Greater Antilles, swamps have been extensively drained.

Bibliography. Allen (1962), Biaggi (1983), Bolen (1979), Bolen & Rylander (1973), Bond (1956, 1971), Collar & Andrew (1988), Dollinger (1988), Evans, P.G.H. (1990), Gooders & Boyer (1986), King (1978/79), Lewis & Renton (1989), Mountfort (1988), Phillips (1922-1926), Scott & Carbonell (1986), Stockton (1978), Vincent (1966), Weller (1980).

9. Black-bellied Whistling-duck

Dendrocygna autumnalis

French: Dendrocygne à bec rouge **German**: Rotschnabel-Pfeifgans **Spanish**: Suirirí Piquirrojo
Other common names: Black-bellied/Red-billed Tree Duck, Red-billed Whistling-duck

Taxonomy. *Anas autumnalis* Linnaeus, 1758, America.
Origin of type specimen unclear, leading to confusion over correct allocation of nominate subspecies; northern race alternatively labelled *fulgens*.
Subspecies and Distribution.
D. a. autumnalis (Linnaeus, 1758) - SE Texas to C Panama.
D. a. discolor P.L. Sclater & Salvin, 1873 - E Panama to South America, S to Ecuador in the W and N Argentina in the E.

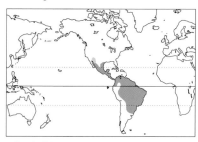

Descriptive notes. 43-53 cm; 650-1020 g. Unmistakable. Race *discolor* has grey lower neck and breast but intermediate individuals occur. Juvenile duller, having greyish-white belly with cross-barring; bare parts dusky or greyer. **Habitat**. Favours tropical lagoons with some tree cover on margins. Often found in vicinity of agricultural land.
Food and Feeding. Eminently vegetarian, basically grass and seeds (grain); small invertebrates (molluscs, insects) also sometimes taken. Feeds mainly on ground by grazing or by wading and dabbling in shallow waters.
Breeding. Season variable according to locality; in S USA starts in Apr. In loose groups; nest usually in tree cavity, occasionally on ground, without material or sometimes with dead grasses woven into shallow bowls. 12-16 eggs; incubation 26-31 days; downy chick is strongly patterned, but mostly black above and yellow below; fledging 53-63 days. Sexual maturity at 1 year. In one study in USA 44% of natural nests hatched; similar success in nestboxes, but 77% in those protected against predators.
Movements. Partially migratory. Northernmost breeding areas deserted in winter, which birds presumably spend in Central America. Otherwise mainly sedentary, but some local movements certainly occur. Regularly reported from West Indies; has occurred N to California.
Status and Conservation. Not globally threatened. Widespread and common. Recent spread over S USA probably favoured by increasing number of small pools provided for cattle to drink at. Large numbers, frequently over 2000 birds, occur in suitable environments. Impressive census results in Mexico, with 47,000 birds nesting at Usumacinta Delta and Tabasco Lagoons. In Costa Rica, 20,000 recorded at Palo Verde National Park and adjacent fauna refuge. Up to 10,000-20,000 birds reported from parts of Venezuela. Like most *Dendrocygna*, not considered important quarry species, but persecuted where concentrates in large numbers and damages crops. CITES III in Honduras.

Bibliography. Allen (1962), Bellrose (1976), Biaggi (1983), Bolen (1967, 1971), Bolen & Forsyth (1967), Bolen & Rylander (1973, 1983), Bolen *et al.* (1964), Cain (1970), Dallmeier (1991), Delnicki (1973), Delnicki & Bolen (1976), Fjeldså & Krabbe (1990), Gómez-Dallmeier & Cringan (1989), Hellmayr & Conover (1948), Hersloff *et al.* (1974), Hilty & Brown (1986), Johnsgard (1975), Markum & Baldassarre (1989b), McCamant & Bolen (1979), Monroe (1968), de la Peña (1986), Ridgely & Gwynne (1989), Ruschi (1979), Rylander & Bolen (1970, 1974a, 1974b, 1980), Schaldach (1963), de Schauensee & Phelps (1978), Scott & Carbonell (1986), Sick (1984), Slud (1964), Wetmore (1965).

Genus *THALASSORNIS* Eyton, 1838

10. White-backed Duck

Thalassornis leuconotos

French: Erismature à dos blanc **German**: Weißrücken-Pfeifgans **Spanish**: Pato Dorsiblanco

Taxonomy. *Thalassornis leuconotus* Eyton, 1838, Cape of Good Hope.
A distinctive species placed in its own genus, it was formerly considered to be closer to stifftails (tribe Oxyurini), but is now usually regarded as an atypical whistling-duck and included in tribe

Dendrocygnini. Some isolate it in its own tribe (Thalassornini) or even subfamily (Thalassorninae). Two subspecies recognized.
Subspecies and Distribution.
T. l. leuconotus Eyton, 1838 - Senegal to Chad; Ethiopia to South Africa.
T. l. insularis Richmond, 1897 - Madagascar.

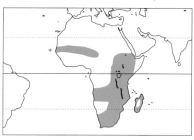

Descriptive notes. 38-40 cm; 625-790 g. Black rump and uppertail-coverts with narrow white barring; mid-back black. Juvenile darker, less distinctively patterned with black spotted sides of face and neck. Race *insularis* is smaller and more vividly marked.
Habitat. Favours a variety of quiet freshwater lakes, pools, lagoons, marshes and swamps with shallow waters and abundant floating vegetation. Not usually found in open waters.
Food and Feeding. Eminently vegetarian, principally seeds and leaves of aquatic plants, especially water-lilies. Young feed mainly on insect larvae (Chironomidae) and *Polygonum* seeds. Virtually all food obtained by diving in shallow waters.
Breeding. Season variable according to locality, generally coincides with period of higher and more stable water levels. In single pairs or loose groups; nest built with weeds, usually lined with fine vegetable matter, rarely with some down or feathers, hidden amidst reedbeds or on small islands of vegetation, often with a ramp leading to water. 4-10 eggs; incubation 29-36 days; downy chicks have olivaceous buff upperparts, with blackish grey underparts and crown; fledging c. 16 weeks.
Movements. Mostly sedentary, with some local movements largely related to availability of water. Seldom flies during day.
Status and Conservation. Not globally threatened. Still locally common, but has declined in parts of range. Difficult to census as fairly solitary, but apparently very scarce; W African population, apparently isolated from other populations, may be near extinction. Census figures give 500 birds at L Nairasha, Kenya, and also at Kafue Flats, Zambia. In South Africa, frequent to uncommon, but presence and numbers unpredictable. Race *insularis* widespread throughout Madagascar except on High Plateau; formerly quite common, but now rather rare, and by 1989 thought to be extinct at L Aloatra; only fairly common now in marshes at Soalala; this decline attributed to trapping and hunting, although species reputed to make rather bad eating.

Bibliography. Benson & Benson (1975), Brickell (1988), Britton (1980), Brown & Britton (1980), Brown *et al.* (1982), Clancey (1967), Clark, A. (1969b, 1979), Delacour (1932), Elgood (1982), Elwell & McIlleron (1978), Johnsgard (1967), Kear (1967), Langrand (1990), Mackworth-Praed & Grant (1957-1973), Maclean (1985), Milon *et al.* (1973), Perennou (1991a, 1991b), Pinto (1983), Raikow (1971), Wintle (1981), Young (1991b).

Tribe ANSERINI

Genus *CYGNUS* Bechstein, 1803

11. Mute Swan

Cygnus olor

French: Cygne tuberculé **German**: Höckerschwan **Spanish**: Cisne Vulgar

Taxonomy. *Anas Olor* Gmelin, 1789, "Russia, Sibiria, Persico etiam littore maris Caspii".
Despite its all-white plumage, apparently linked more closely to Southern Hemisphere species (*C. atratus*, *C. melanocorypha*) than to northern swans. Hybridization with *C. atratus* recorded in captivity. Monotypic.
Distribution. British Is, C and N Europe E through C Asia to E China. Feral populations in North America, Japan, South Africa, SW Australia and New Zealand.

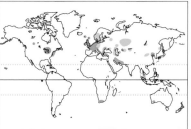

Descriptive notes. 125-160 cm; 6600-15000 g; wingspan 240 cm. Female averages smaller and has less prominent knob on bill. As in all white *Cygnus*, brownish staining on crown, cheeks and neck occurs. Juvenile can be white, but normally has variable amounts of brownish feathers and small knob on bill.
Habitat. Frequently found in a variety of lowland freshwater marshes, lagoons, rivers, etc.; also on estuaries and sheltered coastal sites. Has adapted to living close to man, now occupying many artificial water bodies, like park lakes, reservoirs, gravel pits, etc.
Food and Feeding. Primarily leafy parts of aquatic vegetation and grain; minor quantities of grasses, small amphibians and aquatic invertebrates (molluscs, insects, worms) are also taken; in one study in Sweden over 95% was submerged vegetation in spring and summer. Feeds mostly by dabbling on water surface and upending; seldom dives.
Breeding. During the local spring; generally in isolated pairs in well-defended territories; nest is large mound of vegetation, often floating on water or among reeds. Usually 5-7 eggs (3-12); incubation 35-36 days; chicks have grey down above, white below; fledging 120-150 days. Sexual maturity not until 3 years; annual survival rates of adults 79-94 % in England; oldest ringed bird over 21 years.
Movements. Truly wild populations mainly migratory, particularly where displaced by cold weather; spend winter in more temperate zones. European and feral populations mostly sedentary, males defending territory for most of year. Recorded as vagrant in Pakistan.
Status and Conservation. Not globally threatened. Range increasing due mainly to establishment of feral populations originating from birds introduced for ornamental purposes in urbanized areas. Total Palearctic population numbers c. 500,000 birds. British population stable, estimated at c. 19,000 birds in 1986; increasing in Europe and Asia, with c. 350,000 in USSR by end of breeding season in 1987. Feral populations: c. 200 birds in Japan; c. 20 in Australia; less than 200 in New

Zealand; 4000+ in N America, where noted to be increasing in 1970's; c. 120 in Cape Province, South Africa, in 1970. Lead poisoning due to ingestion of discarded anglers' fishing weights caused decline in British population until use of lead banned. Birds frequently killed or maimed after collisions with overhead wires.

Bibliography. Ali & Ripley (1978), Andersen-Harild (1978), Anon. (1981), Bacon (1980), Bacon & Andersen-Harild (1989), Bauer & Glutz von Blotzheim (1968), Bellrose (1976), Berglund *et al.* (1963), Birkhead (1982a, 1982b, 1983, 1984), Birkhead *et al.* (1983), Birkhead & Perrins (1985, 1986), Brazil (1991), Brickell (1988), Brown *et al.* (1982), Coleman & Minton (1979), Cramp & Simmons (1977), Czapulak & Wieloch (1988), Eltringham (1963a, 1963b, 1966), Etchécopar & Hüe (1978), Fair (1985), Géroudet (1972), Goodman (1989), Grimmett & Jones (1989), Harrison (1988), Huxley (1947), van Ijzendoorn (1951), Jenkins *et al.* (1976), Jogi *et al.* (1974), Kear (1988), Lever (1987), Lüps (1990), Maclean (1985), Marchant, J.H. *et al.* (1990), Marchant, S. & Higgins (1990), Mathiasson (1973), Matthews & Smart (1981), Minton (1971), Monval & Pirot (1989), Munro *et al.* (1968), Muraska & Valius (1968), Ogilvie (1967, 1981, 1986), Paz (1987), de Schneidauer (1961), Scott, D.K. (1984a, 1984b), Scott, D.K. & Birkhead (1983), Scott, P. & Wildfowl Trust (1972), Sears & Bacon (1991), Sokolowski (1960), Sonobe & Izawa (1987), Syroyechkovski (1987), Tenovuo (1976), Ticehurst (1957), Walter (1981), Wieloch (1984).

12. Black Swan

Cygnus atratus

French: Cygne noir **German**: Schwarzschwan **Spanish**: Cisne Negro

Taxonomy. *Anas atrata* Latham, 1790, lakes of Australia.

Sometimes placed in monospecific genus *Chenopis*. Apparently most closely related to *C. olor* and *C. melanocorypha*. Hybridization with *C. olor*, and several species of geese (*Anser*), has been reported in captivity. Monotypic.

Distribution. Australia and Tasmania; introduced and well established in New Zealand.

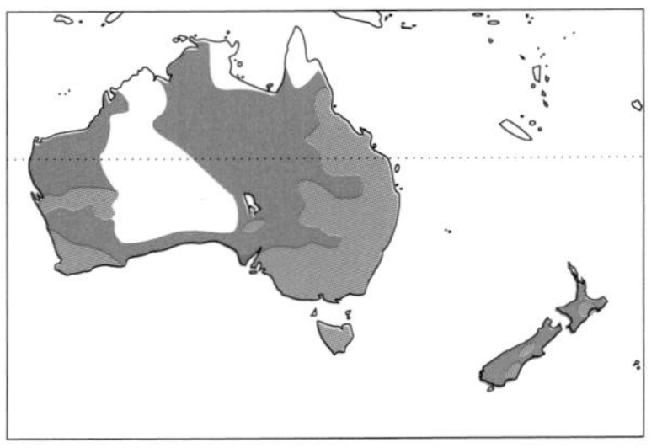

Descriptive notes. 110-140 cm; 3700-8750 g; wingspan 160-200 cm. Unmistakable. Alula, primaries and outer secondaries white, though normally hidden at rest; reddish or pinkish iris. Female averages smaller and has less bright bill and iris. Juvenile brown, mottled greyish with light-tipped feathers and paler bill.

Habitat. Favours large lakes or lagoons of relatively shallow, permanent and fresh or brackish waters. Also, outside the breeding season, on all sorts of water bodies, including rivers, billabongs and even coastal sites.

Food and Feeding. Almost entirely vegetarian diet, consisting of various aquatic plants (*Typha*, *Potamogeton*, *Myriophyllum*, *Ruppia*), algae and pondweeds. Food is obtained largely by dabbling on surface or by upending; also grazes in dry pasture or flooded fields.

Breeding. Season variable with locality, normally adapted to period of highest water levels. Forms colonies; nest is large mound of floating plant matter or on ground. 5-6 eggs (1-14), more than 8-9 usually laid by 2 females; incubation 35-48 days (usually 36-40); chicks have light grey down; fledging 150-170 days, but can be less when food is plentiful. Sexual maturity at 18-36 months. In one study, 75% of eggs hatched and 49% reached fledging.

Movements. Sedentary in permanent suitable habitat; young and adults from ephemeral waters wander extensively; erratic observations outside normal range frequent. Vagrant to New Guinea.

Status and Conservation. Not globally threatened. Widespread and locally very common in both Australia and New Zealand. May have spread to SW Australia during present century. Concentrations of thousands, and sometimes tens of thousands in New South Wales, at L Cowal, L Brewster and L George. Damage to crops has led to establishment of short hunting season in Victoria and Tasmania. Formerly more abundant in New Zealand until end of 1960's, after which sharp drop, partly due to devastation by storm in 1968; numbers have now recovered quite well, with estimates of 60,000 birds; some commercial exploitation of eggs and also hunting pressure; Chatham Is hold c. 3000 birds.

Bibliography. Braithwaite (1970, 1981, 1982), Bull *et al.* (1985), Chambers (1989), Falla *et al.* (1981), Frith (1967), Guiler (1966), Halse & Jaensch (1989), Lever (1987), Marchant & Higgins (1990), Matthews & Smart (1981), Miers & Williams (1969), Schodde & Tidemann (1988), Scott & Wildfowl Trust (1972), Williams, M.J. (1977, 1979a), Wilmore (1974).

13. Black-necked Swan

Cygnus melanocorypha

French: Cygne à cou noir **German**: Schwarzhalsschwan **Spanish**: Cisne Cuellinegro

Taxonomy. *Anas Melanocoripha* [sic] Molina, 1782, Chile.

Believed to form a complex of species with *C. olor* and *C. atratus*. Sometimes placed in monospecific genus *Sthenelides*. Monotypic.

Distribution. S South America from Tierra del Fuego and Falkland Is N to C Chile and Paraguay; in winter N to Paraná, SE Brazil.

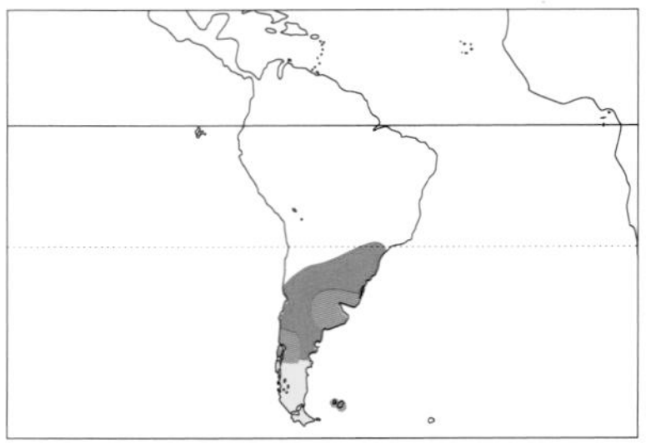

Descriptive notes. 102-124 cm; 3500-6700 g. Unmistakable. Variable white stripe behind eye. Female slightly smaller. Juvenile lacks knob and has varying amounts of greyish- and brownish-tipped feathers.

Habitat. Swamps, freshwater marshes, lagoons of brackish water, shallow lakes and sheltered coastal sites.

Food and Feeding. Eminently vegetarian, mainly stoneworts (*Chara*) and pondweeds (*Potamogeton*); also algae and presumably some aquatic insects and other aquatic invertebrates and fish spawn.

Breeding. Starts in early spring (Jul-Aug). In single pairs or loose groups; nest is large mound of vegetation, in reedbeds or partially floating, preferably on small islets. 4-8 eggs; incubation c. 36 days; chicks have greyish white down; fledging c. 100 days.

Movements. Falkland and northern populations relatively sedentary, but those from higher latitudes descend to lower ones in winter, occurring as far N as Tropic of Capricorn.

Status and Conservation. Not globally threatened. CITES II. Generally common and widespread; has recolonized parts of Chile where had been eradicated by hunting. Largest concentration on record of 5000 birds at Laguna de Chascomús, Argentina. Estimated populations: Brazil, 2000-3000 birds; Uruguay, 20,000; Argentina, 50,000; and Chile, 20,000. Uncommon breeding resident in Falkland Is, with concentrations of c. 100 in most favourable spots. Drainage of marshy areas is main threat; is not a typical quarry species.

Bibliography. Belton (1984), Carp (1991), Dollinger (1988), Fjeldså & Krabbe (1990), Hellmayr & Conover (1948), Humphrey *et al.* (1970), Johnson (1965), Nores & Yzurieta (1980), de la Peña (1986), Ruschi (1979), Salazar (1988), Scott & Carbonell (1986), Scott & Wildfowl Trust (1972), Sears & Bacon (1991), Sick (1984), Weller (1975d), Wilmore (1974), Woods (1988).

14. Trumpeter Swan

Cygnus buccinator

French: Cygne trompette **German**: Trompeterschwan **Spanish**: Cisne Trompetero

Taxonomy. *Cygnus buccinator* Richardson, 1832, Hudson Bay.

Sometimes considered a subspecies of *C. cygnus*, with which it forms a superspecies. Sometimes placed in genus *Olor* with *C. cygnus* and *C. columbianus*. Monotypic.

Distribution. Breeds in Alaska and W Canada, wintering along coastal S Alaska, British Columbia and N USA; also several resident populations in several states of NW USA, mostly from reintroductions.

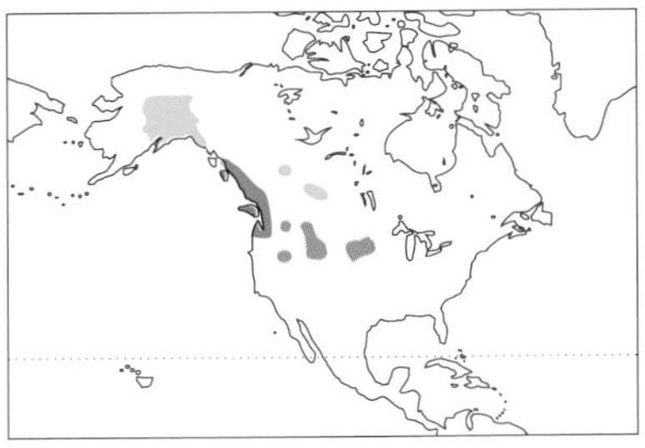

Descriptive notes. 150-180 cm; 7300-1250 g. Black bill larger than in *C. cygnus*. Female averages smaller. Juvenile has some grey feathers.

Habitat. Swamps, marshes and shallow lakes in boreal forest zone; part of the population winters in estuaries and on sheltered coasts.

Food and Feeding. Diet of adults is almost entirely vegetarian, consisting of leafy parts and stems of various aquatic plants (pondweeds, water-lilies, etc.); seeds and tubers (e.g. potato) are also important food. Cygnets feed mainly on aquatic invertebrates for first weeks.

Breeding. Starts Mar-Apr. In solitary pairs; nest built on the ground, with birds uprooting marsh plants surrounding site, preferably on muskrat houses, on islands or along shoreline. 4-8 eggs; incubation 33-37 days; chicks have pale grey down, whitish below; fledging 84-120 days, according to locality. Sexual maturity at 3-4 years; oldest ringed bird over 24 years, in captivity over 32 years.

Movements. US population mostly sedentary, undertaking only short local movements; Alaskan and Canadian birds fly to Pacific sea coast, where they spend the winter.

Status and Conservation. Not globally threatened. Total population estimated at c. 6000 birds in 1975; total with captive birds included, c. 11,000-12,000 birds. Largest population presumably that of Alaska, with 4500 birds in 1975; at least 2700 seen wintering on Vancouver I in 1989; 643 birds counted in Canada in 1985. Species on verge of extinction in early 20th century, with population of USA numbering only 69 birds in 1932; suffered intense shooting pressure, partly due to large-scale trade in swan skins and feathers; full legal protection and establishment of suitable reserves has allowed populations to recover, and still on increase at present; category in USA has passed from endangered to rare. Main cause of mortality amongst birds analysed in Minnesota was lead poisoning.

Bibliography. Anon. (1984a), Banko (1960), Bellrose (1976), Gale (1989), Gale *et al.* (1987), Hampton (1981), Hansen *et al.* (1971), Henson & Grant (1991), Hochbaum (1955), Hodges *et al.* (1986), Holton (1982), Lockman *et al.* (1987), Mackay (1987), Matthews & Smart (1981), McKelvey *et al.* (1988), Rohwer *et al.* (1989), Sears & Bacon (1991), Shea (1979), Vincent (1966).

15. Whooper Swan

Cygnus cygnus

French: Cygne chanteur **German**: Singschwan **Spanish**: Cisne Cantor

Taxonomy. *Anas Cygnus* Linnaeus, 1758, Sweden.

Forms superspecies with *C. buccinator*; this sometimes considered a subspecies of present species. Sometimes placed in genus *Olor* with *C. buccinator* and *C. columbianus*. Population of S Greenland and Iceland has been assigned separate subspecies *islandicus*, though doubtfully valid. Monotypic.

Distribution. Iceland and Scandinavia E to NE Siberia; winters in W and C Europe, around Baltic, North, Black, Caspian and Aral Seas, E to coastal China and Japan.

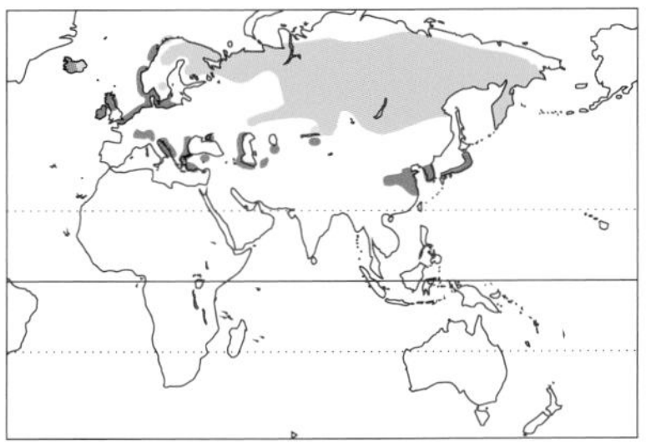

Descriptive notes. 140-165 cm; 7500-12,700 g. Female averages smaller. Juvenile shows greyish feathers and has pinkish rather than yellowish base to bill.

Habitat. Breeds in northern zones, on pools and lakes of shallow fresh waters, preferably in wooded country and only rarely in tundra; also on slow-flowing rivers and sheltered coasts. Winters mainly on low agricultural land, generally not far from coast.

Food and Feeding. Almost entirely vegetarian, mainly aquatic plants (*Zostera*, *Ruppia*, *Potamogeton*) and grass during the breeding season, complemented with grain, potatoes, acorns and other vegetable matter in winter. Forages on water, by head-dipping or upending, or on land.

Breeding. Starts late Apr-May. In solitary pairs in well-defended territories; nests on large mound of plant matter, mainly moss and lichens; 4-5 eggs (3-7); incubation c. 35 days; chicks have pale silvery grey down above, white below; fledging c. 87 days. Sexual maturity at c. 4 years; oldest wild bird over 8 years. Mean annual mortality after fledging c. 17 % in one study.

Movements. Migratory. Part of Icelandic population remains in winter. Migrates southwards to temperate areas, sporadically in more southern latitudes in cold winters; vagrant to USA and Pakistan.

Status and Conservation. Not globally threatened. Slight increase in overall numbers since early 1970's. In Finland, increasing 11% annually since 1950, with 5000 birds at end of 1980's. Apparently abundant in parts of Siberia. Significant concentrations of thousands of wintering birds in Japan, South Korea and Turkmenistan; c. 100,000 reckoned to winter throughout W Palearctic, perhaps 60% of global population. Some reductions or local extinctions, e.g. formerly bred in Greenland; declines caused by excessive hunting and also habitat destruction, especially in Asian part of breeding range.

Bibliography. Ali & Ripley (1978), Arvidsson (1987), Bauer & Glutz von Blotzheim (1968), Bellrose (1976), Black (1988), Blomgren (1974), Brazil (1981, 1991), Brazil & Kirk (1979), Brickell (1988), Brown *et al.* (1982), Cramp & Simmons (1977), Dementiev & Gladkov (1952), Etchécopar & Hüe (1978), Géroudet (1972), Goodman (1989), Grimmett & Jones (1989), Haapanen *et al.* (1973, 1977), Harrison (1988), Henry (1992), Matthews & Smart (1981), Monval & Pirot (1989), Paz (1987), Perennou & Mundkur (1991), Roberts (1991), de Schauensee (1984), de Schneidauer (1961), Scott & Wildfowl Trust (1972), Sears & Bacon (1991), Sonobe & Izawa (1987), Syroyechkovski (1987), Wilmore (1974).

16. **Tundra Swan**
Cygnus columbianus

French: Cygne siffleur　　　**German**: Zwergschwan　　　**Spanish**: Cisne Chico
Other common names: Whistling Swan (*columbianus*); Bewick's Swan (*bewickii*)

Taxonomy. *Anas Columbianus* Ord, 1815, The Dalles, Oregon.
Placed by some in genus *Olor* with *C. buccinator* and *C. cygnus*. Subspecies *bewickii* sometimes regarded as full species. Population of NE Asia has been assigned separate subspecies *jankowskii*, though doubtfully valid. Two subspecies recognized.
Subspecies and Distribution.
C. c. bewickii (Yarrell, 1830) - Kola Peninsula E throughout arctic N Siberia; winters in W Europe, S of Caspian Sea and E China, Korea and Japan.
C. c. columbianus (Ord, 1815) - tundra of Arctic North America; winters in W and coastal E USA.

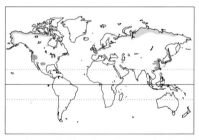

Descriptive notes. 120-150 cm, 4300-9600 g (nominate); 115-140 cm, 3400-7800 g (*bewickii*). Female slightly smaller. Juvenile has some grey feathers and a mostly pinkish bill. Race *bewickii* smaller, with far more yellow on base of bill; considerable variation between individuals in both races.
Habitat. Breeds on shallow pools, lakes and rivers of arctic tundra. Winters on marshes, grasslands or agricultural fields, often in coastal regions.
Food and Feeding. Mainly leaves, roots, rhizomes and stems of aquatic plants (*Potamogeton*, *Zostera*, *Glyceria*) and grasses, complemented with grain and potatoes in winter. Forages by head-dipping and upending in shallow water or by grazing on land. Feeds mostly by day where undisturbed.
Breeding. Starts late May-Jun. In single pairs; nest is large mound of plant matter on elevated ground. 3-5 eggs (2-6); incubation 29-30 (*bewickii*) or 30-32 days (*columbianus*); chicks have pale silvery grey down above, white below; fledging 40-45 (*bewickii*, but few records available) or 60-75 days (*columbianus*). Sexual maturity at 3-4 years; oldest wild bird over 20 years old. Mean annual mortality of birds over 3 years old c. 15 %; so average expectancy of a further c. 6·2 years of life.
Movements. Migratory; winters in temperate areas; sporadically in more southern latitudes during cold winters. Rare vagrant to Pakistan.
Status and Conservation. Not globally threatened. Sizeable populations remain of both races. Winter counts produced 169,300 individuals of nominate *columbianus*; commonest swan in N America, with E population increasing, but W population apparently declining. Race *bewickii* has recently increased in tundra of NE European sector of USSR. Census figures of c. 16,000-17,000 wintering in W Europe, and c. 20,000 wintering in Japan, China and Korea. Illegal hunting continues in NW Europe, and 44% of dead birds analysed contained lead shot; however, population

remains stable. In N America, hunting is the main cause of mortality, annually accounting for 4000 birds; next most important factor is lead poisoning; also 6000-10,000 deaths per year due to subsistence hunting and poaching. Possible race *jankowskii* included in CITES II.

Bibliography. Ali & Ripley (1978), Bauer & Glutz von Blotzheim (1968), Bellrose (1976), Black (1988), Brazil (1991), Brickell (1988), Brown *et al.* (1982), Cramp & Simmons (1977), Dementiev & Gladkov (1952), Dollinger (1988), Etchécopar & Hüe (1978), Evans (1978), Géroudet (1972), Harrison (1988), Higuchi *et al.* (1991), Matthews & Smart (1981), Mikami (1989), Miller *et al.* (1988), Monval & Pirot (1989), Paz (1987), Perennou & Mundkur (1991), Rees (1989), Roberts, T.J. (1989, 1991), de Schauensee (1984), de Schneidauer (1961), Scott, D.K. (1977, 1978a, 1978b, 1980, 1988), Scott, P. & Wildfowl Trust (1972), Sears & Bacon (1991), Syroyechkovski (1987), Wilmore (1974).

Genus *COSCOROBA*　　Reichenbach, 1853

17. **Coscoroba Swan**
Coscoroba coscoroba

French: Coscoroba blanc　　　**German**: Coscorobaschwan　　　**Spanish**: Cisne Coscoroba

Taxonomy. *Anas Coscoroba* Molina, 1782, Chile.
A distinctive species, to some extent intermediate between swans and geese, yet some authors consider it to be most closely related to whistling-ducks (Dendrocygnini). Monotypic.
Distribution. S South America from Tierra del Fuego N to C Chile and N Argentina; winters N to SE Brazil.

Descriptive notes. 90-115 cm; 3200-5400 g. Black tips to 6 external primaries. Breast feathers appear centrally parted. Female has brown iris. Juvenile similar to female, but brownish on head and upperparts; bill greyish.
Habitat. Favours lagoons and large freshwater swamps, preferably those with vegetated margins.
Food and Feeding. Apparently varied diet, consisting of plant matter, small aquatic invertebrates, fish spawn, etc. Forages mainly in shallow water, by swimming or wading, but also grazes on land.
Breeding. During local spring; Oct-Dec in Chile. Usually in single pairs; nest is large mound of aquatic vegetation lined with soft grasses and down situated on small islands, in reedbeds or in long grass, close to water. 4-7 eggs; incubation c. 35 days; downy chicks have three drab grey dorsal bands and black cap.
Movements. Southern breeders migrate to lower latitudes in winter, as far N as Tropic of Capricorn, but other populations mainly sedentary.
Status and Conservation. Not globally threatened. CITES II. Still widespread and quite common locally; decreasing in some areas, especially in Chile, where may now be restricted to extreme S, with total population reckoned at under 1000 birds in 1970's. Partial census of Jul 1990 gave 350 in Uruguay and 12,195 in Argentina. Large numbers occur N of Isla Grande (Tierra del Fuego), but is far less common than sympatric *Cygnus melanocorypha*. Greatest threat seems to be loss of temperate marsh habitats.

Bibliography. Belton (1984), Carp (1991), Dollinger (1988), Fjeldså & Krabbe (1990), Hellmayr & Conover (1948), Humphrey *et al.* (1970), Johnson (1965), Nores & Yzurieta (1980), de la Peña (1986), Ruschi (1979), Scott & Carbonell (1986), Scott & Wildfowl Trust (1972), Sick (1984), Weller (1975d), Wilmore (1974), Woods (1988).

PLATE 41

inches 14
cm 35

18

19

20

21 ssp *flavirostris*

ssp *albifrons*

ssp *anser*

ssp *rubrirostris*

22

23

24

25

blue phase

white phase

26

27

with stained head

28

ssp *leucopareia*

ssp *canadensis*

29

30

31

ssp *minima*

ssp *occidentalis*

ssp *bernicla*

ssp *hrota*

ssp *nigricans*

32

Genus *ANSER* Brisson, 1760

18. Swan Goose

Anser cygnoides

French: Oie cygnoïde   **German**: Schwanengans   **Spanish**: Ansar Cisnal
Other common names: Chinese Goose

Taxonomy. *Anas Cygnoid* Linnaeus, 1758, Asia.
Sometimes placed in monospecific genus *Cygnopsis*. Monotypic.
Distribution. NC Asia from SC Siberia to N China.

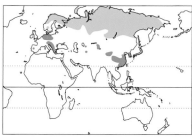

Descriptive notes. 81-94 cm; 2850-3500 g or more. Easily recognized by pattern and shape of head and bill. Female slightly smaller with shorter bill and neck. Juvenile lacks white band around bill and flank markings; upperparts dull greyish brown.
Habitat. Varied, generally in close association with water; also in mountain regions, steppes and floodplains. Breeds in reedbeds along rivers, on grassy hillocks in marshy meadows or on grassy plateaux. Winters in drier ground, often on barren steppes well away from water.
Food and Feeding. Almost exclusively vegetarian diet, partly consisting of sedges. Often grazes on dry land.
Breeding. Starts May. In loose groups or scattered pairs; builds shallow nest of plant matter on ground. Usually 5-6 eggs (5-8); incubation c. 28 days. Sexual maturity at 2-3 years.
Movements. Migratory, winters in E China, formerly also in Korea and Japan where now very rare. Vagrant to Taiwan and SE Siberia.
Status and Conservation. Not globally threatened. Currently considered near-threatened. Range has contracted and numbers have dropped during present century. Population of USSR reckoned to consist of no more than 300-400 pairs. Largest numbers include: 1000 birds in Ogii Nuur, NC Mongolia, in Jun/Jul 1977; 35,000 at Yancheng Marshes, EC China, in Jan 1988; and well over 50,000 recently recorded at Poyang Hu, EC China. Formerly up to 100 wintering in Japan, but continual decrease due to habitat loss culminating in extinction around 1950. Now irregular winter visitor to Japan in insignificant numbers. Severe hunting pressure and habitat destruction at breeding grounds have seriously affected W populations.
Bibliography. Anon. (1984a), Brazil (1991), Dementiev & Gladkov (1952), Etchécopar & Hüe (1978), Ferguson (1966), Flint *et al.* (1984), Perennou & Mundkur (1991), de Schauensee (1984), Sonobe & Izawa (1987), Uspenski (1965).

19. Bean Goose

Anser fabalis

French: Oie des moissons   **German**: Saatgans   **Spanish**: Ansar Campestre

Taxonomy. *Anas Fabalis* Latham, 1787, Great Britain.
Forms superspecies with *A. brachyrhynchus*, which has been considered race of present species. Five subspecies recognized.
Subspecies and Distribution.
A. f. fabalis (Latham, 1787) - taiga from Scandinavia E to Ural Mts.
A. f. johanseni Delacour, 1951 - taiga and wooded tundra from Ural Mts to L Baikal.
A. f. middendorffii Severtsov, 1873 - taiga of E Siberia, E of L Baikal.
A. f. rossicus Buturlin, 1933 - tundra of N Russia and NW Siberia, from Kanin to Taymyr Peninsulas.
A. f. serrirostris Swinhoe, 1871 - tundra of NE Siberia, from Lena Delta to Anadyrland.

Descriptive notes. 66-89 cm; 3171-3948 g; wingspan 142-175 cm. Juvenile as adult though duller and with less conspicuous light edging on mantle. Subspecies vary in colour and structure; two extremes are: *rossicus*, small, strong-billed with short neck and legs; *middendorffii*, large, with longer neck and legs and more slender bill.
Habitat. Breeds on lakes, pools and rivers in high Arctic or taiga zone, according to subspecies. Winters in open country, on marshes or agricultural land.
Food and Feeding. Mostly vegetarian; herbs, grasses and sedges; also berries during breeding season and grain (corn), beans and potatoes in winter. Generally forages on foot on dry land.
Breeding. Starts May/Jun. In single pairs or loose groups; builds shallow nest of vegetation, lined with down, in scrape in ground. Usually 4-6 eggs (3-8); incubation c. 27-29 days; chicks have olive-brown down above, yellowish below; fledging c. 40 days. Sexual maturity at 2-3 years.
Movements. Migratory, winters mostly on coastal plains in NW and Central Europe and E Asia. Sporadically in more southern latitudes during cold winters.
Status and Conservation. Not globally threatened. Widespread and numerous. Winter counts indicate 100,000-200,000 birds in Netherlands. Before 1946, c. 18,000 wintered in Japan, but species has declined markedly due to hunting and habitat loss, e.g. in Norway and Sweden; partial recovery began in 1971 after hunting banned, and at present winter population includes 3000+ of race *serrirostris* and 3000+ of race *middendorffii*. Up to 10,000+ counted in partial winter censuses in China and Korea.

Bibliography. Anon. (1986-1990), Bauer & Glutz von Blotzheim (1968), Boertmann (1991), Brazil (1991), Brickell (1988), Brown *et al.* (1982), Cramp & Simmons (1977), van Eerden (1990), Etchécopar & Hüe (1978), Géroudet (1972), Grimmett & Jones (1989), Harrison (1988), Kurechi (1991), Madsen (1991), Nilsson & Persson (1989a, 1989b), Owen (1976), Owen & Black (1991), Palacios *et al.* (1991), Perennou & Mundkur (1991), Persson (1989), de Schauensee (1984), de Schneidauer (1961), Scott & Fisher (1953).

20. Pink-footed Goose

Anser brachyrhynchus

French: Oie à bec court   **German**: Kurzschnabelgans   **Spanish**: Ansar Piquicorto
Other common names: Pink-footed Bean Goose

Taxonomy. *Anser Brachyrhynchus* Baillon, 1834, Abbeville, lower Somme River, France.
Sometimes considered race of *A. fabalis*, with which forms superspecies. Monotypic.
Distribution. E Greenland, Iceland, Svalbard (Spitzbergen).

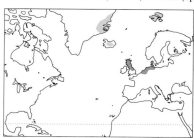

Descriptive notes. 60-75 cm; 2750-3500 g; wingspan 135-170 cm. Reminiscent of *A. fabalis* but smaller, with shorter bill and pink legs. Juvenile similar to adult, but duller and browner.
Habitat. Breeds on rocky outcrops, crags and gorges in very open Arctic tundra. Winters in coastal estuaries and on flat agricultural land.
Food and Feeding. Almost entirely vegetarian; leaves, stems, roots, berries and seedheads of sedges, mosses, lichens, during breeding season; grain, vegetables, potatoes and grasses, in winter. Feeds largely on dry (agricultural) land; also in water.
Breeding. Starts May. In rather loose colonies; builds shallow nest of plant matter on ground. Usually 3-5 eggs; incubation c. 26-27 days; chicks have brownish olive down above, yellowish below; fledging c. 56 days. Sexual maturity at 3 years, occasionally 2.
Movements. Migratory, Greenland and Icelandic populations winter mostly in Scotland and N and E England; Svalbard birds winter along E shores of N Sea. Sporadically in more southern latitudes during cold winters.
Status and Conservation. Not globally threatened. Rather numerous within its limited range. Most of world population winters in British Is, with c. 70,000-100,000. Population of Svalbard numbers c. 30,000 birds, almost all of which winter in Netherlands. Breeding populations of Iceland and Greenland number c. 10,000 pairs and 1000 pairs respectively; marked increase in recent years, probably due to protection of sites and reduction of hunting; in parts of winter quarters, agricultural changes have had negative effects on populations, e.g. in Germany.
Bibliography. Anon. (1986-1990), Bauer & Glutz von Blotzheim (1968), Bell (1988), Bell *et al.* (1988), Cramp & Simmons (1977), Dementiev & Gladkov (1952), van Eerden (1990), Fox, Gitay *et al.* (1989), Fox, Mitchell *et al.* (1989), Géroudet (1972), Hardy (1967), Harrison (1988), Lazarus & Inglis (1978), Lok & Vink (1979), Madsen (1991), Meire *et al.* (1988), Ogilvie (1978), Ogilvie & Boyd (1976), Owen (1976), Owen & Black (1991), Philippona & Smith (1978), de Schneidauer (1961), Scott & Fisher (1953).

21. Greater White-fronted Goose

Anser albifrons

French: Oie rieuse   **German**: Bläßgans   **Spanish**: Ansar Careto
Other common names: Whitefront; European White-fronted Goose (*albifrons*); Pacific White-fronted Goose (*frontalis*); Gambel White-fronted Goose (*gambeli*); Tule White-fronted/Tule Goose (*elgasi*); Greenland White-fronted Goose (*flavirostris*)

Taxonomy. *Branta albifrons* Scopoli, 1769, no locality = ? northern Italy.
Forms superspecies with *A. erythropus*. Validity of race *elgasi* has been questioned. Five subspecies recognized.
Subspecies and Distribution.
A. a. albifrons (Scopoli, 1769) - N Russia and Siberia from Kanin Peninsula to R Kolyma.
A. a. frontalis Baird, 1858 - E Siberia from R Kolyma eastwards to Arctic Canada.
A. a. gambeli Hartlaub, 1852 - taiga of NW Canada.
A. a. elgasi Delacour & Ripley, 1975 - SW Alaska.
A. a. flavirostris Dalgety & Scott, 1948 - W Greenland.

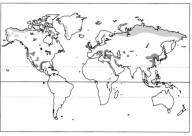

Descriptive notes. 65-86 cm; 1700-3000 g; wingspan 130-165 cm. Only confusion possible with *A. erythropus*, but larger, paler and with less white on forehead. Juvenile lacks black ventral markings and white facial patch and has less conspicuous white markings on flanks and upper surfaces. Subspecies vary mainly in size and coloration; nominate smallest and palest.
Habitat. Breeds in open tundra near marshes, lakes, pools and rivers, near coast as well as inland. Winters in open country, on steppe and farmland, or in marshy habitats.
Food and Feeding. Roots, leaves, stems and seeds of various plants, herbs, berries, grasses and sedges; also grain (corn, oats), potatoes and sprouting cereals in winter. Forages mostly by grazing on dry land.
Breeding. Starts late May/Jun. In single pairs or loose groups; builds shallow nest of vegetation, sparsely lined with down and feathers, on ground. Usually 5-6 eggs (3-7); incubation 22-28 days; chicks have brownish olive down above, pale grey below; fledging c. 40-43 days. Sexual maturity at 3 years.
Movements. Migratory, spends winter months in fixed areas at lower latitudes, mostly in temperate Europe, Asia and North America. Occasionally further S during cold winters.

Status and Conservation. Not globally threatened. Generally widespread and abundant, although some races scarce: *flavirostris* amongst least numerous; only 1200-1500 individuals of *elgasi* located in 1973/74 census; largest known concentration of *gambeli* was 7990 birds at Tamesí and Panuco Deltas, Mexico, in winter 1980, and this race appears to be very uncommon in USA. Mid-continent wintering populations of N America: 102,000 birds in W, where noted to be decreasing in 1989; in C, has increased from 39,300 in 1970 to 116,500 in 1988; in E, 86,000 and increasing. In Japan, has risen from 3000 birds in 1971, when hunting banned, to 19,000 birds in winter 1987/88, almost all of race *frontalis*. Winter population of Netherlands c. 300,000-400,000 (*albifrons*). Intense pressure from hunting in some places. Habitat destruction is main threat, especially significant for less numerous races.

Bibliography. Anon. (1986-1990), Barry (1966), Bauer, R.D. (1979), Bauer, K.M. & Glutz von Blotzheim (1968), Bellrose (1976), Boyd (1953), Brazil (1991), Brickell (1988), Brown *et al.* (1982), Budeau (1989), Cramp & Simmons (1977), Dementiev & Gladkov (1952), van Eerden (1990), Ely (1979), Etchécopar & Hüe (1978), Fox & Stroud (1981), Géroudet (1972), Goodman (1989), Harrison (1988), van Impe (1978), King (1978/79), Krogman (1978, 1979), Lazarus (1978), Madsen (1991), McCabe (1990), Meire *et al.* (1988), Mickelson (1973), Nankinov (1991), Norriss & Wilson (1988), Ogilvie (1978), Owen (1972, 1976), Owen & Black (1991), Perennou & Mundkur (1991), Philipona (1972), Philipona & Mulder (1965), de Schneidauer (1961), Stroud (1982), Terres (1980), Vincent (1966), Würdinger (1970), Ysebaert *et al.* (1988).

22. Lesser White-fronted Goose

Anser erythropus

French: Oie naine   **German**: Zwerggans   **Spanish**: Ansar Chico

Taxonomy. *Anas erythropus* Linnaeus, 1758, "Europa septentrionalis" = northern Sweden. Forms superspecies with *A. albifrons*. Monotypic.
Distribution. Narrow band across Arctic Eurasia.

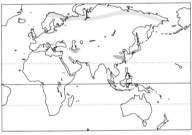

Descriptive notes. 53-66 cm; 1300-2300 g. White forehead reminiscent of *A. albifrons* and also has white claws; however, present species clearly smaller, has yellow eye-ring, more white on forehead and darker head, neck and upperparts. Female slightly smaller. Juvenile lacks white forehead, black spotting underneath and transverse lines on upperparts.
Habitat. Favours variety of Arctic open habitats, particularly scrub-covered and lightly wooded tundra near taiga zone; also lakes and slopes in mountain regions. Winters mostly on dry ground, steppe and agricultural land.
Food and Feeding. Essentially vegetarian; mainly green parts of grasses, plants and small bushes. Feeds mostly on land, by grazing.

Breeding. Starts late May/Jun. In single pairs; nest is shallow depression on ground lined with grass, moss and down. Usually 4-6 eggs (2-8); incubation c. 25-28 days; chicks have dark brown down above, yellowish below; fledging c. 35-40 days. Sexual maturity at 3, occasionally 2, years.
Movements. Migratory, main wintering areas on coastal plains of Caspian and Black Seas and in E China. Occasionally mixes with flocks of *A. albifrons* and occurs much further W than normal range; regular in Britain.
Status and Conservation. RARE. Marked decline during present century, of up to 95% in places; causes not well known. In 1965, total population estimated at 100,000, majority wintering on shores of Caspian Sea; during 1930's was considered most abundant goose wintering on R Yangtze. USSR breeding population perhaps concentrated in region of Yamal Peninsula and lower reaches of Ob, with 6000-10,000 birds. In past was widespread winter visitor to Japan, but now very few birds, normally mixed with groups of *A. albifrons*. Only large concentration in recent years of 14,000 birds at Poyang Hu, EC China, in Jan 1988. Reckoned to be endangered in Europe: best wintering grounds seem to be on Pannoic Plains, Hungary, where species formerly very abundant, but now amasses only a few thousand birds. Very small numbers winter at Evros Delta, N Greece, where threatened by habitat destruction and shooting.
Bibliography. Bauer & Glutz von Blotzheim (1968), Brazil (1991), Brickell (1988), Brown *et al.* (1982), Collar & Andrew (1988), Cramp & Simmons (1977), Dementiev & Gladkov (1952), Etchécopar & Hüe (1978), Géroudet (1972), Grimmett & Jones (1989), Handrinos & Goutner (1990), Hudson (1975), Mountfort (1988), Ogilvie (1978), Owen (1977), Roberts (1991), de Schauensee (1984), de Schneidauer (1961), Sterbetz (1990).

23. Greylag Goose

Anser anser

French: Oie cendrée   **German**: Graugans   **Spanish**: Ansar Común
Other common names: Grey Goose; Western Greylag Goose (*anser*); Eastern Greylag Goose (*rubrirostris*)

Taxonomy. *Anas Anser* Linnaeus, 1758, Europe and northern North America. Two subspecies recognized.
Subspecies and Distribution.
A. a. anser (Linnaeus, 1758) - Iceland, N and C Europe.
A. a. rubrirostris Swinhoe, 1871 - Turkey and USSR to NE China.

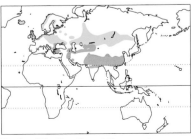

Descriptive notes. 76-89 cm; 2500-4100 g; wingspan 147-180 cm. Distinguished from other *Anser* by basically uniform coloration of body and bill; no black marks on bill; sometimes black spots or blotches present on belly. Juvenile generally less strongly patterned dorsally and overall has more mottled plumage. Subspecies *rubrirostris* has pink bill and paler plumage.
Habitat. Variety of habitats generally associated with water in open country, often with fringe vegetation or near grasslands. Winters on farmland in open country or in swamps, lakes and coastal lagoons.

Food and Feeding. Essentially vegetarian; grass, roots, leaves, stems, seed-heads, fruits and sprouts of wide variety of plants, complemented in winter with grain, potatoes and other vegetables. Forages mainly on land, by grazing, but also on water, where it sometimes upends.

Breeding. Starts Mar/Apr. Often in loose colonies; builds shallow nest of reed stems and grass, lined with down, among reedbeds, on ground or in trees. Usually 4-6 eggs (3-12); incubation c. 27-28 days; chicks have brownish olive down above, yellow below; fledging c. 50-60 days. Sexual maturity at 3, occasionally 2, years.
Movements. A few populations sedentary but most birds move southwards to winter in traditional sites at lower latitudes; many European birds follow French coast and concentrate in large numbers, up to 80,000 in Dec/Jan, in Doñana marshes, SW Spain. Irregular movements often occur as a result of extensive icing over in particularly bad winters.
Status and Conservation. Not globally threatened. Abundant, especially in W Europe, where increasing, with several hundred thousand birds; population of Iceland grew from 3500 pairs in 1960 to c. 18,500 in 1973. Winter census in 1991 gave 48,355 in Iran. Asian race *rubrirostris* not generally abundant, and may be declining due to effects of human pressure which remains intense, but some notable concentrations: 700 birds in wetlands of Dudhwa National Park, N India, in Jan 1987; 2350 birds at Yancheng Marshes, and 10,000 at Dongting Lakes, China, in Jan 1988. Species still suffers considerable hunting pressure throughout much of range; often comes into conflict with farmers, as can cause substantial crop damage. In many areas has been negatively affected by drainage and conversion of wetlands. Interbreeding with feral stock may reduce genetic purity to fair extent. Successfully reintroduced in some areas.
Bibliography. Amat (1986), Anon. (1986-1990), Bauer & Glutz von Blotzheim (1968), Bell (1988), Bell *et al.* (1988), Brazil (1991), Brickell (1988), Brown *et al.* (1982), Cramp & Simmons (1977), Dementiev & Gladkov (1952), Dick (1988a, 1988b), van Eerden (1990), Etchécopar & Hüe (1978), Fisher (1965), Fox, Gitay *et al.* (1989) Géroudet (1972), Harrison (1988), Heath (1971), Hudec & Rooth (1970), Kalas (1979), Lorenz (1950, 1979), Lorenz & Tinbergen (1939), Madsen (1991), Malik (1988), Newton & Kerbes (1974), Ogilvie (1978), Ogilvie & Boyd (1976), Owen (1976), Owen & Black (1991), Parasharya *et al.* (1990), Paz (1987), Raol (1988), Richardson (1990), Roberts (1991), Rooth (1971), de Schneidauer (1961), Thorsteinsson *et al.* (1991), Woods (1988), Young (1972).

24. Bar-headed Goose

Anser indicus

French: Oie à tête barrée   **German**: Streifengans   **Spanish**: Ansar Indio

Taxonomy. *Anas indica* Latham, 1790, India in winter, and Tibet. Sometimes placed in monospecific genus *Eulabeia*. Monotypic.
Distribution. C Asia, mainly Mongolia and China.

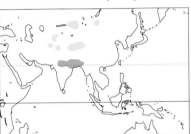

Descriptive notes. 71-76 cm; 2000-3000 g. Unmistakable. Sexes alike. Juvenile has pale grey head and neck with dark brown line through eyes, across crown and backwards down neck.
Habitat. Breeds on variety of wetlands in highland plateaux, generally at 4000-5000 m, preferably near rocky outcrops. Winters in lowland swamps, lakes and rivers.
Food and Feeding. Mainly vegetarian; grasses, roots, stems and green parts of plants and sedges; in winter also grain, tubers and other vegetables, and seaweed on coast. Forages mainly on land, by grazing; also on water.

Breeding. Starts late May/Jun. In colonies; builds shallow nest of vegetation among marshes, on ground or in trees. Usually 4-6 eggs (2-8); incubation 27-30 days; chicks have pale greyish brown down above, pale yellow below; fledging c. 53 days.
Movements. Majority of birds migratory, flying southwards to winter in northern India and adjacent countries.
Status and Conservation. Not globally threatened. Currently considered near-threatened. Has suffered severe reduction in numbers during present century. Fairly numerous in China, with concentrations of more than 1000 in some places, especially in W; in Longbaotan Nature Reserve nesting population increased during 1980's, with 2000 pairs in 1986. Current breeding population of China estimated at c. 20,000 birds, mainly in Qinghai-Tibet Plateau; total number wintering in China estimated at under 8000. Main wintering grounds in India, with 14,112 counted in 1990; also, to lesser extent, in Bangladesh, Nepal, Burma and Pakistan. Threatened by persistent direct human persecution, especially through shooting and egg-collecting, and also by habitat destruction.
Bibliography. Ali & Ripley (1978), Bauer & Glutz von Blotzheim (1968), Chaudhry (1991), Dementiev & Gladkov (1952), Etchécopar & Hüe (1978), Fu Chun-li & Gu Jing-he (1988), Gao Yuan-hong (1988), Gole (1982), Hiebl & Braunitzer (1988), Himmatsinhji & Bapat (1989), Hüe & Etchécopar (1970), Kydyraliew (1967), Lamprecht (1986a, 1986b, 1987), Lamprecht & Buhrow (1987), Lu (1991), Perennou & Mundkur (1991), Raol (1988), Roberts (1991), de Schauensee (1984), Schindler (1983), Schneider & Lamprecht (1990), Wang Xia (1981), Weigmann & Lamprecht (1991), Würdinger (1970, 1973, 1978, 1980), Xian Yao-hua (1964).

25. Snow Goose

Anser caerulescens

French: Oie des neiges   **German**: Schneegans   **Spanish**: Ansar Nival
Other common names: Greater Snow Goose (*atlanticus*); Lesser Snow Goose, Blue Goose (*caerulescens*)

Taxonomy. *Anas caerulescens* Linnaeus, 1758, Hudson Bay. Sometimes placed in genus *Chen* together with *A. rossii*. Two subspecies recognized.
Subspecies and Distribution.
A. c. caerulescens (Linnaeus, 1758) - Wrangel I (off NE USSR); N Alaska E to Baffin I.
A. c. atlanticus (Kennard, 1927) - NW Greenland and islands in N Baffin Bay.
Descriptive notes. 66-84 cm; c. 2500-3300 g; wingspan 132-165 cm. Only possible confusion between white morph and *A. rossii*, but present species larger and with different bill. Blue morph, common in nominate race, only has white on head and upper neck. Head often shows rusty staining. Juveniles of white morph have mottled greyish head and neck, ashy-brown back and scapulars with white edging; secondaries, bill and legs dusky. Blue morph young birds lack white on head; greater secondary coverts are shorter and pale grey and all soft parts are duskily coloured. Subspecies *atlanticus* slightly larger; blue morph is extremely rare.
Habitat. Low, grassy tundra, generally in close association with water or on stony ground. Winters on low agricultural land, usually near coast.
Food and Feeding. Essentially vegetarian; roots, tubers, leaves, grasses, stems and seed-heads of various aquatic plants and sedges; in winter also grain and vegetables. Forages mainly on rough pastures, swamps and dry arable land, by grazing; also feeds while on water.

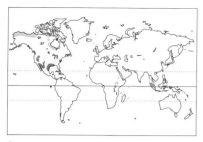

Breeding. Starts Jun. In colonies; nest is shallow depression filled with moss and lined with grass and down, built on ground. Usually 4-5 eggs (2-10); incubation 23-25 days; chicks have olive buff down above, paler below, or mostly olive grey in blue phase; fledging 40-50 days. Sexual maturity at 2 years, though birds do not usually nest until 3-4 years.
Movements. Migratory, departs breeding grounds to winter along Atlantic and Gulf coasts of USA, and in SW states and N Mexico. Irregular in Hawaii and E Asia. Vagrant to NW Europe.

Status and Conservation. Not globally threatened. Numerous, with increase of nominate race in C North America, from 424,600 in 1969 to 1,358,000 in 1988; increase may be due to more rigorous control of hunting. Only Siberian breeding grounds on Wrangel I held 140,000 birds in autumn 1987; said to be declining since recent settlement on island and launching of reindeer farming, as deer cause damage to colony and predatory Arctic fox (*Alopex lagopus*) has increased in number due to surfeit of waste products around farm buildings; hunting on winter quarters in W USA has been regulated. Formerly abundant in winter in Japan, but wintering population suddenly disappeared around 1895, probably due to proliferation of firearms; since 1950's has started to recover and now recorded almost annually, though in very small numbers. Some birds winter in Mexico, with concentrations of up to 2000-3500 in favourable areas. Race *atlanticus* has increased even more than nominate race: 41,800 in 1950, 198,000 in 1988 wintering in E North America; increase due to expansion of range made possible by adaptation to new feeding habitats, such as upland agricultural fields.
Bibliography. Alisauskas *et al.* (1988), Alisauskas & Ankney (1992), Ankney (1977), Ankney & MacInnes (1978), Armstrong (1983), Bartlett (1975), Bauer & Glutz von Blotzheim (1968), Bedard & Lapointe (1991), Bellrose (1976), Brazil (1991), Cooch, F.G. (1958), Cooch, E.G. & Cooke (1991), Cooch E.G. *et al.* (1989), Cooke & McNallay (1975), Cooke, Findlay *et al.* (1985), Cooke, MacInnes & Prevett (1977), Cramp & Simmons (1977), Flint *et al.* (1984), Gallico (1946), Gauthier & Bédard (1985), Gregoire (1985), Harwood (1977), Johnsgard (1974), Kerbes (1988), Kharitonov (1988), Lank, Cooch *et al.* (1989), Lank, Mineau *et al.* (1989), Lessells (1987), McCabe (1990), McKelvey *et al.* (1989), Monroe (1968), Prevett (1973), Prevett & MacInnes (1980), Reed (1990), de Schneidauer (1961), Syroechkovsky (1975), Terres (1980), Thomas (1990), Trauger *et al.* (1971), Turcotte & Bedard (1989a, 1989b), Würdinger (1970).

26. Ross's Goose
Anser rossii

French: Oie de Ross   **German**: Zwergschneegans   **Spanish**: Ansar de Ross

Taxonomy. *Anser Rossii* Cassin, 1861, Great Slave Lake.
Sometimes placed in genus *Chen* together with *A. caerulescens*. Monotypic.
Distribution. Arctic Canada, almost entirely in R Perry region.

Descriptive notes. 53-66 cm; 1224-1633 g. Female averages smaller. Smaller than *A. caerulescens*; shorter bill with different pattern and colour. Very rare blue morph, similar to that of *A. caerulescens*, but apparently with more white on underparts and less on head and neck. Juvenile brownish grey on head, back and scapulars with greyer or browner flight-feathers.
Habitat. Breeds primarily on predator-free rocky or scrubby islands in large lakes of Arctic zone. Winters on low agricultural land.
Food and Feeding. Essentially vegetarian; roots, leaves, stems and green parts of aquatic plants and sedges; also grain (barley, rice) and green grasses, outside breeding season.
Breeding. Starts Jun. In colonies; nest is shallow mound of twigs, grass, moss and lichens, lined with down, built on ground. Usually 4-5 eggs (2-6); incubation c. 21-22 days; chicks have greyish down above, paler below; fledging c. 40 days. Sexual maturity at 2-3 years.
Movements. Migratory, main wintering area in California (Sacramento Valley), but also in New Mexico and along Gulf Coast of USA. Vagrant elsewhere in North America and perhaps to NW Europe, though some escapes certainly involved.
Status and Conservation. Not globally threatened. Total population estimated at 77,300 birds in 1976. Increasing in recent decades, although still legally hunted in places. Average wintering population in N America in period 1956-1974 estimated at 23,400 birds. Potential threats include dependence of large part of population on very limited number of wintering grounds, making it very vulnerable to disease or natural disasters; also fact that species hybridizes with *A. caerulescens*, producing fertile hybrids.
Bibliography. Armstrong (1983), Bellrose (1976), Garner (1991), Haas (1991), MacLandres (1979), McCabe (1990), Plunkett (1989), Robinson (1988, 1991), Ryder, J.P. (1967, 1970, 1972), Scott & Carbonell (1986), Svingen (1991), Terres (1980), Thomas (1990), Trauger *et al.* (1971).

27. Emperor Goose
Anser canagicus

French: Oie empereur   **German**: Kaisergans   **Spanish**: Ansar Emperador
Other common names: Beach Goose

Taxonomy. *Anas canagicus* Sevastianov, 1802, Kanaga Island, Aleutian Islands.
Sometimes placed in monospecific genus *Philacte*. Monotypic.
Distribution. NE Siberia, W Alaska.
Descriptive notes. 66-89 cm; 2766-3129 g. Unmistakable. Very different appearance when strongly stained. Juvenile duller with grey mottling on head and foreneck; brown rather than black barring on back; black bill and olive brown legs.
Habitat. Open sites in Arctic tundra, near coastal lagoons or inland, near freshwater pools and lakes. Winters along rocky coastline and on sheltered sites with soft shores.
Food and Feeding. Grasses, leaves of sedges and berries on breeding grounds; also seaweed and algae along coast, complemented with some animal food (barnacles). Feeds mainly by grazing.

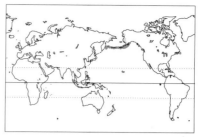

Breeding. Starts late May/Jun. In loose colonies; nest is shallow depression in ground, lined with grass, feathers and down. Usually c. 5 eggs (1-8); incubation c. 24-25 days; chicks have grey down above, whitish below; fledging c. 50-60 days. Sexual maturity at 3, occasionally 2, years.
Movements. Migratory, wintering along Aleutian Is and Gulf of Alaska, with smaller numbers in Kamchatka. Occasionally much further S, having reached California, Hawaii and Japan.
Status and Conservation. Not globally threatened. Has undergone marked decline in recent times. Siberian population poorly known, but apparently numbers 12,000+ individuals; probably never very numerous and currently declining, with significant range reduction in W. Alaskan population has decreased from estimated 150,000 birds in autumn 1976, to 46,000 wintering recently in W North America; factors behind this decline not well known.
Bibliography. Armstrong (1983), Bellrose (1976), Dementiev & Gladkov (1952), Eisenhauer & Kirkpatrick (1977), Eisenhauer *et al.* (1971), Headley (1967), McCabe (1990), Petersen (1990), Petersen & Gill (1982), Quinn *et al.* (1991), Rohwer *et al.* (1989), Terres (1980), Thompson (1987), Thompson & Raveling (1987, 1988).

Genus *BRANTA*   Scopoli, 1769

28. Hawaiian Goose
Branta sandvicensis

French: Bernache néné   **German**: Hawaiigans   **Spanish**: Barnacla Nené
Other common names: Néné, Néné Goose

Taxonomy. *Anser sandvicensis* Vigors, 1833, Hawaiian Islands.
Sometimes placed in monospecific genus *Nesochen*. Monotypic.
Distribution. Hawaii I; reintroduced to Maui I, where may formerly have bred.

Descriptive notes. 56-71 cm; c. 1920-2215 g. Distinctive neck pattern, with noticeable lines of feather grooves on both sides, renders species unmistakable. Female slightly smaller. Juvenile has more mottled body and a dull version of adult head and neck pattern.
Habitat. Lava flows on poorly vegetated volcanic slopes at 1500-2500 m; also, where available, grassland.
Food and Feeding. Essentially vegetarian; grasses, herbs, berries, leaves and green parts of sedges and plants with high water content. Forages almost exclusively on land, by grazing and plucking food items.

Breeding. Starts Oct/Nov. In isolated pairs; nest is depression on ground, sometimes surrounded by fringe of vegetation, lined with down, built between slabs of lava. Usually 3-5 eggs; incubation c. 29 days; chicks have brown down, with whitish markings mainly on underparts; fledging c. 10-12 weeks. Sexual maturity at 2-3 years.
Movements. Mostly sedentary, with only evidence of small-scale, local movements.
Status and Conservation. VULNERABLE. CITES I. Introduction of alien predators to breeding islands resulted in massive decline in numbers: c. 25,000 at end of 18th century, but only 30 by 1952. Captive breeding undertaken by Wildfowl and Wetlands Trust, in England, and Hawaii Division of Fish and Game as early as 1949, with releases into wild of c. 1400 birds between 1960 and 1976; these survived well but have not proliferated, and at present wild population still numbers only c. 350 birds. Haleakala National Park holds c. 150 birds, and numbers appear to be stable in recent years. Of eight areas where birds released: one has stable population; two populations increasing due to intensive control of predators and bolstered food supply; and remaining five decreasing, and dependent on continual reintroductions. Full recovery of species requires elimination, or control, of introduced predators, especially mongooses, and further introductions of birds bred in captivity.
Bibliography. Baldwin (1945, 1947), Banko (1988), Banko & Manuwal (1982), Berger (1972), Black (1991), Collar & Andrew (1988), Devick (1981a, 1981b), Dollinger (1988), Elder & Woodside (1958), Greenway (1967), Hodges (1991), Hoshide *et al.* (1990), Kear & Berger (1980), King (1978/79), Miller (1937), Munro (1960), Pratt *et al.* (1987), Quinn *et al.* (1991), Ripley (1965), Scott & Kepler (1985), Smith (1952), Vincent (1966), Weller (1980), Zimmerman (1974).

29. Canada Goose
Branta canadensis

French: Bernache du Canada   **German**: Kanadagans   **Spanish**: Barnacla Canadiense
Other common names: Aleutian Canada Goose (*leucopareia*); Cackling Canada Goose (*minima*); Taverner Canada Goose (*taverneri*); Dusky Canada Goose (*occidentalis*); Vancouver Canada Goose (*fulva*); Lesser Canada Goose (*parvipes*); Moffitt Canada Goose (*moffitti*); Giant Canada Goose (*maxima*); Baffin Island Canada Goose (*hutchinsii*); Hudson Bay Canada Goose (*interior*); Atlantic Canada Goose (*canadensis*)

Taxonomy. *Anas canadensis* Linnaeus, 1758, Canada.
Hybridized in captivity with several species of *Branta*, *Anser*, *Cygnus*, also with *Alopochen aegyptiacus* and *Cairina moschata*; in the wild only rarely with *Anser caerulescens*. Taxonomic status of subspecies not clear, mainly due to presence of many intergrading zones between two or more races; several, especially *taverneri*, not accepted by some authors, while others split the complex into as many as four distinct species; race *asiatica*, described from Commander and Kuril Is and listed as extinct in first edition of Red Data Book, now considered synonymous with *leucopareia*. Eleven subspecies normally recognized.

Subspecies and Distribution.
B. c. leucopareia (Brandt, 1836) - Aleutian Is.
B. c. minima Ridgway, 1885 - coastal W Alaska.
B. c. taverneri Delacour, 1951 - Alaska Peninsula to Mackenzie Delta.
B. c. occidentalis (Baird, 1858) - SW Alaska.
B. c. fulva Delacour, 1951 - coastal S Alaska, W British Columbia.
B. c. parvipes (Cassin, 1852) - inland Canada.
B. c. moffitti Aldrich, 1946 - Great Basin of Canada.
B. c. maxima Delacour, 1951 - coastal W Alaska.
B. c. hutchinsii (Richardson, 1832) - NC Canada.
B. c. interior Todd, 1938 - C & E Canada.
B. c. canadensis (Linnaeus, 1758) - E Canada.
Introduced and well established in Britain, NW Europe (chiefly race *canadensis*) and New Zealand (mainly race *maxima*).

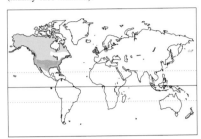

Descriptive notes. 55-110 cm. 2059-6523 g; wingspan 122-183 cm. Unmistakable though very variable. Juvenile duller, especially noticeable in head pattern; breast and flanks mottled rather than barred. Subspecies vary markedly in size, proportions and coloration: *maxima* largest and, with *hutchinsii*, one of palest; *minima* smallest, with most duck-like proportions and, with *occidentalis*, one of darkest; *fulva* is largest of dark forms; *hutchinsii* smallest of pale forms; fairly prominent white neck-ring in *leucopareia*, but also, usually thinner, in some individuals of other races.
Habitat. A very adaptable species, occurring on a diversity of habitats, from tundra to semi-desert and in wooded or open country. However, almost invariably occurs near water.
Food and Feeding. Essentially vegetarian; grasses, roots, stems, leaves, fruits and green parts of aquatic plants and sedges; in winter also grain and seaweed. Feeds mostly by grazing on land; on water, may dip head or upend.
Breeding. Season varies much according to locality but concentrated in spring. In single pairs or in colonies; builds shallow nest of vegetation, lined with down and feathers, on ground. Usually 4-7 eggs (1-12; more than 8 usually by dump laying); incubation c. 24-30 days; chicks have olive brown down above, buffish below; fledging 40-86 days, depending on race; first breeding at 2-3 years.
Movements. Natural populations migratory, flying southwards to winter in southern states of USA and along coasts of N America. Occasional further S and W in cold winters. Feral populations mostly sedentary.
Status and Conservation. Not globally threatened. Total population over 3,000,000 birds. Status of different races variable: large races, e.g. *canadensis* and *maxima*, generally abundant, and in addition, constitute majority of feral populations established outwith natural range; races *hutchinsii* and *parvipes* seem to be stable or increasing, with fairly sizeable populations; *interior* and *moffitti* increasing, at any rate in part of range, and 50,000-60,000 individuals of latter winter in W North America; races *fulva* and *taverneri* probably increasing; *minima* has decreased from 400,000 during 1960's to 25,000 in mid-1980's due to excessive hunting for sport and subsistence harvesting; *occidentalis* has decreased from 25,000 in 1979 to less than 13,000 in 1991, due to ecological changes at breeding grounds and hunting in winter quarters; race *leucopareia* scarce, requires banning of hunting at winter quarters and elimination of introduced Arctic fox (*Alopex lagopus*) from Aleutian Is, and to date with such measures has recovered from 790 birds in 1975 to more than 6400 birds in 1990. Feral populations: c. 50,000 in Britain in 1988; in New Zealand estimated 35,000-40,000 and possibly more, where conflicts with farmers due to damage caused to pastures and crops. In USA and Canada, harvest of 427,400 birds per year is permitted for sport, as is subsistence hunting of E populations which accounts annually for 60,000-80,000 birds on breeding grounds in Canada. Race *leucopareia* on CITES I.
Bibliography. Anon. (1986-1990), Austin (1988, 1990), Badgerow (1988), Bauer & Glutz von Blotzheim (1968), Bell & Klimstra (1970), Bellrose (1976), Bent (1923-1925), Black & Barrow (1985), Brazil (1991), Buchsbaum (1984), Byrd & Springer (1976), Carlsen *et al.* (1990), Clark, K. (1985), Cramp & Simmons (1977), Delacour (1951), Dollinger (1988), Fabricius (1983), Gerell (1985), Hainsworth (1989), Hanson (1965), Harrison (1988), Havel (1985), Havel & Jarvis (1988), Hestbeck *et al.* (1991), Hine & Schoenfeld (1968), Hren (1991), Humburg *et al.* (1985), Johnson & Raveling (1988), King (1978/79), Lever (1987), Madsen (1991), Marchant, J.H. *et al.* (1990), Marchant, S. & Higgins (1990), McCabe (1990), McLandress (1979), McLandress & Raveling (1981), Ogilvie (1978), Owen (1976), Palmer (1976), Petersen (1990), Quinn *et al.* (1991), Raveling (1969, 1970, 1979), Raveling, Crews & Klimstra (1972), Raveling *et al.* (1992), Rusch *et al.* (1985), de Schneidauer (1961), Simpson & Jarvis (1979), Terres (1980), Thompson & Raveling (1988), Vaught & Kirsch (1966), Vincent (1966), Williams, C.S. (1967), Woolington & Springer (1977), Würdinger (1970).

30. **Barnacle Goose**
Branta leucopsis

French: Bernache nonnette   **German**: Weißwangengans   **Spanish**: Barnacla Cariblanca

Taxonomy. *Anas leucopsis* Bechstein, 1803, Germany.
Monotypic.
Distribution. E Greenland, Svalbard (Spitzbergen) and Novaya Zemlya.

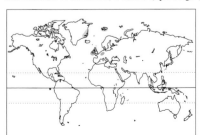

Descriptive notes. 58-71 cm; 1290-2010 g; wingspan 132-145 cm. Unmistakable. Sexes similar though female slightly lighter. Juvenile duller, with greyer neck and grey flecking in white head pattern.
Habitat. Breeds on crags and rocky outcrops in Arctic tundra, preferably near water body. Winters on lowland meadows near coast.
Food and Feeding. Essentially vegetarian; leaves, stems and seed-heads of grasses, sedges and aquatic plants; in winter also grain and some vegetables. Forages by grazing in rough pasture, marshes and arable land.
Breeding. Starts late May/Jun. In colonies; nest is shallow depression lined with grass, moss, lichen and down, on cliff ledges or ground. Usually 4-5 eggs (2-9); incubation c. 24-25 days; chicks have greyish brown down above, whitish below; fledging c. 40-45 days. Sexual maturity at 3, occasionally 2, years.

Movements. Migratory, departs breeding grounds to winter mainly in Britain (Scotland & Ireland) and E coast of North Sea (Netherlands), but has occurred further S (Egypt) and W (N America).
Status and Conservation. Not globally threatened. Has extremely localized breeding and wintering grounds. Total world population c. 80,000-95,000 during 1980's; went through marked decline, with subsequent recovery and now apparently stable or increasing slightly. Breeding population of c. 50,000 birds on Novaya Zemlya, most of which now winter in Netherlands, due to increased habitat and protection, and drainage of German wetlands used in past. Population of Greenland increased from 8000 birds in 1959 to 33,800 in 1978, but then slid back to 25,000 in 1983; c. 35,000 in late 1980's, of which c. 20,000 winter on Islay, SW Scotland. In Mar/Apr 5000-6000 present on Schiermonnikoog salt-marsh in Netherlands.
Bibliography. Anon. (1986-1990), Bauer & Glutz von Blotzheim (1968), Bazely *et al.* (1991), Black (1987), Black & Owen (1984, 1987, 1988, 1989a, 1989b), Boertmann (1991), Brickell (1988), Brown *et al.* (1982), Cabot & West (1973), Cabot *et al.* (1988), Cramp & Simmons (1977), Ebbinge & Ebbinge-Dallmeijer (1977), van Eerden (1990), Ferns & Green (1975), Géroudet (1972), Harrison (1988), Hausberger & Black (1990), Jackson *et al.* (1974), Madsen (1991), McCabe (1990), Ogilvie (1978), Owen (1976, 1984), Owen & Black (1989a, 1989b, 1990b, 1991), Owen, Black, Agger & Campbell (1987), Owen, Black & Liber (1988), Owen, Nugent & Davies (1977), Prestud *et al.* (1989), Prop *et al.* (1984), de Schneidauer (1961), Thorsteinsson *et al.* (1991).

31. **Brent Goose**
Branta bernicla

French: Bernache cravant   **German**: Ringelgans   **Spanish**: Barnacla Carinegra
Other common names: Brant Goose, Brant, Brent; Light-bellied/Atlantic Brent (*hrota*); Dark-bellied/Russian Brent (*bernicla*); Pacific Brent (*orientalis*); Black Brent (*nigricans*)

Taxonomy. *Anas Bernicla* Linnaeus, 1758, Europe.
Race *orientalis* included in *nigricans* by some. Race *nigricans* sometimes considered a full species. Four subspecies recognized.
Subspecies and Distribution.
B. b. hrota (O. F. Müller, 1776) - N Canada, Greenland, Svalbard and Franz Josef Land.
B. b. bernicla (Linnaeus, 1758) - NC Siberia.
B. b. orientalis Tugarinov, 1941 - NE Siberia.
B. b. nigricans (Lawrence, 1846) - extreme NE Siberia to NC Canada.

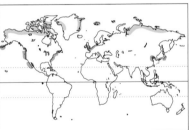

Descriptive notes. 55-66 cm; 1200-2250 g; wingspan 110-120 cm. Unmistakable. Juvenile has conspicuous white fringes on upperparts; acquires white marks on throat gradually. Subspecies vary in coloration, especially on sides; *hrota* has browner upperparts with pale brown and whitish sides; *nigricans* has broader white patches on neck and striking white markings on flanks.
Habitat. Breeds in lowland Arctic tundra, generally near coast. Winters along estuaries and sandy shores.
Food and Feeding. Essentially vegetarian; grasses, mosses, lichens and aquatic plants on breeding grounds; in winter, almost exclusively marine algae, seaweeds and other aquatic plants linked with salt or brackish water. Grazes on land or swims and upends in shallow water.
Breeding. Starts in Jun. In colonies; nest is shallow depression, lined with grass, moss and down, built on ground, often close to water. Usually 3-5 eggs (1-10); incubation c. 24-26 days; chicks have greyish down above, whitish below; fledging c. 40 days. Sexual maturity at 2-3 years.
Movements. Migratory, with main wintering areas in NW Europe, E Asia (Yellow Sea) and Atlantic and Pacific coasts of N America. Unusual occurrences further S normally linked with extent of winter icing.
Status and Conservation. Not globally threatened. Total world population of 400,000-500,000 birds during 1980's, with major fluctuations between years due largely to highly variable breeding success. During early 1930's, nominate *bernicla* declined to c. 10% of previous population, probably due to disease affecting main food plant, eel-grass (*Zostera marina*); subsequently started to recover with 16,500 birds by 1955-1957 and 30,500 in 1966/67; sharp increase from 34,000 in 1971/72 to c. 80,000 in 1973/74; population now stable or still increasing, generally numbering c. 100,000-200,000 birds, with 235,000 in 1988. Race *nigricans* has 185,000 individuals wintering in W North America, and average 139,000 in Mexico in 1978-1982; only small numbers in Japan and China. Race *hrota* undergoes great population fluctuations depending on conditions of breeding grounds, severity of winters, abundance of sea lettuce (*Ulva lactuca*), disturbance and hunting. Species sustains harvest of c. 1000 birds annually for subsistence in Canada.
Bibliography. Anon. (1986-1990), Barry (1966), Bauer & Glutz von Blotzheim (1968), Bellrose (1976), Brazil (1991), Brickell (1988), Brown *et al.* (1982), Cramp & Simmons (1977), Debout & Leclerc (1990), Delacour & Zimmer (1952), Dementiev & Gladkov (1952), Ebbinge (1989), van Eerden (1990), Einarsen (1965), Erskine (1988), Géroudet (1972), Harrison (1988), Inglis & Lazarus (1981), Madsen (1991), Madsen *et al.* (1989), McCabe (1990), Mickelson (1973), Ogilvie (1978), Owen (1976), Owen & Black (1991, 1990b), Quinn *et al.* (1991), Rohwer *et al.* (1989), Rogers (1979), de Schneidauer (1961), Scott & Carbonell (1986), Summers & Underhill (1991), Thomas (1991), Thompson & Raveling (1988), Welsh (1988).

32. **Red-breasted Goose**
Branta ruficollis

French: Bernache à cou roux   **German**: Rothalsgans   **Spanish**: Barnacla Cuelliroja

Taxonomy. *Anser ruficollis* Pallas, 1769, lower Ob, Siberia.
Sometimes placed in monospecific genus *Rufibrenta*. Monotypic.
Distribution. Siberian tundra, almost entirely within Taymyr Peninsula.
Descriptive notes. 53-56 cm; 1150-1625 g; wingspan 116-135 cm. Unmistakable. Juvenile duller with white spotting on sides and mantle; chestnut markings are weaker and less clearly defined.
Habitat. Dry shrub- and lichen-covered tundra not far from water. Winters in low arable land near lakes and reservoirs.
Food and Feeding. Essentially vegetarian; leaves, stems and green parts of grasses, sedges and some aquatic plants, particularly in winter, complemented with green sprouts of cereals, grain and tubers. Forages by grazing on land.
Breeding. Starts Jun. In loose groups; builds shallow nest of vegetation, lined with down, on steep ground, generally in vicinity of raptors' nests. Usually 6-7 eggs (3-7); incubation c. 23-25 days; chicks have dark brown down above, paler below. Sexual maturity at 3-4 years.

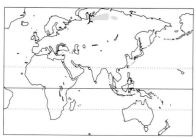

Movements. Highly migratory; leaves breeding quarters in Siberian tundras mid to late Sept. Winters mostly around Black Sea, especially in Romania and Bulgaria, and, to a lesser extent, around Caspian Sea (highest counts in Azerbaydzhan) and Aral Sea; small numbers in SE Europe (Greece, Turkey). Departs from wintering grounds between Mar and early May. Frequent stragglers to W Europe, especially Britain and Netherlands, generally in flocks of *Anser albifrons*; vagrants also as far S as Egypt and as far E as China.

Status and Conservation. INSUFFICIENT-LY KNOWN (under review). CITES II. Alarming decline in numbers during last few decades. Estimated 50,000 birds in mid-1950's, only c. 25,000 from 1960's to 1980's, and possible further decline to c. 20,000 recently, with only c. 6000 breeding pairs. Attendance at wintering grounds fluctuates greatly, e.g. 25,000 in Romania in winter 1968/69, but only 3000-4000 in 1969/70; in 1970/71 9300 were counted in the same country, and only 6000 in 1971/72. In Caspian Sea region several tens of thousands were counted in mid 1950's, but only 1000-2000 since 1968; decline in this area mainly caused by adverse land-use changes, especially conversion of cereal crops to vineyards. Other significant recent counts include 16,000 in Bulgaria in 1980 and 2000 in Greece in 1985. Irregular winter visitor to Israel in very small numbers. In Turkmenistan, 48 recorded in 1991 census. Overall decline of species related with great decline in birds of prey, including Rough-legged Buzzard (*Buteo lagopus*), and especially Peregrine Falcon (*Falco peregrinus*), due to excessive use of pesticides this century; present species nests very close to these raptors, apparently as defence mechanism against foxes. Species continues to suffer hunting pressure at breeding, moulting and wintering grounds.

Bibliography. Bauer & Glutz von Blotzheim (1968), Brown *et al.* (1982), Collar & Andrew (1988), Cramp & Simmons (1977), Dementiev & Gladkov (1952), Dollinger (1988), Flint *et al.* (1984), Géroudet (1972), Hüe & Etchécopar (1970), Hudson (1975), Madsen (1991), Ogilvie (1978), Owen (1977), de Schneidauer (1961), Scott, P. (1970), Zeng Zuo-xin (1960).

PLATE 42

inches 10
cm 25

♀ 34

35

33

white phase ♂

36

♀ 37

barred phase ♂

♀

♂ 38

39

40

41

42

Tribe CEREOPSINI

Genus *CEREOPSIS* Latham, 1801

33. Cape Barren Goose
Cereopsis novaehollandiae

French: Céréope cendrée   **German**: Hühnergans   **Spanish**: Ganso Cenizo
Other common names: Cereopsis Goose

Taxonomy. *Cereopsis N. Hollandiae* Latham, 1801, New South Wales = islands of Bass Strait.
Population of Recherche Archipelago has been assigned subspecies *grisea*, though doubtfully valid.
Monotypic.
Distribution. Islands off S Australia, Tasmania.

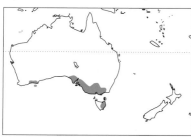

Descriptive notes. 75-100 cm; 3170-6800 g, female lighter. Unmistakable. Juvenile averages slightly lighter with heavier spotting on wings.
Habitat. Breeds in scrub and grassy areas on offshore islands; also frequents beaches, coastal pasture and edges of lakes and lagoons. Does not enter water except when moulting or rearing young.
Food and Feeding. Essentially vegetarian; leaves, stems and seeds of grasses (tussock), sedges and other plants with high water content. A specialist grazer, feeds almost exclusively on land.
Breeding. In winter, starts May/Jun. In single pairs or loose colonies; builds shallow nest of vegetation on ground, lined with down. Average 5 eggs (3-6); incubation c. 34-37 days; chicks have black down above, light grey below; fledging 70-76 days. In one study, 89% of eggs hatched and 54% fledged.
Movements. Partially dispersive after breeding season, with some remaining on nesting islands but others flying to other, larger islands or to adjacent mainland, where species has occurred quite far inland.
Status and Conservation. Not globally threatened. Total population reckoned to be c. 15,000-17,000 birds in 1980's; apparently stable, after major declines earlier in 20th century. Population estimates include: 3500-10,000 birds on Eyre Peninsula, South Australia; 1000 on Recherche Archipelago, Western Australia; and 500 on Wilson's Promontory, Victoria. Furneaux Is, Tasmania, hold large population with 9000 individuals counted in 1988, and numbers increasing; annual production of 4000 goslings from over 3000 breeding geese. Finally extinct in New Zealand, where survived for decades after being introduced. Favourable habitats created for agriculture have assured population recovery after halting of uncontrolled persecution; extensive modifications for agriculture may have negative effects on breeding grounds. Management, perhaps including limited grazing, may be necessary on breeding islands designated as nature reserves, to avoid them reverting to dense scrubland. Extent of damage to pastures is still matter for debate; farmers have been permitted limited amount of shooting in Tasmania.
Bibliography. Bull *et al.* (1985), Delroy *et al.* (1989), Falla *et al.* (1981), Frith (1967), Guiler (1967, 1974), Kear & Murton (1973), Marchant & Higgins (1990), Marriott (1970), Pearse (1975), Robinson *et al.* (1982), Schodde & Tidemann (1988), Velichko (1988), Veselovsky (1973), Vincent (1966), Williams (1968).

Tribe STICTONETTINI

Genus *STICTONETTA* Reichenbach, 1853

34. Freckled Duck
Stictonetta naevosa

French: Stictonette tachetée   **German**: Affengans   **Spanish**: Pato Pecoso

Taxonomy. *Anas naevosa* Gould, 1841, Western Australia.
Monotypic.
Distribution. SE and extreme SW Australia.

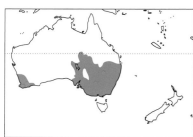

Descriptive notes. 50-55 cm; 691-1130 g. Unmistakable with shape of head and bill diagnostic. Female has paler and less contrasting plumage. Juvenile resembles female but is paler with deeper buff freckles.
Habitat. Freshwater lakes and marshes with abundant emergent and fringe vegetation. Also occurs on coastal lagoons of brackish waters and floodplains.
Food and Feeding. Mainly vegetarian; algae, seeds and green parts of aquatic plants, grasses and minor quantities of aquatic invertebrates (insects). Forages by upending in shallow water, bottom filtering, dabbling and wading along shore and nibbling on surface.

Breeding. Season largely determined by flooding conditions but broadly Jun-Dec. Builds bowl-shaped nest of finely woven twigs among reedbeds or on water. Average 7 eggs (5-10); incubation c. 26-31 days; chicks have buff and brown down; fledging c. 9 weeks. Sexual maturity reached by females at 2 years (in captivity).
Movements. Occurs irregularly outside main centres of distribution, with dispersive movements particularly linked to water availability and extent of flooding. May be encountered almost anywhere in Australia but only exceptionally in Tasmania.
Status and Conservation. INSUFFICIENTLY KNOWN (under review). Total population estimated at 19,000 birds in E Australia, with estimated 3000 birds in Victoria; only c. 1000 in isolated W population. In Jan-Feb 1983, during period of drought, 8000 counted in E Australia, with more than 700 at L Salisbury, New South Wales. Decline in recent decades as many freshwater wetlands which were previously suitable for breeding have been destroyed or modified by drainage, flood mitigation works, clearing, grazing, burning, salinization or increased flooding. Illegal hunting persists, and species under severe pressure, because easy to shoot and tends to form large concentrations in parts of S, in connection with droughts. In Victoria, pre-season counts started in 1987 to identify wetlands with large numbers of present species, in order to establish temporary closure to shooting; waterfowl identification tests for licensed shooters introduced in 1989. Also threatened by human disturbance in areas used for recreation.
Bibliography. Braithwaite (1976), Collar & Andrew (1988), Frith (1964a, 1964b, 1965, 1967), Frith *et al.* (1969), Halse & Jaensch (1989), Johnsgard (1965b), Marchant & Higgins (1990), Schodde & Tidemann (1988).

Subfamily ANATINAE

Tribe TADORNINI

Genus *CYANOCHEN* Bonaparte, 1856

35. Blue-winged Goose
Cyanochen cyanopterus

French: Ouette à ailes bleues   **German**: Blauflügelgans   **Spanish**: Ganso Aliazul
Other common names: Abyssinian Blue-winged/Abyssinian Goose

Taxonomy. *Bernicla cyanoptera* Rüppell, 1845, Shoa, Ethiopia.
Monotypic.
Distribution. Highlands of Ethiopia.

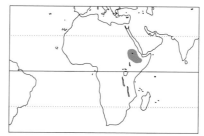

Descriptive notes. 60-75 cm; c. 1520 g (female). Almost unmistakable. Often walks or rests with head held backwards. Upperwing-coverts a distinctive powder blue. Female smaller. Juvenile duller.
Habitat. Grassy meadows and pastures above 1400 m adjacent to rivers, lakes and pools which lack dense marginal vegetation; does not normally enter deep water.
Food and Feeding. Grasses, sedges and green parts of other plants obtained by grazing on dry land in meadows and rough pasture along river banks; invertebrates (worms, adults and larvae of insects, snails) and small reptiles also recorded.
Breeding. Starts Mar. In single pairs; nest built on ground, concealed amidst vegetation. Usually 4-7 eggs (4-12); incubation c. 30-34 days; chicks have black-brown down above, silvery white below; fledging 85-100 days. Sexual maturity probably at 2 years.
Movements. Mostly sedentary, with only a few, small-scale movements recorded, generally related to altitudinal shifts.
Status and Conservation. Not globally threatened. Still considered locally common within its very restricted range. Survey of Web Valley in 1966 produced 30 pairs in 40 km, with extrapolated total of 200-300 pairs for whole valley; density thought to be lower elsewhere. Not threatened by hunting since religious beliefs have prevented its being hunted; probably threatened by growth of human population, with concurrent transformation of habitats. More precise information needed on present numbers and conservation requirements.
Bibliography. Blaauw (1927), Brickell (1988), Brown, L.H. (1966), Brown *et al.* (1982), Delacour (1954-1964), Kolbe (1972), von Loeffler (1977), Mackworth-Praed & Grant (1957-1973), Urban (1980), Veselovsky (1989).

Genus *CHLOEPHAGA* Eyton, 1838

36. Andean Goose
Chloephaga melanoptera

French: Ouette des Andes   **German**: Andengans   **Spanish**: Cauquén Guayata

Taxonomy. *Anser melanopterus* Eyton, 1838, Lake Titicaca. Monotypic.
Distribution. Andes from C Peru to C Argentina.
Descriptive notes. 70-80 cm; 2730-3640 g. Female smaller. Unmistakable. All *Chloephaga* have white wing-coverts and secondaries obvious, in flight. Greater coverts show glossy speculum; purple

On following pages: 37. Upland Goose (*Chloephaga picta*); 38. Kelp Goose (*Chloephaga hybrida*); 39. Ashy-headed Goose (*Chloephaga poliocephala*); 40. Ruddy-headed Goose (*Chloephaga rubidiceps*); 41. Orinoco Goose (*Neochen jubata*); 42. Egyptian Goose (*Alopochen aegyptiacus*).

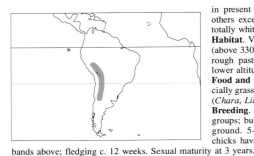

in present species and metallic green in all others except male *C. hybrida* which shows totally white speculum. Juvenile drabber.
Habitat. Variety of wetlands on high ground (above 3300 m), surrounded by grassland and rough pastures. Often forced to descend to lower altitudes by winter snow.
Food and Feeding. Mainly vegetarian, especially grasses, sedges and fleshy aquatic plants (*Chara, Lilaeopsis, Myriophyllum, Nostoc*).
Breeding. Starts Nov. In single pairs or loose groups; builds shallow nest of vegetation on ground. 5-10 eggs; incubation c. 30 days; chicks have white down with three blackish bands above; fledging c. 12 weeks. Sexual maturity at 3 years.
Movements. Mostly sedentary, with only small-scale movements recorded and generally linked to altitudinal shifts.
Status and Conservation. Not globally threatened. Generally widespread and common throughout most of range; common in *puna* of Peru. No information available on size of population. In Feb 1982, 2000 individuals recorded at Laguna Pozuelos, Argentina. Apparently fairly well isolated from typical human threats, because inhabits inaccessible areas; species quite unsuitable for human exploitation.
Bibliography. Blake (1977), Carp (1991), Delacour (1954-1964), Fjeldså & Krabbe (1990), Hellmayr & Conover (1948), Hiebl & Braunitzer (1988), Johnson (1965), Kolbe (1979), Narosky & Yzurieta (1987), de la Peña (1986), Scott & Carbonell (1986), Summers & Castro (1988).

37. **Upland Goose**
Chloephaga picta

French: Ouette de Magellan **German**: Magellangans **Spanish**: Cauquén Común
Other common names: Lesser Magellan Goose (*picta*); Greater/Falkland Magellan Goose (*leucoptera*)

Taxonomy. *Anas picta* Gmelin, 1789, Staten Island.
Two subspecies recognized.
Subspecies and Distribution.
C. p. picta (Gmelin, 1789) - C Chile and C Argentina to Tierra del Fuego.
C. p. leucoptera (Gmelin, 1789) - Falkland Is.

Descriptive notes. 60-72·5 cm; 2721-3200 g. Unmistakable. Strongly barred. Two morphs separated on extension of barring. Juvenile male has dusky brown feathers on head. Race *leucoptera* is larger; male has narrower ventral bars.
Habitat. Continental birds not generally associated with water, frequenting dry pastures and arable land for most of year; on grassy islands or coastal meadows in Falkland Is, often far from water too.
Food and Feeding. Almost exclusively vegetarian; leaves, stems and seed-heads of grasses (*Poa annua, P. pratensis*) and sedges. Feeds mainly by grazing on dry meadows and rough pasture.
Breeding. Starts Sept (Falklands) or Oct/Nov (continent). In single pairs or loose groups; nest on ground, among vegetation, preferably near water. 5-8 eggs; incubation c. 30 days; chicks have olive grey or drab brown down; fledging c. 9-10 weeks. Sexual maturity at 3 years.
Movements. Birds of southernmost part of range descend to lower latitudes (occurring N to Buenos Aires Province, Argentina, and exceptionally to Uruguay) during austral winter. Falkland Is population mostly sedentary.
Status and Conservation. Not globally threatened. Total numbers unknown; formerly very numerous, with records of flocks of thousands. Widely distributed and abundant, both on continent and in Falkland Is, where is especially common on greens and settlements, around ponds and by creeks in coastal areas. During breeding season of 1973, 25,000-30,000 recorded in Tierra del Fuego. Partial census of Meseta de Strobel, Argentina, in Feb 1984 yielded 3700 individuals. Treated as pest and intensely persecuted by farmers and cattle breeders, who destroy eggs and kill large numbers, when birds moulting and therefore flightless.
Bibliography. Blake (1977), Carp (1991), Clark (1986), Fjeldså & Krabbe (1990), Hellmayr & Conover (1948), Humphrey *et al.* (1970), Johnson (1965), Kolbe (1979), Martin, S. (1984), Narosky & Yzurieta (1987), de la Peña (1986), Scott & Carbonell (1986), Siegfried *et al.* (1988), Weller (1972, 1975d), Woods (1988).

38. **Kelp Goose**
Chloephaga hybrida

French: Ouette marine **German**: Kelpgans **Spanish**: Cauquén Caranca

Taxonomy. *Anas Hybrida* Molina, 1782, Chiloé Island.
Two subspecies recognized.

Subspecies and Distribution.
C. h. hybrida (Molina, 1782) - S Chile, Tierra del Fuego.
C. h. malvinarum Phillips, 1916 - Falkland Is.
Descriptive notes. 55-65 cm; c. 2041-2607 g. Female slightly smaller, with totally different plumage. Juvenile male as female but with brown greater coverts and dull greenish yellow legs. Juvenile female has dark uppertail-coverts. Race *malvinarum* is larger, especially evident in bill.
Habitat. Breeds on coastal freshwater lakes but spends most of year along rocky coastlines or on shingle beaches.
Food and Feeding. Almost entirely vegetarian; forages along the coastline feeding on seaweed and algae; also green grasses on breeding grounds and berries in winter.

Breeding. Starts Oct/Nov. In single pairs or loose groups; nest made from grasses, lined with down, situated on low rocky outcrops or on ground among vegetation. 3-7 eggs; incubation c. 30 days; fledging c. 12-13 weeks. Sexual maturity at 3 years.
Movements. Continental race relatively sedentary, with small-scale winter movements along coast of Chile and up Atlantic coast of Argentina. Falkland Is population mostly sedentary.
Status and Conservation. Not globally threatened. Size of total population unknown, but thought to be abundant. Common resident and widely distributed in Falkland Is. In past, population on E coast of Isla Grande (Tierra del Fuego) was reported to number hundreds. Situation similar to that of *C. melanoptera*, as does not compete with human interests due to inaccessibility and types of habitats preferred; no evidence of any significant threats.
Bibliography. Blake (1977), Clark (1986), Gladstone & Martell (1968), Hellmayr & Conover (1948), Humphrey *et al.* (1970), Johnson (1965), Narosky & Yzurieta (1987), Pettingill (1965), Scott & Carbonell (1986), Weller (1972, 1975d), Woods (1975, 1988).

39. **Ashy-headed Goose**
Chloephaga poliocephala

French: Ouette à tête grise **German**: Graukopfgans **Spanish**: Cauquén Cabecigrís

Taxonomy. *Chloëphaga poliocephala* P. L. Sclater, 1857, Chiloé Island.
Monotypic.
Distribution. S Chile and S Argentina to Tierra del Fuego.

Descriptive notes. 50-60 cm; 2200-2267 g. Unmistakable. Sexes alike, female slightly smaller with finely barred breast. Juvenile has much duller rufous areas; mantle and breast more strongly barred; speculum tending towards dark brown rather than metallic green.
Habitat. Favours damp forest clearings on high ground and islands. Winters on more open habitat, frequenting natural meadows and rough pastures.
Food and Feeding. Presumably mainly vegetarian; leaves, stems and seed-heads of grasses and sedges. Feeds by grazing on meadows and rough pasture.

Breeding. Starts Oct/Nov. In single pairs or loose groups; nest abundantly lined with down, and placed in tree-hollows or long grass. 4-6 eggs; incubation c. 30 days; chicks have olive grey or drab brown down.
Movements. Partially migratory, moving N to winter in *pampas* region to Buenos Aires Province, Argentina. Has occurred E to Falkland Is.
Status and Conservation. Not globally threatened. Total population unknown. Considered especially common in Chile; rarer in rest of range; rare in Falklands, and relatively scarce in Tierra del Fuego where 2000-3000 birds counted during breeding season of 1973. Relatively free from human persecution at breeding grounds, but in winter associates with other, more abundant sheldgeese and suffers the same persecution by farmers; possible effects on population should be investigated to prevent risk of significant decline.
Bibliography. Blake (1977), Carp (1991), Clark (1986), Fjeldså & Krabbe (1990), Hellmayr & Conover (1948), Humphrey *et al.* (1970), Johnson (1965), Kolbe (1979), Narosky & Yzurieta (1987), de la Peña (1986), Scott & Carbonell (1986), Siegfried *et al.* (1988), Weller (1975d), Woods (1988).

40. **Ruddy-headed Goose**
Chloephaga rubidiceps

French: Ouette à tête rousse **German**: Rotkopfgans **Spanish**: Cauquén Colorado

Taxonomy. *Chloëphaga rubidiceps* P. L. Sclater, 1861, Falkland Islands.
Monotypic.
Distribution. Extreme S South America, Tierra del Fuego, Falkland Is; formerly more widespread.

Descriptive notes. 45-52·5 cm; c. 2000 g. Female slightly smaller; structure as in *C. picta* but coloration different; considerably smaller with thinner barring on underparts. Juvenile much duller with blackish speculum.
Habitat. Open country, frequenting coastal grassland and meadows; often occurs together with *C. picta*.
Food and Feeding. Almost entirely vegetarian; roots, leaves, stems and seed-heads of grasses and sedges. Feeds mostly on land, often by digging out with bill.
Breeding. Starts Sept/Oct. In single pairs or loose groups; nest lined with down, on ground, among vegetation or boulders. 5-8 eggs; incubation c. 30 days.
Movements. Falkland Is population virtually sedentary; Tierra del Fuego birds move N to winter on grasslands of Buenos Aires Province, Argentina.
Status and Conservation. Not globally threatened. Population of mainland S America in critical state: has decreased dramatically and may now number under 1000 birds, if it still exists. Persecuted by hunters and farmers, as is not distinguished from *C. picta*; considered pest in Argentina, at least until end of 1970's. Was abundant in Tierra del Fuego during 1950's, after which declined sharply, partly due to introduction of Patagonian fox (*Dusicyon griseus*), which occupies same habitat. Census of Tierra del Fuego during breeding season of 1973 only yielded 30 birds. Fairly common resident in Falklands despite being treated as pest; 100,000 killed in period 1905-1912, and fair numbers still killed each year; apparently mobility of species renders efforts to reduce its numbers ineffective. Particularly large numbers in dry coastal grassland on W Falkland. Estimated 38,000-141,000 birds in Falklands during 1970's. Considered Vulnerable in Red Data Book (1978/79), but has been removed from threatened list due to size and stability of population of Falklands, and its apparent resilience in face of persecution.
Bibliography. Bertonatti *et al.* (1991), Blake (1977), Collar & Andrew (1988), Diamond *et al.* (1987), Fjeldså & Krabbe (1990), Hellmayr & Conover (1948), Humphrey *et al.* (1970), Johnson (1965), Johnstone (1985), King (1978/79), Kolbe (1979), de la Peña (1986), Plotnik (1961), Rumboll (1975b, 1991), Scott (1954a), Scott & Carbonell (1986), Siegfried *et al.* (1988), Weller (1972, 1975d), Woods (1975, 1988).

Genus *NEOCHEN* Oberholser, 1918

41. **Orinoco Goose**

Neochen jubata

French: Ouette d'Orénoque   **German**: Orinokogans   **Spanish**: Ganso del Orinoco

Taxonomy. *Anser jubatus* Spix, 1825, "Ad ripam fl. Solimoëns in insula Praya das Onças".
A distinctive species which has been proposed as a possible link between the typical shelducks (*Tadorna*) and sheldgeese (*Chloephaga*). Monotypic.
Distribution. Widespread, though spottily distributed, in N South America E of Andes, from E Colombia, Venezuela and the Guianas, southwards through Amazonian Brazil, extreme E Peru, E and S Bolivia and Paraguay to extreme N Argentina (Salta Province).

Descriptive notes. 61-66 cm; 1250 g (female). Unmistakable; disctinctive pattern of bill, with upper mandible mainly black, lower red. Neck looks broad, often ruffled up. Wings dark green with a broad white band accross secondaries conspicuous in flight; speculum glossy green. Sexes alike, though female slightly smaller. Juvenile is washed out version of adult, with underparts buff; lacks gloss on wings and tail and has paler and duller legs and bill.
Habitat. Forest-covered sides of tropical rivers and damp clearings; also in more open country, on wet savanna and on edges of large, freshwater wetlands. Usually in lowlands, up to 500 m; occasionally recorded up to 2600 m.
Food and Feeding. Information on wild birds not available, but presumed to consume greener parts of grasses, sedges and various plants, as well as invertebrates (insects, worms, molluscs). Forages primarily on land, by grazing.
Breeding. During dry season, mostly Jan, in Colombia and Venezuela. In single pairs; nest lined with down, in hollow trees. 6-10 eggs; incubation c. 30 days.
Movements. Chiefly sedentary throughout range, with only small-scale movements recorded; small moult gatherings, usually not exceeding 20 birds, occur after the breeding season.
Status and Conservation. Not globally threatened. Currently considered near-threatened. Widely distributed but very scarce except in protected or remote areas. Common in parts of Bolivia: groups of up to 250 in Laguna Beni and Laguna Pando; amongst commonest waterbirds along R Yacuma. Common breeder in W Bermejo R, Salta (Argentina), in 1980's. Highly susceptible to hunting pressure.

Bibliography. Bertonatti *et al.* (1991), Blake (1977), Delacour (1954-1964), Fjeldså & Krabbe (1990), Gómez-Dallmeier & Cringan (1989), Hellmayr & Conover (1948), Hilty & Brown (1986), Kolbe (1972), Narosky & Yzurieta (1987), de la Peña (1986), Phillips (1922-1926), Pinto (1964), de Schauensee & Phelps (1978), Scott & Carbonell (1986), Sick (1984).

Genus *ALOPOCHEN* Stejneger, 1885

42. **Egyptian Goose**

Alopochen aegyptiacus

French: Ouette d'Egypte   **German**: Nilgans   **Spanish**: Ganso del Nilo

Taxonomy. *Anas aegyptiaca* Linnaeus, 1766, Egypt. Monotypic.
Distribution. Africa S of Sahara, Nile Valley. Introduced in Britain.

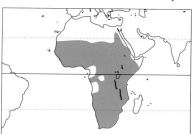

Descriptive notes. 71-73 cm; 1500-2250 g. Facial pattern and variable dark patch on breast distinctive. Fair amount of white on upperwing with iridescent green speculum. Female smaller. Juvenile lacks brown marks around eyes and on breast.
Habitat. Favours a diversity of wetlands in open country, only shunning densely-wooded areas; also occurs on meadows and grassland and, in Ethiopia, in highlands (up to 4000 m).
Food and Feeding. Mostly grass and seeds, leaves and stems of plants, vegetables, grain, shoots and potatoes; also some animal items, such as worms and locusts. Forages mainly by grazing on pasture and arable land; also by dabbling on surface and with head submerged.
Breeding. Season variable, but mostly during local spring or at end of dry season. In single pairs; nest made with reeds, leaves and grass, lined with down, on ground among vegetation, in holes or in trees, sometimes in old nests of other birds. 5-12 eggs; incubation c. 28-30 days; chicks have sooty brown down above, mostly white below; fledging c. 60-75 days. Sexual maturity at 2 years.
Movements. Largely sedentary over much of range, with only some local movements linked with availability of water. Occasional N of Sahara (Algeria, Tunisia) in winter.
Status and Conservation. Not globally threatened. Most widely distributed member of family in Africa. Common to locally abundant, with greatest numbers in S and E Africa; maximum concentration recorded in E Africa was 1740 birds on L Turkana (Kenya) in 1987. In S Africa, 481 counted on L St Lucia. In W Africa maximum recorded was slightly over 3000 birds, and total estimated at over 5000 birds. In parts of range regarded as agricultural pest; also hunted for sport, but has increased in S Africa during present century due to building of dams and irrigation schemes, and since hunting activity curtailed. Introduced to Britain in 17th century, with present feral population of c. 400 birds. Bred in SE Europe until beginning of 18th century and in Israel until c. 1933. CITES III in Ghana.

Bibliography. Bergmann *et al.* (1990), Brickell (1988), Brown & Britton (1980), Brown *et al.* (1982), Clancey (1967), Cramp & Simmons (1977), Dollinger (1988), Edroma & Jumbe (1983), Eltringham (1974), Etchécopar & Hüe (1964), Fraser & McMahon (1991), Geldenhuys (1980, 1981a), Gooders & Boyer (1986), Goodman (1989), Harrison (1988), Lever (1987), Mackworth-Praed & Grant (1957-1973), Maclean (1985), Milstein (1975), Paz (1987), Perennou (1991a, 1991b), Pinto (1983), Pitman (1963), Siegfried (1962a, 1967b), Sutherland & Allport (1991).

43

44

45

46

47

48

49

50

51

52

ssp *niger*

ssp *gambensis*

53

ssp *sylvicola*

54

55

56

ssp *melanotos*

PLATE 43

inches 8

cm 20

Genus *TADORNA* Boie, 1822

43. **Ruddy Shelduck**

Tadorna ferruginea

French: Tadorne casarca   **German**: Rostgans   **Spanish**: Tarro Canelo
Other common names: Brahminy Duck

Taxonomy. *Anas ferruginea* Pallas, 1764, no locality = Tartary.
Sometimes placed in genus *Casarca*, together with *T. cana*, *T. tadornoides* and *T. variegata*. Forms
superspecies with *T. cana*; some also include *T. tadornoides* and *T. variegata*. Hybridization
reported in captivity with several species of *Tadorna*, including *T. radjah*, large species of genus
Anas, and *Alopochen aegyptiacus*. Monotypic.
Distribution. SE Europe E to L Baikal and Mongolia; also in NW Africa, Ethiopian highlands.
Formerly more widespread in W part of range.

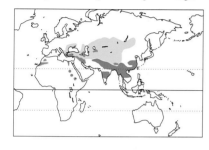

Descriptive notes. 63-66 cm; 925-1640 g.
Upperwing characteristic in flight with white
on coverts, dark primaries and iridescent
green secondaries as in all *Tadorna* species.
Very similar to *T. cana*. Sexes similar, but
female slightly smaller, lacking narrow black
neck-ring; paler face. Juvenile duller with
white upperwing-coverts tinged sooty;
greyish head.
Habitat. Diversity of water bodies of brackish
nature, generally in open country, but also on
sparsely forested, elevated ground in USSR;
these populations descend to lower altitudes
in winter.

Food and Feeding. Grasses, leaves, seeds and stems of plants and sedges, grain, shoots and
vegetables; terrestrial and aquatic invertebrates (worms, insects, crustaceans, molluscs), small fish
and amphibians. Grazes and plucks items on dry land and dabbles, swims and upends in water.
Also frequents rubbish dumps.
Breeding. Starts Mar/Apr. In single pairs or loose groups; nest situated in hole or cavity on ground,
or in tree, lined with feathers and down. Usually 8-9 eggs (6-12); incubation c. 28-29 days; chicks
have dark brown down on upperparts, white below and spots on back; fledging c. 55 days. Sexual
maturity probably at 2 years.
Movements. Asian population largely migratory, moving S to winter at lower latitudes of India
and SE Asia. Other populations chiefly sedentary or only dispersive, with movements linked to
availability of water. Some old records of genuine vagrants in several parts of Europe.
Status and Conservation. Not globally threatened. Has declined markedly in W of range; European
population numbers c. 20,000 birds; c. 1500 birds in NW Africa; c. 12,000 winter regularly in
Turkey. Asian population seems fairly healthy, with significant numbers breeding in China. In Feb
1981, 4000 birds counted wintering at Kosi Barrage and Kosi Tappu Wildlife Reserve, Nepal; 3200
birds in Jan 1988 at Badin and Kadhan Lagoons, Pakistan; census of winter 1991 produced 19,362
birds in Iran. Formerly considered accidental in Japan, but now winters regularly in small numbers.
Reserves established in Europe probably offset decreases caused by wetland drainage, shooting
and human disturbance.

Bibliography. Ali & Ripley (1978), Ash (1977), Bauer & Glutz von Blotzheim (1968), Brazil (1991), Brickell (1988),
Brown *et al*. (1982), Cramp & Simmons (1977), Delacour (1970), Dementiev & Gladkov (1952), Etchécopar & Hüe
(1964, 1978), Gooders & Boyer (1986), Goodman (1989), Grimmett & Jones (1989), Hüe & Etchécopar (1970),
Inskipp & Inskipp (1985), Ledant *et al*. (1981), Liao Yan-fa (1981), Mackworth-Praed & Grant (1957-1973), Monval
& Pirot (1989), Paz (1987), Perennou & Mundkur (1991), Roberts (1991), Smythies (1986), Sugathan *et al*. (1987),
Vieillard (1970).

44. **South African Shelduck**

Tadorna cana

French: Tadorne à tête grise   **German**: Graukopfkasarka   **Spanish**: Tarro Sudafricano
Other common names: African/Cape Shelduck

Taxonomy. *Anas cana* Gmelin, 1789, Cape of Good Hope.
Sometimes placed in genus *Casarca*, together with *T. ferruginea*, *T. tadornoides* and *T. variegata*.
Forms superspecies with *T. ferruginea*; some also include *T. tadornoides* and *T. variegata*. Hybri-
dazation with other *Tadorna* species and *Alopochen aegyptiacus* reported in captivity. Monotypic.
Distribution. S Africa, from C Namibia and S Botswana southwards.
Descriptive notes. 61-66 cm; c. 1400-1750 g. Very similar to *T. ferruginea* but with greyer head.
Upperwing characteristic in flight with white on coverts, dark primaries and iridescent green
secondaries as in all *Tadorna* species. Female slightly smaller with variable amount of white near
eye. Juvenile as male but paler and duller with brownish edging to upperwing-coverts.
Habitat. Favours shallow freshwater and brackish wetlands in open country; moulting flocks
concentrate on deeper waters.
Food and Feeding. Essentially vegetarian during dry season, mainly grain and algae; during rest
of year mostly seeds and also animal items, like insect larvae and crustaceans. Forages by grazing
on land, dabbling and head-dipping in shallow water, and scything on mudflats.
Breeding. Starts Jun/Jul (dry season). In single pairs; nest is lined with plant matter, some feathers
and a thick coat of down, situated in old mammal burrows or in other cavities. Usually about 10

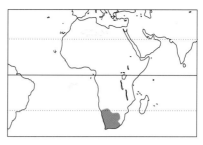

eggs (1-15); incubation c. 30 days; chicks
have dark brown upperparts, silvery white
below with patches on back; fledging c. 10
weeks.
Movements. Basically sedentary, but seasonal
movements related to moulting and to water
availability performed regularly and involving
substantial proportions of total population.
Status and Conservation. Not globally
threatened. Common, with estimated total
population of c. 42,000 in 1981; at present,
population seems fairly stable; species often
found in large flocks of several hundred birds.
Potential threats include: dependence on very
few localities where concentrates in large numbers to moult; requirement of mammal burrows for
nest-sites; and elimination of black-backed jackals (*Canis mesomelas*), which normally kill the
small predators that take eggs of present species. In contrast, construction of dams has provided
potential new sites.

Bibliography. Brickell (1988), Brown *et al*. (1982), Clancey (1967), Delacour (1970), van Ee (1971), Geldenhuys
(1976, 1977, 1979, 1980, 1981a, 1981b), Johnsgard (1965a), Mackworth-Praed & Grant (1957-1973), Perennou
(1991b), Maclean (1985), Siegfried (1966c, 1967b).

45. **Paradise Shelduck**

Tadorna variegata

French: Tadorne de paradis   **German**: Paradieskasarka   **Spanish**: Tarro Maorí
Other common names: Paradise Duck, New Zealand Shelduck

Taxonomy. *Anas variegata* Gmelin, 1789, Dusky Bay, New Zealand.
Sometimes placed in genus *Casarca*, together with *T. ferruginea*, *T. cana* and *T. tadornoides*.
Considered by some to form superspecies with *T. ferruginea*, *T. cana* and *T. tadornoides*. Hybridi-
zation with other *Tadorna* species reported in captivity. Monotypic.
Distribution. North I, South I and Stewart I, New Zealand.

Descriptive notes. 63-71 cm; 1059-2000 g.
Upperwing characteristic in flight with white
on coverts, dark primaries and iridescent green
secondaries as in all *Tadorna* species. Inverted
sexual dimorphism; female has eclipse plumage. Amount of white on female's head variable. Male reminiscent of *T. tadornoides* but
has dark breast and lower neck. Juveniles of
both sexes resemble adult male, but duller, and
females have irregular white feathering on
head.
Habitat. Occupies a diversity of habitats,
from coasts and estuaries to mountain streams,
meadows and lowland flats. As a breeder, most abundant on highland grassy plains of South Island.
Food and Feeding. Highly adaptable to both animal and vegetarian diet; greener parts of grasses,
herbs and sedges as well as several types of invertebrates, like insects, crustaceans.
Breeding. Starts in early Aug, sometimes later; occasionally double-brooded. In single pairs; nest
is lined with a thick layer of down, situated in tree or rock cavity, on cliff ledge or concealed
among vegetation on ground. Usually 8-10 eggs (5-15); incubation c. 32-33 days; chicks have
white down with crown, hindneck and parts of upperbody brown; fledging probably c. 7-10 weeks.
Success of 83% at hatching and of 45% at fledging in one study; average of 4·2 young fledged
per clutch.
Movements. Mainly sedentary, with only small-scale movements reported. Has reached oceanic
archipelago of Chatham Is.
Status and Conservation. Not globally threatened. Generally widespread, with scattered populations; overall population of c. 120,000 birds in 1981. Hunting pressure and introduction of predators, especially stoats and polecats, may have led to some reduction in numbers. Has benefited
from human alterations to environment, in particular clearance of forests to create pastures and
construction of farm dams; range expanded, especially in North I, after arrival of European settlers.

Bibliography. Barker (1990), Bisset (1976), Bull *et al*. (1985), Chambers (1989), Delacour (1970), Falla *et al*.
(1981), Marchant & Higgins (1990), McAllum (1965), Oliver (1955), Soper (1976), Weller (1980), Williams, M.J.
(1971, 1979b, 1981, 1985e), Zander (1967).

46. **Australian Shelduck**

Tadorna tadornoides

French: Tadorne d'Australie   **German**: Halsbandkasarka   **Spanish**: Tarro Australiano
Other common names: Mountain Duck, Chestnut-breasted Shelduck

Taxonomy. *Anas tadornoides* Jardine and Selby, 1828, New South Wales.
Sometimes placed in genus *Casarca*, together with *T. ferruginea*, *T. cana* and *T. variegata*. Considered by some to form superspecies with *T. ferruginea*, *T. cana* and *T. variegata*. Hybridization
with *T. ferruginea* and *T. cana*, and also with *Anser indicus*, reported in captivity. Monotypic.
Distribution. SW and SE Australia, Tasmania.
Descriptive notes. 56-72 cm; 878-1980 g; wingspan 94-132 cm. Unmistakable; contrast between
cinnamon breast and rest of plumage diagnostic. Upperwing characteristic in flight with white on

On following pages: 47. Common Shelduck (*Tadorna tadorna*); 48. Radjah Shelduck (*Tadorna radjah*); 49. Flying Steamerduck (*Tachyeres patachonicus*); 50. Magellanic Steamerduck
(*Tachyeres pteneres*); 51. Falkland Steamerduck (*Tachyeres brachypterus*); 52. White-headed Steamerduck (*Tachyeres leucocephalus*); 53. Spur-winged Goose (*Plectropterus gambensis*);
54. Muscovy Duck (*Cairina moschata*); 55. White-winged Wood Duck (*Cairina scutulata*); 56. Comb Duck (*Sarkidiornis melanotos*)

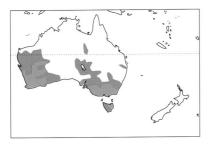

coverts, dark primaries and iridescent green secondaries as in all *Tadorna* species. In non-breeding plumage female has greyish brown body. Juveniles duller than adults, with browner head and lacking well defined neck collar; show some whitish feathering between eye and bill.

Habitat. Shallow freshwater and brackish lakes, lagoons and billabongs, preferably surrounded by scattered trees. Winters on larger water bodies, on estuaries and along sheltered coasts.

Food and Feeding. Combination of vegetable matter (leaves and seeds of plants, sedges and algae) and animal food (aquatic invertebrates, mostly insects, crustaceans, molluscs and small fish), taken by grazing on land and by scything, dabbling and head-dipping in water.

Breeding. Starts Jun/Jul. In single pairs; nest lined only with down, in tree-hollows, cliffs or on ground. Usually 8-10 eggs (5-19); incubation c. 30-33 days (captivity); chicks have white down with crown, hindneck and parts of upperbody brown; fledging c. 50-70 days. Sexual maturity at c. 3 years. In one study at Rottnest I each pair reared 4-5 young per season.

Movements. Largely sedentary in two main breeding centres, with wide-range dispersal after breeding, mainly related to moulting concentrations and availability of water. Has occurred in N Australia and possibly also in New Zealand.

Status and Conservation. Not globally threatened. Widespread and abundant, increasing and expanding in recent years, especially in Western Australia. In SW Australia, 48,802 birds counted at 1398 wetlands in 1988; in Victoria, census yielded 91,558 at 472 wetlands in 1988; at Narrung, SE Australia, c. 15,000 reported in 1983. Almost 75% of population found in waters subject to shooting, but species is not easy to shoot. In places rare, but increasing in several areas due to clearing and conversion to pasture and cropland; may be responsible for substantial crop damage. Construction of freshwater impoundments may have removed constrictions on breeding in some places.

Bibliography. Chambers (1989), Delacour (1954-1964, 1970), Frith (1967), Halse & Jaensch (1989), Kolbe (1979), Macdonald (1988), Marchant & Higgins (1990), Riggert (1977), Robertson (1985), Schodde & Tidemann (1988), Serventy (1985).

47. **Common Shelduck**

Tadorna tadorna

French: Tadorne de Belon   **German**: Brandgans   **Spanish**: Tarro Blanco
Other common names: Shelduck, Northern/Red-billed Shelduck

Taxonomy. *Anas Tadorna* Linnaeus, 1758, coasts of Europe.
One of least typical *Tadorna* species, considered as a link between this genus and *Alopochen*. Hybridization with several species of *Tadorna*, *Alopochen aegyptiacus*, *Anas platyrhynchos* and *Somateria mollissima* recorded in captivity. Monotypic.
Distribution. Coastal NW Europe and scattered Mediterranean sites eastwards through Central Asia to NE China, and south to Iran and Afghanistan.

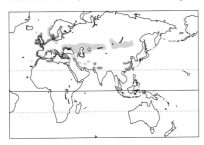

Descriptive notes. 61-63 cm; 801-1450 g. Unmistakable. Upperwing characteristic in flight with white on coverts, dark primaries and iridescent green secondaries as in all *Tadorna* species. Female slightly smaller with less prominent knob on bill and usually some white between bill and eye. Juvenile with largely white underparts and grey or dull black dorsal parts, lacks chestnut breast band, and has white cheeks and throat.

Habitat. Favours coastal mudflats and estuaries, generally occurring in salt water only, particularly in Europe, but often intentionally seeking fresh water as well in order to drink.

Food and Feeding. Mostly aquatic invertebrates (molluscs, insects, crustaceans), with predilection for salt-water snail (*Hydrobia ulvae*), especially in NW Europe; also some small fish and spawn, worms and plant materials. Forages by digging, scything or dabbling on exposed mud and by head-dipping and upending in shallow water.

Breeding. Starts Apr/May. In single pairs or small groups; nest made of grass, moss or bracken, lined with down, in cavities such as hollow trees or rabbit burrows. Usually 8-10 eggs (3-12); incubation c. 29-31 days; chicks have blackish down above and on thighs, white below; fledging c. 45-50 days. Sexual maturity at 2 (female) or 4-5 years (male).

Movements. Most northern and inland populations move southwards to winter at lower latitudes. Even within mainly sedentary populations (e.g. those of Britain and N Sea coasts), some spectacular gatherings at moulting sites, in some cases requiring extensive flights (see page 562).

Status and Conservation. Not globally threatened. Widespread and fairly abundant, especially in W Palearctic, where has increased during last two decades; currently estimated to number c. 325,000 birds, with British population of c. 50,000 birds. In Israel, has become quite common in winter in recent years, with 100-250 birds, and up to 2650 (1983). Winters in large numbers in Iran, with 73,564 individuals recorded in 1991 census. Partial counts in winter 1991 yielded: 3137 in Bangladesh; 4027 in Pakistan; 12,241 in China; and 2333 in South Korea. Large concentrations for moult make species potentially vulnerable to disease or natural disasters.

Bibliography. Ali & Ripley (1978), Bauer & Glutz von Blotzheim (1968), Brazil (1991), Brickell (1988), Brown *et al.* (1982), Bryant & Leng (1975), Clancey (1976), Coombes (1950), Cramp & Simmons (1977), Delacour (1970), Dementiev & Gladkov (1952), Etchécopar & Hüe (1978), Géroudet (1972), Gooders & Boyer (1986), Goodman (1989), Grimmett & Jones (1989), Harrison (1988), Himmatsinhji & Bapat (1989), Hoogerheide & Kraak (1942), Hori (1964, 1969), Jacobs & Ochando (1979), Ledant *et al.* (1981), Marchant *et al.* (1990), Monval & Pirot (1989), Olney (1965), Patterson (1982), Paz (1987), Perennou & Mundkur (1991), Ridgill & Fox (1990), Roberts (1991), Strann (1991), Walmsley (1984, 1987), Young (1970).

48. **Radjah Shelduck**

Tadorna radjah

French: Tadorne radjah   **German**: Radjahgans   **Spanish**: Tarro Rajá
Other common names: White-headed Shelduck, Black-backed Shelduck, Burdekin Duck, Burdekin Shelduck

Taxonomy. *Anas radjah* "Garnot" Lesson, 1828, Buru.
Sometimes placed in monospecific genus *Radjah*. Hybridization recorded in captivity with *T. ferruginea* and *T. tadorna*, producing fertile progeny. Two subspecies recognized.
Subspecies and Distribution.
T. r. radjah (Lesson, 1828) - Moluccas to New Guinea.
T. r. rufitergum Hartert, 1905 - coastal N Australia.

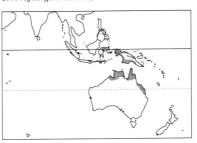

Descriptive notes. 51-61 cm; 600-1130 g. Unmistakable. Upperwing characteristic in flight with white on coverts, dark primaries and iridescent green secondaries as in all *Tadorna*, but present species has narrow blackish subterminal band across white coverts and white trailing edge on secondaries. Juvenile has duller speculum and dirtier white areas of plumage. Subspecies vary mainly in dorsal coloration, more reddish brown in *rufitergum*, blacker in *radjah*.

Habitat. Most commonly found in coastal marshes, lagoons, tidal mudflats, mangrove swamps, sheltered bays and areas of brackish water, but can occur on fresh water during dry season.

Food and Feeding. Mostly animal food, with predominance of aquatic invertebrates, such as molluscs and insects; additionally, some vegetable matter, like algae and sedges. Forages mainly on foot, on land or very shallow water by dabbling or grazing.

Breeding. Laying Feb-May (West of range), Nov-Jan (East), apparently depending on extent and intensity of rainy season. In single pairs; nests in tree-hollows, with probably no material except down, near water. 6-12 eggs; incubation c. 30 days; downy chicks have chestnut crown, brown nape and upperbody and white face, dorsal patches and underparts.

Movements. Mainly sedentary, N Australian race being somewhat dispersive during dry season; has been recorded in S Australia. New Guinea population not recorded far from known breeding range.

Status and Conservation. Not globally threatened. Rather uncommon and absent from several suitable areas within main range; has declined due to excessive hunting pressure, as confiding nature and weak flight make it easy to shoot. In New Guinea, widely distributed but local, normally in pairs or in small flocks of up to 40 birds; 150 recorded in small part of Bensbach River and the Tonda Wildlife Management Area, Papua New Guinea, in Aug 1988. Appears to be fairly numerous in Moluccas. Race *rufitergum* assumed to breed throughout most of range, but unconfirmed in several areas. Until end of 19th century, was widespread in region of Kimberley, Western Australia, and in NE New South Wales, but has disappeared from both areas, probably due to hunting. Local populations tend to decline where settlements, agriculture, mining or roads established; start of rice cultivation in strongholds of species in monsoon zone of Northern Territory may thus represent major threat.

Bibliography. Beehler *et al.* (1986), Coates (1985), Delacour (1954-1964, 1970), Frith (1967), Kolbe (1979), Marchant & Higgins (1990), Morton *et al.* (1990), Schodde & Tidemann (1988), White & Bruce (1986).

Tribe TACHYERINI

Genus *TACHYERES*   Owen, 1875

49. **Flying Steamerduck**

Tachyeres patachonicus

French: Brassemer de Patagonie   **Spanish**: Patovapor Volador
German: Langflügel-Dampfschiffente
Other common names: Canvasback (!)(Falkland Islands)

Taxonomy. *Oidemia Patachonica* King, 1828, Strait of Magellan.
Presumed to be the centre of evolution of genus *Tachyeres*, from which the other species would have radiated. Monotypic.
Distribution. Mainly coasts of S Chile, extreme S Argentina, Tierra del Fuego and Falkland Is.
Descriptive notes. 66-71 cm; 2438-3175 g. Like other *Tachyeres* has white secondaries and greater coverts. More slender and capable of flight than other members of genus. Male has pale head, though less so than *T. leucocephalus*. Female slightly smaller than male; almost identical in plumage to female of *T. brachypterus*, but has less yellow on bill. Juvenile greyish without wine-coloured tones.
Habitat. Most adaptable of *Tachyeres*, occurring both inland, on freshwater lakes, pools and rivers and, especially outside breeding season, on marine inshore waters along rocky coastlines.
Food and Feeding. Consumes primarily aquatic invertebrates (molluscs, crustaceans), captured both in salt and fresh water by diving.
Breeding. Starts Oct/Nov. In single pairs; nests on small islets and well concealed among vegetation. Usually about c. 7 eggs (5-9); incubation c. 30-40 days; chicks have earth-coloured down above, whitish below with broad stripe through eye and behind cheeks; fledging period unknown, but evidently long.

Movements. Mainly sedentary, with only small-scale movements along coast after breeding season. Has occurred N to mouth of R Negro, C Argentina.

Status and Conservation. Not globally threatened. Common in some areas of Argentina, e.g. barren upland plateaux of inland Santa Cruz; one of most frequent nesting birds in several small lakes 40 km E of Calafate, Santa Cruz; in Feb 1984 census, 2500 individuals counted at Laguna del Islote and 118 other lakes on Meseta de Strobel. Scattered population on Falkland Is; numbers unknown due to extensive confusion with *T. brachypte-rus*. Appears to be fairly numerous in S Chile. Throughout range is said to be less common than respective sympatric flightless species. No significant threats known.

Bibliography. Anon. (1991c), Blake (1977), Carp (1991), Corbin *et al.* (1988), Fjeldså & Krabbe (1990), Hellmayr & Conover (1948), Humphrey & Livezey (1982), Humphrey *et al.* (1970), Johnson (1965), Livezey (1989a), Livezey & Humphrey (1983), Moynihan (1958), Murphy (1936), Nuechterlein & Storer (1985), de la Peña (1986), Ryan *et al.* (1988), Scott & Carbonell (1986), Weller (1972, 1975d, 1976, 1980), Woods (1988).

50. **Magellanic Steamerduck**

Tachyeres pteneres

French: Brassemer cendré **Spanish**: Patovapor del Magallanes
German: Magellan-Dampfschiffente
Other common names: Magellanic Flightless/Flightless Steamerduck, Racehorse, Seahorse, Loggerhead

Taxonomy. *Anas pteneres* J. R. Forster, 1844, Tierra del Fuego.
Often considered to form superspecies with *T. brachypterus* and *T. leucocephalus*. Monotypic.
Distribution. Coast from SC Chile to Tierra del Fuego.

Descriptive notes. 74-84 cm; 3629-6180 g. Sturdy bill. Male has grey head, not contrasting with rest of plumage. Sexual dimorphism not as marked as in other *Tachyeres*, as female also has orange bill; female smaller than male, with somewhat darker head. Juvenile grey without wine-coloured tones, and has narrow pale eye-ring.
Habitat. Frequents rocky coasts, where may be found several miles offshore. Breeds along shoreline, in sheltered bays or channels.
Food and Feeding. Dives in rather shallow waters among kelp beds; main diet consists of aquatic molluscs (Mytilidae) and crustaceans; some small fish also taken. Foraging activity mostly during high tide.

Breeding. Starts Sept/Oct. In single pairs; nests near water, well hidden among vegetation. 5-8 eggs; incubation said to be c. 30-40 days; downy chick is smoke-coloured on head and back, whitish on underparts.
Movements. Sedentary, with only small-scale dispersion along adjacent coasts. Essentially flightless.
Status and Conservation. Not globally threatened. Common or fairly abundant within its restricted range. Possible threats may arise from flightlessness and restriction to coastal zone: a tidal wave, for example, could seriously affect population as a whole.
Bibliography. Anon. (1991c), Blake (1977), Carp (1991), Clark (1986), Corbin *et al.* (1988), Hellmayr & Conover (1948), Humphrey *et al.* (1970), Johnson (1965), Livezey (1989a), Livezey & Humphrey (1983), Lowe (1934), Moynihan (1958), Murphy (1936), Ryan *et al.* (1988), Scott & Carbonell (1986), Weller (1975d, 1976).

51. **Falkland Steamerduck**

Tachyeres brachypterus

French: Brassemer des Malouines **Spanish**: Patovapor Malvinero
German: Falkland-Dampfschiffente
Other common names: Falkland Flightless Steamerduck, Logger, Loggerhead

Taxonomy. *Anas brachyptera* Latham, 1790, Falkland Islands.
Often considered to form superspecies with *T. pteneres* and *T. leucocephalus*. Synonymous with *T. brachydactyla*. Monotypic.
Distribution. Restricted to Falkland Is.

Descriptive notes. 61-74 cm; c. 3400-4420 g. Male's grey head contrasts little with rest of plumage; base of foreneck shows faint earth-coloured hue. Female smaller than male; very similar to female of *T. patachonicus*, but has more yellow on bill. Juvenile resembles female but lacks white streak behind eye; adult-like plumage attained by end of first year.
Habitat. Frequents rugged shorelines, being most common on small islands and in sheltered bays.
Food and Feeding. Variety of salt-water molluscs (mussels, limpets) and crustaceans (crabs, shrimps) constitute base of diet. Forages by diving near shore or by upending in shallow waters, generally on incoming tides.

Breeding. Season variable, but most breeding occurs Sept-Dec. In single pairs; nests not far from water, concealed among vegetation or in unoccupied penguin burrow. 5-10 eggs; incubation c. 34 days (28-40); fledging c. 12 weeks.
Movements. Reportedly sedentary, with some small-scale movements within Falkland Is. Essentially flightless.
Status and Conservation. Not globally threatened. Widespread and common to abundant around coasts of Falklands. High mortality of chicks due to predation by Kelp Gulls (*Larus dominicanus*) and skuas (*Catharacta*); adults have no enemies except occasionally sea lions (*Otaria*). No significant threats known.
Bibliography. Corbin *et al.* (1988), Lowe (1934), Livezey (1989a), Livezey & Humphrey (1983), Pettingill (1965), Scott & Carbonell (1986), Weller (1972, 1976, 1980), Woods (1975, 1988).

52. **White-headed Steamerduck**

Tachyeres leucocephalus

French: Brassemer à tête blanche **Spanish**: Patovapor Cabeciblanco
German: Weißkopf-Dampfschiffente
Other common names: White-headed Flightless Steamerduck, Chubut Steamerduck

Taxonomy. *Tachyeres leucocephalus* Humphrey and Thompson, 1981, Chubut Province, Argentina. Although locally abundant, not described until 1981; old records of occurrence of *T. pteneres* on Chubut coast presumably refer to present species. Often considered to form superspecies with *T. pteneres* and *T. brachypterus*. Monotypic.
Distribution. Restricted to S coast of Chubut province, Argentina.

Descriptive notes. 61-74 cm; c. 2950-3800 g. Head of male much whiter than in other *Tachyeres*, contrasting with rest of plumage. Female separable by line behind eye extending as far as foreneck. Juvenile similar to female but with eye-line diffuse and faint.
Habitat. Entirely coastal, has not been recorded in freshwater lagoons; rocky coasts and sheltered bays. Breeds on offshore islands and peninsulas.
Food and Feeding. No specific information, although, as in other members of genus, diet probably based on marine molluscs and crustaceans. Forages mostly by diving in marine inshore waters; also recorded upending.

Breeding. During spring and summer, Oct-Feb. Usually in single pairs, although relatively large, dense colonies located on some offshore islands. Nest is hidden under bushes, not far from water.
Movements. Sedentary, although as in other *Tachyeres*, small-scale movements probably occur outside breeding season, when birds form large concentrations. Essentially flightless.
Status and Conservation. Not globally threatened. Apparently abundant within very restricted range. Minute range and flightlessness could make species vulnerable, although no threats known at present.
Bibliography. Corbin *et al.* (1988), Humphrey & Livezey (1985), Humphrey & Thompson (1981), Livezey (1989a), Livezey & Humphrey (1983), Livezey *et al.* (1985), Narosky & Yzurieta (1987), de la Peña (1986), Scott & Carbonell (1986).

Tribe CAIRININI

Genus *PLECTROPTERUS* Stephens, 1824

53. **Spur-winged Goose**

Plectropterus gambensis

French: Oie-armée de Gambie **German**: Spomgans **Spanish**: Ganso Espolonado
Other common names: Spur-winged Duck

Taxonomy. *Anas gambensis* Linnaeus, 1766, Gambia.
Some authors have proposed isolation of present species in a tribe (Plectropterini), or even in a subfamily (Plectropterinae), of its own. Two subspecies recognized.
Subspecies and Distribution.
P. g. gambensis (Linnaeus, 1766) - Gambia to Ethiopia, S to Angola and Zambezi R.
P. g. niger Sclater, 1877 - S Africa, from Namibia and Zimbabwe to Cape Province.
Descriptive notes. 75-100 cm; 4000-6800 g. Unmistakable. Variable amounts of white on upper-wing-coverts. Female similar to male, but somewhat smaller, with duller facial coloration and smaller bill caruncles. Juvenile lacks bare facial skin, browner on face and neck and body feathers fringed brown; also less white on wings and underparts. Subspecies *niger* has less white on underparts and face, although much individual variation.
Habitat. Common in marshes, rivers, lakes, reservoirs, etc., particularly where they are surrounded by scattered trees and near grassland or arable land.
Food and Feeding. Basically vegetarian diet; greener parts and seeds of grasses, sedges, aquatic vegetation, grain, fruit, vegetables (tubers); occasionally small fish. Forages mostly on land, by grazing. Often considered a local pest for agriculture.
Breeding. Starts during or near end of rainy season. In single pairs; nest is made of twigs, grasses, reed stems and leaves, lined with down, built in trees, often in old nests of other birds, in

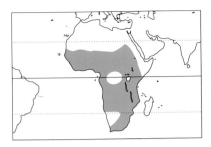

tree-hollows or on ground. 6-14 eggs; incubation c. 30-33 days; chicks have olivaceous brown down on upperparts with silvery white panel on wing and scapulars, yellowish below; fledging c. 10 weeks.
Movements. Undertakes seasonal movements mostly related with availability of water; during dry season, birds congregate to moult, often to N of normal breeding range (Lake Chad, Senegal Delta). Has occurred in Egypt (formerly regular in Abu Simbel area), Oman and Morocco.
Status and Conservation. Not globally threatened. Seasonally common to abundant, occurring on majority of large inland water bodies. In 1987, total of 38,000 birds counted in W Africa, with maximum concentration of 25,000 on reservoir of L Maga (N Cameroon); over 26,000 recorded in E Africa. Race *niger* common to very common in South Africa. Species is neither highly valued by hunters nor easy to hunt, so not under much pressure from hunting. N populations may have been affected by desiccation of Sahel zone. CITES III in Ghana.
Bibliography. Brickell (1988), Britton (1980), Brosset & Erard (1986), Brown & Britton (1980), Brown *et al.* (1982), Browne (1979), Clancey (1967), Clark, A. (1980a), Dollinger (1988), Elgood (1982), Mackworth-Praed & Grant (1957-1973), Maclean (1985), Perennou (1991a, 1991b), Pinto (1983), Pitman (1963), Prozesky (1959), Treca (1979, 1980).

Genus *CAIRINA*   Fleming, 1822

54. **Muscovy Duck**

Cairina moschata

French: Canard musqué   **German**: Moschusente   **Spanish**: Pato Criollo
Other common names: Muscovy, Musky, Musk Duck(!)

Taxonomy. *Anas moschata* Linnaeus, 1758, India = Brazil.
Recently included in tribe Anatini by some authors. Monotypic.
Distribution. Tropical America from Mexico S to E Peru and N Uruguay.
Descriptive notes. 66-84 cm; 1100-4000 g. Unmistakable. Amount of white on upperwing-coverts varies with age. Female smaller with totally feathered face, lacking prominent knob on bill. Juvenile has considerably less iridescent plumage overall, and has little or no white on upperwing.
Habitat. Well wooded tropical wetlands, preferably in lowlands; occasionally on coastal lagoons or marshes. Breeds mostly by or near slow-flowing rivers.
Food and Feeding. Mixture of vegetable and animal foods; roots, seeds, stems and leaves of grasses, sedges and aquatic plants, small vertebrates (fish, reptiles) and invertebrates (insects, arachnids, crustaceans), with special predilection for termites. Feeds by dabbling and upending in shallow water and by grazing on land.
Breeding. Season variable, but mostly during period of rains; Jun in Panama, Jul in Venezuela. In single pairs; nests in tree-hollows or cavities, with little or no down added. Generally 8-15 eggs; incubation c. 35 days (captivity).
Movements. Mainly sedentary, but subject to local movements linked with water availability during dry season, with occasional appearances outside normal breeding range. Has occurred in USA (Texas), Trinidad, coastal Peru and Buenos Aires Province, Argentina.
Status and Conservation. Not globally threatened. Widespread, but only locally common. Has declined somewhat: during early 1960's, up to 1280 recorded in coastal lagoons in Sescapa, Mexico, but at present only small numbers remain; has disappeared from Cauca Valley, W Colombia, due to excessive hunting; in Honduras, has decreased, probably because of habitat destruction and hunting. Common in Nicaragua and parts of Guatemala. Seasonally, up to 400 concentrate in Palo Verde National Park, Costa Rica. Threatened by egg-collecting and natural populations may be subject to hybridization with domestic birds. CITES III in Honduras.
Bibliography. Belton (1984), Bent (1923-1925), Clayton (1984), Donkin (1989), Gómez-Dallmeier & Cringan (1989), Hellmayr & Conover (1948), Hilty & Brown (1986), Johnsgard (1975), Leopold (1959), Markum & Baldassarre (1989a), Monroe (1968), Palmer (1976), de la Peña (1986), Rangel & Bolen (1984), Raud & Faure (1988), Ridgely & Gwynne (1989), Ruschi (1979), Schaldach (1963), de Schauensee & Phelps (1978), Scott & Carbonell (1986), Sick (1984), Slud (1964), Terres (1980), Thibault & Guyot (1988), Wetmore (1965), Woodyard & Bolen (1984).

55. **White-winged Wood Duck**

Cairina scutulata

French: Canard à ailes blanches **German**: Weißflügel-Moschusente   **Spanish**: Pato de Jungla
Other common names: White-winged Duck

Taxonomy. *Anas scutulata* S. Müller, 1842, Java.
Recently included in tribe Anatini by some authors. Sometimes placed in monospecific genus *Asarcornis*. Monotypic.

Distribution. Relict populations in India, Thailand, Bangladesh, Burma, Viet Nam and Sumatra; formerly more widespread throughout range, and also in Java.

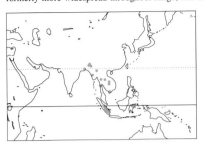

Descriptive notes. 66-81 cm; 1925-3855 g. Unmistakable. Upperwing-coverts, except greater coverts, white. Female smaller, with heavier blackish spotting on head; brownish iris. Juvenile duller and browner.
Habitat. A tropical forest species, inhabiting undisturbed, secluded pools and marshes in dense, swampy forest.
Food and Feeding. Seeds and green parts of various aquatic plants, grain, rice, molluscs (snails) and small vertebrates (fish). Feeds mostly at night, chiefly by dabbling and head-dipping in shallow water; also reported to dive occasionally.
Breeding. During rainy season. In single pairs; nests in tree-hollows, in old nests of other birds or on ground. 6-13 eggs; incubation 33-35 days (captivity).
Movements. Mainly sedentary, with no more than local movements on record.
Status and Conservation. VULNERABLE. CITES I. In 19th century was widespread and locally common. Marked decline due to destruction of lowland tropical forests and also to locally intense hunting pressure. Has become extinct in several countries. Known population in wild numbers only c. 200 birds, with overall total estimated at under 1000 birds. Only c. 40 small, isolated populations known, surviving in forest patches in India, Thailand, Bangladesh, Burma, Viet Nam and Sumatra. In Burma, numbers dropped from 1000 birds in 1971 in Moe-Yum-Gyi Waterfowl Sanctuary, to only 100 in 1978. In one population in Bangladesh, 74% of nestlings taken by hunters. Only 10 populations occur in protected areas; each pair reckoned to require c. 100 ha of well conserved habitat. Urgent need for adequate network of well protected reserves, and strict control of hunting which is still rampant throughout most of range. By 1976, total of c. 70 captive-bred birds released to bolster dwindling wild populations; further reintroductions may offer long-term solution, but underlying causes of decline must first be dealt with. As species tends to be both solitary and secretive, overall numbers very difficult to estimate, but situation is clearly precarious and species should probably be reclassified as Endangered.
Bibliography. Ali & Ripley (1978), Collar & Andrew (1988), Dollinger (1988), Gee (1958), Green (1990, 1991), Holmes (1976, 1977b, 1990b), Hoogerwerf (1950), Humphrey & Bain (1990), King (1978/79), Lambert (1988), Lubbock (1976), Mackenzie (1990), Mackenzie & Kear (1976), van Marle & Voous (1988), Medway & Wells (1976), Mountfort (1988), Nash & Nash (1985), Ounsted (1988), Robinson & Kloss (1910, 1911), Silvius & de Yongh (1989), Smythies (1986), Stanford & Ticehurst (1939).

Genus *SARKIDIORNIS*   Eyton, 1838

56. **Comb Duck**

Sarkidiornis melanotos

French: Canard-à-bosse bronzé   **German**: Glanzente   **Spanish**: Pato Crestudo
Other common names: Knob-billed Duck/Goose, Black-backed Goose; South American Comb Duck (*sylvicola*)

Taxonomy. *Anser melanotos* Pennant, 1769, Ceylon.
Sometimes isolated in its own tribe (Sarkidiornini). Race *sylvicola* sometimes considered full species. Two subspecies recognized.
Subspecies and Distribution.
S. m. melanotos (Pennant, 1769) - Africa S of Sahara and Madagascar; tropical Asia from Pakistan through Indian Subcontinent to extreme S China.
S. m. sylvicola Ihering & Ihering, 1907 - tropical South America from Colombia to N Argentina.

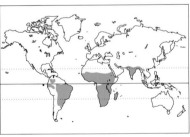

Descriptive notes. 56-76 cm; 1230-2610 g. Unmistakable. Fleshy knob of male smaller outside breeding season. Female smaller without knob over bill; lacks yellowish on head and cinnamon undertail-coverts; flanks different. Juvenile brownish. Subspecies *sylvicola* is a little smaller and has blackish flanks.
Habitat. Swamps, rivers and lakes with thinly scattered trees; also in more open grasslands.
Food and Feeding. Diet based on vegetable matter, mostly seeds of grasses, sedges and aquatic plants and grain, complemented with terrestrial and aquatic invertebrates (insects). Grazes on land and swims, dabbles and wades in shallow water.
Breeding. Season variable, but generally during rainy season. In single pairs or small groups; nest is rough structure of twigs and coarse grass, lined with fine grass, leaves and feathers, built in tree-hollows, occasionally on ground. 6-20 eggs; incubation c. 28-30 days; chicks have sooty brown down above, buffish yellow face and underparts; fledging c. 10 weeks.
Movements. Mainly sedentary, with seasonal movements mostly related to availability of water during dry season. Some extensive journeys performed.
Status and Conservation. Not globally threatened. CITES II. Widespread and locally common. Healthiest populations in Africa, where locally abundant on well watered savanna: 32,800 birds counted in W Africa; 510 birds recorded at Kafue Flats, Zambia, Nov 1970. Widespread throughout Madagascar in small numbers, though abundant in places; has become rare on L Aloatra and generally in E, due to hunting. Generally uncommon in Asia, but locally common; numerous in India, e.g. 200 individuals recorded in Jan 1987 at Dudhwa National Park. Very scarce or extinct in Sri Lanka. S American race *sylvicola* (possibly full species) currently considered near-threatened; widespread, but much scarcer than nominate race, with good populations only in some areas of

Venezuela, e.g. 250 at Hato Masaguaral, in *llanos*; threats include overhunting, deforestation and indiscriminate use of poison in rice fields.

Bibliography. Ali & Ripley (1978), Belton (1984), Bertonatti *et al.* (1991), Blake (1977), Brickell (1988), Brown *et al.* (1982), Clancey (1967), D'Eath (1967), Dollinger (1988), Etchécopar & Hüe (1978), Gómez-Dallmeier & Cringan (1989), Harwin (1971), Hellmayr & Conover (1948), Humphrey & Bain (1990), Langrand (1990), Mackworth-Praed & Grant (1957-1973), Maclean (1985), Milon *et al.* (1973), Nores & Yzurieta (1980), Ortiz (1988), Perennou (1991b), de la Peña (1986), Pinto (1983), Pitman (1963), Ridgely & Gwynne (1989), Roberts (1991), Ruschi (1979), Scott & Carbonell (1986), Sick (1984), Siegfried (1979), Wetmore (1965), Wilson & Wilson (1980).

57 ♀ ♂

58 ♀ ♂

59 ♂ ♀

60 ♂ ♀

61 ♂ ♀

62 ♂ ♀

63 ♀ ♂

64 ♂ ♀

65 ♂ pale phase ♀ dark phase

66 ssp *armata* ♂ ssp *turneri* ♂ ssp *garleppi* ♂

67 ssp *colombiana* ♂ ♀

PLATE 44

inches 8
cm 20

Genus *PTERONETTA* Salvadori, 1895

57. Hartlaub's Duck
Pteronetta hartlaubii

French: Ptéronette de Hartlaub **German**: Hartlaubente **Spanish**: Pato de Hartlaub
Other common names: Hartlaub's Goose/Teal

Taxonomy. *Querquedula Hartlaubii* Cassin, 1859, Camma River, Gabon.
Sometimes placed in genus *Cairina*. Birds with extensive white on head were formerly considered distinct subspecies, *albifrons*. Monotypic.
Distribution. Equatorial W Africa.

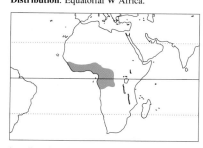

Descriptive notes. 56-58 cm; 800-940 g. Male can have a lot more white on head; bill base becomes swollen in breeding season. Female slightly smaller, duller, with little or no white on forehead; bill does not enlarge; pale markings greyer and less yellow. Juvenile has straw-coloured feather tips on breast and abdomen.
Habitat. Secluded marshes and pools in dense, swampy tropical evergreen forest and small rivers and streams in well-wooded areas.
Food and Feeding. Mostly aquatic invertebrates (insects, arachnids, molluscs, crustaceans) and some vegetable matter (seeds, roots).
Breeding. No nests ever found in wild, but breeding thought to occur during rainy season. Presumably in single pairs or small groups with nests in tree-hollows. 7-11 eggs; incubation c. 30-32 days (captivity); chicks have sooty black down above, yellowish below; fledging c. 8 weeks (captivity). Sexual maturity at 1 year in captivity.
Movements. Mainly sedentary throughout range, with only local movements recorded.
Status and Conservation. Not globally threatened. Widespread in well forested areas, on which is totally dependent; may be locally common. Very little information available, but throughout most of range species is not apparently rare. Uncommon breeding resident in Liberia and Sudan; widespread but scarce resident in Sierra Leone. CITES III in Ghana.
Bibliography. Brickell (1988), Brosset & Erard (1986), Brown *et al.* (1982), Chapin (1932), Dollinger (1988), Elgood (1982), Lernould (1977, 1983), Mackworth-Praed & Grant (1957-1973), Phillips (1922-1926), Pinto (1983).

Genus *NETTAPUS* Brandt, 1836

58. Green Pygmy-goose
Nettapus pulchellus

French: Anserelle élégante **German**: Australische Zwergente **Spanish**: Gansito Australiano
Other common names: Green Dwarf-goose/Goose

Taxonomy. *Nettapus pulchellus* Gould, 1842, Port Essington, Northern Territory. Monotypic.
Distribution. S New Guinea, tropical N Australia.

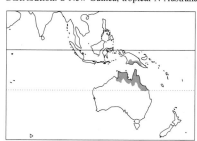

Descriptive notes. 30-36 cm; wingspan 48-60 cm. Female with head similar to female of *N. coromandelianus* but body is different. Juvenile similar to female but with face, chin and neck heavily spotted brown.
Habitat. Lowland tropical lagoons and lakes of rather deep, permanent fresh waters with abundant emergent vegetation, showing a marked preference for waters covered with water-lilies (*Nymphaea*).
Food and Feeding. Essentially vegetarian; seeds, leaves, flowers, buds and stems of water-lilies and other aquatic plants; some aquatic invertebrates also taken. Feeds by grazing, head-dipping and diving while swimming among plants.
Breeding. Starts Nov/Mar, mainly wet season. In single pairs; nests in tree-hollows, probably with no material except down, near water. 8-12 eggs; chicks have brown down above, white below.
Movements. Mainly sedentary, but subject to local dispersive movements favoured by extensive flooding during wet season. Vagrants have been reported at that time from various parts of Australia and from several tropical islands of Banda and Molucca Seas.
Status and Conservation. Not globally threatened. Rather common and locally abundant, but highly dependent on seeds and flowers of water-lilies. Widely distributed and locally abundant in S New Guinea. In Australia, assumed to breed throughout known range, but breeding has only been confirmed in few places. Decline in Kimberley region, Western Australia, attributed to destruction of aquatic vegetation by cattle. Partial census of New Guinea in 1990 yielded 53 birds.
Bibliography. Beehler *et al.* (1986), Coates (1985), Coomans de Ruiter (1955), Delacour (1954-1964), Frith (1967), Marchant & Higgins (1990), Schodde & Tidemann (1988), White & Bruce (1986).

59. Cotton Pygmy-goose
Nettapus coromandelianus

French: Anserelle de Coromandel **German**: Koromandelzwergente **Spanish**: Gansito Asiático
Other common names: White Pygmy-goose, White-quilled Pygmy-goose/Dwarf-goose, Pygmy Goose, Cotton Teal

Taxonomy. *Anas coromandeliana* Gmelin, 1789, Coromandel, India. Two subspecies recognized.
Subspecies and Distribution.
N. c. coromandelianus (Gmelin, 1789) - most of Oriental Region; N New Guinea.
N. c. albipennis Gould, 1842 - E Queensland (Australia).

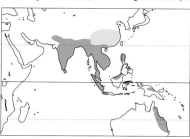

Descriptive notes. 31-38 cm; 380-403 g. Non-breeding male more or less like female but with more white on speculum. Juvenile resembles female but lacks iridescence and has a more distinct eye-stripe. Race *albipennis* larger.
Habitat. Well-vegetated, deep, fresh-water pools, lakes and lagoons in tropical lowlands; also on marshes, rivers and streams.
Food and Feeding. Seeds, grasses, and green parts of aquatic plants, but water-lilies uncommon; also some invertebrates (insects). Forages by dabbling and grazing among floating vegetation.
Breeding. Season variable, generally during rains; laying in Nov-Jan in SE Queensland, Australia. In single pairs; nests in tree-hollows with bottom lined with down and some feathers. 6-16 eggs; chicks have brown down above, white below.
Movements. Mostly sedentary, with some dispersive movements favoured by extensive flooding during rainy season. Northernmost (Chinese) population migratory, descending to lower latitudes in winter.
Status and Conservation. Not globally threatened. Locally rather common, with significant concentrations at favourable sites: in India, 3000 birds recorded in Jan 1980 on Nalsarovar L and Surandranagar Reservoirs (Gujarat), and recently 3600 on L Chilika (Orissa); in Thailand, 2000 in non-breeding season at Sanambin Non-Hunting Area. Partial census in winter 1991 gave 18,967 birds in India. In New Guinea, restricted to few localities, but locally common. Race *albipennis* much less frequent, assumed to breed throughout main range, but few confirmations to date; has declined due to drainage of wetlands for flood control in New South Wales, and introduced water hyacinth (*Eichhornia crassipes*), which has choked surface of some wetlands; population estimated at 1500 birds during 1960's. Requires fresh water with ample vegetation, but not as dependent on water-lilies (*Nymphaea*) as *N. pulchellus*. Scattered distribution facilitates local extinctions.
Bibliography. Alder (1963), Ali (1979), Ali & Ripley (1978), Coates (1985), Dickinson *et al.* (1991), Etchécopar & Hüe (1978), Frith (1967), Harvey (1990), Inskipp & Inskipp (1985), Lekagul & Round (1991), Marchant & Higgins (1990), van Marle & Voous (1988), Mayr & Camras (1938), Medway & Wells (1976), Phillips (1922-1926), Roberts (1991), de Schauensee (1984), Schodde & Tidemann (1988), Smythies (1981, 1986).

60. African Pygmy-goose
Nettapus auritus

French: Anserelle naine **German**: Afrikanische Zwergente **Spanish**: Gansito Africano
Other common names: Dwarf/Pygmy Goose

Taxonomy. *Anas aurita* Boddaert, 1783, Madagascar. Monotypic.
Distribution. Senegal to Ethiopia southwards, except SW Africa; Madagascar.

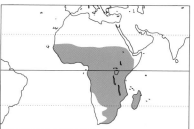

Descriptive notes. 30-33 cm; 260-285 g. Juvenile resembles female but buff on breast and flanks and with a more distinct eye-stripe.
Habitat. Swamps, marshes, shallow lakes and slow-flowing rivers with abundant aquatic vegetation; shows preference for water-lilies.
Food and Feeding. Seeds of water-lilies, seeds and green parts of other aquatic plants, aquatic invertebrates (insects) and small fish. Forages by plucking while swimming among floating vegetation and by diving.
Breeding. Season variable with locality. In single pairs; nest made with grasses and leaves, sometimes lined with down, in tree-holes and other cavities. 6-12 eggs; incubation c. 23-24 days; chicks have blackish down above, white below.
Movements. Mainly sedentary, but subject to dispersive movements dictated by habitat and water availability during dry season.
Status and Conservation. Not globally threatened. Fairly widespread and locally common to abundant. Tied to presence of *Nymphaea* and submerged plants, at least in W Africa where it is uncommon, with only known site of importance at Lagoa de Cufada, in Guinea-Bissau, with 250 birds censused in 1990; widespread but uncommon in Senegal Delta. Abundant on L Tana, Ethiopia. Majority of population in south of continent; very common in Okavango Delta, with estimated c. 10,600 in 1978 and as many as 15,000 more recently; flocks of c. 1000 in N Zululand during dry season; in S Africa it is considered uncommon to rare. In Madagascar, widespread except on High Plateau, but has declined considerably because of hunting (although it is difficult to hunt) and now only common in W and N. CITES III in Ghana.
Bibliography. Alder (1963), Benson & Benson (1975), Brickell (1988), Britton (1980), Brooke (1984), Brown & Britton (1980), Brown *et al.* (1982), Clancey (1964, 1967), Delacour (1959), Dollinger (1988), Elgood (1982), Langrand (1990), Mackworth-Praed & Grant (1957-1973), Maclean (1985), Madge & Burn (1988), Milon *et al.* (1973), de Naurois (1969c), Perennou (1991a, 1991b), Piekarz (1991), Pinto (1983), Pitman (1963), Roux *et al.* (1976-1977), Zaloumis (1976).

Genus *CALLONETTA* Delacour, 1936

61. Ringed Teal
Callonetta leucophrys

French: Callonette à collier noir **German**: Rotschulterente **Spanish**: Pato Acollarado
Other common names: Ring-necked Teal, Red-shouldered Teal

On following pages: 62. American Wood Duck (*Aix sponsa*); 63. Mandarin Duck (*Aix galericulata*); 64. Maned Duck (*Chenonetta jubata*); 65. Brazilian Teal (*Amazonetta brasiliensis*); 66. Torrent Duck (*Merganetta armata*); 67. Blue Duck (*Hymenolaimus malacorhynchos*).

Taxonomy. *Anas leucophrys* Vieillot, 1816, Paraguay. Formerly included in genus *Anas*. Monotypic.
Distribution. Bolivia and S Brazil to N Argentina and Uruguay.

Descriptive notes. 35-38 cm; 190-360 g. Wing pattern characteristic though white oval mark is hidden at rest. Juvenile resembles adult female; young male does not have the barred flanks nor facial pattern of female.
Habitat. Swampy tropical forests and marshy clearings in well-wooded lowlands; also on secluded pools and small streams.
Food and Feeding. Presumably mainly vegetarian diet, including seeds and other small items. Forages by picking from surface and head-dipping, while swimming in shallow water.
Breeding. Season not known, suspected to start late summer. In single pairs; nests in tree-hollows or old stick nests of other birds. 6-12 eggs; incubation 26-28 days (captivity); chicks have dark greyish down above, pale buffish grey below.
Movements. Direction and extent of movements not precisely known, but certainly disperses after breeding, approaching coast and appearing at lower latitudes.
Status and Conservation. Not globally threatened. Very little known about status, but no indication that species is particularly rare. Recorded as fairly common in some places, e.g. Bañados de Figueroa, Argentina, where 800-1000 counted in recent census.
Bibliography. Blake (1977), Brewer (1988, 1989), Carp (1991), Hellmayr & Conover (1948), Johnsgard (1960a, 1965a), Kear (1970), Kolbe (1979), Nores & Yzurieta (1980), Passer *et al.* (1989), de la Peña (1986), Ruschi (1979), Scott & Carbonell (1986), Sick (1984).

Genus *AIX*   Boie, 1828

62. American Wood Duck
Aix sponsa

French: Canard carolin   **German**: Brautente   **Spanish**: Pato Joyuyo
Other common names: Wood Duck, Carolina Duck/Wood Duck

Taxonomy. *Anas Sponsa* Linnaeus, 1758, North America = Carolina *ex* Catesby. Monotypic.
Distribution. W, C and SE North America; W Cuba.

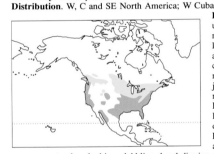

Descriptive notes. 43-51 cm; 482-879 g. Male unmistakable and has eclipse plumage. Female resembles that of *A. galericulata* but with larger white mark around eye, different cheek and browner shades on head; however, these characteristics are variable. Safely separated by more slender bill, with upper part of base projecting towards eyebrow. Juvenile resembles female but with streaked and mottled brown belly.
Habitat. Freshwater swamps, marshes, pools, lakes and slow rivers surrounded by dense deciduous forest; also in secluded parkland.
Food and Feeding. Acorns, nuts and seeds and green parts of various aquatic plants. Forages on water, by plucking, dabbling, head-dipping and upending; also forages on land.
Breeding. Starts Feb-Apr, occasionally double-brooded in S of range. In single pairs; nests in tree-holes, bottom lined with down. 9-15 eggs; incubation c. 30 days; chicks have dark grey-brown down above, dull yellowish below; fledging c. 60 days. Sexual maturity at 1 year. In one study nesting success of 40-55%, but often much less.
Movements. Partially migratory, with northernmost portion of breeding birds flying S to winter at lower latitudes, reaching central Mexico. Has occurred in Bermuda (where regular), Azores and Alaska. Many sightings from Europe, presumably referring to escapes.
Status and Conservation. Not globally threatened. Due to overhunting the world population of this species reached a low in the late 1930's when great concern arose about its future. Legal protection of the species and its preferred haunts, combined with intensive provision of nestboxes, started to give results almost immediately. Numbers increased dramatically to peak of 1,300,000 in 1976; no global estimates made since then, but increase has probably continued, though at slower pace. However, situation in southern part of breeding range far from ideal, as there have been significant decreases resulting mainly from habitat destruction (drainage of wetlands, felling of trees, etc).
Bibliography. Armbruster (1982), Bateman (1977), Bellrose (1976), Bent (1923-1925), Beshears (1974), Brown (1972), Cringan (1971), Cunningham (1968), Decker (1959), Dixon (1924), Drobney (1977), Fredickson *et al.* (1990), Gooders & Boyer (1986), Grice & Rogers (1965), Hansen (1971), Haramis (1975, 1990), Haramis & Malecki (1982), Havera & Kirby (1990), Hepp, Kennamer & Harvey (1990), Hepp, Stangohr *et al.* (1987), Hester & Dermid (1973), Johnsgard (1975), Kennamer & Hepp (1987), Korschgen (1972), Lever (1987), Palmer (1976), Ridlehuber (1980), Ripley (1973), Robb (1986), Savard (1982), Scherpelz (1979), Semel & Sherman (1986), Terres (1980), Townsend (1916), Trefethan (1966), Zipko (1979).

63. Mandarin Duck
Aix galericulata

French: Canard mandarin   **German**: Mandarinente   **Spanish**: Pato Mandarín

Taxonomy. *Anas galericulata* Linnaeus, 1758, China.
Sometimes placed in genus *Dendronessa*. Monotypic.
Distribution. Scattered in SE USSR, NE China, Japan. Introduced in S England.
Descriptive notes. 41-51 cm; 444-500 g. Female separable from that of *A. sponsa* by greener, less blue gloss on flight-feathers and smaller white mark around eye; also different bill shape. Male has eclipse plumage. Juvenile resembles female, though female has pinkish bill.
Habitat. Pools, lakes, rivers, marshes and swamps surrounded by dense deciduous forest. Has a preference for small islands and water bodies with abundant emergent vegetation.

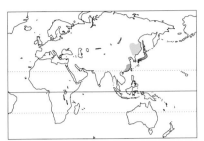

Food and Feeding. Seeds, particularly nuts, acorns and grain, aquatic plants and animal food (land snails, insects, fish). Feeds both by day and at night by dabbling on water surface and by head-dipping and upending in shallow waters.
Breeding. Starts Apr. In single pairs; nests in tree-hollows. 9-12 eggs; incubation 28-30 days; chicks have olive brown down above, yellowish below; fledging c. 40-45 days. Sexual maturity at 1 year (in captivity).
Movements. Asian population essentially migratory, wintering at lower latitudes in eastern China. However, Japanese and British feral birds mostly sedentary. Wild birds have occurred in NE India, Burma and Hong Kong, and escapes throughout Europe and N America.
Status and Conservation. INSUFFICIENTLY KNOWN. Decline of recent decades continues, so considered near-threatened. At present, majority of Asian population (estimated at 6100-6600 pairs in mid-1980's) occurs in Japan. In winter 1990 census, 13,361 birds counted in Japan, and 2332 in partial count in China. Only minimally significant available figures on continental population are: 100 individuals counted during autumn/winter 1986 censuses in Taesong'dong and Panmucnch'om Marshes, South Korea; and flocks of 40-50 occurring in early spring in Changbai Shan Nature Reserve, one of the breeding areas in NE China. In Japan was very common resident but greatly declined due to overhunting, with recovery after protection in 1947; notable increase in wintering population in particular, but not known if this because of increased breeding population or continental visitors; now considered local and uncommon. British feral population of c. 7000 in 1988 significant; currently increasing. Decline in continental Asia related to habitat destruction and exportation in vast numbers during many years.
Bibliography. Ali & Ripley (1978), Austin (1948), Bauer & Glutz von Blotzheim (1968), Brazil (1991), Bruggers (1974), Cramp & Simmons (1977), Davies (1988), Davies & Baggott (1989a, 1989b), Dementiev & Gladkov (1952), Etchécopar & Hüe (1978), Gooders & Boyer (1986), Grimmett & Jones (1989), Harrison (1988), Lai Yong-jin (1987), Lever (1987), Litvinenko (1985), Marchant *et al.* (1990), Perennou & Mundkur (1991), Savage (1952), de Schauensee (1984), Shibnev (1985), Wang Zi-jiang *et al.* (1983), Wu Zhi-kang *et al.* (1983), Yang Jiong-li *et al.* (1985), Zhao Zheng-jie *et al.* (1980).

Genus *CHENONETTA*   Brandt, 1836

64. Maned Duck
Chenonetta jubata

French: Canard à crinière   **German**: Mähnenente   **Spanish**: Pato de Crin
Other common names: Maned Goose, Maned Wood Duck, Australian Wood Duck, Wood Duck

Taxonomy. *Anas jubata* Latham, 1801, New South Wales. Monotypic.
Distribution. SW and E Australia, Tasmania.

Descriptive notes. 44-56 cm; 662-984 g; wingspan 78-80 cm. Structure reminiscent of small *Chloephaga*. Juvenile resembles female, but paler.
Habitat. Favours freshwater marshes and farm dams with abundant grazing, often surrounded by open deciduous forest and swampy open woods; generally inland, moving up rivers.
Food and Feeding. Essentially vegetarian; green grasses, herbs, sedges and, in winter, some aquatic vegetation. Most food is obtained by grazing on dry land, sometimes far from water.
Breeding. Starts mainly Aug, but season variable, depending on rainfall. In single pairs; nests in tree-hollows. 8-11 eggs, up to 18 recorded, probably due to dump-laying; incubation c. 28 days; chicks have grey-brown down above, whitish buff below; fledging 57 days. Probability of survival to fledging varies from 20 to 88% depending on localities.
Movements. Mostly sedentary, perhaps occupying same water body throughout life but also somewhat dispersive; can be found almost anywhere with suitable habitat in Australia and Tasmania. Vagrant to New Zealand.
Status and Conservation. Not globally threatened. Locally very common. Regarded as agricultural pest in some areas, as reputedly causes damage to rice crops and sprouting cereals, and is hunted intensely, especially in SE Australia. However, its exploitation of pastures and crops and its extraordinarily cautious character has allowed expansion of species since European settlement. Partial censuses at end of 1980's yielded 11,667-14,148 in Victoria and 2386-13,911 in SW Australia. 63-82% of population exposed to hunting.
Bibliography. Briggs (1990a, 1990b), Briggs & Thornton (1988), Bull *et al.* (1985), Falla *et al.* (1981), Frith (1967), Halse & Jaensch (1989), Kingsford (1986a, 1986b, 1989), Kingsford *et al.* (1989), Marchant & Higgins (1990), McLaughlin (1989), Roy (1988), Ruschi (1979), Schodde & Tidemann (1988).

Genus *AMAZONETTA*   Boetticher, 1929

65. Brazilian Teal
Amazonetta brasiliensis

French: Canard amazonette   **German**: Amazonasente   **Spanish**: Pato Brasileño
Other common names: Brazilian Duck; Lesser Brazilian Duck/Teal (*brasiliensis*); Greater Brazilian Duck/Teal (*ipecutiri*)

Taxonomy. *Anas brasiliensis* Gmelin, 1789, northeastern Brazil.
Sometimes placed in genus *Anas*. Two subspecies recognized.
Subspecies and Distribution.
A. b. brasiliensis (Gmelin, 1789) - E Colombia, N & E Venezuela, Guyana and N & C Brazil.
A. b. ipecutiri (Vieillot, 1816) - E Bolivia and S Brazil to N Argentina and Uruguay.

Descriptive notes. 35-40 cm; 350-480 g (nominate), 580-600 g (*ipecutiri*). Both subspecies have pale and dark phases. Female separated from male largely by facial pattern; averages smaller. Juvenile as female but duller. Race *ipecutiri* larger.
Habitat. Most commonly found inland, in pools or small lakes in densely wooded country. Occasionally in areas of brackish or saline waters.
Food and Feeding. Little information available suggests varied diet, including fruits and roots of local plants and some invertebrates, e.g. insects.

Breeding. Season variable according to locality. In single pairs; nest is mound of plant matter in rushes or sedge hummocks surrounded by water; occasionally in tree-hollows, abandoned nests in trees or possibly on cliffs. 6-8 eggs; incubation c. 25 days.
Movements. Mostly sedentary throughout northern part of range, but birds of race *ipecutiri* descend to lower latitudes in winter, then occupying part of range of sedentary nominate race.
Status and Conservation. Not globally threatened. Widely distributed and common. Available censuses indicate it does not tend to form large concentrations, but well-represented. Partial censuses in Jul 1990 yielded 696 individuals in Uruguay. Limited human pressure, and species is quite adaptable to wide range of habitats, even after these have been transformed.
Bibliography. Belton (1984), Blake (1977), Carp (1991), Gómez-Dallmeier & Cringan (1989), Hellmayr & Conover (1948), Hilty & Brown (1986), Madriz (1979, 1983), Nores & Yzurieta (1980), de la Peña (1986), Phillips (1922-1926), Ruschi (1979), de Schauensee & Phelps (1978), Scott & Carbonell (1986), Sick (1984).

Tribe MERGANETTINI

Genus *MERGANETTA*   Gould, 1842

66. **Torrent Duck**

Merganetta armata

French: Merganette des torrents   **German**: Sturzbachente   **Spanish**: Pato Torrentero
Other common names: Argentine/Chilean Torrent Duck (*armata*); Colombian Torrent Duck (*colombiana*); Peruvian Torrent Duck (*leucogenis, turneri*)

Taxonomy. *Merganetta armata* Gould, 1842, Andes of Chile, lat. 34°-35° S.
Taxonomic status of races *leucogenis, turneri, garleppi* and *berlepschi* unclear; may be better considered as colour morphs of a single subspecies (*leucogenis*), since birds resembling different races occur together on the same rivers in Peru. Six subspecies normally recognized.
Subspecies and Distribution.
M. a. colombiana Des Murs, 1845 - Andes from Venezuela to N Ecuador.
M. a. leucogenis (Tschudi, 1843) - Andes from C Ecuador to C Peru.
M. a. turneri P. L. Sclater & Salvin, 1869 - Andes of S Peru.
M. a. garleppi Berlepsch, 1894 - Andes of Bolivia.
M. a. berlepschi Hartert, 1909 - Andes of N Chile and NW Argentina.
M. a. armata Gould, 1842 - most of Andes of Chile and Argentina.
Descriptive notes. 43-46 cm; 315-440 g. Unmistakable. Slim and long-tailed. Very variable, even within each subspecies. Juvenile normally greyish above and white below with grey barring on flanks. Subspecies according to variations in pattern and colour, especially in juvenile males. Only nominate race has black "tear". Race *turneri* has blackish body, whereas *colombiana* is palest; *garleppi* intermediate.
Habitat. Mountain rivers and streams of fast-flowing, clear waters. Territory, held year-round, typically consists of a mixture of rapids, boulders, gorges and waterfalls and wider areas of calmer water; situated at anything from over 4500 m (high Andes) to sea level (in S of range).
Food and Feeding. Aquatic invertebrates, mainly insect larvae (*Rheophila, Caddis*) and molluscs; perhaps also some fish. Forages by diving in river waters, head-dipping from surface, upending and probing among rocks.
Breeding. Season variable according to locality; Feb in Colombia. In single pairs; nest made of dry grass, lined with abundant down and some feathers, in hollow or cavity among rocks or in

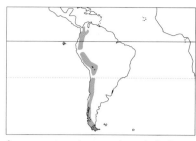

thick vegetation. 3-4 eggs; incubation c. 43-44 days; chicks have boldly striped and spotted black and white down.
Movements. Adult birds virtually sedentary, but displaced from breeding territory by winter weather conditions locally. Young birds may wander widely within range before establishing their own territory.
Status and Conservation. Not globally threatened. Apparently decreasing in many places, especially in N half of range; still locally common, as for example in Lauca National Park, Chile. Formerly inhabited Isla Grande (Tierra del Fuego). Has disappeared from many rivers due to erosion and siltation caused by deforestation, and also to indiscriminate fishing and hunting and pollution from mining activities. Additional causes of regression include hydroelectric schemes and competition for food with introduced trout.
Bibliography. Blake (1977), Carp (1991), Eldridge (1977, 1986b), Fjeldså & Krabbe (1990), Gómez-Dallmeier & Cringan (1989), Hellmayr & Conover (1948), Hilty & Brown (1986), Humphrey *et al.* (1970), Johnsgard (1966a), Johnson (1963, 1965), Kear (1975), Lubbock (1983), Moffett (1970), de la Peña (1986), de Schauensee & Phelps (1978), Scott, D.A. & Carbonell (1986), Scott, P. (1954b), Weller (1968a), Wright (1965).

Tribe ANATINI

Genus *HYMENOLAIMUS*   Gray, 1843

67. **Blue Duck**

Hymenolaimus malacorhynchos

French: Canard bleu   **German**: Saumschnabelente   **Spanish**: Pato Azul
Other common names: Mountain Duck

Taxonomy. *Anas malacorhynchos* Gmelin, 1789, Dusky Sound, South Island, New Zealand.
Race *hymenolaimus* of uncertain status, but recently re-validated. Two subspecies recognized.
Subspecies and Distribution.
H. m. malacorhynchos (Gmelin, 1789) - W South I, New Zealand.
H. m. hymenolaimus Mathews, 1937 - C North I, New Zealand.

Descriptive notes. 53-54 cm; 680-1077 g. Female averages smaller and has less breast spotting. Juvenile lacks breast spotting. Subspecies *hymenolaimus* darker above.
Habitat. Mountain streams and small rivers of clear, fast-flowing waters in well-vegetated areas.
Food and Feeding. Aquatic invertebrates, mainly insect larvae; also some algae. Feeds by probing among rocks, diving; head-dipping and upending in shallow waters.
Breeding. Starts mostly Oct, but season may extend for several months. In single pairs; nests in depression in ground, natural cavity, crevice among rocks, in thick vegetation or on cliff ledge; only a little down added. Usually 5-6 eggs (4-9); incubation c. 31-32 days; chicks have dark brown down above, white below; fledging 70-80 days. Sexual maturity at 1 year. Average of less than 1 young per pair reared in one study during 5 seasons.
Movements. Mainly sedentary, adult birds occurring within breeding territory throughout year unless displaced by adverse weather in winter.
Status and Conservation. Not globally threatened. Currently considered near-threatened, as numbers very reduced and declining; formerly widespread, now rare or absent in majority of territory, dispersed in small, isolated populations in widely scattered locations in North I and South I. Total population estimated recently at 2000-4000 birds. Very sensitive to slightest modification in the torrents of clear water and thus threatened by hydroelectric schemes and mining activities. Breeding success low; suffers high predation from introduced mammals; introduced trout may compete for food, but no studies carried out as yet.
Bibliography. Blackburn (1967), Bull *et al.* (1985), Chambers (1989), Eldridge (1985, 1986a, 1986c), Falla *et al.* (1981), Fordyce (1974, 1976), Fordyce & Tunnicliffe (1973), Harding (1990), Kear (1972b), Kear & Burton (1971), Kear & Steel (1971), Kear & Williams (1978), Marchant & Higgins (1990), McKinney & Bruggers (1983), Phillips (1922-1926), Soper (1976), Steel (1970), Veltman & Williams (1990), Weller (1980), Williams, M.J. (1967, 1985g).

inches 8
cm 20

PLATE 45

68

69 ssp *leucostigma*

ssp *sparsa*

70 ♀

♂

71 ♂

♀

72

73 ♂

♀

74 ♂

75 ♀

76 ♀ ssp *crecca*

♂

77 ssp *flavirostris*

ssp *andium*

ssp *carolinensis* ♂

78

79

80 ♀

♂

ssp *oxyptera*

ssp *albogularis*

ssp *gibberifrons*

Genus *ANAS* Linnaeus, 1758

68. Salvadori's Teal

Anas waigiuensis

French: Canard de Salvadori **German**: Salvadoriente **Spanish**: Anade Papúa
Other common names: Salvadori's Duck

Taxonomy. *Salvadorina waigiuensis* Rothschild and Hartert, 1894, Waigeo.
Sometimes placed in monospecific genus *Salvadorina*; shares several characters with *Hymenolaimus* and *Merganetta*, but possibly due to convergent evolution. Monotypic.
Distribution. Mountains of New Guinea; occurrence on Waigeo I (off NW New Guinea) doubtful.

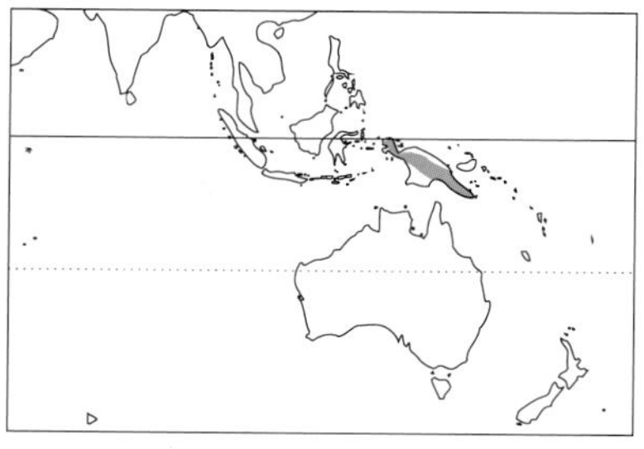

Descriptive notes. 38-43 cm; 400-525 g. Elongated shape; often raises tail. Juvenile duller with darker bill.
Habitat. Mountain torrents, brooks and streams and small lakes in high ground, generally well above 3000 m; also in small rivers of calmer waters down to 500 m.
Food and Feeding. Aquatic invertebrates (mostly insect larvae) and possibly tadpoles and small fish.
Breeding. Very extended season, with suggestions that might be double-brooded. In single pairs; nest usually hidden among vegetation. 3-4 eggs; incubation over 28 days.
Movements. Mainly sedentary; not known to occur outside normal range.
Status and Conservation. Not globally threatened. Restricted range and very specific habitat. Widely distributed in streams and alpine lakes 500-3700 m high, often scarce, but locally fairly common. Hunting by indigenous tribes aggravated by increasing use of firearms. Foreseeable threats to this species are pollution of mountain rivers, predation by alien mammals and competition for food with introduced insectivorous fish.
Bibliography. Beehler *et al.* (1986), Bell (1969), Boetticher & Grummt (1965), Coates (1985), Diamond (1972), Duplaix-Hall (1975), Greenway (1967), Hallstrom (1956), Kear (1975), Kolbe (1972), Mackay (1976), Mayr (1931), Mlíkovsky (1989), Ripley (1964), Weller (1980).

69. African Black Duck

Anas sparsa

French: Canard noir **German**: Schwarzente **Spanish**: Anade Negro
Other common names: Black River Duck, Black Duck; West African/Ethiopian Black Duck (*leucostigma*); South African Black Duck (*sparsa*)

Taxonomy. *Anas sparsa* Eyton, 1838, South Africa.
Sometimes placed in monospecific genus *Melananas*. Population of Gabon and Cameroon has been assigned separate subspecies *maclatchyi*, but doubtfully valid. Two subspecies recognized.
Subspecies and Distribution.
A. s. leucostigma Rüppell, 1845 - W equatorial Africa; E Africa S to Zimbabwe.
A. s. sparsa Eyton, 1838 - S Africa S of Zimbabwe.

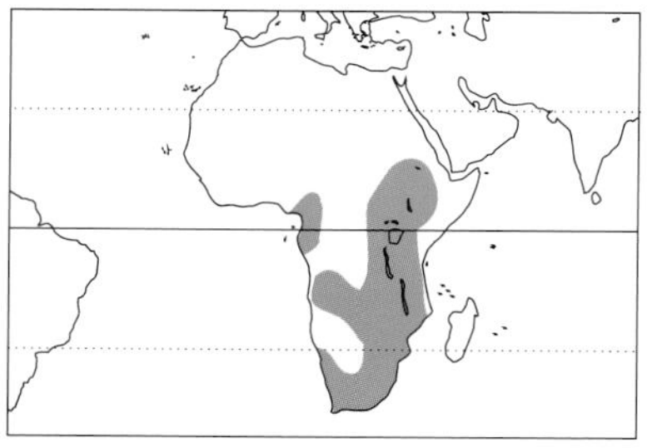

Descriptive notes. 48-58 cm; 952-1077 g. Massive, heavy-looking. Variable marking on flanks; sometimes almost completely black. Female slightly smaller. Juvenile with thin buff barring and white abdomen. Subspecies *leucostigma* with narrower buff bars and spots on upperparts; large part of bill pink or flesh-coloured.
Habitat. Generally in secluded fast-flowing rivers and streams in mountainous and wooded habitat. Also in more open country and more sluggish waters, in lakes, lagoons and reservoirs.
Food and Feeding. Weeds and aquatic vegetation, insect larvae and pupae, and small fish. Forages mostly by dabbling, head-dipping and upending in shallow water, mainly during daylight hours.
Breeding. Season variable with locality. In single pairs; nest thickly lined with down, usually on ground among driftwood, reedbeds or grass on river banks. 4-8 eggs; incubation c. 28 days; chicks have black down above, buffish white below; fledging c. 86 days.
Movements. Mainly sedentary throughout range, with only local movements recorded.
Status and Conservation. Not globally threatened. From fairly common to scarce, but in general considered widespread and nowhere numerous. Nominate subspecies appears the more widely distributed in suitable habitat within range, even though considered uncommon and local in much of South Africa; scarce in Angola and Namibia. Reported as fairly common breeding resident in Sudan, in 1987, although northern populations generally considered least numerous; threatened by deforestation.
Bibliography. Ball *et al.* (1978), Benson & Benson (1975), Brickell (1988), Britton (1980), Brown & Britton (1980), Brown *et al.* (1982), Clancey (1967), Frost *et al.* (1979), Hall (1977), Mackworth-Praed & Grant (1957-1973), Maclean (1985), McKinney *et al.* (1978), Perennou (1991b), Pinto (1983), Siegfried (1968b, 1974), Siegfried *et al.* (1977).

70. Eurasian Wigeon

Anas penelope

French: Canard siffleur **German**: Pfeifente **Spanish**: Silbón Europeo
Other common names: Wigeon, European Wigeon

Taxonomy. *Anas Penelope* Linnaeus, 1758, coasts and swamps of Europe.
Forms superspecies with *A. americana* and *A. sibilatrix*; sometimes placed in genus *Mareca*. Monotypic.
Distribution. Iceland, N Europe, N Asia.
Descriptive notes. 45-51 cm; 415-970 g. Male sometimes has metallic dark-green spot behind eyes; has eclipse plumage. Female slightly smaller with dark head not contrasting with breast and upperparts. Juvenile similar to female.

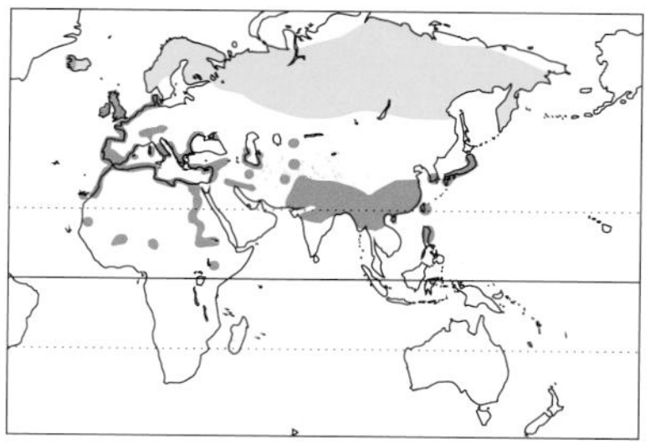

Habitat. Shallow, freshwater marshes, lakes and lagoons surrounded by scattered trees or open forest. Winters in coastal marshes, freshwater and brackish lagoons, estuaries, bays and other sheltered marine habitats.
Food and Feeding. Essentially vegetarian; leaves, stems, roots and seeds of grasses, sedges and aquatic vegetation. Feeds by grazing on dry land, dabbling on water surface and head-dipping in shallow water.
Breeding. Starts Apr/May. In single pairs or small groups; nest is depression on ground, lined with grass and a thick coat of down, hidden among vegetation. Usually 8-9 eggs (6-12); incubation 24-25 days; chicks have dark brown down above, paler below; fledging c. 40-45 days. Sexual maturity at 1, occasionally 2, years.
Movements. Basically migratory, descending to lower latitudes to winter throughout most of W and C Europe, Mediterranean Basin, Middle East, India, SE Asia and Japan; some populations (e.g. British) mostly sedentary. Occurs regularly on Atlantic coast of N America in small numbers.
Status and Conservation. Not globally threatened. Abundant, concentrates in large numbers in wintering grounds. Winter 1991 census yielded 34,403 birds in Iran, 61,900 in Azerbaydzhan, 39,984 in Japan (quite a lot more individuals counted than in other years), and in partial counts in same year 23,355 individuals reported in India, 131,725 in Pakistan and 7946 in China. An estimated 1,350,000 were found wintering in W Palearctic in mid 1980's, this number remaining quite stable in recent years despite intense human pressure from hunting and drainage of habitat, partially compensated by establishment of reserves in many wetlands in W Europe. CITES III in Ghana.
Bibliography. Ali & Ripley (1978), Bauer & Glutz von Blotzheim (1968), Bellrose (1976), Brazil (1991), Brickell (1988), Brown *et al.* (1982), Campredon (1982), Cramp & Simmons (1977), Dementiev & Gladkov (1952), Donker (1959), Etchécopar & Hüe (1978), Géroudet (1972), Gooders & Boyer (1986), Goodman (1989), Grimmett & Jones (1989), Harrison (1988), Mayhew (1987), McClure (1974), Monval & Pirot (1989), Owen (1977), Paz (1987), Perennou (1991a, 1991b), Perennou & Mundkur (1991), Richardson (1990), Ridgill & Fox (1990), Roberts (1991), de Schauensee (1984), Shevareva (1970).

71. American Wigeon

Anas americana

French: Canard d'Amérique **German**: Nordamerikanische Pfeifente **Spanish**: Silbón Americano
Other common names: Baldpate

Taxonomy. *Anas americana* Gmelin, 1789, Louisiana and New York.
Forms superspecies with *A. penelope* and *A. sibilatrix*; sometimes placed in genus *Mareca*. Monotypic.
Distribution. NW to CE North America and S as far as NE California and N Colorado.

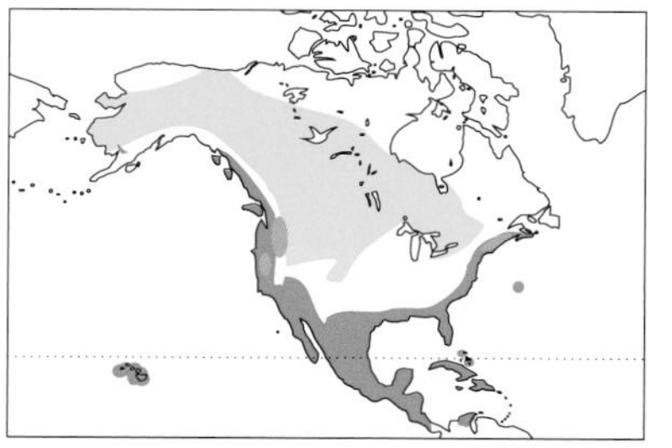

Descriptive notes. 45-56 cm; 680-770 g. Male has eclipse plumage. Female separated from *A. penelope* by lighter-coloured head in contrast with rest of body, and bill slightly longer. Juvenile resembles female but has plainer markings on back.
Habitat. Freshwater swamps, pools and shallow lakes surrounded by good grazing grounds, such as meadows, often in lightly wooded country. Winters in more coastal wetlands.
Food and Feeding. Grasses, sedges, herbs and greener parts of crops and aquatic plants. Grazes by walking in meadows or arable land and by swimming in shallow waters.
Breeding. Starts Apr/May. In single pairs or loose groups; nest is slight depression on ground, lined with grass and down, concealed among vegetation. 7-9 eggs; incubation 23-25 days; chicks have dark brown down above, buffish below; fledging c. 37-48 days. Sexual maturity at 1, occasionally 2, years; oldest ringed bird 9 years old.
Movements. Winters mostly along Atlantic and Pacific coasts of North America and inland S to Panama; also in Bermuda and Hawaii. Occurs in very small numbers on eastern side of N Atlantic, where regular in Britain. Vagrants have also reached NE Siberia.
Status and Conservation. Not globally threatened. Abundant, with large population estimated at over 6,500,000 in early autumn during mid 1970's in North America. Significant numbers also winter in South America, with concentrations of 2000-3550 birds in some areas of Venezuela, and up to 4000 in the Ciénaga Grande de Santa Marta, Colombia. In recent years, regularly wintering in Japan in very reduced numbers (less than 100). Has suffered habitat reduction and intense hunting pressure, but numbers have remained quite stable in last few decades, mainly due to reserves established in the sites of most importance to this species.
Bibliography. Bellrose (1976), Bauer & Glutz von Blotzheim (1968), Biaggi (1983), Blake (1977), Brazil (1991), Cooch (1964), Cramp & Simmons (1977), DuBowy (1987, 1988), Gómez-Dallmeier & Cringan (1989), Gooders & Boyer (1986), Hilty & Brown (1986), Keith (1961), Monroe (1968), Munro (1949b), Ridgely & Gwynne (1989), Scott & Carbonell (1986), Soutiere *et al.* (1972), Sugden (1973), Terres (1980), Townsend (1916), Voous (1983), Wishart (1979, 1983).

72. Chiloe Wigeon

Anas sibilatrix

French: Canard de Chiloé **German**: Chilepfeifente **Spanish**: Silbón Overo
Other common names: Southern/Chilean Wigeon

Taxonomy. *Anas sibilatrix* Poeppig, 1829, Talcahuano, Concepción, Chile.
Forms superspecies with *A. penelope* and *A. americana*; sometimes placed in genus *Mareca*. Monotypic.
Distribution. South America S of C Argentina and C Chile; Falkland Is.
Descriptive notes. 43-54 cm; 828-939 g. Compact, heavier than other wigeons. Flank colour variable. Male has no eclipse plumage. Female somewhat duller, especially on head. Juvenile duller with little iridescence on head.
Habitat. Lakes, lagoons and slow-flowing rivers surrounded by scattered trees not far from grassland and meadows.
Food and Feeding. Essentially vegetarian; grasses, sedges and greener parts of plants and aquatic vegetation. Feeds mainly by grazing on dry land; also by dabbling, head-dipping and upending while swimming in open waters.

On following pages: 73. Falcated Duck (*Anas falcata*); 74. Gadwall (*Anas strepera*); 75. Baikal Teal (*Anas formosa*); 76. Common Teal (*Anas crecca*); 77. Speckled Teal (*Anas flavirostris*); 78. Cape Teal (*Anas capensis*); 79. Madagascar Teal (*Anas bernieri*); 80. Grey Teal (*Anas gibberifrons*).

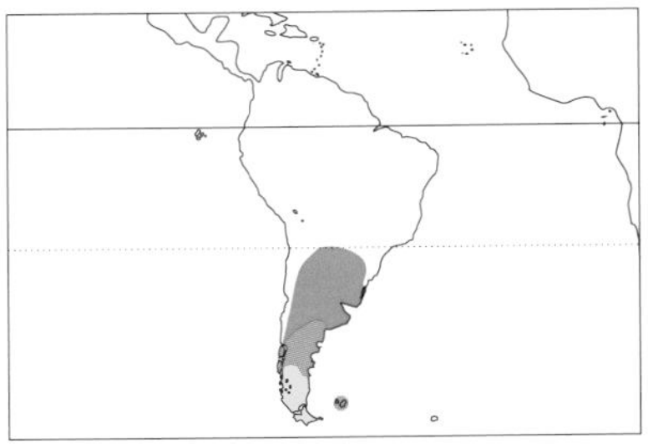

Breeding. Starts Aug/Sept. In single pairs or loose groups; nests on ground among vegetation. 5-8 eggs; incubation c. 26 days; chicks have dark brown down above, buffy below.
Movements. Southernmost breeding populations move to lower latitudes in winter, as far N as Uruguay, Paraguay and S Brazil; sedentary in Falkland Is. Has occurred on South Georgia and South Orkney Is.
Status and Conservation. Not globally threatened. Widely distributed and fairly common in mud of range. Important breeding sites in Argentina include Laguna Blanca, Neuquén Province, with 500 individuals recorded in Jan/Feb census in 1982, and, of particular importance, the Meseta de Strobel, Santa Cruz Province, where an estimated 18,900 individuals were counted recently. In Falkland Is, widely distributed, nowhere very common but locally numerous. Despite hunting pressure and habitat loss, population does not appear to have declined significantly.
Bibliography. Blake (1977), Carp (1991), Fjeldså & Krabbe (1990), Hellmayr & Conover (1948), Humphrey *et al.* (1970), Johnson (1965), Marchant & Higgins (1990), Nores & Yzurieta (1980), de la Peña (1986), Phillips (1922-1926), Scott & Carbonell (1986), Weller (1975d), Woods (1988).

73. Falcated Duck
Anas falcata

French: Canard à faucilles **German**: Sichelente **Spanish**: Cerceta de Alfanjes
Other common names: Falcated/Bronze-capped Teal

Taxonomy. *Anas falcata* Georgi, 1775, Lake Baykal.
Sometimes placed in monospecific genus *Eunetta*. Monotypic.
Distribution. SE Siberia and Mongolia to Kuril Is and N Japan.

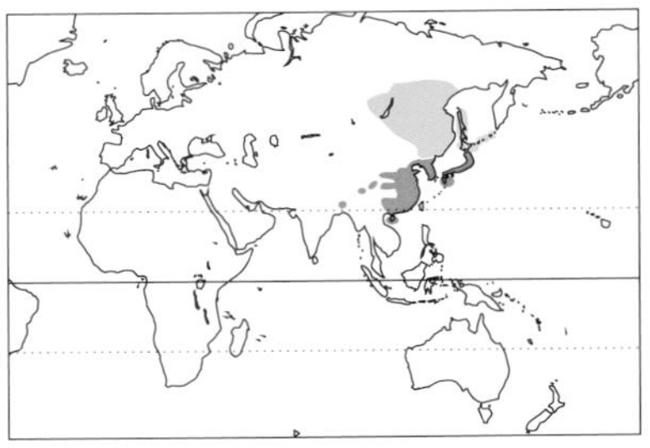

Descriptive notes. 46-54 cm; 422-770 g. Male unmistakable; has eclipse plumage. Female often shows traces of crest on nape; bill long and flat, short tail. Juvenile resembles female but without crest on nape.
Habitat. Breeds on freshwater lakes, rivers, ponds, lagoons, often in wooded country. In winter, also on coast and in larger, shallow water bodies, rice fields and flooded meadows.
Food and Feeding. Essentially vegetarian; seeds of various types (including rice and grain), green parts of aquatic vegetation and crop plants, grasses; also a few aquatic invertebrates (molluscs, insects). Feeds by dabbling and upending in shallow water; also grazes on dry, arable land.
Breeding. Starts May/Jun. In single pairs or loose groups; nests on ground among vegetation, near water. 6-9 eggs; incubation 24-26 days; chicks have dark brown down above, buff below.
Movements. Winters in eastern Asia (China, Japan, Korea, Viet Nam) and scattered localities W to NE India. Vagrants occasionally occur further W (to Iran, Jordan and Turkey) and also E (Aleutian Is), but numerous observations in Europe and N America presumed to refer to escapes.
Status and Conservation. Not globally threatened. Fairly common, even locally abundant. Wintering population in Japan formerly more abundant; in period 1982-1988 censuses yielded 5162-8113 individuals. Significant numbers in South Korea and China: 7000-9000 during migration at Xinghai Hu, NE China. No estimation of total population available. Hunted in large numbers in China, for food and for feathers.
Bibliography. Ali & Ripley (1978), Armstrong (1983), Austin (1948), Bauer & Glutz von Blotzheim (1968), Brazil (1991), Cramp & Simmons (1977), Dementiev & Gladkov (1952), Etchécopar & Hüe (1978), Gooders & Boyer (1986), Inskipp & Inskipp (1985), Lorenz & von de Wall (1960), Perennou & Mundkur (1991), de Schauensee (1984).

74. Gadwall
Anas strepera

French: Canard chipeau **German**: Schnatterente **Spanish**: Anade Friso
Other common names: Gray Duck

Taxonomy. *Anas strepera* Linnaeus, 1758, Europe.
Sometimes placed in monospecific genus *Chaulelasmus*. Race *couesi*, Coues' Gadwall, described from Washington and New York Is, C Pacific, apparently not seen after its discovery in 1874 and considered extinct. Monotypic.
Distribution. Widespread over great part of Palearctic and Nearctic Regions.

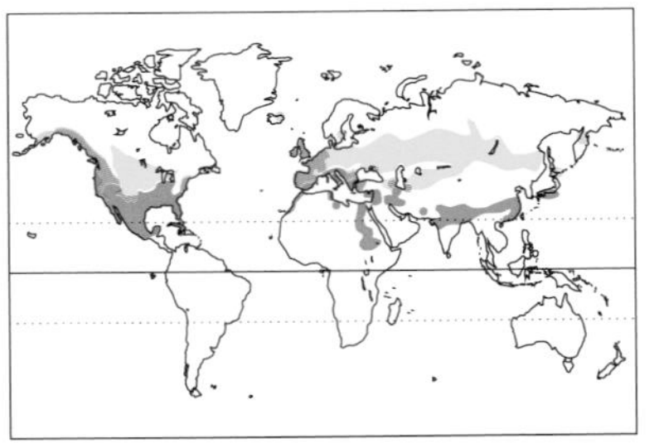

Descriptive notes. 46-58 cm; average 850-990 g. White speculum in both sexes distinguishes this species. Male has eclipse plumage. Female with variable bill, sometimes uniformly dark. Juvenile resembles female but darker and more heavily streaked below.
Habitat. Breeds in various types of freshwater or brackish wetlands, particularly shallow ones with abundant vegetation. Nests preferably on grass-covered islands in such sites. In winter also occasionally on coast.
Food and Feeding. Essentially vegetarian; seeds, leaves, roots and stems of aquatic plants. Food normally obtained under water by head-dipping and upending; occasionally grazes by walking on land. Parasitism of other waterfowl described.
Breeding. Starts Apr/May. In single pairs or loose groups; nest is made with grass and dry leaves, lined with down, built on ground in thick vegetation. Usually 8-12 eggs (5-13, sometimes more by dump-laying); incubation 24-26 days; chicks have sepia-coloured down above, creamy buff below; fledging 45-50 days. Sexual maturity at c. 1 year.
Movements. Partially migratory; northernmost breeding birds descend to lower latitudes in winter, but breeders of more temperate regions mostly sedentary.
Status and Conservation. Not globally threatened. Fairly widespread and locally abundant. In North America, very numerous, with c. 1,500,000 birds in mid-1970's, and range has extended this century; winters in considerable numbers in Mexico, in particular in Topolobampo Lagoons, with censuses of up to 7900, and especially in the Marismas Nacionales, S of Mazatlán, with censuses of up to 29,300. In the Palearctic, also common, but no total estimates available; in W Palearctic, wintering population estimated at 87,000; stable or increasing slightly in NW Europe. About 163,000 pairs estimated in USSR in early 1970's. In winter 1991 census, 38,491 individuals recorded in Iran.
Bibliography. Ali & Ripley (1978), Amat (1980), Bauer & Glutz von Blotzheim (1968), Bellrose (1976), Brazil (1991), Brickell (1988), Brown *et al.* (1982), Cooch (1964), Coronado (1972), Cramp & Simmons (1977), Dementiev & Gladkov (1952), DuBowy (1987, 1988), Duebbert (1966), Etchécopar & Hüe (1978), Fox & Mitchell (1988), Fox & Salmon (1989), Gates (1962), Géroudet (1972), Gooders & Boyer (1986), Goodman (1989), Greenway (1967), Grimmett & Jones (1989), Harrison (1988), Henny & Holgersen (1974), Monval & Pirot (1989), Oring (1969), Parnell & Quay (1962), Paulus (1984a), Paz (1987), Perennou & Mundkur (1991), Richardson (1990), Roberts (1991), Sargeant *et al.* (1984), Schommer (1977), Scott & Carbonell (1986), Shevareva (1970), Sugden (1973), Swanson *et al.* (1979), Terres (1980), Titman & Seymour (1981).

75. Baikal Teal
Anas formosa

French: Sarcelle élégante **German**: Gluckente **Spanish**: Cerceta del Baikal
Other common names: Spectacled/Formosa/Clucking Teal

Taxonomy. *Anas formosa* Georgi, 1775, Irkutsk and Lake Baykal.
Sometimes placed in genus *Nettion*. Monotypic.
Distribution. E Siberia to Kamchatka.

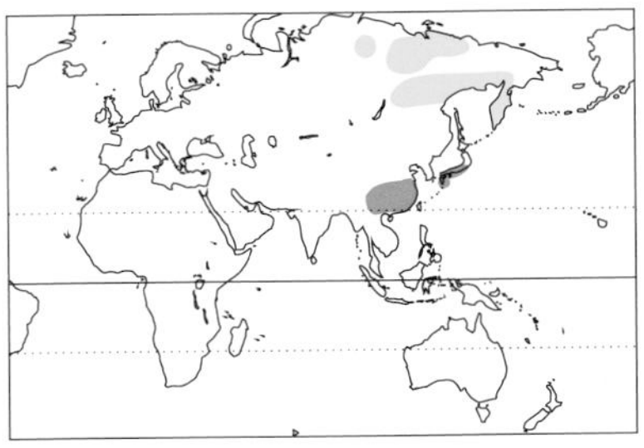

Descriptive notes. 39-43 cm; 360-520 g. Male unmistakable; has eclipse plumage. Female differentiated from other teals by round whitish mark behind bill. Juvenile resembles female and has underparts spotted or streaked brown.
Habitat. Rivers, small lakes, pools and marshes in well-wooded country or in Arctic tundra. Winters in freshwater or brackish wetlands, floodplains and meadows.
Food and Feeding. Seeds, leaves, stems and other vegetative parts of grasses, sedges, aquatic plants and crops; also aquatic invertebrates (molluscs, insects). Feeds by dabbling from water surface, head-dipping and upending; also on foot, looking for acorns in woods and even for grain and seeds on roads at night.
Breeding. Starts May. In single pairs or loose groups; nests on ground, concealed among vegetation, usually near water. 6-9 eggs; incubation c. 24-25 days (captivity); chicks have dark brown down above, yellow below.
Movements. Migratory, winters E and SE China and S Japan, a few individuals regularly venturing as far W as NE India. Vagrants have been reported from W Europe (as far as Britain and Spain) and N America (chiefly Pacific coast), but probably escapes involved.
Status and Conservation. VULNERABLE. Has declined markedly due to overhunting and habitat destruction. Previously widely distributed in Japan where it was common to abundant winter visitor, with flocks of 100,000 near Osaka; now only uncommon winter visitor, with less than 10,000 birds in whole of Japan by 1980, and only around 2000 at end of 1980's. Recently, only large census figures from South Korea, with 18,000 individuals counted in winter 1991. Part of decline can be attributed to changes in breeding grounds.
Bibliography. Ali & Ripley (1978), Bauer & Glutz von Blotzheim (1968), Bellrose (1976), Brazil (1991), Collar & Andrew (1988), Dementiev & Gladkov (1952), Etchécopar & Hüe (1978), Gooders & Boyer (1986), Perennou & Mundkur (1991), Phillips (1922-1926), Poole *et al.* (1990), Roberts (1991), de Schauensee (1984), Shevareva (1970).

76. Common Teal
Anas crecca

French: Sarcelle d'hiver **German**: Krickente **Spanish**: Cerceta Común
Other common names: Teal, Eurasian Teal (*crecca*); Aleutian Green-winged Teal (*nimia*); Green-winged/North American Green-winged Teal (*carolinensis*)

Taxonomy. *Anas Crecca* Linnaeus, 1758, Europe.
Sometimes placed in genus *Nettion*. Forms superspecies with *A. flavirostris*. Race *carolinensis* sometimes considered full species. Three subspecies recognized.
Subspecies and Distribution.
A. c. crecca Linnaeus, 1758 - most of N and C Palearctic.
A. c. nimia Friedmann, 1948 - Aleutian Is.
A. c. carolinensis Gmelin, 1789 - most of Nearctic.

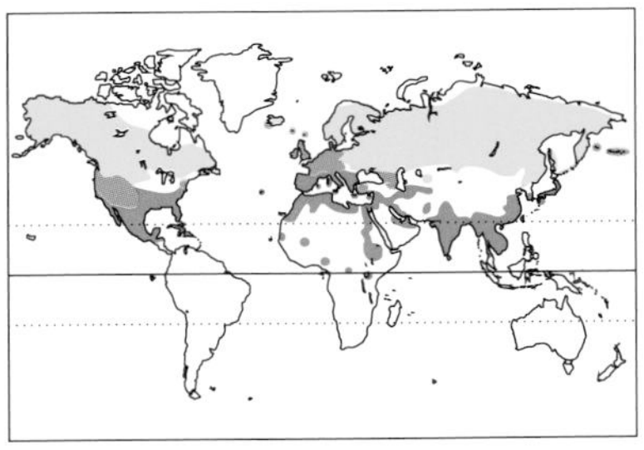

Descriptive notes. 34-43 cm; average 340-360 g. Black and metallic green speculum generally delimited by white lines along front and rear edges. Male has eclipse plumage. Juvenile resembles female but with spots on belly and without buff markings on uppertail-coverts. Subspecies separated according to size and small differences in coloration; *carolinensis* most differentiated, with black line along flanks, white vertical line between breast and flanks and thinner cream-coloured line delimiting facial pattern; female generally has cinnamon instead of white line in front of speculum, though this can vary; even in nominate, shade of cinnamon is not constant.
Habitat. Small freshwater lakes and shallow marshes with abundant fringe vegetation. In winter, also in brackish wetlands and even on coast.
Food and Feeding. Mainly seeds of aquatic plants, grasses, sedges and grain during winter months; many aquatic invertebrates (molluscs, worms, insects, crustaceans) in spring and summer. Feeds by dabbling, head-dipping, upending and diving in shallow water; also filters mud.
Breeding. Starts Mar/May. In single pairs or loose groups; nest is deep hollow in ground, lined with dry leaves and down, built among dense vegetation. Usually 8-11 eggs (5-16); incubation 21-23 days; chicks have dark brown down above, yellow below; fledging 25-30 days. Sexual maturity at c. 1 year.
Movements. Partially migratory, northernmost breeding birds descending to lower latitudes in winter, as far S as equator (Kenya), but breeders of more temperate regions present throughout year.
Status and Conservation. Not globally threatened. One of most abundant ducks. Race *carolinensis* very numerous in North America, with estimate of over 7,000,000; forms large concentrations when wintering, with 42,000 counted in census at Marismas Nacionales, WC Mexico. Nominate subspecies common in Japan (where *carolinensis* rare winter visitor) with population of over 110,000 birds; also common in Taiwan, with 11,780 birds counted in winter 1991 census; partial counts in same period also yielded 37,168 birds in India, 109,170 in Pakistan, 14,406 in Turkmenistan and 77,200 in Azerbaydzhan; in Iran, 211,219 counted in 1990 census; approximately 28,000 wintering in Israel. Also large numbers in Africa, but available data incomplete. Total wintering population in W Palearctic estimated at c. 1,400,000.

Intensive hunting in winter quarters and reduction of suitable habitat appear compensated by establishment of reserves, given apparent stability of population, at least in Europe. CITES III in Ghana.

Bibliography. Ali & Ripley (1978), Baldassarre *et al*. (1988), Bauer & Glutz von Blotzheim (1968), Bellrose (1976), Biaggi (1983), Blake (1977), Brazil (1991), Brickell (1988), Brown *et al*. (1982), Cooch (1964), Cramp & Simmons (1977), Dementiev & Gladkov (1952), DuBowy (1987, 1988), Etchécopar & Hüe (1978), Ferrer (1982), Géroudet (1972), Goodman (1989), Grimmett & Jones (1989), Harrison (1988), Laurie-Ahlberg & McKinney (1979), Lebret (1947), Llorente *et al*. (1987), Marchant *et al*. (1990), McClure (1974), McKinney (1965a), Moisan *et al*. (1967), Monroe (1968), Monval & Pirot (1989), Munro (1949a), Ogilvie (1983), Olney (1963b), Paz (1987), Perennou (1991b), Perennou & Mundkur (1991), Quinlan & Baldassarre (1984), Richardson (1990), Ridgill & Fox (1990), Roberts (1991), Sargeant *et al*. (1984), Scott & Carbonell (1986), Shevareva (1970), Smythies (1986), Tamisier (1971, 1972, 1976).

77. Speckled Teal

Anas flavirostris

French: Sarcelle à bec jaune **German**: Andenente **Spanish**: Cerceta Barcina
Other common names: South American Green-winged/South American Teal; Merida Speckled Teal (*altipetens*); Andean Speckled/Andean Teal (*andium*); Sharp-winged Speckled/Sharp-winged Teal (*oxyptera*); Chilean Speckled/Chilean/Yellow-billed Teal (*flavirostris*)

Taxonomy. *Anas flavirostris* Vieillot, 1816, Buenos Aires.
Sometimes placed in genus *Nettion*. Forms superspecies with *A. crecca*. Two northern races sometimes separated as one full species (*A. andium*). Four subspecies recognized.
Subspecies and Distribution.
A. f. altipetens (Conover, 1941) - E Andes of Colombia to NW Venezuela.
A. f. andium (P. L. Sclater & Salvin, 1873) - Andes of Colombia and N Ecuador.
A. f. oxyptera Meyen, 1834 - Andes from C Peru to NW Argentina.
A. f. flavirostris Vieillot, 1816 - N Argentina S to Tierra del Fuego; Falkland Is, South Georgia.

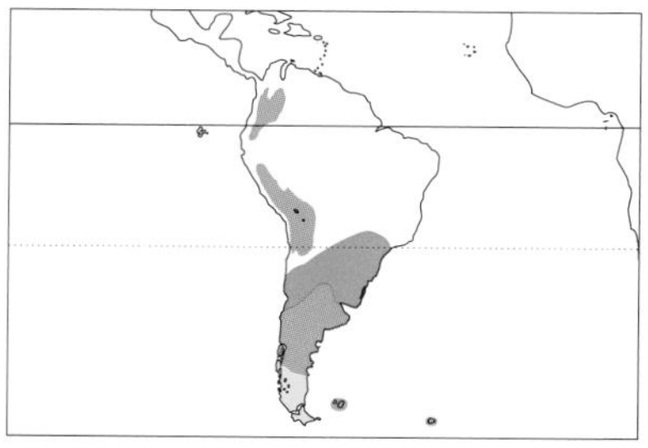

Descriptive notes. 35-45 cm; 600-830 g. Head sometimes paler than in bird depicted. Female slightly smaller and duller. Juvenile with duller bill and spotting on underparts. Subspecies vary in colour: *andium* has longer and bluer bill than others, and dark markings reach further back along flanks; *oxyptera* has dark markings limited to sides of breast, pale parts seem white from a distance.
Habitat. Variety of freshwater lakes, rivers and marshes, generally at high altitude in mountainous country, but also in lower ground. In winter, commonly on coast.
Food and Feeding. Small aquatic invertebrates (insects, crustaceans, amphipods) and seeds and vegetative parts of aquatic plants (seaweed, algae). Filters mud while walking along water's edge, or gathers food items by dabbling, head-dipping or upending in shallow waters.
Breeding. Season variable according to locality; starts Feb in Colombia. Sometimes double-brooded in northern part of range. In single pairs or loose groups; nest well-hidden, often among thick vegetation or in trees, near water. 5-8 eggs; incubation c. 24 days; chicks have dark brown down above, yellowish below; fledging 6-7 weeks.
Movements. Southernmost breeding birds winter in more temperate regions, as far N as Uruguay, Paraguay and southern Brazil. Falkland Is and Andean populations mainly sedentary, the latter perhaps forced to descend to lower altitudes by adverse winter weather.
Status and Conservation. Not globally threatened. Generally common, locally abundant. Races of high Andes less numerous due to more restricted range, but in good state because of inaccessibility of habitat, which remains mostly unchanged; frequently recorded in temperate Ecuador, very frequently in the *paramo* zone. Nominate subspecies widespread within its range; common resident on Falkland Is. Partial counts in Jul 1990 yielded 3019 birds in Argentina, 884 in Chile and 678 in Uruguay. Estimated 40-50 birds in Cumberland Bay, South Georgia, a small breeding population discovered in 1971 and which probably originates from introduction by early whalers. Hunted intensely in winter quarters, but population does not seem seriously affected.

Bibliography. Belton (1984), Blake (1977), Carp (1991), Fjeldså & Krabbe (1990), Gómez-Dallmeier & Cringan (1989), Hellmayr & Conover (1948), Hilty & Brown (1986), Humphrey *et al*. (1970), Johnson (1965), Marchant & Higgins (1990), McKinney & Brewer (1989), Nores & Yzurieta (1980), de la Peña (1986), de Schauensee & Phelps (1978), Scott & Carbonell (1986), Standen (1976, 1980), Vides-Almonacid (1990), Weller (1975d), Weller & Howard (1972), Woods (1975, 1988).

78. Cape Teal

Anas capensis

French: Sarcelle du Cap **German**: Fahlente **Spanish**: Cerceta del Cabo
Other common names: Cape Wigeon, African Cape Teal, Pink-billed Duck/Teal

Taxonomy. *Anas capensis* Gmelin, 1789, Cape of Good Hope.
Sometimes placed in genus *Nettion*. Monotypic.
Distribution. Sudan and Ethiopia to Namibia and South Africa.

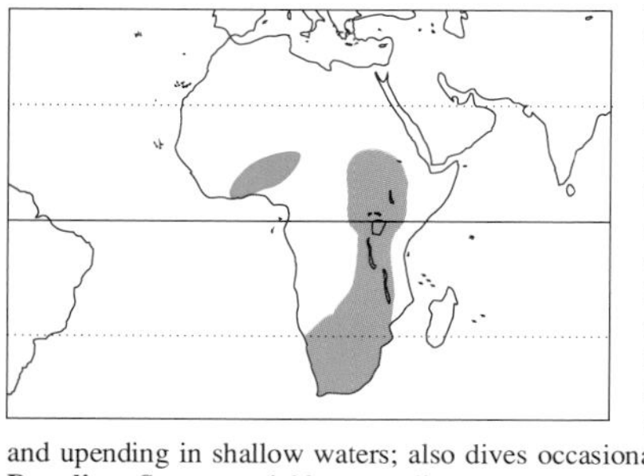

Descriptive notes. 44-48 cm; 316-502 g. Typically shows traces of crest on nape; colours fairly variable and can seem greenish grey. Female with somewhat duller bill, and slightly darker head without traces of crest on nape. Juvenile as adult, though probably with duller bare parts.
Habitat. Strong preference for shallow lagoons of brackish or saline waters. Also in fresh water, on rivers and by coast.
Food and Feeding. Aquatic invertebrates (insects and their larvae, crustaceans) and small amphibians (tadpoles); also plant matter, principally seeds, leaves and stems of aquatic plants. Forages during day by swimming, dabbling, head-dipping and upending in shallow waters; also dives occasionally.
Breeding. Season variable, according to locality and extent of rainfall. In single pairs; nest is hollow scrape in ground, lined with a thick layer of down, concealed among vegetation. 6-11 eggs; incubation 26-30 days; chicks have smoky grey down above, whitish below; fledging c. 8 weeks.
Movements. Mainly sedentary, though may wander widely during droughts and appear well outside normal range. Regular during dry season in Lake Chad area and occasionally N to Libya.
Status and Conservation. Not globally threatened. Widespread and locally common to abundant, though patchily distributed and scarce over much of its range. Total population unknown, but does not appear to have decreased significantly. Rare west of 5° E. In E Africa, common only in Rift Valley soda lakes and in Ethiopia. Fairly common to common in South Africa, where increasing in recent years, except in Natal, where scarce; rare in Mozambique. Highly valued and commonly shot, though benefits from proliferation of artificial water bodies. CITES III in Ghana.

Bibliography. Brand (1961, 1964), Brickell (1988), Britton (1980), Brown & Britton (1980), Brown *et al*. (1982), Clancey (1967), Cramp & Simmons (1977), Elgood (1982), Hall (1977), Macdonald & Taylor (1976), Mackworth-Praed & Grant (1957-1973), Maclean (1985), Perennou (1991b), Pinto (1983), Siegfried (1974), Skead (1977b), Winterbottom (1974).

79. Madagascar Teal

Anas bernieri

French: Sarcelle de Bernier **German**: Bernierente **Spanish**: Cerceta Malgache
Other common names: Bernier's Teal

Taxonomy. *Querquedula Bernieri* "J. Verr." Hartlaub, 1860, Madagascar.
Sometimes placed in genus *Nettion*. Forms superspecies with *A. gibberifrons*. Monotypic.
Distribution. W coastal Madagascar.

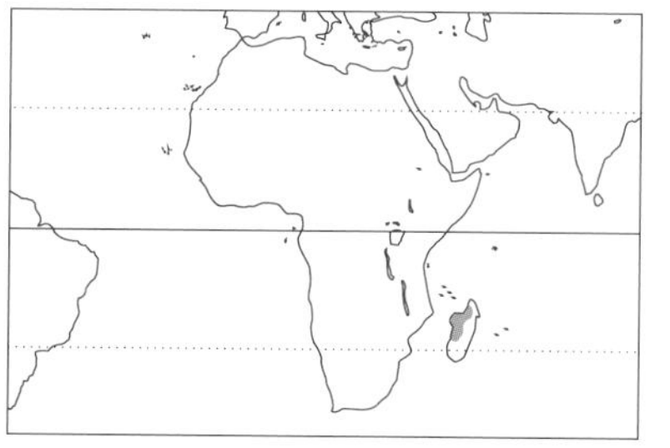

Descriptive notes. 40 cm. Female can have browner bill and legs.
Habitat. Known only from small, saline lakes of shallow waters with emergent reedbeds and adjacent wetlands, marshes, rivers and paddyfields.
Food and Feeding. Diet unknown. Feeds by dabbling and filtering mud while walking on lakeshore. Not seen to dive or upend. Least active during central hours of day.
Breeding. Starts Sept, but clutch found in Apr suggests might be double-brooded. In single pairs or loose groups; nest made with thin reeds or grass, near water; 2-10 eggs; chicks have blackish brown down above, yellowish below.
Movements. Presumably sedentary; not recorded outside regular range.
Status and Conservation. VULNERABLE. CITES II. Poorly known, but seems never to have been numerous. Rare, but well represented in area of Bemamba L and mouth of Tsiribihina R. Only significant recent counts are 60 (13 of which were shot by hunters) on Masama L in 1970 and 61 (total estimate of 120) on Bemamba L in 1973; since then, species seen but no more quantitative data available. Traditionally subjected to intense exploitation through shooting and egg-collecting; also threatened by habitat transformation to create rice-fields. Urgent need to declare adequate protected areas, especially Bemamba L.

Bibliography. Brickell (1988), Collar & Andrew (1988), Collar & Stuart (1985), Dee (1986), Delacour (1929b), Dollinger (1988), King (1978/79), Langrand (1990), Milon *et al*. (1973), Rand (1936), Salvan (1970, 1972b), Scott & Lubbock (1974), Vincent (1966), Young (1991b).

80. Grey Teal

Anas gibberifrons

French: Sarcelle grise **German**: Weißkehlente **Spanish**: Cerceta Grís
Other common names: Slender Teal; Andaman Grey/Andaman Teal (*albogularis*); East Indian/Indonesian Grey Teal, Sunda Teal (*gibberifrons*); Australian/Australasian Grey Teal (*gracilis*)

Taxonomy. *Anas (Mareca) gibberifrons* S. Müller, 1842, Celebes.
Sometimes placed in genus *Nettion*. Forms superspecies with *A. bernieri*. Subspecies *gracilis* often considered full species. Race *remissa* of Rennell I, Solomon Is, extinct. Three living subspecies recognized.
Subspecies and Distribution.
A. g. albogularis (Hume, 1873) - Andaman Is and Great Coco I.
A. g. gibberifrons S. Müller, 1842 - Java and Sulawesi to Timor and Wetar I.
A. g. gracilis Buller, 1869 - New Guinea to New Caledonia and Australia to New Zealand.

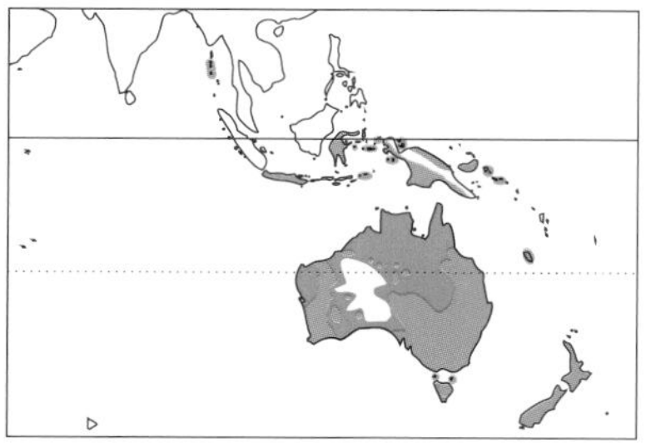

Descriptive notes. 37-47 cm; 395-670 g; wingspan 60-67 cm. Protuberance on forehead variable. Female slightly paler with duller iris. Juvenile paler than female, especially on head and neck. Subspecies vary in structure and colour; *gracilis*, as nominate but with normal forehead, often indistinguishable from female *A. castanea*; *albogularis* has sometimes less, sometimes much more white on face, and colours may be redder.
Habitat. Highly adaptable to all sorts of wetlands, with shallow, fresh, brackish or saline waters; often on temporarily flooded areas and coastal lagoons.
Food and Feeding. Seeds and vegetative parts of aquatic and shoreline vegetation, grasses and sedges; also small aquatic invertebrates (insects and their larvae, molluscs, crustaceans). Feeds by dabbling, mud-filtering in shallow water and by picking up insects and seeds.
Breeding. Season variable, depending on locality and water levels. In single pairs or loose groups; nest is made of plant matter available at site, lined with down, in slight depression on ground among vegetation, sometimes in natural (often tree-) cavity. Usually 7-8 eggs (4-14, up to 30 by dump-laying); incubation c. 26 days; chicks have olive brown down above, whitish buff below; fledging c. 8 weeks. Sexual maturity at 1 year.
Movements. Mostly sedentary but certain populations (particularly Australian) subject to much wandering during dry season. At this time may occur almost anywhere in Australia and surrounding islands.
Status and Conservation. Not globally threatened. Only subspecies on small islands threatened: *remissa* was only known on one lagoon in Rennell I and has recently become extinct after large fish *Tilapia* was introduced into the lagoon; *albogularis* of Andaman Is has an intrinsically small population, possibly in danger through agricultural development and drainage of wetlands, but the total number of individuals is unknown. Nominate subspecies appears locally common but not in large concentrations. Australian *gracilis* is the most abundant subspecies, in general throughout its range; one of the most abundant ducks in Australia; partial censuses in SW Australia yielded 41,280-70,054. In New Guinea, sometimes fairly common but often scarce in widely scattered localities. Colonized New Zealand around 100 years ago, and now widely scattered and increasing, helped by nestboxes; population estimated at fewer than 20,000. Suffers intense hunting pressure; 71-72% of all ducks counted in Victoria, Australia. Breeding on alluvial plains threatened by flood-mitigation schemes.

Bibliography. Ali & Ripley (1978), Balham (1952), Balham & Miers (1959), Beehler *et al*. (1986), Bregulla (1992), Bull *et al*. (1985), Chambers (1989), Coates (1985), Falla *et al*. (1981), Frith (1962, 1963, 1967), Halse & Jaensch (1989), Kear & Williams (1978), Keith & Hines (1958), Lavery (1972), Livezey (1990), Marchant & Higgins (1990), Mees (1982), Mills (1985), Morton *et al*. (1990), Norman (1987, 1990), Norman *et al*. (1979), Roy (1988), Schodde & Tidemann (1988), Soper (1976), Weller (1980), White & Bruce (1986).

81 ♂ ♀

82 ♂ ssp *aucklandica* ♀ ssp *chlorotis*

83 ♂ ssp *platyrhynchos* ♀ ♂ ssp *wyvilliana* ♀

ssp *laysanensis*

83 ssp *diazi* ssp *fulvigula* 84

85 ♀ ssp *poecilorhyncha*

86 ssp *zonorhyncha* 87 ♂ 88

89 90 91 ♀ ssp *acuta* 92 ssp *spinicauda* 93 ssp *georgica*

♂ ssp *eatoni*

PLATE 46

81. Chestnut Teal

Anas castanea

French: Sarcelle rousse **German**: Kastanienente **Spanish**: Cerceta Castaña
Other common names: Red/Chestnut-breasted Teal, Brown Teal (!)

Taxonomy. *Mareca castanea* Eyton, 1838, New South Wales.
Sometimes placed in genus *Nettion*. Forms superspecies with *A. aucklandica*. Hybridization recorded with *A. gibberifrons gracilis*. Monotypic.
Distribution. SW and SE Australia, Tasmania.

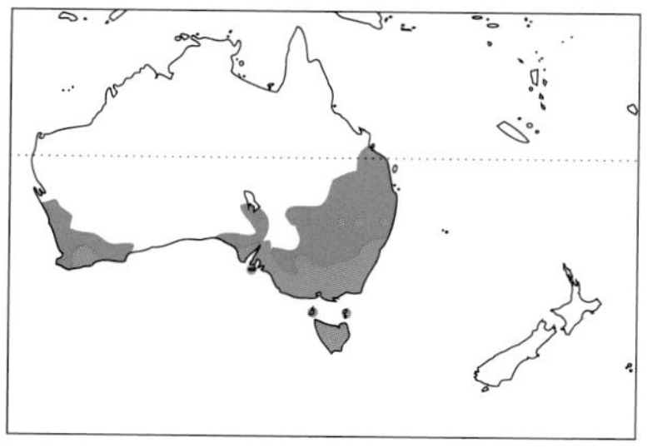

Descriptive notes. 35-46 cm; 600-700 g. No eye-ring; red iris. Non-breeding male slightly duller. Juvenile resembles female but with less spotting.
Habitat. Favours estuaries, coastal lagoons and marshes. Also along coast and, regularly but less commonly, in inland waters.
Food and Feeding. Feeds by dabbling and mud-filtering in very shallow waters, and presumably takes similar kinds of food to that taken by *A. gibberifrons*, with which it often forms mixed flocks.
Breeding. Starts Jun/Nov, mainly about Aug; often double- and perhaps triple-brooded. In single pairs or concentrations; nest is lined with down, situated on ground among vegetation or in natural cavity. Usually 7-10 eggs (5-17); incubation 23-29 days; chicks have brown down on upperparts, paler below and on spot at sides of rump; fledging c. 56 days. Sexual maturity at c. 1 year. Hatching success of 65-78·3% recorded.
Movements. Mostly sedentary, with small-scale dispersion inland and following coast on both sides of Australia. However, vagrants have occurred throughout Australia and in New Guinea.
Status and Conservation. Not globally threatened. Widely scattered, but only locally common, especially in Tasmania and Bass Strait region, scarce or rare elsewhere. Hunting, and destruction or modification of wetlands have caused great decline this century. Partial censuses in Victoria yielded 19,143-31,446, where it represents 6-10% of total ducks counted there, and 465-1140 birds in SW Australia. The nestbox instalment programme has been seen to be very useful in helping this species. Between 58-74% of the population is found in waters open to shooting.
Bibliography. Frith (1967), Kolbe (1979), Livezey (1990), Marchant & Higgins (1990), Norman & McKinney (1987), Norman *et al*. (1979), Ripley (1942), Schodde & Tidemann (1988), van Tets (1965b), Weller (1974).

82. Brown Teal

Anas aucklandica

French: Sarcelle brune **German**: Aucklandente **Spanish**: Cerceta Maorí
Other common names: Brown Duck, New Zealand Teal; Pateke (*chlorotis*); Auckland Duck/Teal (*aucklandica*); Campbell Island Brown/Campbell/Flightless Teal (*nesiotis*)

Taxonomy. *Nesonetta aucklandica* G. R. Gray, 1844, Auckland Islands.
Sometimes placed in genus *Nettion*. Forms superspecies with *A. castanea*. The three races have been proposed as full species, although *nesiotis* doubtfully separable from *aucklandica*. Population of South I has sometimes been assigned separate subspecies, *peculiaris*. Hybridization (race *chlorotis*) recorded with *A. platyrhynchos*. Three subspecies recognized.
Subspecies and Distribution.
A. a. chlorotis G. R. Gray, 1845 - isolated areas of North I and SW South I, New Zealand; formerly more widespread.
A. a. aucklandica (G. R. Gray, 1844) - islets off Auckland Is; formerly Auckland I.
A. a. nesiotis (Fleming, 1935) - Dent I (Campbell I group); formerly in Campbell I.

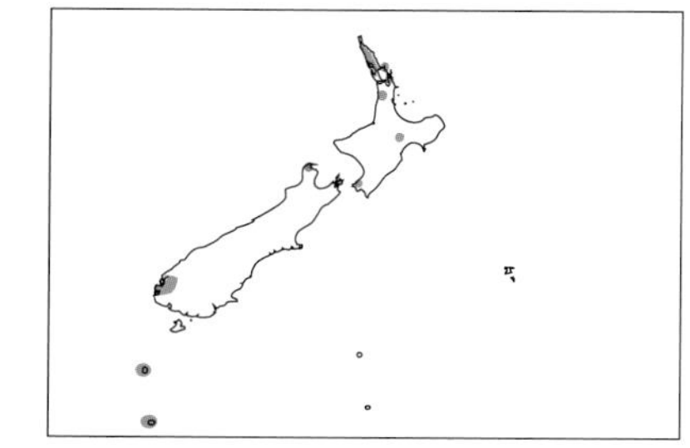

Descriptive notes. 36-48 cm; 375-700 g. Race *chlorotis* resembles *A. castanea*; eclipse plumage similar to female, which some males also exhibit as breeding plumage. Races *aucklandica* and *nesiotis* smaller, short-winged and flightless; little sexual dimorphism; often adopt very upright posture with drooping tail. Juveniles of all races resemble females.
Habitat. Coastal waters in sheltered bays and, inland, on marshes, pools and streams with some tree cover.
Food and Feeding. Mostly aquatic invertebrates (insects and their larvae, crustaceans, molluscs). Forages by probing, dabbling, upending and diving near water's edge or, at low tide, on patches of kelp along shoreline. Often nocturnal, particularly where skuas (*Catharacta*) present.
Breeding. Mainly Jun-Oct, peak Jul-Aug (*chlorotis*); starts Dec-Jan (*aucklandica*). In single pairs; nest is a woven cup made of surrounding grass lined with down, situated on ground among vegetation. Usually 5-6 eggs (4-8); only authenticated record of *aucklandica*, 4 eggs; incubation c. 29-30 days (*chlorotis*); chicks have brown down above, buffish below, with streaked face; fledging 50-55 days (captivity). In one study 27 pairs (44%) out of 68 had broods (*aucklandica*).
Movements. Presumably sedentary; not recorded outside its now much-reduced range. Races *aucklandica* and *nesiotis* flightless.
Status and Conservation. RARE. CITES II. Subspecies *nesiotis* exterminated on Campbell I by alien predators, but rediscovered in 1975 on nearby islet, Dent I, where there are 30-50 birds. Nominate race also eradicated by feral cats and pigs on Auckland I, but still exists on other parts of archipelago, with total of c. 500-600 birds; on Enderby I, suitable habitat inland has probably decreased due to feral cattle and rabbits. Subspecies *chlorotis*, the most common one, has declined markedly since last century because of habitat destruction, introduced predators and overhunting; now is widely distributed but only in small relict populations. In Northland, North I, probably declining, with population of 500-700, maximum 1000; largest population on Great Barrier I, with around 1500, fairly stable. Captive-reared birds have bred successfully, but self-sustaining populations not yet established, although more than 600 freed up to 1989, with annual average of 100. Race *aucklandica* also has good stock of captive breeders; problem is that no predator-free islands can be found to release them. Despite legal protection, some are killed by hunters every year.
Bibliography. Blanshard (1964), Bull *et al*. (1985), Chambers (1989), Collar & Andrew (1988), Cometti (1975), Diamond *et al*. (1987), Dollinger (1988), Dumbell (1986, 1987), Falla & Stead (1938), Falla *et al*. (1981), Gravatt (1966), Hayes & Dumbell (1989), Hayes & Williams (1982), Johnstone (1985), King (1978/79), Livezey (1990), Marchant & Higgins (1990), Mckenzie (1971), McKinney & Bruggers (1983), Mountfort (1988), Pirani (1976, 1979, 1981, 1982), Reid & Roderick (1973), Robertson (1976), Scott (1971), Shephard (1986), Vincent (1966), Weller (1974, 1975b, 1980), Williams, M.J. (1974, 1978, 1985f, 1986).

83. Mallard

Anas platyrhynchos

French: Canard colvert **German**: Stockente **Spanish**: Anade Azulón
Other common names: Greenhead, Common/Green-headed/Northern Mallard (*platyrhynchos*); Greenland Mallard (*conboschas*); Florida Mallard/Duck (*fulvigula*); Mottled Mallard/Duck (*fulvigula*, *maculosa*); Mexican Mallard/Duck (*diazi*); Hawaiian Mallard/Duck, Koloa (*wyvilliana*); Laysan Mallard/Duck/Teal (*laysanensis*)

Taxonomy. *Anas platyrhynchos* Linnaeus, 1758, Europe.
Forms superspecies with *A. rubripes*, *A. melleri* and *A. undulata*. *A. rubripes* sometimes considered subspecies of present species. Probable unstable hybrids of present species and *A. superciliosa*, found on some Micronesian islands, have been considered a different species, Mariana Duck (*A. oustaleti*). Races *fulvigula* and *maculosa* have been partitioned off in a different species, Mottled Duck (*A. fulvigula*). Races *diazi*, *wyvilliana* and *laysanensis* are also often considered full species. Hybridization recorded with at least 23 other species of genus *Anas*, often producing fertile progeny, and also with several species of *Aix*, *Alopochen*, *Anser*, *Branta*, *Tadorna*, *Cairina*, *Aythya* and *Somateria*. Seven subspecies normally recognized.
Subspecies and Distribution.
A. p. platyrhynchos Linnaeus, 1758 - most of Palearctic and Nearctic.
A. p. conboschas C. L. Brehm, 1831 - SW Greenland.
A. p. fulvigula Ridgway, 1874 - Florida.
A. p. maculosa Sennett, 1889 - Atlantic S USA to Mexico.
A. p. diazi Ridgway, 1886 - extreme S USA, from Arizona to Texas, S to C Mexico.
A. p. wyvilliana P. L. Sclater, 1878 - Kauai and Oahu Is (Hawaii).
A. p. laysanensis Rothschild, 1892 - Laysan I (to NW of Hawaii).
Introduced (*platyrhynchos*) to SE Australia and New Zealand.

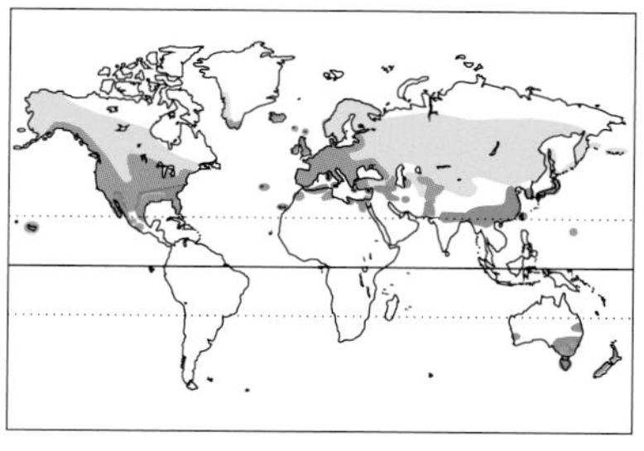

Descriptive notes. 50-65 cm; 750-1575 g; wingspan 75-100 cm (nominate). Blue speculum characteristic. Male has eclipse plumage. Females very variable; can be much darker than illustration. Juvenile resembles female but generally darker with more streaked underparts. Subspecies vary in size and coloration, often with little or no sexual dimorphism. Subspecies *conboschas* similar (male and female) to nominate, paler and larger, but with smaller bill. Subspecies *fulvigula*, 53-58 cm, both sexes resemble nominate female but darker, with uniformly yellow bill; blue-green speculum without white margin to greater coverts. Subspecies *maculosa* like *fulvigula*, but somewhat darker and more heavily marked. Subspecies *diazi*, 51-56 cm, even darker than *fulvigula*, especially on head, which shows less contrast with body; bill uniformly yellowish; dark tail; white lines on speculum narrow. Subspecies *wyvilliana*, 44-49 cm, is only form of *platyrhynchos* complex with whitish eye-ring; male very variable, with some seasonal changes, but never approaches full breeding plumage of nominate; green speculum. Subspecies *laysanensis*, c. 40 cm, very variable, from buff to brown with dark-brown marks; extension of white facial patch very variable; speculum green in male, dull brown in female.
Habitat. Can occur on almost every wetland within range, in fresh, brackish or salt waters, as long as they are relatively shallow and provide some cover; avoids fast-flowing and oligotrophic waters. Very tolerant of human presence; frequent in ornamental waters, irrigation networks and reservoirs. Out of breeding season also on coast, on estuaries, bays and other sheltered sites. Usually in lowlands, occasionally at higher altitudes.
Food and Feeding. Omnivorous and opportunistic. Seeds and vegetative parts of aquatic and crop plants and, in spring and summer, variable amounts of terrestrial and aquatic invertebrates, such as insects, molluscs, crustaceans and worms; occasionally amphibians and fish. Feeds in groups by dabbling, head-dipping and upending in shallow waters; also grazes on land and occasionally dives.
Breeding. Mainly Feb-Jun, but varies depending on latitude, as late as Aug in *fulvigula*. In single pairs or loose groups; nest is bowl of grass lined with feathers and down, situated on ground, concealed among vegetation or in natural (sometimes tree-) cavity. Usually 9-13 eggs (4-18); incubation c. 27-28 days; chicks have dark brown down above and dark eyestripe, yellowish face, underparts and dorsal spots; fledging 50-60 days. Sexual maturity mostly at 1 year. Usually high success; average brood size at fledging 7 from average clutch size 8·1 in one study in Finland.

On following pages: 84. American Black Duck (*Anas rubripes*); 85. Meller's Duck (*Anas melleri*); 86. Yellow-billed Duck (*Anas undulata*); 87. Spot-billed Duck (*Anas poecilorhyncha*); 88. Pacific Black Duck (*Anas superciliosa*); 89. Philippine Duck (*Anas luzonica*); 90. Spectacled Duck (*Anas specularis*); 91. Crested Duck (*Anas specularioides*); 92. Northern Pintail (*Anas acuta*); 93. Yellow-billed Pintail (*Anas georgica*).

Movements. Partially migratory, northernmost breeding populations generally winter much further S, but sedentary in temperate regions (most of Europe, parts of N America). Many records outside range, but perhaps majority attributable to escapes.

Status and Conservation. Not globally threatened. Perhaps most widespread and numerous of all ducks, in good part due to its adaptability to humanized areas, as well as to introductions outside its natural range. Asian population not globally estimated, but high; in winter 1991 census, 158,075 recorded in Japan, 72,583 in Turkmenistan and 187,518 in Iran. Estimated c. 9,000,000 wintering in W Palearctic and c. 17,000,000-18,000,000 in North America, although species hunted intensely almost everywhere. In Australia, small populations from introduction, restricted to humanized areas in temperate zones, increasing in some places, such as in Tasmania. In New Zealand, widespread and abundant, with c. 5,000,000, increasing, in 1981. Subspecies *wyvilliana* rare; at present restricted to Kauai and reintroduced in Oahu and Hawaii; population c. 3000 in 1967; threatened by introduced mongooses and other predators and by habitat reduction. Race *laysanensis* rare; loss of vegetation due to introduced rabbits led it to verge of extinction; now considered stable at around 500 birds, which must be about maximum that the island permits. Subspecies *fulvigula* c. 50,000 in 1960's; average of 3900 counted during winter in Mexico in period 1978-1982, with notable 585 recorded in Tampico Lagoons. Race *diazi* rarest in North America, with 30,000-40,000 in 1975; has important wintering areas in Mexico, especially on L Atotonilco, with maximum of 1690 in winter censuses in period 1977-1982, and on L Chapala and delta of R Lerma, where up to 11,620 individuals counted in winter censuses in period 1978-1982; threatened through hybridization with *platyrhynchos*, which is spreading S in USA. Subspecies *laysanensis* on CITES I.

Bibliography. Aldrich & Baer (1970), Ali & Ripley (1978), Allen (1980), Anderson (1975), Anderson & Burnham (1976), Anderson & Henny (1972), Ankney *et al*. (1987, 1989), Avise *et al*. (1990), Batt (1976), Batt & Prince (1978), Bauer & Glutz von Blotzheim (1968), Bellrose (1976), Berger (1972), Birkhead (1985), Braithwaite & Miller (1975), Brazil (1991), Bregulla (1992), Brodsky & Weatherhead (1984), Brodsky *et al*. (1988), Brown *et al*. (1982), Collar & Andrew (1988), Cooch (1964), Coronado (1972), Cramp & Simmons (1977), Dementiev & Gladkov (1952), Desforges & Wood-Gush (1975a, 1975b), Dollinger (1988), DuBowy (1987, 1988), Engbring & Pratt (1985), Etchécopar & Hüe (1978), Evrard (1990), Géroudet (1972), Gillespie (1985), Goodman (1989), Gordon (1981), Greenway (1967), Heitmeyer (1985), Hestbeck (1990), Johnsgard (1960d), Johnson, D.H. & Sargeant (1977), Johnson, D.H., Nichols *et al*. (1988), Johnson, F.A., Montalbano *et al*. (1991), King (1978/79), Kooloos & Zweers (1989), Kooloos *et al*. (1989), Krapu (1981), Krapu *et al*. (1979), Lever (1987), Marchant & Higgins (1990), Martin & Carney (1977), Moulton & Weller (1984), Mulhern *et al*. (1985), Munro (1960), Munro & Kimball (1982), Nichols, Pospahala & Hines (1982), Owen & Cook (1977), Palmer (1976), Paulus (1984b, 1988), Pehrsson (1979, 1984, 1991), Pospahala *et al*. (1974), Pöysä & Nummi (1990), Raikow (1970), Ripley (1960), Roberts (1991), Scott & Kepler (1985), Shah *et al*. (1988), Shevareva (1970), Stutzenbaker (1984), Swanson *et al*. (1979), Swedberg (1967, 1969), Titman & Seymour (1981), Townsend (1916), Vincent (1966), Warner (1963), Weller (1980), Williams, D.M. (1982), Williams, S.O. (1978), Williams, M.J. & Roderick (1973), Zwank *et al*. (1989).

84. American Black Duck

Anas rubripes

French: Canard noirâtre **German**: Dunkelente **Spanish**: Anade Sombrío
Other common names: North American Black Duck, Black Duck/Mallard

Taxonomy. *Anas obscura rubripes* Brewster, 1902, Lake Umbagog, New Hampshire shore.
Forms superspecies with *A. platyrhynchos*, *A. melleri* and *A. undulata*. Sometimes considered a subspecies of *A. platyrhynchos*, with which frequently interbreeds in the wild. Monotypic.

Distribution. E Canada from Manitoba to Newfoundland, S to E USA as far S as North Carolina.

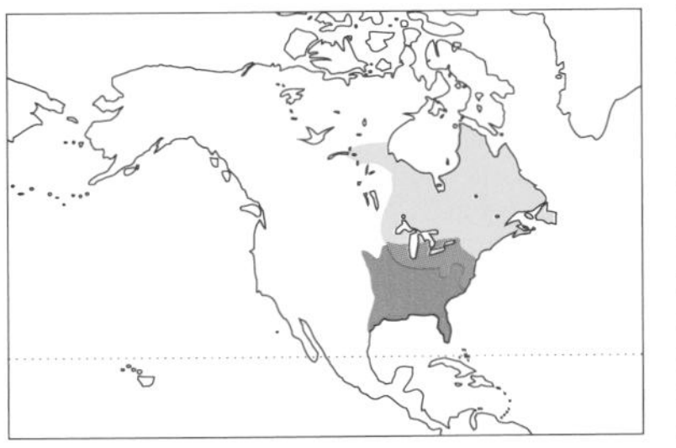

Descriptive notes. 53-61 cm; c. 1150-1350 g. Very dark; face and foreneck lighter than body; violet speculum. Male has eclipse plumage, though only slightly different. Female tends to have more olive-coloured bill and more buff fringes to body; duskier legs. Juvenile more heavily streaked on breast and underparts with buff fringes.

Habitat. Various types of wetlands of fresh or brackish waters, preferably the latter with some tree cover for breeding. Outside breeding season also on large, open lagoons and on coast, even in rough sea waters; more tolerant of salt water than *A. platyrhynchos*.

Food and Feeding. Seeds and vegetative parts of aquatic and crop plants, with rather high proportion of invertebrates (insects, molluscs, crustaceans) in spring and summer. Feeds by grazing, probing, dabbling or upending in shallow waters; occasionally dives.

Breeding. Starts Mar/Apr. In single pairs or loose groups; nest is a scrape on ground, concealed among vegetation, sometimes in tree-cavities or crotches, lined with adjacent plant matter and down. Usually 7-12 eggs (1-17); incubation c. 26-29 days; chicks have blackish down on upperparts and eyestripe, yellowish face, foreneck, underparts and dorsal spots; fledging c. 60 days. Sexual maturity mostly at 1 year; estimated annual mortality, with no hunting losses, of 40% among immatures, 22% among adult birds.

Movements. Northernmost breeders descend to lower latitudes to winter in Atlantic seaboard of North America, usually as far S as Atlanta and Texas. Reported as vagrant to Korea, Puerto Rico and western Europe (particularly Britain), where some have stayed for long time, even hybridizing with local *A. platyrhynchos*.

Status and Conservation. Not globally threatened. Marked decline this century, of approximately 40% in period 1955-1974. Winter censuses yielded 1,311,000 in period 1952-1954 and only 804,000 in period 1959-1962. In Chesapeake Bay, Maryland, c. 200,000 birds wintered in 1955, and only c. 50,000 at the end of the 1980's. Causes of decline unknown, but probably related to habitat loss, deterioration of water and food supplies, intense hunting pressure (is still common quarry species in North America), and competition and hybridization with *A. platyrhynchos*, since the latter's expansion over NE North America.

Bibliography. Albright (1981), Ankney *et al*. (1987, 1989), Avise *et al*. (1990), Barske (1968), Bellrose (1976), Blandin (1982), Brodsky & Weatherhead (1984, 1985), Brodsky *et al*. (1988), Coulter & Miller (1968), Cramp & Simmons (1977), Diefenbach (1988), Diefenbach & Owen (1989), Geis *et al*. (1971), Grandy (1983), Johnsgard (1960d), Krementz *et al*. (1991), Lewis & Garrison (1984), Lewis & Nelson (1988), Longcore *et al*. (1987), Nichols (1991a), Nichols *et al*. (1987), Owen *et al*. (1989), Palmer (1976), Parnell & Quay (1962), Reed (1970), Ringelman (1980), Rusch *et al*. (1989), Seymour & Titman (1978), Terres (1980), Titman & Seymour (1981), Townsend (1916), Wright (1954).

85. Meller's Duck

Anas melleri

French: Canard de Meller **German**: Madagaskarente **Spanish**: Anade Malgache

Taxonomy. *Anas melleri* P. L. Sclater, 1865, Madagascar.
Forms superspecies with *A. platyrhynchos*, *A. rubripes* and *A. undulata*. Clearly derived from *A. platyrhynchos*, but apparently more distantly related than other isolated descendants of that species. Monotypic.

Distribution. E and High Plateau of Madagscar; introduced to Mauritius.

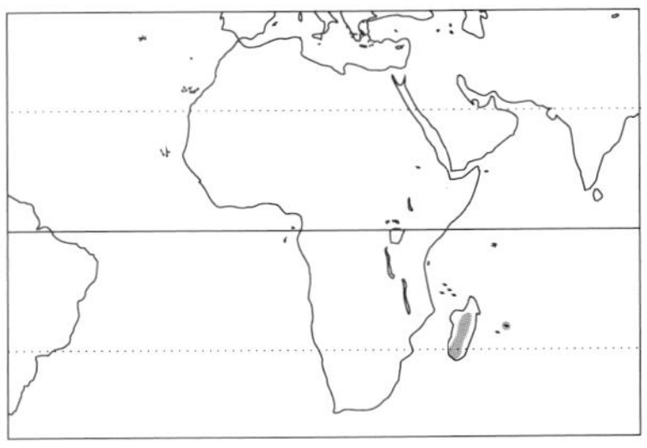

Descriptive notes. 63-68 cm. Reminiscent of female *A. platyrhynchos* but larger and more elongated, with longer bill and head; green speculum with narrow white trailing edge. Sexes alike, but female slightly smaller and a little duller. Juvenile more reddish.

Habitat. Breeds on inland freshwater lakes, pools and marshes in swampy forest country, generally from sea-level to c. 2000 m; also in rivers and streams, even fast-flowing ones; sometimes in rice fields.

Food and Feeding. Not well known, but habits presumably not very different from those of *A. platyrhynchos*; seeds and other parts of aquatic plants recorded; has been seen in rice fields and presumably feeds on stubble. Forages mainly by dabbling.

Breeding. Extended season, nesting has been recorded Sept-Apr. In single pairs or loose groups; nest is bulky structure of dry grass, leaves and other vegetation, lined with down and fine plant matter, situated on ground, usually on banks among tufts of herbaceous vegetation. 5-10 eggs; incubation 28-29 days (captivity); chicks have greyish olive brown down on upperparts, pale chestnut face and underparts, and yellowish dorsal patches; fledging c. 9 weeks.

Movements. Presumably sedentary; some records on W of island where normally does not occur, but not known to wander naturally outside Madagascar.

Status and Conservation. Not globally threatened. Uncommon and not present in any protected areas. Introduced to Mauritius, but overhunting threatens population; only c. 20 pairs thought to exist in late 1970's. In Madagascar, also clear decline over past 20 years due to hunting and poaching. In 1989, count of 1480 birds visiting L Aloatra, where heavily hunted all year. Small captive population seems to be thriving.

Bibliography. Brickell (1988), Darby (1978), Dee (1986), Delacour (1932), Langrand (1990), Lorenz (1951-1953), McKelvey (1977), Milon *et al*. (1973), Weller (1980), Young (1991a, 1991b), Young & Smith (1989).

86. Yellow-billed Duck

Anas undulata

French: Canard à bec jaune **German**: Gelbschnabelente **Spanish**: Anade Picolimón
Other common names: Yellowbill, African Yellow-billed Duck

Taxonomy. *Anas undulata* Dubois, 1839, Cape of Good Hope.
Forms superspecies with *A. platyrhynchos*, *A. rubripes* and *A. melleri*. Two subspecies recognized.

Subspecies and Distribution.
A. u. rueppelli Blyth, 1855 - S Sudan, Ethiopia, Uganda, N Kenya.
A. u. undulata Dubois, 1839 - Kenya SW to Angola and southwards to Cape Province.

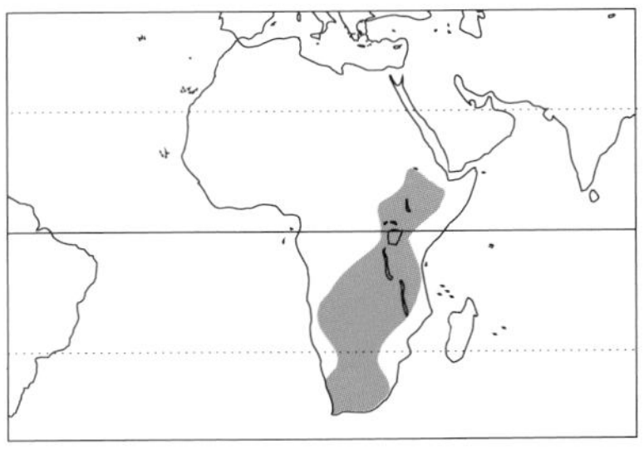

Descriptive notes. 51-58 cm; 630-1208 g. Legs variable, from yellowish through to blackish. Female tends to be slightly paler and smaller with somewhat less bright bill. Juvenile has coarser streaking on head, more buff-fringed body and more heavily spotted underparts. Subspecies *rueppelli* is darker and browner with deeper yellow bill.

Habitat. Freshwater lakes, reservoirs, flooded fields, swamps and marshes, slow-flowing rivers with pools, brackish coastal lagoons and estuaries. Usually lowlands, but locally up to 3890 m in Ethiopia.

Food and Feeding. Seeds, roots, leaves and stems of both aquatic (*Potamogeton*) and terrestrial plants; also animal matter, mainly insects and their larvae (Chironomidae, Dytiscidae), molluscs and crustaceans. Feeds by dabbling, upending and diving in shallow waters and by grazing on land.

Breeding. Season variable, generally coincides with beginning of rains. In single pairs; nest made of grass, rushes and reed stems, lined with down, situated on ground, concealed among rank vegetation. 4-12 eggs; incubation 26-29 days; chicks have greyish olive brown down above, yellowish face, underparts and dorsal panels; fledging c. 68 days.

Movements. Mostly sedentary, with generally only small-scale movements on record, mainly between alternative wetlands within same region, but known to have occurred W to Cameroon (race *rueppelli*); in South Africa movements of up to 1100 km occasionally recorded.

Status and Conservation. Not globally threatened. Common and widespread; most abundant duck in many parts of its range, especially in temperate regions. Very common in southern Africa in general, where commonest duck in agricultural areas; population estimated at 52,000-65,000 birds; in SW Cape, South Africa, abundant, numbers fluctuating. Probably more scattered population towards the N of its range.

Bibliography. Benson & Benson (1975), Brickell (1988), Britton (1980), Brown & Britton (1980), Brown *et al.* (1982), Clancey (1967), Clark (1973), Day (1977), Dean (1978), Dean & Skead (1977, 1989), Elgood (1982), Mackworth-Praed & Grant (1957-1973), Maclean (1985), Middlemiss (1958b), Perennou (1991b), Pinto (1983), Rowan (1963), Siegfried (1970), Skead (1976, 1980b).

87. Spot-billed Duck

Anas poecilorhyncha

French: Canard à bec tacheté   **German**: Fleckschnabelente   **Spanish**: Anade Picopinto
Other common names: Grey Duck, Spotbill, Spot-billed Grey Duck; Chinese Spotbill (*zonorhyncha*); Burmese Spotbill (*haringtoni*); Indian Spotbill (*poecilorhyncha*)

Taxonomy. *Anas poecilorhyncha* J. R. Forster, 1781, Ceylon.
Forms superspecies with *A. superciliosa* and *A. luzonica*. The former is often considered a subspecies of present species. Several cases of hybridization reported in captivity with the two aforementioned species, and also with *A. platyrhynchos*, producing fertile progeny. Three subspecies recognized.
Subspecies and Distribution.
A. p. zonorhyncha Swinhoe, 1866 - SE USSR, Sakhalin and Japan to S China.
A. p. haringtoni (Oates, 1907) - E Assam and Burma eastwards to S China and Laos.
A. p. poecilorhyncha J. R. Forster, 1781 - throughout Indian Subcontinent and E to W Assam.

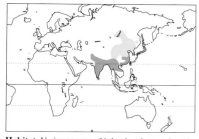

Descriptive notes. 58-63 cm; 750-1500 g. Terminal half of inner tertials white, contrasting strongly with dark plumage. Male has variable red area of bill which becomes large and bright in breeding season. Female averages slightly smaller than male. Juvenile tends to be paler, with spotted underparts. Subspecies *zonorhyncha* resembles *A. superciliosa* more than nominate, but has blue, not green, speculum. Subspecies *haringtoni* similar to nominate, but smaller, with more uniform underparts and less or no red on base of bill.

Habitat. Various types of inland and coastal wetlands, preferably in open low ground, with shallow, fresh waters and abundant emergent vegetation.
Food and Feeding. Essentially vegetarian diet; seeds and vegetative parts of grasses, sedges and aquatic vegetation; occasionally water insects and their larvae, worms and molluscs, like water snails (*Vivipara*). Feeds by dabbling, head-dipping and upending in shallow waters; also by walking about and grubbing in marshland.
Breeding. Season variable, according to locality and water levels; mainly Jul-Oct in N India, Nov-Dec in S India. In single pairs or loose groups; nest is a pad of grass and weeds, usually lined with some feathers and down, situated on ground, concealed among herbaceous vegetation, or in trees. Usually 7-9 eggs (6-12); incubation c. 24 days; chicks have blackish down on upperparts, yellowish below and on dorsal markings; fledging c. 7-8 weeks.
Movements. Partially migratory, with northernmost populations descending to winter at lower latitudes in S and E China. Birds of temperate and tropical regions mainly sedentary, but subject to some degree of dispersal, mainly related with water availability. Has occurred N and E as far as Siberia and Alaska.
Status and Conservation. Not globally threatened. In general widespread and common despite hunting pressure. Adaptable; is only duck common around rice fields during breeding season in Japan, where during 1980's more than 130,000 counted annually in winter. Appears widespread in India, Burma, South Korea and China, in latter two countries recent winter census counts of 15,360 and 23,722 birds respectively.
Bibliography. Ali (1979), Ali & Ripley (1978), Austin (1948), Brazil (1991), Dementiev & Gladkov (1952), Dickinson *et al.* (1991), Etchécopar & Hüe (1978), Frith (1967), Gooders & Boyer (1986), Inskipp & Inskipp (1985), Perennou & Mundkur (1991), Qian Guo-zhen & Xu Hong-fa (1986, 1989), Roberts (1991), de Schauensee (1984), Smythies (1986), Stokes (1988), Uthaman (1990).

88. Pacific Black Duck

Anas superciliosa

French: Canard à sourcils   **German**: Augenbrauenente   **Spanish**: Anade Cejudo
Other common names: Black Duck, Australian Grey/Black Duck

Taxonomy. *Anas superciliosa* Gmelin, 1789, New Zealand.
Often included in *A. poecilorhyncha*. Form superspecies with *A. poecilorhyncha* and *A. luzonica*. Probable unstable hybrids of present species and *A. platyrhynchos*, found on some Micronesian islands, have been considered a different species, Mariana Duck (*A. oustaleti*). Hybridization with several species of genus *Anas* recorded in captivity, and with *A. platyrhynchos*, producing fertile progeny, in the wild; in New Zealand over 25% of populations may be hybrids. Validity of poorly defined subspecies has been questioned. Three subspecies recognized.
Subspecies and Distribution.
A. s. pelewensis Hartlaub & Finsch, 1872 - SW Pacific Is, N New Guinea.
A. s. rogersi Mathews, 1912 - Indonesian region, S New Guinea, Australia.
A. s. superciliosa Gmelin, 1789 - New Zealand and larger offshore islands.
Descriptive notes. 47-61 cm; 700-1340 g; wingspan 82-93 cm. Distinctive boldly streaked face; body colour varies from brown to black; green speculum; dirty yellow legs. Male has no eclipse plumage. Female has browner crown, back and rump; pale buff edges to many feathers making it more strongly marked than male. Juvenile resembles adult but is more streaked on lower foreneck and down to belly. Subspecies based on slight differences in size and plumage coloration.
Habitat. Widespread in variety of wetlands, preferably small, shallow, well vegetated, productive and of low salinity, but can use almost any kind, including channels, sewage ponds, rivers and mountain lakes in New Guinea and New Zealand. Less common in saline habitats like estuaries,

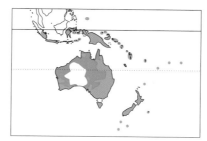

salt-pans, coastal lagoons and sheltered inshore waters. Frequents ornamental wetlands, except in New Zealand, where introduced and well established *A. platyrhynchos* is dominant.
Food and Feeding. Mostly vegetarian diet; seeds of aquatic and fringe vegetation (*Carex*); also dry plants, especially in winter. Animal matter, including bivalve molluscs, freshwater crayfish, aquatic insects and their larvae, probably underestimated in gizzard samples. Forages mostly at night, by dabbling on surface, upending and grazing; occasionally by diving in shallow waters.
Breeding. Starts Jun-Aug. In single pairs; nest is lined with down and surrounding material, if available, and situated in tree-holes, old nests, or occasionally on ground among vegetation. Usually 8-10 eggs (3-15, or more by dump-laying); incubation 26-32 days; chicks have dark brown down on underparts, pale yellowish buff below and on dorsal spots; fledging 52-66 days. Sexual maturity at 1 year. In one study, 20% of hatched young reached fledging.
Movements. Mostly sedentary, but dispersive movements, especially from Australian inland areas, frequent in dry season; many ringing recoveries, some involving distances of more than 400 km. Birds seen crossing Torres Strait; New Guinea population may be swollen seasonally with Australian immigrants.
Status and Conservation. Not globally threatened. Widespread and abundant, at least in Australia and New Zealand. Partial counts in Australia yielded 22,837-40,781 in Victoria (11-13% of total of ducks counted), and 14,245-39,129 in SW; estimated 15,000 at Bool Lagoon, S Australia. Local in New Guinea; 163 birds counted in Papua New Guinea in 1990 partial census out of total of 6596 identified Anatidae. Increase in population of *A. platyrhynchos* causes competition and hybridization, threatening present species in SW Australia, Norfolk I, and in New Zealand where decreased from 1,500,000 in 1970 to 1,200,000 in 1981, parallel to increase of *A. platyrhynchos*; in 1960 present species constituted 95% of all *Anas* in New Zealand, but less than 20% in 1985.
Bibliography. Amadon (1943), Beehler *et al.* (1986), Braithwaite & Miller (1975), Bregulla (1992), Caithness (1985a), Chambers (1989), Coates (1985), Engbring & Pratt (1985), Falla *et al.* (1981), Frith (1963), Gillespie (1985), Hadden (1981), Halse & Jaensch (1989), Marchant & Higgins (1990), van Marle & Voous (1988), Morton *et al.* (1990), Norman (1987, 1990), Norman *et al.* (1979), Roy (1988), Ripley (1964), Schodde & Tidemann (1988), Soper (1976), Watson (1975), White & Bruce (1986), Williams (1969), Williams & Roderick (1973).

89. Philippine Duck

Anas luzonica

French: Canard des Philippines   **German**: Philippinenente   **Spanish**: Anade Filipino
Other common names: Philippine Mallard

Taxonomy. *Anas luzonica* Fraser, 1839, Luzon.
Forms superspecies with *A. poecilorhyncha* and *A. superciliosa*. Monotypic.
Distribution. Luzon, Masbate, Mindoro and Mindanao Is (Philippine Is).

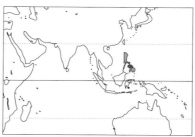

Descriptive notes. 48-58 cm; 725-977 g. Characteristic rusty cinnamon head, contrasting with dark crown and eyestripe; uniform body plumage, but blackish rump and undertail-coverts. Female somewhat smaller, but otherwise as male. Juvenile duller with paler head and throat.
Habitat. Despite restricted range, occurs on a variety of wetlands, from mountain lakes to small pools, rivers and coastal waters.
Food and Feeding. Little known but probably similar to *A. platyrhynchos*. Has been seen to dabble and upend in shallow waters.

Breeding. No nests found in wild as yet, so information available only from captive birds. Ducklings have been recorded in Mindoro in Mar, Apr, May, Sept and Dec. Nests on ground among vegetation. Usually about 10 eggs (8-14); incubation 25-26 days; fledging probably c. 8 weeks.
Movements. Mostly sedentary within restricted range, with only some small-scale movements recorded.
Status and Conservation. Not globally threatened. Adaptable, but under intense pressure from hunting and habitat transformation. Still seems to be fairly common. Was abundant in N Luzon, but no recent data available. 571 counted in 1990 census out of total of 1412 identified Anatidae; 250 roosting and feeding at the mangrove channels in Tayabas Bay, and 200 in Lalaguna Marsh, Quezon Province, Luzon. Breeds well in captivity.
Bibliography. Delacour (1954-1964), Dickinson *et al.* (1991), DuPont (1971), Gonzales (1983), Kolbe (1979), Magsalay (1988), Perennou & Mundkur (1991), Perennou *et al.* (1990), Weller (1980).

90. Spectacled Duck

Anas specularis

French: Canard à lunettes   **German**: Kupferspiegelente   **Spanish**: Anade Anteojillo
Other common names: Bronze-winged Duck

Taxonomy. *Anas specularis* King, 1828, Strait of Magellan.
Sometimes placed in monospecific genus *Speculanas*. Monotypic.
Distribution. S Chile and WC Argentina to Tierra del Fuego.
Descriptive notes. 46-54 cm; c. 960 g. Unmistakable pattern on head; iridescent bronzy pinkish speculum; yellow to yellow-orange legs. Sexes alike, but female slightly duller. Juveniles with little or no white on face; heavily streaked on breast.

Habitat. Breeds by rivers, particularly where these are fast-flowing in wooded country; also on adjacent wetlands with standing waters, e.g. lakes and marshes.

Food and Feeding. Seeds, leaves and stems of aquatic plants (*Batrachium*, *Myriophyllum*) and variable amounts of aquatic invertebrates (insects and their larvae, molluscs). Feeds, usually in pairs or small parties, by wading and probing on foot at water's edge; also grazes on land.

Breeding. Starts Sept/Oct, laying in Oct/Nov. In single pairs; nest abundantly lined with down, situated on ground among vegetation on river islets. 4-6 eggs; incubation c. 30 days (captivity); chicks have black and cinnamon down, with large black spot on cheek.

Movements. Disperses N and E after breeding season, occurring regularly in Buenos Aires Province and Mendoza (Argentina) and Santiago (Chile); some birds remain within nesting territory throughout year.

Status and Conservation. Not globally threatened. Considered widespread, but nowhere numerous. Commoner in valleys in Andean zone, up to 1500 m. Hunted in winter quarters, but does not appear seriously threatened.

Bibliography. Blake (1977), Carp (1991), Clark (1986), Fjeldså & Krabbe (1990), Hellmayr & Conover (1948), Humphrey *et al.* (1970), Johnson (1965), Narosky & Yzurieta (1987), de la Peña (1986), Scott & Carbonell (1986), Woods (1988).

91. Crested Duck
Anas specularioides

French: Canard huppé   **German**: Schopfente   **Spanish**: Anade Juarjal

Taxonomy. *Anas specularioides* King, 1828, Strait of Magellan.
A species of disputed affinities, it is often isolated in monospecific genus *Lophonetta*, and sometimes placed near *Tadorna*, though apparently its closest living relative is *A. specularis*. Two subspecies recognized.

Subspecies and Distribution.
A. s. alticola Ménégaux, 1909 - Andes from S Peru to N Argentina.
A. s. specularioides King, 1828 - C Chile and W Argentina S to Tierra del Fuego; Falkland Is.

Descriptive notes. 51-61 cm; c. 1000 g. Crest and dark mask around eye distinctive. Plumage variable; can be darker than in illustration. Sexes alike but female slightly smaller, with less defined crest. Juvenile has paler face and abdomen, and lacks crest. Subspecies *alticola* larger, with darker, purplish green speculum; browner and less spotted underparts.

Habitat. Freshwater, brackish or saline wetlands such as marshes, swamps, lakes, pools and lagoons, preferably large, from sea-level to high elevations in the Andes; also on coast, commonly in sheltered bays.

Food and Feeding. Principally aquatic invertebrates (insects and their larvae, molluscs, crustaceans) with very few aquatic plants, mainly filamentous algae. Sometimes hundreds of birds assemble on turbid, alkaline lakes with large concentrations of zooplankton. Feeds by wading, dabbling, head-dipping and upending in very shallow water or at water's edge.

Breeding. Season variable according to locality; laying dates in S, mainly Oct-Dec; in Andes, mainly Jan-Mar; double-brooded in some cases. In single pairs; nests on ground on small islets or lakeshores, concealed among vegetation, occasionally far from water. 5-8 eggs; incubation c. 30 days; chicks have blackish down on upperparts, whitish fawn below and on dorsal markings; fledging c. 10-11 weeks.

Movements. Mostly sedentary, but high-altitude or high-latitude breeders commonly disperse following coast in winter.

Status and Conservation. Not globally threatened. Rather common, locally numerous; can concentrate in hundreds on turbid, alkaline lakes with large concentrations of zooplankton. Typically more common in high zones such as *puna* region of Peru and Chile. Significant numbers in some areas of Argentina: 2000 on L Pozuelos in Feb 1982, and estimated 3350 on Meseta de Strobel.

Bibliography. Blake (1977), Buitron & Nuechterleim (1989), Carp (1991), Clark (1986), Fjeldså & Krabbe (1990), Hellmayr & Conover (1948), Humphrey *et al.* (1970), Johnson (1965), de la Peña (1986), Narosky & Yzurieta (1987), Scott & Carbonell (1986), Vides-Almonacid (1990), Weller (1975d), Woods (1975, 1988).

92. Northern Pintail
Anas acuta

French: Canard pilet   **German**: Spießente   **Spanish**: Anade Rabudo
Other common names: Pintail, Common Pintail; Kerguelen/Eaton's/Southern Pintail (*eatoni*); Crozet/Southern Pintail (*drygalskii*)

Taxonomy. *Anas acuta* Linnaeus, 1758, Europe.
Forms superspecies with *A. georgica*, with which is sometimes partitioned off in genus *Dafila*. Southern Hemisphere subspecies sometimes considered to form separate species, Southern Pintail (*A. eatoni*); some consider *drygalskii* not separable from *eatoni*. Three subspecies recognized.

Subspecies and Distribution.
A. a. acuta Linnaeus, 1758 - most of Nearctic and Palearctic.
A. a. eatoni (Sharpe, 1875) - Kerguelen I; introduced to St Paul and Amsterdam Is.
A. a. drygalskii Reichenow, 1904 - Crozet Is.

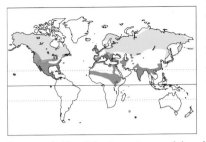

Descriptive notes. 50-65 cm; c. 850 g; wingspan 80-95 cm. Male unmistakable; has eclipse plumage. Female with very dull speculum. Juvenile with plainer, less buffy upperparts and more spotted underneath. Subspecies vary markedly in size and coloration. Subspecies *eatoni* much smaller: 35-45 cm, 400-500 g, wingspan 65-70. Much less marked dimorphism; only a few males show something of nominate race's pattern; normally very brown and like female, although separable by green, not brown, speculum. Subspecies *drygalskii* poorly differentiated from *eatoni*, although has longer tarsus and, in males, shorter wing.

Habitat. Shallow freshwater marshes, small lakes and rivers, preferably with dense vegetation cover in open country. In winter, also on coastal lagoons of brackish waters.

Food and Feeding. Seeds (grain), tubers (potatoes) and vegetative parts of aquatic plants (*Potamogeton*, *Elodea*, *Vallisneria*) and sedges (*Carex*); in spring and summer, also aquatic invertebrates (insects, molluscs, crustaceans), amphibians and some small fish. Feeds by upending, dabbling and head-dipping in shallow water; also grazes on dry land.

Breeding. Starts Apr/May; Nov-Mar in *eatoni*. In single pairs or loose groups; nest is slight hollow lined with grass, leaves and other plant matter, and down, situated on ground, normally among vegetation. Usually 7-9 eggs (6-12); incubation 22-24 days; chicks have dark brown down on upperparts, whitish face, underparts and dorsal markings; fledging 40-45 days. Sexual maturity at 1, occasionally 2, years. Hatching success variable, between 32% and 68%, in different studies.

Movements. Nominate race highly migratory, flying S to winter at lower latitudes, in: Mexico, Central America and West Indies; S Europe, N, W and E Africa; and Middle East, S Asia and Japan. Recorded regularly beyond equator, in E Africa; also small numbers on some oceanic islands (e.g. Hawaii) and frequent stragglers elsewhere outside main range. Moult migrations frequent. Southern Hemisphere subspecies mainly sedentary.

Status and Conservation. Not globally threatened. Nominate subspecies one of commonest ducks in majority of its range. Winter population in North America estimated at 12,000,000 birds in mid-1970's, with enormous concentrations in some areas; up to 131,000 in winter censuses from 1979 and 1982 in coastal lagoons between El Dorado and Dimas, WC Mexico. In W Palearctic c. 370,000 wintering in mid-1980's. Asian Waterfowl Census of mid-winter 1991 yielded 108,208 birds in Iran, 67,831 in Pakistan and 171,281 in India; also 76,000 wintering in c. 2000 ha in lagoons south of Sri Lanka in late 1980's; in Japan, 50,987 were counted in 53 representative wetlands thought to harbour 37% of the waterbirds in the country. Maximum counted in W Africa is 838,000 in winter 1987. In Crozet Is, subspecies *drygalskii* estimated at 1350 birds (800 on Est I), rare on some islands due to introduction of cats and rats last century. Race *eatoni* distributed throughout Kerguelen I and outlying islands, but only abundant in lowlands, estimated 5000-10,000 pairs, suffering annual losses of 200-300 through hunting by sealers and scientific expeditions; on Grande Terre may be seriously threatened in near future by feral cats, once petrels (currently exploited by cats) go extinct. Has not become established on Amsterdam I, where introduced, due to predation by cats and rats (*Rattus norvegicus*); at present, population appears stable. CITES III in Ghana.

Bibliography. Ali & Ripley (1978), Bellrose (1976), Bauer & Glutz von Blotzheim (1968), Blake (1977), Brazil (1991), Brickell (1988), Brown *et al.* (1982), Cooch (1964), Cramp & Simmons (1977), Dementiev & Gladkov (1952), DuBowy (1987, 1988), Etchécopar & Hüe (1978), Ferrer (1982), Fredrickson & Heitmeyer (1991), Géroudet (1972), Gómez-Dallmeier & Cringan (1989), Gooders & Boyer (1986), Goodman (1986), Grimmett & Jones (1989), Gunn & Batt (1985), Harrison (1988), Hudec & Touskova (1969), Krapu (1972, 1974), Krapu & Swanson (1975), Maclean (1985), Marchant & Higgins (1990), McClure (1974), McMahan (1989), Meadows (1984), Medway & Wells (1976), Monroe (1968), Monval & Pirot (1989), Palmer (1976), Paz (1987), Perennou (1991a, 1991b), Perennou & Mundkur (1991), Richardson (1990), Ridgill & Fox (1990), Roberts (1991), Scott & Carbonell (1986), Shevareva (1970), Slud (1964), Smith (1968), Stahl *et al.* (1984), Sugden (1973), Swanson *et al.* (1979), Tamisier (1976), Terres (1980), Thibault & Guyot (1988), Titman & Seymour (1981), Watson (1975), Weller (1980).

93. Yellow-billed Pintail
Anas georgica

French: Canard à queue pointue   **German**: Spitzschwanzente   **Spanish**: Anade Maicero
Other common names: Brown Pintail; Niceforo's Pintail (*niceforoi*); Chilean Pintail (*spinicauda*); South Georgian Teal/Pintail (*georgica*)

Taxonomy. *Anas georgica* Gmelin, 1789, "Georgia Australi America".
Forms superspecies with *A. acuta*, with which is sometimes partitioned off in genus *Dafila*. Subspecies *niceforoi*, described in 1946, considered to be extinct by 1956. Race *spinicauda* sometimes considered full species. Two living subspecies recognized.

Subspecies and Distribution.
A. g. spinicauda Vieillot, 1816 - extreme S Colombia southwards to Tierra del Fuego, and eastwards to E Argentina; Falkland Is.
A. g. georgica Gmelin, 1789 - South Georgia.

Descriptive notes. 43-55 cm, 460-660 g (*georgica*); 65 cm, 663-827 g (*spinicauda*). Both sexes reminiscent of female *A. acuta*, but yellow bill with black ridge very characteristic; female very similar to male, but has duller dark brown speculum and somewhat whiter underparts. Juvenile streaked on underparts and breast. Subspecies vary in plumage coloration and size; nominate is distinctly smaller, darker and more compact than subspecies *spinicauda*.

Habitat. Found in a variety of habitats throughout range, such as freshwater lakes with abundant fringe vegetation on high ground, lowland rivers and lagoons, flooded meadows and sea shores. From sea-level to 4600 m in *puna* zone.

Food and Feeding. Seeds, roots and vegetative parts of grasses, sedges, algae and other aquatic plants, stubble, grain, aquatic invertebrates (crustaceans, molluscs, insects). Feeds by head-dipping and upending with aid of long neck; also dabbles on surface, and often dives; on land, grazes and digs.

Breeding. Season variable with locality; laying Oct-Dec in S of range, Aug-Mar in Peru (*spinicauda*); presumably double-brooded in places. In single pairs or loose groups; nest is shallow platform of stems lined with grass and down, situated on ground, in thick or sparse vegetation, near water. 4-10 eggs; incubation c. 26 days; chicks have dark brown down above, yellowish below and on dorsal markings.

Movements. Partially migratory; southernmost breeders of continental race move N to winter as far as southern Brazil; those of more temperate regions chiefly remain within vicinity of nesting area. Nominate subspecies mostly sedentary, but has occurred in South Shetland Is.

Status and Conservation. Not globally threatened. Widely distributed and locally abundant. Race *spinicauda* is one of most abundant ducks in South America, and also in Falkland Is; recorded frequently but less common N of Junín, C Peru. Forms large concentrations in some parts of Argentina: up to 250,000-300,000 in Cañada de Los Tres Arboles y Los Morteros and 11,600 estimated on Meseta de Strobel in Feb 1984. Nominate subspecies has a minimum population of 2000; was common during 19th century, subsequently scarcer than at present after intense hunting by sealers and whalers; appears to tolerate predation by rats (*Rattus norvegicus*) fairly well.

Bibliography. Antas & Nascimento (1991), Belton (1984), Blake (1977), Carp (1991), Fjeldså & Krabbe (1990), Hilty & Brown (1986), Humphrey *et al.* (1970), Johnson (1965), Klimaitis & Moschione (1987), Marchant & Higgins (1990), McKinney & Brewer (1989), Murphy (1916b, 1936), Nores & Yzurieta (1980), de la Peña (1986), Ruschi (1979), Scott & Carbonell (1986), Sick (1984), Watson (1975), Weller (1975c, 1975d, 1980), Woods (1988).

♀ ♂
94

95

ssp *versicolor*
96

ssp *puna*

97

♂
99

♀

♂
98

♀

ssp *septentrionalium*

♀
100

101

♂

♂
102

ssp *borreroi*

♂

♀

♀
103

♂

104

♀

♂
105

106

94. White-cheeked Pintail

Anas bahamensis

French: Canard des Bahamas **German**: Bahamaente **Spanish**: Anade Gargantillo
Other common names: Bahama Pintail/Duck; Galapagos Pintail (*galapagensis*)

Taxonomy. *Anas bahamensis* Linnaeus, 1758, Bahama Islands.
Considered by some to form superspecies with *A. erythrorhyncha*, with which sometimes partitioned off in genus *Poecilonetta*. Three subspecies recognized.
Subspecies and Distribution.
A. b. bahamensis Linnaeus, 1758 - West Indies, N South America to N Brazil.
A. b. rubrirostris Vieillot, 1816 - E Bolivia and S Brazil to N Argentina and Uruguay.
A. b. galapagensis (Ridgway, 1889) - Galapagos Is.

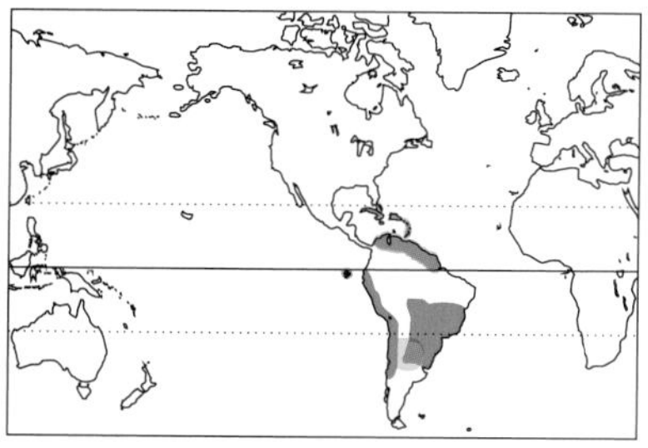

Descriptive notes. 38-51 cm; 474-533 g. Unmistakable. Female slightly duller, with shorter tail. Juvenile resembles female but with less iridescent speculum. Subspecies *galapagensis* duller, with less well-defined patterning, especially on face. Subspecies *rubrirostris* is larger and slightly darker.
Habitat. Mangrove swamps, small pools and lagoons of saline or brackish waters; relatively uncommon on fresh water. May occur on high ground in Andes; regular up to 2500 m and occasionally higher.
Food and Feeding. Presumably essentially vegetarian; seeds, buds, leaves and stems of aquatic plants and grasses. Feeds by diving, head-dipping and upending in shallow waters.
Breeding. Season variable, mainly according to water levels; Jul-Aug in Colombia. In single pairs or loose groups; nests in thick vegetation near water. 5-12 eggs; incubation c. 25 days (captivity).
Movements. Galapagos and West Indian populations mostly sedentary, but race *rubrirostris* somewhat more dispersive, occurring in the lowlands to the N of its range outside breeding season.
Status and Conservation. Not globally threatened. Spottily distributed but fairly common and widespread. Counts of up to 400-500 in some areas of Venezuela, Puerto Rico and Argentina. Common on coast of Peru: c. 1000 at end of 1984 in Playa Chica and El Paraíso Lagoons, several thousand in Mejía Lagoons. In Surinam, more than 1000 pairs nesting in marshes of Bigi Pan and Wageningen and in area between mouth of R Surinam and coast 50 km eastwards. Race *galapagensis* has population of few thousand pairs; widespread but not common on at least the nine major islands, where exposed to predation of introduced mammals.
Bibliography. Allen (1962), Arballo (1990b), Biaggi (1983), Blake (1977), Carp (1991), Evans, P.G.H. (1990), Fjeldså & Krabbe (1990), Gómez-Dallmeier & Cringan (1989), Hellmayr & Conover (1948), Hilty & Brown (1986), Johnson (1965), Lorenz (1951-53), McKinney & Bruggers (1983), Meier *et al.* (1989), Nores & Yzurieta (1980), de la Peña (1986), Ruschi (1979), de Schauensee & Phelps (1978), Scott & Carbonell (1986), Sick (1984), Sorenson (1990), Stockton (1978), Terres (1980), Voous (1983), Weller (1980).

95. Red-billed Duck

Anas erythrorhyncha

French: Canard à bec rouge **German**: Rotschnabelente **Spanish**: Anade Piquirrojo
Other common names: Red-billed Pintail/Teal, African Red-billed Teal

Taxonomy. *Anas erythrorhyncha* Gmelin, 1789, Cape of Good Hope.
Considered by some to form superspecies with *A. bahamensis*, with which sometimes partitioned off in genus *Poecilonetta*. Monotypic.
Distribution. S Sudan and Ethiopia S to Cape Province and W to Angola; Madagascar.

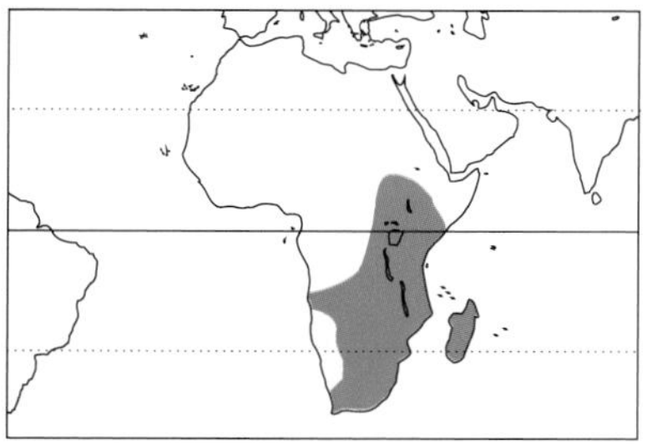

Descriptive notes. 43-48 cm; 345-954 g. Cinnamon-buff speculum; neck variable, can be lighter or darker than in illustration. Female slightly smaller with somewhat duller bill. Juvenile more greyish and more streaked on underparts.
Habitat. Various types of wetland, preferably with shallow, still, fresh water and abundant floating and emergent vegetation.
Food and Feeding. Seeds, fruits, grain, roots and vegetative parts of aquatic plants, grasses and sedges; also aquatic invertebrates, chiefly molluscs, but also insects and crustaceans. Feeds by dabbling, head-dipping and upending in shallow waters; grazes on land and visits fields of stubble.
Breeding. Season variable, generally during rains. In single pairs; nest is mound of grass lined with down, on ground among dense vegetation, near water. 5-12 eggs; incubation 25-28 days; chicks have dark brown down above, yellowish below; fledging c. 8 weeks.
Movements. Mostly sedentary, but somewhat dispersive outside breeding season; movements often linked to extent of flooding. Once recorded on Mediterranean coast of Israel.
Status and Conservation. Not globally threatened. Common to abundant; population appears stable. In S of continent, considered most abundant duck; up to 500,000 estimated on Ngami L, Botswana; 29,000 in 1971 in Kafue Flats, Zambia. In Madagascar, uncommon in E, but one of most common ducks in rest of island. Is a favourite quarry species, and is hunted abundantly.
Bibliography. Brickell (1988), Britton (1980), Brown & Britton (1980), Brown *et al.* (1982), Clancey (1967), Day (1977), Dean & Skead (1977, 1979), Langrand (1990), Mackworth-Praed & Grant (1957-1973), Maclean (1985), Meadows (1984), Milon *et al.* (1973), Perennou (1991b), Pinto (1983), Siegfried (1962a, 1962b, 1974), Skead (1976), Young & Smith (1989).

96. Silver Teal

Anas versicolor

French: Sarcelle bariolée **German**: Silberente **Spanish**: Cerceta Capuchina
Other common names: Puna Teal (*puna*)

Taxonomy. *Anas versicolor* Vieillot, 1816, Paraguay.
Sometimes placed, together with *A. hottentota*, in genus *Punanetta*. Race *puna* often considered a full species. Three subspecies recognized.
Subspecies and Distribution.
A. v. puna Tschudi, 1844 - Andean C Peru to extreme NW Argentina.
A. v. versicolor Vieillot, 1816 - S Bolivia to S Brazil, and S to C Argentina.
A. v. fretensis King, 1831 - C Chile and C Argentina S to Tierra del Fuego; Falkland Is.

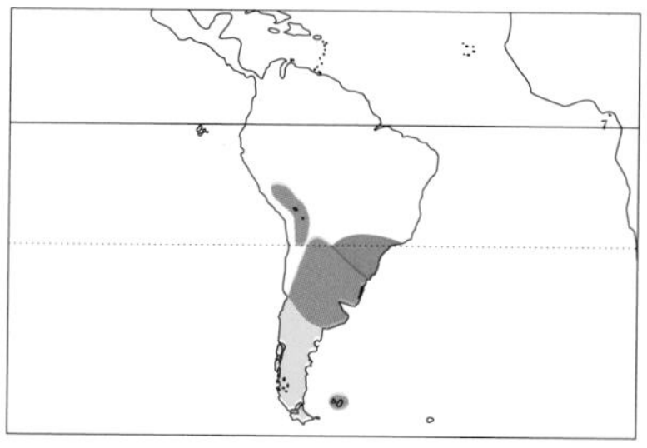

Descriptive notes. 38-43 cm; 442-373 g. Female duller, sometimes lacking yellow on base of bill. Juvenile duller with less iridescent speculum; head less contrastingly patterned. Subspecies vary in colour and size; *puna* much larger, 48-51 cm, c. 550 g; lacks yellow on bill.
Habitat. Shallow freshwater lakes, swamps and pools bordered with abundant vegetation in open country, from *puna* zone of high Andes (up to 4600 m) to *pampas* marshes.
Food and Feeding. Seeds and vegetative parts of aquatic plants, grasses and sedges; also aquatic invertebrates (insects and larvae, molluscs, crustaceans). Feeds by dabbling on surface, head-dipping and upending in shallow waters; occasionally dives.
Breeding. Season variable: starts mainly Oct/Nov in S; Sept-Mar in Peru. In single pairs or loose groups; nests on ground in rough vegetation. 6-10 eggs; incubation 25-26 days; chicks have blackish brown down above, greyish white below.
Movements. Partially migratory; southernmost breeding birds move northwards to winter as far N as S Brazil. Other populations mainly sedentary, but some altitudinal shifts of high Andes birds, appearing in lowlands outside breeding season.
Status and Conservation. Not globally threatened. Fairly widespread and locally abundant. Populations of south cone especially numerous in *pampas* marshes, often in large flocks. Represents 5% of total identified ducks in partial census in Jul 1990 in Uruguay, and approximately 2% in Argentina. On Falkland Is, resident in small numbers. Subspecies *puna* somewhat local, but generally common; notable count of 50,000 in L Junín, Peru, in late 1970's. Under certain amount of pressure from hunting.
Bibliography. Belton (1984), Blake (1977), Carey *et al.* (1989), Carp (1991), Fjeldså & Krabbe (1990), Hellmayr & Conover (1948), Humphrey *et al.* (1970), Johnson (1965), Klimaitis & Moschione (1987), McKinney & Brewer (1989), Nores & Yzurieta (1980), de la Peña (1986), Ruschi (1979), Scott & Carbonell (1986), Sick (1984), Woods (1988).

97. Hottentot Teal

Anas hottentota

French: Sarcelle hottentote **German**: Hottentottenente **Spanish**: Cerceta Hotentote

Taxonomy. *Querquedula hottentota* Eyton, 1838, western coast of South Africa, near Orange River, Cape Province. Sometimes placed, together with *A. versicolor*, in genus *Punanetta*. Synonym *A. punctata* rejected. Monotypic.
Distribution. L Chad; Ethiopia to Cape Province; Madagascar.

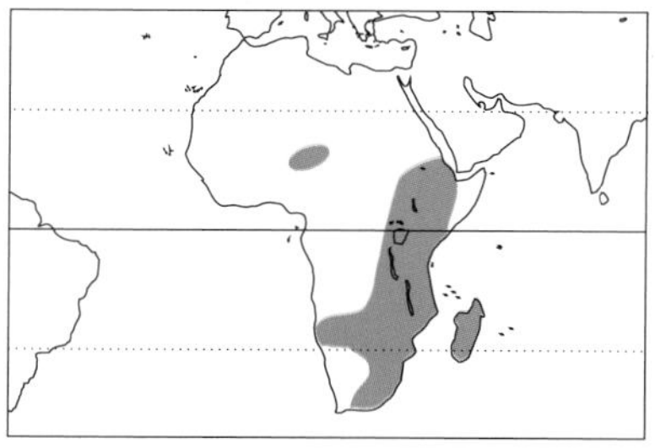

Descriptive notes. 30-36 cm; 216-282 g; wingspan 58-69 cm. Green speculum with black and white terminal lines. Female duller. Juvenile resembles female but duller.
Habitat. Swamps, marshes, small lakes and pools of shallow fresh waters with abundant floating and emergent vegetation.
Food and Feeding. Aquatic invertebrates (crustaceans, molluscs, insects and larvae), seeds, fruits, roots and vegetative parts of aquatic plants; also plant debris. Feeds by dabbling on surface or from shore and by head-dipping and upending in shallow waters.
Breeding. Season variable, mainly according to water levels. In single pairs or loose groups; nest made of grass and reed stems, lined with down, in dense reedbeds. 6-9 eggs; incubation 25-27 days; chicks have sepia brown upperparts, light buff below.
Movements. Mostly sedentary, but subject to seasonal movements of dispersal related with availability of suitable habitat.
Status and Conservation. Not globally threatened. Fairly widespread, though rather inconspicuous. Very abundant in Kenya during northern winter, especially during dry years; thousands in Tanzania; in Kafue Flats, Zambia, small numbers all year, increasing slightly between Oct and May, with maximum of 500 birds. Isolated population in N Nigeria and Chad, more than 1000 km from remaining continental population, may be in decline; maximum of 300 counted in 1972. In South Africa, uncommon to locally common. In Madagascar, common only in W, uncommon to rather rare on rest of island. Does not appear under serious hunting pressure.
Bibliography. Benson & Benson (1975), Brickell (1988), Britton (1980), Brown *et al.* (1982), Clancey (1967), Clark (1969a, 1971, 1974c), Douthwaite (1977), Dowsett (1966b), Elgood (1982), Langrand (1990), Mackworth-Praed & Grant (1957-1973), Maclean (1985), Meadows (1984), Milon *et al.* (1973), Perennou (1991a, 1991b), Pinto (1983), Thomas & Condy (1965), Young & Smith (1989).

98. Garganey

Anas querquedula

French: Sarcelle d'été **German**: Knäkente **Spanish**: Cerceta Carretona

Taxonomy. *Anas Querquedula* Linnaeus, 1758, Europe.
Sometimes placed in monospecific genus *Querquedula*. Monotypic.
Distribution. Palearctic, mostly between 42° N and 65° N.
Descriptive notes. 37-41 cm; 290-480 g; wingspan 58-69 cm. Green speculum with white line along front and rear edges; light grey-blue upperwing-coverts. Male has eclipse plumage. Female has duller upperwing, whitish belly and distinctive striped facial pattern. Juvenile resembles female but has finely streaked and spotted ventral parts.
Habitat. Breeds mostly inland, on swampy meadows, flooded fields and shallow freshwater marshes, pools and small lakes with abundant emergent vegetation. Winters in coastal marshes or lagoons; also at sea.
Food and Feeding. Aquatic invertebrates (worms, insects and their larvae, crustaceans, molluscs), amphibians, small fish, seeds, roots, tubers and green parts of sedges, grasses and aquatic plants. Feeds by dabbling, head-dipping and picking from surface; also upends in shallow waters.
Breeding. Starts Apr/May. In single pairs or loose groups; nest is a depression lined with down and feathers, on ground among grass or reeds, near water. Usually 8-9 eggs (6-14); incubation 21-23 days;

On following pages: 99. Blue-winged Teal (*Anas discors*); 100. Cinnamon Teal (*Anas cyanoptera*); 101. Red Shoveler (*Anas platalea*); 102. Cape Shoveler (*Anas smithii*); 103. Australian Shoveler (*Anas rhynchotis*); 104. Northern Shoveler (*Anas clypeata*); 105. Pink-eared Duck (*Malacorhynchus membranaceus*); 106. Marbled Teal (*Marmaronetta angustirostris*).

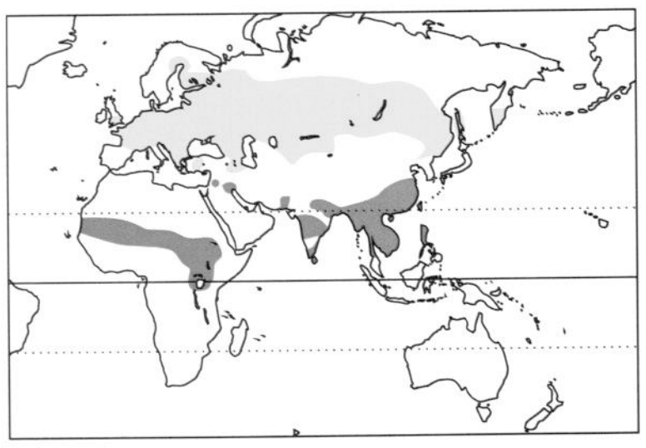

chicks have dark brown down above, pale yellow below; fledging c. 35-40 days. Sexual maturity at c. 1 year.
Movements. Highly migratory, wintering chiefly in sub-Saharan Africa, Indian Subcontinent and SE Asia. Has occurred in Azores, Iceland, Hawaii and Aleutian Is; also a few records from North America, particularly on W coast.
Status and Conservation. Not globally threatened. Common to abundant throughout range. Breeding population in W Europe has not varied significantly despite hunting and habitat destruction in its wintering grounds. In Africa, winter population concentrates especially in Niger Basin; 2,000,000 throughout sub-Saharan W Africa in mid-1980's; 77,310 in Senegal in partial census in winter 1991. In Israel, 100,000-200,000 in autumn. Tens of thousands in partial censuses in India and Thailand; also in Sri Lanka, where notable count of 129,000 in c. 2000 ha of lagoons in S of island, in late 1980's. Possibly regular winter visitor in N Australia but in very small numbers. CITES III in Ghana.
Bibliography. Ali & Ripley (1978), Bauer & Glutz von Blotzheim (1968), Beehler *et al.* (1986), Brazil (1991), Brickell (1988), Brown *et al.* (1982), Cramp & Simmons (1977), Dementiev & Gladkov (1952), Etchécopar & Hüe (1978), Géroudet (1972), Gooders & Boyer (1986), Goodman (1989), Grimmett & Jones (1989), Harrison (1988), Maclean (1985), Marchant & Higgins (1990), Meadows (1984), Monval & Pirot (1989), Nankinov (1981), Owen (1977), Paz (1987), Perennou (1991a, 1991b), Perennou & Mundkur (1991), Pirot (1980), Richardson (1990), Roberts (1991), Shevareva (1970), Smythies (1986), Treca (1981a), White & Bruce (1986).

99. Blue-winged Teal
Anas discors

French: Sarcelle soucrourou **German**: Blauflügelente **Spanish**: Cerceta Aliazul
Other common names: Bluewing

Taxonomy. *Anas discors* Linnaeus, 1766, North America = Carolina *ex* Catesby.
Sometimes placed in genus *Spatula*. E population has been assigned separate subspecies, *orphna*, but doubtfully valid. Monotypic.
Distribution. North America, from S Alaska to Newfoundland, and S to C USA.

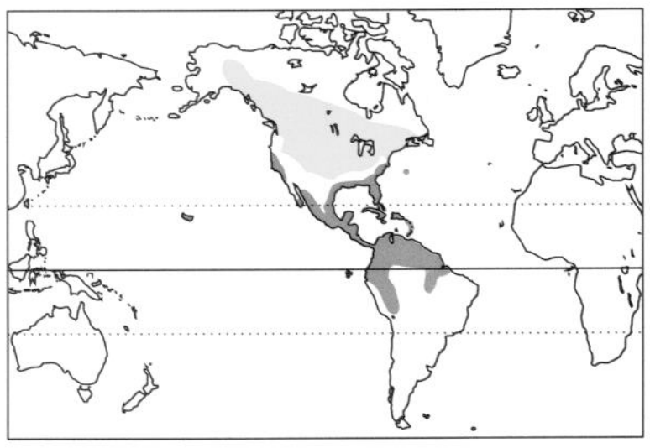

Descriptive notes. 35-41 cm; 266-410 g. Green speculum; light blue upperwing-coverts. Legs vary from yellow to orange. Male has eclipse plumage. Female's speculum more blackish than green. Juvenile resembles female; but has plainer upperparts and more heavily spotted underparts.
Habitat. Marshes, pools and small lakes of shallow fresh waters, swampy grasslands and flooded meadows. Winters on brackish or saline water bodies and on coast, in mangroves.
Food and Feeding. Seeds, roots and vegetative parts of grasses, sedges, algae and other aquatic plants; rice and grain; also aquatic invertebrates, chiefly molluscs but also insects and crustaceans. Feeds mostly by dabbling on surface and head-dipping in shallow water; rarely upends.
Breeding. Starts mainly May. In single pairs or loose groups; nest is scrape lined with adjacent vegetation and down, on ground, among thick vegetation. Usually 8-11 eggs (6-15); incubation 21-27 days; chicks have brown down above, buffish below; fledging 35-44 days. Sexual maturity at 1 year. Nest success from 13 to 72% in several studies.
Movements. Migratory, wintering in N America S of line from California to North Carolina, and through Central to S America, sometimes as far S as northern Chile and Argentina. Vagrant to Europe (regular in Britain), NW Africa, Hawaii, Aleutian and Galapagos Is.
Status and Conservation. Not globally threatened. Abundant in North America, with c. 5,000,000 birds at outset of breeding season and c. 9,000,000 in autumn. Common winter visitor in Central America and in N and NW South America; up to 20,000 in Palo Verde and also 20,000 in Mata Redonda Lagoon, Costa Rica; 3000 in Morrocoy and 60,000 in Cuare Refuge, Venezuela; 20,000 in Ciénaga Grande de Santa Marta, Colombia. Population fluctuates, but does not seem to be in decline despite hunting and transformation of winter habitat.
Bibliography. Bauer & Glutz von Blotzheim (1968), Bellrose (1976), Bennett (1938), Blake (1977), Biaggi (1983), Cooch (1964), Cramp & Simmons (1977), Dane (1965, 1966), DuBowy (1987, 1988), Evans, P.G.H. (1990), Fjeldså & Krabbe (1990), Glover (1956), Gómez-Dallmeier & Cringan (1989), Gooders & Boyer (1986), Hellmayr & Conover (1948), Hilty & Brown (1986), McHenry (1971), Monroe (1968), Mulhern *et al.* (1985), Parnell & Quay (1962), de la Peña (1986), Ridgely & Gwynne (1989), Ruschi (1979), Salvador & Salvador (1990), Sargeant *et al.* (1984), Scott & Carbonell (1986), Sick (1984), Slud (1964), Stewart & Titman (1980), Strohmeyer (1967), Swanson & Meyer (1977), Swanson, Krapu & Serie (1979), Swanson, Meyer & Serie (1974), Titman & Seymour (1981), Urban (1959), Voous (1983), Wetmore (1965).

100. Cinnamon Teal
Anas cyanoptera

French: Sarcelle cannelle **German**: Zimtente **Spanish**: Cerceta Colorada

Taxonomy. *Anas cyanoptera* Vieillot, 1816, Río de la Plata and Buenos Aires.
Sometimes placed in genus *Spatula*. Five subspecies recognized.
Subspecies and Distribution.
A. c. septentrionalium Snyder & Lumsden, 1951 - WC North America, from British Columbia S to NW Mexico.
A. c. tropica Snyder & Lumsden, 1951 - NW Colombia.
A. c. borreroi Snyder & Lumsden, 1951 - E Andes of Colombia.
A. c. orinomus (Oberholser, 1906) - Andes of Peru to N Chile.
A. c. cyanoptera Vieillot, 1816 - S Peru and S Brazil to Tierra del Fuego; Falkland Is.
Descriptive notes. 35-48 cm; c. 400 g. Green speculum; light blue upperwing-coverts. General colour of male varies from rufous-cinnamon to deep chestnut-red; has eclipse plumage; iris yellow-orange tending towards red. Female variable; may resemble that of *A. discors*, but has less contrasted pattern on face, generally warmer buff tones and longer bill. Juvenile as female, but more heavily streaked on underparts. Subspecies vary in size and colour; generally, South American races tend to have more black spots on breast and flanks and a dark belly, as in *borreroi*.
Habitat. Diversity of shallow freshwater or brackish wetlands, with abundant emergent and fringe vegetation in open country; from sea-level up to 5000 m in high Andes (*puna* zone).
Food and Feeding. Seeds, roots and vegetative parts of aquatic plants, complemented with aquatic invertebrates (insects, molluscs, crustaceans). Feeds mostly by dabbling on surface; also head-dips and upends in shallow waters.

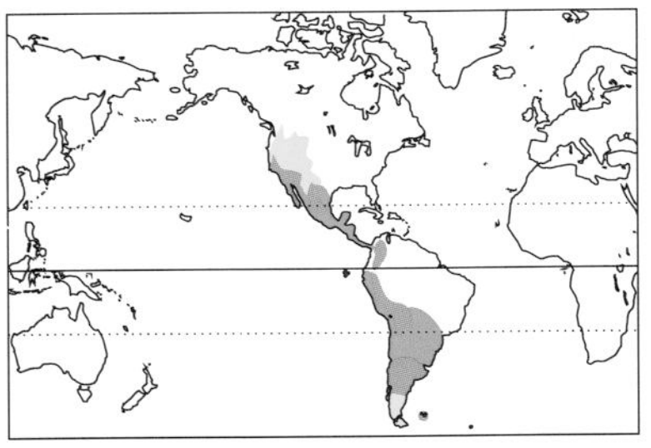

Breeding. Variable depending on locality; starts Apr in N. In single pairs or loose groups; nest is a depression, usually lined with surrounding dead vegetation and down, on ground or water, well-hidden in thick vegetation. Usually 9-12 eggs; incubation 21-25 days; chicks have brown down above, yellowish below; fledging c. 7 weeks. Hatching success of 51% in one study.
Movements. Partially migratory; northernmost and southernmost breeders descend to lower latitudes, to winter generally within subtropical zone; populations of more temperate regions mainly sedentary or with only small-scale dispersive movements. Vagrant to Alaska; records well outside range (e.g. Europe) presumably refer to escapes.
Status and Conservation. Not globally threatened. Fairly common and locally abundant. Subspecies *borreroi* was common in 1950's, now vanishing; no records in recent years. Race *tropica* scarce, possibly at risk. North American population estimated at c. 600,000 birds after breeding. Common on coast of Peru, with thousands of birds recorded in Mejía Lagoons and 1000 in Tilimaco and Pucchun Lagoons, Arequipa Department, and 1000 in Ite Lagoons, Tacna Department. Widespread in Argentina and Chile, where represents respectively 1% and 1·78% of total ducks identified in Jul 1990 partial census; 700-1000 reported in Mar Chiquitita Lagoon, Córdoba Province, Argentina. Considered a rare resident in Falkland Is.
Bibliography. Bellrose (1976), Belton (1984), Blake (1977), Carp (1991), DuBowy (1987, 1988), Fjeldså & Krabbe (1990), Gómez-Dallmeier & Cringan (1989), Gooders & Boyer (1986), Hellmayr & Conover (1948), Hilty & Brown (1986), Humphrey *et al.* (1970), Johnson (1965), McKinney (1970), Nores & Yzurieta (1980), de la Peña (1986), Ridgely & Gwynne (1989), Ruschi (1979), Scott & Carbonell (1986), Sick (1984), Spencer (1953), Wetmore (1965), Woods (1988).

101. Red Shoveler
Anas platalea

French: Canard spatule **German**: Fuchslöffelente **Spanish**: Cuchara Argentino
Other common names: South American/Argentine Shoveler

Taxonomy. *Anas platalea* Vieillot, 1816, Paraguay.
Often placed in genus *Spatula*. Monotypic.
Distribution. S South America, from Tierra del Fuego northwards to C Chile and most of Argentina; small breeding populations may occur isolated in S Peru.

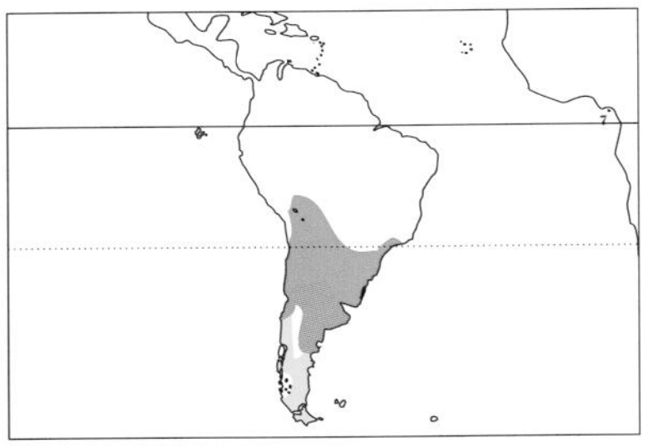

Descriptive notes. 45-56 cm; 523-608 g. Green speculum; light blue upperwing-coverts. Overall tone of male's plumage can be redder or paler; has no eclipse plumage. Female has very large, dark bill. Juveniles resemble female, but with brighter speculum in males.
Habitat. Large coastal lagoons, lakes and estuaries of fresh or, preferably, brackish waters; mostly on low ground but up to 3400 m in Andes.
Food and Feeding. Seeds and other parts of aquatic plants and aquatic invertebrates of planktonic size. Feeds by filtering water or mud by dabbling, head-dipping and upending, presumably also on foot at water's edge; seldom dives.
Breeding. Starts Sept/Oct. In single pairs or loose groups. 5-8 eggs; incubation c. 25 days (captivity); chicks have brown down above, yellowish cinnamon below.
Movements. Partially migratory; southernmost breeding birds disperse northwards to winter as far N as S Peru and Brazil but other populations mainly sedentary. Has occurred in Falkland Is.
Status and Conservation. Not globally threatened. Fairly common and widespread. Large numbers stage and moult around 1000 m on upland plateaux of inland Santa Cruz, Argentina; concentrations of 1000-1500 not rare; up to 4000-5000 on Mar Chiquitita Lagoon, Córdoba Province, and estimated 17,700 on Meseta de Strobel, Santa Cruz Province. Small resident population in highlands of Puno and Cuzco, Peru. Frequent quarry species.
Bibliography. Blake (1977), Carp (1991), Fjeldså & Krabbe (1990), Hellmayr & Conover (1948), Humphrey *et al.* (1970), Johnson (1965), McKinney & Brewer (1989), Narosky & Yzurieta (1987), Nores & Yzurieta (1980), de la Peña (1986), Ruschi (1979), Scott & Carbonell (1986), Sick (1984), Woods (1988).

102. Cape Shoveler
Anas smithii

French: Canard de Smith **German**: Kaplöffelente **Spanish**: Cuchara del Cabo
Other common names: African/South African/Smith's Shoveler

Taxonomy. *Spatula smithii* (nec *capensis* Eyton, 1838) Hartert, 1891, Cape Province.
Often placed in genus *Spatula*, sometimes as *S. capensis*. Monotypic.
Distribution. South Africa N to Namibia and Botswana.

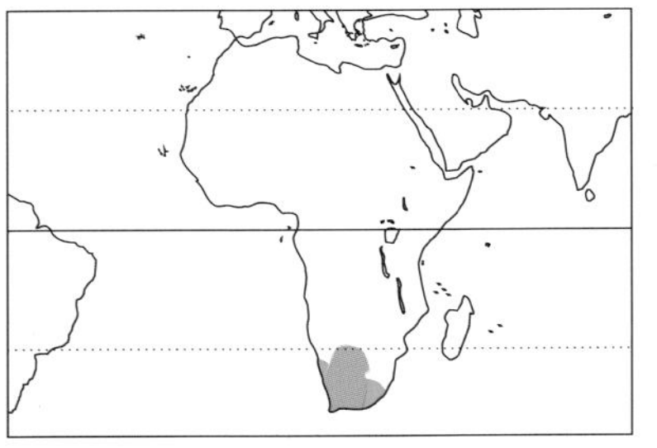

Descriptive notes. 51-53 cm; 584-830 g. Green speculum; light blue upperwing-coverts. Female hard to separate from male at distance, but has duller upperwing and legs, and dark iris. Juvenile resembles female but paler and duller.
Habitat. Favours relatively large, open bodies of fresh or brackish (occasionally saline) waters, provided they are shallow and rich in plankton. Often on temporary ponds or flooded areas.
Food and Feeding. Small aquatic invertebrates (insects, molluscs, crustaceans), and some amphibians (mainly *Xenopus* tadpoles); also seeds and vegetative parts of aquatic plants. Feeds mostly by dabbling, often co-operatively, on surface or from shore, by head-dipping and upending; occasionally dives.
Breeding. Season variable, according to locality and water levels. In single pairs or loose groups; nest is made of reed stems, leaves and grass, lined with down, on ground, in thick or sparse vegetation. 5-12 eggs; incubation 27-28 days; chicks have brown down above, pale yellowish below; fledging c. 8 weeks.
Movements. Mostly sedentary, but somewhat dispersive within its range as availability of suitable habitat varies throughout year. A few records N of Sahara probably attributable to escapes.
Status and Conservation. Not globally threatened. Fairly widespread and locally abundant; probably maintains quite stable numbers. Uncommon in N of range. In Botswana, only common in NW.

Uncommon in Natal and in E Cape, but widespread and common to abundant in SW Cape Province (where has increased greatly in recent years), Orange Free State and Transvaal, South Africa. Only serious threat seems to be reduction of suitable habitat.

Bibliography. Brand (1961, 1964), Brickell (1988), Brown *et al.* (1982), Clancey (1967), Duff (1979), Maclean (1985), McKinney (1970), Perennou (1991b), Pinto (1983), Siegfried (1965, 1971a, 1974), Skead (1977a, 1977c), Skead & Dean (1977a, 1977b).

103. **Australian Shoveler**
Anas rhynchotis

French: Canard bridé **German**: Halbmond-Löffelente **Spanish**: Cuchara Australiano
Other common names: Australasian/Blue-winged/Southern Shoveler

Taxonomy. *Anas Rhynchotis* Latham, 1801, New South Wales.
Often placed in genus *Spatula*. Considered by some to form superspecies with *A. clypeata*. Two subspecies recognized.
Subspecies and Distribution.
A. r. rhynchotis Latham, 1801 - SW and SE Australia, Tasmania.
A. r. variegata (Gould, 1856) - New Zealand.

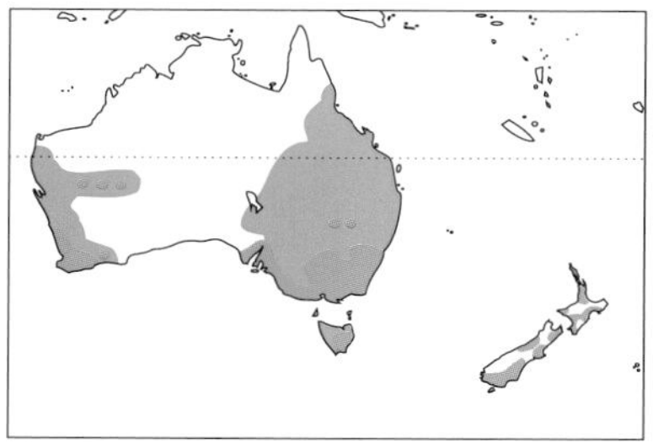

Descriptive notes. 46-56 cm; 545-852 g; wingspan 70-80 cm. Green speculum; light blue upperwing-coverts. Male variable; may have flanks more spotted or more barred, more white on breast and often less distinct white facial crescent; male has eclipse plumage. Female similar to that of *A. clypeata*, but darker, with duller, yellowish legs and lacking clean, fleshy orange bill margins. Juvenile resembles female but paler and less distinctly marked. Subspecies *variegata* somewhat brighter, but difficult to separate given individual variation in both populations.
Habitat. Lakes, marshes, swamps and lagoons of shallow, fresh, permanent waters with abundant emergent vegetation. Outside breeding season, also on temporarily flooded areas and on coast.
Food and Feeding. Small aquatic invertebrates, chiefly insects, but also molluscs and crustaceans; seeds and vegetative parts of aquatic plants. Feeds, often communally, by filtering water or mud by dabbling on surface or at water's edge, head-dipping and upending; also snaps up insects directly.
Breeding. Starts Aug on Australian coast, more variable inland; starts Oct in New Zealand. In single pairs or loose groups; nest is a depression lined with grass and down, on ground, in thick or sparse vegetation, often near water. Usually 9-11 eggs (up to 13); incubation 24-26 days; chicks have dark brown down above, yellow below; fledging probably 8-10 weeks. Sexual maturity at 1 year.
Movements. Mainly sedentary within range, but also somewhat dispersive and nomadic, as some favoured areas may become unsuitable in drought conditions. New Zealand race has occurred in Auckland Is.
Status and Conservation. Not globally threatened. Uncommon to locally abundant. Has decreased in part of its range in relation to population prior to European settlement, but construction of reservoirs and sewage ponds has allowed expansion in other areas. Partial counts in Australia yielded 7618-19,075 in Victoria (representing 4-6% of total ducks counted), and 2365-4554 in SW Australia. 61-68% of population lives in areas open to hunting; bag-limit reduced to two in Victoria in 1987. In New Zealand appears stable, with 100,000-150,000 birds; 30,000 are killed by hunters annually.

Bibliography. Bull *et al.* (1985), Caithness (1985b), Chambers (1989), Falla *et al.* (1981), Frith (1967), Halse & Jaensch (1989), Kingsford *et al.* (1989), Macdonald (1988), Marchant & Higgins (1990), Schodde & Tidemann (1988), Soper (1976).

104. **Northern Shoveler**
Anas clypeata

French: Canard souchet **German**: Löffelente **Spanish**: Cuchara Común
Other common names: Shoveler, European/Common Shoveler

Taxonomy. *Anas clypeata* Linnaeus, 1758, coasts of Europe.
Often placed in genus *Spatula*. Considered by some to form superspecies with *A. rhynchotis*. Monotypic.
Distribution. Most of Nearctic and Palearctic, except high Arctic.

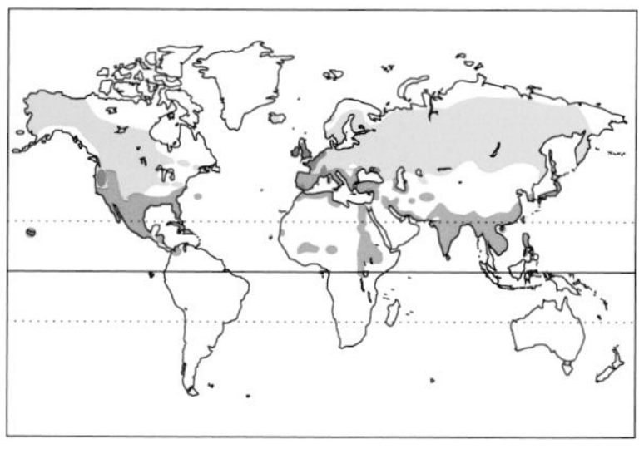

Descriptive notes. 43-56 cm; 410-1100 g; wingspan 70-85 cm. Green speculum; light blue upperwing-coverts. Female similar to that of *A. platyrhynchos*, except in bill and upperwing; orange legs. Juvenile resembles female, though darker above and with a duller upperwing.
Habitat. Wide variety of shallow, freshwater wetlands, preferably well vegetated lakes and marshes with muddy shores in open country. In winter, also on brackish lagoons and tidal mudflats.
Food and Feeding. Varied diet, mostly small-sized aquatic invertebrates (insects and their larvae, molluscs, crustaceans); also seeds and plant remains. Feeds by dabbling and water-filtering from surface, head-dipping and upending; also dives in shallow waters.
Breeding. Starts Apr/May. In single pairs or loose groups; nest is depression in grass lined with down and some feathers. Usually 9-11 eggs (6-14); incubation c. 22-23 days; chicks have dark olivaceous brown down above, buffish below; fledging 40-45 days. Sexual maturity mostly at 1 year. Success of 74% at hatching, but only 17·5% at fledging in one study in Finland.
Movements. Highly migratory, flying S to winter at lower latitudes in southern USA and Central America, Mediterranean basin, tropical Africa, Middle East, Indian Subcontinent and SE Asia; regularly crosses equator in E Africa. Present throughout year in parts of Europe. Vagrant to Australia.
Status and Conservation. Not globally threatened. Fairly widespread and locally abundant. North American population estimated at 3,300,000 birds after breeding, in the mid 1970's. Concentrations of up to 2000 birds in winter in some areas of Colombia, and 110,000 in Marismas Nacionales, WC Mexico. W Palearctic population c. 415,000 in mid 1980's. Partial censuses in winter 1990 yielded 142,407 in India, 76,820 in Pakistan and 18,641 in China. Approximately 10,000-30,000 in Japan. 36,832 in Iran in the winter 1991 census. In Israel wintering population has risen from 1000 in 1966 to 19,500 in 1982, and is now commonest duck in winter in this country. 19,170 wintering in Senegal in 1991. CITES III in Ghana.

Bibliography. Ali & Ripley (1978), Bauer & Glutz von Blotzheim (1968), Bellrose (1976), Blake (1977), Brazil (1991), Brickell (1988), Brown *et al.* (1982), Clark (1977), Cooch (1964), Cramp & Simmons (1977), Dementiev & Gladkov (1952), DuBowy (1987, 1988), Etchécopar & Hüe (1978), Ferrer (1982), Géroudet (1972), Girard (1939), Gómez-Dallmeier & Cringan (1989), Gooders & Boyer (1986), Goodman (1989), Grimmett & Jones (1989), Harrison (1988), Hilty & Brown (1986), Kooloos *et al.* (1989), Maclean (1985), Marchant & Higgins (1990), McClure (1974), McKinney (1967, 1970), Meadows (1984), Monval & Pirot (1989), Monroe (1968), Moreau (1972), Morel (1972), Paz (1987), Perennou (1991a, 1991b), Perennou & Mundkur (1991), Poston (1969), Richardson (1990), Ridgill & Fox (1990), Roberts (1991), Sargeant *et al.* (1984), Scott & Carbonell (1986), Shevareva (1970), Smythies (1986), Swanson *et al.* (1979), Titman & Seymour (1981), Wetmore (1965).

Genus *MALACORHYNCHUS* Swainson, 1831

105. **Pink-eared Duck**
Malacorhynchus membranaceus

French: Canard à oreilles roses **German**: Rosenohrente **Spanish**: Pato Pachón
Other common names: Pink-ear, Zebra Duck/Teal

Taxonomy. *Anas membranacea* Latham, 1801, New South Wales.
Sometimes placed in tribe Tadornini. Monotypic.
Distribution. Australia, with main centres of population in SW and SE.

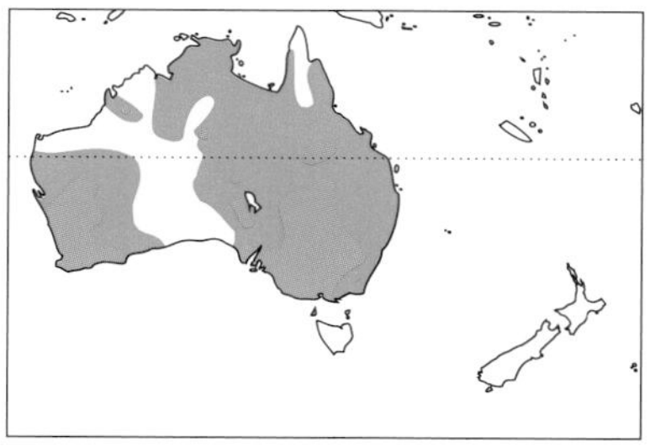

Descriptive notes. 36-45 cm; 272-480 g; wingspan 57-71 cm. Unmistakable. Juvenile duller and browner, with pink spot on face hardly apparent.
Habitat. An ecological specialist, exploiting temporary ponds and lakes of shallow saline or brackish waters of inland Australia. Occasionally found in more permanent, deeper water bodies.
Food and Feeding. Planktonic organisms (algae, microscopic seeds, crustaceans, molluscs, insects, etc.). Feeds mostly on surface by water- and mud-filtering with highly specialized bill; may also dabble.
Breeding. Season variable, much dependent on water levels. In single pairs or loose groups; nest is mound of down, in tree-hollows, crotches or in old nests of other birds, usually over water. Usually 6-8 eggs (3-11); incubation c. 26 days; chicks have light brown down above, whitish below. Average of 6·4 ducklings hatched and 4·7 fledged per nest in one study.
Movements. Somewhat dispersive and nomadic; can be seen almost anywhere in Australia, and even in Tasmania, but only very rarely in dry inland regions. Its distribution clearly reflects extent of flooding in each area.
Status and Conservation. Not globally threatened. Widespread and locally abundant. Total population probably of few hundred thousand individuals, but difficult to calculate given nomadic character of this species which is opportunist breeder on inland floodwaters. In 1988, 45,536 birds counted in 472 wetlands in Victoria, and 6131 in 1398 wetlands in SW Australia. Hunters may kill large numbers, although only 30-40% of population occurs in areas open to hunting.

Bibliography. Eller *et al.* (1991), Frith (1955, 1967), Halse & Jaensch (1989), Hobbs (1957b), Marchant & Higgins (1990), Morton *et al.* (1990), Schodde & Tidemann (1988), Warham (1958d).

Genus *MARMARONETTA* Reichenbach, 1853

106. **Marbled Teal**
Marmaronetta angustirostris

French: Sarcelle marbrée **German**: Marmelente **Spanish**: Cerceta Pardilla
Other common names: Marbled Duck

Taxonomy. *Anas angustirostris* Ménétriés, 1832, Lenkoran.
Often placed in genus *Anas*. Considered to be a link between dabbling ducks and pochards (Aythyini). Monotypic.
Distribution. S Spain and N Africa through Middle East and W Asia to extreme W China.

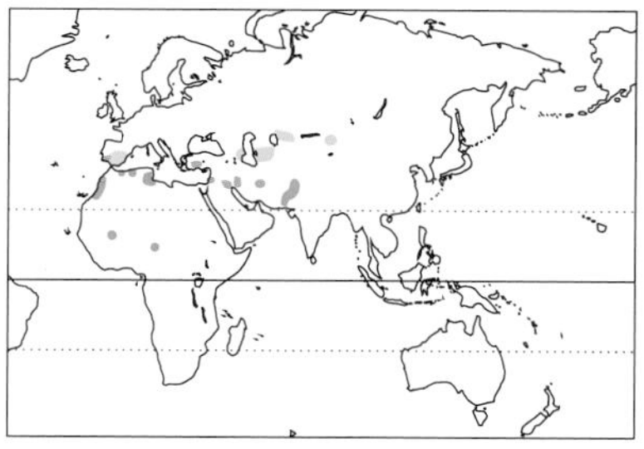

Descriptive notes. 39-48 cm; 450-590 g. Light, uniform speculum, similar to tertials; light-coloured spots can be larger in some individuals. Reminiscent of *A. specularioides*, but smaller and lacks bright speculum. Female with less evident crest on nape and often with a greenish yellow mark at base of bill. Juvenile is more uniform on underparts and has less distinctly mottled sides and upperparts.
Habitat. Shallow brackish or freshwater pools and marshes with abundant vegetation in arid country.
Food and Feeding. Seeds, roots, tubers and green parts of aquatic plants; also aquatic invertebrates (insects and larvae, molluscs, worms). Feeds by mud-filtering from shore, dabbling at water surface, upending and diving in shallow waters.
Breeding. Starts Apr/Jun; May/Jul in N Africa. In single pairs or loose groups; nest is slight depression on ground, lined with adjacent grass and down, concealed among vegetation, not far from water. 7-14 eggs; incubation 25-27 days; chicks have dark fawn brown down above, pale yellowish below. Sexual maturity at 1 year.
Movements. Dispersive and partially migratory; in winter can be found at a number of sites around Mediterranean basin, N and sub-Saharan Africa, Middle East and NW India; subject to certain degree of nomadism during severe late summer drought. Escapes recorded in western Europe.
Status and Conservation. VULNERABLE. Has declined greatly this century. Population of W Palearctic c. 2500, with main breeding populations possibly in Morocco, Iran, Iraq and Turkey, especially in C and S; probably less than 100 pairs in Marismas del Guadalquivir, Spain. Important wintering population in Pakistan, with 2143 birds counted in 1991, and 300 in Jan 1984 in Zangi Nawan L, Baluchistan Province. Winter 1991 partial censuses yielded only 2 birds in Iran; 1161 in India. Also winters in Egypt, Senegal, Mali and Chad, but in general very irregular in number and unpredictable in Africa. Global estimation c. 20,000 birds. Increasingly fragmented range; still threatened by hunting and relentless habitat destruction.

Bibliography. Adamian (1989), Ali & Ripley (1978), Amat (1980), Bauer & Glutz von Blotzheim (1968), Brickell (1988), Brown *et al.* (1982), Collar & Andrew (1988), Cramp & Simmons (1977), Dementiev & Gladkov (1952), Dolz *et al.* (1991), Etchécopar & Hüe (1964), Géroudet (1972), Gooders & Boyer (1986), Goodman (1989), Grimmett & Jones (1989), Hidalgo (1991), Hüe & Etchécopar (1970), Johnsgard (1961c), Ledant *et al.* (1981), Mackworth-Praed & Grant (1957-1973), Monval & Pirot (1989), Perennou (199a), Paz (1987), Roberts (1991), Vieillard (1972).

107 ♂ ♀

108 ♂ ♀

109 ♂ ♀

110 ♂ ♀

111 ♂ ♀

112 ♂ ♀

113 ♂ ♀

114 ♂ ♀

115 ♂ ♀

116 ♂ ♀

117 ♀ ♂

118 ♂ ♀

119 ♀

120 ♂ ♀

121 ♂ ♀

Tribe AYTHYINI

Genus *NETTA* Kaup, 1829

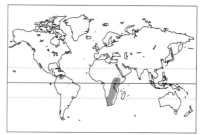

107. **Red-crested Pochard**

Netta rufina

French: Nette rousse **German**: Kolbenente **Spanish**: Pato Colorado
Other common names: Red-crested Duck

Taxonomy. *Anas rufina* Pallas, 1773, Caspian Sea and lakes of the Tartarian Desert.
Usually considered a link between dabbling ducks and *Aythya* pochards. Hybridization recorded in captivity with several species of genera *Anas* and *Aythya*. Monotypic.
Distribution. Scattered populations in W Europe, from S and E Spain and S France eastwards; bulk of population from Black Sea and Turkey E to NW China.

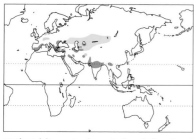

Descriptive notes. 53-58 cm; 830-1320 g; wingspan 84-88 cm. Male unmistakable; has eclipse plumage, similar to that of female, but iris and bill remain red. Female has characteristic pale sides of face and neck, contrasting with dark brown cap and hindneck; reminiscent of female *Melanitta nigra*, but paler, with thinner, bicoloured bill. Juvenile very similar to female, but darker, with more mottled underparts.
Habitat. Favours rather deep, large lakes and lagoons of fresh or brackish waters with abundant border vegetation, mainly inland in open country; also, although less often, near coast, on river deltas, estuaries and other sheltered marine habitats.
Food and Feeding. Essentially vegetarian; roots, seeds and green parts of aquatic plants; *Chara* one of main items, up to 89·7% of stomach contents in one study in Caspian Sea; occasionally, also aquatic invertebrates, amphibians and small fish. Feeds by diving, upending, head-dipping and dabbling on surface.
Breeding. Starts Apr/May. In single pairs or loose groups; nest made of roots, twigs and leaves, lined with thick layer of down, on ground among thick vegetation, near water's edge. Usually 8-10 eggs (6-14); sometimes parasitic, lays eggs in nests of other species; incubation 26-28 days; chicks have olive brown down above, pale yellow to white below and on dorsal spots; fledging 45-50 days. Sexual maturity at 1, occasionally 2, years.
Movements. Partially migratory; winters in Mediterranean basin (where locally sedentary), SW USSR, Middle East, Indian Subcontinent and SE Asia. Has occurred in Japan, Australia and NW Europe, but perhaps some of these records better attributable to escapes.
Status and Conservation. Not globally threatened. Patchily distributed, locally common. Large concentrations of this species hard to find; 1500 breeding pairs in delta of R Ebro, NE Spain; 2000 wintering in Hokarsar, Jamma and Kashmir, India; in winter 1984/85, 2000 on one corner of Erhai L, Yunnan, China. Estimated total number wintering in W Palearctic in mid-1980's was c. 70,000, and c. 400,000 in W USSR. Partial censuses in winter 1991 yielded 1502 in Iran, 13,000 in Kazakhstan, 140,696 in Turkmenistan, 5211 in Pakistan and 5114 in India. Rare to accidental in Israel until 1972; has increased noticeably and now 100 birds winter there regularly. Fairly stable or in slight decline due to hunting and habitat destruction.
Bibliography. Ali & Ripley (1978), Amat *et al.* (1987), Bauer & Glutz von Blotzheim (1969), Brickell (1988), Brown *et al.* (1982), Coronado (1972), Cramp & Simmons (1977), Dementiev & Gladkov (1952), Etchécopar & Hüe (1978), Géroudet (1972), Gooders & Boyer (1986), Goodman (1989), Grimmett & Jones (1989), Monval & Pirot (1989), Olney (1968), Owen (1977), Paz (1987), Platz (1974), Roberts (1991), de Schauensee (1984).

108. **Southern Pochard**

Netta erythrophthalma

French: Nette brune **German**: Rotaugenente **Spanish**: Pato Morado
Other common names: Red-eyed Pochard; African Pochard, South African Pochard (*brunnea*); South American Pochard (*erythrophthalma*)

Taxonomy. *Anas erythrophthalma* Wied, 1832, Lagoa do Braço, Villa de Belmonte, eastern Brazil.
Sometimes placed in monospecific genus *Phaeoaythia*; apparently not closely linked to other members of genus *Netta*. Two subspecies recognized.
Subspecies and Distribution.
N. e. brunnea (Eyton, 1838) - Ethiopia southwards to Cape Province.
N. e. erythrophthalma (Wied, 1832) - Venezuela; E Brazil to NE Argentina.
Descriptive notes. 50-51 cm; 533-1000 g. Broad white wing-band, conspicuous in flight. Male has slight peak to rear of crown; has no eclipse plumage. Juvenile resembles female, but top of head more brownish; whitish eye-stripe less pronounced; body coloration lighter brown. Subspecies *brunnea* paler and browner.
Habitat. Large bodies of rather deep, permanent, standing waters from sea-level to c. 2400 m (Africa); shallow marshes, lakes and pools with abundant submerged vegetation up to 3650 m (South America).
Food and Feeding. Chiefly seeds but also roots and vegetative parts of aquatic plants, grasses and sedges; also aquatic invertebrates (molluscs, insects, crustaceans). Feeds by diving, head-dipping and upending, and by dabbling on surface, often at water's edge.
Breeding. Season variable according to locality and water levels. In single pairs; nest is depression lined with grass, reed stems, down and some feathers, on ground or over water in thick vegetation. 5-15 eggs; incubation 26-28 days; chicks have olive brown down above, yellow on underparts and face; fledging 56-65 days.

Movements. Mainly sedentary, but subject to some dispersive movements during local dry season. This particularly affects S African birds, which move N and concentrate in areas of suitable habitat as far N as Kenya.
Status and Conservation. Not globally threatened. In South America, nominate subspecies scattered and local, apparently vanishing after dramatic decline for unclear reasons. Few observations in Colombia, Ecuador and Peru. May still be numerous in part of Venezuela, but most of recent observations in Brazil: quite common in Jacarepagua, Marapendi, Itaipu and Piratininga Lagoons, Rio de Janeiro, where groups of up to 80 reported; in Piratininga, 120 counted in 1991. Subspecies *brunnea* common to very common in S Africa, with fluctuating numbers; flocks of up to 800-5000 in W Cape, South Africa; 7500 in Kafue Flats, Zambia. Maximum counted in the Sahel and in E Africa is c. 2300 on L Nakuru in 1976; also 1300 on L Naivasha, Kenya. African population scattered; suffering due to transformation of habitat into agricultural land.
Bibliography. Benson & Benson (1975), Bertonatti *et al.* (1991), Blake (1977), Brickell (1988), Britton (1980), Brown & Britton (1980), Brown *et al.* (1982), Casler & Lira (1979), Clancey (1967), Clark, A. (1966, 1973, 1980b), Dean & Skead (1977), ffrench (1992), Fjeldså & Krabbe (1990), Gómez-Dallmeier & Cringan (1989), Hellmayr & Conover (1948), King (1978/79), Mackworth-Praed & Grant (1957-1973), Maclean (1985), Meadows (1984), Middlemiss (1958), de la Peña (1986), Perennou (1991b), Pinto (1983), Ruschi (1979), de Schauensee & Phelps (1978), Scott & Carbonell (1986), Sick (1984), Williams (1956).

109. **Rosy-billed Pochard**

Netta peposaca

French: Nette demi-deuil **German**: Rosenschnabelente **Spanish**: Pato Picazo
Other common names: Rosybill

Taxonomy. *Anas peposaca* Vieillot, 1816, Paraguay and Buenos Aires, Argentina.
Sometimes placed in monospecific genus *Metopiana*. Pronounced tendency to hybridize with *Netta rufina* and other pochards in ornamental wildfowl collections. Monotypic.
Distribution. C Chile, from Atacama to Valdivia; SE South America, from S Brazil and Paraguay southwards to Río Negro, EC Argentina.

Descriptive notes. 55-56 cm; c. 1000-1200 g. Iris of male varies from red to yellowish orange. Legs of female range from orange to yellowish grey. Juvenile resembles female but with browner underparts.
Habitat. Relatively shallow freshwater swamps, marshes and small lakes with abundant floating vegetation on open waters. Occasionally on more open or deeper waters.
Food and Feeding. Little known, but apparently essentially vegetarian diet; seeds, roots and vegetative parts of aquatic plants, grasses and sedges. Feeds by dabbling on surface or from shore, head-dipping and upending in shallow water; frequently grazes on land, and also dives, but less often.
Breeding. Mainly Oct/Nov; Feb/Mar in Paraguay. In single pairs or loose groups; nest is made of fresh herbaceous matter, lined with abundant down, over water or at water's edge, in dense vegetation. Usually 10 eggs (up to 30 by dump nesting); often lays eggs in nests of other species; incubation 27-29 days.
Movements. Partially migratory; southernmost populations descend to lower latitudes to winter as far N as Brazil and southern Bolivia. Has occurred in Falkland Is and there are various records from North America and Europe but these probably attributable to escapes.
Status and Conservation. Not globally threatened. Abundant although usually found in small groups. Notable count of 150,000-200,000 in the Cañada de los Tres Arboles y los Morteros, Córdoba Province, Argentina. In Uruguay, 3529 birds counted in partial census of Jul 1990, representing c. 15·6% of all ducks identified. Not uncommon in Magellanic zone to S Tierra del Fuego, where has probably expanded recently. Frequent quarry species.
Bibliography. Belton (1984), Blake (1977), Carp (1991), Clark (1986), Fjeldså & Krabbe (1990), Hellmayr & Conover (1948), Johnson (1965), Klimaitis & Moschione (1987), Nores & Yzurieta (1980), de la Peña (1986), Phillips (1922-1926), Ruschi (1979), Scott & Carbonell (1986), Sick (1984), Weller (1967a).

Genus *AYTHYA* Boie, 1822

110. **Canvasback**

Aythya valisineria

French: Fuligule à dos blanc **German**: Riesentafelente **Spanish**: Porrón Coacoxtle

Taxonomy. *Anas valisineria* Wilson, 1814, eastern United States.
Forms superspecies with *A. ferina*. Hybridization with other species of *Aythya* and *Netta* frequent in captivity. Monotypic.
Distribution. From C Alaska and W Canada southwards to NE California and Minnesota, USA.
Descriptive notes. 48-61 cm; 850-1600 g. Very similar to *A. ferina* and *A. americana*; separated by general tones of plumage and more specifically by shape and colour of head and bill. Male has

On following pages: 111. Common Pochard (*Aythya ferina*); 112. Redhead (*Aythya americana*); 113. Ring-necked Duck (*Aythya collaris*); 114. Hardhead (*Aythya australis*); 115. Baer's Pochard (*Aythya baeri*); 116. Ferruginous Duck (*Aythya nyroca*); 117. Madagascar Pochard (*Aythya innotata*); 118. Tufted Duck (*Aythya fuligula*); 119. New Zealand Scaup (*Aythya novaeseelandiae*); 120. Greater Scaup (*Aythya marila*); 121. Lesser Scaup (*Aythya affinis*).

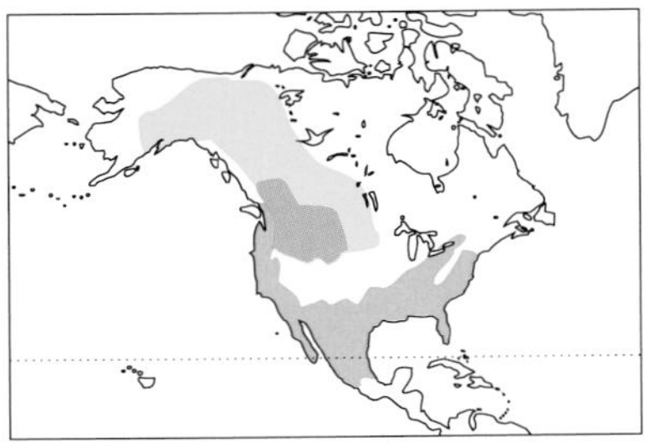

eclipse plumage. Female separable by different, longer bill, head shape, paler flanks and upperparts. Juvenile as female but has darker back and more mottled and browner underparts.
Habitat. Shallow, freshwater marshes and swamps in prairie country, with abundant floating and emergent vegetation and areas of open water. In winter, on larger lakes and coastal lagoons.
Food and Feeding. Seeds, roots, tubers, leaves and stems of aquatic plants, grasses, sedges and stubble; also aquatic invertebrates (insects, molluscs) and small fish. Feeds mostly by diving; also plucks and dabbles on surface and strains shoreline mud.
Breeding. Starts May/Jun. In single pairs or loose groups; nest is bulky structure of surrounding plant matter, lined with down, above shallow water, less often on ground. Usually 9-10 eggs; incubation c. 24 days; chicks have brownish down above, yellowish underparts, face and dorsal spots; fledging 63-77 days. Sexual maturity at 1 year. Nesting success from 21 to 77% found in several localities; in one study low nesting success of 2·7% recorded.
Movements. Migratory; winters in lowlands of USA (both Atlantic and Pacific coasts) and Central America, occasionally S to Guatemala. Vagrants reported from Bermuda, Cuba and several island groups in Pacific Ocean (Japan, Hawaii and Marshall Is).
Status and Conservation. Not globally threatened. Numbers greatly reduced. Drought conditions in 1930's and large-scale destruction of habitat in 1960's and early 1970's have caused a marked decline; over 50% reduction between 1955 and 1974, by which time population estimated at little more than 500,000, with clear predominance of males; during 1950's, average of 250,000 wintered in Chesapeake Bay, Maryland, but only c. 70,000 in recent years. Situation does not appear to have changed much despite hunting restrictions imposed in early 1970's. In winter censuses between 1978 and 1982 in Mexico, maxima of 6350 in L Chapala and delta of R Lerma, 4125 in Alvarado and Camaronera Lagoons and 2100 in Tampico Lagoons. Almost annual winter visitor in Japan, but in very small numbers. Vulnerable to oil spills.
Bibliography. Anderson (1984), Bellrose (1976), Bent (1923-1925), Brazil (1991), Cooch (1964), Erickson (1948), Geis (1974), Gooders & Boyer (1986), Hochbaum (1944), Lagerquist & Ankney (1989), Lovvorn (1989), Monroe (1968), Nichols & Haramis (1980), Olson (1964), Palmer (1976), Perry *et al.* (1988), Stoudt (1971), Terres (1980).

111. Common Pochard

Aythya ferina

French: Fuligule milouin **German**: Tafelente **Spanish**: Porrón Europeo
Other common names: Pochard, European/Eurasian/Northern Pochard

Taxonomy. *Anas ferina* Linnaeus, 1758, Europe.
Forms superspecies with *A. valisineria*. Hybridization with several species of *Aythya* and *Amazonetta brasiliensis* recorded in captivity. Monotypic.
Distribution. Iceland and W Europe E through C Asia to SE USSR; scattered populations from Turkey through S Palearctic to NE China and N Japan.

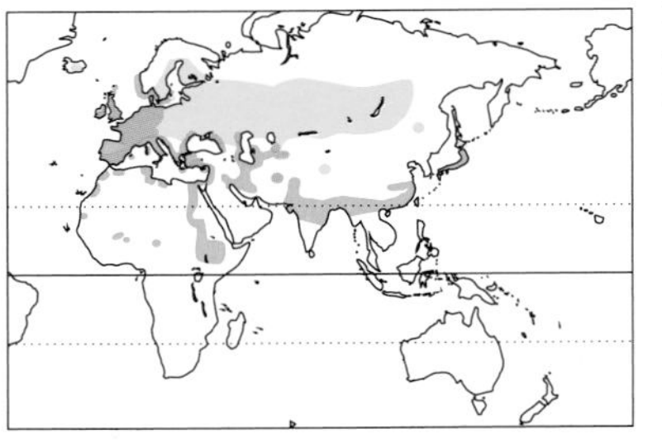

Descriptive notes. 42-58 cm; 900-1100 g. Very similar to *A. americana* but shape of head different. Male has red iris and slightly different pattern on bill; has eclipse plumage. Female has different bill colour and whiter flanks. Juvenile resembles female but has more mottled underparts.
Habitat. Well-vegetated swamps, marshes, lakes and slow-flowing rivers with areas of open water. In winter, often on larger lakes, reservoirs, brackish coastal lagoons and tidal estuaries.
Food and Feeding. Seeds, roots and green parts of grasses, sedges and aquatic plants; also small invertebrates (aquatic insects and their larvae, molluscs, crustaceans, worms), amphibians and small fish. Feeds by diving, upending or dabbling on surface; also filters mud on shore.
Breeding. Starts Apr/May. In single pairs or loose groups; nest is depression in thick heap of grass, reed stems and leaves, lined with down, on ground or water, concealed in thick vegetation. 8-10 eggs; incubation c. 25 days; chicks have brown down on upperparts, and yellow on underparts, face and dorsal spots; fledging 50-55 days. Sexual maturity at 1, occasionally 2, years. Success of 4·42 young reared to fledging per successful pair, and of 1·83 per pair (all pairs) in one study in Germany; hatching success of 56% found in Czechoslovakia.
Movements. Partially migratory; present throughout year in temperate regions (e.g. Central and NW Europe) but northernmost populations winter in Mediterranean basin, sub-Saharan Africa, Middle East, SW USSR, Indian Subcontinent, SE Asia and Japan. Vagrant to Faeroes, Azores, Canary and Cape Verde Is; also to Philippines, Guam and Hawaii.
Status and Conservation. Not globally threatened. Abundant. Wintering population in W Palearctic c. 1,600,000 birds. Important numbers also in Asia: over 100,000 winter in Japan; c. 30,000-40,000 in Iran; partial counts in winter 1991 yielded 22,000 in Kazakhstan, 96,300 in Azerbaydzhan, 72,784 in Turkmenistan, 124,694 in Pakistan and 36,212 in India. Has declined notably in last decades, at least in parts of range, probably due to excessive hunting and habitat destruction.
Bibliography. Ali & Ripley (1978), Bauer & Glutz von Blotzheim (1969), Bent (1923-1925), Bezzel (1969), Brazil (1991), Brickell (1988), Brown *et al.* (1982), Choudhury & Black (1991), Coronado (1972), Cramp & Simmons (1977), Dementiev & Gladkov (1952), Etchécopar & Hüe (1978), Ferrer (1982), Fox (1991), Fox & Salmon (1988), Géroudet (1972), Gooders & Boyer (1986), Goodman (1989), Grimmett & Jones (1989), Harrison (1988), Klima (1966), McClure (174), Monval & Pirot (1989), Olney (1968), Palmer (1976), Paz (1987), Perennou & Mundkur (1991), Richardson (1990), Ridgill & Fox (1990), Roberts (1991).

112. Redhead

Aythya americana

French: Fuligule à tête rouge **German**: Rotkopfente **Spanish**: Porrón Americano
Other common names: Red-headed Pochard

Taxonomy. *Fuligula americana* Eyton, 1838, North America.
Closely linked to *A. valisineria* and *A. ferina*; in spite of greater superficial similarity to latter, apparently closer to former. Monotypic.
Distribution. Main range in SW Canada and W USA, south to California, New Mexico and Nebraska; also populations in Alaska, Great Lakes region and SE Canada.

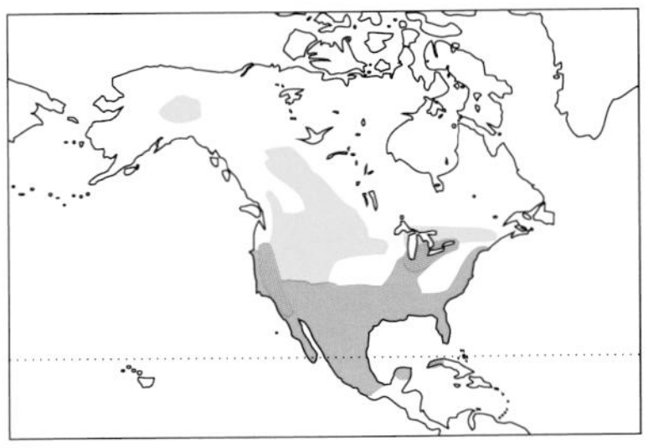

Descriptive notes. 40-56 cm; average 1030-1080 g. Male separable from that of *A. ferina* by yellow iris and different coloration of bill; flanks and wings are more vermiculated and shape of head slightly different; has eclipse plumage. Female also separable by bill and head shape. Juvenile resembles female, but is more heavily mottled.
Habitat. Rather deep freshwater swamps, lakes and marshes with extensive areas of open water. In winter, also on brackish coastal lagoons and other large extensions of standing water.
Food and Feeding. Essentially vegetarian; chiefly seeds, leaves and stems of grasses, sedges, algae and other aquatic plants, tubers, grain, etc.; also insects, molluscs, crustaceans. Feeds mostly by diving in rather deep waters and by dabbling on surface.
Breeding. Starts Apr/May. In single pairs or loose groups; nest made of dry vegetation, lined with down, preferably in dense reedbeds. Usually about 9 eggs (often many more after parasitic nesting, which is frequent in present species); some females sometimes parasitize also other species of waterfowl; incubation 24-28 days; chicks have yellowish brown down above, yellowish below and on face; fledging 56-73 days. Nest success from 15 to 85% in different studies.
Movements. Migratory; moves S to winter in lowlands of southern Canada, USA, Mexico and Central America (to Guatemala) and West Indies (Cuba, Bahamas). Recorded as vagrant in Bermuda and Hawaii.
Status and Conservation. Not globally threatened. Significant decline this century, possibly caused mainly by habitat destruction, especially through drainage of prairie marshes in its breeding grounds. Estimate of c. 600,000 in mid 1970's; now seems stable or slightly increasing, apparently expanding eastwards. Topolobampo Lagoons, NW Mexico, have received in recent years a wintering population of up to 12,200.
Bibliography. Bailey (1982), Bailey & Titman (1984), Bellrose (1976), Bent (1923-1925), Cooch (1964), Gooders & Boyer (1986), Lagerquist & Ankney (1989), Lokomoen (1966), Low (1945), McMahan (1989), Olson (1964), Palmer (1976), Ryder (1991), Sargeant *et al.* (1984), Scott & Carbonell (1986), Terres (1980), Weller (1957, 1959, 1964), Wetmore (1965), Woodin & Swanson (1989).

113. Ring-necked Duck

Aythya collaris

French: Fuligule à collier **German**: Ringschnabelente **Spanish**: Porrón Acollarado
Other common names: Ringneck, Ring-billed Duck

Taxonomy. *Anas collaris* Donovan, 1809, Lincolnshire, England, from specimen found in Leadenhall Market, London.
Considered by some to form superspecies with *A. novaeseelandiae* and *A. fuligula*, although probably affinities closer to *A. valisineria*, *A. ferina* and *A. americana*. Hybridization with *Anas crecca* recorded in captivity. Monotypic.
Distribution. C Alaska and C Canada eastwards to Newfoundland, southwards to C and W USA, as far S as N California, Colorado and Great Lakes region.

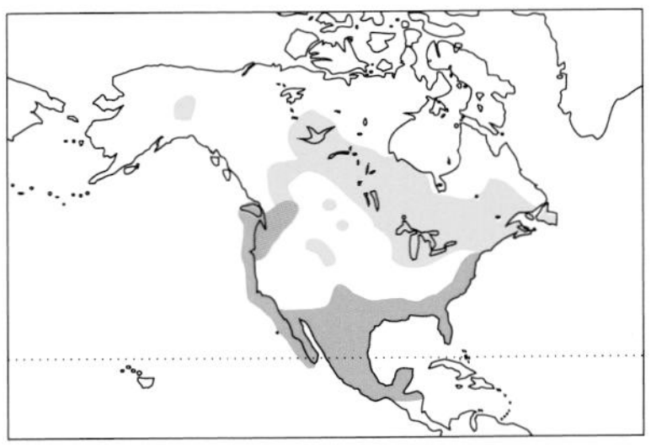

Descriptive notes. 37-46 cm; c. 690-790 g. Male has inconspicuous brown collar and distinctive bill pattern; has eclipse plumage. Juvenile resembles female, being darker above and more mottled below.
Habitat. Shallow marshy areas in open country with extensive cover of floating vegetation and areas of open water. In winter, on larger water bodies, including estuaries and coastal lagoons, but commoner on fresh water.
Food and Feeding. Chiefly seeds, roots, tubers, leaves and stems of grasses, sedges and other aquatic plants; particularly in summer, also aquatic invertebrates (insects, molluscs, crustaceans, arachnids, worms). Feeds mostly by diving; also dabbles on surface and strains mud.
Breeding. Starts May. In single pairs or loose groups; nest made with some plant matter, lined with down, situated on ground or just above water, in dense vegetation. Usually 8-10 eggs (5-14); incubation 25-29 days; chicks have brown down above, and yellowish underparts, face and dorsal spots; fledging 49-56 days. Sexual maturity at 1 year. Nest success of c. 67%, but highly variable depending on location of nests.
Movements. Migratory; winters in lowlands mostly along Atlantic and Gulf coasts, but also following Pacific, and S to Panama and West Indies. A regular trans-Atlantic vagrant, most frequent in Britain, but records from most of Europe; has also occurred in NW Africa (Morocco) and Japan.
Status and Conservation. Not globally threatened. Total population estimated at 460,000 birds at outset of breeding season in mid-1970's, has increased in recent times, as birds have extended their breeding range to E. Average of 4350 birds wintering between 1978 and 1982 in Alvarado and Camaronera Lagoons, Veracruz, Mexico.
Bibliography. Bellrose (1976), Bent (1923-1925), Bergan *et al.* (1989), Biaggi (1983), Blake (1977), Coulter & Miller (1968), Gómez-Dallmeier & Cringan (1989), Gooders & Boyer (1986), Hohman *et al.* (1988), Hoppe *et al.* (1986), Lagerquist & Ankney (1989), Maxson & Pace (1990), McAuley (1986), McAuley & Longcore (1989), Monroe (1968), Montalbano *et al.* (1985), Mendall (1958), Palmer (1976), Ridgely & Gwynne (1989), Sarvis (1972), Slud (1964), Terres (1980), Townsend (1966), Wetmore (1965).

114. Hardhead

Aythya australis

French: Fuligule austral **German**: Tasmanmoorente **Spanish**: Porrón Australiano
Other common names: Australian Hardhead/Pochard/White-eye, White-eyed Duck, Brownhead, Copperhead

Taxonomy. *Nyroca australis* Eyton, 1838, Australia = New South Wales.

Considered by some to form superspecies with *A. baeri*, *A. nyroca* and *A. innotata*. Hybridization with *Anas platyrhynchos* recorded in captivity. Breeding birds collected in Banks Is, Vanuatu, were assigned separate subspecies *extima*, though it has been suggested that this population represented a temporary colonization by nomadic Australian birds. Monotypic.

Distribution. SW and E Australia; isolated population of Banks Is, Vanuatu, may be result of brief colonization by birds of Australian origin.

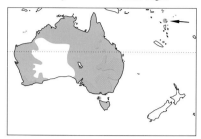

Descriptive notes. 46-49 cm; 525-1100 g; wingspan 65-70 cm. Male very similar to those of *A. nyroca* and *A. innotata*, but has more conspicuous pale subterminal band on bill; plumage browner than the former species. Female paler with brown iris; less well marked subterminal band on bill; chin and throat often pale. No seasonal changes. Juvenile as female, with russet brown on abdomen.

Habitat. Rather large, deep-water lakes and marshes with abundant emergent vegetation. Out of breeding season also found on coastal lagoons and marshes, as well as on mountain lakes.

Food and Feeding. Essentially vegetarian diet; seeds, flowers and vegetative parts of grasses, sedges and other aquatic plants; also aquatic invertebrates (insects, molluscs, crustaceans) and small fish. Feeds by diving, head-dipping, upending and dabbling on surface.

Breeding. Season variable, generally during period of highest water levels. In single pairs; nest is platform made of reeds, sedges and other surrounding plant matter, lined with down, situated on ground or on water, in dense vegetation. Usually 9-13 eggs (6-18); incubation c. 25 days (30-32 also reported); chicks have brown down above, yellowish on underparts, face and dorsal spots.

Movements. Present throughout year in many areas, but dispersive and nomadic during dry season. May wander widely in severe droughts, when it can be seen virtually anywhere in Australia and Tasmania. Has reached New Zealand, Auckland Is, Java, New Guinea and New Caledonia; apparently, sporadic breeding may occur after such irruptions.

Status and Conservation. Not globally threatened. Locally common, though has declined considerably this century. Widespread in Australia, where majority of population can concentrate in few sites during droughts; exceptionally, during severe drought of 1957/58, 80,000 birds counted on L Brewster and 50,000 at Barrenbox Swamp, New South Wales. More recently, up to 6000 birds counted in one lagoon. Partial counts yielded 1980-2584 birds between 1987 and 1989 in Victoria and 483-1351 birds in period 1986-1988 in SW Australia. Regular but scarce in Tasmania; up to 324 in Dulverton L. Breeding habitat markedly reduced by drainage or transformations. Hunted widely but normally represents low proportion of total bag in SE Australia. Very scarce in New Guinea. Common to abundant in parts of New Zealand in 19th century, but now only vagrant.

Bibliography. Beehler *et al.* (1986), Bregulla (1992), Bull *et al.* (1985), Coates (1985), Falla *et al.* (1981), Frith (1967), Halse & Jaensch (1989), Hannecart & Letocart (1980), Macdonald (1988), Marchant & Higgins (1990), Morton *et al.* (1990), Ripley (1964), Roy (1988), Schodde & Tidemann (1988), Weller (1980).

115. **Baer's Pochard**

Aythya baeri

French: Fuligule de Baer   **German**: Baermoorente   **Spanish**: Porrón de Baer
Other common names: Baer's/Siberian White-eye, Asiatic/Eastern White-eyed Pochard

Taxonomy. *Anas (Fuligula) Baeri* Radde, 1863, middle Amur Valley, eastern Siberia.
Considered by some to form superspecies with *A. australis*, *A. nyroca* and *A. innotata*. Monotypic.
Distribution. SE Siberia and NE China, perhaps N Korea.

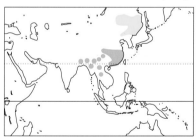

Descriptive notes. 46-47 cm; 680-880 g. Male has small white spot on chin and sometimes pale yellow iris instead of white; has eclipse plumage. Female duller; has dark rufous spot between bill and eye, and inconspicuous small white spots on neck; iris dark brown. Juvenile resembles female with russet-brown on abdomen.

Habitat. Preferably in open country, on well-vegetated pools and small lakes. In winter frequents larger water bodies, including marshes, coastal lagoons and estuaries.

Food and Feeding. Little known, but evidence suggests both plant and animal materials consumed. Probably obtains major part of food by diving.

Breeding. During local spring. In single pairs or loose groups. 6-10 eggs; incubation c. 27 days (captivity).

Movements. Migratory; leaves breeding grounds after moult to winter in coastal plains of SE China and several scattered localities westwards to NE India and southwards to Indochina; a few may winter in South Korea and Japan. Vagrant to Kamchatka.

Status and Conservation. VULNERABLE. Wide range but rather rare. Recently significant numbers recorded in Viet Nam (40 near Hanoi) and especially in Thailand, with some counts of over 100, and up to 426 in Beung Boraphet, Nakhon Sawan Province; in China too, with 100 or more recorded at several sites, and notable 750 birds counted in 23 localities in Yancheng Marshes, coastal Jiangsu Province, in Jan 1988. Partial censuses in winter 1990 yielded: 575 in India; 10 in Bangladesh; 90 in Burma; 192 in Thailand; 853 in China; scarce in Japan, where fairly regular winter visitor in very small numbers. Sharp decline recently in USSR, linked with drainage for rice cultivation and increased disturbance.

Bibliography. Ali & Ripley (1978), Brazil (1991), Collar & Andrew (1988), Dementiev & Gladkov (1952), Etchécopar & Hüe (1978), Gooders & Boyer (1986), Haider (1989), Johnstone (1965), Palmer (1976), Perennou & Mundkur (1991), de Schauensee (1984), Smythies (1986).

116. **Ferruginous Duck**

Aythya nyroca

French: Fuligule nyroca   **German**: Moorente   **Spanish**: Porrón Pardo
Other common names: White-eyed Pochard, Ferruginous White-eye/Pochard, Common White-eye

Taxonomy. *Anas nyroca* Güldenstädt, 1770, southern Russia.

Considered by some to form superspecies with *A. australis*, *A. baeri* and *A. innotata*. Hybridization recorded in captivity with several species of genera *Aythya*, *Anas* and *Netta* and with *Bucephala clangula*. Monotypic.
Distribution. Fragmented from W Europe eastwards to W Mongolia; isolated populations from Libya eastwards to NE Pakistan.

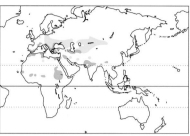

Descriptive notes. 38-42 cm; 410-650 g. Male has small white spot on chin. Differs from *A. innotata* in lack of white on flanks and paler head; blackish collar; has eclipse plumage. Female duller, browner with inconspicuous small white spots on throat. Juvenile as female but lacks white undertail-coverts and has silvery-brown underparts, with blackish barring on breast.

Habitat. Shallow pools and marshes with abundant emergent and shoreline vegetation. Outside breeding season, may frequent larger lakes and lagoons and coastal marshes.

Food and Feeding. Chiefly seeds, roots and green parts of aquatic plants; also aquatic invertebrates (worms, molluscs, crustaceans, insects and larvae), amphibians and small fish. Feeds in shallow water, by diving, head-dipping, upending or dabbling on surface.

Breeding. Starts Apr/May in Central Europe, and apparently similar laying dates in most of range. In single pairs or loose groups; nest is made of reed stems, grass and leaves, lined with down, on ground in thick vegetation or in dense reedbeds on water. Usually 8-10 eggs (6-14); incubation 25-27 days; chicks have dark grey-brown down above, yellowish on underparts, face and dorsal markings; fledging 55-60 days. Sexual maturity at 1 year.

Movements. Migratory; winters around Mediterranean basin (where locally sedentary), sub-Saharan Africa, southern shores of Caspian Sea, Middle East, Indian Subcontinent and a few sites in SE Asia. Records outside regular range, particularly in NW Europe, often better attributable to escapes.

Status and Conservation. Not globally threatened. Has suffered severe reductions in numbers and in several parts of range has become extremely local. Wintering population in W Palearctic estimated at 50,000 in mid-1980's, mostly in C Mediterranean area; average of 300 wintering birds in Israel. USSR breeding population reckoned at c. 140,000 pairs in 1970, but had fallen to c. 5200 pairs by 1984. Winter 1991 census yielded 95 birds in Saudi Arabia, 598 in Iran, 9000 in Azerbaydzhan and 20,833 in Turkmenistan; in several localities of Pakistan, more than 100 birds counted; largest concentrations, from available data, correspond to Hail Haor, Sylhet, Bangladesh, where up to 4000-5000 birds counted in years with good growth of aquatic vegetation; maximum available figures in India of 630 counted in 17 lakes in Central Rajasthan in Nov 1982, and 670 in Khijadia Lakes, Gujarat, recently. Wintering census in tropical Africa yielded maximum of 6450, with estimated 7000-10,000 in W Africa; L Horo, Mali, seems to be the most important refuge. Decline is mainly attributed to habitat destruction; however, species significantly affected by hunting. Urgent need to establish network of suitable reserves. CITES III in Ghana.

Bibliography. Ali & Ripley (1978), Bauer & Glutz von Blotzheim (1969), Brickell (1988), Brown *et al.* (1982), Cramp & Simmons (1977), Dementiev & Gladkov (1952), Dolz *et al.* (1991), Etchécopar & Hüe (1978), Géroudet (1972), Gooders & Boyer (1986), Goodman (1989), Grimmett & Jones (1989), Gustin (1988), Ledant *et al.* (1981), Monval & Pirot (1989), Owen (1977), Paz (1987), Perennou (1991a, 1991b), Perennou & Mundkur (1991), Richardson (1990), Roberts (1991), de Schauensee (1984).

117. **Madagascar Pochard**

Aythya innotata

French: Fuligule de Madagascar   **German**: Madagaskarmoorente   **Spanish**: Porrón Malgache
Other common names: Madagascan Pochard/White-eye

Taxonomy. *Nyroca innotata* Salvadori, 1894, Betsileo, Madagascar.
Considered by some to form superspecies with *A. australis*, *A. baeri* and *A. nyroca*. Monotypic.
Distribution. Restricted to L Aloatra region, Madagascar; may have been more widespread formerly on plateau of C Madagascar.

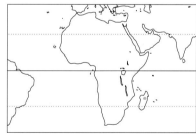

Descriptive notes. 45-56 cm. White on abdomen diffuses towards flanks. Resembles *A. nyroca* but is larger and wings do not appear so white in flight. Female has rounder, darker head than that of *A. nyroca*, and lacks small white spots on throat; iris brown. Juvenile similar to female, but has duller, paler head and body; resembles other closely related *Aythya* juveniles, but has darker scapulars and mantle.

Habitat. Originally freshwater lakes, pools and swamps with areas of open water and many islets of vegetation. L Aloatra combines these with extensive reedbeds and marshy areas.

Food and Feeding. Little known; diet includes aquatic invertebrates and seeds of aquatic plants. Presumably feeds mostly by diving in shallow waters.

Breeding. Little information available. Nesting has been recorded Mar-Apr. In single pairs; nest is structure made of plant matter, lined with down, built in tuft of vegetation on a bank; incubation 26-28 days (captivity); chicks have dark brown down above, yellowish on underparts and face.

Movements. Presumably sedentary within restricted range, as no records from other areas; some local movements may occur.

Status and Conservation. ENDANGERED. On the brink of extinction. Exclusively restricted to L Aloatra region, where has declined sharply since 1930, when was described as common; causes of decline include trapping, hunting, habitat transformation into rice paddies and introduction of exotic fish which have reduced aquatic flora. Last observation was of one pair in 1970, until Oct 1991 when one male was captured alive in fishing gear on L Aloatra and was transported to Antananarivo Botanical Gardens where it now lives. Apparently the species can only be saved by establishment of reserves and prohibiting hunting effectively in its range; probably captive breeding necessary, but can only be attempted if more wild individuals are located.

Bibliography. Brickell (1988), Collar & Andrew (1988), Collar & Stuart (1985), Dee (1986), Delacour (1932, 1954-1964), King (1978/79), Langrand (1990), Milon *et al.* (1973), Rand (1936), Salvan (1970), Webbs (1936, 1953), Weller (1980), Wilmé (1990), Young (1991b), Young & Smith (1989, 1990).

118. **Tufted Duck**

Aythya fuligula

French: Fuligule morillon **German**: Reiherente **Spanish**: Porrón Moñudo
Other common names: Tufted Pochard

Taxonomy. *Anas Fuligula* Linnaeus, 1758, Europe.
Considered by some to form superspecies with *A. collaris* and *A. novaeseelandiae*. Hybridization, particularly with other *Aythya* species, frequently recorded. Monotypic.
Distribution. Across N Palearctic from Iceland eastwards to Kamchatka, southwards to C Europe, N Mongolia and N Japan (Hokkaido).

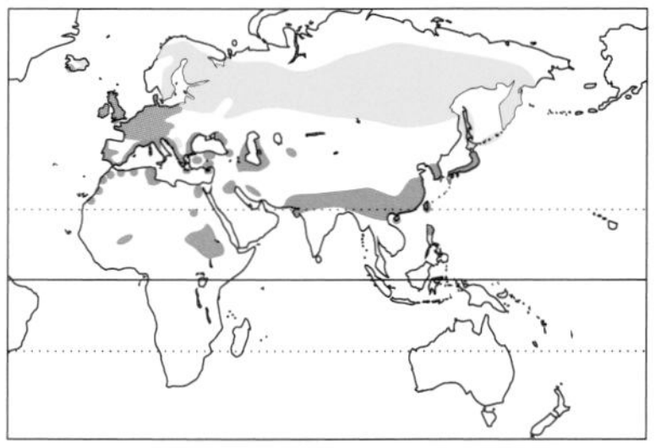

Descriptive notes. 40-47 cm; 1000-1400 g. Long crest of male unique among pochards; also separable from male of *A. collaris* by bill pattern and lack of collar; has eclipse plumage. Female very variable; can have some white on chin, around bill and on undertail-coverts; has short crest, yellow eye and white area on underparts which does not reach as far as flanks. Juvenile resembles female, but young male has darker head and somewhat vermiculated back patterning.
Habitat. Large, deep, freshwater lakes, ponds and reservoirs with open waters and islands for breeding. Also on wide, sluggish rivers and, in winter, on brackish lagoons and tidal bays.
Food and Feeding. Seeds and green parts of aquatic plants, molluscs (often major item in diet, especially *Mytilus*, *Cardium* and gastropods), crustaceans and aquatic insects; also bread and scraps in town parks. Feeds mostly by diving; also upends, dips head or picks items from surface or ashore.
Breeding. Starts May. In single pairs or loose groups; nest made of grass and sedges, lined with thick layer of down, on ground, among vegetation or in open, preferably on islands. Usually 8-11 eggs (6-14); incubation 23-28 days; chicks have sooty brown down above, pale yellowish on underparts and face; fledging 45-50 days. Sexual maturity at 1, occasionally 2, years; oldest ringed bird over 15 years old. Success of 78% at hatching, and 11·4% at fledging recorded in one study in Finland.
Movements. Partially migratory; winters Central and NW Europe (where mainly sedentary), Mediterranean basin, N and sub-Saharan Africa, SW USSR, Middle East, Indian Subcontinent, SE Asia (to Philippines) and Japan. Occasionally in Alaska and North America (mainly W Coast).
Status and Conservation. Not globally threatened. One of few *Aythya* species known to have large populations that are stable or increasing in recent decades. These recently estimated at c. 1,350,000 in W Palearctic in winter; populations in other wintering areas correspondingly high; partial counts in winter 1991 yielded 20,833 in Turkmenistan, 83,640 in India and 38,299 in Japan, where 53 representative wetlands thought to harbour 37% of the waterbirds in the country. Rate of increase remarkable in some areas; in Britain, for example, breeding first recorded in 1849, while in mid-1980's, thought to be over 7000 pairs, and increase still continued. Seemingly, peak winter count nearly trebled in little more than 20 years, and consisted of over 60,000 birds in mid-1980's. Reasons for this outstanding success based mainly on the bird's adaptability to take over new habitats artificially provided by man (parks, reservoirs) and on colonization of NW Europe by exotic molluscs (particularly zebra mussel, *Dreissena polymorpha*), on which present species may rely almost entirely for food at times.
Bibliography. Ali & Ripley (1978), Bauer & Glutz von Blotzheim (1969), Bellrose (1976), Bengtson (1970), Bevan & Butlev (1992), Brazil (1991), Brickell (1988), Brown *et al*. (1982), Cramp & Simmons (1977), Dementiev & Gladkov (1952), Durango (1954), Etchécopar & Hüe (1978), Géroudet (1972), Gillham (1987), Gooders & Boyer (1986), Goodman (1989), Grimmett & Jones (1989), Harrison (1988), Hilden (1964), Marchant *et al*. (1990), Kooloos *et al*. (1989), McClure (1974), Medway & Wells (1976), Mlíkovsky & Buric (1983), Monval & Pirot (1989), Olney (1963a), Owen (1977), Palmer (1976), Paz (1987), Perennou & Mundkur (1991), Richardson (1990), Ridgill & Fox (1990), Roberts (1991).

119. **New Zealand Scaup**

Aythya novaeseelandiae

French: Fuligule de Nouvelle-Zélande **German**: Maoriente **Spanish**: Porrón Maorí
Other common names: Black Scaup/Teal

Taxonomy. *Anas novae Seelandiae* Gmelin, 1789, New Zealand = Dusky Sound, South Island, New Zealand. Considered by some to form superspecies with *A. collaris* and *A. fuligula*. Hybridization with *A. ferina* and *A. nyroca* recorded in captivity. Population of North I has been assigned separate subspecies, *maui*, but not usually accepted. Monotypic.
Distribution. New Zealand; fragmented in North I, but more widespread throughout W South I.

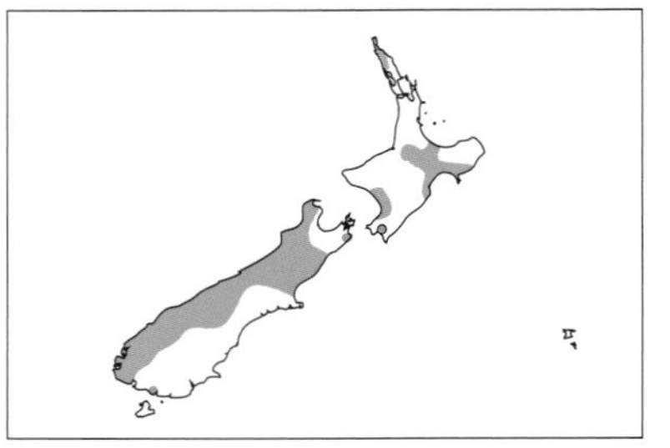

Descriptive notes. 40-46 cm; 550-746 g; wingspan c. 60 cm. Only male of *Aythya* dark overall with yellow eye. Female browner with brown iris; has white triangular patch on chin; c. 50% of females have white feathering around bill. Juvenile as female, without white on face and with whitish abdomen.
Habitat. Fairly deep, large, freshwater lakes and coastal lagoons, from sea-level to c. 1000 m on high ground. Particularly frequent in dams and reservoirs.
Food and Feeding. Apparently mixed diet of aquatic invertebrates, including gastropods and insects, and plant matter, mainly submerged macrophytes. Feeds mostly by diving in relatively shallow water; also chases insects from surface.
Breeding. Starts Oct/Nov. In single pairs or loose groups; nest is cup-like structure made of reed stems, grass and adjacent vegetation, lined with down, on ground, well-concealed among vegetation, near water. 4-8 eggs (2-15); incubation 27-30 days (captivity); chicks have sooty brown down above, brownish white on underparts, face and dorsal spots; fledging c. 75 days (captivity).
Movements. Mostly sedentary, with only small-scale movements recorded.
Status and Conservation. Not globally threatened. Still widespread, though severely reduced during first decades of present century through hunting; has disappeared from lowlands since European settlement. Legal protection since 1934 permitted recovery process, slowed down by large-scale drainage of wetlands. Now increasing in many areas thanks to great adaptability in colonizing artificial water bodies. Total population estimated at only 5000-10,000 birds. A captive breeding and reintroduction programme has proved very successful on North Island.
Bibliography. Bull *et al*. (1985), Chambers (1989), Falla *et al*. (1981), Marchant & Higgins (1990), Oliver (1955), Reid & Roderick (1973), Soper (1976), Weller (1980), Williams (1985h).

120. **Greater Scaup**

Aythya marila

French: Fuligule milouinan **German**: Bergente **Spanish**: Porrón Bastardo
Other common names: Scaup, Bluebill, Broadbill

Taxonomy. *Anas Marila* Linnaeus, 1761, Lapland.
Considered by some to form superspecies with *A. affinis*. Two subspecies recognized.
Subspecies and Distribution.
A. m. marila (Linnaeus, 1761) - N Eurasia from Iceland to R Lena, Siberia.
A. m. mariloides (Vigors, 1839) - NE Siberia, from R Lena eastwards to Bering Sea coast; Aleutian Is; Alaska eastwards through C Canada to Atlantic coast of Canada.

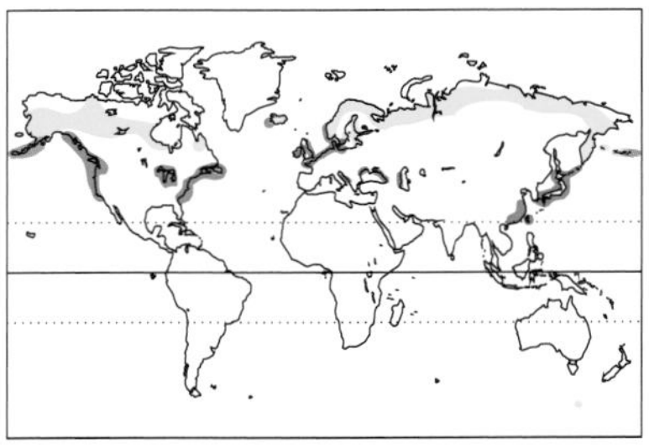

Descriptive notes. 40-51 cm; 900-1250 g. Male separable from *A. affinis* by larger bill, lack of crest and green gloss to head; has eclipse plumage. Legs of female vary from grey-green to dark slate blue. Juvenile resembles female, being duller and with less white on face. Subspecies *mariloides* more boldly vermiculated black.
Habitat. Breeds on shallow, small lakes and tundra pools of high latitudes. Winters mainly on coast, on brackish lagoons, estuaries, sheltered bays and shallow marine waters; also inland, on large lakes.
Food and Feeding. Molluscs often major item in diet; 80-95% of stomach contents, chiefly *Mytilus edulis*, in one study in Denmark; also insects, crustaceans, worms, small fish, roots, seeds and vegetative parts of aquatic plants, including sedges. Feeds mostly by diving; also upends in shallow waters and dabbles on surface.
Breeding. Starts May, occasionally later in N of range. In single pairs or loose groups; nest is depression lined with grass and down, on ground, often in thick vegetation. Usually 8-11 eggs (4-21); incubation 26-28 days; chicks have chestnut brown down above, pale buff on underparts and small dorsal spots; fledging 40-45 days. Sexual maturity at 1 or 2 years; oldest ringed bird 13 years old.
Movements. Migratory; winters along coasts of North America (Atlantic and Pacific), NW Europe, Black and Caspian Seas and Japan, Yellow and East China Seas. At some localities (e.g. Central Europe, Great Lakes of North America) also inland. Males tend to remain much further N than females or immatures.
Status and Conservation. Not globally threatened. Common and widespread. Forms very large concentrations at wintering sites; for example up to 100,000 or more in Tokyo Bay and more than 31,100 in 1986 mid-winter census at L Hamana, Honshu; total wintering population in Japan of up to 262,000 or more in late 1980's. About 30,000 counted in Kazakhstan in winter 1991. Winter population estimated at c. 200,000 in W Palearctic and c. 750,000 in North America in mid-1970's. Its habit of concentrating in large numbers on sewer outlets in winter, places it at a greater risk from pollution than other ducks.
Bibliography. Ali & Ripley (1978), Bauer & Glutz von Blotzheim (1969), Bellrose (1976), Bengtson (1970), Bent (1923-1925), Brazil (1991), Brown *et al*. (1982), Cramp & Simmons (1977), Dementiev & Gladkov (1952), Etchécopar & Hüe (1978), Géroudet (1972), Gooders & Boyer (1986), Grimmett & Jones (1989), Harrison (1988), Hilden (1964), Lagerquist & Ankney (1989), Laursen (1989), Palmer (1976), Perennou & Mundkur (1991), Roberts (1991), Salmon (1988), Weller *et al*. (1969).

121. **Lesser Scaup**

Aythya affinis

French: Fuligule à tête noire **German**: Kleine Bergente **Spanish**: Porrón Bola
Other common names: Bluebill, Little Bluebill, Broadbill

Taxonomy. *Fuligula affinis* Eyton, 1838, North America.
Considered by some to form superspecies with *A. marila*. Hybridization with other species of *Aythya*, particularly *A. marila*, producing fertile progeny, frequent in captivity. Monotypic.
Distribution. C Alaska to NW USA, and E to Great Lakes.

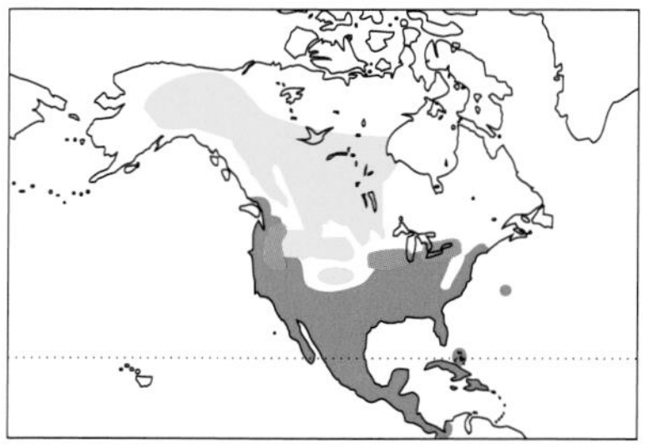

Descriptive notes. 38-48 cm; c. 800-850 g. Small crest, slightly darker vermiculation on wing and lack of green gloss separate male of this species from that of *A. marila*; has eclipse plumage. In addition, female has less white around bill. Juvenile resembles female, but duller and with less white on face.
Habitat. Inland freshwater lakes, pools and marshes in open country and lightly wooded areas during nesting season. Winters on larger lakes and brackish lagoons, but uncommon on sea water.
Food and Feeding. Seeds, roots and vegetative parts of aquatic plants; also aquatic invertebrates (insects, molluscs, crustaceans). Feeds mostly by diving in shallow waters, sieving bottom ooze.
Breeding. Starts May/Jun. In single pairs or loose groups; nest is shallow depression with plant matter, and frequently with down, on ground, among thick vegetation. Usually 9-11 eggs (up to 26 by dump nesting); incubation 21-22 days; chicks have dark brown down above, pale buff on underparts and dorsal spots; fledging 45-50 days. Sexual maturity at 1-2 years; oldest ringed bird over 10 years old. Nesting success about 43%, with 8·33 eggs hatched per successful nest.
Movements. Migratory; winters along coastal plains and Mississippi valley of North America, through Central America and West Indies southwards to N Colombia; also Bermuda and Hawaii. Vagrant S to Ecuador and Surinam, N to Greenland; two recent records from Britain may refer to wild birds.

Status and Conservation. Not globally threatened. Widespread and common, locally abundant. Breeding populations averaged 6,900,000 from 1955 to 1975, appearing stable. Several thousand wintering in Mexico: maximum of 12,300 in Topolobampo Lagoons. Also as far as Colombia: 1000 in Ciénaga Grande de Santa Marta, Magdalena Department. Favourite quarry species. Breeding grounds more secure than those of other duck species breeding further S in N America.

Bibliography. Afton (1984), Afton & Hier (1991), Bartonek & Murdy (1970), Bellrose (1976), Bent (1923-1925), Bergan *et al*. (1989), Biaggi (1983), Fjeldså & Krabbe (1990), Gehrman (1951), Gómez-Dallmeier & Cringan (1989), Gooders & Boyer (1986), Hellmayr & Conover (1948), Hoppe *et al*. (1986), Lagerquist & Ankney (1989), McMahan (1989), Monroe (1968), Palmer (1976), Ridgely & Gwynne (1989), de Schauensee & Phelps (1978), Scott & Carbonell (1986), Slud (1964), Sugden (1973), Trauger (1971), Voous (1983), Wetmore (1965).

ssp *mollissima*

♂

♀ 122

♂ ssp *dresseri*

♂ ssp *v-nigra*

♂ 123

♀

♂

♀ 124

♀ 125

♂

♀ 126

♂

♂ 127

♀

♂ 128

♀

♂ ssp *americana*

ssp *nigra*

♂ 129

♀

♂ 130

♀

♂ ssp *deglandi*

ssp *fusca*

♀ 131

♂

♂ 132

♀

♂ 133

♀

PLATE 49

inches   8

cm   20

Tribe MERGINI

Genus *SOMATERIA* Leach, 1819

122. **Common Eider**

Somateria mollissima

French: Eider à duvet **German**: Eiderente **Spanish**: Eider Común
Other common names: Eider, Eider Duck

Taxonomy. *Anas mollissima* Linnaeus, 1758, northern Europe.
Closely linked to *S. spectabilis*, with which frequently hybridizes in the wild. Six subspecies recognized.
Subspecies and Distribution.
S. m. mollissima (Linnaeus, 1758) - NW Europe E to Novaya Zemlya.
S. m. faeroeensis C. L. Brehm, 1831 - Faeroe Is.
S. m. v-nigra G. R. Gray, 1856 - New Siberian Is (NE Siberia) E to NW North America.
S. m. borealis (C. L. Brehm, 1824) - Arctic Atlantic from Baffin I E through Greenland and Iceland to Franz Josef Land.
S. m. sedentaria Snyder, 1941 - Hudson Bay region.
S. m. dresseri Sharpe, 1871 - Atlantic NE North America.

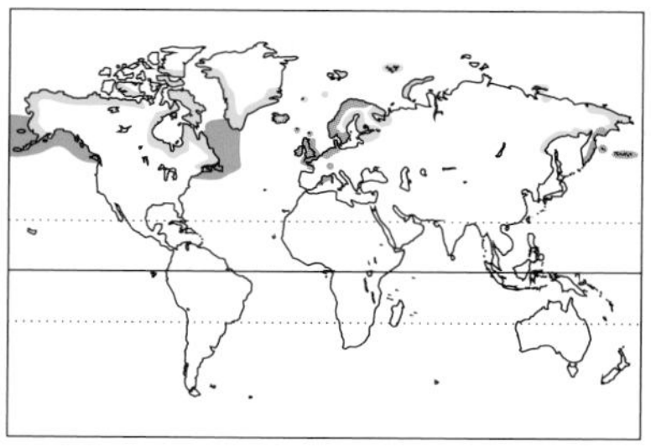

Descriptive notes. 50-71 cm; 1915-2218 g. Male unmistakable; very dark eclipse plumage as in other *Somateria*, but does not resemble females as, for example, in genus *Anas*. Female resembles other *Somateria*; separable by shape of bill and head, and plumage details. Juvenile chiefly dull brown. Subspecies vary mainly in colour and shape of bill, and also have small variations in neck and head colour. Race *v-nigra* has black, V-shaped line on throat. Race *borealis* has bill like *v-nigra* but is grey-green from nostril to nail; frontal shield is orange. Race *faeroeensis* is like nominate but with smaller bill and olive-grey frontal shield; females with darker barring. Race *sedentaria* is like *dresseri* but frontal shield smaller; female paler and greyer than other races.
Habitat. Marine, breeding on islands along low-lying rocky coasts and estuaries; also inland, on tundra pools or rivers. Disperses along shallow seashores in winter, commonly in bays, river mouths, etc.
Food and Feeding. Mostly bottom-lying molluscs, also crustaceans, echinoderms and other marine invertebrates; occasionally fish; on breeding grounds, incubating female takes algae, and berries, seeds and leaves of surrounding plants. Feeds mostly by diving; also by head-dipping and upending in shallow water.
Breeding. Starts Apr/May or even later in N of range. Generally in colonies; nest is slight hollow lined with surrounding material and down, on ground, in shelter of rock or vegetation, sometimes in the open. Usually 4-6 eggs (1-8); incubation 25-28 days; chicks have brown down above, whitish below; fledging 65-75 days. Sexual maturity at 3, occasionally 2, years; oldest ringed bird 23 years old. Nesting success of 15-40% in several studies in North America.
Movements. Partially migratory, wintering at sea in N and NW Europe, Iceland, W Greenland, Hudson Bay, Labrador and NE North America, Alaska, Aleutian Is and Kamchatka. A few (e.g. in C Europe) also inland and in NW Mediterranean. Males tend to remain further N than females or immatures.
Status and Conservation. Not globally threatened. Widespread and locally abundant species in suitable habitat throughout wide range. No global estimates of population size have been made, but must certainly be large. Most numerous breeding sea duck in N Europe, with 100,000 wintering along Norwegian coast. Estimated 1,500,000-2,000,000 wintering birds in North America in mid-1970's, and c. 2,000,000 in the W Palearctic at about same time, with unknown, but seemingly large numbers in E Siberia. Numbers currently stable or increasing in most areas (e.g. Britain, where has increased for most of present century). Main threat for this species comes from risk of major oil spill in one of its favoured haunts, as large flocks (e.g. during moult) not uncommon.
Bibliography. Alerstam *et al*. (1974), Bauer & Glutz von Blotzheim (1969), Bellrose (1976), Bent (1923-1925), Bustnes & Erikstad (1988, 1990, 1991), Cooch (1965), Coulson (1984), Cramp & Simmons (1977), Dementiev & Gladkov (1952), Franzman (1980, 1989), Géroudet (1972), Gooders & Boyer (1986), Götmark (1989), Götmark & Ahlund (1988), Goudie & Ankney (1988), Grimmett & Jones (1989), Hario & Selin (1988), Harrison (1988), Humphrey (1955, 1958), Jenssen & Ekker (1990), Joensen (1973), Laurila & Hario (1988), Laursen (1989), McArthur & Gorman (1978), McKinney (1961), Nehls *et al*. (1988), Palmer (1976), Paludan (1962), Parker & Holm (1990), Reed (1986), Reed & Erskine (1986), Swennen (1976), Swennen, Duiven & Reyrink (1979), Swennen, Nehls & Laursen (1989), Tasker *et al*. (1987), Temme (1974), Terres (1980), Ydenberg & Guillemette (1991).

123. **King Eider**

Somateria spectabilis

French: Eider à tête grise **German**: Prachteiderente **Spanish**: Eider Real

Taxonomy. *Anas spectabilis* Linnaeus, 1758, Canada, Sweden.
Closely linked to *S. mollissima*, with which frequently hybridizes in the wild. Monotypic.
Distribution. Arctic coasts, except Iceland and Scandinavia, where may breed sporadically.
Descriptive notes. 43-63 cm; 1500-2010 g. Male unmistakable; has eclipse plumage. Juvenile similar to female, but duller.
Habitat. Marine; generally breeds on adjacent land, on freshwater lakes, pools, bogs and small rivers of Arctic tundra. Spends rest of year at sea, often in deep waters away from land.
Food and Feeding. Molluscs, crustaceans, insect larvae, echinoderms and other marine invertebrates; little plant material, seeds and green parts of grasses and tundra vegetation. Feeds mostly by diving; also by head-dipping and upending in shallow waters.
Breeding. Starts Jun. In single pairs; nest is slight hollow with little material, lined with down, on ground, often in the open, sometimes in shelter of rock or hummock. Usually 4-5 eggs (2-7); incubation 22-24 days; chicks have brown down above, whitish below. Sexual maturity at 3 years.
Movements. Migratory; winters fairly far N in northern Europe, Iceland, W Greenland, NE North America, Alaska, Aleutian Is and Kamchatka; a few also inland (e.g. on Great Lakes). Stragglers sometimes occur further S than normal range (Italy, Hungary; California and Georgia, USA).
Status and Conservation. Not globally threatened. Common and locally abundant; difficulty of access to areas it frequents gives general idea that is less abundant than it really is. North American breeding

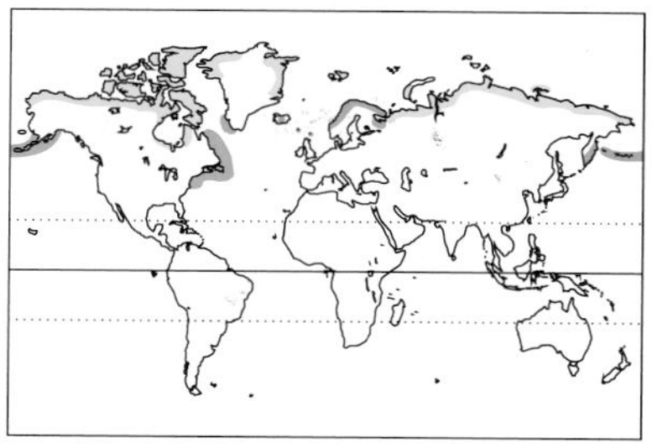

population estimated at 1,000,000-2,000,000 birds, in USSR another 1,000,000-1,500,000 individuals. 45,000 wintering along N Norwegian coast. Formerly common in Kuril Is, where seems to have disappeared. Although hunting pressure on this species high at traditional migration posts, main threat lies in its marine habits outside the breeding season, as often occurs there in large rafts and is thus exposed to massive pollution from potential oil spills.
Bibliography. Armstrong (1983), Bauer & Glutz von Blotzheim (1969), Bellrose (1976), Bent (1923-1925), Brazil (1991), Bustnes & Erikstad (1988), Cramp & Simmons (1977), Dementiev & Gladkov (1952), Gooders & Boyer (1986), Humphrey (1955, 1958), Johnsgard (1975), Palmer (1976), Parmelee *et al*. (1967), Reed (1986), Salomonsen (1968), Terres (1980).

124. **Spectacled Eider**

Somateria fischeri

French: Eider à lunettes **German**: Plüschkopfente **Spanish**: Eider de Anteojos
Other common names: Fischer's Eider

Taxonomy. *Fuligula (Lampronetta) Fischeri* Brandt, 1847, St. Michael, Alaska.
Sometimes placed in monospecific genus *Lampronetta*. Monotypic.
Distribution. Coasts of N Siberia from Lena Delta E to N Alaska.

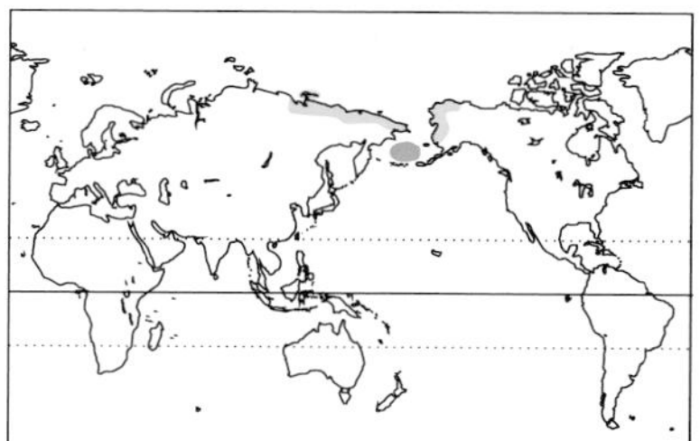

Descriptive notes. 51-58 cm; c. 1630 g. Male unmistakable; has eclipse plumage. Head pattern characteristic, even in female. Juvenile male has "spectacles" slightly developed and resembles female, appearing darker above with faint dusky barring underneath. Juvenile female resembles adult but with spotted rather than barred underparts.
Habitat. Breeds on small lakes, pools, bogs and streams of Arctic tundra, generally not far from sea. In winter, eminently marine, occurring well offshore to pack ice.
Food and Feeding. Chiefly molluscs; also crustaceans and, particularly in summer, insects and larvae, arachnids, seeds and leaves of grasses and sedges, fruits and berries. Feeds mostly by diving; also plucks and dabbles on surface.
Breeding. Starts May/Jun. In single pairs or loose groups; nest is depression covered with layer of plant matter, lined with down. Usually 4-5 eggs; incubation c. 24 days; chicks have brown down above, whitish below; fledging 50-53 days. Sexual maturity probably at 2 years. Nesting success about 73% in one study.
Movements. Winter quarters remain unfound but presumably in Bering Sea area, perhaps variable each year according to extension of pack ice. Exceptional outside normal range, with vagrants in SW Canada (British Columbia), SW USA (California), W Siberia (Kola) and N Norway.
Status and Conservation. Not globally threatened. Total world population estimated at c. 200,000 breeding birds, or c. 400,000 individuals, in mid-1970's. This evaluation probably also valid for the present, as no evidence of any significant change in numbers of this species in recent times. Known to suffer some pressure from hunters, but main potential threat is risk of oil pollution to its large concentrations, particularly since bulk of world population spends most of year in a relatively small geographical area.
Bibliography. Armstrong (1983), Bellrose (1976), Bent (1923-1925), Cramp & Simmons (1977), Dau (1972, 1974, 1976), Dau & Kistchinski (1977), Dementiev & Gladkov (1952), Gooders & Boyer (1986), Humphrey (1955, 1958), Johnsgard (1964a, 1964b), Kistchinski & Flint (1974), Palmer (1976), Reed (1986), Rohwer *et al*. (1989), Terres (1980).

Genus *POLYSTICTA* Eyton, 1836

125. **Steller's Eider**

Polysticta stelleri

French: Eider de Steller **German**: Scheckente **Spanish**: Eider Menor

Taxonomy. *Anas Stelleri* Pallas, 1769, Kamchatka. Monotypic.
Distribution. Arctic coasts of N Alaska westwards to Taymyr Peninsula, Siberia; occasionally further west to extreme N Norway.

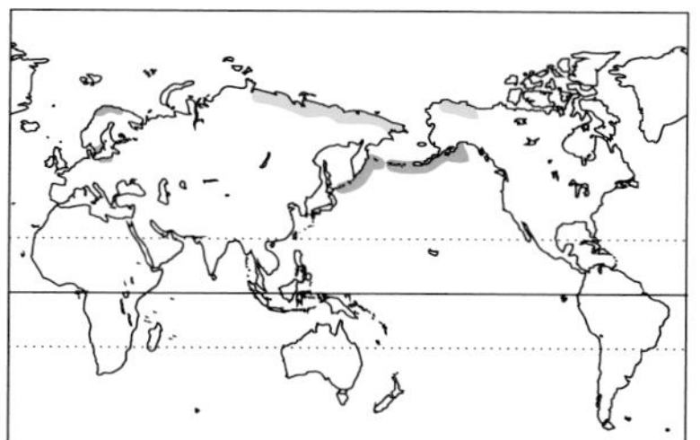

Descriptive notes. 43-48 cm; c. 860 g. Male unmistakable; has eclipse plumage. Female slightly smaller than male. Juvenile resembles female but is paler and more reddish, mottled below.
Habitat. Breeds on Arctic pools, small lakes, rivers and tundra bogs. Mostly on sea water in winter, along low-lying rocky coasts, frequenting bays, river mouths, etc.
Food and Feeding. Chiefly molluscs, crustaceans and other marine invertebrates (worms, echinoderms), small fish and freshwater insects and larvae. Feeds mostly by diving; also dabbles on surface and head-dips and upends in shallow water.
Breeding. Starts Jun/Jul. In single pairs; nest is mound of grass lined with down, on ground, concealed among vegetation, or in the open. Usually 6-8 eggs (5-10); chicks have dark brown down above, paler below. Sexual maturity at 3 years.
Movements. Migratory; winters in southern Bering Sea (Alaska, Kamchatka, Aleutian and Kuril Is) and smaller numbers in N Norway and S Baltic Sea. Stragglers not uncommon in other suitable areas at high latitudes; two in N Scotland stayed for over 12 and nearly 8 years respectively.
Status and Conservation. Not globally threatened. Rather common, locally abundant species with total world population estimated at c. 500,000 birds in early 1970's. No evidence of any significant

On following pages: 126. Harlequin Duck (*Histrionicus histrionicus*); 127. Long-tailed Duck (*Clangula hyemalis*); 128. Black Scoter (*Melanitta nigra*); 129. Surf Scoter (*Melanitta perspicillata*); 130. White-winged Scoter (*Melanitta fusca*); 131. Bufflehead (*Bucephala albeola*); 132. Barrow's Goldeneye (*Bucephala islandica*); 133. Common Goldeneye (*Bucephala clangula*).

changes in population in recent times. In 1971 discovered to be locally uncommon winter visitor off headlands, especially Cape Nosappu, SE Hokkaido, Japan, where normally in small flocks (maximum 40 birds). As in other eiders, some birds known to be killed by hunters, but main threat probably related to habit of occurring in large rafts, particularly during flightless moult period (when up to 200,000 birds observed together), in marine waters. Major oil spill in one of such areas would be catastrophic for future of species.

Bibliography. Armstrong (1983), Bauer & Glutz von Blotzheim (1969), Bellrose (1976), Bent (1923-1925), Brandt (1943), Brazil (1991), Cramp & Simmons (1977), Dementiev & Gladkov (1952), Gooders & Boyer (1986), Grimmett & Jones (1989), Humphrey (1955, 1958), Jones (1965), Kertell (1991), McKinney (1965b), Palmer (1976), Reed (1986), Terres (1980).

Genus *HISTRIONICUS* Lesson, 1828

126. **Harlequin Duck**
Histrionicus histrionicus

French: Arlequin plongeur   **German**: Kragenente   **Spanish**: Pato Arlequín
Other common names: Harlequin

Taxonomy. *Anas histrionicus* Linnaeus, 1758, America = Newfoundland *ex* Edwards.
Pacific population has been assigned separate subspecies *pacificus*, but doubtfully valid. Monotypic.
Distribution. From L Baikal, Siberia, eastwards to Aleutian Is and Alaska, southwards to Colorado, USA; E Canada, Greenland and Iceland.

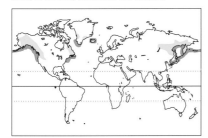

Descriptive notes. 38-51 cm; average 540-680 g. Male unmistakable; has eclipse plumage. Juvenile resembles female but with paler upperparts and more spotted underparts.
Habitat. Breeds on swift torrents and rapid streams of rugged uplands. Winters mostly along rocky coastlines, where dives for food amidst the heavy surf of breaking waves.
Food and Feeding. Mostly molluscs, crustaceans and, in spring and summer, insects and their larvae; also other invertebrates (worms) and small fish; very little plant material recorded. Feeds mostly by diving, but also dabbles and head-dips in shallow waters; occasionally upends.

Breeding. Starts May/Jun. In single pairs; nest is thin layer of grass, occasionally with a few dry twigs and leaves, lined with down, on ground, concealed among vegetation. Usually 5-7 eggs (3-10); incubation 27-29 days; chicks have mostly dark brown down above, whitish below; fledging c. 60-70 days. Sexual maturity at 2 years.
Movements. Not truly migratory; in winter disperses along sea coasts within breeding range. Some birds occur further S (e.g. Florida, Ryukyu Is and Hawaii). Several records in Europe, mostly N USSR and Britain, a few perhaps of Siberian origin.
Status and Conservation. Not globally threatened. Widespread and common, locally abundant species. No global estimates of population size available, but bulk of it known to occur in Aleutian Is, where estimated 1,000,000 birds after breeding in mid-1970's; much smaller Icelandic population currently estimated at c. 3000 pairs. Apart from being common winter visitor, also small breeding population in mountains of N Honshu and central Hokkaido and in Kiritappu, Japan. No evidence of major changes in those populations, so probably little cause for concern about future of this species. However, being specialist feeder, it probably would suffer more from alterations to favoured (particularly breeding) habitat than other species.
Bibliography. Armstrong (1983), Bauer & Glutz von Blotzheim (1969), Bellrose (1976), Bengtson (1966b, 1972), Bent (1923-1925), Brazil (1991), Cramp & Simmons (1977), Dementiev & Gladkov (1952), Etchécopar & Hüe (1978), Gooders & Boyer (1986), Goudie (1989), Goudie & Ankney (1988), Grimmett & Jones (1989), Gudmundsson (1961), Humphrey (1955), Inglis *et al*. (1989), Kuchel (1977), Palmer (1976), Terres (1980), Vickery (1988).

Genus *CLANGULA* Leach, 1819

127. **Long-tailed Duck**
Clangula hyemalis

French: Harelde boréale   **German**: Eisente   **Spanish**: Pato Havelda
Other common names: Oldsquaw

Taxonomy. *Anas hyemalis* Linnaeus, 1758, Arctic Europe and America. Monotypic.
Distribution. Circumpolar, on Arctic coasts.
Descriptive notes. 38-58 cm; c. 650-800 g. Unmistakable. Male has eclipse plumage. Complex seasonal

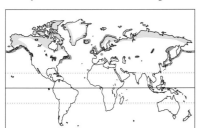

variations; brightest plumage attained in winter (illustrated birds). In summer, darker, with white of head and neck becoming dark brown; also acquires feathers similar to the female's on back. In summer female is darker, especially on face. Superficially, juvenile resembles female, but has sides of breast dark brown and lacks brownish black mark on sides of face.
Habitat. Breeds on small tundra lakes, pools, bogs, rivers and coastal sites of high Arctic. Winters mostly at sea, generally far offshore, but also inland in large, deep freshwater lakes or brackish lagoons.
Food and Feeding. Mostly crustaceans, molluscs, other marine invertebrates (echinoderms, worms), fish and, in fresh water, insects and their larvae; also a little plant material (algae, grasses, seeds, tundra plants and their fruits). Feeds almost exclusively by diving.
Breeding. Starts May/Jun. In single pairs or loose groups; nest is natural depression lined with surrounding plant matter and down, on ground, among vegetation or in the open. Usually 6-9 eggs (2-11); incubation 24-29 days; chicks have dark chestnut brown down above, white below; fledging 35-40 days. Sexual maturity at 2 years. Nesting success of 59% in one study.
Movements. Migratory; winters at sea in northern regions, generally as far S as Britain, South Carolina and Washington in USA, and Korea; also inland in some areas (e.g. Great Lakes or Central Europe). Occurs irregularly further S, often as result of adverse weather conditions.

Status and Conservation. Not globally threatened. Widespread and common species, locally abundant, with total world population that may well exceed 10,000,000 individuals, c. 2,000,000 birds wintering in W Palearctic. Available data suggest that numbers apparently stable in most regions and that no imminent cause for concern about its future. However, is probably seaduck species most exposed to oil pollution, as commonly gathers in large rafts, perhaps of several tens of thousands, to roost or feed in both inshore and offshore waters. In addition, large numbers often drown when entangled in fishing nets; many killed by hunters, as they are commonly shot at while passing on migration over certain regions in Arctic.
Bibliography. Armstrong (1983), Ali & Ripley (1978), Alison (1970, 1975), Bauer & Glutz von Blotzheim (1969), Bellrose (1976), Bent (1923-1925), Bergman & Donner (1964), Brazil (1991), Cramp & Simmons (1977), Dementiev & Gladkov (1952), Ellarson (1956), Géroudet (1972), Gibbs (1961), Gooders & Boyer (1986), Goudie & Ankney (1988), Grimmett & Jones (1989), Humphrey (1955), Harrison (1988), Kondratyev (1989), Laursen (1989), Mathiasson (1970), Nilsson (1980), Palmer (1976), Stewart & Hourston-Wright (1990), Tasker *et al*. (1987), Terres (1980).

Genus *MELANITTA* Boie, 1822

128. **Black Scoter**
Melanitta nigra

French: Macreuse noire   **German**: Trauerente   **Spanish**: Negrón Común
Other common names: Common Scoter; American Scoter (*americana*)

Taxonomy. *Anas nigra* Linnaeus, 1758, Lapland, England.
Races sometimes considered full species. Two subspecies recognized.
Subspecies and Distribution.
M. n. nigra (Linnaeus, 1758) - Iceland and N Britain E to R Olenek, Siberia.
M. n. americana (Swainson, 1832) - R Yana, Siberia, E to Alaska; E Canada to Newfoundland.

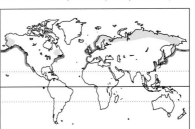

Descriptive notes. 43-54 cm; 703-1363 g. Distinguishable from other *Melanitta* by head and bill pattern. Does not have eclipse plumage like other *Melanitta*. Juvenile resembles female but is paler, especially on underparts and lower half of head. Subspecies *americana* differentiated by shape and pattern of bill.
Habitat. Breeds on freshwater pools, small lakes or streams in tundra or boggy country, sometimes with scattered trees. Winters mostly at sea, preferably in shallow waters of low-lying coasts.
Food and Feeding. Mostly molluscs, occasionally other aquatic invertebrates (crustaceans, worms, insects) and small fish; also some plant material (seeds, roots, tubers). Feeds almost exclusively by diving.

Breeding. Starts May/Jun. In single pairs; nest is scrape on ground, lined with grass and down, hidden among vegetation. Usually 6-8 eggs (5-11); incubation c. 30-31 days; chicks have grey-brown down above, paler greyish below; fledging 45-50 days. Sexual maturity at 2-3 years; oldest ringed bird 16 years old.
Movements. Migratory; winters at sea off Atlantic coast of Europe and N Africa, W Mediterranean, NE North America and, in Pacific, coasts of North America, Aleutian Is, USSR, Japan, Korea and E China; also inland (e.g. Great Lakes). Occurs irregularly further S of normal range.
Status and Conservation. Not globally threatened. Widespread and common over most of range, but probably certain reduction in numbers at present, at least in some areas. This may be due to contraction in extent of suitable breeding habitat (scoters breed further S and thus in less remote places than other seaducks), to oil pollution or to some unknown factors, perhaps related with food or predation on nesting grounds (the latter possibly indirectly induced by man). However, rate of any possible decline not exceedingly rapid at moment, and population still rather large: estimated in mid-1970's at 500,000 in North America before breeding; 800,000 wintering in W Palearctic; and unknown, but maybe even larger numbers in Asia.
Bibliography. Armstrong (1983), Bauer & Glutz von Blotzheim (1969), Bellrose (1976), Bengtson (1966a, 1970), Bent (1923-1925), Bergman & Donner (1964), Brazil (1991), Brickell (1988), Brown *et al*. (1982), Cramp & Simmons (1977), Dean (1989), Dementiev & Gladkov (1952), Géroudet (1972), Gooders & Boyer (1986), Goudie & Ankney (1988), Grimmett & Jones (1989), Harrison (1988), Humphrey (1955), Kondratyev (1989), Laursen (1989), Palmer (1976), Perennou & Mundkur (1991), Ruttledge (1987), Tasker *et al*. (1987).

129. **Surf Scoter**
Melanitta perspicillata

French: Macreuse à lunettes   **German**: Brillenente   **Spanish**: Negrón Careto

Taxonomy. *Anas perspicillata* Linnaeus, 1758, Canada = Hudson Bay *ex* Edwards.
Monotypic.
Distribution. From W Alaska through C Canada to Labrador.

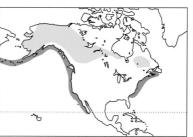

Descriptive notes. 46-55 cm; c. 900-1000 g. Juvenile resembles female but has paler breast, dark brown head from above eyes; lacks whitish nape patch but has more conspicuous whitish markings on head; iris dark, whereas generally pale in adult female.
Habitat. Breeds on small bodies of fresh water in boreal forests or tundra country. Winters mostly at sea, in shallow waters of bays, estuaries and river mouths.
Food and Feeding. Chiefly molluscs; also crustaceans, worms, echinoderms and, mainly in summer, insects and their larvae and plant material, such as seeds and green parts of aquatic plants.

Feeds mostly by diving, often close to shore among breaking waves.
Breeding. Starts May/Jun. In single pairs or loose groups; nest is shallow depression poorly lined with grass and some feathers, on ground among vegetation. 5-8 eggs; chicks have dark brown down above, paler greyish brown below.
Movements. Migratory; winters at sea along Atlantic and Pacific coasts of North America as far S as North Carolina and Baja California respectively; also off Aleutian Is and inland (Great Lakes). Occasionally wanders further S; recorded regularly in NW Europe (Britain).
Status and Conservation. Not globally threatened. Fairly common, although perhaps currently involved in decline. Being North American endemic, is least numerous of the scoters, with total winter population estimated at c. 765,000 individuals in mid-1970's. Reasons for assumed current decline possibly to be

found at breeding grounds, but seems more probable that it may have been suffering slightly higher mortality in marine winter habitat in recent times, perhaps due to oil pollution, as suggested for other seaducks.

Bibliography. Armstrong (1983), Bauer & Glutz von Blotzheim (1969), Bellrose (1976), Bent (1923-1925), Cramp & Simmons (1977), Gooders & Boyer (1986), Humphrey (1955, 1957), Johnsgard (1975), Myres (1959), Palmer (1976).

130. **White-winged Scoter**

Melanitta fusca

French: Macreuse brune **German**: Samtente **Spanish**: Negrón Especulado
Other common names: Velvet Scoter; American/Degland's White-winged Scoter (*deglandi*)

Taxonomy. *Anas fusca* Linnaeus, 1758, "Oceano Europaeo".
Races *deglandi* and *stejnegeri* have been separated by some in a full species, American White-winged Scoter (*M. deglandi*). Three subspecies recognized.
Subspecies and Distribution.
M. f. fusca (Linnaeus, 1758) - Scandinavia E to R Yenisey, C Siberia.
M. f. stejnegeri (Ridgway, 1887) - Siberia, from Yenisey basin E to Kamchatka, S to Mongolia.
M. f. deglandi (Bonaparte, 1850) - Alaska and Canada, E to Hudson Bay.

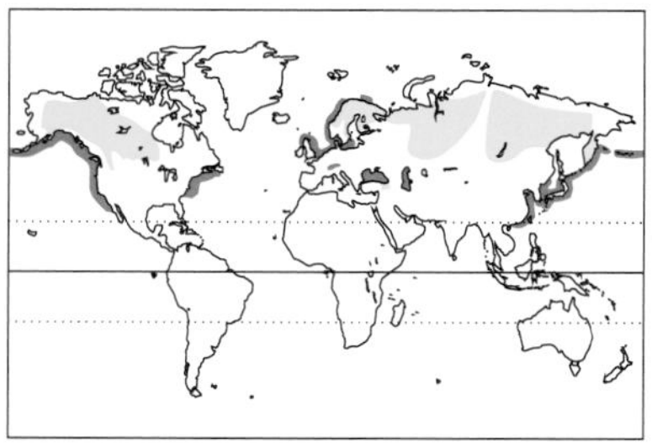

Descriptive notes. 51-58 cm; 1200-1794 g. Large *Melanitta*. Recognizable in flight by conspicuous white secondaries and greater coverts which form square wing bar. Juvenile as female, paler on breast with whiter and larger pale head markings. Subspecies *deglandi* and *stejnegeri* separated mainly by shape and colour of bill.
Habitat. Breeds on small freshwater bodies of boreal forest and Arctic tundra, sometimes well inland. Winters mostly at sea, in shallow waters of littoral zone.
Food and Feeding. Mainly molluscs; also crustaceans, worms, echinoderms, small fish and, in fresh water, insects and their larvae. Little plant material consumed, principally on breeding grounds. Feeds almost exclusively by diving, though occasionally also dabbles on surface.
Breeding. Starts May/Jun. In single pairs or loose groups; nest is shallow depression poorly lined with surrounding plant matter, and also with down, on ground among vegetation. Usually 7-9 eggs (5-12); incubation 27-28 days; chicks have dark brown down above, white below; fledging c. 50-55 days. Sexual maturity at 2-3 years; oldest ringed bird 12 years old.
Movements. Migratory; winters on Atlantic and Pacific coasts of North America as far S as Baja California, also in most of Europe S to Mediterranean, Black and Caspian Seas and NE Asia S to Japan and E China; also inland (e.g. Great Lakes, Central Europe). Irregularly further S.
Status and Conservation. Not globally threatened. May be currently involved in similar downwards trend in numbers as suspected for other *Melanitta* species, at least in part of range, for example in Japan. Winter population estimated at c. 1,000,000 in North America in mid-1970's and 250,000 in W Palearctic, with unknown numbers in Asia. Apart from risk of large congregations of birds being affected by oil spill, threatened because feeds at depths of 30-40 m and thus very prone to being trapped in fishing nets.

Bibliography. Armstrong (1983), Bauer & Glutz von Blotzheim (1969), Bellrose (1976), Bent (1923-1925), Brazil (1991), Brickell (1988), Brown, L.H. *et al.* (1982), Brown, P.W. (1977, 1981), Brown, P.W. & Brown, M.A. (1981), Brown, P.W. & Fredrickson (1986, 1987, 1989), Cramp & Simmons (1977), Dementiev & Gladkov (1952), Etchécopar & Hüe (1978), Géroudet (1972), Gooders & Boyer (1986), Grimmett & Jones (1989), Harrison (1988), Hilden (1964), Humphrey (1955), Kehoe (1989), Kehoe *et al.* (1989), Kondratyev (1989), Koskimies (1975a, 1975b), Koskimies & Routamo (1953), Kurilovich & Tarkhanova (1986), Laursen (1989), Paakspuu (1989), Palmer (1976), Perennou & Mundkur (1991), Rawls (1949), Tasker *et al.* (1987).

Genus *BUCEPHALA* Baird, 1858

131. **Bufflehead**

Bucephala albeola

French: Garrot albéole **German**: Büffelkopfente **Spanish**: Porrón Albeola

Taxonomy. *Anas Albeola* Linnaeus, 1758, America = Newfoundland *ex* Edwards. Monotypic.
Distribution. Alaska E through C Canada to Hudson Bay and Great Lakes, and S to NW USA.

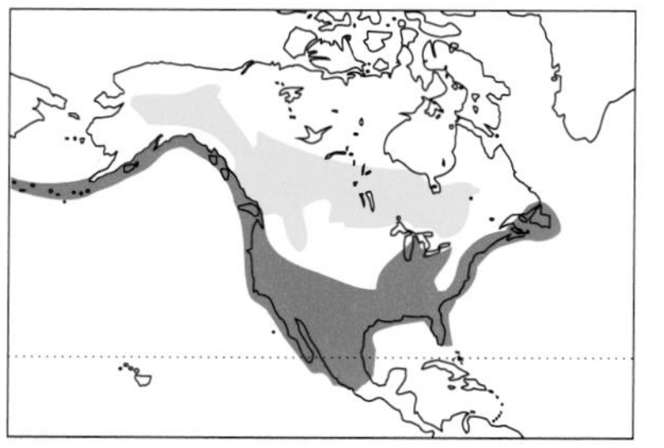

Descriptive notes. 33-40 cm; c. 330-450 g. Unmistakable. Male has eclipse plumage. Juvenile like female; browner and duller, with smaller white head patch.
Habitat. Relatively shallow lakes and pools in or near forested country during breeding season. Winters on larger lakes, brackish waters and along sea coasts.
Food and Feeding. Aquatic invertebrates (insects and their larvae are often main food items in summer; crustaceans, molluscs, arachnids), small fish; also plant material, chiefly seeds of aquatic plants. Feeds mostly by diving.
Breeding. Starts Apr/May. In single pairs; in tree holes. 5-12 eggs; incubation c. 29-31 days; chicks have dark brown down above, white below; fledging 50-55 days. Sexual maturity at 2 years; oldest ringed bird over 13 years old. Nesting success of 78·8% in one study.
Movements. Migratory; winters along Pacific coast of North America from Alaska to Mexico and across S USA to Atlantic seaboard N to New England. Occasionally further S; has occurred in Greenland, NE Siberia, Hawaii and Japan; also in NW Europe (mainly Britain).
Status and Conservation. Not globally threatened. Fairly common. Total world population at onset of breeding season estimated at c. 750,000 birds in mid-1970's, with evident upward trend in NE but significant declines in W. Reasons for these shifts in population numbers remain undiscovered, but may be found on species' breeding grounds (perhaps availability of nest-sites in suitable habitat is limiting factor) or at winter quarters (hunting pressure, extent of ideal wetlands, pollution, etc.). Winters in fair numbers in Mexico: up to 600 counted in Agiabampo Lagoons, and up to 410 in Topolobampo Lagoons, Sinaloa.

Bibliography. Armstrong (1983), Bauer & Glutz von Blotzheim (1969), Bellrose (1976), Bent (1923-1925), Bergan *et al.* (1989), Biaggi (1983), Brazil (1991), Cramp & Simmons (1977), Erskine (1960, 1972b, 1990), Gauthier (1987a, 1987b, 1989), Gauthier & Smith (1987), Gooders & Boyer (1986), Harrison (1988), Humphrey (1955), Myers (1959), Palmer (1976), Savard (1982, 1984), Terres (1980), Townsend (1916), Wienmeyer (1967).

132. **Barrow's Goldeneye**

Bucephala islandica

French: Garrot d'Islande **German**: Spatelente **Spanish**: Porrón Islándico

Taxonomy. *Anas islandica* Gmelin, 1789, Iceland.
Sometimes placed in genus *Glaucionetta*. Infrequent hybridization with *B. clangula* in the wild. Monotypic.
Distribution. S Alaska to N California and Wyoming; Labrador, SW Greenland, Iceland.

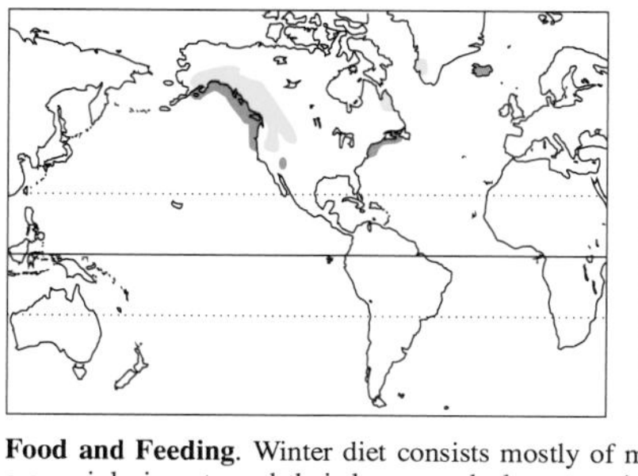

Descriptive notes. 42-53 cm; 737-1304 g. Male very similar to *B. clangula*, but has different pattern on scapulars and greater coverts, small crest, larger spot on cheek, and purple gloss to head; has eclipse plumage. Female even more similar but has brown neck, more yellow on bill (sometimes covering whole bill) and different head shape. Juvenile resembles female but initially has brownish iris.
Habitat. Breeds on freshwater lakes, pools and rivers in open or wooded country, from sea-level to c. 3000 m (Rocky Mts). Winters on larger, unfrozen lakes or brackish coastal lagoons; also on coast.
Food and Feeding. Winter diet consists mostly of molluscs and crustaceans, whereas summer foods are mainly insects and their larvae and plant material (seeds and vegetative parts of aquatic plants). Feeds principally by diving but may also dabble and upend in shallow waters.
Breeding. Starts Apr/May. In single pairs; nest lined with down, well-hidden among vegetation or in natural hole or crevice. Usually 8-11 eggs (6-14); incubation 28-30 days; chicks have dark brown down above, white below. Sexual maturity at c. 2 years.
Movements. Not truly migratory; some populations (e.g. Iceland, southern Rocky Mts) mostly sedentary, whereas others undertake longer trips to winter along Pacific coast of Alaska and Canada and Atlantic coast of NE North America. A few records in W Europe, possibly referring to escapes.
Status and Conservation. Not globally threatened. Entire world population probably in region of 200,000 breeding birds, of which c. 150,000 occur in western North America; Icelandic population estimated at c. 800 breeding pairs and apparently stable. No evidence that population of this species currently undergoing any major changes but presumably is, like *B. clangula*, highly sensitive to alterations in breeding habitat. Thus, where nest-sites less readily available (because of forest destruction), numbers presumably decreasing; in contrast wherever nestboxes provided in suitable habitat, they are promptly occupied by this species, which has increased densities or expanded range in such areas.

Bibliography. Armstrong (1983), Bauer & Glutz von Blotzheim (1969), Bellrose (1976), Bengtson (1971), Bent (1923-1925), Cramp & Simmons (1977), Eadie (1989), Erskine (1990), Gooders & Boyer (1986), Gudmundsson (1961), Humphrey (1955), Munro (1939), Myres (1959), Palmer (1976), Savard (1982, 1984, 1986), Savard & Eadie (1989), Terres (1980).

133. **Common Goldeneye**

Bucephala clangula

French: Garrot à oeil d'or **German**: Schellente **Spanish**: Porrón Osculado
Other common names: Goldeneye, Whistler

Taxonomy. *Anas Clangula* Linnaeus, 1758, Europe.
Sometimes placed in genus *Glaucionetta*. Infrequent hybridization with *B. islandica* in the wild. Validity of subspecies has been questioned. Two subspecies recognized.
Subspecies and Distribution.
B. c. clangula (Linnaeus, 1758) - N and C Europe, Asia E through USSR and N Mongolia to Kamchatka.
B. c. americana (Bonaparte, 1838) - Alaska to Labrador.

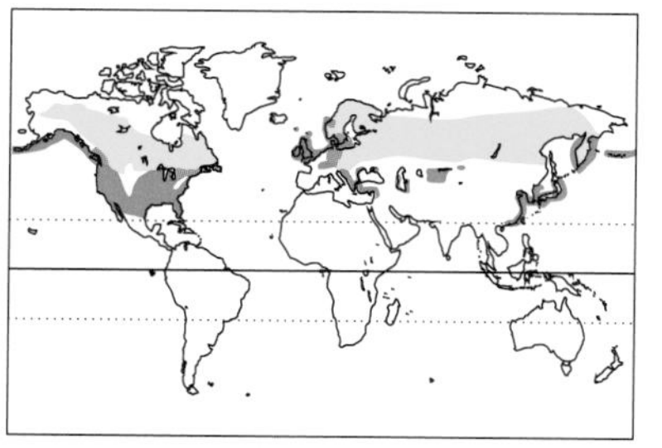

Descriptive notes. 42-50 cm; 770-996 g. Male has smaller and rounder white spot on cheek than *B. islandica*; green gloss on head; has eclipse plumage. Female differs from *B. islandica* in having white neck and different pattern of secondary coverts. Juvenile like female but generally darker on upperwing-coverts; brown iris. Subspecies *americana* separated by small differences in size.
Habitat. Breeds on freshwater lakes, pools and rivers surrounded by coniferous forest. In winter, on coastal lagoons, estuaries and inshore marine waters.
Food and Feeding. Chiefly aquatic invertebrates (molluscs, crustaceans, worms, insects and larvae), amphibians and small fish. Some plant material taken, mainly in autumn (seeds, roots and green parts of aquatic plants). Feeds mostly by diving; occasionally dabbles and upends in shallow waters.
Breeding. Starts Apr/May. In single pairs; nest with only down added, in tree-hollows, often in artificial nestboxes. Usually 8-11 eggs (5-13); incubation 29-30 days; chicks have blackish down above, white below; fledging 57-66 days. Sexual maturity at 2 years; oldest ringed bird 17 years old. Hatching success from 33% to over 80% in several studies.
Movements. Migratory; winters at sea in N of range, or at lower latitudes S to Florida, Mediterranean basin, S USSR and E China, occasionally further S. At times well inland (e.g. Central Europe); present all year in some areas of NW Europe.
Status and Conservation. Not globally threatened. North American spring population clearly exceeds 1,000,000 birds; winter counts in W Palearctic gave total of c. 320,000 birds in mid-1980's and numbers in Asia unknown but seemingly large. This species even more sensitive to habitat alterations than *B. islandica*, as its presence or absence in apparently suitable areas mostly depends on tree holes being available for it to nest in; thus, significant expansions of range and increases in numbers attained through nestbox erection programmes. In winter, main threat for this species from major oil incident near coast or from eating contaminated food, as rather large flocks often gather to feed at sewer outfalls.

Bibliography. Afton & Sayler (1982), Ali & Ripley (1978), Andersson & Eriksson (1982), Armstrong (1983), Bauer & Glutz von Blotzheim (1969), Beattie & Nudds (1989), Bellrose (1976), Bent (1923-1925), Blümel & Krause (1990), Brazil (1991), Brown *et al.* (1982), Carter (1958), Cramp & Simmons (1977), Dane & van der Kloot (1964), Dementiev & Gladkov (1952), Dow & Fredga (1983, 1984), Eriksson, K. (1980), Eriksson, M.O.G. (1982), Etchécopar & Hüe (1978), Géroudet (1972), Gooders & Boyer (1986), Grimmett & Jones (1989), Humphrey (1955), Kondratyev (1986), Kurilovich & Tarkhanova (1986), Monval & Pirot (1989), Nilsson (1965, 1969), Olney & Mills (1963), Palmer (1976), Perennou & Mundkur (1991), Roberts (1991), Savard (1984), Savard & Eadie (1989), Terres (1980), Zicus (1990b).

PLATE 50

inches 10
cm 25

♂ ♀ 134

♂ ♀ 135

136

♂ ♀ 137

♂ ♀ 138

♂ ♀ 139

♂ 140 ♀

♂ ♀ 141

♀ ssp *andina*
♂ ♀
ssp *jamaicensis*
♂ 142
ssp *ferruginea* ♂

♂ ♀ 143

♀ ♂ 144

♂ ♀ 145

♀
♂ 146

♂ ♀ 147

Genus *MERGUS* Linnaeus, 1758

134. **Hooded Merganser**
Mergus cucullatus

French: Harle couronné   **German**: Kappensäger   **Spanish**: Serreta Capuchona

Taxonomy. *Mergus cucullatus* Linnaeus, 1758, America = Virginia and Carolina *ex* Catesby.
Often placed in monospecific genus *Lophodytes*. Hybridization with other species of *Mergus* reported rarely in captivity. Monotypic.
Distribution. SE Alaska S to Oregon; SE Canada S to Mississippi valley.

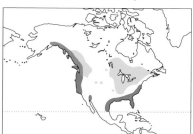

Descriptive notes. 42-50 cm; 453-879 g; wingspan 56-70 cm. Unmistakable. Male has eclipse plumage. Juvenile resembles female, with shorter crest and paler upperparts.
Habitat. Breeds on small lakes, pools and fast-flowing streams with clear waters in wooded country. Winters on larger lakes, rivers, brackish coastal lagoons and estuaries, but uncommon on marine waters.
Food and Feeding. Diet fairly diverse; mostly fish and aquatic invertebrates (crustaceans are often main food item; molluscs, insects and larvae), amphibians, grain and seeds and roots of aquatic plants. Feeds mostly by diving; also by head-dipping and by dabbling on surface.
Breeding. Starts Mar/Apr. In single pairs; nests in tree-hollows, nestboxes or ground cavities, with only down added. Usually 10-12 eggs (6-18); incubation 29-37 days; chicks have dark brown down above, mostly white below; fledging c. 71 days. Sexual maturity at 2 years. Nesting success of 74%, with hatching success of 90·7% in successful nests, in one study.
Movements. Migratory; winters along Pacific coast of North America, sometimes as far N as Alaska and S to Baja California; also along Atlantic coast, generally from Maine S through Florida and Gulf coast to Mexico; occasionally further S. Vagrant to NW Europe (mainly Britain).
Status and Conservation. Not globally threatened. Total world breeding population calculated at c. 76,000 individuals in mid-1970's, with no apparent signs of any major changes. However, method of calculation was rather indirect and so can be taken as indication of magnitude but not as too realistic estimate. Future of this species should not be looked at too optimistically, as it has suffered some reductions on breeding grounds (through forest destruction and pollution of stream waters); besides, although not many birds shot for sport, species subject to persecution by fish-farmers and anglers, allegedly because it destroys all fish wherever it occurs. Reinforcement of hunting regulations and a major nestbox erection programme should produce positive results soon.
Bibliography. Armstrong (1983), Bauer & Glutz von Blotzheim (1969), Bellrose (1976), Bent (1923-1925), Bouvier (1974), Cramp & Simmons (1977), Gooders & Boyer (1986), Humphrey (1955), Johnsgard (1961b), Kennamer *et al.* (1988), Kolbe (1989), Livezey (1989b), Mallory & Weatherhead (1990), Morse *et al.* (1969), Palmer (1976), Zicus (1990a).

135. **Smew**
Mergus albellus

French: Harle piette   **German**: Zwergsäger   **Spanish**: Serreta Chica

Taxonomy. *Mergus Albellus* Linnaeus, 1758, Europe.
Often placed in monospecific genus *Mergellus*. Monotypic.
Distribution. Sweden eastwards to E Siberia.

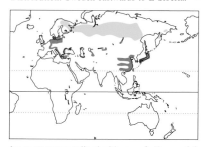

Descriptive notes. 35-44 cm; 515-935 g. wingspan 55-69 cm. Unmistakable. Male has eclipse plumage. Juvenile resembles female, but central wing coverts have brownish edges.
Habitat. Freshwater lakes, pools, rivers and muskegs in taiga zone during breeding season. In winter, on larger lakes, brackish coastal lagoons, estuaries; uncommonly on open sea.
Food and Feeding. Aquatic invertebrates, mainly insects and their larvae, amphibians and some plant material; also fish, mainly in winter and early spring, both in fresh and salt water. Feeds mostly by diving from surface.
Breeding. Starts Apr/May. In single pairs or loose groups; nest lined with some feathers and down, in tree-hollows, often in artificial nestboxes. Usually 7-9 eggs (5-11); incubation 26-28 days; chicks have sooty black down above, white below. Sexual maturity at 2 years.
Movements. Migratory; winters W and C Europe, E Mediterranean basin, Black Sea, S USSR, Middle East, E China, Korea and Japan. Occasionally further S, as sometimes displaced by severely cold winters.
Status and Conservation. Not globally threatened. Not uncommon, but local, winter visitor to Japan, where has bred. Partial winter censuses in 1991, yielded 205 birds in South Korea, 1405 in China and 1646 in Turkmenistan. No global estimates of population size available, but winter population in W Palearctic estimated at c. 80,000 birds in mid-1980's. Much larger numbers presumably winter further E, in several parts of Asia and particularly W Siberia. No indication of significant change in numbers, but these reputed to be much affected locally by availability of nest-sites in suitable habitat. On passage and in winter, subject to certain amount of hunting pressure and exposed to oil pollution where it occurs in numbers in coastal waters.

Bibliography. Ali & Ripley (1978), Allen (1991), Bauer & Glutz von Blotzheim (1969), Bent (1923-1925), Bianki (1989), Brazil (1991), Brickell (1988), Brown *et al*. (1982), Cramp & Simmons (1977), Dennis (1987), Dementiev & Gladkov (1952), Doornbos (1979), Géroudet (1972), Gooders & Boyer (1986), Goodman (1989), Grimmett & Jones (1989), Harrison (1988), Hebb (1991), Humphrey (1955), Kolbe (1989), Kondratyev (1986), Livezey (1989b), Monval & Pirot (1989), Nilsson (1974), Owen (1977), Palmer (1976), Perennou & Mundkur (1991), Roberts (1991).

136. **Brazilian Merganser**
Mergus octosetaceus

French: Harle huppard   **German**: Dunkelsäger   **Spanish**: Serreta Brasileña

Taxonomy. *Mergus octosetaceus* Vieillot, 1817, Brazil.
Monotypic.
Distribution. SE Brazil, E Paraguay (Alto Paraná), NE Argentina (Misiones).

Descriptive notes. 49-56 cm. Sexes similar, but female somewhat browner above, with smaller crest and shorter bill. Juvenile much duller and browner, lacking black on head and neck, and having little or no crest; often lacks barring on breast and abdomen.
Habitat. Rapid, torrential streams and fast-flowing rivers surrounded by dense tropical forest.
Food and Feeding. Mostly fish, complemented with molluscs and insects and their larvae. Feeds usually in pairs, almost exclusively by diving, often in areas of rapids.
Breeding. Little information available. Season apparently starts Jun (rainy season). In single pairs; nests in tree-hollows.
Movements. Mostly sedentary, with only small-scale movements recorded; presumably maintains territory all year round.
Status and Conservation. INDETERMINATE. Small, little-known population, widely scattered over range and everywhere rare. Thought to be extinct until rediscovered in 1948. Recently recorded in Chapada dos Veadeiros National Park, and also in Sena da Canastra National Park, one of most protected parks in Brazil, with breeding population of only 2 pairs in 1990. Main Argentinian population threatened in Misiones by hydro-electric development and other forms of habitat disturbance. Legally protected in Brazil, but small numbers presumably still killed by hunters elsewhere. Possible establishment of captive breeding programme should be considered. In any case, urgent need to halt habitat destruction and establish network of well protected reserves with suitable streams and rivers.
Bibliography. Bartmann (1988), Bertonatti *et al*. (1991), Blake (1977), Collar & Andrew (1988), Forcelli (1987), Granizo & Hayes (1991), Greenway (1967), Hartmann (1988), Hellmayr & Conover (1948), Humphrey (1955), Johnson & Chebez (1985), King (1978/79), Livezey (1989b), Mountfort (1988), Partridge (1956), de la Peña (1986), Pinto (1964), Ruschi (1979), Scott & Carbonell (1986), Sick (1984), Sick & Teixeira (1979), Yamashita & Valle (1990).

137. **Red-breasted Merganser**
Mergus serrator

French: Harle huppé   **German**: Mittelsäger   **Spanish**: Serreta Mediana

Taxonomy. *Mergus Serrator* Linnaeus, 1758, Europe.
Greenland population has been assigned separate subspecies, *schioleri*, but doubtfully valid. Monotypic.
Distribution. Most of N North America, S to Great Lakes; Greenland, Iceland and most of N Eurasia, S to Britain, NE China and N Japan.

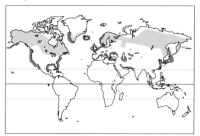

Descriptive notes. 52-58 cm; 780-1350 g; wingspan 70-86 cm. Male has eclipse plumage. Female resembles that of *M. merganser*, but crest and pattern of secondaries different; white on throat reaches breast. Juvenile resembles female but with shorter crest and plumage generally darker grey.
Habitat. Breeds on rather deep lakes and small rivers, often, but not necessarily, in wooded country. Winters mostly at sea, frequenting both inshore and offshore waters, estuaries, bays and brackish lagoons.
Food and Feeding. Small, shoaling, freshwater or marine fish; also aquatic invertebrates and some plant material. Feeds by diving from surface after scanning with head submerged; occasionally on surface.
Breeding. Starts Apr/Jun. In single pairs or larger groups, locally in colonies; nest made of grass, lined with down, on ground, generally well concealed, or in natural cavity or burrow. Usually 8-10 eggs (6-14); incubation 31-32 days; chicks have brownish down above, white below; fledging 60-65 days. Sexual maturity at 2 years. Hatching success of 77% in one study in Finland.
Movements. Partially migratory; winters along Atlantic and Pacific coasts of North America, Mediterranean basin, S USSR, E China, Korea and Japan; present all year round in much of NW Europe, Iceland and W Greenland. Occasionally further S; males tend to remain closer to breeding grounds than females or immatures.
Status and Conservation. Not globally threatened. No total estimates of population size available, but North American spring population calculated at c. 237,000 birds in mid-1970's and c. 150,000 estimated to winter in W Palearctic in mid-1980's; breeding area seems to be slowly expanding S in W Europe. Uncounted but potentially large population winters in various parts of Asia, particularly in Far East. Winters in considerable numbers on coasts of Gulf of California, where numerous localities each hold several hundred birds; notable maximum of 5040 in Topolobampo Lagoons, Sinaloa, and maximum of 2770 in period 1980-1984 in Agiabampo Lagoons. Although not frequent

---

On following pages: 138. Scaly-sided Merganser (*Mergus squamatus*); 139. Goosander (*Mergus merganser*); 140. Black-headed Duck (*Heteronetta atricapilla*); 141. Masked Duck (*Oxyura dominica*); 142. Ruddy Duck (*Oxyura jamaicensis*); 143. White-headed Duck (*Oxyura leucocephala*); 144. Maccoa Duck (*Oxyura maccoa*); 145. Argentine Blue-billed Duck (*Oxyura vittata*); 146. Australian Blue-billed Duck (*Oxyura australis*); 147. Musk Duck (*Biziura lobata*).

quarry species, subject to persecution by fish-farmers and anglers as accused of destroying all fish in rivers and streams they inhabit. Water pollution and human alterations of breeding habitat (construction of dams, forest destruction) also important threats for this species.

Bibliography. Ali & Ripley (1978), Bauer & Glutz von Blotzheim (1969), Bellrose (1976), Bengtson (1971), Bent (1923-1925), Brazil (1991), Brickell (1988), Brown *et al.* (1982), Cramp & Simmons (1977), Curth (1954), Dementiev & Gladkov (1952), Etchécopar & Hüe (1978), Géroudet (1972), Grimmett & Jones (1989), Gooders & Boyer (1986), (1988), Humphrey (1955), Johnsgard (1975), Kolbe (1989), Kondratyev (1986), Livezey (1989b), Monval & Pirot (1989), Palmer (1976), Perennou & Mundkur (1991), Roberts (1991), Tasker *et al.* (1987), Terres (1980), Young & Titman (1988), Zhao Zheng-jie *et al.* (1988).

138. **Scaly-sided Merganser**
Mergus squamatus

French: Harle écaillé   **German**: Schuppensäger   **Spanish**: Serreta China
Other common names: Chinese Merganser

Taxonomy. *Mergus squamatus* Gould, 1864, China.
Monotypic.
Distribution. Extreme SE Siberia, NE China and N Korea.

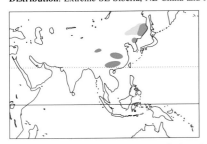

Descriptive notes. 52-62 cm. Male has eclipse plumage. Some females may have more uniform, unmarked white flanks, than depicted bird; patterning on sides and flanks differentiates female from that of *M. merganser* and other species of *Mergus*. Juvenile probably similar to female.
Habitat. Well-forested, fast-flowing mountain rivers and rapid streams in taiga zone during breeding season. Winters on larger lakes, more sluggish rivers and lagoons, but shuns coastal waters.
Food and Feeding. Although little information available, most probably fish form base of diet. as in other *Mergus*. Presumably feeds mainly by diving.
Breeding. Little known. During local spring. In single pairs; nests in tree-hollows. About 10 eggs.
Movements. Partially migratory; in normal winters probably only travels downstream of breeding rivers and mostly remains within same zone. However, occasionally more dispersive, occurring S to Korea and E China. Has occurred in Japan, N Viet Nam and N Burma.
Status and Conservation. RARE. Poorly known, population probably quite small. In USSR, maximum population estimate in Primorskii Krai, one of main breeding areas, c. 1000 breeding pairs; in early 1980's, estimated 482 birds in 3000 km of R Bikin, where intense hunting (around 100 taken annually); one pair, at most, seen every 3·8 km² in Lazovsk protection area, and along Kievka Valley; main breeding site was R Iman, now threatened by high levels of disturbance (logging), and pollution (gold-mining). In Khabarovsk region, c. 100 pairs estimated in 1981. Records indicate that the Soviet population has suffered a drastic decline over past 20 years; has disappeared from some regions and in other areas has dropped to 10% or even 5% of former estimated numbers. In Chonpaek Mountains, NE China, average 3·6 birds per 5 km of river; 28 birds counted wintering in China during 1990 partial census. In North Korea, probably breeds in Mayang Chosuji, where a pair apparently displaying was observed in 1986; the area is protected, and fishing and tree felling prohibited. Throughout most of range, projects for construction of dams, felling of old hollow trees, disturbance of rivers by lumber-carrying motorboats and possibly predation by feral American mink (*Mustela vison*) pose additional threats.

Bibliography. Bocharnikov (1990), Brazil (1991), Collar & Andrew (1988), Dementiev & Gladkov (1952), Etchécopar & Hüe (1978), Gooders & Boyer (1986), He Jing-jie (1985), Hugues (1991), Humphrey (1955), Kazama (1988), King (1978/79), Kolomiitsev (1986), Liu Chang-jiang (1989), Litvinenko (1985), Livezey (1989b), Mountfort (1988), de Schauensee (1984), Shibnev (1985), Sonobe & Izawa (1987), Xu Lin-mu (1988), Zhao Zheng-jie *et al.* (1979).

139. **Goosander**
Mergus merganser

French: Harle bièvre   **German**: Gänsesäger   **Spanish**: Serreta Grande
Other common names: Common Merganser

Taxonomy. *Mergus Merganser* Linnaeus, 1758, Europe.
Race *comatus* synonymous with *orientalis*. Hybridization with *Aythya americana* recorded in captivity. Three subspecies recognized.
Subspecies and Distribution.
M. m. merganser Linnaeus, 1758 - Palearctic, from Iceland E to Kamchatka, S to C Europe, NE China and N Japan.
M. m. orientalis Gould, 1845 - C Asia, from NE Afghanistan E through Tibet and Himalayas to W China.
M. m. americanus Cassin, 1852 - North America, from Alaska to Newfoundland, S to N and W USA.

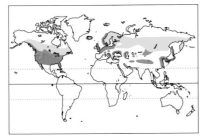

Descriptive notes. 58-66 cm; 898-2160 g; wingspan 82-97 cm. Male has eclipse plumage. Female resemble that of *M. serrator* and *M. squamatus*, but larger and with different pattern of secondaries; white chin; brown of head and upperneck sharply demarcated from white lower neck. Juvenile resembles female, but duller, less distinctly patterned and with shorter neck. Subspecies based on small differences: *orientalis* larger, with thinner bill; *americanus* has darker base to bill, squarer head, and bases of greater coverts form an obvious black band.
Habitat. Breeds on freshwater lakes, pools and in upper reaches of rivers, generally in vicinity of trees. Winters on larger, unfrozen lakes and rivers, lagoons and brackish marshes; uncommonly on coast.
Food and Feeding. Mainly fish; also aquatic invertebrates (molluscs, crustaceans, worms, insects and larvae), amphibians, small mammals and birds; little plant material taken. Feeds mostly by diving from surface, generally after scanning with head submerged; occasionally on surface and may upend.

Breeding. Starts Mar-May. In single pairs or loose groups; nests in tree hole, nestbox or other cavity, with only down added. Usually 8-12 eggs (6-17); incubation 30-32 days; chicks have greyish brown down above, white below; fledging 60-70 days. Sexual maturity at 2 years. Averages of 10·8 ducklings at hatching and 6·8 at fledging in one study in Finland.
Movements. Partially migratory; northernmost breeders descend to winter at lower latitudes, occurring S to Mexico, Mediterranean basin, S USSR, N India and SE Asia, occasionally further S. Breeders in more temperate regions mainly sedentary, usually travelling only short distances.
Status and Conservation. Not globally threatened. North American winter population estimated at c. 165,000 birds in mid 1970's, while 110,000-160,000 estimated to winter in W Palearctic in mid 1980's; unrecorded but seemingly large numbers winter in various parts of Asia. The well-studied populations (North American, W European) seem currently stable or increasing slightly, perhaps recovering from earlier declines caused by human alteration of breeding habitat. Has increased in British Isles, with 2000-3000 pairs in Britain and Ireland. In late Jan 1988, 3000 wintering in R Han, Seoul, South Korea. Also winters in considerable numbers in Japan, where generally uncommon, but locally common, and in China. Still subject to persecution by anglers and fish-farmers, who accuse this (and other fish-eating ducks) of depleting fish stocks wherever they establish a territory.

Bibliography. Ali & Ripley (1978), Anderson & Timken (1972), Bauer & Glutz von Blotzheim (1969), Bellrose (1976), Bent (1923-1925), Brazil (1991), Brickell (1988), Cramp & Simmons (1977), Dementiev & Gladkov (1952), Eriksson & Niittylä (1985), Erskine (1971a, 1971b), Etchécopar & Hüe (1978), Géroudet (1972), Gooders & Boyer (1986), Grimmett & Jones (1989), Hansen (1976a, 1976b, 1980a, 1980b), Harrison (1988), Hofer & Marti (1988), Humphrey (1955), Kiff (1989), Kolbe (1989), Latta & Sharkey (1966), Little & Furness (1985), Livezey (1989b), Meek & Little (1977, 1980), Monval & Pirot (1989), Nilsson (1966), Palmer (1976), Perennou & Mundkur (1991), Roberts (1991), Schmidt, G.A.J. (1980), Sjöberg (1980), Terres (1980), Timken & Anderson (1969), Townsend (1916), Wang Zhong-yu (1984), White (1957).

Tribe OXYURINI
Genus *HETERONETTA*   Salvadori, 1865

140. **Black-headed Duck**
Heteronetta atricapilla

French: Hétéronette à tête noire   **German**: Kuckucksente   **Spanish**: Pato Rinconero

Taxonomy. *Anas atricapilla* Merrem, 1841, Buenos Aires.
Considered to be a link between dabbling ducks and stifftails. Monotypic.
Distribution. C Chile to Paraguay, S to Buenos Aires Province, Argentina.

Descriptive notes. 35-40 cm; 513-565 g. Male sometimes has white patch on throat. Juvenile resembles female but is more rufous above, more yellowish and less mottled below.
Habitat. Swamps, lakes, pools and marshes of permanent fresh waters with abundant emergent vegetation in open or thinly forested country.
Food and Feeding. Diet formed mainly by seeds and vegetative parts of aquatic plants; also aquatic invertebrates (especially molluscs). Feeds by dabbling on surface, head-dipping and upending in shallow waters, and by diving; often filters surface water on mud near shoreline.
Breeding. Adult birds are paired Sept-Dec. Only member of Anatidae that is totally parasitic; lays eggs in nests of other waterfowl (often 2 in each nest), particularly of coots (*Fulica*) and Rosy-billed Pochard (*Netta peposaca*). Young hatch in c. 21 days and can forage for themselves a few hours afterwards, becoming independent almost immediately.
Movements. Partially migratory; southernmost breeding birds disperse northwards in winter, occurring as far N as Bolivia and S Brazil. Other populations chiefly sedentary, as present all year round in breeding grounds.
Status and Conservation. Not globally threatened. Apparently still fairly common but very sensitive to loss of permanent marshes through drainage or pollution. In Jul 1990 censuses, with 26 birds, represented 0·1% of total identified Anatidae in Uruguay, 363 individuals (c. 0·8%) in Argentina and 90 birds (c. 1·4%) in Chile. Only significant concentrations known are maximum of 80-100 in Etruria Lagoons, and maximum of 500 in Bañados del Río Saladillo, Córdoba Province, Argentina. Requires reduction in hunting pressure and establishment of suitable protected areas.

Bibliography. Belton (1984), Blake (1977), Carp (1991), Hellmayr & Conover (1948), Johnson (1965, 1967), Nores & Yzurieta (1980), de la Peña (1986), Raikow (1970), Ruschi (1979), Scott & Carbonell (1986), Sick (1984), Weller (1967b, 1968b).

Genus *OXYURA*   Bonaparte, 1828

141. **Masked Duck**
Oxyura dominica

French: Erismature routoutou   **German**: Maskenruderente   **Spanish**: Malvasía Enmascarada
Other common names: White-winged Lake Duck

Taxonomy. *Anas dominica* Linnaeus, 1766, South America = Santo Domingo *ex* Brisson.
Often placed in monospecific genus *Nomonyx*. Monotypic.

Distribution. West Indies and Mexico S to NW Peru and E of Andes to NE Argentina.

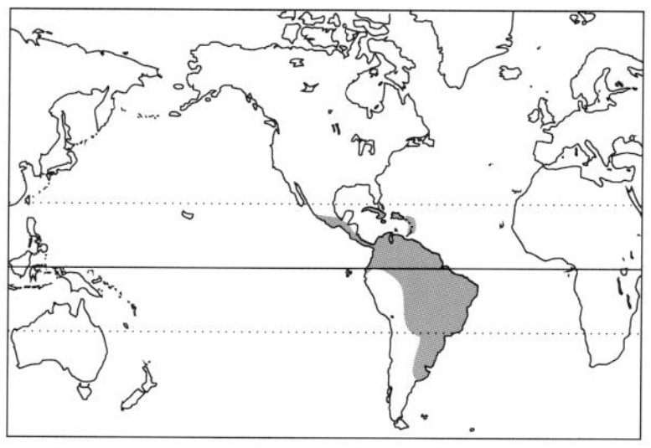

Descriptive notes. 30-36 cm; 339-406 g. Most distinctive member of *Oxyura*; unique, with large white patch on upperwing, conspicuous in flight. Male has strongly spotted flanks and upperparts, chestnut nape and black tip of bill; has eclipse plumage, similar to that of female. Female separable from other *Oxyura* females by small size and by two characteristic dark bands in facial pattern. Juvenile resembles female.

Habitat. Freshwater lakes, pools, swamps and marshes with abundant emergent and floating vegetation and surrounded by dense tree cover; also occurs in mangrove swamps.

Food and Feeding. Chiefly seeds, roots, tubers and vegetative parts of grasses, sedges and aquatic plants; also aquatic invertebrates (insects, crustaceans). Feeds mostly by diving.

Breeding. Starts Nov/Dec. In single pairs; nest is made of reeds or other plants, well hidden in dense vegetation. 3-6 eggs; chicks have dark brown down with striped face pattern.

Movements. Mostly sedentary, but subject to some wide-ranging dispersive movements when it may occur far beyond breeding range; not uncommonly recorded in southern USA (Florida and Texas, where has bred) and occasionally further N in eastern North America (as far as Vermont).

Status and Conservation. Not globally threatened. Widespread and rather uncommon; secretive habits make it seem rarer. Only notable figures available: up to 500 in winter on Jocotal Lagoon, El Salvador, and 80-100 in Bajos Submeridionales, NE Argentina. Like other stifftails, most sensitive to alterations of habitat (particularly through wetland drainage) and to human pressure; may desert area as soon as this becomes too intense.

Bibliography. Bellrose (1976), Belton (1984), Bent (1923-1925), Biaggi (1983), Blake (1977), Carp (1991), Evans, P.G.H. (1990), Fjeldså & Krabbe (1990), Gómez-Dallmeier & Cringan (1989), Gooders & Boyer (1986), Hellmayr & Conover (1948), Hilty & Brown (1986), Howell & Webb (1992), Jenni & Gambs (1974), Johnsgard (1975), Johnsgard & Hagemeyer (1969), Monroe (1968), Navas & Bo (1991), Nores & Yzurieta (1980), Palmer (1976), de la Peña (1986), Ridgely & Gwynne (1989), Ruschi (1979), de Schauensee & Phelps (1978), Scott & Carbonell (1986), Sick (1984), Slud (1964), Stockton (1978), Wetmore (1965).

142. Ruddy Duck

Oxyura jamaicensis

French: Erismature rousse **German**: Schwarzkopf-Ruderente **Spanish**: Malvasía Canela
Other common names: Andean Duck, Peruvian Ruddy Duck (*ferruginea*)

Taxonomy. *Anas jamaicensis* Gmelin, 1789, Jamaica.
Race *ferruginea* often considered a full species; race *andina*, intermediate between *jamaicensis* and *ferruginea*, might be of hybrid origin. Population of North America has been assigned separate subspecies *rubida*, though doubtfully valid. Three subspecies normally recognized.

Subspecies and Distribution.
O. j. jamaicensis (Gmelin, 1789) - Canada, from British Columbia to Manitoba, and S to California and Texas; also scattered in NE USA; West Indies.
O. j. andina Lehmann, 1946 - Andes of C and N Colombia.
O. j. ferruginea (Eyton, 1838) - Andes of S Colombia southwards to Tierra del Fuego.
Introduced (*jamaicensis*) in W England, where well established and spreading.

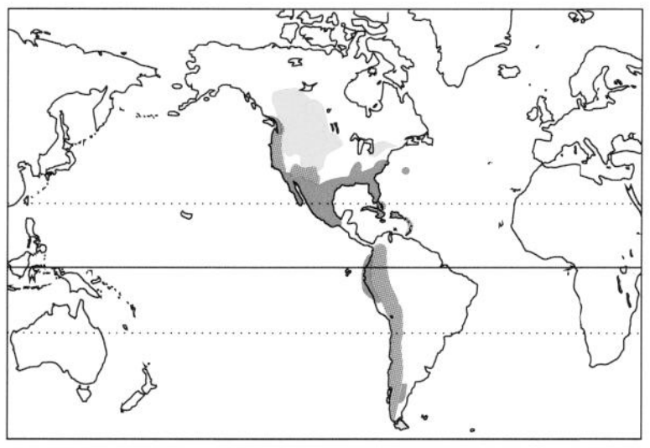

Descriptive notes. 35-43 cm; 310-795 g; wingspan 53-62 cm. Lower half of male's face characteristically white. Female more rufous than in other *Oxyura*, and has rufous marks on scapulars. Male eclipse plumage similar to female; both sexes become duller in non-breeding plumage. Juvenile as non-breeding female, but paler and less boldly patterned. Subspecies *ferruginea* larger and darker; male has black face and white chin. Subspecies *andina* intermediate between *ferruginea* and nominate, but marked individual variation.

Habitat. Freshwater swamps, lakes, pools and marshes with emergent vegetation and areas of open water. Outside breeding season, often on larger lakes, brackish lagoons and estuaries.

Food and Feeding. Aquatic invertebrates (mainly insects and their larvae but also crustaceans, molluscs, worms) and seeds of aquatic plants. Feeds mostly by sieving bottom debris while diving; also dabbles on surface.

Breeding. Starts Apr/May in N of range; apparently most of year in Colombia and coastal Peru. In single pairs; nest is bowl of vegetation, sometimes lined with down, on ground or on water, in dense vegetation. Usually 6-10 eggs (5-15); incubation 25-26 days; chicks have dark grey down above, paler below; fledging 50-55 days. Sexual maturity at 2 years, occasionally 1. Nest success between 55% and 88% in several studies.

Movements. Partially migratory; North American breeders mostly depart breeding grounds to winter in S or near coast. Other populations mainly sedentary or only subject to small-scale movements.

Status and Conservation. Not globally threatened. Locally common. North American population estimated at c. 600,000 breeding birds in mid 1970's; up to 105,000 winter in Mexico; also quite common resident in Caribbean. Has declined recently due to habitat destruction, and to exposure to oil spills in winter quarters; also subject to hunting pressure. Feral British population c. 2400 in late 1980's, after large increase since its establishment. Subspecies *andina*, of Colombia, scarce and local within its restricted range, and declining. Subspecies *ferruginea* uncommon to fairly common, with significant numbers in some places, e.g. estimate of 2000-3000 in 1977-1979 censuses at L Junín, WC Peru. In Bolivia, amongst most common nesting birds at L Uru-Uru, Oruro Department; 500 in Jan 1984 at L Corami, and 2550 at L Alalay, Cochabamba Department.

Bibliography. Barcelona (1976), Bellrose (1976), Bent (1923-1925), Bergan *et al.* (1989), Biaggi (1983), Blake (1977), Briggs (1988), Carp (1991), Cooch (1964), Cramp & Simmons (1977), Evans, P.G.H. (1990), Fjeldså (1986c), Fjeldså & Krabbe (1990), Gooders & Boyer (1986), Gray (1980), Harrison (1988), Hellmayr & Conover (1948), Hilty & Brown (1986), Hoppe *et al.* (1986), Hudson (1976), Johnson (1965), Joyner (1975, 1977), Lagerquist & Ankney (1989), Lever (1987), Misterek (1974), Palmer (1976), Raikow (1970), Scott & Carbonell (1986), Siegfried (1973b, 1976a, 1976b), Siegfried, Burger & Caldwell (1976), Stockton (1978), Terres (1980), Tome (1981, 1989), Went (1975), Woodin & Swanson (1989).

143. White-headed Duck

Oxyura leucocephala

French: Erismature à tête blanche **Spanish**: Malvasía Cabeciblanca
German: Weißkopf-Ruderente
Other common names: White-headed Stifftail

Taxonomy. *Anas leucocephala* Scopoli, 1769, no locality, but probably northern Italy.
Considered by some to form superspecies with *O. jamaicensis*, sometimes including other species, but probably more closely linked to *O. maccoa*; relationships between *Oxyura* species uncertain. Hybridization with *O. jamaicensis* in the wild, producing fertile progeny, has occurred in S Spain, where birds from introduced English population have arrived. Monotypic.

Distribution. SW Mediterranean basin to extreme NW China; main population in S USSR. Formerly more widespread in Mediterranean area.

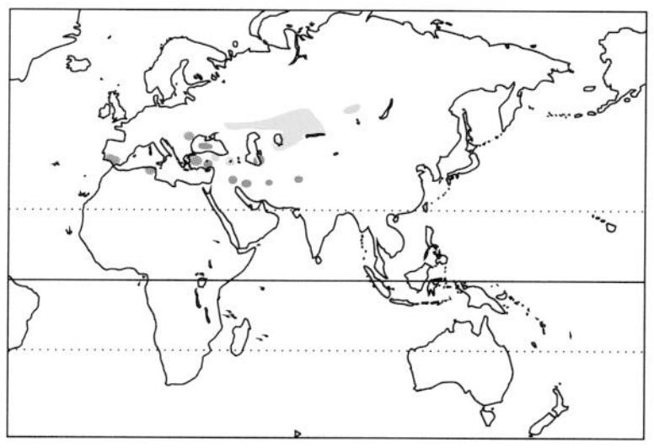

Descriptive notes. 43-48 cm; 510-820 g; wingspan 62-70 cm. Legs can be reddish. According to descriptions, male can have yellow iris. Female distinguished from other related species by shape of head and more robust bill. Both sexes have non-breeding plumage, but male retains white face; female goes duskier. Juvenile resembles non-breeding female but is duller and paler.

Habitat. Small lakes, pools, marshes and lagoons of brackish or fresh waters, bordered by thick cover of vegetation, in arid country. Outside breeding season, also on saline lakes and larger lagoons.

Food and Feeding. Chiefly seeds, leaves and other green parts of aquatic plants; also aquatic invertebrates (insects and their larvae, molluscs, crustaceans). Feeds mostly by diving; sometimes dabbles on surface.

Breeding. Starts mainly May. In single pairs; nest is platform of reed stems and leaves, lined with down, in dense vegetation, on ground or over water, often in old nests of other waterbirds (*Fulica*, *Aythya*, *Tachybaptus*). Usually 5-8 eggs (up to 10); incubation 22-24 days; chicks have dark brown down above, white below; fledging 60-70 days.

Movements. Partially migratory; breeders in Mediterranean area chiefly sedentary, only subject to small-scale dispersion during summer drought. Oriental population strongly migratory, winters at a few sites in S Caspian Sea, Middle East and Pakistan; rarely to NW India.

Status and Conservation. VULNERABLE. CITES II. In recent years, total population has appeared relatively stable, with only c. 14,000 after sharp decline in last few decades which caused generalized rarefication of the species and disappearance from several Mediterranean countries. Western subpopulation undergoing increase and estimated at c. 1000 birds, 500 of which occur in Algeria and Tunisia. No recent breeding records in Morocco. In Spain, the 400 recorded in 1950 had declined to only 22 in 1977, with recovery by protection of last outposts, up to 545 individuals in 1991; currently threatened by hybridization with *O. jamaicensis*, which was introduced to England and is currently expanding southwards. The eastern subpopulation, of c. 12,000 concentrated above all in Turkey and USSR, mainly Kazakhstan, although only 700-900 pairs recorded in USSR in 1984. Largest wintering concentrations in Turkey and Pakistan, and L Ucchali, in Punjab is important for this species, with concentrations of up to 667 birds in Jan 1987. 3520 counted in winter 1991 census in Azerbaydzhan. Threatened by loss of favourable habitat (especially in Turkey, USSR and Pakistan), and by excessive hunting disturbance at primary wintering grounds. Urgent need to establish network of reserves throughout range. Introduced in Hungary and Sardinia through captive breeding programmes.

Bibliography. Ali & Ripley (1978), Amat & Sánchez (1982), Anon. (1991d), Anstey (1989a, 1989b), Arenas & Torres (1988, 1991), Bauer & Glutz von Blotzheim (1969), Brickell (1988), Brown *et al.* (1982), Castro & Nevado (1990), Collar & Andrew (1988), Cramp & Simmons (1977), Dementiev & Gladkov (1952), Dollinger (1988), Dolz *et al.* (1991), Etchécopar & Hüe (1964, 1978), Géroudet (1972), Gooders & Boyer (1986), Grimmett & Jones (1989), Hüe & Etchécopar (1970), Jacobs & Ochando (1979), Kuan Kuan-hsun & Cheng Tso-hin (1962), Ledant *et al.* (1981), Matthews & Evans (1974), Monval & Pirot (1989), Ounsted (1988), Paz (1987), Perennou & Mundkur (1991), Roberts (1991), Torres & Arenas (1985), Torres, Arenas & Ayala (1986), Torres, Raya *et al.* (1985).

144. Maccoa Duck

Oxyura maccoa

French: Erismature maccoa **German**: Afrikaruderente **Spanish**: Malvasía Maccoa

Taxonomy. *Erismatura maccoa* Eyton, 1838, Indian Isles = South Africa, *ex* A. Smith.
Considered by some to be more closely linked to *O. leucocephala* than to the more externally similar *O. vittata* and *O. australis*. Monotypic.

Distribution. E Africa, from Ethiopia and E Sudan to N Tanzania; S Africa, from Namibia and Zimbabwe to Cape Province.

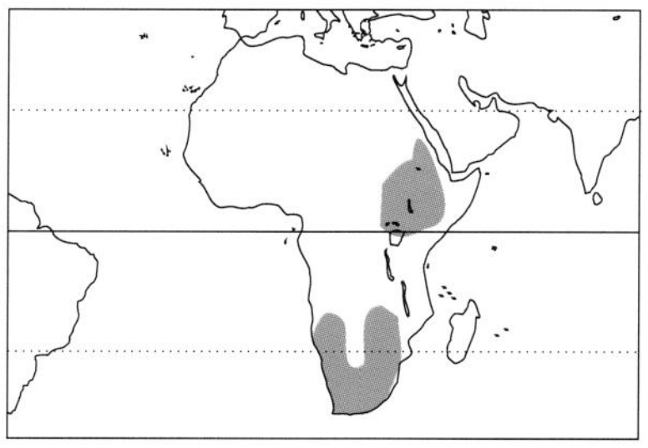

Descriptive notes. 46-51 cm; 516-820 g or more. Male has hindneck and throat black, though foreneck is chestnut, as most of rest of body; head and bill squarer than in *O. jamaicensis*; nail paler; no white on chin; rump spotted with brown. Male in eclipse plumage resembles female. Female has no rufous on scapulars; barring on flanks narrower and more buff-coloured than in *O. jamaicensis*. Juvenile resembles female.

Habitat. Shallow bodies of fresh waters with extensive bordering reedbeds and areas of open water, from sea-level (rare) to c. 3000 m. Wanders about over larger lakes and brackish lagoons after breeding season.

Food and Feeding. Seeds of aquatic plants, plant debris and aquatic invertebrates (insects and their larvae, crustaceans). Feeds almost exclusively by sieving bottom ooze while diving.

Breeding. Season variable according to locality and water levels. In single pairs or loose groups; nest is made with adjacent plant matter, lined with down, over water, in thick vegetation; also in old nests of coots (*Fulica*) and grebes. 4-8 eggs; incubation 25-27 days; chicks have brown down above, white below.

Movements. Mainly sedentary, with only small-scale dispersive movements (mainly South African population), mostly linked to availability of suitable habitat during dry season drought conditions.
Status and Conservation. Not globally threatened. Occurs at fairly low density. Considered fairly common within northern part of range, rare on coastal regions; locally numerous on inland lakes in Kenya and N Tanzania, especially those that are alkaline. Within southern part of range, considered generally uncommon, though locally common; in SW Cape, South Africa, can be locally common resident, but then suddenly disappear completely. Adaptable, colonizing artificial dams and reservoirs. Subject to little hunting pressure.
Bibliography. Brickell (1988), Britton (1980), Brown & Britton (1980), Brown *et al.* (1982), Burger & Berruti (1977), Clark, A. (1964, 1974b, 1974d, 1978b), Clancey (1967), Johnsgard (1968b), Macnae (1959), Mackworth-Praed & Grant (1957-1973), Maclean (1985), Oatley (1971), Perennou (1991b), Santucci & Geber (1971), Siegfried (1968c, 1976a), Siegfried & van der Merwe (1975), Siegfried, Burger & Caldwell (1976), Siegfried, Burger & Frost (1976), Siegfried, Burger & van der Merwe (1976).

145. Argentine Blue-billed Duck
Oxyura vittata

French: Erismature orné   **German**: Bindenruderente   **Spanish**: Malvasía Argentina
Other common names: Lake Duck, Argentine Blue-bill, Argentine Ruddy Duck

Taxonomy. *Erismatura vittata* Philippi, 1860, Chile.
Considered by some to form superspecies with *O. australis*. Monotypic.
Distribution. Most of Chile and Argentina (except highlands), northwards to SE Brazil.

Descriptive notes. 36-46 cm; c. 560-610 g. Male resembles that of *O. jamaicensis ferruginea* but is smaller, lacking white on chin; body colour is slightly darker and black on head continues around whole of neck. Female has more patterned flanks than *O. jamaicensis* and vermiculated reddish buff back. Male non-breeding and juvenile resemble female.
Habitat. Shallow freshwater lakes, small pools and marshes with extensive bordering vegetation. Outside breeding season, also on larger lakes and lagoons.
Food and Feeding. Little information available, but diet presumably based on seeds, plant remains and small aquatic invertebrates. Feeds by sieving bottom debris while diving.
Breeding. Starts Oct. In single pairs or loose groups; nest is flat platform over water, in dense vegetation. 3-5 eggs; chicks have blackish down with white band below eye and pale throat.
Movements. Partially migratory; birds of southernmost populations leave breeding grounds to winter in more temperate regions, occurring as far N as central Brazil and Paraguay. Other populations largely sedentary, with only small-scale movements. Occasionally subject to wide-ranging dispersal during severe droughts.
Status and Conservation. Not globally threatened. Generally local and uncommon throughout its range. Appears only relatively common in N Argentina. Breeds in small numbers in Tierra del Fuego. Population difficult to evaluate due to bird's secretive habits. Not under much hunting pressure, but threatened by habitat transformation; aquatic vegetation being destroyed by fishermen on La Margarita Lagoon, Córdoba Province, where up to 40 birds recorded in 1974 and 1977 censuses; on Blanca Lagoon, Neuquén Province, also in Argentina, 80 individuals counted in Jan/Feb 1982 census, likewise threatened by reduction in aquatic vegetation, in this case due to cattle-rearing activities. Network of reserves with unchanged wetlands should be established to assure continuity of the species.
Bibliography. Blake (1977), Carp (1991), Fjeldså & Krabbe (1990), Hellmayr & Conover (1948), Humphrey *et al.* (1970), Johnsgard (1967), Johnsgard & Nordeen (1981), Johnson (1965), Narosky & Yzurieta (1987), Nores & Yzurieta (1980), de la Peña (1986), Ruschi (1979), Scott & Carbonell (1986), Short (1975), Sick (1984).

146. Australian Blue-billed Duck
Oxyura australis

French: Erismature australe   **German**: Schwarzkinn-Ruderente   **Spanish**: Malvasía Australiana
Other common names: Blue-billed Duck, Australian Stifftail/Blue-bill

Taxonomy. *Oxyura Australis* Gould, 1836, Swan River, Western Australia.
Considered by some to form superspecies with *O. vittata*. Monotypic.
Distribution. SW and SE Australia, Tasmania.
Descriptive notes. 40 cm; 476-1300 g; wingspan 60 cm. Male has somewhat smaller bill and tail than *O. vittata*; plumage darker. Female separated from other *Oxyura* by lack of strong facial pattern. Non-breeding males and juveniles resemble female.
Habitat. Shallow freshwater marshes, swamps and lakes with extensive bordering reedbeds. Outside breeding season, also on larger lakes, lagoons and wide rivers. Very seldom on marine waters.
Food and Feeding. Seeds and vegetative parts of aquatic plants and aquatic insects and their larvae form bulk of diet; also molluscs, crustaceans, arachnids. Feeds mostly by sieving bottom debris whilst diving; also dabbles on surface and strips seeds from overhanging plants.
Breeding. Season variable; continuous, opportunistic breeding probably normal. In single pairs; nest is deep bowl, domed, made usually of dead leaves, sometimes lined with down, in dense

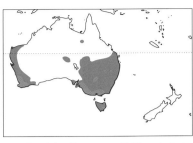

vegetation over water or on islets in lakes. Usually 5-6 eggs; incubation c. 24-27 days; chicks have greyish brown down above, whitish below; fledging c. 8 weeks. Sexual maturity at 1 year; oldest captive bird over 16 years old.
Movements. Somewhat dispersive and partially migratory, as breeding grounds generally abandoned after breeding is completed, birds concentrating in a few favourable areas where they undergo moult and stay until just before the start of next breeding season.
Status and Conservation. Not globally threatened. Widespread and rather uncommon, though locally common. Evidence indicates that numbers have suffered some reductions in recent past. Large concentrations, such as the several thousand reported from L Wyangan, New South Wales, are rare. In Victoria, maximum of 2011, counted in 472 wetlands, in 1988. In SW Australia, 1815 counted in 1398 wetlands, in 1988. Represents less than 1% of all ducks counted. Threatened by drainage or transformation of wetlands. Artificial wetlands may be used for breeding, but many too unstable to develop dense vegetation. A number of birds killed as result of hunting and many drown in gill-nets set for fishing.
Bibliography. Braithwaite & Frith (1969), Briggs (1988), Frith (1967), Frith *et al.* (1969), Halse & Jaensch (1989), Johnsgard (1966b), Macdonald (1988), Marchant & Higgins (1990), Schodde & Tidemann (1988), Serventy (1985), Wheeler (1953).

Genus *BIZIURA*   Stephens, 1824

147. Musk Duck
Biziura lobata

French: Erismature à barbillons   **German**: Lappenente   **Spanish**: Malvasía de Papada
Other common names: Lobed Duck

Taxonomy. *Anas lobata* Shaw, 1796, New South Wales = King George Sound, Western Australia. Eastern population has been assigned separate subspecies *menziesi*, though doubtfully valid. Monotypic.
Distribution. SW and SE Australia, Tasmania.

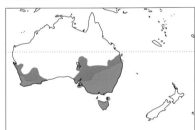

Descriptive notes. Male 66 cm, 1811-3120 g, wingspan c. 87 cm; female 55 cm, 993-1844 g, wingspan c. 72 cm. Female has rudimentary lobe under bill and is often not as dark as male. Plumage gets paler with wear. Juvenile resembles female but has yellowish distal half of lower mandible.
Habitat. Freshwater marshes, swamps and lakes with extensive bordering reedbeds. Outside breeding season, on deeper waters, lagoons, estuaries and along coast, occasionally far offshore.
Food and Feeding. Chiefly aquatic invertebrates (insects and their larvae, molluscs, crustaceans, arachnids), amphibians, some fish and even small ducklings; little plant material (mostly seeds). Feeds almost exclusively by diving in rather deep water.
Breeding. Starts chiefly Sept/Oct, but variable according to water levels. In single pairs; nest is rough cup-like structure of stems, in dense vegetation. Usually 2-3 eggs (1-10); incubation 24 days (captivity); chicks have dark brown down above, whitish below. Oldest captive bird known to have lived over 23 years.
Movements. Mainly sedentary, but many birds, perhaps mostly juveniles, involved in small- or large-scale dispersal after breeding. Their movements often reflect availability of suitable habitat and extent of flooding of a particular area.
Status and Conservation. Not globally threatened. Widespread, assumed to breed throughout main range, but population difficult to estimate; only locally abundant. Counts in 1988 yielded 1947 birds in 472 wetlands in Victoria, and 4247 in 1398 wetlands in SW Australia. Usually one breeding pair per dam in W Australia. Represents less than 1% of all ducks counted, with maximum densities of 0·17-1·99/ha. The 400 reported at L Guraga, represent largest concentration on one lake, according to available data. Has been taken for human consumption; difficult to hunt, but increased mortality as result of drowning in fishing nets. Needs well vegetated swamps; hence, can only use artificial water bodies when they become stable enough to develop dense emergent vegetation. Main threat, transformation or modification of freshwater wetlands.
Bibliography. Braithwaite & Frith (1969), Briggs (1988), Frith (1967), Halse & Jaensch (1989), Johnsgard (1966b), Lowe (1966), Marchant & Higgins (1990), Pycraft (1906), Raikow (1970), Robinson & Robinson (1970), Schodde & Tidemann (1988), Turpin & Dell (1991).

REFERENCES

REFERENCES OF SCIENTIFIC DESCRIPTIONS

Acerbi (1827). *Biblioteca Ital.* **47**: 297.
Afzelius (1804). *K. Vetenskaps Acad. Nya Handlingar, Stockholm* **25**: 264.
Ainley (1980). *Auk* **97**: 837-853.
Aldrich (1937). *Sci. Publ. Cleveland Mus. Nat. Hist.* **7**: 28, 30.
Aldrich (1946). *Wilson Bull.* **58**: 97.
Allen, J.A. (1876). *Bull. Mus. Comp. Zool.* **3**: 355.
Audubon (1835). *Birds Amer.* pls. 252, 281.
Audubon (1838). *Birds Amer.* **4**: 412.
Audubon (1849). *Orn. Biog.* **5**: 327.
Baillon (1834). *Mem. Soc. Royal. Émulation Abbeville (1833)*, sér. 2, **1**: 74.
Baird (1858). in: Baird, Cassin, & Lawrence, *Rep. Explor. Surv. Railroad Mississippi Pacific* **9**: xxiii, L, 762, 766, 788, 795.
Bangs (1903). *Proc. New England Zool. Club* **3**: 100.
Bangs (1905). *Proc. Biol. Soc. Washington* **18**: 151.
Bangs (1910). *Proc. Biol. Soc. Washington* **23**: 107.
Bangs (1913). *Proc. New England Zool. Club* **4**: 89.
Bangs (1918). *Bull. Mus. Comp. Zool.* **61**: 500.
Bangs & Noble (1918). *Auk* **35**: 445.
Bangs & Peters (1927). *Bull. Mus. Comp. Zool.* **67**: 472.
Banks (1977). *Proc. Biol. Soc. Washington* **89**: 536-537.
Banks & Bohl (1968). *Proc. Biol. Soc. Washington* **81**: 486.
Bartlett (1852). *Proc. Zool. Soc. London (1850)*: 275.
Bates (1931). *Ibis*: 302.
Bechtein (1803). *Orn. Taschenbuch Deutschland* **2**: 404, 424.
Berla (1946). *Bol. Mus. Nac. Rio de Janeiro, Zool.* **65**: 2.
Berlepsch (1892). *Bericht. XVII Jahresversammlung Allgemeinen Deutschen Orn. Gesell.*: 13.
Berlepsch (1894). *Orn. Monatsber* **2**: 110.
Berlepsch (1902). *Verh. V Int. Zool. Congr. Berlin (1901)*: 548.
Berlepsch (1906). *Auk* **23**: 185.
Berlepsch (1907). *Ornis* **14**: 371.
Berlepsch & Hartert (1902). *Novit. Zool.* **9**: 131.
Berlepsch & Stolzmann (1894). *Ibis*: 109, 112, 404.
Berlepsch & Stolzmann (1901). *Ornis* **11**: 191-192.
Berlepsch & Stolzmann (1906). *Ornis* **13**: 101.
Billberg (1828). *Synop. Faunae Scand.*, ed. 2, **1(2)**: 166.
Blake (1953). *Fieldiana Zool.* **34**: 199.
Blake (1961). *Fieldiana Zool.* **39**: 573.
Blasius, W. (1896). *Mitt. Geogr. Gesell. Naturhist. Mus. Lübeck* **2(10-11)**: 120.
Blumenbach (1798). *Abbildungen Naturhist. Gegenstände* **25**.
Blyth (1852). *Cat. Birds Mus. Asiatic. Soc. Bengal (1849)*: 281.
Blyth (1855). *J. Asiatic. Soc. Bengal* **24**: 265.
Blyth (1860). *J. Asiatic. Soc. Bengal* **29**: 101, 112.
Boddaert (1783). *Table Planches Enlum.*
Boetticher (1929). *Anzeiger Orn. Gesell. Bayern* **2**: 12.
Boie (1822). *Isis von Oken*, col. 559, 562. [*Hydrobates, Ardeola*]
Boie (1822). *Tagebuch Reise Norwegen*: 140, 308, 351. [*Tadorna, Aythya, Melanitta*]
Boie (1828). *Isis von Oken*, col. 329.
Bonaparte (1828). *Ann. Lyceum Nat. Hyst. New York* **2**: 390.
Bonaparte (1838). *Geogr. Comp. List Birds Europe North Amer.*: 58.
Bonaparte (1843). *Nuov. Ann. Sci. Nat. R. Accademia Sci. Istituto Bologna, (1842)* **8**: 426.
Bonaparte (1850). *Rev. Crit. Orn. Européenne Degland*: 108.
Bonaparte (1852). *Tageblatt* **29**.
Bonaparte (1854). *Compt. Rend. Acad. Sci. Paris* **38**: 662-663.
Bonaparte (1855). *Consp. Gen. Avium* **2**: 106, 127, 129, 134, 139, 141, 151. [*Ardeola bacchus, Butorides striatus chloriceps, Nycticorax nycticorax obscurus, Gorsachius, Ixobrychus minutus podiceps, Ephippiorhynchus, Threskiornis aethiopicus bernieri*]
Bonaparte (1855). *Compt. Rend. Acad. Sci. Paris* **40**: 722-723. [*Bubulcus, Zebrilus*]
Bonaparte (1855). *Compt. Rend. Acad. Sci. Paris* **41**: 1113. [*Fregetta*]
Bonaparte (1856). *Compt. Rend. Acad. Sci. Paris* **42**: 768, 775, 881, 954. [*Nothocercus, Crypturellus cinnamomeus sallaei, Eudyptula, Pagodroma, Pterodroma, Halobaena*]
Bonaparte (1856). *Compt. Rend. Acad. Sci. Paris* **43**: 573, 648, 992. [*Tinamus major peruvianus, Phoenicoparrus, Cyanochen*]
Bonaparte (1857). *Consp. Gen. Avium* **2**: 187, 191, 204-205.
Bond (1955). *Auk* **72**: 208.
Bonnaterre (1791). *Tableau Encycl. Méthod. Trois Règnes Nature, Orn.* **47**: 58, 93.
Bosc (1792). *Actes Soc. Hist. Nat. Paris* **1**: 4.
Bourne (1953). *Bull. Brit. Orn. Club* **73**: 81.
Bourne (1959). *Emu* **59**: 213.
Brabourne & Chubb (1913). *Ann. Mag. Nat. Hist.* (Ser. 8) **12**: 578-579.
Brabourne & Chubb (1914). *Ann. Mag. Nat. Hist.* (Ser. 8) **14**: 319-322.
Brandt (1836). *Descr. Icones Animalium Rossicorum Novorum, Aves* **1**: 5. [*Nettapus, Chenonetta*]
Brandt (1836). *Bull. Sci. Acad. Imp. Sci. St. Pétersbourg* **1**: 37. [*Branta canadensis leucopareia*]
Brandt (1837). *Bull. Sci. Acad. Imp. Sci. St. Pétersbourg* **2** col. 315. [*Eudyptes chrysolophus*]
Brandt (1837). *Bull. Sci. Acad. Imp. Sci. St. Pétersbourg* **3** cols. 55, 56. [*Phalacrocorax auritus cincinatus, Phalacrocorax olivaceus mexicanus, Phalacrocorax sulcirostris, Phalacrocorax penicillatus, Phalacrocorax varius hypoleucos, Phalacrocorax purpurascens*]
Brandt (1840). *Bull. Sci. Acad. Imp. Sci. St. Pétersbourg* **5(2)**, sér. 6, Sci. Nat. **3**: 269.
Brandt (1847). *Fuligulam (Lampronettam) Fischeri Novam Rossicarum Avium Speciem*: 18.
Brasil (1917). *Bull. Mus. Nat. Hist. Nat., Paris* **23**: 432.
Brehm, A.E. (1854). *J. Orn.* **2**: 80.
Brehm, C.L. (1824). *Lehrbuch Naturgeschichte Europäischen Vögel* **2**: 813.
Brehm, C.L. (1831). *Handb. Naturgeschichte Vögel Deutschlands*: 865, 893, 963.
Brewster (1888). *Auk* **5**: 83.
Brewster (1902). *Auk* **19**: 184.
Brisson (1760). *Orn.* **1**: 46, 48, 52, 56, 58, 60. **5**: 10, 361, 503, 506, 518. **6**: 96, 129-130, 261, 476, 494, 511.

Brodkorb (1938). *Occas. Papers Mus. Zool. Univ. Michigan* **367**: 1. [*Rhea americana araneipes*]
Brodkorb (1938). *Occas. Papers Mus. Zool. Univ. Michigan* **382**: 1. [*Eudromia formosa mira*]
Brodkorb (1939). *Proc. Biol. Soc. Washington* **52**: 138. [*Rhea americana nobilis*]
Brodkorb (1939). *Occas. Papers Mus. Zool. Univ. Michigan* **401**: 1. [*Crypturellus cinnamomeus soconuscensis*]
Bruch (1832). *Isis von Oken*, col. 1109.
Brünnich (1764). *Orn. Borealis*: 29, 38.
Buller (1869). *Ibis*: 41.
Buller (1873). *Ibis*: 90.
Buller (1888). *Birds N.Z.* 2nd ed. **2**: 161, 289.
Burmeister (1860). *J. Orn.* **8**: 259.
Buturlin (1933). *Opredelitel Promyslovykh Ptits*: 60.
Cabanis (1869). *J. Orn.* **17**: 212.
Cabanis (1875). *J. Orn.* **23**: 450.
Cabanis (1878). *J. Orn.* **26**: 198.
Carriker (1910). *Ann. Carnegie Mus.* **6**: 379.
Carriker (1933). *Proc. Acad. Nat. Sci. Philadelphia* **85**: 2.
Carriker (1935). *Proc. Acad. Nat. Sci. Philadelphia* **87**: 315.
Carte (1866). *Proc. Zool. Soc. London*: 93.
Cassin (1852). *Proc. Acad. Nat. Sci. Philadelphia*: 187. [*Branta canadensis parvipes*]
Cassin (1852). *Proc. Acad. Nat. Sci. Philadelphia* **6**: 187. [*Mergus merganser americanus*]
Cassin (1859). *Proc. Acad. Nat. Sci. Philadelphia*: 175.
Cassin (1861). *Proc. Acad. Nat. Sci. Philadelphia*: 73.
Cassin (1862). *Proc. Acad. Nat. Sci. Philadelphia*: 326.
Chapin (1923). *Amer. Mus. Novit.* **84**: 5.
Chapman (1899). *Bull. Amer. Mus. Nat. Hist.* **12**: 255-256.
Chapman (1901). *Bull. Amer. Mus. Nat. Hist.* **14**: 87.
Chapman (1912). *Bull. Amer. Mus. Nat. Hist.* **31**: 141, 235.
Chapman (1914). *Bull. Amer. Mus. Nat. Hist.* **33**: 171.
Chapman (1915). *Bull. Amer. Mus. Nat. Hist.* **34**: 635-636.
Chapman (1923). *Amer. Mus. Novit.* **96**: 1.
Chapman (1929). *Amer. Mus. Novit.* **380**: 3.
Chubb (1913). *Bull. Brit. Orn. Cl.* **33**: 79.
Chubb (1917). *Bull. Brit. Orn. Cl.* **28**: 30.
Clancey, Brooke & Sinclair (1981). *Durban Mus. Novit.* **12**: 203-213.
Clark (1907). *Proc. U.S. Nat. Mus.* **32**: 468.
Conover (1924). *Auk* **41**: 334.
Conover (1933). *Proc. Biol. Soc. Washington* **46**: 115.
Conover (1937). *Proc. Biol. Soc. Washington* **50**: 191, 227.
Conover (1941). *Proc. Biol. Soc. Washington* **54**: 143.
Conover (1949). *Fieldiana Zool.* **31**: 263.
Conover (1950). *Fieldiana Zool.* **31**: 351, 353, 357, 364, 367, 369.
Cory (1881). *Bull. Nuttall. Orn. Club* **6**: 84.
Cory (1915). *Publ. Field. Mus. Nat. Hist. Orn. Ser.* **1**: 293.
Coues (1862). *Proc. Acad. Nat. Sci. Philadelphia*: 229.
Coues (1864). *Proc. Acad. Nat. Sci. Philadelphia*: 77-79, 131, 139.
Cuvier (1829). *Règne Animal (Nouv. éd.)* **1**: 520.
Cretzschmar (1827). in: Rüppell, *Atlas Reise Nördl. Afrika, Vögel (1826)*: 39.
Dalgety & Scott (1948). *Bull. Brit. Orn. Club* **68**: 115.
Daudin (1802). in: Buffon, *Hist. Nat. (ed. Didot), Quadr.* **14**: 319.
Delacour (1932). *Oiseau* **2**: 6.
Delacour (1936). *Oiseau* **6**: 369.
Delacour (1951). *Ardea* **39**: 139. [*Anser fabalis johanseni*]
Delacour (1951). *Amer. Mus. Novit.* **1537**: 5, 7. [*Branta canadensis taverneri, Branta canadensis fulva, Branta canadensis maxima*]
Delacour & Ripley (1975). *Amer. Mus. Novit.* **2565**: 2.
Des Murs (1845). *Rev. Zool., Paris*: 179.
Dickerman (1961). *Wilson Bull.* **73**: 333.
Dickerman (1973). *Bull. Brit. Orn. Club* **93**: 113.
Dickerman (1986). *Proc. Biol. Soc. Washington* **99**: 435-436.
Donovan (1809). *Brit. Birds* **6**, pl. 147.
Dubois (1839). *Orn. Gallerie* **1**: 119.
Du Bus de Gisignies (1838). *Bull. Acad. Royal. Sci. Lettres Beaux-Arts Belgique (1837)* **4**: 105.
Dwight (1918). *Auk* **35**: 198.
Dwight & Griscom (1924). *Amer. Mus. Novit.* **142**: 1.
Ehrenberg (1828). *Symbolae Physicae, Aves, London* **2**: 157.
Ehrenberg (1833). *Symbolae Physicae, Aves* **1** sig. m, note 2.
Elliot (1859). *Ibis*: 391.
Eyton (1836). *Cat. Brit. Birds*: 58.
Eyton (1838). *Monogr. Anatidae*: 13, 70, 93, 111, 168.++
Falla (1933). *Rec. Auckland Inst. Mus.* **1**: 176.
Falla (1937). *Brit. Austral. N.Z. Antarctic Res. Exped. Rep.* (Ser. B) **2**: 226.
Falla (1946). *Rec. Canterbury Mus.* **5**: 111.
Filhol (1878). *Bull. Soc. Philomath. Paris*, sér. 7, **2**: 132.
Finch (1874). *Proc. Zool. Soc. London*: 207.
Finch (1876). *Trans N.Z. Inst.* **8**: 204.
Finch (1904). *Orn. Monatsber.* **12**: 94.
Finch & Hartlaub (1867). *Beitr. Fauna Central Polynesiens, Orn.*: 244.
Fleming (1822). *Philos. Zool.* **2**: 260.
Fleming (1935). *Occas. Papers Royal. Ontario Mus. Zool.* **1**: 1.
Fleming & Serventy (1943). *Emu* **43**: 119.
Forbes (1881). *Coll. Sci. Papers Garrod.*: 521.
Forbes (1893). *Ibis*: 533.
Forster, G. (1777). *Voyage World* **1**: 91, 96, 98.
Forster, J.R. (1781). *Ind. Zool.*: 23. [*Anas poecilorhyncha poecilorhyncha*]

Forster, J.R. (1781). *Comment. Phys. Soc. Reg. Sci. Götting (1780)* **3**: 133-135, 140-141, 143, 147. [*Pygoscelis papua, Pygoscelis antarctica, Eudyptes chrysocome, Eudyptula minor minor, Spheniscus magellanicus*]
Forster, J.R. (1785). *Mém. Math. Phys. Acad. Sci., Paris* **10**: 571.
Forster, J.R. (1788). *Enchiridion Hist. Nat.*: 38.
Forster, J.R. (1844). *Descr. Animal. Itinere Maris Australis Terras*: 148, 204, 278, 338.
Forster, T. (1817). *Synop. Cat. Brit. Birds.*: 59.
Fraser (1839). *Proc. Zool. Soc. London*: 113.
Friedmann (1947). *Caldasia* **4**: 472. [*Nothocercus bonapartei discrepans*]
Friedmann (1947). *Condor* **49**: 190. [*Dendrocygna autumnalis fulgens*]
Friedmann (1948). *Proc. Biol. Soc. Washington* **61**: 157.
Friedmann (1949). *Smithsonian Misc. Coll.* **111(9)**: 1.
Gaimard (1823). *Bull. Général Universel Annonces Nouvelles Sci. Paris* **3**: 53.
Garnot (1826). *Ann. Sci. Nat., Paris* **7**: 50, 54.
Geoffroy (1798). *Bull. Sci. Soc. Philomath., Paris* **1(2)**: 98.
Geoffroy Sant-Hilaire, I. (1832). *Mag. Zool., Paris* **2(2)**: 1, 3.
Georgi (1775). *Bemerkungen Reise Russischen Reich*: 167-168.
Giglioli & Salvadori (1869). *Ibis*: 62-63, 68. [*Pterodroma arminjoniana arminjoniana, Pterodroma defilippiana, Puffinus assimilis elegans*]
Giglioli & Salvadori (1869). *Atti Soc. Ital. Sci. Nat., Milan* **11** (1868): 451. [*Pterodroma magentae*]
Gloger (1842). *Gemeinnütziges Hand und Hilfsbuch Naturgeschichte*: 404.
Gmelin (1789). *Syst. Nat.* **1**.
Goss (1888). *Auk* **5**: 242.
Gosse (1847). *Birds Jamaica*: 338.
Gould (1836). *Proc. Zool. Soc. London*: 85.
Gould (1837). *Proc. Zool. Soc. London*: 26.
Gould (1838). *Synop. Birds Austr.* **4** app.: 7.
Gould (1841). *Proc. Zool. Soc. London*: 177-178.
Gould (1842). *Proc. Zool. Soc. London (1841)*: 95. [*Merganetta, Merganetta armata armata*]
Gould (1842). *Birds Austr.* **6**. [*Nettapus pulchellus, Nettapus coromandelianus albipennis*]
Gould (1844). *Proc. Zool. Soc. London*: 57, 135. [*Podiceps cristatus australis, Pterodroma solandri*]
Gould (1844). *Ann. Mag. Nat. Hist.* **13**: 362-365, 366-367. [*Pterodroma mollis mollis, Pterodroma leucoptera, Prodellaria aequinoctialis conspicillata, Puffinus carneipes, Fregetta tropica tropica, Fregetta grallaria leucogaster*]
Gould (1845). *Proc. Zool. Soc. London*: 1, 62.
Gould (1846). *Proc. Zool. Soc. London*: 21. [*Sula dactylatra personata*]
Gould (1846). *Birds Austr.* **25**. [*Egretta garzetta immaculata*]
Gould (1847). *Proc. Zool. Soc. London*: 93.
Gould (1848). *Proc. Zool. Soc. London (1847)*: 221. [*Egretta intermedia plumifera, Butorides striatus stagnatilis*]
Gould (1848). *Proc. Zool. Soc. London*: 39. [*Butorides striatus macrorhynchus*]
Gould (1850). *Athenaeum* **1207**: 1315.
Gould (1856). *Proc. Zool. Soc. London*: 95.
Gould (1857). *Proc. Zool. Soc. London*: 269.
Gould (1868). *Proc. Zool. Soc. London*: 220.
Gould (1864). *Proc. Zool. Soc. London*: 184.
Gray, G.R. (1842). *List. Gen. Birds* **2**: app.: 13.
Gray, G.R. (1843). in: Dieffenbach, *Travels N.Z.* **2**: 198-199. [*Poliocephalus rufopectus, Pterodroma cookii, Sula serrator*]
Gray, G.R. (1843). *Ann. Mag. Nat. Hist.* **11**: 370. [*Hymenolaimus*]
Gray, G.R. (1844). *Gen. Birds* **3**: [627]. [*Anas auklandica auklandica*]
Gray, G.R. (1844). *Ann. Mag. Nat. Hist.* **13**: 315. [*Aptenodytes forsteri*]
Gray, G.R. (1845). in: Richardson & Gray, J.E., eds. *Zool. Voyage Erebus Terror, Birds* **1**: 15, 17, 20. [*Eudyptes pachyrhynchus, Phalacrocorax chalconotus, Anas auklandica chlorotis*]
Gray, G.R. (1845). *Gen. Birds* **3**: 669. [*Fregata ariel ariel*]
Gray, G.R. (1848). *Gen. Birds* **3**: [561].
Gray, G.R. (1854). *Proc. Zool. Soc. London*: 62.
Gray, G.R. (1856). *Proc. Zool. Soc. London (1855)*: 212.
Gray, G.R. (1859). *Proc. Zool. Soc. London*: 167.
Gray, G.R. (1860). *Cat. Birds Tropical Islands Pacific (1859)*: 56.
Gray, G.R. (1861). *Proc. Zool. Soc. London (1860)*: 366.
Gray, G.R. (1862). *Ibis*: 245.
Gray, G.R. (1867). *List Specimens Birds Brit. Mus.* **5**: 97-98, 102, 104.
Gray, G.R. (1869). *Ibis*: 440, 442.
Gray, G.R. (1871). *Hand-list Birds Brit. Mus.* **3**: 2.
Gray, J.E. (1831). *Zool. Misc.*: 19.
Griscom (1926). *Amer. Mus. Novit.* **235**: 11.
Griscom (1929). *Amer. Mus. Novit.* **379**: 5. [*Podilymbus gigas*]
Griscom (1929). *Bull. Mus. Comp. Zool.* **69**: 150, 152. [*Tinamus major saturatus*]
Güldenstädt (1770). *Novi Commentarii Acad. Sci. Imp. Petropolitanae (1969)* **14**: 403.
Gurney (1868). *Ibis*: 253.
Harcourt (1851). *Sketch Madeira*: 123.
Hartert (1891). *Kat. Vogelsammlung Mus. Senckenberg. Naturforschendengesell. Frankfurt*: 231.
Hartert (1905). *Novit. Zool.* **12**: 205.
Hartert (1906). *Bull. Brit. Orn. Club* **16**: 110.
Hartert (1909). *Novit. Zool.* **16**: 216.
Hartert (1914). *Bull. Brit. Orn. Club* **35**: 14.
Hartert (1917). *Bull. Brit. Orn. Club* **38**: 6.
Hartert (1920). *Vögel Pal. Fauna*: 1251.
Hartert (1923). *Novit. Zool.* **30**: 132.
Hartlaub (1852). *Rev. Mag. Zool. Paris*, sér. 2, **4**: 7.
Hartlaub (1858). *J. Orn.* **6**: 42.
Hartlaub (1860). *J. Orn.* **8**: 167, 173.
Hartlaub (1861). *Orn. Madagascar*: 83.
Hartlaub (1880). *Proc. Zool. Soc. London*: 39.
Hartlaub & Finsch (1872). *Proc. Zool. Soc. London*: 108.
Heermann (1854). *Proc. Acad. Nat. Sci. Philadelphia* **7**: 179.
Hellmayr (1903). *Verh. Zool.-Bot. Gesell. Wien* **53**: 247.
Hellmayr (1906). *Abh. K. Bayer. Akad. Wissen., Math.-Phys. Kl.* **22**: 711.
Henshaw (1900). *Auk* **17**: 246.
Hermann (1783). *Tabula Affinitatum Animalium*: 164-165, 235.
Heuglin (1859). *Ibis*: 351.
Hilsenberg (1822). *Froriep, Notizen* **3**: col. 74.
Hodgson (1844). in: Gray, J.E., ed., *Zool. Misc.*: 86.
Hombron & Jacquinot (1841). *Ann. Sci. Nat. Zool. Paris*, sér. 2, **16**: 320.
Horsfield (1821). *Trans. Linn. Soc. London* **12**: 190. [*Ardeola speciosa speciosa, Butorides striatus javanicus*]
Horsfield (1821). *Trans. Linn. Soc. London* **13**: 188-189, 199. [*Leptoptilos javanicus, Dendrocygna javanica*]
Horsfield (1824). *Zool. researches Java* **8**: 64.
Huey (1927). *Condor* **29**: 167.
Humboldt (1805). in: Humboldt & Bonpland, *Recueil Observ. Zool. Anat. Comp.* **1**: 6.
Hume (1873). *Stray Feathers* **1**: 5, 303.
Hume (1875). *Stray Feathers* **3**: 300.
Hume (1876). *Stray Feathers* **4**: 481-483.
Hume (1878). *Stray Feathers* **6**: 470.
Humphrey, P.S. & Thomson, M.C. (1981). A new species of Steamerduck (*Tachyeres*) from Argentina. *Univ. Kansas Mus. Nat. Hist. Occas. Papers* **95**: 1-12.
Hutton (1869). *Ibis*: 351.
Hutton (1879). *Proc. Linn. Soc. New South Wales (1978)* **3**: 334.
Ihering & Ihering (1807). in: Mus. Paulista, São Paulo, *Cat. Fauna Braziliana* **1**: 72.
Illiger (1811). *Prodromus Syst. Mammalium Avium*: 253, 274.
Jameson (1835). *Edinburgh New Philos. J.* **19**: 213.
Jardine (1846). *Ann. Mag. Nat. Hist.* **17**: 86.
Jardine & Selby (1827). *Illus. Orn.* **1**: pl. 13.
Jardine & Selby (1828). *Illus. Orn.* **4**: pl. 62, 65.
Jouanin (1955). *Oiseau* **25**: 155.
Jouanin (1964). *Oiseau* **34**: 84.
Jouanin (1971). *Oiseau (1970)* **40**: 306.
Jouanin & Roux (1963). *Oiseau* **33**: 104.
Kaup (1829). *Skizzirte Entwickelungs-Geschichte Europäisch. Thierwelt*:82, 102.
Kennard (1927). *Proc. New England Zool. Club* **9**: 93.
Keyserling & Blasius, J.H. (1840). *Wirbelthiere Europa's*: xciii, 131, 238.
King (1828). *Zool. J* **4**: 98, 100, 102.
King (1831). *Proc. Com. Sci. Corresp. Zool. Soc. London* **1**: 15.
Kinsky & Falla (1976). *Nat. Mus. N.Z. Rec.* **1**: 116.
Kittlitz (1830). *Mém. Savans Étrangers Acad. Imp. Sci. St. Pétersbourg* **1(2)**: 192.
Koepcke (1968). *Bonner. Zool. Beitr.* **19**: 231.
Kothe (1907). *J. Orn.* **55**: 164.
Kuhl (1820). *Beitr. Zool. Vergl. Anat. Abth.* **1**: 136, 142-143.
Kuroda, Nagamichi (1922). *Ibis*: 311.
Kuroda, Nagamichi (1925). *Tori* **4**: 438.
Lacépède (1799). *Tableaux Mammifères Oiseaux*: 13, 15.
Latham (1787). *General Synop. Birds*, suppl.: 294, 297.
Latham (1790). *Index Orn.*
Latham (1798). *Trans. Linn. Soc. London* **4**: 103.
Latham (1801). *Index Orn.*, suppl.: 45, 67, 69-70.
Lavauden (1929). *Alauda* **1**: 233.
Lawrence (1846). *Ann. Lyceum Nat. Hist. New York* **4**: 171.
Lawrence (1858). in: Baird, Cassin & Lawrence, *Rep. Explor. Surv. Railroad Mississipi Pacific* **9**: 889, 894-895.
Lawrence (1868). *Ann. Lyceum Nat. Hist. New York* **9**: 140.
Leach (1819). in: Ross, *Voyage Discovery*, app.: 48, 1819, ed. 2, **2**: 154.
Lehmann (1946). *Auk* **63**: 221.
Lesson (1825). *Ann. Sci. Nat., Paris* **6**: 95.
Lesson (1828). *Man. Orn.* **2**: 358, 394, 415, 417-418. [*Pelecanoides garnotii, Rollandia rolland chilensis, Anseranas, Tadorna radjah radjah, Histrionicus*]
Lesson (1828). in: Duperrey, *Voyage Coquille, Zool. Atlas* **1(7)** pl. 44. [*Zonerodius heliosylus*]
Lesson (1831). *Traité Orn.* **8**.
Lesson (1837). in: Bougainville, *J. Navig. Thétis Espérance* **2**: 331.
Lesson (1839). *Rev. Zool. Paris* **2**: 102.
Lesson (1842). *Rev. Zool. Paris* **5**: 209-210.
Lesson & Garnot (1828). in: Duperrey, *Voyage Coquille, Zool. Atlas* **1(7)** pl. 48.
Lichtenstein (1819). *Abh. K. Akad. Wissen. Berlin, Phys. Kl.* (1816-17): 163.
Lichtenstein (1823). *Verzeichniss Doubletten Zool. Mus. Berlin*: 75-76, 86.
Lillo (1905). *Rev. Letras Cien. Sociales, Tucumán* **3**: 72.
Linnaeus (1758). *Syst. Nat.* **10**.
Linnaeus (1761). *Fauna Svecica* **2**: [23], 39, 51.
Linnaeus (1766). *Syst. Nat.* **12(1)**.
Lönnberg (1906). *K. Svensk. Vetenskapsakad. Handlingar, Stockholm* **40(5)**: 69.
Lönnberg & Rendahl (1922). *Arkiv. Zool.* **14(25)**: 13.
Louette, M. & Herremans, M. (1985). *Bull. Brit. Orn. Club* **105**: 42-49.
Lowe (1921). *Bull. Brit. Orn. Club* **41**: 140.
Lowe (1925). *Bull. Brit. Orn. Club* **46**: 6.
Lynch Arribálzaga (1877). *La Ley (Buenos Aires), 2 july: 1.* Reprinted 1926, *Bull. U.S. Nat. Mus.* **133**: 44.
Lynch Arribálzaga & Holmberg (1878). *Naturalista Argentina* **1**: 101.
Manghi (1985). *Com. Mus. Arg. Ci. Nat. Bernardino Ribadavia* **14**: 115-119.
Mathews (1911). *Bull. Brit. Orn. Club* **27**: 101. [*Butorides striatus rogersi*]
Mathews (1911). *Birds Austr.* **1**: 272, 286. [*Aptenodytes patagonicus halli, Eudyptula minor iredalei*]
Mathews (1912). *Austral Avian Rec.* **1**: 33, 88. [*Phaethon rubicauda westralis, Anas superciliosa rogersi*]
Mathews (1912). *Birds Austr.* **2**. [*Diomedea melanophris impavida, Diomedea chlororhynchos bassi, Macronectes halli, Pagodroma nivea, Pachyptila salvini macgillivrayi, Pachyptila salvini salvini, Pachyptila desolata alter, Pachyptila crassirostris crassirostris, Pachyptila crassirostris eatoni, Pachyptila belcheri, Puffinus huttoni, Puffinus assimilis boydi, Puffinus assimilis tunneyi, Nesofregetta, Oceanites oceanicus exasperatus, Pelagodroma marina dulciae, Pelagodroma marina maoriana, Pelecanoides urinatrix coppingeri, Pelecanoides magellani*]
Mathews (1912). *Novit. Zool.* **18**: 230-231, 233-234. [*Ardea sumatrana mathewsi, Egretta novaehollandiae parryi, Butorides striatus littleri, Nycticorax caledonicus hilli, Ixobrychus minutus dubius*]
Mathews (1913). *Austral Avian Rec.* **1**: 187. [*Daption capense*]
Mathews (1913). *Austral Avian Rec.* **2**: 7. [*Phaethon lepturus dorotheae*]
Mathews (1914). *Austral Avian Rec.* **2**: 118-121, 199.
Mathews (1915). *Birds Austr.* **4**: 311.
Mathews (1926). *Bull. Brit. Orn. Club* **46**: 60.
Mathews (1929). *Bull. Brit. Orn. Club* **50**: 11.
Mathews (1930). *Trans. Proc. N.Z. Inst.* **61**: 139.
Mathews (1934). *Bull. Brit. Orn. Club* **54**: 179.
Mathews (1935). *Bull. Brit. Orn. Club* **56**: 59.
Mathews (1937). *Emu* **37**: 31-32.
Mathews & Iredale (1915). *Ibis*: 590, 592, 594.
Mathews & Iredale (1921). *Man. Birds Austr.* **1**: 11.
Mayr (1931). *Amer. Mus. Novit.* **486**: 2-3, 6.
Mayr (1943). *Emu* **43**: 5-7, 9-10.
Mayr (1945). *Amer. Mus. Novit.* **1294**: 1, 3.
Mearns (1895). *Auk* **12**: 257.
Ménégaux (1909). *Bull. Soc. Philomath. Paris*, sér. 10, **1**: 224.
Ménétriés (1832). *Cat. Raisonné Objects Zool. Recueillis Voyage Caucase*: 58.
Merrem (1841). in: Ersch & Gruber, *Allgemeine Encycl. Wissen. Künste*, sec. 1, **35**: 26.
Meyen (1834). *Nova Acta Acad. Caes. Leopold.-Carol. Nat. Curiosorum, Halle*, suppl. **16**: 102, 110, 121.
Meyer de Schauensee (1959). *Proc. Acad. Nat. Sci. Philadelphia* **111**: 55.
Milne-Edwards (1880). *Ann. Sci. Nat. Zool. Paris*, sér. 6, **9(9)**: 56. [*Megadyptes*]
Milne-Edwards (1880). *Compt. Rend. Acad. Sci. Paris* **91**: 1037. [*Anastomus lamelligerus madagascariensis*]
Milne-Edwards (1882). *Ann. Sci. Nat. Zool. Paris*, sér. 6, **13(4)**: 37.
Milne-Edwards & Grandidier (1885). *Hist. Nat. Madagascar, Oiseaux* **1**: 546.
Miller, J.F. (1778). *Icones Animalium* **4**: 23.
Miranda-Ribeiro (1919). *Arch. Mus. Nac. Rio de Janeiro.* **22**: 192.
Miranda-Ribero (1938). *Rev. Mus. Paulista* **23**: 763.
Molina (1782). *Saggio Storia Nat. Chili.*
Montagu (1813). *Suppl. Orn. Dict.*: unnumbered.
Moquin-Tandon (1841). in: Webb & Berthelot, *Hist. Nat. Iles Canaries* **2(2)**: 45.
Müller, O.F. (1776). *Zool. Danicae Prodromus*: 14.
Müller, P.L.S. (1776). *Linné Natursystem*, suppl.: 111.
Müller, S. (1842). in: Temminck (ed.), *Verh. Nat. Geschiedenis Nederlandsche Overzeesche Bezittingen, Land-Volkenkunde*: 159.
Murphy (1917). *Bull. Amer. Mus. Nat. Hist.* **37**: 861.
Murphy (1927). *Amer. Mus. Novit.* **276**: 3.
Murphy (1928). *Amer. Mus. Novit.* **322**: 1, 4.
Murphy (1930). *Amer. Mus. Novit.* **419**: 4.
Murphy (1936). *Oceanic Birds South Amer.*: 889.
Murphy (1947). *Auk* **64**: 454.
Murphy (1949). in: Mayr and Schüz, eds., *Orn. Biol. Wissen.*: 89.
Murphy & Harper (1916). *Bull. Amer. Mus. Nat. Hist.* **35**: 65-66.
Murphy & Irving (1951). *Amer. Mus. Novit.* **1506**: 15.
Naumburg (1932). *Amer. Mus. Novit.* **554**: 1.
de Naurois & Roux (1974). *Oiseau* **44**: 77.
Nelson (1901). *Proc. Biol. Soc. Washington* **14**: 169.
Neumann (1898). *J. Orn.* **46**: 243.

Neumann (1909). *Ornis* **13**: 193.
Neumann (1928). *J. Orn.* **76**: 783.
Nichols & Mowbray (1916). *Auk* **33**: 194.
Nicoll (1906). *Bull. Brit. Orn. Club* **16**: 103-105.
O' Brien & Davies (1990). *Marine Orn.* **18(1-2)**: 57-59.
Oates (1907). *J. Bombay Nat. Hist. Soc.* **17**: 558.
Oberholser (1906). *Proc. Biol. Soc. Washington* **19**: 93.
Oberholser (1912). *Smithsonian Misc. Coll.* **60(7)**: 1.
Oberholser (1918). *J. Washington Acad. Sci.* **8**: 571.
Oberholser (1924). *J. Washington Acad. Sci.* **14**: 294.
Ogilvie-Grant (1888). *Proc. Zool. Soc. London*: 203.
Ogilvie-Grant (1899). *Ibis*: 586.
Ogilvie-Grant (1901). *Bull. Brit. Orn. Club.* **11**: 66.
Ogilvie-Grant & Forbes (1899). *Bull. Liverpool Mus.* **2**: 3.
Oken (1816). *Lehrbuch Naturgeschichte* **3(2)**: "939" (= 639).
Oliver (1953). *Emu* **53**: 187.
Olrog (1950). *Acta Zool. Lilloana* **9**: 471.
Olrog (1959). *Neotropica* **5**: 19, 39, 41.
Oort (1910). *Notes Leyden Mus.* **32**: 83.
d'Orbigny (1834). *Voyage Amérique Méridionale livr.* **2**: 67.
Ord (1815). in: Guthrie, *Geogr. (Amer.)*, ed. 2, **2**: 319.
O'Reilly (1818). *Greenland Adjacent Seas North-west Passage*: 140.
Osgood & Conover (1922). *Publ. Field Mus. Nat. Hist. Zool. Ser.* **12**: 24.
Oustalet (1877). *Bull. Soc. Philomath. Paris*, sér. 7, **1**: 25.
Oustalet (1883). *Ann. Sci. Nat. Zool. Paris*, sér. 6, **16(5)**: 1.
Oustalet (1890). *Ann. Sci. Nat. Zool. Paris*, sér. 7, **9**: 18.
Owen (1875). *Trans. Zool. Soc. London* **9**: 254.
Pallas (1764). in: Vroeg, *Cat. Raisonné Coll. Oiseaux, Audumbr.*: 5-6.
Pallas (1769). *Spicilegia Zool.* **1(5)**: 28. [*Diomedea albatrus*]
Pallas (1769). *Spicilegia Zool.* **6**: 21, 35. [*Branta ruficollis, Polysticta stelleri*]
Pallas (1773). *Reise Verschiedene Provinzen Russischen Reichs* **2**: 712-713.
Pallas (1811). *Zoographia Rosso-Asiat.* **2**: 207, 303, 305.
Payraudeau (1826). *Ann. Sci. Nat., Paris* **8**: 464.
Peale (1848). *U.S. Explor. Exped.* **8**: 216, 292, 294, 296.
Pelzeln (1863). *Verh. Zool. Bot. Gesell. Wien* **13**: 1126-1130.
Pennant (1769). *Ind. Zool.*: 11-13.
Peters (1930). *Occas. Papers Boston Soc. Nat. Hist* **5**: 256, 261.
Phelps Jr., W.H. (1976). *Bol. Soc. Venezolana Cien. Nat.* **32**: 16.
Phelps & Phelps (1948). *Bol. Soc. Venezolana Cien. Nat.* **11**: 57.
Phelps & Phelps (1949). *Proc. Biol. Soc. Washington* **62**: 109.
Phelps & Phelps (1952). *Proc. Biol. Soc. Washington* **65**: 39.
Philippi (1854). *Anales. Univ. Chile*: 337.
Philippi (1860). *Archiv Naturgeschichte* **26(1)**: 26.
Philippi & Landbeck (1860). *Archiv Naturgeschichte* **26(1)**: 282.
Phillips (1916). *Auk* **33**: 423.
Poeppig (1829). in: Froriep, *Notizen* **25**, col. 10.
Pontoppidan (1763). *Danske Atlas* **1**: 621.
Potts (1871). *Trans. N.Z. Inst.* **3**: 99.
Potts (1872). *Trans. N.Z. Inst.* **4**: 204.
Quoy & Gaimard (1824). in: Freycinet, *Voyage Uranie Physicienne Zool.* **4**: 133.
Radde (1863). *Reisen Süden Ost-Sibirien* **2**: 376.
Raffles (1822). *Trans. Linn. Soc. London* **13**: 325-327.
Rand (1941). *Amer. Mus. Novit.* **1102**: 1.
Rand (1948). *Fieldiana Zool.* **31**: 201.
Reichenbach (1850). *Avium Syst. Nat.* **4**, novit., col. 7.
Reichenbach (1853). *Avium Syst. Nat. (1852)*.
Reichenow (1877). *J. Orn.* **25**: 253.
Reichenow (1883). *Mitt. Orn. Vereines Wien*: 202.
Reichenow (1898). *Orn. Monatsber.* **6**: 190.
Reichenow (1900). *Orn. Monatsber.* **8**: 140.
Reichenow (1902). *J. Orn.* **50**: 125.
Reichenow (1903). *Orn. Monatsber.* **11**: 134.
Reichenow (1904). *Orn. Monatsber.* **12**: 47.
Reichenow (1907). *Orn. Monatsber.* **15**: 147.
Reichenow (1919). *J. Orn.* **67**: 225.
Reinhardt (1854). *Vidensk. Meddelelser Naturhist. Forening Kjöbenhavn (1853)*: 76.
Reiser (1905). *Anzeiger K. Akad. Wissen. Wien, Math. Naturwissen. Kl.* **42**: 324.
Rensch (1929). *J. Orn.* **77(2)**: 205.
Richardson (1832). in: Swainson & Richardson, *Fauna Boreali-Americana (1831)* **2**: 464, 470.
Richmond (1897). *Proc. U.S. Nat. Mus.* **19**: 679.
Richmond (1905). *Proc. Biol. Soc. Washington* **18**: 76.
Ridgway (1874). *Amer. Naturalist* **8**: 111.
Ridgway (1878). *Bull. U.S. Geol. Geogr. Surv. Territories* **4: 224, 247.**
Ridgway (1882). *Bull. Nuttall Orn. Club* **7**: 5.
Ridgway (1884). in: Baird, Brewer & Ridgway, *Mem. Mus. Comp. Zool.* **13**: 132, 395. [*Pterodroma phaeopygia sandwichensis, Pelecanus occidentalis californicus*]
Ridgway (1884). *Proc. Biol. Soc. Washington* **2**: 95. [*Phalacrocorax auritus albociliatus*]
Ridgway (1885). *Proc. U.S. Nat. Mus.* **8**: 22, 93.
Ridgway (1886). *Auk* **3**: 332.
Ridgway (1887). *Man. North Amer. Birds*: 112.
Ridgway (1889). *Proc. U.S. Nat. Mus.* **12**: 115.
Ridgway (1893). *Proc. U.S. Nat. Mus.* **16**: 599.
Ridgway (1897). *Proc. U.S. Nat. Mus.* **19**: 650.
Roberts (1919). *Ann. Transvaal Mus.* **6**: 118.
van Rossem (1926). *Condor* **28**: 246.
van Rossem (1930). *Trans. San Diego Soc. Nat. Hist.* **6**: 227.
van Rossem (1943). *Occas. Papers Mus. Zool. Louisiana State Univ.* **15**: 266.
van Rossem & Hachisuka (1937). *Trans. San Diego Soc. Nat. Hist.* **8**: 323.
Rothschild (1892). *Bull. Brit. Orn. Club* **1**: 17.
Rothschild (1893). *Bull. Brit. Orn. Club* **1**: 48, 57-58, 61.
Rothschild (1897). *Bull. Brit. Orn. Club* **7**: 5.
Rothschild (1898). *Bull. Brit. Orn. Club* **7**: 52.
Rothschild (1902). *Bull. Brit. Orn. Club* **13**: 7.
Rothschild & Chubb (1914). *Novit. Zool.* **21**: 223.
Rothschild & Hartert (1894). *Novit. Zool.* **1**: 683.
Rothschild, Hartert & Kleinschmidt (1897). *Novit. Zool.* **4**: 377.
Roux, Jouventin, Mougin, Stahl & Weimerskirch (1983). *Oiseau RFO* **53**: 1-11.
Rumboll (1974). *Comunicaciones Mus. Argentino Cien. Nat., Buenos Aires, Zool.* **4**: 33.
Rüppell (1837). *Neue Wirbelthiere Fauna Abyssinien, Vögel*: 49.
Rüppell (1845). *Syst. Uebersicht Vögel Nord-Ost-Afrika's*: 129-130, 138.
Salomonsen (1933). *Orn. Monatsber.* **41**: 41.
Salomonsen (1934). *Proc. Zool. Soc. London*: 219.
Salvadori (1865). *Atti Soc. Ital. Sci. Nat., Milan* **8**: 374.
Salvadori (1882). *Ann. Mus. Civ. Genova* **18**: 336.
Salvadori (1884). *Ann. Mus. Civ. Genova* **21**: 251-252.
Salvadori (1894). *Bull. Brit. Orn. Club* **4**: 2.
Salvadori (1895). *Cat. Birds Brit. Mus.* **27**.
Salvadori (1899). *Ann. Mus. Civ. Genova* **40**: 305.
Salvadori (1908). *Bull. Brit. Orn. Club* **21**: 79.
Salvin (1875). *Ibis*: 373.
Salvin (1876). *Tans. Zool. Soc. London* **9**: 507.
Salvin (1883). *Proc. Zool. Soc. London*: 430.
Salvin (1888). *Ibis*: 354, 357, 359.
Salvin (1891). *Ibis*: 192.
Salvin (1893). *Bull. Brit. Orn. Club* **1**: 33.
Salvin (1896). *Cat. Birds Brit. Mus.* **25**: 347, 354, 437-438.
de Schauensee (1959). see Meyer de Schauensee.
Schlegel (1863). *Mus. Hist. Nat. Pays-Bas, Rev. Méthod. Crit. Coll.* **4**: 9-10. [*Pterodroma incerta, Pterodroma neglecta*]
Schlegel (1863). *Mus. Hist. Nat. Pays-Bas, Rev. Méthod. Crit. Coll.* **3**: 48. [*Botaurus stellaris capensis*]
Schlegel (1866). *Mus. Hist. Nat. Pays-Bas, Rev. Méthod. Crit. Coll.* **8**: 85.
Schrenck (1860). *Reisen Forschungen Amur-Lande* **1**: 441.
Sclater, P.L. (1857). *Proc. Zool. Soc. London*: 128.
Sclater, P.L. (1858). *Proc. Zool. Soc. London (1857)*: 277.
Sclater, P.L. (1859). *Proc. Zool. Soc. London*: 391-392.
Sclater, P.L. (1861). *Proc. Zool. Soc. London (1860)*: 387.
Sclater, P.L. (1865). *Proc. Zool. Soc. London (1864)*: 487.
Sclater, P.L. (1877). *Proc. Zool. Soc. London*: 47.
Sclater, P.L. (1878). *Proc. Zool. Soc. London*: 350.
Sclater, P.L. (1886). *Proc. Zool. Soc. London*: 399-400.
Sclater, P.L. & Salvin (1868). *Exotic Orn.* **6**: 87.
Sclater, P.L. & Salvin (1869). *Exotic Orn.* **13**: 199.
Sclater, P.L. & Salvin (1870). *Proc. Zool. Soc. London*: 327.
Sclater, P.L. & Salvin (1873). *Proc. Zool. Soc. London*: 311, 512. [*Crypturellus obsoletus cerviniventris, Crypturellus bartletti*]
Sclater, P.L. & Salvin (1873). *Nomencl. Avium Neotrop.*: 153, 156, 161-163. [*Nothoprocta, Nothoprocta curvirostris curvirostris, Anas flavirostris andium, Dendrocygna autumnalis discolor*]
Sclater, P.L. & Salvin (1875). *Proc. Zool. Soc. London*: 38, 564.
Sclater, P.L. & Salvin (1878). *Proc. Zool. Soc. London*: 141.
Scopoli (1769). *Annus I Hist.-Nat.*: 65, 67, 69, 74, 88.
Scopoli (1786). *Deliciae Florae Faunae Insubricae* **2**: 92.
Sennett (1889). *Auk* **6**: 263.
Sevastianov (1802). *Nova Acta Acad. Sci. Imp. Petropolitanae* **13**: 349.
Severtsov (1873). *Izvestiia Imp. Obshchestva Liubitelei Estest. Antrop. Etnogr., Moscow* **8(2)**: 113.
Sharpe (1871). *Ann. Mag. Nat. Hist. (Ser. 4)* **8**: 51.
Sharpe (1875). *Ibis*: 328.
Sharpe (1894). *Bull. Brit. Orn. Club* **3**: 17.
Sharpe (1895). *Bull. Brit. Orn. Club* **5**: 13-14.
Shaw (1796). in: Shaw & Nodder, *Nat. Misc.* **8**, pl. 255.
Shaw (1800). *Trans. Linn. Soc. London* **5**: 33, 35.
Shaw (1813). in: Shaw & Nodder, *Nat. Misc.* **24**.
Simmons (1962). *Bull. Brit. Orn. Club* **82**: 93.
Smith, A. (1840). *Illus. Zool. South Africa, Aves*: pls. 51, 52, 55.
Snyder (1941). *Occas. Papers Royal. Ontario Mus. Zool.* **6**: 3.
Snyder & Lumsden (1951). *Occas. Papers Royal. Ontario Mus. Zool.* **10**: 15-16.
Sparrman (1786). *Mus. Carlsonianum* **1(10)**.
Sparrman (1788). *Mus. Carlsonianum* **3(61)**.
Spix (1825). *Avium Species Novae Itinere Brasiliam* **2**.
Stejneger (1885). in: Kingsley, *Standard Nat. Hist.* **4**: 141.
Stejneger (1893). *Proc. U.S. Nat. Mus.* **16**: 618.
Stephens (1819). in: Shaw, *General Zool.* **11(2)**: 592.
Stephens (1824). in: Shaw, *General Zool.* **12(2)**: 6, 221.
Stephens (1826). in: Shaw, *General Zool.* **13(1)**: 18, 68, 91, 93, 236, 239.
Stolzmann (1926). *Ann. Zool. Mus. Polon. Hist. Nat.* **5**: 199.
Streets (1877). *Bull. U.S. Nat. Mus.* **7**: 29.
Such (1825). *Zool. J.* **2**: 117.
Sundevall (1851). *Öfversigt K. Vetenskaps-Akad. Förhandlingar, Stockholm (1850)* **7**: 110.
Sundevall (1871). *Proc. Zool. Soc. London*: 126, 129.
Swainson (1827). *Zool. J.* **3**: 362.
Swainson (1831). *J. Royal. Institution Great Britain* **2**: 18.
Swainson (1832). in: Swainson & Richardson, *Fauna Boreali-Americana (1831)* **2**: 450.
Swainson (1834). in: Murray, *Encycl. Geogr.*: 1383.
Swainson (1837). *Nat. Hist. Class. Birds* **2**: 345, 365.
Swinhoe (1860). *Ibis*: 64.
Swinhoe (1866). *Ibis*: 394.
Swinhoe (1867). *Ibis*: 386.
Swinhoe (1871). *Proc. Zool. Soc. London*: 416-417.
Swinhoe (1873). *Proc. Zool. Soc. London*: 513. [*Ciconia boyciana*]
Swinhoe (1873). *Ibis*: 74 [*Ixobrychus eurhythmus*]
Sykes (1832). *Proc. Com. Sci. Corresp. Zool. Soc. London* **2**: 158.
Taczanowski (1875). *Proc. Zool. Soc. London (1874)*: 563.
Taczanowski (1886). *Orn. Pérou* **3**: 307.
Temminck (1815). *Hist. Nat. Pigeons Gallinacés* **3**.
Temminck (1823). *Planches Color.* **40**: 236.
Temminck (1824). *Planches Color.* **46**: pl. 271. [*Syrigma sibilatrix*]
Temminck (1824). *Planches Color.* **47**: pl. 276. [*Pelecanus conspicillatus*]
Temminck (1824). *Planches Color.* **51**: pl. 304. [*Pseudibis papillosa*]
Temminck (1825). *Planches Color.* **62**: pl. 369.
Temminck (1828). *Planches Color.* **77**: pl. 456.
Temminck (1835). *Planches Color.* **93**: pl. 551. [*Nipponia nippon*]
Temminck (1835). *Planches Color.* **98**: pl. 582. [*Nycticorax goisagi*]
Temminck (1835). *Planches Color.* **99**: pl. 587. [*Calonectris leucomelas, Puffinus tenuirostris*]
Temminck (1840). *Man. Orn.*, ed. 2, **4**: 376.
Temminck & Schlegel (1849). in: Siebold, *Fauna Japonica, Aves*: 120.
Temminck & Schlegel (1850). in: Siebold, *Fauna Japonica, Aves* pl. 83.
Thayer & Bangs (1905). *Bull. Mus. Comp. Zool.* **46**: 92.
Thayer & Bangs (1909). *Proc. New England Zool. Club* **4**: 40.
Ticehurst (1923). *Bull. Brit. Orn. Club* **44**: 28.
Todd (1919). *Proc. Biol. Soc. Washington* **32**: 117.
Todd (1938). *Auk* **55**: 662.
Todd (1948). *Proc. Biol. Soc. Washington* **61**: 49-50.
Townsend, C.H. (1890). *Proc. U.S. Nat. Mus.* **13**: 133-134.
Tschudi (1843). *Archiv Naturgeschichte* **9(1)**: 387, 390.
Tschudi (1844). *Archiv Naturgeschichte* **10(1)**: 307, 315.
Tugarinov (1941). *Fauna SSSr, Ptitsy* **1(4)**: 180.
Van Tyne (1935). *Misc. Publ. Mus. Zool. Univ. Michigan* **27**: 8.
Vieillot (1816). *Analyse*: 54, 67, 70. [*Dromaius, Eudyptes*]
Vieillot (1816). *Nouv. Dict. Hist. Nat. (Nouv. éd.)* **1**: 545. [*Anhinga anhinga leucogaster*]
Vieillot (1816). *Nouv. Dict. Hist. Nat. (Nouv. éd.)* **5**. [*Dendrocygna bicolor, Callonetta leucophrys, Amazonetta brasiliensis ipecutiri, Anas flavirostris flavirostris, Anas georgica spinicauda, Anas bahamensis rubrirostris, Anas versicolor versicolor, Anas cyanoptera cyanoptera, Anas platalea, Netta peposaca*]
Vieillot (1817). *Nouv. Dict. Hist. Nat. (Nouv. éd.)* **8**: 86, 88, 303. [*Phalacrocorax fuscescens, Phalacrocorax melanoleucos melanoleucos, Phalacrocorax niger, Plegadis chihi*]
Vieillot (1817). *Nouv. Dict. Hist. Nat. (Nouv. éd.)* **14**: 222, 415, 422. [*Tigrisoma lineatum marmoratum, Ixobrychus exilis erythromelas, Mergus octosetaceus*]
Vieillot (1817). *Nouv. Dict. Hist. Nat. (Nouv. éd.)* **16**: 18. [*Theristicus caerulescens*]
Vieillot (1817). *Nouv. Dict. Hist. Nat. (Nouv. éd.)* **25**: 418. [*Fregetta grallaria grallaria*]
Vieillot (1818). *Nouv. Dict. Hist. Nat. (Nouv. éd.)* **25** (1817): 422.
Vieillot (1819). *Nouv. Dict. Hist. Nat. (Nouv. éd.)* **34**: 105.
Vieillot (1823). in: Bonnaterre & Vieillot, *Tableau Encycl. Méthod. Trois Règnes Nature Orn.* **93**: 1127.

Vigors / Zimmer

Vigors (1831). *Proc. Com. Sci. Corresp. Zool. Soc. London* **1**: 98.

Vigors (1833). *List Animals Gardens Zool. Soc. London*, ed. 3: 4.

Vigors (1837). *Proc. Zool. Soc. London (1836)*: 79.

Vigors (1839). in: Beechey, *Zool. Voyage Pacific Behring's Straits*: 31.

Vigors & Children (1826). in: Denham & Clapperton, *Narrative Travels Discoveries Northern Central Africa* **21**: 201.

Wagler (1827). *Syst. Avium* [*Nothura*]

Wagler (1827). *Syst. Avium, Crypturus* **13**. [*Crypturellus parvirostris*]

Wagler (1827). *Syst. Avium, Ardea* **20**. [*Egretta ardesiaca*]

Wagler (1827). *Syst. Avium, Ardea* **28**. [*Botaurus poiciloptilus*]

Wagler (1827). *Syst. Avium, Ardea* **33**. [*Nycticorax leuconotus*]

Wagler (1827). *Syst. Avium, Ardea* **37**. [*Ixobrychus sturmii*]

Wagler (1827). *Syst. Avium,* Addit. [*Egretta alba melanorhynchos*]

Wagler (1829). *Isis von Oken*, cols. 659., 662.

Wagler (1832). *Isis von Oken*, cols. 281, 1231, 1232, 1233.

Wahlberg (1855). *Öfversigt K. Vetenskaps-Akad. Förhandlingar, Stockholm* **12**: 214.

Wetmore (1921). *J. Washington Acad. Sci.* **11**: 437.

Wetmore (1945). *Auk* **62**: 582-583.

Wetmore (1946). *Proc. Biol. Soc. Washington* **59**: 49.

Wetmore (1950). *Proc. Biol. Soc. Washington* **63**: 171.

Wetmore (1959). *Proc. Biol. Soc. Washington* **72**: 19-21.

Wetmore (1963). *Proc. Biol. Soc. Washington* **76**: 173.

Wetmore & Phelps (1956). *Proc. Biol. Soc. Washington* **69**: 1.

Wied (1820). *Reise Brasilien* **1**: 160.

Wied (1832). *Beitr. Naturgeschichte Brasilien* **4**: 929.

Wilson (1814). *Amer. Orn.* **8**: 103.

Yarrell (1830). *Trans. Linn. Soc. London* **16**: 453.

Zimmer (1938). *Proc. Biol. Soc. Washington* **51**: 48.

Zimmer & Phelps (1945). *Amer. Mus. Novit.* **1274**: 1.

GENERAL LIST OF REFERENCES

van Aarde, R.J. (1980). The diet and feeding behaviour of feral cats *Felis catus* at Marion Island. *S. Afr. J. Wildl. Res.* **10**: 123-128.

Abduladze, A.V. & Eligulashvili, V.E. (1986). The White Stork (*Ciconia ciconia* L.) in Georgia. *Soobshc Akad. Nauk. Cruz SSR* **124(2)**: 417-420.

Abdulali, H. (1964). On the food and other habits of the Greater Flamingo (*Phoenicopterus roseus* Pallas) in India. *J. Bombay Nat. Hist. Soc.* **61**: 60-68.

Abdulali, H. (1967). On the occurence of the Black-necked Stork, *Xenorhynchus asiaticus* (Latham), in the Bombay Konkan. *J. Bombay Nat. Hist. Soc.* **64**: 367.

Ackerman, R.A., Whittow, C.V., Paganelli, C.V. & Pettit, T.N. (1980). Oxygen consumption, gas exchange and growth of embryonic Wedge-tailed Shearwaters (*Puffinus pacificus chlororhynchus*). *Physiol. Zool.* **53**: 210-221.

Acosta, M., Torres, O. & Valdes, L.M. (1988). Subnicho trófico de *Dendrocygna bicolor* (Vieillot) (Aves: Anatidae) en dos áreas arroceras de Cuba. *Cienc. Biol. Acad. Cienc. Cuba* **19 & 20**: 41-50.

Acosta, M., Valdes, L.M. & Torres, O. (1989a). Ecomorfología de *Dendrocygna bicolor* (Vieillot) (Aves: Anatidae) en Cuba. *Cienc. Biol. Acad. Cienc. Cuba* **21 & 22**: 70-78.

Acosta, M., Valdes, L.M. & Torres, O. (1989b). Ciclo reproductivo de *Dendrocygna bicolor* (Vieillot) (Aves: Anatidae) en Cuba. *Cienc. Biol. Acad. Cienc. Cuba* **21 & 22**: 104-114.

Adamian, M.S. (1989). [On the nidification of the Marble Chirp *Anas angustirostris* Menetries, 1832 in the Armenian SSR]. *Biol. Zh. Arm.* **42 (8)**: 778-780. In Russian.

Adams, N.J. (1987). Foraging range of King Penguins *Aptenodytes patagonica* during summer at Marion Island. *J. Zoology. London* **212**: 475-482.

Adams, N.J. & Brown, C.R. (1983). Diving depths of the Gentoo Penguin *Pygoscelis papua*. *Condor* **85**: 503-504.

Adams, N.J. & Brown, C.R. (1984). Metabolic rates of sub-Antarctic Procellariiformes: a comparative study. *Comp. Biochem. Physiol.* **77 A**: 169-173.

Adams, N.J. & Brown, C.R. (1989). Dietary differentiation and trophic relationships in the sub-Antarctic penguin community at Marion Island. *Marine Ecology Progress Series* **57**: 249-258.

Adams, N.J. & Klages, N.T. (1987). Seasonal variation in the diet of the King Penguin (*Aptenodytes patagonicus*) at sub-Antarctic Marion Island. *J. Zoology. London* **212**: 303-324.

Adams, N.J. & Klages, N.T. (1989). Temporal variation in the diet of the Gentoo Penguin *Pygoscelis papua* at sub-Antarctic Marion Island. *Colonial Waterbirds* **12(1)**: 30-36.

Adams, N.J. & Walter, C.B. (1991). The Occurrence of Second Clutches after Successful Breeding by Cape Gannets (*Morus capensis*). *Colonial Waterbirds* **14(2)**: 173-175.

Adams, N.J. & Wilson, M.P. (1987). Foraging parameters of Gentoo Penguins *Pygoscelis papua* on Marion Island. *Polar. Biol.* **7**: 51-56.

Adams, N.J., Brown, C.R. & Nagy, K.A. (1986). Energy expenditure of free-ranging Wandering Albatrosses *Diomedea exulans*. *Physiol. Zool.* **59**: 583-591.

Adams, R. (1989a). The Least Bittern (*Ixobrychus exilis*) in Michigan. Unpublished Report, Kalamazoo Nat. Cent., Kalamazoo, Michigan.

Adams, R. (1989b). The American Bittern (*Botaurus lentiginosus*) in Michigan. Unpublished Report, Kalamazoo Nat. Cent., Kalamazoo, Michigan.

Aebischer, N.J. (1986). Retrospective investigation of an ecological disaster in the Shag, *Phalacrocorax aristotelis*: a general method based on long-term marking. *J. Anim. Ecol.* **55**: 613-629.

Afton, A.D. (1984). Influence of age time on reproductive performance of female Lesser Scaup. *Auk* **101**: 255-265.

Afton, A.D. & Hier, R.H. (1991). Diets of Lesser Scaup breeding in Manitoba. *J. Field Orn.* **62(3)**: 325-334.

Afton, A.D. & Sayler, R.D. (1982). Social courtship and pairbonding of Common Goldeneyes, *Bucephala clangula*, wintering in Minnesota. *Can. Field-Nat.* **96**: 295-300.

Aguilera, E. (1989). Sperm competition and copulation intervals of the White Spoonbill (*Platalea leucorodia*, Aves, Threskiornithidae). *Ethology* **82**: 230-237.

Aguilera, E. (1990a). Parental infanticide by White Spoonbills *Platalea leucorodia*. *Ibis* **132**: 124-125.

Aguilera, E. (1990b). Sexual differences in nest attendance and chick-feeding rhythms of White Spoonbills. *Auk* **107**: 416-420.

Aguilera, E. & Alvarez, F. (1989). Copulations and mate guarding of the spoonbill (*Platalea leucorodia*). *Behaviour* **110(1-4)**: 1-22.

Aguirre, A. (1957). *Contribuição ao estudo da biologia do macuco*. Divisão de caça e Pesca, Rio de Janeiro.

Aharoni, J. (1929). Zur Brutbiologie von *Comatibis comata* Bp. *Beitr. Fortpfl. Vogel* **5**: 17-19.

Ahlén, I. (1961). Ett fynd af *Podiceps griseigena holboellii* Reinhardt i Sverige. *Vår Fågelvärd* **20**: 296-302.

Ahlén, I. (1966). Studies on the distribution and ecology of the Little Grebe, *Podiceps ruficollis* (Pall.), in Sweden. *Vår Fågelvärld* **4(Suppl.)**: 1-45.

Ahlén, I. (1970). [Breeding population of the Red-necked Grebe *Podiceps grisegena* in Skåne 1960-1968]. In Swedish with English summary. *Vår Fågelvärld* **29**: 57-59.

Ahlquist, J.E., Bledsoe, A.H., Ratti, J.T. & Sibley, C.G. (1987). Divergence of the single-copy DNA-sequences of the Western Grebe (*Aechmophorus occidentalis*) and Clark's Grebe (*A. clarkii*), as indicated by DNA-DNA hybridization. *Postilla* **200**: 1-7.

Aid, C.S., Montgomery, G.G. & Mock, D.W. (1985). Range extension of the Peruvian Booby to Panama during the 1983 El Niño. *Colonial Waterbirds* **8**: 67-68.

Ainley, D.G. (1970). *Communication and Reproductive Cycles in Adelie Penguins*. PhD dissertation, John Hopkins University, Baltimore.

Ainley, D.G. (1972). Flocking in Adelie Penguins. *Ibis* **114**: 388-390.

Ainley, D.G. (1977). Feeding methods in seabirds: a comparison of polar and tropical nesting communities in the eastern Pacific Ocean. Pp. 669-685 in: Llano (1977).

Ainley, D.G. (1978). Activity patterns and social behaviour of non-breeding Adelie Penguins. *Condor* **80**: 138-146.

Ainley, D.G. (1980). Geographic variation in Leach's Storm Petrel. *Auk* **97**: 837-853.

Ainley, D.G. (1983). Further notes on variation in Leach's Storm Petrel. *Auk* **100**: 200-233.

Ainley, D.G. (1984a). Storm-Petrels. Family Oceanitidae. Pp. 58-63 in: Haley (1984).

Ainley, D.G. (1984b). Cormorants. Family Phalacrocoracidae. Pp. 92-101 in: Haley (1984).

Ainley, D.G. & Boekelheide, R.J. (1990). *Seabirds of the Farallon Islands: Ecology, Structure and Dynamics of an Upwelling-system Community*. Stanford University Press, Stanford.

Ainley, D.G. & DeMaster, D.P. (1980). Survival and mortality in a population of Adelie Penguins. *Ecology* **61**: 522-530.

Ainley, D.G. & Emison W.B. (1972). Sexual size dimorphism in Adelie Penguins. *Ibis* **114**: 267-271.

Ainley, D.G. & LeResche, R.E. (1973). The effects of weather and ice conditions on breeding in Adelie Penguins. *Condor* **75**: 235-255.

Ainley, D.G. & Manolis, B. (1979). Occurrence and distribution of the Mottled Petrel. *Western Birds* **10**: 113-123.

Ainley, D.G. & Schlatter, R.P. (1972). Chick raising ability in Adelie Penguins. *Auk* **89**: 559-566.

Ainley, D.G., Anderson, D.W. & Kelly, P.R. (1981). Feeding ecology of marine cormorants in southwestern North America. *Condor* **83**: 120-131.

Ainley, D.G., Henderson, R.P. & Strong, C.S. (1990). Leach's Storm Petrel and Ashy Storm Petrel. Pp. 128-162 in: Ainley, D.G. & Boekelheide, R.J. eds. *Seabirds of the Farallon Islands*. Stanford University Press, Stanford.

Ainley, D.G., LeResche, R.E. & Sladen, W.J.L. (1983). *Breeding Biology of the Adelie Penguin*. University of California Press, Berkeley.

Ainley, D.G., Lewis, T.J. & Morrell, S. (1976). Molt in Leach's and Ashy Storm-petrels. *Wilson Bull.* **88**: 76-95.

Ainley, D.G., Morrell, S. & Lewis, J.T. (1975). Patterns in the life histories of storm petrels on the Farallon Islands. *Living Bird* **13**: 295-312.

Ainley, D.G., O'Connor, E.F. & Boekelheide, R.J. (1984). *The Marine Ecology of Birds in the Ross Sea, Antarctica*. Ornithological Monographs **32**, American Ornithologists Union, Washington, D.C.

Ainley, D.G., Spear, L.B. & Boehkelheide, R.J. (1986). Extended fledging parental care in the Red-tailed Tropicbird and Sooty Tern. *Condor* **88(1)**: 101-102.

Akçakaya, H.R. (1990). Bald Ibis *Geronticus eremita* Population in Turkey: An Evaluation of the Captive Breeding Project for Reintroduction. *Biol. Conserv.* **51**: 225-237.

Akester, A.R., Pomeroy, D.E. & Purton, M.D. (1973). Subcutaneous air pouches in the Marabou Stork (*Leptoptilos crumeniferus*). *J. Zoology. London* **170**: 493-499.

Alam, M. (1982). The flamingos of Sambhar Lake. *J. Bombay Nat. Hist. Soc.* **79(1)**: 194-195.

Alamargot, J. (1976). La nidification du Marabout d'Afrique (*Leptoptilos crumeniferus*) en colonie dans le sud-ouest du L'Ethiopie. *L'Oiseau et la R.F.O.* **46**: 178-182.

Alamargot, J. (1984). New nesting colony of Marabou Storks (*Leptoptilos crumeniferus*). *Eur. Wildl. Nat. Hist. Soc. Newsl.* **188**: 2.

Albright, J.J. (1981). *Behavioral and Physiological Responses of Coastal Wintering Black Ducks (*Anas rubripes*) to Changing Weather in Maine*. MSc thesis, University of Maine, Orono.

Alder, L.P. (1963). The calls and displays of African and Indian Pygmy Geese. *Wildfowl Trust Ann. Rep.* **14**: 174-175.

Aldrich, J.W. & Baer, K.P. (1970). Status and speciation in the Mexican Duck. *Wilson Bull.* **82 (1)**: 63-73.

Alerstam, T., Bauer, C.A. & Ross, G. (1974). Spring migration of Eiders *Somateria mollissima* in southern Scandinavia. *Ibis* **116**: 194-210.

Alerstam, T.H. (1990). *Bird Migration*. Cambridge University Press, Cambridge, England.

Alexander, L.L. (1985). Trouble with loons. *Living Bird Quarterly* **3**: 10-13.

Alexander, W.B., Falla, R.A., Jouanin, C., Murphy, R.C., Salomonsen, F., Voous, K.H., Watson, G.E., Bourne, W.R.P., Fleming, C.A., Kuroda, N.H., Rowan, M.K., Serventy, D.L., Tickell, W.L.N., Warham, J. & Winterbottom, J.M. (1965). The families and genera of the petrels and their names. *Ibis* **107**: 401-405.

Ali, S. (1945). More about the Flamingo *Phoenicopterus ruber roseus* (Pallas) in Kutch. *J. Bombay Nat. Hist. Soc.* **45**: 586-593.

Ali, S. (1960). The Pink-headed Duck *Rhodonessa caryophyllacea* (Latham). *Wildfowl Trust Ann. Rep.* **11**: 55-60.

Ali, S. (1979). *The Book of Indian Birds*. 11th edition. Bombay Natural History Society, Bombay.

Ali, S. & Ripley, S.D. (1978). *Handbook of the Birds of India and Pakistan*. Vol. 1. 2nd edition. Oxford University Press, Delhi.

Alisauskas, R.T. & Ankney, C.D. (1992). Spring habitat use and diets of midcontinent adult Lesser Snow Geese. *J. Wildl. Manage.* **56 (1)**: 43-54.

Alisauskas, R.T., Ankney, C.D. & Klaas, E.E. (1988). Winter diets and nutrition of midcontinental Lesser Snow Geese. *J. Wildl. Manage.* **52(3)**: 403-414.

Alison, R. (1970). *The Behaviour of the Oldsquaw in Winter*. MSc thesis, University of Toronto.

Alison, R. (1975). *Breeding Biology and Behavior of the Oldsquaw (*Clangula hyemalis*)*. Ornithological Monographs **18**. The American Ornithologists' Union, Washington, D.C.

Allan, D. (1983a). Breeding Success of the Bald Ibis, 1983 progress report. Project TN 6/4/4/5. Unpublished report for Nature Conservation Division, Transvaal Provincial Administration, South Africa.

Allan, D. (1983b). The status of the Bald Ibis in the Transvaal, 1983 progress report. Unpublished report for the Transvaal Provincial Administration, Nature Conservation Division.

Allan, D. (1984a). Southern African White Stork census. *Bokmakierie* **36**: 77-80.

Allan, D. (1984b). Saddlebill Stork (R 75) on the Highveld. *Witwatersrand Bird Club News* **125**: 9.

Allan, D. (1984c). A study of coloniality, adaptations to cliff-nesting, productivity, breeding habits, vocalizations and parent-young recognition in the Bald Ibis (*Geronticus calvus*) in southern Africa. Project TN 6/4/4/5. Unpublished report for Nature Conservation Division, Transvaal Provincial Administration, South Africa.

Allan, D. (1985a). White Stork census results 1984/85. *Afr. Wildl.* **39**: 251-252.

Allan, D. (1985b). The Bald Ibis - A false alarm? *Fauna and Flora. Pretoria* **42**: 16-21.

Allan, D. (1989). The Bald Ibis returns to Cape Town. *Quagga* **25**: 18-20.

Allan, R.G. (1962). The Madeiran Storm Petrel *Oceanodroma castro*. *Ibis* **103(b)**: 274-295.

Allen, A.A. (1915). The behavior of Least Bittern. *Bird-Lore* **17**: 425-430.

Allen, G. (1991). Smew. *Game Bird Breeders Avicult. Zool. Conserv. Gazette* **40(7-8)**: 10, 44.

Allen, J.A. (1980). *Nesting and Productivity of Mottled Ducks in Marshlands of Southwest Louisiana*. MSc thesis, Louisiana State University, Baton Rouge, LA.

Allen, R. (1956). *The Flamingos: their Life History and Survival with Special Reference to the American or West Indian Flamingo (Phoenicopterus ruber)*. National Audubon Society Research Report **5**.

Allen, R.P. (1942). *The Roseate Spoonbill*. National Audubon Society Research Report **2**.

Allen, R.P. (1947). *The Flame Birds*. Dodd, Mead & Co., New York.

Allen, R.P. (1954). The Reddish Egret. *Audubon* **56(6)**: 252-255.

Allen, R.P. (1955). The Reddish Egret. *Audubon* 57(1): 24-27.

Allen, R.P. (1962). *Birds of the Caribbean*. Thames and Hudson, London.

Allen, T.T. (1961). Notes on the breeding behavior of the Anhinga. *Wilson Bull.* **73**: 115-125.

Allen-Grimes, A.W. (1982). *Breeding Biology of the White Ibis (*Eudocimus albus*) at Battery Island, North Carolina*. MSc thesis. University of North Carolina, Wilmington, N.C.

Alletson, D.J. (1985). Observations on some piscivorous birds in a trout fishing area of Natal. *Lammergeyer* **35**: 41-46.

Allport, G.A. & Wilson, S.A. (1986). *Results of a Census of the Milky Stork Mycteria cinerea in West Java*. Study Report **14**. ICBP, Cambridge.

Altenburg, W. & van der Kamp, J. (1986). *Oiseaux d'eau dans les zones les zones humides de la Mauritanie du sud, du Sénégal et de la Guinée - Bissau; octobre - désembre 1983*. RIN contributions to research on management of natural resources **1986-1**.

Altenburg, W. & van der Kamp, J. (1989). *Etude Ornithologique Préliminaire de la Zone Côtière du Nord-ouest de la Guinée*. Study report **30**. ICBP, Cambridge.

Altenburg, W., Beintema, A.J. & van der Kamp, J. (1986). *Observations ornithologiques dans le delta intérieur du Niger au Mali pendant les mois de mars et aout 1985 et janvier 1986*. RIN contributions to research on management of natural resources **1986-2**.

Altenburg, W., Engelmoer, M., Mes, R. & Piersma, T. (1982). *Wintering Waders on the Banc d'Arguin*. Communication of the Wadden Sea Working Group **6**.

Alvarez Cotelo, B.J., Fros Fros, T., Puig Bur, J.E. & Sanchez Méndez, J.A. (1989a). Estudio de algunas variables ecoetológicas en una pingüinera de *Pygoscelis papua*, en las Islas Shetland del Sur-Isla Ardley. *Inst. Ant. Uruguayo Act. Cient.* 1987/1988 **3**: 59-75.

Alvarez Cotelo, B.J., Fros Fros, T., Puig Bur, J.E. & Sanchez Méndez, J.A. (1989b). Sindrome general de adaptación en *Pygoscelis papua* a traves de parametros etológicos, biológicos y de productividad en una pingüinera. Islas Shetland del Sur-Isla Ardley. *Inst. Ant. Uruguayo Act. Cient.* 1987/1988 **3**: 77-86.

Alvarez Cotelo, B.J., Fros Fros, T., Puig Bur, J.E. & Sanchez Méndez, J.A. (1989c). Postura y fertilidad en *Pygoscelis papua. Inst. Ant. Uruguayo Act. Cient.* 1987/1988 **3**: 87-100.

Alvo, R. (1985). *The Breeding Success of Common Loons* (Gavia immer) *in Relation to Lake Alcalinity*. MSc thesis. Trent University, Peterborough.

Alvo, R. (1986). Lost loons of the Northern Lakes. *Nat. Hist.* **95**: 58-65.

Alvo, R. (1987). The Acid Test. *Living Bird* **6**(1): 25-30.

Alvo, R. & Prior, K. (1986). Using eggshells to determine the year of a Common Loon, *Gavia immer*, nesting attempt. *Can. Field-Nat.* **100**(1): 114-115.

Alvo, R., Hussell, D.J.T. & Berrill, M. (1988). The breeding success of common loons (*Gavia immer*) in relation to alkalinity and other lake characteristics in Ontario. *Can. J. Zool.* **66**: 746-752.

Amadon, D. (1943). Birds of the Whitney South Sea Expedition 52. Notes on some non-passerine genera, 3. *Amer. Mus. Novitates* **1237**: 1-22.

Amadon, D. (1953). Avian systematics and evolution in the Gulf of Guinea. *Bull. Amer. Mus. Nat. Hist.* **100**: 393-451.

Amadon, D. (1959). The subspecies of *Tinamus tao* and *Tinamus solitarius* (Aves). *Amer. Mus. Novitates* **1955**.

Amat, J.A. (1980). *Biología y ecología de la comunidad de patos del Parque Nacional de Doñana*. Tesis Doctoral, Universidad de Sevilla.

Amat, J.A. (1986). Some aspects of the foraging ecology of a wintering Greylag Goose *Anser anser* population. *Bird Study* **33**: 74-80.

Amat, J.A. & Sánchez, A. (1982). Biología y ecología de la Malvasía (*Oxyura leucocephala*) en Andalucía. *Doñana Acta Vertebrata* **9**: 251-320.

Amat, J.A., Lucientes, J. & Ferrer, X. (1987). La migración de muda del Pato Colorado (*Netta rufina*) en España. *Ardeola* **34**(1): 79-88. In Spanish with English summary.

Ambedkar, V.C. (1959). The occurrence of the White-necked Stork, *Ciconia episcopus* (Boddaert), in the Kashmir Valley. *J. Bombay Nat. Hist. Soc.* **56**: 633.

Ames, P.L. (1971). The Morphology of the Syrinx in Passerine Birds. *Peabody Mus. Nat. Hist. Bull. Yale Univ.* **37**.

Amget, B. (1986). Some information on the Open-billed Stork. Unpublished report. Wildlife Conservation Division, Royal Forest Department, Bangkok.

Amiet, L. (1958). The distribution of *Diomedea* in eastern Australian waters. *Notornis* **7**: 219-230.

Amlaner, C.J. & Ball, N.J. (1983). A synthesis of sleep in wild birds. *Behaviour* **87**: 85-119.

Amundsen, T. & Stokland, J.N. (1988). Adaptative significance of asynchronous hatching in the Shag: a test of the brood reduction hypothesis. *J. Anim. Ecol.* **57**: 329-344.

Amundsen, T. & Stokland, J.N. (1990). Egg size and parental quality influence nestling growth in the Shag. *Auk* **107**(2):410-413.

Andersen-Harild, P. (1978). [*The Mute Swan*]. Copenhagen Skarv. Nature publications. In Danish.

Andersen, K. (1895). *Diomedea melanophrys* in the Faroe Islands. *Proc. R. Phys. Soc.* **13**: 91-114.

Anderson, A. (1982). The establishment and growth of a new Fulmar colony on sand dunes. *Bird Study* **29**: 189-194.

Anderson, A.B. (1949). Marabou nesting colonies of the southern Sudan. *Sudan Notes Rec.* **30**: 114-118.

Anderson, B.W. & Timken, R.L. (1972). Sex and age ratios and weights of Common Merganser. *J. Wildl. Manage.* **36**: 1127-1133.

Anderson, D.J. (1989a). Ecology and behaviour of siblicide in Masked and Blue-footed Boobies. PhD thesis, University of Pennsylvania, PA.

Anderson, D.J. (1989b). The role of hatching asynchrony in siblicidal brood reductin of two booby species. *Beh. Ecol. Sociobiol.* **25**: 363-368.

Anderson, D.J. (1991). Apparent predator-limited distribution of Galápagos Red-footed Boobies *Sula sula. Ibis* **133**: 26-29.

Anderson, D.J. & Horowitz, R.J. (1979). Competitive interactions among vultures and their avian competitors. *Ibis* **121**: 505-509.

Anderson, D.J. & Ricklefs, R.E. (1987). Radio-tracking Masked and Blue-footed Boobies (*Sula* spp.) in the Galápagos Islands. *Natl. Geog. Res.* **3**(2): 152-163.

Anderson, D.R. (1975). *Population Ecology of the Mallard: V. Temporal and Geographic Estimates of Survival, Recovery and Harvest Rates*. US Fish & Wildlife Service Resources Publication **125**.

Anderson, D.R. & Burnham, K.P. (1976). *Population Ecology of the Mallard: VI. The Effect of Exploitation on Survival*. US Fish & Wildlife Service Resources Publication **128**.

Anderson, D.R. & Henny, C.J. (1972). *Population Ecology of the Mallard: I. A Review of Previous Studies and the Distribution and Migration from Breeding Areas*. US Fish & Wildlife Service Resources Publication **105**.

Anderson, D.W. (1984). Pelicans. Family Pelecanidae. Pp. 84-91 in: Haley (1984).

Anderson, D.W. (1988). Dose-response relationship between human disturbance and Brown Pelican nesting success. *Wildl. Soc. Bull.* **16**: 339-345.

Anderson, D.W. & Anderson, I.T. (1976). Distribution and status of Brown Pelicans in the California Current. *Amer. Birds* **30**: 3-12.

Anderson, D.W. & Gress, F. (1981). The politics of pelicans. Pp. 117-143 in: Jackson, T.C. & Reische, D. eds. (1981). *Coast Alert: Scientists Speak Out*. Coast Alliance/Friends of the Earth Press, San Francisco.

Anderson, D.W. & Gress, F. (1982). Brown Pelicans and the anchovy fishery off Southern California. Pp. 128-135 in: Nettleship *et al.* (1982).

Anderson, D.W. & Gress, F. (1983). Status of a northern population of California Brown Pelicans. *Condor* **85**: 79-88.

Anderson, D.W. & Keith, J.O. (1980). The human influence on seabird nesting success: conservation implications. *Biol. Conserv.* **18**: 65-80.

Anderson, D.W., DeWeese, L.R. & Tiller, D.V. (1977). Passive dispersal of California Brown Pelicans. *Bird-Banding* **48**: 228-238.

Anderson, D.W., Gress, F. & Mais, K.F. (1982). Brown Pelicans: influence of food supply on reproduction. *Oikos* **39**: 23-31.

Anderson, D.W., Jehl, J.R., Risebrough, R.W., Woods, L.A., DeWeese, L.R. & Edgecomb, W.G. (1975). Brown Pelicans: improved reproduction off the southern California coast. *Science* **190**: 806-808.

Anderson, D.W., Keith, J.O., Trapp, G.R., Gress, F. & Moreno, L.A. (1989). Introduced small ground predators in California Brown Pelican colonies. *Colonial Waterbirds* **12**: 98-103.

Anderson, J.G.T. (1991). Foraging behavior of the American White Pelican (*Pelecanus erythrorhynchos*) in Western Nevada. *Colonial Waterbirds* **14**(2): 166-172.

Anderson, M.G. (1984). Parental investment and pair-bond behavior among Canvasback Ducks (*Aythya valisineria*, Anatidae). *Behav. Ecol. Sociobiol.* **15**: 81-90.

Andersson, Å., Lindberg, P., Nilsson, P.G. & Pettersson, Å. (1980). Storlommens *Gavia arctica* häckningsframgång i svenska sjöar. *Vår Fågelvärld* **39**(2): 85-94.

Andersson, M. & Eriksson, M.O.G. (1982). Nest parasitism in Goldeneyes *Bucephala clangula*: some evolutionary aspects. *Amer. Naturalist* **120**: 1-16.

Andersson, T. (1954). Simflyttning hos skäggdopping (*Podiceps cristatus*) och gråhakedopping (*P. grisegena*). [Summary: Migration by swimming in two *Podiceps* species]. *Vår Fågelvärld* **3**: 133-142.

André, P. & Johnson, A.R. (1981). Le problème des Flamants roses dans les rizières de Camargue et les résultats de la campagne de dissuasion du printemps 1981. *Courrier Parc Nat. Rég. Camargue* **22/23**: 20-35.

Andrew, P. (1986). Notes on some birds of Timor. *Kukila* **2**(4): 92-95.

Andrew, P. & Holmes, D.A. (1990). Sulawesi Bird Report. *Kukila* **5**(1): 4-26.

Andrewartha, H.G. & Birch, L.C. (1954). *The Distribution and Abundance of Animals*. University of Chicago Press, Chicago.

Andriamampianina, J. & Peyrieras, A. (1972). Les réserves naturelles intégrales de Madagascar. Pp. 103-123 in: *C.R. Conférence Internationale sur la Conservation de la Nature et de ses Ressources à Madagascar*. IUCN, Morges.

Andronov, V.A. (1983). [Status of the populations of cranes and storks in Chinganski Reserve]. Pp. 8-10 in: *Transactions of the Conference of Living Nature*. In Russian.

Angove, R. (1982). Notes on a nesting colony of the Black-faced Shag. *S. Austr. Orn.* **29**: 16.

Aniskowicz, B.T. (1981). Behavior of a male Least Bittern incubation after loss of mate. *Wilson Bull.* **93**: 395-397.

Ankney, C.D. (1977). The use of nutrient reserves by breeding male Lesser Snow Geese *Chen caerulescens. Can. J. Zool.* **55**: 1984-1987.

Ankney, C.D. & MacInnes, C.D. (1978). Nutrient reserves and reproductive performance of female Lesser Snow Geese. *Auk* **95**: 459-471.

Ankney, C.D., Dennis, D.G. & Bailey, R.C. (1987). Increasing Mallards, decreasing American Black Ducks: Coincidence or cause and effect? *J. Wild. Manage.* **51**: 523-529.

Ankney, C.D., Dennis, D.G. & Bailey, R.C. (1989). Increasing Mallards, decreasing American Black Ducks - no evidence for cause and effect: a reply. *J. Wild. Manage.* **53**: 1072-1075.

Anon. (1953). Estudio biológico sobre *Nothercus bonapartei* (Gallina cuero). *Bol. Acad. Cienc. Caracas* **16**(51): 170-192.

Anon. (1974). *Conservation of Endangered Species on Christmas Island*. Australian Government Publishing Service, Canberra.

Anon. (1978). *Sveriges Fåglar*. Sveriges Ornitologiska Förening, Stockholm.

Anon. (1981). *Lead Poisoning in Swans*. Report of the Nature Conservancy Council's Working Group.

Anon. (1982). Nocturnal Birds of Southern Africa: White-Backed Nightheron *Gorsachius leuconotus. Afr. Wildl.* **36**(4-5).

Anon. (1983a). *Guidelines for the Management of the White Pelican, Western Population*. US Fish and Wildlife Service, Portland, OR.

Anon. (1983b). Jabiru nesting in Belize. *Belize Audubon Soc. Bull.* **15**: 1-2.

Anon. (1984a). *North American Management Plan for Trumpeter Swans*. Office of Migratory Bird Management, Washington, D.C.

Anon. (1984b). The Swan Goose, *Anser cygnoides*, selected as City Bird in Mudanjiang (Heilongjiang Province). *Natural Resources Research* 4:48.

Anon. (1985a). Kleptoparasitism of Sea Lions by Magnificent Frigate-birds. *Sea Swallow* **34**: 78-79.

Anon. (1985b). Conservationists battle for Caroni Swamp and Scarlet Ibis. *World Birdwatch* **7**(3): 3.

Anon. (1986-1990). Ganzentellingen in Nederland en Vlaanderen in 1983/84 & 1984/85 & 1985/86 & en België 1987/88. *Limosa* **59**: 25-31; **60**: 31-39, 137-146; **63**: 71-79.

Anon. (1986a). Amendments to Appendices I and II of the Convention. Proposal: inclusion of *Balaeniceps rex* in Appendix I. Report to CITES.

Anon. (1986b). Recovery plan for the US breeding population of the Wood Stork. US Fish & Wildlife Service, Atlanta, Georgia.

Anon. (1986c). Regional reports-Indonesia. *Oriental Bird Club Bull.* **3**: 35.

Anon. (1988). Nest sites of Black Storks (*Ciconia nigra*) in Lasy Janowskie, Prov. Tarnobrzeg. *Notatki Ornitol.* 1988: 227-231.

Anon. (1989a). Milky Stork colonies located in Sumatra. *World Birdwatch* **11**(1): 3.

Anon. (1989b). Captive breeding programme for Milky Storks. *Asian Wetland News* **2**(1): 5.

Anon. (1989c). Storm's Stork discovered breeding in Sumatra. *Asian Wetland News* **2**(1): 14.

Anon. (1989d). A survey of Coastal Wetlands and Shorebirds in South Korea, Spring 1988. *Oryx* 23(3): 176-177.

Anon. (1990a). News from Wat Phai Lom - the Thailand Openbill Stork colony. *Flying Free* **8**: 7-9.

Anon. (1990b). Seabirds of Ascension Island. *World Birdwatch* **12**(4): 5.

Anon. (1990c). New Zealand's population of Royal Spoonbills on the increase. *Specialist Group on Storks, Ibises and Spoonbills Newsletter* 4(1): 7.

Anon. (1990d). Malaysia's Milky Storks breed again. *Asian Wetland News* **2**(2): 1.

Anon. (1991a). Argentinian rainforest bought for conservation. *World Birdwatch* **13**(1): 5.

Anon. (1991b). Asia: almost unnoticed spoonbill slips toward oblivion. *News* May/Jun 1991: 16.

Anon. (1991c). *Micropterus patachonicus* King, 1831 and *Anas pteneres* Forster, 1844 (both currently in *Tachyeres* Owen, 1875; Aves, Anseriformes): specific names conserved. *Bull. Zool. Nomencl.* **48** (29): 187-188.

Anon. (1991d). *Revisión del plan de recuperación de la Malvasía en Andalucía*. Departamento de Protección Fauna y Flora Agencia de Medio Ambiente - Junta de Andalucía, Sevilla.

Anrys, P. & Verhaegen, J.P. (1986). Nidifications du Grèbe à cou noir, *Podiceps nigricollis*, au centre de recherches biologiques d'Harchies. *Gerfaut* **76**: 69-72.

Anstey, S. (1989a). *The Status and Conservation of the White-headed Duck* Oxyura leucocephala. IWRR Special Publication 10.

Anstey, S. (1989b). Progress in the White-headed Duck *Oxyura leucocephala* Action Plan Project. *Wildfowl* **40**: 141.

Antas, P.T.Z. (1979). Breeding the Scarlet Ibis *Eudocimus ruber* at the Rio de Janeiro Zoo. *Int. Zoo Yb.* **19**: 135-139.

Antas, P.T.Z. (1991). Status and Conservation of Seabirds Breeding in Brazilian Waters. Pp. 141-158 in: Croxall (1991).

Antas, P.T.Z. & Cavalcanti, R.B. (1988). *Aves Comunes do Planalto Central*. Editora Universidade de Brasilia, Brasilia.

Antas, P.T.Z. & Nascimento, J.L.X. (1991). Movimentação e situação atual de *Anas georgica* no sul do Brasil. *IV Congreso de Ornitología Neotropical, 3-9 Noviembre 1991*. Quito, Ecuador.

Anthony, A.J. (1977). A further breeding record of the Woolly-necked Stork. *Honeyguide* **89**: 36-40.

Anthony, A.J. (1978a). A further breeding record of the Woolly-necked Stork: the 1977/78 season. *Honeyguide* **95**: 45.

Anthony, A.J. (1978b). Hadedah nesting at Chipinda Pools, Gonarezhou National Park. *Honeyguide* **95**: 33-35.

Anthony, A.J. & Sherry, B.Y. (1980). Openbill Storks breeding in the southeastern lowveld of Zimbabwe Rhodesia. *Ostrich* **51**: 1-6.

Ap-Thomas, D.A. (1986). Pelicans. *Bird Obsr.* **655**: 80.

Appert, O. (1966). Beitrag zur Biologie und zur Kenntnis der Verbreitung des Madagaskar Mahnenibisses, *Lophotibis cristata* (Boddaert). *J. Orn.* **107**: 315-322.

Appert , O. (1971a). Die Taucher (Podidipidae) der Mangokygegend in Südwest-Madagaskar. *J. Orn.* **112**: 61-69.

Appert, O. (1971b). Die Flamingos der Mangokygegend in Südwest-Madagaskar. *Orn. Beob.* **68**(6): 271-276.

Appleby, R.H., Madge, S.C. & Mullarney, K. (1986). Identification of Divers in inmature and winter plumage. *British Birds* **79**(8): 365-391.

Araujo, J., Muñoz-Cobos, J. & Purroy, F.J. (1977). *Las rapaces y aves marinas del archipiélago de Cabrera*. Naturalia Hispánica 12. ICONA, Madrid.

Araya, B. (1983). A preliminary report on the status and distribution of the Humboldt Penguin in Chile. Pp. 125-135 in: *Proceedings of the Jean Delacour/IFCB symposium on Breeding Birds in Captivity*. International Foundation for Conservation of Birds, Los Angeles.

Araya, B. & Millie, G. (1986). *Guía de campo de las aves de Chile*. Editorial Universitaria, Santiago.

Arballo, E. (1990a). Nidificación de *Theristicus caudatus* en Uruguay. *Hornero* **13**: 165-166.

Arballo, E. (1990b). Nuevos registros para avifauna uruguaya. *Hornero* **13**: 179-183.

Archer, A.L. (1978). Marabous breeding at Kiboko, Kenya. *East Afr. Nat. Hist. Soc. Bull.* **Sept/Oct**: 106-107.

Archibald, G.W. (1981). They've captured the Toki! *Int. Wildl.* **11**: 20-24.

Archibald, G.W. & Lantis, S. (1979). Conservation of the Japanese crested ibis. *Proc. Conf. Colonial Waterbirds* **3**: 1-15.

Archibald, G.W., Lantis, S.D.H. Lantis, L.R. & Munetchika, I. (1980). Endangered ibises Threskiornithinae: their future in the wild and in captivity. *Int. Zoo Yb.* **20**: 6-17.

Archibald, K. (1985). Captive management of the Eastern White Stork. *Avicult. Mag.* **91**: 92-101.

Archibald, K. (1989). Recommendations for captive management of the Eastern White Stork (*Ciconia boyciana*). Manuscript, *C. boyciana* proceedings.

Archibald, K. & Luthin, C.S. (1985). Final report on the Eastern White Stork (*Ciconia boyciana*). Manuscript, *C. boyciana* proceedings.

Archibald, K. & Schmidt, B. (1989). Behavioural comparison between the Eastern White Stork (*Ciconia boyciana*) and the European White Stork (*Ciconia c.ciconia*). Manuscript, *C. boyciana* proceedings.

Archibald, K.T. & Nott, T.B. (1987). The breeding success of Flamingos in Etosha National Park, 1986. *Madoqua* **15**: 269-270.

Arenas, R. & Torres, J.A. (1988). La Malvasía (*Oxyura leucocephala*) en las zonas húmedas del sur de Córdoba. Pp. 141-151 in: *Ponencias de las II Jornadas Ibéricas sobre el Estudio y Protección de las Zonas Húmedas*.

Arenas, R. & Torres, J.A. (1991). Biología y situación de la Malvasía en España. *Quercus* **73**: 14-21.

Arendt, W.J. (1988). Range Expansion of the Cattle Egret (*Bubulcus ibis*) in the Greater Caribbean Basin. *Colonial Waterbirds* **11**(2): 252-262.

Arendt, W.J. & Arendt, A.I. (1988). Aspects of the Breeding Biology of the Cattle Egret (*Bubulcus ibis*) in Montserrat, West Indies, and its Impact on Nest Vegetation. *Colonial Waterbirds* **11**(1): 72-84.

Armbruster, J.S. (1982). Wood Duck displays and pairing chronology. *Auk* **99**: 116-122.

Armstrong, E.A. (1958). *The Folklore of Birds*. London.

Armstrong, E.A. (1963). *A Study of Bird Song*. Oxford University Press, London.

Armstrong, E.A. (1965). *Bird Display and Behaviour*. 2nd edition. Dover Publications, New York.

Armstrong, E.A. (1983). *A New, Expanded Guide to the Birds of Alaska*. Alaska Northwest Publishing Company, Anchorage, Alaska.

Arnold, K.A. (1978). A Jabiru (*Jabiru mycteria*) specimen from Texas. *Auk* **95**: 611-612.

Arnold, T.W. (1989). Variation in Size and Composition of Horned and Pied-Billed Grebe Eggs. *Condor* **91**: 987-989.

Arnold, T.W. (1990). Determination of clutch size in Horned and Pied-billed Grebes. *Wilson Bull.* **102**: 336-338.

Arriaga Weiss, S.L. & Hernandez Franyutti, A.A. (1981). Algunas aves de importancia alimentaicia en Balzapote, Veracruz, Mexico. Notas preliminares. *Centzontle Rev. Soc. Mex. Orn.* **1**(3-4): 147-151.

Arvidsson (1987). Distribution and population size of Whooper Swan, *Cygnus cygnus* in Sweden. *Vår Fågelvärld* 46: 248-255.

Asbirk, S. & Dybbro, T. (1978). Bestandsstorrelse og habitatvalg hos Toppet Lappedykker *Podiceps cristatus* i Danmark 1975. [Summary: Population size and habitat selection of the Great Crested Grebe in Denmark, 1975]. *Dan. Orn. Foren. Tidsskr.* **72**: 1-13.

Ash, J. & Rooke, K.B. (1954). Balearic Shearwaters off the Dorset coast in 1953. *Brit. Birds* **47**: 285-296.

Ash, J.S. (1977). First known breeding of the Ruddy Shelduck *Tadorna ferruginea* south of the Sahara. *Bull. Brit. Orn. Club* **97**: 56-59.

Ash, J.S. (1981). Bird-ringing results and ringed bird recoveries in Ethiopia. *Scopus* **5**: 85-101.

Ash, J.S. (1990). Additions to the avifauna of Nigeria, with notes on distributional changes and breeding. *Malimbus* **11**: 104-144.

Ash, J.S. & Howell, T.R. (1977). The Bald Ibis or Waldrapp *Geronticus eremita* in Ethiopia. *Bull. Brit. Orn. Club* **97**: 104.

Ash, J.S. & Miskell, J.E. (1983). *Birds of Somalia. Their Habitat, Status and Distribution.* Scopus Special Supplement Number **1**. Ornithological Sub-Committee of the East African Natural History Society,

Ashby, E. (1933). Detailed observations of the nesting habits of the Black-throated Grebe at "Wittunga", Blackwood, S.A., from August, 1932, until March, 1933. *Emu* **32**: 250-259.

Ashmole, N.P. (1971). Seabird ecology and the marine environment. Pp. 224-286 in: Farner, D.S. & King, J.R. eds. (1971). *Avian Biology.* Vol. 1. Academic Press, London & New York.

Ashmole, N.P. & Ashmole, M.J. (1967). Comparative feeding ecology of seabirds of a tropical oceanic island. *Peabody Mus. Nat. Hist. Yale Univ.* **24**: 1-131.

Assfalg, W. & Schüz, E. (1988). Weissstorch-Dreiergruppe, ein Möglicher Umweg zur Paarbildung. *Orn. Mitt. Jahrg.* **40**(11): 279-286.

Astheimer, L.B., Prince, P.A. & Grau, C.R. (1985). Egg formation and the pre-laying period of Black-browed and Grey-headed Albatrosses at Bird Island, South Georgia. *Ibis* **127**: 523-529.

Atkinson, I. & Daniel, P. (1985). The Weka. Victim or villain. *Forest & Bird* **16**(3): 23-25.

Atkinson, I.A.E. (1985). The Spread of Commensal Species of *Rattus* to Oceanic Islands and their Effects on Island Avifaunas. Pp. 35-81 in: Moors (1985).

Atkinson, P., Dutton, J.S. & Sequeira, V. (1991). UEA Expedition to Sao Tomé e Príncipe June-September 1990. Preliminary report. University of East Anglia Sao Tomé Expedition, Sao Tomé, RDSTP.

Atkinson, P., Peet, N. & Alexander, J. (1991). The status and conservation of the endemic bird species of Sao Tomé and Príncipe, West Africa. *Bird Conserv. Int.* **1**: 255-282.

Atkinson-Willes, G.L. (1972). The International Wildfowl Censuses as a Basis for Wetland Evaluation and Hunting Rationalisation. Pp. 87-110 in: Carp, E. ed. *Proc. Int. Conf. Conserv. Wetlands & Waterfowl, Ramsar 1971.* IWRB, Slimbridge, UK.

Atkinson-Willes, G.L. (1975). The numerical distribution of ducks, swans and coots as a guide in assessing the importance of wetlands. Pp. 199-271 in: Smart, M. ed. *Proc. Int. Conf. Conserv. Wetlands & Waterfowl, Heilingenhafen 1974.* IWRB, Slimbridge, UK.

Austin, J.E. (1988). *Wintering Ecology of Canada Geese Wintering in North Central Missouri.* PhD dissertation, University of Missouri, Columbia, MO.

Austin, J.E. (1990). Comparison of activities within families and pairs of wintering Canada Geese. *Wilson Bull.* **102** (3): 536-542.

Austin, O.L. (1948). *The Birds of Korea.* Bulletin of the Museum of Comparative Zoology **101**: 1-301. Cambridge, MA.

Austin, O.L. (1949). The status of the Steller's Albatross. *Pacific Science* **3**: 283-295.

Austin, O.L. & Singer, A. (1961). *Birds of the World: a Survey of the Twenty-seven Orders and one Hundred and Fifty-five Families.* Golden Press, New York.

Austin, O.L.. & Kuroda, N. (1953). *The Birds of Japan. Their Status and Distribution.* Bulletin of the Museum of Comparative Zoology **109**: 279-637. Cambridge, MA.

Avery, G. (1983). Bank Cormorants *Phalacrocorax neglectus* taking Cape Rock Lobster *Jasus lalandii. Cormorant* **11**: 45-48.

Avery, M., Leslie, R., Fuller, R. & Hope-Jones, P. (1990). *Birds and Forestry.* T & AD Poyser, London.

Avise, J.C., Ankney, C.D. & Nelson, W.S. (1990). Mitochondrial Gene Trees and the Evolutionary Relationship of Mallard and Black Ducks. *Evolution* **44** (4): 1109-1119.

Axelsson, P. (1988). Gråhakedoppingen i trakten av Ystad 1987. *Stenknäcken* **1**: 12-14.

Babko, V.M. (1987). [On the records and breeding of the Black Stork (*Ciconia nigra*) in the southwestern part of Chernigov Region]. *Ornitologiya* **22**: 175. In Russian.

Baccetti, N. (1983). Heronries of Somalia: a Preliminary Report. *Monitore zoologico italiano* **6**: 173-185.

Baccetti, N. (1989). Presenza nei mari italiani di *Puffinus puffinus mauretanicus* Lowe, 1921. *Riv. ital. Orn.* **59**(3-4): 275-278.

Bacon, P. (1974). Observations on the feeding zones of three species of grebes at Lake Tåkern. *Medd. Tåkern fältstation* **10**: 46-53.

Bacon, P.E. (1980). A possible advantage of the "Polish" morph of the Mute Swan. *Wildfowl* **31**: 51-52.

Bacon, P.E. & Andersen-Harild, P. (1989). Mute Swans. Pp. 363-386 in: Newton, I. ed. (1989). *Lifetime Reproductive Success in Birds.* Academic Press, London.

Badano, L.A., Scolaro, J.A. & Upton, J.A. (1982). Distribución espacial de la nidificación de *Spheniscus magellanicus* en Cabo Dos Bahías, Chubut, Argentina (Aves: Spheniscidae). *Historia Nat. Corrientes.* **2**(27): 241-251.

Badgerow, J.P. (1988). An analysis of function in the formation flight of Canada Geese. *Auk* **105**: 749-755.

Badshah, M.A. (1963). Breeding colony of Painted Storks. *Peacock* **3**: 15-17.

Baerends, G.P. & van der Cingel, N.A. (1962). On the phylogenetic origin of the Snap display in the Common Heron (*Ardea cinerea*). *Symp. Zool. Soc. London* **8**: 7-24.

Bagley, F.M. & Grau, G.A. (1979). Aspects of Yellow-crowned Night Heron reproductive behaviour. *Proc. Conf. Colonial Waterbird Group* **3**: 165-175.

Baha El Din, S. (1984). New and interesting records for Egypt 1980-1982. *Courser* **1**: 47-51.

Bahamonde, N. (1955). Alimentación de cormoranes o cuervos marinos (*Phalacrocorax atriceps, Ph. magellanicus* y *Ph. olivaceus olivaceus*). *Invest. Zool. Chil.* **2**: 132-134.

Bahamonde, N. (1974). El piquero blanco de islas Desventuradas. *Not. mensual MNHN* **18** (210): 3-7.

Bahena, A.C.R. (1983). Situación de los flamencos en el Estado de Yucatán. Pp. 108-111 in: *Proc. IWRB Symposium, Edmonton, May 1982.*

Bailey, A.M. & Sorensen, J.H. (1962). Subantarctic Campbell Island. *Proc. Denver. Mus. Nat. His.* **10**.

Bailey, R. (1966). The sea-birds of the southeast coast of Arabia. *Ibis* **108**: 224-264.

Bailey, R.E. (1955). The incubation patch in tinamous. *Condor* **57**: 301-303.

Bailey, R.F. (1934). New nesting records of Glossy Ibis. *Emu* **33**: 279-291.

Bailey, R.O. (1982). *The Postbreeding Ecology of the Redhead Duck (Aythya americana) on Long Island Bay, Lake Winnipegosis, Manitoba.* PhD dissertation, McGill University, Montreal, Quebec.

Bailey, R.O. & Titman, R.D. (1984). Habitat use and feeding ecology of postbreeding Redheads. *J. Wildl. Manage.* **48**: 1144-1155.

Bailey, R.S. (1968). The pelagic distribution of sea-birds in the western Indian Ocean. *Ibis* **110**: 493-519.

Bailey, R.S., Pocklington, R. & Willis, P.R. (1968). Storm-petrels in the Indian Ocean. *Ibis* **110**: 27-34.

Bailey, S.F., Pyle, P. & Spear, L.B. (1989). Dark *Pterodroma* petrels in the North Pacific: identification, status and North American occurrence. *Amer. Birds* **43**(3): 400-415.

Bain, J.R. & Humphrey, S.R. (1980). A profile of the endangered species of Thailand. *Florida State Museum Office of Ecological Services Report* **4**: 173-196.

Bairlein, F. (1981). Analyse der Ringfunde von Weissstörchen (*Ciconia ciconia*) aus Mitteleuropa westlich der Zugscheide: Zug, Winterquartier, Sommerverbreitung vor der Brutreife. *Vogelwarte* **31**: 33-44.

Baker, A.J. & Coleman, J.D. (1977). The breeding cycle of the Westland Black Petrel. *Notornis* **24**: 211-231.

Baker, G. (1982). Review of the status; U.S. breeding populations of the Wood Stork. *Federal Register* **47**: 6675-6677.

Baker, R.R. (1978). *The Evolutionary Ecology of Animal Migration.* Holmes and Meier, New York.

Baker, R.R. (1984). *Bird Navigation: The Solution of a Mystery?.* Hodder & Stoughton, London.

Bakewell, D.N. & Young, L. (1989). *Report on Ornithological Observations from Hangzhou Bay and Yencheng Nature Reserve, East China.* Publication **58**. Asian Wetland Bureau, Kuala Lumpur.

Balança, G. (1987). Etude des strategies alimentaires de l'aigrette garzette *Egretta garzetta,* sur la cote atlantique du Maroc. *Gerfaut* **77**: 443-462.

Baldassarre, G.A., Quinlan, E.E. & Bolen, E.G. (1988). Mobility and Site Fidelity of Green-winged Teal Wintering on the Southern High Plains of Texas. Pp. 483-494 in: Weller (1988).

Baldridge, A. (1973). The status of the Brown Pelican in the Monterey region of California: past and present. *Western Birds* **4**: 93-100.

Baldwin, P.M. (1945). The Hawaiian Goose, its distribution and reduction in numbers. *Condor* **47**: 27-37.

Baldwin, P.M. (1947). Foods of the Hawaiian goose. *Condor* **49**: 108-120.

Balham, R.W. (1952). Grey and Mallard Ducks in the Manawatu District, New Zealand. *Emu* **52**: 163-191.

Balham, R.W. & Miers, K.H. (1959). Mortality and survival of Grey and Mallard Ducks banded in New Zealand. *New Zealand Dept. Intern. Aff. Wildl. Publ.* **1**: 1-56.

Balharry, D., Dennis, R., Mackay, P., Hauter, G., Bell, A. & Wilkie, R. (1989). Aberdeen University ecological expedition to Peru 1986. Unpublished Report. Aberdeen University.

Ball, I.J., Frost, P.G.H., Siegfried, W.R. & McKinney, F.M. (1978). Territories and local movements of African Black Ducks. *Wildfowl* **29**: 61-79.

Ball, S.C. (1934). Hybrid Ducks, including descriptions of two crosses of *Bucephala* and *Lophodytes. Peabody Mus. Nat. Hist. Bull. Yale Univ.* **3**.

Baltzer, M.C. (1990). A report on the wetland avifauna of South Sulawesi. *Kukila* **5**(1): 27-55.

Bamford, O.S. & Maloiy, G.M.O. (1980). Energy metabolism and heart rate during treadmill exercise in the Marabou Stork. *J. Appl. Physiol.* **49**(3): 491-496.

Bandorf, H. (1968). Beiträge zum Verhalten des Zwergtauchers (*Podiceps ruficollis*). *Vogelwelt. Beiheft* **1**: 7-61.

Bandorf, H. (1970). *Der Zwergtaucher* (Tachybaptus ruficollis *Pallas*). Die Neue Brehm-Bucherei **430**. Ziemsen Verlag, Wittenberg-Lutherstadt.

Bang, B.G. (1966). The olfactory apparatus of tubenosed birds. *Acta Anat.* **65**: 391-415.

Bangs, O. & van Tyne, J. (1931). Birds of the Kelley-Roosevelts expedition to French Indo-China. *Field Mus. Nat. Hist. Publ. (Zool. Ser.)* **18**: 39-40.

Banko, P.C. (1988). *Breeding Biology and Conservation of the Nene, Hawaiian Goose (Nesochen sandvicensis).* PhD thesis, University of Wash.

Banko, P.C. & Manuwal, D.A. (1982). *Life History, Ecology and Management of Nene (Branta sandvicensis) in Hawaii Volcanoes and Haleakala National Parks.* Final Report to National Park Service, Hawaii.

Banko, W. (1960). *The Trumpeter Swan: its History, Habits, and Population in the United States.* North American Fauna **63**. US Fish & Wildlife Service.

Banks, R.C. (1975). Development and molt of juvenile primaries in the crested tinamou ("*Eudromia*"). Pp. 628-629 in: *Proc. XV Int. Orn. Congr.*

Banks, R.C. & Clapp, R.B. (1987). Review of wintering by Eared Grebes in the southeastern United States. *Chat* **51**: 29-33.

Banks, R.C. & Dickerman, R.W. (1978). Mexican nesting records for the American Bittern. *Western Birds* **9**(3): 130.

Bannerman, D.A. (1968). *History of the Birds of the Cape Verde Islands.* Oliver & Boyd, Edinburgh.

Barber, J. (1934). Wild Fowl Decoys. Windward House (reissued in 1954 by Dover, New York).

Barber, R.T. & Chavez, F.P. (1983). Biological consequences of El Niño. *Science* **222**: 1203-1210.

Barcelona, F.R. (1976). *Ruddy Duck Food Habits in Northwestern California.* MSc thesis, Humboldt State University, Arcata, CA.

Bardin, P. (1959). Baguage de Cigognes Blanches, *C. ciconia,* de 1950 à 1955, dans la région de Souk-el-Arba (Tunis). *Mem. Soc. Sci. Nat. Tunisie* **4**: 95-101.

Baris, S. (1989). Final report of the Bald Ibis Project. Unpublished Report to the Society for the Protection of Nature, DHKD, Turkey.

Barker, R.J. (1990). Paradise Shelduck band recoveries in the Wanganui District. *Notornis* **37**: 173-181.

Barlow, C.G. & Bock, K. (1984). Predation of fish in farm dams by Cormorants, *Phalacrocorax spp. Austr. Wildl. Res.* **11**(3): 559-566.

Barlow, C.S. (1933). A wonderful nesting colony of Sacred Ibis, herons, and other waders at Johannesberg. *Ostrich* **4**: 5-9.

Barlow, M. (1976). Breeding of the Hoary-headed Grebe in Southland. *Notornis* **23**: 183-187.

Barr, J.F. (1973). *Feeding Biology of the Common Loon* (Gavia immer) *in Oligotrophic Lakes of the Canadian Shield.* PhD thesis. University of Guelph.

Barr, J.F. (1986). *Population Dynamics of the Common Loon* (Gavia immer) *Associated with Mercury-contaminated Waters in Northwestern Ontario.* Canadian Wildlife Service Occasional Papers **56**.

Barrat, A. (1974). Note sur le Petrel Gris. *Com. Natn. Fr. Rech. Antarct.* **33**: 19-23.

Barrat, A. (1976). Quelques aspects de la biologie et de l'écologie du Manchot Royal (*Aptenodytes patagonica*) des Iles Crozet. *Com. Nat. Français Rech. Antarct.* **40**: 9-52.

Barrat, A., Barré, H. & Mougin, J.L. (1976). Données écologiques sur les Grands Albatross de l'île de la Posséssion (Archipel Crozet). *L'Oiseau et la R.F.O.* **46**: 143-155.

Barré, H. (1976). *Pterodroma lessonii* à l'île de la Posséssion (Ile Crozet). *Com. Nat. Français Rech. Antarct.* **40**: 61-75.

Barré, N. & Barau, A. (1982). *Oiseaux de la Réunion.* Authors.

Barrett, J. & Barrett, C.F. (1985). Divers in the Moray Firth, Scotland. *Scottish Birds* **13**: 149-154.

Barrett, R.T. (1988). The dispersal and migration of the gannet from Norwegian breeding colonies. *Ringing & Migration* **9**: 139-145.

Barrett, R.T. & Furness R.W. (1990). The prey and diving depths of seabirds on Hornoy, North Norway after a decrease in the Barents Sea capelin stocks. *Ornis Scand.* **21**: 179-186.

Barrett, R.T. & Strann, K-B. (1987). Two new breeding records of the Storm Petrel *Hydrobates pelagicus* in Norway. *Fauna Norv. (Ser. C) Cinclus* **10**: 115-116.

Barrett, R.T., Rov, N., Loen, J. & Montevecchi, W.A. (1990). Diets of shags *Phalacrocorax aristotelis* and cormorants *P.carbo* in Norway and possible implications for gadoid stock recruitment. *Marine Ecology Progress Series* **66**: 205-218.

Barrett, R.T., Strann, K.B. & Vader, W. (1986). Notes on the eggs and chicks of north Norwegian Shags *Phalacrocorax aristotelis. Seabird* **9**: 3-10.

Barrow, J.H., Black, J.M. & Walter, W. (1986). Behaviour patterns and their function in the Horned Screamer. *Wildfowl* **37**: 156-162.

Barrowclough, G.F., Corbin, K.W. & Zink, R.M. (1981). Genetic differentiation in the Procellariiformes. *Comp. Biochem. Physiol.* **69** B: 629-632.

Barry, T.W. (1966). *Geese of the Anderson River Delta, Northwest Territories, Canada.* PhD dissertation, University of Alberta.

Barske, P. ed. (1968). *The Black Duck. Evaluation, Management and Research: a Symposium.* Wildlife Management Institute, Washington, D.C.

Barthel, P.H. & Mullarney, K. (1988). [Identification of Divers (Gaviidae) in Winter]. *Limicola* **2**(2): 45-69. In German with English summary.

Bartholomew, G.A. (1942). The fishing activities of Double-crested Cormorants in San Francisco Bay. *Condor* **44**: 13-21.

Bartholomew, G.A. & Dawson, W.R. (1954). Temperature regulation in young pelicans, herons and gulls. *Ecology* **35**: 466-472.

Bartholomew, G.A. & Pennycuick, C.J. (1973). The flamingo and pelican populations of the Rift Valley lakes in 1968-9. *East Afr. Wildl. J.* **11**: 189-198.

Bartholomew, G.A., Dawson, W.R. & O'Neill, E.J. (1953). A field study of temperature regulation in young White Pelicans, *Pelecanus erythrorhynchos. Ecology* **34**: 554-560.

Bartle, J.A. (1968). Observations on the breeding habits of Pycroft's Petrel. *Notornis* **15**: 70-99.

Bartle, J.A. (1985). Westland Black Petrel. Page 91 in: Robertson (1985).

Bartle, J.A. (1987). Westland Black Petrel research notes, 10-29/4/87. *O.S.N.Z. News* **44**: 5.

Bartle, J.A. (1990). Sexual segregation of foraging zones in procellariiform birds: implications of accidental capture on commercial fishery longlines of Grey Petrels (*Procellaria cinerea*). *Notornis* **37**: 146-150.

Bartle, J.A. (1991). Incidental capture of seabirds in the New Zealand subantarctic squid trawl fishery, 1990. *Bird Conserv. Int.* **1991**: 351-359.

Bartlett, J. (1975). *The Flight of the Snow Geese.* Stein & Day, New York.

Bartmann, W. (1988). New observations on the Brazilian Merganser. *Wildfowl* **39**: 714.

Barton, D. (1979a). Swimming speed of a Little Penguin. *Emu* **79**: 141-142.

Barton, D. (1979b). Albatrosses in the western Tasman Sea. *Emu* **79**: 31-35.

Bartonek, J.C. & Murdy, H.W. (1970). Summer foods of Lesser Scaup in subarctic Taiga. *Arctic* **23** (1): 35-44.

Batchelor, A.L. (1981). The August 1981 seabird (*Pachyptila* and *Halobaena* spp.) wreck off Port Elizabeth, South Africa. *Cormorant* **9**: 105-112.

Batchelor, A.L. & Ross, G.J.B. (1984). The diet and implications of dietary change of Cape Gannets on Bird Island, Algoa Bay. *Ostrich* **55**: 46-63.

Bateman, D.L. (1970). *Movement-behavior in Three Species of Colonial Nesting Wading Birds: a Radiometric Study.* PhD dissertation. Auburn University, Alabama.

Bateman, H.A. (1977). *The Wood Duck in Louisiana.* Louisiana Dep. Wildl. & Fish, Baton Rouge.

Bates, J.M., Garvin, M.C., Schmitt, D.C. & Schmitt, C.G. (1989). Notes on bird distribution in northeastern Dpto. Danta Cruz, Bolivia, with 15 species new to Bolivia. *Bull. Brit. Orn. Club* **109**(4): 236-244.

Bates, R.S.P. & Lowther, E.H.N. (1952). *Breeding Birds of Kashmir*. Oxford University Press, Delhi.
Batt, B.D.J. (1976). *Reproductive Parameters of Mallards in Relation to Age, Captivity and Geographical Origin*. PhD thesis, Michigan State University, East Lansing.
Batt, B.D.J. & Prince, H.H. (1978). Some reproductive parameters of Mallards in relation to age, captivity, and geographic origin. *J. Wildl. Manage.* **42**: 834-842.
Batten, L.A., Bibby, C.J., Clement, P., Elliott, G.D. & Porter, R.F. eds. (1990). *Red Data Birds in Britain. Action for Rare, Threatened and Important Species*. T & AD Poyser, London.
Baudinette, R.V. & Gill, P. (1985). The energetics of "flying" and "paddling" in water: locomotion in penguins and ducks. *J. Comp. Physiol.* **155**: 373-380.
Baudinette, R.V., Gill, P. & O'Driscoll, M. (1986). Energetics of the Little Penguin, *Eudyptula minor*: Temperature regulation, the calorigenic effect of food, and moulting. *Austr. J. Zool.* **34**: 35-45.
Bauer, K. (1952). Ausbreitung des Schwarzstorches in Österreich. *Vogelwelt* **73**: 125-129.
Bauer, K.M. & Glutz von Blotzheim, U.N. eds. (1966). *Handbuch der Vögel Mitteleuropas*. Vol. 1. Akademische Verlagsgesellschaft, Frankfurt & Main.
Bauer, K.M. & Glutz von Blotzheim, U.N. eds. (1968). *Handbuch der Vögel Mitteleuropas*. Vol. 2. Akademische Verlagsgesellschaft, Frankfurt & Main.
Bauer, K.M. & Glutz von Blotzheim, Urs. N. eds. (1969). *Handbuch der Vögel Mitteleuropas*. Vol. 3. Akademische Verlagsgesellschaft, Frankfurt & Main.
Bauer, R.D. (1979). Historical and status report of the Tule White-fronted Goose. Pp. 44-55 in: Jarvis, R.L. & Bartonek, J.C. eds. *Symp. Manage. Biol. Pacific Flyway Geese*. NW Section, Thel Wildlife Society, Corvallis, Oregon.
Baumel, J.J., King, A.S., Lucas, A.M., Breazile, J.E. & Evans, H.E. eds. (1979). *Nomina Anatomica Avium. An Annotated Anatomical Dictionary of Birds*. Academic Press, London and New York.
Baxter, E.V. & Rintoul, L.J. (1953). *The Birds of Scotland: Their History, Distribution and Migration*. Oliver & Boyd, Edinburgh & London.
Baxter, G.S. & Fairweather, P.G. (1989). Comparison of the Diets of Nestling Cattles Egrets and Intermediate Egrets in the Hunter Valley, New South Wales. *Austr. Wildl. Res.* **16**: 395-404.
Bayer, R.D. (1986). Breeding success of seabirds along the mid-Oregon coast concurrent with the 1983 El Niño. *Murrelet* **67**: 23-26.
Bayliss, P. (1989). Population dynamics of Magpie Geese in relation to rainfall and density: implications for harvest models in a fluctuating environment. *J. Appl. Ecol.* **26(3)**: 913-924.
Bayliss, P. & Yeomans, K.M. (1990). Seasonal distribution and abundance of Magpie Geese, *Anseranas semipalmata* Latham, in the Northern Territory, and their relationship to habitat, 1983-86. *Austr. Wildl. Res.* **17**: 15-38.
Baynard, O.E. (1913). Home life of the Glossy Ibis (*Plegadis autumnalis* Linn.). *Wilson Bull.* **25**: 103-117.
Bazely, D.R., Ewins, P.J. & McCleery, R.H. (1991). Possible effects of local enrichment by gulls on feeding-site selection by wintering Barnacle Geese *Branta leucopsis*. *Ibis* **133**: 111-114.
Beadle, D. & Whittaker, A. (1985). 1985 Sabah survey report. *Interwader Ann. Rep.* **1984**: 79-118, 155.
Beard, D.B., Lincoln, F.C., Cahalane, V.H., Jackson, H.H.T. & Thompson, B.H. (1942). *Fading Trails. The Story of Endangered American Wildlife*. The Macmillan Company, New York.
Beattie, L.A. & Nudds, T.D. (1989). Differential habitat occupancy by Goldeneye Ducklings (*Bucephala clangula*) and fish: predator avoidance or competition?. *Can. J. Zool.* **67**: 475-482.
Beaufort, F. ed. (1983). *Especes Menacées et Exploitées dans le Monde. Guide Pratique pour leur Connaissance et leur Identification*. Inventaires de Faune et de Flore **24**. Secretariat de la Faune et de la Flore, Muséum National d'Histoire Naturelle, Paris.
Beaver, D.L., Osborn, R.G. & Custer, T.W. (1980). Nest-site and colony characteristics of wading birds in selected atlantic coast colonies. *Wilson Bull.* **92(2)**: 200-220.
Beaver, P.W. (1978). Ontogeny of vocalization in the greater rhea. *Auk* **95**: 382-388.
Beaver, R.D. & Lewin, V. (1981). Scheduling censuses of breeding White Pelicans (*Pelecanus erythrorhynchos*) in northern Alberta. *Can. Field-Nat.* **95**: 198-201.
Bech, C., Mehlum, F. & Haftorn, S. (1988). Development of chicks during extreme cold conditions: the Antarctic Petrel. Pp. 1447-1456 in: *Proc. XIX Int. Orn. Congr.*
Becher, L. (1967). Der heilige Ibisvoegel der Aegypter in der Antike. *Acta Antique* **15**: 377-385.
Beck, J.R. (1969). Food, moult and age of first breeding in the Cape Pigeon. *Brit. Antarct. Surv. Bull.* **21**: 33-44.
Beck, J.R. (1970). Breeding seasons and moult in some smaller Antarctic petrels. Pp. 542-550 in Holdgate, M.W. ed. *Antarctic Ecology*. Vol. 1. Academic Press, London.
Beck, J.R. & Brown, D.W. (1971). The breeding biology of the Black-bellied Storm Petrel. *Ibis* **113**: 73-90.
Beck, J.R. & Brown, D.W. (1972). The biology of Wilson's Storm Petrel at Signy Island, South Orkney Islands. *Brit. Antarct. Surv. Scient. Rep.* **69**: 1-54.
Becker, J.J. (1986). Reidentification of *"Phalacrocorax" subvolans* Brodkorb as the earliest record of Anhingidae. *Auk* **103**: 804-808.
Becker, J.J. (1987). Additional material of *Anhinga grandis* Martin and Mengel (Aves: Anhingidae) from the Late Miocene of Florida. *Proc. Biol. Soc. Washington* **100(2)**: 358-363.
Becking, J.H. (1976). Feeding range of Abbott's Booby at the coast of Java. *Ibis* **118(3)**: 589-590.
Becuwe, M. (1971). De Geoorde Fuut (*Podiceps nigricollis*) en de Dodaars (*Podiceps ruficollis*) als doortrecker en wintergast op De Spuikom to Oostende. *Gerfaut* **61**: 303-306.
Bedard, J. & Lapointe, G. (1991). Responses of hayfield vegetation to spring grazing by Greater Snow Geese. *J. Appl. Ecol.* **28 (1)**: 187-193.
Bednorz, J. (1974). The Black Stork, *Ciconia nigra* (L.), in Poland. *Ochr. Przyr.* **39**: 201-243.
Bell, H.L. (1957). Distribution of the Jabiru in south-eastern Australia. *Emu* **63**: 210-206.
Beebe, W. (1925). The variegated tinamou. *Zoologica* **6**: 195-227.
Beebe, W. (1935). Rediscovery of the Bermuda Cahow. *Bull. New York Zool. Soc.* **38**: 187-190.
Beebe, W., Hartley, G.I. & Howes, P.G. (1917). *Tropical Wild Life in British Guiana*. New York Zoological Society, New York.
Beehler, B.M. (1978). *Upland Birds of Northeastern New Guinea*. Wau Ecology Institute Handbook **4**. Wau Ecology Institute, Wau, Papua New Guinea.
Beehler, B.M., Pratt, T.K. & Zimmerman, D.A. (1986). *Birds of New Guinea*. Princeton University Press, Princeton, New Jersey.
de Beer, G.R. (1954). *Archaeopteryx Lithographica*. British Museum (Natural History.
de Beer, G.R. (1956) The evolution of ratites. *Bull. Brit. Mus. Nat. Hist. (Zool.)* **4**: 59-70.
Beesley, J.S.S. (1972). A nesting colony of Black-headed Heron *Ardea melanocephala* in Arusha, Tanzania. *East Afr. Nat. Hist. Soc. Bull.* **March**: 47-48.
Beesley, J.S.S. (1976). Darter *Anhinga rufa*. *Ostrich* **47(4)**: 214.
Bege, L.A.R. & Pauli, B.T. (1988). *As aves nas ilhas Moleques do Sul*. Fundaçao de Amparo à Tecnologia e ao Meio Ambiente (FATMA), Florianópolis, Santa Catarina, Brazil.
Bege, L.A.R. & Pauli, B.T. (1990a). Primer reporte de *Phoenicoparrus andinus* en Brasil. *Volante Migratorio* **14**: 6.
Bege, L.A.R. & Pauli, B.T. (1990b). Two birds new to the Brazilian avifauna. *Bull. Brit. Orn. Club* **110(2)**: 93-94.
Behn, F., Goodall, J.D., Johnson, A.W. & Phillippi B., R.A. (1955). The geographical distribution of the Blue-eyed Shags, *Phalacrocorax albiventer* and *Phalacrocorax atriceps*. *Auk* **72**: 6-13.
Beissmann, W. (1984). Durchzug und Überwinterung des Zwergtauchers *Tachybaptus ruficollis* im Brenztal 1978/79. [Summary: Migration and wintering of the Little Grebe *Tachybaptus ruficollis* in the Brenz Valley (Southern Germany) 1978/79]. *Anz. orn. Ges. Bayern* **23**: 57-64.
Bekle, H. (1982). Sacred Ibis *Threskiornis aethiopica* in Southwestern Australia. *West. Austr. Nat.* **15**: 13-19.
Belant, J.L. & Anderson, R.K. (1991). Winter recoveries and territorial affinities of Common Loons banded in Wisconsin. *Wilson Bull.* **103(1)**: 141-142.
Belknap, H.W. (1957). Observations on the White-faced Ibis, *Plegadis chihi*, in Louisiana. MSc thesis. Lousiana State University, Baton Rouge.
Bell, A. (1984). Native shrubland in an exotic sea. *Forest & Bird* **15(4)**: 22-24.
Bell, B.D. (1986). *The Conservation Status of New Zealand Wildlife*. New Zealand Wildlife Occasional Publications **12**. Wellington.
Bell, H.L. (1967). Bird life of the Balimo Sub-district, Papua. *Emu* **67**: 57-79.
Bell, H.L. (1969). Birds of Ok Tedi, New Guinea. *Emu* **69**: 193-211.
Bell, J., Bruning, D. & Winnegar, A. (1970). Black-necked Screamers seen feeding a chick. *Auk* **87**: 805.
Bell, M.V. (1988). Feeding behaviour of wintering Pink-footed and Greylag Geese in north-east Scotland. *Wildfowl* **39**: 43-53.
Bell, M.V., Dunbar, J. & Parkin, J. (1988). Numbers of wintering Pink-footed and Greylag Geese in north-east Scotland 1950-1986. *Scottish Birds* **15**: 49-60.
Bell, R.Q. & Klimstra, W.D. (1970). Feeding activities of Canada Geese in Southern Illinois. *Trans. Illinois State Acad. Sci.* **63(3)**: 295-304.
Bell, T.R. (1901). (Gorsachius melanolophus). *J. Bombay Nat. Hist. Soc.* **14**: 394-395.
Bell-Cross, G. (1974). Observations on fish-eating birds in central Africa. *Honeyguide* **77**: 23-31.
Bellrose, F.C. (1976). *Ducks, Geese and Swans of North America*. 2nd edition Stackpole Books, Harrisburg, PA.
Belopolsky, L.O. & Laskova, S.V. (1986). [New data on frigate-birds ecology in the tropical eastern part of the Pacific]. *Vestnik Zool.* **1986(2)**: 76-77. In Russian.
Belser, C.G. (1989). A Scarlet Ibis or hybrid White Ibis X Scarlet Ibis in South Carolina. *Chat* **53**: 90-91.
Belton, W. (1982). *Aves silvestres do Rio Grande do Sul*. Fundaçao Zoobotanica do Rio Grande do Sul, Porto Alegre, Brazil.
Belton, W. (1984). *Birds of Rio Grande do Sul, Brazil*. Part 1. Rheidae through Furnariidae. Bulletin of the American Museum of Natural History **178(4)**: 369-636.
Beltrán, J. (1988). A grebe in a tough environment. *Wildfowl World* **99**: 10-11.
Beltzer, A.H. (1983). Fidelidad y participación trófica del "macá grande" (*Podiceps major*) y su relación con el "biguá común" (*Phalacrocorax olivaceus*) en ambientes del Río Paraná medio (Aves: Podicipedidae y Phalacrocoracidae). *Historia Nat. Corrientes* **3(2)**: 17-20.
Bengtson, S.A. (1966a). [Observation on the sexual behavior of the common scoter, *Melanitta nigra*, on the breeding grounds, with special reference to courting parties]. *Vår Fågelvärld* **25**: 202-226. In Swedish with English summary.
Bengtson, S.A. (1966b). Field studies on the harlequin duck in Iceland. *Wildfowl Trust Ann. Rep.* **17**: 79-94.
Bengtson, S.A. (1970). Location of nest-sites of ducks in Lake Myvatn area, north-east Iceland. *Oikos* **21**: 218-229.
Bengtson, S.A. (1971). Variations in clutch-size in ducks in relation to their food supply. *Ibis* **113**: 523-526.
Bengtson, S.A. (1972). Breeding ecology of the Harlequin Duck *Histrionicus histrionicus* (L.) in Iceland. *Ornis Scand.* **3**: 1-19.
Bengtson, S.A. & Ulftrand, S. (1971). Food resources and breeding frequency of the Harlequin Duck *Histrionicus histrionicus* in Iceland. *Oikos* **22**: 235-239.
Benham, W.B. (1906). The olfactory sense in *Apteryx*. *Nature* **74**: 22-223.
Benito-Espinal, E. & Portecop, J. (1935). Installation s'*Ixobrychus e. exilis* (Gmelin) en Guadeloupe et à Marie-Galante (Petites Antilles). *L'Oiseau et la R.F.O.* **5(2)**: 149-152.
Bennett, A.G. (1930). Nesting of the Grey-backed Storm Petrel. *Oologists Record* **10**(4): 79.
Bennett, C. (1987). Breeding and reproduction of the Chilean Flamingo (*Phoenicopterus chilensis*) at the Santa Barbara Zoo. *AAZPA (Amer. Assoc. Zool. Parks & Aquariums) Ann. Conf. Proc.* **1987**: 313-320.
Bennett, G.F., Greiner, E.C. & Campbell, A.G. (1975). Avian haemoproteidae. 5. The haemoproteids of the family of Threskiornithidae. *Can. J. Zool.* **53**: 634-638.
Bennett, K.A. (1990). Molt Patterns of Black-footed Penguins (*Spheniscus demersus*) at Baltimore Zoo. *AAZPA (Amer. Assoc. Zool. Parks & Aquariums) Reg. Conf. Proc.* **1990**: 99-106.
Bennett, K.A. (1991). Behavioral observations of captive magellanic penguins (*Spheniscus magellanicus*) with chicks. *AAZPA (Amer. Assoc. Zool. Parks & Aquariums) Reg. Conf. Proc.* **1991**: 269-276.
Bennett, L.J. (1938). *The Blue-winged Teal, Its Ecology and Management*. Collegiate Press, Ames, Iowa.
Benson, C.W. (1960). The Birds of the Comoro Islands: Results of the British Ornithologists' Union Centenary Expedition, 1958. *Ibis* **103 b**: 1-106.
Benson, C.W. (1961). The breeding of the Whale-headed Stork in Northern Rhodesia. *N. Rhodesia J.* **4**: 557-560.
Benson, C.W. (1967). The birds of Aldabra and their status. *Atoll Res. Bull.* **118**: 63-111.
Benson, C.W. (1971). Quelques spécimens anciens de *Podiceps ruficollis* (Pallas) provenant de Madagascar et des Comores. *L'Oiseau et la R.F.O.* **41**: 88-93.
Benson, C.W. & Benson, F.M. (1975). *The Birds of Malawi*. Montfort Press, Limbe Malawi.
Benson, C.W. & Penny, M.J. (1971). The land birds of Aldabra. *Phil. Trans. Royal Soc. London (Ser. B)* **260**: 417-527.
Benson, C.W. & Pitman, C.R.S. (1962). Some breeding and other records from Madagascar. *Bull. Brit. Orn. Club* **82**: 30-33.
Benson, C.W. & Pitman, C.R.S. (1966). Further breeding reocrds from Zambia (formerly northern Rhodesia). *Bull. Brit. Orn. Club* **86(5)**: 21-23.
Benson, C.W., Brooke, R.K. & Irwin, M.P.S. (1971). The Slatey Egret *Egretta vinaceigula* is a good species. *Bull. Brit. Ornithol. Club* **91**: 131-133.
Benson, C.W., Brooke, R.K., Dowsett, R.J. & Irwin, M.P.S. (1971). *The Birds of Zambia*. Collins, London.
Benson, C.W., Colebrook-Robjent, J.F.R & Williams, A. (1976). Contribution à l'ornithologie de Madagascar. *L'Oiseau et la R.F.O* **41**: 89-93.
Bent, A.C. (1919). *Life Histories of North American Diving Birds*. US National Museum Bulletin **107**. Government Printing Office, Washington, D.C.
Bent, A.C. (1922). *Life Histories of North American Petrels, Pelicans and their Allies*. US National Museum Bulletin **121**. Smithsonian Institution, Washington, D.C.
Bent, A.C. (1923-1925). *Life Histories of North American Wildfowl*. Order Anseres. Parts 1 and 2. US National Museum Bulletin **126 & 130**. Smithsonian Institution, Washington, D.C.
Bent, A.C. (1926). *Life Histories of North American Marsh Birds*. National Museum Bulletin **135**. Smithsonian Institution, Washington, D.C.
Benussi, E. (1985). Osservazioni sulla presenza del marangone minore ("Phalacrocorax pymaeus" Pallas) in Italia. *Atti Mus. civ. Stor. nat. Trieste* **37(3)**: 255-259.
Bereszynski, A. (1977). Spostrzezenia nad zachowaniem sie bocianow bialych (*Ciconia ciconia*) i bocianow czarnych (*Ciconia nigra*) w puszczy bialowieskiej. [Summary: Remarks on behaviour of black storks and white storks in mixed flock]. *Notatki Ornitol.* **18**: 62-63. In Polish with English summary.
van den Berg, A.B. (1989). Bald Ibis. *Dutch Birding* **11**: 128-131.
van den Berg, A.B., Smenk, C., Bosman, C.A.W., Haase, B.J.M., van den Niet, A.M. & Cadee, G.C. (1991). Barau's Petrels *Pterodroma baraui*, Jouanin's Petrels *Bulweria fallax* and other seabirds in the northern Indian Ocean in June-July 1984 and 1985. *Ardea* **79**: 1-14.
Bergan, J.F., Smith, L.M. & Mayer, J.J. (1989). Time-activity budgets of diving ducks wintering in South Carolina. *J. Wildl. Manage.* **53(3)**: 769-776.
Berger, A.J. (1972). *Hawaiian Birdlife*. University Press of Hawaii, Honolulu.
Berger, M. & Hart, J.S. (1974). Physiology and energetics of flight. Pp. 415-477 in: Farner, D.S. & King, J.R. eds. (1974). *Avian Biology*. Vol. 4. Academic Press, London & New York.
Berglund, B.E., Curry-Lindahl, K., Luther, H., Olsson, V., Rodhe, W. & Sellerberg, G. (1963). Ecological studies on the Mute Swan (*Cygnus olor*) in south-eastern Sweden. *Acta Vertebratica* **2**: 163-288.
Bergman, G. & Donner, K.O. (1964). An analysis of the spring migration of the Common Scoter and the Long-tailed Duck in southern Finland. *Ann. Zool. Fennici* **105**: 1-59.
Bergman, R.D. & Derksen, D.V. (1977). Observations on Arctic and Red-throated loons at Storkersen Point, Alaska. *Arctic* **30**: 41-51.
Bergmann, R.F., Kretzschmar, E. & Buchheim, A. (1990). Die Nilgans (*Alopochen aegyptiacus*) als neuer Brutvogel in Westfalen - vom Zooflüchtling zum Kulturfolger?. *Charadrius* **26**: 92-98.
Berndt, R. & Meise, W. (1958). *Naturgeschichte der Vögel*. Franckh'sche Verlagshandlung, Stuttgart.
Bernis, F. (1959). La migración de las cigüeñas españolas y de las otras cigüeñas "occidentales". *Ardeola* **5**: 10-80.
Bernis, F. (1966a). *Migración en Aves. Tratado teórico y práctico*. Sociedad Española de Ornitología, Madrid.
Bernis, F. (1966b). *Aves Migradoras Ibéricas, según anillamientos en Europa*. Vol. 1. Sociedad Española de Ornitología, Madrid.
Bernis, F. (1966c). Presencia de un Flamenco Enano, *Phoeniconaias minor* en el Sur de España. *Ardeola* **12**: 229.
Bernis, F. (1969). Sobre recientes datos de *Platalea leucorodia* en Iberia. *Ardeola* **13**: 239-241.
Bernis, F. (1980). *La migración de las aves en el estrecho de Gibraltar (época posnupcial)*. Universidad Complutense de Madrid, Madrid.
Bernstein, C., Krebs, J.R. & Kalcenik, A. (1991). Distribution of birds amongst habitats: theory and relevance to conservation. Pp. 317-345 in: Perrins *et al.* (1991).
Bernstein, N.P. & Maxson, S.J. (1981). Notes on moult and seasonably variable characters of the Antarctic Blue-eyed Shag (*Phalacrocorax atriceps bransfieldensis*) *Notornis* **28**: 35-39.
Bernstein, N.P. & Maxson, S.J. (1982a). Absence of Wing-spreading Behavior in the Antarctic Blue-eyed Shag (*Phalacrocorax atriceps bransfieldensis*). *Auk* **99**: 588-589.
Bernstein, N.P. & Maxson, S.J. (1982b). Behaviour of the Antarctic Blue-eyed Shag *Phalacrocorax atriceps bransfieldensis*. *Notornis* **29**: 197-207.
Bernstein, N.P. & Maxson, S.J. (1984). Sexually distinct daily activity patterns of Blue-eyed Shags in Antarctica. *Condor* **86**: 151-156.
Bernstein, N.P. & Maxson, S.J. (1985). Reproductive energetics of Blue-eyed Shags in Antarctica. *Wilson Bull.* **97**: 450-462.
Berruti, A. (1979). The breeding biologies of the Sooty albatrosses. *Emu* **79**: 161-175.
Berruti, A. (1980). Status and review of waterbirds breeding at Lake St. Lucia. *Lammergeyer* **28**: 1-19.
Berruti, A. (1981a). The Status of the Royal Penguin and Fairy Prion at Marion Island, with notes on feral cat predation on nestlings of large birds. *Cormorant* **9**: 123-128.
Berruti, A. (1981b). Displays of the sooty albatrosses. *Ostrich* **52**: 98-103.

Berruti, A. (1983). The biomass, energy consumption, and breeding of waterbirds relative to hydrological conditions at Lake St. Lucia. *Ostrich* **54**: 65-82.
Berruti, A. (1986). The predatory impact of feral cats *Felis catus* and their control on Dassen Island. *S. Afr. J. Antarct. Res.* **16(3)**: 123-127
Berruti, A. (1987). Cape Gannets *Sula capensis* feeding a Cape Cormorant *Phalacrocorax capensis* chick. *Cormorant* **15**: 89-90.
Berruti, A. & Harcus, T. (1978). Cephalopod prey of the Sooty Albatrosses, *Phoebetria fusca* and *P. palpebrata* at Marion Island. *S. Afr. J. Antarct. Res.* **8**: 99-103.
Berruti, A. & Hunter, S. (1986). Some aspects of the breeding biology of Salvin's Prion at Marion Island. *Cormorant* **13**: 98-106.
Berruti, A., Adams, N.J. & Brown, C.R. (1985). Chick energy balance in the Whitechinned Petrel, *Procellaria aequinoctialis*. Pp. 360-365 in: Siegfried, W.R., Condy, P.R. & Laws, R.M. eds. *Antarctic Nutrient cycles and Food Webs*. Springer, Berlin.
Berruti, A., Joubert, F., Skinner, M. & Taylor, R.H. (1977). First breeding record of Saddle-billed Stork in Natal. *Lammergeyer* **23**: 48.
Berry, H.H. (1972). Flamingo breeding on the Etosha Pan, South West Africa, during 1971. *Madoqua* **ser 1,5**: 5-31.
Berry, H.H. (1974). The crowned race of Reed Cormorant *P. africanus coronatus* breeding underneath Walvis Bay guano platform, southwest Africa. *Madoqua* **8**: 59-62.
Berry, H.H. (1975). Hand-rearing lesser flamingos. Pp. 109-116 in: Kear & Duplaix-Hall (1975).
Berry, H.H. (1976a). Physiological and behavioural ecology of the Cape Cormorant *Phalacrocorax capensis*. *Madoqua* **9(4)**: 5-55.
Berry, H.H. (1976b). Mass mortality of Cape Cormorants caused by fish oil in the Walvis Bay region of South West Africa. *Madoqua* **9**: 57-62.
Berry, H.H. (1977). Seasonal fidelity of Cape Cormorants to nesting areas. *Cormorant* **2**: 5-6.
Berry, H.H., Stark, H.P. & Van Vuuren, A.S. (1973). White Pelicans *Pelecanus onocrotalus* breeding on the Etosha Pan, South West Africa, during 1971. *Madoqua* **7**: 17-31.
Berry, P.S.M. (1984). Sex and age composition of an unusual gathering of Saddlebills. *Bull. Zamb. Orn. Soc.* **16**: 13-14.
Berthelot, J.Y. & Navizet, G. (1986). Notes sur des herons crabiers nicheurs. *Nos Oiseaux* **38(8)**: 353-358.
Berthold, P. (1975). Migration: control and metabolic physiology. Pp. 77-127 in: Farner, D.S. & King, J.R. eds. (1975). *Avian Biology*. Vol. 5. Academic Press, London & New York.
Bertonatti, C., Canevari, P., Forrester, B.C., Knell, L.A. & Rumboll, M. (1991). Notes on the status of some threatened anatidae in Argentina and Brazil. *IWRB Threatened Waterfowl Research Group Newsletter* **1**: 5-6.
Bertram, B.C.R. (1979a). Ostriches recognize their own eggs and discard others. *Nature* **279**: 233-239.
Bertram, B.C.R. (1979b). Breeding systems and strategies of Ostriches. Pp. 890-894 in: *Proc. XVII Int. Orn. Congr.*
Bertram, B.C.R. (1980). Vigilance and group size in Ostriches. *Anim. Behav.* **28**: 278-286.
Bertram, B.C.R. (1985). Ostrich. Pp. 416-417 in: Campbell & Lack (1985).
Bertram, B.C.R. & Burger, A.E. (1981). Are Ostrich eggs the wrong colour? *Ibis* **123**: 207-210.
Beruldsen, G. (1980). *A Field Guide to Nests and Eggs of Australian Birds*. Rigby, Sidney.
Beruldsen, G.R. (1972). A nest of the Jabiru. *Sunbird* **3**: 40-42.
Beshears, W.W. (1974). *Wood Ducks in Alabama*. Alabama Dep. Conserv. Nat. Resour. Spec. Rep. **4**.
Best, H.A. (1976). First sightings of the Hoary-headed Grebe (*Podiceps poliocephalus*) in New Zealand. *Notornis* **23**: 182-183.
Beteille, G. (1986). [The Spoonbill (*Platalea leucorodia*) in the Seine Estuary (1980-1985)]. *Cormorant* **5**: 473-479.
Betlem, J. (1984). De waarheid over de huidige situatie van de Rode Ibis op Trinidad. *Het Vogeljaar* **32**: 1-7.
Betlem, J. & de Jong, Ben H.J. (1983). De Rode Ibis moord in Frans-Guiana. *Het Vogeljaar* **31**: 192-198.
Beutel, P.M., Davies, S.J.J.F. & Packer, W.C. (1984). Physical and physiological measurements of Emu. *Int. Zoo Yb.* **23**: 175-181.
Bevan, R.M. & Butlev, P.J. (1992). The effects of temperature on the oxygen consumption, heart rate and deep body temperature during diving in the Tufted Duck *Aythya fuligula*. *J. Exp. Biol.* **163**: 139-151.
Bevolscaya, M. & Tikhenov, A. (1985). Early development of acoustic signalling in *Struthio camelus*, *Rhea americana* and *Dromaius novaehollandiae*. Pp. 1082 in: *Proc. XVIII Int. Orn. Congr.*
Bezzel, E. (1969). *Die Tafelente (*Aythya ferina*)*. Neue Brehm-Bücherei **405**. A. Ziemsen Verlag, Wittenberg, Lutherstadt.
Bezzel, E. (1985). Eine Rastplatztradition des Rothalstauchers (*Podiceps grisegena*) in Südbayern. *Vogelwelt* **106**: 202-211.
Bezzel, E. & Engler, U. (1985). Zunahme rastender Kormorane (*Phalacrocorax carbo*) in Südbayern. *Garmischer vogelkdl. Ber.* **14**: 30-42.
Bezzel, E. & Wartmann, B. (1990). Neue Beobachtungen des Waldrapps (*Geronticus eremita*) im Jemen. *J. Orn.* **131**: 456-457.
Bharucha, E. (1987). Some aspects of behaviour observed in the Greater Flamingo at Bhigwan. *J. Bombay Nat. Hist. Soc.* **84(3)**: 677-678.
Bhutia, U. (1985). Chick-feeding in ibises at Keoladeo National Park, Bharatpur. *J. Bombay Nat. Hist. Soc.* **82**: 191-192.
Biaggi, V. (1983). *Las Aves de Puerto Rico*. Editorial de la Universidad de Puerto Rico, Río Piedras, Puerto Rico.
Bianki, V.V. (1989). Smew *Mergus albellus* L.. Pp. 223-225 in: Viksne, J.A. ed. (1989). [*Migrations of birds of eastern Europe and northern Asia. Anseriformes*]. Nauka, Moscow. In Russian.
Bibby, C.J. (1981). Wintering Bitterns in Britain. *British Birds* **74(1)**: 1-10.
Bibby, C.J. & Lunn, J. (1982). Conservation of reed beds and their avifauna in England and Wales. *Biol. Conserv.* **23**: 167-186.
Bibby, C.J. & del Nevo, A.J. (1991). A first record of *Pterodroma feae* from the Azores. *Bull. Brit. Orn. Club* **111(4)**: 183-186.
Biderman, J.D. & Dickerman, R.W. (1978). Feeding behaviour and food habits of the Boat-billed Heron ("*Cochlearius cochlearius*"). *Biotropica* **10(1)**: 33-37.
Bigalke, R. (1948). A note on the breeding of the White-bellied Stork (*Sphenorhynchus abdimii*) in the National Zoological Gardens, Pretoria. *Ostrich* **19**: 200-202.
Bildstein, K.L. (1980). Adult Brown Pelican robs Great Blue Heron's fish. *Wilson Bull.* **92(1)**: 122-123.
Bildstein, K.L. (1983). Age-related Differences in the Flocking and Foraging Behaviour of White Ibises in a South Carolina Salt Marsh. *Colonial Waterbirds* **6**: 45-53.
Bildstein, K.L. (1984). Age-related Differences in the Foraging Behavior of White Ibises and the Question of Deferred Maturity. *Colonial Waterbirds* **7**: 146-148.
Bildstein, K.L. (1987). Energetic Consequences of Sexual Size Dimorphism in White Ibises (*Eudocimus albus*). *Auk* **104**: 771-775.
Bildstein, K.L. (1990a). Status, Conservation and Management of the Scarlet Ibis *Eudocimus ruber* in the Caroni Swamp, Trinidad, West Indies. *Biol. Conserv.* **54**: 61-78.
Bildstein, K.L. (1990b). The use of zoo collections in studies of the feeding ecology and conservation biology of wading birds (Aves: Ciconiiformes). *AAZPA (Amer. Assoc. Zool. Parks & Aquariums) Reg. Conf. Proc.* **1990**: 353-360.
Bildstein, K.L., Post, W., Johnston, J. & Frederick, P. (1990). Freshwater wetlands, rainfall, and the breeding ecology of White Ibises (*Eudocimus albus*) in coastal South Carolina. *Wilson Bull.* **102**: 84-98.
Billing, A.E. (1977). The first occurrence of the Yellow-billed Spoonbill (*Platalea flavipes*) in New Zealand. *Notornis* **24**: 192.
Billings, S.M. (1968). Homing in Leach's Petrel. *Auk* **85**: 36-43.
Binford, L.C.& Zimmerman, D.A. (1974). Rufous-bellied Heron in Kenya. *Bull. Brit. Orn. Club.* **94**: 101.
Birkhead, M.E. (1978). Some aspects of the feeding ecology of the Reed Cormorant and Darter on Lake Kariba, Rhodesia. *Ostrich* **49(1)**: 1-7.
Birkhead, M.E. (1982a). *Population Ecology and Lead Poisoning in the Mute Swan*. PhD thesis, Oxford University.
Birkhead, M.E. (1982b). Causes of mortality in the Mute Swan. *J. Zoology. London* **198**: 1-11.
Birkhead, M.E. (1983). Lead levels in the blood of the Mute Swan. *J. Zoology. London* **199**: 59-73.
Birkhead, M.E. (1984). Variation in the weight and composition of Mute Swan eggs. *Condor* **86**: 489-490.
Birkhead, M.E. (1985). Variation in egg quality and composition in the Mallard *Anas platyrhynchos*. *Ibis* **127**: 467-475.
Birkhead, M.E. & Perrins, C.M. (1985). The breeding biology of the Mute Swan on the river Thames with special reference to lead poisoning. *Biol. Conserv.* **31**: 1-11.
Birkhead, M.E. & Perrins, C.M. (1986). *The Mute Swan*. Croom Helm, London.
Birkhead, M.E., Bacon, P.J. & Walter, P. (1983). Factors affecting the breeding success of the Mute Swan. *J. Anim. Ecol.* **52**: 727-741.
Birkhead, T.R. & Moller, A.P. (1991). *Sperm Competition in Birds*. T & AD Poyser, London.
Birkhead, T.R., Atkin, L. & Moller, A.P. (1987). Copulation behaviour of birds. *Behaviour* **101**: 101-138.
Bishop, K.D. (1984). A preliminary report on the reserves of South-east Irian Jaya (Pulau Kimaam (Dolok), Wasur, Rawa Biru, Kumbe-Merauke, and Danau bian). Unpublished report. ICBP, Cambridge.
Biskup, M.L., Risebrough, R.W. & Dusi, J.L. (1978). Eggshell Measurements and Organochlorine Residues in Little Blue Herons. Pp. 113-116 in: Sprunt *et al.* (1978).
Bisset, S.A. (1976). Foods of the Paradise Shelduck *Tadorna variegata* in the high country of North Canterbury, New Zealand. *Notornis* **23**: 106-119.
Blaauw, F.E. (1917). Some notes on the Black-faced Ibis (*Theristicus melanopis*). *Avicult. Mag.* **8**: 146-148.
Blaauw, F.E. (1927). On the breeding of the Blue-winged Goose of Abyssinia (*Cyanochen cyanopterus*). *Ibis* **3**: 422-424.
Black, J. (1991). The Nene recovery initiative. *IWRB Threatened Waterfowl Research Group Newsletter* **1**: 4.
Black, J.M. (1987). *The Pair-bond, Agonistic Behaviour and Parent-offspring Relationships in Barnacle Geese*. PhD thesis, University College, Cardiff.
Black, J.M. (1988). Preflight signalling in swans: a mechanism for group cohesion and flock formation. *Ethology* **79**: 143-157.
Black, J.M. & Barrow, J.H. (1985). Visual signalling in Canada Geese for the coordination of family units. *Wildfowl* **36**: 35-41.
Black, J.M. & Owen, M. (1984). Importance of the family unit to Barnacle Goose *Branta leucopsis* offspring - a progress report. *Norsk Polarinstitutt Skrifter* **181**: 79-85.
Black, J.M. & Owen, M. (1987). Determinant factors of social rank in goose flocks: acquisition of social rank in youg geese. *Behaviour* **192**: 129-146.
Black, J.M. & Owen, M. (1988). Variations in Pair Bond and Agonistic Behaviors in Barnacle Geese on the Wintering Grounds. Pp. 39-57 in: Weller (1988).
Black, J.M. & Owen, M. (1989a). Parent-offspring relationships in wintering Barnacle Geese. *Animal Behav.* **37**: 187-198.
Black, J.M. & Owen, M. (1989b). Agonistic behaviour in barnacle goose flocks: assessement, investment and reproductive success. *Animal Behav.* **37**: 199-209.
Blackburn, A. (1967). New Zealand's Blue Duck. *Animals* **9**: 620-623.
Blacklock, G.W., Blankenship, D.R., Kennedy, S., King, K.A., Paul, R.T., Slack, R.D., Smith, J.C. & Telfair, R.C. (1978). Texas colonial waterbird census, 1973-1976. F.A. Report Series **15**. Texas Parks and Wildlife Department.
Blair, R.B. (1990). Water Quality and the Summer Distribution of Common Loons in Wisconsin. *Passenger Pigeon* **52(2)**: 119-126.
Blake, E.R. (1953). A Colombian Race of *Tinamus osgoodi*. *Fieldiana (Zool.)* **34(18)**: 199-200.
Blake, E.R. (1955). A collection of Colombian game birds. *Fieldiana (Zool.)* **37**: 9-23.
Blake, E.R. (1959). Two new game birds from Peru. *Fieldiana (Zool.)* **39**: 373-376.
Blake, E.R. (1960). A substitute name for *Crypturellus strigulosus peruvianus*. *Auk* **77**: 92.
Blake, E.R. (1977). *Manual of Neotropical Birds*. Vol. 1. University of Chichago Press, Chicago.
Blake, E.R. (1979). Tinamiformes. Pg. 12-47 in: Mayr & Cottrell (1979).
Blake, R.W. & Smith, M.D. (1988). On penguin porpoising. *Can. J. Zool.* **66**: 2093-2094.
Blaker, D. (1967). Spoonbills in the Western Cape. *Ostrich* **38**: 157-158.
Blaker, D. (1969a). Behaviour of the Cattle Egret *Ardeola ibis*. *Ostrich* **40**: 75-129.
Blaker, D. (1969b). The Behaviour of *Egretta garzetta* and *E. intermedia*. *Ostrich* **40**: 150-155.
Blakers, M., Davies, S.J.J.F. & Reilly, P.N. (1984). *The Atlas of Australian Birds*. Royal Australasian Ornithologist Union & Melbourne University Press, Melbourne.
Blandin, W.W. (1982). *Population Characteristics and Simulation Modelling of Black Ducks*. PhD thesis, Clark University, Worcester, MA.
Blankley, W.O. (1981). Marine food of Kelp Gulls, Lesser Sheathbills and Imperial Cormorants at Marion Island (Subantarctic). *Cormorant* **9**: 77-84.
Blanshard, R.H. (1964). Brown Teal (*Anas castanea chlorotis*) at Little Barrier Island. *Notornis* **11**: 49-51.
Blasco, M., Lucena, J. & Rodriguez, J. (1979). Los flamencos de Fuente Piedra. *Naturalia Hispanica* **23**: 1-55. Instituto para la Conservación de la Naturaleza (ICONA), Madrid.
Blasdale, P. (1984). Some observations on Black-Crowned and White-Backed Night Herons. *Malimbus* **6(1-2)**: 85-89.
Blaser, P. (1985). Der Schwarzhalstaucher *Podiceps nigricollis* auf dem Thunersee im Vergleich zu anderen Gewässern. *Orn. Beob.* **82**: 145-151.
Bledsoe, A.H. (1988). A phylogenetical analysis of postcranial skeletal characters of the ratite birds. *Ann. Carneg. Mus.* **57(2)**: 73-90.
Bleich, V.C. (1975). Diving times and distances in the Pied-billed Grebe. *Wilson Bull.* **87**: 278-280.
Blencowe, E.J. (1962). Abdim's Storks breeding on cliffs. *J. East Afr. Nat. Hist. Soc. Natl. Mus.* **24**: 64.
Bloesch, M. (1980). Drei Jahrzehnte Schweizerischer Storchansiedlungsversuch (*Ciconia ciconia*) in Altreu, 1948-1979. *Orn. Beob.* **77**: 167-194.
Bloesch, M. (1986). Über 33 Jahre alter Weissstorch *Ciconia ciconia* in Altreu. *Orn. Beob.* **83**: 71-76.
Bloesch, M., Boettcher-Streim & Dizerens, M. (1987). Über die Mauser des Grossgefieders beim Schwarzstorch *Ciconia nigra*, [Wing moult in the Black Stork *Ciconia nigra*]. *Orn. Beob.* **84**: 301-315.
Blomgren, A. (1974). *Sangsvan*. Bonniers, Stockholm.
Blümel, H. & Krause, R. (1990). *Die Schellente.* Bucephala clangula. Die Neue Brehm-Bücherei **605**. A. Ziemsen Verlag, Wittenberg Lutherstadt.
Blus, L.J. & Keahey, J.A. (1978). Variation in reproductivity with age in the Brown Pelican. *Auk* **95**: 128.
Blus, L.J., Cromartie, E., McNease, L. & Joanen, T. (1979). Brown Pelican: population status, reproductive success, and organochlorine residues in Louisiana, 1971-1976. *Bull. Environ. Contam. Toxicol.* **22**: 128-135.
Blus, L.J., Lamont, T.G. & Neely, B.S. (1979). Effects of organochlorine residues on eggshell thickness, reproduction, and population status of Brown Pelicans (*Pelecanus occidentalis*) in South Carolina and Florida, 1969-76. *Pestic. Monit. J.* **12**: 172-184.
Blus, L.J., Neely, B.S., Belisle, A.A. & Prouty, R.M. (1982). Further interpretation of the relation of organochlorine residues in Brown Pelican eggs to reproductive success. *Environmental Pollution (Ser. A)* **28**: 15-33.
Bó , N.A. (1956). Observaciones morfológicas y etológicas sobre el Biguá. *Hornero* **10**: 147-157.
Boano, G. (1981). Osservazioni ornitologiche effettuate durante un viaggio in Venezuela. *Doriana* **5(243)**: 1-14.
Board, R.G. & Perrott, H.R. (1979). The plugged pores of tinamou (Tinamidae) and jaçana (Jacanidae) eggshells. *Ibis* **121**: 469-474.
Bocage, J.V.B. (1903). Contribution à la faune des quatre îles du Golfe du Guinée. *J. Acad. Sci. Lisboa* **(2)7**: 25-59, 65-96.
Bocharmikov, V.N. (1990). Current status of the Chinese Merganser *Mergus squamatus* in Russia. *Bull. Inst. Orn. Kyung Hee Univ.* **3**: 23-27.
Bochenski, Z. (1961). Nesting biology of the Black-necked Grebe. *Bird Study* **8**: 6-15.
Bock, K.R. & Medland, R.D. (1988). White-backed Night Heron, *Nycticorax leuconotus*, adopting "bittern" posture. *Nyala* **12(1/2)**: 76.
Bock, W.J. (1956). A Generic Review of the Family Ardeidae (Aves). *Amer. Mus. Novitates* **1779**.
Bock, W.J. (1963). The cranial evidence for ratites affinities. Pp. 39-54 in: *Proc. XIII Int. Orn. Congr.*
Bock, W.J. (1974). The avian skeletomuscular system. Pp. 119-257 in: Farner, D.S. & King, J.R. eds. (1974). *Avian Biology*. Vol. 4. Academic Press, London & New York.
Bock, W.J. & Farrand, J. (1980). The Number of Species and Genera of Recent Birds: a Contribution to Comparative Systematics. *Amer. Mus. Novitates* **2073**: 1-29.
van Bocxstaele, R. (1983). Le Kiwi. Un Oiseau prehistorique au Zoo D'Anvers. *Zoo d'Anvers* **49(2)**: 10-20.
van Bocxstaele, R. (1988). L'autruche: un croisement d'un poulet et d'une girafe? *Zoo d'Anvers* **53(4)**: 57-62.
Boddington, D. (1979). Feeding behaviour of gannets and great black-backed gull with mackerel shoals. *British Birds* **52**: 383-384.
Body, D.N. & Reid, B. (1983). Studies of the lipid, fatty acid, and amino acid composition of the eggs of captive dwarf cassowary (*Cauarius bennetti*) to improve their breeding performance. *New Zealand J. Zool.* **10**: 401-404.
Body, D.N. & Reid, B. (1987). The lipid, fatty acid and amino acid composition of ratite eggs from three different species of kiwis *Apteryx australis australis*, *A.haastii* and *A.owenii* bred in captivity on the same diet. *Biochem. System. & Ecol.* **15**: 625-628.
Boekel, C. (1980). Birds of Victoria River Downs Station and of Yarraldin, Northern Territory. Part 1. *Austr. Bird Watcher* **8**: 171-193.
Boekelheide, R.J. & Ainley, D.G. (1989). Age, resource availability, and breeding effort in Brandt's Cormorant. *Auk* **106**: 389-401.
Boellstorff, D.E., Anderson, D.W., Ohlendorf, H.M. & O'Neill, E.J. (1988). Reproductive effects of nest-marking studies in an American White Pelican colony. *Colonial Waterbirds* **11(2)**: 215-219.
de Boer, B. (1979). *Flamingos on Bonaire and in Venezuela*. Stinapa documentation series **3**. Netherlands Antilles National Parks Foundation, Curaçao, Netherlands Antilles.
de Boer, B. (1981). De Flamingo - Broedkolonie op Bonaire. *Panda (Holland)* **7/8**: 109-111.
de Boer, B. & Johnson, A.R. coord. (1984, 1986, 1988, 1989). *ICBP-IWRB Flamingo Working Group Newsletter* **2, 3, 4, 5**.

de Boer, L.E.M. & Van Brink, J.M. (1982). Cytotaxonomy of the Ciconiiformes (Aves), with karyotypes of eight species new to citology. *Cytogenet. Cell Genet.* **34**: 19-34.
de Boer, L.E.M. (1980). Do the chromosomes of the kiwi provide evidence for a monophyletic origin of the ratites? *Nature. London* **287**: 84-85.
Boersma, P.D. (1974). The Galapagos Penguin: adaptations for life in an unpredictable environment. Ph.D. dissertation The Ohio State University, USA.
Boersma, P.D. (1976). An ecological and behavioural study of the Galapagos Penguin. *Living Bird* **15**: 43-93.
Boersma, P.D. (1978). Breeding patterns of Galapagos Penguins as an indicator of oceanographic conditions. *Science* **200**: 1481-1483.
Boersma, P.D. (1986a). Patagonia's penguin megalopolis. *Animal Kingdom* **89(2)**: 29-39.
Boersma, P.D. (1986b). Body temperature, torpor and growth in chicks of Fork-tailed Storm Petrels. *Physiol. Zool.* **59**: 10-19.
Boersma, P.D. (1987). Penguins oiled in Argentina. *Science* **236**: 135.
Boersma, P.D. (1988). Magellanic Penguins of Patagonia. *Spheniscid Penguin Newsletter* **1**: 2-3.
Boersma, P.D. & Wheelwright, N.T. (1979). Egg neglect in the Procellariiformes: reproductive adaptations in the Fork-tailed Storm-Petrel. *Condor* **81**: 157-165.
Boersma, P.D., Wheelwright, N.T., Nerini, M.K. & Wheelwright, E.S. (1980). The breeding biology of the Fork-tailed Storm-Petrel. *Auk* **97**: 268-282.
Boertmann, D. (1990). Phylogeny of the Divers, Gaviidae (Aves). *Steenstrupia* **16(3)**: 21-36.
Boertmann, D. (1991). Distribution and numbers of moulting non-breeding Geese in Northeast Greenland. *Dan. Ornithol. Foren. Tidsskr.* **85** (1-2): 77-88.
Boesman, P. (1990). Indian Pond Heron in Thailand in March 1989. *Dutch Birding* **12**: 20-21.
Boessneck, J. (1991). [A record of the African Open-bill Stork, *Anastomus lamelligerus*, from ancient Egypt]. *Ecol. Birds* **13(1)**: 83-87. In German with English summary.
von Boetticher, H. (1935). Der Gaimardische Bunt-kormoran. *Vögel ferner Länder* **1935**: 81-83.
von Boetticher, H. (1937). Zur Systematik der Kormorane. *Festschr. f. Prof. Dr. Embrik Strand* **3**: 586-594.
von Boetticher, H. & Grummt, W. (1965). *Gänse- und Entenvögel aus aller Welt.* A. Ziemsen, Wittenberg Lutherstadt.
Boetticher, H.W. (1934). Beitrag zur einem phylogenetisch begrundeten natürlichen System der Steisshuhner (Tinami). *Jena Z. Naturw.* **69**: 169-192.
Boev, N. & Paspaleva-Antonova, M. (1964). Beitrag zur Untersuchung des Schwarzen Storches (*Ciconia nigra* L.) in Bulgarien. *Izv. Zool. Inst. Sofiya* **16**: 5-16.
Boev, Z.N. (1987a). Morphometric Features of the Sexual Dimorphism and Individual Variability of Herons (Aves, Ardeidae) from Bulgaria II. Osteometric Features. *Acta Zool. Bulgarica* **34**: 53-67. In Bulgarian with English summary.
Boev, Z.N. (1987b). Morphometric characteristics of the sexual dimorphism and the individual variability of the Herons (Aves, Ardeidae) in Bulgaria. III. Indices. *Acta Zool. Bulgarica* **35**: 53-64. In Bulgarian with English summary.
Bohl, W.H. (1970). A Study of the Crested Tinamou of Argentina. *US Fish & Wildl. Serv. Spec. Sci. Rep. Wildl.* **131**.
Böhm, M. (1930). Ueber den Bau des jugendlichen Schadels von *Balaeniceps rex* nebst Bemerkungen über dessen systematische Stellun und über dan Gaumenskelett der Vögel. *Zeitschr. Morph. Ökol. Tiere. Berlin* **17**: 677-718.
Bohórquez, G. & Carnevalli, N. (1985). Dimorfismo sexual em *Nothura maculosa* (Temminck, 1815) (Aves, Tinamidae) utilizando a morfometria da pelve. *Iheringia (Misc.)* **1**: 79-85.
Bokermann, W.C.A. (1991). *Observaçes sobre a biologia do Macuco,* Tinamus solitarius *(Aves - Tinamidae).* Doctoral thesis. Universidad de São Paulo.
Bokermann, W.C.A. & Guix, J.C. (1987). Reaparecimiento do guará, *Eudocimus ruber*, no litoral de São Paulo. Pp. 206-207 in: E.P. Coelho, ed. *Anais do II Encontro Nacional de Anilhadores de Aves.* Universidade Federal do Rio de Janeiro.
Bokermann, W.C.A. & Guix, J.C. (1990). Novas observações sobre a ocorrência do guará, *Eudocimus ruber* no litoral paulista (Aves, Threskiornithidae). Page 42 in: Cirne, M.P. ed. *VI Encontro Nacional de Anilhadores de Aves.* Universidade Católica de Pelotas, RS.
Bolen, E.G. (1967). *The Ecology of the Black-bellied Tree Duck in Southern Texas.* PhD dissertation, Utah State University, Logan.
Bolen, E.G. (1971). Pair-bond tenure of the Black-bellied Tree Duck. *J. Wildl. Manage.* **35**: 385-388.
Bolen, E.G. (1973). Breeding whistling ducks *Dendrocygna bicolor* in captivity. *Int. Zoo Yb.* **13**: 32-37.
Bolen, E.G. (1979). The Black Bellied Whistling Duck in South Texas: a review. Pp. 175-185 in: *Proc. First Welder Wildlife Foundation Symp.*
Bolen, E.G. & Forsyth, B.J. (1967). Foods of the Black-bellied Tree Duck in south Texas. *Wilson Bull.* **79**: 43-49.
Bolen, E.G. & Rylander, M.K. (1973). Copulatory behavior in *Dendrocygna*. *Southwestern Nat.* **18**: 348-350.
Bolen, E.G. & Rylander, M.K. (1983). *Whistling-ducks: Zoogeography, Ecology, Anatomy.* Special Publication **20**. The Museum, Texas Tech. University.
Bolen, E.G., McDaniel, B. & Cottam, C. (1964). Natural history of the Black-bellied Tree Duck (*Dendrocugna autumnalis*) in southern Texas. *Southwestern Nat.* **9**: 78-88.
Bolster, R.C. (1923). Note on the breeding season of the Painted Stork *Pseudotantalus leucocephalus*. *J. Bombay Nat. Hist. Soc.* **29**: 561-562.
Bolster, R.C. (1931). Diet and feeding habits of the African Ibidae. *Ostrich* **2**: 18-19.
Bolwig, N. (1973). Agonistic and sexual behaviour of the African Ostrich. *Condor* **75**: 100-105.
Bond, J. (1956). *Check-list of Birds of the West Indies.* Philadelphia Academy Natural Science.
Bond, J. (1971). *Sixteenth supplement to the Check-list of Birds of the West Indies.* Philadelphia Academy Natural Science.
Bonetto, A.A., Pigualberi, C. & Saporito, P. (1961). Acerca de la alimentación de *Nothura maculosa nigroguttata* (Salvadori) con especial referencia a su actividad entomófaga. *Physis. Buenos Aires* **22(63)**: 53-60.
Bonino, N., Bonvissuto, G. Pelliza Sbriller, A. & Somlo, R. (1986). Dietary habits of the herbivores in the central ecological area of Sierras and Mesetas Occidentales of Patagonia. *Rev. Argent. Prod. Anim.* **6(5/6)**: 275-287.
Bonner, W.N. & Hunter, S. (1982). Predatory interactions between Antarctic Fur Seals, Macaroni Penguins and Giant Petrels. *Brit. Antarct. Surv. Bull.* **56**: 75-79.
Bonvallot, J. & Randrianasolo, G. (1975). Présence du Bec-ouvert *Anastomus lamelligerus* sur les Hautes-Terres malgaches. *Alauda* **43**: 323-324.
Bookhout, T.A. ed. (1979). *Waterfowl and Wetlands. An Integrated Review.* The Wildlife Society, Washington, D.C.
Booser, J. & Sprunt, A. (1980). A literature review and annotated bibliography of the Great Basin/Rocky Mountain population of the White-faced Ibis. *US Fish & Wildl. Serv. Rep.* Portland, OR.
Booth, C.J. (1982). Fledging success of some Red-throated Divers in Orkney. *Scottish Birds* **12**: 33-38.
Boothroyd, B. (1987). Additional Marabou colony in Kenya. *Scopus* **11(1)**: 19.
Bordignon, L. (1988). Nidificazione del Mignattaio, *Plegadis falcinellus*, in Piemonte. *Riv. ital. Orn.* **58(3-4)**: 186-188.
Boreiko, V.E., Grischenko, V.N. & Serebryakov, V.V. (1988). [The year of the White Stork in the Ukraine]. *Priroda. Moscow* **1988(6)**: 1114-115. In Russian.
Borg, J. & Zammit, R.C. (1986-87). Arrival dates of Manx Shearwaters at colonies in Malta. *Il-Merill* **24**: 15.
Borin, A.A & Kokshaiskii, N.V. (1983). On the functioning of bird wings. *Doklady (Proc.) Acad. Sci. USSR (Biophys.)* **265-267**: 132-135.
Borodulina, T.L. (1977). Osobennosti stroeniya letateljnogo appara-ta poganok v svyazi s ikh vodnym obrazom zhizni. [Sumary: Specific features of the structure of the flight-apparatus of the grebes in connection with their aquatic mode of life]. *Ornitologiya* **13**: 160-172.
Borrero, J.I. (1971). Notas sobre hábitos alimenticios y comportamiento reproductivo del zambullidor *Podylimbus podiceps* (Aves), en Colombia. *Bol. Soc. Venez. Cienc. Nat.* **29**: 477-486.
Bost, C.A. (1987). Note préliminaire sur le problème de l'étalement des pontes chez le Manchot Papou (*Pygoscelis papua*). *Alauda* **55(4)**: 287-292.
Bost, C.A. & Jouventin, P. (1990). Laying asynchrony in Gentoo Penguins on Crozet Islands: causes and consequences. *Ornis Scand.* **21**: 63-70.
Bost, C.A. & Jouventin, P. (1991). The breeding performance of the Gentoo Penguin *Pygoscelis papua* at the northern edge of its range. *Ibis* **133**: 14-25.
Boswall, J. (1971). Notes from coastal Eritrea on selected species. *Bull. Brit. Orn. Club* **91**: 81-84.
Boswall, J. (1972). The South African Sea Lion *Otaria byronia* as a predator on penguins. *Bull. Brit. Orn. Club* **92**: 129-132.
Boswall, J. (1973). Supplementary notes on the birds of Point Tombo, Argentina. *Bull. Brit. Orn. Club* **93**: 33-36.
Boswall, J. (1989). Some birds at three Chinese zoos (Xi'an, Nanjing and Nanchang). *Avicult. Mag.* **95**: 31-36.
Boswall, J. & Pryterch, R.J. (1972). Some notes on the birds of Point Tombo, Argentina. *Bull. Brit. Orn. Club* **92**: 118-129.
Bottjer, P.D. (1983). *Systematic Relationship among the Anatidae: an Immunological Study with a History of Anatid Classification, and a System of Classification.* PhD dissertation, Yale University, New Haven, Connecticut.
Bourne, W.R.P. (1953). On the races of the Frigate Petrel with a new race from the Cape Verde Islands. *Bull. Brit. Orn. Club* **73**: 79-82.
Bourne, W.R.P. (1955). The birds of the Cape Verde Islands. *Ibis* **97**: 508-556.
Bourne, W.R.P. (1957). Additional notes on the birds of the Cape Verde Islands with particular reference to *Bulweria mollis* and *Fregata magnificens*. *Ibis* **99**: 182-190.
Bourne, W.R.P. (1959). A new Little Shearwater from the Tubuai Islands: *Puffinus assimilis myrtae* subsp. *Emu* **59**: 212-214.
Bourne, W.R.P. (1960). Petrels of the Indian Ocean. *Sea Swallow* **13**: 26-39.
Bourne, W.R.P. (1964). The relationship between the Magenta Petrel and the Chatham Island Taiko. *Notornis* **11**: 139-144.
Bourne, W.R.P. (1965). The missing petrels. *Bull. Brit. Orn. Club* **85**: 95-105.
Bourne, W.R.P. (1967a). Subfossil petrel bones from the Chatham Islands. *Ibis* **109**:1-7.
Bourne, W.R.P. (1967b). Long-distance vagrancy in the petrels. *Ibis* **109**: 141-167.
Bourne, W.R.P. (1968a). The biological effects of oil pollution on littoral communities. *Field Studies* **2(Suppl.)**: 99-121.
Bourne, W.R.P. (1968b). Notes on the diving petrels. *Bull. Brit. Orn. Club* **88(5)**: 77-85.
Bourne, W.R.P. (1976). On subfossil bones of Abbott's Booby *Sula abbotti* from the Mascarene Islands, with a note on the proportion and distribution of the Sulidae. *Ibis* **118**: 119-123.
Bourne, W.R.P. (1977). Half a pair of Black-browed Albatrosses. *British Birds* **70**: 301-303.
Bourne, W.R.P. (1983a). The Soft-plumaged Petrel, the Gon-gon and the Freira, *Pterodroma mollis, P. feae* and *P.madeira*. *Bull. Brit. Orn. Club* **103**: 52-58.
Bourne, W.R.P. (1983b). The appearance and classification of the *Cookilaria* petrels. *Sea Swallow* **32**: 65-71.
Bourne, W.R.P. (1983c). The 'yellow webs' of Wilson's Storm-Petrel. *Brit. Birds* **76**: 316-317.
Bourne, W.R.P. (1985). Petrel. Pp. 451-456 in: Campbell & Lack (1985).
Bourne, W.R.P. (1987a). The classification and nomenclature of the petrels. *Ibis* **129**: 404.
Bourne, W.R.P. (1987b). The affinities, breeding behaviour and distribution of Jouanin's Petrel. *Bull. Brit. Orn. Club* **107**: 4-6.
Bourne, W.R.P. (1989). The evolution, classification and nomenclature of the great albatrosses. *Gerfaut* **79**: 105-116.
Bourne, W.R.P. & David, A.C.F. (1983). Henderson Island, Central South Pacific, and its Birds. *Notornis* **30**: 233-252.
Bourne, W.R.P. & Elliott, H.F.I. (1965). The correct scientific name for the Kerguelen Petrel. *Ibis* **107**: 548-550.
Bourne, W.R.P. & Jehl, J.R. (1982). Variation and nomenclature of Leach's Storm-Petrels. *Auk* **99**(4): 793-797.
Bourne, W.R.P. & Warham, J. (1966). Geographical variation in the giant petrels of the genus *Macronectes*. *Ardea* **54**: 45-67.
Bourne, W.R.P., Bogan, J.A. & Wanless, S. (1978). Pollution in the Sulidae. Pp. 977-983 in: Nelson (1978a).
Bourne, W.R.P., Brooke, M. de L., Clark, G.S. & Stone, T. (1992). Wildlife conservation problems in the Juan Fernández Archipelago, Chile. *Oryx* **26(1)**: 43-51.
Bourne, W.R.P., Mackrill, E.J., Paterson, A.M. & Yésou, P. (1988). The Yelkouan Shearwater *Puffinus (puffinus?) yelkouan*. *British Birds* **81**: 306-319.
Bouvier, J.M. (1974). Breeding biology of the Hooded Merganser in southwestern Quebec, including interactions with common goldeneye and wood duck. *Can. Field-Nat.* **88**: 323-330.
Bowen, W., Gardiner, N., Harris, B.J. & Thomas, J.D. (1962). Communal nesting of *Phalacrocorax africanus, Bubulcus ibis,* and *Anhinga rufa* in southern Ghana. *Ibis* **104**: 246-247.
Bowler, J. & Taylor, J. (1989). An annotated checklist of the birds of Manusela National Park, Seram. Birds recorded on the Operation Raleigh Expedition. *Kukila* **4**: 3-29.
Bowmaker, A.P. (1963). Cormorant predation on two Central African lakes. *Ostrich* **34**: 2-26.
Bowmaker, J.K. & Martin, G.R. (1985). Visual pigments and oil droplets in the penguin, *Spheniscus humboldti*. *J. Comp. Physiol.* **A 156**: 71-77.
Boyd, H. (1953). On encounters between wild white-fronted geese in winter flocks. *Behaviour* **5**: 85-129.
Boyd, H. & Pirot, J.Y. eds. (1989). *Flyways and Reserve Networks for Water Birds.* IWRB, Slimbridge.
Boyd, J.M. (1961). The gannetry of St. Kilda. *J. Anim. Ecol.* **30**: 117-136.
Bradfield, J. (1967). Hadeda Ibis in Rhodesia. *Honeyguide* **53**: 19.
Bradley, J.C., Skira, I.J. & Wooller, R.D. (1991). A Long-term Study of Short-tailed Shearwaters *Puffinus tenuirostris* on Fisher Islands, Australia. *Ibis* **133(Suppl.1)**: 55-61.
Bradley, J.C., Wooller, R.D., Skira, I.J. & Serventy, D.L. (1989). Age-dependent survival of breeding Short-tailed Shearwaters *Puffinus tenuirostris*. *J. Anim. Ecol.* **58**: 175-188.
Bradley, J.C., Wooller, R.D., Skira, I.J. & Serventy, D.L. (1990). The influence of mate retention and divorce upon reproductive success in Short-tailed Shearwaters *Puffinus tenuirostris*. *J. Anim. Ecol.* **59**: 487-496.
Braekevelt, C.R. (1986). Fine structure of the pecten oculi of the Common Loon (*Gavia immer*). *Can. J. Zool.* **64(10)**: 2181-2186.
Braine, J.W.S. (1974). Openbilled storks breeding in South West Africa. *Ostrich* **45**: 255.
Braithwaite, L.W. (1970). *The Black Swan.* Australian Natural History.
Braithwaite, L.W. (1976). Notes on the breeding of the freckled duck in the Lachland River valley. *Emu* 76: 127-132.
Braithwaite, L.W. (1981). Ecological studies of the Black Swan III. Behaviour and social organization. *Austr. Wildl. Res.* **8**: 135-146.
Braithwaite, L.W. (1982). Ecological studies of the Black Swan IV. *Austr. Wildl. Res.* **9**: 261-275.
Braithwarte, W. & Clayton, M. (1976). Breeding of the Nankeen Night Heron "*Nycticorax caledonicus*" while in juvenile plumage. *Ibis* **118(4)**: 584-586.
Braithwaite, L.W. & Frith, H.J. (1969). Waterfowl in an inland swamp in New South Wales. III. Breeding. *CSIRO Wildl. Res.* **14**: 65-109.
Braithwaite, L.W. & Miller, B. (1975). The Mallard, *Anas platyrhynchos*, and Mallard-black duck, *Anas supercil-liosa rogersi*, hybridization. *Austr. Wildl. Res.* **2**: 47-61.
Braithwaite, L.W. & Stewart, D.A. (1975). Dynamics of waterbird populations on the Alice Springs sewage farm. *N.T. Austr. Wild. Res.* **2**: 85-90.
Brand, D.J. (1961). *A comparative study of the Cape teal (*Anas capensis*) and the Cape shoveler (*Spatula capensis*), with special reference to breeding biology, development and food requirements.* PhD dissertation, University of South Africa.
Brand, D.J. (1964). Nesting studies of the Cape shoveler *Spatula capensis* and the Cape teal *Anas capensis* in the western Cape Province, 1957-1959. *Ostrich* **6(Suppl.)**: 217-221.
Brandman, M. (1976). *A Quantitative Analysis of the Annual Cycle of Behavior in the Great Blue Heron.* PhD thesis, UCLA, Los Angeles.
Brandt, C.A. (1984). Age and hunting success in the Brown Pelican: influences of skill and patch choice on foraging efficiency. *Oecologia (Berlin)* **62**: 132-137.
Brandt, H. (1943). *Alaska bird trails.* Bird Research Foundation, Cleveland.
Brasil, L. (1914). The emu of King Island. *Emu* **14**: 88-97.
Bratton, S.P. (1988). Wood Stork use of fresh and salt water habitats on Cumberland Island National Seashore, Georgia. *Inst. Ecol. University Georgia, Cooperative Studies Unit Tech. Rep.* **50**: 1-24.
Bratton, S.P. & Hendricks, S. (1990). Wood Stork nesting, roosting and foraging at Cumberland, Georgia. *Oriole* **53**: 17-24.
Bratton, S.P., Canalos, C. & Bergeron, A. (1989). 1988 surveys for Wood Storks and Least Terns, Cumberland Island National Seashore. *Inst. Ecol. University Georgia, Cooperative Studies Unit Tech. Rep.* **54**.
Bray, M.P. & Klebenow, D.A. (1988). Feeding Ecology of White-faced Ibises in a Great Basin Valley, USA. *Colonial Waterbirds* **11(1)**: 24-31.
Brazil, M.A. (1981). *The Behavioural Ecology of the Whooper Swan* Cygnus cygnus. PhD dissertation, University of Sterling, Sterling.
Brazil, M.A. (1991). *The Birds of Japan.* Christopher Helm, London.
Brazil, M.A. & Kirk, J. (1979). The Current Status of Whooper Swans in Great Britain and Ireland. Unpublished Report, Stirling University.
Brechtel, S. (1983). *The Reproductive Ecology of the Double-crested Cormorant in Southern Alberta.* MSc. thesis, University of Alberta, Edmonton, Alberta.
Bredin, D. (1984). Regime alimentaire du Heron Garde-boeuf a la limite de son expansion geographique recente. *Rev. Ecol. (Terre Vie)* **39**: 431-445.
Breeden, S. & Breeden, B. (1982). The Drought of 1979-1980 at the Keoladeo Ghana Sanctuary, Bharatpur, Rajasthan. *J. Bombay Nat. Hist. Soc.* **79**: 1-37.
Bregulla, H.L. (1992). *Birds of Vanuatu.* Anthony Nelson, Shropshire, UK.
Brelsford, W.V. (1942). Further field notes on northern Rhodesian birds. *Ibis* **6(1)**: 84.
Brelsford, W.V. (1947). Notes on the birds of the Lake Bangweulu in Northern Rhodesia. *Ibis* **89**: 57-77.
Bretagnolle, V. (1988a). Cycles de présence et rhythmes d'activité chez cinq espèces de pétrels antarctiques. *L'Oiseau et la R.F.O* **58**: 44-58.

Bretagnolle, V. (1988b). Social behaviour of the Southern Giant Petrel. *Ostrich* **59**: 116-125.
Bretagnolle, V. (1989a). Temporal Progression of the Giant Petrel Courtship. *Ethology* **80**: 245-254.
Bretagnolle, V. (1989b). Calls of Wilson's Storm Petrel: functions, individual and sexual recognitions, and geographic variation. *Behaviour* **111**: 98-112.
Bretagnolle, V. (1990a). Effects de la lune sur l'activité de pétrels (classe Aves) aux îles Salvages (Portugal). *Can. J. Zool.* **68**: 1404-1409.
Bretagnolle, V. (1990b). Behavioural affinities of the Blue Petrel. *Ibis* **132**: 102-123.
Bretagnolle, V. & Attie, C. (1991). Status of Barau's Petrel (*Pterodroma baraui*): Colony Sites, Breeding Population and Taxonomic Affinities. *Colonial Waterbirds* **14(1)**: 25-33.
Bretagnolle, V. & Lequette, B. (1990). Structural variation in the call of Cory's Shearwater (*Calonectris diomedea*, Aves, Procellariidae). *Ethology* **85**: 313-323.
Bretagnolle, V. & Robisson, P. (1991). Species-specific recognition in birds: an experimental investigation of Wilson's Storm-Petrel (Procellariiformes, Hydrobatidae) by means of digitalized signals. *Can. J. Zool.* **69(6)**: 1669-1673.
Bretagnolle, V. & Thomas, T. (1990). Seabird distribution between Tasmania and Adélie Land (Antarctica), and comparison with nearby Antarctic sectors. *Emu* **90**: 97-107.
Bretagnolle, V., Zotier, R. & Jouventin, P. (1990). Comparative population biology of four prions from the Indian Ocean and consequences for their taxonomic status. *Auk* **107**: 305-316.
Bretagnolle, V., Carruthers, M., Cubitt, M., Bioret, F. & Cuillandre, J.P. (1991). Six captures of a dark-rumped, fork-tailed storm-petrel in the northeastern Atlantic. *Ibis* **133**: 351-356.
Brewer, G. (1988). *Displays and Breeding Behaviour of Captive Ringed Teal* Callonetta leucophrys. MSc thesis, University of Minnesota, Minneapolis.
Brewer, G. (1989). Biparental care behaviour of captive Ringed Teal *Callonetta leucophrys*. *Wildfowl* **40**: 7-13.
Brichetti, P. (1979). Distribuzione geografica degli ucelli nidificanti in Italia, Corsica e Isole Maltesi. 1. Parte introduttiva; Famiglie Podicipedidae, Procellariidae, Hydrobatidae. *Natura Bresciana* **16**: 82-158.
Brichetti, P. (1982). Distribuzione geografica degli Uccelli nidificanti in Italia, Corsica e isole Maltesi. 2. Famiglie Phalacrocoracidae, Ciconiidae, Threskiornithidae. *Natura Bresciana* **19**: 97-157.
Brichetti, P. (1983). Distribuzione geografica degli uccelli nidificanti in Italia, Corsica e Isole Maltesi. 3. Famiglie Phoenicopteridae, Ardeidae (generi *Botaurus*, *Ixobrychus*). *Natura Bresciana* **20**: 197-234.
Brichetti, P. (1986). Nidificazione di Nitticora *Nycticorax nycticorax* e Mignattaio *Plegadis falcinellus* in Puglia. *Avocetta* **10**: 59-60.
Brichetti, P. & Martignoni, C. (1983). Accertata nidificazione di Svasso Maggiore *Podiceps cristatus* sul lago di Mantova e nuovi dati sulla distribuzione in Italia. *Avocetta* **7**: 41-44.
Brickell, N. (1988). *Ducks, Geese and Swans of Africa and its Outlying Islands*. Frandsen Publishers, Sandton.
Briggs, K.T. & Chu, E.W. (1986). Sooty Shearwaters off California: distribution, abundance and habitat use. *Condor* **88**: 355-364.
Briggs, K.T., Lewis, D.B., Tyler, W.B. & Hunt, G.L. (1981). Brown Pelicans in southern California: habitat use and environmental fluctuations. *Condor* **83**: 1-15.
Briggs, K.T., Tyler, W.B., Lewis, D.B., Kelly, P.R. & Croll, D.A. (1983). Brown Pelicans in central and northern California. *J. Field Orn.* **54(4)**: 353-373.
Briggs, S.V. (1977). Variation in waterbird numbers at four swamps on the northern tablelands of New South Wales. *Austr. Wildl. Res.* **4**: 301-309.
Briggs, S.V. (1979). Daytime habitats of waterbirds at four swamps on the Northern Tablelands of New South Wales. *Emu* **79**: 211-214.
Briggs, S.V. (1988). Weight changes and reproduction in female Blue-billed and Musk Ducks, compared with North American Ruddy Ducks. *Wildfowl* **39**: 98-101.
Briggs, S.V. (1990a). Sexual and annual differences in activity budgets of Maned Duck *Chenonetta jubata*. *Emu* **90**: 190-194.
Briggs, S.V. (1990b). *Breeding Ecology of Maned Ducks*. PhD thesis, Australian National University, Canberra.
Briggs, S.V. & Thornton, S.A. (1988). Abdominal fat and percentage water as predictors of body fat in adult Maned Duck, *Chenonetta jubata*. *Austr. Wildl. Res.* **15(3)**: 231-234.
Britton, P.L. (1971). Must the Kisumu Heronry be condemned a second time? *Africana* **4**: 20-22, 32-33.
Britton, P.L. ed. (1980). *Birds of East Africa. Their Habitat, Status and Distribution*. East African Natural History Society, Nairobi.
Britton, R.H., Robert de Groot, E. & Johnson, A.R. (1986). The daily cycle of feeding activity of the Greater Flamingo in relation to the dispersion of the prey *Artemia*. *Wildfowl* **37**: 151-155.
Broad, R.A. (1974). Contamination of birds with Fulmar oil. *Brit. Birds* **67**: 297-301.
Broady, P.A., Adams, C.J., Cleary, P.J. & Weaver, S.D. (1989). Ornithological observations at Edward VII Peninsula, Antarctica, in 1987-88. *Notornis* **36**: 53-61.
Brockman, H.J. & Barnard, C.J. (1979). Kleptoparasitism in birds. *Anim. Behav.* **27**: 487-514.
Brodkorb, P. (1971). Origin and evolution of birds. Pp. 19-55 in: Farner, D.S. & King, J.R. eds. *Avian Biology*. Vol. 1. Academic Press, London & New York.
Brodkorb, P. & Mourer-Chauviré, C. (1982). Fossil anhingas (Aves: Anhingidae) from early Man sites of Hadar and Omo, Ethiopia, and Olduvai Gorge, Tanzania. *Geobios* **15**: 500-515.
Brodsky, L.M. & Weatherkead, P.J. (1984). Behavioral and ecological factors contributing to American Black Duck-Mallard hybridization. *J. Wildl. Manage.* **48**: 846-852.
Brodsky, L.M. & Weatherhead, P.J. (1985). Diving by wintering Black Ducks: and assessement of atypical foraging. *Wildfowl* **36**: 72-76.
Brodsky, L.M., Ankney, C.D. & Dennis, D.G. (1988). The influence of male dominance on social interactions in black ducks and mallards. *Anim. Behav.* **36**: 1371-1378.
Broekhuysen, G.J. (1948). Observations on the great shearwater in the breeding-season. *British Birds* **41**: 338-341.
Broekhuysen, G.J. (1962). Does Black-necked Grebe cover its eggs? *Bokmakierie* **14**: 2-4.
Broekhuysen, G.J. (1973). Behavioural responses of Dabchicks *Podiceps ruficollis* to disturbance while incubating. *Ostrich* **44**: 111-117.
Broekhuysen, G.J. & Frost, P.G.H. (1968a). Nesting Behaviour of the Black-necked Grebe *Podiceps nigricollis* (Brehm) in Southern Africa. I. The reaction of disturbed incubating birds. *Bonn. Zool. Beitr.* **19**: 350-360.
Broekhuysen, G.J. & Frost, P.G.H. (1968b). Nesting Behaviour of the Black-necked Grebe *Podiceps nigricollis* (Brehm) in Southern Africa. II. Laying, clutch size, egg size, incubation and nesting success. *Ostrich* **39**: 242-252.
Broekhuysen, G.J., Liversidge, R. & Rand, R.W. (1961). The South African Gannet. *Ostrich* **32**: 1-19.
Broni, S.C. (1984). *Penguins and Purse-seiners: Competition or Co-existence?* MSc thesis, University of Cape Town.
Broni, S.C. (1985). Social and spatial patterns of foraging by the Jackass Penguin. *S. Afr. J. Zool.* **20**: 241-245.
Brook, D. & Beck, J.R. (1972). Antarctic Petrels, Snow Petrels and South Polar Skuas breeding in the Theron Mountains. *Brit. Antarct. Surv. Bull.* **27**: 131-137.
Brook van Meter, V. (1985). *Florida's Wood storks*. Florida Power & Light Company, Miami.
Brooke, M. & Birkhead, T. eds. (1991). *The Cambridge Encyclopedia of Ornithology*. Cambridge University Press, Cambridge, England.
Brooke, M. de L. (1978a). Some factors affecting the laying date, incubation and breeding success of the Manx Shearwater. *J. Anim. Ecol.* **47**: 477-495.
Brooke, M. de L. (1978b). A test for visual location of the burrow by Manx Shearwaters *Puffinus puffinus*. *Ibis* **120**: 347-349.
Brooke, M. de L. (1978c). The dispersal of female Manx Shearwaters. *Ibis* **120**: 546-551.
Brooke, M. de L. (1978d). Weights and measurements of the Manx Shearwater. *J. Zoology. London* **186**: 359-374.
Brooke, M. de L. (1978e). Sexual differences in the voice and individual recognition in the Manx Shearwater. *Anim. Behav.* **26**: 622-629.
Brooke, M. de L. (1986a). The vocal systems of two nocturnal petrels, the White-chinned *Procellaria aequinoctialis* and the Grey *P. cinerea*. *Ibis* **128**: 502-512.
Brooke, M. de L. (1986b). Manx Shearwater chicks: seasonal, parental and genetic influences on the chick's age and weight at fledging. *Condor* **88**: 324-327.
Brooke, M. de L. (1987a). *The Birds of the Juan Fernández Islands, Chile*. ICBP Study Report **16**. Cambridge, England.
Brooke, M. de L. (1987b). Population estimates and breeding biology of the petrels *Pterodroma externa* and *P. longirostris* on Isla Alejandro Selkirk, Juan Fernandez Archipelago. *Condor* **89**: 581-586.
Brooke, M. de L. (1988). Sexual dimorphism in the voice of the Greater Shearwater. *Wilson Bull.* **100**: 319-323.
Brooke, M. de L. (1989). Determination of the absolute visual threshold of a nocturnal seabird, the Common Diving Petrel. *Ibis* **131**: 290-300.
Brooke, M. de L. (1990). *The Manx Shearwater*. Poyser, London.
Brooke, M. de L. & Prince, P.A. (1991). Nocturnality in Seabirds. Pp. 1113-1121 in: *Proc. XX Int. Orn. Congr.*
Brooke, R.K. (1969). The calls of Abdim's Storks. *Ostrich* **40**: 22.
Brooke, R.K. (1981). Modes of moult of flight feathers in albatrosses. *Cormorant* **9**: 13-18.
Brooke, R.K. (1984). *South African Red Data Book - Birds*. South African National Scientific Programmes Report **97**. Council for Scientific and Industrial Research, Pretoria.
Brooke, R.K. (1986). "Hadeda" in Sightings. *Promerops* 172: 12.
Brooke, R.K. & Furness, B.L. (1982). Reversed modes of moult of flight feathers in the Blackbrowed Albatross *Diomedea melanophris*. *Cormorant* **10**: 27-30.
Brooke, R.K. & Loutit, R. (1984). Marine cormorants using moored boats as nest sites in southern african west coast harbours. *Cormorant* **12**: 55-59.
Brooke, R.K. & Masterson, A.M.B. (1971). Further records of African Marabous breeding south of the Zambesi. *Honeyguide* **67**: 11-14.
Brooke, R.K. & Milton, S.J. (1980). A source of nest material for Cape Cormorants *Phalacrocorax capensis* on Malgas Island. *Cormorant* **8**: 23.
Brooke, R.K., Cooper, J., Shelton, P.A., & Crawford, R.J.M. (1982). Taxonomy, distribution, population size, breeding and conservation of the Whitebreasted Cormorant, *Phalacrocorax carbo*, on the southern African coast. *Gerfaut* **72**: 188-220.
Brooke, R.K., Donelly, B.G. & Irwin, M.P.S. (1982). Comments on cave paintings supposedly depicting Whale-headed Stork in the Matopos, Zimbabwe. *Honeyguide* **110**: 4-7.
Brooks, D.M. (1990). Some notes on the Ciconiiformes in the Paraguayan Chaco. Unpublished Report, Zoological Society of San Diego.
Brooks, D.M. (1991). Some notes on the Ciconiiformes in the Paraguayan Chaco. *Specialist Group on Storks, Ibises and Spoonbills Newsletter* **4(1)**: 4-5.
Brosset, A. (1971). Premières observations sur la reproduction de six oiseaux africains. *Alauda* **39**: 112-126.
Brosset, A. & Erard, C. (1976). [First description of the nesting of four species in Gabon Forest]. *Alauda* **44**: 205-235. In French.
Brosset, A. & Erard, C. (1986). *Les Oiseaux des Régions Forestières du Nord-Est du Gabon*. Vol. 1. Société Nationale de Protection de la Nature, France.
Brothers, N.P. (1983). Seabird Islands: The Thumbs (no. 133) and Blanche Rock (no.135), Tasmania. 135. *Corella* **7(4)**: 83-84, 87-88.
Brothers, N.P. (1984). Breeding, Distribution and Status of Burrow-Nesting Petrels at Macquarie Island. *Austr. Wild. Res.* **11**: 113-131.
Brothers, N.P. (1985). Breeding biology, diet and morphometrics of the King Shag *Phalacrocorax albiventer purpurascens* at Macquarie Island. *str. Wildl. Res.* **12**: 81-94.
Brothers, N.P. & Skira, J. (1983). Seabird Islands no. 132. Hippolyte RocksTasmania. *Corella* **7(4)**: 80-82.
Brouwer, A.C. & van Wieringen, A.M. (1985). *Notes on the Behaviour of Two Colonies of Scarlet Ibis* Eudocimus ruber *in Captivity*. Postgraduate essay. University of Amsterdam, Amsterdam.
Brouwer, A.C. & van Wieringen, A.M. (1986). *De rode ibis. Een onderzoek naar de ethologie en ecologie van de rode ibis* Eudocimus ruber *in het wild*. Postgraduate essay. University of Amsterdam, Amsterdam.
Brouwer, J. & Garnett, S.T. ed. (1990). *Threatened Birds of Australia. An Annotated List*. RAOU Report **68**. Royal Australasian Ornithologists Union.
Brouwer, K. & van Wieringen, M. (1990). Nesting ecology of Scarlet Ibises (*Eudocimus ruber*) in a small colony of mixed ciconiiform birds in the Venezuelan llanos. Pp. 16-27 in: Frederick, Morales *et al.* (1990).
Browder, J.A. (1973). *Studies on the feeding ecology and morphological variation of the Cattle Egret* Bubulcus ibis *(Linnaeus) (Aves: Ardeidae)*. MSc thesis, University of Miami, Coral Gables.
Browder, J.A. (1976). *Water, wetlands and Wood Storks in southwest Florida*. PhD dissertation. University of Florida, Gainsville, Florida.
Browder, J.A. (1978). A modeling study of water, wetlands and Wood Storks. Pp. 325-347 in: Sprunt *et al.* (1978).
Browder, J.A. (1984). Wood Stork feeding areas in southwest Florida. *Florida Field Nature* **12**: 81-96.
Brown, B.W. (1972). The Big Lake Wood Duck: a two-year study of its pre-flight mortality, nesting population growth and migration, 1970-71. *Proc. Annu. Conf. Southeast. Assoc. Game & Fish Comm.* **26**: 195-202.
Brown, C.R. (1984). Resting metabolic rate and energetic cost of incubation in Macaroni Penguins (*Eudyptes chrysolophus*) and Rockhopper Penguins (*E. chrysocome*). *Comp. Biochem. Physiol.* **77A**: 345-350.
Brown, C.R. (1985). Energetic cost of moult in Macaroni Penguins (*Eudyptes chrysolophus*) and Rockhopper Penguins (*Eudyptes chrysocome*). *J. Comp. Physiol.* **B 155**: 515-220.
Brown, C.R. (1986). Feather growth, mass loss and duration of moult in Macaroni and Rockhopper Penguins. *Ostrich* **57**: 180-184.
Brown, C.R. (1987a). Traveling speed and foraging range of Macaroni and Rockhopper Penguins at Marion Island. *J. Field Orn.* **58(2)**: 118-125.
Brown, C.R. (1987b). Energy requirements for growth and maintenance in Macaroni and Rockhopper Penguins. *Polar Biol.* **8**: 95-102.
Brown, C.R. & Adams, N.J. (1984). Female Wandering Albatross raising a chick on its own at Marion Island. *Cormorant* **12**: 103-104.
Brown, C.R. & Klages, N.T. (1987). Seasonal and annual variation in diets of Macaroni (*Eudyptes chrysolophus*) and Southern Rockhopper (*E. chrysocome chrysocome*) Penguins at sub-Antarctic Marion Island. *J. Zoology. London* **212**: 4-28.
Brown, D.A. (1966). Breeding Biology of the Snow Petrel. *Austr. Natl. Antarct. Res. Exped. Sci. Zool.* **89**: 1-63.
Brown, H.D. (1957). The breeding of the Lesser Flamingo in the Mweru Wantipa, Northern Rhodesia. *Ibis* **99**: 688-692.
Brown, J.L. (1987). *Helping and Communal Breeding in Birds. Ecology and Evolution*. Princeton University Press, Princeton, New Jersey.
Brown, L.H. (1955). Breeding of the Lesser and Greater Flamingos in East Africa. *J. East Afr. Nat. Hist. Soc.* **22**: 159-162.
Brown, L.H. (1958). The breeding of the Greater Flamingo *Phoenicopterus ruber* at lake Elmenteita, Kenya Colony. *Ibis* **100**: 388-420.
Brown, L.H. (1959). *The Mystery of the Flamingos*. Country Life, London.
Brown, L.H. (1966). Blue-winged Goose. In: *Report on Nat. Geogr. Soc. W.W.F. Exp. to study Mountain Nyala* Trogelophus buxtoni. Special Mimeo. Report.
Brown, L.H. (1971). The flamingoes of Lake Nakuru. *New Scientist and Sc. J.* **51**: 97-101.
Brown, L.H. (1973). *The Mystery of the Flamingos*. 2nd edition. East African Publishing House, Nairobi.
Brown, L.H. & Britton, P.L. (1980). *The Breeding Seasons of East African Birds*. East African Natural History Society, Nairobi, Kenya.
Brown, L.H. & Pomeroy, D.E. (1984). The age structure of populations of wild birds in tropical Africa, as demonstrated by plumage characters and marking techniques. Pp. 97-119 in: Ledger, J. ed. (1984). *Proceedings of the Fifth Pan-African Ornithological Congress*. Southern African Ornithological Society, Johannesburg.
Brown, L.H. & Root, A. (1971). The breeding behaviour of the Lesser Flamingo *Phoeniconaias minor*. *Ibis* **113**: 147-172.
Brown, L.H. & Urban, E.K. (1969). The breeding biology of the Great White Pelican *Pelecanus onocrotalus roseus* at Lake Shala, Ethiopia. *Ibis* **111**: 199-237.
Brown, L.H., Powell-Cotton, D. & Hopcraft, J.B.D. (1973). The breeding of the Greater Flamingo and Great White Pelican in East Africa. *Ibis* **115**: 352-374.
Brown, L.H., Urban, E.K. & Newman, K. (1982). *The Birds of Africa*. Vol. 1. Academic Press, London & New York.
Brown, P.W. (1977). *Breeding Biology of the White-winged Scoter (*Melanitta fusca deglandi*)*. MSc thesis, Iowa State University, Ames, Iowa.
Brown, P.W. (1981). *Reproductive Ecology and Productivity of White-winged Scoters*. PhD thesis, University of Missouri, Columbia, Missouri.
Brown, P.W. & Brown, M.A. (1981). Nesting biology of the White-winged Scoter. *J. Wildl. Manage.* **45**: 38-45.
Brown, P.W. & Fredrickson, L. (1986). Food habits of breeding White-winged Scoters. *Can. J. Zool.* **64**: 1652-1654.
Brown, P.W. & Fredrickson, L. (1987). Time budget and incubation behavior of breeding White-winged Scoters. *Wilson Bull.* **99**: 50-55.
Brown, P.W. & Fredrickson, L. (1989). White-winged Scoter, *Melanitta fusca*, Populations and Nesting on Redberry Lake, Saskatchewan. *Can. Field-Nat.* **193**: 240-247.
Brown, R.G.B. (1970). Fulmar distribution: a Canadian perspective. *Ibis* **112**: 44-51.
Brown, R.G.B. (1973). Transatlantic migration of dark-phase fulmars from the European Arctic. *Can. Field-Nat.* **87**(3): 312-313.
Brown, R.G.B. (1980). The field identification of Black and Markham's Storm-Petrels. *Am. Birds* **34**: 368.
Brown, R.G.B. (1981). Seabirds in northern Peruvian waters, November-December 1977. *Bol. Instit. Mar. Perú* **1981 (Vol. Extra)**: 34-42.
Brown, R.G.B. (1988a). The Wing-moult of Fulmars and Shearwaters in Canadian Arctic Waters. *Can. Field-Nat.* **102**: 203-208.
Brown, R.G.B. (1988b). Energy requirements for growth of Salvin's Prions *Pachyptila vittata salvini*, Blue Petrels *Halobaena caerulea* and Great-winged Petrels *Pterodroma macroptera*. *Ibis* **130**: 527-534.

Brown, R.G.B. (1988c). The Influence of Oceanographic Anomalies on the Distributions of Storm-Petrels (Hydrobatidae) in Nova Scotian Waters. *Colonial Waterbirds* **11**(1): 1-8.
Brown, R.G.B. (1990). The Wing-moult of Cory's Shearwater, *Calonectris diomedea*, off Nova Scotia. *Can. Field-Nat.* **104**(2): 306-307.
Brown, R.G.B., Barker, S.P., Gaskin, D.E. & Sandeman, M.R. (1981). The foods of Great and Sooty Shearwaters *Puffinus gravis* and *P. griseus* in eastern Canadian waters. *Ibis* **123**: 19-30.
Brown, R.G.B., Bourne, W.R.P. & Wahl, T.R. (1978). Diving by Shearwaters. *Condor* **80**: 123-125.
Brown, R.G.B., Cooke, F. Kinnear, P.K. & Mills, E.L. (1975). Summer seabird distributions in Drake passage, the Chilean fjords and off southern South America. *Ibis.* **117**: 339-356.
Brown, R.S., Norman, F.I. & Eades, D.W. (1986). Notes on Blue and Kerguelen Petrels found beach-washed in Victoria, 1984. *Emu* **86**: 228-238.
Browne, P.W.D. (1979). *Bird Observations in Southwest Mauritania during 1978 and 1979*. Off. Rech. Scient. Tech. Outre-Mer., Senegal.
Browner, G.A. (1964). Some data on the status of the Spoonbill, *Platalea leucorodia* L., in Europe, especially in the Netherlands. *Zool. Meded. Leiden* **39**: 481-521.
Browning, M.R. (1989). The correct name for the Olivaceus Cormorant, "Maiague" of Piso (1658). *Wilson Bull.* **101**: 101-106.
Bruce, M.D. (1982). Occurrence of the Lesser Adjutant Stork *Leptoptilos javanicus* on Bali, Indonesia. *Bull. Brit. Orn. Club* **102(1)**: 39-40.
Bruggers, R.L. (1974). *Nesting biology, social patterns and displays of the mandarin duck,* Aix galericulata. PhD dissertation, Bowling Green University.
Brun, E. (1972). Establishment and populatin increase of the Gannet in Norway. *Ornis Scand.* **3**: 27-38.
Bruning, D.F. (1973a). The greater rhea chick and egg delivery route. *Nat. Hist.* **82**: 68-75.
Bruning, D.F. (1973b). Breeding and rearing rheas in captivity. *Int. Zoo Yb.* **13**: 163-172.
Bruning, D.F. (1974). Social structure and reproductive behavior in the greater rhea. *Living Bird* **1974**: 251-294.
Bruning, D.F. & Dolenzek, E.P. (1986). Ratites (Struthioniformes, Casuariiformes, Rheiformes, Tinamiformes and Apterygiformes). Pp. 277-291 in: Fowler, M.E. ed. *Zoo & Wild animal medecine.* W.B. Saunders Co., Philadelphia.
Brush, A.H. (1976). Waterfowl feather proteins: Analysis of use in taxonomic studies. *J. Zoology. London* **179**: 467-498.
Brush, A.H. & Clark, G.A. eds. (1983). *Perspectives in Ornithology: Essays Presented for the Centennial of the American Ornithologists' Union.* Cambridge University Press, Cambridge, England.
Bryan, A.L. & Coulter, M.C. (1987). Foraging flight characteristics of Wood Storks in east-central Georgia, U.S.A. *Colonial Waterbirds* **10**: 157-161.
Bryant, D.M. & Leng, J. (1975). Feeding distribution and behaviour of Shelduck in relation to food supply. *Wildfowl* **26**: 20-30.
Bub, H. (1991). *Bird Trapping and Bird Banding. A Handbook for Trapping Methods all over the World.* Cornell University Press.
Bucher, E.H. & Nores, M. (1988). Present status of birds in steppes and savannas of northern and central Argentina. Pp. 71-79 in: Goriup (1988).
Buchet, C., Deswasmes, G. & Le Maho, Y. (1986). An electrophysiological and behavioral study of sleep in Emperor Penguins under natural ambient conditions. *Physiol. Behav.* **38**: 331-335.
Buchsbaum, R.N. (1984). *Feeding Ecology of Canada Geese: the Effect of Plant Chemistry on Feeding Selection and Digestion of Salt Marsh Plants.* PhD dissertation, Boston University.
Buckle, A. & Zino, F. (1989). Saving Europe's rarest bird. *Rounder* (ICI) **67**: 112-116.
Buckley, F.G. & Tilger, G.M. (1985). Frigatebird piracy on humans. *Colonial Waterbirds* **6**: 214-218.
Buckley, P.A., Buckley, F.G. (1984). Expanding Double-Crested Cormorant and Laughing Gull populations on Long Island, New York. *Kingbird* **34**: 146-155.
Buckley, P.A., Foster, M.S., Morton, E.S., Ridgely, R.S. & Buckley, F.G. eds. (1985). *Neotropical Ornithology.* Ornithological Monographs **36.** The American Ornithologists' Union, Washington, D.C.
Budd, G.M. (1962). Population studies in rookeries of the Emperor Penguin *Aptenodytes forsteri*. *J. Zoology. London* **139**: 365-388.
Buddle, G.A. (1939). Some notes on the breeding habits of the Dabchick. *Emu* **39**: 77-84.
Budeau, D.A. (1989). *Energy Dynamics, Foraging Ecology and Behavior of Prenesting Greater White-fronted Geese on the Yukon-Kuskokwim Delta, Alaska.* MSc thesis, University of Idaho.
Builles, A., Jullien, J.-M., Yésou, P. & Girard, O. (1986). Rythme d'activité et occupation de l'espace par le Grand Cormorant (*Phalacrocorax carbo*) sur un site d'hivernage: l'exemple de la région d'Olonne, Vendée. *Gibier Faune Sauvage* **3**: 43-65.
Buitron, D. & Nuechterleim, G.L. (1989). Male parental care of Patagonian Crested Duck, *Anas (Lophonetta) specularioides*. *Wildfowl* **40**: 14-21.
Bujnowicz, G. (1977). *Wplyw ingerencji czlowieka na zachowanie sie Perkoza dwuczubego* (Podiceps cristatus *(L.)) w okresie legowym.* MSc thesis. University of Gdansk.
Bulfon, M.E., de Speroni, N.B. & Scolaro, J.A. (1986). An attempt at ageing Magellanic Penguins *Spheniscus magellanicus* by histological analysis of feather follicles. *Cormorant* **13**: 168-171.
Bull, P.C., Gaze, P.D. & Robertson, C.J.R. (1985). *The Atlas of Bird Distribution in New Zealand.* The Ornithological Society of New Zealand, Wellington.
Buller, W.L. (1895). Notes on *Phalacrocorax colensoi*, of the Auckland Islands, and *P. onslowi*, of the Chatham Islands. *Trans. N.Z. Inst.* **27**: 129-132.
Bulmer, R. (1967) Why is the cassowary not a bird? A problem of zoological taxonomy among the Karam of the New Guinea highlands. *Man (New Ser.)* **2**: 5-25.
Bump, G. & Bohl, W.H. (1965). *Some Tinamous of Argentina and Chile.* Interin Report US Department Interior.
Bump, G. & Bump, J.W. (1969). A study of the Spotted Tinamous and Pale Spotted Tinamous of Argentina. *US Fish & Wildl. Serv. Spec. Sci. Rep.* **120**.
Bundy, G. (1976). Breeding biology of the Red-throated Diver. *Bird Study* **23**: 249-256.
Bundy, G. (1979). Breeding and feeding observations on Black-throated Divers. *Bird Study* **26**: 33-46.
Bundy, G., Connor, R.J., Harrison, C.J.O. (1989). *Birds of the Eastern Province of Saudi Arabia.* H.F. & G. Witherby Ltd & Aramco, Dhahran, Saudi Arabia.
Bunn, R.L. (1986). Breeding records for Clark's Grebe in Colorado and Nevada. *Great Basin Naturalist* **46**: 581-582.
Bunnell, F.L., Dunbar, D., Koza, L. & Ryder, G. (1981). Effects of disturbance on the productivity and numbers of White Pelicans in British Columbia - observations and models. *Colonial Waterbirds* **4**: 2-11.
Burbidge, A.A., Fuller, P.J., Lane, J.A.K. & Moore, S.A. (1987). Counts of nesting boobies and Lesser Frigatebirds in Western Australia. *Emu* **87**: 128-129.
Burger, A.E. (1978). Interspecific breeding attempts by *Macronectes giganteus* and *M. halli*. *Emu* **78**: 234-235.
Burger, A.E. (1991). Maximum diving depths and underwater foraging in alcids and penguins. *Canadian Wildlife Service. Occasional paper* **68**: 9-15.
Burger, A.E. & Berruti, A. (1977). Dabchicks *Podiceps ruficollis* feeding in association with Maccoa Ducks *Oxyura maccoa*. *Ostrich* **48(1,2)**.
Burger, A.E. & Cooper, J. (1982). The effects of fisheries on seabirds in South Africa and Namibia. Pp. 150-160 in: Nettleship *et al.* (1982).
Burger, J. (1971). The Western Grebe in Minnesota. *Loon* **43(1)**: 4-9.
Burger, J. (1974). Determinants of colony and nest-site selection in the Silver Grebe (*Podiceps occipitalis*) and Rolland's Grebe (*Rollandia rolland*). *Condor* **76**: 301-306.
Burger, J. (1979). Resource partitioning: nest site selection in mixed species colonies of herons, egrets, and ibises. *Am. Midl. Nat.* **101**: 191-210.
Burger, J. (1980). The transition to independence and postfledging parental care in seabirds. Pp. 367-447 in: Burger *et al.* (1980).
Burger, J. (1982). On the nesting location of Cattle Egrets *Bubulcus ibis* in South African Heronries. *Ibis* **124(4)**: 523-529.
Burger, J. (1984). Grebes nesting in gull colonies: protective associations and early warning. *American Naturalist* **123**: 327-337.
Burger, J. & Gochfeld, M. (1982). Host selection as an adaptation to host-dependent foraging success in the Cattle Egret (*Bubulcus ibis*). *Behaviour* **79(2-4)**: 212-229.
Burger, J. & Gochfeld, M. (1988). Effects of group size and sex on vigilance in ostriches: antipredator strategy or mate competition? *Ostrich* **59(1)**: 14-20.
Burger, J. & Gochfeld, M. (1990). Vertical Nest Stratification in a Heronry in Madagascar. *Colonial Waterbirds* **13(2)**: 143-146.
Burger, J. & Gochfeld, M. (1991). Nest-site selection by the Herald Petrel and White-tailed Tropicbird on Round Island, Indian Ocean. *Wilson Bull.* **103(1)**: 126-130.
Burger, J. & Miller, L.M. (1977). Colony and nest site selection in White-faced and Glossy Ibis. *Auk* **94**: 664-676.
Burger, J., Gladstone, D., Hahn, D. & Miller, L.M. (1977). Intra- and interspecific interactions at a mixed species roost of Ciconiiformes in San Blas, Mexico. *Biol. Behav.* **2**: 309-327.
Burger, J., Miller, L.M. & Hahn, D.C. (1978). Behavior and sex roles of nesting anhingas at San Blas, Mexico. *Wilson Bull.* **90**: 359-375.
Burger, J., Olla, B.L. & Winn H.E. eds. (1980). *Behavior of Marine Animals*. Vol. 4. Plenum Press, New York.
Burger, M.I. (1985). Observações preliminares sobre a variaçao anual no desenvolvimento de testículos de *Nothura maculosa* (Temminck, 1815) (Aves, Tinamidae) no Rio Grande do Sul. *Iheringia* **1**: 71-78.
Burke, V.E.M. & Brown, L.H. (1970). Observations on the breeding of the pink-backed pelican *Pelecanus rufescens*. *Ibis* **112**: 499-512.
Burkholder, G. & Smith, D. (1991). Nest Trees and Productivity of Great Blue Herons (*Ardea herodias*) at Knox Lake, noth-central Ohio. *Colonial Waterbirds* **14(1)**: 61-62.
Burley, R.W. & Vadehra, D.V. (1989). *The Avian Egg. Chemistry and Biology*. Wiley.
Burton, H.R. & Williams, D.L. (1986). Heard Island. *Heard Island ANARE 1985 Rep. Unpublished Rep.*
Burton, M. & Benson, C.W. (1961). The Whale-headed Stork or Shoe-bill: legend and fact. *N. Rhodesia J.* **4**: 411-426.
Burton, R. (1985). *Bird Behaviour*. Granada Publishing, London.
Burton, R. (1987). *Egg: Nature's Miracle of Packaging*. Collins, London.
Burton, R. (1990). *Birdflight. An Illustrated Study of Birds' Aerial Mastery*. Facts on File.
Busnel, R.G. ed. (1963). *Acoustic Behaviour of Animals*. Elsevier, Amsterdam, London and New York
Bustnes, J.O. & Erikstad, K.E. (1988). The diets of sympatric wintering populations of Common Eider *Somateria mollissima* and King Eider *S. spectabilis*. *Ornis Fenn.* **65**: 163-168.
Bustnes, J.O. & Erikstad, K.E. (1990). Size selection of common mussels, *Mytilus edulis*, by Common Eiders, *Somateria mollissima*: energy maximization or shell weight minimization. *Can. J. Zool.* **68 (11)**: 2280-2283.
Bustnes, J.O. & Erikstad, K.E. (1991). Parental care in the common Eider (*Somateria mollissima*): factors affecting abandonment and adoption of young. *Can. J. Zool.* **69(6)**: 1538-1545.
Butler, P.J. & Jones, D.R. (1982). The comparative physiology of diving in vertebrates. Pp. 179-364 in: Lowenstein, O.E. ed. *Advances in Physiology and Biochemistry*. Vol. 8. Academic Press, New York.
Butler, T.Y. (1979). *The Birds of Ecuador and the Galapagos Archipelago*. The Ramphastos Agency, Portsmouth.
Buttemer, W.A. & Dawson, T.J. (1988). Emu winter incubation: thermal, water, and energy relations. In: Bech, C. & Reinertsen, R.E. eds. *Physiology of Cold Adaptations in Birds*. NATO Advanced Research Workshop, Plenum, New York.
Buttemer, W.A., Astheimer, L.B. & Dawson, T.J. (1988). Thermal and water relations of Emu eggs during natural incubation. *Physiol. Zool.* **61(6)**: 483-494.
Büttiker, E. (1985). Die Nahrung der Haubentaucher *Podiceps cristatus* am Untersee (Bodensee) im Jahresverlauf. *Orn. Beob.* **82**: 73-83.
Buxton, L., Slater, J. & Brown, L.H. (1978). The breeding behaviour of the Shoebill or Whale-headed Stork *Balaeniceps rex* in the Bangweulu Swamps, Zambia. *J. East Afr. Wildl.* **16**: 201-220.
Buxton, N.E. (1983). Unnatural mortality of Red-throated Divers. *Scottish Birds* **12**: 227-228.
Bylin, K. (1971). Läten och spel hos smålommen *Gavia stellata*. *Vår Fågelvärld* **30**: 79-83.
Byrd, G.V. & Springer, P.F. (1976). Recovery program for the endangered Aleutian Canada Goose. *Cal.-Nev. Wildl. Trans.* **1976**: 65-73.
Byrd, G.V., Moriarty, D.I. & Brady, B.G. (1983). Breeding biology of Wedge-tailed Shearwaters at Kilauea Point, Hawaii. *Condor* **85**: 292-296.
Byrd, G.V., Sincock, J.L., Telfer, T.C., Moriarty, D.I. & Brady, B.G. (1984). A cross-fostering experiment with Newell's race of the Manx Shearwater. *J. Wildl. Manage.* **48**: 163-168.
Byrd, M.A. (1978). Dispersal and Movements of Six North American Ciconiiforms. Pp. 161-185 in: Sprunt *et al.* (1978).
Cabot, D. & West, B. (1973). Population dynamics of Barnacle Geese *Branta leucopsis* in Iceland. *Proc. Royal Irish Academy (Ser. B)* **73**: 415-443.
Cabot, D., Goodwillie, R. & Viney, M. (1988). *Irish Expedition of North-east Greenland 1987*. Barnacle Books, Dublin.
Cabot, J. & Serrano, P. (1988). Distributional data on some non-passerine species in Bolivia. *Bull. Brit. Orn. Club* **108(4)**: 187-193.
Cade, M. (1983). The possibility of east Mediterranean Manx Shearwaters occurring in British waters. *British Birds* **76**: 413.
Cai Qi-kan (1982). Red-footed Booby *Sula sula* on Xisha Islands (Hainan Province). *Nature* **4**: 32-33.
Cain, B.W. (1970). Growth and plumage development of the Black-bellied Tree Duck, *Dendrocygna autumnalis* (Linnaeus). *Texas A & M University Studies*. **3**: 25-48
Cairns, D.K. (1986). Plumage colour in pursuit-diving seabirds: why do penguins wear tuxedos? *Bird Behav.* **6**: 58-65.
Caithness, T.A. (1985a). Grey Duck. Page 144 in: Robertson (1985).
Caithness, T.A. (1985b). New Zealand Shoveler. Page 148 in: Robertson (1985).
Cajal, J.L. (1988). The Lesser Rhea in the Argentine Puna Region: present situation. *Biol. Conserv.* **45(2)**: 81-91.
Calder, D.R. (1959). Wood Ibis, Ibis ibis. *Ostrich* **30**: 163-164.
Calder, W.A. (1978). The kiwi: a case of compensating divergencies from allometric predictions. Pp. 239-242 in: Piper, J. ed. *Respiratory Function in Birds, Adult and Embryonic*. Spring-Verlag, Berlin.
Calder, W.A. (1979). The kiwi and egg design: evolution as a package deal. *Bioscience* **29**: 461-466.
Calder, W.A. & Dawson, T.J. (1978). Resting metabolic rates of ratite birds: the kiwi and the emu. *Comp. Biochem. Physiol.* **60 A**: 479-481.
Calder, W.A. & Rowe, B.E. (1977). Body mass changes and energetics of the kiwi's egg cycle. *Notornis* **24**: 129-135.
Calder, W.A., Parr, C.R. & Carl, D.P. (1978). Energy contents of the eggs of the brown kiwi *Apteryx australis*; an extreme in avian evolution. *Comp. Biochem. Physiol.* **60 A**: 177-179.
Caldwell, G.S. (1980). Underlying Benefits of Foraging Aggression in Egrets. *Ecology*. **61(4)**: 996-997.
Caldwell, G.S. (1986). Predation as a selective force on foraging Herons: effects of plumage color and flocking. *The Auk* **103**: 494-505.
Caldwell, H.R. & Caldwell, J.C. (1931). *South China Birds*. Vanderburgh, Shangai.
Callister, D. (1991). Exploitation of the Short-tailed Shearwater in Tasmania. *Traffic Bull.* **12(1/2)**: 5-11.
Calvario, E. & Sarrocco, S. (1988). Biologia riproduttiva del Tuffetto *Tachybaptus ruficollis* in una località dell'Italia centrale, Fiume Oeschiera (Lazio). *Avocetta* **12**: 1-11.
Camacho, M.G. (1983). Notes on aquatic birds of Nicaragua, Jabiru *Jabiru mycteria* (Lichtenstein). Unpublished report. Inst. Nicar. Rec. Nat. Ambiente.
Cameron, M. (1981). Cape Gannet photographed at Wedge Light, Port Phillip Bay. *Geelong Nat.* **18**: 34-35.
Campbell, A.G. (1933). The White-faced Storm-Petrel. *Emu* **33**: 86-92.
Campbell, B. & Lack, E. eds. (1985). *A Dictionary of Birds*. T & A D Poyser, Calton, England.
Campbell, J. & Sonter, C. (1985). (*Pelecanus conspicillatus*). *Austr. Birds* **20**: 1-3.
Campbell, K. (1983). Hammerkops. *East Afr. Nat. Hist. Soc. Bull.* **1983 (Jan-Apr)**: 11.
Campbell, K.E., Phillips, A.R. & Olson, S.L. (1986). Comment on the proposed grant of precedence to Threskiornithidae Richmond, 1917 (Aves) over Plataleinae Bonaparte, 1838. *Bull. Zool. Nomencl.* **43**: 10-13.
Campbell, L.H. & Mudge, G.P. (1989). Conservation of Black-throated Divers in Scotland. *RSPB Conserv. Rev.* **3**: 72-74.
Campbell, L.H. & Talbot, T.R. (1987). Breeding status of Black-throated Divers in Scotland. *British Birds* **80**: 1-8.
Campbell, R.W., van der Raay, B.M., Robertson, I. & Petrar, B.J. (1985). Spring and summer distribution, status, and nesting ecology of the Arctic Loon, *Gavia arctica*, in interior British Columbia. *Can. Field-Nat.* **99(3)**: 337-342.
Camphuysen, C.J. & Van Dijk, J. (1983). Zee-en kustvogel langs de Nederlandse kust 1974-79. *Limosa* **56**: 83-230.
Camphuysen, K.C.J. & Derks, P.J.T. (1989). Voorkommen en sterfte van de Fuit *Podiceps cristatus* voor de Nederlandse kust, 1974/86. [Summary: Occurrence and mortality of Great Crested Grebes *Podiceps cristatus* along the Dutch coast, 1974/86]. *Limosa* **62**: 57-62.
Campos, F. & Fernández-Cruz, M. (1989). La población reproductora de Garza Real (*Ardea cinerea*) en la Cuenca del Duero (España), 1988. *Ardeola* **21**: 65-126.
Campos, F. & Fernández-Cruz, M. (1991). The breeding biology of the Grey Heron (*Ardea cinerea*) in the Duero River Basin in Spain. *Colonial Waterbirds* **14(1)**: 57-60.
Campos,F. & Fraile, B. (1990). Les paramètres reproducteurs du Héron cendré (*Ardea cinerea*) dans le nord-ouest de l'Espagne. *L'Oiseau et la R.F.O.* **60(3)**: 212-223.
Campredon, P. (1982). *Demographie et ecologie du Canard Siffleur* Anas penelope *L. pendant son hivernage en France.* PhD thesis, Montpellier, France.
Campredon, P. (1987). La reproduction des oiseaux d'eau sur le Parc National du Banc d'Arguin (Mauritanie) en 1984-1985. *Alauda* **55**: 187-210.
Canales, G.A. (1989). [Activity of *Podiceps occipitalis* on Lake Titicaca]. *Volante Migratorio* **13**: 18. In Spanish.
Canevari, P. & Cabal, G.B. (1988). El flamenco común. Pp. 1-32 in: Cabal, G.B. ed. *Fauna Argentina. Aves.* Vol. 6. Centro Editor de América Latina, Buenos Aires.

Cannon, M.E., Carpenter, R.E. & Ackerman, R.A. (1986). Synchronous hatching and oxygen consumption of Darwin's Rhea eggs (*Pterocnemia pennata*). *Physiol. Zool.* **59(1)**: 95-108.
Canova, L. & Fasola, M. (1989). Prima nidificazione di spatola, *Platalea leucorodia*, in Italia. *Riv. ital. Orn.* **59(3-4)**: 265-267.
Cao Yupu & Xu Tielin (1983). [Ecology of the White Stork, *Ciconia ciconia*]. Pp. 93-94 in: *Proceeding of Heilongjiang Wildlife Society*. In Chinese.
Capanna, E., Civitelli, M.V. & Geralico, C. (1982). The chromosomes of the Hadada Ibis and comments on the karyotype evolution in Threskiornithidae (Aves, Ciconiiformes). *Cytogenet. Cell Genet.* **34**: 35-42.
Capen, D.E. (1977a). Eggshell thickness variability in the White-faced Ibis. *Wilson Bull.* **89**: 99-106.
Capen, D.E. (1977b). *The impact of pesticides on the White-faced Ibis*. PhD Dissertation. Utah State University, Logan, Utah.
Capen, D.E. (1978). Time-lapse Photography and Computer Analysis of Behavior of Nesting White-faced Ibises. Pp. 41-44 in: Sprunt *et al.* (1978).
Capen, D.E. & Leiker, T.J. (1979). DDT residues in blood and other tissues of White-faced Ibis. *Environmental Pollution* **19**: 163-171.
Capurro, A., Frere, E., Gandini, M., Holik, T., Lichtschein, V. & Boersma, P.D. (1988). Nest density and population size of Magellanic Penguins (*Spheniscus magellanicus*) at Cabo Dos Bahías, Argentina. *Auk* **105**: 585-588.
Carey, C., León-Velarde, F., Castro, G. & Monge, C. (1987). Shell conductance, daily water loss, and water content of Andean Gull and Puna Ibis. *J. Exp. Zool.* **1(Suppl.)**: 247-252.
Carey, C., Leon-Valardie, F., Dunin-Borkowskit, O. & Monge, C. (1989). Shell conductance, daily water loss, and water content of Puna Teal eggs. *Physiol. Zool.* **62 (1)**: 83-95.
Carins, M. (1974a). Facial characteristic of Rockhopper Penguins. *Emu* **74**: 55-57.
Carins, M. (1974b). The Blue Petrel in the Falkland Islands. *Ardea* **62**: 239-241.
Carl, R.A. (1987). Age-class variation in foraging techniques by Brown Pelicans. *Condor* **89**: 525-533.
di Carlo, S.A. & Laurenti (1988). Sulla distributione dei componenti la famiglia dei *Podicipedidi* nelle zone umide dell'Italia centrale. *Gli Uccelli d'Italia* **13**: 3-30.
Carlsen, T.L., Eng, R.L., Childress, D.A. & Herbert, J.T. (1990). Response by a Canada Goose population to a high density of man-made nesting islands. *Trans. Congr. Int. Union Game Biol.* **19** (2): 477-482.
Carp, E. compiler (1991). *Censo Neotropical de Aves Acuáticas 1990*. IWRB, Slimbridge, UK.
Carrick, R. (1959). The food and feeding habits of the Straw-necked Ibis *Threskiornis spinicollis* (Jameson) and the White Ibis *Threskiornis molucca* (Cuvier), in Australia. *CSIRO Wildl. Res.* **4**: 69-92.
Carrick, R. (1962). Breeding, movements and conservation of ibises (Threskiornithidae) in Australia. *CSIRO Wildl. Res.* **7**: 71-88.
Carrick, R. & Dunnet, G.M. (1954). Breeding of the fulmar. *Ibis* **96**: 356-370.
Carrick, R.C., Keith, K. & Gwynn, A.M. (1960). Fact and fiction on the breeding of the Wandering Albatross. *Nature. London* **188**: 112-114.
Carriker, M.A. (1955). Notes on the occurrence and distribution of certain species of Colombian birds. *Noved. Colombianas* **2**: 48-64.
Carroll, A.L.K. (1967). Foods of the White-faced Heron. *Notornis* **14**: 11-17.
Carroll, A.L.K. (1970). The White-faced Heron in New Zealand. *Notornis* **17**: 3-24.
Carroll, J.R. (1988). *Population growth of the Double-crested Cormorant Phalacrocorax auritus and its potential for affecting sport fisheries in eastern Lake Ontario*. New York Department of Environmental Conservation, Delmar, New York.
Carroll, S.P. & Cramer, K.L. (1985). Age differences in kleptoparasitism by Laughing Gulls (*Larus atricilla*) on adult and juvenile Brown Pelicans (*Pelecanus occidentalis*). *Anim. Behav.* **33**: 201-205.
Carter, B.C. (1958). *The American Goldeneye in Central New Brunswick*. Wildlife Management Bulletin (Serie 2) **9**, Canadian Wildlife Service.
Carter, H.R. & Hobson, K.H. (1988). Creching Behavior of Brandt's Cormorant chicks. *Condor* **90**: 395-400.
Carter, H.R., Hobson, K.A. & Sealy, S.G. (1984). Colony-site selection by Pelagic Cormorants (*Phalacrocorax pelagicus*) in Barkley Sound, British Columbia. *Colonial Waterbirds* **7**: 25-34.
Carter, M. (1983). The Streaked Shearwater as an Australian Bird. *R.A.O.U. Newsl.* **56**: 5-6.
Carter, M. (1984). Preliminary notice of an invasion and wreck of Blue Petrels, *Halobaena caerulea*, and Kerguelen Petrels, *Pterodroma brevirostris*, during August 1984 in southern Australia. *Australasian Seabird Group Newsletter* **21**: 17-19.
Cash, K.J. & Evans, R.M. (1986a). Brood reduction in the American White Pelican (*Pelecanus erythrorhynchos*). *Behav. Ecol. Sociobiol.* **18**: 413-418.
Cash, K.J. & Evans, R.M. (1986b). The occurrence, context and functional significance of aggressive begging behaviours in young American White Pelicans. *Behaviour* **102(1-2)**: 119-128.
Casler, C.L. (1973). The air-sac systems and buoyancy of the Anhinga and Double-crested Cormorant. *Auk* **90**: 324-340.
Casler, C.L. & Lira, J.R. (1979). El Pato Negro *Netta erythrophthalma* en el Estado Portuguesa, Venezuela. *Bol. Centro Invest. Biol.* **13**: 33-34.
Cassidy, R.J. (1983). The Australian Gannet in African waters. *Ostrich* **54**: 182.
Castan, R. & Olier, A. (1959). Le Tantale ibis, *Ibis ibis* (linne), dans le Sud Tunisien et le Maroc oriental. *Alauda* **27**: 148-150.
Castañera, M. & Mares, M.A. (1986). Algunos aspectos sobre la biología y el comportamiento del suri Pterocnemia pennata garleppi. Unpublished report, Universidad de Buenos Aires.
Castro, H. & Nevado, J.C. (1990). Evolución de la población de malvasía (*Oxyura leucocephala*) en las Albuferas de Adra (Almería) período 1986-1988. *Oxyura* **5(1)**.
Catchpole, C.K. (1979). *Vocal Communication in Birds*. London.
Caughley, G. & Grice, D. (1982). A correction factor for counting emus from the air, and its application to counts in Western Australia. *Austr. Wildl. Res.* **9**: 253-259.
Caughley, G., Grigg, G.C., Caughley, J. & Hill, G.J.E. (1980). Does dingo predation control the densities of kangaroos and emus? *Austr. Wildl. Res.* **7**: 1-12.
Cavalcanti, R.B. (1988). Conservation of birds in the *cerrado* of Central Brazil. Pp. 59-66 in: Goriup (1988).
Cavé, A.J. (1983). Purple Heron survival and drought in tropical West-Africa. *Ardea* **71**: 217-224.
Ceballos-Bendezu, I. (1985). Las aves de la família Tinamidae (Tinamiformes) en el Perú. Pp. 121 in: Stiles, F.G. & Aguilar, F. eds. *Primer Symposio de Ornitología Neotropical, 14-15 octubre 1983. Arequipa, Perú*. Asociación Peruana para la Conservación de la Naturaleza, Lima.
Cezilly, F. & Boy, V. (1988). Age Related Differences in Foraging Little Egrets, *Egretta garzetta*. *Colonial Waterbirds* **11(1)**: 100-106.
Cezilly, F., Boy, V. & Young, L. (1988). Prey selection under the premise of energy maximization: an experimental test in the Little Egret (*Egretta garzetta*). *Colonial Waterbirds* **11(2)**: 315-317.
Chabreck, R.H. (1963). Breeding habits of the Pied-billed Grebe in an impounded coastal marsh in Louisiana. *Auk* **80**: 447-452.
Chamberlain, F.W. (1943). *Atlas of Avian Anatomy*. Michigan State College, East Lansing.
Chamberlain, R.W., Kissling, R.E., Stamm, D.D., Nelson, D.B. & Sikes, R.K. (1956). Venezuelan equine encephalomyelitis in wild birds. *Amer. J. Hyg.* **63**: 261-273.
Chamberlin, M.L. (1977). Observations on the Red-necked Grebe nesting in Michigan. *Wilson Bull.* **89**: 33-46.
Chambers, S. (1989). *Birds of New Zealand. Locality Guide*. Arun Books, Hamilton.
Chance, G.R. (1969). A new bird for New Zealand - Australian Little Grebe, at Arrowtown. *Notornis* **16**: 3-4.
Chandler, R.J. (1981). Influxes into Britain and Ireland of Red-necked Grebes and other water-birds during 1978/79. *British Birds* **74**: 55-81.
Chapdelaine, G., Laporte, P. & Nettleship, D.N. (1987). Population, productivity and DDT contamination trends of Northern Gannets (*Sula bassanus*) at Bonaventure Island, Quebec, 1967-1984. *Can. J. Zool.* **65**: 2922-2926.
Chapin, J.P. (1921). A note on the genus *Lampribis* in east and central Africa. *Ibis (Ser. 11th.)* **3**: 609-610.
Chapin, J.P. (1923). The Olive Ibis of Dubus and its representative on Sao Thomé. *Amer. Mus. Novitates* **84**: 1-9.
Chapin, J.P. (1932). *Birds of the Belgian Congo*. Bulletin of the American Museum of Natural History **65**.
Chapman, B.R. (1988). History of the White Pelican colonies in south Texas and northern Tamaulipas. *Colonial Waterbirds* **11(2)**: 275-283.
Chapman, F.M. (1926). *The Distribution of Bird-life in Ecuador: a Contribution to a Study of the Origin of Andean Bird-life*. Bulletin of the American Museum of Natural History **55**.
Chasen, F.N. (1935). A handlist of Malaysian birds. *Bull. Raffles Mus.* 11.
Chaudhry, A.A. Bar-headed Geese in the Punjab, Pakistan. *IWRB Threatened Waterfowl Research Group Newsletter* **1**: 8.
Chaudhuri, A.B. & Chakrabarti, K. (1973). Wildlife biology of the Sunderbans forests. A study of the birds of the Sunderbans with special reference to the breeding biology of Openbilled Stork, Little Cormorant, and large egrets. *Sci. Cult.* **39**: 8-16.
Chavda, P.B. (1988). *Behavioral and ecological study of the Indian Black Ibis at Junagadh*. MPh dissertation, Saurashtra University, Rajkot, India.
Cheke, A.S. (1968). Copulation in the Hamerkop *Scopus umbretta*. *Ibis* **110**: 201-203.
Cheng Tso-hsin (1973). *A Distributional List of South China Birds*. Vol. 1. Joint Publ. Res. Service, Arlington.
Cheng Tso-hsin (1987). *A Synopsis of the Avifauna of China*. Science Press, Beijing.
Cherel, Y. & Le Maho, Y. (1988). Changes in body mass and plasma metabolites during short-term fasting in the King Penguin. *Condor* **90**: 257-258.
Cherel, Y. & Ridoux, V. (1992). Prey species and nutritive value of food fed during summer to King Penguin *Aptenodytes patagonica* chicks at Possession Island, Crozet Archipelago. *Ibis* **134(2)**: 118-127.
Cherel, Y., Stahl, J.C. & Le Maho, Y. (1987). Ecology and physiology of fasting in King Penguin chicks. *Auk* **104**: 254-262.
Child, G. (1972). (Ardeola rufiventris). *Ostrich* **43**: 60-62.
Chilton, G. & Sealy, S.G. (1987). Species roles in mixed-species feeding flocks of seabirds. *J. Field Orn.* **58(4)**: 456-463.
Cho, P., Brown, R., Anderson, M. (1984). Comparative Gross Anatomy of Ratites. *Zoo Biology* **3**: 133-144.
Choudhury, S. & Black, J.M. (1991). Testing the behavioural dominance and dispersal hypothesis in Pochard. *Ornis Scand.* **22 (2)**: 155-159.
Chozas, P. (1983). *Estudio general sobre la dinámica de la población de cigüeña blanca en España*. Tesis doctoral 227/83. Universidad Complutense, Madrid.
Christenson, B.L. (1981). *Reproductive Ecology and Response to Disturbance by Common Loons in Maine*. MSc thesis, University of Maine, Orono.
Christy, R.L., Bildstein, K.L. & de Coursey, P. (1981). A Preliminary Analysis of Energy Flow in a South Carolina Salt Marsh: Wading Birds. *Colonial Waterbirds* 4: 96-103.
Chubb, C. (1916). *Birds of British Guiana*. Vol. 1. Bernard Quaritch, London.
Chung, J.R. (1986). [First report of North Korean endangered birds]. *Newton Graphic Science Magazine* **6**: 122-129.
Ciarpaglini, V.P. (1983). The reproduction of the Magpie Goose in the Zoological Garden of Cleres, France. Pp. 455-484 in: *Proceedings of the Jean Delacour/IFCB symposium on Breeding Birds in Captivity*. International Foundation for Conservation of Birds, Los Angeles.
Cintra, R. (1986). Nidificação e crescimento do filhote de Curicaca *Harpiprion caerulescens* (Aves: Threskiornithidae) no Pantanal Matogrossense. *Resumos do XIV Congresso Brasileiro de Zoologia*. SBZ, Cuiabá.
Clancey, P.A. (1964). *The Birds of Natal and Zululand*. Oliver & Boyd, Edimburgh.
Clancey, P.A. (1967). *Gamebirds of Southern Africa*. American Elsevier Publishing Co., New York.
Clancey, P.A. (1976). The Shelduck *T. tadorna* in South Africa. *Ostrich* **47**: 145.
Clancey, P.A. (1982). Namibian Ornithological Miscellanea. *Durban Mus. Novit.* **13(6)**: 55-63.
Clancey, P.A. (1985). *The Rare Birds of Southern Africa*. Winchester Press, Johannesburg.
Clancey, P.A. (1990). Variation in *Pterodroma brevirostris* (Lesson), 1831. *Bull. Brit. Orn. Club* **110**(2): 86-90.
Clancey, P.A., Brooke, R.K. & Sinclair, J.C. (1981). Variation in the current nominate subspecies of *Pterodroma mollis*. *Durban Mus. Novit.* **12**: 203-213.
Clapp, R.B. (1971). A specimen of Jouanin's Petrel from Lisianski Island, North-western Hawaiian Islands. *Condor* **73**: 490.
Clapp, R.B. (1974). Specimens of three species of *Pterodroma* from the Pacific Ocean. *Ardea* **62**: 246-427.
Clapp, R.B. & Wirtz, W.O. (1975). The natural history of Lisianski Island, Northwestern Hawaiian Islands. *Atoll Res. Bull.* **186**: 1-196.
Clapp, R.B., Banks, R.C., Morgan-Jacobs, D. & Hoffman, W.A. (1982). *Marine Birds of the Southeastern United States and Gulf of Mexico*. Part 1. Gaviiformes through Pelecaniformes. US Fish & Wildlife Service, Washington, D.C.
Clark, A. (1964). The Maccoa Duck (*Oxyura maccoa* (Eyton)). *Ostrich* **35**: 264-276.
Clark, A. (1966). The social behaviour patterns of the Southern Pochard *Netta erythropthalma brunnea*. *Ostrich* **37**: 45-46.
Clark, A. (1969a). The breeding of the Hottentot teal. *Ostrich* **40**: 33-36.
Clark, A. (1969b). The behaviour of the White-backed Duck. *Wildfowl* 20: 71-74.
Clark, A. (1971). The behaviour of the Hottentot teal. *Ostrich* 42: 131-136.
Clark, A. (1973). Hybrid *Anas undulata* and *Netta erythrophthalma*. *Ostrich* **44**: 265.
Clark, A. (1974a). The status of the Whistling Ducks in South Africa. *Ostrich* **45**: 1-4.
Clark, A. (1974b). Plumage changes in the Maccoa Duck. *Ostrich* **45**: 251-253.
Clark, A. (1974c). The breeding of Hottentot Teal. *Bokmakierie* **26**: 31-32.
Clark, A. (1974d). Plumage changes in the male Maccoa Duck. *Ostrich* **45**: 33-38: 251-253.
Clark, A. (1976). Observations on the breeding of Whistling Ducks in Southern Africa. *Ostrich* **47**: 59-64.
Clark, A. (1977). Review of the records of three Palearctic ducks in Southern Africa: *A. querquedula*, *A. acuta* and *A. clypeata*. *Bull. Brit. Orn. Club* **97**: 107-114.
Clark, A. (1978a). Some aspects of the behaviour of Whistling Ducks in South Africa. *Ostrich* **49**: 31-39.
Clark, A. (1978b). Notes on Maccoa Duck displays. *Ostrich* **49**: 86.
Clark, A. (1979). The breeding of the White-backed Duck on the Witwatersrand. *Ostrich* **50**: 59-60.
Clark, A. (1980a). Notes on the breeding biology of the Spur-winged Goose. *Ostrich* **51**: 179-182.
Clark, A. (1980b). Breeding seasons of Southern Pochard in Southern Africa. *Ostrich* **51**: 122-124.
Clark, B. (1979). The Bald Ibis. *Laniarius* **11**: 4-8.
Clark, C.T. (1982). The Jabiru in the United States. *Birding* **14**: 8-9.
Clark, E.S. (1978). Factors affecting the initiation and success of nesting in an east-central Florida Wood Stork colony. *Proc. Conf. Colonial Waterbird Group* **2**: 178-188.
Clark, E.S. (1979). The attentiveness and time budget of a pair of nesting Wood Storks. *Proc. Conf. Colonial Waterbird Group* **3**: 204-215.
Clark, E.S. (1980). *Attentiveness and time budget of a pair of nesting Wood Storks*. MSc thesis. University Central Florida, Orlando, Florida.
Clark, H. (1985). Storm Petrel ringing in Caithness. *Scott. Birds* **13**(8): 250-257.
Clark, K. (1985). *The Canada Goose Transplant Program in West Virginia*. MSc thesis, West Virginia University.
Clark, L., Ricklefs, R.E. & Schreiber, R.W. (1983). Nest-site selection by the Red-tailed Tropicbird. *Auk* **100**: 953-959.
Clark, L., Schreiber, R.W. & Schreiber, E.A. (199O). Pre- and Post-El Niño Southern Oscillation comparison of nest sites for Red-tailed Tropicbirds breeding in the Central Pacific Ocean. *Condor* **92**: 886-896.
Clark, P. (1968). Lake Atitlan Grebe given secure refuge. *Historia Natural Pro Natura* **2(4)**: 7,11.
Clark, R. (1986). *Aves de Tierra del Fuego y Cabo de Hornos. Guía de Campo*. L.o.l.a. (Literature of Latin America), Buenos Aires.
Clark, R.A. (1979a). The food of the Sacred Ibis at Pretoria, Transvaal. *Ostrich* **50**: 104-111.
Clark, R.A. (1979b). Seasonal levels of body fat, protein, ash and moisture in the Sacred Ibis. *Ostrich* **50**: 129-134.
Clark, R.A. (1979c). DDT contamination of the Sacred Ibis. *Ostrich* **50**: 134-138.
Clark, R.A. & Clark, A. (1979). Daily and seasonal movements of the Sacred Ibis at Pretoria, Transvaal. *Ostrich* **50**: 94-103.
Clarke, G. (1966). Breeding of the Little Grebe. *South Austr. Orn.* **24**: 109-110.
Clarke, M. & Prince, P.A. (1980). Chemical composition and calorific value of food fed to mollymauk chicks Diomedea melanophris and *D. chrysostoma* at Bird Island, South Georgia. *Ibis* **122**: 488-494.
Clarke, M. & Prince, P.A. (1981). Cephalopod remains in regurgitations of Black-browed and Grey-headed Albatrosses at South Georgia. *Brit. Antarct. Surv. Bull.* **54**: 1-7.
Clarke, M., Croxall, J.P. & Prince, P.A. (1981). Cephalopod remains in regurgitations of the Wandering Albatross at South Georgia. *Brit. Antarct. Surv. Bull.* **54**: 9-21.
Clase, H.J., Cooke, F., Hill, T.A. & Roff, W.J. (1960). A survey of the Slavonian Grebe at Myvatn, Iceland. Bird Study **7**: 76-81.
Claugher, D. (1976). A trematode associated with the death of the White-faced Storm Petrel (*Pelagodroma marina*) on the Chatham Islands. *J. Nat. Hist.* **10**: 633-641.
Clay, T. (1976). The species of *Ibidoecus* (Phthiraptera) on *Threskiornis* (Aves). *Systematic Ent.* **1**: 1-7.
Clayton, G.A. (1984). Muscovy Duck, in Mason, I.L. (ed). *Evolution of Domesticated Animals*. Longman, London.
Clements, J.F. (1982). *Birds of the World. A Checklist*. 3rd. edition. Croom Helm, London.
Cloudsley-Thompson, J.L. & Mohamed, E.R. (1967). Water economy of the Ostrich. *Nature* **216**: 1040.
Coate, K. (1989). Red-tailed Tropicbirds return to the Abrolhos Islands. *West. Austr. Nat.* **18(2)**: 64.
Coates, B.J. (1985). *The Birds of Papua New Guinea*. Vol. 1. Dove Publications, Alderley, Australia.
Cobley, N. (1989). First recorded sighting of the Imperial Cormorant *Phalacrocorax atriceps* at Zavadovski Island, South Sandwich Islands. *Cormorant* **17**: 78.
Cock, G.L.A. & Schneider, D.C. (1982). Duration of ship following by Wandering Albatrosses. *Cormorant* **10**: 105-107.
Cody, M.L. (1971). Ecological aspects of reproduction. Pp. 461-512 in: Farner, D.S. & King, J.R. (1971). *Avian Biology*. Vol. 1. Academic Press, London & New York.
Cody, M.L. (1974). *Competition and the Structure of Bird Communities*. Monographs in Population Biology **7**. Princeton University Press, Princeton, New Jersey.

Cody, M.L. ed. (1985). *Habitat Selection in Birds*. Academic Press, London and New York.
Coello, F., Hernandez, C., Ortega, M.L. & de Vries, T. (1977). Reproducción y frecuencia alimenticia de *Fregata minor* en Genovesa y *Fregata magnificens* en Seymour, Galápagos. *Rev. University Católica Quito* **5**: 71-110.
Coimbra-Filho, A.F. (1971). Tres formas de avifauna do nordeste do Brasil ameaçadas de extinçao: *Tinamus solitarius pernambucensis* Berla, 1946, *Mitu m. mitu* (Linnaeus, 1766) e *Procnias a. averano* (Hermann, 1783) (Aves - Tinamidae, Cracidae, Cotingidae). *Rev. Brasil. Biol.* **31**: 239-247.
Colbourne, R. (1981). Why is the kiwi so called? *Notornis* **28(3)**: 216-217.
Colbourne, R. (1982). Surveys of kiwis in four Northland forests. Unpublished report, New Zealand Forest Service.
Colbourne, R. & Kleinpaste, R. (1983). A banding study of North Island Brown Kiwis in an exotic forest. *Notornis* **30(2)**: 109-124.
Colbourne, R. & Kleinpaste, R. (1984). North Island Brown Kiwi vocalisations and their use in censusing populations. *Notornis* **31**: 191-201.
Colbourne, R. & Kleinpaste, R. (1986). Study kiwis in exotic forest. Unpublished report, New Zealand Forest Service.
Colbourne, R. & Powlesland, R.G. (1988). Diet of the Stewart Island Brown Kiwi (*Apteryx australis lawryi*) at Scolley's Flat, southern Stewart Island. *New Zealand Journal of Ecology*. **11**: 99-104.
Coleman, A.E. & Minton, C.D.T. (1979). Pairing and breeding of Mute Swans in relation to natal area. *Wildfowl* **30**: 27-30.
Coles, D. (1986). Record of ratites bred in captivity in the British Isles. *Avicult. Mag.* **92(1)**: 52-54.
Collar, N.J. & Andrew, P. (1988). *Birds to Watch. The ICBP World Checklist of Threatened Birds*. ICBP Technical Publication **8**. Cambridge, England.
Collar, N.J. & Stuart, S.N. (1985). *Threatened Birds of Africa and Related Islands*. The ICBP/IUCN Red Data Book. Part 1. 3rd. edition. ICBP & IUCN, Cambridge, England.
Collar, N.J. & Stuart, S.N. (1988). *Key Forests for Threatened Birds in Africa*. ICPB Monograph **3**. Cambridge, England.
Collias, N.E. & Collias, E.C. (1984). *Nest Building and Bird Behavior*. Princeton University Press, Princeton, New Jersey.
Collins, C.T. (1964). Fossil ibises from the Rexroad fauna of the Upper Pliocene of Kansas. *Wilson Bull.* **76**: 43-49.
Collins, C.T. & Tikasingh, E.S. (1974). Status of the greater shearwater in Trinidad, West Indies. *Bull. Brit. Orn. Club* **94**: 96-99.
Comer, J.A. (1985). *The Movement and Foraging Behaviour of Wood Storks in East-central Georgia*. MSc thesis. University of Georgia, Athens, Georgia.
Comer, J.A., Coulter, M.C. & Bryan, A.L. (1987). Overwintering locations of Wood Storks captured in East-central Georgia. *Colonial Waterbirds* **10(2)**: 162-166.
Cometti, R.H. (1975). Brown Teal on Kawau Island. *Notornis* **22**: 73-76.
Comfort, A. (1962). Survival curves of some birds in the London Zoo. *Ibis* **104**: 115-117.
Commecy, X. (1986). Eco-éthologie du Grèbe huppé (*Podiceps cristatus*) en Picardie. *L'Avocette* **10**: 5-29.
Conant, S. & Collins, M.S. (1983). Frigatebird nests with two chicks. *Elepaio* **44(4)**: 37-38.
Condamin, M. (1979). L'Ibis Rouge de Guyane. *Cour. Nat.* **61**: 7-14.
Condy, J.B. (1965). A technique for capturing Abdim's Storks *Sphenorhynchus abdimii* (Lichtenstein). *Ostrich* **36**: 121-122.
Condy, J.B. (1966). Arrowhead in Abdim's Stork. *Ostrich* **37**: 231-233.
Cone, C.D. (1964). A mathematical analysis of the dynamic soaring flight of the albatross with ecological interpretations. *Virginia Inst. Mar. Sci. Spec. Scient. Rep.* **50**: 1-104.
Connor, M.A. (1979). Feeding association between Little Egret and African Spoonbill. *Ostrich* **50**: 118.
Conroy, J.W.H. (1972). Ecological aspects of the biology of the Giant Petrel in the maritime Antarctic. *Brit. Antarct. Surv. Scient. Rep.* **75**: 1-74.
Conroy, J.W.H. & Twelves, E.L. (1972). Diving depths of the Gentoo Penguin (*Pygoscelis papua*) and Blue-eyed Shag (*Phalacrocorax atriceps*) from the South Orkney Islands. *Bull. Brit. Antarct. Surv.* **38**: 106-108.
Conroy, J.W.H., White, M.G., Furse, J.R. & Bruce, G. (1975). Observations on the breeding biology of the Chinstrap Penguin *Pygoscelis antarctica*, at Elephant Island, South Shetland Islands. *Bull. Brit. Antarct. Surv.* **40**: 23-32.
Contreras, J.R. (1975). Características ponderales de las aves del parque nacional Nahuel Huapi y regiones adyacentes. *Physis. Buenos Aires* **34(88)**: 97-107.
Conway, W.G. (1960). To the high Andes for the rarest flamingo. *Animal Kingdom* **63**: 34-50.
Conway, W.G. (1961). In quest of the rarest flamingo. *Natl. Geogr.* **120**: 91-105.
Conway, W.G. (1965a). The penguin metropolis of Punta Tombo. *Animal Kingdom* **68**: 115-123.
Conway, W.G. (1965b). Care of James's flamingo *Phoenicoparrus jamesi* Sclater and the Andean flamingo *Phoenicoparrus andinus* R. A. Philippi in captivity. *Int. Zoo Yb.* **5**: 162-162.
Conway, W.G. (1971). Predation on penguins at Punta Tombo. *Animal Kingdom* **74**: 2-6.
Conway, W.G. (1980). First Photos of a New Species! The Hooded Grebe. *Animal Kingdom* **83(2)**: 17-19.
Conway, W.G. (1991). The secret lives of the volcano flamingos. *Wildl. Conserv.* **94(6)**: 56-63.
Cooch, E.G. & Cooke, F. (1991). Demographic changes in a Snow Goose population: biological and management implications. Pp. 168-189 in: Perrins *et al.* (1991).
Cooch, E.G., Lank, D.B., Rockbell, R.F. & Cooke, F. (1989). Long-term decline in fecundity in a Snow Goose population: evidence of density dependence?. *J. Anim. Ecol.* **58**: 711-726.
Cooch, F.G. (1958). *The Breeding Biology and Management of the Blue Goose (*Chen caerulescens*)*. PhD thesis, Cornell University, Ithaca, N.Y.
Cooch, F.G. (1964). A preliminary study of the survival value of a functional salt gland in prairie anatidae. *Auk* **81 (3)**: 380-393.
Cooch, F.G. (1965). *The Breeding Biology and Management of the Northern Eider (*Somateria mollissima borealis*) in the Cape Dorset Area, Northwest Territories*. Canadian Wildlife Service, Wildlife Management Bulletin (Ser. 2) **10**.
Cooke, A.S., Bell, A.A. & Prestt, I. (1976). Egg shell characteristics and incidence of shell breakage for Grey Herons *Ardea cinerea* exposed to environmental pollutants. *Environmental Pollution* **11**: 59-84.
Cooke, F. & Buckley, P.A. (1987). *Avian Genetics. A Population and Ecological Approach*. Academic Press, London and New York.
Cooke, F. & McNallay, C.M. (1975). Mate selection and colour preferences in lesser snow geese. *Behaviour* **53**: 151-170.
Cooke, F., Findlay, C.S., Rockwell, R.F. & Smith, J.A. (1985). Life history studies of the Lesser Snow Goose (*Anser caerulescens caerulescens*). III. The selective value of plumage polymorphism: nest fecundity. *Evolution* **39**: 165-177.
Cooke, F., MacInnes, C.D. & Prevett, J.P. (1975). Gene flow between breeding populations of Lesser Snow Geese. *Auk* **92**: 493-510.
Cooke, P., Grobler, J.H. & Irwin, M.P.S. (1978). Notes on Sacred Ibis breeding and other birds at a dam on Aisleby Municipal Sewage Farm, Bulawayo. *Honeyguide* **96**: 5-11.
Coomans de Ruiter, L. (1955). Het voorkomen van het groen dwergganje (*Nettapus pulchellus* Gould) in de Vogelkop (N.W. Nieuw-Guinea). *Limosa* **28**: 7-9.
Coombes, A.H. (1950). The moult-migration of the Shelduck. *Int. Wildl. Res. Ins. Publ.* **2**. British Museum, England.
Cooper, J. (1972). Sexing the Jackass Penguin. Safring **1**: 23-25.
Cooper, J. (1974). The predators of the Jackass Penguin. *Bull. Brit. Orn. Club* **94**: 21-24.
Cooper, J. (1977). Energetic requirements for growth of the Jackass Penguin. *Zoologica Afr.* **12**: 201-213.
Cooper, J. (1978a). Moult of the Black-footed Penguin *Spheniscus demersus*. *Int. Zoo Yb.* **18**: 22-27.
Cooper, J. (1978b). Energetic requirements for growth and maintenance of the Cape Gannet (Aves: Sulidae). *Zool. afr.* **13**: 305-317.
Cooper, J. (1979). Seasonal and spatial distribution of the Antarctic Fulmar in South African waters. *Cormorant* **7**: 15-19.
Cooper, J. (1980a). Breeding biology of the Jackass Penguin with special reference to its conservation. Pp. 227-231 in: Ledger, J. ed. (1984). *Proceedings of the Fifth Pan-African Ornithological Congress*. Southern African Ornithological Society, Johannesburg.
Cooper, J. (1980b). Fatal sibling aggression in pelicans - a review. *Ostrich* **51(3)**: 183-186.
Cooper, J. (1980c). Biology of the Bank Cormorant, Part 1: Distribution, population size, movements and conservation. *Ostrich* **52(4)**: 208-215.
Cooper, J. (1984). Extension of the range of the Bank Cormorant. *Cormorant* **12**: 107-108.
Cooper, J. (1985a). Biology of the Bank Cormorant, Part 2: Morphometrics, plumage, bare parts and moult. *Ostrich* **56**: 79-85.
Cooper, J. (1985b). Biology of the Bank Cormorant, Part 3: Foraging behaviour. *Ostrich* **56**: 86-95.
Cooper, J. (1985c). Foraging behaviour of nonbreeding Imperial Cormorants at the Prince Edward Islands. *Ostrich* **56(1-3)**: 96-100.
Cooper, J. (1986a). Diving patterns of Cormorants Phalacrocoracidae. *Ibis* **128**: 562-570.
Cooper, J. (1986b). Biology of the Bank Cormorant, Part 4: Nest construction and characteristics. *Ostrich* **57(3)**:170-179.
Cooper, J. (1987). Biology of the Bank Cormorant, Part 5: Clutch size, eggs and incubation. *Ostrich* **58(1)**: 1-8.
Cooper, J. & Brooke, R.K. (1986). Cormorants breeding on a wrecked ship near Cape Agulhas, South Africa. *Cormorant* **13**: 178-179.
Cooper, J. & Fourie, A. (1991). Improved breeding success of Great-winged Petrels *Pterodroma macroptera* following control of feral cats *Felis catus* at subantarctic Marion Island. *Bird Conservation International* **1**: 171-175.
Cooper, J. & Morant, P.D. (1981). The design of stainless steel flipper bands for penguins. *Ostrich* **52**: 119-113.
Cooper, J. & Randall, R.M. (1981). Range and movements of the Jackass Penguin *Spheniscus demersus*, with special reference to juvenile dispersal. Pp. 214 in: Cooper, J. ed. *Proc. Symp. Birds on Sea and Shore, 1979*. African Seabird Club, Cape Town.
Cooper, J., Brooke, R.K., Shelton, P.A. & Crawford, R.J.M. (1982). Distribution, population size and conservation of the Cape Cormorant *Phalacrocorax capensis*. *Fish. Bull. S. Afr.* **16**: 121-143.
Cooper, J., Williams, A.J. & Britton, P.L. (1984). Distribution, population sizes and conservation of breeding seabirds in the Afrotropical Region. Pp. 403-419 in: Croxall *et al.* (1984).
Cooper, J.E. (1989). *Disease and Threatened Birds*. ICBP, Cambridge, England.
Cooper, K.N. & Edwards, K.Z. (1969). A survey of Bald Ibis in Natal. *Bokmakierie* **21**: 4-9.
Cooper, S.D., Winkler, D.W. & Lenz, P.H. (1984). The effect of grebe predation on a Brine Shrimp population. *J. Anim. Ecol.* **53**: 51-64.
Copestake, P.C. & Croxall, J.P. (1985). Aspects of the breeding biology of Wilson's Storm Petrel at Bird Island, South Georgia. *Brit. Antarct. Surv. Bull.* **66**: 7-17.
Copson, G.R. & Rousenvell, D.E. (1987). The abundance of Royal Penguins (*Eudyptes schlegeli* Finsch) breeding at Macquarie Island. *ANARE Res. Notes* **41**: 1-11.
Corbett, H., Thode, P. & Reid, B. (1979). A Survey of Kiwis within an Exotic Forest. Unpublished report, New Zealand Forest Service.
Corbin, K.W., Livezey, B.C. & Humphrey, P.S. (1988). Genetic differentiation among Steamer-ducks (Anatidae: Tachyeres): an electrophoretic analysis. *Condor* **90**: 773-781.
Cordier, C. (1965). A la recherche de flamants dans les hautes Andes. *Zoo. Antwerp* **30**: 83-88.
Cordier, C. (1968). Flamingos in Bolivien. *Freunde des Kolner Zoo* **11**: 13-16.
Coronado, R. (1972). *Nidificación, comportamiento y biometría de los huevos y pollos de ánades ibéricos en las Marismas del Guadalquivir (*Anas platyrhynchos, Anas strepera, Netta rufina *y* Aythya ferina*)*. Tesis Doctoral, Universidad Politécnica de Madrid.
Correia, J.G. (1928/29). Field notes and diary from the expedition to San Thome and Principe islands. Unpublished typescript held by the American Museum of Natural History, New York.
Corrick, A.H. & Norman, F.I. (1980). Wetlands and waterbirds of the Snowy River and Gippsland Lakes catchment. *Proc. R. Soc. Vict.* **91**: 1-15.
Costa, D.P., Dann, P. & Disher, W. (1986). Energy requirements of free ranging Little Penguins, *Eudyptula minor*. *Comp. Biochem. Physiol.* **85A(1)**: 135-138.
Cott, H.B. (1953, 1954). The exploitation of wild birds for their eggs. *Ibis* **95**: 409-449, 643-675; **96**: 129-149.
Cottam, C. & Knappen (1939). Food of some uncommon North American birds. *Auk* **56**: 138-169.
Cottam, P.A. (1957). The pelecaniform characters of the skeleton of the Shoe-bill Stork, *Balaeniceps rex. Bull. Brit. Mus. Nat. Hist. (Zool.)* **5**: 51-71.
Cottrille, W.P. & Cottrille, B.D. (1958). *Great Blue Heron: Behavior at the Nest*. Miscellaneous Publications Museum of Zoology, University of Michigan **102**.
Coulson, J.C. (1961). Movements and seasonal variation in mortality of Shags and Cormorants ringed on the Farne Islands, Nothumberland. *British Birds* **54**: 225-235.
Coulson, J.C. (1984). The population dynamics of the Eider Duck *Somateria mollissima* and evidence of extensive non-breeding by adult ducks. *Ibis* **126**: 525-543.
Coulson, J.C. & Brazendale, M.G. (1968). Movements of cormorants ringed in the British Isles and evidence of colony-specific dispersal. *Br. Birds* **61**: 1-21.
Coulson, J.C. & Horobin, J.M. (1972). The annual re-occupation of breeding sites by the fulmar. *Ibis* **114**: 30-42.
Coulson, J.C., Potts, G.R., Deans I.R. & Fraser, S.M. (1968). Exceptional mortality of shags and other seabirds caused by paralytic shellfish poisoning. *British Birds* **61**: 381-404.
Coulson, J.C., Potts, G.R. & Horobin, J. (1969). Variation in the eggs of the Shag (*Phalacrocorax aristotelis*). *Auk* **86**: 232-245.
Coulter, M.C. (1984). Seabird conservation in the Galápagos Islands, Ecuador. Pp. 237-244 in: Croxall *et al.* (1984).
Coulter, M.C. (1986-1990). Wood Storks of the Birdsville Colony and swamps of the Savannah River Plant: 1984, 1985, 1986, 1987, 1988, 1989 annual report. SREL-20/UC-66e, SREL-23/UC-66e, SREL-31/UC-66e, SREL-33/UC-66e, SREL-37/UC-66e, SREL-38/UC-66e. Savannah River Ecology Laboratory, Aiken, South Carolina.
Coulter, M.C. (1987). Foraging and breeding ecology of Wood Storks in east-central Georgia. Pp. 21-27 in: *Proceedings of the III Southeastern Nongame and Endangered Wildlife Symposium*.
Coulter, M.C. (1990). The conservation status of the Oriental White Stork *Ciconia boyciana*. Page 209 in: Matthews, G.V.T. ed. (1990). *Managing waterfowl populations. Proc. IWRB Symp., Astrakhan 1989*. IWRB Special Publication **12**. IWRB, Slimbridge, UK.
Coulter, M.C. & Bryan, A.L. (1988). Field techniques and methods of data collection used in studies of Wood Storks of the Birdsville Colony and swamps of the Savannah River Plant. SREL-34/UC-66e. Savannah River Ecology Laboratory, Aiken, South Carolina.
Coulter, M.C. & Rodgers, J.A. (1987). The ecology and conservation of storks. *Colonial Waterbirds* **10**: 129-130.
Coulter, M.C., Balzano, S., Johnson, R.E., King, C.E., Shannon, P.W. (1989). *Conservation and Captive Management of Storks*. Stork Interest Group. University of Georgia Press, Athens, Georgia.
Coulter, M.C., Beach, T., Cruz, F., Eisele, W. & Martinez, P. (1981). The Dark-rumped Petrel on Isla Floreana, Galápagos. *Charles Darwin Res. Station Ann. Rep.*: **1981**: 170-173.
Coulter, M.C., Bryan, A.L., Young, D.P., Brouwer, K., Kahl, M.P., King, C.E., Kushlan, J.A., Luthin, C.S. & van Wieringen, V. (1991). *A Bibliography of Storks, Ibises and Spoonbills*. Savannah River Ecology Laboratory, Aiken, South Carolina.
Coulter, M.C., Cruz, F. & Cruz, J. (1985). A Programme to Save the Dark-rumped Petrel on Floreana Island, Galapagos, Ecuador. Pp. 177-180 in: Moors (1985).
Coulter, M.C., McCort, W.D. & Bryan, A.L. (1987). Creation of artificial foraging habitat for Wood Storks. *Colonial Waterbirds* **10(2)**: 203-210.
Coulter, M.C., Qishan, W. & Luthin, C.S. (1991). *Biology and Conservation of the Oriental White Stork* Ciconia boyciana. Savannah River Ecology Laboratory, Aiken, South Carolina, USA.
Coulter, M.W. & Miller, W.R. (1968). Nesting biology of black ducks and Mallards in northern New England. *Vermont Fish & Game Dept. Bull.* **68-2**.
Courser, W.D. & Dinsmore, J.J. (1975). Foraging associates of White Ibis. *Auk* **92**: 599-601.
Courtenay-Latimer, M. (1954). Investigation of the Cape Gannet. *Ostrich* **15**: 106-115.
Coverdale, M.A.C., Hancock, J. & Hancock, D.J. (1983). Unusual December-January breeding at the Garsen heronry, Kenya. *Scopus* **7**: 49-50.
Cowan, A.N. (1981). Size variation in the Snow Petrel (*Pagodroma nivea*). *Notornis* **28**: 169-188.
Cowan, A.N. (1983). "Large" Snow Petrels (*Pagodroma nivea*) breeding at the South Sandwich Islands. *Notornis* **30**: 250-252.
Cowles, R.B. (1930). Life history of *Scopus umbretta*. *Auk* **46**: 159-176.
Cowling, S.J. (1974). Observations on ibis feeding on the Australian plague locust. *Emu* **74**: 256-257.
Cowling, S.J. & Lowe, K.W. (1981). Studies of ibises in Victoria, Australia, I: records of breeding since 1955. *Emu* **81**: 33-39.
Cox, J.B. (1980). Some remarks on the breeding distribution and taxonomy of the prions. *Records S. Austr. Mus.* **18**: 91-121.
Crabtree, T. (1985). AOU adds three new Oregon species. *Oregon Birds* **11**: 95-97.
Cracraft, J. (1967). On the systematic position of the Boat-billed Heron. *Auk* **84**: 529-533.
Cracraft, J. (1973). Continental drift, paleoclimatology, and the evolution ande biogeography of birds. *J. Zoology. London* **169**: 455-545.
Cracraft, J. (1974). Phylogeny and evolution of ratite birds. *Ibis* **116**: 494-521.
Cracraft, J. (1981). Towards a phylogenetic classification of the recent birds of the world (Class Aves). *Auk* **98**: 681-714.
Cracraft, J. (1982). Phylogenetic relationships and monophyly of loons, grebes and hesperornithiform birds, with comments on the early history of birds. *Syst. Zool.* **31**: 35-56.
Cracraft, J. (1985). Monophyly and phylogenetic relationships of the Pelecaniformes: a numerical cladistic analysis. *Auk* **102**: 834-853.
Cracraft, J. (1986). The origin and early diversification of birds. *Paleobiology* **12**: 383-399.
Cramp, S. (1983). Studies of west Palearctic birds 185, White Pelican. *British Birds* **76**: 253-262.

Cramp, S. & Simmons, K.E.L. eds. (1977). *The Birds of the Western Palearctic*. Vol. 1. Oxford University Press, Oxford.
Cramp, S., Bourne, W.R.P. & Saunders, D. (1974). *The Seabirds of Britain and Ireland*. Collins, London.
Crandall, L.S. (1927). The storks. *Bull. New York Zool. Soc.* **30**: 149-168.
Crane, J. (1987). Husbandry and behavior of the Hammerkop at the Dallas Zoo. *Animal Keepers' Forum* **14**: 323-326.
Craven, S.R. & Lev, E. (1987). Double-crested Cormorants in the Apostle Islands, Wisconsin, USA: Population Trends, Food Habits, and Fishery Depredations. *Colonial Waterbirds* **10(1)**: 64-71.
Crawford, D.N. (1972). (Ardea pacifica). *Emu* **72**: 131-145.
Crawford, D.N. (1980). Saline coastal swamp in Northern Territory as a habitat for waterbirds. *Emu* **80**: 36-38.
Crawford, E.C. & Schmidt-Nielsen, K. (1967). Temperature regulation and evaporative cooling in the Ostrich. *Amer. J. Physiol.* **212**: 247-353.
Crawford, M. (1987). Predation of Grey Teal by a Pelican. *Bird Obsr.* **663**: 47.
Crawford, R.J.M. & Shelton, P.A. (1978). Pelagic fish and seabird interrelationships off the coast of South West and South Africa. *Biol. Conserv.* **14**: 85-109.
Crawford, R.J.M. & Shelton, P.A. (1981). Population trends for some southern African seabirds related to fish availability. Pp. 15-41 in Cooper, J. ed. *Proceedings of the Symposium on Birds of the Sea and Shore, 1979. African Seabird Group, Cape Town.*
Crawford, R.J.M., Cooper, J. & Shelton, P.A. (1981). The breeding population of White Pelicans *Pelecanus onocrotalus* at Bird Rock platform in Walvis Bay, 1949-1978. *Fish. Bull. S. Afr.* **15**: 67-70.
Crawford, R.J.M., Shelton, P.A., Batchelor, A.L. & Clinning, C.F. (1980). Observations on the mortality of juvenile Cape Cormorants *Phalacrocorax capensis* during 1975 and 1979. *Fish. Bull. S. Afr.* **13**: 69-75.
Crawford, R.J.M., Shelton, P.A., Brooke, R.K. & Cooper, J. (1982). Taxonomy, distribution, population size and conservation of the Crowned Cormorant, *Phalacrocorax coronatus*. *Gerfaut* **72**: 3-30.
Crawford, R.J.M., Shelton, P.A., Cooper, J. & Brooke, R.K. (1983). Distribution, population size and conservation of the Cape Gannet. *S. Afr. J. Mar. Sci.* **1**: 153-174.
Crawford, R.J.M., Williams, A.J., Randall, R.M., Randall, B.M., Berruti, A. & Ross, G.J.B. (1990). Recent population trends of Jackass Penguins *Spheniscus demersus* off Southern Africa. *Biol. Conserv.* **52**: 229-243.
Crawford, W. (1979). Hand-rearing of the Roseate Spoonbill. *Avic. Mag.* **85**: 23-25.
Creutz, G. (1970). Das Vorkommen des Schwarzstorches (*Ciconia nigra* L.) in Brandenburg. *Veröff. Bezirk. Potsdam* **18**: 20-30.
Creutz, G. (1982). Neue Ergebnisse zum Zug des Schwarzstorches. *Falke* **29**: 45-50.
Creutz, G. (1985). *Der Weiss-storch* Ciconia ciconia. Neue Brehm-Bücherei, Bd. **375**. A. Ziemsen Verlag. Wittenberg-Lutherstadt.
Cringan, A.T. (1971). Status of the Wood Duck in Ontario. *Trans. North Amer. Wildl. Nat. Res. Conf.* **36**: 296-311.
Critchley, R.A. & Grimsdell, J.J.R. (1970). Nesting of the Shoebill *Balaeniceps rex* Gould in the Bangweulu swamps. *Bull. Brit. Orn. Club* **90**: 119.
Crivelli, A.J. (1978a). The ecology and behaviour of the Dalmatian Pelican, *Pelecanus crispus* Bruch. A world-endangered species. Unpublished report, Commission of the European Communities and Station Biologique de la Tour de Valat.
Crivelli, A.J. (1978b). Pelicans in Europe. Report to IWRB Symposium on Conservation of Colonially Nesting waterbirds, Carthage, Tunisia.
Crivelli, A.J. (1979). The status of the White Pelican, *Pelecanus onocrotalus*, in Africa. *IWRB, Pelican Research Group Newsletter* **1**: 6-9.
Crivelli, A.J. (1981). The importance of Greece for the conservation of two species of pelicans *Pelecanus onocrotalus* L., and *Pelecanus crispus* Bruch. *Newsletter Hellenic Society for Protection of Nature, Nature* **23-24**: 35-39.
Crivelli, A.J. (1984). European Pelican populations and their conservation. Pp. 123-127 in: *Proc. EEC Contact Group Meeting on Conservation of Birds.* Durham, England, 1983.
Crivelli, A.J. (1987). The ecology and behaviour of the Dalmatian Pelican, *Pelecanus crispus* Bruch: a world endangered species. Final report. Commission of the European Communities, DG XII.
Crivelli, A.J. & Schreiber, R.W. (1984). Status of the Pelecanidae. *Biol. Conserv.* **30**: 147-156.
Crivelli, A.J. & Vizi, O. (1981). The Dalmatian Pelican *Pelecanus crispus* Bruch 1832, a recently world endangered bird species. *Biol. Conserv.* **20**: 297-310.
Crivelli, A.J., Catsadorakis, G., Jerrentrup, H., Hatzilacos, D. & Mitchev, T. (1991). Conservation and management of pelicans nesting in the Palearctic. Pp. 137-152 in: Salathé, T. (1991). *Conserving Migratory Birds.* ICBP Technical Publication **12**. ICBP, Cambridge, England.
Crivelli, A.J., Focardi, S., Fossi, C., Leonzio, C., Massi, A. & Renzoni, A. (1989). Trace elements and chlorinated hydrocarbons in eggs of *Pelecanus crispus*: a world endangered bird species nesting at Lake Mikri Prespa, north-western Greece. *Environ. Pollut.* **61**: 135-247.
Crivelli, A.J., Jerrentrup, H. & Mitchev, T. (1988). Electric power lines: a cause of mortality in *Pelecanus crispus* Bruch, a world endangered bird species, in Porto-Lagos, Greece. *Colonial Waterbirds* **11**: 301-305.
Crivelli, A.J., Leshem, Y, Mitchev, T. & Jerrentrup, H. (1991). Where do Palaearctic Great White Pelicans (*Pelecanus onocrotalus*) presently overwinter? *Rev. Ecol. (Terre Vie)* **46**: 145-171.
Crockett, D.E. (1975). Kermadec Islands Expedition Reports: The Wedge-tailed Shearwater in the northern Kermadecs. *Notornis* **22**: 1-9.
Crockett, D.E. (1979). Rediscovery of the Chatham Island taiko solved century-old-mystery. *Forest and Bird* **13(4)**: 8-13.
Crockett, D.E. (1984). Chatham Island Taiko Expedition 1983-84. *O.S.N.Z. News* **30**: 2.
Crockett, D.E. (1985). Chatham Island Taiko. Page 78 in: Robertson (1985).
Crockett, D.E. (1986). Taiko research project. 1985-1986 expedition report. Unpublished.
Crome, F.H.J. (1976). Some observations on the biology of the Cassowary in Northern Queensland. *Emu* **76**: 8-14
Crome, F.H.J. & Moore, L.A. (1988a). The Cassowary's Casque. *Emu* **88**: 123-124.
Crome, F.H.J. & Moore, L.A. (1988b). *The Southern Cassowary in North Queensland -a Pilot Study*. Vol. 1-4. CSIRO, Atherton, Queensland.
Crome, F.H.J. & Moore, L.A. (1990). Cassowaries in North-Eastern Queensland: report of survey and a review and assessment of their status and conservation and management needs. *Austr. Wildl. Res.* **17(4)**: 369-385.
Croskery, P.R. (1988). Reoccupation of Common Loon, *Gavia immer*, territories following removal of the resident pair. *Can. Field-Nat.* **102(2)**: 264-265.
Croskery, P.R. (1989). Asynchronous hatching pattern of Common Loons, *Gavia immer*, in Northwestern Ontario. *Can. Field-Nat.* **103(4)**: 589-592.
Cross, D.H. compiler (1989). *Waterfowl Management Handbook*. Fish Wild. Leafl. **13**. US Fish & Wildlife Service.
Crossin, R.S. (1974). The storm petrels (Hydrobatidae). Pp. 1-277 in King, W.B. ed. *Pelagic Studies of Seabirds in the Central and Eastern Pacific Oceans. Smithson. Contrib. Zool.* **158**.
Croxall, J.P. (1979). Distribution and population changes in the Wandering Albatross *Diomedea exulans* at South Georgia. *Ardea* **67**: 15-21.
Croxall, J.P. (1982a). Sexual dimorphism in Snow Petrels, *Pagodroma nivea*. *Notornis* **29**: 171-180.
Croxall, J.P. (1982b). Energy costs of incubation and moult in petrels and penguins. *J. Anim. Ecol.* **51**: 177-194.
Croxall, J.P. (1984). Seabirds. Pp. 533-619 in Laws, R.M., *Ecology of the Antarctic*. Academic Press, London and New York.
Croxall, J.P. ed. (1987). *Seabirds Feeding Ecology and Role in Marine Ecosystems.* Cambridge University Press, Cambridge, England.
Croxall, J.P. ed. (1991). *Seabird Status and Conservation: A Supplement*. Technical Publication **11**. ICBP, Cambridge, England.
Croxall, J.P. & Furse, J.R. (1980). Food of Chinstrap Penguins *Pygoscelis antarctica* and Macaroni Penguins *Eudyptes chrysolophus* at Elephant Island group, South Shetland Islands. *Ibis* **122**: 237-245.
Croxall, J.P. & Hunter, I. (1982). The distribution and abundance of burrowing seabirds (procellariiformes) at Bird Island, South Georgia: II. South Georgia Diving Petrel. *Brit. Antarct. Surv. Bull.* **56**: 69-74.
Croxall, J.P. & Kirkwood, D.E. (1979). *The Breeding Distribution of Penguins on the Antarctic Peninsula and Islands of the Scotia Sea.* British Antarctic Survey, Cambridge.
Croxall, J.P. & Lishman, G.S. (1987). The food and feeding ecology of penguins. Pp. 101-133 in: Croxall (1987).
Croxall, J.P. & Prince, P.A. (1980a). The food of Gentoo Penguins *Pygoscelis papua* and Macaroni Penguins *Eudyptes chrysolophus* at South Georgia. *Ibis* **122**: 245-253.
Croxall, J.P. & Prince, P.A. (1980b). Food, feeding ecology and ecological segregation of seabirds at South Georgia. *Biol. J. Linn. Soc.* **14**: 103-131.
Croxall, J.P. & Prince, P.A. (1983). Antarctic Penguins and Albatrosses. *Oceanus* **26(1)**: 18-27.
Croxall, J.P. & Prince, P.A. (1990). Recoveries of Wandering Albatrosses *Diomedea exulans* ringed at South Georgia 1958-1986. *Ringing & Migration* **11**: 43-51.
Croxall, J.P. & Ricketts, C. (1983). Energy costs of incubation in the Wandering Albatross. *Ibis* **125**: 33-39.
Croxall, J.P. & Rothery, P. (1991). Population regulation of seabirds: implications of their demography for conservation. Pp. 272-296 in: Perrins *et al.* (1991).
Croxall, J.P., Davis, R.W. & O'Connell, M.J. (1988). Diving patterns in relation to diet of Gentoo and Macaroni Penguins at South Georgia. *Condor* **90**: 157-167.
Croxall, J.P., Evans, P.G.H. & Schreiber, R.W. eds. (1984). *Status and Conservation of the World's Seabirds.* ICBP Technical Publication **2**. ICBP, Cambridge, England.
Croxall, J.P., Hill, H.J., Lidstone-Scott, R., O'Connel, M.J. & Prince, P.A. (1988). Food and feeding ecology of Wilson's Storm Petrel at South Georgia. *J. Zoology. London* **216**: 83-102.
Croxall, J.P., Prévost, J., Ainley, D.G., Warham, J. & Cooper, J. (1985). Penguin. Pp. 444-449 in: Campbell & Lack (1985).
Croxall, J.P., Prince, P.A., Baird, A. & Ward, P. (1985). The diet of the Southern Rockhopper Penguin *Eudyptes chrysocome chrysocome* at Beauchene Island, Falkland Islands. *J. Zoology. London* **206**: 485-496.
Croxall, J.P., Rothery, P., Pickering, S.P.C. & Prince, P.A. (1990). Reproductive performance, recruitment and survival of Wandering Albatrosses *Diomedea exulans* at Bird Island, South Georgia. *J. Anim. Ecol.* **59**: 775-796.
Crutchfield, P.J. & Whitfield, M.E. (1987). Anhinga, a breeding confirmation from Cumberland County, N.C. *Chat* **51(3)**: 65-68.
Cruz, F. & Cruz, J. (1987a). The Dark-rumped Petrel conservation project. *Charles Darwin Res. Stn. 1984-1985 Ann. Rep.*: 73-78.
Cruz, F. & Cruz, J. (1987b). Control of black rats and its effect on nesting Dark-rumped Petrels in the Galápagos Islands. *Vida Silvestre Neotropical* **2**: 3-13.
Cruz, J.B. & Cruz, F. (1987c). Conservation of the Dark-rumped Petrel in the Galápagos Islands, Ecuador. *Biol. Cons.* **42**: 303-311.
Cruz, F. & Cruz, J.B. (1990a). Breeding, morphology, and growth of the endangered Dark-rumped Petrel. *Auk* **107**: 317-326.
Cruz, J.B. & Cruz, F. (1990b). Effect of El Niño-Southern Oscillation conditions on nestling growth rate in the Dark-rumped Petrel. *Condor* **92**.
Cunningham, D.M. & Moors, P.J. (1985). The birds of the Noises Islands, Hauraki Gulf. *Notornis* **32**: 221-243.
Cunningham, E.R. (1968). A three year study of the Wood Duck on the Yazoo National Wildlife Refuge. *Proc. Annu. Conf. Southeast. Assoc. Game & Fish Comm.* **22**: 145-155.
Cunningham-van Someren, G.R. (1970). Animated perches and feeding associations of birds in the Sudan. *Bull. Brit. Orn. Club* **90**: 120-122.
Curry, P.J. (1979). *The Young Emu and its Family Life in Captivity*. MSc thesis, University of Melbourne, Victoria.
Curry, P.J. (1985). Emu. Pp. 178-179 in: Campbell & Lack (1985).
Curry-Lindahl, K. (1968). Hägrars (Ardeidae) taxonomi belyst av etolgiska studier. En preliminär redögorelse. *Var Fagelvarld* **27(4)**: 289-308.
Curry-Lindahl, K. (1971). Systematic relationships in herons (Ardeidae), based on comparative studies of behaviour and ecology. *Ostrich* **suppl. 9**: 53-70.
Curry-Lindahl, K. (1975). Man in Madagascar. *Defenders of Wildlife* **50(2)**: 164-169.
Curth, P. (1954). *Der Mittelsäger*. Neue Brehm-Bücherei 126. A. Ziemsen Verlag, Wittenberg, Lutherstadt.
Curtis, W.F., Lassey, P.A. & Wallace, D.I.M. (1985). Identifying the smaller shearwaters. *British Birds* **78**: 123-138.
Custer, T.W. & Frederick, P.C. (1990). Egg size and laying order of Snowy Egrets, Great Egrets, and Black-crowned Night-Herons. *Condor* **92**: 772-775.
Custer, T.W. & Mitchell, C.A. (1989). Organochlorine Contaminants in White-faced Ibis Eggs in Southern Texas. *Colonial Waterbirds* **12(1)**: 126-129.
Custer, T.W. & Osborn, R.G. (1978). Feeding habitat use by colonially-breeding herons, egrets, and ibises in North Carolina. *Auk* **95**: 733-743.
Custer, T.W. & Peterson, D.W. (1991). Growth Rates of Great Egret, Snowy Egret and Black-crowned Night-Heron Chicks. *Colonial Waterbirds* **14(1)**: 46-50.
Custer, T.W., Osborn, R.G. & Stout, W.F. (1980). Distribution, species abundance, and nesting-site use of Atlantic Coast colonies of Herons and their allies. *Auk* **97**: 591-600.
Cuvier, G. (1804). Memoire sur l'ibis des anciens Egyptiens. *Annales de Museum D'Histoire Naturelle* **4**: 166-185.
Cyrus, D.P. (1975). Breeding success of Red-throated Divers on Fetlar. *British Birds* **68**: 75-76.
Czapulak, A. & Wieloch, M. (1988). [On "Polish" morph (*immutabilis*) of Mute Swan]. *Notatki Ornitol.* **29(1-2)**: 43-52. In Polish with English summary.
D'Eath, J.O. (1967). The Comb Duck (*Sarkidiornis melanotus melanotus*) in captivity. *Avicult. Mag.* **73**: 197-198.
Dabbene, R. (1920). Sobre la nidificación del flamenco, *Phoenicopterus chilensis* Mol. *Hornero* **2**: 134-135.
Dabbene, R. (1972). *Las aves de caza de la república Argentina*. Albátros, Buenos Aires.
Daciuk, J. (1976a). Notas faunísticas y bioecológicas de Península Valdés y Patagonia, XV. Estudio bioecológico inicial de los esfeníscidos visitantes y colonizadores de Península Valdés y costas aledañas (Prov. Chubut, Argentina). *Physis (Sec. C). Buenos Aires* **35**: 43-56.
Daciuk, J. (1976b). Notas faunísticas y bioecológicas de la Península Valdés y Patagonia XIV. Pingüinos que nidifican y arriban en sus migraciones a las costas de Santa Cruz e Islas Malvinas (*Aves, Spheniscidae*). *Neotropica* **22(68)**: 87-92.
Daciuk, J. (1977). Notas faunísticas y bioecológicas de Península Valdés y Patagonia, VI. Observaciones sobre áreas de nidificación de la avifauna del litoral marítimo Patagónico (Provincias de Chubut y Santa Cruz, Rep. Argentina). *Hornero* **11**: 361-376.
Daciuk, J. (1978). Notas faunísticas y bioecológicas de la Península Valdés y Patagonia. XXIII. Estudio bioecológico y etológico preliminar del ñandú petiso patagónico y de los tinámidos de la Península Valdés, Chubut, Argentina (Aves: Rheidae y Tinamidae). *Physis (Sec. C). Buenos Aires* **38(95)**: 69-85.
Dallinga, J.H. & Schoenmakers, S. (1987). Regional decrease in the number of White Storks (*Ciconia c. ciconia*) in relation to food resources. *Colonial Waterbirds* **10(2)**: 167-177.
Dallmeier, F. (1991). Whistling-ducks as a manageable and sustainable resource in Venezuela: balancing economic costs and benefits. Pp. 266-287 in: Robinson, J.G. & Redford, K.H. eds. (1991). *Neotropical Wildlife Use and Conservation.*
van der Dane, B. & Kloot, W.G. (1964). An analysis of the displays of the goldeneye duck (*Bucephala clangula* L.). *Behaviour* **22**: 282-328.
Dane, C.W. (1965). *The Influence of Age on Development and Reproductive Capability of the Blue-winged Teal (*Anas discors *Linnaeus)*. PhD thesis, Purdue University, West Lafayette, Ind.
Dane, C.W. (1966). Some aspects of breeding biology of the Blue-winged Teal. *Auk* **83**: 389-402.
Danford, C.G. (1880). A further contribution to the ornithology of Asia Minor. *Ibis* **4(4th Ser.)**: 81-99.
Danielsen, F. & Skov, H. (1987). Waterbird survey results from south-east Sumatra. *Bull. Oriental Bird Club* **6**: 8-11.
Dann, P. (1988). An experimental manipulation of clutch size in the Little Penguin *Eudyptula minor*. *Emu* **88**: 101-103.
Dann, P. & Cullen, J.M. (1989). The maximum swimming speed and theoretical foraging range of breeding Little Penguins *Eudyptula minor* at Phillip Island, Victoria. *Corella* **13(2)**: 34-37.
Darby, J.T. (1984). *The Status, Distribution, and Conservation of the Yellow-eyed Penguin* Megadyptes antipodes *in New Zealand together with a Summary of Population Numbers and Distribution on the South East Otago and Southland Coasts.* Report circulated to Government agencies, Otago Museum, New Zealand.
Darby, P.W. (1978). The breeding of Meller's Duck *Anas melleri* (Sclater) at the Jersey Zoological Park. *Dodo* **15**: 29-32.
Darlington, P.J. (1957). *Zoogeography: the Geographical Distribution of Animals.* John Wiley and Sons, New York.
Dathe, H. (1970). Der Argala. *Falke* **17**: 430.
Dau, C.P. (1972). Observations on the natural history of the spectacled eider (*Lampronetta fischeri*). Department Wildlife and Fish, University of Alaska.
Dau, C.P. (1974). *Nesting biology of the spectacled eider* Somateria fischeri *(Brandt) on the Yukon-Kuskokwim delta, Alaska.* MSc thesis, University of Alaska.
Dau, C.P. (1976). Clutch sizes of the spectacled eider on the Yukon-Kuskokwim delta, Alaska. *Wildfowl* **27**: 111-113.
Dau, C.P. & Kistchinski, A.A. (1977). Seasonal movements and distribution of the Spectacled Eider. *Wildfowl* **28**: 65-75.
Daub, B.C. (1989). Behavior of Common Loons in winter. *J. Field Orn.* **60(3)**: 305-311.
Davies, A. (1988). The distribution and status of the Mandarin Duck *Aix galericulata* in Britain. *Bird Study* **35**: 203-208.
Davies, A.K. & Baggott, G.K. (1989a). Clutch size and nesting sites of the Mandarin Ducks *Aix galericulata*. *Bird Study* **36(1)**: 32-36.
Davies, A.K. & Baggott, G.K. (1989b). Egg-laying, incubation and intraspecific nest parasitism by the Mandarin Duck *Aix galericulata*. *Bird Study* **36(2)**: 115-122.
Davies, M. (1938). Partial nidification of the Flightless Cormorant. *Auk* **55**: 596-597.
Davies, R. (1986). Driven to drink. *Bird Obsr.* **648-649**: 10.
Davies, S.J.J.F. (1962a). The nest-building behaviour of the Magpie Goose, *Anseranas semipalmata*. *Ibis* **104**: 147-157.

Davies, S.J.J.F. (1962b). The response of the Magpie Goose to aerial predators. *Emu* **62**: 51-55.
Davies, S.J.J.F. (1963). Aspects of the behaviour of the Magpie Goose, *Anseranas semipalmata*. *Ibis* **105**: 76-98.
Davies, S.J.J.F. (1968). Aspects of a Study of Emus in semi-arid Western Australia. *Proc. Ecol. Soc. Austr.* **3**: 160-166.
Davies, S.J.J.F. (1972). Results of 40 hours continuous watch at five waterpoints in an Australian desert. *Emu* **72**: 8-12.
Davies, S.J.J.F. (1975). Land use by Emus and other wildlife species in the arid shrublands of Western Australia. Pp. 91-98 in: *Arid Shrublands. Proc. 3rd Workshop US/Aust. Rangelands Panel Tucson. Arizona, 1973*.
Davies, S.J.J.F. (1976). The natural history of the emu in comparison with that of other ratites. Pp. 109-120 in: *Proc. XVI Int. Orn. Congr.*
Davies, S.J.J.F. (1977). Man's activities and birds distribution in the arid zone. *Emu* **77**: 169-172.
Davies, S.J.J.F. (1978). The food of Emus. *Austr. J. Ecol.* **3**: 411-422.
Davies, S.J.J.F. (1983). Emus in Western Australia. Pp. 240-247 in: Riney, T. ed. *Wildlife Management in the 80's*. Graduate School of Environmental Science, Monash University.
Davies, S.J.J.F. (1985). Cassowary. Page 82 in: Campbell & Lack (1985).
Davies, S.J.J.F. & Frith, H.J. (1964). Some comments on the taxonomic position of the Magpie Goose, *Anseranas semipalmata* (Latham). *Emu* **63**: 265-272.
Davies, S.J.J.F. & Herd, R.M. (1983). Digestion in the Emu: Low energy and nitrogen requirements of this large ratite bird. *Comp. Biochem. Physiol. (Ser. A)* **75**: 41-45.
Davies, S.J.J.F., Herd, R.M. & Skadhauge, E. (1983). Water turnover and body water distribution during dehydration in a large arid-zone bird, the Emu, *Dromaius novaehollandiae*. *J. Comp. Physiol.* **153 B**: 235-240.
Davies, W.G. (1978). Cluster analysis applied to the classification of postures in the Chilean Flamingo (*Phoenicopterus chilensis*). *Anim. Behav.* **26**: 381-388.
Davis, A.H. & Vinicombe, K.E. (1980). Diving action of Red-necked Grebes. *British Birds* **73**: 31-32.
Davis, D.G. (1961). Western Grebe colonies in northern Colorado. *Condor* **63**: 264-265.
Davis, L.S. (1982). Timing of nest relief and its effect on breeding success in Adelie Penguins (*Pygoscelis adeliae*). *Condor* **84**: 178-183.
Davis, L.S. (1988). Coordination of incubation routines and mate choice in Adelie Penguins (*Pygoscelis adeliae*). *Auk* **105**: 428-432.
Davis, L.S. & Darby, J.T. eds. (1988). First International Conference on penguins. Dunedin, New Zealand, 16-19 August 1988. Abstracts of presented papers and posters. *Cormorant* **16**: 120-137.
Davis, L.S. & Darby, J.T. (1990). *Penguin Biology*. Academic Press, California.
Davis, L.S. & McCaffrey, F.T. (1986). Survival analysis of eggs and chicks of Adelie Penguins (*Pygoscelis adeliae*). *Auk* **103**: 379-388.
Davis, L.S. & McCaffrey, F.T. (1989). Recognition and parental investment in Adelie Penguins. *Emu* **89**: 155-158.
Davis, L.S., Ward, G.D. & Sadleir, R.M.F.S. (1988). Foraging by Adelie Penguins during the incubation period. *Notornis* **35**: 15-23.
Davis, M. (1935). Color changes in the Head of the Single-wattled Cassowary *Casuarius unappendiculatus occipitalis*. *Auk* **52**: 178.
Davis, M. & Friedmann, H. (1936). The courtship display of the Flightless Cormorant. *Sci. Monthly.* **42**: 560-563.
Davis, P. (1957). The breeding of the Storm Petrel. *British Birds* **50**: 85-101; 371-384.
Davis, R.A. (1972). *A Comparative Study of the Use of Habitat by Arctic Loons and Red-throated Loons*. PhD thesis. University of Western Ontario and Dissertation Abstr. Int. **33B(3)**: 1085-1086.
Davis, R.W., Croxall, J.P. & O'Connell, M.J. (1989). The reproductive energetics of Gentoo (*Pygoscelis papua*) and Macaroni (*Eudyptes chrysolophus*) Penguins at South Georgia. *J. Anim. Ecol.* **58**: 59-74.
Davis, R.W., Kooyman, G.L. & Croxall, J.P. (1983). Water flux and estimated metabolism of free-ranging Gentoo and Macaroni Penguins at South Georgia. *Polar Biol.* **2**: 41-46.
Davis, T.A., Platter-Reiger, M.F. & Ackerman, R.A. (1984). Incubation water loss by Pied-billed Grebe eggs: adaptation to a hot, west nest. *Physiol. Zool.* **57**: 384-391.
Davis, W.E. (1979). Analysis of the vocalization of four heron and ibis species. *Proc. Colonial Waterbird Group* **3**: 216-224.
Davis, W.E. (1985a). Foraging White-Faced Herons Follow Australian White Ibises. *Colonial Waterbirds* **8(2)**: 129-134.
Davis, W.E. (1985b). Foraging Behavior of a Western Reef Heron in North America. *Colonial Waterbirds* **8(1)**: 70-73.
Davis, W.E., Donahue, P.K. & Perkins, E.G. (1980). Observations of the Behavior of the Zigzag Heron. *Condor* **82**: 460-461.
Davis, W.M. (1989). Extraordinary aggregation of White-faced Ibises at a playa lake in Texas County, Oklahoma. *Okla. Orn. Soc.* **22(4)**: 27.
Dawson, T.J., Read, D., Russell, E.M. & Herd, R.M. (1984). Seasonal variation in daily activity patterns, water relations and diet of emus. *Emu* **84**: 93-102.
Day, D. (1981). *The Doomsday Book of Animals. A Natural History of Vanished Species*. The Viking Press, New York.
Day, D.H. (1977). A morphological study of Yellowbilled Duck and Redbilled Teal. *Ostrich* **12(Suppl.)**: 86-96.
Day, J.C.U. (1981). Status of Bitterns in Europe since 1976. *British Birds* **74(1)**: 10-16.
Dean, A.R. (1989). Distinguishing Characters of American/East Asian Race of Common Scoter. *British Birds* 82(12): 615-616.
Dean, G.J. (1963). Whale-headed Stork *Balaeniceps rex* Gould. *J. East Afr. Nat. Hist. Soc.* **24**: 77-78.
Dean, G.J.W. (1964). Stork and egret as predators of the red locust in the Rukwa Valley outbreak area. *Ostrich* **36**: 95-100.
Dean, W.R.J. (1977). Breeding of the Great Crested Grebe at Barberspan. *Ostrich* **12(Suppl.)**: 43-48.
Dean, W.R.J. (1978). Moult seasons of some Anatidae in the Western Transvaal. *Ostrich* **49**: 76-84.
Dean, W.R.J. (1988). Breeding of the Goliath Heron at Barberspan Transvaal. *Ostrich* **59(2)**: 75-76.
Dean, W.R.J. & Skead, D.M. (1977). The sex ratio in Yellowbilled Duck, Redbilled Teal and Southern Pochard. *Ostrich* **12(Suppl.)**: 82-85.
Dean, W.R.J. & Skead, D.M. (1979). The weights of some southern African Anatidae. *Wildfowl* **30**: 114-117.
Dean, W.R.J. & Skead, D.M. (1989). Survival and recovery rates of Yellow-billed Ducks. *J. Wildl. Manage.* **53**: 119-122.
Deane, R.A. (1979). Some notes on Hamerkop behaviour. *Honeyguide* **99**: 38-39.
Debout, G. (1987). Le Grand Cormoran, *Phalacrocorax carbo*, en France: les populations nicheuses littorales. *Alauda* **55(1)**: 35-54.
Debout, G. (1988). La biologie de reproduction du Grand Cormoran en Normandie. *L'Oiseau et la R.F.O.* **58(1)**: 1-17.
Debout, G. & Leclerc, F. (1990). La Bernache Cravant à Ventre Clair, *Branta bernicla hrota*, en France: précisions sur son statut. *Alauda* **58 (4)**: 209-215.
Dechambre, E. (1936). Le Balaeniceps. *Terre Vie* **6**: 45-48.
Decker, E. (1959). A 4-year study of Wood Ducks on a Pennsylvania marsh. *J. Wildl. Manage.* **23**: 310-315.
Dee, T.J. (1986). *The Endemic Birds of Madagascar*. ICBP, Cambridge.
Deeming, D.C. & Ferguson, M.W.J. (1991). *Eggs Incubation. Its Effects on Embryonic Development in Birds and Reptiles*. Cambridge University Press, Cambridge, England.
DeGange, A.R. & Nelson, J.W. (1982). Bald Eagle Predation on Nocturnal Seabirds. *J. Field Orn.* **53**(4): 407-409.
Deignan, H.G. (1933). The Jabiru (*Jabiru mycteria*) in western Guatemala. *Auk* **50**: 429.
Deignan, H.G. (1945). The birds of northern Thailand. *US Nat. Mus. Bull.* **186**.
Dejonghe, J.F. (1978). Notes sur les comportements du Grebe castagneux, *Podiceps ruficollis*, en période de nidification. *Nos oiseaux* **34**: 237-244.
Dekeyser, P.L. (1952). Nidification de la cigogne d'Abdim au Senegal. *Notes afr.* **55**: 92-93.
Dekker, D. (1984). Flamingokuiken in de groei. *Artis* **29**: 151-153.
Delacour, J. (1928). On the birds collected during the Third Expedition to French Indo-China. *Ibis* **4(12th Ser.)**: 23-51.
Delacour, J. (1929a). On the birds collected during the Fourth Expedition to French Indo-China. *Ibis* **5(12th Ser.)**: 193-220.
Delacour, J. (1929b). Bird notes from Cleres. *Avic. Mag.* **7 (2)**: 24-27.
Delacour, J. (1932). Les oiseaux de la Mission Franco-Anglo-Américaine à Madagascar. *L'Oiseau et la R.F.O.* **2**: 1-96.
Delacour, J. (1933). Les Grèbes de Madagascar. *L'Oiseau et la R.F.O.* **3**: 4-7.
Delacour, J. (1951). Preliminary note on the taxonomy of Canada Geese, *Branta canadensis*. *Amer. Mus. Novitates* **1537**.
Delacour, J. ed. (1954-1964). *The Waterfowl of the World*. 4 Vols. Country Life, London.
Delacour, J. (1970). Le genre *Tadorna*. *Alauda* **38**: 82-86.
Delacour, J. & Greenway, J. (1940). Liste des oiseaux recueillis dans la Province du Haut-Mekong et la Royaume de Luang-Prabang. *Extrait L'Oiseau et la R.F.O.* **1-2**: 16-27.
Delacour, J. & Jabouille, P. (1931). *Les Oiseau de l'Indochine Française*. Vol. 1. Exposition Coloniale Internationale, Paris.
Delacour, J. & Mayr, E. (1945). The family Anatidae. *Wilson Bull.* **57**: 3-55.
Delacour, J. & Mayr, E. (1946). Supplementary notes on the family Anatidae. *Wilson Bull.* **58**: 104-110.
Delacour, J. & Zimmer, J.T. (1952). The identity of *Anser nigricans* Lawrence 1846. *Auk* **69**: 82-84.
Delgado, F.S. (1985). Present Situation of the Forest Birds of Panama. Pp. 77-94 in: Diamond & Lovejoy (1985).
Delnicki, D.E. (1973). *Renesting, Incubation Behavior and Compound Clutches of the Black-bellied Tree Duck in Southern Texas*. MSc thesis, Texas Tech. University, Lubbock.
Delnicki, D.E. & Bolen, E.G. (1976). Renesting in the Black-bellied Whistling Duck. *Auk* **93**: 535-542.
Delroy, L.B., Robinson, A.C. & Waterman, M.H. (1989). Monitoring of Cape Barren Goose populations in South Australia. 2. The 1987 breeding season and further banding recoveries. *J. Austr. Orn.* **30 (7)**: 184-189.
DeMay, I.S. (1940). A study of the pterylosis and pneumacity of the screamer. *Condor* **42**: 112-118.
Dementiev, G.P., Gladkov, N.A. eds. (1951a). *Birds of the Soviet Union*. Vol. 1 (English translation 1969). Israel Program for Scientific Translation, Jerusalem.
Dementiev, G.P., Gladkov, N.A. eds. (1951b). *Birds of the Soviet Union*. Vol. 2 (English translation 1968). Israel Program for Scientific Translation, Jerusalem.
Dementiev, G.P., Gladkov, N.A. eds. (1951c). *Birds of the Soviet Union*. Vol. 3 (English translation 1968). Israel Program for Scientific Translation, Jerusalem.
Dementiev, G.P. & Gladkov, N.A. eds. (1952). *Birds of the Soviet Union*. Vol. 4. (English translation). Irael Programme for Scientific Translations, Jerusalem.
Dennis, M. (1987). Sawbills Nottinghamshire. *Trent. Val. Bird Watch Ann. Rep.* **1987** [1988]: 39-43.
Dennis, R.H. (1973). Possible interbreeding of Slavonian Grebe and Black-necked Grebe in Scotland. *Scottish Birds* **7**: 307-308.
Derenne, M., Jouventin, P. & Mougin, J.L. (1979). Le chant du Manchot Royal (*Aptenodytes patagonicus*) et sa signification evolutive. *Gerfaut* **69**: 211-224.
Derenne, P. & Mougin, J.L. (1976). Les Procellariiformes à nidification hypogée de l'ile aux Cochons (Archipel Crozet, 46° 06' S, 50° 14' E). *Comité Natl. Français Rech. Antarct.* **40**: 149-175.
Derenne, P., Lufbery, J.X. & Tollu, B. (1974). L'avifaune de l'archipel Kerguelen. *Comité Natl. Français Rech. Antarct.* **33**: 57-87.
Derenne, P., Mary, G. & Mougin, J.L. (1976). Le Cormoran à ventre blanc *Phalacrocorax albiventer melanogenis* (Blyth) de l'archipel Crozet. *Comité Natl. Français Rech. Antarct.* **40**: 191-220.
Derksen, D.V. (1977). A quantitative analysis of the incubation behaviour of the Adelie Penguin. *Auk* **94**: 552-566.
Derksen, D.V., Rothe, T.C. & Eldridge, W.D. (1981). *Use of Wetland Habitats by Birds in the National Petroleum Reserve - Alaska*. US Fish & Wildlife Service Resources Publications **141**. Washington, D.C.
Desai, J.H. (1971). Feeding ecology and nesting of Painted Storks *Ibis leucocephalus* at Delhi Zoo. *Int. Zoo Yb.* **11**: 208-215.
Desai, J.H., Menon, G.K. & Shah, R.V. (1974). Diet and food requirements of Painted Storks at the breeding colony in the Dehli Zoological Park. *Pavo* **12**: 13-23.
Desai, J.H., Menon, G.K. & Shah, R.V. (1979). Studies on the reproductive patterns of the Painted Stork, *Ibis leucocephalus*, Pennant. *Pavo* **15**: 1-32.
DesFayes, M. (1987). Evidence for the ancient presence of Bald Ibis, *Geronticus eremita*, in Greece. *Bull. Brit. Orn. Club* **107**: 93-94.
Desforges, M.F. & Wood-Gush, D.G.M. (1975a). A behavioural comparison of domestic and Mallard Ducks. Habituation and flight reactions. *Anim. Behav.* **23**: 692-697.
Desforges, M.F. & Wood-Gush, D.G.M. (1975b). A behavioural comparison of domestic and Mallard Ducks. Spatial relationships in small flocks. *Anim. Behav.* **23**: 698-705.
Desgranges, J.L. (1982). Weight growth of young Double-crested Cormorants in the St. Lawrence estuary, Quebec. *Colonial Waterbirds* **5**: 79-86.
Desgranges, J.L. & Reed, A. (1981). Disturbance and control of selected colonies of Double-crested Cormorants in Quebec. *Colonial Waterbirds* **4**: 12-19.
Desgranges, J.L., Chapdelaine, G. & Dupuis, P. (1984). Sites de nidification et dynamique des populations du Cormoran à aigrettes au Québec. *Can. J. Zool.* **62(7)**: 1260-1267.
DeSmet, K.D. (1982). Status of the Red-necked Grebe (*Podiceps grisegena*) in Canada. Committee on the Status of Endangered Wildlife in Canada, Ottawa, Ontario.
DeSmet, K.D. (1983). *Breeding ecology and productivity of Red-necked Grebes in Turtle Mountain Provincial Park, Manitoba*. MSc thesis. University of North Dakota, Grand Forks.
DeSmet, K.D. (1987a). Organochlorines, predators and reproductive succes of the Red-necked Grebe in southern Manitoba. *Condor* **89**: 460-467.
DeSmet, K.D. (1987b). First nesting record and status of the Clark's Grebe in Canada. *Blue Jay* **45**: 101-105.
Despin, B. (1972). Note préliminaire sur le Manchot Papou *Pygoscelis papua* de l'Ile de la Possession (Archipel Crozet). *L'Oiseau et la R.F.O.* **42**: 69-83.
Despin, B. (1976). Observations sur le Pétrel gris *Procellaria cinerea*. *L' Oiseau et la R.F.O.* **46**: 432-433.
Despin, B. (1977a). Croissances comparées des poussins chez les manchots du genre *Pygoscelis*. *C. R. Acad. Sci. Paris (Ser. D)* **285**: 1135-1137.
Despin, B. (1977b). Biologie du Damier du Cap à l'Ile de la Possésion (Archipel Crozet). *L'Oiseau et la R.F.O.* **47**: 149-157.
Despin, B. & Mougin, J.L. (1988). Evaluation de la dépense énergetique et de la consommation alimentaire du Puffin Cendré d'après l'étude de la décroissance ponderale au cours du jeune. *L' Oiseau et la R.F.O.* **58**: 28-43.
Despin, B., Mougin, J.L. & Segonzac, M. (1972). Oiseaux et Mammifères de l'Ile de l'Est. *Comité Natl. Français Rech. Antarct.* **31**: 1-106.
Deswasmes, G., Le Maho, Y. & Groscoloas, R. (1980). Resting metabolic rate and cost of locomotion in long term fasting Emperor Penguins. *J. Appl. Physiol.* **49**: 888-896.
Deusing, M. (1939). Nesting habits of the Pied-billed Grebe. *Auk* **56**: 367-373.
Devicenzy, G.J. (1926). (Syrigma sibilatrix). *Ann. Mus. Hist. Nat. Montevideo*.
Devick, W.S. (1981a). Status of the Nene population on the Island of Hawaii between 1975 and 1980. Hawaii Dept. Land & Nat. Res., Honolulu.
Devick, W.S. (1981b). Status of the Nene population on the Island of Maui between 1975 and 1980. Hawaii Dept. Land & Nat. Res., Honolulu.
Devillers, P. & Terschuren, J.A. (1978). Relationships between the Blue-eyed Shags of South America. *Gerfaut* **68**: 53-86.
Devillers, P. & Terschuren, J.A. (1980). Les pétrels géants des Iles Falkland et du Sud de l'Amérique du Sud. *Gerfaut* **70**: 447-454.
Dexter, N. (1988). *The Effect of Experimental Clutch Harvest on Magpie Geese,* Anseranas semipalmata *in Subcoastal Northern Territory, Australia*. M. Appl. Sci. Res. Manage. thesis, Canberra College of Advanced Education, Canberra.
Di Giacomo, A.G. (1988). Nidificación del Chiflón (*Syrigma sibilatrix*) en Salto, Buenos Aires, Argentina. *El Hornero* **13(1)**: 1-7.
Diamond, A.W. (1971). *The Ecology of Seabirds Breeding at Aldabra Atoll, Indian Ocean*. PhD thesis. Aberdeen University.
Diamond, A.W. (1972). Sexual dimorphism in breeding cycles and unequal sex ratio in Magnificent Frigatebirds. *Ibis* **114**: 395-398.
Diamond, A.W. (1973). Notes on the breeding biology and behaviour of the Magnificent Frigatebird. *Condor* **75**: 200-209.
Diamond, A.W. (1974). The Red-footed Booby on Aldraba Atoll, Indian -Ocean. *Ardea* **62**: 196-218.
Diamond, A.W. (1975a). The biology of tropicbirds at Aldabra Atoll, Indian Ocean. *Auk* **92**: 16-39.
Diamond, A.W. (1975b). Biology and behaviour of frigatebirds *Fregata* spp. on Aldabra Atoll. *Ibis* **117**: 302-323.
Diamond, A.W. (1978). Feeding strategies and population size in tropical seabirds. *Amer. Naturalist* **112**: 215-223.
Diamond, A.W. (1979). Dynamic ecology of Aldabran seabird communities. *Phil. Trans. Royal Soc. London (Ser. B)* **286**: 231-240.
Diamond, A.W. (1980). The red-footed booby colony on Little Cayman: size, structure and significance. *Atoll Research Bull.* **241**: 165-170.
Diamond, A.W. & Filion, F.L. eds. (1987). *The Value of Birds*. ICBP Technical Publication **6**. Cambridge, England.
Diamond, A.W. & Lovejoy, T.E. eds. (1985). *Conservation of Tropical Forest Birds*. ICBP Technical Publication **4**. Cambridge, England.
Diamond, A.W., Schreiber, R.L., Attenborough, D. & Presst, I. (1987). *Save the Birds*. Cambridge University Press, Cambridge, England.
Diamond, J.M. (1972). *Avifauna of the Eastern Highlands of New Guinea*. Publications of the Nuttall Ornithological Club **12**. Raymond, A.P. ed. Cambridge, MA.
Dick, G. (1988a). Feeding behaviour of the Greylag Goose (*Anser anser*): A field study. *Ökol. Vögel* **10**: 59-69.
Dick, G. (1988b). Habitat use and group size of the Greylag Goose (*Anser anser*) in Lake Neusiedl area. *Ökol. Vögel* **10**: 71-77.

Dickerman, R.W. (1963). The grebe *Aechmophorus occidentalis clarkii* as a nesting bird of the Mexican Plateau. *Condor* **65**: 66-67.

Dickerman, R.W. (1969). Nesting records of the Eared Grebe in Mexico. *Auk* **86**: 144.

Dickerman, R.W. (1973). Further notes on the Western Grebe in Mexico. *Condor* **75**: 131-132.

Dickerman, R.W. (1986). Two hitherto unnamed populations of *Aechmophorus* (Aves: Podicipitidae). *Proc. Biol. Soc. Washington* **99**: 435-436.

Dickerman, R.W. & Juarez C. (1971). Nesting studies of the Boat-billed Heron *Cochlearius cochlearius* at San Blas, Nayarit, Mexico. *Ardea* **59(1/2)**: 1-16.

Dickerman, R.W. & Parkes, K.C. (1968). Notes on the plumages and generic status of the Little Blue Heron. *Auk* **85**: 437-440.

Dickey, D.R. & van Rossem, A.J. (1938). *The Birds of El Salvador*. Field Museum of Natural History (Zoological Series) **23**.

Dickinson, E.C., Kennedy, R.S. & Parkes, K.C. (1991). *The Birds of the Philippines. An Annotated Check-list*. B.O.U. Check-list **12**. British Ornithologists' Union, Tring, Hertfordshire, U.K.

Dickson, J.G., Conner, R.N., Kroll, J.C., Fleet, R.R. & Jackson, J.A. eds. (1979). *The Role of Insectivorous Birds in Forest Systems*. T & AD Poyser, London.

Diefenbach, D.R. (1988). *Changes in the Wetland Habitats and Population of Breeding Black Ducks in South-central Maine*. MSc thesis, University Maine, Orono.

Diefenbach, D.R. & Owen, R.B. (1989). A model of habitat use by breeding American Black Ducks. *J. Wildl. Manage.* **53**: 383-389.

Diem, K.L. (1979). White Pelican reproductive failures in the Molly Islands breeding colony in Yellowstone National Park. Pp. 489-496 in: *Proc. Res. Nat. Parks Symp.* US National Park Service Transactions and Proceedings Sec. **5**.

Din, N.A. (1979). *Ecology of Pelicans in the Ruwenzori National Park, Uganda*. Starling Press, Tucson, Arizona.

Din, N.A. & Eltringham, S.K. (1974a). Ecological separation between White and Pink-backed Pelicans in the Ruwenzori National Park, Uganda. *Ibis* **116**: 28-43.

Din, N.A. & Eltringham, S.K. (1974b). Breeding of the Pink-backed Pelican *Pelecanus rufescens* in Ruwenzori National Park, Uganda, with notes on Marabou Storks *Leptoptilos crumeniferus*. *Ibis* **116**: 477-493.

Din, N.A. & Eltringham, S.K. (1977). Weights and measures of Uganda pelicans with some seasonal variations. *East Afr. Wildl. J.* **15**: 317-326.

Dinsmore, S. & Dinsmore, J.J. (1986). White-faced Ibis nesting in Dickinson Co., Iowa. *Iowa Bird Life* **56**: 120-121.

Dittberner, H. & Dittberner, W. (1977). Der Ohrentaucher (*Podiceps auritus* Linné) in Berlin und Umgebung. *Orn. Iber. Mus. Hein.* **2**: 5-14.

Dittberner, H. & Dittberner, W. (1984). Zu Ökologie, Brutbiologie und morphologischen Merkmalen des Schwarzhalstauchers (*Podiceps nigricollis*). *Mitt. zool. Mus. Berl.* **60**. Suppl.: *Ann. Orn.* **8**: 57-88.

Dixon, J. (1916). Migration of the Yellow-billed Loon. *Auk* **33**: 370-376.

Dixon, J. (1924). Nesting of the Wood Duck in California. *Condor* **26**: 41-66.

Dixon, J.E.W. (1970). Miscellaneous notes on South West African birds. *Madoqua* **2**: 45-47.

van Dobben, W.H. (1952). The food of the Cormorant in the Netherlands. *Ardea* **40**: 1-63.

Dobrowolski, K. (1969). Structure of the occurrence of waterfowl types and morpho-ecological forms. *Ekol. Polska Ser.* **17**: 29-72.

Doguchi, M. & Ushio, F. (1973). PCB and organochlorine pesticide residues in a White Stork. *Misc. Rep. Yamashina Inst. Orn.* **7**: 202-206.

Doig, V., Hagan, J.M. & Walters, J.R. (1989). Double-Crested Cormorant and Anhinga nesting in the Croatan National Forest. *Chat* **53(1)**:1-4.

Dollinger, P. ed. (1988). *Convention on International Trade in Endangered Species of Wild Fauna and Flora. Identification Manual*. Vol. 2. Aves. Secretariat of the Convention, Lausanne, Switzerland.

Dolz, J.C., Giménez, M. & Huertas, J. (1991). Status of some threatened anatidae species in the Comunidad Valenciana, East Spain. *IWRB Threatened Waterfowl Research Group Newsletter* **1**: 7-8.

Domergue, C. (1950). Le Chott Djérid, station et lieu de ponte du Flamant rose (*Phoenicopterus roseus* Linné). *Bull. Soc. Sci. Nat. Tunis* **2**: 119-128.

Dongchou, S., Xiaoping, Y., Xiuyun, Ch. & Baozhong, L. (1989). [The breeding habits of the Crested Ibis (*Nipponia nippon*)]. *Zool. Res.* **10(4)**: 327-332. In Chinese with English summary.

Donker, J.K. (1959). Migration and distribution of the Wigeon *Anas penelope* L., in Europe, based on ringing results. *Ardea* **47**: 1-27.

Donkin, R.A. (1989). *The Muscovy Duck,* Cairina moschata domestica. Balkema, Rotterdam.

Donnelly, B.G. & Hustler, K. (1986). Notes on the diet of the Reed Cormorant and Darter on Lake Kariba during 1970 and 1971. *Arnoldia Zimbabwe* **9 (24)**: 319-324.

Doornbos, G. (1979). Winter food habits of Smew (*Mergus albellus* L.) on Lake Yssel, the Netherlands: species and size selection in relation to fish stocks. *Ardea* **67**: 42-48.

Dorst, J. (1962). *The Migrations of Birds*. William Heineman, London.

Dorst, J. (1971). *La Vie des Oiseaux*. Éditions Rencontre, Lausanne, Switzerland.

Dorst, J. & Mougin, J.L. (1979). Pelecaniformes. Pp. 155-193 in: Mayr & Cottrell (1979).

Dorst, J. & Roux, F. (1972). Esquisse écologique sur l'avifaune des Monts du Balé, Ethiopie. *L'Oiseau et la R.F.O.* **42**: 203-240.

Dorward, D.F. (1962a). Behaviour of boobies. *Ibis* **103b**: 221-234.

Dorward, D.F. (1962b). Comparative biology of the White Booby and the Brown Booby at Ascension. *Ibis* **103b**: 174-220.

Dostine, P.L. & Morton, S.R. (1988). Notes on the Food and Feeding Habits of Cormorants on a Tropical Floodplain. *Emu* **88**: 263-266.

Dott, H.E.M. (1973). Fulmars at land in summer and autumn. *Bird Study* **20**: 221-225.

Dott, H.E.M. (1975). Fulmars at colonies: time of day and weather. *Bird Study* **22**: 255-259.

Dott, H.E.M. (1984). Range extensions, one new record, and notes on the winter breeding of birds in Bolivia. *Bull. Brit. Orn. Club* **104(3)**: 104-109.

Douglas, S.D. & Reimchen, T.E. (1988a). Habitat characteristics and population estimate of breeding Red-Throated Loons, *Gavia stellata*, on the Queen Charlotte Islands, British Columbia. *Can. Field-Nat.* **102(4)**: 679-684.

Douglas, S.D. & Reimchen, T.E. (1988b). Reproductive phenology and early survivorship in Red-Throated Loons, *Gavia stellata*. *Can. Field-Nat.* **102(4)**: 701-704.

Dourojeanni, M., Hofmann, R., García, R., Malleaux, J. & Tovar, Y.A. (1968). Observaciones preliminares para el manejo de las aves acuáticas del Lago Junín, Peru. *Revista Forestal del Perú* **2**: 3-52.

Douthwaite, R.J. (1977). Filter-feeding ducks of the Kafue Flats, Zambia. *Ibis* **119**: 44-65.

Dover, C. & Basil-Edwards, S. (1921). A note on the habits of the Common Pariah Kite (*Milvus govinda*) and the Adjutant Stork (*Leptoptilus dubius*). *J. Bombay Nat. Hist. Soc.* **27**: 633.

Dow, H. & Fredga, S. (1983). Breeding and natal dispersal of the Goldeneye, *Bucephala clangula*. *J. Anim. Ecol.* **52**: 681-695.

Dow, H. & Fredga, S. (1984). Factors affecting reproductive output of the Goldeneye Duck *Bucephala clangula*. *J. Anim. Ecol.* **53**: 679-692.

Dowding, J.E. & Taylor, M.J. (1987). Genetics of Polymorphism in the Little Shag. *Notornis* **34**: 51-57.

Downes, M.C. (1955). Size variation in eggs and young of the Macaroni Penguin. *Emu* **55**: 19-23.

Downes, M.C., Ealey, E.H.M., Gwynn, A.M. & Young, P.S. (1959). The Birds of Heard Island. *Aust. Natl. Antarct. Res. Exped. Rep. (Ser. B)*

Dowsett, R.J. (1966a). The status of four species of aquatic birds in Zambia as suggested by ringing recoveries. *Puku* **4**: 129-131.

Dowsett, R.J. (1966b). The status and distribution of the Hottentot Teal *Anas punctata* in Zambia. *Puku* **4**: 125-127.

Dowsett, R.J. (1969). Ringed Sacred Ibis *Threskiornis aethiopica* recovered in Zambia. *Puku* **5**: 59-63.

Dowsett, R.J. (1981). Breeding and other observations on the Slaty Egret *Egretta vinaceigula*. *Bull. Brit. Orn. Club* **101**: 323-327.

Dowsett, R.J. & de Vos, A. (1965). The ecology and numbers of aquatic birds on the Kajue Flats, Zambia. *Wildfowl Trust Ann. Rep.* **4**: 67-73.

Dragesco, J. (1861a). Monographies des Oiseaux du Banc d'Arguin: La Spatule blanche (*Platalea leucorodia*). *Science et Nature* **44**: 1-7.

Dragesco, J. (1961b). Observations éthologiques sur les oiseaux du Banc d'Arguin. *Alauda* **29**: 81-98.

Dragesco, J. (1971). Nidification du Pélican blanc (*Pelecanus onocrotalus roseus*) dans le centre africain. *Ann. Fac. Sci. Cameroun* **5**: 103-111.

Draulans, D. (1986). On the distribution and foraging behaviour of the Malagasy Heron *Ardea humbloti*. *Ostrich* **57(4)**: 249-251.

Draulans, D. (1987). The effect of prey density on foraging behaviour and success of adult and first-year Grey Herons (*Ardea cinerea*). *J. Anim. Ecol.* **56**: 479-493.

Draulans, D. (1988). The importance of heronries for mate attraction. *Ardea* **765**: 187-192.

Draulans, D. & van Vessem, J. (1987). Some aspects of population dynamics and habitat choice of Grey Herons (*Ardea cinerea*) in fish-pond areas. *Gerfaut* **77**: 389-404.

Drennen, D.J., Hunt, L.J. & King, T. (1982). Nest characteristics of a Yellow-crowned Night Heron ("*Nyctanassa violacea*" colony. *J. Ala. Acad. Sci.* **53(1-2)**: 5-9.

Drent, R. (1975). Incubation. Pp. 333-420 in: Farner, D.S. & King, J.R. *Avian Biology*. Vol. 5. Academic Press, London & New York.

Drent, R.H. & Stonehouse, B. (1971). Thermoregulatory responses of the Peruvian Penguin, *Spheniscus humboldti*. *Comp. Biochem. Physiol. (Ser. A)* **40**: 689-710.

Drey, B. (1983). The nesting behaviour of a Kiwi. *Notornis* **30**: 135-136.

Drobney, R.D. (1977). *The Feeding Ecology, Nutrition, and Reproductive Bioenergetics of Wood Ducks*. PhD dissertation, University Missouri, Columbia, Missouri.

Drummond, H. (1987). A review of parent-offspring conflict and brood reduction in the Pelecaniformes. *Colonial Waterbirds* **10(1)**: 1-15.

Drummond, H. (1988). Parent-Offspring Conflict and Siblicidal Brood Reduction in Boobies. Pp. 1244-1253 in: *Proc. XIX Int. Orn. Congr.*

Drummond, H., González, E. & Osorno, J.L. (1986). Parent-offspring cooperation in the blue-footed booby (*Sula nebouxii*): social roles in infanticidal brood reduction. *Behav. Ecol. Sociobiol.* **19**: 365-372.

Du Bost, F.D. & Segonzac, M. (1976). Note complementaire sur le cycle reproducteur du Grand Albatross de l'Ile de la Possession, Archipel Crozet. *Com. Natl. Français Rech. Antarct.* **40**: 53-60.

Du Heng-qin (1987). [Ecology of the Pond Heron (*Aredola bacchus*)]. *Chinese Wildlife* **5**: 17, 22-23. In Chinese.

Dubale, M.S. & Mansuri, A.P. (1969). A comparative account of the dimensions of bony elements of the feeding apparatus of certain herons (Family: Ardeidae). *Proc. Natl. Acad. Sci. India* **39**: 226-232.

DuBois, A.D. (1919). An experience with Horned Grebes (*Colymbus auritus*). *Auk* **36**: 170-180.

DuBois, A.D. (1920). Notes on the breeding habits of the Slavonian Grebe. *British Birds* **14**: 2-10.

DuBowy, P.J. (1987). *Seasonal Variation in the Structure of North American Waterfowl Communities*. PhD dissertation. University of California. Davis, California, USA.

DuBowy, P.J. (1988). Waterfowl communities and seasonal environments: temporal variability in interspecific competition. *Ecology* **69 (5)**: 1439-1453.

Dubs, B. (1988). Beobachtungen zur Fortpflanzungsbiologie des Stirnbandsibis, *Harpiprion caerulescens*. *J. Orn.* **129**: 363-365.

Dubus, M. le chevalier. (1838). Note sur l'Ibis Olivacea. *Revue Zoologique* **1838**: 141-142.

Duc, L.D. & Thuy, L.D. (1987). The status of rare bird species in three colonies in Minh Hai Province: Vinh Thanh, Tan Khanh and Tan Hung. *Garrulax* **2**: 3-5.

Duckworth, F. (1974). The Whale-headed Stork in Ethiopia. *Bull. Br. Orn. Club* **94**: 3-4.

Duebbert, H.F. (1966). Island nesting of the gadwall in North Dakota. *Wilson Bull.* **78**: 12-25.

Duebbert, H.F. & Lokemoen, J.T. (1977). Upland nesting of American bitterns, marsh hawks and short-eared owls. *Prairie Nat.* **9**: 33-39.

Duff, A.G. (1979). Sauchets du Cap *Anas smithii* au Maroc. *Alauda* **47**: 216-217.

Duffey, E. (1951). Field studies on the Fulmar. *Ibis* **93**: 237-245.

Duffy, D.C. (1980). *Comparative Reproductive Behavior and Population Regulation of Seabirds of the Peruvian Coastal Current*. PhD thesis, Princeton University.

Duffy, D.C. (1983a). Competition for nesting space among Peruvian guano birds. *Auk* **100**: 680-688.

Duffy, D.C. (1983b). The foraging ecology of Peruvian seabirds. *Auk* **100**: 800-810.

Duffy, D.C. (1983c). Environmental uncertainty and commercial fishing: effects on Peruvian guano birds. *Biol. Conserv.* **26**: 227-238.

Duffy, D.C. (1984). Nest site selection by Masked and Blue-footed boobies on Isla Española, Galapagos. *Condor* **86**: 301-304.

Duffy, D.C. (1985). Plunging Brown Boobies at Copacabana Beach, Rio de Janeiro, Brazil. *Cormorant* **13**: 73-74.

Duffy, D.C (1987a). Ecological implications of intercolony size-variation in Jackass Penguins. *Ostrich* **58**: 54-57.

Duffy, D.C. (1987b). Aspects of the Ecology of Blue-footed and Peruvian Boobies at the Limits of their Ranges on Isla Lobos de tierra, Peru. *Colonial Waterbirds* **101(1)**: 45-49.

Duffy, D.C (1988). Ticks among the seabirds. *Living Bird Quarterly* **7(3)**: 8-13.

Duffy, D.C. (1990a). Field studies of *Spheniscus* penguins. Pp. 87-92 in: *AAZPA (Amer. Assoc. Zool. Parks & Aquariums) Reg. Conf. Proc.*

Duffy, D.C. (1990b). A selected bibliography of the *Spheniscus* penguins. Pp. 93-98 in: *AAZPA (Amer. Assoc. Zool. Parks & Aquariums) Reg. Conf. Proc.*

Duffy, D.C & Laurenson, L.J.B. (1983). Pellets of Cape Cormorant as indicators of diet. *Condor* **85**: 305-307.

Duffy, D.C. & Merlin, G. (1986). Seabird aggregations and densities during the 1983 El Niño in the Galapagos Islands. *Wilson Bull.* **98**: 588-591.

Duffy, D.C. & Ricklefs, R.E. (1981). Observations on growth of Blue-footed Boobies and development of temperature regulation in Peruvian Guano Birds. *J. Field Orn.* **52(4)**: 332-336.

Duffy, D.C & Rudolf, A. (1986). Cape Cormorant mass mortality during a cold-water event off Namibia. *Ostrich* **57(4)**: 247-248.

Duffy, D.C., Berruti, A., Randall, R.M. & Cooper, J. (1984). Effects of the 1982-3 warm water event on the breeding of South African seabirds. *S. Afr. J. Sci.* **80**: 65-69.

Duffy, D.C., Hays, C. & Plenge, M. (1984). The Conservation Status of Peruvian seabirds. Pp. 245-259 in: Croxall *et al.* (1984).

Duffy, D.C., Ryan, P.G., Wilson, R.P. & Wilson, M.P. (1988). Spring seabird distribution in the Straits of Magellan. *Cormorant* **16**: 98-102.

Duffy, D.C., Wilson, R.P., Ricklefs, R.E., Broni, S.C. & Veldhuis, H. (1987). Penguins and purse seiners: competition or coexistence? *Nat. Geogr. Res.* **3(4)**: 480-488.

Duffy, D.C., Wilson, R.P. & Wilson, M.P. (1987). Spatial and temporal patterns of diet in the Cape Cormorant off southern Africa. *Condor* **89**: 830-834.

Duffy, D.C., Wilson, R.P. & Wilson, M.P.T. & Araya, M. (1989). Sympatry of two penguin species on the coast of Chile. *Pacific Seabird Group Bull.* **16(1)**: 25-26.

Dugan, P.J. ed. (1990). *Wetland Conservation: A Review of Current Issues and Required Action*. IUCN, Gland, Switzerland.

Duhautois, L. (1984). Héron pourpré, butors. Le declin. *Le Courrier de la Nature* **92**: 21-29.

Duhautois, L. & Marion, L. (1982). Protection des hérons: des résultats?. *Le Courrier de la Nature* **78**: 23-32.

Duignan, P.J., Nuttall, C., Kirkwood, J.K. & Olney, P.J.S. (1988). Husbandry, breeding and post-embryonic growth of Abdim's Stork *Ciconia abdimii* hand-reared at London Zoo. *Int. Zoo Yb.* **27**:245-252.

Dujardin, J.L. (1987). Statut et conservation de l'Ibis Rouge (*Eudocimus ruber*) en Guyane Française. Unpublished report to the Office de la Recherche Scientifique et Technique Outre-Mer, Cayenne.

Dujardin, J.L. (1991). Scarlet Ibis in French Guiana. *Specialist Group on Storks, Ibises and Spoonbills Newsletter* **4(2)**: 5.

Dujardin, J.L. & Tostain, O. (1990). Les oiseaux de mer nicheurs de Guyane française. *Alauda* **58(2)**: 107-134.

Dulin, G.S. (1988). *Pre-fledging feeding behavior and sibling rivalry in the Common Loon (*Gavia immer*)*. MSc thesis. Central Michigan University.

Dumbell, G. (1986). The New Zealand Brown Teal: 1845-1985. *Wildfowl* **37**: 71-87.

Dumbell, G. (1987). *The Ecology Behaviour and Management of New Zealand Brown Teal or Pateke*. PhD thesis, University of Auckland.

Dunker, H. (1974). Habitat selection and territory size of the Black-throated Diver, *Gavia arctica* (L.). *Norw. J. Zool.* **23**: 149-164.

Dunlop, J.N. (1988). The Status and Biology of the Golden Bosunbirds *Phaethon lepturus fulvus*. Unpublished report to the Australian National Parks and Wildlife Service.

Dunlop, J.N. & Wooller, R.D. (1986). Range extensions and the breeding seasons of seabirds in south Western Australia. *Records W. Austr. Mus.* **12(4)**: 389-394.

Dunlop, J.N., Wooller, R.D. & Cheshire, N.G. (1988). Distribution and abundance of marine birds in the eastern Indian Ocean. *Aust. J. Mar. Freshwater Res.* **39(5)**: 661-669.

Dunn, E.H. (1975). Growth, body components and energy content of nestling Double-crested Cormorants. *Condor* **77**: 431-438.

Dunnet, G.M. (1985). Pycroft's Petrel in the breeding season at Hen and Chickens Islands. *Notornis* **32**: 5-21.

Dunnet, G.M. (1986a). Species accounts: Fulmar. Pp. 50-51 in Lack, P., ed., *The Atlas of Wintering Birds in Britain and Ireland*. Poyser, Calton.

Dunnet, G.M. (1986b). Species Accounts: Gannet. Pp. 52-53 in: Lack, P. ed. *The Atlas of Wintering Birds in Britain and Iceland*. Poyser, Calton.

Dunnet, G.M. (1991). Populations studies of the Fulmar on Eynhallow, Orkney Islands. *Ibis* **133 suppl.1**: 24-27.

Dunnet, G.M. & Ollason, J.C. (1978). The estimation of survival rate in the Fulmar. *J. Anim. Ecol.* **47**: 507-520.

Dunnet, G.M. & Ollason, J.C. (1982). The feeding dispersal of Fulmars in the breeding season. *Ibis* **124**: 359-361.

Dunnet, G.M., Ollason, J.C. & Anderson, A. (1979). A 28-year study of breeding Fulmars in Orkney. *Ibis* **121**: 293-300.

Dunnet, G.M., Anderson, A. & Cormack, R.M. (1963). A study of the survival of adult Fulmars with observations on the pre-laying exodus. *British Birds* **56**: 2-18.

Dunning, J. (1977). Breeding Woolly-necked Stork? *Witwatersrand Bird Club News* **97**: 8.
Dunning, J.S. (1982). *South American Land Birds*. Harrowood Books, Newtown Square, PA.
Dunning, J.S. (1987). *South American Birds. A Photographic Aid to Identification*. Harrowood Books, Newton Square, PA.
Dunstan, F.M. (1976). Roseate Spoonbills nesting in Tampa Bay, Florida. *Fla. Field Nat.* **4**: 25-28.
Duplaix-Hall, N. (1975). Seven days in Papua New Guinea, watching Salvadori's Ducks. *Wildfowl* **71**: 6-7.
DuPont, J.E. (1971). *Philippine Birds*. Delaware Museum of Natural History, Greenville, Delaware, Philippines.
Dupuy, A. (1976). Reproduction des Pélicans Blancs (*Pelecanus onocrotalus*) au Sénégal. *L'Oiseau et la R.F.O.* **46**: 430-432.
Dupuy, A.R. (1979). Reproductions des Pélicans blancs et Flamants roses au Sénégal. *L'Oiseau et la R.F.O.* **49**: 323-324.
Dupuy, A.R. (1982). Reproduction of the Marabou Stork (*Leptoptilos crumeniferus*) in Senegal. *L'Oiseau et la R.F.O.* **52**: 293.
Dupuy, A.R. (1984). Quelques données nouvelles sur l'avifaune du Sénégal ainsi que sur celle des iles de la Madeleine. *Alauda* **52(3)**: 177-183.
Durango, S. (1954). Om viggens häcking i laridsamhällen. [Summary: The Tufted Duck as a breeder in colonies of gulls and terns]. *Ornis Fenn.* **31**: 1-18.
Durham, L. (1955). Effects of cormorants and gars on fish populations of ponds in Illinois. PhD. thesis, University of Illinois, Urbana; Illinois.
Duroselle, T. & Tollu, B. (1977). The Rockhopper Penguin (*Eudyptes chrysocome moseleyi*) of Saint Paul and Amsterdam Islands. Pp. 579-604 in: Llano (1977).
Dutton, T.P. (1972). First nesting record of Openbill stork for the Republic of South Africa. *Lammergeyer* **17**: 36-39.
Dyegtyariov, V.G., Larionov, G.P. & Vinokurov, V.N. (1990). [The second record of the Black-headed Ibis (*Threskiornis melanocephalus*) in the USSR]. *Ornitologiya* **24**: 148. In Russian.
Dyer, B.M. (1990). Eight new records of the Australasian Gannet *Morus serrator* in South Africa. *Marine Orn.* **18**: 60-64.
Dyer, P.K. & Hill, G.J.E. (1991). A solution to the problem of determining occupancy status of Wedge-tailed Shearwater *Puffinus pacificus* burrows. *Emu* **91(1)**: 20-25.
Dymin, V.A. & Pankin, N.S. (1975). Nesting and migration of storks (Ciconidae) and cranes (Gruidae) in the Upper Amur Region. Pp. 263-267 in: Nechaev, V.A. ed. (1975). *Ornithological Studies in the Soviet Far East*. Proceedings of the Institute of Biology and Pedology, New Series **29(132).**
Dymond, J.N., Fraser, P.A. & Gantlett, S.J.M. (1989). *Rare Birds in Britain and Ireland*. Poyser, Calton, England.
Eades, D.W. & Rogers, A.E.F. (1982). Comments on the identification of the Magenta Petrel and similar species. *Notornis* **29**: 81-84.
Eadie, J. (1989). Cost and benefits of brood parasitism to a precocial host. *Bull. Ecol. Soc. Amer.* **70(2)**: 103.
Eagle, M. (1980). Black-winged Petrels on Portland Island. *Notornis* **27**: 171-175.
Eames, J. (1991). White-shouldered Ibis rediscovered. *Specialist Group on Storks, Ibises and Spoonbills Newsletter* **4(2)**: 5.
Earnest, A. (1982). *The Art of the Decoy*. American Bird Carvings. Schiffer, Pennsylvania.
Eason, D. (1988). Breeding of Great Spotted Kiwis in captivity. *Notornis* **35**: 191-193.
Eastman, M. (1968). *The life of the Emu*. Angus & Robertson, Sydney.
Easton, S. (1975). Nesting colony of Marabou Storks at Shinyanga, Tanzania. *East Afr. Nat. Hist. Soc. Bull.* **Oct/Nov**: 110-111.
Ebbinge, B. & Ebbinge-Dallmeijer, D. (1977). Barnacle Geese (*Branta leucopsis*) in the Arctic summer - a reconnaisance trip to Svalbard. *Norsk Polarinstitutt Aarbok* **1975**: 119-138.
Ebbinge, B.S. (1989). A multifactorial explanation for variation in breeding performance of Brent Geese *Branta bernicla*. *Ibis* **131 (2)**: 196-204.
Eberhardt, R.T. (1984). Recent recoveries of Common Loons banded in Minnesota. *Loon* **56**: 202-203.
Eckert, J. (1965). Pelicans breeding near Milang. *S. Aust. Orn.* **24**: 36-37.
Eckert, K. (1986). First spring record of Pacific Loon in Minnesota. *Loon* **58(3)**: 128-129.
Eckert, K. (1988). A White-faced Ibis on Salt Lake weekend. *Loon* **60**: 137.
Eckert, K.R. (1989). Identification and status of Clark's Grebe in Minnesota. *Loon* **61**: 99-108.
Edelson, N.A. (1990). *Foraging Ecology of Wading Birds Using an Altered Landscape in Central Florida*. MSc thesis, University of Florida, Gainesville.
Edgar, A.T. (1962). A note on the diving of the two New Zealand grebes. *Notornis* **10**: 42.
Edgar, A.T. (1978). (Egretta sacra). *Notornis* **25**: 25-58.
Edgington, D. (1989). The Humboldt Penguin (*Spheniscus humboldti*) behavioural and morphological sexing. *Ratel* **16(3)**: 77-85.
Edroma, E.L. & Jumbe, J. (1983). The number and daily activity of the Egyptian Goose in Queen Elizabeth National Park, Uganda. *Wildfowl* **34**: 99-104.
Edwards, E.P. (1989). *A Field Guide to the Birds of Mexico*. E.P. Edwards, Sweet Briar, VA.
van Ee, C.A. (1963). Hamerkops nesting together. *Ostrich* **34**: 252.
van Ee, C.A. (1971). Variations in the head pattern of the female South African Shelduck. *Ostrich* **42**: 149-150.
van Ee, C.A. (1977). Hamerkop. *Bokmakierie* **29**: 51-52.
van Eerden, M.R. (1990). The solution of Goose damage problems in The Netherlands, with special reference to compensation schemes. *Ibis* **132**: 253-261.
van der Eerden, M.R. & Munsterman, M.J. (1986). Importance of the Mediterranean for Wintering Cormorants *Phalacrocorax carbo sinensis*. Pp. 123-141 in MEDMARAVIS & Monbailliu (1986).
Eggleton, P. & Siegfried, W.R. (1979). Displays of the Jackass Penguin. *Ostrich* **50(3)**: 139-167.
Einarsen, A.S. (1965). *Black brant: Sea Goose of the Pacific Coast*. University of Washington Press, Seatlle.
Einarsson, O., Durinck, J., Peterz, M. & Vader, W. (1989). [First record of Black Stork *Ciconia nigra* in Iceland]. *Bliki* **8**: 51-52. In Icelandic.
Eisenhauer, D.I. & Kirkpatrick, C.M. (1977). *Ecology of the Emperor Goose in Alaska*. Wildlife Monographs **57**.
Eisenhauer, D.I., Strang, C.A. & Kirkpatrick, C.M. (1971). Nesting ecology of the emperor goose (*Philacte canagica* Sewastianov) in the Kokechik Bay region, Alaska. Department Forestry & Conservation, Purdue University.
Eisenmann, E. (1965). (Tigrisoma fasciatum). *Hornero* **10**: 225-234.
Eisenmann, E., Mayr, E. & Parkes, K.C. (1984). Threskiornithidae Richmond, 1917 (Aves): application to place on official list of family-group names in zoology and to give precedence over Plataleinae Bonaparte, 1838, and other competing family-group names. *Bull. Zool. Nomencl.* **41**: 240-244.
Elbin, S.B. (1990). Multiple methods of identifying individual Waldrapp Ibis (*Geronticus eremita*). *AAZPA (Amer. Assoc. Zool. Parks & Aquariums) Ann. Conf. Proc.* **1990**: 208-215.
Elder, W.R. & Woodside, D.H. (1958). Biology and management of the Hawaiian goose. Pp. 198-214 in: *Transactions of the 23rd North American Wildlife Conference*.
Eldridge, J.L. (1977). *A Preliminary Ethogram of the Torrent Duck*. MSc thesis, University of Minnesota.
Eldridge, J.L. (1985). Display inventory of Blue Duck. *Wildfowl* **36**: 109-121.
Eldridge, J.L. (1986a). Territoriality in a river specialist: the Blue Duck. *Wildfowl* **37**: 123-135.
Eldridge, J.L. (1986b). Observations on a pair of Torrent Ducks. *Wildfowl* **37**: 113-122.
Eldridge, J.L. (1986c). Territoriality in a river specialist: the Blue Duck. *Wildfowl* **37**: 123-135.
Eldridge, N. & Cracraft, J. (1980). *Phylogenetic Patterns and the Evolutionary Process*. Columbia University Press, New York.
Elgood, J.H. (1982). *The Birds of Nigeria. An Annotated Checklist*. B.O.U Check-list **4**. British Ornithologists' Union, London.
Elgood, J.H., Fry, C.H. & Dowsett, R.J. (1973). African migrants in Nigeria. *Ibis* **108**: 84-116.
Elkins, N. (1988). *Weather and Bird Behaviour*. 2nd edition. T & AD Poyser, London.
Ellarson, R.S. (1956). *A Study of the Old-squaw Duck on Lake Michigan*. PhD dissertation, University of Wisconsin.
Eller, G.J., Haslett, C.M. & Sibson, R.B. (1991). Pink-eared Duck at Mangere. *Notornis* **38(2)**: 109-110.
Elliott, C.C.H. (1970). Ecological considerations and the possible significance of weight variations in the chicks of the Great Shearwater on Gough Island. *Ostrich* **8(Suppl.)**: 385-396.
Elliott, C.C.H. (1983). Unusual breeding records made from a helicopter in Tanzania. *Scopus* **7(2)**: 33-36.
Elliott, D.G. (1877). Review of the Ibidinae, or subfamily of the ibises. *Proc. Zool. Soc. London* **1877**: 477-510.
Ellis, B.A. (1980). New Zealand National Section 1975-1978 Report. ICBP XVIIth World Conference. *ICBP Bull.* **13**: 200-203.
Ellis, R. (1958). Observations on the Straw-necked Ibis. *Emu* **58**: 312.
Ellison, L.N. & Cleary, L. (1978). Effects of human disturbance on breeding of Double-crested Cormorants. *Auk* **95**: 510-517.
van der Elst, D. (1987). Statut des Grebes jougris (*Podiceps grisegena*), esclavon (*Podiceps auritus*), et a cou noir (*Podiceps nigricollis*) en Wallonie et dans le Brabant. *Aves* **24(1)**: 19-33.
van der Elst, D. (1988). Description de la Cigogne Noire (*Ciconia nigra*) et de la Cigogne d'Abdim (*Ciconia abdimii*). *Aves* **25(3-4)**: 171-182.
Eltringham, S.K. (1963a). The British population of the Mute Swan. *Bird Study* **10**: 10-28.
Eltringham, S.K. (1963b). Is the Mute Swan a menace?. *Bird Notes* **30**: 285-289.
Eltringham, S.K. (1966). The survival of Mute Swan cygnets. *Bird Study* 13: 204-207.
Eltringham, S.K. (1974). The survival of broods of Egyptian Goose in Uganda. *Wildfowl* **25**: 41-48.
Eltringham, S.K. & Din, N.A. (1976). Early records of the lesser flamingo *Phoeniconaias minor* in western Uganda with a note on its present status. *East Afr. Wildl. J.* **14**: 171-175.
Elwell, N. (1970). Marabous in winter - by the hundred. *Bokmakierie* **22**: 69-71.
Elwell, N.H. & McIlleron, W.G. (1978). A wild place on the Witwatersrand: Summervlei. *Afr. Wildl.* **32**: 36-38.
Ely, A. (1976). (Egretta picata). *Sunbird* **7**: 77-78.
Ely, C.A. & Clapp, R.B. (1973). The natural history of Laysan Island, Northwestern Hawaiian Islands. *Atoll Res. Bull.* **171**: 1-361.
Ely, C.R. (1979). *Breeding Biology of the White-fronted Goose (*Anser albifrons frontalis*) on the Yukon-Kuskokwim Delta, Alaska*. MSc thesis, University California (Davis).
Elzanowski, A. (1985). The evolution of parental care in birds with reference to fossil embryos. Pp. 178-183 in: Ilyichev, V.D. & Gavrilov, V.M. eds. *Proc. XVIII Int. Orn. Congr.* Vol. 1. Moscow.
Elzanowski, A. (1987). Cranial and eyelid muscles and ligaments of the Tinamous (Aves: Tinamiformes). *Zool. Jb. Anat.* **116**: 63-118.
Elzanowski, A. (1988). Ontogeny and Evolution of the Ratites. Pp. 2037-2046 in: Ouellet, H. ed. *Proc. XIX Int. Orn. Congr.* Vol. 2.
Emerson, K.C. & Proce, R.D. (1969). A new species of Plegadiphilus (Mallophaga: Menoponidae) from the Cayenne Ibis. *Fla. Entomol.* **52**: 161-163.
Emlen, J.T. & Penney, R.L. (1964). Distance navigation in the Adelie Penguin. *Ibis* **106**: 417-431.
Emlen, S.T. (1975). Migration: orientation and navigation. Pp. 129-219 in: Farner, D.S. & King, J.R. (1975). *Avian Biology*. Vol. 5. Academic Press, London & New York.
Emlen, S.T. & Ambrose, H.W. (1970). Feeding interactions of Snowy Egrets and Red-breasted Mergansers. *Auk* **87**: 154-165.
Emmerich, N. (1982). Beobachtungen an einer Population des Haubentauchers (*Podiceps cristatus*) in Berlin (West). *Orn. Ber. Berlin (West)* **7**: 3-15.
Engbring, J. & Pratt, H.D. (1985). Endangered birds in Micronesia: their history, status and future prospects. Pp. 71-106 in: Temple, S.A. ed. (1985). *Bird Conservation ICBP 2* . The University of Wisconsin Press, Wisconsin.
Enquist, M. (1983). How do Arctic Skuas *Stercorarius parasiticus* search for diver eggs? *Ornis Fenn.* **60**: 83-85.
Enquist, M., Plane, E. & Röed, J. (1985). Aggressive communication in fulmars (*Fulmarus glacialis*) competing for food. *Anim. Behav.* **33**: 1007-1020.
Ensor, P.H. & Basset, J.A. (1987). The breeding status of Adélie Penguins and other birds on the coast of George V Land, Antarctica. *ANARE Res. Notes* **50**: 1-16.
Enticott, J.W. (1986). The pelagic distribution of the Royal Albatross *Diomedea epomophora*. *Cormorant* **13**: 143-156.
Enticott, J.W. (1991). Identification of the Soft-plumaged Petrel. *British Birds*. **84(7)**: 245-264.
Enticott, J.W. & O'Connel, M. (1985). The distribution of the spectacled form of the White-chinned Petrel in the South Atlantic Ocean. *Brit. Antarct. Surv. Bull.* **66**: 83-86.
Erard, C., Guillou,J.J. & Mayaud,N. (1986). Le Héron blanc du Banc d'Arguin *Ardea monicae*. Ses affinités morphologiques. Son histoire. *Alauda* **54(3)**: 163-169.
Erasmus, T. & Wessels, E.D. (1985). Heat production studies on normal and oil-covered Jackass Penguins (*Spheniscus demersus*) in air and water. *S. Afr. J. Zool.* **20**: 209-212.
Erasmus, T., Randall R.M. & Randall, B.M. (1981). Oil pollution, insulation and body temperatures in the Jackass Penguin *Spheniscus demersus*. *Comp. Biochem. Physiol. (Ser. A)* **69**: 169-171.
Erftemeijer, P. (1989). The occurrence of nests of Nankeen Night Heron *Nycticorax caledonicus* in East Java. *Kukila* **4(3-4)**: 146-147.
Erftemeijer, P.L.A. & Djuharsa, E. (1988). Survey of coastal wetlands and waterbirds in the Brantas and Solo deltas, East Java. Asian Wetland Bureau (AWB-PHPA)/Interwader Report **5**. Bogor, Indonesia.
Erftemeijer, P.L.A., Allen, G.R. & Zuwendra (1989). Preliminary Resource Inventory of Bintuni Bay and Recommendations for Conservation and Management. Asian Wetland Bureau (AWB-PHPA), Bogor, Indonesia.
Erftemeijer, P.L.A., van Balen, B. & Djuharsa, E. (1988). The importance of Segara Anakan for nature conservation, with special reference to its avifauna. Asian Wetland Bureau (AWB-PHPA)/Interwader Report **5**. Bogor, Indonesia.
Erickson, R.C. (1948). *Life History and Ecology of the Canvasback*, Nyroca valisineria *(Wilson), in South-eastern Oregon*. PhD dissertation, Iowa State College.
Eriksson, K. (1980). *Breeding Biology of the Goldeneye*, Bucephala clangula *L., in S.W. Sweden*. PhD thesis, University Gothenberg.
Eriksson, K. & Niittylä, J. (1985). Breeding performance of the Goosander *Mergus merganser* in the archipelago of the Gulf Finland. *Ornis Fenn.* **62**: 153-157.
Eriksson, M.O.G. (1982). Differences between old and newly established Goldeneye *Bucephala clangula* populations. *Ornis Fenn.* **59**: 13-19.
Eriksson, M.O.G. (1985). Prey detectability for fish-eating birds in relation to fish density and water transparency. *Ornis Scand.* **16**: 1-7.
Eriksson, M.O.G. (1986). Reproduction of Black-throated Diver *Gavia arctica* in relation to fish density in oligotrophic lakes in southwestern Sweden. *Ornis Scand.* **17(3)**: 245-248.
Eriksson, M.O.G. (1987a). Some effects of freshwater acidification on birds in Sweden. Pp. 183-190 in: Diamond & Filion (1987).
Eriksson, M.O.G. (1987b). Storlommens *Gavia arctica* produktion av ungar i sydvästsvenska sjöar. *Vår Fågelvärld* **46(4)**: 172-186.
Eriksson, M.O.G. & Sundberg, P. (1991). The choice of fishing lakes by the Red-Throated Diver *Gavia stellata* and Black-throated Diver *Gavia arctica* during the breeding season in South-west Sweden. *Bird Study* **38(2)**: 135-144.
Eriksson, M.O.G., Arvidsson, B.L. & Johansson, I. (1988). Habitatkaraktärer hos häckningssjöar för smålom *Gavia stellata* i sydvästra Sverige. *Vår Fågelvärld* **47**: 122-132.
Eriksson, M.O.G., Blomqvist, D., Hake, M. & Johansson, O.C. (1990). Parental feeding in the Red-throated Diver *Gavia stellata*. *Ibis* **132**: 1-13.
Erize, F. (1972). The Guanay Cormorant *Phalacrocorax bougainvillii* nesting on the Atlantic coast of South America. *Bull. Brit. Orn. Club* **92**: 117-118.
Erize, F. (1981). El descubrimiento del macá tobiano. *Periplo* **41**: 6-18.
Erize, F. (1983). Observaciones sobre el macá tobiano. *Hornero* **"Número Extraordinario" (1979)**: 256-268.
Erskine, A.J. (1960). *A Discussion of the Distributional Ecology of Bufflehead* (Bucephal albeola*; Anatidae: Aves) Based on Breeding Biology Studies i British Colmubia*. MSc thesis, University of British Columbia.
Erskine, A.J. (1971a). Growth and annual cycle of weights, plumages and reproductive organs of Goosanders in eastern Canada. *Ibis* **113**: 42-58.
Erskine, A.J. (1971b). Parental carrying of young by Goosanders. *Wildfowl* **22**: 60.
Erskine, A.J. (1972a). The Great Cormorant of eastern Canada. *Can. Wildl. Serv. Occ. Pap.* **14.**
Erskine, A.J. (1972b). *Buffleheads*. Canadian Wildlife Service Monograph Series **4**.
Erskine, A.J. (1988). The changing patterns of Brant migration in Eastern North America. *J. Field Orn.* **59 (2)**: 110-119.
Erskine, A.J. (1990). Joint laying in *Bucephala* ducks - "parasitism" or nest-site competition?. *Ornis Scand.* **21**: 52-56.
Erwin, R.M. (1985). Foraging decisions, patch use, and seasonality in Egrets (Aves: Ciconiiformes). *Ecology* **66(3)**: 837-844.
Erwin, R.M., Hafner, H. & Dugan, P. (1985). Differences in the feeding behavior of Little Egrets *Egretta garzetta*) in two habitats in the Camargue, France. *Wilson Bull.* **97(4)**: 534-538.
Escalante, R. (1980). Notas sobre el Macá Grande en el Uruguay. *Com. Zool. Mus. Hist. Nat. Montevideo* **10(143)**: 1-7.
Espino-Barros, R. & Baldassarre, G.A. (1989a). Activity and habitat-use patterns of breeding Caribbean Flamingos in Yucatan, Mexico. *Condor* **91**: 585-591.
Espino-Barros, R. & Baldassarre, G.A. (1989b). Numbers, migration chronology, and activity patterns of non-breeding Caribbean Flamingos in Yucatan, Mexico. *Condor* **91**: 592-597.
Espitalier-Noel, G., Adams, N.J. & Klages, N.T. (1988). Diet of the Imperial Cormorant *Phalacrocorax atriceps* at sub-Antarctic Marion Island. *Emu* **88**: 43-46.
Etchécopar, R.D. & Hüe, F. (1964). *Les Oiseaux du Nord de l'Afrique*. Éditions N. Boubée & Cie, Paris.
Etchécopar, R.D. & Hüe, F. (1978). *Les Oiseaux de Chine, de Mongolie et de Corée. Non Passereaux*. Les éditions du pacifique, Papeete, Tahiti.
Evans, G.R. (1973). Hutton's Shearwaters initiating local soil erosion in the Seaward Kaikoura Range. *New Zealand J. Sci.* **16**: 637-642.

Evans, K. (1983). Hand-rearing a Scarlet ibis *Eudocimus ruber* at Padstow Bird Gardens, Cornwall. *Avicult. Mag.* **89**: 215-217.

Evans, M.E. (1978). *Some Factors Influencing the Use of Wintering Site by Bewick's Swans, Studied through Individual Identification.* MSc thesis, University of Wales.

Evans, P.G.H. (1990). *Birds of the Eastern Caribbean.* Macmillan Education Ltd, London and Basingstoke.

Evans, R.M. (1972). Some effects of water level on the reproductive success of the White Pelican at East Shoal Lake, Manitoba. *Can. Field-Nat.* **86**: 151-153.

Evans, R.M. (1984). Some causal and functional correlates of creching in young White Pelicans. *Can. J. Zool.* **62**: 814-819.

Evans, R.M. (1988a). Embryonic vocalizations and the removal of foot webs from pipped eggs in the American White Pelican. *Condor* **90**: 721-723.

Evans, R.M. (1988b). Embryonic vocalizations as care-soliciting signals, with particular reference to the American White Pelican. Pp. 1467-1475 in: *Proc. XIX Int. Orn. Congr.*

Evans, R.M. (1989). Egg temperatures and parental behaviour during the transition from incubation to brooding in the American White Pelican. *Auk* **106**: 26-33.

Evans, R.M. (1990a). Terminal egg neglect in the American White Pelican. *Wilson Bull.* **102(4)**: 684-692.

Evans, R.M. (1990b). Terminal-egg chilling and hatching intervals in the American White Pelican. *Auk* **107**: 431-434.

Evans, R.M. & Cash, K.J. (1985). Early spring flights of American White Pelicans: timing and functional role in attracting others to the breeding colony. *Condor* **87**: 252-255.

Evans, R.M. & McMahon, B.F. (1987). Within-brood variation in growth and condition in relation to brood reduction in the American White Pelican. *Wilson Bull.* **99(2)**: 190-201.

Evans, S.M., Cantrell, M.A. & Cram, A. (1981). Patterns of arrival and dispersal from a mixed communal roost of Sacred Ibises and Marabou Storks. *Ostrich* **52**: 230-234.

Everett, W.T. (1988). Biology of the Black-vented Shearwater. *Western Birds* **19**: 89-104.

Everett, W.T. & Anderson, D.W. (1991). Status and conservation of the breeding seabirds on offshore Pacific Islands of Baja California and the Gulf of California. Pp. 115-139 in Croxall (1991).

Every, B., Hosten, L.W. & Brooke, R.K. (1981). The Blue Petrel *Halobaena caerulea* in South Africa. *Cormorant* **9**: 19-22.

Evrard, J.O. (1988). Nesting Red-necked Grebes in St.Croix County, Wisconsin. *Passenger Pigeon* **50**: 291-295.

Evrard, J.O. (1990). Male philopatry in Mallards. *Condor* **92**: 247-248.

Ewans, M. (1989). *Bharatpur bird paradise.* H.F. & G. Witherby, London.

Ewins, P.J., Bazely, D.R. & Recher, H.F. (1990). Communal roosting of Eastern Reef Egrets *Egretta sacra*. *Corella* **14(1)**: 29.

Eyton, T.C. (1838). *A Monograph of the Anatidae, or Duck Tribe.* Longman, London.

Ezealour, A.U. (1985). Parasites and diseases of Abdim's Stork *Ciconia abdimii*. *Malimbus* **7(2)**: 120.

Faaborg, J. (1976). Habitat selection and territorial behavior of the small grebes of North Dakota. *Wilson Bull.* **88**: 390-399.

Fabricio, J.A. (1980). Perdiz: una ave solitaria. *Natureza Rev.* **7**: 36-39.

Fabricius, E. (1983). Kanadagåsen i Sverige. [Summary: The Canada Goose in Sweden]. *Statens Naturvårdsverk, PM* **1678**.

Fad, K.W. & Hall, K.P. (1989). Hand-raising Scarlet Ibis. Pp. 78-80 in: *Proceedings of the 15th National Conference of the American Association of Zoo Keepers, Inc. 1989.* Syracuse, New York.

Fair, J. (1985). *The Mute Swan.* Gavin Press, Limington.

Fair, J.S. (1979). Water level fluctuation and Common Loon nest failure. Pp. 57-69 in: Sutcliffe (1979).

Fairchild, L., Mahoney, S.A. & Schreiber, R.W. (1985). Nest material preferences of Great Frigatebirds. *J. Field Orn.* **56(3)**: 236-245.

Falk, L.L. (1989). Clark's Grebe in Clay County. *Loon* **61**: 150-151.

Falla, R.A. (1932). New Zealand cormorants in the collection of the Auckland Museum, with notes on field observations. *Rec. Auck. Inst. Mus.* **1(3)**: 139-145.

Falla, R.A. (1934). The distribution and breeding habits of petrels in northern New Zealand. *Rec. Auckland Inst. Mus.* **1**: 245-259.

Falla, R.A. (1935). Notes on penguins of the genera *Megadyptes* and *Eudyptes* in southern New Zealand. *Rec. Auckland Inst. Mus.* **1**: 319-326.

Falla, R.A. (1937). Birds. *B.A.N.Z. Antarct. Res. Exped. Rep. (Ser. B)* **2**.

Falla, R.A. (1940). The genus *Pachyptila*. *Emu* **40**: 218-236.

Falla, R.A. (1942). Review of the smaller Pacific forms of *Pterodroma* and *Cookilaria*. *Emu* **42**: 111-118.

Falla, R.A. (1946). An undescribed form of the Black Petrel. *Rec. Canterbury Mus.* **5**: 111-113.

Falla, R.A. (1958). Some records of Australian birds in New Zealand. *Notornis* **8**: 28-32.

Falla, R.A. & Mougin, J.L. (1979). Sphenisciformes. Pp. 121-134 in: Mayr & Cottrell (1979).

Falla, R.A. & Stead, E.F. (1938). The plumages of *Nesonetta aucklandica* Gray. *Trans. Royal Soc. New Zealand* **68**: 37-39.

Falla, R.A., Sibson, R.B. & Turbott, E.G. (1981). *The New Guide to the Birds of New Zealand.* Collins, Auckland & London.

Falzone, C.K. (1989). Breeding Goliath Heron, *Ardea goliath* at the Dallas Zoo. Pp. 741-745 in: *AAZPA (Amer. Assoc. Zool. Parks & Aquariums) Reg. Proc.*

Fan, Z. & Song, Y. (1991). Saving a Treasure of the World - Japanese Crested Ibis. *Forestry of China* **1991(5)**: 36-37.

Fan, Z., Song, Y. & Lu, B. (1991). Protection of the Crested Ibis for ten years. *Chinese Wildlife* **59**: 3-5.

Farnell, G. & Shannon, P.W. (1987). The breeding of Abdim's Storks at the Audubon Park Zoo. *Colonial Waterbirds* **10(2)**: 251-254.

Farner, D.S. & King, J.R. (1971-1975). *Avian Biology.* Vols. 1-5. Academic Press, London and New York.

Farner, D.S., King, J.R. & Parkes, K.C. eds. (1982-1985). *Avian Biology.* Vols. 6-8. Academic Press, London and New York.

Fasola, M. (1986). Resource Use of Foraging Herons in Agricultural and Nonagricultural Habitat in Italy. *Colonial Waterbirds* **9(2)**: 130-148.

Fasola, M. & Barbieri, F. (1981). Prima nidificazione di Marangone minore - *Phalacrocorax pygmaeus* - in Italia. *Avocetta* **5**: 155-156.

Fasola, M. & Barbieri, F. (1988). Andamento delle popolazioni svernanti di Garzetta *Egretta garzetta* in Italia. *Avocetta* **12**: 55-58.

Fatio, V. (1906). Sur le Waldrapp "Corvus sylvaticus" de Gesner. *Ibis (Ser. 8th)* **6(21)**: 139-144.

Feare, C.J. (1978). The decline of booby populations in the western Indian Ocean. *Biol. Conserv.* **14**: 295-305.

Feare, C.J. (1984a). Human Exploitation. Pp. 691-699 in: Croxall *et al.* (1984).

Feare, C.J. (1984b). Seabird Status and Conservation in the Tropical Indian Ocean. Pp. 457-471 in: Croxall *et al.* (1984).

Feduccia, A. (1976a). Hypothetical stages in the evolution of modern ducks and flamingos. *Theoret. Biol.* **67**: 715-721.

Feduccia, A. (1976b). Osteological evidence for shorebird affinities of the flamingos. *Auk* **93**: 587-601.

Feduccia, A. (1977). The Whalebill is a stork. *Nature* **266**: 719-20.

Feduccia, A. (1978). *Presbyornis* and the evolution of ducks and flamingos. *Amer. Sci.* **66**: 298-304.

Feduccia, A. (1980). *The Age of Birds.* Harvard University Press, Cambridge, MA.

Feduccia, A. (1985). The morphological evidence for ratites monophyly: fact or fiction. Pp. 184-190 in: Ilyichev, V.D. & Gavrilov, V.M. eds. *Proc. XVIII Int. Orn. Congr.* Vol. 1. Moscow.

Feely, J.M. (1964). Heron and stork breeding colonies in the Luangwa valley. *Puku* **2**: 76-77.

Feerer & Garret (1977). Potential Western Grebe extinction on California lakes. *California-Nevada Wildl. Soc. Trans.* **1977**: 80-89.

Feerer, J.H. (1977). *Niche Partitioning by Western Grebe Polymorphs.* MSc thesis. Humboldt State College, Arcata, California.

Fei Dianjin (1986). [The geographical distribution of Storks (Ciconidae) and their conservation in our country]. *La Animala Mondo* **3(1)**: 71-74. In Chinese.

Fei Dianjin (1989). [An observation and investigation of the breeding situation of Oriental White Storks *Ciconia ciconia* in Qiqihar suburban district (Heilongjiang Province)]. *Zool. Res.* **10(3)**: 263-270. In Chinese.

Fei Dianjin, Wu Guoqing, *et al.* (1983). [Observations of the behavior of the White Stork *Ciconia ciconia* in the suburb of Qiqihar, Heilongjiang Province, China]. *Chinese J. Zool.* **(5)**: 10-13. In Chinese.

Feldman, R. (1965). Der Schwarzstorch in Westfalen. *Decheniana* **118**: 25-30.

Fellows, D.P. & Paton, P.W.C. (1988). Behavioral response on Cattle Egrets to Population Control mesures in Hawaii. Pp. 315-319 in Crabb, A.C. & Marsh, R.E. (1988). *Proc. Vertebr. Pest. Conf.* Davis, California.

Fennel, C.M. & King, B.F. (1964). New occurrences and recent distributional records of Korean birds. *Condor* **66**: 239-246.

Fenwick, G.D. & Browne, W.M.M. (1975). Breeding of the Spotted Shag at Whitewash Head, Banks Peninsula. *J. Royal Soc. New Zeal.* **5**: 31-45.

Ferguson, R.S. (1977). *Adaptations of the Horned Grebe for breeding in prairie pothole marshes.* MSc thesis. University of Manitoba, Winnipeg, Manitoba.

Ferguson, R.S. (1981). Territorial attachment and mate fidelity by Horned Grebes. *Wilson Bull.* **93**: 560-561.

Ferguson, R.S. & Sealy, S.G. (1983). Breeding ecology of the Horned Grebe, *Podiceps auritus*, in southwestern Manitoba. *Can. Field-Nat.* **97**: 401-408.

Ferguson, W.H. (1966). Will my birds nest this year? *Modern Game Breeding* **2**: 18-20, 34-35.

Fernandez, M. (1929). Los pichones de nuestra cigüeña. *Hornero* **2**: 35-38.

Fernández-Cruz, M., Martín-Novella, C., París, M., Izquierdo, E., Camacho, M., Rendón, M. & Rubio, J.C. (1987). Revisión y puesta al día de la invernada del flamenco (*Phoenicopterus ruber roseus*) en la Península Ibérica. Pp. 23-53 in: Tellería, J.L. ed. *Invernada de aves en la Península Ibérica.* Monografías de la S.E.O. **1**. Sociedad Española de Ornitología, Madrid.

Fernández, G. & Fernández-Cruz, M. (1991). Situación actual de las garzas coloniales en España. *Quercus* **60**: 8-16.

Ferns, P.N. & Green, G.H. (1975). Observations of pink-footed and barnacle geese in the Kong Oscar Fjord region of north-east Greenland, 1974. *Wildfowl* **26**: 131-138.

Ferrari, M.A., Olrog, C.C. & Montes, G. (1984). El ñandú. In: Cabal, G.B. ed. *Fauna Argentina. Aves.* Vol. 1. Centro Editor de América Latina, Buenos Aires.

Ferrer, X. (1980). Sobre la nidificación de *Podiceps cristatus* (Linn.) (Aves, Podicipedidae) en el NE de España. *Misc. Zool. Barcelona* **6**: 81-84.

Ferrer, X. (1982). *Anátidas invernantes en el Delta del Ebro.* Tesis doctoral, Universitat de Barcelona, Barcelona, Spain.

ffrench, R. (1985a). A new look at our Scarlet Ibis. *Naturalist* **6**: 23-27.

ffrench, R. (1985b). Changes in the Avifauna of Trinidad. Pp. 986-991 in: Buckley *et al.* (1985).

ffrench, R.P. (1992). *A Guide to the Birds of Trinidad and Tobago.* 2nd edition. Christopher Helm, London.

ffrench, R.P. & Haverschmidt, F. (1970). The Scarlet ibis in Surinam and Trinidad. *Living Bird* **9**: 147-165.

Fiala, V. (1974). Populationsdynamik und Brutbiologie der Lappentaucher (Podicipedidae), im Teichgebiet von Námest' n.Osl./CSSR. *Anz. orn. Ges. Bayern* **13**: 198-218.

Fiala, V. (1976). Beitrag zur Brutbiologie des Schwarzhalstauchers (*Podiceps nigricollis*). *Zoologiké Listy* **25(2)**: 157-173.

Fiedler, B. & Freitag, B. (1989). Zum Brutvorkommen des Rothalstauchers (*Podiceps griseigena*) im Stat- und Landkreis Wismar. *Ornithologischer Rundbrief Mecklenburgs - Neue Folge* **32**: 3-10.

Field, F. (1920).Breeding of the Black-necked Stork (*Xenorhynchus asiaticus*). *J. Bombay Nat. Hist. Soc.* **27**: 171-172.

Fincham, J.E. (1971). Black Storks breeding near Lalapanzi. *Honeyguide* **65**: 25-27.

Findholt, S.L. (1986). New American White Pelican nesting colony in Wyoming. *Western Birds* **17**: 136-138.

Findholt, S.L. (1987). *Population Status, Reproductive Success, Food Habits, Foraging Areas, Prey Availability, Movements, and some Management Considerations of American White Pelicans Nesting at Pathfinder Reservoir, Wyoming.* Nongame Special Report. Wyoming Game and Fish Department, Cheyenne.

Findholt, S.L. (1988). Status, Distribution and Habitat Affinities of Double-crested Cormorant Nesting Colonies in Wyoming. *Colonial Waterbirds* **1(2)**: 245-251.

Findholt, S.L. & Berner, K.L. (1988). Current status and distribution of the Ciconiiforms nesting in Wyoming. *Great Basin Nat.* **48**: 290-297.

Findholt, S.L. & Diem, K.L. (1988). Status and distribution of American White Pelican nesting colonies in Wyoming: an update. *Great Basin Nat.* **48(2)**: 285-289.

Finlayson, C. (1992). *Birds of the Strait of Gibraltar.* Poyser, London.

Fischer, W. (1970). *Der Schuhschnabel.* Neue Brehmen Bücherei 425. A. Ziemsen Verlag, Wittenberg-Lutherstadt.

Fisher, G.D. (1968a). Successful breeding of Cassowaries at the Scottish National Zoological Park, Edinburgh. *Avicult. Mag.* **74**: 181-194.

Fisher, G.D. (1968b). Breeding Australian Cassowaries *Casuarius casuarius* at Edinburgh Zoo. *Int. Zoo Yb.* **8**: 153-156.

Fisher, H. (1965). Das Triumphgeschrei der Graugans *Anser anser*. *Z. Tierpsychol.* **22**: 247-304.

Fisher, H. (1972). The nutrition of birds. Pp. 431-469 in: Farner, D.S. & King, J.R. (1972). *Avian Biology.* Vol. 2. Academic Press, London & New York.

Fisher, H.I. (1961). Weights and measurements of organs of Bonin Island petrels, *Pterodroma leucoptera hypoleuca*. *Auk* **78**: 269-271.

Fisher, H.I. (1967). Body weights in Laysan Albatrosses. *Ibis* **109**: 373-382.

Fisher, H.I. (1968). The 'two-egg clutch' in the Laysan Albatross. *Auk* **85**: 134-136.

Fisher, H.I. (1969). Eggs and egg-laying in the Laysan Albatross. *Condor* **71**: 102-119.

Fisher, H.I. (1971). The Laysan Albatross: its incubation, hatching and associated behaviors. *Living Bird* **10**: 19-78.

Fisher, H.I. (1972). Sympatry of Laysan and Black-footed Albatross. *Auk* **89**: 381-402.

Fisher, H.I. (1975a). Longevity of the Laysan Albatross. *Bird-banding* **46**: 1-6.

Fisher, H.I. (1975b). Mortality and survival in the Laysan Albatross. *Pacif. Sci.* **29**: 279-300.

Fisher, H.I. (1975c). The relationship between deferred breeding and mortality in the Laysan Albatross. *Auk* **92**: 433-441.

Fisher, H.I. (1976). Some dynamics of a breeding colony of Laysan Albatrosses. *Wilson Bull.* **88**: 121-142.

Fisher, H.I. & Baldwin, P.H. (1946). War and the birds of Midway Atoll. *Condor* **48(1)**: 3-15.

Fisher, H.I. & Fisher, J.R. (1972). The oceanic distribution of the Laysan Albatross. *Wilson Bull.* **84**: 7-27.

Fisher, H.I. & Fisher, M.L. (1969). The visits of Laysan Albatrosses to the breeding colony. *Micronesica* **5**: 173-201.

Fisher, J. (1952). *The Fulmar.* Collins, London.

Fisher, J. (1966). The Fulmar population of Britain and Ireland, 1959. *Bird Study* **13**: 5-76.

Fisher, J. & Flegg, J. (1974). *Watching Birds.* Penguin Books, Harmondsworth, Middlesex, U.K.

Fisher, J. & Lockley, R.M. (1954). *Sea-Birds.* Collins, London.

Fisher, J. & Peterson, R.T. (1964). *The World of Birds.* MacDonald, London.

Fisher, J. & Peterson, R.T. (1971). *An Introduction to General Ornithology.* Aldus Books, London.

Fisher, J. & Vevers, H.G. (1943-1944). The Breeding Distribution, History and Population of the North Atlantic Gannet *Sula bassana*. *J. Animal Ecol.* **12**: 173-213 & **13**: 49-62.

Fisher, J., Simon, N. & Vincent, J. eds. (1969). *Wildlife in Danger.* Viking Press, Ney York.

Fishpool, L.D.C., Van Rompaey, B. & Demey, R. (1989). Call of White-Crested Tiger Heron (*Trigiornis leucolophus*) attributed to Rufous Fishing Owl (*Scotopelis ussheri*). *Malimbus* **11(1)**: 96-97.

Fitzgerald, B.M. & Veitch, C.R. (1985). The cats of Herekopare Island, New Zealand; their history, ecology and effects on birdlife. *New Zealand J. Zool.* **12**: 319-330.

Fjeldså, J. (1973a). The distribution and geographical variation of the Horned Grebe *Podiceps auritus*. *Ornis Scand.* **4**: 55-86.

Fjeldså, J. (1973b). Feeding and habitat selection of the Horned Grebe *Podiceps auritus* (Aves) in the breeding season. *Vidensk. Meddr. dansk naturh. Foren.* **136**: 57-95.

Fjeldså, J. (1973c). Territory and the regulation of population density and recruitment in the horned grebe *Podiceps auritus arcticus* Boje, 1822. *Vidensk. Meddr. dansk naturh. Foren.* **136**: 117-189.

Fjeldså, J. (1973d). Antagonistic and heterosexual behaviour of the Horned Grebe, *Podiceps auritus*. *Sterna* **12**: 161-217.

Fjeldså, J. (1974). *Studier over den nordiske lappedykkers* Podiceps auritus *(Linnaeus, 1758) forekomst, forhold til sine omgivelser og sociale adfaerd.* PhD thesis. Universitets Zoologiske Museum, København.

Fjeldså, J. (1978). *Grebes.* AV Media, Copenhagen.

Fjeldså, J. (1980). Post mortem changes in measurements of grebes. *Bull. Brit. Orn. Club* **100**: 151-154.

Fjeldså, J. (1981a). *Podiceps taczanowskii* (Aves, Podicipedidae), the endemic grebe of Lake Junín, Peru. A review. *Steenstrupia* **7(11)**: 237-259.

Fjeldså, J. (1981b). Comparative ecology of Peruvian Grebes - a study of the mechanisms of evolution of ecological isolation. *Vidensk. Meddr. dansk naturh. Foren.* **143**: 125-249.

Fjeldså, J. (1981c). Okologisk isolation mellem lappedykkerarter. *Naturens Verden* **1981**: 33-40.

Fjeldså, J. (1982/83). Geographic variation in the Great Grebe, *Podiceps major* (Aves, Podicipedidae). Unpublished manuscript. Zoological Museum, University of Copenhagen.

Fjeldså, J. (1982a). Some behaviour patterns of four closely related Grebes, *Podiceps nigricollis, P. gallardoi, P. occipitalis* and *P. taczanowskii*, with reflections on phylogeny and adaptative aspects of the evolution of displays. *Dansk Orn. Foren. Tidsskr.* **76**: 37-68.

Fjeldså, J. (1982b). The adaptative significance of local variations in the bill and jaw anatomy of North European Red-necked Grebes *Podiceps grisegena*. *Ornis Fenn.* **59**: 84-98.

Fjeldså, J. (1983a). Social behaviour and displays of the Hoary-headed Grebe *Poliocephalus poliocephalus*. *Emu* **83**: 129-140.

Fjeldså, J. (1983b). Ecological character displacement and character release in grebes Podicipedidae. *Ibis* **125**: 463-481.

Fjeldså, J. (1984a). Three endangered South American grebes (*Podiceps*): case histories and the ethics of saving species by human intervention. *Ann. Zool. Fenn.* **21**: 411-416.

Fjeldså, J. (1984b). Verdens sjaeldneste lappedykkere. *Dyr i Natur og Museum* **1**: 7-16.
Fjeldså, J. (1984c). Haettelappedykkeren - kendt siden 1974. *Naturens Verden* **1984**: 131-142.
Fjeldså, J. (1985a). Origin, evolution, and status of the avifauna of Andean wetlands. Pp. 85-112 in: Buckley *et al.* (1985).
Fjeldså, J. (1985b). Displays of the two primitive grebes *Rollandia rolland* and *Rollandia microptera* and the origin of the complex courtship behaviour of the *Podiceps* species (Aves: Podicipedidae). *Steenstrupia* **11(5)**: 133-155.
Fjeldså, J. (1985c). Classification of waterbird communities in South-eastern Australia. *Emu* 85: 141-149.
Fjeldså, J. (1986a). Management of endangered species of grebes, Podicipedidae: the importance of biological research. Pp. 117-122 in: *Rep. XXXI Annual Meeting IWRB, Paracas*.
Fjeldså, J. (1986b). Feeding ecology and possible life history tactics of the Hooded Grebe *Podiceps gallardoi*. *Ardea* **74(1)**: 40-58.
Fjeldså, J. (1986c). Color variation in the Ruddy Duck *Oxyura jamaicensis andina*. *Wilson Bull.* **98**: 592-594.
Fjeldså, J. (1988a). Status of birds of steppe habitats of the Andean zone and Patagonia. Pp. 81-95 in: Goriup (1988).
Fjeldså, J. (1988b). Comparative ecology of Australian grebes (Aves: Podicipedidae). *RAOU Report* **54**: 1-30. Royal Australasian Ornithologists' Union, Victoria.
Fjeldså, J. (1989a). Slow evolution of neossoptile plumages. Pp. 1476-1485 in: *Proc. XIX Int. Orn. Congr.*
Fjeldså, J. (1989b). Grebe Research Group. Pp. 19-21 in: Pirot, J.Y. compiler. *The IWRB Research Group Report 1987-88*. International Waterfowl Research Bureau, Slimbridge.
Fjeldså, J. & Krabbe, N. (1990). *Birds of the High Andes*. Zoological Museum University of Copenhagen & Apollo Books, Svendborg, Denmark.
Flannery, A.W. (1988). American White Pelicans in northern Utah. *Utah Birds* **4(1-4)**: 11-20.
Fleet, R.R. (1972). Nesting succes of the Red-tailed Tropicbird on Kure Atoll. *Auk* **89**: 651-659.
Fleet, R.R. (1974). *The Red-tailed Tropicbird on Kure Atoll*. Ornithological Monographs **16**. The American Ornithologists' Union.
Fleming, C.A. (1939). Birds of the Chatham Islands. *Emu* **38**: 380-413.
Fleming, C.A. (1941a). The phylogeny of the prions. *Emu* **41**: 134-155.
Fleming, C.A. (1941b). Notes on neozelanic forms of the subgenus *Cookilaria*. *Emu* **41**: 69-80.
Fleming, W.J., Rodgers, J.A. & Stafford, C.J. (1984). Contaminents in Wood Stork eggs and their effects on reproduction, Florida, 1982. *Colonial Waterbirds* **7**: 88-93.
Fletcher, K.C. (1979). Repair of bilateral mandibular fractures in a Shoebill Stork (*Balaeniceps rex*). *J. Zoo An. Med.* **10**: 69-72.
Flickenger, E.L. & Meeker, D.L. (1972). Pesticide mortality of young White-faced Ibis in Texas. *Bull. Environ. Contam. Toxicol.* **8**: 115-168.
Flint, V. ed. (1978). *The Red Data Book of the USSR*. Part 2: Birds. Lesnaya Promyshlennost, Moscow.
Flint, V.E., Boehme, R.L., Kostin, Y.V. & Kuznetsov, A.A. (1984). *A Field Guide to the Birds of the USSR*. Princeton University Press, Princeton, New Jersey.
Flower, S.S. (1922). The Hermit Ibis in the Sudan. *Ibis (Ser. 11th)* **4**: 598-599.
Foers, R. (1984). Greater Flamingo (*Phoenicopterus ruber*) in Cyprus-1978. An analysis of records and migratory trends from 1956-1978. Pp. 46-57 in: *The Birds of Cyprus, 10th Bird Report 1979*. Nicosia, Cyprus.
Folkestad, A.O. (1977). Dvergdykkeren som norsk hekkefugl, status 1973-1977. [Summary: The breeding population of the Little Grebe (*Tachybaptus ruficolis*) in Norway. Status 1973-1977]. *Sterne* **16**: 242-262.
Folkestad, A.O. (1978). Takseringer og studier av Gråstrupedykker i overvintringsområdene på Norskekysten. *Anser* **3(Suppl.)**: 84-89.
Folwell, D. (1988). Kiwi breeding at Auckland Zoo: past, present and future. Pp. 493-499 in: Dresser, B.L., Reece, R.W. & Maruska, E.J. eds. *Proceedings 5th World Conference on Breeding Endangered Species in Captivity*. Cincinnati.
Fooks, P. & Reed, S. (1978). Hoary-headed Grebe in Northland. *Notornis* **25**: 158-159.
Forbes, L.S. (1985a). Extra-pair feeding in Western Grebes. *Wilson Bull.* **97**: 122-123.
Forbes, L.S. (1985b). *The Feeding Ecology of Western Grebes Breeding at Duck Lake, British Colombia*. PhD thesis. University of Manitoba, Winnipeg.
Forbes, L.S. (1987). Feeding behaviour of Great Blue Herons at Creston, British Columbia. *Can. J. Zool.* **65**: 3062-3067.
Forbes, L.S. (1988). Western Grebe nesting in British Colombia. *Murrelet* **69**: 28-33.
Forbes, L. (1989). Coloniality in Herons: Lack's Predation Hypothesis Reconsidered. *Colonial Waterbirds* **12(1)**: 24.29.
Forbes, L.S. & Sealy, S.G. (1988). Diving behaviour of male and female western grebes *Can. J. Zool.* **66**: 2695-2698.
Forbes, L.S. & Sealy, S.G. (1990). Foraging roles of male and female Western Grebes during breeding. *Condor* **92**: 421-426.
Forbes, L.S., Simpson, K., Kelsall, J.P. & Flook, D.R. (1985). Reproductive success of Great Blue Herons in British Columbia. *Can. J. Zool.* **63**: 1110-1113.
Forbes, M.R.L. (1986). *Correlates of Hatching Asynchrony for Pied-billed Grebes,* Podilymbus podiceps. MSc thesis. University of Western Ontario, London.
Forbes, M.R.L. (1987). Extrapair feeding in Pied-billed Grebes. *Wilson Bull.* **99**: 109-111.
Forbes, M.R.L. & Ankney, C.D. (1987). Hatching asynchrony and food allocation within broods of Pied-billed Grebes, *Podilymbus podiceps*. *Can. J. Zool.* **65**: 2782-2877.
Forbes, M.R.L. & Ankney, C.D. (1988a). Intraclutch variation in egg weights of Pied-billed Grebes. *Condor* **90**: 709-711.
Forbes, M.R.L. & Ankney, C.D. (1988b). Nest attendance by adult Pied-billed Grebes, *Podilymbus podiceps* (L.) *Can. J. Zool.* **66**: 2019-2023.
Forbes, M.R.L., Barkhouse, H.P. & Smith, P.C. (1989). Nest-site selection by Pied-billed Grebes *Podilymbus podiceps*. *Ornis Scand.* **20**: 211-218.
Forbes, W.A. (1882). On some points in the anatomy of the Indian Darter (*Plotus melanogaster*) and on the mechanism of the neck in the darters (*Plotus*), in connexion with their habits. *Proc. Zool. Soc. London* **1882**: 208-212.
Forbes-Watson, A.D. (1969). (Ardea humbloti). *Atoll Research. Bull.* **128**.
Forbes-Watson, A.D. (1972). Report on bird preservation in Madagascar. Unpublished report to ICBP.
Forcelli, D.O. (1987). El Pato Esquivo ¿sobrevivirá?. *En Peligro de Extinción* **1(1)**: 2-3.
Ford, E.B. (1943). Wood Ibis at Wepener. *Ostrich* **14**: 183-184.
Ford, H.A. (1989). *Ecology of Birds. An Australian Perspective*. Surrey Beatty & Sons, Chipping Norton, NSW, Australia.
Ford, J. (1963). Dispersal and mortality in the pied cormorant in Western Australia. *West. Aust. Nat.* **8**: 177-181.
Fordyce, R.E. (1974). *Aspects of the Biology of the Blue Duck,* Hymenolaimus malacorhynchus. BSc hons. thesis, University of Canterbury.
Fordyce, R.E. (1976). Distribution and habitat of the Blue Duck (*Hymenolaimus malacorhynchos*), in the South Island, New Zealand. *Mauri Ora* **4**: 79-85.
Fordyce, R.E. & Tunnicliffe, G.A. (1973). The distribution of the Blue Duck (*Hymenolaimus malacorhynchos*), in the South Island: a preliminary survey. *Mauri Ora* **1**: 37-42.
Fordyce, R.E., Jones, C.M. & Field, B.D. (1986). The world's oldest penguin? *Geol. Soc. New Zealand Newsl.* **74**: 56-57.
Forshaw, C.J. (1988). White-backed Night Heron, *Nycticorax leuconotus*, at Lilongwe Nature Sanctuary. *Nyala* **12(1/2)**: 75.
Fossi, C., Focardi, S., Leonzio, C. & Renzoni, A. (1984). Trace-metals and chlorinated hydrocarbons in birds' eggs from the Delta of the Danube. *Environ. Conserv.* **11(4)**: 345-350.
Fothergill, A. (1983). A study of the mixed "heronries" found at Cakanaca, Gcodikwe and Gcobega Lagoons. *Babbler* **5**: 8-14.
Fourage, J. (1987). [Post-nuptial call of the Black Stork (*Ciconia nigra*)]. *Aves* **24**: 152-153. In French.
Fowler, J.A. (1985). Monitoring Storm Petrel activity in Shetland. Pp. 3-4 in: Tasker, M.L. ed. (1985). *Population and Monitoring Studies of Seabirds*. Proceedings of the 2nd. International Conference Seabird Group.
Fowler, J.A. & Swinfen, R. (1984). Scottish storm petrels in Iceland. *Scott. Birds* **13**: 52.
Fowler, J.A., Okill, J.D. & Marshall, B. (1982). A Retrap Analysis of Storm Petrels Tape-lured in Shetland. *Ringing & Migration* **4**: 1-7.
Fox, A.D. (1991). History of the Pochard breeding in Britain. *British Birds* **84 (3)**: 83-98.
Fox, A.D. & Mitchell, C. (1988). Migration and seasonal distribution of Gadwall from Britain and Ireland: a preliminary assessment. *Wilfowld* 145-152.
Fox, A.D. & Salmon, D.G. (1988). Changes in non-breeding distribution and habitat of Pochard *Aythya ferina* in Britain. *Biol. Conserv.* **46**: 303-316.
Fox, A.D. & Salmon, D.G. (1989). The winter status and distribution of Gadwall in Britain and Ireland. *Bird Study* **36**: 37-44.
Fox, A.D. & Stroud, D.A. eds. (1981). *Report of the 1979 Greenland White-Fronted Goose Study Expedition to Eqalungmiut Nunât, West Grennland*. Greenland White-Fronted Goose Study, Aberystwyth.
Fox, A.D., Gitay, H., Owen, M., Salmon, D.G. & Ogilvie, M.A. (1989). Population dynamics of Icelandic-nesting Geese, 1960-1987. *Ornis Scand.* **20**: 289-297.
Fox, A.D., Mitchell, C.R., Fletcher, J.D. & Turner, J.V.N. (1989). Wildfowl and Wetlands Trust Pink-footed Goose *Anser brachyrhynchus* Project: a report on the first three seasons. *Wildfowl* **40**: 153-157.
Fox, G.A., Yonge, K.S. & Sealy, S.G. (1980). Breeding performance, pollutant burden and eggshell thinning in Common Loons *Gavia immer* nesting on a boreal forest lake. *Ornis Scand.* **11**: 243-248.
Fradrich, H. (1969). Der Zoo van Tananarive. *Zool. Garten* **37(1/3)**: 41-47.
Franchimont, J. (1986a). Causes de mortalite aux stades des oeufs et des poussins chez les ardeides. *Aves* **23(1)**: 34-44.
Franchimont, J. (1986b). Aperçú de la situation du Heron Garde-boeuf (*Bubulcus ibis*) en Afrique du Nord dans le contexte de l'expansion mondiale de l'espece. *Aves* **23(2)**: 121-134.
Francis, K. (1982). *The New Zealand Kiwi*. Whitcoulls Publishers, Christchurch & London.
van Franeker, J.A. & Montague, T. (1987). Recoveries of petrels banded near Casey Station, Wilkes Land, Antarctica, 1984 to 1985. *Corella* **11**: 37-43.
van Franeker, J.A. & Wattel, J. (1982). Geographical variation of the Fulmar in the North Atlantic. *Ardea* **70**: 31-44.
van Franeker, J.A., Bell, P.J. & Montague, T.L. (1990). Birds of Ardery and Odbert Islands, Windmill Islands, Antarctica. *Emu* 90: 74-80.
Franke, H. (1969). Die Paarungsbalz des Schwarzhalstauchers. *J. Orn.* **110**: 286-290.
Frantzen, B. (1984). [The Slavonian Grebe (*Podiceps auritus*) as a breeding bird in Finnmark, northern Norway]. *Vår Fuglefauna* **7**: 97-98. In Norwegian.
Franzmann, N.E. (1980). *Ederfuglens (*Somateria m. mollissima*) ynglebiologi og populationsdynamik på Christianso 1973-1977*. Licentiat degree, University of Copenhagen.
Franzmann, N.E. (1989). Status of the Danish breeding population of the Eider *Somateria mollissima* 1980-83, with notes on general population trends in northern Europe. *Dansk Orn. Foren. Tidsskr.* **83**: 62-67.
Fraser, M. & McMahon, L. (1991). Marine Egyptian Geese. *Promerops* **198**: 7-8.
Fraser, M.W. (1984). Foods of Subantarctic Skuas at Inaccessible Island. *Ostrich* **55**: 192-195.
Fraser, M.W., Ryan, P.G. & Watkins, B.P. (1988). The Seabirds of Inaccessible Island, South Atlantic Ocean. *Cormorant* **16**: 7-33.
Fraser, W. (1971). Breeding herons and storks in Botswana. *Ostrich* **42**: 123-127.
Frazier, J. (1982). Marine foraging by Hamerkop in Tanzania. *Ostrich* **53**: 118.
Frédéric, L. (1985). Sous le signe du Bouddha. *L'Univers du Vivant* **4**: 9-13.
Frederick, P.C. (1985a). Intraspecific food piracy in White Ibis. *J. Field Orn.* **56**: 413-414.
Frederick, P.C. (1985b). *Mating strategies of White Ibis (*Eudocimus albus*)*. PhD dissertation. University of North Carolina. Chapel Hill, North Carolina.
Frederick, P.C. (1986a). Extrapair copulations in the mating system of White Ibis (*Eudocimus albus*). *Behaviour* **100(1-4)**: 170-201.
Frederick, P.C. (1986b). Conspecific nest takeovers and egg destruction by White Ibises. *Wilson Bull.* **98**: 156-157.
Frederick, P.C. (1987a). Chronic tidally-induced nest failure in a colony of White Ibises. *Condor* **89**: 413-419.
Frederick, P.C. (1987b). Responses of male White Ibises to their mate's extra-pair copulations. *Behav. Ecol. Sociobiol.* **21**: 223-228.
Frederick, P.C. (1990). Hydrological cues associated with the initiation and abandonment of nesting by White Ibises in the Everglades marshes of Florida, USA. Pp. 64-70 in: Frederick, Morales *et al.* (1990).
Frederick, P.C. & Collopy, M.W. (1989a). The role of predation in determining reproductive success of colonially nesting Wading Birds in the Florida Everglades. *Condor* **91**: 860-867.
Frederick, P.C. & Collopy, M.W. (1989b). Nesting success of five Ciconiiform species in relation to water conditions in the Florida Everglades. *Auk* **106**: 625-634.
Frederick, P.C. & Shields, M.A. (1986). Suspected intraspecific egg dumping in the White Ibis (*Eudocimus albus*). *Wison Bull.* 98(3): 476-478.
Frederick, P.C., Dwyer, N., Fitzgerald, S. & Bennets, R.E. (1990). Relative abundance and habitat preferences of Least Bitterns (*Ixobrychus exilis*) in the Everglades. *Florida Field Nature* **18(1)**: 1-9.
Frederick, P.C., Morales, G., Spaans, A.L. & Luthin, C.S. eds. (1990). *El Corocoro Rojo (*Eudocimus ruber*): Situación Actual, Conservación, e Investigaciones Recientes*. Proceedings of the First International Scarlet Ibis Conservation Workshop, Caracas, Venezuela. IWRB Special Publication **11**.
Fredrickson, L.H. & Heitmeyer, M.E. (1991). Life history strategies and habitat needs of the northern Pintail. *US Fish Wildl. Leafl.* **13.1.3.**
Fredrickson, L.H., Burger, G.V., Havera, S.P., Graber, D.A., Kirby, R.E. & Taylor, T.S. eds. (1990). *Proc. 1988 North Amer. Wood Duck Symp.* St. Louis, MO.
Frieling, H. (1933). Die Ausbreitung des Schwarzhalstauchers, *Podiceps nigricollis nigricollis* Brehm. Ein Beitrag zur kausalanaly-tischen und vergleichenden Tiergeographie. *Zoogeographica* **1**: 485-550.
Friendly, A. (1973). Search for tomb in Egypt uncovers vast animal cult. *Smithsonian* **4**: 66-73.
Frings, H. & Frings, M. (1961). Some biometric studies on the albatrosses of Midway Atoll. *Condor* **63**: 304-312.
Frisch, J.D. (1981). *Aves Brasileiras*. Vol. 1. Dalgas-Ecoltec Ecologia Técnica e Comércio, São Paulo.
Frisch, S. & Frisch, J.D. (1964). *Aves Brasileiras*. Irmaos Vitale, São Paulo.
Frith, C. & Frith, D. (1985). The Cassowary at his nest. A photographic first. *Austr. Nat. Hist.* **21(9)**: 390-393.
Frith, C. & Frith, D. (1986). Cassowary. *Wildlife in Australia* **23(2)**: 8-9.
Frith, H.J. (1955). The downy ducklings of the Pink-eared and White-eyed Ducks. *Emu* **55**: 310-312.
Frith, H.J. (1962). Movements of the Grey Teal, *Anas gibberifrons* (Müller) (Anatidae). *CSIRO Wildl. Res.* **7**: 50-70.
Frith, H.J. (1963). Movements and mortality rates of the Black Duck and Grey Teal in South-eastern Australia. *CSIRO Wildl. Res.* **8**: 119-131.
Frith, H.J. (1964a). Taxonomic relationships of *Stictonetta naevosa* (Gould). *Nature* **202**: 1352-1353.
Frith, H.J. (1964b). The downy young of the Freckled Duck, *Stictonetta naevosa*. *Emu* **64**: 42-47.
Frith, H.J. (1965). Ecology of the Freckled Duck, *Stictonetta naevosa*. *Emu* **64**: 42-47.
Frith, H.J. (1967). *Waterfowl in Australia*. East-West Center Press, Honolulu.
Frith, H.J. & Davies, S.J.J. (1961a). (Egretta picata). *Emu* **61**: 97-111.
Frith, H.J. & Davies, S.J.J.F. (1961b). Ecology of the Magpie Goose, *Anseranas semipalmata* Latham (Anatidae). *CSIRO Wildl. Res.* **6**: 91-141.
Frith, H.J., Braithwaite, L.W. & McKean, J.L. (1969). Waterfowl in an inland swamp in New South Wales. II. Food. *CSIRO Wildlife Res.* **14**: 17-64.
Frost, P.G.H., Ball, I.J., Siegfried, W.R. & McKinney, D.F. (1979). Sex ratios, morphology and growth of the African Black Duck. *Ostrich* **50**: 220-233.
Frost, P.G.H., Shaughnessy, P.D., Semmelink, A., Sketch, M. & Siegfried, W.R. (1975). The response of Jackass Penguins to Killer Whale vocalisations. *J. Afr. J. Sci.* **71**: 158-159.
Frost, P.G.H., Siegfried, W.R. & Burger, A.E. (1976a). Behavioural adaptations of the Jackass Penguin *Spheniscus demersus* to a hot, arid environment. *J. Zoology. London* **179**: 165-187.
Frost, P.G.H., Siegfried, W.R. & Cooper, J. (1976b). Conservation of the Jackass Penguin *Spheniscus demersus* (L.). *Biol. Conserv.* **9**: 79-99.
Fry, C.H., Hosken, J.H. & Skinner, D. (1986). Further observations on the breeding of Slaty Egrets *Egretta vinaceigula* and Rufousbellied Herons *Ardeola rufiventris*. *Ostrich* **57(1)**: 61-64.
Fry, C.H., Keith, S. & Urban, E.K. (1985). Evolutionary expositions from The Birds of Africa: *Halcyon* song phylogeny; Cuckoo host partitioning; systematics of *Aplopelia* and *Bostrychia*. Pp. 163-180 in: Schuchmann, K.L. ed. *African Vertebrates: Systematics, Phylogeny, and Evolutionary Biology*. Zool. Forschungsinstitut und Mus. A. Koenig, Bonn.
Fu Chun-li & Gu Jing-he (1988). Reproductive ecology of the Bar-headed Goose *Anser indicus* at the Yultuz Swamp in the Tianshan (Xinjiang). *Arid Zone Research* **5(3)**: 27-29.
Fuchs, E. (1978). Bestand und Verbreitung des Haubentauchers *Podiceps cristatus* in der Schweiz. *Orn. Beob.* **75**: 19-32.
Fuchs, E. (1982). Bestand, Zugverhalten, Bruterfolg und Mortalität des Haubentauchers *Podiceps cristatus* auf dem Sempachersee. *Orn. Beob.* **79**: 255-264.
Fugle & Rothstein (1977). Clutch size determination, egg size, and eggshell thickness in the Pied-billed Grebe. *Auk* 94: 371-377.
Fugler, S.R., Hunter, S., Newton, I.P. & Steele, W.K. (1987). Breeding biology of Blue Petrels at the Prince Edward Islands. *Emu* **87**: 103-110.
Fujimaki, Y. (1988). [Records of *Ciconia ciconia boyciana* from Hokkaido, Japan.] *Jpn. J. Orn.* **37(1)**: 37-38. In Japanese with English summary.
Fujioka, M. (1984). Asynchronous Hatching, Growth and Survival of Chicks of the Cattle Egret *Bubulcus ibis*. *Tori* **33**: 1-12.
Fujioka, M. (1985). Sibling competition and siblicide in asynchronously-hatching broods of the cattle egret *Bubulcus ibis*. *Anim. Behav.* **33**: 1228-1242.
Fujisawa, K. (1967). *Ahodori,* Diomedea albatrus. Toko Shoin, Tokyo.

Fukuda, M. (1980). Life of the Common Cormorants. *Wild Birds* **45**: 679-684.
Fukuda, M. (1986). [Winter breeding of the Little Grebe, *Podiceps ruficollis*]. *Jpn. J. Orn.* **35**: 81-82. In Japanese.
Fullagar, P.J. (1976). Seabird Islands. No. 35. Cabbage Tree Island, New South Wales. *The Austr. Bird Bander* **14**: 94-97.
Fuller, E. (1987). *Extinct Birds*. Wiking & Rainbird, London.
Fuller, E. ed. (1991). *Kiwis*. Swan-Hill Press, Shrewsbury, England.
Fuller, M.R., Obrecht, H.H., Pennycuick, C.J. & Schaffner, F.C. (1989). Aerial tracking of radio-marked white-tailed tropicbirds over the Caribbean Sea. Pp. 133-137 in: Amlaner, C.J. ed. *Proceedings of 10th International Symposium on Biotelemetry*. University of Arkansas Press, Fayetteville, Arkansas.
Fuller, R.J. (1982). *Bird Habitats in Britain*. Calton.
Fulton, R.V. (1908). The disappearance of New Zealand birds. *Trans. New Zealand Inst.* **40**: 485-500.
Furness, R.W. (1981). The impact of predation by Great Skuas *Catharacta skua* on other seabird populations at a Shetland colony. *Ibis* **123**: 534-539.
Furness, R.W. (1983). *The birds of Foula*. Brathay Hall Trust, Ambleside.
Furness, R.W. (1987). *The Skuas*. Poyser, Calton.
Furness, R.W. & Baillie, S.R. (1981). Factors affecting capture rate and biometrics of Storm Petrels on St Kilda. *Ringing & Migration* **3**: 137-148.
Furness, R.W. & Cooper, J. (1982). Interactions between breeding seabird and pelagic fish populations in the southern Benguela region. *Marine Ecology Progress Series*. **8**: 243-250.
Furness, R.W. & Monaghan, P. (1987). *Seabird Ecology*. Blackie, Glasgow.
Furness, R.W. & Todd, C.M. (1984). Diets and feeding of Fulmars during the breeding season: a comparison between St Kilda and Shetland. *Ibis* **126**: 379-387.
Furniss, S. (1983). Status of the Seabirds of the Culebra Archipelago, Puerto Rico. *Colonial Waterbirds* **6**: 121-125.
Furse, J.R. (1976). The Antarctic Fulmar at home near Elephant Island. *Sea Swallow* **27**: 7-10.
Gabaldón, G. & Ulloa, G. (1980). Holoendemicity of malaria: an avian model. *Trans. Royal Soc. Trop. Med. Hyg.* **74**: 501-507.
Gabrielson, I.N. & Lincoln, F.C. (1959). *The Birds of Alaska*. The Stackpole Company, Harrisburg, PA & Wildlife Management Institute, Washington, D.C.
Gadow, H. (1902). The wings and the skeleton of *Phalacrocorax harrisi*. *Novit. Zool.* **9**: 169-176.
Galarza, A. (1986). Migración de la espátula (*Platalea leucorodia* (Linn.)) por la Península Ibérica. *Ardeola* **33(1-2)**: 195-201.
Galbraith, H., Baillie, S.R., Furness, R.W. & Russell, S. (1986). Regional variations in the dispersal patterns of Shags (*Phalacrocorax aristotelis*) in Northern Europe. *Ornis Scand.* **17**: 68-74.
Galbraith, H., Russell, S. & Furness, R.W. (1981). Movements and mortality of Isle of May Shags as shown by ringing recoveries. *Ringing and Migration* **3**: 181-189.
Galbreath, R. (1989). Short note on "Genetics of polymorphism in the Little Shag". *Notornis* **36**: 62-63.
Galdikas, B.M.F. & King, B. (1989). Lesser Adjutant nests in SW Kalimantan. *Kukila* **4**: 151-152.
Gale, R.S. (1989). Bringing back the Trumpeter Swan. *Utah Birds* **5 (1)**: 1-13.
Gale, R.S., Garton, E.O. & Ball, I.J. (1987). *The History, Ecology and Management of the Rocky Mountain Population of Trumpeter Swans*. Manuscript.
Gales, R.P. (1985). Breeding seasons and double brooding of the Little Penguin *Eudyptula minor* in New Zealand. *Emu* **85**: 127-130.
Gales, R.P. (1987a). Growth strategies in Blue Penguins *Eudyptula minor minor*. *Emu* **87**: 212-219.
Gales, R.P. (1987b). Validation of the stomach flushing technique for obtaining stomach contents of penguins. *Ibis* **129**: 335-343.
Gales, R.P. (1988a). The use of otoliths as indicators of Little Penguin *Eudyptula minor* diet. *Ibis* **130**: 418-426.
Gales, R.P. (1988b). Sexing Blue Penguins by external measurements. *Notornis* **35**: 71-75.
Gales, R.P. (1988c). Free-living energetics of Little Penguins during the annual cycle. *Cormorant* **16(2)**: 127.
Gales, R.P. & Pemberton, D. (1988). Recovery of the King Penguin, *Aptenodytes patagonicus*, population on Heard Island. *Austr. Wild. Res.* **15**: 579-585.
Gales, R.P. & Pemberton, D. (1990). Seasonal and local variation in the diet of the Little Penguin, *Eudyptula minor*, in Tasmania. *Aust. Wild. Res.* **17**: 231-259.
Gales, R.P., Green, B. & Stahel, C. (1988). The energetics of free-living Little Penguins, *Eudyptula minor*, during molt. *Austr. J. Zool.* **36(2)**: 159-167.
Gales, R.P., Williams, C. & Ritz, D. (1990). Foraging behaviour of the Little Penguin *Eudyptula minor*: initial results and an assessment of instrument effect. *J. Zoology. London* **220**: 61-85.
Gallagher, M.D. (1960). Bird notes from Christmas Island, Pacific Ocean. *Ibis* **102**: 489-502.
Gallagher, M.D. (1986). Abdim's Stork in Arabia. *Sandgrouse* **8**: 107-111.
Gallagher, M.D. (1988). The Ostrich in Oman. *Sandgrouse* **10**: 97-101.
Gallagher, M.D., Scott, D.A., Ormond, R.F.G., Connor, R.J. & Jennings, M.C. (1984). The distribution and conservation of seabirds breeding on the coasts and islands of Iran and Arabia. Pp. 421-456 in: Croxall *et al.* (1984).
Gallagher, T. (1990). Courtship of the Red-necked Grebe. *Wildbird* **4**: 44-48.
Gallardo, J. (1970). (Syrigma sibilatrix). *Rev. Mus. Arg. Cienc. Nat. Bernardino Rivadavia.*
Gallardo, J.M. (1984). Observaciones sobre el comportamiento social y reproductivo de "*Eudromia elegans*" (Aves: Tinamiformes). *Rev. Mus. Arg. Cienc. Nat. Bernardino Rivadavia* **13**: 160-170.
Gallet, E. (1949). *Les Flamants Roses de Camargue*. Payot, Lausanne.
Gallico, P. (1946). *The Snow Goose*. Michael Joseph, London.
Gao Yu-ren (1984). Preliminary observations on the ecology of Swinhoe's Petrel *Oceanodroma monorhis* in the Yellow Sea. *Chinese J. Zool.* **5**: 26-29.
Gao Yuan-hong (1988). [A preliminary discussion on several problems of the Bar-headed Goose, *Anser indicus*, on the Bird Island (Qinghai Province)]. *Chinese Wildlife* 2: 21-22. In Chinese.
García Jiménez, F.J. & Calvo Sendín, J.F. (1987). El zampullín cuellinegro, *Podiceps nigricollis*, en la laguna de la Mata (Alicante). *Ardeola* **34(1)**: 102-105.
García, L. (1972). Observaciones sobre aves marinas en las pesquerías del Atlántico sudafricano. *Ardeola* **16**: 159-192.
García, L., Amat, J.A. & Rodriguez, M. (1983). Spoonbills breeding during winter in Sapin. *British Birds* **76(1)**: 32-33.
García-Oliva, J., González Nicolás, M. & Aja, J.J. (1979). Observación de espátulas anilladas en la marisma de Santoña (Santander). *Doñana Acta Vertebrata* **6(2)**: 236-237.
Gardarsson, A. (1979). [A census of breeding Cormorants (*Phalacrocorax carbo*) and Shags (*Phalacrocorax aristotelis*) in Iceland in 1975]. *Náttúrufraeoingurinn* **49(2-3)**: 126-154. In Icelandic with English summary.
Gardarsson, A. (1989). [A survey of gannet *Sula bassana* colonies in Iceland]. *Bliki* **7**: 1-22. In Icelandic with English summary.
Gardner, A.S., Duck, C.D. & Greig, S. (1985). Breeding of the Trindade Petrel *Pterodroma arminjoniana* on Round Island, Mauritius. *Ibis* **127**: 517-522.
Garland, I. (1963). Nesting of the Woolly-necked Stork. *Bokmakierie* **15(2)**: 15-16.
Garner, T. (1991). Second state record of Ross' Goose, *Chen rossii*, Lancaster County. *Pa. Birds* **5 (1)**. 19-20.
Garnett, C.G. (1984). Conservation of Seabirds in the South Pacific Region: a Review. Pp. 547-558 in: Croxall *et al.* (1984).
Garnett, S.T. & Bredl, R. (1985). (*Pelecanus conspicillatus*). *Corella* **15**: 6-23.
Garnett, S.T. & Crowley, G.M. (1987). Manowar Island, Gulf of Carpentaria, Queensland. *Corella* **11(3)**: 73-74.
Garrido, O.H. (1985). Cuban endangered birds. Pp. 992-999 in: Buckley *et al.* (1985).
Garstone, R. (1973). Yellow-billed Spoonbills at Woodanilling. *State Wildlife Advisory News Service* **4**: 39. Published by the Department of Fisheries and Fauna, Perth, Western Australia]
Gartlan, S. (1989). *La Conservation des Ecosystèmes forestiers du Cameroun*. IUCN, Gland, Suisse and Cambridge, England.
Gartshore, N.A., Steele, W.K. & Klages, N.T. (1988). Summer diet of Salvin's Prion at sub-Antarctic Marion Islands. *S. Afr. J. Zool.*
Gassmann-Duvall, R., Loope, L.L. & Duvall, F.II. (1988). Factors affecting groundings of the endangered Dark-rumped Petrel on Maui in 1987. *Elepaio* **48**(10): 85-87.
Gast, S.E. & King, B. (1985). Notes on Philippine birds, 7. Recent records of the Chinese Egret *Egretta eulophotes* from Luzon, Mindoro and Palawan, Philippines. *Bull. Brit. Orn. Club* **105(4)**: 139-141.
Gates, J.M. (1962). Breeding biology of the gadwall in northern Utah. *Wilson Bull.* **74**: 43-67.
Gauckler, A. & Krause, M. (1965). (Botaurus stellaris). *Vogelwelt* **86**: 129-146.
Gauckler, A. & Krause, M. (1968). Zur Vorkommen und zur Brutbiologie des Schwarzhalstauchers (*Podiceps nigricollis*) in Nordbayern. *Anz. orn. Ges. Bayern* **8**: 349-364.
Gauthier, G. (1987a). The adaptative significance of territorial behavior in breeding Buffleheads: a test of three hypotheses. *Anim. Behav.* **35**: 348-360.
Gauthier, G. (1987b). Brood territories in Buffleheads: determinants and correlates of territory size. *Can. J. Zool.* **65**: 1402-1410.
Gauthier, G. (1989). The effect of experience and timing on reproductive performance in Buffleheads. *Auk* **106**: 568-576.
Gauthier, G. & Bédard, J. (1985). Fat reserves and condition indices in Greater Snow Gese. *Can. J. Zool.* **63**: 331-333.
Gauthier, G. & Smith, J.N.M. (1987). Territorial behaviour, nest-site availability and breeding density in Buffleheads. *J. Anim. Ecol.* **56**: 171-184.
Gauthreaux, S.A. (1982). The ecology and evolution of avian migration systems. Pp. 93-168 in: Farner, D.S. & King, J.R. (1982). *Avian Biology*. Vol. 6. Academic Press, London & New York.
Gaymer, R. (1966). Aldabra - The case for conserving this coral atoll. *Oryx* **8**: 348-352.
Gee, E.P. (1958). The present status of the White-winged Wood Duck *Cairina scutulata* (S. Müller). *J. Bombay Nat. Hist. Soc.* **55**: 569-574.
Gee, E.P. (1960). The breeding of the Grey & Spotted billed Pelican (*Pelecanus philippensis philippensis* Gmelin). *J. Bombay Nat. Hist. Soc.* **57(2)**: 245-251.
Gehrman, K.H. (1951). *An ecological study of the lesser scaup duck (Aythya affinis Eyton) at West Medical Lake, Spokane County, Washington*. MSc thesis, Washington State College.
Geiger, W. (1957). Die Nahrung der Haubentaucher (*Podiceps cristatus*) des Bielersees. *Orn. Beob.* **54**: 97-133.
Geis, A.D. (1974). *Breeding and Wintering Areas of Canvasbacks Harvested in Various States and Provinces*. US Fish & Wildlife Sevice, Special Science Report Wildlife **139**.
Geis, A.D., Smith, R.I. & Rogers, J.P. (1971). *Black Duck Distribution, Harvest Characteristics and Survival*. US Fish & Wildlife Service, Special Scientific Report Wildlife **139**.
Geldenhuys, J.G. (1976). Physiognomic characteristics of wetland vegetation in South African Shelduck habitat. *S. Afr. J. Wildl. Res.* **6**: 75-78.
Geldenhuys, J.G. (1977). Feeding habits of South African Shelducks. *S. Afr. J. Wildl. Res.* **7**: 5-9.
Geldenhuys, J.G. (1979). *The population ecology of the South African Shelduck* Tadorna cana *(Gmelin 1789) in the Orange Free State*. MSc thesis (Wildlife Management), University of Pretoria.
Geldenhuys, J.G. (1980). Breeding seasons of Egyptian Geese and South African Shelducks in Central South Africa. Pp. 267-275 in: Johnson, D.N. ed. *Proceedings IV Pan-African Ornithological Congress*. Southern African Ornithological Society.
Geldenhuys, J.G. (1981a). Breeding ecology of the South African Shelduck. *S. Afr. J. Wildl. Res.* **10**.
Geldenhuys, J.G. (1981b). Moults and moult localities of the South African Shelduck. *Ostrich* **52**: 129-133.
Geldenhuys, J.N. (1984). Status of the Fish Eagle and Goliath Heron in the Orange Free State, South Africa. Pp 577-587 in: Ledger, J. ed. (1984). *Proceedings of the Fifth Pan-African Ornithological Congress*. Southern African Ornithological Society, Johannesburg.
Gentis, S. (1976). Co-operative nest building by Hamerkops. *Honeyguide* **88**: 48.
Gentz,K. (1959). Zur Lebensweise der Zwergrohrdommel. *Falke* **6**: 39-47.
Gentz,K. (1965). *Die Grosse Dommel*. Wittnberg Lutherstadt.
George, J.C. & Berger, A.J. (1966). *Avian Miology*. Academic Press, London and New York.
Gerell, R. (1985). Habitat selection and nest predation in a Common Eider population in southern Sweden. *Ornis Scand.* **16**: 129-139.
Gerharts, L.D. & Voous, K.H. (1968). Natural catastrophes in the flamingo colony of Bonaire, Netherlands Antilles. *Ardea* **56**: 188-192.
Géroudet, P. (1965). Du "Waldrapp" de Gessner aux Ibis Chauves du Maroc. *Nos Oiseaux* **28**: 129-143.
Géroudet, P. (1972). *Les Palmipèdes*. Delachaux et Niestlé, Neuchâtel, Switzerland.
Géroudet, P. (1978a). *Grands échassiers gallinacés râles d'Europe*. Delachaux et Niestlé, Paris.
Géroudet, P. (1978b). De nouveau des cigognes en Suisse trente ans d'expérience de réintroduction. *Nos Oiseaux* **34(7)**: 311-318.
Gibbs, H.L. & Gibbs, J.P. (1987). Prey robbery by nonbreeding Magnificent Frigatebirds (*Fregata magnificens*). *Wilson Bull.* **99(1)**: 101-104.
Gibbs, H.L., Latta, S.C. & Gibbs, J.P. (1987). Effects of the 1982-1983 El Niño event on Blue-footed and Masked Booby populations on Isla Daphne Major, Galapagos. *Condor* **89**: 440-442.
Gibbs, R.M. (1961). *Breeding Ecology of the Common goldeneye (*Bucephala clangula*) in Maine*. MSc thesis, University of Maine.
Gibson, E. (1919). Further ornithological notes from the neighbourhood of Cape San Antonio, Province of Buenos Ayres. Part II Trochilidae-Plataleidae. *Ibis* **1(11th Ser.)**: 495-537.
Gibson, J.D. (1963). Third report of the New South Wales Albatross Study Group. *Emu* **63**: 215-223.
Gibson, J.D. (1967). The wandering albatross: results of banding and observations in New South Wales coastal waters and the Tasman Sea. *Notornis* **14**: 47-57.
Gibson-Hill, C.A. (1947a). Notes on the birds of Christmas Island. *Bull. Raffles Mus.* **18**: 87-165.
Gibson-Hill, C.A. (1947b). The normal food of tropicbirds (*Phaëthon* spp.). *Ibis* **89**: 658-661.
Gibson-Hill, C.A. (1948). Display and posturing in the Cape Gannet. *Ibis* **90**: 568-572.
Gibson-Hill, C.A. (1949). Notes on the nesting habits of seven representative tropical sea birds. *J. Bombay Nat. Hist. Soc.* **48**: 214-235.
Gibson-Hill, C.A. (1950). The tropic-birds occurring in the Indian Ocean and adjacent seas. *J. Bombay Nat. Hist. Soc.* **49**: 67-80.
Gill, F.B. (1967). Observations on the pelagic distribution of seabirds in the Western Indian Ocean. *Proc. US Natl. Mus.* **123**: 1-33.
Gill, F.B. (1990). *Ornithology*. W.H. Freeman and Company, New York.
Gill, F.B., Jouanin, C. & Storer, R.W. (1970). Notes on the seabirds of Round Island, Mauritius. *Auk* **87**: 514-521.
Gill, F.B., Stokes, F.J. & Stokes, C.C. (1974). Observations on the Horned Screamer. *Wilson Bull.* **86**: 43-50.
Gillespie, G.D. (1985). Hybridization, introgression and morphometric differentation between Mallard (*Anas platyrhynchos*) and Grey Duck (*Anas superciliosa*) in Otago, New Zealand. *Auk* **102**: 459-469.
Gillespie, T.H. (1932). *A Book of King Penguins*. Jenkins, London.
Gillham, E. (1987). *Tufted Ducks in a Royal Park*. E. Gillham, Romney Marsh.
Gillham, M.E. (1963). Breeding habits of the White-faced Storm Petrel in eastern Bass Strait. *Papers & Proc. Royal Soc. Tasmania* **97**: 33-41.
Gilliard, E.T. (1958). *Living Birds of the World*. Doubleday Garden City, New York.
Gilliard, F.T. & Le Croy, M. (1970). Notes on birds from the Tamrau Mountains, New Guinea. *Amer. Mus. Novitates* **2420**: 1-28.
Gilliéron, G. (1974). Étude des Grèbes castagneux, *Podiceps ruficollis*, hivernant dans la basse-plaine du Rhône. *Nos Oiseaux.* **32**: 207-230.
Ginn, H.B. & Melville, D.S. (1983). *Moult in Birds*. BTO Guide **19**. Tring, UK.
Ginn, P.J. (1984). Feeding of the African Openbill. *Honeyguide* **30(3-4)**: 117.
Giol, A. (1957). Cattura di *Bulweria fallax*. *Riv. ital. Orn.* **27**: 118-121.
Giordani, C. (1988). La véritable politique de l'autruche. *Terre Sauvage* **15**: 68-77.
Girard, G.L. (1939). Notes on the life history of the shoveller. Pp. 364-371 in: *Transactions of the 14th North American Wildlife Conference*.
Girard, O. (1990). La Spatule blanche *Platalea leucorodia* dans le marais d'Olonne (Vendée). *L'Oiseau et la R.F.O.* **60(4)**: 286-297.
Gizels, K. (1969). Systematic position of the Screamers (Anseriformes, Anhimidae): Data on immunological analysis of protein composition in lenses. *So. Zool. Zh.* **45**: 1202-1206.
Glade, A.A. ed. (1988). *Red List of Chilean Terrestrial Vertebrates*. Chilean Forest Service (CONAF), Santiago.
Gladstone, P. & Martell, C. (1968). Some field notes on the breeding of the Greater Kelp Goose. *Wildfowl* **19**: 25-31.
Glas, L. & Porper, D. (1986). [Nesting of storks on the Golan Plateau]. *Tzufit (Sunbird)* **4**: 6-15. In Hebrew.
Glauert, L. (1946). The Little Shearwater's year. *Emu* **46**: 187-192.
Glenny, F.H. (1955). Modifications of pattern in the aortic arch system of birds and their phylogenetic significance. *Proc. US Natl. Mus.* **104**: 525-621.
Gliddon, G.R. (1850). Remarks upon the scarcity of *Ibis religiosa* in Egypt. *Proc. Acad. Nat. Sci. Phila.* **5**: 83-84.
Glover, F.A. (1953). Nesting ecology of the Pied-billed Grebe in northwestern Iowa. *Wilson Bull.* **65**: 32-39.
Glover, F.A. (1956). Nesting and production of the blue-winged teal (*Anas discors* Linnaeus) in northwest Iowa. *J. Wildl. Manage.* **20**: 28-46.
Gnam, R.S. (1981). *Ontogeny of Behavior in the Greater Rhea (*Rhea americana albescens*)*. MSc thesis. Fordham University.
Goc, M. (1982). *Ekologia gniazdowania Perkoza dwuczubego* Podiceps cristatus *(L.) na jezioze Druzno*. Dr thesis. University of Gdansk.
Goc, M. (1986). Colonial versus territorial breeding of the great crested grebe *Podiceps cristatus* on Lake Druzno. *Acta Orn.* **22**: 95-145.
Gochfeld, M. (1973). Observations on new or unusual birds from Trinidad, West Indies and comments on the genus *Plegadis* in Venezuela. *Condor* **75**: 474-478.
Gochfeld, M. (1976). (Egretta picata). *Willson Bull.* **88**: 356-357.

Gochfeld, M. (1980). Timing of breeding and chick mortality in central and peripheral nests of Magellanic Penguins. *Auk* **97**: 191-193.
Gochfeld, M. & Burger, J. (1981). Age-related differences in piracy of frigatebirds from Laughing Gulls. *Condor* **83**: 79-82.
Gochfeld, M., Burger, J., Saliva, J. & Gochfeld, D. (1988). Herald Petrel new to the West Indies. *Am. Birds* **42**: 1254-1258.
Godfrey, W.E. (1966). *The Birds of Canada*. National Museum of Canada Bulletin **203**.
Goenka, D. & Pandit, H. (1986). Intimidation among waterbirds at Bharatpur. *J. Bombay Nat. Hist. Soc.* **83(Suppl.) Centenary issue**: 219-220.
Gole, P. (1982). Status of *Anser indicus* in Asia with special reference to India. *Aquila* **89**: 141-149.
Gollop, J.B. & Marshall, W.H. (1954). *A Guide for Aging Duck Broods in the Field*. Miss. Flyway Tech. Sect.
Golombek, D.A., Calcagno, J.A. & Luquet, C.M. (1991). Circadian activity rhythm of the Chinstrap Penguin of Isla Media Luna, South Shetland Islands, Argentine Antarctica. *J. Field Orn.* **62(3)**: 293-298.
Golovkin, A.N. (1984). Seabirds nesting in the USSR: the status and protection of populations. Pp. 473-486 in: Croxall *et al.* (1984).
Gomersall, C.H. (1982). *Breeding Red-throated Divers in Shetland 1982*. Report to the RSPB, Sandy.
Gomersall, C.H. (1986). Breeding performance of the Red-throated Diver *Gavia stellata* in Shetland. *Holarctic Ecol.* **9(4)**: 277-284.
Gomersall, C.H., Morton, J.S. & Wynde, R.M. (1984). Status of breeding Red-throated Divers in Shetland, 1983. *Bird Study* **31**: 223-229.
Gómez-Dallmeier, F. & Cringan, A.T. (1989). *Biology, Conservation and Management of Waterfowl in Venezuela*. Caracas.
Gómez, F. (1979). *Algunos aspectos sobre la ecología del pato güirí pico negro (*Dendrocygna viduata *L.) en el llano inundable alto Apure de Venezuela*. Trabajo especial de grado, Universidad Central Venezuela, Caracas.
Gómez, F. & Rylander, M.K. (1982). Observations on the feeding ecology and bioenergetics of the White-faced Whistling Duck in Venezuela. *Wildfowl* **33**: 17-21.
Gómez, J.A. & Mendoza, Z. (1981). Aspectos generales sobre la reproducción del Piche Real, *Dendrocygna bicolor*, en la laguna del jojotal. El Salvador. Pp. 807-820 in: Actas del VIII Congreso Latinoamericano de Zoología **II**.
Gonzales, P.C. (1983). Birds of the Catanduanes. *Zool. Pap. Nat. Mus. Manila* **2**.
González, J.L. & Merino, M. (1988). Censo de la población española de Cigüeña Negra. *Quercus* **30**.
Gooders, J. & Boyer, T. (1986). *Ducks of Britain and the Northern Hemisphere*. Dragon's World, Surrey, UK.
Gooders, J. ed. (1969-1971). *Birds of the World*. 9 Vols. IPC, London.
Goodfellow, C.F. (1958). Display of the Hamerkop *Scopus umbretta*. *Ostrich* **29**: 1-4.
Goodman, S.M. (1988). A bird of antiquity. *Birder's World* **2**: 26-29.
Goodman, S.M. ed. (1989). *The Birds of Egypt*. Oxford University Press, Oxford.
Goodman, S.M. & Storer, R.W. (1987). The seabirds of the Egyptian Red Sea and adjacent waters, with notes on selected ciconiiformes. *Gerfaut* **77**: 109-145.
Goodman, S.M., Houlihan, P.F. & Helmy, I. (1984). Recent records of the ostrich in Egypt. *Bull. Brit. Orn. Club.* **104(2)**: 39-44.
Goodwin, J. (1956). Observations on some shags. *Notornis* **7**: 21-22.
Gordienko, N.S. (1981). Ocherk ékologii poganok Severnogo Kazakhstana. *Ornitologiya* **16**: 33-41.
Gordienko, N.S. (1982). Polovoe povedenie cernosejnoj poganki (*Podiceps nigricollis*). *Zool. J. Moskva* **61**: 1104-1107.
Gordillo, T. (1980). Decreciente población de fragatas (*Fregata minor*) en la Isla San Cristóbal, Galápagos. *Rev. Univ. Católica Quito*. **27**: 91-98.
Gordillo, T. (1981). Activities of the representative of the Darwin Station on Isla San Cristobal. *Ann. Rep. Charles Darwin Res. Station* **1980**: 36-38.
Gordon, D.H. (1981). *Condition, feeding ecology and behavior of Mallards wintering in north central Oklahoma*. MSc thesis, Oklahoma State University, Stillwater.
Gordon, H.M. (1959). The Whale-headed Stork at close range. *Afr. Wildl.* **13**: 83.
Gore, M.E.J. & Gepp, A.R.M. (1978). *Las aves del Uruguay*. Mosca Hnos, Montevideo.
Gore, M.E.J. & Won P.O. (1971). *The Birds of Korea*. Royal Asiatic Soc., Seoul.
Goriup, P.D. ed. (1988). *Ecology and Conservation of Grassland Birds*. ICBP Technical Publication **7**. Cambridge, England.
Goriup, P.D. & Schulz, H. (1990). *Conservation Management of the White Stork: an International Opportunity*. ICBP Study Report **37**. ICBP, Cambridge.
Goriup, P.D. & Schulz, H. (1991). Conservation management of the White Stork: an international need and opportunity. Pp. 97-127 in: Salathé (1991).
Gosper, D.G. (1981). Survey of birds on floodplain-estuarine wetlands on the Hunter and Richmond rivers in northern New South Wales. *Corella* **5**: 1-18.
Gosper, D.G. (1983). An avifaunal survey of littoral habitats near Ballina, New South Wales. *Corella* **7**: 7-13.
Gosper, D.G., Briggs, S.V. & Carpenter, S.M. (1983). Waterbird dynamics in the Richmond Valley, New South Wales, 1974-77. *Austr. Wildl. Res.* **10**: 319-327.
Goszawski, J., Lepianka, S. & Zbonikowska, E. (1989). Tumours as cause of death of hatchlings of Crested Screamers sovealers (*Chauna torquata*) at Warsaw Zoo. *ERKR Zootiere* **31**: 367-370.
Gosztonyi, A.E. (1984). La alimentación del Pingüino Magallánico (*Spheniscus magellanicus*) en las adyacencias de Punta Tombo, Chubut, Argentina. *C. Nac. Patag. Contrib.* **95**: 1-19.
Götmark, F. (1989). Costs and benefits to Eiders nesting in gull colonies: a field experiment. *Ornis Scand.* **20**: 283-288.
Götmark, F. & Ahlund, M. (1988). Nest predation and nest site selection among eiders *Somateria mollissima*: the influence of gulls. *Ibis* **130**: 111-123.
Götmark, F., Neergaard, R. & Åhlund, M. (1989). Nesting ecology and management of the Arctic Loon in Sweden. *J. Wildl. Manage.* **53(4)**: 1025-1031.
Götmark, F., Neergaard, R. & Åhlund, M. (1990). Predation of artificial and real Arctic Loon nests in Sweden. *J. Wildl. Manage.* **54(3)**: 429-432.
Gotzman, J. (1965). Environmental preference in the grebes (Podicipedidae) during breeding season. *Ekol. Pol. (Ser. A)* **13**: 289-302.
Goudie, R.I. (1989). Historical status of Harlequin Ducks wintering in eastern North America - a reappraisal. *Wilson Bull.* **101**: 112-114.
Goudie, R.I. & Ankney, C.D. (1988). Patterns of habitat use by sea ducks wintering in Southeastern Newfoundland. *Ornis Scand.* **19 (4)**: 249-256.
Goudswaard, R. (1985). Breeding of the North Island brown kiwi (*Apteyx australis mantelli*) at the Wellington Zoo. *Thylacinus* **10**: 9-19.
Goudswaard, R. (1989). Some new developments on breeding the North Island Brown Kiwi (*Apteryx australis mantelli*) at the Wellington Zoo. *Thylacinus* **14(1)**: 3-6.
Gould, P.J. (1967). Nocturnal feeding of *Sterna fuscata* and *Puffinus pacificus*. *Condor* **69**: 529.
Gould, P.J. (1983). Seabirds between Alaska and Hawaii. *Condor* **85**: 286-291.
Gould, P.J. & King, W.B. (1967). Records of four species of *Pterodroma* from the central Pacific Ocean. *Auk* **84**: 591-594.
Gould, P.J., Forsell, D.J. & Lensink, C.J. (1982). *Pelagic Distribution and Abundance of Seabirds in the Gulf of Alaska and Eastern Bering Sea*. Fish & Wildlife Service, Biol. Serv. Progr., US Department of Interior **294**.
Gould, P.J., King, W.B. & Sanger, G. (1974). The Red-tailed Tropicbird (*Phaethon rubricauda*). Pp. 206-277 in: King, W.B. ed. *Pelagic Studies of Seabirds in the Central and Eastern Pacific Ocean*. Smithsonian Contributions to Zoology **158**.
Gräfe, F. (1973). Verbreitung des Grossen Sturmtauchers (*Puffinus gravis*) vor der SE-Küste Grönlands im August 1966. *Vogelwelt* **94**: 175-182.
Grafton, R.N. (1972). Surveying the Bald Ibis. *Fauna and Flora. Pretoria* **23**: 16-19.
Graham, G.L., Graves, G.R., Sculenberg, T.S. & O'Neill, J.P. (1980). Seventeen bird species new to Peru from the Pampas de Heath. *Auk* **97**: 366-370.
Grandy, J.W. (1983). The North American Black Duck (*Anas rubripes*). A Case study of 28 Years of Failure in American Wildlife Management. *Int. J. Study. Anim. Probl* **4(Suppl.)**: 2-35.
Granizo, T. & Hayes, F.E. (1991). Una especie probablemente extinta en el Paraguay: el pato serrucho *Mergus octosetaceus*. *Proc. IV Congress Ornitología Neotropical*.
Grant, C.B. (1914). (Description of Scopus umbretta bannermani). *Bull. Brit. Orn. Club* **35**: 27.
Grant, C.H.B. (1911). List of birds collected in Argentina, Paraguay, Bolivia, and south Brazil, with Field-notes. *Ibis (Ser. 9th)* **5**: 80-137, 317-349, 459-478.
Grant, G.S. & Whittow, G.C. (1983). Metabolic cost of incubation in the Laysan Albatross and Bonin Petrel. *Comp. Biochem. Physiol. (Ser. A)* **74**: 72-82.
Grant, G.S., Pettit, T.N. & Whittow, G.C. (1981). Rat predation on Bonin Petrel eggs on Midway Atoll. *J. Field Orn.* **52**: 336-338.
Grant. G.S., Warham, J., Pettit, T.N. & Whittow, G.C. (1983). Reproductive behaviour and vocalizations of the Bonin Petrel. *Wilson Bull.* **95**: 522-539.
Grassé, P.P. ed. (1950). *Traité de Zoologie. Tome XV: Les Oiseaux*. Masson, Paris.
Grau, C.R. (1982). Egg formation in Fiorland Crested Penguins (*Eudyptes pachyrhynchus*). *Condor* **84**: 172-177.
Gravatt, D.J. (1966). *Ecological Studies of the New Zealand Brown Teal Duck (*Anas chlorotis*) on Great Barrier Island*. IIIB Zoology Project, University of Auckland, New Zealand.
Graves, G.R. (1985). Elevational correlates of speciation and intraspecific geographical variation in plumage in Andean forest birds. *Auk* **102**: 556-579.
Gray, B.J. (1980). *Reproduction, Energetics and Social Structure of the Ruddy Duck*. PhD dissertation, University California, Davis, California.
Gray, H.H. (1965). Sexual behaviour of the Hammerkop. *Bull. Niger. Orn. Soc.* **2**: 82.
Gray, H.J. (1981). *Christmas Island -Naturally-. The Natural History of An Isolated Oceanic Island*. Howard Gray, Geraldton, Western Australia.
Green, A.J. (1990). Progress in the White-winged Wood Duck *Cairina scutulata* Action Plan Project: a call for information. *Wildfowl* **41**: 161-162.
Green, A.J. (1991). Focus on the White-winged Wood Duck. *Oriental Bird Club Bull.* **14**: 25-27.
Green, K. (1986). Food of the Cape Pigeon (*Daption capense*) from Princess Elizabeth Land, East Antarctica. *Notornis* **33**: 151-154.
Green, K. & Johnstone, G.W. (1988). Changes in the diet of Adelie Penguins breeding in East Antarctica. *Aust. Wildl. Res.* **15**: 103-110.
Green, K., Williams, R. & Slip, D.J. (1990). Diet of the Macquarie Island Cormorant *Phalacrocorax atriceps purpurascens*. *Corella* **14(2)**: 53-55.
Green, K., Williams, R., Woehler, E.J., Burton, H.R., Gales, N.J. & Jones, R.T. (1990). Diet of the Heard Island Cormorant *Phalacrocorax atriceps nivalis*. *Antarctic Science* **2(2)**: 139-141.
Green, R.E., Hirons, G.J.M. & Johnson, A.R. (1989). The origin of long-term cohort differences in the distribution of Greater Flamingos *Phoenicopterus ruber roseus* in winter. *J. Anim. Ecol.* **58**: 543-555.
Green, R.H. (1959a). The White Ibis in Tasmania. *Emu* **59**: 58-60.
Green, R,H. (1959b). Starw-necked Ibis in Tasmania. *Emu* **59**: 221.
Greenewalt, C.H. (1968). *Bird Song: Acoustics and Physiology*. The Smithsonian Institution, Washington, D.C.
Greenewalt, C.H. (1975). The Flight of Birds. *Trans. Amer. Philosoph. Soc. New Series* **65(4)**: 1-67.
Greenquist, E.A. (1982). Displays, vocalizations and breeding biology of the Great Grebe (*Podiceps major*). *Condor* **84**: 370-380.
Greenway, J.C. (1967). *Extinct and Vanishing Birds of the World*. 2nd. edition. Dover Publications, Inc., New York.
Gregoire, P.E.J. (1985). *Behavior of Family and other Social Groups in Wintering and Migrating Lesser Snow Geese*. MS thesis, University of Western Ontario, London, Ontario.
Grenmyr, U. (1984). Gråhakedoppingens *Podiceps grisegena* förekomst i norra Sverige. [Summary: The occurrence of Red-necked Grebe in Northern Sweden]. *Vår Fågelvärld* **43**: 27-34.
Gress, F. & Anderson, D.W. (1982). *A Recovery Plan for the California Brown Pelican*. US Fish & Wildlife Service, Washington D.C.
Gress, F. & Lewis, D.B. (1988). Reproductive success of Brown Pelicans in the Southern California Bight. (Contract Report) Wildlife Management Division, State of California, Dept. of Fish and Game, Sacramento.
Gress, F., Risebrough, R.W., Anderson, D.W., Kiff, L.F. & Jehl, J.R. (1973). Reproductive failures of Double-crested Cormorants in Southern California and Baja California. *Wilson Bull.* **85**: 197-208.
Grice, D. & Rogers, J.P. (1965). *The Wood Duck in Massachusetts*. Massachusetts Division Fisheries & Game, Final Report, Project No. W-19-R.
Grice, D., Caughley, G. & Short, J. (1985). Density and Distribution of Emus. *Austr. Wildl. Res.* **12**: 69-73.
Griffin, D.R. (1940). Homing experiments with Leach's Petrels. *Auk* **57**: 61-74.
Griffin, D.R. (1974). *Bird Migration*. Dover, New York.
Griffith, R.E., Childs, V.L. & Cook, F.W. (1946). Roseate Spoonbill nesting on the Sabine Refuge, Louisiana. *Auk* **63**: 259-260.
Griffiths, A.M. (1981). European Stormpetrels *Hydrobates pelagicus* feeding by diving off South Africa. *Cormorant* **9**: 47.
Griffiths, A.M. (1982). Observations of pelagic seabirds feeding in the African sector of the southern ocean. *Cormorant* **10**: 9-14.
Griffiths, A.M. (1983). Factors affecting the distribution of the Snow Petrel and the Antarctic Petrel. *Ardea* **71**: 145-150.
Griffiths, A.M., Siegfred, W.R. & Abrams, R.W. (1982). Ecological structure of a pelagic seabird community in the Southern Ocean. *Polar Biol.* **1**: 39-46.
Grigera, D.E. (1973). Alimentación de la perdiz chica (*Nothura maculosa*) en la pampasia sudoriental. *Physis. Buenos Aires* **32(84)**: 25-36.
Grimmett, R. (1985). News and views: more news on Sumatran wetlands. *Oriental Bird Club Bull.* **2**: 5.
Grimmett, R.F.A. (1987). *A Review of the Problems Affecting Palearctic Migratory Birds in Africa*. ICBP, Cambridge, England.
Grimmett, R.F.A. & Jones, T.A. (1989). *Important Bird Areas in Europe*. ICBP Technical Publication **9**. Cambridge, England.
Griscom, L. (1932). The distribution of bird life in Guatemala. *Bull. Amer. Mus. Nat. Hist.* **64**: 1-439.
Grobler, N. (1981). Possible breeding attempt by lesser flamingos in western Transvaal. *Bokmakierie* **33(3)**: 67.
Groscolas, R. (1978). Study of molt fasting followed by an experimental forced fasting in the Emperor Penguin: relationship between feather growth, body weight loss, body temperatures and plasma fuel levels. *Comp. Biochem. Physiol. (Ser. A)* **61**: 287-295.
Groscolas, R. & Clément, C. (1976). Utilisation des reserves énergétiques au cours de jeûne de la reproduction chez le Manchot Empereur *Aptenodytes forsteri*. *Comptes Rendus Acad. Scienc. Paris. (Ser. D)* **282**: 297-300.
Gross, A.O. (1912). Observations on the Yellow-billed Tropicbird (*Phaethon americanus* Grant) at the Bermuda Islands. *Auk* **29**: 49-71.
Gross, A.O. (1949). The Antillean Grebe at Central Soledad, Cuba. *Auk* **66**: 42-52.
Gross, W.A.O. (1935). The life history cycle of Leach's Petrel on the outer sea islands of the Bay of Fundy. *Auk* **52**: 382-399.
Grubb, T.C. (1972). Smell and foraging in shearwaters and petrels. *Nature* **237**: 404-405.
Grubb, T.C. (1973). Colony location by Leach's Petrel. *Auk* **90**: 78-82.
Grubb, T.C. (1974). Olfactory navigation to the nesting burrow in Leach's Petrel. *Anim. Behav.* **22**: 192-202.
Grubb, T.C. (1979). Olfactory guidance of Leach's Storm Petrel to the breeding island. *Wilson Bull.* **91**: 141-143.
Grummt, W. (1979). Der Grausteisstao. *Falke* **26**: 250-251.
Grummt, W. (1981). Breeding the Marabou Stork *Leptoptilos crumeniferus* at Tierpark Berlin. *Int. Zoo Yb.* **21**: 96-97.
Grummt, W. (1984). Beiträge zur Biologie, speziell zur Fortpflanzungsbiologie der Pelikane. *Zool. Garten N.F., Jena* **54**: 225-312.
Gruson, E.S. (1976). *A Checklist of the Birds of the World*. Collins, London.
Grussu, M. (1987). Nidificazione e Svernamento del Mignattaio *Plegadis falcinellus*, e nidificazione della Sgarza Ciuffetto, *Ardeola ralloides*, in Sardegna. *Riv. ital. Orn.* **57(1-2)**: 62-68.
Grussu, M. & Secci, A. (1986). Prima nidificazione in Italia dell'Airone guardabuoi *Bubulcus ibis*. *Avocetta* **10**: 131-136.
Grzimek, B. ed. (1972-1973). *Grzimek's Animal Life Encyclopedia*. Vols. 7-9, *Birds*. Van Nostrand Reinhold, New York.
Grzimek, M. & Grzimek, B. (1960). Flamingoes censused in East Africa by aerial photography. *J. Wildl. Manage.* **24(2)**: 215-217.
Gudmundsson, F. (1961). Islank Hrnand (Barrow's Goldeneye) and Stromanden (Harlequin). *Nordens Fugle*: Farver **5**: 220-226, 253-260.
Guiler, E.R. (1966). The Breeding of the Black Swan (*Cygnus atratus* Lathqm) in Tasmania with Special Reference to Some Management Problems. *Papers & Proc. Royal Soc. Tasmania* **100**: 31-52.
Guiler, E.R. (1967). The Cape Barren goose, its environment, numbers and breeding. *Emu* **66**: 211-235.
Guiler, E.R. (1974). The conservation of the Cape Barren goose. *Biol. Conserv.* **6**: 252-257.
Guillet, A. (1978). Distribution and conservation of the Shoebill (*Balaeniceps rex*) in the southern Sudan. *Biol. Conserv.* **13**: 39-49.
Guillet, A. (1979). Aspects of the foraging behaviour of the Shoebill. *Ostrich* **50**: 252-255.
Guillet, A. (1984). Ecological and ethological aspects of the nest of the Shoebill. Pp. 231-236 in: Ledger, J. ed. (1984). *Proceedings of the Fifth Pan-African Ornithological Congress*. Southern African Ornithological Society, Johannesburg.
Guillet, A. (1985). Shoebill. Page 534 in: Campbell & Lack (1985).
Guillet, A. (1987). Aspects of the evolution, ecology and ethology of the Shoebill and their bearing on a captive breeding programme. Pp. 221-229 in: Anon. *Proceedings of the Jean Delacour/IFCB Symposium on Breeding Birds in Captivity*. International Foundation for Conservation of Birds.

Guillet, A. & Crowe, T.M. (1981). Seasonal variation in group size and dispersion in a population of Great White Pelicans. *Gerfaut* **71**: 185-194.
Guillet, A. & Crowe, T.M. (1983). Temporal variation in breeding, foraging and bird sanctuary visitation by a southern African population of Great White Pelicans *Pelecanus onocrotalus*. *Biol. Conserv.* **26**: 15-31.
Guillet, A. & Furness, R.W. (1985). Energy requirements of a Great White Pelican (*Pelecanus onocrotalus*) population and its impact on fish stocks. *J. Zoology. London* **A 205**: 573-583.
Guillotin, M. & Jouventin, P. (1979). La parade nuptiale du Manchot Empereuret sa signification biologique. *Biol. Behav.* **4**: 249-264.
Guillotin, M. & Jouventin, P. (1980). Le Pétrel des Neiges à Pointe Géologie. *Gerfaut* **70**: 51-72.
Guillou, J.J. & Pages, J. (1987). Le Flamant nain *Phoeniconaias minor* pénètre à l'intérieur des terres en Afrique de l'Ouest. *Alauda* **55**: 233-234.
Guillou, J.J. & Vielliard, J. (1969). Sur la signification possible de la première observation du Flamant nain (*Phoeniconaias minor*) dans le domaine paléarctique. *Alauda* **37**: 355-357.
Guittin, P. (1987). Croissance de l'autruche en parc zoologique. *Can. J. Zool.* **65(6)**: 1587-1596.
Gunn, S.J.R. & Batt, B.D.J. (1985). Activity budgets of Northern Pintail hens: influence of brood sizes, brood age and date. *Can. J. Zool.* **63**: 2114-2120.
Gunn, W.W.H. (1951). The changing status of the Red-necked Grebe in southern Ontario. *Can. Field-Nat.* **65**: 143-145.
Gurney, J.H. (1913). *The Gannet, a Bird with a History*. London.
Gustin, M. (1988). [Breeding of a Ferruginous Duck, *Aythya nyroca*, in Province of Oristano, W. Sardinia]. *Riv. ital. Ornitol.* **58(3-4)**: 191. In italian.
Gutmann, K.M. (1989). Aufnahme von Vogeleiprofilen mit hilfe eines Lasertrahls sowie Berechnung von volumen und flache durch rechnergestutzte Daten Bearbeitung. *Vogelwarte* **35(2)**: 85-93.
Guttikar, S.N. (1979). Lost Pelicanry. *J. Bombay Nat. Hist. Soc.* **75**: 482-484.
Guyot, I. (1988). Relationships between Shag feeding areas and human fishing activities in Corsica (Mediterranean Sea). Pp. 22-23 in Tasker, M.L. ed. *Seabird Food and Feeding Ecology. Proceedings 3rd. International Conference* Seabird Group, Sandy.
Guyot, I. & Thibault, J.C. (1988). Les oiseaux marins nicheurs de Mediterranée occidentale: répartition, effectifs et recensements. *Bull. Ecol.* **19(2-3)**: 305-320.
Guzmán, H.M. (1986). Feeding areas and relative abundance of the American Flamingo along the coast of Venezuela. *Amer. Birds* **40(3)**: 535-541.
Guzmán, H.M. & Schreiber, R.W. (1987). Distribution and status of Brown Pelicans in Venezuela in 1983. *Wilson Bull.* **99(2)**: 275-279.
Guzman, J.R. & Myres, M.T. (1983). The occurrence of Shearwaters off the west coast of Canada. *Can. J. Zool.* **61**: 2064-2077.
Gwinner, E. (1975). Circadian and circannual rythms in birds. Pp. 221-285 in: Farner, D.S. & King, J.R. (1975). *Avian Biology*. Vol. 5. Academic Press, London & New York.
Gwinner, E. (1990). *Bird Migration. Physiology and Ecophysiology*. Springer.
Gyldenstolpe, N. (1945a). The Bird Faunas of Rio Jurua in Western Brazil. Kungl. *Svenska Vetenskapsakademiens Handligar. Stockholm (III)*. **23**: 41.
Gyldenstolpe, N. (1945b). *A Contribution to the Ornithology of Northern Bolivia*. Almqvist and Amksells Boktryckeri AB, Stockholm.
Gyllin, R. (1965). Något om avledningsbeteende samt lock- och varningsläten hos smådoppingen. [Summary: On injury-feigning and call- and alarm notes of Little Grebe (*Podiceps ruficollis*)]. *Fauna och Flora. Stockholm* **60**: 148-158.
Gysels, H. (1968). Biochemical approach of the central systematic position of the Ciconiiformes. *Ardea* **56**: 267-280.
Haapanen, A., Helminen, M. & Suomalainen, H.K. (1973). Population growth and breeding biology of the whooper swan, *Cygnus, c. cygnus*, in Finland 1950-1970. *Finnish Game Res.* **33**: 39-60.
Haapanen, A., Helminen, M. & Suomalainen, H.K. (1977). The summer behaviour and habitat use of the whooper swan, *Cygnus, c. cygnus*. *Finnish Game Res.* **36**: 49-81.
Haas, F.C. (1991). First Pennsylvania record of Ross' Goose, *Chen rossii*, Lancaster County. *Pa. Birds* **5 (1)**: 19.
Haavie, J.H. (1962). *A Study of the Phylogenetic Relationships of the Flamingos*. MSc thesis. Cornell University.
Hachisuka, M. & Udagawa, T. (1951). Contribution to the ornithology of Formosa, Part II. *Taiwan Mus. (Taipei)* **4**: 1-180.
Hadden, D. (1981). *Bird of the North Salomons*. Handbook **8**. Wau Ecology Institute, Papua New Guinea.
Haedo Rossi, J.A. (1958). (Behavior in captivity). *Contrib. Cient. Fac. Cienc. Exact. y Nat. Univ. Buenos Aires. (Ser. Zool.)* **1(2)**: 37-62.
Haedo Rossi, J.A. (1969). Notas ornitológicas y observaciones sobre la Cigüeña *Euxenura maguari* (Gmelin). *Acta Zool. Lilloana* **25**: 21-28.
Haffenden, A. (1981). Arboreal foraging by a Straw-necked Ibis (*Threskiornis spinicollis*). *Sunbird* **11(3/4)**: 76.
Haffer, J. (1969). Notes on the wing and tail molt of the screamers, the sunbittern and immature guans. *Auk* **85**: 633-638.
Haffer, J. (1975). *Avifauna of Northwestern Colombia, South America*. Bonner Zoologische Monographien **7**. Bonn.
Hafner, H. (1978). Le secces de reproduction de quatre especes d'ardeides *Egretta g. garzetta* L., *Ardeola r. ralloides* Scop., *Ardeola i. ibis* L., *Nycticorax n. nycticorax* L. en Camargue. *La Terre et la Vie* **32**: 279-289.
Hafner, H. & Britton, R.H. (1983). Changes of Foraging Sites by Nesting Little Egrets (*Egretta garzetta* L.) in Relation to Food Supply. *Colonial Waterbirds* **6**: 24-30.
Hafner, H., Boy, V. & Gory, G. (1982). Feeding methods, flock size and feeding succes in the Little Egret *Egretta garzetta* and the Squacco Heron *Ardeola ralloides* in Camargue, Southern France. *Ardea* **70**: 45-54.
Hafner, H., Dugan, P.J. & Boy, V. (1986). Use of Artificial and Natural Wetlands as Feeding Sites by Little Egrets (*Egretta garzetta* L.) in the Camargue Southern France. *Colonial Waterbirds* **9(2)**: 149-154.
Haftorn, S., Bech, C. & Mehlum, F. (1991). Aspects of the Breeding Biology of the Antarctic Petrel *Thalassoica antarctica* and the Krill Requirement of the Chicks, at Svarthamaren in Muhlig-hofmanfjella, Dronning Maud Land. *Fauna Norv. (Ser. C) Cinclus* **14(1)**: 7-22.
Haftorn, S., Mehlum, F. & Bech, C. (1988). Size variation in the Snow Petrel *Pagodroma nivea*. *Notornis* **35**: 109-116.
Hagen, Y. (1952). Birds of Tristan da Cunha. *Results of the Norwegian Scientific Expedition to Tristan da Cunha 1937-1938*. No. 20. Kommisjon Hos Jacob Dybwad, Oslo.
Hagen, Y. (1982). Migration and longevity of Yellow-nosed Albatrosses banded on Tristan da Cunha in 1938. *Ornis Scand.* **13**: 247-248.
Hagenrath, W. & Ribera, M.O. (1985). Los Ciconiidae de Bolivia. *Ecología en Bolivia* **6**: 73-81.
Hagey, L.R., Schteingart, C.D., Ton-Nu, H-T., Rossi, S.S., Odell, D. & Hofmann, A.F. (1990). ß-phocacholic acid in bile; biochemical evidence that the flamingo is related to an ancient goose. *Condor* **92**: 593-597.
Haider, J. (1989). Baer's Pochard in Pakistan. *J. Bombay Nat. Hist. Soc.* **86(1)**: 96-97.
Hails, C. (1987). *Birds of Singapore*. Times Editions, Singapore.
Hainsworth, F.R. (1989). Wing movements and positioning for aerodynamic benefit by Canada Geese flying in formation. *Can. J. Zool.* **67 (3)**. 585-589.
Halchreuter, H. (1990). The role of IWRB and CIC in waterfowl research and conservation. *Baltic Birds* **5 (1)**: 182-192.
van Halewyn, R. & Norton, R.L. (1984). The Status and Conservation of Seabirds in the Caribbean. Pp. 169-222 in: Croxall *et al.* (1984).
Haley, D. ed. (1984). *Seabirds of Eastern North Pacific and Arctic Waters*. Pacific Search Press, Washington.
Hall, A.J. (1987). The breeding biology of the White-chinned Petrel at South Georgia. J. Zoology. London **212**: 605-617.
Hall, E.R. (1925). Pelicans versus fishes in Pyramid Lake. Condor **27**: 147-160.
Hall, M.R., Gwinner, E. & Bloesch, M. (1987). Annual cycles in moult, body mass, luteinizing hormone, prolactin and gonadal steroids during the development of sexual maturity in the White stork (*Ciconia ciconia*). *J. Zoology. London* **211**: 467-486.
Hall, P. (1976). The status of Cape Wigeon *Anas capensis*, Three-banded Plover *Charadrius tricollaris* and Avocet *Recurvirostra avosetta* in Nigeria. *Bull. Niger. Orn. Soc.* **12**: 43.
Hall, P. (1977). Black Duck *Anas sparsa* on Mambilla Plateau, first record for Nigeria. *Bull. Niger. Orn. Soc.* **13**: 80-81.
Hall-Craggs, J. & Sellar, P.J. (1976). Distinguishing characteristics in the burrow-calling of Storm and Leach's Petrels. *British Birds* **69**: 293-297.
Halliday, T. (1978). *Vanishing Birds. Their Natural History and Conservation*. Sidgwick & Jackson, London.
Hallstrom, E. (1956). Breeding of Salvadori's Duck in New Guinea. *Avicult. Mag.* **62**.
Halse, S.A. (1981). Migration by Hutton's Shearwater. *Emu* **81**: 42-44.
Halse, S.A. & Jaensch, R.P. (1989). Breeding Seasons of Waterbirds in South-western Australia - the importance of Rainfall. *Emu* **89**: 232-249.
Hamel, H.D. (1975). Ein Beitrag zur Populationsdynamik des Waldrapps *Geronticus eremita* (L., 1758). *Die Vogelwelt* **96**: 213-221.
Hamel, P.B. (1977). The Wood Stork in South Carolina, a review. *Chat* **41**: 177-179.
Hamilton, D.C. (1972). Strange Hamerkop behaviour. *Honeyguide* **71**: 33, 35.
Hamilton, J.E. (1951). The breeding place of *Pachyptila belcheri*. *Ibis* **93**: 139-140.
Hamilton, L.S. (1970). More on the Giant Pied-billed Grebe of Lake Atitlán, Guatemala. *Biol. Conserv.* **2**: 142-143.
Hamker, K. & Read, H. (1987). Patterns of return to land in a colony of Cory's Shearwater on Selvagem Grande. *Seabird* **10**: 3-11.
Hammond, D.E. & Wood, R.L. (1976). *New Hampshire and the Disappearing Loon*. The Loon Preservation Committee, Meredith.
Hampton, P.D. (1981). *The Wintering Behavior of the Trumpeter Swan*. MSc thesis, University of Montana, Missoula, Montana.
Hanagarth, W. & Friedhelm, W. (1988). Fauna Boliviana 2: Avestruces de Bolivia. *Ecol. Bolivia (Rev. Inst. Ecol.)* **12**: 1-8.
Hancock, J. (1965). African Pink-backed Pelican. *Nat. Hist. New York* **74**: 24-29.
Hancock, J. (1989). Extinction stalks the storks of Asia. *World Birdwatch* **11(1)**: 1.
Hancock, J. & Elliott, H. (1978). *The Herons of the World*. Harper & Row Publishers, London.
Hancock, J. & Kushlan, J. (1984). *The Herons Handbook*. Croom Helm, London & Sidney.
Handford, P.T. & Mares, M.A. (1982). La distribución de las especies de *Rheidae* (Aves, Rheiformes). *Neotropica* **28(79)**: 47-50.
Handford, P.T. & Mares, M.A. (1985). The mating systems of ratites and tinamous: and evolutionary perspective. *Biol. J. Linn. Soc.* **25(1)**: 77-104.
Handrinos, G.I. & Goutner, V. (1990). On the occurrence of the Lesser White-fronted Goose *Anser erythropus* in Greece. *J. Orn.* **131 (2)**: 160-165.
Hands, H.M., Drobney, R.D. & Ryan, M.R. (1989a). *Status of the Least Bittern in the Northcentral United States*. Report to the US Fish & Wildlife Service, Twin Cities, Minnesota.
Hands, H.M., Drobney, R.D. & Ryan, M.R. (1989b). *Status of the American Bittern in the Northcentral United States*. Report to the US Fish & Wildlife Service, Twin Cities, Minnesota.
Hands, H.M., Drobney, R.D. & Ryan, M.R. (1989c). *Status of the Common Loon in the Northcentral United States*. School of Forestry, Fisheries and Wildlife. University of Missouri.
Haneda, K. & Iwasaki, A. (1982). Population Fluctuation and Spatial Distribution of Little Egrets *Egretta garzetta* in the Zenkoji Plain. *Tori* **31**: 41-56.
Haney, J.C. (1985). Band-rumped Storm-petrel occurrences in relation to upwelling off the coast of the south-eastern United States. *Wilson Bull.* **97**: 543-547.
Haney, J.C. (1987). Aspects of the pelagic ecology and behaviour of the Black-capped Petrel (*Pterodroma hasitata*). *Wilson Bull.* **99**: 153-168.
Haney, J.C. (1988). Foraging by Northern Fulmars (*Fulmarus glacialis*) at a Nearshore, Anticyclonic Tidal Eddy in the Northern Bering Sea, Alaska. *Colonial Waterbirds* **11(2)**: 318-321.
Haney, J.C. (1989). Remote Characterization of Marine Bird Habitats with Satellite Imagery. *Colonial Waterbirds* **12(1)**: 67-77.
Haney, J.C. (1990). Winter habitat of Common Loons on the continental shelf of the southeastern United States. *Wilson Bull.* **102(2)**: 253-263.
Haney, J.C. & McGillivary, P.A. (1985). Aggregations of Cory's Shearwaters at Gulf Stream fronts. *Wilson Bull.* **97**: 191-200.
Hanmer, D.B. (1984). Unusual Hamerkop behaviour. *Witwatersrand Bird Club News* **126**: 16.
Hanmer, D.B. (1985). Feeding of the African Openbill. *Honeyguide* **31(3)**: 168.
Hanmer, D.B. (1989). Comments on the Shoebill in Malawi. *Nyala* **14**: 46.
Hanmer, D.B. & Roseveare, Lady M. (1989). First record of the Shoebill *Balaeniceps rex* in Malawi. *Scopus* **12**: 92-93.
Hannecart, F. & Letocart, Y. (1980). *Oiseaux de Nouvelle Calédonie et des Loyautés*. Volume I. Les Editions Cardinalis, Nouméa, Nouvelle-Calédonie. In French & English.
Hannecart, F. & Letocart, Y. (1983). *Oiseaux de Nouvelle Calédonie et des Loyautés*. Volume II. Les Editions Cardinalis, Nouméa, Nouvelle-Calédonie. In French & English.
Hansen, H.A., Shepherd, P.E.K., King, J.G. & Troyer, W.A. (1971). *The Trumpeter Swan in Alaska*. Wildlife Monographs **26**: 1-83.
Hansen, J.L. (1971). *The role of nest boxes in management of the Wood Duck on Mingo National Wildlife Refuge*. MSc thesis, University Missouri, Columbia.
Hansen, K. (1984). The distribution and numbers of the Southern Cormorant *Phalacrocorax carbo sinensis* in Europe. *Dansk Orn. Foren. Tidsskr.* **78**: 29-40.
Hansen, S.G. (1976a). A survey of the Goosander breeding populations in Northern Europe. *Dansk Fugle* 28: 151-163.
Hansen, S.G. (1976b). Some aspects of the migration biology of the Goosanders populations in Northern Europe on basis of existing ringing data. *Dansk Fugle* **28**: 164-178.
Hansen, S.G. (1980a). Breeding status of the Goosander in Norway. *Danske Fugle* 32: 147-151.
Hansen, S.G. (1980b). Selection of nest-sites of the Goosander (*Mergus m. merganser* L.) in Denmark. *Danske Fugle* **32**: 177-192.
Hanson, H.C. (1965). *The Giant Canada Goose*. Southern Illinois University Press, Carbondale.
Hanzák, J. (1952). The Great Crested Grebe, *Podiceps c. cristatus*, its ecology and economic significance. *Acta Mus. Nat. Pragae* **8(B)**: 1-37.
Haramis, G.M. (1975). *Wood Duck* (Aix sponsa) *ecology and management within the green-timber impoundments at Montezuma National Wildlife Refuge*. MSc thesis, Cornell University, Ithaca, New York.
Haramis, G.M. (1990). Breeding ecology of the Wood Duck: a review. Pp: 45-60 in Fredrickson, L.H., Burger, G.V., Havera, S.P., Graber, D.A., Kirby, R.E. & Taylor, T.S. eds. (1990). *Proceedings of the 1988 North American Wood Duck Symp.* St. Louis, MO.
Haramis, G.M. & Malecki, R.A. (1982). A contributing bibliography on the technical literature of the Wood Duck (*Aix sponsa*). *New York Coop. Wildl. Res. Unit., Nat. Resouc. Res. & Ext. Ser.* **18**.
Harcourt, S.A. (1980). Report on a census of the Flightless Cormorant and Galapagos Penguin. *Noticias Galápagos* **32**: 7-11.
Harding, M.A. (1990). Observations of fruit eating by Blue Duck. *Notornis* **37**: 150-152.
Hardy, D.E. (1967). Observations on the Pink-footed Goose in central Iceland, 1966-1969. *Wildfowl* **21**: 18-21.
Hario, M. & Selin, K. (1988). Thirty-year trends in an eider population: timing of breeding, clutch size, and nest site preferences. *Finnish Game Res.* **45 (3)**: 3-10.
Härkönen, T.J. (1988). Food habitat relationship of harbour seals and black cormorants in Skagerrak and Kattegat. *J. Zool., Lond.* **214**: 673-681.
Harley, K.L.S. (1946). Display and nesting of the Little Pied Cormorant at the Brisbane Botanic Gardens. *Emu* **45**: 298-300.
Harper, E.C. & Drabble, L. (1936). Sobre la nidificación de los flamencos (*Phoenicopterus ruber chilensis* Mol.). *Hornero* **6**: 249-253.
Harper, P.C. (1972). The field identification and distribution of the Thin-billed Prion and the Antarctic Prion. *Notornis* **19**: 140-175.
Harper, P.C. (1973). The field identification and supplementary notes on the Soft-plumaged Petrel. *Notornis* **20**: 193-201.
Harper, P.C. (1976). Breeding biology of the Fairy Prion at the Poor Knights Islands, New Zealand. *N. Z. J. Zool.* **3**: 351-371.
Harper, P.C. (1979). Colour vision in the Procellariiformes. *Mauri Ora* **7**: 151-155.
Harper, P.C. (1980). The field identification and distribution of the prions, with particular reference to the identification of storm-cast material. *Notornis* **27**: 235-286.
Harper, P.C. (1983). Biology of the Buller's Shearwater (*Puffinus bulleri*) at the Poor Knights Islands, New Zealand. *Notornis* **30**: 299-318.
Harper, P.C. (1987). Feeding behaviour and other notes on 20 species of Procellariiformes at sea. *Notornis* **34**: 169-192.
Harper, P.C. & Fowler, J.A. (1987). Plastic pellets in New Zealand storm-killed prions, 1958-1977. *Notornis* **34**: 65-70.
Harper, P.C. & Imber, M.J. (1985). Buller's Shearwater. Page 93 in: Robertson (1985).
Harper, P.C. & Kinsky, F.C. (1978). *Southern Albatrosses and Petrels: an Identification Guide*. Price Milburn, Wellington.
Harper, P.C., Watson, G.E. & Angle, J.P. (1972). New records of the Kerguelen Petrel in the South Atlantic and Pacific Oceans. *Notornis* **19**: 56-60.
Harrington, B.A., Schreiber, R.W. & Woolfenden, G.E. (1972). The distribution of male and female Magnificent Frigate-birds *Fregata magnificens* along the Gulf coast of Florida. *Amer. Birds* **26**: 927-931.
Harriot, M.C. (1970). Breeding behavior of the Anhinga. *Florida Naturalist* **43**: 138-142.
Harris, J. (1988). The Storks of Wat Phai Lom. *I.C.F. Bugle* **14**: 1.

Harris, M.P. (1965). Puffinosis among Manx Shearwaters on Skokholm. *British Birds* **58**: 426-434.
Harris, M.P. (1966). Breeding biology of the Manx Shearwater. *Ibis* **108**: 17-33.
Harris, M.P. (1969a). Age at breeding and other observations on the Waved Albatross. *Ibis* **111**: 97-98.
Harris, M.P. (1969b). Breeding Seasons of sea-birds in the Galápagos Islands. *J. Zoology. London* **159**: 145-165.
Harris, M.P. (1969c). The Biology of Storm Petrels in the Galápagos Islands. *Proc. California Acad. Sci. (4th Ser)* **37(4)**: 95-166.
Harris, M.P. (1969d). Food as a factor controlling the breeding of *Puffinus lherminieri*. *Ibis* **111**: 139-156.
Harris, M.P. (1969e). Factors influencing the breeding cycle of the Red-billed Tropicbird in the Galapagos Islands. *Ardea* **57**: 149-157.
Harris, M.P. (1970). The biology of an endangered species, the Dark-rumped Petrel in the Galápagos Islands. *Condor* **72**: 76-84.
Harris, M.P. (1972). Inter-island movements of Manx Shearwaters. *Bird Study* **19**: 167-171.
Harris, M.P. (1973). The biology of the Waved Albatross of Hood Island, Galápagos. *Ibis* **115**: 483-510.
Harris, M.P. (1974a). *A Field Guide to the Birds of Galápagos*. Collins, London.
Harris, M.P. (1974b). A complete census of the Flightless Cormorant *Nannopterum harrisi*. *Biol. Conserv.* **6(3)**: 188-191.
Harris, M.P. (1977). Comparative ecology of seabirds in the Galápagos Archipelago. Pp. 65-76 in Stonehouse, B. & Perrins, C.M. eds. (1977). *Evolutionary Biology*. Macmillan, London.
Harris, M.P. (1979). Population dynamics of the Flightless Cormorant, *Nannopterum harrisi*. *Ibis* **121**: 135-146.
Harris, M.P. (1981). The waterbirds of Lake Junin, central Peru. *Wildfowl* **32**: 137-145.
Harris, M.P. (1982). Promiscuity in the Shag as shown by time-lapse photography. *Bird Study* **29**: 149-154.
Harris, M.P. (1984). Seabirds of the Galápagos. Pp. 191-206 in: Perry, R. ed. *Galápagos*. Key Environment Series. Pergamon Press, London.
Harris, M.P. & Bode, K.G. (1981). Populations of Little Penguins, Short-tailed Shearwaters and other seabirds on Phillip Island, Victoria, 1978. *Emu* **81**: 20-28.
Harris, M.P. & Hansen, L. (1974). Sea-bird transects between Europe and Rio Plate, South America in autumn 1973. *Dansk Orn. Foren. Tidsskr.* **68**: 117-137.
Harris, S.W. (1974). Status, chronology, and ecology of nesting storm petrels in north western California. *Condor* **76**: 249-261.
Harrison, C.J.O. (1977). The limb osteology of the diving petrels and Little Auk as evidence of the retention of characters in morphologically convergent species. *Ardea* **65**: 43-52.
Harrison, C.J.O. (1978). Osteological differences in the leg bones of two forms of *Anhinga*. *Emu* **78**: 230-231.
Harrison, C.J.O. (1988). *The History of the Birds of Britain*. Collins, London.
Harrison, C.J.O. & Walker, C.A. (1982). Fossil birds from the Upper Miocene of northern Pakistan. *Tertiary Res.* **4(2)**: 53-69.
Harrison, C.S. (1979). Short-tailed Albatross, vigil over Torishima Island. *Oceans* **12**: 24-26.
Harrison, C.S. (1990). *Seabirds of Hawaii. Natural History and Conservation*. Comstock Publishing Associates, Ithaca and London.
Harrison, C.S., Hida, T.S. & Seki, M.P. (1983). *Hawaiian Seabird Feeding Ecology*. Wildlife Monographs **85**: 1-71.
Harrison, C.S., Hida, T.S. & Seki, M.P. (1984). The diet of the Brown Booby and Masked Booby on Rose Atoll, Samoa. *Ibis* **126(4)**: 588-590.
Harrison, C.S., Naughton, M.B. & Fefer, S.I. (1984). The Status and Conservation of Seabirds in the Hawaiian Archipelago and Johnson Atoll. Pp. 513-526 in: Croxall *et al.* (1984).
Harrison, C.S., Telfer, T.C. & Sincock, J.L. (1990). Status of Harcourt's storm-petrel (*Oceanodroma castro cryptoleucura*) in Hawaii. *Elepaio* **50**.
Harrison, J.G. (1958). Skull pneumaticity. *Wildfowl Trust Ann. Rep.* **9**: 193-196.
Harrison, M.J.S. & Steele, P. (1989). ICBP/EEC forest conservation mission to Sao Tomé and Príncipe. January-March 1989. Report on conservation education and training. ICBP, Cambridge, England.
Harrison, P. (1985). *Seabirds. An Identification Guide*. Croom & Helm Ltd, Beckenham.
Harrison, P. (1987). *Seabirds of the World: A Photographic Guide*. Christopher Helm, London.
Harrison, T.H. & Hollom, P.A.D. (1932). The Great Crested Grebe enquiry, 1931. *British Birds* **26**: 62-92, 102-131, 142-155, 174-195.
Harrow, G. (1965). Preliminary report on discovery of nesting site of Hutton's Shearwater. *Notornis* **12**: 59-65.
Harrow, G. (1976). Some observations of Hutton's Shearwater. *Notornis* **23**: 269-288.
Harrow, G. (1985). Hutton's Shearwater. Page 99 in: Robertson (1985).
Hartley, P.H.T. (1937). The sexual display of the Little Grebe. *British Birds* **30**: 266-275.
Hartmann, W. (1988). New observations on the Brazilian Merganser *Wildfowl* **39(1988)**: 7-14.
Harvey, W.G. (1972). Woolly-necked Stork *Ciconia episcopus* near Dar es Salaam. *East Afr. Nat. Hist. Soc. Bull.* **Oct**: 169.
Harvey, W.G. (1990). *Birds in Bangladesh*. University Press Limited, Dhaka, Bangladesh.
Harwin, R.M. (1971). Movements of the Knob-billed Duck. *Honeyguide* **68**: 35-37.
Harwood, J. (1977). Summer feeding ecology of Lesser Snow Geese. *J. Wildl. Manage.* **41**: 48-53.
Hasegawa, H. (1978). Recent observations on the Short-tailed Albatross, *Diomedea albatrus*, on Torishima. *J. Yamashina Inst. Orn.* **10**: 58-69.
Hasegawa, H. (1979). Status of the Short-tailed Albatross of Torishima and the Senkaku Retto in 1978/79. *Pac. Seabird Group Bull.* **6**: 23-25.
Hasegawa, H. (1980). Observations on the status of the Short-tailed Albatross, *Diomedea albatrus*, on Torishima in 1977/78 and 1978/79. *J. Yamashina Inst. Orn.* **12**: 59-67.
Hasegawa, H. (1982). The breeding status of the Short-tailed Albatross on Torishima, 1979/80 - 1980/81. *J. Yamashina Inst. Orn.* **14**: 16-24.
Hasegawa, H. (1984a). [*Short-tailed Albatross - the White-winged Wanderer over the Sea*.] Heibon Sha Co., Tokyo.
Hasegawa, H. (1984b). Status and conservation of seabirds in Japan, with special attention to the Short-tailed Albatross. Pp. 487-500 in: Croxall *et al.* (1984).
Hasegawa, H. & DeGange, A.L. (1982). The Short-tailed Albatross, its status, distribution and natural history. *Amer. Birds* **36**: 806-814.
Haseltine, S.D., Fair, J.S., Sutcliffe, S.A. & Swineford, D.M. (1983). Trends in organochlorine and mercury residues in Common Loon (*Gavia immer*) eggs from New Hampshire. *Trans. Northeast. Sect. Wildl. Soc.* **40**: 131-141.
Hatch, J.J. (1984). Rapid increase of Double-crested Cormorants nesting in southern New England. *American Birds* **38**: 984-988.
Hatch, S.A. (1983). Mechanism and ecological significance of sperm storage in the Northern Fulmar with reference to its occurrence in other birds. *Auk* **100**: 593-600.
Hatch, S.A. (1987). Copulation and male guarding in the Northern Fulmar. *Auk* **104**: 450-461.
Hatch, S.A. (1990a). Incubation rythm in the Fulmar *Fulmarus glacialis*: annual variation and sex roles. *Ibis* **132**: 515-524.
Hatch, S.A. (1990b). Time allocation by Northern Fulmars *Fulmarus glacialis* during the breeding season. *Ornis Scand.* **21**: 89-98.
Hatch, S.A. (1990c). Individual variation in behavior and breeding success of Northern fulmars. *Auk* **107**: 750-755.
Hatch, S.A. & Hatch, M.A. (1990). Breeding seasons of oceanic birds in a subarctic colony. *Can. J. Zool.* **68**: 1664-1679.
Hatzilacos, D. (1986). Preliminary data on the breeding and feeding biology of the White Pelican (*Pelecanus onocrotalus*) at Lake Mikri Prespa. *Biologia Gallo-hellenica* **12**: 497-506.
Hauckl, H.H. & Kiel, W.H. (1973). Jabiru in south Texas. *Auk* **90**: 675-676.
Haupt, H. (1981). Das Vorkommen der Seetaucher (Gaviiformes) und des Ohrentauchers (*Podiceps auritus*) im Süden des Bezirkes Frankfurt/O. *Beitr. Vogelk.* **27**: 197-203.
Hausberger, M. & Black, J.M. (1990). Do females turn males on and off in Barnacle Goose social display? *Ethology* **84**: 232-238.
Havel, L.H. (1985). Formation of Feeding Flocks during Winter by Dusky and Taverner's Canada Geese in Oregon. MSc thesis, Oregon State University, Corvallis.
Havel, L.H. & Jarvis, R. (1988). Formation of Feeding Flocks during Winter by Dusky and Taverner's Canada Geese in Oregon. Pp. 91-101 in: Weller (1988).
Havera, S.P. & Kirby, R.E. (1990). Biology of the species. Pp. 377-379 in: Fredrickson, L.H., Burger, G.V., Havera, S.P., Graber, D.A., Kirby, R.E. & Taylor, T.S. eds. (1990). *Proceedings of the 1988 North American Wood Duck Symposium*. St. Louis, MO.
Haverschmidt, F. (1949). *The Life of the White Stork*. E.J. Brill, Leiden.
Haverschmidt, F. (1958). The feeding habits of the Capped Heron (*Pilherodius pileatus*). *Auk* **75**: 214.
Haverschmidt, F. (1962). Notes on some Suriname breeding birds (II). *Ardea* **50**: 173-179.
Haverschmidt, F. (1966). A partial albino of *Crypturellus soui* (Hermann) from Surinam. *Bull. Brit. Orn. Club* **86**: 101.
Haverschmidt, F. (1967). De broedkolonies van de Rode Ibis (*Eudocimus ruber*) in Suriname in 1966. *Ardea* **55**: 141-143.
Haverschmidt, F. (1968). *Birds of Surinam*. Oliver & Boyd, Edinburgh & London.
Haverschmidt, F. (1969a). Notes on the Boat-billed Heron in Surinam. *Auk* **86**: 130-131.
Haverschmidt, F. (1969b). The Roseate Spoonbill breeding in Surinam. *Auk* **86**: 131.
Haverschmidt, F. (1970). The past and present status of the American Flamingo in the Guianas). *Bull. Brit. Orn. Club* **90**: 74-78.
Hawkins, J.M. (1988). The Farewell Spit Gannetry at New Sea Level Colony. *Notornis* **35(4)**: 249-260.
Hayashi, T. (1983). [Straying of Streaked Shearwaters with special reference to seasonal winds.] *Tori* **32**: 21-29.
Hayes, F.N. & Dumbell, G.S. (1989). Progress in Brown Teal *Anas aucklandica chlorotis* conservation. *Wildfowl* **40**: 137-140.
Hayes, F.N. & Williams, M. (1982). The status, aviculture and re-establishment of Brown Teal in New Zealand. *Wildfowl* **33**: 73-80.
Hays, C. (1984a). The Humboldt Penguin in Perú. *Oryx* **18(2)**: 92-95.
Hays, C. (1984b). The Humboldt Penguin (*Spheniscus humboldti*) in Perú and the effects of the 1982-1983 El Niño. MSc. thesis, University of Florida.
Hays, C. (1985). Informe preliminar sobre el status y la distribución del Pinguino de Humboldt en el Perú. In: *9th. Latin American Congress of Zoology*. Arequipa, Perú.
Hays, C. (1986). Effects of the 1982-83 El Niño on Humboldt Penguin colonies in Perú. *Biol. Conserv.* **36**: 169-180.
Hazevoet, C.J. (1990). Notes on new and rare migrants in the Cape Verde Islands. *Bull. Brit. Orn. Club* **110(4)**: 207-212.
Hazevoet, C.J. (1992). Further notes on migrants in the Cape Verde Islands. *Bull. Brit. Orn. Club* **112(1)**: 61-64.
He, B. (1979). [Preliminary observations on Oriental Ibis breeding and ecology]. Special Report of Scientific Experiment **4**. In Chinese.
He, B. (1987). [Preliminary research on hand-rearing Oriental Ibis]. *Chinese Wildlife* **2**: 25. In Chinese.
He Baoqing (1981). [Conditioned reflex training of the White Stork *Ciconia ciconia* and its behavior differentiating humans]. *Chinese J. Zool.* **(2)**: 11. In Chinese.
He Baoquing, Zhang Fu-di *et al.* (1984). [Observations on the reproductive ecology of Pelicans]. *Chinese J. Zool.* **1984(4)**: 19-21. In Chinese.
He Jing-jie (1985). Chinese Merganser *Mergus squamatus*, a rare bird endemic to China. *Nature* 3: 8-9.
Headley, P.C. (1967). *Ecology of the Emperor Goose*. Report of Alaska Cooperative Wildlife Unit, University of Alaska.
Heath, E.G. (1971). *The Grey Goose Wing*. Osprey.
Heath, R.G.M. (1986). A feasibility study of the Jackass Penguin *Spheniscus demersus* (L.) behaviour at sea using radio tracking. M.Sc. thesis, University of Porth Elizabeth, South Africa.
Heath, R.G.M. & Randall, R.M. (1985). Growth of Jackass Penguin chicks (*Spheniscus demersus*) hand reared on different diets. *J. Zoology. London* **A 205**: 91-105.
Heath, R.G.M. & Randall, R.M. (1989). Foraging ranges and movements of Jackass Penguins (*Spheniscus demersus*) established through radio telemetry. *J. Zoology. London* **217**: 367-379.
Heather, B.D. (1982). The Cattle Egret in New Zealand, 1978-1980. *Notornis* **29(4)**: 241-268.
Heather, B.D. (1985). New Zealand Dabchick. Pp. 54-55 in: Robertson (1985).
Heather, B.D. (1988). A South Island puzzle - Where have all the dabchicks gone? *Notornis* **35**: 185-191.
Heather, B.D. (1991). Cattle Egret Numbers in New Zealand, 1986 to 1990. *Notornis* **38(2)**: 165-169.
Hebb, K. (1991). Raising Smew in Captivity. *AAZPA (Am. Assoc. Zool. Parks Aquariums) Reg. Conf. Proc.* **1991**: 638-642.
Hector, J.A.L. (1988). Reproductive endocrinology of albatrosses. Pp. 1702-1709 in: *Proc. XIX Int. Orn. Congr.*
Hector, J.A.L., Follett, B.K. & Prince, P.A. (1986). Reproductive endocrinology of the Black-browed Albatross and the Grey-headed Albatross. *J. Zoology. London* **208**: 237-253.
van Heezik, Y.M. (1988a). Growth and diet of the Yellow-eyed Penguin, *Megadyptes antipodes*. PhD thesis, University of Otago, Dunedin, New Zealand.
van Heezik, Y.M. (1988b). Diet of Adelie Penguins during the incubation period at Cape Bird, Ross Island, Antarctica. *Notornis* **35**: 23-26.
van Heezik, Y.M. (1989). Diet of the Fiordland Crested Penguin during the post-guard phase of chick growth. *Notornis* **36**: 151-156.
van Heezik, Y.M. (1990a). Patterns and variability of growth in the Yellow-eyed Penguin. *Condor* **92**: 904-912.
van Heezik, Y.M. (1990b). Seasonal, geographical and age-related variation in the diet of the Yellow-eyed Penguin *Megadyptes antipodes*. *N. Z. J. Zool.* **17**: 205-215.
van Heezik, Y.M. (1991). A comparison of the Yellow-eyed penguin's growth rates across fifty years: Richdale revisited. *Notornis* **38(2)**: 117-123.
van Heezik, Y.M. & Davis, L.S. (1990). Effects of food variability on growth rates, fledging sizes and reproductive success in the Yellow-eyed Penguin (*Megadyptes antipodes*). *Ibis* 132: 254-365.
van Heezik, Y.M. & Seddon, P.J. (1989). Stomach sampling in the Yellow-eyed Penguin *Megadyptes antipodes*: erosion of otoliths and squid beaks. *J. Field Orn.* **60**: 451-458.
van der Heiden, J.T. (1973). Openbill Storks nesting near Salisbury. *Honeyguide* **76**: 22-25.
van der Heiden, J.T. (1974). Openbill Storks nesting near Salisbury colony at Prince Edward Dam. *Honeyguide* **77**: 33-36.
Heilmann, G. (1926). *The Origin of Birds*. Witherby, London.
Heim de Balsac, H. (1931). La persistance de l'ibis chauve en Algérie. *Alauda* **3**: 71-71.
Heimberger, M., Euler, D. & Barr, J. (1983). The impact of cottage development on Common Loon reproductive success in Central Ontario. *Wilson Bull.* **95**: 431-439.
Heimendahl, A. (1985). *Untersuchungen zur Nestlingsentwicklung des Scharlachsichlers (*Eudocimus ruber*)*. Thesis. University of Hamburg.
Heinrich, J. (1986). Spoon feeder. *Natl. Wildl.* **24**: 38-41.
Heinroth, O. (1911). Beiträge zur Biologie, namentlich Ethologie und Psychologie der Anatiden. *Proc. V. Internat. Orn. Congr.*, Berlin, 1910, 598-702.
Heinzel, H. & Martinoles, D. (1988). Nouvelle nidification de l'Ibis falcinelle *Plegadis falcinellus* en France. *Alauda* **56(4)**: 429-430.
Heinzman, G. & Heinzman, D. (1965). Nesting of the Wood Stork. *Nat. Hist.* **74**: 30-35.
Heitmeyer, M.E. (1985). *Wintering strategies of female Mallards related to dynamics of lowland hardwood wetlands in the upper Mississippi delta*. PhD dissertation, University of Missouri, Columbia.
Heitmeyer, M.E. (1986). Postbreeding Distribution and Habitat Use of Wading Birds in Oklahoma, USA. *Colonial Waterbirds* **9(2)**: 163-170.
Hellmayr, C.E. & Conover, B. (1942). *Catalogue of Birds of the Americas and the Adjacent Islands*. Publications of the Field Museum of Natural History (Zoological Series) **13 pt 1 (1)**.
Hellmayr, C.E. & Conover, B. (1948). *Catalogue of Birds of the Americas and the Adjacent Islands*. Publications of the Field Museum of Natural History (Zoological Series) **13 pt 1 (2)**.
Hémery, G. (1980). Dynamique de la population basque française de Pétrels tempête (*Hydrobates pelagicus*) de 1974 à 1979. *L'Oiseau et la R.F.O.* **50**: 217-218.
Hémery, G. & Jouanin, C. (1988). Statut et origine géographique des populations de Pétrels Culblanc (*Oceanodroma leucorhoa leucorhoa*) présents dans le golfe de Gascogne. *Alauda* **56**(3): 238-245.
Hemetsberger, J. (1989). Bestandsentwicklung und derzeitige Verbreitung des Schwarzstorches (*Ciconia nigra*) in Oberösterreich. [Summary: Population dynamics and present distribution of the Black Stork (*Ciconia nigra*) in Upper Austria.] *Stapfia* **20**: 119-128. In German with English summary.
Hemming, J.E. (1968). Copulatory behavior of the Red-necked Grebe on open water. *Wilson Bull.* **80**: 326-327.
Hemmings, A.D. & Bailey, E.C. (1985). Pursuit diving by Northern Giant Petrels at the Chatham Islands. *Notornis* **32**: 330-331.
Hemmings, A.D. & Chappell, R.G. (1988). Nesting of White-Faced Herons at the Chatham Islands. *Notornis* **35**: 245-247.
Hemmingsen, A.M. (1951). Observations on the migration of the Eastern White Stork (*Ciconia ciconia boyciana* Swinhoe). Pp. 351-353 in: *Proc. X Int. Orn. Congr.*
Henderson, E.G. (1981). *Behavioral ecology of the searching behavior of the White Ibis (*Eudocimus albus*)*. MSc thesis, University of South Carolina, Colombia, South Carolina.
Hennemann, W.W. (1982). Energetics and spread-winged behavior of Anhingas in Florida. *Condor* **84(1)**: 91-96.
Hennemann, W.W. (1983a). Environmental influences on the energetics and behavior of Anhingas and Double-crested Cormorants. *Physiol. Zool.* **56(2)**: 201-216.
Hennemann, W.W. (1983b). Environmental and behavioural influences on the comparative energetics of Anhingas, Double-crested, and Flightless Cormorants. *Dissertation Abstr. Int. (Ser. B)* **43(9)**: 2824.
Hennemann, W.W. (1984). Spread-winged behaviour of Double-crested and Flightless Cormorants *Phalacrocorax auritus* and *P. harrisi*: wing drying or thermoregulation? *Ibis* **126**: 230-239.
Hennemann, W.W. (1985). Energetics, behavior and the zoogeography of Anhingas and Double-crested Cormorants. *Ornis Scand.* **16(4)**: 319-323.

Hennemann, W.W. (1988). Energetics and spread-winged behaviour in Anhingas and Double-crested Cormorants: the risks of generalization. *Amer. Zool.* **28(3)**: 845-851.
Henny, C.J. & Bennett, J.K. (1990). Comparison of breaking strength and shell thickness as evaluators of White-faced Ibis eggshell quality. *Environ. Toxicol. Chem.* **9**: 797-805.
Henny, C.J. & Bethers, M.R. (1971). Population ecology of the Great Blue Heron with special reference to western Oregon. *Can. Field-Nat.* **85**: 205-209.
Henny, C.J. & Herron, G.B. (1989). DDE, selenium, mercury, and White-faced Ibis reproduction at Carson Lake, Nevada. *J. Wildl. Manage.* **53**: 1032-1045.
Henny, C.J. & Holgersen, N.E. (1974). Range expansion and population increase of the Gadwall in eastern North America. *Wildfowl* **25**: 95-101.
Henny, C.J., Blus, L.J. & Hulse, C.S. (1985). Trends and Effects of Organochlorine Residues on Oregon and Nevada Wading Birds, 1979-1983. *Colonial Waterbirds* **8(2)**: 117-128.
Henry, G.M. (1971). *A Guide to the Birds of Ceylon.* Oxford University Press, London.
Henry, P. (1992). Swan Lake. *Int. Wildl.* **2 (1)**.
Henshaw, H.W. (1881). On *Podiceps occidentalis* and *P. clarkii*. *Bull. Nuttall Orn. Club* **6**: 211-216.
Henson, P. & Grant, T.A. (1991). The effects of human disturbance on Trumpeter Swan breeding behaviour. *Wildl. Soc. Bull.* **19(3)**: 248-257.
Hepburn, I.R. & Randall, R.E. (1975). Nest site distribution of the fulmar within the Monach Isles National Nature Reserve, Outer Hebrides, U.K. *J. Biogeogr.* **2**: 223-228.
Hepp, G.R., Kennamer, R.A. & Harvey, W.F. (1990). Incubation as a reproductive cost in female Wood Ducks. *Auk* **107**: 756-764.
Hepp, G.R., Stangohr, D.J., Baker, L.A. & Kennamer, R.A. (1987). Factors Affecting Variation in the Egg and Duckling Components of Wood Ducks. *Auk* **194**: 435-443.
Herd, R.M. & Dawson, T.J. (1984). Fibre digestion in the emu (*Dromaius novaehollandiae*), a large bird with a simple gut and high rates of passage. *Physiol. Zool.* **57**: 70-84.
Herklots, G.A.C. (1961). *The Birds of Trinidad and Tobago.* Collins, London.
Herklots, G.A.C. (1967). *Hong Kong Birds.* S. China Morning Post, Hong Kong.
Herman, S.G. (1973). *Cyclical fluctuations in feeding rates and body weight in captive Western Grebes,* Aechmophorus occidentalis. PhD thesis. University of California, Davis.
Herman, S.G., Garrett, R.L. & Rudd, R.L. (1969). Pesticides and the Western Grebe: 24-53 in: Miller, M.W. & Berg, G.G. eds. *Chemical fallout/current research on persistent pesticides.* Thomas Springfield, Illinois.
Hermes, N. (1985). *Birds of Norfolk Island.* Wonderland Publications, Norfolk Island.
Hermes, N., Evans, O. & Evans, B. (1986). Norfolk Island birds: a review 1985. *Notornis* **33**: 141-149.
Hernández, C. (1978). Comportamiento reproductivo e impacto del turismo en la población de *Fregata minor* de Bahía Darwin, Isla Genovesa, Galápagos. Tesis de Licenciatura, PUCE, Quito, Ecuador.
Hernández, C. & de Vries, T. (1985). Fluctuaciones en la población de fragatas *Fregata minor* en la Bahía Darwin, Genovesa, durante 1975-1983: 239-244. Pp. 239-244 in: Robinson, G. & del Pino, E.M. eds. *El Niño en las Galápagos: el evento de 1982-1983.* Charles Darwin Foundation for the Galapagos Islands, Quito.
Hernández, E., Nogales, M., Quilis, V. & Delgado, G. (1990). Nesting of the Manx Shearwater (*Puffinus puffinus* Brünnich, 1764) on the island of Tenerife (Canary Islands). *Bonn. zool. Beitr.* **41(1)**: 59-62.
Hernández, M.A. & García, J. (1976). Estudio del flamenco en la península de Yucatán. *Bosques y fauna* **13**: 3-13.
Hernández, M.A. & García, J. (1979). *Reproducción y tamaño de la población de Flamencos en Yucatán.* Instituto Politécnico Nacional (Escuela Nacional de Ciencias Biológicas), Mexico, D.F.
Hersloff, L., Lehner, P.N., Bolen, E.G. & Rylander, M.K. (1974). Visual sensitivity in the Black-bellied Tree Duck (*Dendrocygna autumnalis*) a crepuscular species. *J. Comp. Physiol. Psychol.* **86**: 486-492.
Herter, B.R., Johnston, S.M. & Woodman, A.P. (1989). Molt migration of scoters at Cape Peirce, Alaska. *Arctic* **42 (3)**: 248-252.
Hestbeck, J.B. (1990). North-south gradient in survival rates in midcontinental populations of Mallards. *J. Wildl. Manage.* **54**: 206-210.
Hestbeck, J.B., Nichols, J.D. & Malecki, R.A. (1991). Estimates of movement and site fidelity using mark-resight data of wintering Canada Geese. *Ecology* **72 (2)**: 523-533.
Hester, F.E. & Dermid, J. (1973). *The World of the Wood Duck.* J.P. Lippincott Co., New York.
Heubeck, M. & Richardson, M.G. (1980). Bird mortality following the *Esso Bernicla* oil spill, Shetland, December 1978. *Scottish Birds* **11**: 97-107.
Hick, U. (1966). Hatching and rearing of two Great Crested Grebes *Podiceps cristatus* at Cologna Zoo. *Int. Zoo Yb.* **6**: 212-213.
Hickey, G. (1985). To be or not to be? A cassowary or a bird? *Austr. Nat. Hist.* **21(9)**: 394.
Hickman, G.C. (1980). "Huddling" behaviour of three Hamerkops. *Ostrich* **51**: 123-124.
Hidalgo, J. (1991). The Marbled Teal in the Marismas del Guadalquivir, Spain. *IWRB Threatened Waterfowl Research Group Newsletter* **1**: 6.
Hiebl, I. & Braunitzer, G. (1988). Anpassungen von Hamoglobine von Streifengans (*Anser indicus*), Andengans (*Chloephaga melanoptera*) und Sperbergeier (*Gyps rueppellii*) on hypoxische Bedingungen. *J. Orn.* **129 (2)**: 217-226.
Higuchi, H. (1986). Bait-fishing by the Green-backed Heron *Ardeola striata* in Japan. *Ibis* **128(7)**: 285-290.
Higuchi, H. (1988). Individual differences in bait-fishing by the Green-backed Heron *Ardeola striata* associated with territory quality. *Ibis* **130**: 39-44.
Higuchi, H., Sato, F., Matsui, S., Soma, M. & Kanmuri, N. (1991). Satellite tracking of the migration routes of Whistling Swans *Cygnus columbianus*. *J. Yamashina Inst. Orn.* **23**: 7-13.
Hilden, O. (1964). Ecology of duck populations in the island group of Valassaaret, Gulf of Bothnia. *Ann. Zool. Fennici* **1**: 1-279.
Hill, G.J.E. & Barnes, A. (1989). Census and distribution of Wedge-tailed Shearwater *Puffinus pacificus* burrows on Heron Island, November 1985. *Emu* **89**: 135-139.
Hill, W.C.O. (1943). Intergeneric hybrid storks hatched at semi-liberty. *Avicult. Mag.* **8**: 141-144.
Hilsenbeck, S.G. (1979). Food of Silvery Grebes (*Podiceps occipitalis*) at Lake Cuicocha, Ecuador. *Condor* **81**: 316.
Hilty, S.L. (1985). Distributional changes in the Colombian avifauna: a preliminary Blue List. Pp. 1000-1012 in: Buckley *et al.* (1985).
Hilty, S.L. & Brown, W.L. (1986). *A Guide to the Birds of Colombia.* Princeton, New Jersey.
Himmatsinhji, M.K. & Bapat, N.N. (1989). Reappearance of *Anser indicus* and *Tadorna tadorna* in Kutch, Gujarat. *J. Bombay Nat. Hist. Soc.* **86 (3)**: 445.
Hinde, R.A. ed. (1969). *Bird Vocalizations: Their Relation to Current Problems in Biology and Psychology.* Cambridge University Press, New York.
Hinde, R.A. (1973). Behavior. Pp. 479-535 in: Farner, D.S. & King, J.R. (1973). *Avian Biology.* Vol. 3. Academic Press, London & New York.
Hindell, M.A. (1988a). The diet of the Royal Penguin *Eudyptes schlegeli* at Macquarie Island. *Emu* **88**: 219-226.
Hindell, M.A. (1988b). The diet of the King Penguin *Aptenodytes patagonicus* at Macquarie Island. *Ibis* **130**: 193-203.
Hindell, M.A. (1988c). The diet of the Rockhopper Penguin *Eudyptes chrysocome* at Macquarie Island. *Emu* **88**: 227-233.
Hindell, M.A. (1989). The diet of Gentoo Penguins, *Pygoscelis papua*, at Macquarie Island: winter and early breeding season. *Emu* **89**: 71-78.
Hindwood, K.A. & Serventy, D.L. (1941). The Gould Petrel of Cabbage Tree Island. *Emu* **41**: 1-20.
Hine, R.L. & Schoenfeld, C. eds. (1968). *Canada Goose Management.* Dembar Educational Research Services, Madison, Wisconsin, USA.
Hirsch, U. (1976). Beobachtungen am Waldrapp (*Geronticus eremita*) in Marokko und Versuch zur Bestimmung der Alterszusammensetzung von Brutkolonien. *Orn. Beob.* **73**: 225-235.
Hirsch, U. (1978a). Artificial Nest Ledges for Bald Ibises. Pp.61-69 in: Temple, S.A. ed. *Endangered Birds. Management Techniques for Preserving Threatened Species.* The University of Wisconsin Press, Madison & Croom Helm, London.
Hirsch, U. (1978b). Zum Schutz des Waldrapps (*Geronticus eremita*). *J. Orn.* **119**: 465-466.
Hirsch, U. (1979). Studies of West Palearctic Birds. 183: Bald Ibis. *British Birds* **72**: 313-325.
Hirsch, U. (1980). Der Waldrapp *Geronticus eremita*, ein Beitrag zur Situation in seinem östlichen Verbreitungsgebiet. *Vogelwelt* **101**: 219-236.
Hirsch, U. (1983). Waldrapp Ibis, *Geronticus eremita*. Unpublished report to the World Wildlife Fund International. WWF, Gland.
Hirsch, U. (1991). Northern Bald Ibis. *World Birdwatch* **13(3)**: 13.
Hirsch, U. & Schenker, A. (1977). Der Waldrapp (*Geronticus eremita*): Freilandbeobachtungen und Hinweise für eine artgemässe Haltung. *Z. Kölner Zoo* **20(1)**: 3-11.
Hitchins, P.M. (1974). Breeding localities of the Woollynecked Stork in Zululand game reserves. *Lammergeyer* **21**: 47-49.
Ho, C.Y.K., Prager, E.M., Wilson, A.C., Osuga, D.T. & Feeney, R.E. (1976). Penguin evolution: protein comparisons demonstrate phylogenetic relationship to flying aquatic birds. *J. Mol. Evol.* **8**: 271-282.
Hobbs, J.N. (1957a). Feeding habits of some water birds. *Emu* **57**: 216.
Hobbs, J.N. (1957b). Notes on the Pink-eared Duck. *Emu* **57**: 263-268.
Hobbs, J.N. (1958a). Some notes on grebes. *Emu* **58**: 129-132.
Hobbs, J.N. (1958b). Herons and ibis sun-bathing. *Emu* **58**: 286-287.
Hobbs, J.N. (1959). A feeding association between Little Grebe and Black Duck. *Emu* **59**: 207.
Hobbs, J.N. (1961). The birds of south-west New South Wales. *Emu* **61**: 21-55.
Hobson, K.A. & Sealy, S.G. (1985). Diving rhythms and diurnal roosting times of Pelagic Cormorants. *Wilson Bull.* **97(1)**: 116-119.
Hobson, K.A. & Wilson, D. (1985). Colony establishment by Pelagic Cormorants on man-made structures in southwest coastal British Columbia. *Murrelet* **66**: 84-86.
Hobson, K.A., Knapton, R.W. & Lysack, W. (1989). Population, diet and reproductive success of Double-crested Cormorants breeding on Lake Winnipegosis, Manitoba, in 1987. *Colonial Waterbirds* **12(2)**: 191-197.
Hochbaum, H.A. (1944). *The Canvasback on a Prairie Marsh.* Stackpole, Harrisburg, Pa., and Wildlife Management Institute, Washington, D.C.
Hochbaum, H.A. (1955). *Travels and Traditions of Waterfowl.* University Minnesota Press, Minneapolis.
Hockey, P.A.R. & Hallinan, J. (1981). Effect of human disturbance on the breeding behaviour of Jackass Penguins *Spheniscus demersus*. *S. Afr. J. Wildl. Res.* **11**: 59-62.
Hodder, J. & Graybill, M.R. (1985). Reproduction and survival of seabirds in Oregon during the 1982-1983 El Niño. *Condor* **87**: 535-541.
Hodges, C.S.N. (1991). Survey of Nene (*Nesochen sandvicensis*) at Haleakala National Park 1988 through 1990. *Elepaio* **51 (6)**: 38-39.
Hodges, J.I., Conant, B. & Cain, S.L. (1986). *Alaska Trumpeter Swan status report.* US Fish & Wildlife Service, Juneau.
Hodgson, A. (1975). Some aspects of the ecology of the Fairy Penguin *Eudyptula minor novaehollandiae* (Forster 1781) in Southern Tasmania. PhD. thesis, University of Tasmania, Hobart, Australia.
Hodgson, M.E., Jensen, J.R., Mackey, H.E. & Coulter, M.C.(1988). Monitoring Wood Stork foraging habitat using remote sensing and geographic information systems. *Photogrammetric Engineering and Remote Sensing* **54**: 1601-1607.
Hofer, J. & Marti, C. (1988). Beringungsdaten zur Überwinterung des Gänsesägers *Mergus merganser* am Sempachersee: Herkunft, Zugverhalten und Gewicht. *Orn. Beob.* **85**: 97-122.
Hoffman, L. (1955-63). La nidification des Flamants en 1955, 1956, 1957, 1958, 1959, 1960 & 1961, 1962 & 1963. *Terre Vie* **102**: 315-320, **104**: 179-181, **106**: 74-76, **107**: 118-119, **109**: 78-79, **110**: 289-297, **111**: 331-334.
Högström, S. (1970). Svarthakedoppingen *Podiceps auritus* på Gotland. *Vår Fågelvärld* **29**: 60-66.
Hohman, W.L., Taylor, T.S. & Weller, M.W. (1988). Annual Body Weight Change in Ring-necked Ducks (*Aythia collaris*). Pp. 257-270 in: Weller (1988).
Höhn, E.O. (1975). Notes on Black-headed Ducks, Painted Snipe and Spotted Tinamous. *Auk* **92**: 566-575.
Holdaway, R.N. (1980). Royal Spoonbills nesting near Blenheim. *Notornis* **27(2)**: 169.
Hollom, P.A.D., Porter, R. & Christensen, S. (1988). *The Birds of the Middle East & North Africa.* Poyser, London.
Holm, E.R. & Scott, M.L. (1954). Studies on the nutrition of wild waterfowl. *New York Fish Game J.* **1**: 171-187.
Holmes, D.A. (1969). Bird notes from Brunei: December 1967 - September 1968. *Sarawak Mus. J.* **17**: 399-402.
Holmes, D.A. (1976). Record of the White-winged Wood Duck (*Cairina scutulata*) in Sumatra. *Bull. Brit. Orn. Club* **96**: 88.
Holmes, D.A. (1977a). Faunistic notes and further additions to the Sumatran avifauna. *Bull. Brit. Orn. Club* **97(2)**: 68-71.
Holmes, D.A. (1977b). A report on the White-winged Wood Duck in southern Sumatra. *Wildfowl* **28**: 61-64.
Holmes, D.A. (1990a). *The Birds of Sumatra and Kalimantan.* Oxford University Press, Singapore.
Holmes, D.A. (1990b). Note on the occurrence of the White-winged Wood Duck *Cairina scutulata* on the west coast of North Sumatra. *Kukila* **5(1)**: 69-72.
Holmes, D.A. (1991). Note on the status of the White-shouldered Ibis in Kalimantan. *Kukila* **5(2)**: 145-147.
Holmes, D.A. & Burton, K. (1987). Recent notes on the avifauna of Kalimantan. *Kukila* **3**: 2-7.
Holstein, V. (1929). Skehejren, *Platalea leucorodia*, som ynglende i Danmark. *Dan. Orn. Foren. Tidsskr.* **22**: 111-118.
Holton, G.R. (1982). *Habitat Use by Trumpeter Swans in the Grande Prairie Region of Alberta.* MSc thesis, University Calgary, Calgary, Alberta.
Holt, E. (1928). *The Status of the Great White Heron (*Ardea occidentalis Audubon*) and Würdemann's Heron (*Ardea würdemannii Baird*).* Scientific Publications of the Cleveland Museum of Natural History **1(1)**. Cleveland, Ohio.
Holtz, R.E. (1988). A survey of the American bittern at selected wetlands in Washington County. Unpublished report to Minnesota Department Natural Resources, St. Paul.
Holyoak, D. (1970). Comments on the classification of the Old World Ibises. *Bull. Brit. Orn. Club* **90**: 67-73.
Holyoak, D.T. (1973). Significance of colour dimorphism in polynesian populations of "*Egretta sacra*". *Ibis* **115(3)**: 419-420.
Holyoak, D.T. (1980). *Guide to Cook Islands Birds.* Cook Islands.
Holyoak, D.T. & Thibault, J.C. (1984). Contribution à l'étude des oiseaux de Polynésie orientale. *Mem. Mus. Nat. Hist. Paris (Ser. A) Zool.* **127**: 1-209.
Hölzinger, J. & Schmid, G. eds. (1986). Artenschutzsymposium Weißstorch. *Beih. Veröff. Naturschutz Landschaftspflege Bad.-Württ.* **43**. Landesanstalt für Umweltschutz Baden-Württemburg, Institut f. Ökologie u. Naturschutz.
Hom, C.W. (1983). Foraging Ecology of Herons in a Southern San Francisco Bay Salt Marsh. *Colonial Waterbirds* **6**: 37-44.
Hommonay, N. (1959). The spoonbill colonies on the fishponds of the Hortobagy. *Aquila* **66**: 307.
Hoogerheide, J. & Kraak, W.K. (1942). Voorkomen on trek von de Bergeend, *Tadorna tadorna* L., naar aanleiding van veldobservaties aan de Gooije Kust. *Ardea* **31**: 1-19.
Hoogerwerf, A. (1935a). Ornithologische merkwaardigheden in de Brantas Delta. *De Tropische Natuur* **24(6)**: 89-96.
Hoogerwerf, A. (1935b). Broedende Witte Ibissen in West-Java. *De Tropische Natuur* **24**: 163-171.
Hoogerwerf, A. (1937). Uit het leven der Witte Ibissen *Threskiornis aethiopicus melanocephalus*. *Limosa* **10(4)**: 137-146.
Hoogerwerf, A. (1947). Contribution to the knowledge of the distribution of birds on the island of Java. *Treubia* **19**: 83-137.
Hoogerwerf, A. (1949). Bijdrage tot de oologie van Java. *Limosa* **22**: 1-279.
Hoogerwerf, A. (1950). De Witvleugeleend, *Cairina scutulata*, van de Grote Soenda eilanden. *Ardea* **38**: 64-69.
Hoogerwerf, A. (1951). Nieuwe bijzonderheden over het voorkomen van de lepelaar, *Platalea leucorodia regia* Gould, in west-Java. *Limosa* **24**: 91-99.
Hoogerwerf, A. (1952a). Voorkomen van *Nycticorax caledonicus* in W. Java. *Limosa* **25(1/2)**: 29-31.
Hoogerwerf, A. (1952b). De lepelaars (*Platalea leucorodia regia* Gould) van Pulau Dua (West-Java) gedurende het broedseizoen 1952. *Limosa* **25**: 118-131.
Hoogerwerf, A. (1953). Zwarte ibissen, *Plegadis falcinellus peregrinus* (Bp.), in het vogelreservaat Pulau Dua in de jaren 1951 en 1952. [Summary: The first breeding cases of *Plegadis falcinellus* on West-Java]. *Limosa* **26**: 20-30.
Hoogerwerf, A. (1959). Enkele voorlopige mededelingen over de ekstereend, *Anseranas semipalmatus*, in zuid Nieuw-Guinea. *Ardea* **47**: 192-199.
Hoogerwerf, A. (1962). Some particulars on a research on harmful birds in rice crops in south New Guinea. *Bull. Agric. Res. Stn., Manokwari Agric. Ser.* **7**: 1-8.
Hoogerwerf, A. (1964). On birds new for New Guinea or with a larger range than previously known. *Bull. Brit. Orn. Club* **84**: 70-77.
Hoogerwerf, A. (1966). The occurrence of *Nycticorax caledonicus* in Java. *Ardea* **54**: 81-87.
Hoogerwerf, A. (1971). On the ornithology of the Rhino sanctuary Vajung Kulon in West Java (Indonesia). *Nat. Hist. Bull. Siam Soc.* **24(1&2)**: 79-135.
Hopkins, M.N. & Humphries, R.L. (1983). Observations on a Georgia Wood Stork nesting colony. *Oriole* **48**: 36-39.
Hoppe, R.T., Smith, L.M. & Wester, D.B. (1986). Foods of wintering diving ducks in South Carolina. *J. Field. Orn.* **57 (2)**: 126-134.
Hopwood, J.C. (1909-1910). Occurrence of the spoonbill (*Platalea leucorodia*) in lower Burma. *J. Bombay Nat. Hist. Soc.* **19**: 261.
Hori, J. (1964). The breeding biology of the Shelduck *Tadorna tadorna*. *Ibis* **106**: 333-360.
Hori, J. (1969). Social and populations studies in the Shelduck. *Wildfowl* **20: 5-22.**
Horin, O. & Adar, M. (1986). [Survey of the White Stork migration, Israel, Spring 1984]. *Tzufit (Sunbird)* **4**: 17-38, 138. In Hebrew.
Hornberger, F. (1967). *Der Weiss-Storch.* Die Neue Brehm-Bücherei **375**. Ziemsen Verlag, Wittenberg-Lutherstadt.
Horne, R.S.C. (1985). Diet of Royal and Rockhopper Penguins at Macquarie Island. *Emu* **85**: 150-156.

Horwell, G. (1990). Medical problems of ratites. Pp. 228-230 in: *Proc. SAVMA Symp.*
Hoshide, H.M., Price, A.J. & Katahira, L. (1990). A progress report on Nene *Branta sandvicensis* in Hawaii Volcanoes National Park from 1974-1989. *Wildfowl* **41** 152-155.
Houde, P. (1986). Ostrich ancestors found in the Northern Hemisphere suggest new hypothesis of ratite origins. *Nature* **324**: 563-565.
Houston, D.C. (1980). Interrelations of African scavenging animals. Pp. 307-312 in: Johnson, D.N. ed. *Proceedings of the Fourth Pan-African Ornithological Congress*. Southern African Ornithological Society, Johannesburg.
Howard, G.W. & Aspinwall, D.R. (1984). Aerial censuses of Shoebills, Saddlebilled Storks and Wattled Cranes at the Bangweulu Swamps and Kafue Flats, Zambia. *Ostrich* **55**: 207-212.
Howard, H. (1950). Fossil evidence of avian evolution. *Ibis* **92**: 1-21.
Howard, H. (1975). Fossil anseriformes. Pp: 233-326, 371-378 in Delacour, J. ed. *The Waterfowl of the World*. Vol. 4. Country Life, London.
Howard, H.E. (1920). *Territory in Bird Life*. John Murray, London.
Howard, R. & Moore, A. (1991). *A Complete Checklist of the Birds of the World*. 2nd edition. Academic Press, London & New York.
Howell, S.N.G. & de Montes, B.M. (1989). Status of the Glossy Ibis in Mexico. *American Birds*, **43(1)**: 43-45.
Howell, S.N.G. & Webb, S. (1992). New and noteworthy bird records from Guatemala and Honduras. *Bull. Brit. Orn. Club* **112(1)**: 42-49.
Howell, T.R. (1978). Ecology and reproductive behavior of the Gray Gull of Chile and of the Red-tailed Tropicbird and White Tern of Midway Island. *Natl. Geogr. Soc. Res. Rep.* **1978**: 251-284.
Howell, T.R. (1984). Tropicbirds. Family Phaethontidae. Pp. 66-73 in: Haley (1984).
Howell, T.R. & Bartholomew, G.A. (1961a). Temperature regulation in Laysan and Black-footed Albatrosses. *Condor* **63**: 185-197.
Howell, T.R. & Bartholomew, G.A. (1961b). Temperature regulation in nesting Bonin Petrels, Wedge-tailed Shearwaters and Christmas Island Shearwaters. *Auk* **78**: 343-354.
Howell, T.R. & Bartholomew, G.A. (1962). Temperature regulation in the Red-tailed Tropic Bird and in the Red-footed Booby. *Condor* **64**: 6-18.
Howell, T.R. & Bartholomew, G.A. (1969). Experiments on nesting behavior of the Red-tailed Tropicbird (*Phaethon rubricauda*). *Condor* **71**: 113-119.
Howes, J. (1986). Sarawak. *Interwader* **7**: 6.
Howland, H. & Sivak, J.G. (1984). Penguin vision in air and water. *Vision Res.* **24**: 1905-1909.
Hoy, G. (1980). Notas nidobiologicas del noroeste Argentino. 2. *Physis (Sec. C). Buenos Aires* **39(96)**: 63-66.
Hoyer, E. (1991). [Pairing in *Ixobrychus minutus*]. *Falke* **38(1)**: 6-10. In German.
del Hoyo, J. (1989). Ibis Eremita. El mensajero de Noé al borde de la extinción. *Quercus* **43**: 28-33.
Hoyt, D.F., Board, R.G., Rahn, H. & Paganelli, C.V. (1979). The eggs of the Anatidae: conductance, pore structure, and metabolism. *Physiol. Zool.* **52**: 438-450.
Hoyt, R.D. (1906). Nesting of the Roseate Spoonbill in Florida. *Warbler* **2**: 58-59.
Hren, B.J. (1991). Report on the Dusky Canada Goose. *IWRB Threatened Waterfowl Research Group Newsletter* **1**: 4-5.
Hubaut, D. (1986). Parade aérienne de la Cigogne noire (*Ciconia nigra*). *Aves* **23**: 184.
Hubbard, J.F. (1976). Status of the Night Herons *Nycticorax spp.* of the Philippines and vicinity. *Nemouria* **19**. Delaware Museum.
Hubbs, C.L., Kelly, A.L. & Limbaugh, C. (1970). Diversity in feeding by Brandt's Cormorant near San Diego. *Calif. Fish Game* **53**: 156-165.
Huber, L.N. (1971). Notes on the migration of the Wilson's Storm Petrel near Eniwetok Atoll, Western Pacific Ocean. *Notornis* **18**: 38-42.
Hübner, v.T. & Putzer, D. (1985). Störungsökologische Untersuchungen rastender Kormorane an niederrheinischen Kiessen bei Störungen durch Kiestransport, Segel-, Surf- und Angelsport. *Seevögel* **6**: 122-126. With English summary.
Hudec, K. & Rooth, J. (1970). *Die Graugans (*Anser anser*)*. Neue Brehm-Bücherei **429**. A. Ziemsen Verlag, Wittenberg, Lutherstadt.
Hudec, K. & Touskova, I. (1969). Breeding distribution and biology of the Pintail *Anas acuta* Linnaeus 1758 in Czechoslovakia. *Zool. Listy* **18**: 253-262.
Hudson, G.E., Schreiweis, D.O., Wang, S.Y.C. & Lancaster, D.A. (1972). A numerical study of the wing and leg muscles of tinamous (Tinamidae). *Northwest Sci.* **46(3)**: 207-255.
Hudson, R. (1966). Adult survival estimates for two Antarctic Petrels. *Brit. Antarct. Surv. Bull.* **8**: 63-73.
Hudson, R. (1976). Ruddy Ducks in Britain. *British Birds* **69**: 132-143.
Hudson, R. (ed.) (1975). *Threatened Birds of Europe*. Macmillan, London.
Hudson, W.H. (1920). *Birds of La Plata*. Vol. 2. Dent, London.
Hüe, F. & Etchécopar, R.D. (1962). Comportement sexuel de l'Ombrette (*Scopus umbretta*). *L'Oiseau et la R.F.O.* **32**: 274-275.
Hüe, F. & Etchécopar, R.D. (1970). *Les Oiseaux du Proche et du Moyen Orient*. Éditions N. Boubée & Cie, Paris.
Hughes, M.R. (1984). Further notes on Puna bird species on the coast of Peru. *Condor* **86**: 93.
Hughes, R. & Owen, A. (1988). Hand-rearing the Scarlet Ibis *Eudocimus ruber*. *Avicult. Mag.* **94**: 96-100.
Hughes, R.A. (1970). Notes on the birds of the Mollendo District, southwest Peru. *Ibis* **112**: 229-241.
Hughes, R.A. (1984). Further notes on Puna bird species on the coast of Peru. *Condor* **86**: 93.
Hugues, B. (1991). Status of the Scaly-sided Merganser in the Soviet Far East. *IWRB Threatened Waterfowl Research Group Newsletter* **1**: 9-11.
Hui, C.A. (1983). Swimming in penguins. Ph.D. diss., University of California, Los Angeles.
Hui, C.A. (1985). Maneuverability of the Humbolt Penguin (*Spheniscus humbolti*) during swimming. *Can. J. Zool.* **63**: 2165-2167.
Hui, C.A. (1987). The porpoising of penguins: an energy-conserving behaviour for respiratory ventilation? *Can. J. Zool.* **65**: 209-211.
Hui, C.A. (1988). Penguin swimming. *Physiol. Zool.* **61(4)**: 333-350.
Humburg, D.D., Graber, D.A. & Babcock, K.M. (1985). Factors affecting autumn and winter distribution of Canada Geese. *Trans. North Am. Wildl. Nat. Res. Conf.* **50**: 525-539.
Humphrey, P.S. (1955). *The relationships of the Sea-ducks (tribe Mergini)*. Unpubl. PhD thesis, University of Michigan, Ann Arbor.
Humphrey, P.S. (1957). Observations on the diving of the Surf Scoter (*Melanitta perspicillata*). *Auk* **74**: 392-394.
Humphrey, P.S. (1958). Classification and systematic position of the eiders. *Condor* **60 (2)**: 129-135.
Humphrey, P.S. & Livezey, B.C. (1982). Molts and plumages of flying steamer-ducks (*Tachyeres patachonicus*). *Occas. Pap. Mus. Nat. Hist. Univ. Kansas* **103**.
Humphrey, P.S. & Livezey, B.C. (1983). Giant Petrels nesting in Chubut, Argentina. *Gerfaut* **73**: 3-8.
Humphrey, P.S. & Livezey, B.C. (1985). Nest, eggs, and downy young of the White-headed Flightless Steamer-Duck. Pp. 949-954 in: Buckley *et al.* (1985).
Humphrey, P.S. & Parkes, K.C. (1963). Plumages and systematics of the Whistling Heron (*Syrigma sibilatrix*). Pp. 84-90 in: *Proc. XIII Int. Orn. Congr.*
Humphrey, P.S. & Ripley, S.D. (1962). The affinities of the Pink-headed Duck. *Postilla* **61**: 1-21.
Humphrey, P.S. & Thompson, M.C. (1981). A new species of steamer-duck (*Tachyeres*) from Argentina. *Occas. Pap. Mus. Nat. Hist. Univ. Kansas* **95**.
Humphrey, P.S., Bridge, D., Reynolds, P.W. & Peterson, R.T. (1970). *Birds of Isla Grande (Tierra del Fuego)*. Smithsonian Institution, Washington, D.C.
Humphrey, P.S., Rasmussen, P.C. & López, N. (1988). Fish surface activity and pursuit-plunging by Olivaceus Cormorants. *Wilson Bull.* **100(2)**: 327-328.
Humphrey, R.C. (1987). Range expansion and new breeding record for the Glossy Ibis in Massachusetts. *Bird Obsr. Mass.* **15**: 173-177.
Humphrey, S.R. & Bain, J.R. (1990). *Endangered Animals of Thailand*. Sandhill Crane Press, Gainesville, Florida.
Hunt, G.L., Gould, P.J., Forsell, D.J. & Peterson, H. (1981). Pelagic distribution of marine birds in the eastern Bering Sea. Pp. 689-718 in: *The Eastern Bering Sea Shelf: Oceanography & Resources*. Vol. 2. University Wash. Press, Seattle.
Hunter, E.N. (1970). Great Northern Diver breeding in Scotland. *Scottish Birds* **6**: 195.
Hunter, E.N. & Dennis, R.H. (1972). Hybrid Great Northern x Black-throated Diver in Wester Ross. *Scottish Birds* **7**: 89-91.
Hunter, L.A. (1988). Status of the endemic Atitlan Grebe of Guatemala: Is it extinct? *Condor* **90**: 906-912.
Hunter, M.G. (1985). Status of Clark's Grebe. *Oregon Birds* **11**: 136.
Hunter, S. (1983a). The food and feeding ecology of the giant petrels *Macronectes halli* and *M. giganteus* at South Georgia. *J. Zoology. London* **200**: 521-538.
Hunter, S. (1983b). Interspecific breeding in giant petrels at South Georgia. *Emu* **82** (Suppl.): 312-314.
Hunter, S. (1984a). Moult of the giant petrels *Macronectes halli* and *M. giganteus* at South Georgia. *Ibis* **126**: 119-132.
Hunter, S. (1984b). Breeding biology and population dynamics of giant petrels *Macronectes* at South Georgia (Aves, Procellariiformes). *J. Zoology. London* **203**: 441-460.
Hunter, S. (1984c). Movements of giant petrels ringed at South Georgia. *Ringing & Migration* **5**: 105-112.
Hunter, S. (1987). Species and sexual isolation mechanisms in sibling species of giant petrels. *Polar Biol.* **7**: 295-301.
Hunter, S. (1991). The impact of avian predator-scavengers on King Penguin *Aptenodytes patagonicus* chicks at Marion Island. *Ibis* **133**: 343-350.
Hurlbert, S.H. (1978). Results of five flamingo censuses conducted between November 1975 and December 1977. *Andean Lake & Flamingo Invest. Tech. Rep.* **1**: 1-16. San Diego State University.
Hurlbert, S.H. (1981). Results of three flamingo censuses conducted between December 1978 and July 1980. *Andean Lake & Flamingo Invest. Tech. Rep.* **2**: 1-9. San Diego State University.
Hurlbert, S.H. (1982). Limnological studies of flamingo diets and distributions. *Natl. Geogr. Soc. Res. Rep.* **14**: 351-356.
Hurlbert, S.H. & Chang, C.C. (1983). Ornitholimnology: Effects of grazing by the Andean flamingo (*Phoenicoparrus andinus*). *Proc. Natl. Acad. Sci.* **80**: 4766-4769.
Hurlbert, S.H. & Keith, J.O. (1979). Distribution and spatial patterning of flamingos in the Andean altiplano. *Auk* **96**: 328-342.
Hurlbert, S.H., Loayza, W. & Moreno, T. (1986). Fish-flamingo-plankton interactions in the Peruvian Andes. *Limnol. Oceanogr.* **31(3)**: 457-468.
Hurlbert, S.H., Lopez, M. & Keith, J.O. (1984). Wilson's phalarope in the Central Andes and its interaction with the Chilean flamingo. *Rev. Chilena Hist. Nat.* **57**: 47-57.
Hurxthal, L. (1979). *Breeding behaviour of the Ostrich,* Struthio camelus massaicus, *in Nairobi Park*. PhD thesis. Nairobi University.
Hurxthal, L. (1986). Our Gang, Ostrich Style. *Nat. Hist.* **12**: 34-40.
Hutchinson, L.V. & Wenzel, B.M. (1980). Olfactory guidance in foraging by Procellariiformes. *Condor* **82**: 314-319.
Huxley, J.S. (1914). The courtship habits of the Great Crested Grebe (*Podiceps cristatus*); with an addition to the theory of sexual selection. Pp. 491-562 in: *Proc. Zool. Soc. London. 1914*.
Huxley, J.S. (1924). Some further notes on the courtship behaviour of the Great Crested Grebe. *British Birds* **18**: 129-134.
Huxley, J.S. (1947). Display of the Mute Swan. *British Birds* **40**: 130-134.
Huxley, J.S. (1960). The Open-bill's bill: a teleonomic enquiry. *Zool. Jahrb. Abt. Syst. Oekol. Geogr. Tiere* **88**: 9-30.
Huxley, J.S. (1962). The Openbill Stork *Anastomus oscitans*. *Ibis* **104**: 112.
Huyskens, G. & Maes, P. (1971). La migración de aves marinas en el NW de España. *Ardeola* **(Special vol.)**: 155-180.
Hyde, D.O. ed. (1974). *Raising Wild Ducks in Captivity*. Dutton & Co., New York.
van Ijzendoorn, A.L.J. (1951). The Mute Swan in Holland. *Audubon* **53**: 164-172.
van Ijzendoorn, E.J. (1979). Voorkomen van Geelsnavelduiker *Gavia adamsii* in Nederland. *Dutch Birding* **1(4)**: 90-93.
Ilicev, V.D. & Flint, V.E. (1985). *Handbuch der Vögel der Sowjetunion*. Vol. 1. Aula-Verlag, Wiesbaden.
Im, B.H. & Hafner, H. (1984). Impact des oiseaux piscivores et plus particulièrement du Grand Cormorant *Phalacrocorax carbo sinensis* sur les explotations piscicoles en Camargue, France. Rapport CEE, Station Biologique de la Tour de Valat, Arles.
Imber, M.J. (1973). The food of Grey-faced Petrels, with special reference to diurnal vertical migration of their prey. *J. Anim. Ecol.* **42**: 645-662.
Imber, M.J. (1975). Behaviour of petrels in relation to the moon and artificial lights. *Notornis* **22**: 302-306.
Imber, M.J. (1976a). Comparison of prey of the black *Procellaria* petrels of New Zealand. *New Zealand J. Mar. Freshwater Res.* **10**: 119-130.
Imber, M.J. (1976b). Breeding biology of the Grey-faced Petrel *Pterodroma macroptera gouldi*. *Ibis* **118**: 51-64.
Imber, M.J. (1976c). The origin of petrel stomach oils: a review. *Condor* **78**: 366-369.
Imber, M.J. (1981). Diets of stormpetrels *Pelagodroma* and *Garrodia* and of prions *Pachyptila*. Pp. 63-88 in: Cooper, J. ed. *Proceedings of the Symposium on Birds of the Sea and Shore*. African Seabird Group, Cape Town.
Imber, M.J. (1983). The lesser petrels of Antipodes Islands, with notes from Prince Edward and Gough Island. *Notornis* **30**: 283-298.
Imber, M.J. (1984a). Migration of White-faced Storm-Petrels *Pelagodroma marina* in the South Pacific and the status of the Kermadec subspecies. *Emu* **84**: 32-35.
Imber, M.J. (1984b). Trematode anklets on White-faced Storm-Petrels and Fairy Prions. *Cormorant* **12**: 71-74.
Imber, M.J. (1984c). The age of Kerguelen Petrels found in New Zealand. *Notornis* **31**(2): 89-91.
Imber, M.J. (1984d). Exploitation by rats *Rattus* of eggs neglected by gadfly petrels *Pterodroma*. *Cormorant* **12**: 82-93.
Imber, M.J. (1985a). Origins, phylogeny and taxonomy of the gadfly petrels *Pterodroma* spp. *Ibis* **127**: 197-229.
Imber, M.J. (1985b). Grey-faced Petrel. Page 72 in: Robertson (1985).
Imber, M.J. (1985c). Cook's Petrel. Pp. 80-81 in: Robertson (1985).
Imber, M.J. (1985d). Chatham Island Petrel. Page 81 in: Robertson (1985).
Imber, M.J. (1985e). Black Petrel. Page 90 in: Robertson (1985).
Imber, M.J. (1985f). Fluttering Shearwater. Page 100 in: Robertson (1985).
Imber, M.J. (1985g). Little Shearwater. Page 101 in: Robertson (1985).
Imber, M.J. (1985h). White-faced Storm Petrel. Page 104 in: Robertson (1985).
Imber, M.J. (1987). Breeding ecology and conservation of the Black Petrel (*Procellaria parkinsoni*). *Notornis* **34**: 19-39.
Imber, M.J. & Jenkins, J.A.F. (1981). The New Caledonian Petrel. *Notornis* **28**: 149-160.
Imber, M.J. & Lovegrove, T.G. (1982). Leach's Storm Petrels prospecting for nest sites at the Chatham Islands. *Notornis* **29**: 101-108.
Imber, M.J. & Nilsson, R.J. (1980). South Georgian Diving Petrels breeding on Codfish Island. *Notornis* **27**: 325-330.
Imber, M.J. & Russ, R. (1975). Some foods of the Wandering Albatross. *Notornis* **22**: 27-36.
Imber, M.J., Merton, D.V., West, J.A. & Tennyson, A.J.D. (1991). Juan Fernandez Petrels prospecting at the Chatham Islands. *Notornis* **38(1)**: 60-62.
Imboden, C. & Parish, D. (1986). The Milky Stork recovery action plan. Unpublished project proposal. ICBP.
Immelmann, K. (1971). Ecological aspects of periodic reproduction. Pp. 341-389 in: Farner, S.D. & King, J.R. (1971). *Avian Biology*. Vol. 1. Academic Press, London & New York.
van Impe, J. (1969). Concentration énorme de *Podiceps nigricollis* Brehm, en Dubroudja, Roumanie. *Alauda* **37**: 77-79.
van Impe, J. (1978). La rupture de la cohesion familiale chez l'Oie Rieuse, *Anser albifrons albifrons*, dans les quarties d'hivernage. *Le Gerfaut* **68**: 651-679.
Inglis, I.R. & Lazarus, J. (1981). Vigilance and flock size in Brent Geese: The edge effect. *Z. Tierpsychol.* **57**: 193-200.
Inglis, I.R., Lazarus, J. & Torrance, R. (1989). The pre-nesting behaviour and time budget of the Harlequin Duck *Histrionicus histrionicus*. *Wildfowl* **40**: 55-73.
Ingram, G.S.C. & Salmon, M.H.M. (1941). The diving habits of ducks and grebes. *British Birds* **35**: 22-28.
Inkapatanakul, W. (1986). Factors influencing the survival of the Asian Open-billed Stork *Anastomus oscitans* (Boddaert) fledging at Wat Phai Lom and Wat Umpuwaran Non-Hunting Area, Pathun Thani Province (Thailand). MSc thesis, Kasetsart University, Bangkok.
Innes, J.G., Heather, B.D. & Davies, L.J. (1982). Bird distribution in Tongariro National Park and environs - January 1982. *Notornis* **29**: 93-99.
Inoue, Y. (1981). Food competition and survival of asynchronously hatched siblings in the Little Egret *Egretta garzetta*. *J. Yamashina Inst. Orn.* **13(2)**: 42-57.
Inskipp, C. (1989). *Nepal's Forest Birds: Their Status and Conservation*. ICPB Monograph **4**. Cambridge, England.
Inskipp, C. & Inskipp, T. (1985). *A Guide to the Birds of Nepal*. Croom Helm, Beckenham.
Inskipp, T., Broad, S. & Luxmoore, R. (1988). *Significant Trade in Wildlife: a Review of Selected Species in CITES Appendix II*. Vol. 3: Birds. IUCN & CITES, Cambridge.
Irwin, M.P.S. (1975). Adaptative morphology in the Black and Slaty Egrets *Egretta ardesiaca* and *Egretta vinaceigula*, and relationships within the genus *Egretta* (Aves: Ardeidae). *Bonn. Zool. Beitr.* **26**: 155-163.
Irwin, M.P.S. (1984). Recent reports. *Honeyguide* **30(3-4)**: 133-137.
Isenmann, P. (1970). Contribution à la biologie de reproduction du Pétrel des Neiges. Le problem de la petite et de la grande forme. *L'Oiseau et la R.F.O.* **40** (No. Spéc.): 99-134.
Isenmann, P. (1971). Contribution à l'éthologie et à l'écologie du Manchot Empereur (*Aptenodytes forsteri* Gray) à la colonie de Pointe Géologie (Terre Adélie). *L'Oiseau et la R.F.O.* **41**: 9-64.
Iskander, J. (1985). Survey of waders, herons, egrets, storks, and terns in southeastern coast of Sumatra, Indonesia. Pp. 108-117 in: *Proceedings of the III East-Asian Bird Protection Conference*.
Itoh, S. (1986). [Records of the Oriental Ibis *Threskiornis melanocephalus* in Japan]. *Tori* **34**: 127-143. In Japanese with English summary.

Itzkowitz, M. & Makie, D. (1986). Food provisioning and foraging behavior of the snowy egret, *Egretta thula*. *Biology of Behaviour* **11**: 111-115.
IUCN (1990). *1990 IUCN Red List of Threatened Animals*. IUCN, Gland, Switzerland and Cambridge, England.
Ives, P.P. (1947). *Domestic Geese and Ducks*. New York.
Ivey, G.L. & Severson, D.J. (1984). White-faced ibis nesting in the southern San Joaquin Valley of California. *The Condor* **86**: 492-493.
Ivey, G.L., Stern, M.A. & Carey, C.G. (1988). An increasing White-faced Ibis population in Oregon. *Western Birds* **19**: 105-108.
van Jaarsveld, J. (1979). The Bald Ibis. *Fauna and Flora. Pretoria* 35: 12-13.
van Jaarsveld, J. (1980). Bald Ibis - a master of the air. *Afr. Wildl.* **34(6)**: 20-23.
Jablonski, B. (1985). The diet of penguins on King George Island, South Shetland Islands. *Acta Zool. Cracov.* **29(8)**: 117-186.
Jablonski, B. (1987). Diurnal pattern of changes in the number of penguins on land and the estimation of their abundance (Admiralty Bay, King George I., South Shetland Islands). *Acta Zool. Cracov.* **30(8)**: 97-118.
Jackson, E.E., Ogilvie, M.A., Owen, M. (1974). The Wildfowl Trust expedition to Spitsbergen, 1973. *Wildfowl* **25**: 102-116.
Jackson, F., Siegfried, W.R. & Cooper, J. (1976). A simulation model for the population dynamics of the Jackass Penguin. *Trans. Royal Soc. S. Africa* **42(1)**: 11-21.
Jackson, Sir F.J. (1938). *The Birds of Kenya Colony and the Uganda Protectorate*. 1. Gurney & Jackson, London.
Jackson, J.A. (1983). Establishment and loss of a nesting colony of Anhingas at Noxubee National Wildlife Refuge, Mississippi. *Miss. Kite* **13(2)**: 13-14.
Jackson, R. (1958). The Westland Petrel. *Notornis* **7**: 230-233.
Jackson, S. (1984). Predation by Pied Kingfishers and Whitebreasted Cormorants on fish in the Kosi estuary system. *Ostrich* **55**: 113-132.
Jackson, S. (1986). Assimilation efficiencies of White-chinned Petrels (*Procellaria aequinoctialis*) fed different prey. *Comp. Biochem. Physiol.* **85A**: 301-303.
Jackson, S. (1988). Diets of the White-chinned Petrel and Sooty Shearwater in the southern Benguela Region, South Africa. *Condor* **90**: 20-28.
Jackson, S. & Ryan, P.G. (1986). Differential digestion rates of prey by White-chinned Petrels (*Procellaria aequinoctialis*). *Auk* **103**: 617-619.
Jacob, J. & Glaser, A. (1975). Chemotaxonomy of Anseriformes. *Biochem. System. & Ecology* **2**: 215-220.
Jacob, J. & Pomeroy, D.E. (1979). The feather lipids of the Marabou Stork (*Leptoptilos crumeniferus*). *Comp. Biochem. Physiol.* **64**: 301-303.
Jacob, J.P. (1982). Dénombrement et évolution de la population de Grèbes castagneux (*Tachybaptus ruficollis*) nicheurs en Brabant. *Aves* **19(4)**: 239-244.
Jacob, J.P. (1983). Progression du Grebe huppé (*Podiceps cristatus*) comme nicheur en Wallonie et en Brabant. *Aves* **20(1)**: 1-24.
Jacobs, J. (1953). Nidification du Grèbe oreillard *Podiceps caspicus* (Hablizl) en Campine belge. *Gerfaut* **43**: 2-12.
Jacobs, P. & Ochando, B. (1979). Repartition geographique et importance numerique des Anatidés hivernantes en Algèrie. *Gerfaut* **69**: 239-251.
Jacot-Guillarmod, C. (1965). The Openbill *Anstomus lamelligerus* in the Eastern Cape Province. *Ostrich* **36**: 138.
Jaensch, R.P. (1989). Little Bittern *Ixobrychus minutus* breeding at Bool lagoon, 1984-1986. *S. Austr. Orn.* **30**: 205-209.
Jairaj, A.P. & Sanjeev Kumar, V.K. (1990). Occurrence of Spoonbill *Platalea leucorodia* Linn. in Kerala. *J. Bombay Nat. Hist. Soc.* **87(2)**: 289-290.
James, P. (1963). Freeze loss in the Least Grebe (*Podiceps dominicus*) in the lower Rio Grande Delta of Texas. *Southwestern Naturalist* **8**: 45-46.
James, P.C. (1984). Sexual dimorphism in the voice of the British Storm Petrel. *Ibis* **126**: 89-92.
James, P.C. (1985). The vocal behaviour of the Manx Shearwater. *Z. Tierpsychol.* **67**: 269-283.
James, P.C. (1986a). How do Manx Shearwaters find their burrows? *Ethology* **71**: 287-294.
James, P.C. (1986b). Little Shearwaters in Britain and Ireland. *Brit. Birds* **79**: 28-33.
James, P.C. & Alexander, M. (1984). Madeiran Little Shearwater prospecting on Skomer Island, U.K. *Ardea* **72**: 236-237.
James, P.C. & Robertson, H.A. (1985a). Sexual dimorphism in the voice of the Little Shearwater *Puffinus assimilis*. *Ibis* **127**: 388-390.
James, P.C. & Robertson, H.A. (1985b). The call of male and female Madeiran Storm-Petrels (*Oceanodroma castro*). *Auk* **102**: 391-393.
James, P.C. & Robertson, H.A. (1985c). The call of Bulwer's Petrel and the relationship between intersexual call divergence and aerial calling in the nocturnal Procellariiformes. *Auk* **102**: 878-882.
James, P.C. & Robertson, H.A. (1985d). First record of Swinhoe's Storm Petrel *Oceanodroma monorhis* in the Atlantic Ocean. *Ardea* **73**: 105-106.
James, P.C. & Robertson, H.A. (1985e). Soft-plumaged Petrels (*Pterodroma mollis*) at Great Salvage Island. *Bull. Brit. Orn. Club* **105**: 25-26.
James, R.A. (1989). Mate feeding in wintering Western Grebes. *J. Field Orn.* **60**: 358-360.
Jameson, W. (1958). *The Wandering Albatross*. Hart-Davis, London.
Janda, J. & Mlusil, P. (1990). [Contribution to the Knowledge of Extent of Damage Caused by the Fish-eating Birds in Pounds]. *Tichodroma* **3**: 57-76. In Czech with English summary.
Janez, G. (1987). Black Stork (*C. nigra*) breeding at Ljubljiana Morass. *Acrocephalus* **33**: 37-39.
Janzen, D.H. ed. (1983). *Costa Rican Natural History*. The University of Chicago Press, Chicago & London.
Jarvis, M.J.F. (1971a). *Ethology and Ecology of the South African Gannet*. PhD thesis, Cape Town.
Jarvis, M.J.F. (1971b). The ecological significance of clutch size in the South African Gannet. *J. Anim. Ecol.* **43**: 1-17.
Jarvis, M.J.F. (1971c). Interactions between Man and the South African Gannet. *Ostrich* **8 (Suppl.)**: 497-513.
Jarvis, M.J.F. (1972). The systematic position of the South African Gannet. *Ostrich* **43**: 211-216.
Jarvis, M.J.F., Jarvis, C. & Keffen, R.H. (1985). Breeding seasons and laying patterns of the southern African Ostrich. *Ibis* **127**: 442-449.
Jennings, M.C. (1986). The distribution of the extinct Arabian Ostrich *Struthio camelus syriacus* Rothschild, 1919. *Fauna Saudi Arabia* **8**: 447-461.
Jehl, J.R. (1971). The color patterns of downy young ratites and tinamous. *Trans. San Diego Soc. Nat. Hist.* **16(13)**: 291-302.
Jehl, J.R. (1972). On the cold trail of an extinct petrel. *Pacific Discovery* **25**: 24-29.
Jehl, J.R. (1973a). The distribution of marine birds in Chilean waters in winter. *Auk* **90**: 114-135.
Jehl, J.R. (1973b). Studies of a declining population of Brown Pelicans in northwestern Baja California. *Condor* **75**: 69-79.
Jehl, J.R. (1974a). Aerial feeding by a shearwater. *Auk* **91**: 188-189.
Jehl, J.R. (1974b). The near-shore avifauna of the middle American west coast. *Auk* **91**: 681-699.
Jehl, J.R. (1974c). The distribution and ecology of marine birds over the continental shelf of Argentina in winter. *Trans. San Diego Soc. Nat. Hist.* **17**: 217-234.
Jehl, J.R. (1975). Mortality of Magellanic Penguins in Argentina. *Auk* **92**: 596-598.
Jehl, J.R. (1982). The biology and taxonomy of Townsend's Shearwater, *Puffinus auricularis*. *Gerfaut* **72**: 121-135.
Jehl, J.R. (1984). Conservation problems of seabirds in Baja California and the Pacific Northwest. Pp. 41-48 in: Croxall *et al.* (1984).
Jehl, J.R. (1988). Biology of the Eared Grebe and Wilson's Phalarope in the nonbreeding season: a study of adaptations to saline lakes. *Studies in Avian Biology* **12**: 1-74. Cooper Ornithological Society.
Jehl, J.R. & Bond, S.I. (1983). Mortality of Eared Grebes in winter of 1982-83. A piece of deductive analysis on the causes of a massive grebe die-off on the southern Pacific coast. *Amer. Birds* **37**: 832-835.
Jehl, J.R. & Everett, W.T. (1985). History and status of the avifauna of Isla Guadalupe, Mexico. *Trans. San Diego Soc. Nat. Hist.* **20**: 313-336.
Jehl, J.R. & Yochem, P.K. (1986). Movements of Eared Grebes indicated by banding recoveries. *J. Field Orn.* **57(3)**: 208-212.
Jehl, J.R., Chase, C. & Yochem, P.K. (1987). Survey of Eared Grebe and Wilson's Phalarope staging areas, 1985-1986. *Sea World Research Inst. Tech. Report*: 87-198.
Jehl, J.R., Todd, F.S., Rumboll, M.A.E. & Schwartz, D. (1979). Pelagic birds in the South Atlantic Ocean and at South Georgia in the austral autumn. *Gerfaut* **69**: 13-27.
Jenkin, P.M. (1957). The filter-feeding and food of flamingos (*Phoenicopteri*). *Phil. Trans. Roy. Soc. London* **240B**: 401-493.
Jenkins, D., Newton, I. & Brown, C. (1976). Structure and dynamics of a Mute Swan population. *Wildfowl* **27**: 77-82.
Jenkins, J.A.F. (1974). Local distribution and feeding habits of Buller's Shearwater. *Notornis* **21**: 109-120.
Jenkins, J.A.F. (1979). Observations on the Wedge-tailed Shearwater in the southwest Pacific. *Notornis* **26**: 331-348.
Jenkins, J.A.F. (1982). A note on the winter distribution of the White-headed Petrel. *Sea Swallow* **31**: 37-38.
Jenkins, J.A.F. (1988). The distribution of Buller's Shearwater (*Puffinus bulleri*) in New Zealand coastal waters and in the Tasman Sea. *Notornis* **35**: 203-215.
Jenkins, J.A.F & Cheshire, N.G. (1982). The Black-winged Petrel (*Pterodroma nigripennis*) in the South-West Pacific and the Tasman Sea. *Notornis* **29**: 293-310.
Jenkins, J.M. (1983). *The Native Forest Birds of Guam*. Ornithological Monographs **31**. The American Ornithologists' Union, Washington, D.C.
Jenni, D.A. (1969). Diving times of the Least Grebe and Masked Duck. *Auk* **86**: 355-356.
Jenni, D.A. & Gambs, R.D. (1974). Diving times of grebes and Masked Ducks. *Auk* **91**: 415-417.
Jennings, M.C., Fryer, R.N. & Stagg, A.J. (1982). Birds of Saudi Arabia. First breeding record of the pink-backed pelican, *Pelecanus rufescens* Gmelin, from Arabia. *Fauna of Saudi Arabia* **4**: 478-482.
Jensen, J.R., Hodgson, M.E., Coulter, M.C. & Mackey, H.E. (1989). Feasibility study of Wood Stork foraging habitat mapping using Landsat multispectral data. Pp. 1059-1068 in: Sharitz, R.R. & Gibbons, J.W. eds. *Freshwater Wetlands and Wildlife*. D.O.E. Symposium Series **61**. U.S.D.O.W., Oak Ridge, Tenn.
Jenssen, B.M. & Ekker, M. (1990). Effects of plumage oiling on thermoregulation in Common Eiders residing in air and in water. *Trans. Congr. Int. Union Game Biol.* **19(1)**: 281-287.
Jida, N., Maruyama, N., Oka, N. & Kuroda, N. (1987). [Structure of a Colony of Streaked Shearwaters on Mikura Island. *J. Yamashina Inst. Orn.* **19**: 56-76.
Jimbo, S. (1957). A flora na alimentaçao das aves brasileiras: II alimentaçao da codorna (*Nothura maculosa maculosa*). *Papeis avulsos* **13**: 99-108.
Jing Bo (1982). Visiting the "sacred ibis" on the shores of the Pushi-he (Liaoning Province). *Wildlife* **4**: 66-67.
Jobanek, G.A. (1987). Early records of the White-faced Ibis in Oregon. *Oregon Birds* **13**: 210-215.
Joensen, A.H. (1973). Moult migration and wing-feather moult of seaducks in Denmark. *Danish Rev. Game Biol.* **8**: 1-42.
Jogi, A., Lipsberg, J. & Nedzinskas, V. (1974). Numbers and seasonal distribution of the East Baltic population of the Mute Swan. In: Kumari, E. ed. (1974). *Material of the Conference on the Study and Conservation of Migratory Birds in the Baltic Basin*. Academy Sciences Estonian S.S.R., Tallinn.
Johansen, O. (1975). Forholdet mellom hekke- og overvintringssteder hos toppskarv i Norge som vist ved ringmerkingsgjenfunn. [Summary: The relation between breeding grounds and wintering grounds in the Shag, *Phalacrocorax aristotelis*, in Norway as shown by ringing recoveries]. *Sterna* **14**: 1-21.
Johnsgard, P.A. (1960a). The systematic position of the Ringed Teal. *Bull. Brit. Orn. Club* 80: 165-167
Johnsgard, P.A. (1960b). Comparative behaviour of the Anatidae and its evolutionary implications. *Wildfowl Trust Ann. Rep.* **11**: 31-45.
Johnsgard, P.A. (1960c). Hybridization in the Anatidae and its taxonomic implications. *Condor* **62**: 25-33.
Johnsgard, P.A. (1960d). A quantitative study of sexual behavior of Mallard and Black Ducks. *Wilson Bull.* **72**: 133-155
Johnsgard, P.A. (1961a). The breeding biology of the Magpie Goose. *Wildfowl Trust Ann. Rep.* 12: 92-103.
Johnsgard, P.A. (1961b). The sexual behavior and systematic position of the Hooded Merganser. *Wilson Bull.* **73**: 226-236.
Johnsgard, P.A. (1961c). The systematic position of the Marbled Teal. *Bull. Brit. Orn. Club* **81**: 37-41.
Johnsgard, P.A. (1961d). The taxonomy of the Anatidae. A behavioural analysis. *Ibis* **103a**: 71-85.
Johnsgard, P.A. (1961e). Tracheal anatomy of the Anatidae and its taxonomic significance. *Wildfowl* **12**: 59-69.
Johnsgard, P.A. (1961f). Evolutionary relationships among the North American Mallards. *Auk* **78**: 3-43.
Johnsgard, P.A. (1962). Evolutionary trends in the behaviour and morphology of the Anatidae. *Wildfowl* **13**: 130-148.
Johnsgard, P.A. (1963). Behavioral isolating mechanisms in the family Anatidae. Pp. 531-534 in: Sibley, C.G. (1963). *Proc. XIII Int. Orn. Congr.* American Ornithologists' Union.
Johnsgard, P.A. (1964a). Comparative behavior and relationships of the eiders. *Condor* **66**: 113-129.
Johnsgard, P.A. (1964b). Observations on the breeding biology of the spectacled Eider. *Wildfowl Trust Ann. Rep.* **15**: 104-107.
Johnsgard, P.A. (1965a). *Handbook of Waterfowl Behavior*. Cornell University Press, Ithaca, New York.
Johnsgard, P.A. (1965b). Observations on some aberrant Australian Anatidae. *Wildfowl Trust Ann. Rep.* **16**:73-83.
Johnsgard, P.A. (1966a). The biology and relationships of the Torrent Duck. *Wildfowl* **17**: 66-74.
Johnsgard, P.A. (1966b). Behavior of the Australian Musk Duck and Blue-billed Duck. *Auk* 83: 98-110.
Johnsgard, P.A. (1967). Observations on the behaviour and relationships of the White-backed Duck and the Stiff-tailed Ducks. *Wildfowl Trust Ann. Rep.* **18**: 98-107.
Johnsgard, P.A. (1968a). *Waterfowl: their Biology and Natural History*. University of Nebraska Press, Lincoln.
Johnsgard, P.A. (1968b). Some observations on Maccoa Duck behavior. *Ostrich* **39**: 219-222.
Johnsgard, P.A. (1974). *Song of the North Wind: A Story of the Snow Goose*. Doubleday, New York.
Johnsgard, P.A. (1975). *Waterfowl of North America*. Indiana University Press, Bloomington.
Johnsgard, P.A. (1978). *Ducks, Geese, and Swans of the World*. University of Nebraska Press, Lincoln and London.
Johnsgard, P.A. (1979). Anseriformes. Pp. 425-506 in: Mayr & Cottrell (1979).
Johnsgard, P.A. (1987). *Diving Birds of North America*. University of Nebraska Press, Lincoln & London.
Johnsgard, P.A. & Hagemeyer, D. (1969). The masked duck in the United States. *Auk* **84**: 691-695.
Johnsgard, P.A. & Kear, J. (1968). A review of parental carrying of young by waterfowl. *Living Bird* **7**: 89-102.
Johnsgard, P.A. & Nordeen, C. (1981). Display behaviour and relationships of the Argentine Blue-billed Duck. *Wildfowl* **32**: 5-9.
Johnson, A. & Chebez, J.C. (1985). Sobre la situación de *Mergus octosetaceus* Vieillot (Anseriformes: Anatidae) en la Argentina. *Hist. Nat.* **1(Suppl.)**: 1-16.
Johnson, A.R. (1966). Les Flamants en 1964 et 1965. *Terre Vie* **20**: 255-257.
Johnson, A.R. (1970-1976). La nidification des Flamants de Camargue en 1968 & 1969, 1970 & 1971, 1972 & 1973, 1974 & 1975. *Terre Vie* **24**: 594-603, **27**: 95-101, **29**: 113-115, **30**: 593-598.
Johnson, A.R. (1977). La reproduction des Flamants roses en 1977. *Courrier Parc Nat. Rég. Camargue* **12**: 4-12.
Johnson, A.R. (1978). Les flamants roses: la reproduction en Camargue en 1978 et quelques réflexions sur l'abondance actuelle de l'espèce dans le delta. *Courrier Parc Nat. Rég. Camargue* **16**: 20-25.
Johnson, A.R. (1979a). L'importance des zones humides algériennes pour les Flamants roses (*Phoenicopterus ruber roseus*). In: *Semin. Int. Avifauna Algerienne, 5-11 Juin 1979*.
Johnson, A.R. (1979b). Greater Flamingo (*Phoenicopterus ruber roseus*) ringing in the Camargue and an analysis of recoveries. *Ring* **100**: 53.58.
Johnson, A.R. coord. (1980). ICBP-IWRB Flamingo Working Group. Old World. *Newsletter* **1**: 1-15.
Johnson, A.R. (1983). *Etho-écologie du Flamant Rose (*Phoenicopterus ruber roseus *Pallas) en Camargue et dans l'Ouest Paléarctique*. Doctoral thesis. Université Paul Sabatier de Toulouse.
Johnson, A.R. (1984). La nidification des Flamants roses en Camargue. *Courrier Parc Nat. Rég. Camargue* **27**: 19-21.
Johnson, A.R. (1989a). Movements of greater flamingos in the Western Palearctic. *Rev. Ecol. (Terre Vie)* **44**: 75-94.
Johnson, A.R. (1989b). Population studies and conservation of Greater Flamingos in the Camargue. Pp. 49-63 in: Spaans, A.L. *Wetlands en watervogels*. Pudoc, Wageningen, The Netherlands.
Johnson, A.R., Green, R.E. & Hirons, J.M. (1991). Survival rates of Greater Flamingos in the west Mediterranean region. Pp. 249-271 in: Perrins *et al.* (1991).
Johnson, A.W. (1963). Notes on the distribution, reproduction and display of the Andean torrent duck, *Merganetta armata*. *Ibis* **105**: 114-116.
Johnson, A.W. (1965) *The Birds of Chile and Adjacent Regions of Argentina, Bolivia and Peru*. Vol. 1. Platt Establecimientos gráficos, Buenos Aires.
Johnson, A.W. (1967). *The Birds of Chile and Adjacent Regions of Argentina, Bolivia and Peru*. Vol. 2. Platt Establecimientos Gráficos, Buenos Aires.
Johnson, A.W. (1972). *Supplement to the Birds of Chile and Adjacent Regions of Argentina, Bolivia and Peru*. Platt Establecimientos Gráficos, Buenos Aires.
Johnson, A.W., Behn, F. & Millie, W.R. (1958). The South American Flamingos. *Condor* **60(5)**: 289-299.
Johnson, D.H. & Sargeant, A.B. (1977). *Impact of Red Fox Predation on the Sex Ratio of Prairie Mallards*. Wildlife Research Report **6**. US Fish & Wildlife Service, Washington, D.C.
Johnson, D.H., Nichols, J.D., Conroy, M.J. & Cowardin, L.M. (1988). Some Considerations in Modeling the Mallard Life Cycle. Pp. 9-20 in: Weller (1988).
Johnson, F.A., Montalbano, F., Truitt, J.D. & Eggeman, D.R. (1991). Distribution, abundance, and habitat use by Mottled Ducks in Florida. *J. Wildl. Manage.* **55 (3)**: 476-482.
Johnson, J.C. & Raveling, D.G. (1988). Weak Family Associations in Cackling Geese during Winter: Effects of Body Size and Food Resources on Goose Social Organization. Pp. 71-89 in: Weller (1988).
Johnson, J.M. (1985). A large flock of migrating White Storks. *J. Bombay Nat. Hist. Soc.* **81**: 466-467.
Johnson, K., Bednarz, J.C. & Zack, S. (1987). Crested penguins: why are first eggs smaller? *Oikos* **49(3)**: 347-349.
Johnson, K., Healey, E. & Bednarz, J.C. (1989). Crested penguin egg dimorphism: reply to Williams. *Oikos* **55(1)**: 141-142.
Johnson, R. & Luthin, C.S. (1990). Ciconiidae-current world report and use of Yellow-billed Stork (*Mycteria ibis*) as a model species for captive management of endangered storks. Pp. 93-104 in: Dresser, B.L., Reece, R.W &

Maruska, E.J. eds. *Proceedings 5th World Conference on Breeding Endangered Species in Captivity*. Cincinnati Zoo, Ohio.
Johnson, R.E., Coulter, M.C., Luthin, C.S., King, C.E. & Valenzuela, A.J. (1987). Storks: status, conservation and captive breeding. *Colonial Waterbirds* **10(2)**: 236-241.
Johnson, R.F. & Sloan, N.F. (1976). The effects of human disturbance on the White Pelican colony at Chase Lake National Wildlife Refuge, North Dakota. *Inland Bird Banding News* **48**: 163-170.
Johnson, R.F. & Sloan, N.F. (1978). White Pelican production and survival of young at Chase Lake National Wildlife Refuge, North Dakota. *Wilson Bull.* **90**: 346-352.
Johnson, T.H. (1988). *Biodiversity and Conservation in the Caribbean: Profiles of Selected Islands*. ICBP Monograph **1**. Cambrige, England.
Johnston, J.W. & Bildstein, K.L. (1990). Dietary Salt as a Physiological Constraint in White Ibis Breeding in an Estuary. *Physiol. Zool.* **63**: 190-207.
Johnstone, G.W. (1974). Field characters and behaviour at sea of giant petrels in relation to their oceanic distribution. *Emu* **74**: 209-218.
Johnstone, G.W. (1977). Comparative feeding ecology of the giant petrels *Macronectes giganteus* and *M. halli*. Pp. 647-668 in: Llano (1977).
Johnstone, G.W. (1978). Interbreeding by *Macronectes halli* and *M. giganteus* at Macquarie Island. *Emu* **78**: 235.
Johnstone, G.W. (1982). Zoology. Pp. 33-39 in *Expedition to the Australian territory of Heard and McDonald Islands, 1980*. Canberra: Department of National Development and Energy, Division of National Mapping, Technical Report **31**.
Johnstone, G.W. (1985). Threats to Birds on Subantarctic Islands. Pp. 101-121 in: Moors (1985).
Johnstone, I.G., Harris, M.P., Wanless, S. & Graves, J.A. (1990). The usefulness of pellets for assessing the diet of adult Shags *Phalacrocorax aristotelis*. *Bird Study* **37**: 5-11.
Johnstone, R.E. (1979). Three more records of the Kerguelen Diving-Petrel in Western Australia. *West. Aust. Nat.* **14**: 133.
Johnstone, R.M. & Davis, L.S. (1990). Incubation routines and foraging-trip regulation in the Grey-faced Petrel. *Ibis* **132**: 14-20.
Johnstone, R.M. & Niven, B.E. (1989). Sexing Grey-faced Petrels by discriminant anlysis of measurements. *Notornis* **36**: 261-265.
Johnstone, S.T. (1960). First breeding of the spotted whistling duck (*Dendrocygna guttata*). *Wildfowl Trust Ann. Rep.* **11**: 11-12.
Johnstone, S.T. (1965). 1964 breeding results at the Wildfowl Trust. *Avicult. Mag.* **71**: 20-23.
Johnstone, S.T. (1970). Waterfowl eggs. *Avicult. Mag.* **76**: 52-55.
Jolly, J. (1983). Little spotted Kiwi research on Kapiti Island: 1980-1982. *Wildlife - A Review* **11**: 5-9.
Jolly, J. (1985). Little spotted Kiwi: Paradise Regained or Paradise Lost? *Forest & Bird* **16(1)**: 15-17.
Jolly, J. (1989). A field study of the breeding biology of the little spotted kiwi (*Apteryx owenii*) with emphasis on the causes of nest failures. *J. Royal Soc. New Zealand* **19(4)**: 433-448.
Jones, F.W. (1936). Notes on the breeding of the Short-tailed Shearwater in 1936. *S. Austr. Orn.* **13**: 223-228.
Jones, F.W. (1937a). The diving petrel of Bass Strait. *Victorian Nat.* **54**: 51-55.
Jones, F.W. (1937b). The breeding of the White-faced Storm Petrel on South Australian islands. *S. Austr. Orn.* **14**: 35-41.
Jones, G. (1978). *The Little Blue Penguin (Eudyptula minor) on Tiritiri, Matangi Island*. MSc thesis, University of Auckland, New Zealand.
Jones, M.A. (1978). White-faced Whistling Duck *Dendrocygna viduata* (Linnaeus, 1766) carrying their young. *Honeyguide* **94**: 19-21.
Jones, M.J. (1986). Breeding synchrony of Cory's Shearwater on Selvagem Grande. *Ibis* **128**: 423-426.
Jones, P. (1978). A possible function of the "wing drying" posture in the Reed Cormornt *Phalacrocorax africanus*. *Ibis* **120**: 540-542.
Jones, P.H., Monnat, J.Y., Cadbury, C.J. & Stowe, T.J. (1978). Birds oiled during the Amoco Cadiz incident -an interim report. *Mar. Poll. Bull.* **9**: 307-310.
Jones, P.J. (1979). Variability of egg size and composition in the Great White Pelican (*Pelecanus onocrotalus*). *Auk* **96**: 407-408.
Jones, P.J. (1988). Ibises in the 'OBO'. *World Birdwatch* **10**: 5.
Jones, P.J. (1989). Dwarf Olive Ibis found on Sao Tomé. *Specialist Group on Storks, Ibises and Spoonbills Newsletter* **2**: 9-10.
Jones, P.J. & Tye, A. (1988). *A survey of the Avifauna of Sao Tomé and Príncipe*. ICBP Study Report **24**. ICBP, Cambridge.
Jones, R.D. (1965). Returns from Steller's eiders banded in Izembek Bay, Alaska. *Wildfowl Trust Ann. Rep.* **16**: 83-85.
de Jong, B.H.J. (1983). Inventarisatie Rode Ibis langs de kust van de Guiana's in 1982. *Het Vogeljaar* **31(3)**: 156-157.
de Jong, B.H.J. Spaans, A.L. & Held, M. (1984). Waterfowl and wetlands in Suriname. Contribution to the IWRB/ICBP Neotropical Wetlands Project. *RIN Contributions to Research on Management of Natural Resources* **1984-1**.
Jongejan, W. (1986). [Traditional reaping activities are a threat to the Purple Heron]. *Vogeljaar* **34(6)**: 289-290. In Dutch.
Jordán, R. & Fuentes, H. (1966). Las poblaciones de aves guaneras y su situación actual. *Inf. Inst. Mar Perú - Callao* **10**: 1-31.
Jordán, R. (1959). El fenómeno de las regurgitaciones en el Guanay (*Phalacrocorax bougainvillii* L.) y un método para estimar la ingestión diaria. *Bol. Cia. Adm. Guano* **35(4)**: 23-40.
Jordán, R. & Fuentes, H. (1966). Las poblaciones de aves guaneras y su situación actual. *Inf. Instit. Mar. Perú - Callao.* **10**: 1-31.
Josefik, M. (1969). Studies on the Squacco Heron, *Ardeola ralloides* (Scop.). *Acta Orn. Warsz.* **11**: 135-262.
Josefik, M. (1970). *Acta Orn. Warsz.* **12**: 57-102; 393-443, 445-504. Ardeola ralloides
Jouanin, C. (1955). Une nouvelle espèce de Procellariidé. *L'Oiseau et la R.F.O.* **25**: 155-161.
Jouanin, C. (1957). Les Procellariidés mélaniques signalès en Mer d'Oman. *Oiseau* **27**: 12-27.
Jouanin, C. (1964a). Le comportement en juillet des Petits Puffins de l'Ile Selvagem Grande. *Bolm. Mus. Munic. Funchal* **18**: 142-157.
Jouanin, C. (1964b). Un Pétrel nouveau de la Réunion *Bulweria baraui*. *Bull. Mus. Nat. Hist. Paris* **2(35) 1963**: 593-597.
Jouanin, C. (1970). Le Pétrel Noir de Bourbon. *L'Oiseau et la R.F.O.* **40**: 48-68.
Jouanin, C. (1987). (*Pterodroma baraui*) Pp. 359-363 in: Diamond, A.W. ed. (1987). *Studies of Mascarene Island Birds*.
Jouanin, C. & Gill, F.B. (1967). Recherche du Pétrel de Barau. *L'Oiseau et la R.F.O.* **37**: 1-19.
Jouanin, C. & Mougin, J.L. (1979). Procellariiformes. Pp. 48-121 in: Mayr & Cottrell (1979).
Jouanin, C. & Roux, F. (1966). La colonie de Puffins Cendrés de Selvagem Grande. *Bolm. Mus. Munic. Funchal* **20**: 14-28.
Jouanin, C., Hémery, G., Mougin, J.L. & Roux, F. (1980). Nouvelles précisions sur l'acquisition de l'aptitude à la réproduction chez le Puffin cendré *Calonectris diomedea borealis*. *L'Oiseau et la R.F.O.* **50**: 205-215.
Jouanin, C., Mougin, J.L., Roux, F. & Zino, A. (1979). Le Pétrel de Bulwer dans l'archipel de Madère et aux iles Selvagens. *L'Oiseau et la R.F.O.* **49**: 165-184.
Jouanin, C., Roux, F. & Mougin, J.L. (1992). *Le Puffin Cendre (Calonectris diomedea/ Cory's Shearwater)*. Chabaud.
Jouventin, P. (1977). Olfaction in Snow Petrels. *Condor* **79**: 498-499.
Jouventin, P. (1978). *Ethologie comparée des Sphenisciclés*. Thèse d'État, University of Montpellier, France.
Jouventin, P. (1982). *Visual and Vocal Signals in Penguins, their Evolution and Adaptative Significance*. Parey, Berlin.
Jouventin, P. (1990). Shy Albatrosses breeding on Penguin Island, in the Crozet Archipelago, Indian Ocean. *Ibis* **132**: 126-127.
Jouventin, P. & Lequette, B. (1990). The dance of the Wandering Albatross *Diomedea exulans*. *Emu* **90**: 122-131.
Jouventin, P. & Mougin, J.L. (1981). Les strategies adaptatives des oiseaux de mer. *Rev. Ecol. (Terre Vie)* **35**: 217-272.
Jouventin, P. & Robin, J.P. (1984). Olfactory experiments on some Antarctic birds. *Emu* **84**(1): 46-48.
Jouventin, P. & Viot, C.R. (1985). Morphological and genetic variability of Snow Petrels. *Ibis* **127**: 430-441.
Jouventin, P. & Weimerskirch, H. (1984). L'Albatross Fuligineux à dos sombre, *Phoebetria fusca*, exemple de stratégie d'adaptation extrème à la vie pélagique. *Rev. Ecol. (Terre Vie)* **39**: 401-429.
Jouventin, P. & Weimerskirch, H. (1988). Demographic strategies of southern albatrosses. Pp. 857-868 in: *Proc. XIX Int. Orn. Congr.*
Jouventin, P. & Weimerskirch, H. (1990). Satellite tracking of Wandering Albatrosses. *Nature. London* **343**: 746-748.
Jouventin, P. & Weimerskirch, H. (1991). Changes in the population size and demography of southern seabirds: management implications. Pp. 297-314 in: Perrins *et al.* (1991).
Jouventin, P., Guillotin, M. & Cornet, A. (1979). Le chant du Manchot Empereur (*Aptenodytes forsteri*) et sa signification adaptative. *Behaviour* **70**: 231-250.
Jouventin, P., Martinez, J. & Roux, J.P. (1989). Breeding biology and current status of the Amsterdam Island Albatross. *Ibis* **131**: 171-182.
Jouventin, P., Monicault, G. de & Blosseville, J.M. (1981). La danse de l'Albatross, *Phoebetria fusca*. *Behaviour* **78**: 43-80.
Jouventin, P., Mougin, J.L., Stahl, J.C. & Weimerskirch, H. (1985). Comparative biology of the burrowing petrels of the Crozet Islands. *Notornis* **32**: 157-220.
Jouventin, P., Mougin, J.L., Stahl, J.C. & Weimerskirch, H. (1982). La segregation écologique entre les oiseaux des Iles Crozet. Données préliminaires. *Comité Natl. Français Rech. Antarct.* **51**: 457-467.
Jouventin, P., Roux, J.P., Stahl, J.C. & Weimerskirch, H. (1983). Biologie et fréquence de reproduction chez l'Albatross à Bec Jaune. *Gerfaut* **73**: 161-171.
Jouventin, P., Stahl, J.C. & Weirmerskirch, H. (1988). La conservation des oiseaux des Terres Australes et Atlantiques Françaises. Pp. 225-251 in: Thibault & Guyot (1988).
Jouventin, P., Stahl, J.C., Weimerskirch, H. & Mougin, J.L. (1984). The seabirds of the French subantarctic islands and Adélie Land: their status and conservation. Pp. 609-625 in: Croxall *et al.* (1984).
Joyner, D.E. (1975). *Nest parasitism and brood-related behavior of the ruddy duck (*Oxyura jamaicensis rubida*)*. PhD dissertation, University of Nebraska-Lincoln.
Joyner, D.E. (1977). Nest desertion by Ruddy Ducks in Utah. *Bird-Banding* **48**: 19-24.
Jozefik, M. (1960). Legi podwojne u ibisow kasztanowatych, *Plegadis falcinellus falcinellus* (L.) w delcie Dniestru. [Summary: The double broods of the Glossy Ibises, *Plegadis falcinellus falcinellus* (L.) in the Dniester delta]. *Acta Orn. Warsaw* **5**: 367-377.
de Juana, E. (1984a). The Status and Conservation of Seabirds in the Spanish Mediterranean. Pp. 347-361 in: Croxall *et al.* (1984).
de Juana, E. (1984b). The Conservation of Seabirds at the Chafarinas Islands. Pp. 363-370 in: Croxall *et al.* (1984).
de Juana, E. & Paterson, A.M. (1986). The Status of the Seabirds of the Extreme Western Mediterranean. Pp. 39-106 in MEDMARAVIS & Monbailliu (1986).
de Juana, E. Varela, J. & Witt, H.H. (1980). Le Puffin Cendré nicheur aux Iles Chaffarines. *Alauda* **48**: 27-31.
Jubb, R.A. (1981). Notes on some animals and birds which feed on freshwater mussels. *Naturalist* **25(1)**: 13-15.
Judin, K.A. & Firsova, L.V. (1988). [*Birds of the U.R.S.S.*] Science Press, Moscow. In Russian.
Junor, F.J.R. (1972). Estimation of the daily food intake of piscivorous birds. *Ostrich* **43(4)**: 193-205.
Kahl, M.P. (1962). Bioenergetics and growth of nestling Wood Storks. *Condor* **64**: 169-183.
Kahl, M.P. (1963a). *Food ecology of the Wood Stork in Florida: a study of behavioral and physiological adaptations to seasonal drought*. PhD dissertation, University of Georgia, Athens.
Kahl, M.P. (1963b). Thermoregulation in the Wood Stork, with special reference to the role of the legs. *Physiol. Zool.* **36**: 141-151.
Kahl, M.P. (1964). Food ecology of the Wood Stork (*Mycteria americana*) in Florida. *Ecol. Monogr.* **34(2)**: 97-117.
Kahl, M.P. (1965). Whale-headed Stork: a feathered riddle. *Africana* **2**: 19-20.
Kahl, M.P. (1966a). Comparative ethology of the Ciconiidae. Part 1. The Marabou Stork, *Leptoptilos crumeniferus* Lesson. *Behaviour* **27**: 76-106.
Kahl, M.P. (1966b). A contribution to the ecology and reproductive biology of the Marabou Stork (*Leptoptilos crumeniferus*) in East Africa. *J. Zool.* **148**: 289-311.
Kahl, M.P. (1967a). Observations on the behaviour of the Hamerkop *Scopus umbretta* in Uganda. *Ibis* **109**: 25-32.
Kahl, M.P. (1967b). Behavioural reactions to hyperthermia in *Scopus umbretta* and *Balaeniceps rex*. *Ostrich* **38**: 27-30.
Kahl, M.P. (1968). Recent breeding records of storks in Eastern Africa. *J. East Afr. Nat. Hist. Soc. Natl. Mus.* **27(1)(116)**: 67-72.
Kahl, M.P. (1970). Observations on the breeding of storks in India and Ceylon. *J. Bombay Nat. Hist. Soc.* **67**: 453-461.
Kahl, M.P. (1971a). Social behavior and taxonomic relationships of the storks. *Living Bird* **10**: 151-170.
Kahl, M.P. (1971b). Spread wing postures and their possible functions in the Ciconiidae. *Auk* **88**: 715-722.
Kahl, M.P. (1971c). Observations on the Jabiru and Maguari storks in Argentina, 1969. *Condor* **73**: 220-229.
Kahl, M.P. (1971d). Observations on the breeding of the Abdim's stork at Lake Shala, Ethiopia. *Ostrich* **42**: 233-241.
Kahl, M.P. (1971e). Food and feeding behavior of the Openbill Storks. *J. Orn.* **112**: 21-35.
Kahl, M.P. (1971f). Some observations on the behavior of Whistling Herons. *Willson Bull.* **83**: 302.303.
Kahl, M.P. (1972a). A revision of the family Ciconiidae. *J. Zool.* **167**: 451-461.
Kahl, M.P. (1972b). Comparative ethology of the Ciconiidae. Part 2. The Adjutant storks, *Leptoptilos dubius* and *L. javanicus*. *Ardea* **60**: 97-111.
Kahl, M.P. (1972c). Comparative ethology of the Ciconiidae. Part 3. The wood storks (genera *Mycteria* and *Ibis*). *Ibis* **114**: 15-29.
Kahl, M.P. (1972d). Comparative ethology of the Ciconiidae. Part 4. The "typical" storks (genera *Ciconia*, *Sphenorhynchus*, *Dissoura* and *Euxenura*). *Z. Tierpsychol.* **30**: 225-252.
Kahl, M.P. (1972e). Comparative ethology of the Ciconiidae. Part 5. The Openbill storks (genus *Anastomus*). *J. Orn.* **113**: 121-137.
Kahl, M.P. (1973). Comparative ethology of the Ciconiidae. Part 6. The Black-necked, Saddlebill and Jabiru Storks (genera, *Xenorhynchus*, *Ephippiorhynchus* and *Jabiru*). *Condor* **75**: 17-27.
Kahl, M.P. (1978). *Wonders of Storks*. Dodd, Mead & Co., New York.
Kahl, M.P. (1979a). Ciconiidae. Pp. 245-252 in: Mayr & Cottrell (1979).
Kahl, M.P. (1979b). Phoenicopteriformes. Pp. 269-271 in: Mayr & Cottrell (1979).
Kahl, M.P. (1980). Population ecology of the flamingos of the world. *Natl. Geogr. Soc. Res. Rep.* **12**: 407-415.
Kahl, M.P. (1983). Breeding displays of the African Spoonbill *Platalea alba*. *Ibis* **125**: 324-338.
Kahl, M.P. (1987a). An overview of the storks of the world. *Colonial Waterbirds* **10(2)**: 131-134.
Kahl, M.P. (1987b). The Royal Spoonbill. *Natl. Geogr.* **171**: 280-284.
Kahl, M.P. (1988). Breeding displays of Australian spoonbills. *Natl. Geogr. Res.* **4**: 88-111.
Kahl, M.P. & Peacock, L.J. (1963). The bill-snap reflex: a feeding mechanism in the American wood stork. *Nature* **199**: 505-506.
Kaiser, M.K. & Reid, F.A. (1987). A Comparison of Green-backed Heron Nesting in Two Freshwater Ecosystems. *Colonial Waterbirds* **10(1)**: 78-83.
Kalas, S. (1979). Zur Brutbiologie der Graugans (*A. anser* L.) unter besonderer Berücksichtigung des Verhaltens. *Zool. Anz. Jena* **203**: 193-219.
Kalbe, L. (1990). *Der Gänsesäger*. Die Neue Brehm-Bücherei, A. Ziemsen Verlag, Wittenberg Lutherstadt, Germany.
Kale, H.W. ed. (1978). *Rare and Endangered Biota of Florida*. Vol. 2. Birds. University Presses of Florida, Gainesville.
Kamel, I. (1971). Hybrid between Japanese Stork and European White Stork. *Animals and Zoos* **23(11)(No. 262)**: 370.
Kamil, A.C., Krebs, J.R. & Pulliam, H.R. eds. (1987). *Foraging Behavior*. Plenum, New York.
Kania, W. (1985). [Results of bird ringing in Poland. Migrations of white stork.] *Acta Orn.* **21**: 1-41. In Polish with English summary.
Karlsson, J. & Kjellén, N. (1984). Doppingar i Skåne; historik, nuvarande förekomst och beståndsväxlingar. [Summary: Grebes (Fam. Podicipedidae) in Skåne, Southern Sweden; recent and earlier distribution and short-term fluctuations]. *Anser* **23**: 27-52.
Karpowicz, Z. (1985). *Wetlands in East Asia. A Preliminary Review and Inventory*. Study Report **6**. ICBP, Cambrige, England.
Karr, J.R. (1989). Birds in tropical rainforests: Aspects of zoogeography, species richness, and trophic structure. Pp. 401-416 in: Lieth, H. & Werger, M.J.A. eds. (1989). *Tropical Rainforest Ecosystems*. Vol. 14B. Ecosystems of the World. Elsevier Publ. Co., Amsterdam.
Kasoma, P.M.B. & Pomeroy, D.E. (1987). The status and ecology of storks and the Shoebill in East Africa. *Colonial Waterbirds* **10(2)**: 221-228.
Kasparek, M. (1986). On the age of the colony of the Bald Ibis *Geronticus eremita*, at Birecik, Turkey. *Zool. Middle East* **1**: 42-43.
Katz, E.B. (1986). Problems concerning bird orientation according to the sun. *Ornitologiya* **21**: 103-112.
Katzir, G. & Intrator, N. (1987). Striking of underwater prey by a reef heron, *Egretta gularis schistacea*. *J. Comp. Physiol. (Ser. A)* **160**: 517-523.
Kaufman, K. (1979). The double identity of the Western Grebe. *Continental Birdlife* **1**: 85-89.
Kay, G.T. (1953). The Fulmar's bill. *Scott. Nat.* **65**: 125-127.
Kazama, T. (1988). The First Specimen of Chinese Merganser *Mergus squamatus* Collected from Japan. *J. Yamashina Ist. Orn.* **20**: 116-118.
Keage, P.L. & Johnstone, G.W. (1982). Heard Island and the McDonalds Islands. *Austr. Heritage Comm. Newsl.* **5**: 4-5.
Kear, J. (1964). Colour preference in young Anatidae. *Ibis* **106**: 361-369.

Kear, J. (1967). Notes on the eggs and downy young of *Thalassornis leuconotus*. *Ostrich* **38**: 227-229.
Kear, J. (1970). The Adaptive Radiation of Parental Care in Waterfowl. Pp. 357-392 in: Crook, J.H. (1970). *Social Behaviour in Birds and Mammals*. Academic Press, London.
Kear, J. (1972a). Feeding habits of birds. In: Fiennes, R.N.T.W. ed. *The Biology of Nutrition*. Oxford.
Kear, J. (1972b). The Blue Duck of New Zealand. *Living Bird* **11**: 175-192.
Kear, J. (1975). Salvadori's Duck of New Guinea. *Wildfowl* **26**: 104-111.
Kear, J. (1985). Flamingo. Pp. 217-218 in: Campbell & Lack (1985).
Kear, J. (1986). Captive breeding programmes for waterfowl and flamingos. *Int. Zoo Yb.* **24/25**: 21-25.
Kear, J. (1988). *The Mute Swan*. Shire Natural History **27**, Aylesbury, UK.
Kear, J. (1990). *Man and Wildfowl*. T & AD Poyser, London.
Kear, J. (1991). *Ducks of the World*. Charles Letts and Co Ltd, London.
Kear, J. & Berger, A.J. (1980). *The Hawaiian Goose. An Experiment in Conservation*. Buteo Books, Vermillion, S.D.
Kear, J. & Burton, P.J.K. (1971). The food and feeding apparatus of the Blue Duck *Hymenolaimus*. *Ibis* **113**: 483-493.
Kear, J. & Duplaix-Hall, N. eds. (1975). *Flamingos*. Poyser, Berkhamsted.
Kear, J. & Murton, R.K. (1973). The systematic status of the Cape Barren Goose as judged by its photoresponses. *Wildfowl* **24**: 141-143.
Kear, J. & Palmes, P. (1980). Andean and James' flamingos *Phoenicoparrus andinus* and *P. jamesi* in captivity. *Int. Zoo Yb.* **20**: 17-23.
Kear, J. & Steel, T.H. (1971). Aspects of social behaviour in the Blue Duck. *Notornis* **18**: 187-198.
Kear, J. & Williams, G. (1978). Waterfowl at risk. *Wildfowl* **29**: 5-22.
Keast, A. (1990). *Biogeography and Ecology of Forest Bird Communities*. SPB Academic Publishing, The Hague, The Netherlands.
Keast, J.A. (1985). Heron. Pp. 282-284 in: Campbell & Lack (1985).
Keast, J.A. & D'Ombrain, A.F. (1949). Notes on the Little Pied Cormorant. *Proc. Royal Zool. Soc. NSW.* **1947-1948**: 30-35.
Kehoe, F.P. (1989). The adaptative significance of creching behavior of the White-winged Scoter (*Melanitta fusca deglandi*). *Can. J. Zool.* **67 (2)**: 406-411.
Kehoe, F.P., Brown, P.W. & Houston, C.S. (1989). Survival and longevity of White-winged Scoters nesting in central Saskatchewan. *J. Field Orn.* **60 (2)**: 133-136.
Keith, A.R. (1970). Bird observations from Tierra del Fuego. *Condor* **72**: 361-363.
Keith, G.S., Forbes-Watson, A.D. & Turner, D.A. (1974). The Madagascar Crested Ibis, a threatened species in an endemic and endangered avifauna. *Wilson Bull.* **86**: 197-199.
Keith, K. & Hines, M.P. (1958). New and rare species at Macquarie Island during 1956 and 1957. *CSIRO Wildl. Res.* **3**: 50-53.
Keith, L.B. (1961). *A Study of Waterfowl Ecology on Small Impoundments in Southeastern Alberta*. Wildlife Monographs **6**.
Keller, V. (1989a). Egg-covering behaviour by Great Crested Grebes *Podiceps cristatus*. *Ornis Scand.* **20**: 129-131.
Keller, V. (1989b). Variations in the response of Great Crested Grebes *Podiceps cristatus* to human disturbance - a sign of adaptation? *Biol. Conserv.* **49**: 31-45.
Kemp, A.C. & Kemp, M.I. (1976). Random notes on some Sarawak birds. *Sarawak Mus. J.* **24**: 273-276.
Kemper, J.H. (1985). *Foraging strategy in the Spoonbill (*Platalea leucorodia*)*. Verslagen en Technische Gegevens **44**. Instituut voor Taxonomische Zooelogie, Universiteit van Amsterdam.
Kemper, J.H. (1987). Grote prooien voor de Lepelaar in theorie en praktijk. *Limosa* **60**: 209-210.
Kemper, J.H. (1989). [Fishway for sticklebacks to save the Spoonbill (*Platalea leucorodia*) in Noord-Holland]. *Levende Nat.* **90**: 2-6. In Dutch.
Kennamer, R.A. & Hepp, G.R. (1987). Frequency and timing of second broods in Wood Ducks. *Wilson Bull.* **99 (4)**: 655-662.
Kennamer, R.A., Harvey, W.F. & Hepp, G.R. (1988). Notes on Hooded Merganser nests in the coastal plain of South Carolina. *Wilson Bull.* **100**: 686-688.
Kennerly, P.R. (1987). A survey of the birds of the Poyang Lake Nature Reserve, Jiangxi Province, China, 29 December 1985-4 January 1986. Pp. 97-111 in: *The Hong Kong Bird Report 1984/1985*. Hong Kong Bird Watching Society, Hong Kong.
Kennerly, P.R. (1990a). A summary of the status of the Black-faced Spoonbill. *Specialist Group on Storks, Ibises abnd Spoonbills Newsletter* **3(1/2)**: 3-4.
Kennerly, P.R. (1990b). A review of the status and distribution of Black-faced Spoonbill. Pp. 116-125 in: Picken, V. ed. *The Hong Kong Bird Report 1989*. Hong Kong Bird Watching Society, Hong Kong.
Kent, D.M. (1986). Foraging Efficiency of Sympatric Egrets. *Colonial Waterbirds* **9**: 81-85.
Kent, D.M. (1987). Effects of varying Bahavior and Habitat on the Striking Efficiency of Egrets. *Colonial Waterbirds* **10(1)**: 115-119.
Kenyon, K.W. (1950). Distribution of albatrosses in the North Pacific and adjacent waters. *Condor* **52**: 97-103.
Kenyon, K.W. & Rice, D.W. (1958). Homing of Laysan Albatrosses. *Condor* **60**: 3-6.
Kenyon, K.W., Rice, D.W., Robbins, C.S. & Aldrich, J.W. (1958). Birds and aircraft on Midway Islands: November 1956-June 1957 investigations. *US Fish & Wildl. Serv. Spec. Sci. Rep. Wildl.* **38**: 1-51.
Kenzhegulov, K. (1974). [Distribution and biology of *Pelecanus crispus* in the Amudarya Delta]. *Ornitologiya* **11**: 378-380. In Russian.
Kepler, C.B. (1967). Polynesian rat predation on nesting Laysan Albatrosses and other Pacific seabirds. *Auk* **84**: 426-430.
Kepler, C.B. (1969). *Breeding biology of the Blue-faced Booby* Sula dactylatra personata *on Green Island, Kure Atoll*. Nuttall Pub. **8**. Cambridge, MA.
Kerbes, R. (1988). Progress report: International Snow Goose neckbanding project. Canadian Wildlife Service, Saskatoon.
Kerry, K.R. & Colback, G.C. (1972). Light-mantled Sooty Albatrosses on Macquarie Island. *Austr. Bird Bander* **10**: 61-62.
Kerry, K.R., Horne, R.S.C. & Dorward, D.F. (1983). Records of the Short-tailed Shearwater in Antarctic waters. *Emu* **83**: 35-36.
Kertell, K. (1991). Disappearance of the Steller's Eider from the Yukon-Kuskokwim Delta, Alaska. *Arctic* **44(3)**: 177-187.
Kevan, C.L. (1970). *An Ecological Study of the Red-necked Grebes on Astontin Lake, Alberta*. MSc thesis. University of Alberta.
Khan, M.A.R. (1984). Conservation of storks and ibises in Bangladesh. *Tiger Paper* **11(4)**: 2-4.
Khan, M.A.R. (1987). Conservation of Storks and Other Waterbirds in Bangladesh. *Colonial Waterbirds* **10**: 229-235.
Kharitonov, S.P. [Ethological structure of the local group in the colony of Snow Goose (*Anser caerulescens*). *Zool. Zh.* **67(10)**: 1530-1537.
Kidd, E. (1978). Some notes on the birds of Brunei. *Brunei Mus. J.* **4**: 115-164.
Kieser, G.A. & Kieser, J.A. (1977). Spoonbills breeding in the northern Karoo. *Bokmakierie* **29**: 53.
Kiff, L.F. (1989). Historical breeding records of the Common Merganser in southeastern United States. *Wilson Bull.* **101(1)**: 141-143.
Kilham, L. (1980). Association of Great Egret and the White Ibis. *J. Field Orn.* **51**: 73-74.
Kilham, L. (1984). American Crows Robbing Great Egrets and White Ibis of Large, Eel-like Salamanders. *Colonial Waterbirds* **7**: 143-145.
Kinde, H. (1988). A fatal case of oak poisoning in a Double-Wattled Cassowary (*Casuarius casuarius*). *Avian Dis.* **32(4)**: 849-851.
King, A.S. & McLelland, J. eds. (1980-1988). *Form and Function in Birds*. 4 Vols. Academic Press, London and New York.
King, A.S. & McLelland, J. (1984). *Birds - Their Structure and Function*. 2nd edition. Baillière Tindall, London.
King, B. (1976). Winter feeding behaviour of Great Northern Divers. *Wildl. Rev.* **69**: 497-498.
King, B., Woodcock, M. & Dickinson, E.C. (1975). *A Field Guide to the Birds of South-East Asia*. Collins, London.
King, B.R. & Reimer, D.S. (1991). Breeding and behavior of the Herald Petrel, *Pterodroma arminjoniana*, on Raine Island, Queensland. *Emu* **91(2)**: 122-125.
King, C.E. (1988). An ethological comparison of three storks: *Ciconia boyciana*, *C. ciconia* and *C. maguari*. MSc thesis. Oklahoma State University, Stillwater.
King, C.E. & Brouwer, K. (1991). Conservation and captive management of Indian storks. *Zoo's Print* **6(1)**: 1-3.
King, C.E. & Coulter, M.C. (1989). Status of storks in zoos: 1987 survey. *Int. Zoo Yb.* **28**: 225-229.
King, C.E. & Patzwahl, S. (1987). First successful hatching of the Eastern White Stork outside of China. *Int. Zoo News* **34(4)**: 17-18.
King, K.A., Blankinship, D.R., Payne, E., Krynitsky, A.J. & Hensler, G.L. (1985). Brown Pelican populations and pollutants in Texas (1975-1981). *Wilson Bull.* **92(2)**: 201-214.
King, K.A., Flickinger, E.L. & Hildenbrand, H.H. (1977). The decline of Brown Pelicans on the Louisiana and Texas Gulf Coast. *Southwestern Naturalist* **21**: 417-431.
King, K.A., Keith, J.O., Mitchell, C.A. & Keirans, J.E. (1977). Ticks as a factor in nest desertion of California Brown Pelicans. *Condor* **79**: 507-509.
King, K.A., Meeker, D.L. & Swineford, D.M. (1980). White-faced Ibis populations and pollutants in Texas, 1969-1976. *Southwestern Naturalist* **25**: 225-239.
King, K.A., Stafford, C. J., Cain, B.W., Mueller, A.J. & Hall, H.D. (1987). Industrial, agricultural, and petroleum contaminants in cormorants wintering near the Houston Ship Channel, Texas, USA. *Colonial Waterbirds* **10(1)**: 93-99.
King, W.B. (1970). *The Trade Wind Zone Oceanography Pilot Study. Part VII: Observations of Seabirds, March 1964 to June 1965*. US Fish and Wildlife Service Report: Fisheries **586**.
King, W.B. (1974). Wedge-tailed Shearwater. Pp. 53-95 in King, W.B. ed. *Pelagic Studies of Seabirds in the Central and Eastern Pacific Ocean*. Smithsonian Contributions Zoology **158**. Washington.
King, W.B. compiler (1978/79). *Endangered Birds of the World: The ICBP Bird Red Data Book*. Vol. 2. Aves. 2nd. edition. IUCN, Morges, Switzerland.
King, W.B. (1980). Ecological basis of extinction in birds. Pp. 905-911 in: *Proc. XVII Int. Orn. Congr. (1978)*.
King, W.B. & Gould, P.J. (1967). The status of Newell's race of the Manx Shearwater. *Living Bird* **6**: 163-186.
King, W.B., Brown, R.G.B., & Sanger, G.A. (1979). Mortality to marine birds through commercial fishing. Pp. 195-200 in: Bartonek, J.C. & Nettleship, D.N. eds. *Conservation of Marine Birds of Northern North America*. US Fish & Wildlife Service Research Report **11**.
Kingsford, R.T. (1986a). *Reproductive Biology and Habitat Use of the Maned Duck* Chenonetta jubata *(Latham)*. PhD thesis, University of Sydney, Sydney.
Kingsford, R.T. (1986b). The moults and plumages of the Maned Duck *Chenonetta jubata* on the southern tablelands of New South Wales. *Corella* **10**: 108-113.
Kingsford, R.T. (1989). Food of the Maned Duck *Chenonetta jubata* during the breeding season. *Emu* **89 (2)**: 119-124.
Kingsford, R.T., Flanjak, J. & Black, S. (1989). Lead shot and ducks on Lake Cowal. *Austr. Wildl. Res.* **16 (2)**: 167-172.
Kinsky, F.C. (1960). The yearly cycle of the Northern Blue Penguin *Eudyptula minor novaehollandiae* in the Wellington Harbour area. *Rec. Dom. Mus. Wellington* **3**: 145-218.
Kinsky, F.C. (1971). The consistent presence of paired ovaries in the kiwi (*Apteryx*) with some discussion of this condition in other birds. *J. Orn.* **112**: 334-357.
Kinsky, F.C. & Falla, R.A. (1976). A subspecific revision of the Australasian Blue Penguin (*Eudyptula minor*) in the New Zealand area. *Records Nat. Mus. New Zealand* **1**: 105-126.
Kinsky, F.C. & Yaldwyn, J.C. (1981). The bird fauna of Niue Island, south-west Pacific, with special notes on the white-tailed tropicbird and golden plover. *Natl. Mus. New Zealand (Misc. Ser.)* **2**: 1-49.
Kinsky, F.C., Robertson, C.J.R., Challies, C.N. & Jones, G. (1985). Blue Penguin. Page 46 in: Robertson (1985).
Kinzelbach, R.K. (1986). New records of Goliath Heron, Yellow-billed Stork, Blyth's Reed Warbler and Clamorous Reed Warbler in the Middle East. *Bull. Orn. Soc. Middle East* **17**: 13-17.
Kirby, R.E. (1976). Breeding chronology and interspecific relations of Pied-billed Grebes in northern Minnesota. *Wilson Bull.* **88**: 493-495.
Kirkham, I.R. & Johnson, S.R. (1988). Interspecific aggression in loons. *J. Field Orn.* **59(1)**: 3-6.
Kirkwood, R,J., Woehler, E.J. & Burton, H.R. (1989). Heard Island ANARE 1987-88 Report. Unpublished Report.
Kishchinskij, A.A., Tomkovich, P.S. & Flint, V.E. (1983). The birds of the Kancaalan River Basin, Chukotsk autonomous area. *Sbornik Trud. Zool. Muz. Mgu.* **21**: 3-76.
Kistchinski, A.A. & Flint, V.E. (1974). On the biology of the Spectacled Eider. *Wildfowl* **25**: 5-15.
Klages, N.T.W. (1989). Food and feeding ecology of Emperor Penguins in the Eastern Weddell Sea. *Polar Biol.* **9(6)**: 385-390.
Klages, N.T.W., Brooke, M.L. & Watkins, B.P.(1988). Prey of Rockhopper Penguins at Gough Island, South Atlantic Ocean. *Ostrich* **59**: 162-165.
Klages, N.T.W., Gales, R.P. & Pemberton, D. (1989). Dietary segregation of Macaroni and Rockhopper Penguins at Heard Island. *Austr. Wildl. Res.* **16**: 599-604.
Klages, N.T.W., Pemberton, D. & Gales, R.P. (1990). The diets of King and Gentoo Penguins at Heard Island. *Austr. Wild. Res.* **17**: 53-60.
Klapste, J. (1977). Voice of the Black Cormorant. *Austr. Bird Watcher* **7**: 92.
Klapste, J. (1991). Carrion eating by herons (Ardeinae). *Austr. Bird Watcher* **14(3)**: 108.
Klein, T. (1985). *Loon Magic*. Paper Birch Press, Ashland.
Kleinpaste, R. & Colbourne, R. (1983). Kiwi food study. *New Zealand Journal of Ecology*. **6**: 143-144.
Klima, M. (1966). A study on diurnal activity rhythm in the European Pochard, *Aythya ferina* (L.). *Zool. Listy.* **15**: 317-332.
Klimaitis, J.F. & Moschione, F.N. (1987). *Aves de la Reserva Integral de Selva Marginal de Punta Lara y sus Alrededores*. Dirección de Servicios Generales del Ministerio de Economía de la Provincia de Buenos Aires.
Klockenhoff, H. & Madel, G. (1970). Über die Flamingos (*Phoenicopterus ruber roseus*) der Dasht-r-Nawar in Afghanistan. *J. Orn.* **111**: 78-84.
Klomp, N.I. & Wooller, R.D. (1988a). The size of Little Penguins, *Eudyptula minor*, on Penguin Island, Western Australia. *Records West. Austr. Mus.* **14**: 211-215.
Klomp, N.I. & Wooller, R.D. (1988b). Diet of Little Penguins *Eudyptula minor*, from Penguin Island, Western Australia. *Aust. J. Mar. Freshwater Res.* **39**: 633-639.
Klomp, N.I. & Wooller, R.D. (1991). Patterns of arrival and departure by breeding Little Penguins at Penguin Island, Western Australia. *Emu* **91(1)**: 32-35.
Klomp, N.I., Meathrel, C.E., Wienecke, B.C. & Wooller, R.D. (1991). Surface nesting by Little Penguins on Penguin Island, Western Australia. *Emu* **91(3)**: 190-193.
Klös, C.S. (1985). Bemerkungen zum Haltung des Schuhschnabels im Berliner Zoo. *Gefiederte Welt* **109**: 36-37.
Klös, H.G. (1975). News from the Berlin Zoo (January-June 1975). *Avicult. Mag.* **81**: 170-173.
Klös, H.G. (1976). News from the Berlin Zoo (January-September 1976). *Avicult. Mag.* **82**: 175-177.
Klös, H.G. & Reinhard, R. (1990). Erfahrungen in Haltung und Zucht des Kiwis in Zoologischen Garten Berlin. [Summary: On the maintenance and the rearing of North Island Brown Kiwis (*Apteryx australis mantelli*) in the Berlin Zoo]. *Zool. Garten* **60(3/4)**: 190-196. In German with English summary.
Klug, S. & Boswall, J. (1970). Observations from a water bird colony, Lake Tana, Ethiopia. *Bull. Brit. Orn. Club* **90**: 97-105.
Knaus, R.M. (1990). Estimates of oil-soaked carcasses of the Magellanic Penguin *Spheniscus magellanicus* on the eastern shore of Península Valdés, Chubut Province, Argentina. *Hornero* **13**: 171-173.
Knief, W. & Drenckhahn, D. (1984). [Breeding Status of *Ardea cinerea* in Schleswig-Holstein in 1974-1983 and a Comment on its Breeding There Before 1974]. *Corax* **10(3)**: 334-354. In German.
Knief, W. & Witt, H. (1983). Zur Situation des Kormorans (*Phalacrocorax carbo*) in Schleswig-Holstein uns Vorschläge für seine küntftige Behandlung. *Ber. Dtsch. Sekt. Int. Rat. Vogelschutz* **23**: 67-79.
Knoder, C.E., Plaza, P.D. & Sprunt, A. (1980). Status and distribution of the Jabiru Stork and other water birds in western Mexico. Pp. 58-127 in: Schaeffer & Ehlers (1980).
Knopf, F.L. (1975). Schedule of presupplemental molt of White Pelicans with notes on the bill horn. *Condor* **77**: 356-359.
Knopf, F.L. (1976). Spatial and temporal aspects of colonial nesting in the White Pelican, *Pelecanus erythrorhynchos*. PhD dissertation, Utah State University, Logan, UT.
Knopf, F.L. (1979). Spatial and temporal aspects of colonial nesting of White Pelicans. *Condor* **81**: 353-363.
Knopf, F.L. (1980). On the hatching interval of White Pelican eggs. *Proc. Okla. Acad. Sci.* **60**: 26-28.
Knopf, F.L. & Kennedy, J.L. (1981). Differential predation by two species of piscivorous birds. *Wilson Bull.* **93(4)**: 554-556.
Kochanov, V.D. & Skokova, N.N. (1967). [The Fauna of Birds of the Ainov Islands]. *Trudy Kandlakshskogo Zapovednika* **5**: 185-267. In Russian.
Kock, D. (1991). Renaturierung der Grosstierfauna im tunesischen Sahel. Teil II. Strauß und Perlhuhn. *Natur und Museum* **121(2)**: 50-54.
Koepcke, M. (1968). Die Rassengliederung von *Nothoprocta pentlandi* (Tinamidae) in Peru mit Beschreibung einer neuen subspezies. *Bonn. zool. Beitr.* **19**: 225-234.
Koepcke, M. (1970). *The Birds of the Department of Lima, Peru*. Livingston Publishing Company, Wynnewood, PA.
Kok, O.B. (1980). Voedselinname van volstruise in die Namib-Naukluftpark, Suidwes-Afrika. *Madoqua* **12(3)**: 155-161.
Kokshaisky, N.V. (1959). [Certain differences between the Spoonbill (*Platalea leucorodia* L.) and the Glossy Ibis (*Plegadis falcinellus* L.) connected with flight]. *Doklady Akad. Nauk USSR* **124**: 949-952.
Kolbe, H. (1972). *Die Entenvogel der Welt*. Neumann Verlag, Redebuel.
Kolbe, H. (1979). *Ornamental Waterfowl*. Gresham Books, Surrey.
Kolbe, H. (1988). Spätsommerliche Notizen zur Nordkoreanischen Vogelfauna. *Mitt. Zool. Mus. Berl.* **64(Suppl.) Ann. Orn. 12**: 51-66.

Kolbe, H. (1989). Ergebnisse von Fütterungsversuchen an 4 Säger-(*Mergus-*) Arten. *Beitr. Vogelk.* **35**: 153-162.
Kolbe, U. & Neumann, J. (1987). Der Purpurreiher in der DDR. *Falke* **34(10)**: 331-336.
Kolbe, U. & Neumann, J. (1991a). [The Glossy Ibis in East Germany]. *Falke* **8(2)**: 44-51. In German.
Kolbe, U. & Neumann, J. (1991b). [A Typical Astray Guest? *Platalea leucorodia* in East Germany]. *Falke* **38**(7): 212-223.
Kolichis, N. (1977). Birds of Bedout Island - a visit in May 1975. *West. Austr. Nat.* **13**: 191-194.
Kolomiitsev, N.P. (1986). Factors limiting *Mergus squamatus* and recommendations for conservation of the species. Pp. 306-307 in: *Study of Birds of the USSR. Their Conservation and Management* **1**. Leningrad.
Komine, T. & Sugita, H. (1990). Breeding the Eastern White Stork. *Animals and Zoos* **June**: 212-217.
de Kondo, T. (1987). El ave del mes. "El Pájaro Vaco" *Tigrisoma lineatum. Rupicola* **7(3-4)**: 7-8.
de Kondo, T. (1988). El ave del mes. Las gallinas del monte. *Rupicola* **8(1-2)**: 7-8.
Kondratyev, A.V. (1986). [Comparative analysis of brood behaviour in some species of ducks]. Pp. 163-175 in: Ilichev, V.D. ed. (1986). [*Recent Problems in Ornithology*]. Nauke, Moskow. In Russian.
Kondratyev, A.V. (1989). A comparative ecology of *Melanitta americana, M. deglandi* and *Clangula hyemalis* in the Anadyr River middle stream basin. *Zool. Zh.* **68 (8)**: 93-103.
König, C. (1984). Der Kapuzentaucher - kaum entdeckt - schon bedroht. *Vögel* **16**: 28-29.
Kooloos, J.G.M & Zweers, G.A. (1989). Mechanics of drinking in the Mallard (*Anas platyrhynchos*, Anatidae). *J. Morphol.* **199(3)**: 327-347.
Kooloos, J.G.M., Kraaijeveld, A.R., Langenbach, G.E.J. & Zweers, G.A. (1989). Comparative mechanics of filter feeding in *Anas platyrhynchos, Anas clypeata* and *Aythya fuligula* (Aves, Anseriformes). *Zoomorphology* **108**: 269-290.
Kooyman, G.L. & Davis R.W. (1987). Diving behaviour and performance, with special reference to penguins. Pp. 63-75 in: Croxall, J.P. ed. *Seabirds: Feeding Ecology and Role in Marine Ecosystems.* Cambridge University Press, Cambrige, England.
Kooyman, G.L., Davis, R.W., Croxall, J.P. & Costa, D.P. (1982). Diving depths and energy requirements of King Penguins. *Science* **217**: 726-727.
Kooyman, G.L., Drabek, C.M., Elsner, R. & Campbell, W.B. (1971). Diving behaviour of the Emperor Penguin (*Aptenodytes forsteri*). *Auk* **88**: 775-795.
Kooyman, G.L., Gentry, R.L., Bergman, W.P. & Hammel, H.T. (1976). Heat loss in penguins during immersion and compression. *Comp. Biochem. Physiol.* **54A**: 75-80.
Korn, M. (1989). Ornithologische Beobachtungen auf der Insel Gomera (Kanaren). *Orn. Mitt.* **41(5)**: 105-108.
Korodi, G.J. (1964). Data on the Dalmatian Pelican's territorial extension, biometry and nutrition in Roumania. *Aquila* **69-70**: 79-82.
Korschgen, C. (1972). *Behavior of the Wood Duck.* Unpublished M.A. dissertation, University of Missouri, Columbia.
Korsten, J. & Lukken, H. (1990). *Gedragsstudie rode ibis.* Satageverslag Hogeschool Gelderland.
de Korte, J. & de Vries, T.J. (1978). Moult of primaries and rectrices in the greater frigatebird, *Fregata minor*, on Genovesa, Galápagos. *Bijdragen tot de Dierkunde* **48**: 81-8.
Kortegaard, L. (1973). Skestorken (*Platalea leucorodia*) i Danmark 1900-1971. *Dan. Orn. Foren. Tidsskr.* **67(1-2)**: 3-14.
Kortlandt, A. (1938). De uitdrukkingsbewegingen en geluiden van *Phalacrocorax carbo sinensis* (Shaw and Nodder). *Ardea* **27**: 1-40.
Korzun, L.P. (1981). [On the phylogenetic relations between Gaviiformes and Podicipediformes]. *Zool. Zh.* **60**:1 523-1532. In Russian with English summary.
Koshelev, A.I. (1977). [The colonial nesting habits of the Great Crested Grebe (*Podiceps cristatus* L.) in the northern part of Lake Menzelinskoe (western Siberia)]. In Russian with English summary. *Bull. Moscow Soc. Naturalists (Ser. Biol.)* **82(4)**: 5-9.
Koskimies, J. (1975a). Polymorphic variability in clutch size and laying date in the Velvet Scoter. *Ornis Fennica* **34**: 118-128.
Koskimies, J. (1975b). Variations in size and shape of eggs of the Velvet Scoter, *Melanitta fusca* (L.). *Annales Zoologici Suomalainen Elain-ja Kasvitiesteelinen Seura Vanamo* **12**: 58-69.
Koskimies, J. & Routamo, E. (1953). Zur Fortpflanzungsbiologie der Samtente *Melanitta fusca* L. I. Allgemeine Nistokologie. *Papers on Game Res.* **10**: 1-105.
Kotter, B.L. (1970). *An ecological natural history of the White-faced Ibis (*Plegadis chihi*) in northern Utah.* MSc thesis. University of Utah, Salt Lake City, Utah.
Kral, B. & Figala, J. (1966). Breeding Biology of the Purple Heron in the Valky and Malj Tisy Reserve. *Zool. Listy* **15**: 33-46.
Krapivini, A.P. (1958). [On the intraspecific relationships in White and Black Storks]. *Vestn. Akad. Nauk Belorus. S.S.S.R. Biol.* **1**: 62-70. In Russian.
Krapu, G.L. (1972). *Feeding Ecology of the Pintail (*Anas acuta*) in North Dakota.* PhD thesis, IOwa State University, Ames.
Krapu, G.L. (1974). Feeding ecology of Pintail hens during reproduction. *Auk* **91**: 278-290.
Krapu, G.L. (1981). The role of nutrient reserves in Mallard reproduction. *Auk* **98**: 29-38.
Krapu, G.L. & Swanson, G.A. (1975). Some nutritional aspects of reproduction in prairie nesting Pintails. *J. Wildl. Manage.* **39**: 156-162.
Krapu, G.L., Johnson, D.H. & Dane, C.W. (1979). Age determination of mallards. *J. Wildl. Manage.* **43**: 384-393.
Krebs, J.R. (1974). Colonial nesting and social feeding as strategies for exploiting food resources in the Great Blue Heron (*Ardea herodias*). *Behaviour* **51**: 99-134.
Krebs, J.R. & Davies. N.B. (1991). *Behavioral Ecology.* 3rd. edition. Blackwell Scientific Publications, Oxford.
Krechmar, A.V. (1966). [The birds of the western parts of the Taimyr Peninsula]. *Trudy Zool. Inst. Leningr.* **39**: 185-312. In Russian.
Krementz, D.G., Stotts, V.D., Stotts, D.B., Hines, J.E. & Funderburk, S.L. (1991). Historical changes in laying date, clutch size, and nest succes of American Black Ducks. *J. Wildl. Manage.* **55** (3): 462-466.
Krieg, H. & Schuhmancher, E. (1936). (Comparison of habits of Tinamidae, Cracidae and Phasianidae in the field). *Verh. Orn. Ges. Bay.* **21**: 1-18.
Kriel, F.M, Crawford, R.J.M. & Shelton, P.A. (1980). Seabirds breeding at Robben Island between 1949 and 1980. *Cormorant* **8**: 87-96.
Krogman, B.D. (1978). The Tule Goose mystery - a problem in taxonomy. *Amer. Birds* **32**: 164-166.
Krogman, B.D. (1979). A systematic study of Anser albifrons in California. Pp. 29-43 in: Jarvis, B. (1979). *Symp. Management Biol. Pacific Flyway.*
Kroodsma, D.E. & Miller, E.H. eds. (1983). *Accoustic Communication in Birds.* 2 Vols. Academic Press, London and New York.
Kuan Kuan-hsun & Cheng Tso-hin (1962). a new genus added to the Chinese avifauna - *Oxyura leucocephala* (Scopoli). *Acta Zool. Sinica* **14(3)**: 431.
Kuchel, C.R. (1977). *Some Aspects of the Behavior and Ecology of Harlequin Ducks Breeding in Glacier National Park, Montana.* MSc thesis, University of Montana.
Kuehler, C. & Toone, W. (1989). Zoological Society of San Diego Shoebill Stork management plan (*Balaeniceps rex*). Unpublished report. San Diego Zoological Society, San Diego, California.
Kumar, R.A. (1986). Rise in global mean sea level has it affected the Flamingo breeding grounds? *J. Bombay Nat. Hist. Soc.* **83(2)**: 433-435.
Kumerloeve, H. (1958). Von der Kolonie des Waldrapps *Geronticus eremita* bei Birecik am Euphrat. *Beitr. Vogelk.* **6**: 189-202.
Kumerloeve, H. (1962a). Der Flamingo, *Phoenicopterus ruber*, in Kleinasien und Syrien. *Vogelwelt* **83**: 177-181.
Kumerloeve, H. (1962b). Zur Geschichte der Waldrapp-Kolonie in Birecik am oberen Euphrat. *J. Orn.* **103**: 389-398.
Kumerloeve, H. (1965). Zur Situation der Waldrappkolonie *Geronticus eremita* (L. 1758) in Birecik am Euphrat. *Die Vogelwelt* **86**: 42-48.
Kumerloeve, H. (1966a). Zur Brutverbreitung und Durchzug des Weiss-Storches *C. ciconia* (L.) in Kleinasien. *Vogelwarte* **23**: 221-224.
Kumerloeve, H. (1966b). Zum Zug des Schwarzstorches *Ciconia nigra* (L.) in der Türkei. *Vogelwarte* **23**: 310-311.
Kumerloeve, H. (1966c). Le Lac Djabboul, a l'est d'Alep, Syrie, lieu d'hivernage des Flamants. *Alauda* **34**: 39-44.
Kumerloeve, H. (1967). Nouvelles données sur la situation de la colonie d'Ibis chevelus *Geronticus eremita* (L. 1758), à Birecik sur l'Euphrate (Turquie). *Alauda* **35**: 194-202.
Kumerloeve, H. (1969a). Situation de la colonie d'Ibis chevelus *Geronticus eremita* à Birecik en 1968 et 1969. *Alauda* **37**: 260-261.
Kumerloeve, H. (1969b). Vom Waldrapp, *Geronticus eremita*, dem einstigen Brutvogel der Alpen. *Jb. Ver. Schutz Alpenpfl. Tiere* **34**: 132-138.
Kumerloeve, H. (1971). Zum Brutvorkommen des Sichlers, (*Plegadis falcinellus* L.) im vorderen Orient. *Zool. Abh. Dres.* **30(19)**: 243-246.
Kumerloeve, H. (1978). Waldrapp, *Geronticus eremita* (Linnaeus, 1758) und Glattnackenrapp, *Geronticus calvus* (Boddaert, 1783): zur Geschichte ihrer Erforschung und zur Gegenwärtigen Bestandssituation. *Ann. Nathist. Mus. Wien* **81**: 319-349.
Kumerloeve, H. (1983). Zur Kenntnis altägyptischer Ibis-Darstellungen, unter besonderer Berücksichtigung des Waldrapps, *Geronticus eremita* (Linnaeus, 1758). *Bonn. zool. Beitr.* **34**: 197-234.
Kumerloeve, H. (1984). The Waldrapp, *Geronticus eremita* (Linnaeus, 1758): Historical Review, Taxonomic History, and Present Status. *Biol. Conserv.* **30**: 363-373.
Kurechi, M. (1991). Report on East Asian races of Bean Geese in Japan and Kamchatka. *IWRB Threatened Waterfowl Research Group Newsletter* **1**: 11-12.
Kurilovich, L.Ya. & Tarkhanova, M.A. (1986). [The time budget and daily activity of the female and young *Melanitta fusca* and *Bucephala clangula* in Kandalaksh Bay]. Pp: 176-190 in: Ilichev, V.D. ed. (1986). [*Recent Problems in Ornithology*]. Nauke, Moskow. In Russian.
Kurochkin, E.N. (1963). Distribution of certain species of sea birds in the northern part of the Pacific Ocean. *Zool. J.* **42**(8).
Kuroda, N. (1954). *On the Classification and Phylogeny of the Order Tubinares, Particularly the Shearwaters (*Puffinus*), with Special Consideration on their Osteology and Habit Diferentiation.* Author, Tokyo.
Kuroda, N. (1955). Observation on pelagic birds of the northwest Pacific. *Condor* **57**: 290-300.
Kuroda, N. (1960). Notes on the breeding seasons in the Tubinares. *Japanese J. Zool.* **12**: 449-464.
Kuroda, N. (1967). Morpho-anatomical analysis of parallel evolution between the Diving Petrel and Ancient Auk, with comparative osteological data on other species. *Misc. Rep. Yamashina Inst. Orn. Zool.* **5**: 111-137.
Kuroda, N. (1988). A Distributional Analysis of *Diomedea immutabilis* and *D. nigripes* in the North Pacific. *J. Yamashina Inst. Orn.* **20**: 1-20.
Kury, C.R. & Gochfeld, M. (1975). Human interference and gull predation in cormorant colonies. *Biol. Conserv.* **8**: 23-24.
Kushlan, J.A. (1973a). Least Bittern nesting colonially. *Auk* **90**: 685-686.
Kushlan, J.A. (1973b). Promiscuous mating behaviour in the White Ibis. *Wilson Bull.* **85**: 331-332.
Kushlan, J.A. (1974). *The ecology of the White Ibis in southern Florida. A Regional Study.* PhD dissertation. University of Miami, Florida.
Kushlan, J.A. (1976a). Feeding rhythm in nestling White Ibis. *Wilson Bull.* **88**: 656-658.
Kushlan, J.A. (1976b). Site selection for nesting colonies by the American White Ibis *Eudocimus albus* in Florida. *Ibis* **118**: 590-593.
Kushlan, J.A. (1977a). Growth energetics of the White Ibis. *Condor* **79**: 31-36.
Kushlan, J.A. (1977b). Sexual dimorphism in the White Ibis. *Wilson Bull.* **89**: 92-98.
Kushlan, J.A. (1977c). Foraging behaviour of the White Ibis. *Wilson Bull.* **89**: 342-345.
Kushlan, J.A. (1977d). Populations energetics of the American White Ibis. *Auk* **94**: 114-122.
Kushlan, J.A. (1977e). Differential growth of body parts in the White Ibis. *Auk* **94**: 164-166.
Kushlan, J.A. (1977f). The significance of plumage colour in the formation of feeding aggregations of Ciconiiformes. *Ibis* **119**: 361-364.
Kushlan, J.A. (1978). Feeding Ecology of Wading Birds. Pp 249-297 in: Sprunt *et al.* (1978).
Kushlan, J.A. (1979). Feeding ecology and prey selection in the White Ibis. *Condor* **81**: 376-389.
Kushlan, J.A. (1981). Resource use strategies of wading birds. *Wilson Bull.* **93**: 145-163.
Kushlan, J.A. (1983). Pair formation behavior of the Galapagos Lava Heron. *Wilson Bull.* **95(1)**: 118-121.
Kushlan, J.A. (1985). Heron. Pp. 282-284 in: Campbell & Lack (1985).
Kushlan, J.A. (1986). Responses of Wading Birds to Seasonally Fluctuating Water Levels: Strategies and Their Limits. *Colonial Waterbirds* **9(2)**: 155-162.
Kushlan, J.A. & Frohring, P.C. (1985). Decreases in the Brown Pelican population in southern Florida. *Colonial Waterbirds* **8(2)**: 83-95.
Kushlan, J.A. & Frohring, P.C (1986). The history of the southern Florida Wood stork population. *Wilson Bull.* **98**: 368-386.
Kushlan, J.A. & Kushlan, M.S. (1975). Food of the White Ibis in southern Florida. *Florida Field Nature* **3**: 30-39.
Kushlan, J.A. & McEwan, L.C. (1982). Nesting phenology of the Double-crested Cormorant. *Wilson Bull.* **94**: 201-206.
Kushlan, J.A. & Morales, G. & Frohring, P.C. (1985). Foraging niche relations of wading birds in tropical wet savannahs. Pp. 663-692 in: Buckley *et al.* (1985).
Kushlan, J.A. & Schortemeyer, J.L. (1974). Glossy Ibis nesting in southern Florida. *Florida Field Nature* **2**: 13-14.
Kushlan, J.A. & White, D.A. (1977). Nesting wading bird populations in southern Florida. *Florida Science* **40**: 65-72.
Kushlan J.A., Hancock, J.A. & Pinowski, J. (1982). Behavior of Whistling and Capped Herons in the seasonal savannas of Venezuela and Argentina. *Condor* **84**: 255-260.
Kushlan, J.A., Ogden, J.C. & Higer, A.L. (1975). Relation of water level and fish availability to Wood Stork reproduction in southern Everglades, Florida. US Geol. Survey Open File Report No. 75-434. Tallahassee, Florida.
Kydyraliew, J. (1967). Die Streifengans (*Anser indicus*) im Tienschan Gebirge (Translated from Russian). *Ornithologiya* **8**: 245-253.
Kyllingstad, H.C. (1986). A record of Bald Ibis from the Sinai Mountains. *Bull. Orn. Soc. Middle East* **17**: 1-2.
La Cock, G.D. (1988). Effect of substrate and ambient temperature on burrowing African Penguins. *Wilson Bull.* **100**: 131-132.
La Cock, G.D. & Hänel, C. (1987). Survival of African Penguins *Spheniscus demersus* at Dyer Island, Southern Cape, South Africa. *J. Field. Orn.* **58(3)**: 284-287.
La Cock, G.D., Duffy, D.C. & Cooper, J. (1987). Population dynamics of theAfrican Penguins *Spheniscus demersus* at Marcus Island in the Benguela Upwelling ecosystem: 1979-85. *Biol. Conserv.* **40**: 117-126.
La Cock, G.D., Hecht, T. & Klages, N. (1984). The winter diet of Gentoo Penguins at Marion Island. *Ostrich* **55**: 188-191.
LaBastille, A. (as Bowes) (1965). An ecological investigation of the Giant Pied-billed Grebe, *Podilymbus gigas* Griscom. *Bull. Brit. Orn. Club* **85**: 14-19.
LaBastille, A. (1969). *The life history, ecology and management of the Giant Pied-billed Grebe (*Podilymbus gigas*), Lake Atitlán, Guatemala.* PhD dissertation. Cornell University, Ithaca, N.Y.
LaBastille, A. (1974). *Ecology and Management of the Atitlan Grebe, Lake Atitlán, Guatemala.* Wildlife Monographs **37**: 1-66.
LaBastille, A. (1978). Management of Giant Pied-billed Grebes on Lake Atitlán. Pp 397-401 in: Temple, S.A. ed. *Endangered Birds: Management Techniques for Preserving Threatened Species.* University of Wisconsin Press, Madison.
LaBastille, A. (1983a). Goodbye, Giant Grebe? *Nat. Hist.* **42**: 64-72.
LaBastille, A (1983b). The Guatemalan Giant Grebe: Is there any hope? Pp. 485-493 in: *Proceedings of the Jean Delacour/IFCB Symposium on Breeding Birds in Captivity.* International Foundation for the Conservation of Birds, North Hollywood, California.
LaBastille, A. (1984). Drastic Decline in Guatemala's Giant Pied-billed Grebe Population. *Environ. Conserv.* **11**: 346-348.
LaBastille, A. (1990a). And now they are gone. *Int. Wildl.* **20(4)**: 19-23.
LaBastille, A. (1990b). *Mama Poc: an ecologist's account of the extinction of a species.* Norton, New York.
LaBastille, A. (1992). The Giant Grebes of Atitlán. A Chronicle of Extinction. *Living Bird Quarterly* **11(1)**: 10-15.
LaBastille, A. (as Bowes) **& Bowes, C.V.** (1962). Recent census and observations of the Giant Pied-billed Grebe. *Auk* **79**: 707-709.
LaBastille, A., Ovidio, J. & Bauer, E. (1973). Census in April 1972 of the Atitlán Grebe (*Podilymbus gigas*), Guatemala. *Biol. Conserv.* **5**: 62-63.
Labedz, T.E. (1987). A Nebraska specimen record of Clark's Grebe *Aechmophorus clarkii* (Lawrence). *Nebraska Bird Review* **55**: 68-72.
Lacan, F. (1971). Observations écologiques sur le Pétrel de Wilson en Terre Adélie. *L'Oiseau et la R.F.O.* **41(No. Spéc.)**: 65-89.
Lack, D. (1945). The ecology of closely related species with special reference to Cormorant (*Phalacrocorax carbo*) and Shag (*P. aristotelis*). *J. Anim. Ecol.* **14**: 12-16.
Lack, D. (1947). *Darwin's Finches: An Essay on the General Biological Theory of Evolution.* Cambridge University Press, Cambrige, England.
Lack, D. (1966) *Population Studies of Birds.* Clarendon Press, Oxford.
Lack, D. (1967). The significance of clutch-size in waterfowl. *Wildfowl Trust Ann. Rep.* **18**: 125-128.
Lack, D. (1968). *Ecological Adaptations for Breeding in Birds.* Methuen, London.
Lack, D. (1971). *Ecological Isolation in Birds.* Blackwell Scientific Publications, Oxford.
Lack, D. (1974). *Evolution Illustrated by Waterfowl.* Blackwell Scientific Publications, Oxford.
Lack, D. (1976). *Island Biology, Illustrated by the Land Birds of Jamaica.* Blackwell Scientific Publications, Oxford.
Lack, P. ed. (1986). *The Atlas of Wintering Birds in Britain and Ireland.* T & A D Poyser, Calton, England.
Ladhams, D.E., Prytherch, R.J. & Simmons, K.E.L. (1967). Pied-billed Grebe in Somerset. *British Birds* **60**: 295-299.
Lagerquist, B.A. & Ankney, C.D. (1989). Interspecific Differences in Bill and Tongue Morphology among Diving Ducks (*Aythya* spp., *Oxyura jamaicensis*). *Can. J. Zool.* **67(11)**: 2694-2699.

Lahile, F. (1921). Estudio de las aves en relación a la agricultura. *Hornero* **2**: 214-223.
Lai Yong-jin (1987). A preliminary survey on the population of the Mandarin Duck, *Aix galericulata*, in Pinghe Co., Fujian Province. *Chinese Wildlife* 2: 18-19.
Lalas, C. (1974). Australian Ibis. *Wildl. Austr.* **11**: 30-32.
Lalas, C. (1979). Double breeding season by Pied Shags on Stewart Island. *Notornis* **26**: 94-95.
Lambert, F.R. (1988). *The Status of the White-winged Wood Duck in Sumatra. A Preliminary Report*. Asian Wetland Bureau (AWB-PHPA)/Interwader Report **4**. Bogor, Indonesia.
Lambert, F.R. & Erftemeijer, P.L.A. (1989). The waterbirds of Pulau Rambut, Java. *Kukila* **4**: 109-118.
Lambert, K. (1983). Sturmschwalbe (*Hydrobates pelagicus*) und Schwalbenmöwe (*Xema sabini*) vor der Küste von Moçambique. *Beitr. Vogelk. Jena* **29(1)**: 12-16.
Lambert, K. (1984). Der Kerguelensturmvogel, *Pterodroma brevirostris* Lesson, 1831, im Südatlantik. *Beitr. Vogelk. Jena* **30(3)**: 191-202.
Lambrecht, K. (1933). *Handbuch der Palaeornithologie*. Gebrüder Borntraeger, Berlin.
Lamm, D.W. (1965). Seasonal counts of birds at Lake George, New South Wales. *Emu* **65**: 114-128.
Lamm, D.W. (1974). White Hawk preying on the Great Tinamou. *Auk* **91**: 845-846.
Lammi, E. (1985). *Silkkiuikun* Podiceps cristatus *pesimisbiologia tiheässä eteläsuomalaisessa populaatiossa*. MSc thesis, University Helsinki.
Lamprecht, J. (1986a). Structure and causation of the dominance hierarchy in a flock of Bar-headed Geese (*Anser indicus*). *Behaviour* **96**: 28-48.
Lamprecht, J. (1986b). Social dominance and reproductive success in a Goose Flock (*Anser indicus*). *Behaviour* **97**: 50-65.
Lamprecht, J. (1987). Female reproductive strategies in Bar-headed Geese (*Anser indicus*): why are geese monogamous?. *Behav. Ecol. Sociobiol.* **21**: 297-305.
Lamprecht, J. & Buhrow, H. (1987). Harem polygyny in Bar-headed Geese. *Ardea* **75**: 285-292.
Lancaster, D.A. (1964a). Life history of the Boucard tinamou (*Crypturellus boucardi*) in British Honduras. Part I: distribution and general behavior. *Condor* **66**: 165-181.
Lancaster, D.A. (1964b). Life history of the Boucard tinamou (*Crypturellus boucardi*) in British Honduras. Part II: breeding biology. *Condor* **66**: 253-276.
Lancaster, D.A. (1964c). Biology of the Brushland Tinamou, *Nothoprocta cinerascens*. *Bull. Amer. Mus. Nat. Hist.* **127**: 271-314.
Land, H.C. (1970). *Birds of Guatemala*. Livingston Publishing Company, Wynnewood, PA.
Lane, R. (1978). Cooperative breeding in the Australian Little Grebe. *Sunbird* **9**: 2.
Lane, S.G. (1980). Black-faced Shags breeding on islands off Wilsons Promontory, Victoria. *Austr. Bird Watcher* **8**: 167-168.
Lange, C.E. (1981). Una temporada de observaciones sobre *Podiceps gallardoi* (Aves Podicipediformes). Ecología y etología. *Neotropica* **27**: 39-56.
Langham, N.P. (1984). Observations on the Red-footed Booby on Mabualau Island, Fiji.
Langley, C.H. (1983). Biology of the Little Bittern in the Southwestern Cape. *Ostrich* **54(2)**: 83-94.
Langrand, O. (1981). Nidification du Paille-en queue à queue rouge (*Phaethon rubricauda*) sur le territoire malgache. *L'Oiseau et la R.F.O.* **51**: 338-339.
Langrand, O. (1990). *Guide to the Birds of Madagascar*. Yale University Press, New Haven & London.
Lanham, U.N. (1947). Notes on the phylogeny of the *Pelecaniformes*. *Auk* **64**: 65-70.
Lank, D.B., Cooch, E.G., Rockwell, R.F. & Cooke, F. (1989). Environmental and demographic correlates of intraspecific nest parasitism in Lesser Snow Geese *Chen caerulescens caerulescens*. *J. Anim. Ecol.* **58**: 29-45.
Lank, D.B., Mineau, P., Rockwell, R.F. & Cooke, F. (1989). Intraspecific nest parasitism and extra-pair copulation in Lesser Snow Geese. *Anim. Behav.* **37**: 74-89.
Lansdown, R.V. (1988). Some Calls, Displays and Associated Morphology of the Cinnamon Bittern (*Ixobrychus cinnamomeus*) and their possible functions. *Colonial Waterbirds* **11(2)**: 308-310.
Lansdown, R.V. (1989). Displays of the Sumatran Heron *Ardea sumatrana*. *Colonial Waterbirds* **12(1)**: 113-114.
Lansdown, R.V. (1990). Chinese Egret. *Bull. Oriental Bird Club* **2**: 27-30.
Larkins, D. (1989). Heat regulation in the Great-billed Heron "*Areda sumatrana*". *Corella* **13(1)**: 21-23.
Larsen, J.W. (1967). *The Dark-rumped Petrel in Haleakala Crater*. National Park Service, US Department of the Interior, Hawaii.
Lashmar, A.F.C. (1987). Seabird Islands no. 177. Troubridge Island. *Corella* **11(13)**: 89-92.
Lassus, N.S. (1973). Saddle-bill Storks. *Bull. East Afr. Nat. Hist. Soc.* **May**: 74.
László, S. (1986). Data on the food of the Purple (*Ardea purpurea*), Night (*Nycticorax nycticorax*) and Squacco (*Ardeola ralloides*), Herons on Lake Ludas. *Larus* **36-37**: 175-182.
Lathigara, R. (1989). *Behavioural and ecological studies on population census, roosting, foraging, feeding, and breeding of the Indian Black Ibis at Jamnagar*. MSc dissertation. Saurashtra University, Rajkot, India.
Latta, W.C. & Sharkey, R.F. (1966). Feeding behavior of the American Merganser in captivity. *J. Wildl. Manage.* **30**: 17-30.
Laubhan, M.K. & Frederick, A.R. (1991). Characteristics of Yellow-crowned Night Heron in lowland hardwood forests of Missouri. *Wilson Bull.* **103(3)**: 486-491.
Lauder, C.S. & Murray, D.P. (1978). Breeding of the Australian Little Grebe. *Notornis* **25**: 251-252.
Lauhachinda, V. (1969). *Preliminary study of the life history of the Open-billed Stork,* Anastomus oscitans *(Boddaert)*. MSc thesis. Kasetsart University, Bangkok, Thailand.
Laurie-Ahlberg, C.C. & McKinney, F. (1979). The nod-swim display of male Green-winged Teal (*Anas crecca*). *Anim. Behav.* **27**: 165-172.
Laurila, T. & Hario, M. (1988). Environmental and genetic factors influencing clutch size, egg volume, date of laying and female weight in the Common Eider *Somateria mollissima*. *Finnish Game Res.* **45**: 19-30.
Laursen, K. (1989). Estimates of Sea Duck winter populations of the Western Palearctic. *Dan. Rev. Game Biol.* **13 (6)**: 1-22.
Lavery, H.J. (1972). The gray teal at saline drought-refuges in north Queensland. *Wildfowl* **22**: 56-63.
Law, S.C. (1926). The nesting of the Open-bill Stork (*Anastomus oscitans*) in Purulia, Manbhum District. *J. Bombay Nat. Hist. Soc.* **31**: 223-226.
Lawniczak, D. (1982). Z ekologii i biologii perkoza dwuczubego (*Podiceps cristatus* L.), perkoza rdzawoszyyjego (*Podiceps grisegena* Bodd.) i zausznika (*Podiceps nigricollis* C.L. Brehm) na stawach rybnych kolo Milicza. [Summary: On the ecology and biology of Great Crested Grebe, Red-necked Grebe and Black-necked Grebe breeding in the fish-ponds near Milisz]. *Acta Univ. Wratisl.* **12**: 63-81.
Lawrence, G.E. (1950). The diving and feeding activity of the Western Grebe on the breeding grounds. *Condor* **52**: 3-16.
Laycock, G. (1979). The pelican no one knows. *Audubon* **81(1)**: 36-47.
Lazaro, E., Chozas, P. & Fernandez-Cruz M. (1986). Demografía de la Cigüeña Blanca en España. Censo nacional de 1984. *Ardeola* **33(1-2)**: 131-169.
Lazarus, J. (1978). Vigilance, flock size and domain of danger size in the White-fronted Goose. *Wildfowl* **29**: 135-145.
Lazarus, J. & Inglis, I.R. (1978). The breeding behaviour of the Pink-footed Goose: parental care and vigilant behaviour during the fledgling period. *Behaviour* **65**: 62-88.
Le Maho, Y. (1977). The Emperor Penguin: a strategy to live and breed in the cold. *Amer. Sci.* **65**: 680-693.
Le Maho, Y. (1983). Le Manchot Empereur: une stratégie basée sur l'économie d'énergie. *Courrier CNRS* **50**: 15-21.
Le Maho, Y. & Despin, B. (1976). Réduction de la dépense énergétique au cours du jeûne chez le Manchot Royal (*Aptenodytes patagonica*). *Comptes Rendus Acad. Scienc. Paris. (Ser. D)* **283**: 979-982.
Le Maho, Y., Delclitte, P. & Chatonnet, J. (1976). Thermoregulation in fasting Emperor Penguins under natural conditions. *Amer. J. Physiol.* **231**: 913-922.
Le Maho, Y., Delclitte, P. & Groscolas, R. (1977). Body temperature regulation of the Emperor Penguin (*Aptenodytes forsteri* G.) during physiological fasting. Pp. 501-509 in: Llano (1977).
Lebedeva, M.I. (1958). [The White Stork in Azerbaijan]. *Priroda. Moscow* **9**: 104-105. In Russian.
Lebedeva, M.I. (1959). [Biology of the Black Stork (*Ciconia nigra*) in the Belovezskoi forest]. *Ornitologiya* **2**: 138-142. In Russian.
Lebedeva, M.I. (1960a). [On a number of White Storks in the Soviet Union]. *Ornitologiya* **3**: 413-419. In Russian.
Lebedeva, M.I. (1960b). [Some information on the migration and numbers of the White Stork]. *Migracii Schivotnych 2, Akad. Nauk C.C.C.P.* **2**: 130-139. In Russian.
Lebedeva, M.I. (1977). [The range and numbers of Oriental White Storks in the USSR]. Pp. 228-229 in: Winter, S. ed. *VII All-Soviet Ornithological Conference*. Zoological Institute of the Academy of Science of the Ukranian SSR, Kiev.
Leber, K.K. (1980). Habitat utilization in a tropical heronry. *Brenesia* **17**: 97-136.
Lebret, T. (1947). The migration of the Teal *Anas crecca crecca* L. in western Europe. *Ardea* **35**: 79-131.
Lebreton, J.D., Paucod, J.C. & Coquillart, H. (1983). Sur les relations du Grèbe à cou noir, *Podiceps nigricollis*, et de la Mouette rieuse, *Larus ridibundus*, en période de nidification. *Nos Oiseaux* **37**: 21-24.
Leck, C.F. (1971). Cooperative feeding in *Leucophoyx thula* and *Podilymbus podiceps* (Aves). *Am. Midl. Nat.* **86**: 241-242.
Leck, C.F. (1973). Pelicans in the city of Lima, Peru. *Condor* **75**: 69.
Ledant, J.P., Jacob, J.P., Jacobs, P., Malher, F., Ochando, B. & Roché, J. (1981). Mise à jour de l'avifaune Algérienne. *Gerfaut* **71**: 295-398.
Lee, D.S. (1979). Second record of the south Trinidad Petrel for North America. *Amer. Birds* **33**: 138-139.
Lee, D.S. (1986). Seasonal distribution of marine birds in North Carolina waters. 1975-1986. *Amer. Birds* **40**: 409-412.
Lee, D.S. (1987a). Common Loons wintering in offshore waters. *Chat* **51**: 40-42.
Lee, D.S. (1987b). Long-legged Pink Things: What are they? Where do they come from? *Chat* **51(2)**: 43-48.
Lee, D.S. & Grant, D.S. (1986). An albino Greater Shearwater: feather abrasion and flight energetics. *Wilson Bull.* **98**: 488-490.
Lee, D.S. & Irvin, E.W. (1983). Tropicbirds in the Carolinas: status and period of occurrence of two tropical pelagic species. *Chat* **47(1)**: 1-13.
Lee, D.S., Wingate, D.B. & Kale, H.W. (1981). Records of tropicbirds in the North Atlantic. *Amer. Birds* **35(6)**: 887-890.
Lee, D.T. (1967). Winter breeding of the Western Grebe. *Condor* **69**: 209.
Lefebvre, E.A. (1977). Laysan Albatross breeding behaviour. *Auk* **94**: 270-274.
Léger, C. & McNeil, R. (1985). Nest attendance and care of young in Double-crested Cormorants. *Colonial Waterbirds* **8(2)**: 96-103.
Léger, C. & McNeil, R. (1987a). Choix de l'emplacement des nids de Cormorans à aigrettes (*Phalacrocorax auritus*) aux îles de la Madeleine, Québec. *Can. J. Zool.* **65**: 24-34.
Léger, C. & McNeil, R. (1987b). Brood size and chick position as factors influencing feeding frequency, growth and survival of nesting Double-crested Cormorants (*Phalacrocorax auritus*). *Can. Fiel Nat.* **101**: 351-361.
Lehmann-Nitsche, R. (1921). Aclimatación de la perdiz grande y de la martineta en Alemania. *Hornero* **2**: 292-294.
Lehtonen, L. (1970). Zur biologie des Prachttauchers, *Gavia a. arctica* (L.). *Ann. Zool. Fennici* **7**: 25-60.
Lehtonen, L. (1974). Zur individuellen Erkennung des Prachttauchers, *Gavia a. arctica* im Brutkleid. *Ornis Fenn.* **51(2)**: 117-121.
Lekagul, B. & Round, P.D. (1991). *A Guide to the Birds of Thailand*. Saha Karn Bhaet Co., Bangkok.
Leonovich, V.V. & Nikolyevski, L.A. (1976). [Notes about Far Eastern Stork breeding]. *Trans. Oka. State Nature Reserve* **12**: 17-19.
Leopold, A.S. (1959). *Wildlife of Mexico. The Game Birds and Mammals*. University of California Press, Berkeley, California.
Leopold, M. & Platteeuw, M. (1987). Talrijk voorkomen van Jan van Genten *Sula bassana* bij Texel in de herfst: reactie op lokale voedselsituatie. *Limosa* **60**: 105-110.
Lequette, B. & Jouventin, P. (1991). The dance of the Wandering Albatross II: acoustic signals. *Emu* **91(3)**: 172-178.
Lequette, B. & Weimerskirch, H. (1990). Influence of parental experience on the growth of Wandering Albatross chicks. *Condor* **92**: 726-731.
LeResche, R.W. & Sladen, W.J.L. (1970). Establishment of pair and breeding site bonds by young known-age Adelie Penguins (*Pygoscelis adeliae*). *Anim. Behav.* **18**: 517-526.
Lernould, J.M. (1977). Some notes on Hartlaub's Duck. *A.P. & W.S. Magazine* **77/6**.
Lernould, J.M. (1983). The breeding of Hartlaub's Duck. Pp. 495-501 in: Delacour, J. ed. (1983). *Proceedings of the Jean Delacour/IFCB Symposium on Breeding Birds in Captivity*. International Foundation for the Conservation of Birds, Los Angeles.
Lesniczak, A.B. (1989). The Black Stork, *Ciconia nigra*, in the environs of Rybnik on the Silesian Upland. *Chronmy Przyr. Ojczysta* **45**: 68-70.
LeSouef, W.H.D. (1917). Australian Ibises. *Emu* **17**: 94-95.
Lessells, C.M. (1987). Parental investment, brood-size and time-budgets: behaviour of Lesser Snow Geese families (*Anser c. caerulescens*). *Ardea* **75**: 189-203.
Leuthold, W. (1977). Notes on the breeding biology of the Ostrich *Struthio camelus* in Tsavo East National Park, Kenya. *Ibis* **119**: 541-544.
Leuzinger, H. (1966). Einwirkungen des Polarwinters 1962/63 auf den Bestand des Zwergtauchers, *Podiceps ruficollis*, in der deutschen Schweiz und im Grenzgebiet am Untersee. *Orn. Beob.* **63**: 2-18.
Léveque, R. (1964). Notes on Ecuadorian birds. *Ibis* **106**: 52-62.
Lever, C. (1984). Conservation success for two Bermudan bird species. *Oryx* **18**(3): 138-143.
Lever, C. (1987). *Naturalized Birds of the World*. Longman Scientific & Technical, Essex, England.
Lever, K.K. (1980). Habitat utilization in a tropical Heronry. *Brenesia* **17**: 97-136.
Levy, S.H. (1959). The Least Grebe recorded in Arizona. *Condor* **61**: 226.
Lewis, A.D. (1989). Two commensal feeding associations observed in Kenya. *Scopus* **12**: 101-102.
Lewis, A.D. (1990). Hamerkop *Scopus umbretta* feeding amongst a herd of African Buffalo *Syncerus caffer*. *Scopus* **14**: 17.
Lewis, A.D. & Pearson, D.J. (1981a). Raptor and stork migration at Namanga, southern Kenya. *Scopus* **5**: 83-84.
Lewis, A.D. & Pearson, D.J. (1981b). Stork and raptor migration in South Nyanza, Kenya. *Scopus* **5**: 51.
Lewis, H.F. (1929). *The natural history of the Double-crested Cormorant (*Phalacrocorax auritus auritus *(Lesson))*. Ru-Mi-Lou Books, Ottawa.
Lewis, J.C. & Garrison, R.L. (1984). Habitat suitability index models: American Black Duck (wintering). *US Fish & Wildlife Service FWS/OBS* **82**: 1-16.
Lewis, J.C. & Nelson, M. (1988). Cover Type Relationships and Black Duck Winter Habitat. Pp. 391-398 in: Weller (1988).
Lewis, J.C. & Renton, K. (1989). The status and ecology of the West-Indian Whistling Duck (*Dendrocygna arborea*) on Barbuda. *Neotropical Wetlands Newsletter*. **4**: 10-13.
Leys, H.N. & de Wilde, J.J.F.E. (1971). Het Vorkommen van de fuut *Podiceps cristatus* in Nederland. *Limosa* **44**: 133-183.
Li Cheng-ling, Li Se-dong *et al.* (1986). Preliminary study on the breeding ecology of the Chinese Little Bittern *Ixobrychus sinensis sinensis*. *J. Huazhong Agricultural Univ.* **5(1)**: 28-32.
Li Fulai (1990). First captive breeding of the Crested Ibis *Nipponia nippon* at Beijing Zoo. *Int. Zoo. Yb.* **29**: 90-94.
Li Fulai & Gao Xijing (1989). [Study on the post-nestling moulting of the Crested Ibis *Nipponia nippon*]. *Chinese Wildlife* **5**: 21-22. In Chinese.
Li Fulai & Huang Shiquiang (1986). [A Survey on reproductive habits of *Nipponia nippon*]. *Bull. Biol.* **12**: 6-8. In Chinese.
Li Fulai, Quin, Z. & Ten, H. (1990). [Study on the microstructure and components of eggshell of Japanese Crested Ibis]. *Zool. Res.* **11**: 173-177. In Chinese with English summary.
Li Pei-xun, Zhu Lai-chun (1984). [Life of the Manchurian Green Heron *Butorides striatus* (Northeast of China)]. *Chinese Wildlife* **4**: 23, 26-27. In Chinese.
Li Yung-hsin & Liu Xi-yue. (1963). [On the breeding behaviour of the Pond Heron *Ardeola bacchus* in Yichang (Hubei Province)]. *Acta Zool. Sinica* **15(2)**: 203-210. In Chinese with English summary.
Liao Yan-fa (1981). Observation on the reproductive behavior of the Ruddy Shelduck *Tadorna ferruginea*. *Wildlife* **3**: 34-36, 31.
Liebermann, J. (1936). *Monografía de las Tinamiformes argentinas, problema de su domesticación*. Buenos Aires.
Lies, M.F. & Behle, W.H. (1966). Status of White Pelican in the United States and Canada through 1964. *Condor* **68**: 279-292.
Lieu, Y.Z. (1981). [Discovery of Japanese Crested Ibis in Qinling]. *Acta Zool. Sinica* **27**: 273. In Chinese.
Ligon, J.D. (1967). Relationships of the cathartid vultures. *Occas. Pap. Mus. Zool. Univ. Mich.* **651**.
Lill, A. & Baldwin, J. (1983). Weight changes and the mode of depot fat accumulation in migratory Short-tailed Shearwaters. *Austr. J. Zool.* **31**: 891-902.
Lindberg, P. (1968). Något om storlommens (*Gavia arctica* L.) och smålommens (*Gavia stellata* L.) ekologi. *Zoologisk Revy* **30**: 83-88.
Lindblad, J. (1969). *Journey to Red Birds*. Hill and Wang, New York.
Lindsey, T.R. (1986). *The Seabirds of Australia*. Angus & Robertson publishers, Hong Kong.
Lindstedt, S.L. & Calder, W.A. (1976). Body size and longevity in birds. *Condor* **78**: 91-94.
Lindvall, M.L. (1976). *Breeding biology of pesticide-PCB contamination of Western Grebe at Bear River Migratory Bird Refuge*. MSc thesis. Utah State University, Logan, Utah.
Lindvall, M.L. & Low, J.B. (1980). Effects of DDE, TDE, and PCBs on shell thickness in Western Grebe eggs, Bear River Migratory Bird Refuge, Utah - 1973-1974. *Pestic. Monit. J.* **14**: 108-111.
Lindvall, M.L. & Low, J.B. (1982). Nesting ecology and production of Western Grebes at Bear River Migratory Bird Refuge, Utah. *Condor* **84**: 66-70.
Line, L. (1992). Lord of the Northern Lakes. *Int. Wildl.* **22(3)**: 30-36.
Line, L.J. (1941). Nesting of the Hadada Ibis (*Hagedashia hagedash hagedash*). *Ostrich* **11**: 137-139.
Lint, K.C. (1956). Breeding of the Horned Screamer. *Avicult. Mag.* **62**: 127-128.
Lintermans, M. (1989). The distribution and breeding of the Little Penguin on Bowen Island, Jervis Bay. *Corella* **13(4)**: 123-125.

Linton, A. (1978). *The Food and Feeding Habits of the Leach's Storm-Petrel (*Oceanodroma leucorhoa*) at Pearl I., Nova Scotia, and Middle Lawn I., Newfoundland*. MSc thesis, Dalhousie University.
Lippens, L. (1983). L'agressivité du Grèbe castagneux (*Tachybaptus ruficollis*). *Gerfaut* **73**: 213-214.
Lippens, L. & Wille, H. (1976). *Les Oiseaux du Zaïre*. Editions Lannoo Tielt.
Lishman, G.S. (1983). The comparative breeding biology, feeding ecology and bioenergetics of Adelie and Chinstrap Penguins. PhD thesis, University of Oxford.
Lishman, G.S. (1985a). The comparative breeding biology of Adelie and Chinstrap Penguins, *Pygoscelis adeliae* and *P. antarctica*, at Signy Island, South Orkney Islands. *Ibis* **127**: 84-99.
Lishman, G.S. (1985b). The food and feeding ecology of Adelie and Chinstrap Penguins at Signy Island, South Orkney Islands. *J. Zoology. London* **205**: 245-263.
Lishman, G.S. & Croxall, J.P. (1983). Diving depths of the Chinstrap Penguin *Pygoscelis antarctica*. *Bull. Brit. Antarct. Surv.* **61**: 21-25.
de Lisle, M. (1956). Sur une observation de *Balaeniceps rex* au Cameroun. *L'Oiseau et la R.F.O.* **26**: 1-3.
Little, B. & Furness, R.W. (1985). Long-distance moult migration by British Goosanders *Mergus merganser*. *Ringing and Migration* **6**: 77-82.
Littlejohns, R.T. (1936). Some random notes on the Little Grebe. *Emu* **35**: 350-354.
Litvidinova, N.A., Tkachenko, E.E. & Litvinov, V.P. (1984). Nesting of the flamingo (*Phoenicopterus roseus*) in Kyzyl-Agach nature preserve, Azebaidjan SSR. *Ornitologiya* **19**: 182-183.
Litvinenko, N. (1968). [On distribution of the Oriental White Stork at Lower Amur]. *Ornitologiya* **9**: 356-358. In Russian.
Litvinenko, N. (1982). Nesting of Grey Heron (*Ardea cinerea* L.) on Sea Islands of South Primorye. *J. Yamashina Inst. Orn.* **14**: 220-231.
Litvinenko, N. ed. (1985). [*Rare and Endangered Birds of the Far-East Collection of Scientic Papers*]. Far-East Science Centre, Vladivostok. In Russian.
Litvinenko, N. & Shibaev, Y. (1991). Status and conservation of the seabirds nesting in southeast U.S.S.R. Pp. 175-204 in: Croxall (1991).
Liu Chang-jiang (1989). [A new report on the distribution of the Chinese Merganser *Mergus squamatus* in foreign countries]. *Chinese J. Zool.* **6**: 36-37. In Chinese.
Liu Huan-jin, Feng Jing-yi *et al.* (1982). [Ecological study of the breeding of the Chestnut Bittern *Ixobrychus cinnamomeus*]. *Acta Ecol. Sinica* **2(4)**: 397-401. In Chinese.
Liu Huan-jin, Su Hua-long, *et al.* (1986). [A preliminary study on the reproductive ecology of the Chinese Little Bittern *Ixobrychus sinensis*]. *Chinese J. Zool.* **4**: 13-15. In Chinese.
Liu Huanjin, Su Hualong, *et al.* (1985). [The numerical distribution of the Black Stork *Ciconia nigra* in Shanxi Province]. *Acta Ecol. Sinica* **5(2)**: 193-194. In Chinese.
Liu Yi, Yu Guo-hai, *et al.* (1988). [Reproductive ecology of Shrenk's Bittern *Ixobrychus eurhytmus*]. *Chinese Wildlife* **1988(6)**: 12-14, 22. In Chinese.
Liversidge, R. (1955). Knob-billed Goose, Spoonbill, and Little Swift from the vicinity of Cape Town. *Ostrich* **26**: 45.
Liversidge, R. (1963). The nesting of the Hamerkop, *Scopus umbretta*. *Ostrich* **34**: 55-62.
Liversidge, R. & Le Gras, G.M. (1981). Observations of seabirds off the eastern Cape, South Africa, 1958-1963. In: Cooper, J. ed. *Proceedings of the Symposium on Birds of the Sea and Shore, 1979*. African Seabird Group, Cape Town.
Livezey, B.C. (1986). A phylogenetic analysis of recent Anseriform genera using morphological characters. *Auk* **103**: 737-754.
Livezey, B.C. (1989a). Feeding morphology, foraging behavior and foods of Steamer Ducks (Anatidae: *Tachyeres*). *Occas. Papers Mus. Nat. Hist. Univ. Kansas* **126**: 1-41.
Livezey, B.C. (1989b). Phylogenetic relationships and incipient flightlessness of the extinct Auckland Islands Merganser. *Wilson Bull.* **101 (3)**: 410-435.
Livezey, B.C. (1989c). Flightlessness in Grebes (Aves, Podicipedidae): Its independent evolution in three Genera. *Evolution* **43(1)**: 29-54.
Livezey, B.C. (1990). Evolutionary morphology of Flightlessness in the Auckland Islands Teal. *Condor* **92**: 639-673.
Livezey, B.C. (1991). A phylogenetic analysis and classification of recent dabbling Ducks (Tribe Anatini) based on comparative morphology. *Auk* **108 (3)**: 471-507.
Livezey, B.C. & Humphrey, P.S. (1983). Mechanics of steaming in steamer-ducks. *Auk* **100**: 485-488.
Livezey, B.C., Humphrey, P.S. & Thompson, M.C. (1985). Notes on coastal birds of Puerto Melo, Chubut, Argentina. *Bull. Brit. Orn. Club* **105**: 17-21.
Llano, G.A. ed. (1977). *Adaptations within Antarctic Ecosystems*. Smithsonian Institution, Washington.
Llewellyn, L.C. (1983). Movements of Cormorants in South-Eastern Australia and the Influence of Floods on Breeding. *Austr. Wildl. Res.* **10**: 149-167.
Llorente, G.A., Ruiz, X. & Serra-Cobo, J. (1987). Alimentación otoñal de la Cerceta Común (*Anas crecca*) en el Delta del Ebro. *Misc. Zool.* **11**: 319-330.
Lloyd, C., Tasker, M.L. & Partridge, K. (1991). *The Status of Seabirds in Britain and Ireland*. T & AD Poyser, London.
Lo , P.L. (1982). *Ecological Studies on the White-faced Heron (Ardea novaehollandiae novaehollandiae Latham 1790) in the Manawatu*. MSc thesis, Massey University.
Lo , P.L. (1991). Diet of the White-faced Heron on Manawatu Pastures. *Notornis* **38**: 63-71.
Lo , P.L. & Fordham, R.A. (1986). Seasonal and diurnal time budgets and feeding intensity of the white-faced Heron in pasture. *Notornis* **33**: 233-245.
Lo Valvo, M. & Massa, B. (1988). Considerations on a specimen of Cory's Shearwater ringed at Selvagem Grande and recovered in the central Mediterranean. *Bocagiana* **124**: 1-5.
Lock, A.R. & Ross, R.K. (1973). The nesting of the Great Cormorant (*Phalacrocorax carbo*) and the Double-crested Cormorant (*Phalacrocorax auritus*) in Nova Scotia in 1971. *Can. Field-Nat.* **87**: 43-49.
Lockhart, P.S. (1968). African Darter *Anhinga rufa*. *Ostrich* **39**: 271.
Lockley, R.M. (1930). On the breeding habits of the Manx Shearwater, with special reference to its incubation- and fledging-periods. *British Birds* **23**: 202-218.
Lockley, R.M. (1932). On the breeding habits of the Storm-Petrel, with special reference to its incubation- and fledging-periods. *British Birds* **25**: 206-211.
Lockley, R.M. (1942). *Shearwaters*. Dent, London.
Lockley, R.M. (1952). Notes on the birds of the Berlengas (Portugal), the Desertas and Baixo (Madeira) and the Salvages. *Ibis* **94**: 144-158.
Lockman, D.C., Wood, R., Smith, H., Smith, B. & Burgess, H. (1987). *Rocky Mountain Trumpeter Swan Population - Wyoming flock, 1982-86*. Wyoming Game & Fish Department, Progress Report, Cheyenne.
von Loeffler, H. (1977). Observations on the Anatidae fauna of the Bale Mountains, Ethiopia. *Egretta* 20: 36-44.
Löfgren, L. (1984). *Ocean Birds. Their Breeding, Biology & Behaviour*. Croom Helm, Beckenham.
Lofts, B. & Murton, R.K. (1973). Reproduction in birds. Pp. 1-107 in: Farner, S.D. & King, J.R. (1973). *Avian Biology*. Vol. 3. Academic Press, London & New York.
Logsdon, H.S. (1971). Preliminary results of aerial surveys on Busanga Plain. Department of Wildlife, Chilanga, Zambia.
Lohding, J.A. (1987). Storks and army worms. *East Afr. Nat. His. Soc. Bull.* **17(2)**: 23.
Loiseau, A.J. (1977). Nidification de la cigogne noire (*Ciconia nigra*) en Franche-Comté: première donnée en française. *Alauda* **45**: 335-338.
Lok, C.M. & Vink, J.A.J. (1979). Lodnaver - Kjalkaver (Central Iceland), a hitherto unrecognized important breeding area of the Pink-footed Goose, *Anser brachyrhynchus*. *Le Gerfaut* **69**: 447-459.
Lokki, J. & Eklöf, K. (1984). Breeding success of the Red-throated Diver (*Gavia stellata*) in southern Finland. *Ann. Zool. Fennici* **21**: 417-419.
Lokomoen, J.T. (1966). Breeding ecology of the redhead duck in western Montana. *J. Wildl. Manage.* **30**: 668-681.
Long, J.L. (1959). Some notes on the Emu in the northern wheatbelt of Western Australia. *Emu* **59**: 272-286.
Long, J.L. (1965). Weights, measurements and food of the Emu in the northern wheatbelt of Western Australia. *Emu* **64**: 214-219.
Long, J.L. (1981). *Introduced Birds of the World*. Sydney.
Lönnberg, E. (1936). Några ord om Gråhakedoppingen, *Podiceps griseigena* BODD. och dess variation. *Fauna Flora. Stokholm* **31**: 29-37, 73-78.
Lönnberg, E. (1923). Några ord om Svarthakedoppingen, *Podiceps auritus*, och dess utbredning i Sverige. [Summary: Some words about the Slavonian Grebe *Podiceps auritus*, and its distribution in Sweden]. *Fauna Flora. Stockholm* **18**: 221-227.
Løppenthin, B. (1953). Nordisk Lappedykker (*Podiceps auritus*) som ynglefugl i Danmark. *Dansk Orn. Foren. Tidssk.* **47**: 1-15.
Lorber, P. (1982). Further notes on the Black Stork in Zimbabwe. *Honeyguide* **110**: 8-14.
Lorber, P. (1985). What makes a Hamerskop's nest. *Honeyguide* **31(1)**: 49.
Lorenz, K. (1941). Vergleichende Bewegungsstudien an Anatinae. *J. Orn.* **89**, Sondergeft **3**: 194-284.
Lorenz, K. (1950). *Ethologie der Graugans; aufgenommen 1935-1937*. Film Nr. C560, IWF, Göttingen.
Lorenz, K. (1951-1953). Comparative studies on the behaviour of Anatinae. *Avicult. Mag.* **57**: 157-182; **58**: 8-17, 61-72, 86-94, 172-184; **59**: 24-34, 80-91.
Lorenz, K. (1965). *Evolution and Modification of Behavior*. University of Chicago Press, Chicago.
Lorenz, K. (1979). *The Year of the Greylag Goose*. Methuen, London.
Lorenz, K. & Tinbergen, N. (1939). Taxis und Instinkthandlung in der Eirollbewegung der Graugans. *Z. Tierpsychol.* **2**: 1-29.
Lorenz, K.Z. & von de Wall, W. (1960). Die Ausdrucksbewegungen der Sichelente, *Anas falcata* L. *J. Orn.* **101**: 50-60.
Lotem, A., Schechtman, E. & Katzir, G. (1991). Capture of submerged prey by Little Egrets, *Egretta garzetta garzetta*: strike depth, strike angle and the problem of light reaction. *Anim. Behav.* **42(3)**: 341-346.
Louette, M. (1981). *The Birds of Cameroon. An Annotated Check-list*. Verhandeling Wetenschappen, Jaargang 43, No. **163**. Brussels.
Louisson, V.M. (1972). *Feeding in the White-faced Heron (*Ardea novehollandiae*) at Robinson Bay, Akaroa Harbour*. BSc (Hons) thesis, University of Canterbury.
Louw, G.N., Belonje, P.C. & Coetzee, H.J. (1969). Renal function, respiration, heart rate and thermoregulation in the Ostrich. *Sci. Pap. Namib. Desert Res. Station* **42**: 43-54.
Lovenskiold, H.L. (1960). The Snow Petrel nesting in Dronning Maud Land. *Ibis* **102**: 132-134.
Lovvorn, J.R. (1989). Distributional responses of Canvasback Ducks to weather and habitat change. *J. Appl. Ecol.* **26 (1)**: 113-130.
Low, J.B. (1945). Ecology and management of the red head, *Nyroca americana*, in Iowa. *Ecol. Monogr.* **15**: 35-69.
Lowe, D.W., Matthews, J.R. & Moseley, C.J.eds. (1990). Wood Stork, *Mycteria americana*. Pp. 653-655 in: *The Official World Wildlife Fund Guide to Endangered Species in North America*. World Wildlife Fund/Beecham Publishing Co., Washington D.C.
Lowe, F.A. (1954). *The Heron*. London.
Lowe, K.W. (1981). *Habitat Requirements of Herons, Egrets, Ibis and Spoonbills of the Westernport Region*. Vict. Ministry Conserv. Env. Study Report **347**.
Lowe, K.W. (1982). Feeding behaviour and diet of Royal Spoonbills *Platalea regia* in Westport Bay, Victoria. *Emu* **82**: 163-168.
Lowe, K.W (1983a). Feeding behaviour and diet of the White-faced Heron (*Ardea novehollandiae)* in Westernport Bay, Victoria. *Corella* **7**: 101-108.
Lowe, K.W. (1983b). Egg size, clutch size, and breeding success of the Glossy Ibis *Plegadis falcinellus*. *Emu* **83**: 31-34.
Lowe, K.W. (1984). *The breeding biology of the Sacred Ibis* Threskiornis aethiopicus *in Southern Victoria*. PhD dissertation. University of Melbourne, Parkville, Australia.
Lowe, K.W. (1989). Notes on the breeding of the Pacific Heron *Ardea pacifica* near Balranald, New South Wales. *Corella* **13(3)**: 88-89.
Lowe, K.W. & Richards, G.C. (1991). Morphological variation in the Sacred Ibis *Threskiornis aethiopicus* super-species complex. *Emu* **91(1)**: 41-45.
Lowe, K.W., Clark, A. & Clark, R.A. (1985). Body measurements, plumage and moult of the Sacred Ibis in South Africa. *Ostrich* **56**: 111-116.
Lowe, P.R. (1934). On the evidence for the existence of two species of Steamer Duck (*Tachyeres*) and primary and secondary flightlessness in birds. *Ibis* **4 (13)**: 467-495.
Lowe, V.T. (1966). Notes on the Musk Duck. *Emu* **65**: 279-290.
Lowe, V.T. & Lowe, T.G. (1976). Pelicans feeding on feather *Austr. Bird Watcher* **6(5)**: 169-170.
Lowe-McConnell, R.H. (1967). Notes on the nesting of the Boat-bill, *Cochlearius cochlearius*. *Ibis* **109**: 979.
Lowery, G.H. & Dalquest, W.W. (1951). *Birds from the State of Veracruz, Mexico*. University of Kansas Publications **3(4)**: 531-649. University of Kansas, Lawrence.
Lowery, G.H. & Newman, R.J. (1950). The Mexican Grebe, *Coymbus d. brachypterus*, at Baton Rouge, Louisiana. *Auk* **67**: 505-506.
Loye, J.E. & Zuk, M. *Bird-parasite Interactions*. Oxford University Press.
Lu , J. (1991). Notes on Bar-headed Geese in China. *IWRB Threatened Waterfowl Research Group Newsletter* **1**: 8-9.
Lu Xin, Liu Huan-jin (1987). [The thermoregulation of nestlings of the Yellow Bittern *Ixobrychus sinensis*]. *Sichuan J. Zool.* **6(4)**: 22-23. In Chinese.
Lubbock, M.R. (1976). Breeding the White-winged Wood Duck in Captivity. *Int. Zoo Yb.* **16**: 92-93.
Lubbock, M.R. (1983). Torrent ducks: collecting, rearing and breeding. Pp. 205-209 in: *Proceedings of the Jean Delacour/IFCB Symposium on Breeding Birds in Captivity*. International Foundation for the Conservation of Birds, Los Angeles.
Lucas, A.M. & Stettenheim, P. (1972). *Avian Anatomy: Integument*. 2 Vols. Agriculture Handbook **362**. US Government Printing Office, Washington, D.C.
Luders, D.J. (1977). Behaviour of Antarctic Petrels and Antarctic Fulmars before laying. *Emu* **77**: 208-214.
Ludwig, J.P. (1984). Decline, resurgence and population dynamics of Michigan and Great Lakes Double-crested Cormorants. *Jack-Pine Warbler* **62(4)**: 91-102.
Lugg, D.J., Johnstone, G.W. & Griffith, B.J. (1978). The outlying islands of Macquarie Island. *Geographical J.* **144**: 277-287.
Lugg, D.J., Johnstone, G.W. & Griffith, B.J. (1978). The outlying islands of Macquarie Island. *Geographical J.* **144**: 277-287.
Lumsden, W.H.R. & Haddow, A.J. (1946). The food of the Shag (*Phalacrocorax aristotelis*) in the Clyde Sea area. *J. Anim. Ecol.* **15**: 35-42.
Lüps, P. (1990). Wozu besitzen Höckerschwäne *Cygnus olor* Höcker? *Orn. Beob.* **87**: 1-11.
Lusk, C.H. & Lusk, J.R. (1981). The New Zealand Dabchick on Lake Rotoiti. *Notornis* **28**: 203-208.
Luthin, C.S. (1981). A proposal to study the social behavior and breeding ecology of two subspecies of the Buff-necked Ibis (*Theristicus caudatus*) in Venezuela and Peru. Unpublished report.
Luthin, C.S. (1983a). Breeding ecology of neotropical ibises (Threskiornithidae) in Venezuela, and comments on captive propagation. Pp. 95-124 in: *Proceedings of the Jean Delacour/IFCB Symposium on Breeding birds in Captivity*. International Foundation for the Conservation of Birds, North Hollywood, California.
Luthin, C.S. (1983b). Newsletter of the WWB-Fund for International Bird Conservation. *Flying Free* **1**: 1-12.
Luthin, C.S. (1983c). *Observations on the Breeding Ecology and Behavior of Three Neotropical ibises (Threskiornithidae) on a Ranch in Central Venezuela*. MSc thesis, University of Wisconsin, Madison.
Luthin, C.S. (1983d). World Working Group on Storks, Ibises and Spoonbills, Report 1, Summer 1983. *Flying Free* **1(1) Suppl.**
Luthin, C.S. (1984a). Selected Bibliography on Storks, Ibises and Spoonbills. Supplement to: World Working Group on Storks, Ibises and Spoonbills, Report **2**.
Luthin, C.S. compiler (1984b). World Working Group on Storks, Ibises and Spoonbills, Report 2, 1984. ICBP, W.W. Brehm Fund for International Bird Conservation, Vogelpark, Walsrode, West Germany.
Luthin, C.S. (1984c). Scarlet countdown. *Birds. London* **10(4)**: 26-32.
Luthin, C.S. (1985a). La cigüeña Jabiru. *Dumac* **7**: 6-7.
Luthin, C.S. (1985b). Captive breeding programme for the most endangered ibis in the world. *Avicult. Mag.* **91**: 117.
Luthin, C.S. (1987a). Status of and conservation priorities for the world's stork species. *Colonial Waterbirds* **10(2)**: 181-202.
Luthin, C.S. (1987b). Newsletter of the Brehm Fund for International Bird Conservation. *Flying Free* **5**: 1-11.
Luthin, C.S. (1988). Conservation concerns: Indo-Malayan Realm. Report from the ICBP Specialist Group on Storks, Ibises and Spoonbills. *Tiger Paper* 15(1): 6-7.
Luthin, C.S., Archibald, G.W., Hartman, L., Mirande, C.M. & Swengel, S. (1986). Captive breeding of endangered cranes, storks, ibises and spoonbills. *Int. Zoo. Yb* **24/25**: 25-39.
Luthin, C.S., Frederick, P.C. & Morales, G. (1990). *The Scarlet Ibis* Eudocimus ruber *Action Plan*. IWRB, Slimbridge., UK.
Lyle, G.W. (1973). Australian Little Grebe on Lake Okareka. *Notornis* **20**: 274-280.
MacArthur, R. (1971). Patterns of terrestrial bird communities. Pp. 189-221 in: Farner, S.D. & King, J.R. (1971). *Avian Biology*. Vol. 1. Academic Press, London & New York.
MacArthur, R. (1972). *Geographical Ecology*. Harper and Row, New York.
MacCall, A.D. (1982). Seabird-fishery trophic interactions in eastern Pacific boundary currents: California and Peru. Pp. 136-149 in: Nettleship *et al.* (1982)
Maccarone, A.D. & Parsons, K.C. (1988). Differences in Flight Patterns Among Nesting Ibises and Egrets. *Colonial Waterbirds* **11(1)**: 67-71.
MacConnell, E.S. & McConnell, J.P. (1974). Jabiru Stork in Oklahoma. *Bull. Oklahoma Orn. Soc.* **7**: 9-12.
Macdonald, I.A.W., Brooks, P.M. & Gardner, B.D. (1985). Environmental pollutants as possible factors in the survival of the Openbilled Stork in Southern Africa. *Ostrich* **56**: 280-282.

Macdonald, I.A.W., Richardson, D.M. & Powrie, F.J. (1986). Range expansion of the hadeda ibis *Bostrychia hagedash* in southern Africa. *S. Afr. Tydskr. Dierk.* **21(4)**: 331-342.
Macdonald, J.D. (1988). *Birds of Australia.* Reed, Frenchs Forest, Australia.
Macdonald, M.A. (1975). *The Biology of the Fulmar (*Fulmarus glacialis *L.) in N.E. Scotland with Special Reference to the Pre-egg Laying Period.* PhD thesis, Aberdeen University, Aberdeen.
Macdonald, M.A. (1977a). Adult mortality and fidelity to mate and nest-site in a group of marked fulmars. *Bird Study* **24**: 165-168.
Macdonald, M.A. (1977b). The pre-laying exodus of the Fulmar. *Ornis Scand.* **8**: 33-37.
Macdonald, M.A. (1978). The Yellow-billed Egret in West Africa (Aves: Ardeidae). *Rev. Zool. Afr.* **92**: 191-200.
Macdonald, M.A. (1980). The winter attendance of fulmars at land in NE Scotland. *Ornis Scand.* **11**: 23-29.
Macdonald, M.A. & Taylor, I.R. (1976). First occurrence of the Cape Wigeon *Anas capensis* in Ghana. *Bull. Niger. Orn. Soc.* 12: 44.
MacDonald, R.A. (1987). The breeding population and distribution of the Cormorant in Ireland. *Irish Birds* **3**: 405-416.
MacGillivray, W. (1923). The nesting of the Australian Pelican (*Pelecanus conspicillatus*). *Emu* **22**: 162-174.
Mackay, R.D. & Campbell, R. (1976). Field note on Salvadori's Teal, *Salvadorina waigiuensis* (Rothschild and Hartert). *New Guinea Bird Soc. Newsl.* **122**: 8-9.
Mackay, R.H. (1987). *Trumpeter Swan Investigations, Grande Prairie Area, Alberta, 1953-1975.* Proceedings & Papers 10th Trumpeter Swan Society Conference, Grande Prairie, 1986.
Mackenzie, H.R. (1971). The Brown Teal in the Auckland Province. *Notornis* **18**: 280-286.
Mackenzie, M.J.S. (1990). White-winged Wood Duck *-Cairina scutulata-* the question of Indonesian albinism. *Wildfowl* **41**: 163-166.
Mackenzie, M.J.S. & Kear, J. (1976). The White-winged Wood Duck. *Wildfowl* **27**: 5-17.
MacKinnon, J. (1983). Tanjing Pating National Park management plan for development. World Wildlife Fund Project 1523 Field Report.
Mackinnon, J. (1990). *Field Guide to the Birds of Java and Bali.* Gadjah Mada University Press, Yogyakarta, Indonesia.
Mackowicz, R. & Nowak, E. (1986). Über die Brutmöglichkeit des Prachttauchers (*Gavia arctica*) in Masuren, NO Polen und seine Verbreitungsgrenze in Mitteleuropa. *Vogewelt* **107(3)**: 111-115.
Mackworth-Praed, C.W. & Grant, C.H.B. (1957-1973). *African Handbook of Birds.* Longman, London & New York.
Mackworth-Praed, C.W. & Grant, C.H.B. (1957). *African Handbook of Birds. Series One. Birds of Eastern and North Eastern Africa.* Vol. 1. 2nd. edition. Longman, London & New York.
Mackworth-Praed, C.W. & Grant, C.H.B. (1970). *African Handbook of Birds. Series Three. Birds of West Central and Western Africa.* Vol 1. Longman, London & New York.
MacLandres, M.R. (1979). Status of Ross's Geese in California. Pp. 255-265 in: Jarvis, R.L. & Bartonek, J.C. eds. *Management and Biology of Pacific Flyway Geese.* OSU Book Stores Inc., Corvallis.
Maclean, G.L. (1985). *Roberts' Birds of Southern Africa.* 5th edition. Trustees of the John Voelcker Bird Book Fund, Cape Town.
Macleod, J.G.R., Martin, J. & Uys, C.J. (1960). Grey-headed Gulls and Spoonbills in the Bredasdorp area. *Ostrich* **31**: 80.
MacMillan, B.W.H. (1990). Attempts to re-establish Wekas, Brown Kiwis and Red-Crowned Parakeets in the Waitakere Ranges. *Notornis* **37**: 45-51.
Macnae, W. (1959). Notes on the biology of the Maccoa Duck. *Bokmakierie* **11**: 49-52.
Maddock, M. (1990). Cattle Egret: south to Tasmania and New Zealand for the Winter. *Notornis* **37(1)**: 1-23.
Madge, S. & Burn, H. (1988). *Wildfowl: An Identification Guide to the Ducks, Geese and Swans of the World.* Helm, Bromely, Kent.
Madriz, M. (1979). *Notas sobre la historia natural y energética del Pato Farra-farro (*Amazonetta brasiliensis*) en el alto Apure.* Trabajo especial de grado, Universidad Central Venezuela, Caracas.
Madriz, M. (1982). *Analysis of whistling ducks (*Dendrocygna*, Aves, Anseriformes) hunting in rice fields in Venezuela.* Servicio Nacional de Fauna Silvestre, Maracay.
Madriz, M. (1983). Food habits of the Brazilian Duck in Apure State, Venezuela. *J. Wildl. Manage.* **47**: 531-533.
Madsen, C.S., McHugh, K.P. & de Kloet, S.R. (1988). A partial classification of waterfowl (Anatidae) based on single copy DNA. *Auk* **105**: 452-459.
Madsen, F.J. (1957). On the food habits of some fish eating birds in Denmark. *Dan. Rev. Game Biol.* **3**: 19-83.
Madsen, F.J. & Spärck, R. (1950). On the feeding habits of the southern Cormorant (*Phalacrocorax carbo sinensis* Shaw) in Denmark. *Dan. Rev. Game Biol.* **1**: 45-76.
Madsen, J. (1991). Geese of the Western Palearctic: present status and challenges for research and management in the '90s. *Trans. N. Amer. Wild. Nat. Resourc. Conf.* **56**: 453-463.
Madsen, J., Bregonballe, T. & Mehlum, F. (1989). Study of the breeding ecology and behaviour of the Svalbard population of Light-bellied Brent Goose *Branta bernicla hrota. Polar Res.* **7**: 1-21.
Madsen, S.T. (1990). Black Storks in Nepal and India. *Bull. Oriental Bird Club* **11**: 34-35.
Maesako, Y. (1985). Community structure of *Machilus thunbergii* forests disturbed by birds (Streaked Shearwater) on Kanmurijima Island, Kyoto Prefecture, Japan. *Japanese J. Ecol.* **35**: 387-400.
de Magalhães, J.C.R. (1972). O príncipe macuco. O Gênero Tinamus no Brasil. *Trófeu. São Paulo* **2(14)**: 4-9.
de Magalhães, J.C.R. (1978). Especies cinegeticas e proteçao a fauna na regiao sudeste, com especial referencia ao estade de São Paulo. Pp. 62-67 in: *Seminario sobre caça amadorista.* Fundaçao Brasileira para a Conservaçao da Natureza, Rio de Janeiro.
Magsalay, P. (1988). Wader Survey in Cebu, the Philippines, in 1986/87. Asian Wetland Bureau, Kuala Lumpur and Cebu city.
Maher, W.J. (1962). Breeding biology of the Snow Petrel near Cape Hallett, Antarctica. *Condor* **64**: 488-499.
Mahoney, S.A. (1981). Some aspects of the thermal physiology of Anhingas (*Anhinga anhinga*) and Double-crested Cormorants (*Phalacrocorax auritus*) Pp. 461-470 in: Cooper, J. ed. *Proceedings of the Symposium on Birds of the Sea and Shore, 1979.* African Seabird Group, Cape Town.
Mahoney, S.A. & Jehl, J.R. (1985). Avoidance of salt-loading by a diving bird at a hypersaline and alkaline lake: Eared Grebe. *Condor* **87**: 389-397.
Mahoney, S.A., Fairchild, L. & Shea, R.E. (1985). Temperature regulation in great frigate birds *Fregata minor. Physiol. Zool.* **58(1)**: 138-148.
Mainardi, D. (1962). Immunological data on the phylogenetic relationships and taxonomic position of flamingos. *Ibis* **104(3)**: 426-428.
Mainardi, D. (1963). Immunological distances and phylogenetic relationships in birds. Pp. 103-114 in: *Proc. XIII Int. Orn. Congr.*
Makatsch, W. (1950). *Der Vogel und sein Nest.* Akademische Verlagsgesellschaft, Leipzig.
Malacalza, V.E. (1984a). Biología reproductiva de *Phalacrocorax albiventer*. I. Nidificación en Punta Tombo. *Centro Nacional Patagónico CONICET. Contribución* **98**: 1-13.
Malacalza, V.E. (1984b). Aves Guaneras. Relevamiento de especies en tres cormoraneras continentales de la provincia del Chubut (Argentina). *Centro Nacional Patagónico CONICET. Contribución* **84**: 1-13.
Malacalza, V.E. (1991). External Characters in the Offspring Resulting from Cross-breeding Between Cormorant Species. *Colonial Waterbirds* **14(2)**: 180-183.
Malacalza, V.E. & Hall, M.A. (1988). Sexing Adult King Cormorants (*Phalacrocorax albiventer*) by Discriminant Analysis. *Colonial Waterbirds* **11(1)**: 32-37.
Malhotra, A.K. & Arora, B.M. (1991). Some observations on Painted Storks (*Mycteria leucocephalus*) at National Zoological Park, New Dehli. *Zoos' Print* **6(1)**: 7, 19.
Malik, D. (1988). Eastern Greylag Geese *Anser anser rubrirostris* Swinhoe in Gujarat. *J. Bombay Nat. Hist. Soc.* **85(2)**: 416.
Mallet, M. (1977). Breeding the Waldrapp Ibis *Geronticus eremita* at Jersey Zoo. *Int. Zoo Yb.* **17**: 143-145.
Mallori, M.L. & Weatherhead, P.J. (1990). Effects of nest parasitism and nest location on eggshell strength in waterfowl. *Condor* **92**: 1031-1039.
Manghi, M.S. (1984). Una nueva subespecie de *Podiceps major* Boddaert (Aves, Podicipedidae). *Com. Mus. Arg. Cienc. Nat. Bernardino Rivadavia* **4(14)**: 115-119.
Mann, C.F. (1986). Christmas Island Frigatebirds *Fregata andrewsi* on the Kenya coast. *Bull. Brit. Orn. Club* **106**: 89-90.
Mann, C.F. (1989). More notable bird observations from Brunei, Borneo. *Forktail* **5**: 17-22.
Mann, W., Schmidtke, K. & Brandl, R. (1987). Gibt es einen Bestandsrückgang beim Zwergtaucher *Tachybaptus ruficollis*? *Anz. orn. Ges. Bayern* **26**: 229-235.
Manry, D.E. (1978a). General biology of the African ibises. Unpublished report to the Percy FitzPatrick Institute of African Ornithology, University of Cape Town, Rondebosch, South Africa.
Manry, D.E. (1978b). Life with Schaapen Island's Sacred Ibises - a personal account. *Safring News* **7**: 13-15.
Manry, D.E. (1982). Habitat use by foraging bald ibises *Geronticus calvus* in western Natal. *S. Afr. J. Wildl. Res.* **12**: 86-99.
Manry, D.E. (1983). *Ecology of the Bald Ibis (*Geronticus calvus*) and fire in the South African grassland biome.* MSc thesis. University of Capetown, Cape Town.
Manry, D.E. (1984). Factors influencing the use of winter-burnt grassland by foraging Bald Ibises *Geronticus calvus. S. Afr. J. Zool.* **19**: 12-15.
Manry, D.E. (1985a). Reroductive performance of the Bald Ibis *Geronticus calvus* in relation to rainfall and grass-burning. *Ibis* **127**: 159-173.
Manry, D.E. (1985b). Distribution, Abundance and Conservation of the Bald Ibis *Geronticus calvus* in Southern Africa. *Biol. Conserv.* **33**: 351-362.
Manry, D.E. (1985c). Birds of Fire. *Nat. Hist.* **94(1)**: 39-45.
Manry, D.E. (1986). Ibises in Peril. *Living Bird Quarterly* **5(2)**: 24-27.
Manson, A.J. (1969). Breeding of the Darter. *Honeyguide* **59**: 34-35.
Manuwal, D.A. & Campbell, R.W. (1979). Status and distribution of breeding seabirds of southeastern Alaska, British Columbia and Washington. Pp. 73-91 in: Bartonek, J.C. & Nettleship, D.N. eds. *Conservation of Marine Birds of Northern North America.* Fish and Wildlife Service, Wildlife Research Report **11**. Washington, D.C.
Marchant, J.H., Hudson, R., Carter, S.P. & Whittington, P. (1990). *Population Trends in British Breeding Birds.* British Trust for Ornithology, Tring, Hertfordshire, UK.
Marchant, S. (1960). The breeding of some southwestern Ecuadorian birds. *Ibis* **102**: 349-382.
Marchant, S. (1988). (*Ardea pacifica*). *Austr. Birds* **21**: 61-65.
Marchant, S. & Higgins, P.J. (1990). *Handbook of Australian, New Zealand & Antarctic Birds.* Vol. 1. RAOU/Oxford University Press, Melbourne.
Marchant, S., Fullagar, P.J. & Davey, C.C. (1989). Nesting of the Australian Grebe *Tachybaptus novaehollandiae. Austr. Birds* **23(1)**: 2-6.
Marcondes-Machado, L.O. & Monteiro Filho, E.L.A. (1989). Nota sobre a presença dos guarás, *Eudocimus ruber* (Linné, 1758) (Threskiornithidae, Aves), no litoral de Sao Paulo. Alerta para sua proteçao. *Ciência e Cultura* **41(12)**: 1213-1214.
Marcondes-Machado, L.O. & Monteiro Filho, E.L.A. (1990). The scarlet ibis *Eudocimus ruber* in southeastern Brazil. *Bull. Brit. Orn. Club* **110(3)**: 123-126.
Marin, M. (1989). Notes on the Breeding of Chestnut-bellied Herons (*Agamia agami*) in Costa Rica. *The Condor* **91**: 215-217.
Marion, L. (1983). Problèmes biogéographiques, écologiques et taxonomiques posés par le Grand Cormoran *Phalacrocorax carbo. Rev. Ecol. (Terre Vie)* **38**: 65-99.
Marion, L. (1989). Territorial feeding and colonial breeding are not mutually exclusive: the case of the Grey Heron (*Ardea cinerea*). *J. Anim. Ecol.* **58**: 693-710.
Marion, L. & Marion P. (1982). La spatule blanche (*Platalea leucorodia* L.) niche au Lac de Grand-Lieu. *Alauda* **50(4)**: 241-249.
Marion, L. & Marion, P. (1987). Conséquences de la protection du Héron Cendré sur sa dynamique de population et sur ses stratégies d'occupation de l'espace en France. *Rev. Ecol. (Terre et Vie)* **4**: 261-270.
Markham, B.J. (1971). Censo invernal de cisnes y flamencos en Magallanes. *Anales Inst. Patagonia* **2**: 146-157.
Markum, D.E. & Baldassarre, G.A. (1989a). Breeding Biology of Muscovy Ducks Using Nest Boxes in Mexico. *Wilson Bull.* **101 (4)**: 621-626.
Markum, D.E. & Baldassarre, G.A. (1989b). Ground nesting by Black-bellied Whistling Ducks on Islands in Mexico. *J. Wildl. Manage.* **53**: 707-713.
van Marle, J.G. & Voous, K.H. (1988). *The Birds of Sumatra.* B.O.U. Check-list **10**. British Ornithologists' Union, Tring, Hertfordshire, UK.
Marquiss, M. & Leitch, A.F. (1990). The diet of Grey Herons *Ardea cinerea* breeding at Loch Leven, Scotland, and the importance of their predation on ducklings. *Ibis* **132**: 535-549.
Marriott, R.W. (1970). *The food and water requirements of Cape Barren Geese (*Cereopsis novaehollandiae *Latham).* PhD dissertation, Monash University, Melbourne.
Marshall, A.J. ed. (1960-1961). *Biology and Comparative Physiology of Birds.* 2 Vols. Academic Press, London and New York.
Marshall, A.J. & Serventy, D.L. (1956a). Moult adaptation in relation to long-distance migration in petrels. *Nature. London* **177**: 943.
Marshall, A.J. & Serventy, D.L. (1956b). The breeding cycle of the Short-tailed Shearwater in relation to trans-equatorial migration and its environment. *Proc. Zool. Soc. Lond.* **127**: 489-510.
Marshall, A.J. & Serventy, D.L. (1959). Experimental demonstration of an internal rythm of reproduction in a trans-equatorial migrant (the Short-tailed Shearwater). *Nature. London* **184**: 1704-1705.
Marshall, B. (1972a). Gymnogene feeding on Darter eggs. *Honeyguide* **72**: 34.
Marshall, B. (1972b). Unusual feeding habitat in the Hamerkop. *Honeyguide* **72**: 31.
Marshall, B. (1976). A further note on Hamerkop behaviour. *Honeyguide* **86**: 45-46.
Marshall, B.E. (1982). A possible example of tool usage by Marabou Stork. *Ostrich* **53(3)**: 181.
Martin, A.R. (1989). The diet of Atlantic Puffin *Fratercula arctica* and Northern Gannet *Sula bassana* chicks at a Shetland colony during a period of changing prey availability. *Bird Study* **36**: 170-180.
Martin, E.M. & Carney, S.M. (1977). *Population Ecology of the Mallard. IV. A Review of Duck Hunting Regulations, Activity and Success, with Special Reference to the Mallard.* US Fish & Wildlife Service Resources Publication **130**.
Martin, G.R. & Young, S.R. (1984). The eye of the Humboldt Penguin, *Spheniscus humboldti*: visual fields and schematic optics. *Proc. Royal Soc. Lond. (Ser. B)* **223**: 197-222.
Martin, L. & Mengel, R.M. (1975). A new species of anhinga (Anhingidae) from the Upper Pliocene of Nebraska. *Auk* **92**: 137-140.
Martin, L.D. (1983). The origin and early radiation of birds. Pp. 291-338 in: Brush, H.A. & Clark, G.A. eds. (1983). *Perspectives in Ornithology.* Oxford University Press, Oxford.
Martin, R.J. (1972). Hadeda nesting in the southern entrance of the Seven Weeks Poort. *Ostrich* **43**: 186.
Martin, R.J. (1984). Hadedas in the Karroo. *Promerops* **162**: 6.
Martin, S. (1984). La avutarda magellánica (*Chloephaga picta*) en la Patagonia: su ecología, alimentación, densidad y control. *Idia* **429-432**: 6-24.
Martín, A. (1986). Feeding association between dolphins and shearwaters around the Azores Islands. *Can. J. Zool.* **64**: 1372-1374.
Martín, A., Hernández, E., Delgado, G. & Quilis, V. (1984). Nidificación del Paíño de Madeira *Oceanodroma castro* (Harcourt, 1851) en las Islas Canarias. *Doñana, Acta Vertebrata* **11(2)**: 337-341.
Martínez, E. (1987). *Estudio de la cigüeña blanca en la comunidad de Madrid.* Comunidad de Madrid, Madrid.
Martínez, I. & Elliott, A. (1990). Visit to Riau, July-August 1990. Unpublished report to Asian Wetland Bureau.
Mascher, J.W. (1972). Svarthakedoppingen, *Podiceps auritus* (L.), på Öland. *Calidris* **1972(4)**: 3-11.
Massa, B. & Catalisano, A. (1986). Status and Conservation of the Storm Petrel in Sicily. Pp. 143-151 in: MEDMARAVIS & Monbailliu (1986).
Massa, B. & Lo Valvo, M. (1986). Biometrical and Biological Consideration on the Cory's Shearwater *Calonectris diomedea*. Pp. 293-313 in: MEDMARAVIS & Monbailliu (1986).
Mather, J.R. (1967). Pied-billed Grebe in Yorkshire. *British Birds* **60**: 290-295.
Mathews, G.M. (1933). On *Fregetta* Bonaparte and allied genera. *Novit. Zool.* **39**: 34-54.
Mathews, G.M. (1942). New genus. *Emu* **41**: 305.
Mathews, G.M. (1948). Systematic notes on petrels. *Bull. Brit. Orn. Club* **68**: 155-170.
Mathews, N. & Mcquaid, C.D. (1983). The feeding ecology of the slaty egret (*Egretta vinaceigula*). *Afr. J. Ecol.* **21**: 235-240.
Mathews, N.J.C. (1979). Observations of the Shoebill in the Okavango Swamp. *Ostrich* **50**: 185.
Mathews, N.J.C. & Brooke, R.K. (1988). Notes on the foraging behavior of the Zigzag Heron. *Wilson Bull.* **100(1)**: 147-148.
Mathews, S. & Walker, M. (1983). Ornithological Survey. Pp. 62-66 in: Walker, M.V. & Reynolds, G. eds. *Seram Survey Report 1982/83.* Assoc. Res. Expl. & Aid, Sydney.
Mathiasson, S. (1970). Numbers and distribution of Long-tailed wintering Ducks in Northern Europe. *British Birds* **63**: 414-424.
Mathiasson, S. (1973). Moulting Grounds of Mute Swans (*Cygnus olor*) in Sweden, their origin and Relation to Popular Dynamics, Biology and Distribution of Mute Swans in the Baltic Area. *Viltrevy* **1973**: 399-452.
Matteson, S.W. (1983). A preliminary review of fishery complaints associated with changes in Double-crested Cormorant populations in Maine, Wisconsin, and the Great Lakes region. Wisconsin Endangered Resources Report Wisconsin Departement of Natural Resources, Madison.
Matthews, C.W. & Fordham, R.A. (1986). Behaviour of the Little Pied Cormorant *Phalacrocorax melanoleucos. Emu* **86**: 118-121.
Matthews, G.V.T. (1954). Some aspects of incubation in the Manx Shearwater, with particular reference to chilling resistance in the embryo. *Ibis* **96**: 432-440.
Matthews, G.V.T. (1968). *Bird Navigation.* 2nd edition. Cambridge University Press, Cambrige, England.
Matthews, G.V.T. & Evans, M.E. (1974). On the behaviour of the White-headed Duck with especial reference to breeding. *Wildfowl* **25**: 56-66.

Matthews, G.V.T. & Smart, M. eds. (1981). *Proceedings of the Second International Swan Symposium, Sapporo, Japan, 1980*. IWRB, Slimbridge, UK.
Matthews, L.H. (1949). The origin of stomach oil in the petrels, with comparative observations on the avian proventriculus. *Ibis* **91**: 373-392.
Matthews, L.H. (1951). *Wandering Albatross*. Macgibbon & Kee, London.
Maxson, S.J. & Bernstein, N.P. (1982). Kleptoparasitism by South Polar Skuas on Blue-eyed Shags in Antarctica. *Wilson Bull.* **94(3)**: 269-281.
Maxson, S.J. & Pace, R.M. (1990). Diurnal activity budgets and habitat use of Ring-necked Duck ducklings in Northcentral Minnesota. *Minn. Dep. Nat. Resour. Wildl. Rep.*: 68
Mayaud, N. (1931). Contribution à l'étude de la mue des puffins. *Alauda (2nd. Ser.)* **2**: 230-249.
Mayaud, N. (1932). Considerations sur la morphologie et la systematique de quelques puffins. *Alauda* **4**: 41-78.
Mayaud, N. (1934). Considerations sur la morphologie et la systematique de quelques puffins (addendum). *Alauda* **6**: 87-95.
Mayaud, N. (1949-1950). Nouvelles précisions sur la mue des Procellariens. *Alauda* **17**: 144-155, **18**: 222-233.
Mayhew, P.W. (1987). Vigilance levels in European Wigeon - sexual differences. *Wildfowl* **38**: 77-81.
Mayol, J. (1984). Concentración invernal de Zampullín cuellinegro, *Podiceps nigricollis* C.L. Brehm 1831, en Formentera. *Bol. Estac. Centr. Ecol.* **13**: 63-65.
Mayol, J. (1986). Human Impact on Seabirds in the Balearic Islands. Pp. 379-408 in: MEDMARAVIS & Monbailliu (1986).
Mayr, C. (1986). Häufigkeit, Voraussetzungen und Ursachen von Mehrfachbruten des Haubentauchers (*Podiceps cristatus*). [Summary: Frequency, conditions and causes of multiple broods of the Great Crested Grebe]. *Charadrius* **22**: 55-68.
Mayr, E. (1931). Zur Anatomie und systematischen Stellung der Salvadori-Ente (*Salvadorina waigiuensis* Rothsch. and Hartert). *Orn. Mber.* **39**: 69-70.
Mayr, E. (1945). The downy plumage of the Australian dabchick. *Emu* **44**: 231-233.
Mayr, E. (1969). *Principles of Systematic Zoology*. Mc Graw-Hill, New York.
Mayr, E. (1970). *Populations, Species and Evolution*. Harvard University Press, Cambridge, MA.
Mayr, E. (1979). Struthioniformes. Pp. 7-9 in: Mayr & Cottrell (1979).
Mayr, E. & Amadon, D. (1951). *A Classification of Recent Birds*. American Museum Novitates **1946**. American Museum of Natural History, New York.
Mayr, E. & Camras, S. (1938). Birds of the Crane Pacific Expedition. *Publ. Field Mus. Nat. Hist. Zool. Ser.* **20**: 453-473.
Mayr, E. & Cottrell, G.W. eds. (1979). *Check-list of Birds of the World*. Vol. 1. 2nd. edition. Museum of Comparative Zoology, MA.
Mayr, E. & Short, L.L. (1970). *Species taxa of North American Birds*. Publications of the Nuttall Ornithological Club. **9**. Cambrige, MA.
Mazzeo, R. (1953). Homing of the Manx Shearwater. *Auk* **70**: 200-201.
McAllister, N.M. (1958). Courtship, hostile behaviour, nest establishment and egg laying in the Eared Grebe (*Podiceps caspicus*). *Auk* **75**: 290-311.
McAllister, N.M. & Storer, R.W. (1963). Copulation in the Pied-billed Grebe. *Wilson Bull.* **75**: 166-173.
McAllum, H.J.F. (1965). The adaptation and increase in the Paradise Shelduck (*Tadorna variegata*) within a man-modified environment. *Trans. Royal Soc. New Zealand* **6 (12)**: 115-125.
McAlpine, D.F., Finne, J., Makepeace, S., Gilliland, S. & Phinney, M. (1988). First nesting of the Glossy Ibis, *Plegadis falcinellus*, in Canada. *Can. Field-Nat.* **102**: 536-537.
McArthur, P.D. & Gorman, M.L. (1978). The salt gland of the incubating Eider Duck *Somateria mollissima*: The effects of natural salt deprivation. *J. Zool. London* 184: 83-90.
McAuley, D.G. (1986). Ring-necked Duck Productivity in Relation to Wetland Acidity: Nest Success, Duckling Diet and Survival. MSc thesis, University of Maine, Orono.
McAuley, D.G. & Longcore, J.R. (1989). Nesting phenology and success of Ring-necked Ducks in East-Central Maine. *J. Field Orn.* **60 (1)**: 112-119.
McCabe, R.E. ed. (1990). *Goose Management in the '90s*. Wildlife Management Institute, Washington D.C..
McCamant, R.E. & Bolen, E.G. (1979). A 12-year study of nest box utilization by Black-bellied Whistling Ducks. *J. Wildl. Manage.* **43**: 936-943.
McCann, C. (1930). Nidification of storks. *J. Bombay Nat. Hist. Soc.* **34**: 579-581.
McCann, C. (1973). The tongues of kiwis (*Apteryx* spp.). *Notornis* **20(2)**: 123-127.
McCartan, L. & Simmons, K.E.L. (1956). Territory in the Great Crested Grebe *Podiceps cristatus* re-examined. *Ibis* **98**: 370-378.
McCartney, R.B. (1963). *The Fulvous Tree Duck in Louisiana*. MSc thesis, Louisiana State University.
McCaskie, G. (1990). First record of the Band-rumped Storm Petrel in California. *Western Birds* **21**: 65-68.
McClung, R.M. (1969). *Lost Wild America. The Story of our Extinct and Vanishing Wildlife*. William Morrow and Company, New York.
McClure, H.E. (1974). *Migration and survival of the Birds of Asia*. US Army Component SEATO Medical Research Laboratory. Bangkok, Thailand.
McClure, H.E. (1989). Thailand's sanctuary of struggle. *Birds Int.* **1(3)**: 42-46.
McClure, H.E. & Kwanyuen, P. (1973). The avifaunal complex of an Open-billed Stork colony in Thailand. *Nat. Hist. Bull. Siam Soc.* **25**: 133-155.
McCrimmon, D.A. (1982). Populations of the Great Blue Heron *Ardea herodias* in New York State from 1964 to 1981. *Colonial Waterbirds* **5**: 87-95.
McCulloch, E.M. (1974). Sexual difference in eye-colour of Jabiru, *Xenorhynchus asiaticus*. *Austr. Bird Watcher* **5**: 187-188.
McCulloch, E.M. (1987). Project pelican. *Bird Obsr.* **662**: 26-27.
McDaniel, B., Bogusch, E. & McDaniel, S. (1963). A unique behavior pattern and observations of Roseate Spoonbills (*Ajaia ajaja*) in Kleberg County, Texas. *Tex. J. Sci.* **15**: 354-356.
McGill, L. (1991). A pair of breeding Black Stork in the Baviaanskloof. *Bee-eater* **42(2)**: 32.
McGowan, C. (1982). The wing musculature of the Brown kiwi *Apteryx australis mantelli* and its bearing on ratite affinities. *J. Zoology. London* **197**: 173-219.
McGowan, C. (1985). Tarsal development in birds: evidence for homology with the theropod condition. *J. Zoology. London (Ser. A)* **206**: 53-67.
McHenry, M.G. (1971). *Breeding and post-breeding movements of the Blue-winged Teal (*Anas discors*) in south-western Manitoba*. PhD thesis, University of Oklahoma, Norman.
McHugh (1955). Distribution of Black-footed Albatross, *Diomedea nigripes*, off the coast of North America, 1949 and 1950. *Pacific Science* 9: 375-381.
McIntyre, J.W. (1974). Territorial affinity of a Common Loon. *Bird-Banding* **45**: 178.
McIntyre, J.W. (1975). *Biology and Behavior of the Common Loon (*Gavia immer*) with Reference to its Adaptability in a Man-altered Environment*. PhD thesis, University of Minnesota, St. Paul.
McIntyre, J.W. (1977a). Artificial islands as nest sites for Common Loons. *J. Wildl. Manage.* **41**: 317-319.
McIntyre, J.W. (1977b). The Common Loon: part II. Identification of potential predators on Common Loon nests. *Loon* **49**: 96-99.
McIntyre, J.W. (1978). Wintering behavior of Common Loons. *Auk* **95**: 396-403.
McIntyre, J.W. (1983). Nurseries: a consideration of habitat requirements during the early chick-rearing period in Common Loons. *J. Field Orn.* **54**: 247-253.
McIntyre, J.W. (1986). Common Loon. Pp. 678-695 in: DiSilvestro, R.L. ed. (1986). *Audubon Wildlife Report 1986*. National Audubon Society, New York.
McIntyre, J.W. (1988). *The Common Loon: Spirit of Northern Lakes*. University of Minnesota Press, Minneapolis.
McIntyre, J.W. (1989). The Common Loon Cries for Help. *Natl. Geogr.* **175(4)**: 510-524.
McIntyre, J.W. & Barr, J.F. (1983). Pre-migratory behaviour of Common Loons on the autumn staging grounds. *Wilson Bull.* **95**: 121-125.
McKean, J.L. (1966). Population, status and migration of the gannet of Lawrence Rocks, Victoria. *Emu* **65**: 159-163.
McKelvey, R., Bousfield, M., Reed, A., Baranyuk, V.V. & Canniff, R. (1989). Preliminary results of the Lesser Snow Goose collaring program on the Alaksen National Wildlife Area, 1986 and 1987. *Can. Wildl. Ser.* **183**: 1-5.
McKelvey, R.W., McCormick, K.J. & Shandruk, L.J. (1988). The status of Trumpeter Swans, *Cygnus buccinator*, in Western Canada, 1985. *Can. Field-Nat.* **102 (3)**: 495-499.
McKelvey, S.D. (1977). The Meller's duck on Mauritius: Its status in the wild and captive propagation. *Game Bird Breeders Avicult. Zool. Conserv. Gazette* **May-June 1977**: 11-13.
McKenzie, H.R. (1971). The Brown Teal in the Auckland Province. *Notornis* **18**: 280-286.
McKeown, K.C. (1944). The food of cormorants and other fish-eating birds. *Emu* **43**: 259-269.
McKilligan, N.G. (1975). Breeding and movements of the Straw-necked Ibis in Australia. *Emu* **75**: 199-212.
McKilligan, N.G. (1984). The Food and Feeding Ecology of the Cattle Egret, *Ardeola ibis*, when Nesting in South-East Queensland. *Austr. Wildl. Res.* **11**: 133-144.
McKilligan, N.G. (1990a). Promiscuity in the Cattle Egret (*Bubulcus ibis*). *The Auk* **107**: 334-341.
McKilligan, N.G. (1990b). The Breeding Biology of the Intermediate Egret. Part 1: The Physical and Behavioural Development of the Chick, with Special Reference to Sibling Aggression and Food Intake. *Corella* **14(5)**: 162-169.
McKilligan, N.G. (1991). The Breeding Biology of the Intermediate Egret. Part 2: Parental Behaviour and Nesting Investment by the Male and Female. *Corella* **15(1)**: 8-12.
McKilligan, N.G. & McConnell, P. (1989). Evidence suggesting a case of bygyny in the Intermediate Egret. *Austr. Bird Watcher* **13**:98-99.
McKinney, F. (1953). *Studies on the Behaviour of the Anatidae*. PhD dissertation, University of Bristol, Bristol, UK.
McKinney, F. (1961). An analysis of the displays of the European eider *Somateria mollissima* (Linnaeus) and the Pacific eider *Somateria mollissima v. nigra* (Bonaparte). *Behaviour* **7(Suppl.)**.
McKinney, F. (1965a). The displays of the American green-winged teal. *Wilson Bull.* **77**: 112-121.
McKinney, F. (1965b). The spring behavior of wild Steller's eiders. *Condor* **67**: 273-290.
McKinney, F. (1965c). The comfort movements of Anatidae. *Behaviour* **25**: 120-220.
McKinney, F. (1967). Breeding behaviour of captive shovelers. *Wildfowl Trust Ann. Rep.* **18**: 108-121.
McKinney, F. (1970). Displays of four species of Blue-winged Ducks. *Living Bird* **9**: 29-64.
McKinney, F. (1975). The evolution of duck displays. Pp. 331-357 in: Baerends, G., Beer, C. & Manning, A. eds. *Function and Evolution of Behavior*. Clarendon Press, Oxford.
McKinney, F. (1985). Primary and secondary male reproductive strategies of dabbling Ducks. Pp. 68-82 in: Gowaty, P.A. & Mock, D.W. eds. *Avian Monogamy*. Ornithological Monographs **37**.
McKinney, F. & Brewer, G. (1989). Parental attendance and brood care in four Argentine dabbling ducks. *Condor* **91(1)**: 131-138.
McKinney, F. & Bruggers, D.J. (1983). Status and breeding behavior of the Bahama Pintail and the New Zealand Blue Duck. Pp. 211-221 in: *Proceedings of the Jean Delacour/IFCB Symposium on Breeding Birds in Captivity*. Hollywood, California.
McKinney, F., Siegfried, W.R., Ball, I.J. & Frost, P.G.H. (1978). Behavioral specializations for river life in the African Black Duck (*Anas sparsa* Eyton). *Z. Tierpsychol.* **48**: 349-400.
McKinney, F., Sorenson, L.G. & Hart, M. (1990). Multiple functions of courtship displays in dabbling ducks (Anatini). *Auk* **107**: 188-191.
McLandress, M.R. (1979). *Behavioral and Physiological Changes of Giant Canada Geese (*Branta canadensis maxima*) Prior to Spring Migration*. MSc thesis, University of California (Davis).
McLandress, M.R. & Raveling, D.G. (1981). Hyperphagia and social behavior of Canada Geese prior to spring migration. *Wilson Bull.* **93 (3)**: 310-324.
McLaughlin, J. (1989). Consistent large brood rearing by Maned Ducks. *Austr. Bird Watcher* **13 (4)**: 132-133.
McLean, S. (1986). Saddlebill Stork breeding at St. Lucia. *Lammergeyer* **37**: 55.
McLennan, J.A. (1988). Breeding of North Island Brown Kiwi *Apteryx australis mantelli*, in Hawke's Bay, New Zealand. *New Zealand J. Ecol.* **11**: 89-97.
McLennan, J.A. & McCann, T. (1989). Incubation by female Great Spotted Kiwis. *Notornis* **36**: 325-326.
McLennan, J.A., Rudge, M.R. & Potter, M.A. (1987). Range size and denning behaviour of Brown Kiwi, *Apteryx australis mantelli*, in Hawkes Bay, New Zealand. *New Zealand J. Ecol.* **10**: 97-108.
McMahan, C.A. (1989). *The Food Habits of Ducks Wintering on the Laguna Madre, Texas*. MSc thesis, N.M. State University.
McNally, J. (1957). The feeding habits of cormorants in Victoria. *Victorian Fish Game Dept. Fauna Contrib.* **6**.
McNeil, M.R. & McNeil, R. (1989). Night activity in the Brown Pelican. *Colonial Waterbirds* **12(1)**: 118-119.
McNeil, R. & Léger. C. (1987). Nest-site quality and reproductive success of early- and late-nesting Doublle-crested Cormorants. *Wilson Bull.* **99(2)**: 262-267.
McNeil, R., Limoges, B. & Rodriguez, J.R. (1990). El Corocoro Rojo (*Eudocimus ruber*) y otras aves acuáticas coloniales de las lagunas, ciénagas y salinas de la costa centro-oriental de Venezuela. Pp. 28-45 in: Frederick, Morales *et al.* (1990).
Mead, C. (1983). *Bird Migration*. Country Life Books, Feltham, Middlesex, UK
Meadows, B.S. (1984). Numbers and seasonality of filter-feeding ducks in Kenya. Pp. 441-459 in: Ledger, J. ed. (1984). *Proceedings of the Fifth Pan-African Ornithological Congress*. Southern African Ornithological Society, Johannesburg.
Meanley, B. & Meanley, A.G. (1958). Post-copulatory display in Fulvous and Black-headed Tree Ducks. *Auk* **75**: 95.
Meanley, B. & Meanley, A.G. (1959). Observations on the Fulvous Tree Duck in Louisiana. *Wilson Bull.* **71 (1)**: 33-45.
MEDMARAVIS & Monbailliu, X. eds. (1986). *Mediterranean Marine Avifauna. Population Studies and Conservation*. Springer-Verlag, Berlin.
Medway, M.A. & Wells, D.R. (1971). Diversity and density of birds and mammals at Kuala Lompat, Pahang. *Malay. Nat. J.* **24**: 238-247.
Medway, M.A. & Wells, D.R. (1976). *The Birds of the Malay Peninsula. A General Account of the Birds Inhabiting the Region from the Isthmus of Kra to Singapore with the Adjacent Islands*. Vol 5. Witherby, London & Penerbit Universiti Malaya, Kuala Lumpur.
Meek, E.R. & Little, B. (1977). The spread of the Goosander in Britain and Ireland. *British Birds* **70**: 229-237.
Meek, E.R. & Little, B. (1980). Goosander studies in the British Isles. *Danske Fugle* **32**: 132-146.
Mees, G.F. (1976). Mass mortality of *Puffinus gravis* on the coast of Suriname. *Zoologische Mededelingen* **49**: 269-271.
Mees, G.F. (1982). Bird records from de Moluccas. *Zool. Meded. Leiden* **56(7)**: 91-111.
Meeth, P. & Meeth, K. (1977). Blue Petrels off Peru. *Ardea* **65**: 90-91.
Mehlum, F., Gjessing, Y., Haftorn, S. & Bech, C. (1988). Census of breeding Antarctic Petrels and physical features of the breeding colony at Svarthamaren, D. Maud Land, with notes on the breeding Snow Petrels and S. Polar Skuas. *Polar Res.* **6**: 1-9..
Mehlum, F., Rahn, H., Bech, C. & Haftorn, S. (1986). Interrelationships between egg dimensions, pore numbers, incubation time, and adult body mass in Procellariiformes with special reference to the Antarctic Petrel. *Polar Res.* **5**: 55-58.
Meier, A.J., Noble, R.E., McKenzie, P.M. & Zwank, P.S. (1989). Observations on the nesting ecology of the White-cheeked Pintail. *Caribb. J. Sci.* **25 (1-2)**: 92-93.
Meinertzhagen, R. (1937). Some notes on the birds of Kenya Colony, with especial reference to Mount Kenya. *Ibis (4th. Ser.)* **1**: 731-760.
Meinertzhagen, R. (1954). *Birds of Arabia*. Oliver & Boyd, Edinburgh.
Meire, P.M., Kujiken, E. & Devos,K. (1991). Numbers and distribution of White-fronted and Pink-fronted Geese in Flanders (Belgium) 1981-87 in a North West European context. *Wildfowl* **39**: 71-81.
Melde, M. (1973). *Der Haubentaucher*. Die Neue Brehm-Bücherei **461**. Ziemsen Verlag, Wittenberg-Lutherstadt.
Melville, D.S. (1984). Seabirds of China and the Surrounding Seas. Pp. 501-511 in: Croxall *et al.* (1984).
Mendall, H.L. (1936). *The Home-life and Economic Status of the Double-crested Cormorant* Phalacrocorax auritus auritus *(Lesson)*. University of Maine Bulletin **39 (3)**.
Mendall, H.S. (1958). *The Ring-necked Duck in the North-east*. University of Maine Bulletin **60 (16)**.
Mendelsohn, J. (1981). Movements of prions and low pressure systems at Marion Island. Pp. 223-231 in Cooper, J. ed. (1981). *Proceedins of the Symposium on Birds of the Sea and Shore, 1979*. African Seabird Group, Cape Town.
Mendelssohn, H. (1975). The White Stork (*Ciconia ciconia*) in Israel. *Vogelwarte* **28**: 123-131.
Mendenhall, V.M. & Prouty, R.M. (1979). Recovery of breeding success in a population of Brown Pelicans. *Proc. 1978 Conf. Colonial Waterbird Group* **2**: 65-70.
Mendez, E. (1979). *Las aves de caza de Panamá*. E. Mendez, Panamá.
Menegheti, J.O. (1981). Observaçoes preliminares sobre o acaloramento e recrutamento en "*Nothura maculosa*". *Iheringia (Zool.)* **59**: 65-75.
Menegheti, J.O. (1983). Aspectos da relaçao de coexistencia entre *Nothura maculosa* (Temminck, 1815) e *Rhynchotus rufescens* (Temminck, 1815) (Aves, Tinamidae) no Rio Grande do Sul. *Iheringia (Zool.)* **63**: 27-38.
Menegheti, J.O. (1984). Acasalamiento em *Nothura maculosa* (Temminck, 1815) (Aves, Tinamidae), duraçao o periodo, magnitude e sua variaçao. *Iheringia (Zool.)* **64**: 3-14.
Menegheti, J.O. (1985a). Características de recrutamento em *Nothura maculosa* (Temmick, 1815) (Aves, Tinamidae). *Iheringia (Misc.)* **1**: 5-15.
Menegheti, J.O. (1985b). Densidade de *Nothura maculosa* (Temmick, 1815) (Aves, Tinamidae): variaçao anual. *Iheringia (Misc.)* **1**: 55-69.
Menegheti, J.O. (1985c). Características da caça e seus efeitos sobre a populaçao de *Nothura maculosa* (Temminck, 1815) (Aves, Tinamidae), no Rio Grande do Sul. *Iheringia (Misc.)* **1**: 87-100.
Menegheti, J.O. (1988). Razao de sexo e consideraçoes sobre o sistema de acarolamento en "*Nothura maculosa*" (Temminck, 1815) (Aves, Tinamidae). *Rev. Brasil. Zool.* **5(3)**: 427-440.
Menegheti, J.O. & Arigony, T.H. de A. (1982). Insetos, cuanhus e canapatos na alimentaçao da perdiz. *Natureza Rev.* **9**: 40-45.

Menegheti, J.O. & de Lourdes Abruzzi A. de Oliveira, M. (1982). Vegetais como alimento da perdiz. *Natureza Rev.* **9**: 32-38.
Menegheti, J.O. & Marques, M.I.B. (1981). Reproduçao e mortalidade da perdiz. *Natureza Rev.* **8**: 26-31.
Menegheti, J.O., Frozi, M. & Burger, M.I. (1985). The growth curve of the Red-winged Tinamou (*Rhynchotus rufescens*, Temminck, 1815) (Aves, Tinamidae). *Iheringia (Misc.)* **1**: 47-54.
Menegheti, J.O., Silva, F., Vieira, M.I., Bretschneider, D.S. & Marques, M.I.B. (1981). Spacial and temporal variations of density of "*Nothura maculosa*" (Temmick, 1815) from hunting data 1977, in the Rio Grande do Sul, State, Brazil. *Iheringia (Zool.)* **58**: 23-30.
Menkhorst, P.W., Davey, G.W. & Nicholls, D.G. (1983). Australian Pelicans breeding at Mud Islands, Victoria. *VORG Notes* **19(2)**: 43-44.
Menon, G.K. (1980). Notes on the highly modified bristles of Lesser Adjutant Stork "Leptoptilos javanicus". *J. Yamashina Inst. Orn.* **12(3)**: 213-219.
Menon, G.K., Shah, R.V. & Jani, M.B. (1979). Lipoid secretion by epidermis of bare skin from the head of the Indian White Ibis *Threskiornis melanocephala*. *J. Yamashina Inst. Orn.* **11**: 128-131.
Mercier, G. (1987). Le Fulmar estivant et nicheur en Picardie. *Avocette* **11**: 15-40.
Meredith, M.A.M. & Sin, F.I.T. (1988). Morphometrical analysis of four populations of Little Blue Penguin, *Eudyptula minor*. *J. Nat. Hist.* **22**: 801-809.
Merrie, T.D.H. (1978). Relationship between spatial distribution of breeding divers and the availability of fishing waters. *Bird Study* **25**: 119-122.
Merrie, T.D.H. (1979). Success of artificial island nest-sites for divers. *British Birds* **72**: 32-33.
Merton, D.V. (1970). Kermadec Islands Expedition Reports: a general account of birdlife. *Notornis* **17**: 147-199.
Merz, A. (1980). Marabou stork kills lesser flamingo. *East Afr. Nat. Hist. Soc. Bull.* **1980**: 97-98.
Meseth, E.H. (1975). The dance of the Laysan Albatross. *Behaviour* **54**: 217-257.
Mester, H. (1959). Einige sonderbare Verhaltensweisen des Zwergtauchers (*Podiceps ruficollis*). *J. Orn.* **100**: 352-354.
Meyerriecks, A.J. (1960). *Comparative Breeding Behavior of Four Species of North American Herons*. Publications of the Nuttall Ornithological Club **2**. Cambridge, MA.
Meyers, J.M. (1984). Wood Storks of the Birdsville Colony and swamps of the Savannah River Plant. SREL-15/UC-66e. Savannah River Ecology Laboratory, Aiken, SC.
Michelmore, F. & Oliver, W.L.R. (1982) Hand-rearing and developement of Bare-faced Ibis chicks *Geronticus eremita* at the Jersey Wildlife Preservation Trust; with comparative observations of parent-rearing behaviour. *Dodo* **19**: 51-69.
Michelot, J.L. & Laurent, L. (1988). Observations estivales d'oiseaux marins en mer Méditeranée occidentale. *L'Oiseau et la R.F.O.* **58**(1): 18-27.
Michener, M.C., Weske, J.S. & Clapp, R.B. (1964). A breeding colony of Agami Herons in Veracruz. *Condor* **66**: 77-78.
Mickelson, P.G. (1973). *Breeding Biology of Cackling Geese (*Branta canadensis minima *Ridgway) and Associated Species on the Yukon-Kuskokwim Delta, Alaska*. PhD dissertation, University of Michigan.
Middlemiss, E. (1958a). The Southern Pochard *Netta erythropthalma brunnea*. *Ostrich* **2(Suppl.)**: 1-34
Middlemiss, E. (1958b). Stages in development of *Anas undulata*. *Ostrich* **29**: 126-127.
Middlemiss, E. (1958c). Feeding habits of Lesser Flamingo. *Ostrich* **29**: 5-9.
Middleton, D.S. (1949). Close proximity of two nests of American bitterns. *Wilson Bull.* **61**: 113.
Miers, K.H. & Williams, M. (1969). Nesting of the Black Swan at Lake Ellesmere, New Zealand. *Wildfowl* **20: 23-32.**
Mikami, S. (1989). First Japanese records of crosses between Whistling *Cygnus columbianus columbianus* and Bewick's Swans *C.c. bewickii*. *Wildfowl* **40**: 131-133.
Mikuska, J. (1983). [Contribution to the knowledge of the feeding habits of the Cormorant, *Phalacrocorax carbo* (L., 1758) in the Kopacevski Rit Zoological Reservation]. *Larus* **33-35**: 31-36. In Croatian with English Summary.
Milewski, A.V. (1976). Feeding ecology of the Slaty *Egretta vinaceigula*. *Ostrich* **47**: 132-134.
Milledge, D. (1977). One year's observations of seabirds in continental shelf waters off Sydney, N.S.W. *Corella* **1**: 1-12.
Millener, P.R. (1972). The biology of the New Zealand pied cormorant *P. varius varius*. MSc thesis, Zoology Department, Auckland University.
Miller, A.H. (1937). Structural modifications in the Hawaiian Goose (*Nesochen sandvicensis*). A study in adaptative evolution. *Univ. California Publ. (Zool.)* **42**: 1-80.
Miller, A.H. (1963). Seasonal activity and ecology of the avifauna of an American equatorial cloud forest. *Univ. Calif. Publ. (Zool.)* **66**: 1-74.
Miller, A.H. (1966). An evaluation of the fossil anhingas of Australia. *Condor* **68**: 315-320.
Miller, B. (1976). Environmental control of gonadal cycles and egg laying periodicity in little pied and little black cormorants in inland New South Wales. PhD thesis, University of Sidney.
Miller, B. (1979). Ecology of the little black cormorant, *Phalacrocorax sulcirostris*, and little pied cormorant, *Phalacrocorax melanoleucos*, in inland New South Wales. I. Food and feeding habits. *Austr. Wildl. Res.* **6**: 79-95.
Miller, B. (1980). Ecology of the little black cormorant, *Phalacrocorax sulcirostris*, and little pied cormorant, *Phalacrocorax melanoleucos*, in inland New South Wales. II. Proximate control of reproduction. *Austr. Wildl. Res.* 7: 85-101.
Miller, L. (1940). Observations on the Black-footed Albatross. *Condor* **42**: 229-238.
Miller, L. (1942). Some tagging experiments with Black-footed Albatross. *Condor* **44**: 3-9.
Miller, L.M. (1976). *Expansion dynamics and breeding biology of the Glossy Ibis*, Plegadis falcinellus. MSc thesis. Rutgers University, New Brunswick, New Jersey.
Miller, L.M. & Burger, J. (1978). factors affecting nesting success of the Glossy Ibis. *Auk* **95**: 353-361.
Miller, P. (173). Second record of the Australian Little Grebe in New Zealand. *Notornis* **20**: 272-275.
Miller, P. & Miller, K. (1991). Bitterns using mangrove. *Notornis* **38(1)**: 79.
Miller, S.L., Gregg, M.A., Kuritsubo, A.R., Combs, S.M., Murdock, M.K., Nisson, J.A., Noon, B.R. & Botzler, R.G. (1988). Morphometric variation in Tundra Swans: relationships among sex and age classes. *Condor* **90(4)**: 802-815.
Mills, D. (1965). The distribution and food of the Cormorant in Scottish inland waters. *DAFS Freshwater and Salmon Fisheries Research* **35**: 1-16.
Mills, D. (1969a). The food of the Cormorant at two breeding colonies on the east coast of Scotland. *Scot. Birds* **5**: 268-276.
Mills, D. (1969b). The food of the Shag in Loch Ewe, Ross-shire. *Scottish Birds* **5**: 264-268.
Mills, E.L. (1968). Observations of the Ringed Storm-petrel off the North-West coast of South America. *Condor* **70**: 87-88.
Mills, J.A. (1985). Grey Teal. Page 145 in: Robertson (1985).
Milon, P. (1946). Observation sur quelques oiseaux de Madagascar. *L'Oiseau* **16**: 82-86.
Milon, P. (1948). Notes d'observation à Madagascar. *Alauda* **16**: 55-74.
Milon, P., Petter, J.J. & Randrianalolo, G. (1973). *Faune de Madagascar. Oiseaux*. ORSTOM & CNRS, Tananarive & Paris.
Milstein, P. le S. (1973). Buttons and Bald Ibis. *Bokmakierie* **25**: 57-60.
Milstein, P. le S. (1974). More Bald Ibis buttons. *Bokmakierie* **26**: 88.
Milstein, P. le S. (1975). How baby Egyptian Geese leave a high nest. *Bokmakierie* **27**: 49-51.
Milstein, P. le S. (1984). A waterfowl survey in Southern Moçambique, with conservation implications. Pp. 639-664. in: Ledger, J. ed. (1984). *Proceedings of the Fifth Pan-African Ornithological Congress*. Southern African Ornithological Society, Johannesburg.
Milstein, P. le S. & Hunter, H.C. (1974). The spectacular Black Heron. *Bokmakierie* **26**: 93-97.
Milstein, P. le S. & Siegfried, W.R. (1970). Transvaal status of the Bald Ibis. *Bokmakierie* **22**: 36-39.
Milstein, P. le S. & Wolff, S.W. (1973). Status and Conservations of the Bald Ibis in the Transvaal. *J. S. Afr. Wildl. Manage. Ass.* **3**: 79-83.
Milstein, P. le S., Prestt, I. & Bell, A.A. (1970). The breeding cycle of the Grey Heron. *Ardea* **58**: 171-257.
Milton, G.R. & Austin-Smith, P.J. (1983). Changes in the Abundance and Distribution of Double-crested (*Phalacrocorax auritus*) and Great Cormorants (*P. carbo*) in Nova Scotia. *Colonial Waterbirds* **6**: 130-138.
Milton, G.R & Marhadi, A. (1985). The bird life of the nature reserve Pulau Dua. *Kukila* **2**: 32-41.
Minton, C.D.T (1971). Mute Swan Flocks. *Wildfowl* **22**: 71-80.
Miranda Ribeiro, A. (1938). Notas ornithológicas XIII. Tinamidae. *Rev. Mus. Paulista* **23**: 667-788.
Misquelly, C.M. (1984). Birds of the Western Chain, Snares Islands 1983-84. *Notornis* **31**: 209-223.
Misterek, D. (1974). *The Breeding Ecology of the Ruddy Duck (*Oxyura jamaicensis*) on Rush Lake, Winnebago County, Wisconsin*. MSc thesis, University of Wisconsin, Oshkosh, Wisconsin.
Mitchell, P. (1986). Unusual sighting reports. Series 57. *Bird Obsr.* **653**: 50-51.
Mitchell, P. (1989). Unusual sighting reports. Series 74. *Bird Obsr.* **658**: 26-27.
Mitchell, P.C. (1913). Observations on the anatomy of the Shoe-bill (*Balaeniceps rex*) and allied birds. *Proc. Zool. Soc. Lond.* **1913**: 644-703.
Mitchev, T. (1981). The Dalmatian Pelican (*Pelecanus crispus*) - its numbers and population dynamics in the Srebarna Nature Reserve, south Dobrodgea. Pp. 516-527 in: *Proceedings of the Regional Symposium MAB-UNESCO, 20-24 October 1980, Blagoevgrad, Sofia*. In Bulgarian with English summary.
Mlíkovsky, J. (1989). Note on the osteology and taxonomic position of Salvadori's Duck *Salvadorina waigiuensis* (Aves: Anseridae [Anatidae]). *Bull. Brit. Orn. Club* **109 (1)**: 22-25.
Mlingwa, C. (1989). Notes on Marabou Storks *Leptoptilos crumeniferus* at Shinyanga, Tanzania. *East Afr. Nat. Hist. Soc. Bull.* **19**: 34.
Mocci Demartis, A. (1985). Analisi ricapitolativa sulla distribuzione europea del fenicottero rosa (*Phoenicopterus ruber roseus*) e sua densita in alcuni stagni sardi dal 1977 al 1985. *Rendiconti del Seminario Facolta Sc. Univ. Cagliari* **55**: 85-106.
Mock, D.W. (1975). Social Behavior of the Boat-billed Heron. *Living Bird* **14**: 185-214.
Mock, D.W. (1976a). Pair-formation displays of the Great Blue Heron. *Wilson Bull.* **88**: 185-230.
Mock, D.W. (1976b). *Social Behavior of the Great Blue Heron and Great Egret*. PhD thesis, University of Minnesota, Minneapolis.
Mock, D.W. (1978). Pair-formation displays of the Great Egret. *Condor* **80**: 159-172.
Mock, D.W. (1979). Displays repertoire shifts and "extramarital" courtship in herons. *Behaviour* **69**: 57-71.
Mock, D.W. (1980). Communication strategies of Great Blue Herons and Great Egrets. *Behaviour* **72(3-4)**: 156-170.
Mock, D.W. (1984). Siblicidal Aggression and Resource Monopolization in Birds. *Science* **225**: 731-733
Mock, D.W. (1986). Siblicide, parent-offspring conflict, and unequal parent investment by egrets and herons. *Behav. Ecol. Sociobiol.* **20**: 247-256.
Mock, D.W. & Mock, K.C. (1980). Feeding behavior and ecology of the Goliath Heron. *Auk* **97(3)**: 433-448.
Mock, D.W., Lamey, T.C., Williams, Ch.F. & Pelletier, A. (1987). Flexibility in the development of heron sibling aggression: an intraspecific test of the prey-size hypotesis. *Anim. Behav.* **35**: 1386-1393.
Moerbeek, D.J. van Dobben, W.H., Osieck, E.R., Boere, G.C. & Bungenberg de Jong, C.M. (1987). Cormorant damage prevention at a fish farm in the Netherlands. *Biol. Conserv.* **39**: 23-38.
Moffet, G.M. (1970). A study of nesting torrent ducks in the Andes. *Living Bird* **9**: 5-28.
Moisan, G., Smith, R.I. & Martinson, R.K. (1967). *The Green-winged Teal: its Distribution, Migration and Population Dynamics*. US Department of Interior, Special Scientific Report Wildlife **100**.
Moisley, W.L. (1960). A mixed shag roost at Clevedon. *Notornis* **9**: 58-60.
Moller, A.P. (1991). Sperm Competition, Sperm Depletion, Paternal Care, and Relative Testis Size in Birds. *Amer. Natralist* **137(6)**: 882-906.
Möller, W. (1979). Africa's amazing Shoebill Stork is a whale of a bird. *Wildlife. London* **21**: 38-39.
Möller, W. (1980). *Frilandbeobachtungen am Schuhschnabel* Balaeniceps rex. Diplomarbeit, Zoologisches Institut der Technischen Universitat Braunschweig.
Möller, W. (1982a). Beobachtungen zum Nahrungserwerb der Schuhschnabels. *J. Orn.* **123**: 19-28.
Möller, W. (1982b). Bei den Schuhschnabeln in den Sumpten Ugandas. *Zeitschrift der Zoofreunde Hannover e. V.* **45**: 6-10.
Monroe, B.L. (1968). *A Distributional Survey of the Birds of Honduras*. Ornithological Monographs **7**. The American Ornithologists' Union.
Monroe, B.L. & Browning, M.R. (1992). A re-analysis of *Butorides*. *Bull. Brit. Orn. Club* **112(2)**: 81-85.
Montague, T.L. (1982). The food and feeding ecology of the Little Penguin *Eudyptula minor* at Phillip Island, Victoria, Australia. MSc thesis, Monash University.
Montague, T.L. (1984a). A maximum dive recorder for Little Penguins. *Emu* **85**: 264-268.
Montague, T.L. (1984b). The food of Antarctic Petrels. *Emu* **84**: 244-245.
Montague, T.L. & Cullen, J.M. (1985). Comparison of techniques to recover stomach contents from penguins. *Austr. Wildl. Res.* **12**: 327-330.
Montague, T.L & Cullen, J.M. (1988). The diet of the Little Penguin *Eudyptula minor* at Phillip Island, Victoria. *Emu* **88**: 138-149.
Montague, T.L., Cullen, J.M. & Fitzherbert, K. (1987). The diet of the Short-tailed Shearwater during its breeding season. *Emu*
Montalbano, F., Johnson, F.A. & Conroy, M.J. (1985). Status of wintering Ring-necked Ducks in the southern Atlantic flyway. *J.Wild.Manage.* **49**: 543-546.
Montevecchi, W.A. & Porter, J.M. (1980). Parental investments by seabirds at the breeding area with emphasis on Northern Gannets, *Morus bassanus*. Pp. 323-365 in: Burger *et al.* (1980).
Montevecchi, W.A. & Wells, J. (1984). Fledging success of Northern Gannets from different nest-sites. *Bird Behaviour* **5**: 90-95.
Montevecchi, W.A., Barrett, R.T., Rikardsen, F. & Strann, K.B. (1987). The population and reproductive status of the Gannet in Norway in 1985. *Fauna Norv. (Ser. C.) Cinclus* **10**: 65-72.
Montevecchi, W.A., Kirkham, I.R., Roby, D.D. & Brink, K.L. (1983). Size, organic composition and energy content of Leach's storm-petrel eggs with reference to position in the precocial-altricial spectrum & breeding ecology. *Can. J. Zool.* **61**: 1456-63
Montevecchi, W.A., Ricklefs, R.E., Kirkham, I.R. & Gabaldon, D. (1984). Growth energetics of nestling Northern Gannets (*Sula bassanus*). *Auk* **101**: 334-341.
Montgomery, G.G. & Martínez, M.L. (1984). Timing of Brown Pelican nesting on Taboga Island in relation to upwelling in the Bay of Panama. *Colonial Waterbirds* **7**: 10-21.
Monval, J.Y. & Pirot, J.Y. compilers (1989). *Results of the IWRB International Waterfowl Census 1967-1986*. IWRB, Slimbridge, UK..
Moore, P.J. (1982). *The distribution and Activity of the White-faced Heron (Ardea novaehollandiae) at the Pauatahanui Inlet*. BSc (Hons) thesis, Victoria University.
Moore, P.J. (1984). Foraging and social behaviour of the White-Faced Heron at Pauatahanui Inlet. *Notornis* **31**: 285-299.
Moore, T. de R. (1980). An aerial acrobat practices piracy on the high seas. *Smithsonian* **10(12)**: 82-88.
Moors, P.J. (1980). Southern Great Skuas on Antipodes Island, New Zealand: observations on food, breeding, and growth of chicks. *Notornis* **27**: 133-146.
Moors, P.J. (1985). *Conservation of Island Birds*. ICBP Technical Publication **3**. ICBP, Cambrige, England.
Moors, P.J. (1986). Decline in numbers of Rockhopper Penguins at Campbell Island. *Polar Record* **23**: 69-73.
Moors, P.J. & Atkinson, I.A.E. (1984). Predation on Seabirds by Introduced Animals, and Factors Affecting its Severity. Pp. 667-690 in: Croxall *et al.* (1984).
Mora, M.A. (1989). Predation by a Brown Pelican at a mixed-species heronry. *Condor* **91**: 742-743.
Morales, G. (1990). Conservación de las aves zancudas en los llanos de Venezuela. Pp. 77-84 in: Frederick *et al.* (1990).
Morales, G., Pinowski, J., Pacheco, J., Madriz, M. & Gómez, F. (1981). Densidades poblacionales, flujo de energía y hábitos alimentarios de las aves ictófagas de los módulos de Apure, Venezuela. *Acta Biol. Venez.* **11**: 1-45.
Morant, P.D., Cooper, J. & Randall, R.M. (1981). The rehabilitation of oiled Jackass Penguins *Spheniscus demersus*, 1970-1980. Pp. 267-301 in: Cooper, J. ed. (1981). *Proceedings of the Symposium on Birds of the Sea and Shore, 1979*. African Seabird Group, Cape Town.
Moreau, R.E. (1972). *The Palearctic-African Bird Migration Systems*. Academic Press, London & New York.
Morel, G.J. (1972). *Liste commentée des oiseaux du Sénégal et de la Gambie*. Off. Rech. Scient. Tech. Outre-Mer, Dakar.
Morel, G.J. & Morel, M.Y. (1961). Une hèronnière mixte sur le Bas-Sénégal. *Alauda* **29**: 99-117.
Morel, G.J. & Morel, M.Y. (1962). La reproduction des oiseaux dans une région semi-aride: La Vallée du Sénégal. *Alauda* **30**: 161-203, 241-269.
Morel, G.J. & Morel, M.Y. (1989). Une hèronnière mixte sur le lac de Guier (Sénégal) avec référence spéciale à *Ixobrychus m. minutus* et *Platalea leucorodia*. *L'Oiseau et la R.F.O.* **59(4)**: 290-295.
Moreno, L.A. & Carmona, L.R. (1988). *Ecología Reproductiva de* Fregata magnificens *en Isla Santa Margarita, BCS*. Bachelor's thesis. Universidad Autónoma de Baja California Sur, Mexico.
Morgan, W.L. (1982). Feeding methods of the Short-tailed Shearwaters. *Emu* **82**: 226-227.
Morgan, W.L. & Ritz, D.A. (1982). Comparison of the feeding apparatus in the Muttonbird and the Fairy Prion in relation to the capture of krill. *J. Exp. Mar. Biol. Ecol.* **59**: 61-76.
Morillo, C. (1973). Nueva cita de *Phoeniconaias minor* en España. *Ardeola* **19**: 14-15.
Morman, F.I. (1985). Localised declines in colonies of the Short-tailed Shearwater: an explanation. *Papers & Proc. Royal Soc. Tasmania* **119**: 103-107.
Morony, J.J., Bock, W.J. & Farrand, J. (1975). *Reference List of the Birds of the World*. American Museum of Natural History, New York.
Morris, A. (1979). Saddlebill fishing methods. *Honeyguide* **98**: 33.
Morris, A.K. (1973). White Ibis eats snake. *Emu* **73**: 73.
Morris, A.K. (1990). Colonial Nesting of Striated Herons at Tuggerah, New South Wales. *Corella* **14(1)**: 27-28.
Morris, F.T. (1978). Feeding association between Little Egret and Sacred Ibis. *Emu* **78**: 164.
Morris, G.E. (1988). Recent sight records of birds at nam Cat Tien. *Garrulax* **4**: 11-13.

Morris, G.E. (1989). Further (1988) sight records of birds at nam Cat Tien. *Garrulax* **6**: 2.
Morris, R. & Smith, H. (1988). *Wild South. Saving New Zealand's Endangered Birds*. TVNZ & Century Hutchinson.
Morris, R.D. (1984). Breeding chronology and reproductive success of seabirds on Little Tobago, Trinidad, 1975-1976. *Colonial Waterbirds* **7**: 1-9.
Morrison, A. (1939a). The birds of the department of Huancavelica, Perú. *Ibis* 1939: 453-486.
Morrison, A. (1939b). Notes on the birds of Lake Junín, Central Peru. *Ibis* **1939**: 643-654.
Morrison, M.L. (1977). Life history and status of the Olivaceous Cormorant. MSc thesis, Texas A & M University, College Station, Texas.
Morrison, M.L. & Slack, R.D. (1977a). The role of flock feeding in Olivaceous Cormorants. *Bird Banding* **48**: 277-279.
Morrison, M.L. & Slack, R.D. (1977b). Population trends and status of the Olivaceous Cormorant. *Amer. Birds.* **31**: 954-959.
Morrison, M.L., Hale, B. & Slack, R.D (1983). Recent population trends of cormorants (Aves: Pelecaniformes) in Texas. *Texas J. Sci.* **35**: 239-242.
Morrison, M.L., Ralph, C.J., Verner, J. & Jehl, J.R. eds. (1990). *Avian Foraging: Theory, Methodology and Applications*. Studies in Avian Biology **13**. Cooper Ornithological Society.
Morrison, M.L., Shanley, E. & Slack, R.D. (1977). The food of nesting Olivaceous Cormorants. *Southwestern Naturalist* **22**: 321-326.
Morrison, M.L., Shanley, E. & Slack, R.D. (1979). Breeding biology and age-specific mortality of Olivaceous Cormorants. *Southwestern Naturalist* **24**: 259-266.
Morrison, M.L., Slack, R.D. & Shanley, E. (1978a). Age and foraging ability relationships of Olivaceous Cormorants. *Wilson Bull.* **90**: 414-422.
Morrison, M.L., Slack, R.D. & Shanley, E. (1978b). Interspecific association of Olivaceous Cormorants and Roseate Spoonbills. *Southw. Nat.* **23**: 681-683.
Morrison, T. (1968). Three flamingos of the high Andes. *Animals* **11** 305-309.
Morrison, T. (1972). The rarest flamingo. *Oryx* **11**: 270-272.
Morse, C.M. (1965). Jabiru in north-west New South Wales. *Emu* **64**: 234.
Morse, D.H. (1980). *Behavioral Mechanisms in Ecology*. Harvard University Press, Cambridge, Massachusetts.
Morse, D.H. & Buchheister, C.W. (1977). Age and survival of breeding Leach's Storm-petrels in Maine. *Bird-Banding* **48**: 341-349.
Morse, D.H. & Buchheister, C.W. (1979). Nesting patterns of Leach's Storm-Petrels on Matinicus Rock, Maine. *Bird-Banding* **50**: 145-148.
Morse, T.E., Jakabosky, J.L. & McCrow, V.P. (1969). Some aspects of the breeding biology of the Hooded Merganser. *J. Wildl. Manage.* **33**: 596-604.
Morton, S.R., Brennan, K.G. & Armstrong, M.D. (1990). Distribution and abundance of ducks in the Alligator Rivers Region, Northern Territory. *Austr. Wildl. Res.* **17 (6)**: 573-590.
Moser, M.E. (1986). Breeding strategies of Purple Herons in the Camargue, France. *Ardea* **74**: 91-100.
Moskal, J. & Marszalek, J. (1986). Effect of habitat and nest distribution on the breeding success of the Great Crested Grebe *Podiceps cristatus* on Lake Zarnowieckie. *Acta Orn.* **22(2)**: 147-158.
Mott, L.T. (1965). Water birds of the Gran Chaco of Paraguay. *Game Bird Breeders Gazette* **14**: 14-15.
Mougin, J.L. (1967). Étude écologique des deux espèces de fulmars, le Fulmar Atlantique (*Fulmarus glacialis*) et le Fulmar Antarctique (*Fulmarus glacialoides*). *L'Oiseau et la R.F.O.* **37**: 57-103.
Mougin, J.L. (1968). Étude écologique de quatre espèces de pétrel antarctiques. *L'Oiseau et la R.F.O.* (No. Spéc.) **38**: 1-51.
Mougin, J.L. (1969). Notes écologiques sur le Pétrel de Kerguelen de l'Ile de la Possession (Archipel Crozet). *L'Oiseau et la R.F.O.* **39(No. Spéc.)**: 58-81.
Mougin, J.L. (1970a). Observations écologiques sur le Grand Albatross de l'Ile de la Possession (Archipel Crozet) en 1968. *L'Oiseau et la R.F.O.* **40(No. Spéc.)**: 16-36.
Mougin, J.L. (1970b). Les albatross fuligineux de l'Ile de la Possession (Archipel Crozet). *L'Oiseau et la R.F.O.* **40(No. Spéc.)**: 37-61.
Mougin, J.L. (1970c). Le Pétrel à Menton Blanc de l'Ile de la Possession (Archipel Crozet). *L'Oiseau et la R.F.O.* **40(No. Spéc.)**: 62-96.
Mougin, J.L. (1971). Note complementaire sur le Pétrel à Menton Blanc de l'Ile de la Possession (Archipel Crozet). *L'Oiseau et la R.F.O.* **41**: 82-83.
Mougin, J.L. (1975). Écologie comparée des Procellariidae Antarctiques et Subantarctiques. *Comité Natl. Français Rech. Antarct.* **36**: 1-195.
Mougin, J.L. (1977). Nidification à l'ile Marion d'un Grand Albatross né à l'île de la Possession, Archipel Crozet. *Comptes Rendus Acad. Scienc. Paris* **284**: 2277-2280.
Mougin, J.L. (1984). La ponte du Gorfou Macaroni *Eudyptes chrysolophus* de l'archipel Crozet. *L'Oiseau et la R.F.O.* **54(4)**: 281-291.
Mougin, J.L. (1985). Pétrels, Pétrels-tempête et Pétrels plongeurs de l'île de Croy, îles Nuageuses, Archipel des Kerguelen. *L'Oiseau et la R.F.O.* **55**: 313-349.
Mougin, J.L. (1988). Sur la nidification et l'élevage du poussin chez le Pétrel-frégate *Pelagodroma marina hypoleuca* de l'île Selvagem Grande. *Cyanopica* **4**(2): 167-184.
Mougin, J.L. (1989). Données préliminaires sur la structure et la dynamique de la population de Pétrels de Bulwer de l'ile Selvagem Grande (30° 09' N, 15° 52' W). *Comptes Rendus Acad. Sci. Paris (Ser. III)* **308**: 103-106.
Mougin, J.L. & Prévost, J. (1980). Évolution annuelle des éffectifs et des biomasses des oiseaux antarctiques. *Rev. Ecol. (Terre Vie)* **34**: 101-133.
Mougin, J.L. & Stahl, J.C. (1982). Essai de dénombrement des Puffins Cendrés de l'ile Selvagem Grande (30° 09' N, 15° 52' W) en 1980. *Bocagiana* **63**: 1-17.
Mougin, J.L., Despin, B., Jouanin, C. & Roux, F. (1987). La fidelité au partenaire et au nid chez le Puffin Cendré, *Calonectris diomedea borealis*, de l'ile Selvagem Grande. *Gerfaut* **77**: 353-369.
Mougin, J.L., Jouanin, C., Despin, B. & Roux, F. (1986). The age of first breeding of Cory's Shearwater and problems of ring loss. *Ringing & Migration* **7**: 130-134.
Mougin, J.L., Jouanin, C. & Roux, F. (1987a). Structure et dynamique de la population des Puffins Cendrés de l'ile Selvagem Grande (30° 09' N, 15° 52' W). *L'Oiseau et la R.F.O.* **57**: 201-225.
Mougin, J.L., Jouanin, C. & Roux, F. (1987b). Les paramètres controlant la réussite de l'incubation chez le Puffin Cendré de l'ile Selvagem Grande (30° 09' N, 15° 52' W). *Bocagiana* **112**: 1-11.
Mougin, J.L., Jouanin, C. & Roux, F. (1987c). Les années sabbatiques des Puffins Cendrés de l'ile Selvagem Grande (30° 09' N, 15° 52' W). Influence du sexe et de l'age. *L'Oiseau et la R.F.O.* **57**: 368-381.
Mougin, J.L., Jouanin, C. & Roux, F. (1988a). Les différences d'age et d'expérience entre partenaires chez le Puffin Cendré de l'ile Selvagem Grande (30° 09' N, 15° 52' W). *L'Oiseau et la R.F.O.* **58**: 113-119.
Mougin, J.L., Jouanin, C. & Roux, F. (1988b). Les migrations de Puffin Cendré. *L'Oiseau et la R.F.O.* **58**: 303-318.
Mougin, J.L., Jouanin, C. & Roux, F. (1988c). L'influence des voisins dans la nidification du Puffin Cendré. *Comptes Rendus Acad. Sci. Paris* **307**: 195-198.
Mougin, J.L., Jouanin, C. & Roux, F. (1990a). Le rôle de l'âge et de l'expérience dans le réroulement et la réussite de la reproduction chez le Puffin cendré *Calonectris diomedea borealis* de l'île Selvagem Grande. *L'Oiseau et la R.F.O.* **60**(1): 39-49.
Mougin, J.L., Jouanin, C. & Roux, F. (1990b). Chronologie de la reproduction chez le Pétrel-tempête de Castro *Oceanodroma castro* (Harcourt). *L'Oiseau et la R.F.O.* **60**(2): 136-150.
Mougin, J.L., Jouanin, C., Roux, F. & Stahl, J.C. (1984). Les années sabbatiques des Puffins Cendrés reproducteurs de l'ile Selvagem Grande, océan Atlantique nord-oriental (30° 09' N, 15° 52' W). *C.R. Acad. Sci. Paris* (Ser. III) **299**: 147-150.
Mougin, J.L., Roux, F., Jouanin, C. & Stahl, J.C. (1984a). Quelques aspects de la biologie de reproduction du Puffin Cendré des iles Selvagens (30° 09' N, 15° 52' W). *L'Oiseau et la R.F.O.* **54**: 229-246.
Mougin, J.L., Roux, F., Stahl, J.C. & Jouanin, C. (1984b). L'évolution des éffectifs des Puffins Cendrés de l'ile Selvagem Grande (30° 09' N, 15° 52' W) de 1980 à 1983. *Bocagiana* **75**: 1-8.
Mougin, J.L., Zino, F., Biscoito, M., Despin, B. & Roux, F. (1986). Quelques observations concernant la paraide chez le Puffin Cendré de l'ile Selvagem Grande (30° 09' N, 15° 52' W). *Bol. Mus. Mun. Funchal* **38**: 5-15.
Moulton, D.W. & Weller, M.W. (1984). Biology and conservation of the Laysan Duck (*Anas laysanensis*). *Condor* **86**: 105-117.
Mountfort, G. (1988). *Rare Birds of the World*. Collins, London.
Moynihan, M. (1958). Notes on the behavior of the Flying Steamer Duck. *Auk* **75**: 183-202.
Moynihan, M. (1979). *Geographic Variation in Social Behavior and in Adaptations to Competition Among Andean Birds*. Publications of the Nuttall Ornithological Club **18**. Cambridge, Massachussetts.
Mudge, G.P., Aspinall, S.J. & Crooke, C.H. (1987). A photographic study of seabird attendance at Moray Firth colonies outside the breeding season. *Bird Study* **34**: 28-36.
Mudge, G.P., Dennis, R.H., Talbot, T.R. & Broad, R.A. (1991). Changes in the breeding status of Black-throated Divers in Scotland. *Scot. Birds* **16**: 77-84.
Mukherjee, A.K. (1969). Food Habits of waterbirds of the Sundarban, 24-Parganas District, West Bengal, India - I. *J. Bombay Nat. Hist. Soc.* **66(2)**: 345-360.
Mukherjee, A.K. (1971). Food-habits of waterbirds of the Sundarban, 24-Parganas District, West Bengal, India - II. *J. Bombay Nat. Hist. Soc.* **68**: 17-44.
Mukherjee, A.K. (1974). Food-habits of waterbirds of the Sundarban, 24-Parganas District, West Bengal, India - IV. *J. Bombay Nat. Hist. Soc.* **71**: 188-200.
Mukhopadhyay, A. (1980). Some observations on the biology of the Openbill Stork, *Anastomus oscitans* (Boddaert) in Southern Bengal. *J. Bombay Nat. Hist. Soc.* **77**: 133-137.
Mulhern, J.H., Nudds, T.D. & Neal, B.R. (1985). Wetland selection by Mallards and Blue-winged Teal. *Wilson Bull.* **97**: 473-485.
Müller, A. (1989). Rothalstaucher *Podiceps grisegena* ertrank in mindestens 35 Meter Tiefe im Starnberger See. [Summary: Red-necked Grebe got drowned in a depth of at least 35 metres in the Starnberger See, Bavaria]. *Anz. orn. Ges. Bayern* **28**: 139-142.
Muller, C.Y. (1984). [Breeding Pair Status and Migration of *Platalea leucorodia* L. in Austrian-Hunagarian Areas]. *Egretta* **27(2)**: 45-67. In German.
Muller, C.Y. (1987a). [Contribution to reproduction and rearing of the Spoonbill (*Platalea leucorodia* L.) in the region of Neusiedlersee]. *Egretta* **30**: 13-23. In German.
Muller, C.Y. (1987b). Feeding-sites and resting-places of the Spoonbill *Platalea leucorodia* at Neusiedlersee (Austria). *Orn. Beob.* **84**: 237-245.
Müller, H.H. (1988). Erster Brutnachweis des vom Aussterben bedrohten Taiko-Sturmvogels (*Pterodroma magentae*) auf den Chatham Islands (Neuseeland). *Seevögel* **9**(1): 9-11.
Muller-Scheessel, L. (1964). Zum Brutvorkommen des Schwarztorches in Niedersachsen. *Beitr. Naturkd. Niedersachsens* **18**: 19-20.
Muller-Scheessel, L. (1965). Über Brutvorkommen des Schwarzstorches in Niedersachsen im Jahre 1964. *Beitr. Naturkd. Niedersachsens* **18**: 19-20.
Müller-Schwarze, D. (1984). *The Behaviour of Penguins Adapted to Ice and Tropics*. State University of New York Press, Albany.
Müller-Schwarze, D. & Belanger, P. (1978). Man's impact on Antarctic birds. Pp. 373-383 in: Parker, B.C., ed. *Environmental Impact in Antarctica*. Virginia Polytechnic Inst. and State University, Blacksburg.
Müller-Schwarze, D. & Müller-Schwarze, C. (1977). Interactions between South Polar Skuas and Adelie Penguins. Pp. 619-646 in: Llano (1977).
Müller-Schwarze, D. & Müller-Schwarze, C. (1980). Display rate and speed of nest relief in Antarctic pygoscelid penguins. *Auk* **97**: 825-831.
Mundkur, T. (1984). Occurrence of Lesser Flamingo *Phoeniconaias minor* (Geoffroy) in Poona, Maharashtra. *J. Bombay Nat. Hist. Soc.* **81**: 468.
Mundkur, T. & Pravez, R. (1986). Rediscovery of the Great Crested Grebe (*Podiceps cristatus*) breeding in Gujarat. *J. Bombay Nat. Hist. Soc.* **83**: 429-431.
Mundkur, T., Pravez, R. & Naik, R.M. (1989). A hitherto unreported nest site of the Lesser Flamingo *Phoeniconaias minor* in the Little Rann of Kachchh, Gujarat. *J. Bombay. Nat. Hist. Soc.* **86(3)**: 281-285.
Mundy, P.J. (1985). What brings the African Marabou on? *Honeyguide* **31(4)**: 186.
Mundy, P.J., Cannell, I.C. & Williams, A. (1988). Marabou Storks breeding at Kadoma. *Honeyguide* **34(2)**: 66-69.
Munro, G.C. (1940). Birds of Hawaii - Wedge-tailed Shearwater. *Elepaio* **1**: 7-8.
Munro, J.A. (1939). Studies of waterfowl in British Columbia: Barrow's Goldeneye, American Goldenenye. *Transactions of the Royal Canadian Institute* **22**: 259-318.
Munro, J.A. (1941). The grebes. Studies of waterfowl in British Columbia. *Occ. Papers Brit. Col. Prov. Mus.* **3**: 1-71.
Munro, J.A. (1945). Observations of the loon in the Cariboo Parklands, British Columbia. *Auk* **62**: 38-49.
Munro, J.A. (1949a). Studies of waterfowl in British Columbia: Green-winged Teal. *Can. J. Res. (Sec. D)* **27**: 149-178.
Munro, J.A. (1949b). Studies of waterfowl in British Columbia: Baldpate. *Can. J. Res. (Sec. D)* **27**: 289-307.
Munro, R.E. & Kimball, C.F. (1982). *Population Ecology of the Mallard. VII. Distribution and Derivation of the Harvest*. US Fish & Wildlife Service Resources Publication **147**.
Munro, R.E., Smith, L.T. & Kupa, J.J. (1968). The genetic basis of colour differences observed in the Mute Swan (*Cygnus olor*). *Auk* **85**: 504-505.
Muraska, I.P. & Valius, M.I. (1968). Natural reacclimatization of the Mute Swan in Lithuania and adjacent regions. Pp. 56-64 in: Lusis, Ya.Ya., Spurin, Z.D., Taurins, E.J. & Vilka, E.K. eds. (1968). *Birds of the Baltic Region: Ecology and Migrations*. Israel Program for Scientific Translations, Jerusalem.
Murata, K. (1988). Sex determination in the Eastern White Stork, *Ciconia c. boyciana*, by bill measurements and discriminant analysis. *J. Jpn. Assoc. Zoos & Aquariums* **30**: 43-47.
Murphy, R.C. (1916a). Notes on American subantarctic cormorants. *Bull. Amer. Mus. Nat. Hist.* **35**: 31-48.
Murphy, R.C. (1916b). Anatidae of South Georgia. *Auk* **33**: 270-277.
Murphy, R.C. (1925). *Bird Islands of Peru*. Putnams, New York.
Murphy, R.C. (1936). *Oceanic Birds of South America*. 2 Vols. American Museum of Natural History, New York.
Murphy, R.C. (1947). A new zonal race of the Gentoo Penguin. *Auk* **64**: 454-455.
Murphy, R.C. (1949). A new species of petrel from the Pacific. *Orn. Biol. Wissenschaft*: 89-91.
Murphy, R.C. (1951). The populations of the Wedge-tailed Shearwater. *Amer. Mus. Novitates* **1512**: 1-21.
Murphy, R.C. (1952). The Manx Shearwater as a species of world-wide distribution. *Amer. Mus. Novitates* **1586**: 1-21.
Murphy, R.C. & Harper, F. (1921). A review of the Diving Petrels. *Bull. Amer. Mus. Nat. Hist.* **44**: 495-554.
Murphy, R.C. & Irving, S. (1951). A review of the frigate-petrels (*Pelagodroma*). *Amer. Mus. Novitates* **1506**.
Murphy, R.C. & Mowbray, L.S. (1951). New light on the Cahow. *Auk* **68**: 266-280.
Murphy, R.C. & Pennoyer, J.M. (1952). Larger petrels of the genus *Pterodroma*. *Amer. Mus. Novitates* **1580**: 1-43.
Murphy, R.C. & Snyder, J.P. (1952). The '*Pealea*' phenomenon and other notes on storm petrels. *Amer. Mus. Novitates* **1596**: 1-16.
Murray, S. & Wanless, S. (1984). The status of the Gannet in Scotland 1984 -1985. *Scottish Birds* **14**: 74-85.
Murton, R.K. (1971). Polymorphism in Ardeidae. *Ibis* **113**: 97-99.
Murton, R.K. (1972). The ecology and status of Suringhoes's egret, with notes on other herons in southeastern China. *Biol. Conserv.* **4(2)**: 89-96.
Murton, R.K. & Kear, J. (1978). Photoperiodism in waterfowl: phasing of breeding cycles and zoogeography. *J. Zool. London* **186**: 243-283.
Murton, R.K. & Westwood, N.J. (1976). Birds as pests. Pp. 89-191 in: Coaker, T.H. ed. *Applied Biology*. Vol 1. Academic Press, London and New York.
Murton, R.K. & Westwood, N.J. (1977). *Avian Breeding Cycles*. Clarendon Press, Oxford.
Murton, R.K. & Wright, E.N. (1968). *The Problems of Birds as Pests*. Academic Press, London and New York.
Myers, M.T. (1959). *The Behavior of the Sea-ducks and its Value in the Systematics of the Tribes Mergini and Somateriini, of the family Anatidae*. PhD dissertation, Universiy of British Columbia.
Myong, J.S. (1967). Is the White Stork really extinct? *Korean Nat.* **1967**: 2-3.
Myrberget, S., Johansen, V. & Storjord, O. (1969). Stormsvaler (Fam. Hydrobatidae) i Norge. *Fauna* **22**: 15-26.
Naarding, J.A. (1980). Study of the Short-tailed Shearwater in Tasmania. *Natn. Parks & Wildl. Serv. Tasm. Rep.* 1-78.
Naarding, J.A. (1981). Study of the Short-tailed Shearwater in Tasmania. *Natnl. Parks & Wild. Serv. Tasm. Tech. Rep.* **81/3**: 1-34.
Nagulu, V. & Ramana Rao, J.V. (1981). Andhra Pradesh still the Traditional Home of the Pelicans. *Hornbill* **3**: 30-31.
Nagulu, V. & Ramana Rao, J.V. (1982). Survey of South Indian Pelicanries. *J. Bombay Nat. Hist. Soc.* **80**: 141-143.
Nagulu, V., Suresh Kumar, T. & Ramana Rao, J.V. (1981). Pity the Pelican *Tiger Paper* **8(2)**: 19-20.
Nagy, K.A., Siegfried, W.R. & Wilson, R.P. (1984). Energy utilization by free-ranging Jackass Penguins, *Spheniscus demersus*. *Ecology* **65(5)**: 1648-1655.
Naik, R.M. & Parasharya, B.M. (1987). Impact of the food availability, nesting-habitat destruction and cultural variations of human settlements on the nesting distribution of a coastal bird, *Egretta gularis*, in western India. *J. Bombay Nat. Hist. Soc.* **84(2)**: 350-360.
Naito, Y., Asaga, T. & Ohyama, Y. (1990). Diving behaviour of Adelie Penguins determined by time-depth recorder. *Condor* **92**: 582-586.
Nakamura, K. (1974). [On a mass accidental death of the Streaked Shearwater in Sagami Bay.] *Bull. Nanagawa Prefectural Mus.* **7**: 71-79.
Nakamura, K. (1982). Distribution of the gadfly petrels of the genus *Pterodroma* in the Antarctic and subAntarctic regions of the Australian Sector, Austral summer 1981. *Trans. Tokyo Univ. Fish* **5**: 203-211.
Nakamura, K. & Hasegawa, M. (1979). A brief note on the distribution of Buller's Shearwater, *Puffinus bulleri*, in Japan and adjacent seas. *J. Yamashina Inst. Orn.* **11**(2): 123-127.
Nakamura, K. & Tanaka, Y. (1977). Distribution and migration of two species of the genus *Pterodroma* in the North Pacific. *Misc. Rep. Yamashina Inst. Orn.* **9**: 112-120.

Nakamura, K., Hori, H. & Osaka, Y. (1983). A mass inland drift of Leach's Storm Petrel by a typhoon in the autumn of 1979. *Bull. Kanagawa Prefectural Mus. (Nat. Sci.)* **14**: 37-44.
Nakamura, K., Tanaka, Y. & Hasegawa, M. (1983). Distribution Status of the Wilson's Storm Petrel in Japanese waters. *Bull. Biogeogr. Soc. Japan* **38**: 125-128.
Nakamura, T. (1963). Distribution of the Black-footed Albatross (*Diomedea nigripes*) in the North Pacific Ocean. *J. Yamashina Inst. Orn.* **3**: 239-246.
Nakhasathien, S. (1987). The discovery of Storm's Stork *Ciconia stormi* in Thailand. *Forktail* **3**: 43-49.
Nankinov, D. (1981). [The state of Garganey (*Anas querquedula* L.) breeding population in Bulgaria]. In: [*Regional Symposium to Project 8-May Unesco 20-24-X-1980*]. In Russian.
Nankinov, D. (1991). White-fronted goose (*Anser albifrons*, Scopoli) numbers, migration, conservation. *Sitta* **5**: 27-33.
Napier, R.B. (1968). Erect-crested and Rockhopper Penguins interbreeding in the Falkland Islands. *Bull. Brit. Antarct. Surv.* **16**: 71-72.
Naranjo, L.G. (1986). Aspects of the Biology of the Horned Screamer in southwestern Colombia. *Wilson Bull.* **98(2)**: 243-256.
Narosky, S. (1988). Hallazgos de aves poco comunes en el norte argentino. *Hornero* **13**: 91-93.
Narosky, T. & Yzurieta, D. (1987). *Guía para la identificación de las aves de Argentina y Uruguay*. Vazquez Mazzini, Buenos Aires.
Narosky, T., Montes, G. & de Yoffe, A.E. (1984). El pingüino de Magallanes. Pp. 1-32 in: Cabal, G.B. ed. *Fauna Argentina. Aves*. Vol. 1. Centro Editor de América Latina, Buenos Aires.
Narosky, T., Reig, G. & Battini, M.A. (1988). El macá común. Pp. 1-32 in: Cabal, G.B. ed. *Fauna Argentina. Aves*. Vol. 4. Centro Editor de América Latina, Buenos Aires.
Nash, S.V. & Nash, A.D. (1985). A checklist of the forest and forest edge birds of the Padang-Sugihan Wildlife Reserve, South Sumatra. *Kukila* **2**: 51-59.
Nash, S.V. & Nash, A.D. (1987). Padang-Sugihan's White-winged Wood Ducks: a sign of hope for the Sumatran population. *Biotrop. Spec. Publ.* **30**: 135-140.
Nash, S.V. & Nash, A.D. (1988). An annotated checklist of the birds of Tanjung Puting National Park, Central Kalimantan. *Kukila* **3**: 93-116.
Naumburg, E.M. (1930). Birds of Matto Grosso, Brazil. *Bull. Amer. Mus. Nat. Hist.* **60**.
de Naurois, R. (1965). Une colonie reproductive du petit Flamant *Phoeniconaias minor* dans l'Aftout-es-Sahel (Sud-Ouest mauritanien). *Alauda* **33**: 166-176.
de Naurois, R. (1966a). Le Héron pourpré de l'Archipel du Cap Vert *Ardea purpurea bournei* ssp. nov. *Osiseau* **36**: 89-94.
de Naurois, R. (1966b). Colonies reproductrices de Spatules africaines, Ibis sacrés et lorides, dans L'Archipel des Bijagos (Guinée Portugaise). *Alauda* **34**: 257-278.
de Naurois, R. (1969a). Le Flamant rose (*Phoenicopterus ruber*) a-t-il niché en nombre et réguliérement dans l'archipel du Cap Vert? *L'Oiseau et la R.F.O.* **39**: 28-37.
de Naurois, R. (1969b). Notes breves sur l'avifaune de l'archipel du Cap Vert - Faunistique, endemisme, écologie. *Bull. Inst. Fond. Afr. Noire (Ser. A)* **31**: 143-218.
de Naurois, R. (1969c). *Peuplements et cycles de reproduction des oiseaux de la côte occidentale d'Afrique*. Mem. Mus. Natl. Hist. Nat. (Nouv. Sér A, Zoologie) **56**.
de Naurois, R. (1973). Les ibis des îles de Sao Tomé et du Prince: leur place dans le group des *Bostrychia* (=*Lampribis*). *Arq. Mus. Bocage (2 Ser.)* **4**: 157-173.
de Naurois, R. (1978). Procellariidae reproducteurs en Nouvelle-Calédonie. *Comptes Rendus Acad. Sci. Paris (Ser D)* **287**: 269-271.
de Naurois, R. (1982). Le Statut de l'Aigrette garzette (*Egretta garzetta*) (L.) dans l'Archipel du Cap-Vert. *Cyanopica* **2(4)**: 5-15.
de Naurois, R. (1983). Les oiseaux reproducteurs des îles de Sao Tomé et Príncipe: liste systématique commentée et indications zoogéographiques. *Bonn. zool. Beitr.* **34**: 129-148.
de Naurois, R. (1987). Phalacrocoracidae et Ardeidae dans les Iles de Sao Tomé et du Prince (Golfe de Guinée). *Cyanopica* **4(1)**: 27-54.
de Naurois, R. (1988). *Ardea (purpurea) bournei* endémique de l'Ile de Santiago (Archipel du Cap Vert). *Alauda* **56(3)**: 261-268.
de Naurois, R. & Erard, C. (1979). L'identité subspécifique des populations neo-calédoniennes de *Pterodroma rostrata*. *L'Oiseau et la R.F.O.* **49**: 235-239.
de Naurois, R. & Roux, F. (1974). Précisions concernant la morphologie, les affinités et la position systematique de quelques oiseaux du Banc d'Arguin (Mauritania). *L'Oiseau et la R.F.O.* **44**: 72-84.
Navarro, R.A. (1991). Food Addition and Twinning Experiments in the Cape Gannet: Effects on Breeding Success and Chick Growth and Behavior. *Colonial Waterbirds* **14(2)**: 92-102.
Navas, J.R. & Bó, N.A. (1981). Nuevas aportaciones a la taxionomía de las razas geográficas de *Eudromia elegans* y *Eudromia formosa*. *Rev. Mus. Arg. Cienc. Nat.Bernardino Rivadavia* **11(2)**: 33-59.
Navas, J.R. & Bó, N.A. (1988). Aves nuevas o poco conocidas de Misiones, Argentina. II. *Com. Zool. Mus. Hist. Nat. Montevideo* **166(12)**: 1-9.
Navas, J.R. & Bó, N.A. (1991). Aves nuevas o poco conocidas de Misiones, Argentina, IV. *Rev. Mus. Arg. Cienc. Nat.Bernardino Rivadavia* **15(8)**.
Neame, G.B. (1968). Spoonbill breeding in the Eastern Cape. Ostrich **39**: 265.
Neelakantan, K.K. (1949). A south Indian pelicanry. *J. Bombay Nat. Hist. Soc.* **48**: 565-566.
Neelakantan, K.K. (1980). A Pelican's pathetic plight. *Tiger Paper* **7(2)**: 21-24.
Negere, E. (1980). The effects of religious belief on conservation of birds in Ethiopia. Pp. 361-365 in: Johnson, D.N. ed. (1984). *Proceedings Fourth Pan-African Ornithological Congress*. Southern African Ornithological Society, Johannesburg.
Neginhal, S.G. (1976). Discovery of a Pelicanry in Karnataka. *Newsletter for Birdwatchers* **16**: 14-15.
Nehls, G., Bräger, S., Meissner, J. & Thiel, M. (1988). Zum Bestand der Eiderente (*Somateria mollissima*) an der deutschen Nordseeküste. *Corax* **13**: 41-58.
Nel, J.E. (1966). Nesting Hamerkops. *Bokmakierie* **18**: 70-72.
Nelson, A. (1971). King Shags in the Marlborough Sounds. *Notornis* **18**: 30-37.
Nelson, D. (1975). *Pair-formation displays of the Black-crowned Night Heron*. Honors thesis, University of Minnesota, Minneapolis.
Nelson, E.W. (1903). Notes on the Mexican Cormorant. *Condor* **5**: 137-145.
Nelson, J.B. (1964a).Fledging in the Gannet. *Scot. Nat.* **77**: 47-59.
Nelson, J.B. (1964b). Factors influencing clutch-size and chick growth in the North Atlantic Gannet *Sula bassana Ibis* **106**: 63-77.
Nelson, J.B. (1965). The behavior of the gannet. *Brit. Birds* **58**: 233-288, 313-336
Nelson, J.B. (1966a). The behaviour of the young gannet. *Brit. Birds* **59**: 393-419.
Nelson, J.B. (1966b). Clutch size in the Sulidae. *Nature* **214**: 435-436.
Nelson, J.B. (1966c). The breeding biology of the Gannet on the Bass Rock, Scotland. *Ibis* **108**: 584-626.
Nelson, J.B. (1966d). Population dynamics of the gannet on the Bass Rock, with comparative information from other Sulidae. *J. Anim. Ecol.* **35**: 443-470.
Nelson, J.B. (1967a). The breeding behaviour of the White-footed Booby *Sula dactylatra*. *Ibis* **109**: 194-231.
Nelson, J.B. (1967b). Etho-ecological adaptations in the Great Frigatebird. *Nature. London* **214**: 318.
Nelson, J.B. (1968). *Galapagos: Islands of Birds*. Longmans, London.
Nelson, J.B. (1969a). The breeding behaviour of the Red-footed Booby *Sula sula*. *Ibis* **111**: 357-385.
Nelson, J.B. (1969b). The breeding ecology of the Red-footed Booby in the Galapagos. *J. Anim. Ecol.* **38**; 181-198.
Nelson, J.B. (1970). The relationship between behaviour and ecology in the Sulidae with reference to other seabirds. *Oceanogr. Mar. Biol. Rev.* **8**.
Nelson, J.B. (1971). The biology of the Abbot's Booby. *Ibis* **113**: 429-467.
Nelson, J.B. (1972). The biology of the seabirds of the Indian Ocean Christmas Islands. *J. Mar. Biol. Ass. India* **14**: 643-662.
Nelson, J.B. (1974). The distribution of Abbott's Booby *Sula abbotti*. *Ibis* **116**: 368-369.
Nelson, J.B. (1975). Report on the status and prospects of Abbott's Booby in relation to phosphate mining on the Australian Territory of Christmas Island, August 1974. *Bull. ICBP* **12**: 131-40.
Nelson, J.B. (1976). The breeding biology of frigatebirds - a comparative review. *Living Bird* **14**: 113-155.
Nelson, J.B. (1977a). Some relationships between food and breeding in the marine Pelecaniformes. In: Stonehouse, B. & Perrins, C. eds. (1977). *Evolutionary Ecology*. Macmillan, London.
Nelson, J.B. (1977b). Abbott's Booby and mining. 1977 report. Cyclostyled.
Nelson, J.B. (1978a). *The Sulidae. Gannets and Boobies*. Oxford University Press, Oxford.
Nelson, J.B. (1978b). *The Gannet*. T. & D. Poyser, London.
Nelson, J.B. (1980). *Seabirds. Their Biology and Ecology*. Hamlyn, London.
Nelson, J.B. (1984) [1983]. Contrast in breeding strategies between some tropical and temperate marine Pelecaniformes. Pp. 95-114 in: Schreiber (1984).
Nelson, J.B. (1985a). Frigatebirds, aggression and the colonial habit. *Noticias Galápagos* **41**: 16-19.
Nelson, J.B. (1985b). Gannet. Pp. 245-247 in: Campbell & Lack (1985).
Nelson, J.B. (1986). *Living with Seabirds*. Edinburgh University Press.
Nelson, J.B. & Powell, D. (1986). The breeding ecology of Abbott's Booby. *Emu* **86(1)**: 33-46.
Nero, R.W. (1959). Western Grebe colony. *Nat. Hist.* **68**: 291-295.
Nero, R.W. (1960). Mass Mortality of Western Grebes. *Blue Jay* **18**: 110-112.
Nero, R.W. (1972). Western Grebe fatally entangled in fishing line. *Blue Jay* **30**: 41-42.
Nero, R.W., Lahrman, F.W. & Bard, F.G. (1958). Dry-land nest-site of a Western Grebe colony. *Auk* **75**: 347-349.
Nesbitt, S., Hetrick, W. & Williams, L. (1974). Foods of White Ibis from seven collection sites in Florida. *Proc. Ann. Conf. Southeast. Assoc. Game & Fish Comm.* **28**: 517-532.
Neto, P.S. (1982). Aspectos bioromicos e desenvolvimento de *Theristicus caudatus* (Boddaert 1783) (Aves, Thres-kiornithidae). *Dusenia* **13(4)**: 145-149.
Netschajew, W.A. (1969). Zur Biologie von Swinhoe's Wellenlaufer im Saliw Petra Welikogo. *Falke* **16**: 12-16.
Nettleship, D.N. (1976). Gannets in North America: present numbers and recent population changes. *Wilson Bull.* **88**: 300-313.
Nettleship, D.N. & Chapdelaine, G. (1988). Population size and status of the northern Gannet in North America, 1984. *J. Field Orn.* **59(2)**: 120-127.
Nettleship, D.N., Sanger, G.A. & Springer, P.F. eds. (1982). *Marine Birds: their Feeding Ecology and Commercial Fisheries Relationships*. Canadian Wildlife Service Special Publication, Ottawa.
Neufeldt, I.A. & Wunderlich, K. (1982). *Ciconia boyciana* Swinhoe. In: Stresemann, E. & Portenko, L.A. eds. *Atlas der Verbreitung Palaearktischer Vögel*. Akademie-Verlag, Berlin.
Newlands, W.A. (1975). St Brandon. Fauna Conservation and Management. Cyclostyled report to the Ministry of Agriculture and the Environment, Mauritius.
Newman, D.G. (1978). Tuataras and Petrels. *Wildlife - a Review* **9**: 16-23.
Newman, K. (1982). What colour is the tail of an Ostrich? *Bokmakierie* **33(4)**: 83.
Newman, K. & English, M. (1975). Openbill Storks breeding in the Transvaal. *Ostrich* **46**: 264.
Newton, A. (1896). *A Dictionary of Birds*. A. & C. Black, London.
Newton, I. ed. (1989). *Lifetime Reproduction in Birds*. Academic Press, London.
Newton, I. & Kerbes, R.H. (1974). Breeding of Greylag Geese (*Anser anser*) on the Outer Hebrides, Scotland. *J. Anim. Ecol.* **43**: 771-783.
Newton, I.P. & Fugler, S.R. (1989). Notes on the winter-breeding Greatwinged Petrel *Pterodroma macroptera* and Grey Petrel *Procellaria cinerea* at Marion Island. *Cormorant* **17**: 27-34.
Nichols, J.D. (1990a). Waterfowl mortality factors. Pp. 30-40 in: Beattie, K.H. ed. (1990). *Sixth International Symposium*. Ducks Unlimited, Long Grove.
Nichols, J.D. (1990b). Responses of North American duck populations to exploitation. In: Perrins, C.M., Lebreton, J.D. & Hirons, G.J.M. (eds.)(1990). *Bird Population Studies: their Relevance to Conservation and Management*. Oxford University Press, Oxford, UK.
Nichols, J.D. (1991a). Science, Population Ecology, and the Management of the American Black Duck. *J. Wild. Manage.* **55**(4): 790-799.
Nichols, J.D. (1991b). Extensive monitoring programmes viewed as long-term population studies: the case of North American waterfowl. *Ibis* **133(Suppl. 1)**: 89-98.
Nichols, J.D. & Haramis, G.M. (1980). Inferences regarding survival and recovery of Winter-banded Canvasbacks. *J. Wildl. Manage.* **44 (1)**: 164-173.
Nichols, J.D. & Johnson, F.A. (1989). Evaluation and experimentation with duck management strategies. *Trans. N. Amer. Wildl. Nat. Res. Conf.* **54**: 566-593.
Nichols, J.D. & Johnson, F.A. (1990). Wood Duck population dynamics: a review. Pp. 83-105 in: Fredrickson, L.H., Burger, G.V., Havera, S.P., Graber, D.A., Kirby, R.E. & Taylor, T.S. eds. (1990). *Proc. 1988 North Amer. Wood Duck Symp.* St. Louis, MO.
Nichols, J.D., Conroy, M.J., Anderson, D.R. & Burnham, K.P. (1984). Compensatory mortality in waterfowl populations: a review of the evidence and implications for research and management. *Trans. N. Amer. Wildl. & Nat. Res. Conf.* **49**: 535-554.
Nichols, J.D., Pospahala, R.S. & Hines, J.E. (1982). Breeding-ground habitat conditions and the survival of Mallards. *J. Wildl. Manage.* **46 (1)**: 80-87.
Nichols, J.T. & Mowbray, L.L. (1916). Two new forms of petrels from the Bermudas. *Auk* **33**: 194-195.
Nicholson, E.M. (1952). Shearwaters in the English Channel. *British Birds* **45**:41.
Nicoll, M.J. (1906a). Sacred Ibis from Dassen Island, South Africa. *Avicult. Mag.* **4(2)**: 275-276.
Nicoll, M.J. (1906b). Some notes on the Sacred Ibis, *Ibis aethiopica*. *Avicult. Mag.* **4(9)**: 275-276.
van Niekerk, J.C. (1985). A winter visit. *Witwatersrand Bird Club News* **128**: 3-4.
Nielsen, K. & Tofft, J. (1987). Ynglebestanden af Gråstrubet Lappedykker *Podiceps grisegena* i Sønderjylland. [Summary: The breeding population of Red-necked Grebes *Podiceps grisegena* in Southern Jutland]. *Dansk Orn. Foren. Tidssk.* **81**: 169-170.
Niethammer, G. (1953). Zur Vogelwelt Boliviens. *Bonn. zool. Beitr.* **4**: 195-303.
Niethammer, G. (1967). Storche in Afghanistan. *Vogelwarte* **24**: 42-44.
Niethammer, J. (1970). Die Flamingos am Am-i-Istada in Afghanistan. *Natur und Museum* **100**: 201-210.
Niethammer, K.R. & Kaiser, M.S. (1983). Late Summer Food Habits of Three Heron Species in Northeastern Louisiana. *Colonial Waterbirds* **6**: 148-153.
Nikolaus, G. (1987). *Distribution Atlas of Sudan's Birds with Notes on Habitat and Status*. Bonner zoologische Monographien **25**. Zoologisches Forschungsinstitut und Museum Alexander Koenig, Bonn.
Nilsson, L. (1965). Studies on the preening behaviour of the Goldeneye. *Fågelvärld* **24**: 301-309.
Nilsson, L. (1966). The behaviour of the Goosander in the winter. *Fågelvärld* **25**: 148-160.
Nilsson, L. (1969). The migration of the Goldeneye in north-west Europe. *Wildfowl* **20**: 112-118.
Nilsson, L. (1974). The behaviour of wintering smew in Southern Sweden. *Wildfowl* **25**: 84-88.
Nilsson, L. (1980). De övertintrande alfåglarnas *Clangula hyemalis* antal och utbredning längs den svenska kusten. *Fågelvärld* **39**: 1-14.
Nilsson, L. & Persson, H. (1987). Boplatsval och boöverlevnad hos skäggdopping *Podiceps cristatus* och sothöna *Fulica atra*. [Summary: Choice of nest site and nest survival in Great Crested Grebe and Coot]. *Vår Fågelvärld* **46**: 6-17.
Nilsson, L. & Persson, H. (1989a). Site tenacity and turnover rate of stating and wintering Bean Geese *Anser fabalis* in southern Sweden. Pp. 144-161 in: *Food Selection, Movements and Energy Budgets of Stating and Wintering Geese on South Swedish Farmland*. Lund University, Sweden.
Nilsson, L. & Persson, H. (1989b). Non-breeding distribution numbers and ecology of Bean Geese *Anser fabalis* in Sweden. In: *Food Selection, Movements and Energy Budgets of Stating and Wintering Geese on South Swedish Farmland*. Lund University.
Nilsson, S.G. (1977). Adult survival rate of the Black-throated Diver *Gavia arctica*. *Ornis Scand.* **8**: 193-195.
Nisbet, I.C.T. (1968). The utilization of mangroves by Malayan birds. *Ibis* **110**: 348-352.
Nishikawa, K., Millán, E., Mendoza, R., Jorajuria, A. & Amador, E. (1984). Registro de la mortandad del Colimbo, Zambullidor moñudo (*Podiceps nigricollis*), en Baja California durante el primer trimestre de 1983. *Ciencias Marinas. México* **10(1)**: 77-87.
Niven, B.S. & Abel, C.E. (1991). Logical synthesis of environment of King Penguin, *Aptenodytes patagonicus*. *Ecol. Modell.* **56(1-4)**: 291-311.
Niven, C.K. & Niven, J.P.M. (1966a). Openbill Stork *Anastomus lamelligerus*. *Ostrich* **37**: 58.
Niven, C.K. & Niven, J.P.M. (1966b). Saddlebill Stork feeding young. *Ostrich* **37**: 58-59.
Noble, J.C. (1975). Differences in size of Emus on two contrasting diets on the Riverine Plain of New South Wales. *Emu* **75**: 35-37.
Nökleby, P. (1963). Reirfunn av Horndykker, *Podiceps auritus* (L.), i Stange. [Summary: Breeding of *Podiceps auritus* in SE-Norway]. *Sterna* **5**: 62-64.
Noll, H. (1960). Der Schwarzhalstaucher, *Podiceps nigricollis*, Brutvogel im Kaltbrunner Ried. *Orn. Beob.* **57**: 197-202.
Norberg, J.M. & Norberg, R.A. (1971). Take-off, landing and flight speed during fishing flights of *Gavia stellata*. *Ornis Scand.* **2**: 55-67.
Nores, M. & Yzurieta, D. (1980). *Aves de ambientes acuáticos de Córdoba y centro de Argentina*. Secretaría de Estado de Agricultura y Ganadería de la Provincia de Córdoba.
Norman, F.I. (1970). The effect of sheep on the breeding success and habitat of the Short-tailed Shearwater, *Puffinus tenuirostris* (Temminck). *Austr. J. Zool.* **18**: 215-229.
Norman, F.I. (1974). Notes on the breeding of the Pied Cormorant near Weribee, Victoria in 1971, 1972 and 1973. *Emu* **74**: 223-227.
Norman, F.I. (1987). The ducks of Macquarie Island. *ANARE Res. Notes* **42**.
Norman, F.I. (1990). Macquarie Island Ducks - habitats and hybrids. *Notornis* **37**: 53-58.
Norman, F.I. & Brown, R.S. (1987). Notes on Common Diving-Petrels *Pelecanoides urinatrix* Found Beached-washed in Victoria. *Emu* **87**: 179-185.

Norman, F.I. & McKinney, F. (1987). Clutches, broods and brood care behaviour in Chestnut Teal. *Wildfowl* **38**: 117-126.
Norman, F.I., Brown, R.S. & Deerson, D.M. (1980). Seabird Islands no. 93. Dannevig Island, Glennie Group, Victoria. *Corella* **4(4)**: 91-92.
Norman, F.I., Thomson, L.W. & Hamilton, J.G. (1979). Use of habitat and diurnal activity of Pacific Black Duck, Chesnut Teal and Grey Teal at Serendip, Victoria. *Emu* **79**: 54-62.
Norris, A.Y. (1965). Observations of seabirds in the Tasman Sea and New Zealand waters in October and November, 1962. *Notornis* **12**: 80-105.
Norriss, D.W. & Wilson, H.J. (1988). Disturbance and flock size changes in Greenland Whitefronted Geese wintering in Ireland. *Wildfowl* **39**: 63-70.
North, M.E.W. (1940). Field notes on Abdim's Stork in two Kenya provinces. *J. East Afr. & Uganda Nat. Hist. Soc.* **15**: 1-5.
North, M.E.W. (1943). The breeding of the Marabou Stork in East Africa. *Ibis* **55**: 190-198.
North, M.R. (1986). *Breeding Biology of Yellow-billed Loons on the Colville River Delta, Arctic Alaska.* MSc thesis. North Dakota State University, Fargo.
North, M.R. & Ryan, M.R. (1988). Yellow-billed Loon, *Gavia adamsii*, Breeding Chronology and Reproductive Success in Arctic Alaska. *Can. Field-Nat.* **102(3)**: 485-490.
North, M.R. & Ryan, M.R. (1989). Characteristics of lakes and nest sites used by Yellow-billed Loons in Arctic Alaska. *J. Field Orn.* **60(3)**: 296-304.
Norton, J., Stuart, S. & Johnson, T. compilers. (1990). *World Checklist of Threatened Birds.* NCC, Berkshire, UK.
Norton, R.L. (1988). The density and relative abundance of Pelecaniformes on the eastern Puerto Rico Bank in December 1982. *Caribb. J. Sci.* **24(1-2)**: 28-31.
Nottebohm, F. (1975). Vocal behavior in birds. Pp. 287-332 in: in: Farner, S.D. & King, J.R. (1975). *Avian Biology.* Vol. 5. Academic Press, London & New York.
Novaes, F.C. (1978). Sobre algunas aves pouco conhecidas da Amazonia Brasiliera. *Boletim Mus. Para. Emilio Goeldi (Zool.)* **90**: 1-15.
Novakova, J.M., Veselovsky, Z. & Kucera, K. (1987). [Contribution to phylogeny of the order Anseriformes]. *Gazella* **14**: 105-108. In Czech with English summary.
Nowak, E. (1983). Die Schopfkasarka, *Tadorna cristata* (Kuroda, 1917) - eine vom Aussterben bedrohte Tierart (Wissensstand und Vorschlage zum Schutz) *Bonn. zool. Beitr.* **34**: 235-271.
Nowak, E. (1984a). Ueber das vermutliche Brut - und Ueberwinterungsgebiet der Schopfkasarka, *Tadorna cristata. J. Orn.* **125**: 103-105.
Nowak, E. (1984b). Ueber das vermutliche Brut - un Verhaltensmerkmale der Schopfkasarka. *Falke* **31**: 150-155.
Nowak, E. & Berthold, P. (1987). Die Satelliten - Tellemetrie in der Erforschung von Tierwanderungen: eine Ubersicht. *J. Orn.* **128(4)**: 405-422.
Nudds, T.D. (1982). Ecological separation of grebes and coots: interference competition or microhabitat selection? *Wilson Bull.* **94**: 505-514.
Nuechterlein, G.L. (1975). *Nesting ecology of Western Grebes on the Delta Marsh, Manitoba.* MSc thesis. Colorado State University, Fort Collins.
Nuechterlein, G.L. (1980). *Courtship behavior of the Western Grebe.* PhD dissertation, University of Minnesota, Minneapolis.
Nuechterlein, G.L. (1981a). Asynchronous hatching and sibling competition in Western Grebe broods. *Can. J. Zool.* **59**: 994-998.
Nuechterlein, G.L. (1981b). Variations and multiple functions of the advertising display of Western Grebes. *Behaviour* **76(3-4)**: 289-317.
Nuechterlein, G.L. (1981c). Courtship behavior and reproductive isolation between Western Grebe color morphs. *Auk* **98**: 335-349.
Nuechterlein, G.L. (1981d). 'Information parasitism' in mixed colonies of Western Grebes and Forster's Terns. *Anim. Behav.* **29**: 985-989.
Nuechterlein, G.L. (1981e). Experimental tracking selective pressures on an endangered species: the Hooded Grebe. *A.O.U. Abstracts*: **37**.
Nuechterlein, G.L. (1982). Western Grebes. The Birds that walk on water *Natl. Geogr.* **161(5)**: 624-637.
Nuechterlein, G.L. (1985). Experiments on the functions of the bare crown patch of downy Western Grebe chicks. *Can. J. Zool.* **63**: 464-467.
Nuechterlein, G.L. (1988). Parent-young vocal communication in Western Grebes. *Condor* **90**: 632-636.
Nuechterlein, G.L. & Buitron, D.P. (1989). Diving differences between Western and Clark's Grebes. *Auk* **106**: 467-470.
Nuechterlein, G.L. & Johnson, A. (1980/81). The downy young of the Hooded Grebe. *Living Bird* **19**: 68-71.
Nuechterlein, G.L. & Storer, R.W. (1982). The pair-formation displays of the Western Grebe. *Condor* **84**: 350-369.
Nuechterlein, G.L. & Storer, R.W. (1985). Aggressive behaviour and interspecific killing by Flying Steamer Ducks in Argentina. *Condor* **87**: 87-91.
Nuechterlein, G.L. & Storer, R.W (1989a). Mate feeding by Western and Clark's grebes. *Condor* **91**: 37-42.
Nuechterlein, G.L. & Storer, R.W. (1989b). Reverse mounting in grebes. *Condor* **91**: 341-346.
O Myong Sok (1984). Wiederentdeckung der Schopfkasarka, *Tadorna cristata*, in der Koreanischen Demokratischen Volsrepublik. *J. Orn.* 125: 102-103.
O'Brien, P.J. (1940). Some observation on the breeding habits and general characteristics of the White-flippered Penguin (*Eudyptula albosignata* Finsch). *Rec. Canterbury Mus.* **4**: 311-324.
O'Brien, R.M. & Davies, J. (1990). A new subspecies of Masked Booby *Sula dactylatra* from Lord Howe, Norfolk and Kermadec Islands. *Marine Orn.* **18(1-2)**: 57-59.
O'Connor, R.J. (1984). *The Growth and Development of Birds.* John Wiley and Sons, New York.
O'Connor, R.J. & Shrubb, M. (1990). *Farming and Birds.* Cambridge University Press, Cambridge, England.
O'Connor, T. (1984). A Note on the Diet of nestling Blackheaded Herons. *Ostrich* **55(4)**: 221-222.
O'Donnell, C.F.J. (1980). *The Habitat Preferences, Breeding, Feeding, Behaviour and Population of the Southern Crested Grebe (*Podiceps cristatus australis*) on the Ashburton lakes, 1979-80.* Unpublished BSc (Hons) thesis, University of Canterbury, Christchurch, New Zealand.
O'Donnell, C.F.J. (1982). Food and feeding behaviour of the Southern Crested Grebe on the Ashburton lakes. *Notornis* **29**: 151-156.
O'Malley, J.B.E. (1980). Flight and flocking behaviour of White Pelicans. MSc thesis, University of Manitoba, Winnipeg, Manitoba.
O'Malley, J.B.E. & Evans, R.M. (1980). Variations in measurements among White Pelican eggs and their use as a hatch date predictor. *Can. J. Zool.* **58**: 603-608.
O'Malley, J.B.E. & Evans, R.M. (1982a). Flock formation in White Pelicans. *Can. J. Zool.* **60(5)**: 1024-1031.
O'Malley, J.B.E. & Evans, R.M. (1982b). Structure and behavior of White Pelican formation flocks. *Can. J. Zool.* **60**: 1388-1396.
O'Malley, J.B.E. & Evans, R.M. (1983). Kleptoparasitism and associated foraging behaviors in American White Pelicans. *Colonial Waterbirds* **6**: 126-129.
O'Malley, J.B.E. & Evans, R.M. (1984). Activity of American White Pelicans, *Pelecanus erythrorhynchos*, at a traditional foraging area in Manitoba. *Can. Field-Nat.* **98**: 451-457.
Oatley, T.B. (1971). Distribution of Maccoa Duck *Oxyura punctata. Natal Bird Club News Sheet* **198**.
Obst, B.S. (1986). The ecological energetics of Wilson's Storm-Petrels. PhD thesis, University of California, Berkeley.
Obst, B.S., Nagy, K.A. & Ricklefs, R.E. (1987). Energy utilization by Wilson's Storm-Petrel (*Oceanites oceanicus*). *Physiol. Zool.* **60**(2): 200-210.
Odom, R.R. (1978). Wood Storks nesting on the Georgia coast. *Oriole* **43(1)**: 1-5.
Oelke, H. (1978). Naturliche oder Anthropogene Populationsveranderungen von Adeliepinguinen (*Pygoscelis adeliae*) im Ross-Meer-Sektor der Antarktis. *J. Orn.* **119**: 1-13.
Offredo, C. & Ridoux, V. (1986). The diet of Emperor Penguins *Aptenodytes forsteri* in Adelie Land, Antarctica. *Ibis* **128**: 409-413.
Ogasawara, K. (1985). [Acoustic Sounds of Japanese Crested Ibis *Nipponia nippon* in Japan and China]. *J. Yamashina Inst. Orn.* **17**: 127-134. In Japanese with English summary.
Ogasawara, K. & Izumi, Y. (1977). Japanese White Storks (*Ciconia ciconia boyciana*) appeared in northern Honshu and Hokkaido. *Misc. Rep. Yamashina Inst. Orn.* **9**: 121-127.
Ogden, J.C. (1976a). *An Analysis of Differing Population Trends Between Two Tactile-feeding Wading Birds, Roseate Spoonbill and Wood Stork, on the Southeastern Coastal Plain.* Ms on file, National Audubon Society Research Department, Tavernier, Florida.
Ogden, J.C. (1976b). The pink pause, a previously undescribed behavior by Roseate Spoonbills. *Florida Field Nature* **4**: 34-46.
Ogden, J.C. (1978). Recent population trends of colonial wading birds on the Atlantic and Gulf coastal plains. Pp. 137-153 in: Sprunt *et al.* (1978).
Ogden, J.C. (1981). Nesting distribution and migration of Glossy Ibis *Plegadis falcinellus* in Florida, U.S.A. *Florida Field Nature* **9**: 1-6.
Ogden, J.C. (1985a). Ibis. Pp. 299-300 in: Campbell & Lack (1985).
Ogden, J.C. (1985b). Spoonbill. Page 561 in: Campbell & Lack (1985).
Ogden, J.C. (1985c). Stork. Pp. 563-565 in: Campbell & Lack (1985).
Ogden, J.C. (1985d). The Wood Stork. Pp. 459-470 in: Eno, A.S. & DiSilvestro, R.L. eds. *Audubon Wildlife Report 1985.* National Audubon Society, New York.
Ogden, J.C. & Nesbitt, S.A. (1979). Recent Wood Stork population trends in the United States. *Wilson Bull.* **91**: 512-523.
Ogden, J.C. & Patty, B.W. (1981). The recent status of the Wood Stork in Florida and Georgia. Proceedings of the Georgia Nongame and Endangered Wildlife Symposium. *Georgia Dept. Nat. Res. Game & Fish Div. Tech. Bull.* **5**: 97-103.
Ogden, J.C. & Thomas, B.T. (1985a). A Colonial Wading Bird Survey in the Central Llanos of Venzuela. *Colonial Waterbirds* **8**: 23-31.
Ogden, J.C. & Thomas, B.T. (1985b). An Opened Wing Foraging Behaviour by the Green Ibis. *Colonial Waterbirds* **8(2)**: 181-182.
Ogden, J.C., Kale, H.W. & Nesbitt, S.A. (1980). The influence of annual variation in rainfall and water levels on nesting by Florida populations of wading birds. *Trans. Linn. Soc. New York* **9**: 115-126.
Ogden, J.C., Kushlan, J.A. & Tilmant, J.T. (1976). Prey selectivity by the Wood Stork. *Condor* **78**: 324-330.
Ogden, J.C., Kushlan, J.A. & Tilmant, J.T. (1978). The food habits and nesting success of Wood Storks in Everglades National Park, 1974. *US Natl. Park Serv. Nat. Resour. Publ.* **16**.
Ogden, J.C., McCrimmon, D.A., Bancroft, G.T. & Patty, B.W. (1987). Breeding populations of the Wood Stork in the southeastern United States. *Condor* **89**: 752-759.
Ogi, H. (1982). Feeding ecology of the Sooty Shearwater in the western subarctic North Pacific Ocean. Pp. 78-84 in: Nettleship *et al.* (1982).
Ogi, H. (1984). Seabird Mortality Incidental to the Japanese Salmon Gill-Net Fishery. Pp. 717-721 in: Croxall *et al.* (1984).
Ogi, H., Kubodera, T. & Nakamura, K. (1980). The pelagic feeding ecology of the Short-tailed Shearwater in the Subarctic Pacific Region. *J. Yamashina Inst. Orn.* **12**: 157-182.
Ogilvie, M. & Ogilvie, C. (1986). *Flamingos.* Alan Sutton, Gloucester, UK.
Ogilvie, M.A. (1967). Population changes and mortality of the Mute Swan in Britain. *Wildfowl Trust Ann. Rep.* **18**: 64-73.
Ogilvie, M.A. (1978). *Wild Geese.* T & AD Poyser, Berkhamsted..
Ogilvie, M.A. (1981). The Mute Swan in Britain, 1978. *Bird Study* **28**: 87-106.
Ogilvie, M.A. (1983). *A Migration Study of the Teal* Anas crecca *in Europe using Ringing Recoveries.* PhD thesis, University of Bristol, UK.
Ogilvie, M.A. (1986). The Mute Swan in Britain 1983. *Bird Study* 33: 121-132.
Ogilvie, M.A. & Boyd, H. (1976). The numbers of Pink-footed and Greylag Geese wintering in Britain: observations 1969-1975 and predictions 1976-1980. *Wildfowl* **27**: 63-75.
Ogle, D. (1986). The status and seasonality of birds in Nakhon Sawan Province, Thailand. *Nat. Hist. Bull. Siam Soc.* **34**: 115-143.
Ohanjanian, T.A. (1989). Food fights of Red-necked Grebes during the breeding season. *J. Field Orn.* **60**: 143-153.
Ohashi, T.J. & Kimizuka, K.K. (1988). First Record of Nesting by Cattle Egrets on Maui from Observations Made During Birdstrike Control Operations. *Elepaio* **48(12)**: 111-112.
Ohlendorf, H.M., Klaas, E.E. & Kaiser, T.E. (1978a) Organochlorine residues and eggshell thinning in anhingas and waders. *Proc. Conf. Colonial Waterbird Soc. Natl. Audubon Soc.* **1978**: 185-195.
Ohlendorf, H.M., Klaas, E.E. & Kaiser, T.E. (1978b). Environmental pollutants and eggshell thickness: anhingas and wading birds in the eastern United States. *US Fish & Wildl. Serv. Spec. Sci. Rep. Wildl.* **216**.
Ohlendorf, H.M., Klaas, E.E. & Kaiser, T.E. (1978c). Organochlorine residues and eggshell thinning in wood storks and anhingas. *Wilson Bull.* **90**: 608-618.
Oka, N. (1986). [Observation on the Emaciated and Dead Short-tailed Shearwaters, *Puffinus tenuirostris*, in the North-Western Sea Area of the North Pacific in 1983. *J. Yamashina Inst. Orn.* **18**: 63-67.
Oka, N. (1989). Chick growth and development of the Short-tailed Shearwater in Tasmania. *J. Yamashina Inst. Orn.* **21**: 193-207.
Oka, N. & Maruyama, N. (1986). Mass mortality of Short-tailed Shearwaters along the Japanese coast. *Tori* **34**: 97-104.
Oka, N., Maruyama, N. & Skira, I. (1987). Chick growth and mortality of Short-tailed Shearwaters in comparison with Sooty Shearwaters, as a possible index of fluctuation of Australian Krill abundance. *Proc. Natn. Inst. Polar Res. Tokyo Symp. Polar Biol.* **1**: 166-174.
Okamoto, B. (1972). [Calonectris leucomelas *on Kanmurijima Island.*] Komine Shoten, Tokyo.
Okill, J.D. (1986). Where do all the rain geese go. *Shetl. Bird Club Newsl.* **61**: 1-3.
Olalla, A.M. & Magalhaes, A.C. (1956). (Habits of Tinamidae). *Bibl. Zool.* **3**.
Olivares, A. (1958). Monografía de los Tinamúes Colombianos. *Universidad Nacional de Colombia* **23**: 245-301.
Olivares, A. (1970). Effects of the Environmental Changes on the Avifauna of the Republic of Colombia. Pp. 77-87 in: Buechner, H.K. & Buechner, J.H. eds. *The Avifauna of Northern Latin America: A Symposium Held at the Smithsonian Institution 13-15 April 1966.* Smithsonian Contributions to Zoology **26.** Smithsonian Institution Press, Washington.
Oliver, D.W. (1974). Cormorant and Shag recoveries in first year of life. *Tay Ringing Group 1973 Report*: 1-5
Oliver, W.L.R., Mallet, M., Singleton, D.R. & Ellett, J.S. (1979). Observations on the reproductive behaviour of a captive colony of Bare-faced Ibis *Geronticus eremita. Dodo* **16**: 11-35.
Oliver, W.R.B. (1953). The crested penguins of New Zealand. *Emu* **53**: 185-187.
Oliver, W.R.B. (1955). *New Zealand Birds.* 2nd edition. A.H. & A.W. Reed, Wellington, New Zealand.
Ollason, J.C. & Dunnet, G.M. (1978). Age, experience and other factors affecting the breeding success of the fulmar *Fulmarus glacialis* in Orkney. *J. Anim. Ecol.* **47**: 961-976.
Ollason, J.C. & Dunnet, G.M. (1980). Nest failures in the fulmar: the effect of observers. *J. Field Orn.* **51**: 39-54.
Ollason, J.C. & Dunnet, G.M. (1982). The feeding dispersal of fulmars in the breeding season. *Ibis* **124**: 359-361.
Ollason, J.C. & Dunnet, G.M. (1983). Modelling annual changes in numbers of breeding fulmars at a colony in Orkney. *J. Anim. Ecol.* **52**: 185-198.
Ollason, J.C. & Dunnet, G.M. (1986). Relative effects of parental performance and egg quality on breeding success of fulmars. *Ibis* **128**: 290-296.
Ollason, J.C. & Dunnet, G.M. (1988). Variation in breeding success in fulmars. Pp. 268-287 in: *Reproductive Success.* University of Chicago Press, Chicago.
Olmos, F. (1990). Nest predation of Plumbeous Ibis by Capuchin Monkeys and Black Hawks. *Wilson Bull.* **102**: 169-170.
Olmos, F. & Barbosa, M.F. (1988). A new record of the Streaked Bittern from northeastern Brazil. *Willson Bull.* **100(3)**: 510-511.
Olney, P.J.S. (1963a). The food and feeding habits of the Tufted Duck *Aythya fuligula. Ibis* **105**: 55-62.
Olney, P.J.S. (1963b). The food and feeding habits of Teal *Anas crecca* L.. *Proc. Zool. Soc. London* **140**: 169-210.
Olney, P.J.S. (1965). The food and feeding habits of Shelduck *Tadorna tadorna. Ibis* **107**: 527-532.
Olney, P.J.S. (1968). The food and feeding habits of the Pochard. *Biol. Conserv.* 1: 71-76.
Olney, P.J.S. & Mills, D.H. (1963). The food and feeding habits of the Goldeneye *Bucephala clangula* in Great Britain. *Ibis* **105**: 293-300.
Olrog, C.C. (1956). Contenidos estomacales de aves del noroeste argentino. *Hornero* **10(2)**: 158-163.
Olrog, C.C. (1965). Diferencias en el ciclo sexual de algunas aves. *Hornero* **10**: 269-272.
Olrog, C.C. (1975). Vagrancy of Neotropical cormorants, egrets, and White-faced Ibis. *Bird-Banding* **46**: 207-212.
Olrog, C.C. (1984). *Las aves argentinas.* Administración de Parques Nacionales, Buenos Aires.
Olson, D.P. (1964). *A Study of Canvasback and Redhead Breeding Populations, Nesting Habitat and Productivity.* PhD dissertation, Universiy of Minnesota.
Olson, S.L. (1975a). Paleomithology of St Helena Island, South Atlantic Ocean. *Smithson. Contrib. Paleobiol.* **23**: 1-49.
Olson, S.L. (1975b). Remarks on the generic characters of *Bulweria. Ibis* **117**: 111-113.
Olson, S.L. (1977a). A Lower Eocene frigatebird from the Green River Formation of Wyoming. *Smithson. Contrib. Paleobiol.* **35**.
Olson, S.L. (1977b). Additional notes on subfossil bird remains from Ascension Island. *Ibis* **119**: 37-43.
Olson, S.L. (1978). Multiple origins of the Ciconiiformes. *Proc. Conf. Colonial Waterbird Group.* **1978**: 165-170.
Olson, S.L. (1981a). Natural history of vertebrates on the Brazilian islands of the Mid South Atlantic. *Natl. Geog. Soc. Res. Reports* **13**: 481-492.
Olson, S.L. (1981b). The generic allocation of *Ibis pagana* Milne-Edwards, with a review of fossil ibises (Aves: Threskiornithidae). *J. Vertebr. Paleontol.* **1**: 165-170.
Olson, S.L. (1984). A Hamerkop from the Early Pliocene of South Africa (Aves: Scopidae). *Proc. Biol. Soc. Washington* **97(4)**: 736-740.

Olson, S.L. (1985a). The fossil record of birds. Pp. 79-238 in: Farner, D.S., King, J.R. & Parkes, K.C. (1985). *Avian Biology*. Vol. 8. Academic Press, London & New York.
Olson, S.L. (1985b). The Italian specimen of *Bulweria fallax* (Procellariidae) *Bull. Br. Orn. Club* **105**: 29-30.
Olson, S.L. (1985c). A new genus of tropicbird (Pelecaniformes: Phaethontidae) from the Middle Miocene Calvert Formation of Maryland. *Proc. Biol. Soc. Washington* **98(4)**: 851-855.
Olson, S.L. (1985d). Early Pliocene ibises (Aves, Plataleidae) from South-Western Cape Province, South Africa. *Ann. S. Afr. Mus.* **97(3)**: 57-69.
Olson, S.L. & Feduccia, A. (1980a). Relationships and evolution of flamingos. *Smithson. Contrib. Zool.* **316**: 1-73.
Olson, S.L. & Feduccia, A. (1980b). *Presbyornis* and the Origin of the Anseriformes (Aves: Charadriomorphae). *Smithson. Contrib. Zool.* **323**: 1-24.
Olson, S.L. & den Hartog, J.C. (1990). Former breeding of *Sula dactylatra* in the Cape Verde Islands. *Bull. Brit. Orn. Club.* **110(1)**: 10-12.
Olson, S.L. & Warheit, K.I. (1988). A new genus for *Sula abbotti*. *Bull. Brit. Orn. Club* **108**: 9-12.
Olson, S.T. (1951). *A Study of the Common Loon in the Superior National Forest of Northern Minnesota*. MSc thesis, University of Minnesota.
Olson, S.T. & Marshall, W.H. (1952). The Common Loon in Minnesota. *Occas. Pap. Minn. Mus. Nat. Hist.* **5**: 1-77.
Olsoni, B. (1928). Om Svarthakedoppingens (*Podiceps auritus* L.) häckning. *Ornis Fenn.* **5**: 65-72.
Olver, M.D. (1984). Breeding biology of the Reed Cormorant. *Ostrich* **55(3)**: 133-140.
Olver, M.D. & Kuyper, M.A. (1978). Breeding biology of the Whitebreasted Cormorant in Natal. *Ostrich* **49**: 25-30.
Onno, S. (1960). Zur Ökologie der Lappentaucher (*Podiceps cristatus, griseigena* und *auritus*) in Estland. Pp. 577-582 in: *Proc. XII Int. Orn. Congr.* **2**.
van Oort, E.D. (1912). On *Aestrelata aterrima* (Bonaparte). *Notes Leyden Mus.* **34**: 70.
van Oort, G.J. & Kruijt, J.P. (1953). On the pelagic distribution of some Procellariiformes in the Atlantic and Southern Oceans. *Ibis* **95**: 615-637.
Orejuela, J.E. (1985). Tropical Forest Birds of Colombia: A survey of Problems and a Plan for their Conservation. Pp. 95-114 in: Diamond & Lovejoy (1985).
Orians, G. (1971). Ecological aspects of behavior. Pp. 513-546 in: Farner, D.S. & King, J.R. (1971). *Avian Biology*. Vol. 1. Academic Press, London & New York.
Orians, G.H. (1969). Age and hunting success in the Brown Pelican (*Pelecanus occidentalis*). *Anim. Behav.* **17**: 316-319.
Orians, G.H. & Paulson, D.R. (1969). Notes on Costa Rican birds. *Condor* **71**: 426-431.
Oring, L.W. (1969). Summer biology of the Gadwall at Delta, Manitoba. *Wilson Bull.* **8**: 44-54.
Oring, L.W. (1982). Avian mating systems. Pp. 1-92 in: Farner, D.S. & King, J.R. (1982). *Avian Biology*. Vol. 6. Academic Press, London & New York.
Ortiz, F. (1988). A new locality for the Comb Duck *Sarkidiornis melanotos* from western Ecuador and notes on the distribution of the Horned Screamer *Anhima cornuta*. *Bull. Brit. Orn. Club* **108 (3)**: 141-144.
Osgood, W.H. & Conover, B. (1922). Game Birds from Northwestern Venezuela. *Field Mus. Nat. Hist. (Zool. Ser.)* **12(3)**: 19-47.
Ossowski, L.L.J. (1952). The Hadedah Ibis *Hagedashia hagedash hagedash* (Latham) and its relation to pest control in wattle plantations. *Ann. Natal Mus.* **12**: 279-290.
Ott, J. & Joslin, P. (1981). A helping hand back to mother. *Brookfield Bison* **Feb/Mar**: C1-C8.
Ottenwalder, J.A., Woods, C.A., Rathburn, G.B. & Thorbjarnarson, J.B. (1990). Status of the Greater Flamingo in Haiti. *Colonial Waterbirds* **13(2)**: 115-123.
Otto, J.E. (1983). *Breeding ecology of the Pied-billed Grebe (*Podilymbus podiceps *(Linnaeus)) on Rush Lake, Winnebago County, Wisconsin*. MSc thesis. University of Wisconsin, Oshkosh.
Otto, J.E. & Strohmeyer, D.L. (1985). Wing molt by a nesting Pied-billed Grebe. *Wilson Bull.* **97**: 239-240.
Ounsted, M.L. (1988). Attempts by the Wildfowl Trust to re-establish the White-winged Wood Duck and the White-headed Duck *Cairina scutulata* and *Oxyura leucocephala*. *Int. Zoo Yb.* **27**: 216-222.
Ouweneel, G.L. (1989). Een ruiconcentratie Geoorde Futen (*Podiceps nigricollis*) op de Grevelingen. *Het Vogeljaar* **37**: 100-102.
Ovenden, J.R., Wust-Saucy, A., Bywater, R., Brothers, N. & White, R.W.G. (1991). Genetic Evidence for Philopatry in a Colonially Nesting Seabird, the Fairy Prion (*Pachyptila turtur*). *Auk* **108(3)**: 688-694.
Ovington, D. (1978). *Australian Endangered Species*. Cassell Australia.
Ovington, J.D., Cullen, J.M. & Nelson, J.B. (1981). Appraisal and implications of a survey (1979-80) of Abbott's Booby on Christmas Island. Internal report, Australian National Parks and Wildlife Service.
Owen, M. (1972). Some factors affecting food intake and selection in White-fronted Geese. *J. Anim. Ecol.* **41**: 79-92.
Owen, M. (1976). Factors affecting the distribution of geese in the British Isles. *Wildfowl* **27**.
Owen, M. (1977). *Wildfowl of Europe*. Macmillan, London.
Owen, M. (1980). *Wild Geese of the World*. Batsford, London.
Owen, M. (1984). Dynamics and age structure of an increasing goose population - the Svalbard Barnacle Goose *Branta leucopsis*. *Norsk Polarinstitutt Skrifter* **181**: 37-47.
Owen, M. & Black, J.M. (1989a). Factors affecting the survival of Barnacle Geese on migration from the breeding grounds. *J. Animal Ecol.* **58**: 603-618.
Owen, M. & Black, J.M. (1989b). Barnacle Goose. Pp. 349-362 in: Newton, I. ed. (1989). *Lifetime Reproductive Success in Birds*. Academic Press, London.
Owen, M. & Black, J.M. (1990a). *Waterfowl Ecology*. Blackie, London.
Owen, M. & Black, J.M. (1990b). Migration mortaliy and its significance to goose population dynamics. *Ardea* **78**.
Owen, M. & Black, J.M. (1991). Geese and their future fortune. *Ibis* **133 (Suppl. 1)**: 28-35.
Owen, M. & Cook, W.A. (1977). Variations in body weight, wing length and condition of Mallard *Anas platyrhynchos* and their relationship to environmental changes. *J. Zoology. London* **183**: 377-393.
Owen, M., Black, M. & Liber, H. (1988). Pair Bond Duration and Timing of Its Formation in Barnacle Geese (*Branta leucopsis*). Pp.23-38 in: Weller (1988).
Owen, M., Black, M., Agger, M.C. & Campbell, C.R.G. (1987). The use of the Solway Firth by an increasing population of Barnacle Geese in relation to changes in refuge management. *Biol. Conserv.* **39**: 63-81.
Owen, M., Nugent, M. & Davies, N. (1977). Discrimination between grass species and nitrogen-fertilized vegetation by young Barnacle Geese. *Wildfowl* **28**: 21-26.
Owen, R., Longcore, J., Ringelman, J., Reinecke K., & Hendrix, K. (1989). Breeding biology and habitat use of Black Ducks. *Maine Agric. Exp. Stn. Misc. Rep.* **336**: 261. Abstract only.
Owen, T.R.H. (1958). The Shoebill Stork. *African Wild Life* **12(3)**: 191-195.
Owre, O.T. (1967). *Adaptations for locomotion and feeding in the Anhinga and the Double-crested Cormorant*. Ornithological Monograhs **6**. The American Ornithologists' Union.
Owre, O.T. (1975). A second breeding colony of Waved Albatrosses. *Ibis* **118**: 419-420.
Paakspuu, V. (1989). Velvet Scoter - *Melanitta fusca* (L.). Pp. 217-223 in: Viksne, J.A. ed. (1989). *Migratsii ptits Vostochnoi Europy i Severnoi Azii. Plastinchatoklyuvye* [Migrations of birds of eastern Europe and northern Asia. Anseriformes]. Nauka, Moscow. In Russian.
Pakarinen, R. & Järvinen, O. (1984). [The Red-throated Diver *Gavia stellata* in Finland: a population ecological analysis of its status and population trends.] *Lintumies* **19**: 46-54. In Finnish, with English summary.
Pala, S. (1971). Faydal: kuslarimizdan (*Geronticus - Comatibis - eremita* L.) - ozellikleri, yasayisi ve beslenmesi. *Tabiat ve Insan* **5**: 14-22.
Palacios, J., Regueras, J.I. & Rodríguez, M. (1991). El ocaso del ánsar campestre en España. *Quercus* **63**: 26-29.
Palmer, R.S. ed. (1962). *Handbook of North American Birds*. Vol 1. Yale University Press, New Haven, CT.
Palmer, R.S. (1972). Patterns of molting. Pp. 65-102 in: Farner, D.S. & King, J.R. (1972). *Avian Biology*. Vol. 2. Academic Press, London & New York.
Palmer, R.S. ed. (1976). *Handbook of North American Birds*. Vols. 2 & 3. Yale University Press, New Haven & London.
Palmes, P. (1981). The riddle of the fickle flamingo. *Wildfowl World* **85**: 16-19.
Palmes, P. (1984). Flamingos in Gujarat (India). Pp. 27-28 in: de Boer, B. & Johnson, A.R. coord. (1984). *ICBP-IWRB Flamingo Working Group Newsletter* **2**.
Paludan, K. (1962). Eider-ducks (*Somateria mollissima*) in Danish waters. *Danske Vildtundersogelser* **10**: 1-87.
Panday, J.D. (1974). Storks preying on live birds. *J. Bombay Nat. Hist. Soc.* **71**: 141.
Pankin, N.S. & Neufeldt, I.A. (1976). The Far Eastern White Stork in Amur Region. *Trans. Oka. State Nature Reserve* **12**: 19-31.
Papi, F. & Wallraff, H.G. (1982). *Avian Navigation*. Springer-Verlag, Berlin, Heidelberg and New York.
Paran, Y. & Shluter, P. (1981). The diurnal mass migration of the Little Bittern. *Sandgrouse* **2**: 108-110.
Parasharya, B.M. & Naik, R.M. (1988). Breeding Biology of the Indian Reef Heron. *J. Bombay Nat. Hist. Society.* **86(2)**: 251-262.
Parasharya, B.M., Dodia, J.F., Mathew, K.L., Raol, L. (1990). Status of Greylag Goose *Anser anser* in Gujarat: a Re-evaluation. *J. Bombay Nat. Hist. Soc.* **87**: 140-142.
Parish, D. ed. (1985). Interwader '84 Report. Interwader, Kuala Lumpur, Malaysia.
Parish, D. & Wells, D.R. eds. (1984). Interwader '83 Report. Interwader, Kuala Lumpur, Malaysia.
Parker, H. & Holm, H. (1990). Patterns of nutrient and energy expenditure in female Common Eiders nesting in the high Arctic. *Auk* **107**: 660-668.
Parker, I.S.C. (1982). Two observations of nesting in the eastern race of the Green Ibis *Bostrychia olivacea akleyorum*. *Scopus* **6**: 20.
Parker, I.S.C. (1984a). Shoebill *Balaeniceps rex* and Wattled Crane *Grus carunculatus* in the Moyowosi Swamp, Tanzania. *Scopus* **8**: 24-25.
Parker, I.S.C. (1984b). Shoebill *Balaeniceps rex*: a deletion from the Kenya avifauna. *Scopus* **8**: 79.
Parker, K.E. (1988). Common loon reproduction and chick feeding on acidified lakes in the Adirondack Park, New York. *Can. J. Zool.* **66**: 804-810.
Parker, K.E., Miller, R.L. & Isil, S. (1986). *Status of the Common Loon in New York State*. New York State Department of Environmental Conservation, Delmar.
Parker, S.A. (1984). The extinct Kangaroo Island Emu, a hitherto-unrecognised species. *Bull. Br. Orn. Club* **104**: 19-22.
Parker, T.A. (1982). Observations on some unusual rainforest and marsh birds in Southeastern Peru. *Wilson Bull.* **13(4)**: 477-493.
Parker, T.A., Castillo, U.A., Gell-Mann, M. & Rocha, O.O. (1991). Records of New and Unusual Birds from Northern Bolivia. *Bull. Brit. Orn. Club* **111(3)**: 120-138.
Parker, T.A., Parker, S.A. & Plenge, M.A. (1982). *An Annotated Checklist of Peruvian Birds*. Buteo Books, Vermillion, S.D.
Parkes, K.C. (1952). Geographic variation in the Horned Grebe. *Condor* **54**: 314-315.
Parkes, K.C. (1955). Systematic notes on North American birds. 1. The herons and ibises (Ciconiiformes). *Ann. Carneg. Mus.* **33**: 287-293.
Parkes, K.C. & Clark, G.A. (1966). An additional character linking ratites and tinamous, and an interpretation of their monophyly. *Condor* **68**: 459-471.
Parkin, D.T., Ewing, A.W. & Ford, H.A. (1970). Group diving in the Blue-footed Booby *Sula nebouxii*. *Ibis* **112**: 111-112.
Parmalee, P.W. & Perino, G. (1970). A prehistoric archeological record of the Roseate Spoonbill in Illinois. *Trans. Illinois State Acad. Sci.* **63**: 254-258.
Parmelee, D.F. & Parmelee, J.M. (1987). Movements of Southern Giant Petrels ringed near U.S. Palmer Station, Antarctica. *Ringing & Migration* **8**: 115-118.
Parmelee, D.F., Stephens, H.A. & Schmidt, R.H. (1967). *The Birds of Victoria Island and Adjacent Small Islands*. National Museums of Canada Bulletin **222**.
Parnell, F.I. (1942). The Bald Ibis in Basutoland. *Ostrich* **13**: 100-101.
Parnell, J.F. & Quay, T.L. (1962). The populations, breeding biology and environmental relations of the Black Duck, Gadwall, and Blue-winged Teal at Pea and Bodie Islands, North Carolina. *Proc. S. East Ass. Game Fish Conf.* **16**: 53-67.
Parrack, J.D. (1986a). Red-throated Diver *Gavia stellata*. Pp. 34-35 in: Lack (1986).
Parrack, J.D. (1986b). Black-throated Diver *Gavia arctica*. Pp. 36-37 in: Lack (1986).
Parrack, J.D. (1986c). Great Northern Diver *Gavia immer*. Pp. 38-39 in: Lack (1986).
Parslow, J.L.F. (1973). Organochlorine insecticide residues and food remains in a Bald Ibis (*Geronticus eremita*) chick from Birecik, Turkey. *Bull. Brit. Orn. Club* **93(4)**: 163-166.
Parslow, J.L.F. & Everett, M.J. (1981). *Birds in Need of Special Protection in Europe*. Nature & Environment Series **24**. European Committee for the Conservation of Nature Resources, Council of Europe, Strasbourg.
Parsons, J. (1977). The effect of predation by fish eagles on the breeding success of various Ciconiiformes nesting near Kisumu, Kenya. *J. Nat. Hist.* **11**: 337-353.
Parsons, K.C. & Burger, J. (1981). Nestling Growth in Early- and Late-Nesting Black-Crowned Night Herons. *Colonial Waterbirds* **4**: 120-125.
Parsons, P.F. (1974). Openbill Storks nesting. *Honeyguide* **78**: 41-43.
Partch, M.L. (1990). *Nesting of Great Blue Herons at the Cold Spring Heron Colony*. St. Cloud State University, St. Cloud, Minnesota.
Partridge, W.H. (1953). Observaciones sobre aves de las provincias de Córdoba y San Luis. *Hornero* **10**: 23-73.
Partridge, W.H. (1956). Notes on the Brazilian Merganser in Argentina. *Auk* **73**: 473-488.
Pascal, M. (1979). Données écologiques sur L'Albatross à Sourcils Noirs dans l'Archipel des Kerguelen. *Alauda* 47: 165-172.
Pasquet, E. (1987). *Relation entre les Cormorans huppés de Bretagne et les ressources du milieu marin*. Unpublished Report C.R.B.P.O./Ministère de l'Environnement.
Pasquet, E. & Monnat, J.Y. (1990). Dispersion géographique des Cormorans huppés juvéniles de la mer Celtique. *L'Oiseau et la R.F.O.* **60(2)**: 94-109.
Passer, E.L., Leinaeng, R.H., Birmingham, L.W., Cruz, H., Dupervil, C., Persaud, E.J. & Dolensek, E.P. (1989). Effect of lead on blood photoporphyrin levels of a group of Ring Teal Ducks (*Callonetta leucophrys*). *Zoo Biology* **8 (4)**: 357-365.
Paterson, A.M. & Riddiford, N.J. (1990). Does the Cape Gannet enter European waters? *British Birds* **83**: 519-526.
Paton, P.W.C. & MacIvor, L.H. (1983). Green Heron in Hawaii. *Amer. Bird* **37**: 232-233.
Patrick, R. (1961). Results of researches in the Antofagasta ranges of Chile and Bolivia, II: Diatoms (Bacillariophyceae) from the alimentary tract of *Phoenicoparrus jamesi* (Sclater). *Postilla* **49**: 43-57.
Patterson, I.J. (1982). *The Shelduck*. The University Press, Cambridge, England.
Paul, A. (1969). Survival of Western Grebe in minus fifty degree temperature. *Murrelet* **50**: 36.
Paul, R.T., Kale, H.W.II & Nelson, D.A. (1979). Reddish Egrets nesting on Florida's East Coast. *Florida Field Nature* **7(2)**: 24-25.
Paul, R.T., Meyerriecks, A.J. & Dunstan, F.M. (1975). Return of Reddish Egrets as breeding birds in Tampa Bay, Florida. *Florida Field Nature* **3**: 9-10.
Paulian, P. (1953). Pinnipèdes, cétacés, oiseaux des Iles Kerguelen et Amsterdam. *Mem. Instit. Sci. Madagascar* **A8**: 111-234.
Paulin, C.D. & Sagar, P.M. (1977). A diurnal rhythm of activity by the Adelie Penguin. *Notornis* **24**: 158-160.
Paullin, D.G., Ivey, G.L. & Littlefield, C.D. (1988). The re-establishment of American White Pelican nesting in the Malheur-Harney lakes basin, Oregon. *Murrelet* **69(3)**: 61-64.
Paulraj, S. & Gunasekaran, G. (1988). The Vedanthangal Waterbird Sanctuary: a new breeding ground for pelicans and painted storks. *J. Bombay Nat. Hist. Soc.* **85(2)**: 414-415.
Paulraj, S., Manimozhi, A & Kalyanasundaram, S. (1990). Brooding behavior of the Spot-billed or Grey Pelican (*Pelecanus philippensis*) at Arignar Anna Zoological Park, Madras, India. *Anim. Keepers' Forum* **17**: 163-166.
Paulus, S.L. (1984a). Activity budgets of non-breeding Gadwalls in Louisiana. *J. Wildl. Manage.* **48**: 371-380.
Paulus, S.L. (1984b). *Behavioral Ecology of Mottled Ducks in Lousiana*. PhD thesis, Auburn University, Auburn, Al.
Paulus, S.L. (1988). Social Behavior and Pairing Chronology of Mottled Ducks during Autumn and Winter in Louisiana. Pp. 59-70 in: Weller (1988).
Paxton, R.O. (1968). Wandering Albatross in California. *Auk* **85**: 502-504.
Payne, M.R. and Prince, P.A. (1979). Identification and breeding biology of the diving petrels *Pelecanoides georgicus* and *P. urinatrix exsul* at South Georgia. *New Zealand J. Zool.* **6**: 299-318
Payne, P.M., Powers, K.D. & Bird, J.E. (1983). Opportunistic feeding on whale fat by Wilson's Petrels in the western North Atlantic. *Wilson Bull.* **95**(3): 478-479.
Payne, R.B. (1972). Mechanisms and control of molt. Pp. 103-155 in: Farner, D.S. & King, J.R. (1972). *Avian Biology*. Vol. 2. Academic Press, London & New York.
Payne, R.B. (1974). Species limits and variation of the New World Green Heron *Butorides virescens* and Striated Herons *B. striatus*. *Bull. Br. Orn. Club* **94**: 81-88.
Payne, R.B. (1979). Ardeidae. Pp. 193-244 in: Mayr & Cottrell (1979).
Payne, R.B. & Risley, C.J. (1976). Systematics and Evolutionary Relationships Among the Herons (Ardeidae). *Misc. Publ. Mus. Zool. Univ. Michigan* **150**: 1-115.
Paynter, R.A. (1955). The Ornithogeography of the Yucatan Peninsula. *Peabody Mus. Nat. Hist. Bull.* **9**.
Paynter, R.A. ed. (1974) Avian Energetics. *Publ. Nuttall Orn. Club* **15**. Cambridge, MA.
Paz, U. (1987). *The Birds of Israel*. Christopher Helm (Publishers) Ltd.
Pearse, R.J. (1975). *Cape Barren Geese in Tasmania: Biology and Management to 1975*. National Parks and Wildlife Service, Tasmania, Wildlife Division Technical Report **71/1**.
Pearson, A.K. & Pearson, O.P. (1955). Natural history and breeding behavior of the tinamou *Nothoprocta ornata*. *Auk* **72(2)**: 113-127.
Pearson, B. (1972). *The Avian Brain*. Academic Press, London and New York.
Pearson, D.L. (1975). Un estudio de las aves de Tumi Chucua, Departamento Beni, Bolivia. *Pumapunku* **8**: 50-56.

Pearson, T.G. (1924). Flamingos in Cuba. *Auk* **41**: 599.
Peckover, W.S. & Filewood, L.W.C. (1976). *Birds of New Guinea and Tropical Australia*. A.H. & A.W.Reed, Sydney.
Pefaur, J.E (1974). Egg-neglect in the Wilson's Storm Petrel. *Wilson Bull.* **86**: 16-22.
Pegoraro, K. & Malin, G. (1990). Freilandbeobachtungen am Waldrapp (*Geronticus eremita*) in Marokko: Verhalten immaturer Individuen. *J. Orn.* **131**: 453-456.
Pegoraro, K. & Thaler, E. (1985). Zum Verhalten erstbrütender Waldrapp-Weibchen im Alpenzoo. *Zool. Garten* **55(2/3)**: 113-123.
Pehrsson, O. (1979). Feeding behaviour, feeding habitat utilization, and feeding efficiency of Mallard ducklings (*Anas platyrhynchos* L.) as guided by a domestic Duck. *Viltrevy. Stockholm* **10 (8)**: 193-218.
Pehrsson, O. (1984). Relationships of food to spatial and temporal breeding strategies of Mallard in Sweden. *J. Wildl. Manage.* **48**: 322-339.
Pehrsson, O. (1991). Egg and clutch size in the Mallard as related to food quality. *Can. J. Zool.* **69**: 156-162.
Pemberton, D. & Gales, R.P. (1987). Notes on the status and breeding of the imperial cormorant *Phalarocorax atriceps* at Heard Island. *Cormorant* **15**: 33-40.
Penney, R.L. (1967). Molt in the Adelie Penguin. *Auk* **84**: 61-71.
Penney, R.L. (1968). Territorial and social behaviour in the Adelie Penguin. Pp. 83-131 in: Austin O.L. ed. *Antarctic Bird Studies*. Antarctic Research Series **12**. American Geophysical Union, Washington D.C.
Penney, R.L. & Emlen, J.T. (1967). Further experiments on distance navigation in the Adelie Penguin (*Pygoscelis adeliae*). *Ibis* **109**: 99-109.
Penney, R.L. & Lowry, G. (1967). Leopard seal predation on Adelie Penguins. *Ecology* **48**: 878-882.
Penney, R.L. & Riker, D.K. (1969). Adélie Penguin orientation under the northern sun. *Antarct. J. U. S.* **4**: 116-117.
Pennycuick, C.J. (1960). Gliding flight of the Fulmar Petrel. *J. Exp. Biol.* **37**: 330-338.
Pennycuick, C.J. (1972a). *Animal Flight*. Arnold, London.
Pennycuick, C.J. (1972b). Soaring behaviour and performance of some East African birds, observed from a motor-glider. *Ibis* **114**: 178-218.
Pennycuick, C.J. (1975). Mechanics of flight. Pp. 1-75 in: Farner, D.S. & King, J.R. (1975). *Avian Biology*. Vol. 5. Academic Press, London & New York.
Pennycuick, C.J. (1982). The flight of petrels and albatrosses, observed in South Georgia and its vicinity. *Phil. Trans. Royal Soc. London (Ser. B)* **300**: 75-106.
Pennycuick, C.J. (1983). Thermal soaring compared in three dissimilar tropical bird species, *Fregata magnificens*, *Pelecanus occidentalis* and *Coragyps atratus*. *J. Exp. Biol.* **102**: 307-325.
Pennycuick, C.J. (1987). Flight of seabirds. Pp. 43-62 in: Croxall (1987).
Pennycuick, C.J. (1989). *Bird Flight Performance. A Practical Calculation Manual*. Oxford University Press.
Pennycuick, C.J. & Bartholomew, G.A. (1973). Energy budget of the lesser flamingo. *East Afr. Wildl. J.* **11**: 199-207.
Pennycuick, C.J. & de Santo, T. (1989). Flight Speeds and Energy Requirements for White Ibises on Foraging Flights. *Auk* **106**: 141-144.
Pennycuick, C.J. & Webbe, D. (1959). Observations on the Fulmar in Spitzbergen. *Br Birds* **52**:321-332.
Pennycuick, C.J., Croxall, J.P. & Prince, P.A. (1984). Scaling of foraging radius and growth rate in petrels and albatrosses. *Ornis Scand.* **115**: 145-154..
Pennycuick, C.J., Schaffner, F.C., Fuller, M.R., Obrecht, H.H. & Sternberg, L. (1990). Foraging Flights of the White-tailed Tropicbird (*Phaethon lepturus*): Radiotracking and Doubly-labelled Water. *Colonial Waterbirds* **13(2)**: 96-102.
Penry, E.H. (1975). A year of Dabchick in Kitwe. *Bull. Zambian Orn. Soc.* **7**: 91-98.
Penry, E.H. (1986). Threatened Birds of Botswana. Part 1: The major issues. *Babbler. Gaborone* **11**: 6-8.
Peña, L.E. (1962). Notes on South American flamingos. *Postilla* **69**: 1-8.
de la Peña, M.R. (1980a). Notas nidológicas sobre biguaes y cormoranes (Aves: Anhingidae & Phalacrocoracidae). *Historia Nat. Mendoza* **1(16)**: 109-112.
de la Peña, M.R. (1980b). Notas nidológicas sobre garzas (Aves: Ardeidae). *Historia Natural* **1**: 161-168.
de la Peña, M.R. (1986). *Guía de Aves Argentinas*. Vol. 1. Buenos Aires.
Percy, W. (1951). Three Studies in Bird Character: Bitterns, Herons and Water Rails. Country Life, London.
Perennou, C. (1991a). *Les Recensements Internationaux d'Oiseau d'Eau en Afrique Tropicale*. IWRB Special Publication **15**. BIROE/IWRB, Slimbridge, England.
Perennou, C. (1991b). *African Waterfowl Census 1991 - Les dénombrements internationaux d'oiseaux d'eau en Afrique*. IWRB, Slimbridge, England.
Perennou, C. & Mundkur, T. (1991). Asian Waterfowl Census 1991. IWRB, Slimbridge, UK.
Perennou, C., Rose, P. & Poole, C. (1990). *Asian Waterfowl Census 1990*. International Waterfowl and Wetlands Research Bureau (IWRB)/ Asian Wetland Bureau (AWB), Slimbridge, England.
Pereyra, J.A. (1935). Sobre la perdiz copetona *Eudromia elegans morenoi*. *Hornero* **6**: 74-76.
Perigo, C.A. (1990). The status of storks, ibises and spoonbills in Argentina. *Specialist Group on Storks, Ibises abnd Spoonbills Newsletter* **3(1-2)**: 5.
Perkins, J.S. (1983). Oiled Magellanic Penguins in Golfo San José, Argentina. *Marine Pollution Bull.* **14**: 383-387.
Perkins, J.S. (1984). Breeding ecology of Magellanic Penguins *Spheniscus magellanicus* at Caleta Valdés, Argentina. *Cormorant* **12**: 3-13.
Perrins, C.M. (1966). Survival of young Manx Shearwaters in relation to their presumed date of hatching. *Ibis* **108**: 132-135.
Perrins, C.M. (1990). *The Illustrated Encyclopaedia of Birds*. Headline, London.
Perrins, C.M. & Birkhead, T.R. (1983). *Avian Ecology*. Blackie, Glasgow and London.
Perrins, C.M. & Brooke, M. de L. (1976). Manx Shearwaters in the Bay of Biscay. *Bird Study* **23**: 295-300.
Perrins, C.M. & Middleton, A.A. eds. (1985). *The Encyclopedia of Birds*. Facts on File, New York.
Perrins, C.M., Harris, M.P. & Britton, C.K. (1973). Survival of Manx Shearwaters. *Ibis* **115**: 335-348..
Perrins, C.M., Lebreton, J.D. & Hirons, G.J.M. eds. (1991). *Bird Population Studies*. Relevance to Conservation and Management. Oxford University Press, Oxford.
Perry, M.C., Nichols, D., Conroy, M.J., Obrecht, H.H. & Williams, B.K. (1988). Sex Specificity of Behavioral Dominance and Fasting Endurance in Wintering Canvasbacks: Experimental Results. Pp. 103-122 in: Weller (1988).
Perry, R. (1980). Wildlife conservation in the Line Islands, Republic of Kiribati (formerly Gilbert Islands). *Environ. Conserv.* **7**: 311-318.
Persson, H. (1989). Time and energy budgets of wintering taiga bean geese *Anser fabalis* in Skane, south Sweden. Pp. 169-182 in: *Food Selection, Movements and Energy Budgets of Stating and Wintering Geese on South Swedish Farmland*. Lund University, Sweden.
Persson, J.Å., Lundgren, S. & Johansson, I. (1986). Projekt smålom. *Gavia* **12**: 71-72.
Pescott, T.W. (1980). Seabird Islands no. 100. Lawrence Rocks, Victoria. *Corella* **4(4)**: 107-109.
Peter, H. (1991). *Waldrappdämmerung am Euphrat*. Kasparek Verlag, Heidelberg.
Peters, J.L. (1931-1987). *Checklist of the Birds of the World*. Vols. I-XVI. Harvard University Press, Cambridge, MA.
Peters, L.J. (1991). Ostrich management and propagation. *Game Bird Breeders Avicult. Zool. Conserv. Gazette* **39(1-2)**: 12-14.
Petersen, M.R. (1976). *Breeding Biology of Arctic and Red-throated Loons*. MSc thesis. University of California, Davis.
Petersen, M.R. (1979). Nesting ecology of Arctic Loons. *Wilson Bull.* **91(4)**: 608-617.
Petersen, M.R. (1989). Nesting Biology of Pacific Loons, *Gavia pacifica*, on the Yukon-Kuskokwim Delta, Alaska. *Can. Field-Nat.* **103(2)**: 265-269.
Petersen, M.R. (1990). Nest-site selection by Emperor Geese and Cackling Canada Geese. *Wilson Bull.* **102 (3)**: 413-426.
Petersen, M.R. & Gill, R.E. (1982). Population and status of Emperor Geese along the north side of the Alaska Peninsula. *Wildfowl* **33**: 31-38.
Petersen, S. (1991). A record of White-shouldered Ibis in East Kalimantan. *Kukila* **5(2)**: 144-145.
Peterson, R.T. (1963). *The Birds*. Life Nature Library, Time. New York.
Peterson, R.T. (1979). *Penguins*. Houghton Mifflin Company, Boston.
Peterson, R.T. & Chalif, E.L. (1973). *A Field Guide to Mexican Birds*. Houghton Mifflin Company, Boston.
Peterson, T. (1976). Vit stork (*Ciconia ciconia*) och svart stork (*Ciconia nigra*) pa Oland. *Calidris* **76(3)**: 79-84.
Petit, D.R. & Bildstein, K.L. (1986). Development of formation flying in juvenile White Ibises (*Eudocimus albus*). *Auk* **103**: 244-246.
Petit, D.R. & Bildstein, K.L. (1987). Effect of group size and location within the group on the foraging behavior of White Ibises. *Condor* **89**: 602-609.
Pettingill, O.S. (1960). The effects of climate and weather on the birds of the Falkland Islands. Pp. 604-613 in: *Proc. XII Int. Orn. Congr.*
Pettingill, O.S. (1965). Kelp geese and flightless steamer ducks in the Falkland Islands. *Living Bird* **4**: 65-78.
Pettingill, O.S. (1985). *Ornithology in Laboratory and Field*. 5th edition. T & AD Poyser, London.
Pettit, T.N., Byrd, V.G., Whittow, G.C. & Seki, M.P. (1984). Growth of the Wedgetailed Shearwater in the Hawaiian Islands. *Auk* **101**: 103-109.
Pettit, T.N., Grant, G.S. & Whittow, G.C. (1982). Body temperature and growth of Bonin Petrel chicks. *Wilson Bull* **94**: 358-361.
Philippona, J. (1972). *Die Blessgans*. Die Neu Brehm-Bucherei **457**. Ziemsen Verlag, Wittenberg-Luherstadt.
Philippona, J. & Mulder, Th. (1965). Das Vorkommen der Europaischen Blessgans *Anser a. albifrons*, in Nord un West Europa. *Beitr. Vogelk.* **11**: 1-2, 94-99.
Philippona, J. & Smith, E. (1978). Observations on the Pink-footed Goose, *Anser brachyrhynchus*, in central Iceland in 1975 and 1976. *Gerfaut* **68**: 195-202.
Phillips, C. (1986). *WWF Yearbook 1985/1986*. World Wildlife Fund, Gland, Switzerland.
Phillips, J.C. (1922-1926). *A Natural History of the Ducks*. 4 Vols. Houghton Mifflin, Boston, MA.
Phillips, J.G., Butler, P.J. & Sharp, P.J. (1985). *Physiological Strategies in Avian Biology*. Blackie, Glasgow, Scotland.
Phillips, J.H. (1963). The pelagic distribution of the Sooty Shearwater. *Ibis* **105**(3): 340-353.
Phillips, N.J. (1987). The breeding biology of white-tailed tropicbirds *Phaethon lepturus* at Cousin Islands, Seychelles. *Ibis* **129(1)**: 10-24.
Phillips, W.W.A. (1955). Wilson Petrel in Indo-Ceylon waters, with special reference to the 1954 southward migration. *J. Bombay Nat. Hist. Soc.* **53**: 132-133.
Piatt, J.F., Lensink, C.J., Butler, W., Kendziorek, M. & Nysewander, D.R. (1990). Immediate impact of the "Exxon Valdez" oil spill on marine birds. *Auk* **107**: 387-397.
Pichner, J. & DonCarlos, M.W. (1986). Hatching and rearing of the Common Loon (*Gavia immer*). Pp. 468-472 in: *AAZPA (Amer. Assoc. Zool. Parks & Aquariums) Ann. Conf. Proc.*
Pickering, S.P.C. (1989). Attendance patterns and behaviour in relation to experience and pair-bond formation in the Wandering Albatross at the South Georgia. *Ibis* **131**: 183-195.
Piekarz, D.M. (1991). The current and historical status of the African Pygmy Goosed in captivity and in the wild. Pp. 632-637 in: *AAZPA (Amer. Assoc. Zool. Parks & Aquariums) Reg. Conf. Proc.*
Pierce, R.J. (1980). Seasonal and long-term changes in bird numbers at Lake Wainono. *Notornis* **27**: 21-44.
Pierre, P. (1988). Statut actuel de la Cigogne Noire (*Ciconia nigra*) en Wallonie. *Aves* **25**: 183-189.
Piersma, T. (1984). Estimating energy reserves of Great Crested Grebes *Podiceps cristatus* on the basis of body dimensions. *Ardea* **72**: 119-126.
Piersma, T. (1988a). The annual moult cycle of Great Crested Grebes. *Ardea* **76**: 81-95.
Piersma, T. (1988b). Body size, nutrient reserves and diet of Red-necked and Slavonian Grebes (*Podiceps grisegena* and *P. auritus*) on Lake IJsselmeer, The Netherlands. *Bird Study* **35**: 13-24.
Piersma, T. (1988c). Morphological variation in a European population of Great Crested Grebes *Podiceps cristatus* in relation to age, sex and season. *J. Orn.* **129**: 299-316.
Piersma, T. (1988d). Breast muscle atrophy and constraint on foraging during the flightless period of wing moulting Great Crested Grebes. *Ardea* **76**: 96-106.
Piersma, T. & van Eerden, M.R. (1989). Feather eating in Great Crested Grebes (*Podiceps cristatus*): a unique solution to the problems of debris and gastric parasites in fish-eating birds. *Ibis* **131**: 477-486.
Piersma, T., Lindeboom, R. & van Eerden, M.R. (1988). Foraging rhythm of Great Crested Grebes *Podiceps cristatus* adjusted to diet variations in the vertical distribution of their prey *Osmerus eperlanus* in a shallow eutrophic lake in The Netherlands. *Oecologia* **76**: 481-486.
Pilon, C. (1981). Alimentation et reproduction du Grand Cormoran (*Phalacrocorax carbo*) et du Cormoran à aigrettes (*P. auritus*) aux îles de la Madeleine, Québec. MSc thesis, Université de Montréal, Montréal.
Pilon, C., Burton, J. & McNeil, R. (1983a). Reproduction du Grand Cormoran (*Phalacrocorax carbo*) et du Cormoran à aigrettes (*P. auritus*) aux îles de la Madeleine, Québec. *Can. J. Zool.* **61**: 524-530.
Pilon, C., Burton, J. & McNeil, R. (1983b). Summer food of the Great and Double-crested Cormorants on the Magdalen Islands, Quebec. *Can. J. Zool.* **61**: 2733-2739.
Pinder, R. (1966). The Cape Pigeon at Signy Island, South Orkney Islands. *British Antarct. Surv. Bull.* **8**: 19-47.
Pinshow, B. & Welch, W.R. (1980). Winter breeding in Emperor Penguins: a consequence of the summer heat? *Condor* **82**: 159-163.
Pinshow, B., Fedak, M.A. & Schmidt-Nielsen, K. (1977). Terrestrial locomotion in Penguins: it costs more to waddle. *Science* **195**: 592-594.
Pinshow, B., Fedak, M.A., Battles, D.R. & Schmidt-Nielsen, K. (1976). Energy expenditure for thermoregulation and locomotion in Emperor Penguins. *Amer. J. Physiol.* **231**: 903-912.
Pinto, A.A. da Rosa. (1983). *Ornitologia de Angola*. Vol. 1. Instituto de Investigaçao Científica Tropical, Lisboa.
Pinto, O.M. de Oliveira. (1954). (Range of *Tinamus solitarius pernambucensis*). *Bol. Parque Nac. Itatiáca* **1954**: 18.
Pinto, O.M. de Oliveira. (1964). *Ornitologia Brasiliense*. Vol. 1. Departamento de Zoologia da Secretaria da Agricultura do Estado de São Paulo, São Paulo.
Pirani, C. ed. (1976, 1979, 1981, 1982). Operation Pateke. *Flight* **8**: 5-8, **20**: 4, **27**: 7-9, **32**: 14.
Pitman, C.R.S. (1928). The nesting of *Hagedashia hagedash nilotica* - the Nile Valley Hadada in Uganda. *Oologist's Rec.* **8**: 44-46.
Pirot, J.Y. (1980). *Régime alimentaire de la Sarcelle d'été (*Anas querquedula*) pendant son transit en Camargue*. D.E.A. d'Ecologie, University of Paris. VI rapp. dact.
Pitman, C.R.S. (1931a). The nesting of *Dissoura episcopus microscelis* (Sclater) in Uganda. *Oologist's Record* **11**: 45-46.
Pitman, C.R.S. (1931b). Further notes on the breeding of *Hagedashia hagedash nilotica* - the Nile Valley Hadada in Uganda. *Oologist's Rec.* **11**: 48.
Pitman, C.R.S. (1957). Further notes on aquatic predators of birds. Part 2. *Bull. Brit. Orn. Club* **77**: 105-110.
Pitman, C.R.S. (1963). The nesting and some other habits of *Alopochen*, *Nettapus*, *Plectropterus* and *Sarkidiornis*. *Wildfowl Trust Ann. Rep.* **16**.
Pitman, C.R.S. (1965). The nesting, eggs and young of the Saddle-bill Stork, *Ephippiorhynchus senegalensis* (Shaw). *Bull. Brit. Orn. Club* **85**: 70-80.
Pitman, R.L. (1982). Distribution and foraging habits of Dark-rumped Petrel in the eastern tropical Pacific. *Pacific Seabird Group Bull.* **9**: 72.
Pitman, R.L. (1986). *Atlas of Seabird Abundance and Relative Abundance in the Eastern Tropical Pacific*. Administrative Rep. LJ-86-02C, Southwest Fisheries Center, La Jolla, California.
Pitman, R.L. (1988). Laysan Albatross breeding in the eastern Pacific - and a comment. *Pacific Seabird Group Bull.* **15**: 52.
Pitman, R.L. & Ballance, L.T. (1990). Daytime feeding by Leach's Storm-Petrel on a midwater fish in the eastern Tropical Pacific. *Condor* **92**: 527-530.
Pitman, R.L. & Unitt, P. (1981). Distribution and feeding ecology of Parkinson's Petrel (*Procellaria parkinsoni*) in the eastern tropical Pacific. *Pacific Seabird Group Bull.* **8**: 92.
Place, A.R., Stoyan, N.C., Ricklefs, R.E. & Butler, R.G. (1989). Physiological basis of stomach oil formation in Leach's Storm-Petrel. *Auk* **106**: 687-699.
Plath, K. (1914). With the tropic-birds in Bermuda. *Ibis* **1914**: 552-559.
Platz, F. (1974). Untersuchungen über die Ontogenese von Ausdrucksbewegungen und Latáusserungen bei der Kolbenente (*Netta rufina* Pallas) mit einem Beitrag zur Anatomie des Stimmapparates. *Z. Tierpsychol.* **36**: 293-428.
Plenge, M.A. (1982). The Distribution of the Lesser Rhea in South Perú and North Chile. *Ibis* **124**: 168-172.
Plenge, M.A., Parker, T.A., Hughes, R.A. & O'Neill, J.P. (1989). Additional notes on the distribution of birds in west-central Peru. *Gerfaut* **79**: 55-68.
du Plessis, M. (1986). Observations of kleptoparasitism by the African Fish Eagle. *Bee-Eater* **37(3)**: 31-32.
Ploger, B.J. & Mock, D.W. (1986). Role of Sibling Aggression in Food distribution to Nestling Cattle Egrets (*Bubulcus ibis*). *The Auk* **103**: 768-776.
Plotnik, R. (1961). La Avutarda de Pecho Rayado. *Instituto de Patologia Vegetal IDIA* **157**: 9-22.
Plowes, D.C.H. (1967). Hadeda Ibis in Rhodesia. *Honeyguide* **53**: 19.
Plunkett, A.M. (1989). A county lister's dream come true. *Loon* **61(2)**: 88.
Pocklington, R. (1979). An oceanographic interpretation of distributions in the Indian Ocean. *Mar. Biol.* **51**: 9-21.
Pocock, T.N. & Uys, C.J. (1967). The Bald Ibis in the North-Eastern Orange Free State. *Bokmakierie* **19**: 28-31.
Podolsky, R.H. & Kress, S.W. (1989). Factors affecting colony formation in Leach's Storm-Petrel. *Auk* **106**: 332-336.
Polunin, N. (1969). Conservation of the Giant Pied-billed Grebe of Guatemala. *Biol. Conserv.* **1**: 176.
Polunin, N.V.C. (1979). *Sula leucogaster* and other species in the Iles Mitsios, Madagascar. *Bull. Brit. Orn. Club* **99**: 110-111.
Pomeroy, D.E. (1973). The distribution and abundance of Marabou Storks in Uganda. *East Afr. Wildl. J.* **11**: 227-240.
Pomeroy, D.E. (1977a). The biology of Marabou Storks in Uganda. I. Some characteristics of the species, and the population structure. *Ardea* **65**: 1-24.
Pomeroy, D.E. (1977b). Marabous associated with vulture parties in East Africa. *Scopus* **1(4)**: 103-106.

Pomeroy, D.E. (1978a). The biology of Marabou Storks in Uganda. II. Breeding biology and general review. *Ardea* **66**: 1-23.
Pomeroy, D.E. (1978b). Seasonality of Marabou Storks *Leptoptilos crumeniferus* in eastern Africa. *Ibis* **120**: 313-321.
Pomeroy, D.E. (1978c). Counts of Marabou Storks (*Leptoptilos crumeniferos*) in relation to their movements in eastern Africa. *Scopus* **2(4)**: 92-96.
Pomeroy, D.E. (1986). The Marabou in Kenya. *Scopus* **10**: 1-9.
Poole, C.M., Allport, G.A., Eldrige, M.I., Park, E.M. & Jo, S.R. (1990). *Ch'unam Lake, South Korea and the Conservation of Baikal Teal (*Anas formosa*).* Asian Wetland Bureau, Kuala Lumpur, Malaysia.
Pooley, A.C. (1968). Spoonbill and heron. *Lammergeyer* **8**: 50.
Pooley, H. (1991). Black Egret on west coast. *Promerops* **197**: 10.
Poonswad, P. (1979). *Parasites of Asian Open-billed Stork (*Anastomus oscitans*) and their relationships to Pila and domestic duck.* MSc thesis. Mahidol University, Bangkok, Thailand.
Poorter, E.P.R. (1982). Migration et dispersion des Spatules néerlandaises. *L'Oiseau et la R.F.O.* **52(4)**: 305-334.
Portela, L.I. (1986). Sobre a ocorrência do maçarico-preto *Plegadis falcinellus* (L.) em Portugal. [A review of the status of the Glossy Ibis *Plegadis falcinellus* in Portugal]. *Cyanopica* **3(4)**: 693-712.
Portenko, L.A. (1981). *Birds of the Chukchi Peninsula and Wrangel Island*. Vol. I. Smithsonian Institution and National Science Foundation, Washington, D.C.
Porter, R.N. & Forrest, G.W. (1974). First succesful breeding of greater flamingo in Natal, South Africa. *Lammergeyer* **21**: 26-33.
Poslavski, A.N., Sabinyevski, B.V. & Luri, V.N. (1977). Flamingos in the Northern Caspian. Pp. 209-214 in: Gavrilov *et al*. eds. *Rare and Vanishing Animals and Birds of Kazakhstan*. IWRB translation from Russian to English.
Pospahala, R.S., Anderson, D.R. & Henry, C.J. (1974). *Population Ecology of the Mallard. II. Breeding Habitat Conditions, Size of the Breeding Populations, and Production Indices*. US Fish & Wildlife Service Resources Publication **115**.
Post, J.N.J. (1987). [Living from the dead]. *Dieren* **4(3)**: 92-94. In Dutch.
Post, W. (1988). Spread of the Double-Crested Cormorant into Interior of the Southeastern United States. *Colonial Waterbirds* **11(1)**: 115-116.
Post, W. (1990). Nest Survival in a Large Ibis-Heron Colony during a Three-year Decline to Extinction. *Colonial Waterbirds* **13**: 50-61.
Post, W. & Seals, C.A. (1991). Breeding Biology of a Newly-established Double-crested Cormorant Population in South Carolina, USA. *Colonial Waterbirds*. **14(1)**: 34-38.
Post, W., Enders, F. & Davis, T.H. (1970). The breeding status of the Glossy Ibis in New York. *Kingbird* **20**: 3-8.
Poston, H.J. (1969). Home Range and Breeding Biology of the Shoveler. *Can. Wildl. Serv. Rep. Series* **25**.
Postupalsky, S. (1978). Toxic chemicals and cormorant populations in the Great Lakes. *Wildl. Toxicol. Div. Can. Wildl. Serv. Manuscript Rep.* **40**.
Potter, M.A. (1989). *Ecology and Reproductive Biology of the North Island Brown Kiwi (*Apteryx australis mantelli*).* Unpubl. PhD thesis, Massey University.
Potter, M.A. (1990). Movement of North Island Brown Kiwi (*Apteryx australis mantelli*) between forest remnants. *New Zealand J. Ecol.* **14**: 17-24.
Potts, G.R. (1966). Studies on a marked population of the Shag with special reference to the breeding biology of birds of known age. Unpublished Ph.D. Thesis, University of Durham.
Potts, G.R. (1968). Success of eggs of the Shag on the Farne Islands, Northumberland, in relation to their content of dieldrin and pp'DDE. *Nature* **217**: 1282-1284.
Potts, G.R. (1969). The influence of eruptive movements, age, population size and other factors on the survival of the shag (*Phalacrocorax aristotelis* L.). *J. Anim. Ecol.* **38**: 53-102.
Potts, G.R. (1971). Moult in the Shag *Phalacrocorax aristotelis* and the ontogeny of the "Staffelmauser". *Ibis* **113**: 298-305.
Potts, G.R., Coulson, J.C. & Deans, I.R. (1980). Population dynamics and breeding success of the Shag, *Phalacrocorax aristotelis* on The Farne Islands, Northumberland. *J. Anim. Ecol.* **49**: 465-484.
Potts, K.J. (1977). Food of the Little Shags and Little Black Shags. *Wildlife - A review* **8**: 34-38.
Potts, T.H. (1871). Notes on a new species of *Apteryx* (*A.haastii*, Potts). *Trans. & Proc. New Zealand Inst.* **4**: 204-205.
Potvliege, R. (1978). Origine géographique possible des Grèbes esclavons, *Podiceps auritus*, capturés en Belgique. *Gerfaut* **68**: 121-123.
Powder, D.M. & Ainley, D.C. (1986). Seabird geographic variation: similarity among populations of Leach's Storm-petrel. *Auk* **103**: 575-585.
Powell, G.V.N. (1987). Habitat use by wading birds in a subtropical estuary: implications of hydrography. *Auk* **104**: 740-749.
Powell, G.V.N. & Powell, A.H. (1986). Reproduction by Great White Herons *Ardea herodias* in Florida Bay as an Indicator of Habitat Quality. *Biological Conservation* **36**: 101-113.
Powell, G.V.N., Bjork, R.D., Ogden, J.C., Paul, R.T, Powell, A.H., Robertson, W.B. (1989). Population trends in some Florida Bay wading birds. *Wilson Bull.* **101**: 436-457.
Power, M. E., Dudley, T.L. & Cooper, S.D. (1989). Grazing catfish, fishing birds, and attached algae in a Panamanian stream. *Environ. Biol. Fishes* **26(4)**: 285-294.
Powers, J.E. & LaBastille, A. (1967). Elimination of fish in the Giant Grebe Refuge, Lake Atitlán, Guatemala, using the fish toxicant antimycin. *Trans. Amer. Fish. Soc.* **96(2)**: 210-213.
Powers, K.D. & Cherry, J. (1983). Loon migrations off the northeastern United States. *Wilson Bull.* **95**: 125-132.
Powlesland, R.G. (1983). Seabirds found dead on New Zealand beaches in 1981. *Notornis* **30**: 125-135.
Powlesland, R.G. (1986). Seabirds found dead on New Zealand beaches in 1984, and a review of Fulmar recoveries since 1960. *Notornis* **33**: 171-184.
Powlesland, R.G. (1987). Seabirds found dead on New Zealand beaches in 1985, and a review of *Pterodroma* species recoveries since 1960. *Notornis* **34**: 237-252.
Powlesland, R.G. (1989). Seabirds found dead on New Zealand beaches in 1986, and a review of *Pachyptila* species recoveries since 1960. *Notornis* **36**: 125-140.
Pöysä, H. & Nummi, P. (1990). Sorsien pesimäaikainen elinympäristön valinta. *Suomen Riista* **36**: 97-107.
Prager, E.M., Wilson, A.C., Osuga, D.T. & Feeney, R.E. (1976). Evolution of flightless land birds on southern continents: tranferrin comparison shows monophyletic origin of ratites. *J. Molec. Evol.* **8**: 283-294.
Prall, H.D. (1976). Field identification of White-faced and Glossy Ibis. *Birding* **8**: 1-5.
Prater, A.J. (1981). *Estuary Birds of Britain and Ireland*. T & A D Poyser, Calton, England.
Pratt, H.D., Bruner, P.L. & Berrett, D.G. (1987). *A Field Guide to the Birds of Hawaii and the Tropical Pacific*. Princeton University Press, Princeton, New Jersey.
Pratt, H.M. & Winkler, D.W. (1985). Clutch size, timing of laying, and reproductive success in a colony of Great Blue Herons and Great Egrets. *The Auk* **102**: 49-63.
du Preez, L. (1973). Hand rearing of the lesser flamingo. *Bokmakierie* 25: 105-107.
Preston, I. (1976). Whale-headed Stork. *Bull. East Afr. Nat. Hist. Soc.* **Nov/Dec**: 131-132.
Prestt, I. (1970). Organochlorine pollution of rivers and the heron (*Ardea cinerea* L.). *IUCN Publications (New Ser.)* **17**: 95-102.
Prestt, I. & Jefferies, D.J. (1969). Winter numbers, breeding success, and organochlorine residues in the Great Crested Grebe in Britain. *Bird Study* **16**: 168-185.
Prestud, P. Black, J.M. & Owen, M. (1989). The relationship between an increasing population of Barnacle Geese and the number and size of their colonies in Svalbard. *Wildfowl* **40**: 32-382.
Prestwich, A.A. (1974). The Pink-headed Duck (*Rhodonessa caryophyllacea*) in the wild and in captivity. *Avicult. Mag.* **80**: 47-52.
Prevett, J.P. (1973). *Family Behavior and Age-dependent Breeding Biology of the Blue Goose,* Anser caerulescens. PhD dissertation, University of Western Ontario.
Prevett, J.P. & MacInnes, C.D. (1980). *Family and Other Social Groups in Snow Geese*. Wildlife Monographs **71**.
Prévost, J. (1961). *Ecologie du Manchot Empereur,* Aptenodytes forsteri *Gray*. Paris, Hermann.
Prévost, J. (1964). Remarques écologiques sur quelques Procellarieus antarctiques. *L'Oiseau et la R.F.O.* **34(No. Spéc.)**: 91-112.
Prévost, J. (1969). A propos des Pétrels des neiges de la Terre Adélie. *L'Oiseau et la R.F.O.* **39**: 33-49.
Prévost, J. & Boulière, F. (1975). Vie sociale et thermoregulation chez le Manchot Empereur. *Alauda* **25(3)**: 167-173.
Price, I.M. & Weseloh, D.V. (1986). Increased numbers and productivity of Double-crested Cormorants, *Phalacrocorax auritus*, on Lake Ontario. *Can. Field-Nat.* **100**: 474-482.
Prigioni, C., Galeotti, P. & Fasola, M. (1985). Accrescimiento dei pulli e riuscita della riproduzione nella Nitticora *Nycticorax nycticorax*. *Avocetta* **9**: 127-133.
Priklonskii, S.G. (1958). [Material on the ecology of the Black Stork in the Oka Nature Reserve]. *Trudy Okskogo Gosudarstwennogo Sapowednika II. Raboty Okskoi Orn. St.* **1**: 102-115. In Russian.
Priklonskii, S.G. & Galushin, V.M. (1959). [New data on the ecology of the Black Stork]. *Proc. Baltic Orn. Conf.* **(1957)**3: 231-236. In Russian.
Prince, P.A. (1980a). The food and feeding ecology of the Blue Petrel and Dove Prion. *J. Zool. London* **190**: 59-76.
Prince, P.A. (1980b). The food and feeding ecology of the Grey-headed Albatross and Black-browed Albatross. *Ibis* **122**: 476-488.
Prince, P.A. (1985). Population and energetic aspects of the relationship between Blackbrowed and Greyheaded Albatrosses and the southern Ocean marine environment. Pp. 473-477 in: Siegfried, W.R., Condy, P.R. & Laws, R.M. eds. *Antarctic Nutrient Cycles and Food Webs*. Springer, Berlin.
Prince, P.A. & Copestake, P.G. (1990). Diet and aspects of Fairy Prions breeding at South Georgia. *Notornis* **37**: 59-69.
Prince, P.A. & Croxall, J.P. (1983). Birds of South Georgia: new records and re-evaluations of status. *Brit. Antarct. Surv. Bull.* **59**: 15-27.
Prince, P.A. & Francis, M.D. (1984). Activity budgets of foraging Grey-headed Albatrosses. *Condor* **86**: 297-300.
Prince, P.A. & Morgan, R.A. (1987). Diet and feeding ecology of Procellariiformes. Pp. 135-171 in Croxall (1987).
Prince, P.A. & Ricketts, C. (1981). Relationships between food supply and growth in albatrosses: an interspecies chick fostering experiment. *Ornis Scand.* **12**: 207-210.
Prince, P.A. & Walton, D.W.H. (1984). Automated measurement of meal size and feeding frequency in albatrosses. *J. Appl. Ecol.* **21**: 789-794.
Prince, P.A., Ricketts, C. & Thomas, G. (1981). Weight loss in incubating albatrosses and its implications for their energy and food requirements. *Condor* **83**: 238-242.
Pringle, J.D. (1985). *The Waterbirds of Australia*. Angus & Robertson Publishers, North Ryde.
Prinzinger, R. (1974). Untersuchungen über das Verhalten des Schwarzhalstauchers *Podiceps n. nigricollis*, Brehm (1831). *Anz. orn. Ges. Bayern* **13**: 1-34.
Prinzinger, R. (1979a). *Der Schwarzhalstaucher* Podiceps nigricollis. Die Neue Brehm-Bücherei **521**, Ziemsen Verlag, Wittenberg-Lutherstadt.
Prinzinger, R. (1979b). Ei- und Nestdaten vom Schwarzhalstaucher (*Podiceps nigricollis*) - Eine vergleichend zusammenfassende Darstellung. *Orn. Mitt.* **31**: 35-40.
Profus, P. & Mielczarek, P. (1981). Changes in the numbers of the White Stork *Ciconia ciconia* (Linnaeus 1758) in Southern Poland. *Acta Zool. Cracov* **25**: 139-218.
Prokop, P. (1980). Der Kormoran in Österreich. *Egretta* **23**: 49-55.
Prop, J., van Eerden, M.R. & Drent, R.H. (1984). Reproductive success of the Barnacle Goose *Branta leucopsis* in relation to food exploitation on the breeding grounds, western Spitsbergen. *Norsk Polarinstitutt Skrifter* **181**: 87-117.
Prozesky, O.P.M. (1959). Preliminary observations on clutch laying, incubation and fledging period of Spur-winged Goose. *Bull. S. Afr. Mus. Ass.* **7**: 52-54.
Prys-Jones, R.P. & Peet, C. (1980). Breeding periodicity, nesting success and nest site selection among Red-tailed Tropicbirds *Phaethon rubricauda* and White-tailed Tropicbirds *P. lepturus* on Aldabra Atoll. *Ibis* **122(1)**: 76-81.
Prytherch, R. (1965). Pied-billed Grebe in Somerset: a bird new to Great Britain and Ireland. *British Birds* **58**: 305-309.
Prytherch, R. (1980). Squacco Heron possibly using insects as bait. *British Birds* **73(4)**: 183-184.
Prytherch, R. & Everett, M. (1988). Giant Pied-billed Grebe extinct. *British Birds* **81**: 195.
Pulich, W. (1982). Documentation and status of Cory's Shearwater in the western Gulf of Mexico. *Wilson Bull* **94**: 381-385.
Pundt, G. & Ringleben, H. (1963). Der Loeffler (*Platalea leucorodia*) 1962 erstmals deutscher Brutvogel auf der Insel Memmert. *J. Orn.* **104**: 97-100.
Purchase, D. (1976). The occurrence of *Threskiornis molucca strictipennis* in New Guinea. *Emu* **76(2)**: 89.
Pycraft, W.P. (1906). Notes on a skeleton of the Musk-duck, *Biziura lobata* with special reference to skeletal characters evolved in relation to the diving habits of this bird. *Zool. J. Linn. Soc.* **29**: 396-407.
Pycraft, W.P. (1910). *A History of Birds*. Methuen, London.
Pyle, P., Spear, L. & Engbring, J. (1990). A Previously Unreported Population of Herald Petrel on Ta'u Island, American Samoa. *Colonial Waterbirds* **13**(2): 136-138.
Pyrovetsi, M. (1989). Foraging trips of White Pelicans (*Pelecanus onocrotalus*) breeding on Lake Mikri Prespa, Greece. *Colonial Waterbirds* **12(1)**: 43-50.
Pyrovetsi, M. & Daoutopoulos, G.A. (1989). Conservation - related attitudes of Lake Fishermen in Greece. *Environ. Conserv.* **16(3)**: 245-250.
Qian Guo-zhen & Xu Hong-fa (1986). [Seasonal variation in the energy metabolism of the Common Teal *Anas crecca*, Shoveler *Anas clypeata* and Spotbill Duck *Anas poecilorhyncha* in Taihu Lake (Jiangsu Province)]. *Acta Ecol. Sinica* 6(4): 365-370. In Chinese with English summary.
Qian Guo-zhen & Xu Hong-fa (1989). [Studies of basal metabolic energy in the Common Teal *Anas crecca*, Shoveler *Anas clypeata* and Spotbill Duck *Anas poecilorhyncha* during their wintering period]. *Acta Ecol. Sinica* 9(4): 330-335. In Chinese with English summary.
Qian Guo-zhen & Zhou Hai-zhong (1980). [Some ecological data about the Lesser Whistling Teal *Dendrocygna javanica*]. *Chinese J. Zool.* **3**: 24-27. In Chinese.
Qian Guo-zhen, Wang Tian-hou, *et al*. (1986). [Ecological studies on the breeding habits of inmature Night Herons *Nycticorax nycticorax*]. *Zool. Res.* **7(3)**: 255-261. In Chinese.
Quickelberge, C.D. (1972). Spoonbills breeding in the Eastern Cape Province. *Ostrich* **43**: 67.
Quin, B.R. (1984). *Food Selection and Diet in the* Emu Dromaius novaehollandiae *in the Victoria Valley, Grampians National Park, Victoria*. Unpublished BSc. (Hons) thesis, Latrobe University.
Quinlan, E.E. & Baldassarre, G.A. (1984). Activity budgets of non-breeding Green-winged Teal on playa lakes in Texas. *J. Wildl. Manage.* **48**: 838-845.
Quinlan, S.E. (1983). Avian and River Otter predation on a Storm-Petrel colony. *J. Wildl. Manage.* **47**(4): 1036-1043.
Quinn, T.W., Shields, G.F. & Wilson, A.C. (1991). Affinities of the Hawaiian Goose based on two types of mitochondrial DNA data. *Auk* **108 (3)**: 585-593.
Quinney, T.E. (1982). Growth, diet, and mortality of nestling Great Blue Herons. *Wilson Bull.* **94**: 571-577.
Rabenold, P.P. (1987b). American bitterns (*Botaurus lentiginosus*): 1987 status report for Indiana. Unpublished report to Indiana Department Natural Resources, Indianapolis.
Rabenold, P.P. (1987a). Least Bitterns (*Ixobrychus exilis*): 1987 status report for Indiana. Unpublished report to Indiana Department Natural Resources, Indianapolis.
Rabosée, D. (1983). L'hivernage du Grèbe castagneux (*Tachybaptus ruficollis*) en Wallonie. *Aves* **20**: 121-138.
Rae, B.B. (1969). The food of Cormorants and Shags in Scottish estuaries and coastal waters. *Dept. Agric. Fish. Scotland Mar. Res.* **1**: 1-16.
Rahmani, A.R. (1987). Is the Blacknecked Stork threatened? *Hornbill* **1987(4)**: 18-19.
Rahmani, A.R. (1989a). Status of the Black-necked Stork *Ephippiorhynchus asiaticus* in the Indian subcontinent. *Forktail* **5**: 99-110.
Rahmani, A.R. (1989b). Blacknecked and Greater Adjutant storks in India. *Specialist Group on Storks, Ibis, and Spoonbills Newsletter* **2**: 3-6.
Rahmani, A.R. (1990). Menace to Manas. *World Birdwatch* **12(1-2)**: 3.
Rahmani, A.R., Narayan, G. & Rosalind, L. (1990). Status of the Greater Adjutant (*Leptoptilos dubius*) in the Indian Subcontinent. *Colonial Waterbirds* **13(2)**: 139-142.
Rahn, H. & Whittow, G.C. (1988). Adaptations to a pelagic life: eggs of the albatross, shearwater and petrel. *Comp. Biochem. Physiol. (Ser. A)* **91**: 415-423.
Raikow, R.J. (1968). The maintenance behaviour of the Common Rhea. *Wilson Bull.* **80**: 312-319.
Raikow, R.J. (1969). Sexual and agonistic behaviour of the Common Rhea. *Wilson Bull.* **81**: 196-206.
Raikow, R.J. (1970). *Evolution of Diving Adaptations in the Stifftail Ducks*. University of California Press, Berkeley-Los Angeles-London.
Raikow, R.J. (1971). The osteology and taxonomic position of the White-backed Duck, *Thalassornis leuconotus*. *Wilson Bull.* **83**: 270-277.
Ramo, C. & Busto, B. (1982a). Notes on the Breeding of the Chestnut-bellied Heron (*Agamia agami*) in Venezuela. *Auk* **99(4)**: 784.
Ramo, C. & Busto, B. (1982b). Son *Eudocimus ruber* y *E. albus* distintas especies? *Doñana Acta Vertebrata* **9**: 404-408.
Ramo, C. & Busto, B. (1984). Censo aereo de Corocoros (*Eudocimus ruber*) y otras aves acuáticas en Venezuela. *Bol. Soc. Venez. Cienc. Nat.* **39(142)**: 65-88.
Ramo, C & Busto, B. (1985). Comportamiento reproductivo del Corocoro *Eudocimus ruber*. *Mem. Soc. Cien. Nat. La Salle* **45**: 77-113.
Ramo, C. & Busto, B. (1987). Hybridization Between the Scarlet Ibis (*Eudocimus ruber*) and the White Ibis (*Eudocimus albus*) in Venezuela. *Colonial Waterbirds* **10(1)**: 11-114.
Ramo, C. & Busto, B. (1988). Status of the Nesting Population of the Scarlet Ibis (*Eudocimus ruber*) in the Venezuelan Llanos. *Colonial Waterbirds* **11(2)**: 311-314.

Ramón, R.F. (1987). Aves nuevas para la avifauna española: Colimbo de Adams (*Gavia adamsii*). *La Garcilla* **69**: 24-25.
Ramos, M.A. (1985a). Problems Hindering the Conservation of Tropical Forest Birds in Mexico and Central America. Pp. 67-76 in: Diamond & Lovejoy (1985).
Ramos, M.A. (1985b). Endangered Tropical Birds in Mexico and Northern Central America. Pp. 305-318 in: Diamond & Lovejoy (1985).
Ramsey, J.J. (1968). Roseate Spoonbill chick attacked by ants. *Auk* **85**: 325.
Rand, A.L. (1936). The distribution and habits of Madagascar birds. *Bull. Amer. Mus. Nat. Hist.* **72**: 143-499.
Rand, A.L. (1967). *Ornithology: An Introduction*. Penguin Books, Harmondsworth, Middlesex, UK.
Rand, A.L. & Gilliard, E.T. (1967). *Handbook of New Guinea Birds*. Weidenfeld & Nicolson, London.
Rand, R.W. (1956). Cormorants on Marion Island. *Ostrich* **27**: 127-133.
Rand, R.W. (1959). The biology of guano-producing seabirds. The distribution, abundance and feeding habits of the Cape Gannet off the South-western coast of the Cape Province. *Comm. & Industry Rep.* **39**.
Rand, R.W. (1960). The biology of guano-producing seabirds. Part 1: The distribution, abundance and feeding habits of the Cape Penguin, *Spheniscus demersus* (L.) off the South Western coast of the Cape Province. Part 3: The distribution, abundance, and feeding habits of the cormorants Phalacrocoracidae off the southwest coast of the Cape Province. *Invest. Rep. Div. Fish. Un. S. Afr.* **41**: 1-28, **42**: 1-32.
Rand, R.W. (1963a). The biology of guano-producing seabirds. 4. Composition of colonies on the Cape Islands. *Invest. Rep. Div. Sea Fish S. Afr.* **43**: 1-32.
Rand, R.W. (1963b). The biology of guano-producing seabirds. 5. Composition of colonies on the South West African Islands. *Investl. Rpt. Div. Sea Fish S. Afr.* **46**: 1-26.
Randall, R.M. (1983). Biology of the Jackass Penguin *Spheniscus demersus* (L.) at St. Croix Island, South Africa. PhD thesis, University of Port Elizabeth, South Africa.
Randall, R.M. & Davidson, I.S. (1981). Device for obtaining food samples from the stomachs of Jackass Penguins. *S. Afr. J. Wildl. Res.* **11**: 121-125.
Randall, R.M. & Randall, B.M. (1981). Annual cycle of the Jackass Penguin *Spheniscus demersus* at St. Croix Island, South Africa. Pp. 427-450 in: Cooper, J. ed. *Proc. Symp. Birds on Sea and Shore, 1979*. African Seabird Club, Cape Town.
Randall, R.M. & Randall, B.M. (1986a). The diet of Jackass Penguins *Spheniscus demersus* at Algoa Bay, South Africa, and its bearing on population declines elsewere. *Biol. Conserv.* **37**: 119-134.
Randall, R.M. & Randall, B.M. (1986b). The Kapodistrias affair - another oiling incident affecting seabirds. *Bokmakierie* **38(2)**: 37-40.
Randall, R.M. & Randall, B.M. (1986c). The seasonal occurrence of Leach's Storm Petrel at St. Croix Island, South Africa. *Ostrich* **57**: 157-161.
Randall, R.M. & Randall, B.M. (1990). Cetaceans as predators of Jackass Penguins *Spheniscus demersus*: deductions based on behaviour. *Marine Orn.* **18**: 9-12.
Randall, R.M. & Ross, G.J.B. (1979). Increasing population of Cape Gannet on Bird Island, Algoa, Bay and observations on breeding success. *Ostrich* **50**: 168-175.
Randall, R.M., Randall, B.M. & Baird, D. (1981). Speed of movement Jackass Penguins over long distances and their possible use of ocean currents. *S. Afr. J. Sci.* **77**: 420-421.
Randall, R.M., Randall, B.M. & Bevan, J. (1980). Oil pollution and penguins - is cleaning justified? *Mar. Poll. Bull.* **11**: 234-237.
Randall, R.M., Randall, B.M. & Compagno, L.J.V. (1988). Injuries to Jackass Penguin (*Spheniscus demersus*): evidence for shark involvement. *J. Zoology. London* **214**: 589-599.
Randall, R.M., Randall, B.M., Cooper, J. & Frost, P.G.H. (1986). A new census method for penguins tested on Jackass Penguins *Spheniscus demersus*. *Ostrich* **57(4)**: 211-215.
Randall, R.M., Randall, B.M., Cooper, J., La Cock, D.G. & Ross, G.J.B. (1987). Jackass Penguin *Spheniscus demersus* movements, inter-island visits, and settlement. *J. Field Orn.* **58(4)**: 445-455.
Randall, R.M., Randall, B.M. & Erasmus, T. (1986). Rain-related breeding failures in Jackass Penguins. *Gerfaut* **76**: 281-288.
Randall, R.M., Randall, B.M. & Klingelhoeffer, E.W. (1981). Species diversity and size ranges of cephalopods in the diet of Jackass Penguins from Algoa Bay, South Africa. *S. Afr. J. Zool.* **16**: 163-166.
Rands, M.R.W., Rands, G.F. & Porter, R.F. (1987). *Birds in the Yemen Arab Republic*. A Report of the Expedition of the Ornithological Society of the Middle East October-December 1985. ICBP, Cambridge, England.
Ranftl, H. (1980). Der Haubentaucher (*Podiceps cristatus*) in Bayern. *Schrift. Nat. Lands.* **12**: 159-170.
Rangel, E. & Bolen, E.G. (1984). Ecological studies of Muscovy Ducks in Mexico. *S. West. Nat.* **29**: 453-661.
Rank, M. (1991). Extinct Shelduck rediscovered in China?. *Oriental Bird Club Bull.* **14**: 14-15.
Rao, P. & Murlidharan, S. (1989). Unusual feeding behaviour of the Adjutant Stork, *Leptoptilos dubius* (Gmelin). *J. Bombay Nat. Hist. Soc.* **86**: 97.
Raol, L.M. (1988). Barheaded and Greylag Geese in Gujarat. *J. Bombay Nat. Hist. Soc.* **85(2)**: 416-417.
Rasch, G. & Kayes, P. (1985). The second Survey of the Brown Kiwi in Waitangi State Forest. Unpublished report, New Zealand Forest Service, Auckland.
Raseroka, B.H. (1975a). Diet of the Hadedah Ibis. *Ostrich* **46**: 51-54.
Raseroka, B.H. (1975b). Breeding of the Hadedah Ibis. *Ostrich* **46**: 208-212.
Rasmussen, E.V. (1979). Den sorte storks (*Ciconia nigra*) forekomst i Danmark, isaer i arene 1970-1978. [Summary: The occurrence of the Black Stork (*Ciconia nigra*) in Denmark, 1970-1978]. *Dan. Orn. Foren. Tidsskr.* **73(4)**: 265-270. In Danish with English summary.
Rasmussen, P.C. (1986a). Re-evaluation of cheek patterns of juvenal-plumaged Blue-eyed and King shags. *Condor* **88**: 393-395.
Rasmussen, P.C. (1986b). Reconsideration of the taxonomic status of the King Shag (*Phalacrocorax albiventer*). Mississippi State University: 10th Amer. Orn. Union Abstracts.
Rasmussen, P.C. (1987). Molts of the Rock Shag and new interpretations of the plumage sequence. *Condor* **89**: 760-766.
Rasmussen, P.C. (1988a). Variation in the juvenal plumage of the Red-legged Shag (*Phalacrocorax gaimardi*) and notes on behavior of juveniles. *Wilson Bull.* **100(4)**: 535-544.
Rasmussen, P.C. (1988b) Stepwise molt of the remiges in Blue-eyed and King shags. *Condor* **90**: 220-227.
Rasmussen, P.C. (1988c). Moults of rectrices and body plumage of Blue-eyed and King Shags (*Phalacrocorax atriceps* and *Phalacrocorax albiventer*) and phenology of moults. *Notornis* **35**: 129-142.
Rasmussen, P.C. (1989). Post-landing Displays of Chilean Blue-eyed Shags at a Cliff-nesting Colony. *Bird Behaviour* **8(1)**: 51-54.
Rasmussen, P.C. & Humphrey, P.S. (1988). Wing-spreading in Chilean Blue-eyed Shags (*Phalacrocorax atriceps*). *Wilson Bull.* **100(1)**: 140-144.
Ratti, J.T. (1977). *Reproductive Separation and Isolating Mechanisms between Sympatric Dark- and Light-phase Western Grebes*. PhD dissertation. Utah State University, Logan, Utah.
Ratti, J.T. (1979). Reproductive Separation and Isolating Mechanisms between Sympatric Dark- and Light-phase Western Grebes. *Auk* **96**: 573-586.
Ratti, J.T. (1981). Identification and distribution of Clark's Grebe. *Western Birds* **12**: 41-46.
Ratti, J.T. (1985). A test of water depth niche partitioning by Western Grebe color morphs. *Auk* **102**: 635-637.
Ratti, J.T. (1986). Identification and distribution of Clark's Grebe. *Loon* **58**: 112-116.
Ratti, J.T., McCabe, T.R. & Smith, L.M. (1983). Morphological Divergence between Western Grebe color morphs. *J. Field Orn.* **54(4)**: 424-426.
Raud, H. & Faure, J.M. (1988). Etude descriptive du comportement sexuel du Canard de Barbarie (*Cairina moschata*). *Biol. Behav.* **13**: 175-189.
Rauzon, M.J. (1985). Leucism in a great frigatebird and sooty tern. *Elepaio* **46(3)**: 19-20.
Rauzon, M.J., Harrison, C.S. & Conant, S. (1985). The status of the sooty storm-petrel in Hawaii. *Wilson Bull.* **97**: 390-392.
Raveling, D.G. (1969). Roost sites and flight patterns of Canada Geese in winter. *J. Wildl. Manage.* **33**: 319-330.
Raveling, D.G. (1970). Dominance relationships and agonistic behavior of Canada Geese in winter. *Behaviour* **37**: 291-319.
Raveling, D.G. (1979). The annual cycle of body composition of Canada Geese with special reference to control of reproduction. *Auk* **96**: 234-252.
Raveling, D.G., Crews, W.E. & Klimstra, W.D. (1972). Activity patterns of Canada Geese during winter. *Wilson Bull.* **84**: 278-295.
Raveling, D.G., Nichols, J.D., Hines, J.E., Zezulak, D.S., Silveira, J.G., Johnson, J.C., Aldrich, T.W. & Weldon, J.A. (1992). Survival of cackling Canada Geese, 1982-1988. *J. Wildl. Manage.* **56 (1)**: 63-73.
Rawls, C.K. (1949). *An Investigation of the Life History of the White-winged Scoter (*Melanitta fusca deglandi*).* MSc thesis, University of Minnesota, Minneapolis, MN.
Rayner, J.M.V. (1988). Form and function in avian flight. *Current Ornithology* **5**: 1-77.
Ream, C.H. (1976). Loon productivity, human disturbance, and pesticide residues in northern Minnesota. *Wilson Bull.* **88**: 427-432.
Rech, F.G. (1984). Observaçoes sobre a procriaçao do inambu-guacu ("*Crypturellus obsoletus*") en cativerio. *Subornis* **5**: 5-9.
Recher, H.F. (1972). Territorial and agonistic behaviour of the Reef Heron. *Emu* **72(4)**: 126-130.
Recher, H.F. & Holmes, R.T. (1982). (Nycticorax caledonicus). *Tech. Memo 4 Superv. Scient. Alligator Rs.*
Recher, H.F. & Recher, J.A. (1969). Comparative foraging efficiency of adult and inmature Little Blue Herons (*Florida caerulea*). *Anim. Behav.* **17**: 320-322.
Recher, H.F. & Recher, J.A. (1972). The foraging behaviour of the Reef Heron. *Emu* **72(3)**: 85-90.
Recher, H.F. & Recher, J.A. (1980). (Egretta rufescens). *Trans NY Linnean Soc.* **10**: 135-158.
Recher, H.F., Holmes, R.T., Davis, Jr., W.E. & Morton, S. (1983). Foraging Behavior of Australian Herons. *Colonial Waterbirds* **6**: 1-10.
Rechten, C. (1986). Factors determining the laying date of the Waved Albatross. *Ibis* **128**: 492-502.
Reed, A. (1970). *The Breeding Ecology of the Black Duck in the St. Lawrence Estuary*. Unpublished DSc thesis, Laval University, Quebec.
Reed, A. ed. (1986). Eider Ducks in Canada. *Can. Wildl. Serv. Rep. Series* **47**.
Reed, A. (1990). Population dynamics in a successful species: challenges in managing the increasing population of Greater Snow Geese. *Trans. Congr. Int. Union Game Biol.* **19** (1): 136-142.
Reed, A. & Erskine, A.J. (1986). Populations of the Common Eider in eastern North America: their size and status. *Can. Wildl. Serv. Rep. Ser.* **47**: 156-175.
Reed, C.S. (1919). Breves notas acerca de nidos y huevos de algunas aves de la cordillera de Mendoza. *Hornero* **1(4)**: 267-273.
Rees, E.C. (1989). Consistency in the Timing of Migration for individual Bewick's Swans. *Anim. Behav.* **38(3)**: 384-393.
Regnell, S. (1957). En liten fågelsjö i Östergötland met häckande Svarthalsad dopping (*Podiceps nigricollis*). *Vår Fågelvärld* **16**: 299-303.
Regnell, S. (1981a). Häckningsbeståndet av svarthakedopping *Podiceps auritus* i Sverige. [Summary: The breeding population of the Horned Grebe in Sweden]. *Vår Fågelvärld* **40**: 13-22.
Regnell, S. (1981b). Att taxera häckningsbestånd av Svarthakedopping *Podiceps auritus*. *Vår Fågelvärld* **40**: 23-32.
Reichel, J.D. (1991). Status and Conservation of Seabirds in the Mariana Islands. Pp. 249-262 in: Croxall *et al.* (1991).
Reichholf, J. (1988). Gehört der Zwergtaucher *Tachybaptus ruficollis* in die Rote Liste der gefährdeten Brutvögel Bayerns? [Summary: Should the Little Grebe *Tachybaptus ruficollis* be placed onto the Bavarian "Red List" of endangered breeding birds?]. *Anz. orn. Ges. Bayern* **27**: 275-284.
Reid, B. (1971a). Composition of a kiwi egg. *Notornis* **18**: 250-252.
Reid, B. (1971b). The weight of the kiwi and its egg. *Notornis* **18**: 245-249.
Reid, B. (1977). The energy value of the yolk reserve in a North Island brown kiwi chick. *Notornis* **24**: 194-195.
Reid, B. (1978). The little spotted kiwi - a hunted and destroyed species. *Forest & Bird* **210**: 29-32.
Reid, B. (1979). History of domestication of the Cassowary in Mendi Valley, Papua New Guinea. *Ethnomed* **5**: 407-429.
Reid, B. (1981). Size discrepancy between eggs of wild and captive Brown Kiwi. *Notornis* **28**: 281-287.
Reid, B. (1982a). The Cassowary and the Highlanders. A Present day contribution and value to village life of a traditionally important wildlife resource in New Guinea. *Ethnomed* **7**: 149-240.
Reid, B. (1982b). Cassowaries as currency. *New Zealand J. Ecol.* **5**: 152-153.
Reid, B. (1985). The Kiwi. Pp. 36-39 in: Robertson (1985).
Reid, B. (1987). Food intake and growth rate of Cassowary chicks reared at Mendi, Southern Highland Papua New Guinea. *Int. Zoo Yb.* **26**: 189-198.
Reid, B. & Roderick, C. (1973). New Zealand Scaup *Aythya novae-seelandiae* and Brown Teal *Anas aucklandica chlorotis* in captivity. *Int. Zoo Yb.* **13**: 12-15.
Reid, B. & Rowe, B. (1978). *Management of Kiwis in Captivity*. Otorohanga Zoological Society Progress Report. Otorohanga, New Zealand.
Reid, B. & Williams, G.R. (1975). The kiwi. Pp. 301-330 in: Kuschel, G. ed. *Biogeography and Ecology in New Zealand*. Junk, The Hague.
Reid, B., Ordish, R.G. & Harrison, M. (1982). An analysis of the gizzard contents of 50 North Island brown kiwis, *Apteryx australis mantelli*, and notes on feeding observations. *New Zealand J. Ecol.* **5**: 76-85.
Reig, G. (1988). Los albatros. In: Cabal, G.B. ed. (1988). *Fauna Argentina. Aves*. Vol. 6. Centro Editor de América Latina, Buenos Aires.
Reilly, P.N. & Cullen, J.M. (1979). The Little Penguin, *Eudyptula minor* in Victoria, I: Mortality of adults. *Emu* **79**: 97-102.
Reilly, P.N. & Cullen, J.M. (1981). The Little Penguin, *Eudyptula minor* in Victoria, II: Breeding. *Emu* **81**: 1-19.
Reilly, P.N. & Cullen, J.M. (1982). The Little Penguin, *Eudyptula minor* in Victoria, III: Dispersal of chicks and survival after banding. *Emu* **82**: 137-142.
Reilly, P.N. & Cullen, J.M. (1983). The Little Penguin, *Eudyptula minor* in Victoria, IV: Moult. *Emu* **83**: 94-98.
Reilly, P.N. & Kerle, A. (1981). A study of the Gentoo Penguin *Pygoscelis papua*. *Notornis* **28**: 189-202.
Reimchen, T.E. & Douglas, S. (1984). Feeding schedule and daily consumption in red-throated loons (*Gavia stellata*) over the prefledging period. *Auk* **101**: 593-599.
Reinhard, R. (1983). Andenflamingos gezüchtet!. *Gefiederte Welt* **108**: 24.
Remsen, J.V. (1986). Aves de una localidad en la sabana húmeda del norte de Bolivia. *Ecología en Bolivia* **8**: 21-35.
Remsen, J.V. & Traylor, M.A. (1989). *An Annotated List of the Birds of Bolivia*. Buteo Books, Vermillion, S.D.
Rencurel, P. (1974). L'ibis chauve *Geronticus eremita* dans le Moyen-Atlas. *Alauda* **42**: 143-158.
Renevey, B. (1987). Effectifs et évolution de la population nicheuse de Grèbes huppés, *Podiceps cristatus*, sur la rive Sud-Est du lac de Neuchâtel. *Nos oiseaux* **39**: 113-128.
Renevey, B. (1988). Écologie de la reproduction du Grèbe huppé, *Podiceps cristatus*, sur la rive sud-est du lac de Neuchâtel: 1. partie: la nidification. *Alauda* **56(4)**: 330-349.
Renevey, B. (1989a). Écologie de la reproduction du Grèbe huppé, *Podiceps cristatus*, sur la Rive sud-est du Lac de Neuchâtel: 2. partie: l'élevage des jeunes. *Alauda* **57(2)**: 92-107.
Renevey, B. (1989b). Écologie de l'alimentation du Grèbe huppé, *Podiceps cristatus*, pendant la période de reproduction, sur le lac de Neuchâtel. *Nos Oiseaux* **40**: 141-152.
Renevey, B. (1989c). Budget d'activité et rayon d'action des Grèbes huppés, *Podiceps cristatus*, pendant la période de reproduction sur le lac de Neuchuâtel. *Nos Oiseaux* **40**: 193-202.
Rengstorf, D. (1990). A White-faced Ibis in Dakota and Hennepin counties. *Loon* **62**: 154-156.
van Rensburg, P.J.J. (1985). The feeding ecology of a decreasing Feral House Cat population at Marion Island. Pp. 620-624 in: Siegfried, W.R., Condy, P.R. & Laws, R.M. eds. *Antarctic Nutrient Cycles and Food Webs*. Springer, Berlin.
van Rensburg, P.J.J. & Bester, M.N. (1988). The effect of cat *Felis catus* predation on three breeding Procellariidae species on Marion Island. *S. Afr. J. Zool.* **23**: 301-305.
Rensenbrink, H.P. (1981). [Marabous]. *Artis. Amsterdam* **27(3)**: 100-107. In Dutch.
Reverdin, Y. & Géroudet, P. (1979). Nidifications du Grèbe castagneux, *Podiceps ruficollis* au port de Genève. *Nos Oiseaux* **35**: 25-30.
Reville, B.J. (1980). *Spatial and temporal aspects of breeding in the frigatebirds* Fregata minor *and* F. ariel. PhD thesis, Aberdeen University.
Reville, B.J. (1983). Numbers of nesting frigatebirds, *Fregata minor* and *F. ariel*, on Aldabra Atoll Nature Reserve, Seychelles. *Biol. Conserv.* **27**: 59-76.
Reville, B.J. (1988). Effects of spacing and synchrony on breeding success in the Great Frigatebird (*Fregata minor*). *Auk* **105**: 252-259.
Reville, B.J., Tranter, J.D. & Yorkston, H.D. (1990). Timing of primary moult in the tropical seabird *Sula abbotti*. *Emu* **90(4)**: 266-268.
Reville, R., Tranter, J. & Yorkston, H. (1987). *Monitoring the endangered Abbott's Booby on Christmas Island 1983-1986*. Occasional paper no. 11. Australian National Parks and Wildlife Service, Canberra.
Reynolds, J. (1965). Association between Little Egret and African Spoonbill. *British Birds* **58**: 468.
Rezende, M.A. (1987). Comportamento associativo de *Fregata magnificens* (Fregatidae, Aves) e *Sula leucogaster* (Sulidae, Aves) no litoral centro-norte do Estado de São Paulo. *Bol. Inst. Oceanogr.* **35(1)**: 1-5.
Rheinwald, G., Ogden, J.C. & Schulz, H. eds. (1989). *Proc. Int. Stork Symp.* **1985**. Walsrode, Germany.
Rice, D.W. (1959). Birds and aircraft on Midway Islands: 1957-58 investigations. *US Fish & Wildl. Serv. Spec. Sci. Rep. Wildl.* **44**: 1-49.
Rice, D.W. (1984a). Albatrosses. Family Diomedeidae. Pp. 32-41 in: Haley (1984).
Rice, D.W. (1984b). Boobies. Family Sulidae. Pp. 74-83 in: Haley (1984).
Rice, D.W. & Kenyon, K.W. (1962a). Breeding distribution, history and populations of North Pacific albatrosses. *Auk* **79**: 365-386.
Rice, D.W. & Kenyon, K.W. (1962b). Breeding cycles and behavior of Laysan and Black- footed Albatrosses. *Auk* **79**: 517-567.
Rich, P. & Balouet, J. (1984). The waifs and strays of the bird world or the Ratite problem revisited, one more time. Pp. 447-456 in: Archer, M. & Clayton, G. eds. *Vertebrate Zoogeography and Evolution in Australasia*.

Rich, P.V. (1976). The history of birds on the island continent Australia. Pp. 53-65 in: *Proc. XVI Int. Orn. Congr.*
Richard, E. & Laredo, C. (1988). A *Jabiru mycteria* record outside its usual range, Mendoza Prov. (Argentina). *Nuestras Aves Bol. Asoc. Orn. del Plata* **15**: 12-13.
Richards, A. (1990). *Seabirds of the Northern Hemisphere*. Dragons World.
Richards, D.K. (1979). Unusual feeding habits of Hammerkop, *Scopus umbretta*. *East Afr. Nat. Hist. Bull.* 1979: 93.
Richardson, C. (1990). *The Birds of the United Arab Emirates*. Hobby Publications, Dubai & Warrington.
Richardson, D.M. (1984). Hadeda in the Jonkershoek Valley, Stellenbosch. *Promerops* **162**: 6.
Richardson, F. & Woodside, D.H. (1954). Rediscovery of the nesting of the Dark-rumped Petrel in the Hawaiian Islands. *Condor* **56**: 323-327.
Richardson, M.C., Heubeck, M., Lea, D. & Reynolds, P. (1982). Oil pollution, seabirds and operational consequences around the northern isles of Scotland. *Environ. Conserv.* **9**: 315-321.
Richardson, M.E. (1984). Aspects of the ornithology of the Tristan da Cunha Group and Gough Island, 1972-1974. *Cormorant* **12**: 123-201.
Richdale, L.E. (1939). A Royal Albatross nesting on the Otago Peninsula, New Zealand. *Emu* **38**: 467-488.
Richdale, L.E. (1940). Random notes on the genus *Eudyptula* on the Otago Peninsula, New Zealand. *Emu* **40**: 180-217.
Richdale, L.E. (1941a). The Erect-crested Penguin (*Eudyptes sclateri* Buller). *Emu* **41**: 25-53.
Richdale, L.E. (1941b). A brief summary of the history of the Yellow-eyed Penguin. *Emu* **41**: 265-285.
Richdale, L.E. (1942). Supplementary notes on the Royal Albatross. *Emu* **41**: 169-184; 253-263.
Richdale, L.E. (1943a). The White-faced Storm Petrel or Takahi-kare-moana (*Pelagodroma marina maoriana*, Mathews). *Trans. Proc. Royal Soc. N.Z.* **73**: 97-115, 217-232, 335-350.
Richdale, L.E. (1943b). The Kuaka, or diving petrel. *Emu* **43**: 24-48, 97-107.
Richdale, L.E. (1944a). The Titi Wainui or Fairy Prion. *Trans. Royal Soc. New Zealand* **74**: 32-48; 165-181.
Richdale, L.E. (1944b). The Parara or Broad-billed Prion. *Emu* **43**: 191-217.
Richdale, L.E. (1944c). The Sooty Shearwater in New Zealand. *Condor* **46**: 93-107.
Richdale, L.E. (1945). Supplementary notes on the Diving Petrel. *Trans. Royal Soc. New Zealand* **75**: 42-53.
Richdale, L.E. (1948). *Maori and Mutton-bird*. Author, Dunedin.
Richdale, L.E. (1949). *The Pre-egg Stage in Buller's Mollymawk*. Biological Monographs **2**. Author, Dunedin.
Richdale, L.E. (1950a). Further notes on the Erect-crested Penguin. *Emu* **49**: 153-166.
Richdale, L.E. (1950b). The pre-egg stage in the albatross family. Biological Monographs. **3**. Author, Dunedin.
Richdale, L.E. (1951). *Sexual Behaviour in Penguins*. Lawrence, Kansas, Kansas University.
Richdale, L.E. (1952). *Post-egg Period in Albatrosses*. Biological Monographs. **4**. Author, Dunedin.
Richdale, L.E. (1954). The starvation theory in albatrosses. *Auk* **71**: 239-252.
Richdale, L.E. (1955). Influence of age on size of eggs in Yellow-eyed Penguins. *Ibis* **97**: 266-275.
Richdale, L.E. (1957). *A Population Study of Penguins*. Oxford University Press, Cambridge, England.
Richdale, L.E. (1963). Biology of the Sooty Shearwater. *Proc. Zool. Soc. London* **141**: 1-117.
Richdale, L.E. (1965a). Biology of the birds of Whero Island, New Zealand, with special reference to the diving petrel and the White-faced Storm Petrel. *Trans. Zool. Soc. London* **31**: 1-86.
Richdale, L.E. (1965b). Breeding behavior of the Narrow-billed and the Broad-billed Prion on Whero island, New Zealand. *Trans. Zool. Soc. London* **31**: 87-155.
Richdale, L.E. (1985). Yellow-eyed Penguin. Page 42 in: Robertson (1985).
Richdale, L.E. & Warham, J. (1973). Survival, Pair bond retention and nest-site tenacity in Buller's Mollymawk. *Ibis* **115**: 257-263.
Richter, N.A., Bourne, G.R. & Diebold, E.N. (1991). Gender determination by body weight and linear measurements in American and Chilean Flamingos, previously surgically sexed: within-sex comparison to Greater Flamingo measurements. *Zool. Biol.* **105(4)**: 425-431.
Ricketts, C. & Prince, P.A. (1981). Comparison of growth of albatrosses. *Ornis Scand.* **12**: 120-124.
Ricklefs, R.E. (1983a). Comparative avian demography. *Current Ornithology* **1**: 1-32.
Ricklefs, R.E. (1983b). Avian postnatal development. Pp. 1-83 in: Farner, D.S., King, J.R. & Parkes, K.C. (1983). *Avian Biology*. Vol. 7. Academic Press, London & New York.
Ricklefs, R.E. (1984). Meal sizes and feeding rates of Christmas Shearwaters and Phoenix Petrels on Christmas Island, Central Pacific Ocean. *Ornis Scand* **15**: 16-22.
Ricklefs, R.E. & Roby, D.D. (1983). Development of homeothermy in the diving petrels *Pelecanoides urinatrix exsul* and *P. georgicus* and the Antarctic Prion *Pachyptila desolata*. *Comp Biochem Physiol* **75A**: 307-311.
Ricklefs, R.E., Day, C.H. Huntington, C.E. & Williams, J.B. (1985). Variability in feeding rate and meal size of Leach's Storm-petrel at Kent Island, New Brunswick. *J. Anim. Ecol.* **54**: 566-575.
Ricklefs, R.E., Duffy, D.C. & Coulter, M.C. (1984). Weight gain of Blue-footed Booby chicks: an indicator of marine resources. *Ornis Scand.* **15**: 162-166.
Ricklefs, R.E., Place, A.R. & Anderson, D.J. (1987). An experimental investigation of the influence of diet quality on growth rate in Leach's Storm- Petrel. *Amer. Naturalist* **130**: 300-305.
Ricklefs, R.E., Roby, D.D. & Williams, J.B. (1986). Daily energy expenditure by adult Leach's Storm-Petrels during the nesting cycles. *Physiol. Zool.* **59**: 649-660.
Ricklefs, R.E., White, S. & Cullen, J. (1980). Postnatal development of Leach's Storm-petrel. *Auk* **97**: 768-781.
Ridgely, R.S. & Gwynne, J.A. (1989). *A Guide to the Birds of Panama with Costa Rica, Nicaragua, and Honduras*. 2nd. edition. Princeton University press, Princeton, New Jersey.
Ridgill, S.C. & Fox, A.D. (1990). *Cold Weather Movements of Waterfowl in Western Europe*. IWRB, Slimbridge, England.
Ridgway, R. (1884). Remarks upon the close relationship between the white and scarlet ibises (*Eudocimus albus* and *E. ruber*). *Auk* **1**: 239-240.
Ridlehuber, K.T. (1980). *Wood Duck Production and Habitat Use*. PhD thesis, Texas A & M University, College Station.
Ridley, M.W., Moss, B.L. & Percy, R.C. (1955). The food of the flamingo in Kenya Colony. *J. East Afr. Nat. Hist. Soc.* **22**: 147-158.
Ridoux, V. & Offredo, C. (1989). The diets of five summer breeding seabirds in Adelie Land, Antarctica. *Polar Biol* **9**: 137-145.
Ridoux, V., Jouventin, P., Stahl, J.C. & Weimerskirch, H. (1988). Ecologie alimentaire comparée des manchots nicheurs aux Iles Crozet. *Rev. Ecol. (Terre Vie)* **43**: 17-27.
Riegner, M.F. (1982a). The Diet of Yellow-crowned Night-Herons in the Eastern and Southern United States. *Colonial Waterbirds* **5**: 173-176.
Riegner, M.F. (1982b). Prey Handling in Yellow-crowned Night Herons. *Auk* **99(2)**: 380-381.
Rieta Reig, A. (1969). Sobre un ejemplar de *Aechmophorus major* conservado en Valencia. *Ardeola* **13**: 233-235.
Riggert, T.L. (1977). *The Biology of the Mountain Duck on Rottnest Island, Western Australia*. Wildlife Monographs **52**.
Rijke, A.M. (1968). The water repellency and feather structure of cormorants, Phalacrocoracidae. *J. Exp. Biol.* **48**: 185-189.
Rijke, A.M., Jesser, W.A. & Mahoney, S.A. (1989). Plumage wettability of the African Darter *Anhinga melanogaster* compared with the Double-crested Cormorant *Phalacrocorax auritus*. *Ostrich* **60**: 128-132.
Riley, J.H. (1938). Birds from Siam and the Malay Peninsula in the United States National Museum collected by Drs. Hugh M. Smith and William L. Abbott. *US Natl. Mus. Bull.* **172**.
Ringelman, J.K. (1980). *The Breeding Ecology of the Black Duck in South-central Maine*. PhD thesis, University of Maine, Orono.
Ripley, S.D. (1942). A review of the species *Anas castanea*. *Auk* **59**: 90-99.
Ripley, S.D. (1960). Laysan Teal in captivity. *Wilson Bull.* **72**: 244-247.
Ripley, S.D. (1964). Systematic & Ecolog. N. Guinea.
Ripley, S.D. (1965). Saving the Nene, world's rarest goose. *Natl. Geogr.* **November 1965**: 745-754.
Ripley, S.D. (1973). Saving the Wood Duck *Aix sponsa* through captive breeding. *Int. Zoo Yb* **13**: 55-58.
Ripley, S.D. (1982). *A Synopsis of the Birds of India and Pakistan*. Bombay Natural History Society, Bombay.
Ripley, S.D. & Bond, G.M. (1966). The birds of Socotra and Abd-el-Kuri. *Smithson. Misc. Coll.* **151(7)**: 1-37.
Risdon, D.H.S. (1969). The breeding of Scarlet Ibis. *Avicult. Mag.* **75**: 165-167.
Risdon, D.H.S. (1971). Breeding the Sacred Ibis and the Scarlet Ibis *Threskiornis aethiopica* and *Eudocimus ruber* at the Tropical Bird Gardens, Rode. *Int. Zoo Yb.* **11**: 131-132.
Ristow, D. & Wink, M. (1980). Sexual dimorphism of Cory's Shearwater. *Il-Merill* **21**: 9-12.
Ristow, D., Feldmann, F., Scharlau, W., Wink, M. (1990). Population structure, philopatry and mortality of Cory's Shearwater *Calonectris d. diomedea*. *Vogelwelt* **111**: 172-181.
Riveros-Salcedo, J.C., Aparicio, J.J. & Sanchez, R. (1991). Aves de las islas San Gallan, Paracas; Peru. *Volante Migratorio* **16**: 24-26.
Riveros-Salcedo, J.C. & Aparicio, J.J. (1990). The Peruvian Diving Petrel in Peru. *Pacific Seabird Group Bull.* **17**: 32-33.
Roalkvam, R. (1985). Smålomens *Gavia stellata* og storlomens *G. arctica* hekkeutbredelse i Norge. *Vår Fuglefauna* **8(1)**: 23-27.
Robb, J.R. (1986). *The importance of nesting cavities and brood habitat to Wood Duck production*. MSc thesis, Ohio State University, Columbus.
Robbins, C.S. & Rice, D.W. (1974). Recoveries of banded Laysan Albatrosses and Black-footed Albatrosses. *Smithson. Contr. Zool.* **158**: 232-277.
Robbins, M.B., Parker III, T.A. & Allen, S.E. (1985). The avifauna of Cerro Pirre, Darién, Eastern Panama. Pp. 198-232 in: Buckley *et al.* (1985).
Roberson, D. & Bailey, S. (1991). Cookilaria petrels in the Eastern Pacific Ocean: identification and distribution. Part I of a two-parts series. *Amer. Birds* **45(3)**: 399-403.
Roberts, B. (1940). The life cycle of Wilson's Petrel. *Br. Graham Land Exped. Scient. Rep.* **1**(2): 141-194.
Roberts, C.L. & Roberts, S.L. (1973). Survival rate of Yellow-eyed Penguin egg and chicks on the Otago Peninsula. *Notornis* **20(1)**: 1-5.
Roberts, G.J. (1977). Birds and conservation in Queensland. *Sunbird* **8(4)**: 73-82.
Roberts, R.C. (1979). The evolution of avian food-storing behavior. *Amer. Natur.* **114**: 418-438.
Roberts, T.J. (1969). A note on *Ciconia nigra* (Linnaeus) in West Pakistan. *J. Bombay Nat. Hist. Soc.* **66**: 616-619.
Roberts, T.J. (1989). Recent ornithological records from Pakistan. *J. Bombay Nat. Hist. Soc.* **86 (2)**: 135-140.
Roberts, T.J. (1991). *The Birds of Pakistan*. Vol. 1. Oxford University Press, Karachi.
Robertson, C.J. & Jenkins, J. (1981). Birds seen at sea in southern New Zealand waters, February-June 1981. *Australasian Seabird Group Newsl.* **16**: 17-29.
Robertson, C.J.R. (1974). Albatrosses of the Chatham Islands. *Wildlife - a Review*, Wellington, **5**: 20-22.
Robertson, C.J.R. (1976). The Campbell Island Teal. *Wildflife - a review* **7**: 45-46.
Robertson, C.J.R. ed. (1985). *Complete Book of New Zealand Birds*. Reader's Digest, Sidney.
Robertson, C.J.R. & Bell, B.D. (1984). Seabird Status and Conservation in the New Zealand Region. Pp. 573-586 in: Croxall *et al.* (1984).
Robertson, C.J.R. & James, P.C. (1988). Morphology and egg measurements of seabirds breeding on Grand Salvage Island, North Atlantic. *Bull. Brit. Orn. Club* **108**: 79-87.
Robertson, C.J.R. & Kinsky, F.C. (1972). The dispersal movements of the Royal Albatross. *Notornis* **19**: 289-301.
Robertson, C.J.R. & Kinsky, F.C. (1985). Adélie Penguin. Page 43 in: Robertson (1985).
Robertson, C.J.R. & van Tets, G.F. (1982). The status of birds at the Bounty Islands. *Notornis* **29**: 311-336.
Robertson, C.J.R. & Wright, A. (1973). Successful hand-rearing of an abandoned Royal Albatross chick. *Notornis* **20**: 49-58.
Robertson, G. (1986). Population size and breeding success of the Gentoo Penguin, *Pygoscelis papua*, at Macquarie Island. *Austr. Wild. Res.* **13**: 583-587.
Robertson, G., Green, B. & Newgrain, K. (1988). Estimating feeding rates and energy requirements of Gentoo Penguins *Pygoscelis papua* at Macquarie Island. *Polar Biol.* **9**: 89-93.
Robertson, H.A. & Preece, B.E. (1980). Juvenile Royal Spoonbills at the Manawatu Estuary. *Notornis* **27(2)**: 170-171.
Robertson, H.G. (1981). Group foraging and diurnal activity of Blackheaded Grebes at sea. *Ostrich* **52**: 248-250.
Robertson, H.G. & Johnson, P.G. (1979). First record of greater and lesser flamingos breeding in Botswana. *Botswana Notes Rec.* **11**: 115-119.
Robertson, I. (1971). *The Influence of Brood-size on Reproductive Succes in Two Species of Cormorant*, Phalacrocorax auritus *and* P. pelagicus, *and its relation to the problem of clutch size*. Unpublished MSc. thesis, Vancouver, University British Columbia.
Robertson, I. (1974). The food of nesting Double-crested and Pelagic Cormorants at Mandarte Island, British Columbia, with notes on feeding ecology. *Condor* **76**: 346-348.
Robertson, W.B., Breen, L.L. & Patty, B.W. (1983). Movement of marked Roseate Spoonbills in Florida with a review of present distribution. *J. Field Orn.* **54**: 225-236.
Robiller, F. & Trogisch, K. (1986a). Über den Schwarzstorch und seine Zucht im Vogelpark. *Gefierdete Welt* **110(7)**: 189-191.
Robiller, F. & Trogisch, K. (1986b). Haltung und Zucht von Löfflern im Vogelpark. *Gefiederte Welt* **110**: 266-269.
Robin, P. (1973). Comportement des colonies des *Geronticus eremita* dans le sud Marocain, lors des périodes de sécheresse. *Bonn. zool. Beitr.* **24**: 317-322.
Robinson, A.C., Delroy, L.B. & Jenkins, R.B. (1982). *The Conservation and Management of the Cape Barren Goose* Cereopsis novaehollandiae *Latham in South Australia*. National Parks & Wildlife Service, Department of Environment & Planning South Australia. Special Publication **1**.
Robinson, E.R. & Seely, M.K. (1975). Some food plants of ostriches in the Namib Desert Park, South West Africa. *Madoqua (Ser. II)* **4(74-80)**: 99-100.
Robinson, F.N. & Robinson, A.H. (1970). Regional variation in the visual and acoustic signals of the male Musk Duck, *Biziura lobata*. *CSIRO Wildl. Res.* **15**: 73-78.
Robinson, H.C. & Kloss, C.B. (1910, 1911). On birds from the northern portion of the Malay peninsula including the islands of Langkawi and Teratau. *Ibis* **52**: 659-675; **53**: 10-79.
Robinson, J.C. (1988). First record of Ross' Goose in Tennessee. *Migrant* **59(4)**: 114-115.
Robinson, J.C. (1991). Ross' Goose (*Chen Rossii*). *Passenger Pigeon* **53(2)**: 189.
Robinson, L.N. (1961). The feeding of Fairy Prions. *Austr. Bird Watcher* **1**: 156-157.
Robisson, P. (1990). The importance of the temporal pattern of syllables and the syllable structure of display calls for individual recognition in the genus *Aptenodytes*. *Behav. Processes* **22**: 157-163.
Robisson, P., Aubin, T. Brémond, J.C. (1989). La reconnaissance individuelle chez le Manchot Empereur (*Aptenodytes forsteri*): rôles respectifs du découpage temporel et de la structure sylabique du chant de cour. *C. R. Acad. Sci. Paris* **309(III)**: 383-388.
Roby, D.D. (1989). Chick feeding in the diving petrels *Pelecanoides georgicus* and *P. urinatrix exsul*. *Antarctic Science* **1**(4): 337-342.
Roby, D.D. & Ricklefs, R.E. (1983). Some aspects of the breeding biology of the diving petrels *Pelecanoides georgicus* and *P. urinatrix exsul* at Bird Island, South Georgia. *Brit. Antarct. Surv. Bull.* **59**: 29-34.
Roby, D.D. & Ricklefs, R.E. (1984). Observations on the cooling tolerance of embryos of the Diving Petrel *Pelecanoides georgicus*. *Auk* **101**(1): 160-161.
Rodgers, J.A. (1976). Spread-wing sunbathing by juvenile White-faced Ibis. *Auk* **93**: 375-376.
Rodgers, J.A. (1977). (Egretta tricolor). *Wilson Bull.* **89**: 266-285.
Rodgers, J.A. (1978). Display characteristics and Frequency of Breedings by Subadult Little Blue Herons. Pp. 35-40 in: Sprunt *et al.* (1978).
Rodgers, J.A. (1983). Foraging behaviour of Seven Species of Herons in Tampa Bay, Florida. *Colonial Waterbirds* **6**: 11-23.
Rodgers, J.A. (1990). Breeding chronology and clutch information for the Wood Stork from museum collections. *J. Field Orn.* **61**: 47-53.
Rodgers, J.A., Wenner, A.S. & Schwikert, S.T. (1987). Population Dynamics of Wood Storks in North and Central Florida, USA. *Colonial Waterbirds* **10(2)**: 151-156.
Rodgers, J.A., Wenner, A.S. & Schwikert, S.T. (1988). The uses and function of green nest material by Wood Storks. *Wilson Bull.* **100**: 411-423.
Rodhouse, P.G., Clarke, M.R. & Murray, A.W.A. (1987). Cephalopod prey of the Wandering Albatross. *Mar. Biol.* **96**: 1-10.
Rodriguez dos Santos, M. & Canavate, J.P. (1985). Sélection des proies par le Héron pourpré *Ardea purpurea* pendant la période de reproduction dans les marais du Guadalquivir (Espagne). *L'Oiseau et la R.F.O.* **55(3)**: 195-203.
Rodway, M.S. (1991). Status and Conservation of Breeding Seabirds in British Columbia. Pp. 43-102 in: Croxall (1991).
Rogers, J.P. (1979). *Branta bernicla hrota* in the USA - a management review. Pp. 198-212 in: Smart, M. ed. *Proceedings First Technical Meeting on Western Palearctic Migratory Bird Management, Paris 1977*. IWRB, Slimbridge, England.
Rogers, J.P., Nichols, J.D., Martin, F.W., Kimball, C.F. & Pospahala, R.S. (1979). An examination of harvest and survival rates of ducks in relation to hunting. *Trans. N. Amer. Wildl. & Nat. Res. Conf.* **44**: 114-126.
Rohwer, F.C. (1988). Inter- and intraspecific relationships between egg size and clutch size in waterfowl. *Auk* **105**: 161-176.
Rohwer, F.C. (1989). Egg mass and clutch size relationships in geese, eiders and swans. *Ornis Scand.* **20(1)**: 43-48.
Rohwer, S. (1990). Foraging differences between white and dark morphs of the Pacific Reef Heron *Egretta sacra*. *Ibis* **132**: 21-26.
Romanoff, A.L. & Romanoff, A.J. (1949). *The Avian Egg*. John Wiley and Sons, New York.
Romanov, P.N. (1987). [Pelican Island]. *Priroda. Moscow* **1987(7)**: 34-41. In Russian.
Romer, A.S. (1970). *The Vertebrate Body*. W.B. Saunders, Philadelphia.
Root, A. (1963). Notes on the feeding habits of the Openbill Stork *Anastomus lamelligerus*. *Ibis* **105**: 399-400.
Rooth, J. (1965). *The Flamingos of Bonaire (Netherlands Antilles). Habitat, Diet and Reproduction of* Phoenicopterus ruber ruber. Natuurwetensch. Stud. Suriname en Ned. Antillen, Utrecht **41**: 1-151.
Rooth, J. (1971). The occurrence of the Greylag Goose *Anser anser* in the western part of its distribution area. *Ardea* **59**: 17-27.

Rooth, J. (1976). Ecological aspects of the flamingos on Bonaire. *Stinapa* **11**: 16-33.
Roozendaal, D. (1988). *Waarnemingen aan de paarvorming van de Rode Ibis (*Eudocimus ruber*) in de dierentuin Artis, Amsterdam.* Doctoraal verslag. Afdeling Diergedrag, Universiteit an Amsterdam.
Rose, A.B. (1973). Food of some Australian birds. *Emu* **73**: 177-183.
Rose, P.J. (1974). Some visits to Ascension Island. *Sea Swallow* **23**: 25-28.
Rosenberg, D.K. & Harcourt, S.A. (1987). Population sizes and potential conservation problems of the endemic Galapagos Penguin and Flightless Cormorant. *Noticias de Galápagos* **45**: 24-25.
Rosenberg, D.K., Valle, C.A., Coulter, M.C. & Harcourt, S.A. (1990). Monitoring Galapagos Penguins and Flightless Cormorants in the Galapagos Islands. *Wilson Bull.* **102(3)**: 525-532.
Roseveare, M. (1989). First record of the Shoebill in Malawi. *Nyala* **14**: 45.
Rösler, S. (1980). Zum Verhalten des Eissturmvogels, *Fulmarus glacialis*, auf offener See. *Die Vogelwarte* **30**: 268-270.
Ross, R.K. (1973). A comparison of the feeding and nesting requirements of the Great Cormorant (*Phalacrocorax carbo* L.) and Double-crested Cormorant (*P. auritus* Lesson) in Nova Scotia. MSc. thesis, Dalhousie University, Halifax, Nova Scotia.
Round, P. & Treesucon, U. (1986). Memorandum to Mr. Phairot Suvanakorn (Royal Forest Dept.): Storm's Stork *Ciconia stormi*. Unpublished report. Bangkok, Thailand.
Round, P.D. (1988). *Resident Forest Birds in Thailand: Their Status and Conservation.* ICBP Monograph **2**, Cambridge, England.
Round, P.D. & Swann, R.L. (1977). Aspects of the breeding of Cory's Shearwater in Crete. *Ibis* **119**: 350-353.
Round, P.D., Amget, B., Jintanugol, J. & Treesucon, U. (1988). A summary of the larger waterbirds in Thailand. *Tigerpaper* **15(3)**: 1-7.
Rounds, R.S. (1990). *Men and Birds in South America 1492 to 1900.* Q.E.D. Press. Fort Bragg, California.
Rounsevell, D.E. & Copson, G.R. (1982). Growth rate and recovery of a King Penguin, *Aptenodytes patagonicus*, population after exploitation. *Austr. Wild. Res.* **9(3)**: 519-525.
Roux, F. & Dupuy, A. (1972). L'hivernage de la Cigogne noire en Afrique occidentale. *L'Oiseau et la R.F.O.* **42(1)**: 61-65.
Roux, F., Jarry, G., Maheo, R. & Tamisier, A. (1976-1977). Importance, structure et origine des populations d'Anatidés hivernant dans le delta du Sénegal. *L'Oiseau et la R.F.O.* **46**: 299-336, **47**: 1-24.
Roux, J.P. (1985). Le statut du Puffin à pieds pâles (*Puffinus carneipes*) à l'ile Saint-Paul (38° 48' S, 77° 30' E). *L'Oiseau et la R.F.O.* **55**: 155-157.
Roux, J.P. (1987). Sooty Albatross *Phoebetria fusca* breeding in the Kerguelen archipelago: a confirmation. *Cormorant* **14**: 50-51.
Roux, J.P. & Martinez, J. (1987). Rare, vagrant and introduced birds at Amsterdam and Saint Paul Islands, southern Indian Ocean. *Cormorant* **14**: 3-19.
Roux, J.P., Jouventin, P., Mougin, J.L., Stahl, J.C. & Weimerskirch, H. (1983). Un nouvel albatros *Diomedea amsterdamensis* n. sp. découvert sur l'ile Amsterdam (37° 50' S, 77° 35' E). *L'Oiseau et la R.F.O.* **53**: 1-11.
Roux, J.P., Mougin, J.L. & Bartle, J.A. (1986). Le Prion de MacGillivray. Données taxonomiques. *L'Oiseau et la R.F.O.* **56**: 379-383.
Roux, P. (1977). Ecologie du Fulmar antarctique: biologie et dynamique des populations. D.E.A. d'écophysiologie comparée de la reproduction animale. University Limoges.
Røv, N. (1988). *Bestandsutvikling og produksjon hos storskav i Norge.* Okoforsk, Trondheim.
Røv, N. (1990). *Bestandsforhold hos toppskarv i Norge.* Norwegian Institute for Nature Research, Trondheim.
Røv, N. & Follestad, A. (1983). Toppskarv ringmerket på Sklinna i Nord-Trondelag. *Vår Fuglefauna* **6(3)**: 190-191. Summary: Shags ringed on Sklinna, N. Trondelag.
Røv, N. & Strann, K.B. (1986). The present status, breeding distribution, and colony size of the Cormorant *Phalacrocorax carbo carbo* in Norway. *Fauna Norv. (Ser. C) Cinclus* **10**: 39-44.
Rowan, A.N., Elliott, H.F.I. & Rowan, M.K. (1951). The "spectacled" form of the Shoemaker *Procellaria aequinoctialis* in the Tristan da Cunha Group. *Ibis* **93**: 169-179.
Rowan, M.K. (1951). The Yellow-nosed Albatross *Diomedea chlororhynchos* Gmelin at its breeding grounds in the Tristan da Cunha Group. *Ostrich* **22**: 139-159.
Rowan, M.K. (1952). The Greater Shearwater *Puffinus gravis* at its breeding grounds. *Ibis* **94**: 97-121.
Rowan, M.K. (1963). The Yellowbill Duck *Anas undulata* Dubois in Southern Africa. *Ostrich* **5(Suppl.)**: 1-56.
Rowe, B. (1978). Incubation temperatures of the North Island Brown Kiwi *Apteryx australis mantelli*. *Notornis* **25**: 213-217.
Rowe, B.E. (1985). The New Zealand Kiwis *Apteryx sp. Avicult. Mag.* **91(1-2)**: 59-63.
Rowe, B.W. (1974). Mating behaviour of Brown Kiwi in captivity. *Notornis* **21**: 384-385.
Rozendaal, F.G. (1980). On field identification of Christmas Island Frigatebird. *Dutch Birding* **2(2)**: 48-49.
Ruckdeschel, C. & Shoop, C.P. (1987). Aspects of Wood Stork nesting ecology on Cumberland Island, Georgia. *Oriole* **52**: 1-27, 71.
Rudegeair, T. (1975). *The Reproductive Behavior and Ecology of the White Ibis (*Eudocimus albus*).* PhD thesis. University of Florida, Gainsville, Florida.
Rudinger, A. (1984). [Europe's last pelicans]. *Fauna Flora. Stockholm* **79(2)**: 61-65. In Norwegian.
Ruiz, X. (1983). *Contribución al Conocimiento de la Biología y Ecología de* Bubulcus ibis *(L.1758) en el Delta del Ebro (Tarragona).* Tesis doctoral, Universitat de Barcelona, Barcelona.
Ruiz, X. (1985). An Analysis of the Diet of Cattle Egrets in the Ebro Delta, Spain. *Ardea* **73**: 49-60.
Rumboll, M.A.E. (1974). Una nueva especie de macá (Podicipedidae). *Com. Mus. Arg. Cienc. Nat. Bernardino Rivadavia* **4(5)**: 33-35.
Rumboll, M.A.E. (1975a). Espolones metacarpales del Chajá (*Chauna torquata*). *Hornero* **11**: 316-317.
Rumboll, M.A.E. (1975b). Notas sobre Anseriformes. El Cauqen de Cabeza Colorada (*Chloephaga rubidiceps*). Una nota de alarma. *Hornero* **11 (4)**: 315-316.
Rumboll, M.A.E. & Canevari, P. (1991). Migraciones de anátidos en la Argentina, con énfasis en los Cauquenes (*Chloephaga spp.*). In: *IV Congreso de Ornitología Neotropical, 3-9 Noviembre 1991. Quito, Ecuador.*
Rumboll, M.A.E. & Jehl, J.R. (1977). Observations on pelagic birds in the South Atlantic Ocean in the austral spring. *Trans. San Diego Soc. Nat. Hist.* **19**: 1-16.
Rüppell, G. (1977). *Bird Flight.* Van Nostrand and Reinhold, New York.
Rusch, D.H., Ankney, C.D., Boyd, H., Longcore, J.R., Montalbano, F., Ringelman, J.K. & Stotts, V.D. (1989). Population ecology and harvest of the American Black Duck: a review. *Wildl. Soc. Bull.* **17**: 379-406.
Rusch, D.H., Craven, S.R., Trost, R.E. Cary, J.R., Drieslein, R.L., Ellis, J.W. & Wetzel, J. (1985). Evaluation of efforts to redistribute Canada Geese. *Trans. North Amer. Wildl. Nat. Res. Conf.* **50**: 506-524.
Ruschi, A. (1979). *Aves do Brasil.* Vol. 1. Editora Rios, São Paulo.
Russell, J.K. (1978). Effects of interspecific dominance among egrets commensally following Roseate Spoonbills. *Auk* **95**: 608-610.
Russell, R.P. (1982). Roseate Spoonbills feed on vegetable material. *Florida Field Nature* **10(1)**: 18.
Rutgers, A. & Norris, K.A. eds. (1970). *Encyclopaedia of Aviculture.* Vol. 1. Blandford, London.
Ruthven, J.A. & Zimmerman, W. (1968). *Top Flight Speed Index to Waterfowl.* Milwaukee.
Ruttledge, R.F. (1987). The breeding distribution of the Common Scoter in Ireland. *Irish Birds* **3**: 417-426.
Ruwet, J.C. (1984). La ritualisation des parades chez les oiseaux; le cas du grèbe huppé *Podiceps cristatus* L. *Cahiers d'Ethologie appliquée* **4(4)**: 315-352.
Ryan, M.R. & Heagy, P.A. (1980). Sunbathing behaviour of the Pied-billed Grebe. *Wilson Bull.* **92**: 409-412.
Ryan, P.G. & Cooper, J. (1991). Rockhopper Penguins and other marine life threatened by driftnet fisheries at Tristan da Cunha. *Oryx* **25(2)**: 76-79.
Ryan, P.G. & Hunter, S. (1985). Early breeding of Imperial Cormorants *Phalacrocorax atriceps* at Prince Edward Island. *Cormorant* **13**: 31-34.
Ryan, P.G. & Watkins, B.P. (1989). Snow Petrel breeding biology at an inland site in continental Antarctica. *Colonial Waterbirds* **12**(2): 176-184.
Ryan, P.G., Bosman, A.L. & Hockey, P.A.R. (1988). Notes on the feeding behaviour of Magellanic Flightless Steamer Ducks and Flying Steamer Ducks. *Wildfowl* **39**: 29-33.
Ryan, P.G., Dean, W.R.J., Moloney, C.L., Watkins, B.P. & Milton, S.J. (1990). New Information at Inaccesible Island and other Islands in the Tristan da Cunha Group. *Marine Orn.* **18**: 43-54.
Ryan, P.G., Wilson, R.P. & Cooper, J. (1987). Intraspecific mimicry and status signals in juvenile African Penguins. *Behav. Ecol. Sociobiol.* **20**: 69-76.
Ryder, J.H. & Ryder, B.A. (1978). First breeding records of Black Stork in Malawi. *Ostrich* **49**: 51.
Ryder, J.P. (1967). The breeding biology of Ross's Goose in the Perry River Region, Northwest Territories. *Can. Wildl. Serv. Rep. Series* **3**.
Ryder, J.P. (1970). *Timing and Spacing of Nests and Breeding Biology of Ross's Goose.* PhD dissertation, University of Saskatchewan.
Ryder, J.P. (1972). Biology of nesting Ross's Goose. *Ardea* **60**: 185-215.
Ryder, R.A. (1967). Distribution, migration and mortality of the White-faced Ibis (*Plegadis chihi*) in North America. *Bird-Banding* **38**: 257-277.
Ryder, R.A. (1978). Breeding Distribution, Movements and Mortality of Snowy Egrets in North America. Pp. 197-205 in: Sprunt *et al.* (1978).
Ryder, R.A. (1981). Movements and mortality of White Pelicans fledged in Colorado. *Colonial Waterbirds* **4**: 72-76.
Ryder, R.A. (1991). Distribution, status, migration and harvest of Colorado Redheads. *Colorado Field Orn. J.* **25(4)**: 102.
Rylander, M.K. & Bolen, E.G. (1970). Ecological and anatomical adaptations of North American Tree Ducks. *Auk* **87**: 72-90.
Rylander, M.K. & Bolen, E.G. (1974a). Analysis and comparison of gaits in whistling ducks (*Dendrocygna*). *Wilson Bull.* **86**: 237-245.
Rylander, M.K. & Bolen, E.G. (1974b). Feeding adaptations in whistling ducks (*Dendrocygna*). *Auk* **91**: 86-94.
Rylander, M.K. & Bolen, E.G. (1980). The ecology of Whistling Ducks in the tropics. Pp. 309-314 in: *Tropical Ecology and Development.*
van Ryzin, M.T. & Fisher, H.I. (1976). The age of Laysan Albatrosses at first breeding. *Condor* **78**: 1-9.
Sackl, P. (1982). Ökologie und Brutbiologie einer Population des Zwergtauchers, *Tachybaptus ruficollis*, in der Steiermark. *Egretta* **25**: 1-11.
Sackl, P. (1985). Der Schwarzstorch (*Ciconia nigra*) in Österreich - Arealausweitung, Bestandsentwicklung und Verbreitung. *Vogelwelt* **106**: 121-141.
Sackl, P. (1987). Über saisonale und regionale Unterscheide in der Ernährung und Nahrungswahl des Weißstorches (*Ciconia c. ciconia*) im Verlauf der Brutperiode. *Egretta* **30**: 49-80.
Safford, R. & Duckworth, W. eds. (1990). *A Wildlife Survey of Marojejy Nature Reserve, Madagascar.* ICBP Study Report **40**. ICBP, Cambridge, England.
Safriel, U.N. (1980). Notes on the extinct population of the Bald Ibis *Geronticus eremita* in the Syrian desert. *Ibis* **122**: 82-88.
Sagar, P.M. (1979). Breeding of the Cape Pigeon at the Snares Islands. *Notornis* **26**: 23-36.
Sagar, P.M. (1981). The distribution and numbers of Crested Grebe in New Zealand 1980. *Notornis* **28**: 301-310.
Sagar, P.M. (1985). Cape Pigeon. Page 70 in: Robertson (1985).
Sagar, P.M. (1986). The sexual dimorphism of Snares Cape Pigeons (*Daption capense australe*). *Notornis* **33**: 259-263.
Sage, B.L. (1971). A study of White-billed Divers in Alaska. *British Birds* **64**: 519-528.
Sage, B.L. (1973). Studies of less familiar birds, 169 Red-necked Grebe. *British Birds* **66**: 24-30.
Sahin, R. (1982a). Eltern-Kind-Beziehungen der freilebenden Waldrappe (*Geronticus eremita* L.) in Birecik (Türkei). [Summary: Parent-young relationship of the free-living Bald Ibises (*Geronticus eremita* L.) in Birecik (Turkey)]. *Ökol. Vögel* **4(1)**: 1-7.
Sahin, R. (1982b). Beitrag zum Fortplantzungsverhalten der freilebenden Waldrappe (*Geronticus eremita* L.) in der Türkei. 1. Mitteilung: Ankunft, Paarbildung und Nisten. [Summary: Contribution to the reproductive behaviour of the free-living Bald Ibises (*Geronticus eremita* L.) in Turkey. 1. Communication: Arrival, pair-formation and nesting]. *Ökol. Vögel* **4(2)**: 181-190.
Sahin, R. (1983a). Beitrag zum Fortplantzungsverhalten der freilebenden Waldrappe (*Geronticus eremita* L.) in der Türkei. 2. Mitteilung: Paarung. [Summary: Contribution to the reproductive behaviour of the free-living Bald Ibises (*Geronticus eremita* L.) in Turkey. 2. Communication: Copulation]. *Ökol. Vögel* **5(1)**: 63-72.
Sahin, R. (1983b). Beitrag zum Fortplantzungsverhalten der freilebenden Waldrappe (*Geronticus eremita* L.) in der Türkei. 3. Mitteilung: Eiablage, Brüten und Schlüpfen. [Summary: Contribution to the reproductive behaviour of the free-living Bald Ibises (*Geronticus eremita* L.) in Turkey. 3. Communication: Egg laying, incubation, and hatching]. *Ökol. Vögel* **5**: 255-262.
Sahin, R. (1983c). Beitrag zum Fortplantzungsverhalten der freilebenden Waldrappe (*Geronticus eremita* L.) in der Türkei. 4. Mitteilung: Fortpflanzungskampfe. [Summary: Contribution to the reproductive behaviour of the free-living Bald Ibises (*Geronticus eremita* L.) in Turkey. 4. Communication: Reproductive fighting]. *Ökol. Vögel* **5**: 263-270.
Sahin, R. (1983d). Körper- und Nesthygiene der freilebenden Waldrappe (*Geronticus eremita*). *Orn. Mitt.* **35(6)**: 152-155.
Sahin, R. (1986). Birecik Kelaynaklarin (*Geronticus eremita* L.) ve Yasama Sanslari. *Tabiat ve Insan* **20(3)**: 12-20.
Sahin, R. (1988). Kelaynaklarin (*Geronticus eremita*) Korunmasi ve Yasam Sekilleri. *Tabiat ve Insan* **22(1)**: 21-28.
Sahin, R. (1990). Werdegang und Bedeutung des Kopfnickens beim Waldrapp (*Geronticus eremita*). *J. Orn.* **131**: 445-451.
Saiff, E.J. (1978). The middle ear of the skull of birds: the Pelecaniformes and Ciconiiformes. *Zool. J. Linn. Soc.* **63**: 315-370.
Saiff, E.J. (1988). The anatomy of the middle ear of the Tinamiformes (Aves: Tinamidae). *J. Morphol.* **196(1)**: 1077-116.
Saikia, P. & Bhattacharjee, P.C. (1989a). A preliminary survey of Adjutant Storks in Assam. *Asian Wetland News* **2(2)**: 14-15.
Saikia, P. & Bhattacharjee, P.C. (1989b). Bhattacharjee. 1989. Adjutant Storks at risk in Assam, India. *Specialist Group on Storks, Ibis, and Spoonbills Newsletter* **2**: 6-8.
Saikia, P. & Bhattacharjee, P.C. (1990). Nesting records of Greater Adjutant Storks in Assam, India. *Specialist Group on Storks, Ibises & Spoonbills Newsletter* **3(1/2)**: 2-3.
Saikia, P. & Bhattacharjee, P.C. (1991). Status of ibises and spoonbills in Assam. *Specialist Group on Storks, Ibises and Spoonbills Newsletter* **4(1)**: 3.
Saiz, F. & Hajek, E.R. (1988). Observaciones de Temperatura en Nidos de Petrel Gigante *Macronectes giganteus*. *Inst. Antárt. Chileno* **14**: 1-15.
Sakamoto, M. (1966). *Kohnotori: Japanese Stork,* Ciconia ciconia boyciana *(Swinhoe).* Kobe Newspaper Press, Kobe. 104pp.
Salathé, T. (1983). La predation du flamant rose *Phoenicopterus ruber roseus* par le goeland leucophée *Larus cachinnans* en Camargue. *Rev. Ecol. (Terre Vie)* **37**: 87-115.
Salathé, T. ed. (1991). *Conserving Migratory Birds.* ICBP Technical Publication **12**. ICBP, Cambridge, England.
Salazar, J. (1988). [Census of the Black-neck Swan populations (*Cygnus melancoryphus*) in Valdivia]. *Medio Ambiente* **9(1)**: 78-87.
Salim, A. (1959). The Pink-headed Duck *Rhodonessa caryophyllacea* (Latham). *Wildfowl* **11**: 55-60.
Salimkumar, C. (1982). *Ecology and behaviour of the Indian Black Ibis (*Pseudibis papillosa *Temminck) around Saurashtra University campus: an aerial study.* MSc dissertation. Saurashtra University, Rajkot, India.
Salimkumar, C. & Soni, V.C. (1984). Laboratory observations on the incubation period of the Indian Black Ibis (*Pseudibis papillosa* Temminck). *J. Bombay Nat. Hist. Soc.* **81**: 189-190.
Salmon, D.G. (1988). The numbers and distribution of Scaup *Aythya marila* in Britain and Ireland. *Biol. Conserv.* **43**: 267-278.
Salmon, H.A. (1965). Distribution of the Jabiru in central and northern coastal New South Wales. *Emu* **65**: 149-151.
Salomonsen, F. (1965). The geographical variation of the fulmar and the zones of marine environment in the North Atlantic. *Auk* **82**: 327-335.
Salomonsen, F. (1968). The moult migration. *Wildfowl* **19**: 5-24.
Salonen, V. & Penttinen, A. (1988). Factors affecting nest predation in the Great Crested Grebe: field observations, experiments and their statistical analysis. *Ornis Fenn.* **65**: 13-20.
Salvador, S.A. & Narosky, S. (1984). Notas sobre nidificación de aves andinas, en la Argentina. *Hornero* **12(3)**: 184-188.
Salvador, S.A. & Salvador, L.A. (1988). Nidificación de Aves en Pampa de Achala, Córdoba. *Nuestras Aves* **16**: 20-23.
Salvador, S.A. & Salvador, L.A. (1990). Nuevos hallazgos en Argentina de *Anas discors*, *Lophornis chalybea* y *Tyrannus tyrannus*. *Hornero* **13**: 178-179.
Salvadori, T. (1900). On the ibises of the Genus *Theristicus*. *Ibis (7th Ser.)* **6**: 501-517.
Salvan, J. (1967). Contribution à l'étude des oiseaux du Tchad. *L'Oiseau et la R.F.O.* **37**: 255-284.
Salvan, J. (1970). Remarques sur l'evolution de l'avifauna Malgache depuis 1945. *Alauda* **38**: 191-203.
Salvan, J. (1971). Observations nouvelles à Madagascar. *Alauda* **39**: 37-42.
Salvan, J. (1972a). Statut, recensement, reproduction des oiseaux dulçaquicoles aux environs de Tananarive. *L'Oiseau et la R.F.O.* **42**: 35-51.
Salvan, J. (1972b). Remarques sur l'avifaune malagasy et la protection d'espèces aviennes mal connues ou menacées. Pp. 179-182 in: *C.R. Conférence Internationale sur la Conservation de la Nature et de ses Ressources à Madagascar.* IUCN Document Supplémentaire **36**. IUCN, Morges, Switzerland.
San Martín, P.R. (1959). Nota sobre el contenido estomacal de un *Theristicus caudatus caudatus* (Boddaert), "bandurria", (Ciconiiformes, Threskiornithidae). *Bio. Soc. Cienc. Nat. Taquato* **1(3)**: 79-84.
Sánchez, J.M., Vargas, J.M. & Blasco, M. (1985). Historia y evolución de la colonia de flamenco común *Phoenicopterus ruber* L., de la laguna de Fuentepiedra. *Bol. Estac. Centr. Ecol.* **14**: 9-18.
Sandell, M. (1986). Towards a natural taxonomy or why is the cassowary classified as a bird? *Anser* **25(1)**: 11-14.
Sander, M. (1982). Nota sobre a alimentaçao de perdigao ("*Rhynchotus rufescens*", Temmink, 1815) no Rio Grande do Sul, Brasil. (Aves, Tinamidae). *Pesquizas (Ser. Zool.)* **33**: 17-22.

Sanders, S.W.H. (1967). *The Osteology and Myology of the Pectoral Appendage of Grebes*. PhD thesis, University of Michigan.
Sanger, G.A. (1965). Observations of wildlife off the coast of Washington and Oregon in 1963, with notes on the Laysan Albatross (*Diomedea immutabilis*) in the area. *Murrelet* **46**: 1-6.
Sanger, G.A. (1974a). Black-footed Albatross. *Smithson. Contrib. Zool.* **158**: 96-128.
Sanger, G.A. (1974b). Laysan Albatross. *Smithson. Contrib. Zool.* **158**: 129-153.
Sanson, O., Bell, B.D., Andrews, T. & Wilson, R.A. (1954). Visitation of Glossy Ibis. *Notornis* **6**: 18-19.
de Santo, T. McDowell, S.G. & Bildstein, K.L. (1990). Plumage and behavioral development of nestling White Ibises. *Wilson Bull.* **102(2)**: 226-238.
Santucci, F. & Geber, D. (1971). Distribution of Maccoa Duck. *Natal Bird Club News Sheet* **198**.
Sapetin, Y. V. (1968). [Seasonal distribution and migration of the spoonbills and Glossy Ibis according to ringing data]. *Migratsii Zhivotnykh.* **5**: 94-112.
Sarà, M. (1983). Osservazioni sulla consistenza numerica e sull'allimentazione della Berta Maggiore (*Calonectris diomedea*) del Canale di Sicilia. *Riv. ital. Orn.* **53**: 183-193.
Sargeant, A.B., Allen, S.H. & Eberhardt, R.T. (1984). *Red Fox Predation on Breeding Ducks in Midcontinent North America*. Wildlife Monographs **89**.
Sarrocco, S. (1986). Alcuni dati sulla biologia riproduttiva dello Svasso maggiore, *Podiceps cristatus*, in due bacini dell'Italia centrale, laghi reatini (Rieti). *Riv. ital. Orn.* **56**: 197-202.
Sarvis, J.E. (1972). *The Breeding Biology of the Ring-necked Duck in Northern Michigan*. MSc thesis, Utah State University, Logan.
Sato, H. (1968). A note on the plumage color of the Japanese Crested Ibis. *Tori* **18**: 301-312.
Sauer, E.G.F. (1970). Interspecific behaviour of the South African Ostrich. *Ostrich* **8(Suppl.)**: 91-103.
Sauer, E.G.F. (1971). Zur Biologie der Wilden Strausse Südwestafrikas. *Z. Kölner Zoo* **14**: 43-64.
Sauer, E.G.F. (1972a). Aberrant sexual behaviour in the South African Ostrich. *Auk* **89**: 717-737.
Sauer, E.G.F. (1972b). Ratite eggshells and phylogenetic questions. *Bonn. zool. Beitr.* **23**: 3-48.
Sauer, E.G.F. & Rothe, P. (1972). Ratite eggshells from Lanzarote, Canary Islands. *Science. New York* **176**: 43-45.
Sauer, E.G.F. & Sauer, E.M. (1966a). The behaviour and ecology of the South African Ostrich. *Living Bird* **5**: 45-76.
Sauer, E.G.F. & Sauer, E.M. (1966b). Social behaviour of the South African Ostrich. *Ostrich* **6(Suppl.)**: 183-191.
Sauer, E.G.F. & Sauer, E.M. (1967a). Verhaltensforschung an wilden StrauBen in Südwestafrika. *Umschau in Wissenschaft u. Technik* **67**: 652-657.
Sauer, E.G.F. & Sauer, E.M. (1967b). Yawning and other maintenance activities in the South African Ostrich. *Auk* **84**: 571-587.
Sauer, E.G.F. & Sauer, E.M. (1970). Soziale Kontakte von SatrauBen mit anderem Wild in der inneren Namib. *Namib und Meer* **1**: 5-34.
Savage, C. (1952). *The Mandarin Duck*. A. & C. Black, London.
Savage, C. (1964). Lake Rezaiyeh: a specialised summer habitat for Shelduck and Flamingos. *Wildfowl Trust Ann. Rep.* **15**: 108-113.
Savage, I. (1978). Timing grebe's dives. *Ceelong Nat.* **15(2)**: 38.
Savard, J.P.L. (1982). Intra- and inter-specific competition between Barrow's Goldeneye (*Bucephala islandica*) and Bufflehead (*Bucephala albeola*). *Can. J. Zool.* **60**: 3439-3446.
Savard, J.P.L. (1984). Territorial behaviour of Common Goldeneye, Barrow's Goldeneye and Bufflehead in areas of sympatry. *Ornis Scand.* **15**: 211-216.
Savard, J.P.L. (1986). *Territorial Behaviour, Nesting Success and Brood Survival in Barrow's Goldeneye and its Congeners*. PhD dissertation, University British Columbia, Vancouver.
Savard, J.P.L. & Eadie, J.McA. (1989). Survival and breeding philopatry in Barrow's and Common Goldeneyes. *Condor* **91 (1)**: 198-203.
Saxena, V.S. (1980). Kokkare Bellur Pelicanry. *Cheetal* **21(4)**: 20-24.
Scammell-Tinling, V.L. (1983). *Behavioural ecology of the parent-young relationship of the Western Grebe (*Aechmophorus occidentalis*)*. MSc thesis. University of California, Davis.
Scarlett, R.J. (1962a). Sub-fossils bones of the little grey kiwi on the North Island. *Notornis* **10(2)**: 84-85.
Scarlett, R.J. (1962b). Kiwi courtship. *Notornis* **10(2)**: 93.
Schaefer, M.B. (1970). Men, birds and anchovies in the Peru Current - dynamic interactions. *Trans. Amer. Fish. Soc.* **99**: 461-467.
Schaeffer, P.P. & Ehlers, S.M. eds. (1980). *The Birds of Mexico: Their Ecology and Conservation*. Proceedings of the National Audubon Symposium. National Audubon Society Western Education Center, Tiburon, California.
Schäffer, E. (1954). Zur Biologie des Steisshuhnes *Nothocercus bonapartei*. *J. Orn.* **95**: 219-232.
Schäffer, E. (1975). Der Cuero (Nothocercus bonapartei) Lebensbild eines seltenen Steisshuhns. *Gefiederte Welt* **96(12)**: 222-224.
Schaffner, F.C. (1988). *The Breeding Biology and Energetics of the White-tailed Tropicbird (*Phaethon lepturus*) at Culebra, Puerto Rico*. PhD dissertation. University of Miami.
Schaffner, F.C. (1990a). Food provisioning by White-tailed Tropicbirds: Effects on the developmental pattern of chicks. *Ecology* **71**: 375-390.
Schaffner, F.C. (1990b). Feed Size and Feeding Periodicity in Pelagic Birds: Notes on Metodology. *Colonial Waterbirds* **13(1)**: 7-15.
Schaldach, W.J. (1963). *The Avifauna of Colima and Adjacent Jalisco, Mexico*. Proceedings of the Western Foundation of Vertebrate Zoology **1(1)**. Los Angeles.
Schaller, G.B. (1964). Breeding behavior of the White Pelican at Yellowshore Lake, Wyoming. *Condor* **66**: 3-23.
Schamel, D. & Tracy, D.M. (1985). Replacement Clutches in the Red-throated Loon. *J. Field Orn.* **56(3)**: 282-283.
Scharf, W. & Shugart, G.W. (1981). Recent increases in Double-crested Cormorants in the United States Great Lakes. *American Birds* **35**: 910-911.
de Schauensee, R.M. (1946). On Siamese birds. *Proc. Acad. Nat. Sci. Philadelphia* **98**: 1-82.
de Schauensee, R.M. (1948). The Birds of the Republic of Colombia, part 1. *Caldasia* **5(22)**: 251-380.
de Schauensee, R.M. (1959). *Colymbus caspicus andinus* n, subsp.: 55 *in* Additions to the "Birds of the Republik of Colombia". *Proc. Acad. Nat. Sci. Philadelphia* **111**: 53-75.
de Schauensee, R.M. (1964). *The Birds of Colombia and Adjacent Areas of South and Central America*. The Academy of Natural Sciences of Philadelphia.
de Schauensee, R.M. (1982). *A Guide to the Birds of South America*. Livingston Press, Narbeth, PA.
de Schauensee, R.M. (1984). *The Birds of China*. Oxford University Press, Oxford.
de Schauensee, R.M. & Phelps, W.H. (1978). *A Guide to the Birds of Venezuela*. Princeton, New Jersey.
Schenk, H. (1970). Über Vorkommen, Salztoleranz, Vergesellschaftung und Mauser des Schwarzhalstauchers (*Podiceps nigricollis*) auf Sardinien. *Vogelwelt* **91**: 230-235.
Schenker, A. (1977). Das ehemalige Verbreitungsgebiet des Waldrapps *Geronticus eremita* in Europa. *Orn. Beob.* **74**: 13-30.
Schenker, A. (1979). Beobachtungen zur Brutbiologie des Waldrapps (*Geronticus eremita*) im Zoo Basel. *Zool. Garten* **49**: 104-116.
Schenker, A., Hirsch, U., Mallet, M., Pechlaner, H., Thaler, E. & Wackernagel, H. (1980). Keeping and Breeding the Waldrapp Ibis. *Int. Zoo News* **27(165)**: 9-15.
Scherer Neto, P. (1987). Nota sobre aspectos migratórios de *Fregata magnificens* Mathews (1914) (Fregatidae, Aves). Pp. 202-203 in: *Anais do II Encontro Nacional de Anilhadores de Aves*. Universidade Federal do Rio de Janeiro.
Scherpelz, J.A. (1979). *Chronology of Pair Formation and Breeding Biology in the Wood Duck*. Unpublished MSc dissertation, University of Missouri, Columbia.
Schifferli, A. (1978). Rückstände von Pestiziden und PCB bei schweizerischen Haubentauchern *Podiceps cristatus*. *Orn. Beob.* **75**: 11-18.
Schindler, M. (1983). *Die intrafamiliären Abstandsverhältnisse und ihre Auswirkungen auf Gössel und Elternverhalten bei Streifengänsen (*Anser indicus*)*. Diplomarbeit, Universität München.
Schlatter, R.P. (1984). The status and conservation of seabirds in Chile. Pp. 261-269 in: Croxall *et al.* (1984).
Schlatter, R.P. & Marin, M.A. (1983). Breeding of Elliott's Storm Petrel, *Oceanites gracilis*, in Chile. *Gerfaut* **73**: 197-199.
Schlatter, R.P. & Moreno, C. (1976). Hábitos alimentarios del Cormorán Antártico, *Phalacrocorax atriceps bransfieldensis* (Murphy) en Isla Green, Antártica. *Inst. Antárt. Chileno (Ser. Cient.)* **4**: 69-88.
Schlatter, R.P. & Riveros, M.G. (1981). Ornitocenosis de Islas Diego Ramirez, Chile. Research Project and Report (INACH).
Schlorff, R.W. (1978). Predatory Ecology of the Great Egret at Humboldt Bay, California. Pp. 347-354 in: Sprunt *et al.* (1978).
Schmidt, G.A.J. (1980). *Der Gänsesäger,* Mergus merganser. Monographie der Vogelkundl. Arbeitsgr. Schleswig-Holstein, Kiel.
Schmidt, R.A. (1980). First breeding records of the White-faced Ibis in North Dakota. *Prairie Nat.* **12(1)**: 21-23.
Schmidt, T. (1970). Parringsadfaerden hos Gråstrubet Lappedykker. *Naturens Verden* **1970**: 363-374.
Schmidt-Koenig, K. (1979). *Avian Orientation and Navigation*. Academic Press, London and New York.
Schmidt-Koenig, K. & Keeton, W.T. eds. (1978). *Animal Migration, Navigation and Homing*. Springer-Verlag, Berlin, Heidelberg and New York.
Schneider, J. & Lamprecht, J. (1990). The importance of biparental care in a precocial, monogamous bird, the Bar-headed Goose (*Anser indicus*). *Behav. Ecol. Sociobiol.* **27**: 415-419.
Schneider, K.M. (1952). Vom Kropfstorch (*Leptoptilos*) in Gefangenschaft. *Beitr. Vögelk.* **2**: 196-286.
Schneider, M. (1988). Periodisch überschwemmtes Dauergrünland ermöglicht optimalen Bruterfolg des Weißstorches (*Ciconia ciconia*) in der Save-Stromaue (Kroatien/Jugoslawien). *Vogelwarte* **34**: 164-173.
de Schneidauer, T.R. (1961). *Cygnes et oies sauvages*. Desclée de Brouwer, Belgique.
Schnell, G.D. (1974). Flight speeds and wingbeat frequencies of the Magnificent Frigate Bird. *Auk* **91(3)**: 564-570.
Schnell, G.D., Woods, B.L. & Ploger, B.J. (1983). Brown Pelican foraging success and kleptoparasitism by Laughing Gulls. *Auk* **100**: 636-644.
Schodde, R. & Tidemann, C. eds. (1988). *Reader's Digest Complete Book of Australian Birds*. Reader's Digest Services Pty Ltd, Sydney.
Scholl, D. (1972). Das Vorkommen des Rothalstauchers, *Podiceps grisegena*, in Schleswig-Holstein und Hamburg. *Corax* **4**: 14-29.
Scholten, C.J. (1987). Breeding biology of the Humboldt Penguin *Spheniscus humboldti* at Emmen Zoo. *Int. Zoo Yb.* **26**: 198-204.
Scholten, C.J. (1989a). The timing of moult in relation to age, sex and breeding status in a group of captive Humboldt Penguins (*Spheniscus humboldti*) at Emmen Zoo. The Netherlands. *Netherl. J. Zool.* **39(3-4)**: 113-125.
Scholten, C.J. (1989b). Individual recognition of Humboldt Penguins. *Spheniscid Penguin Newsletter* **2**: 4-8.
Schommer, M. (1977). *On the Social Behaviour of Gadwall (*Anas strepera*): Displays, Pair Bonds and Effects of testosterone Injections*. PhD dissertation, University Leicester, UK.
Schonwetter, M. (1942). Das Ei des *Balaeniceps rex* Gould. *Beitr. Fortpfl. Vogel* **18**: 41-45.
Schramm, M. (1982). Recent records of the dark form of the Softplumaged Petrel *Pterodroma mollis* from the Subantarctic. *Cormorant* **10**: 3-6.
Schramm, M. (1983). The breeding biologies of the petrels *Pterodroma macroptera*, *P. brevirostris* and *P. mollis* at Marion Island. *Emu* **83**: 75-81.
Schramm, M. (1986). The diet of chicks of Greatwinged, Kerguelen and Softplumaged Petrels at the Prince Edward Islands. *Ostrich* **57**: 9-15.
Schreiber, E.A. & Schreiber, R.W. (1988). Great Frigatebird size dimorphism on two central Pacific atolls. *Condor* **90**: 90-99.
Schreiber, R.W. (1975). Bad days for the Brown Pelican. *Natl. Geogr.* **147**: 111-123.
Schreiber, R.W. (1976). Growth and development of nestling Brown Pelicans. *Bird-Banding* **47**: 19-39.
Schreiber, R.W. (1977). Maintenance, behavior, and communication in the Brown Pelican. *Orn. Monogr.* **22**: 1-78.
Schreiber, R.W. (1979). Reproductive performance of the eastern Brown Pelicans (*Pelecanus occidentalis*). *Contrib. Sci. Los Angeles Cty. Mus. Nat. Hist.* **317**.
Schreiber, R.W. (1980). The Brown Pelican: an endangered species? *Bioscience.* **30**: 742-747.
Schreiber, R.W. (1982). Comparative behaviour of the Pelecanidae: *Pelecanus onocrotalus* in South-West Africa (Namibia). *Nat. Geogr. Soc. Res. Rep.* **1977 Projects**: 699-710.
Schreiber, R.W. ed. (1984). *Tropical Seabird Biology.* Studies in Avian Biology **8**. Cooper Ornithological Society, Allen, Kansas.
Schreiber, R.W. & Ashmole, N.P. (1970). Seabird breeding seasons on Christmas Island, Pacific Ocean. *Ibis* **112**: 363-394.
Schreiber, R.W. & Chovan, J.L. (1986). Roosting by pelagic seabirds: energetic, populational, and social considerations. *Condor* **88**: 487-492.
Schreiber, R.W. & Hensley, D.A. (1976). The diets of *Sula dactylatra*, *Sula sula* and *Fregata minor* on Christmas Island, Pacific Ocean. *Pacific Science* **30**: 241-248.
Schreiber, R.W. & Mock, P.J. (1988). Eastern Brown Pelicans: what does 60 years of banding tell us? *J. Field Orn.* **59(2)**: 171-182.
Schreiber, R.W. & Risebrough, R.W. (1972). Studies of the Brown Pelican. I. Status of Brown Pelican populations in the United States. *Wilson Bull.* **84**: 119-135.
Schreiber, R.W. & Schreiber, E.A. (1980). *The Brown Pelican (*Pelecanus occidentalis*): a Bibliography*. Author, Los Angeles.
Schreiber, R.W. & Schreiber, E.A. (1982). Essential habitat of the Brown Pelican in Florida. *Florida Field Nature* **10**: 9-17.
Schreiber, R.W. & Schreiber, E.A. (1983). Use of age-classes in monitoring population stability of Brown Pelicans. *J. Wildl. Manage.* **47(1)**: 105-111.
Schreiber, R.W. & Schreiber, E.A. (1984a). Central Pacific seabirds and the El Niño Southern Oscillation: 1982 to 1983 perspectives. *Science* **225**: 713-716.
Schreiber, R.W. & Schreiber, E.A. (1984b). Frigatebirds. Family Fregatidae. Pp. 102-108 in: Haley (1984).
Schreiber, R.W., Belitski, D.W. & Sorrie, B.A. (1981). Notes on Brown Pelicans in Puerto Rico. *Wilson Bull.* **93(3)**: 397-400.
Schreiber, R.W., Woolfenden, G.E. & Curtsinger, W.E. (1975). Prey capture by the Brown Pelican. *Auk* **92**: 649-654.
Schröder, P. & Burmeister, G. (1974). *Der Schwarzstorch*. Neue Brehm-Bücherei **468**. A. Ziemsen, Wittenberg-Lutherstadt.
Schubart, O., Aguirre, A.C. & Sick, H. (1965). Contribuçao para o conhecimento da alimentaçao das aves brasileiras. *Arq. Zool. São Paulo* **12**: 95-249.
Schulenberg, T.S. & Parker, T.A. (1981). Status and distribution of some northwest Peruvian birds. *Condor* **83**: 209-216.
Schulz, M. (1987). Observations of feeding of a Little Penguin *Eudyptula minor*. *Emu* **87**: 186-187.
Schulz, M. (1989). The Importance of Wetlands in Kakadu National Park to Selected Waterbirds. Report to ANPWS.
Schulze, G.P. & Thinius, L. (1982). Der Rothalstaucher (*Podiceps griseigena* (Boddaert, 1783)) in der nordwestlichen Niederlausitz. *Biol. Stud. Luckau* **11**: 60-68.
Schurmann, A.M.W. (1984). Der Kondor - ein Storch? *Kosmos. Stuttgart* **80(4)**: 60-65.
Schüz, E. (1936). Internationale Bestandsaufnahme am Weißen Storch 1934. *Orn. Monatsber.* **44**: 33-41.
Schüz, E. (1942). Bewegungsnormen des Weissen Storchs. *Z. Tierpsychol.* **5**: 1-37.
Schüz, E. (1960). Die Verteilung des Weiss-Storchs im sudafrikanischen Ruheziel. *Vogelwarte* **20(3)**: 205-222.
Schüz, E. (1970a). Das Ei des Strausses (*Struthio camelus*) als Gebrauchs-und Kultgegenstand. *Tribus* **19**: 79-90.
Schüz, E. (1970b). The riddle of the so-called "Benin Ibis" and the artificial wattled birds. *Ostrich* **8(Suppl.)**: 15-19.
Schüz, E. (1979). Results of the III International Census (1974) of the White Stork. *Bull. ICBP* **13**: 173-179.
Schüz, E. (1984). Über Syngenophagie, besonders Kronismus. Ein Beitrag zur Ethologie speziell des Weißstorchs. *Ökol. Vögel* **6**: 141-158.
Schwartzkopff, J. (1973). Mechanoreception. Pp. 417-477 in: Farner, D.S. & King, J.R. (1973). *Avian Biology*. Vol. 3. Academic Press, London & New York.
Scolaro, J.A. (1978). El Pingüino de Magallanes (*Spheniscus magellanicus*) IV. Notas biológicas y de comportamiento. *Publ. Ocas. Inst. Biol. Animal (Ser. Cient.)* **10**: 1-6.
Scolaro, J.A. (1980). El Pingüino de Magallanes (*Spheniscus magellanicus*) VI. Dinámica de la población de juveniles. *Hist. Nat. Mendoza. Argentina.* **1(25)**: 173-176.
Scolaro, J.A. (1983). Ecology of the Magellanic Penguin *Spheniscus magellanicus*, a long-term breeding study of a temperate-latitude Penguin in Southern Argentina. M.Phil. thesis, University of Bradford, England.
Scolaro, J.A. (1984a). Madurez sexual del Pingüino de Magallanes (*Spheniscus magellanicus*) (Aves: Spheniscidae). *Hist. Nat. Corrientes. Argentina* **4(31)**: 289-292.
Scolaro, J.A. (1984b). Timing of nest relief during incubation and guard stage period of chicks in Magellanic Penguin (*Spheniscus magellanicus*) (Aves: Spheniscidae). *Hist. Nat. Corrientes. Argentina* **4(29)**: 281-284.
Scolaro, J.A. (1984c). Revisión sobre biología de la reproducción del Pingüino de Magallanes (*Spheniscus magellanicus*). El ciclo biológico anual. *C. Nac. Patag. Contrib.* **91**: 1-26.
Scolaro, J.A. (1986). La conservación del Pingüino de Magallanes: un problema de conflicto e intereses que requiere de argumentos científicos. *An. Mus. Hist. Nat. Valparaíso* **17**: 113-119.
Scolaro, J.A. (1987a). Sexing fledglings and yearlings of Magellanic Penguins by discriminant analysis of morphometric measurements. *Colonial Waterbirds* **10(1)**: 50-54.
Scolaro, J.A. (1987b). A Model Life Table for Magellanic Penguins (*Spheniscus magellanicus*) at Punta Tombo, Argentina. *J. Field Orn.* **58(4)**: 432-441.
Scolaro, J.A. (1990). Effects of nest density on breeding success in a colony of Magellanic Penguins (*Spheniscus magellanicus*). *Colonial Waterbirds* **13(1)**: 41-49.
Scolaro, J.A. & Arias de Reyna, L.M. (1984a). Distribución espacial actualizada de la nidificación y tamaño de población de *Spheniscus magellanicus* en Punta Tombo, Chubut, Argentina (*Aves: Spheniscidae*). *Hist. Nat. Corrientes. Argentina.* **4(27)**: 249-256.
Scolaro, J.A. & Arias de Reyna, L.M. (1984b). Principales factores ecológicos que afectan la nidificación del Pingüino de Magallanes (*Spheniscus magellanicus*) en la colonia de Punta Tombo. *C. Nac. Patag. Contrib.* **97**: 1-14.

Scolaro, J.A. & Badano, L.A. (1986). Diet of the Magellanic Penguin *Spheniscus magellanicus* during the chick-rearing period at Punta Clara, Argentina. *Cormorant* **13**: 91-97.
Scolaro, J.A. & Suburo, A.M. (1991). Maximum diving depths of the Magellanic Penguin. *J. Field Orn.* **62(2)**: 204-210.
Scolaro, J.A., Ares, J.O., Alessandria, E., Estecondo, S., Ghersa, C., Gómez, M., Hoffmeyer, M., Orozco Storni, M.S., Pérez, A. & Zavatti, J. (1981). El pingüino de Magallanes (*Spheniscus magellanicus*). VIII. Aspectos de la dinámica de su población en Punta Tombo, Chubut. *Hist. Nat. Corrientes. Argentina* **2(2)**: 5-20.
Scolaro, J.A., Hall, M.A. & Ximénez, I.M. (1983). The Magellanic Penguin (*Spheniscus magellanicus*): sexing adults by discriminant analysis of morphometric characters. *Auk* **100**: 221-224.
Scolaro, J.A., Hall, M.A., Ximénez, I.M. & Kovacs, O. (1979). El Pingüino de Magallanes (*Spheniscus magellanicus*) I. Evaluación y estratificación de densidades de su población en Punta Tombo, Chubut, Argentina. *Rev. Mus. Arg. Cienc. Nat. Bernardino Rivadavia (Ecología)* **2(4)**: 89-102.
Scolaro, J.A., Hall, M.A., Ximénez, I.M. & Kovacs, O. (1980). El Pingüino de Magallanes (*Spheniscus magellanicus*) II. Biología y desarrollo de la incubación en la colonia de Punta Tombo, Chubut, Argentina. *Rev. Mus. Arg. Cienc. Nat. Bernardino Rivadavia (Ecología)* **2(5)**: 103-110.
Scolaro, J.A., Rodríguez, E.N. & Monochio, A.A. (1980). El Pingüino de Magallanes (*Spheniscus magellanicus*) V. Distribución de las colonias de reproducción en el territorio continental argentino. *C. Nac. Patag. Contrib.* **33**: 1-18.
Scott, D. (1971). The Auckland Island flightless Teal. *Wildfowl* **22**: 44-45.
Scott, D. (1984). The feeding success of Cattle Egrets in flocks. *Anim. Behav.* **32**: 1089-1100.
Scott, D. & Lubbock, J. (1974). Preliminary observations on waterfowl of western Madagascar. *Wildfowl* **25**: 117-120.
Scott, D.A. (1970). *The Breeding Biology of the Storm Petrel*. Unpublished PhD thesis, University of Oxford.
Scott, D.A. (1982a). Problems in the management of waterfowl populations. Pp. 89-106 in: Scott, D.A. & Smart, M. eds. (1982). *Proceedings Second Technical Meeting on Western Palaearctic Migratory Bird Management.*
Scott, D.A. ed. (1982b). *Managing Wetlands and their Birds. A Manual of Wetland and Waterfowl Management.* IWRB, Slimbridge, England.
Scott, D.A. ed. (1989). *A Directory of Asian Wetlands*. IUCN, Gland, Switzerland and Cambridge, England.
Scott, D.A. & Brooke, M. de L. (1985). The endangered avifauna of southeastern Brazil: a report on the BOU/WWF expedition of 1980/81 and 1981/82. Pp. 115-139 in: Diamond & Lovejoy (1985).
Scott, D.A. & Carbonell, M. compilers. (1986). *A Directory of Neotropical Wetlands*. IWRB, Slimbridge and UICN, Cambridge, England.
Scott, D.A. & Howes, J.R. (1989). *Xuan Thuy Reserve, Red River Delta, Vietnam. Some Recommendations for Management*. Publication **44**. Asian Wetland Bureau, Kuala Lumpur, Malaysia.
Scott, D.K. (1977). Breeding behaviour of wild whistling swans. *Wildfowl* **28**: 101-106.
Scott, D.K. (1978a). *Social Behaviour of Wintering Bewick's Swans*. PhD thesis, University of Cambridge, England.
Scott, D.K. (1978b). Identification of Individual Bewick's Swans by Bill Patterns. In: Stonehouse, B. ed. *Animal Marking*. Macmillan, London.
Scott, D.K. (1980). Functional aspects of prolonged parental care in Bewick's Swans. *Anim. Behav.* **28**: 938-952.
Scott, D.K. (1984a). Winter territoriality of Mute Swans *Cygnus olor*. *Ibis* **126**: 168-176.
Scott, D.K. (1984b). Parent-offspring association in Mute Swans. *Z. Tierpsychol.* **64**: 74-86.
Scott, D.K. (1988). Reproductive success in Bewick's Swan. Pp. 220-236 in: Clutton-Brock, T.H. ed. (1988). *Reproductive Success*. University Press, Chicago.
Scott, D.K. & Birkhead, M.E. (1983). Resources and reproductive performance in Mute Swans. *J. Zoology. London* **200**: 539-547.
Scott, J.A. (1972). Woolly-necked Stork breeding in Rhodesia. *Ostrich* **43**: 68.
Scott, J.A. (1975). Observations on the breeding of the Woolly-necked Stork. *Ostrich* **46**: 201-207.
Scott, J.M. & Kepler, C.B. (1985). Distribution and abundance of Hawaiian native birds: a status report. Pp. 43-70 in: Temple, S.A. ed. (1985). *Bird Conservation ICBP*. University of Wisconsin Press, Wisconsin.
Scott, J.M., Mountainspring, S., Ramsey, F.L. & Kepler, C.B. (1986). *Forest Bird Communities of the Hawaiian Island: Their Dynamics, Ecology, and Conservation*. Studies in Avian Biology **9**. Cooper Ornithological Society, Allen, Kansas.
Scott, P. (1954a). South America-1953. *Wildfowl Trust Ann. Rep.* **6**: 55-69.
Scott, P. (1954b). Behaviour of the Bolivian Torrent Duck. *Wildfowl Trust Ann. Rep.* **6**: 69-72.
Scott, P. (1970). Redbreasts in Rumania. *Wildfowl* **21**: 37-41.
Scott, P. (1972). *A Coloured Key of the Wildfowl of the World*. The Wildfowl Trust.
Scott, P. (1985). Duck. Pp. 157-161 in: Campbell & Lack (1985).
Scott, P. & Fisher, J. (1953). *A Thousand Geese*. Collins, London.
Scott, P. & Wildfowl Trust (1972). *The Swans*. Michael Joseph, London.
Sealy, S.G. (1978). Clutch size and nest placement of Pied-billed Grebe in Manitoba. *Wilson Bull.* **90**: 301-302.
Sealy, S.G. (1985). Diving times and parental feeding of young in solitarily nesting Eared Grebes. *Colonial Waterbirds* **8**: 63-66.
Sears, J. & Bacon, P.J. eds. (1991). *Third IWRB International Swan Symposium, Oxford 1989. WILDFOWL - Supplement No. 1*. The Wildfowl & Wetlands Trust and the International Waterfowl and Wetlands Research Bureau, Slimbridge, England.
Seddon, P.J. (1988). Patterns of behaviour and nest-site selection in the Yellow-eyed Penguin (*Megadyptes antipodes*). Ph.D. diss., University of Otago, Dunedin, New Zealand.
Seddon, P.J. (1989a). Copulation in the Yellow-eyed Penguin. *Notornis* **36**: 50-51.
Seddon, P.J. (1989b). Patterns of nest relief and incubation: span variability in the Yellow-eyed Penguin. *New Zealand J. Zool.* **16**: 393-400.
Seddon, P.J. (1990). Behaviour of the Yellow-eyed Penguin chick. *J. Zoology. London* **220**: 333-343.
Seddon, P.J. & Davis, L.S. (1989). Nest-site selection by Yellow-eyed Penguins. *Condor* **91**: 653-659.
Seddon, P.J. & van Heezik, Y. (1991a). Effects of hatching order, sibling asymmetries, and nest site on survival analysis of Jackass Penguin chicks. *Auk* **108(3)**: 548-555.
Seddon, P.J. & van Heezik, Y.M. (1991b). Patterns of nest relief during incubation by Jackass Penguin, *Spheniscus demersus*. *Ostrich* **62**: 82-83.
Seddon, P.J. & van Heezik, Y.M. (1991c). Hatching asynchrony and brood reduction in the Jackass Penguin: an experimental study. *Anim. Behav.* **42(3)**: 347-356.
Seddon, P.J., van Heezik, Y.M. & Cooper, J. (1991). Observations of within-colony breeding synchrony in Jackass Penguins. *Wilson Bull.* **103(3)**: 480-485.
Segonzac, M. (1972). Données recentes sur la faune des Iles Saint-Paul et Nouvelle Amsterdam. *L'Oiseau et la R.F.O.* **42(No. Spéc.)**: 1-68.
Seibt, U. & Wickler, W. (1978). Marabou storks wash dung beetles. *Z. Tierpsychol.* **46(3)**: 324-327.
Seki, M.P. & Harrison, C.S. (1989). Feeding ecology of two subtropical seabird species at French Frigate Shoals, Hawaii. *Bull. Mar. Sci.* **45(1)**: 52-67.
Selander, R.K. (1971). Systematics and speciation in birds. Pp. 57-147 in: Farner, D.S. & King, J.R. (1971). *Avian Biology*. Vol. 1. Academic Press, London & New York.
Selous, E. (1915). An observation diary of the domestic habits of the Little Grebe or Dabchick. *Wild Life* **4**: 29-35, 38-42, 98-99, 137-141, 175-178, 219-230.
Semel, B. & Sherman, P.W. (1986). Dynamics of nest parasitism in Wood Ducks. *Auk* **103**: 813-816.
Seriè, P. (1921). Sobre la alimentación de la perdiz común (*Nothura maculosa*). *Hornero* **2**: 230-232.
Sermet, E. (1968). Sur le comportement nocturne de grèbe castagneux *Podiceps ruficollis* à Yuerdon. *Nos Oiseaux* **29**: 269-273.
Serna, M.A. (1990). Algunas aves observadas en la Ciénaga de Ayapel, Córdoba. *Boletin S.A.O.* **1(1)**: 2-21.
Servat, G. & Pearson, D.L. (1991). Natural History and Records for Seven Poorly Known Bird Species from Amazonian Peru. *Bull. Br. Orn. Club* **111(2)**: 92-95.
Serventy, D.L. (1938). The feeding habits of cormorants in south-western Australia. *Emu* **38**: 293-316.
Serventy, D.L. (1939). Notes on cormorants. *Emu* **38**: 357-371.
Serventy, D.L. (1952). Movements of the Wilson Storm-Petrel in Australian seas. *Emu* **52**: 105-116.
Serventy, D.L. (1963). Egg-laying time-table of the Slender-billed Shearwater, *Puffinus tenuirostris*. Pp. 338-343 in: *Proc. XIII Int. Orn. Congr.* **1**.
Serventy, D.L. (1967). Aspects of the population ecology of the Short-tailed Shearwater, *Puffinus tenuirostris*. Pp. 165-190 in: *Proc. XIV Int. Orn. Congr.*
Serventy, D.L. (1974). The biology behind the mutton-bird industry. *Papers & Proc. Royal Soc. Tasmania* **107**: 1-9.
Serventy, D.L. (1985). *The Waterbirds of Australia*. Angus & Robertson Publishers, Australia.
Serventy, D.L. & Curry, P.J. (1984). Observations on colony size, breeding success, recruitment and inter-colony dispersal in a Tasmanian colony of Short-tailed Shearwaters over a 30-year period. *Emu* **84**: 71-79.
Serventy, D.L. & Whittell, H.M. (1962). *Birds of Western Australia*. Paterson, Perth.
Serventy, D.L., Gunn, B.M., Skira, I.J., Bradley, J.S. & Wooller, R.D. (1989). Fledging translocation and philopatry in a seabird. *Oecologia. Heidelb.* **81(3)**: 428-429.
Serventy, D.L., Serventy, V. & Warham, J. (1971). *The Handbook of Australian Seabirds*. A.H. & A.W. Reed, Sydney.
Seth-Smith, D. (1904). On the breeding in captivity of the Tataupa tinamou (*Crypturus tataupa*). *Avicult. Mag.* **2**: 285-292.
Seton, D.H.C. (1973). Observations on breeding of the Great-billed heron in Northern Queensland. *Emu* **73(1)**: 9-11.
Seward, D. (1987). Europe's vanishing storks. *Int. Wildl.* **17(3)**: 4-10.
Seymour, N.R. & Titman, R.D. (1978). Changes in activity patterns, agonistic behavior, and territoriality of Black Ducks (*Anas rubripes*) during the breeding season in a Nova Scotia tidal marsh. *Can. J. Zool.* **56**: 1773-1785.
Sha, G.M. & Qadri, M.Y. (1988). Food of Mallard, *Anas platyrhynchos* at Hokarsar wetland, Kashmir. *J. Bombay Nat. Hist. Soc.* **85(2)**: 325-331.
Shackford, J.S. (1991). The Roseate Spoonbill in Oklahoma. *Bull. Okla. Orn. Soc.* **24**: 1-3.
Shah, R.V. & Desai, J.H. (1972). Possible explanation for voicelessness in the adult stork, *Ibis leucocephalus*. *Pavo* **10**: 21-29.
Shah, R.V. & Desai, J.H. (1975a). Growth and development of the Painted Stork, *Ibis leucocephalus* Pennant. I. Embryonic development. *Pavo* **13**: 83-87.
Shah, R.V. & Desai, J.H. (1975b). Growth and development of the Painted Stork, *Ibis leucocephalus* Pennant. II. Post hatching growth pattern and motor development. *Pavo* **13**: 88-101.
Shah, R.V., Menon, G.K., Desai, J.H. & Jani, M.B. (1977). Feather loss from capital tracts of Painted Storks related to growth and maturity. Part 1. Histo-physiological changes and lipoid secretion in the integument. *J. Anim. Morphol. Physiol.* **24**: 98-107.
Shallenberger, R.J. (1973). *Breeding Biology, Homing Behaviour and Communication Patterns of the Wedge-tailed Shearwater*. PhD thesis, University of California.
Shallenberger, R.J. (1984). Fulmars, Shearwaters, and Gadfly Petrels. Family Procellariidae. Pp. 42-56 in: Haley (1984).
Shanholtzer, G.F. (1970). Breeding records and distribution of the Glossy Ibis on the Georgia coast. *Oriole* **35**: 37-39.
Shannon, P.W. (1981). Social hierarchy in Chilean flamingos (*Phoenicopterus chilensis*) at the Fort Worth Zoo. *Animal Keepers' Forum* **8(8)**: 189-194.
Shannon, P.W. (1987). The Jabiru Stork (*Jabiru mycteria*) in Zoo Collections in the United States. *Colonial Waterbirds* **10(2)**: 242-250.
Sharland, M. (1957a). Royal Spoonbill in Tasmania. *Emu* **57**: 234-235.
Sharland, M. (1957b). White Ibis in Tasmania. *Emu* **57**: 301-302.
Sharrock, J.T.R. (1976). *The Atlas of Breeding Birds in Britain and Ireland*. Poyser, Berkhamsted.
Shaughnessy, G.L. & Shaughnessy, P.D. (1980). A record of the white-backed night heron from the lower Orange River. *Madoqua* **12(2)**: 123.
Shaughnessy, P.D. (1975). Variation in facial colour of the Royal Penguin. *Emu* **75**: 147-152.
Shaughnessy, P.D. (1976). Notes on seabirds at Gough Island. *S. Afr. J. Antarct. Res.* **6**: 23-25.
Shaughnessy, P.D. (1979). Further notes on Crowned Cormorants on the mainland of South West Africa/Namibia. *Cormorant* **6**: 37-38.
Shaughnessy, P.D. (1980). Influence of Cape Fur Seals on Jackass Penguin numbers at Sinclair Island. *S. Afr. J. Wildl. Res.* **10(1)**: 18-21.
Shaughnessy, P.D. (1983). Black-necked Grebes *Podiceps nigricollis* at sea in the vicinity of Lüderitz, South West Africa/Namibia. *Cormorant* **11**: 7-14.
Shaughnessy, P.D. & Shaughnessy, G.L. (1978). Crowned Cormorants on the coast of South West Africa/Namibia. *Cormorant* **5**: 21-25.
Shaw, P. (1985a). Brood reduction in the Blue-eyed Shag *Phalacrocorax atriceps*. *Ibis* **127**: 476-494.
Shaw, P. (1985b). Age-differences within breeding pairs of Blue-eyed Shags *Phalacrocorax atriceps*. *Ibis* **127**: 537-543.
Shaw, P. (1986). Factors affecting the breeding performance of Antarctic Blue-eyed Shags *Phalarocorax atriceps*. *Ornis Scand.* **17**: 141-150.
Shea, R.E. (1979). *The Ecology of the Trumpeter Swan in Yellowstone Park and Vicinity*. MSc thesis, University Montana, Missoula, Montana.
Sheldon, F.H. (1987). Phylogeny of Herons estimated from DNA-DNA hybridization data. *Auk* **104**: 97-108.
Shelley, L.O. (1930). Notes on a Holboell's Grebe in captivity. *Auk* **47**: 238-240.
Shelton, P.A. Crawford, R.J.M., Cooper, J. & Brooke, R.K. (1984). Distribution, population size and conservation of the Jackass Penguin *Spheniscus demersus*. *S. Afr. J. Mar. Sci.* **2**: 217-257.
Shen You-hui, Hu Xi-xing & L. Xu-guang (1987). [A study of the breeding ecology of Chinese Pond Heron, *Ardeola bacchus* in Changsha, Hunan Province]. *Nat. Sci. J. Hunan Normal Univ.* **10(4)**: 65-73. In Chinese with English summary.
Shephard, M. (1986). The benefits of captive breeding in the study and conservation of Australian birds. *RAOU (Royal Australasian Orn. Union) Newsl.* **68**: 6-8.
Shepherd, P., Crockett, T., De Santo, T.L. & Bildstein, K.L. (1991). The Impact of Hurricane Hugo on the Breeding Ecology of Wading Birds at Pumpkinseed Island, Hobcaw Barony, South Carolina. *Colonial Waterbirds* **14(2)**: 150-157.
Sherrit, R. (1969). Junin lagoon marine pollution. Smithsonian Inst. Center for Short-lived Phenomena **562**.
Shevareva, T. (1970). Geographical Distribution of the Main Dabbling Duck Populations in the USSR and the Main Directions of their Migrations. Pp. 46-55 in: Isakov, Y.A. ed. *Proceedings International Regional Meeting on Conservation of Wildfowl Resources, Leningrad*. Moscow.
Shi Dongchou, Yu Xiaoping, Chang Xiuyun & Lu Baozhong (1989). [The breeding habits of the Crested Ibis (*Nipponia nippon*)]. *Zool. Res.* **10(4)**: 327-332. In Chinese with English summary.
Shibaev, I.V., Semenchenko, N.N. & Limin, V.A. (1976). [Nesting area of the White Stork on the right bank of the Ussuri River]. In: [*Nature Conservation in the Soviet Far East*]. In Russian.
Shibnev, Y.B. (1985). Present status of *Aix galericulata* and *Mergus squamatus* on the River Bikin. Pp. 95-99 in: *Rare and Endangered Birds of the Far East*. Far East Sci. Centre, USSR Academy of Science, Vladivostok.
Shields, M.A. (1985). *An analysis of Fish Crow predation on eggs of the White Ibis at Battery Island, North Carolina*. MSc thesis, University of North Carolina, Chapel Hill, N.C.
Shields, M.A. (1987). Internest displacement of White Ibis eggs. *Wilson Bull.* **99(2)**: 273-275.
Shields, M.A. & Parnell, J.F. (1983). Expansion of White Ibis nesting in North Carolina. *Chat* **47**: 101-103.
Shields, M.A. & Parnell, J.F. (1986). Fish Crow predation on eggs of the White Ibis at Battery Island, North Carolina. *Auk* **103**: 531-539.
Shoemaker, V.H. (1972). Osmoregulation and excretion in birds. Pp. 527-574 in: Farner, D.S. & King, J.R. (1972). *Avian Biology*. Vol. 2. Academic Press, London & New York.
Short, L.L. (1975). A zoogeographic analysis of the South American Chaco avifauna. *Bull. Amer. Mus. Nat. Hist.* **154(3)**: 165-352.
Short, L.L. (1976). Notes on a collection of birds from the Paraguayan chaco. *Amer. Mus. Novitates* **2597**: 1-16.
Shoryer, A.W. (1947). The deep diving of the loon and Oldsquaw and its mechanism. *Wilson Bull.* **59**: 151-159.
Shufeldt, R.W. (1915). Comparative osteology of Harris's Flightless Cormorant (*Nannopterum harrisi*). *Emu* **15**. 86-113.
Shufeldt, R.W. (1916). The bird-caves of the Bermudas and their former inhabitants. *Ibis (10th Ser.)* **4**: 623-635.
Shufeldt, R.W. (1922). A comparative study of some subfossil remains of birds from Bermuda, including the "Cahow". *Ann. Carnegie Mus. Nat. Hist.* **13**: 333-418.
Sibley, C.G. (1970). A comparative study of the egg-white proteins of passerine birds. *Bull. Peabody Mus. Nat. Hist. Yale Univ.* **32**.
Sibley, C.G. & Ahlquist, J.E. (1972). A comparative study of the egg white proteins of non-passerine birds. *Bull. Peabody Mus. Nat. Hist. Yale Univ.* **39**: 1-276.
Sibley, C.G. & Ahlquist, J.E. (1981). The phylogeny and classification of the ratite birds as indicated by DNA-DNA hybridization. Pp. 301-335 in: *Evolution Today. Proceedings 2nd. International Congress of Systematics & Evolution of Birds*. Pennsylvania.
Sibley, C.G. & Ahlquist, J.E. (1983). Phylogeny and classification of birds based on the data of DNA-DNA hybridization. *Current Ornithology* **1**: 245-292.
Sibley, C.G. & Ahlquist, J.E. (1985). The relationships of some groups of African birds, based on comparisons of the genetic material, DNA. Pp. 115-161 in: Schuchmann, K.L. ed. *Proceedings of the International Symposium on African Vertebrates: Systematics, Phylogeny and Evolutionary Ecology*. Museum Alexander Koenig, Bonn.
Sibley, C.G. & Ahlquist, J.E. (1990). *Phylogeny and Classification of Birds: A Study in Molecular Evolution*. Yale University Press, New Haven, Connecticut.
Sibley, C.G. & Frelin, C. (1972). Egg white protein evidence for ratite affinities. *Ibis* **114**: 177-387.
Sibley, C.G. & Monroe, B.L. (1990). *Distribution and Taxonomy of Birds of the World*. Yale University Press, New Haven & London.
Sibley, C.G., Ahlquist, J.E. & Monroe, B.L. (1988). A classification of the living birds of the world based on DNA-DNA hybridization studies. *Auk* 105: 409-423.

Sibley, C.G. Corbin, K.W. & Haavie, J.H. (1969). The relationships of the flamingos as indicated by the egg-white proteins and hemoglobins. *Condor* **71(2)**: 155-179.
Sibley, F.C. (1970). Winter wing molt in the Western Grebe. *Condor* **72**: 373.
Sibley, F.C. & Clapp, R.B. (1967). Distribution and dispersal of Central Pacific Lesser Frigatebirds *Fregata ariel*. *Ibis* **109**: 328-337.
Sibson, R.B. (1949). Visit to Little Barrier. *New Zealand Bird Notes* **3**: 151-155.
Sibson, R.B. (1982). *Birds at Risk. Rare or Endangered Species of New Zealand*. Reed, Wellington.
Sibson, R.B. (1988). A black-tailed Australasian Gannet and others with variable tails at Muriwai. *Notornis* **35**: 261-264.
Sichiri, S. (1980). Handraising the Black-headed Ibis. *Animals and Zoos* **32**: 150-151.
Sick, H. (1965). A fauna do cerrado. *Arq. Zool. São Paulo* **12**: 71-93.
Sick, H. (1969). Aves brasileiras ameaçadas de extinçao e noçoes gerais de conservaçao de aves do Brasil. *Anais da Academia Brasileira de Ciências* **41(Suppl.)**: 205-229.
Sick, H. (1972). A ameaça da avifauna brasileira. Pp. 99-153 in: *Especies da Fauna Brasileira Ameaçadas de Extinçao*. Academia Brasileira de Ciências, Rio de Janeiro.
Sick, H. (1984). *Ornitologia brasileira. Uma introduçao*. Vol. 1. Edit. Universidad de Brasília, Brasília.
Sick, H. (1985a). Rhea. Pp. 509-510 in: Campbell & Lack (1985).
Sick, H. (1985b). Tinamou. Pp. 594-595 in: Campbell & Lack (1985).
Sick, H. & Teixeira, D.M. (1979). Notas sobre aves brasileiras raras ou ameaçadas de extinçao. *Publ. Avuls. Mus. Nac.* **62**: 1-39.
Sick, H., Alda do Rosário, L. & Rauh de Azevedo, T. (1981). Aves do Estado de Santa Catarina. Lista sistemática baseada em bibliografia, material de museu e observaçao de campo. *Sellówia (Ser. Zool.)* **1**: 1-51.
Sidle, J.G. & Ferguson, E.L. (1982). White pelican populations at Chase Lake, North Dakota, evaluated by aerial photography. *Prairie Nat.* **14**: 13-26.
Sidle, J.G., Koonz, W.H. & Roney, K. (1985). Status of the American White Pelican: an update. *Amer. Birds* **39**: 859-864.
Siegel-Causey, D. (1986a). The courtship behavior and mixed-species pairing of King and Imperial Blue-eyed shags (*Phalacrocorax albiventer* and *P.atriceps*). *Wilson Bull.* **98(4)**: 571-580.
Siegel-Causey, D. (1986b). Behaviour and affinities of the Magellanic Cormorant. *Notornis* **33**: 249-257.
Siegel-Causey, D. (1988). Philogeny of the Phalacrocoracidae. *Condor* **90**: 885-905.
Siegel-Causey, D. (1989a). Cranial pneumatization in the Phalacrocoracidae. *Wilson Bull.* **101(1)**: 108-112.
Siegel-Causey, D. (1989b). The behaviour of the Red-legged Cormorant (*Phalacrocorax gaimardi*). *Notornis* **34**: 1-9.
Siegel-Causey, D. (1990). Phylogenetic patterns of size and shape of the nasal gland depression in Phalacrocoracidae. *Auk* **107**: 110-118.
Siegel-Causey, D. & Hunt, G.L. (1981). Colonial defense behavior in Double-crested and Pelagic Cormorants. *Auk* **98**: 522-531.
Siegel-Causey, D. & Hunt, G.L. (1986). Breeding-site selection and colony formation in Double-crested and Pelagic Cormorants. *Auk* **103**: 230-234.
Siegfried, W.R. (1962a). Observations on the post-embryonic development of Egyptian Goose *Alopochen aegyptiacus* (L.) and the Redbill Teal *Anas erythrohyncha* Gmelin. *Invest. Rep. Dept. Nat. Cons. (Cape)* **2**: 9-17.
Siegfried, W.R. (1962b). Nesting behaviour of the Redbill Teal *Anas erythrorhyncha* Gmelin. *Invest. Rep. Dept. Nat. Cons. (Cape)* **2**: 19-24.
Siegfried, W.R. (1965). The Cape Shoveler *Anas smithii* (Hartert) in southern Africa. *Ostrich* **37**: 155-198.
Siegfried, W.R. (1966a). The Bald Ibis. *Bokmakierie* **18**: 54-57.
Siegfried, W.R. (1966b). The past and present distribution of the Bald Ibis in the Province of the Cape of Good Hope. *Ostrich* **37**: 216-218.
Siegfried, W.R. (1966c). On the post-embryonic development of the South African Shelduck *Tadorna cana* (Gmel.). *Ostrich* **37**: 149-151.
Siegfried, W.R. (1967a). The distribution and status of the Black Stork in southern Africa. *Ostrich* **38**: 179-185.
Siegfried, W.R. (1967b). Trapping and ringing of Egyptian Geese and African Shelduck at Vogelvlei, Cape. *Ostrich* **38**: 173-178.
Siegfried, W.R. (1968a). Spoonbills breeding at Stellenbosch, Cape Province, South Africa. *Ostrich* **39**: 199.
Siegfried, W.R. (1968b). The Black Duck in the south-western Cape. *Ostrich* **39**: 61-75.
Siegfried, W.R. (1968c). Non-breeding plumage in the adult male Maccoa Duck. *Ostrich* **39**: 91-93.
Siegfried, W.R. (1970). Wildfowl distribution, conservation and research in Southern Africa. *Wildfowl* **21**: 89-98.
Siegfried, W.R. (1971a). Feeding association between *Podiceps ruficollis* and *Anas smithii*. *Ibis* **113**: 236-238.
Siegfried, W.R. (1971b). The nest of the Cattle Egret. *Ostrich* **42**: 193-197.
Siegfried, W.R. (1971c). The food of the Cattle Egret. *J. Applied Ecol.* **8**: 447-468.
Siegfried, W.R. (1971d). The status of the Bald Ibis of southern Africa. *Biol. Conserv.* **3**: 88-91.
Siegfried, W.R. (1972a). Breeding success and reproductive output of the Cattle Egret. *Ostrich* **43(1)**: 43-55.
Siegfried, W.R. (1972b). Aspects of the feeding ecology of Cattle Egrets (*Ardeola ibis*) in South Africa. *J. Anim. Ecol.* **41**: 71-78.
Siegfried, W.R. (1972c). Discrete breeding and wintering areas of the Waldrapp *Geronticus eremita* (L.). *Bull. Brit. Orn. Club* **92**: 102-103.
Siegfried, W.R. (1973a). Morphology and ecology of the southern African whistling ducks (*Dendrocygna*). *Auk* **90**: 198-201.
Siegfried, W.R. (1973b). Post-embryonic development of the Ruddy Duck and some other diving ducks. *Int. Zoo Yb.* **13**.
Siegfried, W.R. (1974). Brood care, pair bonds and plumage in southern African Anatini. *Wildfowl* **25**: 33-40.
Siegfried, W.R. (1975). On the nest of the Hamerkop. *Ostrich* **46**: 267.
Siegfried, W.R. (1976a). Social organization in Ruddy and Maccoa Ducks. *Auk* **93**: 560-570.
Siegfried, W.R. (1976b). Breeding biology and parasitism in the Ruddy Duck. *Wilson Bull.* **88**: 566-574.
Siegfried, W.R. (1978). Habitat and the Modern Range Expansion of the Cattle Egret. Pp. 315-324 in: Sprunt *et al.* (1978).
Siegfried, W.R. (1979). Social behaviour of the African Comb Duck. *Living Bird* **17**: 85-104.
Siegfried, W.R. & Crawford, R.J.M. (1978). Jackass Penguins, eggs and guano: Diminishing resources at Dassen Island. *S. Afr. J. Sci.* **74**: 389-390.
Siegfried, W.R. & Frost, P.G.H. (1974). Egg temperature and incubation behaviour of the ostrich. *Madoqua (Ser. I)* **8**: 63-66.
Siegfried, W.R. & Grimes, L.G. (1985). Hamerkop. Pp. 270-271 in: Campbell & Lack (1985).
Siegfried, W.R. & van der Merwe, F.J. (1975). A description and inventory of the displays of the Maccoa Duck. *Z. Tierpsychol.* **37**: 1-23.
Siegfried, W.R., Burger, A.E. & Caldwell, P.J. (1976). Incubation behaviour of Ruddy and Maccoa Ducks. *Condor* **78**: 512-517.
Siegfried, W.R., Burger, A.E. & Frost, P.G.H. (1976). Energy requirements for breeding in the Maccoa Duck. *Ardea* **64**: 171-191.
Siegfried, W.R., Burger, A.E. & van der Merwe, F.J. (1976). Activity budgets of male Maccoa Duck *Oxyura maccoa*. *Z. Tierpsychol.* **37**: 23.
Siegfried, W.R., Frost, P.G.H., Ball, I.J. & McKinney, F.D.F. (1977). Evening gatherings and night roosting of African Black Ducks. *Ostrich* **48 (1,2)**: 5-16.
Siegfried, W.R., Frost, P.G.H., Cooper, J. & Kemp, A.C. (1976). *South African Red Data Book - Aves*. South African National Science Program Report **7**: 1-108.
Siegfried, W.R., Frost, P.G.H., Kinahan, J.B. & Cooper, J. (1975). Social behaviour of Jackass Penguins at sea. *Zool. Africana* **10**: 87-100.
Siegfried, W.R., Hockey, P.A.R., Ryan, P.G. & Bosman, A.L. (1988). Sex and plumage-type ratios of the Lesser Magellan Goose in Southern Chile. *Wildfowl* **39**: 15-21.
Siegfried, W.R., Williams, A.J., Frost, P.G.H. & Kinahan, J.B. (1975). Plumage and ecology of cormorants. *Zool. Africana* **10**: 183-192.
Sievi, J.R. (1975). Hamerkop breeding. *Honeyguide* **8**: 33-34.
Siewert, H. (1932). *Störche*. D.Reimer & E. Vohsen, Berlin.
Sifgusson, A. (1990). *Studies of Pre-breeding Fulmars (*Fulmarus glacialis*), their Recruitment to Breeding Populations and Intermittent Breeding*. PhD thesis, University of Aberdeen.
Sillman, A.J. (1973). Avian vision. Pp. 349-387 in: Farner, D.S. & King, J.R. (1973). *Avian Biology*. Vol. 3. Academic Press, London & New York.
Silva, F. & Sander, M. (1981). Estudio sobre a alimentaçao de perdiz (*Nothura maculosa*) (Temminck, 1815) no Rio Grande do Sul, Brasil (Aves, Tinamiformes, Tinamidae). *Iheringia* **58**: 65-77.
da Silveira, C.F.B. & Menegheti, J.O. (1981). Estudo sobre a relaçao peso e sexo em "*Nothura maculosa*" (Temmick, 1815) (Aves, Tinamiformes, Tinamidae). *Iheringia (Zool.)* **58**: 7-16.
Silveira, E.K.P. (1967). Distribuçao geográfica do inhambú-carapé no sudeste de Goiás e Brasília, Brasil Central. *Bol. Geo. de Rio de Janeiro* **200**: 38-41.
Silveira, E.K.P. (1968). A brief note on the Little Tinamou, *Taoniscus nanus*, in Brasília Zoo. *Int. Zoo. Yb.* **8**: 212.
Silvius, M.J. (1986). Survey of coastal wetlands in Sumatra Selatan and Jambi, Indonesia. Asian Wetland Bureau (AWB-PHPA)/Interwader Report **1**. Bogor, Indonesia.
Silvius, M.J. & Verheugt, W.J.M. (1989). The status of storks, ibises and spoonbills in Indonesia. *Kukila* **4**: 119-132.
Silvius, M.J. & de Yongh, H. (1989). White-winged Wood Duck, a new site for Jambi Province. *Kukila* **4(3-4)**: 150-151.
Silvius, M.J., Lambert, F.R. & Taufik, A.W. (1991). Conservation of the Wasur Game Reserve and Rawa Biru Nature Reserve, South-east Irian Jaya. Asian Wetland Bureau (AWB-PHPA), Bogor, Indonesia.
Silvius, M.J., Steeman, A.P.J.M., Berczy, E.T., Djuharsa, E. & Taufik, A.W. (1987). *The Indonesian Wetland Inventory. A Preliminary Compilation of Existing Information on Wetlands of Indonesia*. Asian Wetland Bureau (AWB-PHPA), EDWIN, Bogor, Indonesia.
Silvius, M.J., Verheugt, J.M. & Iskandar, J. (1985). Coastal surveys in southeast Sumatra. *Interwader Annual Report* **1984**: 133-142.
Silvius, M.J., Verheugt, J.M. & Iskandar, J. (1986). *Coastal Wetlands Inventory of Southeast Sumatra*. ICBP Study Report **9**. ICBP, Cambridge, England.
Silyn-Roberts, H. (1983). The pore geometry and structure of the eggshell of the North Island brown kiwi, *Apteryx australis mantelli*. *J. Microsc.* **130**: 23-36.
Silyn-Roberts, H. & Sharp, R.M. (1985). Preferred orientation of calcite in the ratite and tinamou eggshells. *J. Zoology. London* **205**: 39-52.
Simmons, K.E.L. (1955). Studies on Great Crested Grebes. 1. Introductory and some general aspects: 3-13. 2. Routine and general habits: 93-102. 3. Threat and fighting and their relation to sexual rivalry, territory, the defence of the young, and courtship: 131-146. 4. The significance of courtship and related behaviour: 294-310. Additional notes: 310-311. Conclusion: The behaviour of other species of grebe: 311-313. Summary of contents: 313-314. References: 315-316. *Avicult. Mag.* **61**.
Simmons, K.E.L. (1962a). Some recommendations for a revised checklist of the genera and species of grebes (Podicipedidae). *Bull. Brit. Orn. Club* **82**: 109-116.
Simmons, K.E.L. (1962b). A new race of the grebe *Podiceps chilensis* from Lake Junín, Peru. *Bull. Brit. Orn. Club* **82**: 92-94.
Simmons, K.E.L. (1965). The ritual world of the Great Crested Grebe. *Animals* **6**: 226-231.
Simmons, K.E.L. (1967a). *The Role of Food Supply in the Biology of the Brown Booby at Ascension Island*. MSc thesis, Bristol University.
Simmons, K.E.L. (1967b). Ecological adaptations in the life history of the Brown Booby at Ascension Island. *Living Bird* **6**: 187-212.
Simmons, K.E.L. (1968a). The taxonomic position of the Little Grebe. *British Birds* **61**: 322-324.
Simmons, K.E.L. (1968b). Occurrence and behaviour of the Redfooted Booby at Ascension Island, 1962-64. *Bull. Brit. Orn. Club* **88**: 15-20.
Simmons, K.E.L. (1969). The Pied-billed Grebe at Blagdon Lake, Somerset, in 1968. *Bristol Orn.* **1**: 21-26.
Simmons, K.E.L. (1970a). Duration of dives in the Red-necked Grebe. *British Birds* **63**: 300-302.
Simmons, K.E.L. (1970b). *The Biology of the Parent-chick Stage in the Great Crested Grebe* Podiceps cristatus. PhD thesis. University of Bristol.
Simmons, K.E.L. (1972). Some adaptive features of seabird plumage types. *British Birds* **65**: 465-479, 510-521.
Simmons, K.E.L. (1974a). Adaptations in the reproductive biology of the Great Crested Grebe. *British Birds* **67**: 413-437.
Simmons, K.E.L. (1974b). Biology of the Brown Booby and conservation at Ascension Island. Report to the Royal Society.
Simmons, K.E.L. (1975). Further Studies on Great Crested Grebes. 1. Courtship. *Bristol Orn.* **8**: 89-107.
Simmons, K.E.L. (1977a). Further Studies on Great Crested Grebes. 2. Maintenance activities and routine. *Bristol Orn.* **10**: 175-196.
Simmons, K.E.L. (1977b). Biology of the Brown Booby and seabird conservation at Ascension Island. Report to the Royal Society.
Simmons, K.E.L. (1983). The Hooded Grebe. *British Birds* **76**: 42.
Simmons, K.E.L. (1985). Grebe. Pp. 254-256 in: Campbell & Lack (1985).
Simmons, K.E.L. (1989). *The Great Crested Grebe*. Shire Natural History series **37**, Aylesbury.
Simon, N. & Géroudet, P. (1970). *Last Survivors. The Natural History of Animals in Danger of Extinction*.
Simons, T.R. (1981). Behavior and attendance patterns of the Fork-tailed Storm-Petrel. *Auk* **98**: 145-158.
Simons, T.R. (1984). A population model of the endangered Hawaiian Dark-rumped Petrel. *J. Wildl. Manage.* **48**: 1065-1076.
Simons, T.R. (1985). Biology and behavior of the endangered Hawaiian Dark-rumped Petrel. *Condor* **87**: 229-245.
Simons, T.R. & Whittow, G.C. (1984). Energetics of breeding Dark-rumped Petrels. Pp. 159-181 in Whittow, G.C. & Rahn, H. eds. *Seabird Energetics*. Plenum, New York.
Simpson, D.M. (1973). Seabird colonies on the rocky islands of Sento Shosho, 28° 48' N, 123° 36' E, and Sekibo Sho Islet, 25° 55' N, 124° 34' E. *Sea Swallow* **22**: 29.
Simpson, G.G. (1946). Fossil penguins. *Bull. Amer. Mus. Nat. Hist.* **87**: 1-100.
Simpson, G.G. (1976). *Penguins: Past and Present, Here and There*. Yale University Press, New Haven.
Simpson, K., Smith, J.N.M. & Kelsall, J.P. (1987). Correlates and consequences of coloniality in great blue herons. *Can. J. Zool.* **65**: 572-577.
Simpson, K.N.G. (1985). A Rockhopper x Royal Penguin hybrid from Macquarie Island. *Austr. Bird Watcher* **11**: 35-45.
Simpson, M.B. (1988). Status of the Scarlet Ibis in South Carolina: historical records from John Abbot and Alexander Wilson. *Chat* **52**: 4-5.
Simpson, S.G. & Jarvis, R.L. (1979). Comparative ecology of several subspecies of Canada Geese during winter in western Oregon. Pp. 233-240 in: Jarvis, R.L. & Bartonek, J.C. eds. *Management and Biology of Pacific Flyway Geese*. Oregon State University Bookstores, Corvallis.
Sinclair, A.R.E. (1978). Factors affecting the food supply and breeding season of resident birds and movements of Palearctic migrants in a tropical African savanna. *Ibis* **120**: 480-497.
Sinclair, J.C., Brooke, R.K. & Randall, R.M. (1982). Races and records of the Little Shearwater *Puffinus assimilis* in South African waters. *Cormorant* **10**: 19-26.
Sincock, J.L. & Swedberg, G.E. (1969). Rediscovery of the nesting grounds of Newell's Manx Shearwater with initial observations. *Condor* **71**: 69-71.
Singh, G. & Singh, C. (1960). The Adjutant Stork, *Leptoptilos dubius* (Gmelin), a destroyer of locusts in Rajasthan. *J. Bombay Nat. Hist. Soc.* **57**: 221-222.
Sitwell, N. (1984). Storks get a helping hand. *Int. Wildl.* **14**: 14-19.
Sivak, J. (1976). The role of a flat cornea in the amphibious behaviours of the Blackfoot Penguin (*Spheniscus demersus*). *Can. J. Zool.* **54**: 1341-1346.
Sivak, J., Howland, H.C. & Mc Gill-Harelstad, P. (1987). Vision of the Humboldt Penguin (*Spheniscus humboldti*) in air and water. *Proc. Royal Soc. London (Ser. B)* **229(1257)**: 467-472.
Sivelle, C. (1984). Management and propagation of Chilean flamingos in a private collection. *Amer. Pheasant Waterfowl Soc. Mag.* **84(10)**: 1-3.
Sjöberg, K. (1980). The Goosander - Relation to Man. *Danske Fugle* **32**: 152-157.
Sjölander, S. (1977). *On the Behaviour of the Red-throated Diver* Gavia stellata *during Reproduction*. Stockholms University, Stockholm.
Sjölander, S. (1978). Reproductive behaviour of the Black-throated Diver *Gavia arctica*. *Ornis Scand.* **9**: 51-65.
Sjölander, S. (1985). Diver. Pp. 149-150 in: Campbell & Lack (1985).
Sjölander, S. & Agren, G. (1972). Reproductive behavior of the Common Loon. *Wilson Bull.* **84**: 296-308.
Sjölander, S. & Agren, G. (1976). Reproductive behavior of the Yellow-billed Loon, *Gavia adamsii*. *Condor* **78**: 454-463.
Skadsen, D. (1988). White-faced Ibis nesting in Day County, South Dakota. *Bird Notes* **40**: 94.
Skead, C.J. (1951). A study of the Hadedah Ibis *Hagedashia h. hagedash*. *Ibis* **93**: 360-382.
Skead, C.J. (1954). African Spoonbills (*Platalea alba*) nesting near Graaf Reinet. *Ostrich* **25**: 41.
Skead, C.J. (1966). Hadedah Ibis *Hagedashia hagedash* (Latham) in the eastern Cape Province. *Ostrich* **37**: 103-108.
Skead, C.J. (1967). Ecology of birds in the eastern Cape Province. *Ostrich Suppl.* **7**: 1-103.
Skead, D.M (1976). *Social Behavior of the Yellow-billed Duck and Red-billed Teal in Relation to Breeding*. MSc thesis, University of Natal.
Skead, D.M. (1977a). Pair-forming and breeding behaviour of the Cape Shoveler at Barberspan. *Ostrich* **12(Suppl.)**.
Skead, D.M. (1977b). Diurnal activity budgets of Anatini during winter. *Ostrich* **12(Suppl.)**: 65-74.
Skead, D.M. (1977c). Pair-bond of the Cape Shoveler. *Ostrich* **12(Suppl.)**: 135-136.
Skead, D.M. (1977d). Feeding association between Dabchicks and four *Anas* species. *Ostrich* **12(Suppl.)**: 132-134.
Skead, D.M. (1980a). Dispersal, life expectancy, and annual mortality of Whitebreasted Cormorants *Phalacrocorax carbo* ringed as nestling at Barberspan. *Cormorant* **8**: 73-80.
Skead, D.M. (1980b). *The Ecological Relationship of the Yellow-billed Duck to its Habitat at Barberspan and Vicinity*. MSc thesis, Potchefstroom University.

Skead, D.M. & Dean, W.R.J. (1977a). Seasonal abundance of Anatidae at Barberspan. *Ostrich* **12(Suppl.)**: 49-64.
Skead, D.M. & Dean, W.R.J. (1977b). Status of the Barberspan avifauna, 1971-1975. *Ostrich* **12(Suppl.)**: 3-42.
Skewes, O.E. (1978). *Determinaciónn de concentraciones de DDT y DDE en lípidos de* Phalacrocorax ol. olivaceus *capturados en la Bahía de Concepción*. Tesis Med. Vet. University Concepción, Chillán.
Skinner, J., Wallace, J.P., Altenburg, W. & Fofana, B. (1987). The status of Heron colonies in the Inner Niger Delta Mali. *Malimbus* **9**: 65-82.
Skira, I.J. (1979). Underwater feeding by Short-tailed Shearwaters. *Emu* **79**: 43.
Skira, I.J. (1991). The Short-tailed Shearwater: a review of its biology. *Corella* **15(2)**: 45-52.
Skira, I.J., Wapstra, J.E., Towney, G.N. & Naarding, J.A. (1985). Conservation of the Short-tailed Shearwater in Tasmania, Australia. *Biol. Conserv.* **37**: 225-236.
Sklepkovych, B.O. & Montevecchi, W.A. (1989). The world's largest known nesting colony of Leach's Storm-Petrels on Baccalieu Island, Newfoundland. *Amer. Birds* **43**(1): 38-42.
Sklyarenko, S.L. & Berezovikov, N.N. (1987). [*Rare and Endangered Animals of Kazakhstan. Storks*]. Kainar, Alma-Ata. In Russian.
Skokova, N.N. (1959). [The Spoonbill in the Volga Delta, its ecology and a role in the fishery]. *Ornitologiya* **2**: 262-270. In Russian.
Skutch, A.F. (1959). The Great Tinamou of the tropical forest. *Animal Kingdom* **62**: 179-183.
Skutch, A.F. (1963). Life history of the little tinamou. *Condor* **65**: 224-231.
Skutch, A.F. (1976). *Parent Birds and Their Young*. University of Texas Press, Austin, Texas.
Skutch, A.F. (1983). *Birds of Tropical America*. University of Texas Press, Austin, Texas.
Skutch, A.F. (1989). *Birds Asleep*. University of Texas Press, Austin, Texas.
Sladen, W.J.L. (1958). The pygoscelid penguins, I: methods of study, II: the Adelie Penguin. *Falkland Is. Depend. Surv. Sci. Rep.* **17**: 1-97.
Slater, C.A. (1990). First arrival dates at two fulmar colonies in Norfolk. *Bird Study* **37**: 1-4.
Slater, P. (1978). *Rare and Vanishing Australian Birds*. Rigby, Adelaide, Australia.
Slater, P. (1987). *Australian Waterbirds*. Reed Books, Frenchs Forest, NSW.
Slater, P. (1991). Learned song variations in British Storm-Petrels? *Wilson Bull.* **103(3)**: 515-517.
Sleptsov, M.M. (1960). Buller's Shearwater in U.S.S.R. waters. *Ornitologiya* **3**: 410-412.
Slipp, J.W. (1952). A record of the Tasmanian White-capped Albatross in American North Pacific waters. *Auk* **69**: 458-459.
Sloan, N.F. (1973). Status of breeding colonies of White Pelicans in the United States through 1972. *Inland Bird Banding News* **45**: 83-96.
Sloan, N.F. (1982). Status of breeding colonies of White Pelicans in the United States through 1979. *American Birds* **36**: 250-254.
Slud, P. (1964). *The Birds of Costa Rica. Distribution and Ecology*. Bulletin of the American Museum of Natural History **128**. New York.
Smart, N. & Andrew, J. (1985). *Birds and Broadleaves Handbook. A Guide to Further the Conservation of Birds in Broadleaved Woodland*. RSPB.
Smirenski, S.M., Andronov, V.A. & Bylkov, A.F. (1987). First results of colour marking of the White Stork ("Ciconia boyciana"). *Ornitologiya* **22**: 219-220.
Smit, D.J.V.Z. (1973). Ostrich farming in the Little Karoo. *Bull. Dept. Agricult. Techn. Services*. **358**. Government Printer, Pretoria.
Smith, E.L. (1981). *Effects of Canoeing on Common Loon Production and Survival on the Kenai National Wildlife Refuge, Alaska*. MSc thesis, University of Wisconsin, Stevens Point.
Smith, G.H. (1943). Parachute action when settling of Sacred Ibis and Spoonbill. *Ostrich* **14**: 192-194.
Smith, J.D. (1952). The Hawaiian Goose (Nene) restoration program. *J. Wildl. Manage.* **16**: 1-9.
Smith, K.D. (1957). An annotated list of the birds of Eritrea. *Ibis* **99**: 1-26, 307-337.
Smith, K.D. (1970). The Waldrapp *Geronticus eremita* (L.). *Bull. Brit. Orn. Club* **90**: 18-24.
Smith, L. (1982). Aerial Survey of Kangaroos and Emus in NW Victoria, 1982. Unpublished Report NPWS, Vic, Australia.
Smith, M.C. (1949). *Notes on Birds of Burma*. Privately printed, Simla.
Smith, R.B. & Breininger, D.R. (1988). Northern breeding range extension for the Roseate Spoonbill in Florida. *Florida Field Nature* **16**: 65-67.
Smith, R.I. (1968). The social aspects of reproductive behavior in the Pintail. *Auk* **85**: 381-396.
Smith, R.I.L. & Prince, P.A. (1985). The natural history of Beauchene Island. *Biol. J. Linn. Soc.* **24**: 233-283.
Smith, S.M. (1983). The ontogeny of avian behavior. Pp. 85-160 in: Farner, S.D., King, J.R. & Parkes, K.C. (1983). *Avian Biology*. Vol. 7.
Smithe, F.B. (1966). *The Birds of Tikal*. The American Museum of Natural History, New York.
Smythies, B.E. (1981). *The Birds of Borneo*. 3rd. edition. The Sabah Society and the Malayan Nature Society, Kuala Lumpur, Malaysia.
Smythies, B.E. (1986). *The Birds of Burma*. 3rd. edition. Nimrod Press Ltd, Liss, Hants, England.
Snow, B.K. (1960). The breeding biology of the Shag *Phalacrocorax aristotelis* on the island of Lundy, Bristol Channel. *Ibis* **102**: 554-575.
Snow, B.K. (1963). The behaviour of the Shag. *British Birds* **56**: 77-103, 164-186.
Snow, B.K. (1966). Observations on the behaviour and ecology of the Flightless Cormorant (*Nannopterum harrisi*). *Ibis* **108**: 265-280.
Snow, D.W. (1950). The birds of Sao Tomé and Príncipe in the Gulf of Guinea. *Ibis* **92**: 579-595.
Snow, D.W. (1965a). The breeding of Audubon's Shearwater in the Galapagos. *Auk* **82**: 591-597.
Snow, D.W. (1965b). The Breeding of the Red-billed Tropicbird in the Galapagos Islands. *Condor* **67**: 210-214.
Snow, D.W. ed. (1978). *An Atlas of Speciation in African Non-passerine Birds*. Trustees of the British Museum (Natural History), London.
Snow, D.W. (1985). The Status of Forest Birds in South America. Pp. 63-66 in: Diamond & Lovejoy (1985).
Snow, D.W. & Snow, B.K. (1966). The breeding season of the Madeiran Storm Petrel in the Galapagos. *Ibis* **108**: 283-284.
Snyder, D. (1966). *The Birds of Guyana*. Peabody Museum, Salem, MA.
Snyder, L.L. (1957). *Arctic Birds of Canada*. University Toronto Press, Toronto.
Sobczyk, R. (1975). Great Crested Grebe (*Podiceps cristatus* L.) on some of the lakes in the Mazurian lakeland. *Pol. Arch. Hydrobiol.* **22**: 181-194.
Sobrinho, G. (1932). (*Tigrisoma lineatum*). *Rev. Mus. Paulista* **17**: 918.
Sodhi, N.S. (1986). Feeding Ecology of Indian Pond Heron and its comparison with that of Little Egret. *Pavo* **24(1-2)**: 97-116.
Sodhi, N.S. & Khera, S. (1986). Feeding Habits of the Median Egret. *Res. Bull. Panjab Univ. Sci.* **37(1-2)**: 9-12.
Sody, H.J.V. (1930). (*Ardeola speciosa*). *Tectona* **23**: 183-198.
Sokolowski, J. (1960). *The Mute Swan in Poland*. State Council for Conservation of Nature, Warsaw.
van Someren, V.D. (1947). Field notes on some Madagascar birds. *Ibis* **89**: 235-267.
van Someren, V.G.L. (1956). *Days with Birds. Studies of Habits of Some East African Species*. Fieldiana (Zool.) **38**: 1-520.
Somme, L. (1977). Observations on the Snow Petrel in Vestfjella, Dronning Maud Land. *Norsk Polarinst. Arbok* **1976**: 285-292.
Soni, V.C., Chavda, P.B. & Vyas, S. (1989). Feeding behaviour of the Indian Black Ibis in various microhabitats at Rajkot and Junagadh. Pp. 39-43 in: Patel, B.H. ed. *The Behaviour. Proceedings of the National Symposium on Animal Behaviour*. Sir P.P. Institute of Science, Bhavnagar, India.
Sonobe, K. & Izawa, N. (1987). *Endangered Bird Species in the Korean Peninsula*. The Museum of Korean Nature & Wild Bird Society of Japan, Japan.
Soothill, E. & Soothill, R. (1982). *Wading Birds of the World*. Blanford Books, Poole.
Soothill, E. & Whitehead, P. (1978). *Wildfowl of the World*. Peerage Books, London.
Soper, M.F. (1976). *New Zealand Birds*. Whitcoulls Publishers, Christchurch, New Zealand.
Sorensen, J.H. (1950). The light-mantled Sooty Albatross at Campbell Island. *Cape Exp. Ser. Bull.* **8**. DSIR, Wellington, New Zealand.
Sorenson, L.G. (1990). *Breeding Behaviour and Ecology of a Sedentary Tropical Duck: the White-checked Pintail (*Anas bahamensis bahamensis*)*. PhD dissertation, University of Minnesota.
Southwood, T.R.E. (1977). Habitat, the templet for ecological strategies? *J. Anim. Ecol.* **46**: 337-365.
Soutiere, E.C., Myrick, H.S. & Bolen, E.G. (1972). Chronology and behavior of American Widgeon wintering in Texas. *J. Wild. Manage.* **36**: 752-758.
de Souza, J.A. & Gómez de la Torre, F. (1980). Algunas notas sobre *Platalea leucorodia* en Galicia. *Doñana Acta Vertebrata* **7**: 111-113.
Sowls, L.K. (1955). *Prairie Ducks. A Study of Their Behavior, Ecology and Management*. Wildlife Management Institute, University of Nebraska Press, Lincoln & London.
Spaans, A.L. (1975a). The status of the Wood Stork, Jabiru and Maguari Stork along the Surinam coast, South America. *Ardea* **63**: 116-130.
Spaans, A.L. (1975b). On the present breeding status of the scarlet ibis *Eudocimus ruber* along the north-eastern coast of South America. *Biol. Conserv.* **7**: 245-253.
Spaans, A.L. (1982). De Rode Ibis: een pronkjuweel van de overstromingsvlaktes van tropisch Zuid-Amerika. *Het Vogeljaar* **30**: 189-193.
Spaans, A.L. & de Jong, B.H.J. (1982). Present Status of Some Colonial Waterbird Species in Surinam, South America. *J. Field Orn.* **53(3)**: 269-272.
Spanier, E. (1980). The use of distress calls to repeal Night Herons (*Nycticorax nycticorax*) from fish ponds. *J. Appl. Ecol.* **17(2)**: 287-294.
Spano, S. (1965). La sula in Italia. *Revista ital. Orn.* **35**: 1-33.
Sparks, J. & Soper, A. (1987). *Penguins*. Davis & Charles, London.
Sparling, D.W. (1977). Sounds of Laysan and Black-footed Albatrosses. *Auk* **94**: 256-269.
Speirs, E.A.H. (1988). Vocal discrimination among individuals by Adelie Penguins (*Pygoscelis adeliae*). MSc thesis, University of Otago, Dunedin, New Zealand.
Spencer, H.E. (1953). *The Cinnamon Teal (*Anas cyanoptera *Vieillot). Its Life History, Ecology and Management*. MSc thesis, Utah State Agricultural College, Logan.
Spendelow, J.A., Erwin, R.M. & Williams, B.K. (1989). Patterns of species co-occurrence of nesting colonial Ciconiformes in Atlantic Coast estuarine areas. *Colonial Waterbirds* **12(1)**: 51-59.
de Speroni, N.B. & Pirlot, P. (1987). Relative size of avian brain components of the Magellanic Penguin, the Greater Rhea and the Tataupa Tinamou. *Cormorant* **15**: 7-22.
Sperry, M.L. (1987). Common Loon attacks on waterfowl. *J. Field Orn.* **58(2)**: 201-205.
Spil, R.E., van Walstijn, M.W. & Albrecht, H. (1985). Observations on the behaviour of the Scarlet Ibis *Eudocimus ruber* in Artis Zoo, Amsterdam. *Bijdragen tot de Dierkunde* **55**: 219-232.
Spreckels, M. (1983). Hand-rearing Ostriches at the Phoenix Zoo (Arizona, USA). *Avicult. Mag.* **89(4)**: 229-233.
Sprunt, A. (1939). The present status of the Roseate Spoonbill in the United States. *Florida Naturalist* **12(3)**: 49-55.
Sprunt, A. (1954). A hybrid between the Little Blue Heron and the Snowy Egret. *Auk* **71**: 314.
Sprunt, A. (1976). A new Colombian site for the American Flamingo. *Stinapa* **11**: 34-39.
Sprunt, A. (1988). The Greater Flamingo. Pp. 553-564 in: *Audubon Wildlife Report 1988*. National Audubon Society, New York.
Sprunt, A. & Knoder, C.E. (1980). Populations of wading birds and other colonially nesting species on the Gulf and Caribbean coasts of Mexico. Pp. 3-6 in: Schaeffer, P.P. & Ehlers, S.M. eds. *The Birds of Mexico: Their Ecology and Conservation*. Proceedings of the National Audubon Symposium, Tiburon, California.
Sprunt, A., Ogden, J.C. & Winckler, S. eds. (1978). *Wading Birds*. Research Report **7**. National Audubon Society, New York.
Spurr, E.B. (1967a). *Observations on the Winter Activities of the White-faced Heron*. BSc (Hons) thesis, University of Canterbury.
Spurr, E.B. (1967b). *Observations on the Winter Feeding of the White-faced Heron*. BSc (Hons) thesis, University of Canterbury.
Spurr, E.B. (1975a). Breeding of the Adelie Penguin *Pygoscelis adeliae* at Cape Bird. *Ibis* **117**: 324-338.
Spurr, E.B. (1975b). Behaviour of the Adelie Penguin chick. *Condor* **77**: 272-280.
Squibb, R.C. & Hunt, G.L. (1983). A comparison of nesting-ledges used by seabirds on St. George Island. *Ecology* **64(4)**: 727-734.
Sridhar, S. (1989). White and Blacknecked Storks in the 1989 census. *Newsletter for Birdwatchers* **29**: 10.
Sridharan, U. (1986). An Adjutant gobbles ducklings. *Hornbill* **1986(2)**: 26, 35.
Stacey, P.B. & Koenig, W.D. eds. (1990). *Cooperative Breeding in Birds*. Cambridge University Press, England.
Stahel, C.D. & Gales, R. (1987). *Little Penguin, Fairy Penguins in Australia*. New South Wales University Press. Kensington, New South Wales.
Stahel, C.D. & Nicol, S.C. (1982). Temperature regulation in the Little Penguin, *Eudyptula minor* in air and water. *J. Comp. Physiol.* **148**: 93-100.
Stahel, C.D., Nicol, S.C. & Walker, G.J. (1987). Heat production and thermal resistance in the Little Penguin *Eudyptula minor* in relation to wind speed. *Physiol. Zool.* **60(4)**: 413-423.
Stahl, J.C., Mougin, J.L., Jouventin, P. & Weimerskirch, H. (1984). Le Canard d'Eaton, *Anas eatoni drygalskii*, des îles Crozet: systématique, comportement alimentaire et biologie de reproduction. *Gerfaut* **74**: 305-326.
Stahl, J.C. (1987). Distribution des oiseaux marins dans le sudouest de l'Océan Indien: données préliminaires de la campaigne Apsara II - Antiprod III. In: Fontugne, M. & Fiala, M. eds. *Les rapports des campagnes à la mer MD38/APSARA II - ANTIPROD III au bord du 'Marion Dufresne' 16 Janvier - 22 Février 1984*. Terre Austr. Antarct. Fr. Publ. Rech. **84**.
Stahl, J.C., Derenne, M., Jouventin, P. Mougin, J.L., Teulières, L. & Weimerskirch, H. (1985). Le cycle reproducteur des gorfous de l'archipel Crozet: *Eudyptes chrysolophus*, le Gorfou Macaroni et *Eudyptes chrysocome*, le Gorfou Sauteur. *L'Oiseau et la R.F.O.* **55(1)**: 27-43.
Stahl, J.C., Jouventin, P., Mougin, J.L., Roux, J.P. & Weimerskirch, H. (1985). The foraging zones of seabirds in the Crozet Islands sector of the Southern Ocean. Pp. 478-485 in: Siegfried, W.R., Condy, P.R. & Laws, R.M. eds. *Antarctic Nutrient Cycles and Food Webs*. Springer, Berlin.
Stahlecker, D.W. (1989). White-faced Ibis breeding in Rio Arriba County: second verified nesting location for New Mexico. *New Mexico Orn. Soc. Bull.* **17**: 2-6.
Standen, P.J. (1976). *The Social Behaviour of the Chilean Teal*. PhD dissertation, University of Leicester, UK.
Standen, P.J. (1980). The social display of the Chilean Teal *Anas flavirostris flavirostris*. *J. Zoology. London* **191**: 293-313.
Stander, G. (1960). Hadeda Ibis nesting in wattles. *Witwatersrand Bird Club News* **33**: 10.
Stanford, J.K. (1954). *A Bewilderment of Birds*. Rupert Hart-Davis, London.
Stanford, J.K. & Ticehurst, C.B. (1939). On the birds of northern Burma. Parts V, VI. *Ibis* **82**: 1-45, 211-258.
Stangel, P.W., Rodgers, J.A. & Bryan, A.L. (1990). Genetic variation and population structure of the Florida Wood Stork. *Auk* **107**: 614-619.
Starett, W.C. & Dixon, K.L. (1946). The scarcity of the Black-footed Albatross in parts of its known range. *Condor* **48**: 268-271.
Staub, F. (1976). *Birds of the Mascarenes and St Brandon*. Organisation Normale des Entreprises Ltée, Port Louis.
Stead, E.F. (1948). Bird life on the Snares. *New Zealand Bird Notes* **3**: 69-80.
Steadman, D.W. & Zousmer, S. (1988). *Galápagos. Discovery on Darwin's Island*. Smithsonian Institution Press, Washington.
Steel, T. (1970). The New Zealand Blue Mountain Duck. *New Zealand Wild Life* **29**: 9-11.
Steele, B.B. (1980). *Reproductive Success of the White-faced Ibis: Effects of Pesticides and Colony Characteristics*. MSc thesis, Utah State University, Logan, Utah.
Steele, B.B. (1984). Effects of Pesticides on Reproductive Success of White-faced Ibis in Utah, 1979. *Colonial Waterbirds* **7**: 80-87.
Steele, W.K. & Klages, N.T. (1986). Diet of the Blue Petrel at Sub-Antarctic Marion Island. *S. Afr. J. Zool.* **21**: 253-256.
Stefferud, A. & Nelson, A.L. eds. (1966). *Birds in Our Lives*. US Fish and Wildlife Service, Washington, D.C.
Stegman, B.K. (1974). [On the phylogenetic relationships between the families of Gaviidae and Podicipedidae]. *Ornitologiya* **11**: 6-19. In Russian.
Stein, P. (1971). Horuhoru revisited. Longevity of the Australian Gannet. *Notornis* **18**: 310-365.
Steinbacher, J. (1979). Threskiornithidae. Pp. 253-268 in: Mayr & Cottrell (1979).
Stephens, D.W. & Krebs, J.R. (1987). *Foraging Theory*. Princeton University Press, Lawrenceville, New Jersey.
Sterbetz, I. (1962). The Squacco Heron in the "Sasér" bird-sanctuary. *Aquila* **67-68**: 39-70.
Sterbetz, I. (1990). Variations in the habitat of the Lesser White-fronted Goose (*Anser erythropus* L., 1758) in Hungary. *Aquila* **96-97**: 11-18.
Stangel, P.W., Rodgers, J.A. & Bryan, A.L. (1991). Low Genetic Differentiation Between Two Disjunct White Ibis Colonies. *Colonial Waterbirds* **14(1)**: 13-16.
Stettenheim, P. (1972). The integument of birds. Pp. 1-63 in: Farner, D.S. & King, J.R. (1972). *Avian Biology*. Vol. 2. Academic Press, London & New York.
Steven, G.A. (1933). The food consumed by Shags and Cormorants around the shores of Cornwall (England). *J. Mar. Biol. Ass. U.K.* **19**: 277-292.
Stevenson, H.M. (1972). Records of the Scarlet Ibis and Red-breasted Blackbird in Ecuador. *Wilson Bull.* **84**: 99.
Stewart, G.R. & Titman, R.D. (1980). Territorial behaviour by prairie pothole Blue-winged Teal. *Can. J. Zool.* **58**: 639-649.
Stewart, T.G. & Hourston-Wright, J. (1990). 6500 BP Oldsquaw Duck (*Clangula hyemalis*) from Northern Ellesmere Island, Arctic Archipelago, Canada. *Arctic* **43 (3)**: 239-243.
Steyn, P. (1972). Hamerkop behaviour. *Honeyguide* **72**: 31.
Steyn, P. (1987). Martial Eagle Kills Woolly-necked stork. *Afr. Wildl.* **41(4)**: 181.
Steyn, P. (1988). Attempted kleptoparasitism of Openbilled Storks by Greyheaded Gulls. *Ostrich* **59(4)**: 182.
Sticklen, E. & Sticklen, R. (1981). Strange behaviour of Black-necked Stork (Jabiru) - Iron Range, Old. *Bird Obsr.* **594**: 59.

Stidolph, R.H.D. & Heather, B.D. (1978). Notes on post-breeding movements of the New Zealand Dabchick in the southern North Island. *Notornis* **25**: 84-88.
Stiles, F.G. (1985). Conservation of Forest Birds in Costa Rica: Problems and Perspectives. Pp. 141-168 in: Diamond & Lovejoy (1985).
Stiles, F.G. & Skutch, A.F. (1989). *A Guide to the Birds of Costa Rica*. Christopher Helm, London.
Stiles, F.G. & Smith, S.M. (1980). Notes on bird distribution in Costa Rica. *Brenesia* **17**: 137-156.
Stirling, D. & Buffam, F. (1966). The first breeding record of Brandt's Cormorant in Canada. *Can. Field-Nat.* **80**: 117-118.
Stocker, G.C. & Irvine, A.K. (1983). Seed dispersal by Cassowaries (*Casuarius casuarius*) in North Queensland's Rainforests. *Biotropica* **15(3)**: 170-176.
Stockton, A. (1978). *Aves de la República Dominicana*. Museo Nacional de Historia Natural, Santo Domingo.
Stoddard, D.R. (1971). Settlement, development and conservation of Aldabra. *Phil. Trans. Royal Soc. London (Ser. B)* **260**: 611-628.
Stoddart, D.R. (1981). Abbott's Booby on Assumption. *Atoll Res. Bull.* **255**: 27-32.
Stokes, T. (1988). *A Review of the Birds of Christmas Island, Indian Ocean*. Occasional Paper **16**. Australian National Parks and Wildlife Service, Canberra.
Stokes, T. (1990). The Post-juvenal plumage of the Red-tailed Tropicbird *Phaeton rubricauda*. *Austr. Bird Watcher*. **13(8)**: 259-260.
Stokes, T. & Dunn, K. (1989). Movements of Least Frigatebirds from the Pacific to the Indian Ocean. *Corella* **13**: 62.
Stokes, T. & Goh, P. (1987). Records of Herald Petrels and the Christmas Frigatebird from North Keeling Island, Indian Ocean. *Austr. Bird Watcher* **12(4)**: 132-133.
Stokes, T., Shiels, W. & Dunn, K.N. (1984). Birds of the Cocos (Keeling) Islands. *Emu* **84**: 23-28.
Stokoe, R. (1958). The spring plumage of the cormorant. *British Birds* **51**: 165-179.
Stone, W. (1965). *Bird Studies at Old Cape May*. Dover Publications, New York.
Stonehouse, B. (1953). The Emperor Penguin *Aptenodytes forsteri*. I. Breeding Behaviour and Development. *Falkland Isl. Depend. Surv. Sci. Rep.* **6**: 1-33.
Stonehouse, B. (1960a). The King Penguin, *Aptenodytes patagonica*, of South Georgia. I. Breeding Behaviour and Development. *Falkland Isl. Depend. Surv. Sci. Rep.* **23**: 1-81.
Stonehouse, B. (1960b). *Wideawake Island*. Hutchinson, London.
Stonehouse, B. (1962a). The tropicbirds (genus *Phaethon*) of Ascension Island. *Ibis* **103b**: 124-161.
Stonehouse, B. (1962b). Ascension Island and the British Ornithologists' Union Centenary Expedition 1957-59. *Ibis* **103b**: 107-123.
Stonehouse, B. (1963). Observations on Adelie Penguins (*Pygoscelis adeliae*) at Cape Royds, Antarctica. Pp. 766-779 in: *Proc. XIII Int. Orn. Congr. (Ithaca, 1962)*.
Stonehouse, B. (1967a). The general biology and thermal balance of penguins. Vol 4: 131-196, in Cragg, J.B. ed. *Adv. Ecol. Res.* Academic Press, London.
Stonehouse, B. (1967b). Feeding behaviour and diving rhythms of some New Zealand shags, Phalacrocoracidae. *Ibis* **109**: 600-605.
Stonehouse, B. (1970a). Adaptation in polar and subpolar penguins (Spheniscidae). Pp. 526-541 in: Holdgate, M.W. ed. *Antarctic Ecology* **1**. Academic Press, London.
Stonehouse, B. (1970b). Geographic variation in Gentoo Penguins *Pygoscelis papua*. *Ibis* **112**: 52-57.
Stonehouse, B. (1971). The Snares Islands Penguin *Eudyptes robustus*. *Ibis* **113**: 1-7.
Stonehouse, B. (1975). *The Biology of Penguins*. Macmillan, London.
Stonehouse, B. (1985a). Tropicbird. Pp. 610-611 in: Campbell & Lack (1985).
Stonehouse, B. (1985b). Frigatebird. Pp. 243-244 in: Campbell & Lack (1985).
Stonehouse, B. & Hempel, G. (1987). Aerial counts of Emperor Penguins, Weddell seals and whales. *Ber. Polarforch.* **39**: 227-230.
Stonehouse, B. & Stonehouse, S. (1963). The frigatebird (*Fregata aquila*) of Ascension island. *Ibis* **103b**: 409-422.
Stonor, C.R. (1939). Notes on the breeding habits of the Common Screamer (*Chauna torquata*). *Ibis* **81**: 45-49.
Storer, J.H. (1948). *The Flight of Birds*. Cranbrook Institute of Science, Bloomfield Hills, Michigan.
Storer, R.W & Jehl, J.R. (1985). Moult patterns and moult migration in the Black-necked Grebe *Podiceps nigricollis*. *Ornis Scand.* **16**: 253-260.
Storer, R.W & Nuechterlein, G.L. (1985). An analysis of plumage and morphological characters of the two color forms of the Western Grebe (*Aechmophorus*). *Auk* **102**: 102-119.
Storer, R.W. (1956). The fossil loon, *Colymbus minutus*. *Condor* **56**: 413-426.
Storer, R.W. (1960). Evolution in the diving birds. Pp. 694-707 in: *Proc. XII Int. Orn. Congr.*
Storer, R.W. (1961). Observations of pellet-casting by Horned and Pied-billed Grebes. *Auk* **78**: 90-92.
Storer, R.W. (1963a). Courtship and mating behaviour and the phylogeny of the grebes. Pp. 562-569 in: *Proc. XIII Int. Orn. Congr.*
Storer, R.W. (1963b). Observations on the Great Grebe. *Condor* **65**: 279-288.
Storer, R.W. (1965). The color phases of the Western Grebe. *Living Bird* **4**: 59-63.
Storer, R.W. (1967a). Observations on Rolland's Grebe. *Hornero* **10**: 339-350.
Storer, R.W. (1967b). The patterns of downy grebes. *Condor* **69**: 469-478.
Storer, R.W. (1969). The behavior of the Horned Grebe in spring. *Condor* **71**: 180-205.
Storer, R.W. (1971a). Adaptive radiation in birds. Pp. 149-188 in: Farner, D.S. & King, J.R. (1971). *Avian Biology*. Vol. 1. Academic Press, London & New York.
Storer, R.W. (1971b). Classification of birds. Pp. 1-18 in: Farner, D.S. & King, J.R. (1971). *Avian Biology*. Vol. 1. Academic Press, London & New York.
Storer, R.W. (1971c). The behaviour of the New Zealand Dabchick. *Notornis* 18: 175-186.
Storer, R.W. (1975). The status of the Least Grebe in Argentina. *Bull. Brit. Orn. Club* **95**: 148-151.
Storer, R.W. (1976a). The behavior and relationships of the Least Grebe. *Trans. San Diego Soc. Nat. Hist.* **18**: 113-126.
Storer, R.W. (1976b). The Pleistocene Pied-billed Grebe (Aves: Podicipedidae). *Smithson. Contrib. Palaeobiol.* **27**: 147-153.
Storer, R.W. (1979). Podicipediformes. Pp. 140-155 in: Mayr & Cottrell (1979).
Storer, R.W. (1980/81). The Hooded Grebe on Laguna de los Escarchados: Ecology and behavior. *Living Bird* **19**: 51-67.
Storer, R.W. (1982). A hybrid between the Hooded and Silver Grebes (*Podiceps gallardoi* and *P. occipitalis*). *Auk* **99**: 168-169.
Storer, R.W. (1987). Morphology and relationships of the Hoary-headed Grebe and the New Zealand Dabchick. *Emu* **87**: 150-7.
Storer, R.W. (1989a). The Pleistocene Western Grebe *Aechmophorus* (Aves, Podicipedidae) from Fossil Lake, Oregon: A comparison with recent material. *Cont. Mus. Paleo. Univ. Mich.* **27**: 321-326.
Storer, R.W. (1989b). Notes on Paraguayan birds. *Occ. Papers Mus. Zool. Univ. Michigan* **719**: 1-21.
Storer, R.W. & Getty, T. (1985). Geographic variation in the Least Grebe (*Tachybaptus dominicus*). *Orn. Monogr.* **36**: 31-39.
Storer, R.W., Siegfried, W.R. & Kinahan, J. (1975). Sunbathing in grebes. *Living Bird* **14**: 45-57.
Storey, A.E. (1984). Function of Manx Shearwater calls in mate attraction. *Behaviour* **89**: 73-89.
Storey, A.E. & Grimmer, B.L. (1986). Effect of illumination on the natural cavities of Manx Shearwaters: colony avoidance or inconspicuous behaviour. *Bird Behaviour* **6**: 85-89.
Storey, A.E. & Lien, J. (1985). Development of the first North American colony of Manx Shearwaters. *Auk* **102**: 395-401.
Stott, J.K.W. (1981). The very wary Cassowary. *Zoonooz* **54(4)**: 5-7.
Stott, K. (1959). Two recent records of the Roseate Spoonbill on the Pacific slope and high Andes of Peru. *Auk* **6**: 244.
Stott, K. & Selsor, C.J. (1960). Least Grebe on the coast of Southern California. *Condor* **62**: 223.
Stott, K.W. (1982). By name and Sound - Screamers. *Zoonooz* **55(6)**: 12-13.
Stoudt, J.H. (1971). *Ecological Factors Affecting Waterfowl Production in the Saskatchewan Parklands*. US Fish & Wildlife Service Resource Publication **99**.
Stowe, T.J. (1982). *Beached Bird Surveys and Surveillance of Cliff-breeding Seabirds*. Report to Nature Conservancy Council on beached bird survey. RSPB, Sandy.
Stowell, R.F. (1954). A note on the behaviour of *Scopus umbretta*. *Ibis* **96**: 150-151.
Strader, R.W. (1978). *Wood Duck nesting behavior and productivity in a South Lousiana beaver pond*. MSc thesis, Louisiana State University, Baton Rouge.
Strait, L.E. & Sloan, N.F. (1974). Life table analysis for the White Pelican. *Inland Bird Banding News* **46**: 20-28.
Straneck, R.J. & Johnson, A. (1984). [Courtship displays of the Hooded Grebe (*Podiceps gallardoi*)]. *Rev. Mus. Arg. Cienc. Nat. Bernardino Rivadavia. Zool.* **13**: 177-188. In Spanish.
Strange, I.J. (1968). A breeding colony of *Pachyptila turtur* in the Falkland Islands. *Ibis* **110**: 358-359.
Strange, I.J. (1980). The Thin-billed Prion at New Island, Falkland Islands. *Gerfaut* **70**: 411-445.
Strange, I.J. (1982). Breeding ecology of the Rockhopper Penguin (*Eudyptes crestatus*) in the Falkland Islands. *Gerfaut* **72**: 137-187.
Strann, K.B. (1991). The status of breeding shelducks *Tadorna tadorna* in North Norway. *Fauna Norv. (Ser. C.) Cinclus* **14(1)**: 1-5.
Stresemann, E. (1934). *Aves*. Vol. 7. Part 2 in: Kukenthal, W. & Krumbach, T. eds. *Handbuch der Zoologie*. Walter de Gruyter, Berlin and Leipzig.
Stresemann, E. (1975). *Ornithology from Aristotle to the Present*. Harvard University Press, Cambridge.
Stresemann, E. & Stresemann, V. (1966). Die Mauser der Vögel. *J. Orn.* **88**: 288-333.
Stresemann, E. & Stresemann, V. (1970). Uber Mauser and Zug von *Puffinus gravis*. *J. Orn.* **111**: 378-393.
Strohmeyer, D.L. (1967). *The Biology of Renesting by Blue-winged Teal (*Anas discors*) in Northwest Iowa*. PhD thesis, University of Minnesota, Minneapolis.
Stronach, B.W. (1968). The Chagana heronry in western Tanzania. *Ibis* **110**: 345-348.
Strong, P.I.V. (1985). *Habitat Selection by Common Loons*. PhD thesis. University of Maine, Orono.
Strong, P.I.V. (1988). ed. *Papers from the 1987 Conference on Loon Research and Management*. North American Loon Fund, Meredith, N.H.
Strong, P.I.V. (1990). The suitability of the Common Loon as an indicator species. *Wildl. Soc. Bull.* **18(3)**: 257-261.
Strong, P.I.V. & Bissonette, J.A. (1989). Feeding and chick-rearing areas of Common Loons. *J. Wildl. Manage.* **53(1)**: 72-76.
Strong, P.I.V., Bissonette, J.A. & Fair, J.S. (1987). Reuse of nesting and nursery areas by Common Loons. *J. Wildl. Manage.* **51(1)**: 123-127.
Strong, P.I.V., Lavalley, S.A. & Burke, R.C. (1987). A colored plastic leg band for Common Loons. *J. Field Orn.* **58**: 218-221.
Stroud, D.A. (1982). Observations on the incubation and post-hatching behaviour of the Greenland White-fronted Goose. *Wildfowl* **33**: 63-72.
Stroud, D.A., Pienkowski, M.W. & Mudge, G.P. (1989). *Review of the Protection Afforded to Bird Species by the Network of Proposed and Designated Special Protection Areas in Great Britain*. Nature Conservancy Council, Peterborough.
Struwe, B. (1985). Brutbestand und Nichtbrüter des Rothalstauchers (*Podiceps grisegena*) an vier schleswig-holsteinischen Brutplätzen 1984. *Corax* **10(4)**: 481-487.
Stuart, C.T. & Dürk, T.E. (1984). Food of the Blackheaded Heron at a breeding colony. *Ostrich* **55(2)**: 103-104.
Stuart, S.N. ed. (1986). *Conservation of Cameroon Montane Forests*. ICBP, Cambridge, England.
Studer-Thiersch, A. (1964). Balzverhalten und Systematik der Gattung Phoenicopterus. *Orn. Beob.* **61**: 99-102.
Studer-Thiersch, A. (1966). Altes und Neues über das Fütterungssekret der Flamingos *Phoenicopterus ruber*. *Orn. Beob.* **63**: 85-89.
Studer-Thiersch, A. (1967). Beiträge zur Brutbiologie der Flamingo (Gattung *Phoenicopterus*). *Zool. Garten* **34**: 149-229.
Stumpf, D. (1978). Zur Brutbiologie des Strohhalsibis (*Threskiornis spinicollis*). *Gefiederte Welt* **102**: 72-76.
Sturkie, P.D. (1986). *Avian Physiology* (4th edn.). Springer-Verlag, Berlin, Heidelberg and New York.
Sturmer, A.T. & Grant, A.D. (1988). Female kiwis incubating. *Notornis* **35**: 193-195.
Stutzenbaker, C.D. (1984). The Mottled Duck, its life history, ecology and management. Draft. Fed. Aid Proj. W-96-R. Texas Parks Wildlife Department.
Su Hualong, Liu Huanjin, *et al.* (1989). [On the breeding ecology of the Black Stork *Ciconia nigra*]. *Acta Zool. Sinica* **35(4)**: 444-446. In Chinese.
Sudbury, A.W., Tompkins, R.J. & Gibson, J.D. (1985). Recurring pairs of Wandering Albatrosses at a New South Wales winter feeding ground? *Emu* **85**: 195-197.
Suetens, W. (1960). De Kuiffuut, *Podiceps cristatus* (L.) in Belgie. *Gerfaut* **50**: 231-264.
Sugathan, R., Melville, D.S. & Alagar Rajan, S. (1987). Further additions to the Avifauna of Point Calimere. *J. Bombay Nat. Hist. Soc.* **84(1)**: 206-207.
Sugden, L.G. (1973). Feeding Ecology of Pintail, Gadwall, American Wigeon and Lesser Scaup ducklings in Southern Alberta. *Can. Wildl. Serv. Rep. Ser.* **24**.
Sugden, L.G. (1977). Horned Grebe breeding habitat in Saskatchewan Parklands. *Can. Field-Nat.* **91**: 372-376.
Sugimori, F., Oka, N. & Ishibashi, Y. (1985). The degree of skull ossification as a mean of ageing Short-tailed Shearwaters. *J. Yamashina Inst. Orn.* **17**: 159-165.
Sullivan, J.P. & Payne, S.M. (1988). Aspects of the history and nestling mortality at a Great Blue Heron, *Ardea herodias*, colony, Quetico Provincial Park, Ontario. *Can. Field-Naturalist* **102**: 237-241.
Summerour, C.W. (1971). *A Quantitative Study of Reproductive Mortality in Cattle Egrets,* Bubulcus ibis, *and Little Blue Herons,* Florida caerulea, *near Cliftonville, Noxubee County, Mississippi*. Thesis, Mississippi State University, Mississippi.
Summers, R.W. & Castro, G. (1988). Population size and feeding behaviour of Andean Geese at Lake Junin, Peru. *Wildfowl* **39**: 22-28.
Summers, R.W. & Laing, S. (1990). Movements of Cormorants from the Lamb, Firth of Forth. *Scottish Birds* **16**: 29-32.
Summers, R.W. & Underhill, L.G. (1991). The growth of the population of Dark-bellied Brent Geese *Branta b. bernicla* between 1955 and 1988. *J. Appl. Ecol.* **28**: 574-585.
Sutcliffe, S.A. (1978). Changes in status and factors affecting Common Loon populations in New Hampshire. *Trans. NE Section. Wildl. Soc. Fish & Wildl. Conf.* **35**: 219-224.
de Sutcliffe, S.A. (1979). *The Common Loon. Proceedings of the 2nd North American Conference on Common Loon Research and Management, Syracuse, New York, 14-16 January 1979*. National Audubon Society, New York.
Sutcliffe, S.A. (1980). *Aspects of the Nesting Ecology of the Common Loon in New Hampshire*. MSc thesis. University of New Hampshire.
Sutherland, W.J. & Allport, G. (1991). The distribution and ecology of naturalized Egyptian Geese *Alopochen aegyptiacus* in Britain. *Bird Study* **38 (2)**: 128-134.
Sutherland, W.J. & Brooks, D.J. (1981). The autumn migration of raptors, storks, pelicans and spoonbills at the Belen Pass, southern Turkey. *Sandgrouse* **2**: 1-21.
Sutter, E.R. (1984). Ontogeny of the wing moult pattern in the White Stork *Ciconia ciconia*. Pp. 543-551 in: Ledger, J. (1984). *Proceedings of the Fifth Pan-African Ornithological Congress*. Southern African Ornithological Society, Johannesburg.
Sutton, G.M. (1951). *Mexican birds*. University of Oklahoma.
Sutton, G.M., Lea, R.B. & Edwards, E.P. (1950). Notes on the ranges and breeding habits of certain Mexican birds. *Bird-Banding* **21**: 45-59.
Sutton, G.M. (1963). On the Yellow-billed Loon. *Wilson Bull.* **75**: 83-87.
Suzuki, S. (1980). Captive reproduction of the Glossy Ibis. *Animals and Zoos* **32**: 155-157.
Svingen, P. (1991). Ross's Goose in Rock Country. *Loon* **63(3)**: 202.
Swales, M.P. (1965). The sea-birds of Gough Island. *Ibis* **107**: 17-42, 215-229.
Swann, R.L. & Ramsay, A.D.K. (1979). An analysis of Shag recoveries from North West Scotland. *Ringing and Migration* **2**: 137-143.
Swanson, G.A. & Meyer, M.I. (1973). The role of invertebrates in the feeding ecology of Anatinae during the breeding season. Pp. 143-184 in: *Proceedings of the Waterfowl Habitat Management Symposium, Moncton, N.B., Canada, 30 July - Aug. 1, 1973*. Atlantic Waterfowl Council, Moncton.
Swanson, G.A. & Meyer, M.I. (1977). Impact of fluctuating water levels on feeding ecology of breeding Blue-winged Teal. *J. Wildl. Manage.* **41**: 426-433.
Swanson, G.A., Krapu, G.L. & Serie, J.R. (1979). Foods of laying female dabbling ducks on the breeding grounds. *Waterfowl & Wetlands Symp.* **1977**: 47-57.
Swanson, G.A., Meyer, M.I. & Serie, J.R. (1974). Feeding ecology of breeding Blue-winged Teal. *J. Wildl. Manage.* **38**: 396-407.
Swanson, N.M. & Merritt, F.D. (1974). The breeding cycle of the Wedge-tailed Shearwater on Mutton Bird Island, N.S.W. *Austr. Bird Bander* **12**: 3-9.
Swedberg, G.E. (1967). *The Koloa: a Preliminary Report on the Life History and Status of the Hawaiian Duck (*Anas wyvilliana*)*. Wildlife Branch, Division of Fish and Game, Department of Lands and Natural Resources, Hawaii.
Swedberg, G.E. (1969). Sighting of wild Koloa on the island of Hawaii and history of a past release. *Elepaio* **29**: 87-88.
Swennen, C. (1976). Populatie-structuur en voedsel van de Eidereend *Somateria m. mollissima* in de Nederlandse Waddenzee. *Ardea* **64**: 311-371.
Swennen, C. & Marteijn, E.C.L. (1987). Notes on the feeding behaviour of the Milky Stork *Mycteria cinerea*. *Forktail* **3**: 63-66.
Swennen, C., Duiven, P. & Reyrink, L.A.F. (1979). Notes on the sex ratio in the Common Eider *Somateria mollissima Ardea* **67**: 54-61.
Swennen, C., Nehls, G. & Laursen, K. (1989). Numbers and distribution of eiders *Somateria mollissima* in the Wadden Sea. *Netherlands J. Sea Res.* **24 (1)**: 83-92.

Swift, B.L., Orman, S.R. & Ozard, J.W. (1988). Response of Least Bitterns to tape-recorded calls. *Wilson Bull.* **100**: 496-499.
Swinhoe, R. (1863). Catalogue of the birds of China, with remarks principally on their geographic distribution. *Proc. Zool. Soc. Lond.* **1863**: 259-339.
Symons, R.E. (1924). The nesting of the Green Ibis, *Theristicus hagedash*, in South Africa. *Comp. Oologist* **1(1)**: 10-13.
Syroyechkovski, Y.V. (1975). [Egg weight and its effect upon mortality of nestlings in *Chen caerulescens* on the Wrangel Island]. *Zool. Zh.* **54**: 408-412. In Russian with English summary.
Syroyechkovski, Y.V. ed. (1987). *Ecology and Migration of Swans in the USSR*. IWRB, Slimbridge, England.
Szijj, L.J. (1967). Notes on the winter distribution of birds in the western Antarctic and adjacent Pacific waters. *Auk* **84**: 366-378.
Taborsky, B. & Taborsky, M. (1991). Social organization of North Island Brown Kiwi: Long-term pairs and three types of male spacing behabiour. *Ethology* **89**: 47-62.
Taborsky, B. & Taborsky, M. (1992). Spatial organization of the North Island Brown Kiwi *Apteryx australis mantelli*: sex, pairing status and territoriality. *Ibis* **134(1)**: 1-10.
Taborsky, M. (1988). Kiwis and dog predation: observations in Waitangi State Forest. *Notornis* **35**: 197-202.
Taibel, A.M. (1938). Sur l'élevage en captivité du *Tinamus major robustus* Sclater et Salvin. Pp. 373-379 in: *Proc. XV Int. Orn. Congr.*
Takashima, H. (1956). The Japanese Stork in the past and present. *Tori* **16**: 35-36.
Takashima, H. (1957). Notes on the Black Stork *Ciconia nigra* in Japan. *Misc. Rep. Yamashina Inst. Orn. Zool.* **11**: 5-9.
Talbot, J.H. (1976). Strange Hamerkop behaviour. *Honeyguide* **86**: 44-45.
Talent, G.F. (1940). Wood Ibis (*Ibis ibis*) in Southern Rhodesia. *Ostrich* **11**: 49.
Talent, L.G. (1984). Food habits of wintering Brandt's Cormorants. *Wilson Bull.* **96(1)**: 130-134.
Tamisier, A. (1971). Régime alimentaire de la Sarcell d'hiver *Anas crecca* (L.) en Camargue. *Alauda* **39**: 261-344.
Tamisier, A. (1972). *Etho-ecologie des Sarcelles d'Hiver* Anas c. crecca *L. pendant leur hivernage en Camargue*. PhD thesis, Université des Sciences et Techniques du Languedoc.
Tamisier, A. (1976). Diurnal activities of Green-winged Teal and Pintail wintering in Lousiana. *Wildfowl* **27**: 19-23.
Tamiya, Y. & Aoyanagi, M. (1982). The significance of reoccupation by non-breeding birds in the Adelie Penguin *Pygoscelis adeliae* during their incubation, guard and creche periods. *J. Yamashina Inst. Orn.* **14**: 35-44.
Tan, N. (1977). [*Streaked Shearwaters and Kanmurijima*.] Tenseisha, Tokyo.
Tanaka, Y. (1986). (*Pterodroma solandri*) *J. Yamashina Inst. Orn.* **18**: 55-62.
Tanaka, Y. & Inaba, F. (1981). [The distribution and migration of the White-necked Petrel, *Pterodroma externa externa*, in the west area of the North Pacific Ocean and the Japanese waters.] *J. Yamashina Inst. Orn.* **13**: 61-68.
Tanaka, Y. & Kaneko, Y. (1983). [Distribution and migration of the Bonin Petrel *Pterodroma hypoleuca* in the Northwest Pacific in relation to sea surface temperatures.] *Tori* **32**: 119-127.
Tanaka, Y., Kaneko, Y. & Sato, S. (1985). [Distribution and Migration of Smaller Petrels of the Genus *Pterodroma* in the Northwest Pacific.] *J. Yamashina Inst. Orn.* **17**: 23-31.
Tandan, B.K. (1976). The species of *Ardeicola* (Phthiraptera) on *Threskiornis* (Aves). *Systematic Ent.* **1**: 75-87.
Tang Zi-ying (1981). [The discovery of a Gould's Petrel *Pterodroma hypoleuca* (Salvin) in Fuding, Fujian Province]. *Acta Zootaxonomica Sinica* **6**(1): 59. In Chinese.
Taoka, M. & Okumura, H. (1990). [Sexual differences in flight calls and the cue for vocal sex recognition of Swinhoe's Storm-Petrels]. *Condor* **92**: 571-575.
Taoka, M., Sato, T., Kamada, T. & Okumura, H. (1988). Situation-specifities of vocalizations in Leach's Storm-Petrel *Oceanodroma leucorhoa*. *J. Yamashina Inst. Orn.* **20**: 82-90.
Taoka, M., Sato, T., Kamada, T. & Okumura, H. (1989). Sexual dimorphism of chatter-calls and vocal sex recognition in Leach's Storm-Petrels. *Auk* **106**: 498-501.
Taoka, M., Won, P. & Okumura, H. (1989). Vocal behavior of Swinhoe's Storm-Petrel. *Auk* **106**: 471-474.
Taranaki, N. & Winter, P. (1987). To catch a Kiwi. *Forest & Bird* **18(1)**: 20-21.
Tarborton, W.R. (1975). Breeding notes on the Darter, *Anhinga rufa*. *Witwatersrand Bird Club News* **88**: 8-9.
Tarborton, W.R. (1977). The status of communal herons, ibis and cormorants on the Witwatersrand. *S. Afr. J. Wildl. Res.* **7**: 19-25.
Tarboton, W. (1967). (*Ixobrychus sturmi*). *Ostrich* **38**: 207.
Tarboton, W. (1977). The Black Stork - one of South Africa's rarest birds. *Fauna Flora. Pretoria* **29**: 14-15.
Tarboton, W. (1982). Breeding status of the Black Stork in the Transvaal. *Ostrich* **53**: 151-156.
Tarburton, M.K. (1977). Nesting of the Red-tailed Tropicbird at Sugarloaf Rock, W.A. *Emu* **77**, 122-126.
Tarburton, M.K. (1981). Notes and measurements of Hutton's and Fluttering Shearwaters found drowned at Kaikoura Peninsula. *Notornis* **28**: 9-10.
Tarburton, M.K. (1984). Incubation behaviour of the red-tailed tropic bird ("*Phaeton rubricauda*") on Norfolk Island. *Notornis* **31(1)**: 92-94.
Tarburton, M.K. (1989). Subspeciation in the Red-tailed Tropicbird. *Notornis* **36**: 39-49.
Tasker, M.L., Jones, P.H., Blake, B.F. & Dixon, T.J. (1985). The marine distribution of the gannet in the North Sea. *Bird Study* **32**: 82-90.
Tasker, M.L., Webb, A., Hall, A.J., Pienkowski, M.W. & Langslow, D.R. (1987). *Seabirds in the North Sea*. Seabirds at Sea Project Final Report. Nature Conservancy Council, Peterborough, UK.
Tate, A.L. & Humphries, R.L. (1980). Humphries. 1980. Wood storks nesting in Jenkins Country, Georgia. *Oriole* **45**: 34-35.
Taylor, J.S. (1948). Notes on the nesting and feeding habits of the black-headed Heron, "*Ardea melanocephala*". *Ostrich* **19**: 203-210.
Taylor, J.S. (1957). Notes on the birds of inland waters in the Eastern Cape Province with special reference to the Karoo. *Ostrich* **28**: 1-80.
Taylor, M.J. (1987). A colony of the Little Shag and the Pied Shag in which the plumage forms of the Little Shag freely interbreed. *Notornis* **34**: 41-50.
Taylor, P.B. & Taylor, C.A. (1988). The status, movements and breeding of some birds in the Kikuyu Escarpment Forest, central Kenya highlands. *Tauraco* **1**: 72-89.
Taylor, R.H. (1962). The Adelie Penguin, *Pygoscelis adeliae*, at Cape Royds. *Ibis* **104**: 176-204.
Taylor, R.H. (1986). Thermal insulation of the down and feathers of pygoscelid penguin chicks and the unique properties of penguin feathers. *Auk* **103**: 160-168.
Taylor, T.B.S. (1989). Unusual nesting site for Little Shag. *Notornis* **36**: 160.
Teixeira, A.M. & Moore, C.C. (1983). The breeding of the Madeiran Petrel *Oceanodroma castro* on Farilhao Grande, Portugal. *Ibis* **125**: 382-384.
Teixeira, D.M. & Carvalho, M.C.S. (1982). Notas sobre a Garcea-Real "*Pilherodius pileatus*" (Boddaert, 1783). *Anais. Soc. Sul-Riograndense Orn.* **3**: 13-15.
Teixeira, D.M. & Negret, A. (1984). The Dwarf Tinamou (*Taoniscus nanus*) of Central Brazil. *Auk* **101**: 188-189.
Teixeira, D.M., Nacimovic, J.B. & Tavares, M.S. (1986). Notes on some Birds from northeastern Brazil. *Bull. Brit. Orn. Club* **106**: 70-74.
Telfair, R.C. (1983). *The Cattle Egret*. Texas.
Telfer, T.C., Sincock, J.L., Byrd, G.V. & Reed, J.R. (1987). Attraction of Hawaiian seabirds to lights: conservation efforts and effects on moon phase. *Wildl. Soc. Bull.* **15**: 406-413.
Tellería, J.L. (1980). Autumn migration of Cory's Shearwater through the Straits of Gibraltar. *Bird Study* **27**: 21-26.
Temme, M. (1974). Zugbewegungen der Eiderente (*Somateria mollissima*) vor der Insel Norderney unter besonderer Berücksichtigung der Wetterverhältnisse. *Vogelwarte* **27**: 252-263.
Temple, S.A. ed. (1978). *Endangered Birds. Management Techniques for Preserving Threatened Species*. The University of Wisconsin Press, Madison & Croom Helm Ltd, London.
Tenaza, R. (1971). Behaviour and nesting success relative to nest location in Adelie Penguins (*Pygoscelis adeliae*). *Condor* **73**: 81-92.
Tennyson, A.J.D. (1991). The Black-winged Petrel on Mangere Island, Chatham Islands. *Notornis* **38(2)**: 111-116.
Tennyson, A.J.D. & Miskelly, C.M. (1989). "Dark-faced" Rockhopper Penguins at the Snares Islands. *Notornis* **36**: 183-189.
Tennyson, A.J.D. & Taylor, G.A. (1990). Behaviour of *Pterodroma* petrels in response to "war-whoops". *Notornis* **37**: 121-128.
Tennyson, A.J.D. & Taylor, G.A. (1991). Variation in leg colour of Black-winged Petrels. *Notornis* **38(1)**: 59.
Tenovuo, R. (1976). the Mute Swan *Cygnus olor* in Finland. *Ornis Fennica* **53**: 147-149.
Terborgh, J. (1989). *Where Have all the Birds Gone?. Essays on the Biology and Conservation of Birds that Migrate to the American Tropics*. Princeton University Press.
Terborgh, J.W., Fitzpatrick, J.W. & Emmons, L. (1984). *Annotated Checklist of Bird and Mammal Species of Cocha Casu Biological Station, Manu National Park, Peru*. Fieldiana Zoology **21**. Field Museum of Natural History.
Terres, J.K. (1980). *The Audubon Society Encyclopedia of North American Birds*. Alfred A. Knopf, New York.
Terry, M.L. (1991). Use of tongue-flicking behavior by the Snowy Egret. *J. Field Orn.* **62(3)**: 399-402.
Tershy, B.R. & Breese, D. (1990). The influence of sexual dimorphism on kleptoparasitism of Blue-footed Boobies by Brown Boobies. *Can. J. Zool.* **68**: 197-199.
Tershy, B.R., Breese, D. & Meyer, G.M. (1990). Kleptoparasitism of adult and immature Brown Pelicans by Heermann's Gulls. *Condor* **92**: 1076-1077.
van Tets, G.F. (1956). *A Comparative Study of the Reproductive Behavior and Natural History of Three Sympatric Species of Cormorants on Mandarte Island*. Unpublished MSc thesis, University of British Columbia.
van Tets, G.F. (1965a). *A Comparative Study of Some Social Communication Patterns in the Pelecaniformes*. Ornithological Monographs **2**. The American Ornithologists' Union.
van Tets, G.F. (1965b). Eastern Swamphen takes a downy from a pair of Chestnut Teal. *Emu* **64**: 100.
van Tets, G.F. (1975). A report on the conservation of resident birds on Christmas Island. *Bull. ICBP* **12**: 238-242.
van Tets, G.F. (1976). Australasia and the origin of shags and cormorants, *Phalacrocoracidae*. Pp. 121-124 in: *Proc. XVI Int. Orn. Congr.*
van Tets, G.F. (1978). (*Pelecanus conspicillatus*). *A'asian Seabird Group Newsl.* **11**: 5-6.
van Tets, G.F. (1980). Preliminary reports of the Campbell Island Expedition 1975-76. Wellington, Department of Lands and Survey Reserve Service **7**.
van Tets, G.F. (1985a). Cormorant. Pp. 110 -111 in: Campbell & Lack (1985).
van Tets, G.F. (1985b). Darter. Page 130 in: Campbell & Lack (1985).
van Tets, G.F. (1985c). King Shag. Page 118 in: Robertson (1985).
van Tets, G.F. (1985d). Stewart Island Shag. Page 119 in: Robertson (1985).
van Tets, G.F. (1985e). Chatham Island Shag. Page 121 in: Robertson (1985).
van Tets, G.F. (1985f). Campbell Island Shag. Page 122 in: Robertson (1985).
van Tets, G.F. (1985g). Auckland Island Shag. Page 123 in: Robertson (1985).
van Tets, G.F. (1985h). Spotted Shag. Page 125 in: Robertson (1985).
van Tets, G.F. (1985i). Pitt Island Shag. Page 126 in: Robertson (1985).
van Tets, G.F. & Fullagar, P.J. (1984). Status of seabirds breeding in Australia. Pp. 559-571 in: Croxall *et al.* (1984).
van Tets G.F. & Marlow, B.J. (1977). Seabirds Islands no. 53. Dangerous Reef, South Australia. *Corella* **1**: 70-71.
van Tets, G.F. & Robertson, C.J.R. (1985). Bounty Island Shag. Page 120 in: Robertson (1985).
van Tets, G.F. & van Tets, P.A. (1967). A report on the resident birds of the Territory of Christmas Island. *Emu* **66**: 304-319.
van Tets, G.F. & Vestjens, W.J.M. (1985). Emperor Shag. Page 124 in: Robertson (1985).
van Tets, G.F. Meredith, C.W., Fullagar, P.J. & Davidson, P.M. (1988). Osteological differences between *Sula* and *Morus*, and a description of an extinct new species of *Sula* from Lord Howe and Norfolk Islands, Tasman Sea. *Notornis* **35**: 35-57.
van Tets, G.F., Milliner, P.R. & Vestjens, W.J.M. (1985). Pied Cormorant. Page 116 in: Robertson (1985).
van Tets, G.F. Waterman, M.H. & Purchase, D. (1976). Dispersal patterns of cormorants banded in South Australia. *Austr. Bird Bander* **14(2)**: 43-46.
Thaler, E., Ettel, E. & Job, S. (1981). Zur Sozialstruktur des Waldrapps *Geronticus eremita* - Beobachtungen an der Brutkolonie des Alpenzoos Innsbruck. *J. Orn.* **122**: 109-128.
Thibault, J.C. (1977). Nouvelles observations sur la disposition helicoidale de l'intestin chez certaines espèces du genre *Pterodroma*. *Alauda* **45**: 237.
Thibault, J.C. (1985). La reproduction du Puffin Cendré *Calonectris diomedea* en Corse. Pp. 49-55 in *Oiseaux marins nicheurs du Midi et de la Corse*. Ann. Centre Rech. Orn. Provence, Aix-en-Provence.
Thibault, J.C. & Guyot, I. (1988). *Livre rouge des oiseaux menaces des regions françaises d'outre-mer*. ICBP, Asnières, France.
Thibault, J.C. & Holyoak, D.T. (1978). Vocal and olfactory displays in the genera *Bulweria* and *Pterodroma*. *Ardea* **66**: 53-56.
Thiede, W. (1987). Bestimmungsmerkmale adulter Flamingos (Phoenicopteridae). *Orn. Mitt.* **39**: 36-38.
Thiede, W. & Gloe, P. (1987). Zwergflamingos (*Phoeniconaias minor*) in Europa. *Orn. Mitt.* **39**: 256-260.
Thiollay, J.M. (1985). Ecology and status of several European raptors and the White Stork in their winter quarters in West Africa. Pp. 5-8 in: MacDonald, A. & Goriup, P. *Migratory Birds: Problems and Prospects in Africa*. ICBP, 14th Conference of the European Continental Section, 1983.
Thom, V.M. (1986). *Birds in Scotland*. T & A D Poyser, Calton, England.
Thomas, B.T. (1979a). The birds of a ranch in the Venezuelan Llanos. Pp. 213-232 in: Eisenberg, J.F. ed. *Vertebrate Ecology of the Northern Neotropics*. Smithsonian Institution Press, Washington, D.C.
Thomas, B.T. (1979b). Plumage succession of nestling Maguari Storks. *Bol. Soc. Venez. Cienc. Nat.* **136**: 239-241.
Thomas, B.T. (1981). Jabiru nest, nest building, and quintuplets. *Condor* **83**: 84-85.
Thomas, B.T. (1984). Maguari Stork nesting: juvenile growth and behavior. *Auk* **101**: 812-823.
Thomas, B.T. (1985). Coexistence and behavior differences among the three Western Hemisphere storks. Pp. 921-931 in: Buckley, P.A., Foster, M.S., Morton, E.S., Ridgely, R.S. & Buckley, F.G. eds. *Neotropical Ornithology*. Ornithological Monographs **36**. American Ornithologists's Union, Washington, D.C.
Thomas, B.T. (1986). The behavior and breeding of adult Maguari Storks. *Condor* **88**: 26-34.
Thomas, B.T. (1987). Philopatry of banded Maguari Storks and their decline in Venezuela. *Bol. Soc. Ven. Cien. Nat.* **41(144)**: 137-157.
Thomas, B.T. (1988). A comparison of the Maguari Stork *Ciconia maguari* with the White Stork *Ciconia ciconia*. *Gerfaut* **78**: 113-119.
Thomas, D.D. & Condy, J.B. (1965). Breeding of Hottentot Teal *Anas punctata* Burchell in Southern Rhodesia. *Ostrich* **36**: 88-89.
Thomas, G. (1982). The food and feeding ecology of the Light-mantled Sooty Albatross at South Georgia. *Emu* **82**: 92-100.
Thomas, G., Croxall, J.P. & Prince, P.A. (1983). Breeding biology of the Light-mantled Sooty Albatross at South Georgia. *J. Zoology. London* **199**: 123-135.
Thomas, T. (1983). Données récentes sur l'avifaune des Kerguelen. *L'Oiseau et la R.F.O.* **53**: 133-141.
Thomas, T. (1986). L'effectif des oiseaux nicheurs de l'archipel de Pointe Géologie (Terre Adélie) et son évolution au cours des trentes dernières années. *L'Oiseau et la R.F.O.* **56**: 349-368.
Thomas, V.G. (1990). Adaptations of breeding Geese to unpredictable environmental conditions of the artic. *Trans. Congr. Int. Union Game Biol.* **19 (1)**: 192-202.
Thomasson, K. (1953). Die Verbreitung des Rothalstauchers, *Podiceps g. griseigena* Bodd. in N.W. Europa. *Zool. Bidrag Uppsala* **30**: 157-168.
Thompson, D.Q. (1951). Notes on distribution of North Pacific albatrosses. *Auk* **68**: 227-235.
Thompson, K.R. (1992). Quantitative analysis of the use of discards from squid trawlers by Black-browed Albatrosses *Diomedea melanophris* in the vicinity of the Falkland Islands. *Ibis* **134**: 11-21.
Thompson, M.C.. (1966). Birds from North Borneo. *Univ. Kansas Publ. Mus. Nat. Hist.* **17**: 377-433.
Thompson, R.B. (1977). Effects of human disturbance on an Adelie Penguin rookery and measures of control. Pp. 1177-1180 in: Llano (1977).
Thompson, S.C. (1987). *Incubation Behavior of Emperor Geese*. MSc thesis, University California (Davis).
Thompson, S.C. & Raveling, D.G. (1987). Incubation behaviour of Emperor Geese compared with other geese: interactions of predation, body-size and energetics. *Auk* **104**: 707-716.
Thompson, S.C. & Raveling, D.G. (1988). Nest insulation and incubation constancy of arctic geese. *Wildfowl* **39**: 124-132.
Thomson, A.L. (1931). On "abmigration" among the ducks: an anomaly shown by the results of bird-marking. Pp. 382-388 in: *Proc. VII Int. Orn. Congr. (Amsterdam, 1930)*.
Thomson, A.L. (1964) *A New Dictionary of Birds*. McGraw-Hill, New York.
Thomson, A.L. (1965). The transequatorial migration of the Manx Shearwater (Puffin des Anglais). *L'Oiseau et la R.F.O.* **35(No. Spéc.)**: 130-140.
Thomson, A.L. (1974). The migration of the gannet: a reassessment of British and Irish ringing data. *British Birds* **67**: 89-103.
Thomson, A.L. (1975). Dispersal of first-year gannets from the Bass Rock. *Scottish Birds* **8**: 295-298.
Thoresen, A.C. (1967). Ecological observations on Stanley and Green Islands, Mercury Group. *Notornis* **14**: 182-200.
Thoresen, A.C. (1969). Observations on the breeding behaviour of the diving petrel *Pelecanoides u. urinatrix*. *Notornis* **16**: 241-260.
Thorpe, W.H. (1961). *Bird Song: The Biology of Vocal Communication and Expression in Birds*. Cambridge University Press, Cambridge, England.
Thorsteinsson, B., Palsdottir, E. & Petersen, A. (1991). [A Barnacle Goose *Branta leucopsis* forming a trio with Greylag Geese *Anser anser*]. *Bliki* **10**: 12-14. In Icelandic with English summary.
Thouless, C.R., Fanshawe, J.H. & Bertram, B.C.R. (1989). Egyptian Vultures *Neophron percnopterus* and Ostrich *Struthio camelus* eggs: the origins of stone-throwing behavior. *Ibis* **131(1)**: 9-15.
Threlfall, W. (1974). Foot injuries in Leach's Storm Petrels. *Wilson Bull.* **86**: 65-67.
Ticehurst, N.F. (1957). *The Mute Swan in England*. Cleaver-Hume Press, London.
Tickell, W.L.N. (1962). *The Dove Prion* Pachyptila desolata. *Falkland Is. Depend. Surv. Sci. Rep.* **33**.

Tickell, W.L.N. (1964). Feeding preferences of the albatrosses *Diomedea melanophris* and *D. chrysostoma* at South Georgia. Pp. 383-387 in: Carrick, R., Holdgate, M.W. & Prévost, J. eds. *Biologie Antarctique*. Hermann, Paris.
Tickell, W.L.N. (1967). Movements of Black-browed and Grey-headed Albatross in the south Atlantic. *Emu* **66**: 357-367.
Tickell, W.L.N. (1968). The biology of the great albatrosses, *Diomedea exulans* and *Diomedea epomophora*. *Antarct. Res. Ser.* **12**: 1-55.
Tickell, W.L.N. (1969). Plumage changes in young albatrosses. *Ibis* **111**: 102-105.
Tickell, W.L.N. (1970). Biennial breeding in albatrosses. Pp. 549-557 in Holdgate, M.W. ed. *Antarctic Ecology*. Vol. 1. Academic Press, London & New York.
Tickell, W.L.N. (1975). Observations on the status of Steller's Albatross (*Diomedea albatrus*) 1973. *Bull. ICBP* **12**: 125-131.
Tickell, W.L.N. (1976). The distribution of Black-browed and Grey-headed Albatrosses. *Emu* **76**: 64-68.
Tickell, W.L.N. (1980). The pink ear stain of Wandering Albatrosses. *Australasian Seabird Group Newsl.* **13**: 12-17.
Tickell, W.L.N. (1984). Behaviour of Blackbrowed and Greyheaded Albatross at Bird Island, South Georgia. *Ostrich* **56**: 64-85.
Tickell, W.L.N. & Gibson, J.D. (1968). Movements of Wandering Albatrosses. *Emu* **68**: 7-20.
Tickell, W.L.N. & Pinder, R. (1966). Two-egg clutches in Albatrosses. *Ibis* **108**: 126-129.
Tickell, W.L.N. & Pinder, R. (1967). Breeding frequencies in the albatrosses *Diomedea melanophris* and *D. chrysostoma*. *Nature. London* **213**: 315-316.
Tickell, W.L.N. & Pinder, R. (1975). Breeding biology of the Black-browed Albatross and Grey-headed Albatross at Bird Island, South Georgia. *Ibis* **117**: 433-451.
Tilson, R.L. & Kok, O.B. (1980). Habitat ecology of Black storks in the Kuiseb River. *Madoqua* **11**: 347-349.
Timken, R.L. & Anderson, B.W. (1969). Food habits of Common Mergansers in the Northcentral United States. *J. Wildl. Manage.* **33**: 87-91.
Tinbergen, N. (1951). *The Study of Instinct*. Oxford University Press, London.
Tindale, N.B. (1953). Cassowary-horn native ornament from Arnhem Land. *S. Austr. Ornithologist* **21**: 11.
Tindle, R. (1978). Studies on the Greater Flamingo *Phoenicopterus ruber* in the Galapagos Islands. *CDRS Annual Report* **1978**.
Tindle, R. (1984). The evolution of breeding strategies in the Flightless Cormorant *Nannopterum harrisi* of the Galapagos. *Biol. J. Linn. Soc.* **21**: 157-164.
Titman, R.D. & Seymour, N.R. (1981). A comparison of pursuits flights by six North American ducks of the genus *Anas*. *Wildfowl* **32**: 11-18.
Titus, J.R. & van Druff, L.W. (1981). *Response of Common Loon to Recreational Pressure in the Boundary Waters Canoe Area, Northeastern Minnesota*. Wildlife Monographs **79**.
Todd, F.S. (1979). *Waterfowl: Ducks, Geese and Swans of the World*. Harcourt Brace Jovanovich, New York.
Todd, F.S. (1980). Factors influencing Emperor Penguin mortality at Cape Crozier and Beaufort Island, Antarctica. *Gerfaut* **70**: 37-49.
Todd, F.S. (1988). Weddell Seal preys on Chinstrap Penguin. *Condor* **90**: 249-250.
Todd, F.S. (1990). Saga of the Brown Pelican. *Birds Int.* **1990**: 75-86.
Todd, W.E.C. (1937). (*Crypturellus variegatus*). *Proc. Biol. Soc. Washington* **50**: 175-178.
Todd, W.E.C. & Carriker, M.A. (1922). (Tigrisoma fasciatum). *Ann. Carneg. Mus.* **14**: 132.
Toft, C.A., Trauger, D.L. & Murdy, H.W. (1984). Seasonal decline in brood sizes of sympatric waterfowl (*Anas* and *Aythya*, Anatidae) and a proposed evolutionary explanation. *J. Anim. Ecol.* **53**: 75-92.
Tollu, B. (1978). *Contribution à l'étude des Spheniscidés du genre Eudyptes dans les Iles australes françaises (Amsterdam, Sant-Paul, Crozet et Kerguelen)*. Thèse Doctorat d'État. Paris.
Tollu, B. (1988). *Les Manchots, Ecologie et Vie Sociale*. Rocher, Monaco.
Tome, M.W. (1981). *The Reproductive Bioenergetics of Female Ruddy Ducks in Manitoba*. MSc thesis University of Maine, Orono.
Tome, M.W. (1989). Search-path characteristics of foraging Ruddy Ducks. *Auk* **106**: 42-48.
Tomek, T. & Dontchev, S. (1987). Materials concerning the avifauna of the Democratic People's Republic of Korea in the postbreeding season. *Acta Zool. Cracov.* **30(4)**: 37-52.
Tomkins, R.J. (1983a). Purple bill flushes and pink ear marks on Wandering Albatrosses on Macquarie Island. *Australasian Seabird Group Newsl.* **18**: 11-15.
Tomkins, R.J. (1983b). Fertilisation of Wandering Albatross eggs on Macquarie Island. *Notornis* **30**: 244-246.
Tomkins, R.J. (1984). Some aspects of the morphology of the Wandering Albatrosses on Macquarie Island. *Emu* **84**: 29-32.
Tomkins, R.J. (1985a). Reproduction and mortality of Wandering Albatrosses on Macquarie Island. *Emu* **85**: 40-42.
Tomkins, R.J. (1985b). Breeding Success and Mortality of Dark-rumped Petrels in the Galápagos, and Control of their Predators. Pp. 159-175 in: Moors (1985).
Tomkins, R.J. & Milne, b.J. (1991). Differences among Dark-rumped Petrel (*Pterodroma phaeopygia*) populations within the Galapagos archipielago. *Notornis* **38(1)**: 1-35.
Tomlinson, D.N.S. (1974a). Studies of the Purple Heron. Part 1: heronry structure, nesting habits and reproductive success. *Ostrich* **45**: 175-181.
Tomlinson, D.N.S. (1974b). Studies on the Purple Heron. Part 2: behaviour patterns. *Ostrich* **45(4)**: 149-160, 209-223.
Tomlinson, D.N.S. (1975). (Ardea melanocephala). *Ostrich* **46**: 157-165.
Tonni, E.P. & Laza, J.H. (1980). Las aves de la fauna local Paso de Otero (Pleistoceno Tardío) en la provincia de Buenos Aires. Su significación ecológica, climática y zoogeográfica. *Ameghiniana* **17(4)**: 313-322.
Torres, J.A. & Arenas, R. (1985). Nuevos datos relativos a la alimentación de *Oxyura leucocephala*. *Ardeola* **32 (1)**: 127-131.
Torres, J.A., Raya, C., Arenas, R. & Ayala, J.M. (1985). Estudio del comportamiento reproductor de la Malvasía (*Oxyura leucocephala*). *Oxyura* **II(1)**: 5-22.
Torres, J.A., Raya, C., Arenas, R. & Ayala, J.M. (1986). Evolución histórica de la población española de Malvasía (*Oxyura leucocephala*). *Oxyura* **III(1)**: 5-17.
Tostain, O., du Plessix, H. & Siblet, J.P. (1981). La nidification du Grèbe jougris (*Podiceps grisegena* Bodd.) en 1978 en Région Parisienne. *L'Oiseau et la R.F.O.* **51**: 205-217.
Tovar, H. (1968). Areas de reproducción y distribución de las aves marinas en el litoral peruano. *Bol. Inst. Mar. Perú-Callao* **1(5)**: 189-304, **1(10)**: 526-545.
Tovar, H. (1978). Las poblaciones de aves guaneras en los ciclos reproductivos de 1969/70 a 1973/74. *Inf. Inst. Mar. Perú-Callao* **45**: 1-13.
Tovar, H. (1983). Fluctuaciones de poblaciones de aves guaneras en el litoral peruano, 1960-1981. *FAO Fish. Rep.* **29(3)**: 957-976.
Tovar, H. & Cabrera, D. (1985). Las aves guaneras y el fenómeno "El Niño". *Bol. Ins. Mar. Perú-Callao* **Vol. Extraordinario**: 181-186.
Tovar, H. & Galarza, N. (1983). Fluctuaciones mensuales de las poblaciones de aves guaneras durante "El Niño" de 1972. *Inf. Inst. Mar. Perú-Callao* **1983**: 1-38.
Tovar, H., Guillén, V. & Cabrera, D. (1987). Reproduction and population levels of Peruvian guano birds, 1980 to 1986. *J. Geophys. Res.* **92(C13)**: 14, 445-14, 448.
Tove, M.H. (1988). First record of a Pacific Loon from North Carolina. *Chat* **53(1)**: 8-11.
Townsend, C.W. (1916). The courtship of the Merganser, Mallard, Black Duck, Baldpate, Wood Duck and Bufflehead. *Auk* **33**: 9-17.
Townsend, C.W. (1924). Diving of grebes and loons. *Auk* **41(1)**: 29-41.
Townsend, G.H. (1966). A Study of Waterfowl Nesting on Saskatchewan River Delta. *Can. Field-Nat.* **80**: 74-88.
Trauger, D.L. (1971). *Population Ecology of Lesser Scaup (*Aythya affinis*) in Subarctic Taiga*. PhD dissertation, Iowa State University, Ames, Iowa.
Trauger, D.L., Dzubin, A. & Ryder, J.P. (1971). White geese intermediate between Ross' Geese and Lesser Snow Geese. *Auk* **88**: 856-875.
Trayler, K.M., Brothers, D.J., Wooller, R.D. & Potter, I.C. (1989). Opportunistic foraging by three species of cormorants in an Australian estuary. *J. Zoology. London* **218**: 87-98.
Traylor, M.A. (1952). Birds of the Marcapata Valley, Peru. *Fieldiana (Zool.)* **34**: 17-19.
Treca, B. (1979). Note sur la reproduction du Canard Arme *Plectropterus gambensis* au Sénégal. *Malimbus* **1**: 29-31.
Treca, B. (1980). Nouvelles données sur la reproduction du Canard Arme *Plectropterus gambensis* au Sénégal. *Malimbus* **2**: 25-28.
Treca, B. (1981a). Régime alimentaire de la Sarcelle d'été (*Anas querquedula* L.) dans le delta du Sénégal. *L'Oiseau et la R.F.O.* **51**: 33-58.
Treca, B. (1981b). Le régime alimentaire du Dendrocygne veuf (*Dendrocygna viduata*) dans le delta du Sénégal. *L'Oiseau et la R.F.O.* **51 (3)**: 219-238.
Tree, A.J. (1982a). The Black Stork in Zimbabwe. *Honeyguide* **109**: 18-19.
Tree, A.J. (1982b). Recent reports. *Honeyguide* **109**: 22-28.
Tree, A.J. (1983). Notes from Mattoffin, Transvaal. *Honeyguide* **114-115**: 57-59.
Treesucon, U. & Round, P.D. (1990). Report on threatened birds in Thailand. *Tiger Paper* **17(3)**: 1-7.
Trefethan, J.B. ed. (1966). *Wood Duck Management and Research: a Symposium*. Wildlife Management Institute, Washington, D.C.
Trillmich, F., Trillmich, K., Limberger, D. & Arnold, W. (1983). The breeding season of the flightless cormorant *Nannopterum harrisi* at Cabo Hammond, Fernandina. *Ibis* **125(29)**: 221-223.
Trivelpiece, S.G. Trivelpiece, W.Z., & Volkman, N.J. (1985). Plumage characteristics of juvenile pygoscelid penguins. *Ibis* **127**: 378-380.
Trivelpiece, W.Z. (1981). Ecological studies of pygoscelid penguins and Antarctic skuas. PhD thesis, State University of New York.
Trivelpiece, W.Z. & Ferraris, J.D. (1987). Notes on the behavioural ecology of the Magnificent Frigatebird *Fregata magnificens*. *Ibis* **129**: 168-174.
Trivelpiece, W.Z. & Volkman, N.J. (1979). Nest site competition between Adelie *Pygoscelis adeliae* and Chinstrap *Pygoscelis antarctica* penguins: ecological interpretation. *Auk* **96**: 675-681.
Trivelpiece, W.Z., Bengston, J.L., Trivelpiece, S.G. & Volkman, N.J. (1986). Foraging behaviour of Gentoo and Chinstrap Penguins as determined by new radiotelemetric techniques. *Auk* **103**: 777-781.
Trivelpiece, W.Z., Trivelpiece, S.G. & Volkman, N.J. (1987). Ecological segregation of Adelie, Gentoo, and Chinstrap Penguins at King George Island, Antarctica. *Ecology* **68**: 351-361.
Trivelpiece, W.Z., Trivelpiece, S.G., Geupel, G., Kjelmyr, J. & Volkman, N.J. (1990). Adelie and Chinstrap Penguins: their potential as monitors of the southern ocean marine ecosystem. Pp. 191-202 in: Kerry, K. & Hempel, G., eds. *Proc. of the Fifth SCAR Symposium on Antarctic Biology*. Springer, Heidelberg.
Trivelpiece, W.Z., Trivelpiece, S.G., Volkman, N.J. & Ware, S.G. (1983). Breeding and feeding ecologies of pygoscelid penguins. *Antarct. J.U.S.* **18**: 209-210.
Trotignon, E. & Trotignon J. (1981). Recensement hivernal 1979-1980 des Spatules, des Flamants et des Pélicans blancs sur le Banc d'Arguin (Mauritanie). *Alauda* **49(3)**: 203-215.
Trotignon, J. (1976). La nidification sur le Banc d'Arguin (Mauritanie) au printemps 1974. *Alauda* **44**: 119-133.
Trottier, G.C., Breneman, R.J. & Young, N.A. (1980). Status and foraging distribution of White Pelicans, Prince Albert National Park, Saskatchewan. *Can. Field-Nat.* **94**: 383-390.
Tuchscherer, K. (1981a). Zum Brutvorkommen des Rothalstauchers, *Podiceps griseigena*, im Bezirk Leipzig. *Actitis* **19**: 2-13.
Tuchscherer, K. (1981b). Zum Vorkommen des Ohrentauchers, *Podiceps auritus* L., im Bezirk Leipzig. *Actitis* **20**: 75-79.
Tuck, G. & Heinzel, H. (1978). *A Field Guide to the Seabirds of Britain and the World*. William Collins Sons & Co Ltd, London.
Tuite, C.H. (1978). *The Lesser Flamingo (*Phoeniconaias minor*, Geoffroy): Aspects of its Ecology and Behaviour in the Eastern Rift Valley of Kenya and Northern Tanzania*. PhD thesis, University of Bristol.
Tuite, C.H. (1979). Population size, distribution and biomass density of the Lesser Flamingo in the Eastern Rift Valley, 1974-76. *J. Appl. Ecol.* **16**: 765-775.
Tuite, C.H. (1980). Le flamant nain en Afrique Orientale. Evolution de la situation entre 1969 et 1976. Pp. 10-12 in: Johnson (1980).
Tuite, C.H. (1981). Flamingos in East Africa. *Swara* **4**: 36-38.
Tulloch, D. (1985). The Magpie Goose (*Anseranas semipalmata*) and the black soil plants: a biological case history of waterbirds in coastal north Australia. Pp. 285-294 in: Bardsley, K.N., Davie, J.D.S. & Woodroffe, C.D. eds. (1985). *Coasts and Tidal Wetlands of the Australian Monsoon Region*. Mangrove Monograph **1**. Australian National University.
Tulloch, D., Cellier, K.M. & Hertog, A.L. (1988). The distribution of the nests of the Magpie Goose (*Anseranas semipalmata* Latham) at Kapalga, N.T.: a four-year study. *Austr. Wildl. Res.* **15 (2)**: 211-221.
Tunnell, J.W. & Chapman, B.R. (1988). First record of Red-footed Boobies nesting in the Gulf of Mexico. *Amer. Birds* **42(3)**: 380-381.
Tunnicliffe, G.A. (1973). The avifauna of the Lake Ellesmere area, Canterbury. *Mauri Ora* **1**: 107-135.
Turbott, E.G. (1956). Notes on the plumages and breeding cycle of the Spotted Shag, *Phalacrocorax (Stictocarbo) punctatus punctatus* (Sparman, 1786). *Rec. Auck. Inst. Mus.* **4(6)**: 343-363.
Turcotte, Y. & Bedard, J. (1989a). Prolonged parental care and foraging of Greater Snow Goose juveniles. *Wilson Bull.* **101 (3)**: 500-503.
Turcotte, Y. & Bedard, J. (1989b). Shared Parental Investment, Parent-offspring conflict and brood size in Greater Snow Geese. *Anim. Behav.* **38(4)**: 703-706.
Turnbull, R.E., Johnson, F.A. & Brakhage, D.H. (1989). Status, distribution, and foods of Fulvous Whistling-duck in South Florida. *J. Wildl. Manage.* **53 (4)**: 1046-1051.
Turner, D. (1980a). Notes on the breeding of the Black-bellied Storm Petrel (*Fregetta tropica*) on Bird Island, South Georgia, 1973/1974. *Notornis* **27**: 94-95.
Turner, D.A. (1980b). The Madagascar Squacco Heron *Ardeola idae* in East Africa, with notes on its field identification. *Scopus* **4**: 42-43.
Turpin, M.C. & Dell, J. (1991). Musk Duck feeding on vertebrates. *West. Austr. Nat.* **18 (6)**: 168.
Tyler, C. (1964). A study of egg shells of the Anatidae. *Proc. Zool. Soc. London* **142**: 547-583.
Tyler, C. & Simkiss, K. (1959). A study of the egg shells of ratite birds. *Proc. Zool. Soc. Lond.* **133**: 201-243.
van Tyne, J. & Berger, A.J. (1976). *Fundamentals of Ornithology*. 2nd edition. John Wiley and Sons, New York.
Uchida, Y. (1970). On the colour change in Japanese Crested Ibis. A new type of cosmetic coloration in birds. *Misc. Rep. Yamashina Inst. Orn.* **6(1/2)**: 54-72.
Uchida, Y. (1974). Feather color of Japanese Crested Ibis. *Animals and Zoos* **12**: 412-414.
Udvardy, M.D.F. (1969). *Dynamic Zoogeography*. Van Nostrand Reinhold, New York.
Ulfvens, J. (1988). Comparative breeding ecology of the Horned Grebe *Podiceps auritus* and the Great Crested Grebe *Podiceps cristatus*: archipelago versus lake habitats. *Acta Zool. Fennica* **183**: 1-75.
Ulfvens, J. (1989a). Egg covering in the Horned Grebe *Podiceps auritus* and the Great Crested Grebe *Podiceps cristatus* in a Finnish archipelago. *Memoranda Soc. Fauna Flora Fennica* **65**: 1-6.
Ulfvens, J. (1989b). Clutch size, productivity and population changes in a population of the Horned Grebe *Podiceps auritus* in an exposed habitat. *Ornis Fenn.* **66**: 75-77.
Urban, E.K. (1959). *Birds of Coahuila, México*. University of Kansas, Lawrence, Kansas.
Urban, E.K. (1967). Possible occurrence of Whale-headed Stork in Ethiopia. *J. East Afr. Nat. Hist. Soc. Natl. Mus.* **26**: 87-88.
Urban, E.K. (1974a). Breeding of sacred ibis *Threskiornis aethiopica* at Lake Shala, Ethiopia. *Ibis* **116**: 263-277.
Urban, E.K. (1974b). Flight speed and wing flapping rate of Sacred Ibis. *Auk* **91**: 423.
Urban, E.K. (1978). *Ethiopia's Endemic Birds*. Ethiopian Tourist Organization, Addis Ababa.
Urban, E.K. (1979). Observations on the nesting of the Great Cormorant in Ethiopia. *Wilson Bull.* **91**: 461-463.
Urban, E.K. (1980). *Ethiopia's Endemics Birds*. Ethiopian Tourism Commission, Addis Adaba.
Urban, E.K. (1984). Time of egg-laying and number of nesting Great White Pelicans at Lake Shala, Ethiopia, and elsewhere in Africa. Pp. 809-823 in: Ledger, J. (1984). *Proceedings of the Fifth Pan-African Ornithological Congress*. Southern African Ornithological Society, Johannesburg.
Urban, E.K. (1985). Pelican. Pp. 442-443 in: Campbell & Lack (1985).
Urban, E.K. & Jefford, T.G. (1974). The status of the cormorants *Phalacrocorax carbo lucidus* and *Phalacrocorax carbo patricki*. *Bull. Br. Orn. Club* **94**: 104-107.
Urfi, A.J. (1989a). Painted Stork *Mycteria leucocephala* (Pennant) swallowing a snake. *J. Bombay Nat. Hist. Soc.* **86**: 96.
Urfi, A.J. (1989b). Painted Storks of Dehli Zoo. *Sanctuary* **9(4)**: 26-33.
Urfi, A.J. (1990). Mysterious disappearance of Painted Storks from Dehli Zoo heronries and abrupt termination of their breeding. *Newsletter for Birdwatchers* **30**: 3-5.
Uspenski, S.M. (1965). *Die Wildgänse Nordeurasiens*. Neue Brehm-Bücherei **352**. A. Ziemsen Verlag, Wittenberg, Lutherstadt.
Uthaman, P.K. (1990). Spotbill Duck *Anas poecilorhyncha* J.R. Forster in Kerala. *J. Bombay Nat. Hist. Soc.* **87 (2)**: 290-291.
Uttley, J. (1987). Survey of Sulawesi Selatan to assess the status of wetlands and to identify key sites for breeding and migratory waterbirds. AWB/PHPA-Interwader Report **2**. Asian Wetland Bureau, Kuala Lumpur, Malaysia.
Utvinenko, N.M. (1968). [On the distribution of the Oriental White Stork in the Lower Amur]. *Ornitologiya* **9**: 356-358. In Russian.
Uusitalo, R. (1969). Mustakurkku-uikun (*Podiceps auritus*) pesimisbiologiasta Etelä-Satakunnassa. [Summary: On the breeding biology of the Horned Grebe in South Satakunta]. *Porin Lintutieteellisen Yhdistyksen Vuosikirja* **1968**: 45-48.
Uusitalo, R. (1976). *Mustakurkku-uikun pesimisbiologiasta, erityisesti habitaatin valinnasta Lounais-Suomessa*. MSc thesis, University Turku.
Uys, C.J. (1967). Hamerkop *Scopus umbretta* nesting on a house. *Ostrich* **38**: 199-200.
Uys, C.J. (1983). Hadeda over Constantia. *Promerops* **161**: 8-9.
Uys, C.J. (1986). Hamerkop takes aquatic prey on the wing. *Promerops* **174**: 10-11.

Uys, C.J. & Broekhuysen, G.J. (1966). Hadeda *Hagedashia hagedash* nesting on telegraph pole. *Ostrich* **37**: 239-240.
Uys, C.J., Broekhuysen, G.J., Martin, J. & Macleod, J.G. (1961). Mass breeding of the Greater Flamingo (*Phoenicopterus ruber roseus*) in the Bredasdorp District. *Ostrich* **32**: 92-93.
Uys, C.J., Broekhuysen, G.J., Martin, J. & Macleod, J.G. (1963). Observations on the breeding of the Greater Flamingo *Phoenicopterus ruber* Linnaeus in the Bredasdorp District, South Africa. *Ostrich* **34**: 129-154.
Vaidya, A.A. (1986). Invasion of White Storks ("Ciconia ciconia") in Kachch (Kutch), Gujarat. *J. Bombay Nat. Hist. Soc.* **83(3)**: 661-662.
Valdes Miro, V. (1984). Datos de nidificación sobre las aves que crían en Cuba. *Poeyana* **282**: 1-27.
Valdivia, J.E. (1978). The anchoveta and El Niño. *Rapports et Proces-verbaux des Reunions du Conseil International pour l'Exploration de la Mer* **173**: 196-202.
Valle, C.A. (1986a). Status of the Galapagos Penguin and Flightless Cormorant populations in 1985. *Noticias Galápagos* **43**: 16-17.
Valle, C.A. (1986b). Natural history, movements and migration of the Great Frigatebird (*Fregata minor*) in Galapagos. *Ann. Rep. Charles Darwin Res. Station* **1983**: 34-36.
Valle, C.A. (1988). Historia natural, movimientos y migraciones de la fragata común (*Fregata minor*) en Galápagos. *Ann. Rep. Charles Darwin Res. Station* **1984/85**: 69-71.
Valle, C.A. & Coulter, M.C. (1987). Present status of the Flightless Cormorant, Galapagos Penguin and Greater Flamingo populations in the Galapagos Islans, Ecuador, after the 1982-83 El Niño. *Condor* **89**: 276-281.
Valley, P.J. (1987). Common Loon productivity and nesting requirements on the whitefish chain of lakes in North-Central Minnesota. *Loon* **59(1)**: 3-11.
Valverde, J.A. (1957). *Aves del Sahara Español*. Instituto de Estudios Africanos, Madrid.
Valverde, J.A. (1960). La nidificación de la Espátula en el sur de España. *Ardeola* **6**: 378.
Van Dijk, K. (1986). Observations on Flamingos. In: Van Dijk, A.J., Van Dijk, K., Dijksen, L.J., van Spanje, T.M. & Wymenga, E. eds. *Wintering Waders and Waterfowl in the Gulf of Gabes, Tunisia, January-March 1984*. W.I.W.O. Report **11**. Zeist.
Vande Weghe, J.F. (1981). L'avifaune des papyraies au Rwanda et au Burundi. *Gerfaut* **71**: 489-536.
Vanden Berge, J.C. (1970). A comparative study of the appendicular musculature of the order Ciconiiformes. *Amer. Midl. Nat.* **84**: 289-364.
Vanden Berge, J.C. (1976). *M. iliotibialis medialis* and a review of the *M. iliotibialis* complex in flamingos. *Auk* **93(3)**: 429-433.
Vandewalle, F.J. (1985). Combined canopying and Foot-stirring functions in the Black Egret. *Bokmakierie* **37(3)**: 73-75.
Vareschi, E. (1978). The ecology of Lake Nakuru (Kenya). 1. Abundance and feeding of the lesser flamingo. *Oecologia* **32**: 11-35.
Varty, N., Adams, J., Espin, P. & Hambler, C. (1986). *An Ornithological Survey of Lake Tota, Colombia, 1982*. ICBP Study Report **12**. ICBP, Cambridge, England.
Vaucoulon, P., Groscolas, R. & Barre, H. (1985). Photoperiodic and food control of moult in the juvenile King Penguin (*Aptenodytes patagonicus*). *Comp. Biochem. Physiol. (Ser. A)* **81(2)**: 347-351.
Vaughan, R. (1980). Notes on Cory's Shearwater and some other birds on Linosa, Pelagic Isles. *Riv. ital. Orn.* **50**: 143-154.
Vaught, R.W. & Kirsch, L.M. (1966). Canada Geese of the Eastern Prairie population, with special reference to the Swan Lake flock. *Missouri Dept. Conserv. Techn. Bull.* **3**.
Vaurie, C. (1972). *Tibet and its Birds*. H.F. and G. Witherby Ltd., London.
Veitch, C.R. (1985). Methods of Eradicating Feral Cats from Offshore Islands in New Zealand. Pp. 125-141 in: Moors (1985).
Velichko, V.P. (1988). [The Cape Barren Goose]. *Priroda. Moscow* **10**: 64-65. In Russian.
Veltman, C.J. & Williams, M. (1990). Diurnal use of time space by breeding Blue Duck *Hymenolaimus malacorhynchos*. *Wildfowl* **41**: 62-74.
Venegas, C. & Jory, J. (1979). *Guía de Campo para las Aves de Magallanes*. Publicación número **11**, Instituto Patagonia Pta. Arenas.
Venn, D.R. (1982). The Cape Gannet, a new record for Australia. *Victorian Nat.* **99**: 56-58.
Vergoossen, W.G. (1983). De Zwarte Ooievaar (*Ciconia nigra*) in de Benelux. [The Black Stork (*Ciconia nigra*) in the Benelux]. *Veldornitol Tijdschr.* **6**: 39-58.
Verheijen, J.A.J. (1964). Breeding season on the island of Flores, Indonesia. *Ardea* **52**: 194-201.
Verheugt, W.J.M. (1987). Conservation status and action programme for the Milky Stork (*Mycteria cinerea*). *Colonial Waterbirds* **10(2)**: 211-220.
Verheugt, W.J.M. (1989). Status of storks in the South Sumatra Province, Indonesia. *Specialist Group on Storks, Ibis, and Spoonbills Newsletter* **2**: 8-9.
Verheyen, R. (1955). La systematique des Anseriformes basée sur l'osteologie comparée. *Bull. Inst. Roy. Sci. Nat. Belgique* **31(35)**: 1-18, **31(36)**: 1-16, **31(37)**: 1-22, **31(38)**: 1-16.
Verheyen, R. (1958). Note sur la classification des Procellariiformes (Tubinares). *Bull. Inst. Roy. Sci. Nat. Belgique* **34**: 1-22.
Verheyen, R. (1959). Contribution à l'anatomie et à la systematique de base des Ciconiiformes (Parker, 1868). *Bull. Inst. Roy. Sci. Nat. Belgique* **35(24)**: 1-34.
Verheyen, R. (1960a). Les kiwis (Apterygiformes) dans les systemes de classification. *Bull. Soc. Royal Zool. d'Anvers* **15**.
Verheyen, R. (1960b). Les tinamous dans les systemes ornithologiques. *Bull. Inst. Royal Sci. Nat. Belgique* **36(1)**: 1-11.
Verheyen, R. (1960c). What are Ciconiiformes? Pp. 741-743 in: *Proc. XII Int. Orn. Congr.*
Vermeer, K. (1970). Distribution and size of colonies of White Pelicans, *Pelecanus erythrorhynchos*, in Canada. *Can. J. Zool.* **48**: 1029-1032.
Vermeer, K. (1973a). Some aspects of the nesting requirements of Common Loons in Alberta. *Wilson Bull.* **85**: 429-435.
Vermeer, K. (1973b). Some aspects of the breeding and mortality of Common Loons in east-central Alberta. *Can. Field-Nat.* **87**: 403-408.
Vermeer, K. & Rankin, L. (1984a). Influence of Habitat Destruction and Disturbance on Nesting Seabirds. Pp. 723-736 in: Croxall *et al.* (1984).
Vermeer, K. & Rankin, L. (1984b). Population trends in nesting Double-crested and Pelagic Cormorants in Canada. *Murrelet* **65**: 1-9.
Vermeer, K. & Sealy, S.G. (1984). Status of the nesting seabirds of British Columbia. Pp. 29-40 in: Croxall *et al.* (1984).
Vermeer, K., Devito, K. & Rankin, L. (1988). Comparison of Nesting Biology of Fork-tailed and Leach's Storm-Petrels. *Colonial Waterbirds* **11**(1): 46-57.
Vermeer, K., Morgan, K.H. & Smith, G.E.J. (1989). Population trends and nesting habitat of Double-crested and Pelagic Cormorants in the Strait of Georgia. In Vermeer, K. & Butler, R.W., eds. *The Status and Ecology of Marine and Shoreline Birds in the Strait of Georgia, British Columbia*. Special Publication **4**. Canadian Wildlife Service, Ottawa.
Verner, J. (1961). Nesting activities of the Red-footed Booby in British Hondura. *Auk* **78**: 573-594.
Verner, J. (1965). Flight behavior of the Red-footed Booby. *Wilson Bull.* **77**: 229-234.
Verney, P. (1979). *Animals in Peril. Man's war against wildlife*. Brigham Young University Press.
Vernon, C.J. (1971). Observations on *Egretta vinaceigula*. *Bull. Brit. Orn. Club* **91**: 157-159.
Vernon, C.J. (1975). Saddlebill Stork breeding at Rainham. *Honeyguide* **83**: 40.
Verschuren, J. & Dupuy, A. (1987). Note sur les Oiseaux des Parcs Nationaux Littoraux du Senegal. *Gerfaut* **77**: 405-442.
Vesall, D.B. (1940). Notes on the nesting habits of the American bittern. *Wilson Bull.* **52**: 207-208.
Veselovsky, Z. (1973). The breeding biology of Cape Barren geese *Cereopsis novaehollandiae*. *Int. Zoo Yb.* **13**: 48-55.
Veselovsky, Z. (1986a). Beitrag zur Kenntnis des Brutverhaltens des Schopfwehrvogels (*Chauna torquata*). *Zool. Garten* **56(4-5)**: 363-384.
Veselovsky, Z. (1986b). Chování a hnízdní biologie cáji chocholaté I. *Ziva* **34(4)**: 154-155.
Veselovsky, Z. (1986c). Chování a hnízdní biologie cáji chocholaté II. *Ziva* **34(5)**: 191-194.
Veselovsky, Z. (1989). Beitrag zur Kenntnis der Blauflugelgans *Cyanochen cyanopterus*. *Zool. Gart.* **59 (2)**: 129-142.
Vesey-Fitzgerald, D. (1957). The breeding of the White Pelican *Pelecanus onocrotalus* in the Rukwa Valley, Tanganyika. *Bull. Brit. Orn. Club* **77**: 127-129.
Vespremeanu, E. (1967). Rolul factorilor abiotici in dinamica populatiilor de lopatar *Platalea leucorodia* L. (Aves, Ciconiiformes) din lunca dunarii. *St. Si Cerc. Biol. Seria Zool. T.* **19**: 279-284.
Vespremeanu, E. (1968). Distribution and biology of the spoonbill in Roumania. *Ardea* **56**: 160-177.
van Vessem, J. & Draulans, D. (1986). Nest attendance by male and female Gray Herons. *J. Field Orn.* **57(1)**: 34-41.
Vestjens, W.J.M. (1973). Feeding of White Ibis on freshwater mussels. *Emu* **73**: 71-72.
Vestjens, W.J.M. (1975a). Feeding behaviour of spoonbills at Lake Cowal, NSW. *Emu* **75**: 132-136.
Vestjens, W.J.M. (1975b). Notes on the tracheae and bronchi of the Australian spoonbills. *Emu* **75**: 87-88.
Vestjens, W.J.M. (1975c). Breeding behavior of the Darter at Lake Cowal. *Emu* **75**: 121-131.
Vestjens, W.J.M. (1977a). Status, habitats and food of vertebrates at Lake Cowal, New South Wales. *CSIRO Division Wildl. Res. Tech. Memo.* **12**.
Vestjens, W.J.M. (1977b). Breeding behaviour of the Australian Pelican, *Pelecanus conspicillatus* in New South Wales. *Austr. Wildl. Res.* **4**: 37-58.
Vestjens, W.J.M. (1977c). Status, habitat and food of vertebrates at Lake Cowal. *CSIRO Division Wildl. Res. Tech. Memo.* **12**: 1-87.
Vestjens, W.J.M. (1983). Australian Pelican "*Pelecanus conspicillatus*". *Corella* **7**: 17-18.
Vestjens, W.J.M. & van Tets, G.F. (1985). Little Black Cormorant. Page 115 in: Robertson (1985).
Vestjens, W.J.M., van Tets, G.F. & Taylor, M.J. (1985). Little Pied Cormorant. Page 117 in: Robertson (1985).
Vicente, R.O. (1984). Nidificaçao da cegonha branca em rochedos da orla marítima Portuguesa. *Cyanopica* **3(2)**: 207-209.
Vickery, P.D. (1988). Distribution and population status of Harlequin Ducks (*Histrionicus histrionicus*) wintering in eastern North America. *Wilson Bull.* **100**: 119-126.
Vidal, P. (1985). Premières observations sur la biologie de la reproduction du Puffin des Anglais yelkouan *Puffinus puffinus yelkouan* dans les îles d'Hyères. In: *Oiseaux marins nicheurs du Midi et de la Corse*. Annales du C.R.O.P. **2**. Aix-en-Provence.
Vides-Almonacid, R. (1988). Aportes sobre la presencia en Tucuman del Hoco oscuro *Trigisoma fasciatum pallescens*. *Olrog. Neotropica (La Plata)* **92**: 123-124.
Vides-Almonacid, R. (1990). Observaciones sobre la utilización del hábitat y la diversidad de especies de aves en una laguna de la puna argentina. *Hornero* **13**: 117-128.
Vieillard, J. (1970). La distribution du Casarca roux *Tadorna ferruginea* (Pallas). *Alauda* **38**: 87-125.
Vieillard, J. (1972). Données biogéographiques sur l'avifaune d'Afrique centrale. *Alauda* **40**: 63-92.
Villavisencio, A. (1988). Conteo de aves en la Reserva Nacional del Titicaca - Sector Puno. *Volante Migratorio* **11**: 25-27.
Vincent, J. (1966). *Red Data Book*. Vol. 2. Aves. 1st. edition. IUCN, Morges, Switzerland.
Vincent, J. & Symons, G. (1948). Some notes on the Bald Ibis *Geronticus calvus* (Boddaert). *Ostrich* **19**: 58-62.
Vinicombe, K. (1982). Breeding and population fluctuations of the Little Grebe. *British Birds* **75**: 204-218.
Vining, R., ed. (1983). Heard Island Expedition 1983. Scientific Reports Garvan Institute of Medical Research, Sidney.
Vinson, J.M. (1976). Notes sur les Procellariens de l'Ile Ronde. *L'Oiseau et la R.F.O.* **46**: 1-24.
Viot C.R. (1987). Différenciation et isolement entre populations chez le Manchot Royal (*Aptenodytes patagonicus*) et le Manchot Papou (*Pygoscelis papua*) des Iles Crozet et Kerguelen. *L'Oiseau et la R.F.O.* **57(3)**: 251-259.
Virchow, H.J.P. (1917). Ueber die Halswirbelsaule von *Plotus anhinga*. *Sitzungsber. Ges. naturf. Freunde. Berlin* **1917**: 454-468.
de Visscher, M.N. (1978). Aspects du comportement du Heron Garde-boeufs, *Bubulcus ibis*, au dortoir dans une region de mangroves du Venezuela. *Gerfaut* **68**: 177-193.
de Visscher, M.N. (1980). La Tijereta de Mar *Fregata magnificens*. *Natura. Venezuela* **69**: 20-22.
Visser, H.T. (1987). *Een karyologische studie van 5 vogelsoorten uit de orden ciconiiformes en phoenicopteriformes, waarvan 4 nieuw beschreven soorten*. Doctoral scriptie, University of Utrecht.
Vizi, O. (1975). O gnezdenju pelikana kudravog (*Pelecanus crispus* Bruch 1832) na Skadarskom jezeru i problem njegove Zastite. *Glas. Republ. Zavoda Zast. prirode. Prirodnajackog muzeja* **8**: 5-13. With English summary.
Vleck, C.M. & Kenagy, G.J. (1980). Embryonic metabolism of the Fork-tailed Storm Petrel: physiological patterns during prolonged and interrupted incubation. *Physiol. Zool.* **53**: 32-42.
Vleck, D., Vleck, C.M. & Hoyt, D.F. (1985). Physiological correlates of synchronous hatching in Rhea eggs (*Rhea americana*). Pp. 864-872 in: *Proc. XVIII Int. Orn. Congr.*
Vlug, J.J. (1976). Zomerconcentraties van de Fuut (*Podiceps cristatus*). *Natura* **73**: 121-132.
Vlug, J.J. (1979). Reproduktie van de Fuut (*Podiceps cristatus*). *Watervogels* **4**: 22-35.
Vlug, J.J. (1980). Broedkolonies van de Fuut (*Podiceps cristatus*). *Watervogels* **5**: 8-17.
Vlug, J.J. (1983). *De Fuut (*Podiceps cristatus*)*. Wet. Med. **160**. Koninklijke Nederlandse Natuurhistorische Vereniging, Hoogwoud.
Vlug, J.J. (1985). Nichtbrüter bei Rothalstaucher (*Podiceps grisegena*) und Haubentaucher (*P. cristatus*). *Corax* **10(4)**: 474-480.
Vlug, J.J. (1986). Der Brutbestand des Rothalstauchers (*Podiceps grisegena*) in Schleswig-Holstein und Hamburg 1969-1984 -mit ergän zenden Bemerkungen zur früheren Situation. *Corax* **12(1)**: 1-33.
Vlug, J.J. & Fjeldså, J. (1990). *Working Bibliography of Grebes of the World with Summaries of Current Taxonomy and of Distributional status*. Zoological Museum, University of Copenhagen.
Vo Quy (1975). Muc Luc. *Chim Vietnam* **1**: 631-649.
Vo Quy (1985). Rare species and protection measures proposed for Vietnam. Pp. 98-102 in: *Proc. 25th Meeting CNPPA, Corbett, India*. IUCN, Gland, Switzerland.
Vo Quy (1990). On the wings of peace. *Natl. Hist.* **Nov/Dec 1990**: 40-41.
Voeks, R. & English, S. (1981). White-faced Ibis (*Plegadis chihi*) populations and distribution in the western United States: 1979-1980. *US Fish and Wildl. Serv. Report*. Portland, OR.
Voet, H. & Maes, P. (1981). Een Broedgeval van Roodhalsfuut, *Podiceps grisegena*, ten noordoosten van Antwerpen. *Gerfaut* **71**: 83-100.
Vogt, W. (1942). Aves guaneras. *Bol. Comp. Admora. Guano* **18**: 1-132.
Voisin, C. (1970). Observations sur le comportement du Heron Bihoreau "*Nycticorax n. nycticorax*" en periode de reproduction. *L'Oiseau et la R.F.O.* **40**: 307-339.
Voisin, C. (1980). Etude du comportement du Héron crabier (*Ardeola ralloides*) en période de reproduction. *L'Oiseau et la R.F.O.* **50(2)**: 149-160.
Voisin, C. (1983). Les Ardéidés du delta du fleuve Sénégal. *L'Oiseau et la R.F.O.* **53(4)**: 335-369.
Voisin, C. (1985). Migration et stabilité des populations chez l'Aigrette garzette *Egretta garzetta*. *L'Oiseau et la R.F.O.* **55(4)**: 291-311.
Voisin, C. (1991). *The Herons of Europe*. Poyser, London.
Voisin, J.F. (1968). Les pétrels géants (*Maconectes halli* et *Macronectes giganteus*) de l'ile de la Possession. *L'Oiseau et la R.F.O.* **38**: 95-122.
Voisin, J.F. (1969). L'Albatros Hurleur *Diomedea exulans* à l'ile de la Possession. *L'Oiseau et la R.F.O.* **39(No. Spéc.)** : 82-106.
Voisin, J.F. (1970). On the specific status of the Kerguelen Shag and its affinities. *Notornis* **17**: 286-290.
Voisin, J.F. (1973). Notes on the blue-eyed shags (genus *Leucocarbo* Bonaparte). *Notornis* **20**: 262-271.
Voisin, J.F. (1976). Observations sur les pétrels géants de l'Ile aux Cochons (Archipel Crozet). *Alauda* **44**: 411-429.
Voisin, J.F. (1978). Observations sur le comportement des pétrels géants de l'Archipel Crozet. *Alauda* **46**: 209-234.
Voisin, J.F. (1979). Observations ornithologiques aux iles Tristan da Cunha et Gough. *Alauda* **47**: 73-82.
Voisin, J.F. (1981). A pursuit plunging Wandering Albatross. *Cormorant* **9**: 136.
Voisin, J.F. (1982). Observations on the Falkland Islands Giant Petrels *Macronectes giganteus solanderi*. *Gerfaut* **72**: 367-380.
Voisin, J.F. (1988). Breeding biology of the Northern Giant Petrel *Macronectes halli* and the Southern Giant Petrel *M. giganteus* at île de la Possession, îles Crozet, 1966-1980. *Cormorant* **16**: 65-97.
Voisin, J.F. (1990). Movements of giant petrels *Macronectes* spp. banded as chicks at îles Crozet and Kerguelen. *Marine Orn.* **18**: 27-36.
Voisin, J.F. & Bester, M.N. (1981). The specific status of giant petrels at Gough Island. Pp. 215-222 in Cooper, J., ed., *Proceedings of the Symposium on Birds of the Sea and Shore*. African Seabird Group, Cape Town.
Voitkevitch, A.A. (1966). *The Feathers and Plumage of Birds*. Sidgwick and Jackson, London.
Volkman, N.J. & Trivelpiece, S.G. (1980). Growth in pygoscelid penguin chicks. *J. Zoology. London* **191**: 521-530.
Volkman, N.J. & Trivelpiece, W.Z. (1981). Nest-site selection among Adelie, Chinstrap and Gentoo Penguins in mixed species rookeries. *Wilson Bull.* **93(2)**: 243-248.
Volkman, N.J., Presler, P. & Trivelpiece, W.Z. (1980). Diets of pygoscelid penguins at King George Island, Antarctica. *Condor* **82**: 373-378.
Volrath, P.G. (1987). European Black Storks. *East Afr. Nat. Hist. Soc. Bull.* **17(2)**: 20.
Vondracek, J. (1983). Zur Wiedereinburgerung des Schwarzstorches in der CSSR. [The recolonization of Czechoslovakia by Black Stork, *C. nigra*, since 1945]. *Falke* **30**: 237-239.
Voous, K.H. (1949). The morphological, anatomical, and distributional relationship of the Arctic and Antarctic Fulmars. *Ardea* **37**: 113-122.
Voous, K.H. (1963). Notes on Seabirds. (2) Royal Penguin (*Eudyptes schlegeli*) on Marion Island. *Ardea* **51**: 251.
Voous, K.H. (1970). Moulting Great Shearwater in Bay of Biscay. *Ardea* **58**: 265-266.
Voous, K.H. (1973). List of recent Holarctic bird species. Nonpasserines. *Ibis* **115**: 612-638.
Voous, K.H. (1983). *Birds of the Netherlands Antilles*. De Walburg Pers, Zutphen.

Voous, K.H. (1986). Striated or Green Herons in the South Caribbean Islands?. *Ann. Naturhist. Mus. Wien* **88/89(B)**: 101-106.
Voous, K.H. & Payne, H.A.W. (1965). The grebes of Madagascar. *Ardea* **53**: 9-31.
Voous, K.H. & Wattel, J. (1963). Distribution and migration of the Greater Shearwater. *Ardea* **51**: 143-157.
de Vries, T. (1981). Natural history of the great frigatebird (*Fregata minor*) on Isla Genovesa. *Ann. Rep. Charles Darwin Res. Station* **1980**: 146.
de Vries, T. (1984). Why are frigatebirds colonial? *Noticias Galápagos* **40**: 19-22.
Vuilleumier, F. (1975). Zoogeography. Pp. 421-496 in: Farner, D.S. & King, J.R. *Avian Biology*. Vol. 5. Academic Press, London & New York.
Waas, J.R. (1988a). Agonistic and sexual communication in the Little Blue Penguin, *Eudyptula minor*. PhD thesis, University of Canterbury, Christchurch, New Zealand.
Waas, J.R. (1988b). Acoustic displays facilitate courtship in Little Blue Penguins, *Eudyptula minor*. *Anim. Behav.* **36**: 366-371.
Waas, J.R. (1990). Intraspecific variation in social repertories: evidence from cave- and burrow-dwelling Little Blue Penguins. *Behaviour* **115(1-2)**: 63-99.
Waas, J.R. (1991a). Do Little Blue Penguins signal their intentions during aggressive interactions with strangers? *Anim. Behav.* **41**: 375-382.
Waas, J.R. (1991b). The risks and benefits on signalling aggressive motivation: a study of cave-dwelling Little Blue-Penguins. *Behav. Ecol. Sociobiol.* **29(2)**: 139-146.
Wackernagel, H. (1959). Ein Bruterfolg beim Chilenischen Flamingo in Zoologischer Garten Basel. *Orn. Beob.* **56**: 33-40.
Wackernagel, H. (1964). Brutbiologische Beobachtungen am Waldrapp, *Geronticus eremita* (L.), im Zoologischen Garten Basel. *Orn. Beob.* **61**: 49-60.
Wahl, T. (1980/81). Identification of Sooty and Short-tailed shearwaters in the North Pacific Ocean. *Sea Swallow* **31**: 42-44.
Wahl, T.R. (1978). Seabirds in the northtwestern Pacific Ocean and south central Bering Sea in June 1975. *Western Birds* **7**: 113-136.
Wahl, T.R. (1985). The distribution of Buller's Shearwater (*Puffinus bulleri*) in the North Pacific Ocean. *Notornis* **32**: 109-117.
Wahl, T.R. (1986). Notes on the feeding behavior of Buller's Shearwater. *Western Birds* **17**: 45-47.
Walcott, F.C. (1925). An expedition to the Laguna Colorada, southern Bolivia. *Geogr. Rev.* **15**: 346-366.
Walker, C.A., Wragg, G.M. & Harrison, C.J.O. (1990). A new shearwater from the Pleistocene of the Canary Islands and its bearing on the evolution of certain Puffinus shearwaters. *Historical Biol.* **3**: 203-224.
Walker, F.J. (1981). Notes on the birds of Dhofar, Oman. *Sandgrouse* **2**: 56-85.
Wallace, A.R. (1876). *The Geographical Distribution of Animals*. Harper and Brothers, New York.
Wallace, G.J. (1963). *An Introduction to Ornithology*. McMillan, London.
Walmsley, J. (1986). The Status of Breeding Storm Petrels on the Mediterranean Coast of France. Pp. 153-160 in MEDMARAVIS & Monbailliu (1986).
Walmsley, J.G. (1975). The development of a breeding population of Grey Herons (*Ardea cinerea*) in the Camargue. *La Terre et la Vie* **29**: 89-99.
Walmsley, J.G. (1984). Wintering Shelduck *Tadorna tadorna* in the West Mediterranean. Pp. 339-354 in: Farina, A. ed. (1984). *Proc. 1st Conf. Birds Wintering in the Med. Region, Aulla*. INBS, Vol. X.
Walmsley, J.G. (1987). Le Tadorne de Belon *Tadorna tadorna* en Mediterranée occidentale. *L'Oiseau et la R.F.O.* **57**: 102-112.
Walravens, M., Fouarge, J.P. & Jacob, J.P. (1990). Le Grèbe huppé (*Podiceps cristatus*) nicheur en Wallonie et Brabant: bilan de la progression en 1987. *Aves* **27(1)**: 1-14.
Walsberg, G.E. (1983). Avian ecological energetics. Pp. 161-220 in: Farner, D.S. King, J.R. & Parkes, K.C. *Avian Biology*. Vol. 7. Academic Press, London & New York.
Walsh, J.F. (1977). Nesting of the Jabiru Stork (*Ephippiorhynchus senegalensis*) in West Africa. *Bull. Brit. Orn. Club* **97(4)**: 136.
Walsh, J.J. (1978). The biological consequences of interaction of the climatic, El Niño, and event scales of variability in the eastern tropical Pacific. *Rapports et Proces-verbaux des Reunions du Conseil International pour l'Exploration de la Mer* **173**: 182-192.
Walsh, J.M. (1990). *Estuarine habitat use and age-specific foraging behaviour of Wood Storks (*Mycteria americana*).* MSc thesis, University of Georgia, Athens, Georgia.
van der Walt, P.T. & Retief, P.F. (1984). Features of habitat selection by larger herbivorous mammals and the Ostrich in the Southern Kalahari conservation areas. *Koedoe* **1984(Suppl.)**: 119-128.
Walter, P. (1981). *A Statistical Study of the Breeding Success of Mute Swan*. MSc thesis, Oxford University.
Walters, M. (1976). Some observations on the eggs of the Great White-bellied Heron, *Ardea insignis*. *J. Bombay Nat. Hist. Soc.* **73**: 213-214.
Walters, M. (1985). Some comments on the distribution of the Ostrich in Asia and North Africa. *J. Bombay Nat. Hist. Soc.* **83(Suppl.)**: 217-218.
Walters, R.C. (1979). Breeding behaviour of the Little Grebe, *Tachybaptus novaehollandiae*. *Tasman. Nat.* **59**: 3-4.
Wang Jian-nan (1986). [Reef Heron *Egretta sacra* discovered in Wenzhou (Zhejiang Province)]. *Chinese J. Zool.* **3**: 41. In Chinese.
Wang Qishan (1987). [A worldwide endangered bird---the Eastern White Stork, *Ciconia ciconia*]. *Chinese Wildl.* (5): 12-14, 21. In Chinese.
Wang Xia (1981). [Observations on the reproductive behavior of the Bar-headed Goose *Anser indicus*]. *Wildlife* **3**: 29-31. In Chinese.
Wang Yongjun & Zhou Wei (1989). [Hunting effects on the number of wintering White Storks *Ciconia ciconia* in Cenhu Lake (Hubei Province)]. *Chinese Wildl.* **(4)**: 16-17. In Chinese.
Wang Zhong-yu (1984). [The wintering habits of the Goosander *Mergus merganser*]. *Chinese Wildlife* **1**: 21-22. In Chinese.
Wang Zi-jiang, Wu Jin-liang *et al.* (1983). The breeding of the Mandarin Duck *Aix galericulata* in Yunnan Province. *Wildlife* **2**: 38-39.
Wanless, S. (1979). *Aspects of the Population Dynamics and Breeding Ecology in the Gannets of Ailsa Craig*. PhD thesis, Aberdeeen.
Wanless, S. (1983). Seasonal variation in the numbers and condition of Gannet dying on Ailsa Craig, Scotland. *Bird Study* **30**: 102-108.
Wanless, S. (1987). *A Survey of the Numbers and Breeding Distribution of the North Atlantic Gannet and and Assessment of the Changes which have occurred since Operation Seafarer 1969/70*. Research & Survey in Nature Conservation Report **4**. NCC, Peterborough, UK.
Wanless, S., Burger, A. E. & Harris, M.P. (1991). Diving depths of Shags *Phalacrocorax aristotelis* breeding on the Isle of May. *Ibis* **133**: 37-42.
Wanless, S., Harris, M.P. & Morris, J.A. (1991). Foraging range and feeding locations of Shags *Phalacrocorax aristotelis* during chick rearing. *Ibis* **133**: 30-36.
Ward, R.A. (1957). A study of the host distribution and some relationships of the mallophaga parasitic of the order Tinamiformes part. 1. *Ann. Ent. Soc. America* **50**: 335-353.
Ward, T.B.S. (1941). Los Flamencos de Mar Chiquita. *Hornero* **8**: 118-120.
Warham, J. (1952). A family of shearwaters. *Country Life* **111**: 1250-1251.
Warham, J. (1955). Observations on the Little Shearwater at the nest. *West Austr. Nat.* **5**: 31-39.
Warham, J. (1956). The breeding of the Great-winged Petrel. *Ibis* **98**: 171-185.
Warham, J. (1957). Additional notes on the Great Winged Petrel. *Ibis* **99**: 511-512.
Warham, J. (1958a). The nesting of the Little Penguin, *Eudyptula minor*. *Ibis* **100**: 605-616.
Warham, J. (1958b). The nesting of the shearwater *Puffinus carneipes*. *Auk* **75**: 1-14.
Warham, J. (1958c). The nesting of the Australian Gannet. *Emu* **58**: 339-369.
Warham, J. (1958d). The nesting of the Pink-eared Duck. *Wildfowl Trust Ann. Rep.* **9**: 118-127.
Warham, J. (1959). The Trinidad Petrel, *Pterodroma arminjoniana*, a new bird for Australia. *Emu* **59**: 153-158.
Warham, J. (1960). Some aspects of breeding behaviour in the Short-tailed Shearwater. *Emu* **60**: 75-87.
Warham, J. (1962). The biology of the Giant Petrel *Macronectes giganteus*. *Auk* **79**: 139-160.
Warham, J. (1963). The Rockhopper Penguin, *Eudyptes chrysocome* at Macquarie Island. *Auk* **80**: 229-256.
Warham, J. (1964). Breeding behaviour in Procellariiformes. Pp. 389-394 in: Carrick, R., Holdgate, M. & Prévost, J. eds. *Biologie Antarctique: Premier Symposium S.C.A.R.*. Hermann, Paris.
Warham, J. (1967). The White-headed Petrel *Pterodroma lessoni* at Macquarie Island. *Emu* **67**: 1-22.
Warham, J. (1968). Biometric studies of birds in the order Procellariiformes. Unpublished MSc thesis, University Durham.
Warham, J. (1971a). Aspects of breeding behaviour in the Royal Penguin, *Eudyptes chrysolophus schlegeli*. *Notornis* **18**: 91-115.
Warham, J. (1971b). Body temperatures of petrels. *Condor* **73**: 214-219.
Warham, J. (1972a). Aspects of the biology of the Erect-crested Penguin, *Eudyptes sclateri*. *Ardea* **60**: 145-184.
Warham, J. (1972b). Breeding seasons and sexual dimorphism in Rockhopper Penguins. *Auk* **89**: 86-105.
Warham, J. (1974a). The Fiordland Crested Penguin, *Eudyptes pachyrhynchus*. *Ibis* **116**: 1-27.
Warham, J. (1974b). The breeding biology and behaviour of the Snares Crested Penguin. *J. Roy. Soc., N.Z.* **4**: 63-108.
Warham, J. (1975). Fulmar behaviour. *Scott. Birds* **8**: 319-321.
Warham, J. (1976). Aerial displays by large petrels. *Notornis* **23**: 255-257.
Warham, J. (1977a). Wing loadings, wing shapes and flight capabilities of Procellariiformes. *N.Z. J. Zool.* **4**: 73-83.
Warham, J. (1977b). The incidence, functions and ecological significance of petrel stomach oils. *Proc. N.Z. Ecol. Soc.* **24**: 84-93.
Warham, J. (1979). The voice of the Soft-plumaged Petrel. *Notornis* **26**: 357-360.
Warham, J. (1981). Does Hutton's Shearwater circumnavigate Australia? *Emu* **81**(1): 44.
Warham, J. (1982). A distant recovery of a Buller's Mollymawk. *Notornis* **29**: 213-214.
Warham, J. (1983). The composition of petrel eggs. *Condor* **85**: 194-199.
Warham, J. (1985a). King Penguin. Page 41 in: Robertson (1985).
Warham, J. (1985b). Emperor Penguin. Page 40 in: Robertson (1985).
Warham, J. (1985c). Gentoo Penguin. Page 44 in: Robertson (1985).
Warham, J. (1985d). Fiorland Crested Penguin. Page. 50 in: Robertson (1985).
Warham, J. (1985e). Erect-crested Penguin. Page 52 in: Robertson (1985).
Warham, J. (1985f). Snares Crested Penguin. Page 51 in: Robertson (1985).
Warham, J. (1985g). Rockhopper Penguin. Page 49 in: Robertson (1985).
Warham, J. (1985h). Royal Penguin. Page 48 in: Robertson (1985).
Warham, J. (1988a). Responses of *Pterodroma* petrels to man-made sounds. *Emu* **88**: 109-111.
Warham, J. (1988b). Vocalisations of *Procellaria* petrels. *Notornis* **35**: 169-183.
Warham, J. (1990). *The Petrels: Their Ecology and Breeding Systems*.Academic Press, London.
Warham, J. & Bell, B.D. (1979). The birds of the Antipodes Island, New Zealand. *Notornis* **26**: 121-169.
Warham, J. & Bennington, S.L. (1983). A census of Buller's Albatross at the Snares Island, New Zealand. *Emu* **83**: 112-114.
Warham, J. & Fitzsimons, C.H. (1987). The vocalisations of Buller's Mollymawk, with some comparative data on other albatrosses. *N.Z. J. Zool.* **14**: 65-79.
Warham, J. & Richdale, L.E. (1973). Survival, pair bond retention and nest-site tenacity in Buller's Mollymawk. *Ibis* **115**: 257-263.
Warham, J. & Wilson, G.J. (1982). The size of the Sooty Shearwater population at the Snares Islands, New Zealand. *Notornis* **29**: 23-30.
Warham, J., Bourne, W.R.P. & Elliott, H.F.I. (1974). Albatross identification in the North Atlantic. *Am. Birds* **28**: 585-603.
Warham, J., Keeley, B.R. & Wilson, G.J. (1977). Breeding of the Mottled Petrel. *Auk* **94**: 1-17.
Warham, J., Watts, R. & Dainty, R.J. (1976). The composition, energy content and function of the stomach oils of petrels. *J. Exp. Mar. Biol. Ecol.* **23**: 1-13.
Warham, J., Wilson, G.J. & Keeley, B.R. (1982). The annual cycle of the Sooty Shearwater at the Snares Islands, New Zealand. *Notornis* **29**: 269-292.
Warheit, K.I. (1990). *The Phylogeny of the Sulidae (Aves: Pelecaniformes) and the Morphometry of Flight-related Structures in Seabirds: a Study of Adaptation*. PhD dissertation, University California (Berkeley).
Warner, R.E. (1963). Recent history and ecology of Laysan Duck. *Condor* **63**: 3-23.
Wasilewski, A. (1986). Ecological aspects of the breeding cycle in the Wilson's Storm Petrel at King George Island (South Shetland Islands, Antarctica). *Polish Polar Res.* **7**: 173-216.
Watanuki, Y. (1985). Food of breeding Leach's Storm Petrels. *Auk* **102**: 884-886
Watanuki, Y. (1986). Moonlight avoidance behavior in Leach's Storm-Petrels as a defense against Slaty-backed Gulls. *Auk* **103**: 14-22.
Waterman, M. (1968). The Black-faced Cormorant breeding at Outer Harbour. *S. Austr. Orn.* **25**: 23.
Waterman, M., Close, D. & Condon, D. (1971). Straw-necked Ibis (*Threskiornis spinicollis*) in South Australia: breeding colonies and movements. *S. Austr. Orn.* **26**: 7-11.
Watkins, B.P. (1987). Population sizes of King, Rockhopper and Macaroni Penguins and Wandering Albatrosses at the Prince Edward Islands and Gough Island, 1951-1986. *S. Afr. J. Antarct. Res.* **17(2)**: 155-162.
Watling, D. (1986a). Rediscovery of a petrel and new faunal records on Gau Island. *Oryx* **20**(1): 31-34.
Watling, D. (1986b). Notes on the Collared Petrel *Pterodroma (leucoptera) brevipes*. *Bull. Brit. Orn. Club* **106(2)**: 63-70.
Watling, D. (1987). The Fiji Petrel: Stranger in Paradise. *Animal Kingdom* **90(1)**: 31-34.
Watling, D. & Lewanavanua, R.F. (1985). A note to record the continuing survival of the Fiji (MacGillivray's) Petrel. *Ibis* **127**: 230-233.
Watmough, B.R. (1978). Observations on nocturnal feeding by Night Herons *Nycticorax nycticorax*. *Ibis* **120**: 356-358.
Watson, G.E. (1968). Synchronous wing and tail molt in diving petrels. *Condor* **70**: 182-183.
Watson, G.E. (1971a). *Eudyptes sclareri* Buller, 1888 and *Eudyptes robustus* Oliver, 1953 (Aves Spheniscidae): proposed preservation under the plenary powers. Z.N. (S.) 1893. *Bull. Zool. Nomencl.* **28**: 92-93.
Watson, G.E. (1971b). Molting Greater Shearwaters off Tierra del Fuego. *Auk* **88**(2): 440-442.
Watson, G.E. (1975). *Birds of the Antarctic and Sub-Antarctic*. American Geophysical Union, Washington, D.C.
Watson, G.E., Lee, D.S. & Backus, E.S. (1986). Status and subspecific identity of White-faced Storm-petrels in the Western North Atlantic Ocean. *Am. Birds* **40**: 401-407.
Watson, G.E., Olson, S.L. & Miller, J.R. (1991). A new subspecies of the Double-crested Cormorant, *Phalacrocorax auritus*, from San Salvador, Bahama Islands. *Proc. Biol. Soc. Wash.* **104(2)**: 356-369.
Watson, J. (1980). Distribution and nesting of the Yellow Bittern in Seychelles. *Ostrich* **51(2)**: 120-122.
Watson, P.S. (1981). Seabird observations from commercial trawlers in the Irish Sea. *British Birds* **74**: 82-90.
Watt, J.C. (1971). The North Island kiwi: a predator of pasture insects. *New Zealand Entomologist* **5**: 25-27.
Watts, B.D. (1988). Foraging implications of food usage patterns in Yellow-crowned Night-Herons. *The Condor* **90**: 860-865.
Watts, B.D. (1989). Nest-site characteristics of Yellow-Crowned Night-Herons in Virginia. *The Condor* **91**: 979-983.
Wayne, A.T. (1922). Discovery of the breeding grounds of the White Ibis in South Carolina. *Bull. Charleston Mus.* **17**: 17-30.
Webbs, C.S. (1936). Collecting waterfowl in Madagascar. *Avicult. Mag.* **1(5)**: 36-39.
Webbs, C.S. (1953). *A Wanderer in the Wind*. Hutchinson, London.
Weeks, S.E. (1973). *Zoologica. New York* **58**: 13-40. (Behaviour).
Weickert, P. (1960). Reproducción de la Espátula en Doñana en 1960. *Ardeola* **6**: 379.
Weigmann, C. & Lampecht, J. (1991). Intraspecific nest parasitism in Bar-headed Geese, *Anser indicus*. *Anim. Behav.* **41 (4)**: 677-688.
Weimerskirch, H. (1982). La strategie de reproduction de l'Albatross Fuligineux à dos Sombre. *Comm. Natl. Français Rech. Antarct.* **51**: 437-447.
Weimerskirch, H. (1990a). Weight loss of Antarctic Fulmars during incubation and chick brooding. *Ibis* **132**: 68-77.
Weimerskirch, H. (1990b). Weight loss in incubating and chick brooding Antarctic Fulmar *Fulmarus glacialoides*. *Ibis* **132**: 68-77.
Weimerskirch, H. (1990c). The Influence of age and experience on breeding performances of the Antarctic Fulmar, *Fulmarus glacialoides*. *J. Anim. Ecol.* **59**: 867-875.
Weimerskirch, H. & Jouventin, P. (1987). Population dynamics of the Wandering Albatros of the Crozet Islands: causes and consequences of the population decline. *Oikos* **49**: 315-322.
Weimerskirch, H., Bartle, J.A., Jouventin, P. & Stahl, J.C. (1988). Foraging ranges and partitioning of feeding zones in three species of southern albatrosses. *Condor* **90**: 214-219.
Weimerskirch, H., Clobert, J. & Jouventin, P. (1987). Survival in five southern albatrosses and its relationship to their life history. *J. Anim. Ecol.* **56**: 1043-1055.
Weimerskirch, H., Jouventin, P., Mougin, J.L., Stahl, J.C. & van Beveren, M. (1985). Banding recoveries and the dispersal of seabirds breeding in French austral and Antarctic Territories. *Emu* **85**: 22-33.
Weimerskirch, H., Jouventin, P. & Stahl, J.C. (1986). Comparative ecology of six albatross species breeding on the Crozet Islands. *Ibis* **128**: 195-213.
Weimerskirch, H., Lequette, B. & Jouventin, P. (1989). Development and maturation of plumage in the Wandering Albatross *Diomedea exulans*. *J. Zoology. London* **219**: 411-421.
Weimerskirch, H., Stahl, J.C. & Jouventin, P. (1992). The breeding biology and population dynamics of King Penguins *Aptenodytes patagonica* on the Crozet Islands. *Ibis* **134(2)**: 107-117.
Weimerskirch, H., Zottier, R. & Jouventin, P. (1989): The avifauna of the Kerguelen Islands. *Emu* **89(1)**: 15-29.
Weinman, A.N. (1940). Breeding of the Indian Painted Stork under semi-domestication. *Ceylon J. Sci. Sect. B Zool.* **22**: 141-144.
Wellenstein, C. & Wiegmann, D.D. (1986). Prey handling by anhingas. *Florida Field Nature* **14(3)**: 74-75.
Weller, M.W. (1957). Growth, weights, and plumages of the Redhead (*Aythya americana*). *Wilson Bull.* **69**: 5-38.

Weller, M.W. (1959). Parasitic egg laying in the Redhead (*Aythya americana*) and other North American Anatidae. *Ecol. Monogr.* **29**: 333-365.
Weller, M.W. (1961). Breeding biology of the Least Bittern. *Wilson Bull.* **73**: 11-35.
Weller, M.W. (1964). Distribution and migration of the Redhead. *J. Wild. Manage.* **28(1)**: 64-103.
Weller, M.W. (1967a). Notes on some marsh birds of Cape San Antonio, Argentina. *Ibis* **109**: 391-411.
Weller, M.W. (1967b). Notes on plumages and weights of the Black-headed Duck, *Heteronetta atricapilla. Condor* **69 (2)**: 133-145.
Weller, M.W. (1968a). Plumages and wings spurs of Torrent Ducks *Merganetta armata. Wildfowl* **19**: 33-40.
Weller, M.W. (1968b). The breeding biology of the parasitic Black-headed Duck. *Living Bird* **7**: 169-270.
Weller, M.W. (1972). Ecological studies of Falkland Islands' waterfowl. *Wildfowl* **23**: 25-44.
Weller, M.W. (1974). Habitat selection and feeding patterns of Brown Teal (*Anas castanea chlorotis*) on Great Barrier Island. *Notornis* **21**: 25-35.
Weller, M.W. (1975a). Migratory waterfowl: a hemispheric perspective. *Publ. Biol. Inst. Invest. Cient. U.A.N.L.* **1(7)**: 89-130.
Weller, M.W. (1975b). Ecological Studies of the Auckland Islands Flightless Teal. *Auk* **92**: 280-297.
Weller, M.W. (1975c). Ecology and Behavior of the South Georgia Pintail *Anas g. georgica. Ibis* **117**: 217-231.
Weller, M.W. (1975d). Habitat selection by waterfowl of Argentine Isla Grande. *Wilson Bull.* **87**: 83-90.
Weller, M.W. (1976). Ecology and Behavior of Steamer Ducks. *Wildfowl* **27**: 45-53.
Weller, M.W. (1980). *The Island Waterfowl.* The Iowa State University Press, Iowa.
Weller, M.W. (1985). Screamer. Page 525 in: Campbell & Lack (1985).
Weller, M.W. ed. (1988). *Waterfowl in Winter.* University of Minnesota Press, Minneapolis.
Weller, M.W. & Howard, R.L. (1972). Breeding of Speckled Teal *Anas flavirostris* on South Georgia. *Bull. Brit. Antarct. Surv.* **30**: 65-68.
Weller, M.W., Trauger, D.L. & Krapu, G.L. (1969). Breeding birds of the West Mirage Islands, Great Slave Lake, N.W.T. *Can. Field-Nat.* **83**: 344-360.
Wells, D.R. (1985). The forest avifauna of western Malaysia and its conservation. Pp. 213-232 in: Diamond & Lovejoy (1985).
Welsh, D. (1988). *The Relationship of Nesting Density to Behavior and Reproductive Success of Black Brant.* MSc thesis, University of Idaho.
Welty, J.C. & Baptista, L. (1988). *The Life of Birds.* 4th edition. T & AD Poyser, London.
Wendt, H. (1956). *Out of Noah's Ark. The Story of Man's Discovery of the Animal Kingdom.* Weidenfeld and Nicolson, London.
Wennrich, G. (1981). Paarungszeremoniell beim Hagedasch (*Hagedashia hagedash*). *Die Voliere* **4**: 27-29.
Wennrich, G. (1982a). Haltung und Welterstzucht des Goldhalskasuars (*Casuarius unappendiculatus auranticus*). *Gefiederte Welt* **106(4)**: 116-118.
Wennrich, G. (1982b). Haltung und Welterstzucht des Goldhalskasuars (*Casuarius unappendiculatus auranticus*). *Gefiederte Welt* **106(5)**: 154-156
Wennrich, G. (1982c). Haltung und Welterstzucht des Goldhalskasuars (*Casuarius unappendiculatus auranticus*). *Gefiederte Welt* **106(6)**: 186-188.
Wennrich, G. (1982d). Keeping Asian White Storks at Vogelpark Walsrode, Germany. *Avicult. Mag.* **88(3)**: 127-129.
Wennrich, G. (1982e). Sunbathing behaviour in five species of ibises (Threskiornithidae) at the Walsrode Bird Park, Germany. *Avic. Mag.* **88**: 96-100.
Wennrich, G. (1983). Haltung und Zucht der Taos (*Tinamus tao*). *Gefiederte Welt* **106(8)**: 243-245.
Went, R. (1975). Rare birds: the North American Ruddy Duck. *Bird Life* **1975**: 18-19.
Wenzel, B.M. (1968). Olfactory prowess in the kiwi. *Nature* **220**: 1133-1134.
Wenzel, B.M. (1973). Chemoreception. Pp. 389-415 in: Farner, D.S. & King, J.R. (1983). *Avian Biology*. Vol. 3. Academic Press, London & New York.
Werding, G. (1972). Vom Vogelleben in Madagaskar. *Gefiederte Welt* **96**: 194-196, 211-213.
Werschkul, D.F. (1982). Parental investment: influence of nest guarding by male little blue herons *Florida caerulea. Ibis* **124(3)**: 343-347.
Weseloh, D.V. & Struger, J. (1985). Massive mortality of juvenile Double-crested Cormorants on Little Galloo Island, July 1984. *Kingbird* **35**: 98-104.
Weseloh, D.V., Brechtel, K.S. & Burns, R.D. (1977). Recent population changes in Double-crested Cormorants and California and Ring-billed Gulls in Alberta, Canada, with a note on White Pelicans. *Proc. 1977 Conf. Colonial Waterbird Group* **1**: 10-18.
Weseloh, D.V., Teeple, S.M. & Gilbertson, M. (1983). Double-crested Cormorants of the Great Lakes: egg-laying parameters, reproductive failure, and contaminant residue in eggs, Lake Huron 1972-1973. *Can. J. Zool.* **61**: 427-436.
West, B., Cabot, D. & Greer-Walker, M. (1975). The food of the Cormorant (*Phalacrocorax carbo*) at some breeding colonies in Ireland. *Proc. Royal Ir. Acad. (Ser. B)* **75**: 285-305.
West, J. & Imber, M.J. (1985). Some foods of Hutton's Shearwater (*Puffinus huttoni*). *Notornis* **32**: 333-336.
West, J. & Imber, M.J. (1989). Surveys of South Georgian Diving Petrels (*Pelecanoides georgicus*) on Codfish Island. *Notornis* **36**: 157-158.
West, J.A. & Imber, M.J. (1986). Some foods of Buller's Mollymawk. *New Zealand J. Zool.* **13**: 169-174
Westerskov, K. (1960). Field identification and sex determination of the Royal Albatross. *Notornis* **9**: 1-6.
Westerskov, K. (1963). Ecological factors affecting distribution of a nesting Royal Albatross population. *Proc. XIII Int. Orn. Congr.*: 795-811.
Westerskov, K.E. (1974). The Grebes. Pp. 489-493 in: *New Zealand's Nature Heritage*. Hamlyn.
Westerskov, K.E. (1977). History of discovery of the Crested Grebe, *Podiceps cristatus*, in New Zealand. *Notornis* **24**: 167-177.
van der Westhuizen, P.M. (1967). Black Kites and Woolly-necked Storks in South West Africa. *Ostrich* **30**: 203.
Westneat, D.F., Sherman, P.W. & Morton, M.L. (1990). The ecology and evolution of extra-pair copulation in birds. *Current Ornithology* **7**.
Westphal, A. & Rowan, M.K. (1971). Some observations on the effects of oil pollution on the Jackass Penguin. *Ostrich* **8((Suppl.)**: 521-526.
Wetmore, A. (1926). *Observations on the Birds of Argentina, Paraguay, Uruguay and Chile.* US National Museum Bulletin **133**.
Wetmore, A. (1941). Notes on birds of the Guatemalan highlands. *Proc. US Nat. Mus.* **89(3105)**: 523-581.
Wetmore, A. (1945). A review of the forms of the Brown Pelican. *Auk* **62**: 577-586.
Wetmore, A. (1949). The Pied-billed Grebe in Ancient Deposits in Mexico. *Condor* **51**: 150.
Wetmore, A. (1960). *A Classification for the Birds of the World.* Smithsonian miscellaneous collections **139(11)**. Smithsonian Institution, Washington.
Wetmore, A. (1965). *The Birds of the Republic of Panamá.* Part. 1. Tinamidae (Tinamous) to Rynchopidae (Skimmers). Smithsonian miscellaneous collections **150**. Smithsonian Institution, Washington.
Wetmore, A. & Galindo, P. (1972). Additions to the birds recorded in Panama. *Proc. Biol. Soc. Washington* **85**: 309-312.
Wetmore, A. & Parkes, K.C. (1954). Notes on the generic affiliations of the Great Grebe of South America. *J. Wash. Acad. Sci.* **44**: 126-127.
van Wetten, J.C.J. (1984). Lepelaar *Platalea leucorodia* met rossige kleur. *Limosa* **57**: 28.
van Wetten, J.C.J. (1985). A census of the Herons, Ibises, Spoonbills and Storks on the south and south-east coast of Sri lanka in December 1984 and January 1985. Unpublished report. Instituut voor Taxonomische Zoologie, Amsterdam.
van Wetten, J.C.J. (1986). The status and distribution of the spoonbill *Platalea leucorodia.* Unpublished Report. Instituut voor Taxonomische Zoologie, Amsterdam.
van Wetten, J.C.J. & Wintermans, G.J.M. (1986). The food ecology of the Spoonbill *Platalea leucorodia.* Unpublished Report. Instituut voor Taxonomische Zoologie, Amsterdam.
Wheeler, J.R. (1953). Notes on the Blue-billed Ducks at Lake Wendouree, Ballarat. *Emu* **53**: 280-282.
Wheelwright, N.T. (1987). Mother Carey's Chickens. *Living Bird Quarterly.* **6**(1): 26-31.
Wheelwright, N.T. & Boersma, P.D. (1979). Egg chilling and the thermal environment of the Fork-tailed Storm Petrel nest. *Physiol. Zool.* **52**: 231-239.
Whistler, H. (1918). The White-necked Stork in the Punjab. *J. Bombay Nat. Hist. Soc.* **25**: 746-747.
White, C.M.N. (1974). Three water birds of Wallacea. *Bull. Brit. Orn. Club* **94**: 9-11.
White, C.M.N. (1975). The problem of the Cassowary in Ceram. *Bull. Brit. Orn. Club* **95**: 165-170.
White, C.M.N. (1976). The problem of the Cassowary in New Britain. *Bull. Brit. Orn. Club* **96**: 66-68.
White, C.M.N. & Bruce, M.D. (1986). *The Birds of Wallacea.* B.O.U. Check-list **7**. British Ornithologists' Union, London.
White, D.H., Fleming, W.J. & Ensor, K.L. (1988). Pesticide contamination and hatching success of waterbirds in Mississippi. *J. Wildl. Manage.* **52(4)**: 724-729.
White, D.H., Mitchell, C.A. & Cromartie, E. (1982). Nesting ecology of Roseate Spoonbills at Nueces Bay, Texas. *Auk* **99**: 275-284.
White, G.C. & Ratti, J.T. (1977). Estimation and testing of parameters in Richards growth model for Western Grebes. *Growth* **41**: 315-323.
White, H.C. (1957). Food and natural history of Mergansers on Salmon waters in the Maritime Provinces of Canada. *Fisheries Research Board of Canada Bulletin* **116**: 1-63.
White, H.L. (1913). Notes on the Cassowary (Casuarius australis, Wall). *Emu* **12**: 172-178.
White, S.J. (1971). Selective responsiveness by the Gannet (*Sula bassana*) to played-back calls. *Anim. Behav.* **19**: 125-131.
White, S.J. & White, R.E.C. (1970). Individual voice production in gannets. *Behaviour* **37**: 40-54.
Whitehead, M. & Masson, G. (1984). Notes on the Double-Wattled Cassowary (*Casuarius casuarius*) at Twycross Zoo, U.K. and elsewhere. Pp. 51-56 in: *Proc. IX Symp. Assoc. Br. Wild. Anim. Keepers.*
Whitehead, M.D. (1989). Maximum diving depths of the Adelie Penguin, *Pygoscelis Adeliae*, during the chick rearing period, in Prydz Bay, Antarctica. *Polar Biol.* **9(5)**: 329-332.
Whitehead, M.D., Johnstone, G.W. & Burton, H.R. (1990). Annual fluctuations in productivity and breeding success of Adelie Penguins and Fulmarine Petrels in Prydz Bay, East Antarctica. Pp. 214-223 in Kerry, K.R. & Hempel, G., eds. *Antarctic Ecosystems, Ecological Change and Conservation.* Springer-Verlag, Heidelberg.
Whitehead, P.J. & Tschirner, K. (1990). Eggs and hatchlings of the Magpie Goose *Anseranas semiñpalmata. Emu* **90**: 154-160.
Whitehead, P.J. & Tschirner, K. (1991). Patterns of egg laying and variation in egg size in the Magpie Goose *Anseranas semipalmata*: evidence for intra-specific nest parasitism. *Emu* **91 (1)**: 26-31.
Whitehead, P.J., Freeland, W.J. & Tschirner, K. (1990). Early growth of Magpie Geese, *Anseranas semipalmata*: sex differences and effects of egg size. *Austr. J. Zool.* **38**: 249-262.
Whitelaw, D. (1968). Notes on the breeding biology of the African Spoonbill *Platalea alba. Ostrich* **39**: 236-241.
Whiteside, A.J. (1989). The behaviour of Bitterns and their use of habitat. *Notornis* **36**: 89-95.
Whitfield, A.K. & Blaber, S.J.M. (1978). Feeding ecology of piscivorous birds at Lake Sta Lucia, part 2: Wading Birds. *Ostrich* **50**: 1-9.
Whitfield, A.K. & Blaber, S.J.M. (1979). Feeding ecology of piscivorous birds at Lake St. Lucia, Part 3: Swimming birds. *Ostrich* **50**: 10-20.
Whitlock, F.L. (1921). Notes on Dirk Hartog Island and Peron Peninsula, Shark Bay, Western Australia. *Emu* **20**: 168-186.
Whittow, G.C., Araki, C.T. & Pepper, R.L. (1978). Body temperature of the great frigatebird *Fregata minor. Ibis* **20**: 358-360.
Whittow, G.C., Pettir, T.N., Ackerman, R.A. & Paganelli, C.V. (1987). Temperature regulation in a burrow-nesting tropical seabird, the Wedge-tailed Shearwater (*Puffinus pacificus*). *Comp. Physiol.* **157B**: 607-614.
Wiegant, W. & van Helvoort, B. (1987). First sighting of *Tachybaptus novaehollandiae* on Bali. *Kukila* **3**: 50-51.
Wieloch, M. (1984). Numbers and distribution of Mute Swan (*Cygnus olor*) in Poland against the situation of this species in Europe. *Acta Orn.* **20**: 187-240.
Wienmeyer, S.N. (1967). *Bufflehead Food Habits, Parasites, and Biology in Northern California.* MSc thesis, Humboldt State College, Arcata, California.
Wiens, J.A. (1989a). Avian community ecology: an iconnoclastic view. Pp. 355-403 in: Brush, A.H. & Clark, G.A. (1983). *Perspectives in Ornithology*. Cambridge Unversity Press, Cambridge, England.
Wiens, J.A. (1989b). *The Ecology of Bird Communities*. 2 Vols. Cambridge University Press, Cambridge, England.
van Wieringen, M. & Brouwer, K. (1990). Morphology and ecology of the Scarlet Ibis (*Eudocimus ruber*) and White Ibis (*E. albus*): a comparative review. Pp. 7-15 in: Frederick, Morales *et al.* (1990).
van Wieringen, M. Brouwer, K. & Spaans, A. (1990). Het kwetsbare leven van de rode ibis. *Panda* **26**: 14-16.
Wiersum, K.F. (1971). *De Rode Ibis. Zijn verspreiding en bescherming in Suriname (Oktober 1970-Januari 1971).* Postgraduate essay. Landbouwhogeschool Wageningen, Netherlands.
Wiese, J.H. (1978). Heron Nest-Site Selection and its Ecological Effects. Pp. 27-34 in: Sprunt *et al.* (1978).
Wiggins, D.A. (1991). Foraging Success and Aggression in Solitary and Group-feeding Great Egrets (*Casmerodius albus*). *Colonial Waterbirds* **14(2)**: 176-179.
Wikramanayake, E.B. (1969). Some rare and vanishing birds of Ceylon. *Loris* **11**: 374-376.
Wilbur, H.M. (1969). The breeding biology of Leach's Petrel. *Auk* **86**: 433-442.
Wildash, P. (1968). *Birds of South Vietnam.* Charles E. Tuttle Co. Inc., Tokyo.
Wiley, J.W. & Wiley, B.N. (1979). Status of the American Flamingo in the Dominican Republic and Eastern Haiti. *Auk* **96**: 615-619.
Wilkins, W.J. & Wilkins, C. (1990). An Abdim's Stork with a broken leg. *Mirafra* **7**: 8-9.
Wilkinson, H.E. (1969). Description of an upper Miocene albatross from Beaumaris, Victoria, Australia, and a review of fossil Diomedeidae. *Mem. Natl. Mus. Victoria* **29**: 41-51.
Wilkinson, R. (1989). Breeding and management of flamingos at Chester Zoo. *Avicult. Mag.* **95(2)**: 51-56.
Willgohs, J.F. (1957). Litt om horndykkeren *Podiceps auritus* i Norge, og et par nye funn. *Naturen* **80**: 24-29.
Williams, A.J. (1977). Nest-scraping behaviour in the Macaroni Penguin. *Cormorant* **3**: 16.
Williams, A.J. (1980a). The breeding biology of *Eudyptes* penguins with particular references to egg-size dimorphism. PhD thesis, University Cape Town.
Williams, A.J. (1980b). Offspring reduction in Macaroni and Rockhopper Penguins. *Auk* **97**: 754-759.
Williams, A.J. (1980c). Rockhopper Penguins *Eudyptes chrysocome* at Gough Island. *Bull. Brit. Orn. Club* **100(4)**: 208-212.
Williams, A.J. (1980d). Penguin proportionate egg weight. *Notornis* **27**: 125-128.
Williams, A.J. (1980e). Aspects of the breeding biology of the Gentoo Penguin, *Pygoscelis papua. Gerfaut* **70**: 283-295.
Williams, A.J. (1980f). Diet and subspeciation in the Gentoo Penguin *Pygoscelis papua. Bull. Brit. Orn. Club* **100**: 173-175.
Williams, A.J. (1981a). The clutch size of Macaroni and Rockhopper Penguins. *Emu* **81**: 87-90.
Williams, A.J. (1981b). Do Rockhopper Penguins *Eudyptes chrysocome* feed their chicks penguin milk? *Cormorant* **9**: 73-75.
Williams, A.J. (1981c). Growth and survival of artificially twinned Rockhopper Penguin twins. *Cormorant* **9**: 8-12.
Williams, A.J. (1981d). The laying interval and incubation period of Rockhopper and Macaroni Penguins. *Ostrich* **52**: 226-229.
Williams, A.J. (1981e). Why do penguins have long laying intervals? *Ibis* **123**: 202-204.
Williams, A.J. (1981f). Factors affecting time of breeding of Gentoo Penguins *Pygoscelis papua* at Marion Island. Pp. 451-459 in: Cooper, J. ed. *Proc. Symp. Birds on Sea and Shore, 1979.* African Seabird Club, Cape Town.
Williams, A.J. (1982). Chick-feeding rates of Macaroni and Rockhopper Penguins at Marion Island. *Ostrich* **53**: 129-134.
Williams, A.J. (1984a). The Status and Conservation of Seabirds on some Islands in the African Sector of the Southern Ocean. Pp. 627-635 in: Croxall *et al.* (1984).
Williams, A.J. (1984b). Breeding distribution, numbers and conservation of tropical seabirds on oceanic islands in the South Atlantic Ocean. Pp. 393-401 in: Croxall *et al.* (1984).
Williams, A.J (1987). New seabird breeding localities, and an extension of Bank Cormorant range, along the Namib coast of southern Africa. *Cormorant* **15**: 98-102.
Williams, A.J. & Burger, A.E. (1978). The ecology of the prey of Cape and Bank Cormorants. *Cormorant* **4**: 28-29.
Williams, A.J. & Burger, A.E. (1979). Aspects of the breeding biology of the Imperial Cormorant, *Phalacrocorax atriceps*, at Marion Island. *Gerfaut* **69**: 407-423.
Williams, A.J. & Cooper, J. (1983). The Crowned Cormorant: breeding biology, diet, and offspring-reduction strategy. *Ostrich* **54(4)**: 213-219.
Williams, A.J. & Cooper, J. (1984). Aspects on the breeding biology of the Jackass Penguin *Spheniscus demersus*. Pp. 841-853 in: Ledger, J. (1984). *Proceedings of the Fifth Pan-African Ornithological Congress.* Southern African Ornithological Society, Johannesburg.
Williams, A.J. & Rowlands, B.W. (1980). Seabirds of the Cargados Carajos shoals, July-August 1971. *Cormorant* **8**: 43-48.
Williams, A.J. & Siegfried, W.R. (1980). Foraging ranges of krill-eating penguins. *Polar Record* **20**: 159-175.
Williams, A.J. & Stone, C. (1981). Rockhopper Penguins *Eudyptes chrysocome* at Tristan da Cunha. *Cormorant* **9**: 59-66.
Williams, A.J., Cooper, J., Newton, I.P., Phillips, C.M. & Watkins, B.P. (1985). *Penguins of the World: a Bibliography.* British Antarctic Survey, Natural Environmental Research Council, Cambridge.
Williams, A.J., Siegfred, W.R., Burger, A.E. & Berruti, A. (1979). The Prince Edward Islands: a sanctuary for seabirds in the Southern Ocean. *Biol. Conserv.* **15**: 59-71.
Williams, A.J., Siegfried, W.R. & Cooper, J. (1982). Egg composition and hatchling precocity in seabirds. *Ibis* **124**: 456-470.
Williams, C.S. (1967). *Honker: a Discussion of the Habits and Needs of the Largest of our Canada Geese.* D. Van Nostrand, Princeton.
Williams, D.M. (1982). *Agonistic Behavior and Mate Selection in the Mallard (*Anas platyrhynchos*).* PhD thesis, University of Leicester, Leicester.

Williams, G.R. (1968). The Cape Barren Goose (*Cereopsis novae-hollandiae* Latham) in New Zealand. *Notornis* **15 (2)**: 66-69.
Williams, G.R. (1985). Kiwis. Page 317 in: Campbell & Lack (1985).
Williams, G.R. & Given, D.R. (1981). *The Red Data Book of New Zealand*. Nature Conservation Council, Wellington.
Williams, J.G. (1956). On the downy young of *Aythya erythrophtalma*. *Bull. Brit. Orn. Club* **76**: 140-141.
Williams, J.W. (1973). *Growth Rate and Nesting Aspects for the Glossy Ibis in Virginia-1972*. MSc thesis, College of William and Mary.
Williams, L. (1942). Display and sexual behavior of the Brandt's Cormorant. *Condor* **44**: 85-104.
Williams, M.D., Bakewell, D.N., Carey, G.J. & Holloway, S.J. (1986). On the bird migration at Beidaihe, Hebei Province, China, during spring 1985. *Forktail* **2**: 3-20.
Williams, M.J. (1967). *Observations on the Behaviour of New Zealand Anatidae in Captivity*. Unpublished B.Sc. (Hons.) thesis, Univerity of Wellington.
Williams, M.J. (1969). Courtship and copulatory behaviour of the New Zealand Grey Duck. *Notornis* **16**: 23-32.
Williams, M.J. (1971). The distribution and abundance of the Paradise Shelduck (*Tadorna variegata*, Gmelin) in New Zealand from pre-European times to the present day. *Notornis* **18**: 71-86.
Williams, M.J. (1974). Conservation of Brown Teal. *Wildlife - a review* **5**: 10-12.
Williams, M.J. (1977). Locations of recoveries of Black Swans, *Cygnus atratus*, Latham, banded at Lake Whangape and Lake Ellesmere, New Zealand. *Austr. Wildl. Res.* **4**: 289-299.
Williams, M.J. (1978). Rehabilitation of Brown Teal. *Wildlife - a review* **9**: 43-45.
Williams, M.J. (1979a). The Status and Management of Black Swans, *Cygnus atratus*, Latham, at Lake Ellesmer since the "Wahine" Storm, April, 1968. *New Zealand J. Ecol.* **2**: 34-41.
Williams, M.J. (1979b). The moult gatherings of Paradise Shelduck in the Gisborne - East Coast District. *Notornis* **26**: 369-390.
Williams, M.J. (1981). Recoveries of Paradise Shelducks banded in the Taihape, Nelson, Marlborough, Waitaki and Southland Districts. *Notornis* **28**: 11-27.
Williams, M.J. (1985a). Family Threskiornithidae, ibises and spoonbills. Pp. 136-137 in: Robertson (1985).
Williams, M.J. (1985b). White-faced Heron. Page 129 in: Robertson (1985).
Williams, M.J. (1985c). Reef Heron. Page 132 in: Robertson (1985).
Williams, M.J. (1985d). Australasian Bittern. Page 135 in: Robertson (1985).
Williams, M.J. (1985e). Paradise Shelduck. Page 142 in: Robertson (1985).
Williams, M.J. (1985f). Brown Teal. Pp. 146-147 in: Robertson (1985).
Williams, M.J. (1985g). Blue Duck. Page 149 in: Robertson (1985).
Williams, M.J. (1985h). Scaup. Page 150 in: Robertson (1985).
Williams, M.J. (1986). The numbers of Auckland Island Teal. *Wildfowl* **37**: 63-70.
Williams, M.J. & Roderick, C. (1973). The breeding performance of Grey Duck, Mallard and their hybrids in captivity. *Int. Zoo Yb.* **13**: 62-69.
Williams, S.O. (1978). *The Mexican Duck in Mexico: Natural History, Distribution and Population Status*. PhD dissertation, Colorado State University.
Williams, S.O. (1982). Notes on the breeding and occurrence of western grebes on the Mexican Plateau. *Condor* **84**: 127-130.
Williams, T.D. (1989). Aggression, incubation behaviour and egg-loss in Macaroni Penguins *Eudyptes chrysolophus* at South Georgia. *Oikos* **55**: 19-22.
Williams, T.D. (1990). Annual variation in the breeding biology of Gentoo Penguins, *Pygoscelis papua*, at Bird Island, South Georgia. *J. Zoology. London* **222**: 247-258.
Williams, T.D. (1991). Foraging ecology and diet of Gentoo Penguins *Pygoscelis papua* at South Georgia during winter and an assessment of their winter prey consumption. *Ibis* **133**: 3-13.
Williams, T.D. & Croxall, J.P. (1991). Annual variation in breeding biology of Macaroni Penguins, *Eudyptes chrysolophus*, at Bird Island, South Georgia. *J. Zoology. London* **223**: 189-202.
Williamson, K., Malcolm, N., MacDougall, C., Norman, D. & Yates, G. (1954). The fledging of a group of young Fulmars. *Scott. Nat.* **66**: 1-12.
Willis, E.O. (1983). Tinamous, chickens, guans, rails and trumpeters and army ants. *Rev. Brasil. Biol.* **43(1)**: 19-22.
Willis, E.O. & Oniki, Y. (1981). Levantamento preliminar de aves em treze areas do Estado de São Paulo. *Rev. Brasil. Biol.* **41**: 121-135.
Willis, E.O. & Oniki, Y. (1988). Bird conservation in open vegetation of São Paulo State, Brazil. Pp. 67-70 in: Goriup (1988).
Willson, M.F. (1989). Gut Retention Times of Experimental Pseudoseeds by Emus. *Biotropica* **21(3)**: 210-213.
Wilmé, L. (1990). Delacour's Grebe (*Tachybaptus rufolavatus*), Madagascar Pochard (*Aythya innotata*), Grey Bamboo Lemur (*Hapalemur griseus aloatrensis*). Status, distribution and proposals for conservation. WWF Project 3918. Unpublished report, Antananarivo, Madagascar.
Wilmore, S.B. (1974). *Swans of the World*. Taplinger, New York.
Wilson, D.B. (1975). Un nido de *Syrigma sibilatrix*. *Hornero* **11**: 319.
Wilson, E.O. (1975). *Sociobiology*. Belknap Press, Cambridge, MA.
Wilson, G.J. (1979). Oiled penguins in Antarctica. *New Zealand Antarct. Rec.* **2**: 3.
Wilson, G.J. (1983). Distribution and abundance of Antarctic and Subantarctic Penguins: a synthesis of current knowledge. *BIOMASS Scientific Series* **4**: 1-46.
Wilson, R.P. (1984). An improved stomach pump for penguins and other seabirds. *J. Field. Orn.* **55**: 109-112.
Wilson, G.R., Hill, G.J. & Barnes, A. (1987). An Aerial Survey of Feral Pigs and Emus in South-Eastern Queensland. *Austr. Wildl. Res.* **14**: 515-520.
Wilson, J.A. (1975). Sweeping flight and soaring by albatrosses. *Nature London* **257**: 307-308.
Wilson, P.J. (1957). Breeding of African spoonbill *Platalea alba* (Scop.) in the South Western Cape. *Ostrich* **28**: 236.
Wilson, R.G., Hernández, C. & Meléndez, A. (1988). Eared Grebes nesting in the valley of Mexico. *Amer. Birds* **42**: 29.
Wilson, R.P. (1985a). The Jackass Penguin (*Spheniscus demersus*) as a pelagic predator. *Mar. Ecol. Prog. Ser.* **25**: 219-227.
Wilson, R.P. (1985b). Seasonality in diet and breeding success of the Jackass Penguin, *Spheniscus demersus*. *J. Orn.* **126 S**: 53-62.
Wilson, R.P. (1985c). Diurnal foraging patterns of the Jackass Penguin. *Ostrich* **56**: 212-214.
Wilson, R.P. (1985d). Breeding Jackass Penguins *Spheniscus demersus* as pelagic predators. PhD thesis, University of Cape Town, South Africa.
Wilson, R.P. (1989). Diving depths of Gentoo *Pygoscelis papua* and Adelie *P. adeliae* Penguins at Esperanza Bay, Antarctic Peninsula. *Cormorant* 17: 1-8.
Wilson, R.P. & Bain, C.A.R. (1984a). An inexpensive speed meter for penguins at sea. *J. Wildl. Manage.* **48**: 1360-1364.
Wilson, R.P. & Bain, C.A.R. (1984b). An inexpensive depth gauge for penguins. *J. Wildl. Manage* **48**: 1077-1084.
Wilson, R.P. & Duffy, D.C. (1986). Prey seizing in African Penguins *Spheniscus demersus*. *Ardea* **74**: 211-214.
Wilson, R.P. & Wilson, M.P.T. (1988). Foraging behaviour in four sympatric cormorants. *J. Anim. Ecol.* **57**: 943-955.
Wilson, R.P. & Wilson, M.P.T. (1989). Substitute burrows for penguins on guano-free islands. *Gerfaut* **79**: 125-131.
Wilson, R.P., Culik, B., Spairani, H.J., Coria, N.R. & Adelung, D. (1991). Depth utilization by penguins and Gentoo Penguin dive patterns. *J. Orn.* **132(1)**: 47-60.
Wilson, R.P., La Cock, G.D., Wilson, M.P.T. & Mollagee, F. (1985). Differential digestion of squid and fish in Jackass Penguins *Spheniscus demersus*. *Ornis Scand.* **16**: 77-79.
Wilson, R.P., Ryan, P.G., James, A. & Wilson, M.P.T. (1987). Conspicuous coloration may enhance prey capture in some piscivores. *Animal Behav.* **35(5)**: 1558-1560.
Wilson, R.P., Wilson, M.P.T. & Duffy, D.C. (1988). Contemporary and historical changes in African Penguin distribution at sea. *Est. Coast. Shelf. Sci.* **26**: 447-458.
Wilson, R.P., Wilson, M.P.T., Duffy, D.C., Araya, B. & Klages, N. (1989). Diving behaviour and prey of the Humboldt Penguin (*Spheniscus humbolti*). *J. Orn.* **130**: 75-79.
Wilson, R.P., Wilson, M.P.T. & McQuaid, L. (1986). Group size in foraging African Penguins (*Spheniscus demersus*). *Ethology* **72**: 338-341.
Wilson, R.T. (1985). *The Ecology and Biology of the Hamerkop "*Scopus umbretta *(Gmelin) in Central Mali*. Doctoral dissertation, Council for National Academic Awards 1985.
Wilson, R.T. (1987). Nest sites, nesting seasons, clutch sizes and eggs sizes of the Hamerkop "*Scopus umbretta*". *Malimbus* **9(1)**: 17-22.
Wilson, R.T. (1988). Birds of the Sahel Zone in Central Mali. Pp. 171-180 in: Goriup (1988).
Wilson, R.T. & Wilson, M.P. (1980). Notes sur la nidification du Canard Casqué (*Sarkidiornis melanotos*) en zone soudano-sahélienne. *L'Oiseau et la R.F.O.* **50**: 117-124.
Wilson, R.T. & Wilson, M.P. (1984). Breeding biology of the Hamerkop in central Mali. Ledger, J. (1984). *Proceedings of the Fifth Pan-African Ornithological Congress*. Southern African Ornithological Society, Johannesburg.
Wilson, R.T. & Wilson, M.P. (1986a). Nest building by the Hamerkop *Scopus umbretta*. *Ostrich* **57**: 224-32.
Wilson, R.T. & Wilson, M.T. (1986b). Nest use by the Hamerkop *Scopus umbretta* and its associates. *Walia* **9**: 24-28.
Wilson, R.T. & Wilson, M.P. (1988). Incubation patterns of the Hamerkop *Scopus umbretta* in central Mali. Pp. 27-30 in: *Proceedings of the Sixth Pan-African Ornithological Congress*. Southern African Ornithological Society, Johannesburg.
Wilson, R.T., Wilson, M.P. & Durkin, J.W. (1987). Aspects of the reproductive ecology of the Hamerkop *Scopus umbretta* in central Mali. *Ibis* **129**: 382-388.
Wilson, R.T., Wilson, M.P. & Durkin, J.W. (1988). Growth of nestling Hamerkops *Scopus umbretta* in central Mali. *Ibis* **130**: 384-392.
Wilson, R.T.A. (1983). Saddlebill stork (Roberts No. 75). *Redwing* 1983: 30-31.
Wilson, S.A. & Allport, G. (1985). Milky Stork (*Ibis cinereus*) and birds of the Java plain. *Oriental Bird Club Bull.* **1**: 12-14.
Wilson, S.V. (1978). The breeding biology of the Oriental White Stork, *Ciconia boyciana* Swinhoe, in the Middle Amur Region. *Tr. Zool. Inst. Akad. Nauk SSSR* **76**: 9-23.
Wingate, D.B. (1964). Discovery of breeding Black-capped Petrels on Hispaniola. *Auk* **81**: 147-159.
Wingate, D.B. (1972). First successful hand rearing of an abandoned Bermuda Petrel chick. *Ibis* **114**: 97-101.
Wingate, D.B. (1977). Excluding competitors from Bermuda Petrel nesting burrows. Pp. 93-102 in Temple, S.A. ed. *Proceedings of Symposium on Management Techniques for Preserving Endangered Birds*. University Wisconsin Press & Croom Helm, Madison.
Wingate, D.B. (1982). Successful Reintroduction of the Yellow-Crowned Night-Heron as a Nesting Resident on Bermuda. *Colonial Waterbirds* **5**: 104-115.
Wingate, D.B. (1985). The Restoration of Nonsuch Island as a Living Museum of Bermuda's Pre-colonial Terrestrial Biome. Pp. 225-238 in: Moors (1985).
Wingham, E.J. (1984a). Breeding biology of the Australian Gannet at Motu Karamarama at Hauraki Gulf, New Zealand I. The egg. *Emu* **84(3)**: 129-136.
Wingham, E.J. (1984b). Breeding biology of the Australian Gannet at Motu Karamara, Hauraki Gulf, New Zealand II. Breeding success and chick growth. *Emu* **84(4)**: 211-224.
Wingham, E.J. (1985). Food and feeding range of the Australasian Gannet. *Emu* **85(4)**: 231-239.
Wink, M., Wink, C. & Ristow, D. (1982). Brutbiologie mediterraner Gelbschnabelsturmtaucher (*Calonectris diomedea diomedea*). *Seevogel* (Spec. No.): 127-135.
Winkler, D.W & Cooper, S.C. (1986). Ecology of migrant Black-necked Grebes *Podiceps nigricollis* at Mono Lake, California. *Ibis* **128**: 483-491.
Winkler, H. (1983a). Das Flügelspreitverhalten der Mohrenscharbe *Phalacrocorax niger*. *J. Orn.* **124**: 177-186.
Winkler, H. (1983b). Das Jagdverhalten des Glockenreihers "*Egretta ardesiaca*" *J.Orn.* **123(3)**: 307-314. In German with English summary.
Winter, S. (1982). Nesting of the Black-billed White Stork (*Ciconia boyciana* Swinhoe) in the Middle Amur Region. Pp. 75-100 in: Gavrilov, V.M. & Potapov, R.L. eds. *Ornithological Studies in the USSR*. Vol. 1. USSR Academy of Sciences, Moscow.
Winterbottom, J.M. (1958). African Spoonbill nesting colony in the Karoo. *Ostrich* **29**: 89.
Winterbottom, J.M. (1972). Range of the Hadeda. *Ostrich* **43**: 186.
Winterbottom, J.M. (1974). The Cape Teal. *Ostrich* **45 (2)**: 110-132.
Wintle, C.C. (1981). Notes on the breeding behaviour of the White-backed Duck. *Honeyguide* **105**: 13-20.
Wirtz, P. (1986). Co-operative prey capture in the Great White Pelican (*Pelecanus onocrotalus*) at Lake Nakuru, Kenya. *Zool. Jb. Syst.* **113**: 37-43.
Wishart, R.A. (1979). Indices of structural size and condition of American Wigeon (*Anas americana*). *Can. J. Zool.* **57**: 2369-2374.
Wishart, R.A. (1983). *The behavioral ecology of the American Wigeon (*Anas americana*) over its annual cycle*. PhD dissertation, University Manitoba.
Withers, P.C., Forbes, R.B. & Hedrick, M.S. (1987). Metabolic, water and thermal relations of the Chilean Tinamou. *Condor* **89**: 424-426.
Wittenberger, J.F. (1981). *Animal Social Behavior*. Wadsworth, Belmont, California.
Wittmann, U. & Ruppert, H. (1984). Kunstliche Erbrutung und Aufzucht des Waldrapp, *Geronticus eremita* (L., 1758). *Zool. Garten.* **54**: 427-438.
Wobus, U. (1964a). Zur Biologie von Haubentaucher (*Podiceps cristatus*) und Rothalstaucher (*Podiceps griseigena*) und ihrer Verbreitung im Kreis Niesky/Oberlausitz. *Abhandlungen und Berichte des Naturkundemuseums Görlitz* **39(12)**: 1-15.
Wobus, U. (1964b). *Der Rothalstaucher*. Die Neue Brehm-Bücherei **330**. Ziemsen Verlag, Wittenberg-Lutherstadt.
Wodzicki, K.A. (1967). The gannets at Cape Kidnappers. *Trans. Roy. Soc. New Zealand* **88**: 149-162.
Wodzicki, K.A. & Robertson, F.H. (1953). Notes of the life history and population trends at the Plateau Gannetry Cape Kidnappers. *Emu* **53**: 152-168.
Wodzicki, K.A. & Robertson, F.H. (1955). Observations on diving of the Australasian Gannet. *Notornis* **67**: 72-76.
Wodzicki, K.A. & Stein, P. (1958). Migration and dispersal of New Zealand gannets. *Emu* **58**: 289-312.
Woehler, E.J. (1990). First records of Kerguelen Petrel *Pterodroma brevirostris* at Heard Island. *Marine Orn.* **18(1-2)**: 70-71.
Woehler, E.J. (1991). Status and conservation of the seabirds of Heard Island and the McDonald Islands. Pp. 263-277 in: Croxall (1991).
Woehler, E.J. & Gilbert, C.A. (1990). Hybrid Rockhopper-Macaroni Penguins, interbreeding and mixed species pairs at Heard and Marion Islands. *Emu* **90**: 198-201.
Woehler, E.J. & Johnstone, G.W. (1991). Status and conservation of the seabirds of the Australian Antarctic territory. Pp. 279-308 in: Croxall (1991).
Wohl, K.D. (1975). Sightings of New Zealand Shearwaters in the northern Gulf of Alaska. *Can. Field-Nat.* **89**: 320-321.
Woldhek, S. (1980). *Bird-killing in the Mediterranean*. European Committee for the Prevention of Mass Destruction of Migratory Birds.
Wolfson, A. ed. (1955). *Recent Studies in Avian Biology*. University of Illinois Press, Urbana, Illinois.
Wolinski, R.A. (1988). Status of the Yellow-crowned Night Heron in Michigan. Jack-Pine Warbler **66(2)** 55-69.
Wolk, K. (1973). Leg Perkoza rogatego, *Podiceps auritus* (L.) w Polsce. [Summary: Nesting of the Slavonian Grebe *Podiceps auritus* (L.) in Poland]. *Przegl. Zool.* **17**: 456-458.
Wolstenhilme, P. (1961). Hadedahs accept humans. *African Wild Life* **15(3)**: 245-250.
Wolters, H.E. (1975-1982). *Die Vogelarten der Erde*. Paul Harey, Hamburg and Berlin.
Won, H.G. (1966). Black-faced Spoonbill and its protection. *Korean Nat.* **1966**: 8-11.
Won, P. & Lee, H. (1986). [The reproductive success of Swinhoe's fork-tailed Petrel on Kugul Islet, Sohuksan Island, Korea.] *Theses Collection, Kyung Hee Univ.* **15**: 15-27.
Won, P.O. (1971). The status of bird conservation in Korea, 1966-1970. *Bull. ICBP* **11**: 242-247.
Wood, C.A. (1923). The Cayenne or River Ibis in British Guiana. *Condor* **25**: 199-201.
Wood, C.J. (1973). The flight of albatrosses (A computer simulation). *Ibis* **115**: 244-256.
Wood, D.S. (1983). Phenetic relationships within the Ciconiidae. *Ann. Carneg. Mus.* **52**: 79-112.
Wood, D.S. (1984). Concordance between classifications of the Ciconiidae based on behavioural and morphological data. *J. Orn.* **125(1)**: 25-37.
Wood, K.A. (1990a). Seasonal abundance and marine habitat of Storm-Petrels (Oceanitidae) off Central New South Wales. *Corella* **14**(2): 37-43.
Wood, K.A. (1990b). Seasonal abundance and marine habitats of *Procellaria* Fulmarine and Gadfly Petrels off Central New South Wales. *Notornis* **37**: 81-105.
Wood, M.G. (1949). A Little Grebe's nest in Kano. *Nigerian Field* **14**: 54-65.
Woodall, P.F. (1985). Waterbird populations in the Brisbane region, 1972-1983, and correlates with rainfall and water heights. *Austr. Wildl. Res.* **12**: 495-506.
Woodall, P.F. (1986). The Cattle Egret, *Ardeola ibis*, in South-east Queensland. *Austr. Wildl. Res.* **13(4)**: 575-582.
Woodin, M.C. & Swanson, G.A. (1989). Foods and dietary strategies of Prairie-nesting Ruddy Ducks and Redheads. *Condor* **91**: 280-287.
Woods, R.W. (1970). Great Shearwater breeding in the Falkland Islands. *Ibis* **112**: 259-260.
Woods, R.W. (1988). *The Birds of the Falkland Islands*. Anthony Nelson, Oswestry, England.
Woodward, P.W. (1972). The natural history of Kure Atoll, Northwestern Hawaiian Islands. *Atoll Res. Bull.* **164**.
Woodyard, E.R. & Bolen, E.G. (1984). Ecological studies of Muscovy Ducks in Mexico. *Southwest. Nat.* **29**: 453-461.
Woolfenden, G.E. (1956). Preening and other behaviour of a captive Horned Grebe. *Wilson Bull.* **68**: 154-156.
Woolfenden, G.E. (1961). Postcranial osteology of the waterfowl. *Bull. Florida State Mus., Biol. Sci.* **6 (1)**: 1-129.
Woolfenden, G.E. (1967). Selection for a delayed simultaneous wing molt in loons (Gaviidae). *Wilson Bull.* **79**: 416-420.
Woolfenden, G.E. & Fitzpatrick, J.W. (1984). *The Florida Scrub Jay. Demography of a Cooperative Breeding Bird*. Princeton University Press, Princeton, New Jersey.

Woolington, D.W. & Springer, P.F. (1977). *Population, distribution and ecology of Aleutian Canada Geese on their migration and wintering areas.* US Fish & Wildlife Service Research Field Station, Humboldt State University, Arcata, California. Unpublished report.
Wooller, R.D. & Dunlop, J.N. (1981). Itinerant breeding by Pied Cormorants on Carnac Island, Western Australia. *Corella* **5**: 97.
Wooller, R.D., Bradley, J.S., Serventy, D.L. & Skira, I.J. (1988). Factors contributing to reproductive success in Short-tailed Shearwaters. Pp. 848-856 in: *Proc. XIX Int. Orn. Congr.* Vol. 1.
Wooller, R.D., Bradley, J.S., Skira, I.J. & Serventy, D.L. (1990). Reproductive success of Short-tailed Shearwaters *Puffinus tenuirostris* in relation to their age and breeding experience. *J. Anim. Ecol.* **59**: 161-170.
Wormell, P. (1976). The Manx Shearwaters of Rhum. *Scottish Birds* **9**: 103-118.
Worrell, E., Drake, B. & Krauss, L. (1975). Breeding the Australian Cassowary *Casuarius casuarius* at the Australian Reptile Park. *Int. Zoo Yb.* **15**: 94-97.
Wrege, P.H. (1980). *Social foraging strategies of White Ibis,* Eudocimus albus. PhD Dissertation. Cornell University. Ithaca, New York.
Wright, B.S. (1954). *High Tide and an East Wind: the Story of the Black Duck.* The Stackpole Company, Harisburg, P.A. & Wildlife Management Institute, Washington, D.C.
Wright, E.N., Inglis, I.R. & Feare, C.J. (1980). *Bird Problems in Agriculture.* British Crop Protection Council Publications, Croydon.
Wright, J.K. (1965). Observations on the behaviour of the Andean Torrent Duck. *Condor* **67**: 535.
Wright, S.M.A. (1988). A three year observational study of the breeding behavior of the Double-wattled Cassowary at the Cleveland Metroparks Zoo. *Animal Keepers' Forum* **15(12)**: 402-406.
Wu Zhi-kang, Xie Jia-hua *et al.* (1983). The breeding of the Mandarin Duck *Aix galericulata* in Guizhou Province. *Wildlife* **2**: 37, 39.
Würdinger, I. (1970). Erzeugung, Ontogenie and Funcktion der Lautäusserungen bei vier Gänsearten (*Anser indicus, A. caerulescens, A. albifrons* and *Branta canadensis*). *Z. Tierpsychol.* **27**: 257-301.
Würdinger, I. (1973). Breeding of Bar-headed Goose *Anser indicus* in captivity. *Int. Zoo Yb.* **13**: 43-47.
Würdinger, I. (1978). Jahres- und tageszeitliche Verteilung von Schlaf, Komfortverhalten, Lokomotion, Nahrungsaufnahme und aggressivem Verhalten bei juvenilen und adulten Streifengänsen (*Anser indicus* vorm. *Eulabeia indica*). *Z. Tierpsychol.* **46**: 306-323.
Würdinger, I. (1980). Die Streifengans (*Anser indicus* vorm. *Eulabeia indica*) - Beschreibung und Analyse des Verhaltens. Unpublished Habil. Hochsch. Hildesheim.
Wylie, S.R. (1982). Breeding the African Spoonbill *Platalea alba* at the St. Louis Zoological Park, USA. *Avicult. Mag.* **88(2)**: 68-70.
Wyndham, E. (1978). Birds of the Milparinka district and Cooper Creek Basin. *Emu* **78**: 179-187.
Wynne-Edwards, V.C. (1939). Intermittent breeding of the Fulmar, with some general observations on non-breeding in sea-birds. *Proc. Zool. Soc. London (Ser. A)* **109**: 127-132.
Xian Yao-hua (1964). [Preliminary observations on the breeding ecology of the Bar-headed Goose *Anser indicus* in the Qinghai-hu (Qinghai Province)]. *Chinese J. Zool.* **6(1)**: 12-14. In Chinese.
Xu Lin-mu (1988). The Chinese Merganser, *Mergus squamatus*, discovered in Feidong, Anhui Province. *Chinese Wildlife* 2: 40.
Yamamoto, H. (1967). *Phalacrocorax capillatus* as a breeding bird on Iwate coast, Honshyu *Misc. Rep. Yamashina Inst. Orn.* **5**: 48-60.
Yamashina, Y. (1952). Classification of the Anatidae based on cytogenetics. *Pap. Coord. Comm. Res. Gen.* **3**: 1-24.
Yamashina, Y. (1962a). Present status of the Japanese White Stork. *Bull. ICBP* **8**: 99-102.
Yamashina, Y. (1962b). History and present status of Japanese Crested Ibis *Nipponia nippon* (Temminck). *ICBP Bulletin* **8**: 99-102.
Yamashina, Y. (1967). The status of endangered species in Japan. *Bull. ICBP* **10**: 100-109.
Yamashina, Y. (1969). Japanese Crested Ibis - protection and propagation on Sado Island, Japan. *Yb. World Wildl. Fund* **1968**: 147-148, 240.
Yamashina, Y. (1977). [The present status of the Japanese Crested Ibis *Nipponia nippon* and the Japanese White Stork *Ciconia ciconia boyciana* in continental Asia]. *Misc. Rep. Yamashina Inst. Orn.* **9**: 131-142. In Japanese.
Yamashina, Y. (1978). The Feeding of Japanese Crested Ibises. Pp. 161-164 in: Temple, S.A. ed. *Endangered Birds. Management Techniques for Preserving Threatened Species.* The University of Wisconsin Press, Madison & Croom Helm, London.
Yamashina, Y. & Takano, S. (1959). Report on the Japanese White Stork census. *Misc. Rep. Yamashina Inst. Orn.* **6**: 505-521.
Yamashita, C. & Valle, M. de P. (1990). Ocorrencia de duas aves raras no Brasil Central: *Mergus octosetaceus* e *Tigrisoma fasciatum fasciatum*. *Ararajuba* **1**: 107-109.
Yan An-hou (1987). [Preliminary observations on the ecology of the Chinese Pond Heron *Ardeola bacchus*]. *Chinese J. Zool.* **22(6)**: 28-30. In Chinese.
Yan An-hou (1988). [A preliminary ecological observation on the Chinese Little Bittern *Ixobrychus sinensis*]. *Chinese J. Zool.* **3**: 20-22. In Chinese.
Yan Fengtao (1987). [A preliminary investigation of the ecology of overwintering of the White Stork, *Ciconia ciconia*]. *Chinese Wildl.* (6): 20-21, 25. In Chinese.
Yang Jiong-li, Zou Xun *et al.* (1985). [Breeding biology of the Mandarin Duck, *Aix galericulata*, in the Fanjin Mountain Region (Guizhou)]. *Chinese Wildlife* **4**: 15-17. In Chinese.
Yapp, B. (1981). *Birds in Medieval Manuscripts.* British Library.
Yasuda, K. (1984). [On a Description about Color Change on Plumage of Japanese Crested Ibis *Nipponia nippon* Observed by M. Berezovsky, 1884-'85]. *J. Yamashina Inst. Orn.* **16**: 174-177. In Japanese with English summary.
Ydenberg, R. & Guillemette, M. (1991). Diving and foraging in the Common Eider. *Ornis Scand.* **22**: 349-352.
Ydenberg, R.C. & Clark (1989). Aerobiosis and anaerobiosis during diving by Western Grebes: and optimal foraging approach. *J. Theor. Biol.* **139**: 437-449.
Ydenberg, R.C. & Forbes, L.S. (1988). Diving and foraging in the Western Grebe. *Ornis Scand.* **19**: 129-133.
Yeates, G.K. (1950a). Field notes on the nesting habits of the Great Northern Diver. *British Birds* **43**: 5-8.
Yeates, G.K. (1950b). *Flamingo City.* Country Life.
Yeates, G.W. (1971). Diurnal activity in the Adelie Penguin (*Pygoscelis adeliae*) at Cape Royds, Antarctica. *J. Nat. Hist.* **5**: 103-112.
Yépez, I. (1979). *Comportamiento reproductivo de Fregata minor en Punta del Este, Isla San Cristóbal, Galápagos.* Tesis de Licenciatura, PUCE, Quito, Ecuador.
Yésou, P. (1982). A propos de la présence remarquable du Puffin Cendré près des côtes du Golfe de Gascogne et de la mer Celtique en 1980. *L'Oiseau et la R.F.O.* **152**: 197-217.
Yésou, P. (1985). Nouvelles données sur la mue de *Puffinus p. mauretanicus*. *L'Oiseau et la R.F.O.* **55**: 177-182.
Yésou, P. (1986). Balearic Shearwaters Summering in Western France. Pp. 515-517 in MEDMARAVIS & Monbailliu (1986).
Yésou, P., Paterson, A.M., Mackrill, E.J. & Bourne, W.R.P. (1990). Plumage variation and identification of the "Yelkouan" Shearwater. *British Birds* **8**: 299-319.
Yinzeng, L. (1982). Search for the crested ibis. *New Scientist* **94(1301)**: 171-172.
Yocom, C. (1947). Notes on behavior and abundance of the Black-footed Albatross in the Pacific waters off the continental North American shores. *Auk* **64**: 507-523.
Yonge, K.S. (1981). *The Breeding Cycle and Annual Production of the Common Loon (*Gavia immer*) in the Boreal Forest Region.* MSc thesis, University of Manitoba, Winnipeg.
Yoshida, N. (1962). [Breeding ecology of the Streaked Shearwater at Kammurijima I., Maizuru in Kyoto.] *Tori* **17**: 83-108.
Yoshida, N. (1973). [A decennial record of fallen Streaked Shearwaters in the Kinki District.] *Tori* **22**: 60-66.
Yoshida, N. (1981). [*Seabirds that Climb Trees.*] Ubunsha, Tokyo.
Yoshida, N. (1986). First record of *Gorsachius melanolophus* for Tokushima Pref, Shikoku. *Japanese J. Orn.* **35(12)**: 37.
Yoshii, M. (1971). The present status of the Japanese Crested Ibis and the Japanese White Stork. *Bull. ICBP* **11**: 168-169.
Young, A.D. & Titman, R.D. (1988). Intraspecific nest parasitism in Red-breasted Mergansers. *Can. J. Zool.* **66**: 2454-2458.
Young, C.G. (1928). A contribution to the ornithology of the coastland of British Guiana. *Ibis* **4(12th Ser.)**: 748-781.
Young, C.M. (1970). Territoriality in the Common Shelduck *Tadorna tadorna*. *Ibis* **112**: 330-335.
Young, E.C. (1978). Behavioural ecology of *lonnbergi* skuas in relation to environment on the Chatham Islands, New Zealand. *New Zealand J. Zool.* **5**: 401-416.
Young, E.C., Jenkins, P.E., Douglas, M.E. & Lovegrove, T.G. (1988). Nocturnal foraging by Chatham Island skuas. *New Zealand J. Ecol.* **11**: 113-117.
Young, H.G. (1991a). Sexual dimorphism in Meller's Duck *Anas melleri*. *Bull. Brit. Orn. Club* **111(4)**: 225-228.
Young, H.G. (1991b). The endemic wildfowl of Madagascar. *IWRB Threatened Waterfowl Research Group Newsletter* **1**: 12-13.
Young, H.G. & Smith, J.G. (1989). The search for the Madgascar Pochard *Aythia innotata*: survey of Lac Alaotra, Madagascar October-November 1989. *Dodo, J. Jersey Preserv. Trust* **26**: 17-34.
Young, H.G. & Smith, J.G. (1990). Notes on an expedition to relocate the Madagascar Pochard *Aythya innotata* - a JWPT, WWT project. *Wildfowl* **41**: 159-160.
Young, J.G. (1972). Breeding biology of feral Graylag Geese in south-west Scotland. *Wildfowl* **23**: 83-87.
Young, W.F. (1972-1975). A series of census reports on *Jabiru mycteria* in Belize. Unpublished report.
Ysebaert, T.J., Meire, P.M. & Dhondt, A.A. (1988). Seasonal changes in habitat use of White-fronted Geese near Antwerp, Belgium. *Wildfowl* **39**: 54-62.
Ytreberg, N.J. (1957). Horndykkerens (*Podiceps auritus* (L.)) forekomst i Norge og noen trekk fra dens biologi. [Summary: The occurrence of the Slavonian Grebe in Norway and some data of its breeding biology]. *Kgl. Norske Vidensk. Selsk. Museet Årbok* **1956-57**: 49-74.
Yu Han (1963). [Observation of a pair of Black Storks *Ciconia nigra* and their chicks in the northern part of Yan'an in Shaanxi Province]. *Chinese J. Zool.* **5(1)**: 17-18. In Chinese.
Yuan Hai-ying. (1984). [Save the Crested Shelduck, *Tadorna cristata*]. *Chinese Wildlife* 2: 55-57. In Chinese.
Zahl, P.A. (1950). Search for the Scarlet Ibis in Venezuela. *Natl. Geogr. Mag.* **97**: 633-661.
Zahl, P.A. (1951). Flamingos' last stand on Andros Island. *Natl. Geogr. Mag.* **99**: 635-652.
Zahl, P.A. (1952). *Flamingo Hunt.* Bobbs-Merrill, Indianapolis.
Zahl, P.A. (1954). *Coro-Coro. The World of the Scarlet Ibis.* Bobbs-Merrill Co., New York.
Zaloumis, E.A. (1976). Incubation period of the African Pygmy Goose. *Ostrich* **47**: 231.
Zander, R.C.W. (1967). *The Paradise Duck (*Tadorna variegata*) in Southland and Otago Acclimatisation Districts.* Unpublished Diploma of Wildlife Management dissertation, University of Otago.
Zang, H. (1977). Zur Frage der Häufigkeit von Zweitbruten beim Haubentaucher (*Podiceps cristatus*). *J. Orn., Berlin* **118**: 261-267.
Zapata, A.R.P. & Martínez, H.S. (1972). Algunas aves no citadas y otras poco frecuentes para el sur de la provincia de Buenos Aires. *Acta Zool. Lilloana* **29**: 181-199.
Zapata, A.R.P. & Martínez, H.S. (1977). Algunas aves no citadas y otras poco frecuentes para el sur de la provincia de Buenos Aires. *Acta Zool. Lilloana* **29**: 181-199.
Zhang, R. (1991). World's first Crested Ibis bred from artificial incubation. *Bird World* **12**: 20-21.
Zhang Xinglu (1983). [The breeding ecology of the Black Stork *Ciconia nigra*]. *Wildlife* **(5)**: 18-19. In Chinese.
Zhao Zheng-jie, Han Xiao-dong *et al.* (1988). New record of the distribution of Red-breasted Merganser, *Mergus serrator*. *Chinese Wildlife* **4**: 45.
Zhao Zheng-jie, Zhang Xing-lu *et al.* (1979). Notes on the ecology of the Chinese Merganser *Mergus squamatus* in the Changbai Shan Area (Jilin Province). *Acta Zool. Sinica* **25(2)**: 189.
Zhao Zheng-jie, Zhang Xing-lu *et al.* (1980). Breeding biology of the Mandarin Duck, *Aix galericulata. Journal of Jilin Normal University (Natural Science)* **2**: 52-58.
Zhao-Qing, C. (1988). Niche Selection of Breeding Seabirds on Chenlushan Island in the Yellow Sea, China. *Colonial Waterbirds* **11**(2): 306-307.
Zheng Zuo-xin (1960). [Discovery of the Red-breasted Goose (*Branta ruficollis*) in China]. *Chinese J. Zool.* **4(6)**: 256. In Chinese.
Zhi-Yen, Z. (1986). Gem of the Orient. *Living Bird Quarterly* **5(2)**: 29-30.
Zhu Xi (1986). The Chinese Pond *Ardeola bacchus* of Zhuxian (Zhejiang Province). *Nature* **3**: 55-57.
Zhu Xi (1989). Studies on the Breeding Ecology of the Pond Heron (*Ardeola bacchus*). *Sci. Silvae* **25(1)**: 93-94.
Zhu Xi & Yang Chun-jiang (1988). [Studies on the breeding biology and ecology of the Chinese Pond Heron *Ardeola bacchus*]. *J. Zhejiang Forestry College* **5(2)**: 197-205. In Chinese.
Zicus, M.C. (1990a). Nesting biology of Hooded Mergansers using nest boxes. *J. Wildl. Manage.* **54 (4)**: 637-643.
Zicus, M.C. (1990b). Renesting by a Common Goldeneye. *J. Field Orn.* **61 (2)**: 245-248.
Zimmer, G.E. (1979). *The Status and Distribution of the Common Loon in Wisconsin.* MSc thesis, University of Wisconsin, Steven Point.
Zimmerman, D.R. (1974). Return of the Nene. *Animal Kingdom* **77 (3)**: 22-28.
Zimmermann, D.A. (1957). Display of the Least Grebe. *Auk* **74**: 390.
Zink, R.M. (1981). Observations of seabirds during a cruise from Ross Island to Anvers Island, Antarctica. *Wilson Bull.* **93**: 1-20.
Zink, R.M. & Eldridge, J.L. (1980). Why does Wilson's Petrel have yellow on the webs of its feet? *British Birds* **73**: 385-387.
Zino, P.A. (1971). The breeding of Cory's Shearwater on the Salvage Islands. *Ibis* **113**: 212-217.
Zino, P.A. (1985). A short history of the Shearwater hunt on the Great Salvage and recent developments on this island. *Bocagiana* **84**: 1-9.
Zino, P.A. & Zino, F. (1986). Contribution to the study of the petrels of the genus *Pterodroma* in the archipelago of Madeira. *Bol. Mus. Mun. Funchal* **180**: 141-165.
Zino, P.A., Zino, F., Maul, T. & Biscoito, J.M. (1987). The laying, incubation and fledging periods of Cory's Shearwater on Selvagem Grande in 1984. *Ibis* **129**: 393-398.
Zipko, S.J. (1979). *Effects of Dump Nests and Habitat on Reproductive Ecology of Wood Ducks,* Aix sponsa, *(Linnaeus).* PhD thesis, Rutgers University, Newark, NJ.
Ziswiler, V. & Farner, D.S. (1972). Digestion and the digestive system. Pp. 343-430 in: Farner, D.S. & King, J.R. (1972). *Avian Biology.* Vol. 2. Academic Press, London & New York.
Zonfrillo, B. (1986). Diet of Bulwer's Petrel *Bulweria bulwerii* in the Madeiran Archipelago. *Ibis* **128**: 570-572.
Zonfrillo, B. (1988). Notes and comments on the taxonomy of Jouanin's Petrel and Bulwer's Petrel. *Bull. Brit. Orn. Club* **108**: 71-75.
Zook-Rimon, Z. & Dotan, A. (1989). The effect of fire on a breeding population of the Glossy Ibis (*Plegadis falcinellus*) at Mishmar Hayam. *Isr. J. Zool.* **36**: 154-155.
Zotier, R. (1990a). Breeding ecology of a subantarctic winter breeder: the Grey Petrel *Procellaria cinerea* on Kerguelen Islands. *Emu* **90**: 180-184.
Zotier, R. (1990b). Breeding ecology of the White-headed Petrel *Pterodroma lessoni* on the Kerguelen Islands. *Ibis* **132**: 525-534.
Zusi, R.L. & Storer, R.W. (1969). Osteology and myology of the head and neck of the pied-billed grebes (*Podilymbus*). *Misc. Publ. Mus. Zool. Univ. Mich.* **139**: 1-49.
Zwank, P.J., McKenzie, P.M. & Moser, E.B. (1989). Mottled Duck habitat use and density indices in agricultural lands. *J. Wildl. Manage.* **53 (1)**: 110-114.
de Zylva, T.S.U. The Spoonbill. *Loris* **11**: 377-378.

INDEX

INDEX